NAVIGATOR SERIES

3000+ PROBLEMS

JEE Main & Advanced

Mechanics I

NAVIGATOR SERIES

3000+ PROBLEMS

JEE Main & Advanced

Mechanics I

PRADEEP BENIWAL
IIT Kharagpur

arihant
SUCCESS AND NOTHING LESS

arihant
SUCCESS AND NOTHING LESS

ARIHANT PRAKASHAN (Series), MEERUT

卐 **Administrative & Production Offices**

Regd. Office
'Ramchhaya' 4577/15, Agarwal Road, Darya Ganj, New Delhi -110002
Tele: 011- 47630600, 43518550

Head Office
Kalindi, TP Nagar, Meerut (UP) - 250002
Tel: 0121-7156203, 7156204

卐 **Sales & Support Offices**
Agra, Ahmedabad, Bengaluru, Bareilly, Chennai, Delhi, Guwahati, Hyderabad, Jaipur, Jhansi, Kolkata, Lucknow, Nagpur & Pune.

卐 **PRICE :** ₹515.00

卐 **PO No :** TXT-XX-XXXXXXX-X-XX

Published by Arihant Publications (India) Ltd.

For further information about the books published by Arihant, log on to www.arihantbooks.com or e-mail at info@arihantbooks.com

Follow us on

PREFACE

Physics is a subject that requires a lot of practice to master it and the best way to practice Physics is to solve more & more problems right from the beginner's level to the most complex ones. That's why the search for a good Physics Problems book has always been the top notch task of each good student.

During the last 15 Years while teaching & mentoring thousands of students preparing for JEE Main, JEE Advanced, KVPY, Olympiads etc. I always felt the need of such a book that can offer quality problems of Physics for all the topics of different chapters. There are many problems books available in the market but unfortunately none of them serve the purpose perfectly.

To fulfil the need of a good Physics Problems book, I have prepared the book **JEE Navigator Mechanics I**. All the problems given in this book are arranged conceptually and systematically in order to test the conceptual understanding & analytical ability of the students.

All the problems given in each chapter of this book have been developed with the utmost care and arranged in a way to enhance the problem-solving skills of the students & to boost their confidence to tackle complex JEE Problems.

The Points given below will help you to learn the basic structure of the book;

- Each chapter is divided into three major heads; **Level 1 'Starter Level', Level 2 'JEE Main Level' & Level 3 'JEE Advanced Level'.**
- **Level 1 'Starter Level'** consists of preliminary questions that test basic concepts. After completing this level student will have a solid understanding of fundamentals of the chapter necessary to solve the problems.
- **Level 2 'JEE Main Level'** has single choice correct questions and numerical value questions aimed especially for JEE Main.
- **Level 3 'JEE Advanced Level'** consists of various types of questions; MCQ with one or more than one correct answer, Comprehension Based Questions, Match the Columns and Numerical Value problems as per JEE Advanced Pattern.
- The problems given in JEE Advanced Level are made to be conceptually challenging resulting in practical and relevant practice for JEE Advanced.
- Detailed solutions to all the problems have been provided at the end of every chapter just to help the students in case they stuck somewhere while solving some questions.

At the end, I can say confidently that if you rigorously practice the problems given in this book, then surely you will get an edge in Physics and will increase your chance of getting good JEE Score.

However, I have taken the utmost care while writing this book but if any error or whatsoever has skipped my attention, then please bring it to my notice so that it can be rectified. I would also like to appeal all my fellow Physics Teachers to have a look at the book and share their valuable suggestions for its further improvement.

Pradeep Beniwal
B.Tech, IIT Kharagpur
problemsinphysics@yahoo.com

CONTENTS

CHAPTER~01

VECTORS

LEVEL 01 Starter Level

1.1 Addition and Subtraction

1 Two vectors have magnitudes 3 unit and 4 unit, respectively. What should be the angle between them if the magnitude of the resultant is

(a) 1 unit (b) 5 unit (c) 7 unit

2 Two forces, each of magnitude F have a resultant of the same magnitude F. Find the angle between them.

3 The resultant of two forces $2p$ and $\sqrt{2}p$ is $\sqrt{10}p$. Find the angle between them.

4 The square of the resultant of two forces 4N and 3N exceeds the square of the resultant of the two forces by 12 when they are mutually perpendicular. Find the angle between the vectors.

5 Two forces of 4 dyne and 3 dyne act upon a body. Find the maximum and minimum value of the resultant force on the body.

6 A vector **A** makes an angle of 20° and **B** makes an angle of 110° with the X-axis. The magnitudes of these vectors are 3m and 4m, respectively. Find their resultant.

7 Two forces each numerically equal to 10 dyne are acting as shown in the following figure, then find their resultant.

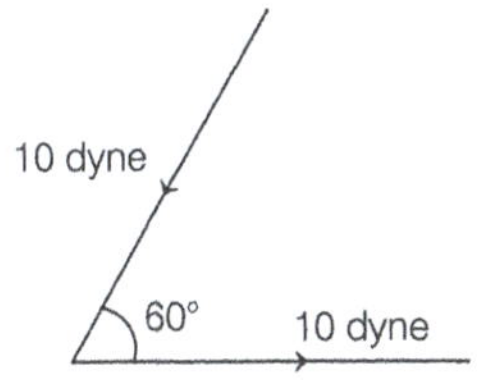

8 Two vectors of 10 units and 5 units make an angle of 120° with each other. Find the magnitude and angle of resultant with vector of 10 unit magnitude.

9 If vectors **P**, **Q** and **R** have magnitudes 5, 12 and 13 units and $\mathbf{P}+\mathbf{Q}=\mathbf{R}$, then find the angle between

(a) **P** and **Q** (b) **Q** and **R** (c) **P** and **R**

10 Five equal forces of 10 N each are applied at one point and all are lying in one plane. If the angles between them are equal, then find the resultant of these forces.

11 Which of the following sets of forces may be in equilibrium?

(a) $F_1 = 3N, F_2 = 5N, F_3 = 1N$
(b) $F_1 = 3N, F_2 = 5N, F_3 = 9N$
(c) $F_1 = 3N, F_1 = 5N, F_3 = 6N$
(d) $F_1 = 3N, F_2 = 5N, F_3 = 15N$

12 The sum of magnitudes of two forces acting at a point is 16N. If the resultant force is 8N and its direction is perpendicular to smaller force, then find the forces.

13 Two vectors **A** and **B** are such that $|\mathbf{A}+\mathbf{B}| = |\mathbf{A}-\mathbf{B}|$. Find the angle between the vectors **A** and **B**.

14 The resultant of two vectors **A** and **B** is perpendicular to the vector **A** and its magnitude is equal to half the magnitude of vector **B**. Find the angle between **A** and **B**.

15 The resultant of two opposite vectors of same magnitude is a ....

16 For the figure write the relation between the three vectors.

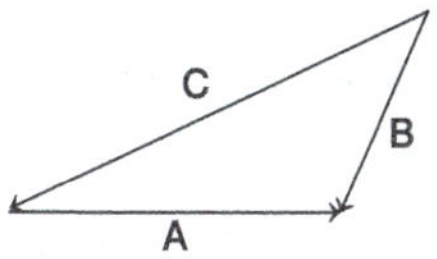

17 A body is moving uniformly on a circle with speed v. Find the magnitude of change in its velocity when it has turned an angle θ.

1.2 Vector Resolution

1 $|\hat{i}| + |\hat{j}| + |\hat{k}| = \ldots\ldots\ldots\ldots$.

2 $\mathbf{A} = 2\hat{i} + \hat{j}, \mathbf{B} = 3\hat{j} - \hat{k}$ and $\mathbf{C} = 6\hat{i} - 2\hat{k}$. Find value of $\mathbf{A} - 2\mathbf{B} + 3\mathbf{C}$.

3 If a unit vector is represented by $(0.5\hat{i} - 0.8\hat{j} + c\hat{k})$, then find the value of c.

4 Forces 3N, 4N and 12N act at a point along *X*, *Y* and *Z*-axis, respectively. Find the magnitude of the resultant force.

5 A force $\mathbf{F} = 6\hat{i} - 8\hat{j} + 10\hat{k}$ N produces an acceleration of 5 ms^{-2} in a body. Find the mass of body.

6 Find the angle that the vector $\mathbf{A} = 2\hat{i} + 3\hat{j}$ makes with (a) *X*-axis (b) *Y*-axis (c) *Z*-axis.

7 If $\mathbf{A} = 3\hat{i} + 4\hat{j}$ and $\mathbf{B} = 7\hat{i} + 24\hat{j}$, find the vector having the same magnitude as **B** and parallel to **A**.

8 If $\mathbf{A} = 2\hat{i} + 4\hat{j} - 5\hat{k}$, then find direction cosines of the vector **A**.

9 If a vector **A** makes angles α, β and γ with the *X*, *Y* and *Z*-axes respectively, then

(a) $\cos^2\alpha + \cos^2\beta + \cos^2\gamma = \ldots$

(b) $\sin^2\alpha + \sin^2\beta + \sin^2\gamma = \ldots$

10 Vector **A** makes equal angles with *X*, *Y* and *Z*-axes. Find value of its components.

11 Find the vector that must be added to the vector $-6\hat{i} - 9\hat{j} + 2\hat{k}$ and $3\hat{i} + 6\hat{j} - 7\hat{k}$, so that the resultant vector is a unit vector along the *Y*-axis.

12 Find the unit vector parallel to the resultant of the vectors $\mathbf{A} = 4\hat{i} + 3\hat{j} + 6\hat{k}$ and $\mathbf{B} = -\hat{i} + 3\hat{j} - 8\hat{k}$.

13 The *x* and *y* components of vector **A** are 4 m and 6 m, respectively. The *x* and *y* components of vector **A** + **B** are 10 m and 9 m, respectively. Calculate for the vector **B** the following

(a) its *x* and *y* components, (b) its length and

(c) the angle it makes with *X*-axis.

14 A particle is acted upon by the forces $\mathbf{F}_1 = 2\hat{i} + a\hat{j} - 3\hat{k}, \mathbf{F}_2 = 5\hat{i} + c\hat{j} - b\hat{k}, \mathbf{F}_3 = b\hat{i} + 5\hat{j} - 7\hat{k}$, $\mathbf{F}_4 = c\hat{i} + 6\hat{j} - a\hat{k}$.

Find the values of the constants a, b, c in order that the particle will be in equilibrium.

15 Add vectors **A**, **B** and **C** each having magnitude of 100 unit and inclined to the *X*-axis at angle 45°, 135° and 315°, respectively.

16 A truck travelling towards North at 50 km/h, then turns West and travels at the same speed. What is the change in velocity?

17 A particle moves from point *P*(2, 3, 5) to point *Q*(3, 4, 5). Find its displacement vector.

18 A bird moves from point (1, −2, 3) to (4, 2, 3). If the speed of the bird is 10m/s, then find the velocity vector of the bird.

19 A person moves 30 m North, then 20 m East and then $30\sqrt{2}$ m South-West. Find his displacement from the original position.

20 A sail boat sails 2 km towards East, 5 km 37° South of East and finally an unknown displacement. If the final displacement of boat from the starting point is 6 km towards East, find the third displacement.

21 A particle moving with initial velocity $2\hat{i} + 3\hat{j} - 4\hat{k}$ has acceleration $-\hat{i} + 2\hat{j} + 5\hat{k}$. Find its velocity at the end of 3 s.

22 Three forces *P*, *Q* and *R* are acting at a point in the plane. The angle between *P* and *Q* and *Q* and *R* are 150° and 120°, respectively. Then for equilibrium, find ratio of forces *P*, *Q* and *R*.

23 Three forces of 3N, 2N and 1N act on a particle as shown in the figure. Calculate the

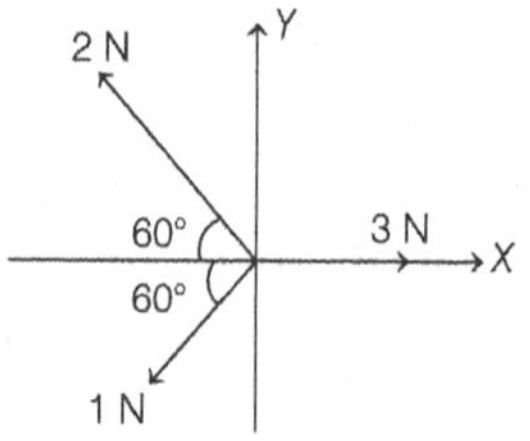

(a) net force along the *X*-axis.

(b) net force along the *Y*-axis.

(c) single additional force required to keep the body in equilibrium.

24 If the four forces as shown in figure are in equilibrium, then express $\mathbf{F}_1$ and $\mathbf{F}_2$ in unit vector form.

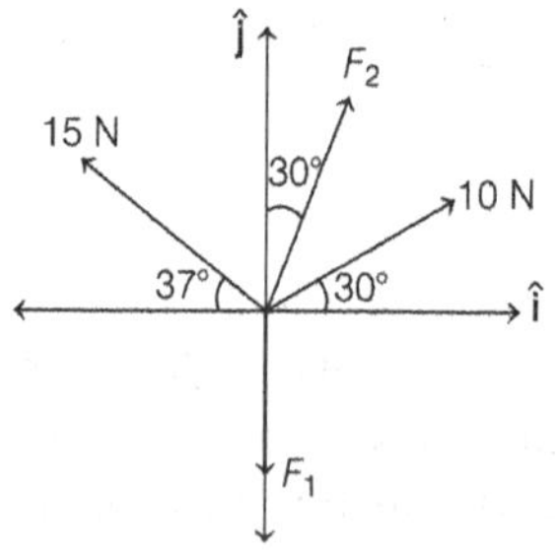

1.3 Dot Product and Cross Product

1 Write the values of the following.

(i) $\hat{j}\cdot\hat{k}$ (ii) $\hat{k}\cdot\hat{k}$ (iii) $\hat{a}\cdot\hat{a}$

(iv) $\hat{k}\cdot(\hat{i}\times\hat{j})$ (v) $(\hat{i}\times\hat{j})\times\hat{k}$

2 Answer the following.

(i) Can 2 similar vectors of different magnitude yield a zero resultant? Can 3 yield?

(ii) Can $\mathbf{a}+\mathbf{b}=\mathbf{a}-\mathbf{b}$?

(iii) Time has a magnitude and direction. Is it a vector?

(iv) When will $\mathbf{a}\times\mathbf{b}=\mathbf{a}\cdot\mathbf{b}$?

(v) Does the unit vectors $\hat{\mathbf{i}}$, $\hat{\mathbf{j}}$ and $\hat{\mathbf{k}}$ have units?

3 Find the scalar product of vectors $\mathbf{A}=2\hat{i}+5\hat{k}$ and $\mathbf{B}=3\hat{j}+5\hat{k}$.

4 Find the angle between the two vectors

(i) $2\hat{i}+2\hat{j}-\hat{k}$ and $\hat{j}-\hat{k}$ (ii) $2\hat{i}+\hat{j}-\hat{k}$ and $\hat{i}-\hat{k}$

(iii) $\hat{i}+\hat{j}+\hat{k}$ and $\hat{i}$ (iv) $2\hat{i}-2\hat{j}-\hat{k}$ and $\hat{i}+\hat{j}$

(v) $\hat{i}+2\hat{j}-\hat{k}$ and $-\hat{i}+\hat{j}-2\hat{k}$

5 If $\mathbf{A}=5\hat{i}+7\hat{j}-3\hat{k}$ and $\mathbf{B}=2\hat{i}+2\hat{j}-c\hat{k}$ are perpendicular vectors, then find the value of c.

6 The scalar product of two vectors is $2\sqrt{3}$ and magnitude of their vector product is 2. Find the angle between them.

7 If $\mathbf{P}\cdot\mathbf{Q}=PQ$, then find the angle between $\mathbf{P}$ and $\mathbf{Q}$.

8 If $|\mathbf{A}\times\mathbf{B}|=\sqrt{3}\mathbf{A}\cdot\mathbf{B}$, then find the value of $|\mathbf{A}+\mathbf{B}|$.

9 Find the value of p for which the vectors $\mathbf{A}=3\hat{i}+2\hat{j}+9\hat{k}$ and $\mathbf{B}=\hat{i}+p\hat{j}+3\hat{k}$ are
(i) perpendicular (ii) parallel.

10 There are two vectors $\mathbf{A}=3\hat{i}+\hat{j}$ and $\mathbf{B}=\hat{j}+2\hat{k}$. For these two vectors, Find

(i) the component of $\mathbf{A}$ along $\mathbf{B}$ and

(ii) the component of $\mathbf{A}$ perpendicular to $\mathbf{B}$ in vector form.

11 Given two vectors $\mathbf{A}=2\hat{i}+2\hat{j}-\hat{k}$ and $\mathbf{B}=3\hat{i}-4\hat{k}$. Find

(a) $\mathbf{A}\cdot\mathbf{B}$

(b) angle between the two vectors

(c) projection of $\mathbf{A}$ on $\mathbf{B}$

(d) projection of $\mathbf{B}$ on $\mathbf{A}$.

12 Find the work done by force $\mathbf{F}=\hat{i}+2\hat{j}-\hat{k}$, when a body is displaced from $\mathbf{r}_1=\hat{i}+\hat{j}$ to $\mathbf{r}_2=2\hat{i}-3\hat{j}+\hat{k}$.

13 The torque of a force $\mathbf{F}$ about a point of position vector $\mathbf{r}$ is given by $\tau=\mathbf{r}\times\mathbf{F}$. Use this formula to find torque of force $2\hat{i}+5\hat{j}$ about a point $2\hat{i}+\hat{j}-\hat{k}$.

14 Find a vector of magnitude 9, which is perpendicular to both the vectors $4\hat{i}+\hat{j}+3\hat{k}$ and $2\hat{i}+\hat{j}+2\hat{k}$.

15 Find the area of the parallelogram whose sides are $\hat{i}+2\hat{j}+3\hat{k}$ and $2\hat{i}+\hat{j}$.

16 Find the area of the parallelogram whose diagonals are given by $\hat{i}+2\hat{j}-\hat{k}$ and $\hat{i}+\hat{j}+2\hat{k}$.

17 $\mathbf{a}=5\hat{i}+4\hat{j}-6\hat{k}$, $\mathbf{b}=-2\hat{i}+2\hat{j}+3\hat{k}$ and $\mathbf{c}=4\hat{i}+3\hat{j}+2\hat{k}$. Find

(a) $\mathbf{a}\times(\mathbf{b}+\mathbf{c})$ (b) $\mathbf{a}\times(\mathbf{b}\times\mathbf{c})$

18 Given that $\mathbf{a}=\hat{i}+\hat{j}+\hat{k}$, $\mathbf{b}=-\hat{i}+\hat{j}-\hat{k}$ and $\mathbf{c}=\hat{i}+\hat{j}-\hat{k}$, then evaluate

(i) $(\mathbf{a}\cdot\mathbf{b})+(\mathbf{b}\cdot\mathbf{c})+(\mathbf{c}\cdot\mathbf{a})$ (ii) $(\mathbf{a}\cdot\mathbf{c})\mathbf{c}+(\mathbf{c}\cdot\mathbf{b})\mathbf{a}$

19 Prove that $(\mathbf{a}+\mathbf{b})\times(\mathbf{a}-\mathbf{b})=-2(\mathbf{a}\times\mathbf{b})$

20 $\mathbf{a}=\hat{i}+\hat{j}$, $\mathbf{b}=\hat{j}+\hat{k}$. Then,

(i) using cross product find the angle between vectors $\mathbf{a}$ and $\mathbf{b}$.

(ii) Find area of the ΔPQS formed by vectors $\mathbf{a}$ and $\mathbf{b}$.

21 (a) If $\mathbf{A}$ points vertically upward and $\mathbf{B}$ points towards East, then what is the direction of $(\mathbf{A}\times\mathbf{B})$?

(b) If $\mathbf{A}$ is vertically downwards and $\mathbf{B}$ is along South, then what is the direction of $(\mathbf{A}\times\mathbf{B})$?

LEVEL 02 JEE Main Level

Single Choice Correct Questions

1 Choose the correct statement.

(a) Electric current is a vector because it has both magnitude and direction.

(b) Time is a vector which has direction always in the forward direction.

(c) All quantities having magnitude and direction are vector quantities.

(d) None of the above

2 A vector may change, if

(a) frame of reference is translated

(b) frame of reference is rotated

(c) vector is translated parallel to itself

(d) vector is rotated

3 At what angle must the two forces $(x+y)$ and $(x-y)$ act, so that the resultant may be $\sqrt{(x^2+y^2)}$?

(a) $\cos^{-1}\left[\frac{-(x^2+y^2)}{2(x^2-y^2)}\right]$ (b) $\cos^{-1}\left[\frac{-2(x^2-y^2)}{x^2+y^2}\right]$

(c) $\cos^{-1}\left[\frac{-(x^2+y^2)}{x^2-y^2}\right]$ (d) $\cos^{-1}\left[\frac{(x^2-y^2)}{x^2+y^2}\right]$

4 If the resultant of two forces of magnitudes P and Q acting at a point at an angle of $60°$ is $\sqrt{7}Q$, then P/Q is

(a) 1 (b) 3/2 (c) 2 (d) 4

5 Square of the resultant of two forces of equal magnitude is equal to three times the product of their magnitudes. The angle between them is

(a) 0° (b) 45° (c) 60° (d) 90°

6 When two vectors of magnitudes P and Q are inclined at an angle θ, the magnitude of their resultant is $2P$. When the inclination is changed to $180° - \theta$, then the magnitude of the resultant is halved. Find the ration $P:Q$.

(a) $\sqrt{2}:\sqrt{3}$ (b) $\sqrt{3}:\sqrt{2}$ (c) $\sqrt{3}:2$ (d) $1:\sqrt{3}$

7 The resultant of two forces $3P$ and $2P$ is R. If the first force is doubled keeping the direction same, then the resultant is also doubled. The angle between the two forces is

(a) 60° (b) 120° (c) 90° (d) 180°

8 Out of the following the resultant of which cannot be 4 N?

(a) 2N and 2N (b) 2N and 4N
(c) 2N and 6N (d) 2N and 8N

9 Maximum and minimum magnitudes of the resultant of two vectors of magnitudes P and Q are in the ratio 3 : 1. Which of the following relations is true?

(a) $P = 2Q$ (b) $P = Q$ (c) $PQ = 1$ (d) None

10 Three forces of magnitudes 30, 60 and P N acting at a point are in equilibrium. If the angle between the first two forces is $60°$, the value of P is

(a) $25\sqrt{2}$ (b) $30\sqrt{3}$ (c) $30\sqrt{6}$ (d) $30\sqrt{7}$

11 Let $\mathbf{C} = \mathbf{A} + \mathbf{B}$, then

(a) $|\mathbf{C}|$ is always greater than $|\mathbf{A}|$
(b) it is possible to have $|\mathbf{C}| < |\mathbf{A}|$ and $|\mathbf{C}| < |\mathbf{B}|$
(c) $\mathbf{C}$ is always equal to $A + B$
(d) $|\mathbf{C}|$ is never equal to $|\mathbf{A}| + |\mathbf{B}|$

12 If $\mathbf{A} = \mathbf{B} + \mathbf{C}$ and the magnitude of $\mathbf{A}, \mathbf{B}$ and $\mathbf{C}$ are 5, 4 and 3 units respectively, the angle between $\mathbf{A}$ and $\mathbf{B}$ is

(a) $\cos^{-1}\left(\frac{3}{5}\right)$ (b) $\cos^{-1}\left(\frac{4}{5}\right)$

(c) $\frac{\pi}{2}$ (d) $\sin^{-1}\left(\frac{3}{4}\right)$

13 The resultant of $\mathbf{P}$ and $\mathbf{Q}$ is perpendicular to $\mathbf{P}$. What is the angle between $\mathbf{P}$ and $\mathbf{Q}$?

(a) $\cos^{-1}\left(\frac{P}{Q}\right)$ (b) $\cos^{-1}\left(-\frac{P}{Q}\right)$

(c) $\sin^{-1}\left(\frac{P}{Q}\right)$ (d) $\sin^{-1}\left(-\frac{P}{Q}\right)$

14 The resultant of two forces acting at an angle of 150° is 10 kg-wt, and is perpendicular to one of the forces. The smaller force is

(a) $10\sqrt{3}$ kg-wt (b) $20\sqrt{3}$ kg-wt
(c) 20 kg-wt (d) $(20/\sqrt{3})$ kg-wt

15 The vectors $\mathbf{P}$, $\mathbf{Q}$ and $\mathbf{R}$ are such that $|\mathbf{P}| = |\mathbf{Q}|$, $|\mathbf{R}| = \sqrt{2}|\mathbf{P}|$ and $\mathbf{P} + \mathbf{Q} + \mathbf{R} = 0$. The angles between $\mathbf{P}$ and $\mathbf{Q}$, $\mathbf{Q}$ and $\mathbf{R}$, $\mathbf{R}$ and $\mathbf{P}$ are respectively (in degrees),

(a) 90°, 135°, 135° (b) 90°, 45°, 45°
(c) 45°, 90°, 90° (d) 45°, 135°, 135°

16 Minimum number of unequal coplanar forces whose vector sum can be equal to zero is

(a) two (b) three
(c) four (d) any

17 How many minimum number of vectors in different planes can be added to give zero resultant?

(a) 2 (b) 3
(c) 4 (d) more than 4

18 Two vectors $\mathbf{A}$ and $\mathbf{B}$ lie in a plane, a third vector lies outside this plane, then the sum of these vectors $\mathbf{A} + \mathbf{B} + \mathbf{C}$

(a) can be zero
(b) can never be zero
(c) lies in a plane containing $\mathbf{A} + \mathbf{B}$
(d) lies in a plane containing $\mathbf{A} - \mathbf{B}$

19 Forces proportional to AB, BC and $2CA$ act along the sides of triangle ABC in order. Their resultant represented in magnitude and direction as

(a) **CA** (b) **AC** (c) **BC** (d) **CB**

20 Figure shows three vectors **a**, **b** and **c**. If $\mathbf{RQ} = 2\mathbf{PR}$. Which of the following relations is correct?

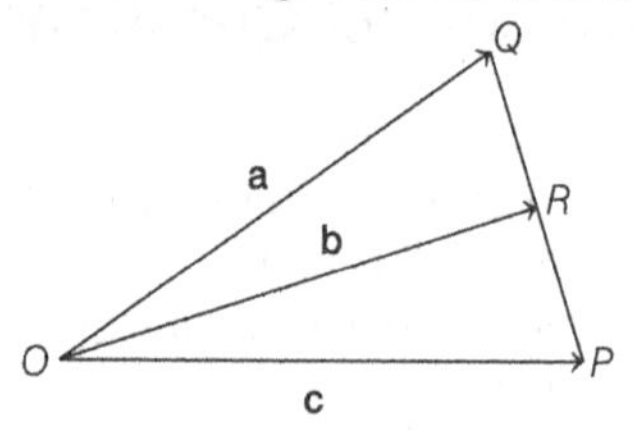

(a) $2\mathbf{a} + \mathbf{c} = 3\mathbf{b}$ (b) $\mathbf{a} + 3\mathbf{c} = 2\mathbf{b}$
(c) $3\mathbf{a} + \mathbf{c} = 2\mathbf{b}$ (d) $\mathbf{a} + 2\mathbf{c} = 3\mathbf{b}$

21 Six vectors, **a** through **f** have the magnitudes and directions indicated in the figure. Which of the following statements is true?

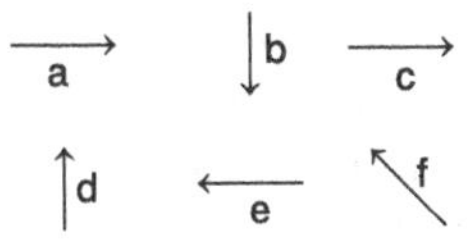

(a) $\mathbf{b}+\mathbf{e}=\mathbf{f}$ (b) $\mathbf{b}+\mathbf{c}=\mathbf{f}$ (c) $\mathbf{d}+\mathbf{c}=\mathbf{f}$ (d) $\mathbf{d}+\mathbf{e}=\mathbf{f}$

22 Which of the following sets of displacements might be capable of returning a car to its starting point?

(a) 4, 6, 8 and 15 km (b) 10, 30, 50 and 120 km
(c) 5, 10, 30 and 50 km (d) 50, 50, 75 and 200 km

23 The direction of a vector **A** is reversed. What are the values of $\Delta\mathbf{A}$ and $\Delta|\mathbf{A}|$?

(a) $+2\mathbf{A}, 0$ (b) $+\mathbf{A}, 0$ (c) $-2\mathbf{A}, 0$ (d) $-\mathbf{A}, 0$

24 The resultant of **A** and **B** is $\mathbf{R}_1$. On reversing the vector **B**, the resultant becomes $\mathbf{R}_2$. The value of $R_1^2+R_2^2$ is

(a) A^2+B^2 (b) A^2-B^2
(c) $2(A^2+B^2)$ (d) $2(A^2-B^2)$

25 **A, B, C, D** and **E** are coplanar vectors having the same magnitude each of 10 units and angle between successive vectors is 72°. If **A** is reversed, then the magnitude of resultant will be

(a) 10 units (b) 20 units
(c) 30 units (d) 40 units

26 Let the angle between two non-zero vectors **A** and **B** be 120° and resultant be C. Then,

(a) C must be equal to $|\mathbf{A}-\mathbf{B}|$
(b) C must be less than $|\mathbf{A}-\mathbf{B}|$
(c) C must be greater than $|\mathbf{A}-\mathbf{B}|$
(d) C may be equal to $|\mathbf{A}-\mathbf{B}|$

27 Arrange the vector subtractions, so that their magnitudes are in decreasing order. If the two vectors **A** and **B** are acting at an angle ($|\mathbf{A}|>|\mathbf{B}|$).

A. 60° B. 90° C. 180° D. 120°

(a) D, C, B, A (b) A, B, D, C
(c) C, D, B, A (d) C, D, A, B

28 If $|\mathbf{a}|=11$, $|\mathbf{b}|=23$, $|\mathbf{a}-\mathbf{b}|=30$, then $|\mathbf{a}+\mathbf{b}|$ is

(a) 10 (b) 20
(c) 30 (d) 40

29 If the sum of two unit vectors is a unit vector, then the magnitude of their difference is

(a) $\sqrt{2}$ (b) $\sqrt{3}$
(c) $\frac{1}{\sqrt{2}}$ (d) $\sqrt{5}$

30 The length of second hand in watch is 1 cm. The change in velocity of its tip in 15 s is

(a) zero (b) $\frac{\pi}{30\sqrt{2}}$ cm/s
(c) $\frac{\pi}{30}$ cm/s (d) $\frac{\pi\sqrt{2}}{30}$ cm/s

31 If $\mathbf{e}_1$ and $\mathbf{e}_2$ are two unit vectors and θ is the angle between them, then $\sin\left(\frac{\theta}{2}\right)$ is

(a) $\frac{1}{2}|\mathbf{e}_1+\mathbf{e}_2|$ (b) $\frac{1}{2}|\mathbf{e}_1-\mathbf{e}_2|$
(c) $\frac{\mathbf{e}_1 \cdot \mathbf{e}_2}{2}$ (d) $\frac{|\mathbf{e}_1\times\mathbf{e}_2|}{2}$

32 An object of m kg with speed of v m/s strikes a wall at an angle θ and rebounds at the same speed and same angle. The magnitude of the change in momentum of the object will be

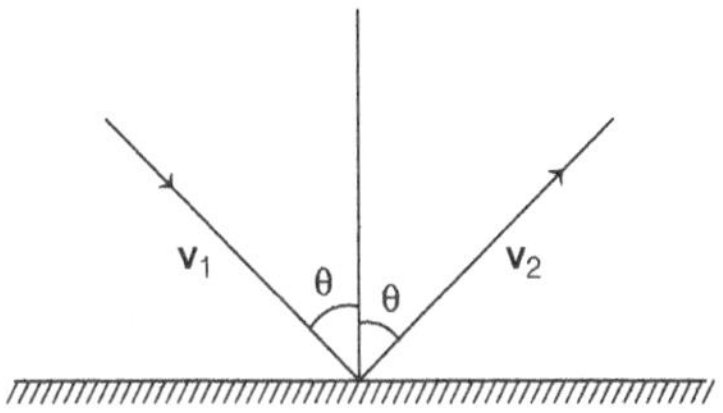

(a) $2mv\cos\theta$ (b) $2mv\sin\theta$
(c) 0 (d) $2mv$

33 x-component of **A** is twice its y-component and $\sqrt{2}$ times of its z-component. What will be the angle made by the vector with the Y-axis?

(a) $\cos^{-1}\left(\frac{2}{\sqrt{7}}\right)$ (b) $\cos^{-1}\left(\frac{1}{\sqrt{7}}\right)$
(c) $\cos^{-1}\left(\frac{1}{\sqrt{6}}\right)$ (d) $\cos^{-1}\left(\frac{2}{\sqrt{6}}\right)$

34 A person pushes a box kept on a horizontal surface with force of 100N. In unit vector notation force **F** can be expressed as

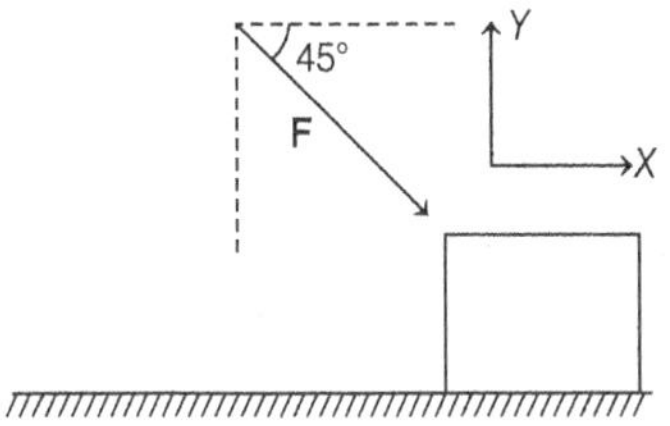

(a) $100(\hat{\mathbf{i}}+\hat{\mathbf{j}})$
(b) $100(\hat{\mathbf{i}}-\hat{\mathbf{j}})$
(c) $50\sqrt{2}(\hat{\mathbf{i}}-\hat{\mathbf{j}})$
(d) $50\sqrt{2}(\hat{\mathbf{i}}+\hat{\mathbf{j}})$

35 The unit vector parallel to the resultant of the vectors $\mathbf{A} = 4\hat{\mathbf{i}} + 3\hat{\mathbf{j}} + 6\hat{\mathbf{k}}$ and $\mathbf{B} = -\hat{\mathbf{i}} + 3\hat{\mathbf{j}} - 8\hat{\mathbf{k}}$ is

(a) $\frac{1}{7}(3\hat{i} + 6\hat{j} - 2\hat{k})$ (b) $\frac{1}{7}(3\hat{i} + 6\hat{j} + 2\hat{k})$

(c) $\frac{1}{49}(3\hat{i} + 6\hat{j} + 2\hat{k})$ (d) $\frac{1}{49}(3\hat{i} + 6\hat{j} - 2\hat{k})$

36 Find the resultant of three vectors **OA**, **OB** and **OC** shown in the following figure. Radius of the circle is R.

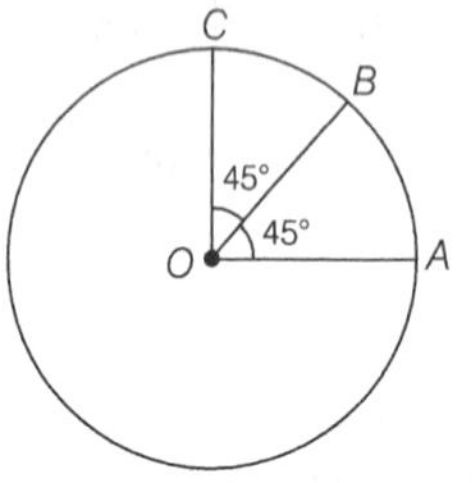

(a) $2R$ (b) $R(1+\sqrt{2})$ (c) $R\sqrt{2}$ (d) $R(\sqrt{2}-1)$

37 Following forces start acting on a particle at rest at the origin of the co-ordinate system simultaneously $\mathbf{F}_1 = -4\hat{\mathbf{i}} - 5\hat{\mathbf{j}} + 5\hat{\mathbf{k}}$, $\mathbf{F}_2 = -5\hat{\mathbf{i}} + 8\hat{\mathbf{j}} + 6\hat{\mathbf{k}}$, $\mathbf{F}_3 = -3\hat{\mathbf{i}} + 4\hat{\mathbf{j}} - 7\hat{\mathbf{k}}$ and $\mathbf{F}_4 = 12\hat{\mathbf{i}} - 3\hat{\mathbf{j}} - 2\hat{\mathbf{k}}$, then the particle will move

(a) in xy-plane (b) in yz-plane
(c) in xz-plane (d) along X-axis

38 Given two vectors $\mathbf{A} = \hat{\mathbf{i}} - 2\hat{\mathbf{j}} - 3\hat{\mathbf{k}}$ and $\mathbf{B} = 4\hat{\mathbf{i}} - 2\hat{\mathbf{j}} + 6\hat{\mathbf{k}}$. The angle made by $(\mathbf{A}+\mathbf{B})$ with the X-axis is

(a) 30° (b) 45°
(c) 60° (d) 90°

39 Given that, $\mathbf{A} = 2\hat{\mathbf{i}} + p\hat{\mathbf{j}} + q\hat{\mathbf{k}}$ and $\mathbf{B} = 5\hat{\mathbf{i}} + 7\hat{\mathbf{j}} + 3\hat{\mathbf{k}}$. If $\mathbf{A} \| \mathbf{B}$, then the values of p and q are

(a) $\frac{14}{5}$ and $\frac{6}{5}$ (b) $\frac{14}{3}$ and $\frac{6}{5}$

(c) $\frac{6}{5}$ and $\frac{1}{3}$ (d) $\frac{3}{4}$ and $\frac{1}{4}$

40 If $\mathbf{A} = 2\hat{\mathbf{i}} - 3\hat{\mathbf{j}} + 4\hat{\mathbf{k}}$, its components in yz-plane and zx-plane are respectively

(a) $\sqrt{13}$ and 5 (b) 5 and $2\sqrt{5}$
(c) $2\sqrt{5}$ and $\sqrt{13}$ (d) $\sqrt{13}$ and $\sqrt{29}$

41 Consider East as positive X-axis, North as positive Y-axis. A girl walks 10 m East first time, then 10 m in a direction 30° West of North for the second time and then third time in unknown direction and magnitude, so as to return to her initial position. What is her third displacement in unit vector notation?

(a) $-5\hat{i} - 5\sqrt{3}\hat{j}$ (b) $5\hat{i} - 5\sqrt{3}\hat{j}$

(c) $-5\hat{i} + 5\sqrt{3}\hat{j}$ (d) She cannot return

42 Find the resultant of the following two vectors **A** and **B**.

A : 40 units due East,

B : 25 units 37° North of West.

(a) 25 units 37° North of West
(b) 25 units 37° North of East
(c) 40 units 53° North of West
(d) 40 units 53° North of East

43 The condition that $(\mathbf{a}\cdot\mathbf{b})^2 = (a^2b^2)$ is satisfied, when

(a) $\mathbf{a} \| \mathbf{b}$ (b) $\mathbf{a} \neq \mathbf{b}$ (c) $\mathbf{a}\cdot\mathbf{b} = 1$ (d) $\mathbf{a} \perp \mathbf{b}$

44 If $\mathbf{a} = 2\hat{\mathbf{i}} - 3\hat{\mathbf{j}}$, $\mathbf{b} = 2\hat{\mathbf{j}} + 3\hat{\mathbf{k}}$, then $(\mathbf{a}+\mathbf{b})\cdot(\mathbf{a}-\mathbf{b})$

(a) 0 (b) -8 (c) 9 (d) -10

45 The angle between two vectors given by $(6\hat{\mathbf{i}} + 6\hat{\mathbf{j}} - 3\hat{\mathbf{k}})$ and $(7\hat{\mathbf{i}} + 4\hat{\mathbf{j}} + 4\hat{\mathbf{k}})$ is

(a) $\cos^{-1}\left(\frac{3}{5}\right)$ (b) $\cos^{-1}\left(\frac{5}{\sqrt{3}}\right)$

(c) $\sin^{-1}\left(\frac{2}{\sqrt{3}}\right)$ (d) $\sin^{-1}\left(\frac{\sqrt{5}}{3}\right)$

46 If $\mathbf{A}+\mathbf{B} = 2\hat{\mathbf{i}}$ and $\mathbf{A}-\mathbf{B} = 4\hat{\mathbf{j}}$, then angle between **A** and **B** is

(a) 127° (b) 143° (c) 53° (d) 37°

47 Given that, $A = B$. Find the angle between $\mathbf{A}+\mathbf{B}$ and $\mathbf{A}-\mathbf{B}$.

(a) 45° (b) 60° (c) 90° (d) 120°

48 $\mathbf{A} = A\cos\theta\,\hat{\mathbf{i}} + A\sin\theta\,\hat{\mathbf{j}}$. Another vector **B** which is perpendicular to **A** is

(a) $B\cos\theta\,\hat{i} + B\sin\theta\,\hat{j}$ (b) $B\sin\theta\,\hat{i} + B\cos\theta\,\hat{j}$

(c) $B\sin\theta\,\hat{i} - B\cos\theta\,\hat{j}$ (d) $A\cos\theta\,\hat{i} - A\sin\theta\,\hat{j}$

49 Vectors $\mathbf{P} = a\hat{\mathbf{i}} + a\hat{\mathbf{j}} + 3\hat{\mathbf{k}}$ and $\mathbf{Q} = a\hat{\mathbf{i}} - 2\hat{\mathbf{j}} - \hat{\mathbf{k}}$ are perpendicular to each other. The positive value of a is

(a) 3 (b) 2 (c) 1 (d) zero

50 The three vectors $\mathbf{A} = 3\hat{\mathbf{i}} - 2\hat{\mathbf{j}} + \hat{\mathbf{k}}$, $\mathbf{B} = \hat{\mathbf{i}} - 3\hat{\mathbf{j}} + 5\hat{\mathbf{k}}$ and $\mathbf{C} = 2\hat{\mathbf{i}} + \hat{\mathbf{j}} - 4\hat{\mathbf{k}}$ form

(a) an equilateral triangle (b) isosceles triangle
(c) a right angled triangle (d) no triangle

51 The vector sum of two forces is perpendicular to their vector difference. In that case, the forces

(a) are equal to each other
(b) are equal to each other in magnitude
(c) are not equal to each other in magnitude
(d) cannot be predicted

52 If $\hat{n} = a\hat{i} + b\hat{j}$ is perpendicular to the vector $(\hat{i} + \hat{j})$, then the value of a and b may be

(a) 1, 0 (b) −2, 0 (c) 3, 0 (d) $\frac{1}{\sqrt{2}}, -\frac{1}{\sqrt{2}}$

53 A vector perpendicular to the vector $(\hat{i} + 2\hat{j})$ and having magnitude $3\sqrt{5}$ units is

(a) $3\hat{i} + 6\hat{j}$ (b) $6\hat{i} - 3\hat{j}$
(c) $4\hat{i} - 2\hat{j}$ (d) $\hat{i} - 2\hat{j}$

54 A body constrained to move in y-direction is subjected to a force given by $\mathbf{F} = (-2\hat{i} + 15\hat{j} + 6\hat{k})$N. What is the work done by this force in moving the body through a distance of 10 m?

(a) 190J (b) 160J (c) 150J (d) 20J

55 The projection of **A** on **B** is

(a) $\mathbf{A} \cdot \mathbf{B}$ (b) $\mathbf{A} \cdot \hat{\mathbf{B}}$ (c) $\mathbf{B} \cdot \mathbf{A}$ (d) $\hat{\mathbf{A}} \cdot \hat{\mathbf{B}}$

56 The velocity of a particle is $\mathbf{v} = 6\hat{i} + 2\hat{j} - 2\hat{k}$. The component of the velocity of a particle parallel to vector $\mathbf{a} = \hat{i} + \hat{j} + \hat{k}$ in vector form is

(a) $6\hat{i} + 2\hat{j} + 2\hat{k}$ (b) $2\hat{i} + 2\hat{j} + 2\hat{k}$
(c) $\hat{i} + \hat{j} + \hat{k}$ (d) $6\hat{i} + 2\hat{j} - 2\hat{k}$

57 In previous problem, the component of **v** in perpendicular direction of **a** in vector form is

(a) $-2\hat{i} - 2\hat{j} - 2\hat{k}$ (b) $4\hat{i} - 4\hat{k}$
(c) $6\hat{i} + 2\hat{j} - 2\hat{k}$ (d) $2\hat{i} + 2\hat{j} + 2\hat{k}$

58 Given $|\mathbf{A}_1| = 2, |\mathbf{A}_2| = 3$ and $|\mathbf{A}_1 + \mathbf{A}_2| = 3$. The magnitude of $(\mathbf{A}_1 + 2\mathbf{A}_2) \cdot (3\mathbf{A}_1 - 4\mathbf{A}_2)$ is

(a) 64 (b) 60
(c) 62 (d) 61

59 If l_1, m_1, n_1 and l_2, m_2, n_2 are the directional cosines of two vectors and θ is the angle between them, then their value of $\cos\theta$ is

(a) $l_1 l_2 + m_1 m_2 + n_1 n_2$ (b) $l_1 m_1 + m_1 n_1 + n_1 l_1$
(c) $l_2 m_2 + m_2 n_2 + n_2 l_2$ (d) $m_1 l_2 + l_2 m_2 + n_1 m_2$

60 Which of the following expression is meaningless?

(a) $(\mathbf{a} \times \mathbf{b}) \cdot \mathbf{c}$ (b) $(\mathbf{a} \cdot \mathbf{b}) \cdot (\mathbf{c} \times \mathbf{d})$
(c) $(\mathbf{a} \times \mathbf{b}) \times (\mathbf{c} \times \mathbf{d})$ (d) $\mathbf{a} \cdot (\mathbf{b} \times \mathbf{c})$

61 $\mathbf{A} \times \mathbf{B}$ is perpendicular to (where **A** and **B** are non-zero and non-collinear vector)

(a) **A** (b) **B**
(c) **A** + **B** (d) All of these

62 Magnetic force on a moving positive charge is defined by $\mathbf{F} = q\mathbf{v} \times \mathbf{B}$.
Here, **v** = velocity of the body and **B** = magnetic field.
If velocity of charged particle is directed vertically upward and magnetic force is directed towards West, the direction of magnetic field is

(a) North (b) East (c) West (d) South

63 The angle between $\mathbf{A} \times \mathbf{B}$ and $\mathbf{B} \times \mathbf{A}$ is

(a) 0 (b) π (c) $\frac{\pi}{2}$ (d) $\frac{\pi}{4}$

64 **A** and **B** are two vectors. Mark the wrong statement in the following.

(a) $\mathbf{A} \cdot \mathbf{B} = \mathbf{B} \cdot \mathbf{A}$ (b) $\mathbf{A} + \mathbf{B} = \mathbf{B} + \mathbf{A}$
(c) $\mathbf{A} \times \mathbf{B} = \mathbf{B} \times \mathbf{A}$ (d) $\mathbf{A} \times \mathbf{B} = -\mathbf{B} \times \mathbf{A}$

65 Let **F** be the force acting on a particle having position vector **r** and τ be the torque of this force about the origin. Then,

(a) $\mathbf{r} \cdot \tau = 0$ and $\mathbf{F} \cdot \tau \neq 0$ (b) $\mathbf{r} \cdot \tau \neq 0$ and $\mathbf{F} \cdot \tau = 0$
(c) $\mathbf{r} \cdot \tau \neq 0$ and $\mathbf{F} \cdot \tau \neq 0$ (d) $\mathbf{r} \cdot \tau = 0$ and $\mathbf{F} \cdot \tau = 0$

66 If three vectors satisfy the relation $\mathbf{A} \cdot \mathbf{B} = 0$ and $\mathbf{A} \cdot \mathbf{C} = 0$, then **A** can be parallel to

(a) **C** (b) **B** (c) $\mathbf{B} \times \mathbf{C}$ (d) $\mathbf{B} \cdot \mathbf{C}$

67 Choose the false statement.

(a) A null vector can have any arbitrary direction.
(b) If $\mathbf{A} \times \mathbf{B} = 0$, then either**A** and **B** or both must have zero magnitude.
(c) The component of a vector is a vector.
(d) All of the above

68 If the angle between the vectors **A** and **B** is θ, then $(\mathbf{B} \times \mathbf{A}) \cdot \mathbf{A}$ is equal to

(a) $BA^2 \cos\theta$ (b) $BA^2 \sin\theta$
(c) $BA^2 \sin\theta \cos\theta$ (d) zero

69 What is the torque of the force $\mathbf{F} = (2\hat{i} - 3\hat{j} + 4\hat{k})$N acting at the point $\mathbf{r} = (3\hat{i} - 2\hat{j} + 3\hat{k})$m about the origin

(a) $6\hat{i} - 6\hat{j} + 12\hat{k}$ (b) $17\hat{i} - 6\hat{j} - 13\hat{k}$
(c) $-6\hat{i} + 6\hat{j} - 12\hat{k}$ (d) $\hat{i} - 6\hat{j} - 5\hat{k}$

70 For a body, angular velocity $\omega = \hat{i} - 2\hat{j} + 3\hat{k}$ and radius vector $\mathbf{r} = \hat{i} + \hat{j} + \hat{k}$. Its velocity $\mathbf{v} = \omega \times \mathbf{r}$ is

(a) $5\hat{i} + 2\hat{j} + 3\hat{k}$ (b) $-5\hat{i} + 2\hat{j} + 3\hat{k}$
(c) $-5\hat{i} - 2\hat{j} + 3\hat{k}$ (d) $-5\hat{i} - 2\hat{j} - 3\hat{k}$

71 If the vectors $(\hat{i} + \hat{j} + \hat{k})$ and $3\hat{i}$ form two sides a triangle, the area of the triangle is

(a) $\sqrt{10}$ units (b) $2\sqrt{3}$ units
(c) $3/\sqrt{2}$ units (d) $3\sqrt{2}$ units

72 The area of the parallelogram formed by $\mathbf{A} = 2\hat{i} + \hat{j} - 3\hat{k}$ and $\mathbf{B} = 12\hat{j} - 2\hat{k}$ is nearly

(a) 72 (b) 56 (c) 38 (d) 42

Numerical Value Questions

1 Sum of the following four forces is zero. If magnitudes of two unknown forces are x and y, then find $x + y$.

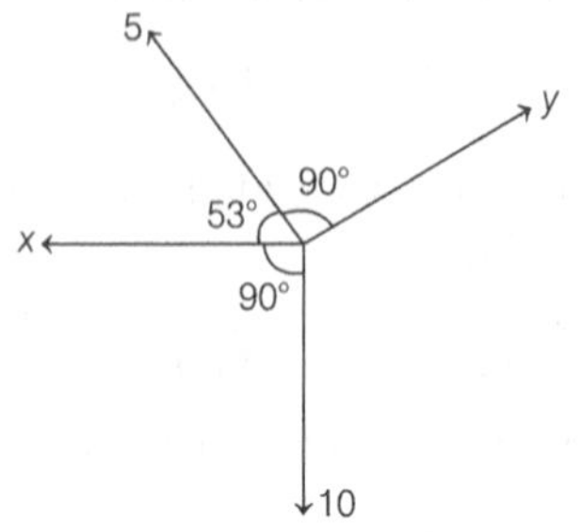

2 If a vector makes angles $\frac{\pi}{3}, \frac{\pi}{3}$ and $\frac{\pi}{n}$ with X-axis, Y-axis and Z-axis respectively, then find the value of n.

3 The magnitude of resultant of two vectors **A** and **B** is 2. The magnitude of **A** is $2\sqrt{3}$ and makes an angle of 30° with the resultant. Find the magnitude of **B**.

4 If a unit vector is represented by $(0.5\hat{i} - 2\alpha\hat{j} + \alpha\hat{k})$, then the value of α is $\sqrt{\frac{3}{\beta}}$. Find β.

5 In the given figure, if the angle between **A** and − **C** is $5\alpha°$, then find the value of α.

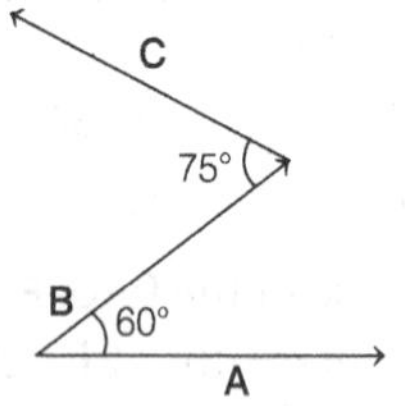

6 Consider the two vectors.
$\mathbf{L} = \hat{i} + 2\hat{j} + 3\hat{k}$ and $\mathbf{l} = 4\hat{i} + 5\hat{j} + 6\hat{k}$
The value of the scalar α such that the vector $\mathbf{L} - \alpha\mathbf{l}$ is perpendicular to **L** is $\frac{n}{16}$. Find n.

7 Angle between two vectors $\hat{i} + \hat{j} + \hat{k}$ and $\hat{i} + \hat{j}$ is θ. Find the value of $2\sec^2\theta$.

8 Area of the parallelogram $ABCD$ formed by point $A(-2, 0)$, $B(0, -2)$, $C(1, 1)$ and $D(-1, 3)$ is η sq. units. Find η.

9 If $|\hat{a} + \hat{b}| = 2$, then what is the value of $\hat{a}\cdot\hat{b} - |\hat{a}\times\hat{b}|$?

10 What is the value of n, so that vectors $2\hat{i} + 3\hat{j} - 2\hat{k}$, $5\hat{i} + n\hat{j} + \hat{k}$ and $-\hat{i} + 2\hat{j} + 3\hat{k}$ may be coplanar?

11 Two constant forces $\mathbf{F}_1 = (2\hat{i} - 3\hat{j} + 3\hat{k})$ N and $\mathbf{F}_2 = (\hat{i} + \hat{j} - 2\hat{k})$ N act on a body and displace it from the position $\mathbf{r}_1 = (\hat{i} + 2\hat{j} - 2\hat{k})$ m to the position $\mathbf{r}_2 = (7\hat{i} + 10\hat{j} + 5\hat{k})$ m. What is the work done (in J)?

12 A particle moving along a straight line with speed 10m/s changes its direction of motion by 60° without changing its speed. Find the magnitude of change in velocity of the particle.

13 An engine exerts a force $\mathbf{F} = (20\hat{i} - 3\hat{j} + 5\hat{k})$ N and moves with velocity $\mathbf{v} = (6\hat{i} + 20\hat{j} - 9\hat{k})$ m/s. What is the power of the engine (in watt)?

14 The diagonals of a parallelogram are represented by vectors $\mathbf{p} = 5\hat{i} - 4\hat{j} + 3\hat{k}$ and $\mathbf{q} = 3\hat{i} + 2\hat{j} - \hat{k}$. Then, the area of the parallelogram is $3\sqrt{n}$. Find n.

15 If $|\mathbf{a}| = 5, |\mathbf{b}| = 13, |\mathbf{a}\times\mathbf{b}| = 25$, then find $\mathbf{a}\cdot\mathbf{b}$.

16 Let $\mathbf{A} = \hat{i} + \hat{j} + \hat{k}$, $\mathbf{B} = a\hat{i} - \hat{j} - \hat{k}$ and $\mathbf{C} = \hat{i} + \hat{j} + b\hat{k}$, given $\mathbf{A} \perp \mathbf{B}$ and $\mathbf{A} \perp \mathbf{C}$. If angle between **B** and **C** is $\frac{\pi}{n}$, then find n.

17 $|\mathbf{a}| = 2$, $|\mathbf{b}| = 3$, $|\mathbf{c}| = 6$. Angle between **a** and **b**, **b** and **c** or **c** and **a** is 120° each.
If $|\mathbf{a} + \mathbf{b} + \mathbf{c}| = \sqrt{n}$, then find n.

18 $\mathbf{A} = 2\hat{i} + \hat{j} + \hat{k}$ and $\mathbf{B} = 10\hat{i} + 5\hat{j} + 5\hat{k}$. If the magnitude of component of $\mathbf{B} - \mathbf{A}$ along **A** is $4\sqrt{x}$, then find the value of x.

19 Consider three vectors $\mathbf{A} = \hat{i} + \hat{j} - 2\hat{k}$, $\mathbf{B} = \hat{i} - \hat{j} + \hat{k}$ and $\mathbf{C} = 2\hat{i} - 3\hat{j} + 4\hat{k}$. A vector **X** of the form $\alpha\mathbf{A} + \beta\mathbf{B}$ (α and β are numbers) is perpendicular to **C**. Find $\frac{\alpha}{\beta}$.

20 Two vectors **P** and **Q** are added, the magnitude of resultant is 15 units. If **Q** is reversed and added to **P**, resultant has a magnitude $\sqrt{113}$ units. The resultant of **P** and a vector perpendicular to **P** and equal in magnitude to **Q** has a magnitude x. Find x.

LEVEL 03 JEE Advanced Level

Single Choice Correct Questions

1 Resultant of two vectors of magnitude P and Q is of magnitude Q. If the magnitude of $\mathbf{Q}$ is doubled now, the angle made by new resultant with $\mathbf{P}$ is

(a) 30° (b) 90° (c) 60° (d) 120°

2 $\mathbf{P}, \mathbf{Q}, \mathbf{R}, \mathbf{S}$ are vectors of equal magnitudes. If $\mathbf{P}+\mathbf{Q}-\mathbf{R}=0$, angle between $\mathbf{P}$ and $\mathbf{Q}$ is θ_1. If $\mathbf{P}+\mathbf{Q}-\mathbf{S}=0$, angle between $\mathbf{P}$ and $\mathbf{S}$ is θ_2. The ratio of θ_1 to θ_2 is

(a) 1 : 2 (b) 2 : 1
(c) 1 : 1 (d) $1:\sqrt{3}$

3 If $\mathbf{a}=\hat{\mathbf{i}}+4\hat{\mathbf{j}}+2\sqrt{2}\,\hat{\mathbf{k}}$ and $\mathbf{b}=(\hat{\mathbf{i}}+\hat{\mathbf{j}})\sqrt{2}$, then find component of $\mathbf{a}$ perpendicular to $\mathbf{b}$.

(a) $\frac{5}{\sqrt{2}}$ (b) $\frac{9}{\sqrt{2}}$ (c) $\frac{10}{\sqrt{2}}$ (d) None of these

4 The angle between the diagonals of a cube with edges of unit length is

(a) $\sin^{-1}(1/3)$ (b) $\cos^{-1}(1/3)$
(c) $\tan^{-1}(1/3)$ (d) $\cot^{-1}(1/3)$

5 A particle is displaced from $A \equiv (2, 2, 4)$ to $B \equiv (5, -3, -1)$. A constant force of 34N acts in the direction of $\mathbf{AP}$, where $P \equiv (10, 2, -11)$. (Co-ordinates are in m). Find work done by the force.

(a) 100 J (b) 198 J
(c) 230 J (d) 248 J

6 When $t=0$, a particle at (1, 0, 0) moves towards (4, 4, 12) with a constant speed of 65 m/s. The position of the particle is measured in metres and time in seconds. Assuming constant velocity, the position of the particle at $t=2$ s is

(a) $(13\hat{\mathbf{i}}-120\hat{\mathbf{j}}+40\hat{\mathbf{k}})$m (b) $(40\hat{\mathbf{i}}+31\hat{\mathbf{j}}-120\hat{\mathbf{k}})$m
(c) $(13\hat{\mathbf{i}}-40\hat{\mathbf{j}}+12\hat{\mathbf{k}})$m (d) $(31\hat{\mathbf{i}}+40\hat{\mathbf{j}}+120\hat{\mathbf{k}})$m

7 Two balloons are moving in air with velocities $\mathbf{v}_1=\{2t\hat{\mathbf{i}}+(t-2)\hat{\mathbf{j}}\}$ m/s and $\mathbf{v}_2=\{(t-4)\hat{\mathbf{i}}+t\,\hat{\mathbf{j}}\}$ m/s, then at what 't' balloons are parallel to each other?

(a) (5/4) s (b) (4/5) s
(c) (10/3) s (d) $(-3+\sqrt{17})$ s

8 The greatest and least resultant of two forces acting at a point are 29 kg-wt and 5 kg-wt, respectively. If each force is increased by 3 kg-wt, the magnitude of the resultant of new forces acting at right angles to each other is

(a) 45 kg-wt (b) 35 kg-wt
(c) 25 kg-wt (d) 15 kg-wt

9 Vector $\mathbf{a}$ is perpendicular to $\mathbf{b}$. Component of $\mathbf{a}-\mathbf{b}$ along $\mathbf{a}+\mathbf{b}$ will be

(a) zero (b) $a-b$
(c) $\frac{a^2-b^2}{\sqrt{a^2+b^2}}$ (d) $\sqrt{a^2+b^2}$

10 The value of $\hat{\mathbf{i}}\times(\mathbf{r}\times\hat{\mathbf{i}})+\hat{\mathbf{j}}\times(\mathbf{r}\times\hat{\mathbf{j}})+\hat{\mathbf{k}}\times(\mathbf{r}\times\hat{\mathbf{k}})$ is

(a) $\mathbf{r}$ (b) $2\mathbf{r}$
(c) $3\mathbf{r}$ (d) $4\mathbf{r}$

11 Figure shows $ABCDEF$ as a regular hexagon. What is the value of $\mathbf{AB}+\mathbf{AC}+\mathbf{AD}+\mathbf{AE}+\mathbf{AF}$?

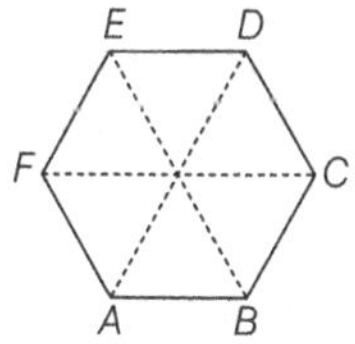

(a) $\mathbf{AO}$ (b) $2\mathbf{AO}$ (c) $4\mathbf{AO}$ (d) $6\mathbf{AO}$

12 From figure, the correct relation is

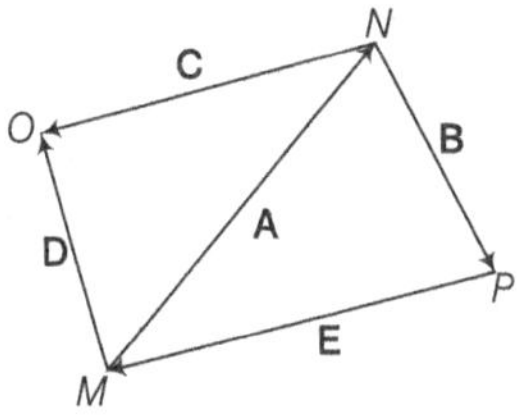

(a) $\mathbf{A}+\mathbf{B}+\mathbf{E}=0$ (b) $\mathbf{C}-\mathbf{D}=-\mathbf{A}$
(c) $\mathbf{B}+\mathbf{E}-\mathbf{C}=-\mathbf{D}$ (d) All of these

13 Let $\mathbf{a}=2\hat{\mathbf{i}}+\hat{\mathbf{j}}-2\hat{\mathbf{k}}$ and $\mathbf{b}=\hat{\mathbf{i}}+\hat{\mathbf{j}}$. If $\mathbf{c}$ is a vector such that $\mathbf{a}\cdot\mathbf{c}=|\mathbf{c}|$, $|\mathbf{c}-\mathbf{a}|=2\sqrt{2}$ and the angle between $\mathbf{a}\times\mathbf{b}$ and $\mathbf{c}$ is 30°, then find $|(\mathbf{a}\times\mathbf{b})\times\mathbf{c}|$.

(a) 2/3 (b) 3/2
(c) 2 (d) 3

14 The resultant of two vectors $(\mathbf{P}+\mathbf{Q})$ and $(\mathbf{P}-\mathbf{Q})$ is a vector of magnitude $\sqrt{3P^2+Q^2}$. The angle between the given two vectors is

(a) $\frac{\pi}{2}$ (b) $\frac{\pi}{4}$
(c) $\frac{\pi}{3}$ (d) None of these

15 If $\mathbf{a}$ and $\mathbf{b}$ are two unit vectors such that $\mathbf{a}+2\mathbf{b}$ and $5\mathbf{a}-4\mathbf{b}$ are perpendicular to each other, then the angle between $\mathbf{a}$ and $\mathbf{b}$ is

(a) $\frac{\pi}{4}$ (b) $\frac{\pi}{3}$ (c) $\cos^{-1}\left(\frac{1}{3}\right)$ (d) $\cos^{-1}\left(\frac{2}{7}\right)$

16 If $\mathbf{a}_1$ and $\mathbf{a}_2$ are two non-collinear unit vectors and if $|\mathbf{a}_1 + \mathbf{a}_2| = \sqrt{3}$, then the value of $(\mathbf{a}_1 - \mathbf{a}_2)\cdot(2\mathbf{a}_1 + \mathbf{a}_2)$ is

(a) 2 (b) $\frac{3}{2}$ (c) $\frac{1}{2}$ (d) 1

17 Three coplanar vectors **A**, **B** and **C** have magnitudes 4, 3 and 2, respectively. If the angle between any two vectors is 120°, then which of the following vector may be equal to $\frac{3\mathbf{A}}{4} + \frac{\mathbf{B}}{3} + \frac{\mathbf{C}}{2} = ?$

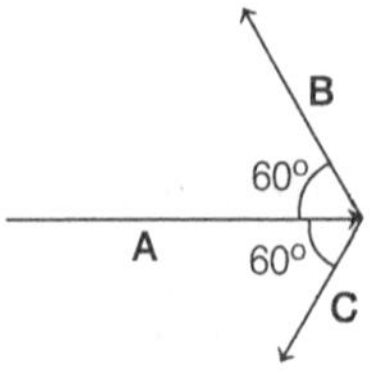

(a)  (b)  (c)  (d) 

18 The resultant of three vectors 1, 2 and 3 units whose directions are those of the sides of an equilateral triangle all taken in the same order is at an angle of

(a) 30° with the first vector
(b) 15° with the first vector
(c) 100° with the first vector
(d) 150° with the first vector

19 **A** and **B** have angle θ between them. If **A** + **B** and **A** − **B**, respectively subtend angles α and β with **A**, then find $(\tan\alpha + \tan\beta)$.

(a) $\frac{AB\sin\theta}{(A^2 + B^2\cos^2\theta)}$ (b) $\frac{2AB\sin\theta}{(A^2 - B^2\cos^2\theta)}$

(c) $\frac{A^2\sin^2\theta}{(A^2 + B^2\cos^2\theta)}$ (d) $\frac{B^2\sin^2\theta}{(A^2 - B^2\cos^2\theta)}$

20 There are three vectors **P**, **Q** and **R**. The angle between **P** and **Q** is 60° and **R** is perpendicular to the plane containing the vectors **P** and **Q**. Consider the following relations.

(1) $\mathbf{P} + \mathbf{Q} + \mathbf{R} = 0$ (2) $\mathbf{P} \times \mathbf{Q} = \mathbf{R}$ (3) $\mathbf{P} \times \mathbf{R} = \mathbf{Q}$

The possible relations are

(a) (1) and (2) (b) (1) and (3)
(c) (2) and (3) (d) only (2)

21 If $|\hat{\mathbf{a}} - \hat{\mathbf{b}}| = \sqrt{2}$, then calculate the value of $|\hat{\mathbf{a}} + \sqrt{3}\hat{\mathbf{b}}|$.

(a) 1 (b) 2 (c) 3 (d) 4

22 The resultant of two vectors **P** and **Q** is **R**. If the magnitude of **Q** is doubled the new resultant becomes perpendicular to **P**, then magnitude of **R** is

(a) $\frac{P^2 - Q^2}{2PQ}$ (b) $\frac{P+Q}{P-Q}$ (c) Q (d) $\frac{P}{Q}$

23 The resultant of **P** and **Q** is **R**. If **Q** is doubled, **R** is doubled, when **Q** is reversed, **R** is again doubled, then $P : Q : R$ is

(a) $\sqrt{2} : \sqrt{3} : \sqrt{2}$ (b) $\sqrt{3} : \sqrt{2} : \sqrt{3}$
(c) $1 : \sqrt{2} : \sqrt{3}$ (d) $\sqrt{3} : 2 : \sqrt{3}$

24 Let **a**, **b**, **c** be vectors of length 3, 4, 5, respectively. Let **a** be perpendicular to **b** + **c**, **b** to **c** + **a** and **c** to **a** + **b**. Then, $|\mathbf{a} + \mathbf{b} + \mathbf{c}|$ is

(a) $2\sqrt{5}$ (b) $2\sqrt{2}$
(c) $10\sqrt{5}$ (d) $5\sqrt{2}$

25 Let **a**, **b** and **c** are three unit vectors such that **a** + **b** + **c** is also a unit vector. If pairwise angles between **a**, **b** and **c** are θ_1, θ_2 and θ_3 respectively, then find $\cos\theta_1 + \cos\theta_2 + \cos\theta_3$.

(a) 3 (b) −3 (c) 1 (d) −1

26 The unit vector which is orthogonal to the vector $3\hat{i} + 2\hat{j} + 6\hat{k}$ and is coplanar with the vectors $2\hat{i} + \hat{j} + \hat{k}$ and $\hat{i} - \hat{j} + \hat{k}$ is

(a) $\frac{2\hat{i} - 6\hat{j} + \hat{k}}{\sqrt{41}}$ (b) $\frac{2\hat{i} - 3\hat{j}}{\sqrt{13}}$

(c) $\frac{3\hat{j} - \hat{k}}{\sqrt{10}}$ (d) $\frac{4\hat{i} + 3\hat{j} - 3\hat{k}}{\sqrt{34}}$

27 x-component of **a** is twice of its y-component. If the magnitude of the vector is $5\sqrt{2}$ and it makes an angle of 135° with Z-axis, then the components of vector is

(a) $2\sqrt{3}, \sqrt{3}, -3$ (b) $2\sqrt{6}, \sqrt{6}, -6$
(c) $2\sqrt{5}, \sqrt{5}, -5$ (d) None of these

28 The vector $(\mathbf{a} + 3\mathbf{b})$ is perpendicular to $(7\mathbf{a} - 5\mathbf{b})$ and $(\mathbf{a} - 4\mathbf{b})$ is perpendicular to $(7\mathbf{a} - 2\mathbf{b})$. The angle between **a** and **b** is

(a) 30° (b) 45°
(c) 60° (d) None of these

29 If the position vector of the vertices of a triangle are $\hat{i} - \hat{j} + 2\hat{k}$, $2\hat{i} + \hat{j} + \hat{k}$ and $3\hat{i} - \hat{j} + 2\hat{k}$, then find the area of the triangle.

(a) $\sqrt{5}$ (b) $\sqrt{3}$
(c) $\sqrt{2}$ (d) $\sqrt{8}$

30 If **A** and **B** are two non-zero vectors such that $|\mathbf{A} + \mathbf{B}| = \frac{|\mathbf{A} - \mathbf{B}|}{2}$ and $|\mathbf{A}| = 2|\mathbf{B}|$, then the angle between **A** and **B** is

(a) 37° (b) 53°
(c) $\cos^{-1}(-3/4)$ (d) $\cos^{-1}(-4/3)$

31 Two forces P and Q act at a point and have resultant R. If Q is replaced by $\frac{(R^2 - P^2)}{Q}$ acting in the direction opposite to that of Q, the resultant

(a) remains same (b) becomes half
(c) becomes twice (d) None of these

32 Two forces P and Q are in ratio $P : Q = 1 : 2$. If their resultant is at an angle $\tan^{-1}\left(\frac{\sqrt{3}}{2}\right)$ to vector P, then angle between P and Q is

(a) $\tan^{-1}\left(\frac{1}{2}\right)$ (b) 45° (c) 30° (d) 60°

33 $ABCD$ is a quadrilateral. Forces **BA**, **BC**, **CD** and **DA** act at a point. Their resultant is

(a) 2**AB** (b) 2**DA** (c) zero vector (d) 2**BA**

34 If $(\mathbf{a}+\mathbf{b})$ is perpendicular to $\mathbf{b}$ and $\mathbf{a}+2\mathbf{b}$ is perpendicular to $\mathbf{a}$ and $|\mathbf{a}| = a, |\mathbf{b}| = b$, then

(a) $a = b$ (b) $a = 2b$ (c) $b = 2a$ (d) $a = b\sqrt{2}$

35 Forces of magnitudes $2P$, $4P$, $3P$ and P act on a particle in directions parallel to the sides **AB**, **BC**, **CD** and **DE** of a regular hexagon. Find the magnitude of their resultant.

(a) $\sqrt{39}\,P$ (b) $\sqrt{30}\,P$ (c) $\sqrt{26}\,P$ (d) $10\,P$

36 If **p** and **q** are unit vectors forming an angle of 30°, find the area of the parallelogram having $\mathbf{a} = \mathbf{p} + 2\mathbf{q}$ and $\mathbf{b} = 2\mathbf{p} + \mathbf{q}$ as its diagonals.

(a) 1/4 sq. units (b) 1/2 sq. units
(c) 3/4 sq. units (d) 2 sq. units

37 Figure shows two vectors **a** (in yz-plane) and **b** (in xy-plane), such that $|\mathbf{a}| = |\mathbf{b}| = 5$ units. What is the angle between **a** and **b**?

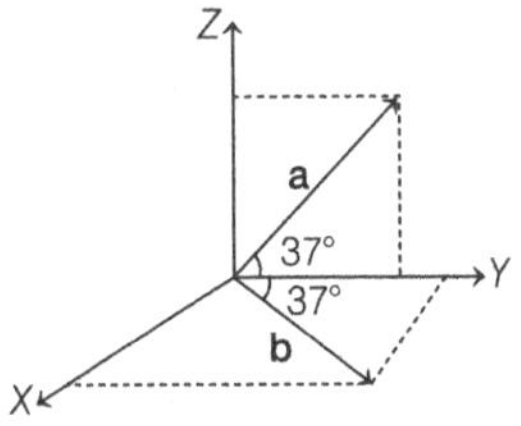

(a) $\theta = \cos^{-1}\left(\frac{12}{25}\right)$ (b) $\theta = \cos^{-1}\left(\frac{16}{25}\right)$

(c) $\theta = \cos^{-1}\left(\frac{9}{25}\right)$ (d) $\theta = 90°$

38 The angle between the vectors $\mathbf{a}+\mathbf{b}$ and $\mathbf{a}-\mathbf{b}$, given $|\mathbf{a}| = 2$, $|\mathbf{b}| = 1$ and angle between **a** and **b** is $\frac{\pi}{3}$, is

(a) $\tan^{-1}\frac{2}{\sqrt{3}}$ (b) $\tan^{-1}\sqrt{\frac{2}{3}}$

(c) $\tan^{-1}\sqrt{\frac{3}{7}}$ (d) None of these

39 Given the vectors **a** and **b** the angle between which equals 120°. If $|\mathbf{a}| = 3$ and $|\mathbf{b}| = 4$, then the length of the vector, $2\mathbf{a} - \frac{3}{2}\mathbf{b}$ is

(a) $6\sqrt{3}$ (b) $7\sqrt{2}$ (c) $4\sqrt{5}$ (d) None of these

40 The volume of the parallelopiped whose edges are represented by the vectors $\mathbf{a} = 2\hat{\mathbf{i}} - 3\hat{\mathbf{j}} + 4\hat{\mathbf{k}}$, $\mathbf{b} = 3\hat{\mathbf{i}} - \hat{\mathbf{j}} + 2\hat{\mathbf{k}}$, $\mathbf{c} = \hat{\mathbf{i}} + 2\hat{\mathbf{j}} - \hat{\mathbf{k}}$ is

(a) 7 (b) 5 (c) 4 (d) None of these

41 Four coplanar forces are applied at a point O. Each of them is equal to F and the angle between two consecutive forces equals 45°. Then, the resultant has the magnitude equal to

(a) $F\sqrt{2+2\sqrt{2}}$ (b) $F\sqrt{3+2\sqrt{2}}$
(c) $F\sqrt{4+2\sqrt{2}}$ (d) None of these

42 If $\mathbf{a}+\mathbf{b}+\mathbf{c} = 0$ and $|\mathbf{a}| = 3$, $|\mathbf{b}| = 5$, $|\mathbf{c}| = 7$, find angle between **a** and **b**.

(a) 30° (b) 45° (c) 60° (d) 120°

43 BC is divided into four equal parts by P, Q and R. The resultant of **AB** and 3**AC** is

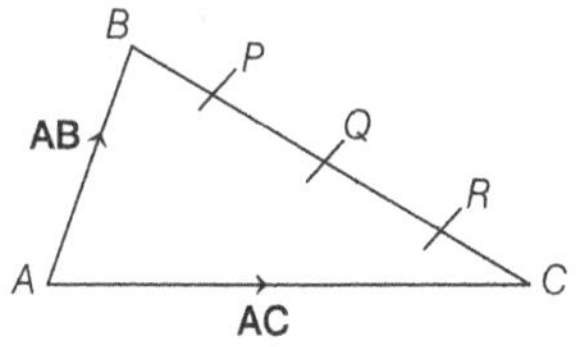

(a) **AR** (b) 4**AR** (c) 4**AP** (d) **PQ**

44 Two vectors of equal magnitude P are inclined at some angle such that the difference in magnitude of resultant and magnitude of either of the vectors is 0.732 times either of the magnitude of vectors. If the angle between them is increased by half of its initial value, then find the magnitude of difference of the vectors.

(a) $2\,P$ (b) $\sqrt{2}\,P$ (c) $3P$ (d) $\sqrt{3}\,P$

45 A bird starts from (1, 0, 0) in the direction ($2\hat{\mathbf{i}} + 3\hat{\mathbf{j}} - 6\hat{\mathbf{k}}$) with a speed 21 m/s for 5 s, then along the direction ($3\hat{\mathbf{i}} + 4\hat{\mathbf{j}} + 5\hat{\mathbf{k}}$) with a speed $5\sqrt{2}$ m/s for 5 s. Find the final displacement of the bird, so that it reaches the origin.

(a) $30\hat{\mathbf{i}} + 45\hat{\mathbf{j}} - 4\hat{\mathbf{k}}$ (b) $-45\hat{\mathbf{i}} - 65\hat{\mathbf{j}} + 65\hat{\mathbf{k}}$
(c) $-46\hat{\mathbf{i}} - 65\hat{\mathbf{j}} + 65\hat{\mathbf{k}}$ (d) $46\hat{\mathbf{i}} - 65\hat{\mathbf{j}} - 65\hat{\mathbf{k}}$

Multiple Choice(s) Correct Questions

1 Which of the following quantities are independent of the choice of orientation of the co-ordinate axes?

(a) $\mathbf{a}+\mathbf{b}$ (b) $a_x + b_y$
(c) $|\mathbf{a}+\mathbf{b}-\mathbf{c}|$ (d) angle between **a** and **b**

2 If $\mathbf{v}_1 + \mathbf{v}_2$ is perpendicular to $\mathbf{v}_1 - \mathbf{v}_2$, then

(a) $\mathbf{v}_1$ is perpendicular to $\mathbf{v}_2$
(b) $|\mathbf{v}_1| = |\mathbf{v}_2|$
(c) $\mathbf{v}_1$ is a null vector
(d) the angle between $\mathbf{v}_1$ and $\mathbf{v}_2$ can have any angle

3 Let **A**, **B** and **C** be unit vectors. Suppose that $\mathbf{A}\cdot\mathbf{B} = \mathbf{A}\cdot\mathbf{C} = 0$ and the angle between **B** and **C** is $\pi/6$, then which of the following is/are possible?

(a) $\mathbf{A} = (\mathbf{B}\times\mathbf{C})$ (b) $\mathbf{A} = 2(\mathbf{B}\times\mathbf{C})$

(c) $\mathbf{A} = 2(\mathbf{C}\times\mathbf{B})$ (d) $|\mathbf{B}\times\mathbf{C}| = \frac{\sqrt{3}}{2}$

4 If the angle between **a** and **b** is 60°, then

(a) the component of $\mathbf{a}-\mathbf{b}$ along $\mathbf{a}+\mathbf{b}$ is $\frac{a^2-b^2}{\sqrt{a^2+b^2+ab}}$

(b) $\mathbf{a}\times\mathbf{b}$ is perpendicular to resultant of $(\mathbf{a}+2\mathbf{b})$ and $(\mathbf{a}-\mathbf{b})$

(c) the component of $\mathbf{a}-\mathbf{b}$ along $\mathbf{a}+\mathbf{b}$ is $\frac{a^2-b^2}{\sqrt{a^2+b^2+2ab}}$

(d) the component of $\mathbf{a}+\mathbf{b}$ along $\mathbf{a}-\mathbf{b}$ is $\frac{a^2-b^2}{\sqrt{a^2+b^2+\sqrt{3}ab}}$

5 Which of the following statements is/are correct?

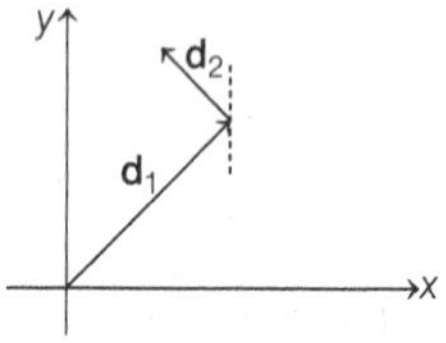

(a) The sign of the x-component of $\mathbf{d}_1$ is positive and that of $\mathbf{d}_2$ is negative.

(b) The signs of the y-components of $\mathbf{d}_1$ and $\mathbf{d}_2$ are positive and negative, respectively.

(c) The signs of the x and y-components of $\mathbf{d}_1+\mathbf{d}_2$ are positive.

(d) None of the above

6 The x-component of the resultant of several vectors

(a) is equal to the sum of the x-components of the vectors

(b) may be smaller than the sum of the magnitudes of the vectors

(c) may be greater than the sum of the magnitudes of the vectors

(d) may be equal to the sum of the magnitudes of the vectors

7 The magnitude of scalar product of two vectors is 8 and of vector product is $8\sqrt{3}$. The angle between them is

(a) 30° (b) 60° (c) 120° (d) 150°

8 If $\lambda\mathbf{a}$ is a vector and λ is a non-zero scalar, then

(a) $\lambda\mathbf{a}$ is a vector in the direction of **a**

(b) $\lambda\mathbf{a}$ is a vector collinear to **a**

(c) $\lambda\mathbf{a}$ and **a** have independent directions

(d) None of the above

9 Given $\mathbf{a}+\mathbf{b}+\mathbf{c}+\mathbf{d}=0$, which of the following statements is/are correct?

(a) **a**, **b**, **c** and **d** each must be a zero vector.

(b) The magnitude of $(\mathbf{a}+\mathbf{c})$ equals the magnitude of $(\mathbf{b}+\mathbf{d})$.

(c) The magnitude of **a** can never be greater than the sum of the magnitudes of **b**, **c** and **d**.

(d) $\mathbf{b}+\mathbf{c}$ must lie in the plane of **a** and **d** if **a** and **d** are not collinear, and in the line of **a** and **d**, if they are collinear

10 The vector $\hat{\mathbf{i}}+x\hat{\mathbf{j}}+3\hat{\mathbf{k}}$ is rotated through an angle θ and doubled in magnitude, then it becomes $4\hat{\mathbf{i}}+(4x-2)\hat{\mathbf{j}}+2\hat{\mathbf{k}}$. The values of x are

(a) $-\frac{2}{3}$ (b) $\frac{1}{3}$ (c) $\frac{2}{3}$ (d) 2

11 Four vectors **A**, **B**, **C** and **D** all have the same magnitude and lie in a plane. The angle between adjacent vectors is 45° as shown. Which of the following equation is/are correct?

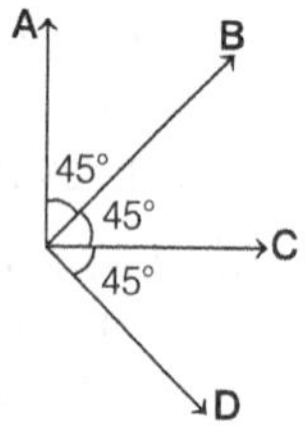

(a) $\mathbf{A}-\mathbf{C} = -\sqrt{2}\mathbf{D}$ (b) $\mathbf{B}+\mathbf{D}-\sqrt{2}\mathbf{C} = 0$

(c) $\mathbf{A}+\mathbf{B} = \mathbf{B}+\mathbf{D}$ (d) $(\mathbf{A}+\mathbf{C})/\sqrt{2} = \mathbf{B}$

12 Angle between the vectors $\mathbf{a} = -\hat{\mathbf{i}}+2\hat{\mathbf{j}}+\hat{\mathbf{k}}$ and $\mathbf{b} = x\hat{\mathbf{i}}+\hat{\mathbf{j}}+(x+1)\hat{\mathbf{k}}$ is

(a) obtuse angle (b) acute angle

(c) 90° (d) depends on x

13 Let **a** and **b** be two non-null vectors such that $|\mathbf{a}+\mathbf{b}| = |\mathbf{a}-2\mathbf{b}|$. Then, the value of $\frac{|\mathbf{a}|}{|\mathbf{b}|}$ may be

(a) $\frac{1}{4}$ (b) $\frac{1}{8}$ (c) 1 (d) 2

14 The vector (s) which is/are coplanar with vectors $\hat{\mathbf{i}}+\hat{\mathbf{j}}+2\hat{\mathbf{k}}$ and $\hat{\mathbf{i}}+2\hat{\mathbf{j}}+\hat{\mathbf{k}}$, and perpendicular to the vector $\hat{\mathbf{i}}+\hat{\mathbf{j}}+\hat{\mathbf{k}}$ is/are

(a) $\hat{\mathbf{j}}-\hat{\mathbf{k}}$ (b) $-\hat{\mathbf{i}}+\hat{\mathbf{j}}$

(c) $\hat{\mathbf{i}}-\hat{\mathbf{j}}$ (d) $-\hat{\mathbf{j}}+\hat{\mathbf{k}}$

15 The vector $\frac{1}{3}(2\hat{\mathbf{i}}-2\hat{\mathbf{j}}+\hat{\mathbf{k}})$ is

(a) a unit vector

(b) makes an angle $\frac{\pi}{3}$ with the vector $2\hat{\mathbf{i}}-4\hat{\mathbf{j}}+3\hat{\mathbf{k}}$

(c) parallel to the vector $-\hat{\mathbf{i}}+\hat{\mathbf{j}}-\frac{1}{2}\hat{\mathbf{k}}$

(d) perpendicular to the vector $3\hat{\mathbf{i}}+2\hat{\mathbf{j}}-2\hat{\mathbf{k}}$

16 Two vectors **A** and **B** lie in one plane. **C** lies in a different plane. Then, **A** + **B** + **C**

(a) can't be null vector
(b) can be a null vector
(c) lies in the plane of **A** or **B**
(d) lies in a plane different from that of any of three vectors

17 Vector product of three vectors **a**, **b** and **c** of the type $\mathbf{a}\times(\mathbf{b}\times\mathbf{c})$ is known as vector triple product. It is defined as $\mathbf{a}\times(\mathbf{b}\times\mathbf{c})=(\mathbf{a}\cdot\mathbf{c})\,\mathbf{b}-(\mathbf{a}\cdot\mathbf{b})\mathbf{c}$. Vector triple product $\mathbf{a}\times(\mathbf{b}\times\mathbf{a})$ is

(a) a null vector
(b) parallel to **b**, if $\mathbf{a}\perp\mathbf{b}$
(c) coplanar with **a** and **b**
(d) normal to the plane containing **a** and **b**

18 If $\mathbf{A}=2\hat{i}+2\hat{j}+\hat{k}$ and $\mathbf{B}=\hat{i}+\hat{j}+\hat{k}$ are two vectors, then the unit vector

(a) parallel to **A** is $\dfrac{2\hat{i}+2\hat{j}+\hat{k}}{3}$
(b) parallel to **B** is $\dfrac{\hat{i}+\hat{j}+\hat{k}}{\sqrt{3}}$
(c) perpendicular to **A** is $\dfrac{\hat{i}-\hat{j}}{\sqrt{2}}$
(d) perpendicular to **B** is $\dfrac{\hat{i}-\hat{j}}{\sqrt{2}}$

19 Two vectors **A** and **B** are drawn from a common point and **C** = **A** + **B**

(a) If $C^2=A^2+B^2$, then the angle between vectors **A** and **B** is 90°
(b) If $C^2<A^2+B^2$, then the angle between **A** and **B** is greater than 90°
(c) If $C^2>A^2+B^2$, then the angle between vectors **A** and **B** is between 0° and 90°
(d) If **C** = **A** − **B**, then the angle between **A** and **B** is 180°

20 Select correct statement(s) for three vectors $\mathbf{a}=-3\hat{i}+2\hat{j}-\hat{k}$, $\mathbf{b}=\hat{i}-3\hat{j}+5\hat{k}$ and $\mathbf{c}=2\hat{i}+\hat{j}-4\hat{k}$.

(a) The above vectors can form triangle.
(b) Component of **a** along **c** is 3.
(c) **a** makes angle $\cos^{-1}\sqrt{\dfrac{2}{7}}$ with *Y*-axis.
(d) A vector having magnitude twice the vector **a** and anti-parallel to vector **b** is $\sqrt{\dfrac{2}{5}}(-2\hat{i}+6\hat{j}-10\hat{k})$.

Comprehension Based Questions

Comprehension-1

Three vectors **A**, **B** and **C** are given as, $\mathbf{A}=3\hat{i}+4\hat{j}+5\hat{k}$, $\mathbf{B}=7\hat{i}+24\hat{j}-25\hat{k}$, $\mathbf{C}=6\hat{i}+8\hat{j}-10\hat{k}$.

1 A bird is flying along **A** with speed $15\sqrt{2}$ m/s, then its velocity (in m/s) will be

(a) $9\hat{i}+12\hat{j}+15\hat{k}$ (b) $3\hat{i}+4\hat{j}-5\hat{k}$
(c) $12\hat{i}+3\hat{j}-15\hat{k}$ (d) $15\hat{i}+12\hat{j}-3\hat{k}$

2 A vector which is parallel to **A** and has magnitude equal to that of **C** is given by

(a) $6\hat{i}+8\hat{j}+10\hat{k}$ (b) $9\hat{i}+12\hat{j}+15\hat{k}$
(c) $9\hat{i}+12\hat{j}-5\hat{k}$ (d) $-6\hat{i}-8\hat{j}-10\hat{k}$

3 What vector should be added to sum of all three vectors **A**, **B** and **C** such that the resultant will be a unit vector along positive *X*-axis?

(a) $-15\hat{i}-36\hat{j}+30\hat{k}$ (b) $-12\hat{i}-34\hat{j}+30\hat{k}$
(c) $-10\hat{i}-16\hat{j}+24\hat{k}$ (d) Not possible

Comprehension-2

If the three successive vertices of a parallelogram have the position vectors as, $A(-3,-2,0)$, $B(3,-3,1)$ and $C(5,0,2)$. Then, find

4 position vector of the fourth vertex *D*.

(a) $-\hat{i}+\hat{j}+\hat{k}$ (b) $-\hat{i}-\hat{j}+\hat{k}$
(c) $-\hat{i}+\hat{j}-\hat{k}$ (d) $\hat{i}+\hat{j}+\hat{k}$

5 a vector having the same direction as that of **AB** but magnitude equal to **AC**.

(a) $\dfrac{6}{\sqrt{19}}(-6\hat{i}+\hat{j}-\hat{k})$ (b) $\dfrac{6}{\sqrt{19}}(6\hat{i}-\hat{j}+\hat{k})$
(c) $\dfrac{6}{\sqrt{38}}(6\hat{i}-\hat{j}+\hat{k})$ (d) $\dfrac{6}{\sqrt{38}}(-6\hat{i}+\hat{j}-\hat{k})$

6 the angle between **AC** and **BD**.

(a) $\dfrac{\pi}{4}$ (b) $\dfrac{\pi}{3}$
(c) $\dfrac{\pi}{2}$ (d) $\dfrac{2\pi}{3}$

Comprehension-3

A body acted upon by three given forces is under equilibrium.

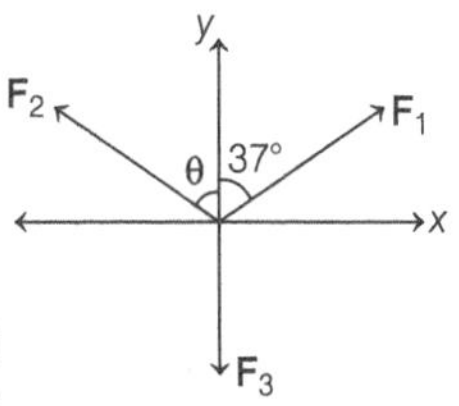

If $|\mathbf{F}_1|=10\text{N}$, $|\mathbf{F}_2|=6\text{N}$, then

7 find the value of $|\mathbf{F}_3|$.

(a) 4 N (b) 5 N
(c) 6 N (d) 8 N

8 find the angle (θ).

(a) 30° (b) 45° (c) 53° (d) 90°

Comprehension-4

For any particle moving with some velocity (**v**) and acceleration (**a**), tangential acceleration and normal acceleration are defined as follows

Tangential acceleration The component of acceleration in the direction of velocity.

Normal acceleration The component of acceleration in the direction perpendicular to velocity.

If at a given instant, velocity and acceleration of a particle are given by

$$\mathbf{v} = 4\hat{i} + 3\hat{j}, \qquad \mathbf{a} = 10\hat{i} + 15\hat{j} + 20\hat{k}$$

9 Find the tangential acceleration of the particle at the given instant.

(a) $17(4\hat{i} + 3\hat{j})$ (b) $\frac{17}{5}(4\hat{i} + 3\hat{j})$

(c) $17(4\hat{i} - 3\hat{j})$ (d) $\frac{17}{5}(4\hat{i} - 3\hat{j})$

10 Find the normal acceleration of the particle at the given instant.

(a) $\frac{-9\hat{i} + 12\hat{j} + 50\hat{k}}{5}$ (b) $\frac{9\hat{i} - 12\hat{j} - 50\hat{k}}{5}$

(c) $\frac{-18\hat{i} + 24\hat{j} + 100\hat{k}}{5}$ (d) $\frac{18\hat{i} - 24\hat{j} - 100\hat{k}}{5}$

Match the Columns Questions

1 Three coplanar forces $\mathbf{F}_1$, $\mathbf{F}_2$ and $\mathbf{F}_3$ are acting simultaneously on a particle. Column I contains different operation between forces and Column II contains their magnitude. Match them.

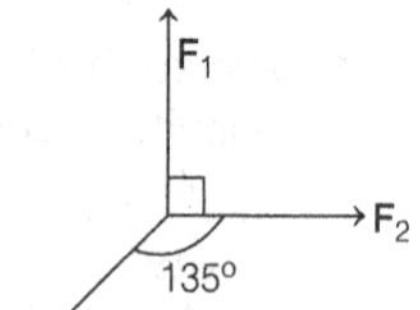

$|F_1| = 10\text{N}$
$|F_2| = 10\text{N}$
$|F_3| = 10\sqrt{2}\text{N}$

Column I	Column II
(A) $\mathbf{F}_1 + \mathbf{F}_2 + \mathbf{F}_3$	(P) 0
(B) $\mathbf{F}_1 + \mathbf{F}_2 - \mathbf{F}_3$	(Q) $1000\sqrt{2}$
(C) $\lvert(\mathbf{F}_1 \times \mathbf{F}_2) \times \mathbf{F}_3\rvert$	(R) $20\sqrt{2}$
(D) $\lvert\mathbf{F}_3 \cdot (\mathbf{F}_1 + \mathbf{F}_2)\rvert$	(S) 200

2 If $\mathbf{A} = 2\hat{i} + 3\hat{j} - \hat{k}$ and $\mathbf{B} = \hat{i} + 2\hat{j} + 2\hat{k}$, then

Column I	Column II
(A) $\lvert\mathbf{A} \times \mathbf{B}\rvert$	(P) $\sqrt{11}$
(B) $\lvert\mathbf{A} - \mathbf{B}\rvert$	(Q) 6
(C) $\mathbf{A} \cdot \mathbf{B}$	(R) $\sqrt{35}$
(D) $\lvert\mathbf{A} + \mathbf{B}\rvert$	(S) $\sqrt{90}$

3 Match the entries in Column I and Column II considering the cube (of side a) shown below

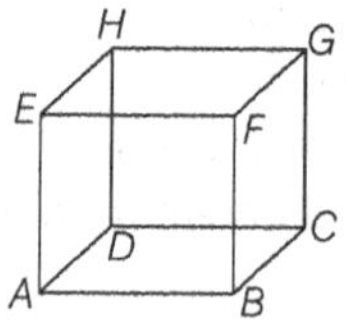

Column I	Column II
(A) **AC** + **BE** + **GB**	(P) is a null vector
(B) **AD** + **EF**	(Q) is a vector with magnitude $a\sqrt{3}$
(C) **AD** + **CD** + **HD**	(R) is a vector with magnitude $a\sqrt{2}$
(D) **AC** + **GF** + **FE**	(S) **EH** − **GH**
	(T) **EH** + **FH** + **HG**

4 A set of 2 vectors is given in each option of Column I. Match Column I and Column II.

Column I	Column II
(A) 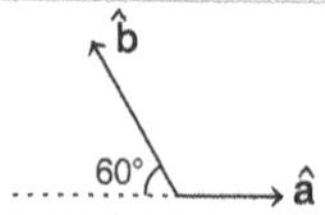	(P) Sum of 2 vectors is a unit vector
(B) 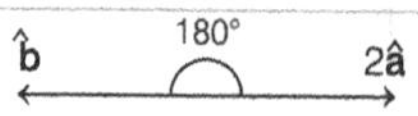	(Q) Magnitude of sum of 2 vectors is $\sqrt{2}$.
(C) 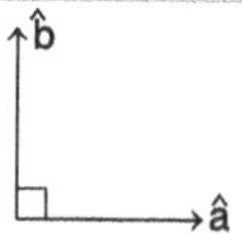	(R) The resultant has a positive rectangular component in the direction of $\hat{\mathbf{a}}$.
(D) 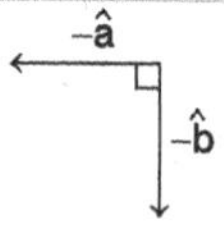	(S) Dot product of two given vectors is zero.
	(T) Magnitude of sum of the two given vectors = magnitude of their subtraction.

5

Column I	Column II
(A) If $\mathbf{a} + \mathbf{b} = \hat{j}$ and $2\mathbf{a} - \mathbf{b} = 3\hat{i} + \frac{\hat{j}}{2}$, then modulus of cosine of the angle between **a** and **b** is	(P) 1
(B) If $\lvert\mathbf{a}\rvert = \lvert\mathbf{b}\rvert = \lvert\mathbf{c}\rvert$, angle between each pair of vectors is $\pi/3$ and $\lvert\mathbf{a} + \mathbf{b} + \mathbf{c}\rvert = \sqrt{6}$, then $\lvert\mathbf{a}\rvert$	(Q) $5\sqrt{3}$
(C) Area of the parallelogram whose diagonals represent the vectors $3\hat{i} + \hat{j} - 2\hat{k}$ and $\hat{i} - 3\hat{j} + 4\hat{k}$ is	(R) 2
(D) If **a** is perpendicular to **b** + **c**, **b** is perpendicular to **c** + **a**, **c** is perpendicular to **a** + **b**, $\lvert\mathbf{a}\rvert = 2$, $\lvert\mathbf{b}\rvert = 3$ and $\lvert\mathbf{c}\rvert = 6$, then $\lvert\mathbf{a} + \mathbf{b} + \mathbf{c}\rvert$	(S) 7
	(T) 3/5

6

Column I (Operation of non-zero vectors **P** and **Q**)		Column II (Possible angle between **P** and **Q**)	
(A)	$\lvert \mathbf{P}\times\mathbf{Q}\rvert = 0$	(P)	90°
(B)	$\lvert \mathbf{P}\times\mathbf{Q}\rvert = \sqrt{3}\mathbf{P}\cdot\mathbf{Q}$	(Q)	180°
(C)	$\mathbf{P}+\mathbf{Q}=\mathbf{R}$ and $P+Q=R$	(R)	60°
(D)	$\lvert \mathbf{P}+\mathbf{Q}\rvert = \lvert \mathbf{P}-\mathbf{Q}\rvert$	(S)	0°

Numerical Value Questions

1 When two forces of magnitude P and Q are perpendicular to each other, their resultant is of magnitude R. When they are at an angle of 180° to each other, their resultant is of magnitude $\frac{R}{\sqrt{2}}$. Find the value of $\frac{P}{Q}+\frac{Q}{P}$.

2 According to Newton's second law of motion, resultant force on a particle is in the direction of acceleration of the particle. Two forces F_1 and F_2 are acting on a particle as shown in the figure. The acceleration of the particle is along X-axis. Find the value of F_1 (in N).

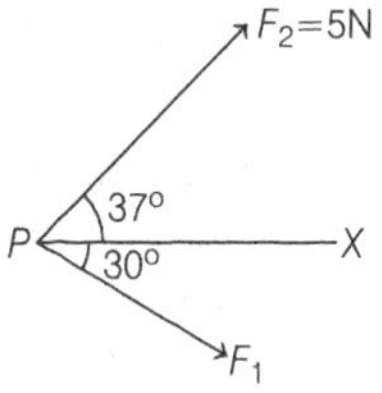

3 A vector **B** which has a magnitude 8.0 is added to a vector **A** which lies along the X-axis. The sum of these two vectors is a third vector which lie along the Y-axis and has a magnitude that is twice the magnitude of **A**. The magnitude of **A** is $p/\sqrt{5}$. Find p.

4 Two forces $\mathbf{F}_1$ and $\mathbf{F}_2$ of magnitude $10\sqrt{10}$ N each are inclined at an angle of 1.8° to each other. What is the magnitude (in N) of vector $\mathbf{F}_1-\mathbf{F}_2$? (Take, $\pi^2=10$)

5 Let $\mathbf{a}=\hat{i}+\hat{j}+\hat{k}$, $\mathbf{b}=\hat{i}-\hat{j}+2\hat{k}$ and $\mathbf{c}=-x\hat{i}-(x+2)\hat{j}-\hat{k}$. If the vector **c** lies in the plane of **a** and **b**, then find the value of x.

6 If **a**, **b** and **c** are unit vectors satisfying $\lvert\mathbf{a}-\mathbf{b}\rvert^2+\lvert\mathbf{b}-\mathbf{c}\rvert^2+\lvert\mathbf{c}-\mathbf{a}\rvert^2=9$, then. Find $\lvert 2\mathbf{a}+5\mathbf{b}+5\mathbf{c}\rvert$.

7 The area of a triangle having vertices at $A(1, 3, 2)$, $B(2, -1, 1)$ and $C(-1, 2, 3)$ is $\sqrt{\frac{107}{n}}$ square units. Find n.

8 Three vectors each of magnitude 1N acts along the sides AB, BC and CD of a regular hexagon $ABCDEF$. Find the magnitude of their resultant (in N).

9 Four forces are acting on a particle and the particle is in equilibrium. One force of magnitude 3 N is directed vertically up. Another is directed 37° East of North having magnitude 5 N. Third force of magnitude $4\sqrt{2}$ N is directed in South-West direction. The fourth force is $\sqrt{n}$ N. Find the value of n.

10 Given $\mathbf{a}+\mathbf{b}+\mathbf{c}=0$ and all vectors have equal magnitude $3\sqrt{3}$. Find the magnitude of $\mathbf{a}+2\mathbf{b}$.

Previous Year's Questions

JEE Main

1 A vector has magnitude same as that of $\mathrm{A}=3\hat{i}+4\hat{j}$ and is parallel to $\mathrm{B}=4\hat{i}+3\hat{j}$. The x and y components of this vector in first quadrant are x and 3, respectively where $x=$......... . **[2024, 30 Jan Shift-II]**

2 If two vectors $\mathbf{P}=\hat{i}+2m\hat{j}+m\hat{k}$ and $\mathbf{Q}=4\hat{i}-2\hat{j}+m\hat{k}$ are perpendicular to each other, then, the value of m will be **[2023, 24 Jan Shift-II]**

(a) 3 (b) -1 (c) 2 (d) 1

3 If $\mathbf{P}=3\hat{i}+\sqrt{3}\hat{j}+2\hat{k}$ and $\mathbf{Q}=4\hat{i}+\sqrt{3}\hat{j}+2.5\hat{k}$, then the unit vector in the direction of $\mathbf{P}\times\mathbf{Q}$ is $\frac{1}{x}(\sqrt{3}\hat{i}+\hat{j}-2\sqrt{3}\hat{k})$. The value of x is **[2023, 25 Jan Shift-I]**

4 **A** is a vector quantity such that $\lvert\mathbf{A}\rvert=$ non-zero constant. Which of the following expressions is true for **A**? **[2022, 25 June Shift-I]**

(a) $\mathbf{A}\cdot\mathbf{A}=0$ (b) $\mathbf{A}\times\mathbf{A}<0$
(c) $\mathbf{A}\times\mathbf{A}=0$ (d) $\mathbf{A}\times\mathbf{A}>0$

5 Projection of $2\hat{i}+4\hat{j}-2\hat{k}$ on $\hat{i}+2\hat{j}-\alpha\hat{k}$ is zero. Then, the value of α will be .... **[2022, 28 JULY Shift-I]**

6 If $\mathbf{A}=(2\hat{i}+3\hat{j}-\hat{k})$ m and $\mathbf{B}=(\hat{i}+2\hat{j}+2\hat{k})$ m. The magnitude of component of vector A along vector B will be .... m. **[2022, 26 JULY Shift-II]**

7 The resultant of these forces OP, OQ, OR, OS and OT is approximately ...... N.
[Take, $\sqrt{3}=1.7$, $\sqrt{2}=1.4$ and given $\hat{i}$ and $\hat{j}$ unit vectors along X, Y axis] **[2021, 27 Aug Shift-I]**

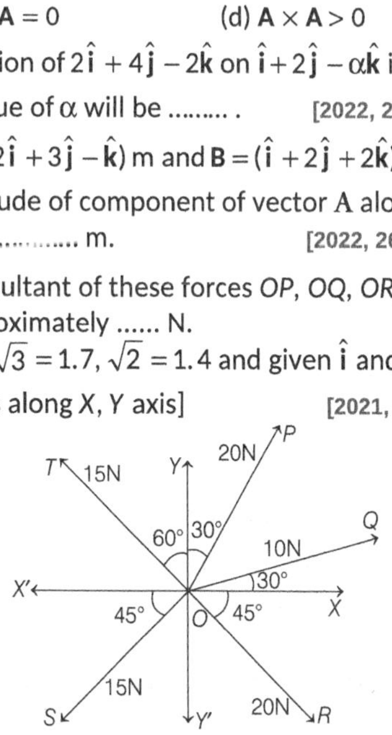

(a) $9.25\hat{i}+5\hat{j}$ (b) $3\hat{i}+15\hat{j}$
(c) $2.5\hat{i}-14.5\hat{j}$ (d) $-1.5\hat{i}-15.5\hat{j}$

8 **Assertion (A)** If A, B, C, D are four points on a semi-circular arc with centre at O such that $|\mathbf{AB}| = |\mathbf{BC}| = |\mathbf{CD}|$, then $\mathrm{AB} + \mathrm{AC} + \mathrm{AD}$ $= 4\mathbf{AO} + \mathbf{OB} + \mathbf{OC}$

Reason (R) Polygon law of vector addition yields

$\mathbf{AB} + \mathbf{BC} + \mathbf{CD} + \mathbf{AD} = 2\mathbf{AO}$ **[2021, 27 July Shift-I]**

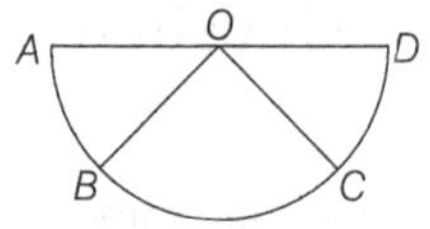

In the light of the above statements, choose the most appropriate answer from the options given below.

(a) Both A and R are correct and R is the correct explanation of A.
(b) Both A and R are correct but R is not the correct explanation of A.
(c) A is correct but R is not correct.
(d) A is not correct but R is correct.

9 Match List I with List II. **[2021, 25 July Shift-1]**

	List I		List II
(A)	$\mathbf{C} - \mathbf{A} - \mathbf{B} = 0$	(i)	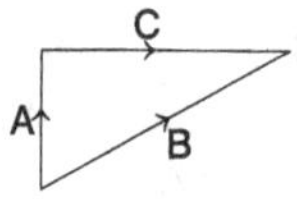
(B)	$\mathbf{A} - \mathbf{C} - \mathbf{B} = 0$	(ii)	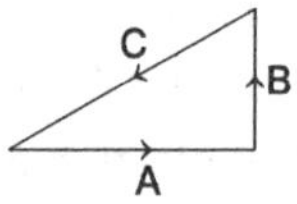
(C)	$\mathbf{B} - \mathbf{A} - \mathbf{C} = 0$	(iii)	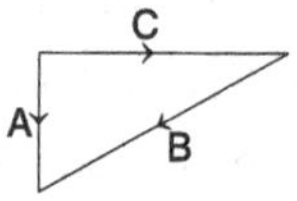
(D)	$\mathbf{A} + \mathbf{B} = -\mathbf{C}$	(iv)	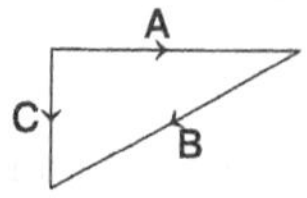

Choose the correct answer from the options given below.

(a) (A) → (iv), (B) → (i), (C) → (iii), (D) → (ii)
(b) (A) → (iv), (B) → (iii), (C) → (i), (D) → (ii)
(c) (A) → (iii), (B) → (ii), (C) → (iv), (D) → (i)
(d) (A) → (i), (B) → (iv), (C) → (ii), (D) → (iii)

10 **Statement I** If three forces $\mathbf{F}_1$, $\mathbf{F}_2$ and $\mathbf{F}_3$ are represented by three sides of a triangle and $\mathbf{F}_1 + \mathbf{F}_2 = -\mathbf{F}_3$, then these three forces are concurrent forces and satisfy the condition for equilibrium.

Statement II A triangle made up of three forces $\mathbf{F}_1$, $\mathbf{F}_2$ and $\mathbf{F}_3$ as its sides taken in the same order, satisfy the condition for translatory equilibrium.

In the light of the above statements, choose the most appropriate answer from the options given below. **[2021, 31 Aug Shift-II]**

(a) Both Statement I and Statement II are true.
(b) Statement I is true but Statement II are false.
(c) Both Statement I and Statement II are false.
(d) Statement I is false but Statement II is true.

11 If $\mathbf{P} \times \mathbf{Q} = \mathbf{Q} \times \mathbf{P}$, the angle between $\mathbf{P}$ and $\mathbf{Q}$ is θ $(0° < \theta < 360°)$. The value of θ will be ....°. **[2021, 25 Feb Shift-II]**

JEE Advanced

1 Two vectors $\mathbf{A}$ and $\mathbf{B}$ are defined as $\mathbf{A} = a\hat{\mathbf{i}}$ and $\mathbf{B} = a(\cos\omega t\hat{\mathbf{i}} + \sin\omega t\hat{\mathbf{j}})$, where a is a constant and $\omega = \pi/6$ rad s^{-1}. If $|\mathbf{A} + \mathbf{B}| = \sqrt{3}|\mathbf{A} - \mathbf{B}|$ at time $t = \tau$ for the first time, the value of τ, in seconds, is .... **[2018 Adv.]**

Answer Key

Level 1

1.1 Addition and Subtraction

1. (a) 180° (b) 90° (c) 0° **2.** 120° **3.** 45°
4. 60° **5.** 7 dyne, 1 dyne
6. 5 m **7.** 10 dyne **8.** 30°
9. (a) 90° (b) $\cos^{-1}\left(\frac{12}{13}\right)$ (c) $\cos^{-1}\left(\frac{5}{13}\right)$ **10.** Zero
11. (c) **12.** 6 N and 10 N **13.** 90° **14.** 150°
15. Null vector **16.** $\mathbf{A} + \mathbf{C} = \mathbf{B}$ **17.** $2v\sin\left(\frac{\theta}{2}\right)$

1.2 Vector Resolution

1. 3 **2.** $20\hat{\mathbf{i}} - 5\hat{\mathbf{j}} - 4\hat{\mathbf{k}}$ **3.** $\sqrt{0.11}$ **4.** 13 N **5.** $2\sqrt{2}$ kg
6. (a) $\tan^{-1}\left(\frac{3}{2}\right)$ (b) $\tan^{-1}\left(\frac{2}{3}\right)$ (c) 90° **7.** $15\hat{\mathbf{i}} + 20\hat{\mathbf{j}}$
8. $\frac{2}{\sqrt{45}}, \frac{4}{\sqrt{45}}, \frac{-5}{\sqrt{45}}$ **9.** 2 **10.** $\frac{A}{\sqrt{3}}$
11. $3\hat{\mathbf{i}} + 4\hat{\mathbf{j}} + 5\hat{\mathbf{k}}$ **12.** $\frac{3\hat{\mathbf{i}} + 6\hat{\mathbf{j}} - 2\hat{\mathbf{k}}}{7}$
13. (a) 6 and 3 (b) $\sqrt{45}$ (c) $\tan^{-1}\left(\frac{1}{2}\right)$

14. $c = -4$ **15.** 100 at an angle of 45° with X-axis
16. $50\sqrt{2}$ km/h (South-West)
17. $\hat{i}+\hat{j}$ **18.** $6\hat{i}+8\hat{j}$ **19.** 10 m (West) **20.** 3 km (North)
21. $-\hat{i}+9\hat{j}+11\hat{k}$ **22.** $\sqrt{3}:2:1$
23.(a) 1.5 N (b) $\sqrt{\frac{3}{2}}$ N (c) $-\frac{3}{2}\hat{i}-\frac{\sqrt{3}}{2}\hat{j}$
24. $F_1 = -(12\sqrt{3}-1)\hat{j}$ and $F_2 = (12-5\sqrt{3})\hat{i}+(12\sqrt{3}-15)\hat{j}$

1.3 Dot Product and Cross Product

1. (i) 0 (ii) 1 (iii) 1 (iv) 1 (v) 0
2. (i) No, Yes (ii) Yes, if **b** is a null vector (iii) No (iv) Never (v) No
3. 25 **4.** (i) 45° (ii) 30° (iii) $\cos^{-1}\left(\frac{1}{\sqrt{3}}\right)$ (iv) 90° (v) 60°
5. -8 **6.** 30° and 150° **7.** 0°
8. $(A^2+B^2+AB)^{1/2}$ **9.** (i) -15 (ii) $\frac{2}{3}$
10. (i) $\frac{1}{5}(\hat{j}+2\hat{k})$ (ii) $3\hat{i}+\frac{4}{5}\hat{j}-\frac{2}{5}\hat{k}$
11. (a) 10 (b) $\cos^{-1}\left(\frac{2}{3}\right)$ (c) $\frac{2}{5}(3\hat{i}-4\hat{k})$ (d) $\frac{10}{9}(2\hat{i}+2\hat{j}-\hat{k})$
12. -8 J
13. $5\hat{i}-2\hat{j}+8\hat{k}$ **14.** $\pm(-3\hat{i}-6\hat{j}+6\hat{k})$
15. $\sqrt{54}$ sq. units **16.** $\frac{\sqrt{35}}{2}$ sq. units
17. (a) $50\hat{i}-37\hat{j}+17\hat{k}$ (b) $40\hat{i}+100\hat{j}+100\hat{k}$
18. (i) 1 (ii) $2\hat{i}+2\hat{j}$ **19.** $-2(\mathbf{a}\times\mathbf{b})$
20. (i) 60° (ii) $\frac{\sqrt{3}}{2}$ sq. units **21.** (a) North (b) West

Level 2

Single Choice Correct Questions

1. (d)	2. (d)	3. (a)	4. (c)	5. (c)
6. (a)	7. (b)	8. (d)	9. (a)	10. (d)
11. (b)	12. (b)	13. (b)	14. (a)	15. (a)
16. (b)	17. (d)	18. (b)	19. (a)	20. (d)
21. (d)	22. (a)	23. (c)	24. (c)	25. (b)
26. (b)	27. (c)	28. (b)	29. (b)	30. (d)
31. (b)	32. (a)	33. (b)	34. (c)	35. (a)
36. (b)	37. (b)	38. (b)	39. (a)	40. (b)
41. (a)	42. (b)	43. (a)	44. (a)	45. (d)
46. (a)	47. (c)	48. (c)	49. (a)	50. (c)
51. (b)	52. (d)	53. (b)	54. (c)	55. (b)
56. (b)	57. (b)	58. (a)	59. (a)	60. (b)
61. (d)	62. (a)	63. (b)	64. (c)	65. (d)
66. (c)	67. (d)	68. (d)	69. (d)	70. (b)
71. (c)	72. (d)			

Numerical Value Questions

1. 15	2. 4	3. 2	4. 20	5. 3
6. 7	7. 3	8. 8	9. 1	10. 18
11. 9	12. 10	13. 15	14. 19	15. 60
16. 3	17. 13	18. 6	19. 1	20. 13

Level 3

Single Choice Correct Questions

1. (b)	2. (b)	3. (a)	4. (b)	5. (b)
6. (d)	7. (d)	8. (c)	9. (c)	10. (b)
11. (d)	12. (d)	13. (b)	14. (a)	15. (b)
16. (c)	17. (b)	18. (d)	19. (b)	20. (d)
21. (h)	22. (c)	23. (b)	24. (d)	25. (d)
26. (c)	27. (c)	28. (c)	29. (a)	30. (c)
31. (a)	32. (d)	33. (d)	34. (d)	35. (a)
36. (c)	37. (b)	38. (a)	39. (a)	40. (a)
41. (c)	42. (c)	43. (b)	44. (b)	45. (c)

Multiple Choice(s) Correct Questions

1. (a, c, d)	2. (b, d)	3. (b, c)	4. (a, b)	5. (a, c)
6. (a, b, d)	7. (b, c)	8. (b)	9. (b)	10. (a, d)
11. (a, b, d)	12. (b, d)	13. (c, d)	14. (a, d)	
15. (a, c, d)	16. (a, d)	17. (b, c)	18. (a, b, c, d)	
19. (a, b, c, d)	20. (a, b, c, d)			

Comprehension Based Questions

1. (a)	2. (a)	3. (a)	4. (a)	5. (b)
6. (d)	7. (d)	8. (d)	9. (b)	10. (c)

Match the Columns Questions

1. A → P; B → R; C → Q; D → S
2. A → S; B → P; C → Q; D → R
3. A → P; B → R; C → Q; D → P
4. A → P; R → P, R; C → Q, R, S; T; D → Q, S, T
5. A → T; B → P; C → Q; D → S
6. A → Q; B → R; C → S; D → P

Numerical Value Questions

1. 4	2. 6	3. 8	4. 1	5. 2
6. 3	7. 4	8. 2	9. 10	10. 9

Previous Year's Questions

JEE Main

1. (4)	2. (c)	3. (4)	4. (a)	5. (5)
6. (2)	7. (a)	8. (c)	9. (b)	10. (a)
11. (180)				

JEE Advanced

1. (2)

SOLUTIONS

Level 1

1.1 Addition and Subtraction

1. (a) $R^2 = A^2 + B^2 + 2AB\cos\theta$

$\Rightarrow \quad 1^2 = 3^2 + 4^2 + 2(3)(4)\cos\theta$

$\Rightarrow \quad \cos\theta = -1 \quad \Rightarrow \quad \theta = 180°$

(b) $5^2 = 3^2 + 4^2 + 2(3)(4)\cos\theta$

$\Rightarrow \quad \cos\theta = 0 \quad \Rightarrow \quad \theta = 90°$

(c) $7^2 = 3^2 + 4^2 + 2(3)(4)\cos\theta$

$\Rightarrow \quad \cos\theta = 1 \quad \Rightarrow \quad \theta = 0°$

2. $F^2 = F^2 + F^2 + 2(F)(F)\cos\theta$

$\Rightarrow \cos\theta = -\frac{1}{2} \quad \Rightarrow \quad \theta = 120°$

3. $(\sqrt{10}p)^2 = (2p)^2 + \sqrt{2}p)^2 + 2(2p)(\sqrt{2}p)\cos\theta$

$\Rightarrow \cos\theta = \frac{1}{\sqrt{2}} \quad \Rightarrow \theta = 45°$

4. Lets take angle between 4N and 3N to be θ.

$$R^2 = A^2 + B^2 + 2AB\cos\theta$$

$\Rightarrow \quad R^2 = 4^2 + 3^2 + 2(4)(3)\cos\theta$

$\Rightarrow \quad R^2 = 25 + 24\cos\theta$

If 4N and 3N are perpendicular, then

$$R^2 = A^2 + B^2 + 2AB\cos\theta$$

$$R'^2 = 4^2 + 3^2 + 2(4)(3)\cos 90° \quad \Rightarrow \quad R'^2 = 25$$

As per question, $R^2 = R'^2 + 12$

$\Rightarrow \quad 25 + 24\cos\theta = 25 + 12$

$\Rightarrow \quad \cos\theta = 1/2 \quad \Rightarrow \quad \theta = 60°$

5. $R_{max} = A + B = 4 + 3 = 7$ dyne

$R_{min} = |A - B| = |4 - 3| = 1$ dyne

6. Angle between **A** and **B** is 90°.

$$R = \sqrt{3^2 + 4^2 + 2(3)(4)\cos 90°} = 5 \text{ m}$$

7. Angle between the two vectors is 120° as they are placed head to tail.

$$R = \sqrt{10^2 + 10^2 + 2(10)(10)\cos 120°} = 10 \text{ dyne}$$

8. $A = 10, B = 5$ and $\theta = 120°$

$$R^2 = A^2 + B^2 + 2AB\cos\theta$$

$\Rightarrow \quad R^2 = 10^2 + 5^2 + 2(10)(5)\cos 120° \quad \Rightarrow \quad R = 5\sqrt{3}$

$$\tan\phi = \frac{B\sin\theta}{A + B\cos\theta}$$

$\Rightarrow \tan\phi = \frac{5\sin 120°}{10 + 5\cos 120°} = \frac{1}{\sqrt{3}} \quad \Rightarrow \phi = 30°$

9. (a) **P** + **Q** = **R**

$\Rightarrow \quad P^2 + Q^2 + 2PQ\cos\theta = R^2$

$\Rightarrow 5^2 + 12^2 + 2(5)(12)\cos\theta = 13^2 \Rightarrow \cos\theta = 0 \Rightarrow \theta = 90°$

So, angle between **P** and **Q** is 90°.

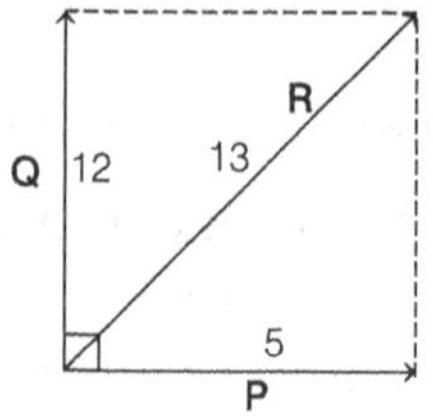

(b) Angle between **Q** and **R** is $\cos^{-1}\left(\frac{12}{13}\right)$.

(c) Angle between **P** and **R** is $\cos^{-1}\left(\frac{5}{13}\right)$.

10.

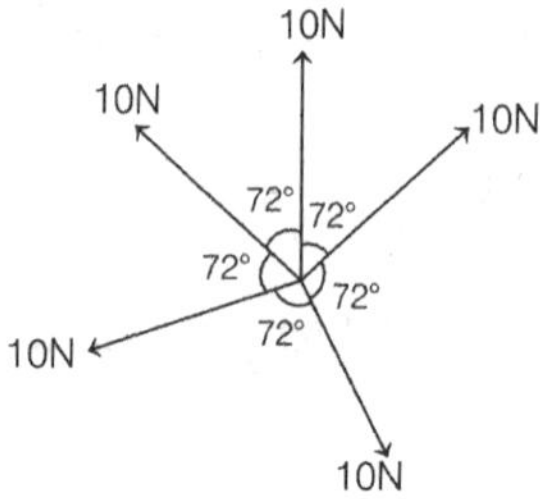

Net force is zero as these five forces will form a closed regular pentagon when rearranged.

11. In option (c) resultant of the first two forces will lie between 2N and 8N (including 2N and 8N).

So, it can cancel out the third force 6N.

12. **R** = **A** + **B** $\Rightarrow$ $A + B = 16$

Let A be x and B be $16 - x$.

$R = 8$

Using Pythagoras theorem,

$x^2 + 8^2 = (16 - x)^2$

$x = 6$N and $16 - x = 10$N

So, forces are 6N and 10N.

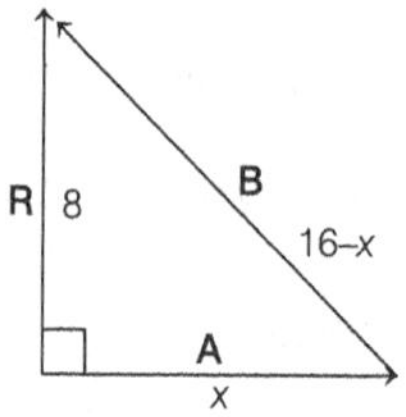

13. |**A** + **B**| = |**A** − **B**|

$\Rightarrow \quad \sqrt{A^2 + B^2 + 2AB\cos\theta} = \sqrt{A^2 + B^2 - 2AB\cos\theta}$

$\Rightarrow \quad A^2 + B^2 + 2AB\cos\theta = A^2 + B^2 - 2AB\cos\theta$

$\Rightarrow \quad 4AB\cos\theta = 0$

Since **A** and **B** are not null vectors,

$$\cos\theta = 0 \quad \Rightarrow \quad \theta = 90°$$

14. **R** = **A** + **B**

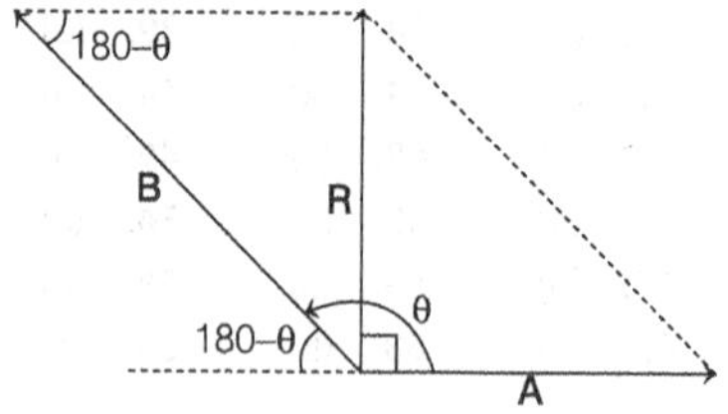

$$R = \frac{B}{2} \Rightarrow \sin(180 - \theta) = \frac{1}{2}$$

$$\Rightarrow 180 - \theta = 30° \Rightarrow \theta = 150°$$

15. Null vector

16. $\mathbf{A} - \mathbf{B} + \mathbf{C} = 0 \Rightarrow \mathbf{A} + \mathbf{C} = \mathbf{B}$

17. $|\Delta \mathbf{v}| = \sqrt{v^2 + v^2 - 2(v)(v)\cos\theta}$

$= \sqrt{2v^2(1 - \cos\theta)}$

$= \sqrt{2v^2 2\sin^2\left(\frac{\theta}{2}\right)} = 2v\sin\left(\frac{\theta}{2}\right)$

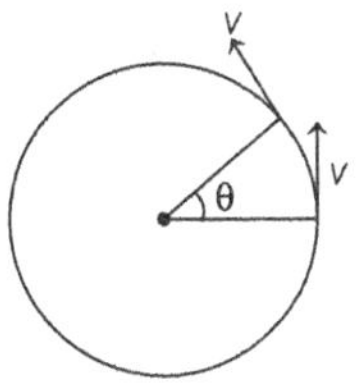

1.2 *Vector Resolution*

1. $1 + 1 + 1 = 3$

2. $\mathbf{A} - 2\mathbf{B} + 3\mathbf{C} = (2\hat{i} + \hat{j}) - 2(3\hat{j} - \hat{k}) + 3(6\hat{i} - 2\hat{k})$

$= 20\hat{i} - 5\hat{j} - 4\hat{k}$

3. $\sqrt{(0.5)^2 + (0.8)^2 + c^2} = 1 \Rightarrow c = \sqrt{0.11}$

4. $\mathbf{R} = 3\hat{i} + 4\hat{j} + 12\hat{k}$

$\Rightarrow R = \sqrt{3^2 + 4^2 + 12^2} \Rightarrow R = 13\text{N}$

5. $\mathbf{F} = m\mathbf{a}$

Given, $\mathbf{F} = 6\hat{i} - 8\hat{j} + 10\hat{k}$

$F = \sqrt{(6)^2 + (-8)^2 + (10)^2} = 10\sqrt{2}$ N

$m = \frac{|\mathbf{F}|}{|\mathbf{a}|} \Rightarrow m = \frac{10\sqrt{2}}{5} \Rightarrow m = 2\sqrt{2}\text{kg}$

6. From figure, $\tan\alpha = \frac{3}{2} \Rightarrow \alpha = \tan^{-1}\left(\frac{3}{2}\right)$

and $\beta = \tan^{-1}\left(\frac{2}{3}\right)$ and $\gamma = 90°$

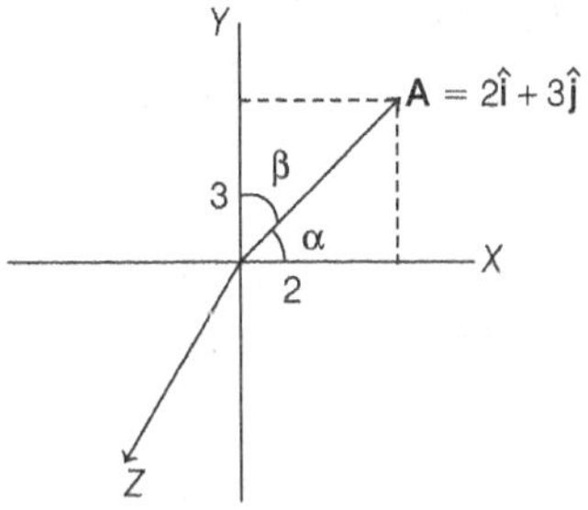

7. $\mathbf{C} = B\hat{\mathbf{A}} = 25\left(\frac{3\hat{i} + 4\hat{j}}{5}\right) = 15\hat{i} + 20\hat{j}$

8. $\cos\alpha = \frac{A_X}{A} = \frac{2}{\sqrt{45}} \Rightarrow \cos\beta = \frac{A_Y}{A} = \frac{4}{\sqrt{45}}$

$\cos\gamma = \frac{A_Z}{A} = \frac{-5}{\sqrt{45}}$

9. (a) $\cos^2\alpha + \cos^2\beta + \cos^2\gamma = 1$

(b) $\sin^2\alpha + \sin^2\beta + \sin^2\gamma$

$= (1 - \cos^2\alpha) + (1 - \cos^2\beta) + (1 - \cos^2\gamma)$

$= 3 - (\cos^2\alpha + \cos^2\beta + \cos^2\gamma) = 3 - 1 = 2$

10. $\alpha = \beta = \gamma$ and $\cos^2\alpha + \cos^2\beta + \cos^2\gamma = 1$

$\Rightarrow 3\cos^2\alpha = 1 \Rightarrow \cos\alpha = \frac{1}{\sqrt{3}}$

$\Rightarrow A_X = A\cos\alpha = \frac{A}{\sqrt{3}}, \; A_Y = \frac{A}{\sqrt{3}}, \; A_Z = \frac{A}{\sqrt{3}}$

11. Lets take the unknown vector to be **A**.

$(-6\hat{i} - 9\hat{j} + 2\hat{k}) + (3\hat{i} + 6\hat{j} - 7\hat{k}) + \mathbf{A} = \hat{j} \Rightarrow \mathbf{A} = 3\hat{i} + 4\hat{j} + 5\hat{k}$

12. $\mathbf{A} + \mathbf{B} = 3\hat{i} + 6\hat{j} - 2\hat{k}$

$\hat{n} = \frac{\mathbf{A} + \mathbf{B}}{|\mathbf{A} + \mathbf{B}|} = \frac{3\hat{i} + 6\hat{j} - 2\hat{k}}{7}$

13. $\mathbf{A} = 4\hat{i} + 6\hat{j}$

$\mathbf{A} + \mathbf{B} = 10\hat{i} + 9\hat{j}$

$\mathbf{B} = 6\hat{i} + 3\hat{j}$

(a) 6 and 3

(b) $\sqrt{6^2 + 3^2} = \sqrt{45}$

(c) $\theta = \tan^{-1}\left(\frac{3}{6}\right) = \tan^{-1}\left(\frac{1}{2}\right)$

14. $\mathbf{F}_1 + \mathbf{F}_2 + \mathbf{F}_3 + \mathbf{F}_4 = 0$

$\Rightarrow (7 + b + c)\hat{i} + (a + c + 11)\hat{j} + (-10 - b - a)\hat{k} = 0$

$7 + b + c = 0 \Rightarrow b + c = -7$

$a + c + 11 = 0 \Rightarrow a + c = -11$

$-10 - b - a = 0 \Rightarrow a + b = -10$

$\Rightarrow 2(a + b + c) = -28$

$\Rightarrow a + b + c = -14$

$\Rightarrow a = -7, \; b = -3, \; c = -4$

15. $\mathbf{A} = 100\cos 45°\,\hat{\mathbf{i}} + 100\sin 45°\,\hat{\mathbf{j}}$

$\mathbf{B} = -100\cos 45°\,\hat{\mathbf{i}} + 100\sin 45°\,\hat{\mathbf{j}}$

$\mathbf{C} = 100\cos 45°\,\hat{\mathbf{i}} - 100\sin 45°$

$\mathbf{A} + \mathbf{B} + \mathbf{C}$

$= 100\cos 45°\,\hat{\mathbf{i}} + 100\sin 45°\,\hat{\mathbf{j}}$

= 100 at an angle of 45° with *X*-axis

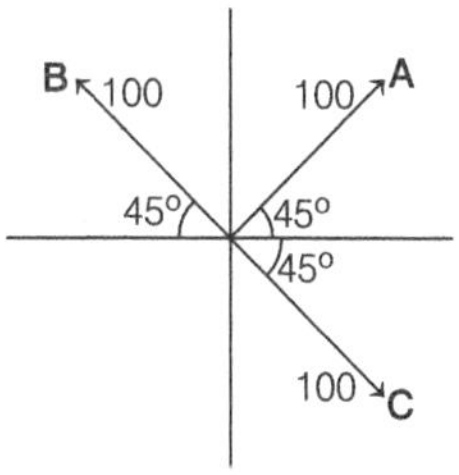

16. $\mathbf{v}_1 = 50\hat{\mathbf{j}}, \mathbf{v}_2 = -50\hat{\mathbf{i}}$

Change in velocity $= \mathbf{v}_2 - \mathbf{v}_1 = -50\hat{\mathbf{i}} - 50\hat{\mathbf{j}}$

$= 50\sqrt{2}$ km/h (South-West)

17. $\mathbf{s} = \mathbf{r}_2 - \mathbf{r}_1 = (3\hat{i} + 4\hat{j} + 5\hat{k}) - (2\hat{i} + 3\hat{j} + 5\hat{k}) = \hat{i} + \hat{j}$

18. $\mathbf{v} = v\hat{\mathbf{n}} = 10\left(\frac{3\hat{i} + 4\hat{j}}{5}\right) = 6\hat{i} + 8\hat{j}$

19. $\mathbf{s}_1 = 30\hat{\mathbf{j}}, \mathbf{s}_2 = 20\hat{\mathbf{i}}$

$\mathbf{s}_3 = -30\sqrt{2}\cos 45°\,\hat{\mathbf{i}} - 30\sqrt{2}\sin 45°\,\hat{\mathbf{j}} = -30\hat{\mathbf{i}} - 30\hat{\mathbf{j}}$

$\mathbf{s} = \mathbf{s}_1 + \mathbf{s}_2 + \mathbf{s}_3 = -10\hat{\mathbf{i}} = 10$ m (West)

20. $\mathbf{s}_1 = 2\hat{\mathbf{i}}, \mathbf{s}_2 = 5\cos 37°\,\hat{\mathbf{i}} - 5\sin 37°\,\hat{\mathbf{j}}, \mathbf{s}_3 = ?$

$\mathbf{s}_1 + \mathbf{s}_2 + \mathbf{s}_3 = 6\hat{\mathbf{i}}$

$\Rightarrow 2\hat{\mathbf{i}} + (4\hat{\mathbf{i}} - 3\hat{\mathbf{j}}) + \mathbf{s}_3 = 6\hat{\mathbf{i}} \Rightarrow \mathbf{s}_3 = 3\hat{\mathbf{j}} = 3$ km (North)

21. $\mathbf{v} = \mathbf{u} + \mathbf{a}t$

$\mathbf{v} = (2\hat{i} + 3\hat{j} - 4\hat{k}) + (-\hat{i} + 2\hat{j} + 5\hat{k})3 = -\hat{i} + 9\hat{j} + 11\hat{k}$

22. Using Lami theorem,

$$\frac{P}{\sin 120^\circ}=\frac{Q}{\sin 90^\circ}=\frac{R}{\sin 150^\circ}$$

$$P:Q:R=\sqrt{3}:2:1$$

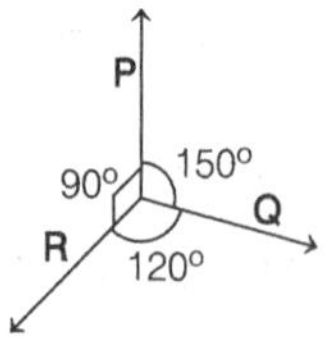

23. (a) $F_x = 3-2\cos 60^\circ - 1\cos 60^\circ = 1.5$ N

(b) $F_y = 2\sin 60^\circ - 1\sin 60^\circ = \frac{\sqrt{3}}{2}$ N

(c) $\mathbf{F} = -\frac{3}{2}\hat{\mathbf{i}} - \frac{\sqrt{3}}{2}\hat{\mathbf{j}}$

24. $\mathbf{F}_1 = F_1(-\hat{\mathbf{j}})$

$\mathbf{F}_2 = F_2\sin 30^\circ\,\hat{\mathbf{i}} + F_2\cos 30^\circ\,\hat{\mathbf{j}}$

$\mathbf{F}_3 = 10\cos 30^\circ\,\hat{\mathbf{i}} + 10\sin 30^\circ\,\hat{\mathbf{j}}$

$\mathbf{F}_4 = -15\cos 37^\circ\,\hat{\mathbf{i}} + 15\sin 37^\circ\,\hat{\mathbf{j}}$

Since the body is in equilibrium, then

$$\mathbf{F}_1+\mathbf{F}_2+\mathbf{F}_3+\mathbf{F}_4 = 0$$

$$\Rightarrow \left(\frac{F_2}{2}+5\sqrt{3}-12\right)\hat{\mathbf{i}} + \left(-F_1+\frac{\sqrt{3}F_2}{2}+5+9\right)\hat{\mathbf{j}} = 0$$

$\Rightarrow \quad F_2 = 24-10\sqrt{3}$ & $F_1 = 12\sqrt{3}-1$

$\mathbf{F}_1 = -(12\sqrt{3}-1)\hat{\mathbf{j}}$ and

$\mathbf{F}_2 = (12-5\sqrt{3})\hat{\mathbf{i}} + (12\sqrt{3}-15)\hat{\mathbf{j}}$

1.3 Dot Product and Cross Product

1. (i) 0 (ii) 1 (iii) 1 (iv) 1 (v) 0

2. (i) No, Yes (ii) Yes, if **b** is a null vector.
(iii) No (iv) Never (v) No

3. $\mathbf{A}\cdot\mathbf{B} = 2\times 0 + 0\times 3 + 5\times 5 = 25$

4. (i) $\theta = \cos^{-1}\left(\frac{\mathbf{A}\cdot\mathbf{B}}{AB}\right) = \cos^{-1}\left(\frac{3}{3\sqrt{2}}\right) = 45^\circ$

(ii) $\theta = \cos^{-1}\left(\frac{3}{\sqrt{6}\sqrt{2}}\right) = \cos^{-1}\left(\frac{\sqrt{3}}{2}\right) = 30^\circ$

(iii) $\theta = \cos^{-1}\left(\frac{1}{\sqrt{3}}\right)$

(iv) $\theta = \cos^{-1}(0) = 90^\circ$

(v) $\mathbf{A} = \hat{\mathbf{i}}+2\hat{\mathbf{j}}-\hat{\mathbf{k}}$ and $\mathbf{B} = -\hat{\mathbf{i}}+\hat{\mathbf{j}}-2\hat{\mathbf{k}}$

$\cos\theta = \frac{\mathbf{A}\cdot\mathbf{B}}{AB} \Rightarrow \cos\theta = \frac{-1+2+2}{\sqrt{6}\sqrt{6}} = \frac{3}{6} = \frac{1}{2}$

$\Rightarrow \quad \theta = 60^\circ$

5. $\mathbf{A}\cdot\mathbf{B} = 0 \Rightarrow 10+14+3c = 0 \Rightarrow c = -8$

6. $\mathbf{A}\cdot\mathbf{B} = AB\cos\theta = 2\sqrt{3}$

$|\mathbf{A}\times\mathbf{B}| = AB\sin\theta = \pm 2$

$\Rightarrow \quad \tan\theta = \pm\frac{1}{\sqrt{3}} \Rightarrow \theta = 30^\circ$ and 150°

7. $\mathbf{P}\cdot\mathbf{Q} = PQ \Rightarrow PQ\cos\theta = PQ$

$\Rightarrow \quad \cos\theta = 1 \Rightarrow \theta = 0^\circ$

8. $|\mathbf{A}\times\mathbf{B}| = \sqrt{3}\mathbf{A}\cdot\mathbf{B} \Rightarrow AB\sin\theta = \sqrt{3}AB\cos\theta$

$\Rightarrow \quad \tan\theta = \sqrt{3} \Rightarrow \theta = 60^\circ$

$|\mathbf{A}+\mathbf{B}| = (A^2+B^2+2AB\cos 60^\circ)^{1/2} = (A^2+B^2+AB)^{1/2}$

9. (i) $\mathbf{A}\cdot\mathbf{B} = 0 \Rightarrow 3+2p+27 = 0 \Rightarrow p = -15$

(ii) $\mathbf{A} = \lambda\mathbf{B}$

$\Rightarrow \quad 3\hat{\mathbf{i}}+2\hat{\mathbf{j}}+9\hat{\mathbf{k}} = \lambda(\hat{\mathbf{i}}+p\hat{\mathbf{j}}+3\hat{\mathbf{k}})$

$\Rightarrow \quad \lambda = 3,\ \lambda p = 2 \Rightarrow p = \frac{2}{3}$

10. (i) $A\cos\theta\hat{\mathbf{B}} = \left(\frac{\mathbf{A}\cdot\mathbf{B}}{B}\right)\frac{\mathbf{B}}{B} = \frac{1}{\sqrt{5}}\frac{(\hat{\mathbf{j}}+2\hat{\mathbf{k}})}{\sqrt{5}} = \frac{1}{5}(\hat{\mathbf{j}}+2\hat{\mathbf{k}})$

(ii) $(3\hat{\mathbf{i}}+\hat{\mathbf{j}}) - \frac{1}{5}(\hat{\mathbf{i}}+2\hat{\mathbf{k}}) = 3\hat{\mathbf{i}}+\frac{4}{5}\hat{\mathbf{j}}-\frac{2}{5}\hat{\mathbf{k}}$

11. (a) $\mathbf{A}\cdot\mathbf{B} = 6+0+4 = 10$

(b) $\theta = \cos^{-1}\left(\frac{\mathbf{A}\cdot\mathbf{B}}{AB}\right) = \cos^{-1}\left(\frac{10}{3\times 5}\right) = \cos^{-1}\left(\frac{2}{3}\right)$

(c) $A\cos\theta\mathbf{B} = \left(\frac{\mathbf{A}\cdot\mathbf{B}}{B}\right)\frac{\mathbf{B}}{B} = \frac{10(3\hat{\mathbf{i}}-4\hat{\mathbf{k}})}{5\times 5} = \frac{2}{5}(3\hat{\mathbf{i}}-4\hat{\mathbf{k}})$

(d) $B\cos\theta\mathbf{A} = \left(\frac{\mathbf{A}\cdot\mathbf{B}}{A}\right)\frac{\mathbf{A}}{A} = \frac{10}{9}(2\hat{\mathbf{i}}+2\hat{\mathbf{j}}-\hat{\mathbf{k}})$

12. $W = \mathbf{F}\cdot\mathbf{s} = \mathbf{F}\cdot(\mathbf{r}_2-\mathbf{r}_1) = (\hat{\mathbf{i}}+2\hat{\mathbf{j}}-\hat{\mathbf{k}})\cdot(\hat{\mathbf{i}}-4\hat{\mathbf{j}}+\hat{\mathbf{k}})$

$= 1-8-1 = -8$ J

13. $\tau = \mathbf{r}\times\mathbf{F} = (2\hat{\mathbf{i}}+\hat{\mathbf{j}}-\hat{\mathbf{k}})\times(2\hat{\mathbf{i}}+5\hat{\mathbf{j}})$

$$= \begin{vmatrix} \hat{\mathbf{i}} & \hat{\mathbf{j}} & \hat{\mathbf{k}} \\ 2 & 1 & -1 \\ 2 & 5 & 0 \end{vmatrix} = 5\hat{\mathbf{i}}-2\hat{\mathbf{j}}+8\hat{\mathbf{k}}$$

14. $\mathbf{A} = 9\hat{\mathbf{n}} = \pm 9\left(\frac{\mathbf{P}\times\mathbf{Q}}{|\mathbf{P}\times\mathbf{Q}|}\right) = \pm(-3\hat{\mathbf{i}}-6\hat{\mathbf{j}}+6\hat{\mathbf{k}})$

15. Area of parallelogram $= AB\sin\theta = |\mathbf{A}\times\mathbf{B}| = \sqrt{54}$ sq. units

16. Area of parallelogram $= \frac{1}{2}|\mathbf{d}_1\times\mathbf{d}_2| = \sqrt{35}/2$ sq. units

17. (a) $\mathbf{a}\times(\mathbf{b}+\mathbf{c})$

$= (5\hat{\mathbf{i}}+4\hat{\mathbf{j}}-6\hat{\mathbf{k}})\times(-2\hat{\mathbf{i}}+2\hat{\mathbf{j}}+3\hat{\mathbf{k}}+4\hat{\mathbf{i}}+3\hat{\mathbf{j}}+2\hat{\mathbf{k}})$

$= (5\hat{\mathbf{i}}+4\hat{\mathbf{j}}-6\hat{\mathbf{k}})\times(2\hat{\mathbf{i}}+5\hat{\mathbf{j}}+5\hat{\mathbf{k}})$

$$= \begin{vmatrix} \hat{\mathbf{i}} & \hat{\mathbf{j}} & \hat{\mathbf{k}} \\ 5 & 4 & -6 \\ 2 & 5 & 5 \end{vmatrix} = 50\hat{\mathbf{i}}-37\hat{\mathbf{j}}+17\hat{\mathbf{k}}$$

(b) $\mathbf{a}\times(\mathbf{b}\times\mathbf{c}) = 40\hat{\mathbf{i}}+100\hat{\mathbf{j}}+100\hat{\mathbf{k}}$

18. (i) $(\mathbf{a}\cdot\mathbf{b})+(\mathbf{b}\cdot\mathbf{c})+(\mathbf{c}\cdot\mathbf{a}) = -1+1+1 = 1$

(ii) $(\mathbf{a}\cdot\mathbf{c})\mathbf{c}+(\mathbf{c}\cdot\mathbf{b})\mathbf{a} = 1(\hat{\mathbf{i}}+\hat{\mathbf{j}}-\hat{\mathbf{k}})+1(\hat{\mathbf{i}}+\hat{\mathbf{j}}+\hat{\mathbf{k}}) = 2\hat{\mathbf{i}}+2\hat{\mathbf{j}}$

19. $(\mathbf{a}+\mathbf{b})\times(\mathbf{a}-\mathbf{b}) = \mathbf{a}\times\mathbf{a}-\mathbf{a}\times\mathbf{b}+\mathbf{b}\times\mathbf{a}-\mathbf{b}\times\mathbf{b}$

$= 0-\mathbf{a}\times\mathbf{b}-\mathbf{a}\times\mathbf{b}-0 = -2(\mathbf{a}\times\mathbf{b})$

20. (i) $\sin\theta = \frac{|\mathbf{A}\times\mathbf{B}|}{AB} = \frac{\sqrt{3}}{\sqrt{2}\sqrt{2}} = \frac{\sqrt{3}}{2} \Rightarrow \theta = 60^\circ$

(ii) Area of $\Delta PQS = \frac{1}{2}|\mathbf{a}\times\mathbf{b}| = \frac{1}{2}(\sqrt{3}) = \frac{\sqrt{3}}{2}$ sq. units

21. (a) North (b) West

Level 2

Single Choice Correct Questions

1. Electric current is scalar despite having both magnitude and direction. Time is also scalar. All quantities having magnitude and direction are not vectors.

2. A vector is independent of choice of reference frame. If a vector is shifted parallel to itself, it does not change. If a vector is rotated by an angle other than a multiple of 2π, it changes.

3. $R^2 = A^2 + B^2 + 2AB\cos\theta$

$$\Rightarrow (\sqrt{x^2+y^2})^2 = (x+y)^2 + (x-y)^2 + 2(x+y)(x-y)\cos\theta$$

$$\Rightarrow \quad \cos\theta = \frac{-(x^2+y^2)}{2(x^2-y^2)} \quad \Rightarrow \quad \theta = \cos^{-1}\left(\frac{-(x^2+y^2)}{2(x^2-y^2)}\right)$$

4. $R^2 = P^2 + Q^2 + 2PQ\cos\theta$

$$\Rightarrow (\sqrt{7}Q)^2 = P^2 + Q^2 + 2PQ\cos 60^\circ \qquad [\because \cos 60^\circ = 1/2]$$

$$\Rightarrow \quad 6Q^2 = P^2 + PQ \Rightarrow 6 = \left(\frac{P}{Q}\right)^2 + \left(\frac{P}{Q}\right)$$

Let, $\frac{P}{Q} = x \quad \Rightarrow \quad 6 = x^2 + x \Rightarrow \quad x^2 + x - 6 = 0$

$$\Rightarrow (x+3)(x-2) = 0 \Rightarrow x = 2 \quad \therefore \frac{P}{Q} = 2$$

5. $R^2 = 3A^2$ and $R^2 = A^2 + A^2 + 2(A)(A)\cos\theta$

$$3A^2 = 2A^2 + 2A^2\cos\theta \Rightarrow \cos\theta = \frac{1}{2} \Rightarrow \theta = 60^\circ$$

6. $(2P)^2 = P^2 + Q^2 + 2PQ\cos\theta \qquad$ ...(i)

$$P^2 = P^2 + Q^2 + 2PQ\cos(180^\circ - \theta)$$

$$\Rightarrow \quad 0 = Q^2 - 2PQ\cos\theta \Rightarrow 2PQ\cos\theta = Q^2 \qquad \text{...(ii)}$$

From Eqs. (i) and (ii), we get

$$4P^2 = P^2 + Q^2 + Q^2 \Rightarrow 3P^2 = 2Q^2 \Rightarrow \frac{P}{Q} = \frac{\sqrt{2}}{\sqrt{3}}$$

7. $R^2 = (3P)^2 + (2P)^2 + 2(3P)(2P)\cos\theta \qquad$ ...(i)

$$(2R)^2 = (6P)^2 + (2P)^2 + 2(6P)(2P)\cos\theta \qquad \text{...(ii)}$$

From Eqs. (i) and (ii), we get

$$\Rightarrow \quad \cos\theta = \frac{-1}{2} \Rightarrow \theta = 120^\circ$$

8. $R_{max} = A + B$ and $R_{min} = |A - B|$

9. $\frac{P+Q}{P-Q} = 3 \quad \Rightarrow P = 2Q$

10. $R = \sqrt{30^2 + 60^2 + 2(30)(60)\cos 60^\circ} = 30\sqrt{7}\text{N}$

11. $\mathbf{C} = \mathbf{A} + \mathbf{B}$

In this figure,

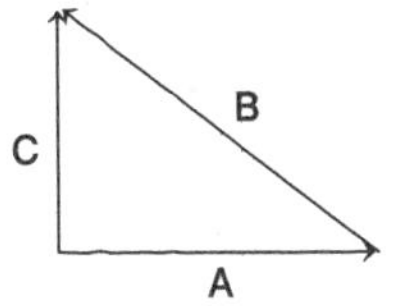

$|\mathbf{C}| < |\mathbf{A}|$ and $|\mathbf{C}| < |\mathbf{B}|$

12. $\mathbf{A} = \mathbf{B} + \mathbf{C}$

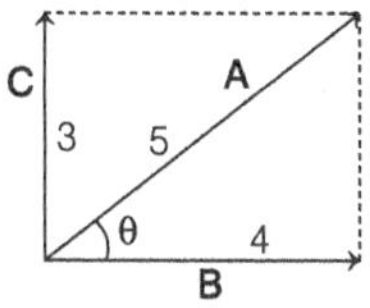

$$\Rightarrow \quad A^2 = B^2 + C^2 + 2BC\cos\theta$$

$$\Rightarrow \quad 5^2 = 4^2 + 3^2 + 2(4)(3)\cos\theta$$

$$\Rightarrow \cos\theta = 0 \Rightarrow \theta = 90^\circ$$

So, angle between **B** and **C** is 90°.

Angle between **A** and **B** = $\cos^{-1}\left(\frac{4}{5}\right)$.

13. $\mathbf{R} = \mathbf{P} + \mathbf{Q}$

R is perpendicular to **P**.

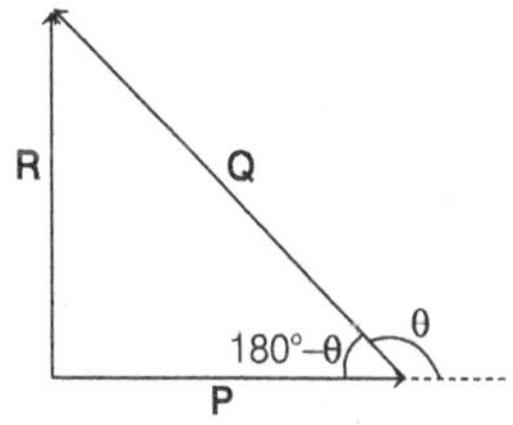

$$\cos(180^\circ - \theta) = \frac{P}{Q} \Rightarrow -\cos\theta = \frac{P}{Q} \Rightarrow \theta = \cos^{-1}\left(-\frac{P}{Q}\right)$$

14. $\mathbf{R} = \mathbf{P} + \mathbf{Q}$

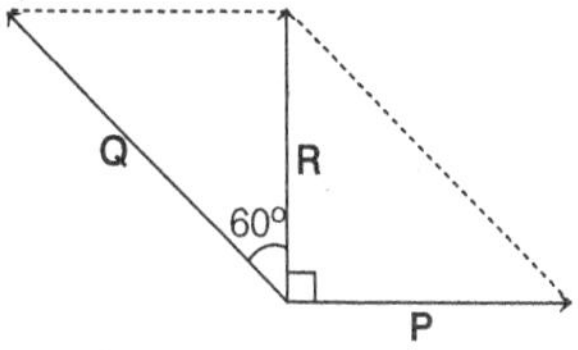

$$\tan 60^\circ = \frac{P}{10} \Rightarrow P = 10\sqrt{3}\text{ kg-wt}$$

15. $\mathbf{R} = -(\mathbf{P} + \mathbf{Q})$

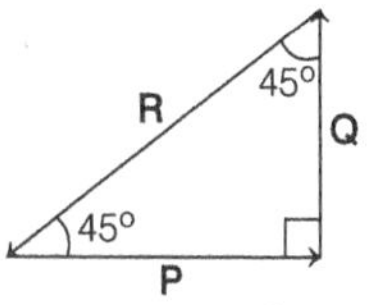

$$\Rightarrow \quad R^2 = P^2 + Q^2 + 2PQ\cos\theta$$

$$\Rightarrow \quad (\sqrt{2}P)^2 = P^2 + P^2 + 2P(P)\cos\theta$$

$$\Rightarrow \quad \cos\theta = 0 \Rightarrow \theta = 90^\circ$$

So, angle between **P** and **Q** is 90°.

Angle between **P** and **R** is 135°.

Angle between **Q** and **R** is 135°.

16. Minimum number of unequal coplanar vectors having zero resultant is three.

17. (d)

18. If $\mathbf{R} = \mathbf{A} + \mathbf{B}$, then **R** lies in the plane containing **A** and **B**.

19. $\mathbf{AB} + \mathbf{BC} + 2\mathbf{CA} = (\mathbf{AB} + \mathbf{BC} + \mathbf{CA}) + \mathbf{CA} = 0 + \mathbf{CA} = \mathbf{CA}$

20. $\mathbf{RQ} = \mathbf{a} - \mathbf{b}$

$\mathbf{PR} = \mathbf{b} - \mathbf{c}$

$\mathbf{RQ} = 2\mathbf{PR}$

$$\Rightarrow \quad \mathbf{a} - \mathbf{b} = 2(\mathbf{b} - \mathbf{c}) \Rightarrow \mathbf{a} + 2\mathbf{c} = 3\mathbf{b}$$

21. $\mathbf{d} + \mathbf{e} = \mathbf{f}$

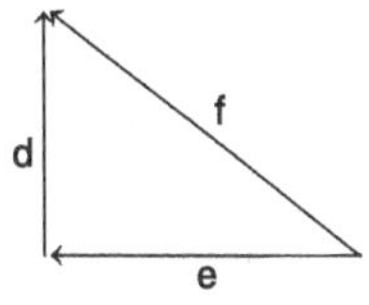

22. Only in option (a), they can form a closed polygon.

23. $\mathbf{A}_1 = \mathbf{A}$ and $\mathbf{A}_2 = -\mathbf{A}$

$$\Delta\mathbf{A} = \mathbf{A}_2 - \mathbf{A}_1 = -\mathbf{A} - \mathbf{A} = -2\mathbf{A}$$
$$\Delta|\mathbf{A}| = |\mathbf{A}_2| - |\mathbf{A}_1| = 0$$

24. $\mathbf{R}_1 = \mathbf{A} + \mathbf{B} \Rightarrow R_1^2 = A^2 + B^2 + 2AB\cos\theta$ ...(i)

$\mathbf{R}_2 = \mathbf{A} - \mathbf{B} \Rightarrow R_2^2 = A^2 + B^2 - 2AB\cos\theta$ ...(ii)

Adding Eqs. (i) and (ii), we get

$$\Rightarrow R_1^2 + R_2^2 = 2(A^2 + B^2)$$

25. $\mathbf{A} + \mathbf{B} + \mathbf{C} + \mathbf{D} + \mathbf{E} = 0$

$\mathbf{R} = (-\mathbf{A}) + \mathbf{B} + \mathbf{C} + \mathbf{D} + \mathbf{E}$ $\because$ (**A** is reversed)

$\Rightarrow \mathbf{R} = (-\mathbf{A}) + (-\mathbf{A})$ $\because (\mathbf{B} + \mathbf{C} + \mathbf{D} + \mathbf{E} = -\mathbf{A})$

$\Rightarrow \mathbf{R} = -2\mathbf{A} \Rightarrow R = 2A$

So, magnitude of resultant will be 20 units.

26. $C^2 = A^2 + B^2 + 2AB\cos 120°$ $[\because \cos 120° = -1/2]$

$$\Rightarrow C = \sqrt{A^2 + B^2 - AB}$$
$$|\mathbf{A} - \mathbf{B}| = \sqrt{A^2 + B^2 - 2AB\cos 120°}$$
$$= \sqrt{A^2 + B^2 + AB} \Rightarrow C < |\mathbf{A} - \mathbf{B}|$$

27. $\mathbf{R} = \mathbf{A} - \mathbf{B} \Rightarrow R = \sqrt{A^2 + B^2 - 2AB\cos\theta}$

28. $|\mathbf{a} - \mathbf{b}| = \sqrt{a^2 + b^2 - 2ab\cos\theta}$

$$\Rightarrow 30^2 = 11^2 + 23^2 - 2(11)(23)\cos\theta$$
$$\Rightarrow \cos\theta = -\frac{250}{2(11)(23)}$$
$$|\mathbf{a} + \mathbf{b}| = \sqrt{a^2 + b^2 + 2ab\cos\theta}$$
$$= \sqrt{11^2 + 23^2 + 2(11)(23)\cos\theta}$$
$$= \sqrt{11^2 + 23^2 - 250}$$
$$= \sqrt{400} = 20$$

29. $1^2 = 1^2 + 1^2 + 2(1)(1)\cos\theta$

$$\cos\theta = -\frac{1}{2} \Rightarrow \theta = 120°$$
$$|\mathbf{A} - \mathbf{B}| = R = \sqrt{A^2 + B^2 - 2AB\cos\theta}$$
$$R = \sqrt{1^2 + 1^2 - 2\left(-\frac{1}{2}\right)} = \sqrt{3}$$

30. Speed of tip of second hand $= v = \dfrac{2\pi(1\text{ cm})}{60\ s} = \dfrac{\pi}{30}$ cm/s

$$|\Delta\mathbf{v}| = 2v\sin\left(\frac{\theta}{2}\right) = 2\left(\frac{\pi}{30}\right)\sin 45° = \frac{\pi\sqrt{2}}{30}\text{ cm/s}$$

31. $|\hat{\mathbf{e}}_1 - \hat{\mathbf{e}}_2| = \sqrt{1^2 + 1^2 - 2\times1\times1(\cos\theta)}$

$$= \sqrt{2 - 2\cos\theta} = \sqrt{2(1 - \cos\theta)}$$
$$= \sqrt{2\cdot 2\sin^2\left(\frac{\theta}{2}\right)} = 2\sin\left(\frac{\theta}{2}\right)$$

32.

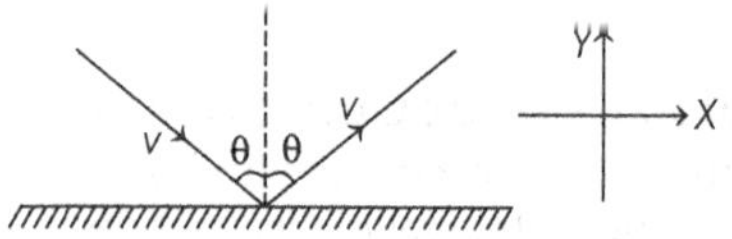

$$\mathbf{p}_1 = mv\sin\theta\hat{\mathbf{i}} - mv\cos\theta\hat{\mathbf{j}}$$
$$\mathbf{p}_2 = mv\sin\theta\hat{\mathbf{i}} + mv\cos\theta\hat{\mathbf{j}}$$
$$\Delta\mathbf{p} = \mathbf{p}_2 - \mathbf{p}_1 = 2mv\cos\theta\hat{\mathbf{j}}$$
$$|\Delta\mathbf{p}| = 2mv\cos\theta$$

33. $A_x = 2A_y$ and $A_x = \sqrt{2}A_z \Rightarrow A_z = \sqrt{2}A_y$

$$\cos\beta = \frac{A_y}{A} = \frac{A_y}{\sqrt{A_x^2 + A_y^2 + A_z^2}}$$
$$= \frac{A_y}{\sqrt{(2A_y)^2 + A_y^2 + (\sqrt{2}A_y)^2}} = \frac{1}{\sqrt{7}}$$
$$\Rightarrow \beta = \cos^{-1}\left(\frac{1}{\sqrt{7}}\right)$$

34. $\mathbf{F} = 100\cos 45°\hat{\mathbf{i}} - 100\sin 45°\hat{\mathbf{j}} = 50\sqrt{2}(\hat{\mathbf{i}} - \hat{\mathbf{j}})$

35. $\hat{\mathbf{n}} = \dfrac{\mathbf{A} + \mathbf{B}}{|\mathbf{A} + \mathbf{B}|} = \dfrac{3\hat{\mathbf{i}} + 6\hat{\mathbf{j}} - 2\hat{\mathbf{k}}}{7}$

36. $\mathbf{OA} = R\hat{\mathbf{i}}$

$$\mathbf{OB} = R\cos 45°\hat{\mathbf{i}} + R\sin 45°\hat{\mathbf{j}}$$
$$\mathbf{OC} = R\hat{\mathbf{j}}$$
$$\mathbf{OA} + \mathbf{OB} + \mathbf{OC} = R\left(1 + \frac{1}{\sqrt{2}}\right)\hat{\mathbf{i}} + R\left(1 + \frac{1}{\sqrt{2}}\right)\hat{\mathbf{j}}$$
$$|\mathbf{OA} + \mathbf{OB} + \mathbf{OC}| = (\sqrt{2} + 1)R$$

37. $\mathbf{F}_1 + \mathbf{F}_2 + \mathbf{F}_3 + \mathbf{F}_4 = 4\hat{\mathbf{j}} + 2\hat{\mathbf{k}}$

So, the particle will move in yz-plane.

38. $\mathbf{A} + \mathbf{B} = (\hat{\mathbf{i}} - 2\hat{\mathbf{j}} - 3\hat{\mathbf{k}}) + (4\hat{\mathbf{i}} - 2\hat{\mathbf{j}} + 6\hat{\mathbf{k}}) = 5\hat{\mathbf{i}} - 4\hat{\mathbf{j}} + 3\hat{\mathbf{k}}$

$$\cos\alpha = \frac{A_x}{A} \Rightarrow \cos\alpha = \frac{5}{5\sqrt{2}} \Rightarrow \alpha = 45°$$

39. $\mathbf{A} = \lambda\mathbf{B}$

$$2\hat{\mathbf{i}} + p\hat{\mathbf{j}} + q\hat{\mathbf{k}} = \lambda(5\hat{\mathbf{i}} + 7\hat{\mathbf{j}} + 3\hat{\mathbf{k}})$$
$$\Rightarrow 5\lambda = 2, p = 7\lambda, q = 3\lambda$$
$$p = \frac{14}{5} \text{ and } q = \frac{6}{5}$$

40. $\mathbf{A} = 2\hat{\mathbf{i}} - 3\hat{\mathbf{j}} + 4\hat{\mathbf{k}}$

Component in yz-plane $= \sqrt{(-3)^2 + 4^2} = 5$

Component in zx-plane $= \sqrt{2^2 + 4^2} = 2\sqrt{5}$

41. $\mathbf{s}_1 = 10\hat{\mathbf{i}}$; $\mathbf{s}_2 = -5\hat{\mathbf{i}} + 5\sqrt{3}\hat{\mathbf{j}}$; $\mathbf{s}_3 = ?$

$$\mathbf{s} = \mathbf{s}_1 + \mathbf{s}_2 + \mathbf{s}_3 = 0$$
$$\Rightarrow 10\hat{\mathbf{i}} - 5\hat{\mathbf{i}} + 5\sqrt{3}\hat{\mathbf{j}} + \mathbf{s}_3 = 0$$
$$\Rightarrow \mathbf{s}_3 = -5\hat{\mathbf{i}} - 5\sqrt{3}\hat{\mathbf{j}}$$

42. $\mathbf{A} = 40\hat{\mathbf{i}}$

$\mathbf{B} = -25\cos 37°\,\hat{\mathbf{i}} + 25\sin 37°\,\hat{\mathbf{j}} = -20\hat{\mathbf{i}} + 15\hat{\mathbf{j}}$

$\mathbf{R} = \mathbf{A} + \mathbf{B} = (40\hat{\mathbf{i}}) + (-20\hat{\mathbf{i}} + 15\hat{\mathbf{j}}) = 20\hat{\mathbf{i}} + 15\hat{\mathbf{j}}$

$= 25$ units 37° North of East

43. $(\mathbf{a}\cdot\mathbf{b})^2 = a^2b^2 \Rightarrow \mathbf{a}\cdot\mathbf{b} = ab$

$\Rightarrow ab\cos\theta = ab \Rightarrow \cos\theta = 1 \Rightarrow \theta = 0° \Rightarrow \mathbf{a}\,||\,\mathbf{b}$

44. $(\mathbf{a}+\mathbf{b})\cdot(\mathbf{a}-\mathbf{b}) = (2\hat{\mathbf{i}} - \hat{\mathbf{j}} + 3\hat{\mathbf{k}})\cdot(2\hat{\mathbf{i}} - 5\hat{\mathbf{j}} - 3\hat{\mathbf{k}}) = 4 + 5 - 9 = 0$

45. $\theta = \cos^{-1}\left(\frac{\mathbf{A}\cdot\mathbf{B}}{AB}\right) = \cos^{-1}\left(\frac{54}{9\times 9}\right) = \cos^{-1}\left(\frac{2}{3}\right)$

$\Rightarrow \cos\theta = 2/3$

$\sin\theta = \sqrt{1-\cos^2\theta} = \frac{\sqrt{5}}{3} \Rightarrow \theta = \sin^{-1}\left(\frac{\sqrt{5}}{3}\right)$

46. $\mathbf{A} + \mathbf{B} = 2\hat{\mathbf{i}}$ ...(i)

$\mathbf{A} - \mathbf{B} = 4\hat{\mathbf{j}}$ ...(ii)

Solving Eqs. (i) and (ii), we get

$\mathbf{A} = \hat{\mathbf{i}} + 2\hat{\mathbf{j}}$ & $\mathbf{B} = \hat{\mathbf{i}} - 2\hat{\mathbf{j}}$

$\cos\theta = \frac{\mathbf{A}\cdot\mathbf{B}}{AB} = \frac{1+2(-2)}{\sqrt{5}\sqrt{5}} = -\frac{3}{5} \Rightarrow \theta = 127°$

47. $\theta = \cos^{-1}\left(\frac{\mathbf{P}\cdot\mathbf{Q}}{PQ}\right) = \cos^{-1}\left(\frac{(\mathbf{A}+\mathbf{B})\cdot(\mathbf{A}-\mathbf{B})}{|\mathbf{A}+\mathbf{B}||\mathbf{A}-\mathbf{B}|}\right)$

$= \cos^{-1}\left(\frac{A^2 - B^2}{|\mathbf{A}+\mathbf{B}||\mathbf{A}-\mathbf{B}|}\right) = \cos^{-1}(0) = 90°$

48. $\mathbf{A} = A\cos\hat{\mathbf{i}} + A\sin\theta\hat{\mathbf{j}}$

$\mathbf{B} = B\sin\theta\hat{\mathbf{i}} - B\cos\theta\hat{\mathbf{j}}$

$\mathbf{A}\cdot\mathbf{B} = AB\sin\theta\cos\theta - AB\sin\theta\cos\theta = 0$

So, **A** and **B** are perpendicular to each other.

49. $\mathbf{P}\cdot\mathbf{Q} = 0 \Rightarrow a^2 - 2a - 3 = 0$

$\Rightarrow (a-3)(a+1) = 0 \Rightarrow a = 3$ and $a = -1$

50. $\mathbf{A}\cdot\mathbf{C} = 0$, so $\mathbf{A}\perp\mathbf{C}$ and it will be a right angled triangle.

51. $\mathbf{A}+\mathbf{B}$ is perpendicular to $\mathbf{A}-\mathbf{B}$.

$\Rightarrow (\mathbf{A}+\mathbf{B})\cdot(\mathbf{A}-\mathbf{B}) = 0$

$\Rightarrow \mathbf{A}\cdot\mathbf{A} - \mathbf{A}\cdot\mathbf{B} + \mathbf{B}\cdot\mathbf{A} - \mathbf{B}\cdot\mathbf{B} = 0$

$\Rightarrow A^2 - \mathbf{A}\cdot\mathbf{B} + \mathbf{A}\cdot\mathbf{B} - B^2 = 0$

$\Rightarrow A^2 - B^2 = 0 \Rightarrow A = B$

52. $(a\hat{\mathbf{i}} + b\hat{\mathbf{j}})\cdot(\hat{\mathbf{i}} + \hat{\mathbf{j}}) = 0 \Rightarrow a + b = 0$

$\hat{\mathbf{n}}$ is a unit vector $\Rightarrow \sqrt{a^2+b^2} = 1 \Rightarrow a = \pm\frac{1}{\sqrt{2}}, b = \mp\frac{1}{\sqrt{2}}$

53. Unit vector perpendicular to $(\hat{\mathbf{i}} + 2\hat{\mathbf{j}})$ will be $(\pm 2\hat{\mathbf{i}} \mp \hat{\mathbf{j}})/\sqrt{5}$.

So, our required vector will be $3\sqrt{5}\left(\frac{\pm 2\hat{\mathbf{i}} \mp \hat{\mathbf{j}}}{\sqrt{5}}\right)$

$= \pm 6\hat{\mathbf{i}} \mp 3\hat{\mathbf{j}} = (6\hat{\mathbf{i}} - 3\hat{\mathbf{j}})$ or $(-6\hat{\mathbf{i}} + 3\hat{\mathbf{j}})$

54. $W = \mathbf{F}\cdot\mathbf{s} = (-2\hat{\mathbf{i}} + 15\hat{\mathbf{j}} + 6\hat{\mathbf{k}})\cdot(10\hat{\mathbf{j}}) = 150$ J

55. $A\cos\theta = \mathbf{A}\cdot\hat{\mathbf{B}}$

56. $\left(\frac{\mathbf{v}\cdot\mathbf{a}}{a}\right)\frac{\mathbf{a}}{a} = \frac{6}{\sqrt{3}}\left(\frac{\hat{\mathbf{i}} + \hat{\mathbf{j}} + \hat{\mathbf{k}}}{\sqrt{3}}\right) = 2\hat{\mathbf{i}} + 2\hat{\mathbf{j}} + 2\hat{\mathbf{k}}$

57. $(6\hat{\mathbf{i}} + 2\hat{\mathbf{j}} - 2\hat{\mathbf{k}}) - (2\hat{\mathbf{i}} + 2\hat{\mathbf{j}} + 2\hat{\mathbf{k}}) = 4\hat{\mathbf{i}} - 4\hat{\mathbf{k}}$

58. Given $|\mathbf{A}_1| = 2, |\mathbf{A}_2| = 3$ and $|\mathbf{A}_1 + \mathbf{A}_2| = 3$

$|\mathbf{A}_1 + \mathbf{A}_2| = \sqrt{A_1^2 + A_2^2 + 2A_1A_2\cos\theta} = 3$

$\Rightarrow (2)^2 + (3)^2 + 2(\mathbf{A}_1\cdot\mathbf{A}_2) = 9 \Rightarrow \mathbf{A}_1\cdot\mathbf{A}_2 = -2$

$(\mathbf{A}_1 + 2\mathbf{A}_2)\cdot(3\mathbf{A}_1 - 4\mathbf{A}_2)$

$= 3\mathbf{A}_1\cdot\mathbf{A}_1 - 4\mathbf{A}_1\cdot\mathbf{A}_2 + 6\mathbf{A}_1\cdot\mathbf{A}_2 - 8\mathbf{A}_2\cdot\mathbf{A}_2$

$= 3A_1^2 + 2\mathbf{A}_1\cdot\mathbf{A}_2 - 8A_2^2 = 3(2)^2 + 2(-2) - 8(3)^2 = -64$

Magnitude will be 64.

59. $\mathbf{A} = A(l_1\hat{\mathbf{i}} + m_1\hat{\mathbf{j}} + n_1\hat{\mathbf{k}})$

$\mathbf{B} = B(l_2\hat{\mathbf{i}} + m_2\hat{\mathbf{j}} + n_2\hat{\mathbf{k}})$

$\cos\theta = \frac{\mathbf{A}\cdot\mathbf{B}}{AB} = \frac{AB(l_1l_2 + m_1m_2 + n_1n_2)}{AB}$

$= l_1l_2 + m_1m_2 + n_1n_2$

60. (b)

61. $\mathbf{A}\times\mathbf{B}$ is perpendicular to the plane containing **A** and **B**. So $\mathbf{A}\times\mathbf{B}$ is perpendicular to $\mathbf{A}, \mathbf{B}$ and $\mathbf{A}+\mathbf{B}$.

62. Using right hand thumb rule for finding $\mathbf{A}\times\mathbf{B}$, magnetic field will be directed North.

63. Angle between $\mathbf{A}\times\mathbf{B}$ and $\mathbf{B}\times\mathbf{A}$ is π.

64. Cross-product is not commutative.

65. $\boldsymbol{\tau} = \mathbf{r}\times\mathbf{F} \Rightarrow \boldsymbol{\tau}\perp\mathbf{r}$ and $\boldsymbol{\tau}\perp\mathbf{F}$

$\Rightarrow \boldsymbol{\tau}\cdot\mathbf{r} = 0$ and $\boldsymbol{\tau}\cdot\mathbf{F} = 0$

66. $\mathbf{A}\perp\mathbf{B}$ and $\mathbf{A}\perp\mathbf{C}$

So, $\mathbf{A}\,||\,(\mathbf{B}\times\mathbf{C})$

67. $\mathbf{A}\times\mathbf{B} = 0$

$\Rightarrow$ Either $A = 0$, or $B = 0$, or **A** and **B** are parallel/anti-parallel.

68. $(\mathbf{B}\times\mathbf{A})\perp\mathbf{A}$

So, $(\mathbf{B}\times\mathbf{A})\cdot\mathbf{A} = 0$

69. $\boldsymbol{\tau} = \mathbf{r}\times\mathbf{F} = (3\hat{\mathbf{i}} - 2\hat{\mathbf{j}} + 3\hat{\mathbf{k}})\times(2\hat{\mathbf{i}} - 3\hat{\mathbf{j}} + 4\hat{\mathbf{k}})$

$$= \begin{vmatrix} \hat{\mathbf{i}} & \hat{\mathbf{j}} & \hat{\mathbf{k}} \\ 3 & -2 & 3 \\ 2 & -3 & 4 \end{vmatrix} = \hat{\mathbf{i}} - 6\hat{\mathbf{j}} - 5\hat{\mathbf{k}}$$

70. $\mathbf{v} = \boldsymbol{\omega}\times\mathbf{r}$

$$\mathbf{v} = \begin{vmatrix} \hat{\mathbf{i}} & \hat{\mathbf{j}} & \hat{\mathbf{k}} \\ 1 & -2 & 3 \\ 1 & 1 & 1 \end{vmatrix} = -5\hat{\mathbf{i}} + 2\hat{\mathbf{j}} + 3\hat{\mathbf{k}}$$

71. $\mathbf{A} = \hat{\mathbf{i}} + \hat{\mathbf{j}} + \hat{\mathbf{k}}, \quad \mathbf{B} = 3\hat{\mathbf{i}}$

$$\mathbf{A}\times\mathbf{B} = \begin{vmatrix} \hat{\mathbf{i}} & \hat{\mathbf{j}} & \hat{\mathbf{k}} \\ 1 & 1 & 1 \\ 3 & 0 & 0 \end{vmatrix} = 3\hat{\mathbf{j}} - 3\hat{\mathbf{k}}$$

Area of triangle $= \frac{1}{2}AB\sin\theta = \frac{1}{2}|\mathbf{A}\times\mathbf{B}| = \frac{3\sqrt{2}}{2} = \frac{3}{\sqrt{2}}$ units

72. Area of parallelogram $= AB\sin\theta = |\mathbf{A}\times\mathbf{B}| = \left\|\begin{matrix}\hat{\mathbf{i}} & \hat{\mathbf{j}} & \hat{\mathbf{k}}\\ 2 & 1 & -3\\ 0 & 12 & -2\end{matrix}\right\|$

$= |34\hat{\mathbf{i}} + 4\hat{\mathbf{j}} + 24\hat{\mathbf{k}}| = \sqrt{1748} = 41.8$

Numerical Value Questions

1. $\Sigma F_x = y\cos 37° - x - 5\cos 53° = 0$

$\Rightarrow \quad 5x - 4y = -15 \quad$ ...(i)

$\Sigma F_y = y\sin 37° + 5\sin 53° - 10 = 0 \quad$ ...(ii)

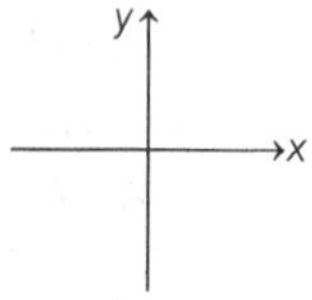

From Eqs. (i) and (ii), we get

$y = 10$ and $x = 5$

So, $x + y = 15$

2. $\cos^2\alpha + \cos^2\beta + \cos^2\gamma = 1$

$\Rightarrow \quad \cos^2\frac{\pi}{3} + \cos^2\frac{\pi}{3} + \cos^2\frac{\pi}{n} = 1$

$\Rightarrow \quad \cos^2\frac{\pi}{n} = \frac{1}{2} \Rightarrow \cos\frac{\pi}{n} = \frac{1}{\sqrt{2}} \Rightarrow \frac{\pi}{n} = \frac{\pi}{4} \Rightarrow n = 4$

3. $B\cos\alpha + 2\sqrt{3}\cos 30° = 2$

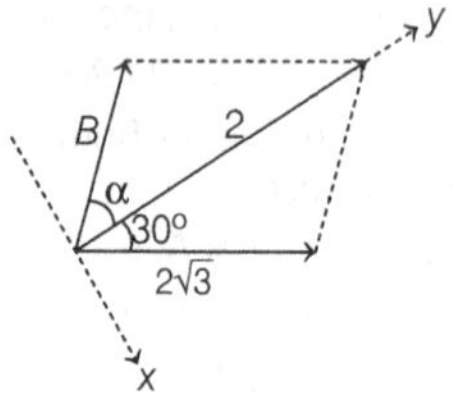

$\Rightarrow \quad B\cos\alpha = -1 \quad$ ...(i)

$B\sin\alpha = 2\sqrt{3}\sin 30° \Rightarrow B\sin\alpha = \sqrt{3} \quad$ ...(ii)

Now, adding Eqs. (i)^2 + (ii)^2, we get

$\Rightarrow \quad B^2 = 4 \Rightarrow B = 2$

4. Magnitude of a unit vector is unity.

$\sqrt{(0.5)^2 + (2\alpha)^2 + \alpha^2} = 1$

$\Rightarrow \quad 5\alpha^2 = 0.75 \Rightarrow \alpha^2 = 0.15$

$\Rightarrow \quad \alpha = \sqrt{\frac{15}{100}} = \sqrt{\frac{3}{20}}$

5. Angle between **A** and **−C** is 15°.

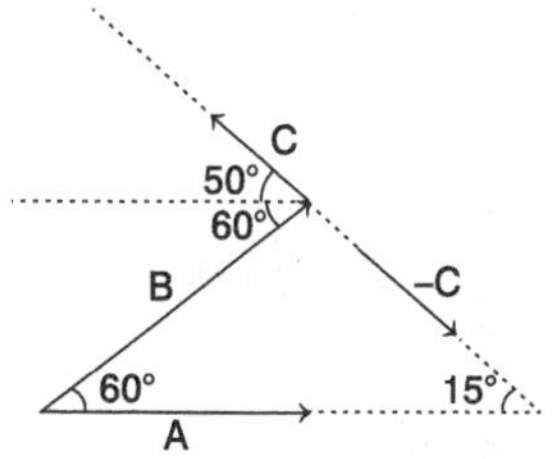

6. $(\mathbf{L} - \alpha\mathbf{I})\cdot\mathbf{L} = 0$

$[(\hat{\mathbf{i}} + 2\hat{\mathbf{j}} + 3\hat{\mathbf{k}}) - (4\alpha\hat{\mathbf{i}} + 5\alpha\hat{\mathbf{j}} + 6\alpha\hat{\mathbf{k}})]\cdot(\hat{\mathbf{i}} + 2\hat{\mathbf{j}} + 3\hat{\mathbf{k}}) = 0$

$\Rightarrow [(1 - 4\alpha)\hat{\mathbf{i}} + (2 - 5\alpha)\hat{\mathbf{j}} + (3 - 6\alpha)\hat{\mathbf{k}}]\cdot(\hat{\mathbf{i}} + 2\hat{\mathbf{j}} + 3\hat{\mathbf{k}}) = 0$

$\Rightarrow 1 - 4\alpha + (2 - 5\alpha)2 + (3 - 6\alpha)3 = 0$

$\Rightarrow \quad 1 - 4\alpha + 4 - 10\alpha + 9 - 18\alpha = 0$

$\Rightarrow \quad 32\alpha = 14 \Rightarrow \alpha = \frac{7}{16}$

7. $\cos\theta = \frac{\mathbf{A}\cdot\mathbf{B}}{AB} = \frac{2}{\sqrt{3}\sqrt{2}} = \sqrt{\frac{2}{3}}$

$2\sec^2\theta = 2\times\frac{3}{2} = 3$

8. $\mathbf{P} = 2\hat{\mathbf{i}} - 2\hat{\mathbf{j}}$

$\mathbf{Q} = \hat{\mathbf{i}} + 3\hat{\mathbf{j}}$

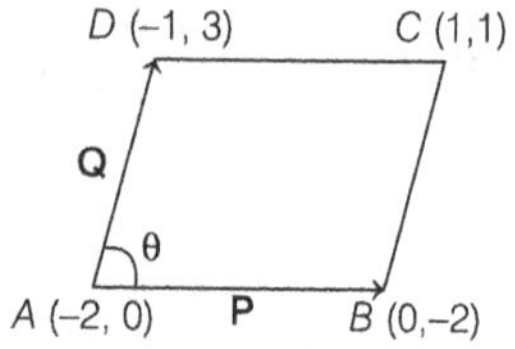

Area of parallelogram

$= PQ\sin\theta = |\mathbf{P}\times\mathbf{Q}|$

$= \left\|\begin{matrix}\hat{\mathbf{i}} & \hat{\mathbf{j}} & \hat{\mathbf{k}}\\ 2 & -2 & 0\\ 1 & 3 & 0\end{matrix}\right\| = |8\hat{\mathbf{k}}| = 8$ sq. units

9. $|\hat{\mathbf{a}} + \hat{\mathbf{b}}| = 2$

$\Rightarrow 1^2 + 1^2 + 2(1)(1)\cos\theta = 4$

$\Rightarrow \quad 2 + 2\cos\theta = 4 \Rightarrow 2\cos\theta = 2$

$\Rightarrow \quad \cos\theta = 1 \Rightarrow \theta = 0°$

$\hat{\mathbf{a}}\cdot\hat{\mathbf{b}} - |\hat{\mathbf{a}}\times\hat{\mathbf{b}}| = (1)(1)\cos 0° - (1)(1)\sin 0° = 1$

10. $(\mathbf{A}\times\mathbf{B})\cdot\mathbf{C} = 0$

$\begin{vmatrix}2 & 3 & -2\\ 5 & n & 1\\ -1 & 2 & 3\end{vmatrix} = 0$

$\Rightarrow 2(3n - 2) - 3(15 + 1) - 2(10 + n) = 0$

$\Rightarrow \quad 6n - 4 - 45 - 3 - 20 - 2n = 0$

$\Rightarrow \quad 4n = 72 \Rightarrow n = 18$

11. $W = \mathbf{F}\cdot\mathbf{s} = (\mathbf{F}_1 + \mathbf{F}_2)\cdot(\mathbf{r}_2 - \mathbf{r}_1)$

$= (3\hat{\mathbf{i}} - 2\hat{\mathbf{j}} + \hat{\mathbf{k}})\cdot(6\hat{\mathbf{i}} + 8\hat{\mathbf{j}} + 7\hat{\mathbf{k}})$

$= 18 - 16 + 7 = 9$ J

12. $|\Delta\mathbf{v}| = 2v\sin\left(\frac{\theta}{2}\right) = 2(10)\sin\left(\frac{60°}{2}\right) = 10$

13. $P = \mathbf{F}\cdot\mathbf{v} = 120 - 60 - 45 = 15$ W

14. Area of parallelogram

$= \frac{1}{2}|\mathbf{d}_1\times\mathbf{d}_2| = \frac{1}{2}\left\|\begin{matrix}\hat{\mathbf{i}} & \hat{\mathbf{j}} & \hat{\mathbf{k}}\\ 5 & -4 & 3\\ 3 & 2 & -1\end{matrix}\right\|$

$= \frac{1}{2}[-2\hat{\mathbf{i}} + 14\hat{\mathbf{j}} + 22\hat{\mathbf{k}}]$

$= \frac{1}{2}\sqrt{2^2 + 14^2 + 22^2}$

$= \frac{1}{2}\sqrt{684} = 3\sqrt{19}$

15. $|\mathbf{a}\times\mathbf{b}|=25$

$\Rightarrow \quad ab\sin\theta=25 \quad \Rightarrow \quad (5)(13)\sin\theta=25$

$\Rightarrow \quad \sin\theta=\dfrac{5}{13} \quad \Rightarrow \quad \cos\theta=\dfrac{12}{13}$

$$\mathbf{a}\cdot\mathbf{b}=ab\cos\theta=(5)(13)\left(\frac{12}{13}\right)=60$$

16. $\mathbf{A}\cdot\mathbf{B}=0 \quad \Rightarrow \quad a-1-1=0 \quad \Rightarrow \quad a=2$

$\mathbf{A}\cdot\mathbf{C}=0 \quad \Rightarrow \quad 1+1+b=0 \quad \Rightarrow \quad b=-2$

$$\cos\theta=\frac{\mathbf{B}\cdot\mathbf{C}}{BC}=\frac{a-1-b}{\sqrt{6}\sqrt{6}}=\frac{3}{6}=\frac{1}{2} \quad \Rightarrow \quad \theta=\frac{\pi}{3}$$

17. $|\mathbf{a}+\mathbf{b}+\mathbf{c}|=\sqrt{(\mathbf{a}\cdot\mathbf{a}+\mathbf{b}\cdot\mathbf{b}+\mathbf{c}\cdot\mathbf{c}+2\mathbf{a}\cdot\mathbf{b}+2\mathbf{b}\cdot\mathbf{c}+2\mathbf{c}\cdot\mathbf{a})}$

$=\sqrt{a^2+b^2+c^2+2ab\cos\theta_1+2bc\cos\theta_2+2ca\cos\theta_3}$

$=\sqrt{2^2+3^2+6^2+(2\times2\times3+2\times3\times6+2\times6\times2)\left(\dfrac{-1}{2}\right)}$

$=\sqrt{13}$

18. $\mathbf{C}=\mathbf{B}-\mathbf{A}=8\hat{\mathbf{i}}+4\hat{\mathbf{j}}+4\hat{\mathbf{k}}$

$\mathbf{A}=2\hat{\mathbf{i}}+\hat{\mathbf{j}}+\hat{\mathbf{k}}$

Component of **C** along **A** $=C\cos\theta$

$$=\frac{\mathbf{C}\cdot\mathbf{A}}{A}=\frac{16+4+4}{\sqrt{6}}=\frac{24}{\sqrt{6}}=4\sqrt{6}$$

19. Since **X** and **C** are perpendicular

$\mathbf{X}\cdot\mathbf{C}=0 \quad \Rightarrow \quad (\alpha\mathbf{A}+\beta\mathbf{B})\cdot\mathbf{C}=0$

$\Rightarrow (\alpha(\hat{\mathbf{i}}+\hat{\mathbf{j}}-2\hat{\mathbf{k}})+\beta(\hat{\mathbf{i}}-\hat{\mathbf{j}}+\hat{\mathbf{k}}))\cdot(2\hat{\mathbf{i}}-3\hat{\mathbf{j}}+4\hat{\mathbf{k}})=0$

$\Rightarrow [(\alpha+\beta)\hat{\mathbf{i}}+(\alpha-\beta)\hat{\mathbf{j}}+(\beta-2\alpha)\hat{\mathbf{k}}]\cdot(2\hat{\mathbf{i}}-3\hat{\mathbf{j}}+4\hat{\mathbf{k}})=0$

$\Rightarrow 2(\alpha+\beta)-3(\alpha-\beta)+4(\beta-2\alpha)=0$

$\Rightarrow -9\alpha+9\beta=0 \Rightarrow \alpha=\beta$

So, $\dfrac{\alpha}{\beta}=1$

20. $\mathbf{R}=\mathbf{P}+\mathbf{Q}$

$\Rightarrow \quad R^2=P^2+Q^2+2PQ\cos\theta$

$\Rightarrow \quad 15^2=P^2+Q^2+2PQ\cos\theta \quad$ ...(i)

$\mathbf{R}=\mathbf{P}+(-\mathbf{Q})$

$\Rightarrow \quad R^2=P^2+Q^2+2PQ\cos(180°-\theta)$

$\Rightarrow \quad (\sqrt{113})^2=P^2+Q^2-2PQ\cos\theta$

$\Rightarrow \quad 113=P^2+Q^2-2PQ\cos\theta \quad$ ...(ii)

Solving Eqs. (i) and (ii), we get

$$P^2+Q^2=169$$

$\mathbf{R}=\mathbf{P}+\mathbf{S}$,

where **S** is perpendicular to **P** and magnitude of **S** is equal to magnitude of **Q**.

$\Rightarrow \quad R^2=P^2+S^2+2PS\cos 90°$

$\Rightarrow \quad R=\sqrt{P^2+Q^2}$

$\Rightarrow \quad R=\sqrt{169}=13$

Level 3

Single Choice Correct Questions

1. $\mathbf{R}=\mathbf{P}+\mathbf{Q}$

$\Rightarrow \quad R^2=P^2+Q^2+2PQ\cos\theta$

$\Rightarrow \quad Q^2=P^2+Q^2+2PQ\cos\theta \Rightarrow P+2Q\cos\theta=0$

$\tan\phi=\dfrac{Q\sin\theta}{P+Q\cos\theta} \quad \Rightarrow \tan\phi=\dfrac{2Q\sin\theta}{P+2Q\cos\theta}$

$\Rightarrow \quad \tan\phi=\infty \qquad [\because P+2Q\cos\theta=0]$

$\Rightarrow \quad \phi=90°$

2. $P=Q=R=S=x$

$\mathbf{P}+\mathbf{Q}-\mathbf{R}=0 \quad \Rightarrow \mathbf{R}=\mathbf{P}+\mathbf{Q}$

$\Rightarrow \quad R^2=P^2+Q^2+2PQ\cos\theta_1$

$\Rightarrow \quad x^2=x^2+x^2+2xx\cos\theta_1$

$\Rightarrow \quad \cos\theta_1=-\dfrac{1}{2} \Rightarrow \theta_1=120°$

$\mathbf{P}+\mathbf{Q}-\mathbf{S}=0 \quad \Rightarrow \quad \mathbf{S}=\mathbf{P}+\mathbf{Q}$

Angle between **S** and **P** is θ_2.

$$\tan\phi=\frac{B\sin\theta}{A+B\cos\theta}$$

$$\tan\theta_2=\frac{x\sin 120°}{x+x\cos 120°}=\sqrt{3} \Rightarrow \theta_2=60°$$

So, $\dfrac{\theta_1}{\theta_2}=\dfrac{120°}{60°}=\dfrac{2}{1}$

3. Component of **a** along **b** $=(a\cos\theta)\hat{\mathbf{b}}$

$$=\left(\frac{\mathbf{a}\cdot\mathbf{b}}{b}\right)\left(\frac{\mathbf{b}}{b}\right)=\left(\frac{\sqrt{2}+4\sqrt{2}}{2}\right)\left(\frac{(\hat{\mathbf{i}}+\hat{\mathbf{j}})\sqrt{2}}{2}\right)=\frac{5}{2}(\hat{\mathbf{i}}+\hat{\mathbf{j}})$$

a = (component of **a** along **b**) + (component of **a** perpendicular to **b**)

$\hat{\mathbf{i}}+4\hat{\mathbf{j}}+2\sqrt{2}\hat{\mathbf{k}}=\dfrac{5}{2}(\hat{\mathbf{i}}+\hat{\mathbf{j}})$ + (component of **a** perpendicular to **b**)

$\Rightarrow$ Component of **a** perpendicular to **b**

$$=-\frac{3}{2}\hat{\mathbf{i}}+\frac{3}{2}\hat{\mathbf{j}}+2\sqrt{2}\hat{\mathbf{k}}$$

$$\Rightarrow \text{Magnitude}=\sqrt{\left(\frac{3}{2}\right)^2+\left(\frac{3}{2}\right)^2+(2\sqrt{2})^2}=\frac{5}{\sqrt{2}}$$

4. Side of cube = 1 m

Co-ordinates of $A=(0,0,0)$

Co-ordinates of $F=(1,1,1)$

Co-ordinates of $D=(0,0,1)$

Co-ordinates of $G=(1,1,0)$

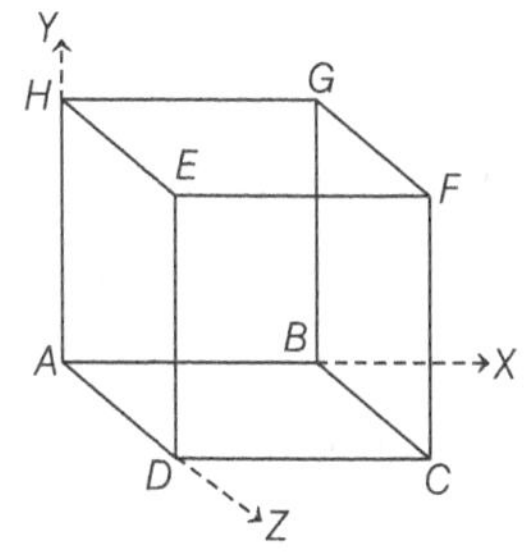

$\mathbf{AF}=\hat{\mathbf{i}}+\hat{\mathbf{j}}+\hat{\mathbf{k}}$

$\mathbf{DG}=\hat{\mathbf{i}}+\hat{\mathbf{j}}-\hat{\mathbf{k}}$

$\cos\theta=\dfrac{\mathbf{A}\cdot\mathbf{B}}{AB}=\dfrac{1+1-1}{\sqrt{3}\sqrt{3}}$

$\Rightarrow \theta=\cos^{-1}\left(\dfrac{1}{3}\right)$

5. $\mathbf{AP} = (10\hat{i} + 2\hat{j} - 11\hat{k}) - (2\hat{i} + 2\hat{j} + 4\hat{k}) = 8\hat{i} - 15\hat{k}$

$$\mathbf{F} = 34\left(\frac{8\hat{i} - 15\hat{k}}{17}\right) = 16\hat{i} - 30\hat{k}$$

$$\mathbf{s} = (5\hat{i} - 3\hat{j} - \hat{k}) - (2\hat{i} + 2\hat{j} + 4\hat{k}) = 3\hat{i} - 5\hat{j} - 5\hat{k}$$

$$W = \mathbf{F} \cdot \mathbf{s} = 16(3) + 0(-5) - 30(-5) = 198 \text{ J}$$

6. $\mathbf{v} = v\hat{\mathbf{v}} = 65\left(\frac{3\hat{i} + 4\hat{j} + 12\hat{k}}{13}\right) \Rightarrow \mathbf{v} = 15\hat{i} + 20\hat{j} + 60\hat{k}$

$$\mathbf{s} = \mathbf{u}t + \frac{1}{2}\mathbf{a}t^2 \Rightarrow \mathbf{r}_2 - \mathbf{r}_1 = \mathbf{u}t, \text{ since } \mathbf{a} = 0$$

$$\Rightarrow \mathbf{r}_2 - (\hat{i}) = (15\hat{i} + 20\hat{j} + 60\hat{k}) \times 2$$

$$\Rightarrow \quad \mathbf{r}_2 = 31\hat{i} + 40\hat{j} + 120\hat{k}$$

7. If $\mathbf{v}_1$ and $\mathbf{v}_2$ are parallel, then $\mathbf{v}_1 = \lambda \mathbf{v}_2$

$$2t\hat{i} + (t-2)\hat{j} = \lambda(t-4)\hat{i} + t\hat{j})$$

$$\Rightarrow \quad 2t = \lambda(t-4) \quad \text{...(i)}$$

$$t - 2 = \lambda t \quad \text{...(ii)}$$

Dividing Eq. (i) by Eq. (ii), we get

$$\frac{2t}{t-2} = \frac{t-4}{t}$$

$$\Rightarrow \quad 2t^2 = t^2 - 6t + 8 \Rightarrow t^2 + 6t - 8 = 0$$

$$\Rightarrow \quad t = \frac{-6 + \sqrt{36+32}}{2} \Rightarrow t = (-3 + \sqrt{17})\text{s}$$

8. $R_{max} = A + B = 29$ ...(i)

$R_{min} = A - B = 5$ ...(ii)

Solving Eqs. (i) and (ii), we get

$A = 17$ and $B = 12$

Now each force is increased by 3 units.

$$A' = 17 + 3 = 20$$

$$B' = 12 + 3 = 15$$

$$R^2 = A^2 + B^2 + 2AB\cos\theta$$

$$\Rightarrow R^2 = (20^2) + (15)^2 + 2(20)(15)\cos 90^\circ \Rightarrow R = 25 \text{ kg-wt}$$

9. Component of **A** along **B** $= A\cos\theta = \dfrac{\mathbf{A} \cdot \mathbf{B}}{B}$

$$= \frac{(\mathbf{a} - \mathbf{b}) \cdot (\mathbf{a} + \mathbf{b})}{(\mathbf{a} + \mathbf{b})}$$

$$= \frac{a^2 - b^2}{\sqrt{a^2 + b^2}}$$

10. Let $\mathbf{r} = a\hat{i} + b\hat{j} + c\hat{k}$

$$\hat{i} \times (\mathbf{r} \times \hat{i}) = \hat{i} \times ((a\hat{i} + b\hat{j} + c\hat{k}) \times \hat{i})$$

$$= \hat{i} \times (b(-\hat{k}) + c\hat{j}) = b\hat{j} + c\hat{k} \quad \text{...(i)}$$

Similarly, $\hat{j} \times (\mathbf{r} \times \hat{j}) = a\hat{i} + c\hat{k}$ ...(ii)

$\hat{k} \times (\mathbf{r} \times \hat{k}) = a\hat{i} + b\hat{j}$ ...(iii)

Adding Eqs. (i), (ii) and (iii), we get

$$\Rightarrow \quad = 2(a\hat{i} + b\hat{j} + c\hat{k}) \Rightarrow = 2\mathbf{r}$$

11. $\mathbf{AB} + \mathbf{AC} + \mathbf{AD} + \mathbf{AE} + \mathbf{AF}$

$$= \mathbf{AB} + (\mathbf{AD} - \mathbf{CD}) + \mathbf{AD} + (\mathbf{AD} + \mathbf{DE}) + \mathbf{AF}$$

$$= 3\mathbf{AD} + \mathbf{AB} - \mathbf{CD} + \mathbf{DE} + \mathbf{AF}$$

$$= 3\mathbf{AD} + \mathbf{AB} - \mathbf{CD} + (-\mathbf{AB}) + \mathbf{CD}$$

$$= 3\mathbf{AD} = 3(2\mathbf{AO}) = 6\mathbf{AO}$$

12. Use triangle law and polygon law of vector addition.

13. $\mathbf{a} = 2\hat{i} + \hat{j} - 2\hat{k} \Rightarrow a = 3$

$\mathbf{b} = \hat{i} + \hat{j} \Rightarrow b = \sqrt{2}$

$$\mathbf{a} \cdot \mathbf{c} = c$$

$$\Rightarrow \quad ac\cos\theta = c \Rightarrow 3\cos\theta = 1 \Rightarrow \cos\theta = \frac{1}{3}$$

$$|\mathbf{c} - \mathbf{a}| = 2\sqrt{2} \Rightarrow c^2 + a^2 - 2ac\cos\theta = 8$$

$$\Rightarrow \quad c^2 + 9 - 2c = 8 \Rightarrow c^2 - 2c + 1 = 0$$

$$\Rightarrow \quad (c-1)^2 = 0 \Rightarrow c = 1$$

$$|(\mathbf{a} \times \mathbf{b}) \times \mathbf{c}| = |\mathbf{a} \times \mathbf{b}|c\sin 30^\circ = 3 \times 1 \times \frac{1}{2} = \frac{3}{2}$$

14. Resultant of **P** + **Q** and **P** − **Q** is 2**P**.

$$2P = \sqrt{3P^2 + Q^2}$$

$$4P^2 = 3P^2 + Q^2 \Rightarrow P^2 = Q^2$$

$$\Rightarrow \quad P = Q$$

$$\cos\theta = \frac{(\mathbf{P} + \mathbf{Q}) \cdot (\mathbf{P} - \mathbf{Q})}{|\mathbf{P} + \mathbf{Q}||\mathbf{P} - \mathbf{Q}|} = \frac{P^2 - Q^2}{|\mathbf{P} + \mathbf{Q}||\mathbf{P} - \mathbf{Q}|} = 0$$

$$\Rightarrow \quad \theta = \frac{\pi}{2}$$

15. $(\mathbf{a} + 2\mathbf{b}) \cdot (5\mathbf{a} - 4\mathbf{b}) = 0$

$$\Rightarrow 5\mathbf{a} \cdot \mathbf{a} - 4\mathbf{a} \cdot \mathbf{b} + 10\mathbf{b} \cdot \mathbf{a} - 8\mathbf{b} \cdot \mathbf{b} = 0$$

$$\Rightarrow \quad 5a^2 + 6\mathbf{a} \cdot \mathbf{b} - 8b^2 = 0$$

$$\Rightarrow \quad 5(1)^2 + 6(1)(1)\cos\theta - 8(1)^2 = 0$$

$$\Rightarrow \quad 6\cos\theta = 3$$

$$\Rightarrow \quad \cos\theta = \frac{1}{2} \Rightarrow \theta = \frac{\pi}{3}$$

16. $|\mathbf{a}_1 + \mathbf{a}_2| = \sqrt{3}$

$$\Rightarrow 1^2 + 1^2 + 2(1)(1)\cos\theta = 3 \Rightarrow \cos\theta = \frac{1}{2}$$

$$(\mathbf{a}_1 - \mathbf{a}_2) \cdot (2\mathbf{a}_1 + \mathbf{a}_2) = 2\mathbf{a}_1 \cdot \mathbf{a}_1 - \mathbf{a}_1 \cdot \mathbf{a}_2 - \mathbf{a}_2 \cdot \mathbf{a}_2$$

$$= 2(1)^2 - (1)(1)\cos\theta - (1)^2$$

$$= 1 - \frac{1}{2} = \frac{1}{2}$$

17. $\hat{\mathbf{A}} + \hat{\mathbf{B}} + \hat{\mathbf{C}} = 0$

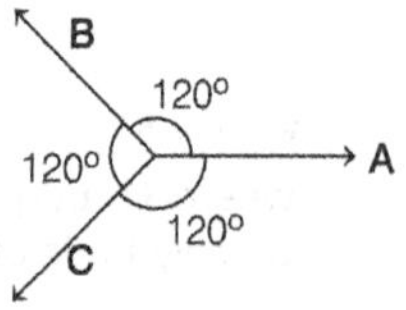

$$\frac{\mathbf{A}}{4} + \frac{\mathbf{B}}{3} + \frac{\mathbf{C}}{2} = 0$$

$$\frac{3\mathbf{A}}{4} + \frac{\mathbf{B}}{3} + \frac{\mathbf{C}}{2} = \frac{\mathbf{A}}{2} + \left(\frac{\mathbf{A}}{4} + \frac{\mathbf{B}}{3} + \frac{\mathbf{C}}{2}\right)$$

$$= \frac{\mathbf{A}}{2} + 0 = \frac{\mathbf{A}}{2}$$

18. $\mathbf{A} = 1\hat{\mathbf{i}}$

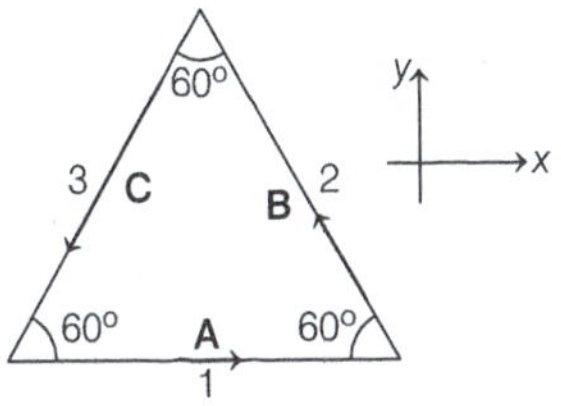

$$\mathbf{B} = -2\cos 60°\,\hat{\mathbf{i}} + 2\sin 60°\,\hat{\mathbf{j}}$$

$$\mathbf{C} = -3\cos 60°\,\hat{\mathbf{i}} - 3\sin 60°\,\hat{\mathbf{j}}$$

$$\mathbf{R} = \mathbf{A} + \mathbf{B} + \mathbf{C} = -\frac{3}{2}\hat{\mathbf{i}} - \frac{\sqrt{3}}{2}\hat{\mathbf{j}}$$

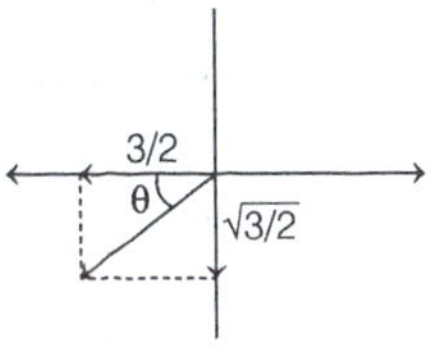

$$\tan\theta = \frac{\sqrt{3}/2}{3/2} = \frac{1}{\sqrt{3}} \Rightarrow$$

$\theta = 30°$

So, angle between **R** and **A** is 150°.

19. $\tan\alpha = \dfrac{B\sin\theta}{A + B\cos\theta}$

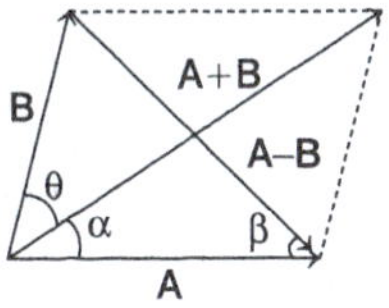

$$\Rightarrow \tan\beta = \frac{B\sin\theta}{A - B\cos\theta}$$

$$\tan\alpha + \tan\beta = \frac{2AB\sin\theta}{A^2 - B^2\cos^2\theta}$$

20. (1) Since **P**, **Q** and **R** are not coplanar, so their sum cannot be zero.

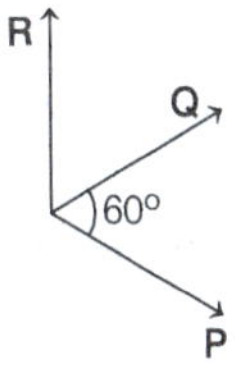

(2) **R** is perpendicular to both **P** and **Q**. So, **R** may be equal to **P** × **Q**.

(3) **P** × **R** can never be **Q** because angle between **P** and **Q** is not 90°.

21. $|\hat{\mathbf{a}} - \hat{\mathbf{b}}| = \sqrt{2}$

$$\Rightarrow 1^2 + 1^2 - 2(1)(1)\cos\theta = 2 \Rightarrow \cos\theta = 0 \Rightarrow \theta = 90°$$

$$|\hat{\mathbf{a}} + \sqrt{3}\hat{\mathbf{b}}| = \sqrt{1^2 + (\sqrt{3})^2 + 2(1)(\sqrt{3})\cos 90°} = 2$$

22. $\mathbf{R} = \mathbf{P} + \mathbf{Q}$ and $\mathbf{S} = \mathbf{P} + 2\mathbf{Q}$

S is perpendicular to **P**.

$$\Rightarrow \mathbf{S}\cdot\mathbf{P} = 0 \Rightarrow (\mathbf{P} + 2\mathbf{Q})\cdot\mathbf{P} = 0$$

$$\Rightarrow \mathbf{P}\cdot\mathbf{P} + 2\mathbf{P}\cdot\mathbf{Q} = 0 \Rightarrow \mathbf{P}^2 + 2PQ\cos\theta = 0 \qquad ...(i)$$

Since, $\mathbf{R} = \mathbf{P} + \mathbf{Q}$

$$\Rightarrow R^2 = P^2 + Q^2 + 2PQ\cos\theta \qquad ...(ii)$$

Solving Eqs. (i) and (ii), we get

$$R = Q$$

23. $R^2 = P^2 + Q^2 + 2PQ\cos\theta$ ...(i)

$$(2R)^2 = P^2 + (2Q)^2 + 2P(2Q)\cos\theta \qquad ...(ii)$$

$$(2R)^2 = P^2 + Q^2 + 2PQ\cos(180° - \theta) \qquad ...(iii)$$

Solving Eqs. (i), (ii) and (iii), we get

$$P : Q : R :: \sqrt{3} : \sqrt{2} : \sqrt{3}$$

24. $\mathbf{a} \perp \mathbf{b} + \mathbf{C}$

$$\Rightarrow \mathbf{a}\cdot(\mathbf{b} + \mathbf{c}) = 0 \Rightarrow \mathbf{a}\cdot\mathbf{b} + \mathbf{a}\cdot\mathbf{c} = 0 \qquad ...(i)$$

$$\mathbf{b} \perp \mathbf{c} + \mathbf{a} \Rightarrow \mathbf{b}\cdot(\mathbf{c} + \mathbf{a}) = 0$$

$$\Rightarrow \mathbf{b}\cdot\mathbf{c} + \mathbf{a}\cdot\mathbf{b} = 0 \qquad ...(ii)$$

$$\mathbf{c} \perp \mathbf{a} + \mathbf{b} \Rightarrow \mathbf{c}\cdot(\mathbf{a} + \mathbf{b}) = 0$$

$$\Rightarrow \mathbf{c}\cdot\mathbf{a} + \mathbf{c}\cdot\mathbf{b} = 0 \qquad ...(iii)$$

Adding Eqs. (i), (ii) and (iii), we get

$$2(\mathbf{a}\cdot\mathbf{b} + \mathbf{b}\cdot\mathbf{c} + \mathbf{c}\cdot\mathbf{a}) = 0$$

$$|\mathbf{a} + \mathbf{b} + \mathbf{c}| = \sqrt{a^2 + b^2 + c^2 + 2(\mathbf{a}\cdot\mathbf{b} + \mathbf{b}\cdot\mathbf{c} + \mathbf{c}\cdot\mathbf{a})}$$

$$= \sqrt{50} = 5\sqrt{2}$$

25. $|\mathbf{a} + \mathbf{b} + \mathbf{c}| = \sqrt{\mathbf{a}\cdot\mathbf{a} + \mathbf{b}\cdot\mathbf{b} + \mathbf{c}\cdot\mathbf{c} + 2(\mathbf{a}\cdot\mathbf{b} + \mathbf{b}\cdot\mathbf{c} + \mathbf{c}\cdot\mathbf{a})}$

$$1 = \sqrt{1^2 + 1^2 + 1^2 + 2(\cos\theta_1 + \cos\theta_2 + \cos\theta_3)}$$

$$\cos\theta_1 + \cos\theta_2 + \cos\theta_3 = -1$$

26. Let $\hat{\mathbf{A}} = a\hat{\mathbf{i}} + b\hat{\mathbf{j}} + c\hat{\mathbf{k}}$

$\hat{\mathbf{A}}$ is orthogonal to $3\hat{\mathbf{i}} + 2\hat{\mathbf{j}} + 6\hat{\mathbf{k}}$

$$\Rightarrow (a\hat{\mathbf{i}} + b\hat{\mathbf{j}} + c\hat{\mathbf{k}})\cdot(3\hat{\mathbf{i}} + 2\hat{\mathbf{j}} + 6\hat{\mathbf{k}}) = 0$$

$$\Rightarrow 3a + 2b + 6c = 0 \qquad ...(i)$$

A is coplanar with $2\hat{\mathbf{i}} + \hat{\mathbf{j}} + \hat{\mathbf{k}}$ and $\hat{\mathbf{i}} - \hat{\mathbf{j}} + \hat{\mathbf{k}}$.

$$\Rightarrow \begin{vmatrix} a & b & c \\ 2 & 1 & 1 \\ 1 & -1 & 1 \end{vmatrix} = 0 \Rightarrow 2a - b - 3c = 0 \qquad ...(ii)$$

From Eqs. (i) and (ii), we get

$$a = 0 \text{ and } b = -3c$$

$\hat{\mathbf{A}}$ is a unit vector $\Rightarrow a^2 + b^2 + c^2 = 1$

$$\Rightarrow 0 + 9c^2 + c^2 = 1$$

$$\Rightarrow c = \frac{1}{\sqrt{10}} \text{ and } b = \frac{-3}{\sqrt{10}}$$

27. $A\cos\alpha = 2(A\cos\beta)$ ...(i)

$$A = 5\sqrt{2}$$

$$\cos^2\alpha + \cos^2\beta + \cos^2\gamma = 1 \qquad ...(ii)$$

$$\Rightarrow 4\cos^2\beta + \cos^2\beta + \frac{1}{2} = 1 \Rightarrow 5\cos^2\beta = \frac{1}{2}$$

$$\Rightarrow \cos\beta = \frac{1}{\sqrt{10}} \text{ and } \cos\alpha = \frac{2}{\sqrt{10}}$$

$$A_x = A\cos\alpha = 2\sqrt{5}$$

$$A_y = A\cos\beta = \sqrt{5}$$

$$A_z = A\cos\gamma = 5\sqrt{2}\cos 135° = -5$$

28. $(\mathbf{a} + 3\mathbf{b})\cdot(7\mathbf{a} - 5\mathbf{b}) = 0$

$$\Rightarrow 7\mathbf{a}\cdot\mathbf{a} + 16\mathbf{a}\cdot\mathbf{b} - 15\mathbf{b}\cdot\mathbf{b} = 0$$

$$\Rightarrow 15b^2 - 7a^2 = 16ab\cos\theta \qquad ...(i)$$

$$(\mathbf{a} - 4\mathbf{b})\cdot(7\mathbf{a} - 2\mathbf{b}) = 0$$

$$\Rightarrow 7\mathbf{a}\cdot\mathbf{a} - 30\mathbf{a}\cdot\mathbf{b} + 8\mathbf{b}\cdot\mathbf{b} = 0$$

$$\Rightarrow 7a^2 + 8b^2 = 30ab\cos\theta \qquad ...(ii)$$

Solving Eqs. (i) and (ii), we get

$$a = b \text{ and } \cos\theta = \frac{1}{2} \Rightarrow \theta = 60°$$

29. $\mathbf{A} = \hat{\mathbf{i}} + 2\hat{\mathbf{j}} - \hat{\mathbf{k}}$; $\mathbf{B} = 2\hat{\mathbf{i}}$

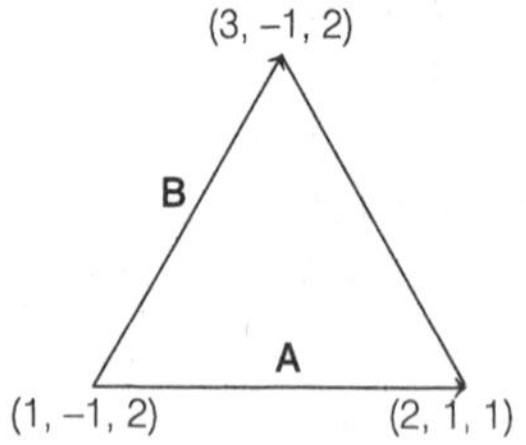

$$\text{Area of triangle} = \frac{1}{2}|\mathbf{A}\times\mathbf{B}| = \frac{1}{2}\left\|\begin{matrix}\hat{\mathbf{i}} & \hat{\mathbf{j}} & \hat{\mathbf{k}}\\ 1 & 2 & -1\\ 2 & 0 & 0\end{matrix}\right\|$$

$$= \frac{1}{2}|-2\hat{\mathbf{j}} - 4\hat{\mathbf{k}}| = \frac{1}{2}(\sqrt{20}) = \sqrt{5}$$

30. $|\mathbf{A}+\mathbf{B}| = \dfrac{|\mathbf{A}-\mathbf{B}|}{2}$

$$\Rightarrow \sqrt{A^2+B^2+2AB\cos\theta} = \frac{\sqrt{A^2+B^2-2AB\cos\theta}}{2}$$

$$\Rightarrow 4A^2+4B^2+8AB\cos\theta = A^2+B^2-2AB\cos\theta$$

$$\Rightarrow 3A^2+3B^2+10AB\cos\theta = 0 \quad \text{...(i)}$$

$$A = 2B \quad \text{...(ii)}$$

From Eqs. (i) and (ii), we get

$$\cos\theta = -\frac{3}{4}$$

31. $\mathbf{R} = \mathbf{P}+\mathbf{Q}$

$$R^2 = P^2+Q^2+2PQ\cos\theta \quad \text{...(i)}$$

$$R'^2 = P^2 + \left(\frac{R^2-P^2}{Q}\right)^2 + 2P\left(\frac{R^2-P^2}{Q}\right)\cos(180^\circ-\theta) \quad \text{...(ii)}$$

Solving Eqs. (i) and (ii), we get

$$R' = R$$

32.
$$\frac{P}{Q} = \frac{1}{2} \quad \text{...(i)}$$

$$\frac{\sqrt{3}}{2} = \frac{Q\sin\theta}{P+Q\cos\theta} \quad \text{...(ii)}$$

From Eqs. (i) and (ii), we get

$$\theta = 60^\circ$$

33.

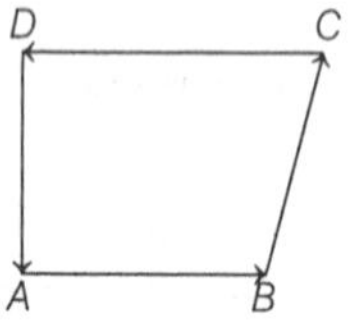

$\mathbf{AB}+\mathbf{BC}+\mathbf{CD}+\mathbf{DA} = 0$

$\mathbf{BA}+\mathbf{BC}+\mathbf{CD}+\mathbf{DA} = 2\mathbf{BA}$

34. $(\mathbf{a}+\mathbf{b})\cdot\mathbf{b} = 0 \Rightarrow ab\cos\theta + b^2 = 0$ ...(i)

$(\mathbf{a}+2\mathbf{b})\cdot\mathbf{a} = 0 \Rightarrow a^2 + 2ab\cos\theta = 0$ ...(ii)

From Eqs. (i) and (ii), we get

$$a = \sqrt{2}b$$

35.

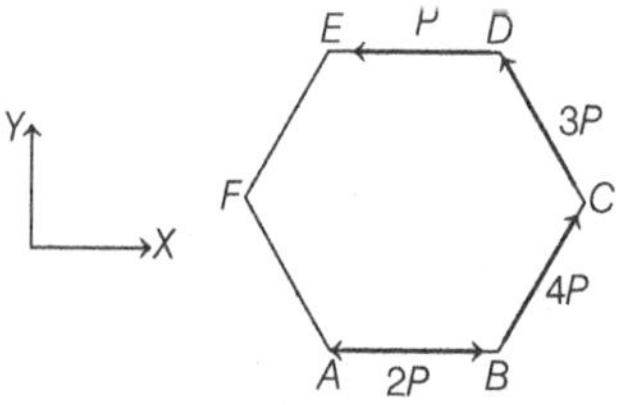

$$\mathbf{F}_1 = 2P\hat{\mathbf{i}}$$

$$\mathbf{F}_2 = 4P\cos60^\circ\,\hat{\mathbf{i}} + 4P\sin60^\circ\,\hat{\mathbf{j}}$$

$$\mathbf{F}_3 = -3P\cos60^\circ\,\hat{\mathbf{i}} + 3P\sin60^\circ\,\hat{\mathbf{j}}$$

$$\mathbf{F}_4 = -P\hat{\mathbf{i}}$$

$$\mathbf{R} = \mathbf{F}_1+\mathbf{F}_2+\mathbf{F}_3+\mathbf{F}_4 = \frac{3P}{2}\hat{\mathbf{i}} + \frac{7\sqrt{3}}{2}P\hat{\mathbf{j}}$$

$$R = \sqrt{39}P$$

36. Area of parallelogram $= \dfrac{1}{2}|\mathbf{a}\times\mathbf{b}|$

$$= \frac{1}{2}|(\mathbf{p}+2\mathbf{q})\times(2\mathbf{p}+\mathbf{q})| = \frac{1}{2}|(\mathbf{p}\times\mathbf{q})+4(\mathbf{q}\times\mathbf{p})|$$

$$= \frac{1}{2}|3(\mathbf{q}\times\mathbf{p})| = \frac{3}{2}\times1\times1\times\sin30^\circ = \frac{3}{4}$$

37. $\mathbf{a} = 5\cos37^\circ\,\hat{\mathbf{j}} + 5\sin37^\circ\,\hat{\mathbf{k}}$

$$\Rightarrow \quad \mathbf{a} = 4\hat{\mathbf{j}} + 3\hat{\mathbf{k}}$$

$$\mathbf{b} = 5\cos37^\circ\,\hat{\mathbf{j}} + 5\sin37^\circ\,\hat{\mathbf{i}} \Rightarrow \mathbf{b} = 3\hat{\mathbf{i}} + 4\hat{\mathbf{j}}$$

$$\cos\theta = \frac{\mathbf{a}\cdot\mathbf{b}}{ab} = \frac{16}{5(5)} = \frac{16}{25}$$

38. $\cos\theta = \dfrac{(\mathbf{a}+\mathbf{b})\cdot(\mathbf{a}-\mathbf{b})}{|\mathbf{a}+\mathbf{b}||\mathbf{a}-\mathbf{b}|} = \dfrac{a^2-b^2}{|\mathbf{a}+\mathbf{b}||\mathbf{a}-\mathbf{b}|}$

$$\Rightarrow \cos\theta = \frac{3}{\sqrt{7}\sqrt{3}} = \sqrt{\frac{3}{7}} \Rightarrow \tan\theta = \frac{2}{\sqrt{3}}$$

39. $\left|2\mathbf{a} - \dfrac{3}{2}\mathbf{b}\right| = \sqrt{4a^2 + \dfrac{9}{4}b^2 - 2(2a)\left(\dfrac{3b}{2}\right)\cos120^\circ}$

$$= \sqrt{4(3)^2 + \frac{9}{4}(4)^2 - 2(6)(6)\left(-\frac{1}{2}\right)}$$

$$= \sqrt{36+36+36} = 6\sqrt{3}$$

40. Volume of parallelopiped $= (\mathbf{a}\times\mathbf{b})\cdot\mathbf{c}$

$$= \begin{vmatrix}\hat{\mathbf{i}} & \hat{\mathbf{j}} & \hat{\mathbf{k}}\\ 2 & -3 & 4\\ 3 & -1 & 2\end{vmatrix}\cdot(\hat{\mathbf{i}}+2\hat{\mathbf{j}}-\hat{\mathbf{k}})$$

$$= (-2\hat{\mathbf{i}}+8\hat{\mathbf{j}}+7\hat{\mathbf{k}})\cdot(\hat{\mathbf{i}}+2\hat{\mathbf{j}}-\hat{\mathbf{k}}) = -2+16-7 = 7$$

41.

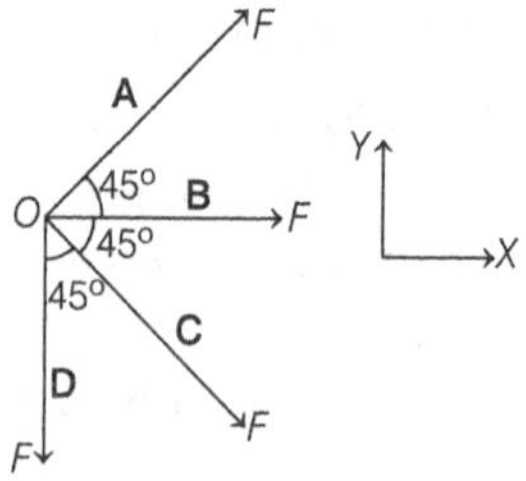

$$A = \frac{F}{\sqrt{2}}\hat{\mathbf{i}} + \frac{F}{\sqrt{2}}\hat{\mathbf{j}}$$
$$B = F\hat{\mathbf{i}}$$
$$C = \frac{F}{\sqrt{2}}\hat{\mathbf{i}} - \frac{F}{\sqrt{2}}\hat{\mathbf{j}}$$
$$D = -F\hat{\mathbf{j}}$$
$$\mathbf{R} = \mathbf{A} + \mathbf{B} + \mathbf{C} + \mathbf{D} = F(\sqrt{2}+1)\hat{\mathbf{i}} - F\hat{\mathbf{j}}$$
$$R = F\sqrt{4+2\sqrt{2}}$$

42. $\mathbf{a} + \mathbf{b} + \mathbf{c} = 0$

$\Rightarrow \quad \mathbf{c} = -(\mathbf{a} + \mathbf{b})$

$\Rightarrow \quad c^2 = a^2 + b^2 + 2ab\cos\theta$

$\Rightarrow \quad 7^2 = 3^2 + 5^2 + 2(3)(5)\cos\theta$

$\Rightarrow \quad \cos\theta = \frac{1}{2} \Rightarrow \theta = 60°$

43. $\mathbf{AB} + 3\mathbf{AC} = (\mathbf{AC} + \mathbf{CB}) + 3\mathbf{AC} = 4\mathbf{AC} + \mathbf{CB} = 4\mathbf{AC} + 4\mathbf{CR}$

$= 4(\mathbf{AC} + \mathbf{CR}) = 4\,\mathbf{AR}$

44. $\mathbf{R} = \mathbf{P} + \mathbf{Q}$

$\Rightarrow R^2 = P^2 + Q^2 + 2PQ\cos\theta$

$\Rightarrow R^2 = P^2 + P^2 + 2(P)(P)\cos\theta \qquad (\because P = Q)$

$\Rightarrow R = 2P\cos\left(\frac{\theta}{2}\right) \qquad$ ...(i)

$R - P = 0.732P \Rightarrow R = \sqrt{3}P \qquad$ ...(ii)

From Eqs. (i) and (ii), we get

$$\sqrt{3}P = 2P\cos\left(\frac{\theta}{2}\right) \Rightarrow \cos\left(\frac{\theta}{2}\right) = \frac{\sqrt{3}}{2} \Rightarrow \frac{\theta}{2} = 30°$$

$\Rightarrow \quad \theta = 60°$

$$\theta' = \theta + \frac{\theta}{2} = 60° + \frac{60°}{2} = 90°$$

$$\mathbf{R} = \mathbf{P} - \mathbf{Q}$$

$\Rightarrow \quad R = \sqrt{P^2 + Q^2 - 2PQ\cos\theta'} \Rightarrow R = \sqrt{2}P$

45. $\mathbf{s} = \mathbf{u}t + \frac{1}{2}\mathbf{a}t^2$

$\mathbf{s} = \mathbf{u}t \qquad (\because \mathbf{a} = 0)$

$$\mathbf{s}_1 = \left(21\left(\frac{2\hat{\mathbf{i}} + 3\hat{\mathbf{j}} - 6\hat{\mathbf{k}}}{7}\right)\right)5 = 30\hat{\mathbf{i}} + 45\hat{\mathbf{j}} - 90\hat{\mathbf{k}}$$

$$\mathbf{s}_2 = 5\sqrt{2}\left(\frac{3\hat{\mathbf{i}} + 4\hat{\mathbf{j}} + 5\hat{\mathbf{k}}}{5\sqrt{2}}\right)5 = 15\hat{\mathbf{i}} + 20\hat{\mathbf{j}} + 25\hat{\mathbf{k}}$$

$$\mathbf{s} = \mathbf{s}_1 + \mathbf{s}_2 + \mathbf{s}_3$$

$\Rightarrow 0 - \hat{\mathbf{i}} = (30\hat{\mathbf{i}} + 45\hat{\mathbf{j}} - 90\hat{\mathbf{k}}) + (15\hat{\mathbf{i}} + 20\hat{\mathbf{j}} + 25\hat{\mathbf{k}}) + \mathbf{s}_3$

$\Rightarrow \quad \mathbf{s}_3 = -46\hat{\mathbf{i}} - 65\hat{\mathbf{j}} + 65\hat{\mathbf{k}}$

Multiple Choice Correct Questions

1. Components of a vector depend on the choice of co-ordinate system.

2. $(\mathbf{v}_1 + \mathbf{v}_2)\cdot(\mathbf{v}_1 - \mathbf{v}_2) = 0$

$\Rightarrow \mathbf{v}_1\cdot\mathbf{v}_1 - \mathbf{v}_1\cdot\mathbf{v}_2 + \mathbf{v}_2\cdot\mathbf{v}_1 - \mathbf{v}_2\cdot\mathbf{v}_2 = 0$

$\Rightarrow \quad v_1^2 - v_2^2 = 0$

$\Rightarrow \quad v_1 = v_2$

3. $\mathbf{A}\cdot\mathbf{B} = 0 \Rightarrow \mathbf{A} \perp \mathbf{B}$

$\mathbf{A}\cdot\mathbf{C} = 0 \Rightarrow \mathbf{A} \perp \mathbf{C}$

$|\mathbf{C}\times\mathbf{B}| = |\mathbf{B}\times\mathbf{C}| = 1\times1\times\sin 30° = \frac{1}{2}$

4. Component of $\mathbf{a} - \mathbf{b}$ along $\mathbf{a} + \mathbf{b}$

$$= \frac{(\mathbf{a}-\mathbf{b})\cdot(\mathbf{a}+\mathbf{b})}{|\mathbf{a}+\mathbf{b}|} = \frac{a^2 - b^2}{\sqrt{a^2 + b^2 + ab}}$$

Component of $\mathbf{a} + \mathbf{b}$ along $\mathbf{a} - \mathbf{b}$

$$= \frac{(\mathbf{a}+\mathbf{b})\cdot(\mathbf{a}-\mathbf{b})}{|\mathbf{a}-\mathbf{b}|} = \frac{a^2 - b^2}{\sqrt{a^2 + b^2 - ab}}$$

5. (a, c)

6. The x-component of the resultant of several vectors is always less than or equal to the sum of the magnitudes of the vectors.

7. $AB\cos\theta = 8$

$AB\sin\theta = \pm 8\sqrt{3} \Rightarrow \tan\theta = \pm\sqrt{3}$

$\Rightarrow \quad \theta = 60°$ and $\theta = 120°$

8. If λ is positive scalar, then $\lambda\mathbf{a}$ will be parallel to $\mathbf{a}$.

If λ is negative scalar, then $\lambda\mathbf{a}$ will be anti-parallel to $\mathbf{a}$.

9. (b) $\mathbf{a} + \mathbf{b} + \mathbf{c} + \mathbf{d} = 0$

$\Rightarrow \mathbf{a} + \mathbf{c} = -(\mathbf{b} + \mathbf{d}) \Rightarrow |\mathbf{a} + \mathbf{c}| = |\mathbf{b} + \mathbf{d}|$

(c) $\mathbf{a} + \mathbf{b} + \mathbf{c} + \mathbf{d} = 0 \Rightarrow \mathbf{a} = -(\mathbf{b} + \mathbf{c} + \mathbf{d})$

$\Rightarrow |\mathbf{a}| = |\mathbf{b} + \mathbf{c} + \mathbf{d}|$ and $|\mathbf{b} + \mathbf{c} + \mathbf{d}| \le |\mathbf{b}| + |\mathbf{c}| + |\mathbf{d}|$

So, $|\mathbf{a}| \le |\mathbf{b}| + |\mathbf{c}| + |\mathbf{d}|$

(d) $\mathbf{a} + \mathbf{b} + \mathbf{c} + \mathbf{d} = 0 \Rightarrow \mathbf{b} + \mathbf{c} = -(\mathbf{a} + \mathbf{d})$

So, $\mathbf{b} + \mathbf{c}$ and $\mathbf{a} + \mathbf{d}$ are in the same plane.

10. $\sqrt{4^2 + (4x-2)^2 + 2^2} = 2\sqrt{1^2 + x^2 + 3^2}$

$\Rightarrow \quad 3x^2 - 4x - 4 = 0$

$\Rightarrow \quad 3x(x-2) + 2(x-2) = 0 \Rightarrow x = 2$ and $x = -\frac{2}{3}$

11. Lets take magnitude of each of them to be x.

$\mathbf{A} = x\hat{\mathbf{j}}, \mathbf{B} = x\cos 45°\,\hat{\mathbf{i}} + x\sin 45°\,\hat{\mathbf{j}}$,

$\mathbf{C} = x\hat{\mathbf{i}}, \mathbf{D} = x\cos 45°\,\hat{\mathbf{i}} - x\sin 45°\,\hat{\mathbf{j}}$

$\mathbf{A} - \mathbf{C} = x\hat{\mathbf{j}} - x\hat{\mathbf{i}} = -\sqrt{2}\mathbf{D}$

$$\mathbf{B} + \mathbf{D} - \sqrt{2}\mathbf{C} = \left(\frac{x}{\sqrt{2}}\hat{\mathbf{i}} + \frac{x}{\sqrt{2}}\hat{\mathbf{j}}\right) + \left(\frac{x}{\sqrt{2}}\hat{\mathbf{i}} - \frac{x}{\sqrt{2}}\hat{\mathbf{j}}\right) - \sqrt{2}x\hat{\mathbf{i}} = 0$$

$$\frac{\mathbf{A} + \mathbf{C}}{\sqrt{2}} = \frac{x\hat{\mathbf{j}} + x\hat{\mathbf{i}}}{\sqrt{2}} = \mathbf{B}$$

12. $$\cos\theta = \frac{\mathbf{a}\cdot\mathbf{b}}{ab} = \frac{-x + 2 + x + 1}{\sqrt{6}\sqrt{x^2 + 1^2 + (x+1)^2}}$$

$$\cos\theta = \frac{3}{\sqrt{6}\sqrt{2x^2 + 2 + 2x}}$$

$\Rightarrow \theta$ is acute and depends on x.

13. $|\mathbf{a} + \mathbf{b}| = |\mathbf{a} - 2\mathbf{b}|$

$\Rightarrow \sqrt{a^2 + b^2 + 2ab\cos\theta} = \sqrt{a^2 + 4b^2 - 4ab\cos\theta}$

$$\Rightarrow \quad a^2 + b^2 + 2ab\cos\theta = a^2 + 4b^2 - 4ab\cos\theta$$

$$\Rightarrow \quad 3b^2 = 6ab\cos\theta$$

$$\Rightarrow \quad \frac{a}{b} = \frac{1}{2\cos\theta}$$

Since, $\cos\theta \le 1$

$$\frac{a}{b} \ge \frac{1}{2}$$

14. $\mathbf{A} = \hat{\mathbf{i}} + \hat{\mathbf{j}} + 2\hat{\mathbf{k}}$

$\mathbf{B} = \hat{\mathbf{i}} + 2\hat{\mathbf{j}} + \hat{\mathbf{k}}$

$\mathbf{C} = \hat{\mathbf{i}} + \hat{\mathbf{j}} + \hat{\mathbf{k}}$

Vectors coplanar with **A** and $\mathbf{B} = \mathbf{A} + \lambda\mathbf{B}$

Since, $(\mathbf{A} + \lambda\mathbf{B}) \perp \mathbf{C}$

$$(\mathbf{A} + \lambda\mathbf{B}) \cdot \mathbf{C} = 0$$

$$[(\lambda + 1)\hat{\mathbf{i}} + (2\lambda + 1)\hat{\mathbf{j}} + (\lambda + 2)\hat{\mathbf{k}}] \cdot (\hat{\mathbf{i}} + \hat{\mathbf{j}} + \hat{\mathbf{k}}) = 0$$

$$\lambda + 1 + 2\lambda + 1 + \lambda + 2 = 0$$

$$4\lambda + 4 = 0$$

$$\lambda = -1$$

15. (a,c,d) **16.** (a,d)

17. $\mathbf{a} \times (\mathbf{b} \times \mathbf{a}) = (\mathbf{a} \cdot \mathbf{a})\mathbf{b} - (\mathbf{a} \cdot \mathbf{b})\mathbf{a}$

(a) Not a null vector.

(b) If $\mathbf{a} \perp \mathbf{b}$, it is parallel to **b**.

(c) Coplanar with **a** and **b**.

18. (a,b,c,d)

19. $\mathbf{C} = \mathbf{A} + \mathbf{B}$

$\Rightarrow C^2 = A^2 + B^2 + 2AB\cos\theta$

20. (a) Since, $\mathbf{a} + \mathbf{b} + \mathbf{c} = 0$, these vectors can form triangle.

(b) Component of **a** along $\mathbf{c} = a\cos\theta = \dfrac{\mathbf{a} \cdot \mathbf{c}}{c} = \dfrac{-6 + 2 + 4}{\sqrt{21}} = 0$

(c) $\cos\beta = \dfrac{A_Y}{A} = \dfrac{2}{\sqrt{14}} \quad \Rightarrow \beta = \cos^{-1}\left(\sqrt{\dfrac{2}{7}}\right)$

(d) Magnitude of $\mathbf{a} = \sqrt{3^2 + 2^2 + 1^2} = 14$

Required vector $= (2\sqrt{14})(-\mathbf{b})$

$$= 2\sqrt{14}\left(\frac{-(\hat{\mathbf{i}} - 3\hat{\mathbf{j}} + 5\hat{\mathbf{k}})}{\sqrt{35}}\right)$$

$$= \sqrt{\frac{2}{5}}(-2\hat{\mathbf{i}} + 6\hat{\mathbf{j}} - 10\hat{\mathbf{k}})$$

Comprehension Based Questions

1. $\mathbf{v} = v\hat{\mathbf{A}} = 15\sqrt{2}\left(\dfrac{3\hat{\mathbf{i}} + 4\hat{\mathbf{j}} + 5\hat{\mathbf{k}}}{5\sqrt{2}}\right) = 9\hat{\mathbf{i}} + 12\hat{\mathbf{j}} + 15\hat{\mathbf{k}}$

2. $C\hat{\mathbf{A}} = 10\sqrt{2}\left(\dfrac{3\hat{\mathbf{i}} + 4\hat{\mathbf{j}} + 5\hat{\mathbf{k}}}{5\sqrt{2}}\right) = 6\hat{\mathbf{i}} + 8\hat{\mathbf{j}} + 10\hat{\mathbf{k}}$

3. $\mathbf{A} + \mathbf{B} + \mathbf{C} + \mathbf{D} = \hat{\mathbf{i}}$

$$\mathbf{D} = -15\hat{\mathbf{i}} - 36\hat{\mathbf{j}} + 30\hat{\mathbf{k}}$$

4.

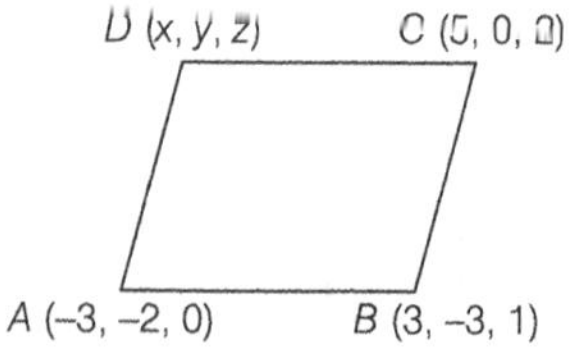

$$\mathbf{BC} = 2\hat{\mathbf{i}} + 3\hat{\mathbf{j}} + \hat{\mathbf{k}}$$

$$\mathbf{AD} = (x + 3)\hat{\mathbf{i}} + (y + 2)\hat{\mathbf{j}} + z\hat{\mathbf{k}}$$

$$\mathbf{AD} = \mathbf{BC}$$

$$(x + 3)\hat{\mathbf{i}} + (y + 2)\hat{\mathbf{j}} + z\hat{\mathbf{k}} = 2\hat{\mathbf{i}} + 3\hat{\mathbf{j}} + \hat{\mathbf{k}}$$

$$x + 3 = 2 \Rightarrow x = -1$$

$$y + 2 = 3 \Rightarrow y = 1$$

$$z = 1$$

5. $AC\,\hat{\mathbf{AB}} = \sqrt{72}\left(\dfrac{6\hat{\mathbf{i}} - \hat{\mathbf{j}} + \hat{\mathbf{k}}}{\sqrt{38}}\right) = \dfrac{6(6\hat{\mathbf{i}} - \hat{\mathbf{j}} + \hat{\mathbf{k}})}{\sqrt{19}}$

6. $\cos\theta = \dfrac{\mathbf{AC} \cdot \mathbf{BD}}{(AC)(BD)} = -\dfrac{1}{2} \quad \Rightarrow \quad \theta = \dfrac{2\pi}{3}$

7. (d)

8. $\mathbf{F}_1 = 6\hat{\mathbf{i}} + 8\hat{\mathbf{j}}$

$$\mathbf{F}_2 = -6\sin\theta\hat{\mathbf{i}} + 6\cos\theta\hat{\mathbf{j}}$$

$$\mathbf{F}_3 = -F_3\hat{\mathbf{j}}$$

$$\mathbf{F}_1 + \mathbf{F}_2 + \mathbf{F}_3 = (6 - 6\sin\theta)\hat{\mathbf{i}} + (8 + 6\cos\theta - F_3)\hat{\mathbf{j}}$$

$$6 - 6\sin\theta = 0 \quad \Rightarrow \quad \sin\theta = 1 \quad \Rightarrow \quad \theta = 90°$$

$$8 + 6\cos\theta - F_3 = 0 \quad \Rightarrow \quad F_3 = 8\text{ N}$$

9. Tangential acceleration $= \left(\dfrac{\mathbf{a} \cdot \mathbf{v}}{v}\right)\hat{\mathbf{v}} = \left(\dfrac{40 + 45}{5}\right)\left(\dfrac{4\hat{\mathbf{i}} + 3\hat{\mathbf{j}}}{5}\right)$

$$= \frac{17}{5}(4\hat{\mathbf{i}} + 3\hat{\mathbf{j}})$$

10. Normal acceleration = **a** – (tangential acceleration)

$$= (10\hat{\mathbf{i}} + 15\hat{\mathbf{j}} + 20\hat{\mathbf{k}}) - \frac{17}{5}(4\hat{\mathbf{i}} + 3\hat{\mathbf{j}})$$

$$= \frac{-18\hat{\mathbf{i}} + 24\hat{\mathbf{j}} + 100\hat{\mathbf{k}}}{5}$$

Match the Columns Questions

1. $\mathbf{F}_1 = 10\hat{\mathbf{j}}$

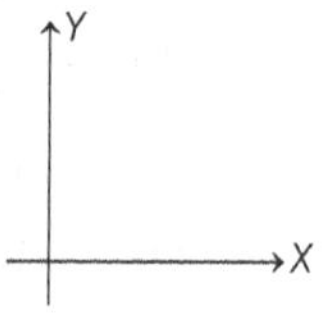

$\mathbf{F}_2 = 10\hat{\mathbf{i}}$

$\mathbf{F}_3 = -10\sqrt{2}\cos 45°\,\hat{\mathbf{i}} - 10\sqrt{2}\sin 45°\,\hat{\mathbf{j}}$

$= -10\hat{\mathbf{i}} - 10\hat{\mathbf{j}}$

$\mathbf{F}_1 + \mathbf{F}_2 + \mathbf{F}_3 = 0$

$\mathbf{F}_1 + \mathbf{F}_2 - \mathbf{F}_3 = 20\hat{\mathbf{i}} + 20\hat{\mathbf{j}}$

$(\mathbf{F}_1 \times \mathbf{F}_2) \times \mathbf{F}_3 = (-100\hat{\mathbf{k}}) \times (-10\hat{\mathbf{i}} - 10\hat{\mathbf{j}}) = 1000\hat{\mathbf{j}} - 1000\hat{\mathbf{i}}$

$\mathbf{F}_3 \cdot (\mathbf{F}_1 + \mathbf{F}_2) = (-10\hat{\mathbf{i}} - 10\hat{\mathbf{j}}) \cdot (10\hat{\mathbf{i}} + 10\hat{\mathbf{j}}) = -200$

2. $|\mathbf{A} \times \mathbf{B}| = |(2\hat{\mathbf{i}} + 3\hat{\mathbf{j}} - \hat{\mathbf{k}}) \times (\hat{\mathbf{i}} + 2\hat{\mathbf{j}} + 2\hat{\mathbf{k}})|$

$$= |8\hat{i} - 5\hat{j} + \hat{k}| = \sqrt{90}$$

$$|\mathbf{A} - \mathbf{B}| = |\hat{i} + \hat{j} - 3\hat{k}| = \sqrt{11}$$

$$\mathbf{A} \cdot \mathbf{B} = 2 + 6 - 2 = 6$$

$$|\mathbf{A} + \mathbf{B}| = |3\hat{i} + 5\hat{j} + \hat{k}| = \sqrt{35}$$

3.

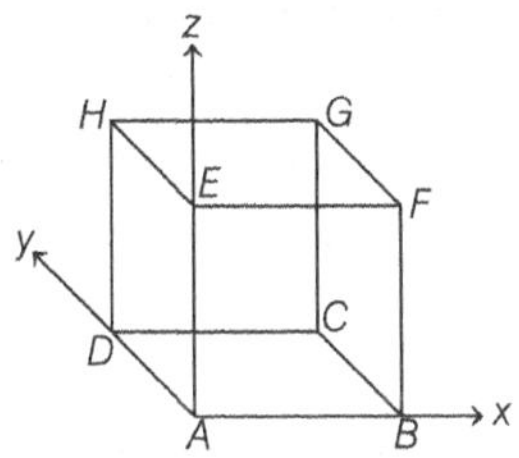

Point	Co-ordinates
A	(0, 0, 0)
B	(a, 0, 0)
C	(a, a, 0)
D	(0, a, 0)
E	(0, 0, a)
F	(a, 0, a)
G	(a, a, a)
H	(0, a, a)

$\mathbf{AC} = a\hat{i} + a\hat{j}$; $\mathbf{BE} = -a\hat{i} + a\hat{k}$

$\mathbf{GB} = -a\hat{j} - a\hat{k}$; $\mathbf{AD} = a\hat{j}$

$\mathbf{EF} = a\hat{i}$; $\mathbf{CD} = -a\hat{i}$

$\mathbf{HD} = -a\hat{k}$; $\mathbf{AC} = a\hat{i} + a\hat{j}$

$\mathbf{GF} = -a\hat{j}$; $\mathbf{FE} = -a\hat{i}$

$\mathbf{EH} = a\hat{j}$; $\mathbf{GH} = -a\hat{i}$

$\mathbf{FH} = -a\hat{i} + a\hat{j}$; $\mathbf{HG} = a\hat{i}$

4. (a) $|\hat{a} + \hat{b}| = \sqrt{(1)^2 + (1)^2 + 2(1)(1)\cos 120°} = 1$

$$\hat{a} = \hat{i} \text{ and } \hat{b} = -\cos 60° \hat{i} + \sin 60° \hat{j}$$

$$\hat{a} + \hat{b} = \hat{i} + (-\cos 60° \hat{i} + \sin 60° \hat{j})$$

$$= \frac{1}{2}\hat{i} + \frac{\sqrt{3}}{2}\hat{j}$$

So, the resultant has positive rectangular component in the direction of $\hat{\mathbf{a}}$.

$$\hat{a} \cdot \hat{b} = \hat{i} \cdot \left(-\frac{1}{2}\hat{i} + \frac{\sqrt{3}}{2}\hat{j}\right) = -\frac{1}{2}$$

$$|\hat{a} - \hat{b}| = \sqrt{1^2 + 1^2 - 2(1)(1)\cos 120°} = \sqrt{3}$$

(b) $2\hat{a} = 2\hat{i}$ and $\hat{b} = = -\hat{i}$

$$2\hat{a} + \hat{b} = 2\hat{i} + (-\hat{i}) = \hat{i}$$

$$|2\hat{a} + \hat{b}| = 1$$

$$2\hat{a} + \hat{b} = 2\hat{i} \cdot (-\hat{i}) = -2$$

$$|2\hat{a} - \hat{b}| = 3$$

(c) $\hat{a} = \hat{i}$ and $\hat{b} = \hat{j}$

$$\hat{a} + \hat{b} = \hat{i} + \hat{j} \Rightarrow |\hat{a} + \hat{b}| = \sqrt{2}$$

$$\hat{a} \cdot \hat{b} = 0 \Rightarrow |\hat{a} - \hat{b}| = \sqrt{2}$$

(d) $-\hat{a} = -\hat{i}$ and $-\hat{b} = -\hat{j}$

$$-\hat{a} - \hat{b} = -\hat{i} - \hat{j} \Rightarrow |-\hat{a} - \hat{b}| = \sqrt{2}$$

$$(-\hat{a}) \cdot (-\hat{b}) = 0$$

$$|-\hat{a} - (-\hat{b})| = \sqrt{2}$$

5. (a) $\mathbf{a} + \mathbf{b} = \hat{j}$ ...(i)

$2\mathbf{a} - \mathbf{b} = 3\hat{i} + \dfrac{\hat{j}}{2}$ ...(ii)

Solving Eqs. (i) and (ii), we get

$$\mathbf{a} = \hat{i} + \frac{\hat{j}}{2} \text{ and } \mathbf{b} = -\hat{i} + \frac{\hat{j}}{2}$$

$$\cos\theta = \frac{\mathbf{a} \cdot \mathbf{b}}{\mathbf{ab}} = \frac{-1 + \frac{1}{4}}{\frac{\sqrt{5}}{2}\frac{\sqrt{5}}{2}} = \frac{3}{5}$$

(b) $|\mathbf{a} + \mathbf{b} + \mathbf{c}|^2 = (\mathbf{a} + \mathbf{b} + \mathbf{c}) \cdot (\mathbf{a} + \mathbf{b} + \mathbf{c})$

$$= \mathbf{a} \cdot \mathbf{a} + \mathbf{b} \cdot \mathbf{b} + \mathbf{c} \cdot \mathbf{c} + 2\mathbf{a} \cdot \mathbf{b} + 2\mathbf{b} \cdot \mathbf{c} + 2\mathbf{c} \cdot \mathbf{a}$$

$$\Rightarrow (\sqrt{6})^2 = a^2 + a^2 + a^2 + 2a^2 \cos\frac{\pi}{3}$$

$$+ 2a^2 \cos\frac{\pi}{3} + 2a^2 \cos\frac{\pi}{3}$$

$$\Rightarrow \quad 6 = 6a^2 \Rightarrow a = 1$$

(c) Area of parallelogram $= \dfrac{1}{2}|\mathbf{d}_1 \times \mathbf{d}_2| = \dfrac{1}{2}|-2\hat{i} - 14\hat{j} - 10\hat{k}|$

$$= 5\sqrt{3}$$

(d) $|\mathbf{a} + \mathbf{b} + \mathbf{c}|^2 = (\mathbf{a} + \mathbf{b} + \mathbf{c}) \cdot (\mathbf{a} + \mathbf{b} + \mathbf{c})$

$$= \mathbf{a} \cdot \mathbf{a} + \mathbf{b} \cdot \mathbf{b} + \mathbf{c} \cdot \mathbf{c} + 2(\mathbf{a} \cdot \mathbf{b}) + 2(\mathbf{b} \cdot \mathbf{c}) + 2(\mathbf{c} \cdot \mathbf{a})$$

$\mathbf{a} \perp \mathbf{b} + \mathbf{c} \Rightarrow \mathbf{a} \cdot (\mathbf{b} + \mathbf{c}) = 0$ ...(i)

$\mathbf{b} \perp \mathbf{c} + \mathbf{a} \Rightarrow \mathbf{b} \cdot (\mathbf{c} + \mathbf{a}) = 0$ ...(ii)

$\mathbf{c} \perp \mathbf{a} + \mathbf{b} \Rightarrow \mathbf{c} \cdot (\mathbf{a} + \mathbf{b}) = 0$ ...(iii)

Adding Eqs. (i), (ii) and (iii), we get

$\Rightarrow \mathbf{a} \cdot (\mathbf{b} + \mathbf{c}) + \mathbf{b} \cdot (\mathbf{c} + \mathbf{a}) + \mathbf{c} \cdot (\mathbf{a} + \mathbf{b}) = 0$

$\Rightarrow 2\mathbf{a} \cdot \mathbf{b} + 2\mathbf{b} \cdot \mathbf{c} + 2\mathbf{c} \cdot \mathbf{a} = 0$

Now $|\mathbf{a} + \mathbf{b} + \mathbf{c}|^2 = a^2 + b^2 + c^2 + 0 = 2^2 + 3^2 + 6^2 = 49$

$$|\mathbf{a} + \mathbf{b} + \mathbf{c}| = \sqrt{49} = 7$$

6. (a) $|\mathbf{P} \times \mathbf{Q}| = 0 \Rightarrow PQ\sin\theta = 0 \Rightarrow \theta = 0°$ or $180°$

(b) $|\mathbf{P} \times \mathbf{Q}| = \sqrt{3}\mathbf{P} \cdot \mathbf{Q}$

$$\Rightarrow PQ\sin\theta = \sqrt{3}PQ\cos\theta$$

$$\Rightarrow \quad \tan\theta = \sqrt{3} \Rightarrow \theta = 60°$$

(c) $\mathbf{P} + \mathbf{Q} = \mathbf{R}$

$$\Rightarrow R^2 = P^2 + Q^2 + 2PQ\cos\theta \text{ and } P + Q = R$$

$$\Rightarrow \cos\theta = 1 \Rightarrow \theta = 0°$$

(d) $|\mathbf{P}+\mathbf{Q}| = |\mathbf{P}-\mathbf{Q}|$

$$\Rightarrow \sqrt{P^2+Q^2+2PQ\cos\theta} = \sqrt{P^2+Q^2-2PQ\cos\theta}$$

$$\Rightarrow \cos\theta = 0 \Rightarrow \theta = 90°$$

Numerical Value Questions

1. $$R^2 = P^2 + Q^2 \quad \text{...(i)}$$

$$\frac{R}{\sqrt{2}} = P - Q \quad \text{...(ii)}$$

$$\Rightarrow [\sqrt{2}(P-Q)]^2 = P^2 + Q^2$$

$$\Rightarrow 2(P^2+Q^2-2PQ) = P^2+Q^2$$

$$\Rightarrow P^2+Q^2-4PQ = 0$$

$$\Rightarrow P^2+Q^2 = 4PQ$$

$$\Rightarrow \frac{P}{Q}+\frac{Q}{P} = 4$$

2. $\mathbf{F}_1 = F_1\cos 30°\,\hat{\mathbf{i}} - F_1\sin 30°\,\hat{\mathbf{j}}$

$\mathbf{F}_2 = 5\cos 37°\,\hat{\mathbf{i}} + 5\sin 37°\,\hat{\mathbf{j}}$

$$\mathbf{F}_1+\mathbf{F}_2 = \left(\frac{\sqrt{3}F_1}{2}+4\right)\hat{\mathbf{i}} + \left(3-\frac{F_1}{2}\right)\hat{\mathbf{j}}$$

$$\Sigma F_y = 0 \Rightarrow \left(3-\frac{F_1}{2}\right) = 0 \Rightarrow F_1 = 6\text{ N}$$

3.

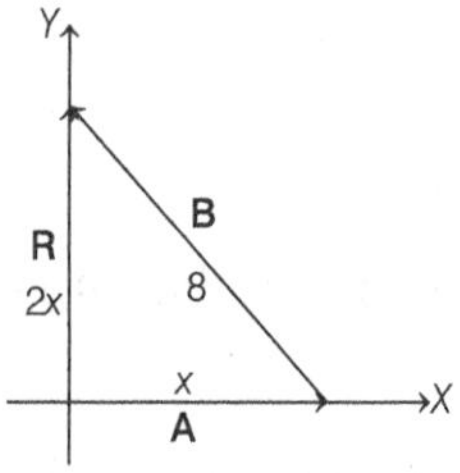

$$x^2 + (2x)^2 = 8^2 \Rightarrow 5x^2 = 64 \Rightarrow x = \frac{8}{\sqrt{5}}$$

4. $$|\mathbf{F}_1-\mathbf{F}_2| = \sqrt{F_1^2+F_2^2-2F_1F_2\cos\theta}$$

$$= \sqrt{1000+1000-2(10\sqrt{10})(10\sqrt{10})\cos(\theta)}$$

$$= \sqrt{2000(1-\cos\theta)}$$

$$= \sqrt{4000\sin^2\left(\frac{\theta}{2}\right)} = \sqrt{4000}\sin\left(\frac{\theta}{2}\right)$$

$$= (\sqrt{4000})\frac{\theta}{2} = \sqrt{4000}\left(\frac{1.8\pi}{180}\right)\frac{1}{2}$$

$$= \sqrt{4000}\,\frac{\pi}{200} = 1$$

5. $$\begin{vmatrix} 1 & 1 & 1 \\ 1 & -1 & 2 \\ -x & -(x+2) & -1 \end{vmatrix} = 0$$

$$\Rightarrow 1 + 2(x+2) - (-1+2x) + 1[-(x+2)-x] = 0$$

$$\Rightarrow 1+2x+4+1-2x-x-2-x = 0$$

$$\Rightarrow 4-2x = 0 \Rightarrow x = 2$$

6. $|\mathbf{a}-\mathbf{b}|^2 + |\mathbf{b}-\mathbf{c}|^2 + |\mathbf{c}-\mathbf{a}|^2 = 9$

$$|\mathbf{a}-\mathbf{b}|^2 = 1^2+1^2-2\mathbf{a}\cdot\mathbf{b} = 2(1-\mathbf{a}\cdot\mathbf{b})$$

$$|\mathbf{b}-\mathbf{c}|^2 = 2(1-\mathbf{b}\cdot\mathbf{c})$$

$$|\mathbf{c}-\mathbf{a}|^2 = 2(1-\mathbf{c}\cdot\mathbf{a})$$

$$\Rightarrow 6-2(\mathbf{a}\cdot\mathbf{b}+\mathbf{b}\cdot\mathbf{c}+\mathbf{c}\cdot\mathbf{a}) = 9$$

$$\Rightarrow 2(\mathbf{a}\cdot\mathbf{b}+\mathbf{b}\cdot\mathbf{c}+\mathbf{c}\cdot\mathbf{a}) = -3$$

Also, $|\mathbf{a}+\mathbf{b}+\mathbf{c}|^2 = |\mathbf{a}^2|+|\mathbf{b}^2|+|\mathbf{c}^2| + 2(\mathbf{a}\cdot\mathbf{b}+\mathbf{b}\cdot\mathbf{c}+\mathbf{c}\cdot\mathbf{a})$

$$= 1^2+1^2+1^2+(-3) = 0$$

$$\Rightarrow \mathbf{a}+\mathbf{b}+\mathbf{c} = 0$$

$$\Rightarrow \mathbf{b}+\mathbf{c} = -\mathbf{a}$$

$$\therefore |2\mathbf{a}+5(\mathbf{b}+\mathbf{c})| = |2\mathbf{a}+5(-\mathbf{a})| = |-3\mathbf{a}| = 3$$

7. $\mathbf{AB} = \hat{\mathbf{i}} - 4\hat{\mathbf{j}} - \hat{\mathbf{k}}$

$\mathbf{AC} = -2\hat{\mathbf{i}} - \hat{\mathbf{j}} + \hat{\mathbf{k}}$

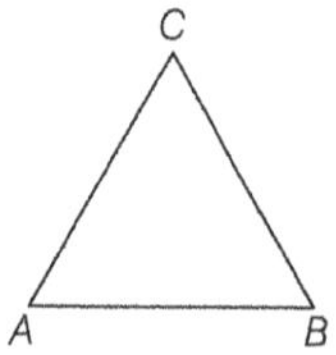

Area of triangle $= \frac{1}{2}|\mathbf{AB}\times\mathbf{AC}|$

$$= \frac{1}{2}|-5\hat{\mathbf{i}}+\hat{\mathbf{j}}-9\hat{\mathbf{k}}|$$

$$= \frac{\sqrt{107}}{2} = \sqrt{\frac{107}{4}}$$

8. $\mathbf{AD} = \mathbf{AB}+\mathbf{BC}+\mathbf{CD}$

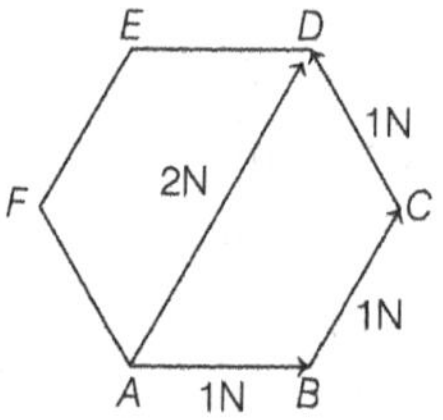

$$|\mathbf{AD}| = 2$$

9. $\mathbf{F}_1 = 3\hat{\mathbf{k}},\ \mathbf{F}_2 = 3\hat{\mathbf{i}}+4\hat{\mathbf{j}},\ \mathbf{F}_3 = -4\hat{\mathbf{i}}-4\hat{\mathbf{j}}$

$$\mathbf{F}_1+\mathbf{F}_2+\mathbf{F}_3+\mathbf{F}_4 = 0$$

$$\Rightarrow -\hat{\mathbf{i}}+3\hat{\mathbf{k}}+\mathbf{F}_4 = 0$$

$$\Rightarrow \mathbf{F}_4 = \hat{\mathbf{i}}-3\hat{\mathbf{k}}$$

$$\Rightarrow F_4 = \sqrt{10}\text{ N}$$

10. $\mathbf{a}+\mathbf{b}+\mathbf{c} = 0$

$$\Rightarrow \mathbf{a}+\mathbf{b} = -\mathbf{c}$$

$$\Rightarrow a^2+b^2+2ab\cos\theta = c^2$$

$$\Rightarrow (3\sqrt{3})^2+(3\sqrt{3})^2+2(3\sqrt{3})(3\sqrt{3})\cos\theta = (3\sqrt{3})^2$$

$$\Rightarrow 27+27+54\cos\theta = 27$$

$$\Rightarrow \cos\theta = -\frac{1}{2} \Rightarrow \theta = 120°$$

$$|\mathbf{a}+2\mathbf{b}| = \sqrt{(3\sqrt{3})^2+4(3\sqrt{3})^2+2(3\sqrt{3})(2)(3\sqrt{3})\left(-\frac{1}{2}\right)}$$

$$= \sqrt{27+4(27)-2(27)}$$

$$= \sqrt{3\times 27}$$

$$= \sqrt{81} = 9$$

Previous Year's Questions

JEE Main

1. Magnitude of vector $A = \sqrt{3^2 + 4^2} = 5$

   Direction of $\mathbf{B} = \hat{\mathbf{B}} = \dfrac{\mathbf{B}}{|\mathbf{B}|} = \dfrac{4\hat{i} + 3\hat{j}}{\sqrt{4^2 + 3^2}} = \dfrac{4\hat{i} + 3\hat{j}}{5}$

   Required vector has direction of B and magnitude of A. So, required vector is;

   Vector = magnitude × direction

   $$= 5 \times \left(\frac{4\hat{i} + 3\hat{j}}{5}\right) = 4\hat{i} + 3\hat{j}$$

2. Given vectors,

   $$\mathbf{P} = \hat{i} + 2m\hat{j} + m\hat{k} \quad \text{and} \quad \mathbf{Q} = 4\hat{i} - 2\hat{j} + m\hat{k}$$

   As, **P** and **Q** are given perpendicular vectors, so $\mathbf{P} \cdot \mathbf{Q} = 0$

   $\Rightarrow \; (\hat{i} + 2m\hat{j} + m\hat{k}) \cdot (4\hat{i} - 2\hat{j} + m\hat{k}) = 0$

   $\Rightarrow \quad 4 - 4m + m^2 = 0 \;\Rightarrow\; m = 2$

3. Given, $\mathbf{P} = 3\hat{i} + \sqrt{3}\hat{j} + 2\hat{k}$

   $\mathbf{Q} = 4\hat{i} + \sqrt{3}\hat{j} + 2.5\hat{k}$

   $$\therefore \quad \mathbf{P} \times \mathbf{Q} = \begin{vmatrix} \hat{i} & \hat{j} & \hat{k} \\ 3 & \sqrt{3} & 2 \\ 4 & \sqrt{3} & 2.5 \end{vmatrix}$$

   $$= \hat{i}(2.5\sqrt{3} - 2\sqrt{3}) - \hat{j}(7.5 - 8) + \hat{k}(3\sqrt{3} - 4\sqrt{3})$$

   $$\Rightarrow \mathbf{P} \times \mathbf{Q} = \frac{\sqrt{3}}{2}\hat{i} + \frac{1}{2}\hat{j} - \sqrt{3}\hat{k}$$

   $$\therefore |\mathbf{P} \times \mathbf{Q}| = \sqrt{\left(\frac{\sqrt{3}}{2}\right)^2 + \left(\frac{1}{2}\right)^2 + (-\sqrt{3})^2}$$

   $$= \sqrt{\frac{3}{4} + \frac{1}{4} + 3} = \sqrt{4} = 2$$

   $\therefore$ Unit vector in the direction of

   $$\mathbf{P} \times \mathbf{Q} = \frac{\mathbf{P} \times \mathbf{Q}}{|\mathbf{P} \times \mathbf{Q}|}$$

   $$= \frac{1}{2}\left(\frac{\sqrt{3}}{2}\hat{i} + \frac{1}{2}\hat{j} - \sqrt{3}\hat{k}\right)$$

   $$= \frac{1}{4}(\sqrt{3}\hat{i} + \hat{j} - 2\sqrt{3}\hat{k})$$

   $$= \frac{1}{x}(\sqrt{3}\hat{i} + \hat{j} - 2\sqrt{3}\hat{k}) \quad \text{(given)}$$

4. $\mathbf{A} \times \mathbf{A} = |\mathbf{A}||\mathbf{A}| \sin 0° \hat{\mathbf{n}}$

   $= |\mathbf{A}|^2 \times 0 \times \hat{\mathbf{n}} \quad [\because |\mathbf{A}| \neq 0]$

   $= 0$

5. Given, $\mathbf{a} = 2\hat{i} + 4\hat{j} - 2\hat{k}$ and $\mathbf{b} = \hat{i} + 2\hat{j} + \alpha\hat{k}$

   $\therefore$ Projection of **a** and **b** is given as,

   $$a\cos\theta = \frac{\mathbf{a} \cdot \mathbf{b}}{|\mathbf{b}|}$$

   $$\Rightarrow \quad 0 = \frac{2.1 + 4.2 + (-2).(\alpha)}{\sqrt{1^2 + 2^2 + (-\alpha)^2}} \quad [\text{given, } a\cos\theta = 0]$$

   $\Rightarrow \quad 0 = 2 + 8 - 2\alpha$

   $\Rightarrow \quad 2\alpha = 10 \;\Rightarrow\; \alpha = 5$

6. Given, $\mathbf{A} = (2\hat{i} + 3\hat{j} - \hat{k})\,\text{m}$

   $\mathbf{B} = (\hat{i} + 2\hat{j} + 2\hat{k})\,\text{m}$

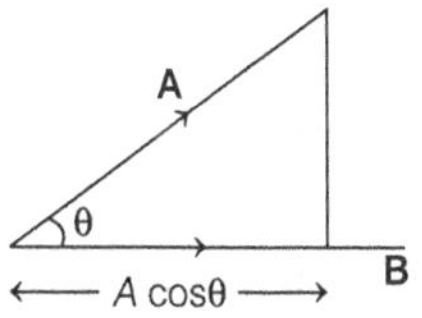

   We know that,

   $$\mathbf{A} \cdot \mathbf{B} = AB\cos\theta \quad \text{...(i)}$$

   The magnitude of component of **A** along **B**

   $$A\cos\theta = \frac{\mathbf{A} \cdot \mathbf{B}}{B} \quad \text{[From Eq. (i)]}$$

   $$= \frac{2.1 + 3.2 + (-1).2}{\sqrt{1^2 + 2^2 + 2^2}}$$

   $$= \frac{2 + 6 - 2}{\sqrt{9}} = \frac{6}{3} = 2$$

7. From given figure, we can write all the forces in vector notation as

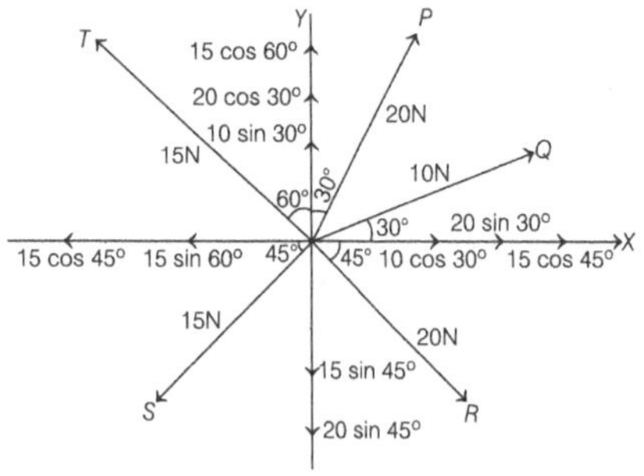

   $\mathbf{OP} = (20\sin 30°\,\hat{i} + 20\cos 30°\,\hat{j})\,\text{N} = (10\hat{i} + 17.32\hat{j})\,\text{N}$

   $\mathbf{OQ} = (10\cos 30°\,\hat{i} + 10\sin 30°\,\hat{j})\,\text{N} = (8.66\hat{i} + 5\hat{j})\,\text{N}$

   $\mathbf{OR} = (20\cos 45°\,\hat{i} - 20\sin 45°\,\hat{j})\,\text{N} = (14.14\hat{i} - 14.14\hat{j})\,\text{N}$

   $\mathbf{OS} = (-15\cos 45°\,\hat{i} - 15\sin 45°\,\hat{j})\,\text{N} = (-10.60\hat{i} - 10.60\hat{j})\,\text{N}$

   $\mathbf{OT} = (-15\sin 60°\,\hat{i} + 15\cos 60°\,\hat{j})\,\text{N} = (-12.99\hat{i} + 7.5\hat{j})\,\text{N}$

   The resultant of these forces is given as

   $$\mathbf{F} = \mathbf{OP} + \mathbf{OQ} + \mathbf{OR} + \mathbf{OS} + \mathbf{OT}$$

   $$\mathbf{F} = [(10\hat{i} + 17.32\hat{j}) + (8.66\hat{i} + 5\hat{j}) + (14.14\hat{i} - 14.14\hat{j}) + (-10.60\hat{i} - 10.60\hat{j}) + (-12.99\hat{i} + 7.5\hat{j})]$$

   $$\mathbf{F} = 9.21\hat{i} + 5.08\hat{j} \approx 9.25\hat{i} + 5\hat{j}\,\text{N}$$

   Thus, the resultant force is $\mathbf{F} \approx 9.25\hat{i} + 5\hat{j}$ N

8. Applying triangular law of vector addition in the given figure in question, we can write

$$\mathbf{OA} + \mathbf{AB} = \mathbf{OB} \quad \text{...(i)}$$

$$\mathbf{OB} + \mathbf{BC} = \mathbf{OC} \quad \text{...(ii)}$$

$$\mathbf{OC} + \mathbf{CD} = \mathbf{OD} \quad \text{..(iii)}$$

Also, $$\mathbf{AB} = \mathbf{OB} - \mathbf{OA} \quad \text{...(iv)}$$

$$\mathbf{AC} = \mathbf{OC} - \mathbf{OA} \quad \text{...(v)}$$

$$\mathbf{AD} = \mathbf{OD} - \mathbf{OA} = -\mathbf{OA} - \mathbf{OA} \quad \text{...(vi)}$$

On adding Eqs. (iv), (v) and (vi), we get

$$\mathbf{AB} + \mathbf{AC} + \mathbf{AD} = \mathbf{OB} + \mathbf{OC} - 4\mathbf{OA}$$

$$= 4\mathbf{AO} + \mathbf{OB} + \mathbf{OC} \quad \text{...(vii)}$$

According to polygon law of vector addition,

$$\mathbf{AB} + \mathbf{BC} + \mathbf{CD} + \mathbf{AD} = (\mathbf{OB} - \mathbf{OA}) + (\mathbf{OC} - \mathbf{OB}) + (\mathbf{OD} - \mathbf{OA}) + 2\mathbf{OA}$$

$$= \mathbf{OC} + \mathbf{OD} = \mathbf{OC} + \mathbf{AO}$$

9. Using triangular law of vector addition for each case,

(A) $\mathbf{C} - \mathbf{A} - \mathbf{B} = 0$

$\Rightarrow \mathbf{C} = \mathbf{A} + \mathbf{B}$ i.e. **C** is resultant vector.

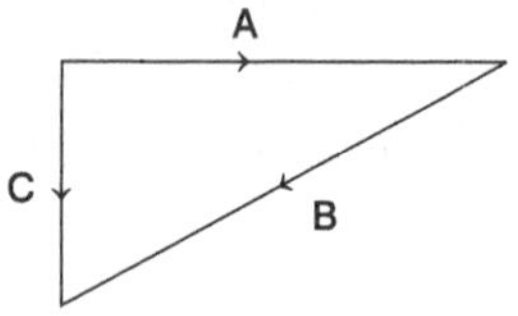

(B) $\mathbf{A} - \mathbf{C} - \mathbf{B} = 0$

$\Rightarrow \mathbf{A} = \mathbf{C} + \mathbf{B}$ i.e. **A** is resultant vector.

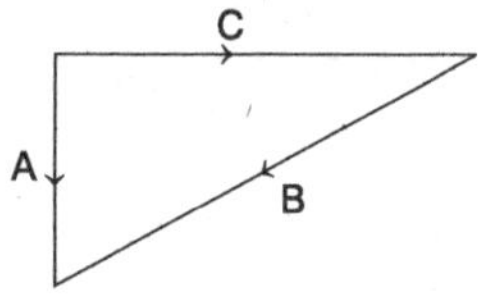

(C) $\mathbf{B} - \mathbf{A} - \mathbf{C} = 0$

$\Rightarrow \mathbf{B} = \mathbf{A} + \mathbf{C}$ i.e. **B** is resultant vector.

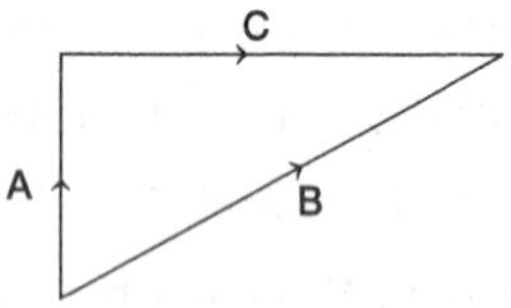

(D) $\mathbf{A} + \mathbf{B} = -\mathbf{C}$

$\mathbf{A} + \mathbf{B} + \mathbf{C} = 0$ i.e. these are cyclic vectors.

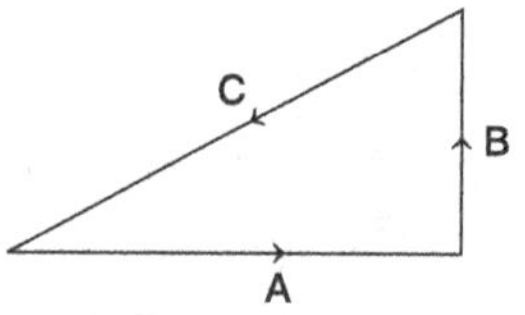

10. For the forces represented by the sides of a triangle and they are concurrent in nature is given as,

$$\mathbf{F}_1 + \mathbf{F}_2 + \mathbf{F}_3 = 0$$

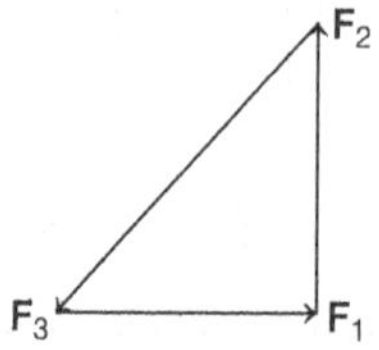

$\mathbf{F}_1, \mathbf{F}_2$ and $\mathbf{F}_3$ as the sides taken in the same order satisfy the condition for translatory equilibrium.

11. Given, $\mathbf{P} \times \mathbf{Q} = \mathbf{Q} \times \mathbf{P}$

$\Rightarrow \quad \mathbf{P} \times \mathbf{Q} = -\mathbf{P} \times \mathbf{Q}$

$\Rightarrow \quad 2(\mathbf{P} \times \mathbf{Q}) = 0$ or $\mathbf{P} \times \mathbf{Q} = 0$

It is possible only, if $\mathbf{P} = 0$ or $\mathbf{Q} = 0$,

angle between them is 180°.

$\therefore \quad \theta = 180°$

JEE Advanced

1. $\mathbf{A} = a\hat{\mathbf{i}}$ and $\mathbf{B} = a\cos\omega\hat{\mathbf{i}} + a\sin\omega t\hat{\mathbf{j}}$

$$\mathbf{A} + \mathbf{B} = (a + a\cos\omega t)\hat{\mathbf{i}} + a\sin\omega t\hat{\mathbf{j}}$$

$$\mathbf{A} - \mathbf{B} = (a - a\cos\omega t)\hat{\mathbf{i}} + a\sin\omega t\hat{\mathbf{j}}$$

$$|\mathbf{A} + \mathbf{B}| = \sqrt{3}|\mathbf{A} - \mathbf{B}|$$

$$\sqrt{(a + a\cos\omega t)^2 + (a\sin\omega t)^2} = \sqrt{3}\sqrt{(a - a\cos\omega t)^2 + (a\sin\omega t)^2}$$

$$\Rightarrow \quad 2\cos\frac{\omega t}{2} = \pm\sqrt{3} \times 2\sin\frac{\omega t}{2}$$

$$\Rightarrow \quad \tan\frac{\omega t}{2} = \pm\frac{1}{\sqrt{3}} \quad \Rightarrow \quad \frac{\omega t}{2} = n\pi \pm \frac{\pi}{6}$$

$$\Rightarrow \quad \frac{\pi}{12}t = n\pi \pm \frac{\pi}{6}$$

$$\Rightarrow \quad t = (12n \pm 2)\text{ s} = 2\text{ s}, 10\text{ s}, 14\text{ s} \text{ and so on.}$$

CHAPTER~02

CALCULUS IN PHYSICS

LEVEL 01 Starter Level

2.1 Power Rule

Find first derivative of dependent variable w.r.t. independent variable

1 $y = x^2 + x + 3$

2 $y = 5x^3 - 6x + \frac{7}{x} + 8$

3 $s = \frac{4t^3}{3} - 10t^{10} + 9t$

4 $r = \frac{12}{\theta} - \frac{4}{\theta^3} + \frac{1}{\theta^4}$

5 $y = 8\sqrt{x} - \frac{4}{\sqrt{x}} + 5x + 6$

6 $y = x\sqrt{x} + 18\sqrt[3]{x} - \frac{3}{x^2}$

2.2 Product Rule

Find derivative of functions

1 $y = (3 - x^2)(x^3 - x + 1)$

2 $y = (x^2 + 1)\left(x + 5 + \frac{1}{x}\right)$

3 $y = \left(x^2 + \frac{1}{x^2}\right)(5x^6 + 3)$

2.3 Quotient Rule

Find the derivative of functions

1 $y = \frac{2x + 5}{3x - 2}$

2 $z = \frac{2x + 1}{x^2 - 1}$

3 $g(x) = \frac{x^2 - 4}{x + 0.5}$

4 $f(t) = \frac{t^2 - 1}{t^2 + t - 2}$

2.4 Derivative of Trigonometric Functions,

Find $\frac{dy}{dx}$

1 $y = -10x + 3\cos x$

2 $y = \frac{3}{x} + 5\sin x$

3 $y = \operatorname{cosec} x - 4\sqrt{x} + 7$

4 $y = x^2 - \sec x + x$

5 $y = (\sin x + \cos x)\sec x$

6 $y = 4\sqrt{x}\sin x$

7 $y = \frac{\cos x}{1 + \sin x}$

8 $y = \frac{4}{\cos x} + \frac{1}{\tan x}$

9 $y = x^3 \tan x$

10 $y = x^2 \sin x + 2x\cos x - 2\sin x$

11 $y = (\sec x + \tan x)(\sec x - \tan x)$

12 $y = \frac{\cos x}{x} + \frac{x}{\cos x}$

2.5 Derivative of Exponential and Logarithmic Functions

Find $\frac{dy}{dx}$ as a function of x.

1 $y = \ln x + e^x$

2 $y = e^x \ln x$

3 $y = x^2 \ln x$

4 $y = e^x \tan x$

5 $y = x^2 e^x + 5e^x + 6x$

6 $\frac{\ln x}{x} + \frac{x}{\ln x}$

2.6 Chain Rule

Find $\frac{dy}{dx}$ as a function of x

1 $y = \cos 5x$

2 $y = 2\sin(\omega x + \phi)$

3 $y = (4 - 3x)^9$

4 $y = \ln(\sin x) + \sin(\ln x)$

5 $y = \sqrt{5x + 3}$

6 $y = 2e^{x^2} + x^2 e^x + 2x^2 + 3$

7 $y = \sqrt{\tan\sqrt{x}}$

8 $y = \cos 2x + \ln(x^2)$

9 $y = \sin^3 x + \sin 3x$

10 $\cos^2(x^2 + 1)$

11 $y = x(x^2 + 1)^{-1/2}$

12 $y = 2\tan^2 x + 2x\tan 2x$

13 $y = \dfrac{x}{\sqrt{x^2+4}}$

14 $y = \ln(2x+3) + x^2 \ln 2x$

15 $y = 2\sin\left(\dfrac{x}{2}\right) - 4\cos\left(\dfrac{x}{2}\right)$

16 $y = 7e^{3x} - 5e^{-2x} + 6e^{x}$

17 $y = e^{\sqrt{x}} + e^{\sin\left(\frac{3}{x}\right)} + x^{e}$

18 $y = \sin \sin \sin x$

19 $y = e^{e^{e^{x}}}$

20 $y = 7\ln^2(\sec 2x)$

2.7 Value of Derivatives at a Point

Suppose u and v are functions of x that are differentiable at $x = 0$ and that

$u(0) = 5, u'(0) = -3, v(0) = -1 \quad v'(0) = 2$

Find the values of the following derivatives at $x = 0$.

1 $\dfrac{d}{dx}(uv)$ 2 $\dfrac{d}{dx}\left(\dfrac{u}{v}\right)$

3 $\dfrac{d}{dx}\left(\dfrac{v}{u}\right)$ 4 $\dfrac{d}{dx}(7v - 2u)$

2.8 Derivative of Implicit Functions

Find $\dfrac{dy}{dx}$

1 $(x+y)^2 = 4$ 2 $x^2y + xy^2 = 6$

3 $x^3 + y^3 = 18xy$

2.9 Derivative as Rate of Change

1 The sides of a square sheet are increasing at the rate of 4 cm per minute. At what rate is the area increasing when the side is 8 cm long?

2 The radius r and height h of a circular cylinder are related to the cylinder's volume V by the formula $V = \pi r^2 h$. Find rate of increase of volume of cylinder,

(a) if height is increasing at a rate of 5 m/s while radius is constant.

(b) if radius is increasing at a rate of 5 m/s while height is constant.

(c) if height is increasing at a rate of 5 m/s and radius is increasing at a rate of 5 m/s.

3 A 13 m ladder is leaning against a wall when its base starts to slide away. By the time, the base is 12 m from the wall, the base is moving at the rate of 2 m/s.

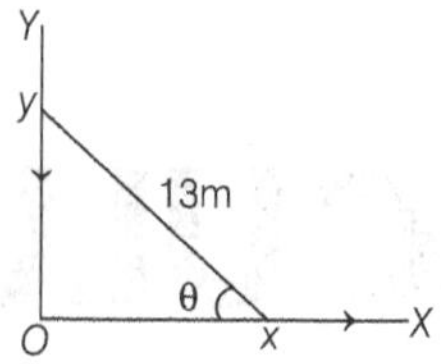

(a) How fast is the top of the ladder sliding down the wall then?

(b) At what rate is the area of the triangle formed by the ladder, wall and the ground changing?

(c) At what rate is the angle θ between the ladder and the ground changing then?

4 A balloon, which always remains spherical, has a variable radius. Find the rate at which its volume is increasing w.r.t. its radius when the radius is 7 cm.

5 Sand is pouring from a pipe at the rate of 12 cm^3/s. The falling sand forms a cone on the ground in such a way that the height of the cone is always one-sixth of the radius of the base. How fast is the height of the sand-cone increasing when the height is 4 cm?

2.10 Local Maxima and Minima

1 Particle's position as a function of time is given by $x = -t^2 + 4t + 4$, find the maximum value of position co-ordinate of particle.

2 Find the values of function $2x^3 - 15x^2 + 36x + 11$ at the points of maximum and minimum.

3 Find the point of maxima and minima for the function $2x^3 - 9x^2 + 100$.

4 Sum of two positive numbers is 60. Find the numbers, so that their product is maximum.

5 Find x, so that $\sin x(1 + \cos x)$ is minimum.

6 Electric field due a uniformly charged ring carrying charge Q and of radius R at a point on its axis at a distance x from its centre is given as
$E = \dfrac{KQx}{(R^2+x^2)^{3/2}}$, where K is Coulomb's constant.

Find x, where electric field is maximum.

7 A square piece of tin of side 18 cm is to be made into a box without top, by cutting a square from each corner and folding up the flaps to form the box. What should be the side of the square to be cut-off, so that the volume of the box is the maximum possible.

8 Find the height of a right circular cylinder of maximum volume inscribed in a sphere of radius a.

2.11 Integration of Elementary Functions

Find integrals of given functions.

1 $\int (2x^3 - 5x + 7)\,dx$ 2 $\int \left(\frac{1}{5} - \frac{2}{x^3} + 2x\right) dx$

3 $\int (\sqrt{x} + \sqrt[3]{x})\,dx$ 4 $\int x^{-3}(x+1)\,dx$

5 $\int \frac{t\sqrt{t} + \sqrt{t}}{t^2}\,dt$ 6 $\int \frac{4 + \sqrt{t}}{t^3}\,dt$

7 $\int \left(8y - \frac{2}{y^{1/4}}\right) dy$ 8 $\int \left(\frac{\sqrt{x}}{2} + \frac{2}{\sqrt{x}}\right) dx$

9 $\int (-2\cos t)\,dt$ 10 $\int (7e^x + 4\sin x + ex)dx$

11 $\int \frac{1}{2}(\text{cosec}^2 x - \text{cosec}\, x \cot x)\,dx$

12 $\int \left(-\frac{\sec^2 x}{3}\right) dx$ 13 $\int \tan^2 x\,dx$

14 $\int \cos\theta(\tan\theta + \sec\theta)\,d\theta$

15 $\int \frac{dx}{\sin^2 x \cos^2 x}$ 16 $\int \left(x^2 + \sin x + \frac{1}{x} + 3\right) dx$

17 $\int (4\sec x \tan x - 2\sec^2 x)\,dx$

18 $\int (1 - \cot^2 x)dx$

2.12 Integration by Substitution Method

1 $\int \sin 3x\,dx$ 2 $\int x\cos(2x^2)dx$

3 $\int \sec 2t \tan 2t\,dt$ 4 $\int \left(1 - \cos\frac{t}{2}\right)^2 \sin\frac{t}{2}dt$

5 $\int x^3(x^4 - 1)^2\,dx$ 6 $\int \frac{9r^2}{\sqrt{1 - r^3}}\,dr$

7 $\int 4\sin^2 y\,dy$ 8 $\int (2x+1)^3\,dx$

9 $\int \frac{3}{(2-x)^2}dx$ 10 $\int \frac{4y}{\sqrt{2y^2 + 1}}\,dy$

11 $\int 7\sin\frac{\theta}{3}\,d\theta$ 12 $\int \sin(8z - 5)\,dz$

13 $\int \frac{1}{\sqrt{t}}\cos(\sqrt{t} + 3)dt$ 14 $\int 28(7x - 2)^{-5}dx$

15 $\int \frac{6\cos t}{(2 + \sin t)^3}\,dt$ 16 $\int \frac{\ln x}{x}\,dx$

17 $\int \tan^7 \frac{x}{2} \sec^2 \frac{x}{2} dx$ 18 $\int \frac{1}{\sqrt{x}(1 + \sqrt{x})^2}\,dx$

19 $\int \frac{\cos^2 y}{7}\,dy$ 20 $\int \sec^2(3x + 2)\,dx$

21 $\int \tan^2 x \sec^2 x\,dx$ 22 $\int e^{2x-3}dx$

23 $\int \frac{x\,dx}{\sqrt{a^2 + x^2}}$ 24 $\int \frac{\sin(2t+1)}{\cos^2(2t+1)}\,dt$

25 $\int \sqrt{3 - 2s}\,ds$ 26 $\int (\sin 2x - \text{cosec}^2 x)\,dx$

27 $\int (2\cos 2x - 3\sin 3x)\,dx$

28 $\int \frac{1}{x^2}\cos^2\left(\frac{1}{x}\right) dx$ 29 $\int \sqrt{x}\,\sin^2(x^{3/2} - 1)\,dx$

30 $\int \cos^3 x\,dx$ 31 $\int \frac{1 - \cos 6t}{2}\,dt$

32 $\int \frac{\cos x}{\sin^3 x}\,dx$ 33 $\int \frac{\text{cosec}\,\theta}{\text{cosec}\,\theta - \sin\theta}\,d\theta$

34 $\int \frac{1}{\sqrt{5s + 4}}\,ds$ 35 $\int (e^{3x} + e^{-5x} + e)\,dx$

36 $\int \sqrt{\cot y}\ \text{cosec}^2 y\,dy$

2.13 Definite Integration

1 $\int_{-4}^{-1} \frac{\pi}{2}d\theta$ 2 $\int_{\sqrt{2}}^{5\sqrt{2}} r\,dr$

3 $\int_0^1 e^{2x}dx$ 4 $\int_0^4 \frac{dx}{\sqrt{x}}$

5 $\int_1^2 \left(6x^2 + \frac{2}{x^2}\right) dx$ 6 $\int_0^{3\pi/4} \sec^2\left(\frac{x}{3}\right) dx$

7 $\int_0^1 \frac{dx}{3x + 2}$ 8 $\int_0^{\pi/2} \sin\left(\frac{x}{2}\right) dx$

9 $\int_0^{\pi/2} (\sin x + \cos x)\,dx$ 10 $\int_0^{\pi/4} \cos 2x\,dx$

11 $\int_0^{\infty} e^{-x}dx$ 12 $\int_0^1 \frac{x}{x^2 + 1}\,dx$

2.14 Calculation of Area

1. Find the area of the region bounded by $y = x^2$, $x = 1$, $x = 3$ and the X-axis.
2. Find the area of the region between the curve $y = \sin x$ and the X-axis on the interval $[0, 2\pi]$.

LEVEL 02 JEE Main Level

Single Choice Correct Questions

1 $\frac{d}{dx}(x^2+4)=$

(a) $2x^2$ (b) $2x$ (c) 0 (d) $2x+4$

2 $\frac{d}{dx}\left(x^2-\frac{1}{x}+\ln 2\right)=$

(a) $2x+\frac{1}{x^2}+\frac{1}{2}$ (b) $2x-\frac{1}{x^2}+\frac{1}{2}$

(c) $2x-1$ (d) None of these

3 $y=x^{10}+\frac{1}{x^{10}}+\frac{1}{x}+3$, then $\frac{dy}{dx}$ is

(a) $10x^9+\frac{10}{x^9}+\ln x$ (b) $10x^9-\frac{10}{x^{11}}+\ln x$

(c) $10x^9-\frac{10}{x^{10}}+\ln x$ (d) $10x^9-\frac{10}{x^{11}}-\frac{1}{x^2}$

4 If $\frac{d}{dx}(\sqrt{x})=\frac{1}{k\sqrt{x}}$, then $k=$

(a) 3 (b) 1 (c) $\frac{1}{2}$ (d) 2

5 If $y=\tan x$, then $\sqrt{\frac{dy}{dx}-1}=$

(a) $\sec^2 x$ (b) $\sec x$ (c) $\tan x$ (d) None of these

6 $\frac{d}{dx}(x^4-2\sin x+3\cos x)=$

(a) $4x^3-2\cos x+3\sin x$ (b) $3x^2+2\cos x+3\sin x$

(c) $4x^3+2\cos x-3\sin x$ (d) $4x^3-2\cos x-3\sin x$

7 $\frac{d}{dx}\left(\frac{x^2+1}{x+1}\right)$

(a) $\frac{x^2+2x-1}{(x+1)^2}$ (b) $\frac{x^2-2x+1}{(x+1)^2}$

(c) $\frac{x^2+2x-1}{x+1}$ (d) $\frac{x^2+2x+1}{(x+1)^2}$

8 If $y=x^2\sin x$, then $\frac{dy}{dx}$ will be,

(a) $x^2\cos x+2x\sin x$ (b) $2x\sin x$

(c) $x^2\cos x$ (d) $2x\cos x$

9 $\frac{d}{dx}(x^2e^x)=$

(a) $2xe^x$ (b) x^2e^x+2x (c) e^x+2x (d) $e^x(x^2+2x)$

10 $\frac{d}{dx}[(1+x^2)e^x]=$

(a) $(x+1)^2e^x$ (b) $(x+1)^3e^x$

(c) $(x^2+1)^2e^x$ (d) None of these

11 $\frac{d}{dx}(x\ln 2x)=$

(a) $\frac{1}{2}$ (b) $1+\ln x$

(c) $1+\ln 2x$ (d) $\frac{1}{2}+\ln 2x$

12 $\frac{d}{dx}(x\sin x)=$

(a) $x\cos x$ (b) $\sin x$

(c) $x\cos x+\sin x$ (d) None of these

13 $y=x\ln x+\sqrt{x}$, then $\frac{dy}{dx}$ is

(a) $1+\ln x+\frac{1}{\sqrt{x}}$ (b) $1+\ln x+\frac{1}{2\sqrt{x}}$

(c) $x+\ln x+\frac{1}{2\sqrt{x}}$ (d) $x+\ln x+\frac{1}{\sqrt{x}}$

14 $\frac{d}{dx}(xe^x\sin x)=$

(a) $e^x(x\cos x+x\sin x+\sin x)$

(b) $e^x(x\cos x+\sin x)$

(c) $e^x(x\sin x+\cos x)$

(d) None of the above

15 $y=\ln x+e^{-x}$, then $\frac{dy}{dx}$ is

(a) $\frac{1}{x}+e^{-x}$ (b) $\frac{1}{x}-e^{-x}$ (c) $x+e^{-x}$ (d) $\frac{1}{x}+e^x$

16 If $y=2\tan\sqrt{x}$, find $\frac{dy}{dx}$

(a) $2\sec^2\sqrt{x}$ (b) $\frac{\sec^2\sqrt{x}}{\sqrt{x}}$ (c) $\sqrt{x}\sec^2\sqrt{x}$ (d) $\frac{\tan\sqrt{x}}{\sqrt{x}}$

17 If $a=\sec(3b)$, then $\frac{da}{db}$ will be

(a) $3\sec(3b)\tan(3b)$ (b) $3a^2\sin(3b)$

(c) $\sec(3b)\tan(3b)$ (d) $3\sec^2(3b)$

18 If $y=\sin 2x$, then $\left(\frac{dy}{dx}\right)_{x=\pi}=$

(a) -2 (b) 2 (c) $\frac{1}{2}$ (d) 1

19 $y=\cos(3x)+\sin(1-x)$, then $\frac{dy}{dx}$ will be

(a) $-\sin(3)+\cos(-1)$ (b) $-\sin(3x)+\cos(1-x)$

(c) $-3\sin(3x)-\cos(1-x)$ (d) $-3\sin(3x)+\cos(1-x)$

20 $y=e^{\sin 3x}$, then $\frac{dy}{dx}$ is

(a) $e^{\sin 3x}\cos 3x$ (b) $3e^{\sin 3x}\cos 3x$

(c) $3e^{\sin 3x}$ (d) $3e^{\sin 3x}\cos x$

21 $y = 3\tan\left(\frac{x}{3}\right)$, then $\frac{dy}{dx}$ is

(a) $\sec^2\left(\frac{x}{3}\right)$ (b) $3\sec^2\left(\frac{x}{3}\right)$

(c) $9\sec^2\left(\frac{x}{3}\right)$ (d) $\frac{1}{3}\sec^2\left(\frac{x}{3}\right)$

22 $y = \sin^3 x + \sin 3x$, then $\frac{dy}{dx}$ is

(a) $3\sin^2 x + 3\cos 3x$ (b) $3\sin^2 x\cos x + 3\cos 3x$

(c) $3\sin^2 x\cos x + \cos 3x$ (d) $3\sin^3 x\cos x + 3\cos 3x$

23 Find the derivative for the function $y = x\sin^2 x$.

(a) $\sin x(2x + \sin x)$ (b) $\sin x(x\cos x + \sin x)$
(c) $(2x\cos x + \sin x)$ (d) $x\sin 2x + \sin^2 x$

24 $\frac{d}{dx}(\sqrt{2x+3}) =$

(a) $\frac{1}{2\sqrt{2x+3}}$ (b) $\frac{2x}{\sqrt{2x+3}}$

(c) $\frac{1}{\sqrt{2x+3}}$ (d) None of these

25 Calculate the rate of change for the function $y = \sqrt{x^2+2}$ w.r.t. x.

(a) $\frac{dy}{dx} = \frac{2x}{\sqrt{x^2+2}}$ (b) $\frac{dy}{dx} = \frac{1}{\sqrt{x^2+2}}$

(c) $\frac{dy}{dx} = \frac{x}{2\sqrt{x^2+2}}$ (d) $\frac{dy}{dx} = \frac{x}{\sqrt{x^2+2}}$

26 Calculate the rate of change for the function $y = e^{\sqrt{2x}}$.

(a) $\frac{dy}{dx} = \frac{1}{\sqrt{x}}e^{\sqrt{2x}}$ (b) $\frac{dy}{dx} = \frac{2}{\sqrt{x}}e^{\sqrt{2x}}$

(c) $\frac{dy}{dx} = \frac{1}{\sqrt{2x}}e^{\sqrt{2x}}$ (d) $\frac{dy}{dx} = \sqrt{x}\,e^{\sqrt{2x}}$

27 $y = e^{\sin(3-x)}$, then find y'.

(a) $e^{\sin(3-x)}\cos(3-x)$ (b) $-e^{\sin(3-x)}\cos(3-x)$

(c) $e^{\sin(3-x)}$ (d) $-e^{\sin(3-x)}$

28 $\frac{d}{dx}(x^3 - 3x^2 + 3x - 1)^{100} =$

(a) $30(X-1)^{29}$ (b) $300(x-1)^{99}$
(c) $300(x-1)^{299}$ (d) $100(x-1)^{99}$

29 $f(x) = (x^3 + 6x^2 + 12x - 13)^{100}$, then $f'(x) =$

(a) $100(x^3 + 6x^2 + 12x - 13)^{99}$
(b) $300(x+2)^2(x^3 + 6x^2 + 12x - 13)^{99}$
(c) $100x^{99}$
(d) None of the above

30 Find the derivative of $y = \sin^2(\ln x)$.

(a) $2\sin(\ln x)\cos(\ln x)\cdot\frac{1}{x}$ (b) $-2\cos(\ln x)\cos(\ln x)\frac{1}{x}$

(c) $\frac{2\cos(\ln x)}{x}$ (d) $\frac{-2\sin(\ln x)\cos x}{x}$

31 $y = \sin(\cos^2(e^x))$, then $\frac{dy}{dx} =$

(a) $-2e^x\sin(e^x)\cos(e^x)\times\cos(\cos^2(e^x))$
(b) $e^x\sin(e^x)\cos(e^x)\times\sin(\cos(e^x))$
(c) $e^{2x}\sin e^x\cos e^x\times\cos(\cos^2(e^x))$
(d) None of the above

32 $y = \log_e(\tan(x^3))$, find $\frac{dy}{dx} =$

(a) $3x^2\frac{\sec^2(x^3)}{\tan(x^3)}$ (b) $x^2\sec(x)$

(c) $3x^2\frac{\sec(x^3)}{\tan(x)}$ (d) None of these

33 $\frac{d}{dx}(\sqrt{1+\sin 2x}) =$

(a) $\cos x$ (b) $\cos x + \sin x$
(c) $\cos x - \sin x$ (d) $\sin x$

34 $\frac{d}{dx}\left(\sqrt{\frac{1-\cos 2x}{1+\cos 2x}}\right) =$

(a) $\tan x$ (b) $\sec^2 x$
(c) $\tan^2 x$ (d) None of these

35 If $y = \sin x$ and $x = 3t$, then $\frac{dy}{dt}$ will be

(a) $3\cos(3x)$ (b) $\cos x$ (c) $3\cos(3t)$ (d) $-\cos x$

36 For what values of x is the derivative of the function $2x - \frac{3}{x}$ equal to 14?

(a) 1 (b) $\frac{1}{3}$ (c) $\frac{1}{2}$ (d) $\frac{2}{3}$

37 Find derivative of $x^2 + 4x + 5$ with respect to $2x + 7$.

(a) $x + 4$ (b) $x + 2$ (c) $2x + 4$ (d) $4x + 8$

38 Suppose u and v are functions of x that are differentiable at $x = 0$ and that
$u(0) = 5,\ u'(0) = -3,\ v(0) = -1,\ v'(0) = 2$
Find $\frac{d}{dx}(uv)$ at $x = 0$.

(a) 7 (b) 10 (c) 13 (d) -5

39 The slope of curve $y = 2\sec x - \tan x$ at $x = \frac{\pi}{6}$ will be

(a) 0 (b) 1
(c) $\frac{8}{3}$ (d) None of these

40 Find points at which the tangent to the curve $y = x^3 - 3x^2 - 9x + 7$ is parallel to the X-axis

(a) $(3, -20)$ and $(-1, 12)$ (b) $(3, 20)$ and $(1, 12)$
(c) $(3, -10)$ and $(1, 12)$ (d) None of these

41 A particle moves along the curve $x^2 + 4 = y$. The point on the curve at which the y-coordinates changes twice as fast as the x-coordinate, is

(a) $(1, 5)$ (b) $(5, 29)$
(c) $(2, 8)$ (d) None of these

42 A hot air balloon rising straight up from a level field is tracked by a range finder 500 ft from the lift-off point. At the moment the range finder's elevation angle is $\frac{\pi}{4}$, the angle is increasing at the rate of 0.14 rad/min. How fast is the balloon rising at the moment?

(a) 50 ft/min (b) 70 ft/min
(c) 100 ft/min (d) 140 ft/min

43 The sides of a certain closed cube are increasing at a constant rate uniformly such that at the instant when the side-length is 25 cm, the rate of change for the volume enclosed within the cube is exactly equal to 3 cc/s. The rate of change for the total surface area of the cube is

(a) $12 \text{ cm}^2/\text{s}$ (b) $0.12 \text{ cm}^2/\text{s}$
(c) $4.8 \text{ cm}^2/\text{s}$ (d) $0.48 \text{ cm}^2/\text{s}$

44 A stone is dropped into a quiet lake and waves move in circles at the speed of 5 cm/s. At the instant when the radius of the circular wave is 8 cm, how fast is the enclosed area increasing?

(a) $80\pi \text{ cm}^2/\text{s}$ (b) $90\pi \text{ cm}^2/\text{s}$
(c) $85\pi \text{ cm}^2/\text{s}$ (d) $89\pi \text{ cm}^2/\text{s}$

45 A ladder 5m long is leaning against a wall. The foot of the ladder is pulled out along the ground away from the wall at a rate of 2 m/s. How fast is the height of ladder on the wall decreasing at the instant when the foot of the ladder is 4 m away from the wall?

(a) 10 m/s (b) $\frac{3}{2}$ m/s
(c) $\frac{8}{3}$ m/s (d) None of these

46 A kite is 120 m high and 130 m of string is out. If the kite is moving away horizontally at the rate of 52 m/s, find the rate at which the string is being pulled out.

(a) 20 m/s (b) 30 m/s
(c) 40 m/s (d) 50 m/s

47 The charge flowing through a conductor beginning with time $t = 0$ is given by the formula $q = 2t^2 - 3t + 1$ (coulomb). Find the current $i = dq/dt$ at $t = 5$ s.

(a) 36 (b) 17
(c) 20 (d) 40

48 The momentum of a moving particle given by $P = t \ln t$. Net force acting on this particle is defined by equation $F = \frac{dp}{dt}$. The net force acting on the particle is zero at time

(a) $t = 0$ (b) $t = \frac{1}{e}$ (c) $t = \frac{1}{e^2}$ (d) None of these

49 Find the point of minima for the function $y = 2x^3 - 9x^2 + 100$.

(a) 0 (b) 1 (c) 2 (d) 3

50 If $y = \sqrt{3} \sin x + \cos x$, then there will be maxima corresponding to

(a) 0 (b) $\frac{\pi}{3}$ (c) $\frac{\pi}{6}$ (d) $\frac{\pi}{2}$

51 Minimum value of function $x^2 - 2x + 3$ is

(a) 1 (b) 2 (c) -2 (d) 3

52 Find the minimum value of the function $y = x^3 - 7x^2 + 8x + 5$.

(a) -7 (b) 4 (c) -11 (d) -5

53 A 2m wide truck is moving with a uniform speed of 8 m/s along a straight horizontal road. A pedestrian starts crossing the road at an instant when the truck is 4m away from him. The minimum constant velocity with which he should run to avoid an accident is

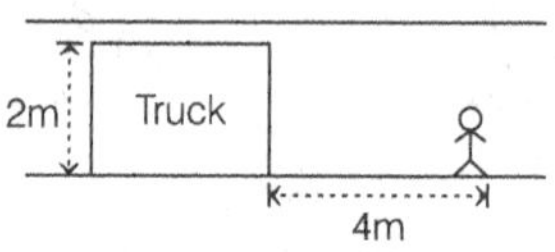

(a) $1.6\sqrt{5}$ m/s (b) $1.2\sqrt{5}$ m/s
(c) $1.2\sqrt{7}$ m/s (d) $1.6\sqrt{7}$ m/s

54 $\int 5x^4 \, dx =$

(a) $x^4 + C$ (b) $x^5 + C$
(c) $x^6 + C$ (d) $x^8 + C$

55 $\int \left(x^2 + \frac{1}{x^2} + 2 \right) dx$

(a) $x^3 + \frac{1}{2x^3} + 2x + C$ (b) $\frac{x^3}{3} + \frac{1}{2x^3} + 2x + C$
(c) $\frac{x^3}{3} - \frac{1}{x} + 2x + C$ (d) $\frac{x^3}{3} - \frac{2}{x^3} + 2x + C$

56 $\int \frac{3x^2+7x-11}{x^3}dx =$

(a) $-\frac{3}{x^2}-\frac{7}{x}-\frac{11}{2x^2}+C$ (b) $3\ln|x|-\frac{7}{x}+\frac{11}{2x^2}+C$

(c) $-\frac{3}{x^2}+\frac{7}{x}+\frac{22}{x^2}+C$ (d) $3\ln|x|+\frac{7}{x}+\frac{22}{x^2}+C$

57 $\int\left(x+\frac{1}{x}\right)\left(x^2+\frac{1}{x^2}\right)dx =$

(a) $\frac{x^4}{4}-\frac{x^2}{2}-\ln|x|-\frac{1}{2x^2}+C$

(b) $\frac{x^4}{4}+\frac{x^2}{2}+\ln|x|+\frac{1}{2x^2}+C$

(c) $\frac{x^4}{4}+\frac{x^2}{2}+\ln|x|-\frac{1}{2x^2}+C$

(d) $\frac{x^4}{4}-\frac{x}{2}+\ln|x|-\frac{1}{2x^2}+C$

58 $\int\frac{(x^2-1)^2}{x^3}dx =$

(a) $\frac{x^2}{2}-\frac{1}{x^2}-\ln x+C$ (b) $\frac{x}{2}-\frac{1}{2x}+2\ln x+C$

(c) $\frac{x^2}{2}-\frac{1}{2x^2}-2\ln x+C$ (d) None of these

59 $\int\left(\sqrt{x}-\frac{1}{\sqrt{x}}\right)dx$

(a) $\frac{1}{3}x^{3/2}+2\sqrt{x}+C$ (b) $\frac{1}{3}x^{3/2}-2\sqrt{x}+C$

(c) $\frac{2}{3}x^{3/2}+2\sqrt{x}+C$ (d) $\frac{2}{3}x^{3/2}-2\sqrt{x}+C$

60 Calculate the indefinite integral $\int(x\sqrt{x}+2)dx$.

(a) $\frac{2}{5}x\sqrt{x}+2x+C$ (b) $\frac{2}{5}x^2\sqrt{x}+2+C$

(c) $\frac{2}{5}x^2\sqrt{x}+2x+C$ (d) $\frac{2}{5}x\sqrt{x}+2x^2+C$

61 $\int\sin\left(\frac{x}{2}\right)dx$

(a) $-\cos(x/2)+C$ (b) $\cos(x/2)+C$

(c) $2\cos(x/2)+C$ (d) $-2\cos(x/2)+C$

62 $\int\operatorname{cosec}^2 x\,dx$

(a) $\cot x+C$ (b) $-\cot^2 x+C$

(c) $-\cot x+C$ (d) $\cot^2 x+C$

63 $\int e^{2x}dx$ is equal to

(a) $e^{2x}+C$ (b) $\frac{e^{2x}}{2}+C$

(c) $2e^{2x}+C$ (d) $2e^{x}+C$

64 $\int(3x-4)^3\,dx =$

(a) $\frac{(3x-4)^4}{12}+C$ (b) $\frac{(3x+4)^4}{12}+C$

(c) $\frac{(3x-4)^4}{4}+C$ (d) $\frac{(3x+4)^4}{4}+C$

65 $\int\sqrt{1+x}\,dx =$

(a) $\frac{2}{3}(1+x)^{3/2}+C$ (b) $\frac{3}{2}(1+x)^{3/2}+C$

(c) $\frac{2}{3}(1-x)^{3/2}+C$ (d) $\frac{2}{3}(1+x)+C$

66 $\int\frac{dx}{(3x+1)^5}$

(a) $-\frac{1}{4(3x+1)^4}+C$ (b) $-\frac{1}{12(3x+1)^4}+C$

(c) $-\frac{1}{18(3x+1)^6}+C$ (d) $-\frac{1}{6(3x+1)^6}+C$

67 $\int\frac{5}{3x-7}dx =$

(a) $\frac{5}{3}\ln|3x-7|+C$ (b) $\frac{3}{5}\ln|5x-7|+C$

(c) $\frac{5}{3}\ln|5x-7|+C$ (d) $\frac{3}{5}\ln|3x-7|+C$

68 $\int\frac{\ln^2 x}{x}\cdot dx$

(a) $\ln(x)+C$ (b) $\frac{\ln^3 x}{3}+C$ (c) $\frac{\ln^2 x}{2}+C$ (d) $-\ln(x)+C$

69 $I=\int\frac{1+2\sin x}{\cos^2 x}dx$; then I is equal to

(a) $\tan x+\sec x+C$ (b) $\tan x-\sec x+C$

(c) $\tan x-2\sec x+C$ (d) $\tan x+2\sec x+C$

70 $\int\cos^2 y\,dy$

(a) $\frac{y}{2}+\frac{\sin 2y}{2}+C$ (b) $\frac{y}{2}+\frac{\sin 2y}{4}+C$

(c) $\frac{y}{4}+\frac{\sin 2y}{4}+C$ (d) $\frac{y}{2}-\frac{\sin 2y}{4}+C$

71 $\int\cos(x^3)\cdot x^2dx$ will be

(a) $\sin(x^3)+C$ (b) $\cos(x^3)\cdot\frac{x^3}{3}+C$

(c) $-\frac{\sin(x^3)}{3}+C$ (d) $\frac{\sin(x^3)}{3}+C$

72 $\int_{-2}^{4}\left(\frac{x}{2}+3\right)dx$

(a) 24 (b) 21 (c) 18 (d) 15

73 $\int_{\pi}^{2\pi}\theta d\theta$

(a) $\frac{\pi^2}{2}$ (b) $\frac{3\pi^2}{2}$ (c) $2\pi^2$ (d) $3\pi^2$

74 If $I = \int_0^{\pi/2} \sin 2x \, dx$, the value of I is

(a) 1 (b) -1 (c) $\frac{1}{2}$ (d) $-\frac{1}{2}$

75 $\int_{x=0}^{x=\frac{\pi}{4}} 2\cos x \cdot dx$

(a) 1/2 (b) $\sqrt{2}$ (c) 1 (d) $1/\sqrt{2}$

76 $\int_0^1 \sqrt{\frac{x}{4}} dx =$

(a) 1 (b) -1 (c) $\frac{1}{3}$ (d) $-\frac{1}{3}$

77 Value of $\int_0^{\pi/2} \cos(3t) \, dt$ is

(a) $\frac{2}{3}$ (b) $-\frac{1}{3}$ (c) $-\frac{2}{3}$ (d) $\frac{1}{3}$

78 $\int_0^{\infty} e^{-x} \, dx$

(a) 1 (b) 0
(c) -1 (d) None of these

79 $\int_{x=0}^{x=\pi/8} 2\cos 2x \, dx$

(a) 1/2 (b) $\sqrt{2}$ (c) 1 (d) $1/\sqrt{2}$

80 $\int_{x=0}^{x=\pi/4} 2\sin 4x \cdot dx$

(a) 0 (b) $\sqrt{2}$ (c) 1 (d) None of these

81 $\int_0^{\pi/2} \sin^2 x \, dx =$

(a) $\frac{\pi}{2}$ (b) $\frac{\pi}{4}$ (c) $\frac{\pi}{8}$ (d) π

82 $\int_0^{\pi/4} (\sin 2x + \cos 2x) \, dx$

(a) 2 (b) 1 (c) -2 (d) -1

83 $\int_0^{\sqrt{\pi}} x \sin x^2 \, dx$

(a) 1 (b) 2 (c) $\frac{1}{2}$ (d) None of these

84 Area of curve $y = 2x^3 - 3x^2 + 4$ from $x_1 = -1$ to $x_2 = 1$ will be

(a) 0 (b) 2 (c) 6 (d) 10

85 The area of region between $y = \sin x$ and X-axis in the interval $\left[0, \frac{3\pi}{2}\right]$ will be

(a) 3 (b) 0 (c) 1 (d) -1

86 Consider the parabola $y = x^2$

The shaded area is

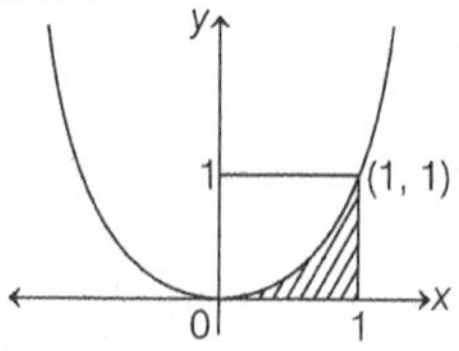

(a) 1 (b) $\frac{1}{3}$ (c) $\frac{1}{2}$ (d) $\frac{2}{3}$

Previous Year's Questions

JEE Advanced

1 A person of height 1.6 m is walking away from a lamp post of height 4 m along a straight path on the flat ground. The lamp post and the person are always perpendicular to the ground. If the speed of the person is 60 cm s^{-1}, the speed of the tip of the person's shadow on the ground with respect to the person is ……… cm s^{-1}. **[2023 Adv.]**

Answer Key

Level-1

2.1 Power Rule

1. $2x + 1$
2. $15x^2 - 6 - \frac{7}{x^2}$
3. $4t^2 - 100t^9 + 9$
4. $-\frac{12}{\theta^2} + \frac{12}{\theta^4} - \frac{4}{\theta^5}$
5. $\frac{4}{\sqrt{x}} + 2x^{-3/2} + 5$
6. $\frac{3}{2}\sqrt{x} + 6x^{-2/3} + \frac{6}{x^3}$

2.2 Product Rule

1. $-5x^4 + 12x^2 - 2x - 3$
2. $3x^2 + 10x + 2 - \frac{1}{x^2}$
3. $40x^7 + 20x^3 + 6x - \frac{6}{x^3}$

2.3 Quotient Rule

1. $-\dfrac{19}{(3x-2)^2}$
2. $\dfrac{-2(x^2+x+1)}{(x^2-1)^2}$
3. $g'(x)=\dfrac{x^2+x+4}{(x+0.5)^2}$
4. $f'(t)=\dfrac{t^2-2t+1}{(t^2+t-2)^2}$

2.4 Derivative of Trigonometric Functons

1. $-10-3\sin x$
2. $-\dfrac{3}{x^2}+5\cos x$
3. $-\text{cosec } x\cdot\cot x-\dfrac{2}{\sqrt{x}}$
4. $2x-\sec x\tan x+1$
5. $\sec^2 x$
6. $4\left(\sqrt{x}\cos x+\dfrac{1}{2\sqrt{x}}\sin x\right)$
7. $\dfrac{-1}{1+\sin x}$
8. $4\tan x\sec x-\text{cosec}^2 x$
9. $x^3\sec^2 x+3x^2\tan x$
10. $x^2\cos x$
11. 0
12. $\dfrac{-x\sin x-\cos x}{x^2}+\dfrac{x\sin x+\cos x}{\cos^2 x}$

2.5 Derivative of Exponential and Logarithmic Functions

1. $\dfrac{1}{x}+e^x$
2. $e^x\ln x+\dfrac{e^x}{x}$
3. $x(1+2\ln x)$
4. $e^x(\tan x+\sec^2 x)$
5. $x^2e^x+2xe^x+5e^x+6$
6. $\dfrac{1-\ln x}{x^2}+\dfrac{\ln x-1}{\ln^2 x}$

2.6 Chain Rule

1. $-5\sin 5x$
2. $2\omega\cos(\omega x+\phi)$
3. $-27(4-3x)^8$
4. $\cot x+\dfrac{\cos(\ln x)}{x}$
5. $\dfrac{5}{2\sqrt{5x+3}}$
6. $4xe^{x^2}+x^2e^x+2xe^x+4x$
7. $\dfrac{\sec^2\sqrt{x}}{4\sqrt{x}\tan\sqrt{x}}$
8. $-2\sin 2x+\dfrac{2}{x}$
9. $3\sin^2 x\cos x+3\cos 3x$
10. $-2x\sin 2(x^2+1)$
11. $\dfrac{1}{(x^2+1)^{3/2}}$
12. $4\tan x\sec^2 x+2\tan 2x+4x\sec^2 2x$
13. $\dfrac{4}{(x^2+4)^{3/2}}$
14. $\dfrac{2}{2x+3}+x+2x\ln 2x$
15. $\cos\left(\dfrac{x}{2}\right)+2\sin\left(\dfrac{x}{2}\right)$
16. $21e^{3x}+10e^{-2x}+6e^x$
17. $\dfrac{e^{\sqrt{x}}}{2\sqrt{x}}-\dfrac{3e^{\sin\left(\frac{3}{x}\right)}}{x^2}\cos\left(\dfrac{3}{x}\right)+ex^{e-1}$
18. $\cos\sin\sin x\cdot\cos\sin x\cdot\cos x$
19. $e^{e^{e^x}}\cdot e^{e^x}\cdot e^x$
20. $28\tan 2x\ln(\sec 2x)$

2.7 Value of Derivatives at a Point

1. 13
2. -7
3. $\dfrac{7}{25}$
4. 20

2.8 Derivative of Implicit Functions

1. $\dfrac{dy}{dx}=-1$
2. $\dfrac{-(2xy-y)^2}{x^2+2xy}$
3. $\dfrac{dy}{dx}=\dfrac{6y-x^2}{y^2-6x}$

2.9 Derivative as Rate of Change

1. $64\text{ cm}^2/\text{min}$
2. (a) $\dfrac{dV}{dt}=5\pi r^2$ (b) $\dfrac{dV}{dt}=10\pi rh$
   (c) $\dfrac{dV}{dt}=5\pi r^2+10\pi rh$
3. (a) -4.8 m/s (b) $-23.8\text{ m}^2/\text{s}$ (c) -0.4 rad/s
4. 616
5. $\dfrac{1}{48\pi}$ cm/s

2.10 Local Maxima and Minima

1. 8
2. At local maxima $y=39$ and at local minima $y=38$
3. $x=0$ is a point of maxima and $x=3$ is a point of minima.
4. 30 and 30
5. $x=\pi/3$
6. $\dfrac{R}{\sqrt{2}}$
7. 3 cm
8. $\dfrac{2a}{\sqrt{3}}$

2.11 Integration of Elementary Functions

1. $\dfrac{x^4}{2}-\dfrac{5x^2}{2}+7x+C$
2. $\dfrac{x}{5}+\dfrac{1}{x^2}+x^2+C$
3. $\dfrac{2}{3}x^{3/2}+\dfrac{3}{4}x^{4/3}+C$
4. $-\dfrac{1}{x}-\dfrac{1}{2x^2}+C$
5. $2\sqrt{t}-\dfrac{2}{\sqrt{t}}+C$
6. $-2t^{-2}-\dfrac{2}{3}t^{-3/2}+C$
7. $4y^2-\dfrac{8}{3}y^{3/4}+C$
8. $\dfrac{x^{3/2}}{3}+4x^{1/2}+C$
9. $-2\sin t+C$
10. $7e^x-4\cos x+\dfrac{ex^2}{2}+C$
11. $-\dfrac{1}{2}\cot x+\dfrac{1}{2}\text{cosec } x+C$
12. $-\dfrac{1}{3}\tan x+C$

13. $\tan x - x + C$

14. $-\cos\theta + \theta + C$

15. $\tan x - \cot x + C$

16. $\frac{x^3}{3} - \cos x + \log_e x + 3x + C$

17. $4\sec x - 2\tan x + C$

18. $2x + \cot x + C$

2.12 Integration by Substitution Method

1. $-\frac{1}{3}\cos 3x + C$

2. $\frac{1}{4}\sin(2x^2) + C$

3. $\frac{1}{2}\sec 2t + C$

4. $\frac{2}{3}\left(1 - \cos\frac{t}{2}\right)^3 + C$

5. $\frac{1}{12}(x^4 - 1)^3 + C$

6. $-6(1 - r^3)^{1/2} + C$

7. $2y - \sin 2y + C$

8. $\frac{(2x+1)^4}{8} + C$

9. $\frac{3}{2-x} + C$

10. $2\sqrt{2y^2 + 1} + C$

11. $-21\cos\frac{\theta}{3} + C$

12. $-\frac{\cos(8z-5)}{8} + C$

13. $2\sin(\sqrt{t} + 3) + C$

14. $-(7x-2)^{-4} + C$

15. $\frac{-3}{(2 + \sin t)^2} + C$

16. $\frac{1}{2}\ln^2 x + C$

17. $\frac{1}{4}\tan^8\frac{x}{2} + C$

18. $\frac{(-2)}{(1+\sqrt{x})} + C$

19. $\frac{y}{14} + \frac{\sin 2y}{28} + C$

20. $\frac{1}{3}\tan(3x+2) + C$

21. $\frac{\tan^3 x}{3} + C$

22. $\frac{1}{2}e^{2x-3} + C$

23. $\sqrt{a^2 + x^2} + C$

24. $\frac{1}{2\cos(2t+1)} + C$

25. $-\frac{1}{3}(3-2s)^{3/2} + C$

26. $-\frac{1}{2}\cos 2x + \cot x + C$

27. $\sin 2x + \cos 3x + C$

28. $-\frac{1}{2x} - \frac{1}{4}\sin\frac{2}{x} + C$

29. $\frac{1}{3}(x^{3/2} - 1) - \frac{1}{6}\sin(2x^{3/2} - 2) + C$

30. $\frac{3}{4}\sin x + \frac{1}{12}\sin 3x + C$

31. $\frac{t}{2} - \frac{\sin 6t}{12} + C$

32. $\frac{-1}{2\sin^2 x}$

33. $\tan\theta + C$

34. $\frac{2}{5}(5s+4)^{1/2} + C$

35. $\frac{e^{3x}}{3} - \frac{e^{-5x}}{5} + ex + C$

36. $-\frac{2}{3}(\cot^3 y)^{1/2} + C$

2.13 Definite Integration

1. $\frac{3\pi}{2}$

2. 24

3. $\frac{e^2 - 1}{2}$

4. 4

5. 15

6. 3

7. $\frac{1}{3}\ln\frac{5}{2}$

8. $2 - \sqrt{2}$

9. 2

10. 1/2

11. 1

12. $\frac{1}{2}\ln 2$

2.14 Calculation of Area

1. Area = 26 / 3 units

2. 4 units

Level 2

Single Choice Correct Questions

1. (b)	2. (d)	3. (d)	4. (d)	5. (c)
6. (d)	7. (a)	8. (a)	9. (d)	10. (a)
11. (c)	12. (c)	13. (b)	14. (a)	15. (b)
16. (b)	17. (a)	18. (b)	19. (c)	20. (b)
21. (a)	22. (b)	23. (d)	24. (c)	25. (d)
26. (c)	27. (b)	28. (c)	29. (b)	30. (a)
31. (a)	32. (a)	33. (c)	34. (b)	35. (c)
36. (c)	37. (b)	38. (c)	39. (a)	40. (a)
41. (a)	42. (d)	43. (d)	44. (a)	45. (c)
46. (a)	47. (b)	48. (b)	49. (d)	50. (b)
51. (b)	52. (c)	53. (a)	54. (b)	55. (c)
56. (b)	57. (c)	58. (c)	59. (d)	60. (c)
61. (d)	62. (c)	63. (b)	64. (a)	65. (a)
66. (b)	67. (a)	68. (b)	69. (d)	70. (b)
71. (d)	72. (b)	73. (b)	74. (a)	75. (b)
76. (c)	77. (b)	78. (a)	79. (d)	80. (c)
81. (b)	82. (b)	83. (a)	84. (c)	85. (a)
86. (b)				

Previous Year's Questions

JEE Advanced

1. (40)

SOLUTIONS

Level 1

2.1 Power Rule

1. $\frac{dy}{dx} = 2x + 1$
2. $\frac{dy}{dx} = 15x^2 - 6 - \frac{7}{x^2}$
3. $\frac{ds}{dt} = 4t^2 - 100t^9 + 9$
4. $\frac{dr}{d\theta} = -\frac{12}{\theta^2} + \frac{12}{\theta^4} - \frac{4}{\theta^5}$
5. $\frac{dy}{dx} = \frac{4}{\sqrt{x}} + 2x^{-3/2} + 5$
6. $\frac{dy}{dx} = \frac{3}{2}\sqrt{x} + 6x^{-2/3} + \frac{6}{x^3}$

2.2 Product Rule

1. $y = (3 - x^2)(x^3 - x + 1)$

$$\frac{dy}{dx} = (3 - x^2)(3x^2 - 1) + (x^3 - x + 1)(-2x)$$
$$= -5x^4 + 12x^2 - 2x - 3$$

2. $y = (x^2 + 1)\left(x + 5 + \frac{1}{x}\right)$

$$\frac{dy}{dx} = (x^2 + 1)\left(1 - \frac{1}{x^2}\right) + 2x\left(x + 5 + \frac{1}{x}\right)$$
$$= 3x^2 + 10x + 2 - \frac{1}{x^2}$$

3. $\frac{dy}{dx} = \left(x^2 + \frac{1}{x^2}\right)(30x^5) + (5x^6 + 3)\left(2x - \frac{2}{x^3}\right)$

$$= 40x^7 + 20x^3 + 6x - \frac{6}{x^3}$$

2.3 Quotient Rule

1. $\frac{dy}{dx} = \frac{(3x - 2)(2) - (2x + 5)(3)}{(3x - 2)^2} = \frac{-19}{(3x - 2)^2}$
2. $\frac{dz}{dx} = \frac{(x^2 - 1)(2) - (2x + 1)(2x)}{(x^2 - 1)^2} = \frac{-2(x^2 + x + 1)}{(x^2 - 1)^2}$
3. $g'(x) = \frac{(x + 0.5)(2x) - (x^2 - 4)(1)}{(x + 0.5)^2} = \frac{x^2 + x + 4}{(x + 0.5)^2}$
4. $f'(t) = \frac{(t^2 + t - 2)(2t) - (t^2 - 1)(2t + 1)}{(t^2 + t - 2)^2} = \frac{t^2 - 2t + 1}{(t^2 + t - 2)^2}$

2.4 Derivative of Trigonometric Functions

1. $\frac{dy}{dx} = -10 - 3\sin x$
2. $\frac{dy}{dx} = -\frac{3}{x^2} + 5\cos x$
3. $\frac{dy}{dx} = -\operatorname{cosec} x \cot x - \frac{2}{\sqrt{x}}$
4. $\frac{dy}{dx} = 2x - \sec x \tan x + 1$
5. $\frac{dy}{dx} = \sec^2 x$
6. $\frac{dy}{dx} = 4\left(\sqrt{x}\cos x + \frac{1}{2\sqrt{x}}\sin x\right)$
7. $\frac{dy}{dx} = \frac{(1 + \sin x)(-\sin x) - (\cos x)(\cos x)}{(1 + \sin x)^2} = \frac{-1}{1 + \sin x}$
8. $\frac{dy}{dx} = 4\sec x \tan x - \operatorname{cosec}^2 x$
9. $\frac{dy}{dx} = x^3 \sec^2 x + 3x^2 \tan x$
10. $\frac{dy}{dx} = (x^2 \cos x + 2x \sin x) + [2(x(-\sin x)) + (\cos x)(1)]$

$2\cos x$

$$= x^2 \cos x$$

11. $y = \sec^2 x - \tan^2 x = 1 \Rightarrow \frac{dy}{dx} = 0$
12. $\frac{dy}{dx} = \frac{-x\sin x - \cos x}{x^2} + \frac{\cos x + x\sin x}{\cos^2 x}$

2.5 Derivative of Exponential and Logarithmic Functions

1. $\frac{dy}{dx} = \frac{1}{x} + e^x$
2. $\frac{dy}{dx} = e^x\left(\frac{1}{x}\right) + e^x \ln x$
3. $\frac{dy}{dx} = x^2\left(\frac{1}{x}\right) + 2x\ln x = x(1 + 2\ln x)$
4. $\frac{dy}{dx} = e^x \sec^2 x + e^x \tan x$
5. $\frac{dy}{dx} = (x^2 e^x + 2xe^x) + 5e^x + 6 = e^x(x^2 + 2x + 5) + 6$
6. $\frac{dy}{dx} = \frac{x\left(\frac{1}{x}\right) - (\ln x)(1)}{x^2} + \frac{\ln x - x\left(\frac{1}{x}\right)}{\ln^2 x} = \frac{1 - \ln x}{x^2} + \frac{\ln x - 1}{\ln^2 x}$

2.6 Chain Rule

1. $\frac{dy}{dx} = -(\sin 5x)(5) = -5\sin 5x$
2. $\frac{dy}{dx} = (2\cos(\omega x + \phi))(\omega) = 2\omega\cos(\omega x + \phi)$
3. $\frac{dy}{dx} = 9(4 - 3x)^8(-3) = -27(4 - 3x)^8$
4. $\frac{dy}{dx} = \frac{1}{\sin x}\cos x + \frac{\cos(\ln x)}{x} = \cot x + \frac{\cos(\ln x)}{x}$
5. $\frac{dy}{dx} = \frac{1}{2\sqrt{5x + 3}}(5) = \frac{5}{2\sqrt{5x + 3}}$

6. $\dfrac{dy}{dx} = 2e^{x^2}(2x) + (x^2e^x + 2xe^x) + 4x$

7. $\dfrac{dy}{dx} = \dfrac{1}{2\sqrt{\tan\sqrt{x}}}(\sec^2\sqrt{x})\left(\dfrac{1}{2\sqrt{x}}\right)$

8. $\dfrac{dy}{dx} = (-\sin 2x)(2) + \left(\dfrac{1}{x^2}\right)(2x) = -2\sin 2x + \dfrac{2}{x}$

9. $\dfrac{dy}{dx} = 3\sin^2 x\cos x + (\cos 3x)(3)$

10. $\dfrac{dy}{dx} = [2\cos(x^2+1)][-\sin(x^2+1)](2x)$

$= -2x\sin 2(x^2+1)$

11. $\dfrac{dy}{dx} = x\left(\dfrac{-1}{2}\right)(x^2+1)^{-3/2}(2x) + (x^2+1)^{-1/2}$

$= -x^2(x^2+1)^{-3/2} + (x^2+1)^{-1/2} = (x^2+1)^{-3/2}$

12. $\dfrac{dy}{dx} = 2(2\tan x\sec^2 x) + 2[x(\sec^2 2x)(2) + \tan 2x]$

$= 4\tan x\sec^2 x + 4x\sec^2 2x + 2\tan 2x$

13. $\dfrac{dy}{dx} = \dfrac{(\sqrt{x^2+4})(1) - \dfrac{x}{2\sqrt{x^2+4}}(2x)}{x^2+4} = \dfrac{4}{(x^2+4)^{3/2}}$

14. $\dfrac{dy}{dx} = \dfrac{1}{2x+3}(2) + \left(x^2\left(\dfrac{1}{2x}\right)(2) + 2x\ln 2x\right)$

$= \dfrac{2}{2x+3} + x + 2x\ln 2x$

15. $\dfrac{dy}{dx} = \left(2\cos\left(\dfrac{x}{2}\right)\right)\left(\dfrac{1}{2}\right) - 4\left(-\sin\left(\dfrac{x}{2}\right)\right)\left(\dfrac{1}{2}\right)$

$= \cos\left(\dfrac{x}{2}\right) + 2\sin\left(\dfrac{x}{2}\right)$

16. $\dfrac{dy}{dx} = 7e^{3x}(3) - 5e^{-2x}(-2) + 6e^x$

$= 21e^{3x} + 10e^{-2x} + 6e^x$

17. $\dfrac{dy}{dx} = e^{\sqrt{x}}\left(\dfrac{1}{2\sqrt{x}}\right) + e^{\sin\left(\frac{3}{x}\right)}\left(\cos\left(\dfrac{3}{x}\right)\right)\left(\dfrac{-3}{x^2}\right) + ex^{e-1}$

18. $y = \sin\sin\sin x$

$\dfrac{dy}{dx} = \cos(\sin\sin x) \times \cos(\sin x) \times \cos x$

19. $y = e^{e^{e^x}}$

$\dfrac{dy}{dx} = e^{e^{e^x}} \times e^{e^x} \times e^x$

20. $y = 7\ln^2(\sec 2x)$

$\dfrac{dy}{dx} = (7)(2\ln(\sec 2x))\dfrac{1}{\sec 2x}(\sec 2x\tan 2x)(2)$

$= 28\tan 2x\ln(\sec 2x)$

2.7 Value of Derivatives at a Point

1. $\dfrac{d}{dx}(uv) = u(x)v'(x) + v(x)u'(x)$

At $x = 0$

$\dfrac{d}{dx}(uv) = u(0)v'(0) + v(0)u'(0) = 5(2) + (-1)(-3) = 13$

2. $\dfrac{d}{dx}\left(\dfrac{u}{v}\right) = \dfrac{v(x)u'(x) - v'(x)u(x)}{v^2(x)}$

At $x = 0$

$\dfrac{d}{dx}\left(\dfrac{u}{v}\right) = \dfrac{v(0)u'(0) - u(0)v'(0)}{v^2(0)} = \dfrac{(-1)(-3) - 5(2)}{(-1)^2} = -7$

3. $\dfrac{d}{dx}\left(\dfrac{v}{u}\right) = \dfrac{u(x)v'(x) - v(x)u'(x)}{u^2(x)}$

At $x = 0$

$\dfrac{d}{dx}\left(\dfrac{v}{u}\right) = \dfrac{u(0)v'(0) - v(0)u'(0)}{u^2(0)} = \dfrac{5(2) - (-1)(-3)}{5^2} = \dfrac{7}{25}$

4. $\dfrac{d}{dx}(7v - 2u) = 7\dfrac{dv}{dx} - 2\dfrac{du}{dx} = 7v'(x) - 2u'(x)$

At $x = 0$

$\dfrac{d}{dx}(7v - 2u) = 7v'(0) - 2u'(0) = 7(2) - 2(-3) = 20$

2.8 Derivative of Implicit Functions

1. $(x+y)^2 = 4 \;\Rightarrow\; x + y = \pm 2$

Differentiating both sides w.r.t. x,

$1 + \dfrac{dy}{dx} = 0 \;\Rightarrow\; \dfrac{dy}{dx} = -1$

2. $x^2y + xy^2 = 6$

Differentiating both sides w.r.t. x,

$\left(x^2\dfrac{dy}{dx} + 2xy\right) + \left(2xy\dfrac{dy}{dx} + y^2\right) = 0 \;\Rightarrow\; \dfrac{dy}{dx} = -\dfrac{2xy + y^2}{2xy + x^2}$

3. $x^3 + y^3 = 18xy$

Differentiating both sides w.r.t. x,

$3x^2 + 3y^2\dfrac{dy}{dx} = 18\left(x\dfrac{dy}{dx} + y\right) \;\Rightarrow \dfrac{dy}{dx} = \dfrac{6y - x^2}{-6x + y^2} = \dfrac{6y - x^2}{y^2 - 6x}$

2.9 Derivative as Rate of Change

1. $A = l^2$

$\dfrac{dA}{dt} = 2l\dfrac{dl}{dt} = 2(8\text{ cm})(4\text{ cm/min}) = 64\text{ cm}^2/\text{min}$

2. (a) $V = \pi r^2 h$

$\dfrac{dV}{dt} = \pi r^2\dfrac{dh}{dt} = \pi r^2(5) = 5\pi r^2$

(b) $V = \pi r^2 h$

$\dfrac{dV}{dt} = \pi\left(2r\dfrac{dr}{dt}\right)h = 10\,\pi rh$

(c) $V = \pi r^2 h$

$$\frac{dV}{dt} = \pi r^2 \frac{dh}{dt} + \pi\left(2r\frac{dr}{dt}\right)h = 5\pi r^2 + 10\pi rh$$

3. (a) $x^2 + y^2 = l^2$

Differentiating both sides w.r.t. time (*t*)

$$2x\frac{dx}{dt} + 2y\frac{dy}{dt} = 0$$

$$\Rightarrow \quad \frac{dy}{dt} = -\frac{x}{y}\frac{dx}{dt} = -\frac{12}{5}(2) = -4.8\,\text{m/s}$$

(b) $A = \frac{1}{2}xy$

Differentiating both sides w.r.t. *t*

$$\frac{dA}{dt} = \frac{1}{2}x\frac{dy}{dt} + \frac{1}{2}y\frac{dx}{dt} = \frac{1}{2}\times 12\times(-4.8) + \frac{1}{2}\times 5\times 2$$

$$= -23.8\,\text{m}^2/\text{s}$$

(c) $\cos\theta = \frac{x}{13}$

Differentiating both sides w.r.t. *t*

$$-\sin\theta\frac{d\theta}{dt} = \frac{1}{13}\frac{dx}{dt}$$

$$\frac{d\theta}{dt} = -\frac{1}{13\sin\theta}\frac{dx}{dt} = -\frac{1}{13\left(\frac{5}{13}\right)}\times 2 = -0.4\,\text{rad/s}$$

4. $V = \frac{4}{3}\pi r^3 \Rightarrow \frac{dV}{dr} = \frac{4}{3}\pi(3r^2) = 4\pi r^2 = 4\times\frac{22}{7}\times 7^2 = 616$

5. $h = \frac{r}{6} \Rightarrow V = \frac{1}{3}\pi r^2 h \Rightarrow V = \frac{1}{3}\pi(6h)^2 h = 12\pi h^3$

Differentiating both sides w.r.t *t*

$$\frac{dV}{dt} = 12\pi(3h^2)\frac{dh}{dt}$$

$$\Rightarrow 12\,\text{cm}^3/\text{s} = 36\pi(4)^2\frac{dh}{dt} \Rightarrow \frac{dh}{dt} = \frac{1}{48\pi}\,\text{cm/s}$$

2.10 Local Maxima and Minima

1. $x = -t^2 + 4t + 4$

$$\frac{dx}{dt} = -2t + 4 = 0 \Rightarrow t = 2$$

At $t = 2$

$$x_{max} = -(2)^2 + 4(2) + 4 = 8$$

2. $y = 2x^3 - 15x^2 + 36x + 11$

$$\frac{dy}{dx} = 6x^2 - 30x + 36 = 0$$

$$\Rightarrow 6(x^2 - 5x + 6) = 0 \Rightarrow x = 2 \text{ and } x = 3$$

$$\frac{d^2y}{dx^2} = 12x - 30$$

At $x = 2, \frac{d^2y}{dx^2} = 12(2) - 30 < 0$

$\Rightarrow x = 2$ is point of local maxima.

At $x = 2, y = 2(2)^3 - 15(2)^2 + 36(2) + 11 = 39$

At $x = 3, \frac{d^2y}{dx^2} = 12(3) - 30 > 0$

$\Rightarrow x = 3$ is point of local minima.

At $x = 3, y = 2(3)^3 - 15(3)^2 + 36(3) + 11 = 38$

3. $y = 2x^3 - 9x^2 + 100$

$$\frac{dy}{dx} = 6x^2 - 18x = 0$$

$$\Rightarrow \quad 6x(x-3) = 0 \Rightarrow x = 0 \text{ and } x = 3$$

At $x = 0, \frac{d^2y}{dx^2} = 12(0) - 18 < 0$

$\Rightarrow x = 0$ is point of local maxima.

At $x = 3, \frac{d^2y}{dx^2} = 12(3) - 18 > 0$

$\Rightarrow x = 3$, is point of local minima.

4. $x + y = 60 \Rightarrow y = 60 - x$

Product of numbers $= p = xy$

$$p = x(60 - x)$$

To maximise *p*

$$\frac{dp}{dx} = 60 - 2x = 0 \Rightarrow x = 30$$

So, numbers will be $x = 30$ and $y = 30$.

5. $y = \sin x(1 + \cos x)$

$$\frac{dy}{dx} = \sin x(-\sin x) + (1 + \cos x)\cos x = 0$$

$$\Rightarrow \quad \cos^2 x + \cos x - (1 - \cos^2 x) = 0$$

$$\Rightarrow \quad 2\cos^2 x + \cos x - 1 = 0$$

$$\Rightarrow \quad 2\cos^2 x + 2\cos x - \cos x - 1 = 0$$

$$\Rightarrow \quad 2\cos x(\cos x + 1) - (\cos x + 1) = 0$$

$$\Rightarrow \quad \cos x = -1 \text{ and } \cos x = \frac{1}{2}$$

At $\cos x = \frac{1}{2}, \frac{d^2y}{dx^2} > 0 \Rightarrow$ So, at $x = \cos^{-1}\left(\frac{1}{2}\right)$, *y* is minimum.

6. $E = \frac{kQx}{(R^2 + x^2)^{3/2}}$

$$\frac{dE}{dx} = kQ\left(\frac{(R^2+x^2)^{3/2}(1) - \frac{3}{2}(R^2+x^2)^{1/2}(2x)(x)}{(R^2+x^2)^3}\right) = 0$$

$$= \frac{kQ(R^2+x^2)^{1/2}}{(R^2+x^2)^3}(R^2 - 2x^2) = 0$$

$$\Rightarrow \quad x = \pm\frac{R}{\sqrt{2}}$$

7. Lets take side of square cut from each corner to be *x*.

Volume of box $= (18 - 2x)^2 x$

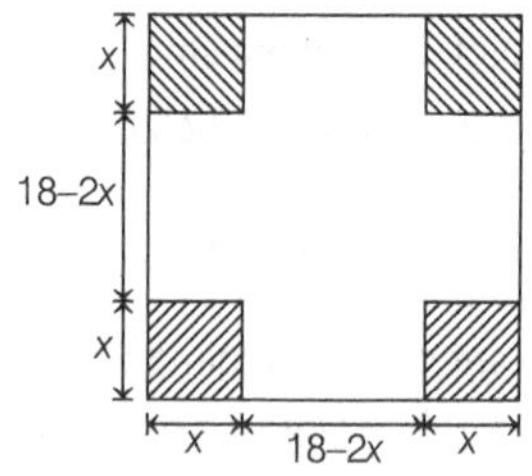

$$V=(18-2x)^2x$$

$$\frac{dV}{dx}=(18-2x)^2(1)+x(2)(18-2x)(-2)=0$$

$$\Rightarrow (18-2x)(18-6x)=0 \quad \Rightarrow x=3$$

8. Volume of cylinder $=\pi r^2 2(\sqrt{a^2-r^2}) \Rightarrow V=2\pi r^2(\sqrt{a^2-r^2})$

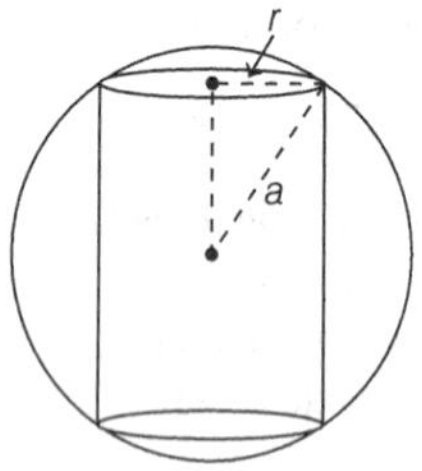

$$\frac{dV}{dr}=2\pi\left(\frac{r^2(-2r)}{2\sqrt{a^2-r^2}}+2r\sqrt{a^2-r^2}\right)=0$$

$$\Rightarrow \quad r^2=\frac{2a^2}{3} \quad \Rightarrow h=2\sqrt{a^2-r^2}=\frac{2a}{\sqrt{3}}$$

2.11 Integration of Elementary Functions

1. $\int (2x^3-5x+7)\,dx=2\left(\frac{x^4}{4}\right)-5\left(\frac{x^2}{2}\right)+7x+C$

$$=\frac{x^4}{2}-\frac{5x^2}{2}+7x+C$$

2. $\int\left(\frac{1}{5}-\frac{2}{x^3}+2x\right)dx=\frac{x}{5}+\frac{1}{x^2}+x^2+C$

3. $\int(\sqrt{x}+\sqrt[3]{x})\,dx=\frac{x^{3/2}}{(3/2)}+\frac{x^{4/3}}{(4/3)}+C=\frac{2}{3}x^{3/2}+\frac{3}{4}x^{4/3}+C$

4. $\int x^{-3}(x+1)\,dx=\int(x^{-2}+x^{-3})\,dx$

$$=\frac{x^{-1}}{(-1)}+\frac{x^{-2}}{(-2)}+C=\frac{-1}{x}-\frac{1}{2x^2}+C$$

5. $\int\left(\frac{t\sqrt{t}+\sqrt{t}}{t^2}\right)dt=\int(t^{-1/2}+t^{-3/2})\,dt=2\sqrt{t}-\frac{2}{\sqrt{t}}+C$

6. $\int\frac{4+\sqrt{t}}{t^3}\,dt=\int\left(\frac{4}{t^3}+t^{-5/2}\right)dt=-\frac{2}{t^2}-\frac{2}{3}t^{-3/2}+C$

7. $\int\left(8y-\frac{2}{y^{1/4}}\right)dy=4y^2-\frac{8}{3}y^{3/4}+C$

8. $\int\left(\frac{\sqrt{x}}{2}+\frac{2}{\sqrt{x}}\right)dx=\frac{x^{3/2}}{3}+4\sqrt{x}+C$

9. $\int(-2\cos t)\,dt=-2\sin t+C$

10. $\int(7e^x+4\sin x+ex)\,dx=7e^x-4\cos x+\frac{ex^2}{2}+C$

11. $\int\frac{1}{2}(\text{cosec}^2 x-\text{cosec}\,x\cot x)\,dx=-\frac{1}{2}\cot x+\frac{1}{2}\text{cosec}\,x+C$

12. $\int\frac{-\sec^2 x}{3}\,dx=-\frac{\tan x}{3}+C$

13. $\int\tan^2 x\,dx=\int(\sec^2 x-1)\,dx=\tan x-x+C$

14. $\int\cos\theta(\tan\theta+\sec\theta)\,d\theta=\int(\sin\theta+1)\,d\theta=-\cos\theta+\theta+C$

15. $\int\frac{dx}{\sin^2 x\cos^2 x}=\int\left(\frac{\sin^2 x+\cos^2 x}{\sin^2 x\,\cos^2 x}\right)dx$

$$=\int(\sec^2 x+\text{cosec}^2 x)\,dx=\tan x-\cot x+C$$

16. $\int\left(x^2+\sin x+\frac{1}{x}+3\right)dx=\frac{x^3}{3}-\cos x+\ln x+3x+C$

17. $\int(4\sec x\tan x-2\sec^2 x)\,dx=4\sec x-2\tan x+C$

18. $\int(1-\cot^2 x)\,dx=\int[1-(\text{cosec}^2 x-1)]\,dx$

$$=\int(2-\text{cosec}^2 x)\,dx=2x+\cot x+C$$

2.12 Integration by Substitution Method

1. $\int\sin 3x\,dx$

Let's take $t=3x$,

$$\Rightarrow \quad \frac{dt}{dx}=3 \quad \Rightarrow \frac{1}{3}dt=dx$$

$$\int\sin 3x\,dx=\frac{1}{3}\int\sin t\,dt=-\frac{1}{3}\cos t+C=-\frac{1}{3}\cos 3x+C$$

2. $\int x\cos(2x^2)\,dx$

Let's take $t=2x^2$,

$$\Rightarrow \quad \frac{dt}{dx}=4x \Rightarrow x\,dx=\frac{1}{4}dt$$

$$\int x\cos(2x^2)\,dx=\frac{1}{4}\int\cos t\,dt=\frac{1}{4}\sin t+C=\frac{1}{4}\sin(2x^2)+C$$

3. $\int\sec 2t\tan 2t\,dt$

Lets take $x=2t$

$$\frac{dx}{dt}=2 \Rightarrow \frac{1}{2}dx=dt$$

$$\frac{1}{2}\int\sec x\tan x\,dx=\frac{1}{2}\sec x+C=\frac{1}{2}\sec 2t+C$$

4. $\int\left(1-\cos\left(\frac{t}{2}\right)^2\right)\sin\left(\frac{t}{2}\right)dt$

Lets take $x=1-\cos\left(\frac{t}{2}\right)$

$$\frac{dx}{dt} = \frac{1}{2}\sin\left(\frac{t}{2}\right) \quad \Rightarrow 2\,dx = \sin\left(\frac{t}{2}\right)dt$$

$$2\int x^2\,dx = \frac{2x^3}{3} + C = \frac{2}{3}\left(1 - \cos\left(\frac{t}{2}\right)\right)^3 + C$$

5. $\int x^3(x^4-1)^2\,dx$

Lets take $t = x^4 - 1 \Rightarrow \frac{dt}{dx} = 4x^3 \Rightarrow x^3\,dx = \frac{1}{4}dt$

$$\frac{1}{4}\int t^2\,dt = \frac{t^3}{12} + C = \frac{(x^4-1)^3}{12} + C$$

6. $\int \frac{9r^2}{\sqrt{1-r^3}}\,dr$

Lets take $t = 1 - r^3$

$$\frac{dt}{dr} = -3r^2 \Rightarrow \quad r^2\,dr = -\frac{1}{3}dt$$

$$-\int 3\frac{dt}{\sqrt{t}} = -6\sqrt{t} + C = -6\sqrt{1-r^3} + C$$

7. $\int 4\sin^2 y\,dy = 2\int(1-\cos 2y)\,dy = 2y - \sin 2y + C$

8. $\int (2x+1)^3\,dx$

Lets take $t = 2x + 1$

$$\frac{dt}{dx} = 2 \quad \Rightarrow dx = \frac{1}{2}dt \quad \Rightarrow \frac{1}{2}\int t^3\,dt = \frac{t^4}{8} + C = \frac{(2x+1)^4}{8} + C$$

9. $\int \frac{3}{(2-x)^2}\,dx$

Lets take $t = 2 - x$

$$\frac{dt}{dx} = -1 \quad \Rightarrow dx = -\,dt \quad \Rightarrow -3\int\frac{dt}{t^2} = \frac{3}{t} + C = \frac{3}{2-x} + C$$

10. $\int \frac{4y}{\sqrt{2y^2+1}}\,dy$

Lets take $t = \sqrt{2y^2+1}$

$$\frac{dt}{dy} = \frac{1}{2\sqrt{2y^2+1}}(4y) \quad \Rightarrow \quad \frac{4y\,dy}{\sqrt{2y^2+1}} = 2\,dt$$

$$\int 2\,dt = 2t + C = 2\sqrt{2y^2+1} + C$$

11. $\int 7\sin\left(\frac{\theta}{3}\right)d\theta$

Lets take $t = \frac{\theta}{3} \quad \Rightarrow \quad \frac{dt}{d\theta} = \frac{1}{3} \quad \Rightarrow 3\,dt = d\theta$

$$21\int \sin t\,dt = -21\cos t + C = -21\cos\left(\frac{\theta}{3}\right) + C$$

12. $\int \sin(8z-5)\,dz$

Lets take $t = 8z - 5$

$$\frac{dt}{dz} = 8 \quad \Rightarrow dz = \frac{1}{8}dt$$

$$\frac{1}{8}\int \sin t\,dt = -\frac{1}{8}\cos t + C = -\frac{1}{8}\cos(8z-5) + C$$

13. $\int \frac{1}{\sqrt{t}}\cos(\sqrt{t}+3)\,dt$

Lets take $x = \sqrt{t} + 3$

$$\frac{dx}{dt} = \frac{1}{2\sqrt{t}} \quad \Rightarrow \frac{dt}{\sqrt{t}} = 2\,dx$$

$$2\int \cos x\,dx = 2\sin x + C = 2\sin(\sqrt{t}+3) + C$$

14. $\int 28(7x-2)^{-5}\,dx$

Lets take $t = 7x - 2$

$$\frac{dt}{dx} = 7 \Rightarrow dx = \frac{1}{7}dt$$

$$\int 28t^{-5}\left(\frac{1}{7}\right)dt = 4\int t^{-5}\,dt = -t^{-4} + C = \frac{-1}{(7x-2)^4} + C$$

15. $\int \frac{6\cos t}{(2+\sin t)^3}\,dt$

Lets take $y = 2 + \sin t$

$$\frac{dy}{dt} = \cos t \quad \Rightarrow \cos t\,dt = dy$$

$$\Rightarrow \quad \int\frac{6\,dy}{y^3} = -\frac{3}{y^2} + C = \frac{-3}{(2+\sin t)^2} + C$$

16. $\int \frac{\ln x}{x}\,dx$

Lets take $t = \ln x$

$$\frac{dt}{dx} = \frac{1}{x} \quad \Rightarrow \frac{dx}{x} = dt \quad \Rightarrow \quad \int t\,dt = \frac{t^2}{2} + C = \frac{\ln^2 x}{2} + C$$

17. $\int \tan^7\left(\frac{x}{2}\right)\sec^2\left(\frac{x}{2}\right)dx$

Lets take $t = \tan\left(\frac{x}{2}\right)$

$$\frac{dt}{dx} = \frac{1}{2}\sec^2\left(\frac{x}{2}\right) \quad \Rightarrow \sec^2\left(\frac{x}{2}\right)dx = 2\,dt$$

$$2\int t^7\,dt = 2\left(\frac{t^8}{8}\right) + C = \frac{1}{4}\tan^8\left(\frac{x}{2}\right) + C$$

18. $\int \frac{1}{\sqrt{x}\,(1+\sqrt{x})^2}\,dx$

Lets take $t = 1 + \sqrt{x}$

$$\frac{dt}{dx} = \frac{1}{2\sqrt{x}} \quad \Rightarrow \frac{dx}{\sqrt{x}} = 2\,dt \Rightarrow 2\int\frac{dt}{t^2} = -\frac{2}{t} + C = \frac{-2}{1+\sqrt{x}} + C$$

19. $\int \frac{\cos^2 y}{7} = \frac{1}{14}\int(1+\cos 2y)\,dy = \frac{1}{14}\left[y + \frac{\sin 2y}{2}\right] + C$

20. $\int \sec^2(3x+2)\,dx$

Lets take $3x + 2 = t$

$$\frac{dt}{dx} = 3 \Rightarrow dx = \frac{1}{3}dt$$

$$\frac{1}{3}\int \sec^2 t\,dt = \frac{1}{3}\tan t + C = \frac{1}{3}\tan(3x+2) + C$$

21. $\int \tan^2 x \sec^2 x\, dx$

Lets take $t = \tan x \Rightarrow dt = \sec^2 x\, dx$

$$\int t^2\, dt = \frac{t^3}{3} + C = \frac{1}{3}\tan^3 x + C$$

22. $\int e^{2x-3}\, dx$

Lets take $t = 2x - 3$

$$\frac{dt}{dx} = 2 \Rightarrow dx = \frac{1}{2}dt \Rightarrow \frac{1}{2}\int e^t\, dt = \frac{1}{2}e^t + C = \frac{1}{2}e^{2x-3} + C$$

23. $\int \frac{x\, dx}{\sqrt{x^2 + a^2}}$

Lets take $t = x^2 + a^2$

$$\frac{dt}{dx} = 2x \Rightarrow x\, dx = \frac{1}{2}dt \Rightarrow \frac{1}{2}\int \frac{dt}{\sqrt{t}} = \sqrt{t} + C = \sqrt{x^2 + a^2} + C$$

24. $\int \frac{\sin(2t+1)}{\cos^2(2t+1)}dt$

Lets take $x = \cos(2t+1)$

$$\frac{dx}{dt} = -2\sin(2t+1) \Rightarrow \sin(2t+1)\, dt = -\frac{1}{2}dx$$

$$-\frac{1}{2}\int \frac{dx}{x^2} = \frac{1}{2x} + C = \frac{1}{2\cos(2t+1)} + C$$

25. $\int \sqrt{3 - 2s}\, ds$

Lets take $t = 3 - 2s$

$$\frac{dt}{ds} = -2 \Rightarrow ds = -\frac{1}{2}dt$$

$$-\frac{1}{2}\int \sqrt{t}\, dt = -\frac{1}{2}\frac{t^{3/2}}{3/2} + C = \frac{-1}{3}(3 - 2s)^{3/2} + C$$

26. $\int (\sin 2x - \operatorname{cosec}^2 x)\, dx = -\frac{\cos 2x}{2} + \cot x + C$

27. $\int (2\cos 2x - 3\sin 3x)\, dx = \sin 2x + \cos 3x + C$

28. $\int \frac{1}{x^2}\cos^2\left(\frac{1}{x}\right)dx$

Lets take $t = \frac{1}{x} \Rightarrow \frac{dt}{dx} = -\frac{1}{x^2} \Rightarrow \frac{dx}{x^2} = -dt$

$$-\int \cos^2 t\, dt = \frac{-1}{2}\int (1 + \cos 2t)\, dt$$

$$= -\frac{1}{2}\left[t + \frac{\sin 2t}{2}\right] + C = -\frac{1}{2}\left(\frac{1}{x} + \frac{1}{2}\sin\left(\frac{2}{x}\right)\right) + C$$

29. $\int \sqrt{x}\sin^2(x^{3/2} - 1)\, dx$

Lets take $t = x^{3/2} - 1$

$$\frac{dt}{dx} = \frac{3}{2}\sqrt{x} \Rightarrow \sqrt{x}\, dx = \frac{2}{3}dt$$

$$\frac{2}{3}\int \sin^2 t\, dt = \frac{1}{3}\int (1 - \cos 2t)\, dt = \frac{1}{3}\left[t - \frac{\sin 2t}{2}\right] + C$$

$$= \frac{1}{3}\left[(x^{3/2} - 1) - \frac{\sin[2(x^{3/2} - 1)]}{2}\right] + C$$

30. $\int \cos^3 x\, dx = \frac{1}{4}\int (\cos 3x + 3\cos x)\, dx$

$$= \frac{1}{4}\left(\frac{\sin 3x}{3}\right) + \frac{3}{4}\sin x + C = \frac{1}{12}\sin 3x + \frac{3}{4}\sin x + C$$

31. $\int \left(\frac{1 - \cos 6t}{2}\right)dt = \frac{t}{2} - \frac{\sin 6t}{12} + C$

32. $\int \frac{\cos x}{\sin^3 x}dx$

Lets take $t = \sin x$,

$$\frac{dt}{dx} = \cos x \Rightarrow dt = \cos x\, dx$$

$$\int \frac{dt}{t^3} = -\frac{1}{2t^2} + C = -\frac{1}{2\sin^2 x} + C$$

33. $\int \frac{\operatorname{cosec}\theta}{\operatorname{cosec}\theta - \sin\theta}d\theta = \int \frac{1}{1 - \sin^2\theta}d\theta = \int \sec^2\theta\, d\theta = \tan\theta + C$

34. $\int \frac{1}{\sqrt{5s + 4}}ds$

Lets take $t = 5s + 4$

$$\frac{dt}{ds} = 5 \Rightarrow ds = \frac{1}{5}dt \Rightarrow \frac{1}{5}\int \frac{dt}{\sqrt{t}} = \frac{1}{5}(2\sqrt{t}) + C = \frac{2}{5}\sqrt{5s + 4} + C$$

35. $\int (e^{3x} + e^{-5x} + e)\, dx = \frac{e^{3x}}{3} - \frac{e^{-5x}}{5} + ex + C$

36. $\int \sqrt{\cot y}\operatorname{cosec}^2 y\, dy$

Lets take $t = \cot y$, $\frac{dt}{dy} = -\operatorname{cosec}^2 y$

$\operatorname{cosec}^2 y\, dy = -dt$

$$-\int \sqrt{t}\, dt = -\frac{t^{3/2}}{\left(\frac{3}{2}\right)} + C = -\frac{2}{3}(\cot y)^{3/2} + C$$

2.13 Definite Integration

1. $\int_{-4}^{-1}\frac{\pi}{2}d\theta = \frac{\pi}{2}[\theta]_{-4}^{-1} = \frac{\pi}{2}[(-1) - (-4)] = \frac{3\pi}{2}$

2. $\int_{\sqrt{2}}^{5\sqrt{2}} r\, dr = \left[\frac{r^2}{2}\right]_{\sqrt{2}}^{5\sqrt{2}} = \frac{(5\sqrt{2})^2 - (\sqrt{2})^2}{2} = 24$

3. $\int_0^1 e^{2x}\, dx = \left[\frac{e^{2x}}{2}\right]_0^1 = \frac{e^2 - e^0}{2} = \frac{e^2 - 1}{2}$

4. $\int_0^4 \frac{dx}{\sqrt{x}} = [2\sqrt{x}]_0^4 = 2(\sqrt{4} - \sqrt{0}) = 4$

5. $\int_1^2 \left(6x^2 + \frac{2}{x^2}\right)dx = \left[2x^3 - \frac{2}{x}\right]_1^2 = (16 - 1) - (2 - 2) = 15$

6. $\int_0^{3\pi/4} \sec^2\left(\frac{x}{3}\right)dx = \left[\frac{\tan\left(\frac{x}{3}\right)}{\left(\frac{1}{3}\right)}\right]_0^{\frac{3\pi}{4}} = 3(1 - 0) = 3$

7. $\int_0^1 \frac{dx}{3x+2} = \frac{1}{3}[\ln(3x+2)]_0^1 = \frac{1}{3}(\ln 5 - \ln 2) = \frac{1}{3}\ln\left(\frac{5}{2}\right)$

8. $\int_0^{\pi/2} \sin\left(\frac{x}{2}\right) dx = \left[\frac{-\cos\left(\frac{x}{2}\right)}{\frac{1}{2}}\right]_0^{\pi/2} = -2\left(\frac{1}{\sqrt{2}} - 1\right) = 2 - \sqrt{2}$

9. $\int_0^{\pi/2} (\sin x + \cos x)\, dx = [-\cos x + \sin x]_0^{\pi/2}$

$= (-0+1) - (-1+0) = 2$

10. $\int_0^{\pi/4} \cos 2x\, dx = \left[\frac{\sin 2x}{2}\right]_0^{\frac{\pi}{4}} = \frac{1}{2}$

11. $\int_0^{\infty} e^{-x}\, dx = \left[\frac{e^{-x}}{(-1)}\right]_0^{\infty} = -(e^{-\infty} - e^0) = -(0-1) = 1$

12. $\int_0^1 \frac{x}{x^2+1} dx$

Lets take $t = x^2 + 1$

$\Rightarrow \frac{dt}{dx} = 2x \Rightarrow x\, dx = \frac{1}{2} dt \Rightarrow \frac{1}{2}\int_1^2 \frac{dt}{t} = \frac{1}{2}[\ln t]_1^2 = \frac{1}{2}\ln 2$

2.14 Calculation of Area

1.

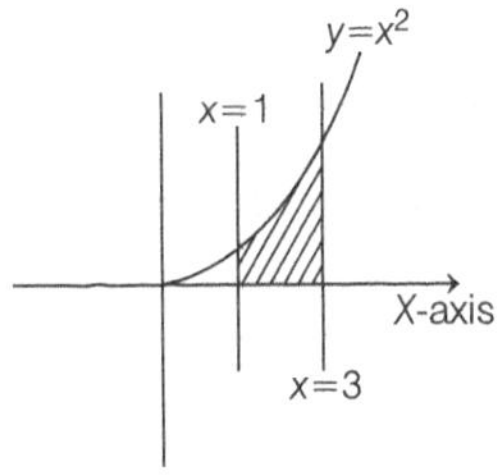

$\text{Area} = \int_1^3 y\, dx = \int_1^3 x^2\, dx = \left[\frac{x^3}{3}\right]_1^3 = \frac{26}{3}$ sq. units

2.

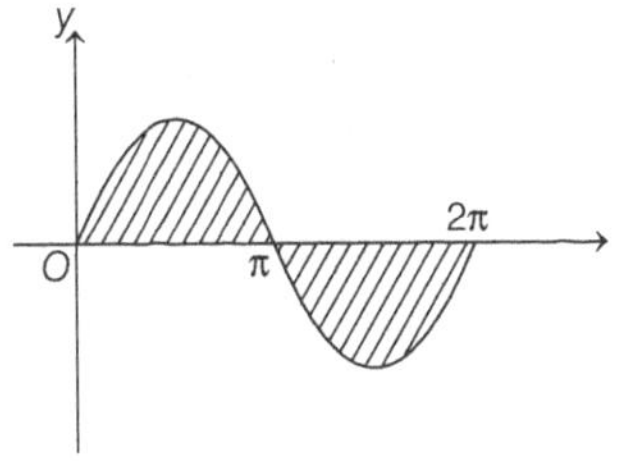

$\int_0^{\pi} \sin x\, dx = 2 \Rightarrow \int_{\pi}^{2\pi} \sin x\, dx = -2$

Area = 2 + 2 = 4 sq. units

Level 2

Single Correct Choice Questions

1. $\frac{d}{dx}(x^2 + 4) = 2x$

2. $\frac{d}{dx}\left(x^2 - \frac{1}{x} + \ln 2\right) = 2x + \frac{1}{x^2}$

3. $y = x^{10} + \frac{1}{x^{10}} + \frac{1}{x} + 3$

$\frac{dy}{dx} = 10x^9 - \frac{10}{x^{11}} - \frac{1}{x^2}$

4. $\frac{d}{dx}(\sqrt{x}) = \frac{1}{2\sqrt{x}}$

5. $y = \tan x \Rightarrow \frac{dy}{dx} = \sec^2 x$

$\sqrt{\frac{dy}{dx} - 1} = \sqrt{\sec^2 x - 1} = \tan x$

6. $\frac{d}{dx}(x^4 - 2\sin x + 3\cos x) = 4x^3 - 2\cos x - 3\sin x$

7. $\frac{d}{dx}\left(\frac{x^2+1}{x+1}\right) = \frac{(x+1)(2x) - (x^2+1)(1)}{(x+1)^2} = \frac{x^2+2x-1}{(x+1)^2}$

8. $y = x^2 \sin x \Rightarrow \frac{dy}{dx} = x^2 \cos x + 2x \sin x$

9. $\frac{d}{dx} = (x^2 e^x) = x^2 e^x + 2x\, e^x = e^x(x^2 + 2x)$

10. $\frac{d}{dx}[(1+x^2)\, e^x] = (1+x^2)\, e^x + 2xe^x = (x+1)^2\, e^x$

11. $\frac{d}{dx}(x \ln 2x) = x\left(\frac{1}{2x}\right)(2) + \ln 2x\,(1) = 1 + \ln 2x$

12. $\frac{d}{dx}(x \sin x) = x\cos x + (\sin x)(1) = x\cos x + \sin x$

13. $y = x\ln x + \sqrt{x}$

$\frac{dy}{dx} = x\left(\frac{1}{x}\right) + (\ln x)(1) + \frac{1}{2\sqrt{x}} = 1 + \ln x + \frac{1}{2\sqrt{x}}$

14. $\frac{d}{dx}(xe^x \sin x) = x[e^x \cos x + e^x \sin x] + (e^x \sin x)(1)$

$= e^x[x\cos x + x\sin x + \sin x]$

15. $y = \ln x + e^{-x}$

$\frac{dy}{dx} = \frac{1}{x} - e^{-x}$

16. $y = 2\tan\sqrt{x}$

$\frac{dy}{dx} = 2(\sec^2\sqrt{x})\left(\frac{1}{2\sqrt{x}}\right) = \frac{\sec^2\sqrt{x}}{\sqrt{x}}$

17. $a = \sec(3b)$

$\frac{da}{db} = [\sec(3b)\tan(3b)](3) = 3\sec 3b \tan 3b$

18. $y = \sin 2x$

$\frac{dy}{dx} = (\cos 2x)(2) \Rightarrow \left(\frac{dy}{dx}\right)_{x=\pi} = (\cos 2\pi)(2) = 2$

19. $y = \cos 3x + \sin(1-x)$

$\frac{dy}{dx} = -3\sin 3x - \cos(1-x)$

20. $y = e^{\sin 3x}$

$$\frac{dy}{dx} = e^{\sin 3x}(\cos 3x)(3) = 3e^{\sin 3x}\cos 3x$$

21. $y = 3\tan\left(\frac{x}{3}\right)$

$$\frac{dy}{dx} = 3\left(\sec^2\left(\frac{x}{3}\right)\right)\left(\frac{1}{3}\right) = \sec^2\left(\frac{x}{3}\right)$$

22. $y = \sin^3 x + \sin 3x$

$$\frac{dy}{dx} = 3\sin^2 x\cos x + 3\cos 3x$$

23. $y = x\sin^2 x$

$$\frac{dy}{dx} = x(2\sin x\cos x) + \sin^2 x(1) = x\sin 2x + \sin^2 x$$

24. $\frac{d}{dx}(\sqrt{2x+3}) = \frac{1}{2}\frac{1}{\sqrt{2x+3}}(2) = \frac{1}{\sqrt{2x+3}}$

25. $y = \sqrt{x^2+2} \Rightarrow \frac{dy}{dx} = \frac{1}{2\sqrt{x^2+2}}(2x) = \frac{x}{\sqrt{x^2+2}}$

26. $y = e^{\sqrt{2x}} \Rightarrow \frac{dy}{dx} = e^{\sqrt{2x}} \times \left(\frac{1}{2\sqrt{2x}}\right) \times 2 = \frac{e^{\sqrt{2x}}}{\sqrt{2x}}$

27. $y = e^{\sin(3-x)}$

$$\frac{dy}{dx} = e^{\sin(3-x)}[\cos(3-x)](-1) = -e^{\sin(3-x)}\cos(3-x)$$

28. $\frac{d}{dx}(x^3 - 3x^2 + 3x - 1)^{100}$

$$= 100(x^3 - 3x^2 + 3x - 1)^{99}(3x^2 - 6x + 3) = 300(x-1)^{299}$$

29. $f(x) = (x^3 + 6x^2 + 12x - 13)^{100}$

$$f'(x) = 100(x^3 + 6x^2 + 12x - 13)^{99}(3x^2 + 12x + 12)$$

$$= 300(x+2)^2(x^3 + 6x^2 + 12x - 13)^{99}$$

30. $y = \sin^2(\ln x)$

$$\frac{dy}{dx} = 2\sin(\ln x)(\cos(\ln x))\left(\frac{1}{x}\right)$$

31. $y = \sin[\cos^2(e^x)]$

$$\frac{dy}{dx} = [\cos(\cos^2(e^x))](2\cos e^x)(-\sin e^x)(e^x)$$

$$= -2e^x\sin e^x\cos e^x\cos[\cos^2(e^x)]$$

32. $y = \ln[\tan(x^3)]$

$$\frac{dy}{dx} = \frac{1}{\tan(x^3)}[\sec^2(x^3)](3x^2) = \frac{3x^2\sec^2(x^3)}{\tan(x^3)}$$

33. $\frac{d}{dx}(\sqrt{1+\sin 2x}) = \frac{d}{dx}(\sqrt{\sin^2 x + \cos^2 x + 2\sin x\cos x})$

$$= \frac{d}{dx}\left(\sqrt{(\sin x + \cos x)^2}\right)$$

$$= \frac{d}{dx}(\sin x + \cos x) = \cos x - \sin x$$

34. $\frac{d}{dx}\left(\sqrt{\frac{1-\cos 2x}{1+\cos 2x}}\right) = \frac{d}{dx}\left(\sqrt{\frac{2\sin^2 x}{2\cos^2 x}}\right) = \frac{d}{dx}(\tan x) = \sec^2 x$

35. $y = \sin x \Rightarrow \frac{dy}{dx} = \cos x$

$x = 3t \Rightarrow \frac{dx}{dt} = 3$

$$\frac{dy}{dt} = \frac{dy}{dx}\frac{dx}{dt} = (\cos x)(3) = 3\cos x = 3\cos(3t)$$

36. $y = 2x - \frac{3}{x}$

$$\frac{dy}{dx} = 2 + \frac{3}{x^2} = 14 \Rightarrow \frac{3}{x^2} = 12 \Rightarrow x = \pm\frac{1}{2}$$

37. $y = x^2 + 4x + 5 \Rightarrow \frac{dy}{dx} = 2x + 4$

$t = 2x + 7 \Rightarrow \frac{dt}{dx} = 2$

$$\frac{dy}{dt} = \frac{dy/dx}{dt/dx} = \frac{2x+4}{2} = x + 2$$

38. $\frac{d}{dx}(uv) = u(x)v'(x) + v(x)u'(x)$

At $x = 0$,

$$= u(0)v'(0) + v(0)u'(0) = 5(2) + (-1)(-3) = 13$$

39. $y = 2\sec x - \tan x$

Slope $= \frac{dy}{dx} = 2\sec x\tan x - \sec^2 x$

At $x = \frac{\pi}{6}$, slope $= 0$

40. $y = x^3 - 3x^2 - 9x + 7 \Rightarrow \frac{dy}{dx} = 3x^2 - 6x - 9 = 0$

$\Rightarrow \quad 3(x^2 - 2x - 3) = 0 \Rightarrow x = 3$ and $x = -1$

41. $y = x^2 + 4 \Rightarrow \frac{dy}{dt} = 2x\left(\frac{dx}{dt}\right)$

and as per question, $\frac{dy}{dt} = 2\left(\frac{dx}{dt}\right) \Rightarrow x = 1$ and $y = 5$

42. $\tan\theta = \frac{y}{500} \Rightarrow y = 500\tan\theta$

$$\frac{dy}{dt} = 500\sec^2\theta\frac{d\theta}{dt}$$

$$= 500\sec^2 45°(0.14)$$

$$= 140 \text{ ft/min}$$

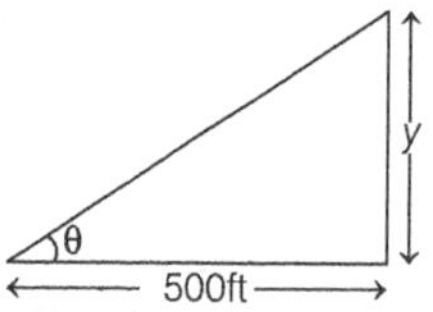

43. $V = l^3 \Rightarrow \frac{dV}{dt} = 3l^2\frac{dl}{dt} \Rightarrow 3 = 3(25)^2\frac{dl}{dt}$

$$\Rightarrow \frac{dl}{dt} = \frac{1}{625} \Rightarrow A = 6l^2$$

$$\Rightarrow \frac{dA}{dt} = 6(2l)\frac{dl}{dt} = 12(25)\left(\frac{1}{625}\right) = 0.48 \text{ cm}^2/\text{s}$$

44. $A = \pi r^2 \Rightarrow \frac{dA}{dt} = \pi(2r)\frac{dr}{dt} = \pi(2\times 8)(5) = 80\pi \text{ cm}^2/\text{s}$

45. $x^2 + y^2 = 25$

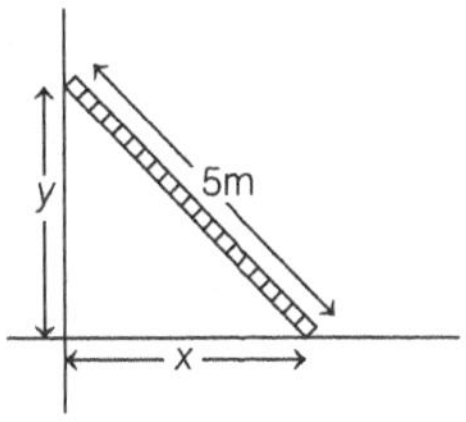

Differentiating both sides w.r.t. t

$$2x\frac{dx}{dt} + 2y\frac{dy}{dt} = 0$$

$$\Rightarrow \quad \frac{dy}{dt} = -\frac{x}{y}\frac{dx}{dt}$$

$$= -\frac{4}{3}(2) = \frac{8}{3}\,\text{m/s}$$

46. $l^2 = (120)^2 + x^2$

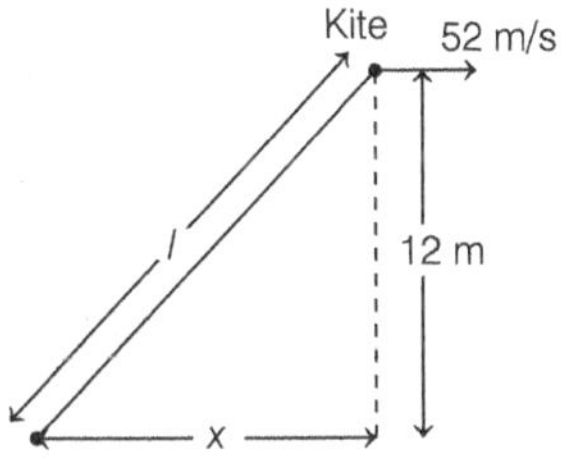

$$\Rightarrow \quad 2l\frac{dl}{dt} = 2x\frac{dx}{dt}$$

$$\frac{dl}{dt} = \frac{x}{l}\frac{dx}{dt}$$

$$= \frac{50}{130}(52) = 20\,\text{m/s}$$

47. $q = 2t^2 - 3t + 1$

$$i = \frac{dq}{dt} = 4t - 3$$

At $t = 5, i = 4(5) - 3 = 17\text{A}$

48. $p = t\ln t$

$$F = \frac{dp}{dt} = t\left(\frac{1}{t}\right) + (\ln t)(1) \quad \Rightarrow \quad F = 1 + \ln t = 0$$

$$\Rightarrow \ln t = -1 \quad \Rightarrow t = e^{-1} = \frac{1}{e}$$

49. $y = 2x^3 - 9x^2 + 100 \quad \Rightarrow \frac{dy}{dx} = 6x^2 - 18x = 0$

$$\Rightarrow x = 0 \text{ and } x = 3 \quad \Rightarrow \quad \frac{d^2y}{dx^2} = 12x - 18$$

At $x = 3, \frac{d^2y}{dx^2} = 12(3) - 18 > 0$

So, $x = 3$ is point of minima.

50. $y = \sqrt{3}\sin x + \cos x$

$$\frac{dy}{dx} = \sqrt{3}\cos x - \sin x = 0 \Rightarrow \tan x = \sqrt{3} \quad \Rightarrow x = \frac{\pi}{3}$$

51. $y = x^2 - 2x + 3 \quad \Rightarrow \frac{dy}{dx} = 2x - 2 = 0 \quad \Rightarrow \quad x = 1$

At $x = 1, y_{min} = 1^2 - 2(1) + 3 = 2$

52. $y = x^3 - 7x^2 + 8x + 5 \quad \Rightarrow \frac{dy}{dx} = 3x^2 - 14x + 8 = 0$

$$\Rightarrow 3x^2 - 12x - 2x + 8 = 0 \quad \Rightarrow 3x(x-4) - 2(x-4) = 0$$

$$\Rightarrow \quad x = \frac{2}{3} \text{ and } x = 4$$

At $x = 4, \frac{d^2y}{dx^2} = 6(4) - 14 > 0$

So, $x = 4$ is point of local minima.

$$y_{min} = 4^3 - 7(4)^2 + 8(4) + 5 = -11$$

53.

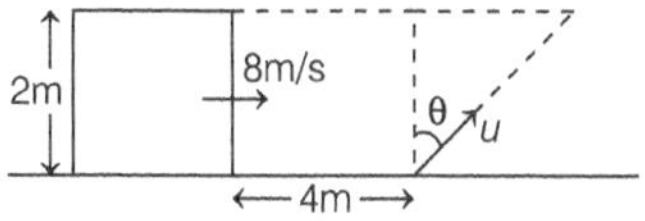

Time taken to cross the road $= t = \frac{2}{u\cos\theta}$

Distance travelled by truck in time $t = 8t$

Displacement of pedestrain along the road $= 4 + (u\sin\theta)t$

$$8t = 4 + (u\sin\theta)t \quad \Rightarrow \quad (8 - u\sin\theta)t = 4$$

$$\Rightarrow \quad (8 - u\sin\theta)\left(\frac{2}{u\cos\theta}\right) = 4$$

$$\Rightarrow \quad 8 - u\sin\theta = 2u\cos\theta \quad \Rightarrow \quad u = \frac{8}{\sin\theta + 2\cos\theta}$$

u will be minimum when $\sin\theta + 2\cos\theta$ is maximum.

$$y = \sin\theta + 2\cos\theta$$

$$\frac{dy}{d\theta} = \cos\theta - 2\sin\theta = 0$$

$$\Rightarrow \quad \tan\theta = \frac{1}{2} \quad \Rightarrow y_{max} = \frac{1}{\sqrt{5}} + 2 \times \frac{2}{\sqrt{5}} = \sqrt{5}$$

$$u_{min} = \frac{8}{\sqrt{5}} = 1.6\sqrt{5}\,\text{m/s}$$

54. $\int 5x^4\,dx = 5\left(\frac{x^5}{5}\right) + C = x^5 + C$

55. $\int\left(x^2 + \frac{1}{x^2} + 2\right)dx = \frac{x^3}{3} - \frac{1}{x} + 2x + C$

56. $\int\left(\frac{3x^2 + 7x - 11}{x^3}\right)dx = \int\left(\frac{3}{x} + \frac{7}{x^2} - \frac{11}{x^3}\right)dx$

$$= 3\ln x - \frac{7}{x} + \frac{11}{2x^2} + C$$

57. $\int\left(x + \frac{1}{x}\right)\left(x^2 + \frac{1}{x^2}\right)dx$

$$\int\left(x^3 + \frac{1}{x} + x + \frac{1}{x^3}\right)dx = \frac{x^4}{4} + \ln x + \frac{x^2}{2} - \frac{1}{2x^2} + C$$

58. $\int\frac{(x^2-1)^2}{x^3}dx = \int\left(\frac{x^4 + 1 - 2x^2}{x^3}\right)dx = \int\left(x + \frac{1}{x^3} - \frac{2}{x}\right)dx$

$$= \frac{x^2}{2} - \frac{1}{2x^2} - 2\ln x + C$$

59. $\int\left(\sqrt{x} - \frac{1}{\sqrt{x}}\right)dx = \frac{2}{3}x^{3/2} - 2\sqrt{x} + C$

60. $\int(x\sqrt{x} + 2)\,dx = \frac{x^{5/2}}{\left(\frac{5}{2}\right)} + 2x + C = \frac{2}{5}x^2\sqrt{x} + 2x + C$

61. $\int\sin\left(\frac{x}{2}\right)dx = -\frac{\cos\left(\frac{x}{2}\right)}{\frac{1}{2}} + C = -2\cos\left(\frac{x}{2}\right) + C$

62. $\int \text{cosec}^2 x\, dx = -\cot x + C$

63. $\int e^{2x}\, dx = \dfrac{e^{2x}}{2} + C$

64. $\int (3x-4)^3\, dx = \dfrac{1}{3}\dfrac{(3x-4)^4}{4} + C = \dfrac{1}{12}(3x-4)^4 + C$

65. $\int (\sqrt{1+x})\, dx = \dfrac{2}{3}(1+x)^{3/2} + C$

66. $\int \dfrac{dx}{(3x+1)^5} = \dfrac{1}{3}\dfrac{(3x+1)^{-4}}{(-4)} + C = -\dfrac{1}{12}\dfrac{1}{(3x+1)^4} + C$

67. $\int \dfrac{5}{3x-7}\, dx = \dfrac{5}{3}\ln(3x-7) + C$

68. $\int \dfrac{\ln^2 x}{x}\, dx$

Lets take $t = \ln x$

$$\frac{dt}{dx} = \frac{1}{x} \Rightarrow \frac{dx}{x} = dt \Rightarrow \int t^2\, dt = \frac{t^3}{3} + C = \frac{\ln^3 x}{3} + C$$

69. $\int \left(\dfrac{1+2\sin x}{\cos^2 x}\right) dx = \int (\sec^2 x + 2\sec x \tan x)\, dx$

$$= \tan x + 2\sec x + C$$

70. $\int \cos^2 y\, dy = \int \left(\dfrac{1+\cos 2y}{2}\right) dy = \dfrac{y}{2} + \dfrac{\sin 2y}{4} + C$

71. $\int x^2 \cos(x^3)\, dx$

Lets take $t = x^3$

$$\frac{dt}{dx} = 3x^2 \Rightarrow x^2\, dx = \frac{1}{3}dt$$

$$\frac{1}{3}\int \cos t\, dt = \frac{1}{3}\sin t + C = \frac{1}{3}\sin(x^3) + C$$

72. $\int_{-2}^{4} \left(\dfrac{x}{2} + 3\right) dx = \left[\dfrac{x^2}{4} + 3x\right]_{-2}^{4}$

$$= \left(\frac{4^2}{4} + 3(4)\right) - \left(\frac{(-2)^2}{4} + 3(-2)\right) = 16 + 5 = 21$$

73. $\int_{\pi}^{2\pi} \theta\, d\theta = \left[\dfrac{\theta^2}{2}\right]_{\pi}^{2\pi} = \dfrac{(2\pi)^2 - \pi^2}{2} = \dfrac{3\pi^2}{2}$

74. $I = \int_0^{\pi/2} \sin 2x\, dx = \left[\dfrac{-\cos 2x}{2}\right]_0^{\pi/2}$

$$= -\frac{1}{2}(\cos \pi - \cos 0°) = 1$$

75. $\int_0^{\pi/4} 2\cos x\, dx = 2[\sin x]_0^{\pi/4}$

$$= 2\left(\sin\frac{\pi}{4} - \sin 0°\right) = 2\left(\frac{1}{\sqrt{2}} - 0\right) = \sqrt{2}$$

76. $\int_0^1 \sqrt{\dfrac{x}{4}}\, dx = \dfrac{1}{2}\int_0^1 \sqrt{x}\, dx = \dfrac{1}{2}\left[\dfrac{x^{3/2}}{3/2}\right]_0^1 = \dfrac{1}{3}$

77. $\int_0^{\frac{\pi}{2}} \cos 3t\, dt = \left[\dfrac{\sin 3t}{3}\right]_0^{\pi/2} = -\dfrac{1}{3}$

78. $\int_0^{\infty} e^{-x}\, dx = [-e^{-x}]_0^{\infty} = -(e^{-\infty} - e^0) = -(0-1) = 1$

79. $\int_0^{\pi/8} 2\cos 2x\, dx = 2\left[\dfrac{\sin 2x}{2}\right]_0^{\pi/8} = \sin\dfrac{\pi}{4} - \sin 0° = \dfrac{1}{\sqrt{2}}$

80. $\int_0^{\pi/4} 2\sin 4x\, dx = -2\left[\dfrac{\cos 4x}{4}\right]_0^{\pi/4} = -\dfrac{1}{2}(-1-1) = 1$

81. $\int_0^{\frac{\pi}{2}} \sin^2 x\, dx = \int_0^{\frac{\pi}{2}} \left(\dfrac{1-\cos 2x}{2}\right) dx = \left[\dfrac{1}{2}x - \dfrac{\sin 2x}{4}\right]_0^{\pi/2} = \dfrac{\pi}{4}$

82. $\int_0^{\pi/4} (\sin 2x + \cos 2x)\, dx$

$$= \left[\frac{-\cos 2x}{2} + \frac{\sin 2x}{2}\right]_0^{\pi/4}$$

$$= \frac{1}{2}\left(-\cos\left(\frac{\pi}{2}\right) + \sin\left(\frac{\pi}{2}\right)\right) - \frac{1}{2}(-\cos 0° + \sin 0°) = 1$$

83. $\int_0^{\sqrt{\pi}} x \sin x^2\, dx$

Lets take $t = x^2$

$$\frac{dt}{dx} = 2x \Rightarrow x\, dx = \frac{1}{2}dt$$

$$\frac{1}{2}\int_0^{\pi} \sin t\, dt = \frac{1}{2}[-\cos t]_0^{\pi} = -\frac{1}{2}(\cos \pi - \cos 0°) = 1$$

84. Area $= \int y\, dx = \int_{-1}^{1} (2x^3 - 3x^2 + 4)\, dx$

$$= \left[\frac{x^4}{2} - x^3 + 4x\right]_{-1}^{1} = 6$$

85. $A_1 = \int_0^{\pi} \sin x\, dx = -[\cos x]_0^{\pi} = 2$

$$A_2 = \int_{\pi}^{3\pi/2} \sin x\, dx = -[\cos x]_0^{\pi} = -1$$

Area $= |A_1| + |A_2| = 2 + 1 = 3$

86. Area $= \int y\, dx = \int_0^1 x^2\, dx = \left[\dfrac{x^3}{3}\right]_0^1 = \dfrac{1}{3}$

Previous Year's Questions

JEE Advanced

1.

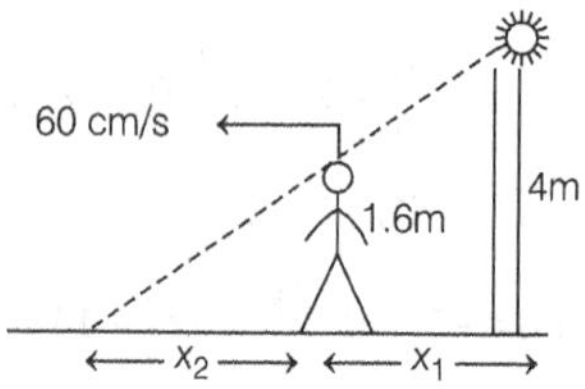

$$\frac{x_1 + x_2}{x_2} = \frac{4}{1.6} = \frac{5}{2}$$

$$\Rightarrow \quad x_2 = \frac{2}{3}x_1 \Rightarrow \frac{dx_2}{dt} = \frac{2}{3}\frac{dx_1}{dt}$$

where, $\dfrac{dx_1}{dt} = 60$ cm/s

$$\frac{dx_2}{dt} = \left(\frac{2}{3}\right)(60) = 40 \text{ cm/s}$$

CHAPTER~03

UNITS & DIMENSIONS

LEVEL 01 Starter Level

3.1 To Find Dimensional Formula of Unknown Quantities

1 The velocity v of a particle depends upon the time t according to the equation $v = a + bt + \frac{c}{d - t}$. Write the dimensions of a, b, c and d.

2 The equation of state of some gases can be expressed as $\left(p + \frac{a}{V^2}\right)(V - b) = nRT$, where p is pressure, V the volume, T the absolute temperature and a, b & R are constants. Find the dimensions of a and b.

3 If $\alpha = \frac{F}{v^2}\sin(\beta t)$ (where, v = velocity, F = force and t = time), then find the dimensions of α and β.

4 Force F is given in terms of time t and distance x by $F = A\sin Ct + B\cos Dx$. Then, find the dimensions of $\frac{A}{B}$ and $\frac{C}{D}$.

5 A particle is in a uni-directional potential field, where the potential energy U of a particle depends on the x-coordinate given by $U = k(1 - \cos\alpha x)$, where k and α are constants. Find the physical dimensions of α and k.

6 The position of a particle at time t is given by the relation $x(t) = \left(\frac{v_0}{\alpha}\right)(1 - e^{-\alpha t})$, where v_0 is a constant and $\alpha > 0$. Find the dimensions of v_0 and α.

7 An unknown quantity α is expressed as $\alpha = \frac{2ma}{\beta}\log\left(1 + \frac{2\beta l}{ma}\right)$, where m = mass, a = acceleration and l = length. Find the unit of α.

3.2 To Verify Correctness of a Given Equation

1 Check whether this equation may be correct or not.

$$p_0 = \frac{3\,Fv^2}{\pi^2 t^2 x}$$

where, p_0 = pressure, F = force, v = velocity, t = time and x = distance.

2 Test if the following equations are dimensionally correct.

(i) $h = \frac{2S\cos\theta}{\rho g}$ (ii) $v = \sqrt{\frac{p}{\rho}}$

(iii) $V = \frac{\pi p r^4}{8\eta l}$ (iv) $f = \frac{1}{2\pi}\sqrt{\frac{mgl}{I}}$

where, h = height, S = surface tension, v = speed of sound, ρ = density, p = pressure, V = volume, η = coefficient of viscosity, l = length, f = frequency, t = time and I = moment of inertia.

3.3 To Convert a Physical Quantity From One System to Another

1 If unit of length is doubled, then find the numerical value of area.

2 Force acting on a particle is 5 N. If unit of length and time are doubled and unit of mass is halved, then find the numerical value of the force in the new unit.

3 The value of acceleration due to gravity is 980 cm/s^2. What will be its value, if the unit of length is kilometre and that of time is minute?

4 In system called the star system we have 1 star kilogram = 10^{20} kg. 1 starmetre = 10^8 m, 1 starsecond = 10^3 second, then calculate the value of 1 joule in this system.

5 In a certain system of units, 1 unit of time is 5 s, 1 unit of mass is 20 kg and 1 unit of length is 10m. In this system, one unit of power will correspond to how many watts?

3.4 To Find Dimensional Formula in Terms of New Fundamental Set of Quantities

1 If the velocity of light c, gravitational constant G and Planck constant h be chosen as fundamental units, then find the dimensions of mass, length and time in this new system.

2 Can pressure (p), density (ρ) and velocity (v) be taken as fundamental quantities?

3 If velocity (v), force (F) and time (T) are chosen as fundamental quantities, then express energy in terms of v, F and T.

4 If instead of mass, length and time as fundamental quantities we choose velocity (v), acceleration (a) and force (F) as fundamental quantities, then find dimensional formula of Young's modulus.

5 If energy (E), density (ρ) and time (T) are fundamental quantities, then what will be the dimensional formula of surface tension?

3.5 To Derive New Relations

1 It has been observed that velocity of ripple waves produced in water depends upon their wavelength (λ), density of water (ρ) and surface tension (T). Obtain an expression for velocity of ripple waves.

2 The mass m of the heaviest stone that can be moved by the water flowing in a river varies as with the speed of water (v), density of water (ρ) and the acceleration due to gravity (g). Prove that the heaviest mass moved is proportional to the sixth power of speed. Also, find the complete dependence.

3 The critical velocity of flow of a liquid through a pipe depends upon the diameter (d) of the pipe, density (ρ) and the coefficient of viscosity (η) of the liquid. Obtain an expression for the critical velocity.

4 Consider a planet of mass (m), revolving round the sun. The time period (T) of revolution of the planet depends upon the radius of the orbit (r), mass of the sun (M) and the gravitational constant (G). Using dimensional analysis, find an expression for time period (T).

5 Experiment shows that two perfectly neutral parallel metal plates separated by a small distance d, attract each other *via* a very weak force, known as the Casimir force. The force per unit area of the plates, P, depends only on the Planck constant h, on the speed of light c and on d. Find the correct expression for P by dimensional analysis [useful formula $E = hf$].

LEVEL 02 JEE Main Level / JEE Advanced Level

Single Choice Correct Questions

1 In a new system of units, the fundamental quantities mass, length and time are replaced by acceleration a, density ρ and frequency f. The dimensional formula for force in this system is

(a) $[\rho a^4 f]$ (b) $[\rho a^4 f^{-6}]$ (c) $[\rho^{-1} a^{-4} f^6]$ (d) $[\rho^{-1} a^{-4} f^{-1}]$

2 A dimensionless quantity

(a) never has a unit (b) always has a unit
(c) may have a unit (d) does not exit

3 A unit less quantity

(a) never has a non-zero dimension
(b) always has a non-zero dimension
(c) may have a non-zero dimension
(d) does not exit

4 Which pair of following quantities has dimensions different from each other?

(a) Impulse and linear momentum
(b) Planck's constant and angular momentum
(c) Moment of inertia and moment of force
(d) Young's modulus and pressure

5 The velocity of water waves may depend on their wavelength λ, the density of water ρ and the acceleration due to gravity g. The method of dimensions gives the relation between these quantities as

(a) $v^2 = k\lambda^{-1}\rho^{-1}g^{-1}$
(b) $v^2 = k\lambda g$
(c) $v^2 = k\lambda\rho g$
(d) $v^2 = k\lambda^3\rho^{-1}g^{-1}$

where, k is a dimensionless constant.

6 The value of $G = 6.67 \times 10^{-11}$ N-m^2/kg^2. Its numerical value in CGS system will be

(a) 6.67×10^{-8} (b) 6.67×10^{-6}
(c) 6.67×10^{-7} (d) 6.67×10^{-5}

7 Force applied by water stream depends on density of water (ρ), velocity of the stream (v) and cross-sectional area of the stream (A). The expression of the force should be

(a) $\rho A v$ (b) $\rho A v^2$ (c) $\rho^2 A v$ (d) $\rho A^2 v$

8 If unit of length and time is doubled, the numerical value of g (acceleration due to gravity) will be
(a) doubled (b) halved (c) four times
(d) remain same

9 Force on a particle in one-dimensional motion is given by $F = Av + Bt + \frac{Cx}{At + D}$, where F = force, v = speed, t = time, x = position and A, B, C and D are constants. Dimensions of C will be
(a) $[M^2L^{-2}T^0]$ (b) $[M L^{-1}T^0]$
(c) $[M^2L^0T^{-2}]$ (d) None of these

10 The velocity v of a particle at time t is given by $v = at + \frac{b}{t + c}$, where a, b and c are constants. The dimensions of a, b and c are respectively,
(a) $[LT^{-2}]$, $[L]$ and $[T]$ (b) $[L^2]$, $[T]$ and $[LT^2]$
(c) $[LT^2]$, $[LT]$ and $[L]$ (d) $[L]$, $[LT]$ and $[T^2]$

11 The units of length, velocity and force are doubled. Which of the following is the correct change in the other units?
(a) Unit of time is doubled
(b) Unit of mass is doubled
(c) Unit of momentum is doubled
(d) Unit of energy is doubled

12 Choose the incorrect statement.
(a) A dimensionally correct equation may be correct.
(b) A dimensionally correct equation may be incorrect.
(c) A dimensionally incorrect equation may be correct.
(d) A dimensionally incorrect equation must be incorrect.

13 The potential energy of a particle varies with distance x from a fixed origin as $U = \frac{A\sqrt{x}}{x^2 + B}$, where A and B are dimensional constants, then dimensional formula for AB is
(a) $[M L^{7/2} T^{-2}]$ (b) $[M L^{11/2} T^{-2}]$
(c) $[M^2 L^{9/2} T^{-2}]$ (d) $[M L^{13/2} T^{-3}]$

14 The equation of the stationary wave is $y = 2a\sin\left(\frac{2\pi ct}{\lambda}\right)\cos\left(\frac{2\pi x}{\lambda}\right)$, which of the following statement is wrong?
(a) The unit of ct is same as that of λ.
(b) The unit of x is same as that of λ.
(c) The unit of $\frac{2\pi c}{\lambda}$ is same as that of $\frac{2\pi x}{\lambda t}$.
(d) The unit of $\frac{c}{\lambda}$ is same as that of $\frac{x}{\lambda}$.

15 Calorie is a unit of heat or energy whose value is 4.2 J, where $J = 1\,kgm^2s^{-2}$. If one uses a unit system in which units of mass, length and time are taken as a kilogram, b metre and g second respectively, then the value of calorie in this system will be
(a) $4.2\,a^{-1}b^{-2}g^{2}$ (b) $4.2\,a^{1}b^{2}g^{-2}$
(c) $a^{1}b^{-2}g^{-2}$ (d) $a^{-1}b^{2}g^{-2}$

16 In a particular system, the units of length, mass and time are chosen to be 10 cm, 10g and 0.1 s, respectively. The unit of force in this system will be equal to
(a) 0.1 N (b) 1 N (c) 10 N (d) 100 N

17 The time dependence of a physical quantity p is given by $p = p_0 \exp(-\alpha t^2)$, where α is a constant and t is time. The constant α
(a) is dimensionless (b) has dimensions $[T^{-2}]$
(c) has dimensions of $[p]$ (d) has dimensions $[T^2]$

18 Which of the following pairs does not have similar dimensions?
(a) Planck's constant and angular momentum
(b) Tension and surface tension
(c) Angle and strain
(d) Stress and pressure

19 Which of the following combinations of three dimensionally different physical quantities P, Q and R can never be a meaningful quantity?
(a) $PQ - R$ (b) $\frac{PQ}{R}$ (c) $\frac{(P - Q)}{R}$ (d) $\frac{(PR - Q^2)}{QR}$

20 If force acceleration and time are taken as fundamental quantities, then the dimensions of length will be
(a) $[FT^2]$ (b) $[F^{-1}A^2T^{-1}]$
(c) $[FA^2T]$ (d) $[AT^2]$

21 The method of dimensional analysis can be used to derive which of the following relations?
(a) $N_0e^{-\lambda t}$ (b) $A\sin(\omega t + kx)$
(c) $\frac{1}{2}mv^2 + \frac{1}{2}I\omega^2$ (d) None of these

22 The dimensions of $\frac{a}{b}$ in the equation $p = \frac{a - t^2}{bx}$, where p is pressure, x is distance and t is time, are
(a) $[M^2LT^{-3}]$ (b) $[MT^{-2}]$ (c) $[L T^{-3}]$ (d) $[M L^3T^{-1}]$

23 E, m, L and G denote energy, mass, angular momentum and gravitational constant, respectively. The dimensions of $\frac{EL^2}{m^5G^2}$ will be that of
(a) angle (b) length (c) mass (d) time

24 Which of the following can be a set of fundamental quantities?
(a) Length, velocity and time
(b) Momentum, mass and velocity
(c) Force, mass and velocity
(d) Momentum, time and frequency

25 $\frac{\alpha}{t^2} = Fv + \frac{\beta}{x^2}$. Find dimensional formula for $\frac{\alpha}{\beta}$ (here, t = time, F = force, v = velocity and x = distance).
(a) $[M^0L^2T^{-2}]$ (b) $[M^0L^{-2}T^2]$
(c) $[ML^2T^2]$ (c) None of these

26 If the acceleration due to gravity is 10 ms^{-2} and the units of length and time are changed to kilometre and hour respectively, the numerical value of the acceleration is
(a) 360000 (b) 72000
(c) 36000 (d) 129600

27 Conversion of 1MW power on a new system having basic units of mass, length and time as 10 kg, 1 dm and 1min respectively is
(a) 2.16×10^{12} unit (b) 1.26×10^{12} unit
(c) 2.16×10^{10} unit (d) 2×10^{14} unit

28 If the speed of light (c), acceleration due to gravity (g) and pressure (p) are taken as fundamental units, the dimensions of gravitational constant (G) are
(a) $[c^2g^3p^2]$ (b) $[c^0g^2p^{-1}]$
(c) $[c^2g^2p^{-2}]$ (d) $[c^0gp^{-3}]$

29 $\int \frac{dx}{\sqrt{2ax - x^2}} = a^n \sin^{-1}\left[\frac{x}{a} - 1\right]$. The value of n is
(a) 0 (b) −1
(c) 1 (d) None of these
You may use dimensional analysis to solve the problem.

30 Consider the equation $\frac{d}{dt}(\int \mathbf{F} \cdot d\mathbf{s}) = A(\mathbf{F} \cdot \mathbf{p})$, where $\mathbf{F}$ = force, $\mathbf{s}$ = displacement, t = time and $\mathbf{p}$ = momentum. The dimensional formula of A will be
(a) $[M^0L^0T^0]$ (b) $[M\,L^0T^0]$
(c) $[M^{-1}L^0T^0]$ (d) $[M^0L^0T^{-1}]$

31 When a wave traverses a medium, the displacement of a particle located at x at time t is given by $y = a\sin(bt - cx)$, where a, b and c are constants of the wave. The dimensions of b are the same as those of
(a) wave velocity
(b) amplitude
(c) wavelength
(d) wave frequency

32 In the above question dimensions of $\frac{b}{c}$ are the same as those of
(a) wave velocity (b) wavelength
(c) wave amplitude (d) wave frequency

33 In two different systems of units, an acceleration is represented by the same number, while a velocity is represented by numbers in the ratio 1 : 3. The ratio of unit of length and time are
(a) $\frac{1}{3}, \frac{1}{9}$ (b) $\frac{1}{9}, \frac{1}{3}$ (c) 1, 1 (d) None of these

34 Suppose we employ a system in which the unit of mass equals 100 kg, the unit of length equals 1 km and the unit of time 100 s and call the unit of energy eluoj (joule written in reverse order), then
(a) 1 eluoj = 10^4 joule (b) 1 eluoj = 10^{-3} joule
(c) 1 eluoj = 10^{-4} joule (d) 1 eluoj = 10^3 joule

35 If in a system, the force of attraction between two point masses of 1 kg each situated 1 km apart is taken as a unit of force and is called notwen (newton written in reverse order) and if $G = 6.67 \times 10^{-11}$ N-m^2 kg^{-2} in SI units, then which of the following is true?
(a) 1 notwen = 6.67×10^{-11} newton
(b) 1 newton = 6.67×10^{-17} notwen
(c) 1 notwen = 6.67×10^{-17} newton
(d) 1 newton = 6.67×10^{-12} notwen

36 In the given expression $A = ax - ce^{-at/b}$, if A is in m^2/s, x is in metre and t is in second, then dimension of a and b will be, respectively
(a) metre/second and metre
(b) metre /second and metre/second
(c) metre and metre/second
(d) metre/second and metre/second^2

37 The Van der Waal's equation of a gas is $\left(P + \frac{aT^2}{V}\right)V^c = (RT + b)$, where a, b, c and R are constants. If the isotherm is represented by $P = AV^m - BV^n$, where A and B depend on temperature
(a) $m = -c, n = -1$ (b) $m = +c, n = 1$
(c) $m = -c, n = +1$ (d) $m = c, n = -1$

38 Of the following quantities, which one has dimension different from the remaining three?
(a) Energy per unit volume
(b) Force per unit area
(c) Product of voltage and charge per unit volume
(d) Angular momentum per unit mass

39 If $A =$ amplitude, $t =$ time, $y =$ displacement, $c =$ speed of wave, $T =$ time period, $\omega = \frac{2\pi}{T}$. Then, on the basis of dimensional analysis, which of the following expression is correct?

(a) $y = \frac{At}{T}\sin ct$ (b) $y = \frac{At}{T}\cos\frac{ct}{A}$
(c) $y = \frac{A}{T}\sin\frac{ct}{A}$ (d) $y = A\omega t\cos ct$

40 A Boomerang has mass m, surface area A, radius of curvature of lower surface r and it is moving with velocity v in air of density ρ. The resistive force on it should be

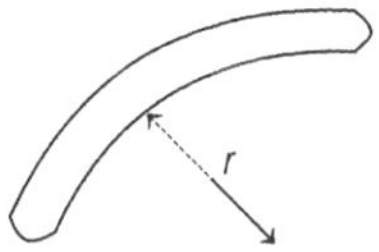

(a) $\frac{2\rho vA}{r^2}\log\left(\frac{\rho m}{\pi Ar}\right)$ (b) $\frac{2\rho v^2 A}{r}\log\left(\frac{\rho A}{\pi m}\right)$
(c) $2\rho v^2 A\log\left(\frac{\rho Ar}{\pi m}\right)$ (d) $\frac{2\rho Av^2}{r^2}A\log\left(\frac{\rho Ar}{\pi m}\right)$

41 The number of particles crossing per unit area perpendicular to X-axis in unit time is $N = -D\frac{n_2 - n_1}{x_2 - x_1}$, where n_1 and n_2 are number of particles per unit volume for the value of x_1 and x_2, respectively. The dimensions of diffusion constant D are

(a) $[M^0LT^2]$ (b) $[M^0L^2T^{-4}]$
(c) $[M^0LT^{-3}]$ (d) $[M^0L^2T^{-1}]$

42 A highly rigid cubical block A of small mass M and side L is fixed rigidly onto another cubical block B of the same dimensions and of low modulus of rigidity η such that the lower face of A completely covers the upper face of B. The lower face of B is rigidly held on a horizontal surface. A small force F is applied perpendicular to one of the side faces of A. After the force is withdrawn block A executes small oscillations. The time period of which is given by

(a) $2\pi\sqrt{\frac{M\eta}{L}}$ (b) $2\pi\sqrt{\frac{L}{M\eta}}$ (c) $2\pi\sqrt{\frac{ML}{\eta}}$ (d) $2\pi\sqrt{\frac{M}{\eta L}}$

Multiple Choice(s) Correct Questions

1 Which of the following sets cannot enter into the list of fundamental quantities in any newly proposed system of units?

(a) Length, mass and velocity
(b) Pressure, density and velocity
(c) Force, velocity and time
(d) Force, momentum and time

2 If A and B are two physical quantities having different dimensions, then which of the following can denote a new physical quantity?

(a) $A + \frac{A^3}{B}$ (b) $\exp\left(-\frac{A}{B}\right)$ (c) AB^2 (d) $\frac{A}{B^4}$

3 The Van der Waal's equation for n moles of a real gas is given by $\left(p + \frac{n^2 a}{V^2}\right)(V - nb) = nRT$, where

$p =$ pressure of gas, $V =$ volume of gas,
$R =$ molar gas constant, $T =$ temperature of gas
and a and $b =$ Van der Waal's constants.
Which of the following have the same dimensions as those of nRT?

(a) pV (b) $\frac{aV}{b^2}$ (c) $\frac{pV^2}{nb}$ (d) $\frac{na}{b}$

4 In damped simple harmonic motion, displacement $x = a_0 e^{\frac{bt}{2m}}\sin(\omega t + \phi)$, where t is in second. Choose the correct statement (s).

(a) Dimensions of m/b are same as t.
(b) Dimensions of $a_0\omega$ are $[LT^{-1}]$
(c) b is dimensionless constant.
(d) ϕ is dimensionless and unitless.

5 In a certain system of units, unit of time is 5 s, unit of mass is 20 kg and unit of length is 10m. In this system, unit of power, unit of force, unit of velocity and unit of energy will correspond to

(a) $P = 16$ W (b) $F = 8$ N (c) $v = 2$ m/s (d) $E = 40$ J

6 If $y = a^3\sin^{-1}\left(\frac{x}{b} - 1\right)$, where y is in metre, then

(a) dimensional formula of a is $[M^0L^{1/3}T^0]$
(b) the unit of $\sin^{-1}\left(\frac{x}{b} - 1\right)$ is radian
(c) the dimensions of x are same as those of b
(d) the unit of a is metre

7 The speed of a particle depends on the time t as $v = \sqrt{AB} + Bt + \frac{C}{D + t}$. Then,

(a) A represents distance (b) B represents acceleration
(c) C represents distance (d) D represents time

8 If pressure p of a gas is given in terms of time t and distance x as $p = A\sin bt + B\sin ct$, then

(a) dimensions of $\frac{A}{B}$ are same as $\frac{b}{c}$
(b) dimensions of A is $[ML^{-1}T^{-2}]$
(c) dimensions of A and B are same
(d) dimensions of b and c are same

9 If $\left(A+\frac{B}{C^2}\right)(D-x)=y$, then
(a) dimensions of A and B must be same
(b) dimensions of A and B may be same
(c) dimensions of D and x must be same
(d) dimensions of AD and y must be same

10 In two systems of relations among velocity, acceleration and force are respectively $v_2=\frac{\alpha^2}{\beta}v_1$, $a_2=\alpha\beta a_1$ and $F_2=\frac{F_1}{\alpha\beta}$. If α and β are constants, then relations among mass, length, time and momentum in two systems are
(a) $M_2=\frac{1}{\alpha^2\beta^2}M_1$ (b) $L_2=\frac{\alpha^2}{\beta^2}L_1$
(c) $T_2=T_1\frac{\alpha}{\beta^2}$ (d) $p_2=\frac{1}{\beta^3}p_1$

Comprehension Based Questions

Comprehension-1

A physical quantity X depends on another physical quantities as $X=YFe^{-\beta r^2}+ZW\sin(\alpha r)$ where r, F and W represents distance, force and work respectively and Y and Z are unknown physical quantities and α, β are positive constants.

1 If Y represents displacement, then dim $\left(\frac{\alpha YZ}{\beta F}\right)$ is equal to
(a) $[M^{-1}LT^2]$ (b) $[M^{-1}L^2T^{-2}]$
(c) $[M^1L^1T^{-2}]$ (d) None of these

2 If Y represents velocity, then dim (X) is equal to
(a) $[ML^2T^{-3}]$ (b) $[M^{-1}L^2T^{-3}]$
(c) $[ML^2T^{-2}]$ (d) None of these

3 If Z represents frequency, then choose the correct alternative.
(a) The dimensional formula of X is $[ML^1T^{-3}]$.
(b) The dimensional formula of Y is $[M^0LT^{-1}]$.
(c) The dimensional formula of β is $[M^0L^{-1}T^0]$.
(d) The dimensional formula of α is $[M^0L^1T^0]$.

Comprehension-2

In a certain system of absolute units, the acceleration produced by gravity in a body falling freely is denoted by 3, the kinetic energy of a 272.1 kg shot moving with velocity 448 m/s is denoted by 100, and its momentum by 10.

4 The unit of length is
(a) 15.36 m (b) 153.6 m
(c) 68.57 m (d) None of these

5 The unit of time is
(a) 68.57 s (b) 0.6857 s
(c) 6.857 s (d) None of these

6 The unit of mass is
(a) 544.2 kg (b) 54.42 kg
(c) 5442 kg (d) None of these

Comprehension-3

A student forgot Newton's formula for speed of sound but he knows there were speed (v), pressure (p) and density (d) in the formula. He then starts using dimensional analysis method to find the actual relation.

$$v=k\,p^x\,d^y$$

where, k is a dimensionless constant. On the basis of above passage answer the following questions.

7 The value of x is
(a) 1 (b) $\frac{1}{2}$ (c) $-\frac{1}{2}$ (d) 2

8 The value of y is
(a) 1 (b) $\frac{1}{2}$ (c) $-\frac{1}{2}$ (d) 2

9 If the density will increase, then the speed of sound will
(a) increase (b) decrease
(c) unchanged (d) None of these

Comprehension-4

According to Newton's laws of gravitation, force between two particles of masses m_1 and m_2 separated by a distance r is given by $F=\frac{Gm_1m_2}{r^2}$. Here, G is universal gravitational constant.

10 What is the dimensional formula of G if M, L and T are taken as fundamental physical quantities?
(a) $[ML^3T^{-1}]$ (b) $[M^{-1}L^{-3}T^{-2}]$
(c) $[M^{-1}L^3T^{-2}]$ (d) $[MLT^{-2}]$

Now, suppose we take density (ρ), length (L) and universal gravitational constant (G) as fundamental physical quantities, then

11 dimensional formula of pressure will be
(a) ρ^2L^2G (b) ρL^2G
(c) ρLG (d) Cannot be derived

12 dimensional formula of velocity will be
(a) $L\sqrt{\frac{G}{\rho}}$ (b) $L\sqrt{G\rho}$
(c) $L\sqrt{\frac{\rho}{G}}$ (d) Cannot be derived

Comprehension-5

A piston of mass m is at rest enclosing a cavity of volume V. It is slightly displaced and released. A dimensionless quantity γ known as adiabatic exponent of the gas depends on time period T of small oscillations of piston, the mass m of piston, cross-sectional area A of piston and pressure p. If $\gamma = k\left(\frac{m}{p}\right)^x A^y T^z$, where k is dimensionless constant.

13 Find the value of x.
(a) -1 (b) -2
(c) 3 (d) Cannot be calculated

14 Find the value of y.
(a) 1 (b) -1
(b) 2 (d) Cannot be calculated

15 Find the value of z.
(a) 1 (b) -1
(c) 2 (d) Cannot be calculated

Match the Columns Questions

1 In a new system (say ABG system) of measurement, the fundamental quantities length, mass and time are measured in alpha, beta and gamma, respectively. 1 alpha = 1 km, 1 beta = 1 quintal (100 kg) 1 gamma = 1 min

	Column I		Column II
A.	One unit of acceleration in ABG system	P.	$\frac{5}{18}\times 10^{-4}$ SI unit
B.	One unit of kinetic energy in ABG system	Q.	$\frac{5}{18}\times 10^{-3}$ MKS unit
C.	One unit of pressure in ABG system	R.	$\frac{5}{18}\times 10^{0}$ MKS unit
D.	One unit of work in ABG system	S.	$\frac{5}{18}\times 10^{4}$ MKS unit
		T.	$\frac{5}{18}\times 10^{5}$ SI unit

2 Considering force (F), velocity (v) and energy (E) as fundamental quantities, match the correct dimensions of following quantities.

	Column I		Column II
A.	Mass	P.	$[F^{-1} v^0 E^1]$
B.	Light year	Q.	$[F^1 v^1 E^{-1}]$
C.	Frequency	R.	$[F^3 v^0 E^{-2}]$
D.	Pressure	S.	$[F^0 v^{-2} E^1]$

Numerical Value Questions

1 A gas bubble, from an explosion under water, oscillates with a period T proportional to $p^a d^b E^c$, where p is the pressure, d is the density of water and E is the total energy of the explosion. Find the value of $\frac{6a^2}{b+c}$.

2 In relativistic energy-momentum relation $E^n = p^2c^2 + m_0^2c^4$. Find the value of n. (Here, E = energy, p = linear momentum, c = speed of light and m_0 = rest mass of the particle.

3 The power for a hovering helicopter depends on its linear size, the density of air and weight per unit volume of the helicopter as power $\propto$ (linear size)^x (density of air)^y (weight per unit volume of helicopter)^z. What is the value of $x + 2y + z$?

4 $\int \frac{dx}{\left(\frac{1}{a}\right)^2 + x^2} = a^n \tan^{-1}(ax)$. Find the value of n.

5 If unit of mass becomes 2 times, the unit of length becomes 4 times and the unit of time becomes 4 times, then unit of Planck's constant becomes n times. Find the value of n.

6 In a new system of units, the unit of mass is 100 g, unit of length is 4 m and unit of time is 2 s. Find the numerical value of 10 J in this system.

7 If the speed of light (c), acceleration due to gravity (g) and pressure (p) taken as base quantities, then find dimension of g in the dimensional formula of universal gravitational constant.

8 If volume is written as $V = kG^x c^y h^z$, where k is dimensionless constant and G, c and h are universal gravitational constant, speed of light and Planck's constant, respectively. Find the value of $x - 2y + z$.

9 In system called the star system we have 1 star kilogram = 10^{20} kg. 1 starmeter = 10^8 m, 1 starsecond = 10^3 second, then the value of 1 watt in this system is 10^{-n} starwatt. Find n.

10 In a new system of units, the speed of light in vacuum is 90000 and acceleration due to gravity is 1. What is the numerical value of distance between the Sun and Earth in terms of the new unit, if light takes 8 min and 20 s to cover this distance?

Previous Year's Questions

JEE Main

01 Given below are two statements:

Statement I Planck's constant and angular momentum have same dimensions.

Statement II Linear momentum and moment of force have same dimensions.

In the light of the above statements, choose the correct answer from the options given below [2024, 27 Jan Shift-I]

(a) Both Statement I and Statement II are false.
(b) Both Statement I and Statement II are true.
(c) Statement I is true but Statement II is false.
(d) Statement I is false but Statement II is true.

02 The equation of state of a real gas is given by $\left(p+\frac{a}{V^2}\right)(V-b)=RT$, where p, V and T are pressure, volume and temperature respectively and R is the universal gas constant. The dimensions of $\frac{a}{b^2}$ is similar to that of [2024, 27 Jan Shift-II]

(a) RT (b) p
(c) pV (d) R

03 Match List I with List II.

	List I		List II
(A)	Coefficient of viscosity	(I)	$[ML^2T^{-2}]$
(B)	Surface tension	(II)	$[ML^2T^{-1}]$
(C)	Angular momentum	(III)	$[ML^{-1}T^{-1}]$
(D)	Rotational kinetic energy	(IV)	$[ML^0T^{-2}]$

Choose the correct answer from the options given below. [2024, 30 Jan Shift-I]

(a) (A)-(I), (B)-(II), (C)-(III), (D)-(IV)
(b) (A)-(III), (B)-(IV), (C)-(II), (D)-(I)
(c) (A)-(II), (B)-(I), (C)-(IV), (D)-(III)
(d) (A)-(IV), (B)-(III), (C)-(II), (D)-(I)

04 If mass is written as $m=k\,c^P G^{\frac{-1}{2}} h^{\frac{1}{2}}$, then the value of P will be (Constants have their usual meaning with k a dimensionless constant) [2024, 30 Jan Shift-II]

(a) $\frac{-1}{3}$ (b) 2 (c) $\frac{1}{2}$ (d) $\frac{1}{3}$

05 In the equation $\left[x+\frac{a}{y^2}\right][y-b]=RT$, x is pressure, y is volume, R is universal gas constant and T is temperature. The physical quantity equivalent to the ratio a/b is [2023, 13 April Shift-II]

(a) Coefficient of viscosity (b) Impulse
(c) Energy (d) Pressure gradient

06 Given below are two statements :

Statement I Astronomical unit (Au), Parsec (Pc) and Light year (ly) are units for measuring astronomical distances.

Statement II Au < Parsec (Pc) < ly

In the light of above statements, choose the most appropriate answer from the options given below. [2023, 11 April Shift-I]

(a) Both Statement I and Statements II are correct.
(b) Statements I is correct but Statements II is incorrect.
(c) Statements I is incorrect but Statements II is correct.
(d) Both Statements I and Statements II are incorrect.

07 Match List-I with List-II

	List-I		List-II
A.	Torque	I.	kg $m^{-1}s^{-2}$
B.	Energy density	II.	kg ms^{-1}
C.	Pressure gradient	III.	kg $m^{-2}s^{-2}$
D.	Impulse	IV.	kg $m^2\,s^{-2}$

Choose the correct answer from the options given below [2023, 30 Jan Shift-II]

(a) A-IV, B-I, C-II, D-III
(b) A-IV, B-I, C-III, D-II
(c) A-IV, B-III, C-I, D-II
(d) A-I, B-IV, C-III, D-II

08 Match List-I with List-II.

	List-I		List-II
A.	Spring constant	I.	$[T^{-1}]$
B.	Angular speed	II.	$[ML^{-2}]$
C.	Angular momentum	III.	$[ML^2]$
D.	Moment of inertia	IV.	$[ML^2T^{-1}]$

Choose the correct answer from the options given below. [2023, 12 April Shift-I]

(a) A-II, B-I, C-IV, D-III (b) A-I, B-III, C-II, D-IV
(c) A-II, B-III, C-I, D-IV (d) A-IV, B-I, C-III, D-II

09 Match List I with List II.

	List I		List II
A.	Torque	I.	$[ML^{-2}T^{-2}]$
B.	Stress	II.	$[ML^2T^{-2}]$
C.	Pressure gradient	III.	$[ML^{-1}T^{-1}]$
D.	Coefficient of viscosity	IV.	$[ML^{-1}T^{-2}]$

Choose the correct answer from the options given below **[2023, 8 April Shift-I]**

(a) A-IV, B-II, C-III, D-I (b) A-II, B-I, C-IV, D-III
(c) A-II, B-IV, C-I, D-III (d) A-III, B-IV, C-I, D-II

10 If force (F), velocity (V) and time (T) are considered as fundamental physical quantity, then dimensional formula of density will be **[2023, 11 April Shift-II]**

(a) $FV^{-4}T^{-2}$ (b) $FV^{4}T^{-6}$
(c) $F^{2}V^{-2}T^{6}$ (d) $FV^{-2}T^{2}$

11 Dimension of $\frac{1}{\mu_0\varepsilon_0}$ should be equal to **[2023, 8 April Shift-I]**

(a) $\frac{L^2}{T^2}$ (b) $\frac{T^2}{L^2}$ (c) $\frac{T}{L}$ (d) $\frac{L}{T}$

12 The speed of a wave produced in water is given by $v=\lambda^a g^b \rho^c$. Where λ, g and ρ are wavelength of wave, acceleration due to gravity and density of water respectively. The values of a, b and c respectively, are **[2023, 15 April Shift-I]**

(a) $\frac{1}{2}, \frac{1}{2}, 0$ (b) $\frac{1}{2}, 0, \frac{1}{2}$
(c) $1, -1, 0$ (d) $1, 1, 0$

13 Match List-I with List-II.

List-I		List-II	
A.	Planck's constant (h)	I.	$[M^1L^2T^{-2}]$
B.	Stopping potential (V_s)	II.	$[M^1L^1T^{-1}]$
C.	Work function (ϕ)	III.	$[M^1L^2T^{-1}]$
D.	Momentum (p)	IV.	$[M^1L^2T^{-3}A^{-1}]$

Choose the correct answer from the options given below **[2023, 24 Jan Shift-I]**

(a) A-I, B-III, C-IV, D-II (b) A-II, B-IV, C-III, D-I
(c) A-III, B-IV, C-I, D-II (d) A-III, B-I, C-II, D-IV

14 Match List I with List II

List I		List II	
A.	Torque	I.	Nms^{-1}
B.	Stress	II.	$J kg^{-1}$
C.	Latent Heat	III.	Nm
D.	Power	IV.	Nm^{-2}

Choose the correct answer from the optns given below **[2022, 29 July Shift-II]**

(a) A-III, B-II,C-I, D-IV (b) A-III, B-IV, C-II, D-I
(c) A-IV, B-I, C-III, D-II (d) A-II, B-III, C-I, D-IV

15 Velocity (v) and acceleration (a) in two systems of units 1 and 2 are related as $v_2=\frac{n}{m^2}v_1$ and $a_2=\frac{a_1}{mn}$, respectively. Here, m and n are constants. The relations for distance and time in two systems respectively are: **[2022, 28 June Shift-II]**

(a) $\frac{n^3}{m^3}L_1=L_2$ and $\frac{n^2}{m}T_1=T_2$
(b) $L_1=\frac{n^4}{m^2}L_2$ and $T_1=\frac{n^2}{m}T_2$
(c) $L_1=\frac{n^2}{m}L_2$ and $T_1=\frac{n^4}{m^2}=T_2$
(d) $\frac{n^2}{m}L_1=L_2$ and $\frac{n^4}{m^2}T_1=T_2$

16 The distance of the Sun from Earth is 1.5×10^{11} m and its angular diameter is (2000) s when observed from the earth. The diameter of the Sun will be **[2022, 27 June Shift-II]**

(a) 2.45×10^{10} m (b) 1.45×10^{10} m
(c) 1.45×10^{9} m (d) 0.14×10^{9} m

17 If E and H represent the intensity of electric field and magnetising field respectively, then the unit of E/H will be **[2021, 27 Aug Shift-I]**

(a) ohm (b) mho (c) joule (d) newton

18 If L, C and R are the self inductance, capacitance and resistance respectively, which of the following does not have the dimension of time? **[2022, 27 June Shift-II]**

(a) RC (b) L/R (c) $\sqrt{LC}$ (d) L/C

19 Identify the pair of physical quantities which have different dimensions **[2022, 24 June Shift-I]**

(a) Wave number and Rydberg's constant
(b) Stress and coefficient of elasticity
(c) Coercivity and Magnetisation
(d) Specific heat capacity and latent heat

20 An expression of energy density is given by $u=\frac{\alpha}{\beta}\sin\left(\frac{\alpha x}{kt}\right)$, where α, β are constants, x is displacement, k is Boltzmann constant and t is the temperature. The dimensions of β will be **[2022, 27 July Shift-II]**

(a) $[ML^{-2}T^{-1}q^{-1}]$ (b) $[M^0L^2T^{-2}]$
(c) $[M^0L^0T^0]$ (d) $[M^0L^2T^0]$

21 In vander Waal's equation $\left[p+\frac{a}{V^2}\right][V-b]=RT$ where, p is pressure, V is volume, R is universal gas constant and T is temperature. The ratio of constants a/b is dimensionally equal to **[2022, 29 June Shift-I]**

(a) $\frac{p}{V}$ (b) $\frac{V}{p}$ (c) pV (d) pV^3

22 Given below are two statements One is labelled as Assertion (A) and other is labelled as Reason (R).

Assertion (A) Time period of oscillation of a liquid drop depends on surface tension (S), if density of the liquid is ρ and radius of the drop is r, then $T = k\sqrt{\frac{\rho r^3}{S^{3/2}}}$ is dimensionally correct, where k is dimensionless.

Reason (R) Using dimensional analysis we get RHS having different dimension than that of time period.

In the light of above statements, choose the correct answer from the options given below. **[2022, 29 July Shift-I]**

(a) Both (A) and (R) are true and (R) is the correct explanation of (A).
(b) Both (A) and (R) are true but (R) is not the correct explanation of (A).
(c) (A) is true but (R) is false.
(d) (A) is false but (R) is true.

23 Consider the efficiency of carnot's engine is given by $\eta = \frac{\alpha\beta}{\sin\theta}\log_e\frac{\beta x}{kT}$, where α and β are constants. If T is temperature, k is Boltzmann constant, θ is angular displacement and x has the dimensions of length. Then, choose the incorrect option. **[2022, 28 July Shift-II]**

(a) Dimensions of β is same as that of force.
(b) Dimensions of $\alpha^{-1}x$ is same as that of energy.
(c) Dimensions of $\eta^{-1}\sin\theta$ is same as that of $\alpha\beta$.
(d) Dimensions of α is same as that of β.

24 If momentum (p), area (A) and time (t) are taken as fundamental quantities, then the dimensional formula for coefficient of viscosity is **[2022, 25 July Shift-I]**

(a) $[PA^{-1}T^0]$
(b) $[PAT^{-1}]$
(c) $[PA^{-1}T]$
(d) $[PA^{-1}T^{-1}]$

25 Which of the following physical quantities have the same dimensions? **[2022, 25 July Shift-I]**

(a) Electric displacement (D) and surface charge density
(b) Displacement current and electric field
(c) Current density and surface charge density
(d) Electric potential and energy

26 Given below are two statements One is labelled as Assertion (A) and the other is labelled as Reason (R).

Assertion (A) Product of Pressure p and time t has the same dimension as that of coefficient of viscosity.

Reason (R) Coefficient of viscosity $= \frac{\text{Force}}{\text{Velocity gradient}}$

Choose the correct answer from the options given below : **[2022, 28 June Shift-I]**

(a) Both A and R true, and R is correct explanation of A.
(b) Both A and R are true but R is NOT the correct explanation of A.
(c) A is true but R is false.
(d) A is false but R is true.

27 The SI unit of a physical quantity is pascal-second. The dimensional formula of this quantity will be **[2022, 27 June Shift-II]**

(a) $[ML^{-1}T^{-1}]$
(b) $[ML^{-1}T^{-2}]$
(c) $[ML^2T^{-1}]$
(d) $[M^{-1}L^3T^0]$

28 The dimension of mutual inductance is **[2022, 26 June Shift-II]**

(a) $[ML^2T^{-2}A^{-1}]$
(b) $[ML^2T^{-3}A^{-1}]$
(c) $[ML^2T^{-2}A^{-2}]$
(d) $[ML^2T^{-3}A^{-2}]$

29 An expression for a dimensionless quantity P is given by $P = \frac{\alpha}{\beta}\log_e\left(\frac{kt}{\beta x}\right)$, where α and β are constants, x is distance, k is Boltzmann constant and t is the temperature. Then, the dimensions of α will be **[2022, 26 June Shift-I]**

(a) $[M^0L^{-1}T^0]$
(b) $[ML^0T^{-2}]$
(c) $[MLT^{-2}]$
(d) $[ML^2T^{-2}]$

30 Identify the pair of physical quantities that have same dimensions. **[2022, 24 June Shift-II]**

(a) Velocity gradient and decay constant
(b) Wien's constant and Stefan constant
(c) Angular frequency and angular momentum
(d) Wave number and Avogadro number

31 Match List-I with List-II. **[2021, 31 Aug Shift-I]**

	List-I		List-II
(A)	Torque	(i)	MLT^{-1}
(B)	Impulse	(ii)	MT^{-2}
(C)	Tension	(iii)	ML^2T^{-2}
(D)	Surface tension	(iv)	MLT^{-2}

Choose the most appropriate answer from the options given below.

(a) (A)-(iii), (B)-(i), (C)-(iv), (D)-(ii)
(b) (A)-(ii), (B)-(i), (C)-(iv), (D)-(iii)
(c) (A)-(i), (B)-(iii), (C)-(iv), (D)-(ii)
(d) (A)-(iii), (B)-(iv), (C)-(i), (D)-(ii)

32 Match List-I with List-II. [2021, 31 Aug Shift-I]

List-I	List-II
(A) Capacitance, C	(i) $M^1L^1T^{-3}A^{-1}$
(B) Permittivity of free space, ε_0	(ii) $M^{-1}L^{-3}T^4A^2$
(C) Permiability of free space, μ_0	(iii) $M^{-1}L^{-2}T^4A^2$
(D) Electric field, E	(iv) $M^1L^1T^{-2}A^{-2}$

Choose the most appropriate answer from the options given below.

(a) (A)-(iii), (B)-(ii), (C)-(iv), (D)-(i)
(b) (A)-(iii), (B)-(iv), (C)-(ii), (D)-(i)
(c) (A)-(iv), (B)-(ii), (C)-(iii), (D)-(i)
(d) (A)-(iv), (B)-(iiii), (C)-(ii), (D)-(i)

33 Which of the following equations is dimensionally incorrect ?

Where, t = time, h = height, s = surface tension, θ = angle, ρ = density, a, r = radius, g = acceleration due to gravity, V = volume, p = pressure, W = work done, τ = torque, ε = permittivity, E = electric field, J = current density, L = length. [2021, 31 Aug Shift-I]

(a) $V = \frac{\pi p a^4}{8\eta L}$
(b) $h = \frac{2s\cos\theta}{\rho r g}$
(c) $J = \varepsilon\frac{\partial E}{\partial t}$
(d) $W = \tau\theta$

34 If velocity $[v]$, time $[T]$ and force $[F]$ are choosen as the base quantities, the dimensions of the mass will be [2021, 31 Aug Shift-II]

(a) $[FT^{-1}v^{-1}]$
(b) $[FTv^{-1}]$
(c) $[FT^2v]$
(d) $[FvT^{-1}]$

35 If force (F), length (L) and time (T) are taken as the fundamental quantities. Then what will be the dimension of density? [2021, 27 Aug Shift-II]

(a) $[FL^{-4}T^2]$
(b) $[FL^{-3}T^2]$
(c) $[FL^{-5}T^2]$
(d) $[FL^{-3}T^3]$

36 Which of the following is not a dimensionless quantity ? [2021, 27 Aug Shift-I]

(a) Relative magnetic permeability (μ_r)
(b) Power factor
(c) Permeability of free space (μ_0)
(d) Quality factor

37 If E, L, M and G denote the quantities as energy, angular momentum, mass and constant of gravitation respectively, then the dimension of P in the formula $P = EL^2M^{-5}G^{-2}$ is [2021, 26 Aug Shift-I]

(a) $[M^0L^1T^0]$
(b) $[M^{-1}L^{-1}T^2]$
(c) $[M^1L^1T^{-2}]$
(d) $[M^0L^0T^0]$

38 The force is given in terms of time t and displacement x by the equation $F = A\cos Bx + C\sin Dt$

The dimensional formula of AD/B is [2021, 25 July Shift-II]

(a) $[M^0LT^{-1}]$
(b) $[ML^2T^{-3}]$
(c) $[M^1L^1T^{-2}]$
(d) $[M^2L^2T^{-3}]$

39 If time (t), velocity (v) and angular momentum (l) are taken as the fundamental units, then the dimension of mass (m) in terms of t, v and l is [2021, 20 July Shift-II]

(a) $[t^{-1}v^1l^{-2}]$
(b) $[t^1v^2l^{-1}]$
(c) $[t^{-2}v^{-1}l^1]$
(d) $[t^{-1}v^{-2}l^1]$

JEE Advanced

1. Young's modulus of elasticity Y is expressed in terms of three derived quantities, namely, the gravitational constant G, planck's constant h and the speed of light c, as $Y = c^\alpha h^\beta G^\gamma$. Which of the following is the correct option? (2023 Adv.)

(a) $\alpha = 7, \beta = -1, \gamma = -2$
(b) $\alpha = -7, \beta = -1, \gamma = -2$
(c) $\alpha = 7, \beta = -1, \gamma = 2$
(d) $\alpha = -7, \beta = 1, \gamma = -2$

2. In a particular system of units, a physical quantity can be expressed in terms of the electric charge e, electron mass m_e, Planck's constant h and Coulomb's constant $k = \frac{1}{4\pi\varepsilon_0}$, where ε_0 is the permittivity of vacuum. In terms of these physical constants, the dimension of the magnetic field is $[B] = [e]^\alpha [m_e]^\beta [h]^\gamma [k]^\delta$. The value of $\alpha + \beta + \gamma + \delta$ is .... (2022 Adv.)

3. A physical quantity **S** is defined as $\mathbf{S} = (\mathbf{E} \times \mathbf{B})/\mu_0$, where **E** is electric field, **B** is magnetic field and μ_0 is the permeability of free space. The dimensions of **S** are the same as the dimensions of which of the following quantity(ies) ? (2021 Adv.)

(a) $\frac{\text{Energy}}{\text{Charge} \times \text{Current}}$
(b) $\frac{\text{Force}}{\text{Length} \times \text{Time}}$
(c) $\frac{\text{Energy}}{\text{Volume}}$
(d) $\frac{\text{Power}}{\text{Area}}$

4. Sometimes it is convenient to construct a system of units so that all quantities can be expressed in terms of only one physical quantity. In one such system, dimensions of different quantities are given in terms of a quantity X as follows: [position] = $[X^\alpha]$; [speed] = $[X^\beta]$; [acceleration] = $[X^p]$; [linear momentum] = $[X^q]$; [force] = $[X^r]$. Then, (2020 Adv.)

(a) $\alpha + p = 2\beta$
(b) $p + q - r = \beta$
(c) $p - q + r = \alpha$
(d) $p + q + r = \beta$

5. A length-scale (l) depends on the permittivity (ε) of a dielectric material, Boltzmann's constant (k_B), the absolute temperature (T), the number per unit volume (n) of certain charged particles, and the charge (q) carried by each of the particles. Which of the following expression (s) for l is (are) dimensionally correct? (2016 Adv.)

(a) $l=\sqrt{\left(\frac{nq^2}{\varepsilon k_B T}\right)}$ (b) $l=\sqrt{\left(\frac{\varepsilon k_B T}{nq^2}\right)}$

(c) $l=\sqrt{\left(\frac{q^2}{\varepsilon n^{2/3} k_B T}\right)}$ (d) $l=\sqrt{\left(\frac{q^2}{\varepsilon n^{1/3} k_B T}\right)}$

6. In terms of potential difference V, electric current I, permittivity ε_0, permeability μ_0 and speed of light c, the dimensionally correct equations is/are (2015 Adv.)

(a) $\mu_0 I^2 = \varepsilon_0 V^2$ (b) $\varepsilon_0 I = \mu_0 V$

(c) $I = \varepsilon_0 cV$ (d) $\mu_0 cI = \varepsilon_0 V$

Answer Key

Level 1

3.1 To Find Dimensional Formula of Unknown Quantities

1. $[a]=[LT^{-1}]$; $[b]=[LT^{-2}]$; $[c]=[L]$; $[d]=[T]$
2. $[a]=[M^1 L^5 T^{-2}]$; $[b]=[L^3]$ 3. $\alpha=[ML^{-1}], \beta=[T^{-1}]$
4. $[M^0L^0T^0]$, $[M^0L^1T^{-1}]$ 5. $\alpha=[L^{-1}], k=[ML^2T^{-2}]$
6. $v_0=[LT^{-1}]$, $\alpha=[T^{-1}]$ 7. metre

3.2 To Verify Correctness of a Given Equation

1. Dimensionally incorrect
2. (i) Dimensionally incorrect (ii) Dimensionally correct (iii) Dimensionally incorrect (iv) Dimensionally correct

3.3 To Convert a Physical Quantity From One System to Another

1. $\frac{1}{4}$ 2. 20 units 3. 35.28 4. 10^{-30} star joule 5. 16 W

3.4 To Find Dimensional Formula in Terms of New Fundamental Set of Quantities

1. $[\text{Mass}]=[c^{1/2}\, G^{-1/2}\, h^{1/2}]$; $[\text{Length}]=[c^{-3/2}\, G^{1/2}\, h^{1/2}]$; $[\text{Time}]=[c^{-5/2}\, G^{1/2}\, h^{1/2}]$
2. No 3. Energy $= kvFT$ 4. $[Y]=[v^{-4}\, a^2\, F]$
5. $[\text{Surface tension}]=[E^{3/5}\, \rho^{2/5}\, T^{-4/5}]$

3.5 To Derive New Relations

1. $v^2 \propto \frac{T}{\lambda\rho}$ 2. $m \propto \frac{\rho v^6}{g^3}$ 3. $v = k\, d^{-3} \rho^{-1} \eta$
4. $T = k\sqrt{\frac{r^3}{GM}}$ 5. $P = k\frac{hc}{d^3}$

Level 2

Single Choice Correct Questions

1. (b)	2. (c)	3. (a)	4. (c)	5. (b)
6. (a)	7. (b)	8. (a)	9. (c)	10. (a)
11. (c)	12. (d)	13. (b)	14. (d)	15. (a)
16. (a)	17. (b)	18. (b)	19. (c)	20. (d)
21. (d)	22. (b)	23. (a)	24. (c)	25. (b)
26. (d)	27. (a)	28. (b)	29. (a)	30. (c)
31. (d)	32. (a)	33. (b)	34. (a)	35. (c)
36. (a)	37. (a)	38. (d)	39. (b)	40. (c)
41. (d)	42. (d)			

Multiple Choice(s) Correct Questions

1. bd	2. acd	3. abcd	4. ab
5. abc	6. abc	7. abcd	8. abcd
9. bcd	10. acd		

Comprehension Based Questions

1. (a)	2. (a)	3. (b)	4. (b)	5. (c)
6. (a)	7. (b)	8. (c)	9. (a)	10. (c)
11. (a)	12. (b)	13. (d)	14. (d)	15. (d)

Match the Columns Questions

1. A-R, B-T, C-P, D-T 2. A-S, B-P, C-Q, D-R

Numerical Value Questions

1. (5)	2. (2)	3. (4)	4. (1)	5. (8)
6. (25)	7. (2)	8. (12)	9. (27)	10. (1.5)

Previous Year's Questions

JEE Main

1. (c)	2. (b)	3. (b)	4. (c)	5. (c)
6. (b)	7. (b)	8. (a)	9. (c)	10. (a)
11. (a)	12. (a)	13. (c)	14. (b)	15. (a)
16. (c)	17. (a)	18. (d)	19. (d)	20. (d)
21. (c)	22. (d)	23. (d)	24. (a)	25. (a)
26. (c)	27. (a)	28. (c)	29. (c)	30. (a)
31. (a)	32. (a)	33. (a)	34. (b)	35. (a)
36. (c)	37. (d)	38. (b)	39. (d)	

JEE Advanced

1. (a)	2. (4)	3. (b, d)	4. (b)	5. (b,d)
6. (a)				

SOLUTIONS

Level 1

3.1 To Find Dimensional Formula of Unknown Quantities

1. $v = a + bt + \dfrac{c}{d-t}$

$$[v] = [a] = [bt] = \left[\frac{c}{d-t}\right] \text{ and } [d] = [t]$$

$$[a] = [v] = [LT^{-1}]$$

$$[b] = \left[\frac{v}{t}\right] = [LT^{-2}]$$

$$[c] = [vt] = [L]$$

$$[d] = [T]$$

2. $\left(p + \dfrac{a}{V^2}\right)(V - b) = nRT$

$$[p] = \left[\frac{a}{V^2}\right] \Rightarrow [a] = [pV^2] = [ML^{-1}T^{-2}(L^3)^2] = [ML^5T^{-2}]$$

and $[V] = [b] \Rightarrow [b] = [L^3]$

3. $\alpha = \dfrac{F}{v^2}\sin(\beta t)$

$$[\beta t] = [M^0L^0T^0] \Rightarrow [\beta] = [T^{-1}]$$

and $\left[\dfrac{F}{v^2}\right] = [\alpha] \Rightarrow [\alpha] = \left[\dfrac{MLT^{-2}}{(LT^{-1})^2}\right] = [ML^{-1}T^0]$

4. $F = A\sin Ct + B\cos Dx$

$$[Ct] = [M^0L^0T^0] \Rightarrow [C] = [T^{-1}]$$

$$[Dx] = [M^0L^0T^0] \Rightarrow [D] = [L^{-1}]$$

$$[A] = [B] = [F] = [M\,L\,T^{-2}]$$

$$\left[\frac{A}{B}\right] = [M^0L^0T^0], \quad \left[\frac{C}{D}\right] = \left[\frac{T^{-1}}{L^{-1}}\right] = [LT^{-1}]$$

5. $U = k(1 - \cos\alpha x)$

$$[\alpha x] = [M^0L^0T^0] \Rightarrow [\alpha] = [L^{-1}]$$

$$[k] = [U] = [M\,L^2T^{-2}]$$

6. $x = \dfrac{v_0}{\alpha}(1 - e^{-\alpha t})$

$$[\alpha t] = [M^0L^0T^0] \Rightarrow [\alpha] = [T^{-1}]$$

$$\left[\frac{v_0}{\alpha}\right] = [x] \Rightarrow [v_0] = [\alpha\, x] = [LT^{-1}]$$

7. $\alpha = \dfrac{2ma}{\beta}\log\left(1 + \dfrac{2\beta l}{ma}\right)$

$$\left[\frac{2\beta l}{ma}\right] = [M^0L^0T^0]$$

$$\Rightarrow \left[\frac{ma}{\beta}\right] = [l] = [L] \text{ and } \left[\frac{2ma}{\beta}\right] = [\alpha] \Rightarrow [\alpha] = \left[\frac{ma}{\beta}\right] = [l] = [L]$$

3.2 To Verify Correctness of a Given Equation

1. $p_0 = \dfrac{3Fv^2}{\pi^2t^2x} \Rightarrow [p_0] = [ML^{-1}T^{-2}]$

$$\left[\frac{3Fv^2}{\pi^2t^2x}\right] = \left[\frac{[MLT^{-2}][LT^{-1}]^2}{T^2L}\right] = [ML^2T^{-6}]$$

So, this equation is dimensionally incorrect.

2. (i) $h = \dfrac{2S\cos\theta}{\rho g} \Rightarrow [h] = [L]$

$$\left[\frac{2S\cos\theta}{\rho g}\right] = \frac{[MT^{-2}]}{[ML^{-3}][LT^{-2}]} = [L^2]$$

It is dimensionally incorrect.

(ii) $v = \sqrt{\dfrac{p}{\rho}} \Rightarrow [v] = [LT^{-1}]$

$$\left[\sqrt{\frac{p}{\rho}}\right] = \sqrt{\frac{[ML^{-1}T^{-2}]}{[ML^{-3}]}} = [LT^{-1}]$$

It is dimensionally correct.

(iii) $V = \dfrac{\pi pr^4}{8\eta l} \Rightarrow [V] = [L^3]$

$$\left[\frac{\pi pr^4}{8\eta l}\right] = \frac{[ML^{-1}T^{-2}]\,[L^4]}{[ML^{-1}T^{-1}]\,[L]} = [L^3T^{-1}]$$

This equation is dimensionally incorrect.

(iv) $f = \dfrac{1}{2\pi}\sqrt{\dfrac{mgl}{I}} \Rightarrow [f] = [T^{-1}]$

$$\left[\frac{1}{2\pi}\sqrt{\frac{mgl}{I}}\right] = \sqrt{\frac{[M][LT^{-2}]\,[L]}{[ML^2]}} = [T^{-1}]$$

This equation is dimensionally correct.

3.3 To Convert a Physical Quantity From One System to Another

1. $[A] = [L^2] \Rightarrow nu = \text{constant} \Rightarrow n \propto \dfrac{1}{u}$

If unit of length is doubled, unit of area will become four times. So, numerical value of area will become one fourth.

2. $[F] = [MLT^{-2}]$

Unit of force will become $\dfrac{1}{2}(2)(2)^{-2} = \dfrac{1}{4}$ times.

So, numerical value will become four times.

So, new force will be 20 units.

3. $g = 980\ \text{cm/s}^2$

$$= 980\,(10^{-2} \times 10^{-3}\ \text{km}) \,/ \left(\frac{1}{60}\right)^2 \text{min}^2$$

$$= 980 \times 10^{-5} \times 3600\ \text{km/min}^2 = 35.28\ \text{km/min}^2$$

4. $1\text{ J} = 1\text{ kg-m}^2/\text{s}^2$
$= 1(10^{-20})$ star kg $(10^{-8})^2$ star $m^2/(10^{-3}$ star s$)^2$
$= 10^{-20} \times 10^{-16} \times 10^6$ (star kg) star m^2/star s^2
$= 10^{-30}$ (star kg) (star m)^2/(star s)$^2 = 10^{-30}$ star J

5. In new system,
1 ma = 1 unit of mass = 20 kg
1 le = 1 unit of length = 10 m
1 ti = 1 unit of time = 5 s
1 unit of power = 1 ma le^{2}ti^{-3} = $(20)\,(10)^2\,(5)^{-3} = 16$ W

3.4 To Find Dimensional Formula in Terms of New Fundamental Set of Quantities

1. Mass $= C^x G^y h^z$

$[M^1L^0T^0] = [(LT^{-1})^x (M^{-1}L^3T^{-2})^y (ML^2T^{-1})^z]$

$[M^1L^0T^0] = [M^{-y+z} L^{x+3y+2z} T^{-x-2y-z}]$

$\Rightarrow \quad -y + z = 1 \quad ...(i)$

$x + 3y + 2z = 0 \quad ...(ii)$

$-x - 2y - z = 0 \quad ...(iii)$

Solving Eqs. (i), (ii) and (iii), we get

$$x = \frac{1}{2}, y = -\frac{1}{2} \text{ and } z = \frac{1}{2}$$

So, [Mass] $= C^{1/2} G^{-1/2} h^{1/2}$

[Length] $= C^x G^y h^z$

$[M^0L^1T^0] = [M^{-y+z} L^{x+3y+2z} T^{-x-2y-z}]$

$\Rightarrow \quad -y + z = 0 \quad ...(i)$

$x + 3y + 2z = 1 \quad ...(ii)$

$-x - 2y - z = 0 \quad ...(iii)$

Solving Eqs. (i), (ii) and (iii), we get

$$x = -\frac{3}{2}, y = \frac{1}{2} \text{ and } z = \frac{1}{2}$$

So, [length] $= C^{-3/2} G^{1/2} h^{1/2}$

[Time] $= C^x G^y h^z$

$[M^0L^0T^1] = [M^{-y+z} L^{x+3y+2z} T^{-x-2y-z}]$

$-y + z = 0 \quad ...(i)$

$x + 3y + 2z = 0 \quad ...(ii)$

$-x - 2y - z = 1 \quad ...(iii)$

Solving Eqs. (i), (ii) and (iii), we get

$$x = -\frac{5}{2}, y = \frac{1}{2} \text{ and } z = \frac{1}{2}$$

So, [time] $= C^{-5/2} G^{1/2} h^{1/2}$

2. Since, pressure can be expressed in terms of density and velocity, they cannot be taken as fundamental quantities.

3. Energy $\propto v^a F^b T^c$

Energy $= k\, v^a F^b T^c$

[Energy] $= [v^a F^b T^c]$

$[ML^2T^{-2}] = [LT^{-1}]^a\, [MLT^{-2}]^b\, [T]^c$

$[ML^2T^{-2}] = [M^b L^{a+b}\, T^{-a-2b+c}]$

$\Rightarrow \quad b = 1 \quad ...(i)$

$\Rightarrow \quad a + b = 2 \quad ...(ii)$

$-a - 2b + c = -2 \quad ...(iii)$

Solving Eqs. (i), (ii) and (iii), we get

$$a = 1, b = 1 \text{ and } c = 1$$

So, [energy] $= k\,vFT$

4. $[Y] = v^x\, a^y\, F^z$

$[ML^{-1}T^{-2}] = [LT^{-1}]^x\, [LT^{-2}]^y [MLT^{-2}]^z$

$[ML^{-1}T^{-2}] = [M^z L^{x+y+z} T^{-x-2y-2z}]$

$\Rightarrow \quad z = 1 \quad ...(i)$

$x + y + z = -1 \quad ...(ii)$

$-x - 2y - 2z = -2 \quad ...(iii)$

Solving Eqs. (i), (ii) and (iii), we get

$$x = -4, y = 2 \text{ and } z = 1$$

So, $[Y] = v^{-4} a^2 F$

5. [Surface tension] $= E^x \rho^y T^z$

$[MT^{-2}] = [ML^2T^{-2}]^x\, [ML^{-3}]^y\, [T]^z$

$[M^1L^0T^{-2}] = [M^{x+y}\, L^{2x-3y}\, T^{-2x+z}]$

$\Rightarrow \quad x + y = 1 \quad ...(i)$

$2x - 3y = 0 \quad ...(ii)$

$-2x + z = -2 \quad ...(iii)$

Solving Eqs. (i), (ii) and (iii), we get

$$x = \frac{3}{5}, y = \frac{2}{5} \text{ and } z = -\frac{4}{5}$$

[Surface tension] $= E^{3/5} \rho^{2/5}\, T^{-4/5}$

3.5 To Derive New Relations

1. $v = k\,\lambda^a\, \rho^b\, T^c$

$[v] = [\lambda^a\, \rho^b\, T^c] \Rightarrow [LT^{-1}] = [L]^a [ML^{-3}]^b\, [MT^{-2}]^c$

$[M^0L^1T^{-1}] = [M^{b+c}\, L^{a-3b}\, T^{-2c}]$

$\Rightarrow \quad b + c = 0 \quad ...(i)$

$\Rightarrow \quad a - 3b = 1 \quad ...(ii)$

$\Rightarrow \quad -2c = -1 \quad ...(iii)$

Solving Eqs. (i), (ii) and (iii), we get

$$c = \frac{1}{2}, b = -\frac{1}{2} \text{ and } a = -\frac{1}{2}$$

So, $v \propto \lambda^{-1/2}\, \rho^{-1/2}\, T^{1/2} \Rightarrow v^2 \propto \dfrac{T}{\lambda\rho}$

2. $m \propto v^a\, \rho^b\, g^c$

$[m] = [v^a \rho^b g^c]$

$[M^1L^0T^0] = [LT^{-1}]^a\, [ML^{-3}]^b\, [LT^{-2}]^c$

$[M^1L^0T^0] = [M^b\, L^{a-3b+c}\, T^{-a-2c}]$

$\Rightarrow \quad b = 1 \quad ...(i)$

$a - 3b + c = 0 \quad ...(ii)$

$-a - 2c = 0 \quad ...(iii)$

Solving Eqs. (i), (ii) and (iii), we get

$$a = 6, b = 1 \text{ and } c = -3$$

$$\therefore \quad m \propto \frac{v^6 \rho}{g^3}$$

3. $v \propto d^a \rho^b \eta^c$

$$[v] = [d^a \rho^b \eta^c]$$

$$[M^0L^1T^{-1}] = [L]^a [ML^{-3}]^b [ML^{-1}T^{-1}]^c$$

$$[M^0L^1T^{-1}] = [M^{b+c}L^{a-3b+c}T^{-c}]$$

$\Rightarrow \quad b + c = 0$ ...(i)

$a - 3b + c = 1$ ...(ii)

$-c = -1$ ...(iii)

Solving Eqs. (i), (ii) and (iii), we get

$$c = 1, b = -1 \text{ and } a = -3$$

$$v \propto d^{-3}\rho^{-1}\eta$$

4. $T \propto r^a M^b G^c$

$$[T] = [r^a M^b G^c]$$

$$[M^0L^0T^1] = [L]^a [M]^b [M^{-1}L^3T^{-2}]^c$$

$$[M^0L^0T^1] = [M^{b-c}L^{a+3c}T^{-2c}]$$

$b - c = 0$ ...(i)

$a + 3c = 0$ ...(ii)

$-2c = 1$ ...(iii)

Solving Eqs. (i), (ii) and (iii), we get

$$c = -\frac{1}{2}, b = -\frac{1}{2} \text{ and } a = \frac{3}{2}$$

So, $T \propto r^{\frac{3}{2}} M^{-\frac{1}{2}} G^{-\frac{1}{2}}$

$$T \propto \left(\frac{r^3}{GM}\right)^{\frac{1}{2}} \Rightarrow T \propto \sqrt{\frac{r^3}{GM}} \Rightarrow T = k\sqrt{\frac{r^3}{GM}}$$

5. $P \propto h^a c^b d^c$

$$\left[\frac{MLT^{-2}}{L^2}\right] = [ML^2T^{-1}]^a [LT^{-1}]^b [L]^c$$

$$[ML^{-1}T^{-2}] = [M^aL^{a+b+c}T^{-a-b}]$$

$a - 1$ ...(i)

$a + b + c = -1$ ...(ii)

$-a - b = -2$ ...(iii)

Solving Eqs. (i), (ii) and (iii), we get

$$a = 1, b = 1 \text{ and } c = -3$$

So, $P \propto hcd^{-3} \Rightarrow P = \dfrac{khc}{d^3}$

Level 2

Single Choice Correct Questions

1. $[F] = a^x \rho^y f^z$

$$[MLT^{-2}] = [LT^{-2}]^x [ML^{-3}]^y [T^{-1}]^z$$

$$[MLT^{-2}] = [M^yL^{x-3y}T^{-2x-z}]$$

$y = 1$ ...(i)

$x - 3y = 1$ ...(ii)

$-2x - z = -2$ ...(iii)

Solving Eqs. (i), (ii) and (iii), we get

$$x = 4, y = 1 \text{ and } z = -6$$

So, $[F] = [\rho a^4 f^{-6}]$

2. A dimensionless quantity may have a unit. e.g., angle which is dimensionless has a unit radian.

3. Unitless quantity is always dimensionless.

4. (A) [Impulse] = [Linear momentum] = $[MLT^{-1}]$

(B) [Planck's constant] = [Angular momentum = $[ML^2T^{-1}]$

(C) [Moment of inertia] = $[ML^2]$

[Moment of force] = $[ML^2T^{-2}]$

(D) [Young's modulus]= [Pressure] = $[ML^{-1}T^{-2}]$

5. $v \propto \lambda^a \rho^b g^c \Rightarrow [v] = [\lambda^a \rho^b g^c]$

$$[LT^{-1}] = [L]^a [ML^{-3}]^b [LT^{-2}]^c$$

$$[M^0L^1T^{-1}] = [M^bL^{a-3b+c}T^{-2c}]$$

$\Rightarrow \quad b = 0$ ...(i)

$\Rightarrow \quad a - 3b + c = 1$ ...(ii)

$\Rightarrow \quad -2c = -1$ ...(iii)

Solving Eqs. (i), (ii) and (iii), we get

$$a = \frac{1}{2}, b = 0, c = \frac{1}{2}$$

$$v \propto \lambda^{\frac{1}{2}} \rho^0 g^{\frac{1}{2}}$$

$$v^2 \propto \lambda g \Rightarrow v^2 = k\lambda g$$

6. $G = 6.67 \times 10^{-11}$ N-m^2/kg^2

$= 6.67 \times 10^{-11} \times (10^5 \text{ dyne}) (100 \text{ cm})^2/(1000 \text{ gm})^2$

$= 6.67 \times 10^{-8}$

7. $F \propto \rho^a v^b A^c$

$$[F] = [ML^{-3}]^a [LT^{-1}]^b [L^2]^c$$

$$[MLT^{-2}] = [M^aL^{-3a+b+2c}T^{-b}]$$

$\Rightarrow \quad a = 1$ ...(i)

$-3a + b + 2c = 1$ ...(ii)

$-b = -2$ ...(iii)

Solving Eqs. (i), (ii) and (iii), we get

$$a = 1, b = 2, c = 1$$

$$[F] = \rho A v^2$$

8. $n_1 u_1 = n_2 u_2$

$$[g] = [LT^{-2}]$$

If length is doubled and time is doubled, then unit will become half. So, numerical value will get doubled.

9. $F = Av + Bt + \dfrac{Cx}{At + D}$

$$[Av] = [F] \Rightarrow [A] = \left[\frac{F}{v}\right] = [MT^{-1}]$$

$$[At] = [MT^{-1}][T] = [M]$$

$$[F] = \left[\frac{Cx}{At}\right] \Rightarrow [C] = \left[\frac{FAt}{x}\right] = \frac{[MLT^{-2}][M]}{[L]} = [M^2L^0T^{-2}]$$

10. $v = at + \dfrac{b}{t+c}$

$[t] = [c] \Rightarrow [c] = [M^0L^0T^1]$

$[at] = [v] \Rightarrow [a] = \left[\dfrac{v}{t}\right] = [LT^{-2}]$

$\left[\dfrac{b}{t}\right] = [v] \Rightarrow [b] = [vt] = [L]$

11. Momentum $= \dfrac{F}{t} = \dfrac{F}{l/v} = \dfrac{Fv}{l}$

If F, v and l are doubled, then unit of momentum will also get doubled.

12. A dimensionally correct equation may or may not be correct but a dimensionally incorrect equation is certainly incorrect.

13. $U = \dfrac{A\sqrt{x}}{B + x^2}$

$[B] = [x^2] = [L^2]$

$\left[\dfrac{A\sqrt{x}}{x^2}\right] = [U] \Rightarrow [A] = [Ux^{3/2}]$

$[A] = [ML^{7/2}T^{-2}]$

$[AB] = [ML^{7/2}T^{-2}][L^2] = [ML^{11/2}T^{-2}]$

14. (d)

15. In new system; 1 ma $= a$ kg

1 le $= b$ m

1 ti $= g$ s

1 cal $= 4.2$ J $= 4.2$ kgm^2/s^2

$= 4.2\left(\dfrac{1}{a}\right)\text{ma}\left(\dfrac{1}{b}\right)^2 \text{le}^2 / \left(\dfrac{1}{g}\right)^2 \text{ti}^2$

$= 4.2\, a^{-1}b^{-2}g^2$ ma-le^2/ti^2

16. 1 ma = 10 gm, 1 le = 10 cm, 1 ti = 0.1 s

1 unit of force = 1 ma-le/ti^2

$= (10 \text{ gm}) (10 \text{ cm})/(0.1 \text{ s})^2$

$= 10^4$ gm-cm/s^2

$= 10^4$ dyne $= 0.1$ N

17. $p = p_0 e^{-\alpha t^2}$

Powers are dimensionless.

So, $[\alpha t^2] = [M^0L^0T^0] \Rightarrow [\alpha] = [T^{-2}]$

18. [Tension] $= [MLT^{-2}]$

[Surface tension] $= [MT^{-2}]$

19. According to principle of homogeneity of dimensions, only quantities with same dimensions can be added, subtracted or compared.

20. [Length] $= F^x A^y T^z$

$[L] = [MLT^{-2}]^x [LT^{-2}]^y [T]^z$

$[L] = [M^x L^{x+y} T^{-2x-2y+z}]$

$\Rightarrow \qquad x = 0 \qquad$ ...(i)

$x + y = 1 \qquad$ ...(ii)

$-2x - 2y + z = 0 \qquad$ ...(iii)

Solving Eqs. (i), (ii) and (iii), we get

$x = 0, y = 1$ and $z = 2$

So, [length] $= F^0A^1T^2$

21. (d)

22. $[a] = [t^2] = [T^2]$ and $\left[\dfrac{t^2}{bx}\right] = [p]$

$\Rightarrow [b] = \left[\dfrac{t^2}{px}\right] \Rightarrow [b] = \left[\dfrac{T^2}{ML^{-1}T^{-2}L}\right] = [M^{-1}T^4]$

So, $\left[\dfrac{a}{b}\right] = \left[\dfrac{T^2}{M^{-1}T^4}\right] = [MT^{-2}]$

23. $\left[\dfrac{EL^2}{m^5G^2}\right] = \left[\dfrac{ML^2T^{-2}(ML^2T^{-1})^2}{M^5(M^{-1}L^3T^{-2})^2}\right] = [M^0L^0T^0]$

[Angle] $= [M^0L^0T^0]$

24. Force, mass and velocity as none of them can be expressed in terms of the other two quantities.

25. $\left[\dfrac{\alpha}{t^2}\right] = \left[\dfrac{\beta}{x^2}\right] \Rightarrow \left[\dfrac{\alpha}{\beta}\right] = \left[\dfrac{t^2}{x^2}\right] = [M^0L^{-2}T^2]$

26. $g = 10$ m/s^2

$= 10\,(10^{-3} \text{ km})/\left(\dfrac{1}{3600}\text{h}\right)^2 = 129600$ km/h^2

27. 1 MW $= 10^6$ W $= 10^6$ kg-m^2/s^3

$= 10^6 \left(\dfrac{1}{10}\right)\text{Ma}\,(10)^2\text{Le}^2 / \left(\dfrac{1}{60}\right)^3 \text{Ti}^3$

$= 2.16 \times 10^{12}$ u

28. $[G] = c^a g^b p^c$

$[M^{-1}L^3T^{-2}] = [LT^{-1}]^a [LT^{-2}]^b [ML^{-1}T^{-2}]^c$

$[M^{-1}L^3T^{-2}] = [M^cL^{a+b-c}T^{-a-2b-2c}]$

$c = -1 \qquad$ ...(i)

$a + b - c = 3 \qquad$ ...(ii)

$-a - 2b - 2c = -2 \qquad$ ...(iii)

Solving Eqs. (i), (ii) and (iii), we get

$a = 0, b = 2, c = -1$

$[G] = [c^0 g^2 p^{-1}]$

29. (a)

30. $\left[\dfrac{d}{dt}\int \mathbf{F}\cdot ds)\right] = [A(\mathbf{F}\cdot\mathbf{p}]$

$\left[\dfrac{Fs}{t}\right] = [AFp] \Rightarrow [A] = \left[\dfrac{s}{pt}\right] = \left[\dfrac{L}{MLT^{-1}T}\right] = [M^{-1}L^0T^0]$

31. $[bt] = [M^0L^0T^0]$

$[b] = [T^{-1}] =$ [Frequency]

32. $\left[\frac{b}{c}\right]=\left[\frac{T^{-1}}{L^{-1}}\right]=[LT^{-1}]=[\text{Velocity}]$

33. $a_1=a_2 \quad\Rightarrow\quad [L_1T_1^{-2}]=[L_2T_2^{-2}]$ ...(i)

$v_1=\frac{v_2}{3} \quad\Rightarrow\quad [L_1T_1^{-1}]=\frac{[L_2T_2^{-1}]}{3}$ ...(ii)

From Eqs. (i) and (ii), we get

$\Rightarrow \quad \frac{T_1}{T_2}=\frac{1}{3}$ and $\frac{L_1}{L_2}=\frac{1}{9}$

34. 1 eluoj = 1 Ma-Le^2/Ti^2

$=1\,(100\text{ kg})\,(10^3\text{ m})^2/(100\text{ s})^2$

$=10^4\text{ kg-m}^2/\text{s}^2=10^4$ joule

35. $F=\frac{Gm_1m_2}{r^2}$

$1\text{ notwen}=\frac{(6.67\times10^{-11}\text{ Nm}^2/\text{kg}^2)\,(1\text{ kg})\,(1\text{ kg})}{(1000\text{ m})^2}$

1 notwen = 6.67×10^{-17} newton

36. $[A]=[ax] \quad\Rightarrow\quad [a]=\left[\frac{A}{x}\right]$

$[a]=\left[\frac{L^2T^{-1}}{L}\right]=[LT^{-1}] \quad\Rightarrow\quad \left[\frac{at}{b}\right]=[M^0L^0T^0]$

$[b]=[at]=[LT^{-1}T]=[L]$

37. $\left(p+\frac{aT^2}{V}\right)V^m=RT+b \quad\Rightarrow\quad p+\frac{aT^2}{V}=(RT+b)V^{-c}$

$\Rightarrow\quad p=(RT+b)V^{-c}-aT^2V^{-1} \quad\Rightarrow\quad m=-c$ and $n=-1$

38. (d)

39. (b)

40. Only (c) is dimensionally correct.

41. $N=-D\frac{n_2-n_1}{x_2-x_1}$

$[N]=\left[\frac{Dn}{x}\right]$

$[D]=\left[\frac{Nx}{n}\right]=\left[\frac{\frac{1}{AT}x}{\frac{1}{V}}\right]=\left[\frac{\frac{1}{[L^2T]}\,[L]}{\left[\frac{1}{[L^3]}\right]}\right]=[L^2T^{-1}]$

42. $\left[2\pi\sqrt{\frac{M}{\eta L}}\right]=\left[\sqrt{\frac{[M]}{[ML^{-1}T^{-1}L]}}\right]=[T]$

Only option (d) has dimension of time-period.

Multiple Choice(s) Correct Questions

1. (b) Since, pressure can be expressed in terms of density and velocity as

pressure $\propto$ (density) (velocity)^2.

(d) Since, force can be expressed in terms of momentum and time as

force $\propto \frac{\text{momentum}}{\text{time}}$.

2. (a,c,d)

3. $[p]=\left[\frac{n^2a}{V^2}\right]$ and $[V]=[nb]$ and $[pV]=[nRT]$

4. $\left[\frac{bt}{2m}\right]=[M^0L^0T^0]$ as powers are dimensionless.

$\Rightarrow \quad \left[\frac{m}{b}\right]=[t]$

$[\omega t]=[M^0L^0T^0]$ as angle is dimensionless.

$\Rightarrow \quad [\omega]=[T^{-1}]$

$[a_0\omega]=[LT^{-1}]$

5. 1 Ma = 20 kg

1 Le = 10 m

1 Ti = 5 s

$[\text{Power}]=[ML^2T^{-3}]$

(a) Unit of power = 1 Ma-Le^2/Ti^3

$=(20\text{ kg})\,(10\text{ m})^2/(5\text{ s})^3$

$=8\text{ kg m}^2/\text{s}^3=8\text{ W}$

(b) Unit of force = 1 Ma-Le/Ti^2

$=(20\text{ kg})\,(10\text{ m})/(5\text{ s})^2$

$=8\text{ kg-m/s}^2=8\text{ N}$

(c) Unit of velocity = Le/Ti = (10 m)/ 5 s = 2 m/s

(d) Unit of energy = 1 Ma-Le^2/Ti^2

$=(20\text{ kg})\,(10\text{ m})^2/(5\text{ s})^2$

$=80\text{ kg-m}^2/\text{s}^2=80\text{ J}$

6. $\left[\sin^{-1}\left(\frac{x}{b}-1\right)\right]=[M^0L^0T^0]$

$\left[\frac{x}{b}\right]=[M^0L^0T^0]$

$[y]=[a^3] \quad\Rightarrow\quad [a]=[y^{1/3}]=[M^0L^{1/3}T^0]$

7. $v=\sqrt{AB}+Bt+\frac{C}{D+t}$

$[v]=[\sqrt{AB}]=[Bt]=\left[\frac{C}{D}\right]$ and $[D]=[t]$

$[D]=[M^0L^0T^1]$

$[C]=[vD]=[vt]=[L]$

$[B]=\left[\frac{v}{t}\right]=[LT^{-2}]$

$[A]=\left[\frac{v^2}{B}\right]=\frac{[L^2T^{-2}]}{[LT^{-2}]}=[L]$

8. $[p]=[A]=[B]=[ML^{-1}T^{-2}]$

and $\quad [bt]=[Ct]=[M^0L^0T^0]$

9. $[A]=\left[\frac{B}{C^2}\right]$ and $[D]=[x]$ and $[AD]=[y]$

10. (a) $m=\frac{F}{a} \Rightarrow \frac{m_2}{m_1}=\frac{\frac{F_2}{a_2}}{\frac{F_1}{a_1}} \Rightarrow \frac{m_2}{m_1}=\frac{1}{\alpha^2\beta^2}$

(b) $L=\frac{v^2}{a} \Rightarrow \frac{L_2}{L_1}=\frac{\alpha^3}{\beta^3}$

(c) $T=\frac{v}{a} \Rightarrow \frac{T_2}{T_1}=\frac{\alpha}{\beta^2}$

(d) $p=mv \Rightarrow \frac{p_2}{p_1}=\frac{1}{\beta^3}$

Comprehension Based Questions

1. $[X]=[YF]=[ZW]$

and $[\beta r^2]=[M^0L^0T^0] \Rightarrow [\beta]=[L^{-2}]$

and $[\alpha r]=[M^0L^0T^0] \Rightarrow [\alpha]=[L^{-1}]$

$$\left[\frac{\alpha YZ}{\beta F}\right]=\left[\frac{L^{-1}L\left(\frac{YF}{W}\right)}{L^{-2}F}\right]=\left[\frac{L^2L}{ML^2T^{-2}}\right]=[M^{-1}LT^2]$$

2. $[X]=[YF] \Rightarrow [X]=[LT^{-1}MLT^{-2}]=[ML^2T^{-3}]$

3. $[YF]=[ZW] \Rightarrow [Y]=\left[\frac{ZW}{F}\right]=\left[\frac{T^{-1}ML^2T^{-2}}{MLT^{-2}}\right]=[M^0LT^{-1}]$

4, 5 and 6

$g=9.8\ \text{m/s}^2=3\ \text{Le/Ti}^2$ ...(i)

$K=\frac{1}{2}(272.1)\ \text{kg}\ (448\ \text{m/s})^2=100\ \text{Ma Le}^2/\text{Ti}^2$ ...(ii)

$p=(272.1\ \text{kg})\ (448\ \text{m/s})=10\ \text{Ma Le/Ti}$ ...(iii)

From Eqs. (ii) and (iii), we get

$\frac{K}{p}=\frac{1}{2}\times 448\ \text{m/s}=10\ \text{Le/Ti}$

$v=224\ \text{m/s}=10\ \text{Le/Ti}$ ...(iv)

From Eqs. (iv) and (i)

$\Rightarrow \frac{v}{g}=\frac{224\ \text{m/s}}{9.8\ \text{m/s}^2}=\frac{10}{3}\text{Ti} \Rightarrow 1\ \text{Ti}=\frac{224\times 3}{9.8}=6.857\ \text{s}$

$\text{Length}=\frac{v^2}{g}=\frac{(224\ \text{m/s})^2}{9.8\ \text{m/s}^2}=\frac{(10\ \text{Le/Ti})^2}{3\ \text{Le/Ti}^2}$

$\Rightarrow 1\ \text{Le}=\frac{(224)^2\times 3}{980}=153.6\ \text{m}$

$\text{Mass}=\frac{p}{v}=\frac{(272.1\ \text{kg})\ (448\ \text{m/s})}{224\ \text{m/s}}=\frac{10\ \text{Ma Le/Ti}}{10\ \text{Le/Ti}}$

$1\ \text{Ma}=544.2\ \text{kg}$

7, 8 and 9

$v=kp^xd^y \Rightarrow [v]=[p^xd^y]$

$[LT^{-1}]=[ML^{-1}T^{-2}]^x\ [ML^{-3}]^y$

$[M^0L^1T^{-1}]=[M^{x+y}L^{-x-3y}T^{-2x}]$

$\Rightarrow x+y=0$ ...(i)

$-x-3y=1$ ...(ii)

$-2x=-1$ ...(iii)

Solving Eqs. (i), (ii) and (iii), we get

$x=\frac{1}{2}$ and $y=-\frac{1}{2}$

10. $[G]=[M^{-1}L^3T^{-2}]$

11. $[p]=\rho^aL^bG^c$

$[ML^{-1}T^{-2}]=[ML^{-3}]^a\ [L]^b\ [M^{-1}L^3T^{-2}]^c$

$[ML^{-1}T^{-2}]=[M^{a-c}L^{-3a+b+3c}T^{-2c}]$

$\Rightarrow a-c=1$ ...(i)

$-3a+b+3c=-1$ ...(ii)

$-2c=-2$ ...(iii)

Solving Eqs. (i), (ii) and (iii), we get

$c=1, a=2$ and $b=2$

So, $[p]=\rho^2L^2G$

12. $[v]=\rho^aL^bG^c$

$[M^0L^1T^{-1}]=[M^{a-c}L^{-3a+b+3c}T^{-2c}]$

$\Rightarrow a-c=0$ ...(i)

$-3a+b+3c=1$ ...(ii)

$-2c=-1$ ...(iii)

Solving Eqs. (i), (ii) and (iii), we get

$a=\frac{1}{2}, b=1$ and $c=\frac{1}{2}$

So, $[v]=L\sqrt{G\rho}$

13, 14 and 15

$\gamma=k\left(\frac{m}{p}\right)^xA^yT^z \Rightarrow [\gamma]=\left[\frac{M}{ML^{-1}T^{-2}}\right]^x[L^2]^y\ [T]^z$

$[M^0L^0T^0]=[L^{x+2y}T^{2x+z}]$

$\Rightarrow x+2y=0$ ...(i)

$2x+z=0$ ...(ii)

We have three variables and two equations.

So, we cannot find value of x, y and z.

Match the Columns Questions

1. $[\text{Acceleration}]=[LT^{-2}]$

(A) 1 unit of acceleration = 1 alpha/(gamma)^2

$=10^3\ \text{m}/(60\ \text{s})^2=\frac{5}{18}\text{m/s}^2$

(B) 1 unit of KE = 1 beta (alpha)^2/(gamma)^2

$=100\ \text{kg}\ (10^3\ \text{m})^2/(60\ \text{s})^2$

$=\frac{5}{18}\times 10^5\ \text{kg-m}^2/\text{s}^2$

(C) 1 unit of pressure = 1 beta/alpha-(gamma)^2

$=\frac{100\ \text{kg}}{10^3\ \text{m}-(60\ \text{s})^2}=\frac{5}{18}\times 10^{-4}\ \text{kg/m-s}^2$

(D) 1 unit of work = beta (alpha)^2/(gamma)^2

$$= 100\text{ kg } (10^3\text{ m})^2/(60\text{ s})^2$$

$$= \frac{5}{18} \times 10^5\text{ kg-m}^2/\text{s}^2$$

2. (A) $[\text{Mass}] = [F^a v^b E^c]$

$$[M^1L^0T^0] = [MLT^{-2}]^a [LT^{-1}]^b [ML^2T^{-2}]^c$$

$$[M^1L^0T^0] = [M^{a+c}L^{a+b+2c}T^{-2a-b-2c}]$$

$\Rightarrow \quad a + c = 1 \quad$ ...(i)

$a + b + 2c = 0 \quad$ ...(ii)

$-2a - b - 2c = 0 \quad$ ...(iii)

Solving Eqs. (i), (ii) and (iii), we get

$a = 0, b = -2$ and $c = 1$

So, $[\text{mass}] = F^0 v^{-2} E^1$

(B) $[\text{Light year}] = F^a v^b E^c$

$$[M^0L^1T^0] = [M^{a+c}L^{a+b+2c}T^{-2a-b-2c}]$$

$\Rightarrow \quad a + c = 0 \quad$ ...(i)

$a + b + 2c = 1 \quad$ ...(ii)

$-2a - b - 2c = 0 \quad$ ...(iii)

Solving Eqs. (i), (ii) and (iii), we get

$\Rightarrow \quad a = -1, b = 0$ and $c = 1$

So, $[\text{light year}] = F^{-1} v^0 E^1$

(C) $[\text{Frequency}] = [F^a v^b E^c]$

$$[M^0L^0T^{-1}] = M^{a+c}L^{a+b+2c}T^{-2a-b-2c}$$

$\Rightarrow \quad a + c = 0 \quad$ ...(i)

$a + b + 2c = 0 \quad$ ...(ii)

$-2a - b - 2c = 0 \quad$ ...(iii)

Solving Eqs. (i), (ii) and (iii), we get

$a = 1, b = 1$ and $c = -1$

So, $[\text{frequency}] = F^1 v^1 E^{-1}$

(D) $[\text{Pressure}] = F^a v^b E^c$

$$[ML^{-1}T^{-2}] = [M^{a+c}L^{a+b+2c}T^{-2a-b-2c}]$$

$\Rightarrow \quad a + c = 1 \quad$ ...(i)

$a + b + 2c = -1 \quad$ ...(ii)

$-2a - b - 2c = -2 \quad$ ...(iii)

Solving Eqs. (i), (ii) and (iii), we get

$a = 3, b = 0$ and $c = -2$

So, $[\text{pressure}] = F^3 v^0 E^{-2}$

Numerical Value Questions

1. $T \propto p^a d^b E^c \quad \Rightarrow \quad [T] = [p^a d^b E^c]$

$\Rightarrow \quad [M^0L^0T^1] = [ML^{-1}T^{-2}]^a [ML^{-3}]^b [ML^2T^{-2}]^c$

$\Rightarrow \quad [M^0L^0T^1] = [M^{a+b+c}L^{-a-3b+2c}T^{-2a-2c}]$

$\Rightarrow \quad a + b + c = 0 \quad$ ...(i)

$-a - 3b + 2c = 0 \quad$ ...(ii)

$-2a - 2c = 1 \quad$ ...(iii)

Solving Eqs. (i), (ii) and (iii), we get

$$a = -\frac{5}{6}, b = \frac{1}{2} \text{ and } c = \frac{1}{3} \quad \Rightarrow \quad \frac{6a^2}{b+c} = \frac{6\left(-\frac{5}{6}\right)^2}{\frac{1}{2}+\frac{1}{3}} = 5$$

2. $E^n = p^2c^2 + m_0^2c^4 \quad \Rightarrow [E^n] = [p^2c^2] = [m_0^2c^4]$

$\Rightarrow \quad [ML^2T^{-2}]^n = [M]^2[LT^{-1}]^4$

$\Rightarrow \quad [ML^2T^{-2}]^n = [ML^2T^{-2}]^2 \Rightarrow n = 2$

3. $\text{Power} \propto l^x d^y \left(\frac{w}{V}\right)^z$

$$\Rightarrow \quad [\text{Power}] = \left[l^x d^y \left(\frac{w}{V}\right)^z\right]$$

$$\Rightarrow \quad [ML^2T^{-3}] = [L]^x[ML^{-3}]^y \left[\frac{MLT^{-2}}{L^3}\right]^z$$

$$\Rightarrow \quad [ML^2T^{-3}] = [M^{y+z}L^{x-3y-2z}T^{-2z}]$$

$\Rightarrow \quad y + z = 1 \quad$ ...(i)

$\Rightarrow \quad x - 3y - 2z = 2 \quad$ ...(ii)

$\Rightarrow \quad -2z = -3 \quad$ ...(iii)

Solving Eqs. (i), (ii) and (iii), we get

$z = \frac{3}{2}, y = -\frac{1}{2}$ and $x = \frac{7}{2} \quad \Rightarrow$

$$x + 2y + z = \frac{7}{2} + 2\left(-\frac{1}{2}\right) + \frac{3}{2} = 4$$

4. $\left[\left(\frac{1}{a}\right)^2\right] = [x^2]$ and $[a^n] = \left[\frac{x}{x^2}\right]$

$\Rightarrow \quad [a] = [L^{-1}]$ and $[a^n] = [L^{-1}]$

So, $n = 1$

5. $[\text{Planck's constant}] = [ML^2T^{-1}]$

Unit of Planck's constant will become $(2)^1 \times (4)^2 \times (4)^{-1} = 8$ times

6. 1 unit of mass = 1 Ma = 100 gm

1 unit of length = 1 Le = 4 m

1 unit of time = 1 Ti = 2 s

$$10\text{ J} = 10\text{ kg-m}^2/\text{s}^2 = 10\,(10\text{ Ma})\left(\frac{1}{4}\text{ Le}\right)^2/\left(\frac{\text{Ti}}{2}\right)^2$$

$$= 100 \times \frac{1}{16} \times 4\text{ Ma-Le}^2/\text{Ti}^2 = 25\text{ Ma Le}^2/\text{Ti}^2$$

7. $[G] = c^x g^y p^z$

$$[M^{-1}L^3T^{-2}] = [LT^{-1}]^x [LT^{-2}]^y [ML^{-1}T^{-2}]^z$$

$$[M^{-1}L^3T^{-2}] = [M^zL^{x+y-z}T^{-x-2y-2z}]$$

$\Rightarrow \quad z = -1 \quad$ ...(i)

$x + y - z = 3 \quad$ ...(ii)

$-x - 2y - 2z = -2 \quad$ ...(iii)

Solving Eqs. (i), (ii) and (iii), we get

$x = 0, y = 2, z = -1$

So, $\quad y = 2$

8. $V = kG^x c^y h^z$

$[V] = [G^x c^y h^z]$

$[L^3] = [M^{-1}L^3T^{-2}]^x[LT^{-1}]^y[ML^2T^{-1}]^z$

$[L^3] = [M^{-x+z}L^{3x+y+2z}T^{-2x-y-z}]$

$\Rightarrow \quad -x + z = 0 \quad ...(i)$

$3x + y + 2z = 3 \quad ...(ii)$

$-2x - y - z = 0 \quad ...(iii)$

Solving Eqs. (i), (ii) and (iii), we get

$$x = \frac{3}{2}, y = -\frac{9}{2} \text{ and } z = \frac{3}{2}$$

So, $x - 2y + z = 12$

9. $1\text{ W} = 1\text{ kg-m}^2/\text{s}^3$

$$= \frac{(10^{-20}\text{ star kilogram})(10^{-8}\text{ star metre})^2}{(10^{-3}\text{ star second})^3}$$

$$= 10^{-27}\frac{\text{star kilogram (star metre)}^2}{(\text{star second})^3} \Rightarrow n = 27$$

10. Speed of light in vacuum $= 3 \times 10^8$ m/s

Acceleration due to gravity $= 10\text{ m/s}^2$

$$\frac{v^2}{a} = \frac{(3\times10^8\text{ m/s})^2}{10\text{ m/s}^2} = \frac{90000\text{ Le}^2/\text{Ti}^2}{1\text{ Le/Ti}^2}$$

1 unit of length $= 1\text{ Le} = 10^{11}$ m

Distance between sun and earth $= (3\times10^8\text{ m/s})(500\text{ s})$

$$= 3\times10^8\times500\text{ m}$$

$$= 3\times10^8\times500\left(\frac{\text{Le}}{10^{11}}\right) = 1.5\text{ Le}$$

Previous Year's Questions

JEE Main

1. Angular momentum of an electron in Bohr's atom is,

$$L = \frac{nh}{2\pi}$$

As n = a whole number, 2π = constant

$\therefore \quad [L] = [h]$

Statement I is true

Linear momentum

$$p = mv \Rightarrow [p] = [\text{MLT}^{-1}]$$

moment of force,

$$\tau = F\cdot d \Rightarrow [\tau] = [\text{ML}^2\text{T}^{-2}]$$

$\therefore \quad [p] \neq [\tau]$

Statement II is false.

2. $\left(p - \frac{a}{V^2}\right)(V - b) = RT$

As $[V] = [b]$

$\therefore \quad [b] = [L^3]$ and $[p] = \frac{[a]}{[V^2]}$

$\Rightarrow \quad [a] = [V^2][p] = [\text{ML}^{-1}\text{T}^{-2}][\text{L}^6] = [\text{ML}^5\text{T}^{-2}]$

$\therefore$ Dimension of $\left[\frac{a}{b^2}\right] = \frac{[\text{ML}^5\text{T}^{-2}]}{[\text{L}^3]^2} = \frac{[\text{ML}^5\text{T}^{-2}]}{[\text{L}^6]}$

$= [\text{ML}^5\text{T}^{-2}][\text{L}^{-6}]$

$= [\text{ML}^{-1}\text{T}^{-2}] = [p]$

3.

Term	SI unit	Dimension
Coefficient of viscosity	N.s m^{-2}	$\text{ML}^{-1}\text{T}^{-1}$
Surface tension	Nm^{-1}	ML^0T^{-2}
Angular momentum	$\text{kg m}^2\text{s}^{-1}$	ML^2T^{-1}
Rotational kinetic energy	(J) or $\text{kg m}^2\text{s}^{-2}$	ML^2T^{-2}

Therefore, the correct match is

A-III, B-IV, C-II, D-I

4. Given,

$$m = k\,c^p\cdot G^{-1/2}\cdot h^{1/2}$$

Substituting dimensions of different quantities on both sides we get,

$$[M] = [L^pT^{-p}][M^{-1}L^3T^{-2}]^{\frac{-1}{2}}[ML^2T^{-1}]^{1/2}$$

$$\Rightarrow \quad [M] = M\left(L^{p-\frac{1}{2}}\right)\cdot\left(T^{\frac{1}{2}-x}\right)$$

Equating dimensions of length on both sides, we get

$$p - \frac{1}{2} = 0 \text{ or } p = \frac{1}{2}$$

5. $\left[x + \frac{a}{y^2}\right][y - b] = RT$

$\left(p + \frac{a}{V^2}\right)(V - b) = RT \rightarrow$ Compare

$[a] = [p][V^2] \Rightarrow [b] = [V]$

$\frac{[a]}{[b]} = \frac{[p][V^2]}{[V]} = [p][V]$

$p = \frac{[F]}{[A]} = \frac{[\text{MLT}^{-2}]}{[\text{L}^2]} = [\text{ML}^{-1}\text{T}^{-2}]$

$Y = [L^3]$

So $\frac{[a]}{[b]} = [\text{ML}^{-1}\text{T}^{-2}][\text{L}^3] = [\text{ML}^2\text{T}^{-2}] = $ Energy

6. Astronomical unit (Au), Parses and Light year are the unit of distance.

Light year $\rightarrow$ distance travelled by light in one year

1 Light year $= 9.5\times1.0^{15}$ m

Parsec = 3.262 light year

Astronomical unit (Au) $= 1.58\times10^{-5}$ light year

Au < 1Y < Parsec

Statement I correct and Statement II incorrect.

7. A $\rightarrow$ IV

Torque = Force $\times$ perpendicular distance

= Mass $\times$ acceleration $\times$ perpendicular distance

$= \text{kg} \times \text{ms}^{-2} \times \text{m} = \text{kg m}^2\text{s}^{-2}$

B $\rightarrow$ I Energy density $= \frac{\text{Energy}}{\text{Volume}} = \frac{\text{kg m}^2\text{s}^{-2}}{\text{m}^3} = \text{kg m}^{-1}\text{s}^{-2}$

C $\rightarrow$ III Pressure gradient

$$p = \frac{\text{Pressure}}{\text{distance}} = \frac{\text{Force}}{\text{Area} \times \text{distance}}$$

$$= \frac{\text{kg ms}^{-2}}{\text{m}^2 \times \text{m}} = \text{kg m}^{-2}\text{s}^{-2}$$

D $\rightarrow$ II, Impulse = Force $\times$ time

$= \text{kg ms}^{-2} \times \text{s} = \text{kg ms}^{-1}$

8. Spring constant

$$(k) = \frac{[F]}{[x]} = \frac{[\text{MLT}^{-2}]}{[\text{L}]} = [\text{MT}^{-2}]$$

Angular speed $(\omega) = \frac{[\theta]}{[t]} = \frac{1}{[\text{T}]} = [\text{T}^{-1}]$

Angular momentum $(L) = mvr$

$= [\text{M}]\,[\text{LT}^{-1}] \times [\text{L}]$

$= [\text{ML}^2\text{T}^{-1}]$

Moment of inertia $(I) = [Mr^2] = [\text{M}]\,[\text{L}^2] = [\text{ML}^2]$

Hence the correct match is

A $\rightarrow$ II, B $\rightarrow$ I, C $\rightarrow$ IV, D $\rightarrow$ III

9. Torque = Force $\times$ Distance

$= \text{MLT}^{-2} \times \text{L} = \text{ML}^2\text{T}^{-2}$

Stress $= \frac{\text{Force}}{\text{Area}} = \frac{\text{MLT}^{-2}}{\text{L}^2} = \text{ML}^{-1}\text{T}^{-2}$

Pressure gradient $= \frac{\text{pressure}}{\text{length}} = \frac{F}{A \times L}$

$= \frac{\text{MLT}^{-2}}{\text{L}^3} = \text{ML}^{-2}\text{T}^{-2}$

Coefficient of viscosity $= \frac{\text{force} \times \text{length}}{\text{area} \times \text{velocity}}$

$= \frac{\text{MLT}^{-2} \times \text{L}}{\text{L}^2 \times \text{LT}^{-1}} = [\text{ML}^{-1}\text{T}^{-1}]$

10. $\rho = KF^aV^bT^c$

K is dimensionless constant

$[\text{ML}^{-3}] = [\text{MLT}^{-2}]^a[\text{LT}^{-1}]^b[\text{T}]^c$

$[\text{ML}^{-3}] = [\text{M}^a\text{L}^{a+b}\text{T}^{-2a-b+c}]$

$a = 1 \quad \Rightarrow \quad a + b = -3$

$1 + b = -3$

$b = -4$

$-2a - b + c = 0$

$-2 \times 1 - \times(-4) + c = 0$

$-2 + 4 + c = 0$

$2 + c = 0, \quad c = -2$

$\rho = KF^1V^{-4}T^{-2}$

11. Speed of light in vacuum is given by

$$c = \frac{1}{\sqrt{\mu_0\varepsilon_0}} \quad \Rightarrow \quad c^2 = \frac{1}{\mu_0\varepsilon_0}$$

Hence dimensions of $\frac{1}{\mu_0\varepsilon_0}$ are dimensions of

$$c^2 = [\text{LT}^{-1}]^2 = [\text{L}^2\text{T}^{-2}]$$

12. Speed of wave produced in water,

$$v = \lambda^a g^b \rho^c \quad \text{...(i)}$$

where, λ = wavelength, ρ = density,

$\therefore$ Writing the dimensions of each term of Eq. (i), we get

$[\text{LT}^{-1}] = [\text{L}]^a[\text{LT}^{-2}]^b[\text{ML}^{-3}]^c$

$\Rightarrow \quad [\text{LT}^{-1}] = [\text{M}^c\text{L}^{a+b-3c}\text{T}^{-2b}]$

Comparing the powers, we get

$c = 0, -2b = -1 \quad \Rightarrow \quad b = \frac{1}{2}$

$a + b - 3c = 1$

$\Rightarrow \quad a + b - 0 = 1$

$\Rightarrow \quad a + \frac{1}{2} = 1 \quad \Rightarrow \quad a = \frac{1}{2}$

13. Planck's constant, $h = \frac{E}{f} = \frac{[\text{ML}^2\text{T}^{-2}]}{[\text{T}^{-1}]} = [\text{ML}^2\text{T}^{-1}]$

So, A $\rightarrow$ III.

Stopping potential, $V = \frac{U}{q} = \frac{[\text{ML}^2\text{T}^{-2}]}{[\text{A}]\cdot[\text{T}]} = [\text{ML}^2\text{T}^{-3}\text{A}^{-1}]$

So, B $\rightarrow$ IV

Work function = Minimum energy $= [\text{ML}^2\text{T}^{-2}]$

So, C $\rightarrow$ I

Momentum = Mass $\times$ Velocity $= [\text{MLT}^{-1}]$

So, D $\rightarrow$ II

14. As we know,

Torque $= F(N) \times r_\perp(m) \rightarrow \text{Nm}$

Stress $= \frac{\text{Force (N)}}{\text{Area (m}^2)} \rightarrow \text{N/m}^2$

Latent heat $= \frac{\text{Energy (J)}}{\text{Mass (kg)}} \rightarrow \text{J kg}^{-1}$

Power $= \frac{\text{Work (Nm)}}{\text{Time (s)}} \rightarrow \text{N ms}^{-1}$

15. Given, $v_2 = \frac{n}{m^2} v_1$

$\because$ Velocity, $v = \frac{\text{Displacement}}{\text{Time}}$

$$\therefore \quad \frac{L_2}{T_2} = \frac{n}{m^2} \cdot \frac{L_1}{T_1} \quad \text{...(i)}$$

and $\quad a_2 = \frac{a_1}{mn}$

$\therefore \qquad \dfrac{L_2}{T_2^2} = \dfrac{L_1}{T_1^2} \cdot \dfrac{1}{mn}$ ...(ii)

On dividing Eq. (ii) by Eq. (i), we get

$$\frac{L_2 / T_2^2}{L_2 / T_2} = \frac{L_1 / T_1^2 \cdot 1 / mn}{n / m^2 \cdot L_1 / T_1}$$

$$\Rightarrow \qquad T_2 = \frac{n^2}{m} T_1$$

as, $L_2 = \dfrac{T_2}{T_1} \cdot L_1 \dfrac{n}{m^2} = \dfrac{n^2}{m} L_1 \dfrac{n}{m^2} = \dfrac{n^3}{m^3} L_1$

16. As we know, $1\,s = \dfrac{1}{3600^\circ}$ and $\pi = 180^\circ$

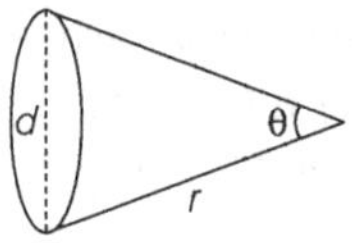

Thus, $2000\,s = \left(\dfrac{2000}{3600}\right)^\circ = \left(\dfrac{2000}{3600} \times \dfrac{\pi}{180}\right)$ rad

$\because$ Angle $(\theta) = \dfrac{\text{Arc } (d)}{\text{Radius } (r)}$

$$\therefore \qquad d = r\,\theta = 1.5 \times 10^{11} \times \frac{2000}{3600} \times \frac{\pi}{180}$$

$$= \frac{3000 \times 10^{11} \times \pi}{3600 \times 180} = 1.45 \times 10^9 \text{ m}$$

17. Unit of intensity of electric field E is Vm^{-1}. Unit of intensity of magnetising field H is Am^{-1}.
Unit of E / H can be calculated as

$$\frac{\text{Unit of } E}{\text{Unit of } H} = \frac{\text{Vm}^{-1}}{\text{Am}^{-1}} = \frac{\text{V}}{\text{A}} = \text{ohm.}$$

Thus, the unit of E / H will be ohm.

18. Since we know, RC and $\dfrac{L}{R}$ are time constants. Where, $\sqrt{LC}$ is reciprocal of angular frequency and has dimension of time.
Thus, $\left(\dfrac{L}{C}\right)$ does not have the dimension of time.

19. Since we know, wave number and Rydberg constant have same unit m^{-1}. Stress and coefficient of elasticity have same unit Pascal (P).
Coercivity and magnetisation have same unit A/m.
Whereas, specific heat capacity, $S = \dfrac{\Delta Q}{m\Delta T}$ has unit $\dfrac{\text{J}}{\text{Kg K}}$ and latent heat, $L = \dfrac{\Delta Q}{m}$ has unit $\dfrac{\text{J}}{\text{Kg}}$.

20. Energy density, $u = \dfrac{\alpha}{\beta} \sin\left(\dfrac{\alpha x}{kt}\right)$

Where, α, β = constants.
x = Displacement
k = Boltzmann constant
t = Temperature

We know that, energy density $= \dfrac{\text{energy}}{\text{volume}}$

and $\dfrac{\alpha x}{kt}$ = dimensionless

$$\alpha = \frac{kt}{x} = \frac{[\text{ML}^2\text{T}^{-2}\text{K}^{-1}]\,[\text{K}]}{[\text{L}]} = [\text{MLT}^{-2}]$$

Now, $\dfrac{\alpha}{\beta} = \dfrac{\text{energy}}{\text{volume}}$

$$\Rightarrow \qquad \beta = \frac{\alpha \times \text{volume}}{\text{energy}} = \frac{\alpha\,[\text{L}^3]}{[\text{ML}^2\text{T}^{-2}]}$$

$$\Rightarrow \qquad \beta = \frac{[\text{MLT}^{-2}]\,[\text{L}^3]}{[\text{ML}^2\text{T}^{-2}]} \qquad \text{[From Eq. (i)]}$$

$$\Rightarrow \quad \beta = [\text{L}^2] \quad \Rightarrow \quad \beta = [\text{M}^0\text{L}^2\text{T}^0]$$

21. As a / V^2 is added to pressure, so dimensions of a / V^2 must be that of pressure.
Also, dimensions of b must be that of volume

$$\Rightarrow \qquad \left[\frac{a}{V^2}\right] = [p] \qquad \Rightarrow \qquad \frac{[a]}{[\text{L}^6]} = \frac{[\text{MLT}^{-2}]}{[\text{L}^2]}$$

$$\Rightarrow \qquad [a] = [\text{ML}^5\,\text{T}^{-2}]$$

and $[b] = [V] = [\text{L}^3]$

So, $\left[\dfrac{a}{b}\right] = \dfrac{[\text{ML}^5\text{T}^{-2}]}{[\text{L}^3]} = [\text{ML}^2\text{T}^{-2}]$

These are dimensions of work or energy and pV = work due to pressure. Hence, $\dfrac{a}{b} = pV$

22. We know,

$[S] = [\text{MT}^{-2}] \quad \Rightarrow \quad [\rho] = [\text{ML}^{-3}]$

$[r] = [\text{L}]$

$$\therefore \text{ Dimension of RHS} = \frac{\left[\text{M}^{\frac{1}{2}}\text{L}^{-\frac{3}{2}}\right]\left[\text{L}^{\frac{3}{2}}\right]}{[\text{MT}^{-2}]^{\frac{3}{4}}}$$

$$= \left[\text{M}^{\left(\frac{1}{2} - \frac{3}{4}\right)}\,\text{L}^{\left(-\frac{3}{2} + \frac{3}{2}\right)}\,\text{T}^{\frac{6}{4}}\right] = \text{M}^{-\frac{1}{4}}\text{L}^0\text{T}^{\frac{3}{2}}$$

dimension of L.H.S. = [T]

$\therefore$ Dimension of LHS $\neq$ Dimension of RHS.

23. Since, ratios of trigonometric function and logarithmic function are dimensionless quantities.

$$\therefore \qquad [\eta] = [\text{M}^0\text{L}^0\text{T}^0]$$

Also, dimensions of temperature,

$$[T] = [\text{M}^0\text{L}^0\text{T}^0\text{K}]$$

Dimensions of Boltzmann constant,

$$[k] = [\text{ML}^2\text{T}^{-2}\,\text{K}^{-1}]$$

Dimension of $x = [\text{M}^0\text{LT}^0]$

$\therefore \quad \left[\frac{\beta x}{kT}\right] = [\eta] = [M^0L^0T^0]$

$\Rightarrow \quad [\beta] = \frac{[kT]}{[x]} = \frac{[ML^2\ T^{-2}\ K^{-1}][K]}{[L]}$

$= [MLT^{-2}] = [\text{Force}]$

Hence, dimensions of β is same as that of force.

Also, $\quad [\eta] = [\alpha\beta]$

$[\alpha\beta] = [M^0L^0T^0]$

$\Rightarrow \quad [\alpha] = \frac{1}{[\beta]} = \frac{1}{[MLT^{-2}]}$

or $\quad [\alpha^{-1}] = [\beta] = [MLT^{-2}]$

$\therefore \quad [\alpha^{-1}x] = [MLT^{-2}][L] = [ML^2T^{-2}] = [\text{Energy}]$

i.e. Dimensions of $\alpha^{-1}x$ is same as that of energy.

Since, the quantity $\alpha\beta$ is dimensionless, so dimensions of α cannot be same as that of β.

24. Fundamental quantities taken are momentum (p), area (A) and time (t).

Let coefficient of viscosity (η) depends on p, A and t are

$\eta = k \cdot p^a \cdot A^b \cdot t^c$, where k is a constant

Then writing dimensions of all quantities and comparing, we get $[ML^{-1}T^{-1}] = [MLT^{-1}]^a[L^2]^b[T]^c$

$\Rightarrow \quad M = M^a \Rightarrow a = 1$

$L^{-1} = L^{a+2b}$

$\Rightarrow \quad a + 2b = -1 \quad \text{or} \quad 2b = -2$

$\Rightarrow \quad b = -1 \quad \text{and} \quad T^{-1} = T^{-a+c}$

$\Rightarrow \quad -a + c = -1 \quad \text{or} \quad -1 + c = -1$

$c = 0$

So, coefficient of viscosity has dimension

$[\eta] = [p^1A^{-1}t^0] = [pA^{-1}t^0]$

25. Surface charge density,

$\sigma = \frac{Q}{A} = \frac{I.t}{A}$

$\Rightarrow \quad [\sigma] = \frac{[I][t]}{[A]} = \frac{[AT]}{[L^2]}$

$\Rightarrow \quad [\sigma] = [L^{-2}TA] \quad \text{...(i)}$

Electric displacement, $\mathbf{D} = \varepsilon_0\mathbf{E}$

$\Rightarrow \quad D = \frac{Q^2}{F \cdot r^2} \cdot \frac{F}{Q} = \frac{Q}{r^2}$

$\because \quad \varepsilon_0 = \frac{Q^2}{F \cdot r^2} \quad \text{and} \quad \mathbf{E} = \frac{\mathbf{F}}{Q}$

$\Rightarrow \quad D = \frac{I \cdot t}{r^2} \Rightarrow [D] = \frac{[I][t]}{[r^2]} = \frac{[A][T]}{[L^2]}$

$\Rightarrow \quad [D] = [L^{-2}TA] \quad \text{...(ii)}$

From Eqs. (i) and (ii) we can observe that dimensions of surface charge density and electric displacement are same.

26. Viscous force is given by

$F = -\eta A \frac{dv}{dx}$

So, coefficient of viscosity,

$\eta = \frac{F}{A \cdot \left(\frac{dv}{dx}\right)}$

Hence, reason is false.

Also, $[\eta] = \frac{[F]}{[A]\left[\frac{dv}{dx}\right]} = \frac{[MLT^{-2}]}{[L^2]\left[\frac{LT^{-1}}{L}\right]} = [ML^{-1}T^{-1}]$

And $[p \times t] = \frac{[F][t]}{[A]} = \frac{[MLT^{-2}][T]}{L^2} = [ML^{-1}T^{-1}]$

Hence, assertion is true.

27. Given, SI unit of a quantity is pascal-second.

Pressure × Time = $[ML^{-1}T^{-2}]\,[T]$

$= [ML^{-1}T^{-1}]$

28. We know that induced emf across the coil due to change of current flowing through it

i.e. $\quad e = -M\frac{di}{dt}$

$\Rightarrow \quad M = -\frac{e}{\left[\frac{di}{dt}\right]} \Rightarrow M = -e \cdot \frac{dt}{di}$

$\Rightarrow \quad [M] = [e]\frac{[dt]}{[di]} = \left[\frac{W}{q}\right]\frac{[dt]}{[di]}$

$= \left[\frac{ML^2T^{-2}}{AT}\right]\frac{[T]}{[A]}$

$= [ML^2T^{-2}A^{-2}]$

29. Given, $P = \frac{\alpha}{\beta}\log_e\left[\frac{kt}{\beta x}\right]$

The logarithmic term is dimensionless.

Thus, $[kt/\beta x]$ is also dimensionless.

i.e. $\quad \frac{[k][t]}{[\beta][x]} = [M^0\ L^0\ T^0] \quad \text{... (i)}$

We have, $\quad E = kt$

Thus, Eq. (i) becomes,

$\frac{[M^1L^2T^{-2}]}{[\beta][L^1]} = [M^0L^0T^0]$

$\therefore \quad [\beta] = [MLT^{-2}]$

Since, P is also a dimensionless quantity.

$\frac{[\alpha]}{[\beta]} = [M^0L^0T^0]$

$\Rightarrow \quad [\alpha] = [\beta][M^0L^0T^0]$

$\therefore \quad [\alpha] = [M^1L^1T^{-2}] = [MLT^{-2}]$

30. Velocity gradient $=\dfrac{\Delta v}{\Delta x}$

$$[\text{Velocity gradient}]=\frac{[\Delta v]}{[\Delta x]}=\frac{[LT^{-1}]}{[L]}=[T^{-1}]$$

Decay constant, $\lambda=\dfrac{1}{\tau}$

where, τ is average life time.

$$\therefore \quad [\lambda]=\frac{1}{[\tau]}=\frac{1}{[T]}=[T^{-1}]$$

Therefore, velocity gradient and decay constant have same dimensional formula.

According to Stefan's Boltzmann law,

$$\frac{E}{At}=\sigma T^4,$$

where σ is Stefan's constant.

$$\Rightarrow \quad \sigma=\frac{E}{AtT^4} \Rightarrow [\sigma]=\frac{[ML^2T^{-2}]}{[L^2][T][K^4]}$$

$$[\sigma]=[MT^{-3}K^{-4}]$$

Wien's constant, $b=\lambda_m T$

$$\therefore \quad [b]=[LK]$$

Therefore, Wien's constant and Stefan's constant have different dimensions.

Angular frequency, $\omega=\dfrac{2\pi}{T}$

$$\therefore \quad [\omega]=[T^{-1}]$$

Angular momentum,

$$L=mvr$$

$$[L]=[M]\,[LT^{-1}]\,[L]=[ML^2T^{-1}]$$

Thus, angular frequency and angular momentum have different dimensions.

Wave number, $\bar{v}=\dfrac{1}{\lambda}$

$$[\bar{v}]=\frac{1}{[\lambda]}=\frac{1}{[L]}=[L^{-1}]$$

Avogadro number is a dimensionless constant,

Hence, wave number and Avogadro number also have different dimensions.

31. Since we know,

Torque τ = force $\times$ perpendicular distance
$= [MLT^{-2}]\,[L] = [ML^2T^{-2}]$

Impulse I = force $\times$ time $= [MLT^{-2}]\,[T] = [MLT^{-1}]$

Tension force $= MLT^{-2}$

Surface tension $S=\dfrac{F}{L}=MT^{-2}$

32. Charge $Q=CV$

$$\Rightarrow \quad C=\frac{Q}{V}=\frac{(A\times T)^2}{ML^2T^{-2}}=M^{-1}L^{-2}T^4A^2$$

Electric Field, $E=\dfrac{F}{q}=\dfrac{MLT^{-2}}{AT}=MLT^{-3}A^{-1}$

Force, $F=\dfrac{q_1q_2}{4\pi\varepsilon_0 r^2}$

$$\Rightarrow \quad \epsilon_0=M^{-1}L^{-3}T^4A^2$$

Speed of light, $C=\dfrac{1}{\sqrt{\mu_0\epsilon_0}}$

$$\Rightarrow \quad \mu_0=\frac{1}{\epsilon_0 C^2}=\frac{1}{[M^{-1}L^{-3}T^4A^2]\,[LT^{-1}]^2}$$
$$=[M^1L^1T^{-2}A^{-2}]$$

33. According to question,

$$\left[\frac{\pi p a^4}{8\eta L}\right]=\frac{[M\,L^{-1}\,T^{-2}]\,[L^4]}{[ML^{-1}\,T^{-1}]\,[L^1]}=[M^0\,L^3\,T^{-1}] \quad \text{...(ii)}$$

Thus, option (a) is wrong .

Now, since formula of capillary rise in tube, $h=\dfrac{2s\cos\theta}{\rho g r}$

Thus, $=\dfrac{[s]}{[\rho][g][r]}=\dfrac{[MT^{-2}]}{[ML^{-3}]\,[LT^{-2}]\,[L]}=[L]$

Hence, $h=\dfrac{2s\cos\theta}{\rho r g}$ is dimensionally correct.

So, option (b) will also be dimensionally correct.

In option (c),

$$J=\varepsilon\frac{dE}{\partial t} \quad \text{...(iii)}$$

$$\Rightarrow \quad J=\varepsilon\frac{E}{t}$$

Since, $\quad J=\dfrac{I}{A}$

$$\therefore \quad [J]=\frac{[I]}{[A]}=\frac{[A]}{[L^2]}$$

$$\Rightarrow \quad [J]=[AL^{-2}] \quad \text{...(iv)}$$

Again, we know that

$$E=\frac{1}{4\pi\varepsilon}\cdot\frac{q}{r^2}$$

$$\Rightarrow \quad \varepsilon E=\frac{1}{4\pi}\cdot\frac{q}{r^2} \Rightarrow \frac{\varepsilon E}{t}=\frac{1}{4\pi}\cdot\frac{q}{tr^2}$$

$$\Rightarrow \quad \left[\frac{\varepsilon E}{t}\right]=\frac{[q]}{[t][r^2]}=\frac{[AT]}{[T]\,[L^2]}$$

$$\Rightarrow \quad \left[\frac{\varepsilon E}{t}\right]=[AL^{-2}] \quad \text{...(v)}$$

Form Eqs. (iv) and (v), we see that Eq. (iii) is dimensionally correct.

In option (d) $W=\tau\theta$ and $\tau=r\times F$

So, dimensional formula of

$$[\tau][\theta]=[r][F]=[L]\,[MLT^{-2}]$$
$$=[ML^2T^{-2}]=[\text{Work}]$$

34. As per question

$$m\propto v^xT^yF^z \quad \text{...(i)}$$

Thus, we have,

$$[ML^0T^0] = [LT^{-1}]^x [T]^y [MLT^{-2}]^z$$
$$[M^1L^0T^0] = [M^zL^{x+z}T^{-x+y-2z}]$$

On Comparing we get, $z = 1$

$$x + z = 0 \text{ and } -x + y - 2z = 0$$

$\Rightarrow$ $x + 1 = 0 \Rightarrow x = -1$

and $-(-1) + y - 2(1) = 0$

$\Rightarrow$ $1 + y - 2 = 0 \Rightarrow y = 1$

Substituting these values in Eq. (i), we get

$$m \propto v^{-1}T^1F^1 \Rightarrow m = [FTv^{-1}]$$

35. According to the question,

$$\rho \propto F^aL^bT^c$$

Thus,

$\therefore$ $[\rho] = [F]^a [L]^b [T]^c$

$\Rightarrow$ $[ML^{-3}T^0] = [MLT^{-2}]^a$

$$[M^0L^1T^0]^b[M^0L^0T^1]^c = [M^aL^{a+b}T^{-2a+c}]$$

Comparing powers of dimensions on both sides, we get

$$a = 1$$
$$a + b = -3 \Rightarrow b = -3 - 1 = -4$$

and $-2a + c = 0$

$$c = 2a \Rightarrow c = 2 \times 1 = 2$$

$\therefore$ Dimensional formula of density will be $[F^1L^{-4}T^2]$.

36. Relative magnetic permeability is given by $\mu_r = \frac{\mu_m}{\mu_0}$

As, it is a ratio of permeabilities. So, it is unitless and dimensionless quantity.

Power factor = cos ϕ, so it is also a unitless and dimensionless

Permeability of free space,

$$\mu_0 = \frac{B}{H} \Rightarrow [\mu_0] = \frac{[B]}{[H]} \quad ...(i)$$

$$[H] = [n][I] = [L^{-1}][A] = [AL^{-1}]$$

$\because n$: number of terms per unit length

B = magnetic field, $[ML^{-2}A^{-1}]$

$$[\mu_0] = \frac{[MT^{-2}A^{-1}]}{[AL^{-1}]} = [MLT^{-2}A^{-2}]$$

Hence, permeability of free space is not a dimensionless quantity.

$$\text{Quality factor} = \frac{\text{Energy stored}}{\text{Energy dissipated per cycle}}$$

So, it will be unitless and dimensionless quantity.

37. According to the question

$$P = EL^2M^{-5}G^{-2}$$

$$\therefore \quad [P] = \frac{[E][L^2]}{[M^5][G^2]} = \frac{[ML^2T^{-2}] \times [M^2L^4T^{-2}]}{[M^5][M^{-2}L^6T^{-4}]} = [M^0L^0T^0]$$

38. Given,

Equation of force,

$$F = A\cos Bx + C\sin Dt$$

where, x is displacement and t is time.

Now, trigonometric ratios are dimensionless,

$\therefore$ $[Bx] = [M^0L^0T^0]$

$\Rightarrow$ $[B][L^1] = [M^0L^0T^0]$

$\Rightarrow$ $[B] = [M^0L^{-1}T^0]$ ...(i)

Similarly,

$$[Dt] = [M^0L^0T^0]$$

$\Rightarrow$ $[D] = \frac{[M^0L^0T^0]}{[t]} = [M^0L^0T^{-1}]$ ...(ii)

and $[A] = [F] = [MLT^{-2}]$ ...(iii)

From Eqs. (i), (ii) and (iii), we get

$$\frac{[AD]}{[B]} = \frac{[MLT^{-2}][M^0L^0T^{-1}]}{[M^0L^{-1}T^0]}$$
$$= \frac{[MLT^{-3}]}{[L^{-1}]} = [ML^2T^{-3}]$$

39. As per question,

$$m \propto t^av^bl^c$$

or $m = kt^av^bl^c$ ...(i)

Where, k is constant.

Substituting all these dimensions in Eq. (i), we get

$$[M^1L^0T^0] = [M^0L^0T^1]^a [M^0L^1T^{-1}]^b[M^1L^2T^{-1}]^c$$
$$[M^1L^0T^0] = [M^cL^{b+2c}T^{a-b-c}]$$

On comparing powers, we get

$$c = 1,$$
$$b + 2c = 0$$
$$b + 2 = 0 \Rightarrow b = -2$$
$$a - b - c = 0$$

$\Rightarrow$ $a - (-2) - 1 = 0 \Rightarrow a = -1$

$\therefore$ We can write $[m] = [t^{-1}v^{-2}l^1]$

JEE Advanced

1. Given, $Y = c^\alpha h^\beta G^\gamma$

Writing the dimensional formula of Y, c, h, and G, we get

$$[ML^{-1}T^{-2}] = [M^0L^1T^{-1}]^\alpha [ML^2T^{-1}]^\beta [M^{-1}L^3T^{-2}]^\gamma$$

$\Rightarrow$ $[ML^{-1}T^{-2}] = [M^{\beta-\gamma} L^{\alpha+2\beta+3\gamma} T^{-\alpha-\beta-2\gamma}]$

$\therefore$ $\beta - \gamma = 1$ ...(i)

$\alpha + 2\beta + 3\gamma = -1$ ...(ii)

$$-\alpha - \beta - 2\gamma = -2$$

$\Rightarrow$ $\alpha + \beta + 2\gamma = 2$ ...(iii)

Solving Eqs. (i), (ii) and (iii), we get

$$\alpha = 7, \beta = -1, \gamma = -2$$

2. $[B] = [e]^\alpha [m_e]^\beta [h^\gamma][k]^\delta$

$$[M^1T^{-2}I^{-1}] = [IT]^\alpha [M]^\beta [ML^2T^{-1}]^\gamma [ML^3T^{-4}]^\delta$$

So, $\beta + \gamma + \delta = 1$ ...(i)

$2\gamma + 3\delta = 0$ ...(ii)

$$\alpha - \gamma - 4\delta = -2 \quad \text{...(iii)}$$
$$\alpha - 2\delta = -1 \quad \text{...(iv)}$$

Solving Eqs. (i) and (iv), we get

So, $\alpha + \beta + \gamma + \delta = 4$

3. $S = \dfrac{E \times B}{\mu_0}$

$\Rightarrow \dfrac{E \times B}{\mu_0}$ is poynting vector and its dimension is same as that of intensity $\left(\dfrac{W}{m^2}\right)$.

$$\text{Dimension} = \frac{[ML^2T^{-2}]}{[TL^2]} = [MT^{-3}]$$

Alternate solutions

Dimension of electric field $[E] = [MA^{-1}LT^{-3}]$

Dimensions of magnetic field $[B]$

$$[B] = [MA^{-1}T^{-2}]$$

Dimensions of magnetic permeability

$$[\mu_0] = [MA^{-2}T^{-2}L]$$

$$[S] = \frac{EB}{\mu_0} = \frac{[MA^{-1}LT^{-3})(MA^{-1}T^{-2}]}{[MA^{-2}T^{-2}L]} = [MT^{-3}]$$

4. $[x] = x^\alpha \quad \Rightarrow \quad \dfrac{p}{v} = \text{time}$

$[v] = x^\beta$

$[a] = x^p \quad \Rightarrow \quad \dfrac{v}{a} = \text{time}$

$[p] = x^q$

$[F] = x^r$

$$\Rightarrow \left(\frac{\text{position}}{\text{speed}}\right) = \left(\frac{\text{speed}}{\text{acceleration}}\right) = \left(\frac{p}{F}\right)$$

$$\Rightarrow \frac{x^\alpha}{x^\beta} = \frac{x^\beta}{x^p} = \frac{x^q}{x^r}$$

$$\Rightarrow x^{\alpha - \beta} = x^{\beta - p} = x^{q - r}$$

$$\alpha - \beta = \beta - p = q - r$$
$$\alpha + p = 2\beta$$
$$q + p = \beta + r$$
$$p + q - r = \beta$$

5. $[n] = [L^{-3}], [q] = [AT]$

$$[\varepsilon] = [M^{-1}L^{-3}T^4A^2] \Rightarrow [T] = [K]$$
$$[l] = [L] \Rightarrow [k_B] = [M^1L^2T^{-2}K^{-1}]$$

(a) $\text{RHS} = \sqrt{\dfrac{[L^{-3}A^2T^2]}{[M^{-1}L^{-3}T^4A^2][M^1L^2T^{-2}K^{-1}][K]}}$

$= \sqrt{\dfrac{[L^{-3}A^2T^2]}{[L^{-1}T^2A^2]}} = \sqrt{[L^{-2}]} = [L^{-1}]$ Wrong

(b) $\text{RHS} = \sqrt{\dfrac{[M^{-1}L^{-3}T^4A^2][M^1L^2T^{-2}K^{-1}][K]}{[L^{-3}][A^2T^2]}}$

$= \sqrt{\dfrac{[L^{-1}T^2A^2]}{[L^{-3}T^2A^2]}} = [L]$ Correct

(c) $\text{RHS} = \sqrt{\dfrac{[A^2T^2]}{[M^{-1}L^{-3}T^4A^2][L^{-2}][M^1L^2T^{-2}K^{-1}][K]}}$

$= \sqrt{[L^3]}$ Wrong

(d) $\text{RHS} = \sqrt{\dfrac{[A^2T^2]}{[M^{-1}L^{-3}T^4A^2][L^{-1}][M^1L^2T^{-2}K^{-1}][K]}}$

$= \sqrt{\dfrac{[A^2T^2]}{[L^{-2}T^2A^2]}} = [L]$ Correct

6. Energy $U = \dfrac{1}{2}LI^2 = \left(\dfrac{1}{2}\dfrac{\mu_0 N^2 A}{l}\right)I^2$

Energy $U = \dfrac{1}{2}CV^2 = \left(\dfrac{1}{2}\varepsilon_0 \dfrac{A}{d}\right)V^2$

$\Rightarrow \mu_0 \dfrac{A}{l} I^2$ and $\varepsilon_0 \dfrac{A}{d} V^2$ have same dimension.

So, $\mu_0 I^2$ and $\varepsilon_0 V^2$ have same dimension.

(c) $Q = CV, \dfrac{Q}{t} = I = \dfrac{CV}{t} = \left(\dfrac{\varepsilon_0 A}{l}\right)\dfrac{V}{t}$

$\therefore \quad I = \varepsilon_0 \left(\dfrac{A}{lt}\right)V$

But, A/lt have units of speed.

So, $\quad I = \varepsilon_0 cV$

CHAPTER~04

SIGNIFICANT FIGURES & ERRORS IN MEASUREMENT

LEVEL 01 Starter Level

4.1 Significant Figures

1 How many significant figures are given in the following quantities?

(i) 343 g (ii) 2002 (iii) 1.103 N
(iv) 6000 m (v) 0.0145 m (vi) 0.0080 V
(vii) 9.1×10^4 km (viii) 1.124×10^{-3} V (ix) 0.5000 kg

2 Round off the following numbers to three significant figures.

(i) 16468 (ii) 12.745 (iii) 11.650
(iv) 20.350 (v) 0.0008568 (vi) 12.456

3 Perform the following operations

(i) $5.8 + 0.125$ (ii) $9.15 + 3.8$ (iii) $3.5 - 2.51$
(iv) $703 + 7 + 0.66$ (v) 2.21×0.3 (vi) 12.4×84
(vii) $14.28 / 0.714$ (viii) 142.06×0.23
(ix) $\dfrac{2.91 \times 0.3842}{0.080}$ (x) $\dfrac{0.9996 \times 3.54}{1.638}$

4 The mass of a box is 2.3 kg. Two gold pieces of masses 2.15 g and 12.39 g are added to it. Find the total mass of the box to the correct number of significant figures.

5 5.74 gm of a substance occupies a volume of 1.2 cm^3. Calculate its density with due regard for significant figures.

6 A man runs 100.5 m in 10.3 s. Find his average speed upto appropriate significant figures.

7 The length of a rectangular path is 10.52 m and its width is only 0.041 m. Find its area upto appropriate significant figures.

8 In Ohm's law experiment, reading of voltmeter across the resistor is 12.5 V and reading of current $i = 0.20$ A. Estimate the resistance in correct significant figures.

9 State True/False

(i) All non-zero digits are significant.
(ii) All zeros occurring between two non-zeroes digits are significant.
(iii) Leading zeroes are always insignificant.
(iv) Trailing zeroes in a measurement without decimal are insignificant.
(v) Trailing zeroes in a measurement with decimal are significant.
(vi) Change of unit can change the number of significant figures.
(vii) Number of signficant figures in 4000 is 4.
(viii) Number of signficant figures in π is infinite.

10 What are the orders of magnitude of the following numbers?

(i) 147 (ii) 501
(iii) 8346002 (iv) 0.00025432

4.2 Errors in Measurement

1 In an experiment, the value of refractive index of glass was found to be 1.54, 1.53, 1.44, 1.56 and 1.45 in successive measurements. Calculate

(i) the mean value of refractive index of glass,
(ii) absolute error in each measurement,
(iii) mean absolute error,
(iv) relative error and
(v) percentage error.

2 Two resistances $R_1 = (10.0 \pm 0.5)\,\Omega$ and $R_2 = (5.00 \pm 1.5)\,\Omega$ are connected in series. Find the equivalent resistance of the series combination.

3 The initial and final temperatures of liquid in a container are observed to be 76.3 ± 0.4°C and 67.7 ± 0.3°C. Determine the fall in the temperature of the liquid.

4 The length and breadth of a rectangle are (5.7 ± 0.1) cm and (3.4 ± 0.2) cm. Find the area of the rectangle.

5 A capacitor of capacitance $C = 2.0 \pm 0.1\mu F$ is charged to a voltage $V = 20 \pm 0.2$ V. What will be the percentage error in measurement of charge Q on the capacitor? Use, $Q = CV$.

6 The resistance $R = \frac{V}{I}$, where $V = (100 \pm 5)$ V and $I = (10 \pm 0.2)$ A. Find R.

7 The error in the measurement of the radius of a sphere is 0.5%. What is the permissible percentage error in the measurement of its (a) surface area and (b) volume?

8 The edge of a cube is measured to be (2.1 ± 0.05) cm. Calculate the surface area with error limits.

9 A physical quantity P is related to a, b, c and d as follows : $P = \frac{a^3 b^2}{\sqrt{c}\, d}$. The percentage errors of measurement in a, b, c and d are 1%, 3%, 4% and 2%, respectively. What is the percentage error in the quantity P ?

10 The centripetal force is given by $F = \frac{mv^2}{r}$. The mass, velocity and radius of the circular path of an object are 0.5 kg, 10 m/s and 0.4, m respectively. Find the percentage error in the force. Given, m, v and r are measured to accuracies of 0.005 kg, 0.01 m/s and 0.01 m, respectively.

11 An experiment to determine the density ρ of a metal wire provided the following observations mass of wire $(m) = (88 \pm 2)$ g, length $(l) = (100 \pm 0.1)$ cm, radius $(r) = (0.28 \pm 0.02)$ cm. Find ρ.

12 Two resistors have resistances $R_1 = (24 \pm 0.5)\Omega$ and $R_2 = (8 \pm 0.3)\ \Omega$. Calculate the absolute error and the percentage relative error in calculating the equivalent resistance when they are in parallel.

13 The period of oscillation of a simple pendulum is $T = 2\pi\sqrt{\frac{L}{g}}$. L is about 10 cm and is known to 1 mm accuracy. The period of oscillation is about 0.5 s. The time of 100 oscillations is measured with a wrist watch of 1 s resolution. What is the percentage error in the determination of g ?

14 Calculate focal length of a spherical mirror from the following observations object distance $u = (50.1 \pm 0.5)$ cm and image distance $v = (20.1 \pm 0.2)$ cm.

15 If percentage error in the measurement of speed of a body is 30 %, then what will be percentage error in the measurement of its kinetic energy?

4.3 Vernier Callipers

1 Main scale of a vernier calliper has 100 divisions in 5 cm. Its vernier scale has 25 divisions in 1 cm. What is the least count?

2 1 cm on the main scale of vernier callipers is divided into 10 equal parts. If 20 divisions of vernier scale coincide with 8 small divisions of the main scale, what will be the least count of callipers?

3 In a vernier callipers, 10 VSD = 9 MSD and 1 cm on main scale is divided into 10 parts. While measuring the length of a line, the zero of VS is just ahead of 1.8 cm mark and 4th division of VS coincides with a main scale division. What is the length of line?

4 The smallest division on the main scale of a vernier callipers is 1 mm and 10 vernier divisions coincide with 9 scale divisions. While measuring the diameter of a sphere, the zero mark of the vernier scale lies between 2.0 and 2.1 cm and the fifth division of the vernier scale coincide with a scale division.
(a) Determine the vernier constant (b) Find the diameter of the sphere

5 The length of a cylinder is measured with vernier callipers whose smallest division on main scale is 0.5 mm and 10 vernier divisions is equal to 9 main scale divisions. It is observed that 80th division of the main scale coincides with the 4th division of the vernier scale. What is the length of the cylinder?

6 When nothing is placed between jaws of a vernier callipers of MSD = 1 mm then sixth vernier scale division coincides with a main scale division and zero of main scale is on left of zero of vernier scale. If 9 main scale divisions equals 10 vernier scale divisions, then calculate
(a) zero error
(b) zero correction

7 The main scale of a vernier callipers reads in millimeter and its vernier in divided into 10 divisions which coincide with a division of the main scale. When the two jaws of the instrument touch each other the seventh division of the vernier scale coincide with a scale divisions and the zero of the vernier lies to the right of the zero of mains scale. Furthermore when a cylinder is tightly placed along its length between the two jaws, the zero of the vernier scale lies slightly to the left of 3.2 cm and the fourth vernier division coincides with a scale division. What is the length of the cylinder?

4.4 Screw Gauge

1 The pitch of a screw gauge 0.5 mm and there are 50 divisions on the circular scale. In measuring the thickness of a metal plate, there are 5 divisions on the pitch scale (or main scale) and 34th division coincides with the reference line. Calculate the thickness of the metal plate.

2 The distance advanced by the screw of a screw gauge is 2 mm in four rotations. Its cap is divided into 50 divisions. There is no zero error.
(a) Find the pitch of the screw gauge
(b) Find the least count of the instrument
(c) Find the diameter of a wire, if the screw reads 3 divisions on the main scale and 32 divisions on the cap

3 The pitch of a screw gauge is 1 mm and there are 50 divisions on its cap. When nothing is put in between the studs, 44th division of the circular scale coincides with the reference line and zero of the main scale is not visible. When a glass plate is placed between the studs, the main scale reads 3 divisions and the circular scale reads 26 divisions. Calculate the thickness of the plate.

4 The circular scale of a micrometer has 200 divisions and pitch of 2 mm. Find the measured value of thickness of a thin sheet.

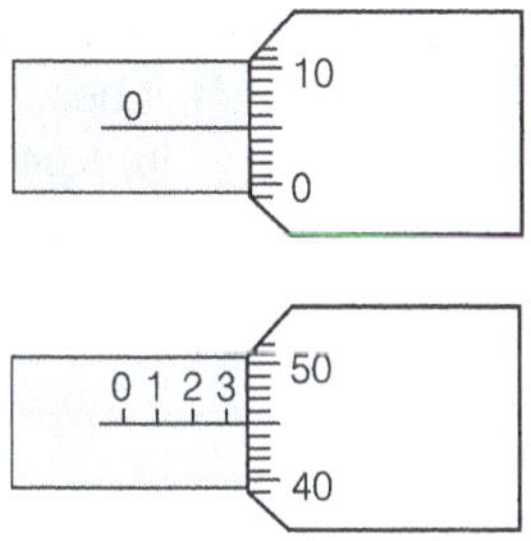

LEVEL 02 JEE Main Level / JEE Advanced Level

Single Choice Correct Questions

1 The result after adding 3.8×10^{-6} with 4.2×10^{-5} with due regard to significant figures is
(a) 4.58×10^{-5} (b) 0.458×10^{-4}
(c) 4.6×10^{-6} (d) 45.8×10^{-6}

2 The volume of a sphere is 2.42 cm^3. The volume of 12 such spheres taking into account the significant figure is
(a) 29.04 cm^3 (b) 29 cm^3
(c) 29.0 cm^3 (d) 29.1 cm^3

3 The radius of a thin wire is 0.16 mm. The area of cross-section taking significant figure into consideration in square mm^2 is
(a) 0.0804 (b) 0.080
(c) 0.08 (d) 0.080384

4 After rounding off the number 4621 to 2 significant digits, the value becomes
(a) 4600 (b) 4620
(c) 4700 (d) 4720

5 The area of a rectangle of size 1.23 cm × 2.345 cm is
(a) 2.88 cm^2
(b) 2.884 cm^2
(c) 2.9 cm^2
(d) 2.88435 cm^2

6 The length, breadth and thickness of a block are given by $l = 12$ cm, $b = 6$ cm and $t = 2.45$ cm. The volume of the block according to the idea of significant figures should be
(a) 1×10^2 cm^3 (b) 2×10^2 cm^3
(c) 1.763×10^2 cm^3 (d) None of these

7 If 97.52 is divided by 2.54, the correct result in terms of significant figures is
(a) 38.4 (b) 38.3937 (c) 38.394 (d) 38.3

8 The decimal equivalent of 1/20 upto three significant figures is
(a) 0.0500 (b) 0.05000
(c) 0.0050 (d) 5.0×10^{-2}

9 If $L = 2.331$ cm, $B = 2.1$ cm, then $L + B$
(a) 4.431 cm (b) 4.43 cm
(c) 4.4 cm (d) 4 cm

10 The number of significant figures in all the given numbers 25.12, 2009, 4.156 and 1.217×10^{-4} is
(a) 1 (b) 2
(c) 3 (d) 4

11 The edge of a cube is $a = 1.2 \times 10^{-2}$ m. Then, its volume will be recorded as
(a) 1.72×10^{-6} m^3 (b) 1.728×10^{-6} m^3
(c) 1.7×10^{-6} m^3 (d) 1.73×10^{-6} m^3

12 The respective number of significant figures for the numbers 20.003, 0.0003 and 2.0×10^{-3} are
(a) 5, 1, 2 (b) 5, 1, 5
(c) 2, 1, 1 (d) 2, 4, 2

13 A body of mass $m = 3.513$ kg is moving along the X-axis with a speed of 5.00 ms^{-1}. The magnitude of its momentum is recorded as
(a) 17.6 kg-ms^{-1} (b) 17.565 kg-ms^{-1}
(c) 17.56 kg-ms^{-1} (d) 17.5 kg-ms^{-1}

14 When the number 6.03587 is rounded off up to the second place of decimals, it becomes
(a) 6.035 (b) 6.04
(c) 6.03 (d) None

15 Using significant figures, match the following columns.

	Column I		Column II
A.	0.12345	P.	5
B.	0.12100 cm	Q.	4
C.	$47.23 \div 2.3$	R.	1
D.	3×10^8	S.	2

(a) A → P, B → P, C → S, D → R
(b) A → P, B → Q, C → S, D → R
(c) A → P, B → Q, C → R, D → S
(d) A → Q, B → R, C → S, D → R

16 The external and internal diameters of a hollow cylinder are measured to be (4.23 ± 0.01) cm and (3.89 ± 0.01) cm. The thickness of the wall of the cylinder is
(a) (0.34 ± 0.02) cm
(b) (0.17 ± 0.02) cm
(c) (0.17 ± 0.01) cm
(d) (0.34 ± 0.01) cm

17 The measure of radius of a sphere is $(4.22 \pm 2\%)$ cm. The volume of the sphere is
(a) $(315 \pm 6\%)$ (b) $(315 \pm 2\%)$
(c) $(315 \pm 4\%)$ (d) $(315 \pm 5\%)$

18 Two resistors $R_1 = (24 \pm 0.5)\,\Omega$ and $R_2 = (8 \pm 0.3)\,\Omega$ are joined in series. The equivalent resistance is
(a) $32 \pm 0.33\,\Omega$ (b) $32 \pm 0.8\,\Omega$
(c) $32 \pm 0.2\,\Omega$ (d) $32 \pm 0.5\,\Omega$

19 The length, breadth and thickness of a strip are (10.0 ± 0.1) cm, (1.00 ± 0.01) cm and (0.100 ± 0.001) cm, respectively. The most probable error in its volume will be
(a) $\pm 0.03\ cm^3$ (b) $\pm 0.111\ cm^3$
(c) $\pm 0.012\ cm^3$ (d) None of these

20 The heat generated in a circuit is given by $H = I^2 Rt$ joule, where I is current, R is resistance and t is time. If the percentage errors in measuring I, R and t are 2%, 1% and 1%, respectively, then maximum error in measuring heat will be
(a) 2% (b) 3% (c) 4% (d) 6%

21 If the length of rod A is 3.25 ± 0.01 cm and that of B is 4.19 ± 0.01 cm, then the rod B is longer than rod A by
(a) 0.94 ± 0.00 cm (b) 0.94 ± 0.01 cm
(c) 0.94 ± 0.02 cm (d) 0.94 ± 0.005 cm

22 A physical quantity is represented by $X = [M^a L^b T^{-c}]$. If percentage error in the measurement of [M], [L] and [T] are $\alpha\%$, $\beta\%$ and $\gamma\%$ respectively, then total percentage error is
(a) $(\alpha a + \beta b - \gamma c)\%$ (b) $(\alpha a + \beta b + \gamma c)\%$
(c) $(\alpha + \beta + \gamma)\%$ (d) $(\alpha + \beta - \gamma)\%$

23 The volume of a sphere is $(1.76 \pm 0.02)\ cm^3$. The volume of 25 such spheres will be
(a) $(44.0 \pm 0.02)\ cm^3$ (b) $(44 \pm 0.02)\ cm^3$
(c) $(44.0 \pm 0.5)\ cm^3$ (d) $(44 \pm 0.5)\ cm^3$

24 In the measurement of n from the formula $n = \dfrac{2Wg^2\ell^3}{\pi r^4 \theta}$, the quantity which should be measured with best care is
(a) W (b) ℓ
(c) r (d) θ

25 While measuring acceleration due to gravity by simple pendulum, a student makes a positive error of 1% in the length of the pendulum and a negative error of 3% in the value of the time period. His actual percentage error in the measurement of the value of g will be
(a) 2% (b) 4%
(c) 5% (d) 7%

26 The density of cube is measured by measuring its mass and the length of its sides. If the maximum errors in the measurement of mass and length are 3% and 2% respectively, then the maximum error in the measurement of density is
(a) 9% (b) 7%
(c) 5% (d) 1%

27 The least count of a stopwatch is 0.2 s. The time for 20 oscillations of a pendulum is measured to be 25 s. The percentage error in the measurement of time will be
(a) 0.1% (b) 8%
(c) 1.8% (d) 0.8%

28 Which of the following measurements is most accurate?

(a) 0.005 mm (b) 5.00 mm
(c) 50.00 mm (d) 5.0 mm

29 The period of oscillation of a simple pendulum in the experiment is recorded as 2.63 s, 2.56 s, 2.42 s, 2.71 s, 2.80 s, respectively. Find the mean absolute error in the measurement of time period.

(a) 0.11 s (b) 0.13 s
(c) 0.15 s (d) 0.08 s

30 An experiment measured quantities a, b, c and then x is calculated from $x = \frac{a^2\sqrt{b}}{2c^3}$. If the percentage errors in a, b, c are $\pm 2\%$, $\pm 4\%$ and $\pm 1\%$ respectively, the maximum percentage error in x will be

(a) $\pm 3\%$ (b) $\pm 9\%$
(c) $\pm 12\%$ (d) $\pm 0\%$

31 A body travels uniformly a distance of (20.0 ± 0.2) m in a time (5.0 ± 0.1) s. The velocity of the body within error limits is

(a) $(4.0 \pm 0.05)\ \text{ms}^{-1}$ (b) $(4.0 \pm 0.15)\ \text{ms}^{-1}$
(c) $(4.0 \pm 0.2)\ \text{ms}^{-1}$ (d) $(4.0 \pm 0.3)\ \text{ms}^{-1}$

32 The pressure on a square plate is measured by measuring the force on the plate and the length of the side of the plate. The errors in the measurement of force and length are 4% and 2%, respectively. The maximum error in the value of the pressure would be

(a) 1 % (b) 2%
(c) 6% (d) 8%

33 What is the maximum percentage error in the measurement of acceleration due to gravity, if maximum errors in the measurement of time period and length of a simple-pendulum are 4% and 2%, respectively?

(a) 2% (b) 6%
(c) 8% (d) 10%

34 A glass plate is of length 2.0 cm and width 1.5 cm. The maximum probable error in measuring the area of the plate is

(a) $0.15\ \text{cm}^2$ (b) $0.25\ \text{cm}^2$
(c) $0.35\ \text{cm}^2$ (d) $0.45\ \text{cm}^2$

35 If there is a positive error of 50% in the measurement of velocity of a body, then the error in the measurement of kinetic energy is

(a) 25% (b) 50%
(c) 100% (d) 125%

36 A wire has a mass (0.3 ± 0.003) g, radius (0.5 ± 0.005) mm and length (6 ± 0.06) cm. The maximum percentage error in the measurement of its density is

(a) 1% (b) 2 %
(c) 3 % (d) 4 %

37 The least count of a screw gauge is 0.01 mm. The percentage error in measuring 5 mm thickness will be

(a) 0.01% (b) 0.1%
(c) 0.2% (d) 0.02%

38 Percentage error in measurement of mass and speed of a body are 2% and 3%, respectively. If we calculate kinetic energy of this body by using mass and velocity, then percentage error in kinetic energy is

(a) 11% (b) 8%
(c) 5% (d) 1%

39 Position of a particle is given by $y = \frac{t^2 + t^3}{8}$. If % error in calculating time is 0.1% at $t = 2$ s, find % error in calculating position of the particle at $t = 2$ s.

(a) 0.267%
(b) 0.4%
(c) 0.8%
(d) None of the above

40 A projectile is thrown with velocity $u = 20$ m/s $\pm 3\%$ at an angle of 15°. If the projectile falls back on the ground at the same level, then which of following cannot be a possible answer for range? [Consider, $g = 10\ \text{m/s}^2$]

(a) 21.3 m (b) 21.0 m
(c) 19.6 m (d) 18.9 m

41 For finding the specific resistance of a wire, a student took the following readings by using a metre scale, a micrometer and a resistance box. Length of the wire $(L) = 100.0$ cm, Radius $(r) = 0.100$ cm and $R = 10\Omega$. What is the maximum possible percentage error in the value of the specific resistance?

(a) 9.8 % (b) 12.1 %
(c) 15.5% (d) 18%

42 If $(n+1)$th division of vernier scale coincides with nth division of main scale then the least count of the vernier scale is [Given one main scale division is equal to 'a' units]–

(a) $\frac{a}{n-1}$ (b) $\frac{a}{n}$
(c) $\frac{a}{n+1}$ (d) $\frac{a+1}{n}$

43 The vernier of a circular scale is divided into 30 divisions which coincide against 29 divisions of main scale. Each main scale division is 0.5°. The least count of the instrument is–

(a) 10' (b) 0.1'
(c) 1' (d) 30'

44 A spectrometer gives the following reading when used to measure the angle of a prism.
Main scale reading : 58.5 degree
Vernier scale reading : 09 divisions
Given that 1 division on main scale corresponds to 0.5 degree. Total divisions on the vernier scale is 30 and match with 29 divisions of the main scale. The angle of the prism from the above data:

(a) 59 degree
(b) 58.59 degree
(c) 58.77 degree
(d) 58.65 degree

45 The diameter of a cylinder is measured using a Vernier callipers with no zero error. It is found that the zero of the Vernier scale lies between 5.10 cm and 5.15 cm of the main scale. The Vernier scale has 50 divisions equivalent to 2.45 cm. The 24th division of the Vernier scale exactly coincides with one of the main scale divisions. The diameter of the cylinder is:

(a) 5.112 cm (b) 5.124 cm
(c) 5.136 cm (d) 5.148 cm

46 The main scale of a vernier callipers reads in millimeter and its vernier is divided into 10 divisions which coincides with 9 divisions of the main scale. What is the reading for the situation shown?

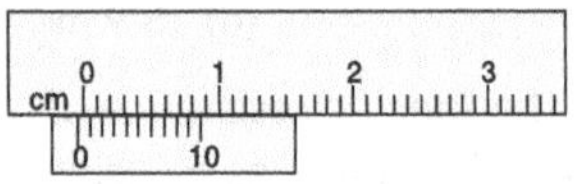

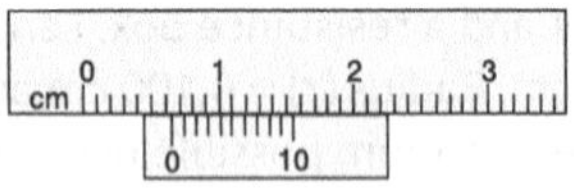

(a) 6.0 mm (b) 6.1 mm
(c) 6.5 mm (d) 6.9 mm

47 A screw gauge gives the following reading when used to measure the diameter of a wire.
Main scale reading : 0 mm.
Circular scale reading : 52 divisions
Given that 1 mm on main scale corresponds to 100 divisions of the circular scale.
The diameter of wire from the above data is :

(a) 0.025 cm (b) 0.005 cm
(c) 0.52 cm (d) 0.052 cm

48 The circular scale of a screw gauge has 50 divisions and pitch of 0.5 mm. Find the diameter of sphere. Main scale reading is 2 –

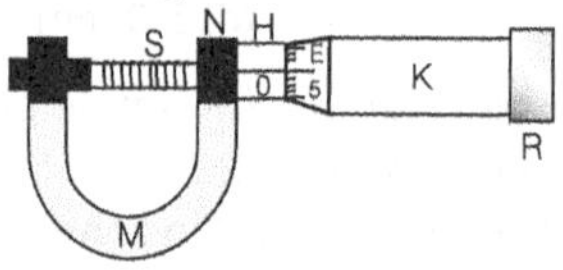

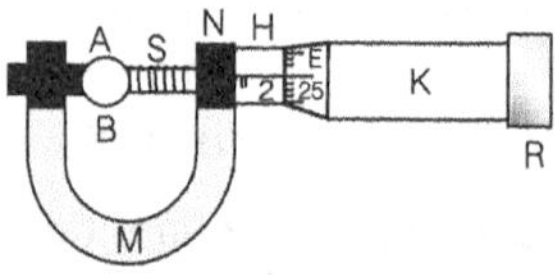

(a) 1.2 (b) 1.25 (c) 2.207 (d) 2.25

49. Two full turns of the circular scale of gauge cover a distance of 1 mm on scale. The total number of divisions on circular scale is 50. Further, it is found that screw gauge has a zero error of – 0.3 mm. While measuring the diameter of a thin wire a student notes the main scale reading of 3 mm and the number of circular scale division in line, with the main scale as 35. The diameter of the wire is

(a) 3.32 mm (b) 3.73 mm
(c) 3.67 mm (d) 3.38 mm

50. A screw gauge having 100 equal divisions and pitch of length 1 mm is used to measure the diameter of a wire of length 5.6 cm. The main scale reading is 1 mm and 47th circular division coincides with the main scale. The surface area of wire to appropriate significant figure is equal to (use $\pi = \frac{22}{7}$)

(a) 2.1 cm^2 (b) 2.6 cm^2 (c) 5. 2 cm^2 (d) 1. 3 cm^2

Multiple Choice(s) Correct Questions

1 Error in the measurement of radius of a sphere is 1 %. Then,

(a) the error in the measurement of its surface area is 2%
(b) the error in the measurement of its surface area is 4%
(c) the error in the measurement of its volume is 2%
(d) the error in the measurement of its volume is 3%

2 Error in the measurement of surface area of a cube is 4 %. Then,

(a) the error in the measurement of its side is 1%
(b) the error in the measurement of its side is 2%
(c) the error in the measurement of its volume is 4%
(d) the error in the measurement of its volume is 6%

3 Two resistances are given as $R_1 = (3 \pm 0.2)\,\Omega$ and $R_2 = (6 \pm 0.3)\,\Omega$. Then,

(a) equivalent resistance in series combination is $(9 \pm 0.5)\,\Omega$

(b) equivalent resistance in series combination is $(9 \pm 0.1)\,\Omega$

(c) equivalent resistance in parallel combination is $(2 \pm 0.5)\,\Omega$

(d) equivalent resistance in parallel combination is $(2 \pm 0.12)\,\Omega$

Previous Year's Questions

JEE Main

1 Given below are two statements : one is labelled as **Assertion (A)** and other is labelled as **Reason (R).**

Assertion (A) In vernier calliper if positive zero error exists, then while taking measurements, the reading taken will be more than the actual reading.

Reason (R) The zero error in vernier calliper might have happened due to manufacturing defect or due to rough handling.

In the light of the above statements, choose the **correct** answer from the options given below **[2024, 27 Jan Shift-II]**

(a) Both (A) and (R) are correct but (R) is not the correct explanation of (A).
(b) (A) is true but (R) is false.
(c) Both (A) and (R) are correct and (R) is the correct explanation of (A).
(c) (A) is false but (R) is true.

2 The resistance $R = \frac{V}{I}$ where $V = (200 \pm 5)$ V and $I = (20 \pm 0.2)$ A, the percentage error in the measurement of R is **[2024, 29 Jan Shift-I]**

(a) 3% (b) 7%
(c) 3.5% (d) 5.5%

3 A physical quantity Q is found to depend on quantities a, b, c by the relation $Q = \frac{a^4 b^3}{c^2}$. The percentage error in a, b and c are 3%, 4% and 5% respectively. Then, the percentage error in Q is **[2024, 29 Jan Shift-II]**

(a) 14% (b) 43% (c) 34% (d) 66%

4 If 50 vernier divisions are equal to 49 main scale divisions of a travelling microscope and one smallest reading of main scale is 0.5 mm, the vernier constant of travelling microscope is **[2024, 30 Jan Shift-II]**

(a) 0.1 cm (b) 0.01 mm (c) 0.1 mm (d) 0.01 cm

5 A physical quantity P is given as $P = \frac{a^2 b^3}{c\sqrt{d}}$

The percentage error in the measurement of a, b, c and d are 1%, 2%, 3% and 4% respectively. The percentage error in the measurement of quantity P will be **[2023, 10 April Shift-I]**

(a) 14% (b) 13% (c) 16% (d) 12%

6 A cylindrical wire of mass (0.4 ± 0.01) g has length (8 ± 0.04) cm and radius (6 ± 0.03) mm. The maximum error in its density will be **[2023, 8 April Shift-I]**

(a) 5% (b) 3.5% (c) 4% (d) 1%

7 A silver wire has mass (0.6 ± 0.006) g, radius (0.5 ± 0.005) mm and length (4 ± 0.04) cm. The maximum percentage error in the measurement of its density will be: **[2022, 27 June Shift-I]**

(a) 4% (b) 3% (c) 6% (d) 7%

8 In an experiment to find acceleration due to gravity (g) using simple pendulum, time period of 0.5 s is measured from time of 100 oscillation with a watch of 1s resolution. If measured value of length is 10 cm known to 1 mm accuracy. The accuracy in the determination of g is found to be x%. The value of x is **[2022, 28 July Shift-II]**

9 A travelling microscope is used to determine the refractive index of a glass slab. If 40 divisions are there in 1 cm on main scale and 50 vernier scale divisions are equal to 49 main scale divisions, then least count of the travelling microscope is .... $\times 10^{-6}$ m. **[2022, 26 June Shift-II]**

10 Two resistors $R_1 = (4 \pm 0.8)\,\Omega$ and $R_2 = (4 \pm 0.4)\,\Omega$ are connected in parallel. The equivalent resistance of their parallel combination will be **[2021, 1 Sep Shift-II]**

(a) $(4 \pm 0.4)\,\Omega$ (b) $(2 \pm 0.4)\,\Omega$
(c) $(2 \pm 0.3)\,\Omega$ (d) $(4 \pm 0.3)\,\Omega$

11 A student determined Young's modulus of elasticity using the formula $Y = \frac{MgL^3}{4bd^3\delta}$. The value of g is taken to be 9.8 m/s^2, without any significant error, his observations are as following.

Physical quantity	Least count of the equipment used for measurement	Observed value
Mass (M)	1 g	2 kg
Length of bar (L)	1 mm	1 m
Breadth of bar (b)	0.1 mm	4 cm
Thickness of bar (d)	0.01 mm	0.4 cm
Depression (δ)	0.01 mm	5 mm

Then, the fractional error in the measurement of Y is **[2021, 1 Sep Shift-II]**

(a) 0.0083 (b) 0.0155 (c) 0.155 (d) 0.083

12 If the length of the pendulum in pendulum clock increases by 0.1%, then the error in time per day is **[2021, 26 Aug Shift-II]**

(a) 86.4 s (b) 4.32 s (c) 43.2 s (d) 8.64 s

13 In order to determine the Young's modulus of a wire of radius 0.2 cm (measured using a scale of least count = 0.001 cm) and length 1m (measured using a scale of least count = 1 mm), a weight of mass 1kg (measured using a scale of least count = 1g) was hanged to get the elongation of 0.5 cm (measured using a scale of least count 0.001 cm). What will be the fractional error in the value of Young's modulus determined by this experiment ? **[2021, 16 March Shift-II]**

(a) 0.14% (b) 0.9%
(c) 9% (d) 1.4%

14 The period of oscillation of a simple pendulum is $T = 2\pi\sqrt{\frac{L}{g}}$. Measured value of L is 1.0 m from metre scale having a minimum division of 1 mm and time of one complete oscillation is 1.95 s measured from stopwatch of 0.01 s resolution. The percentage error in the determination of g will be **[2021, 24 Feb Shift-II]**

(a) 1.13% (b) 1.03%
(c) 1.33% (d) 1.30%

15 The resistance $R = \frac{V}{I}$, where $V = (50 \pm 2)$ V and $I = (20 \pm 0.2)$ A. The percentage error in R is x %. The value of x to the nearest integer is......... . **[2021, 16 March Shift-I]**

16 The radius of a sphere is measured to be (7.50 + 0.85) cm. Suppose, the percentage error in its volume is x. The value of x, to the nearest x, is .... **[2021, 18 March Shift-II]**

17 The density of a solid metal sphere is determined by measuring its mass and its diameter. The maximum error in the density of the sphere is $\left(\frac{x}{100}\right)$%. If the relative errors in measuring the mass and the diameter are 6.0% and 1.5% respectively, the value of x is .... **[2020, 6 Sep Shift-I]**

JEE Advanced

1. Area of the cross-section of a wire is measured using a screw gauge. The pitch of the main scale is 0.5 mm. The circular scale has 100 divisions and for one full rotation of the circular scale, the main scale shifts by two divisions.

The measured readings are listed below.

Measurement condition	Main scale reading	Circular scale reading
Two arms of gauge touching each other without wire	0 division	4 divisions
Attempt-1: With wire	4 divisions	20 divisions
Attempt-2: With wire	4 divisions	16 divisions

What are the diameter and cross-sectional area of the wire measured using the screw gauge? **(2022 Adv.)**

(a) 2.22 ± 0.02 mm, $\pi(1.23 \pm 0.02)$ mm^2
(b) 2.22 ± 0.01 mm, $\pi(1.23 \pm 0.01)$ mm^2
(c) 2.14 ± 0.02 mm, $\pi(1.14 \pm 0.02)$ mm^2
(d) 2.14 ± 0.01 mm, $\pi(1.14 \pm 0.01)$ mm^2

2. The smallest division on the main scale of a Vernier calipers is 0.1 cm. Ten divisions of the Vernier scale correspond to nine divisions of the main scale. The figure below on the left shows the reading of this calipers with no gap between its two jaws. The figure on the right shows the reading with a solid sphere held between the jaws. The correct diameter of the sphere is **(2021 Adv.)**

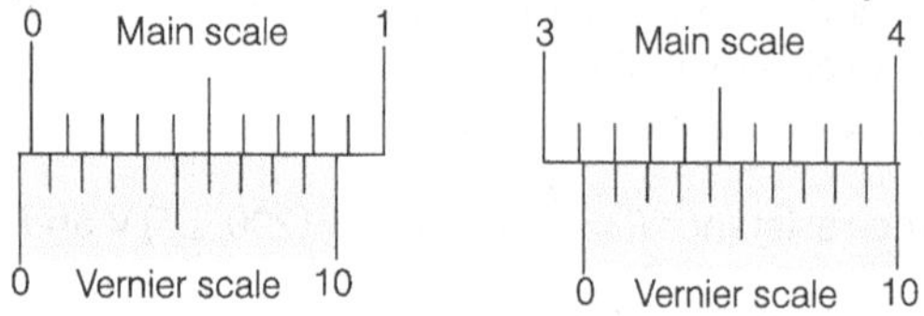

(a) 3.07 cm (b) 3.11 cm
(c) 3.15 cm (d) 3.17 cm

3. Two capacitors with capacitance values $C_1 = 2000 \pm 10$pF and $C_2 = 3000 \pm 15$ pF are connected in series. The voltage applied across this combination is $C = 5.00 \pm 0.02$ V. The percentage error in the calculation of the energy stored in this combination of capacitors is ________. **(2020 Adv.)**

Passage

If the measurement errors in all the independent quantities are known, then it is possible to determine the error in any dependent quantity. This is done by the use of series expansion and truncating the expansion at the first power of the error. For example, consider the relation $z = x/y$. If the errors in x, y and z are Δx, Δy and Δz respectively, then

$$z \pm \Delta z = \frac{x \pm \Delta x}{y \pm \Delta y} = \frac{x}{y}\left(1 \pm \frac{\Delta x}{x}\right)\left(1 \pm \frac{\Delta y}{y}\right)^{-1}$$

The series expansion for $\left(1 \pm \frac{\Delta y}{y}\right)^{-1}$ to first power in $\Delta y/y$, is $1 \mp (\Delta y/y)$. The relative errors in independent variables are always added. So, the error in z will be

$$\Delta z = z\left(\frac{\Delta x}{x} + \frac{\Delta y}{y}\right)$$

The above derivation makes the assumption that $\Delta x / x \ll 1$, $\Delta y/y \ll 1$. Therefore, the higher powers of these quantities are neglected.

(There are two questions based on above paragraph.) **(2018 Adv.)**

4. Consider the ratio $r = \frac{(1-a)}{(1+a)}$ to be determined by measuring a dimensionless quantity a. If the error in the measurement of a is Δa ($\Delta a / a \ll 1$), then what is the error Δr in determining r?

(a) $\frac{\Delta a}{(1+a)^2}$ (b) $\frac{-2\Delta a}{(1+a)^2}$

(c) $\frac{2\Delta a}{(1-a)^2}$ (d) $\frac{2a\Delta a}{(1-a^2)}$

5. In an experiment, the initial number of radioactive nuclei is 3000. It is found that 1000 ± 40 nuclei decayed in the first 1.0 s. For $|x| \ll 1$, $\ln(1+x) = x$ up to first power in x. The error $\Delta\lambda$, in the determination of the decay constant λ in s^{-1}, is

(a) 0.04 (b) 0.03

(c) 0.02 (d) 0.01

6. A person measures the depth of a well by measuring the time interval between dropping a stone and receiving the sound of impact with the bottom of the well. The error in his measurement of time is $\delta T = 0.01$ s and he measures the depth of the well to be $L = 20$ m. Take the acceleration due to gravity $g = 10$ ms^{-2} and the velocity of sound is 300 ms^{-1}. Then, the percentage error in the measurement, $\frac{\delta L}{L}$, is closest to **(2017 Adv.)**

(a) 1% (b) 5%

(c) 3% (d) 0.2%

7. In an experiment to determine the acceleration due to gravity g, the formula used for the time period of a periodic motion is $T = 2\pi\sqrt{\frac{7(R-r)}{5g}}$. The values of R and r are measured to be (60 ± 1) mm and (10 ± 1) mm, respectively. In five successive measurements, the time period is found to be 0.52 s, 0.56 s, 0.57 s, 0.54 s and 0.59 s. The least count of the watch used for the measurement of time period is 0.01 s. Which of the following statement(s) is (are) true? **(2016 Adv.)**

(a) The error in the measurement of r is 10%

(b) The error in the measurement of T is 3.57%

(c) The error in the measurement of T is 2%

(d) The error in the measurement of g is 11%

8. There are two vernier calipers both of which have 1 cm divided into 10 equal divisions on the main scale. The vernier scale of one of the calipers (C_1) has 10 equal divisions that correspond to 9 main scale divisions. The vernier scale of the other caliper (C_2) has 10 equal divisions that correspond to 11 main scale divisions. The readings of the two calipers are shown in the figure. The measured values (in cm) by calipers C_1 and C_2 respectively, are **(2016 Adv.)**

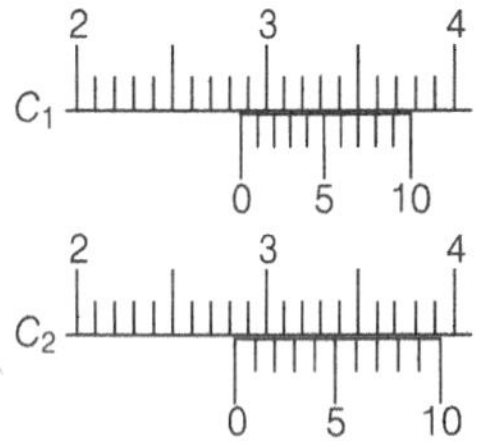

(a) 2.87 and 2.87 (b) 2.87 and 2.83

(c) 2.85 and 2.82 (d) 2.87 and 2.86

9. The energy of a system as a function of time t is given as $E(t) = A^2 \exp(-\alpha t)$, where $\alpha = 0.2$ s^{-1}. The measurement of A has an error of 1.25%. If the error in the measurement of time is 1.50%, the percentage error in the value of $E(t)$ at $t = 5$ s is **(2015 Adv.)**

10. During Searle's experiment, zero of the vernier scale lies between 3.20×10^{-2} m and 3.25×10^{-2} m of the main scale. The 20th division of the vernier scale exactly coincides with one of the main scale divisions. When an additional load of 2 kg is applied to the wire, the zero of the vernier scale still lies between 3.20×10^{-2} m and 3.25×10^{-2} m of the main scale but now the 45th division of vernier scale coincides with one of the main scale divisions. The length of the thin metallic wire is 2 m and its cross-sectional area is 8×10^{-7} m^2. The least count of the vernier scale is 1.0×10^{-5} m. The maximum percentage error in the Young's modulus of the wire is **(2014 Adv.)**

Answer Key

Level 1

4.1 Significant Figures

1. (i) 3, (ii) 4, (iii) 4, (iv) 1, (v) 3, (vi) 2, (vii) 2, (viii) 4, (ix) 4
2. (i) 16500, (ii) 12.7 , (iii) 11.6, (iv) 20.4 (v) 0.00857, (vi) 12.5
3. (i) 5.9, (ii) 13.0, (iii) 1.0, (iv) 711, (v) 0.7, (vi) 1.0×10^3, (vii) 20.0, (viii) 33 , (ix) 14, (x) 2.16
4. 2.3 kg **5.** 4.8 g/cm^3 **6.** 9.76 m/s **7.** 0.43 m^2 **8.** 62 ohm
9. (i) True (ii) True (iii) True (iv) True (v) True (vi) False (vii) False (viii) True
10. (i) 2 (ii) 3 (iii) 7 (iv) – 4

4.2 Errors in Measuement

1. (i) 1.50 (ii) –0.04, – 0.03, + 0.06, – 0.06, + 0.05 (iii) 0.048 (iv) $\pm$ 0.032 (v) $\pm$3.2%
2. $15.0 \pm 2.0\,\Omega$ **3.** $8.6 \pm 0.7°C$ **4.** Area $= 19 \pm 1.4$ cm^2
5. 6% **6.** $(10 \pm 0.7)\,\Omega$
7. (a) 1% (b) 1.5% **8.** $A = (26.46 \pm 1.26)$ cm^2 **9.** 13%
10. 3.7% **11.** (3.6 ± 0.6) gm/cm^3
12. $R_{eq} = (6 \pm 0.2)\,\Omega$ or $R_{eq} = (6\,\Omega \pm 3.33\%)$ **13.** 5%
14. $f = (14.3 \pm 0.14)$ cm **15.** 69%

4.3 Vernier Callipers

1. 0.01 cm **2.** 0.06 cm
3. 1.804 cm **4.** (a) $x = 0.10$ cm (b) $d = 2.05$ cm
5. 3.82 cm **6.** (a) + 0.6 mm (b) – 0.6 mm
7. 3.07 cm

4.4 Screw Gauge

1. 2.84 mm **2.** (a) 0.01 mm (b) 0.01 mm (c) 1.82 mm
3. 3.64 mm **4.** 6.41mm

Level 2

Single Choice Correct Questions

1. (c)	2. (c)	3. (b)	4. (a)	5. (a)
6. (b)	7. (a)	8. (a)	9. (c)	10. (d)
11. (c)	12. (a)	13. (a)	14. (b)	15. (a)
16. (c)	17. (a)	18. (b)	19. (a)	20. (d)
21. (c)	22. (b)	23. (c)	24. (c)	25. (d)
26. (a)	27. (d)	28. (c)	29. (a)	30. (b)
31. (b)	32. (d)	33. (d)	34. (c)	35. (d)
36. (d)	37. (c)	38. (b)	39. (a)	40. (a)
41. (b)	42. (c)	43. (c)	44. (d)	45. (b)
46. (d)	47. (d)	48. (a)	49. (d)	50. (b)

Multiple Choice(s) Correct Questions

1. (a,d) **2.** (b,d) **3.** (a,d)

Previous Year's Questions

JEE Main

1. (a)	2. (c)	3. (c)	4. (b)	5. (b)
6. (c)	7. (a)	8. (5)	9. (5)	10. (c)
11. (b)	12. (c)	13. (d)	14. (a)	15. (5)
16. (34)	17. (1050)			

JEE Advanced

1. (*)	2. (c)	3. (1.3)	4. (b)	5. (c)
6. (1)	7. (d)	8. (b)	9. (4)	10. (4)

SOLUTIONS

Level 1

4.1 Significant Figures

1. (i) 3 (ii) 4 (iii) 4 (iv) 1 (v) 3 (vi) 2 (vii) 2 (viii) 4 (ix) 4

2. (i) $164\underline{6}8 = 16500$ (ii) $12.7\underline{4}5 = 12.7$
(iii) $11.6\underline{5}0 = 11.6$ (iv) $20.3\underline{5}0 = 20.4$
(v) $0.0085\underline{6}8 = 0.00857$ (vi) $12.4\underline{5}6 = 12.5$

3. (i) $5.8 + 0.125 = 5.9\underline{2}5 = 5.9$
(ii) $9.15 + 3.8 = 12.9\underline{5} = 13.0$
(iii) $3.5 - 2.51 = 0.9\underline{9} = 1.0$
(iv) $703 + 7 + 0.66 = 710.\underline{6}6 = 711$
(v) $2.21 \times 0.3 = 0.\underline{6}63 = 0.7$
(vi) $12.4 \times 84 = 10\underline{4}1.6 = 1.0 \times 10^3$
(vii) $14.28 / 0.714 = 20 = 20.0$
(viii) $142.06 \times 0.23 = 32.\underline{6}738 = 33$
(ix) $\dfrac{2.91 \times 0.3842}{0.080} = 13.\underline{9}75 = 14$
(x) $\dfrac{0.9996 \times 3.54}{1.638} = 2.16\underline{0}3 = 2.16$

4. $2.3 + 0.00215 + 0.01239 = 2.3\underline{1}454 = 2.3$ kg

5. Density $= \dfrac{\text{Mass}}{\text{Volume}} = \dfrac{5.74}{1.2} = 4.7\underline{8}33 \text{ gm/cm}^3 = 4.8 \text{ g/cm}^3$

6. Average speed $= \dfrac{100.5 \text{ m}}{10.3 \text{ s}} = 9.75\underline{7}28 \text{ m/s} = 9.76 \text{ m/s}$

7. Area $= 10.52 \times 0.041 = 0.4\underline{3}132 \text{ m}^2 = 0.43 \text{ m}^2$

8. $R = \dfrac{V}{i} \Rightarrow R = \dfrac{12.5}{0.20} = 62.\underline{5} = 62\,\Omega$

9. (i) True, (ii) True, (iii) True, (iv) True, (v) True, (vi) False, (vii) False, (viii) True

10. (i) $147 = 1.47 \times 10^2$
Since, $1.47 < 5$, order of magnitude $= 2$
(ii) $501 = 5.01 \times 10^2$
Since, $5.01 > 5$, order of magnitude $= 2 + 1 = 3$
(iii) $8346002 = 8.34 \times 10^6$
Since, $8.34 > 5$, order of magnitude $= 6 + 1 = 7$
(iv) $0.00025432 = 2.54 \times 10^{-4}$
Since, $2.54 < 5$, order of magnitude $= -4$

4.2 Errors in Measurement

1. (i) Mean value $= \dfrac{1.54 + 1.53 + 1.44 + 1.56 + 1.45}{5}$
$= \dfrac{7.52}{5} = 1.50\underline{4} = 1.50$

(ii) $\Delta x_1 = 1.50 - 1.54 = -0.04$
$\Delta x_2 = 1.50 - 1.53 = -0.03$
$\Delta x_3 = 1.50 - 1.44 = 0.06$
$\Delta x_4 = 1.50 - 1.56 = -0.06$
$\Delta x_5 = 1.50 - 1.45 = 0.05$

(iii) $\Delta x = \dfrac{|\Delta x_1| + |\Delta x_2| + |\Delta x_3| + |\Delta x_4| + |\Delta x_5|}{5}$
$= \dfrac{0.24}{5} = 0.048$

(iv) Relative error $= \dfrac{\Delta x}{x_m} = \dfrac{0.048}{1.50} = \pm 0.032$

(v) Percentage error $= \dfrac{\Delta x}{x_m} \times 100 = \pm 3.2\%$

2. $R_{eq} = R_1 + R_2$
$R_{eq} = (10.0 \pm 0.5) + (5.00 \pm 1.5) = (15.0 \pm 2.0)\,\Omega$

3. $\Delta T = T_1 - T_2 = (76.3 \pm 0.4)°\text{C} - (67.7 \pm 0.3)°\text{C} = (8.6 \pm 0.7)°\text{ C}$

4. Area $= A \pm \Delta A$
$A = 5.7 \times 3.4 = 19.\underline{3}8 = 19 \text{ cm}^2$ and $\dfrac{\Delta A}{A} = \dfrac{\Delta l}{l} + \dfrac{\Delta b}{b}$
$\dfrac{\Delta A}{19} = \dfrac{0.1}{5.7} + \dfrac{0.2}{3.4}$
$\Rightarrow \Delta A = 19\left(\dfrac{0.1}{5.7} + \dfrac{0.2}{3.4}\right) = 1.4\underline{5} \text{ cm}^2 = 1.4 \text{ cm}^2$
Area $= (19 \pm 1.4) \text{ cm}^2$

5. $Q = CV$
$Q = 2.0 \times 20 = 40$
$\dfrac{\Delta Q}{Q} = \dfrac{\Delta C}{C} + \dfrac{\Delta V}{V} \Rightarrow \dfrac{\Delta Q}{40} = \dfrac{0.1}{2.0} + \dfrac{0.2}{20}$
$\Rightarrow \Delta Q = 2.4\,\mu\text{C} \Rightarrow Q = (40 \pm 2.4)\,\mu\text{C}$
$\Rightarrow$ % error $= \dfrac{2.4}{40} \times 100 = 6\%$

6. $R = \dfrac{V}{I} \Rightarrow R = \dfrac{100}{10} = 10\,\Omega$
$\dfrac{\Delta R}{R} = \dfrac{\Delta V}{V} + \dfrac{\Delta I}{I}$
$\Rightarrow \dfrac{\Delta R}{10} = \dfrac{5}{100} + \dfrac{0.2}{10} \Rightarrow \Delta R = 0.7\,\Omega$
$R = (10 \pm 0.7)\,\Omega$

7. $A = 4\pi r^2 \Rightarrow \dfrac{\Delta A}{A} = \dfrac{2\Delta r}{r}$
$\Rightarrow \dfrac{\Delta A}{A} \times 100 = 2\left(\dfrac{\Delta r}{r} \times 100\right) = 2(0.5\%) = 1\%$
$V = \dfrac{4}{3}\pi r^3 \Rightarrow \dfrac{\Delta V}{V} = 3\dfrac{\Delta r}{r}$
$\Rightarrow \dfrac{\Delta V}{V} \times 100 = 3\left(\dfrac{\Delta r}{r} \times 100\right) = 3(0.5\%) = 1.5\%$

8. $A = 6l^2$

$A = 6(2.1)^2 = 26.46 \text{ cm}^2$

and $\frac{\Delta A}{A} = \frac{2\Delta l}{l} \Rightarrow \frac{\Delta A}{26.46} = 2\left(\frac{0.05}{2.1}\right) \Rightarrow \Delta A = 1.26 \text{ cm}^2$

$A = (26.46 \pm 1.26) \text{ cm}^2$

9. $P = \frac{a^3 b^2}{\sqrt{cd}}$

$\frac{\Delta P}{P} = \frac{3\Delta a}{a} + \frac{2\Delta b}{b} + \frac{1}{2}\frac{\Delta c}{c} + \frac{\Delta d}{d}$

$\frac{\Delta P}{P} \times 100 = 3\left(\frac{\Delta a}{a} \times 100\right) + 2\left(\frac{\Delta b}{b} \times 100\right) + \frac{1}{2}\left(\frac{\Delta c}{c} \times 100\right) + \left(\frac{\Delta d}{d} \times 100\right)$

$= 3(1\%) + 2(3\%) + \frac{1}{2}(4\%) + (2\%) = 13\%$

10. $F = \frac{mv^2}{r} \Rightarrow F = \frac{(0.5)(10)^2}{(0.4)} = 125 \text{ N}$

and $\frac{\Delta F}{F} = \frac{\Delta m}{m} + \frac{2\Delta v}{v} + \frac{\Delta r}{r}$

$\Rightarrow \frac{\Delta F}{125} = \frac{0.005}{0.5} + 2\left(\frac{0.01}{10}\right) + \frac{0.01}{0.4} \Rightarrow \Delta F = 4.625$

$\therefore$ % error in $F = \frac{\Delta F}{F} \times 100 = \frac{4.625}{125} \times 100 = 3.7\%$

11. $\rho = \frac{m}{V} = \frac{m}{\pi r^2 l} = \frac{88}{\frac{22}{7} \times (0.28)^2 (100)} = 3.5\underline{7}1 \text{ gm/cm}^3$

$= 3.6 \text{ gm/cm}^3$ and $\frac{\Delta \rho}{\rho} = \frac{\Delta m}{m} + \frac{2\Delta r}{r} + \frac{\Delta l}{l}$

$\frac{\Delta \rho}{3.6} = \frac{2}{88} + 2\left(\frac{0.02}{0.28}\right) + \frac{0.1}{100}$

$\Rightarrow \Delta \rho = 0.5\underline{9}9 \text{ gm/cm}^3 = 0.6 \text{ gm/cm}^3$

$\rho = (3.6 \pm 0.6) \text{ gm/cm}^3$

12. $R_{eq} = \frac{R_1 R_2}{R_1 + R_2} = \frac{24(8)}{24 + 8} = 6\,\Omega$

$\frac{1}{R_{eq}} = \frac{1}{R_1} + \frac{1}{R_2} \Rightarrow \frac{\Delta R_{eq}}{R_{eq}^2} = \frac{\Delta R_1}{R_1^2} + \frac{\Delta R_2}{R_2^2}$

$\Rightarrow \frac{\Delta R_{eq}}{6^2} = \frac{0.5}{(24)^2} + \frac{0.3}{8^2} \Rightarrow \Delta R_{eq} = 0.2\,\Omega$

$R_{eq} = (6 \pm 0.2)\,\Omega$

13. $T = 2\pi\sqrt{\frac{l}{g}} \Rightarrow g = \frac{4\pi^2 l}{T^2} \Rightarrow \frac{\Delta g}{g} = \frac{\Delta l}{l} + \frac{2\Delta T}{T}$

$\frac{\Delta g}{g} = \frac{0.1}{10} + \frac{2\left(\frac{1}{100}\right)}{0.5} = 0.05 \Rightarrow \frac{\Delta g}{g} \times 100 = 0.05 \times 100 = 5\%$

14. $\frac{1}{v} + \frac{1}{u} = \frac{1}{f} \Rightarrow f = 14.3 \text{ cm}$

and $\frac{\Delta v}{v^2} + \frac{\Delta u}{u^2} = \frac{\Delta f}{f^2} \Rightarrow \frac{\Delta f}{(14.3)^2} = \frac{0.2}{(20.1)^2} + \frac{0.5}{(50.1)^2}$

$\Rightarrow \Delta f = 0.14 \Rightarrow f = (14.3 \pm 0.14) \text{ cm}$

15. $K = \frac{1}{2}mv^2; K' = \frac{1}{2}m(1.3v)^2 \Rightarrow K' = 1.69\left(\frac{1}{2}mv^2\right) = 1.69K$

% error in KE $= \frac{\Delta K}{K} \times 100 = \frac{1.69K - K}{K} \times 100 = 69\%$

4.3 Vernier Callipers

1. $\text{MSD} = \frac{5}{100} = 0.05 \text{ cm},$

$\text{VSD} = \frac{1}{25} = 0.04 \text{ cm}$

$\text{LC} = \text{MSD} - \text{VSD} = 0.01 \text{ cm}$

2. $\left(1 \text{ M. S. D.} = \left(\frac{1}{10}\right) \text{cm} = 0.1 \text{ cm}\right)$

20 division of vernier scale = 8 division of main scale

$\Rightarrow \quad 1 \text{ V. S. D.} = \left(\frac{8}{20}\right) \text{M. S. D.}$

$= \left(\frac{2}{5}\right) \times 0.1 = 0.04 \text{ cm}$

L. C. = 1 M. S. D. – 1 V. S. D. = 0.1 cm – 0.04 cm = 0.06 cm.

3. Least count $= \frac{1}{10}$ cm = 0.01 cm,

Length of line = 1.8 + 4 × (0.01) = 1.804 cm

4. (a) LC $= \frac{1}{10}$ mm = 0.01 cm,

(b) diameter = 2 + 5 × (0.01) = 2.05 cm

5. Least count = 0.05 mm

Main scale reading = 76 × 0.5 = 38 mm

Vernier scale reading = 4 × 0.05 = 0.2 mm.

length = 38.2 mm = 3.82 cm

6. (a) LC $= \frac{1}{10}$ = 0.1 mm,

zero error = + 6 × 0.1 = + 0.6 mm

(b) zero correction = – 0.6 mm

7. LC = 0.1 mm

The error = 7 × 0.1 = 0.7 mm = 0.07 cm

True reading = 3.1 + 4 (0.01) – 0.07 = 3.07 cm

4.4 Screw Gauge

1. Least count $= \frac{0.5 \text{ mm}}{50} = 0.01 \text{ mm}$

Diameter,

D = 5 × 0.5 mm + (34) (0.01) mm = 2.84 mm

2. (a) Pitch $= \frac{2}{4} = 0.5$ mm,

(b) LC $= \frac{\frac{2}{4}}{50} = 0.01$ mm

(c) Diameter $= 3 \times 0.5 + 32 \times 0.01 = 1.5 + 0.32 = 1.82$ mm

3. Zero error $= -(50-44)\left(\frac{1\,mm}{50}\right) = -0.12$mm,

Thickness of plate $= 3 + 26 \times \frac{1}{50} + 0.12$ mm $= 3.64$ mm

4. Least count $= \frac{\text{pitch}}{\text{No. of division}} = \frac{2}{200} = 0.01$ mm;

Reading $= 3 \times 2 + (46-5)(0.01) = 6.41$ mm

Level 2

Single Choice Correct Questions

1. $3.8 \times 10^{-6} + 4.2 \times 10^{-5} = 4.5\underline{8} \times 10^{-6} = 4.6 \times 10^{-6}$

2. $V = 12 \times 2.42 = 29.0\underline{4}$ cm^3 $= 29.0$ cm^3

3. $A = \pi r^2 = 3.14\,(0.16)^2 = 0.080\underline{3}84$ mm^2 $= 0.080$ mm^2

4. $46\underline{2}1 = 4600$

5. Area $= 1.23 \times 2.345 = 2.88\underline{4}35$ cm^2 $= 2.88$ cm^2

6. $V = 12 \times 6 \times 2.45 = 1\underline{7}6.4$ cm^3 $= 2 \times 10^2$ cm^3

7. $\frac{97.52}{2.54} = 38.3\underline{9}37008 = 38.4$

8. $\frac{1}{20} = 0.0500$

9. $L + B = 2.331 + 2.1 = 4.4\underline{3}1 = 4.4$ cm

10. 4

11. $V = l^3 = (1.2 \times 10^{-2})^3 = 1.7\underline{2}8 \times 10^{-6}$ m^3 $= 1.7 \times 10^{-6}$ m^3

12. 5, 1, 2

13. $p = mv = 3.513 \times 5.00 = 17.5\underline{6}5$ kg-m/s $= 17.6$ kg-m/s

14. $6.03\underline{5}87 = 6.04$

15. (A) 0.12345 has 5 significant figures.
(B) 0.12100 has 5 significant figures.
(C) $47.23 \div 2.3$ has 2 significant figures.
(D) 3×10^8 has 1 significant figures.

16. $d_1 = (4.23 \pm 0.01)$ cm $\Rightarrow d_2 = (3.89 \pm 0.01)$ cm

Mean thickness $= \frac{d_1 - d_2}{2} = \frac{4.23 - 3.89}{2} = 0.17$ cm

Thickness $= (0.17 \pm 0.01)$ cm

17. $r = (4.22 \pm 2\%)$ cm

Mean value of volume $= \frac{4}{3}\pi r^3 = \frac{4}{3}\pi(4.22)^3 = 315$ cm^3

% error in volume $= \frac{\Delta V}{V} \times 100 = 3\left(\frac{\Delta r}{r} \times 100\right) = 6\%$

So, $V = (315 \pm 6\%)$ cm^3

18. $R_{eq} = R_1 + R_2 = (24 \pm 0.5) + (8 \pm 0.3) = (32 \pm 0.8)\,\Omega$

19. $V = lbh$

$$\frac{\Delta V}{V} = \frac{\Delta l}{l} + \frac{\Delta b}{b} + \frac{\Delta h}{h}$$

$$\Rightarrow \frac{\Delta V}{1.00} = \frac{0.1}{10.0} + \frac{0.01}{1.00} + \frac{0.001}{0.100}$$

$$\Rightarrow \frac{\Delta V}{1.00} = 0.01 + 0.01 + 0.01$$

$$\Rightarrow \Delta V = 1.00(0.03) \Rightarrow \Delta V = 0.03 \text{ cm}^3$$

20. $H = I^2Rt$

$$\frac{\Delta H}{H} \times 100 = \left(\frac{2\Delta I}{I} + \frac{\Delta R}{R} + \frac{\Delta t}{t}\right) \times 100 = 2(2\%) + 1\% + 1\% = 6\%$$

21. $I_B - I_A = (4.19 \pm 0.01) \pm (3.25 \pm 0.01) = 0.94 \pm 0.02$

22. $[X] = [M^a L^b T^{-c}]$

$$\frac{\Delta X}{X} \times 100 = \left[a\frac{\Delta M}{M} + b\frac{\Delta L}{L} + \frac{c\Delta T}{T}\right] \times 100 = (\alpha a + \beta b + c\gamma)\%$$

23. $V = (1.76 \pm 0.02)$ cm^3

$V' = 25\,V$

$V' = 1.76 \times 25 \pm 0.02 \times 25$

$V' = (44.0 \pm 0.5)$ cm^3

24. $n = \frac{2Wg^2 l^3}{\pi r^4 \theta}$

$$\frac{\Delta n}{n} = \frac{\Delta W}{W} + 2\frac{\Delta g}{g} + 3\frac{\Delta l}{l} + 4\frac{\Delta r}{r} + \frac{\Delta\theta}{\theta}$$

So, r should be measured with best care.

25. $T = 2\pi\sqrt{\frac{l}{g}} \Rightarrow g = \frac{4\pi^2 l}{T^2}$

$$\frac{\Delta g}{g} = \frac{\Delta l}{l} - \frac{2\Delta T}{T} = 1 - 2(-3) = 7\%$$

26. $\rho = \frac{m}{V} = \frac{m}{l^3}$

$$\frac{\Delta\rho}{\rho} \times 100 = \left(\frac{\Delta m}{m} + 3\frac{\Delta l}{l}\right) \times 100 = 3 + 3(2) = 9\%$$

27. % error in time $= \frac{\Delta t}{t} \times 100 = \frac{0.2}{25} \times 100 = 0.8\%$

28. One with maximum significant figures will be most accurate.

29. $T_m = \frac{2.63 + 2.56 + 2.42 + 2.71 + 2.80}{5} = 2.62$ s

$\Delta T_1 = 2.62 - 2.63 = -0.01$

$\Delta T_2 = 2.62 - 2.56 = 0.06$

$\Delta T_3 = 2.62 - 2.42 = 0.20$

$\Delta T_4 = 2.62 - 2.71 = -0.09$

$$\Delta T_5 = 2.62 - 2.80 = -0.18$$

$$\Delta T_m = \frac{(|-0.01| + |0.06| + |0.20| + |-0.09| + |-0.18|)}{5} = 0.11 \text{ s}$$

30. $x = \dfrac{a^2\sqrt{b}}{2c^3}$

$$100 \times \frac{\Delta x}{x} = \left(2\frac{\Delta a}{a} + \frac{1}{2}\frac{\Delta b}{b} + 3\frac{\Delta c}{c}\right) \times 100$$

$$= \left(2(2) + \frac{1}{2}(4) + 3(1)\right)\% = 9\%$$

31. $v = \dfrac{s}{t} \Rightarrow v = \dfrac{20.0}{5.0} = 4.0 \Rightarrow \dfrac{\Delta v}{v} = \dfrac{\Delta s}{s} + \dfrac{\Delta t}{t}$

$$\frac{\Delta v}{5.0} = \frac{0.2}{20.0} + \frac{0.1}{5.0} \Rightarrow \Delta v = \left(\frac{1}{100} + \frac{1}{50}\right)5$$

$$\Delta v = 0.15$$

32. $P = \dfrac{F}{A} = \dfrac{F}{l^2}$

$$\frac{\Delta P}{P} \times 100 = \frac{\Delta F}{F} \times 100 + 2\left(\frac{\Delta l}{l} \times 100\right) = 4\% + 2(2\%) = 8\%$$

33. $T = 2\pi\sqrt{\dfrac{l}{g}} \Rightarrow g = \dfrac{4\pi^2 l}{T^2}$

$$100 \times \frac{\Delta g}{g} = \left(\frac{\Delta l}{l} + 2\frac{\Delta T}{T}\right) \times 100 = [2 + 2(4)]\% = 10\%$$

34. $A = lb$

$$\frac{\Delta A}{A} = \frac{\Delta l}{l} + \frac{\Delta b}{b} \Rightarrow \frac{\Delta A}{2.0 \times 1.5} = \frac{0.1}{2.0} + \frac{0.1}{1.5}$$

$$\Rightarrow \Delta A = 0.35 \text{ cm}^2$$

35. $K = \dfrac{1}{2}mv^2$

$$K' = \frac{1}{2}m(1.5v)^2 = 2.25\left(\frac{1}{2}mv^2\right) = 2.25K$$

$$\%\text{ error in KE} = \frac{K' - K}{K} \times 100 = 125\%$$

36. $\rho = \dfrac{m}{V} = \dfrac{m}{\pi r^2 l}$

$$100 \times \frac{\Delta\rho}{\rho} = \left(\frac{\Delta m}{m} + 2\frac{\Delta r}{r} + \frac{\Delta l}{l}\right) \times 100$$

$$= \left(\frac{0.003}{0.3} + 2\left(\frac{0.005}{0.5}\right) + \frac{0.06}{6}\right) \times 100 = 4\%$$

37. $\%\text{ error} = \dfrac{0.01}{5} \times 100 = 0.2\%$

38. $K = \dfrac{1}{2}mv^2$

$$100 \times \frac{\Delta K}{K} = \left(\frac{\Delta m}{m} + 2\frac{\Delta v}{v}\right) \times 100 = [2 + 2(3)]\% = 8\%$$

39. $y = \dfrac{t^2 + t^3}{8} \Rightarrow \dfrac{dy}{dt} = \dfrac{2t + 3t^2}{8} \Rightarrow dy = \left(\dfrac{2t + 3t^2}{8}\right)dt$

$$100 \times \frac{dy}{y} = \frac{\left(\dfrac{2t + 3t^2}{8}\right)t}{y}\left(\frac{dt}{t}\right) \times 100$$

$$\%\text{ error in } y = \left(\frac{2t^2 + 3t^3}{8y}\right)\left(\frac{dt}{t} \times 100\right)$$

$$= \frac{32}{8\left(\dfrac{12}{8}\right)} \times (0.1\%) = 0.267\%$$

40. $R = \dfrac{u^2 \sin 2\theta}{g}$

$$\Rightarrow R = \frac{(20)^2 \sin 30°}{10} = 20 \text{ m}$$

$$100 \times \frac{\Delta R}{R} = 2\frac{\Delta u}{u} \times 100$$

$\Rightarrow$ % error in $R = 2(3\%) = 6\%$

So, $R = (20 \pm 6\%) = (20 \pm 1.2)$ m

41. Least count of radius = 0.001 cm

Least count of resistance = 1Ω,

Least count of length = 0.1 cm

$$R = \frac{\rho L}{\pi r^2} \Rightarrow \rho = \frac{\pi r^2 R}{L}$$

$$\therefore \frac{\Delta\rho}{\rho} \times 100 = \left[2\left(\frac{\Delta r}{r}\right) + \frac{\Delta R}{R} + \frac{\Delta L}{L}\right] \times 100$$

$$= \left[2\left(\frac{0.001}{0.100}\right) + \frac{1}{10} + \frac{0.1}{100.0}\right] \times 100 = 12.1\%$$

42. $(n+1)$ VSD = n MSD

$$\Rightarrow 1 \text{ VSD} = \left(\frac{n}{n+1}\right)\text{MSD}$$

$$\text{L. C.} = 1 \text{ MSD} - 1 \text{ VSD} = a - \left(\frac{n}{n+1}\right)a = \frac{a}{n+1}$$

43. Least count = 1 MSD − 1 VSD

but 30 VSD = 29 MSD

$$\Rightarrow 1 \text{ VSD} = \left(\frac{29}{30}\right)\text{MSD}$$

$$\text{Therefore L. C.} = 1 \text{ MSD} - \frac{29}{30}\text{MSD} = \frac{\text{MSD}}{30} = \frac{0.5°}{30} = 1'$$

44. $1 \text{ VSD} = \dfrac{29}{30} \times 0.5° = \left(\dfrac{29}{60}\right)^\circ$ and $1 \text{ MSD} = \left(\dfrac{1}{2}\right)^\circ = \left(\dfrac{30}{60}\right)^\circ$

$$\text{Least count} = 1 \text{ MSD} - 1 \text{ VSD} = \left(\frac{1}{60}\right)^\circ,$$

$$\text{Reading} = 58.5° + 9 \times \left(\frac{1}{60}\right)^\circ = 58.65°$$

45. 50 divisions = 2.45 cm

$\Rightarrow$ 1 division $= \frac{2.45}{50} = 0.049$ cm.

Least count = 1 MSD − 1 VSD

$= 0.05 - 0.049 = 0.001$ cm

So vernier reading $= 0.001 \times 24 = 0.024$ cm.

Therefore diameter of cylinder

$= 5.10 + 0.024 = 5.124$ cm

46. Least count $= \frac{1\text{mm}}{1} = 0.01$ mm ;

Zero error $= -(10-6)\times 0.1 = -0.4$ mm

Reading $= 6 + 5 \times (0.1) - (-0.4) = 6.9$ mm

47. Least count $= \frac{1\text{mm}}{10} = 0.01$ mm

Diameter of the wire

$= 0 + 52 \times 0.01$ mm $= 0.52$ mm $= 0.052$ cm

48. Least count $= \frac{0.5}{50} = 0.01$ mm

Diameter of sphere

$= 2 \times 0.5 + (25-5) \times 0.01 = 1.2$ cm

49. Diameter = M. S. R. + C. S. R. × L. C. + Z. E.

$= 3 + 35 \times \left(\frac{0.5}{50}\right) + 0.03 = 3.38$ mm

50. Diameter $= 1 + 47 \times \left(\frac{1}{100}\right) = 1.47$ mm $= 0.147$ cm

$s = l \times \pi \times d = 5.6\text{ cm} \times \frac{22}{7} \times 0.147$ cm

$= 2.5872\text{ cm}^2 = 2.6\text{ cm}^2$

Multiple Choice(s) Correct Questions

1. $V = \frac{4}{3}\pi r^3 \Rightarrow \frac{\Delta V}{V} = 3\frac{\Delta r}{r}$

$\Rightarrow \frac{\Delta V}{V} \times 100 = 3\left(\frac{\Delta r}{r} \times 100\right) = 3\%$ and $A = 4\pi r^2$

$\frac{\Delta A}{A} = 2\frac{\Delta r}{r} \Rightarrow \frac{\Delta A}{A} \times 100 = 2\left(\frac{\Delta r}{r} \times 100\right) = 2\%$

2. $A = l^2$

$\frac{\Delta A}{A} \times 100 = 2\left(\frac{\Delta l}{l} \times 100\right) \Rightarrow 4 = 2\left(\frac{\Delta l}{l} \times 100\right)$

$\Rightarrow \frac{\Delta l}{l} \times 100 = 2\%$ and $V = l^3 \Rightarrow \frac{\Delta V}{V} = \frac{3\Delta l}{l}$

$\frac{\Delta V}{V} \times 100 = 3\left(\frac{\Delta l}{l} \times 100\right) = 3(2\%) = 6\%$

3. In series combination, $R_{eq} = R_1 + R_2$

$= (3 \pm 0.2) \pm (6 \pm 0.3)\Omega = (9 \pm 0.5)\Omega$

In parallel combination, $\frac{1}{R_{eq}} = \frac{1}{R_1} + \frac{1}{R_2}$

$\Rightarrow \frac{\Delta R_{eq}}{R_{eq}^2} = \frac{\Delta R_1}{R_1^2} + \frac{\Delta R_2}{R_2^2}$

$\Rightarrow \frac{\Delta R_{eq}}{2^2} = \frac{0.2}{3^2} + \frac{0.3}{6^2} \Rightarrow \Delta R_{eq} = 0.12$

So, $R_{eq} = (2 \pm 0.12)\Omega$

Previous Year's Questions

JEE Main

1. Positive zero error subtracted from actual reading, hence reading taken is more than actual reading.

2. $R = \frac{V}{I}$

$\Rightarrow V = (200 \pm 5)\text{ V} \Rightarrow I = (20 \pm 0.2)\text{ A}$

The percentage error in the measurement of R

$R = \frac{V}{I}$

Fractional error in R is

$\frac{dR}{R} = \frac{dV}{V} + \frac{dI}{I}$

$\frac{dR}{R} = \frac{5}{200} + \frac{0.2}{20}$

$\frac{dR}{R} = \frac{5}{200} + \frac{0.2 \times 10}{20 \times 10} = \frac{5}{200} + \frac{2}{200}$

$\frac{dR}{R} = \frac{7}{200}$

Percentage error, $\frac{dR}{R} \times 100 = \frac{7}{200} \times 100 = 3.5\%$

Percentage error = 3.5%

3. $Q = \frac{a^4 b^3}{c^2}$

$\therefore \frac{\Delta Q}{Q} = 4\frac{\Delta a}{a} + 3\frac{\Delta b}{b} + 2\frac{\Delta c}{c}$

$\Rightarrow \frac{\Delta Q}{Q} \times 100 = 4 \times \frac{\Delta a}{a} \times 100 + 3 \times \frac{\Delta b}{b} \times 100 + 2 \times \frac{\Delta c}{c} \times 100$

$= 4 \times 3\% + 3 \times 4\% + 2 \times 5\%$

$= 34\%$

4. Given, 50 vernier scale divisions = 49 main scale divisions.

Also, 1 main scale division = 0.5 mm

Now, 1 vernier scale division $= \frac{49}{50}$ MSD

$= \frac{49}{50} \times 0.5\text{ mm} = 0.49$ mm

Least count of instrument is

LC = 1 MSD − 1 VSD

$= 0.5 - 0.49\text{ (mm)} = 0.01$ mm

$\therefore$ Vernier constant = Least count = 0.01 mm

5. Given, $P = \dfrac{a^2b^3}{c\sqrt{d}}$

So, maximum % error in measurement of P is;

$$\frac{\Delta P}{P}\times 100 = 2\left(\frac{\Delta a}{a}\times 100\right)+3\left(\frac{\Delta b}{b}\times 100\right)+\left(\frac{\Delta c}{c}\times 100\right)+\frac{1}{2}\left(\frac{\Delta d}{d}\times 100\right)$$

$$= 2\times 1 + 3\times 2 + 3 + \frac{1}{2}\times 4$$

$$= 2 + 6 + 3 + 2 = 13\%$$

6. Density of wire (ρ)

$$= \frac{\text{Mass}}{\text{Volume}} \text{ or } \rho = \frac{m}{\pi r^2 l}$$

Hence, maximum error in ensity is

$$\Rightarrow \frac{\Delta\rho}{\rho}\times 100 = \frac{\Delta m}{m}\times 100 + \frac{2\Delta r}{r}\times 100 + \frac{\Delta l}{l}\times 100$$

So, $$\frac{\Delta\rho}{\rho}\times 100 = \frac{0.01}{0.4}\times 100 + \frac{2\times 0.03}{6}\times 100 + \frac{0.04}{8}\times 100$$

$$= 2.5 + 1 + 0.5 = 4\%$$

7. We know,

$$\rho = \frac{m}{V} = \frac{m}{\frac{1}{3}\pi r^2 h}$$

$$\Rightarrow \frac{\Delta\rho}{\rho} = \frac{\Delta m}{m} + \frac{2\Delta r}{r} + \frac{\Delta h}{h}$$

$$= \frac{0.006}{0.6} + \frac{2\times 0.005}{0.5} + \frac{0.04}{4}$$

$$= 0.01 + 2\times 0.01 + 0.01$$

$$= 0.01 + 0.02 + 0.01 = 0.04$$

So, $\dfrac{\Delta\rho}{\rho}\times 100 = 4\%$

8. For a simple pendulum

$$T = 2\pi\sqrt{\frac{l}{g}} \Rightarrow g = \frac{4\pi^2 l}{T^2}$$

$$\Rightarrow \frac{\Delta g}{g} = \frac{2\Delta T}{T} + \frac{\Delta l}{l}$$

$$\Rightarrow \frac{\Delta g}{g} = 2\cdot\frac{1}{100\times 0.5} + \frac{1\text{ mm}}{10\text{ cm}}$$

$$\Rightarrow \frac{\Delta g}{g} = \frac{5}{100} \text{ or } 5\%$$

9. Given, 49 MSD = 50 VSD

$$1\text{ VSD} = \frac{49}{50}\text{ MSD}$$

Thus, L.C. = 1 MSD – 1 VSD

$$= 1\text{ MSD} - \frac{49}{50}\text{ MSD}$$

$$= \frac{1}{50}\text{ MSD} = \frac{1}{50}\times\frac{1}{40}\text{ cm}$$

$$= \frac{1}{2000}\text{ cm} = \frac{10000}{2000\times 10^4}$$

$$= 5\times 10^{-4}\text{ cm} = 5\times 10^{-6}\text{ m}$$

10. In parallel combination,

$$\frac{1}{R_{eq}} = \frac{1}{R_1} + \frac{1}{R_2} \Rightarrow \frac{1}{R_{eq}} = \frac{1}{4} + \frac{1}{4}$$

$$\Rightarrow R_{eq} = 2\,\Omega$$

Now, $$\frac{\Delta R_{eq}}{R_{eq}^2} = \frac{\Delta R_1}{R_1^2} + \frac{\Delta R_2}{R_2^2}$$

Substituting the values in the above equation, we get

$$\frac{\Delta R_{eq}}{4} = \frac{0.8}{16} + \frac{0.4}{16} \Rightarrow \Delta R_{eq} = 0.3\,\Omega$$

$\therefore$ The equivalent resistance in parallel combination is $R_{eq} = (2\pm 0.3)\,\Omega$.

11. The formula of Young's modulus of elasticity is given by,

$$Y = \frac{MgL^3}{4bd^3\delta}$$

where, symbols have their usual meaning

There is no error in the value of the g.

The fractional error in Y,

$$\frac{\Delta Y}{Y} = \frac{\Delta M}{M} + 3\frac{\Delta L}{L} + \frac{\Delta b}{b} + 3\frac{\Delta d}{d} + \frac{\Delta\delta}{\delta}$$

$$\therefore \frac{\Delta Y}{Y} = \frac{10^{-3}}{2} + 3\frac{(1\times 10^{-3})}{1} + \frac{0.1\times 10^{-3}}{4\times 10^{-2}} + 3\frac{(0.01\times 10^{-3})}{0.4\times 10^{-2}} + \frac{(0.01\times 10^{-3})}{5\times 10^{-3}}$$

$$\frac{\Delta Y}{Y} = 0.0155$$

The fractional error in is 0.0155.

12. Given, $\dfrac{\Delta L}{L}\times 100 = 0.1$

$$\therefore T = 2\pi\sqrt{\frac{l}{g}}$$

$\therefore$ The % change in T,

$$\frac{\Delta T}{T}\times 100 = \frac{1}{2}\frac{\Delta L}{L}\times 100$$

$$\Rightarrow \frac{\Delta T}{T}\times 100 = \frac{1}{2}\times 0.1$$

$$\Rightarrow \Delta T = 0.05\times\frac{T}{100}$$

In one single day,

$$T = 24\times 60\times 60 = 86400\text{s}$$

$$\therefore \Delta T = 0.05\times\frac{86400}{100} = 43.2\text{ s}$$

Thus, the error in time per day is 43.2 s.

13. Young's modulus,

$$Y = \frac{\text{Stress}}{\text{Strain}} = \frac{FL}{Al}$$

$$\Rightarrow Y = \frac{mgL}{\pi R^2 l} \quad \text{...(i)}$$

$[\because F = mg \text{ and } A = \pi R^2]$

$\therefore$ The fractional errors, in Y

$$\frac{\Delta Y}{Y}=\frac{\Delta m}{m}+\frac{\Delta L}{L}+\frac{2\cdot\Delta R}{R}+\frac{\Delta l}{l}$$

$$\Rightarrow \quad \frac{\Delta Y}{Y}\times 100=100\left[\frac{\Delta m}{m}+\frac{\Delta L}{L}+\frac{2\Delta R}{R}+\frac{\Delta l}{l}\right]$$

$$=100\left[\frac{1}{1000}+\frac{1}{1000}+2\left(\frac{0.001}{0.2}\right)+\frac{0.001}{0.5}\right]$$

$$=\frac{1}{10}+\frac{1}{10}+1+\frac{1}{5}=\frac{14}{10}=1.4\%$$

14. Given,

Time period, $T=1.95$ s

Length of string, $l=1$ m

Error in time period, $\Delta T=0.01\text{ s}=10^{-2}$ s

Error in length,

$$\Delta L=1\text{ mm}=1\times 10^{-3}\text{ m}$$

$$\because \quad T=2\pi\sqrt{\frac{L}{g}}$$

Thus, we have,

$$\Rightarrow \quad \frac{\Delta g}{g}=\frac{\Delta L}{L}+\frac{2\Delta T}{T}=\frac{10^{-3}}{1}+\frac{2\times 10^{-2}}{1.95}$$

$$=10^{-3}+1.025\times 10^{-2}$$

$$=10^{-3}+10.25\times 10^{-3}=11.25\times 10^{-3}$$

$$\because \quad \Delta g/g\times 100=11.25\times 10^{-3}\times 10^{2}=1.125\%\simeq 1.13\%$$

15. Given, $R=V/I$ ...(i)

where, $V=(50\pm 2)$ V

$I=(20\pm 0.2)$ A

From Eq. (i)

$$\frac{\Delta R}{R}\times 100=\frac{\Delta V}{V}\times 100+\frac{\Delta I}{I}\times 100$$

$$\%\text{ error in } R=\left[\frac{2}{50}\times 100+\frac{0.2}{20}\times 100\right]\%$$

$$=[2\times 2+0.2\times 5]\%=5\%$$

Thus, the value of $x=5$.

16. We know volume of sphere,

$$V=\frac{4}{3}\pi R^3$$

Percentage error in volume

$$\frac{\Delta V}{V}\times 100=(3)\times\frac{\Delta R}{R}\times 100$$

$$=(3)\times\frac{0.85}{7.5}\times 100=34$$

Hence, $x=34$

17. Given, relative error in mass,

$$\frac{\Delta m}{m}\times 100=6\%$$

Relative error in diameter,

$$\frac{\Delta d}{d}\times 100=1.5\%$$

Density of sphere, $\rho=\dfrac{\text{Mass}}{\text{Volume}}$

$$=\frac{M}{\frac{4}{3}\pi r^3}=\frac{M}{\frac{4}{3}\pi\left(\frac{d}{2}\right)^3}$$

$$\rho=\frac{6}{\pi}Md^{-3}\text{ or }\rho\propto Md^{-3}$$

For maximum error in density,

$$\frac{\Delta\rho}{\rho}\times 100=\frac{\Delta M}{M}\times 100+3\times\frac{\Delta d}{d}\times 100$$

$$=6\%+3\times 1.5\%$$

$$\frac{\Delta\rho}{\rho}\times 100=10.5\%$$

$$\Rightarrow \quad \frac{1050}{100}\%=\frac{x}{100}\% \quad \text{(given)}$$

$$\therefore \quad x=1050$$

JEE Advanced

1. Question was dropped

2. Least count $=\left(1-\dfrac{9}{10}\right)(0.1)=0.01$ cm

Zero error $=-0.1+0.06=-0.04$ cm

Final reading $=3.1+0.01\times 1=3.11$ cm

So, correct measurement $=3.11+0.04=3.15$ cm

3. $\because \quad \dfrac{1}{C_{eq}}=\dfrac{1}{C_1}+\dfrac{1}{C_2}$

$$\Rightarrow C_{eq}=\frac{2000\times 3000}{5000}=1200\text{ pF}$$

$$\frac{-dC_{eq}}{C_{eq}^2}=\frac{-dC_1}{C_1^2}-\frac{dC_2}{C_2^2} \quad\Rightarrow\quad dC_{eq}=6\text{ pF}$$

$$\therefore \quad \varepsilon=\frac{1}{2}CV^2$$

$$\frac{d\varepsilon}{q}\times 100=\left(\frac{dC}{C}+\frac{2dV}{V}\right)\times 100$$

$$=\left(\frac{6}{1200}+2\times\frac{0.02}{5}\right)\times 100=1.3\%$$

4. $r=\dfrac{1-a}{1+a}$

$\ln r=\ln(1-a)-\ln(1+a)$

Differentiating, we get

$$\frac{dr}{r}=-\frac{da}{1-a}-\frac{da}{1+a}$$

or, we can write

$$\frac{\Delta r}{r}=-\left[\frac{\Delta a}{1-a}+\frac{\Delta a}{1+a}\right]$$

$$\frac{\Delta r}{r}=\frac{-2\Delta a}{1-a^2}$$

or $$\Delta r = -\left(\frac{2\Delta a}{1-a^2}\right)(r) = \frac{-2\Delta a}{(1+a)^2}$$

5. $N = N_0 e^{-\lambda t}$

$\ln N = \ln N_0 - \lambda t$

Differentiating w.r.t λ, we get

$$\frac{1}{N} \cdot \frac{dN}{d\lambda} = 0 - t$$

$\Rightarrow$ $$|d\lambda| = \frac{dN}{Nt}$$

or $$|\Delta\lambda| = \frac{\Delta N}{Nt}$$

Here, $N = 3000 - 1000 = 2000$

$\therefore$ $$|\Delta\lambda| = \frac{40}{2000 \times 1} = 0.02$$

6. $T = t_1 + t_2$ or $T = \sqrt{\frac{2L}{g}} + \frac{L}{V_s}$, $g = 10\,m/s^2$

$$T = \sqrt{\frac{L}{5}} + \frac{L}{300}$$

Differentiating equations, we get

$$dT = \frac{1}{\sqrt{5}}\frac{1}{2}L^{-1/2}dL + \left(\frac{1}{300}dL\right)$$

$$dT \text{ or } \delta T = \frac{1}{2\sqrt{5}}\frac{1}{\sqrt{20}}dL + \frac{dL}{300} = 0.01$$

$$dL\left(\frac{1}{20} + \frac{1}{300}\right) = 0.01$$

$$dL\left[\frac{16}{300}\right] = 0.01,\ dL = \frac{3}{16}$$

$$\frac{dL}{L} \times 100 = \frac{3}{16} \times \frac{1}{20} \times 100 = \frac{15}{16} \simeq 1\%$$

7. Mean time period $= \dfrac{0.52 + 0.56 + 0.57 + 0.54 + 0.59}{5}$

$= 0.556 \cong 0.56$ sec as per significant figures

Error in readings : $|T_{mean} - T_1| = 0.04$ s

$|T_{mean} - T_2| = 0.00$ s

$|T_{mean} - T_3| = 0.01$ s

$|T_{mean} - T_4| = 0.02$ s

$|T_{mean} - T_5| = 0.03$ s

Mean error $= \dfrac{0.04 + 0.00 + 0.01 + 0.02 + 0.03}{5} = 0.02$ s

% error in $T = \dfrac{\Delta T}{T} \times 100 = \dfrac{0.02}{0.56} \times 100 = 3.57\%$

% error in $r = \dfrac{1}{10} \times 100 = 10\%$

% error in $R = \dfrac{1}{60} \times 100 = 1.67\%$

$$g \propto \frac{(R-r)}{T^2}$$

Here, $R - r = 50$ mm and $\Delta(R-r) = (1+1)$ mm $= 2$ mm

% error in g is: $\dfrac{\Delta g}{g} \times 100 = \dfrac{\Delta(R-r)}{R-r} \times 100 + 2 \times \dfrac{\Delta T}{T} \times 100$

$$= \frac{2 \times 100}{50} + 2 \times 3.57$$

$$\approx 4\% + 7\% \approx 11\%$$

8. Reading of vernier scale C_1 can be calculated by the usual method.

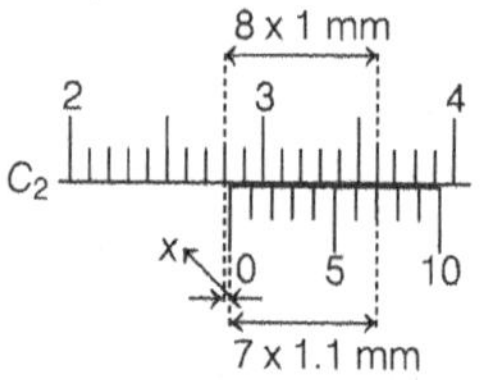

Reading = MSD + LC × VSR = 2.8 + 0.1 × 7 = 2.87 cm

In second scale C_2, length of VSD is greater than MSD

So, usual formula will not be applicable.

Let the point where scales coincide be P.

Total reading = 2.8 mm + x

From figure, x = (8 × 1) mm − (7 × 1.1) mm = 0.3 mm

So, reading = 2.83 mm

9. $$E(t) = A^2 e^{-\alpha t} \quad \text{...(i)}$$

$$\alpha = 0.2\ s^{-1}$$

$$\left(\frac{dA}{A}\right) \times 100 = 1.25\%$$

$$\left(\frac{dt}{t}\right) \times 100 = 1.50$$

$\Rightarrow$ $$(dt \times 100) = 1.5t$$

$$= 1.5 \times 5 = 7.5\ s$$

Taking log on both sides of Eq. (i), we get

$$\log E = 2\log A - \alpha t$$

Now, differentiating equations, we get,

$$\frac{dE}{E} = \pm 2\frac{dA}{A} \pm \alpha dt$$

$\therefore$ $$\left(\frac{dE}{E}\right) \times 100 = \pm\left[2\left(\frac{dA}{A}\right) \times 100 + \alpha(dt \times 100)\right]$$

$$= \pm[2(1.25) + 0.2(7.5)]$$

$$= \pm[2.5 + 1.5] = \pm 4\%$$

10. $Y = \dfrac{FL}{Al}$

Here, l is change in length.

$\therefore$ $$Y \propto \frac{1}{l} \text{ or } \frac{\Delta Y}{Y} \times 100$$

$$= \frac{\Delta l}{l} \times 100 = \frac{(LC)}{(45-20)\,LC} \times 100$$

$$= 4\%$$

CHAPTER~05

RECTILINEAR MOTION

LEVEL 01 Starter Level

5.1 Average Speed and Average Velocity

1 It is 220 km from Delhi to Sirsa by air and 250 km by road. An aeroplane takes 30 min to go from Delhi to Sirsa whereas a deluxe bus takes 5 h.

(a) Find the average speed of the aeroplane.

(b) Find the average speed of the bus.

(c) Find the average velocity of the aeroplane.

(d) Find the average velocity of the bus.

2 When a person leaves his home for sightseeing by his car, the meter reads 12352 km. When he returns home after two hours the reading is 12416 km.

(a) What is the average speed of the car during this period?

(b) What is the average velocity?

3 A particle travels half of total distance with speed v_1 and next half with speed v_2 along a straight line. Find out the average speed of the particle.

4 A person travelling on a straight line moves with a uniform velocity v_1 for sometime and with uniform velocity v_2 for the next equal time. Find the average speed of the particle.

5 A particle travels one-third of total distance with speed v_1 and next one-third with speed v_2 and remaining distance with speed v_3 along a straight line. Find out the average speed of the particle.

5.2 Motion Along a Horizontal Line

1 A roller coaster car is travelling at a constant 6 m/s when it reaches a downward slope. On the slope, the car accelerates at a constant rate of 2.5 m/s^2. The length of the slope is 44 m.

(a) Find the velocity of the car at the bottom of the hill.

(b) Find the time of travel.

2 A bullet travelling with a velocity of 16 m/s penetrates a tree trunk and comes to rest in 0.4 m. Find the time taken during the retardation.

3 An airplane starts at rest on a runway. It takes the airplane 50 s until it takes off. If the airplane had a constant acceleration and an average velocity of 60 m/s during the take off. Find

(a) the final velocity,

(b) the acceleration,

(c) the minimum length the runway needs to be

(d) and at what time the plane is halfway down the runway.

4 The brakes are applied to a car traveling on a dry, level highway. A typical value for the magnitude of the car's acceleration is 5.00 m/s^2.

(a) If the car's initial speed is 30.0 m/s, how long does it take to stop and how far does it travel, starting from the moment the brakes are applied?

(b) How do these quantities change, if we double the initial speed?

5 A woman and her dog are out for a morning run to the river which is located 4.0 km away. The woman runs at a constant speed of 2.5 m/s. The dog is unleashed and runs back and forth between his owner and the river at constant speed of 4.5 m/s until she reaches the river. What is the total distance that the dog runs?

6 A train starts from rest and moves with a constant acceleration of 2.0 m/s^2 for half a minute. The brakes are then applied and the train comes to rest in one minute. Find

(a) the total distance moved by the train,

(b) the maximum speed attained by the train

(c) and the position (s) of the train at half the maximum speed.

7 A ball is rolling at 2 m/s East when it encounters a steady breeze that causes it to change its velocity at a constant rate until it is finally going 4 m/s West. This takes 0.75 s.

(a) What is the acceleration?

(b) At what time does the ball stop?

(c) What is the total displacement?

(d) What is the total distance travelled?

(e) What is the average velocity?

(f) What is the average speed?

8 A car travelling at 72 km/h decelerates uniformly at 2 m/s^2. Calculate (a) the distance it goes before it stops, (b) the time it takes to stop and (c) the distance it travels during the first and third seconds.

9 A tiger running 100 m race, accelerates for one-third time of the total time and then moves with uniform speed. Find the total time taken by the tiger to run 100 m, if the acceleration of the tiger is 8 m/s^2.

10 A body travels for 15 s starting from rest with constant acceleration. If it travels distance s_1, s_2 and s_3 in the first 5 s, second 5 s and next 5 s, respectively. Find the ratio $s_1 : s_2 : s_3$.

11 A particle moving along a straight line with uniform acceleration travels 20m and 24m in the 7th and 9th seconds, respectively. Find distance travelled by the particle in the 15th second.

12 A particle is moving along a straight line with constant acceleration. At the end of 10th second, its velocity becomes 20 m/s and in 10th second, it travels a distance of 10 m. Find the acceleration of the particle.

13 A driver takes 0.2s to apply the brakes after he sees a need for it. This is called the reaction time of the driver. If he is driving a car at a speed of 54 km/h and the brakes cause a deceleration of 6.0 m/s^2, find the distance travelled by the car after he sees the need to put the brakes on.

14 A particle travelling along a straight line PQ with uniform acceleration has velocities 7 m/s and 17 m/s at P and Q, respectively. Find
(a) velocity at R, where R is the mid-point of PQ
(b) average velocity between P and Q.

15 A police jeep is chasing a culprit going on a motorbike. The motorbike crosses a turning at a speed of 72 km/h. The jeep follows it at a speed of 90 km/h crossing the turning ten seconds later than the bike. Assuming that they travel at constant speeds, how far from the turning will the jeep catch up with the bike?

16 A man is standing 40 m behind the bus. Bus starts with 1 m/s^2 constant acceleration and also at the same instant the man starts moving with constant speed 9 m/s. Find the time taken by man to catch the bus.

5.3 Motion Under Gravity

1 A stone is dropped from a tower of height 80 m. Find .
(a) time taken to reach ground ,
(b) speed just before striking the ground,
(c) speed and time when it is mid-way,
(d) speed when it is at a height of 35 m from ground
(e) and distance covered in last two seconds of its journey. (Take, $g = 10\ m/s^2$)

2 A stone is thrown vertically down from a building of height 160 m with initial speed of 20 m/s. Find
(a) time taken to reach ground,
(b) speed just before hitting the ground,
(c) time when it is at a height of 100 m from ground ,
(d) height when its speed is 45 m/s
(e) and distance covered during last second of its journey. (Take, $g = 10\ m/s^2$)

3 A ball is projected vertically upward with a speed of 50 m/s. Find
(a) the maximum height,
(b) the time taken to reach the maximum height,
(c) the speed at half the maximum height,
(d) average speed and velocity over first 7 s
(e) and time(s) when it is at a height of 105 m from ground. (Take, $g = 10\ m/s^2$)

4 A ball is thrown vertically upwards with a velocity of 20 m/s from the top of a tower. The height of the tower is 160 m from the ground. How
(a) high will the ball rise,
(b) long will it be before the ball hits the ground
(c) and average speed over entire journey? (Take, $g = 10\ m/s^2$)

5 A balloon starts rising from the ground with an acceleration of 1.25 m/s^2. After 8s, a stone is released from the balloon. Find
(a) time taken by stone to reach after it is dropped,
(b) height of the balloon when it hits the ground
(c) and distance travelled by stone after it is dropped. (Take, $g = 10\ m/s^2$)

6 A ball is dropped from a certain height. If it takes 0.200 s to cross the last 5.8 m before hitting the ground, find the height from which it was dropped. (Take, $g = 10\ m/s^2$)

7 A rocket is fired vertically up from the ground with a resultant vertical acceleration of 20 m/s^2 The fuel is finished in 1 min and it continues to move up. Find
(a) the maximum height reached
(b) and after how much time from then will the maximum height be reached. (Take, $g = 10\ m/s^2$)

8 A parachutist after bailing out falls 500 m without friction. When the parachute opens, she decelerates at 2 m/s^2 and reaches the ground with a speed of 8 m/s.
(a) How long has been the parachutist in the air?
(b) At what height did the fall begin?

9 When a particle is projected upward with speed u from the top of a tower, it reaches the ground in time t_1. When it is projected downward with the same

9 When a particle is projected upward with speed u from the top of a tower, it reaches the ground in time t_1. When it is projected downward with the same speed, it reaches the ground in time t_2. How long does it take to reach the ground, if it is just dropped?

10 A stone is dropped from the top of a tower of height h. After 1 s, another stone is dropped from the balcony 20 m below the top. Both reach the bottom simultaneously. What is the value of h? (Take, $g = 10 \text{ m/s}^2$)

11 A stone is dropped from a tower and 2 s later another stone is thrown vertically down with initial speed 30 m/s from the same tower. When and where will they meet?

12 A particle is dropped from height 100 m and another particle is projected vertically up with velocity 50 m/s from the ground along the same line. Find out the position where the two particles will meet. (Take, $g = 10 \text{ m/s}^2$)

13 A lift accelerates downwards from rest at rate of 4 m/s^2, starting 200 m above the ground. After 5 s, an object falls out of the lift. Which will reach the ground first, lift or object? What is the time interval between their striking the ground?

LEVEL 02\ JEE Main Level

Single Choice Correct Questions

1 The correct statement from the following.

(a) A body having zero velocity will not necessarily have zero acceleration.

(b) A body having zero velocity will necessarily have zero acceleration.

(c) A body having uniform speed can have only uniform acceleration.

(d) A body having non-uniform velocity will have zero acceleration.

2 A particle moves along the sides AB, BC, CD of a square of side 25 m with a velocity of 15 m/s. Its average velocity is

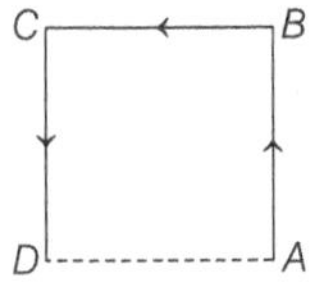

(a) 15 m/s (b) 10 m/s (c) 7.5 m/s (d) 5 m/s

3 A car travels from A and B at a speed of 20 km h^{-1} and returns at a speed fo 30 km h^{-1}. The average speed of the car for the whole journey is

(a) 5 km h^{-1} (b) 24 km h^{-1} (c) 25 km h^{-1} (d) 50 km h^{-1}

4 A body has speed v, $2v$ and $3v$ in first (1/3)rd of distance s, second (1/3)rd of s and third (1/3)rd of s respectively. Its average speed will be

(a) v (b) $2v$ (c) $\frac{18}{11}v$ (d) $\frac{11}{18}v$

5 A body travelling along a straight line traversed one-third of the total distance with a velocity 4 m/s. The remaining part of the distance was covered with a velocity 2 m/s for half the time and with velocity 6 m/s for the other half of time. The mean velocity averaged over the whole time of motion is

(a) 5 m/s (b) 4 m/s (c) 4.5 m/s (d) 3.5 m/s

6 The speed of a body is doubled when it moves over a distance of 10 m. If the initial speed be u, what will be the speed after further coverage of distance 10 m?

(a) $\sqrt{5}\,u$ (b) $\sqrt{6}\,u$ (c) $\sqrt{7}\,u$ (d) $\sqrt{8}\,u$

7 When the speed of a car is v, the minimum distance over which it can be stopped is s. If the speed becomes nv, what will be the minimum distance over which it can be stopped?

(a) s/n (b) ns (c) s/n^2 (d) $n^2 s$

8 A bullet moving with a velocity of 200 cm/s penetrates a wooden block and comes to rest after traversing 4 cm inside it. What velocity is needed for travelling distance of 9 cm in same block?

(a) 100 cm/s (b) 136.2 cm/s

(c) 300 cm/s (d) 250 cm/s

9 An engine of a train moving with uniform acceleration passes an electric pole with velocity u and the last compartment with velocity v. The middle point of the train passes past the same pole with a velocity of

(a) $\frac{u+v}{2}$ (b) $\frac{u^2+v^2}{2}$

(c) $\sqrt{\frac{u^2+v^2}{2}}$ (d) $\sqrt{\frac{v^2-u^2}{2}}$

10 A body starts with some initial velocity along a straight line. After 3 s, it is found to be at distance of 15 m from the starting point and at 4 s, it is at the starting point. What is the initial velocity? (Assume constant acceleration)

(a) 5 m/s (b) 10 m/s (c) 15 m/s (d) 20 m/s

11 A body moving with uniform acceleration describes 40 m in the first 5 s and 65 m in next 5 s. Its initial velocity will be

(a) 4 m/s (b) 2.5 m/s (c) 5.5 m/s (d) 11 m/s

12 A body moves with uniformly accelerated motion and travels 200 cm in the first two second and 220 cm in the next four seconds. What will be the velocity at the end of 7 s from start?

(a) 10 cm/s (b) 20 cm/s (c) 30 cm/s (d) 40 cm/s

13 A body starts from rest and moves with uniform acceleration. The ratio of distance covered by the body in the *n*th second to that covered in *n* second is

(a) $\frac{1}{n}$ (b) $\frac{2n-1}{n^2}$ (c) $\frac{n^2}{2n-1}$ (d) $\frac{2n-1}{2n^2}$

14 A body is moving from rest under constant acceleration and let s_1 be the displacement in the first $(p-1)$ seconds and s_2 be the displacement is the first *p* seconds. The displacement in (p^2-p+1)th second will be

(a) s_1+s_2 (b) s_1s_2 (c) s_1-s_2 (d) s_1/s_2

15 A body starts from rest with uniform acceleration. If its velocity after *n*-second is *v*, then its displacement in the last two seconds is

(a) $\frac{2v(n+1)}{n}$ (b) $\frac{v(n+1)}{n}$ (c) $\frac{v(n-1)}{n}$ (d) $\frac{2v(n-1)}{n}$

16 A body moving with uniform acceleration covers 12 m in the 2nd second and 20 m in the 4th second of its motion. How much distance will it cover is 5 s after the 4th second?

(a) 160 m (b) 80 m (c) 120 m (d) 150 m

17 A particle is moving along straight line with initial velocity 48 m/s and acceleration $-10\ m/s^2$. The distance travelled by particle in 5th second is

(a) 3m (b) 115 m (c) $\frac{17}{5}$ m (d) $\frac{14}{5}$ m

18 A particle move for 8 s. It first accelerates from rest and then retards to rest. If the retardation be 3 times the acceleration, then time for which it accelerates will be

(a) 2 s (b) 3 s (c) 4 s (d) 6 s

19 A car accelerates from rest at a constant rate of $2\ m/s^2$ for sometime, then its retards at a constant rate of $4\ m/s^2$ and comes to rest. What is the maximum speed attained by the car, if it remains in motion for 3 s?

(a) 2 m/s (b) 3 m/s
(c) 4 m/s (d) 6 m/s

20 Acceleration of a particle is a_0 from $t=0$ to $t=t_0$, then it is $-a_0$ from $t=t_0$ to $t=2t_0$. The again it is a_0 from $t=2t_0$ to $t=3t_0$ and so on. Initial velocity of particle was zero. At time $t=9t_0$, velocity of particle is

(a) zero (b) a_0t_0
(c) $4.5\,a_0t_0$ (d) $9\,a_0t_0$

21 Between two stations a train starting from rest first accelerates uniformly, then moves with constant velocity and finally retards uniformly to come to rest. If the ratio of the time taken be 1 : 8 : 1 and the maximum speed achieved be 60 km/h, then what is the average speed over the whole journey?

(a) 48 km/h (b) 52 km/h
(c) 54 km/h (d) 56 km/h

22 A car starting from rest, accelerates at the rate *f* through a distance *s*, then continues at constant speed for time *t* and then the decelerates at the rate of $\frac{f}{2}$ to comes to rest. if the total distance traversed is 15*s*, then

(a) $s=\frac{1}{36}ft^2$ (b) $s=\frac{1}{18}ft^2$
(c) $s=\frac{1}{4}ft^2$ (d) $s=\frac{1}{72}ft^2$

23 A point starts moving in a straight line with a certain acceleration. At a time *t* after beginning of motion, the acceleration suddenly becomes retardation of the same value. The time in which the point return to the initial point is

(a) $\sqrt{2}t$ (b) $(2+\sqrt{2})t$ (c) $\frac{t}{\sqrt{2}}$

(d) Cannot be predicted unless acceleration is given

24 Two cars start off to race with velocities 4m/s and 2m/s and travel in straight live with uniform accelerations $1\ m/s^2$ and $2m/s^2$, respectively. If they reach the final point at the same instant, then the length of the path is

(a) 30 m (b) 32 m
(c) 20 m (d) 24 m

25 A motorcycle thief speeding at 126 km/h is shot at by a stationary policemen 65 m behind him. If the speed of the bullet is 100 m/s, how far from the policemen does he get shot?

(a) 50 m (b) 100 m (c) 150 m (d) 200 m

26 A thief is running away on a straight road in jeep moving with a speed of 9 m/s. A policeman chases him on a motorcycle moving at a speed of 10 m/s. If the instantaneous separation of the jeep from the motorcycle is 100 m, how long will it take for the police to catch the thief?

(a) 1 s (b) 19 s (c) 90 s (d) 100 s

27 A truck starts from rest with an acceleration of 1.5 m/s^2 while a car 100 m behind starts from rest with an acceleration of $2\ m/s^2$. How long will it take before both the truck and car to be side?

(a) 2.45 s (b) 5 s (c) 20 s (d) 5.3 s

28 A bus starts moving with acceleration 2 m/s^2. A cyclist 96 m behind the bus starts simultaneously towards the bus at 20 m/s, after what time will he be able to overtake the bus?
(a) 4 s (b) 8 s (c) 12 s (d) 16 s

29 A passenger is at distance of x from a bus when the bus begins to move with constant acceleration a. What is the minimum velocity with which the passenger should run towards the bus, so as to reach it?
(a) $\sqrt{2ax}$ (b) $2ax$ (c) $\sqrt{ax}$ (d) ax

30 On a foggy day, two drivers spot each other when 80 m apart. They were travelling at 70 km/h and 60 km/h. Both apply brakes simultaneously which retard the cars at the rate of 5 ms^{-2}. Which of the following statements is correct?
(a) The collision will be averted
(b) The collision will take place
(c) They will cross each other
(d) They will just collide

31 The splash is heard after 2.05 s after the stone is dropped into a well of depth 19.6 m. The velocity of sound is
(a) 342 m/s (b) 372 m/s (c) 392 m/s (d) 352 m/s

32 A body is dropped from a height of 100 m. At what height the velocity of the body will be equal to one-half of velocity when it hits the ground?
(a) 45 m (b) 55 m (c) 65 m (d) 75 m

33 A body is dropped from a height 39.2 m. After it crosses half distance, the accelertion due to gravity ceases to act. The body wil hit the ground with velocity
(a) 19.6 m/s (b) 20 m/s (c) 1.96 m/s (d) 196 m/s

34 A stone is dropped from a certain height, which can reach the ground in 5 s. It is stopped after three seconds of its fall and then is again released. The total time taken by the stone to reach the ground will be
(a) 6s (b) 6.5s (c) 7s (d) 7.5s

35 The distances travelled by a body falling freely from rest in the first, second and third seconds are in the ratio
(a) 1 : 2 : 3 (b) 1 : 3 : 5 (c) 1 : 4 : 9 (d) None of these

36 A particle is dropped vertically from rest, from a height. The time taken by it to fall through successive distances of 1 m each will then be
(a) all equal, being equal to $\sqrt{2/g}$ second
(b) in the ratio of the square roots of the integers 1,2,3, ...
(c) in the ratio of the difference in the square roots of the integers, i.e. $\sqrt{1}, (\sqrt{2}-\sqrt{1}), (\sqrt{3}-\sqrt{2}), (\sqrt{4}-\sqrt{3})$, ...
(d) in the ratio of the reciprocals of the square roots of the integers, i.e. $\frac{1}{\sqrt{1}}, \frac{1}{\sqrt{2}}, \frac{1}{\sqrt{3}} \ldots$

37 A particle is falling freely. If the sum of the distances travelled in the tth and $(t+1)^{th}$ second is 100 m, then its velocity after t seconds (in m/s) is
(a) 20 (b) 30 (c) 50 (d) 60

38 A body falling from a high Minaret travels 40 m in the last 2 s of its fall to ground. Height of Minaret (in metre) is (Take, $g = 10 m/s^2$)
(a) 60 (b) 45 (c) 80 (d) 50

39 A hail is dropped from the roof of a tower of height h. The total distance covered by it in the last second of its motion is equal to the distance covered by it in first three seconds. The value of h (in metre) is (Take, $g = 10 m/s^2$)
(a) 125 (b) 200 (c) 100 (d) 80

40 A stone is dropped from a point 0.4 m above the top of a 0.5 m long window. Find time taken by the stone to cross the window.
(a) $\frac{1}{4}$ s (b) $\frac{1}{5}$ s (c) $\frac{1}{6}$ s (d) $\frac{1}{7}$ s

41 Drops of water fall from the roof of a building 9 m high at regular intervals of time, the first drop reaching the ground at the same instant fourth drop starts its fall. What are the distances of the third and second drops from the roof?
(a) 1m and 3m (b) 1m and 4m
(c) 3m and 5m (d) None of these

42 A stone is dropped from the top of a tower. When it has fallen by 5m from the top, another stone is dropped from a point 25m below the top. If both stones reach the ground at the same moment, then height of the tower from ground is (take, $g = 10 m/s^2$)
(a) 45 m (b) 50 m (c) 60 m (d) 65 m

43 A ball is thrown downwards with velocity v from the top of a tower and it reaches the ground with speed $3v$. What is the height of the tower?
(a) $\frac{v^2}{g}$ (b) $\frac{v^2}{2g}$ (c) $\frac{2v^2}{g}$ (d) $\frac{4v^2}{g}$

44 A body dropped from a height h, with an initial speed zero, strikes the ground with a velocity 3 km/h. Another body of same mass is dropped from the same height h with an initial speed of 4 km/h. Find the final velocity of second body with which it strikes the ground.
(a) 3 km/h (b) 4 km/h (c) 5 km/h (d) 12km/h

45 A parachutist drops freely from an aeroplane for 10 s before the parachute opens out, then he descends with a net retardation of 2.5 m/s^2. If he bails out of the plane at a height of 2495 m and $g = 10$ m/s^2, his velocity on reaching the ground will be
(a) 5 m/s (b) 10 m/s (c) 15 m/s (d) 20 m/s

46 A man thrown a ball vertically upward and it rises through 20 m and returns to his hands. What was the initial velocity (u) of the ball and for how much time (T) it remains in the air? (Take, $g = 10 \text{m/s}^2$)

(a) $u = 10$ m/s, $T = 2$ s (b) $u = 10$ m/s, $T = 4$ s
(c) $u = 20$ m/s, $T = 2$ s (d) $u = 20$ m/s, $T = 4$ s

47 The acceleration due to gravity on the planet A is 9 times the acceleration due to gravity on planet B. A man jumps to a height of 2m on the surface of A. What is the height of jump by the same person on the planet B?

(a) 18m (b) 6m (c) $\frac{2}{3}$ m (d) $\frac{2}{9}$ m

48 An object projected upwards acquires a velocity of 9.8 m/s when it reaches half of the maximum height. The maximum height reached is

(a) 4.9 m (b) 7.8 m (c) 8.8 m (d) 9.8 m

49 A person is throwing balls into the air one after the other. He throws the second ball when first ball is at the highest point. If he is throwing two balls every second, how high do they rise?

(a) 5m (b) 3.75 m (c) 2.50 m (d) 1.25m

50 A rocket is fired vertically from the ground. It moves upwards with a constant acceleration 10 m/s^2 for 30 s after which the fuel is finished. After what time from the instant of firing the rocket will attain the maximum height? (Take, $g = 10$ m/s^2)

(a) 30 s (b) 45 s (c) 60 s (d) 75 s

51 A body thrown vertically upwards with an initial velocity u reaches maximum height in 6 s. The ratio of the distances travelled by the body in the 1st second and the 7th second is

(a) 1 : 1 (b) 11 : 1 (c) 1 : 2 (d) 1 : 11

52 A particle when thrown moves, such that it passes from same height at 2s and 10 s, the height is

(a) 10 m (b) 20 m (c) 100 m (d) 180 m

53 A body is thrown with a certain velocity. It crosses the 80 m height mark on its upward as well as the downward journey with a time difference of 6 s. The initial velocity of the body is

(a) 30m/s (b) 40 m/s
(c) 50 m/s (d) Data insufficient

54 With what speed should a body be thrown upwards, so that the distances traversed in the 5th second and 6th second are equal?

(a) 58.4 m/s (b) 49 m/s (c) $\sqrt{98}$ m/s (d) 98 m/s

55 A ball is projected upwards from the foot of a tower. The ball crosses the top of the tower twice after an interval of 6s and the ball reaches the ground after 12s. The height of the tower is (take, $g = 10 \text{m/s}^2$)

(a) 120 m (b) 135 m (c) 175 m (d) 80 m

56 A particle is projected vertically upwards from a points A on the ground. It takes time t_1 to reach a point B but it still continues to move up. If it takes further t_2 time to reach the ground from point B, then height of point B from the ground is

(a) $\frac{1}{2}g(t_1 + t_2)^2$ (b) gt_1t_2 (c) $\frac{1}{8}g(t_1 + t_2)^2$ (d) $\frac{1}{2}gt_1t_2$

57 A particle is projected from ground in vertical direction at $t = 0$ .At $t = 0.8$ s, it reaches $h = 14$m. It will again come to same height at $t =$ (Take, $g = 10 \text{m/s}^2$)

(a) 2 s (b) $\frac{14}{5}$ s (c) 3 s (d) $\frac{7}{2}$ s

58 Two bodies A and B are thrown simultaneously. A is projected vertically upwards with 20 m/s speed from ground and B is projected vertically downwards from a height of 40 m with the same speed and along the same line of motion. At what point, do the 2 bodies collide? (Take, $g = 10$ m/s^2)

(a) 20 m from ground (b) 15 m from ground
(c) 30 m from ground (d) 5 m from ground

59 Ball A is dropped from the top of a building. At the same instant, ball B is thrown vertically upwards from the ground. When the balls collide, they are moving in opposite directions and the speed of A is twice the speed of B. At what fraction of the height of the building did the collision occurs?

(a) $\frac{1}{3}$ (b) $\frac{2}{3}$ (c) $\frac{1}{4}$ (d) $\frac{2}{5}$

60 A ball is thrown vertically upwards from the top of a tower at 4.9 m/s. It strikes the pond near the base of the tower after 3 s. The height of the tower is

(a) 73.5 m (b) 44.1 m
(c) 29.4 m (d) None of these

61 A balloon is moving vertically with a velocity of 4 m/s. When it is at a height of h, a body is gently released from it. If it reaches the ground in 4 s, the height of the balloon, when the body is released, is

(a) 62.4 m (b) 42.4 m (c) 78.4 m (d) 82.2 m

62 A stone is dropped from a rising balloon at a height of 76 m above the ground and reaches the ground in 6 s. What was the approximate velocity of the balloon when the stone was dropped?

(a) (52/3) m/s, upwards (b) (52/3) m/s, downwards
(c) 3 m/s (d) 9.8 m/s

63 From the top of a tower, a stone is thrown up and it reaches the ground in 9 s. A second stone is thrown down with the same speed and reaches the ground in 4 s. A third stone is released from rest and reaches the ground in

(a) 5 s (b) 6 s (c) 7 s (d) 8 s

Numerical Value Questions

1 A driver travelling at speed 36 kmh^{-1} sees the light turn red at the intersection. His reaction time is 0.6s and the car can decelerate at $4ms^{-2}$. Find the stopping distance (in m) of the car.

2 A bullet loses 25% of its speed while travelling 14 cm inside a wooden block. How much further (in cm) will it travel before stopping?

3 Two cars *A* and *B* cross a point *P* with velocities 10 m/s and 15 m/s. After that they move with different uniform accelerations and the car *A* overtakes *B* with a speed of 25 m/s. What is the speed (in m/s) of *B* at that instant?

4 A particle moving along a straight line with a constant acceleration of $-4\ m/s^2$ passes through a point *A* on the line with a velocity of 8 m/s at some moment. Find the distance (in m) travelled by the particle in 5 s after that moment.

5 A particle is projected vertically up with initially velocity 45 m/s. Find distance travelled in the fifth (5th) second. (Take, $g = 10 m/s^2$)

6 A dog sees a flower pot sail up and then back down past a window 5 ft high. If the total time the pot is in sight is 1 s, then the height above the window that the pot rises is $1/\beta$ ft.
Find the value of β. (Use, $g = 32 ft/s^2$)

7 A stone is dropped from a height *h*. Simultaneously another stone is thrown up from the ground with such a velocity that it can reach a height of 4*h*. The time when two stones cross each other is $\sqrt{\frac{h}{ng}}$. Find the value of *n*.

8 A healthy young man standing at a distance of 6 m from a 11.5 m high building sees a kid slipping from the top floor. With what uniform acceleration (starting from rest) should he run to catch the kid at the arms height (1.5 m)? (Take, $g = 10 m/s^2$)

9 To measure height of a building a student dropped a watermelon from it and 4.25 s later he heard the sound of watermelon hitting the ground. Find height (in m) of the building. (Neglect air resistance; $g = 10 m/s^2$ and speed of sound = 320 m/s)

10 A body is thrown vertically up with a velocity *u*. It passes three points *A*, *B* and *C* in its upwards journey with velocities $\frac{u}{2}, \frac{u}{3}$ and $\frac{u}{4}$ respectively. The ratio of the separations between points *A* and *B* and between *B* and *C*, i.e. $\frac{AB}{BC}$ is $\frac{20}{n}$. Find the value of *n*.

11 A particle is dropped from point A at a certain height from ground. It falls freely and passes through points *B*, *C* and *D* with $BC = CD$. The time taken by the particle to move from *B* to *C* is 2 s and from *C* to *D* is 1 s. If the time taken by the particle to move from *A* to *B* is $\frac{n}{10}$ seconds, then find the value of *n*.

12 A uniformly accelerated body passes two points *P* and *Q* with speeds of 10 m/s and 20 m/s, respectively. If *O* is mid-point of *P* and *Q*, then find the speed (in m/s) at point *O*.

13 With what speed (in m/s) must a ball be thrown down for it to bounce 10 m higher than its original level? Neglect any loss of energy in striking the ground.

14 The vertical height of P above the ground is twice that of Q. A particle is projected downward with a speed of 9.8 m/s from *P* and simultaneously another particle is projected upwards with the same speed of 9.8 m/s from Q. Both particles reach the ground simultaneously. Find the time (in seconds) taken to reach the ground.

15 A man in a balloon rising vertically with an acceleration of 4.9 m/s^2 releases a ball 2 s after the balloon is let go from the ground. Find the greatest height (in metre) above the ground reached by the ball.

LEVEL 03\ JEE Advanced Level

Single Choice Correct Questions

1 An ant is at a corner of a cubical room of side a. The ant can move with a constant speed u. The minimum time taken to reach the farthest corner of the cube is

(a) $\frac{3a}{u}$ (b) $\frac{\sqrt{3}a}{u}$ (c) $\frac{\sqrt{5}a}{u}$ (d) $\frac{(\sqrt{2}+1)a}{u}$

2 In a car race, car A takes t_0 time less to finish than car B and passes the finishing point with a velocity v_0 more than car B. The cars start from rest and travel with constant accelerations a_1 and a_2. Then, the ratio of $\frac{v_0}{t_0}$ is equal to

(a) $\frac{a_1^2}{a_2}$ (b) $\frac{a_1+a_2}{2}$ (c) $\sqrt{a_1 a_2}$ (d) $\frac{a_2^2}{a_1}$

3 A body starts with an initial velocity of 10 m/s and moves along a straight line with a constant acceleration. When the velocity of the particle becomes 50 m/s, the acceleration is reversed in direction without changing magnitude. Find the velocity of the particle when it reaches the starting point.

(a) 50 m/s (b) 60 m/s
(c) 70 m/s (d) 80 m/s

4 A helicopter takes off along the vertical with acceleration of 4 m/s^2 and zero initial velocity at $t = 0$. In a certain time, the pilot switches off the engine. At the point of take-off, the sound dies away at $t = 50$ s. Determine the velocity of the helicopter at the moment when its engine is switched off, assuming the velocity of sound is 320 m/s.

(a) 120 m/s (b) 160 m/s
(c) 180 m/s (d) 200 m/s

5 A speeder in an automobile passes a stationary policeman who is hiding behind a bill board with a motorcycle. After a 2.0 s delay (reaction time), the policeman accelerates to his maximum speed of 150 km/h in 12 s and catches the speeder 1.5 km beyond the billboard. Find the speed of speeder in km/h.

(a) 100 km/h (b) 122.7 km/h
(c) 135.2 km/h (d) 140 km/h

6 A balloon starts ascending from the ground at a constant speed of 25 m/s. After 5 s, a bullet is shot vertically upwards from the ground. What should be the minimum speed of the bullet, so that it may reach the balloon?

(a) 25 m/s (b) 50 m/s
(c) 75 m/s (d) 100 m/s

7 Two particles start from rest and move in a straight line for the same time. The first particle has an acceleration a for half the time and an acceleration $2a$ for the remaining time. The second particle has acceleration $2a$ for half the total distance traveled by it and acceleration a for the remaining distance. Find the ratio of the distances travelled by the particles.

(a) $(35-10\sqrt{6}):16$ (b) $(25-10\sqrt{6}):16$
(c) $(35-10\sqrt{6}):8$ (d) $(25-10\sqrt{6}):8$

8 Two bikes A and B start from a point. A moves with uniform speed 40 m/s and B starts from rest with uniform acceleration 2 m/s^2. If B starts at $t = 0$ and A starts from the same point at $t = 10$ s, then the time during the journey in which A was ahead of B is

(a) 20 s (b) 8 s
(c) 10 s (d) A was never ahead of B

9 A particle moving in straight line, traversed half the distance with a velocity v_1. The remaining part of the distance was covered with velocity v_2 for half the time and with velocity v_3 for the other half of the time. Find the mean velocity of the particle averaged over the whole time of motion.

(a) $\frac{2v_1(v_2+v_3)}{2v_1+v_2+v_3}$ (b) $\frac{2v_1(v_2v_3+v_3v_1)}{2v_1v_2+v_2v_3+v_3v_1}$
(c) $\frac{v_1(v_2+v_3)}{v_1+2v_2+2v_3}$ (d) $\frac{2v_1v_2v_3}{v_1v_2+v_2v_3+v_3v_1}$

10 For a particle undergoing rectilinear motion with uniform acceleration, the magnitude of displacement is one-third the distance covered in some time interval. The magnitude of final velocity is less than magnitude of initial velocity for this time interval, then the ratio of initial speed to the final speed for this time interval is

(a) $\sqrt{2}$ (b) 2
(c) $\sqrt{3}$ (d) 3

11 A particle moving in a straight line with uniform acceleration is observed to be at a distance a from a fixed point initially. It is at distance b, c, d from the same point after n, $2n$, $3n$ second. The acceleration of the particle is

(a) $\frac{c-2b+a}{n^2}$ (b) $\frac{c+b+a}{9n^2}$
(c) $\frac{c+2b+a}{4n^2}$ (d) $\frac{c-b+a}{n^2}$

12 Three particles start from the origin at the same time, one with a velocity v_1 along X-axis, the second along the Y-axis with a velocity v_2 and the third along $x = y$ line. The velocity of the third, so that the three may always lie on the same line is

(a) $\frac{v_1 v_2}{v_1 + v_2}$ (b) $\frac{\sqrt{2} v_1 v_2}{v_1 + v_2}$ (c) $\frac{\sqrt{3} v_1 v_2}{v_1 + v_2}$ (d) zero

13 A particle moves on a straight line with uniform acceleration of -5 m/s^2. Distance travelled by it in three consecutive intervals of 1 s each are in the ratio 3:1:1. Find total distance travelled by the particle in 3 s.

(a) 15 m (b) 12.5 m (c) 22.5 m (d) 20 m

14 A particle is moving with uniform acceleration along a straight line. The average velocity of the particle from P to Q is 20 m/s and that of Q to S is 30 m/s. If $PQ = QS$, then find average velocity from P to S.

(a) 24 m/s (b) 25 m/s (c) 26 m/s (d) 27 m/s

15 From the top of a tower, a ball is thrown vertically upwards. When the ball reaches h below the tower, its speed is double of what it was at height h above the tower. Find the greatest height attained by the ball from the tower.

(a) $\frac{5h}{3}$ (b) $\frac{4h}{3}$ (c) $2h$ (d) $\frac{3h}{2}$

16 A stone is thrown vertically upward with an initial velocity v_0. Find the distance travelled in time $\frac{3v_0}{2g}$.

(a) $\frac{5v_0^2}{4g}$ (b) $\frac{5v_0^2}{8g}$ (c) $\frac{3v_0^2}{8g}$ (d) $\frac{3v_0^2}{4g}$

17 A particle is projected vertically upwards and it attains maximum height H. The particle appears at height h ($<H$) twice at time t_1 and t_2. If $\frac{t_1}{t_2} = \frac{1}{3}$, then $h =$

(a) $\frac{2H}{3}$ (b) $\frac{3H}{4}$ (c) $\frac{4H}{5}$ (d) $\frac{5H}{6}$

18 A particle is projected vertically upwards with a velocity u m/s and after t second, another particle is projected upwards from the same point with the same velocity. Find the time at which they meet after the first particle is projected.

(a) $\left(\frac{u}{g} + t\right)$ (b) $\left(\frac{2u}{g} + t\right)$ (c) $\left(\frac{u}{g} + \frac{t}{2}\right)$ (d) $\left(\frac{u}{g} + 2t\right)$

19 A balloon is rising vertically upwards with uniform acceleration 2 m/s^2. A stone is dropped from it. After 4s, another stone is dropped from it. Find the distance between the two stones 6 s after the second stone is dropped. (Take, $g = 10 \text{ m/s}^2$)

(a) 288 m (b) 384 m
(c) 216 m (d) 600 m

20 A ball is thrown vertically upward from the ground. It crosses a point at the height of 25m twice at an interval of 4 s. The ball was thrown with the velocity of

(a) 20 m/s (b) 25 m/s
(c) 30 m/s (d) 35 m/s

21 A particle is thrown upwards from the ground. It experiences a constant air resistance which can produce a retardation of 2 m/s^2 opposite to the direction of velocity of particle. The ratio of time of ascent to the time of descent is (take, $g = 10 \text{ m/s}^2$)

(a) 1:1 (b) $\sqrt{\frac{2}{3}}$ (c) $\frac{2}{3}$ (d) $\sqrt{\frac{3}{2}}$

22 A stone is thrown up vertically with a speed of 50 m/s. 2 s later, another stone is thrown up vertically and the stones pass each other at a height of 45 m. Find the speed of the second stone.

(a) (230/7) m/s (b) (250/7) m/s
(c) (270/7) m/s (d) (290/7) m/s

23 A juggler projects a ball upward in a room of height $H = 20$ m. Ball's projection speed was such that it can just reach the ceiling. Now the ball is projected with two times of the previous velocity. After what time interval in second, does this ball return to hand of juggler? [Assume collision with roof results in reversal in direction of velocity with no change in magnitude.]

(a) $8 - 4\sqrt{3}$ (b) $8 + 4\sqrt{3}$ (c) $4 - 2\sqrt{3}$ (d) $4 + 2\sqrt{3}$

24 A student determined to test the law of gravity for himself walks off a skyscraper 320 m high with a stopwatch in hand and starts his free fall (zero initial velocity). 5 s later, superman arrives at the scene and dives off the roof to save the student. What must be superman's initial velocity in order that he catches the student just before reaching the ground? [Assume that, the superman's acceleration is that of any freely falling body.] (Take, $g = 10 \text{ m/s}^2$)

(a) 67.23 m/s (b) 91.66 m/s
(c) 102.91 m/s (d) It is not possible

25 In the above question, what must be the maximum height of the skyscraper so that even superman cannot save him?

(a) 65 m (b) 85 m
(c) 125 m (d) 145 m

26 A stone is dropped from a certain height into a lake 10 m deep. The stone reaches the bed of the lake 7 seconds after it was dropped. Assume that both the velocity and the acceleration of the stone are halved on entering the water. Find the height from which the stone was dropped.

(a) 35 m (b) 45 m (c) 55 m (d) 75 m

27 A steel ball bearing is released from the roof of a building. An observer standing infront of a window 180 cm high observes that the ball takes 0.2 s to fall from top to the bottom of the window. The ball continues to fall and makes a completely elastic collision (no change in speed) with side walk and reappears at the bottom of the window 2 s after passing it on the way down. How tall is the building? (Take, $g = 10 \text{ m/s}^2$)

(a) 10 m (b) 15 m
(c) 18.75 m (d) 20 m

28 A stone is dropped from the top of building and at the same time a second stone is thrown vertically upward from the bottom of the building with a speed of 20 m/s. They pass each other 3 s later. Find the height of the building.

(a) 40 m (b) 60 m (c) 65 m (d) 80 m

29 The driver of a car moving on a straight road applies brakes to come to rest with a constant retardation a. Assuming that the time of motion is more than 2 s, the distance covered by the car in second last second of its motion is

(a) a (b) $\frac{a}{2}$ (c) $\frac{3a}{2}$ (d) $\frac{5a}{2}$

30 An astronaut on the starship Enterprise is roaming around on a distant planet. He drops a rock from the top of a cliff and observes that it takes time $t_1 = \sqrt{2}$ s to reach the bottom. He now throws another rock vertically upwards, so that it reaches a height $h = 10$ m above the cliff before dropping down the cliff. The second rock takes a total time $t_2 = 2$ s to reach the bottom of the cliff, starting from the time it leaves the astronaut's hand. The planet has a very thin atmosphere which offers negligible air resistance. What is the value of acceleration (in m/s^2) due to gravity on this planet?

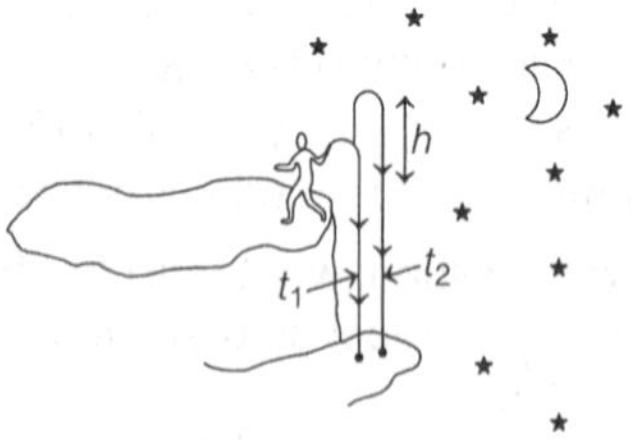

(a) 80 (b) 50 (c) 20 (d) 10

31 A particle is thrown vertically upwards from the surface of the earth. Let T_p be the time taken by the particle to travel from a point P above the earth to its highest point and back to the point P. Similarly, let T_Q be the time taken by the particle to travel from another point Q above the earth to its highest point and back to the same point Q. If the distance between the points P and Q is H, the expression for acceleration due to gravity in terms of T_P, T_Q and H is

(a) $\frac{6H}{T_P^2 + T_Q^2}$ (b) $\frac{8H}{T_P^2 - T_Q^2}$ (c) $\frac{2H}{T_P^2 + T_Q^2}$ (d) $\frac{H}{T_P^2 - T_Q^2}$

32 A lift on the ground starts from rest and accelerates uniformly upward at 1.25 m/s^2, reaching its maximum velocity in 10 s. When it has attained a height of 40 m, a bolt gas gets loosened and falls to the ground. What is the height of the lift when th bolt hits the ground?

(a) 75 m (b) 80.25 m
(c) 84.50 m (d) 87.5 m

Multiple Choice(s) Correct Questions

1 Mark the correct statement(s) for a particle going on a straight line.

(a) If the velocity and acceleration have opposite sign, the object is slowing down.
(b) If the position and velocity have opposite sign, the particle is moving towards the origin.
(c) If the velocity is zero at an instant, the acceleration should also be zero at that instant.
(d) If the velocity is zero for a time interval, the acceleration is zero at any instant within the time interval.

2 Mark the correct statement(s).

(a) The magnitude of the instantaneous velocity of a particle is equal to its instantaneous speed.
(b) The magnitude of average velocity in an interval is equal to its average speed in that interval.
(c) It is possible to have a situation in which the speed of a particle is always zero but the average speed is not zero.
(d) It is possible to have a situation in which the speed of the particle is never zero but the average velocity in an interval is zero.

3 A particle moves with constant speed v along a regular hexagon ABCDEF in the same order, then the magnitude of the average velocity for its motion from A to

(a) F is $\frac{v}{5}$ (b) D is $\frac{v}{3}$ (c) C is $v\frac{\sqrt{3}}{2}$ (d) B is v

4 A car is accelerating uniformly as it passes two check points that are 30 m apart. The time taken between check points is 4 s and the speed of the car at the first check point is 5 m/s, then

(a) the speed of the car at the second check point is 10 m/s
(b) the speed of the car at the second check point is 20 m/s
(c) the acceleration of the car is 2.5 m/s^2
(d) the acceleration of the car is 1.25 m/s^2

5 A ball is dropped from the top of a building. The ball takes 0.5 s to fall the 3 m length of a window which is located some distance from the top of the building. If the velocities of the ball at the top and at the bottom of the window are v_T and v_B respectively, then (take, $g = 10\,m/s^2$)

(a) $v_T + v_B = 12\text{ms}^{-1}$ (b) $v_B - v_T = 5\text{ms}^{-1}$
(c) $v_B v_T = 1\text{ms}^{-1}$ (d) $\frac{v_B}{v_T} = 1\text{ms}^{-1}$

6 A particle is projected vertically upwards in vacuum with a speed u,
(a) when it rises to half its maximum height, its speed becomes $u/2$
(b) when it rises to half its maximum height, its speed becomes $\frac{u}{\sqrt{2}}$
(c) the time taken to rise to half its maximum height is half the time taken to reach its maximum height.
(d) the time taken to rise to three-fourth of its maximum height is half the time taken to reach its maximum height.

7 A ball is thrown upward from the ground with velocity u. It is at a height 100 m at two times t_1 and t_2 respectively. If $g = 10\,m/s^2$, then
(a) $t_1 t_2 = 20$ (b) $t_1 + t_2 = 20$
(c) $t_1 t_2 = \frac{u}{5}$ (d) $t_1 + t_2 = \frac{u}{5}$

8 The vertical height of point P above the ground is twice that of point Q. A particle is projected downward with a speed of 5 m/s from P and at the same time another particle is projected upward with the same speed from Q. Both particles reach the ground simultaneously, if PQ lies on same vertical line, then
(a) $PQ = 30$ m
(b) $PQ = 60$ m
(c) time of flight of the stones = 3 s
(d) time of flight of the stones = (1/3) s

9 A particle is thrown in vertically upward direction and passes three equally spaced windows of equal heights, then

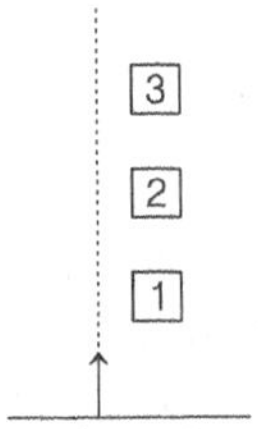

(a) the average speed of the particle while passing the windows satisfy the relation $v_{av_1} > v_{av_2} > v_{av_3}$
(b) the time taken by the particle to cross the windows satisfies the relation $t_1 < t_2 < t_3$
(c) the magnitude of the acceleration of the particle while crossing the windows, satisfies the relation $a_1 = a_2 \neq a_3$
(d) the change in the speed of the particle, while crossing the windows, would satisfy the relation $\Delta v_1 < \Delta v_2 < \Delta v_3$

10 Which of the following statement(s) is/are true for a moving body?
(a) If its speed changes, its velocity must change and it must have some acceleration.
(b) If its velocity changes, its speed must change and it must have some acceleration.
(c) If its velocity changes, its speed may or may not change and it must have some acceleration.
(d) If its speed changes but direction of motion does not change, its velocity may remains constant.

11 A motorist is travelling at 54 km/h when he observes a traffic signal at a distance of 280 m ahead turning red at time $t = 0$. If he decides to decelerate and then accelerate by the same magnitude so as to pass the signal at 54 km/h at $t = 28$ s, when the signal turns green, then
(a) magnitude of deceleration is (5/7) m/s^2
(b) magnitude of deceleration is 1 m/s^2
(c) minimum speed reached is 5 m/s
(d) minimum speed reached is 10 m/s

12 A particle has initial velocity 10 m/s. It moves against a constant retarding force along the line of velocity which produces a retardation of 5 m/s^2, then
(a) the maximum displacement in the direction of the initial velocity is 10 m
(b) the distance travelled in the first three seconds is 12.5 m
(c) the particle returns to its initial position in 4 s
(d) average velocity over first 4 s in 5 m/s

13 A body moving with uniform acceleration in a straight line covers 25 m in the 5th second and 33 m in the 7th second, so
(a) initial velocity is 6 m/s
(b) initial velocity is 7 m/s
(c) acceleration is 2 m/s^2
(d) acceleration is 4 m/s^2

14 Choose the correct option(s):
(a) If $\hat{\mathbf{a}} \cdot \hat{\mathbf{v}} = 1$, then object is moving with increasing speed without change in direction.
(b) If $\hat{\mathbf{a}} \cdot \hat{\mathbf{v}} = -1$, then object definitely changes in its direction.
(c) If $\mathbf{r} \cdot \mathbf{v} < 0$, then object is moving towards origin.
(d) If $\mathbf{r} \cdot \mathbf{v} < 0$, then object is moving away from origin.

Comprehension Based Questions

Comprehension-1

A particle is moving along X-axis. Its initial velocity is 40 m/s along positive X-axis and an acceleration of 10 m/s^2 along negative X-axis. Particle starts from $x = 10$ m.

1 Velocity of particle is zero at .... s.
(a) 6 (b) 4
(c) 5 (d) 2

2 Maximum x-coordinate of particle (in positive direction) is .... m.
(a) 90 (b) 60
(c) 120 (d) 30

3 Velocity of particle at origin is .... m/s.
(a) $30\sqrt{2}$ (b) $20\sqrt{2}$
(c) $-20\sqrt{2}$ (d) $-30\sqrt{2}$

4 Particle is at time .... s at origin.
(a) $4+3\sqrt{2}$ (b) $4+\sqrt{2}$
(c) $2+3\sqrt{2}$ (d) $3+2\sqrt{2}$

Comprehension-2

A spaceship ferrying walks to Moon base. It takes a straight line path from the Earth to the Moon, a distance of 384000 km. Suppose it accelerates at 20 m/s^2 for the first 15 min of the trip, then travels with same speed until the last 15 min, when it decelerates at 20 m/s^2 just coming to rest as it reaches the Moon.

5 What distance does it travel while decelerating?
(a) 6.1×10^3 km
(b) 5.1×10^3 km
(c) 3.1×10^3 km
(d) 8.1×10^3 km

6 What fraction of the total distance it travelled at constant speed?
(a) 0.95 (b) 0.23
(c) 0.40 (d) 0.52

7 What total time is required for the trip?
(a) 170 min (b) 270 min
(c) 370 min (d) 470 min

Comprehension-3

A particle moving with uniform acceleration passes the point $x = 2$ m with velocity 20 m/s at the instant $t = 0$. Sometime later, it is observed at the point $x = 32$ m moving with velocity 10 m/s.

8 What is its acceleration?
(a) -2 m/s^2 (b) -4 m/s^2
(c) -5 m/s^2 (d) -10 m/s^2

9 Find the velocity at the instant $t = 8$ s.
(a) 0 (b) 10 m/s
(c) -10 m/s (d) -20 m/s

10 What is the distance travelled during the interval $t = 0$ to 8 s?
(a) 80 m (b) 60 m
(c) 40 m (d) 20 m

Comprehension-4

Two balls A and B are thrown with same speed u from the top of a tower. Ball A is thrown vertically upwards and the ball B is thrown vertically downwards.

t_A = time taken by A to reach ground
t_B = time taken by B to reach ground

11 If $t_A = 6$ s and $t_B = 2$ s, then height of the tower is
(a) 80 m
(b) 60 m
(c) 45 m
(d) None of the above

12 The velocity u of each ball is
(a) 10 m/s
(b) 15 m/s
(c) 20 m/s
(d) None of the above

Match the Columns Questions

1 A car accelerates from rest at a constant rate of 10 m/s^2 for sometime after which it retards at a constant rate of 5 m/s^2 to come to rest. The total time taken is 15 s. Match the following columns.

	Column I		Column II
(A)	Maximum speed of car (in m/s)	(P)	10
(B)	Distance (in m) travelled by the car till its speed becomes half of the maximum speed for the second time	(Q)	25
(C)	Average speed (in m/s) during entire journey	(R)	50
(D)	Time during which car is retarding	(S)	312.5

2 A juggler throws 20 balls using only one hand. He throws each ball vertically upward with the same speed at equal interval of time. When he is about to throw the 20th ball, the first ball reaches his hand after being in air for 10 s.

Match the following columns.

	Column I		Column II
(A)	The speed (in m/s) of projection of ball	(P)	93.75
(B)	The height (in m) of the 15th ball when 20th ball is in hand	(Q)	50
(C)	Speed (in m/s) of the 10th ball when 20th ball is in hand	(R)	120
(D)	The number of balls thrown by juggler per minute	(S)	zero

3 For a body projected vertically up with a velocity $\mathbf{v}_0$ from the ground, match the following columns.

	Column I		Column II
(A)	$\mathbf{v}_{av}$ (average velocity)	(P)	zero for round trip
(B)	u_{av} (average speed)	(Q)	$\frac{\mathbf{v}_1 + \mathbf{v}_2}{2}$ over any time interval
(C)	T_{ascent}	(R)	$\frac{v_0}{2}$ over the total time of its flight
(D)	$T_{descent}$	(S)	$\frac{v_0}{g}$

4 In Column I, the description of change in velocity of a body moving with constant acceleration (or retardation) in a 10 s interval is given, while Column II gives the information about the acceleration in the corresponding time interval. Match the entries of Column I with the entries of Column II.

	Column I		Column II
(A)	At the beginning of the interval, the body is moving towards the right along the X-axis at 5 m/s and at the end of the interval, it is moving towards right at 20 m/s	(P)	magnitude of acceleration is 1.5 m/s^2
(B)	At the beginning, the body is moving towards right at 20 m/s and at the end, it is moving towards right at 5 m/s	(Q)	average acceleration is towards right
(C)	At the beginning, the body is moving towards left at 5 m/s and at the end, it is moving towards left at 20 m/s	(R)	average acceleration is towards left
(D)	At the beginning, the body is moving towards right at 5 m/s and at the end, it is moving towards left at 10 m/s	(S)	body is decelerated for at last some part of its motion

Numerical Value Questions

1 A bullet enters a thick wooden block with a certain velocity and loses (1/10)th of its velocity when it emerges from the opposite face of the block. What is the maximum number of such identical blocks that must be placed in series (in contact one after the other), so that the bullet fired into the first of the blocks will not come out of the blocks? Assume that, all blocks offer uniform retardation to the bullet.

2 A particle beginning from rest, travels a distance s with uniform acceleration and immediately after travels a distance of $3s$ with uniform speed followed by a distance $5s$ with uniform deceleration and comes to rest. The ratio of average speed to the maximum speed of the particle is $\frac{n}{5}$. Find the value of n.

3 A point moving with constant acceleration from A to B in the straight line AB has velocities u & v at A & B respectively and C is the mid-point of AB. If the time from A to C is twice the time taks from C to B, then $v = \lambda u$. Find the value of λ.

4 A train stopping at two stations 2 km apart on a straight line takes 4 min for the journey. Assuming that, its motion is first uniformly accelerated and then uniformly retarded. If $\frac{1}{x} + \frac{1}{y} = n$, where x and y are the magnitude of the acceleration and retardation respectively. Find the value of n.

5 Two particles P and Q start simultaneously from point A with velocities 15 m/s and 20 m/s, respectively. The two particles move with accelerations equal in magnitude but opposite in direction. When P overtakes Q at B, then its velocity is 30 m/s. Find velocity of Q at point B (in m/s).

6 A small electric car has a maximum acceleration of 1 m/s^2, a maximum retardation of 2 m/s^2, and a maximum speed of 20 m/s. Find the minimum time (in seconds), it would take to drive this car 1 km starting from rest and finally bringing it to rest.

7 A ball is dropped from a height of 20 m from ground and it loses 75% of its kinetic energy during its collision with ground. Find total time of flight of ball.

8 A boy throws a ball with speed u in a well, of depth 14 m as shown in figure. On bounce with bottom of the well, the speed of the ball gets halved. What should be the minimum value of u (in m/s), such that the ball may be able to reach his hand again? It is given that his hands are at 1 m height from top of the well while throwing and catching.

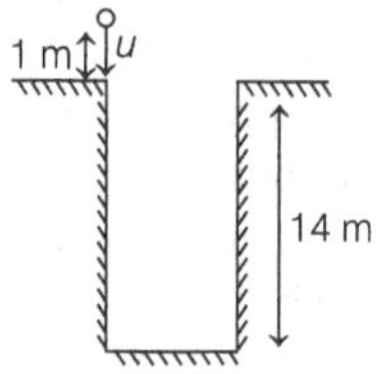

9 A big Diwali rocket is projected vertically upward, so as to attain a maximum height of 160 m. The rocket explodes just as it reaches the top of its trajectory sending out luminous particles in all possible directions all with same speed v. The display, consisting of the luminous particles, spreads out as an expanding, brilliant sphere. The bottom of this sphere just touches the ground when its radius is 80 m. With what speed (in m/s) are the luminous particles ejected by the explosion?

10 A stone is thrown vertically upward. When the stone is at point A, its distance from a certain point O is $6\sqrt{5}$ m at $t=0$ and the component of velocity along OA is non-zero. When it is at point B ($OB = 10$ m), the component of velocity along OB is zero. When it is at point C ($OC = 6$ m), the component of velocity of the particle along OC is zero. Find the speed (in m/s) of projection.

11 Four small stones A, B, C and D are dropped from the top of a tower after 1 s intervals. First stone A hits the ground 4 s after it is dropped. Find the value of $3\left(\frac{AB+BC}{2CD}\right)$ at that instant when the first stone A reaches the ground.

12 Balls P and Q are released from rest from roof of a building at $t=0$ and $t=2$ s, respectively. Ball P strikes the ground and rebounds with the same speed. After sometime, both balls P and Q meet each other at a height of 55 m from the ground. Find the height (in m) of the building.

13 If a particle takes t seconds less and acquires a velocity of v m/s more in falling through the same distance on two planets where acceleration due to gravity are $2g$ and $8g$ respectively, then $v = x\,gt$. Find the value of x.

14 A ball is thrown upwards with a speed of 40 m/s. When the speed becomes half of the initial speed, gravity is switched off for the next two seconds, then gravity is again switched on but magnitude of gravity is doubled. Find the total distance (in m) travelled by the ball from the beginning till it reaches the maximum height.

15 A passenger who just missed the train stands on the platform, sadly watching the last two boggies of the train. The second last boggy takes 3 s to pass by the passenger and the last one takes 2 s to pass by. If the passenger is late by 'T' s for departure of the train, calculate the value of T.

(Assume that the train accelerates at constant rate)

Previous Year's Questions

JEE Main

1 A bullet is fired into a fixed target looses one third of its velocity after travelling 4 cm. It penetrates further $D \times 10^{-3}$ m before coming to rest. The value of D is **[2024, 27 Jan Shift-II]**

(a) 2 (b) 3 (c) 4 (d) 5

2 A body falling under gravity covers two points A and B separated by 80 m in 2 s. The distance of upper point A from the starting point is .... m (use $g = 10\ \text{ms}^{-2}$). **[2024, 27 Jan Shift-II]**

3 A body starts moving from rest with constant acceleration covers displacement S_1 in first $(p-1)$ seconds and S_2 in first p seconds. The displacement $S_1 + S_2$ will be made in time **[2024, 29 Jan Shift-I]**

(a) $(2p^2 - 2p + 1)$ s (b) $(2p + 1)$ s

(c) $(2p - 1)$ s (d) $\sqrt{(2p^2 - 2p + 1)}$ s

4 A person travels x distance with velocity v_1 and then x distance with velocity v_2 in the same direction. The average velocity of the person is v, then the relation between v, v_1 and v_2 will be **[2023, 10 April Shift-II]**

(a) $v = \frac{v_1 + v_2}{2}$ (b) $\frac{2}{v} = \frac{1}{v_1} + \frac{1}{v_2}$

(c) $v = v_1 + v_2$ (d) $\frac{1}{v} = \frac{1}{v_1} + \frac{1}{v_2}$

5 An object moves with speed v_1, v_2 and v_3 along a line segment AB, BC and CD, respectively as shown in figure. where $AB = BC$ and $AD = 3AB$, then average speed of the object will be **[2023, 1 Feb Shift-I]**

(a) $\frac{v_1 v_2 v_3}{3(v_1 v_2 + v_2 v_3 + v_3 v_1)}$

(b) $\frac{3 v_1 v_2 v_3}{(v_1 v_2 + v_2 v_3 + v_3 v_1)}$

(c) $\frac{(v_1 + v_2 + v_3)}{3 v_1 v_2 v_3}$

(d) $\frac{(v_1 + v_2 + v_3)}{3}$

6 A car travels a distance of x with speed v_1 and then same distance x with speed v_2 in the same direction. The average speed of the car is **[2023, 25 Jan Shift-I]**

(a) $\dfrac{2x}{v_1 + v_2}$

(b) $\dfrac{2v_1 v_2}{v_1 + v_2}$

(c) $\dfrac{v_1 v_2}{2(v_1 + v_2)}$

(d) $\dfrac{v_1 + v_2}{2}$

7 A vehicle travels 4 km with speed of 3 km/h and another 4 km with speed of 5 km/h, then its average speed is **[2023, 30 Jan Shift-II]**

(a) 3.50 km/h (b) 3.75 km/h
(c) 4.00 km/h (d) 4.25 km/h

8 A horse rider covers half the distance with 5 m/s speed. The remaining part of the distance was travelled with speed 10 m/s for half the time and with speed 15 m/s for other half of the time. The mean speed of the rider averaged over the whole time of motion is $x/7$ m/s. The value of x is......... . **[2023, 30 Jan Shift-I]**

9 A ball is thrown vertically upward with an initial velocity of 150 m/s. The ratio of velocity after 3s and 5s is $\dfrac{x+1}{x}$. The value of x is {Take, $g = 10 \text{ m/s}^2$} **[2023, 12 April Shift-I]**

(a) 10 (b) 5
(c) 6 (d) – 5

10 A particle starts with an initial velocity of 10.0 ms^{-1} along x-direction and accelerates uniformly at the rate of 2.0 ms^{-2}. The time taken by the particle to reach the velocity of 60.0 ms^{-1} is **[2023, 6 April Shift-II]**

(a) 25 s (b) 3 s
(c) 30 s (d) 6 s

11 A tennis ball is dropped on to the floor from a height of 9.8 m. It rebounds to a height 5.0 m. Ball comes in contact with the floor for 0.2 s. The average acceleration during contact is .... ms^{-2} (Given, $g = 10 \text{ ms}^{-2}$) **[2023, 29 Jan Shift-I]**

12 A car covers AB distance with first one-third at velocity $v_1 \text{ ms}^{-1}$, second one-third at $v_2 \text{ ms}^{-1}$ and last one-third at $v_3 \text{ ms}^{-1}$. If $v_3 = 3v_1$, $v_2 = 2v_1$ and $v_1 = 11 \text{ ms}^{-1}$ then the average velocity of the car is .... ms^{-1}. **[2022, 28 June Shift-II]**

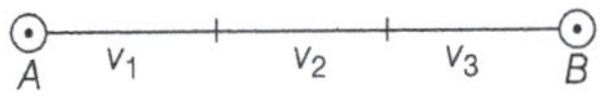

13 When a ball is dropped into a lake from a height 4.9 m above the water level, it hits the water with a velocity v and then sinks to the bottom with the constant velocity v. If reaches the bottom of the lake 4.0 s after it is dropped. The approximate depth of the lake is **[2022, 27 June Shift-II]**

(a) 19.6 m (b) 29.4 m
(c) 39.2 m (d) 73.5 m

14 A juggler throws balls vertically upwards with same initial velocity in air. When the first ball reaches its highest position, he throws the next ball. Assuming the juggler throws n balls per second, the maximum height the balls can reach is **[2022, 29 July Shift-II]**

(a) $g/2n$ (b) g/n
(c) $2gn$ (d) $g/2n^2$

15 Two balls A and B are placed at the top of 180 m tall tower. Ball A is released from the top at $t = 0$ s. Ball B is thrown vertically down with an initial velocity u at $t = 2$ s. After a certain time, both balls meet 100 m above the ground. Find the value of u (in ms^{-1}). [Use $g = 10 \text{ ms}^{-2}$] **[2022, 29 June Shift-I]**

(a) 10 (b) 15
(c) 20 (d) 30

16 A ball is thrown vertically upwards with a velocity of 19.6 ms^{-1} from the top of a tower. The ball strikes the ground after 6 s. The height from the ground up to which the ball can rise will be $\left(\dfrac{k}{5}\right)$m. The value of k is .... (Use, $g = 9.8 \text{ m/s}^2$) **[2022, 28 July Shift-II]**

17 A particle is moving in a straight line such that its velocity is increasing at 5 ms^{-1} per metre. The acceleration of the particle is ...... ms^{-2} at a point where its velocity is 20 ms^{-1}. **[2022, 25 July Shift-II]**

18 A car is moving with speed of 150 km/h and after applying the break it will move 27 m before it stops. If the same car is moving with a speed of one-third the reported speed, then it will stop after travelling ...... m distance. **[2022, 25 July Shift-I]**

19 A ball is projected vertically upward with an initial velocity of 50 ms^{-1} at $t = 0$ s. At $t = 2$ s, another ball is projected vertically upward with same velocity. At $t =$...... s, second ball will meet the first ball (Take, $g = 10 \text{ ms}^{-2}$). **[2022, 26 June Shift-II]**

20 A ball of mass 0.5 kg is dropped from the height of 10 m. The height, at which the magnitude of velocity becomes equal to the magnitude of acceleration due to gravity, is .... m. (Use, $g = 10 \text{ m/s}^2$) **[2022, 26 June Shift-I]**

21 From the top of a tower, a ball is thrown vertically upward which reaches the ground in 6 s. A second ball thrown vertically downward from the same position with the same speed reaches the ground in 1.5 s. A third ball released, from the rest from the same location, will reach the ground in .... s.
[2022, 24 June Shift-I]

22 Water drops are falling from a nozzle of a shower onto the floor, from a height of 9.8 m. The drops fall at a regular interval of time. When the first drop strikes the floor, at that instant, the third drop begins to fall. Locate the position of second drop from the floor when the first drop strikes the floor.
[2021, 27 Aug Shift-II]

(a) 4.18 m (b) 2.94 m
(c) 2.45 m (d) 7.35 m

23 A balloon was moving upwards with a uniform velocity of 10 m/s. An object of finite mass is dropped from the balloon when it was at a height of 75 m from the ground level. The height of the balloon from the ground when object strikes the ground was around, is
(Take, the value of $g = 10\ \text{m/s}^2$) [2021, 25 July Shift-II]

(a) 300 m (b) 200 m
(c) 125 m (d) 250 m

24 Water droplets are coming from an open tap at a particular rate. The spacing between a droplet observed at 4th second after its fall to the next droplet is 34.3 m. At what rate, the droplets are coming from the tap? (Take, $g = 9.8\ \text{m/s}^2$)
[2021, 25 July Shift-I]

(a) 3 drops / 2 s (b) 2 drops / s
(c) 1 drop / s (d) 1 drop / 7 s

25 A scooter accelerates from rest for time t_1 at constant rate a_1 and then retards at constant rate a_2 for time t_2 and comes to rest. The correct value of $\frac{t_1}{t_2}$ will be [2021, 26 Feb Shift-II]

(a) $\frac{a_1 + a_2}{a_2}$ (b) $\frac{a_2}{a_1}$
(c) $\frac{a_1}{a_2}$ (d) $\frac{a_1 + a_2}{a_1}$

26 A stone is dropped from the top of a building. When it crosses a point 5 m below the top, another stone starts to fall from a point 25 m below the top. Both stones reach the bottom of building simultaneously. The height of the building is [2021, 25 Feb Shift-II]

(a) 45 m (b) 25 m
(c) 35 m (d) 50 m

27 An engine of a train moving with uniform acceleration, passes the signal-post with velocity u and the last compartment with velocity v. The velocity with which middle point of the train passes the signal post is [2021, 25 Feb Shift-I]

(a) $\sqrt{\frac{v^2 + u^2}{2}}$ (b) $\frac{v - u}{2}$
(c) $\frac{u + v}{2}$ (d) $\sqrt{\frac{v^2 - u^2}{2}}$

28 Two spherical balls having equal masses with radius of 5 cm each are thrown upwards along the same vertical direction at an interval of 3s with the same initial velocity of 35 m/s, then these balls collide at a height of .... m. (Take, $g = 10\ \text{m/s}^2$)
[2021, 26 Aug Shift-I]

Answer Key

Level 1

5.1 Average Speed and Average Velocity

1. (a) 440 km/h (b) 50 km/h (c) 440 km/h (d) 44 km/h
2. (a) 32 km/h (b) zero
3. $\frac{2v_1v_2}{v_1+v_2}$ 4. $\frac{v_1+v_2}{2}$ 5. $\frac{3v_1v_2v_3}{v_1v_2+v_2v_3+v_3v_1}$

5.2 Motion Along a horizontal Line

1. (a) 16 m/s (b) 4 s 2. 0.05 s
3. (a) 120 m/s (b) 2.4 m/s^2 (c) 3 km (d) $25\sqrt{2}$ s
4. (a) 6 s and 90 m (b) 12 s and 360 m. Time gets doubled while stopping distance becomes four tlmes.
5. 7.2 km
6. (a) 2700 m (b) 60 m/s (c) 225 m and 2250 m
7. (a) 8 m/s^2, West (b) 0.25 s (c) 0.75 m, West (d) 1.25m (e) 1 m/s, West (f) 1.67 m/s
8. (a) 100 m (b) 10 s (c) 19m, 15m 9. $3\sqrt{5}$ s 10. 1:3:5
11. 36 m 12. 20 m/s^2 13. 21.75 m
14. (a) 13 m/s (b) 12 m/s 15. 1.25 km 16. 8 s and 10 s

5.3 Motion Under Gravity

1. (a) 4 s (b) 40 m/s (c) $20\sqrt{2}$ m/s, $2\sqrt{2}$ s (d) 30 m/s (e) 60 m
2. (a) 4 s (b) 60 m/s (c) 2 s (d) 78.75 m (e) 55 m
3. (a) 125 m (b) 5 s (c) $25\sqrt{2}$ m/s (d) $\frac{145}{7}$ m/s, 15 m/s (e) 3 s and 7 s
4. (a) 180 m from ground (b) 8 s (c) 25 m/s
5. (a) 4 s (b) 90 m (c) 50 m 6. 45 m
7. (a) 108 km (b) 3 min 8. (a) 56 s (b) 2984 m
9. $\sqrt{t_1t_2}$ 10. 31.25 m
11. 4 s after first stone is dropped, 80 m from tower
12. 80 m from ground 13. Object, $(7-\sqrt{34})$ s

Level 2

Single Choice Correct Questions

1. (a)	2. (d)	3. (b)	4. (c)	5. (b)
6. (c)	7. (d)	8. (c)	9. (c)	10. (d)
11. (c)	12. (a)	13. (b)	14. (a)	15. (d)
16. (a)	17. (c)	18. (d)	19. (c)	20. (b)
21. (c)	22. (d)	23. (b)	24. (d)	25. (b)
26. (d)	27. (c)	28. (b)	29. (a)	30. (a)
31. (c)	32. (d)	33. (a)	34. (c)	35. (b)
36. (c)	37. (c)	38. (b)	39. (a)	40. (d)
41. (b)	42. (a)	43. (d)	44. (c)	45. (a)
46. (d)	47. (a)	48. (d)	49. (d)	50. (c)
51. (b)	52. (c)	53. (c)	54. (b)	55. (b)
56. (d)	57. (d)	58. (b)	59. (b)	60. (c)
61. (a)	62. (a)	63. (b)		

Numerical Value Questions

1. 18.5	2. 18	3. 20	4. 26	5. 2.5
6. 16	7. 8	8. 6	9. 80	10. 7
11. 5	12. 15.8	13. 14	14. 6	15. 14.70

Level 3

Single Choice Correct Questions

1. (c)	2. (c)	3. (c)	4. (b)	5. (b)
6. (c)	7. (a)	8. (d)	9. (a)	10. (a)
11. (a)	12. (b)	13. (b)	14. (a)	15. (a)
16. (b)	17. (b)	18. (c)	19. (b)	20. (c)
21. (b)	22. (d)	23. (a)	24. (b)	25. (c)
26. (b)	27. (d)	28. (b)	29. (c)	30. (a)
31. (b)	32. (d)			

Multiple Choice(s) Correct Questions

1. acd	2. ad	3. acd	4. ad	5. ab
6. bd	7. ad	8. ac	9. abd	10. ac
11. ac	12. abc	13. bd	14. abc	

Comprehension Based Questions

1. (b)	2. (a)	3. (d)	4. (a)	5. (d)
6. (a)	7. (c)	8. (c)	9. (d)	10. (a)
11. (b)	12. (c)			

Match the Columns Questions

1. A→ R B→ S C→ Q D→ P
2. A→ Q B→ P C→ S D→ R
3. A→ PQ B→ R C→ S D→ S
4. A→ PQ B→ PRS C→ PR D→ PRS

Numerical Value Questions

1. 5	2. 3	3. 7	4. 4	5. 5
6. 65	7. 6	8. 30	9. 20	10. 20
11. 6	12. 180	13. 4	14. 110	15. 3.50

Previous Year's Questions

JEE Main

1. (*)	2. (45)	3. (d)	4. (b)	5. (b)
6. (b)	7. (b)	8. (50)	9. (b)	10. (a)
11. (20)	12. (18)	13. (b)	14. (d)	15. (d)
16. (392)	17. (100)	18. (3)	19. (6)	20. (5)
21. (3)	22. (d)	23. (c)	24. (c)	25. (b)
26. (a)	27. (a)	28. (50)		

SOLUTIONS

Level 1

5.1 Average Speed and Average Velocity

1. (a) Average speed of aeroplane $= \dfrac{220}{\frac{1}{2}} = 440$ km/h

   (b) Average speed of bus $= \dfrac{250}{5} = 50$ km/h

   (c) Average velocity of aeroplane $= \dfrac{220}{\frac{1}{2}} = 440$ km/h

   (d) Average velocity of bus $= \dfrac{220}{5} = 44$ km/h

2. (a) Average speed $= \dfrac{\text{Distance travelled}}{\text{Time taken}} = \dfrac{64}{2} = 32$ km/h

   (b) Average velocity = 0

3. Let total distance to be $2d$.

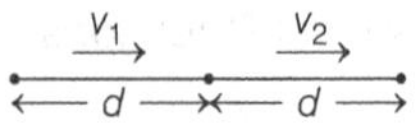

   Total time taken $= \dfrac{d}{v_1} + \dfrac{d}{v_2}$

   Average speed $= \dfrac{\text{Total distance}}{\text{Total time}} = \dfrac{2d}{\frac{d}{v_1} + \frac{d}{v_2}} = \dfrac{2v_1v_2}{v_1 + v_2}$

4. Let total time of journey to be $2t$.

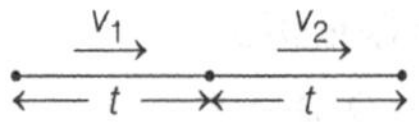

   Total distance travelled $= v_1t + v_2t$

   Average speed $= \dfrac{v_1t + v_2t}{2t} = \dfrac{v_1 + v_2}{2}$

5. Let total distance to be $3d$.

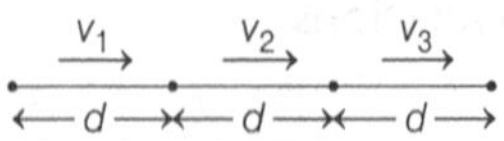

   Total time taken $= \dfrac{d}{v_1} + \dfrac{d}{v_2} + \dfrac{d}{v_3}$

   Average speed $= \dfrac{3d}{\frac{d}{v_1} + \frac{d}{v_2} + \frac{d}{v_3}} = \dfrac{3v_1v_2v_3}{v_1v_2 + v_2v_3 + v_3v_1}$

5.2 Motion Along a Horizontal Line

1. $u = 6\text{ m/s},\ a = 2.5\text{ m/s}^2, s = 44\text{ m}$

   (a) $v^2 = u^2 + 2as \Rightarrow v^2 = 6^2 + 2(2.5)(44)$

   $v = \sqrt{256} = 16\text{ m/s}$

   (b) $v = u + at \Rightarrow 16 = 6 + 2.5t \Rightarrow t = 4\text{ s}$

2. $u = 16\text{ m/s},\ s = 0.4\text{ m},\ v = 0$

   $v^2 = u^2 + 2as \Rightarrow 0^2 = 16^2 + 2a(0.4)$

   $\Rightarrow a = -\dfrac{256}{0.8} = -320\text{ m/s}^2$

   $v = u + at \Rightarrow 0 = 16 - 320t$

   $\Rightarrow t = \dfrac{1}{20}\text{ s} = 0.05\text{ s}$

3. Average velocity $= \dfrac{s}{t}$

   $60 = \dfrac{s}{50} \Rightarrow s = 3000\text{ m}$

   (a) $v = u + at \Rightarrow v = 0 + 2.4 \times 50 = 120\text{ m/s}$

   (b) $s = ut + \dfrac{1}{2}at^2$

   $\Rightarrow 3000 = 0 + \dfrac{1}{2}(a)(50)^2 \Rightarrow a = 2.4\text{ m/s}^2$

   (c) Length of runway = 3000 m = 3 km

   (d) $1500 = \dfrac{1}{2}(2.4)t^2 \Rightarrow t = 25\sqrt{2}\text{ s}$

4. $u = 30\text{ m/s}, a = -5\text{ m/s}^2$

   (a) $v^2 = u^2 + 2as \Rightarrow 0^2 = 30^2 + 2(-5)s \Rightarrow s = 90\text{ m}$

   $v = u + at \Rightarrow 0 = 30 + (-5)t \Rightarrow t = 6\text{ s}$

   (b) If initial speed is doubled stopping distance will become 4 times and stopping time will get doubled.

5. Time taken by the woman to reach river $= \dfrac{4\text{ km}}{2.5\text{ km/h}}$

   Distance travelled by dog $= ut = (4.5)\left(\dfrac{4}{2.5}\right) = 7.2\text{ km}$

6.

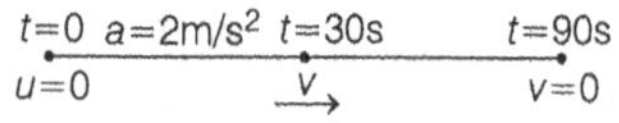

   From $t = 0$ to $t = 30$ s,

   $v = u + at \Rightarrow v = 0 + 2(30) \Rightarrow v = 60\text{ m/s}$

   $v^2 = u^2 + 2as \Rightarrow 60^2 = 0^2 + 2(2)s \Rightarrow s = 900\text{ m}$

   From $t = 30$ s to $t = 90$ s,

   $v = u + at \Rightarrow 0 = 60 + a(60) \Rightarrow a = -1\text{ m/s}^2$

   $v^2 = u^2 + 2as \Rightarrow 0^2 = 60^2 + 2(-1)s \Rightarrow s = 1800\text{ m}$

   (a) Total distance = 900 + 1800 = 2700 m

   (b) Maximum speed = 60 m/s $[\because v = 60\text{ m/s}]$

   (c) $v^2 = u^2 + 2as \Rightarrow 30^2 = 0^2 + 2(2)s \Rightarrow s = 225\text{ m}$

   $v^2 = u^2 + 2as \Rightarrow 30^2 = 60^2 + 2(-1)s \Rightarrow s = 1350\text{ m}$

   So, position of train at half the maximum speed = 225 m and (1350 + 900) m = 225 m and 2250 m

7. $u = 2\,m/s, v = -4\,m/s, t = 0.75\,s$

(a) $v = u + at \Rightarrow -4 = 2 + a(0.75)$

$\Rightarrow a = -8\,m/s^2 = 8 m/s^2$, West

(b) $v = u + at \Rightarrow 0 = 2 - 8t \Rightarrow t = 0.25\,s$

(c) $v^2 = u^2 + 2as \Rightarrow (-4)^2 = 2^2 + 2(-8)\,s \Rightarrow s = -0.75\,m$

(d) $v^2 = u^2 + 2as \Rightarrow 0^2 = 2^2 + 2(-8)\,s \Rightarrow s = 0.25\,m$

Total distance $= 0.25 + 0.25 + 0.75 = 1.25\,m$

(e) Average velocity $= \dfrac{s}{t} = \dfrac{-0.75}{0.75}$

$= -1\,m/s = 1\,m/s$, West

(f) Average speed $= \dfrac{1.25}{0.75} = \dfrac{5}{3}\,m/s$

8. $u = 72\,km/h = 20\,m/s, v = 0, a = -2\,m/s^2$

(a) $v^2 = u^2 + 2as \Rightarrow 0^2 = 20^2 + 2(-2)\,s \Rightarrow s = 100\,m$

(b) $v = u + at \Rightarrow 0 = 20 + (-2)t \Rightarrow t = 10\,s$

(c) $s_{nth} = u + \dfrac{1}{2}a\,(2n - 1)$

$s_{1st} = 20 + \dfrac{1}{2}(-2)\,[2(1) - 1] = 19\,m$

$s_{3rd} = 20 + \dfrac{1}{2}(-2)\,[2(3) - 1] = 15\,m$

9. Let total time to be T

$$s = ut + \frac{1}{2}at^2 \Rightarrow s = 0 + \frac{1}{2} \times 8\left(\frac{T}{3}\right)^2 = \frac{4T^2}{9}$$

$$v = u + at = 0 + 8\left(\frac{T}{3}\right) = \frac{8T}{3}$$

Remaining distance $= 100 - \dfrac{4T^2}{9}$

$$s = ut + \frac{1}{2}at^2$$

$$100 - \frac{4T^2}{9} = \frac{8T}{3}\left(\frac{2T}{3}\right) \Rightarrow \frac{20T^2}{9} = 100$$

$\Rightarrow \quad T^2 = 45 = 3\sqrt{5}\,s$

10. Distance travelled in first 5 s $= ut + \dfrac{1}{2}at^2 = 0 + \dfrac{1}{2}(a)(5)^2 = \dfrac{25a}{2}$

Distance travelled in first 10 s $= 0 + \dfrac{1}{2}a(10)^2 = \dfrac{100a}{2}$

Distance travelled in first 15 s $= 0 + \dfrac{1}{2}a(15)^2 = \dfrac{225a}{2}$

$$s_1 = \frac{25a}{2}$$

$$s_2 = \frac{100a}{2} - \frac{25a}{2} = \frac{75a}{2} \Rightarrow s_3 = \frac{225a}{2} - \frac{100a}{2} = \frac{125a}{2}$$

$s_1 : s_2 : s_3 = 1 : 3 : 5$

11. $s_{nth} = u + \dfrac{1}{2}a(2n - 1) \Rightarrow 20 = u + \dfrac{1}{2}a(2 \times 7 - 1)$

$\Rightarrow \quad 2u + 13a = 40 \quad$ ...(i)

$$24 = u + \frac{1}{2}a(2 \times 9 - 1)$$

$\Rightarrow 2u + 17a = 48 \quad$ ...(ii)

Solving Eqs. (i) and (ii), we get

$u = 7\,m/s, a = 2\,m/s^2$

$$s_{15th} = 7 + \frac{1}{2} \times 2[2(15) - 1] = 36\,m$$

12. $v = u + at$

$\Rightarrow \quad 20 = u + a(10) \quad$ ...(i)

$s_{nth} = u + \dfrac{1}{2}a(2n - 1) \Rightarrow 10 = u + \dfrac{1}{2}a(19)$

$\Rightarrow 2u + 19a = 20 \quad$ ...(ii)

Solving Eqs. (i) and (ii), we get

$u = -180\,m/s$ and $a = 20\,m/s^2$

13. $u = 54\,km/h = 15\,m/s$

Distance travelled before brakes start acting

$= 15 \times 0.2 = 3\,m$

After brakes start acting,

$v^2 = u^2 + 2as \Rightarrow 0^2 = 15^2 + 2(-6)\,s \Rightarrow s = 18.75\,m$

Total distance $= 3 + 18.75 = 21.75\,m$

14.

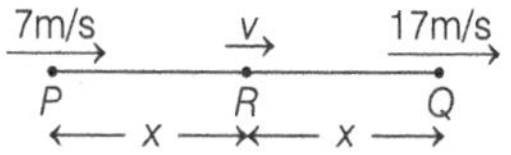

(a) $v^2 = u^2 + 2as \Rightarrow v^2 = 7^2 + 2ax \Rightarrow 2ax = v^2 - 49$ ...(i)

$v^2 = u^2 + 2as \Rightarrow 17^2 = v^2 + 2ax \Rightarrow 2ax = 289 - v^2$ ...(ii)

From Eqs. (i) and (ii), we get

$2v^2 = 49 + 289 \Rightarrow v^2 = 169 \Rightarrow v = 13\,m/s$

(b) $v_{avg} = \left(\dfrac{v + u}{2}\right) = \left(\dfrac{17 + 7}{2}\right) = 12\,m/s$

15. Distance travelled by bike in 10 s $= 20 \times 10 = 200\,m$

Lets say bike travels a further x distance before it is caught by police,

$x = 20t \quad$ ...(i)

and $200 + x = 25t \quad$ ...(ii)

Solving Eqs. (i) and (ii), we get

$t = 40\,s \Rightarrow x = 800\,m$

Distance from turning $= 200 + 800 = 1000\,m$

16. Lets say bus travel a distance x. In the same time boy will travel $(40 + x)$m.

Boy,

$s = ut + \dfrac{1}{2}at^2 \Rightarrow 40 + x = 9t \quad$ ...(i)

Bus,

$s = ut + \dfrac{1}{2}at^2 \Rightarrow x = \dfrac{1}{2}(1)t^2 \quad$ ...(ii)

Solving Eqs. (i) and (ii), we get

$t^2 - 18t + 80 = 0 \Rightarrow t = 8\,s$ and $t = 10\,s$

5.3 Motion Under Gravity

1. (a) $s = ut + \frac{1}{2}at^2 \Rightarrow 80 = 0 + \frac{1}{2}(10)t^2 \Rightarrow t = 4\text{ s}$

(b) $v^2 = u^2 + 2as \Rightarrow v^2 = 0^2 + 2(10)(80) \Rightarrow v = 40\text{ m/s}$

(c) $s = ut + \frac{1}{2}at^2 \Rightarrow 40 = 0 + \frac{1}{2}(10)t^2 \Rightarrow t = 2\sqrt{2}\text{ s}$

$v^2 = u^2 + 2as \Rightarrow v^2 = 0^2 + 2(10)(40) \Rightarrow v = 20\sqrt{2}\text{ m/s}$

(d) $v^2 = u^2 + 2as \Rightarrow v^2 = 0^2 + 2(10)(45) \Rightarrow v = 30\text{ m/s}$

(e) $s_4 = 80\text{ m} \Rightarrow s_2 = ut + \frac{1}{2}at^2 = \frac{1}{2}(10)(2) = 20\text{ m}$

Distance travelled in last 2 s $= s_4 - s_2 = 60\text{ m}$

2. (a) $s = ut + \frac{1}{2}at^2 \Rightarrow 160 = 20t + \frac{1}{2}(10)t^2 \Rightarrow t = 4\text{ s}$

(b) $v^2 = u^2 + 2as \Rightarrow v^2 = 20^2 + 2(10)(160) \Rightarrow v = 60\text{ m/s}$

(c) $s = ut + \frac{1}{2}at^2 \Rightarrow 60 = 20t + \frac{1}{2}(10)t^2 \Rightarrow t = 2\text{ s}$

(d) $v^2 = u^2 + 2as \Rightarrow 45^2 = 20^2 + 2(10)s \Rightarrow s = 81.25\text{ m}$

Height from ground $= 160 - 81.25 = 78.75\text{ m}$

(e) $s_{nth} = u + \frac{1}{2}a(2n - 1) = 20 + \frac{1}{2}(10)(2(4) - 1) = 55\text{ m}$

3. (a) $v^2 = u^2 + 2as \Rightarrow 0^2 = 50^2 + 2(-10)H_{max} \Rightarrow H_{max} = 125\text{ m}$

(b) $v = u + at \Rightarrow 0 = 50 + (-10)t \Rightarrow t = 5\text{ s}$

(c) $v^2 = u^2 + 2as \Rightarrow v^2 = 50^2 + 2(-10)\left(\frac{125}{2}\right)$

$v^2 = 3750 \Rightarrow v = \sqrt{3750}\text{ m/s or } 25\sqrt{2}\text{ m/s}$

(d)

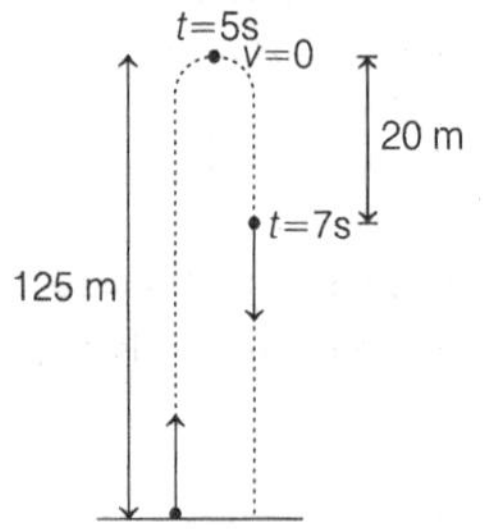

Average speed $= \frac{145}{7}\text{ m/s}$

Average velocity $= \frac{105}{7}\text{ m/s} = 15\text{ m/s}$

(e) $s = ut + \frac{1}{2}at^2$

$\Rightarrow \quad 105 = 50t + \frac{1}{2}(-10)t^2 \Rightarrow t = 3\text{ s and } 7\text{ s}$

4. (a) $v^2 = u^2 + 2as \Rightarrow 0^2 = 20^2 + 2(-10)(H)$

$H = 20\text{ m}$ from tower or 180 m from ground.

(b) $s = ut + \frac{1}{2}at^2 \Rightarrow -160 = 20T + \frac{1}{2}(-10)T^2$

$\Rightarrow \quad T = -4\text{ s and } T = 8\text{ s}$

(c) Average speed $= \frac{200}{8} = 25\text{ m/s}$

5. At $t = 8$ s

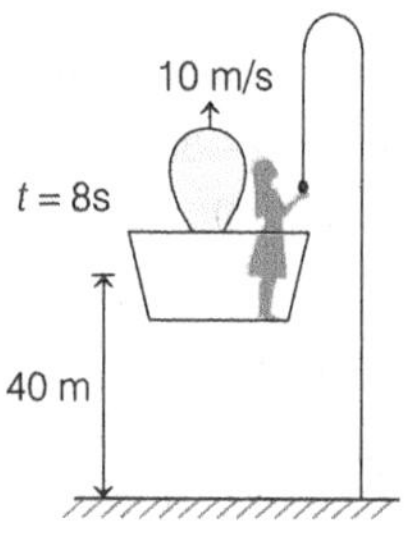

For balloon,

$v = u + at \Rightarrow v = 0 + 1.25 \times 8 \Rightarrow v = 10\text{ m/s}$

$s = ut + \frac{1}{2}at^2 \Rightarrow s = 0 + \frac{1}{2}(1.25)(8)^2 \Rightarrow s = 40\text{ m}$

(a) For stone,

$s = ut + \frac{1}{2}at^2 \Rightarrow -40 = 10T + \frac{1}{2}(-10)T^2 \Rightarrow T = 4\text{ s}$

(b) For balloon,

$s = ut + \frac{1}{2}at^2 \Rightarrow s = \frac{1}{2} \times 1.25 \times 12^2 = 90\text{ m}$

(c) Distance $= 40 + 2\left(\frac{u^2}{2g}\right) = 40 + 10 = 50\text{ m}$

6.
$$H = \frac{1}{2}gT^2 \quad \text{...(i)}$$
$$H - 5.8 = \frac{1}{2}g(T - 0.2)^2 \quad \text{...(ii)}$$

Solving Eqs. (i) and (ii), we get

$H = 45\text{ m}$

7. $s = ut + \frac{1}{2}at^2 \Rightarrow s = ut + \frac{1}{2}(20)(60)^2 = 36\text{ km}$

$v = u + at \Rightarrow v = 0 + 20(60) = 1200\text{ m/s}$

$v^2 = u^2 + 2as \Rightarrow 0^2 = (1200)^2 + 2(-10)H$

$H = 72\text{ km}$

(a) Maximum height reached $= 36 + 72 = 108\text{ km}$

(b) $v = u + at \Rightarrow 0 = 1200 + (-10)t \Rightarrow t = 120\text{ s}$

Total time $= 60 + 120 = 180\text{ s} = 3\text{ min}$

8. For free fall,

$v^2 = u^2 + 2as \Rightarrow v^2 = 0^2 + 2(10)(500) \Rightarrow v = 100\text{ m/s}$

$v = u + at \Rightarrow 100 = 0 + 10t \Rightarrow t = 10\text{ s}$

After parachute opens, $v^2 = u^2 + 2as$

$8^2 = 100^2 + 2(-2)s \Rightarrow s = 2484\text{ m}$

$v = u + at \Rightarrow 8 = 100 + (-2)t \Rightarrow t = 46\text{ s}$

(a) Total time $= 10 + 46 = 56\text{ s}$

(b) Height $= 500 + 2484 = 2984\text{ m}$

9. $s = ut + \frac{1}{2}at^2 \Rightarrow -H = ut_1 + \frac{1}{2}(-g)t_1^2$ ...(i)

$+H = ut_2 + \frac{1}{2}(+g)t_2^2$ ...(ii)

$$+H = \frac{1}{2} g t_3^2 \qquad \text{...(iii)}$$

Solving Eqs. (i), (ii) and (iii), we get

$$t_3^2 = t_1 t_2 \quad \Rightarrow \quad t_3 = \sqrt{t_1 t_2}$$

10. First stone,

$$h = \frac{1}{2} g T^2 \qquad \text{...(i)}$$

Second stone,

$$h - 20 = \frac{1}{2} g (T-1)^2 \qquad \text{...(ii)}$$

Solving Eqs. (i) and (ii), we get

$$h = 31.25\ \text{m}$$

11. First stone,

$$s = 0 + \frac{1}{2} g t^2 \qquad \text{...(i)}$$

Second stone,

$$s = 30(t-2) + \frac{1}{2} g (t-2)^2 \qquad \text{...(ii)}$$

Solving Eqs. (i) and (ii), we get

$$t = 4\ \text{s}$$

12. For first particle, $x = \frac{1}{2} g t^2$ ...(i)

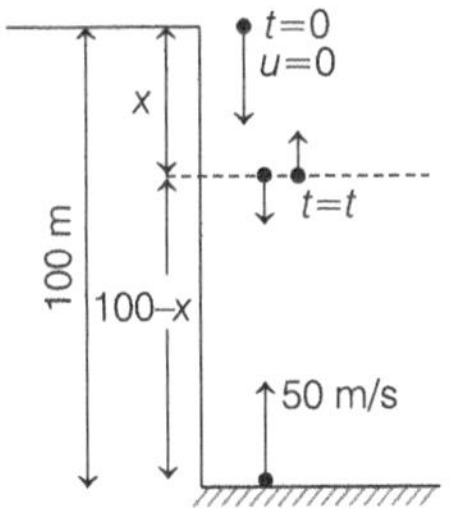

For second particle,

$$100 - x = 50t - \frac{1}{2} g t^2 \qquad \text{...(ii)}$$

Solving Eqs. (i) and (ii), we get

$$100 = 50t \Rightarrow t = 2\ \text{s} \Rightarrow x = 20\ \text{m}$$

13. Lift,

$$s = ut + \frac{1}{2} a t^2 \Rightarrow 200 = \frac{1}{2}(4) t^2 \Rightarrow t = 10\ \text{s}$$

Object,

At $t = 5$s,

$$v_{\text{lift}} = u + at = 0 + 4(5) = 20\ \text{m/s}$$

$$s_{\text{lift}} = 0 + \frac{1}{2}(4)(5)^2 = 50\ \text{m} \Rightarrow s = ut + \frac{1}{2} a t^2$$

$$150 = 20t + \frac{1}{2}(10) t^2 \Rightarrow t^2 + 4t - 30 = 0$$

$$t = \frac{-4 + \sqrt{16 + 120}}{2} \Rightarrow t = -2 + \sqrt{34}$$

Time taken by object to reach ground

$$= (-2 + \sqrt{34}) + 5 = (3 + \sqrt{34})\ \text{s}$$

Level 2

Single Choice Correct Questions

1. A body having zero velocity can have acceleration.

2. Time taken $= \frac{75}{15} = 5$ s

Displacement $= 25$ m

Average velocity $= \frac{25}{5} = 5$ m/s

3. Let distance between A and $B = d$

Total time taken $= \frac{d}{20} + \frac{d}{30}$

$$\text{Average speed} = \frac{2d}{\frac{d}{20} + \frac{d}{30}} = 24\ \text{km/h}$$

4. Total time $= \frac{s/3}{v} + \frac{s/3}{2v} + \frac{s/3}{3v}$

$$\text{Average speed} = \frac{s}{\frac{s/3}{v} + \frac{s/3}{2v} + \frac{s/3}{3v}} = \frac{18v}{11}$$

5. Let the total distance to be $3d$

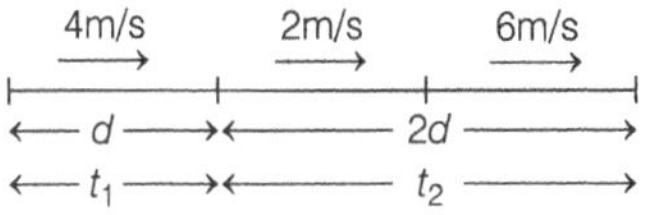

$$t_1 = \frac{d}{4}$$

$$2d = 2\left(\frac{t_2}{2}\right) + 6\left(\frac{t_2}{2}\right)$$

$$\Rightarrow \quad t_2 = \frac{d}{2}$$

$$\text{Average velocity} = \frac{3d}{t_1 + t_2} = \frac{3d}{\frac{d}{4} + \frac{d}{2}} = 4\ \text{m/s}$$

6.

$$v^2 = u^2 + 2as$$

$$\Rightarrow \quad (2u)^2 = u^2 + 2a(10) \qquad \text{...(i)}$$

$$v^2 = (2u)^2 + 2a(10) \qquad \text{...(ii)}$$

Solving Eqs. (i) and (ii), we get $v = \sqrt{7}\, u$

7.

$$v^2 = u^2 + 2as$$

$$0^2 = v^2 + 2as \qquad \text{...(i)}$$

$$0^2 = (nv)^2 + 2as' \qquad \text{...(ii)}$$

Solving Eqs. (i) and (ii), we get

$$s' = n^2 s$$

8.

$$v^2 = u^2 + 2as$$

$$0^2 = (200)^2 + 2a(4) \qquad \text{...(i)}$$

$$0^2 = u^2 + 2a(9) \qquad \text{...(ii)}$$

Solving Eqs. (i) and (ii), we get

$$u = 300\ \text{cm/s}$$

9.

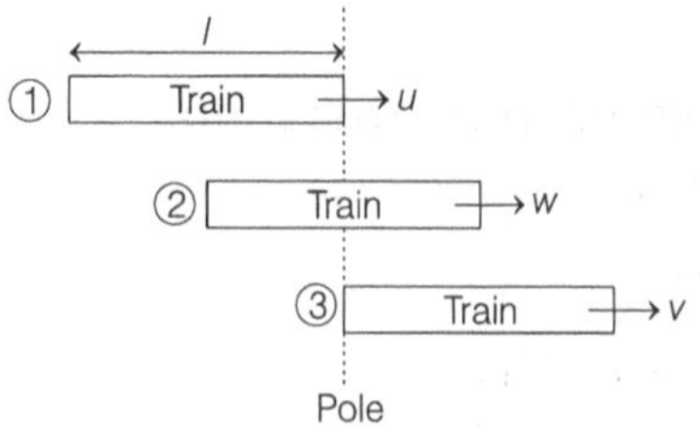

Between (1) and (2),

$$v^2 = u^2 + 2as \Rightarrow w^2 = u^2 + \frac{2al}{2} \quad \text{...(i)}$$

Between (2) and (3),

$$v^2 = u^2 + 2as \Rightarrow u^2 = w^2 + 2a\left(\frac{l}{2}\right) \quad \text{...(ii)}$$

Solving Eqs. (i) and (ii), we get

$$w = \sqrt{\frac{u^2 + v^2}{2}}$$

10.
$$15 = u(3) + \frac{1}{2}a(3)^2 \quad \text{...(i)}$$
$$0 = 4(4) + \frac{1}{2}a(4)^2 \quad \text{...(ii)}$$

Solving Eqs. (i) and (ii), we get

$$u = 20 \text{ m/s}$$

11. In first 5 s, distance travelled is 40 m,

$$s = ut + \frac{1}{2}at^2 \Rightarrow 40 = u(5) + \frac{1}{2}a(5)^2 \quad \text{...(i)}$$

In first 10 s, distance travelled is $(40 + 65 = 105 \text{ m})$.

$$105 = u(10) + \frac{1}{2}a(10)^2 \quad \text{...(ii)}$$

Solving Eqs. (i) and (ii), we get

$$u = 5.5 \text{ m/s and } a = 1 \text{ m/s}^2$$

12.
$$s_2 = u(2) + \frac{1}{2}a(2)^2 = 200 \text{ cm} \quad \text{...(i)}$$
$$s_6 = u(6) + \frac{1}{2}a(6)^2 = 420 \text{ cm} \quad \text{...(ii)}$$

Solving Eqs. (i) and (ii), we get

$$u = 115 \text{ cm/s and } a = -15 \text{ cm/s}^2$$
$$v = u + at \Rightarrow v = 115 + (-15)(7) \Rightarrow v = 10 \text{ cm/s}$$

13. $s_{nth} = 0 + \frac{1}{2}a(2n-1)$ and $s_n = 0 + \frac{1}{2}an^2$

$$\therefore \quad \frac{s_{nth}}{s_n} = \frac{2n-1}{n^2}$$

14. $s_1 = 0 + \frac{1}{2}a(p-1)^2$ and $s_2 = 0 + \frac{1}{2}ap^2$

$$s_{(p^2-p+1)th} = 0 + \frac{1}{2}a[2(p^2 - p + 1) - 1]$$
$$= \frac{1}{2}a(2p^2 - 2p + 1)$$
$$= s_1 + s_2$$

15.
$$v = u + at$$
$$v = 0 + an \quad \text{...(i)}$$
$$s_n = un + \frac{1}{2}a(n)^2 \Rightarrow s_{(n-2)} = u(n-2) + \frac{1}{2}a(n-2)^2$$

Displacement in last 2 s

$$= s_n - s_{(n-2)} = \frac{1}{2}a[n^2 - (n-2)^2]$$
$$= \frac{1}{2}\frac{v}{n}(2n-2)(2) = \frac{2v(n-1)}{n}$$

16.
$$s_{nth} = u + \frac{1}{2}a(2n-1)$$
$$12 = u + \frac{1}{2}a[2(2) - 1] \quad \text{...(i)}$$
$$20 = u + \frac{1}{2}a(2(4) - 1) \quad \text{...(ii)}$$

Solving Eqs. (i) and (ii), we get

$$u = 6 \text{ m/s and } a = 4 \text{ m/s}^2$$
$$s_4 = ut + \frac{1}{2}at^2 = 6(4) + \frac{1}{2}(4)(4)^2 = 56 \text{ m}$$
$$s_9 = 6(9) + \frac{1}{2} \times 4 \times 9^2 = 216 \text{ m}$$
$$s_9 - s_4 = 216 - 56 = 160 \text{ m}$$

17. $v = u + at \Rightarrow 0 = 48 + (-10)t \Rightarrow t = 4.8$ s

$t = 4$ s to $t = 4.8$ s, $v^2 = u^2 + 2as$

$$\Rightarrow \quad 0 = 8^2 + 2(-10)s_1 \Rightarrow s_1 = \frac{16}{5} \text{ m}$$

$$t = 4.8 \text{ s to } t = 5 \text{ s}, \; s_2 = 0 + \frac{1}{2}(-10)(0.2)^2$$

$$\Rightarrow \quad s_2 = -\frac{1}{5} \text{ m}$$

$$\text{Total distance in the 5th second} = \frac{16}{5} + \frac{1}{5} = \frac{17}{5} \text{ m}$$

18.

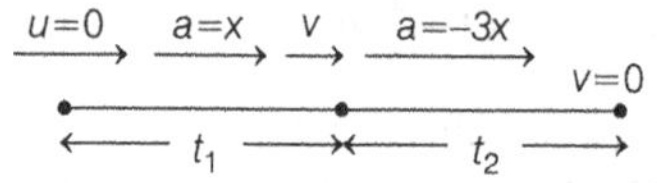

$$v = u + at \Rightarrow v = 0 + xt_1 \quad \text{...(i)}$$
$$v = u + at \Rightarrow 0 = v - 3xt_2 \quad \text{...(ii)}$$

Solving Eqs. (i) and (ii), we get

$$t_1 = 3t_2 \text{ and } t_1 + t_2 = 8 \Rightarrow t_1 = 2 \text{ s and } t_2 = 6 \text{ s}$$

19.

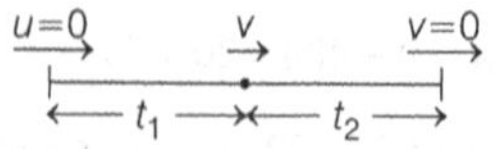

$$v = 0 + 2t_1 \quad \text{...(i)}$$
$$0 = v - 4t_2 \quad \text{...(ii)}$$

Solving Eqs. (i) and (ii), we get

$$t_1 = 2t_2 \quad \text{and} \quad t_1 + t_2 = 3$$
$$\Rightarrow \quad t_1 = 2\text{s} \quad \text{and} \quad t_2 = 1\text{s}$$
$$\Rightarrow \quad v = 4 \text{ m/s}$$

20. At $t = t_0$; $v = u + at \Rightarrow v = 0 + a_0 t_0$

At $t = 2t_0$, $v = u + at \Rightarrow v = a_0 t_0 - a_0 t_0 = 0$

At $t = 3t_0$, $v = u + at \Rightarrow v = 0 + a_0 t_0$

$\vdots$

At $t = 9t_0$, $v = a_0 t_0$

21. Lets take time are $t, 8t$ and t.

$$\text{Total distance} = \frac{1}{2}at^2 + 60(8t) + \left(60t - \frac{1}{2}at^2\right)$$

$$\text{Average speed} = \frac{540t}{10t} = 54 \text{ km/h}$$

22.
$$s = \frac{1}{2}ft^2 \Rightarrow t = \sqrt{\frac{2s}{f}}$$

$$v^2 = u^2 + 2as \Rightarrow v = \sqrt{2fs}$$

$$s_2 = (\sqrt{2fs})t$$

$$v^2 = u^2 + 2as \Rightarrow 0^2 = (\sqrt{2fs})^2 - 2\left(\frac{f}{2}\right)s_3$$

$$\Rightarrow s_3 = 2s$$

$$s_2 = 15s - s - 2s = 12s = \sqrt{2fs}\,t$$

$$\Rightarrow s = \frac{1}{72}ft^2$$

23. $s = ut + \frac{1}{2}at^2 = 0 + \frac{1}{2}at^2$

$$v = u + at = at$$

$$s = ut + \frac{1}{2}at^2$$

$$\Rightarrow -\frac{1}{2}at^2 = (at)t_1 + \frac{1}{2}(-a)t_1^2$$

$$\Rightarrow t_1^2 - 2tt_1 - t^2 = 0$$

$$\Rightarrow t_1 = \frac{2t + \sqrt{4t^2 + 4t^2}}{2} = t + \sqrt{2}t$$

Total time $= t + (t + \sqrt{2}t) = (2 + \sqrt{2})t$

24. $s = ut + \frac{1}{2}at^2$

first car, $s = 4t + \frac{1}{2}(1)t^2$ ...(1)

second car, $s = 2t + \frac{1}{2}(2)t^2$ ...(2)

From Eqs. (i) and (ii), we get

$$4t + \frac{t^2}{2} = 2t + t^2 \Rightarrow t = 4\text{ s} \Rightarrow s = 4(4) + \frac{1}{2}(1)(4)^2 = 24 \text{ m}$$

25. $u_{\text{thief}} = 126 \text{ km/h} = 35 \text{ m/s}$

$x = 35t$ ...(i)

$65 + x = 100t$ ...(ii)

Solving Eqs. (i) and (ii), we get

$$t = 1\text{ s} \Rightarrow 65 + x = 100 \text{ m}$$

26. $x = 9t$ ...(i)

$100 + x = 10t$ ...(ii)

Solving Eqs. (i) and (ii), we get

$$t = 100 \text{ s}$$

27. $x = \frac{1}{2}(1.5)t^2$ ...(i)

$100 + x = \frac{1}{2}(2)t^2$ ...(ii)

Solving Eqs. (i) and (ii), we get

$$t = 20 \text{ s}$$

28. Let bus travels a distance x.

In the same time, cyclist will travel $(96 + x)$.

Cyclist,

$s = ut + \frac{1}{2}at^2 \Rightarrow 96 + x = 20t$ ...(i)

Bus,

$s = ut + \frac{1}{2}at^2 \Rightarrow x = \frac{1}{2}(2)t^2$ ...(ii)

Solving Eqs. (i) and (ii), we get

$$t = 8 \text{ s and } t = 12 \text{ s}$$

29. Let bus travels a distance y and in the same time passenger travels $y + x$

$$y = \frac{1}{2}at^2 \text{ and } x + y = ut$$

$$x + \frac{1}{2}at^2 = ut \Rightarrow t^2 - \frac{2u}{a}t + \frac{2x}{a} = 0$$

For real roots $D > 0$

$$\left(\frac{2y}{a}\right)^2 - 4\left(\frac{2x}{a}\right) > 0 \Rightarrow u^2 > 2ax \Rightarrow u > \sqrt{2ax}$$

30.
$$v^2 = u^2 + 2as$$

$0^2 = \left(70 \times \frac{5}{18}\right)^2 + 2(-5)s_1$ ...(i)

$0^2 = \left(60 \times \frac{5}{18}\right)^2 + 2(-5)s_2$ ...(ii)

Since, $s_1 + s_2 < 80$ m

Collision will be averted.

31. Time taken by stone to hit water $= \sqrt{\frac{2h}{g}} = 2$ s

$$\text{Velocity of sound} = \frac{\text{Distance}}{\text{Time}} = \frac{19.6}{2.05 - 2} = 392 \text{ m/s}$$

32.
$$v^2 = u^2 + 2as \Rightarrow v^2 = 0^2 + 2 \times 10 \times 100$$

$$\Rightarrow v = \sqrt{2000} \text{ m/s}$$

$$v^2 = u^2 + 2as$$

$$\Rightarrow \left(\frac{\sqrt{2000}}{2}\right)^2 = 0^2 + 2 \times 10 \times h$$

$$\Rightarrow h = 25 \text{ m from tower} = 75 \text{ m from ground}$$

33. $v^2 = u^2 + 2as$

$$\Rightarrow v^2 = 0^2 + 2(9.8)\left(\frac{39.2}{2}\right) \Rightarrow v = 19.6 \text{ m/s}$$

34. $s = ut + \frac{1}{2}at^2 \Rightarrow H = 0 + \frac{1}{2} \times 10 \times 5^2 = 125\,\text{m}$

Distance travelled in first 3 s $= 0 + \frac{1}{2}(10)(3)^2 = 45\,\text{m}$

Remaining distance $= 125 - 45 = 80\,\text{m}$

$$s = ut + \frac{1}{2}at^2 \Rightarrow 80 = 0 + \frac{1}{2}(10)t^2 \Rightarrow t = 4\,\text{s}$$

Total time $= 3 + 4 = 7\,\text{s}$

35. $s_{Ist} = 0 + \frac{1}{2}(10)(1)^2 = 5\,\text{m}$

$s_{2nd} = 0 + \frac{1}{2} \times 10\,(2(2) - 1) = 15\,\text{m}$

$s_{3rd} = 0 + \frac{1}{2} \times 10(2(3) - 1) = 25\,\text{m}$

$s_{Ist} : s_{2nd} : s_{3rd} :: 1:3:5$

36. $1 = 0 + \frac{1}{2}gt_1^2 \Rightarrow t_1 = \sqrt{\frac{2}{g}}$

$$2 = 0 + \frac{1}{2}gt_2^2 \Rightarrow t_2 = \sqrt{\frac{4}{g}}$$

$$3 = 0 + \frac{1}{2}gt_3^2 \Rightarrow t_3 = \sqrt{\frac{6}{g}}$$

Time taken for successive 1m distance

$$= t_1 : (t_2 - t_1) : (t_3 - t_2)$$

37. $s_{tth} = 0 + \frac{1}{2} \times 10(2t - 1) = 5(2t - 1)$

$$s_{(t+1)th} = 0 + \frac{1}{2} \times 10[2(t + 1) - 1] = 5(2t + 1)$$

$$100 = 5(2t - 1) + 5(2t + 1)$$

$\Rightarrow$ $t = 5\,\text{s}$

$$v = u + at \Rightarrow v = 0 + 10(5) = 50\,\text{m/s}$$

38. $H = \frac{1}{2}gT^2$ ...(i)

$H - 40 = \frac{1}{2}g\,(T - 2)^2$ ...(ii)

Solving Eqs. (i) and (ii), we get

$H = 45\,\text{m}$

39. Distance covered in first 3 s $= 0 + \frac{1}{2}(10)(3)^2 = 45\,\text{m}$

$H = \frac{1}{2}gT^2$ ...(i)

$H - 45 = \frac{1}{2}g(T - 1)^2$ ...(ii)

Solving Eqs. (i) and (ii), we get

$H = 125\,\text{m}$

40. $0.4 = 0 + \frac{1}{2} \times 9.8\,t_1^2 \Rightarrow t_1 = \sqrt{\frac{0.8}{9.8}}$

$$0.9 = 0 + \frac{1}{2} \times 9.8\,t_2^2 \Rightarrow t_2 = \sqrt{\frac{1.8}{9.8}}$$

$$t_2 - t_1 = \sqrt{\frac{1.8}{9.8}} - \sqrt{\frac{0.8}{9.8}} = \sqrt{\frac{9}{49}} - \sqrt{\frac{4}{49}} = \frac{3}{7} - \frac{2}{7} = \frac{1}{7}\,\text{s}$$

41. Time taken by a drop to reach ground $= \sqrt{\frac{2h}{g}} = \sqrt{\frac{2(9)}{10}}$

Time interval between successive dropping $= \frac{1}{3}\sqrt{\frac{2h}{g}}$

Distance of 2nd drop $= 0 + \frac{1}{2}g\left(\frac{1}{3}\sqrt{\frac{2h}{g}}\right)^2 = 1\,\text{m}$

Distance of 3rd drop $= 0 + \frac{1}{2}g\left(\frac{2}{3}\sqrt{\frac{2h}{g}}\right)^2 = 4\,\text{m}$

42. $H = 0 + \frac{1}{2}gT^2$ ...(i)

$H - 25 = 0 + \frac{1}{2}g(T - 1)^2$ ...(ii)

Solving Eqs. (i) and (ii), we get

$H = 45\,\text{m}$

43. $v^2 = u^2 + 2as \Rightarrow (3v)^2 = v^2 + 2gh \Rightarrow h = \frac{4v^2}{g}$

44. $3^2 = 0^2 + 2gh$ ...(i)

$v^2 = 4^2 + 2gh$ ...(ii)

Solving Eqs. (i) and (ii), we get

$v = 5\,\text{km/h}$

45. For first 10 s,

$$v = u + at \Rightarrow v = 0 + 10(10) = 100\,\text{m/s}$$

$$s = ut + \frac{1}{2}at^2 \Rightarrow s = 0 + \frac{1}{2}(10)(10)^2 = 500\,\text{m}$$

After parachute opens,

$$v^2 = u^2 + 2as \Rightarrow v^2 = 100^2 + 2(-2.5)(2495 - 500)$$

$$v^2 = 100^2 - 9975 = 25 \Rightarrow v = 5\,\text{m/s}$$

46. $\frac{u^2}{2g} = 20 \Rightarrow u = 20\,\text{m/s} \Rightarrow T = \frac{2u}{g} = 4\,\text{s}$

47. $g_A = 9g_B \Rightarrow H = \frac{u^2}{2g} \Rightarrow 2 = \frac{u^2}{2g_A}$ ...(i)

$h = \frac{u^2}{2g_B}$ ...(ii)

Solving Eqs. (i) and (ii), we get

$h = 18\,\text{m}$

48. $v^2 = u^2 + 2as \Rightarrow (9.8)^2 = u^2 - 2(9.8)\left(\frac{H}{2}\right)$ ...(i)

$0^2 = u^2 - 2(9.8)(H)$ ...(ii)

Solving Eqs. (i) and (ii), we get

$H = 9.8\,\text{m}$

49. Since he is throwing two balls every second, time interval between two throwings $= \frac{1}{2}\,\text{s} = 0.5\,\text{s}$

$$v = u + at \Rightarrow 0 = u + (-10)(0.5)$$

$$u = 5\,\text{m/s} \Rightarrow H_{max} = \frac{u^2}{2g} = \frac{5^2}{20} = 1.25\,\text{m}$$

50. $v = u + at \Rightarrow v = 0 + 10(30) = 300$ m/s

$v = u + at \Rightarrow 0 = 300 + (-10)t \Rightarrow t = 30$ s

Total time = 30 + 30 = 60 s

51. $\frac{u}{g} = 6 \Rightarrow u = 60$ m/s

$$s_{1st} = 60 + \frac{1}{2}(-10)[2(1) - 1] = 55 \text{ m}$$

$$s_{7th} = 60 + \frac{1}{2}(-10)[2(7) - 1] = -5 \text{ m}$$

Ratio = 11 : 1

52. $s = ut + \frac{1}{2}at^2 \Rightarrow h = ut - \frac{1}{2}gt^2 \Rightarrow t^2 - \frac{2u}{g}t + \frac{2h}{g} = 0$

Lets take roots of the quadratic equation to be t_1 and t_2.

$t_1 + t_2 = \frac{2u}{g} = 12 \Rightarrow u = 60$ m/s

At $t = 2$ s,

$$s = ut + \frac{1}{2}at^2 \Rightarrow h' = 60(2) + \frac{1}{2}(-10)(2)^2 = 100 \text{ m}$$

53. $$v^2 = u^2 + 2as$$

$$\Rightarrow 30^2 = u^2 + 2(-10)(80) \Rightarrow u = 50 \text{ m/s}$$

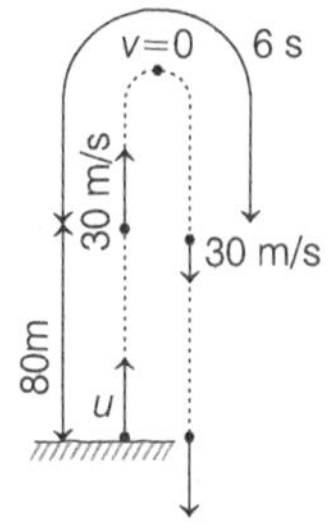

54. At $t = 5$s, it will be at its highest point

$$\frac{u}{g} = 5$$

$$u = 49 \text{ m/s}$$

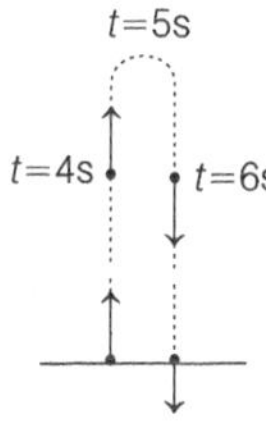

55. $$\frac{2u}{g} = 12$$

$$u = 60 \text{ m/s}$$

$$s = ut + \frac{1}{2}at^2$$

$$\Rightarrow H = 60(3) + \frac{1}{2}(-10)(3)^2$$

$$\Rightarrow H = 135 \text{ m}$$

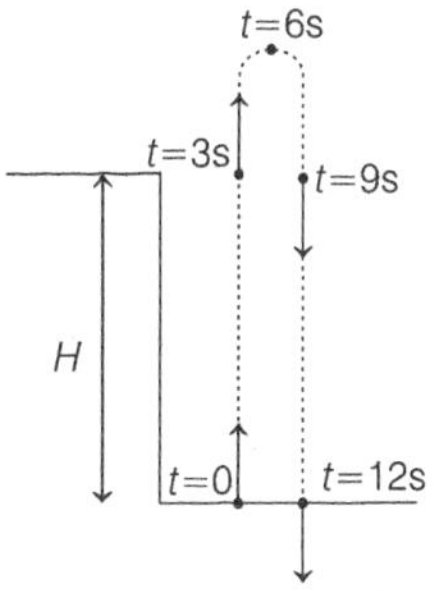

56. Total time of flight $= t_1 + t_2$

$$\frac{2u}{g} = t_1 + t_2 \Rightarrow u = \frac{g(t_1 + t_2)}{2}$$

$$s = ut + \frac{1}{2}at^2$$

$$\Rightarrow h = \left(\frac{g(t_1 + t_2)}{2}\right)t_1 - \frac{1}{2}gt_1^2 \Rightarrow h = \frac{1}{2}gt_1t_2$$

57. $$s = ut + \frac{1}{2}at^2 \Rightarrow 14 = u(0.8) + \frac{1}{2}(-10)(0.8)^2$$

$$\Rightarrow u = \frac{17.2}{0.8} = \frac{43}{2}$$

$$T = \frac{2u}{g} = \frac{2}{10}\left(\frac{43}{2}\right) = \frac{43}{10} \text{s}$$

$$t_1 + t_2 = T \Rightarrow 0.8 + t_2 = \frac{43}{10}$$

$$\Rightarrow t_2 = \frac{43}{10} - \frac{4}{5} = \frac{35}{10} = \frac{7}{2} \text{ s}$$

58. $$x = 20t + \frac{1}{2} \times 10 \times t^2$$

$$40 - x = 20t - \frac{1}{2} \times 10t^2$$

Solving equations, we get

$$t = 1 \text{ s} \quad \text{and} \quad x = 25 \text{ m}$$

∴ Height from ground = 15 m

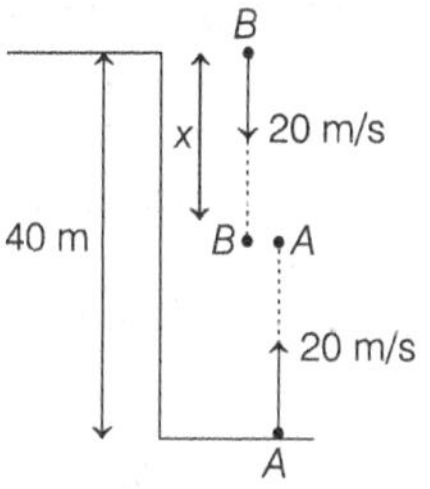

59. $v^2 = u^2 + 2as \Rightarrow (2v)^2 = 0^2 + 2gx$ ...(i)

$v^2 = u^2 - 2g(H - x)$ ...(ii)

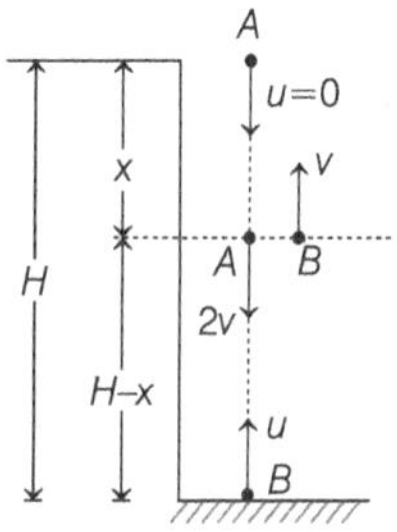

$$s = ut + \frac{1}{2}at^2 \Rightarrow x = 0 + \frac{1}{2}gt^2 \quad \text{...(iii)}$$

$$H - x = ut - \frac{1}{2}gt^2 \quad \text{...(iv)}$$

Solving Eqs. (i), (ii), (iii) and (iv), we get

$$\frac{H - x}{H} = \frac{2}{3}$$

60. $s = ut + \frac{1}{2}at^2 \Rightarrow -h = 4.9(3) + \frac{1}{2}(-9.8)(3)^2$

$$\Rightarrow h = 29.4 \text{ m}$$

61. $s = ut + \frac{1}{2}at^2 - h = 4(4) + \frac{1}{2}(-9.8)(4)^2 \Rightarrow h = 62.4$ m

62. For stone,

$$s = ut + \frac{1}{2}at^2 \Rightarrow -76 = u(6) + \frac{1}{2}(-10)6^2$$

$$\Rightarrow u = \frac{52}{3} \text{ m/s upwards}$$

So, initial velocity of balloon $= \frac{52}{3}$ m/s upwards

63. $$s = ut + \frac{1}{2}at^2$$

$$\Rightarrow \quad -H = u(9) + \frac{1}{2}(-10)(9)^2 \quad \text{...(i)}$$

$$+H = u(4) + \frac{1}{2}(+10)(4)^2 \quad \text{...(ii)}$$

$$+H = \frac{1}{2}(+10)t^2 \quad \text{...(iii)}$$

Solving Eqs. (i), (ii) and (iii), we get

$$t = 6\text{ s}$$

Numerical Value Questions

1. $u = 36\text{ km/h} = 10\text{ m/s}$

   Before brakes, $s = 10 \times 0.6 = 6\text{ m}$

   After brakes, $v^2 = u^2 + 2as \Rightarrow 0^2 = 10^2 + 12(-4)s$

   $\Rightarrow \quad s = 12.5\text{ s}$

   Total distance $= 6 + 12.5 = 18.5\text{ m}$

2. $$v^2 = u^2 + 2as$$

   $$\left(\frac{3u}{4}\right)^2 = u^2 + 2a(14) \quad \text{...(i)}$$

   $$0^2 = \left(\frac{3u}{4}\right)^2 + 2ax \quad \text{...(ii)}$$

   Solving Eqs. (i) and (ii), we get

   $$x = 18\text{ cm}$$

3. $$s = \left(\frac{v+u}{2}\right)t \Rightarrow s_A = \left(\frac{25+10}{2}\right)t$$

   $$s_B = \left(\frac{v+15}{2}\right)t$$

   $$s_A = s_B \Rightarrow v = 20\text{ m/s}$$

4. 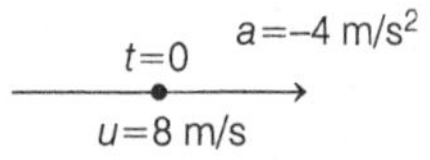

   When particle comes to rest momentarily

   $$v = u + at \Rightarrow 0 = 8 - 4t \Rightarrow t = 2\text{ s}$$

   $$v^2 = u^2 + 2as \Rightarrow 0^2 = 8^2 + 2(-4)s \Rightarrow s = 8\text{m}$$

   Now, from $t = 2$ to $t = 5$,

   $$s = ut + \frac{1}{2}at^2 \Rightarrow s = 0 + \frac{1}{2}(-4)(3)^2 = -18\text{ m}$$

   Total distance $= 8 + 18 = 26\text{ m}$

5. Time taken to reach max. height $= \frac{4}{g} = 4.5\text{ s}$

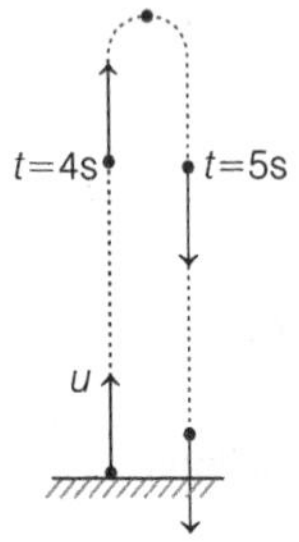

From $t = 4.5\text{s}$ to $t = 5\text{s}$,

$$s = ut + \frac{1}{2}at^2 = \frac{1}{2}(10)(0.5)^2 = 1.25\text{ m}$$

Distance travelled in the 5th second $= 2 \times 1.25 = 2.5\text{ m}$

6. 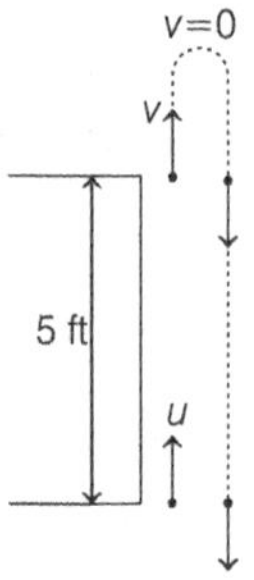

   $$s = ut + \frac{1}{2}at^2 \Rightarrow 5 = u(0.5) + \frac{1}{2}(-32)(0.5)^2$$

   $$\Rightarrow \quad u = 18\text{ ft/s}$$

   $$v^2 = u^2 + 2as$$

   $$\Rightarrow \quad v^2 = 18^2 + 2(-32)(5)$$

   $$\Rightarrow \quad v^2 = 324 - 320 \Rightarrow v = 2\text{ ft/s}$$

   Height above the window $= \frac{v^2}{2g} = \frac{2^2}{2 \times 32} = \frac{1}{16}$ ft

7. 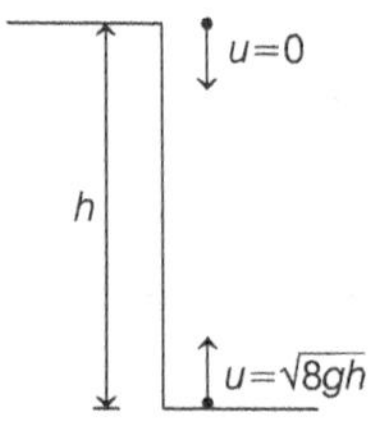

   $$\frac{u^2}{2g} = 4h \Rightarrow u = \sqrt{8gh}$$

   $$s = ut + \frac{1}{2}at^2$$

   $$x = \frac{1}{2}gt^2 \quad \text{...(i)}$$

   $$h - x = (\sqrt{8gh})t - \frac{1}{2}gt^2 \quad \text{...(ii)}$$

   Solving Eqs. (i) and (ii), we get

   $$t = \frac{h}{\sqrt{8gh}} = \sqrt{\frac{h}{8g}}$$

8. $$t = \sqrt{\frac{2h}{g}} = \sqrt{\frac{2(11.5-1.5)}{10}} = \sqrt{2}\text{ s}$$

   $$s = ut + \frac{1}{2}at^2$$

   $$\Rightarrow \quad 6 = 0 + \frac{1}{2}a(\sqrt{2})^2 \Rightarrow a = 6\text{ m/s}^2$$

9. $4.25 = \sqrt{\frac{2h}{g} + \frac{h}{320}} \Rightarrow h = 80\,\text{m}$

10. Between A and B,

$$v^2 = u^2 + 2as$$

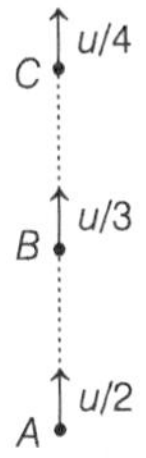

$$\left(\frac{u}{3}\right)^2 = \left(\frac{u}{2}\right)^2 + 2a\,(AB) \quad \text{...(i)}$$

Between B and C,

$$\left(\frac{u}{4}\right)^2 = \left(\frac{u}{3}\right)^2 + 2a(BC) \quad \text{...(ii)}$$

Solving Eqs. (i) and (ii), we get

$$\frac{AB}{BC} = \frac{20}{7}$$

11. $AB = \frac{1}{2}gt^2,\ AC = \frac{1}{2}g(t+2)^2,\ AD = \frac{1}{2}g(t+3)^2$

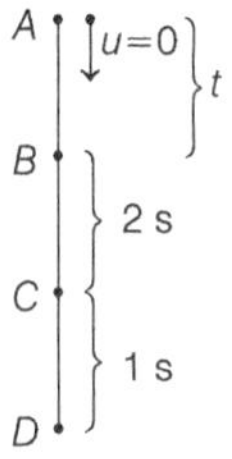

$$BC = CD \Rightarrow AC - AB = AD - AC$$

$$\Rightarrow \quad 2AC = AB + AD$$

$$\Rightarrow \quad 2\left(\frac{1}{2}g(t+2)^2\right) = \frac{1}{2}gt^2 + \frac{1}{2}g(t+3)^2$$

$$\Rightarrow \quad 2t^2 + 8t + 8 = t^2 + t^2 + 9 + 6t$$

$$\Rightarrow \quad 2t = 1 \Rightarrow t = \frac{1}{2}$$

12.

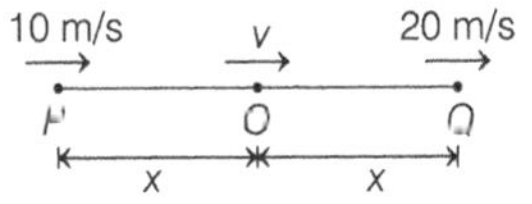

Between P and O,

$$v^2 = u^2 + 2as \Rightarrow v^2 = 10^2 + 2(a)(x) \quad \text{...(i)}$$

Between O and Q,

$$v^2 = u^2 + 2as \Rightarrow 20^2 = v^2 + 2ax \quad \text{...(ii)}$$

Solving Eqs. (i) and (ii), we get

$$v = \sqrt{250} = 15.8\,\text{m/s}$$

13. $\frac{u^2}{2g} = 10 \Rightarrow u^2 = 196 \Rightarrow u = 14\,\text{m/s}$

14.

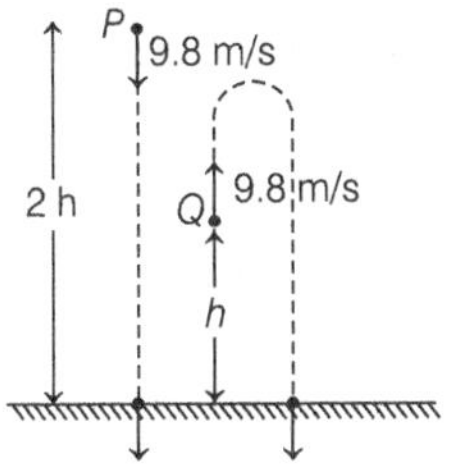

For P, $s = ut + \frac{1}{2}at^2$

$$\Rightarrow \quad 2h = (9.8)T + \frac{1}{2}(+9.8)T^2 \quad \text{...(i)}$$

For Q, $s = ut + \frac{1}{2}at^2$

$$\Rightarrow \quad -h = 9.8T + \frac{1}{2}(-9.8)T^2 \quad \text{...(ii)}$$

Solving Eqs. (i) and (ii), we get

$$T = 6\,\text{s}$$

15. For balloon, $u = 0$, $a = 4.9\,\text{m/s}^2$

$$v = u + at$$

At $t = 2$, $v = 0 + (4.9)2 = 9.8\,\text{m/s}$

$$s = ut + \frac{1}{2}at^2$$

At $t = 2$; $s = 0 + \frac{1}{2}(4.9)(2)^2 = 9.8\,\text{m}$

Initial velocity of ball will be same as that of the balloon.

For ball, $v^2 = u^2 + 2as$

$$\Rightarrow \quad 0^2 = (9.8)^2 + 2(-9.8)(+h) \Rightarrow h = 4.9\,\text{m}$$

Maximum height of ball from ground $= 9.8 + 4.9 = 14.70\,\text{m}$

Level 3

Single Choice Correct Questions

1.

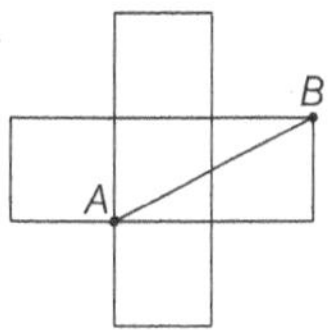

We can open the cube as shown in figure.

Shortest path length $= \sqrt{(2a)^2 + a^2} = \sqrt{5}a$

Time taken by ant $= \frac{\sqrt{5}a}{u}$

2. Let s be distance covered by each car. Let times taken by the 2 cars to complete journey be t_1 and t_2 and velocities at finishing point be v_1 and v_2.

$$v_1 - v_2 = v_0,\ t_2 - t_1 = t_0$$

$$\frac{v_0}{t_0} = \frac{v_1 - v_2}{t_2 - t_1} = \frac{\sqrt{2a_1 s} - \sqrt{2a_2 s}}{\sqrt{\frac{2s}{a_2}} - \sqrt{\frac{2s}{a_1}}} = \sqrt{a_1 a_2}$$

3. $v^2 = u^2 + 2as \Rightarrow 50^2 = 10^2 + 2as$ ...(i)

$v^2 = 50^2 + 2(-a)(-s)$ ...(ii)

Solving Eqs. (i) and (ii), we get

$v = \sqrt{4900} = 70\,\text{m/s}$

4. Lets t be time when engine is switched off.

$$s = ut + \frac{1}{2}at^2$$

Height of helicopter $= s = 0 + \frac{1}{2}(4)t^2$

Time taken by sound $= \dfrac{\frac{1}{2}(4)t^2}{320} = 50 - t$

$\Rightarrow \quad t^2 + 160t - 8000 = 0 \quad \Rightarrow \quad t = 40\text{ s}$

For helicopter, $v = u + at$

$\Rightarrow \qquad v = 0 + 4(40) = 160\text{ m/s}$

5. Distance travelled by policeman in 12 s

$$= \left(\frac{v+u}{2}\right)t = \left(\frac{150 \times \frac{5}{18} + 0}{2}\right)12 = 250\text{ m}$$

Thereafter, policeman travel with constant speed.

$$1500 = 250 + \left(150 \times \frac{5}{18}\right)(T - 12 - 2) \Rightarrow T = 44\text{ s}$$

Speed of speeder $= \dfrac{1500}{44}\text{ m/s} = \dfrac{1500}{44} \times \dfrac{18}{5}\text{ km/h}$

$= 122.7\text{ km/h}$

6. At $t = 5$ s, balloon will be at a height of $25 \times 5 = 125$ m

Lets say bullet hits balloon in further time t and balloon travels 'x' distance further.

For bullet,

$$s = ut + \frac{1}{2}at^2 \quad \Rightarrow 125 + x = ut - 5t^2$$

For balloon,

$$s = ut + \frac{1}{2}at^2 \quad \Rightarrow \quad x = 25t$$

$$125 + 25t = ut - 5t^2 \quad \Rightarrow \quad 5t^2 + (25 - u)t + 125 \geq 0$$

For real roots $D \geq 0$

$$\sqrt{(25-u)^2 - 2500} \geq 0 \quad \Rightarrow \quad (25-u)^2 \geq 2500$$

$$|25 - u| \geq 50 \quad \Rightarrow \quad u - 25 \geq 50 \quad \Rightarrow \quad u \geq 75\text{ m/s}$$

7. Lets T be time taken by each of them.

Distance travelled by first particle

$$s_1 = \left(0 + \frac{1}{2}a\left(\frac{T}{2}\right)^2\right) + \left(\left(a\frac{T}{2}\right)\frac{T}{2} + \frac{1}{2}(2a)\left(\frac{T}{2}\right)\right)^2$$

$$\Rightarrow \qquad s_1 = \frac{5}{8}aT^2$$

Distance travelled by second particle $= s_2$

$$\frac{s_2}{2} = 0 + \frac{1}{2}(2a)T_1^2 \qquad \text{...(i)}$$

$$\frac{s_2}{2} = [(2a)T_1]T_2 + \frac{1}{2}aT_2^2 \qquad \text{...(ii)}$$

$$T_1 + T_2 = T \qquad \text{...(iii)}$$

Solving Eqs. (i), (ii) and (iii), we get

$$5T_1^2 - 2TT_1 - T^2 = 0$$

$$T_1 = \frac{(1+\sqrt{6})T}{5}$$

$$\frac{s_2}{2} = \frac{1}{2}(2a)T_1^2 \quad \Rightarrow \quad s_2 = \frac{2a(7+2\sqrt{6})}{25}T^2$$

$$\therefore \qquad \frac{s_1}{s_2} = \frac{\frac{5}{8}aT^2}{\frac{2a(7+2\sqrt{6})}{25}T^2} = \frac{35 - 10\sqrt{6}}{16}$$

8.

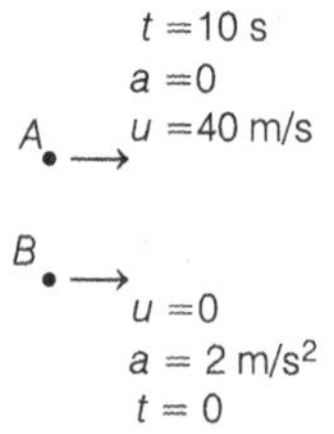

$$v_B = u_B + a_B t \quad \Rightarrow \quad 40 = 0 + 2(t) \quad \Rightarrow \quad t = 20\text{ s}$$

In 20 s, distance travelled by $B = \frac{1}{2}(2)(20)^2 = 400$ m

Distance travelled by $A = 40 \times 10 = 400$ m

So, A will be never ahead of B.

9.

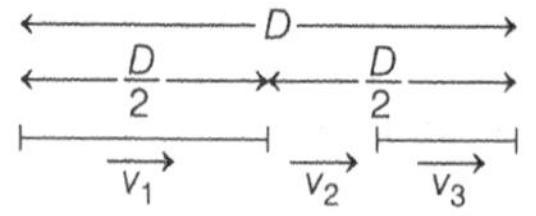

Total distance $= D$

Total time $= T$

Time taken to cover first $\frac{D}{2}$ distance $= \dfrac{D/2}{v_1}$

Remaining time $= T - \dfrac{D}{2v_1}$

$$\frac{D}{2} = v_2\left(\frac{1}{2}\left(T - \frac{D}{2v_1}\right)\right) + v_3\left(\frac{1}{2}\left(T - \frac{D}{2v_2}\right)\right)$$

$$\text{Average speed} = \frac{D}{T} = \frac{2v_1(v_2 + v_3)}{2v_1 + v_2 + v_3}$$

10.

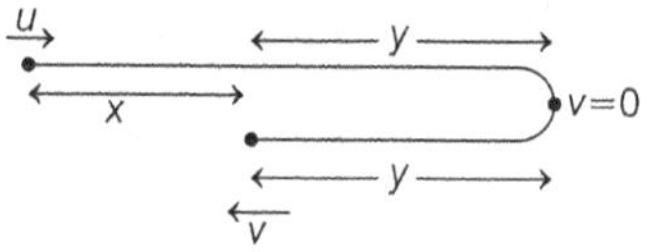

Displacement $= \frac{1}{3}$ (Distance)

$$x = \frac{x + 2y}{3} \quad \Rightarrow \quad x = y$$

$$\frac{u}{v} = \frac{\sqrt{2a(x+y)}}{\sqrt{2ay}} = \sqrt{2}$$

11. $b - a = un + \frac{1}{2}a'n^2 \qquad \text{...(i)}$

$$c - a = u(2n) + \frac{1}{2}a'(2n)^2 \qquad \text{...(ii)}$$

$$d - a = u(3n) + \frac{1}{2}a'(3n)^2$$

Solving Eqs. (i) and (ii), we get

$$a' = \frac{c - 2b + a}{n^2}$$

12.

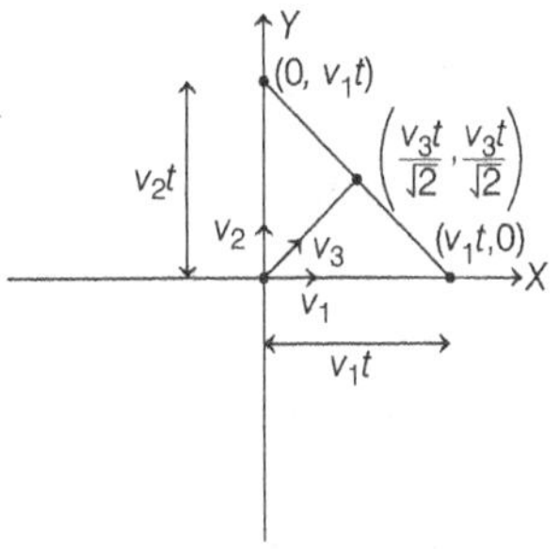

$$\frac{\frac{v_3t}{\sqrt{2}}-0}{\frac{v_3t}{\sqrt{2}}-v_1t}=\frac{\frac{v_3t}{\sqrt{2}}-v_2t}{\frac{v_3t}{\sqrt{2}}-0} \Rightarrow \frac{v_3}{v_3-\sqrt{2}v_1}=\frac{v_3-\sqrt{2}v_2}{v_3}$$

$$\Rightarrow \quad v_3^2=v_3^2-\sqrt{2}v_1v_3-\sqrt{2}v_2v_3+2v_1v_2$$

$$\Rightarrow \quad v_3=\frac{\sqrt{2}v_1v_2}{v_1+v_2}$$

13.

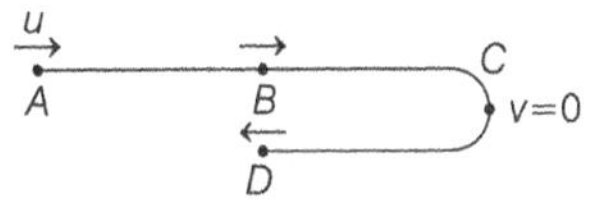

Between B and C,

$$v=u+at \Rightarrow 0=u_B+(-5)(1) \Rightarrow u_B=5\,\text{m/s}$$

Between A and B,

$$v=u+at \Rightarrow s=u_A-5(1) \Rightarrow u_A=10\,\text{m/s}$$

Between A and B,

$$v^2=u^2+2as \Rightarrow 5^2=10^2+2(-5)s_1 \Rightarrow s_1=7.5\,\text{m}$$

Between B and C,

$$v^2=u^2+2as \Rightarrow 0^2=5^2+2(-5)s_2 \Rightarrow s_2=2.5\,\text{m}$$

Total distance $=7.5+2.5+2.5=12.5\,\text{m}$

14. $s=\left(\frac{v+u}{2}\right)t=v_{avg}\cdot t$

For P to Q, $PQ=20t_1$

For Q to S, $QS=30t_2$

$$PQ=QS=20t_1=30t_2$$

For P to S, $(PQ+QS)=v_{avg}(t_1+t_2)$

$$\Rightarrow \quad 2PQ=v_{avg}\left(\frac{PQ}{20}+\frac{PQ}{30}\right) \Rightarrow v_{avg}=24\,\text{m/s}$$

15. $\sqrt{u^2+2gh}=2\sqrt{u^2-2gh} \Rightarrow u^2+2gh=4u^2-8gh$

$$\Rightarrow \quad 3u^2=10gh \Rightarrow \frac{u^2}{2g}=\frac{5h}{3}$$

16. Maximum height $=\frac{v_0^2}{2g}$

$$s=ut+\frac{1}{2}at^2 \Rightarrow s=0+\frac{1}{2}g\left(\frac{3v_0}{2g}-\frac{v_0}{g}\right)^2 \Rightarrow s=\frac{1}{8}\frac{v_0^2}{g}$$

Total distance $=\frac{v_0^2}{2g}+\frac{v_0^2}{8g}=\frac{5v_0^2}{8g}$

17. $\frac{u^2}{2g}=H$

$$\Rightarrow \quad t_1+t_2=\frac{2u}{g} \quad \text{...(i)}$$

and $\frac{t_1}{t_2}=\frac{1}{3}$ ...(ii)

Solving Eqs. (i) and (ii), we get

$$t_1=\frac{u}{2g} \quad \text{and} \quad t_2=\frac{3u}{2g}$$

$$s=ut+\frac{1}{2}at^2=u\left(\frac{u}{2g}\right)+\frac{1}{2}(-g)\left(\frac{u}{2g}\right)^2=\frac{3}{8}\frac{u^2}{g}=\frac{3H}{4}$$

18. Lets say time taken is T.

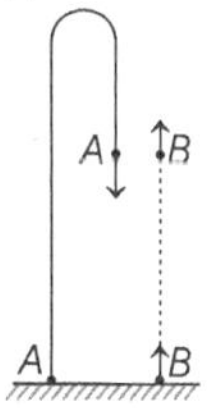

$$s_A=uT-\frac{1}{2}gT^2, \quad s_B=u(T-t)-\frac{1}{2}g(T-t)^2$$

$$s_A=s_B$$

$$\Rightarrow uT-\frac{1}{2}gT^2=u(T-t)-\frac{1}{2}g(T-t)^2$$

$$\Rightarrow \quad ut=\frac{1}{2}g(2T-t)(t) \Rightarrow 2T-t=\frac{2u}{g}$$

$$\Rightarrow \quad T=\frac{1}{2}\left(\frac{2u}{g}+t\right) \Rightarrow T=\frac{u}{g}+\frac{t}{2}$$

19. $s_A=u(10)-\frac{1}{2}g(10)^2$

$$s_B=\left((u+8)6-\frac{1}{2}g(6)^2\right)+\left(u(4)+\frac{1}{2}\times 2\times 4^2\right)$$

$$s_B=(u(10)+64)-\frac{1}{2}g(6)^2$$

$$s_B-s_A=64+5(64)=64+320=384\,\text{m}$$

20. $v^2=u^2+2as$

$$\Rightarrow \quad (20)^2=u^2-2(10)(25) \Rightarrow u=30\,\text{m/s}$$

21. $\frac{T_1}{T_2}=\frac{\sqrt{\frac{2h}{12}}}{\sqrt{\frac{2h}{8}}}=\sqrt{\frac{8}{12}}=\sqrt{\frac{2}{3}}$

22. $50T-\frac{1}{2}gT^2=45$

$$\Rightarrow \quad T^2-10T+9=0 \Rightarrow T=1 \text{ and } T=9$$

$$u(9-2)-\frac{1}{2}g(9-2)^2=45$$

$$\Rightarrow \quad 7u-245=45 \Rightarrow u=\frac{290}{7}\,\text{m/s}$$

23. $\dfrac{u^2}{2g} = 20 \quad \Rightarrow \quad u = 20\,\text{m/s}$

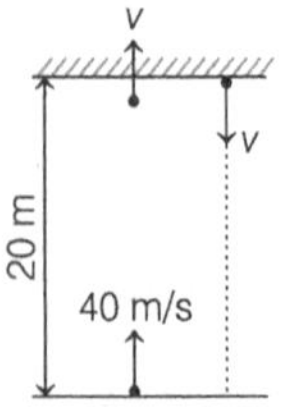

$v^2 = u^2 + 2as \quad \Rightarrow \quad v^2 = 40^2 + 2(-10)(20)$

$\Rightarrow \quad v = 20\sqrt{3}\,\text{m/s}$

$v = u + at \quad \Rightarrow \quad 20\sqrt{3} = 40 - 10t_1 \quad \Rightarrow t_1 = 4 - 2\sqrt{3}$

Total time $= 8 - 4\sqrt{3}$

24. $T = \sqrt{\dfrac{2h}{g}} = \sqrt{\dfrac{2(320)}{10}} = 8\,\text{s}$

$s = ut + \dfrac{1}{2}at^2$

$\Rightarrow \quad 320 = u(3) + \dfrac{1}{2}(10)(3)^2 \quad \Rightarrow \quad u(3) = 275$

$\Rightarrow \quad u = \dfrac{275}{3} = 91.66\,\text{m/s}$

25. $s = ut + \dfrac{1}{2}at^2$

$s = 0 + \dfrac{1}{2} \times 10 \times 5^2 = 125\,\text{m}$

26.

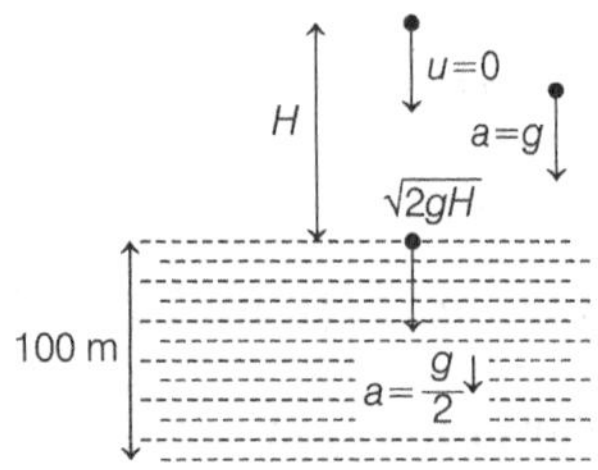

Inside lake, $s = ut + \dfrac{1}{2}at^2$

$$\Rightarrow \quad 100 = \left(\frac{\sqrt{2gH}}{2}\right)\left(7 - \sqrt{\frac{2H}{g}}\right) + \frac{1}{2}\left(\frac{g}{2}\right)\left(7 - \sqrt{\frac{2H}{g}}\right)^2$$

$\Rightarrow \quad H = 45\,\text{m}$

27.

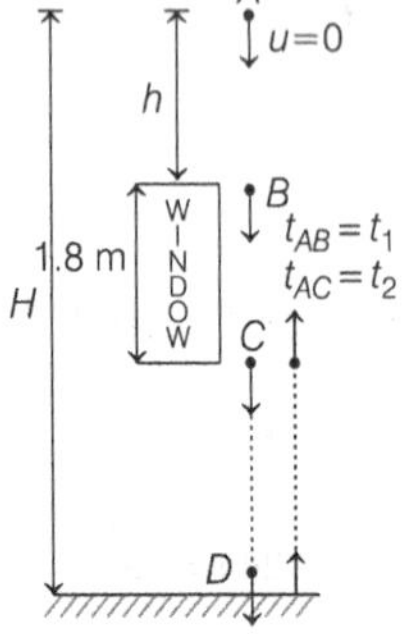

$s = ut + \dfrac{1}{2}at^2$

For A to B, $h = 0 + \dfrac{1}{2}(10)(t_1^2)$ ...(i)

For A to C, $h + 1.8 = 0 + \dfrac{1}{2}(10)t_2^2$ ...(ii)

Solving Eqs. (i) and (ii), we get

$5(t_2^2 - t_1^2) = 1.8$ ...(iii)

$t_2 - t_1 = 0.2$ ...(iv)

Solving Eqs. (iii) and (iv), we get

$t_2 = 1\,\text{s}$ and $t_1 = 0.8\,\text{s}$ and $t_{CD} = t_{DC} = 1\,\text{s}$

So, $t_{AD} = 2\,\text{s}$

28. $H = \left(\dfrac{1}{2}gt^2\right) + \left(20(3) - \dfrac{1}{2}gt^2\right) \quad \Rightarrow \quad H = 60\,\text{m}$

29. $s_{nth} = u + \dfrac{1}{2}a(2n-1) = u + \dfrac{1}{2}(-a)\left(2\left(\dfrac{u}{a} - 1\right) - 1\right) = \dfrac{3a}{2}$

30. $H = \dfrac{1}{2}g(\sqrt{2})^2$ ...(i)

$u = \sqrt{2g(10)} = \sqrt{20g}$

$-H = (\sqrt{20g})(2) - \dfrac{1}{2}g(2)^2$ ...(ii)

Solving Eqs. (i) and (ii), we get

$0 = 2\sqrt{20g} - g$

$\Rightarrow \quad g = 80\,\text{m/s}^2$

31.

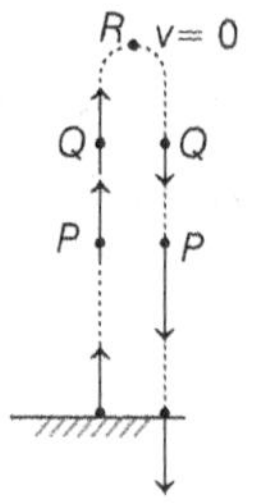

$RP = \dfrac{1}{2}g\left(\dfrac{T_P}{2}\right)^2, \quad RQ = \dfrac{1}{2}g\left(\dfrac{T_Q}{2}\right)^2$

$PQ = RP - RQ = \dfrac{g(T_P^2 - T_Q^2)}{8} = H \quad \Rightarrow g = \dfrac{8H}{T_P^2 - T_Q^2}$

32. $s = ut + \dfrac{1}{2}at^2 \quad \Rightarrow s = 0 + \dfrac{1}{2}(1.25)(10)^2 \Rightarrow s = 62.5\,\text{m}$

$v = u + at \Rightarrow v = 0 + 1.25 \times 10 \quad \Rightarrow \quad v = 12.5\,\text{m/s}$

$s = ut + \dfrac{1}{2}at^2 \quad \Rightarrow 40 = \dfrac{1}{2}(1.25)t^2 \Rightarrow t = 8\,\text{s}$

$v = u + at \Rightarrow v = 0 + 1.25 \times 8 \quad \Rightarrow \quad v = 10\,\text{m/s}$

For bolt, $s = ut + \dfrac{1}{2}at^2 \quad \Rightarrow \quad -40 = 10t - 5t^2$

$\Rightarrow \quad t^2 - 2t - 8 = 0 \quad \Rightarrow \quad t = 4\,\text{s}$

Distance travelled by lift from $t = 10$ s to $t = 12$ s

$$s = ut + \frac{1}{2}at^2 \Rightarrow s = 12.5 \times 2 = 25 \text{ m}$$

Height of lift $= 62.5 + 25 = 87.5$ m

Multiple Choice(s) Correct Questions

1. $\mathbf{v} \cdot \mathbf{a} > 0$ object is speeding up.
   $\mathbf{v} \cdot \mathbf{a} < 0$ object is slowing down.

2. (a) |Instantaneous velocity| = Instantaneous speed
   (d) In circular motion average velocity is zero in one revolution.

3. For A to C,

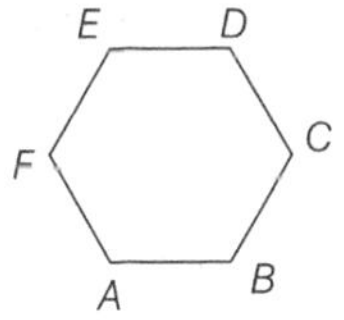

$$v_{avg} = \frac{s}{t} = \frac{\sqrt{3}a}{\frac{2a}{v}} = \frac{\sqrt{3}v}{2}$$

For A to D,

$$v_{avg} = \frac{s}{t} = \frac{2a}{\frac{3a}{v}} = \frac{2v}{3}$$

For A to F,

$$v_{avg} = \frac{s}{t} = \frac{a}{\frac{5a}{v}} = \frac{v}{5}$$

For A to B,

$$v_{avg} = \frac{s}{t} = \frac{a}{\frac{a}{v}} = v$$

4. $s = \left(\frac{v+u}{2}\right)t \Rightarrow 30 = \left(\frac{v+5}{2}\right)4 \Rightarrow v = 10 \text{ m/s}$

$$v = u + at$$

$$\Rightarrow \quad 10 = 5 + a(4) \Rightarrow a = 1.25 \text{ m/s}^2$$

5. $v = u + at \Rightarrow v_B = v_T + 10(0.5) \Rightarrow v_B - v_T = 5$

$$s = \left(\frac{u+v}{2}\right)t \Rightarrow 3 = \left(\frac{v_T + v_B}{2}\right)(0.5)$$

$$v_T + v_B = 12 \Rightarrow v_B = 8.5 \text{ m/s} \text{ and } v_T = 3.5 \text{ m/s}$$

6. $$H_{max} = \frac{u^2}{2g}$$

$$v^2 = u^2 + 2as$$

$$\Rightarrow \quad v^2 = u^2 + 2(-g)\left(\frac{1}{2}\left(\frac{u^2}{2g}\right)\right) \Rightarrow v = \frac{u}{\sqrt{2}}$$

7. $s = ut + \frac{1}{2}at^2 \Rightarrow 100 = ut - 5t^2$

$$5t^2 - ut + 100 = 0 \quad \begin{cases} t_1 \\ t_2 \end{cases}$$

$$t_1 + t_2 = \frac{u}{5} \text{ and } t_1 t_2 = 20$$

8. Lets take time taken to reach ground to be t.
   For P,

$$s = ut + \frac{1}{2}at^2 \Rightarrow 2h = 5t + 5t^2 \quad \text{...(i)}$$

For Q,

$$s = ut + \frac{1}{2}at^2 \Rightarrow h = 5t - 5t^2 \quad \text{...(ii)}$$

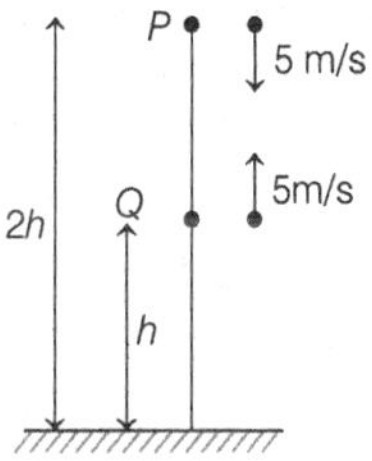

Solving Eqs. (i) and (ii), we get

$$-2 = \frac{5t(1+t)}{5t(1-t)} \Rightarrow -2 + 2t = 1 + t \Rightarrow t = 3\text{s}$$

$$h = 30 \text{ m}$$

9. As the particle goes up, it slows down.
   So, $t_3 > t_2 > t_1$.

$$\text{Average speed} = \frac{\text{Distance}}{\text{Time}} = \frac{d}{t}$$

Since, distances are same, average speed is inversely proportional to time.

So, $v_{av_1} > v_{av_2} > v_{av_3}$

Acceleration is constant.

So, $a_1 = a_2 = a_3 = g$

$$v = u + at \Rightarrow v - u = at$$

$$\Rightarrow \quad \Delta v = at \Rightarrow \Delta v \propto t$$

So, $\Delta v_3 > \Delta v_2 > \Delta v_1$

10. Velocity is vector quantity. It has both magnitude and direction. If either magnitude or direction changes, velocity changes.
    Acceleration is rate of change of velocity.
    So, when velocity changes, body has acceleration.

11. $140 = 15(14) - \frac{1}{2}a(14)^2 \Rightarrow a = \frac{5}{7} \text{ m/s}^2$

$$v = u + at \Rightarrow v = 15 - \frac{5}{7}(14) = 5 \text{ m/s}$$

12. $v^2 = u^2 + 2as \Rightarrow 0^2 = 10^2 + 2(-5)s \Rightarrow s = 10 \text{ m}$

$$v = u + at \Rightarrow 0 = 10 - 5t$$

$$\Rightarrow \quad t = 2 \text{ s}$$

From $t = 2$ s to $t = 3$ s

$$s = ut + \frac{1}{2}at^2 \Rightarrow s = \frac{1}{2}(-5)(1)^2 = 2.5 \text{ m}$$

So distance travelled from $t = 0$ to $t = 3$

$$= 10 + 2.5 = 12.5 \text{ m}$$

13. $$s_{nth} = u + \frac{1}{2}a(2n - 1)$$

$$25 = u + \frac{1}{2}a[(2(5) - 1)] \qquad \text{... (i)}$$

$$33 = u + \frac{1}{2}a[(2(7) - 1)] \qquad \text{... (ii)}$$

Solving Eqs. (i) and (ii), we get

$$u = 7\,\text{m/s}, a = 4\,\text{m/s}^2$$

14. If acceleration has a component in the direction of velocity, then body speeds up. If acceleration has a component in the direction opposite to velocity, then body slows down.

Comprehension Based Questions

1. $v = u + at \Rightarrow 0 = 40 - 10t \Rightarrow t = 4\,\text{s}$

2. $v^2 = u^2 + 2as \Rightarrow 0^2 = 40^2 + 2(-10)(x - 10) \Rightarrow x = 90\,\text{m}$

3. $v^2 = u^2 + 2as \Rightarrow v^2 = 40^2 + 2(-10)(-10)$

$\Rightarrow v = -30\sqrt{2}\,\text{m/s}$

4. $s = ut + \frac{1}{2}at^2 \Rightarrow -10 = 40t - 5t^2 \Rightarrow t = 4 + 3\sqrt{2}$

5. $s = ut + \frac{1}{2}at^2$

$\Rightarrow s = \frac{1}{2} \times 20 \times (15 \times 60)^2 = 8100\,\text{km or } 8.1 \times 10^3\,\text{km}$

6. $\frac{384000 - 8100 - 8100}{384000} = 0.95$

7. $v = u + at \Rightarrow v = 0 + 20(15 \times 60) = 18000\,\text{m/s}$

$t = \frac{384000 \times 10^3}{18000} = 340\,\text{min}$

Total time $= 15 + 340 + 15 = 370\,\text{min}$

8. $v^2 = u^2 + 2as \Rightarrow 10^2 = 20^2 + 2a(30) \Rightarrow a = -5\,\text{m/s}^2$

9. $v = u + at \Rightarrow v = 20 + (-5)(8) = -20\,\text{m/s}$

10. $v = u + at \Rightarrow 0 = 20 + (-5)t \Rightarrow t = 4\,\text{s}$

From $t = 0\text{s}$ to $t = 4\text{s}$; $s = \frac{20^2}{2(5)} = 40\,\text{m}$

From $t = 4\text{s}$ to $t = 8\text{s}$; $s = \frac{20^2}{2(5)} = 40\,\text{m}$

Total distance $= 40 + 40 = 80\,\text{m}$

11. and **12.** $-h = u(6) - \frac{1}{2}g(6)^2 \qquad \text{...(i)}$

$$+h = u(2) + \frac{1}{2}g(2)^2 \qquad \text{...(ii)}$$

Solving Eqs. (i) and (ii), we get

$$h = 60\,\text{m and } u = 20\,\text{m/s}$$

Match the Columns Questions

1. $v = u + at \Rightarrow v = 0 + 10t \qquad \text{...(i)}$

$v = u + at \Rightarrow 0 = v - 5(15 - t) \qquad \text{...(ii)}$

Solving Eqs. (i) and (ii), we get

$$t = 5 \quad \text{and} \quad v = 50\,\text{m/s}$$

$$s = ut + \frac{1}{2}at^2$$

$$\Rightarrow \quad s = \frac{1}{2}(10)(5)^2 = 125\,\text{m}$$

$$s = ut + \frac{1}{2}at^2$$

$$\Rightarrow \quad s = 50(10) + \frac{1}{2}(-5)(10)^2 \Rightarrow s = 250\,\text{m}$$

$$v^2 = u^2 + 2as$$

$$\Rightarrow \quad 25^2 = 50^2 + 2(-5)s \Rightarrow s = 187.5\,\text{m}$$

Distance $= 125 + 187.5 = 312.5\,\text{m}$

Average speed $= \frac{125 + 250}{15} = \frac{375}{15} = 25\,\text{m/s}$

2. $\frac{2u}{g} = 10 \Rightarrow u = 50\,\text{m/s}$

Time between two successive throwings $= \frac{10}{20} = 0.5\,\text{s}$

Height of 15th ball when 20th ball is in hand

$$= ut + \frac{1}{2}at^2 = 50(2.5) + \frac{1}{2}(-10)(2.5)^2 = 93.75\,\text{m}$$

Speed of 10th ball when 20th ball is in hand $= u + at$

$$= 50 + (-10)5 = 0$$

Number of balls thrown per minute $= \frac{60}{0.5} = 120$ balls/min

3. A → PQ, B → R, C → S, D → S

4. A → PQ, B → PRS, C → PR, D → PRS

Numerical Value Questions

1. $v^2 = u^2 + 2as$

$\left(\frac{9u}{10}\right)^2 = u^2 + 2al$ (For a single plank)

$0^2 = u^2 + 2a(nl)$ (For n planks)

2.

First part	Second part	Third part
$v^2 = u^2 + 2as$ $\Rightarrow v = \sqrt{2as}$ $s = ut + \frac{1}{2}at^2$ $\Rightarrow t_1 = \sqrt{\frac{2s}{a}}$	$t_2 = \frac{3s}{\sqrt{2as}}$	$v^2 = u^2 + 2as$ $\Rightarrow 0^2 = (\sqrt{2as})^2 + 2a'(5s)$ $\Rightarrow a' = -\frac{a}{5}$ $v = u + at$ $\Rightarrow 0 = \sqrt{2as} - \frac{a}{5}t_3 \Rightarrow t_3 = 5\sqrt{\frac{2s}{a}}$

$$v_{avg} = \frac{\text{Total distance}}{\text{Total time}} = \frac{s + 3s + 5s}{\sqrt{\frac{2s}{a}} + \frac{3s}{\sqrt{2as}} + 5\sqrt{\frac{2s}{a}}}$$

$$= \frac{9s}{\frac{15}{\sqrt{2}}\sqrt{\frac{s}{a}}} = \frac{9\sqrt{2}}{15}\sqrt{as} = 3\sqrt{2as}$$

$$\therefore \quad \frac{v_{avg}}{v_{max}} = \frac{\frac{3}{5}\sqrt{2as}}{\sqrt{2as}} = \frac{3}{5}$$

3.

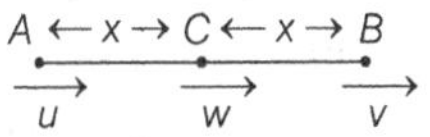

$$\left.\begin{aligned} w^2 &= u^2 + 2ax \\ v^2 &= w^2 + 2ax \end{aligned}\right\} \text{Solving them, we get}$$

$$w = \sqrt{\frac{v^2 + u^2}{2}}$$

$$v = u + at \Rightarrow w = u + at_1 \Rightarrow t_1 = \frac{w-u}{a}$$

$$v = u + at \Rightarrow v = w + at_2 \Rightarrow t_2 = \frac{v-w}{a}$$

$$t_1 = 2t_2 \Rightarrow \frac{w-u}{a} = 2\left(\frac{v-w}{a}\right) \Rightarrow w = \frac{2v+u}{3}$$

$$w = \frac{2v+u}{3} = \sqrt{\frac{v^2+u^2}{2}} \Rightarrow \frac{4v^2+u^2+4uv}{9} = \frac{u^2+v^2}{2}$$

$$\Rightarrow \quad v^2 - 8uv + 7u^2 = 0$$

$$\Rightarrow \quad \left(\frac{v}{u}\right)^2 - 8\left(\frac{v}{u}\right) + 7 = 0$$

$$\Rightarrow \quad \lambda^2 - 8\lambda + 7 = 0 \Rightarrow \lambda = 1 \text{ and } \lambda = 7$$

4. Accelerating, $v = u + at \Rightarrow v_{max} = xt_1 \Rightarrow t_1 = \frac{v_{max}}{x}$

$$v^2 = u^2 + 2as$$

$$\Rightarrow \quad v_{max}^2 = 2xs_1 \Rightarrow s_1 = \frac{v_{max}^2}{2x}$$

Retarding, $v = u + at \Rightarrow 0 = v_{max} - yt_2 \Rightarrow t_2 = \frac{v_{max}}{y}$

$$v^2 = u^2 + 2as$$

$$\Rightarrow \quad 0^2 = v_{max}^2 - 2ys_2 \Rightarrow s_2 = \frac{v_{max}^2}{2y}$$

$$t_1 + t_2 = 4\,\text{min} \Rightarrow v_{max}\left(\frac{1}{x} + \frac{1}{y}\right) = 4 \qquad \text{...(i)}$$

$$s_1 + s_2 = 2\,\text{km} \Rightarrow \frac{v_{max}^2}{2}\left(\frac{1}{x} + \frac{1}{y}\right) = 2 \qquad \text{...(ii)}$$

From Eqs. (i) and (ii), we get

$$v_{max} = 1$$

Put $v_{max} = 1$ in Eq. (i), we get

$$\frac{1}{x} + \frac{1}{y} = 4$$

5. For P, $v = u + at \Rightarrow 30 = 15 + at \Rightarrow at = 15$

For Q, $v = u + at \Rightarrow v = 20 + (-a)t$

$$\Rightarrow \quad v = 20 - at = 20 - 15 = 5$$

6. Time taken for reaching maximum speed $= t$

$$v = u + at \Rightarrow 20 = 0 + 1t \Rightarrow t = 20\,\text{s}$$

$$s = ut + \frac{1}{2}at^2 \Rightarrow s = \frac{1}{2}(1)(20)^2 = 200\,\text{m}$$

Time taken for retardation $= t'$

$$v = u + at \Rightarrow 0 = 20 + (-2)t' \Rightarrow t' = 10\,\text{s}$$

$$s = ut + \frac{1}{2}at^2 \Rightarrow s' = 20(10) + \frac{1}{2}(-2)(10)^2 \Rightarrow s' = 100\,\text{m}$$

Remaining distance will be covered with constant speed of 20 m/s.

$$t = \frac{1000 - 200 - 100}{20} = 35\,\text{s}$$

Total time $= 20 + 35 + 10 = 65$ s

7. On each collision speed will get halved.

$$T = \sqrt{\frac{2h}{g}} + \frac{2\left(\frac{\sqrt{2gh}}{2}\right)}{g} + \frac{2\left(\frac{\sqrt{2gh}}{2^2}\right)}{g} + \ldots$$

$$T = \sqrt{\frac{2h}{g}} + \sqrt{\frac{2h}{g}}\left(1 + \frac{1}{2} + \frac{1}{2^2} + \frac{1}{2^3} + \ldots\infty\right)$$

$$T = \sqrt{\frac{2h}{g}}\left(1 + \frac{1}{1-(1/2)}\right) = 6\,\text{s}$$

8. $H_{max} = \frac{u^2}{2g} \Rightarrow 15 = \frac{\left(\frac{\sqrt{u^2 + 2g(15)}}{2}\right)^2}{2g} \Rightarrow u = 30\,\text{m/s}$

9. $0 = vt - \frac{1}{2}gt^2 \qquad \text{...(i)}$

$160 = vt + \frac{1}{2}gt^2 \qquad \text{...(ii)}$

$\Rightarrow v = 20\,\text{m/s}$

10.

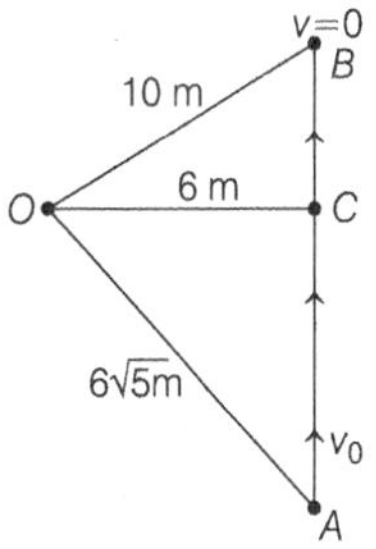

$$AC = \sqrt{6(\sqrt{5})^2 - 6^2} = 12\,\text{m} \quad \text{and} \quad CB = \sqrt{10^2 - 6^2} = 8\,\text{m}$$

The maximum height attained by the ball

$$H = AB = 12 + 8 = 20\,\text{m}$$

$$v^2 = u^2 - 2gH$$

$$\Rightarrow \quad 0^2 = v_0^2 - 2gH \Rightarrow v_0 = \sqrt{2gH} = 20\,\text{m/s}$$

11. Stone A takes 4 s from O to A

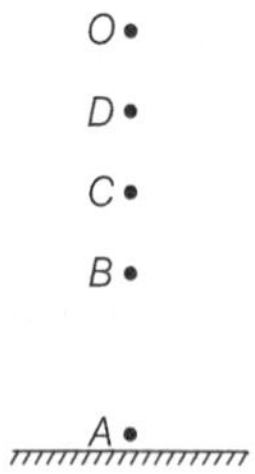

$$\Rightarrow \quad s = ut + \frac{1}{2}at^2$$

$$\Rightarrow \quad OA = 0 + \frac{1}{2}(10)(4)^2 = 80\,\text{m}$$

Stone B is travelling for 3 s

$$OB = 0 + \frac{1}{2}(10)(3)^2 = 45\,\text{m}$$

$$OC = 0 + \frac{1}{2}(10)(2)^2 = 20\,\text{m}$$

$$OD = 0 + \frac{1}{2}(10)(1)^2 = 5\,\text{m}$$

So, $AB = OA - OB = 80 - 45 = 35\,\text{m}$

$BC = OB - OC = 45 - 20 = 25\,\text{m}$

$CD = OC - OD = 20 - 5 = 15\,\text{m}$

$$\frac{3(AB+BC)}{2CD} = \frac{3(35+25)}{2(15)} = 6$$

12. Lets say they collide after time t

$$\left[\sqrt{2gh}\left(t-\sqrt{\frac{2h}{g}}\right)-\frac{1}{2}g\left(t-\sqrt{\frac{2h}{g}}\right)^2\right]=55 \quad \text{...(i)}$$

$$\frac{1}{2}g(t-2)^2 = h - 55 \quad \text{...(ii)}$$

Solving Eqs. (i) and (ii), we get

$t = 7\text{s}$ and $h = 180\,\text{m}$

13. Planet A

$$s = ut + \frac{1}{2}at^2 \Rightarrow h = 0 + \frac{1}{2}(2g)t_1^2 \Rightarrow t_1 = \sqrt{\frac{h}{g}}$$

$$v^2 = u^2 + 2as \Rightarrow v_1^2 = 0^2 + 2(2g)h \Rightarrow v_1 = 2\sqrt{gh}$$

Planet B

$$s = ut + \frac{1}{2}at^2 \Rightarrow h = 0 + \frac{1}{2}(8g)t_2^2 \Rightarrow t_2 = \frac{h}{4g}$$

$$v^2 = u^2 + 2as \Rightarrow v_2^2 = 0^2 + 2(8g)h \Rightarrow v_2 = 4\sqrt{gh}$$

$$v_2 - v_1 = v \Rightarrow 4\sqrt{gh} - 2\sqrt{gh} = u \Rightarrow u = 2\sqrt{gh}$$

$$t_1 - t_2 = t \Rightarrow \sqrt{\frac{h}{g}} - \sqrt{\frac{h}{4g}} = t \Rightarrow t = \frac{1}{2}\sqrt{\frac{h}{g}}$$

$$\frac{v}{t} = \frac{2\sqrt{gh}}{\frac{1}{2}\sqrt{\frac{h}{g}}} = 4g \Rightarrow u = 4gt$$

14.

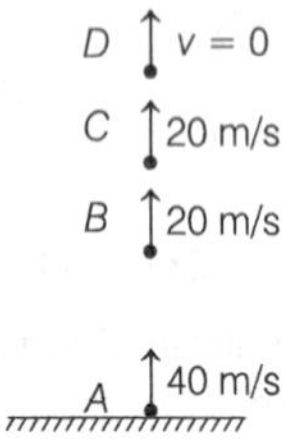

From A to B,

$$v^2 = u^2 + 2as \Rightarrow 20^2 = 40^2 + 2(-10)(AB) \Rightarrow AB = 60\,\text{m}$$

For next 2s,

$$s = ut + \frac{1}{2}at^2 \Rightarrow BC = 20 \times 2 + \frac{1}{2}(0)(2)^2 \Rightarrow BC = 40\,\text{m}$$

From C to D,

$$v^2 = u^2 + 2as \Rightarrow 0^2 = 20^2 + 2(-20)(CD) \Rightarrow CD = 10\,\text{m}$$

$$AB + BC + CD = 60 + 40 + 10 = 110\,\text{m}$$

15. Lets say passenger is late by T second for departure.

For train, $u = 0$

$v = u + at$

$\Rightarrow \quad v = 0 + aT \Rightarrow v = aT$

For second last boggy,

$$s = ut + \frac{1}{2}at^2$$

$$l = (aT)(3) + \frac{1}{2}a(3)^2 \quad \text{...(i)}$$

For (last boggy + second last boggy),

$$s = ut + \frac{1}{2}at^2$$

$$2l = aT(5) + \frac{1}{2}a(5)^2 \quad \text{...(ii)}$$

Solving Eqs. (i) and (ii), we get

$T = 3.50\,\text{s}$

Previous Year's Questions

JEE Main

1. As, we know,

$$v^2 = u^2 - 2ax$$

When bullet looses one-third velocity,

$$v = u - \frac{u}{3} = \frac{2u}{3}$$

$$\therefore \quad \left(\frac{2u}{3}\right)^2 = u^2 - 2a(4)$$

$$\left(\frac{4u^2}{9} - u^2\right) = -8a$$

$$\frac{5u^2}{9} = 8a \quad \text{...(i)}$$

When bullet coming to rest,

$$0 = \left(\frac{2u}{3}\right)^2 - 2ax$$

$$\frac{4u^2}{9} = 2ax \quad \text{...(ii)}$$

Using Eqs. (i) and (ii),

$$\frac{5}{4} = \frac{4}{x}$$

$$\Rightarrow \quad x = \frac{16}{5} = 3.2\,\text{cm} = 32 \times 10^{-3}\,\text{m}$$

Therefore, $D = 32$

2. Top most point

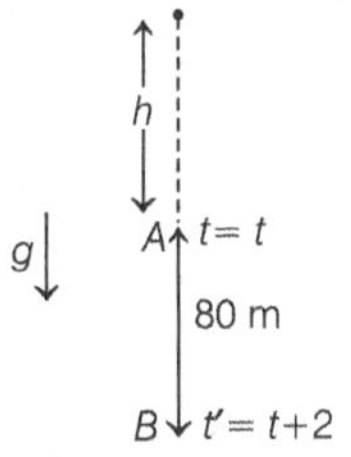

$$h = ut + \frac{1}{2}gt^2$$

$$h = \frac{1}{2}gt^2 \qquad [\because u = 0]$$

$$h = \frac{1}{2}\times 10t^2$$

$$h = 5t^2 \qquad \text{...(i)}$$

Now $\quad h + 80 = u(t+2) + \frac{1}{2}g(t+2)^2$

$$h + 80 = \frac{1}{2}g(t+2)^2$$

$$5t^2 + 80 = \frac{10}{2}(t+2)^2$$

$$5t^2 + 80 = 5(t+2)^2$$

$$5t^2 + 80 = 5t^2 + 20 + 20t$$

$$60 = 20t$$

$$t = 3\text{ s}$$

From Eq. (i), we get

$$h = 5\times(3)^2 = 5\times 9 = 45\text{ m}$$

$$h = 45\text{ m}$$

3. s_1 in first $(p-1)$ s

s_2 in first p s

$$s_1 = \frac{1}{2}a(p-1)^2,\ 2s_1 = a(p-1)^2$$

$$s_2 = \frac{1}{2}ap^2,\ 2s_2 = ap^2$$

Let $s_1 + s_2$ displacement is in time t s then,

$$s_1 + s_2 = \frac{1}{2}at^2$$

$$2(s_1 + s_2) = at^2$$

$$2s_1 + 2s_2 = at^2$$

$$a(p-1)^2 + ap^2 = at^2$$

$$(p-1)^2 + p^2 = t^2$$

$$t = \sqrt{(p-1)^2 + p^2} = \sqrt{p^2 + 1 - 2p + p^2}$$

$$= \sqrt{2p^2 - 2p + 1}$$

4. Average velocity is given by formula as

Average velocity,

$$= \frac{x + x}{\frac{x}{v_1} + \frac{x}{v_2}} = v = \frac{2x}{x\left(\frac{1}{v_1} + \frac{1}{v_2}\right)} = v$$

$$\Rightarrow \quad \frac{2}{v} = \frac{1}{v_1} + \frac{1}{v_2}$$

5. From given figure,

$$AB = BC \text{ and } AD = 3AB$$

$$(AB + BC + CD) = 3AB$$

$$CD = AB \qquad [\because AB = BC]$$

Average speed,

$$v_{avg} = \frac{\text{Total distance}}{\text{Total time}}$$

$$= \frac{AB + BC + CD}{t_1 + t_2 + t_3} = \frac{x + x + x}{\frac{x}{v_1} + \frac{x}{v_2} + \frac{x}{v_3}}$$

$$= \frac{3x}{x\left(\frac{1}{v_1} + \frac{1}{v_2} + \frac{1}{v_3}\right)}$$

$$v_{avg} = \frac{3v_1v_2v_3}{v_1v_2 + v_2v_3 + v_1v_3}$$

6. When car travels a distance x with speed v_1, then time taken,

$$t_1 = \frac{x}{v_1}$$

Similarly, $\quad t_2 = \frac{x}{v_2}$

$\therefore$ Average speed, $\quad v_{avg} = \dfrac{\text{total distance}}{\text{total time taken}}$

$$= \frac{x + x}{\frac{x}{v_1} + \frac{x}{v_2}} = \frac{2}{\left(\frac{v_1 + v_2}{v_1v_2}\right)} = \frac{2v_1v_2}{v_1 + v_2}$$

7. Time taken by vehicle to travel first 4 km with speed of 3 km/h.

$$t_1 = \frac{4}{3}\text{ hour}$$

Time taken by the vehicle to travel second 4 km with speed of 5 km/h,

$$t_2 = \frac{4}{5}\text{ hour}$$

$\therefore$ Average speed $= \dfrac{\text{Total distance travelled}}{\text{Total time taken}}$

$$= \frac{4 + 4}{t_1 + t_2} = \frac{8}{\frac{4}{3} + \frac{4}{5}}$$

$$= \frac{8\times 15}{32}$$

$$= 3.75\text{ km/h}$$

8. Let $AB = BD = a$

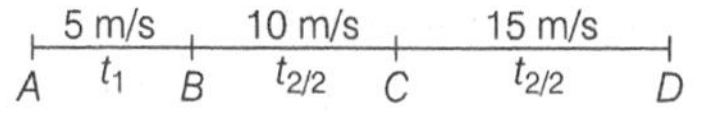

Then, time to cover distance a with speed of 5 m/s is,

$$t_1 = \frac{\text{Distance}}{\text{Speed}} = \frac{a}{5}$$

Now, in second part of journey let in time t_2, rider covers distance a.

$$BC = 10 \times \frac{t_2}{2}$$

Similarly, $CD = 15 \times \frac{t_2}{2}$

But, $BC + CD = a$

$$\Rightarrow \quad 10\frac{t_2}{2} + 15\frac{t_2}{2} = a \quad \Rightarrow \quad t_2 = \frac{a}{12.5}$$

So, total time of journey $= t_1 + t_2$

$$= \frac{a}{5} + \frac{a}{12.5}$$

Hence, average speed for entire journey.

$$= \frac{\text{Total distance}}{\text{Total time}}$$

$$= \frac{a + a}{\frac{a}{5} + \frac{a}{12.5}} = \frac{5 \times 12.5 \times 2}{12.5 + 5}$$

$$= \frac{5 \times 12.5 \times 2}{17.5} = \frac{50}{7} \text{ m/s}$$

Given, average speed $= \frac{5}{7}$ m/s

$$\therefore \quad x = 50$$

9. Given, initial velocity $(v) = 150$ m/s

From $v = u + at$, we have

$$v = 150 - 10t \quad (\because a = -g \text{ for vertically thrown object})$$

$$v_{(3)} = 150 - 30 = 120 \text{ m/s}$$

$$v_{(5)} = 150 - 50 = 100 \text{ m/s}$$

According to question,

$$\frac{x+1}{x} = \frac{120}{100} = \frac{6}{5} \Rightarrow x = 5$$

10. Using first equation of motion

$$v = u + at$$

$$v - u = at$$

$$t = \frac{v-u}{a} = \frac{60-10}{2} = \frac{50}{2} = 25 \text{ s}$$

11. Velocity with which ball strikes from v_1

$$= \sqrt{2gh} = \sqrt{2 \times 9.8 \times 10} = 14 \text{ m/s}$$

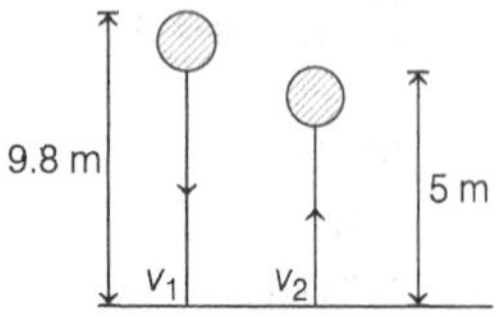

$$\Delta t = 0.2 \text{ s}$$

Velocity with which ball rebounces,

$$v_2 = \sqrt{2gh} = \sqrt{2 \times 10 \times 5} = 10 \text{ m/s}$$

$$\text{Acceleration of ball} = \frac{14-10}{0.2} = 20 \text{ m/s}^2$$

12. Given situation is

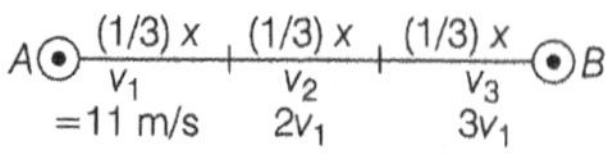

Now, let total displacement $= x$

Then, time to cover first $\frac{x}{3}$ Displacement,

$$t_1 = \frac{\text{displacement}}{\text{velocity}}$$

$$\Rightarrow \quad t_1 = \frac{x}{3 \times 11}$$

Similarly, $t_2 = \frac{x}{3 \times 22}$ and $t_3 = \frac{x}{3 \times 33}$

Now, $v_{\text{average}} = \frac{\text{Total displacement}}{\text{Total time}}$

$$= \frac{x}{\frac{x}{33} + \frac{x}{66} + \frac{x}{99}}$$

$$= \frac{1}{\frac{1}{33}\left(1 + \frac{1}{2} + \frac{1}{3}\right)} = \frac{33}{\left(\frac{6+3+2}{6}\right)}$$

$$= \frac{33 \times 6}{11} = 18 \text{ m/s}$$

13. The time taken by the ball to reach at the surface of water is given by

$$t_1 = \sqrt{\frac{2h}{g}}$$

$$\therefore \quad t_1 = \sqrt{\frac{2 \times 4.9}{9.8}} = 1.0 \text{ s}$$

Now, the velocity acquired by the ball to reach water surface,

$$v = gt_1 = 9.8 \times 1.0 = 9.8 \text{ ms}^{-1}$$

Now, time taken by the ball to reach the bottom of the lake from the water surface is $t_2 = 4.0 - 1.0 = 3.0$ s

Given that, velocity of the ball in water is constant, therefore depth of the lake will be,

$$d = vt_2 = 9.8 \times 3.0 = 29.4 \text{ m}$$

14. Let initial speed of the ball is u

Time taken by the ball to reach maximum height is given as,

$$0 = u - gt \quad \Rightarrow \quad t = \frac{u}{g} \quad \text{... (i)}$$

According to question, $t = \frac{1}{n}$ ...(ii)

Form Eqs. (i) and (ii), $\frac{u}{g} = \frac{1}{n}$

$$\Rightarrow \quad u = \frac{g}{n}$$

$\therefore$ Maximum height, $h = \dfrac{u^2}{2g} = \dfrac{g^2}{2gn^2} = \dfrac{g}{2n^2}$

15. Let both balls meet after t seconds.

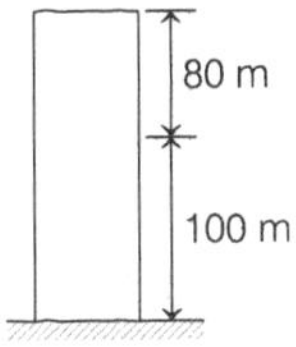

Then, displacement of ball A in t seconds = displacement of ball B in $(t-2)$ seconds

$\Rightarrow \quad \frac{1}{2}gt^2 = x(t-2) + \frac{1}{2}g(t-2)^2$

$\Rightarrow \quad g[t^2 - (t-2)]^2 = 2u(t-2)$

$\Rightarrow \quad g(2)(2t-2) = 2u(t-2)$

$\Rightarrow \quad g(2t-2) = u(t-2)$ ...(i)

Also, displacement of ball A in t seconds = 80 m

$\Rightarrow \quad \frac{1}{2}gt^2 = 80$

$\Rightarrow \quad t = 4\text{s}$ ...(ii)

Substituting $t = 4\text{s}$ in Eq. (i), we get

$g(8-2) = u(4-2)$

$\Rightarrow \quad u = 3 \times g = 30$ m/s

16. Given, $v = 19.6 \text{ ms}^{-1}$

$t = 6\text{ s}, g = 9.8 \text{ ms}^{-2}$

Let t' be the time taken by the ball to reach B from position A, then using equation of motion,

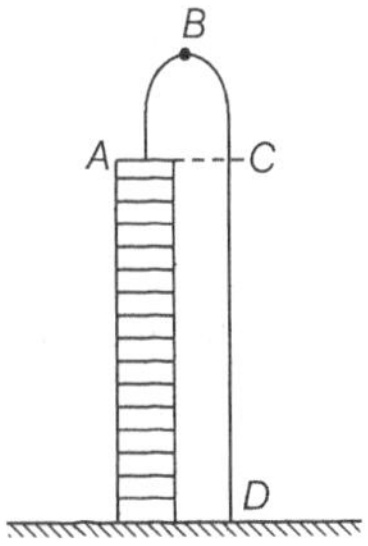

$v = u + gt'$

$\Rightarrow \quad 0 = 19.6 + (-9.8)t'$

$\Rightarrow \quad t' = \frac{19.6}{9.8} = 2\text{ s}$

So, time taken from B to D,

$t'' = (6-2)\text{ s} = 4\text{ s}$

If h be the height from the ground to the top, then

$h = ut + \frac{1}{2}gt^2$

$\Rightarrow \quad h = 0 + \frac{1}{2}(gt'')^2 = \frac{1}{2} \times 9.8 \times (4)^2 = 78.4$ m

Given, $\quad h = \frac{k}{5}$

$\Rightarrow \quad k = h \times 5 = 78.4 \times 5 = 392$

17. Given, increase of velocity of particle with respect to distance

$\frac{dv}{dx} = 5 \text{ ms}^{-1}\text{/m}$

$\therefore$ Acceleration of particle,

$a = \frac{dv}{dt} = \frac{dv}{dx} \cdot \frac{dx}{dt} = \frac{dv}{dx} \times v \quad \left(\because v = \frac{dx}{dt}\right)$

$= 5 \times 20 \quad (\because v = 20 \text{ m/s})$

$= 100 \text{ m/s}^2$

18. Given, $s = 27$ m, $v = 0$

$u = 150 \text{ km/h} = 150 \times \frac{5}{18} = \frac{125}{3}$ m/s

Using $v^2 - u^2 = 2as$, we get

$0 - \frac{125^2}{9} = 2 \times a \times 27$

$\Rightarrow \quad a = \frac{-125^2}{2 \times 27 \times 9} \text{ m/s}^2$

Now, when car is moving with one-third of its initial speed, we have

$v = 0$

$u = \frac{1}{3} \times 150$ km/h

or $\quad u = 50 \times \frac{5}{18} = \frac{125}{9}$ m/s

Now again using

$v^2 - u^2 = 2as$

we get

$0 - \frac{125^2}{9^2} = 2 \times \left(\frac{-125^2}{2 \times 27 \times 9}\right) \times s$

$\Rightarrow \quad s = \frac{125^2}{9^2} \times \frac{27 \times 9}{125^2} \Rightarrow s = 3$ m

19. Initial velocity of ball,

$u = 50$ m/s

Let both balls meet together after t seconds.

For the first ball, height attained by it in t seconds,

$h_1 = ut - \frac{1}{2}gt^2$

$\Rightarrow \quad h_1 = 50t - \frac{1}{2}gt^2$ ...(i)

After 2 s, second ball is projected vertically upward with $u = 50$ m/s,

i.e. $\quad t' = t - 2$

$\therefore$ Height attained by second ball,

$h_2 = u(t-2) - \frac{1}{2}g(t-2)^2$

$\Rightarrow \quad h_2 = 50(t-2) - \frac{1}{2}g(t-2)^2$ ...(ii)

Both balls will meet, if

$$h_1 = h_2 50t - \frac{1}{2}gt^2 = 50(t-2) - \frac{1}{2}g(t-2)^2$$

$$\Rightarrow 50t - 50(t-2) = \frac{1}{2}gt^2 - \frac{1}{2}g(t-2)^2$$

$$\Rightarrow \quad t = 6 \text{ s}$$

20.

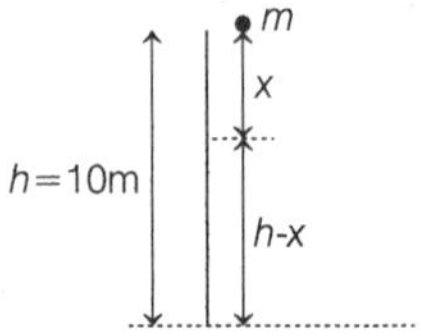

After falling a distance x,

$$|v| = |g| = 10$$

$\therefore$ $$v^2 = 2gx$$

$$\Rightarrow \quad 10^2 = 2 \times 10 \times x \Rightarrow x = 5 \text{ m}$$

21. Let h be the height of tower.

Situation for the first condition is shown in the figure.

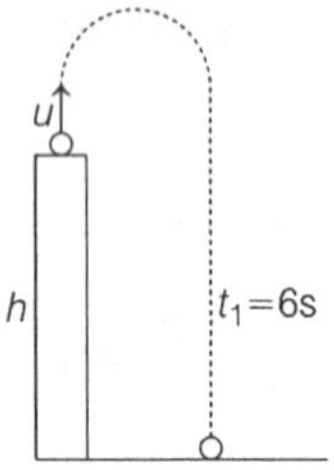

By using equation of motion,

$$h = -ut_1 + \frac{1}{2}gt_1^2$$

$$h = -6u + \frac{1}{2}g(6)^2$$

$$h = -6u + 18g \quad \text{... (i)}$$

Situation for the second condition is shown in the figure.

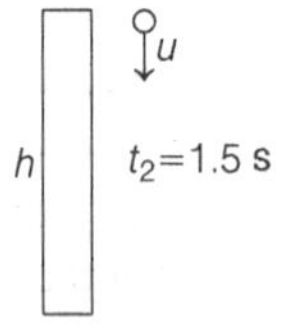

Now, using equation of motion,

$$h = ut_2 + \frac{1}{2}gt_2^2$$

$$h = 1.5u + \frac{1}{2}g(1.5)^2$$

$$h = 1.5u + \frac{2.25}{2}g \quad \text{...(ii)}$$

Solving Eqs. (i) and (ii), we get

$$h = 4.5 \text{ gm}$$

For the third case, when ball is released from rest, i.e. $u = 0$

In this case,

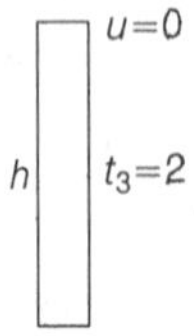

$$h = 0 \times t_3 + \frac{1}{2}gt_3^2 = \frac{1}{2}gt_3^2$$

$$\Rightarrow \quad t_3 = \sqrt{\frac{2h}{g}} = \sqrt{\frac{2 \times 4.5g}{g}} = \sqrt{9} = 3 \text{ s}$$

22. Given, height of nozzle from floor, $H = 9.8$ m

Let, t_1 = time taken by first drop to reach the ground and t_2 = time taken by 2nd drop.

$$t_2 = \frac{t_1}{2}$$

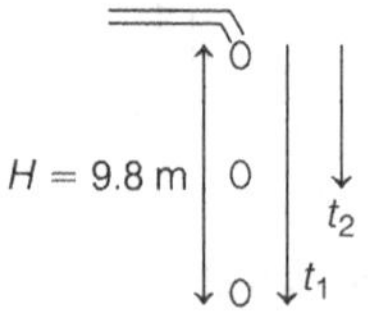

g = acceleration due to gravity (9.8 ms^{-2})

$$u = \text{initial speed} = 0$$

Since, $$H = ut + \frac{1}{2}gt_1^2 \quad \text{...(i)}$$

$$\therefore \quad t_1 = \sqrt{\frac{2H}{g}}$$

$$\Rightarrow \quad t_1 = \sqrt{\frac{2 \times 9.8}{9.8}} = \sqrt{2} \text{ s}$$

$$\therefore \quad t_2 = \frac{\sqrt{2}}{2} = \frac{1}{\sqrt{2}} \text{ s}$$

Again from Eq. (i)

Distance covered by 2nd drop,

$$x = \frac{1}{2}gt_2^2$$

$$\therefore \quad x = \frac{1}{2} \times 9.8 \times \left(\frac{1}{\sqrt{2}}\right)^2 = 2.45 \text{m}$$

and position of second drop from ground,

$$H_2 = H_1 - x = 9.8 - 2.45 = 7.35 \text{ m}$$

23. Given, $u_b = 10$ ms, $h = 75$ m

Initial speed of object, $u_a = -10 \text{ ms}^{-1}$

Let the time taken by object to reach ground be t.

As, $$h = ut + \frac{1}{2}gt^2$$

For object a,

$$\Rightarrow \quad 75 = -10t + \frac{1}{2} \times 10 \times t^2 = -10t + 5t^2$$

$$\Rightarrow \quad t^2 - 2t - 15 = 0$$

$$\Rightarrow t^2 - 5t + 3t - 15 = 0$$

$$\Rightarrow t(t-5) + 3(t-5) = 0$$

$$\Rightarrow \quad t = 5, -3$$

$$\therefore \quad t = 5 \text{ s} \quad (\because t \neq -\text{ve})$$

Also, $$u_b = \frac{s}{t}$$

where, s is distance covered by balloon and t is time taken by object to reach ground

$\therefore$ Final height, $h_f = h + s = h + u_b \times t$

$$= 75 + 10 \times 5$$

$$= 75 + 50 = 125 \text{ m}$$

24. Given, distance travelled in 4th second,

$$s_2 = 34.3 \text{ m},$$

Acceleration due to gravity, $g = 9.8 \text{ ms}^{-2}$

Let distance covered by 1st drop in time $t\,(= 4 \text{ s})$ be s_1.

As we know that,

$$s = ut + \frac{1}{2}gt^2 \quad \text{...(i)}$$

where, u = initial speed of drop $= 0 \text{ ms}^{-1}$

$$\Rightarrow \quad s_1 = \frac{1}{2}gt^2 = \frac{1}{2} \times 9.8 \times 4^2$$

$$= \frac{1}{2} \times 9.8 \times 16 = 9.8 \times 8 = 78.4 \text{ m}$$

Now, distance covered by 2nd drop will be s.

$$s = s_1 - s_2 = 78.4 - 34.3 = 44.1 \text{ m}$$

Again, By using Eq. (i)

$$s = \frac{1}{2} 9.8 t'^2$$

where, t' is the time taken by 2nd drop to cover 44.1 m.

$$\therefore \quad 44.1 = 4.9t'^2 \Rightarrow t'^2 = \frac{44.1}{4.9}$$

$$\Rightarrow \quad t' = \sqrt{\frac{441}{49}} = \sqrt{9} = 3 \text{ s} \quad \text{...(ii)}$$

Since, time taken by 1st drop is 4 s, and time taken by 2nd drop is 3 s, so one drop is falling per second.

25. By using first equation of motion,

$$v_1 = u + a_1t_1$$

$$\Rightarrow \quad v_1 = a_1t_1 \quad \text{... (i)}$$

and for second case,

$$v_2 = v_1 - a_2t_2$$

$$\Rightarrow \quad 0 = v_1 - a_2t_2$$

$$\Rightarrow \quad v_1 = a_2t_2 \quad \text{...(ii)}$$

On dividing Eq. (i) by Eq. (ii), we get

$$v_1 / v_1 = 1 = \frac{a_1t_1}{a_2t_2}$$

$$\Rightarrow \quad a_2t_2 = a_1t_1 \Rightarrow t_1 / t_2 = a_2 / a_1$$

26. Let the total height of building be x.

$$TA = 5 \text{ m} \Rightarrow TB = 25 \text{ m}$$

$$\therefore \quad AG = x - 5 \quad \text{and} \quad BG = x - 25$$

Since, $s = ut + 1/2gt^2$

where, $g = 10 \text{ ms}^{-2}$

$$\therefore \quad 5 = 0 + 1/2 \times 10t^2 \Rightarrow t = 1 \text{ s}$$

Thus, $v_A = u + gt = 0 + 10 = 10 \text{ ms}^{-1}$

From second equation of motion,

$$x - 5 = v_At + 1/2gt^2 \quad \text{... (i)}$$

Similarly, $x - 25 = 1/2gt^2$

Put the above value in Eq. (i), we get

$$x - 5 = 10t + x - 25$$

$$20 = 10t \Rightarrow t = 2\text{s}$$

Put the value of t in Eq. (i), we get

$$x - 5 = 10 \times 2 + 1/2 \times 10 \times 4$$

$$\Rightarrow \quad x - 5 = 20 + 20$$

$$\Rightarrow \quad x = 45 \text{ m}$$

27. Let the length of train be l and the speed of mid-point of train be v'.

Using third equation of motion,

$$\Rightarrow \quad v'^2 = u^2 + 2al/2$$

$$\Rightarrow \quad v'^2 - u^2 = al \quad \text{...(i)}$$

Also, $v^2 - u^2 = 2al$

$$\Rightarrow \quad a = \frac{v^2 - u^2}{2l}$$

From Eq. (i), we get

$$v'^2 - u^2 = \frac{v^2 - u^2}{2l} \cdot l = \frac{v^2 - u^2}{2}$$

$$\Rightarrow \quad v' = \sqrt{\frac{v^2 - u^2}{2} + u^2}$$

$$= \sqrt{\frac{v^2 + u^2}{2}}$$

28. Given,

$$m_1 = m_2 = m$$

$$r_1 = r_2 = r = 5 \text{ cm} = 5 \times 10^{-2} \text{ m}$$

$$u_1 = u_2 = 35 \text{ m/s}$$

$$t_1 = 0 \text{ and } t_2 = 3 \text{ s}$$

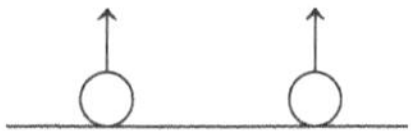

When both ball will collide,

$$(S_1)_{\text{vertical}} = (S_2)_{\text{vertical}} \quad \text{...(i)}$$

Let after time t both ball will collide.

$$(S_1)_{\text{vertical}} = u_1t - \frac{1}{2}gt^2$$

$$(S_2)_{\text{vertical}} = u_2(t-3) - \frac{1}{2}g(t-3)^2$$

From Eq. (i), we have

$$\Rightarrow \quad u_1t - \frac{1}{2}gt^2 = u_2(t-3) - \frac{1}{2}g(t-3)^2$$

$$\Rightarrow \quad 35t - \frac{1}{2} \times 10 \times t^2 \Rightarrow t = 5 \text{ s}$$

So, the height at which ball will collide is

$$(S_1)_{\text{vertical}} = u_1t - \frac{1}{2}gt^2$$

$$= 35 \times 5 - \frac{1}{2} \times 10 \times (5)^2$$

$$= 175 - 125 = 50 \text{ m}$$

CHAPTER~06

PROJECTILE MOTION

LEVEL 01 Starter Level

6.1 Ground-to-Ground Projectile

1 A particle is projected with speed 10 m/s at an angle 60° with horizontal. Find
(a) time of flight,
(b) range,
(c) maximum height,
(d) speed of particle after one second
(e) and velocity when height of the particle is 1 m.

2 A body is projected with a speed of 30 ms^{-1} at an angle of 30° with the vertical. Find the maximum height, time of flight and the horizontal range of the motion. [Take, $g = 10 \text{ m/s}^2$]

3 The velocity of projection of a projectile is given by $\mathbf{u} = 5\hat{\mathbf{i}} + 10\hat{\mathbf{j}}$. Find
(a) time of flight, (b) maximum height
(c) and range.

4 A particle is projected with velocity 20 m/s at an angle of 45° with horizontal. Find out
(a) for which angle is T maximum, $T_{max} = ?$
(b) for which angle is R maximum, $R_{max} = ?$

5 Two bodies are projected at angles θ and $(90° - \theta)$ to the horizontal with the same speed. Find the ratio of their
(a) times of flight (b) maximum heights
(c) and horizontal ranges.

6 A body is so projected in the air that the horizontal range covered by the body is equal to the vertical height attained by the body. Find the angle of projection.

7 A projectile can have the same range R for two angles of projections.
(a) If T_1 and T_2 be the times of flight in two cases, then find out relation between T_1, T_2 and R.
(b) If H_1 and H_2 are maximum heights in two cases, find the sum of the maximum heights.
(c) Find product of H_1 and H_2.

8 A cricketer can throw a ball to a maximum horizontal distance of 100 m. How much high above the ground can the cricketer throw the same ball?

9 The equation of a projectile is $y = \sqrt{3}x - \frac{1}{2}gx^2$, find the angle of projection and also find the speed of projection.

10 A ball is thrown upward at an angle of 45° with the horizontal and lands on the top edge of a building that is 20 m away. The top edge is 12 m above the throwing point. Find the initial speed of the ball in m/s. (Take, $g = 10 \text{ m/s}^2$)

11 Find the value of θ in the diagram given below, so that the projectile can hit the target.

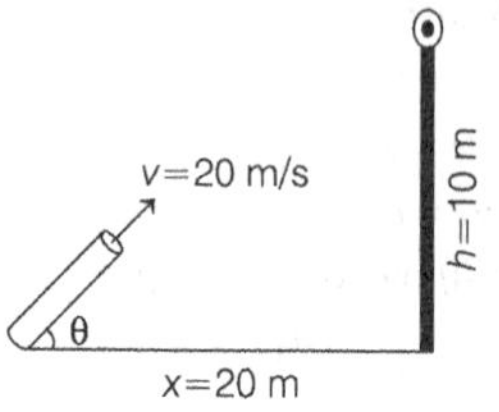

12 A projectile is thrown with a speed of 100 m/s making an angle of 60° with the horizontal. Find the time after which its inclination with the horizontal is 45°.

13 A stone is thrown with a velocity u at an angle α with horizontal. Find its speed when it makes an angle β with the horizontal.

14 A particle is thrown with initial speed u at an angle θ w.r.t. horizontal. Find the time after which velocity of the projectile becomes perpendicular to the initial velocity.

15 A large number of bullets are fired in all directions with the same speed v. What is the maximum area on the ground on which these bullets will spread?

16 A particle is projected at an angle of 30° w.r.t. horizontal speed 20 m/s. Find

(a) the position vector of the particle after 1 s.

(b) the angle between velocity vector and position vector at $t = 1$s.

17 A player kicks a football at an angle of 45° with an initial speed of 20 m/s. A second player on the goal line 60 m away in the direction of kick starts running to receive the ball at that instant. Find the speed of the second player with which he should run to catch the ball before it hits the ground. [Take, $g = 10 \text{ m/s}^2$]

18 A man is sitting on the shore of a river. He is in the line of a 1.0 m long boat and is 5.5 m away from the centre of the boat. He wishes to throw an apple into the boat. If he can throw the apple only with a speed of 10 m/s, find the minimum and maximum angles of projection for successful shot. Assume that, the point of projection and the edge of the boat are in the same horizontal level.

19 A ball is thrown from ground level so as to just clear a wall 4 m high at a distance of 4 m and falls at a distance of 14 m from the wall. Find the magnitude and direction of initial velocity of the ball.

6.2 Projection from Certain Height

1 A projectile is fired horizontally with a speed of 98 ms^{-1} from the top of a hill 490 m high. Find (a) the time taken to reach the ground, (b) the distance of the target from the hill (c) and the velocity with which the projectile hits the ground. (Take, $g = 9.8 \text{ m/s}^2$)

2 Two stones A and B are projected simultaneously from the top of a 100 m high tower. Stone B is projected horizontally with speed 10 m/s and stone A is dropped from the tower. Find out the following (Take, $g = 10 \text{ m/s}^2$)

(a) time of flight of the two stones,

(b) distance between two stones after 3 s,

(c) angle of strike of B with ground

(d) and horizontal range of particle B.

3 Two paper screens A and B are separated by a distance of 100 m. A bullet pierced A and then B. The hole in B is 10 cm below the hole in A. If the bullet is travelling horizontally at the time of hitting the screen A, calculate the velocity of the bullet when it hits the screen A. Neglect the resistance of paper and air.

4 A motorcycle stunt rider rides off the edge of a cliff. Just at the edge his velocity is horizontal with magnitude 9.0 m/s. Find the motorcycle's position, distance from the edge of the cliff and velocity after 0.5 s.

5 An object is thrown between two tall buildings 180 m from each other. The object is thrown horizontally from a window 55 m above ground from one building to a window 10.9 m above ground in the other building. Find out the speed of projection. (Use, $g = 9.8 \text{ m/s}^2$)

6 From the top of a 11 m high tower, a stone is projected with speed 10 m/s at an angle of 37° as shown in figure. Find

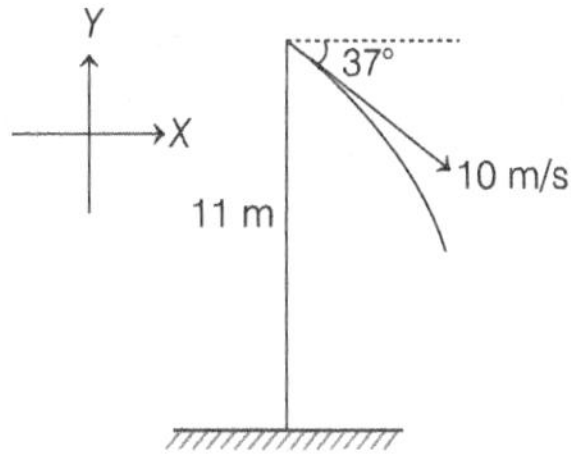

(a) time of flight,

(b) horizontal range

(c) and speed just before striking the ground.

7 From the top of a 11 m high tower, a stone is projected with speed 10 m/s at an angle of 37° as shown in figure. Find

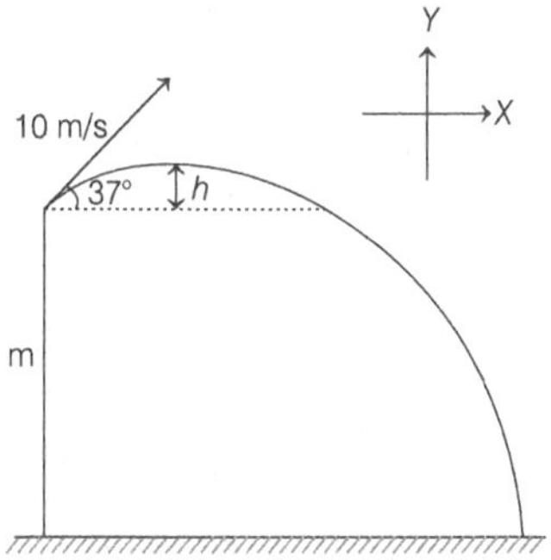

(a) speed after 2 s,

(b) time of flight,

(c) horizontal range,

(d) the maximum height attained by the particle

(e) and speed just before striking the ground.

8 An object is thrown horizontally from a point A from a tower and hits the ground 3 s later at B. The line from A to B makes an angle of 30° with the horizontal. Find the initial velocity of the object. (Take, $g = 10 \text{ m/s}^2$)

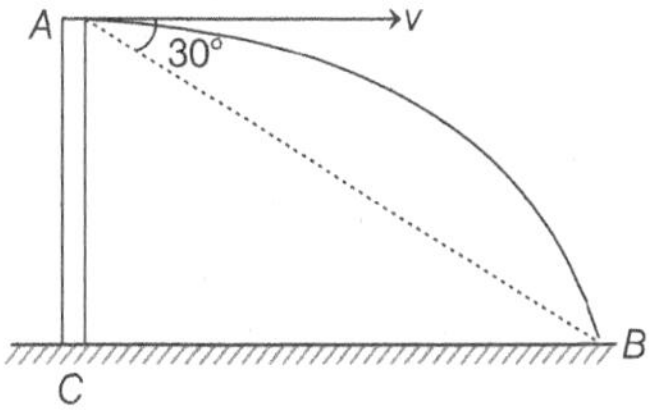

9 A body is projected horizontally from the top of a tower with initial velocity 18 ms^{-1}. It hits the ground at angle 45°. What is the vertical component of velocity when it strikes the ground?

10 A bomber flying upward at an angle of 53° with the vertical releases a bomb at an altitude of 800 m. The bomb strikes the ground 20 s after its release. Find
(a) the velocity of the bomber at the time of release of the bomb,
(b) the maximum height attained by the bomb,
(c) the horizontal distance travelled by the bomb before it strikes the ground
(d) and the velocity (magnitude and direction) of the bomb just when it strikes the ground.
[Given, $\sin 53° = 0.8$, $g = 10\ ms^{-2}$]

6.3 Projection on Inclined Plane

1 A bullet is fired from the bottom of the incline plane with speed 50 m/s at an angle $\theta = 37°$ with the inclined plane. The angle of incline is 30° with the horizontal. Find (a) the position of the maximum height of the bullet from inclined plane, (b) time of flight, (c) horizontal range along the incline, (d) for what value of θ will range be maximum (e) and maximum range.

2 A particle is projected horizontally with speed u from the top of a plane inclined at an angle θ with horizontal. How far from the point of projection will the particle strike the plane?

3 A projectile is thrown at an angle θ with an inclined plane of inclination β as shown in figure. Find the relation between β and θ, if
(a) projectile strikes the inclined plane perpendicularly
(b) and projectile strikes the inclined plane horizontally.

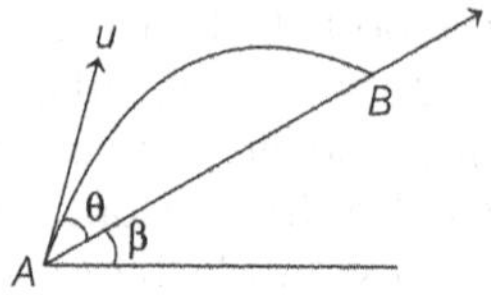

4 A particle is projected at an angle θ with an inclined plane making an angle β with the horizontal as shown in figure. Initial speed of the particle is u. After time t, find

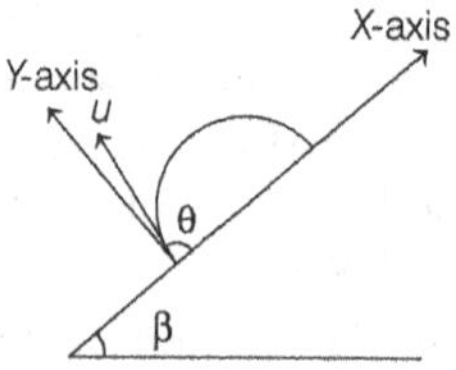

(a) x-component of acceleration,
(b) y-component of acceleration,
(c) x-component of velocity,
(d) y-component of velocity,
(e) x-component of displacement,
(f) y-component of displacement
(g) and y-component of velocity when particle is at maximum distance from the incline plane.

LEVEL 02 JEE Main Level

Single Choice Correct Questions

1 The horizontal range of a projectile is $4\sqrt{3}$ times its maximum height. Its angle of projection will be
(a) 45° (b) 60°
(c) 90° (d) 30°

2 A particle is projected with a velocity v such that its range on the horizontal plane is twice the greatest height attained by it. The range of the projectile is (where g is acceleration due to gravity)
(a) $\frac{4v^2}{5g}$ (b) $\frac{5v^2}{4g}$ (c) $\frac{v^2}{4g}$ (d) $\frac{4v^2}{\sqrt{5}g}$

3 At what angle with the horizontal should a ball be thrown, so that its range R is related to the time of flight as $R = 5T^2$? (Take, $g = 10\ ms^{-2}$)
(a) 30° (b) 45°
(c) 60° (d) 90°

4 A projectile is thrown with an initial velocity of $\mathbf{v} = a\hat{i} + b\hat{j}$. If the range of projectile is double of maximum height reached by it, then
(a) $a = 2b$ (b) $b = a$ (c) $b = 2a$ (d) $b = 4a$

5 A stone is thrown at an angle θ to the horizontal reaches a maximum height H, then the time of flight of stone will be
(a) $\sqrt{\frac{2H}{g}}$ (b) $2\sqrt{\frac{2H}{g}}$ (c) $2\sqrt{\frac{2H\sin\theta}{g}}$ (d) $\sqrt{\frac{2H\sin\theta}{g}}$

6 A shot is fired at an angle θ to the horizontal such that it strikes the hill while moving horizontally. Find initial angle of projection θ.

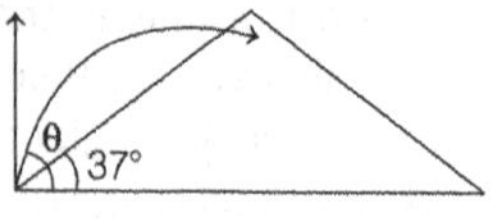

(a) $\tan\theta = \frac{2}{5}$ (b) $\tan\theta = \frac{3}{8}$
(c) $\tan\theta = \frac{3}{2}$ (d) None of these

7 Galileo writes that for angles of projection of a projectile at angles $(45° + \theta)$ and $(45° - \theta)$, the horizontal ranges described by the projectile are in the ratio of $(\theta < 45°)$

(a) 2 : 1 (b) 1 : 2 (c) 1 : 1 (d) 2 : 3

8 The range of a particle when launched at an angle of 15° with the horizontal is 1.5 km. What is the range of the projectile when launched at an angle of 45° to the horizontal?

(a) 1.5 km (b) 3.0 km (c) 6.0 km (d) 0.75 km

9 The greatest height to which a man can throw a stone is h. The greatest distance to which he can throw it, will be

(a) $\frac{h}{2}$ (b) h (c) $2h$ (d) $3h$

10 A cricketer can thrown a ball to a maximum horizontal distance of 100 m. The speed with which he throws the ball is (to the nearest integer)

(a) 25 ms^{-1} (b) 42 ms^{-1} (c) 31 ms^{-1} (d) 35 ms^{-1}

11 The ceiling of a hall is 40 m high. For maximum horizontal distance, the angle at which the ball can be thrown with a speed of 56 ms^{-1} without hitting the ceiling of the hall is

(a) 25° (b) 30° (c) 45° (d) 60°

12 Distance between a frog and an insect on a horizontal plane is 10 m. Frog can jump with a maximum speed of $\sqrt{10}$ m/s. Minimum number of jumps require by the frog to catch the insect is (take, $g = 10\ m/s^2$)

(a) 5 (b) 10
(c) 100 (d) 50

13 A projectile is aimed at a mark on a horizontal plane through the point of projection and falls 3 m short when its elevation is 15° but overshoots the mark by 12 m when its elevation is 45°. The angle of elevation to hit the target on the horizontal plane is

(a) 18.5° (b) 26.5°
(c) 30° (d) 37°

14 A particle is fired with velocity u making angle θ with the horizontal. What is the change in velocity when it is at the highest point?

(a) $-u \cos\theta$ (b) u
(c) $-u \sin\theta$ (d) $(u \cos\theta - u)$

15 A body of mass 0.5 kg is projected under gravity with a speed of 98 m/s at an angle of 30° with the horizontal. The magnitude of change in momentum of the body by the time it hits the ground is

(a) 24.5 N-s (b) 49.0 N-s
(c) 98.0 N-s (d) 50.0 N-s

16 A projectile is projected at an angle α (> 45°) with an initial velocity u. The time (t) at which its vertical component of its velocity will be equal to the horizontal component of its velocity is

(a) $\frac{u}{g}(\cos\alpha - \sin\alpha)$ (b) $\frac{u}{g}(\cos\alpha + \sin\alpha)$

(c) $\frac{u}{g}(\sin\alpha - \cos\alpha)$ (d) $\frac{u}{g}(\sin^2\alpha - \cos^2\alpha)$

17 Three projectiles A, B and C are thrown from the same point in the same plane. Their trajectories are shown in the figure, then which of the following statement is true?

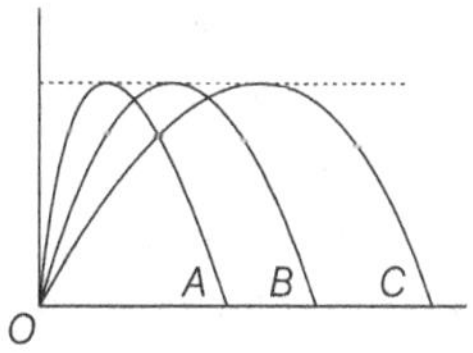

(a) The time of flight is the same for all the three.
(b) The launch speed is greatest for particle C.
(c) The horizontal velocity component is greatest for particle C.
(d) All of the above

18 A projectile is thrown with a speed v at an angle θ with the vertical. Its average velocity between the instants it crosses half the maximum height is

(a) $v \sin\theta$, horizontal and in the plane of projection
(b) $v \cos\theta$, horizontal and in the plane of projection
(c) $2v \sin\theta$, horizontal and perpendicular to the plane of projection
(d) $2v \cos\theta$, vertical and in the plane of projection

19 One second after projection, a stone moves at an angle 45° with horizontal. 2s after projection, it moves horizontally, its angle of projection is [take, $g = 10\ m/s^2$]

(a) $\tan^{-1}(\sqrt{3})$ (b) $\tan^{-1}(4)$

(c) $\tan^{-1}(3)$ (d) $\tan^{-1}(2)$

20 A particle is projected from ground with velocity u at an angle θ to horizontal. Average velocity of particle between point of projection and maximum height of projectile is

(a) $\frac{u}{2}\sqrt{1 + 2\cos^2\theta}$ (b) $\frac{u}{2}\sqrt{1 + \cos^2\theta}$

(c) $\frac{u}{2}\sqrt{1 + 3\cos^2\theta}$ (d) $u \cos\theta$

21 A particle is projected with a velocity u making an angle θ with the horizontal. At any instant, its velocity v is at right angles to its initial velocity u, then v is

(a) $u \cos\theta$ (b) $u \tan\theta$ (c) $u \cot\theta$ (d) $u \sec\theta$

22 A particle is projected from a horizontal floor with speed 10 m/s at an angle 30° with the floor and striking the floor after sometime. State which is correct.

(a) Velocity of particle will be perpendicular to initial direction two seconds after projection.
(b) Minimum speed of particle will be 5 m/s.
(c) Displacement of particle after half second will be $\frac{35}{4}$ m.
(d) None of the above

23 A particle is projected speed 50 m/s at an angle of 53°, find out the time when velocity vector makes an angle of 83° with the initial vector.

(a) $\sqrt{3}$ s (b) $4+\sqrt{3}$ s (c) $4-\sqrt{3}$ s (d) 4 s

24 Velocity of a stone projected, 2 s before it reaches the maximum height, makes angle 53° with the horizontal, then the velocity at highest point will be

(a) 20 m/s (b) 15 m/s (c) 22 m/s (d) $\frac{80}{3}$ m/s

25 A particle is projected from point A with velocity $u\sqrt{2}$ at angle 45° to horizontal as shown in diagram. It strikes the plane BC at right angle. What is the velocity of particle at the time of impact?

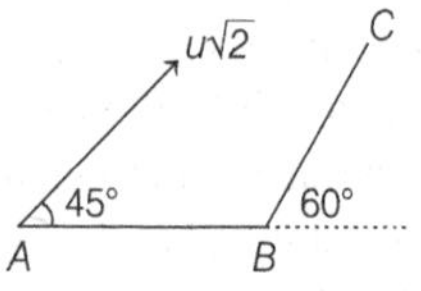

(a) $\frac{\sqrt{3}u}{2}$ (b) $\frac{u}{2}$ (c) $\frac{2u}{\sqrt{3}}$ (d) u

26 In above question, calculate time after which particle strikes the plane.

(a) $\left(\frac{\sqrt{3}+1}{\sqrt{3}}\right)\frac{u}{g}$ (b) $\frac{u}{g}$

(c) $\frac{\sqrt{3}u}{g}$ (d) $\left(\frac{\sqrt{3}}{\sqrt{3}-1}\right)\frac{u}{g}$

27 A cricket ball is hit at 30° with the horizontal with kinetic energy K. The kinetic energy at the highest point is

(a) zero (b) $K/4$ (c) $K/2$ (d) $3K/4$

28 A ball is thrown at an angle θ with the horizontal. Its initial kinetic energy is 100 J and it becomes 75 J at half the maximum height. The angle of projection is

(a) 45° (b) 30°

(c) $\cos^{-1}\left(\frac{3}{4}\right)$ (d) $\tan^{-1}\left(\frac{4}{3}\right)$

29 A stone is projected from the ground with velocity 25 m/s. 2 s later, it just clear a wall 5 m high. The angle of projection of the stone is (Take, g=10 m/s^2)

(a) 30° (b) 45°
(c) 50.2° (d) 60°

30 A stone is projected from the ground with velocity 50 m/s at an angle of 30°. It crosses a wall after 3 s. How far beyond the wall the stone will strike the ground? (Take, $g = 10$ m/s^2)

(a) 90.2 m (b) 89.6 m
(c) 86.6 m (d) 70.2 m

31 A ball is thrown up with a certain velocity at an angle θ to the horizontal. The kinetic energy (KE) of the ball varies with height h as

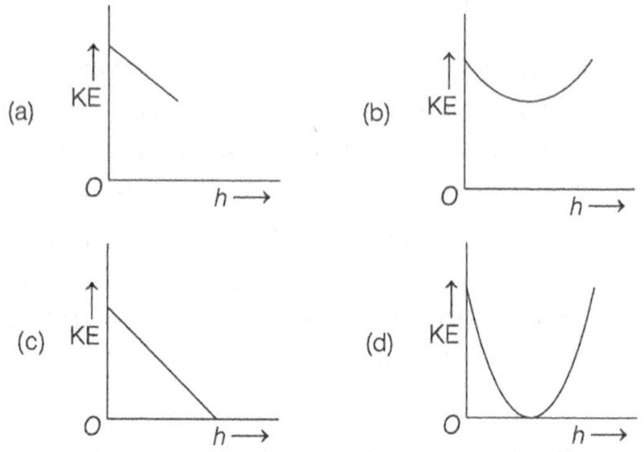

32 A ball is thrown up with a certain velocity at an angle θ to the horizontal. The kinetic energy (KE) of the ball varies with horizontal displacement x as

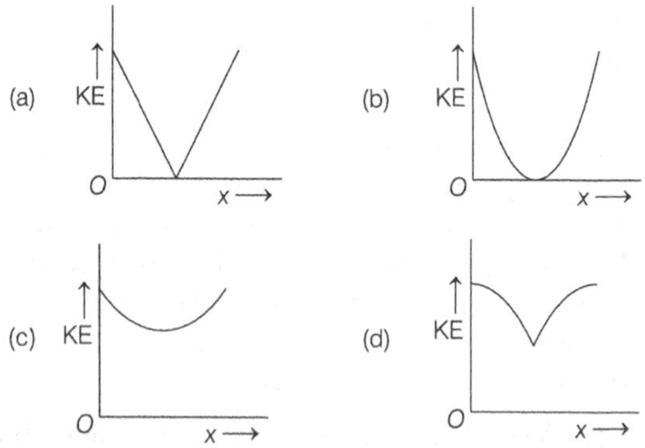

33 Horizontal range and maximum height of a projectile are R and H. If a constant horizontal acceleration $a = \frac{g}{4}$ is given to projectile due to air, then what will be the horizontal range and maximum height of projectile?

(a) $(R + H), \frac{H}{2}$ (b) $\left(R + \frac{H}{2}\right), 2H$

(c) $(R + 2H), H$ (d) $(R + H), H$

34 A particle is projected at an angle of elevation α and after t seconds it appears to have an angle of elevation β as seen from the point of projection. The initial velocity will be

(a) $\frac{2g \sin(\alpha - \beta)}{\cos \beta}$ (b) $\frac{\sin(\alpha - \beta)}{2gt}$

(c) $\frac{gt \cos \beta}{2 \sin(\alpha - \beta)}$ (d) $\frac{gt}{2 \sin(\alpha - \beta)}$

35 An object is projected with a velocity of 20 m/s making an angle of 45° with horizontal. The equation for the trajectory is $h = Ax - Bx^2$, where h is height, x is horizontal distance and A and B are constants. The ratio $A : B$ is (Take, $g = 10 \text{ ms}^{-2}$)

(a) 1 : 5 (b) 5 : 1

(c) 1 : 40 (d) 40 : 1

36 A cricketer hits a ball with a velocity of 25 m/s at 60° above the horizontal. How far above the ground it passes over a fielder 50 m from the bat? (Assume the ball is struck very close to the ground)

(a) 8.2 m (b) 9.0 m

(c) 11.6 m (d) 12.7 m

37 A particle is projected at an angle of 45° from 8 m before the foot of a wall, just touches the top of the wall and falls on the ground of the opposite side at a distance 4 m from it. The height of wall is

(a) $\frac{2}{3}$ m (b) $\frac{4}{3}$ m

(c) $\frac{8}{3}$ m (d) $\frac{3}{4}$ m

38 A stone is just released from the window of a train moving along a horizontal straight track. The stone will hit the ground following a

(a) straight line path (b) circular path

(c) parabolic path (d) hyperbolic path

39 An aeroplane moving horizontally with a speed of 720 km/h drops a food pocket, while flying at a height of 396.9 m. The time taken by a food pocket to reach the ground and its horizontal range is (Take, $g = 9.8 \text{ ms}^{-1}$)

(a) 3 s and 2000 m (b) 5 s and 500 m

(c) 8 s and 1500 m (d) 9 s and 1800 m

40 A body is thrown horizontally from the top of a tower of height 5 m. It touches the ground at a distance of 10 m from the foot of the tower. The initial velocity of the body is (take, $g = 10 \text{ ms}^{-2}$)

(a) 2.5 ms^{-1} (b) 5 ms^{-1}

(c) 10 ms^{-1} (d) 20 ms^{-1}

41 A ball is rolled off the edge of horizontal table at a speed of 4 m/s. It hits the ground after 0.4 s. Which is statement given below is true ?

(a) It hits the ground at a horizontal distance 2.6m from the edge of the table.

(b) The speed with which it hits the ground is 4.0 m/s.

(c) Height of the table is 0.8 m.

(d) It hits the ground at an angle of 60° to the horizontal.

42 A body is projected horizontal from a height with speed 20 m/s. What will be its speed after 5 s? (Take, $g = 10 \text{ m/s}^2$)

(a) 54 m/s (b) 20 m/s

(c) 50 m/s (d) 70 m/s

43 A boy aims at a bird from a point at a horizontal distance of 100 m . The gun can impart a velocity of 500 ms^{-1} to the bullet. At what height above the bird must he aim his gun in order to hit? (Take, $g = 10 \text{ ms}^{-2}$)

(a) 20 cm (b) 40 cm

(c) 50 cm (d) 100 cm

44 From the top of a tower 19.6 m high, a ball is thrown horizontally. If the line joining the point of projection to the point where it hits the ground makes an angle of 45° with the horizontal, then the initial velocity of the ball is

(a) 9.8 ms^{-1} (b) 4.9 ms^{-1}

(c) 14.7 ms^{-1} (d) 2.8 ms^{-1}

45 A ball rolls off the top of a stairway with a horizontal velocity u m/s. If the steps are h metres high and w metres wide, then the ball will just hit the edge of the nth step is

(a) $n = \frac{2hu^2}{gw^2}$ (b) $n = \frac{2hu}{gw}$

(c) $n = \frac{2h^2u^2}{g^2w^2}$ (d) $n = \frac{2h^2}{gu}$

46 From the top of a tower of height h, a body of mass m is projected in the horizontal direction with a velocity v. It falls on the ground at a distance x from the tower. If a body of mass 2 m is projected from the top of another tower of height $2h$ in the horizontal direction so that it falls on the ground at a distance $2x$ from the tower, the horizontal velocity of the second body is

(a) $2v$ (b) $\sqrt{2}v$ (c) $\frac{v}{2}$ (d) $\frac{v}{\sqrt{2}}$

47 A particle is projected upwards from the top of a tower with an initial velocity 40 m/s and angle of projection 30° with the horizontal falls at a distance of $200\sqrt{3}$ from foot of tower. The height of tower is (take, $g = 10 \text{ m/s}^2$)

(a) 160 m (b) 200 m (c) 300 m (d) None of these

48 A body has an initial velocity of 3 ms^{-1} and has an acceleration of 1 ms^{-2} normal to the direction of the initial velocity. Then its velocity, 4 s after the start is

(a) 7 ms^{-1} along the direction of initial velocity

(b) 7 ms^{-1} along the normal to the direction of the initial velocity

(c) 7 ms^{-1} mid-way between the two directions

(d) 5 ms^{-1} at an angle of $\tan^{-1}\frac{4}{3}$ with the direction of the initial velocity

49 The trajectory of a projectile fired horizontally with velocity u is parabola given by

(a) $y = \frac{g}{2u^2}x^2$ (b) $y = \frac{g}{u^2}x^2$

(c) $x = \frac{g}{2u^2}y^2$ (d) $x = \frac{g}{u^2}y^2$

50 A ball is projected upwards from the top of tower with a velocity 50 ms^{-1} making an angle 30° with the horizontal. The height of tower is 70 m. After how many second from the instant of throwing will the ball reach the ground?

(a) 2 s (b) 5 s (c) 7 s (d) 9 s

51 At what speed (in m/s) must a pebble be thrown at a height of $h = 1.6$ m and at an angle of 30° with the horizontal, if it is to hit the ground at angle of 45°?

(a) 5 m/s (b) 8 m/s

(c) 10 m/s (d) 12 m/s

52 A ball is projected from the top of a tower with a velocity $3\hat{i} + 4\hat{j} + 5\hat{k}$ ms^{-1}, where $\hat{i}$, $\hat{j}$ and $\hat{k}$ are unit vectors along east, north and vertical upwards, respectively. If the height of the tower is 30 m, its range is ($g = 10$ ms^2)

(b) 12 m (b) 9 m (c) 15 m (d) 25 m

53 Two bodies are thrown simultaneously from the same point. One straight up and the other at an angle θ to the horizontal. The initial speed of each body is equal to u. The distance between the two besides t seconds later is

(a) $ut\sqrt{2(1+\sin\theta)}$ (b) $ut\sqrt{2(1-\sin\theta)}$

(c) $ut\sqrt{2(1+\cot\theta)}$ (d) $\sqrt{2ut(1-\sin\theta)}$

54 A plane surface is inclined making an angle θ with the horizontal. From the bottom of this inclined plane, a bullet is fired with velocity v. The maximum possible range of the bullet on the inclined plane is

(a) $\frac{v^2}{g}$ (b) $\frac{v^2}{g(1+\sin\theta)}$

(c) $\frac{v^2}{g(1-\sin\theta)}$ (d) $\frac{v^2}{g(1+\cos\theta)}$

55 A ball is horizontally projected with a speed v from the top of a plane inclined at an angle 45° with the horizontal. How far from the point of projection will the ball strike the plane?

(a) $\frac{v^2}{g}$ (b) $\frac{\sqrt{2}v^2}{g}$

(c) $\frac{2v^2}{g}$ (d) $\frac{2\sqrt{2}v^2}{g}$

56 A particle is projected at angle 37° with the incline plane in upward direction with speed 10 m/s. The angle of incline plane is 53°, then the maximum distance from the incline plane attained by the particle will be

(a) 3 m (b) 4 m

(c) 5 m (d) zero

57 On an inclined plane of inclination 30°, a ball is thrown at an angle of 60° with the horizontal from the foot of the incline with a velocity of $10\sqrt{3}$ ms^{-1}. If $g = 10$ ms^{-2}, then the time in which ball will hit the inclined plane is

(a) 1 s (b) 6 s

(c) 2 s (d) 4 s

58 A projectile is fired at an angle θ with the horizontal. Find the condition under which it lands perpendicular on an inclined plane of inclination α as shown in figure.

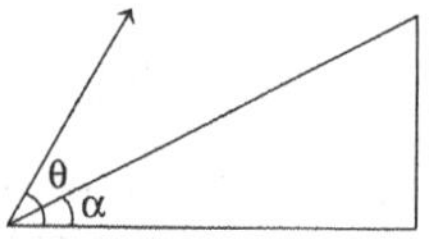

(a) $\sin\alpha = \cos(\theta - \alpha)$

(b) $\cos\alpha = \sin(\theta - \alpha)$

(c) $\tan\theta = \cot(\theta - \alpha)$

(d) $2\tan\alpha = \cot(\theta - \alpha)$

Numerical Value Questions

1 The speed of a particle when it is at its greatest height is $\sqrt{\frac{3}{5}}$ times of its speed when it is at its one-third of the maximum height. If the angle of projection is $\frac{2\pi}{n}$, then find the value of n.

2 A stone is thrown horizontally from a tower. In 0.5 s after the stone began to move, the numerical value of its velocity was 1.5 times its initial velocity. If the initial velocity of stone is $\sqrt{p}$ m/s, find the value of p. [Take, $g = 10$ m/s^2]

3 A bullet is fired with speed 50 m/s at 45° angle, find the height (in m) of the bullet when its direction of motion makes angle 30° with the horizontal. [Take, $g = 10 \text{ m/s}^2$]

4 A ball is projected at an angle of 37° above with the horizontal from the top of a tower and strikes the ground in 7 s at an angle of 45° with the horizontal. Find the height (in m) of the tower. [Take, $g = 10 \text{ m/s}^2$]

5 A projectile is thrown with speed u making angle θ with horizontal at $t = 0$. It just crosses the two points at equal height at time $t = 1$ s and $t = 3$ s, respectively. Calculate maximum height attained by it. [Take, $g = 10 \text{ m/s}^2$]

6 A building 7.5 m high and $2b$ meters wide has a flat roof. A ball is projected from a point on the horizontal ground 28.4 m away from the building along its width. If projected with velocity 20 m/s at an angle of 45° with the ground, the ball hits the roof in the middle, find the width $2b$ (in m). [Take, $g = 10 \text{ m/s}^2$]

7 A gun kept on a straight horizontal road is used to hit a car, travelling along the same road away from the gun with a uniform speed of 72 km/h. The car is at a distance of 120 m from the gun, when the gun is fired at an angle of 37° with the horizontal. Find the speed (in m/s) of projection of the shell from the gun. [Take, $g = 10 \text{ m/s}^2$]

8 A particle is projected from point P with velocity $5\sqrt{2}$ ms^{-1} perpendicular to the surface of a hollow right angle cone whose axis is vertical. It collides at Q normally, find the time of the flight (in s) of the particle.

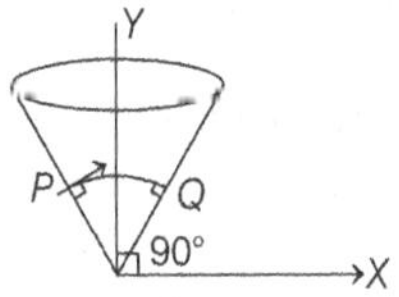

9 A shell is fired from point O on the level ground with velocity 50 m/s at an angle 53°. A hill of uniform slope 37° starts from point A that is 100 m away from the point O as shown in the figure. Calculate the time of flight (in seconds).

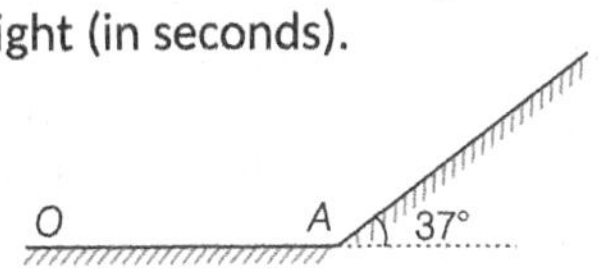

10 A body is projected with speed $40\sqrt{2}$ m/s at an angle of 45° with horizontal. If displacement of the particle in the 4th second is $5\sqrt{x}$, then find the value of x.

11 A particle is projected with speed 30 m/s at angle of 22.5° with horizontal from ground as shown in figure. AB and CD are parallel to Y-axis and B is the highest point of trajectory of the particle. Find the ratio of $\frac{CD}{AB}$.

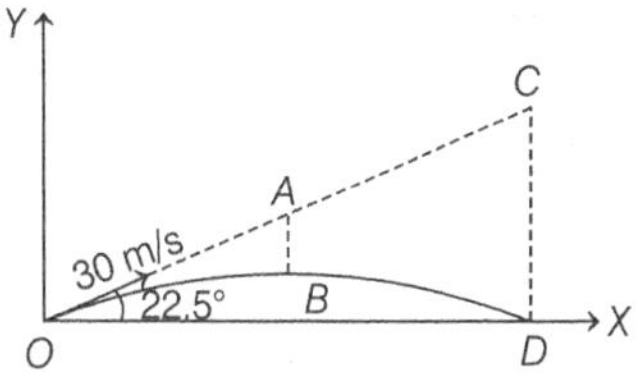

12 A particle is projected from a point O with an initial speed of 30 m/s to pass through a point which is 40 m from O horizontally and 10 m above. There are two angles of projection with horizontal for which this is possible. If these angles are α and β, then find the value of $\tan[-\{\alpha + \beta\}]$.

13 A particle is projected upwards with a velocity of 100 m/s at an angle of 60° with the vertical. Find the time when the particle will move perpendicular to its initial direction. [Take, $g = 10 \text{ m/s}^2$]

14 A ball is projected on smooth inclined plane in direction perpendicular to line of greatest slope with velocity of 8 m/s. Find its speed (in m/s) after 1 s.

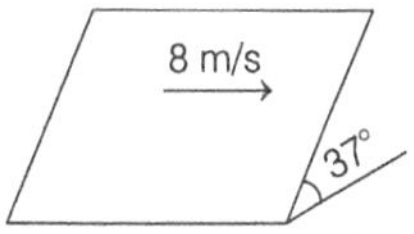

15 A projectile is fired into the air from the edge of a 100 m high cliff at angle of 37° above the horizontal. The projectile hits a target 400 m away from the base of the cliff. If initial velocity of the projectile v_0 is $x\sqrt{5}$ m/s, then find the value of x. (Neglect air friction and assume X-axis to be horizontal and Y-axis to be vertical).

16 Find range of projectile on the inclined plane which is projected perpendicular to the inclined plane with velocity 20 m/s as shown in figure.

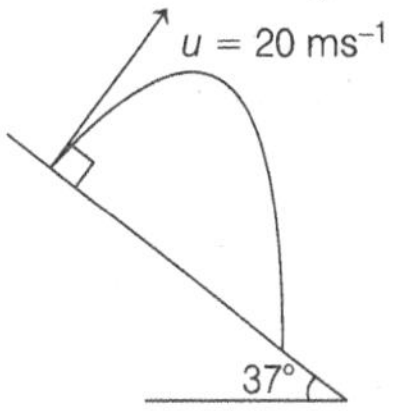

17 A particle starts from the origin at $t = 0$ and moves in the xy-plane with constant acceleration a in the y-direction. Its equation of motion is $y = bx^2$. If the x component of its velocity is given by $\sqrt{\frac{a}{nb}}$, then calculate the value of n.

18 A is the highest point on the path of a projectile and average velocity of the projectile between O and A is $8\hat{i}+3\hat{j}$. If $\tan\alpha$ is given by $\frac{n}{4}$, then calculate the value of n.

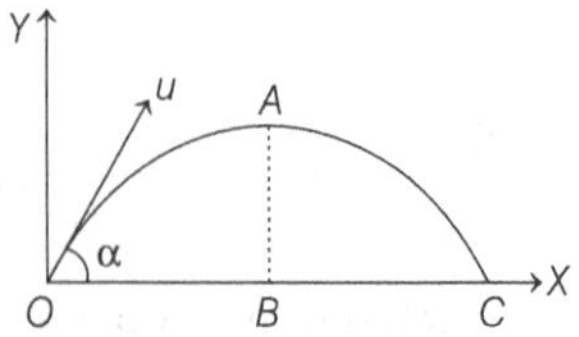

19 A cylinder is placed on a horizontal surface. A particle is projected with speed u and it crosses the cylinder by just touching it at two points as shown in figure. Then, the initial speed with which the mass projected is $\sqrt{5x}$ m/s. Find the value of x.

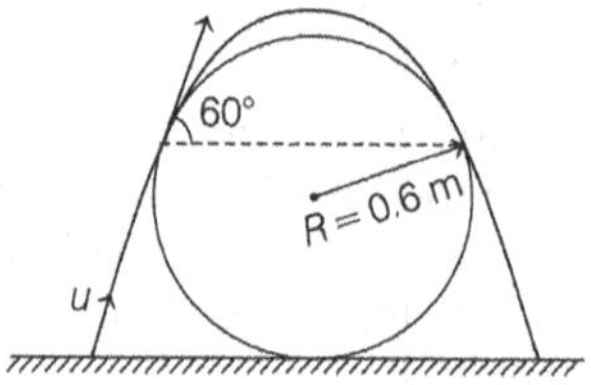

20 Two cliffs of height 120 m and 100.4 m are separated by a horizontal distance of 16m. If a car has to reach from the first cliff to the second, find the minimum horizontal velocity (in m/s) of car.

LEVEL 03 JEE Advanced Level

Single Choice Correct Questions

1 A projectile is thrown with velocity $10\sqrt{2}$ m/s at an angle 45° to horizontal. Calculate time interval between the moments when velocity is $\sqrt{125}$ m/s. (Take, $g = 10$ m/s^2)

(a) 1.0 s (b) 1.5 s
(c) 2.0 s (d) 0.5 s

2 An object is projected so that it just clears two vertical walls each of height 7.5 m and separation 50 m. If time of passing between the two walls is 2.5 s, then find horizontal range of the object.

(a) 70 m
(b) 75 m
(c) 105 m
(d) 150 m

3 A fixed rifle is aimed at a point on a vertical wall 1440 m horizontally away and 1080 m high above the point of the rifle end. A bullet is fired at 150 m/s towards the target. 10 s after the firing, the gravitational field vanishes. At what height from ground the bullet will hit the vertical wall? ($g = 10$ m/s^2)

(a) 400 m (b) 420 m
(c) 380 m (d) 250 m

4 A shot is fired with a velocity u at a very high vertical wall whose distance from the point of projection is x. The greatest height above the level of the point of project at which the bullet can hit the wall is

(a) $\frac{u^4+g^2x^2}{2gu^2}$ (b) $\frac{u^4-g^2x^2}{gu^2}$
(c) $\frac{u^4-g^2x^2}{4gu^2}$ (d) $\frac{u^4-g^2x^2}{2gu^2}$

5 A stone projected at an angle of 60° from the ground level strikes at an angle of 30° on the roof of a building of height h, then the speed of projection of the stone is

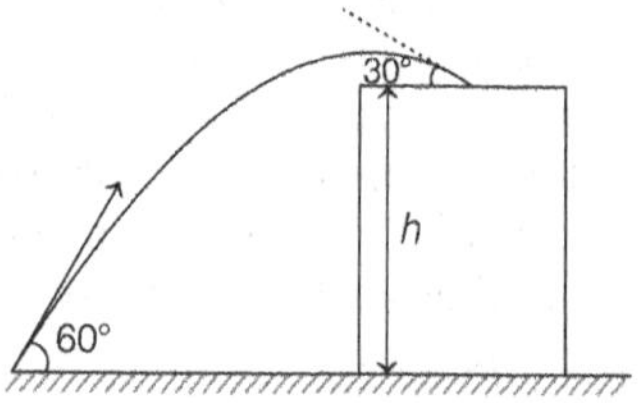

(a) $\sqrt{2gh}$ (b) $\sqrt{6gh}$
(c) $\sqrt{3gh}$ (d) $\sqrt{gh}$

6 A ball is thrown eastward across level ground. A wind blows horizontally to the east and assume that the effect of wind is to provide is constant force to the east, equal in magnitude to the weight of the ball. The angle θ (with respect to horizontal) at which the ball should be projected, so that it travels maximum horizontal distance is

(a) 45° (b) 37°
(c) 53° (d) 67.5°

7 If 4 s be the time in which a projectile reaches a point P of the its path and 5 s the time from P till it reaches the horizontal plane through the point of projection. The height of P above the horizontal plane will be [take, $g = 9.8$ m/s^2]

(a) 98 m (b) 49 m
(c) 196 m (d) 147 m

8 From the ground level, a ball is to be shot with a certain speed. Graph shows the range R it will have *versus* the launch angle θ. The least speed the ball will have during its flight, if θ is chosen such that the flight time is half of its maximum possible value, is equal to (take, $g = 10\text{ m/s}^2$)

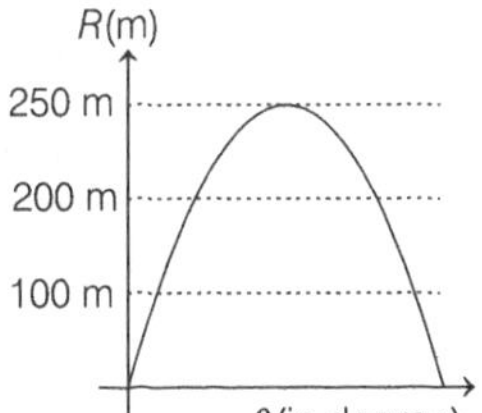

(a) 250 m/s (b) $50\sqrt{3}$ m/s

(c) 50 m/s (d) $25\sqrt{3}$ m/s

9 From the top of a tower, two balls are thrown horizontally with velocities u_1 and u_2 in opposite directions. If their velocities are perpendicular to each other just before they strike the ground, then find the height of tower.

(a) $\frac{u_1u_2}{2g}$ (b) $\frac{2u_1u_2}{g}$

(b) $\frac{4u_1u_2}{g}$ (d) $\frac{u_1u_2}{4g}$

10 A particle move along the parabolic path $x = y^2 + 2y + 2$ in such a way that the y-component of velocity vector remains 5 m/s during the motion. The magnitude of the acceleration of the particle is

(a) 50 m/s^2 (b) 100 m/s^2

(c) $10\sqrt{2}\text{ m/s}^2$ (d) 0.1 m/s^2

11 A stone is projected horizontally with speed 10 m/s from a height h above ground. A horizontal wind is blowing in direction opposite to velocity of projection and gives the stone a constant horizontal acceleration 10 m/s^2 (in direction opposite to initial velocity). As a result, the stone falls on ground at a point vertically below of projection. Then, the value of height h is (take, $g = 10\text{ m/s}^2$)

(a) 10 m (b) 20 m

(c) 50 m (d) None of these

12 A projectile is required to hit a target whose coordinates relative to the horizontal and vertical axes through the point of projection are (α, β). If the projection velocity is $\sqrt{2g\alpha}$, it is impossible to hit the target, if

(a) $\beta < \frac{3}{4}\alpha$ (b) $\beta < \frac{1}{4}\alpha$

(c) $\beta > \frac{3}{4}\alpha$ (d) $\beta > \frac{1}{4}\alpha$

13 Two projectiles are projected with velocity v_A, v_B at an angle θ_A (from horizontal) and θ_B (from vertical) as shown in the figure below, such that $v_A > v_B$ but having same horizontal component of velocity. Which of the following cannot be correct?

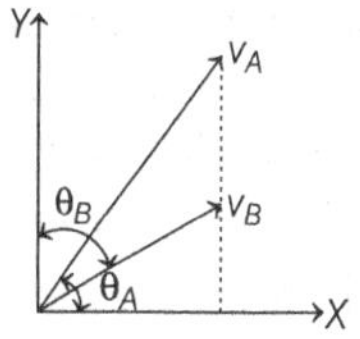

(a) $T_A > T_B$ (b) $H_A > H_B$

(c) $R_A > R_B$ (d) $R_B > R_A$

14 A particle is projected with a velocity 20 m/s, so that it just clears two walls of equal height 10 m which are at a distance 20 m apart. Find the time (in seconds) of passing between the walls.

(a) $\sqrt{2}$ s (b) 2 s

(c) $\frac{2}{\sqrt{3}}$ s (d) None of these

15 Speed of ground-to-ground projectile at height h from ground is half of its speed at height $\frac{h}{2}$ from ground. Find the maximum range possible for the projectile with the same speed.

(a) $\frac{13h}{4}$ (b) $\frac{7h}{3}$ (c) $\frac{15h}{7}$ (d) None of these

16 For a projectile launched upwards from level ground, with initial velocity u and angle of projection 30° with vertical, height of projectile above ground will be greater than horizontal distance covered upto time

(a) $\frac{u}{g\sqrt{3}}$ (b) $\frac{u}{g\sqrt{2}}$

(c) $\frac{u}{g}(\sqrt{3} - 1)$ (d) None of these

17 A ball is thrown with a velocity whose horizontal component is 12 ms^{-1} from a point 15 m above the ground and 6 m away from a vertical wall 18.75 m high in such a way to just clear the wall. At what time (in seconds) will the ball reach the ground? [Take, $g = 10\text{ ms}^{-2}$]

(a) 1 (b) 2 (c) 3 (d) 4

18 A particle at a height h from the ground is projected with an angle 30° from the horizontal, it strikes the ground making an angle 45° with horizontal. It is again projected from the same point at height h with the same speed but with an angle of 60° with horizontal. Find the angle it makes with the horizontal when it strikes the ground.

(a) $\tan^{-1}(4)$ (b) $\tan^{-1}(5)$

(c) $\tan^{-1}(\sqrt{5})$ (d) $\tan^{-1}(\sqrt{3})$

19 A projectile of mass 2 kg has velocities 3 m/s and 4 m/s at two points during its flight in the uniform gravitational field of the earth. If these two velocities are perpendicular to each other, then the minimum kinetic energy of particle during its fight is

(a) 7 J (b) 25 J (c) 16.32 J (d) 5.76 J

20 A particle is projected from the horizontal *xz*-plane, in vertical *xy*-plane where *X*-axis is horizontal and positive *Y*-axis vertically upwards. The graph of *y* coordinate of the particle *versus* time is as shown in figure. The range of the particle is $\sqrt{3}$ m, then the speed of the projected particle is

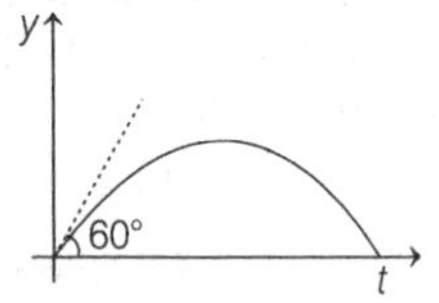

(a) $\sqrt{3}$ m/s (b) $\sqrt{\frac{403}{4}}$ m/s

(c) $2\sqrt{5}$ m/s (d) $\sqrt{28}$ m/s

21 Two balls are thrown with the same speed v_0 from the top of a cliff. The angle of their initial velocities are θ above and below the horizontal, as shown in figure. How much farther along the ground does the top ball hit than that of the bottom ball?

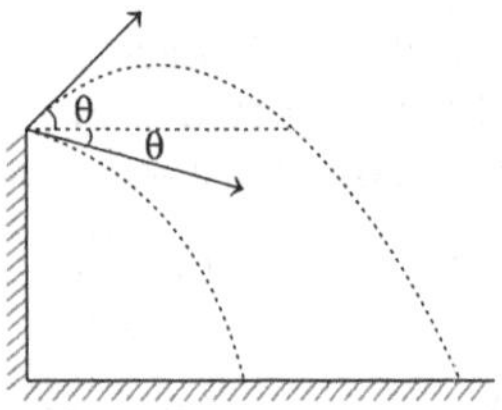

(a) $\frac{v_0^2 \sin^2 2\theta}{2g}$ (b) $\frac{2v_0^2 \sin 2\theta}{g}$

(c) $\frac{2v_0^2 \cos\theta}{g}$ (d) $\frac{v_0^2 \sin 2\theta}{g}$

22 A ball is projected from origin with speed 20 m/s at an angle 30° with *X*-axis. The *X*-coordinate of the ball at the instant when the velocity of the ball becomes perpendicular to the velocity of projection will be

(a) $40\sqrt{3}$ m (b) 40 m

(c) $20\sqrt{3}$ m (d) 20 m

23 A particle is projected from a point (0, 1) on *Y*-axis (assume +*y* direction vertically upwards) aiming towards a point (4, 9). It fell on ground on *X*-axis in 1 s. Taking , $g = 10\ \text{m/s}^2$ and all coordinate in metres. Find the coordinates of the point where it fell on the *X*-axis.

(a) (3, 0) (b) (4, 0)

(c) (2, 0) (d) $(2\sqrt{5}, 0)$

24 A heavy particle is projected with a velocity *u* at an angle θ with the horizontal into a uniform gravitational field. The slope of the trajectory of the particle varies as

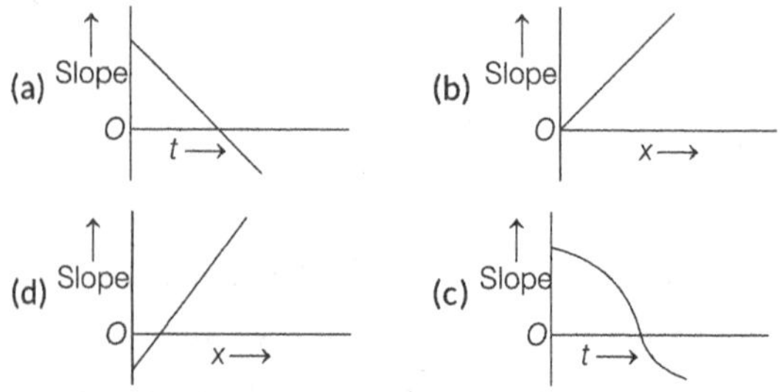

25 A boy *A* is running on a circular track of radius *R*. His friend standing at a point *O* on the circumference of the track is throwing balls at speed $u = \sqrt{gR}$. Balls are being thrown randomly in all possible directions. Find the length of the circumference of the circle on which the boy is completely safe from being hit by a ball.

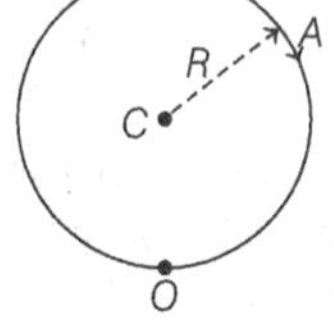

(a) $\frac{\pi R}{3}$ (b) $\frac{2\pi R}{3}$ (c) πR (d) $\frac{4\pi R}{3}$

26 A ball thrown down the incline strikes at a point on the incline 25 m below the horizontal as shown in the figure. If the ball rises to a maximum height of 20 m above the point of projection, the angle of projection α (with horizontal *X*-axis) is

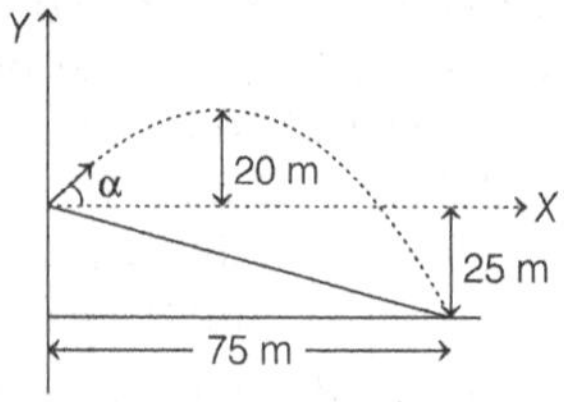

(a) $\tan^{-1}\frac{4}{3}$ (b) $\tan^{-1}\frac{3}{4}$

(c) $\tan^{-1}\frac{3}{2}$ (d) $\tan^{-1}\frac{2}{3}$

27 A bomber plane moving at a horizontal speed of 20 m/s releases a bomb at a height of 80 m above ground as shown in figure. At the same instant, a hunter of negligible height starts running from a point below it, to catch the bomb with speed 10 m/s. After 2s, he realised that he cannot make it, he stops running and immediately holds his gun and fires in such direction so that just before bomb hits the ground, bullet will hit it. What should be the firing speed speed of bullet? (Take, $g = 10\ m/s^2$)

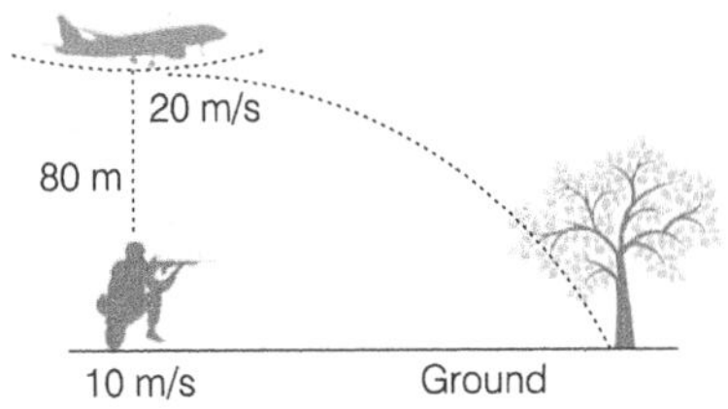

(a) 10 m/s (b) $20\sqrt{10}$ m/s
(c) $10\sqrt{10}$ m/s (d) None of these

28 A projectile is launched from point A with the initial conditions shown in figure. BC part is circular with radius 150 m. Determine the x and y-coordinates of the point of impact.

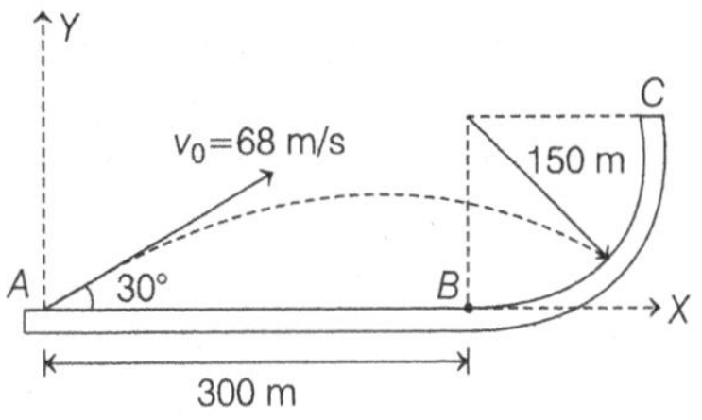

(a) $x = 373$ m, $y = 18.75$ m (b) $x = 393$ m, $y = 15.75$ m
(c) $x = 350$ m, $y = 15$ m (d) $x = 380$ m, $y = 20.55$ m

29 A hunter tries to hunt a monkey with a small, very poisonous arrow, blown from a pipe with initial speed v_0. The monkey is hanging on a branch of a tree at height H above the ground. The hunter is at a distance L from the bottom of the tree. The monkey sees the arrow leaving the blow pipe and immediately loses the grip on the tree, falling freely down with zero initial velocity. The minimum initial speed v_0 of the arrow for hunter to succeed while monkey is in air, is

(a) $\sqrt{\dfrac{g(H^2 + L^2)}{2H}}$ (b) $\sqrt{\dfrac{gH^2}{\sqrt{H^2 + L^2}}}$

(c) $\sqrt{\dfrac{g(H^2 + L^2)}{H}}$ (d) $\sqrt{\dfrac{2gH^2}{\sqrt{H^2 + L^2}}}$

30 A particle is thrown over a triangle from one end of a horizontal base and grazing the vertex falls on the other end of the base. If α and β be the base angles and θ the angle of projection, then

(a) $\tan^2 \theta = \tan^2 \alpha + \tan^2 \beta$
(b) $\tan \theta = \tan \alpha + \tan \beta$
(c) $\tan \theta = \sqrt{\tan \alpha \tan \beta}$
(d) $\tan \theta = \dfrac{\tan \alpha \tan \beta}{\tan \alpha + \tan \beta}$

31 A cannon fires successively two shells with velocity $v_0 = 250$ m/s; the first at the angle $\theta_1 = 53°$ and the second at the angle $\theta_2 = 37°$ to the horizontal, in the same vertical plane. Neglecting the air drag, find the time interval in seconds between firing leading to the collision of the shells. (Take, $g = 10\ m/s^2$)

(a) 5 (b) 10 (c) 20 (d) 25

32 A particle is projected from point A. A fly is sitting at a tower at point B as shown in the figure. When particle passes from B, fly starts flying in horizontal direction with constant speed of 2 m/s. Both will meet at the same horizontal level at point C, then (take, $g = 10\ m/s^2$)

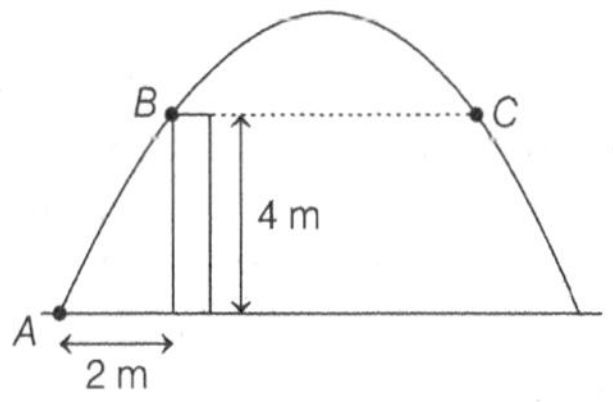

(a) angle of projection is $\tan^{-1}\left(\dfrac{9}{2}\right)$
(b) angle of projection is $\tan^{-1}$ (2)
(c) angle of projection is 45°
(d) None of these

33 Three stones A, B and C are projected from surface of very long inclined plane with equal speeds and different angles of projection as shown in figure. The incline makes an angle θ with horizontal. If H_A, H_B and H_C are maximum height attained by A, B and C respectively above inclined plane, then (neglect air friction)

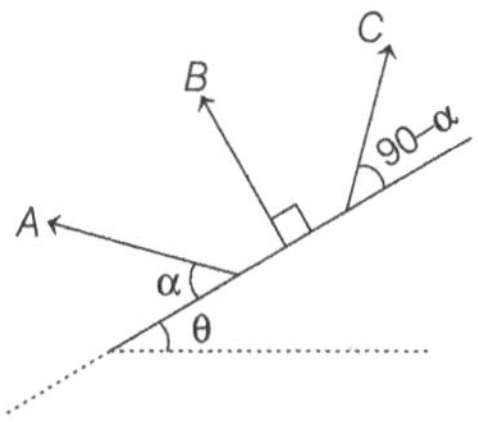

(a) $H_A + H_C = H_B$ (b) $H_A^2 + H_C^2 = H_B^2$
(c) $H_A + H_C = 2H_B$ (d) $H_A^2 + H_C^2 = 2H_B^2$

34 A particle is projected from surface of the inclined plane with speed u and at an angle θ with the horizontal. After sometime, the particle collides elastically with the smooth fixed inclined plane for the first time and subsequently moves in vertical direction. Starting from projection, find the time taken by the particle to reach maximum height. (Neglect time of collision).

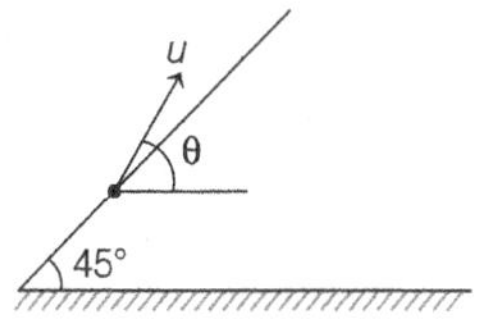

(a) $\dfrac{2u \cos \theta}{2}$ (b) $\dfrac{2u \sin \theta}{g}$

(c) $\dfrac{u(\sin \theta + \cos \theta)}{g}$ (d) $\dfrac{2u}{g}$

35 A ball is projected horizontally from a table such that it collides with the wall and then with ground. After collision, component of velocity perpendicular to the surface is reversed in direction without change in magnitude and component of velocity parallel to surface remains unchanged. At what distance from the wall does the ball collide with the ground? ($H = 500$ m, $v_0 = 20$ m/s and $D = 140$ m)

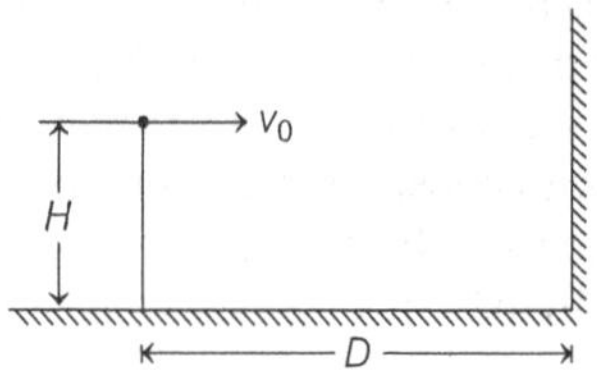

(a) 50 m (b) 60 m (c) 80 m (d) 150 m

36 A ball is fired from point P, with an initial speed of 50m/s at an angle of 53°, with the horizontal. At the same time, a long wall AB at 200 m from point P, starts moving towards P with a constant speed of 10 m/s. Find the coordinate of point C, where the ball collides. Taking point P as origin.

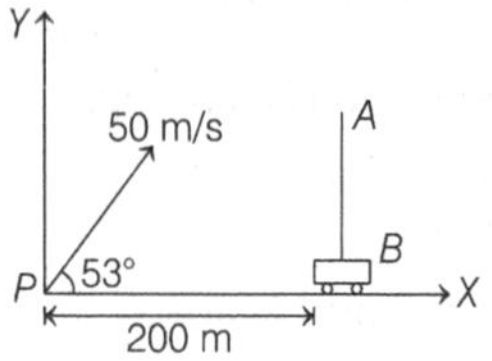

(a) (90, 75) (b) (120, 80) (c) (150, 75) (d) (180, 60)

37 A particle is projected horizontally as shown in figure from the rim of a large hemispherical bowl. The displacement of the particle when it strikes the bowl the first time is R. Find the time taken.

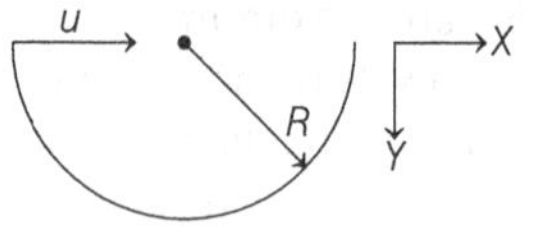

(a) $\sqrt{\frac{3R}{g}}$ (b) $\sqrt{\frac{\sqrt{3}R}{g}}$ (c) $\sqrt{\frac{\sqrt{2}R}{g}}$ (d) $\sqrt{\frac{2R}{g}}$

38 If the maximum range down an inclined plane is three times the maximum range up the inclined plane, then the angle of inclination of the plane to the horizontal is

(a) 30° (b) 45° (c) 60° (d) 15°

39 A particle is projected under gravity with velocity $\sqrt{2ag}$ from a point at a height h above the level plane at an angle θ to it. The maximum range R on the ground is

(a) $\sqrt{(a^2+1)h}$ (b) $\sqrt{a^2h}$

(c) $\sqrt{ah}$ (d) $2\sqrt{a(a+h)}$

40 Shots are fired from the top of a tower and from bottom simultaneously at angles 45° and 60° respectively as shown in the figure. If horizontal distance of the point of collision is at a distance $(\sqrt{3}+1)$ m from the tower, then find height h of tower (in metre).

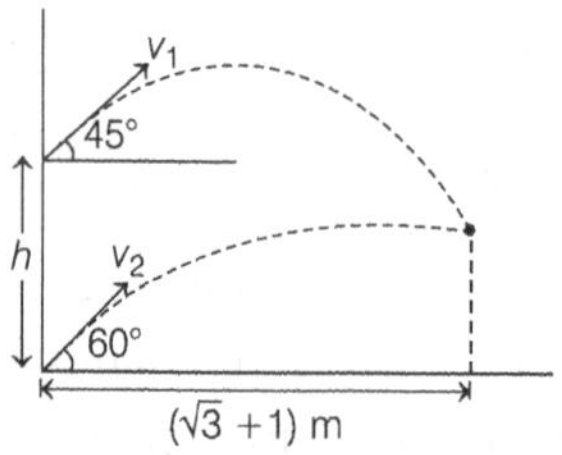

(a) 1 m (b) 2 m (c) 3 m (d) 4 m

Multiple Choice(s) Correct Questions

1 Two particles A and B projected along different directions from the same point P on the ground with the same velocity of 70 m/s in the same vertical plane. They hit the ground at the same point Q such that $PQ = 480$ m, then (take, $g = 9.8\text{ m/s}^2$)

(a) ratio of their times of flight is 4 : 5

(b) ratio of their maximum heights is 9 : 16

(c) ratio of their minimum speeds during flights is 4 : 3

(d) the bisector of the angle between their directions of projection makes 45° with horizontal

2 A projectile is fired on a horizontal ground. Variation of slope of its trajectory with horizontal displacement is shown in figure. (Take, $g = 10\text{ m/s}^2$)

Choose the correct statement(s).

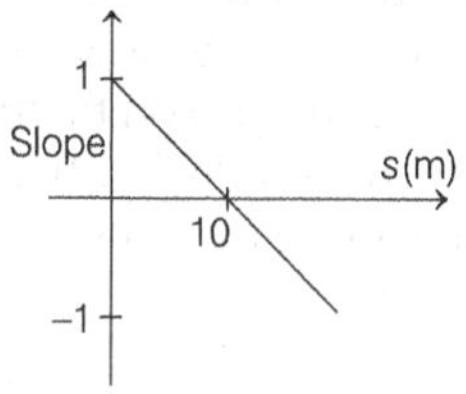

(a) Angle of projection of projectile is 60°.

(b) Horizontal range of projectile is 20 m.

(c) Time of flight of projectile is 2 s.

(d) Area under curve gives vertical displacement of projectile.

3 Equation of trajectory of a particle moving in xy-plane is given by $y = 10x - 2x^2$ (x and y are in meters). Assume acceleration of gravity as 10 m/s^2 in negative y-direction. Choose correct statement(s).

(a) Maximum height of the particle is 12.5 m.

(b) Range of the particle is $x = 5$ m.

(c) At $x = 2.25$ m, particle is moving at an angle of 45° with X-axis.

(d) Initially particle is projected at an angle of 53°.

4 For a ground-to-ground projectile with zero air resistance, choose the correct statement(s).

(a) A projectile is freely falling body.

(b) Acceleration of projectile is maximum at the highest point in its flight.

(c) Time of flight is maximum when the range of projectile is maximum.

(d) Acceleration perpendicular to the velocity of projectile is maximum at its highest position.

5 Choose the correct statement(s).

(a) If the greatest height to which a man can throw a stone is h, then the greatest horizontal distance upto which he can throw the stone is $2h$.

(b) The angle of projection for a projectile motion whose range R is n times the maximum height is $\tan^{-1}(4/n)$.

(c) The time of flight T and the horizontal range R of a projectile are connected by the equation $gT^2 = 2R\tan\theta$, where θ is the angle of projection.

(d) A ball is thrown vertically up. Another ball is thrown at an angle θ with the vertical. Both of them remain in air for the same period of time, then the ratio of heights attained by the two balls is 1 : 1.

6 At what angle should a body be projected with a velocity 24 ms^{-1} just to pass over the obstacle 14 m high at a distance of 24 m? [Take, $g = 10\text{ ms}^{-2}$]

(a) $\tan^{-1}(3.8)$ (b) $\tan^{-1}(1)$

(c) $\tan^{-1}(3.2)$ (d) $\tan^{-1}(2)$

7 A particle is projected from a point O with a velocity u at an angle α (upwards) to the horizontal. At a certain point P, it moves at right angles to its initial direction. It follows that

(a) OP makes an angle $\tan^{-1}(u/2g)$ to the horizontal

(b) the distance of P from O is $u/(2g\sin\alpha)$

(c) the time of flight from O to P is $u/(g\sin\alpha)$

(d) the velocity of the particle at P is $u\cot\alpha$

8 A ball is dropped onto a pad at A and rebounds with a velocity v_0 at an angle 60° with horizontal as shown in the figure. The ball would not enter the opening BC, if v_0 is

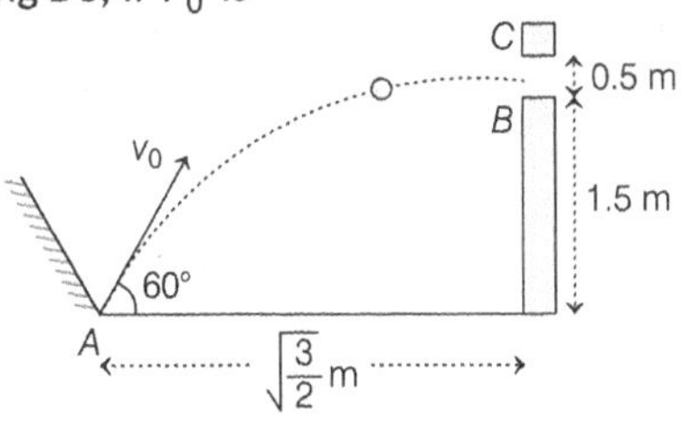

(a) 5 ms^{-1} (b) 6 ms^{-1}

(c) 7 ms^{-1} (d) 50 ms^{-1}

9 Two NCC cadets simultaneously aim their guns at a target put on a tower. The first cadet fired the bullet with speed of 100 ms^{-1} at an angle of 37° with the horizontal, the second cadet ahead of first cadet by a distance 70 m, fired the bullet with a speed of 75 ms^{-1} at an angle of θ with the horizontal. Both the bullets hit the target simultaneously. Which of the following is/are correct?

(a) $\theta = 53°$ (b) $\theta = \sin^{-1}\left(\frac{3}{4}\right)$

(c) Time taken to hit the target is 2 s.

(d) Time taken to hit the target is 4 s.

10 A ball is rolled off along the edge of a horizontal table with velocity 4 m/s. It hits the ground after time 0.4 s. Which of the following statements are correct? ($g = 10\text{ m/s}^2$)

(a) The height of the table is 0.8 m.

(b) It hits the ground at an angle of 60° with the vertical.

(c) It covers a horizontal distance 1.6 m from the table.

(d) It hits the ground with vertical component of velocity 4 m/s.

11 In a projectile motion assuming no air drag let $t_{OA} = t_1$ and $t_{AB} = t_2$. The horizontal displacement from O to A is R_1 and from A to B is R_2. Maximum height is H and time of flight is T. Now if air drag is to be considered, then choose the correct alternative(s).

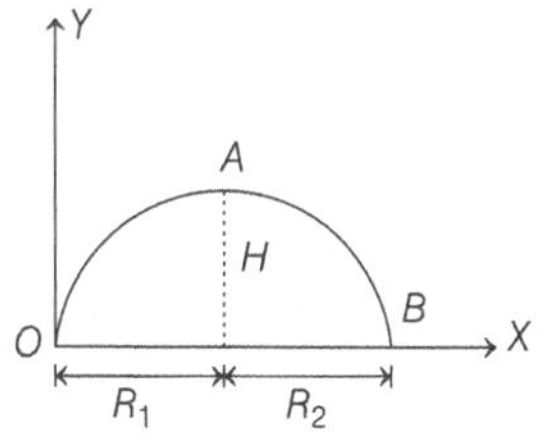

(a) t_1 will decrease while t_2 will increase

(b) H will increase

(c) R_1 will decrease while R_2 will increase

(d) T may increase or decrease

12 Two particles were projected one by one with the same initial velocity from the same point on level ground. They follow the same parabolic trajectory and are found to be in the same horizontal level, separated by a distance of 1 m, 2 s after the second particle was projected. Assume that, the horizontal component of their velocities is 0.5 m/s. Which of the following statements will be true about their motion?

(a) The horizontal range of the parabolic path is 3 m.

(b) The maximum height for the parabolic path is 45 m.

(c) The total time of flight in the parabolic path for each particle is 4s.

(d) The horizontal range of the parabolic path is 6m.

13 A projectile is projected as shown in figure. A proper light arrangement makes a shadow on the wall as well as on the floor. Which of the following graph(s) is/are correct?

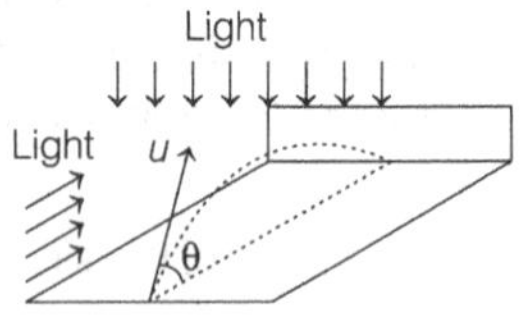

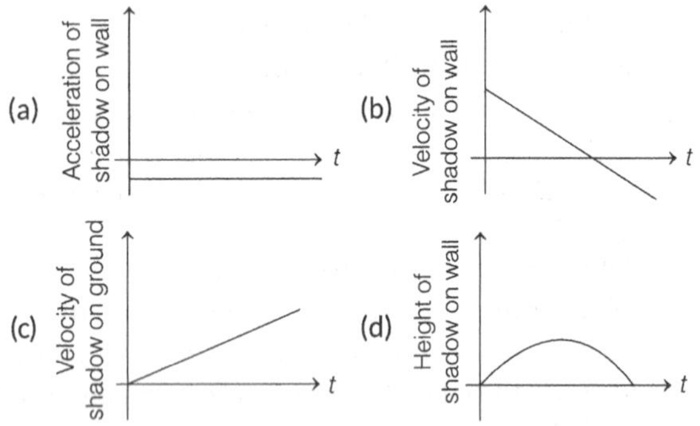

14 A particle is projected from a point on the ground with an initial velocity of $u = 100$ m/s at angle of 53° with the horizontal. (Take, $\tan 53° = \frac{4}{3}$, $g = 10$ m/s^2)

(a) The velocity will make an angle of 45° with the horizontal after time 2s.

(b) The velocity will make an angle of 45° with the horizontal after time 14s.

(c) The average velocity between $t = 6$ s and $t = 10$ s is 60 m/s horizontal.

(d) Displacement of particle from $t = 4$ to $t = 12$ s is 480 m.

Comprehension Based Questions

Comprehension-1

Velocity of a projectile at a height of 15 m from ground is $\mathbf{v} = (20\hat{\mathbf{i}} + 10\hat{\mathbf{j}})$ m/s. Here, $\hat{\mathbf{i}}$ is in horizontal direction and $\hat{\mathbf{j}}$ is vertically upwards, then

1 Maximum height from the ground is .... m.

(a) 30 (b) 60

(c) 40 (d) 20

2 Horizontal range on the ground is .... m.

(a) 60 (b) 50

(c) 80 (d) 70

Comprehension-2

AB is a pipe fixed to the ground at an inclination of 37°. A ball is projected from point *O* at a speed of $u = 20$ m/s at an angle of 53° to the horizontal and it smoothly enters into the pipe with its velocity parallel to the axis of the pipe. (Take, $g = 10$ m/s^2)

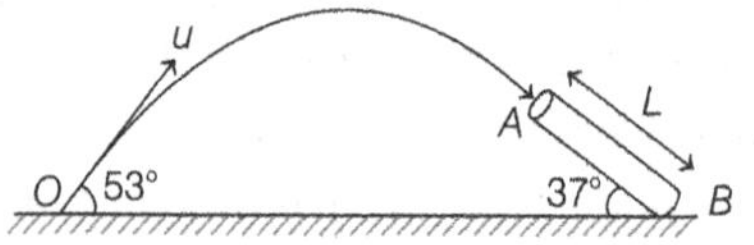

3 Find the length of the pipe.

(a) $\frac{175}{12}$ m (b) $\frac{337}{12}$ m (c) $\frac{150}{13}$ m (d) $\frac{125}{13}$ m

4 Find the distance of end *B* of the pipe from point *O*.

(a) $\frac{175}{3}$ m (b) $\frac{337}{3}$ m (c) $\frac{150}{7}$ m (d) $\frac{125}{3}$ m

Comprehension-3

A ball is projected from the floor a long having a roof height of $H = 10$ m. The ball is projected with a velocity of $u = 25$ m/s making an angle of 37° to the horizontal. On hitting the roof, the ball loses its entire vertical component of velocity but there is no change in the horizontal component of its velocity. The ball was projected from point *A* and it hit the floor at *B*.

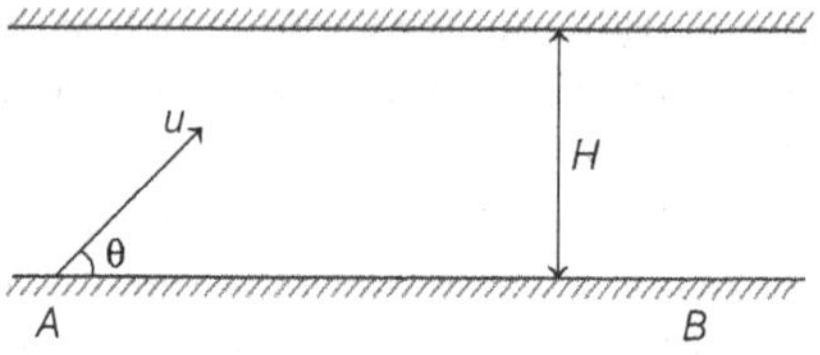

5 Find total time taken to reach *B* after projection.

(a) $(1.5 + \sqrt{2})$ s (b) 3 s

(c) $(1 + \sqrt{2})$ s (d) $(1 + 2\sqrt{2})$ s

6 Find distance *AB*.

(a) $20(1 + \sqrt{2})$ m (b) 60 m

(c) $30(1 + \sqrt{2})$ m (d) $20 + 40\sqrt{2}$ m

Comprehension-4

In the figure shown there is a long horizontal bridge over a river 75 m high from water surface. A strong man throws a stone in the parallel plane of the bridge. An observer in a car travelling on the bridge finds the stone going pass by the car while ascending and also while descending between two points on the road 30 m away. The car is travelling at a speed of 15 m/s. The stone is thrown from the bank of river just at the same level of water.

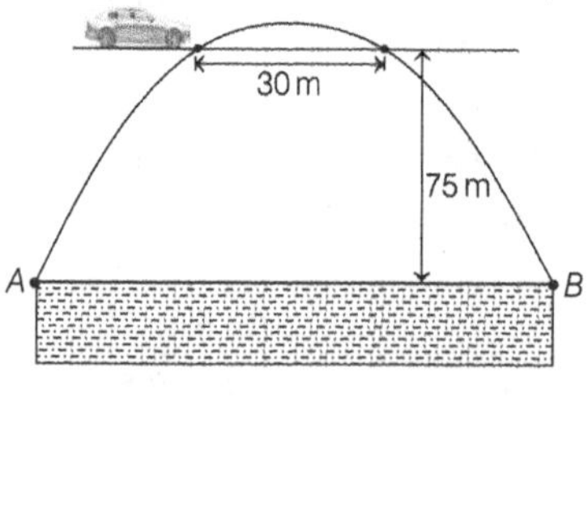

7 What is the angle, the velocity makes with the bridge when it goes past the car while ascending?

(a) 30° (b) 45° (c) $\tan^{-1}\left(\frac{2}{3}\right)$ (d) $\tan^{-1}\left(\frac{3}{2}\right)$

8 Horizontal distance *AB* travelled by stone is

(a) 0 m (b) 75 m (c) 120 m (d) 240 m

9 What is the distance between car and stone at the instant when particle reaches at point *B*?

(a) 0 m (b) 75 m (c) 120 m (d) 240 m

Comprehension-5

From a tower of height 40 m, two bodies are simultaneously projected horizontally in opposite direction, with velocities of 2 m/s and 8 m/s respectively.

10 The time taken for the velocity vectors of two bodies to become perpendicular to each other is

(a) 0.1 s (b) 0.2 s (c) 0.4 s (d) 0.8 s

11 The distance between two bodies, when their velocity vectors are perpendicular to each other is

(a) 1 m (b) 0.5 m (c) 2 m (d) 4 m

12 The time taken for the displacement vectors of two bodies to become perpendicular to each other is

(a) 0.1 s (b) 0.2 s (c) 0.8 s (d) $\sqrt{0.8}$ s

Comprehension-6

In IPL Chris Gayle hit a six which lands on the roof of stadium situated at a distance of 60 m from Gayle. If time of flight of ball is 4 s and ball hits the stadium of at an angle of 45° with horizontal in downward direction, then

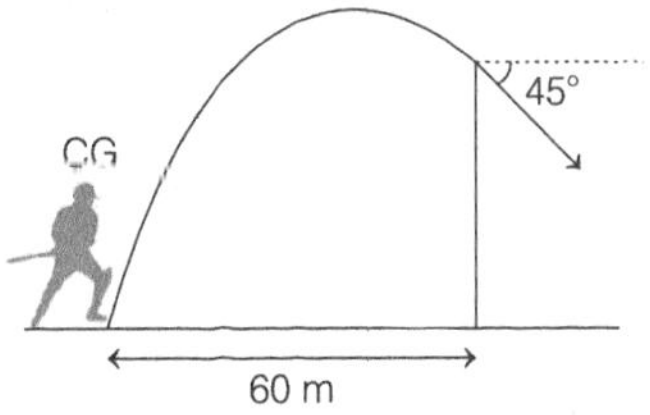

13 Height of roof of stadium where ball hits from the ground is

(a) 60 m (b) 40 m (c) 20 m (d) None of these

14 Initial speed of the ball when Gayle hit the ball was

(a) $\sqrt{150}$ m/s (b) $\sqrt{1250}$ m/s

(c) $\sqrt{850}$ m/s (d) $\sqrt{1050}$ m/s

Comprehension-7

An observer having a gun observes a remotely controlled balloon. When he first noticed the balloon, it was at an altitude of 800 m and moving vertically upward at a constant velocity of 5 m/s. The horizontal displacement of balloon from the observer is 1600 m. Shells fired from the gun have an initial velocity of 400 m/s at a fixed angle 37°. The observer having gun waits (for sometime after observing balloon) and fires so as to destroy the balloon. Assume, $g = 10 \text{ m/s}^2$. Neglect air resistance.

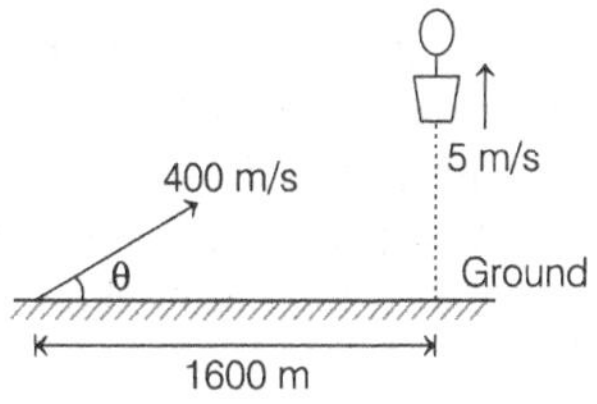

15 The flight time of the shell before it strikes the balloon is

(a) 2 s (b) 5 s

(c) 10 s (d) 15 s

16 The altitude of the collision above ground level is

(a) 1075 m (b) 1200 m

(c) 1250 m (d) 1325 m

17 After noticing the balloon, the time for which observer having gun waits before firing the shell is

(a) 45 s (b) 50 s

(c) 55 s (d) 60 s

Comprehension-8

Two inclined planes *OA* and *OB* having inclinations 30° and 60° with the horizontal respectively intersect each other at *O*, as shown in figure. A particle is projected from point *P* with velocity $u = 10\sqrt{3}$ m/s along a direction perpendicular to plane *OA*. If the particle strikes plane *OB* perpendicular at *Q*, then (take, $g = 10 \text{ m/s}^2$)

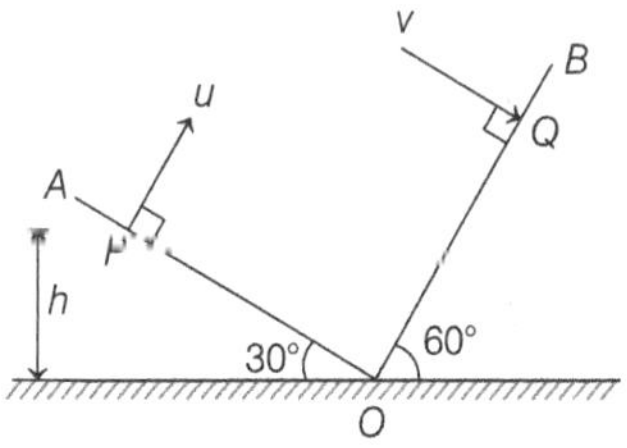

18 The time of flight from *P* to *Q* is

(a) 5 s (b) 2 s

(c) 1 s (d) None of these

19 The speed with which the particle strikes the plane *OB* is

(a) 10 m/s (b) 20 m/s (c) 30 m/s (d) 40 m/s

20 The height *h* of point *P* from the ground is

(a) $10\sqrt{3}$ m (b) 10 m

(c) 5 m (d) 20 m

21 The distance *PQ* is

(a) 20 m (b) $10\sqrt{3}$ m

(c) 10 m (d) 5 m

Match the Columns Questions

1 A particle is projected from level ground. Assuming projection point as origin, X-axis along horizontal and Y-axis along vertical upwards. If particle moves in xy-plane and its path is given by $y = ax - bx^2$, where a and b are positive constants. Then match the physical quantities given in Column I with the values given in Column II. (g in Column II is acceleration due to gravity)

	Column I		Column II
(A)	Horizontal component of velocity	(P)	$\frac{a}{b}$
(B)	Time of flight	(Q)	$\frac{a^2}{4b}$
(C)	Maximum height	(R)	$\sqrt{\frac{g}{2b}}$
(D)	Horizontal range	(S)	$\sqrt{\frac{2a^2}{bg}}$

2 Trajectories are shown in figure for three kicked footballs. Initial vertical and horizontal velocity components are u_y and u_x respectively. Ignoring air resistance, choose the correct statement from Column II for the value of variable in Column I.

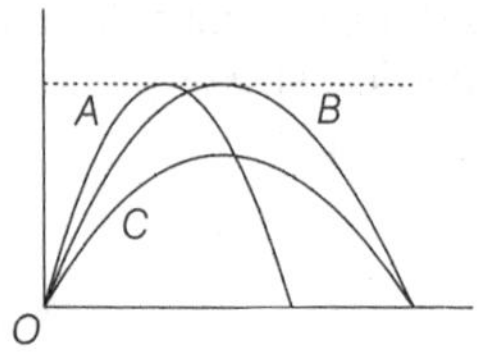

	Column I		Column II
(A)	Time of flight	(P)	greatest for A only
(B)	u_y / u_x	(Q)	greatest for C only
(C)	u_x	(R)	equal for A and B
(D)	$u_x u_y$	(S)	equal for B and C

3 On a planet particle is thrown with a velocity as a function of time $\mathbf{v} = 6\hat{i} + (20 - 4t)\hat{j}$, then match the Column I with Column II.

	Column I		Column II
(A)	Time of flight	(P)	3
(B)	Time when particle is moving at an angle of 53° with horizontal in upwards direction	(Q)	10
(C)	Range of the particle	(R)	50
(D)	Maximum height of the particle	(S)	60

4

	Column I		Column II
(A)	Particles are projected at same speed from same point on level ground such that their range is same.	(P)	Time of flight will be same.
(B)	Particles are projected from same point on ground such that maximum height reached is same.	(Q)	Speed just before reaching ground will be same.
(C)	Particles are projected horizontally from same point at a height with different initial velocities.	(R)	Vertical component of velocity just before reaching ground will be same.
(D)	Particles are projected from the same point at a height with same initial speed, direction of velocity makes equal angle with horizontal one below and the other above horizontal.	(S)	Minimum kinetic energy during the flight will be equal.

5 An inclined plane makes an angle $\theta = 45°$ with horizontal. A stone is projected normally from the inclined plane, with speed u m/s at $t = 0$ s. X and Y-axes are drawn from point of projection along and normal to inclined plane as shown in figure. The length of incline is sufficient for stone to land on it and neglect air friction. Match the statements given in Column I with the results in Column II. (g in Column II is acceleration due to gravity)

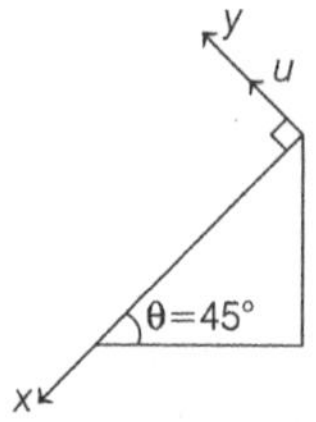

	Column I		Column II
(A)	The instant of time at which velocity of stone is parallel to X-axis	(P)	$\frac{2\sqrt{2}u}{g}$
(B)	The instant of time at which velocity of stone makes an angle $\theta = 45°$ with positive X-axis in clockwise direction	(Q)	$\frac{2u}{g}$
(C)	The instant of time till which (starting from $t = 0$) component of displacement along X-axis become half the range on inclined plane is	(R)	$\frac{\sqrt{2}u}{g}$
(D)	Time of flight on inclined plane is	(S)	$\frac{u}{\sqrt{2}g}$

6 The projectile collides perpendicularly with the inclined plane. (Refer the figure)

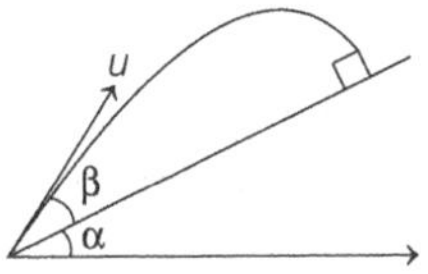

	Column I		Column II
(A)	Maximum height attained by the projectile from the ground	(P)	$\dfrac{u^2 \cos^2 \beta}{2g \sin \alpha}$
(B)	Maximum height attained by the projectile from inclined plane	(Q)	$\dfrac{3u^2 \cos^2 \beta}{8g \sin \alpha}$
(C)	Displacement along the inclined plane by the time the projectile achieves maximum height from the inclined plane	(R)	$\dfrac{u^2 \sin^2 \beta}{2g \cos \alpha}$
(D)	Displacement along the inclined plane	(S)	$\dfrac{u^2 \sin^2 (\alpha + \beta)}{2g}$

Numerical Value Questions

1 A body is projected upwards from level ground with certain speed at an angle θ with horizontal such that at half the maximum height, the velocity vector makes angle 45° with horizontal. Find the value of $\tan^2 \theta$.

2 A cannon fires a projectile as shown in figure. The dashed line shows the trajectory in the absence of gravity. The points M, N, O and P correspond to time at $t = 0$, 1 s, 2 s and 3 s, respectively. Find the sum of lengths of X, Y and Z. (Take, $g = 10 \text{ ms}^{-2}$)

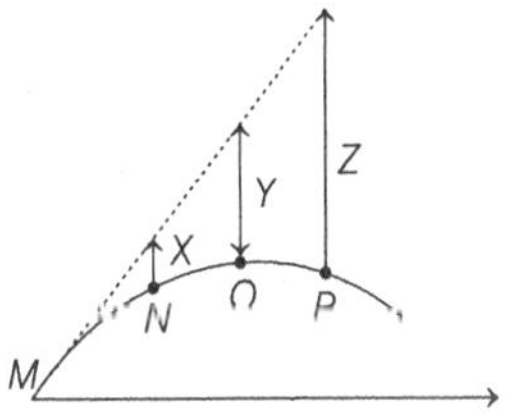

3 Ball A is projected from tower of height 30 m and B is projected horizontally at 6 m/s from tower of height 60m. If A and B collide in air, then find the separation d between the towers in meters.

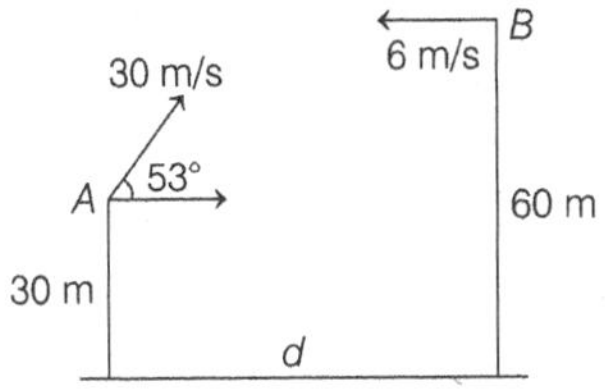

4 A stone is thrown from the top of a vertical column at a certain angle above the horizontal. It strikes the ground twice as far as it would have struck it, if it had been thrown from the bottom of the column with the same initial velocity. In this latter case, the stone would fly during a time $T = 2$ s. Find the height of the column (in m) (Use, $g = 10 \text{ m/s}^2$)

5 Two persons Ram and Shyam are throwing ball at each other as shown in the figure. The maximum horizontal distance from the building where Ram can stand and still throw a ball at Shyam is d_1. The maximum horizontal distance of Ram from the building where Shyam can throw a ball is d_2. If both of them can throw ball with a velocity of $2\sqrt{gh}$, find out the ratio of $\dfrac{d_2^2}{d_1^2}$.

Neglect the height of each person.

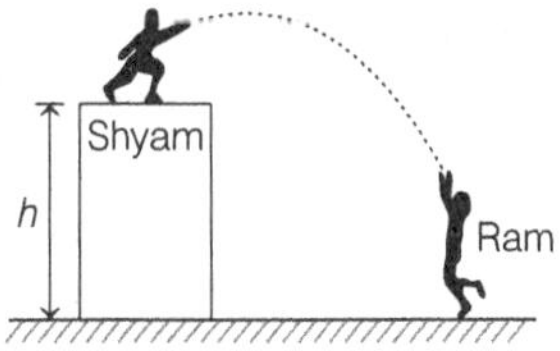

6 A person standing on the top of a cliff 171 ft. high has to throw a packet to his friend standing on the ground 228 ft horizontally away. If he throws the packet directly aiming at the friend with a speed of 15.0 ft/s, how short (in ft) will the packet fall? [Use, $g = 32 \text{ ft/s}^2$]

7 A particle is projected with a velocity u in horizontal direction as shown in figure. Find u (in m/s), so that the particle collides orthogonally with the inclined plane of the fixed wedge.

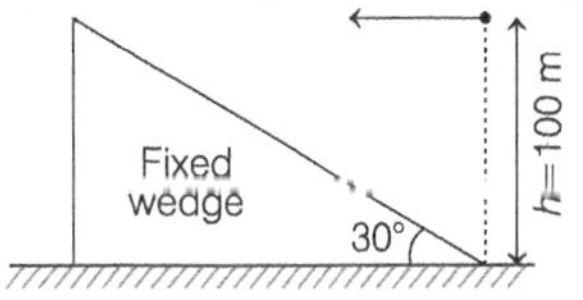

8 A commander fires a shell at a certain angle of projection from A which clears the building (cuboid) of dimensions $(20 \times 15 \times 12.5) \text{ m}^3$ in its diagonal plane. Shell just clears the roof diagonally at point P and Q and falls on the other side of the building at B and makes 45° angle with horizontal at P and Q as shown in figure. If range AB of the shell is $N \times \sqrt{3}$m, then find the value of N.

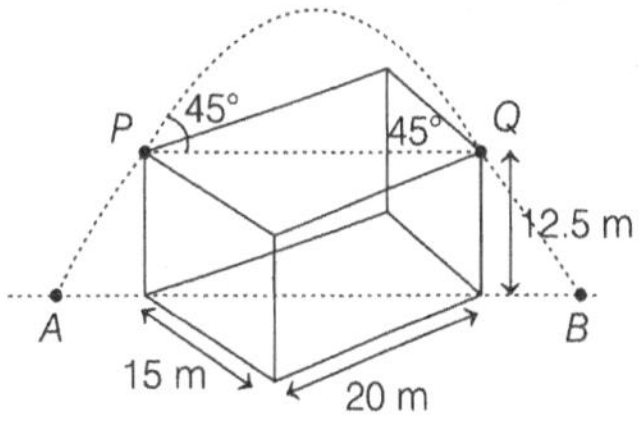

9 If the maximum angle to the horizontal at which a stone can be thrown such that its distance from the thrower is always increasing is α, then find the value of $9\sin^2\alpha$.

10 A shell is fired from a point O at an angle of 60° with a speed of 40 m/s and it strikes a horizontal plane through O, at a point A. The gun is fired a second time with the same angle of elevation but a different speed v. If it hits the target which starts to rise vertically from A with a constant speed $9\sqrt{3}$ m/s at the same instant as the shell is fired, find the value of v (in m/s).

11 A particle is projected from the ground level. It just passes through upper end of vertical poles A, B, C of height 20 m, 30 m & 20 m, respectively. The time taken by the particle to travel from B to C is double of the time taken from A to B. Find the maximum height (in m) attained by the particle from the ground level.

12 A gun is mounted on an elevated platform AB. The distance of the gun at A from the edge B is $AB = 960$ m. Height of the platform is $OB = 960$ m. The gun can fire shells with a velocity of $u = 100$ m/s at any angle. What is the minimum distance (OP) from the foot of the platform where the shell of the gun can reach?

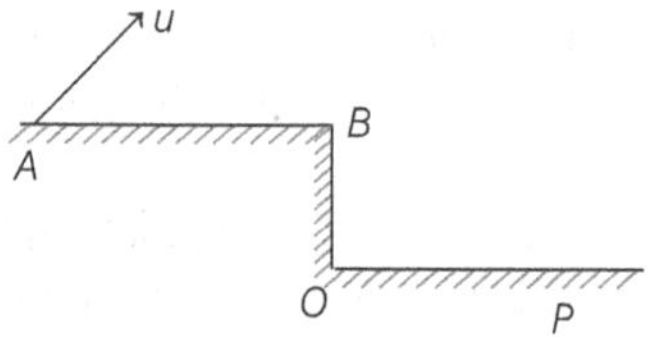

13 A shell bursts on contact with the ground and pieces from it fly in all directions with all velocities up to 80 feet per second. If a man 100 ft away is in danger for $\frac{p}{\sqrt{2}}$ seconds, then find the value of p.

[Take, $g = 32$ ft/s^2]

14 Some students are playing cricket on the roof of a building of height 20 m. While playing, ball falls on the ground. A person on the ground returns their ball with the minimum possible speed at an angle 45° with the horizontal, find out the speed of projection (in m/s).

15 A stone is projected from top of a vertical pole of height 3 m with initial velocity 10 ms^{-1}. The maximum range on the ground is $x\sqrt{10}$ m. Find the value of x.

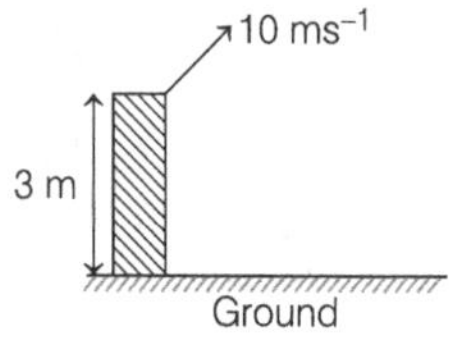

16 A particle is moving in xy-plane. It starts to move from origin O at an angle α with X-axis. It has a constant acceleration in negative y-direction. After sometime it passes through a point B in a direction making angle β with the X-axis. If OB makes $\theta = 45°$ angle with the X-axis, find the value of $\tan\alpha + \tan\beta$.

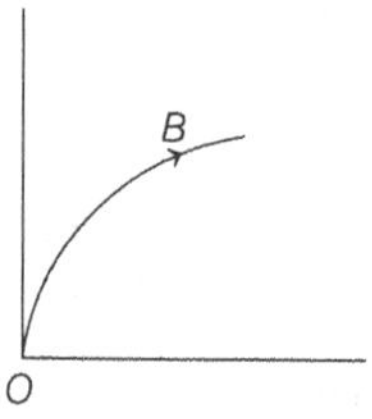

17 A ball is thrown at speed v from zero height on level ground. The angle at which the particle is thrown is such that the area under the trajectory is maximum. If the angle of projection is $\frac{\pi}{k}$, then find the value of k.

18 Two balls are projected from a point in two mutually perpendicular vertical planes. Speed of projection of both the balls is 400 ms^{-1}. Angle of projection with horizontal is 53° for both the balls. After how much time (in second), their velocities will be the angle 60° from each other? [Take, $g = 10$ ms^{-2}]

Previous Year's Questions

JEE Main

1 A particle starts from origin at $t = 0$ with a velocity $5\hat{i}$ m/s and moves in XY-plane under action of a force which produces a constant acceleration of $(3\hat{i} + 2\hat{j})$ m/s^2. If the x-coordinate of the particle at that instant is 84 m, then the speed of the particle at this time is $\sqrt{\alpha}$ m/s. The value of α is .... **[2024, 27 Jan Shift-I]**

2 A ball rolls off the top of a stairway with horizontal velocity u. The steps are 0.1 m high and 0.1 m wide. The minimum velocity u with which that ball just hits the step 5 of the stairway will be $\sqrt{x}$ ms^{-1} where $x =$ .... [use $g = 10$ m / s^2]. **[2024, 29 Jan Shift-I]**

3 Projectiles A and B are thrown at angles of 45° and 60° with vertical respectively from top of a 400 m high tower. If their ranges and times of flight are same, the ratio of their speeds of projection $v_A : v_B$ is [Take, $g = 10$ ms^{-2}] **[2024, 30 Jan Shift-II]**

(a) $\sqrt{2} : 1$

(b) $1 : 2$

(c) $1 : \sqrt{3}$

(d) $1 : \sqrt{2}$

4 The maximum vertical height to which a man can throw a ball is 136 m. The maximum horizontal distance upto which he can throw the same ball is **[2023, 24 Jan Shift-I]**

(a) 136 m (b) 192 m (c) 68 m (d) 272 m

5 A child stands on the edge of the cliff 10 m above the ground and throws a stone horizontally with an initial speed of 5 ms^{-1}. Neglecting the air resistance, the speed with which the stone hits the ground will be ______ ms^{-1}. (given, $g = 10\ ms^{-2}$). **[2023, 1 Feb Shift-I]**

(a) 25 (b) 30 (c) 15 (d) 20

6 The initial speed of a projectile fired from ground is u. At the highest point during its motion, the speed of projectile is $\sqrt{3}/2u$. The time of flight of the projectile is **[2023, 31 Jan Shift-I]**

(a) $\frac{2u}{g}$ (b) $\frac{u}{2g}$ (c) $\frac{u}{g}$ (d) $\frac{\sqrt{3}u}{g}$

7 The range of the projectile projected at an angle of 15° with horizontal is 50 m. If the projectile is projected with same velocity at an angle of 45° with horizontal, then its range will be **[2023, 10 April Shift-I]**

(a) $100\sqrt{2}$ m (b) 50 m
(c) $50\sqrt{2}$ m (d) 100 m

8 Two projectiles are projected at 30° and 60° with the horizontal with the same speed. The ratio of the maximum height attained by the two projectiles respectively is **[2023, 10 April Shift-II]**

(a) $1:\sqrt{3}$ (b) $1:3$ (c) $2:\sqrt{3}$ (d) $\sqrt{3}:1$

9 A projectile is projected at 30° from horizontal with initial velocity 40 ms^{-1}. The velocity of the projectile at $t = 2$ s from the start will be (Given, $g = 10\ m/s^2$) **[2023, 11 April Shift-II]**

(a) $40\sqrt{3}\ ms^{-1}$ (b) $20\ ms^{-1}$
(c) $20\sqrt{3}\ ms^{-1}$ (d) zero

10 The trajectory of projectile, projected from the ground is given by $y = x - \frac{x^2}{20}$. Where x and y are measured in meter. The maximum height attained by the projectile will be. **[2023, 8 April Shift-II]**

(a) 200 m (b) 5 m
(c) 10 m (d) $10\sqrt{2}$ m

11 Two bodies are projected from ground with same speeds 40 ms^{-1} at two different angles with respect to horizontal. The bodies were found to have same range. If one of the body was projected at an angle of 60°, with horizontal then sum of the maximum heights, attained by the two projectiles, is .... m. (Given, $g = 10\ ms^{-2}$) **[2023, 31 Jan Shift-II]**

12 A projectile fired at 30° to the ground is observed to be at same height at time 3s and 5s after projection, during its flight. The speed of projection of the projectile is .... ms^{-1} (Given, $g = 10\ ms^{-2}$) **[2023, 11 April Shift-I]**

13 Two projectiles are thrown with same initial velocity making an angle of 45° and 30° with the horizontal, respectively. The ratio of their respective ranges will be **[2022, 26 July Shift-II]**

(a) $1:\sqrt{2}$ (b) $\sqrt{2}:1$ (c) $2:\sqrt{3}$ (d) $\sqrt{3}:2$

14 Two projectiles thrown at 30° and 45° with the horizontal respectively, reach the maximum height in same time. The ratio of their initial velocities is **[2022, 26 July Shift-I]**

(a) $1:\sqrt{2}$ (b) $2:1$
(c) $\sqrt{2}:1$ (d) $1:2$

15 A ball is projected from the ground with a speed 15 ms^{-1} at an angle θ with horizontal so that its range and maximum height are equal, then tanθ will be equal to **[2022, 25 July Shift-II]**

(a) 1/4 (b) 1/2
(c) 2 (d) 4

16 A projectile is projected with velocity of 25 m/s at an angle θ with the horizontal. After t seconds its inclination with horizontal becomes zero. If R represents horizontal range of the projectile, the value of θ will be [use, $g = 10\ m/s^2$] **[2022, 24 June Shift-I]**

(a) $\frac{1}{2}\sin^{-1}\left(\frac{5t^2}{4R}\right)$ (b) $\frac{1}{2}\sin^{-1}\left(\frac{4R}{5t^2}\right)$
(c) $\tan^{-1}\left(\frac{4t^2}{5R}\right)$ (d) $\cot^{-1}\left(\frac{R}{20t^2}\right)$

17 A fighter jet is flying horizontally at a certain altitude with a speed of 200 ms^{-1}. When it passes directly overhead an anti-aircraft gun, a bullet is fired from the gun, at an angle θ with the horizontal, to hit the jet. If the bullet speed is 400 m/s, then the value of θ will be ....°. **[2022, 26 June Shift-I]**

18 A body is projected from the ground at an angle of 45° with the horizontal. Its velocity after 2s is 20 ms^{-1}. The maximum height reached by the body during its motion is ...... m. (Use, $g = 10\ ms^{-2}$) **[2022, 24 June Shift-II]**

19 If the initial velocity in horizontal direction of a projectile is unit vector $\hat{i}$ and the equation of trajectory is $y = 5x(1-x)$. The y component vector of the initial velocity is ......$\hat{j}$ [Take, $g = 10\ m/s^2$] **[2022, 26 July Shift-I]**

20 A player kicks a football with an initial speed of 25 ms^{-1} at an angle of 45° from the ground. What are the maximum height and the time taken by the football to reach at the highest point during motion? (Take, $g = 10 \text{ ms}^{-2}$) [2021, 27 Aug Shift-II]

(a) $h_{max} = 10 \text{ m}, T = 2.5 \text{ s}$

(b) $h_{max} = 15.625 \text{ m}, T = 3.54 \text{ s}$

(c) $h_{max} = 15.625 \text{ m}, T = 1.77 \text{ s}$

(d) $h_{max} = 3.54 \text{ m}, T = 0.125 \text{ s}$

21 The projectile motion of a particle of mass 5 g is shown in the figure.

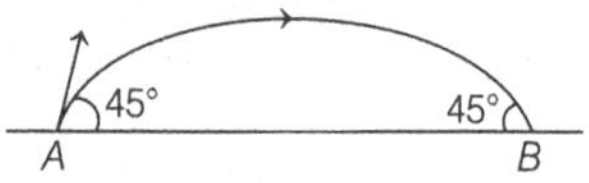

The initial velocity of the particle is $5\sqrt{2} \text{ ms}^{-1}$ and the air resistance is assumed to be negligible. The magnitude of the change in momentum between the points A and B is $x \times 10^{-2}$ kg-ms^{-1}. The value of x to the nearest integer, is .... [2021, 18 March Shift-II]

JEE Advanced

1 A projectile is fired from horizontal ground with speed v and projection angle θ. When the acceleration due to gravity is g, the range of the projectile is d. If at the highest point in its trajectory, the projectile enters a different region, where the effective acceleration due to gravity is $g' = \frac{g}{0.81}$, then the new range is $d' = nd$. The value of n is .... (2022 Adv.)

2 A ball is thrown from ground at an angle θ with horizontal and with an initial speed u_0. For the resulting projectile motion, the magnitude of average velocity of the ball up to the point when it hits the ground for the first time is v_1. After hitting the ground, the ball rebounds at the same angle θ but with a reduced speed of $\frac{u_0}{\alpha}$. Its motion continues for a long time as shown in figure.

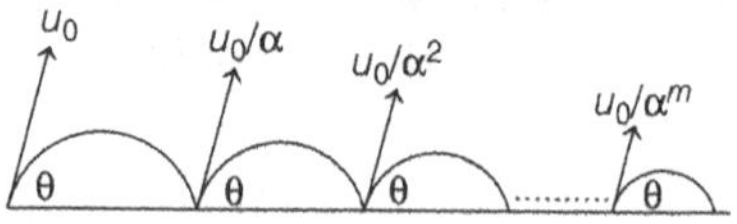

If the magnitude of average velocity of the ball for entire duration of motion is $0.8v_1$, the value of α is .... (2019 Adv.)

3 A ball is projected from the ground at an angle of 45° with the horizontal surface. It reaches a maximum height of 120 m and returns to the ground. Upon hitting the ground for the first time, it loses half of its kinetic energy. Immediately after the bounce, the velocity of the ball makes an angle of 30° with the horizontal surface. The maximum height it reaches after the bounce, in metres, is .... (2018 Adv.)

Answer Key

Level 1

6.1 Ground-to-Ground Projectile

1. (a) $\sqrt{3}$ s (b) $5\sqrt{3}$ m (c) $\frac{15}{4}$ m (d) $10\sqrt{2-\sqrt{3}}$ m/s (e) $\mathbf{v} = 5\hat{\mathbf{i}} + \sqrt{55}\hat{\mathbf{j}}$
2. $\frac{135}{4}$ m, $3\sqrt{3}$ s, $45\sqrt{3}$ m
3. (a) 2 s (b) 5 m (c) 10 m
4. (a) $\theta = 90°$, 4 s (b) $\theta = 45°$, 40 m
5. (a) $\tan\theta : 1$ (b) $\tan^2\theta : 1$ (c) $1:1$
6. $\theta = \tan^{-1}(4)$
7. (a) $T_1T_2 = \frac{2R}{g}$ (b) $\frac{u^2}{2g}$ (c) $\frac{R^2}{16}$
8. 50 m
9. $\theta = 60°$, 2 m/s
10. $10\sqrt{5}$ m/s
11. $\theta = 45°, \tan^{-1}(3)$
12. $t = 5(\sqrt{3}-1)$ s
13. $u \cos\alpha \sec\beta$
14. $t = \frac{u \operatorname{cosec}\theta}{g}$
15. Maximum area $= \frac{\pi v^4}{g^2}$
16. (a) $\mathbf{r} = 10\sqrt{3}\,\hat{\mathbf{i}} + 5\hat{\mathbf{j}}$, $|\mathbf{r}| = \sqrt{(10\sqrt{3})^2 + 5^2}$ (b) $\theta = \cos^{-1}\left(2\sqrt{\frac{3}{13}}\right)$
17. $5\sqrt{2}$ m/s
18. $\theta \in [15°, 18.5°] \cup [71.5°, 75°]$
19. $\theta = \tan^{-1}\left(\frac{9}{7}\right) u = \sqrt{182}$

6.2 Projection from Certain Height

1. (a) 10 s (b) 980 m (c) $98\sqrt{2} \text{ ms}^{-1}$ at an angle of 45°
2. (a) $\sqrt{20}$ s (b) 30 m (c) $\tan^{-1} 2\sqrt{5}$ (d) $20\sqrt{5}$ m
3. 700 m/s
4. $x = 4.5 \text{ m}, y = \frac{5}{4} \text{ m}, r = \frac{\sqrt{349}}{4}$ m. The component of velocity at this time are $v_x = 9.0$ m/s and $v_y = 5$ m/s.
5. $u = 60$ m/s
6. (a) 1 s (b) 8 m (c) $8\sqrt{5}$ m/s

7. (a) $8\hat{i} - 14\hat{j}$ (b) $T = \frac{11}{5}$ s (c) Range $= \frac{88}{5}$ m (d) 12.8 m

   (e) $8\sqrt{5}$ m/s

8. $15\sqrt{3}$ m/s

9. 18 m/s

10. (a) 100 m/s (b) 980 m (c) 1600 m (d) $\theta = \tan^{-1}\left(\frac{7}{4}\right)$,

    $v = 20\sqrt{65}$ m/s

6.3 Projection on Inclined Plane

1. (a) $30\sqrt{3}$ m (b) $4\sqrt{3}$ s (c) $40(4\sqrt{3} - 3)$ m (d) 30° (e) $\frac{500}{3}$ m

2. $R = \dfrac{2u^2 \sin\theta}{g \cos^2\theta}$

3. (a) $2\tan\theta = \cot\beta$ (b) $2\sin\theta = \sin(\theta+\beta)\cos\beta$

4. (a) $-g\sin\beta$ (b) $-g\cos\beta$, (c) $u\cos\theta - g\sin\beta \times t$

   (d) $u\sin\theta - g\cos\beta \times t$ (e) $u\cos\theta \times t - \frac{1}{2}g\sin\beta \times t^2$

   (f) $u\sin\theta \times t - \frac{1}{2}g\cos\beta \times t^2$ (g) zero

Level 2

Single Choice Correct Questions

1. (d)	2. (a)	3. (b)	4. (c)	5. (b)
6. (c)	7. (c)	8. (b)	9. (c)	10. (c)
11. (b)	12. (b)	13. (a)	14. (c)	15. (b)
16. (c)	17. (d)	18. (b)	19. (d)	20. (c)
21. (c)	22. (a)	23. (b)	24. (b)	25. (b)
26. (a)	27. (d)	28. (a)	29. (a)	30. (c)
31. (a)	32. (c)	33. (d)	34. (c)	35. (d)
36. (a)	37. (c)	38. (c)	39. (d)	40. (c)
41. (c)	42. (a)	43. (a)	44. (a)	45. (a)
46. (b)	47. (c)	48. (d)	49. (a)	50. (c)
51. (b)	52. (c)	53. (b)	54. (b)	55. (d)
56. (a)	57. (c)	58. (d)		

Numerical Value Questions

1. 8	2. 20	3. 41.67	4. 35	5. 20
6. 1.6	7. 50	8. 1	9. 6	10. 65
11. 4	12. 4	13. 20	14. 10	15. 25
16. 75	17. 2	18. 3	19. 6	20. 8

LEVEL 3

Single Choice Correct Questions

1. (b)	2. (a)	3. (c)	4. (d)	5. (c)
6. (d)	7. (a)	8. (d)	9. (a)	10. (a)
11. (b)	12. (c)	13. (d)	14. (b)	15. (b)
16. (d)	17. (c)	18. (c)	19. (d)	20. (d)
21. (d)	22. (a)	23. (c)	24. (a)	25. (d)
26. (a)	27. (c)	28. (a)	29. (a)	30. (b)
31. (b)	32. (a)	33. (a)	34. (c)	35. (b)
36. (c)	37. (b)	38. (a)	39. (d)	40. (b)

Multiple Choice(s) Correct Quesions

1. (b,c,d)	2. (b,c,d)	3. (a,b,c)	4. (a,d)	5. (a,b,c,d)
6. (a,b)	7. (c,d)	8. (a,b,d)	9. (a,c)	10. (a,c,d)
11. (a,d)	12. (a,b)	13. (a,b,d)	14. (a,b,c,d)	

Comprehension Based Questions

1. (d)	2. (c)	3. (a)	4. (d)	5. (c)
6. (a)	7. (c)	8. (c)	9. (b)	10. (c)
11. (d)	12. (c)	13. (c)	14. (c)	15. (b)
16. (a)	17. (b)	18. (b)	19. (a)	20. (c)
21. (a)				

Match the Columns Questions

1. (A) R (B) S (C) Q (D) P	2. (A) R (B) P (C) Q (D) S
3. (A) Q (B) P (C) S (D) R	4. (A) Q (B) P, R (C) P, R (D) Q, R
5. (A) R (B) S (C) Q (D) P	6. (A) S (B) R (C) Q (D) P

Numerical Value Questions

1. (2)	2. (70)	3. (30)	4. (40.00)	5. (3)
6. (192)	7. (20)	8. (25)	9. (8)	10. (50)
11. (2)	12. (3)	13. (480)	14. (28.28)	15. (4)
16. (2)	17. (3)	18. (8)		

Previous Year's Questions

JEE Main

1. (673)	2. (2)	3. (d)	4. (d)	5. (c)
6. (c)	7. (d)	8. (b)	9. (c)	10. (b)
11. (80)	12. (80)	13. (c)	14. (c)	15. (d)
16. (d)	17. (60)	18. (20)	19. (5)	20. (c)
21. (5)				

JEE Advanced

1. (0.95)	2. (4)	3. (30.00)

SOLUTIONS

Level 1

6.1 Ground to Ground Projectile

1. $u = 10$ m/s

$\theta = 60°$

(a) $T = \dfrac{2u \sin\theta}{g} = \sqrt{3}$ s

(b) $R = \dfrac{u^2 \sin 2\theta}{g} = 5\sqrt{3}$ m

(c) $H = \dfrac{u^2 \sin^2\theta}{2g} = \dfrac{15}{4}$ m

(d) $\mathbf{v} = u\cos\theta\,\hat{\mathbf{i}} + (u\sin\theta - gt)\,\hat{\mathbf{j}}$

$\mathbf{v} = 5\hat{\mathbf{i}} + (5\sqrt{3} - 10)\,\hat{\mathbf{j}}$

Speed $= \sqrt{5^2 + (5\sqrt{3} - 10)^2} = 10\sqrt{2 - \sqrt{3}}$ m/s

(e) $\mathbf{v} = u\cos\theta\,\hat{\mathbf{i}} + (\sqrt{u^2\sin^2\theta - 2gh})\,\hat{\mathbf{j}} = 5\hat{\mathbf{i}} + \sqrt{55}\,\hat{\mathbf{j}}$

2. $u = 30$ m/s, $\theta = 60°$ with horizontal

$$H = \frac{u^2\sin^2\theta}{2g} = \frac{135}{4}\text{ m} \Rightarrow T = \frac{2u\sin\theta}{g} = 3\sqrt{3}\text{ s}$$

$$R = \frac{u^2 \sin 2\theta}{g} = 45\sqrt{3}\text{ m}$$

3. $\mathbf{u} = 5\hat{\mathbf{i}} + 10\hat{\mathbf{j}}$

(a) $T = \dfrac{2u_y}{g} = 2$ s

(b) $H = \dfrac{u_y^2}{2g} = 5$ m

(c) $R = \dfrac{2u_x \times u_y}{g} = 10$ m

4. $T = \dfrac{2u\sin\theta}{g} \Rightarrow T_{max} = 4$ s when $\theta = 90°$

$R = \dfrac{u^2\sin 2\theta}{g} \Rightarrow R_{max} = 40$ m when $\theta = 45°$

5. (a) $\dfrac{T_1}{T_2} = \dfrac{\dfrac{2u\sin\theta}{g}}{\dfrac{2u\cos\theta}{g}} = \tan\theta : 1$

(b) $\dfrac{H_1}{H_2} = \dfrac{u^2\sin^2\theta/2g}{u^2\cos^2\theta/2g} = \tan^2\theta : 1$

(c) $\dfrac{R_1}{R_2} = \dfrac{u^2\sin 2\theta/g}{u^2\sin 2\theta/g} = 1:1$

6. $R = H \Rightarrow \dfrac{u^2\sin 2\theta}{g} = \dfrac{u^2\sin^2\theta}{2g}$

$$2\sin\theta\cos\theta = \frac{\sin^2\theta}{2} \Rightarrow \tan\theta = 4 \Rightarrow \theta = \tan^{-1}(4)$$

7. Angles of projection will be θ and $90° - \theta$.

(a) $T_1T_2 = \left(\dfrac{2u\sin\theta}{g}\right)\left(\dfrac{2u\cos\theta}{g}\right) = \dfrac{2u^2\sin 2\theta}{g} = \dfrac{2R}{g}$

(b) $H_1 + H_2 = \dfrac{u^2\sin^2\theta}{2g} + \dfrac{u^2\cos^2\theta}{2g} = \dfrac{u^2}{2g}$

(c) $H_1H_2 = \sqrt{\dfrac{u^2\sin^2\theta}{2g}\,\dfrac{u^2\cos^2\theta}{2g}} = \dfrac{R^2}{16}$

8. $R_{max} = \dfrac{u^2}{g} = 100\text{ m} \Rightarrow H_{max} = \dfrac{u^2}{2g} = \dfrac{100}{2} = 50$ m

9. $y = \sqrt{3}x - \dfrac{1}{2}gx^2$ ...(i)

$y = x\tan\theta - \dfrac{gx^2}{2u^2\cos^2\theta}$ ...(ii)

Comparing Eqs. (i) and (ii), we get

$\tan\theta = \sqrt{3}, u^2\cos^2\theta = 1 \Rightarrow \theta = 60°, u = 2$ m/s

10.

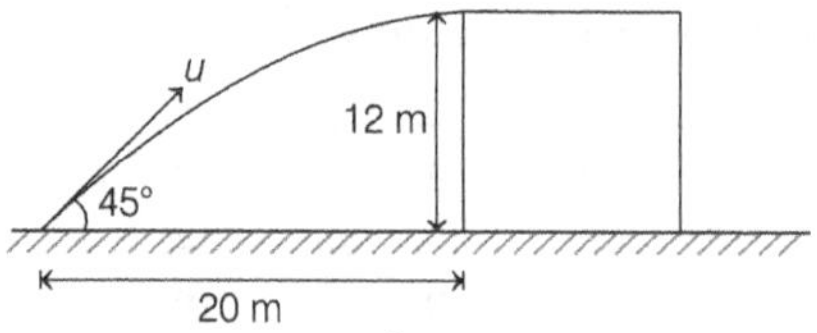

$$y = x\tan\theta - \frac{gx^2}{2u^2\cos^2\theta}$$

$$\Rightarrow \quad 12 = 20\tan 45° - \frac{10\,(20)^2}{2u^2\cos^2 45°}$$

$$\Rightarrow \quad 12 = 20 - \frac{4000}{u^2} \Rightarrow \frac{4000}{u^2} = 8$$

$$\Rightarrow \quad u^2 = 500 \Rightarrow u = 10\sqrt{5}\text{ m/s}$$

11. $y = x\tan\theta - \dfrac{gx^2}{2u^2\cos^2\theta} \Rightarrow 10 = 20\tan\theta - \dfrac{10(20)^2}{2(20)^2}\sec^2\theta$

$\Rightarrow 10 = 20\tan\theta - 5\sec^2\theta \Rightarrow \sec^2\theta - 4\tan\theta + 2 = 0$

$\Rightarrow \tan^2\theta - 4\tan\theta + 3 = 0 \Rightarrow \tan\theta = 3$ and $\tan\theta = 1$

$\Rightarrow \theta = \tan^{-1}(3)$ and $\theta = 45°$

12. $\tan\phi = \dfrac{u\sin\theta - gt}{u\cos\theta} \Rightarrow \tan 45° = \dfrac{100\sin 60° - 10t}{100\cos 60°}$

$t = 5(\sqrt{3} - 1)$ s

13. Horizontal component of velocity remains constant.

$\Rightarrow u\cos\alpha = v\cos\beta$

$\Rightarrow v = u\cos\alpha\sec\beta$

14.

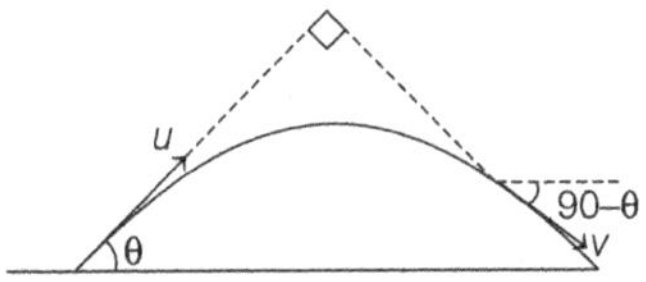

$$\tan\phi = \frac{u\sin\theta - gt}{u\cos\theta}$$

$$\tan(-(90-\theta)) = \frac{u\sin\theta - gt}{u\cos\theta} \Rightarrow t = \frac{u}{g}\operatorname{cosec}\theta$$

15. $R_{max} = \frac{v^2}{g}$, Area of circle $= \pi R_{max}^2 = \frac{\pi v^4}{g^2}$

16. $u = 20$ m/s, $\theta = 30°$

(a) $\mathbf{r} = (u\cos\theta t)\hat{\mathbf{i}} + (u\sin\theta t - \frac{1}{2}gt^2)\hat{\mathbf{j}} \Rightarrow \mathbf{r} = 10\sqrt{3}\,\hat{\mathbf{i}} + 5\,\hat{\mathbf{j}}$

(b) $\mathbf{v} = u\cos\theta\,\hat{\mathbf{i}} + (u\sin\theta - gt)\hat{\mathbf{j}} \Rightarrow \mathbf{v} = 10\sqrt{3}\,\hat{\mathbf{i}}$

$$\theta = \cos^{-1}\left(\frac{\mathbf{r}\cdot\mathbf{v}}{rv}\right) = \cos^{-1}\left(2\sqrt{\frac{3}{13}}\right)$$

17. $T = \frac{2u\sin\theta}{g} = \frac{2(20)\frac{1}{\sqrt{2}}}{10} = 2\sqrt{2}$ s

$$R = \frac{u^2\sin 2\theta}{g} = \frac{20^2\sin 90°}{10} = 40 \text{ m}$$

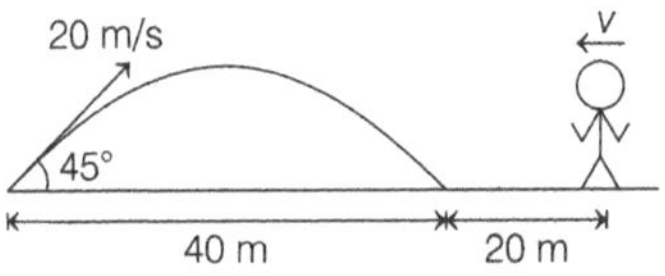

$$20 = v(2\sqrt{2}) \Rightarrow v = 5\sqrt{2} \text{ m/s}$$

18.

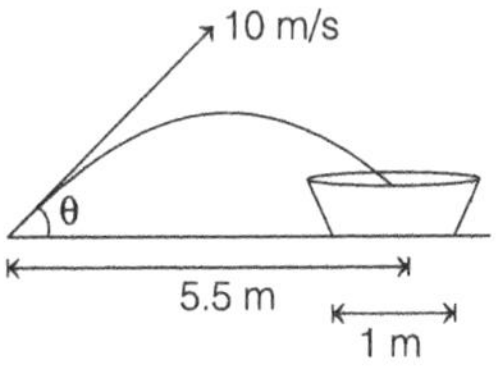

$$R_{max} = 6 \Rightarrow \frac{10^2\sin 2\theta}{10} = 6$$

$\Rightarrow \quad \sin 2\theta = \frac{3}{5}$

$\Rightarrow \quad 2\theta = 37°$ or $2\theta = 143°$

$\Rightarrow \quad \theta = 18.5°$ or $\theta = 71.5°$

$R_{min} = 5$

$\Rightarrow \quad \frac{10^2\sin 2\theta}{10} = 5 \Rightarrow \sin 2\theta = \frac{1}{2}$

$\Rightarrow \quad 2\theta = 30°$ or $2\theta = 150°$

$\Rightarrow \quad \theta = 15°$ or $\theta = 75°$

$\theta = [15°, 18.5°] \cup [71.5°, 75°]$

19.

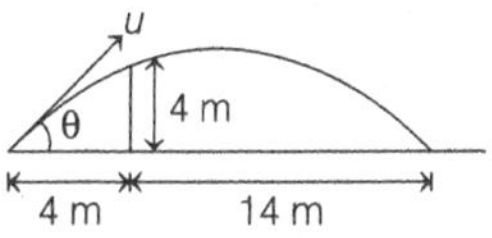

$$y = x\tan\theta\left(1 - \frac{x}{R}\right) \Rightarrow 4 = 4\tan\theta\left(1 - \frac{4}{18}\right)$$

$\Rightarrow \quad \tan\theta = \frac{9}{7}$

$$R = \frac{u^2\sin 2\theta}{g} = 18$$

$$\Rightarrow \frac{u^2\, 2\left(\frac{9}{\sqrt{130}}\,\frac{7}{\sqrt{130}}\right)}{9.8} = 18 \Rightarrow u = \sqrt{182} \text{ m/s}$$

$\Rightarrow$ Initial velocity $= \sqrt{182}$ m/s at an angle of $\tan^{-1}\left(\frac{9}{7}\right)$ with horizontal.

6.2 Projection from Certain Height

1. (a) $T = \sqrt{\frac{2h}{g}} = \sqrt{\frac{2\times 490}{9.8}} = 10$ s

(b) $R = uT = 98 \times 10 = 980$ m

(c) $\mathbf{v} = u\hat{\mathbf{i}} + \sqrt{2gH}\,\hat{\mathbf{j}} = 98\hat{\mathbf{i}} + 98\hat{\mathbf{j}}$

$= 98\sqrt{2}$ m/s at an angle of 45°

2. (a) $\sqrt{\frac{2H}{g}} = \sqrt{20}$ s for each of them

(b) $x = ut = 10(3) = 30$ m

(c) $\mathbf{v} = 10\hat{\mathbf{i}} + 20\sqrt{5}\hat{\mathbf{j}}$

$$\phi = \tan^{-1}\left(\frac{20\sqrt{5}}{10}\right) = \tan^{-1}(2\sqrt{5})$$

(d) $R = uT = 10(2\sqrt{5}) = 20\sqrt{5}$ m

3.

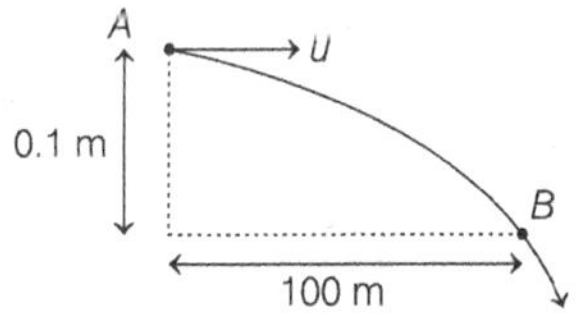

$$R = ut \Rightarrow 100 = u\sqrt{\frac{2(0.1)}{9.8}} \Rightarrow u = 700 \text{ m/s}$$

4. $x = ut = 9(0.5) = 4.5$ m $\Rightarrow y = \frac{1}{2}gt^2 = \frac{5}{4}$ m

$\mathbf{r} = 4.5\hat{\mathbf{i}} + 1.25\hat{\mathbf{j}} \Rightarrow r = \sqrt{(4.5)^2 + (1.25)^2} = \frac{\sqrt{349}}{2}$ m

$\mathbf{v} = u\hat{\mathbf{i}} + gt\hat{\mathbf{j}} \Rightarrow \mathbf{v} = (9\hat{\mathbf{i}} + 5\hat{\mathbf{j}})$ m/s

5. $R = uT = u\sqrt{\frac{2H}{g}} \Rightarrow 180 = u\sqrt{\frac{2(55-10.9)}{9.8}} \Rightarrow u = 60$ m/s

6. (a) $s_y = u_y t + \frac{1}{2}a_y t^2 \Rightarrow +11 = (+10\sin 37°)T + \frac{1}{2}(+10)T^2$

$\Rightarrow 5T^2 + 6T - 11 = 0 \Rightarrow T = 1$ s

(b) $R = u_x T = (10\cos 37°)\times 1 = 8m$

(c) $\mathbf{v} = u\cos\theta\,\hat{\mathbf{i}} + (u\sin\theta + gt)\,\hat{\mathbf{j}} \Rightarrow \mathbf{v} = 8\hat{\mathbf{i}} + 16\hat{\mathbf{j}}$

Speed $= 8\sqrt{5}$ m/s

7. (a) $\mathbf{v} = u\cos\theta\,\hat{\mathbf{i}} + (u\sin\theta - gt)\,\hat{\mathbf{j}}$

$= 8\hat{\mathbf{i}} + (6 - 2(10))\,\hat{\mathbf{j}} = 8\hat{\mathbf{i}} - 14\hat{\mathbf{j}}$

(b) $s_y = u_y t + \frac{1}{2}a_y t^2 \Rightarrow -11 = 6T - 5T^2$

$5T^2 - 6T - 11 = 0 \Rightarrow T = \frac{11}{5}$ s

(c) $R = u_x T = 8\left(\frac{11}{5}\right) = \frac{88}{5}$ m

(d) $H = 11 + \frac{u^2\sin^2\theta}{2g} = 11 + 1.8 = 12.8$ m

(e) $\mathbf{v} = u\cos\theta\,\hat{\mathbf{i}} + (u\sin\theta - gt)\,\hat{\mathbf{j}}$

$= 8\hat{\mathbf{i}} + \left(6 - 10\left(\frac{11}{5}\right)\right)\hat{\mathbf{j}} = 8\hat{\mathbf{i}} - 16\hat{\mathbf{j}}$

Speed $= 8\sqrt{5}$ m/s

8. $\tan 30° = \frac{H}{R} \Rightarrow \frac{1}{\sqrt{3}} = \frac{\frac{1}{2}g(3)^2}{u(3)} \Rightarrow u = 15\sqrt{3}$ m/s

9. $\mathbf{v} = 18\hat{\mathbf{i}} + v_y\hat{\mathbf{j}} \Rightarrow \tan 45° = \frac{v_y}{18} \Rightarrow v_y = 18$ m/s

10.

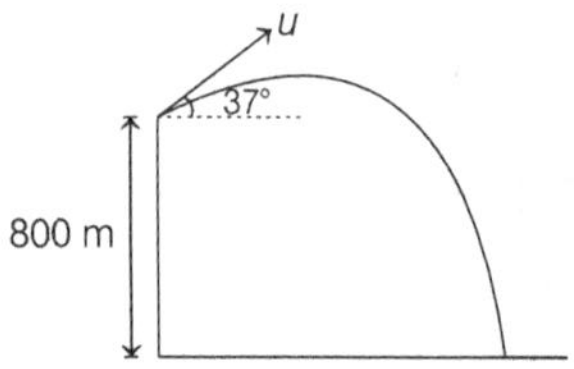

(a) $s_y = u_y t + \frac{1}{2}a_y t^2$

$-800 = (u\sin 37°)(20) + \frac{1}{2}(-10)(20)^2 \Rightarrow u = 100$ m/s

(b) $H_{max} = 800 + \frac{u^2\sin^2\theta}{2g} = 980$ m

(c) $R = (u\cos 37°)T = 80 \times 20 = 1600$ m

(d) $\mathbf{v} = u\cos\theta\,\hat{\mathbf{i}} + (u\sin\theta - gt)\,\hat{\mathbf{j}}$

$= 80\hat{\mathbf{i}} + (60 - 20\times 10)\,\hat{\mathbf{j}} = 80\hat{\mathbf{i}} - 140\hat{\mathbf{j}}$

$\tan\phi = \frac{140}{80} = \frac{7}{4} \Rightarrow \phi = \tan^{-1}\left(\frac{7}{4}\right)$

Speed $= \sqrt{80^2 + 140^2} = 20\sqrt{65}$ m/s

6.3 Projection on Inclined Plane

1. (a) $H = \frac{u^2\sin^2\theta}{2g\cos\alpha} = \frac{50^2\sin^2 37°}{2(10)\cos 30°} = 30\sqrt{3}$ m

(b) $T = \frac{2u\sin\theta}{g\cos\alpha} = \frac{2\times 50\times\frac{3}{5}}{10\cos 30°} = 4\sqrt{3}$ s

(c) $s_x = u_x t + \frac{1}{2}a_x t^2$

$\Rightarrow R = 40(4\sqrt{3}) + \frac{1}{2}(-g\sin 30°)(4\sqrt{3})^2$

$\Rightarrow R = 160\sqrt{3} - 120 = 40(4\sqrt{3} - 3)$ m

(d) $\theta = \frac{\pi}{4} - \frac{\alpha}{2} = 45° - 15° = 30°$

(e) $R_{max} = \frac{u^2}{g(1+\sin\alpha)} = \frac{500}{3}$ m

2.

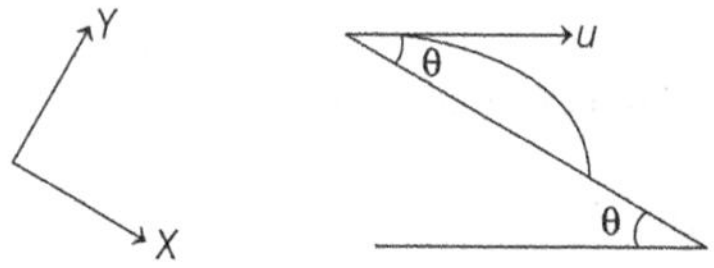

$s_x = u_x t + \frac{1}{2}a_x t^2$

$\Rightarrow R = (u\cos\theta)\left(\frac{2u\sin\theta}{g\cos\theta}\right) + \frac{1}{2}(g\sin\theta)\left(\frac{2u\sin\theta}{g\cos\theta}\right)^2$

$\Rightarrow R = \frac{2u^2\sin\theta}{g} + \frac{2u^2\sin^3\theta}{g\cos^2\theta} = \frac{2u^2\sin\theta}{g\cos^2\theta}$

3.

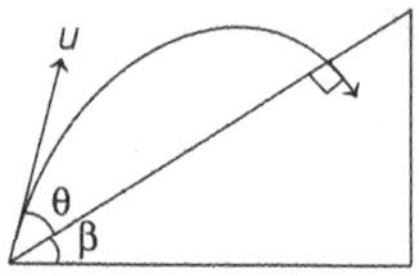

(a) $T = \frac{2u\sin\theta}{g\cos\beta}$

$v_x = u_x + a_x t$

$\Rightarrow 0 = u\cos\theta - g\sin\beta\left(\frac{2u\sin\theta}{g\cos\beta}\right) \Rightarrow 2\tan\theta = \cot\beta$

(b)

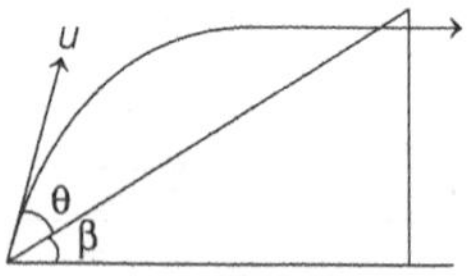

$\frac{u\sin(\theta+\beta)}{g} = \frac{2u\sin\theta}{g\cos\beta} \Rightarrow 2\sin\theta = \sin(\theta+\beta)\cos\beta$

4. (a) $a_x = -g\sin\beta$

(b) $a_y = -g\cos\beta$

(c) $v_x = u\cos\theta - (g\sin\beta)t$

(d) $v_y = u\sin\theta - (g\cos\beta)t$

(e) $x = (u\cos\theta)t - \frac{1}{2}(g\sin\beta)t^2$

(f) $y = (u\sin\theta)t - \frac{1}{2}(g\cos\beta)t^2$

(g) $v_y = 0$

Level 2

Single Choice Correct Questions

1. $R = 4\sqrt{3}H$

$$\Rightarrow \frac{u^2 \sin 2\theta}{g} = \frac{4\sqrt{3}\, u^2 \sin^2\theta}{2g} \Rightarrow \tan\theta = \frac{1}{\sqrt{3}} \Rightarrow \theta = 30°$$

2. $R = 2H$

$$\Rightarrow \frac{v^2 \sin 2\theta}{g} = 2\frac{v^2 \sin^2\theta}{2g} \Rightarrow \tan\theta = \frac{1}{2}$$

$$R = \frac{v^2 \sin 2\theta}{g} = \frac{v^2\, 2\sin\theta\cos\theta}{g}$$

$$= \frac{v^2\, 2\left(\frac{1}{\sqrt{5}}\right)\left(\frac{2}{\sqrt{5}}\right)}{g} = \frac{4v^2}{5g}$$

3. $R = 5T^2$

$$\Rightarrow \frac{u^2 \sin 2\theta}{g} = 5\left(\frac{2u\sin\theta}{g}\right)^2 \Rightarrow \tan\theta = 1 \Rightarrow \theta = 45°$$

4. $R = 2H$

$$\Rightarrow \frac{u^2 \sin 2\theta}{g} = 2\left(\frac{u^2\sin^2\theta}{2g}\right) \Rightarrow \tan\theta = 2$$

$$\tan\theta = \frac{b}{a} = 2 \Rightarrow b = 2a$$

5. $H = \frac{u_y^2}{2g} \Rightarrow u_y = \sqrt{2gH}$

$$T = \frac{2u_y}{g} = \frac{2\sqrt{2gH}}{g} = 2\sqrt{\frac{2H}{g}}$$

6. $\tan 37° = \frac{H}{\left(\frac{R}{2}\right)} \Rightarrow \frac{3}{4} = \frac{\frac{u^2\sin^2\theta}{2g}}{\frac{(u^2\sin 2\theta/g)}{2}}$

$$\frac{3}{4} = \frac{\tan\theta}{2} \Rightarrow \tan\theta = \frac{3}{2}$$

7. $45° + \theta$ and $45° - \theta$ are complementary angle. So, the range will be same.

8. $R = \frac{u^2 \sin 2\theta}{g} \Rightarrow 1.5\,\text{km} = \frac{u^2 \sin 30°}{g} \Rightarrow \frac{u^2}{g} = 3\,\text{km}$

$$R = \frac{u^2}{g}\sin(2\times 45°) = \frac{u^2}{g} = 3\,\text{km}$$

9. $H_{max} = \frac{u^2}{2g} = h \Rightarrow \frac{u^2}{g} = 2h \Rightarrow R_{max} = \frac{u^2}{g} = 2h$

10. $R_{max} = \frac{u^2}{g} = 100 \Rightarrow u = \sqrt{980}\,\text{m/s} = 31\,\text{m/s}$

11. $H = \frac{u^2\sin^2\theta}{2g} \Rightarrow 40 = \frac{(56)^2\sin^2\theta}{2\times 9.8}$

$$\Rightarrow \sin^2\theta = \frac{1}{4} \Rightarrow \sin\theta = \frac{1}{2} \Rightarrow \theta = 30°$$

12. $R_{max} = \frac{u^2}{g} = \frac{(\sqrt{10})^2}{10} = 1\,\text{m}$

Minimum number of jumps $= \frac{10}{1} = 10$

13. $R = \frac{u^2 \sin 2\theta}{g} \Rightarrow R - 3 = \frac{u^2\sin(2\times 15°)}{g}$ ...(i)

$$R + 12 = \frac{u^2 \sin(2\times 45°)}{g} \quad \text{...(ii)}$$

Solving Eqs. (i) and (ii), we get

$$R = 18\text{ m and } \frac{u^2}{g} = 30\text{ m}$$

Now, $R = \frac{u^2\sin 2\theta}{g} \Rightarrow 18 = 30\sin 2\theta$

$$\Rightarrow \sin 2\theta = \frac{3}{5} \Rightarrow 2\theta = 37° \Rightarrow \theta = 18.5°$$

14. $\mathbf{u} = u\cos\theta\,\hat{\mathbf{i}} + u\sin\theta\,\hat{\mathbf{j}} \Rightarrow \mathbf{v} = u\cos\theta\,\hat{\mathbf{i}}$

$$\Delta\mathbf{v} = \mathbf{v} - \mathbf{u} = -u\sin\theta\,\hat{\mathbf{j}}$$

15. $\mathbf{p}_1 = m(u\cos\theta\,\hat{\mathbf{i}} + u\sin\theta\,\hat{\mathbf{j}})$

$$\mathbf{p}_2 = m(u\cos\theta\,\hat{\mathbf{i}} - u\sin\theta\,\hat{\mathbf{j}})$$

$$\Delta\mathbf{p} = \mathbf{p}_2 - \mathbf{p}_1 = -2mu\sin\theta\,\hat{\mathbf{j}}$$

$$|\Delta\mathbf{p}| = 2mu\sin\theta = 2\times 0.5\times 98\times\sin 30° = 49\text{ N-s}$$

16. $v_y = v_x \Rightarrow u\sin\alpha - gt = u\cos\alpha$

$$\Rightarrow t = \frac{u}{g}(\sin\alpha - \cos\alpha)$$

17. $H = \frac{u_y^2}{2g}, T = \frac{2u_y}{g}, R = \frac{2u_x u_y}{g}$

Since, all three have same maximum heights they will have same vertical component of velocity (v_y).

Time of flight of all three will be same.

C has the greatest range. So, horizontal component of velocity will be greatest for *C*.

18. $v_{avg} = \frac{s}{t} = \frac{v\cos\theta\, t}{t} = v\cos\theta$

19. $\tan 45° = \frac{u\sin\theta - g(1)}{u\cos\theta}$ ...(i)

$$\tan 0° = \frac{u\sin\theta - g(2)}{u\cos\theta} \quad \text{...(ii)}$$

Solving Eqs. (i) and (ii), we get

$$u\sin\theta = 20 \text{ and } u\cos\theta = 10$$

$$\Rightarrow \tan\theta = 2 \Rightarrow \theta = \tan^{-1}(2)$$

20. $\mathbf{u} = u\cos\theta\,\hat{\mathbf{i}} + u\sin\theta\,\hat{\mathbf{j}}$

$$\mathbf{v} = u\cos\theta\,\hat{\mathbf{i}}$$

$$\mathbf{v}_{avg} = \frac{\mathbf{u}+\mathbf{v}}{2} = u\cos\theta\,\hat{\mathbf{i}} + \frac{u\sin\theta}{2}\hat{\mathbf{j}}$$

$$|\mathbf{v}_{avg}| = \sqrt{(u\cos\theta)^2 + \left(\frac{u\sin\theta}{2}\right)^2} = \frac{u}{2}\sqrt{1 + 3\cos^2\theta}$$

21. $u \cos\theta = v \cos(90 - \theta)$

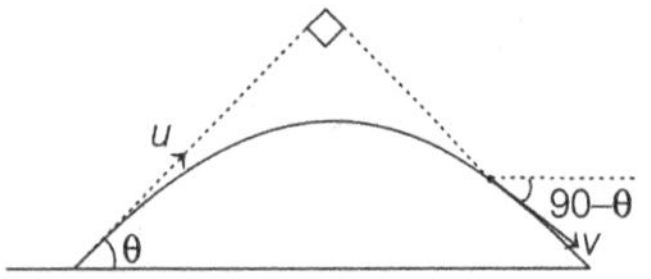

$v = u \cot\theta$

22. $\tan(-60°) = \dfrac{10 \sin 30° - 10t}{10 \cos 30°} \Rightarrow t = 2\text{ s}$

23. $\tan(-30°) = \dfrac{50 \sin 53° - 10t}{50 \cos 53°} \Rightarrow -\dfrac{1}{\sqrt{3}} = \dfrac{40 - 10t}{30}$

$\Rightarrow 10t - 40 = 10\sqrt{3} \Rightarrow t = (4 + \sqrt{3})\text{ s}$

24. $\tan 53° = \dfrac{20}{u \cos\theta}$

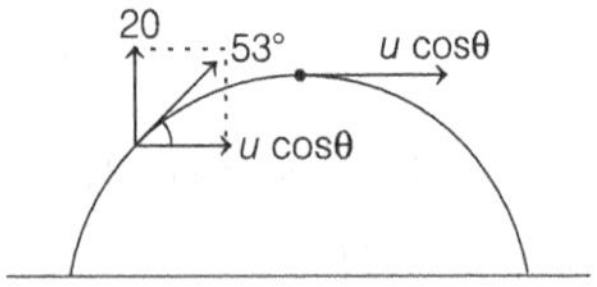

$u \cos\theta = 15\text{ m/s}$

25.

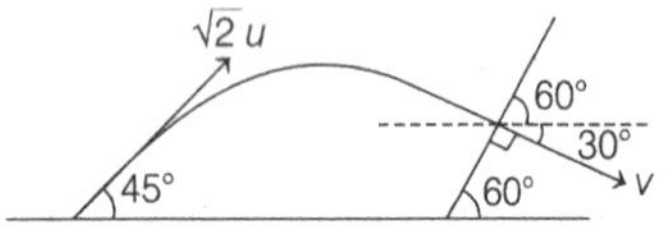

$\sqrt{2}u \cos 45° = v \cos 30° \Rightarrow v = \dfrac{2u}{\sqrt{3}}$

26. $v_y = u_y + a_y t$

$\Rightarrow -\left(\dfrac{2u}{\sqrt{3}} \sin 30°\right) = (\sqrt{2}u \sin 45°) - gt \Rightarrow t = \dfrac{u}{g}\left(1 + \dfrac{1}{\sqrt{3}}\right)$

27. $K = \dfrac{1}{2} mu^2 \Rightarrow K' = \dfrac{1}{2} m (u \cos 30°)^2 = \dfrac{3K}{4}$

28. $\dfrac{1}{2} mu^2 = 100$ ...(i)

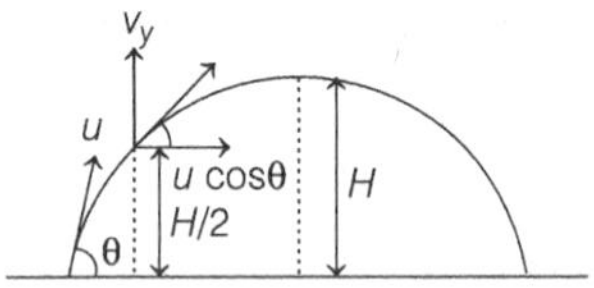

$v_y^2 = u_y^2 + 2a_y s_y$

$\Rightarrow v_y^2 = u^2 \sin^2\theta - 2g\left[\left(\dfrac{u^2 \sin^2\theta}{2g}\right)\dfrac{1}{2}\right]$

$\Rightarrow v_y = \dfrac{u \sin\theta}{\sqrt{2}}$

$\text{Speed} = \sqrt{(u \cos\theta)^2 + \dfrac{u^2 \sin^2\theta}{2}} = u\sqrt{\dfrac{1 + \cos^2\theta}{2}}$

$K = \dfrac{1}{2} mu^2 \left(\dfrac{1 + \cos^2\theta}{2}\right) = 75$ ...(ii)

From Eqs. (i) and (ii), we get

$\dfrac{1 + \cos^2\theta}{2} = \dfrac{75}{100} = \dfrac{3}{4} \Rightarrow 4 + 4\cos^2\theta = 6$

$\Rightarrow \cos\theta = \dfrac{1}{\sqrt{2}} \Rightarrow \theta = 45°$

29. $s_y = u_y t + \dfrac{1}{2} a_y t^2$

$5 = (25 \sin\theta)(2) + \dfrac{1}{2}(-10)(2)^2 \Rightarrow \sin\theta = \dfrac{1}{2} \Rightarrow \theta = 30°$

30. $R = \dfrac{u^2 \sin 2\theta}{g} = \dfrac{(50)^2 \sin 60°}{10} = 125\sqrt{3}\text{ m}$

$x = (u \cos\theta)t = (50 \cos 30°)3 = 75\sqrt{3}\text{ m}$

Distance beyond wall $= R - x = 125\sqrt{3} - 75\sqrt{3}$

$= 50\sqrt{3} = 86.6\text{ m}$

31. $K + U = \text{constant}$

$K + mgh = \text{constant}$

and at the maximum height, kinetic energy is not zero.

32. Kinetic energy first decreases and then increases and at the highest point it is minimum.

33. Maximum height and time of flight will be unchanged as they depend only on y-direction.

$s_x = u_x t + \dfrac{1}{2} a_x t^2$

$\Rightarrow R' = (u \cos\theta)\left(\dfrac{2u \sin\theta}{g}\right) + \dfrac{1}{2}\left(\dfrac{g}{4}\right)\left(\dfrac{2u \sin\theta}{g}\right)^2$

$\Rightarrow R' = R + H$

34. $\tan\beta = \dfrac{y}{x} = \dfrac{u \sin\alpha t - \dfrac{1}{2} gt^2}{u \cos\alpha}$

$\Rightarrow \tan\beta = \tan\alpha - \dfrac{gt}{2u \cos\alpha}$

$\Rightarrow \dfrac{gt}{2u \cos\alpha} = \tan\alpha - \tan\beta$

$\Rightarrow u = \dfrac{gt}{2 \cos\alpha\left(\dfrac{\sin\alpha}{\cos\alpha} - \dfrac{\sin\beta}{\cos\beta}\right)}$

$\Rightarrow u = \dfrac{gt \cos\beta}{2 \sin(\alpha - \beta)}$

35. $y = x \tan\theta - \dfrac{gx^2}{2u^2 \cos^2\theta}$

$\dfrac{A}{B} = \dfrac{\tan\theta}{\left(\dfrac{g}{2u^2 \cos^2\theta}\right)} = \dfrac{2u^2 \cos\theta \sin\theta}{g} = \dfrac{u^2 \sin 2\theta}{g}$

$\Rightarrow \dfrac{A}{B} = \dfrac{(20)^2}{10} \sin 90° = 40 : 1$

36. $y = x \tan\theta - \dfrac{gx^2}{2u^2 \cos^2\theta}$

$\Rightarrow y = 50 \tan 60° - \dfrac{(9.8)(50)^2}{2(25)^2 \cos^2 60°}$

$\Rightarrow y = 50\sqrt{3} - 78.4 = 8.2\text{ m}$

37. $R = 12$ m

$$y = x\tan\theta\left(1 - \frac{x}{R}\right)$$

$$y = 8\tan 45^\circ\left(1 - \frac{8}{12}\right) = \frac{8}{3}\text{ m}$$

38. Parabolic path.

39. $T = \sqrt{\frac{2H}{g}} = \sqrt{\frac{2(396.9)}{9.8}} = 9$ s

$$R = u\sqrt{\frac{2H}{g}} = \left(720 \times \frac{5}{18}\right)9 = 1800\text{ m}$$

40. $R = u\sqrt{\frac{2H}{g}} \Rightarrow 10 = u\sqrt{\frac{2(5)}{10}} \Rightarrow u = 10$ m/s

41. Height of table $- h = \frac{1}{2}gt^2 = \frac{1}{2}\times 10 \times (0.4)^2 = 0.8$ m

$$\mathbf{v} = u\hat{\mathbf{i}} + gt\hat{\mathbf{j}} = 4\hat{\mathbf{i}} + 4\hat{\mathbf{j}}$$

Speed $= 4\sqrt{2}$ m/s

$$\tan\phi = \frac{4}{4} = 1 \Rightarrow \phi = 45^\circ$$

It hits the ground at angle of 45°.

42. $\mathbf{v} = u\hat{\mathbf{i}} + gt\,\hat{\mathbf{j}} \Rightarrow \mathbf{v} = 20\hat{\mathbf{i}} + 50\hat{\mathbf{j}}$

Speed $= \sqrt{20^2 + 50^2} = 10\sqrt{29} = 53.8$ m/s ≃ 54m/s

43. Time taken by bullet to cover horizontal distance

$$= \frac{100}{500} = 0.2\text{ s.}$$

Distance covered by bullet in vertical

$$= ut + \frac{1}{2}at^2 = 0 + \frac{1}{2}\times 10 \times (0.2)^2 = 0.2\text{ m} = 20\text{ cm}$$

44. $\tan 45^\circ = \frac{H}{R} = \frac{19.6}{u\sqrt{\frac{2(19.6)}{9.8}}} \Rightarrow u = 9.8$ m/s

45. $R = u\sqrt{\frac{2H}{g}} \Rightarrow nw = u\sqrt{\frac{2(nh)}{g}}$

$$n^2w^2 = \frac{u^2 2nh}{g} \Rightarrow n = \frac{2hu^2}{gw^2}$$

46. $R = u\sqrt{\frac{2H}{g}} \Rightarrow x = v\sqrt{\frac{2h}{g}}$ ...(i)

$$2x = v\sqrt{\frac{2(2h)}{g}} \quad \text{...(ii)}$$

Solving Eqs. (i) and (ii), we get

$$v' = \sqrt{2}v$$

47. $R = (u\cos\theta)T$

$$\Rightarrow 200\sqrt{3} = (40\cos 30^\circ)T \Rightarrow T = 10\text{ s}$$

$$s_y = u_y t + \frac{1}{2}a_y t^2$$

$$\Rightarrow -H = (40\sin 30^\circ)(10) + \frac{1}{2}(-10)(10)^2 \Rightarrow H = 300\text{ m}$$

48. $u_x = 3$ m/s, $u_y = 0$, $a_x = 0, a_y = 1$ m/s^2

$$v_x = u_x + a_x t \Rightarrow v_x = 3\text{ m/s}^2$$

$$v_y = u_y + a_y t \Rightarrow v_y = 1(4) = 4\text{ m/s}$$

$$\mathbf{v} = 3\hat{\mathbf{i}} + 4\hat{\mathbf{j}} = 5\text{ m/s at angle of } \tan^{-1}\left(\frac{4}{3}\right).$$

49. $y = \frac{1}{2}gt^2 \Rightarrow x = ut \Rightarrow y = \frac{gx^2}{2u^2}$

50. $s_y = u_y t + \frac{1}{2}a_y t^2 \Rightarrow -70 = (50\sin 30^\circ)T + \frac{1}{2}(-10)T^2$

$$\Rightarrow T^2 - 5T - 14 = 0 \Rightarrow T = 7\text{ s}$$

51. $\tan 45^\circ = \frac{v_y}{v_x}$

$$1 = \frac{\sqrt{u^2\sin^2 30^\circ + 2(-10)(-1.6)}}{u\cos 30^\circ} \Rightarrow u = 8\text{ m/s}$$

52. Along vertical,

$$s_z = u_z t + \frac{1}{2}a_z t^2 \Rightarrow -30 = 5T + \frac{1}{2}(-10)T^2$$

$$\Rightarrow T^2 - T - 6 = 0 \Rightarrow T = -2 \text{ and } T = 3$$

In horizontal plane,

$$s = ut + \frac{1}{2}at^2 \Rightarrow R = (\sqrt{3^2 + 4^2})(3) + 0 = 15\text{ m}$$

53. $\mathbf{r}_1 = \left(ut - \frac{1}{2}gt^2\right)\hat{\mathbf{j}}$

$$\mathbf{r}_2 = (u\cos\theta\, t)\,\hat{\mathbf{i}} + \left(u\sin\theta t - \frac{1}{2}gt^2\right)\hat{\mathbf{j}}$$

$$\mathbf{r}_2 - \mathbf{r}_1 = (u\cos\theta\, t)\,\hat{\mathbf{i}} + (u\sin\theta - u)\,t\,\hat{\mathbf{j}}$$

$$|\mathbf{r}_1 - \mathbf{r}_1| = ut\sqrt{\cos^2\theta + (\sin\theta - 1)^2} = ut\sqrt{2(1 - \sin\theta)}$$

54. $R_{max} = \frac{v^2}{g(1 + \sin\theta)}$

55. $s_x = u_x t + \frac{1}{2}a_x t^2$

$$\Rightarrow R = (v\cos 45^\circ)\left(\frac{2v\sin 45^\circ}{g\cos 45^\circ}\right) + \frac{1}{2}(g\sin 45^\circ)\left(\frac{2v\sin 45^\circ}{g\cos 45^\circ}\right)^2$$

$$\Rightarrow R = \frac{\sqrt{2}v^2}{g} + \frac{\sqrt{2}v^2}{g} = \frac{2\sqrt{2}v^2}{g}$$

56. $H_{max} = \frac{u^2\sin^2\theta}{2g\cos\alpha} = \frac{10^2\sin^2 37^\circ}{2\times 10\cos 53^\circ} = 3$ m

57. $T = \frac{2u\sin\theta}{g\cos\alpha} = \frac{2(10\sqrt{3})\sin 30^\circ}{10\cos 30^\circ} = 2$ s

58. $T = \frac{2u\sin(\theta - \alpha)}{g\cos\alpha}$

$$v_x = u_x + a_x t$$

$$\Rightarrow 0 = u\cos(\theta - \alpha) - g\sin\alpha\left(\frac{2u\sin(\theta - \alpha)}{g\cos\alpha}\right)$$

$$\Rightarrow 2\tan\alpha = \cot(\theta - \alpha)$$

Numerical Value Questions

1.

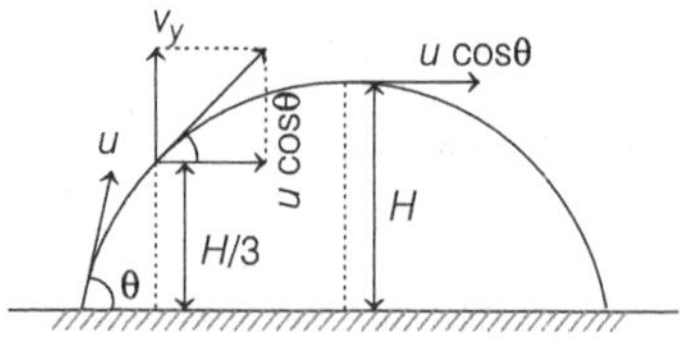

$$v_y^2 = u_y^2 + 2a_y s_y$$

$$\Rightarrow \quad v_y^2 = u^2\sin^2\theta - 2g\left[\frac{1}{3}\left(\frac{u^2\sin^2\theta}{2g}\right)\right]$$

$$\Rightarrow \quad v_y^2 = \frac{2}{3}u^2\sin^2\theta$$

$$\Rightarrow \quad v_y = \sqrt{\frac{2}{3}}\,u\sin\theta$$

$$u\cos\theta = \sqrt{\frac{3}{5}}\sqrt{(u\cos\theta)^2 + \left(\sqrt{\frac{2}{3}}\sin\theta\right)^2}$$

$$\Rightarrow \quad u^2\cos^2\theta = \frac{3}{5}u^2\left(\cos^2\theta + \frac{2}{3}\sin^2\theta\right)$$

$$\Rightarrow \quad 5^2\cos^2\theta = 3\cos^2\theta + 2\sin^2\theta \Rightarrow 2\cos^2\theta = 2\sin^2\theta$$

$$\Rightarrow \quad \tan^2\theta = 1 \Rightarrow \tan\theta = 1 \Rightarrow \theta = 45° = \frac{\pi}{4}$$

2

$$\mathbf{v} = u\hat{\mathbf{i}} + gt\hat{\mathbf{j}}$$

$$\sqrt{u^2 + g^2t^2} = 1.5u$$

$$\Rightarrow u^2 + 10^2(0.5)^2 = 2.25u^2 \Rightarrow u = \sqrt{20}\text{ m/s}$$

3. $\tan 30° = \dfrac{\sqrt{50^2\sin^2 45° - 2gH}}{50\cos 45°}$

$$\Rightarrow \quad \frac{2500}{6} = \frac{2500}{2} - 20H$$

$$\Rightarrow \quad 20H = \frac{5000}{6}$$

$$\Rightarrow \quad H = \frac{125}{3}\text{ m} = 41.67\text{ m}$$

4. $\dfrac{u\sin 37° - 10t}{u\cos 37°} = \tan(-45°)$

$$\Rightarrow \quad \frac{3u - 350}{4u} = -1$$

$$\Rightarrow \quad u = 50\text{ m/s}$$

$$s_y = u_y t + \frac{1}{2}a_y t^2$$

$$\Rightarrow \quad -H = (50\sin 37°)(7) + \frac{1}{2}(-10)(7)^2$$

$$\Rightarrow \quad -H = 210 - 245 \Rightarrow H = 35\text{ m}$$

5. $s_y = u_y t + \dfrac{1}{2}a_y t^2 \Rightarrow +h = (u\sin\theta)t - \dfrac{1}{2}gt^2$

$$\Rightarrow \quad t^2 - \left(\frac{2u\sin\theta}{g}\right)t + \frac{2h}{g} = 0$$

Lets say roots of the equation are t_1 and t_2.

$$t_1 + t_2 = \frac{2u\sin\theta}{g} = 4 \Rightarrow u\sin\theta = 20\text{ m/s}$$

$$H_{max} = \frac{u^2\sin^2\theta}{2g} = 20\text{ m}$$

6. $y = x\tan\theta - \dfrac{gx^2}{2u^2\cos^2\theta}$

$$\Rightarrow 7.5 = x\tan 45° - \frac{10x^2}{2(20)^2\cos^2 45°}$$

$$\Rightarrow \quad x^2 - 40x + 300 = 0 \Rightarrow x = 10 \text{ and } x = 30$$

$$28.4 + b = 30 \Rightarrow b = 1.6\text{ m}$$

7. $\dfrac{u^2(2\sin 37°\cos 37°)}{10} = 120 + 20\left(\dfrac{2u\sin 37°}{10}\right)$

$$\Rightarrow \quad \frac{24u^2}{250} = 120 + \frac{12u}{5}$$

$$\Rightarrow \quad u^2 - 25u - 1250 = 0$$

$$\Rightarrow u(u - 50) + 25(u - 50) = 0$$

$$\Rightarrow \quad u = 50\text{ m/s}$$

8. $T = \dfrac{2u\sin\theta}{g} = \dfrac{2(5\sqrt{2})\sin 45°}{10} = 1\text{ s}$

9.

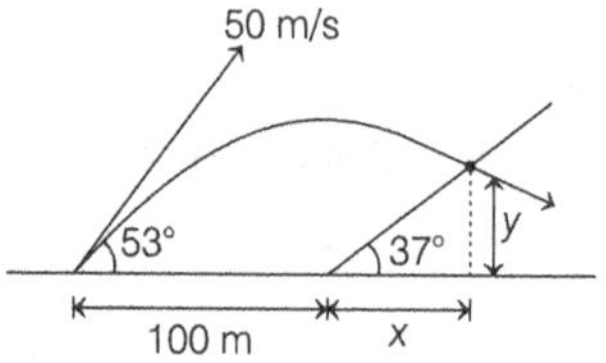

$$R = \frac{50^2\sin 106°}{10} \Rightarrow R = 240\text{ m}$$

$$\tan 37° = \frac{y}{x} = \frac{3}{4} \Rightarrow y = \frac{3x}{4}$$

$$y = (100 + x)\tan 53°\left(1 - \frac{100 + x}{240}\right)$$

$$\Rightarrow \quad \frac{3x}{4} = \frac{4}{3}(100 + x)\left(1 - \frac{100 + x}{240}\right)$$

$$\Rightarrow \quad \frac{9x}{16} = \frac{(100 + x)(140 - x)}{240} \Rightarrow x = 80\text{ m}$$

$$y = \frac{3}{4}(80) = 60\text{ m}$$

$$y = u\sin\theta t - \frac{1}{2}gt^2$$

$$\Rightarrow \quad 60 = 40t - 5t^2 \Rightarrow t^2 - 8t + 12 = 0 \Rightarrow t = 6, 2$$

10.

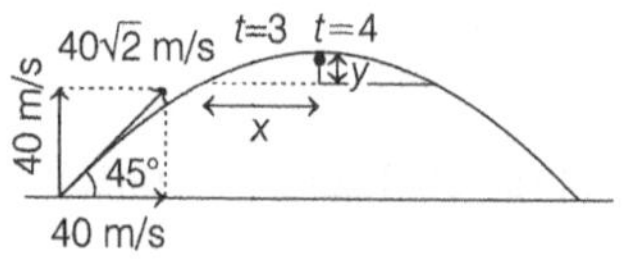

$$x = u\cos\theta t = 40(1) = 40\text{ m} \quad \text{and} \quad y = \frac{1}{2}gt^2 = 5\text{ m}$$

Displacement $= \sqrt{40^2 + 5^2} = \sqrt{1625} = 5\sqrt{65}$ m

11. $$\frac{CD}{AB} = \frac{R\tan\theta}{\frac{R}{2}\tan\theta - H} = \frac{2}{1 - \frac{2H}{R\tan\theta}} = \frac{2}{1 - \frac{2(u^2\sin^2\theta/2g)}{(u^2\sin 2\theta/g)\tan\theta}} = 4$$

12. $$y = x\tan\theta - \frac{gx^2}{2u^2\cos^2\theta} \Rightarrow 10 = 40\tan\theta - \frac{10(40)^2}{2(30)^2}\sec^2\theta$$

$$\Rightarrow 10 = 40\tan\theta - \frac{80}{9}\sec^2\theta \Rightarrow 8\sec^2\theta - 36\tan\theta + 9 = 0$$

$$8\tan^2\theta - 36\tan\theta + 17 = 0 \quad (\text{roots } \alpha, \beta)$$

$$\tan(\alpha+\beta) = \frac{\tan\alpha + \tan\beta}{1 - \tan\alpha\tan\beta} = \frac{\frac{36}{8}}{1 - \frac{17}{8}} = -\frac{36}{9} = -4$$

13.

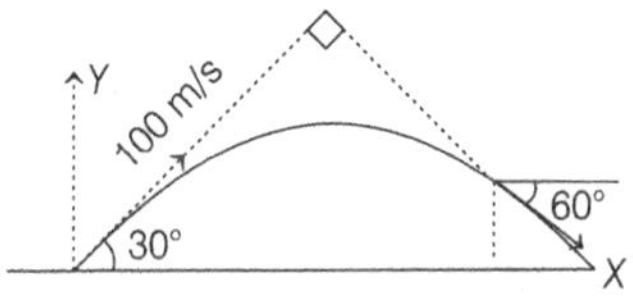

$$\tan\phi = \frac{u\sin\theta - gt}{u\cos\theta} \Rightarrow \tan(-60°) = \frac{100\sin 30° - 10t}{100\cos 30°}$$

$$\Rightarrow -150 = 50 - 10t \Rightarrow t = 20\text{ s}$$

14.

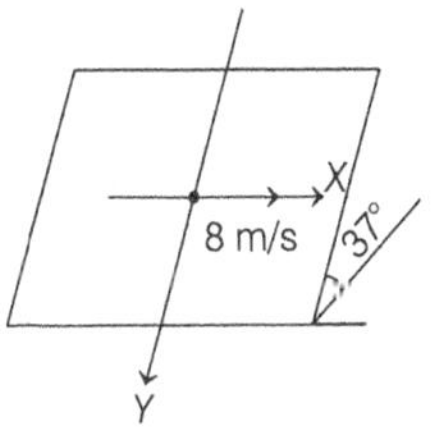

$$u_x = 8\text{ m/s}, \quad u_y = 0, \quad a_x = 0, \; a_y = g\sin 37°$$

$$v_x = u_x + a_x t = 8 + 0 = 8\text{ m/s}$$

$$v_y = u_y + a_y t = 0 + 6(1) = 6\text{ m/s}$$

$$\therefore \quad \mathbf{v} = 8\hat{\mathbf{i}} + 6\hat{\mathbf{j}}$$

Speed $= \sqrt{8^2 + 6^2} = 10$ m/s

15. $$R = (u\cos\theta)T \Rightarrow 400 = (v_0\cos 37°)T$$

$$\Rightarrow T = \frac{500}{v_0}$$

$$s_y = u_y t + \frac{1}{2}a_y t^2$$

$$\Rightarrow -100 = (v_0\sin 37°)T + \frac{1}{2}(-g)T^2$$

$$\Rightarrow -100 = 500 \times \frac{3}{5} + \frac{1}{2}(-10)\left(\frac{500}{v_0}\right)^2 \Rightarrow v_0 = 25\sqrt{5}\text{ m/s}$$

16. $$T = \frac{2u\sin\theta}{g\cos\alpha} = \frac{2 \times 20 \times \sin 90°}{10(\cos 37°)} \Rightarrow T = 5\text{ s}$$

$$s_x = u_x t + \frac{1}{2}a_x t^2 \Rightarrow R = 0 + \frac{1}{2}(10\sin 37°)(5)^2 \Rightarrow R = 75\text{ m}$$

17. $$y = bx^2 \Rightarrow \frac{dy}{dt} = b(2x)\frac{dx}{dt}$$

$$\Rightarrow \frac{d^2y}{dt^2} = \left(2b\frac{dx}{dt}\right)\left(\frac{dx}{dt}\right) + 2bx\left(\frac{d^2x}{dt^2}\right)$$

$$\Rightarrow a = 2b\left(\frac{dx}{dt}\right)^2 \qquad \left(\because \frac{d^2x}{dt^2} = a_x = 0\right)$$

$$\Rightarrow \frac{dx}{dt} = \sqrt{\frac{a}{2b}}$$

18. $$\mathbf{u} = u\cos\theta\hat{\mathbf{i}} + u\sin\theta\hat{\mathbf{j}} \Rightarrow \mathbf{v} = u\cos\theta\hat{\mathbf{i}}$$

$$\mathbf{v}_{avg} = \frac{\mathbf{v}+\mathbf{u}}{2} = u\cos\theta\hat{\mathbf{i}} + \frac{u\sin\theta}{2}\hat{\mathbf{j}} \Rightarrow \mathbf{v}_{avg} = 8\hat{\mathbf{i}} + 3\hat{\mathbf{j}}$$

$$\Rightarrow u\cos\theta = 8 \Rightarrow u\sin\theta = 6 \Rightarrow \tan\theta = \frac{3}{4}$$

19.

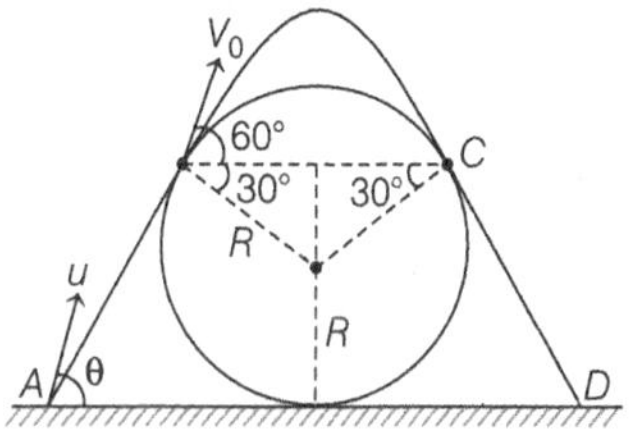

From B to C,

$$R = \frac{u^2\sin 2\theta}{g}$$

$$\Rightarrow 2R\cos 30° = \frac{u_0^2\sin 120°}{g} \Rightarrow v_0 = \sqrt{2gR}$$

From A to B,

$$v_y^2 = u_y^2 + 2a_y s_y$$

$$\Rightarrow (v_0\sin 60°)^2 = u^2\sin^2\theta - 2g(R + R\sin 30°)$$

$$\Rightarrow u\sin\theta = \sqrt{\frac{9gR}{2}} \quad \text{...(i)}$$

and $$v_x = u_x \Rightarrow v_0\cos 60° = u\cos\theta$$

$$\Rightarrow u\cos\theta = \sqrt{\frac{gR}{2}} \quad \text{...(ii)}$$

Squaring and adding Eqs. (i) and (ii), we get

$$u^2 = 5gR \Rightarrow u = \sqrt{5gR}$$

20. $$s_y = u_y t + \frac{1}{2}a_y t^2$$

$$\Rightarrow 120 - 100.4 = 0 + \frac{1}{2}(9.8)T^2$$

$$\Rightarrow T = 2\text{ s}$$

$$s_x = u_x t + \frac{1}{2}a_x t^2$$

$$\Rightarrow 16 = u_x(2) + 0 \Rightarrow u_x = 8\text{ m/s}$$

Level 3

Single Choice Correct Questions

1. $\mathbf{v} = u\cos\theta\,\hat{\mathbf{i}} + (u\sin\theta - gt)\,\hat{\mathbf{j}}$

$$\text{Speed} = \sqrt{(u\cos\theta)^2 + (u\sin\theta - gt)^2}$$

$$\Rightarrow \quad \sqrt{125} = \sqrt{(10\sqrt{2}\cos 45^\circ)^2 + (10\sqrt{2}\sin 45^\circ - 10t)^2}$$

$$\Rightarrow \quad 125 = 100 + (10 - 10t)^2 \quad \Rightarrow (10 - 10t)^2 = 25$$

$$\Rightarrow \quad |10 - 10t| = 5 \quad \Rightarrow \quad 10 - 10t = 5$$

$$\Rightarrow \quad t = 0.5\text{ s} \quad \Rightarrow \quad 10 - 10t = -5 \quad \Rightarrow \quad t = 1.5\text{ s}$$

2.

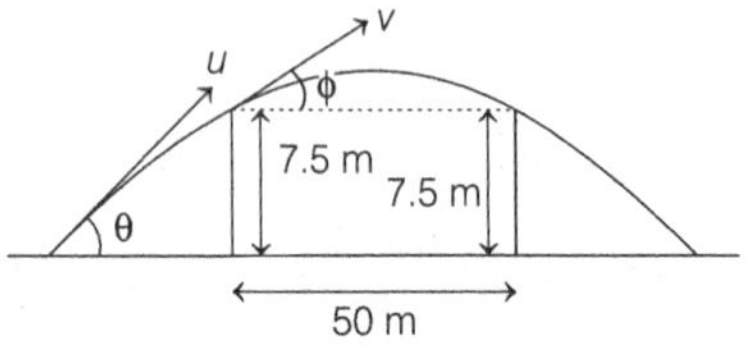

$$x = u\cos\theta\, t \quad \Rightarrow \quad 50 = u\cos\theta\,(2.5) \quad \Rightarrow \quad u\cos\theta = 20\text{ m/s}$$

$$\frac{2v\sin\phi}{g} = 2.5 \quad \Rightarrow \quad v\sin\phi = 12.5$$

$$v_y^2 = u_y^2 + 2a_y s_y$$

$$\Rightarrow \quad (12.5)^2 = u^2\sin^2\theta - 2\times 10\times 7.5$$

$$u\sin\theta = \sqrt{\frac{1225}{4}} = 17.5\text{ m/s}$$

$$R = \frac{2u_x u_y}{g} = \frac{2(20)(17.5)}{10} = 70\text{ m}$$

3. $\tan\theta = \dfrac{1080}{1440} = \dfrac{3}{4}$

$$u_x = 150\cos\theta = 120\text{ m/s}$$

$$u_y = 150\sin\theta = 90\text{ m/s}$$

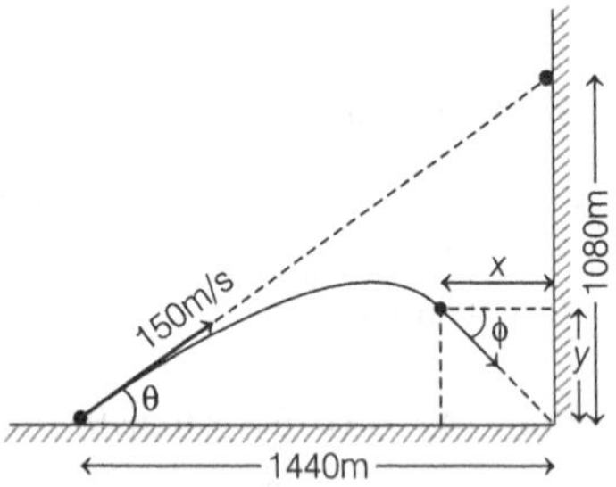

$$s_x = u_x t + \frac{1}{2}a_x t^2$$

At $t = 10$ s, $s_x = 120 \times 10 = 1200$ m

$$s_y = u_y t + \frac{1}{2}a_y t^2$$

At $t = 10$ s, $s_y = 90\times 10 + \frac{1}{2}(-10)(10)^2 = 400$ m

$$\tan\phi = \frac{v_y}{v_x} = \frac{u\sin\theta - gt}{u\cos\theta}$$

$$\Rightarrow \quad \tan\phi = \frac{90 - 10(10)}{120} = -\frac{1}{12}$$

$$\tan\phi = \frac{1}{12} = \frac{y}{x} \quad \Rightarrow \quad \frac{1}{12} = \frac{y}{1440 - 1200} \quad \Rightarrow \quad y = 20\text{ m}$$

Height from ground $= 400 - 20 = 380$ m

4. $y = x\tan\theta - \dfrac{gx^2}{2u^2}\sec^2\theta$

$$\frac{dy}{d\theta} = x\sec^2\theta - \frac{gx^2}{2u^2}(2\sec\theta)(\sec\theta\tan\theta) = 0$$

$$\Rightarrow \quad \tan\theta = \frac{u^2}{gx}$$

$$\Rightarrow \quad y_{max} = x\left(\frac{u^2}{gx}\right) - \frac{gx^2}{2u^2}\left(1 + \left(\frac{u^2}{gx}\right)^2\right)$$

$$\Rightarrow \quad y_{max} = \frac{u^4 - g^2x^2}{2gu^2}$$

5. $$\tan\phi = \frac{v_y}{v_x} = \frac{\sqrt{u^2\sin^2\theta - 2gh}}{u\cos\theta}$$

$$\tan(-30^\circ) = \frac{\sqrt{u^2\sin^2 60^\circ - 2gh}}{u\cos 60^\circ}$$

$$-\frac{u}{2\sqrt{3}} = \sqrt{\frac{3u^2}{4} - 2gh} \quad \Rightarrow \quad \frac{u^2}{12} = \frac{3u^2}{4} - 2gh$$

$$\Rightarrow \quad u = \sqrt{3gh}$$

6. $s_x = u_x t + \dfrac{1}{2}a_x t$

$$\Rightarrow \quad R = (u\cos\theta)\left(\frac{2u\sin\theta}{g}\right) + \frac{1}{2}g\left(\frac{2u\sin\theta}{g}\right)^2$$

$$\Rightarrow \quad R = \frac{u^2\sin 2\theta}{g} + \frac{2u^2}{g}\sin^2\theta$$

For R to be maximum.

$$\frac{dR}{d\theta} = \frac{u^2}{g}(2\cos 2\theta + 4\sin\theta\cos\theta) = 0$$

$$\Rightarrow \quad \tan 2\theta = -1 \quad \Rightarrow \quad 2\theta = 135^\circ \quad \Rightarrow \quad \theta = 67.5^\circ$$

7. $T = 4 + 5 = 9$

Time of flight $= \dfrac{2u\sin\theta}{g} = 9$

$$\Rightarrow \quad s_y = u_y t + \frac{1}{2}a_y t^2$$

$$\Rightarrow \quad h = (u\sin\theta)(4) - \frac{1}{2}g(4)^2$$

$$= \left(\frac{9g}{2}\right)4 - 8g = 10g = 98\text{ m}$$

8. $R_{max} = \dfrac{u^2}{g} = 250 \quad \Rightarrow \quad u = 50\text{ m/s} \quad \Rightarrow \quad T = \dfrac{T_{max}}{2}$

$$\frac{2u\sin\theta}{g} = \frac{\left(\frac{2u}{g}\right)}{2} \quad \Rightarrow \theta = 30^\circ$$

Least speed $= u\cos 30^\circ = 50\left(\dfrac{\sqrt{3}}{2}\right) = 25\sqrt{3}$ m/s

9. $\mathbf{v}_1 = u_1\hat{\mathbf{i}} + \sqrt{2gh}\,\hat{\mathbf{j}}$ and $\mathbf{v}_2 = -u_2\hat{\mathbf{i}} + \sqrt{2gh}\,\hat{\mathbf{j}}$

Since $\mathbf{v}_1 \perp \mathbf{v}_2 \Rightarrow \mathbf{v}_1 \cdot \mathbf{v}_2 = 0 \Rightarrow -u_1u_2 + 2gh = 0$

$$\Rightarrow \quad h = \frac{u_1u_2}{2g}$$

10. $$\frac{dx}{dt} = 2y\left(\frac{dy}{dt}\right) + 2\frac{dy}{dt} = 10y + 10$$

$$a_x = \frac{d^2x}{dt^2} = 10\left(\frac{dy}{dt}\right) = 50 \text{ and } a_y = 0$$

11. $$T = \sqrt{\frac{2H}{g}}$$

$$s_x = u_x t + \frac{1}{2}a_x t^2$$

$$\Rightarrow \quad 0 = 10\left(\sqrt{\frac{2H}{g}}\right) + \frac{1}{2}(-10)\left(\sqrt{\frac{2H}{g}}\right)^2 \quad \Rightarrow \sqrt{\frac{2H}{g}} = 2$$

$\Rightarrow H = 20\,\text{m}$

12. $$y = x\tan\theta - \frac{gx^2}{2u^2\cos^2\theta} \quad \Rightarrow \beta = \alpha\tan\theta - \frac{g\alpha^2}{2(\sqrt{2g\alpha})^2}\sec^2\theta$$

$$\Rightarrow \beta = \alpha\tan\theta - \frac{\alpha\sec^2\theta}{4} \quad \Rightarrow 4\beta = 4\alpha\tan\theta - \alpha - \alpha\tan^2\theta$$

$$\Rightarrow \quad \alpha\tan^2\theta - 4\alpha\tan\theta + (4\beta + \alpha) = 0$$

For θ not to exist,

$$D < 0 \quad \Rightarrow \quad b^2 - 4ac < 0$$

$$\Rightarrow \quad (4\alpha)^2 - 4\alpha(4\beta + \alpha) < 0 \quad \Rightarrow \beta > \frac{3\alpha}{4}$$

13. $v_A\cos\theta_A = v_B\cos(90 - \theta_B)$

$v_A\sin\theta_A > v_B\sin(90 - \theta_B)$

$$T = \frac{2u_y}{g}; H = \frac{u_y^2}{2g}; R = \frac{2u_xu_y}{g}$$

$$\Rightarrow \quad T_A > T_B, \quad H_A > H_B, \quad R_A > R_B$$

14. $20 = (20\cos\theta)(t_2 - t_1)$

$$s_y = u_yt + \frac{1}{2}a_y t^2$$

$$\Rightarrow +10 = (20\sin\theta)t - 5t^2 \quad \Rightarrow t^2 - 4\sin\theta\, t + 2 = 0 \quad (t_1, t_2)$$

$$(t_2 - t_1)^2 = (t_2 + t_1)^2 - 4t_1t_2$$

$$\Rightarrow \left(\frac{20}{20\cos\theta}\right)^2 = (4\sin\theta)^2 - 4(2)$$

$$\Rightarrow \quad 1 = 16\sin^2\theta\cos^2\theta - 8\cos^2\theta$$

$$\Rightarrow \quad 1 = 16(1 - \cos^2\theta)\cos^2\theta - 8\cos^2\theta$$

$$\Rightarrow \quad 16\cos^4\theta - 8\cos^2\theta + 1 = 0$$

$$\Rightarrow \cos^2\theta = \frac{1}{4} \quad \Rightarrow \cos\theta = \frac{1}{2} \quad \Rightarrow \theta = 60°$$

$$t_2 - t_1 = \frac{20}{20\cos 60°} = 2\,\text{s}$$

15. $\mathbf{v} = u\cos\theta\,\hat{\mathbf{i}} + (\sqrt{u^2\sin^2\theta - 2gh})\,\hat{\mathbf{j}}$

$$\sqrt{u^2\cos^2\theta + \sqrt{(u^2\sin^2\theta - 2gh)^2}}$$

$$= \frac{1}{2}\sqrt{u^2\cos^2\theta + (\sqrt{u^2\sin^2\theta - gh})^2}$$

$$\Rightarrow \quad u^2 - 2gh = \frac{1}{4}(u^2 - gh) \quad \Rightarrow \quad \frac{u^2}{g} = \frac{7h}{3}$$

$$R_{\max} = \frac{u^2}{g} = \frac{7h}{3}$$

16. $$y = x\tan\theta - \frac{gx^2}{2u^2\cos^2\theta} = \sqrt{3}x - \frac{2gx^2}{u^2} > x$$

$$\Rightarrow \quad \frac{2gx^2}{u^2} < (\sqrt{3} - 1)\,x \quad \Rightarrow \left(\frac{x}{u\cos 60°}\right) < (\sqrt{3} - 1)\,u$$

$$\Rightarrow \quad t < (\sqrt{3} - 1)\frac{u}{g}$$

17.

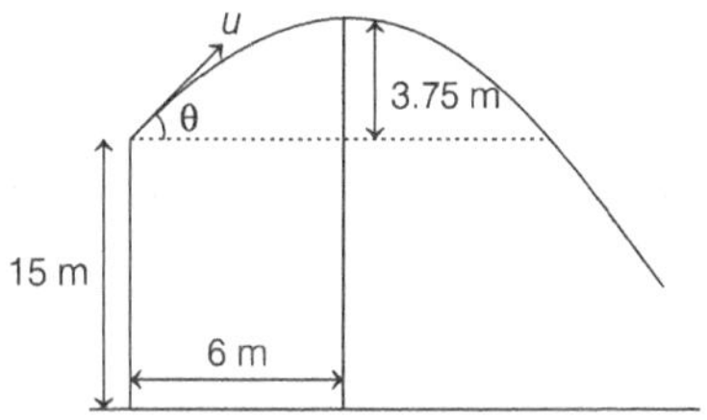

$$y = x\tan\theta - \frac{gx^2}{2u^2\cos^2\theta} \quad \Rightarrow 3.75 = 6\tan\theta - \frac{5(6)^2}{(12)^2}$$

$$\Rightarrow \quad 6\tan\theta = 3.75 + \frac{5}{4} \quad \Rightarrow \tan\theta = \frac{20}{24} = \frac{5}{6} \quad \Rightarrow \quad u\cos\theta = 12$$

$$\Rightarrow \quad u\left(\frac{6}{\sqrt{61}}\right) = 12 \quad \Rightarrow \quad u = 2\sqrt{61}\,\text{m/s}$$

$$s_y = u_yt + \frac{1}{2}a_yt$$

$$\Rightarrow \quad -15 = (2\sqrt{61}\sin\theta)T + \frac{1}{2}(-10)T^2$$

$$\Rightarrow \quad -15 = 2\sqrt{61}\left(\frac{5}{\sqrt{61}}\right)T - 5T^2$$

$$\Rightarrow \quad -15 = 10T - 5T^2 \quad \Rightarrow \quad T^2 - 2T - 3 = 0$$

$$\Rightarrow (T - 3)(T + 1) = 0 \quad \Rightarrow \quad T = 3\,\text{s}$$

18. $$\tan\phi = \frac{v_y}{v_x}$$

$$\Rightarrow \quad \tan 45° = \frac{\sqrt{u^2\sin^2 30° + 2gh}}{u\cos 30°}$$

$$\Rightarrow \quad u^2\cos^2 30° = u^2\sin^2 30° + 2gh$$

$$\Rightarrow \quad u^2 = 4gh$$

$$\Rightarrow \quad u = 2\sqrt{gh}$$

$$\tan\phi = \frac{\sqrt{u^2\sin^2 60° + 2gh}}{u\cos 60°}$$

$$\Rightarrow \quad \tan\phi = \sqrt{5} \quad \Rightarrow \quad \phi = \tan^{-1}(\sqrt{5})$$

19.

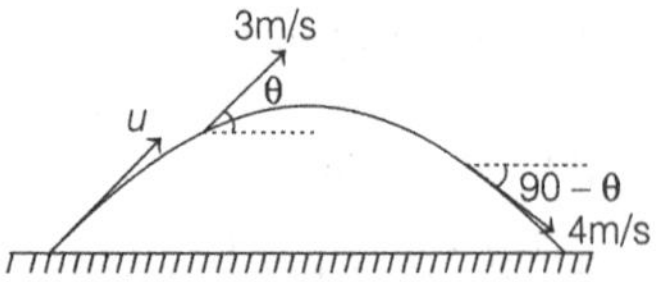

$$v_x = 3\cos\theta = 4\cos(90° - \theta)$$

$$\Rightarrow \quad \tan\theta = \frac{3}{4} \quad \Rightarrow \quad v_x = 3\left(\frac{4}{5}\right) = \frac{12}{5}\,\text{m/s}$$

$$K_{min} = \frac{1}{2}mv_x^2 = \frac{1}{2}\times 2\times\left(\frac{12}{5}\right)^2 = 5.76\text{ J}$$

20. $u_y = \tan 60° = \sqrt{3}\,\text{m/s}$

$$R = \frac{2u_xu_y}{g} \quad \Rightarrow \quad \sqrt{3} = \frac{2u_x(\sqrt{3})}{g} \quad \Rightarrow \quad u_x = 5\,\text{m/s}$$

$$\text{Speed} = \sqrt{5^2 + (\sqrt{3})^2} = \sqrt{28}\,\text{m/s}$$

21. $\Delta T = T_2 - T_1 = \dfrac{2v_0\sin\theta}{g}$

$$\Delta R = (v_0\cos\theta)\left(\frac{2v_0\sin\theta}{g}\right) = \frac{v_0^2\sin 2\theta}{g}$$

22. $\tan\phi = \dfrac{u\sin\theta - gt}{u\cos\theta} \quad \Rightarrow \quad \tan(-60°) = \dfrac{20\sin 30° - 10t}{20\cos 30°}$

$\Rightarrow \quad t = 4\text{ s}$

$$x = (u\cos\theta)t = \left(20\frac{\sqrt{3}}{2}\right)(4) = 40\sqrt{3}\text{ m}$$

23. $\sin\theta = \dfrac{8}{\sqrt{8^2 + 4^2}} \quad \Rightarrow \sin\theta = \dfrac{8}{\sqrt{80}} = \dfrac{2}{\sqrt{5}}$

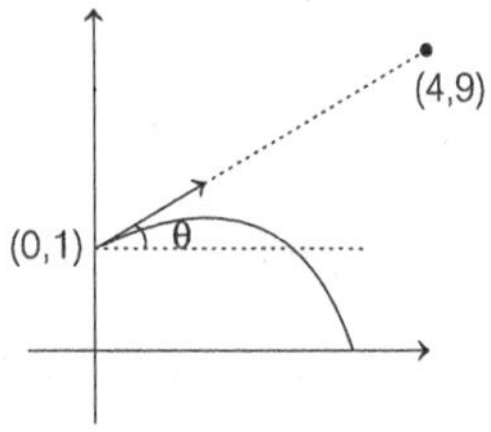

$$s_y = u_yt + \frac{1}{2}a_yt^2 \quad \Rightarrow \quad -1 = \left(u\frac{2}{\sqrt{5}}\right)(1) + \frac{1}{2}(-10)(1)^2$$

$\Rightarrow \quad u = 2\sqrt{5}\,\text{m/s}$

$$x = (u\cos\theta)t = (2\sqrt{5})\frac{(4)}{\sqrt{80}}(1) = 2\text{ m}$$

24. $y = x\tan\theta - \dfrac{gx^2}{2u^2\cos^2\theta}$

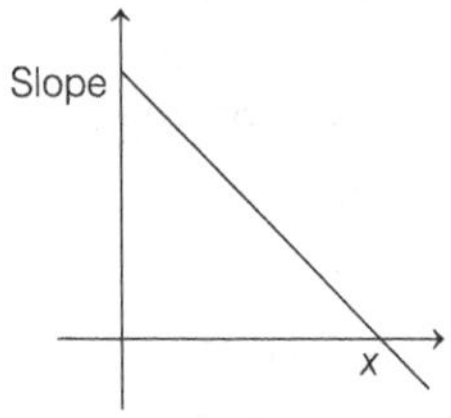

$$\text{Slope} = \frac{dy}{dx} = \tan\theta - \frac{gx}{u^2\cos^2\theta}$$

So, slope *versus* x graph will be a straight line as shown in figure.

$$\text{Slope} = \tan\theta - \frac{g(u\cos\theta)t}{u^2\cos^2\theta} = \tan\theta - \frac{gt}{u\cos\theta}$$

So, slope *versus* t graph will be a straight line as shown in figure.

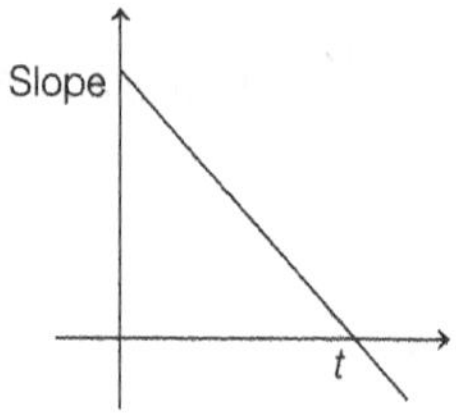

25. $R_{max} = \dfrac{u^2}{g} = \dfrac{(\sqrt{gR})^2}{g} = R$

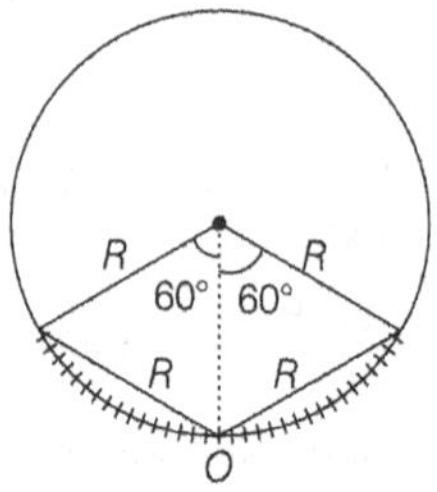

Angle subtended by arc of circle, where no ball will land $= 240°$

Length of arc $= \dfrac{4\pi R}{3}$

26. $y = x\tan\theta - \dfrac{gx^2}{2u^2\cos^2\theta}$

$$-25 = 75\tan\alpha - \frac{5(75)^2}{u^2\cos^2\alpha} \qquad \text{...(i)}$$

$$\frac{u^2\sin^2\alpha}{2g} = 20 \qquad \text{...(ii)}$$

From Eqs. (i) and (ii), we get

$$\Rightarrow \quad -25 = 75\tan\alpha - \frac{5(75)^2\sin^2\alpha}{400\cos^2\alpha}$$

$$\Rightarrow \quad \frac{45}{16}\tan^2\alpha - 3\tan\alpha - 1 = 0$$

$$\Rightarrow 45\tan^2\alpha - 48\tan\alpha - 16 = 0 \quad \Rightarrow \tan\alpha = \frac{4}{3}$$

27. $T = \sqrt{\dfrac{2H}{g}} = \sqrt{\dfrac{2(80)}{10}} = 4\text{ s}$

$$R = uT = 20\times 4 = 80\text{ m}$$

In 2 s, hunter will travel $10\times 2 = 20\text{ m}$

For bullet, $T = \dfrac{2u\sin\theta}{g} = 4 - 2 = 2\text{ s}$ ...(i)

$$R = \frac{u^2\sin 2\theta}{g} = 80 - 20 = 60\text{ m} \qquad \text{...(ii)}$$

From Eqs. (i) and (ii), we get

$$\tan\theta = \frac{1}{3} \text{ and } u = 10\sqrt{10} \text{ m/s}$$

28. $y = R(1 - \sin\theta)$ ...(i)

$x = 300 + R\cos\theta$ ...(ii)

$$y = x\tan 30° - \frac{gx^2}{2(68)^2\cos^2 30°} \quad ...(iii)$$

Solving Eqs. (i), (ii) and (iii), we get

$$x = 373 \text{ m and } y = 18.75 \text{ m}$$

29.

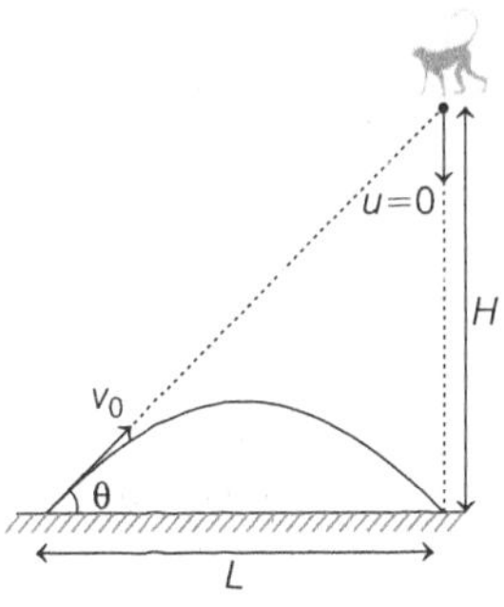

For minimum speed,arrow will hit the monkey just at ground.

$$T = \frac{2v_0\sin\theta}{g} = \sqrt{\frac{2H}{g}} \Rightarrow v_0\sin\theta = \sqrt{\frac{gH}{2}} \quad ...(i)$$

$$R = L = (v_0\cos\theta)\sqrt{\frac{2H}{g}} \Rightarrow v_0\cos\theta = \sqrt{\frac{gL^2}{2H}} \quad ...(ii)$$

Adding and squaring Eqs. (i) and (ii), we get

$$v_0 = \sqrt{\frac{g(H^2 + L^2)}{2H}}$$

30.

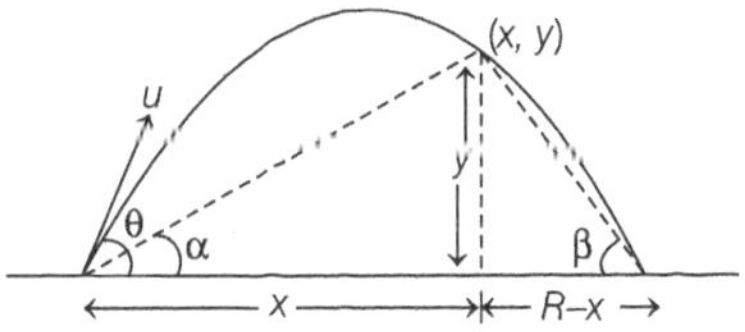

$$y = x\tan\theta\left(1 - \frac{x}{R}\right) \quad ...(i)$$

$$\tan\alpha = \frac{y}{x} \quad ...(ii)$$

$$\tan\beta = \frac{y}{R - x} \quad ...(iii)$$

Solving Eqs. (i), (ii) and (iii), we get

$$\tan\theta = \tan\alpha + \tan\beta$$

31. Both will have same range

$$T_1 = \frac{2u\sin 53°}{g}, T_2 = \frac{2u\sin 37°}{g}$$

$$T_1 - T_2 = \frac{2u}{g}(\sin 53° - \sin 37°) = 10 \text{ s}$$

32. $y = x\tan\theta - \dfrac{gx^2}{2u^2\cos^2\theta} \Rightarrow 4 = 2\tan\theta - \dfrac{5(2)^2}{(2)^2}$

$$\Rightarrow \tan\theta = \frac{9}{2} \Rightarrow \theta = \tan^{-1}\left(\frac{9}{2}\right)$$

33. $H_A = \dfrac{u^2\sin^2\alpha}{2g\cos\theta}, \; H_B = \dfrac{u^2}{2g\cos\theta}, \; H_C = \dfrac{u^2\cos^2\alpha}{2g\cos\theta}$

$$\Rightarrow H_A + H_C = H_B$$

34.

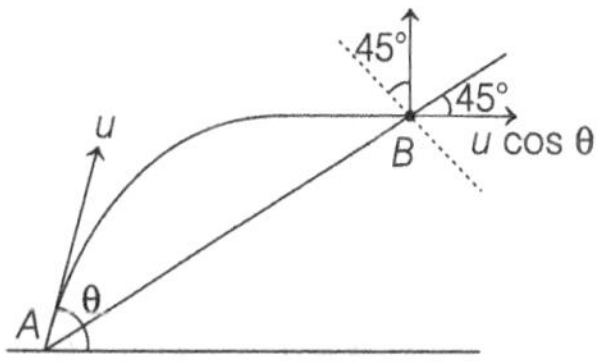

After the elastic collision with the inclined plane, the particle moves in vertical direction.

The inclination of plane with horizontal is 45°, hence velocity of particle just before collision should be horizontal.

$$T = T_{AB} + T_{BC} = \frac{u\sin\theta}{g} + \frac{u\cos\theta}{g} = \frac{u(\sin\theta + \cos\theta)}{g}$$

35.

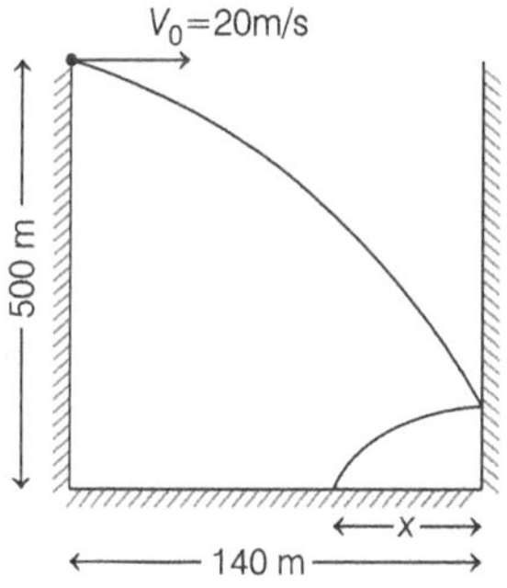

Since, v_y is not affected in collision, time of flight will be unchanged.

$$T = \sqrt{\frac{2H}{g}} = \sqrt{\frac{2 \times 500}{10}} = 10 \text{ s}$$

$$s_x = u_x t + \frac{1}{2}a_x t^2$$

$\Rightarrow \quad 140 = 20t + 0 \quad \Rightarrow t = 7 \text{ s}$

So, collision will take place at $t = 7$ s.

Remaining time $= 10 - 7 = 3$ s

$$s_x = u_x t + \frac{1}{2}a_x t^2 \Rightarrow x = 20 \times 3 + 0 = 60 \text{ m}$$

36. $x = (50\cos 53°)t \Rightarrow y = (50\sin 53°)t - \dfrac{1}{2}gt^2$

Distance travelled by ball in horizontal + distance travelled by wall = 200

$\Rightarrow \quad x + 10t = 200$

$\Rightarrow \; 30t + 10t = 200 \quad \Rightarrow \quad t = 5$ s

Coordinates = (150, 75)

37.

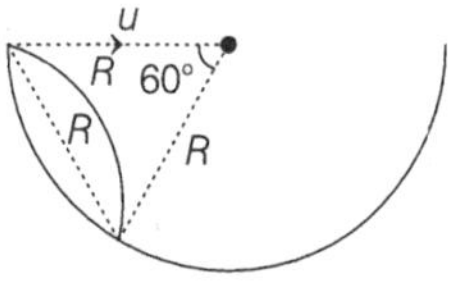

$$T=\sqrt{\frac{2H}{g}} \Rightarrow T=\sqrt{\frac{2(R\sin 60°)}{g}} \Rightarrow T=\sqrt{\frac{\sqrt{3}R}{g}}$$

38. $$\frac{u^2}{g(1-\sin\theta)}=\frac{3u^2}{g\,(1+\sin\theta)}$$

$\Rightarrow \quad 1+\sin\theta=3-3\sin\theta \Rightarrow 4\sin\theta=2$

$\Rightarrow \quad \sin\theta=\frac{1}{2} \Rightarrow \theta=30°$

39. $s_x=u_xt+\frac{1}{2}a_xt^2 \Rightarrow R=[(\sqrt{2ag})\cos\theta]T$ ...(i)

$s_y=u_yt+\frac{1}{2}a_yt^2$

$\Rightarrow \quad -h=(\sqrt{2ag}\,\sin\theta)T+\frac{1}{2}(-g)(T)^2$ ...(ii)

From Eqs. (i) and (ii), we get

$$-h=\sqrt{2ag}\,\sin\theta\frac{R}{\sqrt{2ag}\,\cos\theta}-\frac{1}{2}g\left(\frac{R}{\sqrt{2ag}\,\cos\theta}\right)^2$$

$\Rightarrow \quad -h=R\tan\theta-\frac{R^2}{4a}\sec^2\theta$

$\Rightarrow \quad R^2\tan^2\theta-4aR\tan\theta+(R^2-4ah)=0$

For θ to be real

$D\geq 0 \Rightarrow (4aR)^2-4R^2(R^2-4ah)\geq 0$

$\Rightarrow \quad 4a\geq R^2-4ah \Rightarrow R\leq 2\sqrt{a(a+h)}$

$\Rightarrow \quad R_{max}=2\sqrt{a(a+h)}$

40. $s_x=u_xt+\frac{1}{2}a_xt^2$

$(\sqrt{3}+1)=(v_1\cos 45°)t$ ...(i)

$(\sqrt{3}+1)=(v_2\cos 60°)t$ ...(ii)

$s_y=u_yt+\frac{1}{2}a_yt^2$

$-y=(v_1\sin 45°)t-\frac{1}{2}gt^2$ ...(iii)

$h-y=(v_2\sin 60°)t-\frac{1}{2}gt^2$ ...(iv)

From Eq. (i), we get $v_1t=(\sqrt{3}+1)\sqrt{2}$

From Eq. (ii), we get $v_2t=(\sqrt{3}+1)2$

Subtracting Eq. (iii) from Eq. (iv), we get

$h=(v_2t\sin 60°-v_1t\sin 45°)$

$\Rightarrow \quad h=(\sqrt{3}+1)2\left(\frac{\sqrt{3}}{2}\right)-(\sqrt{3}+1)\sqrt{2}\left(\frac{1}{\sqrt{2}}\right)$

$\Rightarrow \quad h=(\sqrt{3}+1)(\sqrt{3}-1)=2\text{ m}$

Multiple Choice(s) Correct Questions

1. $R=\frac{u^2\sin 2\theta}{g}=480\text{ m} \Rightarrow \frac{70^2\sin 2\theta}{9.8}=480$

$\Rightarrow \quad \sin 2\theta=\frac{480\times 9.8}{70\times 70}=\frac{24}{25} \Rightarrow \cos 2\theta=\frac{7}{25}$

$\Rightarrow 2\cos^2\theta-1=\frac{7}{25} \Rightarrow \cos^2\theta=\frac{16}{25} \Rightarrow \cos\theta=\frac{4}{5}$

$\Rightarrow \quad \theta=37°$

So, angles of projection will be 37° and 53°.

$$\frac{T_1}{T_2}=\frac{\frac{2u\sin 37°}{g}}{\frac{2u\sin 53°}{g}}=\frac{3}{4} \text{ and } \frac{H_1}{H_2}=\frac{9}{16}$$

$$\frac{u_{\min 1}}{u_{\min 2}}=\frac{u\cos 37°}{u\cos 53°}=\frac{4}{3}$$

2. $$y=x\tan\theta-\frac{gx^2}{2u^2\cos^2\theta}$$

$$\text{Slope}=\frac{dy}{dx}=\tan\theta-\frac{gx}{u^2\cos^2\theta}$$

At $x=0$; Slope $=\tan\theta=1 \Rightarrow \theta=45°$

At $x=10$; Slope $=1-\frac{g(10)}{u^2\cos^2\theta}=0$

$\Rightarrow \quad u^2\cos^2\theta=100 \Rightarrow u\cos\theta=10$

$\Rightarrow \quad u=10\sqrt{2}\text{ m/s}$

$$R=\frac{u^2\sin 2\theta}{g}=20\text{ m},\quad T=\frac{2u\sin\theta}{g}=2\text{ s}$$

$\int(\text{slope})\,dx=\int dy=$ vertical displacement

3. $y=10x-2x^2=10x\left(1-\frac{x}{5}\right)$

Comparing it with $y=x\tan\theta\left(1-\frac{x}{R}\right)$

$R=5\text{ m}$ and $\tan\theta=10$

$\frac{u^2\sin 2\theta}{g}=5 \Rightarrow u^2\,2\sin\theta\cos\theta=50$

$\Rightarrow 2u^2\frac{10}{\sqrt{101}}\frac{1}{\sqrt{101}}=50 \Rightarrow u^2=25\times 10.1$

$\Rightarrow \quad u=5\sqrt{10.1}\text{ m/s}$

$$H=\frac{u^2\sin^2\theta}{2g}=\frac{25(10.1)}{20}\frac{100}{101}=12.5\text{ m}$$

$$\tan\phi=\frac{u\sin\theta-gt}{u\cos\theta}$$

$$\tan\phi=\frac{u\sin\theta-g\left(\frac{x}{u\cos\theta}\right)}{u\cos\theta}=\frac{u^2\sin\theta\cos\theta-gx}{u^2\cos^2\theta}=1$$

4. (a) A projectile is freely falling body, since the only force acting on the body is due to gravity.

(b) Acceleration at every point on the trajectory is g.

(c) Time of flight will be maximum when $\theta = 90°$ and Range is maximum when $\theta = 45°$ for a given speed of projection.

(d) Tangential acceleration is maximum at the highest position.

5. (a) $$H_{max} = \frac{u^2}{2g} = h \Rightarrow R_{max} = \frac{u^2}{g} = 2h$$

(b) $$R = nH$$

$$\frac{u^2 \sin 2\theta}{g} = n\frac{u^2 \sin^2\theta}{2g} \Rightarrow \tan\theta = \frac{4}{n} \Rightarrow \theta = \tan^{-1}\left(\frac{4}{n}\right)$$

(c) $$\left.\begin{aligned} R &= \frac{u^2 \sin 2\theta}{g} \\ T &= \frac{2u\sin\theta}{g} \end{aligned}\right\} \Rightarrow R\tan\theta = \frac{1}{2}gt^2$$

(d) $$T = \frac{2u_y}{g}, H = \frac{u_y^2}{2g}$$

$T_1 : T_2 :: 1 : 1,\quad H_1 : H_2 :: 1 : 1$

6. $$y = x\tan\theta - \frac{gx^2}{2u^2\cos^2\theta}$$

$$\Rightarrow \quad 14 = 24\tan\theta - \frac{5(24)^2}{(24)^2}\sec^2\theta$$

$$\Rightarrow \quad 5\tan^2\theta - 24\tan\theta + 19 = 0$$

$$\Rightarrow \quad \tan\theta = 1 \text{ and } \tan\theta = \frac{19}{5} = 3.8$$

$$\Rightarrow \quad \theta = \tan^{-1}(1) \text{ and } \theta = \tan^{-1}(3.8)$$

7.

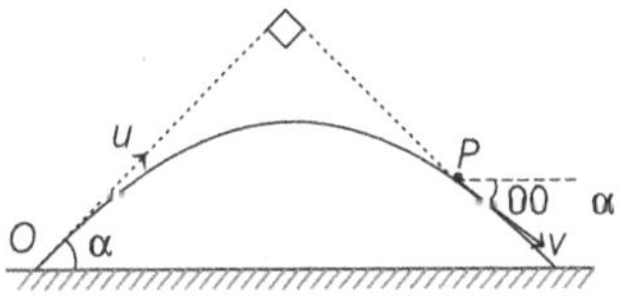

(d) $v\cos(90 - \alpha) = u\cos\alpha \Rightarrow v = u\cot\alpha$

(c) $\tan(-(90-\alpha)) = \dfrac{u\sin\alpha - gt}{u\cos\alpha} \Rightarrow t = \dfrac{u}{g\sin\alpha}$

(b) $$\mathbf{r} = (u\cos\alpha)\left(\frac{u}{g\sin\alpha}\right)\hat{\mathbf{i}} + \left(u\sin\alpha\left(\frac{u}{g\sin\alpha}\right) - \frac{1}{2}g\left(\frac{u}{g\sin\alpha}\right)^2\right)\hat{\mathbf{j}}$$

$$\mathbf{r} = \frac{u^2}{g}\cot\alpha\,\hat{\mathbf{i}} + \left(\frac{u^2}{g} - \frac{u^2}{2g}\mathrm{cosec}^2\alpha\right)\hat{\mathbf{j}}$$

$$\mathbf{r} = \frac{u^2}{g}\cot\alpha\,\hat{\mathbf{i}} + \frac{u^2}{g}\left(1 - \frac{\mathrm{cosec}^2\alpha}{2}\right)\hat{\mathbf{j}}$$

$$OP = \sqrt{\left(\frac{u^2}{g}\cot\alpha\right)^2 + \left(\frac{u^2}{g}\left(1 - \frac{\mathrm{cosec}^2\alpha}{2}\right)\right)^2}$$

(a) $$\tan\theta = \frac{\dfrac{u^2}{g}\left(1 - \dfrac{\mathrm{cosec}^2\alpha}{2}\right)}{\dfrac{u^2}{2}\cot\alpha}$$

8. $$y = x\tan\theta - \frac{gx^2}{2u^2\cos^2\theta}$$

$$\Rightarrow \quad y = \sqrt{\frac{3}{2}}\tan 60° - \frac{9.8\left(\sqrt{\frac{3}{2}}\right)^2}{2v^2\cos^2 60°}$$

$$\Rightarrow \quad y = \frac{3}{\sqrt{2}} - \frac{29.4}{v^2} \quad \Rightarrow \quad v = \sqrt{\frac{29.4\sqrt{2}}{3 - \sqrt{2}y}}$$

$1.5 < y < 2$

9.

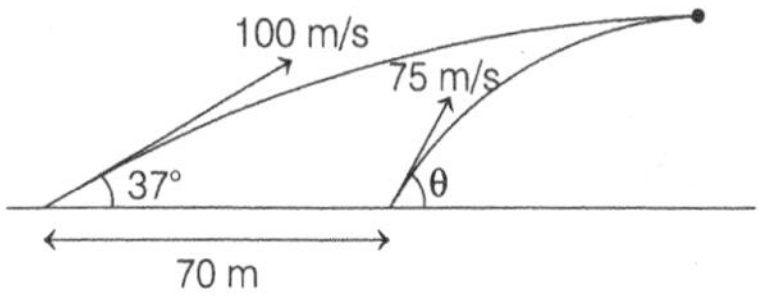

$$100\sin 37° = 75\sin\theta \Rightarrow \sin\theta = \frac{4}{5} \Rightarrow \theta = 53°$$

$$t = \frac{70}{(100\cos 37° - 75\cos\theta)} = \frac{70}{80 - 45} = 2\text{ s}$$

10. $\mathbf{u} = 4\hat{\mathbf{i}} \Rightarrow \mathbf{v} = u\hat{\mathbf{i}} + gt\hat{\mathbf{j}} = 4\hat{\mathbf{i}} + 10t\hat{\mathbf{j}}$

When it hits the ground at $t = 0.4$s, $\mathbf{v} = 4\hat{\mathbf{i}} + 10(0.4)\hat{\mathbf{j}} = 4\hat{\mathbf{i}} + 4\hat{\mathbf{j}}$

Vertical component of velocity when it hits ground = 4m/s

Angle at which it hits the ground $= \tan^{-1}\left(\dfrac{4}{4}\right)$

$= \tan^{-1}(1) = 45°$

$$s_y = u_y t + \frac{1}{2}a_y t^2 \Rightarrow +H = 0 + \frac{1}{2}(+10)(0.4)^2$$

$$\Rightarrow \quad H = 0.8\text{ m}$$

$$s_x = u_x t + \frac{1}{2}a_x t^2$$

$$\Rightarrow \quad R = 4 \times 0.4 = 1.6\text{ m}$$

11. During ascent, retardation will be more than g and during descent acceleration will be less than g.

So, t_1 will decrease and t_2 will increase. But $T = t_1 + t_2$, may increase or decrease.

12.

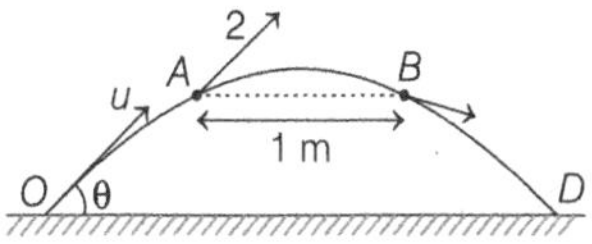

Time taken by particle 2 to go from O to $A = 2$ s

Time taken by particle 1 to go from A to $B = \dfrac{1}{0.5} = 2$ s

Time taken by them to go from B to $D = 2$ s

$T = 2 + 2 + 2 = 6$ s

$\Rightarrow \quad \frac{2u \sin\theta}{g} = 6 \Rightarrow u \sin\theta = 30$

$$H_{max} = \frac{u^2 \sin^2\theta}{2g} = \frac{30^2}{20} = 45 \text{ m}$$

$$R = (u \cos\theta) T = 0.5 \times 6 = 3 \text{ m}$$

13. $y = (u \sin\theta)t - \frac{1}{2}gt^2$

Velocity of shadow on wall $= \frac{dy}{dt} = u \sin\theta - gt$

Acceleration of shadow on wall $= \frac{d^2y}{dt^2} = -g$

$$x = (u \cos\theta)\, t$$

Velocity of shadow on floor $= \frac{dx}{dt} = v = u \cos\theta$

14. $\tan\phi = \frac{u \sin\theta - gt}{u \cos\theta} \Rightarrow \tan(\pm 45^\circ) = \frac{100 \sin 53^\circ - 10t}{100 \cos 53^\circ}$

$\Rightarrow t = 2$ s and $t = 14$ s

$$\mathbf{v} = u \cos\theta \hat{\mathbf{i}} + (u \sin\theta - gt)\hat{\mathbf{j}}$$

At $t = 6$ s, $\mathbf{v}_1 = 60\hat{\mathbf{i}} + 20\hat{\mathbf{j}}$

At $t = 10$ s, $\mathbf{v}_2 = 60\hat{\mathbf{i}} - 20\hat{\mathbf{j}}$

$$\mathbf{v}_{avg} = \frac{\mathbf{v}_1 + \mathbf{v}_2}{2} = 60\hat{\mathbf{i}}$$

$$\mathbf{r} = (u \cos\theta)t\,\hat{\mathbf{i}} + \left(u \sin\theta t - \frac{1}{2}gt^2\right)\hat{\mathbf{j}}$$

At $t = 4$ s, $\mathbf{r}_1 = 240\hat{\mathbf{i}} + 240\hat{\mathbf{j}}$

At $t = 12$ s, $\mathbf{r}_2 = 720\hat{\mathbf{i}} + 240\hat{\mathbf{j}}$

Displacement $= |\mathbf{r}_2 - \mathbf{r}_1| = 480$ m

Comprehension Based Questions

1. $H = \frac{u^2 \sin^2\theta}{2g} = \frac{(20\sqrt{2})^2 \sin^2 45}{20} = 20 \text{ m}$

2. $R = \frac{u^2 \sin 2\theta}{g} = 80 \text{ m}$

3. $\tan(+37^\circ) = \frac{\sqrt{20^2 \sin^2 53^\circ - 2 \times 10 \times (L \sin 37^\circ)}}{20 \cos 53^\circ}$

$\Rightarrow \quad \frac{3}{4} = \frac{\sqrt{256 - 12L}}{12} \Rightarrow 256 - 12L = 81$

$\Rightarrow \quad L = \frac{175}{12} \text{ m}$

4. $\tan(-37^\circ) = \frac{u \sin\theta - gt}{u \cos\theta} \Rightarrow -\frac{3}{4} = \frac{20 \sin 53^\circ - 10t}{20 \cos 53^\circ}$

$\Rightarrow \quad -\frac{3}{4} = \frac{16 - 10t}{12} \Rightarrow t = 2.5 \text{ s}$

$$x = (u \cos\theta)\,t = (20 \cos 53^\circ)(2.5) = 30 \text{ m}$$

$$OB = 30 + L \cos 37^\circ$$

$$= 30 + \frac{175}{12} \times \frac{4}{5} = 30 + \frac{35}{3} = \frac{125}{3} \text{ m}$$

5.

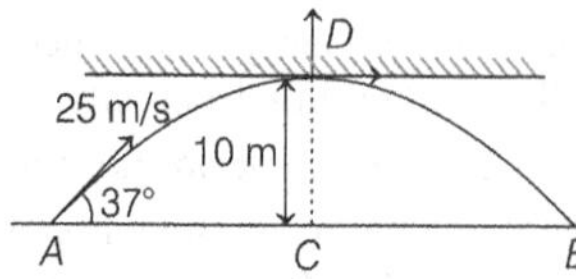

$$s_y = u_y t + \frac{1}{2}a_y t^2 \Rightarrow 10 = (25 \sin 37^\circ)t + \frac{1}{2}(-10)t^2$$

$\Rightarrow t^2 - 3t + 2 = 0 \Rightarrow t = 1$ and $t = 2$

$$T_{AD} = 1 \text{ s} \Rightarrow T_{DB} = \sqrt{\frac{2H}{g}} = \sqrt{\frac{2(10)}{10}} = \sqrt{2} \text{ s}$$

$$T = T_{AD} + T_{DB} = (1 + \sqrt{2}) \text{ s}$$

6. $AC = (25 \cos 37^\circ)(1) = 20 \text{ m}$

$CB = (25 \cos 37^\circ)\sqrt{\frac{2H}{g}} = 20\sqrt{2} \text{ m}$

$AB = AC + CB = 20(1 + \sqrt{2}) \text{ m}$

7.

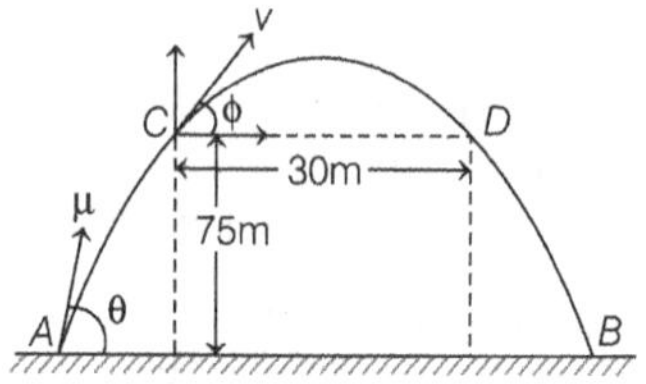

From C to D, $T = \frac{2v \sin\phi}{g} \Rightarrow 2 = \frac{2v \sin\phi}{10}$

$\Rightarrow \quad v \sin\phi = 10$ ...(i)

Horizontal component of velocity of stone will be same as velocity of car.

$\Rightarrow \quad v \cos\phi = 15$ ...(ii)

Solving Eqs. (i) and (ii), we get

$$\tan\phi = \frac{10}{15} = \frac{2}{3} \Rightarrow \phi = \tan^{-1}\left(\frac{2}{3}\right)$$

8. Between A and C, $v_y^2 = u_y^2 + 2a_y s_y$

$\Rightarrow \quad 10^2 = (u \sin\theta)^2 + 2(-10)(+75) \Rightarrow u \sin\theta = 40$

Horizontal range $= AB = \frac{2u_x u_y}{g} = \frac{2(15)(40)}{10} = 120 \text{ m}$

9. Since, horizontal velocity of stone and car is same, horizontal separation will be zero. So, separation will be 75 m vertical.

10. $\mathbf{v}_1 = 8\hat{\mathbf{i}} + 10t\hat{\mathbf{j}} \Rightarrow \mathbf{v}_2 = -2\hat{\mathbf{i}} + 10t\hat{\mathbf{j}}$

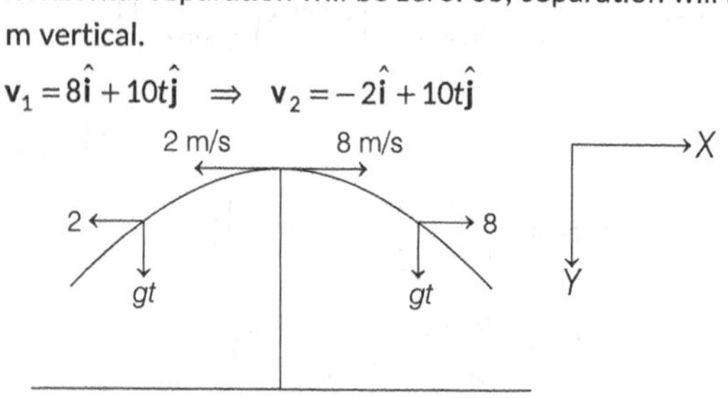

$$\mathbf{v}_1 \cdot \mathbf{v}_2 = 0 \Rightarrow -16 + 100t^2 = 0$$

$\Rightarrow \quad t^2 = \frac{16}{100} \Rightarrow t = \frac{4}{10} = 0.4 \text{ s}$

11. Horizontal distance $= 8(0.4) + 2(0.4) = 4\,\text{m}$

12. $\mathbf{r}_1 = 8t\hat{\mathbf{i}} + 5t^2\hat{\mathbf{j}}, \quad \mathbf{r}_2 = -2t\hat{\mathbf{i}} + 5t^2\hat{\mathbf{j}}$

$$\mathbf{r}_1 \cdot \mathbf{r}_2 = 0 \Rightarrow -16t^2 + 25t^4 = 0 \Rightarrow t = \frac{4}{5} = 0.8\,\text{s}$$

13. $x = u\cos\theta t \Rightarrow 60 = (u\cos\theta)(4) \Rightarrow u\cos\theta = 15$ ...(i)

$$\tan(-45°) = \frac{u\sin\theta - 10(4)}{15}$$

$\Rightarrow u\sin\theta = 25$ ...(ii)

$$\mathbf{u} = 15\hat{\mathbf{i}} + 25\hat{\mathbf{j}}$$

$$s_y = u_y t + \frac{1}{2}a_y t^2$$

$$\Rightarrow h = 25(4) + \frac{1}{2}(-10)(4)^2 = 20\,\text{m}$$

14. Initial speed $= \sqrt{15^2 + 25^2} = \sqrt{850}\,\text{m/s}$

15. $(400\cos\theta)t = 1600$

$$\Rightarrow 400\left(\frac{4}{5}\right)t = 1600 \Rightarrow t = 5\,\text{s}$$

16. $s_y = u_y t + \frac{1}{2}a_y t^2 \Rightarrow h = 400\left(\frac{3}{5}\right)(5) + \frac{1}{2}(-10)(5)^2$

$$\Rightarrow h = 1200 - 125 = 1075\,\text{m}$$

17. Time taken by balloon $= \frac{1075 - 800}{5} = 55\,\text{s}$

Waiting time $= 55 - 5 = 50\,\text{s}$

18.

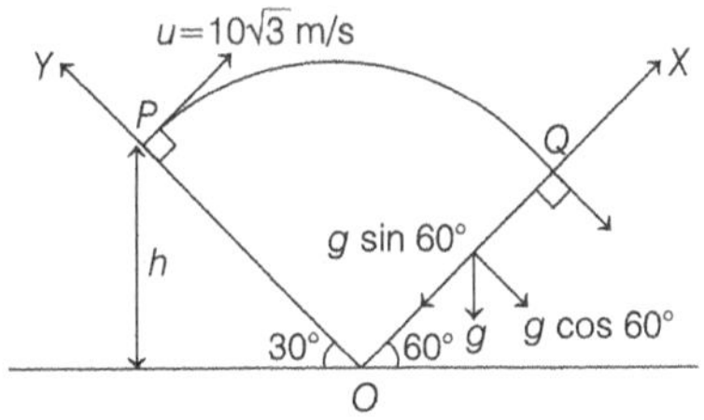

At P, $u_x = 10\sqrt{3}, u_y = 0$

At Q, $v_x = 0$, $v_y = ?$

$$a_x = -g\sin 60°, a_y = -g\cos 60°$$

$$v_x = u_x + a_x t \Rightarrow 0 = 10\sqrt{3} - \frac{10\sqrt{3}}{2}t \Rightarrow t = 2\,\text{s}$$

19. $v_y = u_y + a_y t \Rightarrow v_y = 0 - (g\cos 60°) \times 2$

$$\Rightarrow v_y = -10\,\text{m/s}$$

20. $s_x = u_x t + \frac{1}{2}a_x t^2$

$$\Rightarrow OQ = (10\sqrt{3})(2) + \frac{1}{2}\left(-\frac{10\sqrt{3}}{2}\right)(2)^2 \Rightarrow OQ = 10\sqrt{3}\,\text{m}$$

$$s_y = u_y t + \frac{1}{2}a_y t^2 \Rightarrow -OP = 0 + \frac{1}{2}(-g\cos 60°)(2)^2$$

$\Rightarrow OP = 10\,\text{m}$

$$h = OP\sin 30° = 10\left(\frac{1}{2}\right) = 5\,\text{m}$$

21. $PQ = \sqrt{OP^2 + OQ^2} = \sqrt{10^2 + (10\sqrt{3})^2} = 20\,\text{m}$

Match the Columns Questions

1. $y = ax - bx^2$ ...(i)

$$y = x\tan\theta - \frac{gx^2}{2u^2\cos^2\theta}$$ ...(ii)

Comparing Eqs. (i) and (ii), we get

$$\tan\theta = a, \quad \frac{g}{2u^2\cos^2\theta} = b$$

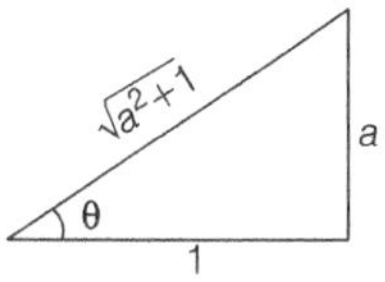

$$u\cos\theta = \sqrt{\frac{g}{2b}}$$

$$\Rightarrow u\left(\frac{1}{\sqrt{a^2+1}}\right) = \sqrt{\frac{g}{2b}} \Rightarrow u = \left(\sqrt{\frac{g}{2b}}\right)\sqrt{a^2+1}$$

(A) $u\cos\theta = \sqrt{\frac{g}{2b}}$

(B) $T = \frac{2u\sin\theta}{g} = \frac{2\left(\sqrt{\frac{g}{2b}}\sqrt{a^2+1}\right)\left(\frac{a}{\sqrt{a^2+1}}\right)}{g} = \sqrt{\frac{2a^2}{bg}}$

(C) $H = \frac{u^2\sin^2\theta}{2g} = \frac{\left(\sqrt{\frac{g}{2b}}\sqrt{a^2+1}\right)^2 \frac{a^2}{a^2+1}}{2g} = \frac{a^2}{4b}$

(D) $R = \frac{u^2\sin 2\theta}{g} = \frac{u^2\, 2\sin\theta\cos\theta}{g}$

$$= \frac{\left(\sqrt{\frac{g}{2b}}\sqrt{a^2+1}\right)^2 2\left(\frac{a}{\sqrt{a^2+1}}\right)\left(\frac{1}{\sqrt{a^2+1}}\right)}{g} = \frac{a}{b}$$

2. $T = \frac{2u_y}{g}, \quad H = \frac{u_y^2}{2g}, \quad R = \frac{2u_x u_y}{g}$

$$H_A = H_B > H_C \Rightarrow (u_y)_A = (u_y)_B > (u_y)_C \Rightarrow T_A = T_B > T_C$$

$$R_B = R_C > R_A$$

$$\Rightarrow (u_x u_y)_B = (u_x u_y)_C > (u_x u_y)_A$$

3. $\mathbf{v} = 6\hat{\mathbf{i}} + (20 - 4t)\hat{\mathbf{j}}$

$\Rightarrow v_x = 6;\ v_y = 20 - 4t$

$\Rightarrow u_x = 6;\ u_y = 20$ and $a_y = -4 \Rightarrow g = 4$

$$T = \frac{2u_y}{g} = \frac{2(20)}{4} = 10\,\text{s}, \quad H = \frac{u_y^2}{2g} = \frac{(20)^2}{2(4)} = 50\,\text{m}$$

$$R = \frac{2u_x u_y}{g} = \frac{2(6)(20)}{4} = 60\,\text{m}$$

$$\tan\phi = \frac{u\sin\theta - gt}{u\cos\theta} \Rightarrow \tan 53° = \frac{20 - 4t}{6}$$

$$\Rightarrow \frac{4}{3} = \frac{20 - 4t}{6} \Rightarrow t = 3\,\text{s}$$

4. A → Q, B → P,R; C → P,R; D → Q, R

5. $u_x = 0, u_y = u, a_x = g \sin 45°;\ a_y = -g \cos 45°$

(A) $v_y = u_y + a_y t \Rightarrow 0 = u - \frac{g}{\sqrt{2}} t \Rightarrow t = \frac{\sqrt{2}u}{g}$

(B) $\tan\phi = \frac{u_y + a_y t}{u_x + a_x t} \Rightarrow 1 = \frac{u - \frac{g}{\sqrt{2}}t}{\frac{g}{\sqrt{2}}t} \Rightarrow t = \frac{u}{\sqrt{2}g}$

(C) $s_x = u_x t + \frac{1}{2} a_x t^2 \Rightarrow R = 0 + \frac{1}{2}\left(\frac{g}{\sqrt{2}}\right)\left(\frac{2u}{g/\sqrt{2}}\right)^2$

$$\Rightarrow R = \frac{2\sqrt{2}u^2}{g}$$

$$s_x = u_x t + \frac{1}{2} a_x t^2$$

$$\Rightarrow \frac{1}{2}\left(\frac{2\sqrt{2}u^2}{g}\right) = 0 + \frac{1}{2}\left(\frac{g}{\sqrt{2}}\right)t^2 \Rightarrow t = \frac{2u}{g}$$

(D) $s_y = u_y t + \frac{1}{2} a_y t^2 \Rightarrow 0 = u(T) + \frac{1}{2}\left(-\frac{g}{\sqrt{2}}\right)T^2$

$$\Rightarrow T = \frac{2\sqrt{2}u}{g}$$

6. $u_x = u\cos\beta; u_y = u\sin\beta;\ a_x = -g\sin\alpha, a_y = -g\cos\alpha$

(A) $H = \frac{u^2 \sin^2(\alpha+\beta)}{2g}$

(B) $H = \frac{u^2 \sin^2\beta}{2g\cos\alpha}$

(C) $s_x = u_x t + \frac{1}{2} a_x t^2$

$$\Rightarrow s_x = (u\cos\beta)\left(\frac{1}{2}\frac{u\cos\beta}{g\sin\alpha}\right) + \frac{1}{2}(-g\sin\alpha)\left(\frac{1}{2}\frac{u\cos\beta}{g\sin\alpha}\right)^2$$

$$\Rightarrow s_x = \frac{3}{8}\frac{u^2\cos^2\beta}{g\sin\alpha}$$

(D) $v_x^2 = u_x^2 + 2a_x s_x \Rightarrow 0^2 = (u\cos\beta)^2 - 2g\sin\alpha\, s_x$

$$\Rightarrow s_x = \frac{u^2\cos^2\beta}{2g\sin\alpha}$$

Numerical Value Questions

1. $\tan\phi = \frac{v_y}{v_x} = \frac{\sqrt{u^2\sin^2\theta - 2gh}}{u\cos\theta}$

$$\Rightarrow \tan 45° = \frac{\sqrt{u^2\sin^2\theta - 2g\frac{1}{2}\left(\frac{u^2\sin^2\theta}{2g}\right)}}{u\cos\theta}$$

$$\Rightarrow u^2\cos^2\theta = \frac{u^2\sin^2\theta}{2} \Rightarrow \tan^2\theta = 2$$

2. $\tan\theta = \frac{X+y}{x} \Rightarrow X = x\tan\theta - y$ ...(i)

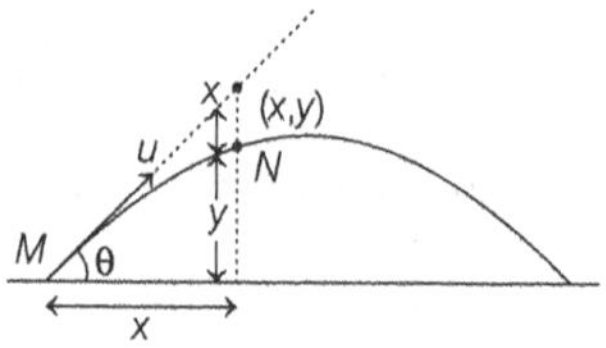

$$y = x\tan\theta - \frac{1}{2}g\left(\frac{x}{u\cos\theta}\right)^2 \quad \text{...(ii)}$$

From Eqs. (i) and (ii), we get

$$X = \frac{1}{2}g\left(\frac{x}{u\cos\theta}\right)^2 \Rightarrow X = \frac{1}{2}gt^2 = 5t^2$$

So, $x + y + z = 5(1^2 + 2^2 + 3^2) = 70$

3. $\left((30\sin 53°)t - \frac{1}{2}gt^2\right) + \left(\frac{1}{2}gt^2\right) = 30$

$$\Rightarrow 30 \times \frac{4}{5}t = 30 \Rightarrow t = \frac{5}{4}\text{ s}$$

$$d = (30\cos 53°)t + 6t$$

$$\Rightarrow d = 24t = 24\left(\frac{5}{4}\right) = 30\text{ m}$$

4.

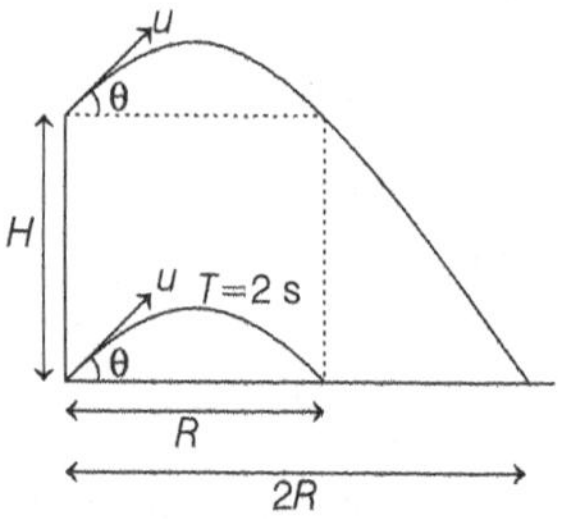

$$R = (u\cos\theta)2 \Rightarrow 2R = (u\cos\theta)T' \Rightarrow T' = 4\text{ s}$$

$$\frac{2u\sin\theta}{g} = 2 \Rightarrow u\sin\theta = 10$$

$$s_y = u_y t + \frac{1}{2}a_y t^2$$

$$\Rightarrow -H = 10(4) + \frac{1}{2}(-10)(4)^2$$

$$\Rightarrow -H = 40 - 80 \Rightarrow H = 40\text{ m}$$

5. $y = x\tan\theta - \frac{gx^2}{2u^2}\sec^2\theta$

When Ram throws the ball,

$$h = x\tan\theta - \frac{gx^2}{2(2\sqrt{gh})^2}(1+\tan^2\theta)$$

$$\Rightarrow \tan^2\theta - \frac{8h}{x}\tan\theta + \left(1 + \frac{8h^2}{x^2}\right) = 0$$

For real roots, $D \geq 0$

$$\Rightarrow \left(\frac{8h}{x}\right)^2 - 4\left(1 + \frac{8h^2}{x^2}\right)^2 \geq 0$$

$\Rightarrow \quad x \le \sqrt{8h} \quad \Rightarrow \quad x_{max} = \sqrt{8h} \quad \Rightarrow \quad d_1 = \sqrt{8h}$

When Shyam throws the ball,

$$y = x\tan\theta - \frac{gx^2}{2u^2\cos^2\theta}$$

$$\Rightarrow \quad -h = x\tan\theta - \frac{gx^2}{2(2\sqrt{gh})^2}\sec^2\theta$$

$$\Rightarrow \tan^2\theta - \frac{8h}{x}\tan\theta + \left(1 - \frac{8h^2}{x^2}\right) = 0$$

For real roots, $D \ge 0$

$$\left(\frac{8h}{x}\right)^2 - 4\left(1 - \frac{8h^2}{x^2}\right) \ge 0 \quad \Rightarrow \quad x \le \sqrt{24h}$$

$$x_{max} = \sqrt{24h} \quad \Rightarrow \quad d_2 = \sqrt{24h}$$

$$\therefore \quad \frac{d_2^2}{d_1^2} = \left(\frac{\sqrt{24h}}{\sqrt{8h}}\right)^2 = 3$$

6.

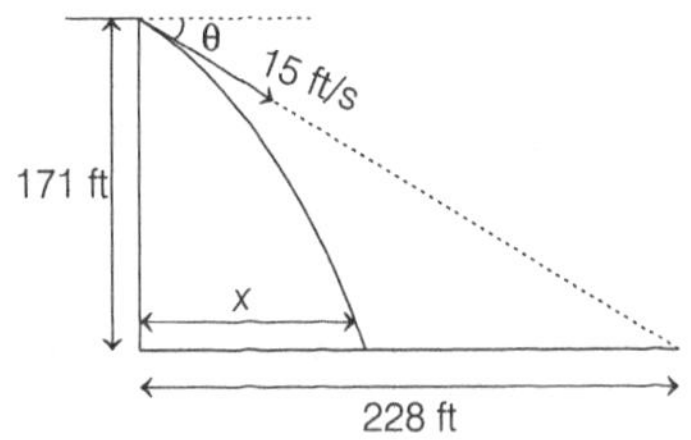

$$\tan\theta = \frac{171}{228} = \frac{3}{4}$$

$$s_y = u_y t + \frac{1}{2}a_y t^2$$

$$\Rightarrow \quad +171 = +(15\sin\theta)T + \frac{1}{2}(+32)T^2$$

$$\Rightarrow \quad 171 = 15\left(\frac{3}{5}\right)T + 16T^2 \quad \Rightarrow \quad 16T^2 + 9T - 171 = 0$$

$$\Rightarrow \quad 16T^2 + 57T - 48T - 171 = 0$$

$$\Rightarrow \quad T(16T + 57) - 3(16T + 57) = 0 \quad \Rightarrow \quad T = 3\text{ s}$$

$$s_x = u_x t + \frac{1}{2}a_x t^2$$

$$\Rightarrow \quad s_x = (15\cos\theta)T = \left(15 \times \frac{4}{5}\right)(3) = 36\text{ ft} \quad \Rightarrow \quad x = 36\text{ ft}$$

So, packet will tall short by $(228 - 36) = 192$ ft

7.

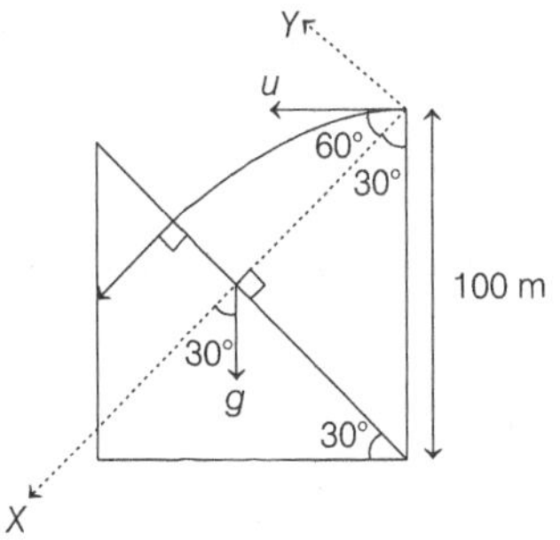

We have taken a new co-ordinate system as shown in figure.

$u_x = u\cos 60°$ and $u_y = u\sin 60°$

$a_x = g\cos 30°$ and $a_y = -g\sin 30°$

$v_y = u_y + a_y t \quad \Rightarrow 0 = u\sin 60° - (g\sin 30°)t$

$$\Rightarrow \quad t = \frac{\sqrt{3}u}{g}$$

$$s_x = u_x t + \frac{1}{2}a_x t^2$$

$$\Rightarrow 100\cos 30° = (u\cos 60°)\left(\frac{\sqrt{3}u}{g}\right) + \frac{1}{2}(g\cos 30°)\left(\frac{\sqrt{3}u}{g}\right)$$

$$\Rightarrow \quad 50\sqrt{3} = \frac{\sqrt{3}u^2}{2g} + \frac{3\sqrt{3}u^2}{4g} \quad \Rightarrow \quad \frac{5\sqrt{3}u^2}{4g} = 50\sqrt{3}$$

$$\Rightarrow \quad u = 20\text{ m/s}$$

8. $PQ = \sqrt{15^2 + 20^2} = 25\text{ m} \quad \Rightarrow \quad PQ = \dfrac{v^2\sin 2\theta}{g} = 25$

$\Rightarrow \quad v^2 = 250 \quad \Rightarrow \quad v = \sqrt{250}$ m

$v_y = \sqrt{250}\sin 45° = \sqrt{125}$

$v_y^2 = u_y^2 + 2a_y s_y \quad \Rightarrow \quad (\sqrt{125})^2 = u_y^2 + 2(-10)(12.5)$

$\Rightarrow \quad u_y = \sqrt{375}$ m/s

$$AB = R = \frac{2u_x u_y}{g} = \frac{2\sqrt{125}\sqrt{375}}{10} = 25\sqrt{3}\text{ m}$$

9. $\mathbf{v} = u\cos\theta\,\hat{\mathbf{i}} + (u\sin\theta - gt)\,\hat{\mathbf{j}}$

$\mathbf{r} = (u\cos\theta)t\,\hat{\mathbf{i}} + \left((u\sin\theta)t - \dfrac{1}{2}gt^2\right)\hat{\mathbf{j}}$

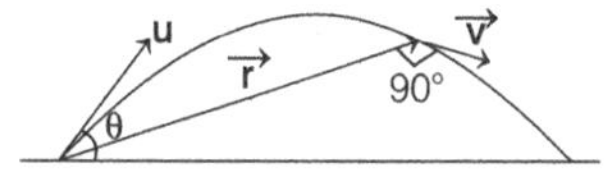

$$\mathbf{v}\cdot\mathbf{r} = 0$$

$$\Rightarrow \quad (u^2\cos^2\theta)t + (u\sin\theta - gt)\left(u\sin\theta\, t - \frac{1}{2}gt^2\right) = 0$$

$\Rightarrow \quad g^2t^2 - 3gu\sin\theta t + 2u^2 = 0$

For single solution, $D = 0$

$\Rightarrow (3gu\sin\theta)^2 - 4(2u^2)(g^2t^2) = 0 \quad \Rightarrow \quad \sin^2\theta = \dfrac{8}{9}$

10. $R = \dfrac{u^2\sin 2\theta}{g} = \dfrac{(40)^2\sin 120°}{10} = 80\sqrt{3}$ m

$x = (u\cos\theta)t \quad \Rightarrow \quad 80\sqrt{3} = v\cos 60°\, t$

$$\Rightarrow \quad t = \frac{160\sqrt{3}}{v}$$

$$s_y = u_y t + \frac{1}{2}a_y t^2$$

$$\Rightarrow (9\sqrt{3})\left(\frac{160\sqrt{3}}{v}\right) = (v\sin 60°)\left(\frac{160\sqrt{3}}{v}\right) + \frac{1}{2}(-10)\left(\frac{160\sqrt{3}}{v}\right)^2$$

$$\Rightarrow \quad v^2 - 18v - 1600 = 0$$

$$\Rightarrow \quad v(v - 50) + 32(v - 50) = 0$$

$$\Rightarrow \quad v = 50\text{ m/s}$$

11.

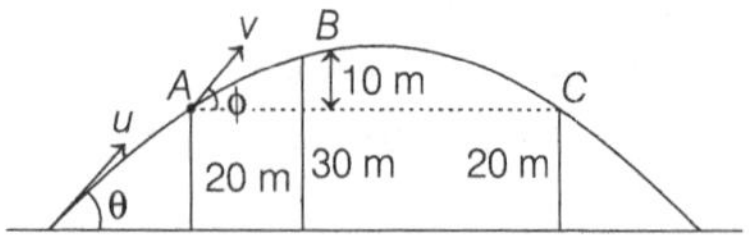

$$T_{BC}=2T_{AB} \Rightarrow T_{AB}+T_{BC}=\frac{2v\sin\phi}{g}$$

$$\Rightarrow 3T_{AB}=\frac{2v\sin\phi}{g} \Rightarrow T_{AB}=\frac{2v\sin\phi}{3g}$$

$$s_y=u_y t+\frac{1}{2}a_y t^2$$

$$\Rightarrow 10=(v\sin\phi)\left(\frac{2v\sin\phi}{3g}\right)-\frac{1}{2}g\left(\frac{2v\sin\phi}{3g}\right)^2$$

$$\Rightarrow 10=\frac{2}{3}\frac{v^2\sin^2\phi}{g}-\frac{2}{9}\frac{v^2\sin^2\phi}{g}$$

$$\Rightarrow \frac{4}{9}\frac{v^2\sin^2\phi}{g}=10 \Rightarrow \frac{v^2\sin^2\phi}{2g}=\frac{45}{4}$$

Maximum height from ground $=20+\frac{45}{4}=31.25\text{ m}$

12.

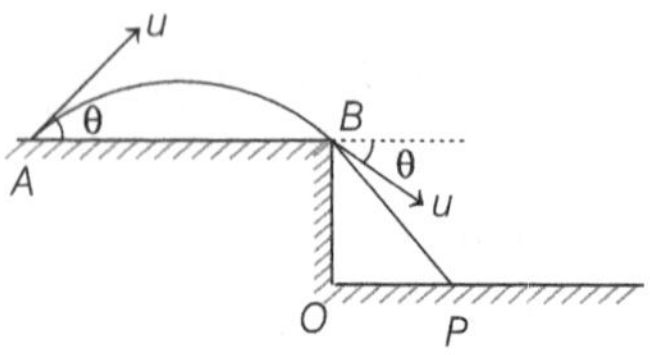

$$AB=\frac{u^2\sin 2\theta}{g}=960 \Rightarrow \frac{100^2\sin 2\theta}{10}=960$$

$$\Rightarrow \sin 2\theta=\frac{24}{25} \Rightarrow \theta=37^\circ \text{ or } 53^\circ$$

OP will be minimum when $\theta=53^\circ$

$$y=(u\sin\theta)t-\frac{1}{2}gt^2$$

$$\Rightarrow +960=100(\sin 53^\circ)t+5t^2$$

$$\Rightarrow t^2+16t-192=0 \Rightarrow t=8\text{ s}$$

$$OP=(u\cos\theta)t \Rightarrow OP=(100\cos 53^\circ)8=480\text{ m}$$

13. $R=\frac{u^2\sin 2\theta}{g} \Rightarrow 100=\frac{(80)^2\sin 2\theta}{32} \Rightarrow \sin 2\theta=\frac{1}{2}$

$$\Rightarrow 2\theta=30^\circ \text{ or } 2\theta=150^\circ \Rightarrow \theta=15^\circ \text{ or } \theta=75^\circ$$

$$T_1=\frac{2u\sin 15^\circ}{g} \text{ and } T_2=\frac{2u\sin 75^\circ}{g}$$

The man will be in danger for time $=T_2-T_1$

$$=\frac{2u}{g}(\sin 75^\circ-\sin 15^\circ)=\frac{2u}{g}(2\sin 30^\circ\cos 45^\circ)=\frac{5}{\sqrt{2}}\text{ s}$$

14. $s_y=u_y t+\frac{1}{2}a_y t^2 \Rightarrow 20=(u\sin 45^\circ)t-\frac{1}{2}(10)t^2$

$$\Rightarrow 5t^2-\frac{u}{\sqrt{2}}t+20=0$$

For real roots, $D\geq 0$

$$\Rightarrow \left(\frac{u}{\sqrt{2}}\right)^2-400\geq 0 \Rightarrow u^2\geq 800 \Rightarrow u\geq 20\sqrt{2}$$

$$\Rightarrow u_{min}=20\sqrt{2}\text{ m/s}=28.28\text{ m/s}$$

15. $y=x\tan\theta-\frac{gx^2}{2u^2}\sec^2\theta$

$$\Rightarrow -3=x\tan\theta-\frac{5x^2}{100}(1+\tan^2\theta)$$

$$\Rightarrow x^2\tan^2\theta-20x\tan\theta+(x^2-60)=0$$

For real roots, $D\geq 0$

$$\Rightarrow (20x)^2-4x^2(x^2-60)\geq 0$$

$$\Rightarrow 400x^2-4x^2(x^2-60)\geq 0$$

$$\Rightarrow 100-(x^2-60)\geq 0$$

$$x^2\leq 160 \Rightarrow x=\sqrt{160}$$

16. $\tan\phi=\frac{u\sin\theta-gt}{u\cos\theta} \Rightarrow \tan\beta=\frac{u\sin\alpha-gt}{u\cos\alpha}$

$$\Rightarrow u\cos\alpha\tan\beta=u\sin\alpha-gt$$

$$\Rightarrow t=\frac{u}{g}(\sin\alpha-\cos\alpha\tan\beta) \quad \text{...(i)}$$

$$x=(u\cos\alpha)t, \quad y=u\sin\alpha t-\frac{1}{2}gt^2$$

$$\Rightarrow \tan 45^\circ=\frac{y}{x}=\frac{u\sin\alpha t-\frac{1}{2}gt^2}{(u\cos\alpha)t}$$

$$\Rightarrow u\cos\alpha=u\sin\alpha-\frac{1}{2}gt$$

$$\Rightarrow t=\frac{2u}{g}(\sin\alpha-\cos\alpha) \quad \text{...(ii)}$$

From Eqs. (i) and (ii), we get

$$\frac{u}{g}(\sin\alpha-\cos\alpha\tan\beta)=\frac{2u}{g}(\sin\alpha-\cos\alpha)$$

$$\Rightarrow \sin\alpha-\cos\alpha\tan\beta=2\sin\alpha-2\cos\alpha$$

$$\Rightarrow 2\cos\alpha-\cos\alpha\tan\beta=\sin\alpha$$

$$\Rightarrow 2\cos\alpha=\sin\alpha+\cos\alpha\tan\beta \Rightarrow 2=\tan\alpha+\tan\beta$$

17.

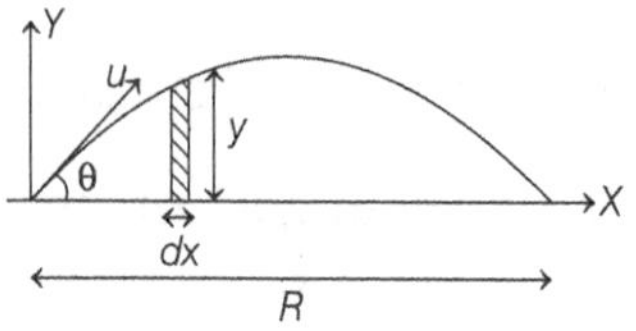

Equation of trajectory,

$$y=x\tan\theta\left(1-\frac{x}{R}\right)$$

$$A=\text{Area under trajectory}=\int_0^R y\,dx$$

$$A=\int_0^R\left(x\tan\theta-\frac{x^2\tan\theta}{R}\right)dx$$

$$A=\left[\frac{x^2\tan\theta}{2}-\frac{x^3\tan\theta}{3R}\right]_0^R=\frac{R^2\tan\theta}{6}$$

$$A = \frac{\left(\frac{u^2\, 2\sin\theta\cos\theta}{g}\right)^2 \tan\theta}{6} = \frac{2}{3}\frac{u^4}{g^2}\sin^3\theta\cos\theta$$

To maximise area,

$$\frac{dA}{d\theta} = 0 \Rightarrow \tan\theta = \sqrt{3} \Rightarrow \theta = \frac{\pi}{3}$$

18. $\mathbf{u}_1 = 400\cos 53°\,\hat{\mathbf{i}} + 400\sin 53°\,\hat{\mathbf{j}} \Rightarrow \mathbf{u}_1 = 240\,\hat{\mathbf{i}} + 320\hat{\mathbf{j}}$

$\mathbf{u}_2 = 400\cos 53°\,\hat{\mathbf{k}} + 400\sin 53°\,\hat{\mathbf{j}} \Rightarrow \mathbf{u}_2 = 240\,\hat{\mathbf{k}} + 320\hat{\mathbf{j}}$

$\mathbf{v}_1 = 240\hat{\mathbf{i}} + (320 - 10t)\,\hat{\mathbf{j}}$

$\mathbf{v}_2 = 240\hat{\mathbf{k}} + (320 - 10t)\,\hat{\mathbf{j}}$

$$\cos\theta = \frac{\mathbf{v}_1 \cdot \mathbf{v}_2}{v_1 v_2} \Rightarrow \cos 60° = \frac{(320-10t)^2}{(\sqrt{240^2 + (320-10t)^2})^2}$$

$$\Rightarrow \frac{1}{2} = \frac{(320-10t)^2}{240^2 + (320-10t)^2}$$

$$\Rightarrow 2(320-10t)^2 = 240^2 + (320-10t)^2$$

$$\Rightarrow (320-10t)^2 = (240)^2 \Rightarrow 320 - 10t = 240 \Rightarrow t = 8\text{ s}$$

Previous Year's Questions

JEE Main

1. $u_x = 5\hat{i}$ m/s, $a_x = 3\hat{i} + 2\hat{j}$

$$x = u_x t + \frac{1}{2}a_x t^2$$

When x coordinate is 84 m,

$$84 = 5t + \frac{3}{2}t^2 \Rightarrow t = 6\text{ s}$$

Using, $v = u + at$ $\mathbf{v} = 5\hat{i} + (3\hat{i} + 2\hat{j})6$

$$= 5\hat{i} + 18\hat{i} + 12\hat{j}$$

$$\mathbf{v} = 23\hat{i} + 12\hat{j}$$

$$|\mathbf{v}| = \sqrt{(23)^2 + (12)^2} = \sqrt{529 + 144} = \sqrt{673}\text{ m/s}$$

$$\alpha = 673$$

2.

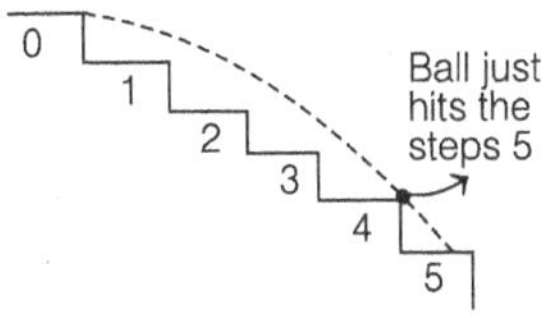

The ball needs to just cross 4 steps to just hit 5th step. therefore, horizontal range, $R = 0.4$ m

$$R = ut, t = R/u$$

Similarly, in vertical direction

$$h = \frac{1}{2}gt^2 \Rightarrow 0.4 = \frac{1}{2}gt^2$$

$$0.4 = \frac{1}{2}g\left(\frac{R}{u}\right)^2$$

$$0.4 = \frac{1}{2} \times \frac{0.4 \times 0.4}{u^2} \times 10$$

$$u^2 = 0.2 \times 10 = 2$$

$$u = \sqrt{2}\text{ m/s}$$

Therefore, $x = 2$

3.

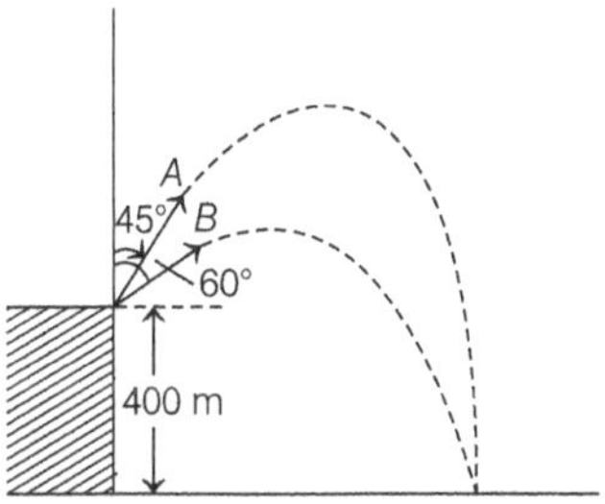

In vertical direction,

For projectile A,

$$u_{yA} = v_A \cdot \cos 45° = \frac{v_A}{\sqrt{2}}$$

$$s_{yA} = -400\text{ m}, a_{yA} = -10\text{ m/s}^2$$

Using $s = ut + \frac{1}{2}at^2$ we have,

$$-400 = \frac{v_A}{\sqrt{2}} \times t + \frac{1}{2}(-10)t^2 \quad \text{...(i)}$$

Similarly for projectile B,

$$-400 = \frac{v_B}{2} \times t + \frac{1}{2}(-10)t^2 \quad \text{...(ii)}$$

From Eqs. (i) and (ii),

$$\frac{v_A}{\sqrt{2}}t = \frac{v_B}{2}t \text{ or } v_A : v_B = 1 : \sqrt{2}$$

4. Maximum horizontal distance

$$= \text{Maximum range} = \left.\frac{u^2 \sin 2\theta}{g}\right|_{(\theta = 45°)} = \frac{u^2}{g}$$

Maximum vertical height (from $v^2 - u^2 = 2gh$) is

$$H_{max} = \frac{u^2}{2g} = 136\text{ m} \quad \text{(given)}$$

Hence, maximum horizontal distance

$$= 2 \times H_{max} = 2 \times 136 = 272\text{ m}$$

5. The given situation in question is as follows

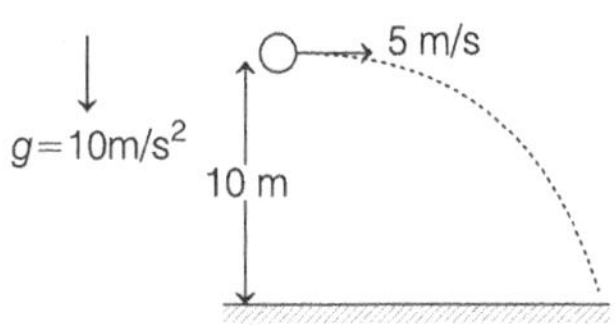

Let, the striking speed be v.

Using third equation of motion,

$$v^2 = u^2 + 2as = ((5\hat{i})^2 + 2(-10\hat{j})(-10\hat{j})$$

$$= 5^2 + 200 = 225$$

$$\Rightarrow \quad v = \sqrt{225}$$

$$\Rightarrow \quad v = 15\text{ m/s}$$

6. During the projectile motion, horizontal component of velocity does not change.

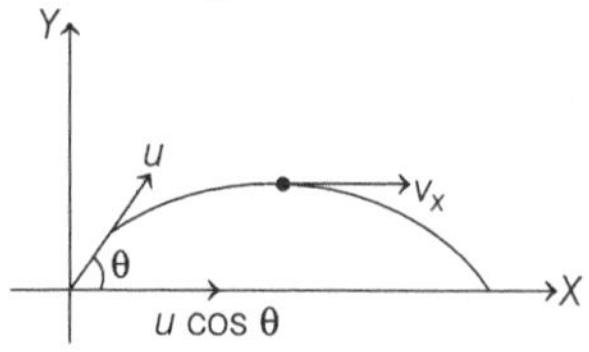

Given that, $v_x = \frac{\sqrt{3}}{2}u$

$$u\cos\theta = \frac{\sqrt{3}}{2}u \Rightarrow \cos\theta = \frac{\sqrt{3}}{2}$$

$$\theta = 30°$$

Time of flight,

$$T = \frac{2u\sin\theta}{g} = \frac{2u\sin 30°}{g} = \frac{2u}{g} \times \frac{1}{2}$$

$$\Rightarrow \qquad T = \frac{u}{g}$$

7.

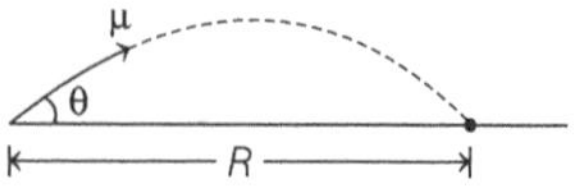

Range of a projectile, $R = \frac{u^2 \sin 2\theta}{g}$

⇒ Ratio of ranges of a projectile thrown at two different angles θ_2 and θ_1 is;

$$\frac{R_2}{R_1} = \frac{\sin(2\theta_2)}{\sin(2\theta_1)}$$

Here $R_1 = 50$ m, $\theta_1 = 15°$ and $\theta_2 = 45°$

So, $R_2 = R_1 \cdot \frac{\sin(2\theta_2)}{\sin(2\theta_1)} = 50 \times \frac{\sin 2(45°)}{\sin 2(15°)} = \frac{50 \times \sin 90°}{\sin 30°} = 100$ m

8. Maximum height of projectile is given by,

$$H_{max} = \frac{u^2 \sin^2\theta}{2g}$$

Therefore, $\frac{H_{max_1}}{H_{max_2}} = \frac{(u^2 \sin^2 30°)/2g}{(u^2 \sin^2 60°)/2g}$

$$= \frac{\sin^2 30°}{\sin^2 60°} = \frac{\left(\frac{1}{2}\right)^2}{\left(\frac{\sqrt{3}}{2}\right)^2} = \frac{1}{3}$$

9. At $t = 2$ s, $g = 10$ m/s^2

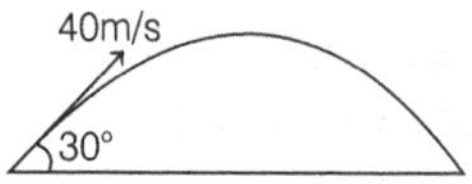

$$u_x = 40\cos 30°, \quad u_y = 40\sin 30°$$

At h_{max}, $u_y = 0$ and $u_x = 40\cos 30° = 40 \times \frac{\sqrt{3}}{2}$

$$\Rightarrow \qquad u_x = 20\sqrt{3} \text{ m/s}$$

10.

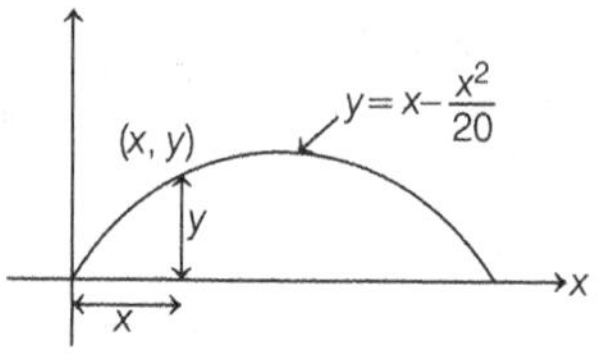

Height above ground is $y = x - \frac{x^2}{20}$

For maximum height,

$$\frac{dy}{dx} = 0 \Rightarrow \frac{d}{dx}\left(x - \frac{x^2}{20}\right) = 0$$

$$\Rightarrow \qquad 1 - \frac{x}{10} = 0$$

$$\Rightarrow \qquad x = 10 \text{ m}$$

So, y_{max} (at $x = 10$ m) $= 10 - \frac{10^2}{20} = 10 - 5 = 5$ m

11. For same range if projection speed for two projectiles are same, then angles are complementary.

For projectile-1,

$$\theta_1 = 60°, u = 40 \text{ m/s}$$

Maximum height,

$$H_1 = \frac{u^2 \sin^2\theta}{2g} = \frac{(40)^2 \times \sin^2 60°}{2 \times 10}$$

$$H_1 = 60 \text{ m}$$

For projectile-2,

$$\theta_2 = 90° - \theta_1 = 90° - 60° = 30°,$$
$$u = 40 \text{ m/s}$$

Maximum height,

$$H_2 = \frac{u^2 \sin^2 30°}{2g} = \frac{(40)^2}{2 \times 10} \times \frac{1}{4} = 20 \text{ m}$$

Sum of heights, $H_1 + H_2 = 60 + 20 = 80$ m

12. Time of flight $= 5 + 3 = 8$ s

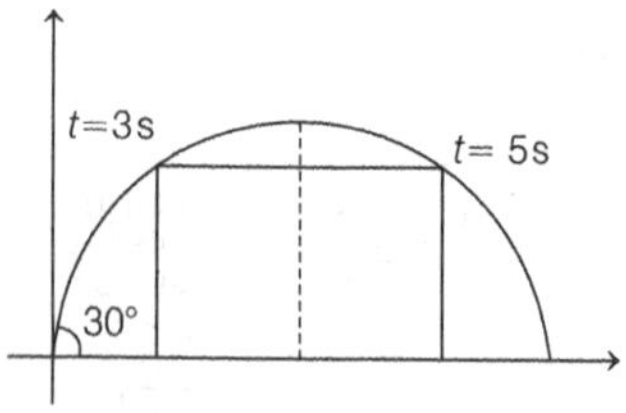

$$T = \frac{2u\sin\theta}{g} \Rightarrow 8 = \frac{2u\sin 30°}{10}$$

$$\Rightarrow \qquad u\sin 30° = 40 \Rightarrow u \times \frac{1}{2} = 40$$

$$\Rightarrow \qquad u = 80 \text{ m/s}$$

13. Given, angle of projection for the two projectile are given as $\theta_1 = 45°$ and $\theta_2 = 30°$

Initial speeds, $u_1 = u_2 = u$

Range of projectile, $R = \frac{u^2 \sin 2\theta}{g}$

$$\Rightarrow \frac{R_1}{R_2}=\frac{u_1^2}{u_2^2}\times\frac{\sin 2\theta_1}{\sin 2\theta_2}=\frac{u^2}{u^2}\times\frac{\sin(2\times 45^\circ)}{\sin(2\times 30^\circ)}=\frac{\sin 90^\circ}{\sin 60^\circ}=\frac{1}{\frac{\sqrt{3}}{2}}$$

$$\Rightarrow \quad R_1/R_2=2/\sqrt{3}$$

$$\Rightarrow \quad R_1:R_2=2:\sqrt{3}$$

14. If T be the time of flight, then time taken by the projectile to reach at maximum height,

$$t=\frac{T}{2}=\frac{1}{2}\cdot\frac{2u\sin\theta}{g}=\frac{u\sin\theta}{g}$$

According to question,

$$t_1=t_2$$

$$\Rightarrow \quad \frac{u_1\sin\theta_1}{g}=\frac{u_2\sin\theta_2}{g}$$

$$\Rightarrow \quad u_1\sin\theta_1=u_2\sin\theta_2$$

$$\Rightarrow \quad \frac{u_1}{u_2}=\frac{\sin\theta_2}{\sin\theta_1}=\frac{\sin 45^\circ}{\sin 30^\circ}=\frac{1/\sqrt{2}}{1/2}=\frac{\sqrt{2}}{1}$$

$$\therefore \quad u_1:u_2=\sqrt{2}:1$$

15. Projection speed of ball, $u=15\text{ ms}^{-1}$

Given that, $R=H$

$$\Rightarrow \quad \frac{u^2\sin 2\theta}{g}=\frac{u^2\sin^2\theta}{2g}$$

$$\Rightarrow \quad \frac{\sin 2\theta}{1}=\frac{\sin^2\theta}{2}$$

$$\Rightarrow \quad 2\sin\theta.\cos\theta=\frac{\sin^2\theta}{2} \qquad [\because \sin 2\theta=2\sin\theta\cdot\cos\theta]$$

$$\Rightarrow \quad 4=\frac{\sin\theta}{\cos\theta} \Rightarrow 4=\tan\theta$$

$$\Rightarrow \quad \tan\theta=4$$

16. Since, after t seconds, its inclination becomes 0° i.e., $\theta=0^\circ$, hence it concludes that projectile reaches at maximum height after t seconds.

$$\therefore \quad t=\frac{\text{time of flight}}{2}=\frac{2u\sin\theta}{2g}$$

$$t=\frac{u\sin\theta}{g} \Rightarrow u=\frac{tg}{\sin\theta} \qquad \text{...(i)}$$

Again we know that, horizontal range,

$$R=\frac{u^2\sin 2\theta}{g}=\frac{\frac{t^2g^2}{\sin^2\theta}\times 2\sin\theta\cos\theta}{g} \qquad \text{[From Eq. (i)]}$$

$$\Rightarrow \quad R=2t^2g\cot\theta$$

$$\Rightarrow \quad \frac{1}{\cot\theta}=\frac{2t^2g}{R}=\frac{2t^2\times 10}{R}=\frac{20t^2}{R}$$

$$\Rightarrow \cot\theta=\frac{R}{20t^2} \quad \Rightarrow \quad \theta=\cot^{-1}\left(\frac{R}{20t^2}\right)$$

17. Given,

speed of jet, $v=200$ m/s

Velocity of bullet, $u=400$ m/s

Let the time taken by the bullet to hit jet be t.

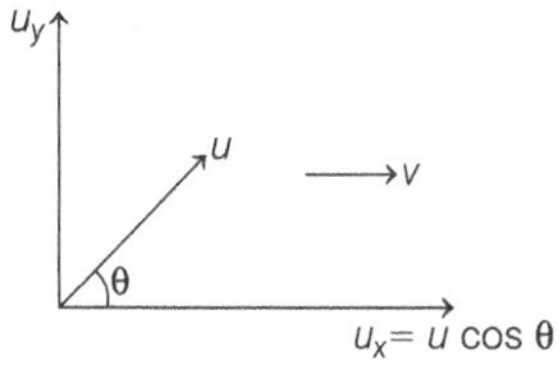

Distance travelled by plane should be equal to that of bullet.

$$\therefore \quad u_xt=vt$$

$$\Rightarrow \quad t\cdot u\cos\theta=vt$$

$$\Rightarrow \quad u\cos\theta=v \Rightarrow \theta=\cos^{-1}(v/u)$$

$$\Rightarrow \quad \theta=\cos^{-1}(200/400)=\cos^{-1}\left(\frac{1}{2}\right)=60^\circ$$

18. Given, angle of projection,

$$\theta=45^\circ$$

Velocity after $t=2$ s, $v'=20$ m/s

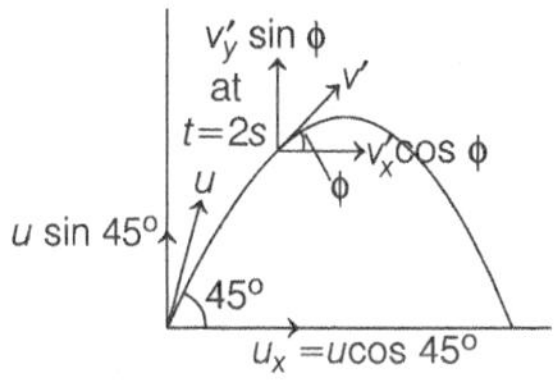

The resultant velocity at time t after the projection,

$$v'=\sqrt{u^2+g^2t^2-2ugt\sin 45^\circ}$$

$$20=\sqrt{u^2+10^2\times 2^2-2u\times 10\times 2\times\frac{1}{\sqrt{2}}}$$

$$\Rightarrow \quad 400=u^2+400-20\sqrt{2}u$$

$$\Rightarrow \quad u^2-20\sqrt{2}u=0$$

$$\Rightarrow \quad u(u-20\sqrt{2})=0$$

But $u\neq 0$,

$$\therefore \quad u \quad 20\sqrt{2}-0$$

$$\Rightarrow \quad u=20\sqrt{2}\text{ m/s}$$

$\therefore$ Maximum height,

$$H_{max}=\frac{u^2\sin^2\theta}{2g}=\frac{(20\sqrt{2})^2\sin^2 45^\circ}{2\times 10}=\frac{800\times\frac{1}{2}}{20}=20\text{ m}$$

19. Given, equation of projectile motion,

$$y=5x(1-x)$$

$$\Rightarrow \quad y=5x-5x^2 \qquad \text{...(i)}$$

But we know that, equation of projectile motion is given as

$$y=x\tan\theta-\frac{1}{2}\frac{gx^2}{u^2} \qquad \text{...(ii)}$$

Comparing Eqs. (i) and (ii), we get

$$\tan\theta=5$$

$$\Rightarrow \quad \frac{u_y}{u_x}=5 \Rightarrow u_y=5u_x$$

Since, $\mathbf{u}_x = \hat{i}$

$$u_x = |\mathbf{u}_x| = 1\text{ m/s}^2$$

$$u_y = 5 \times 1 = 5\text{ m/s}^2$$

$$\therefore \quad \mathbf{u}_y = u_y\hat{j} = 5\hat{j}$$

20.

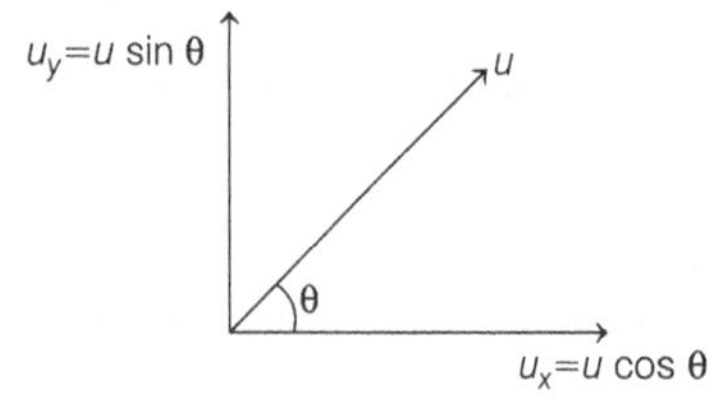

Velocity at maximum height along Y-axis, $v_y = 0\text{ ms}^{-1}$

As we know that, for motion along Y-axis,

$$\because \quad v_y^2 - u_y^2 = 2gH$$

$$\therefore \quad 0^2 - (25\sin 45°)^2 = -2 \times 10 \times H$$

$$\Rightarrow \quad -312.5 = -20H$$

$$\Rightarrow \quad H = 15.625\text{ m}$$

$$\because \quad H = \frac{1}{2}gt^2$$

$$\therefore \quad t = \sqrt{\frac{2H}{g}} = \sqrt{\frac{2 \times 15.625}{10}}$$

$$= 1.767 \simeq 1.77\text{ s}$$

21. The given situation is shown below

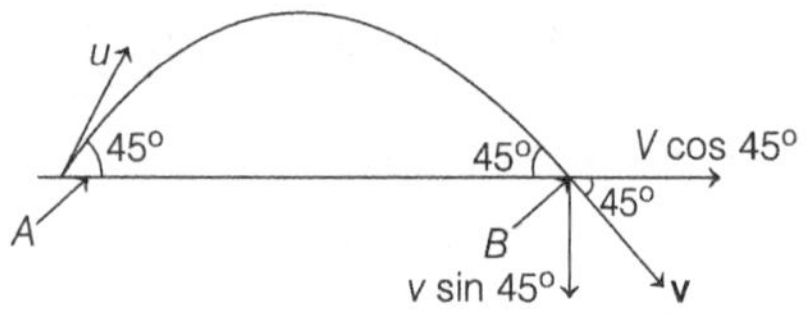

Initial velocity of the projectile,

$$\mathbf{u} = u\cos 45°\,\hat{i} + u\sin 45°\,\hat{j}$$

Final velocity of the projectile,

$$\mathbf{v} = v\cos 45°\,\hat{i} - v\sin 45°\,\hat{j}$$

At point B, $v\cos 45° = u\cos 45°$

and $v\sin 45° = u\sin 45°$

$$\mathbf{v} = u\cos 45°\,\hat{i} - u\sin 45°\,\hat{j}$$

The magnitude of change in the momentum between the points A and B

$$|\Delta p| = |m(v - u)|$$

$$\Rightarrow \quad \Delta p = 2mu\sin 45°$$

$$\Rightarrow \quad \Delta p = 2 \times 0.005 \times 5\sqrt{2} \times \frac{1}{\sqrt{2}}$$

$$\Rightarrow \quad \Delta p = 5 \times 10^{-2}\text{ kg-m/s}$$

Hence, the value of the x is 5.

JEE Advanced

1. $d = \dfrac{u^2 \sin 2\theta}{g}$, $\quad H = \dfrac{u^2 \sin^2\theta}{2g}$

So, after entering in the new region, time taken by projectile to reach ground,

$$t = \sqrt{\frac{2H}{g'}} = \sqrt{\frac{2u^2\sin^2\theta \times 0.81}{2g \times g}} = \frac{0.94\sin\theta}{g}$$

So, horizontal displacement of the projectile in new region in reaching from topmost point to ground,

$$x = (t)(u\cos\theta) = \frac{0.9u\sin\theta}{g} \times u\cos\theta = 0.9\frac{u^2\sin 2\theta}{2g}$$

So, $d' = \dfrac{d}{2} + x = 0.95d$

So, $n = 0.95d$

2. Let $\dfrac{2u\sin\theta}{g} = T_0$ and $u_0\cos\theta = v_1$

Average velocity

$$= \frac{(u_0\cos\theta)T_0 + \left(\frac{u_0}{\alpha}\cos\theta\right)\left(\frac{T_0}{\alpha}\right) +}{T_0 + \frac{T_0}{\alpha} + \frac{T_0}{\alpha^2}}$$

$$\Rightarrow \quad v_{avg} = \frac{u_0\cos\theta\, T_0\left(1 + \frac{1}{\alpha^2} + \frac{1}{\alpha^4} + \ldots\right)}{T_0\left(1 + \frac{1}{\alpha} + \frac{1}{\alpha^2} + \ldots\right)}$$

$$\Rightarrow \quad 0.8v_1 = v_1\left(\frac{\alpha}{1+\alpha}\right)$$

$$\Rightarrow \quad \alpha = 4$$

3. $\dfrac{u_y^2}{2g} = 120$

$$\Rightarrow \quad u_y = \sqrt{240g}$$

and $\tan 45° = \dfrac{u_y}{u_x}$

$$\Rightarrow \quad u_x = \sqrt{240g}$$

$$\mathbf{u} = \sqrt{240g}\,\hat{i} + \sqrt{240g}\,\hat{j}$$

$$\Rightarrow \quad u = \sqrt{480g}$$

After hitting ground $u' = \dfrac{1}{\sqrt{2}}(\sqrt{480g})$

$$u' = \sqrt{240g}$$

$$H_{max} = \frac{u'^2_y}{2g} = \frac{(\sqrt{240g}\sin 30°)^2}{2g} = \frac{240g \times \frac{1}{4}}{2g} = 30\text{ m}$$

CHAPTER~07

RELATIVE MOTION

LEVEL 01 Starter Level

7.1 Relative Motion in One Dimension

1 Two parallel rail tracks run north-south. Train A moves due north with a speed of 54 km h^{-1} and train B moves due south with a speed of 90 km h^{-1}. A monkey runs on the roof of train A with a velocity of 18 km/h w.r.t. train A in a direction opposite to that of A. Calculate (a) the relative velocity of B with respect to A, (b) relative velocity of ground with respect to B, (c) velocity of a monkey as observed by a man standing on the ground and (d) velocity of monkey as observed by a passenger of train B.

2 Two trains A and B, of lengths 300 m and 100 m respectively, are running on parallel tracks with velocities 108 km/h and 72 km/h, respectively.

(a) If both the trains are travelling in the same directions, then how long will A take to overtake B?

(b) If both the trains are travelling in the opposite directions, then how long will they take to cross each other?

3 Two cars A and B moving in the same direction on a straight single lane road with velocities 90 km/h and 72 km/h, respectively. When the separation between the two was 10 m, 'A' started decelerating to avoid collision. What is the minimum deceleration of car A, so that they don't collide?

4 A ball is thrown downwards with a speed of 20 m/s from the top of a building 200 m high and simultaneously another ball is thrown vertically upwards with a speed of 30 m/s from the foot of the building. Find the time after which both the balls will meet. ($g = 10\ m/s^2$)

5 A lift is moving up with acceleration a. A person inside the lift throws the ball upwards with a velocity u relative to hand.

(a) What is the time of flight of the ball?

(b) What is the maximum height reached by the ball in the lift?

7.2 Relative Motion in Two Dimensions

1 A particle A moves with a velocity $4\hat{i}$ and another particle B moves with a velocity $3\hat{j}$. Find $\mathbf{v}_{AB}$, $\mathbf{v}_{BA}$ and their magnitudes.

2 A ship is steaming due east at 12 ms^{-1}. A woman runs across the deck at 5ms^{-1} in a direction at right angles to the direction of motion of the ship towards north. Calculate the velocity of the woman relative to sea.

3 Two perpendicular rail tracks have two trains A and B respectively. Train A moves north with a speed of 54 km h^{-1} and train B moves west with a speed of 72 km h^{-1}. Assume that both trains starts from same point. Calculate the

(a) relative velocity of ground with respect to B,

(b) relative velocity of A with respect to B

(c) and rate of separation of the two trains.

4 A man is swimming in a lake in a direction of 30° east of north with a speed of 5 km/h and a cyclist is going on a road along the lake shore towards east at a speed of 10 km/h. In what direction and with what speed would the man appear to swim to the cyclist?

7.3 River Flow Problems

1 A swimmer's speed in the direction of flow of river is 16 km h^{-1}. Against the direction of flow of river; the swimmer's speed is 8 km h^{-1}. Calculate the swimmer's speed in still water and the velocity of flow of the river.

2 A man wishing to cross a river flowing with velocity u jumps at an angle θ with the river flow.

(a) Find the net velocity of the man with respect to ground if he can swim with speed v in still water.

(b) In what direction does the man actually move?

(c) Find how far from the point directly opposite to the starting point does the man reach the opposite bank, if the width of the river is d. (i.e. drift)

3 A man can swim with a speed of 4 km h^{-1} in still water. He wants to cross a river 1 km wide in the shortest time possible. River flows steadily at 3 km h^{-1}?

(a) Along what direction must the man make his strokes?

(b) How much time will he take to cross the river?

(c) What will be his drift?

4 A man can swim at the rate of 5 km/h in still water. A 1 km wide river flows at the rate of 3 km/h. The man wishes to swim across the river directly opposite to the starting point.

(a) Along what direction must the man swim?

(b) What will be his resultant velocity?

(c) How much time will he take to cross the river?

5 A 400 m wide river is flowing at a rate of 10 m/s. A boy can swim with a velocity of 5 m/s with respect to the water. The boy wants to cross the river along the shortest route.

(a) Along what direction should the boy swim?

(b) How much time will he take to cross the river?

(c) What distance will he have to walk after reaching the other bank to reach a point directly opposite his starting point?

7.4 Air Flow Problems

1 An aeroplane pilot sets a compass course due west and maintains an air speed of 240 km/h. After flying for $\frac{1}{2}$ h, he finds himself over a town that is 150 km west and 40 km south of his starting point. Find the wind velocity, in magnitude and direction.

2 An aeroplane flies along a straight path *A* to *B* and returns back again. The distance between *A* and *B* is *l* and the aeroplane maintains the constant speed *v* w.r.t. wind. There is a steady wind with a speed *u* at an angle θ with line *AB*. Determine the expression for the total time of the trip.

3 Find the time an aeroplane having velocity v, takes to fly around a square of side *l*, if the wind is blowing at a velocity *u* along one of the sides of the square.

4 An aeroplane has to go from a point *A* to another point *B*, 500 km away due 30° east of north. A wind is blowing due north at a speed of 20 m/s. The air-speed of the plane is 150 m/s.

(a) Find the direction in which the pilot should head the plane to reach the point *B*.

(b) Find the time taken by the plane to go from *A* to *B*.

5 A man holding a flag is running in north-east direction with speed 10 m/s. Wind is blowing in east direction with speed $5\sqrt{2}$ m/s. Find the direction in which flag will flutter.

7.5 Rain Problems

1 A pipe which can rotate in a vertical plane is mounted on a cart. The cart moves uniformly along a horizontal path with a speed $v_1 = 2$ m/s. At what angle θ to the horizontal should the pipe be placed so that drops of rain falling vertically with a velocity $v_2 = 4$ m/s move parallel to the axis of the pipe without touching its walls? Consider the velocity of the drops as constant due to the resistance of the air.

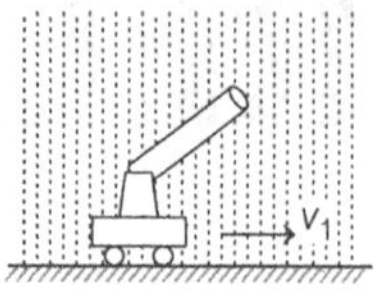

2 Rain seems to be falling vertically to a person sitting in a bus which is moving uniformly eastwards with 10 m/s. It appears to come from vertical at a velocity 20 m/s. Find the speed of rain drops with respect to ground.

3 To a man walking at the rate of 2 km/h with respect to ground, the rain appears to fall vertically. When he increases his speed to 4 km/h in same direction of his motion, rain appears to meet him at an angle of 45° with horizontal, find the real direction and speed of the rain.

4 A man standing on a horizontal road has to hold his umbrella at 30° to the vertical to keep rain away. When he walks on the road at 10 km/h, he has to hold his umbrella vertically to keep himself dry. Find the speed of the rain drops with respect to ground.

5 In the absence of wind, rain is falling vertically with 20 m/s speed. A person is running in the rain at a speed of 5 m/s on straight horizontal road. Wind starts blowing with 15 m/s speed. Directions of both wind and person is from west to east. Find the angle with the vertical that a person should hold his umbrella to keep the rain away.

7.6 Velocity of Separation and Approach

1 Particles *A* and *B* are moving as shown in the diagram at $t = 0$. Find their velocity of separation

(a) at $t = 0$

(b) at $t = 1$ s

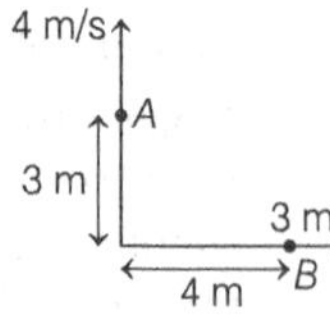

2 Two particles *A* and *B* are moving with constant velocities v_1 and v_2. At $t = 0$, v_1 makes an angle θ_1 with the line joining *A* and *B* and v_2 makes an angle θ_2 with the line joining *A* and *B*.

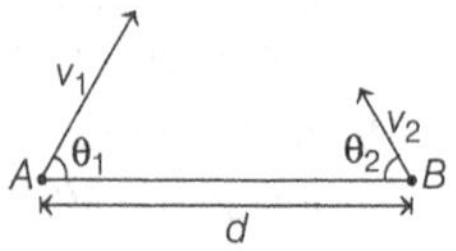

(a) Find the condition for *A* and *B* to collide.

(b) Find the time after which *A* and *B* will collide if separation between them is *d* at $t = 0$.

3 Two ships are 10 km apart on a line joining south to north. The one farther north is steaming west at 20 km h^{-1}. The other is steaming north at 20 km h^{-1}. What is their distance of closest approach? How long do they take to reach it?

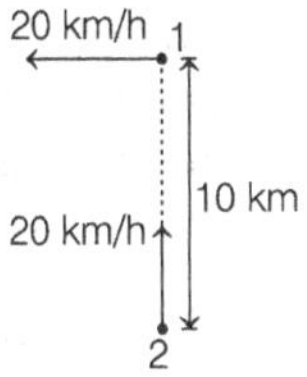

4 Three particles A, B and C are situated at the vertices of an equilateral triangle of side a at $t = 0$. Each of the particles moves with constant speed v. A always has its velocity along AB, B along BC and C along CA. At what time will the particles meet each other?

5 'n' number of particles are located at the vertices of a regular polygon of 'n' sides having the edge length 'a'. They all start moving simultaneously with equal constant speed 'v' heading towards the particle next to it all the time. How long will the particles take to collide?

LEVEL 02 JEE Main Level

Single Choice Correct Questions

1 A stone is thrown upwards from a tower with a velocity 50 ms^{-1}. Another stone is simultaneously thrown downwards from the same location with a velocity 50 ms^{-1}. When the first stone is at the highest point, the relative velocity of the second stone w.r.t. the first stone is (assume that second stone has not yet reached the ground):

(a) zero (b) 50 ms^{-1}
(c) 100 ms^{-1} (d) 150 ms^{-1}

2 A car is going eastwards with a velocity of 8 ms^{-1}. To the passengers in the car, a train appears to be moving northwards with a velocity 15 ms^{-1}. What is the actual velocity of the train?

(a) 7 ms^{-1} (b) 17 ms^{-1}
(c) 23 ms^{-1} (d) None of these

3 For four particles A, B, C and D, the velocities of one with respect to other are given as; $\mathbf{v}_{DC}$ is 20 m/s towards north, $\mathbf{v}_{BC}$ is 20 m/s towards east and $\mathbf{v}_{BA}$ is 20 m/s towards south. Then $\mathbf{v}_{DA}$ is

(a) 20 m/s towards north (b) 20 m/s towards south
(c) 20 m/s towards east (d) 20 m/s towards west

4 Three elephants A, B and C are moving along a straight line with constant speed in same direction as shown in figure. Speed of A is 5 m/s and speed of C is 10 m/s. Initially separation between A and B is d and between B and C is also d. When 'B' catches 'C' separation between A and C becomes $3d$. Then, the speed of B will be

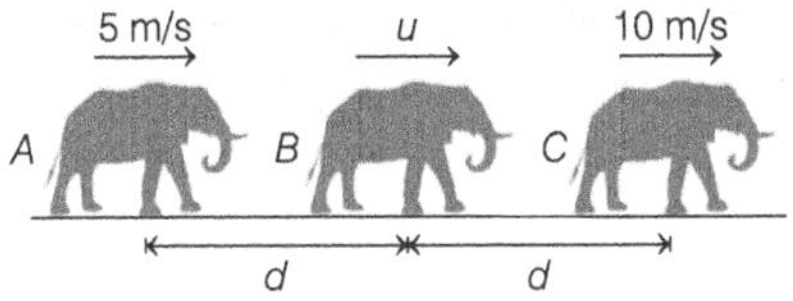

(a) 7.5 m/s (b) 15 m/s (c) 20 m/s (d) 5 m/s

5 Two trains A and B 100 km apart are travelling towards each other on different tracks with starting speed of 50 km/h for both. The train A accelerates at 20 km/h^2 and the train B retards at the rate 20 km/h^2. The distance covered by the train A when they cross each other is

(a) 45 km (b) 55 km (c) 65 km (d) 60 km

6 Two cars get closer by 8 m every second while travelling in the opposite directions. They get closer by 0.8 m every second while travelling in the same directions. What are the speeds of the cars?

(a) 4 ms^{-1} and 4.4 ms^{-1}
(b) 4.4 ms^{-1} and 3.6 ms^{-1}
(c) 4 ms^{-1} and 3.6 ms^{-1}
(d) 4 ms^{-1} and 3 ms^{-1}

7 A helicopter is flying south with a speed of 50 km h^{-1}. A train is moving with the same speed towards East. The relative velocity of the helicopter as seen by the passengers in the train will be towards

(a) North-East (b) South-East
(c) North-West (d) South-West

8 An aeroplane is flying vertically upwards. When it is at a height of 1000 m above the ground and moving at a speed of 367 m/s, a shot is fired at it with a speed of 567 m/s from a point directly below it. What should be the acceleration of aeroplane, so that it may escape from being hit?

(a) > 5 m/s^2 (b) > 10 m/s^2
(c) <10 m/s^2 (d) Not possible

9 A ship is travelling due east at 10 km/h. A ship heading 30° east of north is always north from the first ship. The speed of the second ship in km/h is

(a) $20\sqrt{2}$ (b) $10\sqrt{3}$
(c) 20 (d) $20/\sqrt{2}$

10 A coin is released inside a lift at a height of 2 m from the floor of the lift. The height of the lift is 10 m. The lift is moving with an acceleration of 11 m/s^2 downwards. The time after which the coin will strike with the lift is

(a) 4 s (b) 2 s (c) $\frac{4}{\sqrt{21}}$ s (d) $\frac{2}{\sqrt{11}}$ s

11 Two transparent elevator cars *A* and *B* are moving in front of each other. Car *A* is moving up and retarding at a_1, while car *B* is moving down and retarding at a_2. Person in car *A* drops a coin inside the car. What is the acceleration of coin observed by person in car *B*.

(a) $g + a_2$ downward (b) $g - a_1 - a_2$ downward
(c) $g - a_1 + a_2$ downward (d) None of these

12 At a given instant, an observer stationary on the ground sees a package falling with speed v_1 at certain angle with the vertical. A pilot flying at a constant horizontal velocity relative to the ground sees the package falling vertically with a speed v_2 at the same instant. What is the speed of the pilot relative to the ground?

(a) $v_1 + v_2$ (b) $v_1 - v_2$ (c) $\sqrt{v_1^2 - v_2^2}$ (d) $\sqrt{v_1^2 + v_2^2}$

13 Three ships *A*, *B* and *C* are in motion. The motion of *A* as seen by *B* is with speed *v* towards North-East. The motion of *B* as seen by *C* is with speed *v* towards the North-West. Then as seen by *A*, *C* will be moving towards

(a) North (b) South (c) East (d) West

14 A man in a balloon, throws a stone downwards with a speed of 5 m/s with respect to balloon. The balloon is moving upwards with a constant acceleration of 5 m/s^2. Then velocity of the stone relative to the man after 2 s is

(a) 10 m/s (b) 30 m/s (c) 15 m/s (d) 35 m/s

15 A jet aeroplane travelling from east to west at a speed of 500 km h^{-1} ejected out gases of combustion at a speed of 1500 km h^{-1} with respect to the jet plane. What is the velocity of the gases with respect to an observer on the ground?

(a) 1000 km h^{-1} in the direction west to east
(b) 1000 km h^{-1} in the direction east to west
(c) 2000 km h^{-1} in the direction west to east
(d) 2000 km h^{-1} in the direction east to west

16 A boat, which has a speed of 5 km/h in still water, crosses a river of width 1 km along the shortest possible path in 15 min. The velocity of the river water in km/h is

(a) 1 (b) 3 (c) 4 (d) $\sqrt{41}$

17 To cross the river in shortest distance, a swimmer should swim making angle θ with the upstream. What is the ratio of the time taken to swim across in the shortest time to that in swimming across over shortest distance. [Assume speed of swimmer in still water is greater than the speed of river flow]

(a) $\cos\theta$ (b) $\sin\theta$ (c) $\tan\theta$ (d) $\cot\theta$

18 A swimmer crosses the river along the line making an angle of 45° with the direction of flow. Velocity of the river water is 5 m/s. Swimmer takes 6 seconds to cross the river of width 60 m. The velocity of the swimmer with respect to water will be

(a) 10 m/s (b) 12 m/s (c) $5\sqrt{5}$ m/s (d) $10\sqrt{2}$ m/s

19 A boat is rowed across a river (perpendicular to river flow) at the rate of 4.5 km/h. The river flows at the rate of 6 km/h. The velocity of boat (in m/s) is

(a) 3.1 (b) 2.1 (c) 2.9 (d) 5

20 A boat which can move with a speed of 5 m/s relative to water crosses a river of width 480 m flowing with a constant speed of 4 m/s. What is the time taken by the boat to cross the river along the shortest path.

(a) 80 s (b) 160 s (c) 240 s (d) 320 s

21 A man who can swim at the rate of 2 km/h (in still river) crosses a river to a point exactly opposite on the other bank by swimming in a direction of 120° to the flow of the water in the river. The velocity of the water current (in km/h) is

(a) 1 (b) 2 (c) $\frac{1}{2}$ (d) $\frac{3}{2}$

22 A battalion of soldiers is ordered to swim across a river 500 ft wide. At what minimum rate should they swim perpendicular to river flow in order to avoid being washed away by the waterfall 300 ft downstream. The speed of current is 3 mph.

(a) 6 mph (b) 5 mph
(c) 4 mph (d) 2 mph

23 A man crosses the river perpendicular to river flow in time *t* seconds and travels an equal distance down the stream in *T* seconds. The ratio of man's speed in still water to the speed of river water will be

(a) $\frac{t^2 - T^2}{t^2 + T^2}$ (b) $\frac{T^2 - t^2}{T^2 + t^2}$
(c) $\frac{t^2 + T^2}{t^2 - T^2}$ (d) $\frac{T^2 + t^2}{T^2 - t^2}$

24 An aeroplane flies between two cities separated by a distance d. Assume the wind blows directly from one city to the other at a speed v_A (as shown) and the speed of the aeroplane is v_0 relative to the air. Find the time taken by the aeroplane to make a round trip between the two cities (that is, to fly from city A to city B and then back to city A)?

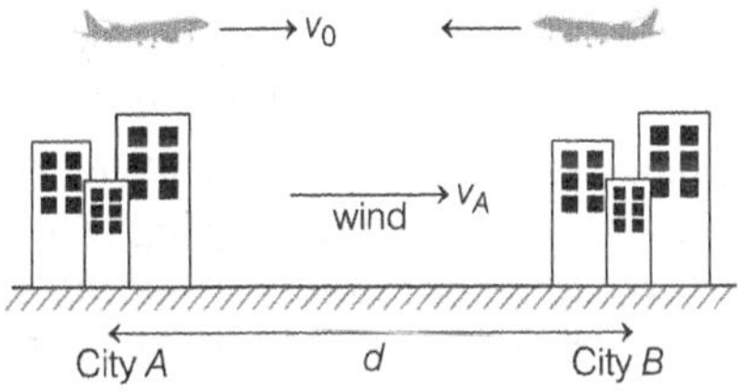

(a) $\frac{2dv_0}{v_0^2 - v_A^2}$ (b) $\frac{dv_0}{v_0^2 - v_A^2}$ (c) $\frac{2dv_0}{v_0^2 + v_A^2}$ (d) $\frac{dv_0}{v_0^2 + v_A^2}$

25 A man standing, observes rain falling with velocity of 20 m/s at an angle of 30° with the vertical. Find out velocity of man, so that rain again appears to fall at 30° with the vertical.

(a) 20 m/s (b) 30 m/s (c) 40 m/s (d) 10 m/s

26 A boy starts from rest with an acceleration of $\sqrt{3}$ m/s^2 at $t = 0$. At $t = 3$ s, it appears to him that rain falls with the velocity 3 m/s in vertically downward direction. The actual velocity of rain is

(a) $3\sqrt{3}$ m/s (b) 3 m/s (c) 6 m/s (d) $3\sqrt{5}$ m/s

27 Raindrops are falling vertically with a velocity of 10 m/s. To a cyclist moving on a straight road the raindrops appear to be coming with a velocity of 20 m/s. The velocity of cyclist is

(a) 10 m/s (b) $10\sqrt{3}$ m/s
(c) 20 m/s (d) $10\sqrt{5}$ m/s

28 For two particles A and B, given that $\mathbf{r}_A = 2\hat{\mathbf{i}} + 3\hat{\mathbf{j}}$, $\mathbf{r}_B = 6\hat{\mathbf{i}} + 7\hat{\mathbf{j}}$, $\mathbf{v}_A = 3\hat{\mathbf{i}} - \hat{\mathbf{j}}$ and $\mathbf{v}_B = x\hat{\mathbf{i}} - 5\hat{\mathbf{j}}$. What is the value of x, if they collide?

(a) 1 (b) -1 (c) 2 (d) -2

29 Two particles A and B move with velocities v_1 and v_2 respectively along the X and Y-axis. The initial separation between them is d as shown in the figure. Find the least distance between them during their motion.

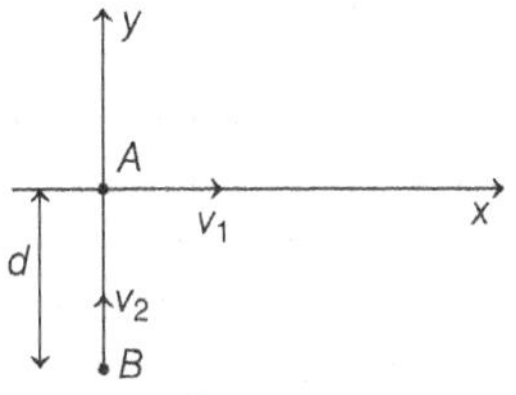

(a) $\frac{dv_1^2}{v_1^2 + v_2^2}$ (b) $\frac{dv_2^2}{v_1^2 + v_2^2}$ (c) $\frac{dv_1}{\sqrt{v_1^2 + v_2^2}}$ (d) $\frac{dv_2}{\sqrt{v_1^2 + v_2^2}}$

30 A boat has a velocity 4 m/s towards east with respect to river and river is flowing towards north with velocity 2 m/s. Wind is blowing towards north with velocity 6 m/s. The direction of the flag blown over by the wind hoisted on the boat is

(a) north-west (b) south-east
(c) $\tan^{-1}\left(\frac{1}{2}\right)$ with east (d) north

31 A motorboat is observed to travel 10 kmh^{-1} relative to the earth in the direction 37° north of east. If the velocity of the boat due to the wind only is 2 km h^{-1} westwards and that due to the current only is 4 kmh^{-1} southwards, what is the magnitude and direction of the velocity of the boat due to its own power?

(a) $10\sqrt{2}$ km/h, north-east (b) $10\sqrt{2}$ km/h, north-west
(c) 20 km/h, north-east (d) 20 km/h, north-west

32 Two cars are moving in the same direction with a speed of 30 km h^{-1}. They are separated from each other by 5 km. Third car moving in the opposite direction meets the two cars after an interval of 4 min. What is the speed of the third car?

(a) 30 km h^{-1} (b) 35 km h^{-1}
(c) 40 km h^{-1} (d) 45 km h^{-1}

33 Two identical trains take 3 s to pass one another when going in the opposite direction but only 2.5 s, if the speed of one is increased by 50%. The time one would take to pass the other when going in the same direction at their original speed is

(a) 10 s (b) 12 s
(c) 15 s (d) 18 s

34 A particle A is at rest and particle B moves in a circle with A at its centre. The particle A will appear

(a) at rest if seen from B
(b) to move in straight line if seen from B
(c) to move in a circle if seen from B
(d) to move in parabola if seen from B

35 A person standing on the escalator takes time t_1 to reach the top of the tower when the escalator is moving. He takes time t_2 to reach the top of the tower when the escalator is standing. How long will he take if he walks up a moving escalator?

(a) $t_2 - t_1$ (b) $t_1 + t_2$
(c) $t_1t_2/(t_1 - t_2)$ (d) $t_1t_2/(t_1 + t_2)$

36 A body is thrown up in a lift with a velocity u relative to the lift and the time of flight is found to be 't'. The acceleration with which the lift is moving up is

(a) $\frac{u - gt}{t}$ (b) $\frac{2u - gt}{t}$ (c) $\frac{u + gt}{t}$ (d) $\frac{2u + gt}{t}$

37 A girl inside a moving train observes the objects outside of the train. Choose the correct choice from the following statements.

(a) Stationary objects near the train will move with greater velocity and object far from train will move with lesser velocity with respect to the girl.

(b) All stationary objects outside the train will move with same velocity in opposite direction of the train with respect to the girl.

(c) Large objects like the moon or mountains will move with same velocity as that of the train.

(d) All of the above

38 A stationary man observes that the rain strikes him at an angle of 60° to the horizontal. When he begins to move with a velocity of 25 m/s, then the drops appear to strike him at an angle of 30° from horizontal. The velocity of the rain drops is

(a) 25 m/s (b) 50 m/s (c) 12.5 m/s (d) $24\sqrt{2}$ m/s

Numerical Value Questions

1 A train is moving with a speed of 36 km/h takes 14 s to cross a bridge of length 100 m. Find the length of the train (in metre).

2 A sailor in a boat, which is going due east with a speed of 8 m/s, observes that a submarine is heading towards north at a speed of 12 m/s and sinking at a rate of 2 m/s. The commander of submarine observes a helicopter ascending at a rate of 5 m/s and heading towards west with 4 m/s. Find the actual speed of the helicopter.

3 On a 2-lane road, car A is travelling with a speed of 36 km/h. Two car B and C approach car A in opposite directions with a speed of 54 km/h each. At a certain instant, when the distance AB is equal to AC, both being 1 km, B decides to overtake A before C does. The minimum acceleration of car B required to avoid an accident is x m/s^2. Therefore, find x.

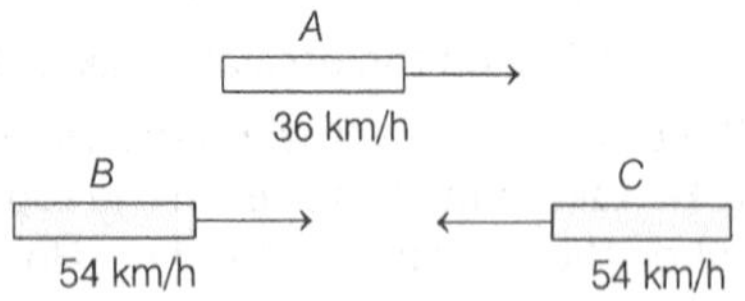

4 An aeroplane is observed by two persons travelling at 60 km/hr in two vehicles moving in opposite directions on a straight road. To an observer in one vehicle the plane appears to cross the road track at right angle while to the observer in the other vehicle the angle appears to be 45°. If the angle does the plane actually cross the road track is given by $\tan^{-1}(N)$, then find the value of N.

5 A boat is travelling east at 12 m/s. A flag flaps at 53° north of west at the bow of the boat. Another flag on shore flaps due north. Find the speed (in m/s) of the wind as measured on land.

6 A man swimming downstream overcomes a float at a point M. After travelling distance d he turned back and passed the float at a distance of $d/2$ from the point M, then find the ratio of speed of swimmer with respect to still water to the speed of the river.

7 Rain appears to be falling at an angle of 37° with vertical to the driver of a car moving with a velocity of 7 m/s. When he increases the velocity of the car to 25 m/s, the rain again appears to fall at an angle 37°. What is the actual velocity (in m/s) of rain?

8 The driver of a car travelling at a speed of 20 m/s, wishes to overtake a truck that is moving with a constant speed of 20 m s^{-1} in the same lane. The car's maximum acceleration is 0.5 ms^{-2}. Initially the vehicles are separated by 40 m, and the car returns back into its lane after it is 40 m ahead of the truck. The car is 3 m long and the truck 17 m. Find the minimum time (in seconds) required for the car to pass the truck and return back to its lane.

9 A police van moving on a highway with a speed of 30 km h^{-1} fires a bullet at a thief's car speeding away in the same direction with a speed of 192 km h^{-1}. If the muzzle speed of the bullet is 150 ms^{-1}, with what speed (in m/s) does the bullet hit the thief's car?

10 A boat man finds that he can save 6 s in crossing a river by quicker path, then by shortest path, if the velocity of boat in still water and river be respectively 17 m/s and 8 m/s, then find the river width (in metre).

11 Width of a river is 60 m. A swimmer wants to cross the river such that he reaches from A to B directly. Point B is 45 m ahead of line AC (perpendicular to river). Assume speed of river and speed of swimmer as equal. Swimmer must try to swim at angle θ with the line AC. Find the value of θ in degree.

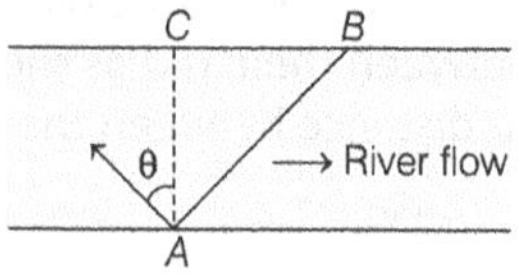

12 A straight railway track has trains plying on it at a constant speed of 100 km/h. Two trains which are one after another pass a certain point on the track at an interval of 6 min. On a straight road parallel to the track, a car is moving in the same direction as the trains, at a speed of 60 km/h. What is the interval between time (in min) when consecutive trains pass by the car?

LEVEL 03 JEE Advanced Level

Single Choice Correct Questions

1 A, B and C are three objects each moving with constant velocity. A's speed is 10 m/s in a direction **PQ**. The velocity of B relative to A is 6 m/s at an angle of, $\cos^{-1}(15/24)$ to PQ. The velocity of C relative to B is 12 m/sec in a direction **QP**, then find the magnitude of the velocity of C.

(a) 5 m/s (b) 13 m/s
(c) 17 m/s (d) None of these

2 Men are running along a road at 15 km/h behind one another at equal intervals of 20 m. Cyclists are riding in the same direction at 25 km/h at equal intervals of 30 m. At what speed an observer travel along the road in opposite direction, so that whenever he meets a runner he also meets a cyclist?

(a) 30 km/h (b) 20 km/h
(c) 10 km/h (d) 5 km/h

3 A student is standing on a train travelling along a straight horizontal track a speed of $2\sqrt{5}$ m/s. The student throws a ball into the air along a path, that he sees to make an initial angle of 60° with the horizontal along the track. The professor standing on ground observes the ball to rise vertically. What is the maximum height (in m) reached by the ball with respect to the point of projection?

(a) 0.25 m (b) 0.33 m
(c) 1 m (d) 3 m

4 During a rainy day, rain is falling vertically with a velocity 2 m/s. A boy at rest starts his motion with a constant acceleration of 2 m/s^2 along a straight road. If the angle of the axis of umbrella with vertical is changed at such a rate that relative to the boy rain always falls parallel to the axis of the umbrella. Find the rate at $t = \frac{1}{2}$ s.

(a) (3/5) rad/s (b) (4/5) rad/s
(c) (6/5) rad/s (d) (8/5) rad/s

5 A hunter is riding an elephant of height 4 m moving in straight line with uniform speed of 2 m/s. A deer running with a speed v in front at a distance of $4\sqrt{5}$ m moving perpendicular to the direction of motion of the elephant. If hunter can throw his spear with a speed of 10 m/s relative to the elephant, then at what angle θ to its direction of motion must he throw his spear horizontally for a successful hit. Find also the speed v of the deer.

(a) 37°, 6 m/s (b) 53°, 8 m/s
(c) 45°, $10\sqrt{2}$ m/s (d) 60°, $10\sqrt{3}$ m/s

6 Hailstones falling vertically with a speed of 10 m/s, hit the wind screen (wind screen makes an angle 30° with the horizontal) of a moving car and rebound elastically. The velocity of the car if the driver finds the hailstones rebound vertically after striking is

(a) $10\sqrt{3}$ m/s (b) $20\sqrt{3}$ m/s
(c) 10 m/s (d) $\frac{10}{\sqrt{3}}$ m/s

7 Two observers A and B are moving opposite to each other on a parallel track, separated by a distance d, with same speed. When they are at the shortest distance, a particle is thrown horizontally from some height from ground by A toward B with respect to itself. The path of the particle observed by B is

(a) horizontal straight line
(b) vertical straight line
(c) straight line at some angle with the horizontal
(d) parabolic

8 Two particles are projected from the same point, with the same speed, in the same vertical plane, at different angles with the horizontal. A frame of reference is fixed to one particle. The position vector of the other particle, as observed from this frame, is **r**. Which of the following statement is correct?

(a) **r** is a constant vector.
(b) **r** changes in magnitude and direction with time.
(c) The magnitude of **r** increases linearly with time; its direction does not change.
(d) The direction of **r** changes with time; its magnitude may or may not change, depending on the angles of projection.

9 A particle is thrown up inside a stationary lift of sufficient height. The time of flight is T. Now it is thrown again with same initial speed u with respect to lift. At the time of second throw, lift is moving up with speed u and uniform acceleration g upward (the acceleration due to gravity). The new time of flight is

(a) $\frac{T}{4}$ (b) $\frac{T}{2}$
(c) T (d) $2T$

10 A taxi leaves the station X for station Y every 10 min. Simultaneously, a taxi also leaves the station Y for station X every 10 min. The taxis move at the same constant speed and go from X to Y or *vice-versa* in 2h. How many taxis coming from the other side will meet each taxi enroute from Y to X.

(a) 11 (b) 12
(c) 23 (d) 24

11 While standing in an elevator, you see a screw fall from the ceiling of elevator. The celing of elevator is 9 m above the floor of the elevator. If the elevator is moving upward with a constant speed of 4 m/s, how long does it take for the screw to hit the floor? ($g = 10\ m/s^2$)

(a) 1 (b) $\sqrt{\frac{9}{5}}$ (c) $\sqrt{\frac{5}{9}}$ (d) 3

12 In the above question, how long is the screw in air if the elevator starts from rest when the screw falls, and moves downward with a constant acceleration of $5.5\ m/s^2$?

(a) 1 s (b) 2 s (c) 3 s (d) 4 s

13 In the above question, the time of screw in the air is always

(a) independent of the speed of the elevator

(b) independent of the speed of the elevator as long as the elevator does not accelerate.

(c) independent of the speed of the elevator as long as the elevator does not accelerate horizontally

(d) None of the above

14 Ram moves with a velocity of 10 m/s in west direction. Shyam moves a direction 23° east of north. Ram is 100 m away from Shyam in directon 53° east of north of him. What should be the speed of Shyam, so that he collides with Ram?

(a) $4\sqrt{3}$ m/s (b) 10 m/s

(c) 12 m/s (d) None of these

15 Two swimmers start from point A on one bank of a river to reach point B on the other bank, lying directly opposite to point A. One of them crosses the river along the straight line AB, while the other swims at right angles to the stream and then walks the distance which he has been carried away by the stream to get to point B. What was the velocity (assumed uniform) of his walking if both the swimmers reached point B simultaneously. Velocity of each swimmer in still water is 2.5 km h^{-1} and the stream velocity is 2 km h^{-1}.

(a) 1.5 km/h (b) 2 km/h (c) 2.5 km/h (d) 3 km/h

16 A man can swim in still water with a speed of 3 m/s. x and y axis are drawn along and normal to the bank of river flowing to right with a speed of 1 m/s. The man starts swimming from origin O at $t = 0$. Assume size of man to be negligible. Find the equation of locus of all the possible points where man can reach at $t = 1$ s.

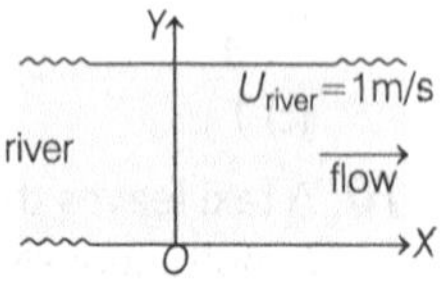

(a) $(x-1)^2 + y^2 = 3$ (b) $(x-1)^2 + y^2 = 9$

(c) $x^2 + (y-1)^2 = 3$ (d) $x^2 + (y-1)^2 = 9$

17 A swimmer crosses a river with minimum possible time 10 s. And when he reaches the other end, he starts swimming in the direction from where he started swimming. Keeping the direction fixed, the swimmer crosses the river in 15 s. The ratio of speed of swimmer with respect to water and the speed of river flow is (Assume constant speed of river and swimmer)-

(a) $\frac{3}{2}$ (b) $\frac{9}{4}$

(c) $\frac{2}{\sqrt{5}}$ (d) $\frac{\sqrt{5}}{2}$

18 A river of width 100 m is flowing with a velocity of 1.5 m/s. A man starts from one end from rest relative to the river. He rows with an acceleration of $2 m/s^2$ relative to the river. If the man wants to cross the river in the minimum time, by how much distance will he be drifted in the direction of river flow during crossing?

(a) 15 m (b) 20 m

(c) 25 m (d) 30 m

19 A man wearing a hat of extended length 12 cm is running in rain falling downwards with speed 10 m/s. The maximum speed with which man can run, so that rain drops does not fall on his face (the length of his face below the extended part of the hat is 16 cm) will be

(a) 7.5 m/s (b) 13.33 m/s

(c) 10 m/s (d) zero

20 A flag on a bus is fluttering in north direction and wind is blowing in east direction. Which of the following will be true?

(a) Bus is moving in south direction.

(b) Bus is moving in north-east direction.

(c) Bus may be moving in any direction between south and east.

(d) Bus may be moving in any direction between south and west.

21 A man starts running along a straight road with uniform velocity $u\hat{i}$ observes that the rain is falling vertically downward. If he doubles his speed, he finds that the rain is coming at an angle θ to the vertical. The velocity of rain with respect to the ground is

(a) $u\hat{i} - u\tan\theta\hat{j}$ (b) $u\hat{i} + u\tan\theta\hat{j}$

(c) $u\hat{i} + u\cot\theta\hat{j}$ (d) $\frac{u}{\tan\theta}\hat{i} - u\hat{j}$

22 An aeroplane flies along a straight path from town A to town B, 500 km away. Town B is due east of town A and a strong wind blows from north to south at

300 km/h. If the plane's airspeed is 900 km/h, which of the following statements is true?

(a) Trip time is $\frac{5}{3\sqrt{8}}$ h.

(b) Plane's speed with respect to ground is 600 km/h.

(c) Plane's heading is 30° north of east.

(d) None of the above

23 A passenger on a ship travelling due east with a speed of 18 km/h observes that the smoke from the ship makes an angle of 30° with the ship's direction of motion. The wind is blowing from south to north. Assume that the smoke acquires a velocity (with respect to the earth) equal to the velocity of the wind, as soon as it leaves the ship. Find the speed of the wind.

(a) $18\sqrt{3}$ km/h (b) $\frac{18}{\sqrt{3}}$ km/h

(c) 9 km/h (d) None of these

24 A man is standing on incline which makes θ with horizontal and rain is falling vertically with respect to man. Now man starts walking along the incline. Mark the correct option.

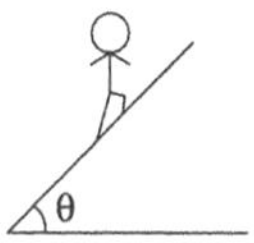

(a) If man walks up the incline, rain may appear to come horizontally.

(b) If man walks down the incline, rain may appear to come horizontally.

(c) No matter whether man walks up or down, rain can never appear to come horizontally.

(d) If man walks (up or down) along incline rain may appear to come along the incline.

25 Particles A and B are moving with constant velocities along X and Y-axis respectively, the graph of separation between them with time is

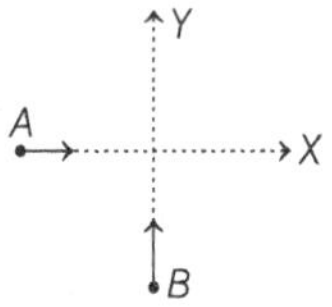

(a)

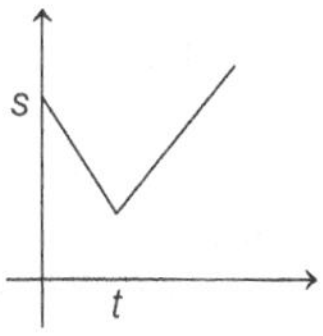

(b)

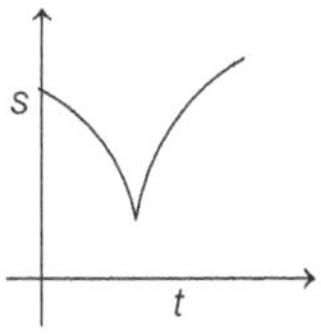

(c)

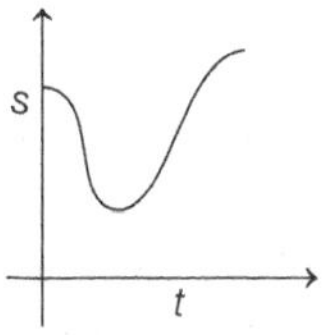

(d)

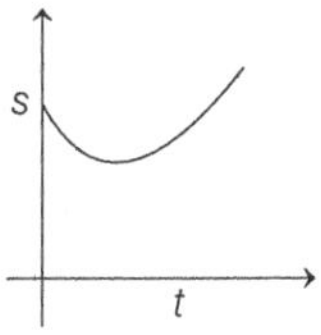

26 A motor boat is to reach at a point 30° upstream (w.r.t. normal) on other side of a river flowing with velocity 5 m/s. Velocity of motorboat w.r.t. water is $5\sqrt{3}$ m/s. The driver should steer the boat at an angle

(a) 120° w.r.t. stream direction

(b) 30° w.r.t. normal to the bank

(c) 30° w.r.t. the line of destination from starting point

(d) None of the above

27 At a harbour, a boat is standing and wind is blowing at a speed of $\sqrt{2}$ m/s due to which, the flag on the boat flutters along north-east. Now the boat enters in to river, which is flowing with a velocity of 2 m/s due north. The boat starts with zero velocity relative to the river and its constant acceleration relative to the river is 0.2 m/s^2 due east. In which direction will the flag flutter at 10 s?

(a) south-east (b) south-west

(c) 30° south of west (d) west

28 A man is on ship which is moving in east direction with speed 60 km/h. Waves of ocean is taking ship towards west with speed 20 km/h. Man start running on ship with flag in his hand in north direction with speed 30 km/h and wind is blowing with 50 km/h, 37° towards south of west then find the direction of flutter of the flag as seen by man on ground.

(a) 37° south of west (b) 53° south of west

(c) 37° west of north (d) flag will not flutter

29 A swimmer crosses a flowing stream of breadth 'd' to and fro along the shortest path in time T_1. The time taken to cover the same distance up and down the stream is T_2. If T_3 is the time the swimmer would take to swim a distance $2d$ in still water, then

(a) $T_3 = T_1 + T_2$ (b) $T_1^2 = T_2 T_3$

(c) $T_2^2 = T_1 T_3$ (d) $T_3^2 = T_1 T_2$

30 A motorboat going downstream in a river overcame a raft at a point A; 60 min later it turned back and after some time passed the raft at a distance 6 km from the point A. Find the flow velocity of the river assuming the duty of the engine to be constant?

(a) 2 km/h (b) 4 km/h (c) 6 km/h (d) 3 km/h

31 A glass wind screen whose inclination with the vertical can be changed is mounted on a car. The car moves horizontally with a speed of 2 m/s. At what angle θ with the vertical should the wind screen be placed so that the rain drops falling vertically downwards with velocity 6 m/s strike the wind screen perpendicularly?

(a) $\tan^{-1}\left(\frac{1}{3}\right)$ (b) $\tan^{-1}(3)$

(c) $\cos^{-1}(3)$ (d) $\sin^{-1}\left(\frac{1}{3}\right)$

32 A bird can fly in still air at 15 km/h. Wind is blowing at 5 km/h due east. What is the time it takes to reach a point 5 km due north east of its starting point.

(a) $t = \left(\frac{\sqrt{34}+\sqrt{2}}{16}\right)$h (b) $t = \left(\frac{\sqrt{34}-\sqrt{2}}{16}\right)$h

(c) $t = \left(\frac{\sqrt{17}+\sqrt{2}}{16}\right)$h (d) $t = \left(\frac{\sqrt{17}-\sqrt{2}}{16}\right)$h

33 Two points, A and B, are located on the ground a certain distance $d = 10\sqrt{2}$ m apart. Two rocks are launched simultaneously from points A and B with equal speeds but at different angles. Each rock lands at the launch point of the other. Knowing that one of the rocks is launched at an angle $\theta = 37°$, with the horizontal, what is the minimum distance between the rocks during the flight? (given $\cos 37° = \frac{4}{5}$)

(a) 2 m (b) $2\sqrt{2}$ m

(c) 5 m (d) $5\sqrt{2}$ m

34 The last soldier of an 80 m long marching troop runs from the end to its front, and then it runs back to the end with the same speed. During this, the marching troop covers a distance of 150 m. The distance covered by the soldier is

(a) 0 (b) 250 m

(c) 330 m (d) 70 m

35 Two particles A and B are moving with uniform velocity as shown in the figure given below at $t = 0$. Find out shortest distance between two particles

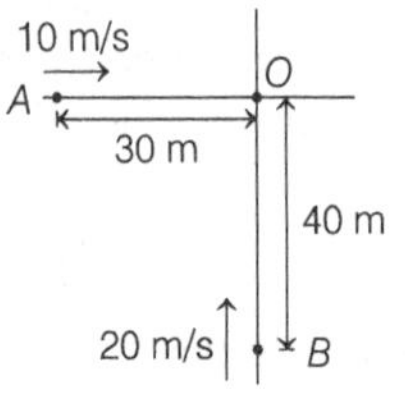

(a) 10 m (b) $10\sqrt{2}$ m (c) $2\sqrt{5}$ m (d) $4\sqrt{5}$ m

36 A ball is projected in the vertical x-y plane from a train moving in horizontal x direction with constant positive acceleration. The trajectory of the ball as seen from frame of train cannot be (point of projection is origin)

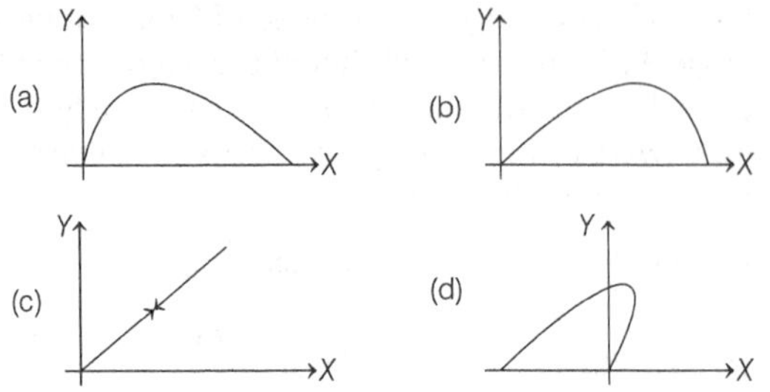

37 Two cars A and B are travelling with the same speed 108 km/h on a road. The car A is 3 m behind the car B. The driver of the car B suddenly applies brakes causing it to decelerate at a constant rate of 3 m/s^2. One second later the driver of car A applies brakes and just manages to avoid a rear end collision. Find the magnitude of constant retardation of the car A.

(a) 4 m/s^2 (b) 5 m/s^2 (c) 6 m/s^2 (d) 8 m/s^2

38 A transparent lift A is going upwards with velocity 20 m/s and retarding at the rate of 8 m/s^2. Second transparent lift B is located in front of it and is going down at 10 m/s with retardation of 2 m/s^2. At the same instant, a bolt from the ceiling of lift A drops inside lift. If height of car of lift A is 16 m, then find the distance travelled by bolt as observed by a person in lift B till the time, it hits the floor of lift A.

(a) 56 m (b) 51 m (c) 75 m (d) 24 m

Multiple Choice(s) Correct Questions

1 A man standing on the edge of the terrace of a high rise building throws a stone vertically up with a speed of 20 m/s. Two seconds later an identical stone is thrown vertically downwards with the same speed of 20 m/s. Then

(a) the relative velocity between the two stones remains constant till one hits the ground

(b) both will have the same kinetic energy when they hit the ground

(c) the time interval between their hitting the ground is 2 s

(d) if the collisions on the ground are perfectly elastic both will rise to the same height above the ground

2 A ball is thrown vertically upward in a compartment of a moving train.

(a) The ball will maintain the same horizontal velocity as that of the person (or the compartment) at the time of throwing.

(b) If the train is accelerating then the horizontal velocity of the ball will be different from that of the train velocity, at the time of throwing.

(c) If the ball appears to be moving backward to the person sitting in the compartment it means that speed of the train is increasing.

(d) If the ball appears to be moving ahead of the person sitting in the compartment it means the train's motion is retarding.

3 A man in a lift which is ascending with an upward acceleration a throws a ball vertically upwards with a velocity v with respect to himself and catches it after t_1 seconds. Afterwards when the lift is descending with the same acceleration a acting downwards the man again throws the ball vertically upwards with the same velocity with respect to him and catches it after 't_2' seconds

(a) the acceleration of the ball with respect to ground is g when it is in air

(b) the velocity v of the ball relative to the lift is $\frac{g(t_1 + t_2)}{t_1 t_2}$

(c) the acceleration a of the lift is $\frac{g(t_2 - t_1)}{t_1 + t_2}$

(d) the velocity v of the ball relative to the man is $\frac{g t_1 t_2}{(t_1 + t_2)}$

4 Eight particles are situated at the vertices of a regular octagon having side 10 cm. They all start moving simultaneously with constant speed of 1 cm/s heading towards each other all the time. Choose the correct option (s).

(a) They will converge at the centroid.

(b) They will converge after time $\frac{10\sqrt{2}}{\sqrt{2}-1}$ s.

(c) The distance travelled by each particle is $\frac{10\sqrt{2}}{\sqrt{2}-1}$ m.

(d) Acceleration of each particle is directed perpendicular to its velocity.

5 Several particles are projected simultaneously in the same vertical plane from a fixed point O, all with the same initial speed but with different angles of projection with the horizontal.

(a) After time t, all the particles lie in a circle whose centre C is vertically below O, and as t increases C falls with acceleration g.

(b) After time t, all the particles lie in a circle whose centre C is vertically below O, and as t increases C falls with constant velocity.

(c) Products of the times for which any particular particle at the height h above the horizontal surface is $\frac{2h}{g}$.

(d) Products of the times for which any particular particle at the height h above the horizontal surface is $\frac{h}{g}$.

6 The wind is blowing towards east with a speed of 30 m/s. Speed of aeroplane in still air in 50 m/s. The aeroplane has to go from city A to city B 720 km away due north. Choose the correct option(s).

(a) The direction in which the pilot should head the aeroplane to reach the city B is 53° north of west.

(b) The time taken by the aeroplane to fly from city A to city B is 5 h.

(c) The time taken by the aeroplane to fly from city A to city B is 6.67 h.

(d) None of the above

7 A stationary person observers that rain is falling vertically down at 30 kmh^{-1}. A cyclist is moving up on an inclined plane making an angle 30° with horizontal at 10 km h^{-1}. In which direction should the cyclist hold his umbrella to prevent himself from the rain?

(a) At an angle $\tan^{-1}\left(\frac{3\sqrt{3}}{5}\right)$ with inclined plane

(b) At an angle $\tan^{-1}\left(\frac{3\sqrt{3}}{5}\right)$ with horizontal

(c) At an angle $\tan^{-1}\left(\frac{\sqrt{3}}{7}\right)$ with inclined plane

(d) At an angle $\tan^{-1}\left(\frac{\sqrt{3}}{7}\right)$ with vertical

8 Suppose two particles 1 an 2 are projected in vertical plane simultaneously.

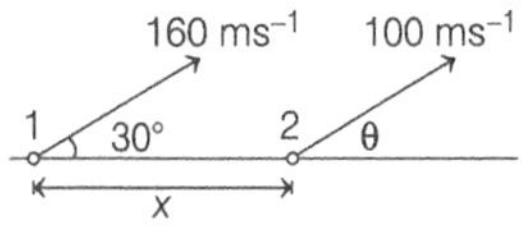

Their angles of projection are 30° and θ, respectively, with the horizontal. Let they collide after a time t in air. Then

(a) $\theta = \sin^{-1}\left(\frac{4}{5}\right)$ and they will have same speed just before the collision

(b) $\theta = \sin^{-1}\left(\frac{4}{5}\right)$ and they will have different speed just before the collision

(c) $x < 1280\sqrt{3} - 960$ m

(d) It is possible that the particles collide when both of them are at their highest point

9 Two particles A and B are located in x-y plane at points (0, 0) and (0, 4m). They simultaneously start moving with velocities. $\mathbf{v}_A = 2\hat{\mathbf{j}}$ m/s and $\mathbf{v}_B = 2\hat{\mathbf{i}}$ m/s. Select the correct alternative (s).

(a) The distance between them is constant.

(b) The distance between them first decreases and then increases.

(c) The shortest distance between them is $2\sqrt{2}$ m.

(d) Time after which they are at minimum distance is 1 s.

10 A river is flowing with a speed of 1 km/h. A swimmer wants to go to point 'C' starting from 'A'. He swims with a speed of 5 km/h, at an angle θ, w.r.t. t river. If $AB = BC = 400$ m. Then

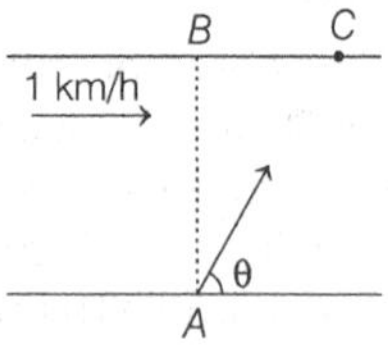

(a) the value of θ is 53°
(b) time taken by the man is 6 min
(c) time taken by the man is 8 min
(d) the value of θ is 45°

11 A boy holding an umbrella at an angle 30° with vertical with lower end towards himself, which is appropriate angle to protect him from rain for his horizontal velocity 10 m/s. Then which of the following can be true?

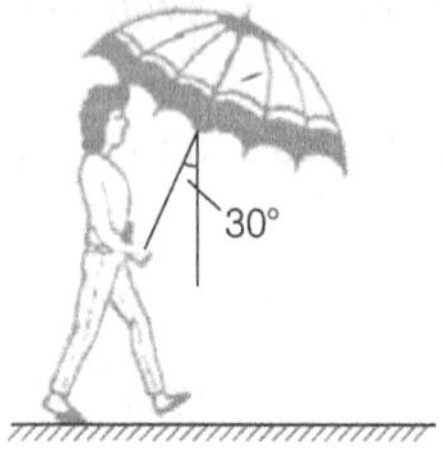

(a) Rain is falling at angle 30° with vertical towards him.
(b) Rain may be falling at angle 30° with vertical, away from him
(c) Rain may be falling vertically with a speed of nearly 17.3 m/s
(d) Rain is falling obliquely with some speed towards him.

12 Two swimmers A and B start swimming from different positions on the same bank as shown in figure. The swimmer A swims at angle 90° with respect to the river to reach point P. He takes 120 s to cross the river of width 10m. The swimmer B also takes the same time to reach the point P.

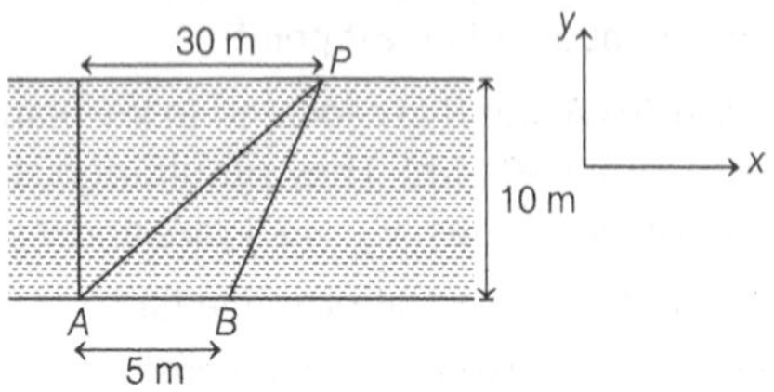

(a) velocity of A with respect to river is 1/6 m/s.
(b) river flow velocity is 1/4 m/s.
(c) velocity of B along Y-axis with respect to earth is 1/3 m/s.
(d) velocity of B along X-axis with respect to earth is 5/24 m/s.

Comprehension Based Questions

Comprehension-1

Two swimmers start a race. One who reaches the point C first on the other bank wins the race. A makes his strokes in a direction of 37° to the river flow with velocity 5 km/h relative to water. B makes his strokes in a direction 127° to the river flow with same relative velocity. River is flowing with speed of 2 km/h and is 100 m wide. Speeds of A and B on the ground are 8 km/h and 6 km/h, respectively.

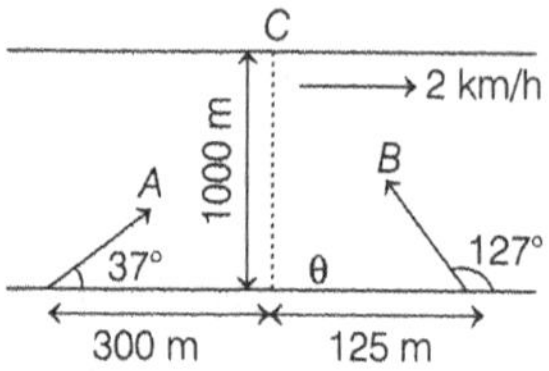

1 Time taken by A to reach C is
(a) 135 s (b) 150 s (c) 165 s (d) 175 s

2 Time taken by B to reach C is
(a) 135 s (b) 150 s (c) 165 s (d) 175 s

3 Velocity of B with respect to ground is
(a) $\sqrt{17}$ km/h (b) $\sqrt{41}$ km/h
(c) $\sqrt{45}$ km/h (d) 5 km/h

Comprehension-2

A man with some passengers in his boat, starts perpendicular to flow of river 200 m wide and flowing with 2 m/s. Boat speed in still water is 4 m/s. When he reaches half the width of river the passengers asked him they want to reach the just opposite end from where they have started.

4 Find the direction due to which he must row now to reach the required end.
(a) 30° with upstream (b) 37° with upstream
(c) 45° with upstream (d) 53° with upstream

5 How many times more total time, it would take to that if he would have denied the passengers?
(a) $\frac{2}{3}$ (b) $\frac{7}{4}$ (c) $\frac{4}{3}$ (d) $\frac{5}{3}$

Comprehension-3

On a frictionless horizontal surface, assumed to be the xy-plane a small trolley A is moving along a straight line parallel to the y-axis as shown in the figure with a constant velocity of $(\sqrt{3}-1)$ m/s. At a particular instant, when the line OA makes an angle of 45° with the x-axis, a ball is thrown along the surface from the origin O. Its velocity makes an angle ϕ with the x-axis when it hits the trolley.

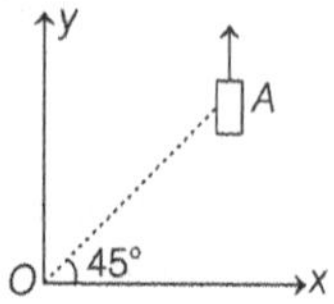

6 The motion of the ball is observed from the frame of the trolley. Calculate the angle θ made by the velocity of the ball with the x-axis in this frame.
(a) 30° (b) 45° (c) 60° (d) 75°

7 Find the speed of the ball with respect to the surface, if $\phi = \frac{4\theta}{3}$.

(a) 2 m/s (b) $2\sqrt{3}$ m/s
(c) 3 m/s (d) 4 m/s

Comprehension-4

Raindrops are falling with a velocity $10\sqrt{2}$ m/s making an angle of 45° with the vertical. The drops appear to be falling vertically to a man running with constant velocity. The velocity of rain drops change such that the rain drops now appear to be falling vertically with $\sqrt{3}$ times the velocity it appeared earlier to the same person running with same velocity.

8 The magnitude of velocity of man with respect to ground is

(a) $10\sqrt{2}$ m/s (b) $10\sqrt{3}$ m/s
(c) 20 m/s (d) 10 m/s

9 After the velocity of rain drops change, the magnitude of velocity of raindrops with respect to ground is

(a) 20 m/s (b) $20\sqrt{3}$ m/s
(c) 10 m/s (d) $10\sqrt{3}$ m/s

10 The angle (in degrees) between the initial and the final velocity vectors of the raindrops with respect to the ground is

(a) 8 (b) 15 (c) 22.5 (d) 37

Match the Columns Questions

1 Two particles A and B moving in x-y plane are at origin at $t = 0$. The initial velocity vectors of A and B are $\mathbf{u}_A = 8\hat{\mathbf{i}}$ m/s and $\mathbf{u}_B = 8\hat{\mathbf{j}}$ m/s. The acceleration of A and B are constant and are $\mathbf{a}_A = -2\hat{\mathbf{i}}$ m/s^2 and $\mathbf{a}_B = -2\hat{\mathbf{j}}$ m/s^2. Column I gives certain statements regarding particle A and B. Column II gives corresponding result. Match the statements in Column I with corresponding results in Column II.

	Column I		Column II
(A)	The time (in seconds) at which velocity of A relative to B is zero	(P)	$16\sqrt{2}$
(B)	The distance (in metres) between A and B when their relative velocity is zero	(Q)	$8\sqrt{2}$
(C)	The time (in seconds) after $t = 0$ s, at which A and B are at same position	(R)	8
(D)	The magnitude of relative velocity of A and B (in m/s) at the instant they are at same position	(S)	4

2

	Column I		Column II
(A)	If swimmer can swim at 5 m/s in still water and if velocity of water flow is 4 m/s, then angle between direction of swimming and direction of river flow to minimize drift.	(P)	53°
(B)	If swimmer can swim at 5 m/s in still water and velocity of flow in 3 m/s, then angle between direction of velocity of swimmer with respect to river and the direction of river flow if swimmer crosses the river in minimum time.	(Q)	127°
(C)	If swimmer can swim at 4 m/s, and velocity of flow in 3 m/s then angle of resultant velocity (w.r.t. ground) with the direction of river flow if swimmer swims perpendicular to flow of river	(R)	143°
(D)	Angle between direction of fluttering of flag and north if wind blows towards south west direction with a velocity $3\sqrt{2}$ m/s. Man moves with a velocity 7 m/s along west, holding flag in his hand.	(S)	90°

3 Two particles A and B are projected as shown in figure in xy-plane under the effect of force which provides a constant acceleration $a = 11$ m/s^2 in negative y-direction. Then match situation in Column I with the corresponding results in Column II (All positions are given in metre) ($\mathbf{v}_{AB}$ = velocity of A w.r.t. B; $\mathbf{r}_{AB}$ = Position of A w.r.t B)

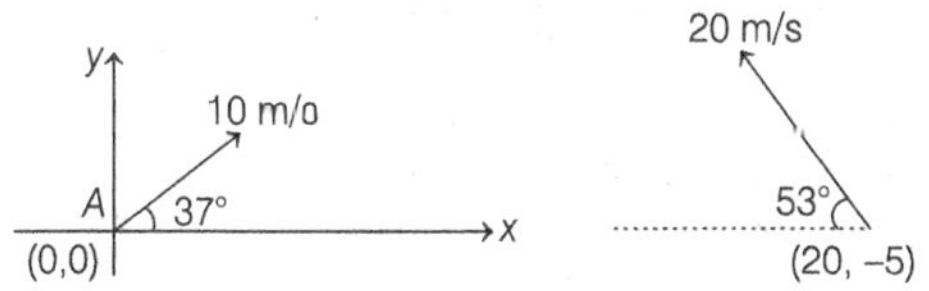

	Column I		Column II
(A)	Separation between the two particles is minimum at .... s.	(P)	0
(B)	Minimum separation between the two particles is .... m.	(Q)	0.5
(C)	Time when velocities of both particles are perpendicular to each other is .... s.	(R)	0.9
(D)	At the time of minimum separation $\mathbf{v}_{AB} \cdot \mathbf{r}_{AB} =$	(S)	2
		(T)	$2\sqrt{5}$

4 A square platform of side length 8m is situated in xz-plane such that it is at 16 m from the X-axis and 8 m from the Z-axis as shown in figure. A particle is projected with velocity $\mathbf{v} = (v_2\hat{\mathbf{i}} + 25\hat{\mathbf{j}})$ m/s relative to wind from origin and at the same instant the platform starts with acceleration $\mathbf{a} = (2\hat{\mathbf{i}} + 2.5\hat{\mathbf{j}})$ m/s^2. Wind is blowing with velocity $\mathbf{v}_w = (v_1\hat{\mathbf{k}})$ m/s.

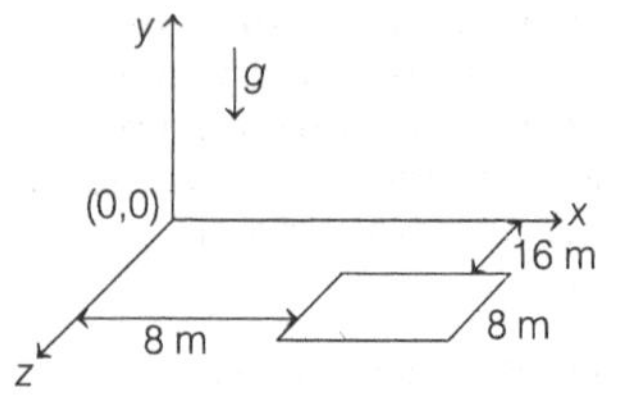

Column I		Column II
(A)	Least possible value of v_2 (in m/s) so that particle hits the platform or edge of platform is	(P) 4
(B)	Least possible value of v_1 (in m/s) so that particle hits the platform or edge or platform is	(Q) 6
(C)	If t is the time (in second) after particle hits the platform, then $2t$ is equal to	(R) 8
(D)	Value of displacement with respect to ground (in metre) of the particle in y-direction, when v_2 has its minimum possible value is (till particle hits the platform or edge of platform)	(S) 20

Numerical Value Questions

1 A man is coming down an incline of angle 30°. When he walks with speed $2\sqrt{3}$ m/s he has to keep his umbrella vertical to protect himself from rain. The actual speed of rain is 5 m/s. At what angle (in degrees) with vertical should he keep his umbrella when he is at rest so that he does not get drenched?

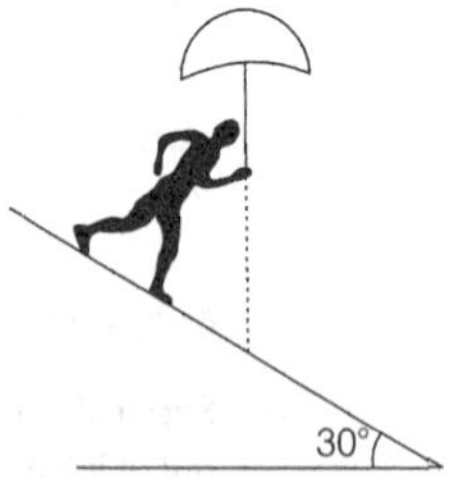

2 A swimmer swims in still water at a speed = 5 km/h. He enters a 200 m wide river, having river flow speed = 4 km/h at point A and proceeds to swim at an angle of 127° with the river flow direction. Another point B is located directly across A on the other side. The swimmer lands on the other bank at a point C, from which he walks the distance CB with a speed = 3 km/h. The total time (in minutes) in which he reaches from A to B is

3 A man is crossing a river flowing with velocity of 5 m/s. He reaches a point directly across at a distance of 60 m in 5 s. His velocity (in m/s) in still water should be

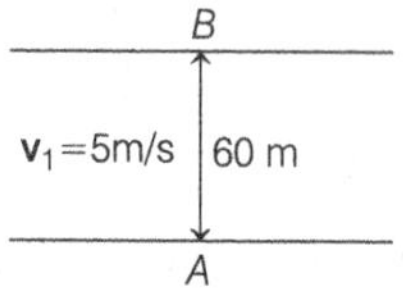

4 A lift is moving up with a constant retardation of 2 ms^{-2}. When its upward velocity is 5 m/s, a body in the lift tosses a coin, imparting it an upward initial velocity of 3 m/s with respect to himself. His fingers at the moment of toss are midway between the floor and the ceiling of the lift whose total height is 2 m. After how many time (in second) will the coin hit the floor or the ceiling of the lift?

5 Two particles P and Q are launched simultaneously as shown in figure. Find the minimum distance (in metre) between particles.

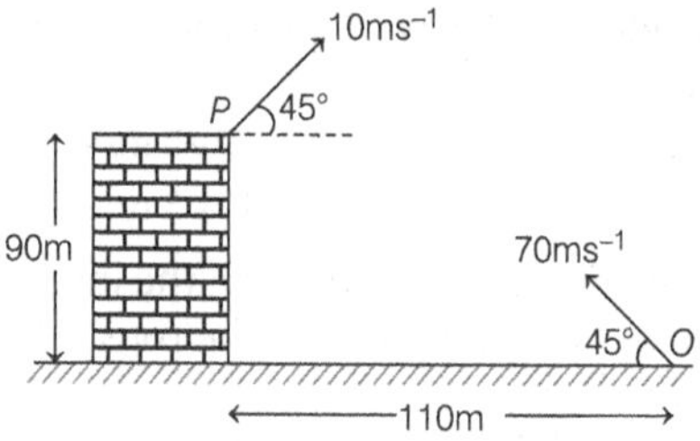

6 A vertical wind screen of a car is made up of 2 parts, where the upper one A is 20 cm vertically long and covers the top 5 cm of the lower piece B (see figure). The upper one is hinged at the top, so that it can be opened outward, inclining to the vertical.

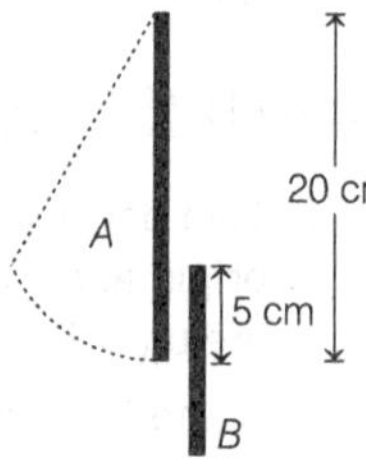

The car is running on the horizontal road at 60 km/h in the rain which is falling vertically at $10\sqrt{3}$ km h^{-1}. The maximum angle (in degrees), through which the upper part A can be opened outward, such that the rain drops do not enter the car is

7 Two cars A and B are moving west to east and south to north respectively, along crossroads. A moves with a speed of 72 kmh^{-1} and is 500 m away from point of intersection of cross roads and B moves with a speed of 54 kmh^{-1} and is 400 m away from point of intersection of cross roads. Find the shortest distance (in m) between them.

8 A swimmer jumps from a bridge over a canal and swims 1 km upstream. After that 1 km, he passes a floating cork. He continues swimming for half an hour and then turns around and swims back to the bridge. The swimmer and the cork reach the bridge at the same time. The swimmer has been swimming at a constant speed. How fast (in km/h) does the water in the canal flow?

9 A dog moves uniformly with speed 5 m/s, so that it is always headed towards a cat moving on a straight line with constant velocity of 3 m/s. Initially their velocities are perpendicular to each other and they are separated by a distance 16 m apart. Find the time (in s) after which the dog will catch the cat.

10 Velocity of river flow grows in proportion to the distance from the bank and reaches its maximum velocity of 2 m/s in the middle. Near the bank, velocity is zero. The velocity of a swimmer in still water is 5 m/s and is directed perpendicular to river flow. The width of the river is 100 m. Find the drift (in m) of the swimmer.

11 A boat travels across a river from a point A to a point B of opposite bank along the line AB forming angle 60° with the bank. A flag on the pole (mounted on the boat) flutters at an angle of 60° with the line AB as shown in figure. If velocity of wind ($5\sqrt{3}$ m/s) is perpendicular to the flow of river, find the speed (in m/s) of boat with respect to the bank.

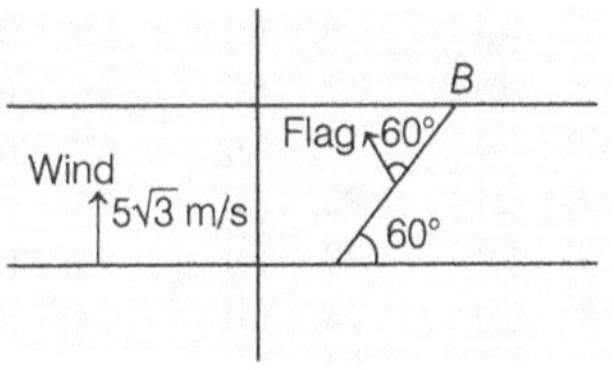

12 An armored car 2 m long and 3 m wide is moving at 20 m/s. A bullet hits the car in a direction making an angle of $\tan^{-1}\left(\frac{1}{2}\right)$ with the X-axis as seen from the street. The bullet enters one edge of the corner and passes out at the diagonally opposite corner. Neglecting any interaction between the bullet and the car, find the time taken (in seconds) by the bullet to cross the car.

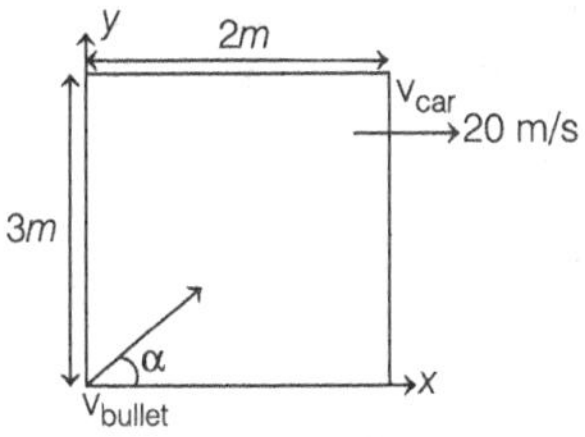

Previous Year's Questions

JEE Main

1 A passenger sitting in a train A moving at 90 km/h observes another train B moving in the opposite direction for 8s. If the velocity of the train B is 54 km/h, then length of train B is **[2023, 13 April Shift-II]**

(a) 200 m (b) 320 m
(c) 120 m (d) 80 m

2 Two trains A and B of length l and $4l$ are travelling into a tunnel of length L in parallel tracks from opposite directions with velocities 108 km/h and 72 km/h, respectively. If train A takes 35 s less time than train B to cross the tunnel then, length L of tunnel is (Given, $L = 60l$) **[2023, 13 April Shift-I]**

(a) 1200 m (b) 1800 m
(c) 2700 m (d) 900 m

3 The speed of a swimmer is 4 km h^{-1} in still water. If the swimmer makes his strokes normal to the flow of river of width 1 km, he reaches a point 750 m down the stream on the opposite bank. **[2023, 31 Jan Shift-I]**
The speed of the river water is .... km h^{-1}.

JEE Advanced

1 Airplanes A and B are flying with constant velocity in the same vertical plane at angles 30° and 60° with respect to the horizontal respectively as shown in figure. The speed of A is $100\sqrt{3}$ ms^{-1}. At time $t = 0$ s, an observer in A finds B at a distance of 500 m. This observer sees B moving with a constant velocity perpendicular to the line of motion of A. If at $t = t_0$, A just escapes being hit by B, t_0 in seconds is **(2014 Adv.)**

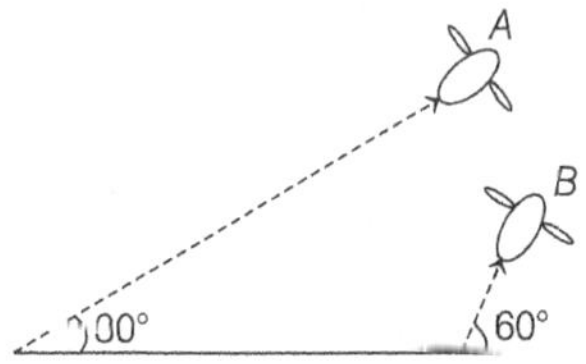

2 A rocket is moving in a gravity free space with a constant acceleration of 2 ms^{-2} along $+x$-direction (see figure). The length of a chamber inside the rocket is 4 m. A ball is thrown from the left end of the chamber in $+x$-direction with a speed of 0.3 ms^{-1} relative to the rocket. At the same time, another ball is thrown in $-x$-direction with a speed of 0.2 ms^{-1} from its right end relative to the rocket. The time in seconds when the two balls hit each. [**Question was Wrong**] **(2014 Adv)**

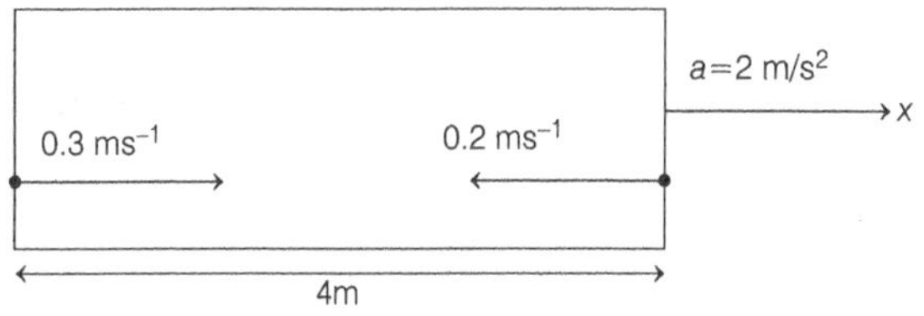

Answer Key

Level 1

7.1 Relative Motion in One Dimension

1. (a) 144 km/h due, south (b) 90 km/h, due north (c) 36 km/h, due north (d) 126 km/h, due north
2. (a) 40 s (b) 8 s 3. 1.25 ms^{-2} 4. 4s
5. (a) $T=\frac{2u}{(g+a)}$ (b) $H=\frac{u^2}{2(g+a)}$

7.2 Relative Motion in Two Dimensions

1. $-4\hat{i}-3\hat{j}, 4\hat{i}+3\hat{j}$, 5 unit, 5 unit
2. 13 m/s, $\tan^{-1}\left(\frac{5}{12}\right)$ north of east
3. (a) 20 m/s of 72 km/h, due east (b) 25 m/s or 90 km/h at 37°N of E (c) 25 m/s or 90 km/h
4. 30° N of W at $5\sqrt{3}$ km/h.

7.3 River Flow Problems

1. 12 km/h, 4 km/h
2. (a) $v_M=\sqrt{u^2+v^2+2vu\cos\theta}$ (b) $\tan\phi=\frac{v\sin\theta}{u+v\cos\theta}$

   (c) $(u+v\cos\theta)\frac{d}{v\sin\theta}$
3. (a) perpendicular to river flow (b) $\frac{1}{4}$ h (c) 0.75 km
4. (a) 127° w.r.t. the river flow or 37° w.r.t. perpendicular in backward direction.

   (b) 4 km/h along the direction perpendicular to the river flow.

   (c) 15 min
5. (a) 120° with the river flow (b) $\frac{160}{\sqrt{3}}$ s (c) $\frac{560}{\sqrt{3}}$ m

7.4 Air Flow Problems

1. 100 km/h, 37° W of S 2. $\frac{2l\sqrt{v^2-u^2\sin^2\theta}}{v^2-u^2}$
3. $\frac{2l}{v^2-u^2}(v+\sqrt{v^2-u^2})$
4. (a) $\sin^{-1}\left(\frac{1}{15}\right)$ east of the line *AB* (b) 50 min 5. South

7.5 Rain Problems

1. $\theta=\tan^{-1}(2)$ 2. $10\sqrt{5}$ m/s
3. $2\sqrt{2}$ km/h, 45° with vertically away from the man.
4. 20 km/h 5. $\tan^{-1}\left(\frac{1}{2}\right)$

7.6 Velocity of Separation and Approach

1. (a) 4.8 m/s (b) $\frac{7}{\sqrt{2}}$ m/s 2. (a) $v_1\sin\theta_1=v_2\sin\theta_2$

   (b) $t=\frac{d}{v_{app}}=\frac{d}{v_1\cos\theta_1+v_2\cos\theta_2}$
3. $5\sqrt{2}$ km, $t=15$ min 4. $\frac{2a}{3v}$ 5. $\frac{a}{v\left(1-\cos\frac{2\pi}{n}\right)}$

LEVEL 2

Single Choice Correct Questions

1. (c)	2. (b)	3. (d)	4. (b)	5. (d)
6. (b)	7. (d)	8. (b)	9. (c)	10. (a)
11. (a)	12. (c)	13. (b)	14. (d)	15. (a)
16. (b)	17. (b)	18. (c)	19. (b)	20. (b)
21. (a)	22. (b)	23. (c)	24. (a)	25. (a)
26. (c)	27. (b)	28. (b)	29. (c)	30. (a)
31. (a)	32. (d)	33. (c)	34. (c)	35. (d)
36. (b)	37. (b)	38. (c)		

Numerical Value Questions

1. 40	2. 13	3. 1	4. 2	5. 16
6. 3	7. 20	8. 20	9. 105	10. 765
11. 16	12. 15			

LEVEL 3

Single Choice Correct Questions

1. (a)	2. (d)	3. (d)	4. (b)	5. (a)
6. (a)	7. (d)	8. (c)	9. (b)	10. (c)
11. (b)	12. (b)	13. (a)	14. (c)	15. (d)
16. (b)	17. (c)	18. (a)	19. (a)	20. (c)
21. (c)	22. (a)	23. (b)	24. (b)	25. (d)
26. (c)	27. (b)	28. (a)	29. (b)	30. (d)
31. (b)	32. (b)	33. (a)	34. (b)	35. (d)
36. (a)	37. (c)	38. (b)		

Multiple Choice(s) Correct Quesions

1. (a,b,c,d)	2. (a,c,d)	3. (a,c,d)	4. (a,b,c,d)	5. (a,c)
6. (a,b)	7. (a,d)	8. (b,c,d)	9. (b,c,d)	10. (a,b)
11. (c,d)	12. (b,d)			

Comprehension Based Questions

1. (c)	2. (b)	3. (a)	4. (b)	5. (c)
6. (b)	7. (a)	8. (d)	9. (a)	10. (b)

Match the Columns Questions

1. A→S, B→P, C→R, D→Q 2. A→R, B→S, C→P, D→Q
3. A→R, B→T, C→P, S, D→P 4. A→Q, B→P, C→R, D→S

Numerical Value Questions

1. 37	2. 4	3. 13	4. 1	5. 6
6. 60	7. 20	8. 1	9. 5	10. 20
11. 5	12. 0.20			

Previous Year's Questions

JEE Main

1. (b) 2. (b) 3. (3)

JEE Advanced

1. (5) 2. (*)

SOLUTIONS

Level 1

7.1 Relative Motion in One Dimension

1.

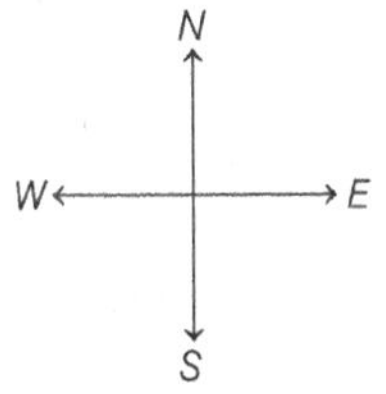

$\mathbf{v}_A = (54\,\text{km/h})\hat{\mathbf{j}}, \quad \mathbf{v}_B = (-90\,\text{km/h})\hat{\mathbf{j}}$

$\mathbf{v}_{\text{monkey}, A} = -18\hat{\mathbf{j}}$

(a) $\mathbf{v}_{BA} = \mathbf{v}_B - \mathbf{v}_A = -(144\,\text{km/h})\hat{\mathbf{j}} = 144$ km/h, South

(b) $\mathbf{v}_{\text{ground}, B} = \mathbf{v}_{\text{ground}} - \mathbf{v}_B = 0 - (-90)\hat{\mathbf{j}} = 90$ km/h, North

(c) $\mathbf{v}_{\text{monkey}} = \mathbf{v}_{\text{monkey}, A} + \mathbf{v}_A$
$= -18\hat{\mathbf{j}} + 54\hat{\mathbf{j}} = 36\hat{\mathbf{j}} = 36$ km/h, North

(d) $\mathbf{v}_{\text{monkey}, B} = \mathbf{v}_{\text{monkey}} - \mathbf{v}_B$
$= 36\hat{\mathbf{j}} - (-90)\hat{\mathbf{j}} = 126$ km/h, North

2. (a) $t_1 = \dfrac{l_1 + l_2}{v_{\text{rel}}} = \dfrac{300 + 100}{30 - 20} = 40$ s

(b) $t_2 = \dfrac{l_1 + l_2}{v_{\text{rel}}} = \dfrac{300 + 100}{30 + 20} = 8$ s

3. $v_{AB} = 25 - 20 = 5$ m/s, $\quad a_{AB} = a_A - 0 = a_A$

$v_{AB}^2 = u_{AB}^2 + 2a_{AB}\, s_{AB} \quad \Rightarrow \quad 0^2 = 5^2 + 2a_A(10)$

$\Rightarrow \; a_A = -1.25\,\text{m/s}^2$

4.

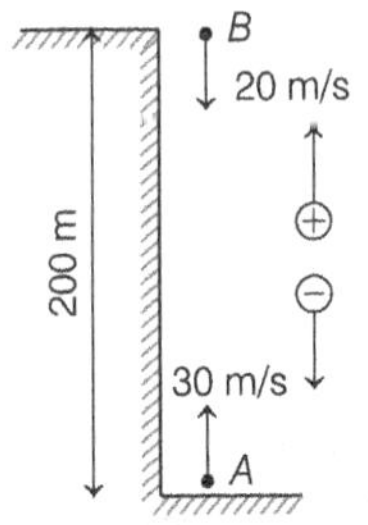

$u_{AB} = 30 - (-20) = 50$ m/s, $\quad s_{AB} = 200$ m

$a_{AB} = (-g) - (-g) = 0$

$s_{AB} = u_{AB}t + \dfrac{1}{2}a_{AB}t^2$

$\Rightarrow \quad 200 = 50t \quad \Rightarrow \quad t = 4$ s

5. (a) $u_{\text{ball, lift}} = u$

$a_{\text{ball, lift}} = a_{\text{ball}} - a_{\text{lift}} = -g - (+a) = -(g + a)$

$s_{\text{ball, lift}} = u_{\text{ball, lift}}t + \dfrac{1}{2}a_{\text{ball, lift}}t^2$

$$0 = uT + \frac{1}{2}(-(g+a))T^2 \quad \Rightarrow \quad T = \frac{2u}{g+a}$$

(b) $v_{\text{ball, lift}}^2 = u_{\text{ball, lift}}^2 + 2a_{\text{ball, lift}}\, s_{\text{ball, lift}}$

$$0^2 = u^2 + 2(-(g+a))H_{\max} \quad \Rightarrow \quad H_{\max} = \frac{u^2}{2(g+a)}$$

7.2 Relative Motion in Two Dimensions

1. $\mathbf{v}_A = 4\hat{\mathbf{i}}, \quad \mathbf{v}_B = -3\hat{\mathbf{j}}$

$\mathbf{v}_{AB} = \mathbf{v}_A - \mathbf{v}_B = 4\hat{\mathbf{i}} - (-3\hat{\mathbf{j}}) = 4\hat{\mathbf{i}} + 3\hat{\mathbf{j}}$

$|\mathbf{v}_{AB}| = 5,$

$\mathbf{v}_{BA} = \mathbf{v}_B - \mathbf{v}_A = -4\hat{\mathbf{i}} - 3\hat{\mathbf{j}}$

$\Rightarrow \quad |\mathbf{v}_{BA}| = 5$

2. $\mathbf{v}_{\text{ship}} = 12\hat{\mathbf{i}}, \; \mathbf{v}_{\text{woman, ship}} = 5\hat{\mathbf{j}}$

$\mathbf{v}_{\text{woman}} = \mathbf{v}_{\text{woman, ship}} + \mathbf{v}_{\text{ship}} = 5\hat{\mathbf{j}} + 12\hat{\mathbf{i}} = 12\hat{\mathbf{i}} + 5\hat{\mathbf{j}}$

$= 13$ m/s, $\tan^{-1}\left(\dfrac{5}{12}\right)$ North of East

3. $\mathbf{v}_A = 54\hat{\mathbf{j}}, \quad \mathbf{v}_B = -72\hat{\mathbf{i}}$

(a) $\mathbf{v}_{\text{ground}, B} = \mathbf{v}_{\text{ground}} - \mathbf{v}_B = 72\hat{\mathbf{i}} = 72$ km/h, East

(b) $\mathbf{v}_{AB} = \mathbf{v}_A - \mathbf{v}_B = 54\hat{\mathbf{j}} - (-72\hat{\mathbf{i}}) = 72\hat{\mathbf{i}} + 54\hat{\mathbf{j}}$
$= 90$ km/h, 37° North of East

(c) Rate of separation $= v_{AB} = 90$ km/h

4. $\mathbf{v}_{\text{man}} = 5\sin 30°\,\hat{\mathbf{i}} + 5\cos 30°\,\hat{\mathbf{j}} = 2.5\hat{\mathbf{i}} + \dfrac{5\sqrt{3}}{2}\hat{\mathbf{j}}$

$\mathbf{v}_{\text{cyclist}} = 10\hat{\mathbf{i}}$

$\mathbf{v}_{\text{man, cyclist}} = (2.5\hat{\mathbf{i}} + \dfrac{5\sqrt{3}}{2}\hat{\mathbf{j}}) - 10\hat{\mathbf{i}} = \dfrac{-15}{2}\hat{\mathbf{i}} + \dfrac{5\sqrt{3}}{2}\hat{\mathbf{j}}$

$= 5\sqrt{3}$ km/h, 30° North of West

7.3 River Flow Problems

1. $v + u = 16$ ...(i)

$v - u = 8$ ...(ii)

$\Rightarrow v = 12$ km/h and $u = 4$ km/h

2. (a) $\mathbf{v}_{MR} = v\cos\theta\,\hat{\mathbf{i}} + v\sin\theta\,\hat{\mathbf{j}}, \; \mathbf{v}_R = u\hat{\mathbf{i}}$

$\mathbf{v}_M = \mathbf{v}_{MR} + \mathbf{v}_R = (v\cos\theta + u)\,\hat{\mathbf{i}} + (v\sin\theta)\,\hat{\mathbf{j}}$

(b) $\tan\phi = \dfrac{v\sin\theta}{u + v\cos\theta} \quad \Rightarrow \quad \phi = \tan^{-1}\left(\dfrac{v\sin\theta}{u + v\cos\theta}\right)$

(c) Drift $= (v\cos\theta + u)T = (v\cos\theta + u)\left(\dfrac{d}{v\sin\theta}\right)$

3. (a) Perpendicular to river flow.

(b) $\mathbf{v}_{MR} = 4\hat{\mathbf{j}}, \quad \mathbf{v}_R = 3\hat{\mathbf{i}}$

$\mathbf{v}_M = \mathbf{v}_{MR} + \mathbf{v}_R = 3\hat{\mathbf{i}} + 4\hat{\mathbf{j}}$

$$\text{Time} = \frac{1\,\text{km}}{4\,\text{km/h}} = 15\,\text{min}$$

(c) $\text{Drift} = 3\left(\frac{1}{4}\right) = \frac{3}{4}\,\text{km} = 0.75\,\text{km}$

4.

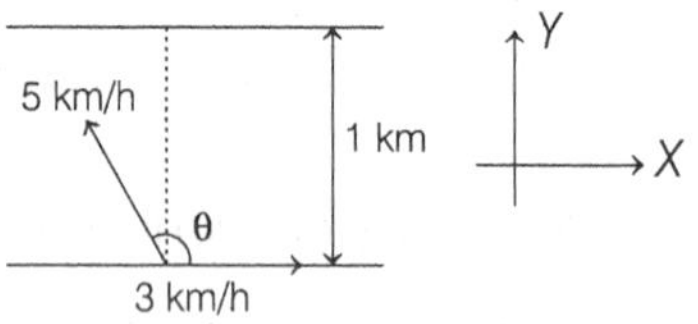

$$\mathbf{v}_R = 3\hat{\mathbf{i}}, \quad \mathbf{v}_{MR} = 5\cos\theta\,\hat{\mathbf{i}} + 5\sin\theta\,\hat{\mathbf{j}}$$

$$\mathbf{v}_M = \mathbf{v}_{MR} + \mathbf{v}_R = (5\cos\theta + 3)\,\hat{\mathbf{i}} + 5\sin\theta\,\hat{\mathbf{j}}$$

(a) $5\cos\theta + 3 = 0$

$\cos\theta = -\frac{3}{5} \Rightarrow \theta = 127°$ with the river flow.

(b) $\mathbf{v}_M = 5\sin\theta\,\hat{\mathbf{j}} = 5\left(\frac{4}{5}\right) = 4\hat{\mathbf{j}}$

$= 4$ km/h, perpendicular to river flow.

(c) $\text{Time} = \frac{1\,\text{km}}{4\,\text{km/h}} = 15$ min

5. (a)

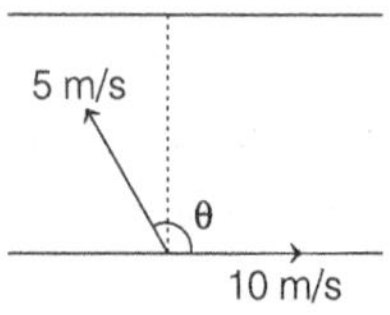

$$\mathbf{v}_R = 10\hat{\mathbf{i}}, \quad \mathbf{v}_{MR} = 5\cos\theta\,\hat{\mathbf{i}} + 5\sin\theta\,\hat{\mathbf{j}}$$

$$\mathbf{v}_M = \mathbf{v}_{MR} + \mathbf{v}_R \quad \Rightarrow \quad \mathbf{v}_M = (5\cos\theta + 10)\,\hat{\mathbf{i}} + 5\sin\theta\,\hat{\mathbf{j}}$$

$$\text{Time taken} = \frac{400}{5\sin\theta}$$

$$\text{Drift} = x = (5\cos\theta + 10)\left(\frac{400}{5\sin\theta}\right) = (\cos\theta + 2)\frac{400}{\sin\theta}$$

We have to minimise drift

$$\frac{dx}{d\theta} = -\text{cosec}^2\theta - 2\cot\theta\,\text{cosec}\theta = 0 \quad \Rightarrow \cos\theta = -\frac{1}{2}$$

$\Rightarrow \quad \theta = 120°$ with river flow

(b) $T = \dfrac{400}{5\sin 120°} = \dfrac{80}{\frac{\sqrt{3}}{2}} = \dfrac{160}{\sqrt{3}}$ s

(c) $\text{Drift} = (5\cos\theta + 10)\,T$

$$= \left(5\left(\frac{-1}{2}\right) + 10\right)\left(\frac{160}{\sqrt{3}}\right) = \frac{560}{\sqrt{3}}\,\text{m}$$

7.4 Air Flow Problems

1. $\mathbf{v}_{\text{plane, wind}} = -240\,\hat{\mathbf{i}}, \quad \mathbf{v}_{\text{plane}} = -300\,\hat{\mathbf{i}} - 80\hat{\mathbf{j}}$

$$\mathbf{v}_{\text{plane, wind}} = \mathbf{v}_{\text{plane}} - \mathbf{v}_{\text{wind}}$$

$$-240\,\hat{\mathbf{i}} = (-300\,\hat{\mathbf{i}} - 80\,\hat{\mathbf{j}}) - \mathbf{v}_{\text{wind}}$$

$\mathbf{v}_{\text{wind}} = -60\,\hat{\mathbf{i}} - 80\,\hat{\mathbf{j}} = 100$ km/h, 53° South of West

2.

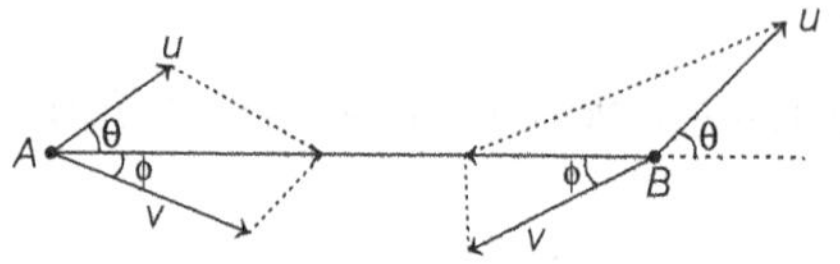

$$u\sin\theta = v\sin\phi \quad \Rightarrow \quad \sin\phi = \frac{u\sin\theta}{v}$$

$$T = \frac{l}{u\cos\theta + v\cos\phi} + \frac{l}{v\cos\phi - u\cos\theta}$$

$$T = \frac{2l\,v\cos\phi}{v^2\cos^2\phi - u^2\cos^2\theta} = \frac{2lv\left(\sqrt{1 - \frac{u^2\sin^2\theta}{v^2}}\right)}{v^2\left(1 - \frac{u^2\sin^2\theta}{v^2}\right) - u^2\cos^2\theta}$$

$$T = \frac{2l\sqrt{v^2 - u^2\sin^2\theta}}{v^2 - u^2}$$

3.

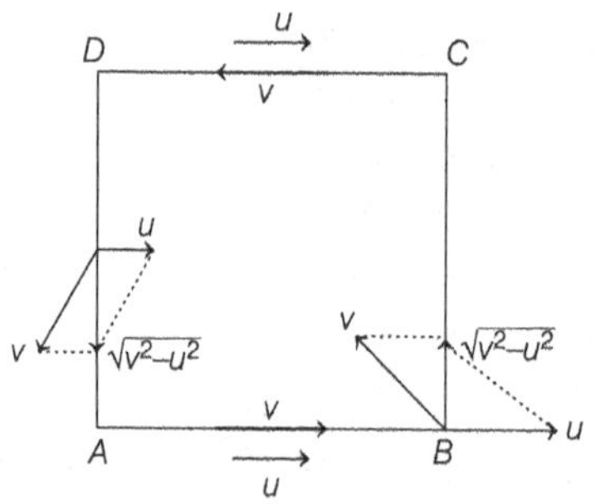

$$T = T_{AB} + T_{BC} + T_{CD} + T_{DA}$$

$$\Rightarrow \quad T = \frac{l}{v+u} + \frac{l}{\sqrt{v^2 - u^2}} + \frac{l}{v-u} + \frac{l}{\sqrt{v^2 - u^2}}$$

$$\Rightarrow \quad T = \frac{2lv}{v^2 - u^2} + \frac{2l}{\sqrt{v^2 - u^2}}$$

4.

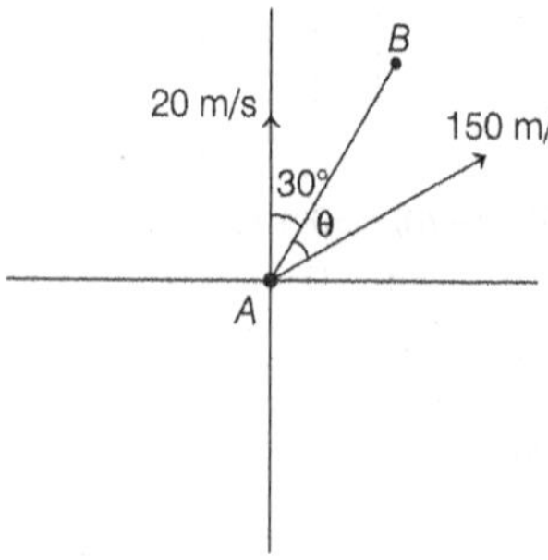

(a) $150\sin\theta = 20\sin 30°$

$$\Rightarrow \sin\theta = \frac{1}{15} \quad \Rightarrow \theta = \sin^{-1}\left(\frac{1}{15}\right)$$

(b) $T = \dfrac{l}{150\cos\theta + 20\cos 30°} \quad \Rightarrow \quad T \approx 50$ min

5. $\mathbf{v}_{\text{flag}} = \mathbf{v}_M = 10 \cos 45° \hat{\mathbf{i}} + 10 \sin 45° \hat{\mathbf{j}}$, $\mathbf{v}_{\text{wind}} = 5\sqrt{2}\,\hat{\mathbf{i}}$

$\mathbf{v}_{\text{wind, flag}} = \mathbf{v}_{\text{wind}} - \mathbf{v}_{\text{flag}} = 5\sqrt{2}\,\hat{\mathbf{i}} - (5\sqrt{2}\,\hat{\mathbf{i}} + 5\sqrt{2}\,\hat{\mathbf{j}}) = -5\sqrt{2}\,\hat{\mathbf{j}}$

So, flag will flutter in South direction.

7.5 Rain Problems

1.

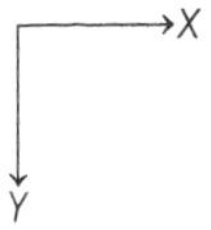

$$\mathbf{v}_R = 4\hat{\mathbf{j}}, \quad \mathbf{v}_C = 2\hat{\mathbf{i}}$$

$$\mathbf{v}_{RC} = \mathbf{v}_R - \mathbf{v}_C = 4\hat{\mathbf{j}} - 2\hat{\mathbf{i}} = -2\hat{\mathbf{i}} + 4\hat{\mathbf{j}}$$

$\theta = \tan^{-1}(2)$ with horizontal.

2.

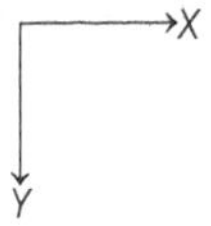

$$\mathbf{v}_{\text{person}} = 10\hat{\mathbf{i}}, \quad \mathbf{v}_{\text{rain, person}} = 20\hat{\mathbf{j}}$$

$$\mathbf{v}_{\text{rain, person}} = \mathbf{v}_{\text{rain}} - \mathbf{v}_{\text{person}} \Rightarrow 20\hat{\mathbf{j}} = \mathbf{v}_{\text{rain}} - 10\hat{\mathbf{i}}$$

$$\Rightarrow \quad \mathbf{v}_{\text{rain}} = 10\hat{\mathbf{i}} + 20\hat{\mathbf{j}} \Rightarrow |\mathbf{v}_{\text{rain}}| = 10\sqrt{5} \text{ m/s}$$

3. $\mathbf{v}_M = (2 \text{ km/h})\hat{\mathbf{i}}$, $\mathbf{v}_R = v_R \sin\theta\,\hat{\mathbf{i}} + v_R \cos\theta\,\hat{\mathbf{j}}$

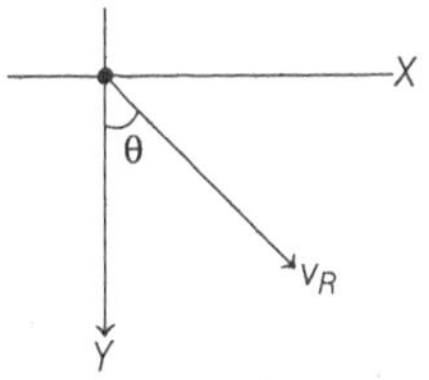

$$\mathbf{v}_{RM} = \mathbf{v}_R - \mathbf{v}_M = (v_R \sin\theta - 2)\hat{\mathbf{i}} + v_R \cos\theta\,\hat{\mathbf{j}}$$

Since, rain appears to fall vertically,

$$v_R \sin\theta - 2 = 0 \Rightarrow v_R \sin\theta = 2$$

$$\mathbf{v}_M = 4\hat{\mathbf{i}}, \quad \mathbf{v}_R = 2\hat{\mathbf{i}} + v_R \cos\theta\,\hat{\mathbf{j}}$$

$$\mathbf{v}_{RM} = -2\hat{\mathbf{i}} + v_R \cos\theta\,\hat{\mathbf{j}}$$

$$\tan\phi = \frac{v_R \cos\theta}{2} = 1 \Rightarrow v_R \cos\theta = 2$$

$$\mathbf{v}_R = 2\hat{\mathbf{i}} + 2\hat{\mathbf{j}} = 2\sqrt{2} \text{ km/h, at 45° with vertical}$$

4.

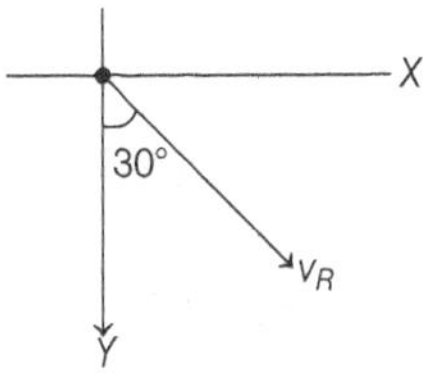

$$\mathbf{v}_R = v_R \sin 30° \hat{\mathbf{i}} + v_R \cos 30° \hat{\mathbf{j}}, \quad \mathbf{v}_M = 10\hat{\mathbf{i}}$$

$$\mathbf{v}_{RM} = \mathbf{v}_R - \mathbf{v}_M = (v_R \sin 30° - 10)\hat{\mathbf{i}} + v_R \cos 30°$$

Since, rain appears to fall vertically

$v_R \sin 30° - 10 = 0 \Rightarrow v_R = 20$ km/h

5.

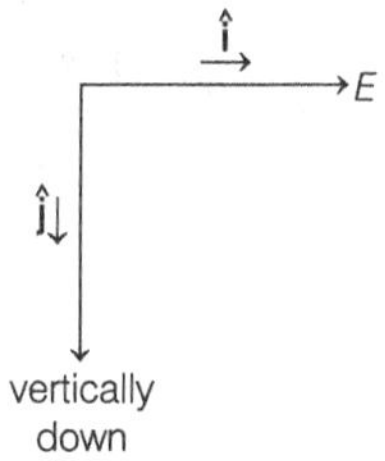

$$\mathbf{v}_{RW} = 20\hat{\mathbf{j}}, \quad \mathbf{v}_W = 15\hat{\mathbf{i}}$$

$$\mathbf{v}_R = \mathbf{v}_{RW} + \mathbf{v}_W \Rightarrow \mathbf{v}_R = 15\hat{\mathbf{i}} + 20\hat{\mathbf{j}}$$

$$\mathbf{v}_M = 5\hat{\mathbf{i}}$$

$$\mathbf{v}_{RM} = \mathbf{v}_R - \mathbf{v}_M = (15\hat{\mathbf{i}} + 20\hat{\mathbf{j}}) - 5\hat{\mathbf{i}} = 10\hat{\mathbf{i}} + 20\hat{\mathbf{j}}$$

So, he should hold his umbrella at an angle of $\tan^{-1}\left(\frac{1}{2}\right)$ with vertical.

7.6 Velocity of Separation and Approach

1.

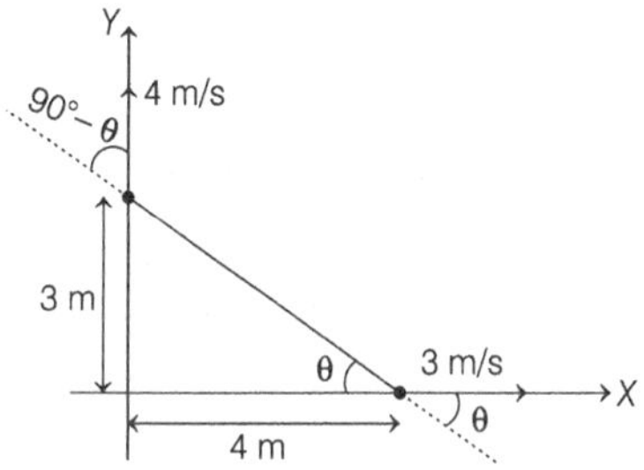

$\tan\theta = \frac{3}{4}$

(a) At $t = 0$,

$$v_{\text{sep}} = 3\cos\theta + 4\sin\theta = 3\left(\frac{4}{5}\right) + 4\left(\frac{3}{5}\right) = \frac{24}{5} = 4.8 \text{ m/s}$$

(b) At $t = 1$, $\tan\theta = \frac{7}{7} = 1$

$$v_{\text{sep}} = 3\cos\theta + 4\sin\theta = 3\left(\frac{1}{\sqrt{2}}\right) + 4\left(\frac{1}{\sqrt{2}}\right) = \frac{7}{\sqrt{2}} \text{ m/s}$$

2. (a) $v_1 \sin\theta_1 = v_2 \sin\theta_2$

(b) $t = \dfrac{d}{v_{\text{app}}} = \dfrac{d}{v_1 \cos\theta_1 + v_2 \cos\theta_2}$

3. $\mathbf{v}_1 = -20\hat{\mathbf{i}}$, $\mathbf{v}_2 = 20\hat{\mathbf{j}} \Rightarrow \mathbf{v}_{12} = -20\hat{\mathbf{i}} - 20\hat{\mathbf{j}}$

$$\tan\theta = \frac{20}{20} = 1$$

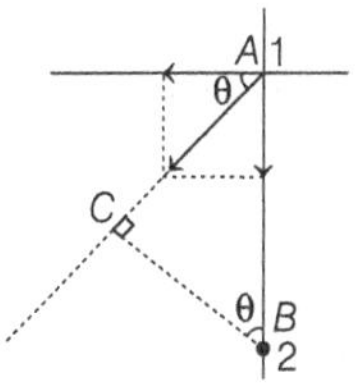

$$BC = AB\cos\theta = (10 \text{ km})\left(\frac{1}{\sqrt{2}}\right) = 5\sqrt{2} \text{ km}$$

$$t = \frac{AC}{20\sqrt{2}} = \frac{AB\sin\theta}{20\sqrt{2}} = \frac{(10\,\text{km})\left(\frac{1}{\sqrt{2}}\right)}{20\sqrt{2}} = \frac{1}{4}\,\text{h} = 15\,\text{min}$$

4.

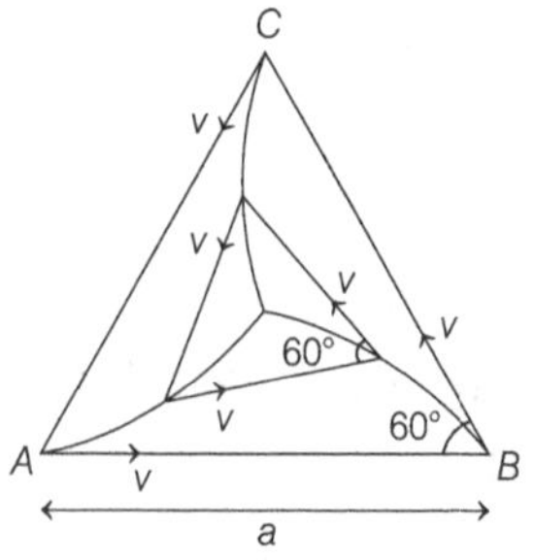

At any time,

$$v_{app} = v + v\cos 60° = \frac{3v}{2},\quad T = \frac{a}{3v/2} = \frac{2v}{3a}$$

5.

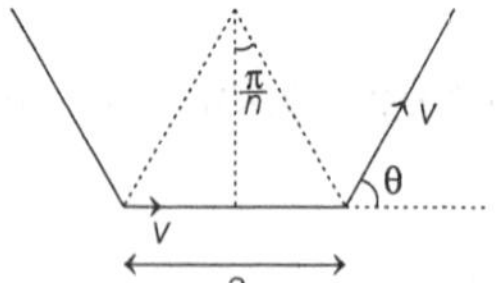

$$v_{app} = v - v\cos\theta = v(1-\cos\theta)$$

$$t = \frac{a}{v(1-\cos\theta)} = \frac{a}{v\left(1-\cos\frac{2\pi}{n}\right)}$$

Level 2

Single Choice Correct Questions

1. $u_{12} = 50 - (-50) = 100$ m/s, $a_{12} = g - (g) = 0$

So, relative velocity is constant till both of them are in air.

2. $\mathbf{v}_{car} = (8\,\text{m/s})\,\hat{\mathbf{i}}$, $\mathbf{v}_{train,\,car} = 15\,\hat{\mathbf{j}}$

$\mathbf{v}_{train} = \mathbf{v}_{train,\,car} + \mathbf{v}_{car} = 15\,\hat{\mathbf{j}} + 8\,\hat{\mathbf{i}}$

$|\mathbf{v}_{train}| = \sqrt{15^2 + 8^2} = 17$ m/s

3. $\mathbf{v}_{DC} = 20\,\hat{\mathbf{j}} = \mathbf{v}_D - \mathbf{v}_C$, $\mathbf{v}_{BC} = 20\,\hat{\mathbf{i}} = \mathbf{v}_B - \mathbf{v}_C$

$\mathbf{v}_{BA} = -20\,\hat{\mathbf{j}} = \mathbf{v}_B - \mathbf{v}_A$

$\mathbf{v}_{DA} = \mathbf{v}_D - \mathbf{v}_A = \mathbf{v}_{DC} - \mathbf{v}_{BC} + \mathbf{v}_{BA}$

$= -20\,\hat{\mathbf{i}} = 20$ m/s, towards west

4. $v_{CA} = 10 - 5 = 5$ m/s, $v_{BC} = u - 10$

$$\frac{d}{5} = \frac{d}{u-10} \Rightarrow u = 15\,\text{m/s}$$

5. $u_{AB} = 50 - (-50) = 100$ km/h

$a_{AB} = 20 - 20 = 0$, $s_{AB} = 100$ km

$$s_{AB} = u_{AB}t + \frac{1}{2}a_{AB}t^2 \Rightarrow 100 = 100t + \frac{1}{2}(0)t^2 \Rightarrow t = 1\,\text{h}$$

$$s_A = u_A t + \frac{1}{2}a_A t^2 \Rightarrow s_A = 50(1) + \frac{1}{2}(20)(1)^2 = 60\,\text{km}$$

6. $v_1 + v_2 = 8$ m/s ...(i)

$v_1 - v_2 = 0.8$ m/s ...(ii)

From Eqs. (i) and (ii), we get

$v_1 = 4.4$ m/s and $v_2 = 3.6$ m/s

7. $\mathbf{v}_{helicopter} = -50\,\hat{\mathbf{j}}$, $\mathbf{v}_{train} = 50\,\hat{\mathbf{i}}$

$\mathbf{v}_{helicopter,\,train} = \mathbf{v}_{helicopter} - \mathbf{v}_{train} = -50\,\hat{\mathbf{j}} - 50\,\hat{\mathbf{i}}$

$= 50\sqrt{2}$ km/h, South-West

8. $u_{rel} = 567 - 367 = 200$ m/s

$a_{rel} = -10 - a = -(a+10)$

$$s_{rel} = u_{rel}t + \frac{1}{2}a_{rel}t^2$$

$$\Rightarrow \quad 1000 = 200t - \frac{1}{2}(a+10)t^2$$

$\Rightarrow (a+10)t^2 - 400t + 2000 = 0$

For aeroplane to escape from being hit,

$D < 0$

$\Rightarrow (400)^2 - 4(a+10)(2000) < 0$

$\Rightarrow \quad a + 10 > 20 \;\Rightarrow\; a > 10\,\text{m/s}^2$

9. $\mathbf{v}_1 = (10\,\text{km/h})\,\hat{\mathbf{i}}$

$\mathbf{v}_2 = v\sin 30°\,\hat{\mathbf{i}} + v\cos 30°\,\hat{\mathbf{j}}$

$\mathbf{v}_{21} = (v\sin 30° - 10)\,\hat{\mathbf{i}} + v\cos 30°\,\hat{\mathbf{j}}$

$v\sin 30° - 10 = 0 \;\Rightarrow v = 20$ km/h

10. $u_{coin,\,lift} = 0$

$a_{coin,\,lift} = 10 - 11 = -1\,\text{m/s}^2 = 1\,\text{m/s}^2$, up

$$s_{coin,\,lift} = u_{coin,\,lift}t + \frac{1}{2}a_{coin,\,lift}t^2$$

$$\Rightarrow \quad 10 - 2 = \frac{1}{2}(1)t^2 \;\Rightarrow\; t = 4\,\text{s}$$

At $t = 4$ s, coin will strike the ceiling of the lift.

11. $\mathbf{a}_{coin,B} = \mathbf{a}_{coin} - \mathbf{a}_B = g - (-a_2) = (g + a_2)$, down

12.

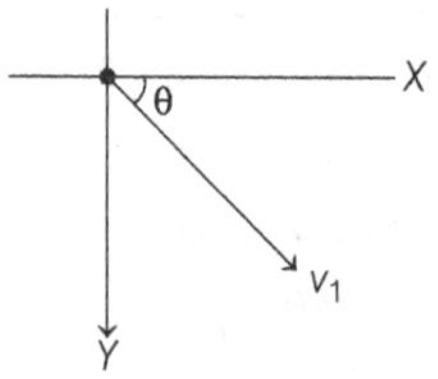

$\mathbf{v}_{packet} = v_1\cos\theta\,\hat{\mathbf{i}} + v_1\sin\theta\,\hat{\mathbf{j}}$, $\mathbf{v}_{packet,\,pilot} = v_2\,\hat{\mathbf{j}}$

$\mathbf{v}_{packet,\,pilot} = \mathbf{v}_{packet} - \mathbf{v}_{pilot}$

$\Rightarrow \quad v_2\hat{\mathbf{j}} = v_1\cos\theta\,\hat{\mathbf{i}} + v_1\sin\theta\,\hat{\mathbf{j}} - \mathbf{v}_{pilot}$

$\Rightarrow \quad \mathbf{v}_{pilot} = v_1\cos\theta\,\hat{\mathbf{i}} + (v_1\sin\theta - v_2)\,\hat{\mathbf{j}}$

Since, pilot is flying horizontally.

$$v_1\sin\theta - v_2 = 0 \;\Rightarrow\; \sin\theta = \frac{v_2}{v_1}$$

$$\mathbf{v}_{pilot} = v_1\sqrt{1 - \frac{v_2^2}{v_1^2}}\,\hat{\mathbf{i}} = \left(\sqrt{v_1^2 - v_2^2}\right)\hat{\mathbf{i}}$$

13. $\mathbf{v}_{AB} = v\cos 45°\,\hat{\mathbf{i}} + v\sin 45°\,\hat{\mathbf{j}}$

$\mathbf{v}_{BC} = -v\cos 45°\,\hat{\mathbf{i}} + v\sin 45°\,\hat{\mathbf{j}}$

$$\mathbf{v}_{CA} = \mathbf{v}_C - \mathbf{v}_A = (\mathbf{v}_C - \mathbf{v}_B) + (\mathbf{v}_B - \mathbf{v}_A)$$
$$= \mathbf{v}_{CB} + \mathbf{v}_{BA} = -(\mathbf{v}_{BC} + \mathbf{v}_{AB})$$
$$= -2v \sin 45^\circ \hat{\mathbf{j}} = \sqrt{2}v, \text{ South}$$

14. $u_{\text{stone, man}} = -5 \text{ m/s}$

$a_{\text{stone, man}} = a_{\text{stone}} - a_{\text{man}} = -10 - 5 = -15 \text{ m/s}^2$

$v_{\text{rel}} = u_{\text{rel}} + a_{\text{rel}} t = -5 + (-15)(2) = -35 \text{ m/s}$

15. $\mathbf{v}_{\text{jet}} = (500 \text{ km/h}) \text{ West} = -500 \text{ km/h}$

$\mathbf{v}_{\text{gas, jet}} = (1500 \text{ km/h}) \text{ East} = 1500 \text{ km/h}$

$\mathbf{v}_{\text{gas}} = \mathbf{v}_{\text{gas, jet}} + \mathbf{v}_{\text{jet}} = 1500 - 500 = 1000 \text{ km/h, East}$

16. $\sqrt{v_{MR}^2 - v_R^2} = \dfrac{1 \text{ km}}{\frac{1}{4} \text{ h}} \Rightarrow \sqrt{5^2 - v_R^2} = 4 \Rightarrow v_R = 3 \text{ km/h}$

17. $v_{MR} \cos\theta = v_R$ ...(i)

$$\frac{T_1}{T_2} = \frac{\dfrac{d}{v_{MR}}}{\dfrac{d}{(v_{MR} \sin\theta)}} = \sin\theta$$

18. $t = \dfrac{d}{v_{MR} \sin\theta} \Rightarrow v_{MR} \sin\theta = \dfrac{60}{6} = 10 \text{ m/s}$

$\tan\phi = \dfrac{v_{MR} \sin\theta}{v_R + v_{MR} \cos\theta} \Rightarrow \tan 45^\circ = \dfrac{10}{5 + v_{MR} \cos\theta}$

$\Rightarrow v_{MR} \cos\theta = 5 \Rightarrow v_{MR} = \sqrt{10^2 + 5^2} = 5\sqrt{5} \text{ m/s}$

19. $v_{MR} = (4.5 \text{ km/h}) \hat{\mathbf{j}} \Rightarrow \mathbf{v}_R = (6 \text{ km/h}) \hat{\mathbf{i}}$

$\mathbf{v}_M = \mathbf{v}_{MR} + \mathbf{v}_R = (4.5\hat{\mathbf{j}} + 6\hat{\mathbf{i}}) \text{ km/h}$

$v_m = (\sqrt{(4.5)^2 + 6^2}) \text{ km/h} = \dfrac{15}{2} \text{ km/h} = \dfrac{15}{2} \times \dfrac{5}{18} \text{ m/s}$

20. $v_{MR} = 5 \text{ m/s}, \quad v_R = 4 \text{ m/s}$

$t = \dfrac{d}{\sqrt{v_{MR}^2 - v_R^2}} = \dfrac{480}{3} = 160 \text{ s}$

21. $v_{MR} \cos\theta + v_R = 0 \Rightarrow 2\cos(120^\circ) + v_R = 0$

$\Rightarrow v_R = 1 \text{ km/h}$

22. $\text{Drift} = v_R \left(\dfrac{d}{v_{MR}}\right) \Rightarrow 300 = 3\left(\dfrac{500}{v_{MR}}\right)$

$\Rightarrow v_{MR} = 5 \text{ mph}$

23. $t = \dfrac{d}{\sqrt{v^2 - u^2}}$ and $T = \dfrac{d}{v + u} \Rightarrow \dfrac{v}{u} = \dfrac{t^2 + T^2}{t^2 - T^2}$

24. $\text{Total time} = \dfrac{d}{v_0 + v_A} + \dfrac{d}{v_0 - v_A} = \dfrac{2dv_0}{v_0^2 - v_A^2}$

25. $\mathbf{v}_M = v_M \hat{\mathbf{i}}$

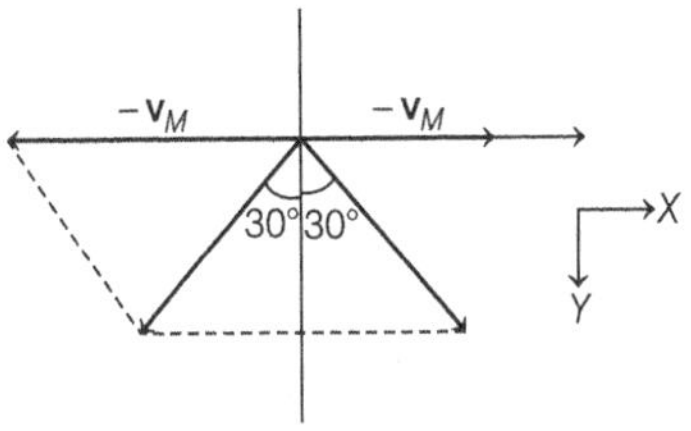

$\mathbf{v}_R = 20 \sin 30^\circ \hat{\mathbf{i}} + 20 \cos 30^\circ \hat{\mathbf{j}} = 10\hat{\mathbf{i}} + 10\sqrt{3}\hat{\mathbf{j}}$

$\mathbf{v}_{RM} = \mathbf{v}_R + (-\mathbf{v}_M) = (10 - v_M)\hat{\mathbf{i}} + 10\sqrt{3}\hat{\mathbf{j}}$

$\tan(-30^\circ) = \dfrac{10 - v_M}{10\sqrt{3}}$

$\Rightarrow 10 - v_M = -10 \Rightarrow v_M = 20 \text{ m/s}$

26. For boy,

$v = u + at \Rightarrow v_{\text{boy}} = 0 + \sqrt{3}(3) = 3\sqrt{3} \text{ m/s}$

$\mathbf{v}_{\text{boy}} = 3\sqrt{3}\hat{\mathbf{i}}, \quad \mathbf{v}_{\text{rain, boy}} = 3\hat{\mathbf{j}}$

$\mathbf{v}_{\text{rain}} = \mathbf{v}_{\text{rain, boy}} + \mathbf{v}_{\text{boy}} = 3\hat{\mathbf{j}} + 3\sqrt{3}\hat{\mathbf{i}}$

$v_{\text{rain}} = \sqrt{3^2 + (3\sqrt{3})^2} = 6 \text{ m/s}$

27. $\mathbf{v}_{\text{cyclist}} = v\hat{\mathbf{i}}, \quad \mathbf{v}_{\text{rain}} = 10\hat{\mathbf{j}}$

$\mathbf{v}_{\text{rain, cyclist}} = 10\hat{\mathbf{j}} - v\hat{\mathbf{i}} \; \sqrt{10^2 + v^2} = 20$

$\Rightarrow v = 10\sqrt{3} \text{ m/s}$

28. $\mathbf{v}_{AB}$ and $\mathbf{r}_{AB}$ should be anti-parallel

$\mathbf{v}_{AB} = (3 - x)\hat{\mathbf{i}} + 4\hat{\mathbf{j}}, \quad \mathbf{r}_{AB} = -4\hat{\mathbf{i}} - 4\hat{\mathbf{j}}$

$\mathbf{v}_{AB} \times \mathbf{r}_{AB} = 0$

$$\begin{vmatrix} \hat{\mathbf{i}} & \hat{\mathbf{j}} & \hat{\mathbf{k}} \\ 3 - x & 4 & 0 \\ -4 & -4 & 0 \end{vmatrix} = 0$$

$\Rightarrow -4(3 - x) - (-16) = 0 \Rightarrow -12 + 4x + 16 = 0$

$\Rightarrow 4x + 4 = 0 \Rightarrow x = -1$

29. $\mathbf{v}_{AB} = \mathbf{v}_A - \mathbf{v}_B = v_1\hat{\mathbf{i}} - v_2\hat{\mathbf{j}}$

$\tan\theta = \dfrac{v_2}{v_1}$

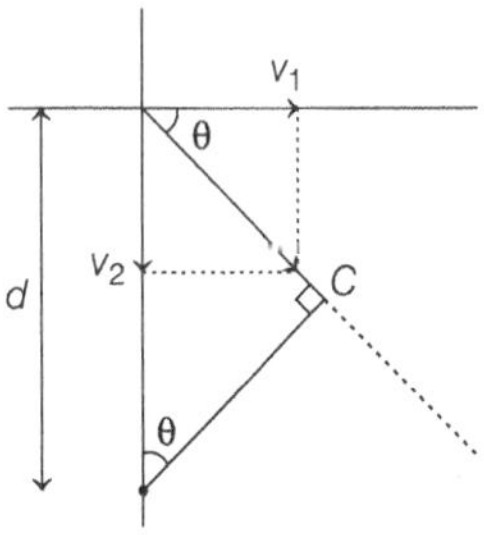

$\text{Least distance} = d\cos\theta = \dfrac{dv_1}{\sqrt{v_1^2 + v_2^2}}$

30. $\mathbf{v}_{bR} = 4\hat{\mathbf{i}}, \quad \mathbf{v}_R = 2\hat{\mathbf{j}}, \quad \mathbf{v}_w = 6\hat{\mathbf{j}}$

$\mathbf{v}_b = \mathbf{v}_{bR} + \mathbf{v}_R \Rightarrow \mathbf{v}_b = 4\hat{\mathbf{i}} + 2\hat{\mathbf{j}} \Rightarrow \mathbf{v}_{\text{flag}} = 4\hat{\mathbf{i}} + 2\hat{\mathbf{j}}$

$\mathbf{v}_{\text{wind, flag}} = \mathbf{v}_{\text{wind}} - \mathbf{v}_{\text{flag}} = 6\hat{\mathbf{j}} - (4\hat{\mathbf{i}} + 2\hat{\mathbf{j}})$

$= -4\hat{\mathbf{i}} + 4\hat{\mathbf{j}} = 4\sqrt{2} \text{ m/s, N-W}$

31. $\mathbf{v}_b = 10\cos 37^\circ \hat{\mathbf{i}} + 10 \sin 37^\circ \hat{\mathbf{j}} = 8\hat{\mathbf{i}} + 6\hat{\mathbf{j}}$

$\mathbf{v}_{bw} = -2\hat{\mathbf{i}}, \quad \mathbf{v}_{bR} = -4\hat{\mathbf{j}}$

$$\mathbf{v}_b = \mathbf{v}_{\text{due to own power}} + \mathbf{v}_{bw} + \mathbf{b}_{bR}$$
$$8\hat{\mathbf{i}} + 6\hat{\mathbf{j}} = \mathbf{v}_{\text{due to own power}} - 2\hat{\mathbf{i}} - 4\hat{\mathbf{j}}$$
$$\mathbf{v}_{\text{due to own power}} = 10\hat{\mathbf{i}} + 10\hat{\mathbf{j}} = 10\sqrt{2}\text{ km/h, N-E}$$

32. $v + 30 = \dfrac{5\text{ km}}{\dfrac{4}{60}\text{h}} \Rightarrow v + 30 = 75 \Rightarrow v = 45\text{ km/h}$

33. $\dfrac{l}{v_1 + v_2} = 3\text{ s}$ ...(i)

$\dfrac{l}{1.5v_1 + v_2} = 2.5\text{ s}$ ...(ii)

$\dfrac{l}{v_1 - v_2} = t$ ...(ii)

Solving Eqs. (i), (ii) and (iii), we get

$t = 15\text{ s}$

34. The particle *A* will appear to move in a circle, if seen from *B*.

35. $\dfrac{l}{u} = t_1, \quad \dfrac{l}{v} = t_2$

$$t = \frac{l}{v+u} = \frac{l}{\dfrac{l}{t_2} + \dfrac{l}{t_1}} = \frac{t_1 t_2}{t_1 + t_2}$$

36. $t = \dfrac{2u}{g+a} \Rightarrow a = \dfrac{2u}{t} - g = \dfrac{2u - gt}{t}$

37. $\mathbf{v}_{\text{object, girl}} = \mathbf{v}_{\text{object}} - \mathbf{v}_{\text{girl}}$

For stationary objects outside the train

$\mathbf{v}_{\text{object, girl}} = -\mathbf{v}_{\text{girl}}$

38. $\mathbf{v}_R = v_R \cos 60° \hat{\mathbf{i}} + v_R \sin 60° \hat{\mathbf{j}}, \quad \mathbf{v}_m = 25\hat{\mathbf{i}}$

$$\mathbf{v}_{RM} = \mathbf{v}_R - \mathbf{v}_M = (v_R \cos 60° - 25)\hat{\mathbf{i}} + (v_R \sin 60°)\hat{\mathbf{j}}$$

$$\tan(-30°) = \frac{v_R \sin 60°}{v_R \cos 60° - 25} \Rightarrow -\frac{1}{\sqrt{3}} = \frac{v_R(\sqrt{3}/2)}{\dfrac{v_R}{2} - 25}$$

$\Rightarrow \quad v_R = 12.5\text{ m/s}$

Numerical Value Questions

1. $100 + l = \left(36 \times \dfrac{5}{18}\right)(14) \Rightarrow l = 140 - 100 = 40\text{ m}$

2. $\mathbf{v}_{\text{sailor}} = 8\hat{\mathbf{i}}$

$\mathbf{v}_{\text{submarine, sailor}} = 12\hat{\mathbf{j}} - 2\hat{\mathbf{k}}$

$\mathbf{v}_{\text{helicopter, submarine}} = -4\hat{\mathbf{i}} + 5\hat{\mathbf{k}}$

$$\mathbf{v}_{\text{helicopter}} = \mathbf{v}_{\text{helicopter, submarine}} + \mathbf{v}_{\text{submarine, sailor}} + \mathbf{v}_{\text{sailor}}$$
$$= (-4\hat{\mathbf{i}} + 5\hat{\mathbf{k}}) + (12\hat{\mathbf{j}} - 2\hat{\mathbf{k}}) + 8\hat{\mathbf{i}} = 4\hat{\mathbf{i}} + 12\hat{\mathbf{j}} + 3\hat{\mathbf{k}}$$

$|\mathbf{v}_{\text{helicopter}}| = \sqrt{4^2 + 12^2 + 3^2} = 13\text{ m/s}$

3. Time when *A* and *C* cross each other $= \dfrac{1\text{ km}}{90\text{ km/h}} = \dfrac{1}{90}\text{h}$

$s_{BA} = 1\text{ km}, \quad u_{BA} = 54 - 36 = 18\text{ km/h}$

$a_{BA} = a_B - 0 = a_B$

$s_{BA} = u_{BA}t + \dfrac{1}{2}a_{BA}t^2$

$$\Rightarrow 1\text{ km} = (18\text{ km/h})\left(\frac{1}{90}\text{h}\right) + \frac{1}{2}a_B\left(\frac{1}{90}\text{h}\right)^2$$

$\Rightarrow \quad a_B = 1\text{ m/s}^2$

4.

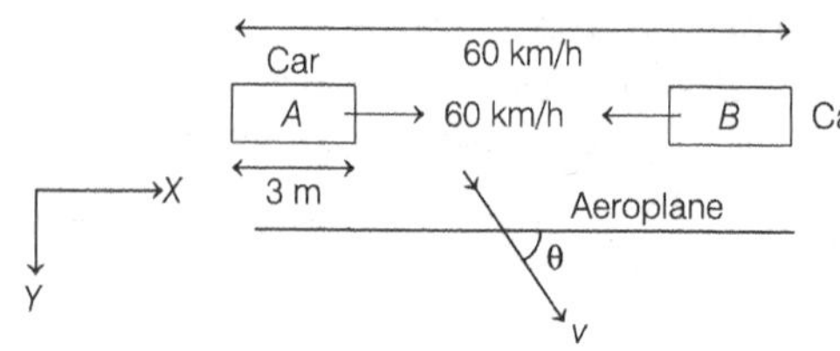

$\mathbf{v}_A = 60\hat{\mathbf{i}}, \quad \mathbf{v}_B = -60\hat{\mathbf{j}}$

$\mathbf{v}_P = v\cos\theta\hat{\mathbf{i}} + v\sin\theta\hat{\mathbf{j}}$

$\mathbf{v}_{PA} = (v\cos\theta - 60)\hat{\mathbf{i}} + v\sin\theta\hat{\mathbf{j}}$

$v\cos\theta - 60 = 0 \Rightarrow v\cos\theta = 60$

$\mathbf{v}_{PB} = (v\cos\theta + 60)\hat{\mathbf{i}} + v\sin\theta\hat{\mathbf{j}}$

$\tan 45° = \dfrac{v\sin\theta}{v\cos\theta + 60} \Rightarrow v\sin\theta = 120$

$\therefore \quad \mathbf{v}_P = 60\hat{\mathbf{i}} + 120\hat{\mathbf{j}} \Rightarrow \tan\theta = \dfrac{120}{60} = 2$

5. $\mathbf{v}_b = (12\text{ m/s})\hat{\mathbf{i}}, \quad \mathbf{v}_w = v\hat{\mathbf{j}}$

$\mathbf{v}_{wb} = \mathbf{v}_w - \mathbf{v}_b = v\hat{\mathbf{j}} - 12\hat{\mathbf{i}}$

$\tan 53° = \dfrac{v}{12} \Rightarrow \dfrac{4}{3} = \dfrac{v}{12} \Rightarrow v = 16\text{ m/s}$

6. $\dfrac{D}{v+u} + \dfrac{\left(\dfrac{D}{2}\right)}{v-u} = \dfrac{\left(\dfrac{D}{2}\right)}{u} \Rightarrow \dfrac{2v - 2u + v + u}{2(v^2 - u^2)} = \dfrac{1}{2u}$

$\Rightarrow \quad (3v - u)u = v^2 - u^2 \Rightarrow 3vu - u^2 = v^2 - u^2$

$\Rightarrow \quad \dfrac{v}{u} = 3$

7. $\mathbf{v}_M = 7\hat{\mathbf{i}}$

$\mathbf{v}_R = v_R\sin\theta\hat{\mathbf{i}} + v_R\cos\theta\hat{\mathbf{j}}$

$\mathbf{v}_{RM} = (v_R\sin\theta - 7)\hat{\mathbf{i}} + v_R\cos\theta\hat{\mathbf{j}}$

$\tan 37° = \dfrac{v_R\sin\theta - 7}{v_R\cos\theta} \Rightarrow \dfrac{3}{4} = \dfrac{v_R\sin\theta - 7}{v_R\cos\theta}$

$\Rightarrow \quad 4v_R\sin\theta - 3v_R\cos\theta = 28$ ...(i)

$\mathbf{v}_{M'} = 25\hat{\mathbf{i}}, \quad \mathbf{v}_{RM'} = (v_R\sin\theta - 25)\hat{\mathbf{i}} + v_R\cos\theta\hat{\mathbf{j}}$

$\tan(-37°) = \dfrac{v_R\sin\theta - 25}{v_R\cos\theta}$

$4v_R\sin\theta + 3v_R\cos\theta = 100$ ...(i)

Solving Eqs. (i) and (ii), we get

$v_R\cos\theta = 12$ and $v_R\sin\theta = 16$

$\therefore \quad \mathbf{v}_R = 16\hat{\mathbf{i}} + 12\hat{\mathbf{j}}$

8.

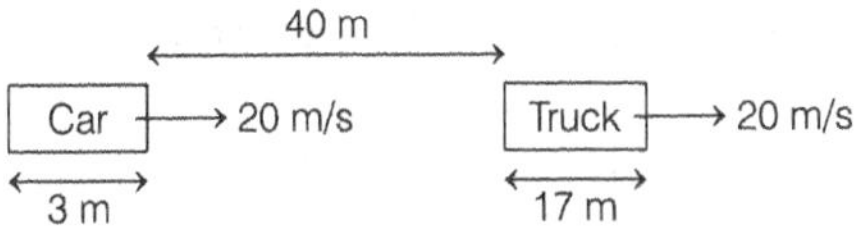

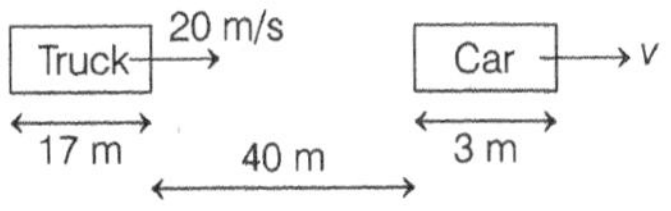

$$s_{rel} = u_{rel}\, t + \frac{1}{2} a_{rel}\, t^2$$

$$\Rightarrow \quad (40 + 40 + 17 + 3) = 0 + \frac{1}{2}(0.5)t^2 \Rightarrow t = 20 \text{ s}$$

9. $\mathbf{v}_{\text{bullet, van}} = 150 \text{ m/s} = 150 \times \frac{18}{5} = 540 \text{ km/h}$

$$v_{van} = 30 \text{ km/h}$$

$$v_{bullet} = v_{\text{bullet, van}} + v_{van} = 540 + 30 = 570 \text{ km/h}$$

$$v_{car} = 192 \text{ km/h}$$

$$v_{\text{bullet, car}} = v_{bullet} - v_{car} = 570 - 192 = 378 \text{ km/h} = 105 \text{ m/s}$$

10. $T_1 = \frac{d}{v_{MR}} = \frac{d}{17}$

$$T_2 = \frac{d}{\sqrt{v_{MR}^2 - v_R^2}} = \frac{d}{\sqrt{17^2 - 8^2}} = \frac{d}{15}$$

$$T_2 - T_1 = 6 \text{ s}$$

$$\Rightarrow \quad \frac{d}{15} - \frac{d}{17} = 6 \Rightarrow d = 765$$

11.

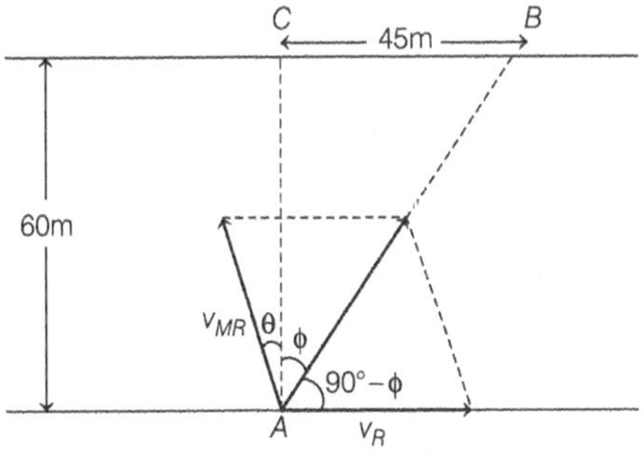

$$\tan\phi = \frac{BC}{AC} = \frac{45}{60} = \frac{3}{4} \Rightarrow \phi = 37°$$

Since, $v_R = v_{MR}$

$$\Rightarrow \theta + \phi = 90° - \phi$$

$$\Rightarrow \quad \theta = 90° - 2\phi$$

$$\Rightarrow \quad \theta = 90° - 2(37°) \Rightarrow \theta = 16°$$

12. Separation between the train = (100 km / h) × 6 min = 10 km

Velocity of train w.r.t. car = 100 − 60 = 40 km/h

If t is the interval of time passing through cars, then

$$40 \times t = 10 \Rightarrow t = \frac{1}{4} \text{ h} = 15 \text{ min}$$

Level 3

Single Choice Correct Questions

1. $\mathbf{v}_A = 10\hat{i}, \quad \mathbf{v}_{BA} = (6\cos\theta\,\hat{i} + 6\sin\theta\,\hat{j})$

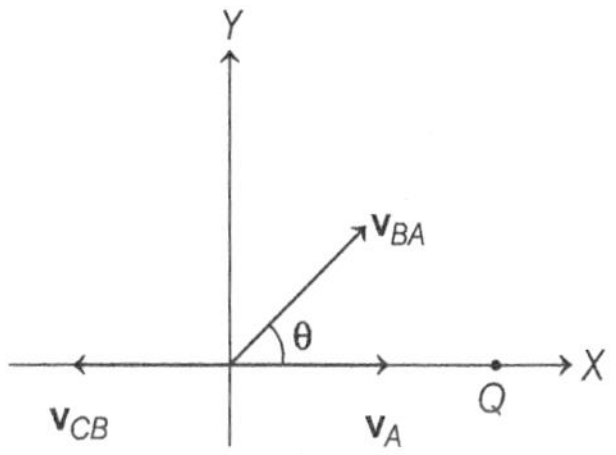

$$\mathbf{v}_{CB} = -12\hat{i}$$

$$\mathbf{v}_C = \mathbf{v}_{CB} + \mathbf{v}_{BA} + \mathbf{v}_A$$

$$= -12\hat{i} + \left(6\left(\frac{15}{24}\right)\hat{i} + 6\left(\frac{\sqrt{351}}{24}\right)\hat{j}\right) + 10\hat{i}$$

$$= \frac{7\hat{i}}{4} + \frac{\sqrt{351}}{4}\hat{j}$$

$$|\mathbf{v}_C| = \sqrt{\left(\frac{7}{4}\right)^2 + \left(\frac{\sqrt{351}}{4}\right)^2} = 5 \text{ m/s}$$

2. $\frac{20}{v + 15} = \frac{30}{v + 25} \Rightarrow 2v + 50 = 3v + 45 \Rightarrow v = 5 \text{ km/h}$

3.

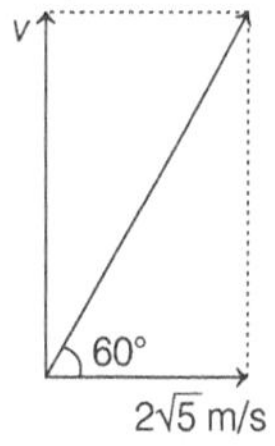

$$\tan 60° = \frac{v}{2\sqrt{5}} \Rightarrow v = (2\sqrt{5})(\sqrt{3}) \Rightarrow v = 2\sqrt{15} \text{ m/s}$$

$$H_{max} = \frac{v^2}{2g} = \frac{(2\sqrt{15})^2}{20} = 3 \text{ m}$$

4. $v = u + at \Rightarrow v_{boy} = 2t$

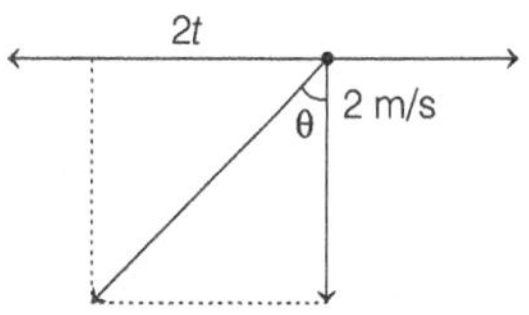

$$\tan\theta = \frac{2t}{2} \Rightarrow \sec^2\theta \frac{d\theta}{dt} = 1$$

$$\Rightarrow \quad \frac{d\theta}{dt} = \cos^2\theta \Rightarrow \frac{d\theta}{dt} = \frac{1}{1 + t^2}$$

At $t = \frac{1}{2}$, $\frac{d\theta}{dt} = \frac{1}{1 + \left(\frac{1}{2}\right)^2} = \frac{4}{5} \text{ rad/s}$

5. $T = \sqrt{\frac{2H}{g}} = \sqrt{\frac{2(4)}{10}} = \frac{2}{\sqrt{5}}$ s

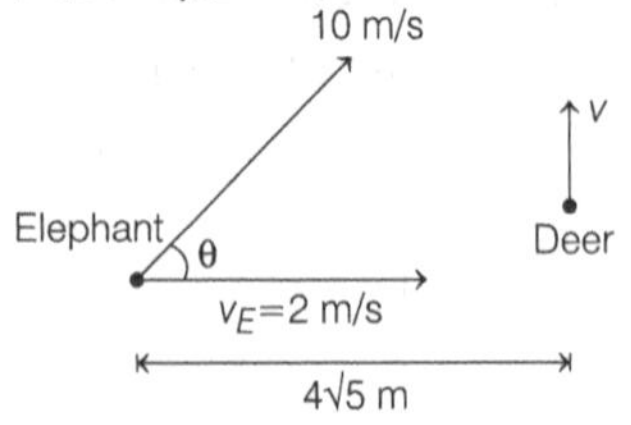

$$(10\cos\theta + 2)\frac{2}{\sqrt{5}} = 4\sqrt{5} \Rightarrow 10\cos\theta + 2 = 10$$

$$\Rightarrow \quad 10\cos\theta = 8 \Rightarrow \cos\theta = \frac{4}{5} \Rightarrow \theta = 37^\circ$$

$$v_{deer} = 10\sin\theta = 10\left(\frac{3}{5}\right) = 6\,\text{m/s}$$

6.

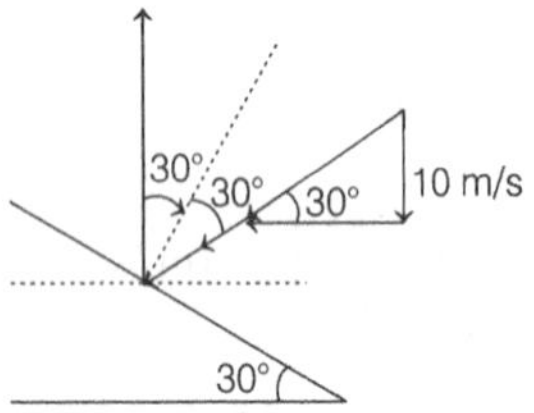

$$\tan 30^\circ = \frac{10}{v_{car}} \Rightarrow v_{car} = 10\sqrt{3}\,\text{m/s}$$

7.

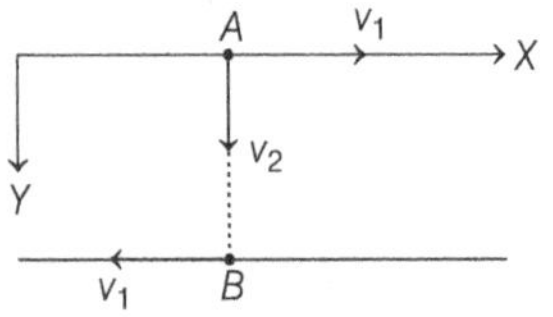

Velocity of particle w.r.t. *B* will be $2v_1\hat{\mathbf{i}} + v_2\hat{\mathbf{j}}$ in horizontal plane and acceleration will be $g\hat{\mathbf{k}}$.

So, it will follow a parabolic path.

8. Since, their relative acceleration is zero, their relative velocity is constant. So, magnitude of **r** will increase linearly with time.

9. $T = \frac{2u_{rel}}{g_{rel}}$

$$\Rightarrow \quad T = \frac{2u}{g} \text{ and } T' = \frac{2u}{g+g} \quad \therefore \; T' = \frac{T}{2}$$

10. Number of taxis $= \frac{240}{10} = 24$

But when 24th taxi starts motion it reaches the destination. So, it will meet 23 only.

11. $T = \sqrt{\frac{2H}{g}} = \sqrt{\frac{2(9)}{10}} = \sqrt{\frac{9}{5}}$ s

12. $T = \sqrt{\frac{2(9)}{10 - 5.5}} = 2$ s

13. Independent of the speed of the elevation as u_{rel} is zero.

14.

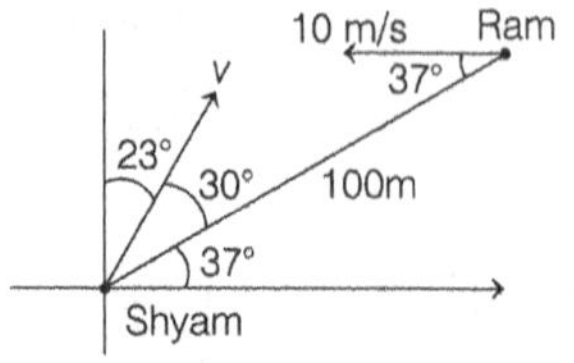

$$v\sin 30^\circ = 10\sin 37^\circ \Rightarrow v = 12\,\text{m/s}$$

15. $\frac{d}{\sqrt{v^2 - u^2}} = \frac{d}{v} + \frac{u\left(\frac{d}{v}\right)}{v_{walking}}$

$$\frac{d}{\sqrt{2.5^2 - 2^2}} = \frac{d}{2.5} + \frac{2d}{2.5\,v_{walking}} \Rightarrow v_{walking} = 3\,\text{km/h}$$

16. $x = (1 + 3\cos\theta)t$ ...(i)

$y = (3\sin\theta)t$ ...(ii)

From Eqs. (i) and (ii), we get

$(x-1)^2 + y^2 = 9t^2$

17.

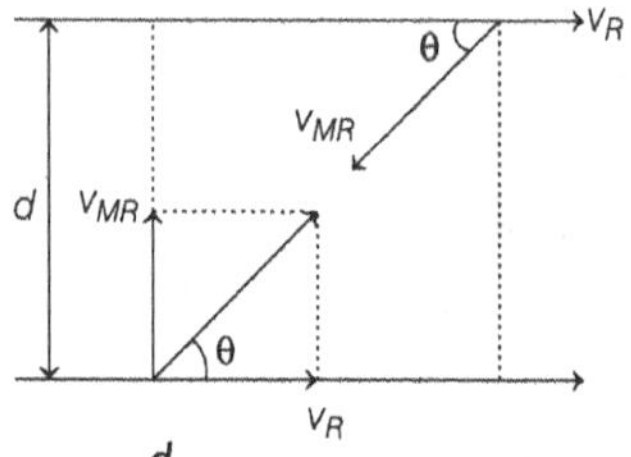

$$10 = \frac{d}{v_{MR}} \quad \text{...(i)}$$

$$15 = \frac{d}{v_{MR}\sin\theta} \quad \text{...(ii)}$$

From Eqs. (i) and (ii), we get

$$\sin\theta = \frac{2}{3}$$

Now, $\tan\theta = \frac{v_{MR}}{v_R} \Rightarrow \frac{v_{MR}}{v_R} = \frac{2}{\sqrt{5}}$

18. $s_y = u_y t + \frac{1}{2}a_y t^2$

$$\Rightarrow \quad 100 = 0 + \frac{1}{2}(2)t^2 = 10\text{ s}$$

Drift $= 1.5 \times 10 = 15$ m

19.

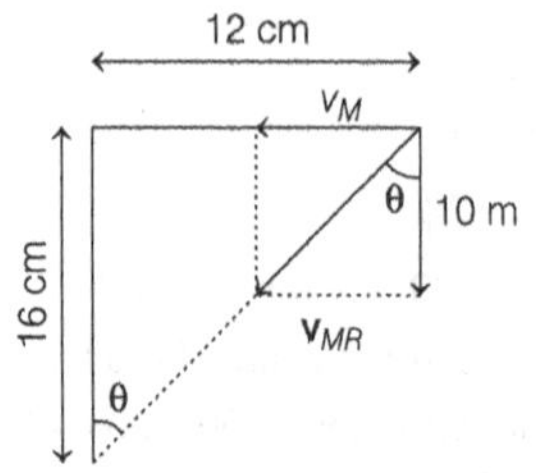

$$\tan\theta = \frac{12}{16} = \frac{v_M}{10} \Rightarrow v_M = 7.5\,\text{m/s}$$

20.

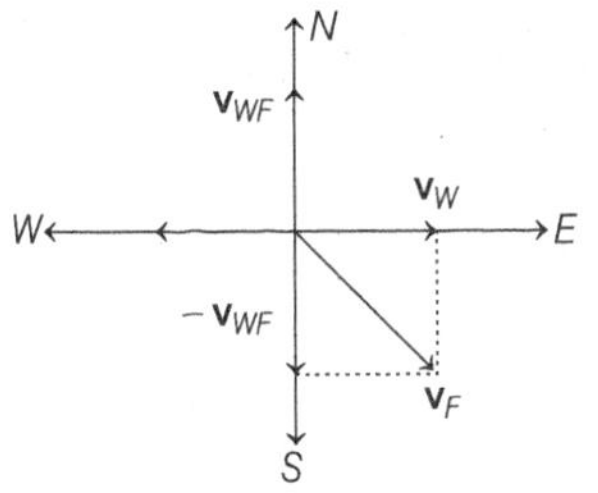

$$\mathbf{v}_{WF} = \mathbf{v}_W - \mathbf{v}_F \Rightarrow \mathbf{v}_F = \mathbf{v}_W - \mathbf{v}_{WF}$$

So, velocity of bus will be in any direction between South and East.

21. $\mathbf{v}_M = u\hat{\mathbf{i}}, \quad \mathbf{v}_R = v_R \sin\phi\,\hat{\mathbf{i}} + v_R \cos\phi\,\hat{\mathbf{j}}$

$$\mathbf{v}_{RM} = (v_R \sin\phi - u)\,\hat{\mathbf{i}} + v_R \cos\phi\,\hat{\mathbf{j}}$$

$$v_R \sin\phi - u = 0 \Rightarrow v_R \sin\phi = u \quad \text{...(i)}$$

$$\mathbf{v}_{RM} = (v_R \sin\phi - 2u)\,\hat{\mathbf{i}} + v_R \cos\phi\,\hat{\mathbf{j}}$$

$$\mathbf{v}_{RM} = -u\hat{\mathbf{i}} + v_R \cos\phi\,\hat{\mathbf{j}}$$

$$\tan\theta = \frac{u}{v_R \cos\phi} \Rightarrow v_R \cos\phi = \frac{u}{\tan\theta} = u\cot\theta \quad \text{...(ii)}$$

$$\therefore \quad \mathbf{v}_R = u\hat{\mathbf{i}} + u\cot\theta\,\hat{\mathbf{j}}$$

22.

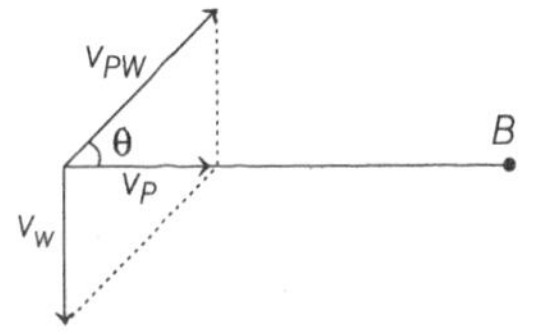

$$v_W = 300\text{ km/h}, \; v_{PW} = 900\text{km/h}$$

$$v_{PW} \sin\theta = v_W \Rightarrow 900 \sin\theta = 300 \Rightarrow \sin\theta = \frac{1}{3}$$

$$v_P = 900\cos\theta = 900\left(\frac{2\sqrt{2}}{3}\right) = 600\sqrt{2}\text{ km/h}$$

$$\text{Time taken} = \frac{500}{600\sqrt{2}} = \frac{5}{3\sqrt{8}}\text{ h}$$

23. $\mathbf{v}_{ship} = 18\,\hat{\mathbf{i}}, \quad \mathbf{v}_{wind} = \mathbf{v}_{wind}\hat{\mathbf{j}}$

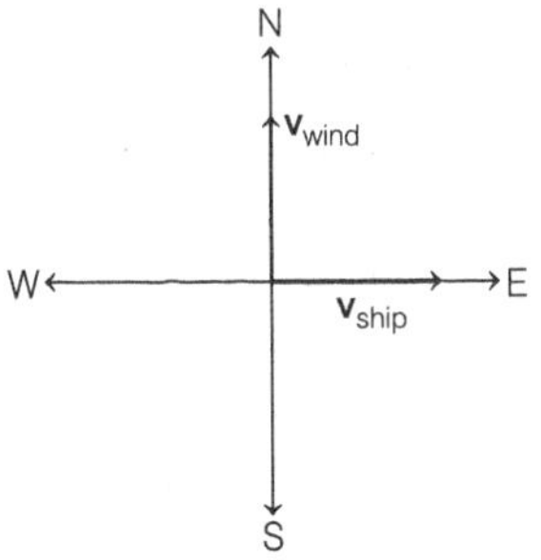

$$\mathbf{v}_{wind,\,ship} = \mathbf{v}_{wind} - \mathbf{v}_{ship} = \mathbf{v}_{wind}\,\hat{\mathbf{j}} - 18\,\hat{\mathbf{i}}$$

$$\tan 30^\circ = \frac{v_{wind}}{18}$$

$$\Rightarrow \quad v_{wind} = \frac{18}{\sqrt{3}}\text{ km/h}$$

24.

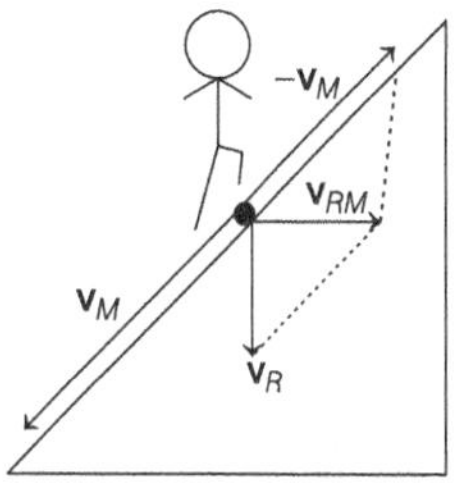

When the man is walking down the incline, rain may appear to come horizontally.

25.

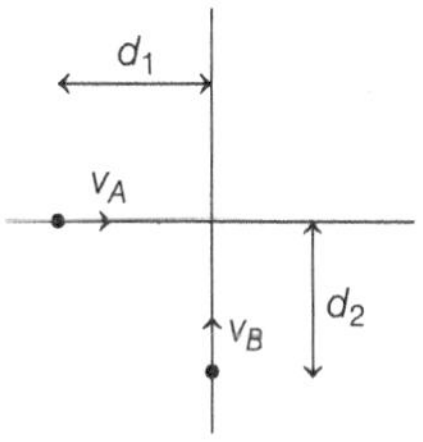

$$\text{Separation} = \sqrt{(d_1 - v_A t)^2 + (d_2 - v_B t)^2}$$

26.

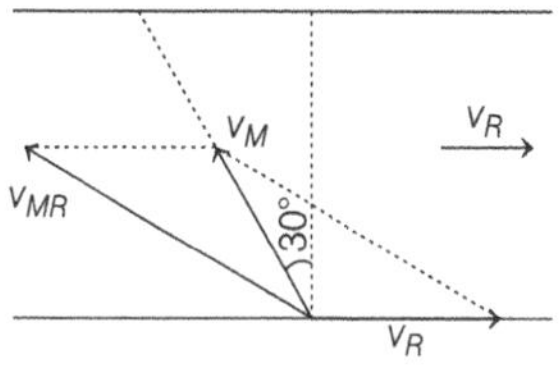

$$\tan\phi = \frac{v_{MR}\sin\theta}{v_R + v_{MR}\cos\theta} \Rightarrow \tan(120^\circ) = \frac{5\sqrt{3}\sin\theta}{5 + 5\sqrt{3}\cos\theta}$$

$$\Rightarrow \; -5\sin\theta = 5 + 5\sqrt{3}\cos\theta \Rightarrow 5(\sqrt{3}\cos\theta + \sin\theta) = -5$$

$$\Rightarrow \; 2\sin(\theta + 60^\circ) = -1 \Rightarrow \theta + 60^\circ = 210^\circ \Rightarrow \theta = 150^\circ$$

27. $\mathbf{v}_w = \sqrt{2}\cos 45^\circ\,\hat{\mathbf{i}} + \sqrt{2}\sin 45^\circ\,\hat{\mathbf{j}} = \hat{\mathbf{i}} + \hat{\mathbf{j}}$

$$\mathbf{v}_R = 2\hat{\mathbf{j}}, \quad \mathbf{v}_{bR} = 0 + 0.2t\hat{\mathbf{i}}$$

At $\quad t = 10\text{ s}, \; \mathbf{v}_{bR} = 2\hat{\mathbf{i}}$

$$\mathbf{v}_b = \mathbf{v}_{bR} + \mathbf{v}_R \Rightarrow \mathbf{v}_b = 2\hat{\mathbf{i}} + 2\hat{\mathbf{j}} = \mathbf{v}_{flag}$$

$$\mathbf{v}_{wind,\,flag} = (\hat{\mathbf{i}} + \hat{\mathbf{j}}) - 2(\hat{\mathbf{i}} + \hat{\mathbf{j}}) = -\hat{\mathbf{i}} - \hat{\mathbf{j}} = \sqrt{2}\text{ m/s, S - W}$$

28. $\mathbf{v}_{sw} = 60\hat{\mathbf{i}}, \quad \mathbf{v}_w = -20\hat{\mathbf{i}}$

$$\mathbf{v}_s = \mathbf{v}_{sw} + \mathbf{v}_w = 60\hat{\mathbf{i}} - 20\hat{\mathbf{i}} = 40\hat{\mathbf{i}}$$

$$\mathbf{v}_{man,\,ship} = 30\,\hat{\mathbf{j}}$$

$$\mathbf{v}_{man} = \mathbf{v}_{man,\,ship} + \mathbf{v}_{ship} = 30\,\hat{\mathbf{j}} + 40\hat{\mathbf{i}}$$

$$\mathbf{v}_{flag} = \mathbf{v}_{man} = 30\hat{\mathbf{j}} + 40\hat{\mathbf{i}}$$

$$\mathbf{v}_{wind} = -50\cos 37^\circ\,\hat{\mathbf{i}} - 50\sin 37^\circ\,\hat{\mathbf{j}} = -40\,\hat{\mathbf{i}} - 30\hat{\mathbf{j}}$$

$$\mathbf{v}_{wind\ flag} = \mathbf{v}_{wind} - \mathbf{v}_{flag}$$

$$= (-40\hat{\mathbf{i}} - 30\hat{\mathbf{j}}) - (40\hat{\mathbf{i}} + 30\hat{\mathbf{j}}) = -80\hat{\mathbf{i}} - 60\hat{\mathbf{j}}$$

$$= 100\text{ km/h, 37° South of West}$$

29. $T_1 = 2\left(\dfrac{d}{\sqrt{v^2 - u^2}}\right)$ ...(i)

$T_2 = \dfrac{d}{v+u} + \dfrac{d}{v-u} = \dfrac{2\,dv}{v^2 - u^2}$ ...(ii)

$T_3 = \dfrac{2d}{v}$ ...(iii)

From Eqs. (i), (ii) and (iii), we get

$T_1^2 = T_2 T_3$

30. $(v+u)(1\text{ h}) - (v-u)\left(\dfrac{6}{u} - 1\right) = 6$

$\Rightarrow\ v + u - \left(\dfrac{6v}{u} - v - 6 + 4\right) = 6$

$\Rightarrow\quad 2v - \dfrac{6v}{u} = 0 \quad \Rightarrow\ u = 3\text{ km/h}$

31.

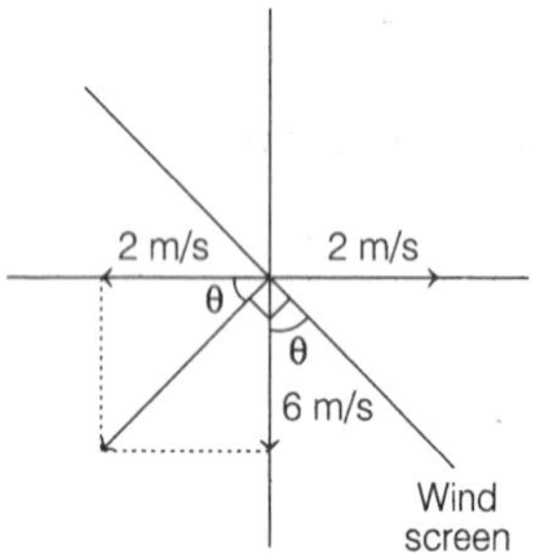

$\tan\theta = \dfrac{6}{2} = 3 \ \Rightarrow\ \theta = \tan^{-1}(3)$

32.

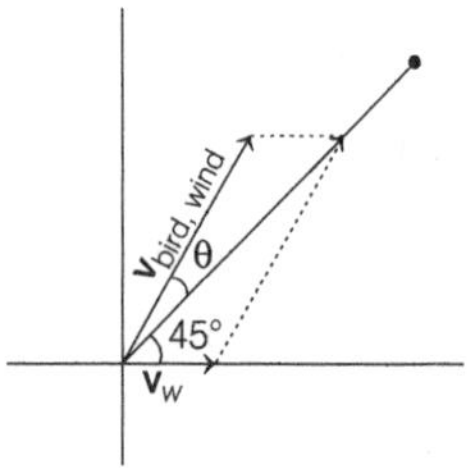

$v_w \sin 45° = v_{bw} \sin\theta$

$\Rightarrow\quad 5\left(\dfrac{1}{\sqrt{2}}\right) = 15\sin\theta \ \Rightarrow\ \sin\theta = \dfrac{1}{3\sqrt{2}}$

$t = \dfrac{5\text{ km}}{(15\cos\theta + 5\cos 45°)}$

$= \dfrac{5}{15\dfrac{\sqrt{17}}{3\sqrt{2}} + \dfrac{5}{\sqrt{2}}} = \dfrac{\sqrt{2}}{\sqrt{17}+1}\text{h}$

33.

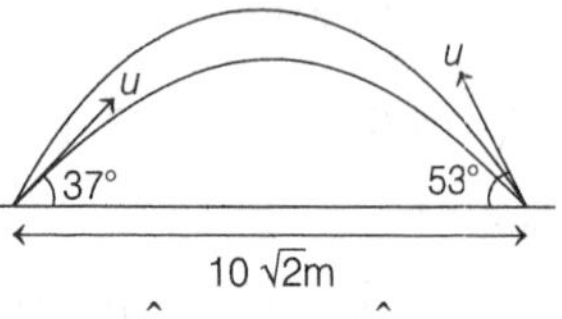

$\mathbf{v}_1 = u\cos 37°\,\hat{\mathbf{i}} + u\sin 37°\,\hat{\mathbf{j}}$

$\mathbf{v}_2 = -u\cos 53°\,\hat{\mathbf{i}} + u\sin 53°\,\hat{\mathbf{j}}$

$\mathbf{v}_{12} = \mathbf{v}_1 - \mathbf{v}_2 = \dfrac{7u}{5}\hat{\mathbf{i}} - \dfrac{u}{5}\hat{\mathbf{j}}$

$\tan\phi = \dfrac{\dfrac{u}{5}}{\dfrac{7u}{5}} = \dfrac{1}{7}$

$r_{\min} = d\sin\phi = 10\sqrt{2}\left(\dfrac{1}{5\sqrt{2}}\right) = 2\text{ m}$

34. $\dfrac{80}{v-u} + \dfrac{80}{v+u}$ = Time taken by soldier to run from the end to its front and then back to the end

$\dfrac{150}{u}$ = Time taken by the troop

$\dfrac{80}{v-u} + \dfrac{80}{v+u} = \dfrac{150}{u}$

$\Rightarrow\quad 15v^2 - 16vu - 15u^2 = 0$

$\Rightarrow\quad (5v+3u)(3v-5u) = 0 \ \Rightarrow\ 3v - 5u = 0$

$\Rightarrow\quad v = \dfrac{5u}{3} \ \Rightarrow\ \dfrac{v}{u} = \dfrac{5}{3}$

Distance covered by soldier $= v\left(\dfrac{150}{u}\right) = \dfrac{5}{3}(150) = 250\text{m}$

35.

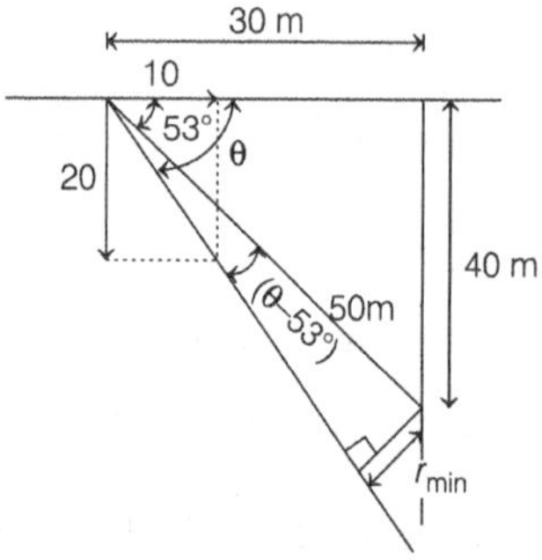

$\mathbf{v}_1 = 10\hat{\mathbf{i}},\quad \mathbf{v}_2 = 20\hat{\mathbf{j}}$

$\mathbf{v}_{12} = 10\hat{\mathbf{i}} - 20\hat{\mathbf{j}}$

$\tan\theta = \dfrac{20}{10} = 2$

$r_{\min} = 50\sin(\theta - 53°)$

$= 50\left[\sin\theta\left(\dfrac{3}{5}\right) - \cos\theta\left(\dfrac{4}{5}\right)\right]$

$= 10\left[3\left(\dfrac{2}{\sqrt{5}}\right) - \dfrac{4}{\sqrt{5}}\right] = \dfrac{20}{\sqrt{5}} = 4\sqrt{5}\text{ m}$

36. Horizontal component of velocity of ball with respect to train will keep decreasing. So, graph *A* is not possible

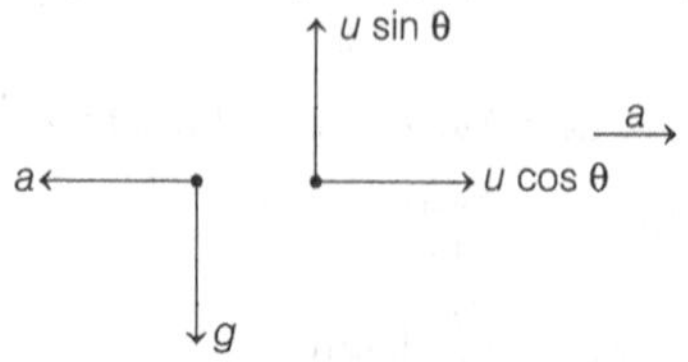

$v_x = u\cos\theta - at \ \Rightarrow\ v_y = u\sin\theta - gt$

37. At $t = 0, u_A = 30\,m/s, \quad u_B = 30\,m/s$

$$a_A = 0, \quad a_B = 3\,m/s^2$$

and separation $= 3\,m$

At $t = 1\,s, u_A = 30\,m/s, \quad u_B = 30 - 3(1) = 27\,m/s$

$$s_{rel} = u_{rel}\,t + \frac{1}{2}a_{rel}\,t^2$$

$$\Rightarrow \quad s_{rel} = 0 + \frac{1}{2}(-3)(1)^2 = 1.5\,m$$

So, separation at $t = 1$ is 1.5 m.

After $t = 1$,

$$u_A = 30\,m/s, \quad u_B = 27\,m/s$$

$$a_A = -a, \quad a_B = -3\,m/s^2$$

$$v_{rel}^2 = u_{rel}^2 + 2a_{rel}\,s_{rel}$$

$$\Rightarrow \quad 0^2 = (30 - 27)^2 + 2[-a - (-3)](1.5)$$

$$\Rightarrow \quad a = 6\,m/s^2$$

38. $u_A = 20$ m/s, $a_A = -8$ m/s^2

Lets say time taken by the bolt to hit the floor of lift A is t.

$$s_{bolt,\,A} = u_{bolt,\,A}t + \frac{1}{2}a_{bolt,\,A}t^2$$

$$\Rightarrow \quad -16 = 0 + \frac{1}{2}[-10 - (-8)]t^2$$

$$\Rightarrow \quad t = 4\,s$$

$$s_{AB} = U_{AB}t + \frac{1}{2}a_{AB}t^2$$

$$= (20 - (-10))4 + \frac{1}{2}(-8 - 2)(4)^2 = 40m$$

$$u_{bolt,\,B} = 20 - (-10) = 30\text{ m/s}$$

$$a_{bolt,\,B} = -10 - 2 = -12\text{ m/s}^2$$

$$H_{max} = \frac{u_{bolt,\,B}^2}{2a_{bolt,\,B}} = \frac{30^2}{2(12)} = 37.5\text{ m}$$

Distance travelled by the bolt as observed by a person in lift $B = 75 + 16 - 40 = 51$ m.

Multiple Choice(s) Correct Questions

1. (a) Since, their relative acceleration is zero, their relative velocity will be constant till one hits the ground.

(b) Both will hit the ground with the same speed.

(c) Second stone is thrown when the first stone is at its highest point.

(d) Since, they hit the ground with same speed, in case of elastic collisions they will rebound to the same height.

2. (a, c, d)

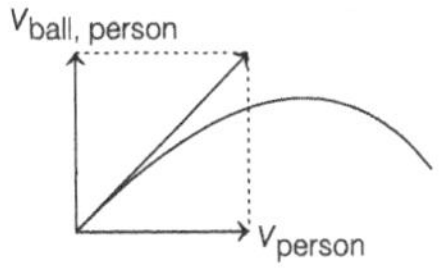

3. $t_1 = \frac{2u_{rel}}{g + a} \quad \Rightarrow \quad g + a = \frac{2u_{rel}}{t_1}$ ...(i)

$t_2 = \frac{2u_{rel}}{g - a} \quad \Rightarrow \quad g - a = \frac{2u_{rel}}{t_2}$ ...(ii)

Solving Eqs. (i) and (ii), we get

$$u_{rel} = \frac{gt_1t_2}{t_1 + t_2} \quad \text{and} \quad a = \frac{g(t_2 - t_1)}{t_1 + t_2}$$

4. They will always lie on a regular octagon but side of octagon will keep decreasing. Velocity of approach of two adjacent particle is $v - v\cos\left(\frac{2\pi}{8}\right)$

$$v_{app} = v\left(1 - \frac{1}{\sqrt{2}}\right)$$

Finally all will meet at the centroid,

$$t = \frac{a}{v_{app}} = \frac{10}{1 - \frac{1}{\sqrt{2}}} = \frac{10\sqrt{2}}{\sqrt{2} - 1}\,s$$

5.

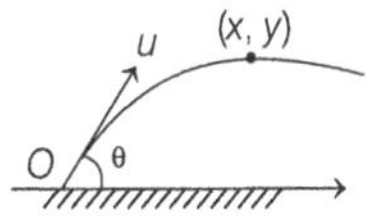

$x = (u\cos\theta)t$ ...(i)

$y = u\sin\theta\,t - \frac{1}{2}gt^2$ ...(ii)

From Eqs. (i) and (ii), we get

$$x^2 + \left(y + \frac{1}{2}gt^2\right)^2 = u^2t^2$$

Coordinates of centre of circle $= \left(0, -\frac{1}{2}gt^2\right)$

r = radius of circle $= ut$

$$y_C = -\frac{1}{2}gt^2, \quad \frac{dy_C}{dt} = -gt \quad \Rightarrow \quad \frac{d^2y_C}{dt^2} = -g$$

So, centre is vertically below O and it falls with acceleration g

$$h = (u\sin\theta)t - \frac{1}{2}gt^2$$

$$\Rightarrow t^2 - \left(\frac{2u\sin\theta}{g}\right)t + \frac{2h}{g} = 0 \begin{cases} t_1 \\ t_2 \end{cases} \quad \Rightarrow \quad t_1t_2 = \frac{2h}{g}$$

6.

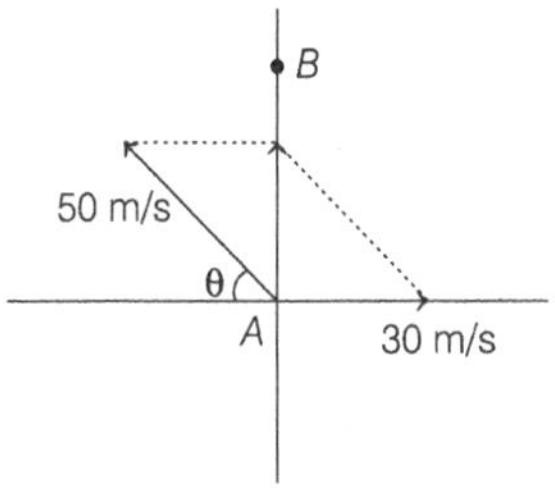

$$50\cos\theta = 30 \quad \Rightarrow \quad \theta = 53° \text{ North of West}$$

$$\text{Time taken} = \frac{720}{50\sin\theta \times \frac{18}{5}} = 5\text{ h}$$

7.

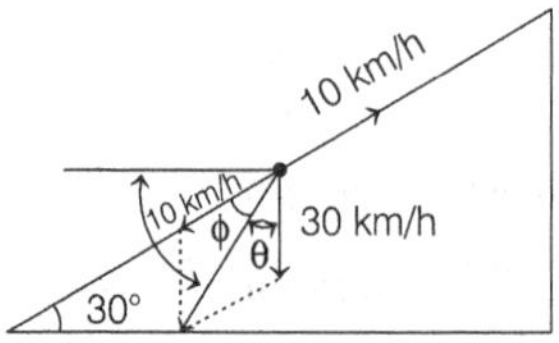

$\mathbf{v}_{RM} = \mathbf{v}_R - \mathbf{v}_M = \mathbf{v}_R + (-\mathbf{v}_M)$

$$\tan\phi = \frac{30\sin 60°}{10 + 30\cos 60°} \Rightarrow \phi = \tan^{-1}\left(\frac{3\sqrt{3}}{5}\right) \text{ with vertical}$$

$$\tan\theta = \frac{10\cos 30°}{30 + 10\sin 30°}$$

$$\theta = \tan^{-1}\left(\frac{\sqrt{3}}{7}\right) \text{ with vertical}$$

8. For them to collide

$160\sin 30° = 100\sin\theta$

$$\Rightarrow \quad \sin\theta = \frac{4}{5}$$

$$T = \frac{2u\sin\theta}{g} = \frac{2(100)\left(\frac{4}{5}\right)}{10} = 16 \text{ s}$$

$x < (160\cos 30° - 100\cos\theta)16$

$x < (1280\sqrt{3} - 960)$ m

9. $\mathbf{v}_{AB} = 2\hat{\mathbf{j}} - 2\hat{\mathbf{i}} = -2\hat{\mathbf{i}} + 2\hat{\mathbf{j}}$

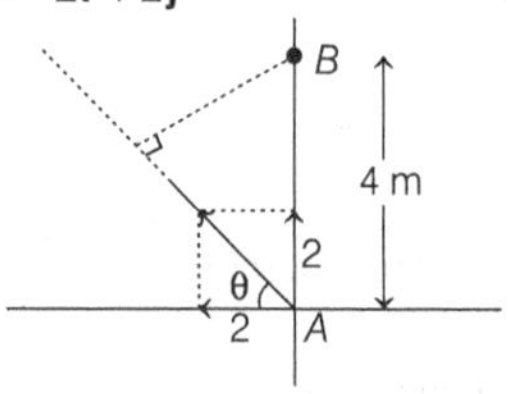

$\tan\theta = 1, \quad r_{min} = 4\cos\theta = 2\sqrt{2}$ m

$$t = \frac{4\sin\theta}{2\sqrt{2}} = 1 \text{ s}$$

10. $\mathbf{v}_M = (1 + 5\cos\theta)\hat{\mathbf{i}} + 5\sin\theta\,\hat{\mathbf{j}}$

$$\text{Drift} = (1 + 5\cos\theta)\frac{0.4}{5\sin\theta} = 0.4$$

$\Rightarrow 5(\sin\theta - \cos\theta) = 1 \Rightarrow \theta = 53°$

$$\text{Time} = \frac{0.4}{5\left(\frac{4}{5}\right)} = 0.1 \text{ h} = 6 \text{ min}$$

11. $\tan 30° = \frac{v_M}{v_R} \Rightarrow v_R = 10\sqrt{3}$ m/s, if the rain is falling vertically.

12. For A, $t = \frac{d}{v_{MR}} \Rightarrow 120 = \frac{10}{v_{MR}} \Rightarrow v_{MR} = \frac{1}{12}$ m/s

$\text{Drift} = v_R t \Rightarrow 30 = v_R(120) \Rightarrow v_R = \frac{1}{4}$ m/s

For B,

Along Y-axis, $s_y = u_y t + \frac{1}{2}a_y t^2$

$$\Rightarrow \quad 10 = u_y(120) \Rightarrow u_y = \frac{1}{12} \text{ m/s}$$

Along X-axis, $s_x = u_x t + \frac{1}{2}a_x t^2$

$$\Rightarrow \quad 25 = u_x(120) \Rightarrow u_x = \frac{5}{24} \text{ m/s}$$

Comprehension Based Questions

1, 2 and 3.

For *A*

$\mathbf{v}_{MR} = 5\cos 37°\,\hat{\mathbf{i}} + 5\sin 37°\,\hat{\mathbf{j}} = 4\hat{\mathbf{i}} + 3\hat{\mathbf{j}}$

$\mathbf{v}_R = 2\hat{\mathbf{i}}, \quad \mathbf{v}_M = \mathbf{v}_{MR} + \mathbf{v}_R = 6\hat{\mathbf{i}} + 3\hat{\mathbf{j}}$

Time taken by A to cross the river $= \frac{0.1}{3}$ h

$$\text{Drift} = 6\left(\frac{0.1}{3}\right) = 0.2 \text{ km}$$

$$\text{Time taken to walk to reach } C = \frac{0.3 - 0.2}{8} = \frac{1}{80} \text{ h}$$

$$\text{Total time} = \left(\frac{1}{30} + \frac{1}{80}\right) \text{h} = 165 \text{ s}$$

For *B*

$\mathbf{v}_{MR} = 5\cos 127°\,\hat{\mathbf{i}} + 5\sin 127°\,\hat{\mathbf{j}}$

$\mathbf{v}_M = \mathbf{v}_{MR} + \mathbf{v}_R = -\hat{\mathbf{i}} + 4\hat{\mathbf{j}}$

$$\text{Total time taken by } B = \frac{0.1}{4} + \frac{0.125 - 1\left(\frac{0.1}{4}\right)}{6} = \frac{1}{24} \text{ h} = 150 \text{ s}$$

$|\mathbf{v}_B| = \sqrt{1^2 + 4^2} = \sqrt{17}$ km/h

4.

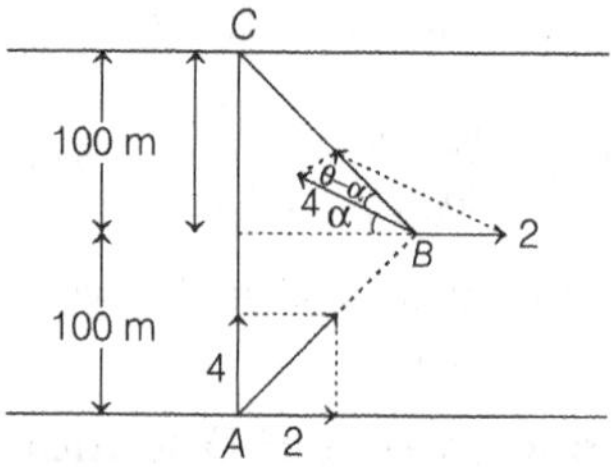

$$\tan\theta = \frac{100}{50} \Rightarrow \tan\theta = 2$$

$4\sin(\theta - \alpha) = 2\sin\theta$

$$\Rightarrow 4\left(\frac{2}{\sqrt{5}}\cos\alpha - \frac{1}{\sqrt{5}}\sin\alpha\right) = 2\left(\frac{2}{\sqrt{5}}\right)$$

$\Rightarrow 2\cos\alpha - \sin\alpha = 1 \Rightarrow (2\cos\alpha)^2 = (1 + \sin\alpha)^2$

$\Rightarrow 4(1 - \sin^2\alpha) = 1 + \sin^2\alpha + 2\sin\alpha$

$$\Rightarrow \quad \sin\alpha = \frac{3}{5} \quad \Rightarrow \quad \alpha = 37° \text{ with upstream}$$

5. $T_1 = \frac{200}{4} = 50 \text{ s} \Rightarrow T_2 = \frac{100}{4} + \frac{100}{4\sin\alpha} = 25 + \frac{125}{3} = \frac{200}{3}$ s

6. With respect to trolley the ball will appear to be coming at an angle of 45° with X-axis.

7. $$\phi = \frac{4\theta}{3} = \frac{4}{3}(45°) = 60°$$

$$\mathbf{v}_{ball} = v\cos 60°\,\hat{\mathbf{i}} + v\sin 60°\,\hat{\mathbf{j}}$$

$$\mathbf{v}_{trolley} = (\sqrt{3}-1)\hat{\mathbf{j}}$$

$$\mathbf{v}_{ball,\ trolley} = v\cos 60°\,\hat{\mathbf{i}} + (v\sin 60° - \sqrt{3}+1)\,\hat{\mathbf{j}}$$

$$\tan 45° = \frac{v\sin 60° - \sqrt{3}+1}{v\cos 60°}$$

$$\Rightarrow \quad \frac{v}{2} = \frac{\sqrt{3}v}{2} - \sqrt{3}+1 \quad \Rightarrow \quad \frac{\sqrt{3}v}{2} - \frac{v}{2} = \sqrt{3}-1 \quad \Rightarrow v = 2$$

m/s

8. $\mathbf{v}_M = v_M\hat{\mathbf{i}}$

$$\mathbf{v}_R = 10\sqrt{2}\cos 45°\,\hat{\mathbf{i}} + 10\sqrt{2}\sin 45°\,\hat{\mathbf{j}} = 10\,\hat{\mathbf{i}} + 10\,\hat{\mathbf{j}}$$

$$\mathbf{v}_{RM} = (10 - v_M)\,\hat{\mathbf{i}} + 10\,\hat{\mathbf{j}}$$

$$10 - v_M = 0 \quad \Rightarrow \quad v_M = 10 \text{ m/s}$$

9. $\mathbf{v}_{RM} = \sqrt{3}\,(10\,\hat{\mathbf{j}}) = 10\sqrt{3}\,\hat{\mathbf{j}}$

$$\mathbf{v}_R = 10\,\hat{\mathbf{i}} + 10\sqrt{3}\,\hat{\mathbf{j}}$$

$$|\mathbf{v}_R| = \sqrt{10^2 + (10\sqrt{3})^2} = 20 \text{ m/s}$$

10. Initial angle $= \tan^{-1}\left(\frac{10}{10}\right) = 45°$

Final angle $= \tan^{-1}\left(\frac{10\sqrt{3}}{10}\right) = 60°$

Change in angle $= 60° - 45° = 15°$

Match the Columns Questions

1. $\mathbf{v}_A = \mathbf{u}_A + \mathbf{a}_A t = (8-2t)\hat{\mathbf{i}}$

$\mathbf{v}_B = \mathbf{u}_B + \mathbf{a}_B t = (8-2t)\,\hat{\mathbf{j}}$

(A) $\mathbf{v}_{AB} = \mathbf{v}_A - \mathbf{v}_B = (8-2t)\hat{\mathbf{i}} - (8-2t)\hat{\mathbf{j}} = 0$

$\Rightarrow 8 - 2t = 0 \quad \Rightarrow \quad t = 4\text{ s}$

(B) $\mathbf{s}_{AB} = (8t - t^2)\,\hat{\mathbf{i}} - (8t - t^2)\,\hat{\mathbf{j}}$

At $t = 4$, $\mathbf{s}_{AB} = 16\,\hat{\mathbf{i}} - 16\hat{\mathbf{j}} \quad \Rightarrow \quad |\mathbf{s}_{AB}| = 16\sqrt{2}$ m

(C) $\mathbf{s}_A = \mathbf{s}_B$

$$(8t - t^2)\,\hat{\mathbf{i}} = (8t - t^2)\,\hat{\mathbf{j}}$$

$\Rightarrow \; 8t - t^2 = 0 \quad \Rightarrow \quad t(8-t) = 0 \quad \Rightarrow \quad t = 8\text{ s}$

(D) $\mathbf{v}_{AB} = (8 - 2(8))\,\hat{\mathbf{i}} - (8 - 2(8))\hat{\mathbf{j}} = -8\hat{\mathbf{i}} + 8\hat{\mathbf{j}}$

$|\mathbf{v}_{AB}| = 8\sqrt{2}$ m/s

2. (A) $\mathbf{v}_M = (4 + 5\cos\theta)\,\hat{\mathbf{i}} + 5\sin\theta\,\hat{\mathbf{j}}$

$$4 + 5\cos\theta = 0 \quad \Rightarrow \quad \theta = \cos^{-1}\left(-\frac{4}{5}\right) = 143°$$

(B) $T = \dfrac{d}{v_{MR}\sin\theta}$

For T to be minimum $\theta = 90°$

(C) $\tan\theta = \dfrac{v_{MR}}{v_R} = \dfrac{4}{3} \quad \Rightarrow \quad \theta = 53°$

(D) $\mathbf{v}_{wind} = -3\sqrt{2}\cos 45°\,\hat{\mathbf{i}} - 3\sqrt{2}\sin 45°\,\hat{\mathbf{j}} = -3\hat{\mathbf{i}} - 3\hat{\mathbf{j}}$

$$\mathbf{v}_{flag} = -7\hat{\mathbf{i}}$$

$$\mathbf{v}_{wind,\ flag} = (-3\hat{\mathbf{i}} - 3\hat{\mathbf{j}}) - (-7\hat{\mathbf{i}}) = 4\hat{\mathbf{i}} - 3\hat{\mathbf{j}}$$

$= 5$ m/s, 37° South of East

3. $\mathbf{u}_A = 10\cos 37°\,\hat{\mathbf{i}} + 10\sin 37°\,\hat{\mathbf{j}} = 8\hat{\mathbf{i}} + 6\hat{\mathbf{j}}$

$\mathbf{u}_B = -20\cos 53°\,\hat{\mathbf{i}} + 20\sin 53°\,\hat{\mathbf{j}} = -12\hat{\mathbf{i}} + 16\hat{\mathbf{j}}$

$\mathbf{u}_{AB} = \mathbf{u}_A - \mathbf{u}_B = 20\,\hat{\mathbf{i}} - 10\hat{\mathbf{j}}$

$\tan\alpha = \frac{5}{20} = \frac{1}{4}$

$\tan\beta = \frac{10}{20} = \frac{1}{2}$

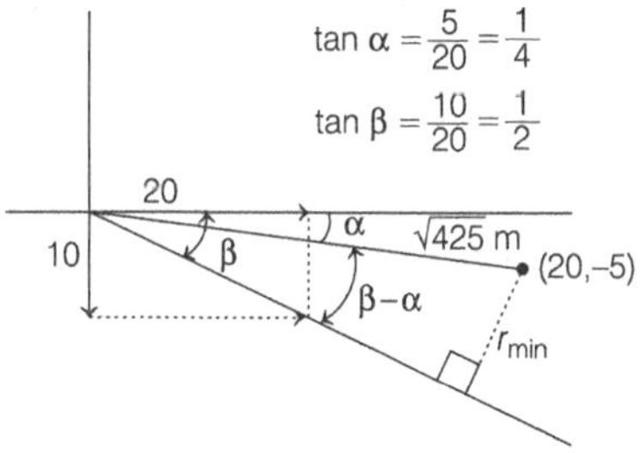

(A) $r_{min} = \sqrt{425}\sin(\beta - \alpha) = \sqrt{425}\,(\sin\beta\cos\alpha - \cos\beta\sin\alpha)$

$$= \sqrt{425}\left(\frac{1}{\sqrt{5}}\frac{4}{\sqrt{17}} - \frac{2}{\sqrt{5}}\frac{1}{\sqrt{17}}\right)$$

$$= \frac{\sqrt{425}\times 2}{\sqrt{85}} = 2\sqrt{5}\text{ m}$$

(B) Time taken $= \sqrt{\dfrac{425}{500}}$

(C) $\mathbf{v}_A = 8\hat{\mathbf{i}} + (6 - 11t)\hat{\mathbf{j}},\; \mathbf{v}_B = -12\hat{\mathbf{i}} + (6 - 11t)\,\hat{\mathbf{j}}$

$$\mathbf{v}_A \cdot \mathbf{v}_B = 0$$

$$\Rightarrow \quad -96 + (6 - 11t)(16 - 11t) = 0$$

$$\Rightarrow \quad -96 + 96 - 242t + 121t^2 = 0$$

$$\Rightarrow \quad 121t(t-2) = 0 \quad \Rightarrow \quad t = 0 \text{ and } t = 2$$

(D) At the time of minimum separation

$$\mathbf{v}_{AB} \cdot \mathbf{r}_{AB} = 0$$

4. $\mathbf{v}_{particle,\ platform} = v_2\hat{\mathbf{i}} + 25\,\hat{\mathbf{j}} + v_1\hat{\mathbf{k}}$

$\mathbf{a}_{particle,\ platform} = -2\hat{\mathbf{i}} - 12.5\hat{\mathbf{j}}$

Time $= \dfrac{2\times 25}{12.5} = 4$ s

$$8 \le v_2 \times 4 - \frac{1}{2}\times 2\times 4^2 \le 16$$

$$\Rightarrow \quad 6 \le v_2 \le 8$$

$$16 \le v_1 \times 4 \le 24 \quad \Rightarrow \quad 4 \le v_1 \le 6$$

$$Y = 25\times 4 - \frac{1}{2}\times 10\times 4^2 = 100 - 80 = 20\text{ m}$$

Numerical Value Questions

1. $\mathbf{v}_{RM} = \mathbf{v}_R + (-\mathbf{v}_M)$

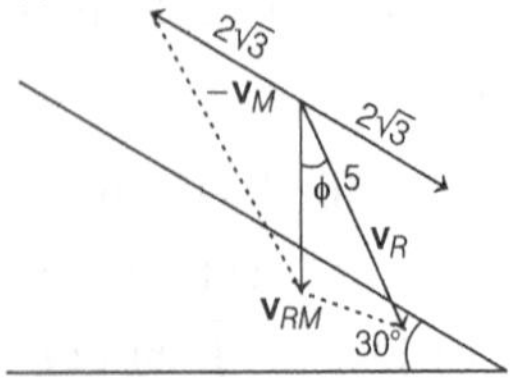

Since, $\mathbf{v}_{RM}$ is vertical, horizontal components of $\mathbf{v}_R$ and $-\mathbf{v}_M$ will cancel out each other.

So, $5\sin\phi = 2\sqrt{3}\cos 30° \Rightarrow \sin\phi = \dfrac{3}{5} \Rightarrow \phi = 37°$

2. $\mathbf{v}_{RM} = 5\cos 127°\,\hat{\mathbf{i}} + 5\sin 127°\,\hat{\mathbf{j}} = -3\hat{\mathbf{i}} + 4\hat{\mathbf{j}}$

$\mathbf{v}_R = 4\hat{\mathbf{i}}$

$\Rightarrow \mathbf{v}_M = \mathbf{v}_{MR} + \mathbf{v}_R = \hat{\mathbf{i}} + 4\hat{\mathbf{j}}$

Time taken to cross the river $= \dfrac{0.2}{4} \times 60 = 3$ min

Drift $= 1\left(\dfrac{0.2}{4}\right) = \dfrac{1}{20}$ km

Walking time $= \dfrac{1/20}{3} = \dfrac{1}{60}$ h $= 1$ min

Total time $= 3 + 1 = 4$ min

3. $5 = \dfrac{60}{\sqrt{v_{MR}^2 - 5^2}} \Rightarrow v_{MR} = 13$ m/s

4. $s_{rel} = u_{rel}t + \dfrac{1}{2}a_{rel}t^2 \Rightarrow -1 = 3t + \dfrac{1}{2}(-8)t^2$

$\Rightarrow 4t^2 - 3t - 1 = 0 \Rightarrow t = 1$ s

5. $\mathbf{u}_P = 10\cos 45°\,\hat{\mathbf{i}} + 10\sin 45°\,\hat{\mathbf{j}}$

$\mathbf{u}_Q = -70\cos 45°\,\hat{\mathbf{i}} + 70\sin 45°\,\hat{\mathbf{j}}$

$\mathbf{u}_{PQ} = \mathbf{u}_P - \mathbf{u}_Q = 80\cos 45°\,\hat{\mathbf{i}} - 60\sin 45°\,\hat{\mathbf{j}}$

$= 40\sqrt{2}\,\hat{\mathbf{i}} - 30\sqrt{2}\,\hat{\mathbf{j}}$

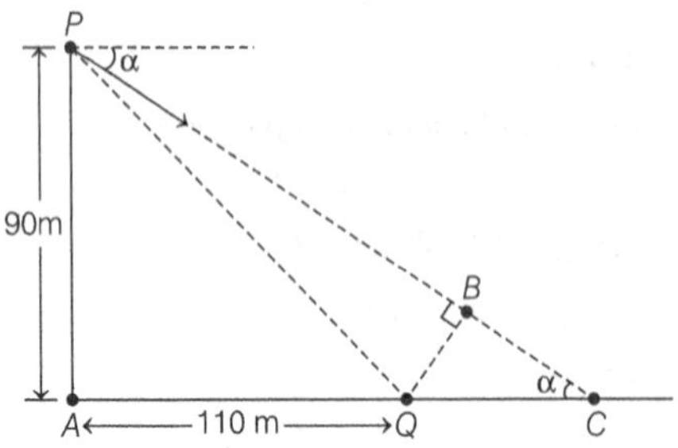

$\tan\alpha = \dfrac{30\sqrt{2}}{40\sqrt{2}} = \dfrac{3}{4} \Rightarrow \alpha = 37°$

Also, $\tan\alpha = \dfrac{AP}{AC} \Rightarrow \dfrac{3}{4} = \dfrac{90}{AC}$

$\Rightarrow AC = 120$ m

$QC = AC - AQ = 120 - 110 = 10$ m

$r_{min} = QB = QC\sin\alpha = 10\sin 37° = 6$ m

6.

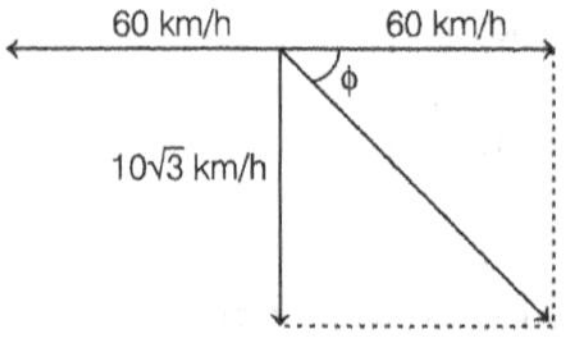

$\tan\phi = \dfrac{10\sqrt{3}}{60}$

$\Rightarrow \tan\phi = \dfrac{\sqrt{3}}{6}$ ...(i)

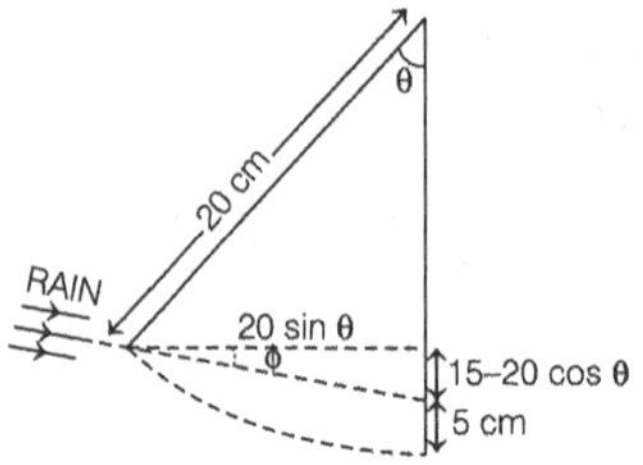

$\tan\phi = \dfrac{15 - 20\cos\theta}{20\sin\theta}$ ...(ii)

Solving Eqs. (i) and (ii), we get

$\theta = 60°$

7. $\mathbf{v}_A = 20\,\hat{\mathbf{i}}, \quad \mathbf{v}_B = 15\,\hat{\mathbf{j}}$

$\Rightarrow \mathbf{v}_{AB} = \mathbf{v}_A - \mathbf{v}_B = 20\,\hat{\mathbf{i}} - 15\,\hat{\mathbf{j}}$

$\tan\theta = \dfrac{15}{20} = \dfrac{3}{4}$

$\tan\alpha = \dfrac{4}{5}$

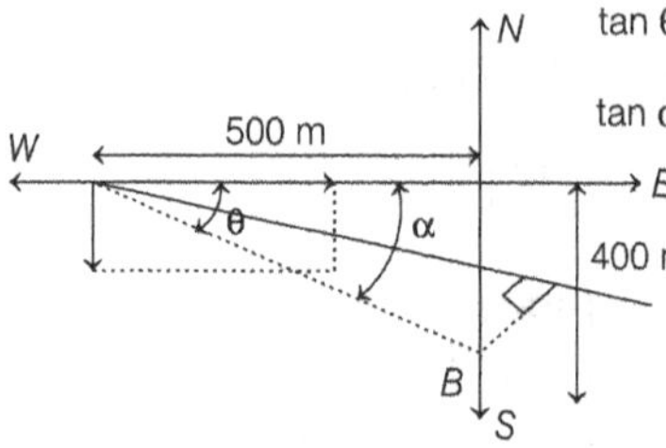

$r_{min} = \sqrt{500^2 + 400^2}\,\sin(\alpha - \theta)$

$= 100\sqrt{41}\left(\dfrac{4}{\sqrt{41}} \times \dfrac{4}{5} - \dfrac{5}{\sqrt{41}} \times \dfrac{3}{5}\right) = 20$ m

8. $\dfrac{1}{2} + \dfrac{1 + \dfrac{v-u}{2}}{v+u} = \dfrac{1}{u} \Rightarrow u = 1$ km/h

9. $\dfrac{dx}{dt} = v\cos\theta$

$\int_0^{uT} dx = v\int_0^T \cos\theta\, dt$

$\Rightarrow \int \cos\theta\, dt = \dfrac{uT}{v}$

$-\dfrac{dr}{dt} = v - u\cos\theta$

$\Rightarrow -\int_l^0 dr = \int_0^T (v - u\cos\theta)\, dt$

$\Rightarrow l = vT - \int_0^T u\cos\theta\, dt \Rightarrow l = vT - u\left(\dfrac{uT}{v}\right)$

$\Rightarrow T = \dfrac{lv}{v^2 - u^2} = \dfrac{16 \times 5}{5^2 - 3^2} = 5$ s

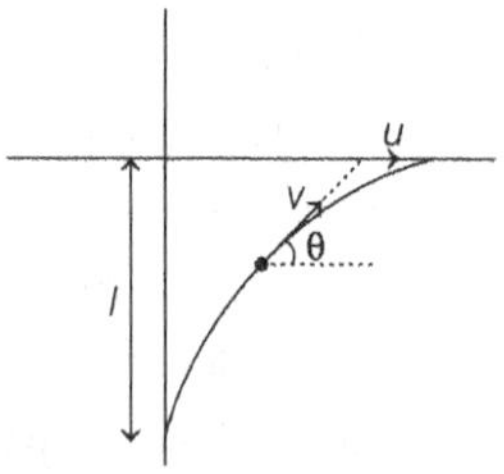

10. $T = \dfrac{100}{5} = 20$ s

$v_R = ky$

$\Rightarrow 2 = k(50) \Rightarrow k = \dfrac{1}{25}$

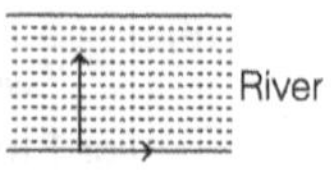

$$v_R = \frac{y}{25} = \frac{5t}{25}$$

$$\Rightarrow \quad v_R = \frac{t}{5} \quad \Rightarrow \quad \frac{dx}{dt} = \frac{t}{5} \quad \Rightarrow \quad \int dx = \int_0^{10} \frac{t}{5}\,dt \quad \Rightarrow \quad x = 10\text{ m}$$

So, drift in 20 s will be 20 m.

11. $\mathbf{v}_{boat} = \mathbf{v}_b \cos 60° \hat{\mathbf{i}} + \mathbf{v}_b \sin 60° \hat{\mathbf{j}}$

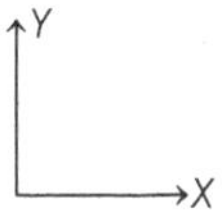

$$\mathbf{v}_{wind} = 5\sqrt{3}\,\hat{\mathbf{j}}$$

$$\mathbf{v}_{wind,\ flag} = \mathbf{v}_{wind,\ boat} = \mathbf{v}_{wind} - \mathbf{v}_{boat}$$

$$= 5\sqrt{3}\,\hat{\mathbf{j}} - (v_b \cos 60° \hat{\mathbf{i}} + v_b \sin 60° \hat{\mathbf{j}})$$

$$= -\frac{v_b}{2}\hat{\mathbf{i}} + \left(5\sqrt{3} - \frac{\sqrt{3}}{2}v_b\right)\hat{\mathbf{j}}$$

$$\tan 60° = \frac{5\sqrt{3} - \frac{\sqrt{3}}{2}v_b}{\frac{v_b}{2}} \quad \Rightarrow \quad \frac{\sqrt{3}v_b}{2} = 5\sqrt{3} - \frac{\sqrt{3}}{2}v_b$$

$$\Rightarrow \quad v_b = 5\text{ m/s}$$

12. $\mathbf{v}_{bullet} = v_1\hat{\mathbf{i}} + v_2\hat{\mathbf{j}}$ and $\mathbf{v}_{car} = 20\hat{\mathbf{i}}$

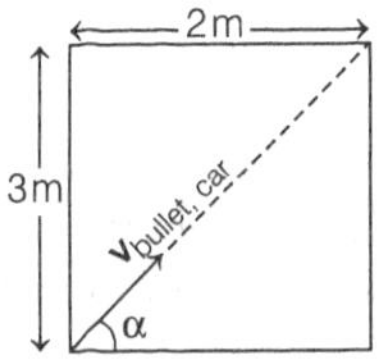

$$\tan\theta = \frac{1}{2} = \frac{v_2}{v_1} \quad \Rightarrow \quad v_1 = 2v_2$$

$$\mathbf{v}_{bullet,\ car} = \mathbf{v}_{bullet} - \mathbf{v}_{car} = (v_1 - 20)\,\hat{\mathbf{i}} + v_2\hat{\mathbf{j}}$$

Also, $\tan\alpha = \frac{3}{2} = \frac{v_2}{v_1 - 20} \quad \Rightarrow \quad v_2 = 15\text{ m/s}$

Time taken $= \frac{s_y}{u_y} = \frac{3}{15} = \frac{1}{5} = 0.2\text{ s}$

Previous Year's Questions

JEE Main

1. $v_A = 90\text{ km/hr} = \frac{90 \times 5}{18} = 25\text{ m/s}$

$$v_B = 54\text{ km/hr} = \frac{54 \times 5}{18} = 15\text{ m/s}$$

$v_{BA} = v_B - v_A = 15 - (-25)$ (Move opposite to each other)

$= 15 + 25 = 40\text{ m/s}$

$$\text{Time of crossing} = \frac{\text{Length of train}}{\text{Relative velocity}}$$

$$8 = \frac{l}{40} \quad \Rightarrow \quad l = 8 \times 40 = 320 \quad \Rightarrow \quad l = 320\text{ m}$$

2. Velocity of train A,

$$v_A = 108\text{ km/h} = 180 \times \frac{5}{18}\text{ m/s} = 30\text{ m/s}$$

Velocity of train B,

$$v_B = 72\text{ km/h} = 72 \times \frac{5}{18} = 20\text{ m/s}$$

According to given situation,

time taken to cross the tunnel by train B – time taken to cross the tunnel by train A = 35 s

$$\Rightarrow \quad \frac{L + 4l}{20} - \frac{L + l}{30} = 35$$

$$\Rightarrow \quad \frac{60l + 4l}{20} - \frac{60l + l}{30} = 35 \qquad (\because L = 60l)$$

$$\Rightarrow \quad \frac{180l + 12l - 120l - 2l}{60} = 35 \quad \Rightarrow \quad l = 30\text{ m}$$

$\therefore$ Length of the tunnel, $L = 60l = 60 \times 30 = 1800\text{ m}$

3. Given that, Speed of swimmer, $v_{MR} = 4\text{km/h}$

Width of river, $w = 1\text{ km}$

Drift in downstream, $x = 750\text{ m}$ or 0.75 km

Swimmer makes his strokes normal to the flow of river and due to addition of river velocity to swimmer, man has drift.

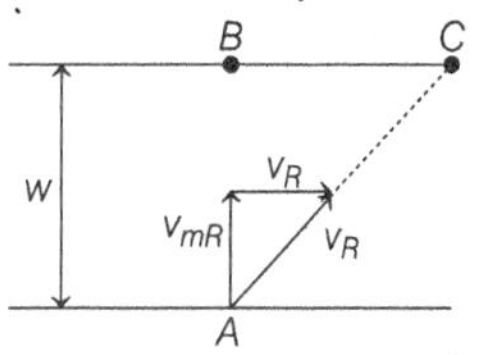

$$\text{Time of crossing,} \quad t = \frac{w}{v_{MR}} \quad \Rightarrow \quad t = \frac{1}{4}\text{ h}$$

Drift, $x = v_R \times t$

or $\quad v_R = \frac{x}{t} = \frac{0.75}{1/4} = 3\text{ km/h}$

JEE Advanced

1. Relative velocity of B with respect to A is perpendicular to line PA. Therefore, along line PA, velocity components of A and B should be same.

AP and BM are parallel and AB is perpendicular to both

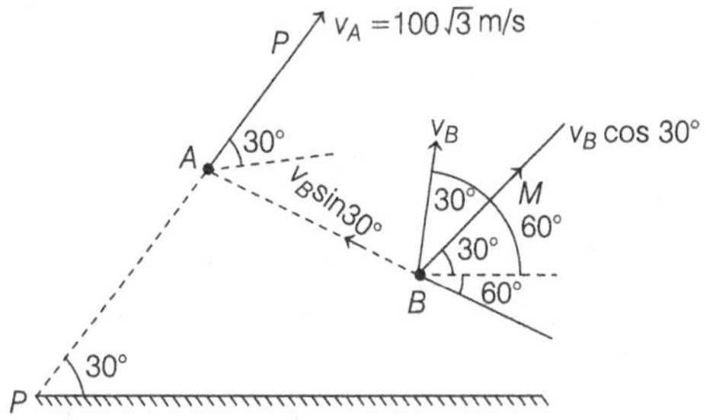

$$\Rightarrow \quad v_A = 100\sqrt{3} = v_B \cos 30°$$

$$\Rightarrow \quad v_B = 200\text{ m/s}$$

$$t_0 = \frac{500}{v_B \sin 30°} = \frac{500}{200 \times 1/2} = 5\text{ s}$$

2. Question was wrong as the ball moving with 0.3 m/s will collide with the left wall of the rocket before two balls collide.

CHAPTER~08

KINEMATICS WITH CALCULUS

LEVEL 01 Starter Level

1 The displacement of a particle is given by $y = a + bt + ct^2 - dt^4$. Find the initial velocity and acceleration.

2 Displacement for any particle is $s = (3t^3 + 7t^2 + 14t + 8)$ m. Find its acceleration at time $t = 1$ s.

3 A particle moves along a straight line such that its displacement at any time t is given by $s = (t^3 - 6t^2 + 3t + 4)$ m. Find the velocity when the acceleration is zero.

4 A particle starts moving such that displacement with respect to origin O varies with time t as $s = t^2(t-1)$. Find

(a) velocity and acceleration when the particle is passing through origin,

(b) displacement when the particle is momentarily at rest and

(c) velocity when net force acting on the particle is zero.

5 Velocity of a particle is given by the equation $v = 2t^2 + 5$ cm/s. Find

(a) average acceleration during the time interval $t_1 = 2$ s and $t_2 = 4$ s and

(b) instantaneous acceleration at $t_2 = 4$ s.

6 The displacement of a particle moving in a straight line is given by $x = (16t - 2t^2)$ m. Find out

(a) displacement and distance travelled in first 2 s and

(b) displacement and distance travelled in first 6 s.

7 Velocity v of a particle moving along X-axis varies as $v = \sqrt{(8x - 5)}$ m/s. Find acceleration of the particle.

8 The motion of a particle is described by the equation $u = at$. Find the distance travelled by the particle in the first 4 s.

9 The acceleration of a particle is increasing linearly with time t as bt. The particle starts from the origin with an initial velocity v_0. Find the distance travelled by the particle in time t.

10 The acceleration of the particle moving in straight line is given by $a = 4t - 30$, where a is in m/s^2 and t is in second. Determine the position as function of time. The initial position at $t = 0$ is $s_0 = -5$ m and the initial velocity is $v_0 = 3$ m/s.

11 The instantaneous velocity of a particle varies with position x as $v = 2x + 7$. Assuming that particle was at origin at $t = 0$, find the relation between x and t.

12 For a particle moving along $+X$-axis, acceleration is given as $a = 6x + 5$. Find the velocity as a function of position? Given that, initially particle is at origin and moving with velocity 2 m/s.

13 For a particle moving along X-axis, acceleration is given as $a = v$. Find the position as a function of time. Given that, at $t = 0$, $x = 0$ and $v = 2$.

14 For a particle moving along X-axis, acceleration is given as $a = 2v^2$. If the speed of the particle is v_0 at $x = 0$, then find speed as a function of x.

15 A particle travels, so that its acceleration is given by $\mathbf{a} = 5\cos t\,\hat{\mathbf{i}} - 3\sin t\,\hat{\mathbf{j}}$. If the particle is located at $(-2, 5)$ at time $t = 0$ and is moving with a velocity given by $(-3\hat{\mathbf{i}} + 2\hat{\mathbf{j}})$. Find

(a) the velocity at time t and

(b) the position vector of the particle at time $(t > 0)$.

LEVEL 02 JEE Main Level

Single Choice Correct Questions

1 If the velocity of a particle is $(10 + 2t^2)$ m/s, then the average acceleration of the particle between 2s and 5 s is

(a) 2 m/s^2 (b) 4 m/s^2 (c) 12 m/s^2 (d) 14 m/s^2

2 The relation $3t = \sqrt{3x} + 6$ describes the displacement of a particle in one direction, where x is in metre and t in second. The displacement, when velocity is zero, is

(a) 25 m (b) 12 m (c) 5 m (d) zero

3 The displacement x of a particle varies with time t, $x = ae^{-\alpha t} + be^{\beta t}$, where a, b, α and β are positive constants. The velocity of the particle will

(a) go on decreasing with time
(b) be independent of α and β
(c) drop to zero when $\alpha = \beta$
(d) go on increasing with time

4 If the velocity of a particle is given by $v = (180 - 16x)^{1/2}$ m/s, then its acceleration will be

(a) 0.5 m/s^2 (b) 8 m/s^2
(c) -8 m/s^2 (d) 4 m/s^2

5 The velocity v of a moving particle varies with displacement as $x = \sqrt{v + 1}$, the acceleration of the particle at $x = 5$ unit will be

(a) $\sqrt{6}$ unit (b) 24 unit
(c) 240 unit (d) 25 unit

6 In the one-dimensional motion of a particle, the relation between position x and time t is given by $x^2 + 2x = t$. Choose the correct statement.

(a) The retardation of the particle is $\frac{1}{4(x+1)^3}$.

(b) The acceleration of the particle is $\frac{1}{(x+1)^3}$.

(c) The uniform velocity of the particle is $\frac{1}{(x+1)^3}$.

(d) The particle has an acceleration of $4t + 6$.

7 Position of a particle moving along X-axis is given by $x = 2 + 8t - 4t^2$. The distance travelled by the particle (in metre) from $t = 0$ to $t = 3$ is

(a) 10 (b) 8
(c) 12 (d) 20

8 The position x of a particle with respect to time t along X-axis is given by $x = 9t^2 - t^3$, where x is in metres and t in seconds. What will be the position of this particle when it achieves maximum speed along the $+x$-direction?

(a) 24 m (b) 32 m (c) 54 m (d) 81 m

9 A particle starts moving rectilinearly at time $t = 0$ such that its velocity v changes with time t according to the equation $v = t^2 - t$, where t is in seconds and v is in metre/second. The time interval for which the particle retards is

(a) $t < \frac{1}{2}$ (b) $\frac{1}{2} < t < 1$ (c) $t > 1$ (d) $t < \frac{1}{2}$ and $t > 1$

10 An object is moving along the X-axis with position as a function of time given by $x = x(t)$. Point O is at $x = 0$. The object is definitely moving towards O, when

(a) $\frac{dx}{dt} < 0$ (b) $\frac{dx}{dt} > 0$ (c) $\frac{d(x^2)}{dt} < 0$ (d) $\frac{d(x^2)}{dt} > 0$

11 The position vector of a particle is given as $\mathbf{r} = (t^2 - 4t + 6)\hat{\mathbf{i}} + (t^2)\hat{\mathbf{j}}$. The time after which the velocity vector and acceleration vector becomes perpendicular to each other is equal to

(a) 1 s (b) 2 s (c) 1.5 s (d) Not possible

12 The coordinates of a moving particle at a time t, are given by $x = 5\sin 10t$, $y = 5\cos 10t$. The acceleration of the particle (in m/s^2) is

(a) 5 (b) 50
(c) 500 (d) None of these

13 A particle moves in the xy-plane and its coordinates are given by $x = k \sin\omega t$ and $y = k(1 - \cos\omega t)$, where k and ω are constants. What is the magnitude of acceleration of the particle?

(a) Zero (b) $k\omega$ (c) $k\omega^2$ (d) $k^2\omega$

14 Starting from rest, the acceleration of a particle is $a = 2(t - 1)$. The velocity of the particle at $t = 5$s is

(a) 15 m/s (b) 25 m/s
(c) 5 m/s (d) None of these

15 The velocity of a particle is dependent on the time as $v = k(t - 1)$, where $k = 2 \text{ m/s}^2$. The distance covered in first 3 s will be

(a) 18 m (b) 5 m (c) 3 m (d) 6 m

16 A particle moving along X-axis has acceleration f, at time t, given by $f = f_0\left(1 - \frac{t}{T}\right)$, where f_0 and T are constants. The particle at $t = 0$ has zero velocity. Find the maximum velocity of the particle.

(a) $\frac{1}{2} f_0 T$ (b) $f_0 T$ (c) $\frac{1}{2} f_0 T^2$ (d) $f_0 T^2$

17 The acceleration of a particle starting from rest, varies with time according to the relation $A = -a\omega^2 \sin\omega t$. The displacement of this particle at a time t will be

(a) $-\frac{1}{2}(a\omega^2 \sin\omega t)t^2$ (b) $a\omega \sin\omega t$

(c) $a\omega \cos\omega t$ (d) $a \sin\omega t - a\omega t$

18 The velocity of a particle moving in the positive direction of the X-axis varies as $v = \alpha\sqrt{x}$, where α is a positive constant. Assuming that at the moment $t = 0$, the particle was located at the point $x = 0$, find the time dependence of velocity.

(a) $v = \frac{\alpha^2 t}{2}$ (b) $v = \alpha^2 t$ (c) $v = \frac{\alpha t}{2}$ (d) $v = \alpha t$

19 The velocity of a particle moving along positive X-axis varies as $v = \alpha\sqrt{x}$, where a is a constant. If particle is at $x = 0$ at $t = 0$, what will be the average velocity of particle during the time, it moves a distance s?

(a) $\frac{\alpha}{2}\sqrt{s}$ (b) $\frac{2}{\alpha}\sqrt{s}$ (c) $\alpha\sqrt{s}$ (d) $\frac{\sqrt{s}}{\alpha}$

20 A body starts from the origin and moves along the X-axis such that the velocity at any instant is given by $(4t^3 - 2t)$, where t is in second and velocity in m/s. What is acceleration of the particle, when it is 2 m from the origin.

(a) 28 m/s^2 (b) 22 m/s^2

(c) 12 m/s^2 (d) 10 m/s^2

21 For the motion of a particle, velocity v depends on displacement x as $v = \frac{20}{3x-2}$. If at $t = 0$, $x = 0$, then at what time t, $x = 20$?

(a) 7 s (b) 14 s

(c) 28 s (d) 35 s

22 Velocity vector of a particle is given as $\mathbf{v} = 4t\hat{i} + 3\hat{j}$. At $t = 0$, position of the particle is given as $\mathbf{r}_0 = 2\hat{j}$. Find the position vector of the particle at $t = 2$ s.

(a) $\mathbf{r} = 8\hat{i} + 4\hat{j}$ (b) $\mathbf{r} = 4\hat{i} + 4\hat{j}$

(c) $\mathbf{r} = 8\hat{i} + 8\hat{j}$ (d) $\mathbf{r} = 4\hat{i} + 8\hat{j}$

23 A force $\mathbf{F} = 6t^2\hat{i} + 4t\hat{j}$ is acting on a particle of mass 3 kg, then what will be velocity of particle at $t = 3$ s if at $t = 0$, particle is at rest?

(a) $18\hat{i} + 6\hat{j}$ (b) $18\hat{i} + 12\hat{j}$

(c) $12\hat{i} + 6\hat{j}$ (d) None of these

24 The deceleration experienced by a moving motor boat, after its engine is cut-off is given by $\frac{dv}{dt} = -kv^3$, where k is constant. If v_0 is the magnitude of the velocity at cut-off, the magnitude of the velocity at a time t after the cut-off is

(a) $\frac{v_0}{2}$ (b) v_0 (c) $v_0 e^{-k/t}$ (d) $\frac{v_0}{\sqrt{(2v_0^2 kt + 1)}}$

25 A particle of mass m moves on the X-axis under the influence of a force of attraction towards the origin O given by $F = -\frac{k}{x^2}\hat{i}$. If the particle starts from rest at $x = a$, the speed it will attain to reach at distance x from the origin O will be

(a) $\sqrt{\frac{2k}{m}\left[\frac{x-a}{ax}\right]}^{1/2}$ (b) $\sqrt{\frac{2k}{m}\left[\frac{x+k}{ax}\right]}^{1/2}$

(c) $\sqrt{\frac{k}{m}\left[\frac{ax}{x-a}\right]}$ (d) $\sqrt{\frac{m}{2k}\left[\frac{a-x}{ax}\right]}^{1/2}$

26 A particle is projected with velocity v_0 along X-axis. The deceleration of the particle is proportional to the square of the distance from the origin, i.e. $a = \alpha x^2$. The distance at which the particle stops is

(a) $\sqrt[3]{\frac{3v_0^2}{\alpha}}$ (b) $\sqrt[3]{\frac{v_0^2}{2\alpha}}$ (c) $\sqrt[3]{\frac{3v_0^2}{2\alpha}}$ (d) $\sqrt[3]{\frac{v_0^2}{\alpha}}$

27 A point moves in a straight line with retardation d which depends on velocity of particle v as $d = C\sqrt{v}$, where C is a positive constant. If initial velocity of the particle is v_0, then total distance travelled by the particle before stopping is

(a) $\frac{1}{3C}v_0^{1/2}$ (b) $\frac{2}{3C}v_0^{3/2}$ (c) $\frac{2}{C}v_0^{3/2}$ (d) $\frac{v_0}{C}$

Numerical Value Questions

1 A particle, initially at rest, starts moving in a straight line with an acceleration $a = (6t + 4)$ m/s^2. The distance (in m) covered by it in 3 s is ....

2 An object moving with a speed of 5 m/s is decelerated at a rate given by $\frac{dv}{dt} = -\frac{1}{30}v^2$, where v is the instantaneous speed. The time(in s) when its speed becomes 3 m/s is ....

3 A particle moves along a straight line according to the law $s^2 = at^2 + bt + c$. The acceleration of the particle varies as $s^{-\alpha}$. Find α.

4 The motion of a body is given by the equation $\frac{dv}{dt} = 6 - 3v$, where v is speed in m/s and t is time in second. If the body was at rest at $t = 0$, its terminal velocity (in m/s) is ....

5 The acceleration of a particle moving rectilinearly varies with the magnitude of its velocity as $a = -\sqrt{v}$. Find its initial speed (in m/s), if it stops after $t_0 = 4$ s from starting.

6 Starting from rest, a particle moving in a straight line is accelerated by an acceleration

$a = (4 - t^2)$ m/s^2 for $0 \le t \le 2$ s

$a = \frac{1}{3}$ m/s^2 for $t > 2$ s

What is the velocity (in m/s) of the particle after 4 s?

7 A point moves in the xy-plane according to the law $x = 3t$ and $y = 3t\left(1 - \frac{t}{4}\right)$, where x, y are in metre and t is in second. What is the time(in second) after which velocity makes an angle of $\frac{\pi}{2}$ with the acceleration?

8 A particle projected from the origin ($x = y = 0$) moves in xy-plane, so that its velocity is $\mathbf{v} = (2\hat{\mathbf{i}} + 4x\hat{\mathbf{j}})$ m/s, when it is at the point (x, y) m. What is the value of y when x = 3?

9 Velocity of a particle moving along a straight line at any time t is given by $v = \cos\left(\frac{\pi}{3}t\right)$. If the magnitude of displacement of the particle in the first two seconds is $\frac{\sqrt{k}}{2\pi}$. Find k.

10 From point A located on a highway (figure) one has to get by car as soon as possible to point B located in the field at a distance $l = 3\sqrt{2}$ km from the highway. It is known that the car moves in the field 3 times slower than on the highway. At what distance (in km) from point D one must turn off the highway?

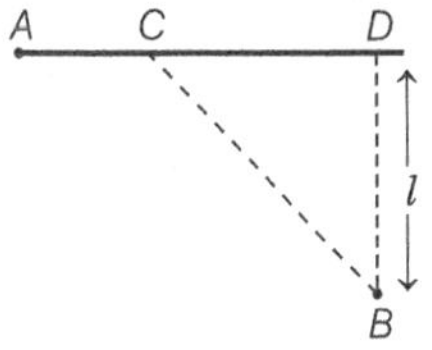

LEVEL 03 JEE Advanced Level

Single Choice Correct Questions

1 A point moves in the xy-plane according to the law $x = \alpha t$ and $y = \alpha t(1 - \beta t)$, where α and β are positive constants. The time after which the velocity makes an angle $\frac{\pi}{4}$ with the acceleration is

(a) $\frac{1}{\alpha}$ (b) $\frac{1}{\beta}$ (c) $\frac{2}{\beta}$ (d) $\frac{2}{\alpha}$

2 A particle starts from rest. Its acceleration at an instant t is $a = \frac{1.5}{v+1}$ m/s^2, v is the instantaneous velocity. The distance travelled till t = 5 s is

(a) 5 m (b) 9 m (c) 15 m (d) 20 m

3 A motor boat of mass m moves along a lake with velocity v_0. At $t = 0$, the engine of the boat is shut down. Magnitude of resistance force offered to the boat is equal to rv. (v is instantaneous speed). What is the total distance covered till it stops completely?

(a) mv_0/r (b) $3mv_0/2r$

(c) $mv_0/2r$ (d) $2mv_0/r$

4 A particle is moving in a plane with velocity given by $\mathbf{u} = u_0\hat{\mathbf{i}} + (a\omega\cos\omega t)\hat{\mathbf{j}}$, where $\hat{\mathbf{i}}$ and $\hat{\mathbf{j}}$ are unit vectors along X and Y-axes, respectively. If particle is at the origin at t = 0, the trajectory of the particle is

(a) $y = a\sin\left(\frac{u_0}{\omega x}\right)$ (b) $y = a\sin\left(\frac{\omega x}{u_0}\right)$

(c) $y = \frac{1}{a}\sin\left(\frac{u_0}{\omega x}\right)$ (d) $y = \frac{1}{a}\sin\left(\frac{\omega x}{u_0}\right)$

5 A point moves in a straight line under the retardation av^2. If the initial velocity is u, the distance covered in t seconds, is

(a) aut (b) $\frac{1}{a}\ln(aut)$

(c) $\frac{1}{a}\ln(1 + aut)$ (d) $a\ln(aut)$

6 Starting from rest, a particle moves in a straight line with acceleration,

$a = (25 - t^2)^{1/2}$ m/s^2 for $0 \le t \le 5$s; $a = \frac{3\pi}{8}$ m/s^2 for $t > 5$s

The velocity of particle at t = 7 s is

(a) 11 m/s (b) 22 m/s (c) 33 m/s (d) 44 m/s

7 A body is in rectilinear motion with an acceleration given by $a = 2v^{3/2}$. If the particle starts its motion from origin with a velocity of 4 m/s, the position x of the particle at t = 1/4 s is

(a) $x = 2$ m (b) $x = 4$ m (c) $x = 6$ m (d) $x = 8$ m

8 A particle moves uniformly with speed v along the parabolic path $y = kx^2$, where k is a positive constant. The acceleration of the particle at $x = 0$ is given by

(a) $2kv^2$ (b) kv^2 (c) $\frac{1}{2}kv^2$ (d) $2kv$

9 The displacement x and time of travel t for a particle moving on a straight line are related as $t = \sqrt{(x+1)(x-1)}$. Its acceleration at a time t is

(a) $\frac{1}{x} - \frac{1}{x^2}$ (b) $\frac{1}{x^3}$ (c) $\frac{-t^2}{x^3}$ (d) $\frac{-t}{x^2}$

10 The acceleration of a particle is given by

$$\mathbf{a} = \left[2\hat{\mathbf{i}} + 6t\hat{\mathbf{j}} + \frac{2\pi^2}{9}\cos\frac{\pi t}{3}\hat{\mathbf{k}}\right] \text{ms}^{-2}.$$

At $t = 0$, $\mathbf{r} = 0$ and $\mathbf{v} = (2\hat{\mathbf{i}} + \hat{\mathbf{j}})$ m/s. The position vector at $t = 2$ s will be

(a) $(8\hat{\mathbf{i}} + 10\hat{\mathbf{j}} + \hat{\mathbf{k}})$ m (b) $(8\hat{\mathbf{i}} + 10\hat{\mathbf{j}} + 3\hat{\mathbf{k}})$ m
(c) $(3\hat{\mathbf{i}} + 8\hat{\mathbf{j}} + 10\hat{\mathbf{k}})$ m (d) $(10\hat{\mathbf{i}} + 3\hat{\mathbf{j}} + 8\hat{\mathbf{k}})$ m

11 A particle moves in xy-plane with a velocity given by $\mathbf{v} = (8t - 2)\hat{\mathbf{i}} + 2\hat{\mathbf{j}}$. If it passes through the point (14, 4) at $t = 2$ s, then find equation of the path.

(a) $x = y^2 + y - 6$ (b) $x = y^2 - y + 2$
(c) $y = x^2 - 14x + 4$ (d) $y = x - 10$

12 The velocities in x and y-direction of a particle moving in xy-plane is given by $v_x = a_0 t$, $v_y = \lambda x$, where a_0 and λ are some constants, t is time and x is the displacement in x-direction at any time t. The trajectory of the particle will be

(a) $y^3 = \frac{2\lambda^2}{9a_0}x^2$ (b) $y^3 = \frac{9\lambda^2}{2a_0}x^2$
(c) $y^2 = \frac{9\lambda^2}{2a_0^2}x^2$ (d) $y^2 = \frac{2\lambda^2}{9a_0}x^3$

13 A particle moves in the xy-plane with velocity $\mathbf{v} = k_1\hat{\mathbf{i}} + k_2 x\hat{\mathbf{j}}$, where $\hat{\mathbf{i}}$ and $\hat{\mathbf{j}}$ are the unit vectors along the X and Y-axes and k_1 and k_2 are constants. At the initial moment, the particle was located at the point $x = y = 0$. The equation of the particle's trajectory is

(a) $y = \frac{k_1}{2k_2}x^2$ (b) $y = \frac{k_2}{2k_1}x^2$
(c) $y = \frac{2k_1}{k_2}x^2$ (d) $y = \frac{2k_2}{k_1}x^2$

14 The velocity of a point moving in straight line changes according to the equation $v = (3t^2 - 2t - 1)$ m/s. The path covered by the point during 10 s from the start is

(a) 890 m (b) 892 m (c) 1110 m (d) 1100 m

15 A particle moves along a straight line. The relation between the position of particle and time is

$$x^2 = (8t^2 + 8t + 4)\text{ m}^2$$

Find acceleration of particle at $x = 2$ m.

(a) 2 m/s^2 (b) 4 m/s^2 (c) Zero (d) 8 m/s^2

16 A particle is moving on a straight line. Its acceleration as a function of displacement is $a = \left(2 + \frac{100}{s^2}\right)$ m/s^2.

If the velocity of particle is 5 m/s at $s = 10$ m, then the velocity of the particle at $s = 25$ m is

(a) 9.84 m/s (b) 10 m/s (c) 20 m/s (d) 8 m/s

17 A balloon starts rising from the earth's surface with constant vertical velocity of v_0. Due to wind, balloon gathers horizontal velocity component $v_x = ky$, where k is a constant and y is height through which balloon has risen. With respect to the point of start, find horizontal displacement of balloon when it has ascended through a vertical height h.

(a) $\frac{kh^2}{v_0}$ (b) $\frac{kh^2}{2v_0}$ (c) $\frac{kh^2}{3v_0}$ (d) $\frac{2kh^2}{v_0}$

18 A particle is moving in xy-plane. At certain instant, the components of its velocity and acceleration are as follows $v_x = 3$ m/s, $v_y = 4$ m/s, $a_x = 2$ m/s^2 and $a_y = 1$ m/s^2. The rate of change of speed at this moment is

(a) 4 m/s^2 (b) 2 m/s^2 (c) $\sqrt{3}$ m/s^2 (d) $\sqrt{5}$ m/s^2

19 A particle is moving along the locus : $y = k\sqrt{x}$ $(k > 0)$ with a constant speed v. At $t = 0$, it is at origin and about to enter the first quadrant of xy-axes. At some time later $t > 0$, $v_x = v_y$. At this moment, $(a_y - a_x)$ is

(a) $\frac{v^2}{k^2}$ (b) $\frac{v^2}{2k^2}$ (c) $-\frac{v^2}{k^2}$ (d) $-\frac{v^2}{4k^2}$

20 A point moves in xy-plane according to the law $x = 3\cos 4t$ and $y = 3(1 - \sin 4t)$. The distance travelled by the particle in 2 s is (where x and y are in metre)

(a) 48m (b) 24m (c) $48\sqrt{2}$m (d) $24\sqrt{2}$m

Multiple Choice(s) Correct Questions

1 A particle moves with an initial velocity v_0 and retardation bv, where v is its velocity at any time t,

(a) the particle will cover a total distance of v_0/b
(b) the particle will continue for a very long time
(c) the particle will stop shortly
(d) the velocity of particle will become $v_0/2$ after time $1/b$

2 The coordinates of the particle in xy-plane are given as $x = 2 + 2t + 4t^2$ and $y = 4t + 8t^2$.
The motion of the particle is
(a) along a straight line
(b) uniformly accelerated
(c) along a parabolic path
(d) non-uniformly accelerated

3 A particle moves on straight line whose velocity and displacement relation is $v^2 = 400 - 4x$.
Which of the following statement(s) is/(are) correct?
(a) The time in which particle stops is 10 s.
(b) The distance travelled by the particle in last 2 s before coming to rest is 4 m.
(c) This is an example of non-uniformly accelerated motion.
(d) This is an example of uniformly accelerated motion.

4 A particle moves in the xy-plane and at time t is at the point $(t^2, t^3 - 2t)$. Then,
(a) at $t = 2/3$ s, directions of velocity and acceleration are perpendicular
(b) at $t = 0$, directions of velocity and acceleration are perpendicular
(c) at $t = \sqrt{\frac{2}{3}}$ s, particle is moving parallel to X-axis
(d) acceleration of the particle when it is at point (4, 4) is $2\hat{i} + 24\hat{j}$

5 A particle moves along X-axis according to the law $x = (t^3 - 3t^2 - 9t + 5)$ m. Then,
(a) in the interval $3<t<5$, the particle is moving in $+x$-direction
(b) the particle reverses its direction of motion twice in entire motion, if it starts at $t = 0$
(c) the average acceleration from $1 < t < 2$ s is $6 m/s^2$
(d) in the interval $5 < t < 6$ s, the distance travelled is equal to the magnitude of the displacement

6 Pick the correct statements.
(a) Average speed of a particle in a given time is never less than the magnitude of the average velocity.
(b) It is possible to have a situation in which $\left|\frac{d\mathbf{u}}{dt}\right| \neq 0$ but $\frac{d}{dt}|\mathbf{u}| = 0$.
(c) The average velocity of a particle is zero in a time interval. It is possible that the instantaneous velocity is never zero in the interval.
(d) The average velocity of a particle moving on a straight line is zero in a time interval. It is possible that the instantaneous velocity is never zero in the interval. (Infinite acceleration is not allowed)

7 A particle starts rectilinearly from station A with acceleration varying according to $a = \alpha - \beta s$ and comes to halt at station B. α and β are positive constants and s is the distance from station A.
(a) Distance between station A and B is $\frac{2\alpha}{\beta}$
(b) Maximum velocity of particle is $\frac{\alpha}{\sqrt{\beta}}$
(c) Distance yet to covered when particle attains its maximum velocity is $\frac{\alpha}{\beta}$
(d) Maximum velocity is 2α

8 A particle of mass m moves along a curve $y = x^2$. When particle has x-coordinate as 1/2 and x-component of velocity as 4 m/s and x-component of acceleration as 8 ms^{-2}, then
(a) the position coordinate of particles are (1/2, l/4)
(b) the velocity of particle will be along the line $4x - 4y - 1 = 0$
(c) the magnitude of velocity at that instant is $4\sqrt{2}$ m/s
(d) the acceleration is $\mathbf{a} = (8\hat{i} + 40\hat{j}) \text{ ms}^{-2}$

9 A particle is moving along the X-axis whose position is given by $x = 4 - 9t + \frac{t^3}{3}$. Mark the correct statement(s) in relation to its motion.
(a) The direction of motion is never changing.
(b) The direction of motion is changing at $t = 3$ s.
(c) For $0 < t < 3$ s, the particle is slowing down.
(d) For $0 < t < 3$s, the particle is speeding up.

10 Velocity v of a moving particle on X-axis varies with x-coordinate varies as $v = \beta x^{1/3}$, where β is a positive constant. Assume that the particle starts from origin.
(a) Acceleration of particle is variable.
(b) Mean velocity of point averaged over time T from starting is $\left(\frac{2\beta}{3}\right)^{3/2}\sqrt{T}$.
(c) Mean velocity of point averaged over the time taken by the particle to move from origin to the point, where its x-coordinate becomes x_0 is $\frac{2\beta x_0^{1/3}}{3}$.
(d) All above statements are false

11 At time $t = 0$, a car moving along a straight line has a velocity of 16 m/s. It slows down with an acceleration of $(-0.5\,t)\text{ms}^{-2}$, where t is in seconds. Mark the correct statement(s).
(a) The velocity at $t = 10$ s is 9m/s.
(b) The distance travelled in 6 s is 78 m.
(c) The distance travelled by the particle in 10 s is 94m.
(d) The direction of velocity changes at $t = 8$ s.

12 An object moves with constant acceleration **a**. Which of the following expressions is/are also constant?

(a) $\frac{d|\mathbf{v}|}{dt}$ (b) $\left|\frac{d\mathbf{v}}{dt}\right|$

(c) $\frac{d(v^2)}{dt}$ (d) $\frac{d\left(\frac{\mathbf{v}}{|\mathbf{v}|}\right)}{dt}$

13 A particle moves along a straight line and its velocity depends on time t as $v = 4t - t^2$. Here v is in m/s and t is in s. Then for the first 5 s,

(a) magnitude of average velocity is 5/3 m/s
(b) average speed is 13/5 m/s
(c) average speed is 11/5 m/s
(d) average acceleration is 1 m/s^2

14 Two balloons are simultaneously released from two buildings A and B. Balloon A rises with constant velocity 10 m/s, while the other one rises with constant velocity of 20 m/s. Due to the wind, the balloons gather horizontal velocity $v_x = 0.5y$, where y is the height from the point of release. The buildings are at a distance of 250 m and after some time t, the balloons collide. Then,

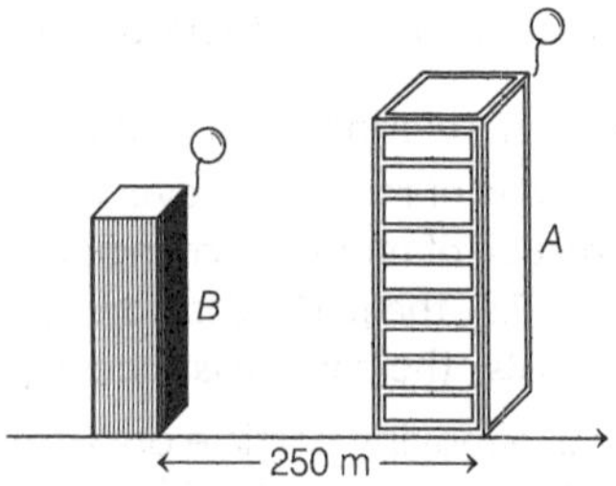

(a) $t = 5$ s
(b) difference in heights of buildings is 100m
(c) difference in heights of buildings is 50 m
(d) $t = 10$ s

Comprehension Based Questions

Comprehension-1

For a particle moving along X-axis, the acceleration a of the particle in terms of its x-coordinate, x is given by $a = -9x$, where x is in m and a is in m/s^2. Take, acceleration, velocity and displacement in positive x-direction as positive. The initial velocity of particle at $x = 0$ is $u = +6$ m/s.

1 The velocity of particle at $x = 2$ m will be

(a) $+6\sqrt{2}$ m/s (b) $-6\sqrt{2}$ m/s
(c) 72 m/s (d) zero

2 The maximum distance of particle from origin will be

(a) 1 m (b) 2 m (c) 3 m (d) 4 m

3 The plot of velocity *versus* x-coordinate of particle in the duration it moves from origin towards the positive x-direction, is best represented by

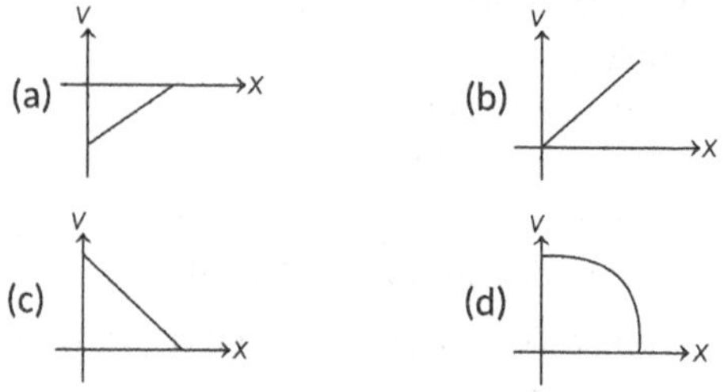

Comprehension-2

The velocity v of a particle moving along straight line is given in terms of time t as $v = 3(t^2 - t)$, where t is in s and v is in m/s.

4 The distance travelled by particle from $t = 0$ to $t = 2$ s is

(a) 2m (b) 3 m (c) 4 m (d) 6 m

5 The displacement of particle from $t = 0$ to $t = 2$ s is

(a) 1 m (b) 2 m (c) 3 m (d) 4 m

6 The velocity is minimum after $t = 0$ s at instant of time

(a) 0.5 s (b) 1 s
(c) 2 s (d) None of these

Comprehension-3

A point moves in xy-plane according to the law $x = a \sin \omega t$ and $y = a - a \cos\omega t$, where a is a positive constant and t is the time.

7 The magnitude of velocity of the body at any instant of time t is

(a) $a\omega \cos\omega t$ (b) $a\omega$
(c) $a\omega \sin\omega t$ (d) None of these

8 The trajectory represents

(a) $x = \sqrt{2ay}$ (b) $x = \pm\sqrt{2ay\left(1 - \frac{y}{2a}\right)}$
(c) $x \propto y^2$ (d) None of these

Comprehension-4

At $t = 0$ on the planet "Gravitus Increasicus", a projectile is fired with speed 6 m/s at an angle 30° above the horizontal. This planet is a strange one, in that the acceleration due to gravity increases linearly with time, starting with a value of zero when the projectile is fired. In other words, $g(t) = 2t$.

9 The time of flight of the projectile is

(a) 1 s (b) 2 s
(c) 3 s (d) $3\sqrt{3}$ s

10 Range of the projectile is

(a) 9 m (b) $\frac{9}{\sqrt{3}}$ m (c) $6\sqrt{3}$ m (d) $9\sqrt{3}$ m

Match the Columns Question

1 The equation of one dimensional motion of the particle is described in Column I. At $t = 0$, particle is at origin and at rest. Match the Column I with the statements in Column II.

	Column I		Column II
A.	$x = (3t^2 + 2)$m	P.	Velocity of particle at t = 1s is 8 m/s
B.	$v = 8t$ m/s	Q.	Particle moves with uniform acceleration
C.	$a = 16t\,\text{m/s}^2$	R.	Particle moves with variable acceleration
D.	$v = (6t - 3t^2)$ m/s	S.	Particle will change its direction at some time

Numerical Value Questions

1 A particle starts from rest with an acceleration of 2 ms^{-2}. The acceleration of the particle decreases down to zero linearly in 4 s. Find the velocity (in m/s) of the particle after 2 s.

2 A ball is released from rest from top of a tower. The retardation due to air resistance is bv, where b is 10 per second and velocity v is in m/s. The velocity of ball at $t = \frac{1}{10}$ s is $\frac{n}{27}$ m/s. Find the value of n.
(Given, e = 2.7)

3 A ball is projected upward with initial velocity v_0. The retardation due to air resistance is bv where b is a positive constant. The time taken by particle to reach maximum height is t_0. If $\frac{bv_0}{g} = 2$, then find the value of e^{bt_0}.

4 A balloon moves up vertically such that if a stone is thrown from it with a horizontal velocity u relative to it, the stone always hits the ground at a fixed point $\frac{2u^2}{g}$ horizontally away from it. If the height of balloon as a function of time t is expressed $h = \frac{2u^2}{g}[1 - e^{-gt/xu}]$, then find the value of x.

5 The acceleration of a marble in a certain fluid is proportional to the speed of the marble squared and is given (in SI units) by $a = -\frac{v^2}{3}$ for $v > 0$. If the marble enters this fluid with a speed of 1.50 m/s, how long will it take before the marble's speed is reduced to half of its initial value?

6 A body is projected vertically upwards with a velocity u = 5 m/s. After time t another body is projected vertically upward from the same point with a velocity v = 3 m/s. If they meet in minimum time duration measured from the projection of first body, then find the minimum time(in s). (g =10 ms^{-2})

7 A particle is moving along a straight line. Its velocity varies as $v = 6 - 2t$, where v is in metre/second and t in s. Find the difference between distance covered and magnitude of displacement in first 4 s.

8 A projectile is fired with a speed 6.25 m/s at an angle $\theta = 53°$ above horizontal. This planet is strange one, in that acceleration due to gravity increases linearly with time starting with a value zero, when projectile is fired. In other words $g = \beta t$, where β is a constant. If horizontal range of projectile remains same as obtained, if $g = 10\ \text{ms}^{-2}$ (under same initial velocity), then find the value of β in ms^{-3}.

9 The velocity of water current varies as

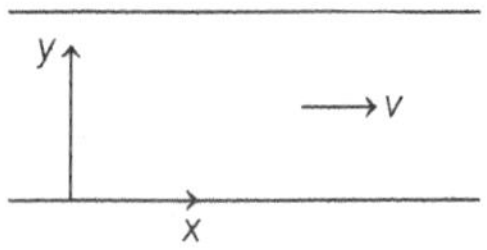

$$v = \left(\frac{4}{25}\right)y \text{ for } y \le 250 \text{ m}$$

$$v = 80 - \left(\frac{4}{25}\right)y \text{ for } y > 250 \text{ m}$$

where, y is the perpendicular distance from one bank. The width of the river is 500 m. A swimmer is crossing the river with constant velocity 5 m/s relative to water and heading perpendicular to the current. Find the drift of the swimmer (in km).

Previous Year's Questions

JEE Main

1 The position of a particle related to time is given by $x = (5t^2 - 4t + 5)$ m. The magnitude of velocity of the particle at $t = 2$ s will be **[2023, 15 April Shift-I]**

(a) 06 ms^{-1} (b) 10 ms^{-1} (c) 14 ms^{-1} (d) 16 ms^{-1}

2 The distance travelled by an object in time t is given by $s = (2.5)t^2$. The instantaneous speed of the object at $t = 5$ s will be **[2023, 13 April Shift-II]**

(a) 25 ms^{-1} (b) 5 ms^{-1}
(c) 62.5 ms^{-1} (d) 12.5 ms^{-1}

3 The distance travelled by a particle is related to time t as $x = 4t^2$. The velocity of the particle at $t = 5$s is **[2023, 25 Jan Shift-II]**

(a) $8\ ms^{-1}$ (b) $40\ ms^{-1}$
(c) $20\ ms^{-1}$ (d) $25\ ms^{-1}$

4 Two buses P and Q start from a point at the same time and move in a straight line and their positions are represented by $X_P(t) = \alpha t + \beta t^2$ and $X_Q(t) = ft - t^2$. At what time, both the buses have same velocity? **[2022, 25 June Shift-II]**

(a) $\frac{\alpha - f}{1+\beta}$ (b) $\frac{\alpha + f}{2(\beta - 1)}$ (c) $\frac{\alpha + f}{2(1+\beta)}$ (d) $\frac{f - \alpha}{2(1+\beta)}$

JEE Advanced

1 A particle of mass m is moving in the XY-plane such that its velocity at a point (x, y) is given as $\mathbf{v} = \alpha(y\hat{\mathbf{x}} + 2x\hat{\mathbf{y}})$, where α is a non-zero constant. What is the force $\mathbf{F}$ acting on the particle? **(2023 Adv.)**

(a) $\mathbf{F} = 2m\alpha^2(x\hat{\mathbf{x}} + y\hat{\mathbf{y}})$ (b) $\mathbf{F} = m\alpha^2(y\hat{\mathbf{x}} + 2x\hat{\mathbf{y}})$
(c) $\mathbf{F} = 2m\alpha^2(y\hat{\mathbf{x}} + x\hat{\mathbf{y}})$ (d) $\mathbf{F} = m\alpha^2(x\hat{\mathbf{x}} + 2y\hat{\mathbf{y}})$

2 Starting at time $t = 0$ from the origin with speed $1\ ms^{-1}$, a particle follows a two-dimensional trajectory in the xy-plane so that its coordinates are related by the equation $y = \frac{x^2}{2}$. The x and y components of its acceleration are denoted by a_x and a_y, respectively. Then, **(2020 Adv)**

(a) $a_x = 1\ ms^{-2}$ implies that when the particle is at the origin, $a_y = 1\ ms^{-2}$

(b) $a_x = 0$ implies $a_y = 1\ ms^{-2}$ at all times

(c) at $t = 0$, the particle's velocity points in the x-direction

(d) $a_x = 0$ implies that at $t = 1$ s, the angle between the particle's velocity and the x axis is 45°

Answer Key

Level 1

1. $b, 2c$ 2. $32\ m/s^2$ 3. -9 m/s
4. (a) Velocity = 0 and 1 m/s, acceleration = $-2\ m/s^2$ and $4\ m/s^2$ (b) $-4/27$ m (c) $-1/3$ m/s
5. (a) $12\ cm^2/s$ (b) $16\ cm^2/s$
6. (a) 24 m and 24 m (b) 24 m and 40 m 7. $4\ m/s^2$
8. $8a$ 9. $v_0 t + \frac{bt^3}{6}$ 10. $\frac{2t^3}{3} - 15t^2 + 3t - 5$
11. $\frac{7}{2}(e^{2t} - 1)$ 12. $\sqrt{6x^2 + 10x + 4}$ 13. $x = 2(e^t - 1)$
14. $v = v_0 e^{2x}$
15. (a) $\mathbf{v} = (5\sin t - 3)\hat{i} + (3\cos t - 1)\hat{j}$ (b) $\mathbf{r} = (-5\cos t - 3t + 3)\hat{i} + (3\sin t - t + 5)\hat{j}$

Level 2

Single Choice Correct Questions

1. (d)	2. (d)	3. (d)	4. (c)	5. (c)
6. (a)	7. (d)	8. (c)	9. (b)	10. (c)
11. (a)	12. (c)	13. (c)	14. (a)	15. (c)
16. (a)	17. (d)	18. (a)	19. (a)	20. (b)
21. (c)	22. (c)	23. (a)	24. (d)	25. (a)
26. (c)	27. (b)			

Numerical Value Questions

1. (45)	2. (4)	3. (3)	4. (2)	5. (4)
6. (6)	7. (2)	8. (9)	9. (27)	10. (1.50)

Level 3

Single Choice Correct Questions

1. (b)	2. (b)	3. (a)	4. (b)	5. (c)
6. (b)	7. (a)	8. (a)	9. (b)	10. (b)
11. (b)	12. (d)	13. (b)	14. (b)	15. (a)
16. (a)	17. (b)	18. (b)	19. (c)	20. (b)

Multiple Choice(s) Correct Questions

1. (ab)	2. (ab)	3. (abd)	4. (abc)	5. (ad)
6. (abc)	7. (abc)	8. (abcd)	9. (bc)	10. (abc)
11. (bcd)	12. (ab)	13. (abd)	14. (bd)	

Comprehension Based Questions

1. (d)	2. (b)	3. (d)	4. (b)	5. (b)
6. (a)	7. (b)	8. (b)	9. (c)	10. (d)

Match the Columns Question

1. A → Q, B → PQ, C → PR, D → RS

Numerical Value Questions

1. (3)	2. (17)	3. (3)	4. (2)	5. (5)
6. (0.6)	7. (2)	8. (5)	9. (2)	

Previous Year's Questions

JEE Main

1. (d) 2. (a) 3. (b) 4. (d)

JEE Advanced

1. (a) 2. (a,b,c,d)

SOLUTIONS

Level 1

1. $y = a + bt + ct^2 - dt^4$

$$v = \frac{dy}{dt} = b + 2ct - 4dt^3$$

At $t = 0$; $v = b$

$$\Rightarrow \quad a = \frac{d^2y}{dt^2} = 2c - 12dt^2$$

At $t = 0$; $\quad a = 2c$

2. $s = 3t^3 + 7t^2 + 14t + 8$

$$v = \frac{ds}{dt} = 9t^2 + 14t + 14, \quad a = \frac{dv}{dt} = 18t + 14$$

At $t = 1$; $\quad a = 18(1) + 14 = 32 \text{ m/s}^2$

3. $s = t^3 - 6t^2 + 3t + 4$

$$v = \frac{ds}{dt} = 3t^2 - 12t + 3, \quad a = \frac{dv}{dt} = 6t - 12$$

$$a = 6t - 12 = 0 \quad \Rightarrow \quad t = 2 \text{ s}$$

At $t = 2$; $\quad v = 3(2)^2 - 12(2) + 3 = -9 \text{m/s}$

4. $s = t^2(t-1) = t^3 - t^2$

$$v = \frac{ds}{dt} = 3t^2 - 2t = t(3t-2), \quad a = \frac{dv}{dt} = 6t - 2$$

(a) When particle passing through the origin

$$s = t^2(t-1) = 0 \quad \Rightarrow \quad t = 0 \text{ and } t = 1$$

At $t = 0$; $\quad v = 0$ and $a = -2 \text{ m/s}^2$

At $t = 1$; $\quad v = 1$ m/s and $a = 4 \text{ m/s}^2$

(b) $v = t(3t - 2) = 0 \quad \Rightarrow \quad t = 0$ and $t = \frac{2}{3}$

At $t = \frac{2}{3}$; $\quad s = \left(\frac{2}{3}\right)^3 - \left(\frac{2}{3}\right)^2 = -\frac{4}{27}$ m

(c) Net force $= ma \quad \Rightarrow \quad 0 = ma \quad \Rightarrow \quad a = 0$

$$a = 6t - 2 = 0 \quad \Rightarrow \quad t = \frac{1}{3} \text{ s}$$

$$v = 3t^2 - 2t = 3\left(\frac{1}{3}\right)^2 - 2\left(\frac{1}{3}\right) = -\frac{1}{3} \text{ m/s}$$

5. $v = 2t^2 + 5$

At $t = 2$; $\quad v_1 = 2(2)^2 + 5 = 13$ cm/s

At $t = 4$; $\quad v_2 = 2(4)^2 + 5 = 37$ cm/s

Average acceleration $= \frac{v_2 - v_1}{t_2 - t_1} = \frac{37 - 13}{2} = 12 \text{ cm}^2/\text{s}$

(b) $a = \frac{dv}{dt} = 4t$

At $t = 4$; $a = 4(4) = 16 \text{ cm}^2/\text{s}$

6. $x = 16t - 2t^2$

At $t = 0$; $\quad x = 0$

$t = 2$; $\quad x = 24$

$t = 6$; $\quad x = 24$

$$v = \frac{dx}{dt} = 16 - 4t = 0 \quad \Rightarrow \quad t = 4$$

At $t = 4$; $x = 32$

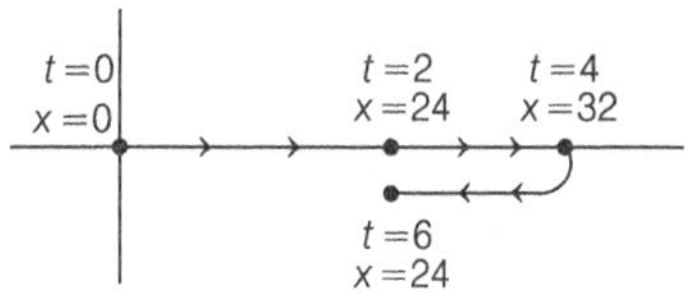

From $t = 0$ to $t = 2$

Displacement = 24 m, Distance = 24 m

From $t = 0$ to $t = 6$

Displacement = 24 m, Distance = 24 + 8 + 8 = 40 m

7. $\quad v = \sqrt{8x - 5}$

$$a = v\frac{dv}{dx} = (\sqrt{8x-5})\left(\frac{1}{2\sqrt{8x-5}} \times 8\right) = 4 \text{ m/s}^2$$

8. $u = at$

$$\Rightarrow \quad \frac{dx}{dt} = at \quad \Rightarrow \quad \int_0^x dx = \int_0^4 at\, dt$$

$$\Rightarrow \quad x - 0 = \left[\frac{at^2}{2}\right]_0^4 \quad \Rightarrow \quad x = 8a$$

9. $a = bt$

$$\Rightarrow \quad \frac{dv}{dt} = bt \quad \Rightarrow \quad \int_{v_0}^{v} dv = \int_0^t bt\, dt \quad \Rightarrow \quad [v]_{v_0}^{v} = b\left[\frac{t^2}{2}\right]_0^t$$

$$\Rightarrow \quad v = v_0 + \frac{bt^2}{2} \quad \Rightarrow \quad \frac{dx}{dt} = v_0 + \frac{bt^2}{2}$$

$$\Rightarrow \int_0^x dx = \int_0^t \left(v_0 + \frac{bt^2}{2}\right) dt \quad \Rightarrow \quad x = v_0 t + \frac{bt^3}{6}$$

10. $a = 4t - 30$

$$\Rightarrow \int_3^v dv = \int_0^t (4t - 30)\, dt \quad \Rightarrow \quad [v]_3^v = [2t^2 - 30t]_0^t$$

$$\Rightarrow \quad v = 2t^2 - 30t + 3 \quad \Rightarrow \quad \int_{-5}^{x} dx = \int_0^t (2t^2 - 30t + 3)\, dt$$

$$\Rightarrow \quad x = \frac{2t^3}{3} - 15t^2 + 3t - 5$$

11. $v = 2x + 7$

$$\Rightarrow \quad \frac{dx}{dt} = 2x + 7 \Rightarrow \int_0^x \frac{dx}{2x+7} = \int_0^t dt$$

$$\Rightarrow \quad \frac{1}{2}[\ln(2x+7)]_0^x = [t]_0^t$$

$$\Rightarrow \quad \frac{1}{2}[\ln(2x+7) - \ln 7] = t \quad \Rightarrow \ln\left(\frac{2x+7}{7}\right) = 2t$$

$$\Rightarrow \quad 2x + 7 = 7e^{2t} \quad \Rightarrow x = \frac{7}{2}(e^{2t} - 1)$$

12. $a = 6x + 5$

$$\Rightarrow \quad v\frac{dv}{dx} = 6x + 5 \Rightarrow \int_2^u v\,dv = \int_0^x (6x+5)dx$$

$$\Rightarrow \quad \left[\frac{v^2}{2}\right]_2^V = [3x^2 + 5x]_0^x$$

$$\Rightarrow \quad \frac{v^2 - 4}{2} = 3x^2 + 5x$$

$$\Rightarrow \quad v = \sqrt{6x^2 + 10x + 4}$$

13. $a = v$

$$\Rightarrow \quad \frac{dv}{dt} = v \Rightarrow \int_2^v \frac{dv}{v} = \int_0^t dt \Rightarrow [\ln v]_2^v = [t]_0^t$$

$$\Rightarrow \quad \ln v - \ln 2 = t \Rightarrow \ln\left(\frac{v}{2}\right) = t \Rightarrow v = 2e^t$$

$$\frac{dx}{dt} = 2e^t \quad \Rightarrow \int_0^x dx = \int_0^t 2e^t dt$$

$$\Rightarrow \quad [x]_0^x = 2[e^t]_0^t \quad \Rightarrow x = 2(e^t - 1)$$

14. $a = 2v^2$

$$\Rightarrow \quad v\frac{dv}{dx} = 2v^2 \Rightarrow \int_{v_0}^{v} \frac{dv}{v} = 2\int_0^x dx$$

$$\Rightarrow \quad [\ln v]_{v_0}^{v} = 2[x]_0^x \quad \Rightarrow \ln\left(\frac{v}{v_0}\right) = 2x$$

$$\Rightarrow \quad v = v_0 e^{2x}$$

15. $\mathbf{a} = 5\cos t\,\hat{\mathbf{i}} - 3\sin t\,\hat{\mathbf{j}}$

$$\Rightarrow \quad d\mathbf{v} = (5\cos t\,\hat{\mathbf{i}} - 3\sin t\,\hat{\mathbf{j}})dt$$

$$\Rightarrow \quad \int_{(-3\hat{i}+2\hat{j})}^{v} d\mathbf{v} = \int_0^t (5\cos t\,\hat{\mathbf{i}} - 3\cos t\,\hat{\mathbf{j}})dt$$

$$\Rightarrow \quad [\mathbf{v}]_{-3\hat{i}+2\hat{j}}^{v} = [5\cos t\,\hat{\mathbf{i}} - 3\sin t\,\hat{\mathbf{j}}]_0^t$$

$$\Rightarrow \quad \mathbf{v} = 5\sin t\,\hat{\mathbf{i}} + 3\cos t\,\hat{\mathbf{j}} - 3\hat{\mathbf{i}} - \hat{\mathbf{j}}$$

$$\Rightarrow \quad \mathbf{v} = (5\sin t - 3)\hat{\mathbf{i}} + (3\cos t - 1)\hat{\mathbf{j}}$$

$$\Rightarrow \quad d\mathbf{r} = [(5\sin t - 3)\hat{\mathbf{i}} + (3\cos t - 1)\hat{\mathbf{j}}]\,dt$$

$$\Rightarrow \quad \int_{-2\hat{i}+5\hat{j}}^{r} d\mathbf{r} = \int_0^t [(5\sin t - 3)\hat{\mathbf{i}} + (3\cos t - 1)\hat{\mathbf{j}})]dt$$

$$\Rightarrow \quad \mathbf{r} = (-5\cos t - 3t + 3)\,\hat{\mathbf{i}} + (3\sin t - t + 5)\hat{\mathbf{j}}$$

Level 2

Single Choice Correct Questions

1. $v = 10 + 2t^2$

At $t = 2$; $v_1 = 10 + 2(2)^2 = 18$ m/s

At $t = 5$; $v_2 = 10 + 2(5)^2 = 60$ m/s

$$\text{Average acceleration} = \frac{v_2 - v_1}{t_2 - t_1} = \frac{60 - 18}{3} = 14 \text{ m/s}^2$$

2. $3t = \sqrt{3x} + 6 \quad \Rightarrow 3x = (3t - 6)^2$

$$\Rightarrow \quad x = \frac{1}{3}(3t-6)^2 \quad \Rightarrow v = \frac{dx}{dt} = \left(\frac{1}{3}\right) \times 2(3t-6)(3) = 6t - 12$$

$v = 0 = 6t - 12 \quad \Rightarrow t = 2$ s

At $t = 2$; $x = 0$

3. $x = ae^{-\alpha t} + be^{\beta t}$

$$v = \frac{dx}{dt} = ae^{-\alpha t}(-\alpha) + be^{\beta t}(\beta)$$

$$v = -a\alpha e^{-\alpha t} + b\beta e^{\beta t}$$

Since a, b, α and β are positive constants as time increases, v increases.

4. $v = (180 - 16x)^{1/2}$

$$a = v\frac{dv}{dx} = (180 - 16x)^{1/2} \frac{1}{2(180 - 16x)^{1/2}} \times (-16)$$

$$= -8 \text{ m/s}^2$$

5. $x = \sqrt{v + 1} \Rightarrow v + 1 = x^2 \Rightarrow v = x^2 - 1$

$$\Rightarrow \quad a = v\frac{dv}{dx} = (x^2 - 1)(2x) \Rightarrow a = 2x(x^2 - 1)$$

At $x = 5$, $a = 2(5)(5^2 - 1) \Rightarrow a = 240$

6. $x^2 + 2x = t$

Differentiating both sides w.r.t. t

$$2x\frac{dx}{dt} + 2\frac{dx}{dt} = 1 \Rightarrow v = \frac{dx}{dt} = \frac{1}{2(x+1)}$$

$$a = v\frac{dv}{dx} = \frac{1}{2(x+1)} \times \frac{1}{2} \times \frac{-1}{(x+1)^2} = -\frac{1}{4(x+1)^3}$$

$$\therefore \text{ Retardation} = \frac{1}{4(x+1)^3}$$

7. $x = 2 + 8t - 4t^2 \Rightarrow v = 8 - 8t = 0 \Rightarrow t = 1$

At $t = 0$, $x = 2$

At $t = 1$, $x = 6$

At $t = 3$, $x = -10$

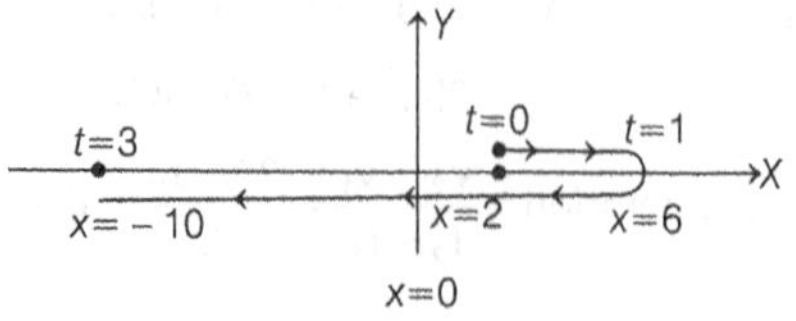

Distance travelled = 4 + 4 + 12 = 20 m

8. $x = 9t^2 - t^3 \Rightarrow v = 18t - 3t^2 \Rightarrow a = 18 - 6t$

Speed will be maximum when $a = 0$.

$$a = 18 - 6t = 0 \Rightarrow t = 3$$

At $t = 3, x = 9(3)^3 - 3^3 = 54$ m

9. $v = t^2 - t = t(t-1) \Rightarrow a = 2t - 1$

Particle retards when $\mathbf{v} \cdot \mathbf{a} < 0$.

When velocity and acceleration are in opposite directions.

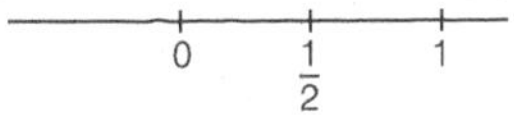

$v > 0, a < 0 \Rightarrow$ No time interval

$v < 0, a > 0 \Rightarrow \frac{1}{2} < t < 1$

10. If object is moving towards origin,

then $\mathbf{v} \cdot \mathbf{r} < 0 \Rightarrow x\frac{dx}{dt} < 0 \Rightarrow \frac{d(x)^2}{dt} < 0$

11. $\mathbf{r} = (t^2 - 4t + 6)\hat{\mathbf{i}} + t^2\hat{\mathbf{j}}$

$$\mathbf{v} = \frac{d\mathbf{r}}{dt} = (2t-4)\hat{\mathbf{i}} + 2t\hat{\mathbf{j}} \Rightarrow \mathbf{a} = \frac{d\mathbf{v}}{dt} = 2\hat{\mathbf{i}} + 2\hat{\mathbf{j}}$$

Since, $\mathbf{v} \perp \mathbf{a} \Rightarrow \mathbf{v} \cdot \mathbf{a} = 0$

$$[(2t-4)\hat{\mathbf{i}} + 2t\hat{\mathbf{j}}) \cdot (2\hat{\mathbf{i}} + 2\hat{\mathbf{j}}) = 0$$

$$\Rightarrow 2(2t-4) + 2(2t) = 0 \Rightarrow 4t - 4 = 0 \Rightarrow t = 1 \text{ s}$$

12. $x = 5\sin 10t, \quad y = 5\cos 10t$

$v_x = 50\cos 10t, \quad v_y = -50\sin 10t$

$a_x = -500\sin 10t, \quad a_y = -500\cos 10t$

$$\therefore \quad \mathbf{a} = -500\sin 10t\,\hat{\mathbf{i}} - 500\cos 10t\,\hat{\mathbf{j}}$$

$$a = \sqrt{(500\sin 10t)^2 + (500\cos 10t)^2}$$

$$a = 500 \text{ m/s}^2$$

13. $x = k\sin\omega t, \quad y = k(1 - \cos\omega t)$

$$\mathbf{r} = k\sin\omega t\,\hat{\mathbf{i}} + k(1-\cos\omega t)\hat{\mathbf{j}}$$

$$\mathbf{v} = k\omega\cos\omega t\,\hat{\mathbf{i}} + k\omega\sin\omega t\,\hat{\mathbf{j}}$$

$$\mathbf{a} = -k\omega^2\sin\omega t\,\hat{\mathbf{i}} + k\omega^2\cos\omega t\,\hat{\mathbf{j}}$$

$$|\mathbf{a}| = \sqrt{(k\omega^2\sin\omega t)^2 + (k\omega^2\cos\omega t)^2}$$

$$a = k\omega^2$$

14. $a = 2(t-1)$

$$\Rightarrow \frac{dv}{dt} = 2(t-1) \Rightarrow \int_0^v dv = 2\int_0^t (t-1)dt$$

$$\Rightarrow [v]_0^v = \left[2\left(\frac{t^2}{2} - t\right)\right]_0^t \Rightarrow v = t^2 - 2t$$

At $t = 5, v = 5^2 - 2(5) = 15$ m/s

15. $v = 2(t-1)$

$$\int_0^x dx = \int_0^t 2(t-1)dt \Rightarrow [x]_0^x = [t^2 - 2t]_0^t \Rightarrow x = t^2 - 2t$$

At $t = 3, x = 3^2 - 2(3) = 3$ m

16. $f = f_0\left(1 - \frac{t}{T}\right) \Rightarrow \frac{dv}{dt} = f_0\left(1 - \frac{t}{T}\right)$

$$\Rightarrow \int_0^v dv = \int_0^t f_0\left(1 - \frac{t}{T}\right)dt \Rightarrow [v]_0^v = f_0\left[t - \frac{t^2}{2T}\right]_0^t$$

$$\Rightarrow \quad v = f_0\left(t - \frac{t^2}{2T}\right)$$

Velocity is maximum, when $a = 0$.

$$\therefore \quad 0 = f_0\left(1 - \frac{t}{T}\right) \Rightarrow t = T$$

At $t = T$, $\quad v_{max} = f_0\left(T - \frac{T^2}{2T}\right) = \frac{f_0 T}{2}$

17. Acceleration $= -a\omega^2\sin\omega t$

$$\frac{dv}{dt} = -a\omega^2\sin\omega t \Rightarrow \int_0^v dv = -\int_0^t a\omega^2\sin\omega t\,dt$$

$$\Rightarrow \quad [v]_0^v = -\frac{a\omega^2}{\omega}[-\cos\omega t]_0^t \Rightarrow v - 0 = a\omega(\cos\omega t - 1)$$

$$\Rightarrow \quad v = a\omega(\cos\omega t - 1)$$

$$v = \frac{ds}{dt} = a\omega(\cos\omega t - 1)$$

$$\Rightarrow \quad \int_0^s ds = \int_0^t a\omega(\cos\omega t - 1)dt$$

$$\Rightarrow \quad [s]_0^s = \left[\frac{a\omega\sin\omega t}{\omega} - a\omega t\right]_0^t$$

$$s = a\sin\omega t - a\omega t$$

18. $v = \alpha\sqrt{x} \Rightarrow \frac{dx}{dt} = \alpha\sqrt{x} \Rightarrow \int_0^x \frac{dx}{\sqrt{x}} = \alpha\int_0^t dt$

$$\Rightarrow [2\sqrt{x}]_0^x = \alpha[t]_0^t \Rightarrow x = \frac{\alpha^2 t^2}{4}$$

$$\Rightarrow \quad v = \frac{dx}{dt} = \frac{\alpha^2}{4}(2t) = \frac{1}{2}\alpha^2 t$$

19. $v = \alpha\sqrt{x} \Rightarrow \frac{dx}{dt} = \alpha\sqrt{x} \Rightarrow \int_0^x \frac{dx}{\sqrt{x}} = \alpha\int_0^t dt$

$$\Rightarrow \quad [2\sqrt{x}]_0^x = \alpha[t]_0^t \Rightarrow t = \frac{2\sqrt{x}}{\alpha}$$

$$v_{avg} = \frac{s}{t} = \frac{s}{\left(\frac{2\sqrt{s}}{\alpha}\right)} = \frac{1}{2}\alpha\sqrt{s}$$

20. $v = 4t^3 - 2t$

$$\Rightarrow \quad \frac{dx}{dt} = 4t^3 - 2t \Rightarrow \int_0^x dx = \int_0^t (4t^3 - 2t)dt$$

$$\Rightarrow \quad x = t^4 - t^2$$

At $x = 2$, $\quad t^4 - t^2 = 2 \Rightarrow t^4 - t^2 - 2 = 0$

$\Rightarrow (t^2 + 1)(t^2 - 2) = 0 \Rightarrow t = \sqrt{2}$

$$a = 12t^2 - 2$$

At $t = \sqrt{2}, a = 12(\sqrt{2})^2 - 2 = 22 \text{ m/s}^2$

21. $v = \frac{20}{3x-2} \Rightarrow \frac{dx}{dt} = \frac{20}{3x-2}$

$\Rightarrow \int_0^x (3x-2)\,dx = 20\int_0^t dt \Rightarrow \frac{3x^2}{2} - 2x = 20t$

At $x = 20$, $\frac{3(20)^2}{2} - 2(20) = 20t \Rightarrow t = 28\text{ s}$

22. $\mathbf{v} = 4t\hat{i} + 3\hat{j} \Rightarrow \frac{d\mathbf{r}}{dt} = 4t\hat{i} + 3\hat{j}$

$\Rightarrow \int_{2\hat{j}}^{\mathbf{r}} d\mathbf{r} = \int_0^t (4t\hat{i} + 3\hat{j})dt \Rightarrow [\mathbf{r}]_{2\hat{j}}^{\mathbf{r}} = [2t^2\hat{i} + 3t\hat{j}]_0^t$

$\Rightarrow \mathbf{r} - 2\hat{j} = 2t^2\hat{i} + 3t\hat{j} \Rightarrow \mathbf{r} = 2t^2\hat{i} + (3t+2)\hat{j}$

At $t = 2 \Rightarrow \mathbf{r} = 8\hat{i} + 8\hat{j}$

23. $\mathbf{F} = 6t^2\hat{i} + 4t\hat{j} = m\mathbf{a} \Rightarrow \mathbf{a} = 2t^2\hat{i} + \frac{4t}{3}\hat{j}$

$\Rightarrow \frac{d\mathbf{v}}{dt} = 2t^2\hat{i} + \frac{4t}{3}\hat{j} \Rightarrow \int_0^{\mathbf{v}} d\mathbf{v} = \int_0^3 \left(2t^2\hat{i} + \frac{4t}{3}\hat{j}\right)dt$

$\Rightarrow \mathbf{v} = \frac{2t^3}{3}\hat{i} + \frac{2t^2}{3}\hat{j}$

At $t = 3$, $\mathbf{v} = 18\hat{i} + 6\hat{j}$

24. $\frac{dv}{dt} = -kv^3 \Rightarrow \int_{v_0}^{v} v^{-3}dv = -\int_0^t k\,dt$

$\Rightarrow \left[\frac{v^{-2}}{(-2)}\right]_{v_0}^{v} = -k[t]_0^t \Rightarrow \frac{1}{v^2} - \frac{1}{v_0^2} = 2kt$

$\Rightarrow \frac{1}{v^2} = \frac{1}{v_0^2} + 2kt \Rightarrow v = \frac{v_0}{\sqrt{1 + 2kv_0^2 t}}$

25. $F = \frac{k}{x^2} \Rightarrow ma = \frac{k}{x^2} \Rightarrow mv\frac{dv}{dx} = \frac{k}{x^2}$

$\Rightarrow m\int_0^v v\,dv = k\int_a^x \frac{dx}{x^2} \Rightarrow m\left(\frac{v^2}{2}\right)_0^v = k\left(\frac{-1}{x}\right)_a^x$

$\Rightarrow \frac{mv^2}{2} = k\left(\frac{1}{a} - \frac{1}{x}\right) \Rightarrow v = \sqrt{\frac{2k}{m}\left(\frac{1}{a} - \frac{1}{x}\right)}$

26. $a = -\alpha x^2 \Rightarrow v\frac{dv}{dx} = -\alpha x^2$

$\Rightarrow \int_{v_0}^{v} v\,dv = -\int_0^x \alpha x^2 dx \Rightarrow \left[\frac{v^2}{2}\right]_{v_0}^{v} = -\left[\frac{\alpha x^3}{3}\right]_0^x$

$\Rightarrow \frac{v^2}{2} - \frac{v_0^2}{2} = -\frac{\alpha x^3}{3} \Rightarrow v = \sqrt{v_0^2 - \frac{2\alpha x^3}{3}}$

$v = 0 \Rightarrow x = \left(\frac{3v_0^2}{2\alpha}\right)^{1/3}$

27. Retardation $= C\sqrt{v} \Rightarrow a = -C\sqrt{v}$

$\Rightarrow v\frac{dv}{dx} = -C\sqrt{v} \Rightarrow \int_{v_0}^{v} \sqrt{v}\,dv = -\int_0^x C\,dx$

$\Rightarrow \left[\frac{v^{3/2}}{\frac{3}{2}}\right]_{v_0}^{v} = -C[x]_0^x \Rightarrow v^{3/2} - v_0^{3/2} = -\frac{3Cx}{2}$

$\Rightarrow v = \left(v_0^{3/2} - \frac{3Cx}{2}\right)^{2/3}$

When the particle stops, $v = 0$

$\Rightarrow 0 = \left(v_0^{3/2} - \frac{3Cx}{2}\right)^{2/3} \Rightarrow x = \frac{2v_0^{3/2}}{3C}$

Numerical Value Questions

1. $a = 6t + 4$

$\Rightarrow \frac{dv}{dt} = 6t + 4 \Rightarrow \int_0^v dv = \int_0^t (6t+4)dt$

$\Rightarrow [v]_0^v = [3t^2 + 4t]_0^t \Rightarrow v - 0 = 3t^2 + 4t$

$\Rightarrow v = 3t^2 + 4t \Rightarrow v = \frac{dx}{dt} = 3t^2 + 4t$

$\Rightarrow \int_0^x dx = \int_0^t (3t^2 + 4t)dt \Rightarrow [x]_0^x = (t^3 + 2t^2)_0^t$

$\Rightarrow x - 0 = t^3 + 2t^2 \Rightarrow x = t^3 + 2t^2$

At $t = 3, x = 45$

2. $\frac{dv}{dt} = -\frac{1}{30}v^2 \Rightarrow \int_5^v v^{-2}dv = -\frac{1}{30}\int_0^t dt$

$\Rightarrow \left[-\frac{1}{v}\right]_5^v = -\frac{1}{30}[t]_0^t \Rightarrow \frac{1}{v} - \frac{1}{5} = \frac{t}{30}$

$\Rightarrow \frac{1}{v} = \frac{t}{30} + \frac{1}{5} \Rightarrow v = \frac{30}{t+6}$

When $v = 3$, $\frac{30}{t+6} = 3 \Rightarrow t = 4\text{ s}$

3. $s = \sqrt{at^2 + bt + c}$

$v = \frac{ds}{dt} = \frac{2at + b}{\sqrt{at^2 + bt + c}}$

Acceleration $= \frac{dv}{dt}$

$\Rightarrow$ Acceleration $= \frac{(\sqrt{at^2 + bt + c})(2a) - \frac{(2at+b)(2at+b)}{2\sqrt{at^2 + bt + c}}}{(\sqrt{at^2 + bt + c})^2}$

$\Rightarrow$ Acceleration $= \frac{4a(at^2 + bt + c) - (2at+b)^2}{2(at^2 + bt + c)^{3/2}}$

$\Rightarrow$ Acceleration $= \frac{4ac - b^2}{(\sqrt{at^2 + bt + c})^3} = (4ac - b^2)s^{-3}$

Acceleration $\propto s^{-3}$

4. $\dfrac{dv}{dt} = 6 - 3v$

At $v\uparrow$, acceleration decreases

when $a = 0$, object achieves terminal velocity

$$\frac{dv}{dt} = 6 - 3v_T = 0 \Rightarrow v_T = 2\text{ m/s}$$

5. $a = -\sqrt{v} \Rightarrow \dfrac{dv}{dt} = -\sqrt{v} \Rightarrow \displaystyle\int_{v_0}^{v} \frac{dv}{\sqrt{v}} = -\int_0^t dt$

$$\Rightarrow [2\sqrt{v}]_{v_0}^{v} = -[t]_0^t \Rightarrow 2(\sqrt{v} - \sqrt{v_0}) = -t$$

$$\Rightarrow \sqrt{v} = \frac{-t}{2} + \sqrt{v_0} \Rightarrow v = \left(-\frac{t}{2} + \sqrt{v_0}\right)^2$$

At $t = 4$, $v = \left(-\dfrac{4}{2} + \sqrt{v_0}\right)^2 = 0 \Rightarrow v_0 = 4\text{ m/s}$

6. $a = 4 - t^2$

$$\Rightarrow \frac{dv}{dt} = 4 - t^2 \Rightarrow \int_0^v dv = \int_0^2 (4 - t^2)dt$$

$$\Rightarrow [v]_0^v = \left[4t - \frac{t^3}{3}\right]_0^2 \Rightarrow v - 0 = 8 - \frac{8}{3} = \frac{16}{3}$$

For $t > 2$, $a = \dfrac{1}{3}$

$$v = u + at$$

At $t = 4$, $v = \dfrac{16}{3} + \dfrac{1}{3}(2) = 6\text{ m/s}$

7. $\mathbf{r} = 3t\hat{\mathbf{i}} + 3t\left(1 - \dfrac{t}{4}\right)\hat{\mathbf{j}} \Rightarrow \mathbf{v} = 3\hat{\mathbf{i}} + \left(3 - \dfrac{3t}{2}\right)\hat{\mathbf{j}}$

$$\mathbf{a} = -\frac{3}{2}\hat{\mathbf{j}}$$

$$\mathbf{v}\cdot\mathbf{a} = 0$$

$$\Rightarrow \left(3 - \frac{3t}{2}\right)\left(-\frac{3}{2}\right) = 0 \Rightarrow t = 2\text{ s}$$

8. $\mathbf{v} = 2\hat{\mathbf{i}} + 4x\hat{\mathbf{j}}$

$v_x = 2,$	$v_y = 4x$
$\Rightarrow \dfrac{dx}{dt} = 2,$	$\Rightarrow v_y = 4(2t)$
$\Rightarrow \displaystyle\int_0^x dx = 2\int_0^t dt$	$\Rightarrow \dfrac{dy}{dt} = 8t$
$\Rightarrow [x] = 2[t]_0^t,$	$\Rightarrow \displaystyle\int_0^y dy = 8\int_0^t t\,dt$
$\Rightarrow x = 2t,$	$\Rightarrow y = 4t^2$

When $x = 3$, $3 = 2t \Rightarrow t = \dfrac{3}{2}$

At $t = \dfrac{3}{2}$, $y = 4\left(\dfrac{3}{2}\right)^2 = 9$

9. $v = \cos\left(\dfrac{\pi t}{3}\right) \Rightarrow \dfrac{dx}{dt} = \cos\left(\dfrac{\pi t}{3}\right)$

$$\Rightarrow \int_0^x dx = \int_0^2 \cos\left(\frac{\pi t}{3}\right)dt \Rightarrow [x]_0^x = \left[\frac{\sin\left(\frac{\pi}{3}t\right)}{\frac{\pi}{3}}\right]_0^2$$

$$x = \frac{3\sqrt{3}}{2\pi} = \frac{\sqrt{27}}{2\pi}$$

10. $T = \dfrac{AC}{v} + \dfrac{\sqrt{(CD)^2 + l^2}}{v/3} \Rightarrow T = \dfrac{AD - CD}{v} + \dfrac{3\sqrt{(CD)^2 + l^2}}{v}$

$$\frac{dT}{d(CD)} = \frac{1}{v}\left(-1 + \frac{3}{2\sqrt{(CD)^2 + l^2}}(2CD)\right) = 0$$

$$\Rightarrow 3CD = \sqrt{CD^2 + l^2} \Rightarrow 9(CD)^2 = (CD)^2 + l^2$$

$$\Rightarrow CD = \frac{l}{2\sqrt{2}}$$

Level 3

Single Choice Correct Questions

1. $\mathbf{r} = \alpha t\,\hat{\mathbf{i}} + \alpha t(1 - \beta t)\hat{\mathbf{j}}$

$$\mathbf{v} = \alpha\hat{\mathbf{i}} + \alpha(1 - 2\beta t)\hat{\mathbf{j}} \Rightarrow \mathbf{a} = -2\alpha\beta\hat{\mathbf{j}}$$

$$\cos\theta = \frac{\mathbf{v}\cdot\mathbf{a}}{va}$$

$$\Rightarrow \cos\left(\frac{\pi}{4}\right) = \frac{\alpha(1 - 2\beta t)(-2\alpha\beta)}{\sqrt{\alpha^2 + \alpha^2(1 - 2\beta t)^2}\,(2\alpha\beta)}$$

$$\Rightarrow \frac{1}{\sqrt{2}} = -\frac{\alpha(1 - 2\beta t)}{\alpha\sqrt{1 + (1 - 2\beta t)^2}}$$

$$\Rightarrow 1 + (1 - 2\beta t)^2 = 2(1 - 2\beta t)^2$$

$$\Rightarrow 1 - 2\beta t = \pm 1$$

$$\Rightarrow t = \frac{1}{\beta} \text{ and } t = 0$$

2. $a = \dfrac{1.5}{v + 1} \Rightarrow \dfrac{dv}{dt} = \dfrac{1.5}{v + 1} \Rightarrow \displaystyle\int_0^v (v + 1)dv = 1.5\int_0^t dt$

$$\Rightarrow \frac{v^2}{2} + v = 1.5t$$

At $t = 5$,

$$\frac{v^2}{2} + v = 7.5$$

$$\Rightarrow v^2 + 2v - 15 = 0 \Rightarrow v = 3 \text{ and } v = -5$$

$$a = v\frac{dv}{dx} = \frac{1.5}{v + 1}$$

$$\Rightarrow \int_0^v (v + 1)\,v\,dv = 1.5\int_0^x dx$$

$$\Rightarrow \left[\frac{v^3}{3} + \frac{v^2}{2}\right]_0^v = 1.5\,[x]_0^x \Rightarrow \frac{v^3}{3} + \frac{v^2}{2} = 1.5x$$

At $v = 3 \Rightarrow \dfrac{3^3}{3} + \dfrac{3^2}{2} = 1.5x \Rightarrow x = 9\text{ m}$

3. $F = -rv \Rightarrow ma = -rv \Rightarrow mv\dfrac{dv}{dx} = -rv$

$$\Rightarrow m\int_{v_0}^{v} dv = -r\int_0^x dx \Rightarrow m(v - v_0) = -rx \Rightarrow v = v_0 - \frac{rx}{m}$$

When it comes to rest,

$$\Rightarrow \quad 0 = v_0 - \frac{rx}{m} \Rightarrow x = \frac{mv_0}{r}$$

4. $v_x = u_0$, $\dfrac{dx}{dt} = u_0$, $\displaystyle\int_0^x dx = u_0\int_0^t dt$, $x = u_0 t$ ...(i),

$v_y = a\omega\cos\omega t$, $\dfrac{dy}{dt} = a\omega\cos\omega t$, $\displaystyle\int_0^y dy = a\omega\int_0^t \cos\omega t dt$, $y = a\sin\omega t$ ...(ii)

From Eqs. (i) and (ii), we get

$$\Rightarrow \quad y = a\sin\left(\frac{\omega x}{u_0}\right)$$

5. Retardation $= av^2$

$$\Rightarrow \quad \frac{dv}{dt} = -av^2 \Rightarrow \int_u^v \frac{dv}{v^2} = -a\int_0^t dt$$

$$\Rightarrow \quad \left[-\frac{1}{v}\right]_u^v = -a[t]_0^t \Rightarrow \frac{1}{v} - \frac{1}{u} = at$$

$$\Rightarrow \quad v = \frac{u}{1 + uat}$$

$$v = \frac{dx}{dt} = \frac{u}{1 + uat} \Rightarrow \int_0^x dx = u\int_0^t \frac{dt}{1 + uat}$$

$$\Rightarrow \quad [x]_0^x = \frac{u}{ua}[\ln(1 + uat)]_0^t \Rightarrow x = \frac{1}{a}\ln(1 + uat)$$

6.

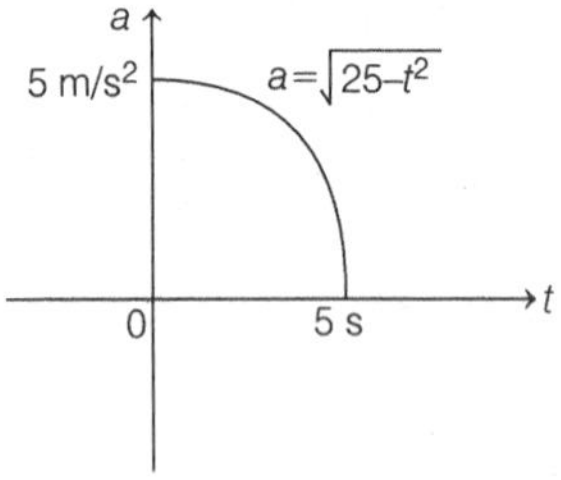

$$\text{Area under } a\text{-}t \text{ curve} = \frac{\pi(5)^2}{4} = \frac{25\pi}{4}$$

$$v_2 - v_1 = \frac{25\pi}{4} \Rightarrow v_2 - 0 = \frac{25\pi}{4}$$

So, velocity at $t = 5$ is $\dfrac{25\pi}{4}$ m/s.

For $t = 5$ to $t = 7$, $a = \dfrac{3\pi}{8}$ m / s^2

$$v = u + at$$

$$\Rightarrow \quad v = \frac{25\pi}{4} + \frac{3\pi}{8}(2) = 7\pi = 7 \times \frac{22}{7} = 22 \text{ m/s}$$

7. $a = 2v^{3/2} \Rightarrow \dfrac{dv}{dt} = 2v^{3/2} \Rightarrow \displaystyle\int_4^v v^{-3/2}dv = 2\int_0^t dt$

$$\Rightarrow \quad \left[\frac{v^{-1/2}}{\left(\frac{-1}{2}\right)}\right]_4^v = 2[t_0]^t \Rightarrow -2\left[\frac{1}{\sqrt{v}} - \frac{1}{2}\right] = 2t$$

$$\Rightarrow \quad v = \frac{4}{(1 - 2t)^2}$$

$$\frac{dx}{dt} = \frac{4}{(1 - 2t)^2} \Rightarrow \int_0^x dx = 4\int_0^t \frac{dt}{(1 - 2t)^2}$$

$$\Rightarrow \quad [x]_0^x = 4\left[\frac{1}{(1 - 2t)(-1)(-2)}\right]_0^t$$

$$\Rightarrow \quad x = \frac{2}{1 - 2t} - 2 \Rightarrow x = \frac{4t}{1 - 2t}$$

At $t = \dfrac{1}{4}$, $x = 2$m

8. $\sqrt{v_x^2 + v_y^2} = v$ ...(i)

$$y = kx^2 \Rightarrow \frac{dy}{dt} = 2kx\frac{dx}{dt} \Rightarrow v_y = 2kxv_x \quad \text{...(ii)}$$

From Eqs. (i) and (ii), we get

$$\sqrt{v_x^2 + (2kxv_x)^2} = v \Rightarrow v_x = \frac{v}{\sqrt{1 + 4k^2x^2}}$$

$$a_x = \frac{dv_x}{dt} = \frac{-v}{(1 + 4k^2x^2)^{3/2}}(4k^2)(2x)\frac{dx}{dt}$$

At $x = 0, a_x = 0$

$$v_y = 2kxv_x$$

$$\Rightarrow \quad \frac{dv_y}{dt} = 2k\left[x\frac{dv_x}{dt} + v_x\frac{dx}{dt}\right]$$

At $x = 0, a_y = 2kv_x^2$ and $v_y = 0 \Rightarrow a_y = 2kv^2$

9. $t = \sqrt{x^2 - 1} \Rightarrow x = \sqrt{t^2 + 1}$

$$v = \frac{dx}{dt} = \frac{1}{2\sqrt{t^2 + 1}}2t = \frac{t}{\sqrt{t^2 + 1}}$$

$$a = \frac{dv}{dt} = \frac{(\sqrt{t^2 + 1})(1) - t\left(\frac{2t}{2\sqrt{t^2 + 1}}\right)}{(\sqrt{t^2 + 1})^2} = \frac{1}{(t^2 + 1)^{3/2}} = \frac{1}{x^3}$$

10. $\dfrac{d\mathbf{v}}{dt} = \mathbf{a} = 2\hat{\mathbf{i}} + 6t\hat{\mathbf{j}} + \dfrac{2\pi^2}{9}\cos\left(\dfrac{\pi t}{3}\right)\hat{\mathbf{k}}$

$$\int_{2\hat{i}+\hat{j}}^{v} dv = \int_0^t \left(2\hat{\mathbf{i}} + 6t\hat{\mathbf{j}} + \frac{2\pi^2}{9}\cos\left(\frac{\pi t}{3}\right)\hat{\mathbf{k}}\right)dt$$

$$[\mathbf{v}]_{2\hat{i}+\hat{j}}^{v} = \left[[2t\hat{\mathbf{i}} + 3t^2\hat{\mathbf{j}}] + \frac{2\pi}{3}\sin\frac{(\pi t)}{3}\hat{\mathbf{k}}\right]_0^t$$

$$\mathbf{v} = (2t + 2)\hat{\mathbf{i}} + (3t^2 + 1)\hat{\mathbf{j}} + \frac{2\pi}{3}\sin\left(\frac{\pi t}{3}\right)\hat{\mathbf{k}}$$

$$\mathbf{v} = \frac{d\mathbf{r}}{dt}$$

$$\int_0^{\mathbf{r}} d\mathbf{r} = \int_0^t \left((2t+2)\hat{\mathbf{i}} + (3t^2+1)\hat{\mathbf{j}} + \frac{2\pi}{3}\sin\left(\frac{\pi t}{3}\right)\hat{\mathbf{k}} \right) dt$$

$$\Rightarrow [\mathbf{r}]_0^{\mathbf{r}} = \left[(t^2+2t)\hat{\mathbf{i}} + (t^3+t)\hat{\mathbf{j}} - 2\cos\left(\frac{\pi t}{3}\right)\hat{\mathbf{k}} \right]_0^t$$

$$\Rightarrow \quad \mathbf{r} = (t^2+2t)\hat{\mathbf{i}} + (t^3+t)\hat{\mathbf{j}} - 2\left(\cos\left(\frac{\pi t}{3}\right) - 1\right)\hat{\mathbf{k}}$$

At $t = 2$, $\mathbf{r} = (8\hat{\mathbf{i}} + 10\hat{\mathbf{j}} + 3\hat{\mathbf{k}})$ m

11. $v_x = 8t - 2,$ | $v_y = 2$

$\frac{dx}{dt} = 8t - 2,$ | $\frac{dy}{dt} = 2$

$\int_{14}^{x} dx = \int_2^t (8t-2)\,dt,$ | $\int_4^y dy = \int_y^t 2\,dt$

$x - 14 = 4t^2 - 2t - 12,$ | $y - 4 = 2t - 4$

$x = 4t^2 - 2t + 2$ ....(i), | $y = 2t$ ...(ii)

From Eqs. (i) and (ii), we get

$$x = 4\left(\frac{y}{2}\right)^2 - 2\left(\frac{y}{2}\right) + 2 \Rightarrow x = y^2 - y + 2$$

12. $v_x = a_0 t$ | $v_y = \lambda x$

$\frac{dx}{dt} = a_0 t$ | $\frac{dy}{dt} = \lambda \frac{a_0 t^2}{2}$

$\int_0^x dx = a_0 \int_0^t t\,dt$ | $\int_0^y dy = \frac{\lambda a_0}{2}\int_0^t t^2\,dt$

$x = \frac{a_0 t^2}{2}$ ....(i) | $y = \frac{\lambda a_0 t^3}{6}$ ....(ii)

From Eqs. (i) and (ii), we get

$$y = \frac{\lambda a_0}{6}\left(\frac{2x}{a_0}\right)^{3/2} \Rightarrow y^2 = \frac{\lambda^2 a_0^2}{36}\left(\frac{2x}{a_0}\right)^3 = \frac{2\lambda^2}{9a_0}x^3$$

13. $\mathbf{v} = k_1\hat{\mathbf{i}} + k_2 x\hat{\mathbf{j}}$

$v_x = k_1$ | $v_y = k_2 x$

$\Rightarrow \frac{dx}{dt} = k_1$ | $\Rightarrow \frac{dy}{dt} = k_2(k_1 t)$

$\Rightarrow \int_0^x dx = k_1\int_0^t dt$ | $\Rightarrow \int_0^y dy = k_1 k_2 \int_0^t t\,dt$

$\Rightarrow x = k_1 t$ ... (i) | $\Rightarrow y = \frac{k_1 k_2 t^2}{2}$ ...(ii)

From Eqs. (i) and (ii), we get

$$y = \frac{k_1 k_2}{2}\left(\frac{x}{k_1}\right)^2$$

$$\Rightarrow \quad y = \left(\frac{k_2}{2k_1}\right)x^2$$

14. $v = 3t^2 - 2t - 1 \Rightarrow x = t^3 - t^2 - t$

$v = 3t^2 - 2t - 1 = 0 \Rightarrow 3t^2 - 3t + t - 1 = 0$

$\Rightarrow 3t(t-1) + 1(t-1) = 0 \Rightarrow t = 1$ s

At $t = 0$, $x = 0$

At $t = 1$; $x = -1$

At $t = 10$, $x = 890$

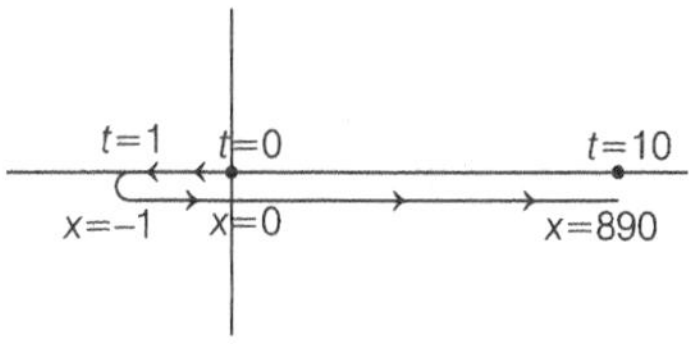

Distance travelled $= 890 + 1 + 1 = 892$m

15. $x = \sqrt{8t^2 + 8t + 4}$

$$v = \frac{dx}{dt} \Rightarrow v = \frac{1}{2\sqrt{8t^2+8t+4}}(16t+8) \Rightarrow v = \frac{8t+4}{\sqrt{8t^2+8t+4}}$$

$$a = \frac{dv}{dt} \Rightarrow a = \frac{(\sqrt{8t^2+8t+4})(8) - (8t+4)\frac{(16t+8)}{2\sqrt{8t^2+8t+4}}}{\sqrt{(8t^2+8t+4)^2}}$$

$$\Rightarrow \quad a = \frac{8(8t^2+8t+4) - 64t^2 - 16 - 64t}{(8t^2+8t+4)^{3/2}}$$

$$a = \frac{16}{(8t^2+8t+4)^{3/2}} = \frac{16}{x^3}$$

At $x = 2$, $a = 2\text{ m/s}^2$

16. $a = 2 + \frac{100}{s^2} \Rightarrow v\frac{dv}{ds} = 2 + \frac{100}{s^2}$

$$\int_5^v v\,dv = \int_{10}^s \left(2 + \frac{100}{s^2}\right)ds \Rightarrow \left[\frac{v^2}{2}\right]_5^v = \left[2s - \frac{100}{s}\right]_{10}^5$$

$$\Rightarrow \frac{v^2}{2} - \frac{25}{2} = \left(2s - \frac{100}{s}\right) - \left(20 - \frac{100}{10}\right)$$

$$\Rightarrow \quad v = \sqrt{4s - \frac{200}{s} + 5}$$

At $s = 25 \Rightarrow v = \sqrt{100 - 8 + 5} = \sqrt{97} = 9.84$ m/s

17. $y = v_0 t \Rightarrow v_x = ky = kv_0 t$

$$\int_0^x dx = \int_0^t kv_0 t\,dt \Rightarrow x = \frac{kv_0 t^2}{2}$$

$$\Rightarrow \quad x = \frac{kv_0}{2}\left(\frac{h}{v_0}\right)^2 = \frac{kh^2}{2v_0}$$

18. $v = \sqrt{v_x^2 + v_y^2}$

$$\frac{dv}{dt} = \frac{1}{2\sqrt{v_x^2+v_y^2}}\left(2v_x\frac{dv_x}{dt} + 2v_y\frac{dy}{dt}\right)$$

$$= \frac{1}{2\sqrt{3^2+4^2}}(2\times 3\times 2 + 2\times 4\times 1) = 2\text{ m/s}^2$$

19. $y = k\sqrt{x}$

Differentiating with respect to time,

$$\frac{dy}{dt} = \frac{k}{2\sqrt{x}}\frac{dx}{dt} \Rightarrow v_y = \frac{k}{2\sqrt{x}}v_x$$

and $$a_y = \frac{k}{2}\left[\left(\frac{1}{\sqrt{x}}\right)a_x - \frac{v_x^2}{2x\sqrt{x}}\right]$$

When $v_x = v_y$, then $\frac{k}{2\sqrt{x}} = 1$

$$a_y = \frac{k}{2}\left[\frac{a_x(2)}{k} - \frac{v_x^2}{2\left(\frac{k^3}{8}\right)}\right] \Rightarrow a_y = a_x - \frac{4v_x^2}{k^3}\times\frac{k}{2}$$

$$\Rightarrow \quad a_y - a_x = \frac{-2v_x^2}{k^2}$$

When $v_x = v_y = \frac{v}{\sqrt{2}}$, then $a_y - a_x = -\left(\frac{2}{k^2}\right)\left(\frac{v^2}{2}\right) = -\frac{v^2}{k^2}$

20. $x = 3\cos 4t,\ y = 3(1-\sin 4t)$

$$v_x = \frac{dx}{dt} = 3(-\sin 4t)\times 4 = -12\sin 4t$$

$$v_y = \frac{dy}{dt} = 3(-\cos 4t)\times 4 = -12\cos 4t$$

$$v = \sqrt{v_x^2 + v_y^2} = \sqrt{(-12\sin 4t)^2 + (12\cos 4t)^2}$$

$$= 12 \text{ m/s}$$

Since, speed of particle is constant.

Distance = speed × time = $12\times 2 = 24$ m

Multiple Choice(s) Correct Questions

1.

$a = -bv$,	$a = -bv$
$\frac{dv}{dt} = -bv$,	$\Rightarrow v\frac{dv}{dx} = -bv$
$\Rightarrow \int_{v_0}^{v}\frac{dv}{v} = -b\int_0^t dt$,	$\Rightarrow \int_{v_0}^{v} dv = -b\int_0^x dx$
$\Rightarrow \ln\left(\frac{v}{v_0}\right) = -bt$,	$\Rightarrow v - v_0 = -bx$
$\Rightarrow v = v_0e^{-bt}$	$\Rightarrow v = v_0 - bx$
$\Rightarrow 0 = v_0e^{-bt}$	$\Rightarrow 0 = v_0 - bx$
$\Rightarrow t = \infty$	$\Rightarrow x = \frac{v_0}{b}$

2.

$x = 2 + 2t + 4t^2$,	$y = 4t + 8t^2$
$v_x = 2 + 8t$,	$v_y = 4 + 16t$
$a_x = 8$,	$a_y = 16$

$\mathbf{a} = 8\hat{i} + 16\hat{j}$

$y = 2(2t + 4t^2) \Rightarrow y = 2(x-2) \Rightarrow y = 2x - 4$

3. $v = \sqrt{400 - 4x}$

$$a = v\frac{dv}{dx} = \sqrt{400-4x}\,\frac{1(-4)}{2\sqrt{400-4x}} \Rightarrow a = -2 \text{ m/s}^2$$

At $x = 0$, $v = 20$ m/s

(a) $v = u + at \Rightarrow 0 = 20 + (-2)t \Rightarrow t = 10$ s

(b) $v = u + at \Rightarrow v = 20 + (-2)(8) = 4$ m/s

$v^2 = u^2 + 2as \Rightarrow 0^2 = 4^2 + 2(-2)s \Rightarrow s = 4$ m

(c) Acceleration is uniform

4. $\mathbf{r} = t^2\hat{i} + (t^3 - 2t)\hat{j} \Rightarrow \mathbf{v} = 2t\hat{i} + (3t^2 - 2)\hat{j} \Rightarrow \mathbf{a} = 2\hat{i} + 6t\hat{j}$

$$\mathbf{v} \perp \mathbf{a} \Rightarrow \mathbf{v}\cdot\mathbf{a} = 0$$

$\Rightarrow (2t\mathbf{i} + (3t^2 - 2)\hat{\mathbf{j}})\cdot(2\hat{i} + 6t\hat{j}) = 0$

$\Rightarrow \quad 4t + 6t(3t^2 - 2) = 0$

$\Rightarrow \quad t(18t^2 - 8) = 0 \Rightarrow t = 0$ and $t = \frac{2}{3}$ s

At $t = \sqrt{\frac{2}{3}}$, $\mathbf{v} = 2\sqrt{\frac{2}{3}}\hat{i}$

So, particle is moving parallel to X-axis.

When particle is at (4, 4), $t = 2$

At $t = 2$, $\mathbf{a} = 2\hat{i} + 12\hat{j}$

5. $x = t^3 - 3t^2 - 9t + 5$

$v = 3t^2 - 6t - 9 = 3(t^2 - 2t - 3) = 3(t-3)(t+1)$

(a) In interval $3 < t < 5$ velocity is positive. So, it is moving in positive direction.

(b) $v = 3(t-3)(t+1) = 0 \Rightarrow t = 3$

So, particle reverses its direction of motion once.

(c) $a_{avg} = \frac{v_2 - v_1}{t_2 - t_1} = \frac{-9-(-12)}{1} = 3 \text{ m/s}^2$

(d) In interval $5 < t < 6$, velocity is positive, so particle is not changing its direction of motion. So, distance is equal to magnitude of displacement.

6. (a) Average speed ≥ |Average velocity|

(b) A particle moving with constant speed may have variable velocity.

(c) It can happen in a round trip.

(d) Particle must take a turn.

7. (a) $a = \alpha - \beta s$

$$\frac{v\,dv}{ds} = \alpha - \beta s \Rightarrow \int_0^v v\,dv = \int_0^s(\alpha - \beta s)ds$$

$$\Rightarrow \frac{v^2}{2} = \alpha s - \frac{\beta s^2}{2} \Rightarrow v = \sqrt{2\alpha s - \beta s^2}$$

At station B, $v = 0 = \sqrt{2\alpha d - \beta d^2} \Rightarrow d = \frac{2\alpha}{\beta}$

(b) Velocity is maximum when $a = 0$

$$a = \alpha - \beta s = 0 \Rightarrow s = \frac{\alpha}{\beta}$$

At $s = \frac{\alpha}{\beta}$, $v_{max} = \sqrt{2\alpha\left(\frac{\alpha}{\beta}\right) - \beta\left(\frac{\alpha}{\beta}\right)^2} = \frac{\alpha}{\sqrt{\beta}}$

(c) Distance to be covered after attaining maximum velocity $= \frac{2\alpha}{\beta} - \frac{\alpha}{\beta} = \frac{\alpha}{\beta}$

8. $y = x^2 \Rightarrow \frac{dy}{dt} = 2x\frac{dx}{dt}$

At $x = \frac{1}{2}, v_y = 2\left(\frac{1}{2}\right)(4) = 4$

So, $\mathbf{r} = \frac{1}{2}\hat{\mathbf{i}} + \frac{1}{4}\hat{\mathbf{j}}$, $\mathbf{v} = 4\hat{\mathbf{i}} + 4\hat{\mathbf{j}}$

$$\frac{d^2y}{dt^2} = 2x\frac{d^2x}{dt^2} + 2\left(\frac{dx}{dt}\right)\left(\frac{dx}{dt}\right) = 2\left(\frac{1}{2}(8) + (4)^2\right) = 40 \text{ m/s}^2$$

$\mathbf{a} = 8\hat{\mathbf{i}} + 40\hat{\mathbf{j}}$

9. $x = 4 - 9t + \frac{t^3}{3}$

$v = -9 + t^2 = (t+3)(t-3)$

$a = 2t$

(a) Direction of motion is changing at $t = 3$.

(c) $0 < t < 3, v < 0$ and $a > 0$.

So, particle is slowing down.

10. $v = \beta x^{1/3}$

$\frac{dx}{dt} = \beta x^{1/3}$

$\int_0^x x^{-1/3} dx = \beta \int_0^t dt$

$\frac{3}{2}x^{2/3} = \beta t$

$a = v\frac{dv}{dx}$

$a = \beta x^{1/3} \frac{1}{3}\beta x^{-2/3}$

$a = \frac{\beta^2}{3}x^{-1/3}$

So, acceleration is variable.

(b) Mean velocity $= \frac{x}{T} = \frac{\left(\frac{2\beta T}{3}\right)^{3/2}}{T} = \left(\frac{2\beta}{3}\right)^{3/2}\sqrt{T}$

(c) Mean velocity $= \frac{x_0}{t} = \frac{x_0}{\frac{3}{2\beta}x_0^{2/3}} = \frac{2\beta}{3}x_0^{1/3}$

11. $a = -0.5t$

$v = \frac{-t^2}{4} + 16 = 0 \Rightarrow t = 8\text{ s}$

$s = \frac{-t^3}{12} + 16t$

At $t = 0, s = 0$

At $t = 8, s = \frac{256}{3}$ m

At $t = 10; s = \frac{230}{3}$ m

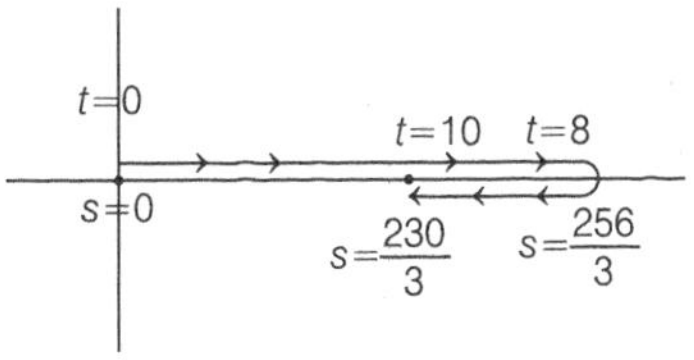

Distance travelled in 10 s $= \frac{256}{3} + \left(\frac{256}{3} - \frac{230}{3}\right) = 94$ m

12. $\mathbf{a}$ = constant

(a) $\frac{d|\mathbf{v}|}{dt}$ = tangential acceleration

So, it will remain constant.

(b) $\left|\frac{d\mathbf{v}}{dt}\right|$ = magnitude of acceleration which is constant.

(c) $\frac{d(v^2)}{dt} = 2v\frac{dv}{dt}$

Here, $\frac{dv}{dt}$ = tangential acceleration = constant

but v will keep changing.

So, overall it will be variable.

(d) $\frac{d(\hat{\mathbf{v}})}{dt}$ is variable as direction of velocity will keep changing.

13. $v = 4t - t^2$

$\frac{dx}{dt} = 4t - t^2 \Rightarrow \int_0^x dx = \int_0^t (4t - t^2)dt$

$\Rightarrow x = 2t^2 - \frac{t^3}{3} \Rightarrow v = (4-t)t = 0 \Rightarrow t = 4\text{s}$

At $t = 0$; $x = 0$

At $t = 4$; $x = 2(4)^2 - \frac{4^3}{3} = \frac{32}{3}$

At $t = 5$; $x = 2(5)^2 - \frac{5^3}{3} = \frac{25}{3}$

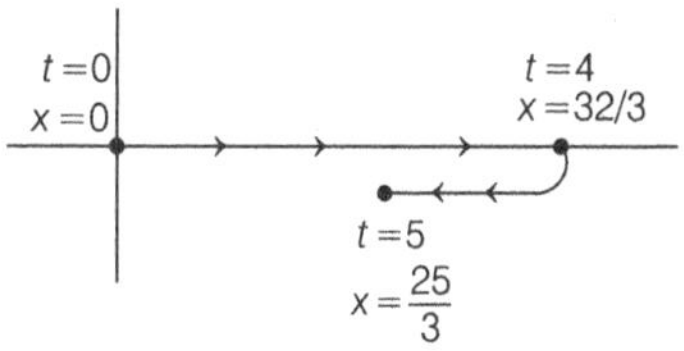

From $t = 0$ to $t = 5$,

displacement $= \frac{25}{3}$, distance $= \frac{25}{3} + \frac{7}{3} + \frac{7}{3} = 13$

$$|\text{Average velocity}| = \frac{|\text{Displacement}|}{\text{Time}} = \frac{25/3}{5} = \frac{5}{3}\text{m/s}$$

$$\text{Average speed} = \frac{\text{Distance}}{\text{Time}} = \frac{13}{5}\text{ m/s}$$

$$\text{Average acceleration} = \frac{v_2 - v_1}{t_2 - t_1} = \frac{-5-0}{5} = -1\text{m/s}^2$$

14.

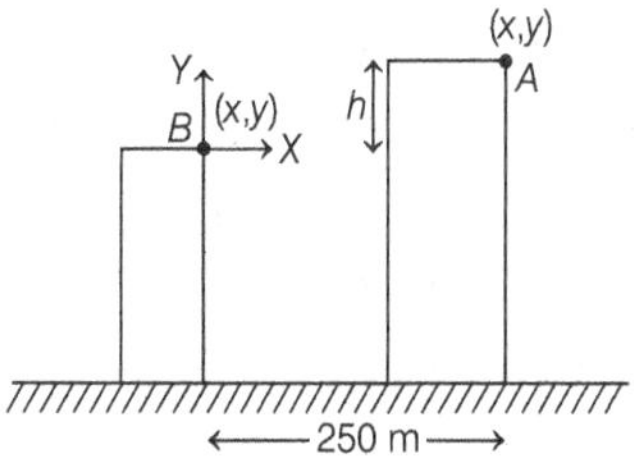

Lets say the balloons collide at point (x, y) at time t.

For Balloon B	For Balloon A
$s_y = u_y t + \frac{1}{2} a_y t^2$	$s_y = u_y t + \frac{1}{2} a_y t^2$
$\Rightarrow \; y = 20t$	$\Rightarrow y - h = 10t$
$v_x = 0.5\,y$	$v_x = 0.5(10t)$
$\Rightarrow \; v_x = 0.5(20t)$	$v_x = 5t$
$\Rightarrow \int_0^x dx = 10\int_0^t t\,dt$	$\int_{250}^{x} dx = \int_0^t 5t\,dt$
$\Rightarrow \; x = 5t^2 \quad \ldots\text{(i)}$	$x = 250 + \frac{5t^2}{2} \quad \ldots\text{(ii)}$

Solving Eqs. (i) and (ii), we get

$$t = 10\text{ s}$$

Now $y = 20 \times 10 = 200$ and $y - h = 10 \times 10 \;\Rightarrow\; h = 100$ m

Comprehension Based Questions

1. $a = -9x$

$$\Rightarrow \quad v\frac{dv}{dx} = -9x \;\Rightarrow\; \int_6^v v\,dv = -9\int_0^x x\,dx$$

$$\Rightarrow \quad \left[\frac{v^2}{2}\right]_6^v = -9\left[\frac{x^2}{2}\right]_0^x \;\Rightarrow\; \frac{v^2 - 36}{2} = -\frac{9x^2}{2}$$

$$\Rightarrow \quad v = \sqrt{36 - 9x^2}$$

At $x = 2$, $v = \sqrt{36 - 9(2)^2} = 0$

2. Distance will be maximum when $v = 0$.

$$0 = \sqrt{36 - 9x^2} \Rightarrow x = 2$$

3. (*d*)

4. $v = 3(t^2 - t) = 3t(t-1)$

$$x = t^3 - \frac{3t^2}{2} = t^2\left(t - \frac{3}{2}\right)$$

$v = 3t(t-1) = 0 \quad \Rightarrow \quad t = 0$ and $t = 1$

At $t = 0, x = 0, \quad t = 1, x = \frac{-1}{2}, \quad t = 2, x = 2$

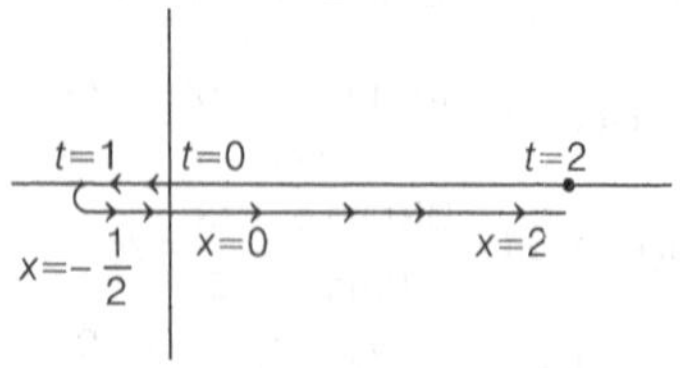

Distance travelled $= \frac{1}{2} + \frac{1}{2} + 2 = 3$ m

5. Displacement $= 2 - 0 = 2$ m

6. $v = 3(t^2 - t) \;\Rightarrow\; a = 3(2t - 1) = 0 \;\Rightarrow\; t = 0.5$ s

7. $x = a\sin\omega t \;\Rightarrow\; y = a(1 - \cos\omega t)$

$\mathbf{r} = a\sin\omega t\,\hat{\mathbf{i}} + a(1 - \cos\omega t)\hat{\mathbf{j}}$

$\mathbf{v} = a\omega\cos\omega t\,\hat{\mathbf{i}} + a\omega\sin\omega t\,\hat{\mathbf{j}}$

$|\mathbf{v}| = \sqrt{(a\omega\cos\omega t)^2 + (a\omega\sin\omega t)^2} = a\omega$

8. $\sin\omega t = \frac{x}{a}, \quad \cos\omega t = 1 - \frac{y}{a}$

$$\sin^2\omega t + \cos^2\omega t = 1$$

$$\Rightarrow \quad \frac{x^2}{a^2} + \left(1 - \frac{y}{a}\right)^2 = 1$$

$$\Rightarrow \quad x^2 = 2ay - y^2$$

$$\Rightarrow \quad x = \pm\sqrt{2ay - y^2}$$

$$\Rightarrow \quad x = \pm\sqrt{2ay\left(1 - \frac{y}{2a}\right)}$$

9. $a_y = -2t$

$$\Rightarrow \quad \int_{6\sin 30^\circ}^{v_y} dv_y = -\int_0^t 2t\,dt \;\Rightarrow\; v_y - 3 = -t^2 \;\Rightarrow\; v_y = 3 - t^2$$

$$v_y = \frac{dy}{dt} \;\Rightarrow\; \int_0^y dy = \int_0^t (3 - t^2)\,dt \;\Rightarrow\; y = 3t - \frac{t^3}{3}$$

Lets say time of flight is T,

$$0 = 3T - \frac{T^3}{3} \;\Rightarrow\; T = 3\text{ s}$$

10. $s_x = u_x t + \frac{1}{2} a_x t$

$$R = (6\cos 30^\circ)3 + 0 \;\Rightarrow\; R = 9\sqrt{3}\text{ m}$$

Match the Columns Question

1. (A) $x = 3t^2 + 2$, $v = 6t$, $a = 6$ — at $t = 1$, $v = 6$ m/s, acceleration is uniform.

(B) $v = 8t$, $a = 8$ — at $t = 1$, $v = 8$ m/s, acceleration is uniform.

(C) $a = 16t$, $v = 8t^2$ — at $t = 1$, $v = 8$ m/s, acceleration is variable.

(D) $v = 6t - 3t^2$, $a = 6 - 6t$ — at $t = 1$, $v = 3$ m/s, acceleration is variable and particle changes its direction.

Numerical Value Questions

1. $a = -\frac{t}{2} + 2$

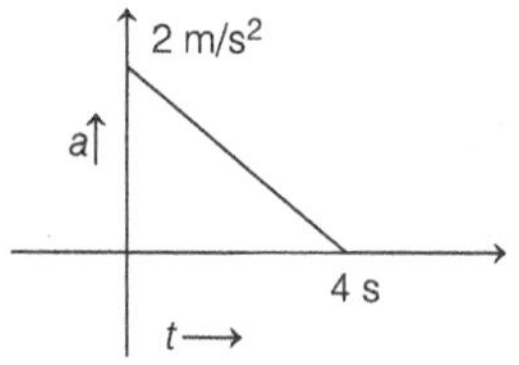

$$\frac{dv}{dt} = -\frac{t}{2} + 2 \;\Rightarrow\; \int_0^v dv = \int_0^t \left(-\frac{t}{2} + 2\right)dt$$

$$\Rightarrow \quad [v]_0^v = \left[-\frac{t^2}{4} + 2t\right]_0^t \;\Rightarrow\; v = \frac{-t^4}{4} + 2t$$

At $t=2$, $v=-\frac{2^2}{4}+2(2)=3$ m/s

2. $a=g-bv \Rightarrow \frac{dv}{dt}=g-bv \Rightarrow \int_0^v \frac{dv}{g-bv}=\int_0^t dt$

$$\Rightarrow \frac{1}{(-b)}[\ln(g-bv)]_0^v=[t]_0^t \Rightarrow \ln(g-bv)-\ln g=-bt$$

$$\Rightarrow \ln\left(\frac{g-bv}{g}\right)=-bt \Rightarrow \frac{g-bv}{g}=e^{-bt}$$

$$\Rightarrow g-bv=ge^{-bt} \Rightarrow v=\frac{g}{b}(1-e^{-bt})$$

At $t=1/10$ s

$$v=\frac{g}{10}\left(1-e^{-10\left(\frac{1}{10}\right)}\right) \rightarrow v=\frac{g}{10}\left(1-\frac{1}{2.7}\right)=\frac{17}{27}$$

So, $n=17$

3. $a=-(g+bv) \Rightarrow \frac{dv}{dt}=-(g+bv)$

$$\Rightarrow \int_{v_0}^{v}\frac{dv}{g+bv}=-\int_0^t dt \Rightarrow \frac{1}{b}[\ln(g+bv)]_{v_0}^{v}=-[t]_0^t$$

$$\Rightarrow [\ln(g+bv)]-\ln(g+bv_0)=-bt \Rightarrow \ln\left(\frac{g+bv}{g+bv_0}\right)=-bt$$

At maximum height $v=0$, $t=t_0$

$$\Rightarrow \ln\left(\frac{g}{g+bv_0}\right)=-bt_0 \Rightarrow \frac{g}{g+bv_0}=e^{-bt_0}$$

$$\Rightarrow e^{bt_0}=\frac{g+bv_0}{g}=\frac{g+2g}{g}=3$$

4. $R=\frac{2u^2}{g}$

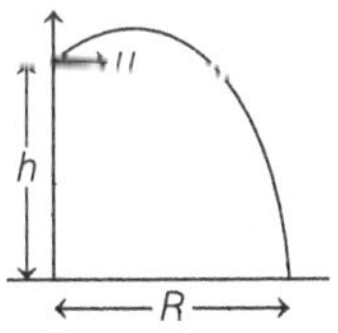

$$R=uT=\frac{2u^2}{g} \Rightarrow T=\frac{2u}{g}$$

$$s_y=u_yt+\frac{1}{2}a_yt^2$$

$$\Rightarrow -h=\frac{dh}{dt}\left(\frac{2u}{g}\right)+\frac{1}{2}(-g)\left(\frac{2u}{g}\right)^2$$

$$\Rightarrow \left(\frac{2u}{g}\right)\frac{dh}{dt}=\frac{2u^2}{g}-h \Rightarrow \int_0^h \frac{dh}{\frac{2u^2}{g}-h}=\left(\frac{g}{2u}\right)\int_0^t dt$$

$$\Rightarrow \frac{1}{(-1)}\left[\ln\left(\frac{2u^2}{g}-h\right)\right]_0^h=\frac{g}{2u}[t]_0^t \Rightarrow \ln\left(\frac{\frac{2u^2}{g}-h}{\frac{2u^2}{g}}\right)=-\frac{gt}{2u}$$

$$\Rightarrow h=\frac{2u^2}{g}\left(1-e^{-\frac{gt}{2u}}\right)$$

5. $a=-\frac{v^2}{3} \Rightarrow \frac{dv}{dt}=-\frac{v^2}{3} \Rightarrow \int_{1.5}^{v} v^{-2}dv=-\frac{1}{3}\int_0^t dt$

$$\Rightarrow \frac{1}{-1}[v^{-1}]_{1.5}^{v}=-\frac{1}{3}[t]_0^t \Rightarrow \frac{1}{v}-\frac{1}{1.5}=\frac{t}{3}$$

$$\Rightarrow \frac{1}{v}=\frac{t}{3}+\frac{2}{3} \Rightarrow v=\frac{3}{t+2}$$

When $v=\frac{1.5}{2}$ m/s, $\frac{3}{t+2}=\frac{1.5}{2} \Rightarrow t+2=4$

$t=2$ s

6. Lets say they collide in time T.

$$5T-\frac{1}{2}gT^2=3(T-t)-\frac{1}{2}g(T-t)^2$$

$$\Rightarrow T=\frac{5t^2+3t}{10t-2}$$

We have to minimize T,

$$\frac{dT}{dt}=\frac{(10t-2)(10t+3)-(5t^2+3t)10}{(10t-2)^2}=0$$

$$\Rightarrow 100t^2-6+10t-50t^2-30t=0$$

$$\Rightarrow 50t^2-20t-6=0$$

$$\Rightarrow 25t^2-10t-3=0 \Rightarrow t=0.6 \text{ s}$$

7. $v=6-2t=0 \Rightarrow t=3$ s

$x=6t-t^2$

At $t=0, x=0$; $t=3, x=9$; $t=4, x=8$

Distance $=9+1=10$ m

Displacment $=8-0=8$ m

8. $a_y=-g \Rightarrow a_y=-\beta t$

$$\frac{dv_y}{dt}=-\beta t \Rightarrow \int_5^{v_y} dv_y=-\beta\int_0^t t\,dt \Rightarrow v_y=5-\frac{\beta t^2}{2}$$

$$\frac{dy}{dt}=5-\frac{\beta t^2}{2} \Rightarrow \int_0^y dy=\int_0^t\left(5-\frac{\beta t^2}{2}\right)dt \Rightarrow y=5t-\frac{\beta t^3}{6}$$

At $t=T$, $y=0=5T-\frac{\beta T^3}{6} \Rightarrow T^2=\frac{30}{\beta} \Rightarrow T=\sqrt{\frac{30}{\beta}}$

Time of flight with $g=10$ m/s^2

$$T=\frac{2u\sin\theta}{g}=1 \text{ s} \Rightarrow \sqrt{\frac{30}{\beta}}=1 \Rightarrow \beta=30$$

9. $s_y=u_yt+\frac{1}{2}a_yt^2 \Rightarrow y=5t$

$$v_x=\left(\frac{4}{25}\right)y \text{ for } y\le 250 \text{ m} \Rightarrow \frac{dx}{dt}=\left(\frac{4}{25}\right)5t$$

$$\Rightarrow \int_0^x dx=\frac{4}{5}\int_0^{50} t\,dt \Rightarrow x=\frac{4}{5}\frac{(50)^2}{2}=1000 \text{ m}$$

$$v_x=80-\left(\frac{4}{25}\right)y \text{ for } y>250$$

$$\Rightarrow \quad \frac{dx}{dt} = 80 - \left(\frac{4}{25}\right)(5t)$$

$$\Rightarrow \quad \int_{1000}^{x} dx = \int_{50}^{100} \left(80 - \frac{4t}{5}\right) dt$$

$$\Rightarrow \quad x - 1000 = 80(100 - 50) - \frac{4}{5}\left(\frac{100^2 - 50^2}{2}\right)$$

$$\Rightarrow \quad x = 2000 \text{ m}$$

$$\Rightarrow \quad \text{Drift} = 2000 \text{ m} = 2 \text{ km}$$

Previous Year's Questions

JEE Main

1. Given, $x = 5t^2 - 4t + 5$

$\therefore$ Velocity, $v = \frac{dx}{dt} = \frac{d}{dt}(5t^2 - 4t + 5)$

$\Rightarrow \quad v = 10t - 4$

at $t = 2$ s, $v = 10 \times 2 - 4 = 16$ m/s

2. Given,

$$s = 2.5t^2$$

$$\frac{ds}{dt} = 2.5 \times 2t$$

$$v_1 = 5t, t = 5 \text{ s}$$

$$v = 5 \times 5 = 25 \text{ m/s}$$

3. Distance travelled $x = 4t^2$

$\therefore$ Velocity of the particle is given as

$$v = \frac{dx}{dt} = \frac{d}{dt}(4t^2) = 8t$$

At $t = 5$ s, $v = 8 \times 5 = 40 \text{ ms}^{-1}$

4. Given, position of bus P,

$$X_P(t) = \alpha t + \beta t^2$$

Its velocity, $v_P = \frac{d}{dt}X_P(t) = \frac{d}{dt}(\alpha t + \beta t^2)$

$\Rightarrow \quad v_P = \alpha + 2\beta t$

Position of bus Q,

$$X_Q(t) = ft - t^2$$

Its velocity, $v_Q = \frac{d}{dt}X_Q(t) = \frac{d}{dt}(ft - t^2) = f - 2t$

Since, $\quad v_P = v_Q$

$$\alpha + 2\beta t = f - 2t$$

$\Rightarrow \quad 2\beta t + 2t = f - \alpha$

$\Rightarrow \quad t(2\beta + 2) = f - \alpha$

$\Rightarrow \quad t = \frac{f - \alpha}{2\beta + 2} = \frac{f - \alpha}{2(\beta + 1)}$

JEE Advanced

1. Given, $\quad \mathbf{v} = \alpha(y\hat{\mathbf{x}} + 2x\hat{\mathbf{y}})$ ...(i)

$\therefore$ Acceleration on the particle,

$$\mathbf{a} = \frac{dv}{dt}$$

$$= \frac{d}{dt}[2y\hat{\mathbf{x}} + 2\alpha x\hat{\mathbf{y}}]$$

$$= \alpha\frac{dy}{dt}\hat{\mathbf{x}} + 2\alpha\frac{dx}{dt}\hat{\mathbf{y}}$$

$\Rightarrow \quad \mathbf{a} = \alpha v_y\hat{\mathbf{x}} + 2\alpha v_x\hat{\mathbf{y}}$ ...(ii)

from Eq. (i), $v_x = \alpha y$

and $\quad v_y = 2x\alpha$

Putting these values in Eq. (ii), we get

$$\mathbf{a} = \alpha(2x\alpha)\hat{\mathbf{x}} + 2\alpha(\alpha y)\hat{\mathbf{y}}$$

$\Rightarrow \quad \mathbf{a} = 2x\alpha^2\hat{\mathbf{x}} + 2\alpha^2 y\hat{\mathbf{y}}$

$\therefore$ Force, $\mathbf{F} = m\mathbf{a}$

$$= 2m\alpha^2\hat{\mathbf{x}} + 2m\alpha^2 y\hat{\mathbf{y}}$$

$$= 2m\alpha^2(x\hat{\mathbf{x}} + y\hat{\mathbf{y}})$$

2. Given, equation $y = \frac{x^2}{2}$

$$\frac{dy}{dt} = \frac{2x}{2}\frac{dx}{dt}$$

$$v_y = xv_x$$

$$\frac{dv_y}{dt} = x\frac{dv_x}{dt} + \frac{dx}{dt}v_x$$

$$a_y = xa_x + v_x^2$$

Put the condition of option you get the answer.

CHAPTER 09

KINEMATICS GRAPHS

LEVEL 01 Starter Level

1 In the following position-time graphs, comment on the nature of motion of body.

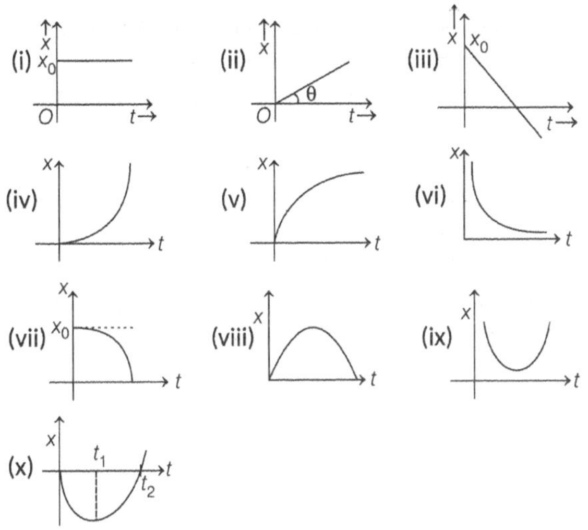

2 In the following velocity-time graphs, comment on the nature of motion of the body.

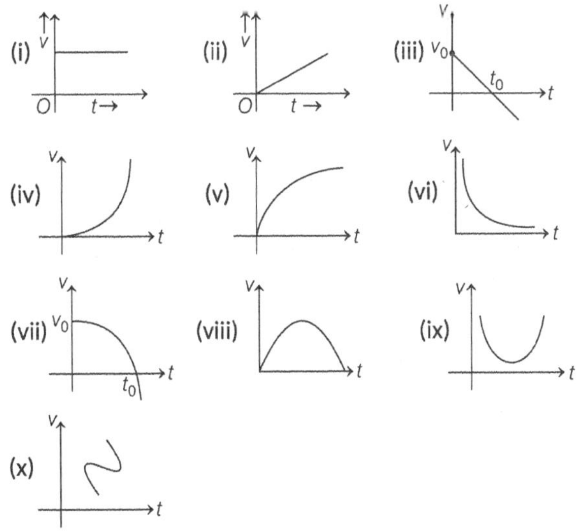

3 In the following acceleration-time graphs, comment on the nature of motion.

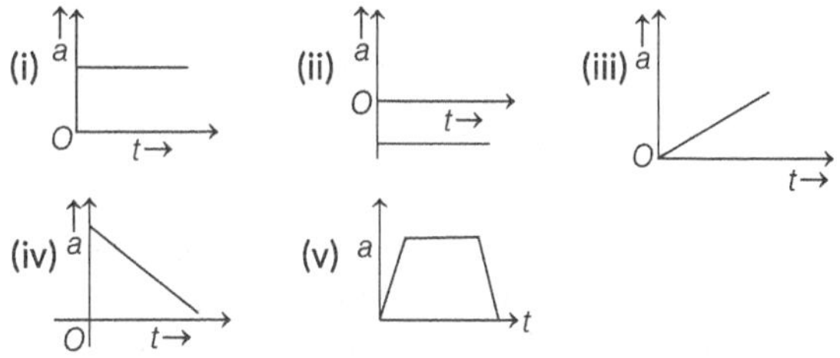

4 For a particle moving along X-axis, velocity-time graph is as shown in figure.

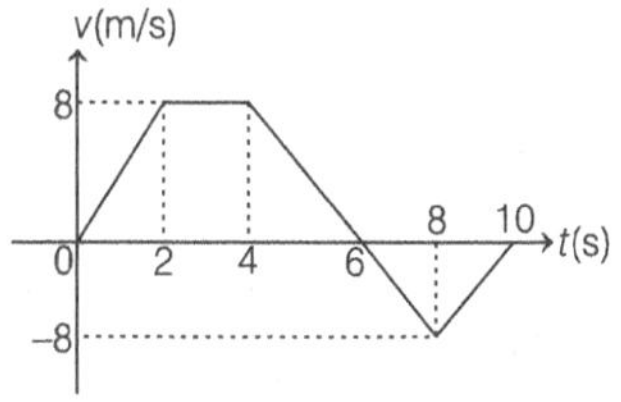

(a) Find the distance travelled and displacement from $t = 0$ to $t = 10$.
(b) Find acceleration at $t = 1, 3, 5, 7$ and 9.
(c) Find average velocity and speed from $t = 0$ to $t = 10$.
(d) Find average acceleration over interval from $t = 2$ to $t = 7$.

5 For a particle moving along X-axis acceleration-time graph is given. At $t = 0$, velocity of particle is 2 m/s. Find

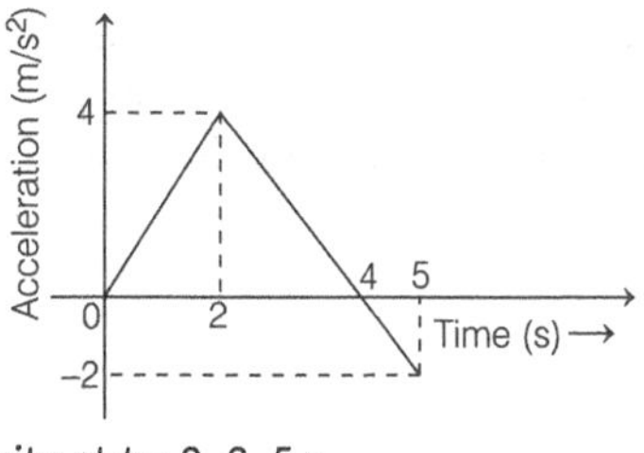

(a) velocity at $t = 2, 3, 5$ s
(b) average acceleration between $t = 0$ and $t = 5$ s
(c) Plot v-t curve

6 The acceleration of a particle which moves along the positive X-axis varies with its position as shown. The velocity of the particle is 0.8 m/s at $x = 0$, find the velocity of the particle at $x = 1.4$.

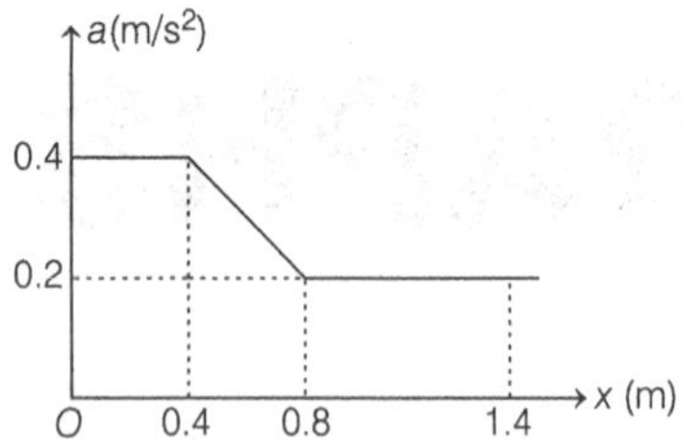

7 The accompanying figure shows the velocity v of a particle moving on a coordinate line.

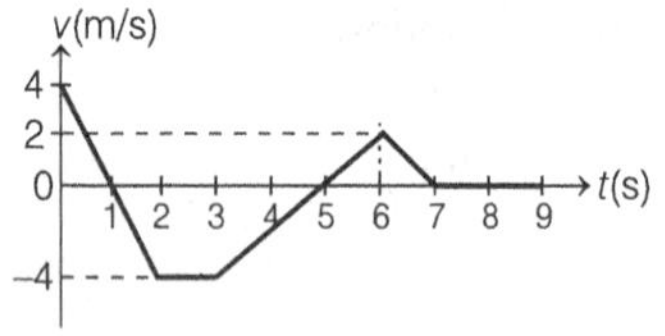

(a) When does the particle move forward? move backward? speed up? slow down?
(b) When is the particle's acceleration positive? negative? zero?
(c) When does the particle move at its greatest speed?
(d) When does the particle stand still for more than an instant?

8 A car starting from rest accelerates uniformly at $2\ ms^{-2}$ for 5 s and then moves with constant speed acquired for the next 5 s and then comes to rest retarding at $2\ ms^{-2}$.

Draw its
(a) acceleration *versus* time graph,
(b) velocity *versus* time graph and
(c) position *versus* time graph.

9 A particle starts from $x = 0$ and initial speed $10\ ms^{-1}$ and moves with constant speed $10\ ms^{-1}$ for 20 s and then retarding uniformly comes to rest in next 10 s.

Draw its
(a) position *versus* time graph,
(b) velocity *versus* time graph and
(c) acceleration *versus* time graph.

10 A particle is thrown vertically up from ground with initial speed 19.6 m/s. Taking, upward direction positive and initial point as origin plot the following graphs till it comes back to ground
(a) acceleration-time (b) velocity-time
(c) speed-time (d) displacement-time
(e) distance-time

11. A particle is dropped from height 19.6 m. After hitting the ground it reaches a height of 4.9 m. Taking downward direction positive and initial point as origin plot the following graphs.
(a) acceleration-time
(b) velocity-time
(c) speed-time
(d) displacement-time

12 The velocity-displacement graph of a particle moving along a straight line is shown in figure.

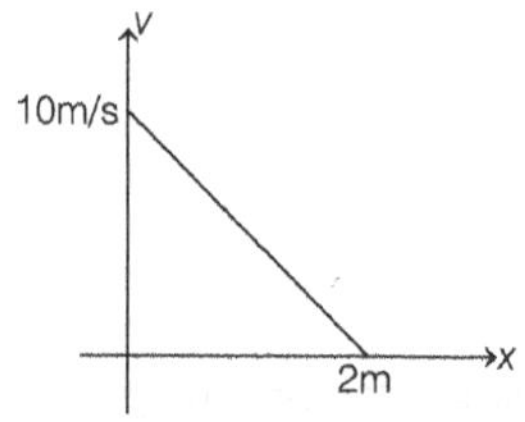

Draw the acceleration-displacement graph.

LEVEL 02 JEE Main Level

Single Choice Correct Questions

1 A particle starts from rest. Its acceleration (a) *versus* time (t) is as shown in the figure below. The maximum speed of the particle will be

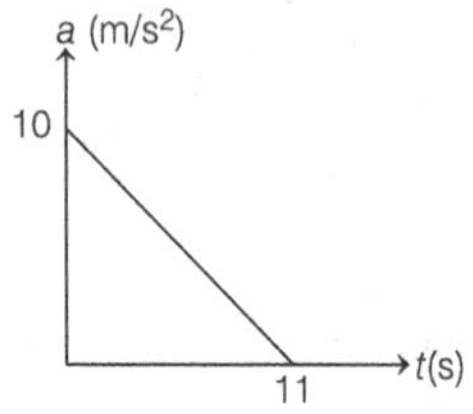

(a) 110 m/s (b) 55 m/s
(c) 550 m/s (d) 660 m/s

2 The variation of velocity of a particle with time moving along a straight line is illustrated in the following figure. The distance travelled by the particle in 4 s is

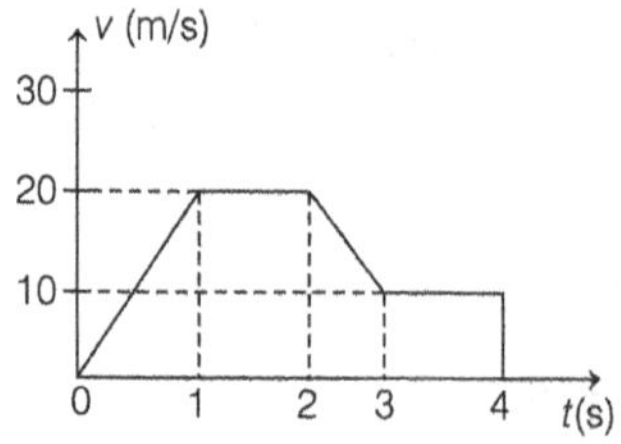

(a) 60 m (b) 50 m (c) 25 m (d) 30 m

3 The displacement of a particle as a function of time is shown in the figure. The figure shows that

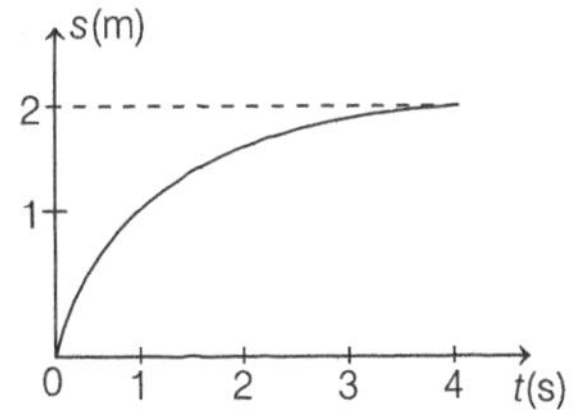

(a) the particle starts with certain velocity but the motion is retarded and finally the particle stops.
(b) the velocity of the particle is constant throughout.
(c) the acceleration of the particle is constant throughout.
(d) the particle starts with constant velocity, then motion is accelerated and finally the particle moves with another constant velocity.

4 A ball is thrown vertically upwards. Which of the following graph represents velocity-time graph of the ball during its flight (air resistance is neglected).

(a) 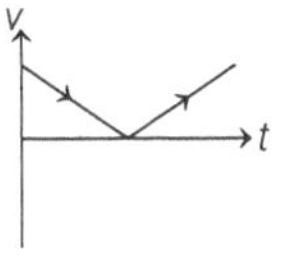
(b) 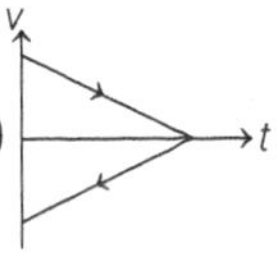
(c) 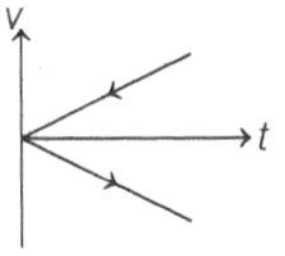
(d) 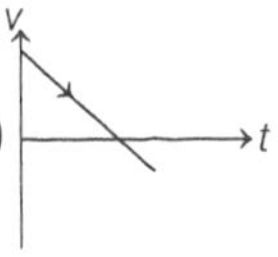

5 The displacement-time graph of moving particle is shown below. The instantaneous velocity of the particle is negative at the point.

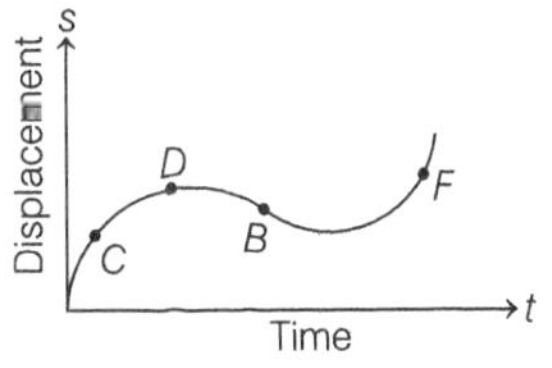

(a) *D* (b) *B* (c) *C* (d) *F*

6 The displacement *versus* time graph for a body moving in straight line is shown in figure. Which of the following regions represents the motion when no force is acting on the body?

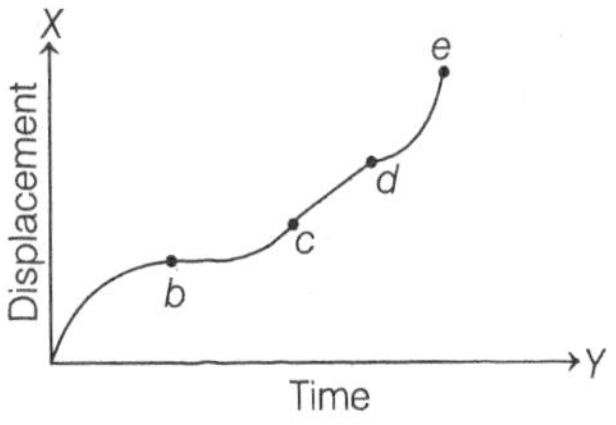

(a) *ab* (b) *bc* (c) *cd* (d) *de*

7 The graph of displacement *versus* time is given below, its corresponding velocity-time graph will be

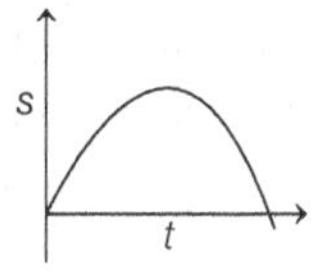

(a) 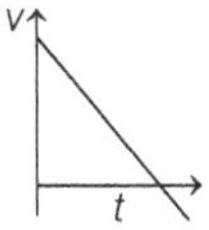
(b) 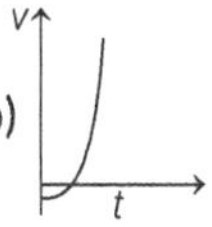
(c) 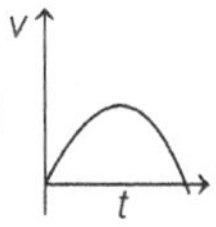
(d) 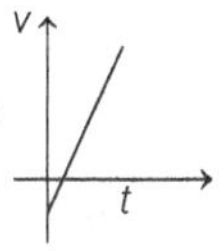

8 Acceleration-time graph of a body is shown. The corresponding velocity-time graph of the same body is

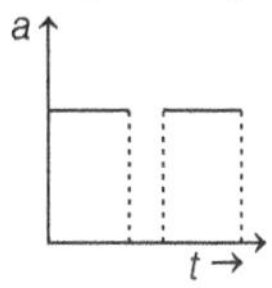

(a) 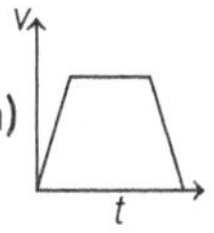
(b) 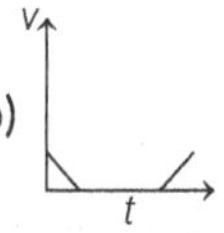
(c) 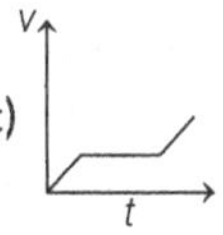
(d) 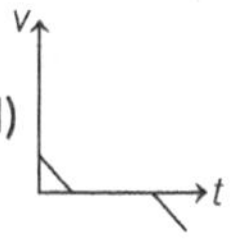

9 A lift is going up. The variation in the speed of the lift is as given in the graph. What is the height to which the lift takes the passengers?

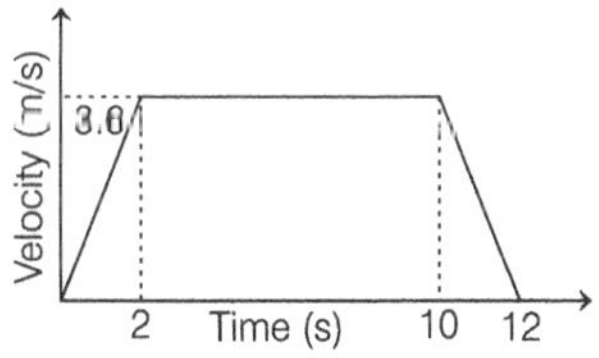

(a) 3.6 m (b) 28.8 m
(c) 36.0 m (d) Cannot be calculated

10 The velocity-time graph of a body moving in a straight line is shown in the figure. The displacement and distance travelled by the body in 6 s are respectively,

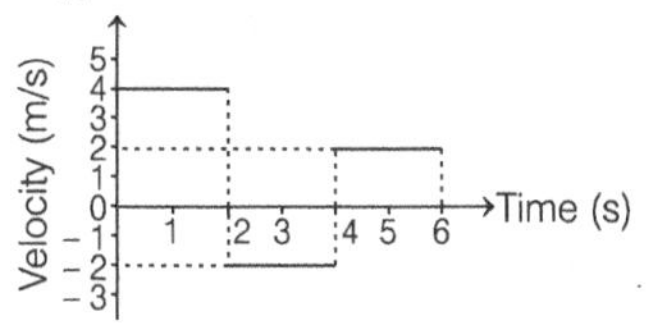

(a) 8 m, 16 m (b) 16 m, 8 m
(c) 16 m, 16 m (d) 8 m, 8m

11 For the velocity-time graph shown in figure below, the distance covered by the body in last two seconds of its motion is what fraction of the total distance covered by it in all the seven seconds?

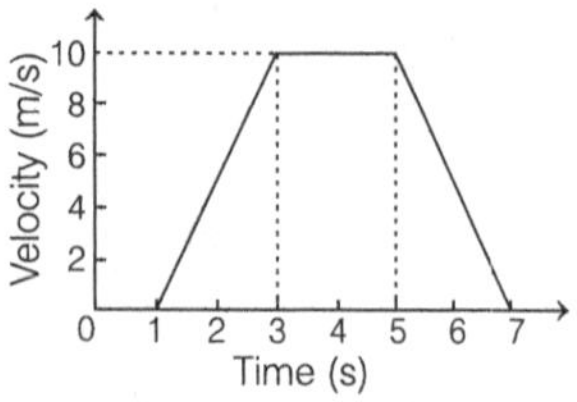

(a) $\frac{1}{2}$ (b) $\frac{1}{4}$ (c) $\frac{1}{3}$ (d) $\frac{2}{3}$

12 Which of the following graph represents uniform motion?

(a) 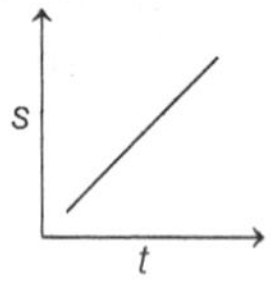

(b) 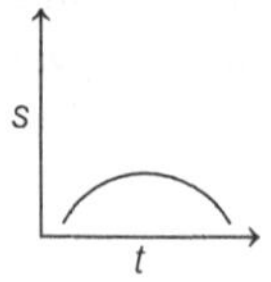

(c) 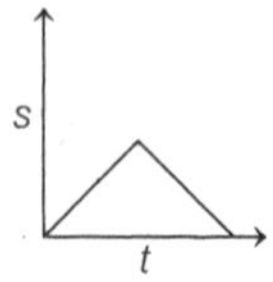

(d) 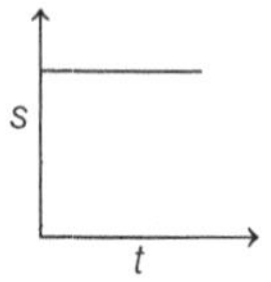

13 A ball is dropped vertically from a height d above the ground. It hits the ground and bounces up vertically to a height $d/2$. Neglecting subsequent motion and air resistance, its velocity v varies with the height h above the ground is

(a) 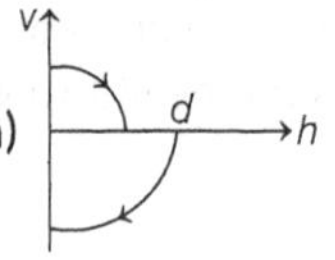

(b) 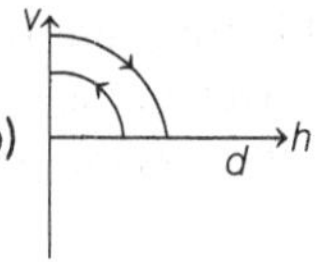

(c) 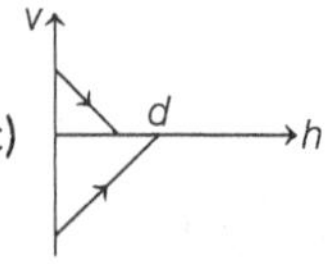

(d) 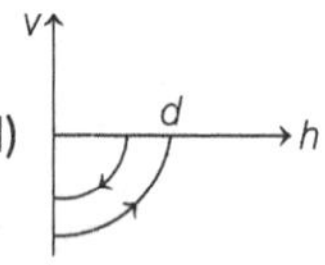

14 The area under acceleration-time graph gives
(a) distance travelled (b) change in acceleration
(c) force acting (d) change in velocity

15 Which graph may represent uniform acceleration?

(a) 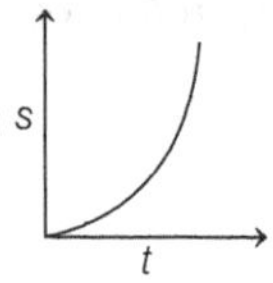

(b) 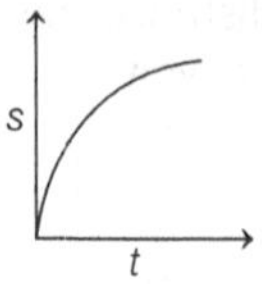

(c) 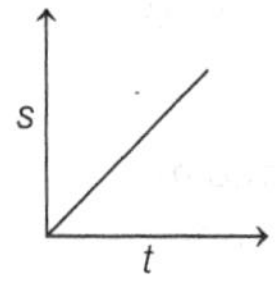

(d) 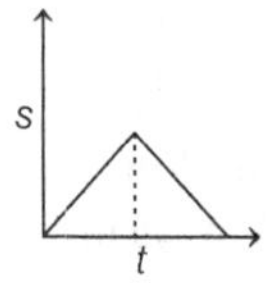

16 Which of the following velocity-time graph represents uniform motion?

(a) 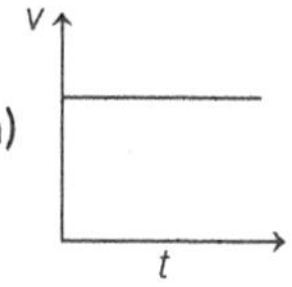

(b) 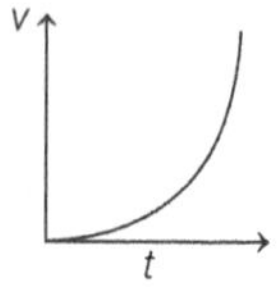

(c) 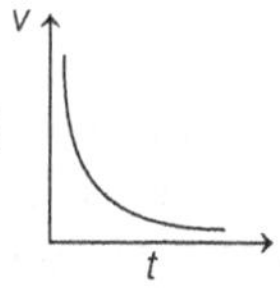

(d) 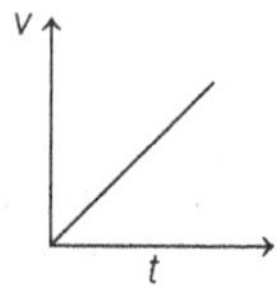

17 The given graph shows the variation of velocity with displacement. Which one of the graphs given below correctly represents the variation of acceleration with displacement.

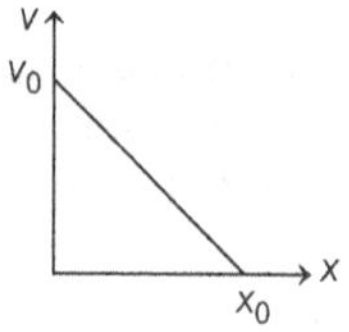

(a) 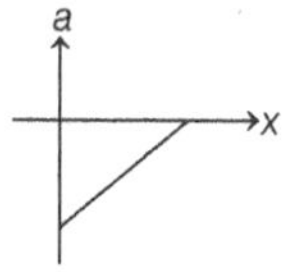

(b) 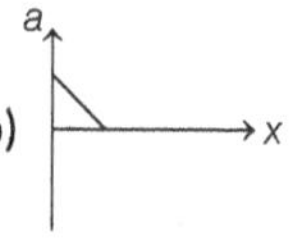

(c) 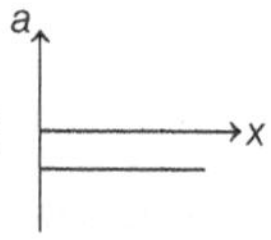

(d) 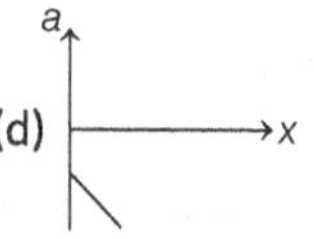

18 From the following displacement-time graph, find out the velocity of a moving body.

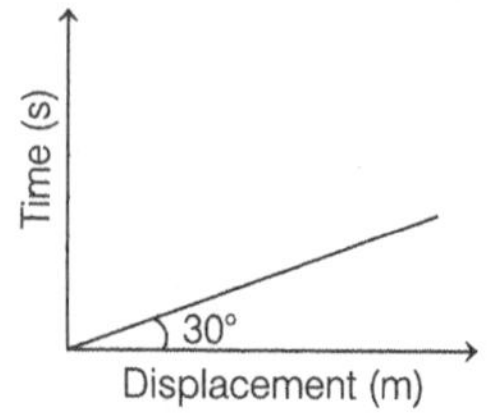

(a) $\frac{1}{\sqrt{3}}$ m/s (b) 3 m/s (c) $\sqrt{3}$ m/s (d) $\frac{1}{3}$ m/s

19 The v-t plot of a moving object is shown in the figure. The average velocity of the object during the first 10 s is

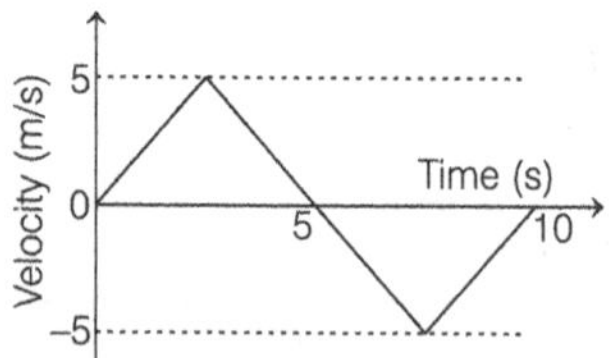

(a) 0 (b) 2.5 ms^{-1} (c) 5 ms^{-1} (d) 2 ms^{-1}

20 Which of the following velocity-time graph shows a realistic situation for a body in motion?

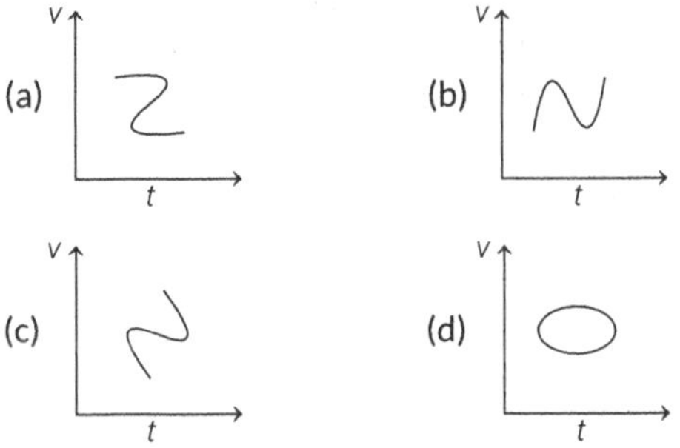

21 If position-time graph of a particle is sine curve as shown, what will be its velocity-time graph?

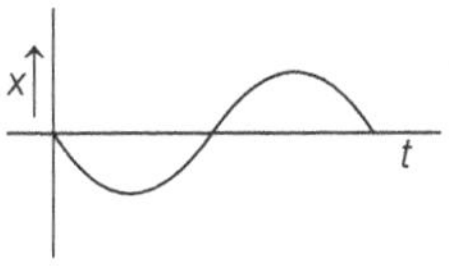

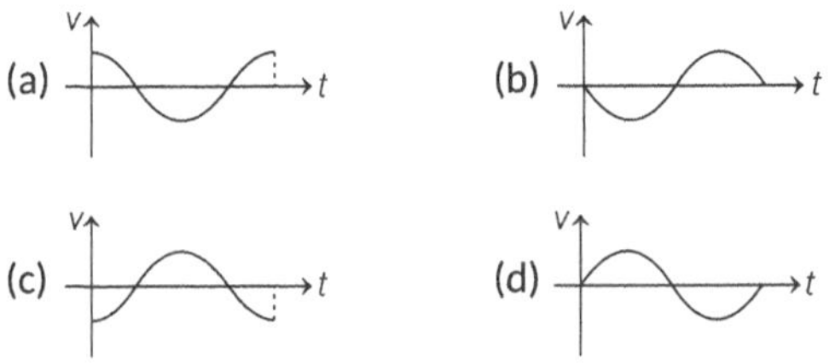

22 A particle starts from rest and moves along a straight line with constant acceleration. The variation of velocity v with displacement s is

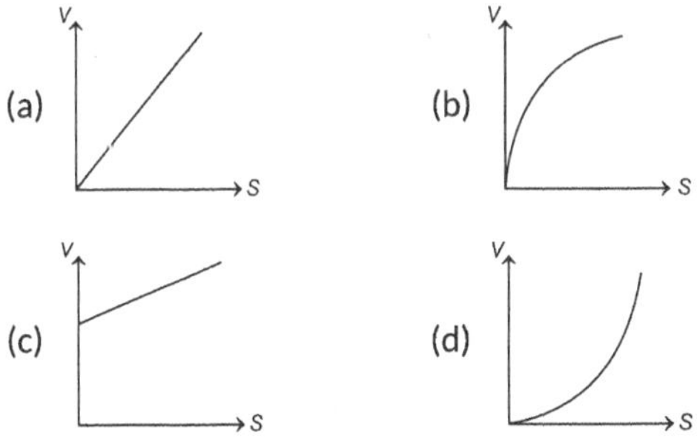

23 The displacement time graphs of two particles A and B are straight lines making angles of respectively 30° and 60° with the time axis. If the velocity of A is v_A and that of B is v_B, then the value of $\frac{v_A}{v_B}$ is

(a) 3

(b) $\frac{1}{\sqrt{3}}$

(c) $\sqrt{3}$

(d) $\frac{1}{3}$

24 For a particle moving along X-axis, velocity-time graph is as shown in figure.

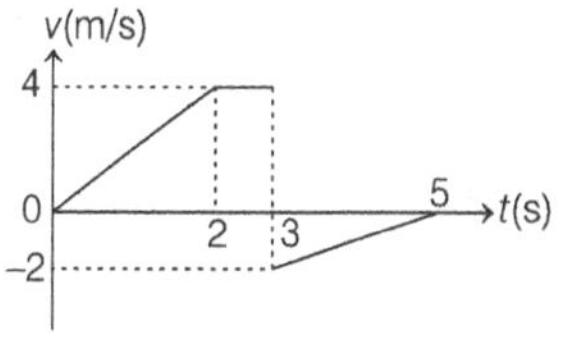

Find the ratio of average speed to magnitude of average velocity of the particle in interval 0 to 5 s.

(a) 5/3 (b) 4/3 (c) 6/5 (d) 7/5

25 A body initially at rest, starts moving along X-axis in such a way, so that its acceleration *versus* displacement plot is as shown in figure. The maximum velocity of particle is

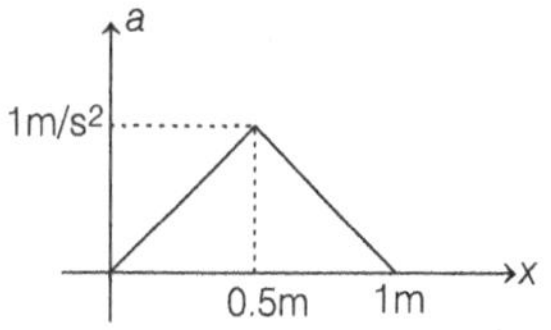

(a) 1 m/s (b) 0.25 m/s

(c) 0.5 m/s . (d) None of these

26 Figure shows position-time graph of two cars A and B. Lines are parallel.

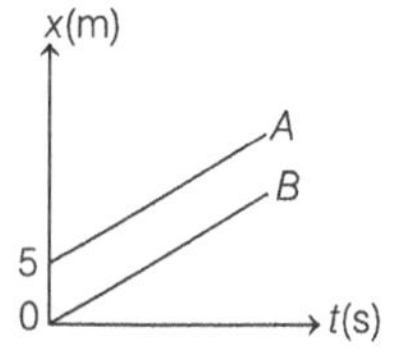

(a) Car A is faster than Car B

(b) Car B always leads Car A.

(c) Both cars are moving with same velocity.

(d) Both cars have positive acceleration

27 Figure shows position-time graph of a particle moving on the X-axis.

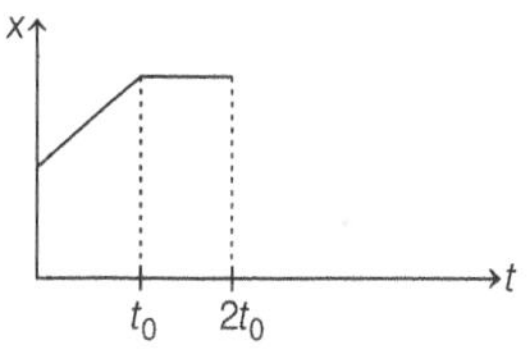

(a) The particle is continuously going in positive x-direction

(b) Area under x-t curve shows the displacement of particle

(c) The velocity increases up to a time t_0, and then becomes constant

(d) The particle moves at a constant velocity upto a time t_0, and then stops

28. The graph gives the position as a function of time for a train on a straight and level track. The average acceleration of the train between interval 5 s to 35 s is

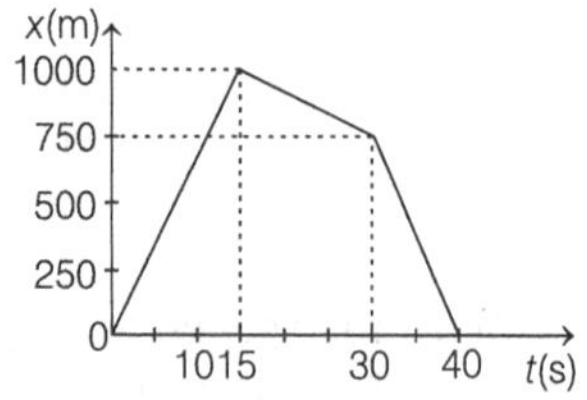

(a) $(85/18)\ m/s^2$ (b) $(-85/18)\ m/s^2$
(c) $(-15/18)\ m/s^2$ (d) $(15/18)\ m/s^2$

29 The velocity-time graph of a stone thrown vertically upward with an initially velocity of $30\ ms^{-1}$ is as shown in figure. The velocity in the upward direction is taken as positive and that in the downward direction as negative.

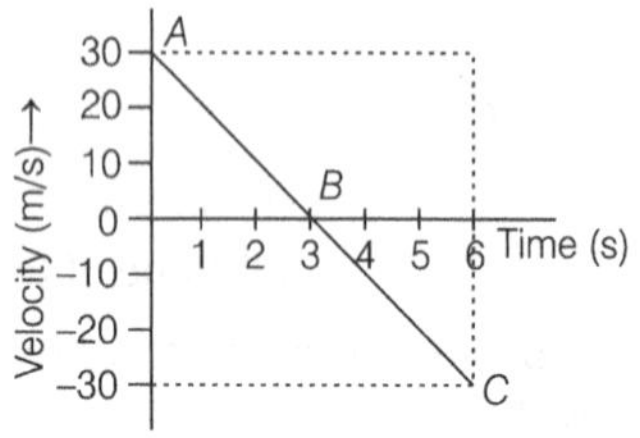

What is the maximum height to which the stone rises?

(a) 30 m (b) 45 m
(c) 60 m (d) 90 m

30 A particle moves in one-dimension. Its velocity is given by v and its acceleration by a. The figure shows its measured acceleration *versus* time graph.Which of the graph (v *versus* t) below are consistent with measured acceleration?

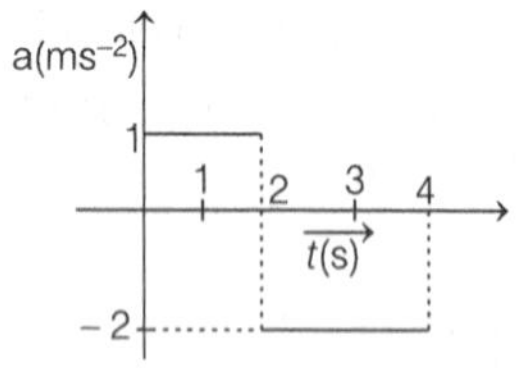

(a) 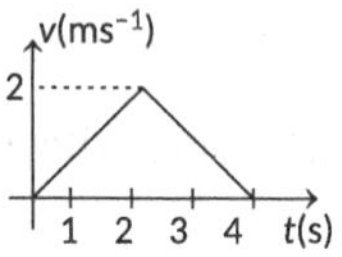

(b) 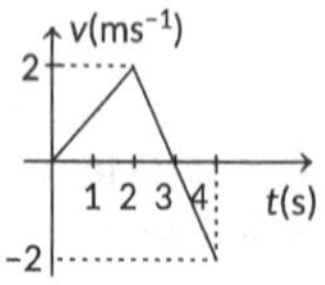

(c) 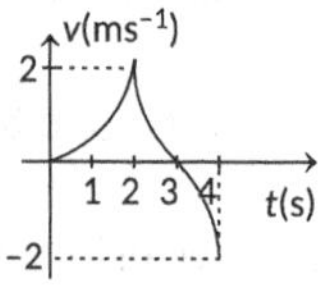

(d) 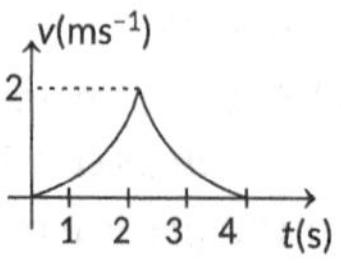

31 The displacement-time graph of a particle moving with constant acceleration is shown in the figure below. The velocity-time graph is best given by

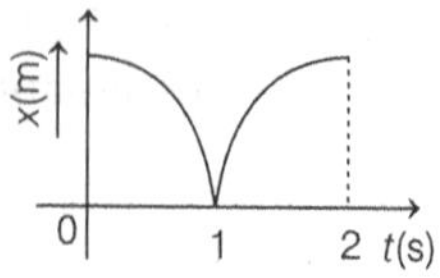

(a) 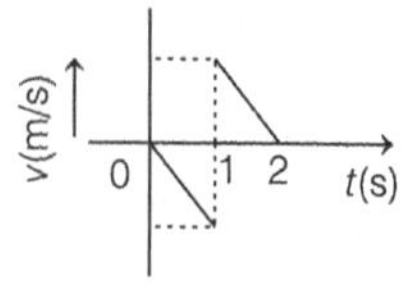

(b) 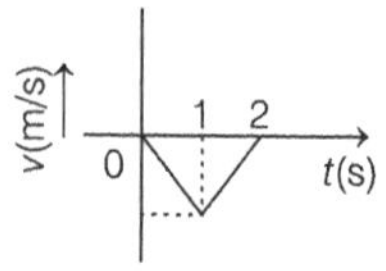

(c) 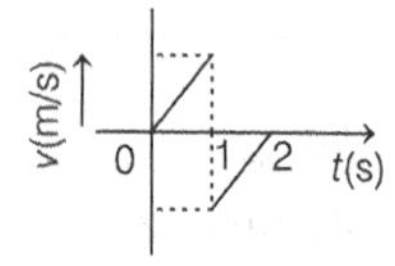

(d) 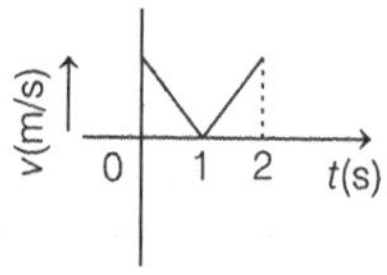

32 The velocity of particle (whose displacement-time graph is shown) at $t = 3$ is

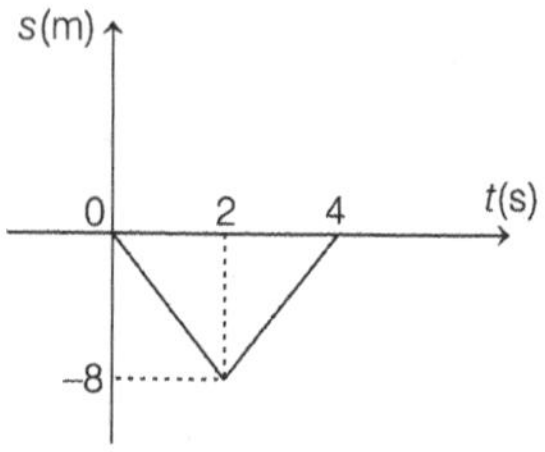

(a) 4 m/s (b) −4 m/s
(c) 8 m/s (d) 2 m/s

33 Figure shows the acceleration-time graph for a particle in rectilinear motion. The average acceleration in first 20 s is

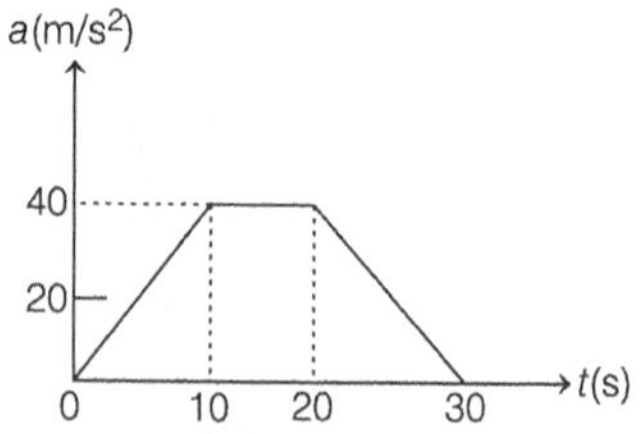

(a) $45\ m/s^2$ (b) $40\ m/s^2$
(c) $30\ m/s^2$ (d) $20\ m/s^2$

34 The velocity-time graph of a body is given in figure. The maximum acceleration in m/s^2 is

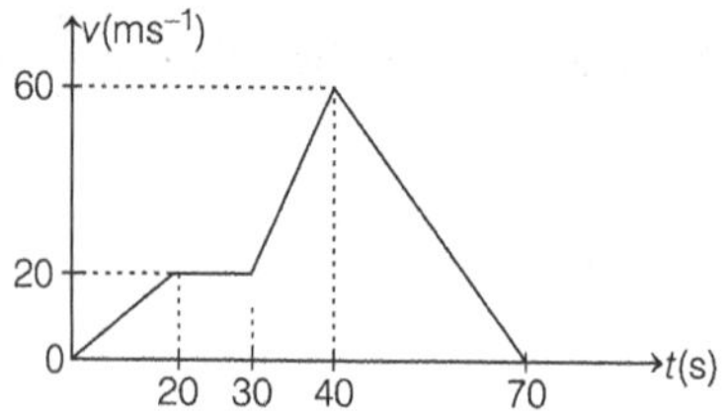

(a) 4 (b) 3 (c) 2 (d) 1

35 Acceleration-time graph of a particle moving in a straight line is shown in the figure. If velocity of particle at $t = 0$ is 1 m/s, then its velocity at the end of 10 s will be

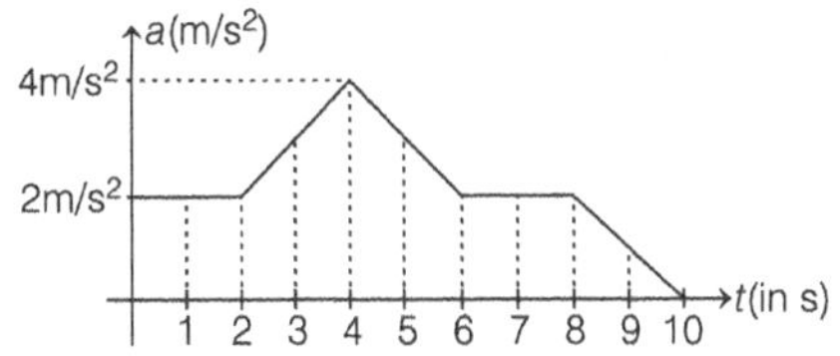

(a) 22 m/s opposite to the initial direction
(b) 23 m/s along the initial direction
(c) 22 m/s along the initial direction
(d) 23 m/s in the opposite direction

36 Position-time graph is shown which is a semicircle from $t = 2$ to $t = 8$ s. Find time t at which the instantaneous velocity, is equal to average velocity over first t seconds.

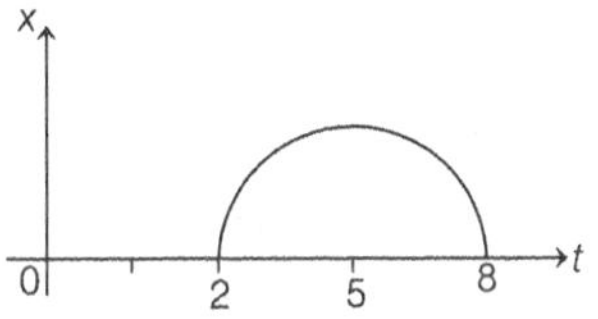

(a) 4.8 s (b) 3.2 s (c) 2.4 s (d) 5 s

37 A particle is moving along a straight line whose velocity-displacement curve is as shown in figure. The acceleration of particle when its displacement is 3 m is

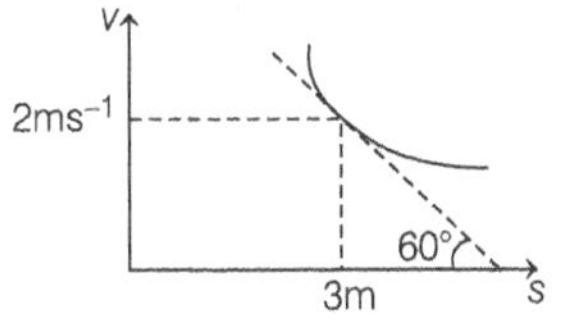

(a) $-2\sqrt{3}$ m/s^2 (b) $2\sqrt{3}$ m/s^2
(c) $-\sqrt{3}$ m/s^2 (d) $\sqrt{3}$ m/s^2

38 A particle starts from origin, accelerates for t_0 second, then decelerates with same acceleration till $2t_0$ second along the x-direction. The graph representing variation of displacement (x) with time (t) is

(a)
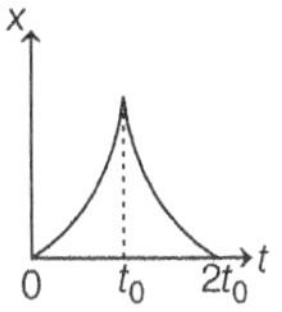

(b)
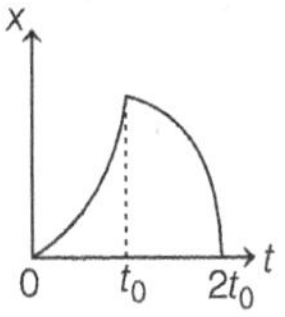

(c)
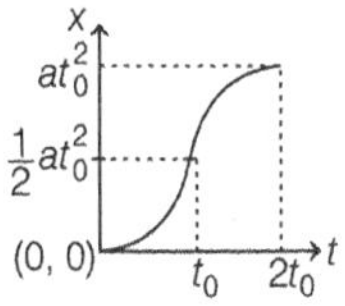

(d)
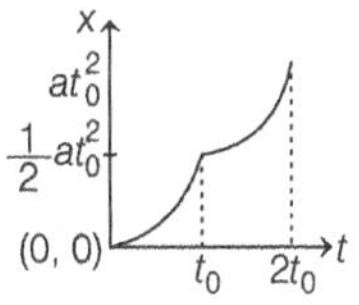

39 The velocity-time graph of a body is shown in figure. The ratio of magnitude of average acceleration during the intervals OA and AB is

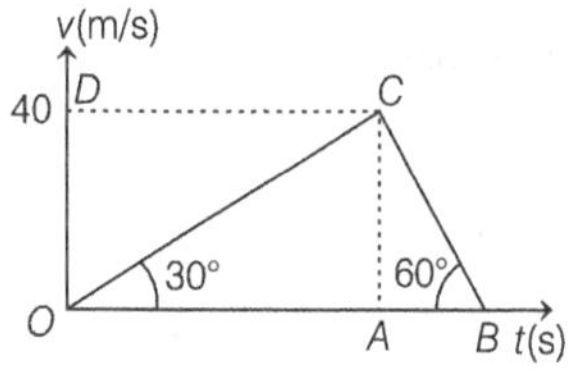

(a) 1 (b) 1/ 2
(c) 1/3 (d) 3

40 Shown in the figure are the velocity-time graphs of the two particles P_1 and P_2. Which of the following statements about their relative motion is true?

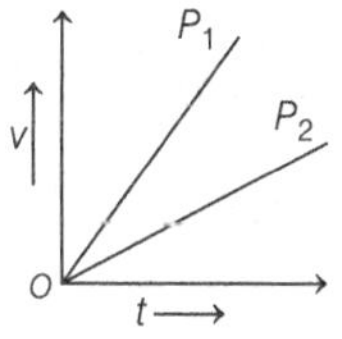

The magnitude of their relative velocity
(a) is zero
(b) is non-zero but constant
(c) continuously decreases
(d) continuously increases

Numerical Value Questions

1 Acceleration of a particle is varying with x according to curve. Velocity of particle at A is 2 m/s. What is the velocity (in m/s) of particle at point B?

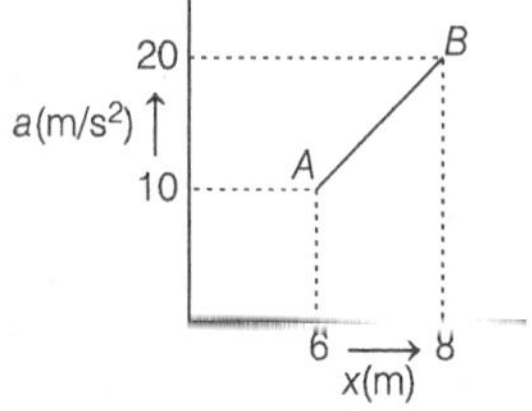

2 The figure shows the graph of velocity-time for a particle moving in a straight line. If the average speed for 6 s is b and the average acceleration from 0 s to 4 s is c, find magnitude of bc (in m^2/s^3).

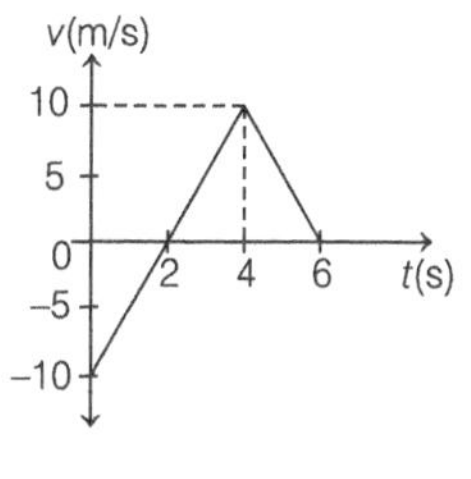

3 A car starts moving rectilinearly, first with constant acceleration $a = 5.0$ m/s^2 (the initial velocity is equal to zero), then uniformly and finally decelerating at the same constant rate a, comes to a stop. The total time of motion equals $\tau = 25$ s. The average velocity during that time is equal to $\langle v \rangle = 72$ km per hour. How long (in seconds) does the car move uniformly ?

4 The acceleration-time graph of the motion of a particle from A to B is semicircle with radius of $\sqrt{7}$ unit. Find the velocity (in m/s) of particle at t_2 if at t_1, velocity is 3 m/s. $[\pi = \frac{22}{7}]$

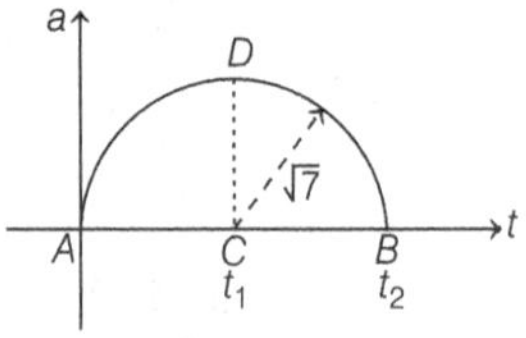

5 A lift starts going up from rest. Its acceleration is shown in figure, plotted against time. Time (in seconds) when lift comes to instantaneous rest is

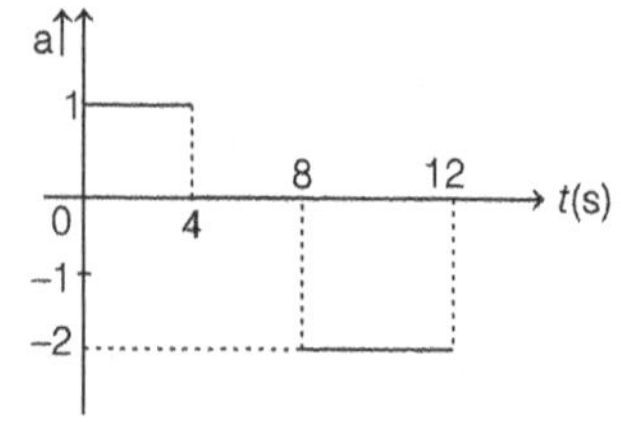

LEVEL 03 JEE Advanced Level

Single Choice Correct Questions

1 Velocity (v) *versus* displacement (x) graph for motion of a particle along x-axis is as shown in figure. The average acceleration over the time interval for journey from $x = 0$ to $x = L$ is

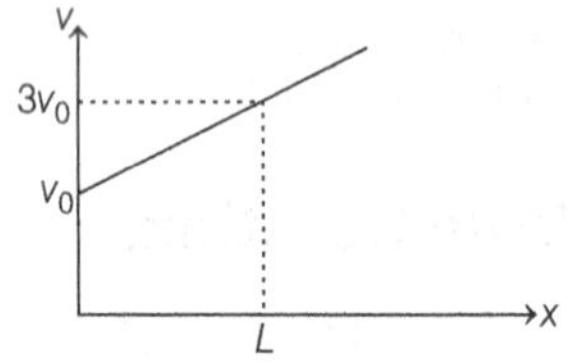

(a) $\frac{2v_0^2}{L}$ (b) $\frac{Lv_0^2}{\ln 3}$

(c) $\frac{4v_0^2}{L\ln 3}$ (d) None of these

2 Acceleration *versus* time graph is given below for motion of an object on a straight line. Find average velocity for the motion $t = 0$ to $t = 10$ s. (Given that, velocity at $t = 0$ is 2/3 m/s)

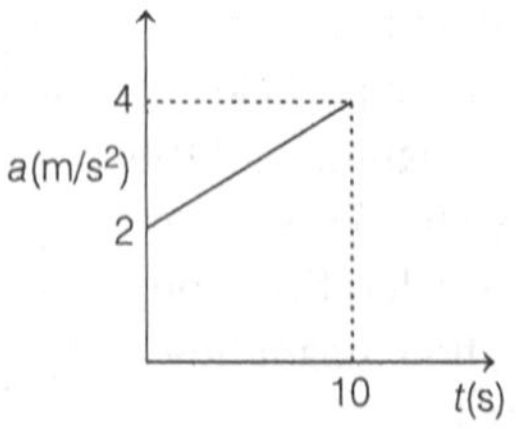

(a) 12 m/s (b) 14 m/s
(c) 6m/s (d) 18 m/s

3 Figure shows $\frac{2}{v}$ *versus* s curve for a particle of mass 2 kg moving in a straight line. Find the time (in seconds) taken by the particle to acheive a displacement of 10 m.
(v = velocity and s = displacement)

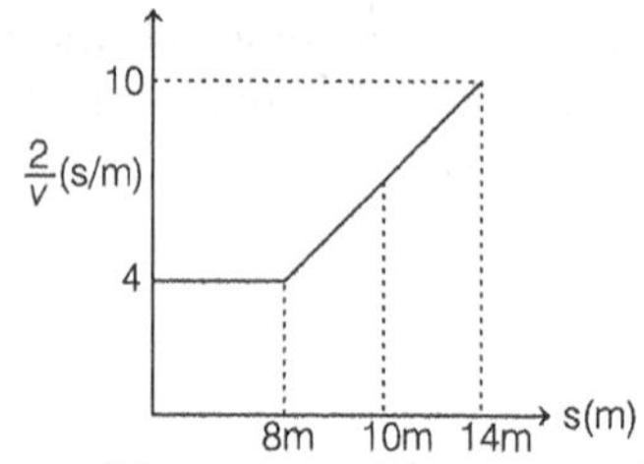

(a) 20 s (b) 21 s (c) 24 s (d) 25 s

4 The figure shows the v-t graph of a particle moving in straight line. Find the time when particle returns to the starting point.

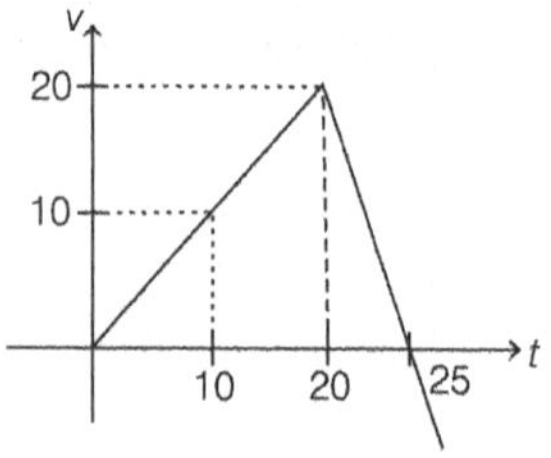

(a) 36.2 s (b) 40 s (c) 45 s (d) 50 s

5 A particle moves in xy-plane, starting from A, along straight line paths AB and then BC, as shown in the graph. When it is at point P, angle between directions of its average velocity and instantaneous velocity is $\left[\tan 37° = \frac{3}{4}\right]$

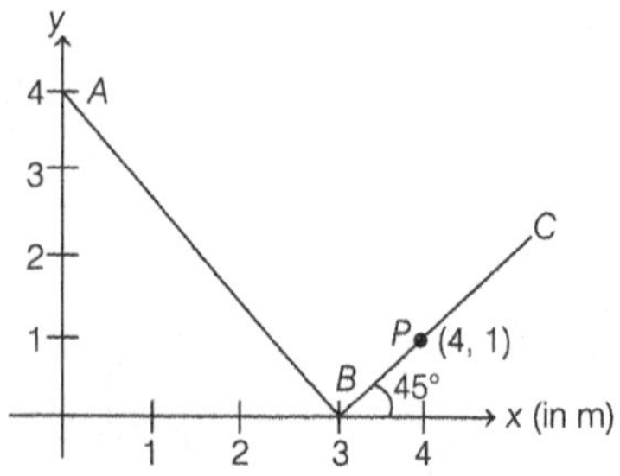

(a) 90° (b) 82° (c) 98° (d) 74°

6 Figure shows the velocity- time graph for a particle in rectilinear motion. The average acceleration in first $2\sqrt{3}$ s is

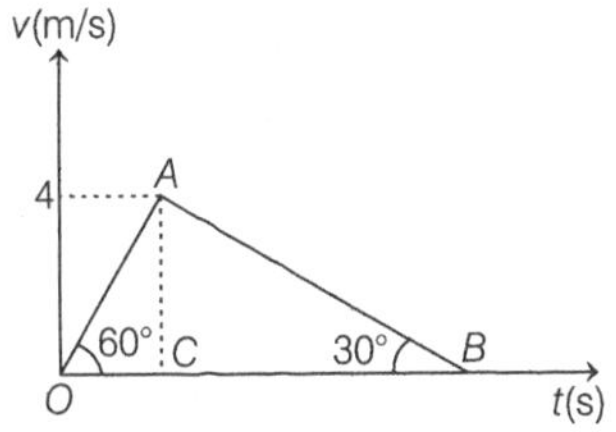

(a) $\frac{2}{3\sqrt{3}}$ m/s^2 (b) $\frac{1}{\sqrt{3}}$ m/s^2

(c) $\frac{4}{3\sqrt{3}}$ m/s^2 (d) $\frac{5}{3\sqrt{3}}$ m/s^2

7 Acceleration *versus* velocity graph of a particle moving in a straight line starting from rest is as shown in figure. The corresponding velocity-time graph would be

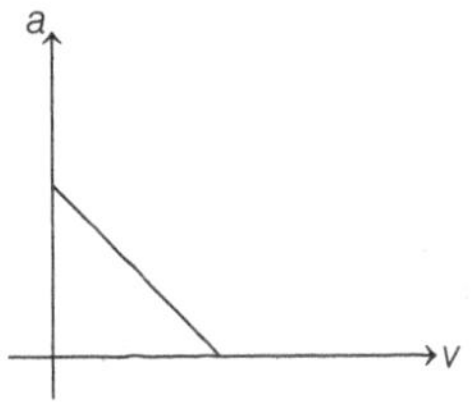

(a)
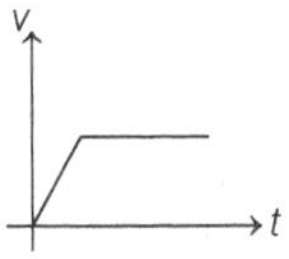

(b)
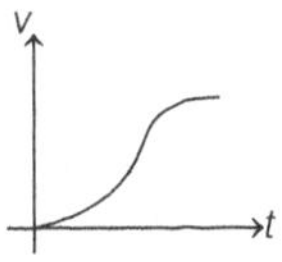

(c)
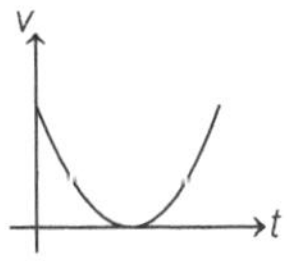

(d)
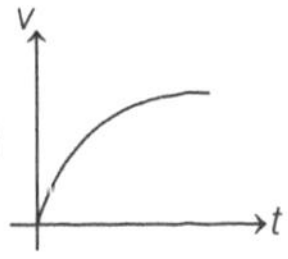

8 Velocity-time graph for a car is semicircle as shown here. Which of the following is correct ?

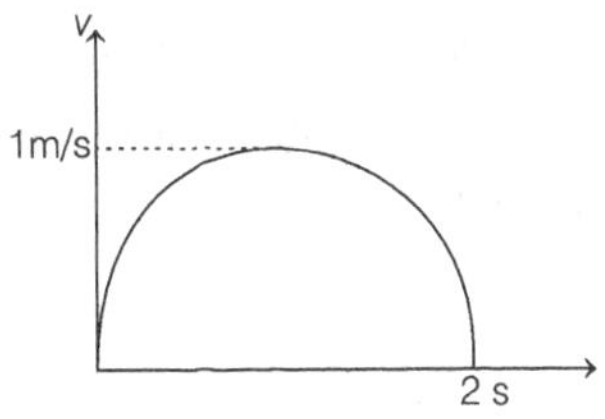

(a) Car must move in circular path

(b) Acceleration of car is never zero

(c) Mean speed of the particle is $\frac{\pi}{4}$ m/s

(d) The car makes a turn once during its motion

9 Initially Car *A* is 10.5 m ahead of Car *B*. Both start moving at time $t = 0$ in the same direction along a straight line. The velocity-time graph of two cars is shown in figure. The time when the Car *B* will catch the Car *A*, will be

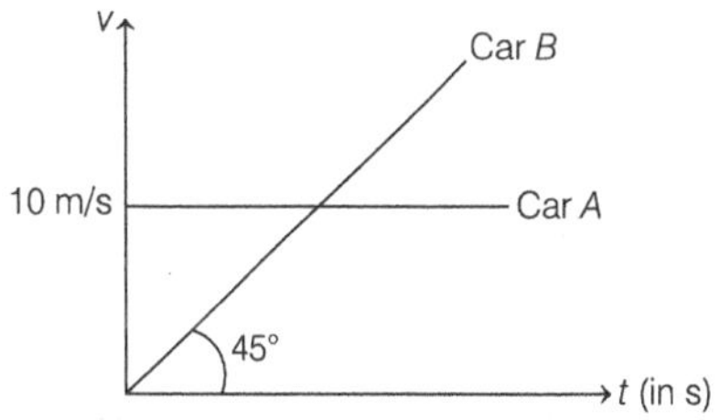

(a) $t = 21$ s (b) $t = 2\sqrt{5}$ s

(c) 20 s (d) None of these

10 A graph between the square of speed of a particle moving along a straight line and the distance *s* moved is shown in the figure. The acceleration of the particle in km/ h^2 is

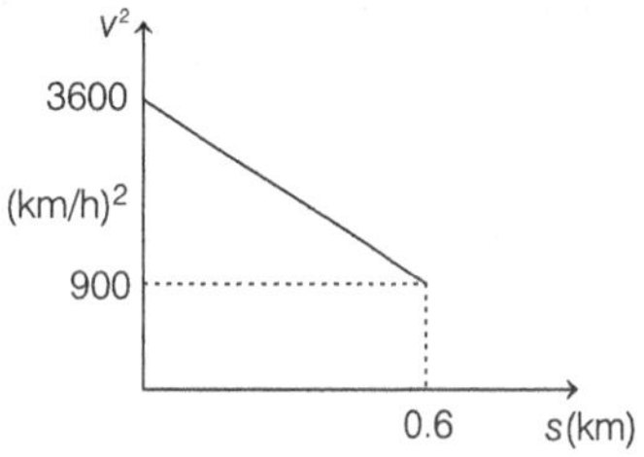

(a) 2250 (b) 225 (c) – 2250 (d) – 225

11 Acceleration-time graph is given. The particle starts from rest at t = 0 from origin. Find distance travelled by the particle in first 12 s.

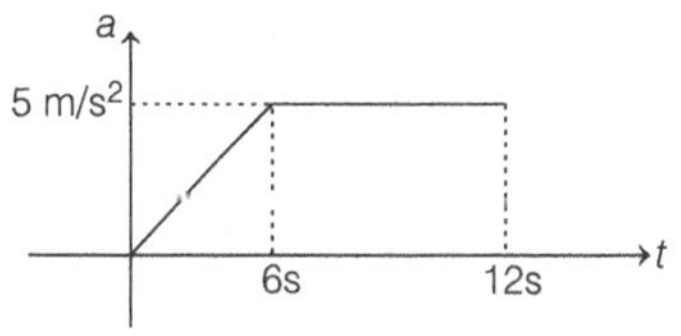

(a) 180 m (b) 200 m (c) 210 m (d) 240 m

12 The velocity-displacement graph describing the motion of a motorcycle is shown in figure.

Calculate the time needed by the motorcycle to reach *s* =120 m. (In 5 = 1.6)

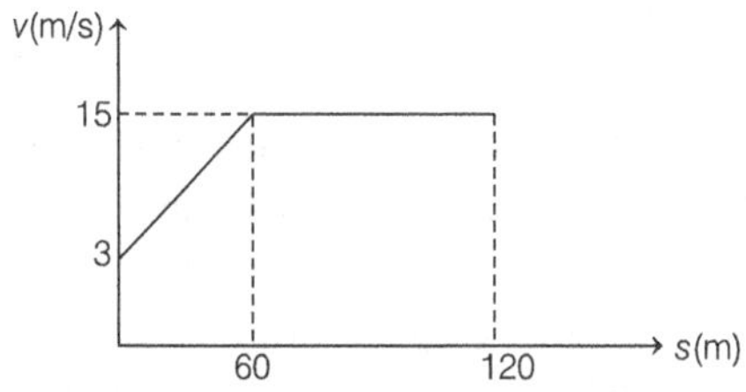

(a)9s (b) 12s (c) 15s (d) 18s

13 The graph shows the variation of 1/acceleration *versus* velocity of a particle moving on a straight line, find out the time of motion of the particle when its velocity changes from 0 m/s to 15 m/s.

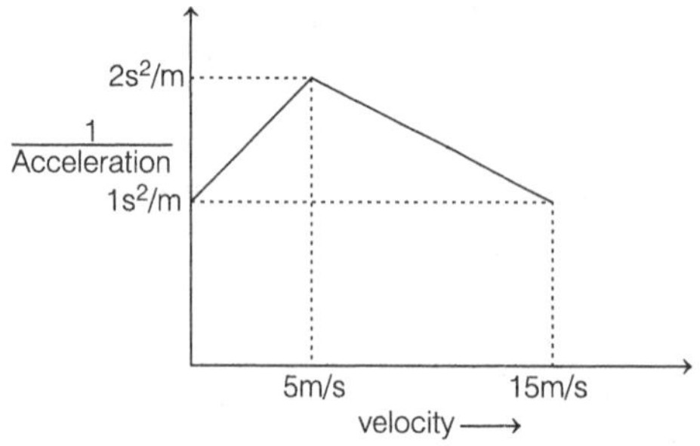

(a) 15 s (b) 20 s (c) 22.5 s (d) 25 s

14 A particle moves along X-axis in positive direction. Its acceleration a is given as $a = cx + d$, where x denotes the x-coordinate of particle, c and d are positive constants. For velocity-position graph of particle to be of type as shown in figure, the value of speed of particle at $x = 0$ should be

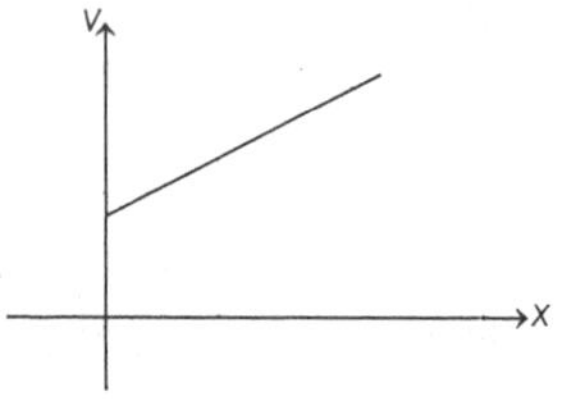

(a) $\sqrt{\frac{4d^2}{c}}$ (b) $\sqrt{\frac{d^2}{c}}$ (c) $\sqrt{\frac{2d^2}{c}}$ (d) $\sqrt{\frac{8d^2}{c}}$

15 The drawing shows velocity (v) *versus* time (t) graphs for two cyclists moving along the same straight segment of a highway from the same point. The first cyclist starts at $t = 0$ min and the second cyclist starts moving at $t = 3.0$ min. The time at which the two cyclists meet is

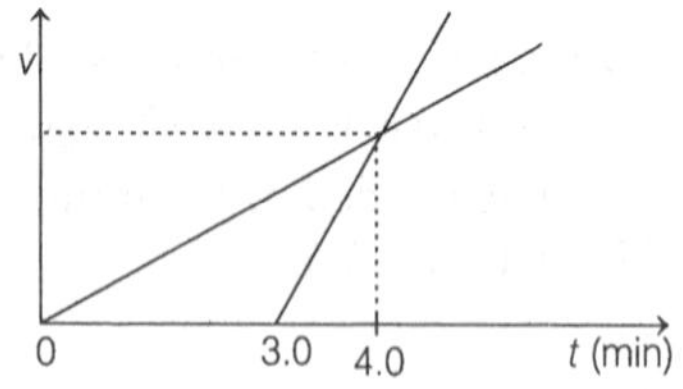

(Both velocity-time curves intersect at $t = 4$ min)

(a) 4.0 min (b) 6.0 min
(c) 8 min (d) 12 min

16 Each of the three graphs represents acceleration *versus* time for an object that already has a positive velocity at time t_1. Which graphs show an object whose speed is increasing for the entire time interval between t_1 and t_2?

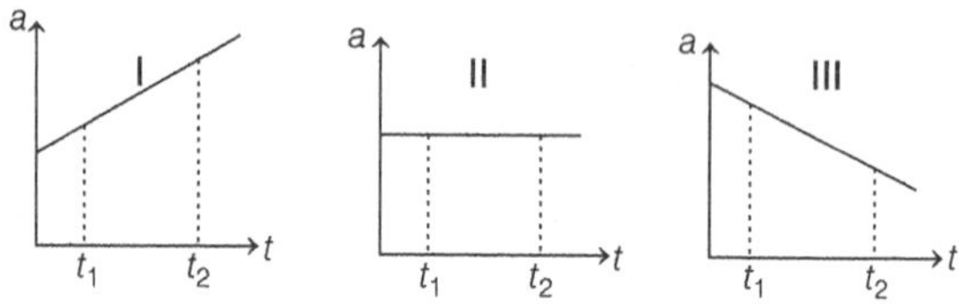

(a) graph I, only (b) graphs I and II, only
(c) graphs I and III, only (d) graphs I, II, and III

17 Two trains, which are moving along different tracks in opposite directions towards each other, are put on the same track by mistake. Their drivers, on noticing the mistake, start slowing down the trains when the trains are 300 m apart.

Graphs given below show their velocities as function of time as the trains slow down. The separation between the trains after both have stopped, is

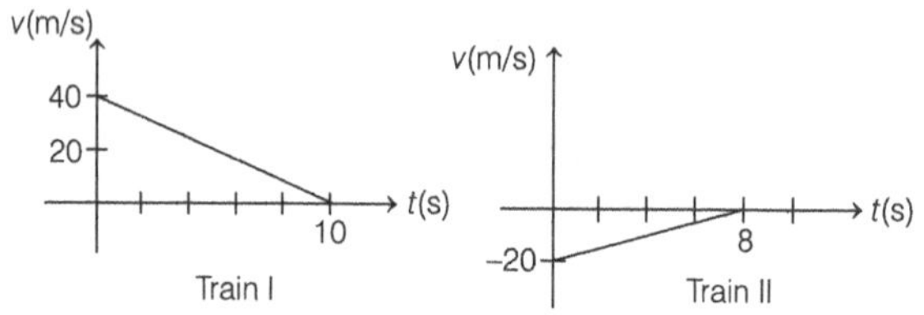

(a) 120 m (b) 280 m (c) 60 m (d) 20 m

18 A jet plane is subjected to the acceleration shown. Determine the speed of the plane when it has travelled 60 m. At $s = 0$, velocity of jet plane is 7 m/s.

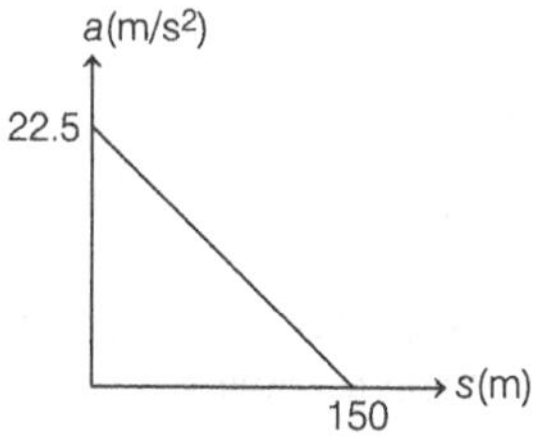

(a) 47 m/s (b) 50 m/s (c) 54 m/s (d) 60 m/s

19 For shown graph, magnitude of acceleration of particle at point P is

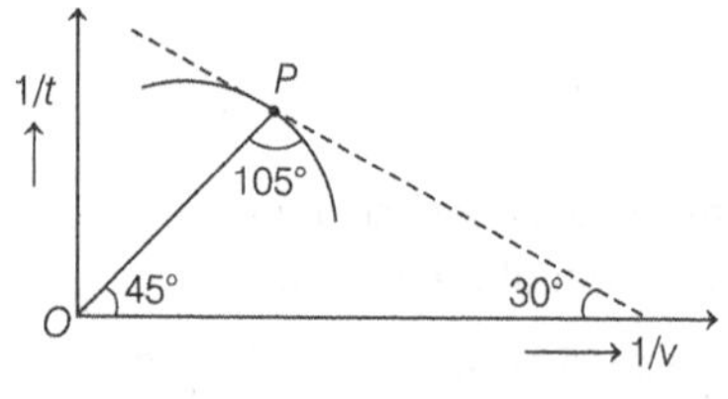

(a) $\sqrt{3}$ units (b) $\frac{1}{\sqrt{3}}$ units

(c) $3\sqrt{3}$ units (d) Cannot determine

Multiple Choice(s) Correct Questions

1 For a body moving in a straight line, choose the incorrect statement(s).

(a) When the net area of acceleration-time graph is negative, it always means that final velocity of body is negative.

(b) When the net area of velocity-time graph is negative, it always means that final position of the body is negative.

(c) When net area of velocity-time graph is negative, it may happen that body returns to its original position.

(d) When net area of acceleration -time graph is negative, it may happen that final velocity of particle is zero.

2 A particle is moving in a straight line whose acceleration *versus* time graph is given. Assume that, initial velocity is in the direction of acceleration. Then, which of the statement is correct between time $t = 0$ to $t = t_0$?

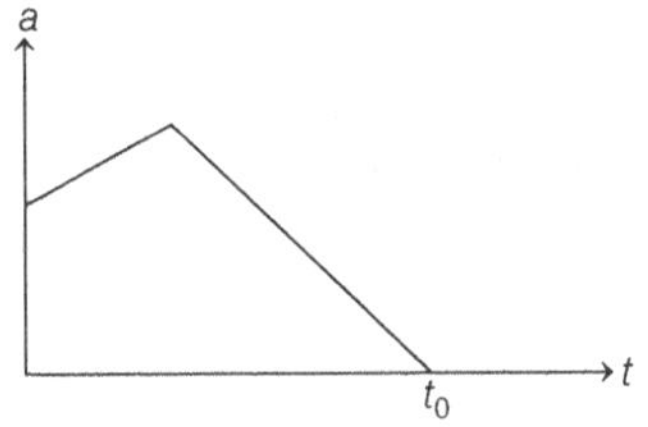

(a) Velocity first increases then decreases, displacement always increases.

(b) Velocity and displacement both, first increase and then decrease.

(c) Displacement increases and velocity decrease.

(d) Displacement and velocity both always increase.

3 The velocity-time plot for a particle moving on a straight line is shown in figure. Then,

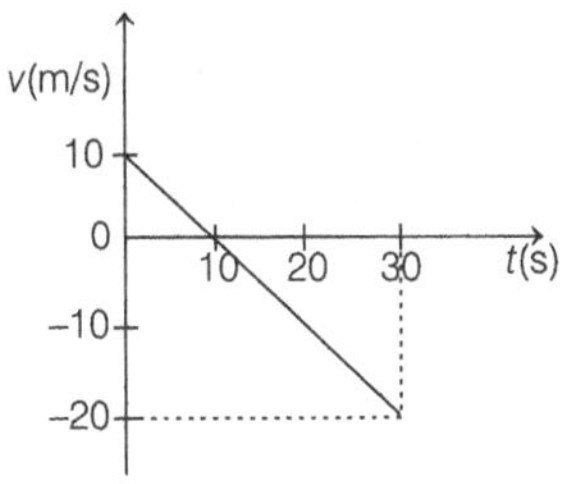

(a) the particle has a constant acceleration

(b) the particle has never turned around

(c) the particle has zero displacement

(d) the average speed in the interval 0 to 10 s is the same as the average speed in the interval 10s to 20 s

4 Which of the following graphs can be possibly representing one-dimensional motion of a particle?

(a)

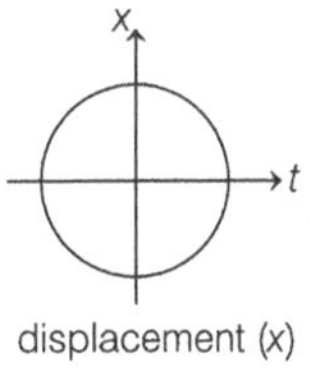

displacement (x)

(b)

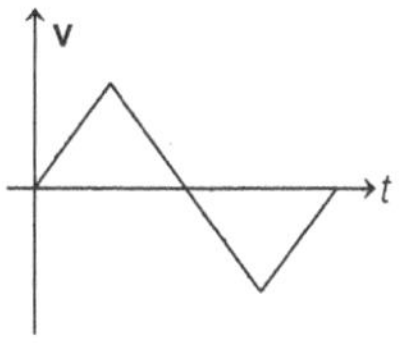

(c)

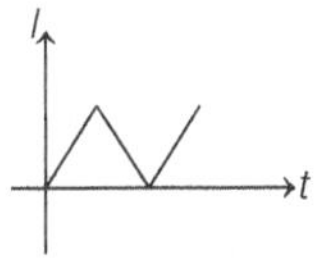

length of path (*l*)

(d) None of these

5 The figure shows the velocity-time graph of a particle which moves along a straight line starting with velocity at 5 m/s and coming to rest at $t = 30$s. Then

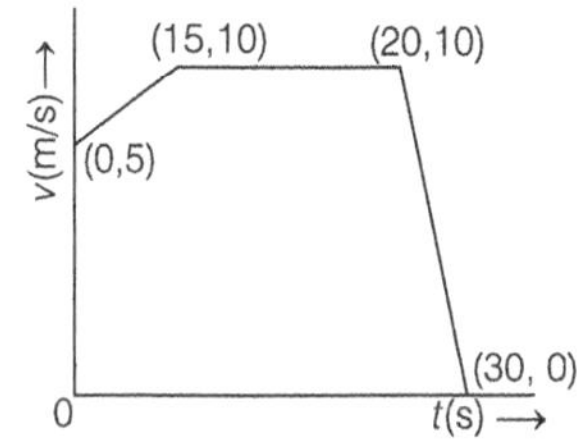

(a) distance travelled by the particle is 212.5 m.

(b) distance covered by the particle when it moves with constant velocity is 100 m.

(c) average acceleration of the particle from $t = 15$ to $t = 25$ s is -0.5 m/s^2.

(d) acceleration at $t = 25$ is 1 m/s^2.

6 The velocity-time graph of 2 bodies *A* and *B* is given here. Choose the correct statement(s).

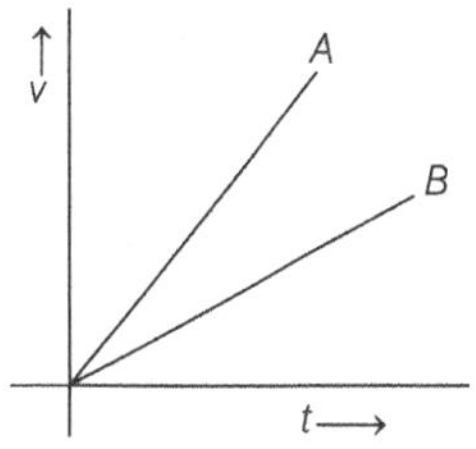

(a) Acceleration of *B* > Acceleration of *A*

(b) Acceleration of *A* > Acceleration of *B*

(c) Both are starting from same point.

(d) *A* covers greater distance than *B* in the same time.

7 At the instant a motorbike starts from rest in a given direction, a car overtakes the motorbike, both moving in the same direction.

The speed-time graphs for motorbike and car are represented by *OAB* and *CD*, respectively. Then,

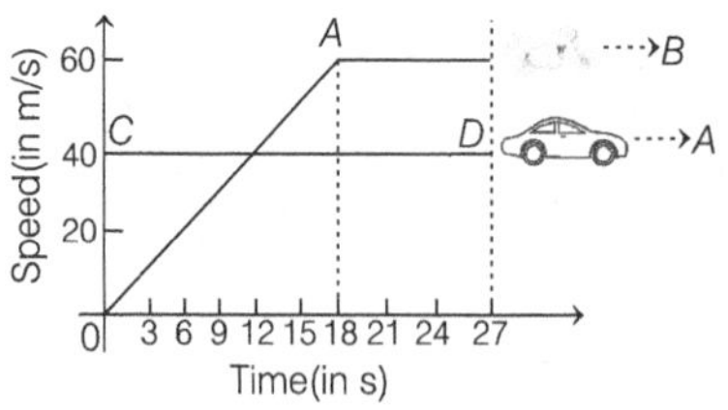

(a) at $t = 18$ s, the motorbike and car are 180 m apart
(b) at $t = 18$ s, the motorbike and car are 720 m apart
(c) the relative distance between motorbike and car reduces to zero at $t = 27$ s and both are 1080 m far from origin
(d) the relative distance between motorbike and car always remains same

8 A particle moves in a straight line with the velocity as shown in the figure.
At $t = 0$, $x = -16$ m. Then,

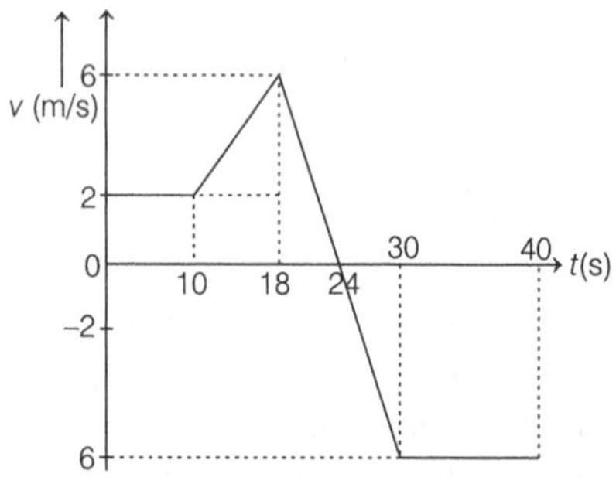

(a) the maximum value of the position coordinate of the particle is 54 m
(b) the maximum value of the position coordinate of the particle is 70 m
(c) the particle is at the position of 36 m at $t = 18$ s
(d) the particle is at the position of 36 m at $t = 30$ s

9 For the velocity-time graph as shown in figure, the correct statement(s) is/are

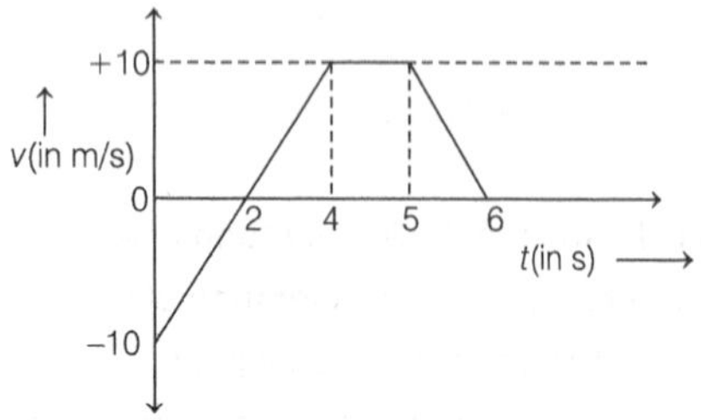

(a) the average velocity for the entire journey is 2.5 m/s.
(b) the average acceleration from 1 s to 4 s is 5 m/s^2.
(c) the average speed for the first 4 s is zero.
(d) the acceleration at $t = 3$ s is 5 m/s^2.

10 A particle is dropped from a finite height H above the ground level under gravity. Due to air resistance acceleration of particle become $a = g - kv$ in the direction of velocity, where k is a positive constant and v = speed of particle. Then, which of the following graph(s) is/are possible (t_0 = time when particle touches the ground)

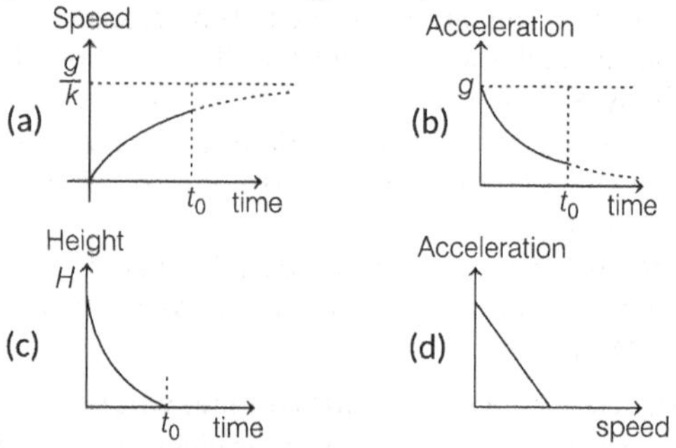

11 Two stones are thrown vertically upwards simultaneously from the same point on the ground with initial speed $u_1 = 30$ m/s and $u_2 = 50$ m/s. For the time interval in which both reach the ground, which of the curve represent correct variation of
$(x_2 - x_1)$ = the relative position of second stone with respect to first with time (t)?
$(v_2 - v_1)$ = the relative velocity of second stone with respect to first with time (t)?
Assume that stones do not rebound after hitting.

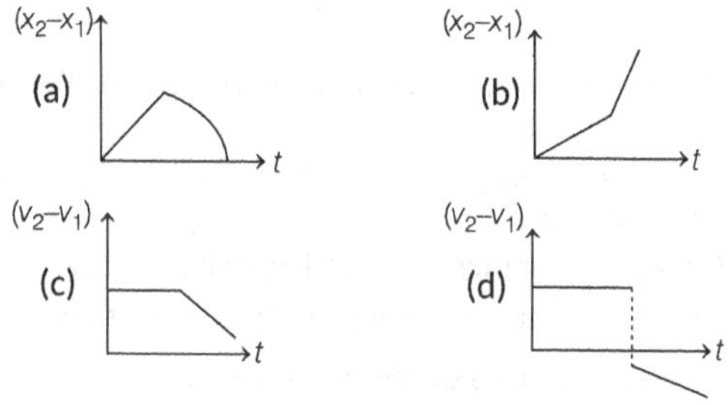

12 The graph given shows the position of two cars, *A* and *B*, as a function of time. The cars move along the *X*-axis on parallel but separate tracks, so that they can pass each other's position without colliding. Mark the correct statement(s)

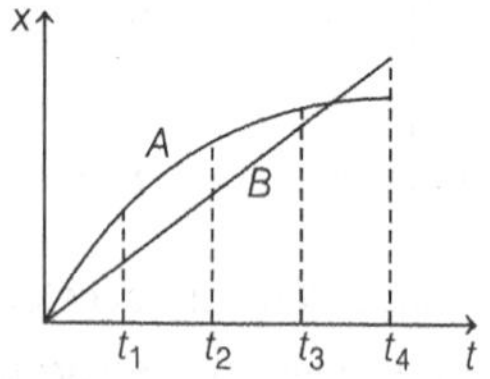

(a) At time t_1, car *A* is overtaking the car *B*.
(b) At time t_3, car *B* is moving faster.
(c) At time t_2, the two cars may have the same velocity.
(d) The motion of car *A* as shown on the graphs shows that it is slowing down.

Comprehension Based Questions

Comprehension-1

A car is moving on a straight road. The velocity of the car varies with time as shown in the figure. Initially (at $t = 0$), the car was at $x = 0$, where x is the position of the car at any time t.

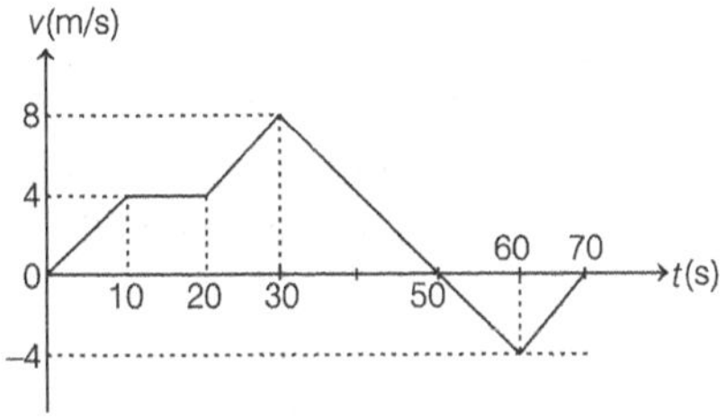

1 The variation of acceleration (a) with time (t) will be best represented by

(a) 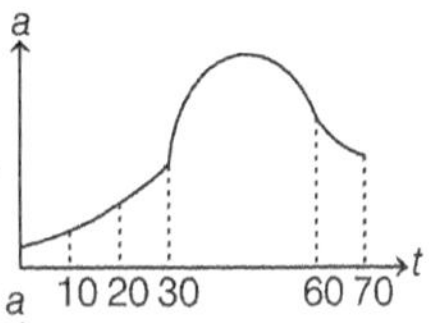

(b) 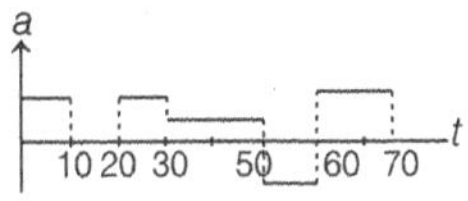

(c) 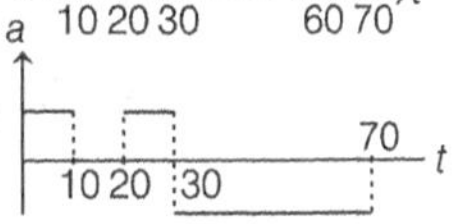

(d) 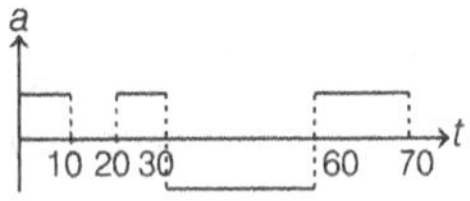

2 The displacement-time graph will be best represented by

(a) 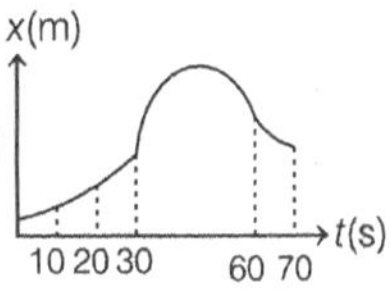

(b) 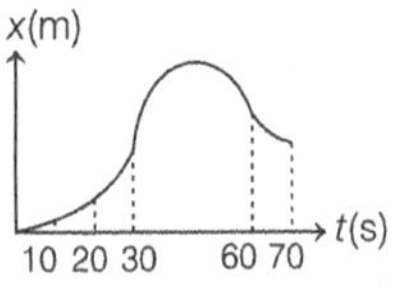

(c) 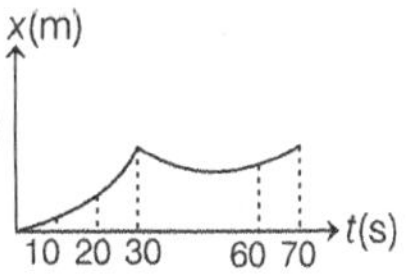

(d) 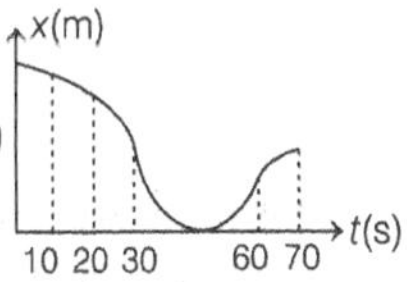

3 The maximum displacement from the starting position will be

(a) 200 m (b) 250 m (c) 160 m (d) 165 m

4 Average speed from $t = 0$ to $t = 70$ s will be

(a) $\frac{16}{7}$ m/s (b) $\frac{24}{7}$ m/s

(c) $\frac{20}{7}$ m/s (d) zero

5 The time interval during which the car is retarding can be

(a) $t = 50$s to $t = 70$s (b) $t = 30$s to $t = 50$s

(c) $t = 30$s to $t = 60$ s (d) $t = 10$s to $t = 20$s

Comprehension-2

The figure shows a velocity-time graph of a particle moving along a straight line

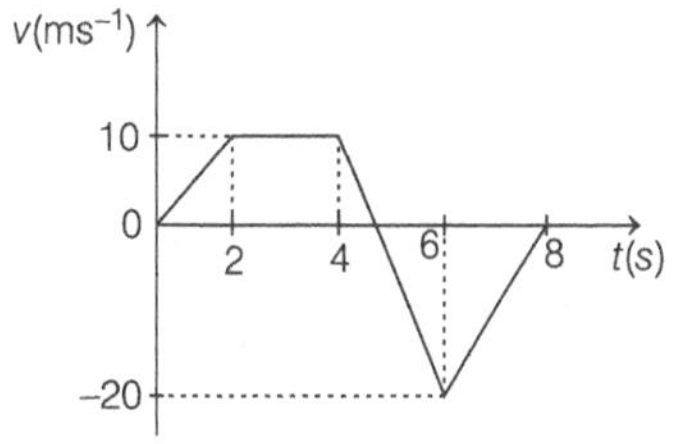

6 Choose the incorrect statement. The particle comes to rest at

(a) $t = 0$ (b) $t = 5$s

(c) $t = 8$ s (d) None of these

7 Identify the region in which the rate of change of velocity $\left|\frac{\Delta \mathbf{v}}{\Delta t}\right|$ of the particle is maximum.

(a) 0 to 2s (b) 2 to 4s (c) 4 to 6s (d) 6 to 8s

8 If the particle starts from the position $x_0 = -15$ m, then its position at $t = 2$s will be

(a) – 5 m (b) 5 m (c) 10 m (d) 15m

9 The maximum displacement of the particle is

(a) 33.3 m (b) 23.3 m

(c) 18.3 m (d) zero

10 The total distance travelled by the particle is

(a) 66.6 m (b) 51.6 m (c) zero (d) 36.6 m

Comprehension-3

The x-t graph of a particle moving along a straight line is shown in figure

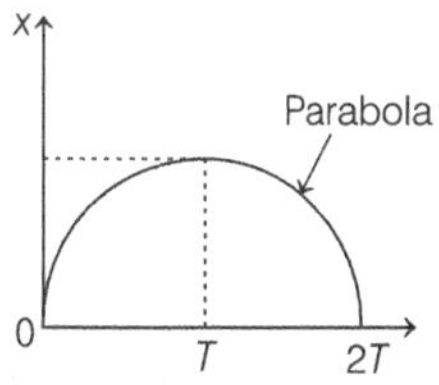

11 The velocity-time graph of the particle is correctly shown by

(a) 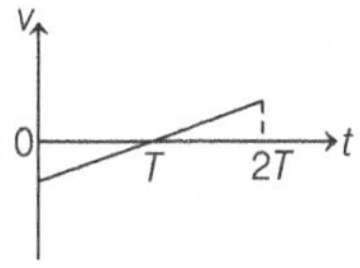

(b) 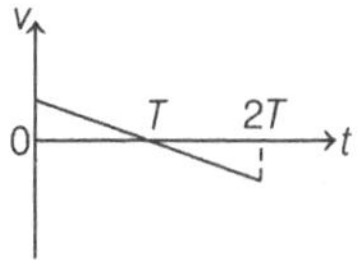

(c) 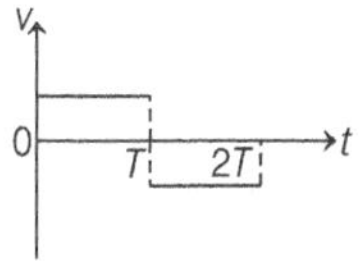

(d) 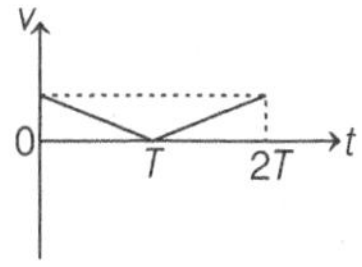

12 The acceleration-time graph of the particle is correctly shown by

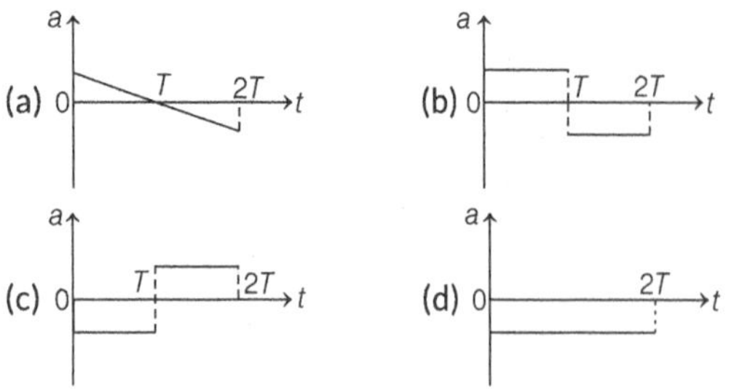

13 The speed-time graph of the particle is correctly shown by

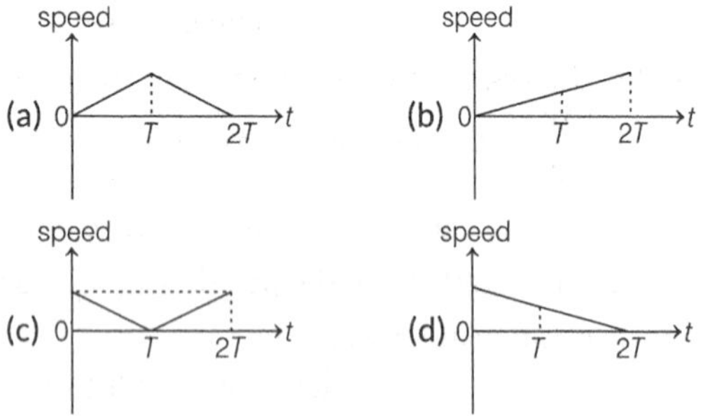

Comprehension-4

The graph below gives the coordinate of a particle travelling along the X-axis as a function of time. AM is the tangent to the curve at the starting moment and BN is tangent at the end moment ($\theta_1 = \theta_2 = 120°$).

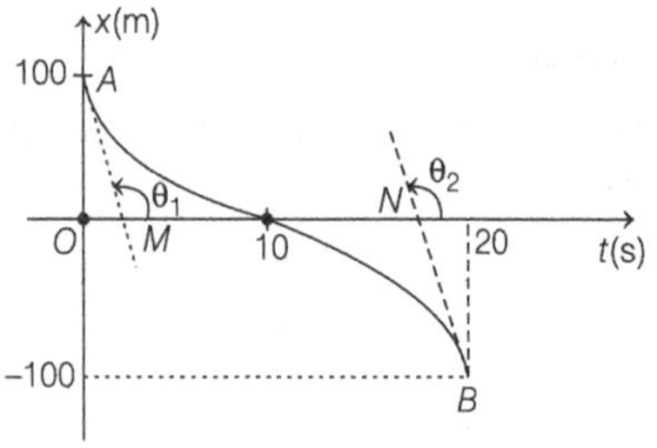

14 The average velocity during the first 20 s is

(a) – 10 m/s (b) 10 m/s

(c) zero (d) 20 m/s

15 The average acceleration during the first 20 s is

(a) $-1\ m/s^2$ (b) $1\ m/s^2$

(c) zero (d) $2\ m/s^2$

16 The direction ($\hat{i}$ or $-\hat{i}$) of acceleration during the first 10 s is

(a) $\hat{i}$ (b) $-\hat{i}$

(c) first $\hat{i}$, then $-\hat{i}$ (d) first $-\hat{i}$, then $\hat{i}$

17 Time interval during which the motion is retarded.

(a) 0 to 20s (b) 10 to 20s

(c) 0 to 10s (d) None of these

Comprehension-5

Two cars are travelling on a straight road. The car C_1 is going at a constant speed of 9 m/s. 40 m ahead of C_1 is car C_2 initially at rest, but starts moving with an acceleration of $1\ m/s^2$.

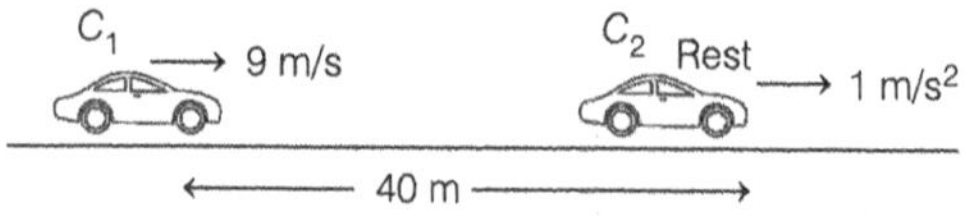

18 The graph correctly representing the position of two cars with time w.r.t. initial position of C_1 is

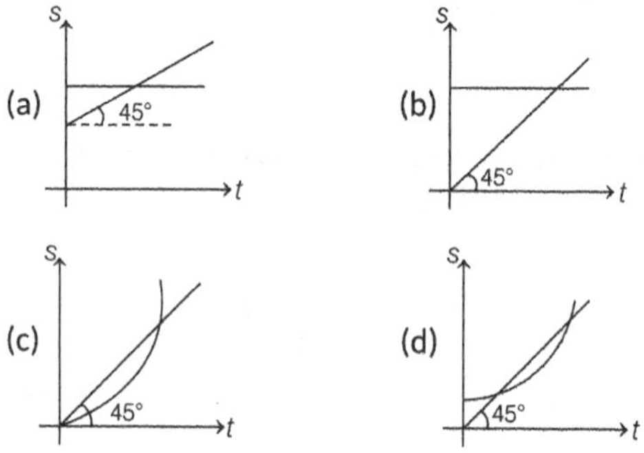

19 The graph correctly representing the velocity of the two cars with time

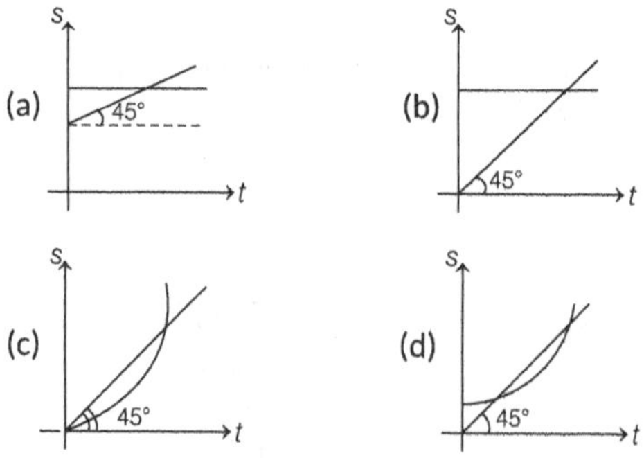

20 During their motion, the car C_1 over takes the car C_2. But soon C_2 overtakes C_1, so determine the maximum lead that C_1 can have from C_2.

(a) 0.5 m (b) 9.5 m

(c) 81 m (d) 90 m

Comprehension-6

A particle which is initially at rest at the origin, is subjected to an acceleration with x and y-components as shown. After time $t = 5$, the particle has no acceleration

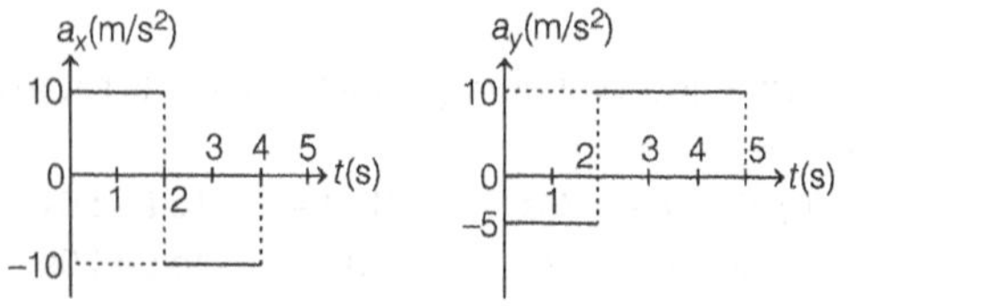

21 What is the magnitude of velocity of the particle at $t = 2$ s?

(a) $10\sqrt{5}$ m/s (b) $5\sqrt{10}$ m/s
(c) $5\sqrt{5}$ m/s (d) None of these

22 What is the magnitude of average velocity of the particle between $t = 0$ and $t = 4$ s?

(a) $\frac{5}{2}\sqrt{13}$ m/s (b) $\frac{5}{2}\sqrt{17}$ m/s
(c) 30 m/s (d) None of these

23 When is the particle at its farthest distance from the Y-axis?

(a) 3 s (b) 2 s
(c) 4 s (d) 1 s

Comprehension-7

The velocity-time graph of a particle moving along a straight line is as shown. The rate of acceleration and deceleration is constant and it is equal to 5 m/s^2. If the average velocity during the motion is 20 ms^{-1}, then

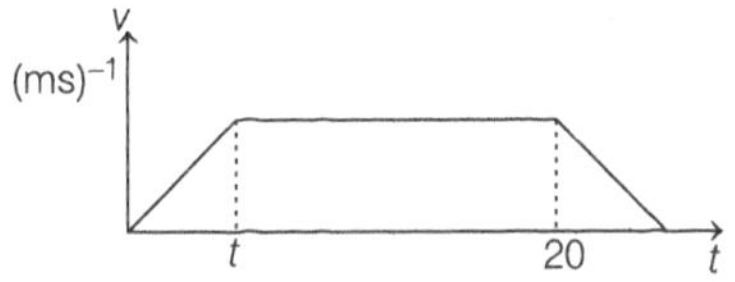

24 the value of t is

(a) 5 s (b) 10 s
(c) 20 s (d) $5\sqrt{2}$ s

25 the maximum velocity of the particle is

(a) 20 m/s (b) 25 m/s
(c) 30 m/s (d) 40 m/s

26 the distance travelled with uniform velocity is

(a) 375 m (b) 125 m
(c) 300 m (d) 450 m

Match the Columns Questions

1 Column I gives some graphs for a particle moving along X-axis in positive x-direction. The variables v, x and t represent velocity of particle, x-coordinate of particle and time, respectively. Column II gives certain resulting interpretation. Match the graphs in Column I with the statements in Column II.

Column I	Column II
(A) 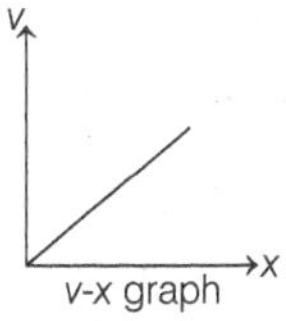	(P) Acceleration of particle is uniform.
(B) 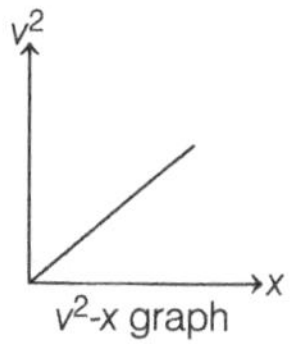	(Q) Acceleration of particle is non-uniform.
(C) 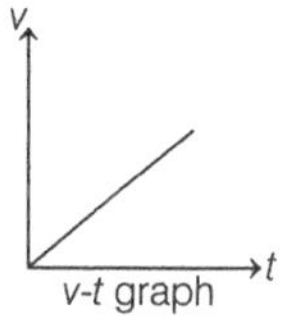	(R) Acceleration of particle is directly proportional to t.
(D) 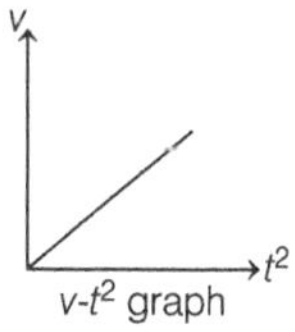	(S) Acceleration of particle is directly proportional to x.

2 For the velocity-time graph shown in figure, in a time interval from $t = 0$ to $t = 6$ s, match the following.

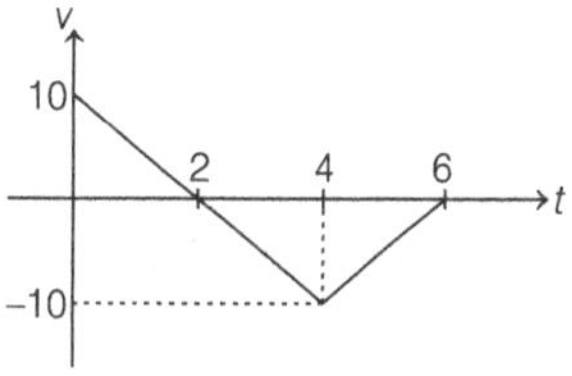

	Column I		Column II
(A)	Change in velocity	(P)	– 5/3 SI unit
(B)	Average acceleration	(Q)	– 20 SI unit
(C)	Total displacement	(R)	– 10 SI unit
(D)	Acceleration at t = 3s	(S)	– 5 SI unit

3 Match the Column I with Column II and mark the correct option given below.

Column I	Column II
(A) Zero acceleration	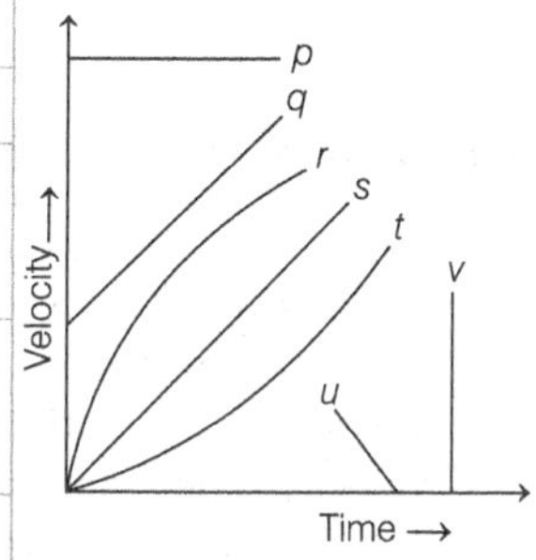
(B) Infinite acceleration	
(C) Constant positive acceleration, with zero initial velocity	
(D) Constant positive acceleration, with non-zero initial velocity	
(E) Constant negative acceleration	
(F) Increasing acceleration	
(G) Decreasing acceleration	

4 Match the Column I with Column II and mark the correct option given below.

Column I	Column II
(A) Deceleration decreasing with time	(P) 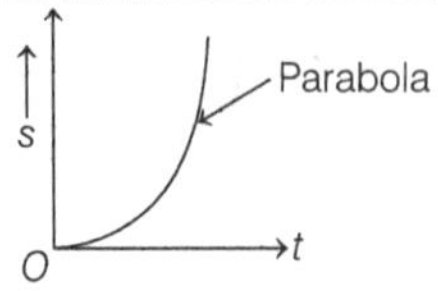
(B) Velocity increasing with time	(Q) 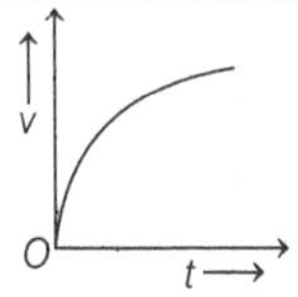
(C) Magnitude of acceleration increasing with time	(R) 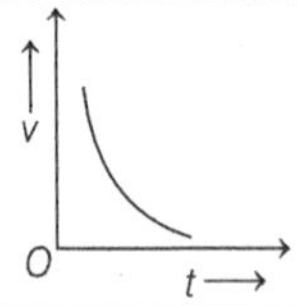
(D) Body going farther away from the starting point with time	(S) 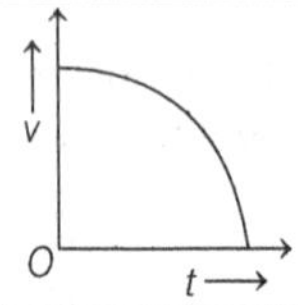

5 Figure shows a graph of position *versus* time graph for a particle moving along X-axis

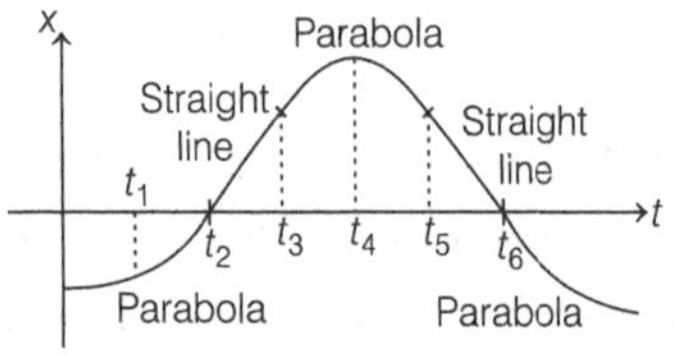

Column I	Column II
(A) Slowing down	(P) $t_1 \to t_2$
(B) Returning towards origin	(Q) $t_2 \to t_3$
(C) Moving away from origin	(R) $t_3 \to t_4$
(D) Speeding up	(S) $t_4 \to t_5$
	(T) $t_5 \to t_6$

Numerical Value Questions

1 A particle starts moving with velocity 10 m/s in a straight line under an acceleration varying linearly with time. Its velocity-time graph is shown in the figure. Its velocity is maximum at $t = 3$ s. The time (in s) when the particle stops is
(tan 37° = 3/4)

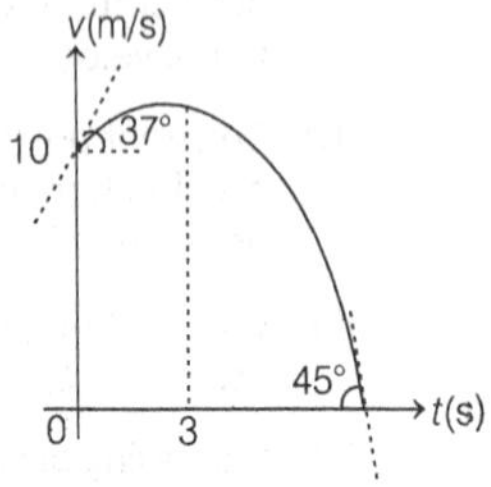

2 The graph shows the variation of $\frac{1}{v}$ (where v is the velocity of the particle) with respect to time. Then, find the value of acceleration at $t = 3$ s in m/s^2.

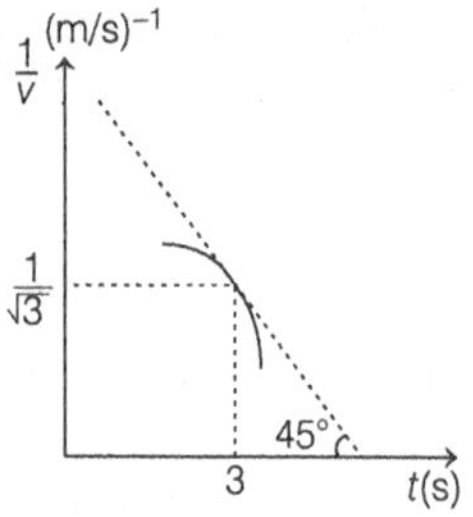

3 Graph of (1/v) *versus* x for a particle under motion is as shown, where v is velocity and x is position. The time (in second) taken by particle to move from x = 4m to x = 12m is

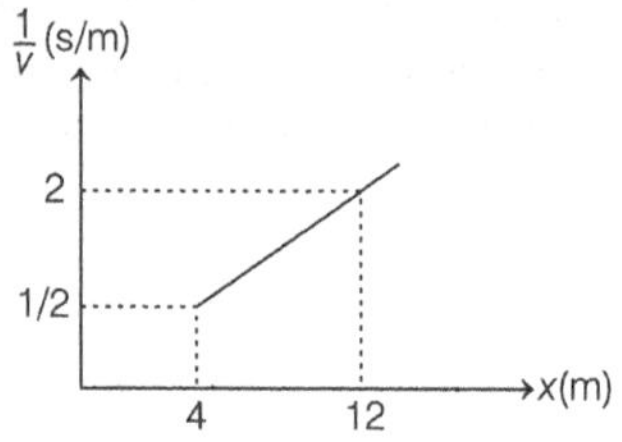

4 An experiment on the take-off performance of a toy aeroplane shows that the acceleration varies as shown in the figure, and that it takes 10s to take off from rest position. The distance(in m) along the runway covered by the aeroplane is

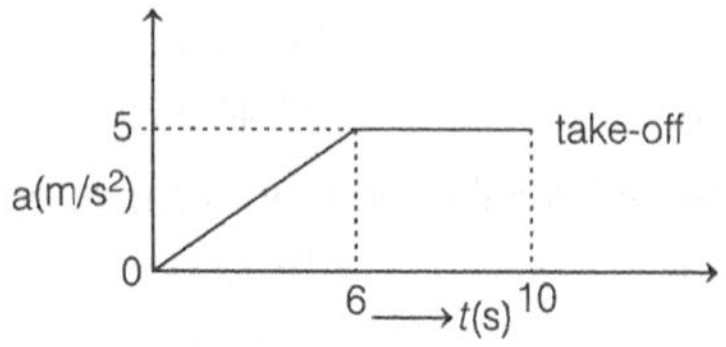

5 Velocity of a particle changes with position according to the following curve. Acceleration (in m/s^2) of the particle at $s = 1$ m is

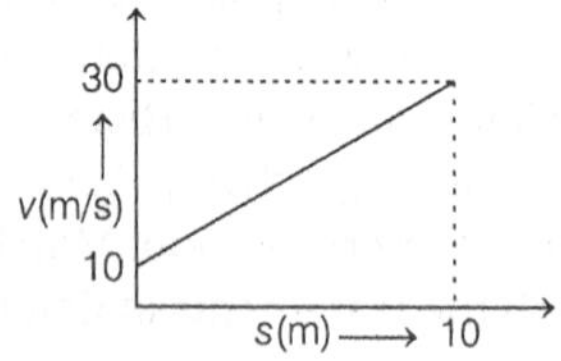

6 An automobile can accelerate or decelerate at a maximum value of $\frac{5}{3}$ m/s^2 and can attain a maximum speed of 90 km/h. If it starts from rest, what is the shortest time (in s) in which it can travel 1 km, if it is to come to rest at the end of the kilometre run?

Previous Year's Questions

JEE Main

1 Given below are two statements :

Statement I Area under velocity-time graph gives the distance travelled by the body in a given time.

Statement II Area under acceleration- time graph is equal to the change in velocity in the given time.

In the light of given statements, choose the correct answer from the options given below. **[2023, 8 April Shift-II]**

(a) Statement I is incorrect but Statement II is true.
(b) Statement I is correct but Statement II is false.
(c) Both Statement I and Statement II are true.
(d) Both Statement I and Statement II are False.

2 The position-time graphs for two students *A* and *B* returning from the school to their homes are shown in figure.

(A) *A* lives closer to the school
(B) *B* lives closer to the school
(C) *A* takes lesser time to reach home
(D) *A* travels faster than *B*
(E) *B* travels faster than *A*

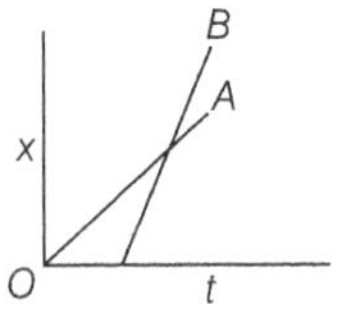

Choose the correct answer from the options given below **[2023, 10 April Shift-I]**

(a) (A), (C) and (E) only (b) (A), (C) and (D) only
(c) (A) and (E) only (d) (B) and (E) only

3 From the *v*-*t* graph shown, the ratio of distance to displacement in 25 s of motion is **[2023, 11 April Shift-I]**

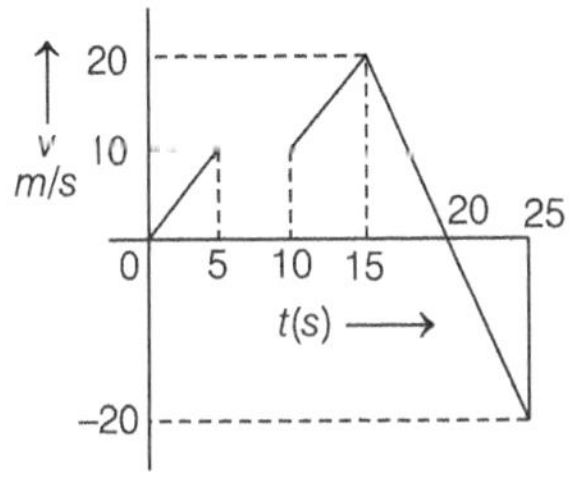

(a) $\frac{5}{3}$ (b) $\frac{3}{5}$ (c) $\frac{1}{2}$ (d) 1

4 The velocity-time graph of a body moving in a straight line is shown in figure.

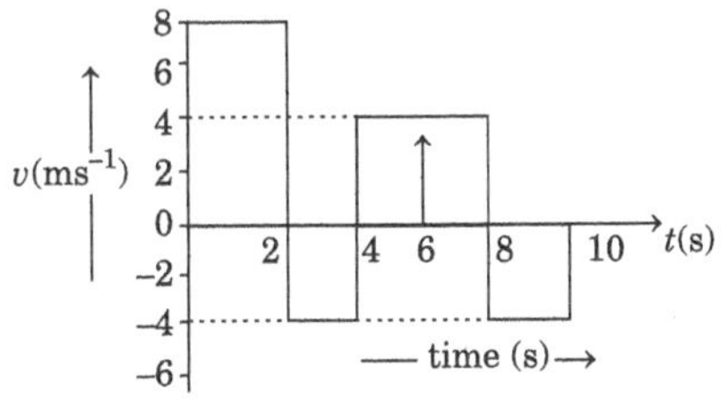

The ratio of displacement to distance travelled by the body in time 0 to 10s is **[2023, 24 Jan Shift -II]**

(a) 1 : 2 (b) 1 : 3 (c) 1 : 1 (d) 1 : 4

5 If the velocity-time graph has the shape *AMB*, what would be the shape of the corresponding acceleration time graph? **[2021, 24 Feb Shift-I]**

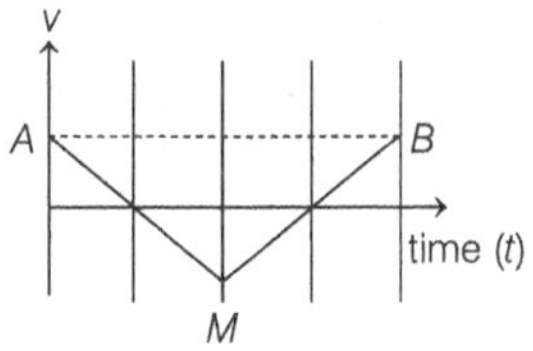

(a)
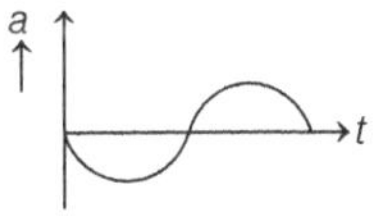

(b)
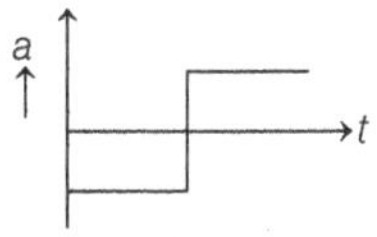

(c)
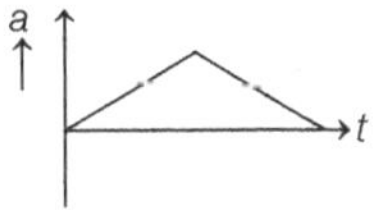

(d)
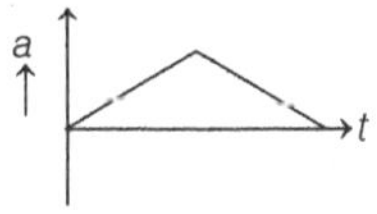

6 The velocity- displacement graph of a particle is shown in the figure.

The acceleration-displacement graph of the same particle is represented by **[2021, 18 March Shift-II]**

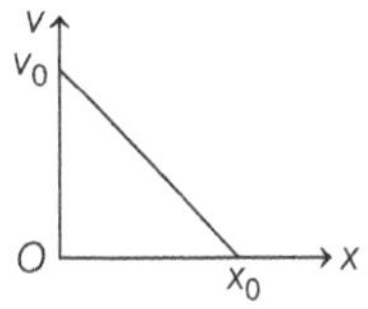

(a)
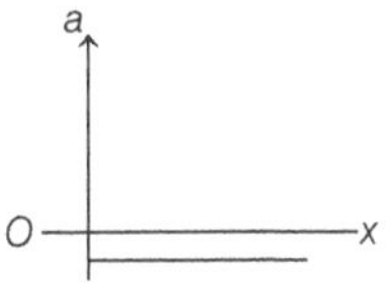

(b)
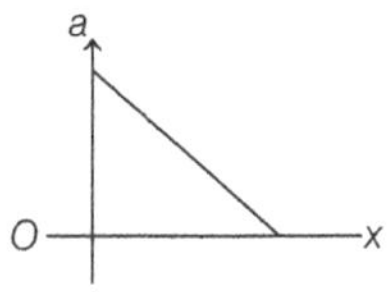

(c)
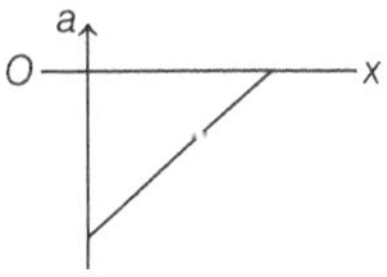

(d)
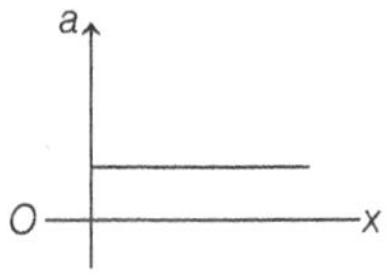

7 A particle is moving with constant acceleration *a*. Following graph shows v^2 *versus* *x* (displacement) plot. The acceleration of the particle is .... m/s^2 **[2021, 31 Aug Shift-II]**

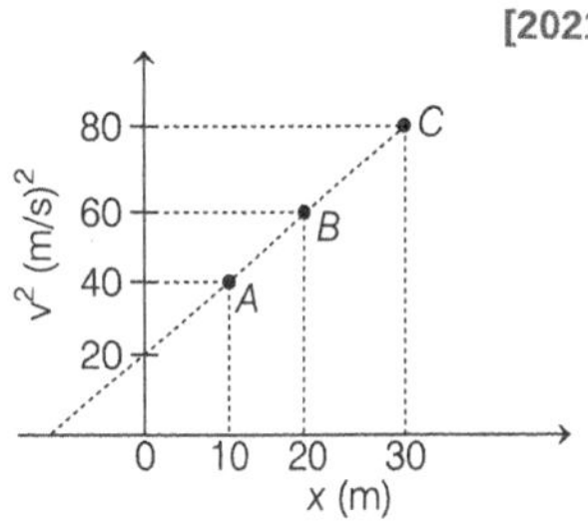

(a) 1 (b) 2 (c) 3 (d) 4

Answer Key

Level 1

4. (a) 48 m, 16 m (b) (4, 0, – 4, – 4, 4) m/s^2
   (c) 1.6 m/s, 4.8 m/s (d) – 2.4 m/s^2
5. (a) 6 m/s, 9 m/s, 9 m/s (b) 1.4 ms^{-2}
6. 1.2 m/s
7. (a) Moving forward → (0, 1) s and (5, 7) s;
   Moving backward → (1, 5) s; Speeding up (1, 2) s;
   and (5, 6) s; Slowing down → (0, 1) s, (3, 5) s and (6, 7) s
   (b) Positive acceleration → (3, 6) s;
   Negative acceleration → (0, 2) s and (6, 7) s
   Zero acceleration → (2, 3) s and (7, 9) s
   (c) 0 s and (2, 3) s (d) (7, 9) s
8.

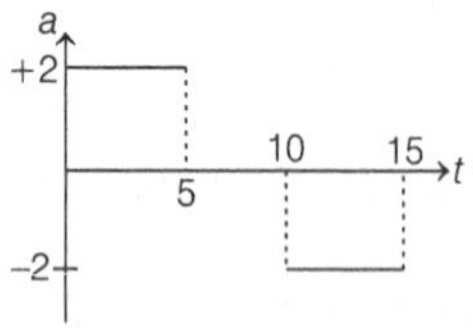

Acceleration *versus* time graph

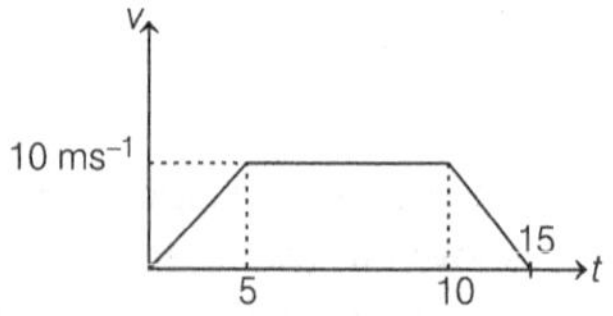

Velocity *versus* time graph

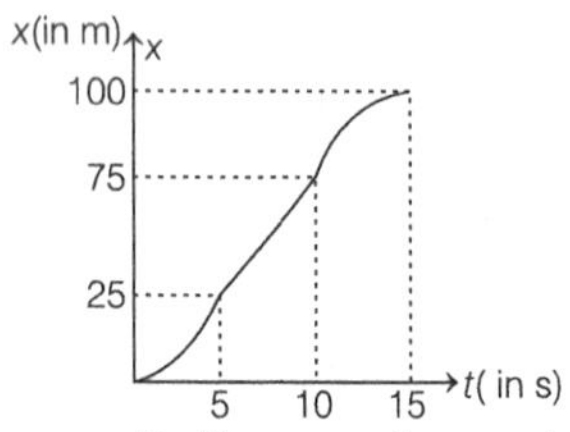

Position *versus* time graph

9.

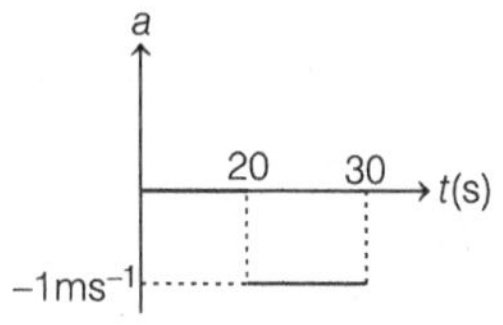

Acceleration *versus* time graph

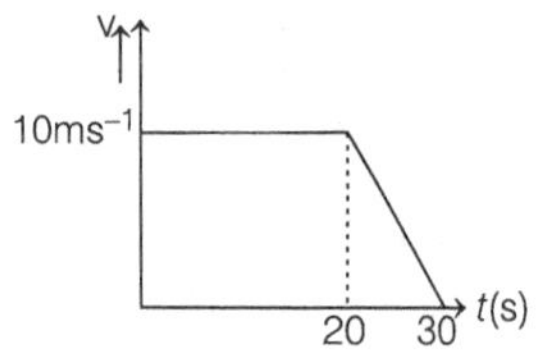

Velocity *versus* time graph

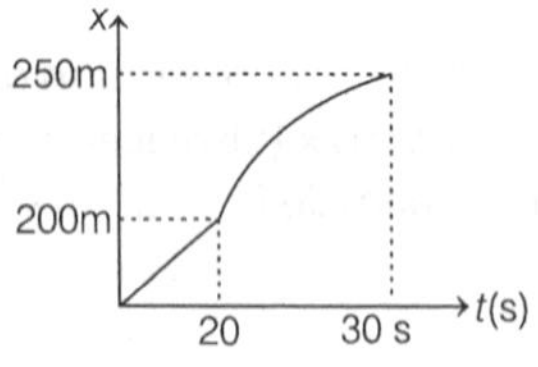

Position *versus* time graph

10. (a)

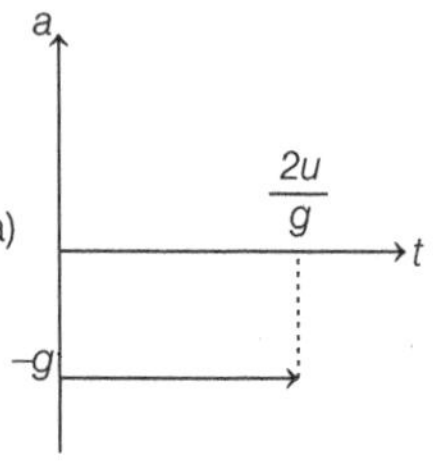

(b)

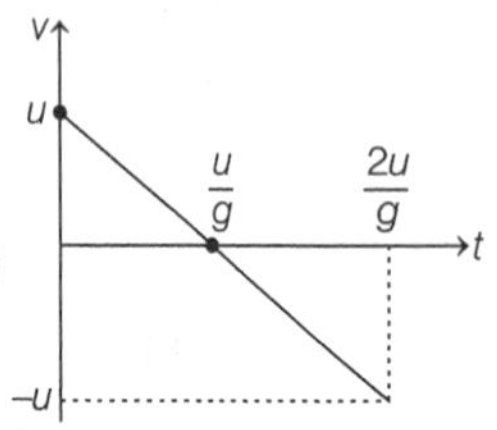

(c)

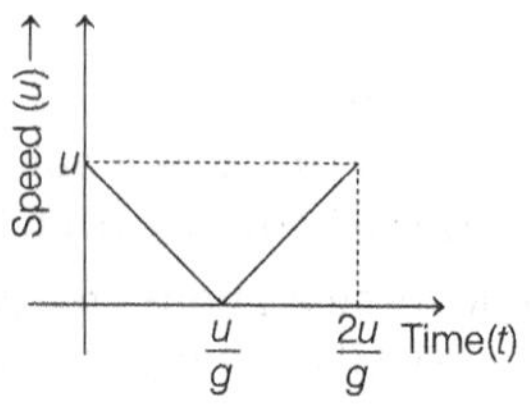

(d)

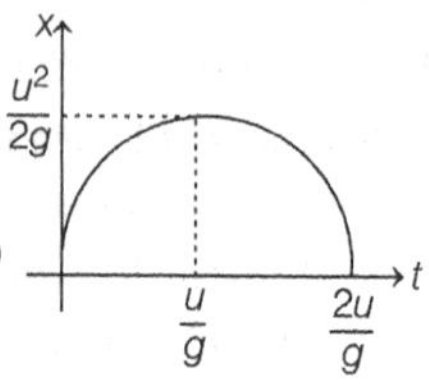

(e)

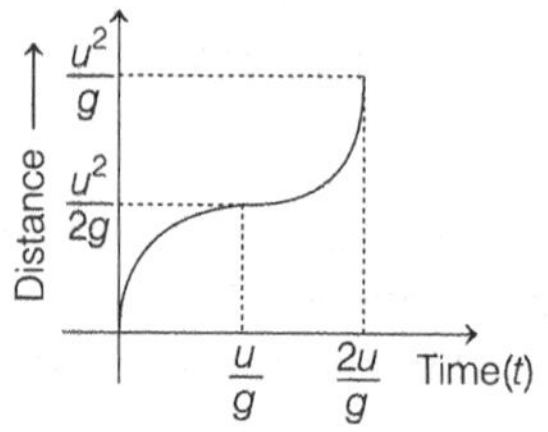

11. (a)

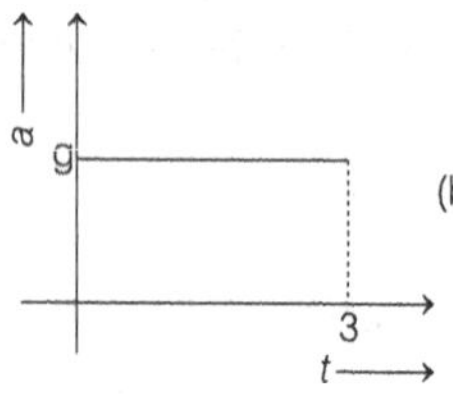

(b)

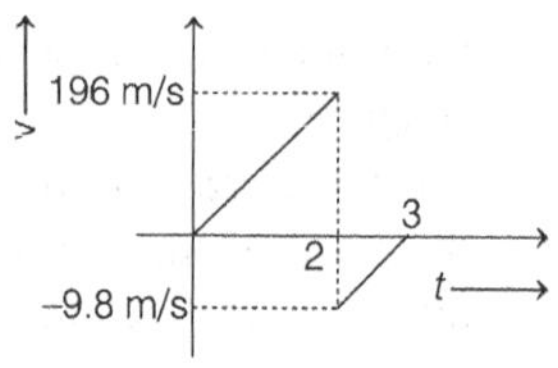

(c)

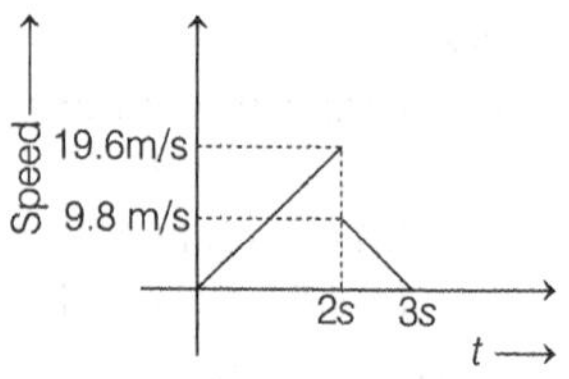

(d)

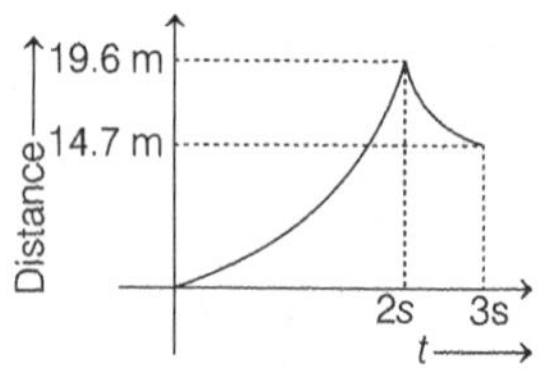

(e)

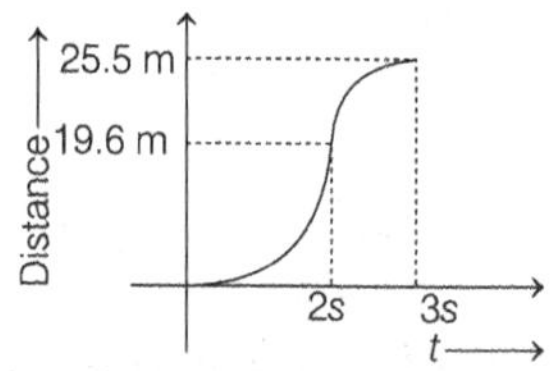

12.

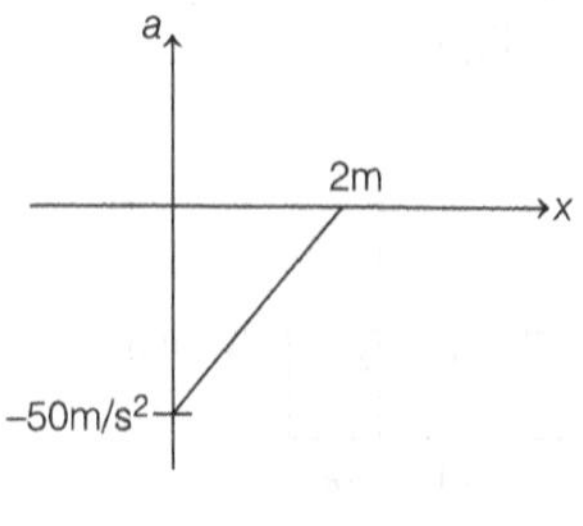

Level 2

Single Choice Correct Questions

1. (b)	**2.** (b)	**3.** (a)	**4.** (d)	**5.** (d)
6. (c)	**7.** (a)	**8.** (c)	**9.** (c)	**10.** (a)
11. (b)	**12.** (a)	**13.** (a)	**14.** (d)	**15.** (a)
16. (a)	**17.** (a)	**18.** (c)	**19.** (a)	**20.** (b)
21. (c)	**22.** (b)	**23.** (d)	**24.** (a)	**25.** (a)
26. (c)	**27.** (d)	**28.** (b)	**29.** (b)	**30.** (b)
31. (a)	**32.** (a)	**33.** (c)	**34.** (a)	**35.** (b)
36. (b)	**37.** (a)	**38.** (c)	**39.** (c)	**40.** (d)

Numerical Value Questions

1. (8)	**2.** (25)	**3.** (15)	**4.** (8.5)	**5.** (8)

Level 3

Single Choice Correct Questions

1. (c)	**2.** (b)	**3.** (b)	**4.** (a)	**5.** (b)
6. (b)	**7.** (d)	**8.** (c)	**9.** (a)	**10.** (c)
11. (c)	**12.** (b)	**13.** (c)	**14.** (b)	**15.** (b)
16. (d)	**17.** (d)	**18.** (a)	**19.** (a)	

Multiple Choice(s) Correct Questions

1. (abc)	**2.** (d)	**3.** (ad)	**4.** (d)	**5.** (ac)
6. (bd)	**7.** (ac)	**8.** (acd)	**9.** (abd)	**10.** (abd)
11. (ad)	**12.** (abcd)			

Comprehension Based Questions

1. (d)	**2.** (b)	**3.** (a)	**4.** (b)	**5.** (c)
6. (b)	**7.** (c)	**8.** (a)	**9.** (a)	**10.** (a)
11. (b)	**12.** (d)	**13.** (c)	**14.** (a)	**15.** (c)
16. (a)	**17.** (c)	**18.** (d)	**19.** (b)	**20.** (a)
21. (a)	**22.** (b)	**23.** (c)	**24.** (a)	**25.** (b)
26. (a)				

Match the Columns Questions

1. (A) → Q, S (B) → P (C) → P (D) → Q,R

2. (A) → R (B) → P, (C) → R (D) → S

3. (A) → P, (B) → V, (C) → S, (D) → Q (E) → U, (F) → T, (G) → R

4. (A) → R; (B) → P,Q (C) → S; (D) → P,Q,R,S

5. (A) → R (B) → P,S,T (C) → Q,R (D) → P,S

Numerical Value Questions

1. (7)	**2.** (3)	**3.** (10)	**4.** (24)	**5.** (55)

Previous Year's Questions

JEE Main

1. (c)	**2.** (c)	**3.** (a)	**4.** (b)	**5.** (b)
6. (c)	**7.** (a)			

SOLUTIONS

Level 1

1. (i) Body is at rest at $x = x_0$
   (ii) Body starts from origin and is moving with speed $\tan\theta$ away from origin.
   (iii) Body starts from $x = x_0$ and it moves towards the origin with constant velocity. After some time, it passes through the origin and then continues to moves along negative X-axis with the same constant velocity.
   (iv) Body starts from rest from origin and moves away from origin with increasing speed and positive acceleration.
   (v) Body starts from origin with certain initial velocity along the positive X-axis. It moves with decreasing speed and negative acceleration.
   (vi) Body starts from somewhere on the positive X-axis and moves towards origin with decreasing speed.
   (vii) Body starts from rest at $x = x_0$ and then moves with increasing speed towards origin. Therefore, acceleration is negative.
   (viii) Body starts from origin with some initial velocity along positive X-axis. Speed of body is decreasing and it becomes zero momentarily and at this instant it reverses its direction of motion and then moves towards the origin with increasing speed.
   (ix) Body starts from somewhere on the positive X-axis with certain initial velocity directed towards origin. Speed of body first decreases and it becomes zero momentarily and at this instant it reverses its direction of motion and then moves away from the origin with increasing speed.
   (x) Body starts from origin with certain initial velocity directed along the negative X-axis. It slows down and comes to rest $t = t_1$ momentarily. Then it reverses its direction and moves towards the origin with increasing speed. It crosses the origin at $t = t_2$ and continues to move along the positive X-axis with increasing speed.
2. (i) Body is moving with constant velocity. Acceleration is zero.
   (ii) Body is at rest initially. Then it starts moving with its velocity increasing at a constant rate, i.e. body is moving with constant acceleration.
   (iii) Body starts its motion with initial velocity v_0. Then its velocity decreases at a constant rate, i.e. acceleration of the body is negative and constant. At $t = t_0$ the body comes to rest for a moment and it reverses its direction of motion and then continues to move with increasing speed.
   (iv) Body is at rest initially. As time progress, its velocity and acceleration both increase in magnitude.
   (v) Body starts with certain initial velocity. As time progresses, its velocity increases but magnitude of acceleration decreases.
   (vi) Body starts with certain initial velocity. As time progresses, its velocity and magnitude of acceleration both decrease.
   (vii) Body starts its motion with initial velocity v_0. Its velocity is decreasing with time and at $t = t_0$ it comes to rest for an instant and after that the body reverses its direction of motion and continues to move with decreasing velocity or increasing speed. Since, velocity of the body is decreasing for whole motion, therefore its acceleration is negative. For $0 < t < t_0$ motion of the body is deaccelerated (speed is decreassing) and for $t > t_0$ motion of the body is accelerated (speed is increasing).
   (viii) Body starts from rest. First it speeds up (with decreasing acceleration) and then slows down (with increasing retardation).
   (Ix) Body first slows down (with decreasing retardation) and then speeds up (with increasing acceleration).
   (x) This motion is not possible as a body cannot have multiple velocities at a particular instant of time.
3. (i) Acceleration of the body is constant and positive. The body will speed up at constant rate if initial velocity is zero or positive. The body will slow down at constant rate if initial velocity is negative.
   (ii) Acceleration of the body is constant and negative. The body will slow down at constant rate if initial velocity is positive. The body will speed up at constant rate if initial velocity is zero or negative.
   (iii) Initially the acceleration of the body is zero. Then its acceleration increases at a constant rate.
   (iv) Acceleration decreases at a constant rate.
   (v) Acceleration first increases at a constant rate, then acceleration is constant and finally acceleration decreases at a constant rate. If initial velocity is positive or zero, then the body will speed up throughout the journey.
4. (a) Area from $(t = 0)$ to $(t = 6) = 32$

   Area from $(t = 6)$ to $(t = 10) = 16$

   Distance $= 32 + 16 = 48$ m

   Displacement $= 32 - 16 = 16$ m

   (b) $a = \dfrac{dv}{dt}$ = slope of v-t curve

   At $t = 1$, $a = \dfrac{8}{2} = 4\ \text{m/s}^2$

   At $t = 3, a = 0$

   At $t = 5, a = -4\ \text{m/s}^2$

   At $t = 7, a = -4\ \text{m/s}^2$

   At $t = 9, a = 4\ \text{m/s}^2$

(c) Average velocity $= \frac{16}{10} = 1.6$ m/s

Average speed $= \frac{48}{10} = 4.8$ m/s

(d) Average acceleration $= \frac{\Delta v}{\Delta t} = \frac{-4-8}{5} = -2.4 \text{ m/s}^2$

5. Area under a-t curve gives change in velocity.

(a) Area from $t=0$ to $t=2$ is 4

So, $\Delta v = 4 \Rightarrow v-2=4 \Rightarrow v=6$ m/s

Area from $t=0$ to $t=3$ is 7

$\Rightarrow \Delta v = 7 \Rightarrow v-2=7 \Rightarrow v=9$ m/s

Area from $t=0$ to $t=5$ is (8 – 1) = 7

$\Rightarrow \Delta v = 7 \Rightarrow v-2=7 \Rightarrow v=9$ m/s

(b) Average acceleration $= \frac{\Delta v}{\Delta t} = \frac{9-2}{5} = 1.4 \text{ m/s}^2$

(c)

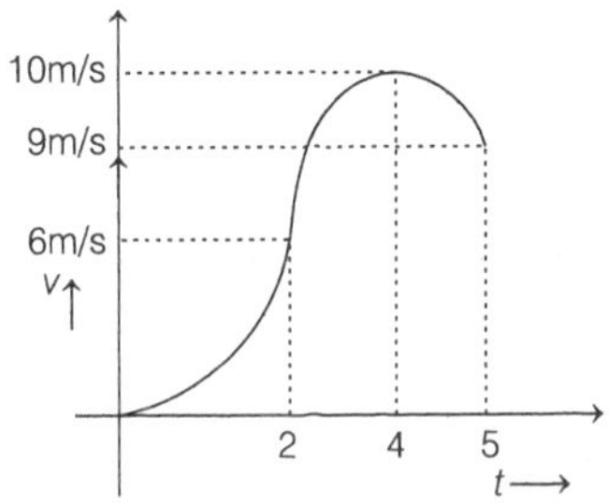

6. Area under a-x curve = 0.4

$$\frac{v_2^2 - v_1^2}{2} = 0.4 \Rightarrow v_2^2 - (0.8)^2 = 0.8 \Rightarrow v_2 = 1.2 \text{ m/s}$$

7. (a) Moving forward ⟶ (0, 1) s and (5, 7) s;

Moving backward ⟶ (1, 5) s;

Speeding up (1, 2) s; and (5, 6) s; Slowing down ⟶ (0, 1) s, (3, 5) s and (6, 7) s

(b) Positive acceleration ⟶ (3, 6) s; Negative acceleration ⟶ (0, 2) s and (6, 7) s

Zero acceleration ⟶ (2, 3) s and (7, 9) s

(c) 0 s and (2, 3) s

(d) (7, 9) s

12. $v = -5x + 10$

$$a = v\frac{dv}{dx} = (-5x+10)(-5) = 25x - 50$$

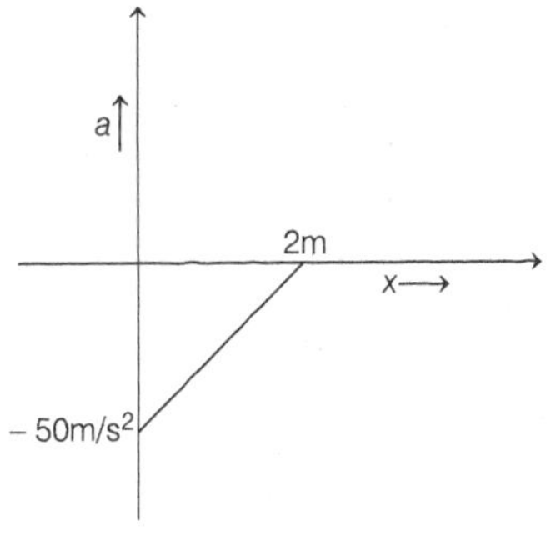

Level 2

Single Choice Correct Questions

1. Speed will be maximum at $t = 11$ s

Area under a-t curve $= \frac{1}{2} \times 11 \times 10 = 55$

So, $\Delta v = 55 \Rightarrow v_2 - v_1 = 55 \Rightarrow v = 55$ m/s

2. Distance = Area under v-t curve from $t = 0$ to $t = 4$

= 50 m

3. $v = \frac{ds}{dt}$ = slope of displacement-time graph.

As time progresses slope of graph is decreasing, so velocity is decreasing.

4. $v = u + at \Rightarrow v = u - 10t$

5. $v = \frac{ds}{dt}$ = slope of displacement-time curve.

6. In cd region, velocity is constant.

7. Velocity first decreases, becomes zero and then becomes negative.

8. First velocity increases at constant rate, then velocity is uniform and finally increases again at constant rate.

9. Area = 36m

10. Displacement $= +8 - 4 + 4 = 8$ m

Distance $= 8 + 4 + 4 = 16$ m

11. Total distance travelled = 40 m

Distance covered in last 2 s =10m

Fraction $= \frac{10}{40} = \frac{1}{4}$

12. In option (a) velocity is constant.

13. $v = \sqrt{u^2 + 2g(d-h)}$

14. Area under acceleration-time graph gives change in velocity.

15. In option (a), $s \propto t^2 \rightarrow v \propto t \Rightarrow a =$ constant

16. In option (a), velocity is constant. So, the body is in uniform motion.

17. $v = \left(\frac{-v_0}{x_0}\right)x + v_0$

$$a = \frac{v\,dv}{dx} = \left[\left(\frac{-v_0}{x_0}\right)x + v_0\right]\left(\frac{-v_0}{x_0}\right) = \frac{v_0^2}{x_0^2}x - \frac{v_0^2}{x_0}$$

So, acceleration-displacement graph will be straight line with positive slope and negative y-intercept.

18. v = slope of displacement-time graph

$= \tan 60° = \sqrt{3}$ m/s

19. Average velocity $= \frac{\text{Displacement}}{\text{Time}}$

$= \frac{\text{Area under } v\text{-}t \text{ graph}}{\text{Time}} = 0$

20. A body cannot have multiple velocities at an instant.

21. $x = -\sin t \Rightarrow v = -\cos t$

22. $v^2 = u^2 + 2as \Rightarrow v^2 = 0^2 + 2as \Rightarrow v = \sqrt{2as}$

23. $\frac{v_A}{v_B} = \frac{\tan 30°}{\tan 60°} = \frac{1}{3}$

24. Average speed $= \frac{\text{Distance}}{\text{Time}} = \frac{\text{Area}}{\text{Time}} = \frac{8+2}{5} = 2\text{m/s}$

Average velocity $= \frac{\text{Displacement}}{\text{Time}} = \frac{\text{Area}}{\text{Time}} = \frac{8-2}{5} = 1.2 \text{ m/s}$

$\frac{\text{Average speed}}{\text{Average velocity}} = \frac{2}{1.2} = \frac{5}{3}$

25. Area under a-x graph $= \frac{v_2^2 - v_1^2}{2}$

$$\frac{1}{2} \times 1 \times 1 = \frac{v_2^2 - 0}{2} \Rightarrow v_2 = 1\text{m/s}$$

26. Both cars have same velocity. As both lines have same slope.

27. The particle moves at a constant velocity upto time t_0, and then stops.

28. Average acceleration $= \frac{\Delta v}{\Delta t} = \frac{v_2 - v_1}{t_2 - t_1} = \frac{\frac{-750}{10} - \frac{1000}{15}}{35-5}$

$$= \frac{-85}{18} \text{ m/s}^2$$

29. Height will be maximum when $v = 0$.

Area from A to $B = \frac{1}{2} \times 3 \times 30 = 45$ m

So, maximum height reached = 45 m

30. (b) For $t = 0$ to $t = 2$,

$$a = 1 \Rightarrow \frac{dv}{dt} = 1 \Rightarrow \int_0^v dv = \int_0^t dt \Rightarrow v = 1$$

For $t = 2$ to $t = 4$,

$$a = -2 \Rightarrow \frac{dv}{dt} = -2 \Rightarrow \int_2^v dv = -2\int_2^t dt$$

$$\Rightarrow v - 2 = -2(t-2) \Rightarrow v = -2t + 6$$

31. Velocity is first negative and increasing in magnitude and then positive and decreasing in magnitude.

32. $v = \frac{ds}{dt}$ = slope of s-t graph $= \frac{8}{2} = 4\text{m/s}$

33. Average acceleration $= \frac{\Delta v}{\Delta t} = \frac{\text{Area under } a\text{-}t \text{ curve}}{\Delta t}$

$$= \frac{600}{20} = 30 \text{ m/s}^2$$

34. $a = \frac{dv}{dt}$ = Slope of v-t curve

Slope is maximum in interval $t = 30$ to $t = 40$

$$a_{max} = \frac{40}{10} = 4 \text{ m/s}^2$$

35. Area under a-t curve $= \Delta v$

$22 = v - 1 \Rightarrow v = 23$ m/s along the initial direction.

36.

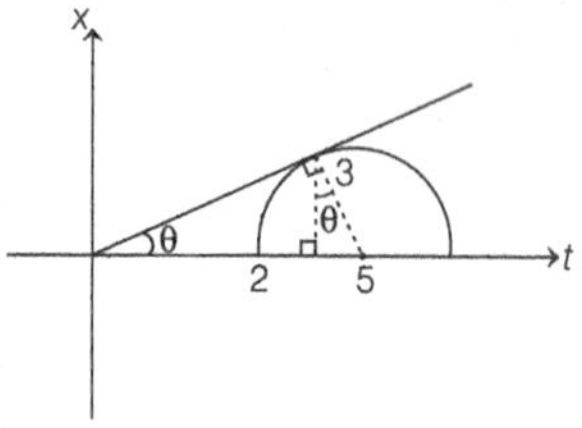

$$\sin\theta = \frac{3}{5}$$

$$\text{Time} = 5 - 3\sin\theta = 5 - 3\left(\frac{3}{5}\right) = \frac{16}{5} = 3.2 \text{ s}$$

37. $a = v\frac{dv}{dx} \Rightarrow a = 2\tan(120°) = -2\sqrt{3} \text{ m/s}^2$

38. For $t < t_0$,

$$s = ut + \frac{1}{2}at^2 \Rightarrow x - 0 = 0 + \frac{1}{2}at^2 \Rightarrow x = \frac{1}{2}at^2$$

At $t = t_0$, $x_0 = \frac{1}{2}at_0^2$

For $t_0 < t < 2t_0$,

$$s = ut + \frac{1}{2}at^2 \Rightarrow x - x_0 = (at_0)t + \frac{1}{2}(-a)t^2$$

$$\Rightarrow x = x_0 + (at)t_0 - \frac{1}{2}at^2$$

39. Average acceleration $= \frac{\Delta v}{\Delta t}$

During interval OA, $a_{avg} = \frac{v_2 - v_1}{t_2 - t_1} = \frac{40-0}{40\cot 30°} = \tan 30°$

During interval AB,

$$a'_{avg} = \frac{v_2 - v_1}{t_2 - t_1} = \frac{0-40}{40\cot 60°} = -\tan 60°$$

$$\therefore \frac{a_{avg}}{|a'_{avg}|} = \frac{1/\sqrt{3}}{\sqrt{3}} = \frac{1}{3}$$

40. $a_{rel} = a_1 - a_2 = \frac{dv_1}{dt} - \frac{dv_2}{dt}$

= Slope of P_1 – Slope of P_2

Since, a_{rel} is constant, magnitude of relative velocity continuously increases.

Numerical Value Questions

1. Area under a-x curve $= \frac{v_2^2 - v_1^2}{2} \Rightarrow 30 = \frac{v_2^2 - 2^2}{2}$

$$\Rightarrow v_2^2 = 64 \Rightarrow v_2 = 8 \text{ m/s}$$

2. Average speed $= \frac{\text{Distance}}{\text{Time}} = \frac{\text{Area under } v\text{-}t \text{ curve}}{\text{Time}}$

$$= \frac{30}{6} = 5 \text{ m/s}$$

Average acceleration, $= \frac{\Delta v}{\Delta t} = \frac{v_2 - v_1}{t_2 - t_1} = \frac{10-(-10)}{4} = 5 \text{ m/s}$

3. Average velocity $= \frac{\text{Displacement}}{\text{Time}}$

$$72 \times \frac{5}{18} = \frac{\text{Displacement}}{25}$$

$\Rightarrow$ Displacement $= 25 \times 20 = 500$ m

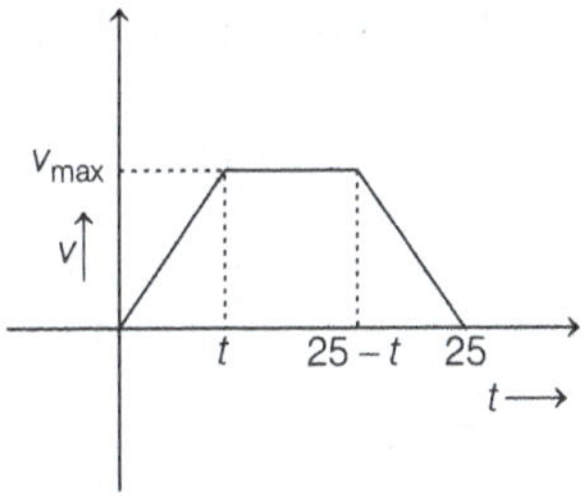

Area under v-t curve $= \frac{1}{2}(25 + (25-2t) \times v_{max}$

$$500 = \frac{1}{2}(50-2t)v_{max} \quad \text{...(i)}$$

$$a = 5 = \frac{v_{max}}{t} \quad \text{...(ii)}$$

From Eqs. (i) and (ii), we get

$$t = 5$$

So, particle is moving with uniform velocity for time

$$= 25 - 5 - 5 = 15 \text{ s}$$

4. Area under a-t curve $= v_2 - v_1$

$$\frac{\pi r^2}{4} = v_2 - v_1 \Rightarrow \frac{22}{7} \times \frac{(\sqrt{7})^2}{4} = v_2 - 3$$

$$\Rightarrow \quad v_2 = \frac{11}{2} + 3 = \frac{17}{2} = 8.5 \text{ m/s}$$

5. Area from $(t=0)$ to $(t=4) = 4$

Area from $(t=4)$ to $(t=8) = 0$

Lets say lift comes to rest at time t

Area from $(t=8)$ to $(t=t) = (t-8)2$

$$\Rightarrow \quad (t-8)2 = 4 \Rightarrow t = 10 \text{ s}$$

Level 3

Single Choice Correct Questions

1. $v = \frac{2v_0}{L}x + v_0 \Rightarrow \frac{dx}{dt} = \left(\frac{2v_0}{L}\right)x + v_0$

$$\Rightarrow \int_0^x \frac{dx}{\left(\frac{2v_0}{L}\right)x + v_0} = \int_0^t dt$$

$$\Rightarrow \frac{1}{\left(\frac{2v_0}{L}\right)}\left[\ln\left(\left(\frac{2v_0}{L}\right)x + v_0\right)\right]_0^x = [t]_0^t$$

$$\frac{L}{2v_0}\ln\left(\frac{\left(\frac{2v_0}{L}\right)x + v_0}{v_0}\right) = t$$

At $x = L$

$$\frac{L}{2v_0}\ln\left(\frac{\left(\frac{2v_0}{L}\right)L + v_0}{v_0}\right) = t \Rightarrow t = \frac{\ln 3}{2v_0}$$

$$\text{Average acceleration} = \frac{\Delta v}{\Delta t} = \frac{3v_0 - v_0}{\left(\frac{L\ln 3}{2v_0}\right)} = \frac{4v_0^2}{L\ln 3}$$

2. $a = \left(\frac{2}{10}\right)t + 2 \Rightarrow \frac{dv}{dt} = (0.2)t + 2$

$$\Rightarrow \int_{2/3}^{v} dv = \int_0^t (0.2)t + 2)dt \Rightarrow [v]_{2/3}^v = [0.1t^2 + 2t]_0^t$$

$$\Rightarrow v = (0.1)t^2 + 2t + \frac{2}{3} \Rightarrow \frac{dx}{dt} = (0.1)t^2 + 2t + \frac{2}{3}$$

$$\Rightarrow \int_0^x dx = \int_0^t \left((0.1)t^2 + 2t + \frac{2}{3}\right)dt$$

$$\Rightarrow [x]_0^x = \left[\frac{0.1t^3}{3} + t^2 + \frac{2}{3}t\right]_0^t \Rightarrow x = \frac{0.1t^3}{3} + t^2 + \frac{2t}{3}$$

At $t = 10$, $x = \frac{(0.1)(10)^3}{3} + 10^2 + \frac{2(10)}{3} \Rightarrow x = 140$ m

Average velocity $= \frac{140}{10} = 14$ m/s

3. For $s = 0$ to $s = 8$ m

$$\frac{2}{v} = 4 \Rightarrow v = \frac{1}{2} \text{ m/s}$$

Time taken $= \frac{8}{1/2} = 16$ s

For $s > 8$ m

$$\frac{2}{v} = \left(\frac{6}{6}\right)s - 4 \Rightarrow v = \frac{2}{s-4} \Rightarrow \frac{ds}{dt} = \frac{2}{s-4}$$

$$\Rightarrow \quad 2\int_{16}^{t} dt = \int_8^s (s-4)ds$$

$$\Rightarrow \quad 2(t-16) = \left(\frac{s^2}{2} - 4s\right) - \left(\frac{8^2}{2} - 4(8)\right)$$

$$\Rightarrow \quad t = 16 + \frac{s^2}{4} - 2s$$

At $s = 10$

$$t = 16 + \frac{(10)^2}{4} - 2(10) \Rightarrow t = 16 + 25 - 20 = 21 \text{ s}$$

4.

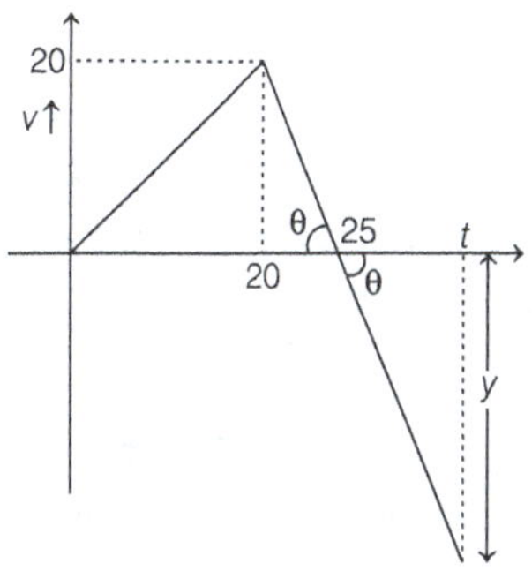

$$\tan\theta = \frac{20}{5} = \frac{y}{t-25} \Rightarrow y = 4(t-25)$$

Area from $t = 0$ to $t = 25 = \frac{1}{2} \times 25 \times 20 = 250$ m

Area from $t = 25$ to $t = t = \frac{1}{2}(t-25)[4(t-25)] = 2(t-25)^2$

$$250 = 2(t-25)^2 \Rightarrow (t-25)^2 = 125$$

$$\Rightarrow \quad t = 25 + 5\sqrt{5} \Rightarrow t = 25 + 11.2 = 36.2 \text{ s}$$

5.

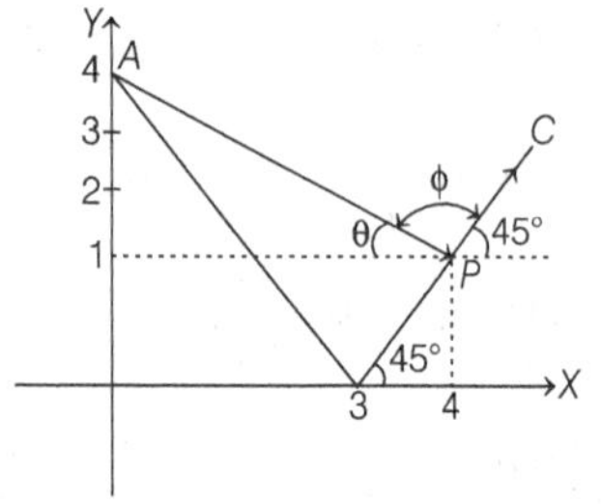

$$\tan\theta = \frac{3}{4} \Rightarrow \theta = 37°$$

$$\phi = 180° - 37° - 45° = 98°$$

Angle between AP and PC $= 180° - 98° = 82°$

6. $\tan 60° = \frac{AC}{OC} \Rightarrow OC = \frac{AC}{\sqrt{3}} = \frac{4}{\sqrt{3}} = \frac{4\sqrt{3}}{3}$

$\tan 30° = \frac{AC}{BC} \Rightarrow BC = 4\sqrt{3}$

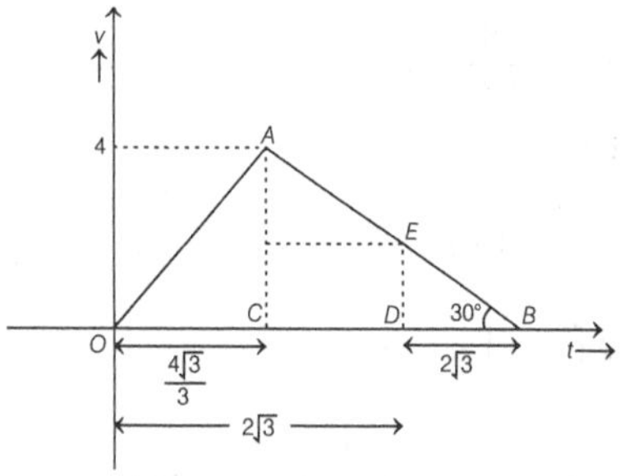

$\tan 30° = \frac{DE}{DB} = \frac{DE}{2\sqrt{3}} = DE = 2$

Average acceleration $= \frac{2-0}{2\sqrt{3}} = \frac{1}{\sqrt{3}}$ m/s^2

7. $a = mv + c \Rightarrow \frac{dv}{dt} = mv + c \Rightarrow \int_0^v \frac{dv}{mv+c} = \int_0^t dt$

$\Rightarrow \frac{1}{m}[\ln(mv+c)]_0^v = [t]_0^t \Rightarrow \ln\left(\frac{mv+c}{c}\right) = mt$

$\Rightarrow \frac{mv+c}{C} = e^{mt} \Rightarrow v = \frac{1}{m}(e^{mt} - 1)$

Velocity is varying with time exponentially.

8. Velocity of car is first increasing and then decreasing. At $t = 1$, Car velocity is maximum. So, at $t = 1$, acceleration is zero.

Mean speed $= \frac{\text{Distance}}{\text{time}} = \frac{\text{Area under } v\text{-}t \text{ curve}}{\text{Time}}$

$= \frac{\pi(1)^2/2}{2} = \frac{\pi}{4}$ m/s

9. Distance travelled by car A in time $t = 10t$

Distance travelled by car B in time $t = \frac{1}{2}(t)t = \frac{1}{2}t^2$

$$\frac{1}{2}t^2 = 10t + 10.5$$

$\Rightarrow \quad t^2 - 20t - 21 = 0 \Rightarrow t^2 - 21t + t - 21 = 0$

$\Rightarrow \quad t(t-21) + (t-21) = 0 \Rightarrow t = -1$ and $t = 21$

10. $v^2 = -\left(\frac{2700}{0.6}\right)s + 3600 \Rightarrow v = \sqrt{-\left(\frac{2700}{0.6}\right)s + 3600}$

$a = v\frac{dv}{ds} = \frac{(\sqrt{-4500s + 3600})}{2\sqrt{-4500s + 3600}} \times -4500$

$a = -\frac{4500}{2} = -2250$ km/h^2

11. From $t = 0$ to $t = 6$

$a = \frac{5}{6}t \Rightarrow \frac{dv}{dt} = \frac{5t}{6} \Rightarrow \int_0^v dv = \int_0^t \frac{5t}{6}dt$

$\Rightarrow [v]_0^v = \left[\frac{5t^2}{12}\right]_0^t \Rightarrow v = \frac{5t^2}{12} \Rightarrow \frac{dx}{dt} = \frac{5t^2}{12}$

$\Rightarrow \int_0^x dx = \int_0^t \frac{5t^2}{12}dt \Rightarrow x = \frac{5t^3}{36}$

At $t = 6, x = \frac{5(6)^3}{36} = 30$m and $v = \frac{5(6)^2}{12} = 15$ m/s

From $t = 6$ to $t = 12$,

$s = ut + \frac{1}{2}at^2 \Rightarrow s = 15(6) + \frac{1}{2}(5)(6)^2 \Rightarrow s = 180$ m

Total distance $= 30 + 180 = 210$ m

12. From $s = 0$ to $s = 60$

$v = \left(\frac{12}{60}\right)s + 3 \Rightarrow v = \frac{s}{5} + 3 \Rightarrow \frac{ds}{dt} = \frac{s}{5} + 3 \Rightarrow \int_0^s \frac{ds}{\frac{s}{5} + 3} = \int_0^t dt$

$\Rightarrow \left[\frac{\ln\left(\frac{s}{5} + 3\right)}{(1/5)}\right]_0^s = [t]_0^t \Rightarrow 5\ln\left(\frac{s/5 + 3}{3}\right) = t$

At $s = 60 \Rightarrow 5\ln\left(\frac{60/5 + 3}{3}\right) = t$

$\Rightarrow \quad t = 5 \ln 5 \Rightarrow t = 5(1.6) = 8$ s

From $s = 60$ to $s = 120 \Rightarrow t = \frac{60}{15} = 4$

Total time $= 8 + 4 = 12$ s

13. Area under $\frac{1}{a}$ *versus* v curve $= \int \frac{1}{a}dv = \int \frac{1}{dv/dt}dv$

$= \int dt = \Delta t$

Area $= 15 \times 1 + \frac{1}{2} \times 15 \times 1 = 22.5$

So, $\Delta t = 22.5$ s

14. $a = cx + d \Rightarrow v\frac{dv}{dx} = cx + d$

$$\int_{v_0}^{v} v\,dv = \int_0^x (cx+d)dx \Rightarrow \frac{v^2 - v_0^2}{2} = \frac{cx^2}{2} + dx$$

$$\Rightarrow \quad v = \sqrt{cx^2 + 2dx + v_0^2}$$

For v-x graph to be linear as given

Discriminant of $(cx^2 + 2dx + v_0^2) = 0$

$$\Rightarrow \quad (2d)^2 - 4cv_0^2 = 0 \Rightarrow v_0 = \sqrt{\frac{d^2}{c}}$$

15. Distance covered by cyclist 1 in time $t = \frac{1}{2}t\left(\frac{v_0 t}{4}\right) = \frac{v_0 t^2}{8}$

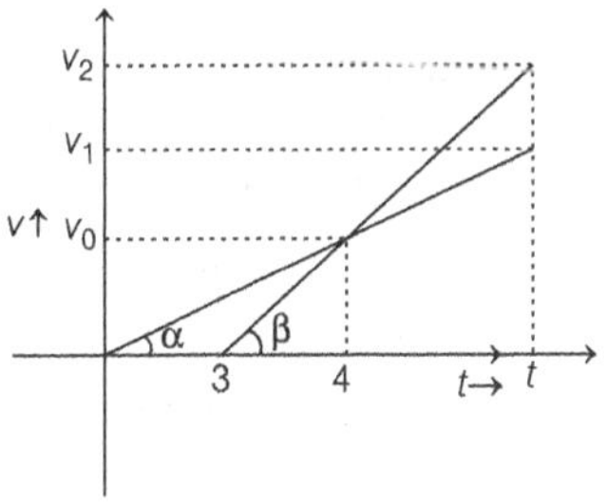

$$\tan\alpha = \frac{v_0}{4} = \frac{v_1}{t}, \quad \tan\beta = \frac{v_0}{1} = \frac{v_2}{t-3}$$

Distance covered by cyclist 2 in time t

$$= \frac{1}{2}(t-3)[v_0(t-3)] = \frac{v_0}{2}(t-3)^2$$

$$\frac{v_0 t^2}{8} = \frac{v_0}{2}(t-3)^2 \Rightarrow t^2 = 4(t-3)^2$$

$$\Rightarrow \quad t = 2(t-3) \Rightarrow 2t - 6 = t \Rightarrow t = 6 \text{ min}$$

16. In all three graphs, acceleration is positive. So, particle will speed up.

17 Distance travelled by train I $= \frac{1}{2} \times 10 \times 40 = 200$ m

Distance travelled by train II $= \frac{1}{2} \times 8 \times 20 = 80$ m

So, separation = (300 – 200 – 80) m = 70 m

18. $\tan\theta = \frac{22.5}{150} = \frac{y}{90}$

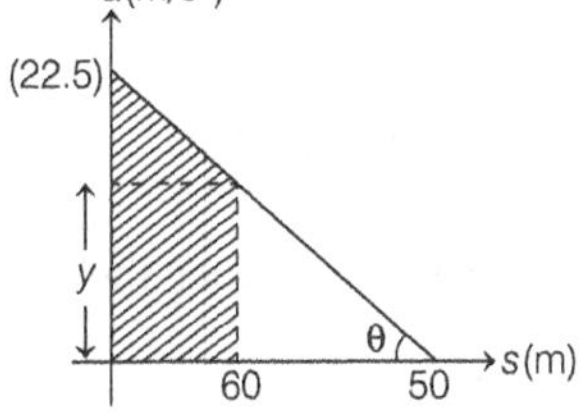

$$\Rightarrow \quad y = \frac{90 \times 22.5}{150} = 13.5$$

Area under a-s curve $= \frac{v_2^2 - v_1^2}{2}$

$$\Rightarrow \frac{1}{2}(22.5 + 13.5) \times 60 = \frac{v_2^2 - 7^2}{2} \Rightarrow v_2 = \sqrt{2209} = 47 \text{ m/s}$$

19. Slope $= \frac{dy}{dx} = \frac{d\left(\frac{1}{t}\right)}{d\left(\frac{1}{v}\right)} \Rightarrow -\tan 30° = \frac{(-1/t^2)dt}{(-1/v^2)dv}$

$$\Rightarrow \quad \frac{dv}{dt} = -\sqrt{3}\frac{v^2}{t^2}$$

At point P, $\tan 45° = \frac{y}{x} \Rightarrow 1 = \frac{1/t}{1/v} \Rightarrow v = t$

$$a = -\sqrt{3}\left(\frac{v^2}{t^2}\right) \Rightarrow a = -\sqrt{3}\text{units}$$

Multiple Choice(s) Correct Questions

1. Area under a-t graph $= \Delta v = v_2 - v_1$
   Area under v-t graph $= \Delta x = x_2 - x_1$
2. Since, particle has positive acceleration upto time t_0, both velocity and displacement will increase.
3. (a) $a = \frac{dv}{dt}$ = slope of v-t graph.
   (b) Direction of velocity of changes at $t = 10$ s
   (c) Net area is non-zero.
   (d) Distance travelled is same in the two intervals. So, average speed will be equal.
4. Speed cannot be negative. Length of path can never decrease.
5. (a) Distance = Area under v-t graph
   $$= \frac{1}{2} \times 15 \times 15 + 10 \times 5 + \frac{1}{2} \times 10 \times 10 = 212.5 \text{ m}$$
   (b) $10 \times 5 = 50$ m
   (c) Average acceleration $= \frac{\Delta v}{\Delta t} = \frac{5-10}{10} = -0.5 \text{ m/s}^2$
6. $a_A > a_B$
   Their initial positions may be different.
7. (a) Upto 18 s
   $s_A = 40 \times 18 = 720$ m, $s_B = \frac{1}{2} \times 18 \times 60 = 540$ m
   Separation = 720 – 540 = 180 m
   (c) At $t = 27$, $s_A = 40 \times 27 = 1080$ m
   $s_B = \frac{1}{2} \times 18 \times 60 + 60 \times 9 = 1080$ m
8. From $t = 0$ to $t = 24$
   Area $= 70 = x_2 - x_1 \Rightarrow 70 = x_2 - (-16) \Rightarrow x_2 = 54$
   From $t = 0$ to $t = 18$ and $t = 0$ to $t = 30$
   Area $= 52 = x_2 - (-16) \Rightarrow x_2 = 36$ m
9. Average velocity $= \frac{\text{Displacement}}{\text{Time}} = \frac{-10+25}{6} = 2.5$ m/s
   Average acceleration $= \frac{\Delta v}{\Delta t} = \frac{10-(-5)}{3} = 5 \text{ m/s}^2$
   Average speed $= \frac{\text{Distance}}{\text{Time}} \neq 0$
   $a = \frac{dv}{dt}$ = slope of v-t graph $= \frac{10}{2} = 5 \text{ m/s}^2$

10. $a = g - kv$

$$\Rightarrow \int_0^v \frac{dv}{g-kv} = \int_0^t dt \Rightarrow \ln\left(\frac{g-kv}{g}\right) = -kt$$

$$\Rightarrow \quad v = \frac{g}{k}(1-e^{-kt}) \Rightarrow \frac{dh}{dt} = \frac{g}{k}(1-e^{-kt})$$

$$\Rightarrow \int_H^h dh = \int_0^t \frac{g}{k}(1-e^{-kt})dt \Rightarrow h - H = \left[\frac{g}{k}\left(t + \frac{e^{-kt}}{k}\right)\right]_0^t$$

$$\Rightarrow \quad h = H + \frac{g}{k}\left(t + \frac{e^{-kt}}{k} - 1\right)$$

$$a = \frac{dv}{dt} \Rightarrow a = ge^{-kt}$$

11. When both the balls in the air,their relative acceleration is zero. So, their relative velocity will be constant.

When the first stone reaches ground and does not rebound, relative acceleration of second stone w.r.t. the first stone is g. So, their relative velocity will increase linearly and their separation parabollically.

12. $v = \frac{dx}{dt}$ = slope of x-t graph

(a) At $t = t_1$, slope of graph is more for A than B. So, $v_A > v_B$.

(b) At $t = t_3$, slope of graph is more for B than A. So, $v_B > v_A$.

(c) At $t = t_2$, slopes may be equal. So, they may have same velocity.

(D) For car A, slope is continuously decreasing. So, it is slowing down.

Comprehension Based Questions

1. $a = \frac{dv}{dt}$ = slope of v-t graph.

2. Acceleration motion having positive area on v-t graph has concave shape.

3. Maximum displacement = Total area upto $t = 50$

$= 20 + 40 + 60 + 80 = 200$ m

4. Average speed $= \frac{\text{Distance}}{\text{Time}} = \frac{20+40+60+80+40}{70} = \frac{24}{7}$ m/s

5. Time interval of retardation = 30 to 60 s

6.

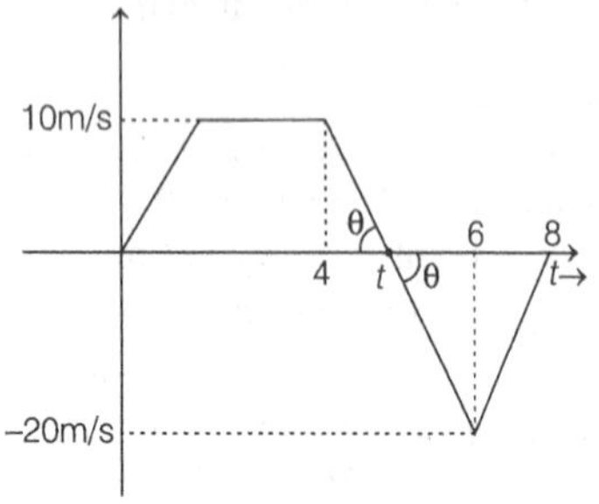

$$\tan\theta = \frac{10}{t-4} = \frac{20}{6-t} \Rightarrow 6 - t = 2(t-4) \Rightarrow t = \frac{14}{3}\text{ s}$$

7. $t = 0$ to $t = 2$; $\frac{\Delta v}{\Delta t} = \frac{10-0}{2-0} = 5\text{ m/s}^2$

$t = 2$ to $t = 4$; $\frac{\Delta v}{\Delta t} = 0$

$t = 4$ to $t = 6$; $\frac{\Delta v}{\Delta t} = \frac{-20-10}{2} = -15\text{ m/s}^2$

$t = 6$ to $t = 8$; $\frac{\Delta v}{\Delta t} = \frac{0-(-20)}{2} = 10\text{ m/s}^2$

8. Area under v-t graph $= \int_0^2 v\,dt = \Delta x \Rightarrow 10 = x - (-15)$

$\Rightarrow \quad x = -5$ m

9. Maximum displacement is at $t = \frac{14}{3}$ s

Maximum displacement $= \frac{1}{2}\left(\frac{14}{3} + 2\right)(10) = \frac{100}{3}$ m

10. Total distance = Total area

$= \frac{100}{3} + \frac{1}{2}\left(8 - \frac{14}{3}\right)(20) = \frac{200}{3}$ m

11. $x = -k(t-0)(t-2T) \Rightarrow x = -k(t^2 - 2Tt)$

$x = -kt^2 + 2kTt \Rightarrow v = -2kt + 2kT$

So, v-t graph will be straight line with negative slope.

12. $a = \frac{dv}{dt} = -2k$

So, acceleration is negative and constant.

13. In v-t graph, where velocity is negative, shift that branch up as speed cannot be negative.

14. Average velocity $= \frac{\Delta x}{\Delta t} = \frac{-100-100}{20} = -10$ m/s

15. Average acceleration $= \frac{\Delta v}{\Delta t} = \frac{\tan 120° - \tan 120°}{20-0} = 0$

16. From $t = 0$ to $t = 10$, particle is slowing down as magnitude of slope of x-t graph is decreasing.

Since, initial velocity is negative, for particle to retard acceleration will be positive.

17. Particle is slowing down from $t = 0$ and $t = 10$ and from $t = 10$ to $t = 20$ is speeding up.

18. and **19.**

For C_1,	For C_2,
$s = 9t$,	$s = 40 + \frac{1}{2}(1)t^2$
$v = 9$,	$v = 0 + 1(t) = t$
$a = 0$,	$a = 1\text{ m/s}^2$

20. Separation will be maximum when their relative velocity is zero.

$$v_1 = v_2 \Rightarrow 9 = t \Rightarrow t = 9\text{ s}$$

$$s_1 = 9(9) = 81\text{ m}, \quad s_2 = 40 + \frac{1}{2}(1)(9)^2 = 80.5\text{ m}$$

So, maximum lead will be $(81 - 80.5) = 0.5$ m

21. $\Delta v_x = \int_0^2 a_x dx$ = Area= 10×2 = 20 m/s

$\Rightarrow \quad v_x - 0 = 20 \quad \Rightarrow \quad v_x = 20$ m/s

$$\Delta v_y = \int_0^2 a_y d_y = \text{Area} = 2 \times (-5) = -10 \text{ m/s}$$

$v_y = -10$ m/s $\Rightarrow$ $\mathbf{v} = 20\hat{\mathbf{i}} - 10\hat{\mathbf{j}}$

Speed $= \sqrt{20^2 + 10^2} = 10\sqrt{5}$ m/s

22. From $t = 0$ to $t = 2$,

$a_x = 10$

$\Rightarrow v_x = 10t$

$\Rightarrow s_x = 5t^2$

At $t = 2$

$v_x = 20$

$s_x = 5(2)^2 = 20$ m

From $t = 2$ to $t = 4$,

$a_x = -10$

$\Rightarrow \dfrac{dv_x}{dt} = -10$

$\Rightarrow \int_{20}^{v_x} dv_x = -10\int_2^t dt$

$\Rightarrow v_x = 20 - 10(t-2)$

$\Rightarrow \dfrac{ds_x}{dt} = 40 - 10t$

$\Rightarrow s_x = 40t - 5t^2 - 40$

At $t = 4$, $s_x = 40$ m

From $t = 0$ to $t = 2$

$a_y = -5$

$\Rightarrow \dfrac{dv_y}{dt} = -5$

$\Rightarrow v_y = -5t$

$\Rightarrow s_y = -\dfrac{5t^2}{2}$

At $t = 2$

$v_y = -10$ m/s

$s_y = -10$ m

From $t = 2$ to $t = 4$

$a_y = 10$

$\Rightarrow \dfrac{dv_y}{dt} = 10$

$\Rightarrow \int_{-10}^{v_y} dv_y = 10\int_2^t dt$

$\Rightarrow v_y = 10(t-2) - 10$

$\Rightarrow v_y = 10t - 30$

$\Rightarrow s_y = 5t^2 - 30t + 30$

At $t = 4$

$s_y = 5(4)^2 - 30(4) + 30 = -10$ m

At $t = 4$, $\mathbf{s} = 40\hat{\mathbf{i}} - 10\hat{\mathbf{j}}$

$$|\text{Average velocity}| = \frac{\sqrt{40^2 + 10^2}}{4} = \frac{5}{2}\sqrt{17} \text{ m/s}$$

23. x will be maximum when,

$v_x = 0 \quad \Rightarrow \quad 40 - 10t = 0 \quad \Rightarrow \quad t = 4$ s

24. 25. and **26.**

Lets say maximum velocity is v_{max}

$$\frac{v_{max}}{t} = 5 \Rightarrow v_{max} = 5t$$

Distance = Area under v-t graph $= \dfrac{1}{2}\{(20+t) + (20-t)\}v_{max}$

$$\text{Average velocity} = \frac{\text{Displacement}}{\text{Time}} \Rightarrow 20 = \frac{\frac{1}{2}(40)(v_{max})}{20+t}$$

$$20 = \frac{20(5t)}{20+t} \Rightarrow t = 5 \text{ s} \Rightarrow v_{max} = 25 \text{ m/s}$$

Distance travelled with uniform velocity $= 25 \times 15 = 375$ m

Match the Columns Questions

1. From graph (A), $v = kx \quad \Rightarrow \quad a = v\dfrac{dv}{dx} = k^2x$

So, acceleration is non-uniform and directly proportional to x.

From graph (B), $v^2 = kx$

Differentiating both sides w.r.t. x,

$$\Rightarrow \quad 2v\frac{dv}{dx} = k \quad \Rightarrow \quad v\frac{dv}{dx} = \frac{k}{2}$$

Hence, acceleration is uniform.

From graph (C), $v = kt \quad \Rightarrow \quad a = \dfrac{dv}{dt} = k$

So, acceleration is uniform.

From graph (D), $v = kt^2 \quad \Rightarrow \quad a = \dfrac{dv}{dt} = 2kt$

So, acceleration is non-uniform and directly proportional to t.

2. (A) Change in velocity $= v_2 - v_1 = 0 - 10 = -10$

(B) Average acceleration $= \dfrac{\Delta v}{\Delta t} = \dfrac{-10}{6} = \dfrac{-5}{3}$

(C) Total displacement = Net area

$$= \frac{1}{2} \times 2 \times 10 - \frac{1}{2} \times 4 \times 10 = -10$$

(D) Acceleration at $t = 3$, $\dfrac{dv}{dt}$ = slope $= -\dfrac{10}{2} = -5$

3. Acceleration $= \dfrac{dv}{dt}$ = slope of v-t graph

4. $a = \dfrac{dv}{dt}$ = slope of v-t graph, $v = \dfrac{ds}{dt}$ = slope of s-t graph

5. (A) Slowing down

$\Rightarrow$ magnitude of slope of x-t graph decreases

(B) Returning towards origin $\Rightarrow \mathbf{v} \cdot \mathbf{r} < 0$

So, when velocity is positive and position is negative.

or velocity is negative and position is positive.

(C) Moving away from origin $\Rightarrow \mathbf{v} \cdot \mathbf{r} > 0$

(D) Speeding up $\Rightarrow$ magnitude of slope of x-t graph increases.

Numerical Value Questions

1. At $t = 0$; $v = 10$ m/s, $a = \dfrac{dv}{dt} = \tan 37° = \dfrac{3}{4}$ m/s^2

At $t = 3$; velocity is maximum $\Rightarrow a = 0$

Acceleration is varying linearly with time

$\Rightarrow \quad a = kt + c$

At $\quad t = 0$; $a = \dfrac{3}{4} \quad \Rightarrow \quad a = kt + \dfrac{3}{4}$

At $\quad t = 3$; $a = 0 \quad \Rightarrow \quad 0 = k(3) + \dfrac{3}{4} \quad \Rightarrow \quad k = -\dfrac{1}{4}$

So, $\quad a = \dfrac{-t}{4} + \dfrac{3}{4}$

When, $v = 0 \quad \Rightarrow \quad a = -\tan 45° \quad \Rightarrow \quad a = -1$

$$-1 = -\frac{t}{4} + \frac{3}{4} \quad \Rightarrow \quad t = 7 \text{ s}$$

2. $\dfrac{d\left(\frac{1}{v}\right)}{dt}$ = slope of $\dfrac{1}{v}$ *versus* t graph

$$-\frac{1}{v^2}\frac{dv}{dt} = -1 \quad \Rightarrow \quad \frac{dv}{dt} = v^2 = (\sqrt{3})^2 = 3$$

3. Slope $= \dfrac{2 - \frac{1}{2}}{8} = \dfrac{3}{16}$

$$\left(\frac{1}{v}-\frac{1}{2}\right)=\frac{3}{16}(x-4)$$

$$\Rightarrow \quad v=\frac{16}{3x-4} \Rightarrow \frac{dx}{dt}=\frac{16}{3x-4}$$

$$\int_4^{12}(3x-4)dx=16\int_{t_1}^{t_2}dt$$

$$\Rightarrow \quad 16(t_2-t_1)=\left[\frac{3x^2}{2}-4x\right]_4^{12}$$

$$\Rightarrow \quad 16(t_2-t_1)=(216-48)-(24-16)$$

$$\Rightarrow \quad t_2-t_1=\frac{160}{16}=10\text{ s}$$

4. For $t=0$ to $t=6$

$$a=\frac{5t}{6} \Rightarrow \frac{dv}{dt}=\frac{5t}{6} \Rightarrow \int_0^v dv=\frac{5}{6}\int_0^t tdt$$

$$\Rightarrow \quad v=\frac{5}{12}t^2 \Rightarrow \int_0^x dx=\frac{5}{12}\int_0^t t^2dt \Rightarrow x=\frac{5}{36}t^3$$

At $t=6$; $x=\frac{5}{36}(6)^3=30$ m

At $t=6$; $v=\frac{5}{12}(6)^2=15$ m/s

From $t=6$ to $t=10$, $a=5$

$$s=ut+\frac{1}{2}at^2$$

$$\Rightarrow \quad s=15(4)+\frac{1}{2}(5)(4)^2=100\text{ m}$$

Total distance = 30 + 100 = 130 m

5. $v=2s+10 \Rightarrow a=v\frac{dv}{ds}=(2s+10)(2)=24\text{ m/s}^2$

6.

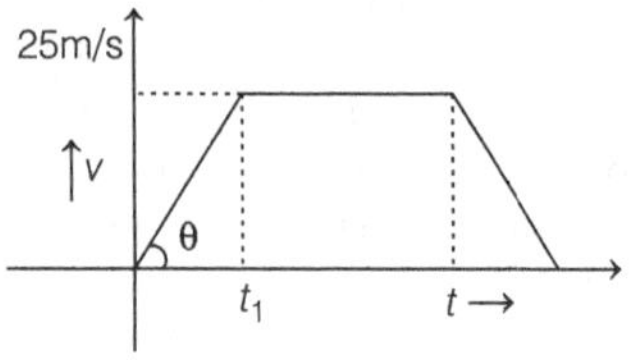

From $t=0$ to $t=t_1$

$$a=\frac{5}{3}\text{ m/s}^2$$

$$\Rightarrow \quad a=\frac{dv}{dt}=\tan\theta=\frac{25}{t_1}=\frac{5}{3} \Rightarrow t_1=15\text{ s}$$

Distance travelled = Area under v-t curve

$$=\frac{1}{2}\times 15\times 25=\frac{375}{2}\text{ m}$$

Distance covered with uniform velocity

$$=1000-\frac{375}{2}-\frac{375}{2}=625\text{ m}$$

Time taken $=\frac{625}{25}=25$ s

Total time $=15+25+15=55$ s

Previous Year's Questions

JEE Main

1.

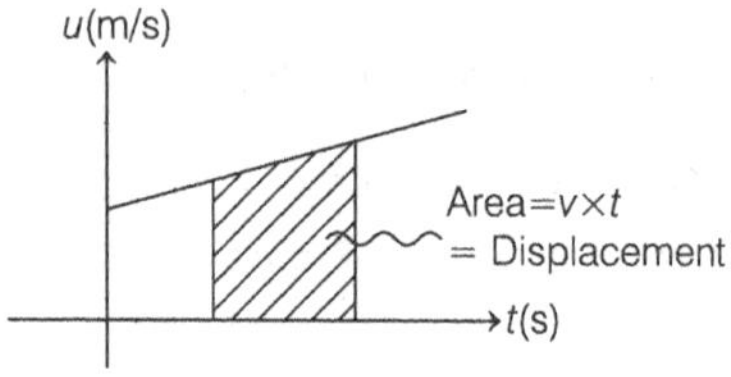

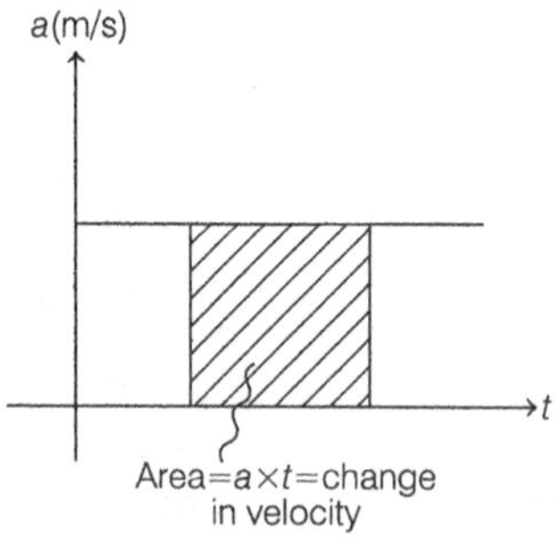

Area = $a\times t$ = change in velocity.

So, both statements I and II are correct.

2.

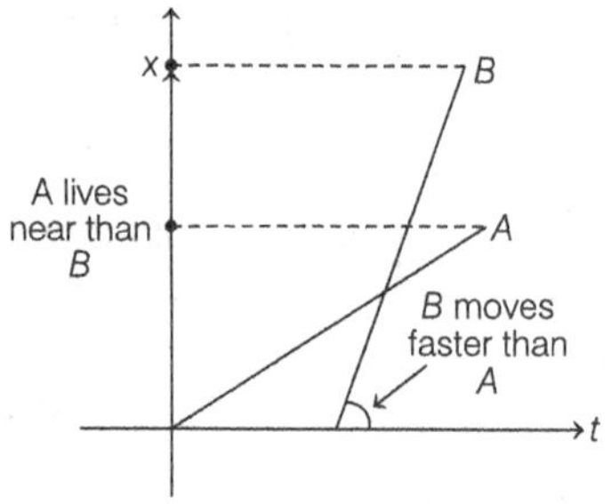

Given, slope of $B>$ slope of A. So, B is fast.

Projection of A on X-axis is less than projection of B. So, A lives near to school.

Therefore, option (c) is correct.

3.

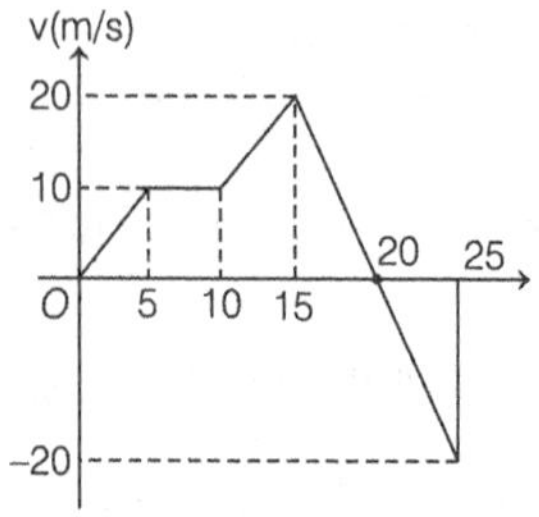

Displacement = Area of graph

$$\therefore \text{ Displacement}=\left(\frac{1}{2}\times 10\times 5\right)+(10\times 5)+\left(\frac{1}{2}\times 5\times 30\right)+\left(\frac{1}{2}\times 5\times 20\right)-\frac{1}{2}(5)(20)$$

$$=25+50+75+50-50=150\text{ m}$$

Distance $\rightarrow$ Area of graph with the value

Distance $= 25 + 50 + 75 + 50 = 250$

$$\frac{\text{Distance}}{\text{Displacement}} = \frac{250}{150} = \frac{5}{3}$$

4. Displacement = Net area of velocity-time graph

$$= 8 \times 2 + 4 \times 4 - 4 \times 2 - 4 \times 2$$
$$= 16 + 16 - 8 - 8 = 16 \text{ m}$$

Distance = Magnitude of total area under velocity-time graph

$$= 16 + 16 + 8 + 8 = 48 \text{ m}$$

Hence, ratio $= \dfrac{\text{Displacement}}{\text{Distance}} = \dfrac{16}{48} = \dfrac{1}{3}$

5. The slope of velocity-time graph gives the value of acceleration.

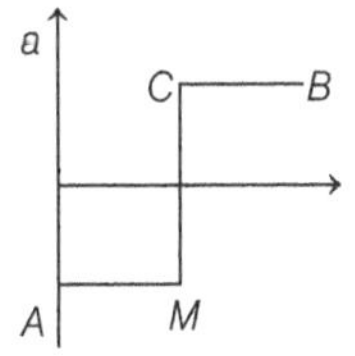

In Part AM, acceleration is constant and negative. In Part CB acceleration is constant and positive.

6. For the given velocity-displacement graph,

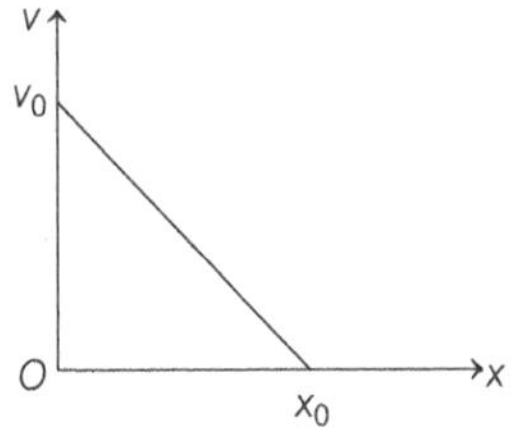

Intercept, $\quad c = v_0$

Slope, $\quad m = -\dfrac{v_0}{x_0}$

$\therefore$ Slope, $\quad m = \dfrac{dv}{dx} = -\dfrac{v_0}{x_0}$ ...(i)

For given diagram, the equation of line,

$$y = mx + c$$
$$v = -\frac{v_0}{x_0}x + v_0 \quad \text{...(ii)}$$

Acceleration, $a = \dfrac{dv}{dx} \times \dfrac{dx}{dt}$

$\Rightarrow \quad a = v\dfrac{dv}{dx}$

$\Rightarrow \quad a = \left(-\dfrac{v_0}{x_0}x + v_0\right)\left(-\dfrac{v_0}{x_0}\right)$ [From Eqs. (i) and (ii)]

$\Rightarrow \quad a = \left(\dfrac{v_0}{x_0}\right)^2 x - \dfrac{v_0^2}{x_0}$

Hence, the intercept is negative and the slope is positive, so the correct graph is given in option (c).

7. A v^2 *versus* x graph is shown below.

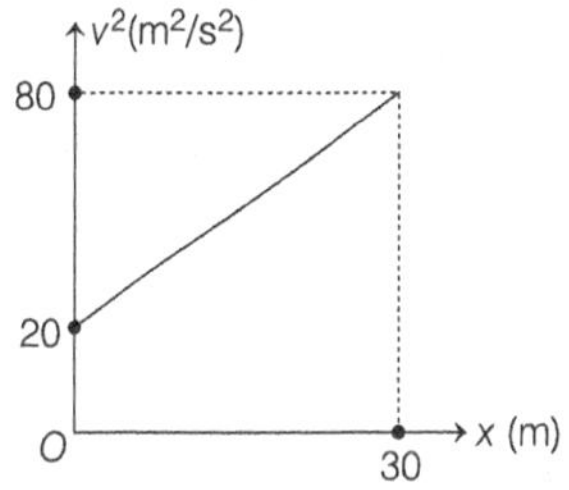

Using equation of motion,

$$v^2 = u^2 + 2ax \quad \text{...(i)}$$

We know that, the equation of straight line.

$$y = mx + c \quad \text{...(ii)}$$

Comparing Eqs. (i) and (ii),

Slope, $m = 2a = \dfrac{80 - 20}{30 - 0} = \dfrac{60}{30} = 2$

Now, the acceleration,

$$a = 2/2 = 1 \text{ m/s}^2$$

CHAPTER~10

NEWTON'S LAWS OF MOTION

LEVEL 01 Starter Level

10.1 Normal Force

For Q. No. 1 to 4 Make free body diagram of each block and Earth. Also find normal forces at all contacts.

1
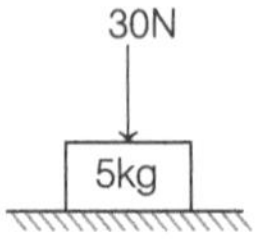

2
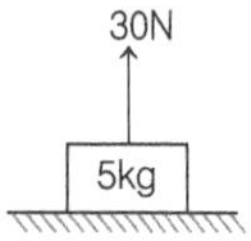

3
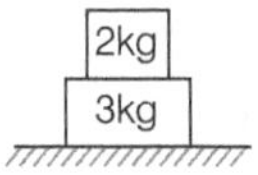

4
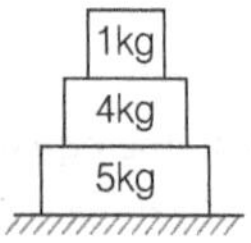

For Q. No. 5 to 11 The following systems are in equilibrium. Find normal forces at all contacts.

5
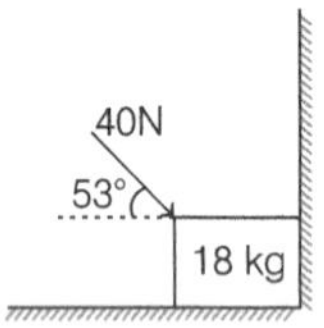

6
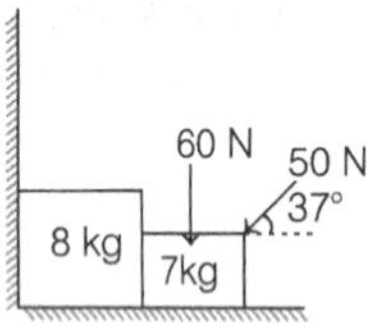

7
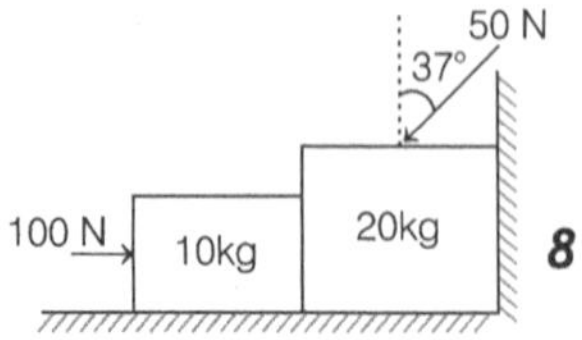

8
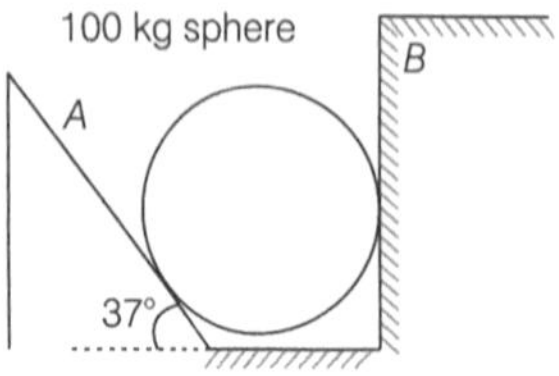

9
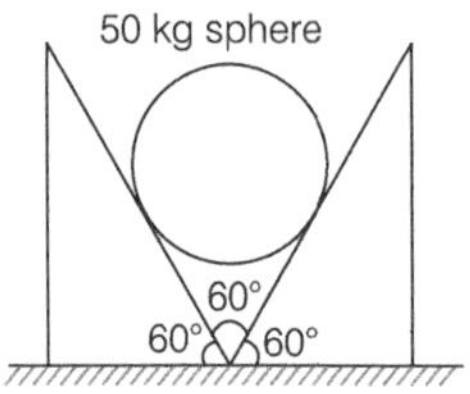

10
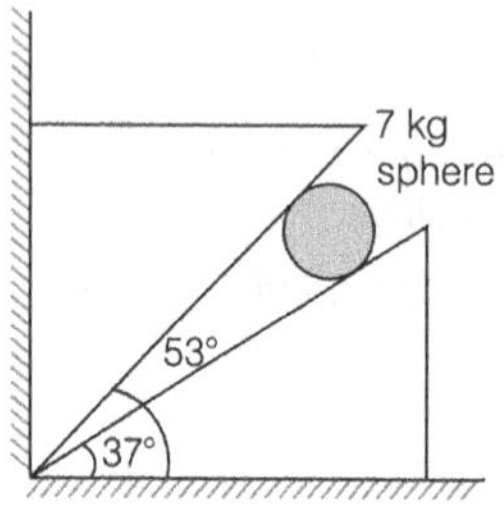

11
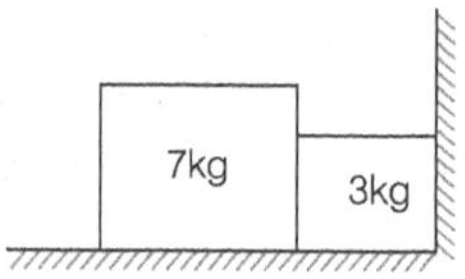

For Q. No. 12 to 19 Find acceleration and normal forces.

12
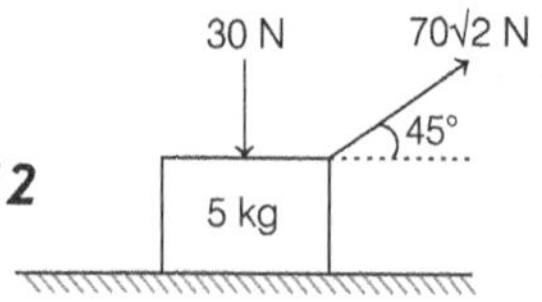

13
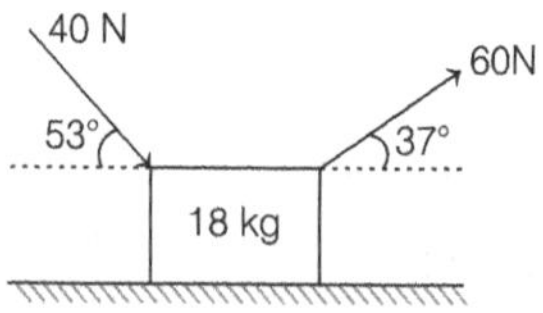

14
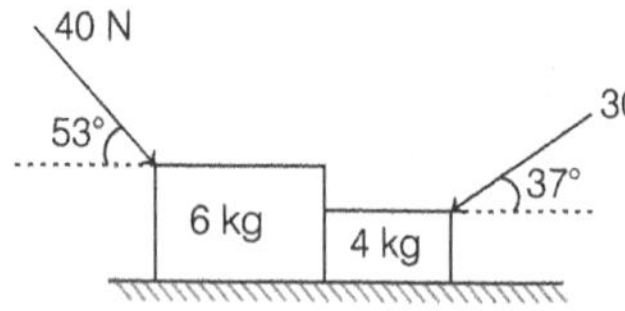

15
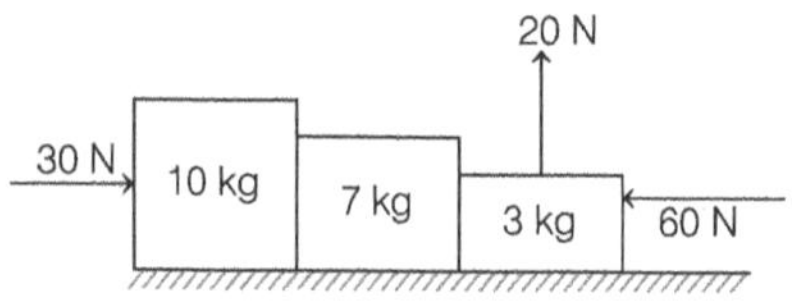

16
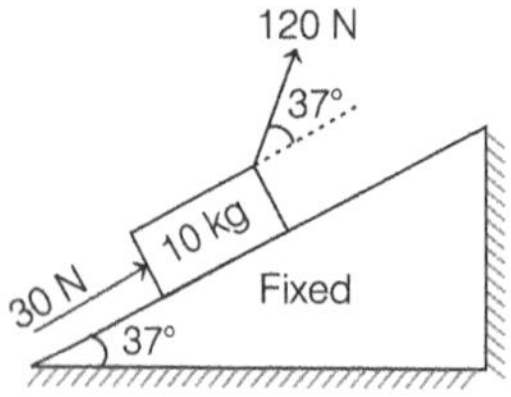

17

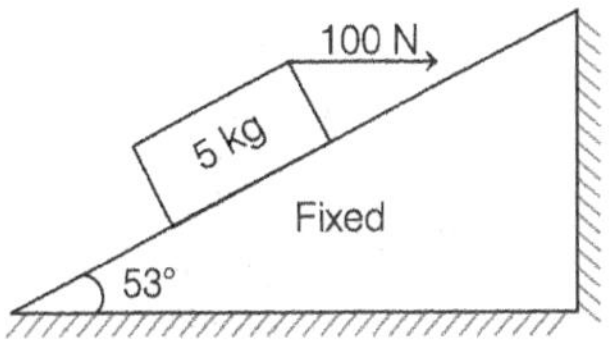

18

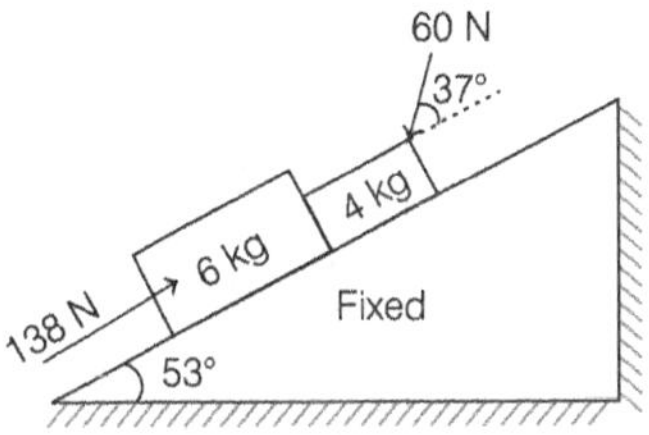

19

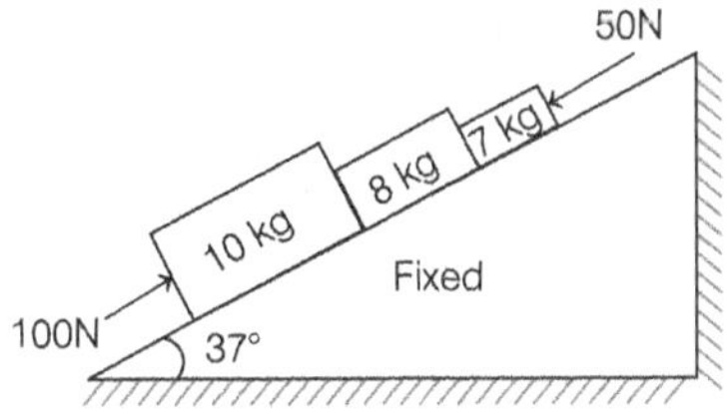

For. Q. No. 8 to 10 All the strings are massless. Find acceleration of blocks and tension in all the strings.

8

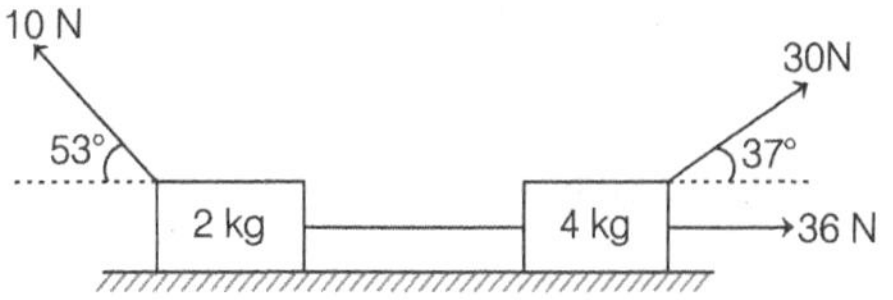

9

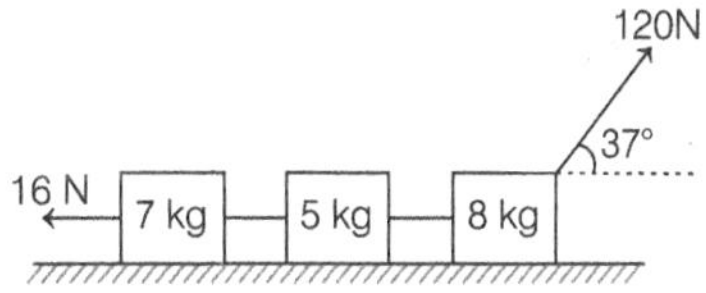

10

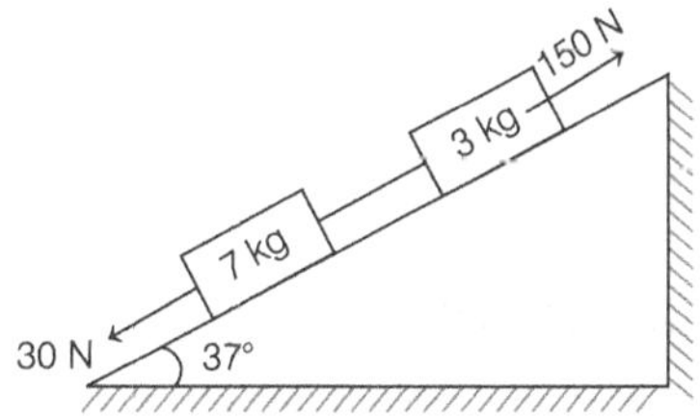

10.2 Tension Force

For Q. No. 1 to 7 The following systems are in equilibrium. Strings are massless unless mentioned. Find tension in all the strings.

1

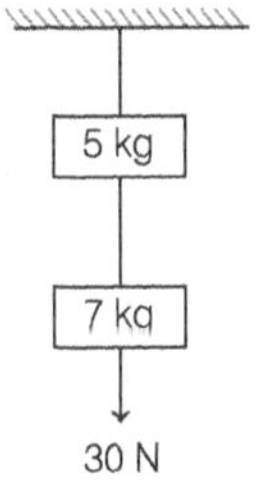

2

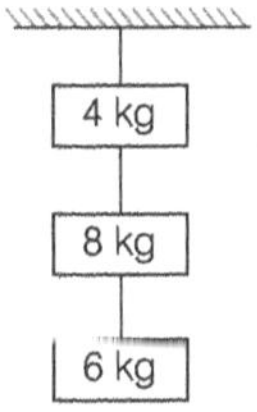

3

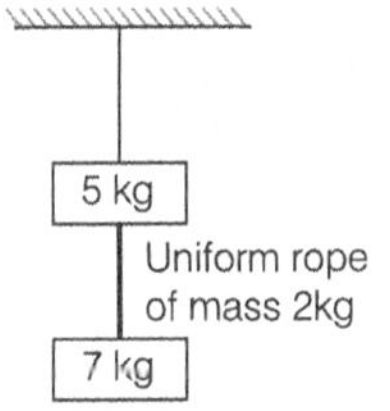

4

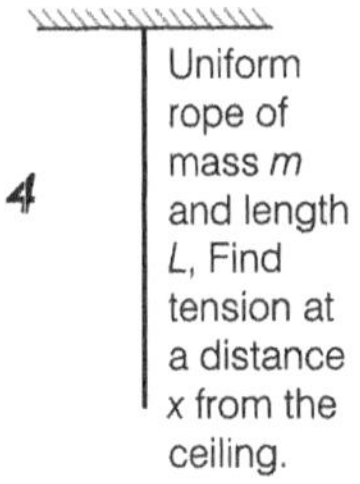

5

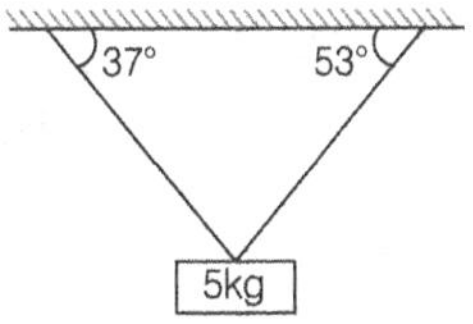

6

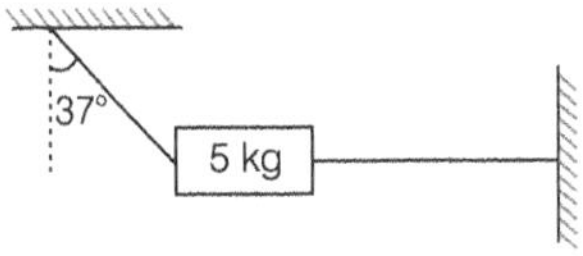

7

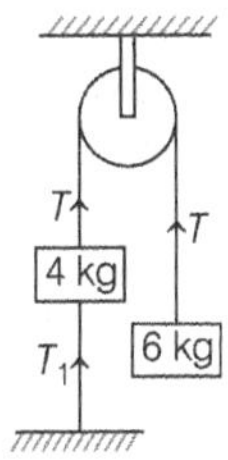

10.3 Fixed Pulleys

For Q. No. 1 to 10 All strings are massless and pulleys are fixed and smooth. Find acceleration of blocks.

1

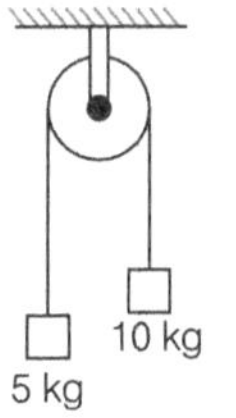

2

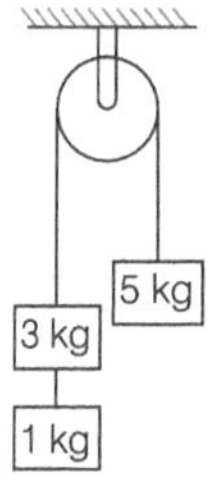

3

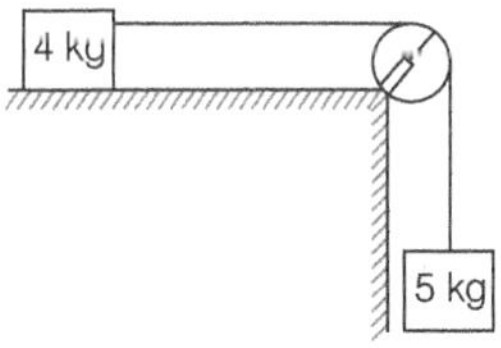

4

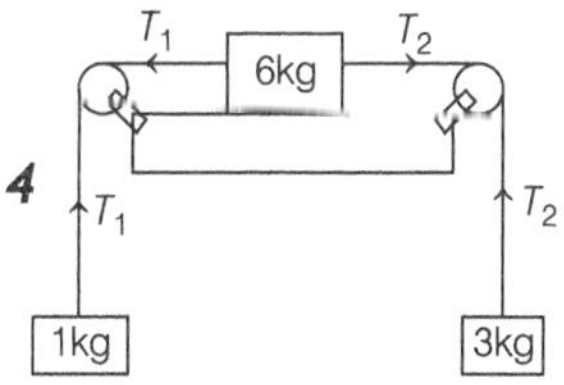

5

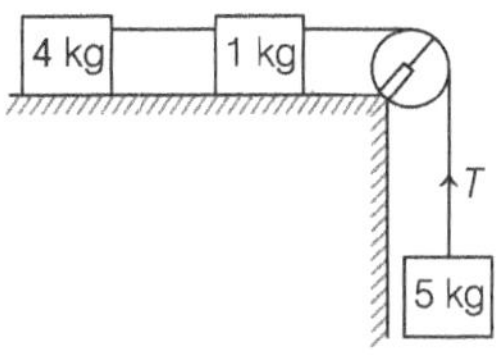

6

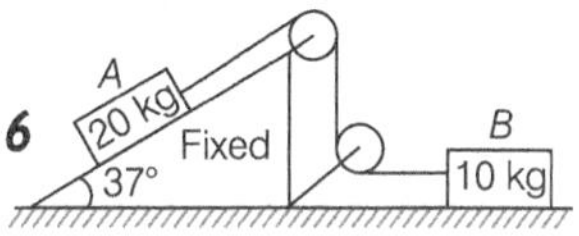

7

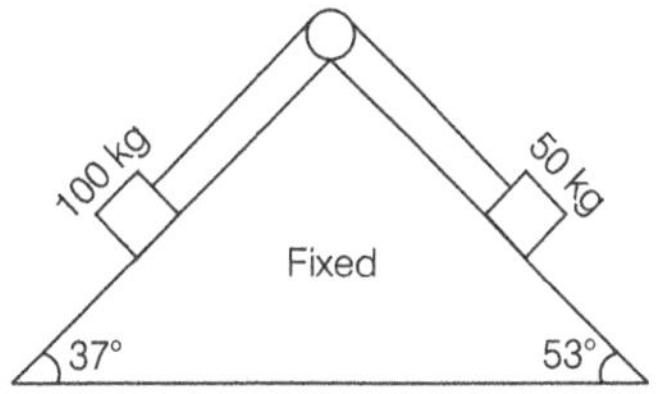

8

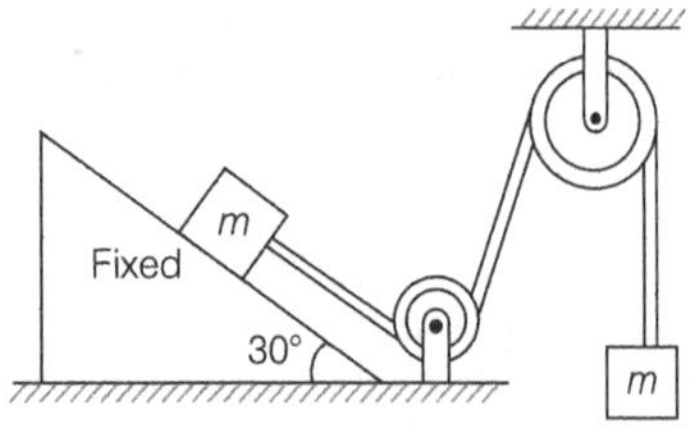

9

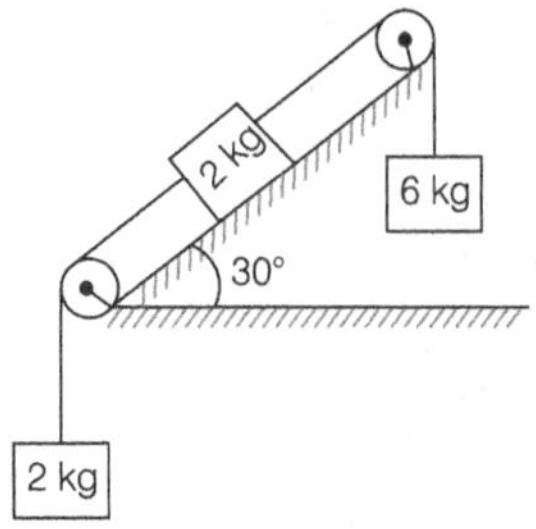

10

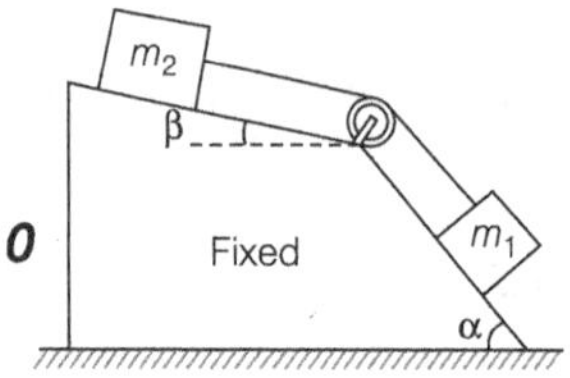

10.4 String Constraint

In the following questions, find unknown velocity and acceleration using string constraints. All strings are inextensible.

1

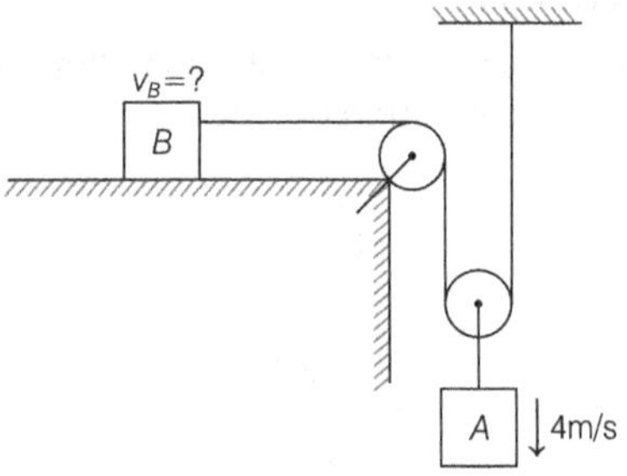

2

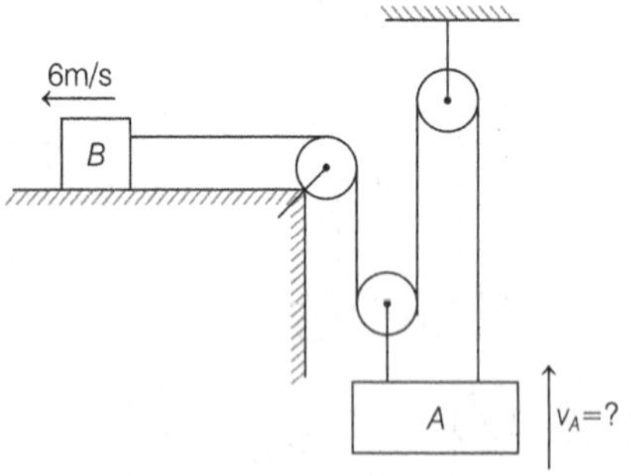

3

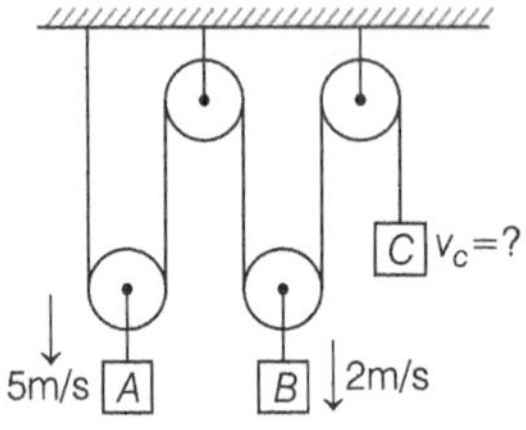

4

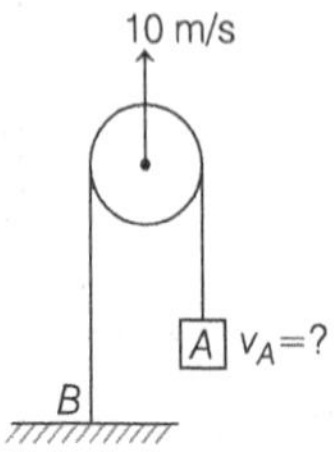

5

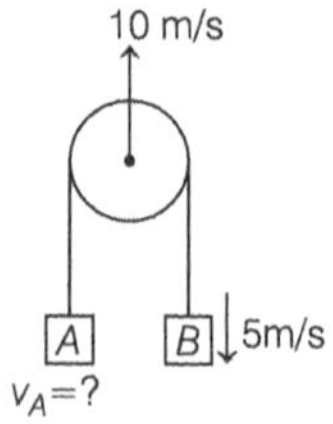

6

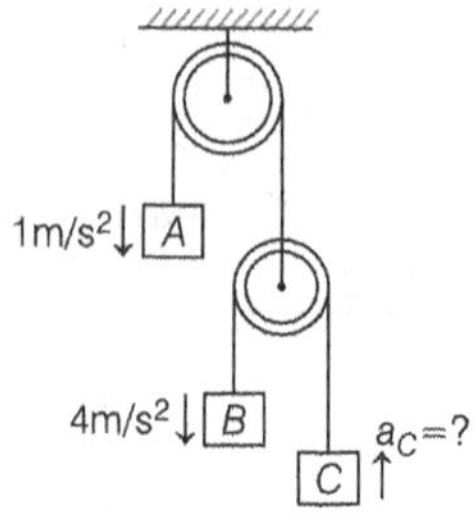

7

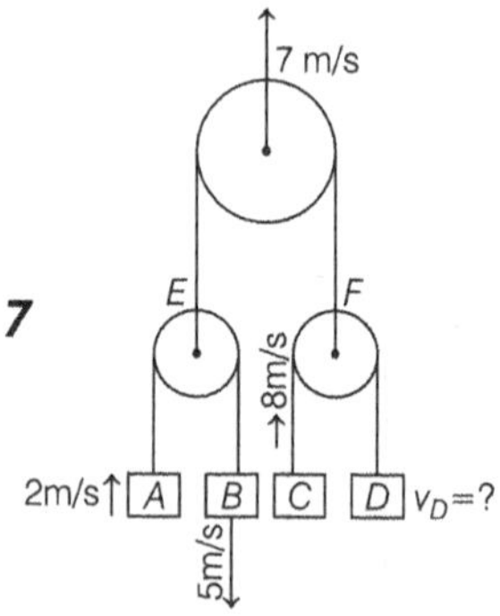

8

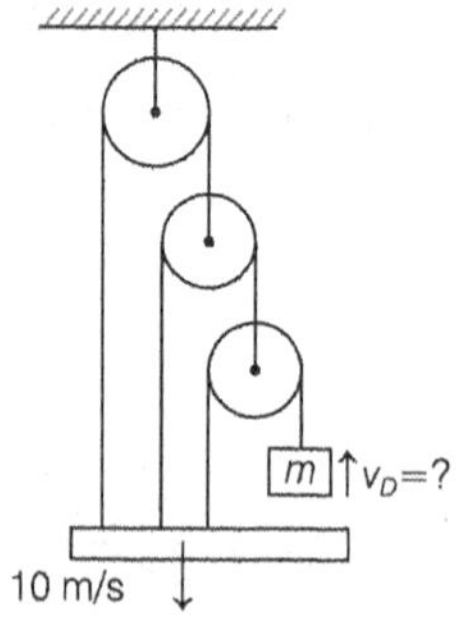

9

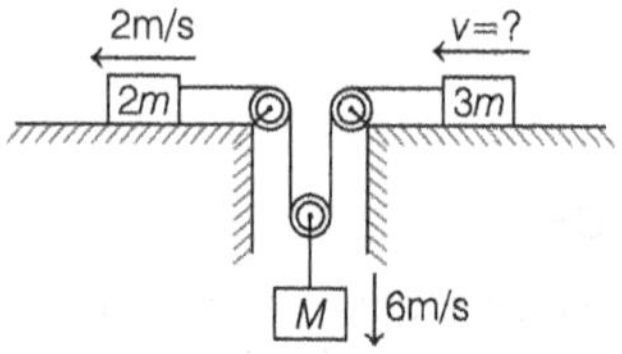

10

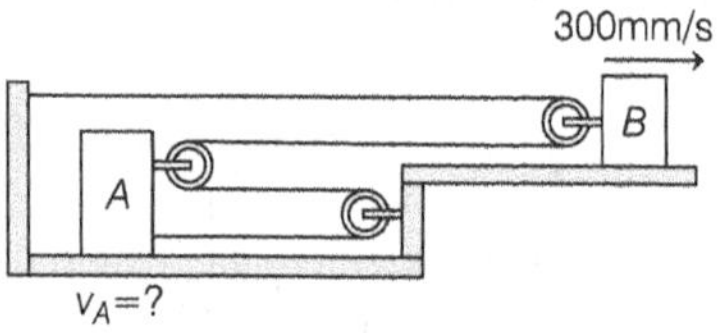

11

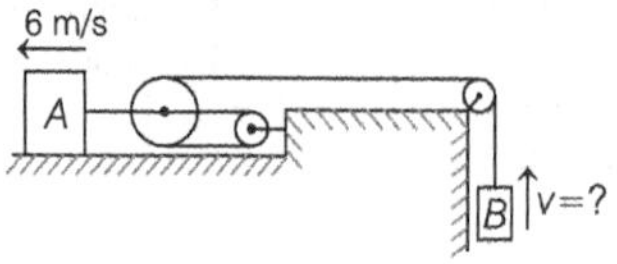

12

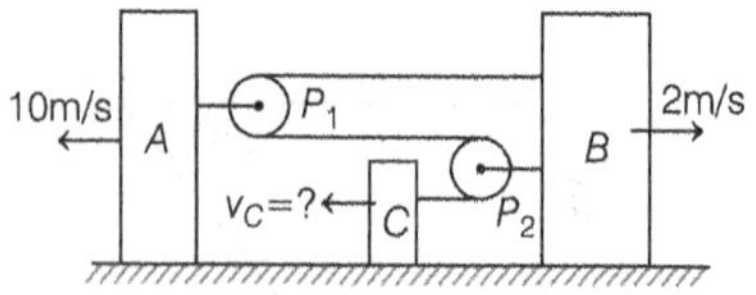

13

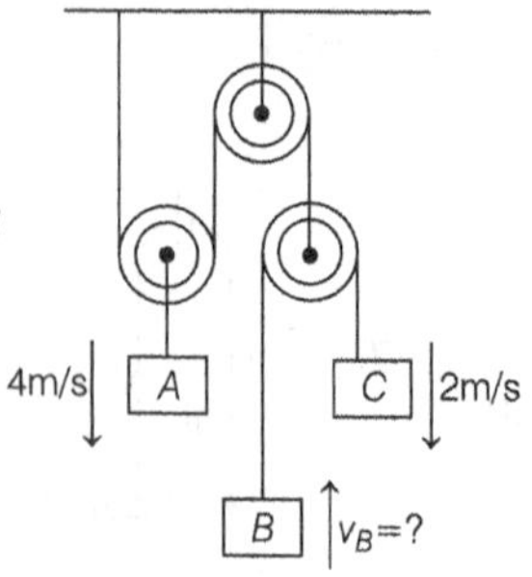

14

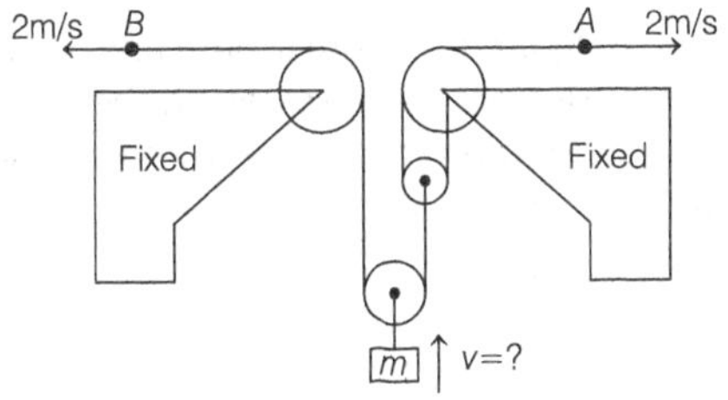

15

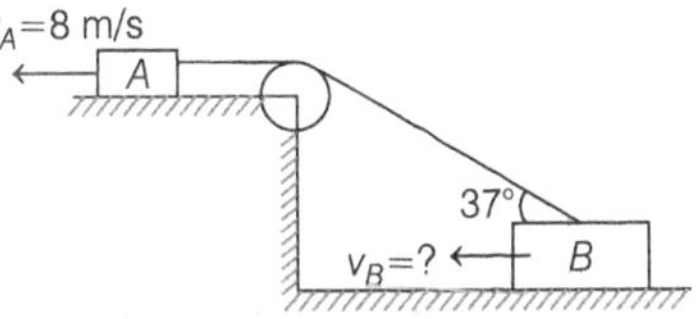

16

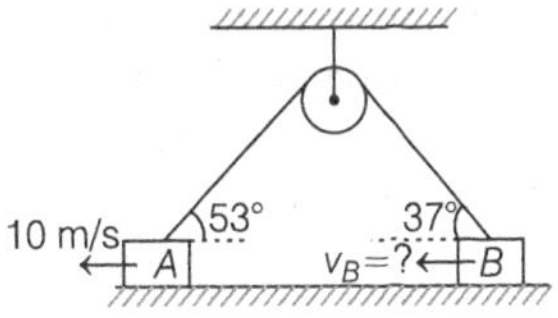

17

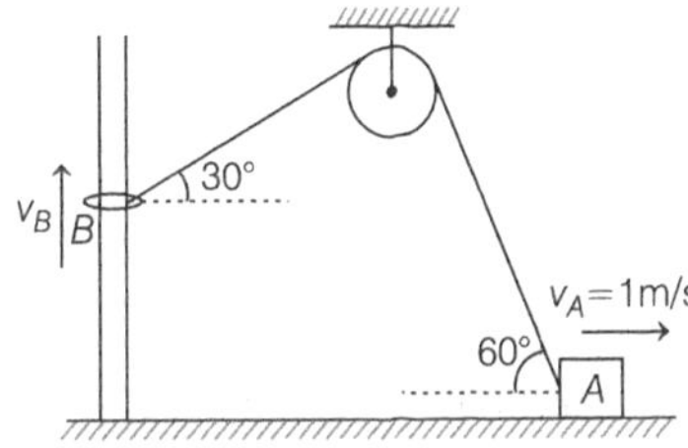

18 If the string is inextensible, determine the velocity *u* of each block in terms of *v* and θ.

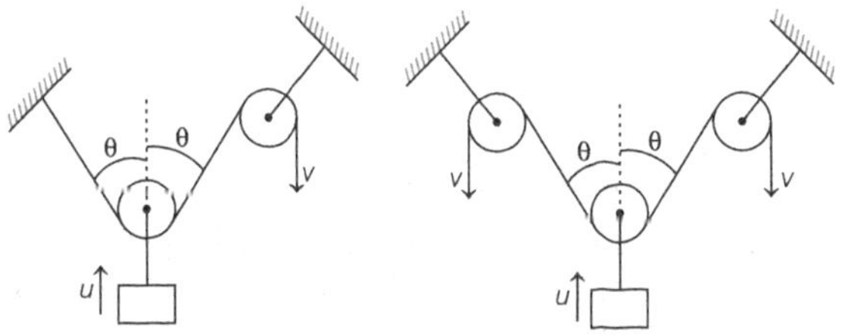

(a) Fig. (A) *u* = ... (b) Fig. (B) *u* = ...

19 Slider block *A* moves to the left with a constant velocity of 6 m/s. Determine

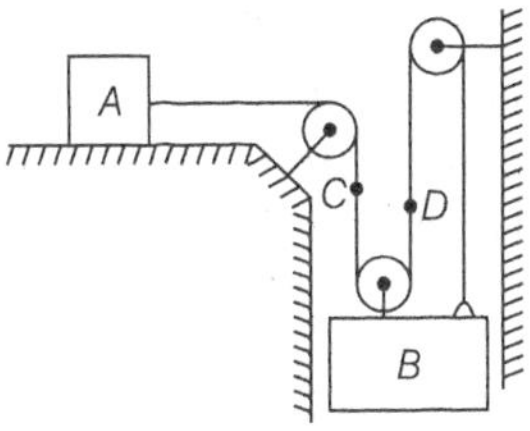

(a) the velocity of block *B*
(b) the velocity of portion *D* of the cable
(c) the relative velocity of portion *C* of the cable with respect to portion *D*

10.5 Moveable Pulleys

All strings are massless and inextensible. All pulleys are smooth and moveable pulleys are massless. Find acceleration of all the blocks.

1

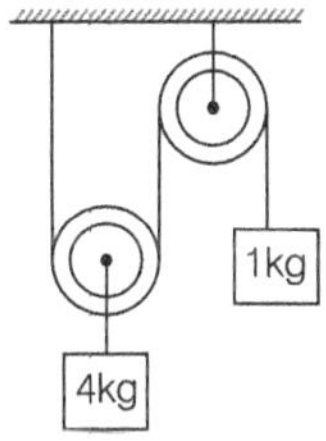

2

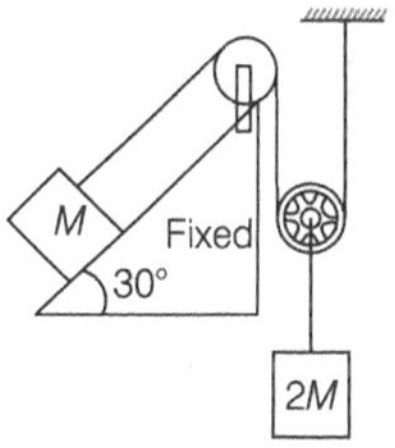

3

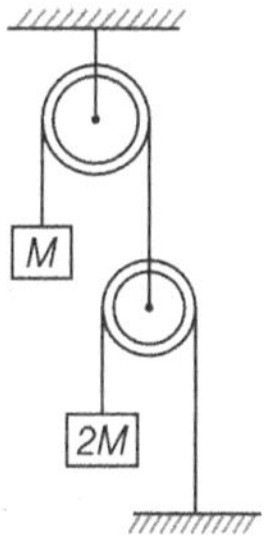

4

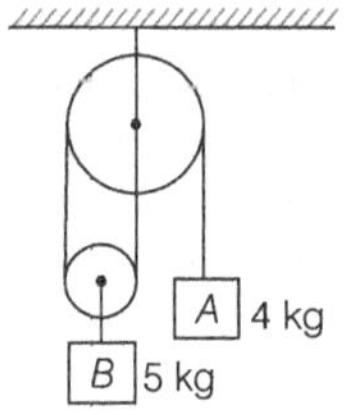

5

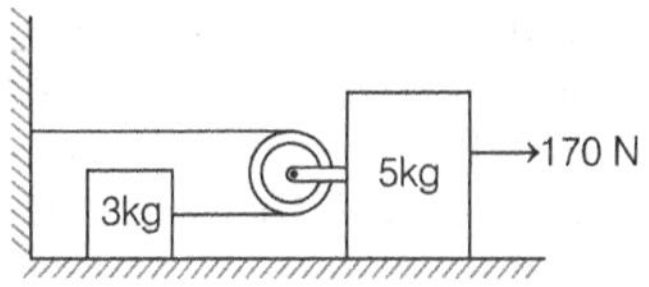

6

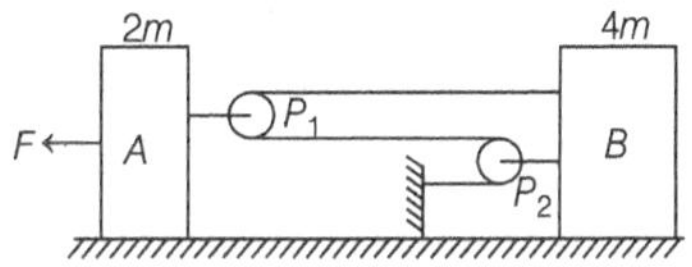

7

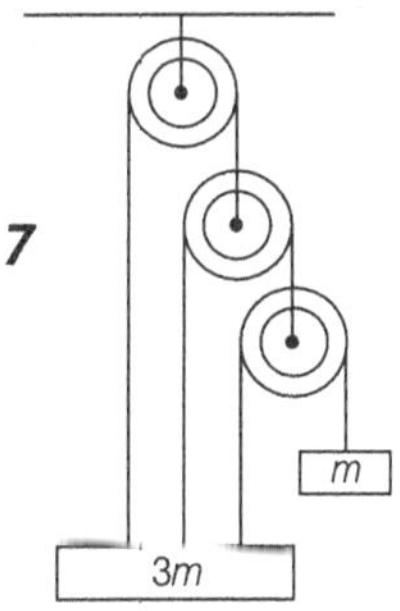

8

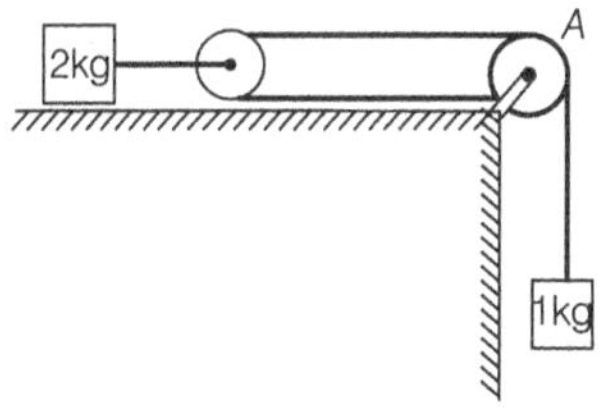

9

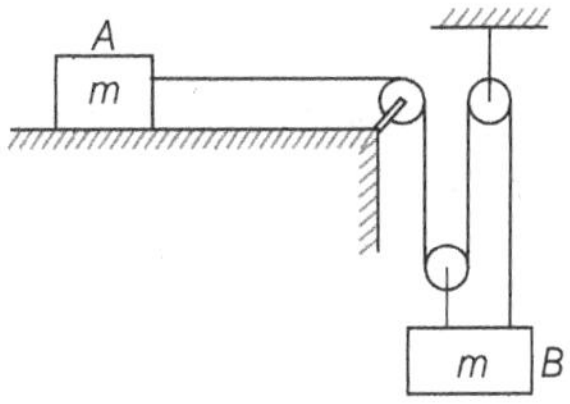

10

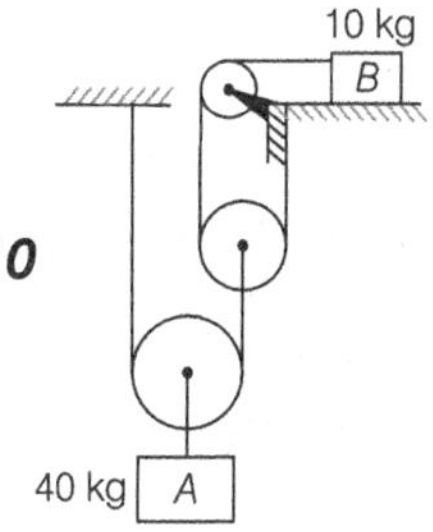

11

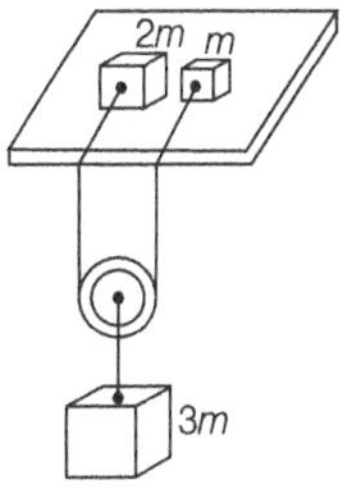

12

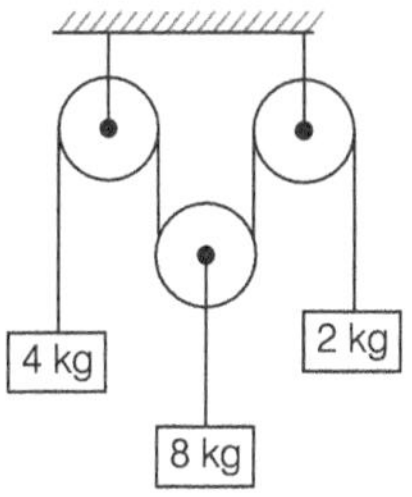

13
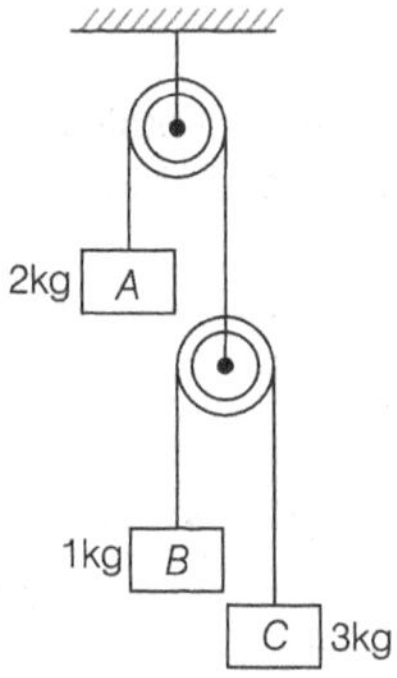

10.6 Spring Force

1 Two masses of 10 kg and 20 kg respectively, are connected by a massless spring as shown in figure. A force of 200 N acts on the 20 kg mass at the instant when the 10 kg mass has an acceleration of 12 ms^{-2} towards right, then find the acceleration of the 20 kg mass.

2 In the given figures, what is the reading of the spring balances? (Springs and strings are massless)

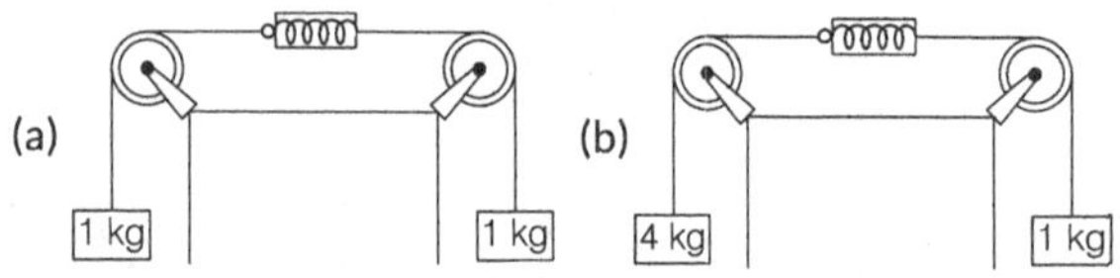

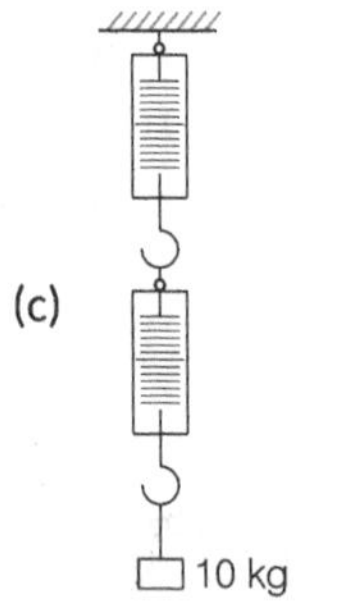

3 From the fixed pulley, masses 2 kg, 1 kg and 3 kg are suspended as shown in the figure. Find the extension in the spring if $k = 100$ N/m. (Neglect oscillations due to spring)

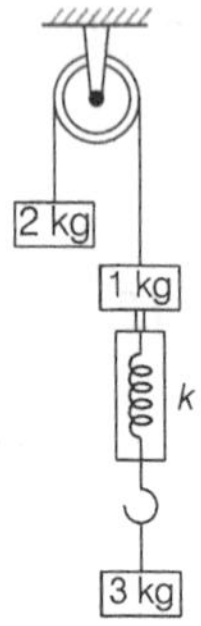

4 System shown in figure is in equilibrium and at rest. The spring and string are massless. Now, the string is cut. Find the accelerations of mass $2m$ and m just after the string is cut.

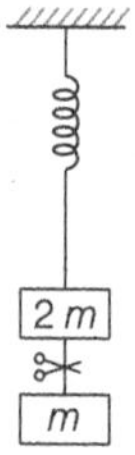

5 Two identical blocks are connected by a spring. The combination is suspended, at rest, from a string attached to the ceiling, as shown in the figure. The string breaks suddenly. Immediately after the string breaks, what is the initial acceleration of the upper and lower blocks?

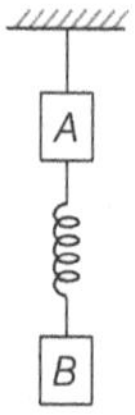

6 Find out the acceleration of 1 kg, 2 kg and 3 kg block and tension in the string between 1 kg and 2 kg block just after cutting the string as shown in figure.

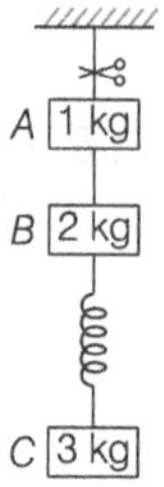

10.7 Pseudo Force

1 A pendulum is hanging from a ceiling of a car having an acceleration a_0 with respect to the road. Find the angle made by the string with vertical at equilibrium.

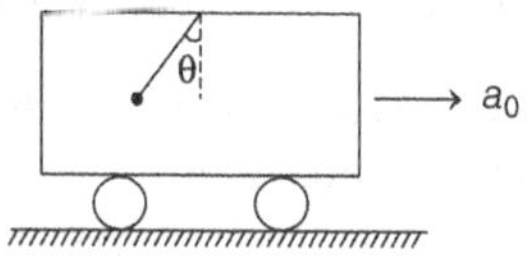

2 A block of mass m resting on a wedge of angle θ as shown in the figure. The wedge is given an acceleration a. What is the minimum value of a, so that the mass falls freely?

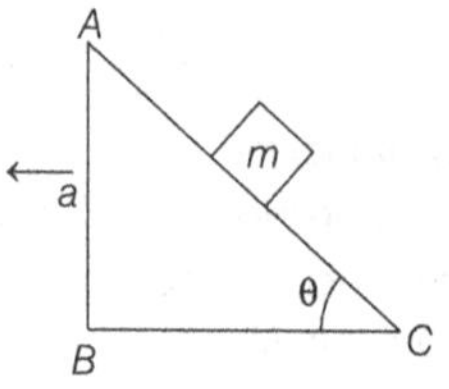

3 A triangular block of mass M rests on a smooth surface as shown in figure. A cubical block of mass m rests on the inclined surface. If all surfaces are frictionless, find the force that must be applied to M, so as to keep m stationary relative to M.

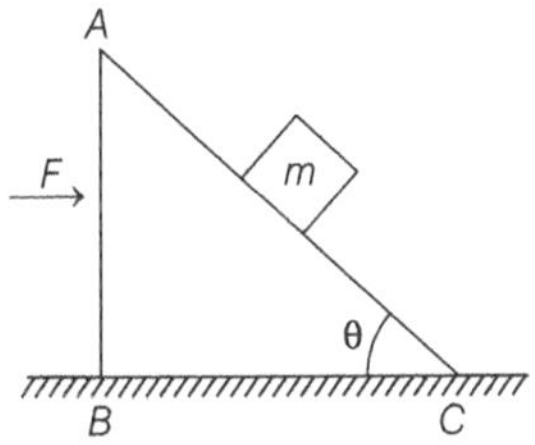

4 A block slides down from top of a smooth inclined plane of elevation θ fixed in an elevator going up with an acceleration a_0. The base of incline has length L. Find the time taken by the block to reach the bottom.

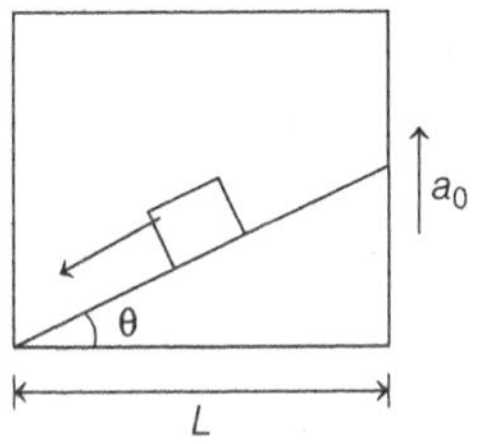

5 A bead of mass m is fitted on a rod and can move on it without friction. Initially the bead is at the middle of the rod and the rod moves horizontally in a vertical plane with an acceleration a_0 in a direction forming an angle α with the rod. Find the acceleration of bead with respect to rod.

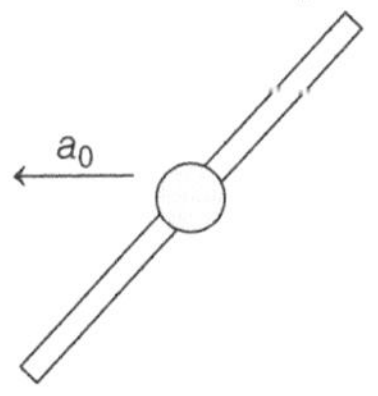

6 Two cubes of masses m_1 and m_2 lie on frictionless slopes of a block A which rests on a horizontal table. The cubes are connected by a string which passes over a pulley as shown in figure. If a be the horizontal acceleration to which the whole system (block + masses) is subjected, so that m_1 and m_2 do not move, then find a.

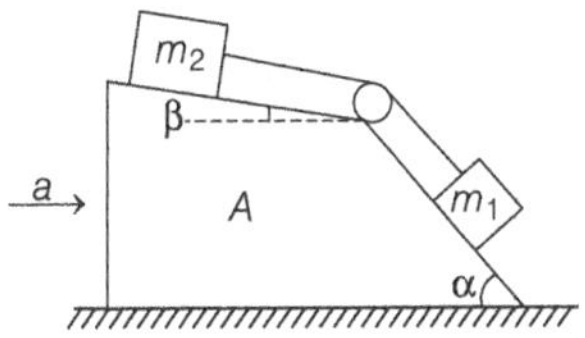

10.8 Wedge Constraint

1 In the questions below take the unit vectors as follows. Find the acceleration of smaller block (B) w.r.t. ground in terms of accelerations of other blocks.

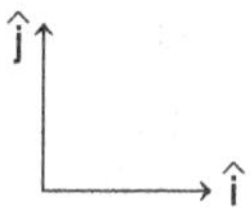

(a)

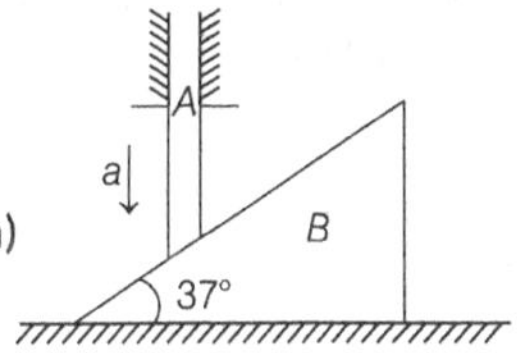

(b)

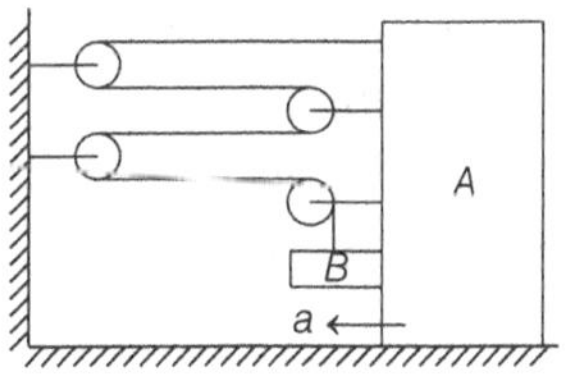

(c)

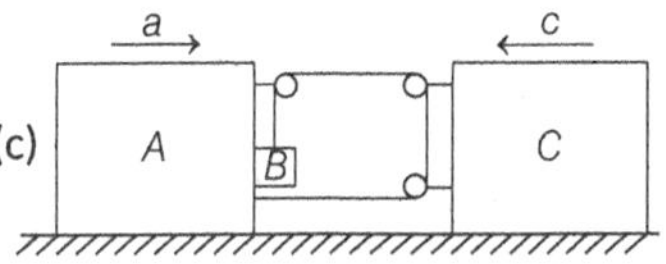

(d)

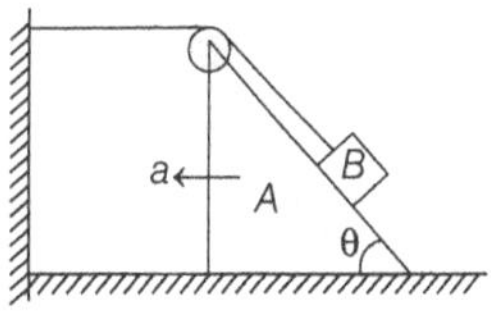

2 The masses of blocks A and B are same and equal to m. Friction is absent everywhere. Find the magnitude of accelerations of the blocks A and B.

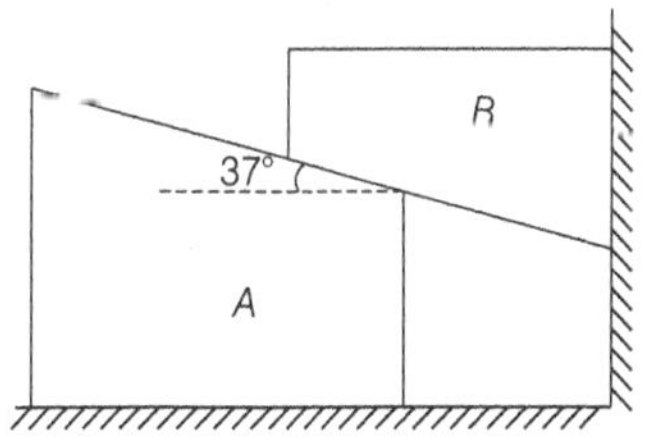

3 The system shown in figure is released from rest, calculate the value of accelerations a and b. (where b is w.r.t. to A)

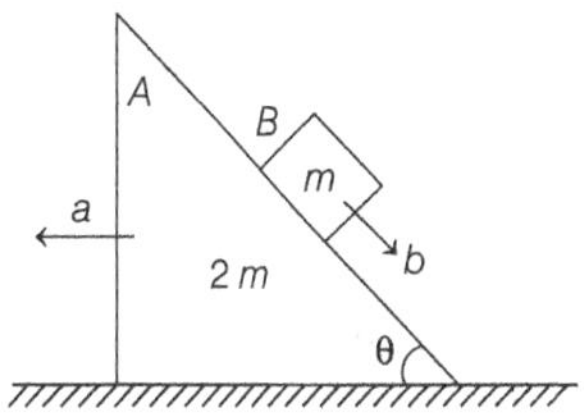

LEVEL 02 JEE Main Level

Single Choice Correct Questions

1 n-blocks of different masses are placed on the frictionless inclined plane in contact. They are released at the same time. The force of interaction between $(n-1)^{th}$ and n^{th} blocks is

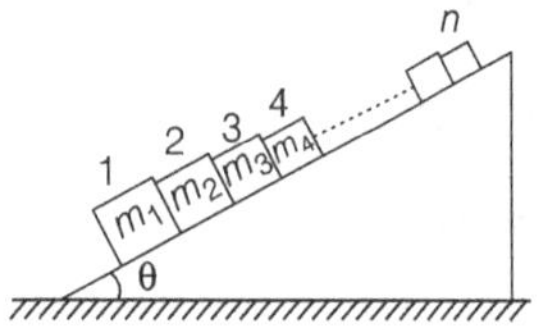

(a) $(m_{n-1} - m_n)\, g \sin\theta$ (b) zero
(c) $m_{n-1} m_n g \cos\theta$ (d) None of these

2 Find the acceleration of each block. 100 N is applied horizontally.

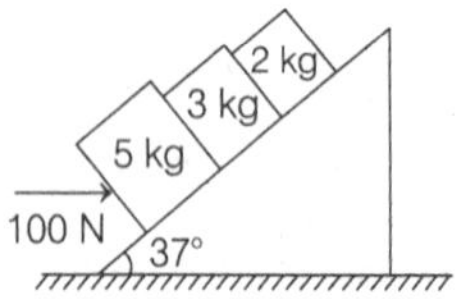

(a) 2 m/s^2 (b) 3 m/s^2
(c) 4 m/s^2 (d) 5 m/s^2

3 Five identical cubes each of mass m are on a straight line with two adjacent faces in contact on a horizontal surface as shown in the figure. Suppose the surface is frictionless and a constant force P is applied from left to right to the end face of A; which of the following statements is incorrect?

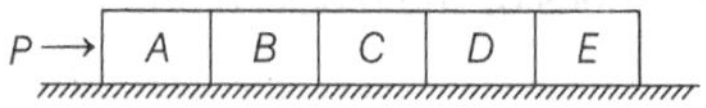

(a) The acceleration of the system is $\frac{P}{5m}$.

(b) The resultant force acting on each cube is $\frac{P}{5}$.

(c) The force exerted by C on D is $\frac{2P}{5}$.

(d) The force exerted on A by B is $\frac{3P}{5}$.

4 A ball of mass $m = 10$ kg is suspended with the help of three strings as shown in the figure. Find the tension T_3.

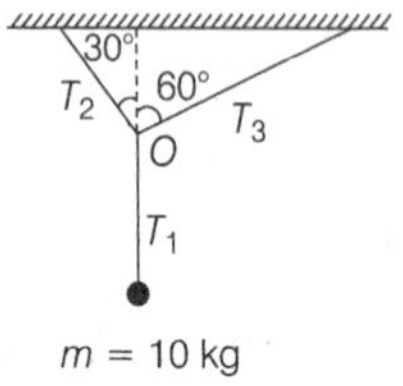

(a) 60 N (b) 30 N (c) 80 N (d) 50 N

5 In the situation shown blocks are connected with the help of ropes. Find tension at the middle of each rope. Masses of blocks and ropes are indicated in figure. ($g = 10\ m/s^2$)

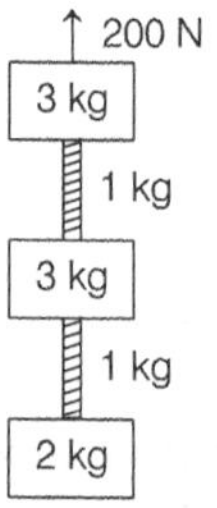

(a) 90 N, 160 N (b) 60 N, 140 N
(c) 50 N, 130 N (d) 70 N, 150 N

6 In a hemispherical shell of radius R, a rod of mass $\frac{\sqrt{3}}{2}$ kg is placed horizontally. The length of rod is R. Find the normal reaction at any end of the rod.

(a) 5 N (b) $5\sqrt{3}$ N (c) $\frac{5}{\sqrt{3}}$ N (d) 2.5 N

7 Two objects of mass m are connected by a thread that passes over a light, frictionless pulley as shown. The objects are at rest. If a third object with mass m_1 is added on top of one of the objects and objects are released, the tension in the string becomes $\frac{4}{3}$ times of the initial tension. Find the value of m_1.

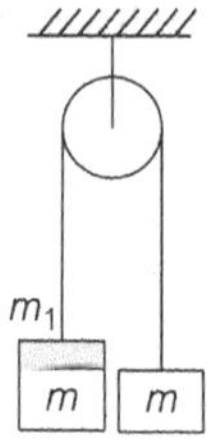

(a) $\frac{m}{2}$ (b) m (c) $2m$ (d) $3m$

8 Three equal weights of mass 2 kg each are hanging by a string passing over a fixed pulley. The tension in the string (in N) connecting B and C is

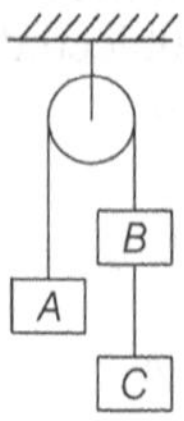

(a) $\frac{4g}{3}$ (b) $\frac{g}{3}$ (c) $\frac{2g}{3}$ (d) $\frac{g}{2}$

9 Find tension acting on 10 kg block.

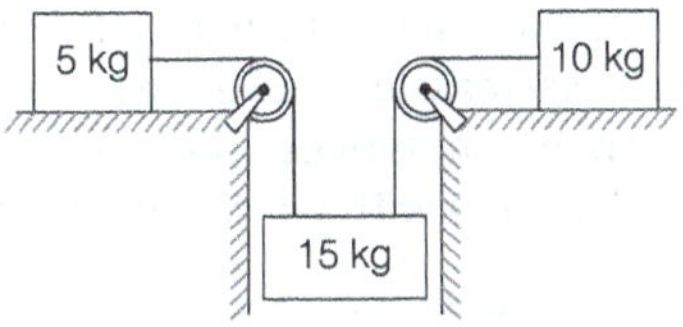

(a) 30 N (b) 40 N
(c) 50 N (d) 60 N

10 Find acceleration of each block.

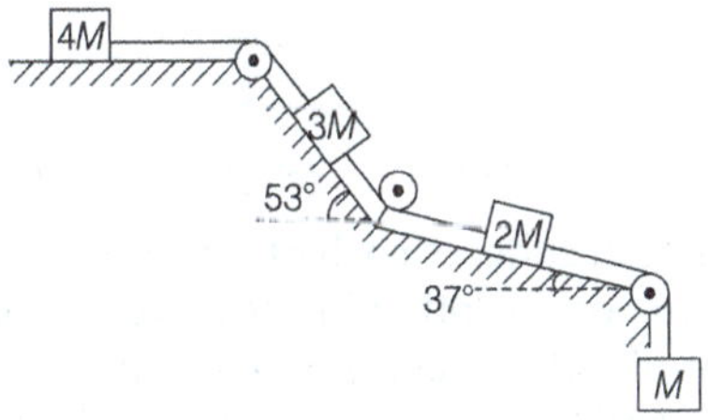

(a) 3.6 m/s^2 (b) 4.6 m/s^2
(c) 5.6 m/s^2 (d) 6.6 m/s^2

11 Two bodies of masses 5 kg and 4 kg are arranged in two positions as shown in Figs. (A) and (B). If the pulleys and the table are perfectly smooth, the accelerations of the 5 kg body in case (A) and (B) are

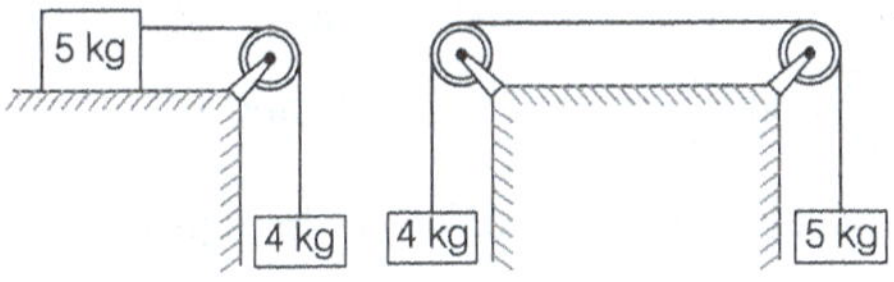

(A) (B)

(a) g and $\left(\frac{5}{9}\right)g$
(b) $\left(\frac{4}{9}\right)g$ and $\left(\frac{1}{9}\right)g$
(c) $\frac{g}{5}$ and $\frac{g}{5}$
(d) $\left(\frac{5}{9}\right)g$ and $\left(\frac{1}{9}\right)g$

12 Two blocks are in contact on a frictionless table. One has mass m and the other $2m$. A force F is applied on $2\,m$ as shown in the figure. Now, the same force F is applied from the right on m. In the two cases respectively, the ratio of force of contact between the two blocks will be

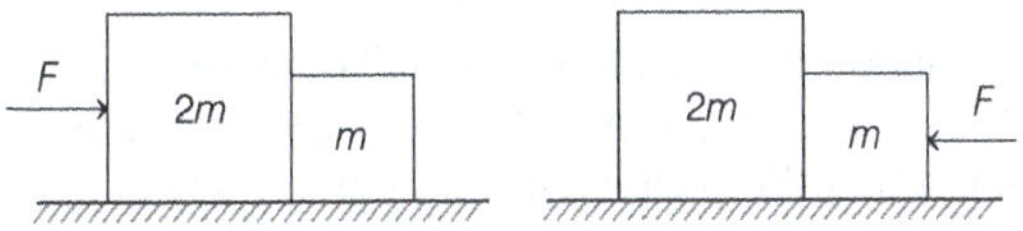

(a) Same (b) 1 : 2 (c) 2 : 1 (d) 1 : 3

13 Two masses of 8 kg and 4 kg are connected by a string as shown in the figure over a frictionless pulley. The acceleration of the system and tension are

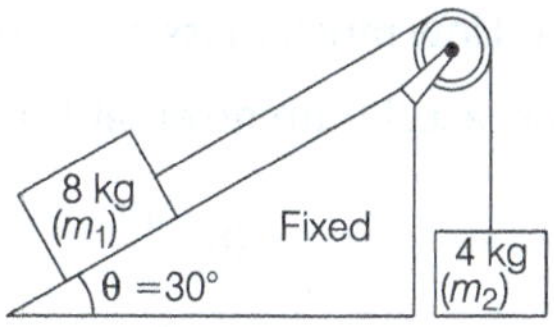

(a) $\frac{g}{3}, \frac{16}{3}$ kgf (b) $\frac{g}{4}$, 5 kgf
(c) zero, 4 kgf (d) zero, zero

14 A ball weighing 10 g hits a hard surface with a speed of 5 m/s at an angle of 53° with the surface and rebounds with the same speed. The ball remains in contact with the surface for 0.01 s. The average force exerted by the surface on the ball is
(a) 100 N (b) 10 N
(c) 8 N (d) 6 N

15 A chain consisting of six links each with mass 100 g is lifted vertically with constant force $F = 7.2$ N, as shown in figure. Find the force acting between the 4th and 5th link from the top.

(a) 1.0 N (b) 2.0 N (c) 2.1 N (d) 2.4 N

16 A rope of length L is pulled by a constant force F. What is the tension in the rope at a distance x from one end, where the force is applied?
(a) $\frac{FL}{x}$ (b) $\frac{F(L-x)}{L}$ (c) $\frac{FL}{(L-x)}$ (d) $\frac{Fx}{(L-x)}$

17 With what acceleration a should the box in the figure descend, so that a body of mass M placed in it exerts a force $\frac{Mg}{4}$ on the base of the box?

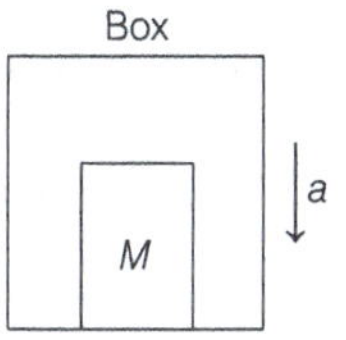

(a) $\frac{3g}{4}$ (b) $\frac{g}{4}$ (c) $\frac{g}{2}$ (d) $\frac{g}{8}$

18 An elevator weighing 6000 kg is pulled upward by a cable with an acceleration of 4.9 m/s^2. The tension in the cable is (take, $g = 9.8\ m/s^2$)
(a) 6000 N (b) 6000 gN (c) 9000 N (d) 9000 gN

19 An empty plastic box of mass m is found to accelerateg up at the rate of $\frac{g}{6}$ when placed deep inside water. How much mass of sand be filled in it, so that it may accelerate down at the rate of $\frac{g}{6}$?

(a) $\frac{m}{6}$ (b) $\frac{5m}{6}$

(c) $\frac{2m}{5}$ (d) $\frac{3m}{5}$

20 Two masses M_1 and M_2 are attached to the ends of a light string which passes over a massless pulley attached to the top of a double inclined smooth plane of angle of inclination α and β. The tension in the string is

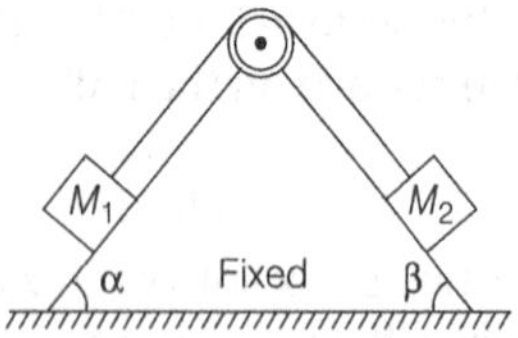

(a) $\frac{M_2(\sin\beta)\,g}{M_1+M_2}$ (b) $\frac{M_1(\sin\alpha)\,g}{M_1+M_2}$

(c) $\frac{M_1M_2(\sin\beta+\sin\alpha)g}{M_1+M_2}$ (d) zero

21 A monkey of mass 20 kg is climbing up on the rope to balance the cage of 25 kg. What is the acceleration of monkey? [$g = 10\ \text{ms}^{-2}$]

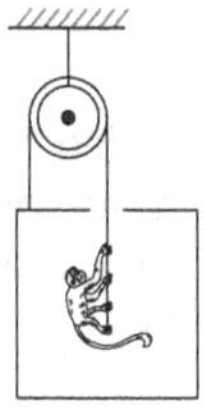

(a) 5 m/s^2 (b) 11.5 m/s^2

(c) 22.5 m/s^2 (d) 2.5 m/s^2

22 Figure shows a uniform block of length 30 cm having a mass of 3 kg. The strings shows in figure are pulled by constant force of 20 N and 32 N. All the surfaces are smooth and the strings and the pulley are light. The force exerted by the 20 cm part of the rod on the 10 cm part is

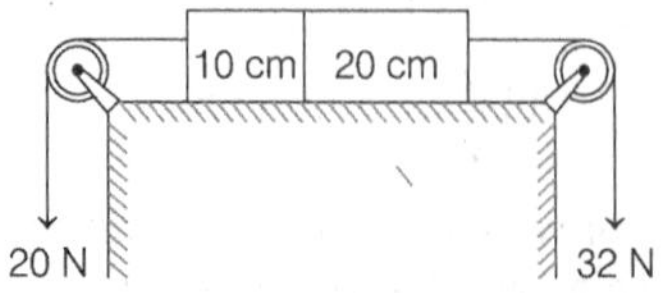

(a) 16 N (b) 20 N

(c) 24 N (d) 25 N

23 A 50 kg person stands on a 25 kg platform. She pulls massless rope which is attached to the platform *via* the frictionless, massless pulleys as shown in the figure. The platform moves upwards at a steady velocity if the force with which the person pulls the rope is

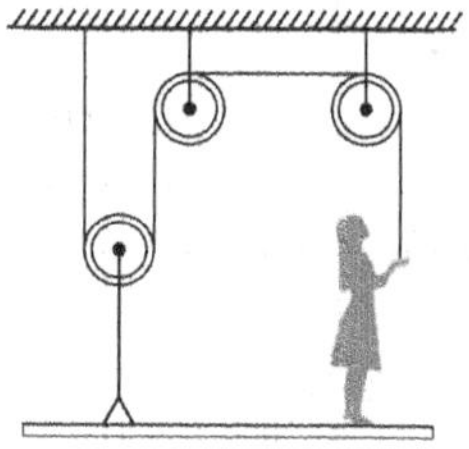

(a) 500 N (b) 250 N (c) 25 N (d) 50 N

24 Two smooth spheres each of radius 5 cm and weight w rest one on the other inside a fixed smooth cylinder of radius 8 cm. The reactions between the spheres and the vertical side of the cylinder are

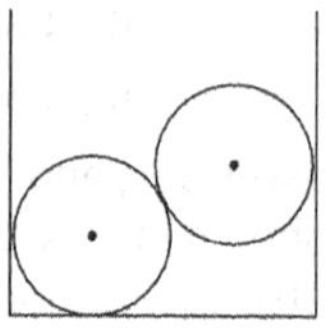

(a) $\frac{w}{4}$ and $\frac{3w}{4}$ (b) $\frac{w}{4}$ and $\frac{w}{4}$

(c) $\frac{3w}{4}$ and $\frac{3w}{4}$ (d) w and w

25 The acceleration of block B in the figure will be

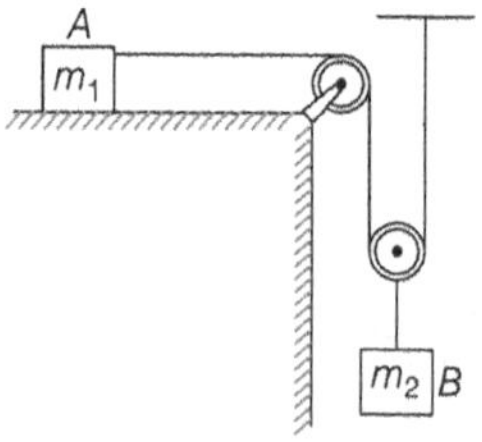

(a) $\frac{m_2g}{(4m_1+m_2)}$ (b) $\frac{2m_2g}{(4m_1+m_2)}$

(c) $\frac{2m_1g}{(m_1+4m_2)}$ (d) $\frac{2m_1g}{(m_1+m_2)}$

26 A 10 kg wagon is pushed with a force of 7 N for 1.5 s, then with a force of 5 N for 1.7 s, and then with a force of 10 N for 3 s in the same direction. What is the change in velocity brought about?

(a) 9.8 m/s (b) 19.6 m/s (c) 4.9 m/s (d) 10 m/s

27 A balloon has 5 g of air. A small hole is pierced into it. The air escapes at a uniform rate with a velocity of 4 cm/s. If the balloon shrinks completely in 2.5 s, then the mean force acting on the balloon is

(a) 5 dyne (b) 8 dyne (c) 10 dyne (d) 20 dyne

28 In figure shown, both blocks are released from rest. Find the time to cross each other?

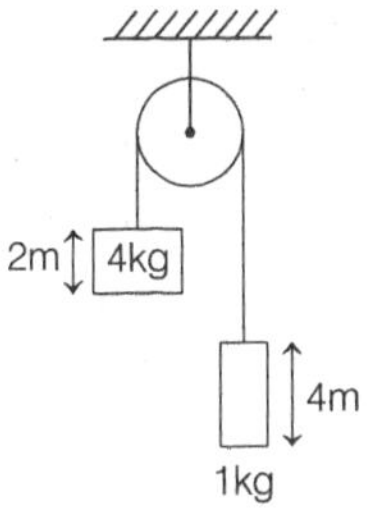

(a) 1 s (b) 2 s
(c) 3 s (d) 4 s

29 Two blocks, each having mass M, rest on frictionless surfaces as shown in the figure. If the pulleys are light and frictionless, and M on the incline is allowed to move down, then the tension in the string will be

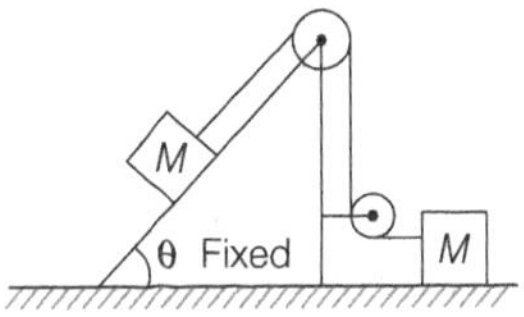

(a) $\frac{2}{3} Mg \sin\theta$ (b) $\frac{3}{2} Mg \sin\theta$
(c) $\frac{Mg \sin\theta}{2}$ (d) $2 Mg \sin\theta$

30 A block slides down a frictionless incline making an angle θ with the floor at an elevator. The elevator is descending with an acceleration a. The value of normal reaction acting on the block is

(a) $mg \sin\theta$
(b) $m(g-a)\cos\theta$
(c) $mg \cos\theta$
(d) $m(g-a)\sin\theta$

31 Figure shows two pulley arrangements for lifting a mass m. In (a) the mass is lifted by attaching a mass $2m$, while in (*b*) the mass is lifted by pulling the other end with a downward force $F = 2mg$. If f_a and f_b are the accelerations of the two masses, then

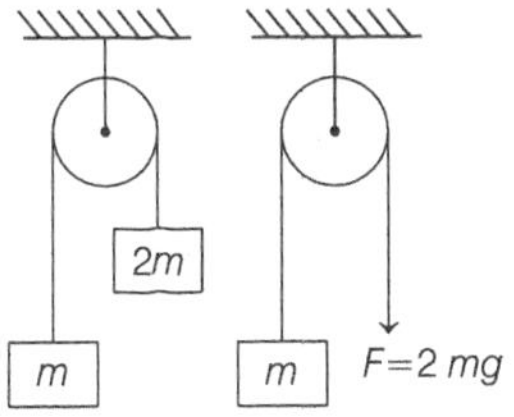

(a) $f_a = f_b$ (b) $f_a = \frac{f_b}{2}$
(c) $f_a = \frac{f_b}{3}$ (d) $f_a = 2f_b$

32 To paint the side of a building, painter normally hoists himself up by pulling on the rope A as in figure. The masses of painter and platform are 60 kg and 20 kg, respectively. The rope B can withstand 1000 N. Find the maximum acceleration of the painter.

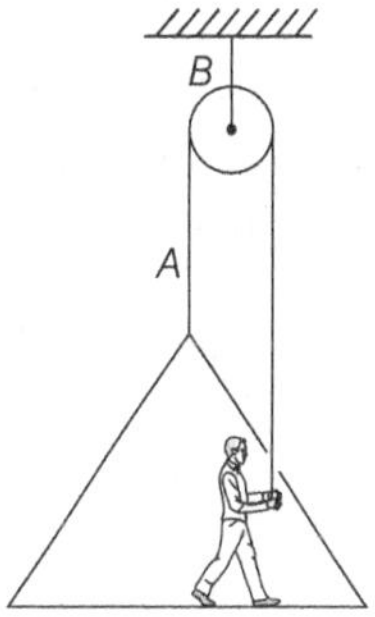

(a) 3 ms^{-2} (b) 2.5 ms^{-2} (c) 5 ms^{-2} (d) zero

33 A uniform sphere of weight w and radius 3 m is being held by a string of length 2 m attached to a frictionless wall as shown in the figure. Normal reaction by wall will be

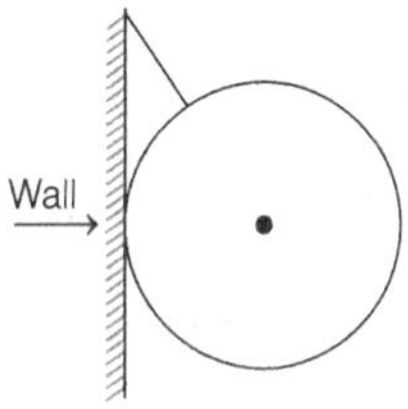

(a) $\frac{5w}{4}$ (b) $\frac{15w}{4}$ (c) $\frac{15w}{16}$ (d) $\frac{3w}{4}$

34 A man is standing in a lift which goes up and comes down with the same constant acceleration. If the ratio of the apparent weights in the two cases is 2 : 1, then the acceleration of the lift is

(a) 3.33 ms^{-2} (b) 2.50 ms^{-2}
(c) 2.00 ms^{-2} (d) 1.67 ms^{-2}

35 In the figure at the free end of the light string, a force F is applied to keep the suspended mass of 18 kg at rest. Assuming, pulley is light then the force exerted by the ceiling on the system is

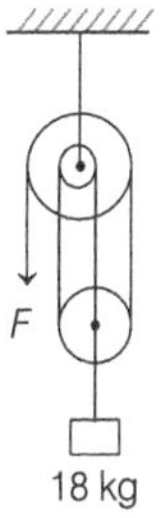

(a) 200 N (b) 120 N (c) 180 N (d) 240 N

36 A spring has length l and spring constant k. It is cut into two pieces of length l_1 and l_2 such that $l_1 = nl_2$. The force constant of spring of length l_1 is

(a) $k(l+n)$ (b) $\left(\frac{k(l+n)}{n}\right)$ (c) k (d) $\frac{k}{(l+n)}$

37 Three masses m_1, m_2 and m_3 are attached to a string-pulley system as shown. All the three masses are held at rest and then released. To keep m_3 at rest, m_3 should be

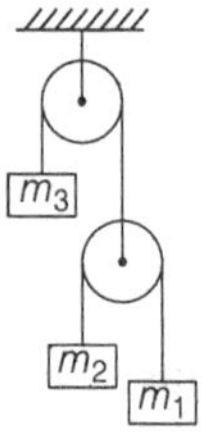

(a) $\frac{4m_1m_2}{m_1+m_2}$ (b) $2(m_1+m_2)$

(c) (m_1+m_2) (d) $\frac{2m_1m_2}{m_1+m_2}$

38 Three planes coincide with the chords of the same circle of radius R. A small body slides down each of them without friction and without initial velocity. If t_1, t_2 and t_3 are time taken by the body to reach the bottom of planes denoted by 1, 2 and 3 respectively, then

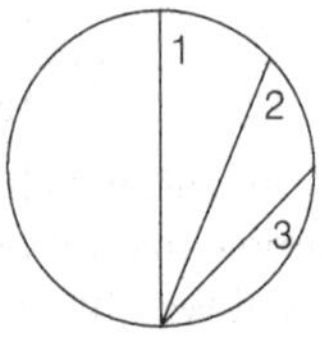

(a) $t_1 > t_2 > t_3$ (b) $t_1 < t_2 < t_3$

(c) $t_1 = t_2 = t_3$ (d) Cannot be decided

39 The wedge is moved towards right with acceleration a which is slowly increased from zero. Find tension in the string just when the small block breaks contact with the surface of the wedge. (Assume all surfaces are smooth and string is inextensible)

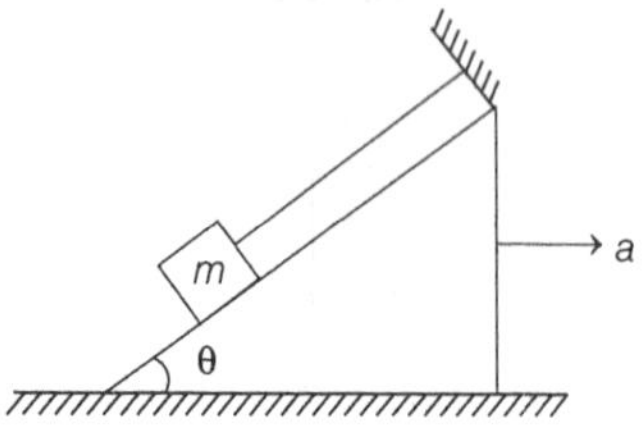

(a) $2mg \sin\theta$ (b) $mg \operatorname{cosec}\theta$

(c) $mg \tan\theta$ (d) $mg \cot\theta$

40 What will be the displacement of a block in first 0.2 s, if the block is kept on the floor of an elevator at rest. Suddenly, elevator starts descending with an acceleration 13 m/s^2. Take, $g = 10$ m/s^2.

(a) 26 cm (b) 6 cm

(c) 46 cm (d) 20 cm

41 A trolley is being pulled up an inclined plane by a man sitting on it (as shown in figure). He applies a force of 250 N. If the combined mass of the man and trolley is 100 kg, the acceleration of the trolley will be [Use, $\sin 15° = 0.26$, $g = 10$ m / s^2]

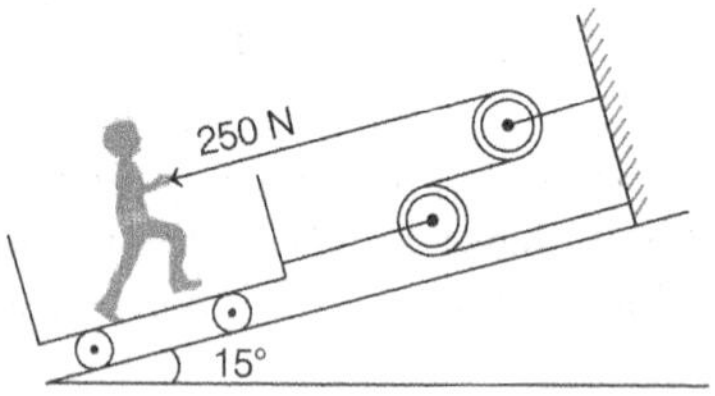

(a) 2.4 ms^{-2} (b) 4 ms^{-2}

(c) 4.9 ms^{-2} (d) 0.1 ms^{-2}

42 The pulley shown is frictionless. A monkey of mass 1 kg moves up on the massless string, so as to just lift a block of mass 2 kg. After sometime, the monkey stops moving with respect to string. The change in magnitude of monkey's acceleration is

(a) $\frac{g}{3}$ (b) $\frac{2g}{3}$ (c) g (d) $2g$

43 A trolley T of mass 5 kg on a horizontal smooth surface is pulled by a load of 2 kg through a uniform rope ABC of length 2m and mass 1 kg. As the load falls from $BC = 0$ to $BC = $ 2m, its acceleration (in m/s^2) changes from

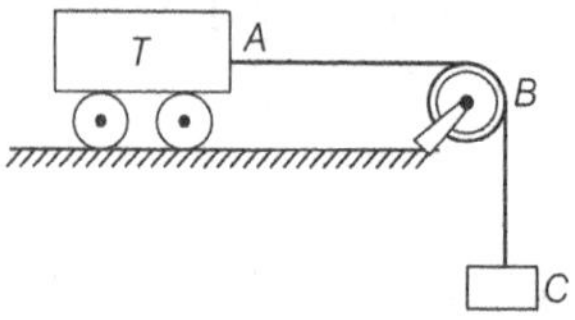

(a) $\frac{20}{6}$ to $\frac{30}{5}$ (b) $\frac{20}{8}$ to $\frac{30}{8}$

(c) $\frac{20}{5}$ to $\frac{30}{6}$ (d) None of these

44 Two unequal masses are connected on two sides of a light string passing over a light and smooth pulley as shown in figure. The system is released from rest. The larger mass is stopped 1.0 s after the system is set into motion. The time elapsed before the string is tight again is ($g = 10 \text{ m/s}^2$)

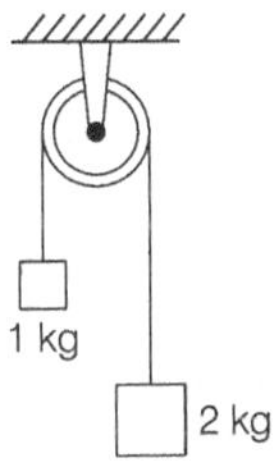

(a) $\frac{1}{4}$ s (b) $\frac{1}{2}$ s (c) $\frac{2}{3}$ s (d) $\frac{1}{3}$ s

45 A string of negligible mass going over a clamped pulley of mass m supports a block of mass M as shown in the figure. The force on the pulley by the clamp is given by

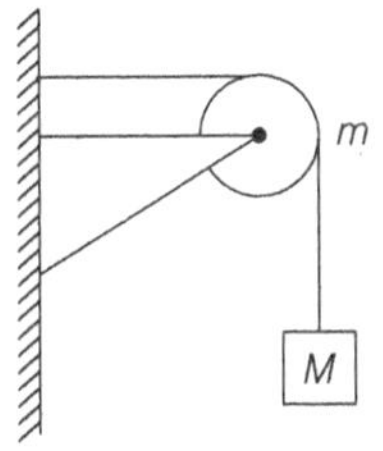

(a) $\sqrt{2}mg$ (b) $\sqrt{2}Mg$
(c) $\left(\sqrt{(M+m)^2 + m^2}\right)g$ (d) $\left(\sqrt{(M+m)^2 + M^2}\right)g$

46 In the figure shown acceleration of monkey relative to the rope if it exerts a force of 80 N on string will be

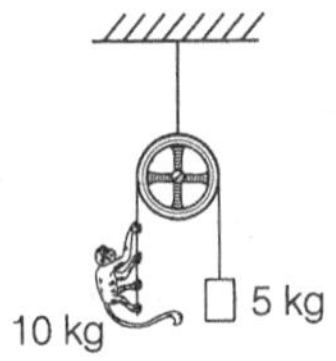

(a) 2 ms^{-2} (b) 4 ms^{-2} (c) 6 ms^{-2} (d) 8 ms^{-2}

47 Find mass (M) of the hanging block, if the string in steady state makes an angle of 53° with normal to the trolley as shown in figure.

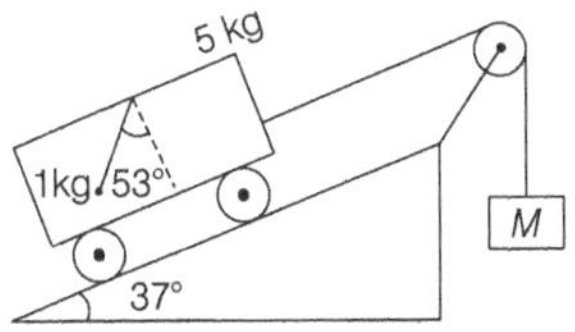

(a) 8 kg (b) 10 kg (c) 12 kg (d) 16 kg

48 Inclined plane of length 4m is moved towards right with an acceleration of 10 ms^{-2} starting from rest as shown in figure. Find time taken by the block to reach top of the inclined plane.

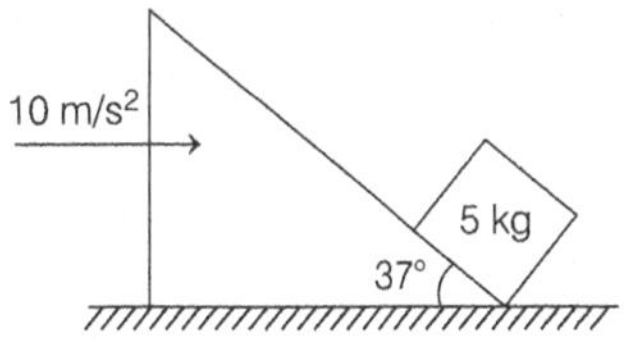

(a) 1 s (b) 2 s
(c) 3 s (d) 4 s

49 Force F is applied on upper pulley. If $F = 30t$ N, where t is time in second. Find the time when m_1 loses contact with floor. ($m_1 = 4$kg and $m_2 = 1$kg)

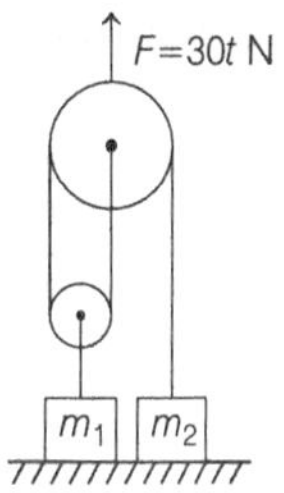

(a) 1s (b) 2 s
(c) 3 s (d) 4 s

50 A block is dragged on smooth plane with the help of a rope which moves with velocity v. The horizontal velocity of the block is

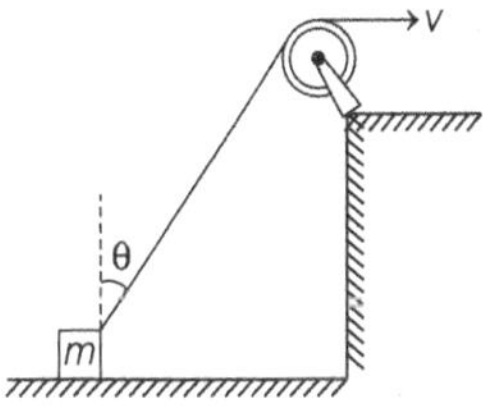

(a) v (b) $\frac{v}{\sin\theta}$ (c) $v \sin\theta$ (d) $\frac{v}{\cos\theta}$

51 In the figure shown, the speed of the car is v to the right. The speed with which the block is moving up at $\theta = 60°$ is

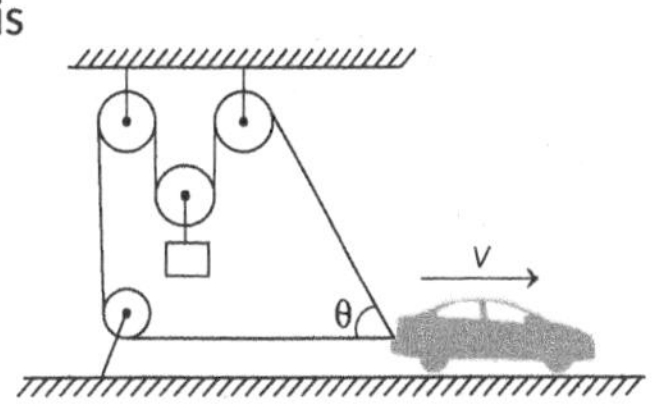

(a) v (b) $\frac{2v}{3}$
(c) $\frac{3v}{4}$ (d) None of these

52 A mass m_1, placed on top of a trolley of mass m_3, is connected to another mass m_2 by means of a string passing over a smooth pulley as shown in the figure. The friction between surfaces is negligible. For m_1 and m_2 not to move with respect to trolley, the horizontal force F to be applied on trolley is

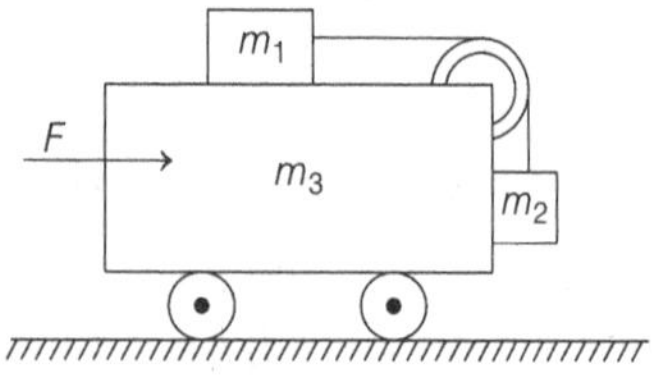

(a) $F = m_3 g$ (b) $F = (m_1 + m_2)g$

(c) $F = (m_1 + m_2 + m_3)\dfrac{m_2 g}{m_1}$ (d) $F = m_1 g$

53 What should be the minimum force P to be applied to the string, so that block of mass m just begins to move up the frictionless plane?

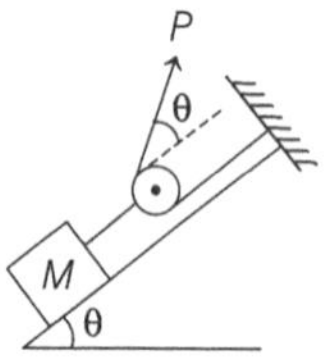

(a) $Mg \tan \dfrac{\theta}{2}$ (b) $Mg \cot \dfrac{\theta}{2}$

(c) $\dfrac{Mg \cos \theta}{1 + \sin \theta}$ (d) None of these

54 A man uses two pulleys to raise himself with an acceleration 2 m/s^2, as in figure. Man stands on a light weighing machine fitted in horizontal platform. Determine the reading of weighing machine. (Mass of man = 75 kg, mass of platform = 25 kg.

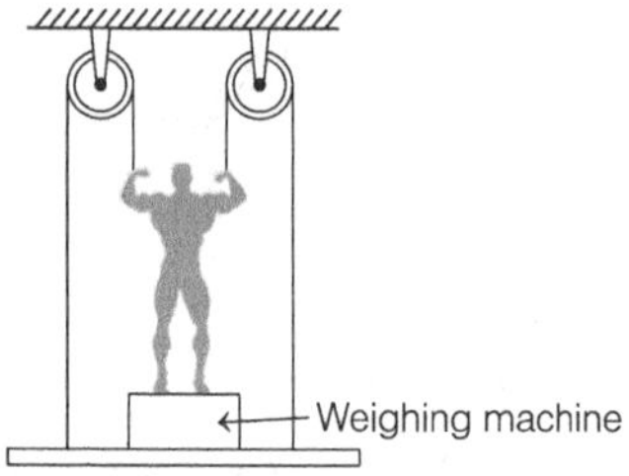

(a) 15 kg (b) 30 kg

(c) 60 kg (d) 90 kg

55 Two blocks A and B with masses 4 kg and 6 kg respectively are connected by a stretched spring of negligible mass as in figure. When the two blocks are released simultaneously, the initial acceleration of B is 1.5 m/s^2 westward. The acceleration of A is

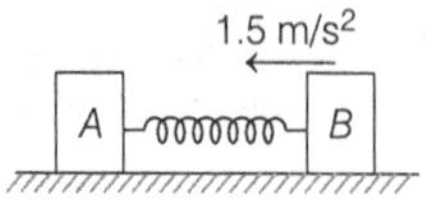

(a) 1 m/s^2, westward (b) 2.25 m/s^2, eastward

(c) 1 m/s^2, eastward (d) 2.75 m/s^2, westward

56 The block shown in the figure is equilibrium. Find acceleration of the block just after the string burns.

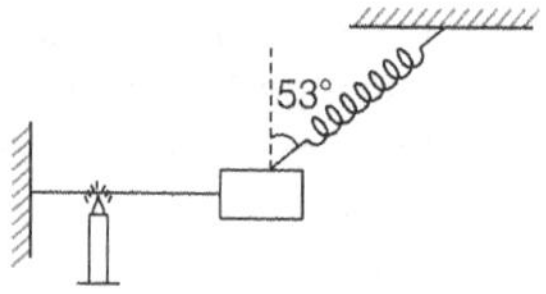

(a) $\dfrac{3g}{5}$ (b) $\dfrac{4g}{5}$

(c) $\dfrac{4g}{3}$ (d) None of these

57 Find the reading of spring balance as shown in figure. Assume that, mass M is in equilibrium

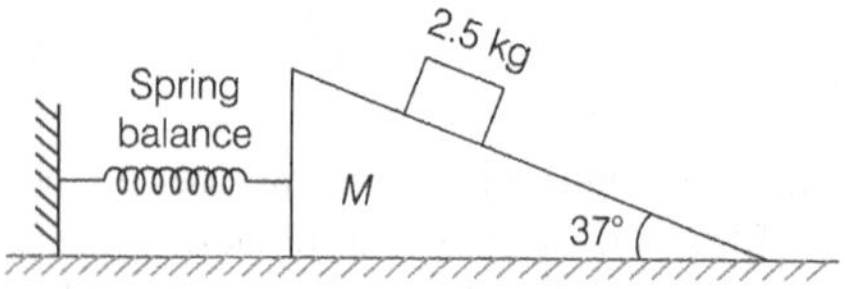

(a) 40 N (b) 15 N

(c) 20 N (d) 12 N

58 Find the reading of the spring balance as shown in figure. The elevator is going up with an acceleration of $\dfrac{g}{10}$, the pulley and the string are light and the pulley is smooth.

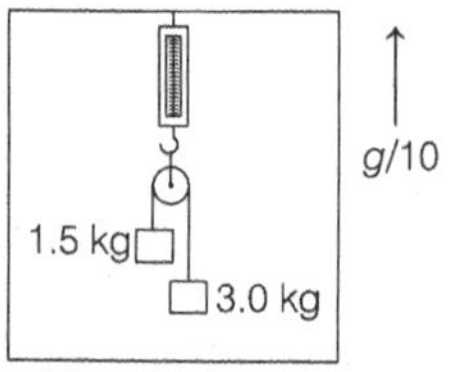

(a) 4 kg (b) 4.3 kg (c) 4.4 kg (d) 4.5 kg

59 A block tied between two springs is in equilibrium. If upper spring is cut, then the acceleration of the block just after cut is 6 m/s^2 downwards. Now, if instead of upper spring, lower spring is cut, then the magnitude of acceleration of the block just after the cut will be (take, $g = 10$ m/s^2)

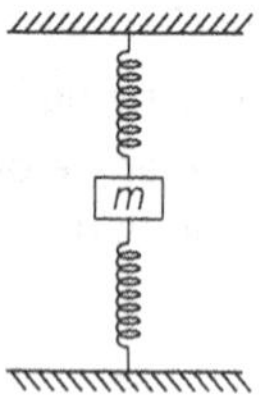

(a) 16 m/s^2

(b) 4 m/s^2

(c) Cannot be determined

(d) None of the above

60 Figure shows a 5 kg ladder hanging from a string from ceiling. A boy of mass 25 kg is climbing up the ladder at acceleration 2 m/s^2. Find the reading of spring balance in the upper string. Assume, spring balance and string are light.

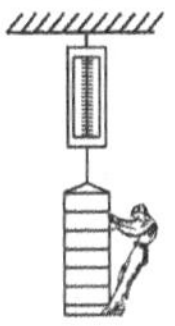

(a) 25 kg (b) 30 kg
(c) 35 kg (d) 37.5 kg

61 Two masses are connected by a string which passes over a pulley accelerating upward at a rate A as shown. If a_1 and a_2 be the acceleration of bodies 1 and 2 respectively, then

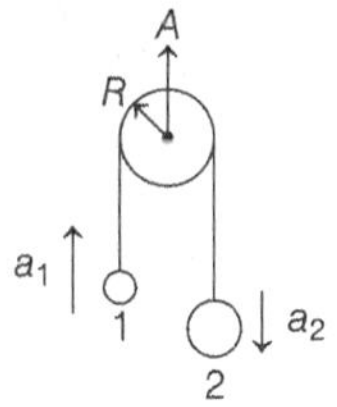

(a) $A = a_1 - a_2$ (b) $A = a_1 + a_2$
(c) $A = \dfrac{a_1 - a_2}{2}$ (d) $A = \dfrac{a_1 + a_2}{2}$

62 A monkey of mass m climbs a rope slung over a light frictionless pulley. The opposite end of the rope is tied to a block of mass M lying on a smooth horizontal plane. Then, the acceleration of block, when monkey moves upwards with an acceleration a relative to rope is

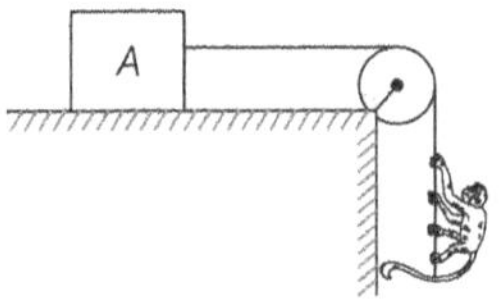

(a) $\dfrac{m}{M+2m}(g+a)$ (b) $\dfrac{m}{M+3m}(g+a)$
(c) $\dfrac{m}{M+m}(g+a)$ (d) $\dfrac{2m}{M+m}(g+a)$

63 Two masses m and M are attached with strings as shown. For the system to be in equilibrium we have

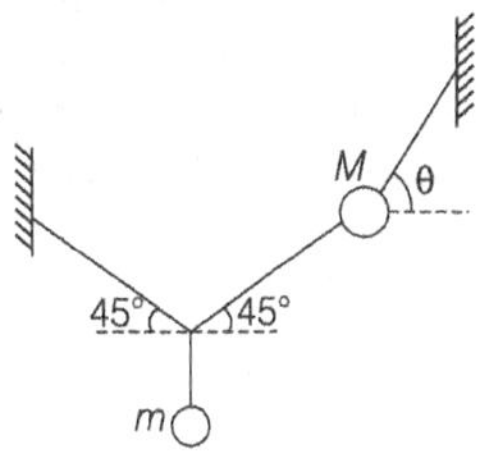

(a) $\tan\theta = 1 + \dfrac{2M}{m}$ (b) $\tan\theta = 1 + \dfrac{2m}{M}$
(c) $\tan\theta = 1 + \dfrac{M}{2m}$ (d) $\tan\theta = 1 + \dfrac{m}{2M}$

64 A block of mass $m_1 = 8$ kg on a smooth, horizontal surface is connected to a second mass $m_2 = 2$ kg by a light cord over a light, frictionless pulley as shown. (Neglect the mass of the cord and of the pulley). A force of magnitude $F_0 = 80$ N is applied to mass m_1 as shown. Neglect any friction. Find the tension in string attached to m_2.

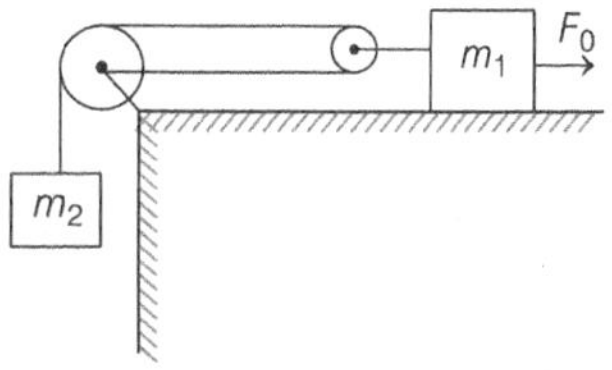

(a) 40 N (b) 30 N
(c) 20 N (d) 10 N

Numerical Value Questions

1 Figure shows N identical blocks connected with identical strings on a smooth horizontal surface. A constant force is pulling the blocks horizontally. If tension in string connecting 4th and 5th block is two times that between 8th and 9th block, what is the total number of blocks?

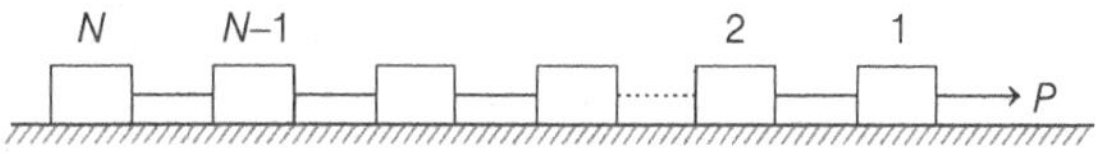

2 Three monkeys A, B and C with masses 10 kg, 15 kg and 8 kg respectively are climbing up and down the rope suspended from D. At the instant represented A is descending the rope with acceleration of 2 m/s^2 and C is pulling himself up with an acceleration of 1.5 m/s^2. Moneky D is climbing up with a constant speed of 0.8 m/s. What is the tension (in N) in the rope at D? (Take, $g = 10$ m/s^2)

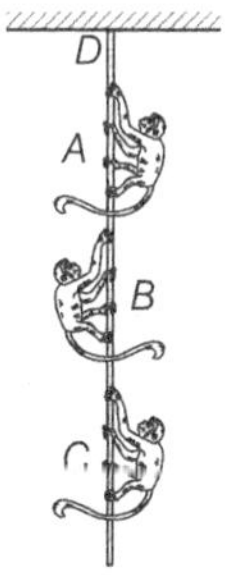

3 The monkey A shown in the figure climbing on a rope, while monkey B holding tail of the monkey A which is climbing on a rope. The masses of the monkeys A and B are 7 kg and 3 kg, respectively. If A can tolerate a tension of 45 N in its tail, what maximum force (in N) should monkey A apply on the rope in order to carry the monkey B with it? (Take, $g = 10$ m/s^2)

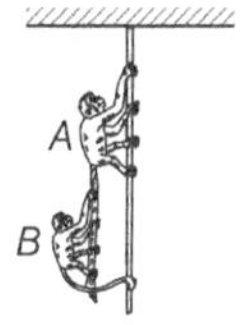

4 A block of mass 1 kg is kept on the tilted floor of a lift moving down with 3 m/s^2. If the block is released from rest as shown, what will be the time (in s) taken by block to reach the bottom?

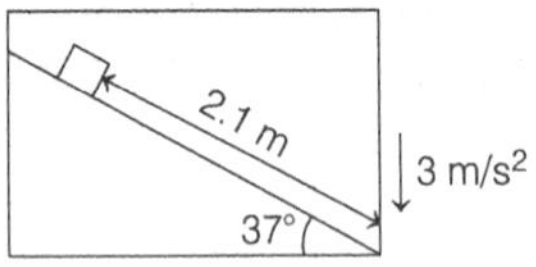

5 A solid sphere of mass 2 kg is resting inside a cube as shown in figure. The cube is moving with a velocity $\mathbf{v} = (5t\hat{\mathbf{i}} + 2t\hat{\mathbf{j}})$ m/s. Here, t is the time in second. All surfaces are smooth. The sphere is at rest with respect to the cube. What is the total force (in N) exerted by the sphere on the cube? (Take, $g = 10$ ms^{-2} and positive Y-axis is vertically up)

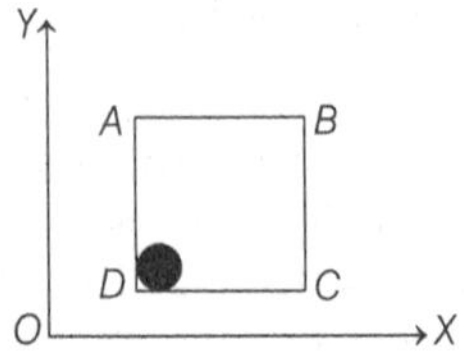

6 Blocks A and B each have same mass, $m = 1$ kg. Determine the largest horizontal force P (in newton) which can be applied to B, so that A will not slip up on B. Neglect any friction.

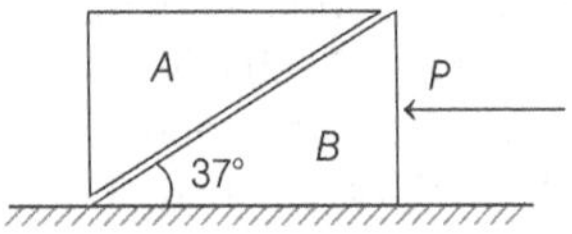

7 A bead of mass 2 kg is fitted on to a rod of a length L and can move on it without friction. The rod moves translationally in a horizontal plane with an acceleration 5 ms^{-2} in a direction forming an angle of 37° with the rod. Find the reaction force (in N) exerted by the rod on the bead.

8 Monkey of mass 10 kg starts going up on a rope hanging on a pulley system as shown with acceleration of 11.5 ms^{-2} with respect to the rope. What is the acceleration (in m/s^2) of the 11 kg mass? ($g = 10$ m/s^2)

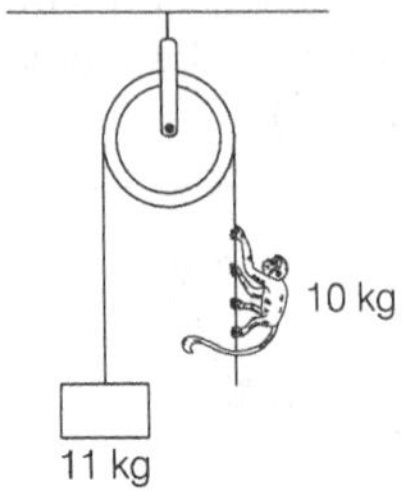

9 Consider the situation as shown in figure [all the pulleys and string are ideal and surfaces are smooth]. Find the magnitude of acceleration of 10 kg block in ms^{-2}.

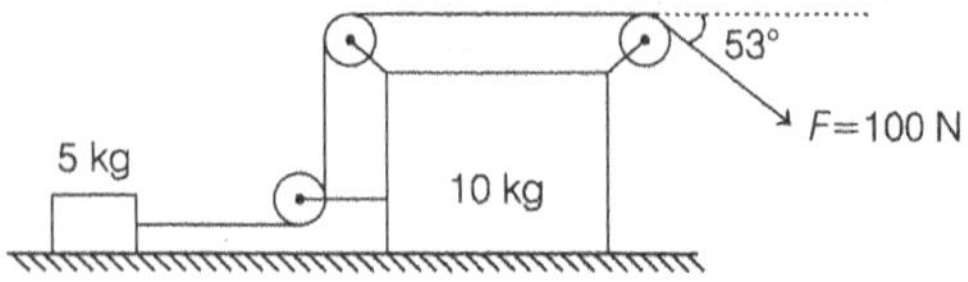

10 A 80 kg person standing on a light weighing machine in a 40 kg lift pulls on the rope, which supports the lift as shown in the figure. Find the force (in N) with which the person should pull on the rope, so that the weighing machine shows his actual weight.

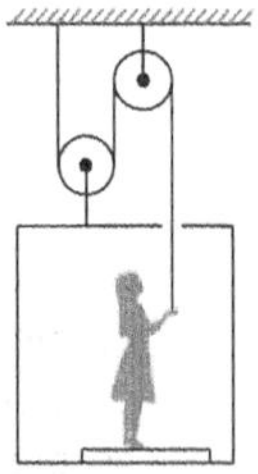

11 There is a trolley with fixed inclined surface on which a smooth block of mass 10 kg is placed. There is no friction anywhere. If trolley is at rest, then tension (in N) in the string is

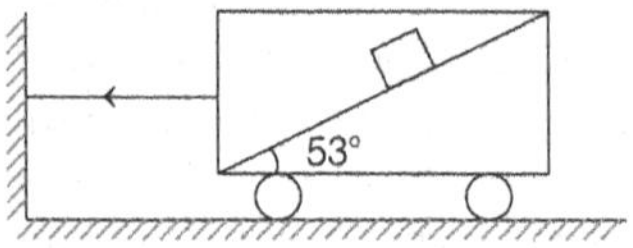

12 A steel ball is suspended from the ceiling of an accelerating carriage by means of two cords A and B. The acceleration of the carriage which will cause the tension in A to be twice that in B is $\frac{g}{\sqrt{p}}$. Find p.

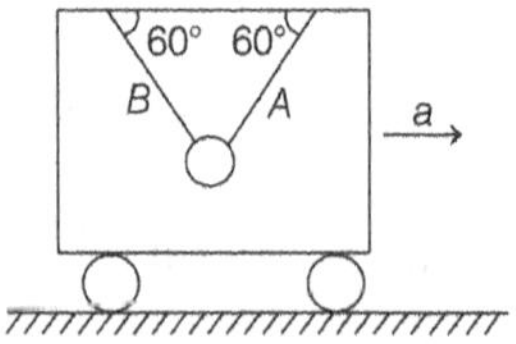

13 The system of two weights with masses m_1 and m_2 are connected with weightless spring as shown. The system is resting on the support S. The support S is quickly removed. Find the acceleration (in m/s^2) of 5 kg right after the support S is removed.

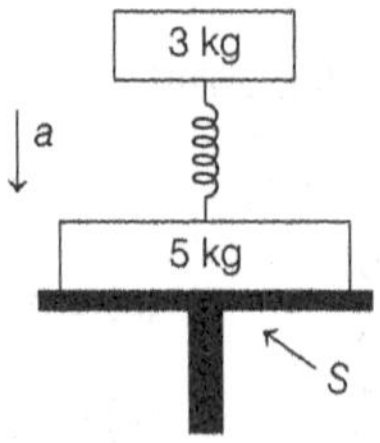

14 Find F (in N), so that the system is in equilibrium. (Neglect friction)

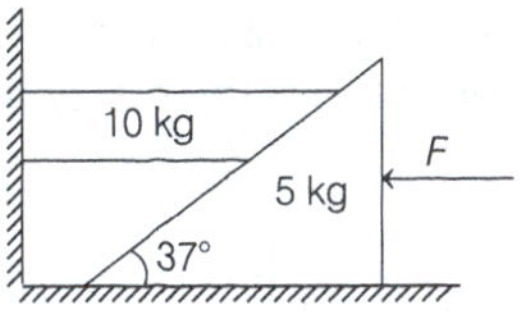

15 A sphere of radius R is in contact with a wedge. The point of contact is $\frac{R}{5}$ from the ground as shown in the figure. Wedge is moving with velocity 20 m/s, then the velocity (in m/s) of the sphere at this instant will be

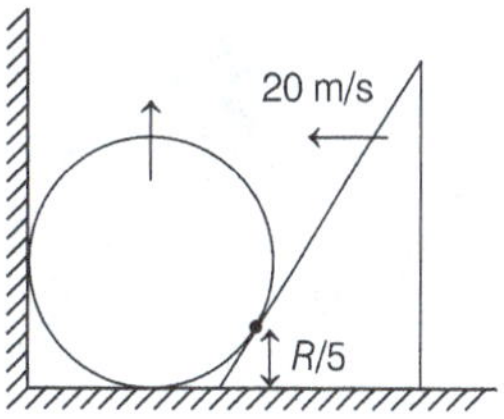

LEVEL 03 JEE Advanced Level

Single Choice Correct Questions

1 A truck shown in the figure is driven with an acceleration $a = 3\ \text{m/s}^2$. Masses of bodies A and B are 10 kg and 5 kg, respectively. Assuming pulleys are massless and friction is absent everywhere, find acceleration of body A.

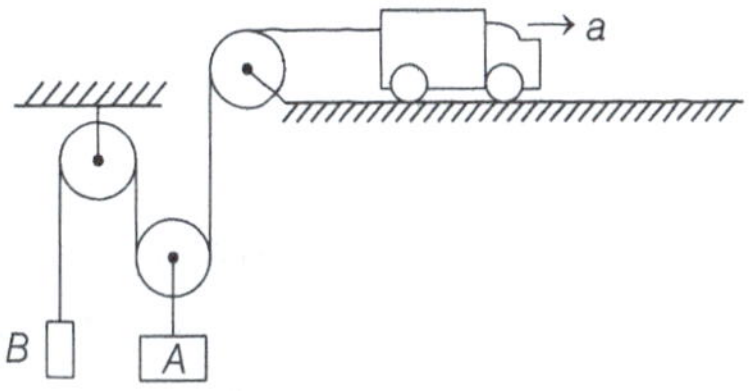

(a) $1\ \text{ms}^{-2}$ (b) $2\ \text{ms}^{-2}$
(c) $3\ \text{ms}^{-2}$ (d) $4\ \text{ms}^{-2}$

2 A smooth pulley P of mass $M = 2$ kg is lying on a smooth table. A light string passes round the pulley and has mass $m = 1$ kg and $m' = 2$ kg attached to its ends, the two portions of the string being perpendicular to the edge of the table, so that the masses hang vertically. Acceleration of pulley is

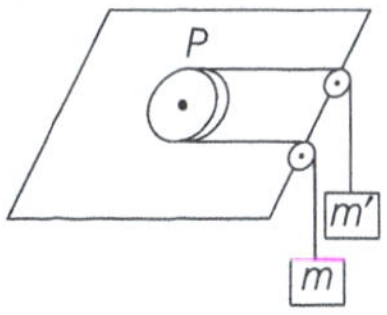

(a) $\frac{g}{2}$ (b) $\frac{2g}{3}$ (c) $\frac{4g}{9}$ (d) $\frac{4g}{7}$

3 Two identical blocks each of mass m are kept on a table in an elevator as shown. Find acceleration of elevator, so that acceleration of the block on the table is minimum as seen from ground frame.

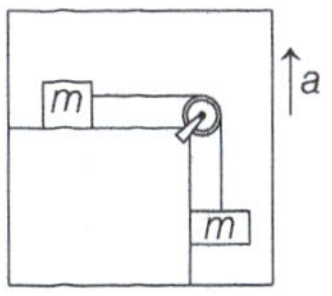

(a) Zero (b) $\frac{g}{2}$ (c) g (d) $\frac{g}{5}$

4 In the figure shown pulley and string are massless. Friction is absent everywhere, m kg is the mass of the hanging block, so that the 1 kg block remains at rest with respect to the 2 kg wedge. The angle of wedge is 37°. Find m.

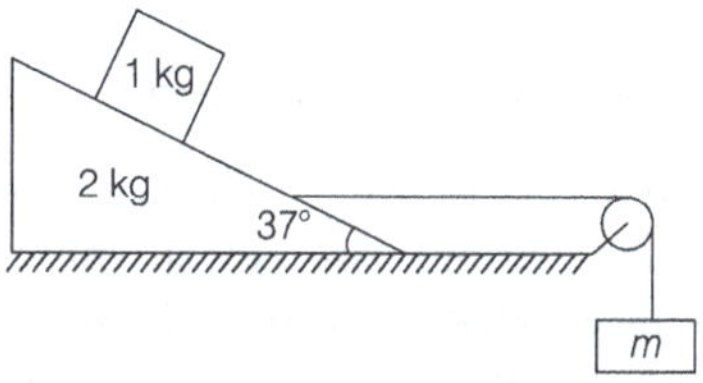

(a) 5 kg (b) 6 kg (c) 8 kg (d) 9 kg

5 B is moving towards right with acceleration $8\ \text{ms}^{-2}$. Find mass of A (in kg).

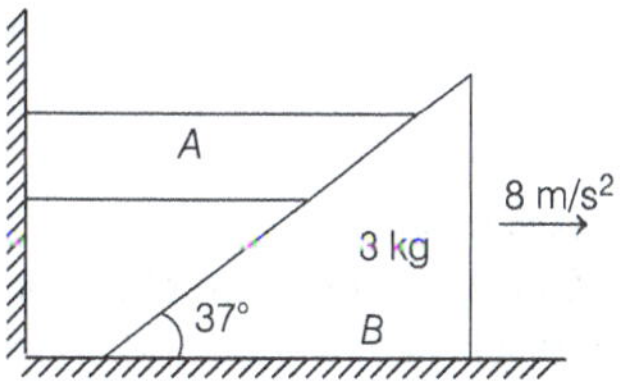

(a) 5 kg (b) 6 kg (c) 8 kg (d) 9 kg

6 A uniform string AB of length 10 m and mass 20 kg lies on a smooth frictionless inclined plane. A force of 200 N is applied as shown in the figure. Find the tension in the string at 2 m from end A.

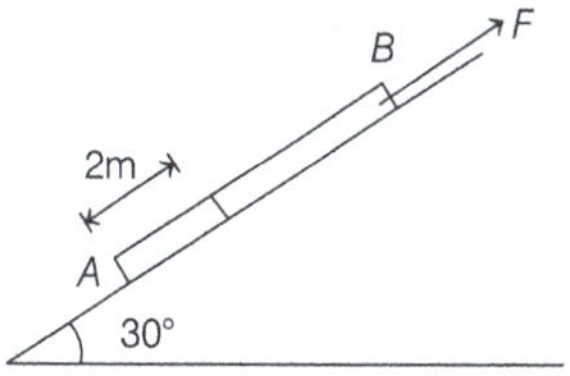

(a) 40 N (b) 55 N
(c) 75 N (d) 105 N

7 System is shown in the figure and man is pulling the rope from both sides with constant speed u. Then, the velocity of the block will be

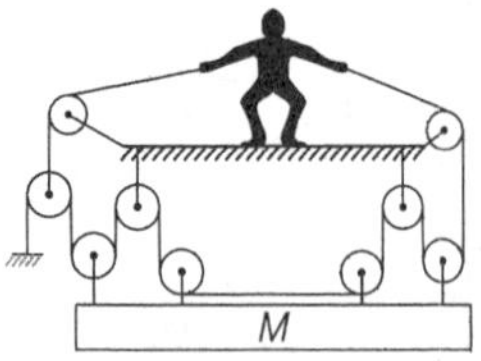

(a) $\frac{3u}{4}$ (b) $\frac{3u}{2}$ (c) $\frac{u}{4}$ (d) $\frac{u}{2}$

8 At a given instant wedge A is moving towards left with acceleration a. Find acceleration of block B at this instant.

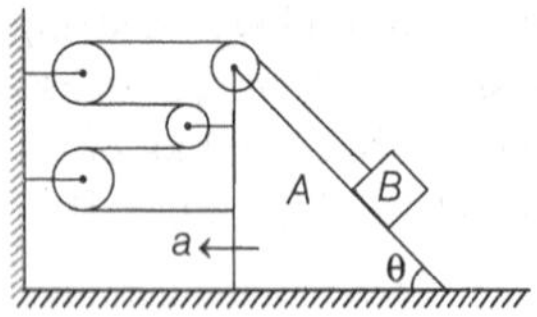

(a) $4a$ (b) $a\sqrt{17+8\cos\theta}$
(c) $a\sqrt{17-8\cos\theta}$ (d) $a\sqrt{17}$

9 Three blocks A, B and C are arranged as shown. Pulleys and strings are ideal. All surfaces are frictionless. If block C is observed moving down along the incline at 1 m/s^2, find mass of block B.

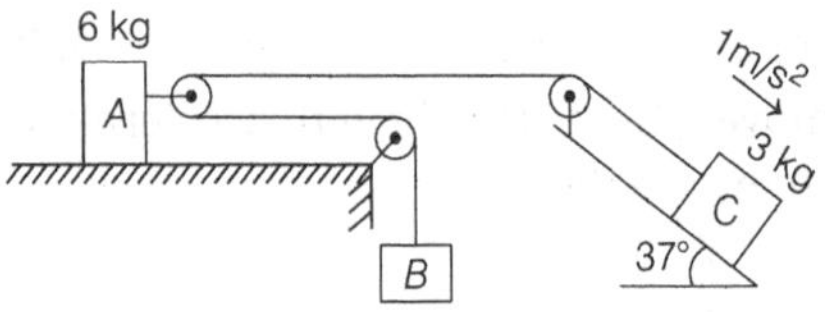

(a) 10 kg (b) 20 kg (c) 25 kg (d) 15 kg

10 A man of mass m slides down along a rope which is connected to the ceiling of an elevator with declaration a relative to the rope. If elevator is going upwards with an acceleration a relative to the ground, then tension in the rope is

(a) mg (b) $m(g+2a)$
(c) $m(g+a)$ (d) $m(g+3a)$

11 All surfaces are smooth. Free end P of the string is pulled with constant horizontal force F. Find acceleration of the point P.

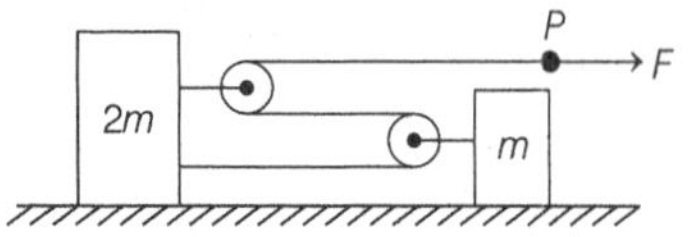

(a) $\frac{F}{3m}$ (b) $\frac{F}{m}$
(c) $\frac{17F}{2m}$ (d) None of these

12 In the figure shown, girl is balanced by counter weight of same mass. She starts to climb the rope with an acceleration of 2 m/s^2 w.r.t. rope. The time after which she reaches the pulley will be

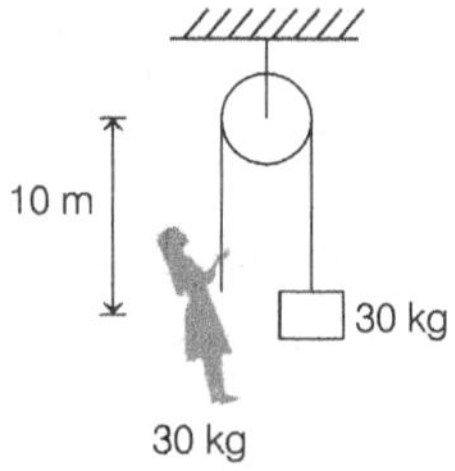

(a) $\sqrt{10}$ s (b) $2\sqrt{5}$ s
(c) infinity (d) None of these

13 In the figure, $m_1 = 4m_2$. Pulleys are smooth and thread is light. At $t = 0$ system is released from rest. Find maximum height reached by m_2.

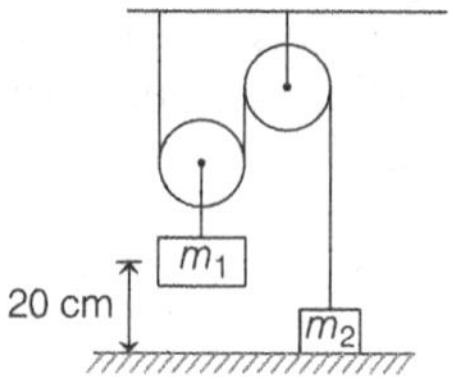

(a) 0.6 m (b) 0.4 m
(c) 0.8 m (d) None of these

14 Three identical rigid circular cylinders A, B and C are arranged on smooth inclined surfaces as shown in figure. The least value of θ that prevent the arrangement from collapse is

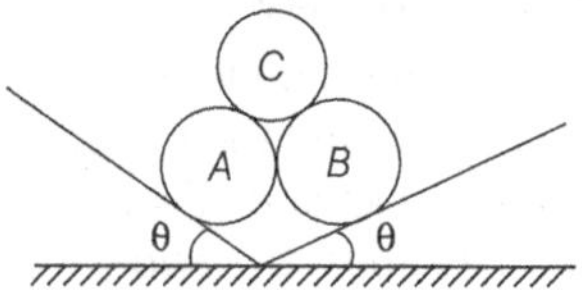

(a) $\tan^{-1}\left(\frac{1}{\sqrt{3}}\right)$ (b) $\tan^{-1}\left(\frac{1}{2\sqrt{3}}\right)$
(c) $\tan^{-1}\left(\frac{1}{3\sqrt{3}}\right)$ (d) $\tan^{-1}(\sqrt{3})$

15 A 1 kg block B rests as shown on a bracket A of same mass. Constant forces $F_1 = 20$ N and $F_2 = 8$ N start to act at time $t = 0$ when the distance of block B from pulley is 50 cm. Time when block B reaches the pulley is

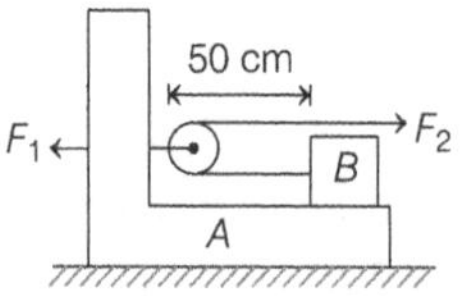

(a) 0.5 s (b) 1 s (c) 1.5 s (d) 2 s

16 In the figure shown, the block B moves down with a velocity 10 m/s. The velocity of A in the position shown is

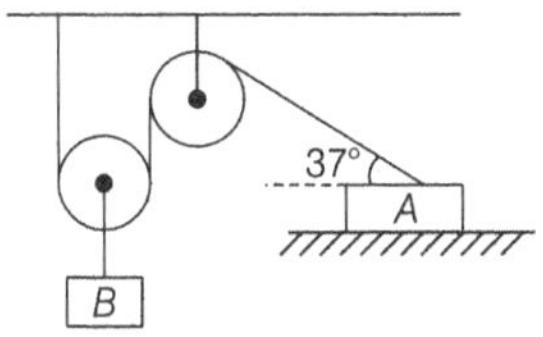

(a) 12.5 m/s (b) 25 m/s (c) 8 m/s (d) 16 m/s

17 In the figure shown, all pulleys are massless and frictionless. The time taken by the ball to reach the upper end of the rod is

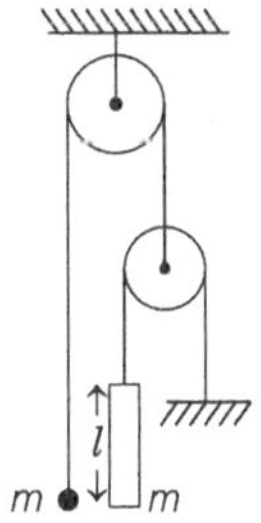

(a) $\sqrt{\frac{10l}{3g}}$ (b) $\sqrt{\frac{5l}{3g}}$

(c) $\sqrt{\frac{3l}{4g}}$ (d) $\sqrt{\frac{3l}{10g}}$

18 In the figure shown, the velocity of different blocks is shown. The velocity of C is

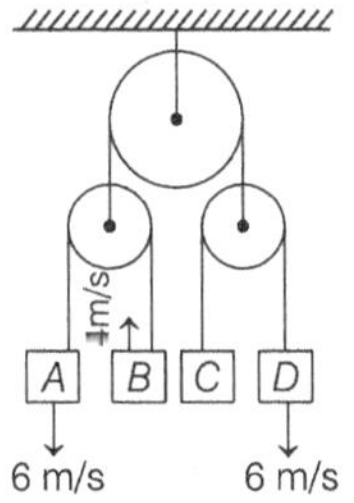

(a) 6 m/s (b) 4 m/s

(c) 8 m/s (d) None of these

19 All the surfaces are frictionless, then acceleration of the block B is

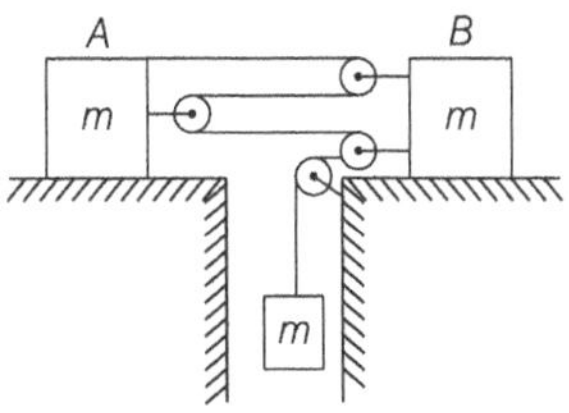

(a) $\frac{2g}{13}$ (b) $\frac{3g}{13}$ (c) $\frac{4g}{13}$ (d) $\frac{g}{13}$

20 A flexible chain of weight w hangs between two fixed points A and B at the same level. The inclination of the chain with the horizontal at the two points of support is θ. What is the tension of the chain at the midpoint?

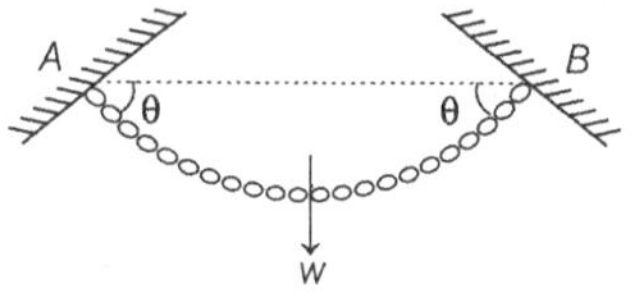

(a) $\frac{w}{2}\cot\theta$ (b) $\frac{w}{2}\operatorname{cosec}\theta$

(c) $\frac{w}{2}\cos\theta$ (d) $\frac{w}{2}\sin\theta$

21 Blocks A and C start from rest and move to the right with acceleration $a_A = \frac{t}{2}$ m/s^2 and $a_C = 2$ m/s^2. Here, t is in seconds. The time when block B again comes to rest is

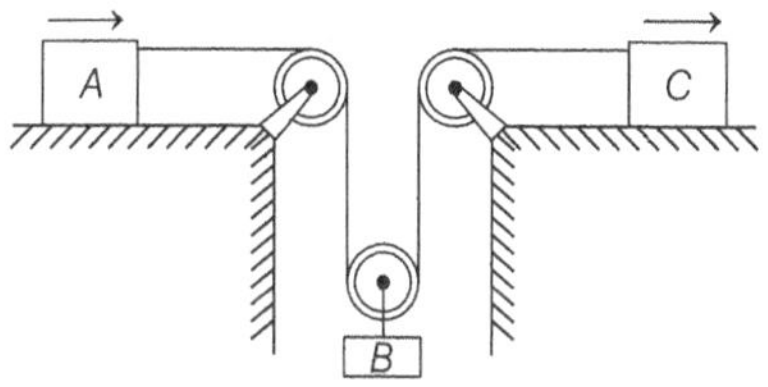

(a) 2 s (b) 4 s (c) 8 s (d) 6 s

22 An inclined plane makes an angle 30° with the horizontal. A groove $OA = 5$ m cut in the plane makes an angle 30° with OX as shown in the figure. A short smooth cylinder is free to slide down the influence of gravity. The time taken by the cylinder to reach from A to O is

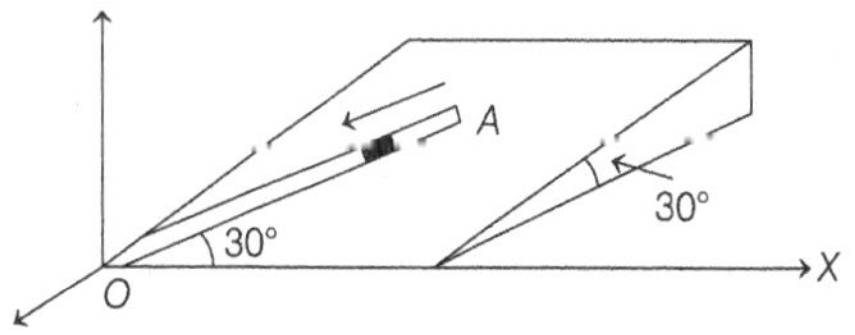

(a) 4 s (b) 2 s (c) $2\sqrt{2}$ s (d) 1 s

23 The system shown in the figure is given an acceleration $a = 1.5$ ms^{-2} towards left. Assuming, all the surfaces to be frictionless and the sphere of mass 1 kg to be at rest w.r.t. the wedge, find the normal force exerted on the sphere by the vertical surface of the wedge. (Take, $g = 10$ m / s^2)

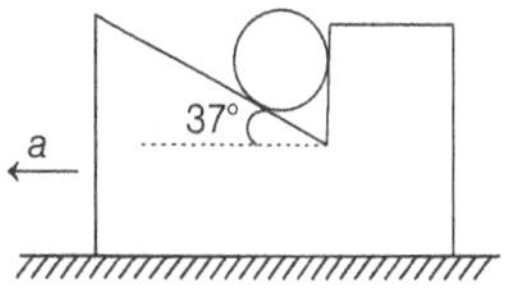

(a) 5 N (b) 6 N (c) 8 N (d) 9 N

24 Two blocks A and B each of mass m are placed on a smooth horizontal surface. Two horizontal forces F and $2F$ are applied on the two blocks A and B respectively as shown in figure. The block A does not slide on block B. Then, the normal reaction acting between the two blocks is

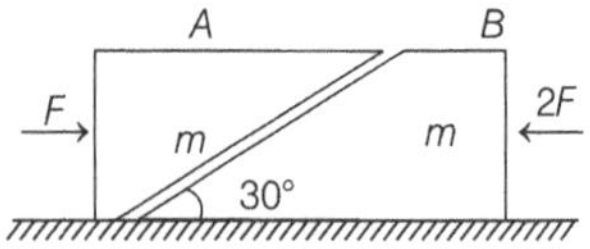

(a) F (b) $\frac{F}{2}$ (c) $\frac{F}{\sqrt{3}}$ (d) $3F$

25 System is shown in the figure. Velocity of sphere A is 9 m/s. Then, speed of sphere B will be

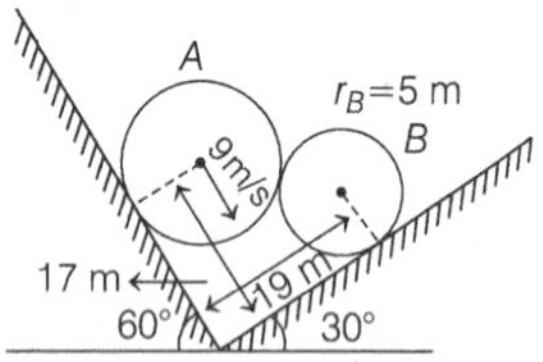

(a) 9 m/s (b) 12 m/s

(c) $9 \times \frac{5}{4}$ m/s (d) None of these

26 Block A of mass m is placed over a wedge B of same mass m. Assuming, all surfaces to be smooth, the displacement of block A in 1 s, if the system is released from rest is

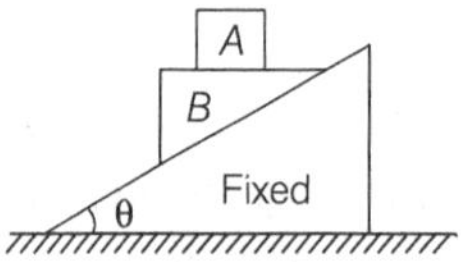

(a) $g \frac{(1+\sin^2\theta)}{(1-\sin^2\theta)}$ (b) $\frac{g\sin\theta}{2}$

(c) $g\frac{\cos^2\theta}{1+\sin^2\theta}$ (d) $g\frac{\sin^2\theta}{1+\sin^2\theta}$

27 Two monkeys Ronit and Yatin of equal mass m can climb strings of a pulley arrangement as shown in figure. Find magnitude of acceleration of Ronit with respect to rope, so that the block remains stationary. It is given that, Yatin is just holding the string. Assume pulley is frictionless and string is massless and inextensible.

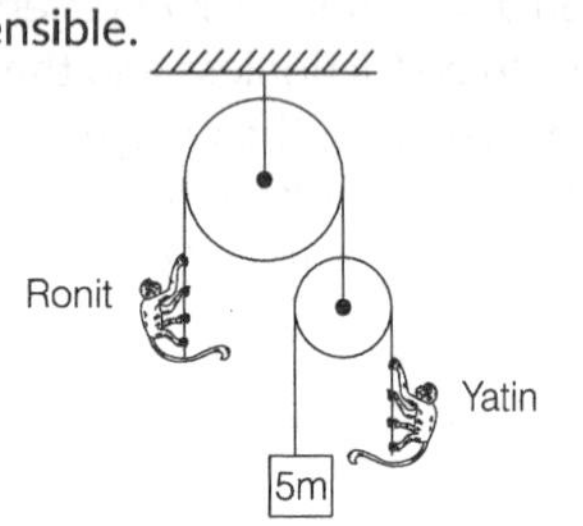

(a) 90 m/s^2 (b) 100 m/s^2

(c) 110 m/s^2 (d) 70 m/s^2

28 The velocities of A and B are marked in the figure. The velocity of block C is (assume that the pulleys are ideal and string inextensible.)

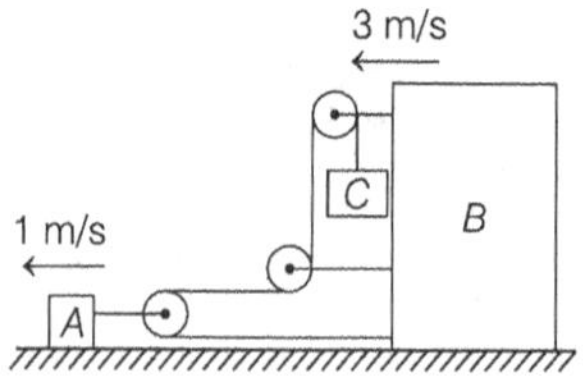

(a) 5 m/s (b) 2 m/s (c) 3 m/s (d) 4 m/s

29 In the figure shown the velocity of lift is 2 m/s, while string is winding on the motor shaft with velocity 2 m/s and block A is moving downwards with a velocity of 2 m/s, then find out the velocity of block B.

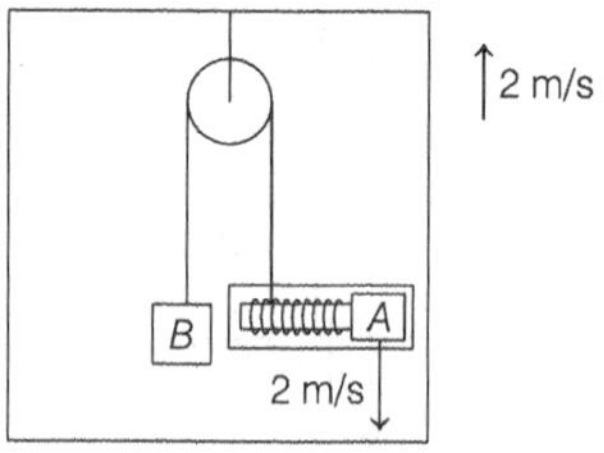

(a) 2 m/s↑ (b) 2 m/s↓ (c) 4 m/s↑ (d) 8 m/s↑

30 Two rods AC and BC are hinged at the end C and the ends A and B are moving along the surface with velocities $v_A = 8$ m/s and $v_B = 4\sqrt{3}$ m/s, respectively as shown. The velocity of hinged point C is

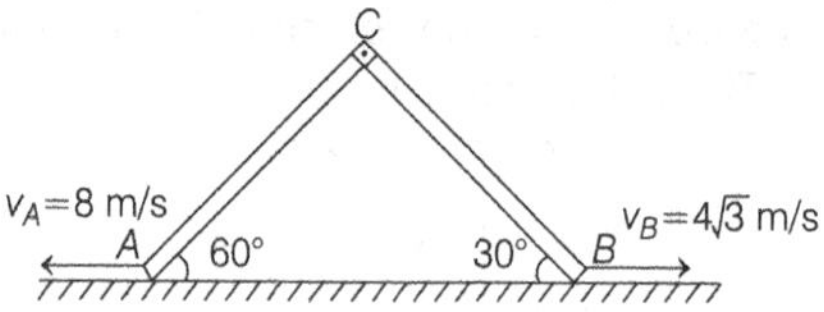

(a) $\sqrt{13}$ m/s (b) $2\sqrt{13}$ m/s

(c) $3\sqrt{13}$ m/s (d) $4\sqrt{13}$ m/s

31 Two objects A and B are connected by a light string and these blocks are further connected to block C by thread that passes over a light frictionless pulley as shown. The objects are at rest. At $t = 0$, block B is given a velocity 40 m/s in vertical upward direction. Find the time after which string between A and B again becomes tight (string is very long, blocks do not collide with each other or with pulley)

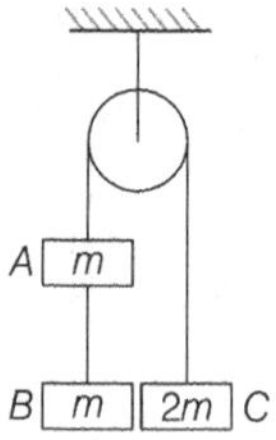

(a) 4 s (b) 5 s (c) 6 s (d) 8 s

32 A force F is applied on block A of mass M, so that the tension in light string also becomes F when block B of mass m acquires an equilibrium state with respect to block A. Find value of F.
$(m = M = \sqrt{3}\text{ kg})$

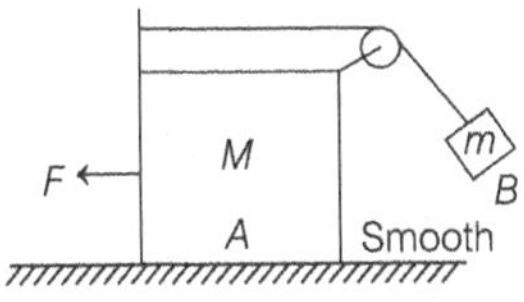

(a) 10 N (b) 20 N (c) 30 N (d) 40 N

33 In the figure shown, the pulleys and string are massless. The acceleration of the block of mass 4m just after the system is released from rest is
$\left(\theta = \sin^{-1}\frac{3}{5}\right)$

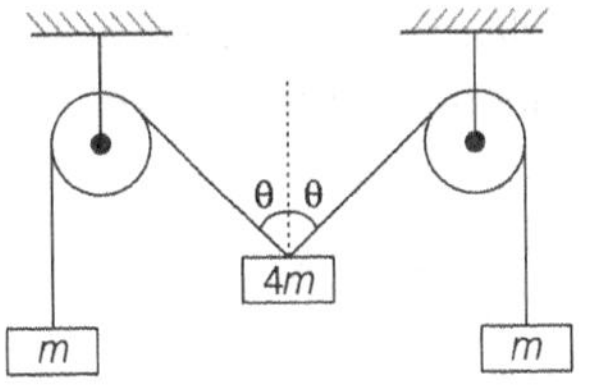

(a) $\frac{2g}{5}$, downwards (b) $\frac{2g}{5}$, upwards
(d) $\frac{5g}{11}$, upwards (d) $\frac{5g}{11}$, downwards

34 A force mg is applied horizontally on a wedge of mass m. Mass of block is also m. All surfaces are smooth . Find acceleration of the wedge.

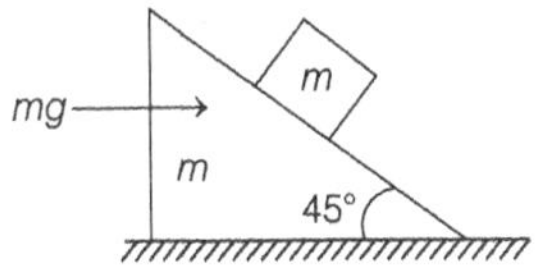

(a) $\frac{g}{2}$ (b) $\frac{g}{3}$ (c) $\frac{g}{4}$ (d) $\frac{g}{5}$

35 In the system shown in figure $m_A = 4\,m, m_B = 3\,m$ and $m_C = 8\,m$. Friction is absent everywhere. String is light and inextensible. If the system is released from rest, find the acceleration of block B.

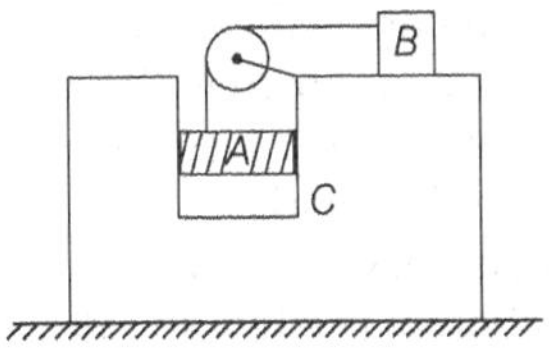

(a) $\frac{g}{8}$ (leftward) (b) $\frac{g}{2}$ (leftward)
(c) $\frac{g}{6}$ (rightward) (d) $\frac{g}{4}$ (rightward)

36 A motor is mounted rigidly on block B which is moving horizontally with velocity 10 m/s as shown in figure. The motor winds the light inelastic string on the shaft of the motor at a constant rate of 1 m/s. The pulley P is moving horizontally with speed $v_P = 5$ m/s. If none of the blocks leave the contact with the ground during motion, then find the speed of block A at the given instant. (Neglect friction and size of blocks and motor).

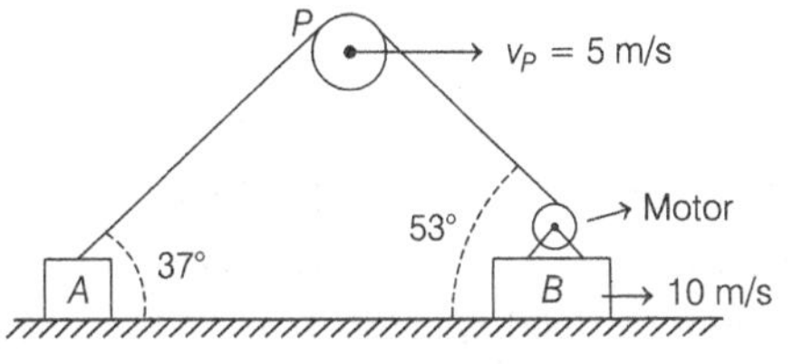

(a) 8 m/s (b) 10 m/s (c)12 m/s (d) 15 m/s

37 Two blocks A and B are connected by an ideal spring of force constant 100 N/m and moving on a smooth horizontal surface under the influence of a force 36 N. What is the extension in the spring, when acceleration of 2 kg is twice that of 5 kg?

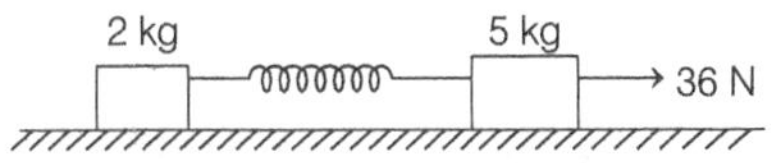

(a) 4 cm (b) $\frac{36}{7}$ cm (c) $\frac{72}{7}$ cm (d) 16 cm

38 System shown in figure is in equilibrium. Find the magnitude of net change in the string tension just before and just after, when one of the springs is cut. Mass of both the blocks is same and equal to m and spring constant of both springs is k.

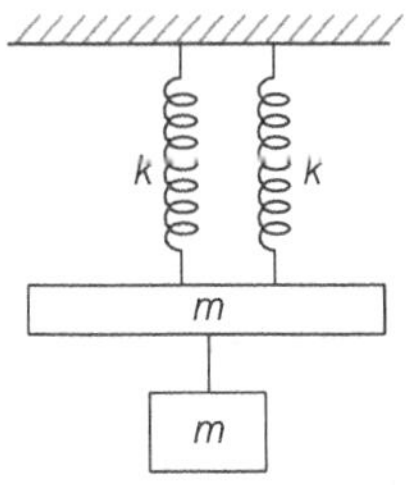

(a) $\frac{mg}{2}$ (b) $\frac{mg}{4}$ (c) $\frac{3mg}{4}$ (d) $\frac{3mg}{2}$

39 According to figure, the reading of the spring balance will be (all contacts are smooth) $[g = 10\text{ m/s}^2]$

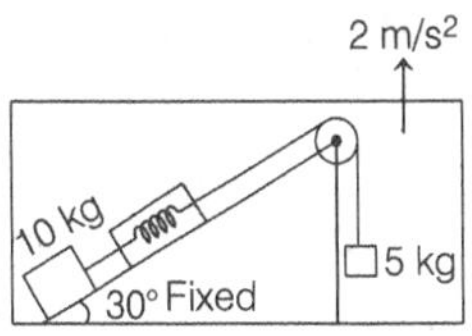

(a) 5 kgf (b) 6 kgf (c) 7 kgf (d) 8 kgf

40 The system shown is in equilibrium. All the strings and pulleys are massless. Instantaneous acceleration of A, B and C, when string above B is cut are respectively,

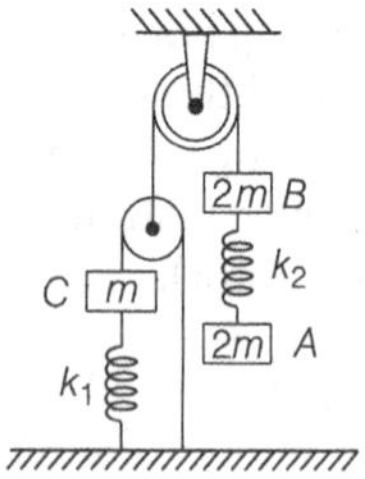

(a) $0, 2g, 2g$ (b) $0, 2g, g$
(c) $0, 2g, 0$ (d) $g, g, 2g$

41 Two uniform solid cylinders A and B each of mass 1 kg are connected by a spring of constant 200 N/m at their axles and are placed on a fixed wedge as shown in the figure. All contacts are frictionless. The angle made by the line AB with the horizontal in equilibrium, is

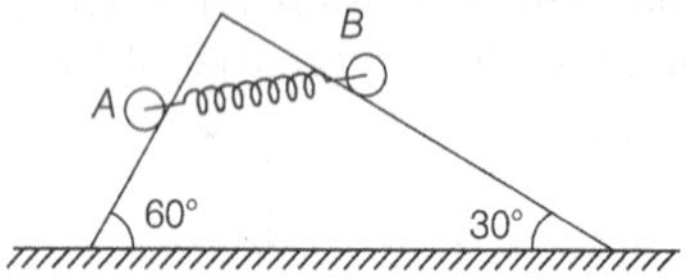

(a) 0° (b) 15° (c) 30° (d) None of these

42 System is shown in the figure. Assume that cylinder remains in contact with the two wedges. The velocity of cylinder is

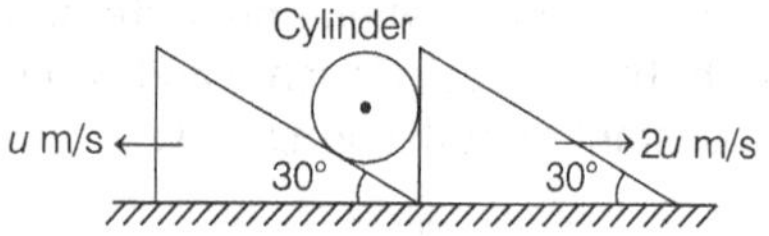

(a) $\sqrt{19 - 4\sqrt{3}}\,\frac{u}{2}$ m/s (b) $\frac{\sqrt{13}u}{2}$ m/s
(c) $\sqrt{3}u$ m/s (d) $\sqrt{7}u$ m/s

43 A plank of mass m rests symmetrically on two movable identical wedges B and C of mass M as shown in the figure. Neglecting frictional effects between all the surfaces in contact, the acceleration of the plank is

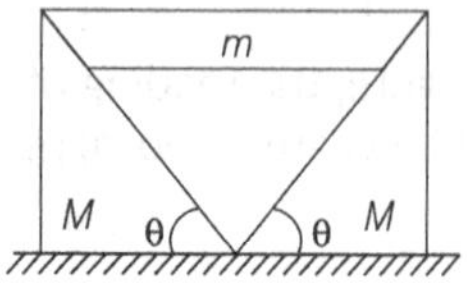

(a) $\frac{Mg \sin^2 \theta}{m \sin^2 \theta + 2M \cos^2 \theta}$ (b) $\frac{mg \sin^2 \theta}{2M \sin^2 \theta + m \cos^2 \theta}$
(c) $\frac{mg \sin^2 \theta}{m \sin^2 \theta + 2M \cos^2 \theta}$ (d) $\frac{Mg \sin^2 \theta}{2M \sin^2 \theta + m \cos^2 \theta}$

44 In the system shown. Find the initial acceleration of the wedge of mass $5M$. The pulleys are ideal and the cords are inextensible. (there is no friction anywhere)

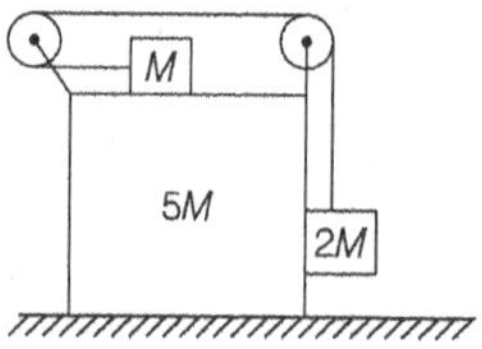

(a) Zero (b) $\frac{2g}{21}$ (c) $\frac{2g}{23}$ (d) $\frac{2g}{25}$

45 A trolley car of mass 8 kg is connected with a hanging block of mass 10 kg by an inextensible string that passes over a pulley. A ball of mass 2 kg is hanging from the roof of the trolley car by another inextensible string. If all the surfaces are smooth, then find angle made by the string with normal to the inclined plane in steady state.

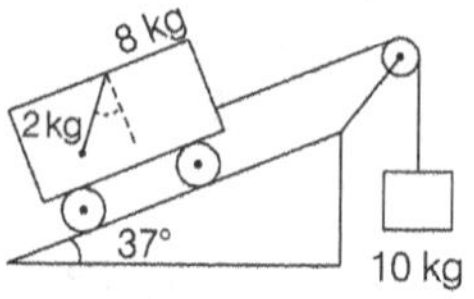

(a) $\tan^{-1}(1)$ (b) $\tan^{-1}(2)$ (c) $\tan^{-1}\left(\frac{1}{2}\right)$ (d) $\tan^{-1}\left(\frac{1}{4}\right)$

46 All surfaces are smooth and pulley, string are ideal. System is released from rest. If $m_1 = 10$ kg, $m_2 = 5$ kg and $m = 3$ kg, then find acceleration of m.

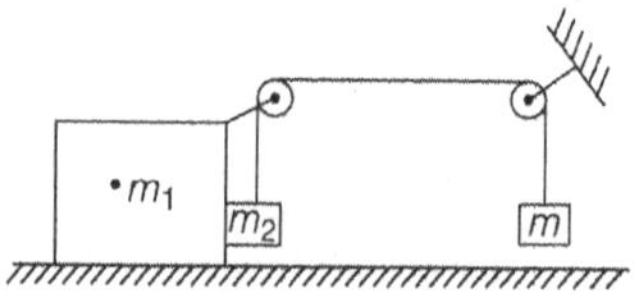

(a) $\frac{4g}{9}$ (b) $\frac{2g}{3}$
(c) $\frac{g}{3}$ (d) $\frac{g}{9}$

47 A block of mass m resting on the ground is tied to a light string of length $2l$ which passes through a fixed light pulley as shown in the figure. The free end of the string is pulled to the right with uniform horizontal velocity v_0.

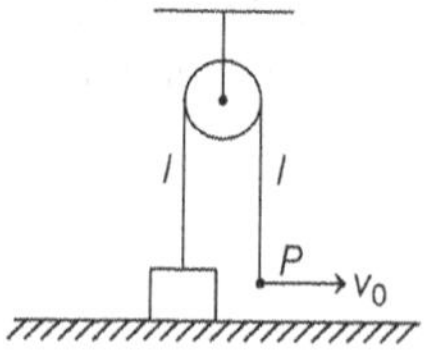

The acceleration of the block at the instant when P is horizontally displaced through x can be

(a) $\frac{2v_0^2 l^2}{(x^2 + l^2)^{3/2}}$ (b) $\frac{v_0^2 l^2}{(x^2 + l^2)^{3/2}}$
(c) zero (d) None of these

48 Block B has a downward velocity in m/s and given by $v_B = \frac{t^2}{2} + \frac{t^3}{6}$, where t is in second. Acceleration of A at $t = 2$ s is

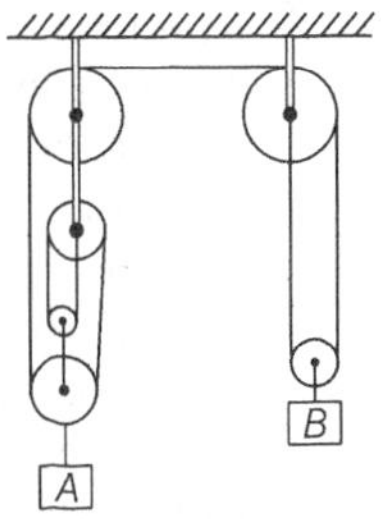

(a) 2 m/s^2
(b) 4 m/s^2
(c) 6 m/s^2
(d) None of the above

49 In the figure shown, the blocks A and C are pulled down with constant velocities u. Acceleration of block B is

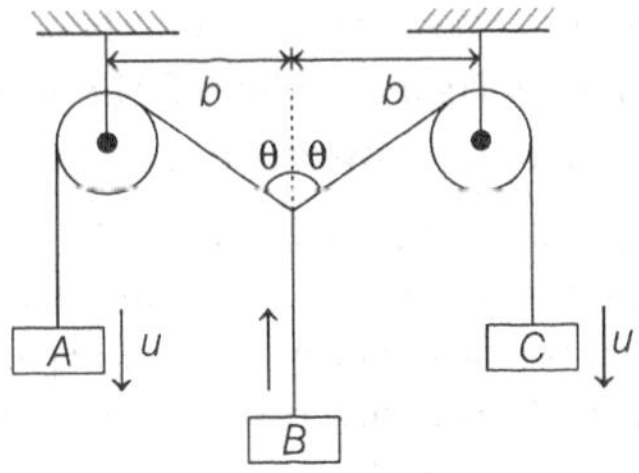

(a) $\frac{u^2}{b}\tan^2\theta\sec\theta$ (b) $\frac{u^2}{b}\tan^3\theta$
(c) $\frac{u^2}{b}\sec^3\theta\tan\theta$ (d) zero

50 In the figure shown the acceleration of A is, $\mathbf{a}_A = 15\hat{i} + 15\hat{j}$, then the acceleration of B is (A remains in contact with B)

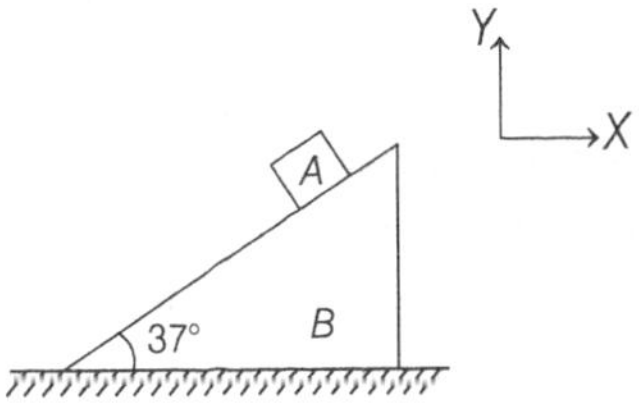

(a) $6\hat{i}$ (b) $-15\hat{i}$ (c) $-10\hat{i}$ (d) $-5\hat{i}$

Multiple Choice(s) Correct Questions

1 A situation is shown in the figure. Suppose, $M = 6m$. All the strings used are light and pulleys are light and smooth. Now select the correct alternative(s).

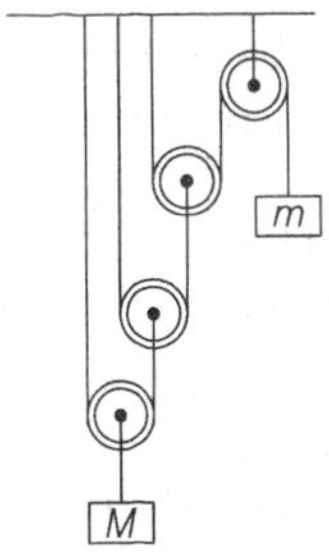

(a) Acceleration of m is $\frac{8g}{35}$ along downward.
(b) Acceleration of M is $\frac{4g}{35}$ along downward.
(c) If speed of m at some instant is v, then speed of M at that instant is $\frac{v}{4}$.
(d) If speed of m at some instant is v, then speed of M at that instant is $\frac{v}{8}$.

2 A trolley of mass 8 kg is standing on a frictionless surface inside which an object of mass 2 kg is suspended. A constant force F starts acting on the trolley as a result of which the string stood at an angle of 37° from the vertical (bob at rest relative to trolley). Then,

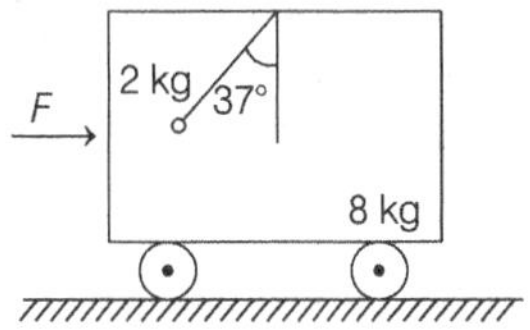

(a) acceleration of the trolley is $\frac{40}{3}$ m/s^2
(b) force applied is 60 N
(c) force applied is 75 N
(d) tension in the string is 25 N

3 In the pulley system shown in figure, the moveable pulleys A, B and C are of mass m each. D and E are fixed pulleys. The strings are light and inextensible. Choose the correct alternative(s).

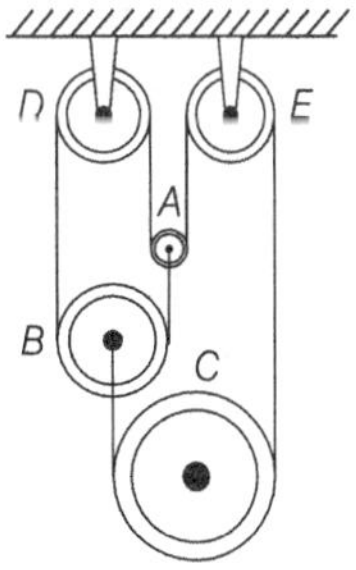

(a) Tension in the string is $\frac{5mg}{6}$.
(b) Acceleration of pulley A is $\frac{g}{3}$ downward.
(c) Acceleration of pulley B is $\frac{g}{6}$ upward.
(d) Acceleration of pulley C is $\frac{g}{3}$ upward.

4 An iron sphere weighing 10 N rests in a V-shaped smooth trough whose sides form an angle of 60° as shown in the figure. The reaction forces are R_A and R_B.

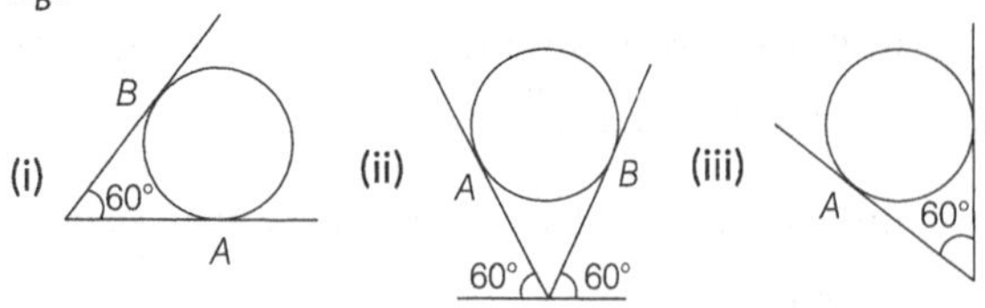

(a) $R_A = 10$ N and $R_B = 0$ in case (i)
(b) $R_A = 10$ N and $R_B = 10$ N in case (ii)
(c) $R_A = \frac{20}{\sqrt{3}}$ N and $R_B = \frac{10}{\sqrt{3}}$ N in case (iii)
(d) $R_A = 10$ N and $R_B = 10$ N in all the three cases

5 The blocks B and C in the figure have mass m each. The strings AB and BC are light, having tensions T_1 and T_2, respectively. The system is in equilibrium with a constant horizontal force mg acting on C

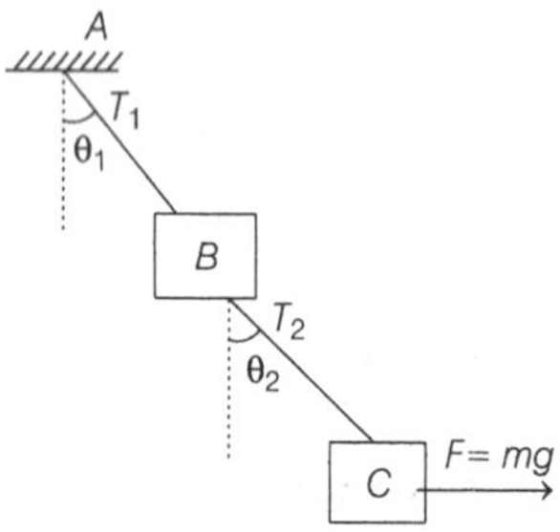

(a) $\tan\theta_1 = 2$
(b) $\tan\theta_2 = 1$
(c) $T_1 = \sqrt{5}\,mg$
(d) $T_2 = \sqrt{2}mg$

6 Two blocks A and B of mass 10 kg and 40 kg are connected by an ideal string as shown in the figure. Neglect the masses of the pulleys and effect of friction. ($g = 10$ m/s^2)

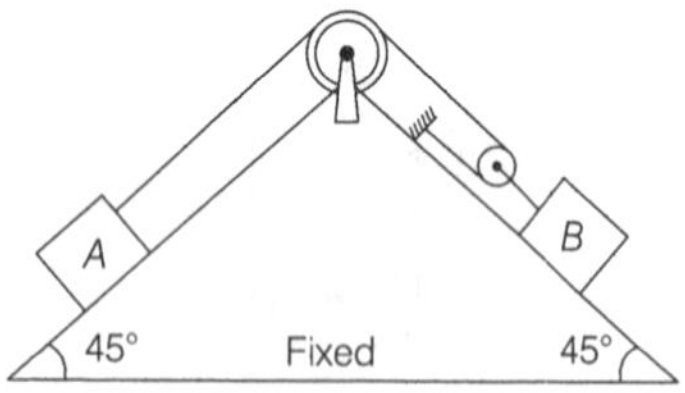

(a) The acceleration of block A is $\frac{5}{\sqrt{2}}$ ms^{-2}

(b) The acceleration of block B is $\frac{5}{2\sqrt{2}}$ ms^{-2}

(c) The tension in the string is $\frac{125}{\sqrt{2}}$ N

(d) The tension in the string is $\frac{150}{\sqrt{2}}$ N

7 A particle is found to be at rest when seen from a frame S_1 and moving with a constant velocity when seen from another frame S_2. Choose the possible options.
(a) Both the frames are inertial
(b) Both the frames are non-inertial
(c) S_1 is inertial and S_2 is non-inertial
(d) S_1 is non-inertial and S_2 is inertial

8 A block of weight 9.8 N is placed on a table. The table surface exerts an upward force of 10 N on the block. Assume, $g = 9.8$ m / s^2.
(a) The block exerts a force of 10 N on the table
(b) The block exerts a force of 19.8 N on the table
(c) The block exerts a force of 9.8 N on the table
(d) The block has an upward acceleration

9 Three blocks a, b and c of masses 10 kg, 10 kg and 20 kg respectively are arranged as shown in figure. All the surfaces are frictionless and string is inextensible. A constant force $F = 20$ N is applied on block a as shown. Pulleys and string are light. Part of the string connecting both pulleys is vertical and part of the strings connecting pulleys with masses a and b are horizontal

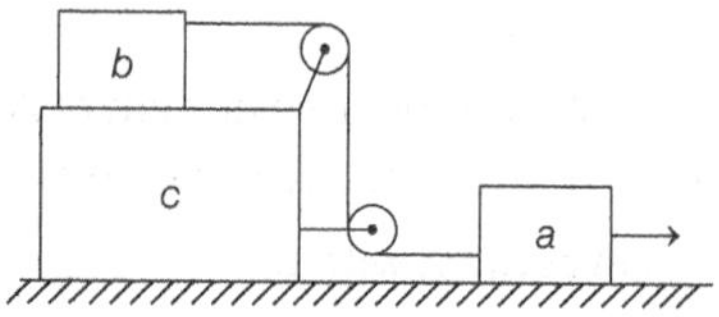

(a) Acceleration of mass blocks a, b and c is 0.5 m/s^2
(b) Acceleration of mass block b is 1 m/s^2
(c) Tension in the string is 10 N
(d) Acceleration of mass block c is 0.5 m/s^2

10 All surfaces are smooth, string is light and pulley is frictionless. At given instant, mark the correct statement(s).

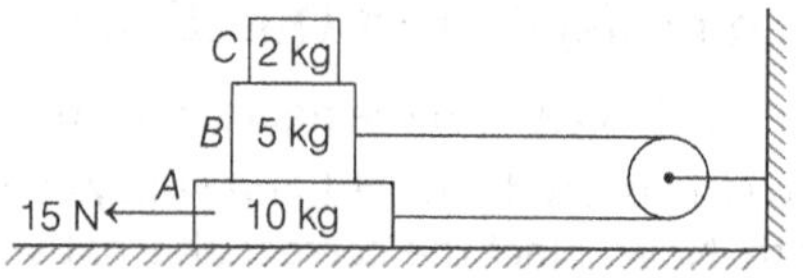

(a) Acceleration of block A is 1 m/s^2.
(b) Magnitudes of acceleration of blocks A and B are same.
(c) Acceleration of block C is zero.
(d) Tension in the string between pulley and wall is 10 N.

11 In the given diagram, pulley is frictionless and massless. Both the springs are having same force constant 10 N/m. Initially, with the string attached to the grounds, the total system is at rest. Now, if the left spring is cut, then immediately after cutting the left spring $[g = 10\ m/s^2]$

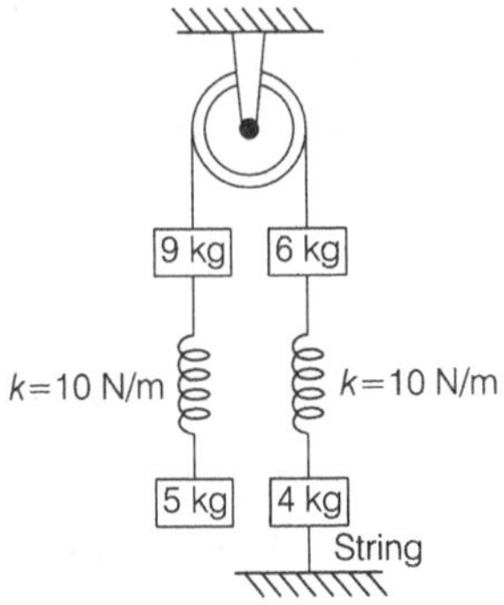

(a) acceleration of 5 kg block is zero

(b) acceleration of 6 kg block is $\frac{10}{3}\ m/s^2$

(c) tension in the string connecting 6 kg and 7 kg blocks is 120 N

(d) tension in the string connected to ground is 40 N

12 An elastic spring of force constant k and natural length $3L$ is cut into two parts, so that their natural length are $2L$ and L. One end of these parts are attached to point P and Q on a fixed vertical wall and tied with a block of mass m.

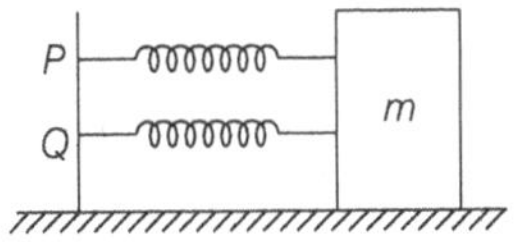

(a) In equilibrium, distance of the block from the vertical wall is $\frac{4L}{3}$

(b) In equilibrium, distance of the block from the vertical wall is $\frac{5L}{3}$

(c) The force constant of the shorter part of the spring is $3k$

(d) The force constant of the longer part of the spring is $\frac{2k}{3}$

13 A block B of mass 0.6 kg slides down the smooth face PR of a wedge A of mass 1.7 kg which can move freely on a smooth horizontal surface. The inclination of the face PR to the horizontal is 45°. Then,

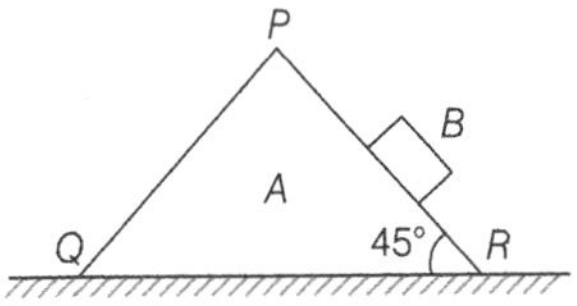

(a) the acceleration of A is $\frac{3g}{20}$

(b) the vertical component of the acceleration of B is $\frac{23g}{40}$

(c) the horizontal component of the acceleration of B is $\frac{17g}{40}$

(d) None of the above

14 In the figure shown, all the surfaces are smooth. All the blocks A, B and C are moveable. X-axis is horizontal and Y-axis vertical as shown. Just after the system is released from the position as shown,

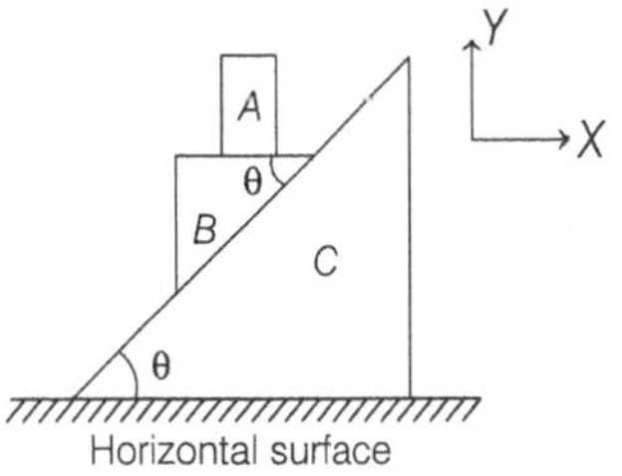

(a) acceleration of A relative to ground is in negative Y-direction

(b) acceleration of A relative to B is in positive X-direction

(c) the horizontal acceleration of B relative to ground is in negative X-direction

(d) the acceleration of B relative to ground directed along the inclined surface of C is greater than $g \sin\theta$

15 For given figure m_A is 30 kg, $m_B = m_C = 5$ kg, respectively. All contact surfaces are smooth. $(g = 10\ m/s^2)$. Select the correct statements.

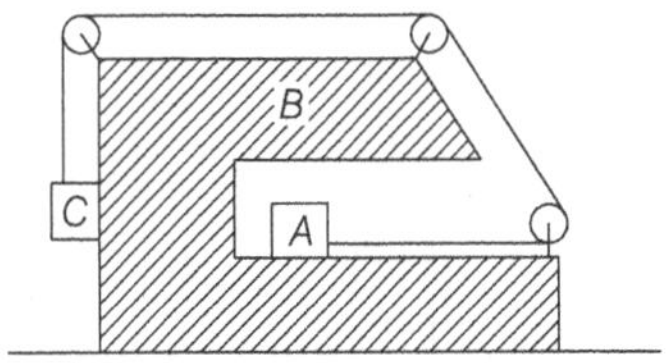

(a) Acceleration of blocks A, B and C are $1\ m/s^2$, $3\ m/s^2$ and $5\ m/s^2$, respectively.

(b) Contact force between B and ground is 350 N.

(c) Tension in string is 30 N.

(d) Contact force between B and C is 15 N.

Comprehension Based Questions

Comprehension 1

For all situations, strings are light and inextensible, all pulleys are light and smooth, all surfaces are frictionless. Find, in each case, acceleration of *A*.

1

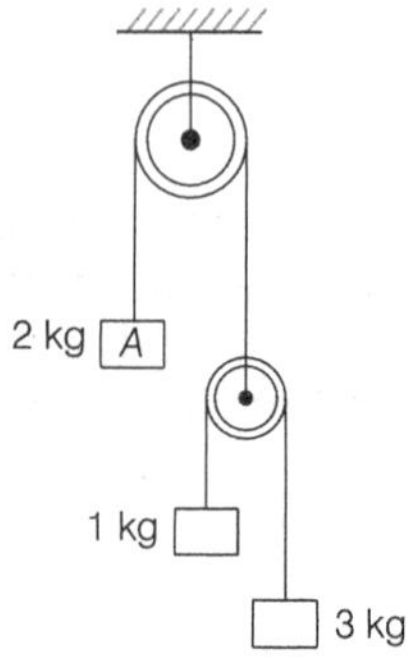

(a) $\frac{g}{5}$ down (b) $\frac{g}{5}$ up (c) $\frac{g}{3}$ down (d) $\frac{g}{3}$ up

2

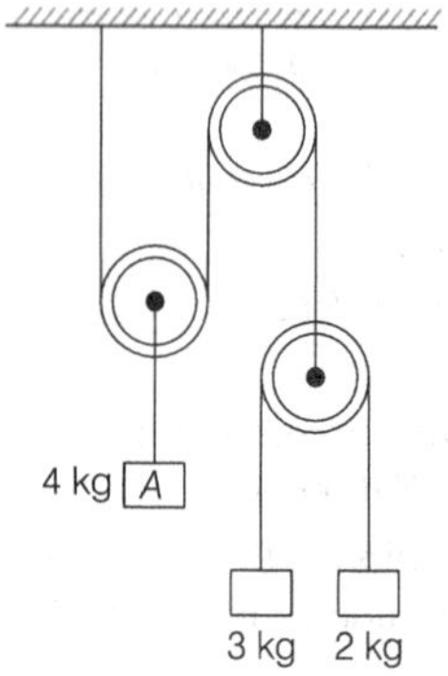

(a) $\frac{7g}{23}$ up (b) $\frac{7g}{22}$ up (c) $\frac{7g}{29}$ up (d) $\frac{g}{2}$ up

3

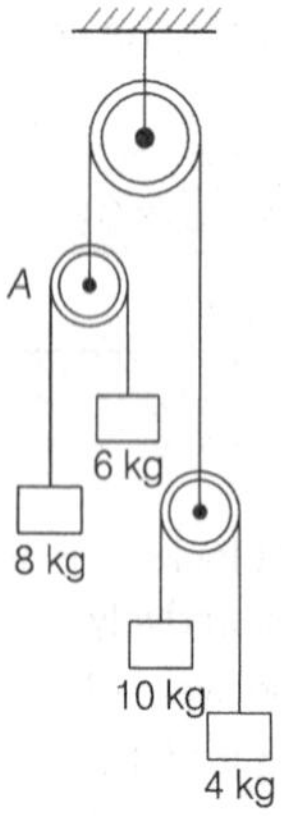

(a) $\frac{g}{10}$ down (b) $\frac{g}{11}$ down (c) $\frac{g}{13}$ down (d) $\frac{g}{17}$ up

Comprehension 2

A body of mass $m = 1.8$ kg is placed on an inclined plane, the angle of inclination is $\alpha = 37°$ and is attached to the top end of the slope with a thread which is parallel to the slope. Then, the slope is moved with a horizontal acceleration *a*. Friction is negligible.

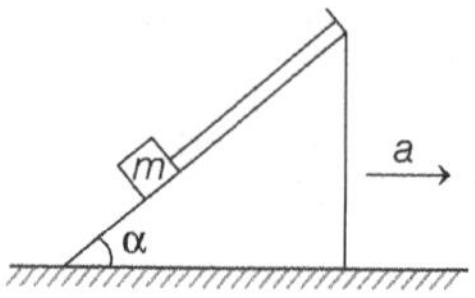

4 Find the acceleration, if the body pushes the slope with a force of $\frac{3}{4}mg$.

(a) $\frac{5}{3}$ m/s^2 (b) 0.5 m/s^2
(c) 0.75 m/s^2 (d) $\frac{5}{6}$ m/s^2

5 In the above question, also find the tension in thread.

(a) 12 N (b) 10 N
(c) 8 N (d) 4 N

6 At what acceleration will the body lose contact with plane?

(a) $\frac{40}{3}$ m/s^2 (b) 7.5 m/s^2
(c) 10 m/s^2 (d) 5 m/s^2

Comprehension 3

Two smooth blocks are placed at a smooth corner as shown. Both the blocks are having mass *m*. We apply a force *F* on the small block *m*. Block *A* presses the block *B* in the normal direction, due to which pressing force on vertical wall will increase, and pressing force on the horizontal wall decrease, as we increase *F*. As soon as the pressing force on the horizontal wall by block *B* becomes zero, it will loose the contact with the ground. If the value of *F* is further increased, the block *B* will accelerate in upward direction and simultaneously the block *A* will move towards right. ($\theta = 37°$ with horizontal)

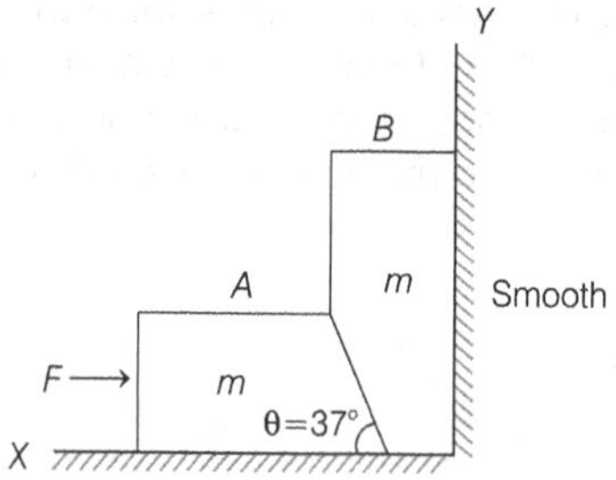

7 What is minimum value of F to lift block B from ground?

(a) $\frac{25}{12}mg$ (b) $\frac{5}{4}mg$

(c) $\frac{3}{4}mg$ (d) $\frac{4}{3}mg$

8 If both the blocks are stationary, the force exerted by ground on block A is

(a) $mg+\frac{3F}{4}$ (b) $mg-\frac{3F}{4}$

(c) $mg+\frac{4F}{3}$ (d) $mg-\frac{4F}{3}$

9 If acceleration of block A is 'a' rightward, then acceleration of block B will be

(a) $\frac{3a}{4}$ upwards (b) $\frac{4a}{3}$ upwards

(c) $\frac{3a}{5}$ upwards (d) $\frac{4a}{5}$ upwards

Comprehension 4

Two blocks A and B of equal masses m kg each are connected by a light thread, which passes over a massless pulley as shown. Both the blocks lie on wedge of mass m kg. Assume friction to be absent everywhere and both the blocks to be always in contact with the wedge. The wedge lying over smooth horizontal surface is pulled towards right with constant acceleration a (m/s^2). (g is acceleration due to gravity).

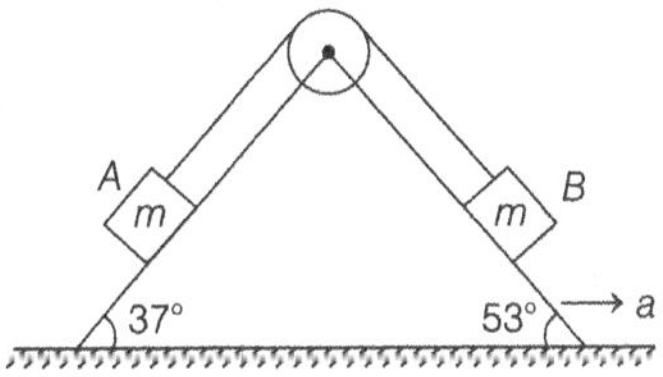

10 Normal reaction (in N) acting on block A is

(a) $\frac{m}{5}(3g+4a)$ (b) $\frac{m}{5}(3g-4a)$

(c) $\frac{m}{5}(4g+3a)$ (d) $\frac{m}{5}(4g-3a)$

11 Normal reaction (in N) acting on block B.

(a) $\frac{m}{5}(3g+4a)$ (b) $\frac{m}{5}(3g-4a)$

(c) $\frac{m}{5}(4g+3a)$ (d) $\frac{m}{5}(4g-3a)$

12 The maximum value of acceleration a (in m/s^2) for which normal reactions acting on the block A and block B are non-zero, is

(a) $\frac{3}{4}g$ (b) $\frac{4}{3}g$ (c) $\frac{3}{5}g$ (d) $\frac{5}{3}g$

Comprehension 5

Masses of blocks A, B and C are 7 kg, 4 kg and 1 kg, respectively. String and pulleys are ideal. All surfaces are smooth. Answer the following questions.

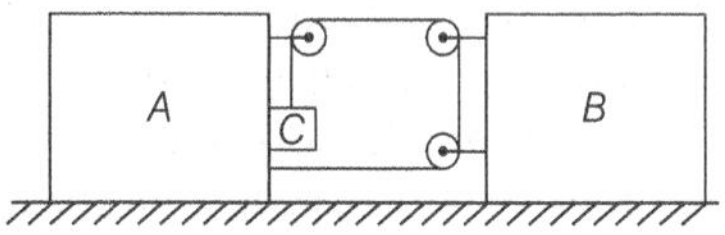

13 Find tension in the string.

(a) 4 N (b) 5 N (c) 6 N (d) 8 N

14 Find acceleration of block B.

(a) 2 m/s^2 (b) 2.5 m/s^2

(c) 3 m/s^2 (d) 4 m/s^2

15 Find acceleration of block C.

(a) 6 m/s^2 (b) $\sqrt{26}$ m/s^2

(c) $\sqrt{37}$ m/s^2 (d) $\sqrt{60}$ m/s^2

Comprehension 6

The system shown adjacent is in equilibrium. Find the acceleration of the blocks A, B and C all of equal masses m at the instant (Assume springs to be ideal)

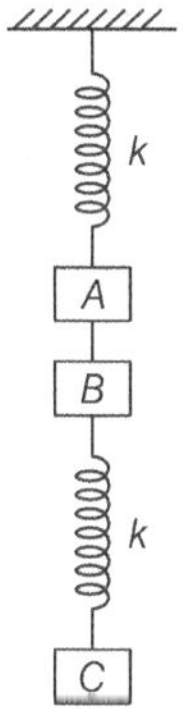

16 when the spring between ceiling and A is cut.

(a) $a_A=a_B=g\downarrow; a_C=0$ (b) $a_A=a_B=\frac{3g}{2}\downarrow; a_C=0$

(c) $a_A=g\downarrow; a_B=a_C=0$ (d) $a_A=\frac{3g}{2}\downarrow; a_B=a_C=0$

17 when the string (inextensible) between A and B is cut.

(a) $a_A=g\uparrow, a_B=g\downarrow, a_C=0$

(b) $a_A=2g\uparrow, a_B=g\downarrow, a_c=g\downarrow$

(c) $a_A=2g\uparrow, a_B=2g\downarrow, a_C=0$

(d) $a_A=g\downarrow, a_B=2g\uparrow, a_c=0$

18 when the spring between B and C is cut.

(a) $a_A=a_B=\frac{g}{2}\downarrow, a_C=g\downarrow$ (b) $a_A=a_B=g\uparrow, a_C=g\downarrow$

(c) $a_A=g\uparrow, a_B=g\downarrow, a_C=0$ (d) $a_A=a_B=\frac{g}{2}\downarrow, a_C=0$

Comprehension 7

In the arrangement shown in figure, a wedge of mass $m_3 = 3.45$ kg is placed on a smooth horizontal surface. A small and light pulley is connected on its top edge. A light flexible thread passes over the pulley. The blocks having mass $m_1 = 1.3$ kg and $m_2 = 1.5$kg are connected at the end of the thread, m_1 is on smooth horizontal surface and m_2 rests on inclined surface of the wedge. All surfaces are smooth, $g = 10\ \text{m/s}^2$. If the whole system is released from rest, calculate

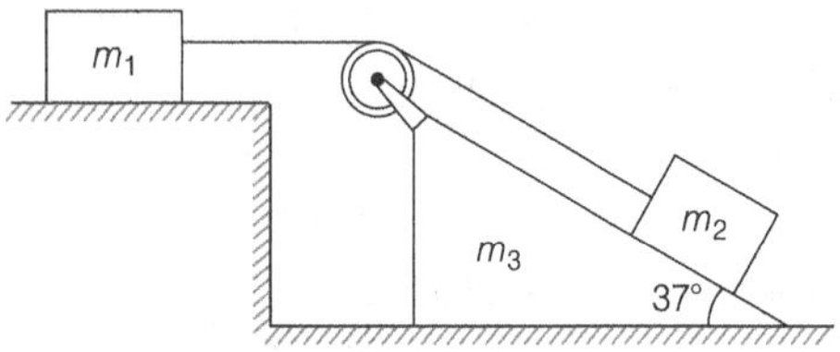

19 the tension in the string.
(a) 1.9 N (b) 2.9 N (c) 3.9 N (d) 4.9 N

20 the acceleration of m_1.
(a) $2\ \text{m/s}^2$ (b) $3\ \text{m/s}^2$
(c) $4\ \text{m/s}^2$ (d) $5\ \text{m/s}^2$

21 the acceleration of m_3.
(a) $2\ \text{m/s}^2$ (b) $3\ \text{m/s}^2$
(c) $4\ \text{m/s}^2$ (d) $5\ \text{m/s}^2$

Match the Columns Questions

1 Match the column I with column II

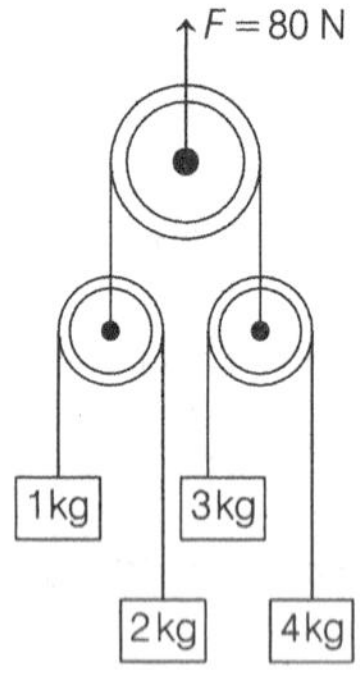

Column I	Column II
(A) 1 kg block	(P) will remain stationary
(B) 2 kg block	(Q) will move down
(C) 3 kg block	(R) will move up
(D) 4 kg block	(S) has acceleration $5\ \text{m/s}^2$

2 All surfaces are smooth. If *A*, *B* and *C* all have the same mass *m*, then match the **Column I** with **Column II.**

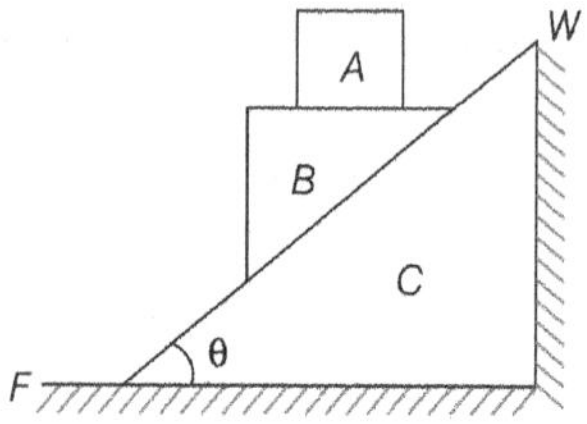

Column I	Column II
(A) N_{AB}	(P) $N_{BC} \sin\theta$
(B) N_{BC}	(Q) $mg\dfrac{(2+\cos^2\theta)}{1+\sin^2\theta}$
(C) N_{CW}	(R) $\dfrac{mg\cos^2\theta}{1+\sin^2\theta}$
(D) N_{FC}	(S) $\dfrac{2mg\cos\theta}{1+\sin^2\theta}$

3 **Column I** gives four different situations involving two blocks of mass m_1 and m_2 placed in different ways on a smooth horizontal surface as shown. In each of the situations horizontal forces F_1 and F_2 are applied on blocks of mass m_1 and m_2 respectively and also $m_2F_1 < m_1F_2$.

Match the statements in **Column I** with corresponding results in **Column II.**

Column I	Column II
(A) 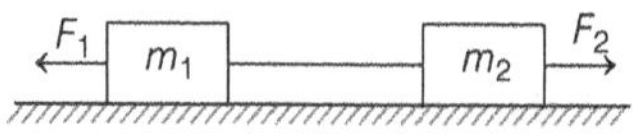 Both the blocks are connected by massless inelastic string. The magnitude of tension in the string is	(P) $\dfrac{m_1m_2}{m_1+m_2}\left(\dfrac{F_1}{m_1}-\dfrac{F_2}{m_2}\right)$
(B) 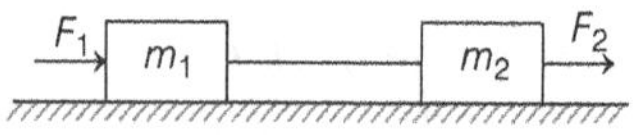 Both the blocks are connected by massless inelastic string. The magnitude of tension in the string is	(Q) $\dfrac{m_1m_2}{m_1+m_2}\left(\dfrac{F_1}{m_1}+\dfrac{F_2}{m_2}\right)$
(C) 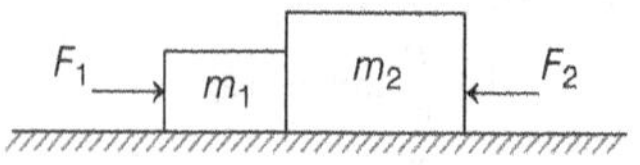 The magnitude of normal reaction between the blocks is	(R) $\dfrac{m_1m_2}{m_1+m_2}\left(\dfrac{F_2}{m_2}-\dfrac{F_1}{m_1}\right)$
(D) 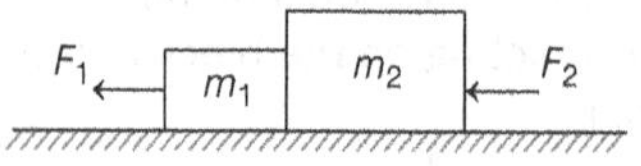 The magnitude of normal reaction between the blocks is	(S) $m_1m_2\left(\dfrac{F_1+F_2}{m_1+m_2}\right)$

4 The system shown in figure is initially in equilibrium. The masses of blocks *A*, *B*, *C*, *D* and *E* are 3*m*, 3*m*, 2*m*, 2*m* and 2*m*, respectively. Match the condition in **Column I** with the immediately effects in **Column II.**

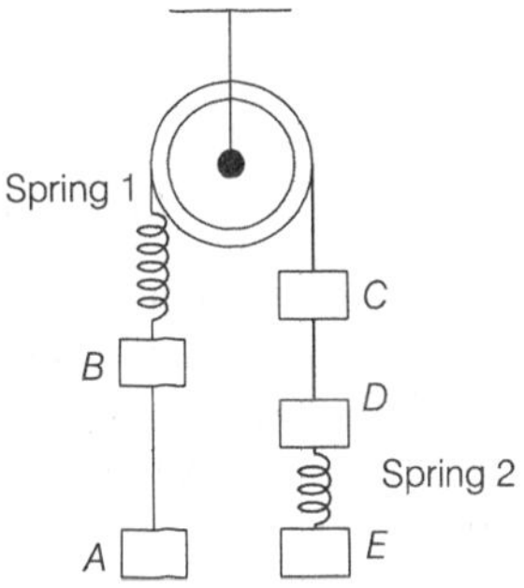

Column I	Column II
(A) After spring 2 is cut, tension in string *AB*	(P) increases
(B) After spring 2 is cut, tension in string *CD*	(Q) decreases
(C) After string between *C* and pulley is cut, tension in string *AB*	(R) does not change
(D) After string between *C* and pulley is cut, tension in string *CD*	(S) is zero

Numerical Value Questions

1 The system starts from rest and *A* attains a velocity of 5 m/s after it has moved 5 m towards right. Assuming the arrangement to be frictionless everywhere and pulley and strings to be light, find the value of the constant force *F* (in N) applied on *A*. $(g = 10 \text{ m/s}^2)$

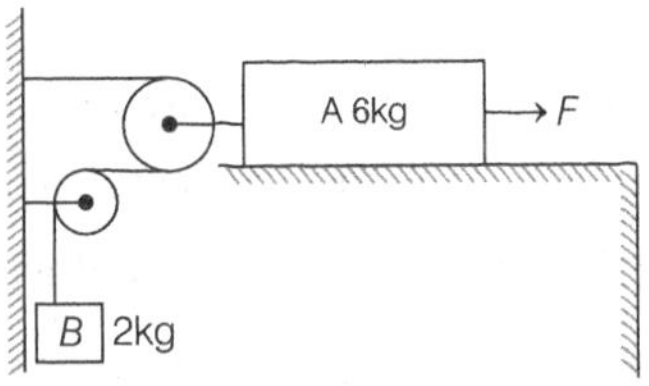

2 In the figure shown, string is winding on the motor shaft with velocity 5 m/s. Find velocity of platform (in m/s).

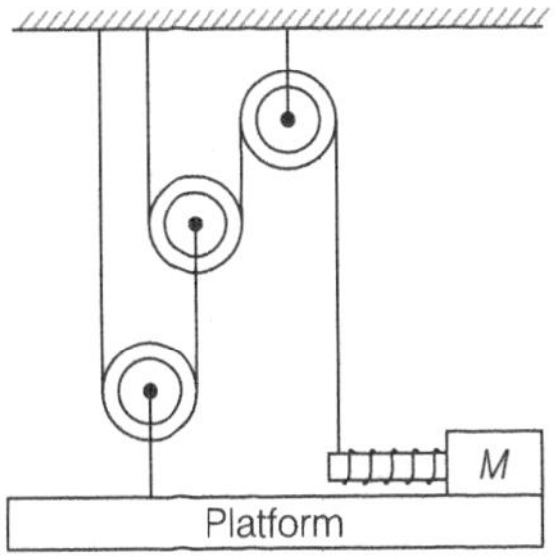

3 A smooth ring *A* of mass *m* can slide on a fixed horizontal rod. A string tied to the ring passes over a fixed pulley *B* and carries a block *C* of mass 2*m* as shown in figure. At an instant the string between the ring and the pulley makes an angle θ with the rod. Find acceleration (in m/s^2) of ring, if the system is released from rest with $\theta = 60°$. $(g = 10 \text{ m/s}^2)$

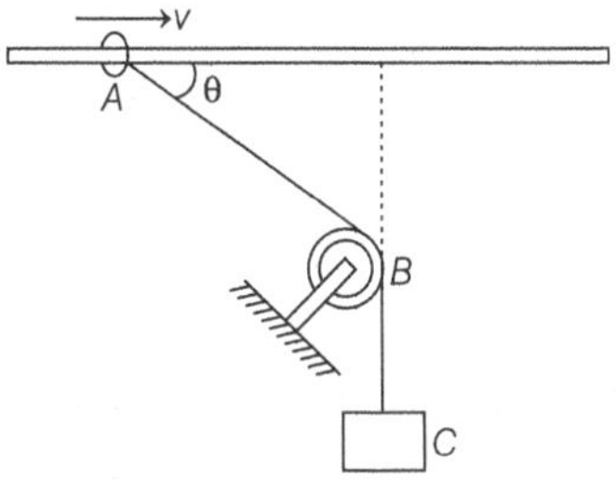

4 Two masses *A* and *B*, lie on a frictionless table. They are attached to either end of a light rope which passes around a horizontal moveable pulley of negligible mass. $M_A = 1 \text{ kg}, M_B = 2 \text{ kg}, M_C = 4 \text{ kg}$. The pulley P_2 is vertical.Find the acceleration (in m/s^2) of block *C*.

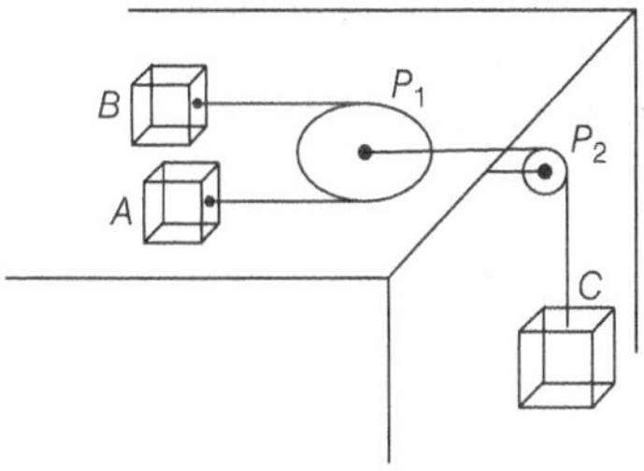

5 One end of a light inextensible string is attached to a ceiling. The string passes under a smooth light pulley carrying a weight *C* and then over a fixed smooth light pulley. To the free end of the string is attached a light scale pan in which two weights *A* and *B* are placed with *A* on top of *B* as shown. The portions of the string not in contact with the pulleys are vertical. Each of the weights *A* and *B* has a mass *M* and the weight *C* has a mass 5*M*. If the system is released from rest, the reaction force between the weights *A* and *B* is $\frac{\beta Mg}{13}$. Find β.

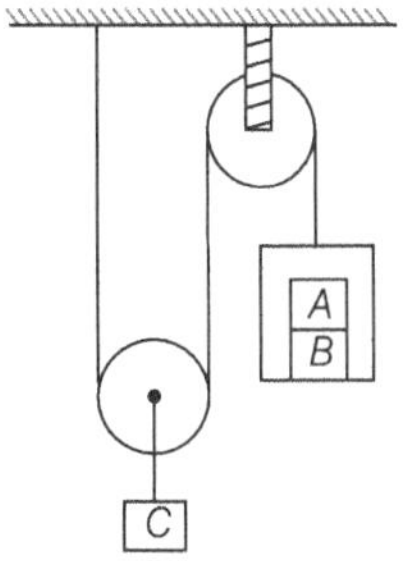

6 Blocks A, B and C have masses $2m$, $4m$ and m, respectively. Assume that the surfaces and the pulleys P_1 and P_2 are all smooth and pulleys and string are light. Acceleration of block B is $\frac{F}{\lambda m}$. Find λ.

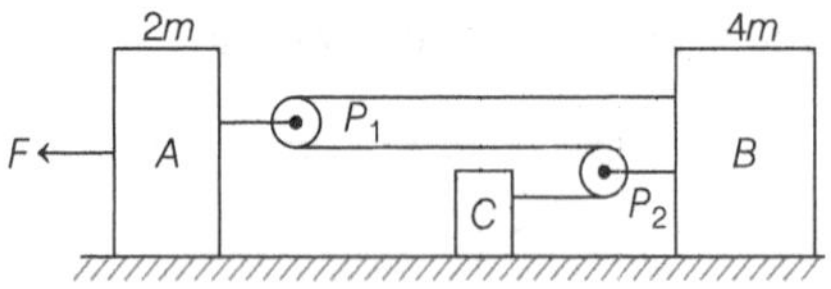

7 In the situation shown in figure pulleys P_1, P_2 and P_4 are fixed and pulley P_3 is moving horizontally with 10 m/s. Find speed of block B in m/s.

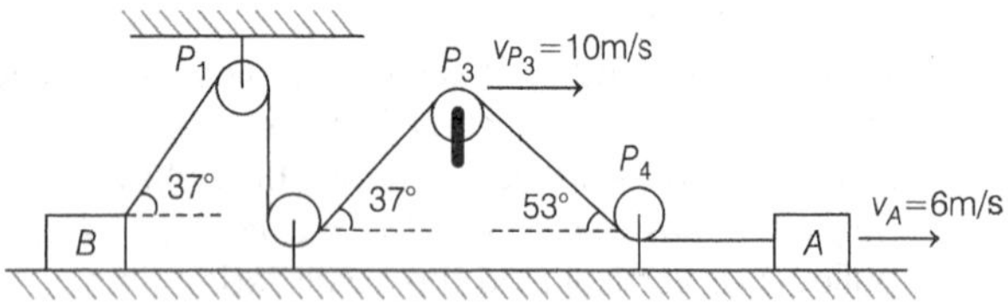

8 The system shown in figure is in equilibrium, find the tension (in N) in the string connecting 1 kg and 1 kg blocks just after string S is cut.

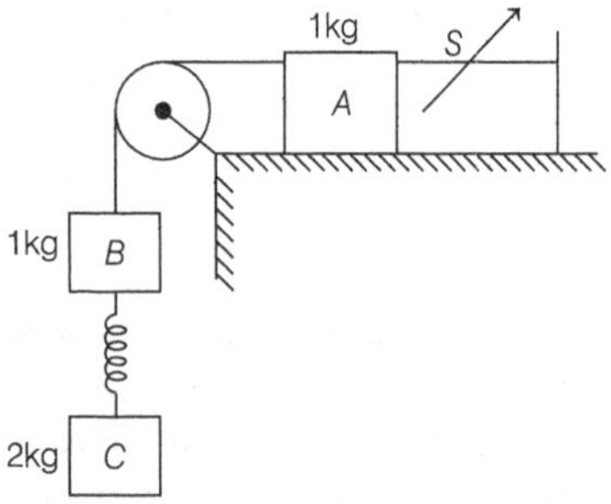

9 In the figure shown, pulley and spring are ideal and strings are light and inextensible. Initially all the bodies are at rest when string connecting A and B is cut. Find initial acceleration (in m/s^2) of pulley.

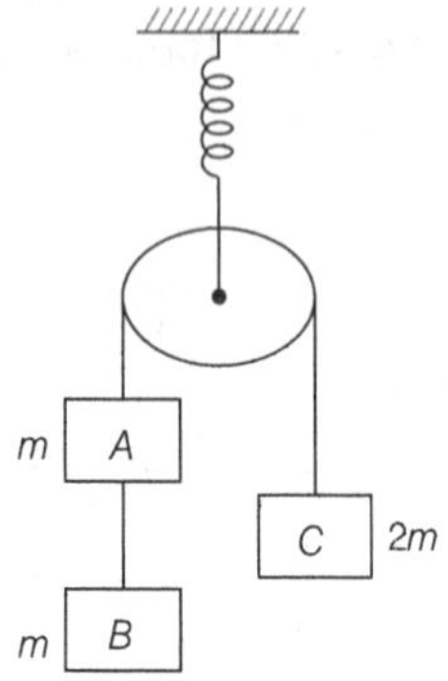

10 The system is in equilibrium. There is no friction anywhere. Spring, string, pulley are massless. Spring compression is x cm. Find x.

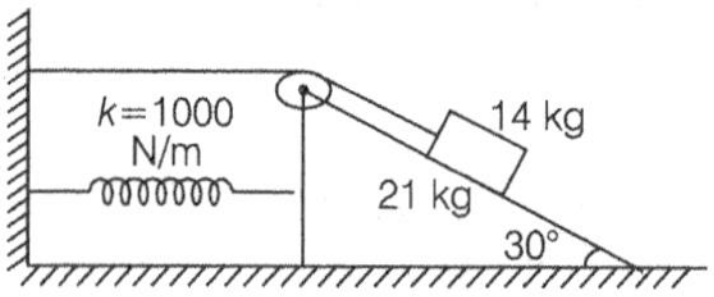

11 Figure shows a ball of mass m connected with two ideal springs of force constant k, kept in equilibrium on a smooth incline, suddenly right spring is cut. What is the magnitude of instantaneous acceleration (in m/s^2) of ball?

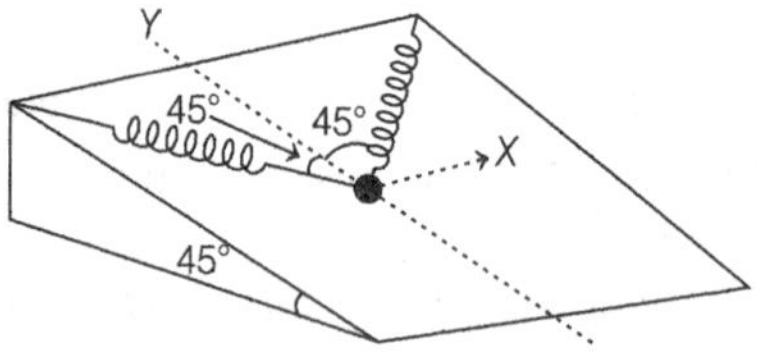

12 A small block of mass $m = 1$ kg is pulled on a frictionless horizontal surface by means of a light rope at a rate of $u = 10$ m/s with a pulley situated at a height h (= 10 m) above the level of block. The block was initially placed at a very large distance from the pulley. If the angle θ of rope with horizontal, when the block leaves the surface is $\frac{2\pi}{n}$, then find n.

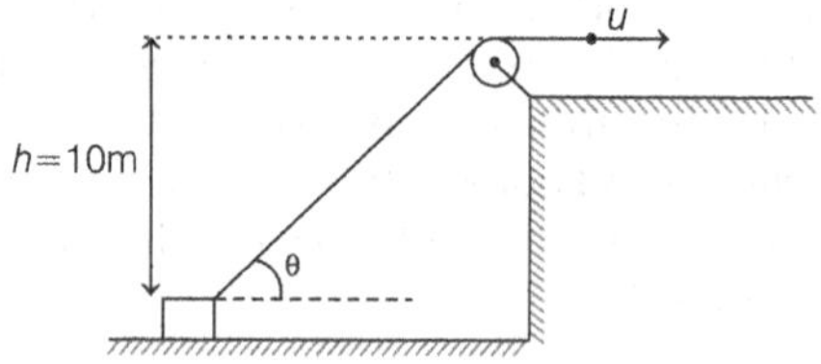

13 In the figure shown P_1 and P_2 are massless pulleys. P_1 is fixed and P_2 can move. Masses of A, B and C are $\frac{9m}{64}$, $2m$ and m, respectively. All contacts are smooth and the string is massless. Find the acceleration (in m/s^2) of block C. $\left[\theta = \tan^{-1}\left(\frac{3}{4}\right)\right]$

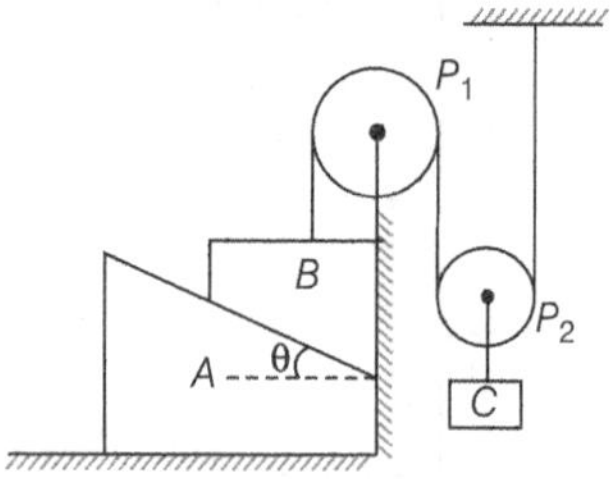

14 In the figure shown C is a fixed wedge. A block B is kept on the inclined surface of the wedge C. Another block A is inserted in a slot in the block B as shown in figure. A light inextensible string passes over a light pulley which is fixed to the block B through a light rod. One end of the string is fixed and other end of the string is fixed to A. S is a fixed support on the wedge. All the surfaces are smooth. Masses of A and B are same. If the magnitude of acceleration of A is $\frac{\sqrt{n}}{3}$ m/s^2, then find n. $\left(\sin 37° = \frac{3}{5}\right)$

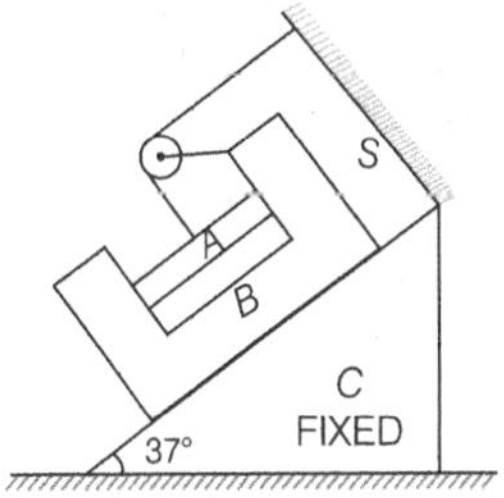

15 Two particles A and B of masses 3 kg and 2 kg are connected by a light inextensible string. The particles are in contact with the smooth faces of a wedge DCE of mass 10 kg resting on a smooth horizontal plane. When the system is moving freely, find the acceleration (in m/s^2) of the wedge.

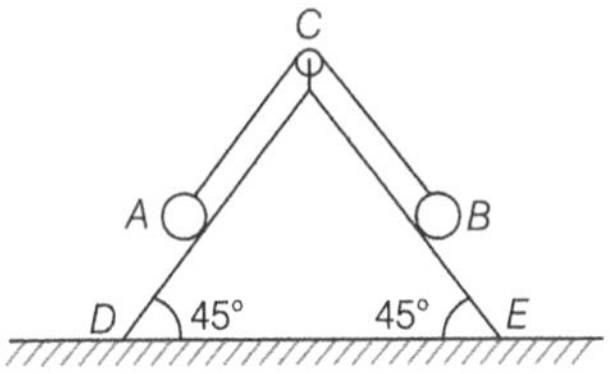

16 A system is shown in the figure. All contact surfaces are smooth and string is tight and inextensible. Wedge A moves towards right with speed 10 m/s and velocity of B relative to A is in downward direction along the incline having magnitude 5 m/s. If the velocity of block C is $2\sqrt{p}$ m/s, then find p.

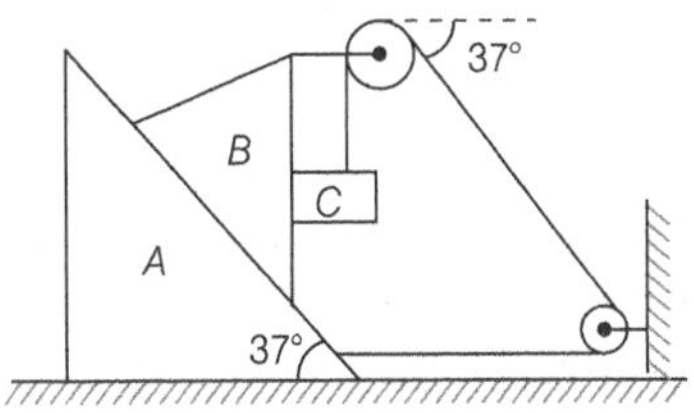

17 All surfaces are smooth. The system is released from rest. If initial acceleration of 5 kg block is $\frac{g}{\eta}$. Find η.

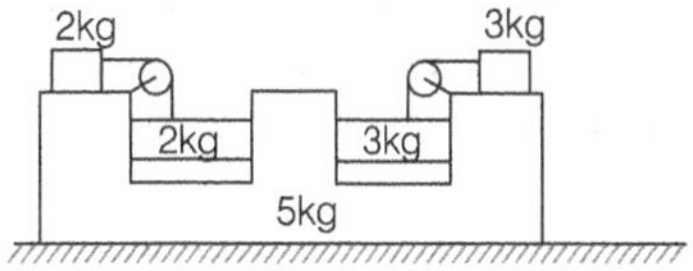

18 The smooth cylindrical bars weighing $20\sqrt{3}$ N each lie next to each other in contact. A similar third bar is placed over the two bars as shown in figure. Find the minimum horizontal force (in newton) on each lower bar necessary to keep them in contact. Neglect friction everywhere.

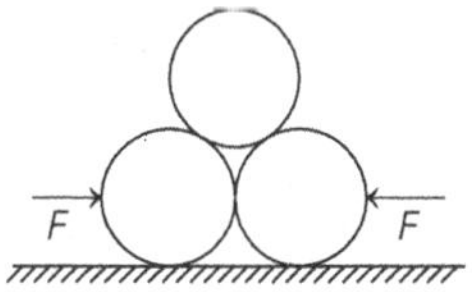

19 In the given situation all surfaces are frictionless. Both blocks have mass M. If $F = \frac{Mg}{2}$ then ratio of accelerations of blocks A and B is $\frac{n}{\sqrt{5}}$. Find n.

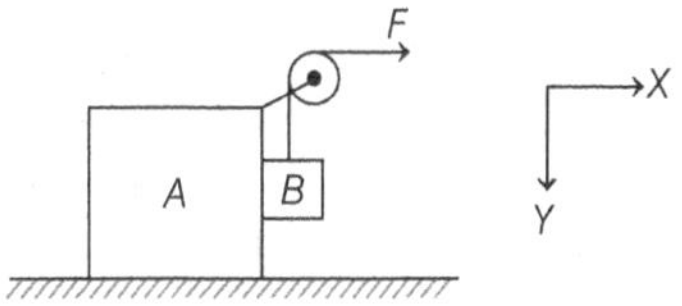

20 System is shown in the figure. All the surfaces are smooth. Rod is moved by external agent with acceleration 9 m/s^2 vertically downwards. Find the force (in newton) exerted on the ground by the wedge.

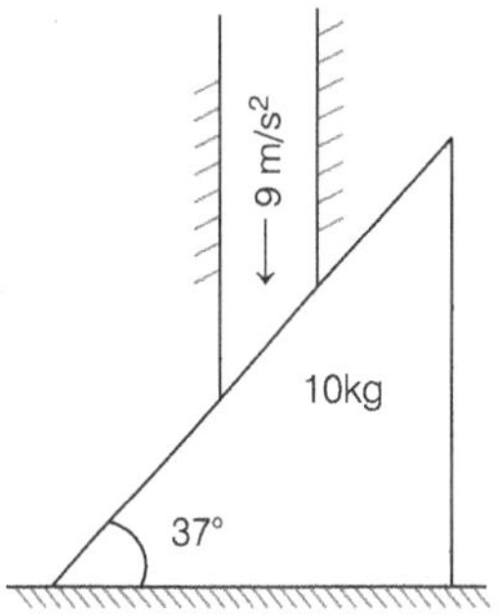

Previous Year's Questions

JEE Main

1 All surfaces shown in figure are assumed to be frictionless and the pulleys and the string are light. The acceleration of the block of mass 2 kg is [2024, 30 Jan Shift-I]

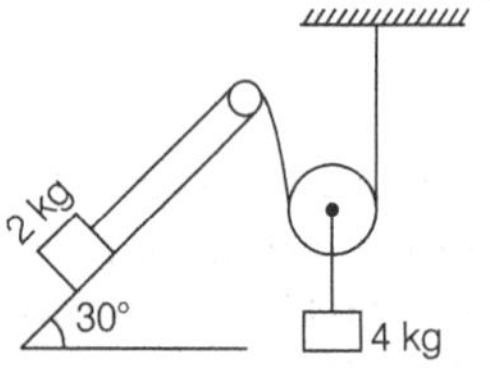

(a) $\frac{g}{3}$ (b) g
(c) $\frac{g}{2}$ (d) $\frac{g}{4}$

2 Three blocks A, B and C are pulled on a horizontal smooth surface by a force of 80 N as shown in figure

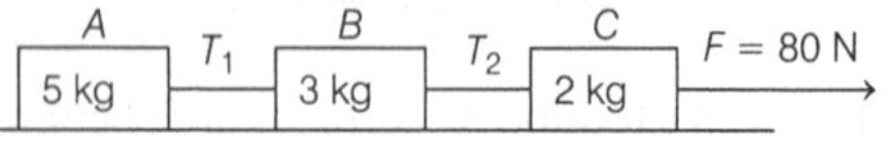

The tensions T_1 and T_2 in the string are respectively [2024, 30 Jan Shift-II]

(a) 60 N, 80 N (b) 88 N, 96 N
(c) 40 N, 64 N (d) 80 N, 100 N

3 An average force of 125 N is applied on a machine gun firing bullets each of mass 10 g at the speed of 250 m/s to keep it in position. The number of bullets fired per second by the machine gun is [2023, 11 April Shift-I]

(a) 25 (b) 5
(c) 50 (d) 100

4 Three forces $F_1 = 10$ N, $F_2 = 8$ N, $F_3 = 6$ N are acting on a particle of mass 5 kg. The forces F_2 and F_3 are applied perpendicularly, so that particle remains at rest. If the force F_1 is removed, then the acceleration of the particle is [2023, 12 April Shift-I]

(a) 0.5 ms^{-2} (b) 4.8 ms^{-2}
(c) 2 ms^{-2} (d) 7 ms^{-2}

5 The position vector of a particle related to time t is given by $\mathbf{r} = (10t\hat{\mathbf{i}} + 15t^2\hat{\mathbf{j}} + 7\hat{\mathbf{k}})$ m

The direction of net force experienced by the particle is [2023, 15 April Shift-I]

(a) Positive X-axis (b) Positive Z-axis
(c) Positive Y-axis (d) In x-y plane

6 The figure represents the momentum time (p-t) curve for a particle moving along an axis under the influence of a force. Identify the regions on the graph where the magnitude of the force is maximum and minimum respectively? [2023, 30 Jan Shift-I]

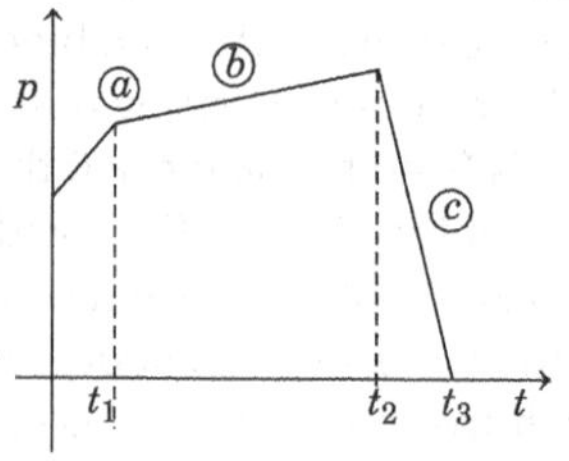

(a) a and b (b) c and b (c) c and a (d) b and c

7 As shown in figure, a 70 kg garden roller is pushed with a force of $\mathbf{F} = 200$ N at an angle of 30° with horizontal. The normal reaction on the roller is (Given, $g = 10$ ms^{-2}) [2023, 31 Jan Shift-I]

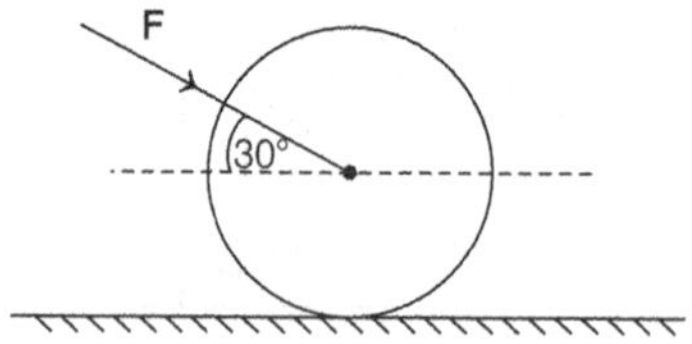

(a) $800\sqrt{2}$ N (b) 800 N (c) $200\sqrt{3}$ N (d) 600 N

8 A block of $\sqrt{3}$ kg is attached to a string whose other end is attached to the wall. An unknown force F is applied so that the string makes an angle of 30° with the wall. The tension T is (Given, $g = 10$ ms^{-2}) [2023, 30 Jan Shift-II]

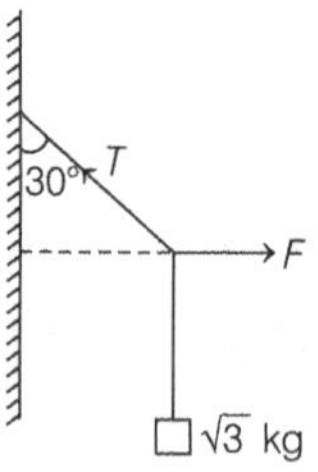

(a) 15 N (b) 25 N (c) 10 N (d) 20 N

9 A balloon has mass of 10 g in air. The air escapes from the balloon at a uniform rate with velocity 4.5 cm/s. If the balloon shrinks in 5 s completely, the average force acting on that balloon will be (in dyne). [2022, 28 July Shift-I]

(a) 3 (b) 9
(c) 12 (d) 18

10 A ball of mass 0.15 kg hits the wall with its initial speed of 12 ms^{-1} and bounces back without changing its initial speed. If the force applied by the wall on the ball during the contact is 100 N, calculate the time duration of the contact of ball with the wall. [2022, 26 July Shift-II]

(a) 0.018 s (b) 0.036 s
(c) 0.009 s (d) 0.072 s

11 A block A takes 2 s to slide down a frictionless incline of 30° and length l kept inside a lift going up with uniform velocity v. If the incline is changed to 45°, the time taken by the block, to slide down the incline, will be approximately. [2022, 27 July Shift-II]

(a) 2.66 s (b) 0.83 s
(c) 1.68 s (d) 0.70 s

12 In the arrangement shown in figure a_1, a_2, a_3 and a_4 are the accelerations of masses m_1, m_2, m_3 and m_4, respectively. Which of the following relation is true for this arrangement? [2022, 26 June Shift-II]

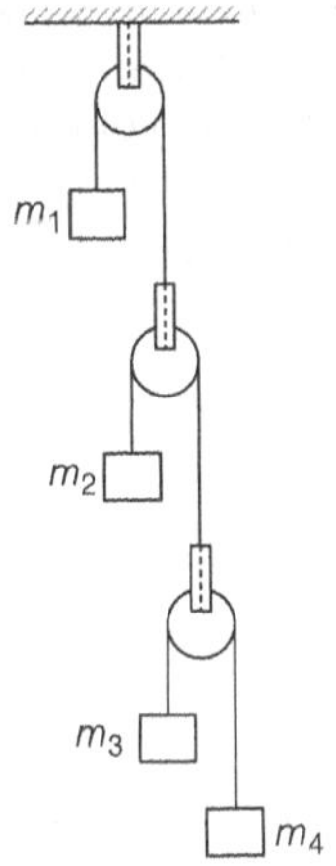

(a) $4a_1 + 2a_2 + a_3 + a_4 = 0$
(b) $a_1 + 4a_2 + 3a_3 + a_4 = 0$
(c) $a_1 + 4a_2 + 3a_3 + 2a_4 = 0$
(d) $2a_1 + 2a_2 + 3a_3 + a_4 = 0$

13 A block of metal weighing 2 kg is resting on a frictionless plane (as shown in figure). It is struck by a jet releasing water at a rate of 1 kg s^{-1} and at a speed of 10 m s^{-1}. Then, the initial acceleration of the block, in m s^{-2}, will be [2022, 29 June Shift-I]

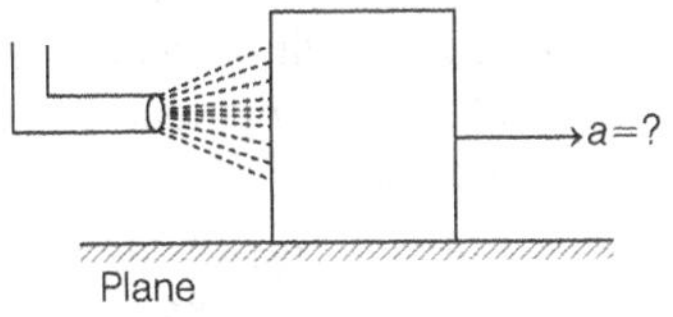

(a) 3 (b) 6 (c) 5 (d) 4

14 A block of mass M placed inside a box descends vertically with acceleration a. The block exerts a force equal to one-fourth of its weight on the floor of the box. The value of a will be [2022, 29 June Shift-I]

(a) $\frac{g}{4}$ (b) $\frac{g}{2}$
(c) $\frac{3g}{4}$ (d) g

15 A pressure-pump has a horizontal tube of cross sectional area 10 cm^2 for the outflow of water at a speed of 20 m/s. The force exerted on the vertical wall just in front of the tube which stops water horizontally flowing out of the tube, is
[Given : density of water = 1000 kg/m^3] [2022, 28 July Shift-II]

(a) 300 N (b) 500 N (c) 250 N (d) 400 N

16 A uniform metal chain of mass m and length L passes over a massless and frictionless pulley. It is released from rest with a part of its length l is hanging on one side and rest of its length $L-l$ is hanging on the other side of the pulley. At a certain point of time, when $l = \frac{L}{x}$, the acceleration of the chain is $\frac{g}{2}$. The value of x is .... [2022, 28 July Shift-II]

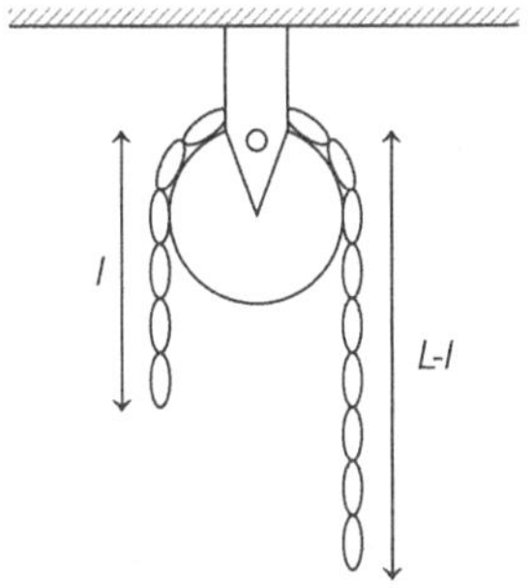

(a) 6 (b) 2
(c) 1.5 (d) 4

17 A force on an object of mass 100g is $(10\hat{i} + 5\hat{j})$ N. The position of that object at $t = 2$ s is $(a\hat{i} + b\hat{j})$ m after starting from rest.
The value of a/b will be.... [2022, 25 June Shift-I]

18 Four forces are acting at a point P in the equilibrium as shown in figure. The ratio of force F_1 to F_2 is $1 : x$, where x is [2022, 25July Shift-I]

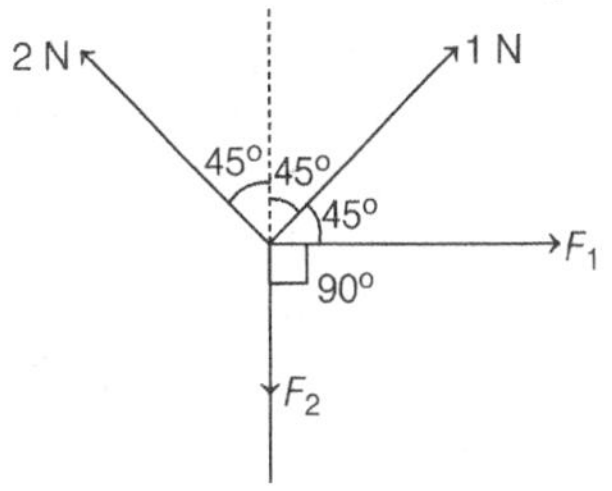

19 A mass of 10 kg is suspended vertically by a rope of length 5m from the roof. A force of 30 N is applied at the middle point of rope in horizontal direction. The angle made by upper half of the rope with vertical is $\theta = \tan^{-1}(x \times 10^{-1})$. The value of x is ______ . (Given, $g = 10$ m/s^2) [2022, 27 June Shift-II]

20 A system of 10 balls each of mass 2 kg are connected *via* massless and unstretchable string. The system is allowed to slip over the edge of a smooth table as shown in figure. Tension on the string between the 7th and 8th ball is ...... N, when 6th ball just leaves the table. **[2022, 26 June Shift-II]**

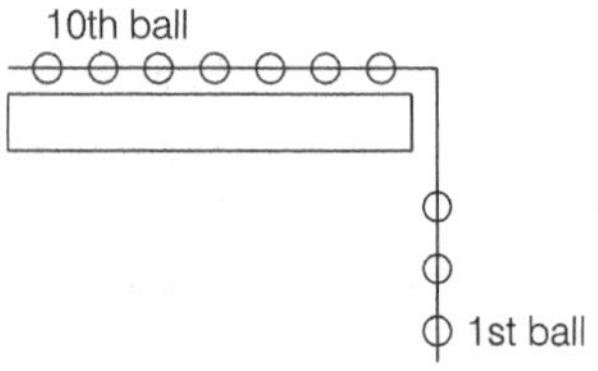

21 A block of mass 200 g is kept stationary on a smooth inclined plane by applying a minimum horizontal force $F = \sqrt{x}N$ as shown in figure. The value of $x =$ .... **[2022, 25 June Shift-II]**

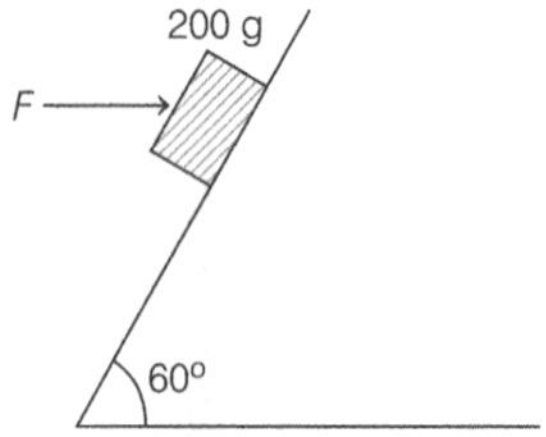

22 Two masses A and B, each of mass M are fixed together by a massless spring. A force acts on the mass B as shown in figure. If the mass A starts moving away from mass B with acceleration a, then the acceleration of mass B will be **[2021, 26 Feb Shift-II]**

(a) $\frac{Ma-F}{M}$ (b) $\frac{MF}{F+Ma}$

(c) $\frac{F+Ma}{M}$ (d) $\frac{F-Ma}{M}$

23 A bullet of mass 0.1 kg is fired on a wooden block to pierce through it, but it stops after moving a distance of 50 cm into it. If the velocity of bullet before hitting the wood is 10 m/s and it slows down with uniform deceleration, then the magnitude of effective retarding force on the bullet is x N. The value of x to the nearest integer is .... **[2021, 18 March Shift-I]**

24 A body of mass 2 kg moves under a force of $(2\hat{i}+3\hat{j}+5\hat{k})$N. It starts from rest and was at the origin initially. After 4 s, its new coordinates are $(8, b, 20)$. The value of b is .... (Round off to the nearest integer) **[2021, 16 March Shift-II]**

25 A boy pushes a box of mass 2 kg with a force $\mathbf{F} = (20\hat{i}+10\hat{j})$ N on a frictionless surface. If the box was initially at rest, then .... m is displacement along the X-axis after 10 s. **[2021, 26 Feb Shift-I]**

26 A block of mass m slides on the wooden wedge, which in turn slides backward on the horizontal surface. The acceleration of the block with respect to the wedge is [Given, $m = 8$ kg, $M = 16$ kg]
Assume all the surfaces shown in the figure to be frictionless. **[2021, 1 Sep Shift-II]**

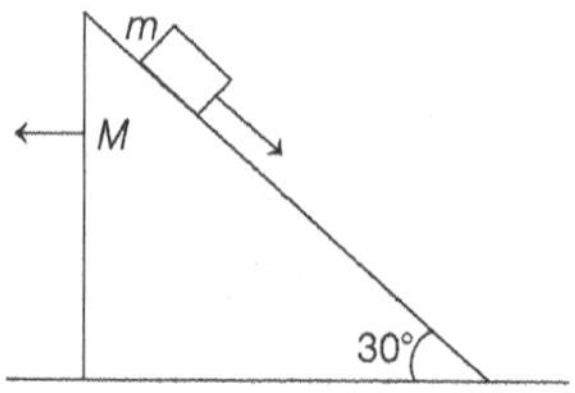

(a) $\frac{4}{3}g$ (b) $\frac{6}{5}g$

(c) $\frac{3}{5}g$ (d) $\frac{2}{3}g$

JEE Advanced

1. A piece of wire is bent in the shape of a parabola $y = kx^2$ (y-axis vertical) with a bead of mass m on it. The bead can slide on the wire without friction. It stays at the lowest point of the parabola when the wire is at rest. The wire is now accelerated parallel to the x-axis with a constant acceleration a. The distance of the new equilibrium position from the y-axis of the bead, where the bead can stay at rest with respect to the wire, **(2009)**

(a) $\frac{a}{gk}$ (b) $\frac{a}{2gk}$

(c) $\frac{2a}{gk}$ (d) $\frac{a}{4gk}$

Answer Key

Level 1

10.1 Normal Force

1. Normal force = 80 N
2. Normal force = 20 N
3. Normal force between (3 kg and ground) = 50 N and between (3 kg and 2 kg) = 20 N
4. Normal force (4 kg and 1 kg = 10 N) (4 kg and 5 kg = 50 N) (5kg and ground) = 100 N
5. Normal force between (block and ground = 212 N) (block and wall = 24 N)
6. Normal force (7 kg and ground = 160 N) (8 kg and ground = 80 N) (8 kg and wall = 40 N) (7 kg and 8 kg = 40 N)
7. Normal force (10 kg and ground = 100 N) (20 kg and ground = 240 N) (20 kg and wall = 70 N) (10 kg and 20 kg = 100 N)
8. Normal force between (sphere and wedge $A = 1250$ N) (sphere and wedge $B = 750$ N)
9. Normal force between sphere and either wedge = 500 N
10. 200 N and 150 N
11. Normal force (7 kg and ground = 70 N) (3 kg and ground = 30 N) (7 kg and wall = 0 N) (7 kg and 3 kg = 0 N)
12. $a = 14$ m/s^2 and normal force = 10 N
13. Acceleration = 4 m/s^2, Normal force = 176 N
14. $a = 3$ m/s^2, Normal force (6 kg and ground = 132 N) (4 kg and ground = 58 N) (6 kg and 4 kg = 36 N)
15. $a = -1.5$ m/s^2, left Normal force (10 kg and ground = 100 N) (7 kg and ground = 70 N) (3 kg and ground = 10 N) (10 kg and 7 kg = 45 N) (7 kg and 3 kg = 55.5 N)
16. $a = 6.6$ m/s^2 up, Normal force = 8 N
17. $a = 4$ m/s^2 up, Normal force = 110 N
18. $a = 1$ m/s^2 up, Normal force (6 kg and wedge = 36 N) (4 kg and wedge = 60 N) (6 kg and 4 kg = 84 N)
19. $a = 4$ m/s^2 down, Normal force (10 kg and wedge = 80 N) (8 kg and wedge = 64 N) (7 kg and wedge = 56 N) (10 kg and 8 kg = 80 N) (8 kg and 7 kg = 64 N)

10.2 Tension Force

1. Tension in lower string = 100 N and Tension in upper string = 150 N
2. Tension in lower string = 60 N, Tension in middle string = 140 N, Tension in upper string = 180 N
3. Tension in lower string will vary between 70 N and 90 N, Tension in upper string = 140 N
4. $T = \frac{M(L-x)}{L}g$
5. Tension in left string = 30 N, Tension in the right string = 40 N
6. Tension in left string = 62.5 N, Tension in the right string = 37.5 N
7. $T_1 = 20$ N, $T = 60$ N **8.** $a = 9$ m/s^2, $T = 24$ N **9.** $a = 4$ m/s^2, $T_1 = 44$ N and $T_2 = 64$ N **10.** $a = 6$ m/s^2, $T = 114$ N

10.3 Fixed Pulleys

1. $\frac{g}{3}$ **2.** $\frac{g}{9}$ **3.** $\frac{5g}{9}$ **4.** $\frac{g}{5}$ **5.** $\frac{g}{2}$
6. $\frac{2g}{5}$ **7.** $\frac{2g}{15}$ **8.** $\frac{3g}{4}$ **9.** $\frac{3g}{10}$
10. $\frac{(m_1 \sin\alpha + m_2 \sin\beta)g}{m_1 + m_2}$

10.4 String Constraint

1. 8 m/s **2.** 2 m/s **3.** 14 m/s up **4.** 20 m/s up
5. 25 m/s up **6.** 6 m/s^{2}up **7.** 23 m/s up **8.** 70 m/s up
9. 14 m/s **10.** 200 mm/s **11.** 18 m/s **12.** 26 m/s right
13. 18 m/s **14.** 1.5 m/s **15.** 10 m/s **16.** 7.5 m/s
19.(a) 2 m/s up (b) 2m/s down, (c) 8 m/s up

10.5 Moveable Pulleys

1. acceleration of 4 kg = 2.5 m/s^2 down, acceleration of 1 kg = 5 m/s^2 up
2. acceleration of $2M = \frac{g}{6}$ down, acceleration of $M = \frac{g}{3}$ up the plane
3. acceleration of $2M = \frac{2g}{3}$ down, acceleration of $M = \frac{g}{3}$ up
4. acceleration of 4 kg = $\frac{2g}{7}$ down, acceleration of 5 kg = $\frac{g}{7}$ up
5. acceleration of 3 kg = 20 m/s^2 and acceleration of 5 kg = 10 m/s^2
6. acceleration of $A = \frac{9F}{34m}$, acceleration of $B = \frac{3F}{17m}$
7. acceleration of $3m$ and m are $\frac{g}{13}$ and $\frac{7g}{13}$, respectively.
8. acceleration of 1 kg and 2 kg are $\frac{2g}{3}$ and $\frac{g}{3}$, respectively.
9. acceleration of $B = 1$ m/s^2 and acceleration of $A = 3$ m/s^2
10. acceleration of $A = 2$ m/s^2 and acceleration of $B = 8$ m/s^2
11. acceleration of m, $2m$ and $3m$ are $\frac{12g}{17}$, $\frac{6g}{17}$ and $\frac{9g}{17}$, respectively.
12. acceleration of 8 kg, 4 kg and 2 kg are 2 m/s^2 up, 2 m/s^2 down, 6 m/s^2 up, respectively.
13. acceleration of 1 kg, 2 kg and 3 kg are 2 m/s^2 down, 2 m/s^2 up and 6 m/s^2 up, respectively.

10.6 Spring Force

1. 4 ms^{-2} 2. (a) 10 N (b) 16 N (c) Each will read 10 kg.

3. 0.2 m 4. $\frac{g}{2}$ upwards, g downwards

5. $2g$ downwards, 0

6. 20 m/s^2, 20 m/s^2, 0 m/s^2 and $T = 10$ N

10.7 Pseudo Force

1. $\tan^{-1}\left(\frac{a_0}{g}\right)$ 2. $g\cot\theta$ 3. $(M+m)g\tan\theta$

4. $\sqrt{\left(\frac{2L}{(g+a_0)\sin\theta\cos\theta}\right)}$

5. $g\sin\alpha - a_0\cos\alpha$

6. $a = \left(\frac{m_1\sin\alpha + m_2\sin\beta}{m_1\cos\alpha + m_2\cos\beta}\right)g$

10.8 Wedge Constraint

1. (a) $\frac{4a}{3}\hat{i}$ (b) $-a\hat{i} - 4a\hat{j}$ (c) $a\hat{i} - 2(a+c)\hat{j}$

(d) $a(\cos\theta - 1)\hat{i} - a\sin\theta\,\hat{j}$

2. $a = \frac{12g}{25}; b = \frac{9g}{25}$

3. $a = \frac{b\cos\theta}{3}; b = \frac{3g\sin\theta}{3-\cos^2\theta}$

Level 2

Single Choice Correct Questions

1. (b)	2. (a)	3. (d)	4. (d)	5. (c)
6. (a)	7. (b)	8. (a)	9. (c)	10. (b)
11. (b)	12. (b)	13. (c)	14. (c)	15. (d)
16. (b)	17. (a)	18. (d)	19. (c)	20. (c)
21. (d)	22. (c)	23. (b)	24. (c)	25. (a)
26. (c)	27. (b)	28. (a)	29. (c)	30. (b)
31. (c)	32. (b)	33. (d)	34. (a)	35. (d)
36. (b)	37. (a)	38. (c)	39. (b)	40. (d)
41. (c)	42. (b)	43. (b)	44. (d)	45. (d)
46. (b)	47. (c)	48. (b)	49. (b)	50. (b)
51. (c)	52. (c)	53. (a)	54. (b)	55. (b)
56. (c)	57. (d)	58. (c)	59. (b)	60. (c)
61. (c)	62. (c)	63. (a)	64. (b)	

Numerical Value Questions

1. (12)	2. (322)	3. (150)	4. (1)	5. (26)
6. (15)	7. (20.88)	8. (5)	9. (4)	10. (800)
11. (48)	12. (27)	13. (16)	14. (75)	15. (15)

Level 3

Single Choice Correct Questions

1. (a)	2. (d)	3. (d)	4. (d)	5. (c)
6. (a)	7. (d)	8. (c)	9. (d)	10. (b)
11. (c)	12. (b)	13. (a)	14. (c)	15. (a)
16. (b)	17. (a)	18. (c)	19. (a)	20. (a)
21. (c)	22. (b)	23. (d)	24. (d)	25. (b)
26. (d)	27. (c)	28. (a)	29. (d)	30. (b)
31. (c)	32. (b)	33. (d)	34. (b)	35. (b)
36. (b)	37. (d)	38. (a)	39. (b)	40. (a)
41. (c)	42. (d)	43. (c)	44. (c)	45. (a)
46. (d)	47. (b)	48. (a)	49. (b)	50. (d)

Mulltiple Choice(s) Correct Questions

1. (ad)	2. (cd)	3. (bd)	4. (abc)	5. (bcd)
6. (abd)	7. (ab)	8. (ad)	9. (bc)	10. (abcd)
11. (bcd)	12. (ac)	13. (abc)	14. (abcd)	15. (acd)

Comprehension Based Questions

1. (b)	2. (c)	3. (b)	4. (d)	5. (a)
6. (a)	7. (c)	8. (c)	9. (a)	10. (d)
11. (a)	12. (b)	13. (a)	14. (a)	15. (c)
16. (b)	17. (c)	18. (a)	19. (c)	20. (b)
21. (a)				

Match the Columns Questions

1. (A-R, B-P, C-Q, D-QS) 2. (A-R B-S, C-P, D-Q)
3. (A-Q, B-R, C-Q, D-R) 4. (A-R, B-Q, C-Q, D-Q)

Numerical Value Questions

1. (75)	2. (1)	3. (6.67)	4. (6)	5. (15)
6. (7)	7. (10)	8. (15)	9. (5)	10. (7)
11. (5)	12. (8)	13. (3)	14. (32)	15. (0.4)
16. (218)	17. (25)	18. (10)	19. (1)	20. (260)

Previous Year's Questions

JEE Main

1. (a)	2. (c)	3. (c)	4. (c)	5. (c)
6. (b)	7. (b)	8. (d)	9. (b)	10. (b)
11. (c)	12. (a)	13. (c)	14. (c)	15. (d)
16. (d)	17. (2)	18. (3)	19. (3)	20. (36)
21. (12)	22. (d)	23. (10)	24. (12)	25. (500)
26. (d)				

JEE Advanced

1. (b)

SOLUTIONS

Level 1

10.1 Normal Force

1.

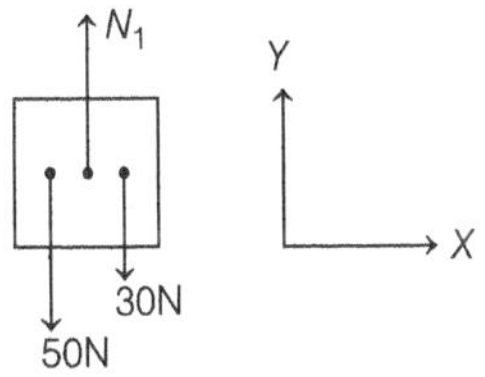

FBD of 5 kg block

$$\Sigma F_y = 0 \Rightarrow +N_1 - 50 - 30 = 0 \Rightarrow N_1 = 80\,\text{N}$$

2.

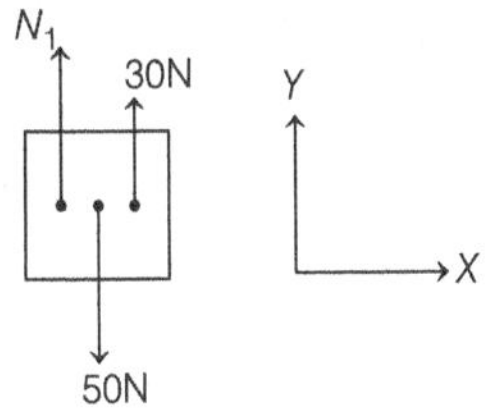

FBD of 5 kg block

$$\Sigma F_y = 0 \Rightarrow +N_1 + 30 - 50 = 0 \Rightarrow N_1 = 20\,\text{N}$$

3.

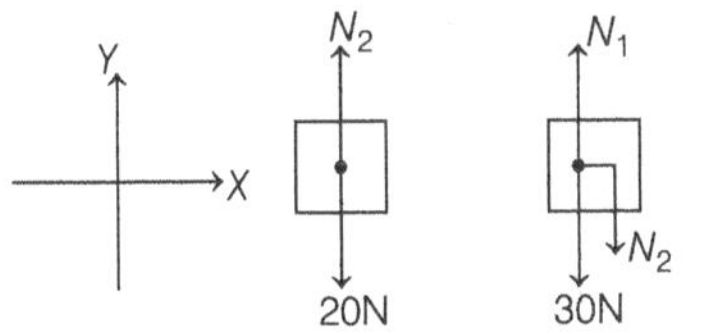

FBD of 2 kg block   FBD of 3 kg block

$$\Sigma F_y = 0$$

For 2 kg block; $+N_2 - 20 = 0 \Rightarrow N_2 = 20\,\text{N}$

For 3 kg block; $+N_1 - 30 - N_2 = 0 \Rightarrow N_1 = 50\,\text{N}$

4.

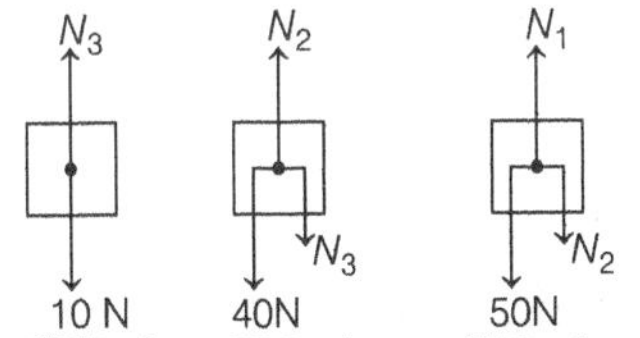

FBD of 1kg block   FBD of 4kg block   FBD of 5kg block

$$\Sigma F_y = 0 \Rightarrow +N_3 - 10 = 0 \Rightarrow N_3 = 10\,\text{N}$$

$$+N_2 - N_3 - 40 = 0 \Rightarrow N_2 = 50\,\text{N}$$

$$+N_1 - 50 - N_2 = 0 \Rightarrow N_1 = 100\,\text{N}$$

5.

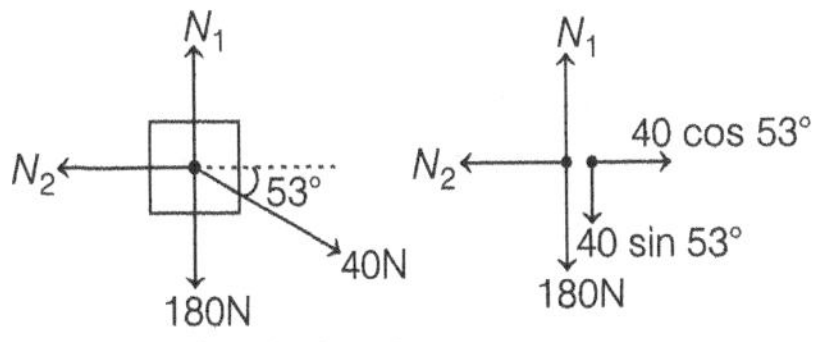

FBD of 18 kg block

$$\Sigma F_x = 0 \Rightarrow 40\cos 53^\circ - N_2 = 0 \Rightarrow N_2 = 24\,\text{N}$$

$$\Sigma F_y = 0 \Rightarrow +N_1 - 180 - 40\sin 53^\circ = 0 \Rightarrow N_1 = 212\,\text{N}$$

6.

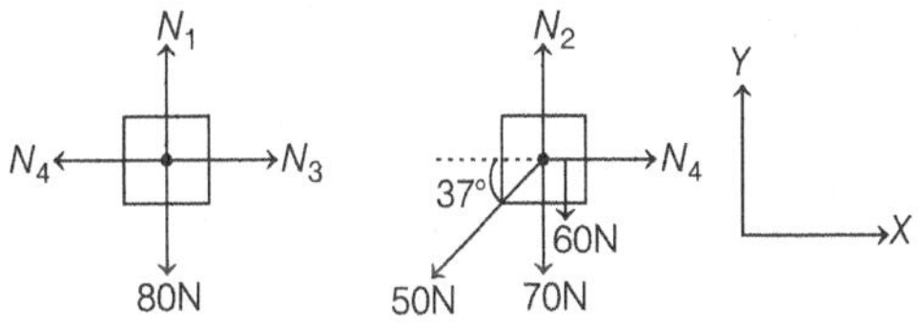

FBD of 8kg block   FBD of 7kg block

$$\Sigma F_x = 0 \Rightarrow N_4 - 50\cos 37^\circ = 0 \Rightarrow N_4 = 40\,\text{N}$$

$$\Rightarrow N_3 - N_4 - 0 \Rightarrow N_3 - 40\,\text{N}$$

$$\Sigma F_y = 0 \Rightarrow +N_2 - 70 - 60 - 50\sin 37^\circ = 0$$

$$\Rightarrow N_2 = 160\,\text{N}$$

$$+N_1 - 80 = 0 \Rightarrow N_1 = 80\,\text{N}$$

7.

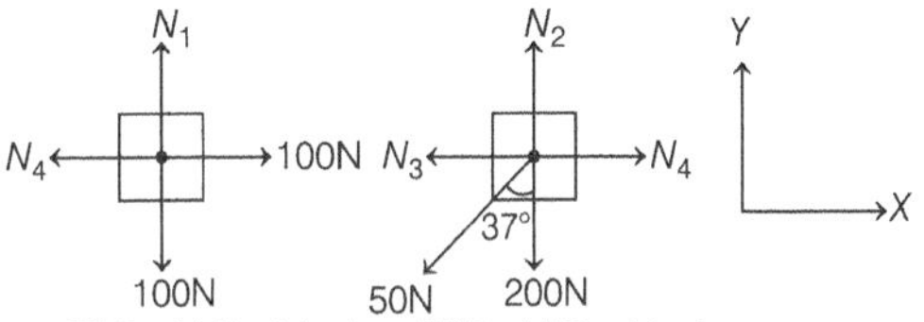

FBD of 10kg block   FBD of 20kg block

$$\Sigma F_x = 0 \Rightarrow +100 - N_4 = 0 \Rightarrow N_4 = 100\,\text{N}$$

$$+N_4 - N_3 - 50\sin 37^\circ = 0 \Rightarrow N_3 = 70\,\text{N}$$

$$\Sigma F_y = 0 \Rightarrow +N_1 - 100 = 0 \Rightarrow N_1 = 100\,\text{N}$$

$$+N_2 - 200 - 50\cos 37^\circ = 0 \Rightarrow N_2 = 240\,\text{N}$$

8.

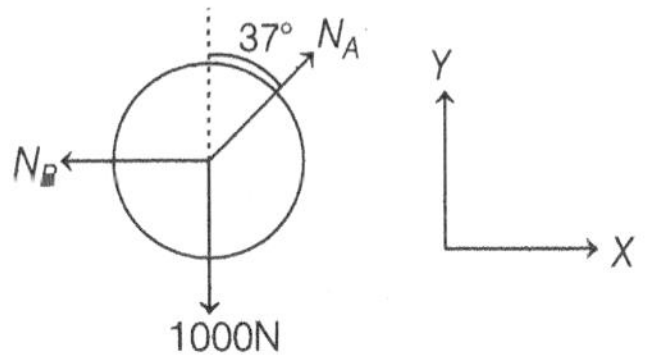

$$\Sigma F_y = 0 \Rightarrow +N_A\cos 37^\circ - 1000 = 0 \Rightarrow N_A = 1250\,\text{N}$$

$$\Sigma F_x = 0 \Rightarrow +N_A\sin 37^\circ - N_B = 0 \Rightarrow N_B = 750\,\text{N}$$

9.

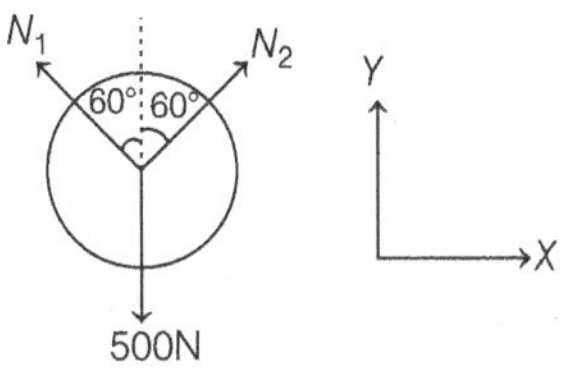

$$\Sigma F_x = 0 \Rightarrow N_2\sin 60^\circ - N_1\sin 60^\circ = 0 \Rightarrow N_1 = N_2$$

$$\Sigma F_y = 0 \Rightarrow N_1\cos 60^\circ + N_2\cos 60^\circ - 500 = 0$$

$$\Rightarrow N_1 = N_2 = 500\,\text{N}$$

10.

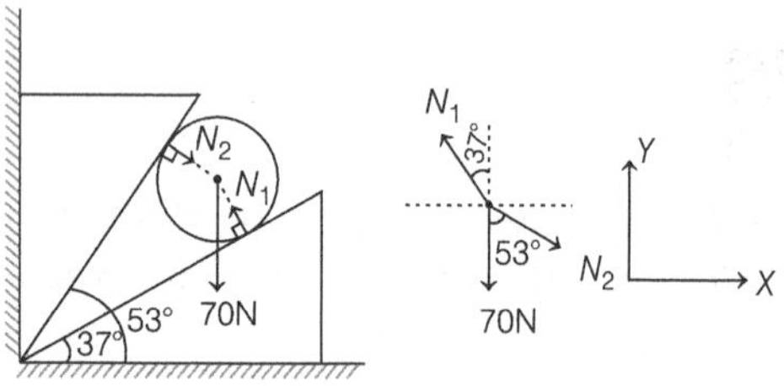

$\Sigma F_y = 0 \Rightarrow +N_1 \cos 37° - 70 - N_2 \cos 53° = 0$ ...(i)

$\Sigma F_x = 0 \Rightarrow N_2 \sin 53° - N_1 \sin 37° = 0$ ...(ii)

Solving Eqs. (i) and (ii), we get

$N_2 = 150\,\text{N}$ and $N_1 = 200\,\text{N}$

11.

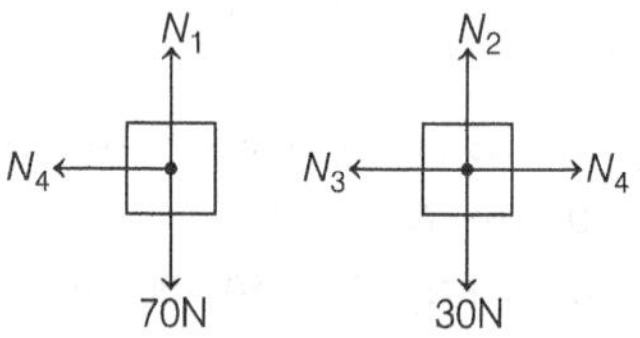

$\Sigma F_x = 0 \Rightarrow N_4 = 0 \Rightarrow N_3 = N_4 = 0$

$\Sigma F_y = 0 \Rightarrow N_1 = 70\,\text{N}$ and $N_2 = 30\,\text{N}$

12.

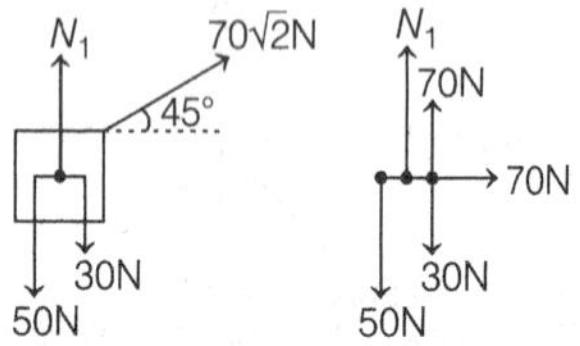

$\Sigma F_y = 0 \Rightarrow +N_1 + 70 - 50 - 30 = 0 \Rightarrow N_1 = 10\,\text{N}$

$\Sigma F_x = ma_x \Rightarrow 70 = 5a_x \Rightarrow a_x = 14\,\text{m/s}^2$

13.

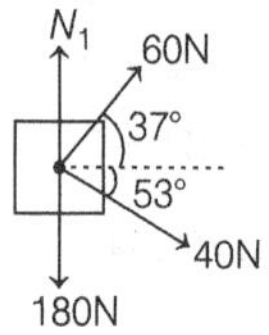

$\Sigma F_y = 0 \Rightarrow +N_1 + 60 \sin 37° - 40 \sin 53° - 180 = 0$

$\Rightarrow N_1 = 176\,\text{N}$

$\Sigma F_x = ma_x \Rightarrow 60 \cos 37° + 40 \cos 53° = 18a_x$

$\Rightarrow a_x = 4\,\text{m/s}^2$

14.

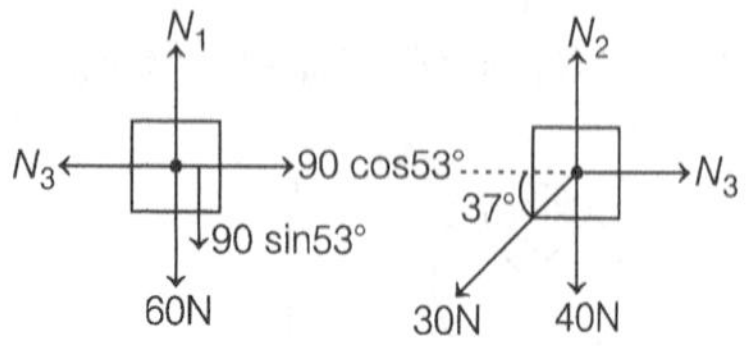

FBD of 6kg block

FBD of 4kg block

$\Sigma F_y = 0 \Rightarrow +N_1 - 60 - 90 \sin 53° = 0 \Rightarrow N_1 = 132\,\text{N}$

$\Sigma F_y = 0 \Rightarrow +N_2 - 40 - 30 \sin 37° = 0 \Rightarrow N_2 = 58\,\text{N}$

$\Sigma F_x = ma_x \Rightarrow 90 \cos 53° - N_3 = 6a$ ...(i)

$N_3 - 30 \cos 37° = 4a$ ...(ii)

Solving Eqs. (i) and (ii), we get

$\Rightarrow a = 3\,\text{m/s}^2$ and $N_3 = 36\,\text{N}$

15.

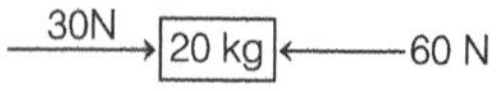

FBD of system,

$\Sigma F_x = ma_x \Rightarrow -60 + 30 = 20a_x \Rightarrow a_x = -1.5\,\text{m/s}^2$

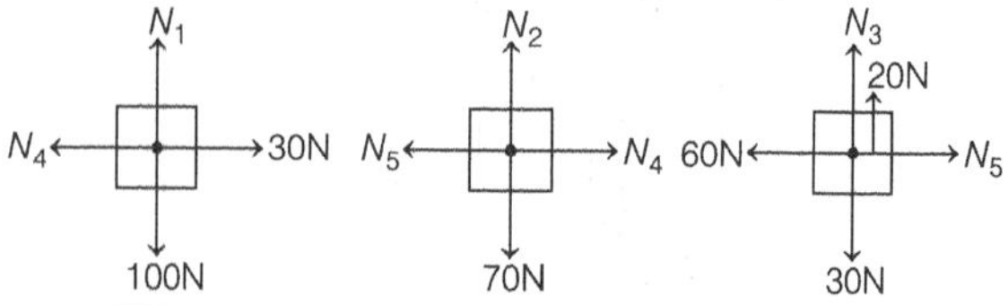

FBD of 10 kg block

FBD of 7 kg block

FBD of 3 kg block

$\Sigma F_y = 0$

For 10 kg block; $+N_1 - 100 = 0 \Rightarrow N_1 = 100\,\text{N}$

For 7 kg block; $+N_2 - 70 = 0 \Rightarrow N_2 = 70\,\text{N}$

For 3 kg block; $N_3 + 20 - 30 = 0 \Rightarrow N_3 = 10\,\text{N}$

$\Sigma F_x = ma_x$

For 10 kg block; $30 - N_4 = 10(-1.5) \Rightarrow N_4 = 45\,\text{N}$

For 10 kg block; $N_4 - N_5 = 7(-1.5) \Rightarrow N_5 = 55.5\,\text{N}$

16.

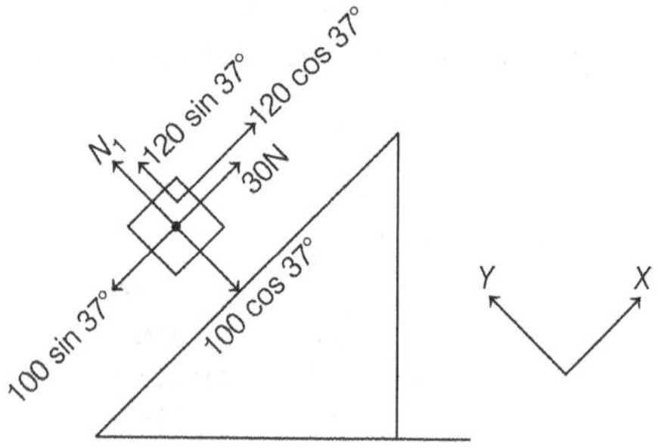

$\Sigma F_y = 0$

$\Rightarrow +N_1 + 120 \sin 37° - 100 \cos 37° = 0 \Rightarrow N_1 = 8\,\text{N}$

$\Sigma F_x = ma_x$

$+120 \cos 37° + 30 - 100 \sin 37° = 10a_x \Rightarrow a_x = 6.6\,\text{m/s}^2$

17.

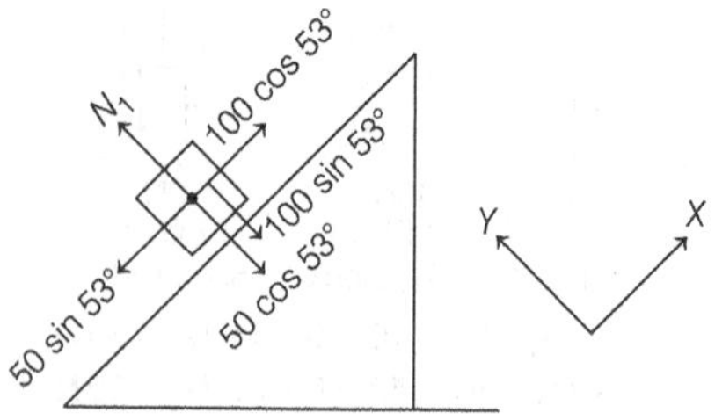

$\Sigma F_y = 0$

$\Rightarrow +N_1 - 50 \cos 53° - 100 \sin 53° = 0 \Rightarrow N_1 = 110\,\text{N}$

$\Sigma F_x = 0$

$\Rightarrow 100 \cos 53° - 50 \sin 53° = 5a_x \Rightarrow a_x = 4\,\text{m/s}^2$

18.

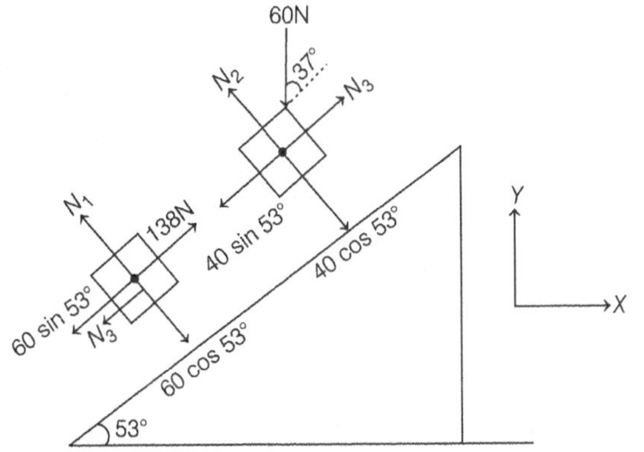

$$\Sigma F_y = 0$$

For 6 kg block, $+N_1 - 60\cos 53° = 0$

$\Rightarrow \qquad N_1 = 36\,\text{N}$

For 4 kg block, $+N_2 - 40\cos 53° - 60\sin 37° = 0$

$\Rightarrow \qquad N_2 = 60\,\text{N}$

$$\Sigma F_x = 0$$

$\Rightarrow \; 138 - N_3 - 60\sin 53° = 6a$ ...(i)

$N_3 - 40\sin 53° - 60\cos 37° = 4a$ ...(ii)

From Eqs. (i) and (ii), we get

$a = 1\,\text{m/s}^2$ and $N_3 = 84\,\text{N}$

19.

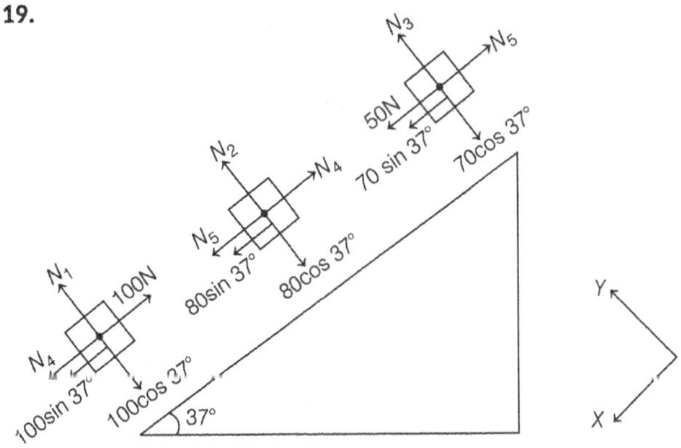

$$\Sigma F_y = 0$$

For 10 kg block, $+N_1 - 100\cos 37° = 0 \Rightarrow N_1 = 80\,\text{N}$

For 8 kg block, $+N_2 - 80\cos 37° = 0 \Rightarrow N_2 = 64\,\text{N}$

For 7 kg block, $N_3 - 70\cos 37° = 0$

$\Rightarrow \qquad N_3 = 56\,\text{N}$

$$\Sigma F_x = ma_x$$

$\Rightarrow \qquad N_4 + 60 - 100 = 10a$ ...(i)

$N_5 + 48 - N_4 = 8a$ ...(ii)

$50 + 42 - N_5 = 7a$ ...(iii)

From Eqs. (i), (ii) and (iii), we get

$a = 4\,\text{m/s}^2$

$N_4 = 80\,\text{N}$

$N_5 = 64\,\text{N}$

10.2 Tension Force

1.

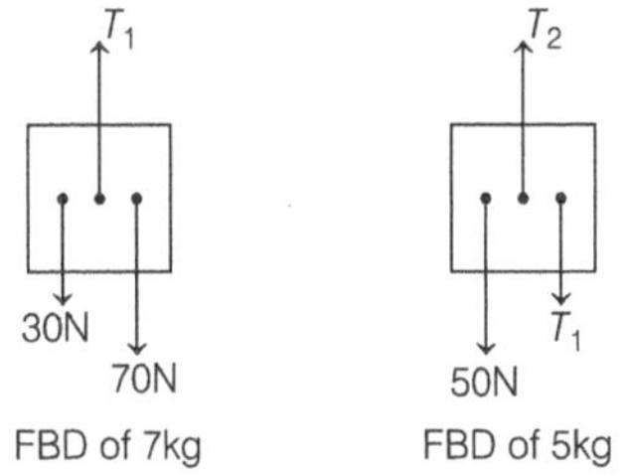

$$\Sigma F_y = 0$$

For 7 kg block; $+T_1 - 30 - 70 = 0 \Rightarrow T_1 = 100\,\text{N}$

For 5 kg block; $+T_2 - T_1 - 50 = 0 \Rightarrow T_2 = 150\,\text{N}$

2.

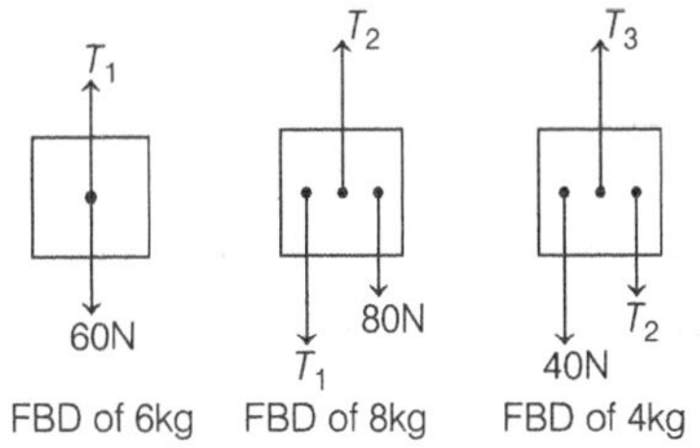

$$\Sigma F_y = 0$$

For 6 kg block; $T_1 - 60 = 0 \Rightarrow T_1 = 60\,\text{N}$

For 8 kg block; $T_2 - T_1 - 80 = 0 \Rightarrow T_2 = 140\,\text{N}$

For 4 kg block; $+T_3 - 40 - T_2 = 0 \Rightarrow T_3 = 180\,\text{N}$

3.

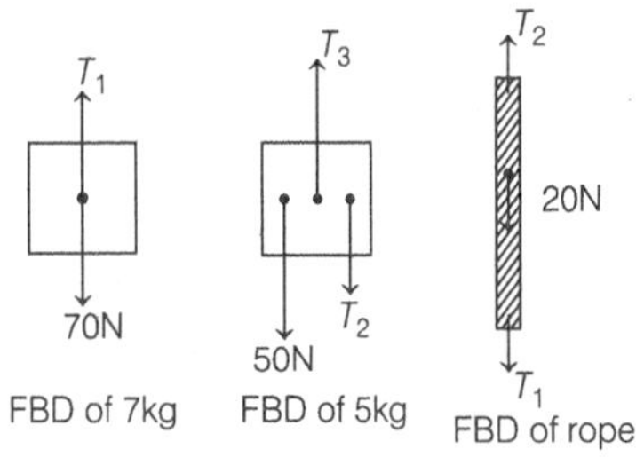

$$\Sigma F_y = 0$$

For 7 kg block; $+T_1 - 70 = 0 \Rightarrow T_1 = 70\,\text{N}$

For rope; $+T_2 - 20 - T_1 = 0 \Rightarrow T_2 = 90\,\text{N}$

For 5 kg block; $+T_3 - T_2 - 50 = 0 \Rightarrow T_3 = 140\,\text{N}$

Tension in rope will vary between 70 N and 90 N.

4.

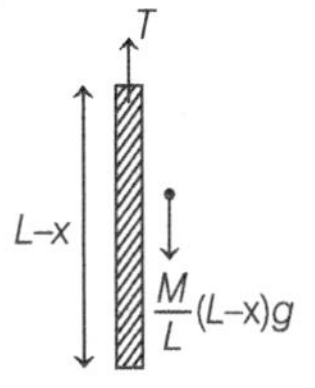

FBD of $(L - x)$ length of rope

$$\Sigma F_y = 0$$

$$\Rightarrow \qquad T - \frac{M}{L}(L - x)g = 0 \Rightarrow T = \frac{M}{L}(L - x)g$$

5.

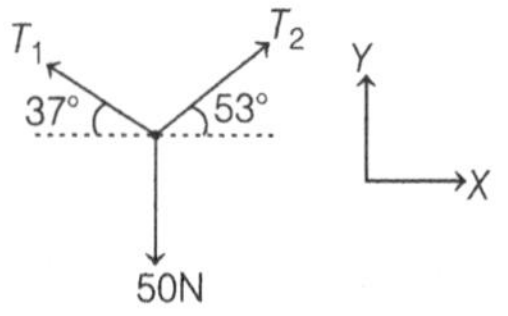

$$\Sigma F_x = 0 \quad \Rightarrow T_2 \cos 53° - T_1 \cos 37° = 0 \qquad \text{...(i)}$$

$$\Sigma F_y = 0 \quad \Rightarrow T_1 \sin 37° + T_2 \sin 53° - 50 = 0 \qquad \text{...(ii)}$$

Solving Eqs. (i) and (ii), we get

$$T_1 = 30\,\text{N} \text{ and } T_2 = 40\,\text{N}$$

6.

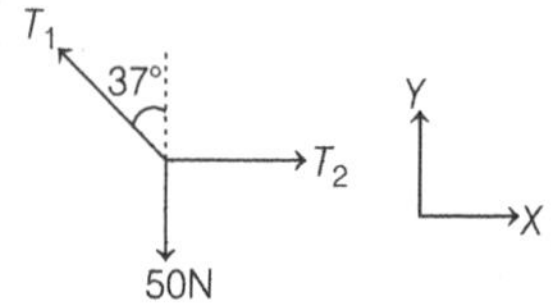

$$\Sigma F_x = 0 \quad \Rightarrow \quad +T_2 - T_1 \sin 37° = 0 \qquad \text{...(i)}$$

$$\Sigma F_y = 0 \quad \Rightarrow T_1 \cos 37° - 50 = 0 \qquad \text{...(ii)}$$

From Eqs. (i) and (ii), we get

$$T_1 = 62.5\,\text{N} \quad \text{and} \quad T_2 = 37.5\,\text{N}$$

7.

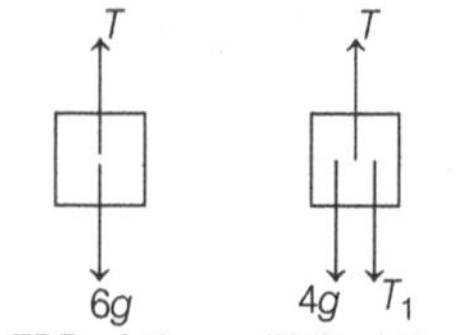

FBD of 6kg   FBD of 4kg

$$\Sigma F_y = 0$$

For 6 kg block; $T - 6g = 0 \quad \Rightarrow T = 60\,\text{N}$

For 4 kg block, $T - 4g - T_1 = 0 \Rightarrow T_1 = 20\,\text{N}$

8.

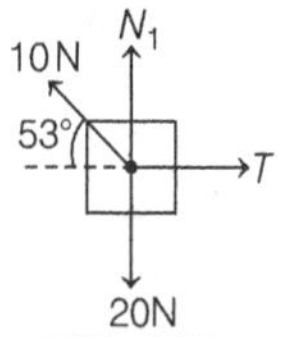

FBD of 2 kg

$$\Sigma F_x = ma_x \quad \Rightarrow \quad T - 10 \cos 53° = 2a \qquad \text{...(i)}$$

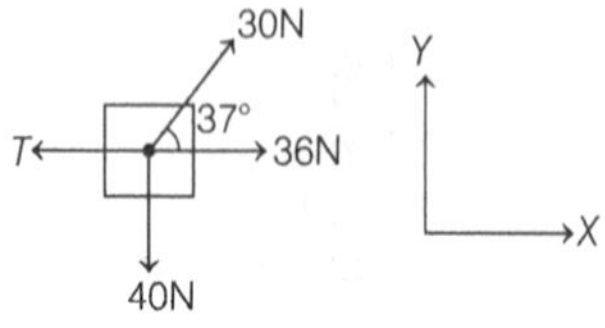

FBD of 4 kg

$$\Sigma F_x = ma_x$$

$$36 + 30 \cos 37° - T = 4a \qquad \text{...(ii)}$$

Solving Eqs. (i) and (ii), we get

$$a = 9\,\text{m/s}^2 \text{ and } T = 24\,\text{N}$$

9.

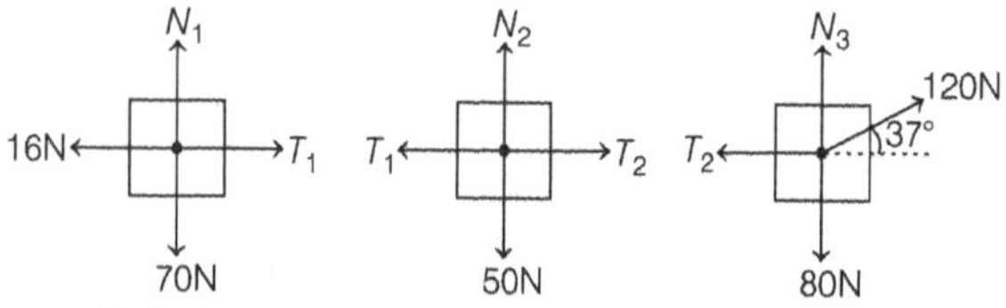

FBD of 7 kg   FBD of 5 kg   FBD of 8 kg

$$\Sigma F_x = ma_x \quad \Rightarrow \quad T_1 - 16 = 7a \qquad \text{...(i)}$$

$$T_2 - T_1 = 5a \qquad \text{...(ii)}$$

$$96 - T_2 = 8a \qquad \text{...(iii)}$$

From Eqs. (i), (ii) and (iii), we get

$$a = 4\,\text{m/s}^2 \quad \Rightarrow \quad T_1 = 44\,\text{N} \quad \Rightarrow \quad T_2 = 64\,\text{N}$$

10.

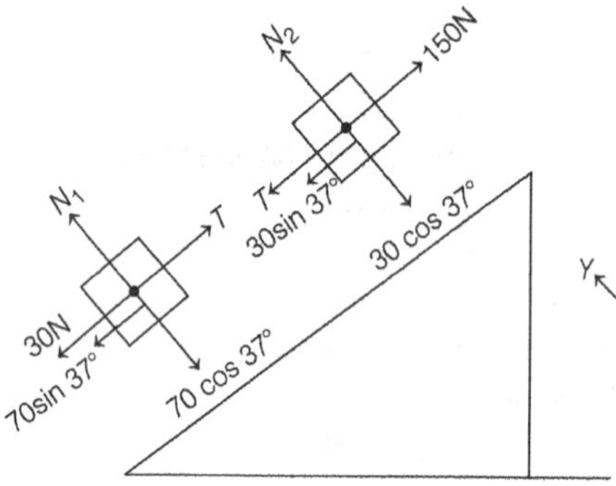

$$\Sigma F_x = ma_x \quad \Rightarrow \quad T - 30 - 70 \sin 37° = 7a \qquad \text{...(i)}$$

$$150 - T - 30 \sin 37° = 3a \qquad \text{...(ii)}$$

Solving Eqs. (i) and (ii), we get

$$a = 6\,\text{m/s}^2 \text{ and } T = 114\text{N}$$

10.3 Fixed Pulleys

1.

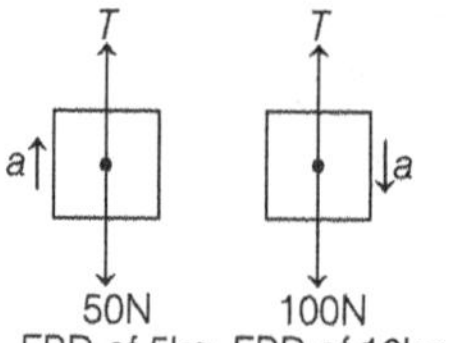

FBD of 5kg FBD of 10kg

$$\Sigma F_y = ma_y \quad \Rightarrow 100 - T = 10a \qquad \text{...(i)}$$

$$T - 50 = 5a \qquad \text{...(ii)}$$

Solving Eqs. (i) and (ii), we get

$$a = \frac{10}{3}\,\text{m/s}^2 \quad \text{and} \quad T = \frac{200}{3}\,\text{N}$$

2.

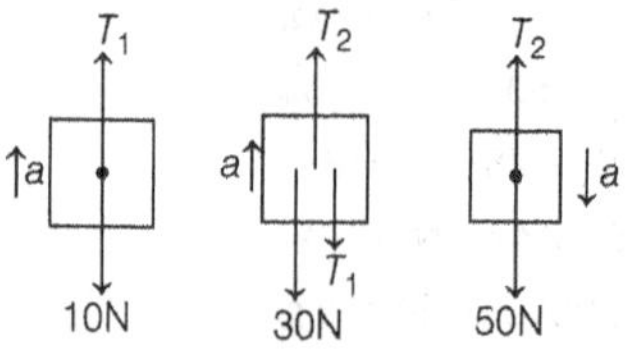

$$50 - T_2 = 5a \qquad \text{...(i)}$$

$$T_2 - 30 - T_1 = 3a \qquad \text{...(ii)}$$

$$T_1 - 10 = 1\,a \qquad \text{...(iii)}$$

Solving Eqs. (i), (ii)and (iii), we get

$$a=\frac{g}{9}$$

3.

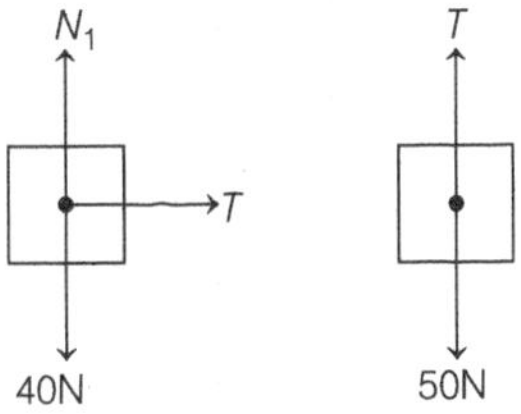

$$50-T=5a \quad \text{...(i)}$$

$$T=4a \quad \text{...(ii)}$$

Solving Eqs. (i) and (ii), we get

$$\Rightarrow \quad a=\frac{50}{9}\,\text{m/s}^2$$

4.

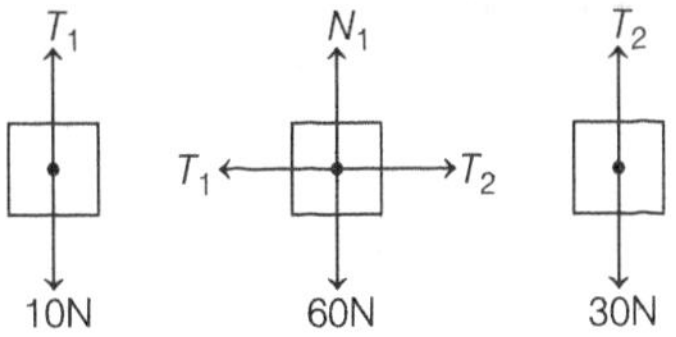

$$30-T_2=3a \quad \text{...(i)}$$

$$T_2-T_1=6a \quad \text{...(ii)}$$

$$T_1-10=1\,a \quad \text{...(iii)}$$

Adding Eqs. (i), (ii) and (iii), we get

$$\Rightarrow \quad 10a=20 \Rightarrow a=2\,\text{m/s}^2$$

5.

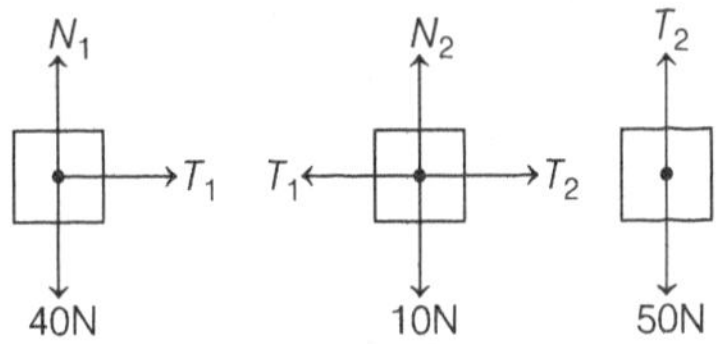

$$50-T_2=5a \quad \text{...(i)}$$

$$T_2-T_1=1\,a \quad \text{...(ii)}$$

$$T_1=4a \quad \text{...(iii)}$$

From Eqs. (i), (ii) and (iii), we get

$$\Rightarrow \quad a=5\,\text{m/s}^2$$

6.

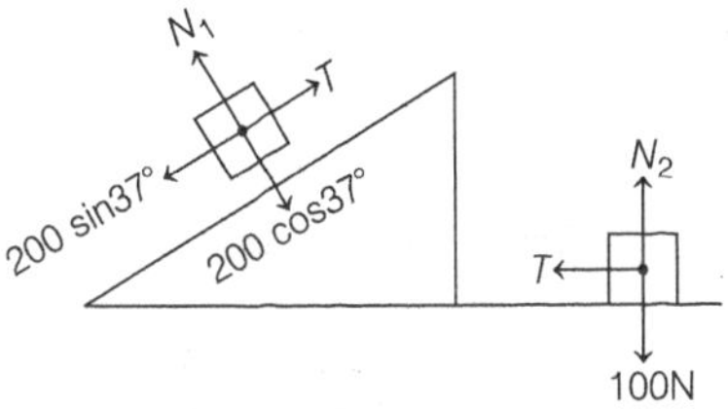

$$200\sin 37°-T=20a \quad \text{...(i)}$$

$$T=10a \quad \text{...(ii)}$$

Adding Eqs. (i) and (ii), we get

$$\Rightarrow \quad a=4\,\text{m/s}^2$$

7.

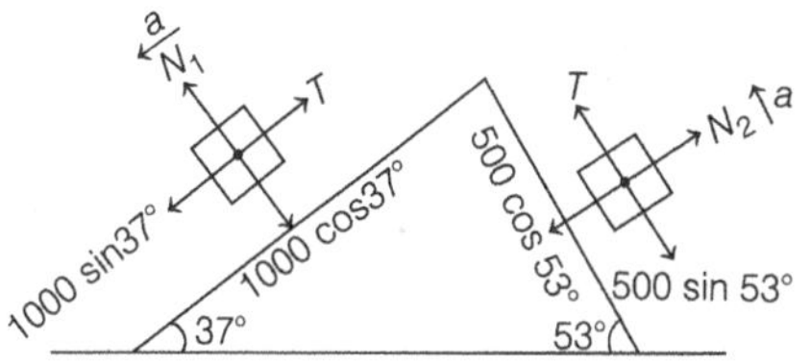

$$1000\sin 37°-T=100a \quad \text{...(i)}$$

$$T-500\sin 53°=50a \quad \text{...(ii)}$$

Adding Eqs. (i) and (ii), we get

$$\Rightarrow \quad a=\frac{4}{3}\,\text{m/s}^2$$

8.

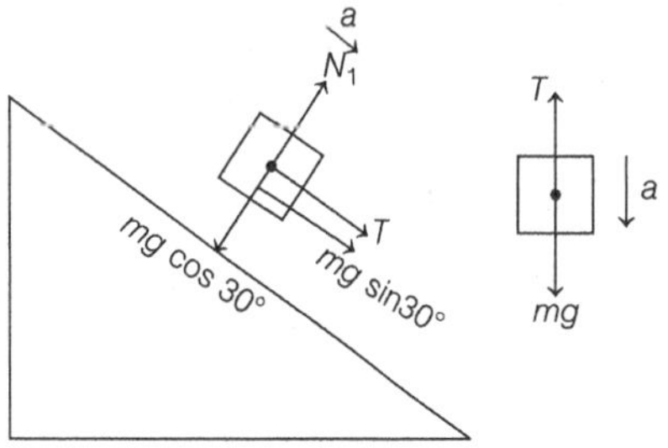

$$mg-T=ma \quad \text{...(i)}$$

$$T+mg\sin 30°=ma \quad \text{...(ii)}$$

Adding Eqs. (i) and (ii), we get

$$\Rightarrow \quad a=\frac{3g}{4}$$

9.

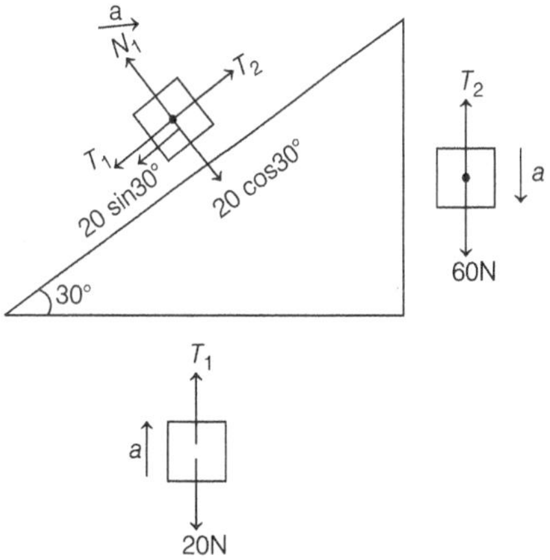

$$60-T_2=6a \quad \text{...(i)}$$

$$T_2-T_1-10=2a \quad \text{...(ii)}$$

$$T_1-20=2a \quad \text{...(iii)}$$

Adding Eqs. (i), (ii) and (iii), we get

$$\Rightarrow \quad a=3\,\text{m/s}^2$$

10.

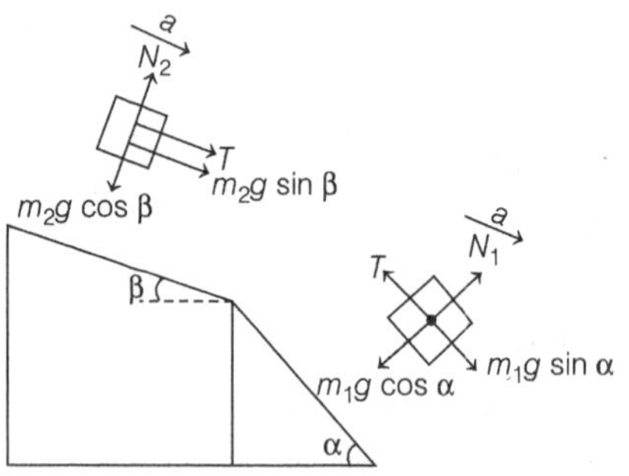

$$m_1 g \sin\alpha - T = m_1 a \quad \text{...(i)}$$
$$T + m_2 g \sin\beta = m_2 a \quad \text{...(ii)}$$

Adding Eqs. (i) and (ii), we get

$$\Rightarrow \quad a = \frac{(m_1 \sin\alpha + m_2 \sin\beta)g}{m_1 + m_2}$$

10.4 String Constraint

1. $-v+4+4=0 \Rightarrow v=8\,\text{m/s}$
2. $+6-v-v-v=0 \Rightarrow v=2\,\text{m/s}$
3. $+5+5+2+2-v_C=0 \Rightarrow v_C=14\,\text{m/s}$, up
4. $+10+10-v_A=0 \Rightarrow v_A=20\,\text{m/s}$, up
5. $+10+10+5-v_A=0 \Rightarrow v_A=25\,\text{m/s}$, up
6.

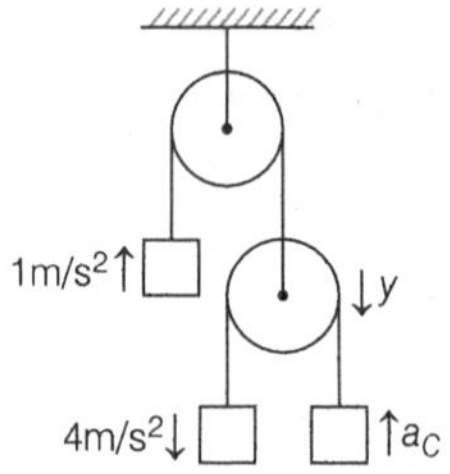

$$+1+y=0 \quad \text{...(i)}$$
$$-y-y+4-a_C=0 \quad \text{...(ii)}$$

From Eqs. (i) and (ii), we get

$$a_C = 6\,\text{m/s}^2, \text{up}$$

7.

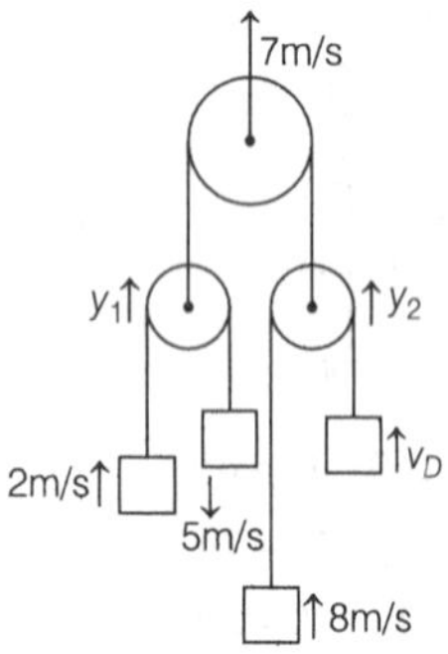

$$+7+7-y_1-y_2=0 \quad \text{...(i)}$$
$$-2+y_1+y_1+5=0 \quad \text{...(ii)}$$
$$-8+y_2+y_2-v_D=0 \quad \text{...(iii)}$$

From Eqs. (i), (ii) and (iii), we get

$$v_D = 23\,\text{m/s}, \text{up}$$

8.

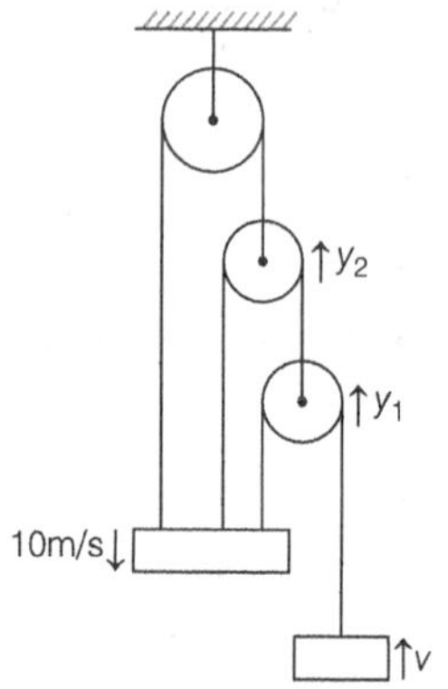

$$-y_2+10=0 \quad \text{...(i)}$$
$$+y_2+y_2+10-y_1=0 \quad \text{...(ii)}$$
$$+y_1+y_1+10-v=0 \quad \text{...(iii)}$$
$$v=70\,\text{m/s}, \text{up}$$

9.

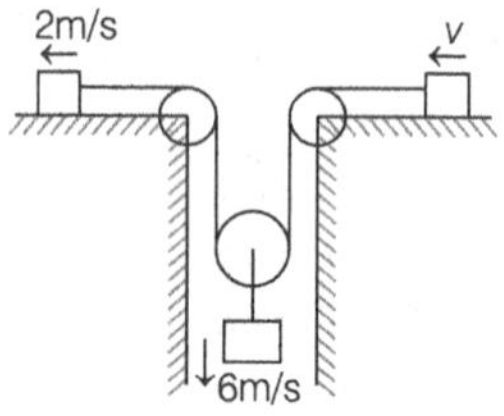

$$+2-v+6+6=0 \Rightarrow v=14\,\text{m/s}$$

10. $-v-v-v+300+300=0 \Rightarrow v=200\,\text{mm/s}$
11. $+6+6+6-v=0 \Rightarrow v=18\,\text{m/s}$
12. $+10+10+2+2+2+v_C=0$
    $v_C = -26\,\text{m/s} = 26\,\text{m/s right}$
13.

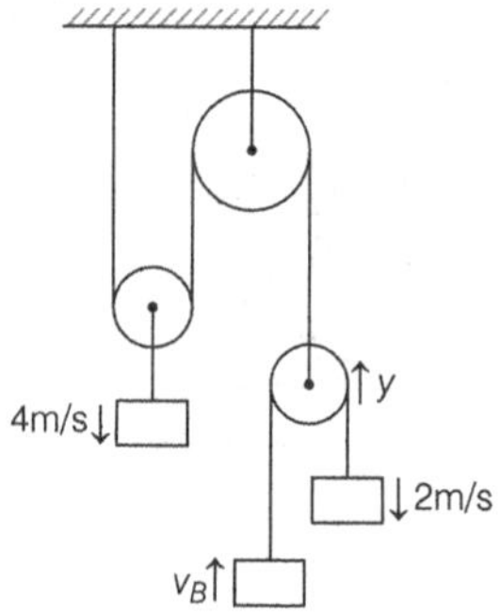

$$+4+4-y=0 \Rightarrow y=8\,\text{m/s}$$
$$+y+y-v_B+2=0 \Rightarrow v_B=18\,\text{m/s}$$

14.

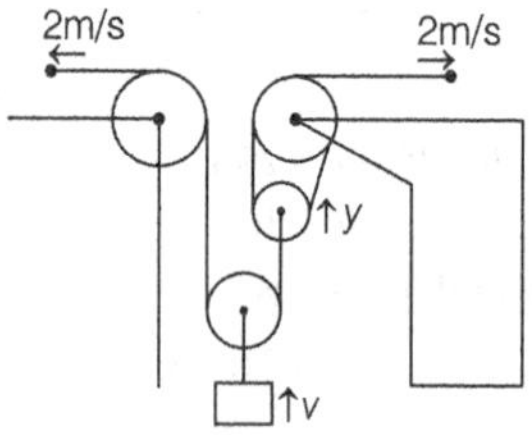

$$-y-y+2=0 \Rightarrow y=1\,\text{m/s}$$
$$+2-v-v+y=0 \Rightarrow v=1.5\,\text{m/s}$$

15. $+8 - v_B \cos 37° = 0 \Rightarrow v_B = 10\,\text{m/s}$

16. $+10\cos 53° - v_B \cos 37° = 0 \Rightarrow v = 7.5\,\text{m/s}$

17. $-v_B \cos 60° + 1 \cdot \cos 60° = 0 \Rightarrow v_B = 1\,\text{m/s}$

18. (a) $-u\cos\theta - u\cos\theta + v = 0 \Rightarrow u = \dfrac{v}{2\cos\theta}$

(b) $-u\cos\theta - u\cos\theta + v + v = 0 \Rightarrow u = \dfrac{v}{\cos\theta}$

19. (a) $+6 - v_B - v_B - v_B = 0 \Rightarrow v_B = 2\,\text{m/s, up}$

(b) $+6 - 2 - 2 - v_D = 0 \Rightarrow v_D = 2\,\text{m/s, down}$

(c) $+6 - v_C = 0$

$\Rightarrow v_C = 6\,\text{m/s, up} \Rightarrow V_{CD} = v_C - v_D = 8\,\text{m/s, up}$

10.5 Moveable Pulleys

1.

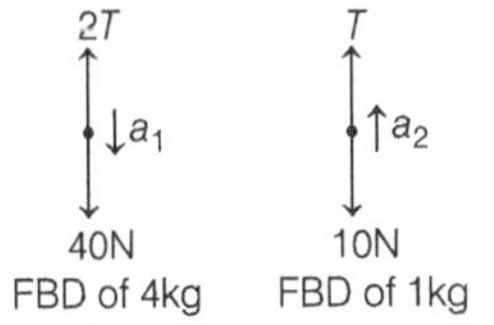

$$40 - 2T = 4a_1 \quad \text{...(i)}$$
$$T - 10 = 1\,a_2 \quad \text{...(ii)}$$
$$2a_1 = a_2 \quad \text{...(iii)}$$

Solving Eqs. (i), (ii) and (iii), we get

$$a_1 = 2.5\,\text{m/s}^2\text{, down} \quad \text{and} \quad a_2 = 5\,\text{m/s}^2\text{, up}$$

2.

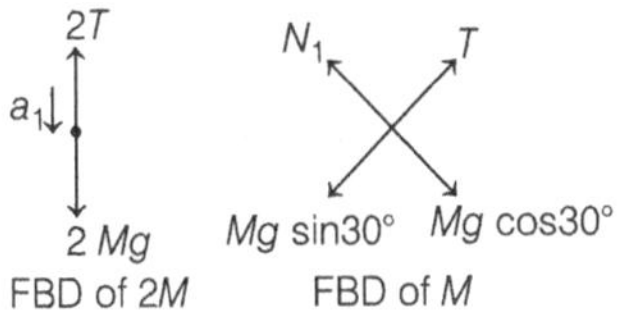

$$2Mg - 2T = 2Ma_1 \quad \text{...(i)}$$
$$T - Mg\sin 30° = Ma_2 \quad \text{...(ii)}$$
$$2a_1 = a_2 \quad \text{...(iii)}$$

Solving Eqs. (i), (ii) and (iii), we get

$$a_1 = \frac{g}{6}\text{, down} \quad \text{and} \quad a_2 = \frac{g}{3}\text{, up the plane}$$

3.

$$2Mg - T = 2Ma_1 \quad \text{...(i)}$$
$$2T - Mg = Ma_2 \quad \text{...(ii)}$$
$$2a_2 = a_1 \quad \text{...(iii)}$$
$$a_2 = \frac{g}{3}\text{, up and } a_1 = \frac{2g}{3}\text{, down}$$

4.

$$50 - 2T = 5a_1 \quad \text{...(i)}$$
$$T - 40 = 4a_2 \quad \text{...(ii)}$$
$$a_2 = 2a_1 \quad \text{...(iii)}$$

Solving Eqs. (i), (ii) and (iii), we get

$$a_1 = -\frac{10}{7}\,\text{m/s}^2 = \frac{10}{7}\,\text{m/s}^2\text{, up}$$
$$a_2 = -\frac{20}{7}\,\text{m/s}^2 = \frac{20}{7}\,\text{m/s}^2\text{, down}$$

5.

$$170 - 2T = 5a_1 \quad \text{...(i)}$$
$$T = 3a_2 \quad \text{...(ii)}$$
$$a_2 = 2a_1 \quad \text{...(iii)}$$

Solving Eqs. (i), (ii) and (iii), we get

$$a_1 = 10\,\text{m/s}^2 \text{ and } a_2 = 20\,\text{m/s}^2$$

6.

$$F - 2T = 2ma_1 \quad \text{...(i)}$$
$$3T = 4ma_2 \quad \text{...(ii)}$$
$$2a_1 = 3a_2 \quad \text{...(iii)}$$

Solving Eqs. (i), (ii) and (iii), we get

$$a_2 = \frac{3F}{17m} \text{ and } a_1 = \frac{9F}{34m}$$

7.

$$mg - T = ma_1 \quad \text{...(i)}$$
$$7T - 3mg = 3ma_2 \quad \text{...(ii)}$$
$$a_1 = 7a_2 \quad \text{...(iii)}$$

Solving, Eqs. (i), (ii) and (iii), we get

$$a_1 = \frac{7g}{13} \text{ and } a_2 = \frac{g}{13}$$

8.

$$10 - T = a_1 \quad \text{...(i)}$$
$$2T = 2a_2 \quad \text{...(ii)}$$
$$a_1 = 2a_2 \quad \text{...(iii)}$$

From Eqs. (i), (ii) and (iii), we get

$$a_2 = \frac{g}{3} \text{ and } a_1 = \frac{2g}{3}$$

9.

$$mg - 3T = ma_1 \quad \text{...(i)}$$
$$T = ma_2 \quad \text{...(ii)}$$
$$a_2 = 3a_1 \quad \text{...(iii)}$$

From Eqs. (i), (ii) and (iii), we get

$$a_1 = \frac{g}{10} \text{ and } a_2 = \frac{3g}{10}$$

10.

$$400 - 4T = 40a_1 \quad \text{...(i)}$$
$$T = 10a_2 \quad \text{...(ii)}$$
$$a_2 = 4a_1 \quad \text{...(iii)}$$

Solving Eqs. (i), (ii) and (iii), we get

$$a_1 = 2\,\text{m/s}^2 \quad \text{and} \quad a_2 = 8\,\text{m/s}^2$$

11.

$$3mg - 2T = 3ma_3 \quad \text{...(i)}$$
$$T = ma_1 \quad \text{...(ii)}$$
$$T = 2ma_2 \quad \text{...(iii)}$$
$$a_1 + a_2 = 2a_3 \quad \text{...(iv)}$$

Solving Eqs. (i), (ii), (iii) and (iv), we get

$$a_1 = \frac{12g}{17} \text{ and } a_2 = \frac{6g}{17} \text{ and } a_3 = \frac{9g}{17}$$

12.

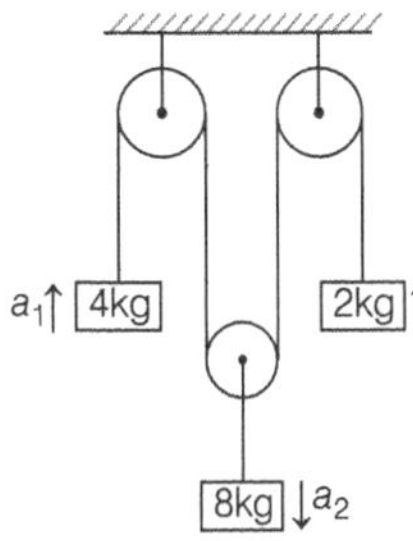

$$T-40=4a_1 \quad \text{...(i)}$$
$$80-2T=8a_2 \quad \text{...(ii)}$$
$$T-20=2a_3 \quad \text{...(iii)}$$
$$2a_2=a_1+a_3 \quad \text{...(iv)}$$
$$a_1=-2\,\text{m/s}^2 \Rightarrow a_2=+2\,\text{m/s}^2 \Rightarrow a_3=+6\,\text{m/s}^2$$

13.

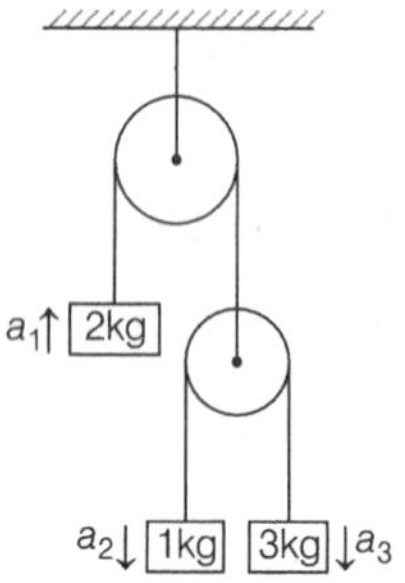

$$2T-20=2a_1 \quad \text{...(i)}$$
$$10-T=a_2 \quad \text{...(ii)}$$
$$30-T=3a_3 \quad \text{...(iii)}$$
$$2a_1=a_2+a_3 \quad \text{...(iv)}$$

Solving Eqs. (i), (ii), (iii) and (iv), we get

$$a_1=2\,\text{m/s}^2, a_2=-2\,\text{m/s}^2\ a_3=6\,\text{m/s}^2$$

10.6 Spring Force

1.

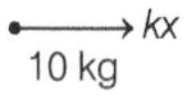

$\Rightarrow \quad kx=10(12) \Rightarrow kx=120\,\text{N}$

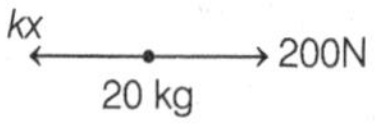

$$200-kx=20a \Rightarrow 200-120=20a \Rightarrow a=4\,\text{m/s}^2$$

2. (a) System is in equilibrium. Tension in the string will be 10 N, so spring balance reading will be 10 N.

(b) $\quad 40-T=4a \quad \text{...(i)}$

$T-10=1\,a \quad \text{...(ii)}$

From Eqs. (i) and (ii), we get

$$a=6\,\text{m/s}^2 \text{ and } T=16\,\text{N}$$

Spring balance reading $=T=16\,\text{N}$

(c) Both of them will read 100 N.

3.
$$30-T_1=3a \quad \text{...(i)}$$
$$10+T_1-T_2=a \quad \text{...(ii)}$$
$$T_2-20=2a \quad \text{...(iii)}$$

Solving Eqs. (i), (ii) and (iii), we get

$$a=\frac{10}{3}\,\text{m/s}^2 \quad \text{and} \quad T_1=20\,\text{N}$$

Spring force $=kx=T_1$

$\Rightarrow \quad 100x=20$

$\Rightarrow \quad x=0.2\,\text{m}$

4. Just after cutting the string

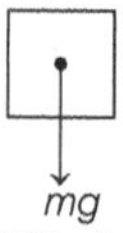

FBD of m

$$F=ma \Rightarrow mg=ma \Rightarrow a=g\downarrow$$

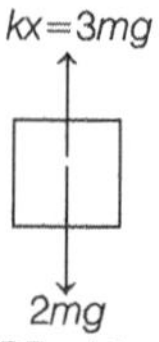

FBD of $2m$

$$F=ma \Rightarrow 3mg-2mg=2ma \Rightarrow a=\frac{g}{2}\uparrow$$

5.

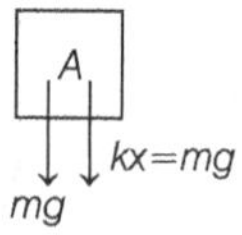

For A, $\quad mg+mg=ma_A \Rightarrow a_A=2g\downarrow$

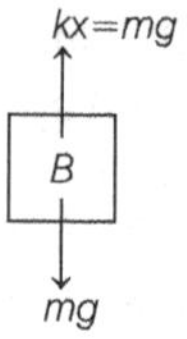

For B, $\quad a_B=0$

6. Just after cutting the string, $a_{3\text{kg}}=0$

1 kg and 2 kg will have common acceleration, lets say a downward.

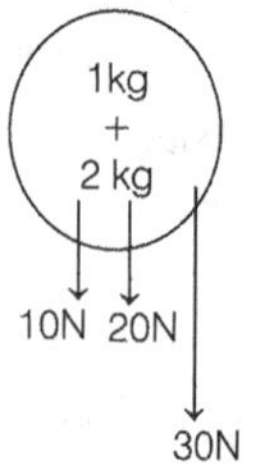

$$F=ma \Rightarrow 10+20+30=3a \Rightarrow a=20\,\text{m/s}^2\downarrow$$

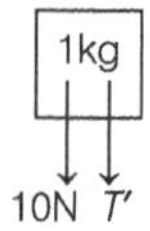

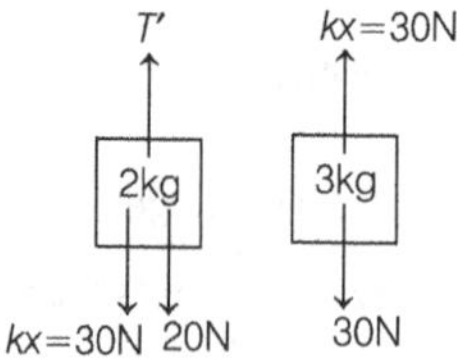

$$T'+10=1(20)$$

$\Rightarrow \quad T'=10\,\text{N}$

10.7 Pseudo Force

1.

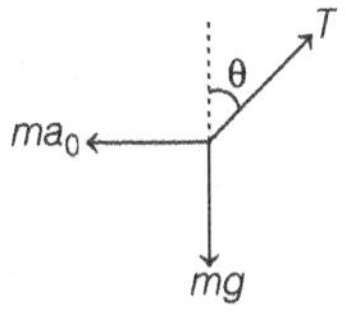

FBD of m

$$\Sigma F_x = 0 \Rightarrow T\sin\theta = ma_0 \quad \text{...(i)}$$

$$\Sigma F_y = 0 \Rightarrow T\cos\theta = mg \quad \text{...(ii)}$$

Dividing Eq. (i) by Eq. (ii), we get

$$\Rightarrow \quad \tan\theta = \frac{a_0}{g} \Rightarrow \theta = \tan^{-1}\left(\frac{a_0}{g}\right)$$

2.

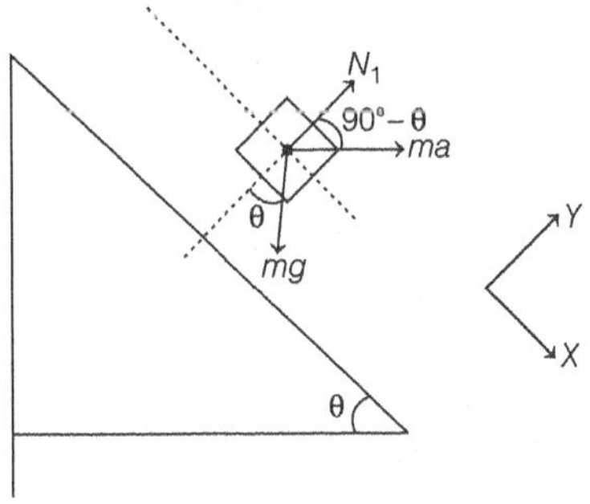

$$\Sigma F_y = 0 \Rightarrow N_1 + ma\sin\theta = mg\cos\theta$$

$$\Rightarrow \quad N_1 = mg\cos\theta - ma\sin\theta$$

When block loses contact with the wedge

$$N_1 = mg\cos\theta - ma\sin\theta = 0 \Rightarrow a = g\cot\theta$$

3. Lets take acceleration of wedge to be a.

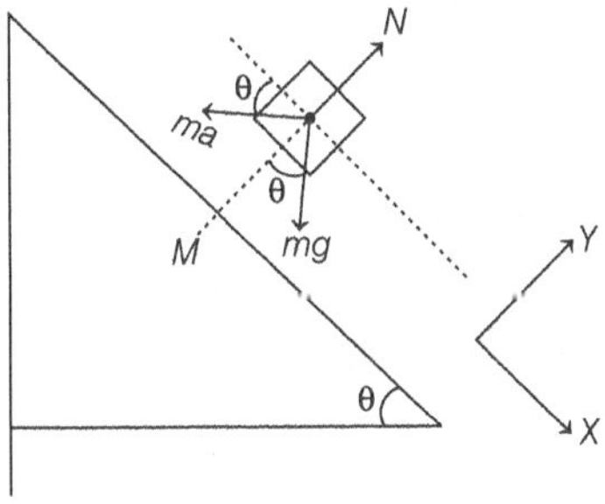

$$\Sigma F_x = 0$$

$$\Rightarrow \quad mg\sin\theta - ma\cos\theta = 0 \Rightarrow a = g\tan\theta$$

For $(M + m)$ system,

$$\Sigma F_x = ma \Rightarrow F = (M + m)g\tan\theta$$

4.

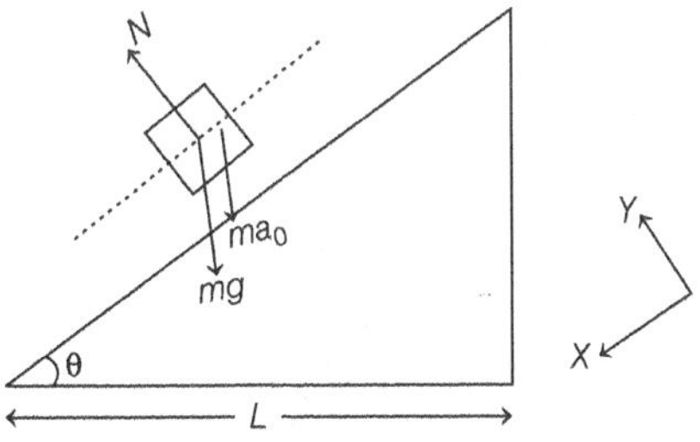

$$\Sigma F_x = ma_x \Rightarrow (mg + ma_0)\sin\theta = ma_x$$

$$\Rightarrow \quad a_x = (g + a_0)\sin\theta \Rightarrow s = ut + \frac{1}{2}at^2$$

$$\Rightarrow \quad \frac{L}{\cos\theta} = 0 + \frac{1}{2}(g + a_0)\sin\theta T^2$$

$$T = \sqrt{\frac{2L}{(g + a_0)\sin\theta\cos\theta}}$$

5.

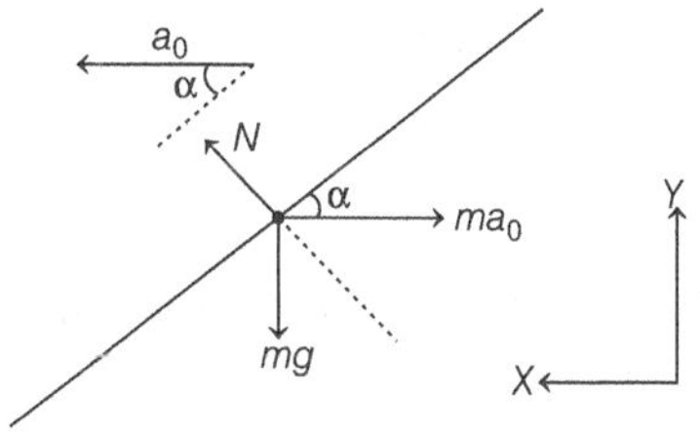

$$\Sigma F_x = ma_x \Rightarrow mg\sin\alpha - ma_0\cos\alpha = ma_x$$

$$\Rightarrow \quad a_x = g\sin\alpha - a_0\cos\alpha$$

6.

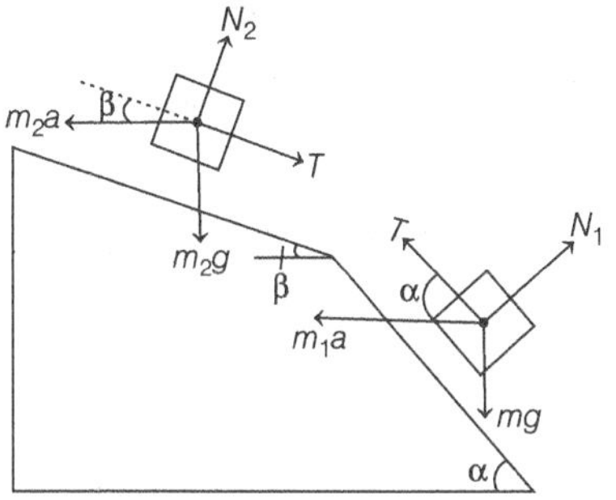

Since m_1 is at rest w.r.t. wedge

$$\Rightarrow \quad m_1 g\sin\alpha = T + m_1 a\cos\alpha \quad \text{...(i)}$$

m_2 is also at rest w.r.t. wedge

$$\Rightarrow \quad T + m_2 g\sin\beta = m_2 a\cos\beta \quad \text{...(ii)}$$

From Eqs. (i) and (ii), we get

$$u = \frac{m_1 g\sin\alpha + m_2 g\sin\beta}{m_1\cos\alpha + m_2\cos\beta}$$

10.8 Wedge Constraint

1. (a)

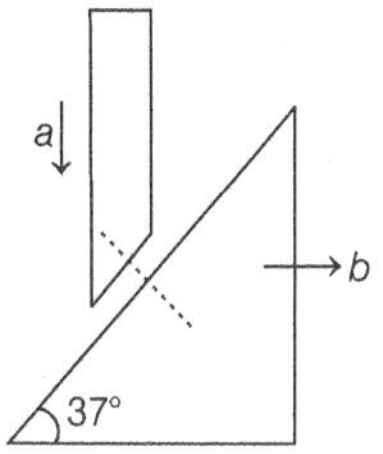

From wedge constraint their acceleration will be same along the common normal at contact.

$$\Rightarrow \quad a\cos 37° = b\sin 37° \Rightarrow b = \frac{4a}{3}$$

So, $$\mathbf{a}_B = \left(\frac{4a}{3}\right)\hat{\mathbf{i}}$$

(b) From string constraint,

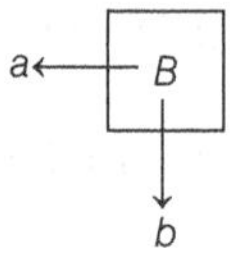

$$-4a + b = 0 \Rightarrow b = 4a \Rightarrow \mathbf{a}_B = -a\hat{\mathbf{i}} - 4a\hat{\mathbf{j}}$$

(c) From string constraint,

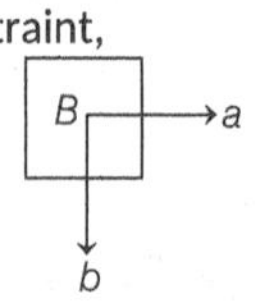

$$-2a - 2c + b = 0 \Rightarrow b = 2(a+c) \Rightarrow \mathbf{a}_B = a\hat{\mathbf{i}} - 2(a+c)\hat{\mathbf{j}}$$

(d) From string constraint,

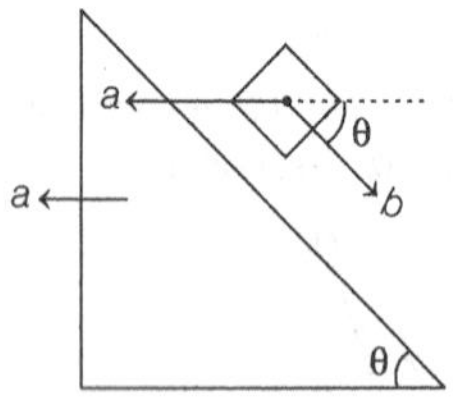

$$-a + b = 0 \Rightarrow b = a$$

$$\mathbf{a}_B = (b\cos\theta - a)\hat{\mathbf{i}} - b\sin\theta\,\hat{\mathbf{j}} = a(\cos\theta - 1)\hat{\mathbf{i}} - a\sin\theta\,\hat{\mathbf{j}}$$

2.

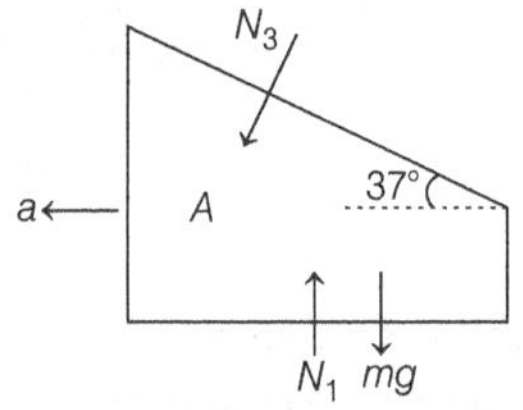

For A, $\Sigma F_x = ma_x \Rightarrow N_3 \sin 37° = ma$ ...(i)

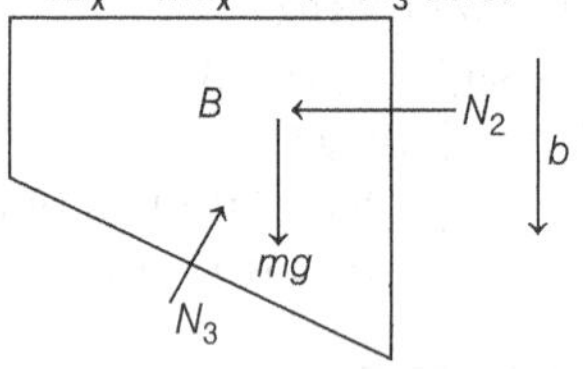

For B, $\Sigma F_y = ma_y \Rightarrow mg - N_3\cos 37° = mb$ ...(ii)

From wedge constraint,

$\Rightarrow a\sin 37° = b\cos 37° \Rightarrow a = 4b/3$ ...(iii)

Solving Eqs. (i), (ii) and (iii),

$$a = \frac{12g}{25} \text{ and } b = \frac{9g}{25}$$

3.

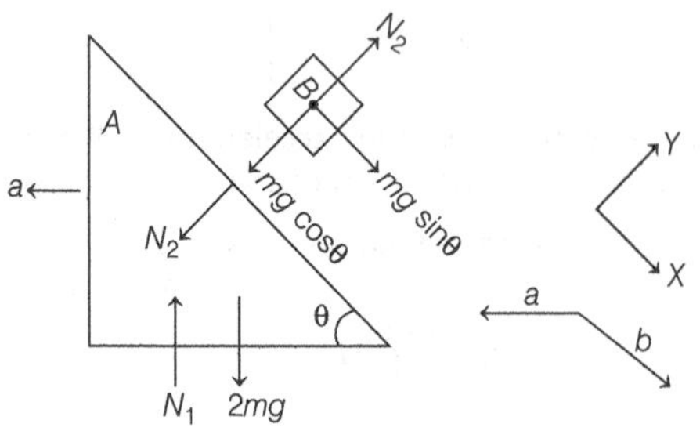

For A, $\Sigma F_x = ma_x \Rightarrow N_2 \sin\theta = 2ma$ ...(i)

For B, $\Sigma F_x = ma_x \Rightarrow mg\sin\theta = m(b - a\cos\theta)$ ...(ii)

$\Sigma F_y = ma_y \Rightarrow mg\cos\theta - N_2 = ma\sin\theta$ ...(iii)

Solving Eqs. (i), (ii) and (iii), we get

$$a = \frac{b\cos\theta}{3};\ b = \frac{3g\sin\theta}{3 - \cos^2\theta}$$

Level 2

Single Choice Correct Questions

1. Taking all blocks as a system

$$\Sigma F_x = ma_x$$

$$(m_1 + m_2 + m_3 + \ldots)g\sin\theta = (m_1 + m_2 + \ldots)a$$

$$a = g\sin\theta$$

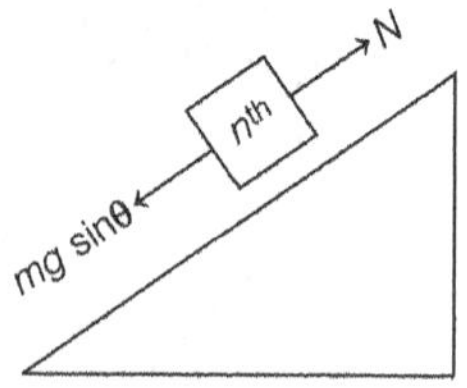

For nth block, $\Sigma F_x = ma_x$

$\Rightarrow mg\sin\theta - N = m(g\sin\theta) \Rightarrow N = 0$

2.

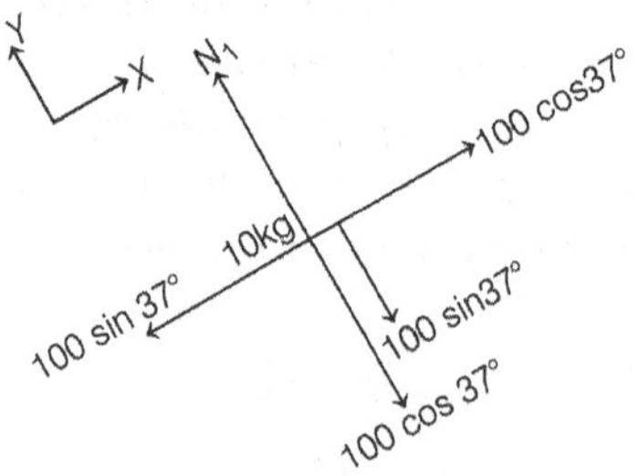

$$\Sigma F_x = ma_x$$

$$\Rightarrow 100\cos 37° - 100\sin 37° = 10a \Rightarrow a = 2\,\text{m/s}^2$$

3. (a) For system, $\Sigma F_x = ma_x$

$$P = 5ma \Rightarrow a = \frac{P}{5m}$$

(b) Resultant force on each cube $= ma = \dfrac{P}{5}$

(c)

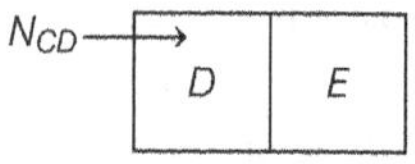

$$N_{CD} = 2ma = \frac{2P}{5}$$

4.

FBD of 10 kg

$\Sigma F_y = 0 \Rightarrow +T_1 - 100 = 0 \Rightarrow T_1 = 100\,\text{N}$

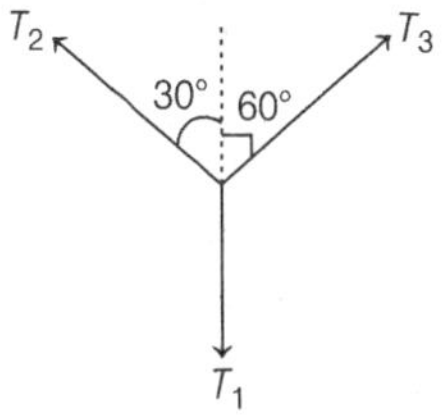

FBD of *O*

$$\Sigma F_y = 0 \Rightarrow T_2 \cos 30° + T_3 \cos 60° = 100 \quad \text{...(i)}$$

$$\Sigma F_x = 0 \Rightarrow T_3 \sin 60° - T_2 \sin 30° = 0 \quad \text{...(ii)}$$

From Eqs. (i) and (ii), we get

$$T_3 = 50\,\text{N}$$

5.

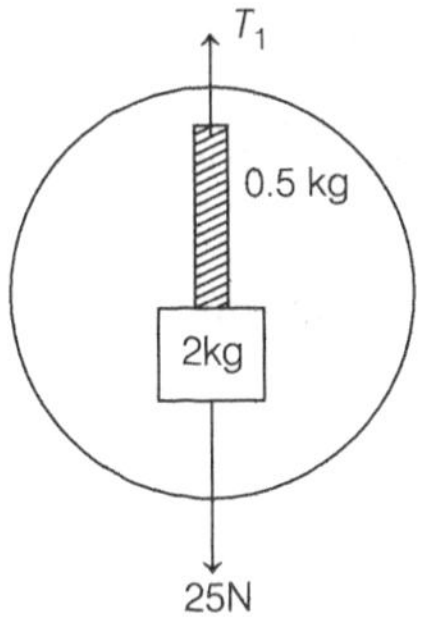

$$\Sigma F_y = ma_y \Rightarrow T_1 - 25 = 2.5(10) \Rightarrow T_1 = 50\text{N}$$

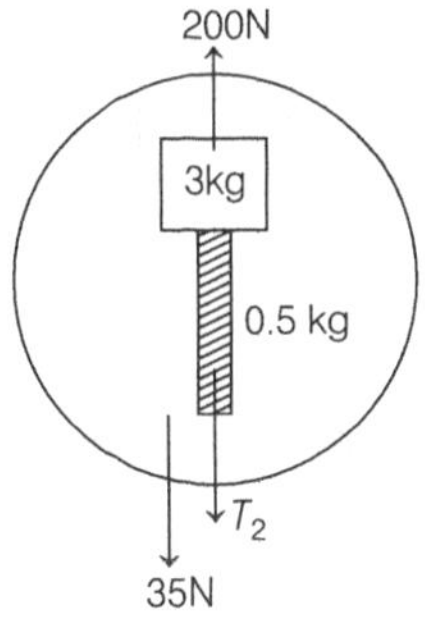

$$\Sigma F_y = ma_y \Rightarrow 200 - 35 - T_2 = 3.5(10)$$

$$\Rightarrow \quad T_2 = 130\,\text{N}$$

6.

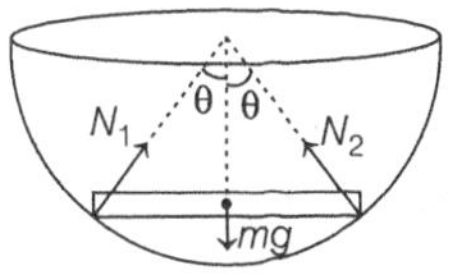

$$\sin\theta = \frac{R/2}{R}$$

$$\Rightarrow \theta = 30°$$

$$\Sigma F_x = 0 \Rightarrow N_1 \sin\theta = N_2 \sin\theta \Rightarrow N_1 = N_2$$

$$\Sigma F_y = 0 \Rightarrow N_1 \cos\theta + N_2 \cos\theta = mg$$

$$\Rightarrow N_1 = N_2 = \frac{mg}{2\cos\theta} = 5\,\text{N}$$

7. $T_1 = mg, \quad T_2 = \dfrac{2(m+m_1)\,m}{(m+m_1)+m}\,g$

$$T_2 = \frac{4}{3}T_1$$

$$\Rightarrow \frac{2m(m+m_1)}{2m+m_1} = \frac{4}{3}mg$$

$$\Rightarrow 3m + 3m_1 = 4m + 2m_1 \Rightarrow m_1 = m$$

8. Acceleration $= \dfrac{\text{Net driving force}}{\text{Total mass}} = \dfrac{20+20-20}{6} = \dfrac{10}{3}\,\text{m/s}^2$

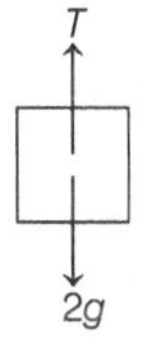

FBD of *C*

$$2g - T = 2\left(\frac{g}{3}\right) \Rightarrow T = \frac{4g}{3}$$

9.

$$150 - T_1 - T_2 = 15a \quad \text{...(i)}$$

$$T_1 = 5a \quad \text{...(ii)}$$

$$T_2 = 10a \quad \text{...(iii)}$$

From Eqs. (i), (ii)and (iii), we get

$$a = 5\,\text{m/s}^2 \text{ and } T_2 = 50\,\text{N}$$

10. Acceleration $= \dfrac{\text{Net driving force}}{\text{Total mass}}$

$$= \frac{mg + 2mg\sin 37° + 3\,mg\sin 53°}{10m} = \frac{23}{5}\,\text{m/s}^2$$

11. $a_1 = \dfrac{40}{9}\,\text{m/s}^2, \quad a_2 = \dfrac{50-40}{9} = \dfrac{10}{9}\,\text{m/s}^2$

12. $N_1 = ma = m\left(\dfrac{F}{3m}\right), \quad N_2 = 2ma = 2m\left(\dfrac{F}{3m}\right)$

$$N_1 : N_2 :: 1 : 2$$

13.

$$8g\sin 30° - T = 8a \quad \text{...(i)}$$

$$T - 4g = 4a \quad \text{...(ii)}$$

From Eqs. (i) and (ii), we get

$$a = 0$$

14. $F_{avg} = \dfrac{\Delta p}{\Delta t} = \dfrac{2\,mv\sin 53°}{\Delta t} = 8\,\text{N}$

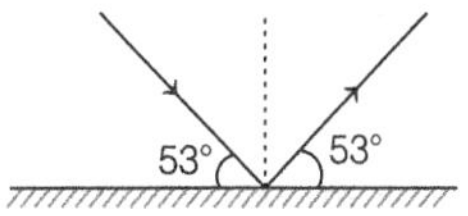

15.

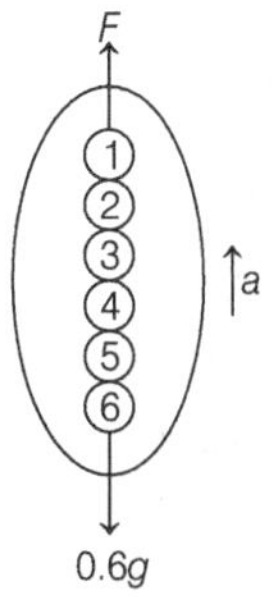

$F - 0.6g = 0.6a \Rightarrow 7.2 - 6 = 0.6a \Rightarrow a = 2\,\text{m/s}^2$

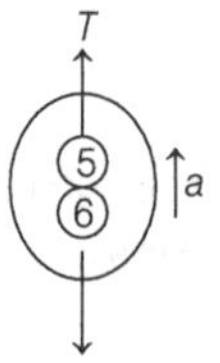

$T - 0.2g = 0.2(2) \Rightarrow T = 2.4\,\text{N}$

16.

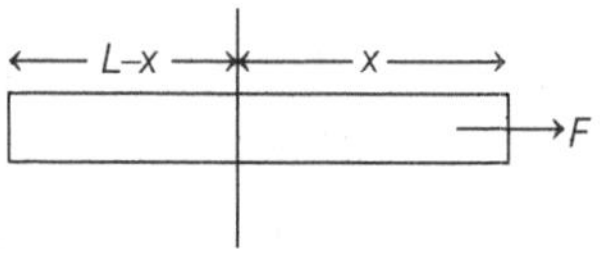

$F = Ma \Rightarrow a = \dfrac{F}{M}$

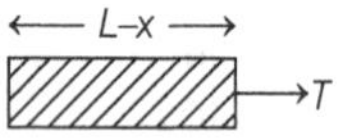

$T = \left(\dfrac{M}{L}(L-x)\right)\left(\dfrac{F}{M}\right) = \dfrac{F(L-x)}{L}$

17.

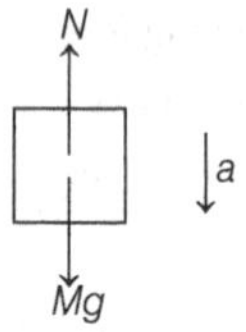

FBD of block

$Mg - N = ma \Rightarrow Mg - \dfrac{Mg}{4} = Ma \Rightarrow a = \dfrac{3g}{4}$

18. $T - 6000g = 6000\left(\dfrac{g}{2}\right)$

$\Rightarrow T = 9000\,g$

19. $B - mg = m\left(\dfrac{g}{6}\right)$ ...(i)

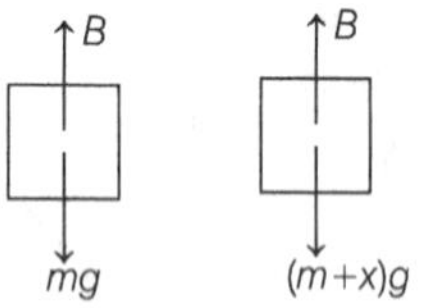

$(m+x)g - B = (m+x)\dfrac{g}{6}$ ...(ii)

From Eqs. (i) and (ii), we get

$x = \dfrac{2m}{5}$

20. $M_1 g \sin\alpha - T = M_1 a$ ...(i)

$T - M_2 g \sin\beta = M_2 a$ ...(ii)

From Eqs. (i) and (ii), we get

$T = \dfrac{M_1 M_2(\sin\alpha + \sin\beta)\,g}{M_1 + M_2}$

21.

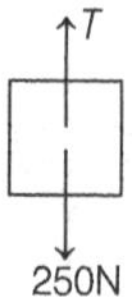

FBD of cage

$\Sigma F_y = 0 \Rightarrow T = 250\,\text{N}$

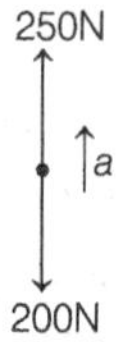

FBD of monkey

$250 - 200 = 20a \Rightarrow a = 2.5\,\text{m/s}^2$

22.

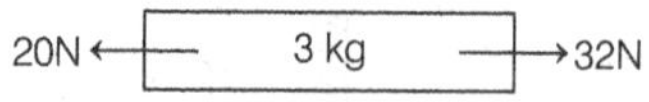

FBD of 3kg

$\Sigma F_x = ma_x \Rightarrow 32 - 20 = 3a \Rightarrow a = 4\,\text{m/s}^2$

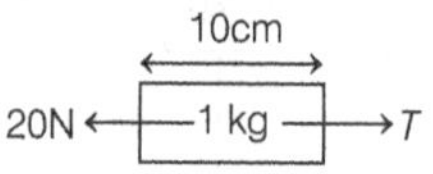

FBD of 10cm part

$\Sigma F_x = ma_x \Rightarrow T - 20 = 1(4) \Rightarrow T = 24\,\text{N}$

23.

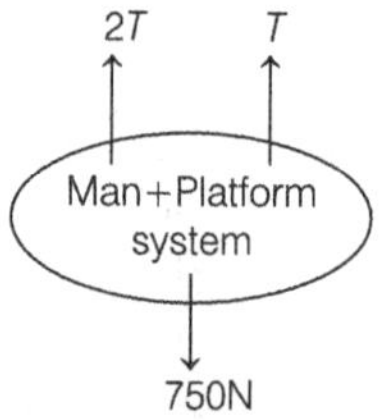

$\Sigma F_y = ma_y \Rightarrow 3T - 750 = 75(0) \Rightarrow T = 250\,\text{N}$

24. For right sphere,

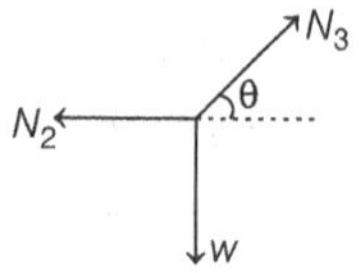

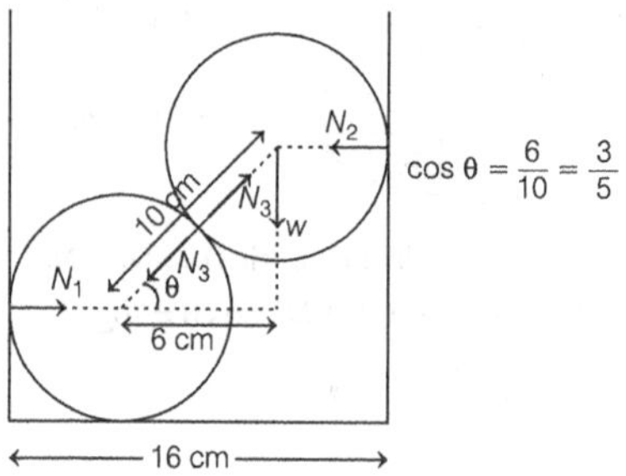

$\Sigma F_y = 0 \Rightarrow N_3 \sin\theta = w$

$\Sigma F_x = 0 \Rightarrow N_3 \cos\theta = N_2$

$\Rightarrow N_2 = W\cot\theta = \dfrac{3w}{4} \Rightarrow N_1 = N_2 = \dfrac{3w}{4}$

25. $m_2g - 2T = m_2a_2$ ...(i)

$T = m_1a_1$ ...(ii)

$a_1 = 2a_2$ ...(iii)

From Eqs. (i), (ii) and (iii), we get

$$a_2 = \frac{m_2g}{4m_1 + m_2}$$

26. $\Delta p = \Sigma F\Delta t \Rightarrow m\Delta v = 7(1.5) + 5(1.7) + 10(3) \Rightarrow \Delta v = 4.9\ \text{m/s}$

27. $F = \frac{dm}{dt}v \Rightarrow F_{avg} = \frac{\Delta m}{\Delta t}v = \frac{5}{2.5} \times 4 = 8$ dyne

28. $a = \frac{(m_1 - m_2)g}{m_1 + m_2} = \frac{3 \times 10}{5} = 6\ \text{m/s}^2$

$s_{rel} = u_{rel}t + \frac{1}{2}a_{rel}t^2 \Rightarrow 6 = 0 + \frac{1}{2}\{6 - (-6)\}t^2 \Rightarrow t = 1\ \text{s}$

29. $Mg\sin\theta - T = Ma$ ...(i)

$T = Ma$ ...(ii)

Solving Eqs. (i) and (ii), we get

$$a = \frac{g\sin\theta}{2} \quad \text{and} \quad T = \frac{Mg\sin\theta}{2}$$

30.

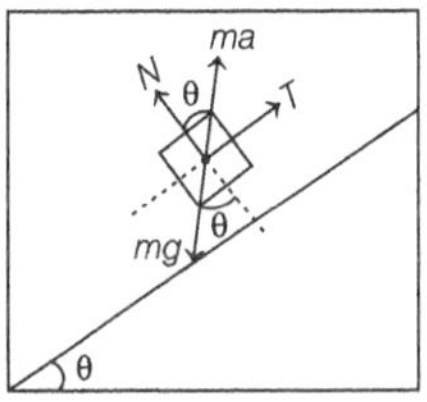

$\Sigma F_y = 0 \Rightarrow N + ma\cos\theta = mg\cos\theta$

$\Rightarrow N = m(g - a)\cos\theta$

31. $f_a = \frac{(2m - m)g}{2m + m} = \frac{g}{3}, \quad f_b = \frac{2mg - mg}{m} = g$

32. For (man + platform) system,

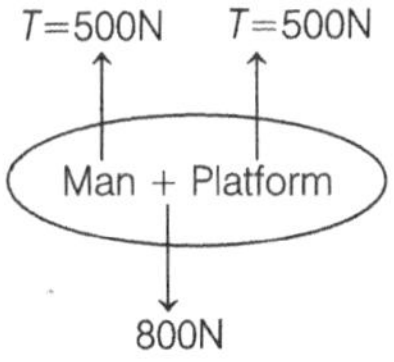

$\Sigma F_y = ma_y \Rightarrow 2T - 800 = 80a \Rightarrow a = 2.5\ \text{m/s}^2$

33. $\sin\theta = \frac{3}{5} \Rightarrow T\cos\theta = mg$ ...(i)

$T\sin\theta = N$ ...(ii)

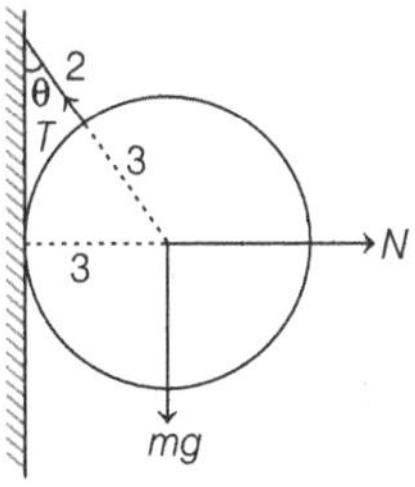

From Eqs. (i) and (ii), we get

$\Rightarrow N = mg\tan\theta \Rightarrow N = \frac{3mg}{4}$

34. $\frac{N_1}{N_2} = \frac{m(g + a)}{m(g - a)} = 2 \Rightarrow g + a = 2g - 2a \Rightarrow a = \frac{g}{3}$

35. $3T = 180 \Rightarrow T = 60\ \text{N}$

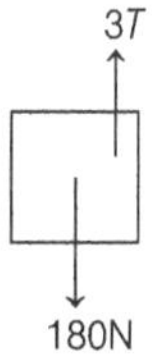

Force exerted by the ceiling $= 4T = 240$ N

36. $kl = k_1l_1 = k_2l_2$

$\Rightarrow k_1 = \frac{kl}{l_1} = \frac{k(l_1 + l_2)}{l_1} = k\left(1 + \frac{1}{n}\right) = \frac{k(1 + n)}{n}$

37. Since, m_3 is at rest.

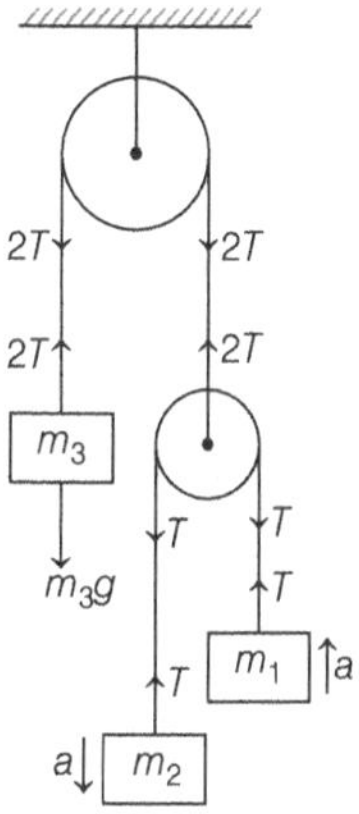

$\Rightarrow 2T = m_3g$

For m_1 and m_2,

$m_2g - T = m_2a$ ...(i)

$T - m_1g = m_1a$ ...(ii)

From Eqs. (i) and (ii), we get

$$\frac{m_2g - T}{m_2} = \frac{T - m_1g}{m_1} \Rightarrow T = \frac{2m_1m_2g}{m_1 + m_2} = \frac{m_3g}{2}$$

$$\Rightarrow m_3 = \frac{4m_1m_2}{m_1 + m_2}$$

38.

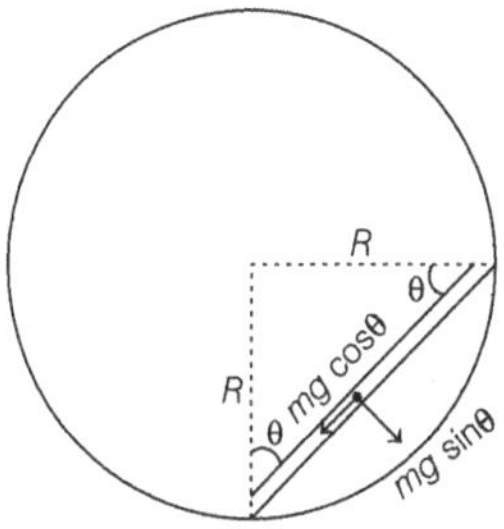

$$s = ut + \frac{1}{2}at^2 \Rightarrow 2R\cos\theta = \frac{1}{2}(g\cos\theta)t^2 \Rightarrow t = \sqrt{\frac{4R}{g}}$$

So, time taken is independent of θ.

39.

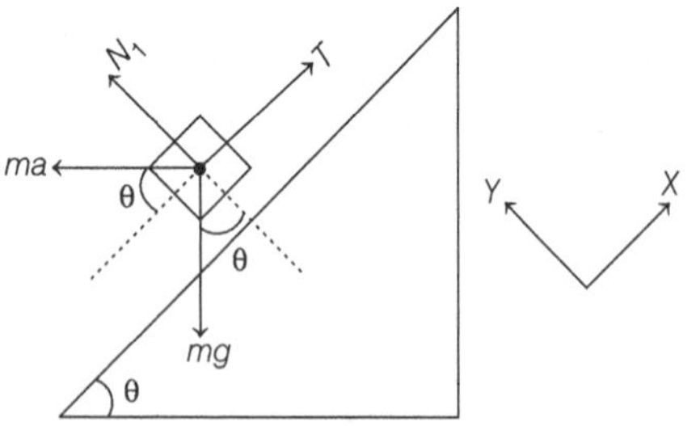

$\Sigma F_y = 0 \Rightarrow N_1 + ma\sin\theta = mg\cos\theta$

$\Rightarrow \quad N_1 = mg\cos\theta - ma\sin\theta = 0 \Rightarrow a = g\cot\theta$

$\Sigma F_x = 0 \Rightarrow T - mg\sin\theta - ma\cos\theta = 0$

$\Rightarrow \quad T = mg\sin\theta + ma\cos\theta$

$\Rightarrow \quad T = mg\sin\theta + m(g\cot\theta)\cos\theta$

$\Rightarrow \quad T = mg\,\text{cosec}\,\theta$

40.

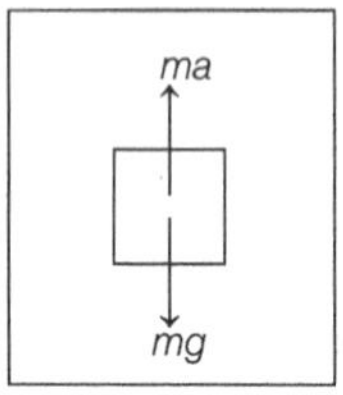

Since, pseudo force is more than the weight of block, it will lose contact with the floor of the elevator.

$$s = ut + \frac{1}{2}at^2 = 0 + \frac{1}{2}(10)(0.2)^2 = 0.2 \text{ m} = 20 \text{ cm}$$

41.

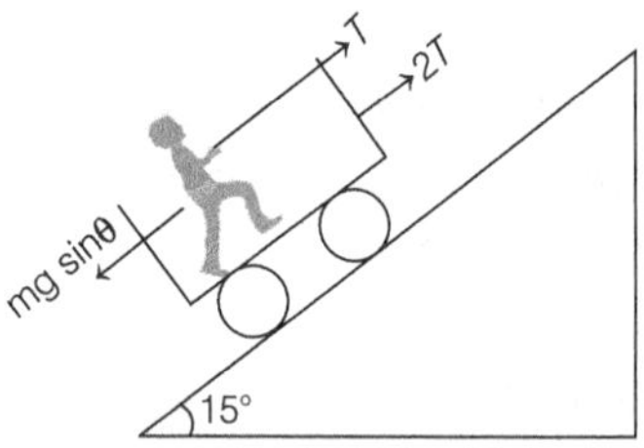

$3T - mg\sin\theta = ma \Rightarrow 750 - 1000(0.26) = 100a$

$\Rightarrow \quad a = 4.9 \text{ m/s}^2$

42. To just lift the block, tension in the string will be 20 N.

$F = ma \Rightarrow 20 - 10 = 1 \cdot a_1 \Rightarrow a_1 = 10 \text{ m/s}^2$

When monkey stops moving w.r.t. the string

$20 - T = 2a_2$ ...(i)

$T - 10 = 1\,a_2$ ...(ii)

From Eqs. (i) and (ii), we get

$\Rightarrow \quad a_2 = \frac{10}{3} \text{ m/s}^2$

Change in acceleration $= a_1 - a_2 = 10 - \frac{10}{3} = \frac{20}{3} \text{ m/s}^2$

43. $a = \frac{\text{Net pulling force}}{\text{Total mass}} \Rightarrow a_1 = \frac{20}{8}$ and $a_2 = \frac{30}{8}$

44. $20 - T = 2a$ ...(i)

$T - 10 = 1\,a$ ...(ii)

From Eqs. (i)and (ii), we get

$a = \frac{10}{3} \text{ m/s}^2$

$v = u + at$

$\Rightarrow \quad v = 0 + \frac{10}{3}(1) = \frac{10}{3} \text{ m/s}$

Now the larger mass is stopped momentarily, so the string will become slack.

Lets assume that string gets taut t time later.

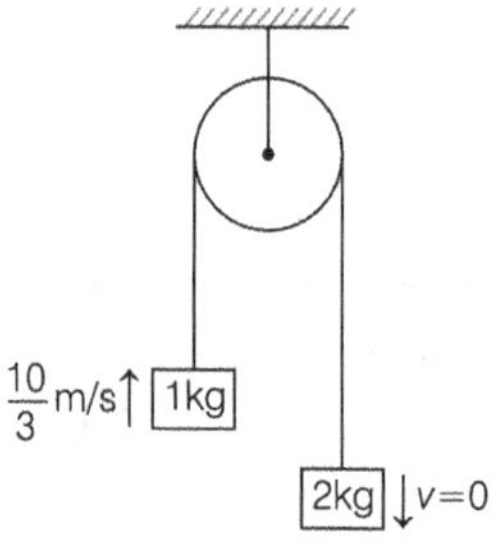

$$s = ut + \frac{1}{2}at^2 \Rightarrow \frac{10}{3}t - \frac{1}{2}\times 10 \times t^2 = 0 + \frac{1}{2}(10)t^2 \Rightarrow t = \frac{1}{3} \text{ s}$$

45.

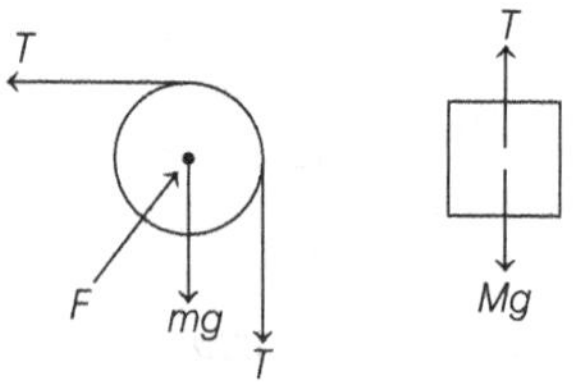

Since, the block is in equilibrium,

$\Rightarrow \quad T = Mg$

Force due to clamp on the pulley

$$= \sqrt{(T + mg)^2 + T^2} = \sqrt{(Mg + mg)^2 + (Mg)^2}$$

46. Tension in the string will be 80 N.

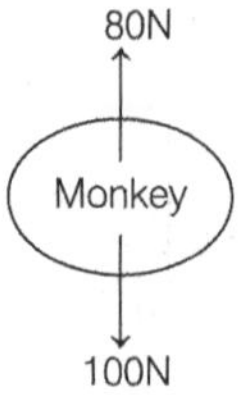

$\Sigma F_y = ma_y \Rightarrow 100 - 80 = 10a_1 \Rightarrow a_1 = 2\,\text{m/s}^2$, down

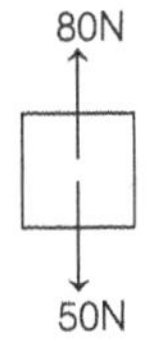

$\Sigma F_y = ma_y \Rightarrow 80 - 50 = 5a_2 \Rightarrow a_2 = 6\,\text{m/s}^2$, up

Hence, the rope in monkey's hand will be going down with 6 m/s², so relative acceleration $= 6 - (+2) = 4\,\text{m/s}^2$.

47. $\tan 53° = \dfrac{mg \sin 37° + ma}{mg \cos 37°}$

$\Rightarrow \dfrac{4}{3} = \dfrac{3g/5 + a}{4g/5} \Rightarrow a + \dfrac{3g}{5} = \dfrac{16g}{15} \Rightarrow a = \dfrac{7g}{15}$

$$Mg - T = Ma \quad \text{...(i)}$$

$$T - 60 \sin 37° = 6a \quad \text{...(ii)}$$

From Eqs. (i) and (ii), we get

$$a = \frac{10M - 36}{M + 6} = \frac{7g}{15}$$

$\Rightarrow 30M - 108 = 14M + 84 \Rightarrow 16M = 192 \Rightarrow M = 12\,\text{kg}$

48.

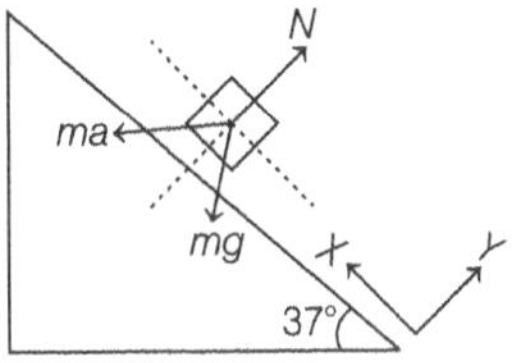

$$\Sigma F_x = ma_x$$

$\Rightarrow ma \cos 37° - mg \sin 37° = ma_x \Rightarrow a_x = 2\,\text{m/s}^2$

$$s_x = u_x t + \frac{1}{2} a_x t^2 \Rightarrow 4 = \frac{1}{2}(2)t^2 \Rightarrow t = 2\,\text{s}$$

49.

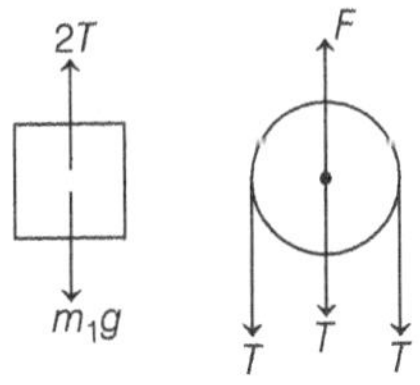

Since pulley is massless,

$\Rightarrow F - 3T = 0 \Rightarrow F = 3T$

For m_1 to lose contact, $2T = m_1 g \Rightarrow 2T = 40 \Rightarrow T = 20\,\text{N}$

So, $F = 3T = 3(20) = 60\,\text{N}$

$F = 30t = 60 \Rightarrow t = 2\,\text{s}$

50.

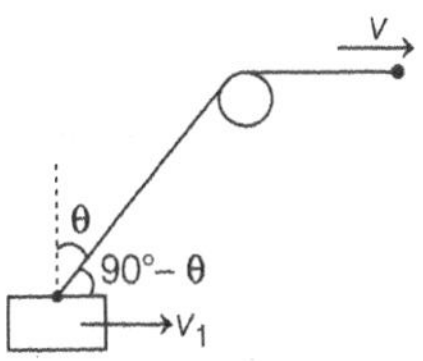

$+v - v_1 \cos(90° - \theta) = 0 \Rightarrow v_1 = \dfrac{v}{\sin\theta}$

51.

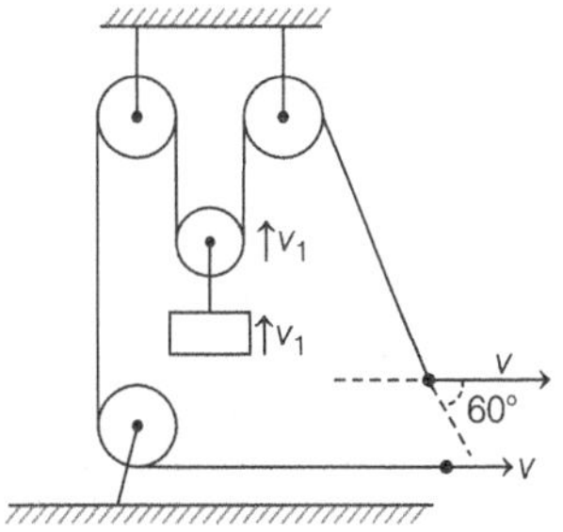

$+v + v\cos 60° - v_1 - v_1 = 0 \Rightarrow 2v_1 = \dfrac{3v}{2} \Rightarrow v_1 = \dfrac{3v}{4}$

52. Lets say acceleration of system is a and m_1, m_2 are at rest w.r.t trolley.

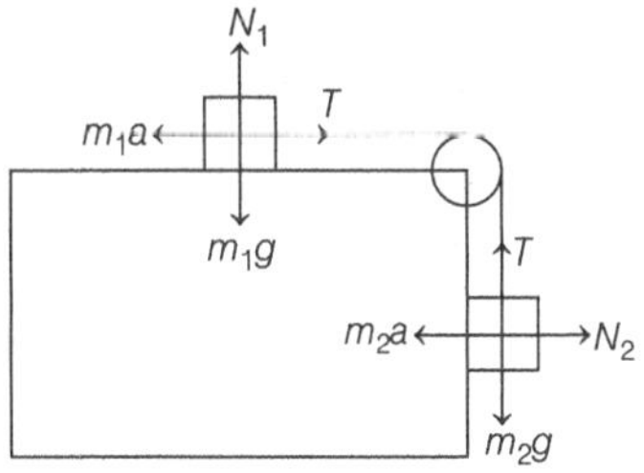

Net force on m_1 and m_2 along the string = 0

$\Rightarrow m_1 a = m_2 g \Rightarrow a = \dfrac{m_2 g}{m_1}$

For $(m_1 + m_2 + m_3)$ system,

$$\Sigma F_X = ma \Rightarrow F = (m_1 + m_2 + m_3)\left(\frac{m_2 g}{m_1}\right)$$

53. $T = P$

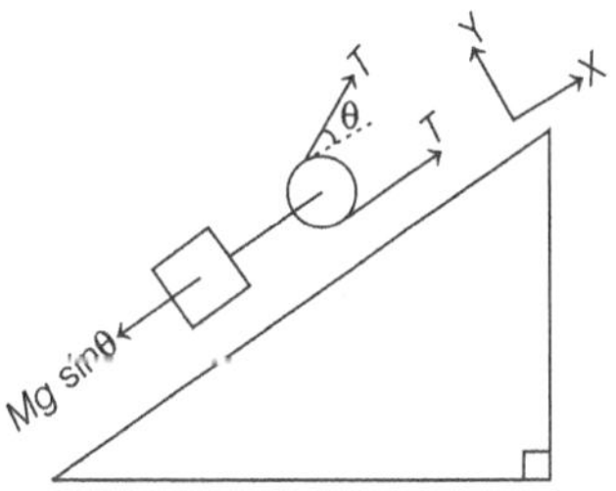

$\Sigma F_x = ma_x \Rightarrow T + T\cos\theta - Mg\sin\theta = 0$

$$T = \frac{Mg \sin\theta}{1 + \cos\theta} = Mg \tan\left(\frac{\theta}{2}\right)$$

54. For (man + platform) system

$\Sigma F = ma \Rightarrow 4T - 750 - 250 = 100 \times 2 \Rightarrow T = 300\,\text{N}$

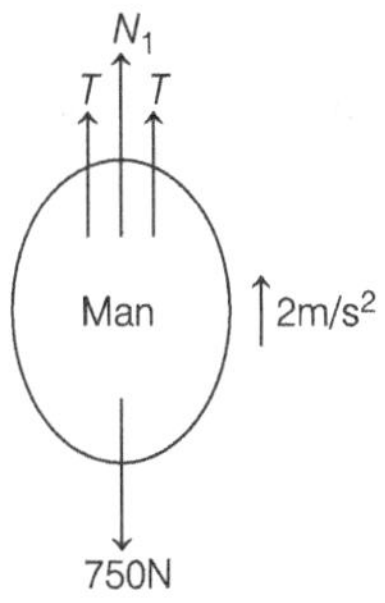

For only man, $\Sigma F = ma \Rightarrow 2T + N_1 - 750 = 75(2)$

$\Rightarrow \quad N_1 = 300\,\text{N}$

Reading $= \dfrac{N_1}{g} = 30\,\text{kg}$

55. Since acceleration of B is westward, spring will be elongated.

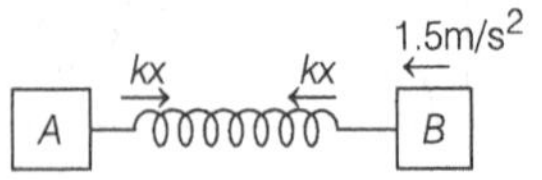

For B, $kx = 6 \times 1.5 = 9\,\text{N}$

For A, $kx = ma \quad \Rightarrow \quad 9 = 4a \Rightarrow a = 2.25\,\text{m/s}^2$, eastward

56. Before burning the string,

$\Sigma F_x = 0 \quad \Rightarrow \quad T = kx \sin 53°$

$\Sigma F_y = 0 \quad \Rightarrow \quad kx \cos 53° = mg$

$\Rightarrow \quad kx = \dfrac{5mg}{3}$

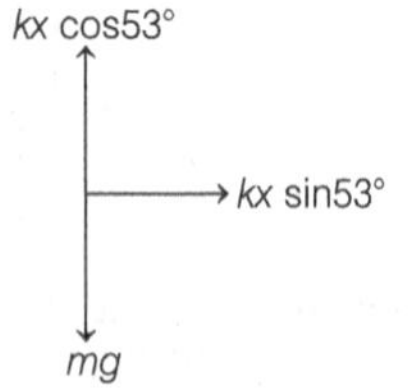

After burning the string,

$\Sigma F_x = ma_x \quad \Rightarrow \quad kx \sin 53° = ma_x \quad \Rightarrow \quad a_x = \dfrac{4g}{3}$

$\Sigma F_y = ma_y \quad \Rightarrow mg - kx \cos 53° = ma_y \quad \Rightarrow \quad a_y = 0$

57. $N_1 = mg \cos 37° \quad \Rightarrow \quad kx = N_1 \sin 37°$

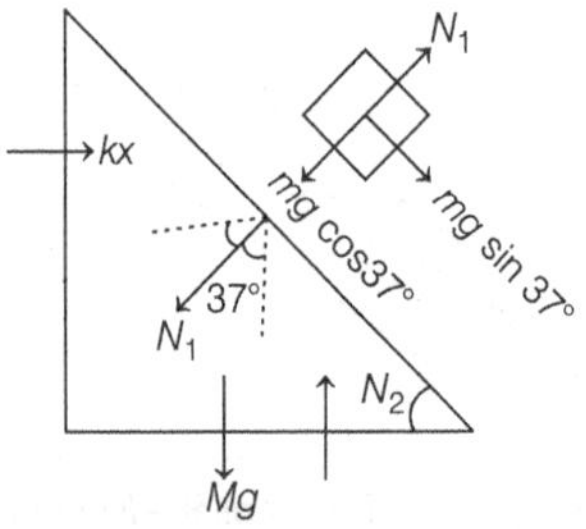

$$kx = mg \cos 37° \sin 37° = 2.5 \times 10 \times \frac{4}{5} \times \frac{3}{5} = 12\,\text{N}$$

58. $$T = \frac{2m_1 m_2 g_{\text{eff}}}{m_1 + m_2} = \frac{2(3)(1.5)}{4.5}\left(g + \frac{g}{10}\right) = \frac{11g}{5} = 22\,\text{N}$$

$kx = 2T = 2(22) = 44\,\text{N}$

Reading of spring balance $= \dfrac{44}{g} = 4.4\,\text{kg}$

59. $k_1x_1 + k_2x_2 = mg$

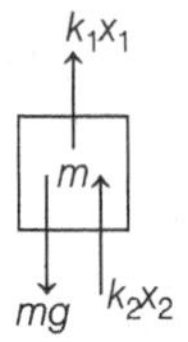

If upper spring is cut, $mg - k_2x_2 = ma$

$\Rightarrow \quad mg - k_2x_2 = m(6) \quad \Rightarrow \quad k_2x_2 = 4\,m$

If lower spring is cut,

$mg - k_1x_1 = ma \quad \Rightarrow \quad mg - 6m = ma \Rightarrow a = 4\,\text{m/s}^2$, down

60.

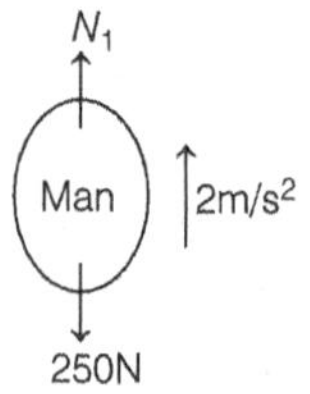

For boy, $\Sigma F = ma \quad \Rightarrow \quad N_1 - 250 = 25(2) \quad \Rightarrow \quad N_1 = 300\,\text{N}$

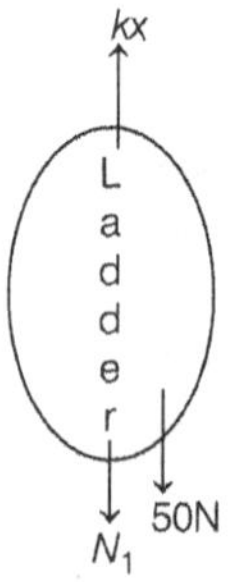

For ladder, $kx = 50 + N_1 \quad \Rightarrow \quad kx = 350\,\text{N}$

Reading of spring balance $= 35$ kg

61. $l_1 + l_2 = \text{constant}$

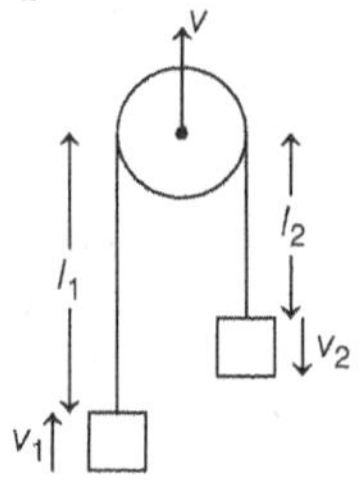

$$\frac{dl_1}{dt} + \frac{dl_2}{dt} = 0 \quad \Rightarrow \quad (-v_1 + v) + (v + v_2) = 0$$

$$\Rightarrow \quad v = \frac{v_1 - v_2}{2} \quad \Rightarrow \quad A = \frac{a_1 - a_2}{2}$$

62.

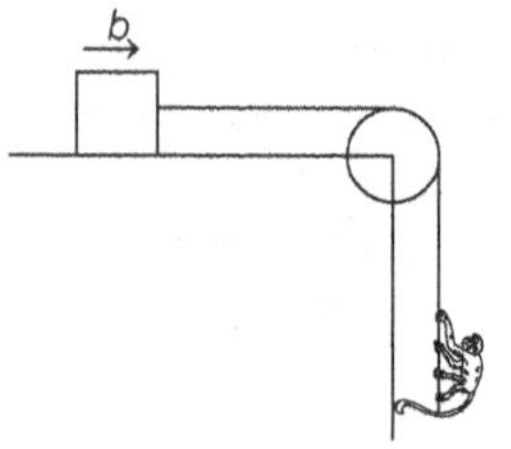

$a_{mR} = a \quad \Rightarrow \quad a_m = a + a_R \quad \Rightarrow \quad a_m = a - b$

$T = Mb$ ...(i)

$T - mg = m(a - b)$ ...(ii)

From Eqs. (i) and (ii), we get

$$mg = -ma + (M + m)b \quad \Rightarrow \quad b = \frac{m(g + a)}{M + m}$$

63.

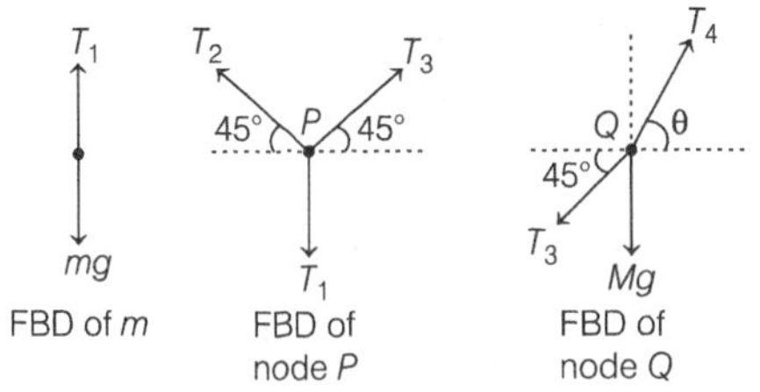

For m, $\Sigma F_y = 0 \Rightarrow T_1 - mg = 0 \Rightarrow T_1 = mg$

For node P, $\Sigma F_x = 0$

$\Rightarrow T_3 \cos 45° - T_2 \cos 45° = 0 \Rightarrow T_3 = T_2$

$\Sigma F_y = 0 \Rightarrow T_2 \sin 45° + T_3 \sin 45° = T_1$

$$\Rightarrow 2T_3 \sin 45° = T_1 \Rightarrow T_3 \sin 45° = \frac{T_1}{2} = \frac{mg}{2}$$

For node Q,

$\Sigma F_y = 0 \Rightarrow T_4 \sin\theta = Mg + T_3 \sin 45°$ ...(i)

$\Sigma F_x = 0 \Rightarrow T_4 \cos\theta = T_3 \cos 45°$ ...(ii)

Dividing Eq. (i) by Eq. (ii), we get

$$\Rightarrow \tan\theta = \frac{M + \frac{m}{2}}{\frac{m}{2}} = 1 + \frac{2M}{m}$$

64. $80 - 2T = 8a_1$ ...(i)

$T - 20 = 2a_2$ ...(ii)

$a_2 = 2a_1$ ...(iii)

Solving Eqs. (i), (ii) and (iii), we get

$T = 30\,N$

Numerical Value Questions

1.

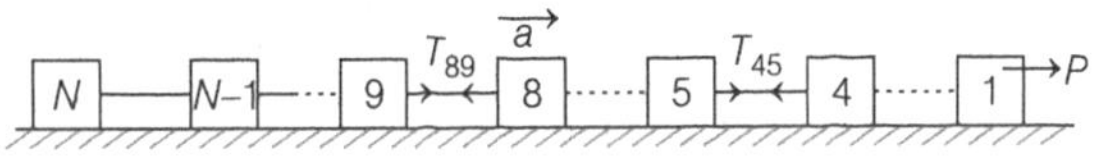

$T_{89} = (N - 8)\,ma, \quad T_{45} = (N - 4)ma$

$T_{45} = 2T_{89}$

$\Rightarrow (N - 4)ma = 2(N - 8)ma \Rightarrow N - 4 = 2N - 16 \Rightarrow N = 12$

2. For $(A + B + C)$ system, $\Sigma F = \Sigma ma$

$T_D - 100 - 150 - 80 = [10(-2) + 15(0) + 8(1.5)] \Rightarrow T_D = 322\,N$

3. For monkey B, $T - mg = ma \Rightarrow 45 - 30 = 3a_{max}$

$\Rightarrow a_{max} = 5\,m/s^2$

For $(A + B)$ system, $\Sigma F = ma$

$T' - 70 - 30 = 10(5) \Rightarrow T' = 150\,N$

4. $\Sigma F_x = ma_x$

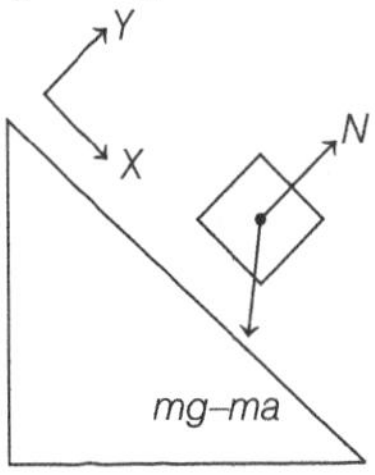

$(mg - ma) \sin 37° = ma_x$

$$\Rightarrow a_x = 7 \times \frac{3}{5} = \frac{21}{5}\,m/s^2$$

$$s = ut + \frac{1}{2}at^2$$

$$\Rightarrow 2.1 = \frac{1}{2}\left(\frac{21}{5}\right)t^2 \Rightarrow t = 1\,s$$

5. $\mathbf{v} = 5t\hat{\mathbf{i}} + 2t\hat{\mathbf{j}} \Rightarrow \mathbf{a} = 5\hat{\mathbf{i}} + 2\hat{\mathbf{j}}$

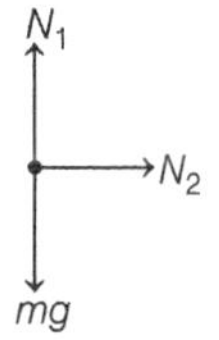

$\Sigma F_x = ma_x \Rightarrow N_2 = m(5) = 10\,N$

$\Sigma F_y = ma_y \Rightarrow N_1 - mg = m(2) \Rightarrow N_1 = 24\,N$

Net force by the cube on the sphere $= \sqrt{N_1^2 + N_2^2}$

$= \sqrt{10^2 + 24^2} = 26\,N$

6.

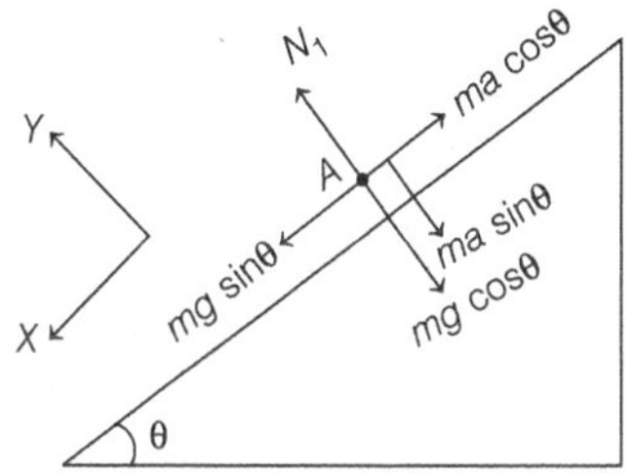

$\Sigma F_x = 0 \Rightarrow mg \sin\theta = ma \cos\theta \Rightarrow \Rightarrow a = g \tan\theta$

For $(A + B)$ system, $p = 2ma$

$$\Rightarrow p = 2mg \tan\theta = 2 \times 1 \times 10 \times \frac{3}{4} = 15\,N$$

7.

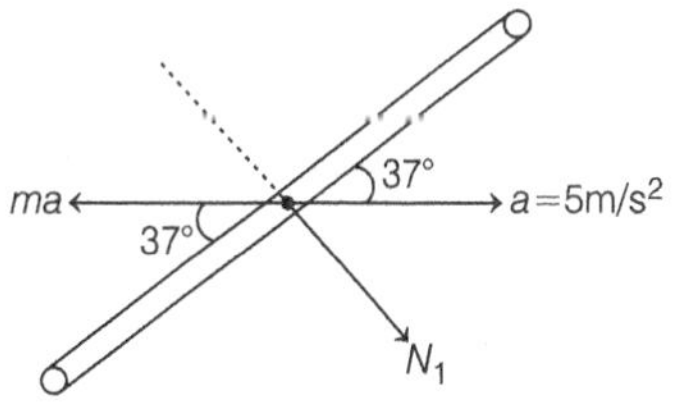

$N_1 = \sqrt{(mg)^2 + (ma \sin 37°)^2}$

$N_1 = \sqrt{(20)^2 + (6)^2} = \sqrt{436}\,N = 20.88\,N$

8. $a_{mR} = 11.5\,m/s^2 \Rightarrow a_m = 11.5 + a_R$

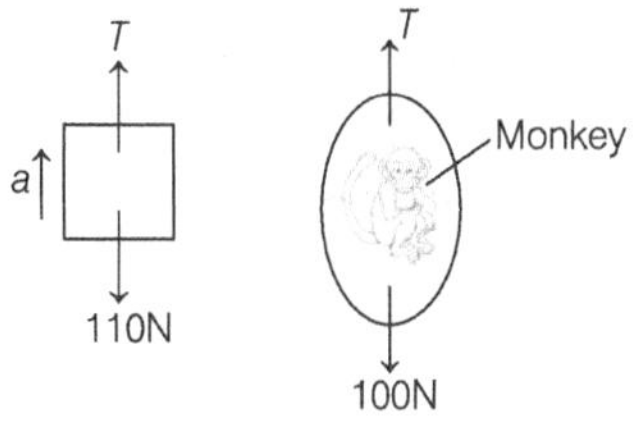

The rope in monkey's hand is going down with acceleration a.

$$T - 110 = 11a \quad \text{...(i)}$$

$$T - 100 = 10[11.5 + (-a)] \quad \text{...(ii)}$$

From Eqs. (i) and (ii), we get

$$a = 5\ \text{m/s}^2$$

9.

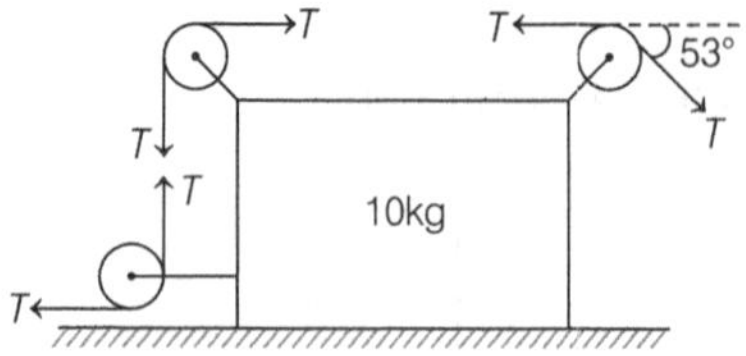

$$T = 100\ \text{N}$$

$$\Sigma F_x = ma_x \Rightarrow T - T\cos 53° = 10a$$

$$100 - 100\left(\frac{3}{5}\right) = 10a \Rightarrow a = 4\ \text{m/s}^2 \text{ left}$$

10. For man only,

$$N_1 + T - mg = ma \Rightarrow 800 + T - 800 = 80a \Rightarrow T = 80a \quad \text{...(i)}$$

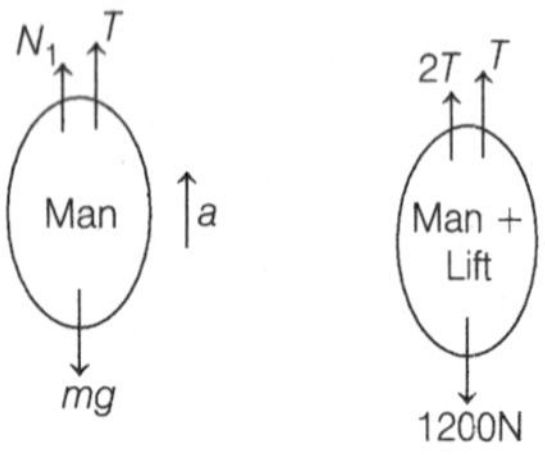

For (man + lift) system,

$$3T - 1200 = 120a \quad \text{...(ii)}$$

From Eqs. (i) and (ii), we get

$$a = 10 \text{ and } T = 800\ \text{N}$$

11.

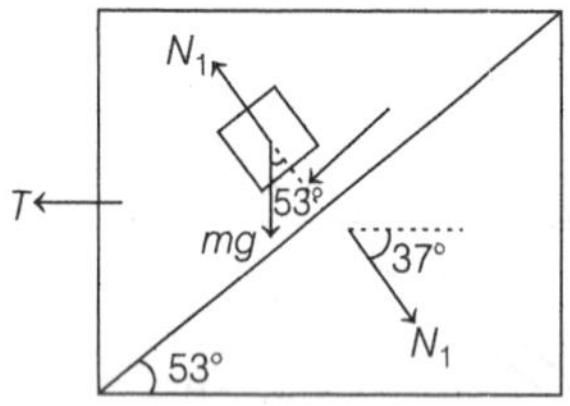

For block, $N_1 = mg\cos 53°$

For trolley, $T = N_1 \cos 37° \Rightarrow T = mg\cos 53° \cos 37°$

$$T = 100 \times \frac{3}{5} \times \frac{4}{5} = 48\ \text{N}$$

12. $\Sigma F_y = 0$

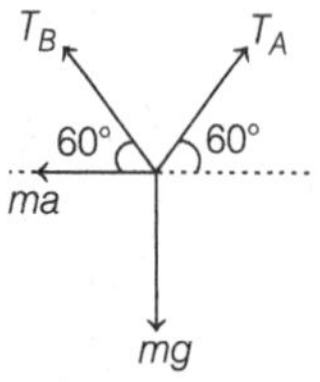

$$T_A \sin 60° + T_B \sin 60° = mg \quad \text{...(i)}$$

$$\Sigma F_x = 0 \Rightarrow T_A \cos 60° - T_B \cos 60° - ma = 0 \quad \text{...(ii)}$$

Solving Eqs. (i) and (ii), we get

$$a = \frac{g}{3\sqrt{3}}$$

13. $\Sigma F_y = 0 \Rightarrow kx = 30\ \text{N}$

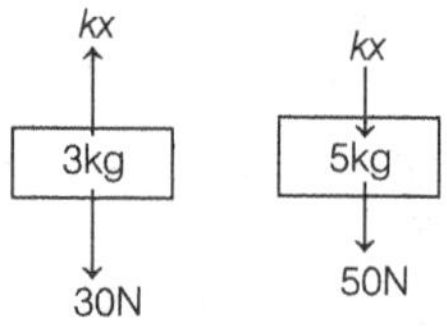

$$\Sigma F_y = ma_y \Rightarrow 50 + 30 = 5a$$

$$a = 16\ \text{m/s}^2 \downarrow$$

14. $\Sigma F_y = 0$

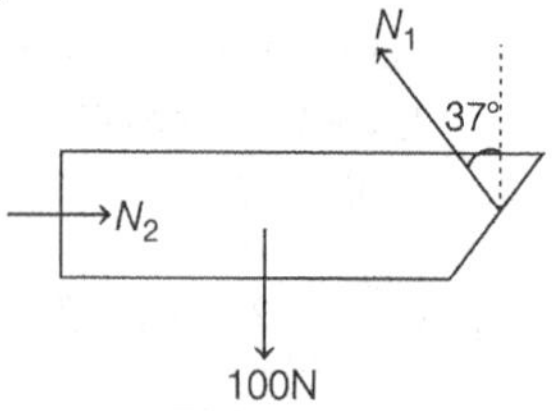

FBD of 10 kg

$$\Rightarrow N_1 \cos 37° = 100 \Rightarrow N_1 = \frac{500}{4} = 125\ \text{N}$$

$$\Sigma F_x = 0$$

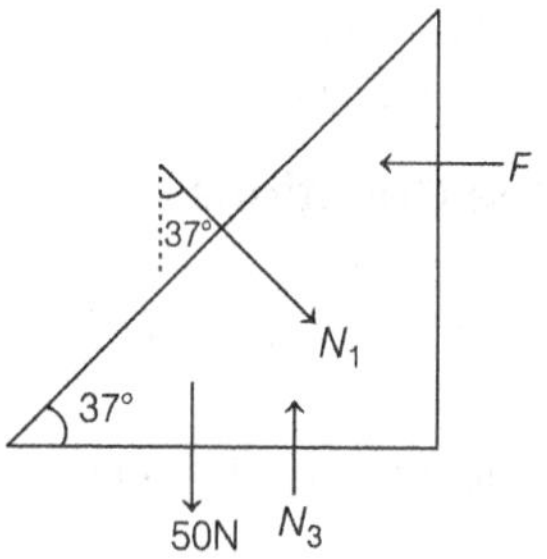

FBD of 5 kg

$$F = N_1 \sin 37°$$

$$\Rightarrow \quad F = 125\left(\frac{3}{5}\right) \Rightarrow F = 75\ \text{N}$$

15. $\cos\theta = \dfrac{4R/5}{R} = \dfrac{4}{5} \Rightarrow \theta = 37°$

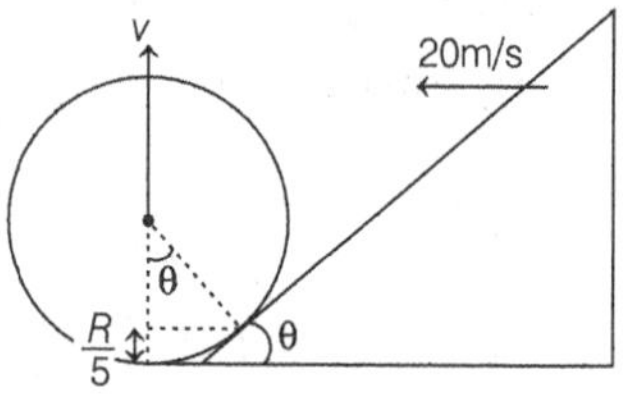

From wedge constraint, $v\cos\theta = 20\sin\theta$

$$\Rightarrow \quad v = 20\tan\theta = 20\left(\frac{3}{4}\right) = 15\ \text{m/s}$$

Level 3

Single Choice Correct Questions

1. $T - 50 = 5a_1$ ...(i)

$2T - 100 = 10a_2$ ...(ii)

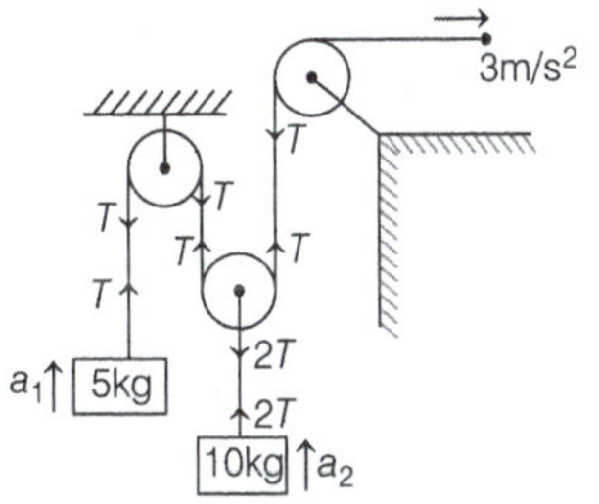

$$-a_1 - a_2 - a_2 + 3 = 0$$

$\Rightarrow \quad a_1 + 2a_2 = 3$ ...(iii)

Solving Eqs. (i), (ii) and (iii), we get

$$a_1 = 1\,\text{m/s}^2 \quad \text{and} \quad a_2 = 1\,\text{m/s}^2$$

2. $10 - T = 1\,a_1$ ...(i)

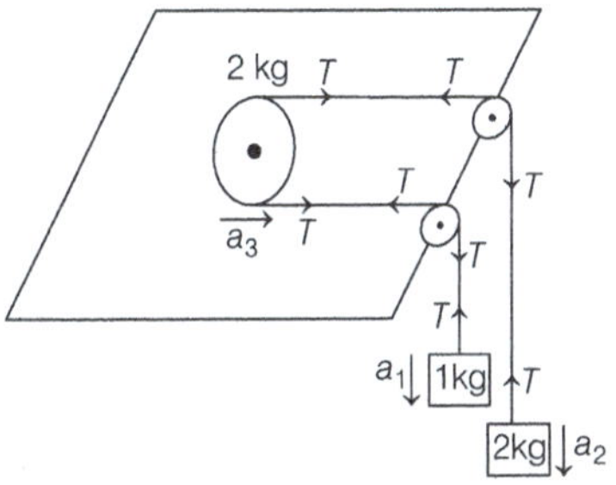

$20 - T = 2a_2$ ...(ii)

$2T = 2a_3$ ...(iii)

$-a_3 - a_3 + a_1 + a_2 = 0 \quad \Rightarrow \quad a_1 + a_2 = 2a_3$ ...(iv)

Solving Eqs. (i), (ii), (iii) and (iv), we get

$$a_3 = \frac{4g}{7}$$

3.

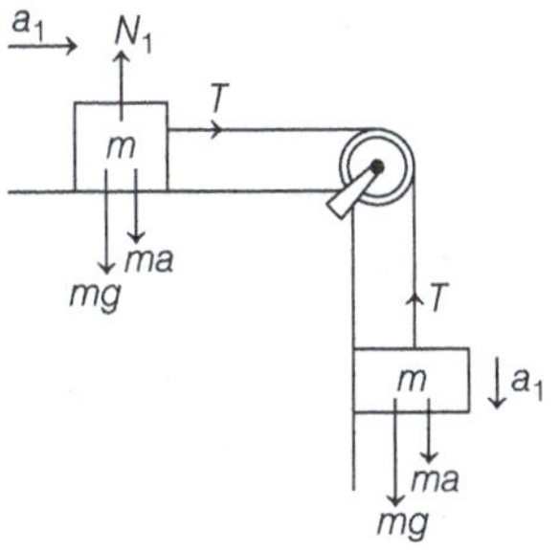

$\Sigma F = ma \quad \Rightarrow \quad mg + ma - T = ma_1$ ...(i)

$T = ma_1$ ...(ii)

From Eqs. (i) and (ii), we get

$$a_1 = \frac{g + a}{2}$$

Acceleration of block on the table as seen from ground

$$(A) = \sqrt{a^2 + a_1^2} \quad \Rightarrow \quad A = \sqrt{a^2 + \left(\frac{g+a}{2}\right)^2}$$

$$\frac{dA}{da} = \frac{1}{2\sqrt{a^2 + \left(\frac{g+a}{2}\right)^2}}\left(2a + 2\left(\frac{g+a}{2}\right)\left(\frac{1}{2}\right)\right) = 0$$

$$\Rightarrow \quad 4a + g + a = 0 \quad \Rightarrow \quad a = \frac{-g}{5}$$

$$\Rightarrow \quad a = \frac{g}{5} \text{ vertically down}$$

4.

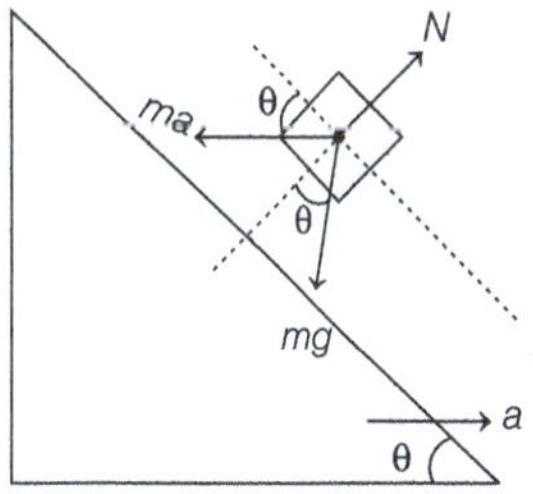

Since, 1 kg is not sliding down the wedge.

$$\Rightarrow \quad mg \sin\theta = ma\cos\theta \quad \Rightarrow \quad a = g\tan\theta = \frac{3g}{4}$$

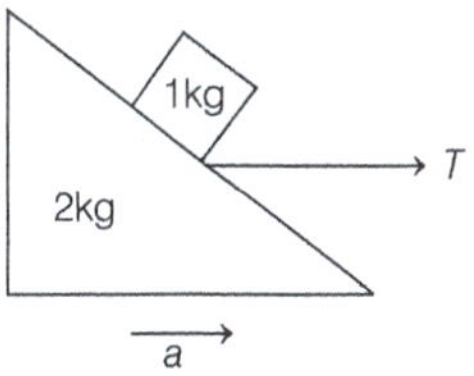

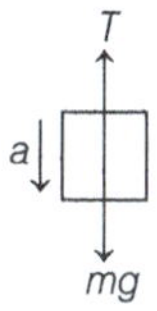

For (2 kg + 1 kg) system,

$\Sigma F_x = ma_x \quad \Rightarrow \quad T = 3a$ ...(i)

For hanging block

$mg - T = ma$ ...(ii)

From Eqs. (i) and (ii), we get

$$a = \frac{mg}{3+m} \quad \Rightarrow a = \frac{mg}{3+m} = \frac{3g}{4} \Rightarrow 4m = 9 + 3m \Rightarrow$$

$m = 9\,\text{kg}$

5.

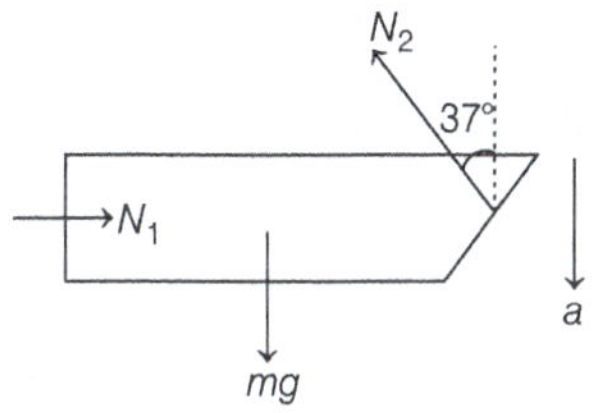

FBD of A

For A,

$$\Sigma F_y = ma_y$$

$\Rightarrow \quad mg - N_2\cos 37° = ma$ ...(i)

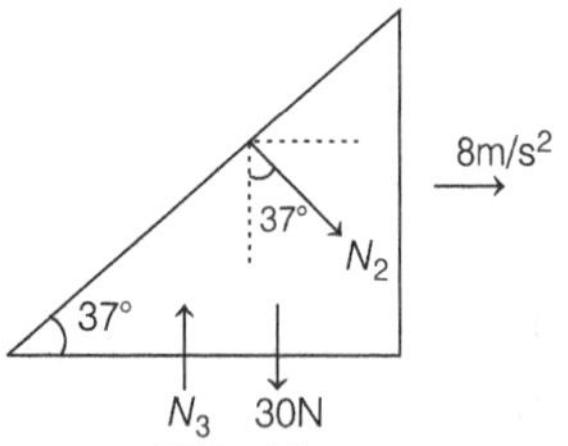

FBD of B

For B, $\Sigma F_x = ma_x \Rightarrow N_2 \sin 37° = 3(8)$ ...(ii)

and from wedge constraint,

$8 \sin 37° = a \cos 37°$ ...(iii)

From Eqs. (i), (ii) and (iii), we get

$m = 8\,\text{kg}$

6.

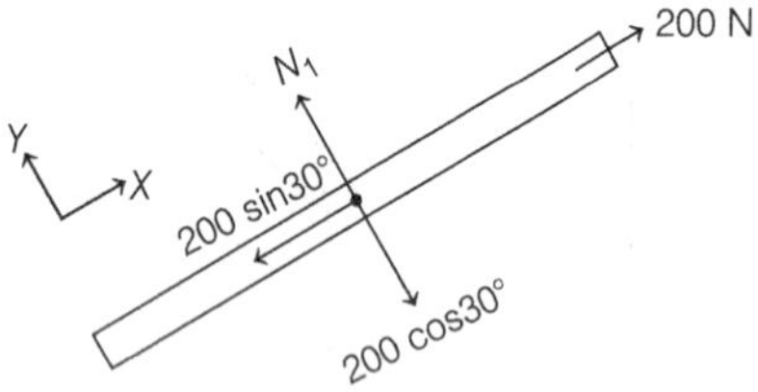

FBD of full rope

For entire string, $\Sigma F_x = ma_x$

$\Rightarrow 200 - 200 \sin 37° = 20a \Rightarrow a = 5\,\text{m/s}^2$

For $2m$ part of rope, $\Sigma F_x = ma_x$

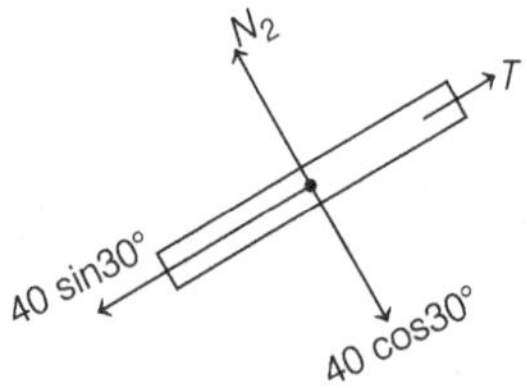

FBD of $2m$ part of rope

$\Rightarrow T - 40 \sin 30° = 4(5) \Rightarrow T = 40\,\text{N}$

7.

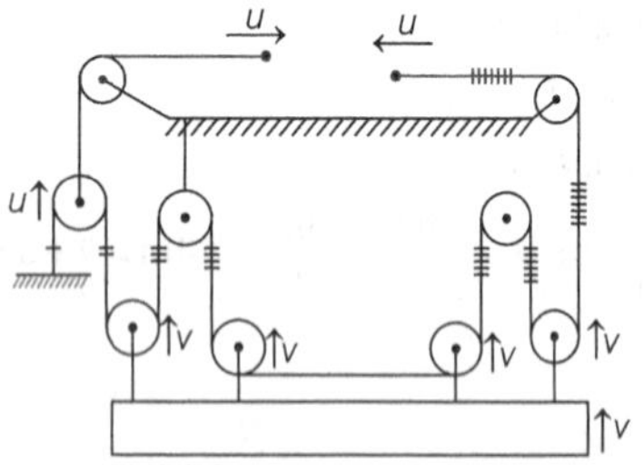

$+u + u - v - v - v - v - v - v + u = 0 \Rightarrow 6v = 3u \Rightarrow v = \dfrac{u}{2}$

8. $-a - a - a - a + a_1 = 0 \Rightarrow a_1 = 4a$

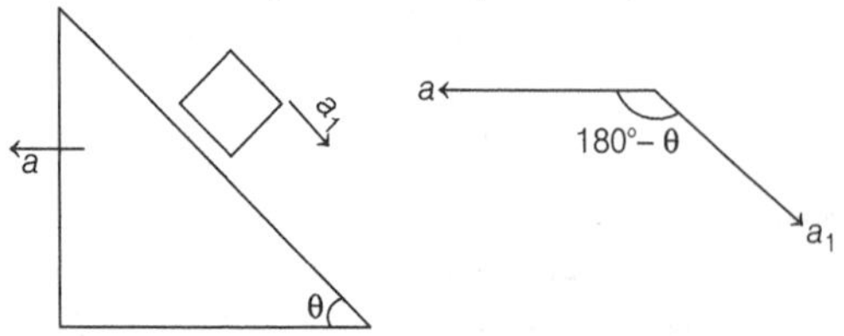

Acceleration of block in ground frame

$$= \sqrt{a^2 + a_1^2 + 2aa_1 \cos(180° - \theta)}$$

$$= \sqrt{a^2 + (4a)^2 - 2(a)(4a)\cos\theta} = a\sqrt{17 - 8\cos\theta}$$

9.

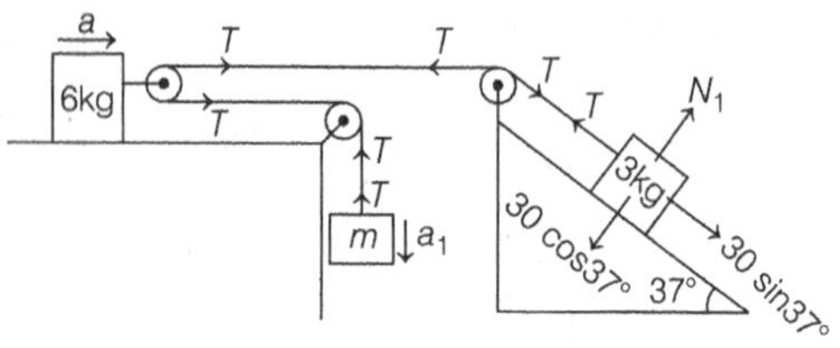

For 3 kg block,

$\Rightarrow 30 \sin 37° - T = 3(1) \Rightarrow T = 15\,\text{N}$

For 6 kg block,

$\Rightarrow \quad 2T = 6a \Rightarrow 2(15) = 6a \Rightarrow a = 5\,\text{m/s}^2$

From string constraint,

$\Rightarrow \quad -a - a + a_1 + 1 = 0 \Rightarrow a_1 = 9\,\text{m/s}^2$

For block B,

$\Rightarrow \quad mg - T = ma_1 \Rightarrow 10m - 15 = m(9) \Rightarrow m = 15\,\text{kg}$

10. $a_{mR} = a \Rightarrow a_m = a + a_R \Rightarrow a_m = a + a = 2a$

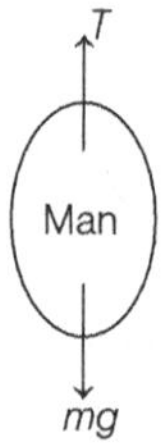

For man, $T - mg = m(2a) \Rightarrow T = m(g + 2a)$

11.

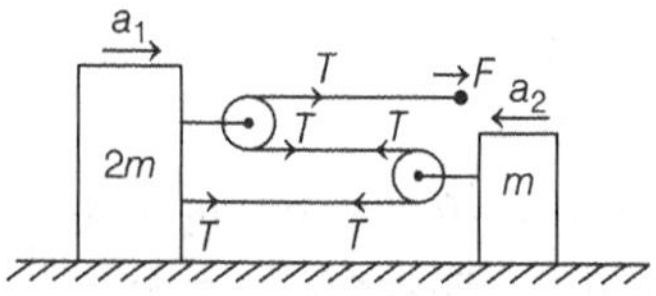

$T = F$

For $2m$,

$\Rightarrow \quad 3T = 2ma_1 \Rightarrow a_1 = \dfrac{3F}{2m}$

For m,

$\Rightarrow \quad 2T = ma_2 \Rightarrow a_2 = \dfrac{2F}{m}$

From string constraint,

$-3a_1 - 2a_2 + a_p = 0 \Rightarrow a_p = \dfrac{17F}{2m}$

12. $a_{mR} = 2 \Rightarrow a_m = 2 + a_R$

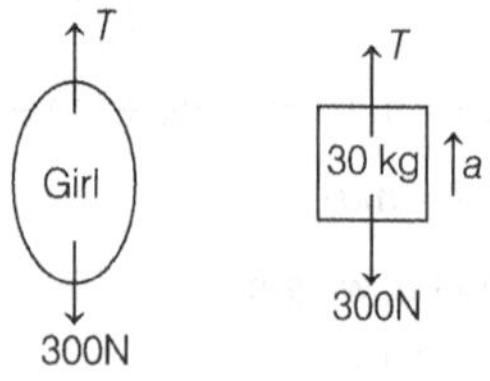

For block,

$$T - 300 = 30a \quad \text{...(i)}$$

For girl,

$$T - 300 = 30(2 - a) \quad \text{...(ii)}$$

From Eqs. (i) and (ii), we get

$$a = 1\,\text{m/s}^2$$

So, acceleration of girl $= 2 - 1 = 1\,\text{m/s}^2$

For girl, $s = ut + \frac{1}{2}at^2 \Rightarrow 10 = 0 + \frac{1}{2}(1)t^2$

$$t = \sqrt{20}\,\text{s} = 2\sqrt{5}\,\text{s}$$

13. $m_1 g - 2T = m_1 a_1$ ...(i)

$$T - m_2 g = m_2 a_2 \quad \text{...(ii)}$$

$$2a_1 = a_2 \quad \text{...(iii)}$$

From Eqs. (i), (ii) and (iii), we get

$$a_1 = \frac{(m_1 - 2m_2)g}{m_1 + 4m_2} = \frac{g}{4} \text{ and } a_2 = \frac{g}{2}$$

When m_1 strikes floor, string becomes slack and at this instant.

For block m_2,

$$v^2 = u^2 + 2as \Rightarrow v^2 = 0^2 + 2\left(\frac{g}{2}\right)(0.4) \Rightarrow v = 2\,\text{m/s}$$

Maximum height reached by m_2 from ground

$$= 40 + \frac{u^2}{2g} = 40 + \left(\frac{2^2}{20} \times 100\right) = 60 \text{ cm} = 0.6 \text{ cm}$$

14.

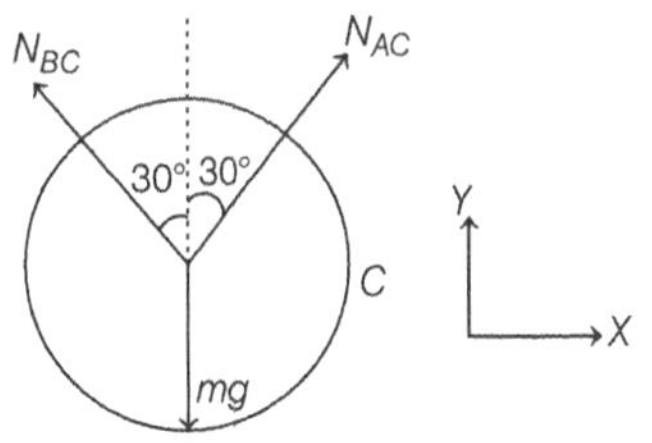

For A,

$$\Sigma F_x = 0 \Rightarrow N_{AC} \sin 30° = N_{BC} \sin 30° \Rightarrow N_{AC} = N_{BC}$$

$$\Sigma F_y = 0 \Rightarrow N_{BC} \cos 30° + N_{AC} \cos 30° = mg$$

$$\Rightarrow \quad N_{AC} = N_{BC} = \frac{mg}{\sqrt{3}}$$

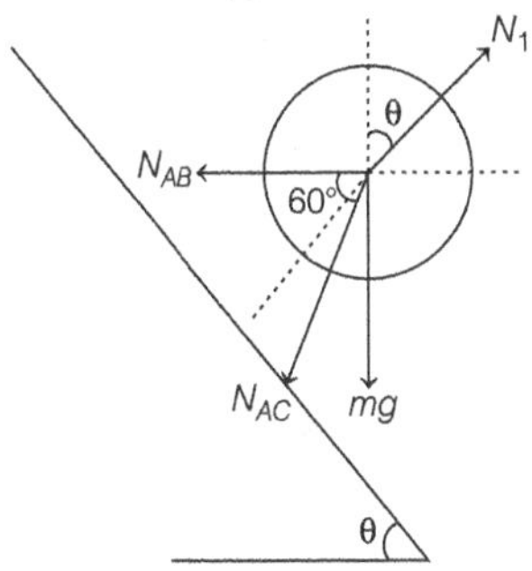

FBD of sphere *A*

$$\Sigma F_y = 0$$

$$\Rightarrow \quad N_1 \cos\theta = mg + N_{AC} \sin 60° \quad \text{...(i)}$$

$$\Sigma F_x = 0 \Rightarrow N_1 \sin\theta = N_{AB} + N_{AC} \cos 60° \quad \text{...(ii)}$$

Dividing Eq. (ii) by Eq. (i), we get

$$\tan\theta = \frac{N_{AB} + N_{AC}\cos 60°}{mg + N_{AC}\sin 60°}$$

When arrangement is on the verge of collapsing

$$\Rightarrow \quad N_{AB} = 0 \Rightarrow \tan\theta = \frac{1}{3\sqrt{3}}$$

15.

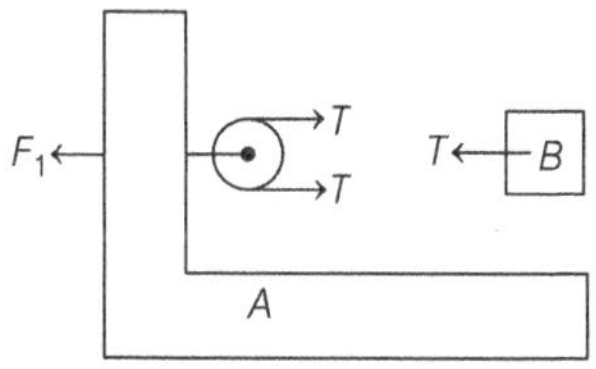

For block B, $\Sigma F = ma \Rightarrow 8 = 1\,a_B \Rightarrow a_B = 8\,\text{m/s}^2$

For block A,

$$\Sigma F = ma \Rightarrow F_1 - 2T = 1\,a_A \Rightarrow a_A = 4\,\text{m/s}^2$$

$$a_{BA} = a_B - a_A = 8 - 4 = 4\,\text{m/s}^2$$

$$s_{BA} = u_{BA}t + \frac{1}{2}a_{BA}t^2$$

$$\Rightarrow \quad 0.5 = 0 + \frac{1}{2} \times 4 \times t^2 \Rightarrow t = 0.5\,\text{s}$$

16.

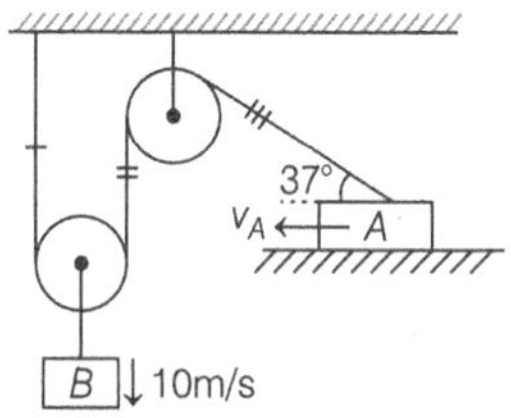

From string constraint,

$$+10 + 10 - v_A \cos 37° = 0 \Rightarrow v_A = 25\,\text{m/s}$$

17.

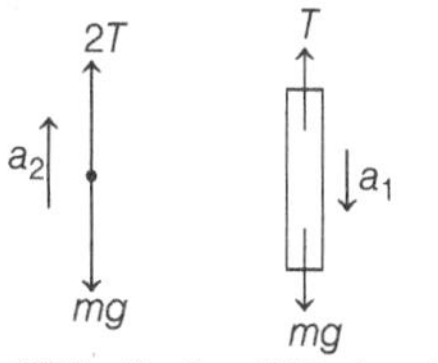

FBD of ball   FBD of rod

$$mg - T = ma_1 \quad \text{...(i)}$$

$$2T - mg = ma_2 \quad \text{...(ii)}$$

$$a_1 = 2a_2 \quad \text{...(iii)}$$

From Eqs. (i), (ii) and (iii), we get

$$a_2 = \frac{g}{5} \text{ and } a_1 = \frac{2g}{5}$$

$$\Rightarrow \quad s_{rel} = u_{rel}t + \frac{1}{2}a_{rel}t^2$$

$$\Rightarrow \quad l = \frac{1}{2}\left(\frac{3g}{5}\right)t^2$$

$$\Rightarrow \quad t = \sqrt{\frac{10l}{3g}}$$

18.

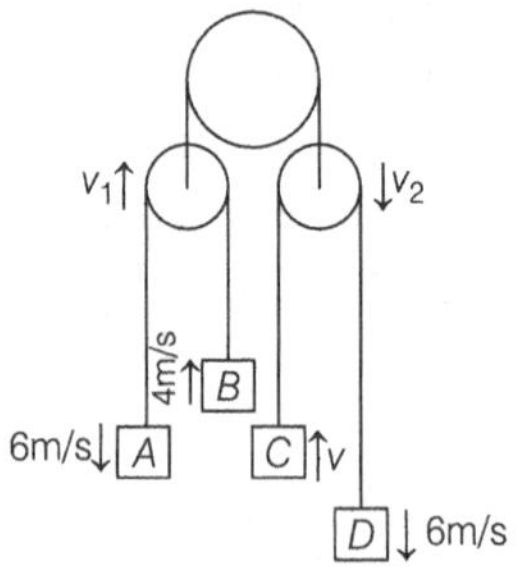

$$+6+v_1+v_1-4=0 \quad \text{...(i)}$$
$$-v_1+v_2=0 \quad \text{...(ii)}$$
$$-v_2-v_2-v_C+6=0 \quad \text{...(iii)}$$

Solving Eqs. (i), (ii) and (iii), we get

$$v_C = 8\,\text{m/s}$$

19.

$$mg - T = ma_C \quad \text{...(i)}$$
$$3T = ma_A \quad \text{...(ii)}$$
$$4T = ma_B \quad \text{...(iii)}$$
$$3a_A + 4a_B = a_C \quad \text{...(iv)}$$

Solving Eqs. (i), (ii), (iii) and (iv), we get

$$a_B = \frac{2g}{13}$$

20.

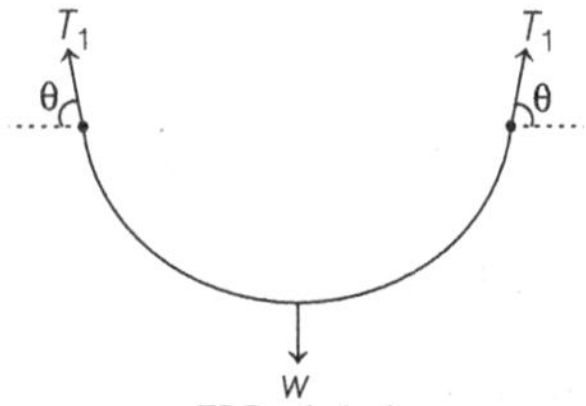

FBD of chain

$$\Sigma F_y = 0 \;\Rightarrow\; 2T_1 \sin\theta = w \;\Rightarrow\; T_1 = \frac{w}{2\sin\theta}$$

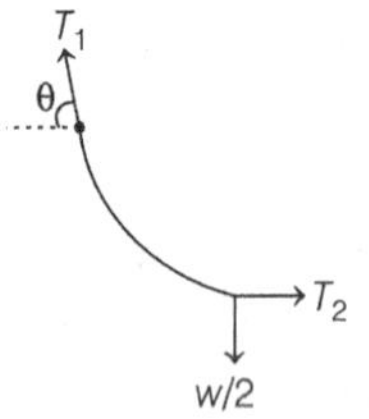

FBD of half chain

$$\Sigma F_x = 0 \;\Rightarrow\; T_2 = T_1\cos\theta \;\Rightarrow\; T_2 = \frac{w}{2}\cot\theta$$

21.

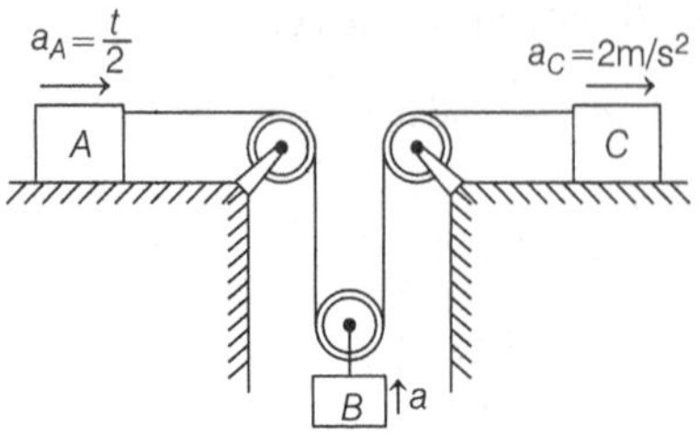

From string constraint,

$$-\frac{t}{2} - a - a + 2 = 0 \;\Rightarrow\; 2a = 2 - \frac{t}{2} \;\Rightarrow\; a = 1 - \frac{t}{4}$$

$$\Rightarrow\; \frac{dv}{dt} = 1 - \frac{t}{4} \;\Rightarrow\; \int_0^v dv = \int_0^t \left(1 - \frac{t}{4}\right) dt \;\Rightarrow\; v = t - \frac{t^2}{8}$$

When B again comes to rest,

$$v = t - \frac{t^2}{8} = 0 \;\Rightarrow\; t = 8\text{ s}$$

22.

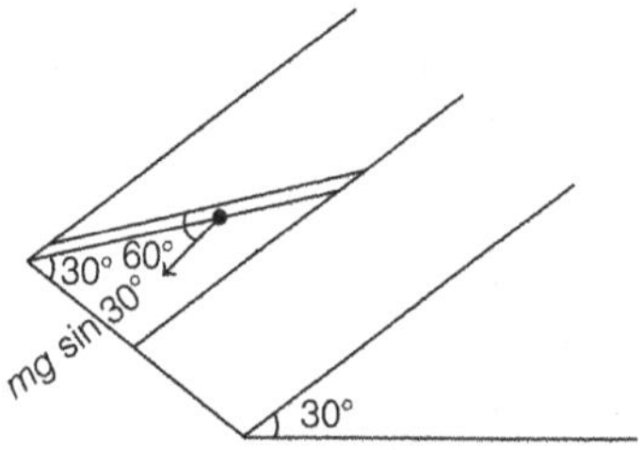

Force on the particle along the groove

$$= (mg\sin 30°)\cos 60° = \frac{mg}{4}$$

$$F = ma \;\Rightarrow\; a = \frac{g}{4}$$

$$s = ut + \frac{1}{2}at^2 \;\Rightarrow\; 5 = \frac{1}{2}\left(\frac{10}{4}\right)t^2 \;\Rightarrow\; t = 2\text{ s}$$

23. $\Sigma F_y = 0$

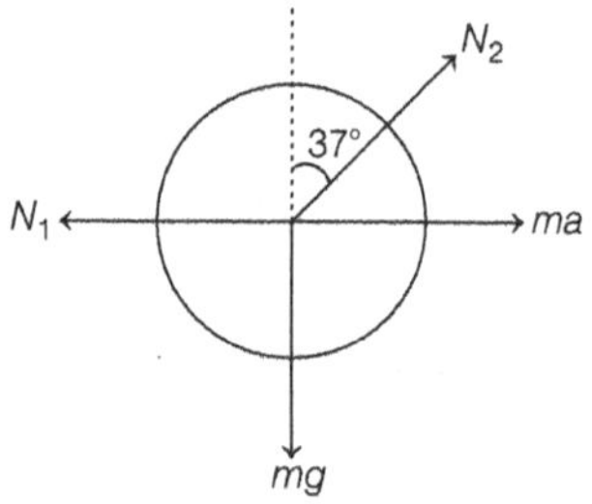

$$N_2\cos 37° - mg = 0 \;\Rightarrow\; N_2 = \frac{5mg}{4}$$

$$\Sigma F_x = 0 \;\Rightarrow\; N_1 = N_2 \sin 37° + ma$$

$$\Rightarrow \quad N_1 = \frac{3mg}{4} + ma = 9\text{ N}$$

24.

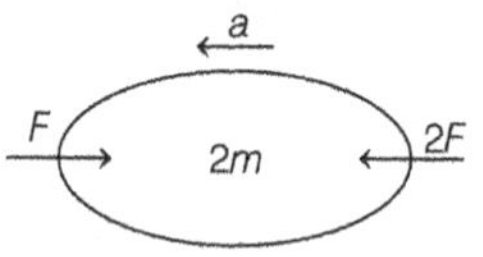

FBD of (A+B) system

$$\Sigma F = ma \;\Rightarrow\; 2F - F = 2ma \;\Rightarrow\; a = \frac{F}{2m}$$

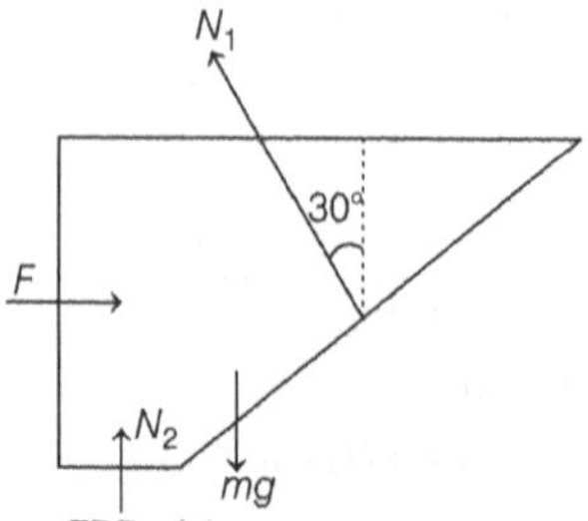

FBD of A

For A,

$$\Sigma F_x = ma \Rightarrow N_1 \sin 30° - F = m\left(\frac{F}{2m}\right)$$

$$N_1 = 3F$$

25.

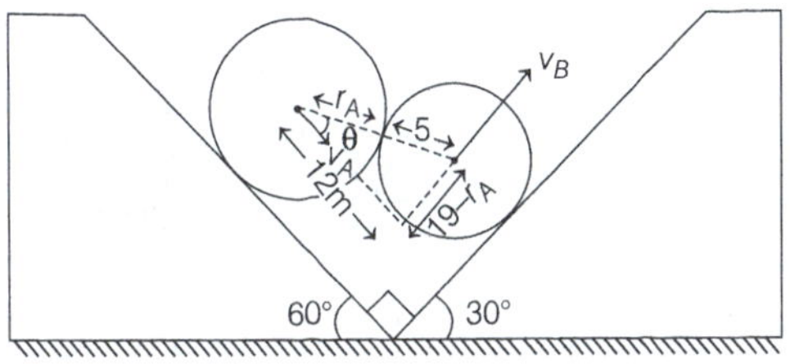

$$(r_A + 5)^2 = 12^2 + (19 - r_A)^2 \Rightarrow r_A = 10\,\text{m}$$

From wedge constraint,

$$v_A \cos\theta - v_B \sin\theta \Rightarrow v_B = v_A \cot\theta = 9 \times \frac{12}{9} = 12\,\text{m/s}$$

26.

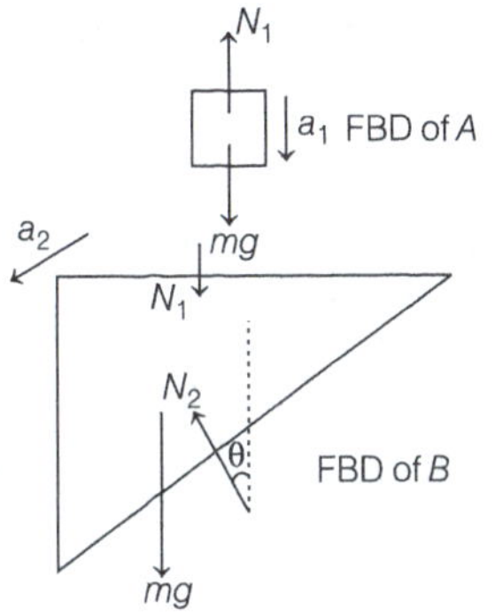

For A, $\Sigma F_y = ma_y$

$\Rightarrow \quad mg - N_1 = ma_1$ ...(i)

For B, $mg \sin\theta + N_1 \sin\theta = ma_2$ ...(ii)

For wedge constraint,

$a_1 = a_2 \sin\theta$ ...(iii)

From Eqs. (i), (ii) and (iii), we get

$$a_1 = \frac{2g \sin^2\theta}{1 + \sin^2\theta}$$

$$s_A = u_A t + \frac{1}{2} a_A t^2$$

$$\Rightarrow \quad s_A = 0 + \frac{1}{2}\left(\frac{2g \sin^2\theta}{1 + \sin^2\theta}\right)(1)^2 = \frac{g \sin^2\theta}{1 + \sin^2\theta}$$

27.

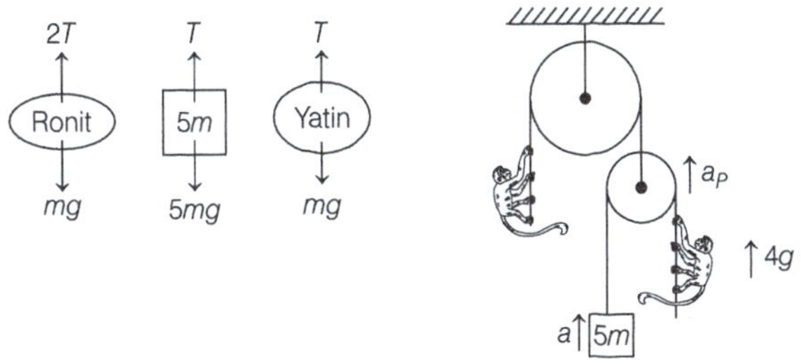

Since, block is stationary

$$\Sigma F_y = 0 \Rightarrow T = 5\,mg$$

For Yatin $\Rightarrow \Sigma F_y = ma_y \Rightarrow T - mg = ma$

$\Rightarrow \quad 5mg - mg = ma \Rightarrow a = 4g \uparrow$

From string constraint,

$$0 + a_P + a_P - 4g = 0 \Rightarrow a_P = 2g \uparrow$$

For Ronit, $\Sigma F_y = ma_y \Rightarrow 2T - mg = ma$

$\Rightarrow \quad 10mg - mg = ma \Rightarrow a = 9g$

$$a_{\text{Ronit, Rope}} = a_{\text{Ronit}} - a_{\text{Rope}} = 9g - (-2g) = 11\,g$$

28. $v_x = 3\,\text{m/s}$

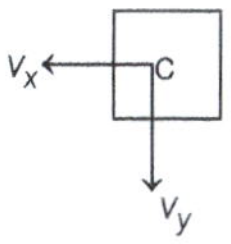

From string constraint, $-3 - 3 + 1 + 1 + v_y = 0$

$$\Rightarrow \quad v_y = 4\,\text{m/s} \Rightarrow \mathbf{v}_C = 3\hat{\mathbf{i}} + 4\hat{\mathbf{j}}$$

$$|\mathbf{v}_C| = \sqrt{3^2 + 4^2} = 5\,\text{m/s}$$

29.

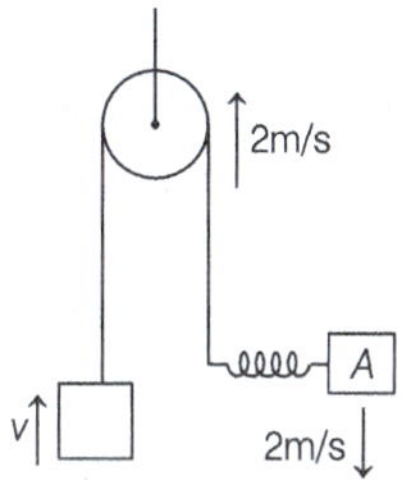

$$l = \text{length of string} \Rightarrow \frac{dl}{dt} = -v + 2 + 2 + 2 = -2$$

$\Rightarrow \quad v = 8\,\text{m/s} \uparrow$

30.

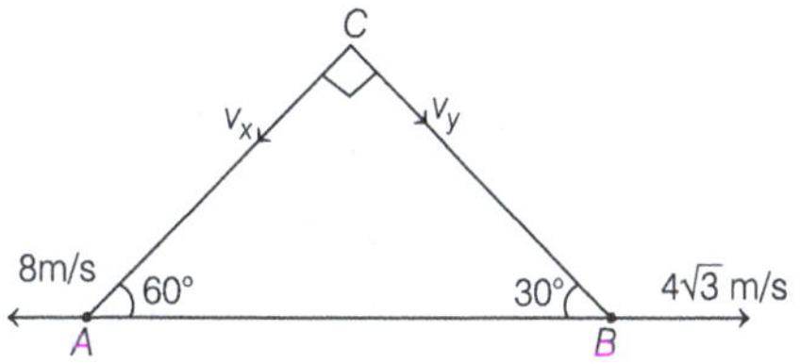

$$v_x = 8 \cos 60° = 4, \quad v_y = 4\sqrt{3} \cos 30° = 6$$

$$\mathbf{v}_C = 4\hat{\mathbf{i}} + 6\hat{\mathbf{j}} \Rightarrow |\mathbf{v}_C| = \sqrt{4^2 + 6^2} = 2\sqrt{13}\,\text{m/s}$$

31.

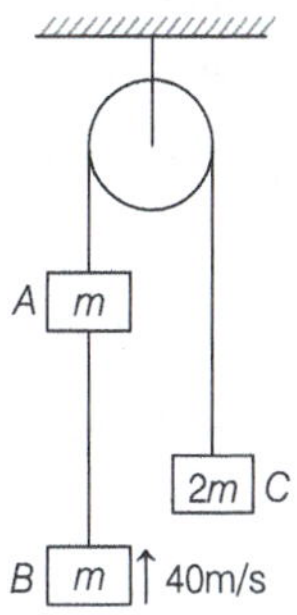

For A and C,

$$2mg - T = 2ma \Rightarrow T - mg = ma \Rightarrow a = \frac{g}{3}$$

Lets say string gets taut in time t.

$$s_B = 40t - \frac{1}{2}gt^2, \quad s_A = \frac{1}{2}\left(\frac{g}{3}\right)t^2$$

$$s_A = s_B$$

$$\Rightarrow \quad \frac{1}{2}\left(\frac{g}{3}\right)t^2 = 40t - \frac{1}{2}gt^2 \Rightarrow t = 6\text{ s}$$

32. $T = F$

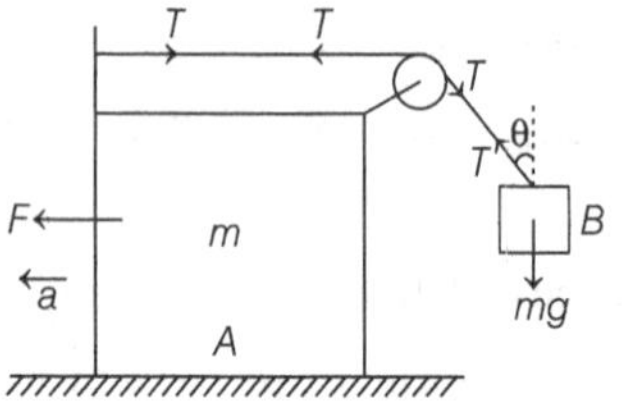

For Block B,

$$\Sigma F_y = 0 \Rightarrow T\cos\theta = mg \quad \text{...(i)}$$

$$\Sigma F_x = ma_x \Rightarrow T\sin\theta = ma \quad \text{...(ii)}$$

Squaring + adding Eqs. (i) and (ii), we get

$$T = m\sqrt{g^2 + a^2} = F \quad \text{...(iii)}$$

For $(A + B)$ system,

$$\Sigma F_x = ma_x \Rightarrow F = (2m)a \quad \text{...(iv)}$$

From (iii) and (iv), we get

$$F = m\sqrt{g^2 + a^2} = 2ma \Rightarrow a = \frac{g}{\sqrt{3}}$$

So, $F = 2ma = 2m\left(\frac{g}{\sqrt{3}}\right) = 20\text{ N}$

33.

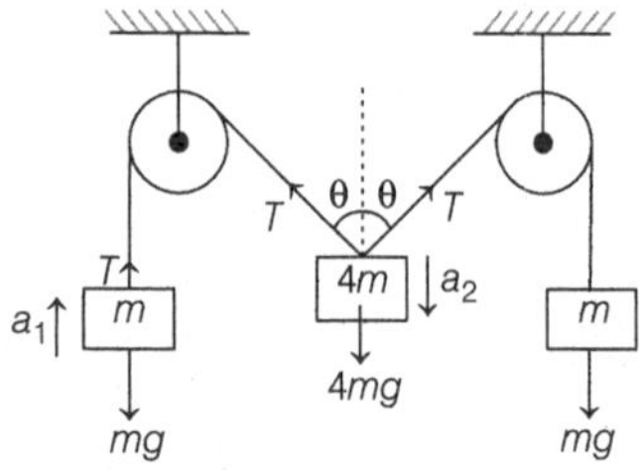

$$4mg - 2T\cos\theta = 4ma_2 \quad \text{...(i)}$$

$$T - mg = ma_1 \quad \text{...(ii)}$$

$$a_1 = a_2\cos\theta \quad \text{...(iii)}$$

Solving Eqs. (i), (ii) and (iii), we get

$$a_2 = \frac{5g}{11}, \text{ downwards}$$

34.

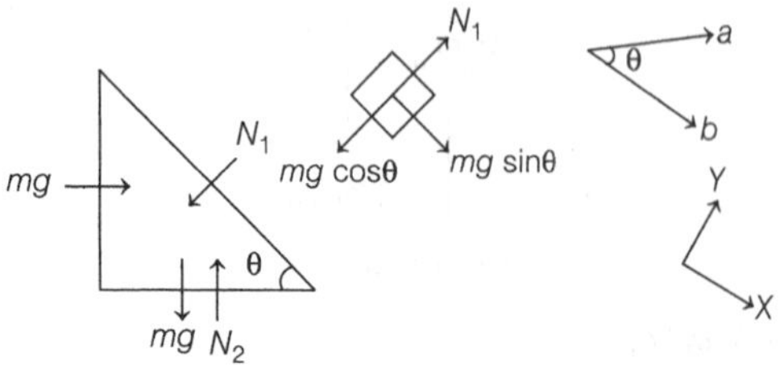

For block, $mg\sin\theta = m(b + a\cos\theta)$ ...(i)

$$N_1 - mg\cos\theta = ma\sin\theta \quad \text{...(ii)}$$

For wedge, $mg - N_1\sin\theta = ma$ ...(iii)

From Eqs. (ii) and (iii), we get

$$a = \frac{(1 - \sin\theta\cos\theta)g}{1 + \sin^2\theta} = \frac{g}{3}$$

35.

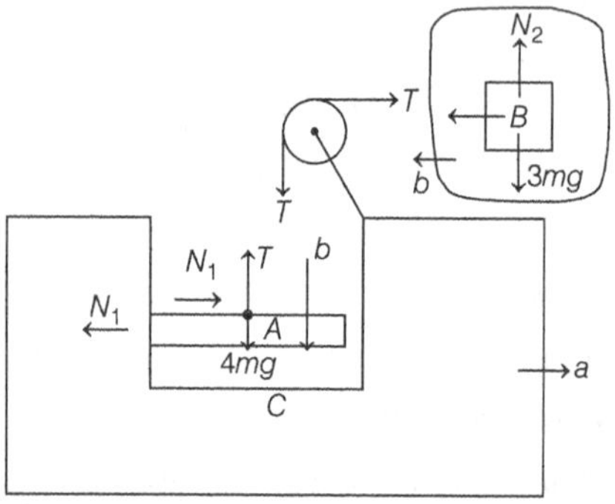

For $(A + C)$ system,

$$\Sigma F_x = ma_x \Rightarrow T = 12ma \quad \text{...(i)}$$

For B,

$$\Sigma F_x = ma_x \Rightarrow T = 3m(b - a) \quad \text{...(ii)}$$

For A,

$$\Sigma F_y = ma_y \Rightarrow 4mg - T = 4mb \quad \text{...(iii)}$$

Solving Eqs. (i), (ii) and (iii), we get

$$a = \frac{g}{8} \text{ and } b = \frac{5g}{8}$$

Acceleration of $B = b - a = \frac{5g}{8} - \frac{g}{8} = \frac{g}{2}$, leftward

36. Length of string at any time $= l$

$$\frac{dl}{dt} = -v_A\cos 37° + 5\cos 37° - 5\cos 53° + 10\cos 53°$$

$$\Rightarrow \quad \frac{dl}{dt} = -\frac{4v_A}{5} + 7 = -1 \Rightarrow v_A = 10\text{ m/s}$$

37.

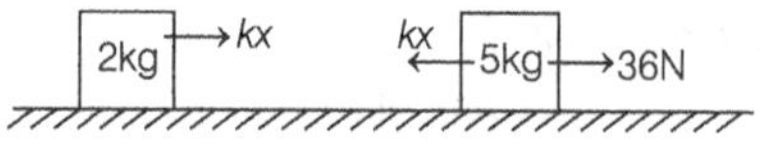

$$kx = 2a_1 \text{ and } 36 - kx = 5a_2$$

Given that, $a_1 = 2a_2$

$$\Rightarrow \quad \frac{kx}{2} = 2\left(\frac{36 - kx}{5}\right) \Rightarrow 5kx = 144 - 4kx$$

$$\Rightarrow \quad 9kx = 144 \Rightarrow kx = 16$$

$$\Rightarrow \quad 100x = 16 \Rightarrow x = 0.16\text{ m} \Rightarrow x = 16\text{ cm}$$

38. Before cutting one of the springs,

$$T_1 = mg \text{ and } 2kx = 2mg \Rightarrow kx = mg$$

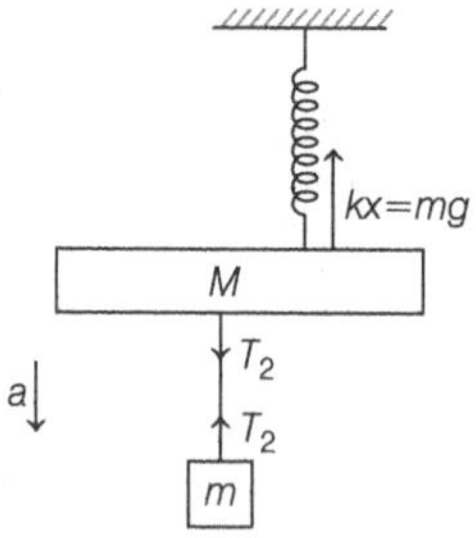

After cutting one of the spring, taking both blocks as a system

$$\Sigma F_y = ma_y$$

$\Rightarrow \quad 2mg - kx = 2ma \Rightarrow a = \frac{g}{2}$

For lower block $\Rightarrow \quad mg - T_2 = m\left(\frac{g}{2}\right)$

$\Rightarrow \quad T_2 = \frac{mg}{2}$

So, $\quad T_1 - T_2 = mg - \frac{mg}{2} = \frac{mg}{2}$

39.

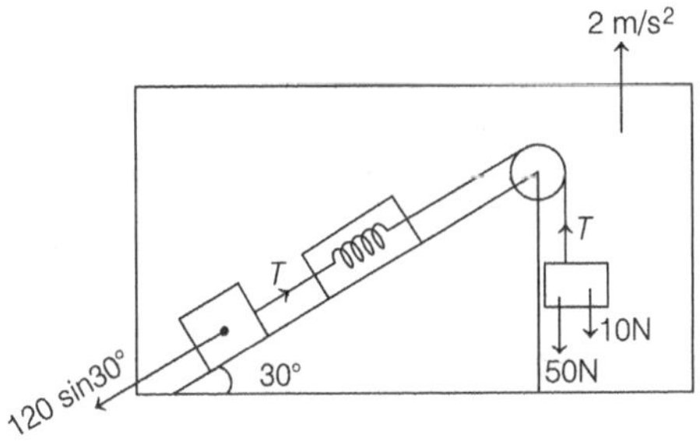

Net force along the string is zero.

So, blocks are in equilibrium with respect ot the inclined plane.

$$T = 60\,\text{N} = \text{spring force}$$

40. Before string is cut, all are in equilibrium.

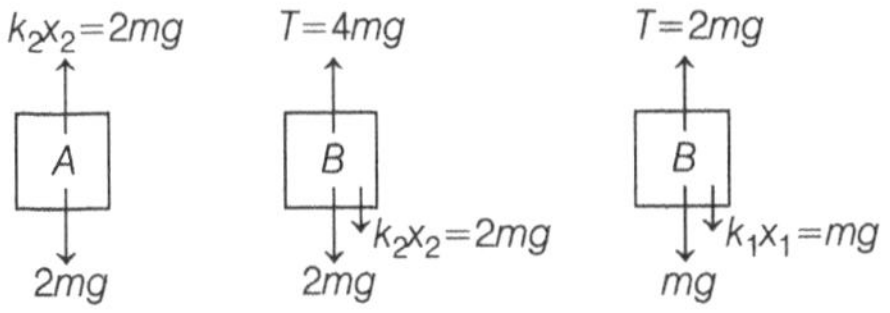

Just after the string is cut.

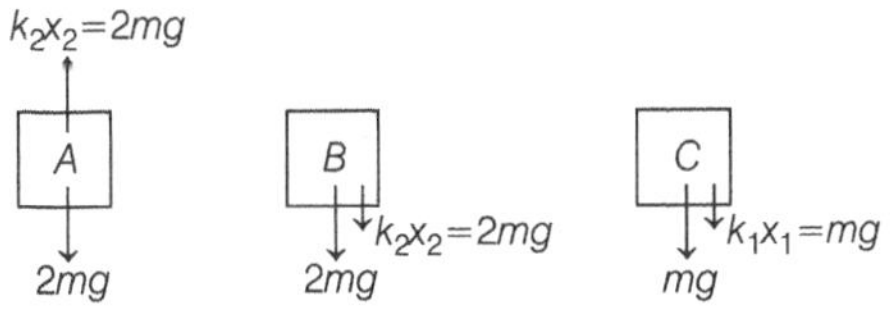

Hence, $\quad a_A = 0,\ a_B = 2g\downarrow,\ a_C = 2g\downarrow$

41. For equilibrium of cylinder A,

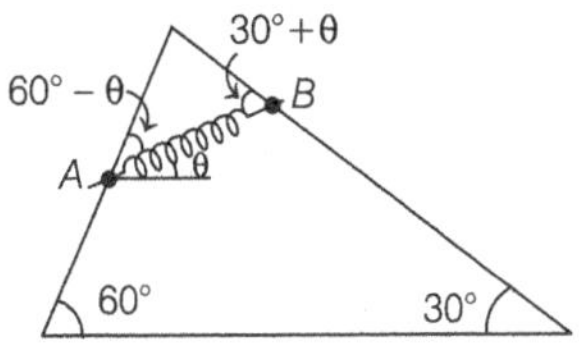

$$mg \sin 60° = kx \cos(60° - \theta) \quad \text{...(i)}$$

Cylinder B,

$$mg \sin 30° = kx \cos(30° + \theta) \quad \text{...(ii)}$$

Solving Eqs. (i) and (ii), we get

$$\theta = 30°$$

42.

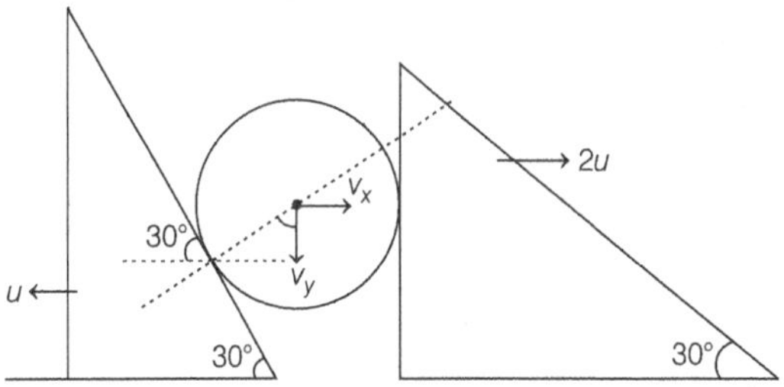

As cylinder is in contact with right wedge, from wedge constraint $\Rightarrow v_x = 2u$

As cylinder is in contact with left wedge, from wedge constraint,

$\Rightarrow \quad u\sin 30° = v_y \cos 30° - v_x \sin 30° \Rightarrow v_y = \sqrt{3}u$

So, velocity of cylinder $= \sqrt{(2u)^2 + (\sqrt{3}u)^2} = \sqrt{7}u$ m/s

43.

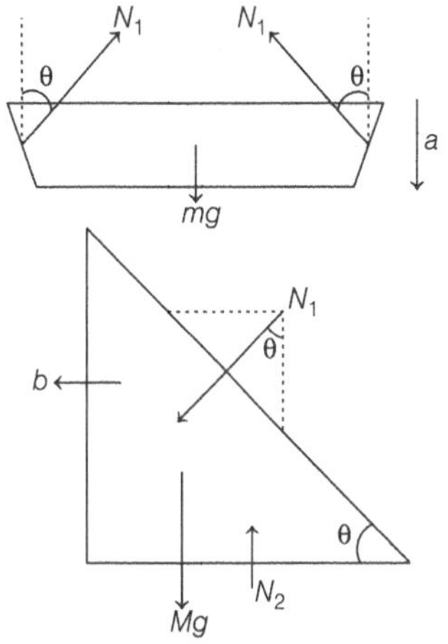

For plank $\Rightarrow mg - 2N_1 \cos\theta = ma$ ...(i)

For wedge $\Rightarrow N_1 \sin\theta = Mb$ ...(ii)

Wedge constraint $\Rightarrow a\cos\theta = b\sin\theta$ ...(iii)

Solving Eqs. (i), (ii) and (iii), we get

$$a = \frac{mg\sin^2\theta}{m\sin^2\theta + 2M\cos^2\theta}$$

44.

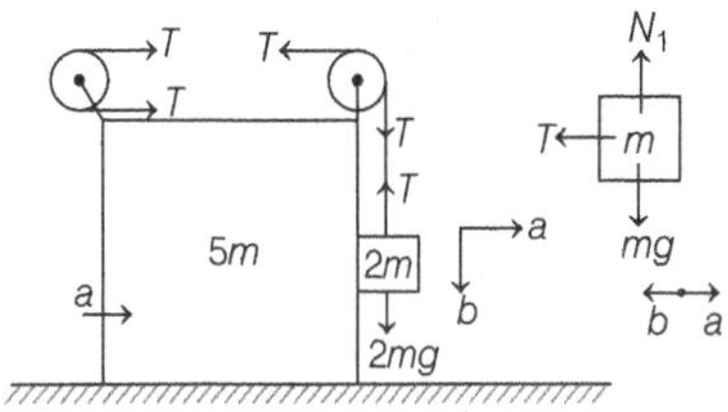

For ($5m$ and $2m$) system,

$$\Sigma F_x = ma_x \Rightarrow T = 7ma \quad \text{...(i)}$$

For $2m \quad \Rightarrow \quad 2mg - T = 2mb$ ...(ii)

For $m \quad \Rightarrow \quad T = m(b - a)$ ...(iii)

Solving Eqs. (i), (ii) and (iii), we get

$$a = \frac{2g}{23}$$

45. $100 - T = 10a$ ...(i)

$T - 100 \sin 37° = 10a$ ...(ii)

Solving Eqs. (i) and (ii)

$$a = 2\,m/s^2$$

$$\tan\phi = \frac{mg \sin 37° + ma}{mg \cos 37°} = \frac{6+2}{8} = 1 \Rightarrow \phi = \tan^{-1}(1)$$

46. $T = 15a$ ...(i)

$50 - T = 5b$ ...(ii)

$T - 30 = 3c$ ...(iii)

$-a + b - c = 0 \Rightarrow b = a + c$ ...(iv)

Solving Eqs. (i), (ii) and (iii), we get

$$a = \frac{2g}{9},\ b = \frac{g}{3} \text{ and } c = \frac{g}{9}$$

47.

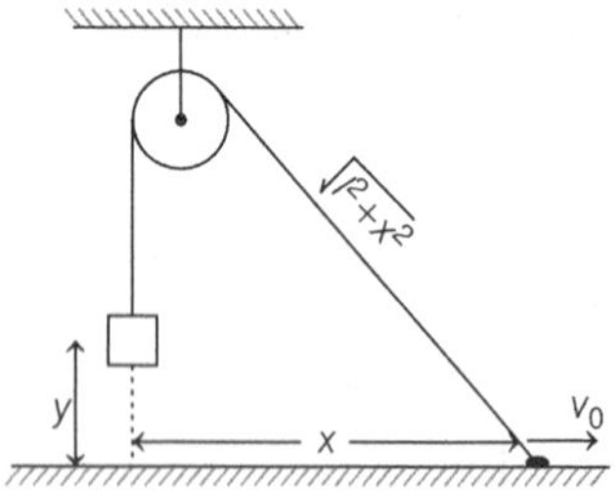

$$y = \sqrt{l^2 + x^2} - l \Rightarrow \frac{dy}{dt} = \frac{1}{2\sqrt{l^2+x^2}} 2x \frac{dx}{dt}$$

$$\Rightarrow \quad v = \frac{xv_0}{\sqrt{l^2+x^2}}$$

$$a = \frac{dv}{dt} = \left(\frac{\sqrt{l^2+x^2}\frac{dx}{dt} - \frac{x(2x)}{2\sqrt{l^2+x^2}}\frac{dx}{dt}}{(\sqrt{l^2+x^2})^2} \right) v_0$$

$$= \frac{v_0^2 l^2}{(l^2+x^2)^{3/2}}$$

48. From string constraint,

$$+v_B + v_B - v_A - v_A - v_A - v_A = 0 \Rightarrow 4v_A = 2v_B$$

$$\Rightarrow v_A = \frac{v_B}{2} \Rightarrow a_A = \frac{a_B}{2}$$

$$a_B = \frac{dv_B}{dt} = t + \frac{t^2}{2}$$

At, $t = 2, a_B = 2 + \frac{2^2}{2} = 4$

$$\therefore \quad a_A = \frac{a_B}{2} = 2\,m/s^2$$

49. From string constraint,

$v \cos\theta = u \Rightarrow v = u \sec\theta$ ...(i)

$\frac{dv}{dt} = u \sec\theta \tan\theta \frac{d\theta}{dt}$ ...(ii)

$$x = b \cot\theta \Rightarrow \frac{dx}{dt} = -b \operatorname{cosec}^2\theta \frac{d\theta}{dt}$$

$\Rightarrow \quad v = -b \operatorname{cosec}^2\theta \frac{d\theta}{dt}$ ...(iii)

Solving Eqs. (i), (ii) and (iii), we get

$$\text{acceleration} = \frac{u^2}{b}\tan^3\theta$$

50.

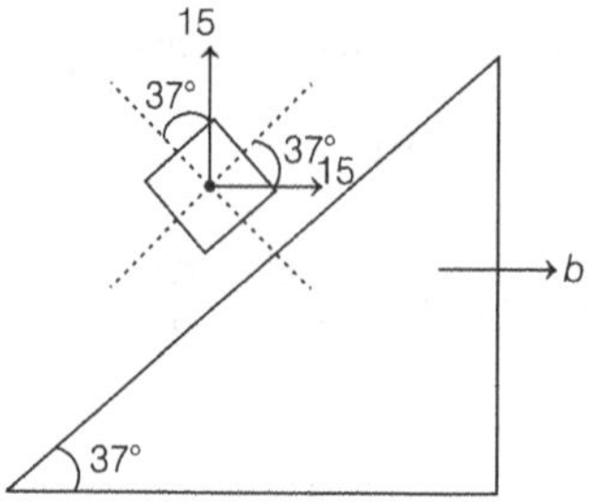

From wedge constraint,

$$b \sin 37° = 15 \sin 37° - 15 \cos 37°$$

$$\Rightarrow \quad \frac{3b}{5} = -15\left(\frac{1}{5}\right) \Rightarrow b = -5\hat{i}$$

Multiple Choice(s) Correct Questions

1. $6mg - 8T = 6ma_2$ ...(i)

$T - mg = ma_1$ ...(ii)

$a_1 = 8a_2$ ...(iii)

Soving Eqs. (i), (ii) and (iii), we get

$$a_2 = -\frac{g}{35}, a_1 = -\frac{8g}{35} \text{ and } v_1 = 8v_2$$

2. $F = 10a,\ T \sin\theta = ma,\ T \cos\theta = mg$

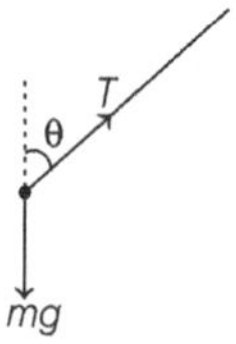

$$\Rightarrow \quad \tan\theta = \frac{a}{g} \Rightarrow \frac{3}{4} = \frac{a}{10} \Rightarrow a = 7.5\,m/s^2$$

$$\Rightarrow \quad F = 10 \times 7.5 = 75\,N,\quad T = 20 \times \frac{5}{4} = 25\,N$$

3.

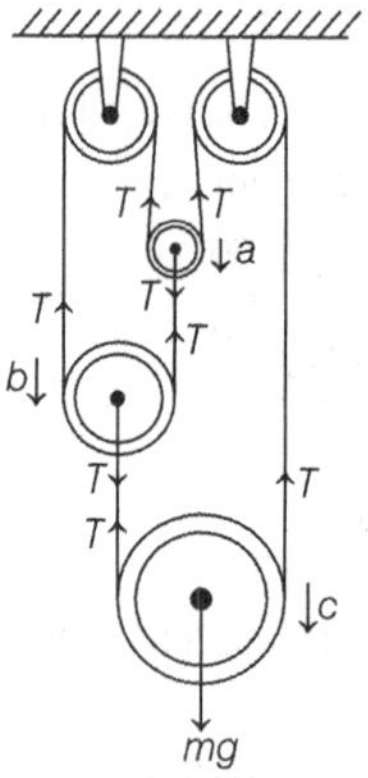

$T + mg - 2T = ma$ ...(i)

$T + mg - 2T = mb$ ...(ii)

$$mg - 2T = mc \quad \text{...(iii)}$$

From string constraint,

$$+2a - a + 2b - b + 2c = 0$$

$$a + b + 2c = 0 \quad \text{...(iv)}$$

Solving Eqs. (i), (ii) and (iii), we get

$$T = \frac{2mg}{3} \text{ and } a = \frac{g}{3}\downarrow,\ b = \frac{g}{3}\downarrow \text{ and } c = -\frac{g}{3} = \frac{g}{3}\uparrow$$

4. (i) $R_B \sin 60° = 0 \Rightarrow R_A = mg + R_B \cos 60°$

(ii) $R_A \sin 60° = R_B \sin 60° \Rightarrow R_A \cos 60° + R_B \cos 60° = mg$

(iii) $R_A \cos 30° = mg \Rightarrow R_A \sin 30° = R_B$

5.

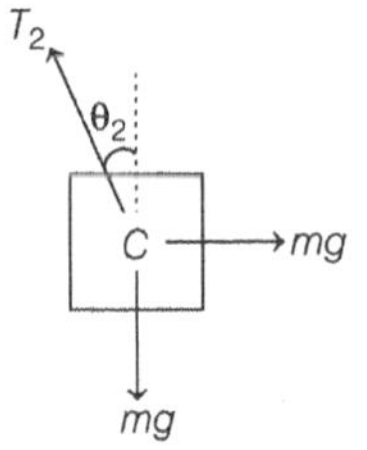

For C,

$$\Sigma F_x = 0 \Rightarrow T_2 \sin\theta_2 = mg \quad \text{...(i)}$$

$$\Sigma F_y = 0 \Rightarrow T_2 \cos\theta_2 = mg \quad \text{...(ii)}$$

From Eqs. (i) and (ii), we get

$$\tan\theta_2 = 1 \Rightarrow T_2 = \sqrt{2}mg$$

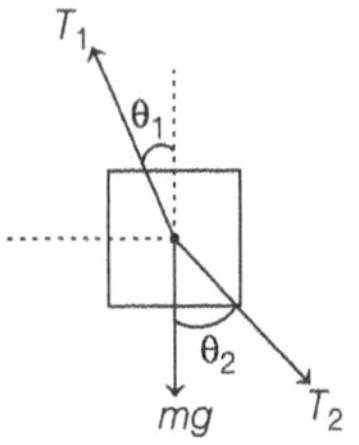

For B,

$$\Sigma F_x = 0$$

$$\Sigma F_y = 0$$

$$T_1 \sin\theta_1 = T_2 \sin\theta_2 \quad \text{...(iii)}$$

$$T_1 \cos\theta_1 = mg + T_2 \cos\theta_2 \quad \text{...(iv)}$$

From Eqs. (iii) and (iv), we get

$$\tan\theta_1 = \frac{1}{2} \text{ and } T_2 = \sqrt{5}\,mg$$

6. $400 \sin 45° - 2T = 40a_2$ ...(i)

$T - 100 \sin 45° = 10a_1$ ...(ii)

$a_1 = 2a_2$ ...(iii)

From Eqs. (i), (ii) and (iii), we get

$$a_2 = \frac{5}{2\sqrt{2}}\,\text{m/s}^2 \text{ and } a_1 = \frac{5}{\sqrt{2}}\,\text{m/s}^2 \text{ and } T = \frac{150}{\sqrt{2}}\,\text{N}$$

7. S_1 is moving with constant velocity w.r.t. frame S_2. So, if S_1 is inertial, then S_2 will be inertial and if S_1 is non-inertial, then S_2 will be non-inertial.

8. Since, the table surface exerts an upward force of 10N on the block, the block will also exert 10N on the table in downward direction as they are action-reaction pair. Net force on the block is in upward direction. So, the block will have upward acceleration.

9.

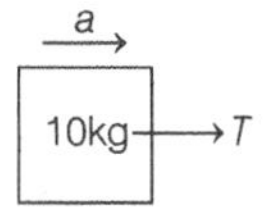

FBD of B

$$T = 10a \quad \text{...(i)}$$

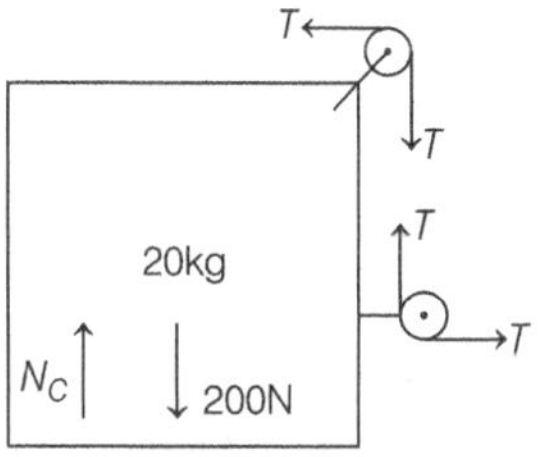

FDB of C

$$\Sigma F_x = ma \Rightarrow a_c = 0$$

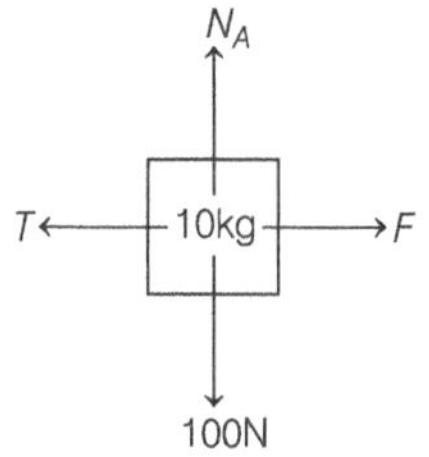

$$20 - T = 10a \quad \text{...(ii)}$$

From Eqs. (i) and (ii), we get

$$a = 1\,\text{m/s}^2 \text{ and } T = 10\,\text{N}$$

10.

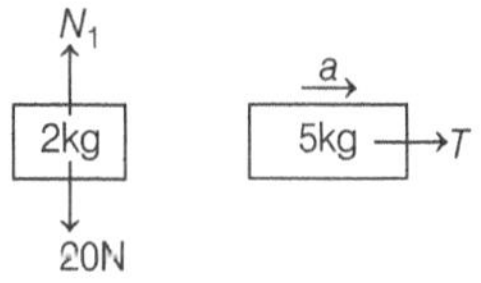

$$a_c = 0$$

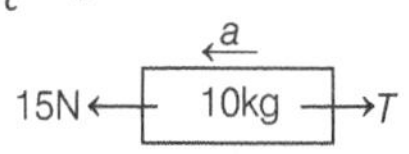

$$15 - T = 10a \Rightarrow T = 5a$$

$$\Rightarrow \quad a = 1\,\text{m/s}^2 \text{ and } T = 5\,\text{N}$$

So, tension in the string between pulley and wall $= 2T = 10\,\text{N}$

11.

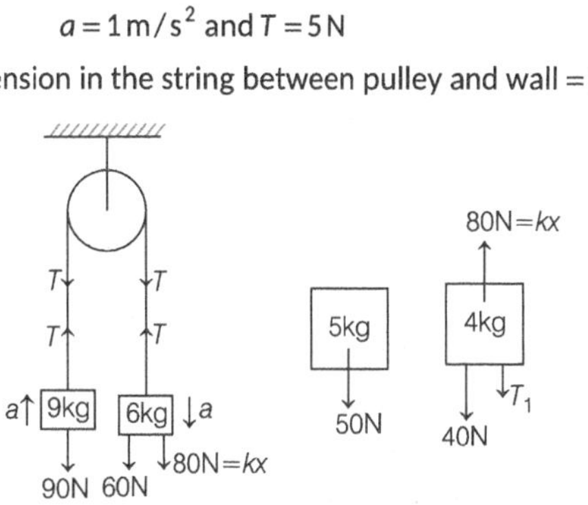

Just after cutting the left spring, for 5 kg block,

$$a_{5\,kg} = g \downarrow$$

For (9 kg + 6 kg) system

$$140 - T = 6a \Rightarrow T - 90 = 9a$$

$$a = \frac{50}{15} = \frac{10}{3}\,m/s^2 \text{ and } T = 120\,N$$

For 4 kg,

$$80 = 40 + T_1 \Rightarrow T_1 = 40\,N$$

12. $k(3L) = k_1(2L) = k_2(L) \Rightarrow k_1 = \frac{3k}{2}$ and $k_2 = 3k$

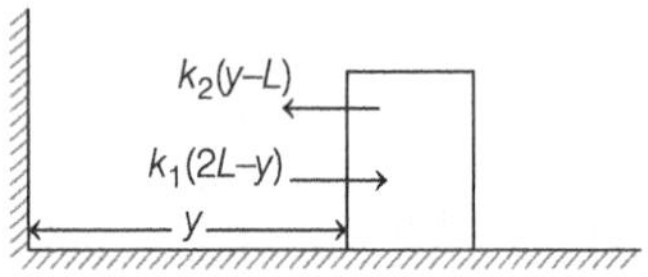

$$k_1(2L - y) = k_2(y - L)$$

$$\Rightarrow \frac{k_2}{k_1} = \frac{2L - y}{y - L} = \frac{3k}{3k/2}$$

$$\Rightarrow 2y - 2L = 2L - y \Rightarrow 3y = 4L \Rightarrow y = \frac{4L}{3}$$

13. For wedge,

$$N_1 \sin 45° = m_2 b \qquad \text{...(i)}$$

For block,

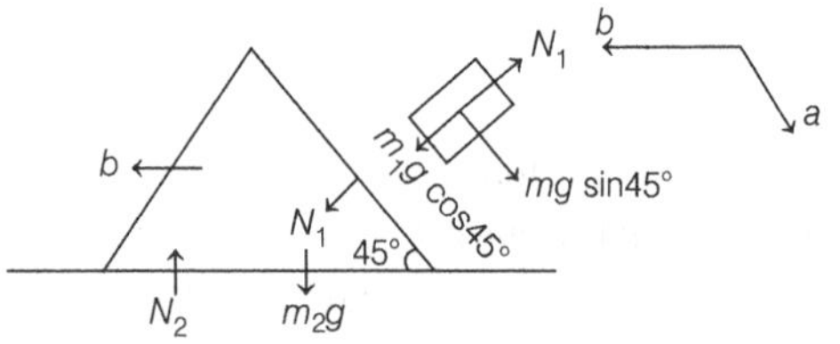

$$m_1 g \sin 45° = m_1(a - b\cos 45°) \qquad \text{...(ii)}$$

$$m_1 g \cos 45° - N_1 = m_1 b \sin 45° \qquad \text{...(iii)}$$

Solving Eqs. (i), (ii) and (iii), we get

$$b = \frac{m_1 g}{m_1 + 2m_2} = \frac{3g}{20} \text{ and } a = \frac{23\sqrt{2}g}{20}$$

14.

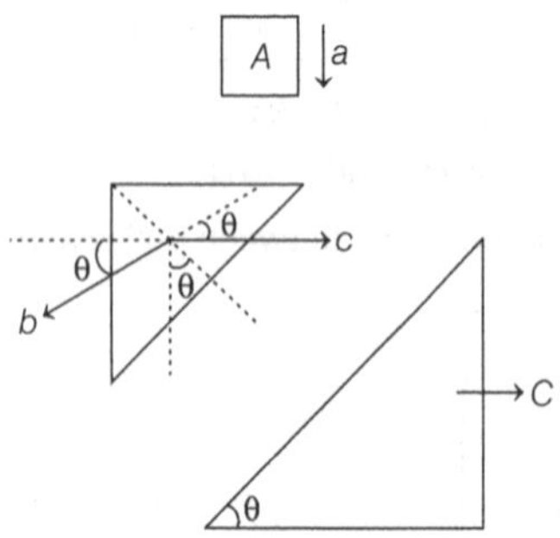

a = acceleration of A w.r.t ground

b = acceleration of B w.r.t. C

c = acceleration of C w.r.t. ground

From wedge constraint between A and B

$$a = b\sin\theta$$

$$\mathbf{a}_A = -a\hat{\mathbf{j}}$$

$$\mathbf{a}_B = (c - b\cos\theta)\,\hat{\mathbf{i}} - b\sin\theta\,\hat{\mathbf{j}}$$

$$\mathbf{a}_C = c\hat{\mathbf{i}}$$

$$\mathbf{a}_{AB} = -(c - b\cos\theta)\,\hat{\mathbf{i}}$$

For B,

$$(mg + N_1)\sin\theta = m(b - c\cos\theta)$$

So, $b - c\cos\theta > g\sin\theta$

15.

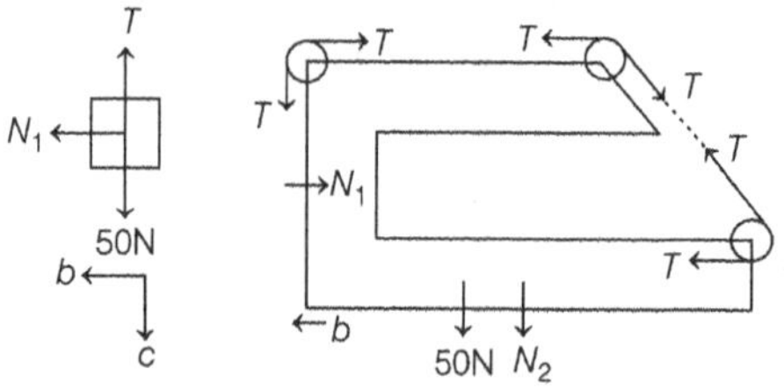

For (B + C),

$$T = 10b \qquad \text{...(i)}$$

$$50 - T = 5c \qquad \text{...(ii)}$$

$$T = 30(c - b) \qquad \text{...(iii)}$$

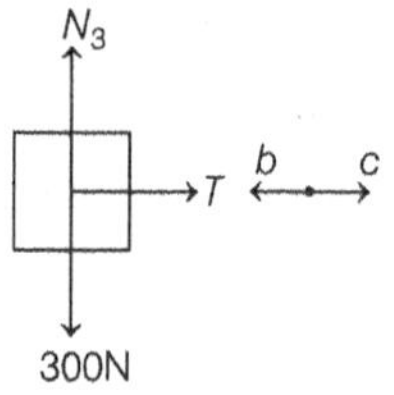

Solving Eqs. (i), (ii) and (iii), we get

$$B = 3\,m/s^2 \text{ and } C = 4\,m/s^2 \text{ and } T = 30\,N$$

$$\mathbf{a}_A = (c - b)\,\hat{\mathbf{i}} = \hat{\mathbf{i}}$$

$$\mathbf{a}_B = -3\hat{\mathbf{i}}$$

$$\mathbf{a}_C = -3\hat{\mathbf{i}} + 4\hat{\mathbf{j}}$$

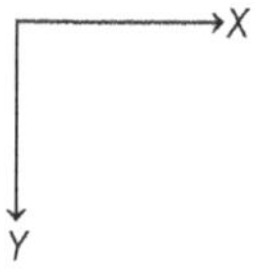

For C, $\Sigma F_x = ma_x$

$$N_1 = 5(3) = 15\,N$$

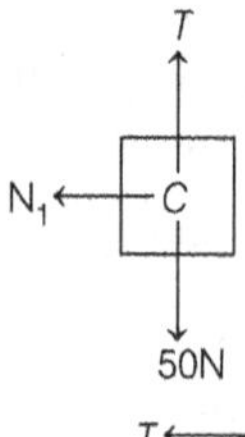

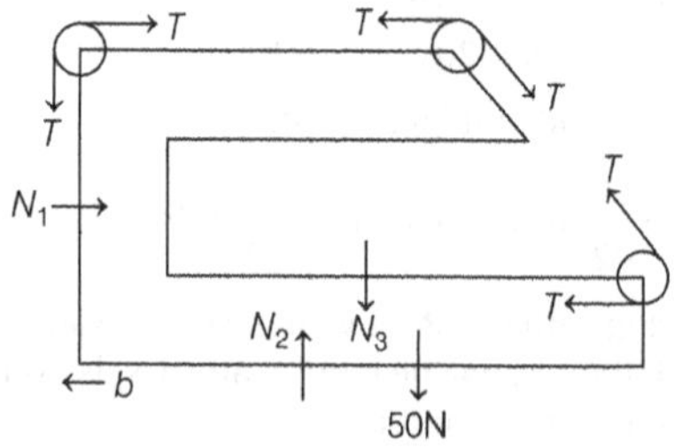

For B,

$$\Sigma F_y = 0 \Rightarrow N_2 - 50 - N_3 - T = 0$$

$$N_2 = 50 + N_3 + T = 50 + 300 + 30 = 380\,\text{N}$$

Comprehension Based Questions

1.

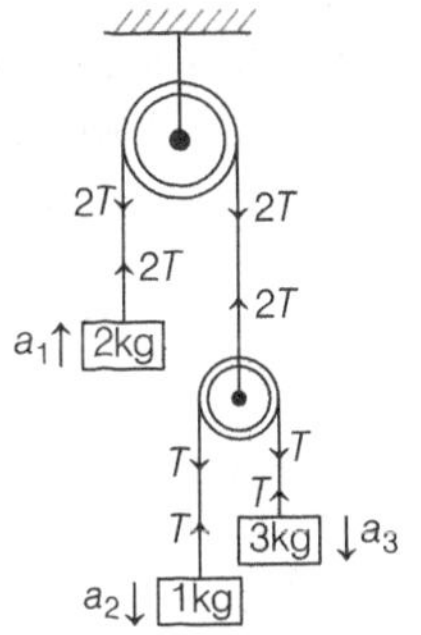

$$2T - 20 = 2a_1 \quad \text{...(i)}$$

$$10 - T = 1\,a_2 \quad \text{...(ii)}$$

$$30 - T = 3a_3 \quad \text{...(iii)}$$

$$2a_1 = a_2 + a_3 \quad \text{...(iv)}$$

$$\Rightarrow \quad 2\left(\frac{2T-20}{2}\right) = \left(\frac{10-T}{1}\right) + \left(\frac{30-T}{3}\right)$$

$$\Rightarrow \quad 3(2T - 20) = 3(10 - T) + 30 - T$$

$$\Rightarrow \quad 6T - 60 = 30 - 3T + 30 - T$$

$$\Rightarrow \quad 10T = 120 \Rightarrow T = 12\,\text{N}$$

$$2(12) - 20 = 2a_1 \Rightarrow a_1 = 2\,\text{m/s}^2 \uparrow$$

2.

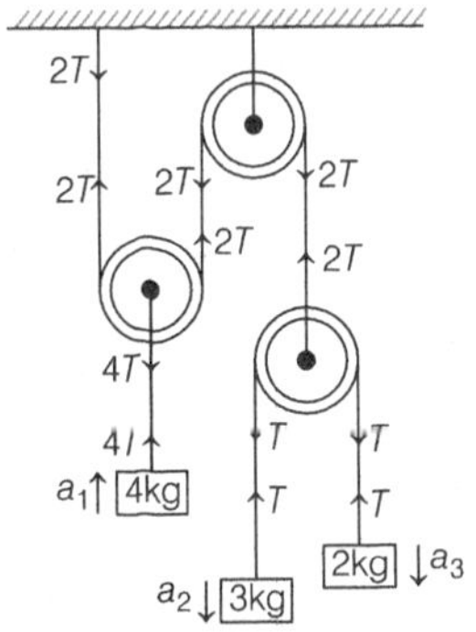

$$4T - 40 = 4a_1 \quad \text{...(i)}$$

$$30 - T = 3a_2 \quad \text{...(ii)}$$

$$20 - T = 2a_3 \quad \text{...(iii)}$$

$$4a_1 = a_2 + a_3 \quad \text{...(iv)}$$

$$\Rightarrow \quad 4T - 40 = \frac{30-T}{3} + \frac{20-T}{2}$$

$$\Rightarrow \quad 24T - 240 = 60 - 2T + 60 - 3T$$

$$\Rightarrow \quad 29T = 360 \quad \Rightarrow \quad T = \frac{360}{29}\,\text{N}$$

$$4\left(\frac{360}{29}\right) - 40 = 4a_1$$

$$\Rightarrow \quad a_1 = \frac{70}{29}\,\text{m/s}^2 \uparrow$$

3.

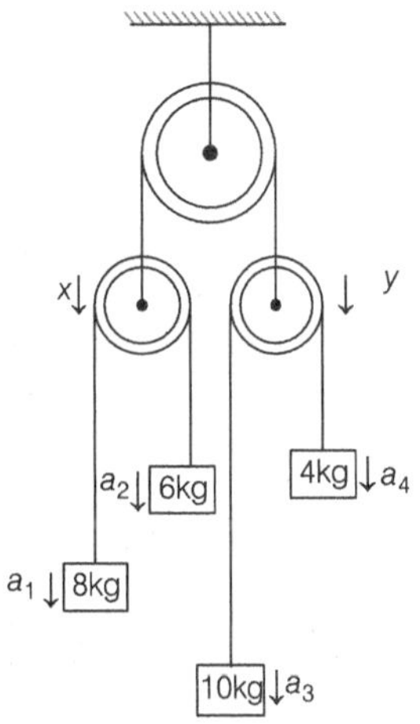

$$80 - T = 8a_1 \quad \text{...(i)}$$

$$60 - T = 6a_2 \quad \text{...(ii)}$$

$$100 - T = 10a_3 \quad \text{...(iii)}$$

$$40 - T = 4a_4 \quad \text{...(iv)}$$

$$+a_1 + a_2 - x - x = 0 \quad \Rightarrow \quad 2x = a_1 + a_2 \quad \text{...(v)}$$

$$+x + y = 0 \quad \text{...(vi)}$$

$$+a_3 + a_4 - y - y = 0 \quad \text{...(vii)}$$

From Eqs. (v), (vi) and (vii), we get

$$a_1 + a_2 + a_3 + a_4 = 0 \quad \text{...(viii)}$$

$$\frac{80-T}{8} + \frac{60-T}{6} + \frac{100-T}{10} + \frac{40-T}{4} = 0$$

$$\Rightarrow \quad T = \frac{4800}{77}\,\text{N} \quad \Rightarrow \quad x = \frac{a_1 + a_2}{2} = \frac{10}{11}\,\text{m/s}^2 \downarrow$$

4.

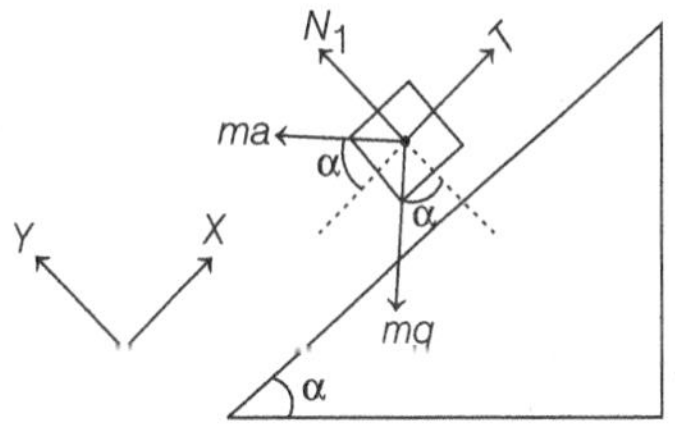

$$\Sigma F_y = 0$$

$$\Rightarrow N_1 - mg\cos\alpha + ma\sin\alpha = 0$$

$$\Rightarrow \quad N_1 = mg\cos\alpha - ma\sin\alpha$$

$$\Rightarrow \quad \frac{3}{4}mg = \frac{4mg}{5} - ma\left(\frac{3}{5}\right) \quad \Rightarrow \quad a = \frac{5}{6}\,\text{m/s}^2$$

5.

$$\Sigma F_x = 0$$

$$\Rightarrow \quad +T - mg\sin\alpha - ma\cos\alpha = 0$$

$$\Rightarrow \quad T = mg\sin\alpha + ma\cos\alpha$$

$$\Rightarrow \quad T = 1.8\left(10 \times \frac{3}{5} + \frac{5}{6} \times \frac{4}{5}\right) \quad \Rightarrow \quad T = 12\,\text{N}$$

6.

$$N_1 = mg\cos\alpha - ma\sin\alpha = 0$$

$$\Rightarrow \quad a = g\cot\alpha = 10 \times \frac{4}{3} = \frac{40}{3}\,\text{m/s}^2$$

7.

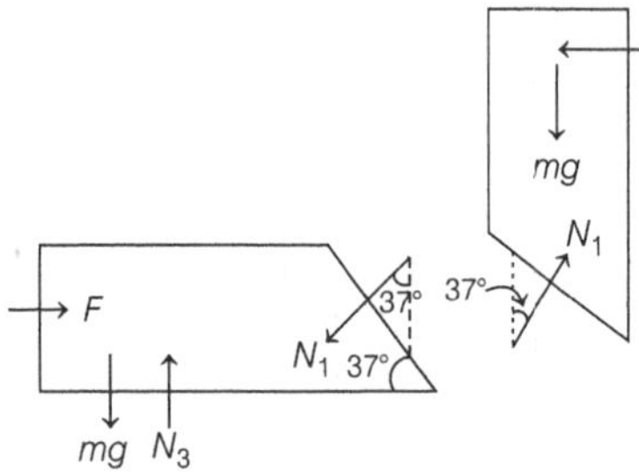

When m_2 gets just lifted

$$N_1 \cos 37° = mg \Rightarrow N_1 = \frac{5mg}{4}$$

For m_1, $F = N_1 \sin 37° \Rightarrow F = \frac{5mg}{4}\left(\frac{3}{5}\right) = \frac{3mg}{4}$

8. For m_1, $\Sigma F_y = 0 \Rightarrow N_3 = mg + N_1 \cos 37°$

$$\Rightarrow \quad N_3 = mg + \left(\frac{5F}{3}\right)\left(\frac{4}{5}\right) \Rightarrow N_3 = mg + \frac{4F}{3}$$

9. From wedge constraint, $a_1 \sin 37° = a_2 \cos 37°$

$$\Rightarrow \quad a_2 = \frac{3a}{4}, \text{ upwards}$$

10.

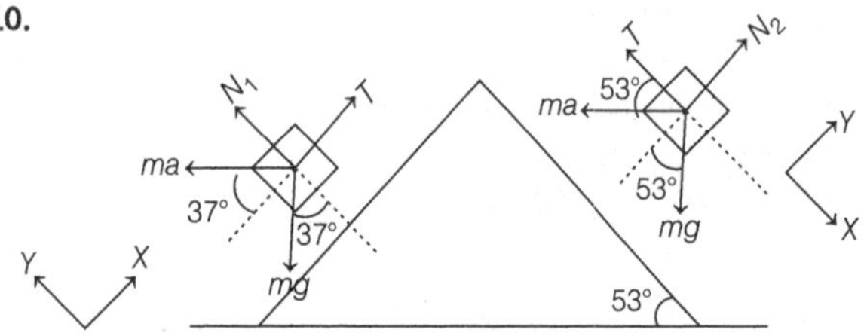

For A, $\Sigma F_y = 0 \Rightarrow N_1 + ma \sin 37° - mg \cos 37° = 0$

$$\Rightarrow \quad N_1 = \frac{m}{5}(4g - 3a)$$

11. For B, $\Sigma F_y = 0 \Rightarrow N_2 - mg \cos 53° - ma \sin 53° = 0$

$$\Rightarrow \quad N_2 = \frac{m}{5}(3g + 4a)$$

12. $N_1 = \frac{m}{5}(4g - 3a) > 0 \Rightarrow a < \frac{4g}{3} \Rightarrow a_{max} = \frac{4g}{3}$

13. 14. and **15.**

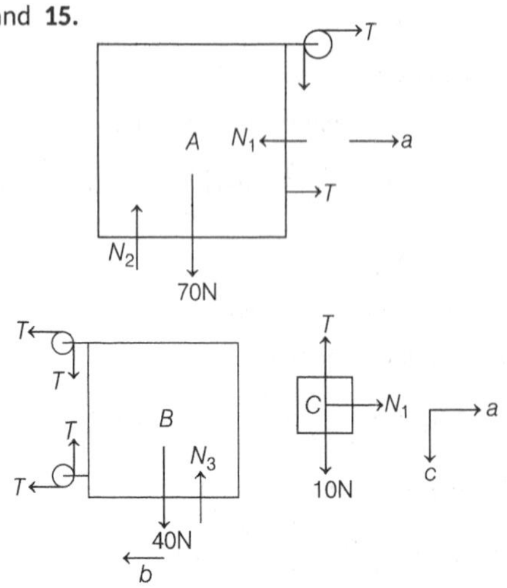

For $(A + C)$ system,

$$\Sigma F_x = ma \Rightarrow 2T = 8a \quad \text{...(i)}$$

For B, $\Sigma F_x = ma_x \Rightarrow 2T = 4b$ ...(ii)

For C, $\Sigma F_y = ma_y$ ...(iii)

$$10 - T = 1(c)$$

From string constant, $-2a - 2b + c = 0$ ...(iv)

Solving Eqs. (i), (ii), (iii) and (iv), we get

$$T = 4\text{N}, \quad a = 1\text{ m/s}^2, \quad b = 2\text{ m/s}^2, c = 6\text{ m/s}^2$$

$$\mathbf{a}_c = \hat{\mathbf{i}} + 6\hat{\mathbf{j}}$$

$$\Rightarrow \quad a_c = \sqrt{37}\text{ m/s}^2$$

16.

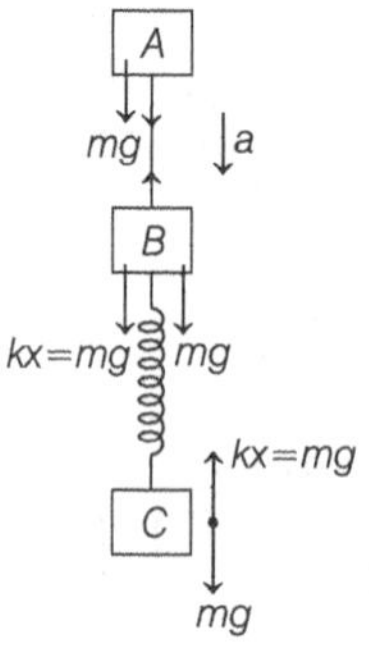

$$a_C = 0$$

For $(A + B)$ system,

$$kx + mg + mg = 2ma \Rightarrow a = \frac{3g}{2} \downarrow$$

$$a_A = a_B = \frac{3g}{2} \downarrow$$

17.

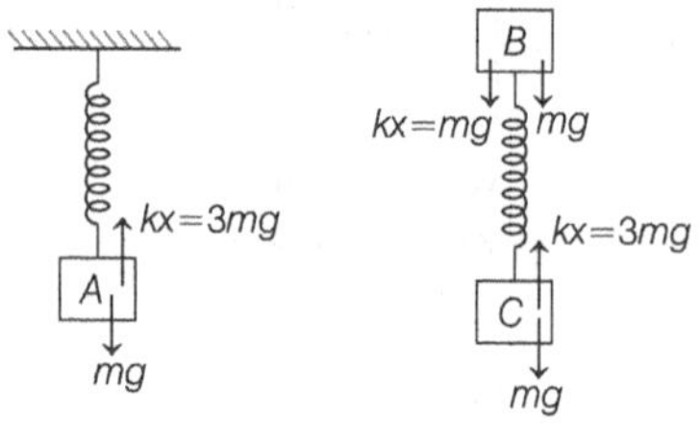

$$a_A = \frac{3mg - mg}{m} = 2g \uparrow, \quad a_B = \frac{mg + mg}{m} = 2g \downarrow, \quad a_C = 0$$

18.

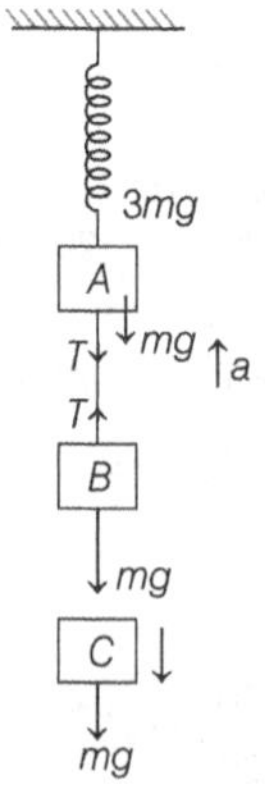

For $(A+B)$ system, $\Sigma F_y = ma_y$

$$\Rightarrow \quad 3mg - 2mg = 2ma \quad \Rightarrow \quad a = \frac{g}{2}\uparrow$$

$$a_A = a_B = \frac{g}{2}\uparrow$$

For C,

$$mg = ma_C \quad \Rightarrow \quad a_C = g\downarrow$$

19., **20.** and **21.**

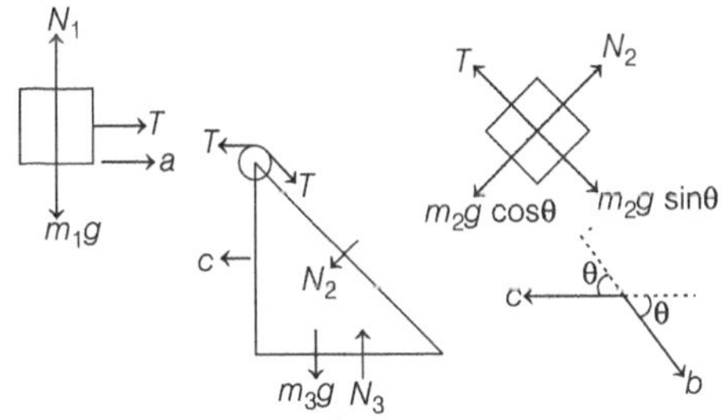

For m_1, $T = m_1 a$ ...(i)

For $(m_2 + m_3)$ in horizontal,

$\Rightarrow \qquad T = m_3 c + m_2(c - b\cos\theta)$ ...(ii)

For m_2, $m_2 g\sin\theta - T = m_2(b - c\cos\theta)$ ...(iii)

From string constraint,

$\Rightarrow -a - c + b = 0$ ...(iv)

Solving Eqs. (i), (ii), (iii) and (iv), we get

$$a = 3\,\text{m/s}^2, \quad T = 3.9\text{N}, \quad c = 2\,\text{m/s}^2$$

Match the Columns Questions

1.

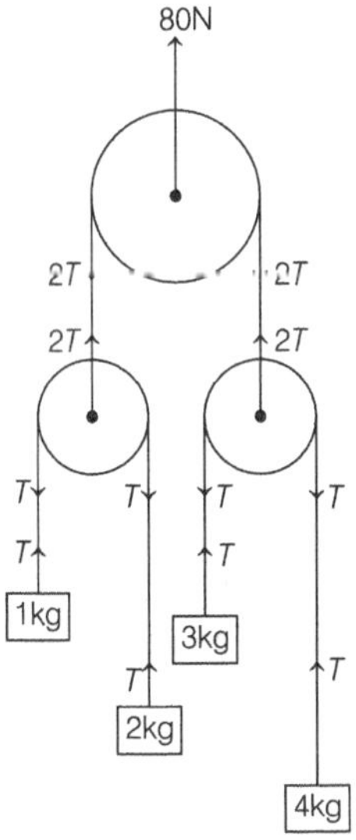

For the top pulley,

$\Sigma F_y = 0 \quad \Rightarrow \quad 80 - 2T - 2T = 0 \quad \Rightarrow \quad T = 20\text{ N}$

For 1 kg block,

$\Sigma F_y = ma_y \quad \Rightarrow T - 10 = 1\times a \quad \Rightarrow a = 10\text{ m/s}^2\uparrow$

For 2kg block,

$\Sigma F_y = ma_y \quad \Rightarrow \quad T - 20 = 2a \quad \Rightarrow \quad a = 0$

For 3 kg block.

$\Sigma F_y = ma_y \quad \Rightarrow \quad 30 - T = 3a \quad \Rightarrow \quad a = \frac{10}{3}\text{ m/s}^2\downarrow$

For 4 kg block,

$\Sigma F_y = ma_y \quad \Rightarrow \quad 40 - T = 4a \quad \Rightarrow \quad a = 5\text{ m/s}^2\downarrow$

2.

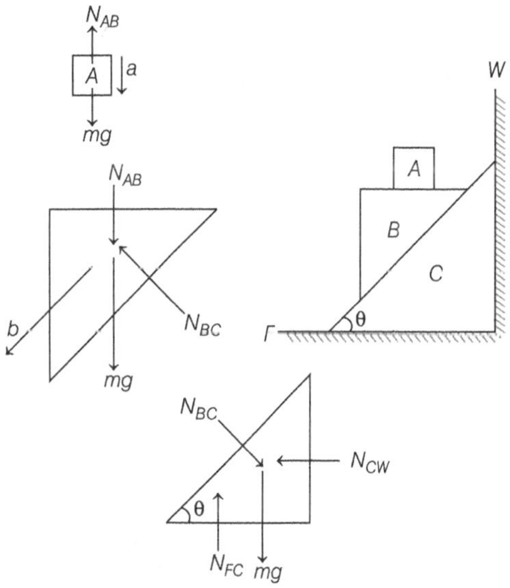

For A; $\quad \Sigma F_y = ma_y \Rightarrow \quad mg - N_{AB} = ma$ ...(i)

For B; $\quad (mg + N_{AB})\sin\theta = mb$ ...(ii)

From wedge constraint; $\quad a = b\sin\theta$ ...(iii)

Solving Eqs. (i), (ii) and (iii), we get

$$b = \frac{2g\sin\theta}{1+\sin^2\theta};\ a = \frac{2g\sin^2\theta}{1+\sin^2\theta} \text{ and } N_{AB} = \frac{mg\cos^2\theta}{1+\sin^2\theta}$$

For B; Perpendicular to the inclined surface of C.

$$\Sigma F = 0 \quad \Rightarrow N_{BC} - (mg + N_{AB})\cos\theta = 0$$

$$\Rightarrow \quad N_{BC} = (mg + N_{AB})\cos\theta \quad \Rightarrow N_{BC} = \frac{2mg\cos\theta}{1+\sin^2\theta}$$

For C; $\Sigma F_x = 0 \quad \Rightarrow N_{CW} - N_{BC}\sin\theta = 0$

$$\Rightarrow \ N_{CW} = N_{BC}\sin\theta = \frac{2mg\sin\theta\cos\theta}{1+\sin^2\theta}$$

$$\Sigma F_y = 0 \quad \Rightarrow N_{FC} - mg - N_{BC}\cos\theta = 0$$

$$\Rightarrow \quad N_{FC} = mg + \left(\frac{2mg\cos\theta}{1+\sin^2\theta}\right)\cos\theta = mg\left(\frac{2+\cos^2\theta}{1+\sin^2\theta}\right)$$

3. A. Taking both the blocks as a system,

$$\Sigma F = ma$$

$$\Rightarrow \qquad F_2 - F_1 = (m_1+m_2)a \quad \Rightarrow \quad a = \frac{F_2 - F_1}{m_1+m_2}$$

For m_2; $\quad \Sigma F = ma \quad \Rightarrow \quad F_2 - T = m_2\left(\frac{F_2 - F_1}{m_1+m_2}\right)$

$$\Rightarrow \qquad T = \frac{m_1 m_2}{m_1+m_2}\left(\frac{F_1}{m_1} + \frac{F_2}{m_2}\right)$$

B. Taking both the blocks as a system,

$$\Sigma F = ma \Rightarrow F_1 + F_2 = (m_1 + m_2)\,a$$

$$\Rightarrow \quad a = \frac{F_1 + F_2}{m_1 + m_2}$$

For m_2 ; $\Sigma F = ma$

$$\Rightarrow \quad F_2 - T = m_2\left(\frac{F_1 + F_2}{m_1 + m_1}\right) \Rightarrow T = \frac{m_1 m_2}{m_1 + m_2}\left(\frac{F_2}{m_2} - \frac{F_1}{m_1}\right)$$

C. Taking both the blocks as a system,

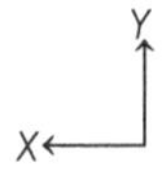

$$\Sigma F = ma \Rightarrow F_2 - F_1 = (m_1 + m_2)\,a$$

$$\Rightarrow \quad a = \frac{F_2 - F_1}{m_1 + m_2}$$

For m_2; $\quad \Sigma F = ma$

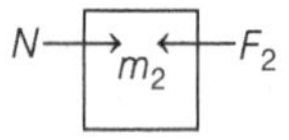

$$\Rightarrow \quad F_2 - N = m_2\left(\frac{F_2 - F_1}{m_1 + m_2}\right)$$

$$\Rightarrow \quad N = \frac{m_1 m_2}{m_1 + m_2}\left(\frac{F_1}{m_1} + \frac{F_2}{m_2}\right)$$

D. Taking both the blocks as a system,

$$\Sigma F = ma \Rightarrow (F_1 + F_2) = (m_1 + m_2)\,a$$

$$\Rightarrow \quad a = \frac{F_1 + F_2}{m_1 + m_2}$$

For m_2 ; $\Sigma F = ma$

$$\Rightarrow \quad F_2 - N = m_2\left(\frac{F_1 + F_2}{m_1 + m_2}\right)$$

$$\Rightarrow \quad N = \frac{m_1 m_2}{m_1 + m_2}\left(\frac{F_2}{m_2} - \frac{F_1}{m_1}\right)$$

4. Initially, the system is in equilibrium.

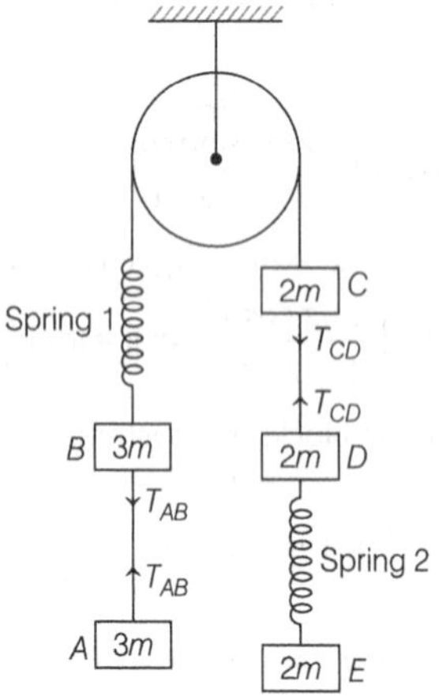

For A; $\Sigma F_y = 0 \Rightarrow T_{AB} - 3mg = 0 \quad \Rightarrow T_{AB} = 3mg$

For $(D + E)$ system,

$$\Sigma F_y = 0 \Rightarrow T_{CD} - 2mg - 2mg = 0 \Rightarrow T_{CD} = 4\,mg$$

Just after spring 2 is cut, spring force in spring 1 remains unchanged.

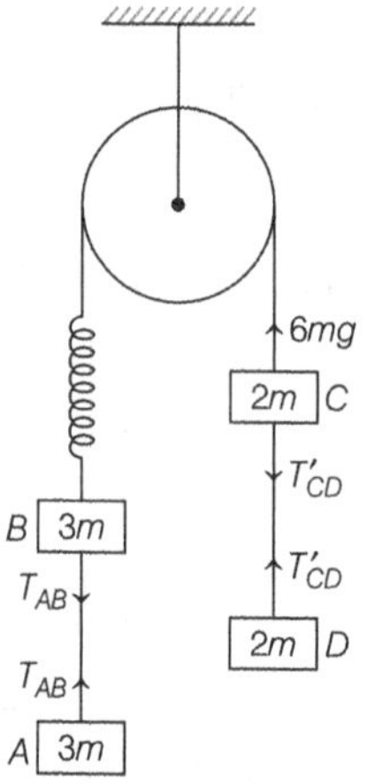

So, tension in AB does not change.

For $(C + D)$ system,

$$\Sigma F = ma \Rightarrow 6mg - 2mg - 2mg = 4ma \Rightarrow a = \frac{g}{2}\uparrow$$

For D; $\quad \Sigma F = ma$

$$T'_{CD} - 2mg = 2m\left(\frac{g}{2}\right) \Rightarrow T'_{CD} = 3mg$$

Since, $T'_{CD} < T_{CD}$; tension in the string CD decreases.

Just after string between C and pulley is cut, spring force in spring 1 becomes zero and spring force in spring 2 remains unchanged.

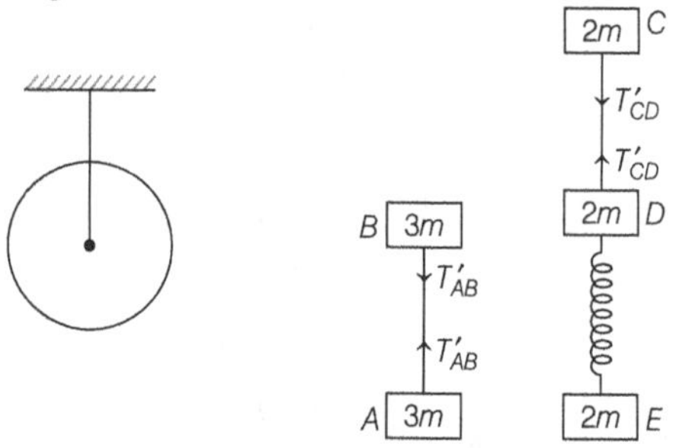

For $(A + B)$ system,

$$\Sigma F = ma \Rightarrow 3mg + 3mg = 6ma \Rightarrow a = g\downarrow$$

For A ; $\Sigma F = ma \Rightarrow 3mg - T'_{AB} = 3mg \quad \Rightarrow T'_{AB} = 0$

So, tension in the string AB decreases.

For $(C + D)$ system,

$$\Sigma F = ma \Rightarrow 2mg + 2mg + kx = 4ma$$

$$\Rightarrow \quad a = \frac{3g}{2}\downarrow \qquad [\because kx = 2mg]$$

For C; $\Sigma F = ma \Rightarrow 2mg + T'_{CD} = 2ma$

$$\Rightarrow \quad 2mg + T'_{CD} = 2m\left(\frac{3g}{2}\right) \Rightarrow T'_{CD} = mg$$

Since $T'_{CD} < T_{CD}$; tension in the string CD decreases.

Numerical Value Questions

1. $v^2 = u^2 + 2as \Rightarrow 5^2 + 0^2 + 2a(5) \Rightarrow a_A = 2.5\,\text{m/s}^2$

$a_B = 2a_A = 5\,\text{m/s}^2$

For block B, $T - 20 = 2(5) \Rightarrow T = 30\,\text{N}$

For block A, $F - 2(30) = 6(2.5) \Rightarrow F = 75\,\text{N}$

2.

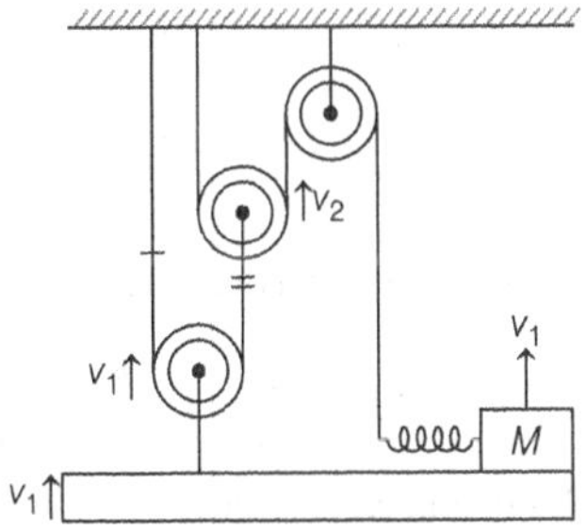

From string constraint,

$$-v_1 - v_1 + v_2 = 0 \Rightarrow v_2 = 2v_1 \quad \text{...(i)}$$

Lets say length of string is l.

$$\frac{dl}{dt} = -v_2 - v_2 - v_1 \Rightarrow -5 = -2v_2 - v_1 \quad \text{...(ii)}$$

From Eqs. (i) and (ii), we get

$$v_1 = 1\,\text{m/s}$$

3.

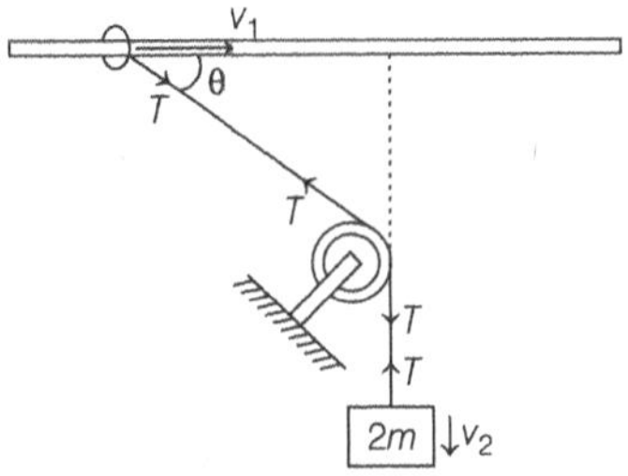

From string constraint,

$$v_2 = v_1 \cos\theta$$

$$\frac{dv_2}{dt} = v_1\left(-\sin\theta \frac{d\theta}{dt}\right) + \cos\theta \frac{dv_1}{dt}$$

Since, system is released from rest ($v_1 = 0$)

$$a_2 = a_1 \cos\theta \quad \text{...(i)}$$

$$2mg - T = 2ma_2 \quad \text{...(ii)}$$

$$T\cos\theta = ma_1 \quad \text{...(iii)}$$

Solving Eqs. (i), (ii) and (iii), we get

$$a_1 = \frac{2g}{3} = 6.67\,\text{m/s}^2$$

4.

$$T = 1a_1 \quad \text{...(i)}$$

$$T = 2a_2 \quad \text{...(ii)}$$

$$40 - 2T = 4a_3 \quad \text{...(iii)}$$

$$-a_1 - a_2 + a_3 + a_3 = 0 \quad \text{...(iv)}$$

Solving Eqs. (i), (ii), (iii) and (iv), we get

$$a_3 = 6\,\text{m/s}^2$$

5.

$$5mg - 2T = 5ma_2 \quad \text{...(i)}$$

$$T - 2mg = 2ma_1 \quad \text{...(ii)}$$

$$a_1 = 2a_2 \quad \text{...(iii)}$$

Solving Eqs. (i), (ii) and (iii), we get

$$a_2 = \frac{g}{13} \text{ and } a_1 = \frac{2g}{13}$$

$$N_1 - mg = m\left(\frac{2g}{13}\right)$$

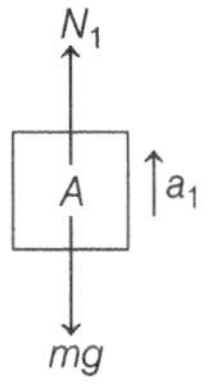

$$\Rightarrow \quad N_1 = \frac{15mg}{13}$$

6.

$$F - 2T = 2ma_1 \quad \text{...(i)}$$

$$3T = 4ma_2 \quad \text{...(ii)}$$

$$T = ma_3 \quad \text{...(iii)}$$

$$+a_1 + a_1 - a_2 - a_2 - a_2 - a_3 = 0 \Rightarrow 2a_1 = 3a_2 + a_3 \quad \text{...(iv)}$$

Solving Eqs. (i), (ii), (iii) and (iv), we get

$$a_2 = \frac{F}{7m}$$

7. From string constraint,

$$-v_B\cos 37^\circ + v_{P_3}\cos 37^\circ - v_{P_3}\cos 53^\circ + v_A = 0$$

$$\Rightarrow -\frac{4v_B}{5} + 8 - 6 + 6 = 0 \Rightarrow v_B = 10\,\text{m/s}$$

8.

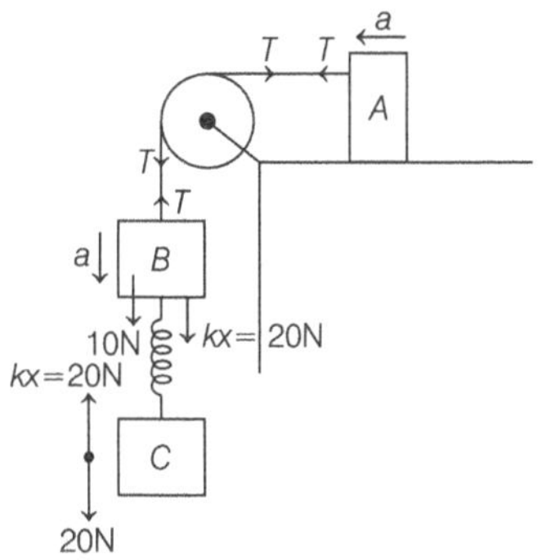

$$30 - T = 1a \quad \text{...(i)}$$

$$T = a \quad \text{...(ii)}$$

Solving Eqs. (i) and (ii), we get

$$a = 15\,\text{m/s}^2 \quad \text{and} \quad T = 15\,\text{N}$$

9.

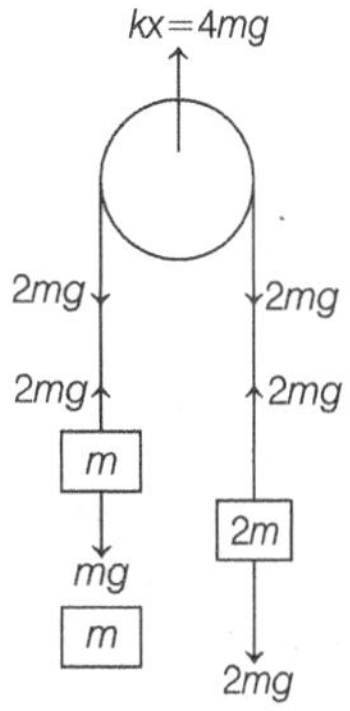

Spring force does not change instantly. Just after cutting the string, spring force will be 4 mg. Since, pulley is massless, tension in the string will be still 2 mg.

$$a_A = \frac{2mg - mg}{m} = g \uparrow \text{ and } a_C = 0$$

So, $a_{\text{pulley}} = \dfrac{(g+0)}{2} = 5 \text{ m/s}^2$

10.

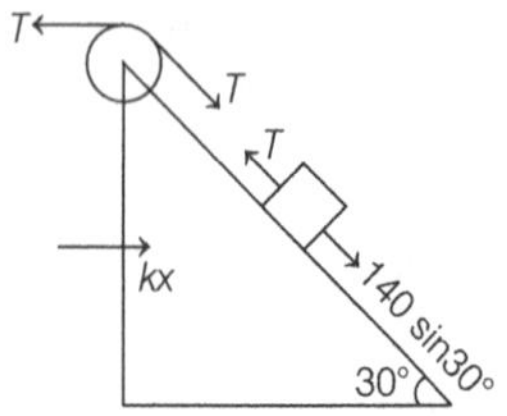

For 14 kg block,

$$T = 140 \sin 30° = 70 \text{ N}$$

For (wedge + block) system, $\Sigma F_x = 0$

$\Rightarrow \quad T = kx = 70\text{N}, \quad 1000x = 70 \quad \Rightarrow \quad x = \dfrac{7}{100} \text{ m} = 7\text{cm}$

11.

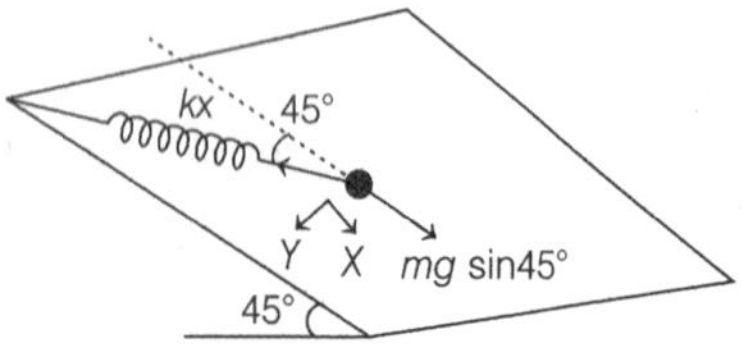

Initially $mg \sin 45° = 2kx \cos 45° \quad \Rightarrow \quad kx = \dfrac{mg}{2}$ ...(i)

$$\Sigma F_x = ma_x \quad \Rightarrow mg \sin 45° - kx \cos 45° = ma_x$$

$$a_x = \frac{g}{2\sqrt{2}}$$

$$\Sigma F_y = ma_y \quad \Rightarrow \quad kx \sin 45° = ma_y$$

$$\Rightarrow \quad a_y = \frac{g}{2\sqrt{2}}$$

$$\mathbf{a} = \frac{g}{2\sqrt{2}}(\hat{\mathbf{i}} + \hat{\mathbf{j}})$$

Magnitude of acceleration $= \dfrac{g}{2} = 5 \text{m}/\text{s}^2$

12. From string constraint,

$v \cos\theta = 10 \quad \Rightarrow \quad v = 10 \sec\theta$ ...(i)

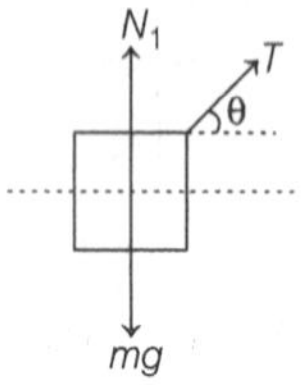

$a = \dfrac{dv}{dt} = 10 \sec\theta \tan\theta \dfrac{d\theta}{dt}$ ...(ii)

$\Sigma F_x = ma \quad \Rightarrow T \cos\theta = ma$ ...(iii)

$\Sigma F_y = 0 \quad \Rightarrow \quad T \sin\theta + N_1 = mg$

When block loses contact,

$T \sin\theta = mg$ ...(iv)

From Eqs. (iii) and (iv), we get

$a = g \cot\theta$ ...(v)

Also,

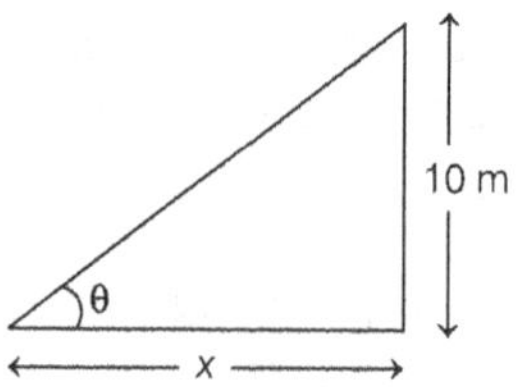

$$\cot\theta = \frac{x}{10} \Rightarrow x = 10 \cot\theta \Rightarrow \frac{dx}{dt} = -10 \operatorname{cosec}^2\theta \frac{d\theta}{dt}$$

$\Rightarrow -10 \sec\theta = -10 \operatorname{cosec}^2\theta \dfrac{d\theta}{dt} \Rightarrow \dfrac{d\theta}{dt} = \dfrac{\sec\theta}{\operatorname{cosec}^2\theta}$ ...(vi)

From Eqs. (ii), (iv) and (vi), we get

$$\tan^4\theta = 1 \Rightarrow \theta = \frac{\pi}{4}$$

13.

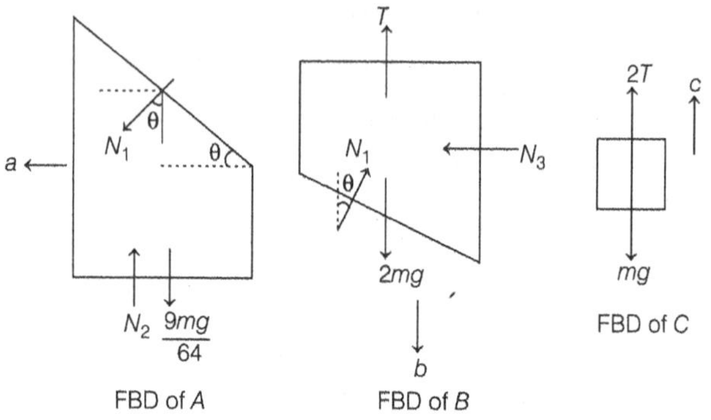

For A,

$\Sigma F_x = ma \Rightarrow N_1 \sin\theta = \dfrac{9ma}{64}$ ...(i)

For B,

$\Sigma F_y = ma_y \Rightarrow 2mg - T - N_1 \cos\theta = 2mb$ ...(ii)

For C,

$2T - mg = mc$ ...(iii)

From wedge constraint,

$\Rightarrow a \sin\theta = b \cos\theta$ ...(iv)

From string constraint ,

$\Rightarrow \quad +b - c - c = 0 \Rightarrow b = 2c$ ...(v)

Solving Eqs. (i), (ii), (iii), (iv) and (v), we get

$$a = 8 \text{m}/\text{s}^2 \Rightarrow b = 6 \text{m}/\text{s}^2 \Rightarrow c = 3 \text{m}/\text{s}^2$$

14.

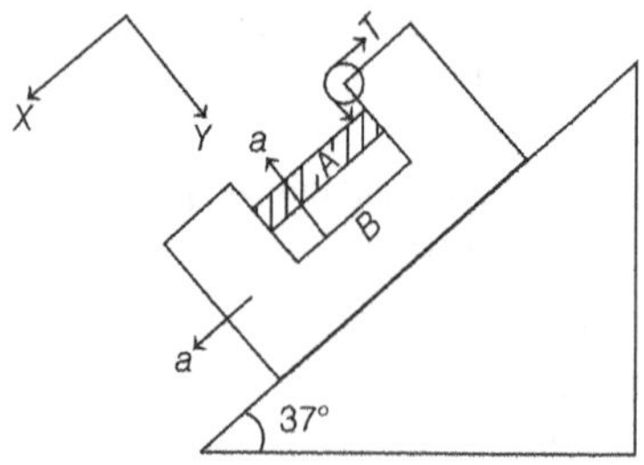

For $(A+B)$ system,

$$\Sigma F_x = ma_x$$

$$2mg\sin 37^\circ - T = 2ma \quad \text{...(i)}$$

For A,

$$\Sigma F_y = ma_y \Rightarrow T - mg\cos 37^\circ = ma \quad \text{...(ii)}$$

From Eqs. (i) and (ii), we get

$$a = \frac{4}{3}\ \text{m/s}^2$$

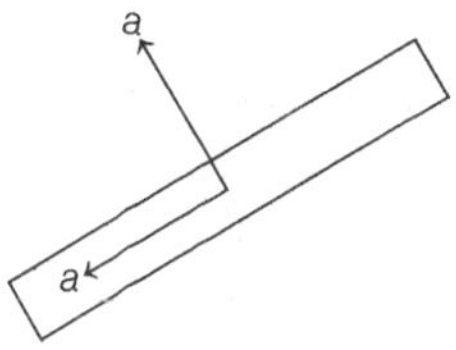

$$\mathbf{a}_A = a\hat{\mathbf{i}} - a\hat{\mathbf{j}} \Rightarrow \mathbf{a}_A = \frac{4}{3}\hat{\mathbf{i}} - \frac{4}{3}\hat{\mathbf{j}} \Rightarrow a_A = \frac{4\sqrt{2}}{3}\ \text{m/s}^2$$

15.

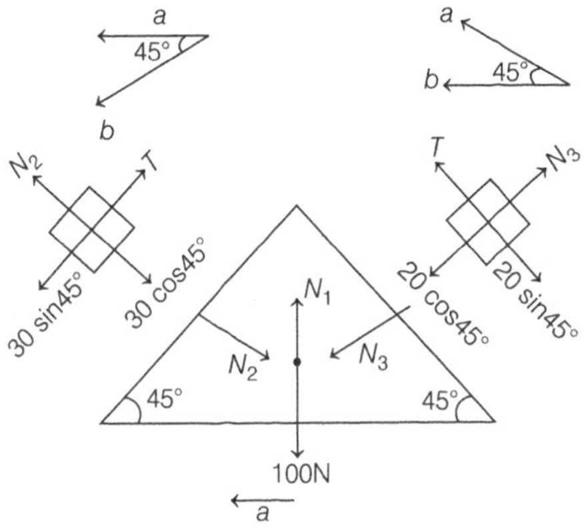

For wedge,

$$\Sigma F_x = ma_x$$

$$\Rightarrow N_3\sin 45^\circ - N_2\sin 45^\circ = 10a \quad \text{...(i)}$$

For A, $\Sigma F_x = ma_x$

$$\Rightarrow 30\sin 45^\circ - T = 3(b + a\cos 45^\circ) \quad \text{...(ii)}$$

$$\Sigma F_y = ma_y \Rightarrow N_2 - 30\cos 45^\circ = 3(a\sin 45^\circ) \quad \text{...(iii)}$$

For B, $\Sigma F_x = ma_x$

$$\Rightarrow T - 20\sin 45^\circ = 2(b + a\cos 45^\circ) \quad \text{...(iv)}$$

$$\Sigma F_y = ma_y \Rightarrow 20\cos 45^\circ - N_3 = 2(a\sin 45^\circ) \quad \text{...(v)}$$

Solving Eqs. (i), (ii), (iii), (iv) and (v), we get

$$a = -\frac{2}{5}\ \text{m/s}^2$$

16.

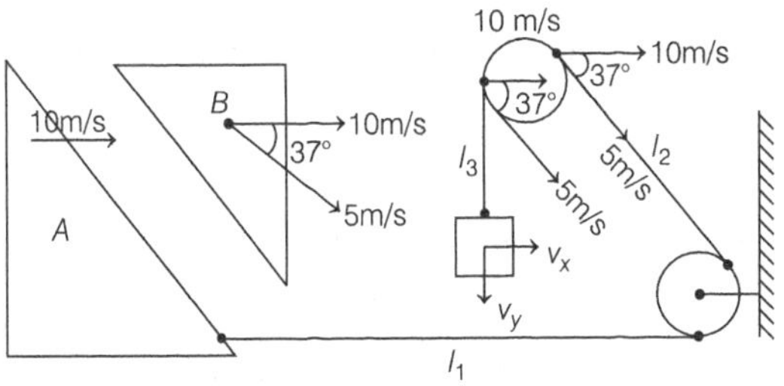

String constraint, $l_1 + l_2 + l_3 = \text{constant}$

$$\frac{dl_1}{dt} + \frac{dl_2}{dt} + \frac{dl_3}{dt} = 0$$

$$-10 + (-5 - 10\cos 37^\circ) + (-5\sin 37^\circ + v_y) = 0$$

$$\Rightarrow \quad v_y = 26\ \text{m/s}$$

Wedge constraint for (B and C)

$$10 + 5\cos 37^\circ = v_x \Rightarrow v_x = 14\ \text{m/s}$$

$$\mathbf{v}_c = 14\hat{\mathbf{i}} + 26\hat{\mathbf{j}} \Rightarrow v_c = \sqrt{14^2 + 26^2} = \sqrt{872}\ \text{m/s}$$

17.

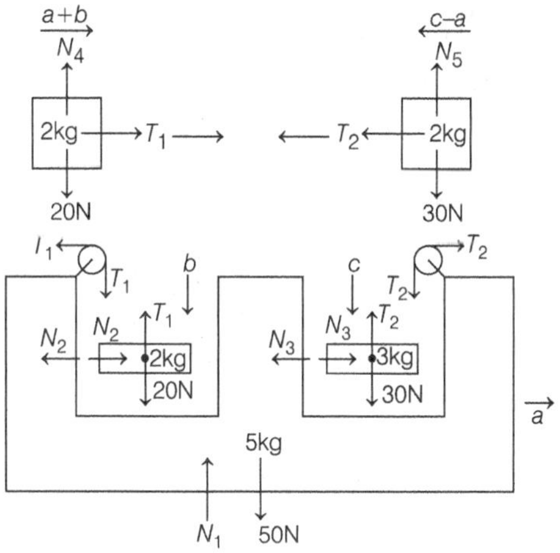

$$T_1 = 2(a+b) \quad \text{...(i)}$$

$$T_2 = 3(c-a) \quad \text{...(ii)}$$

$$20 - T_1 = 2b \quad \text{...(iii)}$$

$$30 - T_2 = 3c \quad \text{...(iv)}$$

$$T_2 - T_1 = 10a \quad \text{...(v)}$$

Solving Eqs. (i), (ii), (iii), (iv) and (v), we get

$$a = \frac{g}{25}$$

18. For top bar, $\Sigma F_y = 0$

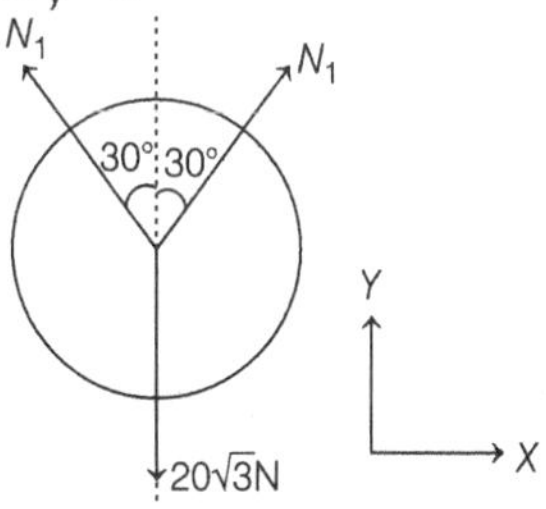

$$\Rightarrow 2N_1\cos 30^\circ = 20\sqrt{3} \Rightarrow N_1 = 20\ \text{N}$$

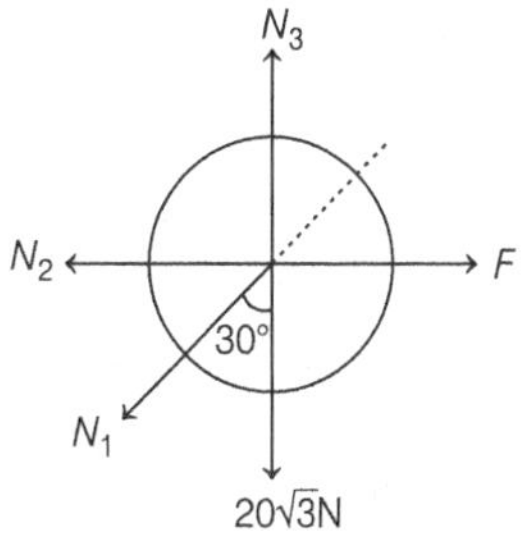

$$\Sigma F_x = 0 \Rightarrow F = N_2 + N_1\sin 30^\circ$$

F will be minimum when $N_2 = 0$

$\Rightarrow \quad F_{min} = N_1 \sin 30° = 20\left(\frac{1}{2}\right) = 10\,N$

19. For $(A+B)$ system, $\Sigma F_x = ma_x$

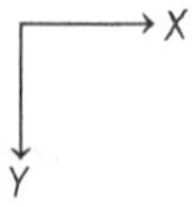

$\Rightarrow \quad F = 2ma$

$\Rightarrow \quad \frac{mg}{2} = 2ma$

$\Rightarrow \quad a = \frac{g}{4}$

For B,

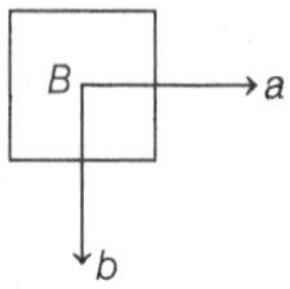

$\Sigma F_y = ma_y$

$\Rightarrow \quad mg - F = mb$

$\Rightarrow \quad mg - \frac{mg}{2} = mb \quad \Rightarrow \quad b = \frac{g}{2}$

$a_A = a = \frac{g}{4}$

$a_B = \sqrt{a^2 + b^2} = \sqrt{\left(\frac{g}{4}\right)^2 + \left(\frac{g}{2}\right)^2} = \frac{\sqrt{5}g}{4}$

$\therefore \quad \frac{a_A}{a_B} = \frac{1}{\sqrt{5}}$

20.

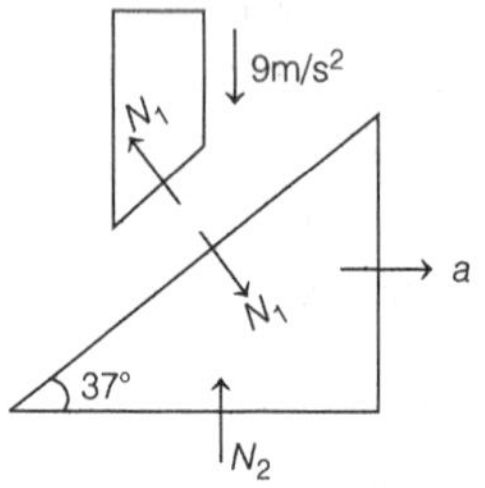

From wedge constraint,

$9 \cos 37° = a \sin 37° \quad \Rightarrow a = 12\,m/s^2$

For wedge,

$\Sigma F_x = ma_x \quad \Rightarrow \quad N_1 \sin 37° = 10(12) \quad \Rightarrow \quad N_1 = 200\,N$

$\Sigma F_y = 0 \quad \Rightarrow N_2 = N_1 \cos 37° + mg$

$= 200\left(\frac{4}{5}\right) + 100$

$= 160 + 100 = 260\,N$

Previous Year's Questions

JEE Main

1. Given,

Slope of inclined, $\theta = 30°$

Mass on inclined plane, $m = 2$ kg

Mass hanging = 4 kg

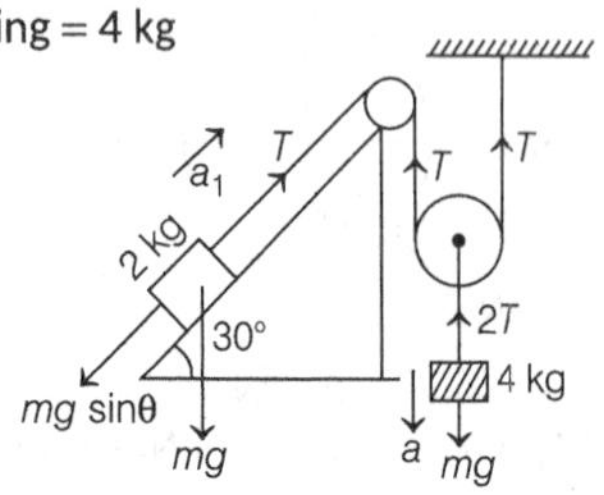

Using the relation

$$\Sigma \mathbf{T} \cdot \mathbf{a} = 0$$

$$Ta_1 - 2Ta = 0$$

$$a_1 = 2a$$

Net force on 2 kg mass

$$T - mg \sin 30° = 4a$$

$$T - g = 4a \quad \text{...(i)}$$

Net force on 4 kg mass

$$4g - 2T = 4a \quad \text{...(ii)}$$

From Eq. (i) and (ii), we get

$$4g - 2g = 12a$$

$$a = \frac{g}{6}$$

Now, $a_1 = 2a = 2 \times \frac{g}{6} = \frac{g}{3}$

2.

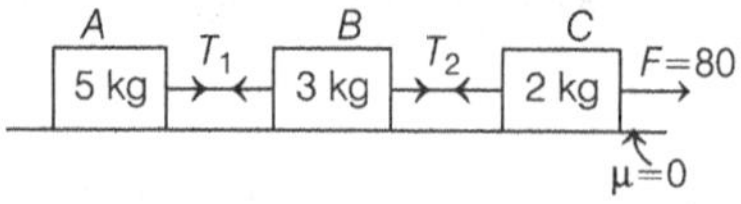

Acceleration of system

$$= \frac{\text{Net force}}{\text{Total mass}} = \frac{80\,N}{10\,kg} = 8\,m/s^2$$

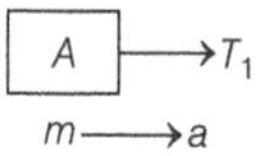

Force on block A,

$$T_1 = m_A \times a = 5 \times 8 = 40\,N$$

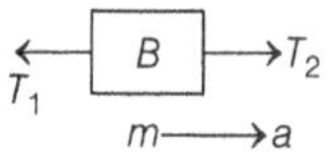

Force on block B,

$$T_2 - T_1 = m_B a$$

$$T_2 - 40 = 3 \times 8$$

$$T_2 = 64\,N$$

3. Given, $F = 125\,N$

$$F = \frac{dp}{dt}$$

$$p = nmv$$

$$F = \frac{d}{dt}(nmv) = mv\frac{dn}{dt}$$

$$125 = \frac{10}{1000} \times 250 \times \frac{dn}{dt}$$

$$\frac{dn}{dt} = \frac{125 \times 100}{250} \quad \Rightarrow \quad \frac{dn}{dt} = 50$$

4. Given,

$F_1 = 10\,N, F_2 = 8\,N,$

$F_3 = 6\,N$

mass, $m = 5$ kg

According to question, resultant of $\mathbf{F}_2$ and $\mathbf{F}_3$ should be opposite of $\mathbf{F}_1$.

$\Rightarrow \quad \mathbf{a} = \frac{\mathbf{F}}{m} = \frac{10}{5} = 2\,m/s^2$

5. Given, position vector of particle

$$\mathbf{r} = (10t\hat{\mathbf{i}} + 15t^2\hat{\mathbf{j}} + 7\hat{\mathbf{k}})\,m$$

$\therefore$ Velocity of particle, $\mathbf{v} = \frac{d\mathbf{r}}{dt} = 10\hat{\mathbf{i}} + 30t\hat{\mathbf{j}}$

Acceleration of particle,

$$a = \frac{dv}{dt} = 30\hat{j}$$

∴ Net force applied on the particle,

$$F = ma = 30m\hat{j}$$

Clearly, net force is applied along Y-axis.

6. Force $= \frac{d}{dt}(p) =$ Slope of p-t graph.

From the graph, it is clear that slope of line C is maximum while slope of line b is minimum, therefore, in region C, magnitude of force is maximum whereas in region b, magnitude of force is minimum.

7. FBD of the sphere

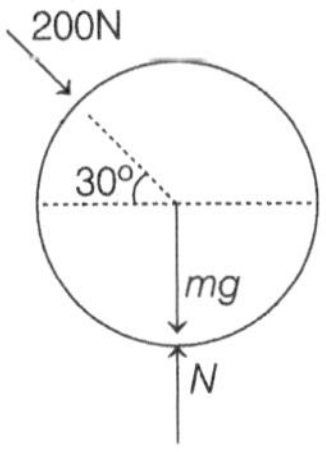

Therefore,

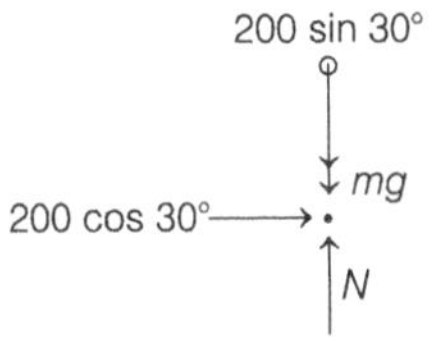

Since, $a_y = 0$

Thus, $N = mg + 200 \sin 30°$

$$N = 70 \times 10 + 200 \times \sin 30° = 800 \text{ N}$$

8. From the given free body diagram.

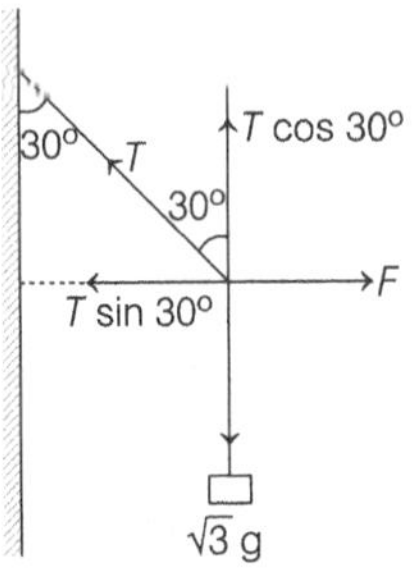

$$T \cos 30° = \sqrt{3}\, g$$

$$\Rightarrow \quad T\frac{\sqrt{3}}{2} = \sqrt{3}\, g$$

$$\Rightarrow \quad T = 2g = 2 \times 10 \; (\because g = 10 \text{ ms}^{-2})$$

$$= 20 \text{ N}$$

9. Given, $m = 10$ g

Air escaping rate from balloon,

$$v = 4.5 \text{ cm/s}, t = 5 \text{ s}$$

$$F_{avg} = ma = m \cdot \frac{dv}{dt} = v\frac{dm}{dt} = 4.5 \times \frac{10}{5} = 9 \text{ dyne}$$

10. Given, $m = 0.15$ kg

$u = 12 \text{ ms}^{-1}$

The final velocity $v = -u = -12$ m/s

According to Newton's second law of motion,

$$F = \frac{\Delta p}{\Delta t} = \frac{m(v-u)}{\Delta t} = \frac{0.15(-12-12)}{\Delta t}$$

$$\Rightarrow \quad 100 = \frac{3.6}{\Delta t} \Rightarrow |\Delta t| = \frac{3.6}{100} = 0.036 \text{ s}$$

11. For the block's motion,

$$l = 0 + \frac{1}{2}(g \sin 30°)(2)^2 \quad \text{...(i)}$$

$$l = 0 + \frac{1}{2}(g \sin 45°)(t)^2 \quad \text{...(ii)}$$

From Eqs. (i) and (ii), we get

$$\Rightarrow \quad 0 + \frac{1}{2}(g \sin 30°)(2)^2 = 0 + \frac{1}{2}(g \sin 45°)(t)^2$$

By solving, $t = (2)^{3/4} = 1.68$ s

12. By the method of virtual work,

$$\Rightarrow \quad T \cdot a = 0;$$

So, $4Ta_1 + 2Ta_2 + Ta_3 + Ta_4 = 0$

Hence, $4a_1 + 2a_2 + a_3 + a_4 = 0$

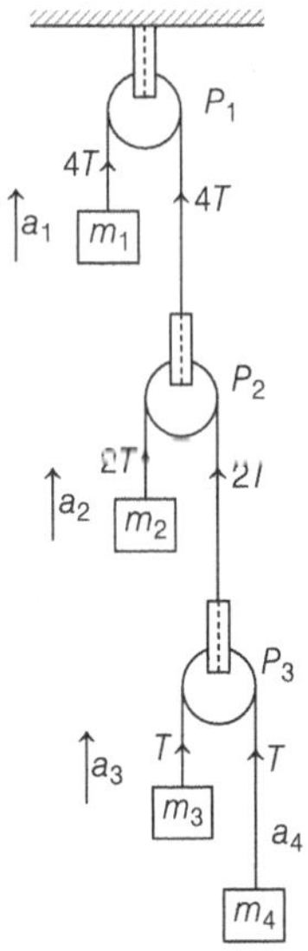

13. Given, $m = 2$ kg

Rate of water striking the block,

$$\frac{dm}{dt} = 1 \text{ kg s}^{-1}$$

Water released by the jet striking the block with a rate of 1 kg s^{-1} at a speed of 10 m/s will exert a force on the block given by, $F = v\frac{dm}{dt} = 10 \times 1 = 10$ N

According to Newton's second law of motion,

$$a = \frac{F}{m} = \frac{10}{2} = 5 \text{ m s}^{-2}$$

14. As per question, $N = \frac{Mg}{4}$

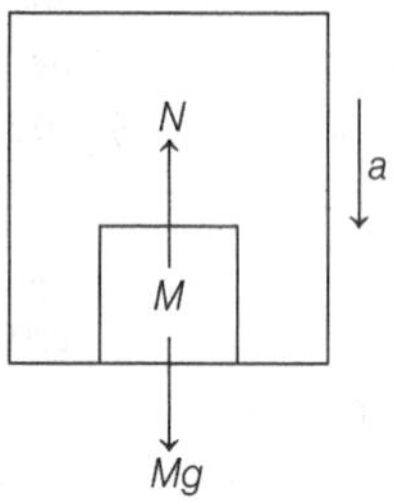

By using Newton's second law,

$$Mg - N = Ma$$

$$Mg - \frac{Mg}{4} = Ma \; ; \; a = \frac{3g}{4}$$

15. Given area,

$$A = 10 \text{ cm}^2 = 10^{-4} \text{ m}^2$$

Speed, $v = 20$ m/s,

Density of water, $\rho = 1000$ kg/m^3

We know that force,

$$F = v\frac{dm}{dt}, \; F = v\rho A\frac{dx}{dt}$$

$$F = \rho A v^2,$$

$$F = 10^3 \times 10 \times 10^{-4} \times 400 = 400 \text{ N}$$

16. Mass of complete chain $= m$

Length of chain $= L$

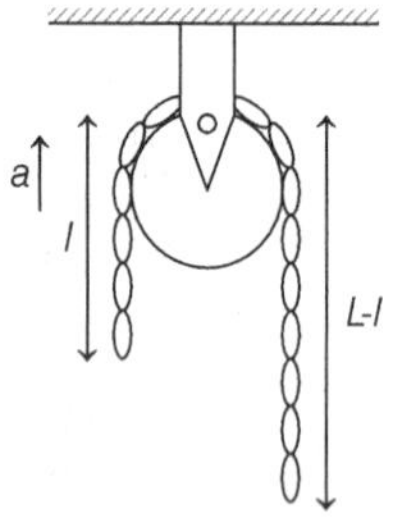

Mass of $(L - l)$ length chain $= \frac{m}{L}(L - l)$

Force on $(L - l)$ length chain $= \frac{m}{L}(L - l)\,g$

Mass of l length chain $= \frac{ml}{L}$

Force on l length chain $= \frac{ml}{L}g$

Now, $\frac{m(L - l)}{L}g - \frac{ml}{L}g = ma$

$$a = \frac{(L - 2l)}{L}g \Rightarrow \frac{g}{2} = \frac{L - 2l}{L}g$$

$$L = 4l \Rightarrow l = \frac{L}{4} = \frac{1}{x}$$

$$x = 4$$

17. Given, $m = 100 \text{ g} = 0.1$ kg

Force, $\mathbf{F} = (10\hat{\mathbf{i}} + 5\hat{\mathbf{j}})$ N

$\therefore \quad \mathbf{a} = \frac{\mathbf{F}}{m} = \frac{10\hat{\mathbf{i}} + 5\hat{\mathbf{j}}}{0.1} = 100\hat{\mathbf{i}} + 50\hat{\mathbf{j}}$

$\therefore$ Position of object,

$$\mathbf{s} = \mathbf{u}t + \frac{1}{2}\mathbf{a}t^2 = 0 \cdot t + \frac{1}{2}\mathbf{a}t^2$$

$$= \frac{1}{2}(100\hat{\mathbf{i}} + 50\hat{\mathbf{j}}) \cdot 2^2 \qquad [\because t = 2\text{s}]$$

$$= 200\hat{\mathbf{i}} + 100\hat{\mathbf{j}} = a\hat{\mathbf{i}} + b\hat{\mathbf{j}} \qquad \text{[given]}$$

$\therefore \quad a = 200, b = 100$

$\therefore \quad \frac{a}{b} = \frac{200}{100} = 2$

18. Resolving the forces components along X-axis

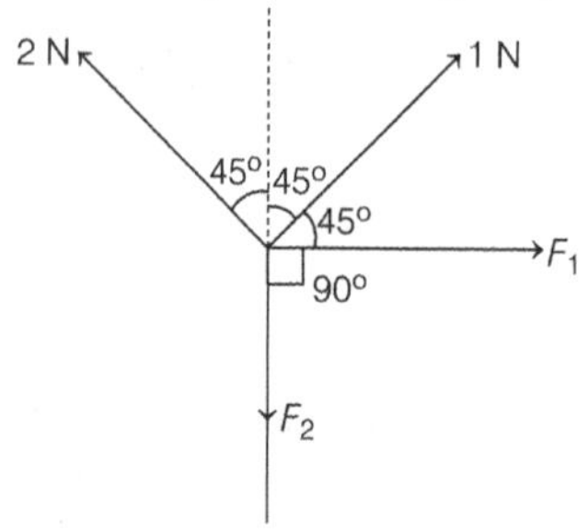

$$F_x = F_1 + 1\cos 45° - 2\cos 45°$$

$F_x = 0$ for equilibrium

$$F_1 = -\cos 45° \qquad \text{...(i)}$$

$$F_y = 1\sin 45° + 2\sin 45° - F_2$$

$$F_y = 0$$

$$F_2 = 3\sin 45° \qquad \text{...(ii)}$$

From Eqs. (i) and (ii), we get

$$\frac{F_1}{F_2} = -\frac{\cos 45°}{3\sin 45°} = -\frac{1}{3}$$

So, $x = 3$ (ignore negative sign)

19. Given, $m = 10$ kg, $L = 5$ m

$F = 30$ N

According to the question FBD of the system,

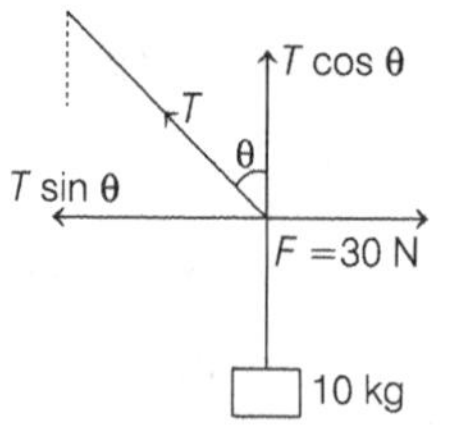

$$T\cos\theta = 10\,g \qquad \text{...(i)}$$

$\Rightarrow \quad T\cos\theta = 100 \text{ N} \qquad \text{...(ii)}$

$$T\sin\theta = 30$$

On dividing Eq. (ii) by Eq. (i), we get

$$\frac{T\sin\theta}{T\cos\theta} = \tan\theta = \frac{30}{100} = \frac{3}{10}$$

$\therefore$ $$\theta = \tan^{-1}(3\times 10^{-1})$$

Thus, $x = 3$

20. Given, each ball, $m = 2$ kg

The given situation is shown below.

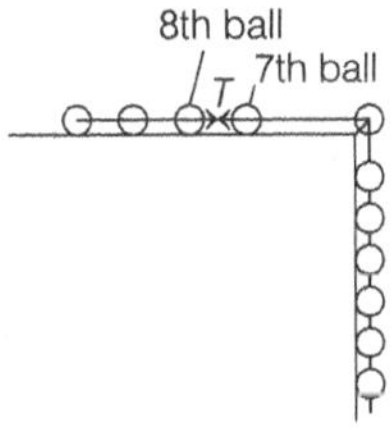

If a be the resultant acceleration, then

$$a = \frac{\text{net force } (F_{net})}{\text{mass of total ball}} = \frac{6mg}{10m}$$

($\because F_{net}$ = weight of balls below the 7th ball $= 6\,mg$)

$\Rightarrow$ $a = 3g/5$

But, according to diagram,

$$T = 3ma = 3m\times\frac{3g}{5} = \frac{9}{5}mg$$

$$= \frac{9}{5}\times 2\times 10 = 36 \text{ N}$$

21. From free body diagram,

$F\cos 60° = mg\sin 60°$

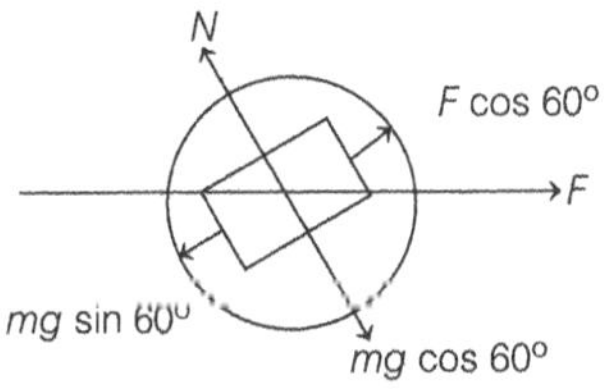

$$F = mg\tan 60°$$
$$= 0.2\times 10\times\sqrt{3} = 2\sqrt{3}$$
$$F = \sqrt{12} \text{ N}$$

So, $x = 12$ $(\because F = \sqrt{x}\text{ N})$

22. Here, the two masses are not tied by inextensible string. So, acceleration in different blocks will be different.

Net force on block $A = Ma$

Remaining force on $B = F - Ma$

Acceleration on block $B = \dfrac{F - Ma}{M}$

23. Given,

The mass of the bullet, $m = 0.1$ kg

The initial velocity of the bullet

$u = 10$ m/s

The final velocity of the bullet

$$v = 0$$
$$v^2 - u^2 = 2as$$

$\Rightarrow$ $$0^2 - (10)^2 = 2a(0.50)$$

$\Rightarrow$ $$a = -100 \text{ m/s}^2$$

The retarding force on the bullet,

$$F = ma$$
$$F = 0.1(-100)$$
$$F = -10 \text{ N}$$

Hence, the value of x to the nearest integer is 10.

24. Given,

$$m = 2\text{ kg } t = 4\text{ s}$$

Force, $\mathbf{F} = (2\hat{\mathbf{i}} + 3\hat{\mathbf{j}} + 5\hat{\mathbf{k}})$ N

$\Rightarrow$ $$\mathbf{a} = \frac{\mathbf{F}}{m}$$

$\Rightarrow$ $$\mathbf{a} = \frac{2\hat{\mathbf{i}} + 3\hat{\mathbf{j}} + 5\hat{\mathbf{k}}}{2}$$

Using, $\mathbf{s} = \mathbf{u}t + \frac{1}{2}\mathbf{a}t^2$

$$\mathbf{s} = \mathbf{u}t + \frac{1}{2}\frac{(2\hat{\mathbf{i}} + 3\hat{\mathbf{j}} + 5\hat{\mathbf{k}})}{2}\cdot t^2$$

$$= 0 + \frac{1}{4}(2\hat{\mathbf{i}} + 3\hat{\mathbf{j}} + 5\hat{\mathbf{k}})\cdot(4)^2 \quad [\because \mathbf{u} = 0 \text{ and } t = 4\text{ s}]$$

$$= 8\hat{\mathbf{i}} + 12\hat{\mathbf{j}} + 20\hat{\mathbf{k}}$$

Let $s = x\hat{\mathbf{i}} + y\hat{\mathbf{j}} + z\hat{\mathbf{k}}$

$\Rightarrow$ $$x\hat{\mathbf{i}} + y\hat{\mathbf{j}} + z\hat{\mathbf{k}} = 8\hat{\mathbf{i}} + 12\hat{\mathbf{j}} + 20\hat{\mathbf{k}}$$

Thus, we get (8, 12, 20)

$\therefore$ $$b = 12$$

25. Given, $m = 2$ kg

Force, $F = 20\hat{\mathbf{i}} + 10\hat{\mathbf{j}}$ N

$$u = 0\text{ ms}^{-1}, t = 10\text{ s}$$

As, $F = ma$

$\Rightarrow$ $$a = F/m = \frac{20\hat{\mathbf{i}} + 10\hat{\mathbf{j}}}{2} = (10\hat{\mathbf{i}} + 5\hat{\mathbf{j}})\text{ ms}^{-2}$$

The motion along X- axis,

$$s_x = u_x t + \frac{1}{2}a_x t^2$$

$$= 0 + \frac{1}{2}\times 10\times(10)^2 = 500\text{ m}$$

Hence, displacement along X-axis after 10 s is 500 m.

26. Here, both block and wedge are moving.

Consider the acceleration of the block with respect to the wedge is a_1 and the acceleration of the wedge is a_2.

Given, $M = 16$ kg

$m = 8$ kg

FBD of the wedge

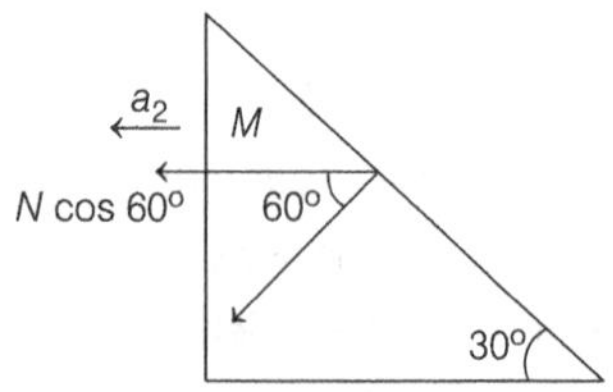

In the x-directions,

$$N\cos 60° = Ma_2$$
$$N(0.5) = 16 \times a_2$$
$$\Rightarrow \quad N = 32a_2$$

Now, FBD of the block with respect to the wedge.

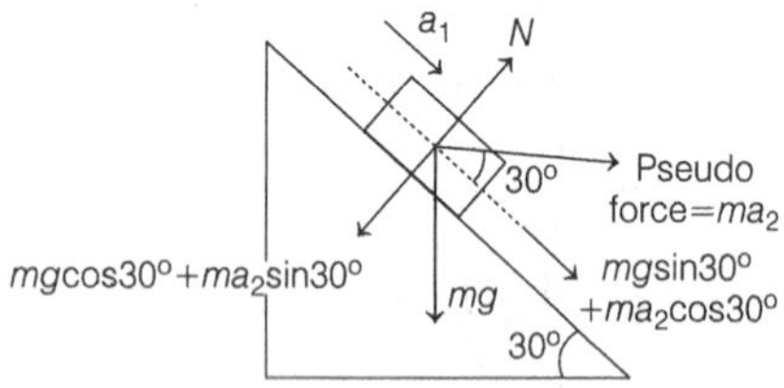

Along the perpendicular to the inclined plane,

$$N = 8g\cos 30° - 8a_2\sin 30°$$
$$32a_2 = 4\sqrt{3}g - 4a_2$$
$$36a_2 = 4\sqrt{3}g$$
$$\Rightarrow \quad a_2 = \frac{\sqrt{3}}{9}g$$

Along the inclined plane,

$$mg\sin 30° + ma_2\cos 30° = ma_1$$
$$8g \times \frac{1}{2} + 8 \times \frac{\sqrt{3}}{9}g \times \frac{\sqrt{3}}{2} = 8a_1$$
$$\Rightarrow \quad a_1 = \frac{2g}{3}$$

JEE Advanced

1. $N\sin\theta = mg \quad \Rightarrow N\cos\theta = ma$

$$\tan\theta = \frac{g}{a}$$
$$\Rightarrow \quad \cot\theta = \frac{a}{g} = \tan(90° - \theta) = \frac{dy}{dx} = 2kx$$
$$\therefore \quad x = \frac{a}{2kg}$$

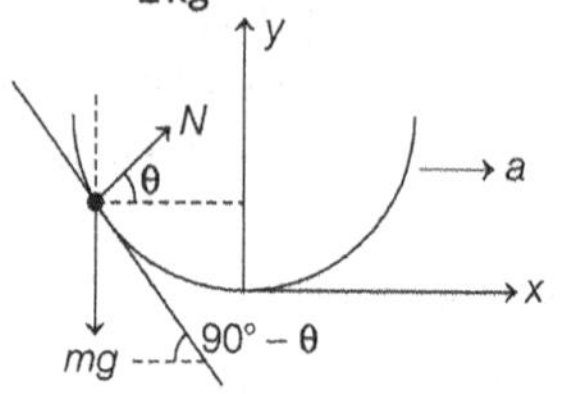

CHAPTER~11

FRICTION

LEVEL 01 Starter Level

1 Find the direction of kinetic friction force
(a) on the block, exerted by the ground,
(b) on the ground, exerted by the block.

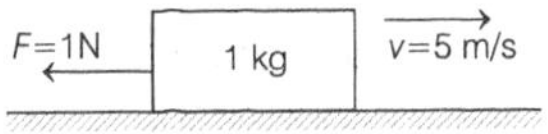

2 In the given diagram, find the direction of friction forces on each block and the ground (assume all surfaces are rough and all velocities are with respect to ground).

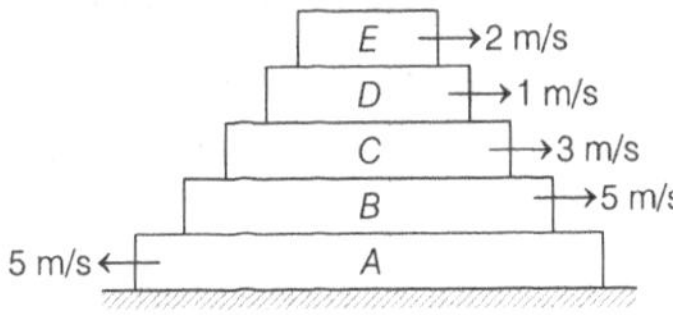

3 Find the distance travelled by the block shown in the figure before it stops.

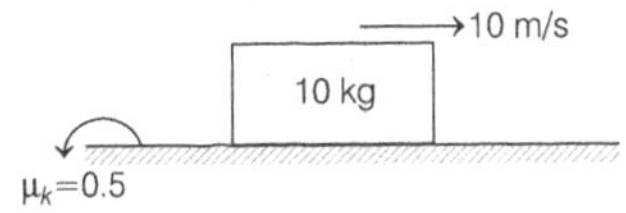

4 Initial velocity of the block is 10 m/s and coefficient of friction between the block and incline is $\mu = 0.5$.
(a) Find the distance travelled by the block on incline before it stops.
(b) Find the total time taken by the block to reach the initial position.

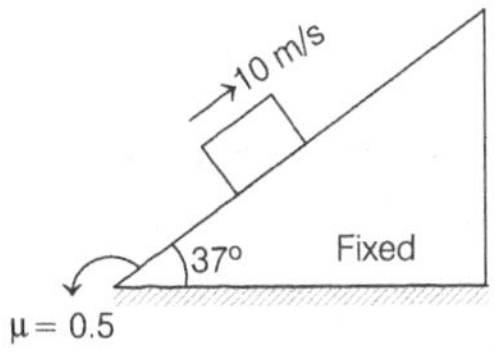

5 A horizontal force of 20 N is applied to a block of mass 4 kg resting on a rough horizontal table. If the block does not move on the table, how much frictional force the table is applying on the block? What can be said about the coefficient of static friction between the block and the table? (Take, $g = 10\ m/s^2$)

6 A block of mass 5 kg is resting on a rough surface as shown in the figure. It is acted upon by a force F towards right. Find acceleration and frictional force acting on block when
($\mu_s = 0.6$, $\mu_k = 0.5$ and $g = 10\ m/s^2$)

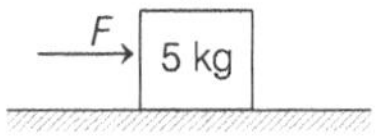

(a) $F = 0$ (b) $F = 25$ N
(c) $F = 30$ N (d) $F = 31$ N

7 In the figure, the block rests on a horizontal surface and weighs 20 N. The horizontal tension T can be increased to 8 N before the block starts to slide along the horizontal surface. A force of 7 N will keep the block in uniform motion, once it has been set in motion. Find the coefficients of static and kinetic friction.

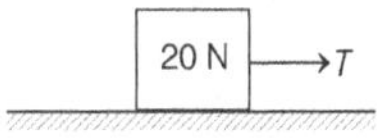

8 Find out acceleration of the block. Initially the block is at rest.

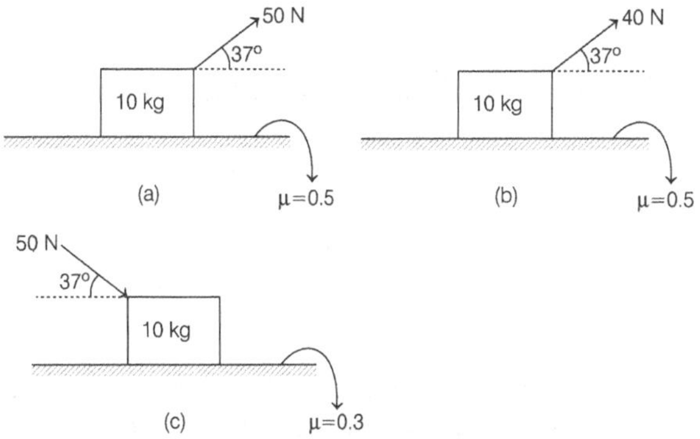

9 Consider a block pressed against a vertical wall as shown. Find the magnitude of acceleration of block.

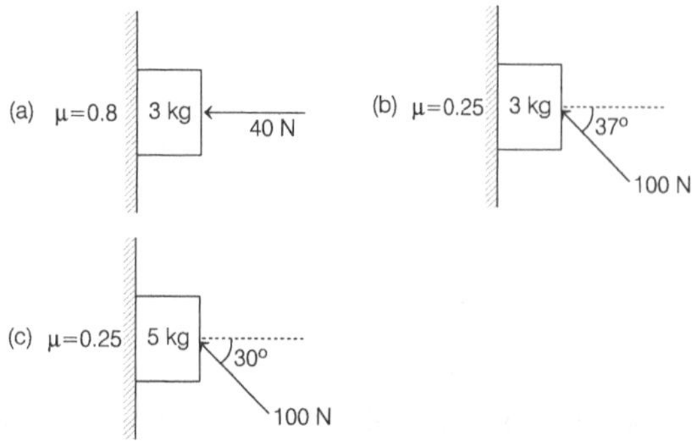

10 Find the acceleration of the block and friction force for different values of F. The block is initially at rest.

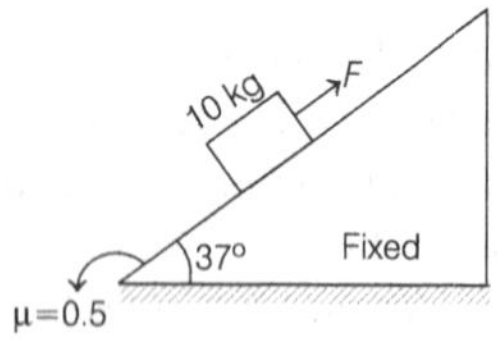

(a) $F = 0$ (b) $F = 10$ N
(c) $F = 20$ N (d) $F = 40$ N
(e) $F = 60$ N (f) $F = 70$ N
(g) $F = 100$ N (h) $F = 110$ N

11 Find the minimum force that must be applied on the block vertically downwards, so that the block doesn't move.

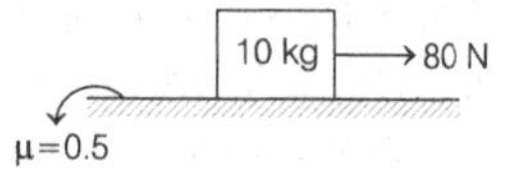

12 Top view of a block on a table is shown ($g = 10$ m/s^2). Find the acceleration of the block.

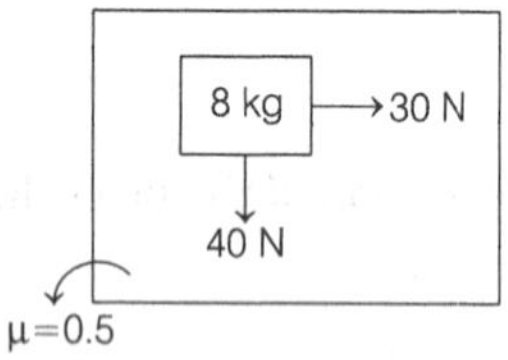

13 Find μ, so that the blocks remain stationary.

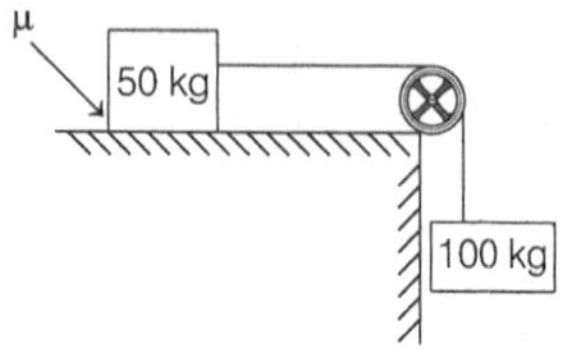

14 A cart of mass M has a block of mass m attached to it as shown in the figure. Coefficient of friction between the block and cart is μ. What is the minimum acceleration of the cart, so that the block m does not fall?

15 A block B slides with a constant speed on a rough horizontal floor acted upon by a force which is 1.5 times the weight of the block. The line of action of F makes 37° with the ground. Find the coefficient of friction between the block and the ground.

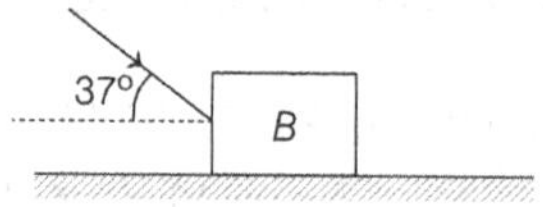

16. The coefficient of static friction between a block of mass m and an inclined plane is μ.

(a) What can be the maximum angle θ of the incline with the horizontal, so that the block does not slip on the plane?

(b) If the incline makes an angle $\frac{\theta}{2}$ with the horizontal, find the friction force on the block.

17 A block slides down an incline of angle 30° with an acceleration $g/4$. Find the dynamic friction coefficient.

18 What is the minimum value af force required to pull a block of mass M on a horizontal surface having coefficient of friction μ? Also, find the angle that force makes with the horizontal.

19 A block of mass m is at rest on a rough inclined plane of inclination θ with horizontal. The coefficient of friction between block and inclined plane is μ. Find

(a) minimum force to applied on the block parallel to inclined plane, so that it just starts moving up,

(b) minimum force to be applied on the block parallel to inclined plane to prevent the block from slipping down the inclined plane

(c) and minimum force to be applied on the block perpendicular to the inclined plane to prevent the block from slipping down the inclined plane.

20 In the figure shown below, the friction between the 5 kg block and the incline as μ_1 and between 10 kg and incline is μ_2. Calculate the accelerations of the blocks (a) $\mu_1 = 0.7$ and $\mu_2 = 0.5$ (b) $\mu_1 = 0.5$ and $\mu_2 = 0.7$. ($g = 10$ m/s^2)

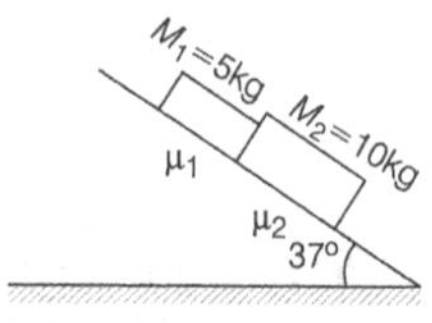

21 Find acceleration of blocks and frictional force acting on 10 kg block.

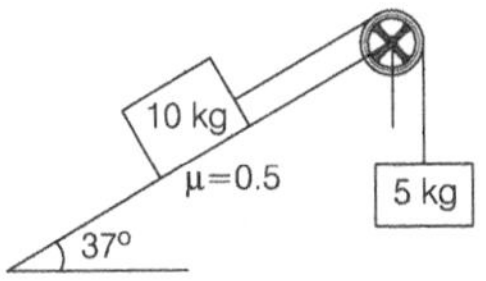

22 Block A has a mass of 2 kg and block B has 20 kg. If the coefficient of kinetic friction between block B and the horizontal surface is 0.1 and B is accelerating towards the right with $a = 2\ \text{m/s}^2$, then find the mass of the block C.

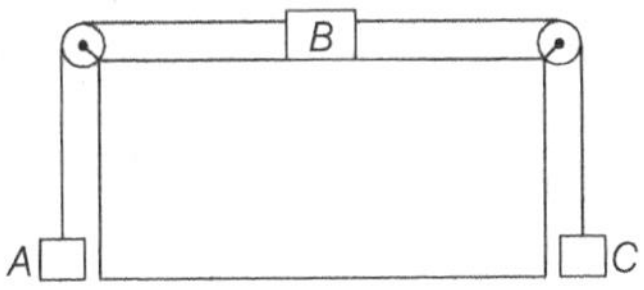

23 Block A of mass M in the system shown in the figure slides down the incline at a constant speed. The coefficient of friction between block A and the surface is $\frac{1}{3\sqrt{3}}$. Find the mass of block B.

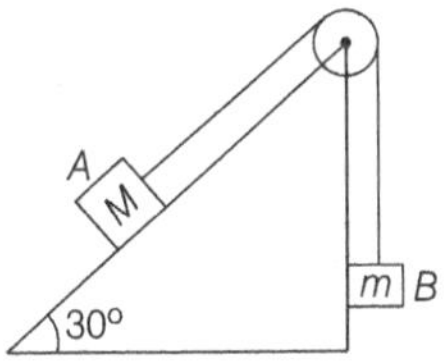

24 A uniform rope, so lies on a table that part of it lays over. The rope begins to slide when the length of hanging part is 25% of entire length. Find the coefficient of friction between rope and table.

25 A block lying on a long horizontal conveyor belt moving at a constant velocity receives a velocity 5 m/s at $t = 0$ relative to the ground in the direction opposite to the direction of motion of the coveyor. At $t = 4$ s, the relative motion between the block and the belt stops. The coefficient of friction between the block and the belt is 0.2. Find the velocity of the conveyor belt. ($g = 10\ \text{m/s}^2$)

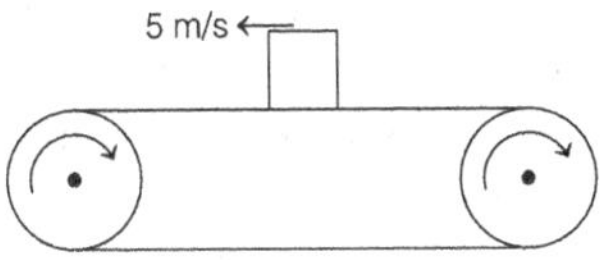

26 Find acceleration of both the blocks in the following problems.

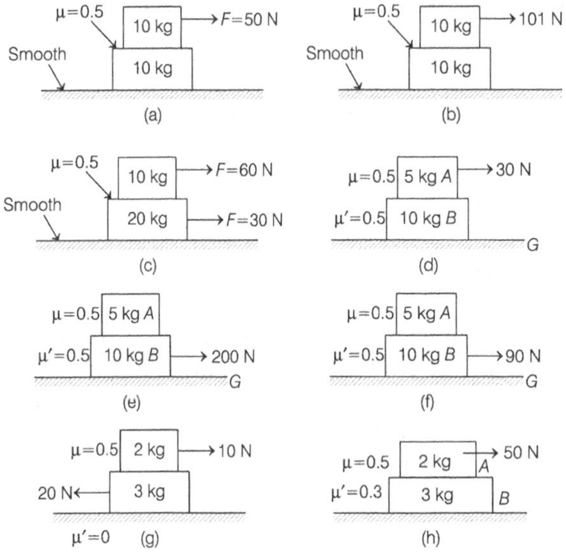

27 **True or False Statements**

(a) Force of friction always opposes motion.
(b) The direction of frictional force always opposes the tendency of relative motion of body.
(c) The coefficient of static friction is usually greater than the coefficient of kinetic friction
(d) Friction force depends on the surface area of contact.
(e) The coefficient of friction depends on the nature of the surface in contact.
(f) The coefficient of friction can exceed unity.
(g) Pushing on a rough surface is always easier than pulling.
(h) A body slides down an inclined plane if angle of friction is more than the angle of inclined plane.
(i) The force of friction can on a body be zero even if it is on a rough surface.
(j) A large brake on a bicycle wheel is more effective than a smaller one.
(k) Static friction is a self-adjusting force with no upper limit.
(l) The origin of friction lies in the irregularities of surface at the molecular level.
(m) When a person walks on a rough surface, the frictional force exerted by the surface on the person is opposite to direction of his motion.

LEVEL 02 JEE Main Level

Single Choice Correct Questions

1 A smooth block is released from rest on a 45° incline and then slides a distance d. The time taken to slide is n times as much to slide on rough incline than on a smooth incline. The coefficient of friction is

(a) $\mu_s = 1 - \frac{1}{n^2}$ (b) $\mu_s = \sqrt{1 - \frac{1}{n^2}}$

(c) $\mu_k = 1 - \frac{1}{n^2}$ (d) $\mu_k = \sqrt{1 - \frac{1}{n^2}}$

2 The upper half of an incline plane with inclination θ is perfectly smooth while the lower half is rough. A body starting from rest at the top will again come to rest at the bottom, if the coefficient of friction for the lower half is given by

(a) $2\tan\theta$ (b) $\tan\theta$

(c) $2\cot\theta$ (d) $\cot\theta$

3 A wooden block of mass m resting on a rough horizontal table (coefficient of friction $= \mu$) is pulled by a force F as shown in figure. The acceleration of the block moving horizontally is

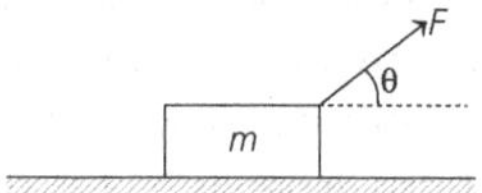

(a) $\frac{F\cos\theta}{m}$ (b) $\frac{\mu F\sin\theta}{m}$

(c) $\frac{F}{m}(\cos\theta + \mu\sin\theta) - \mu g$ (d) None of these

4 The force (along incline) required to just move a body up the inclined plane is double the force required to just prevent the body from sliding down the plane. The coefficient of friction is μ. The inclination θ of the plane is

(a) $\tan^{-1}(\mu)$ (b) $\tan^{-1}(\mu/2)$

(c) $\tan^{-1}(2\mu)$ (d) $\tan^{-1}(3\mu)$

5 What is the maximum value of the force F such that the block shown in the arrangement, does not move?

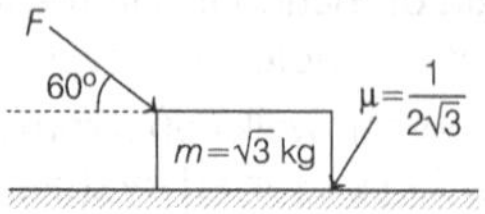

(a) 20 N (b) 10 N

(c) 12 N (d) 15 N

6 A block of mass 3 kg is at rest on a rough fixed inclined plane as shown in the figure. The magnitude of net force exerted by the surface on the block will be ($g = 10 \text{ m/s}^2$)

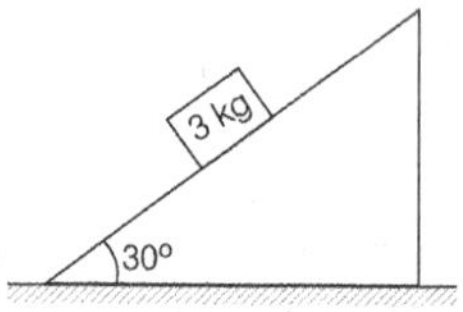

(a) 26 N (b) $15\sqrt{3}$ N (c) 15 N (d) 30 N

7 A block of mass $m = 2\sqrt{3}$ kg is resting on a rough inclined plane of inclination 30° as shown in figure. The coefficient of friction between the block and the plane is $\mu = \frac{\sqrt{3}}{4}$. What minimum force F should be applied perpendicular to the plane on the block, so that block does not slip on the plane? ($g = 10 \text{ m/s}^2$)

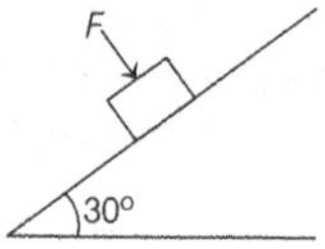

(a) Zero (b) 5 N (c) 10 N (d) 20 N

8 A block of mass 1 kg lies on a horizontal surface in a truck. The coefficient of static friction between the block and the surface is 0.6. If the acceleration of the truck is 5 m/s^2, the frictional force acting on the block is

(a) 5 N (b) 6 N (c) 10 N (d) 15 N

9 What is the minimum value of mass of block A, so that B starts moving on rough horizontal surface?

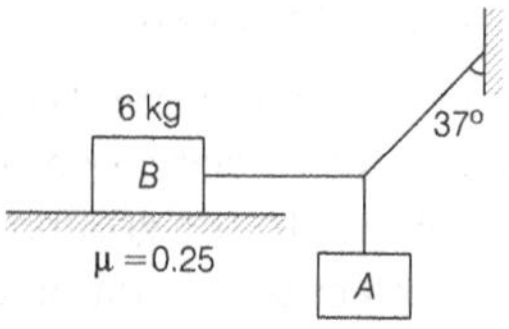

(a) 1 kg (b) 1.5 kg (c) 2 kg (d) 2.5 kg

10 The two blocks, $m = 10$ kg and $M = 50$ kg are free to move as shown in the figure. The coefficient of static friction between the blocks is 0.5 and there is no friction between M and the ground. Find the minimum horizontal force F to be applied to prevent 10 kg block from falling down.

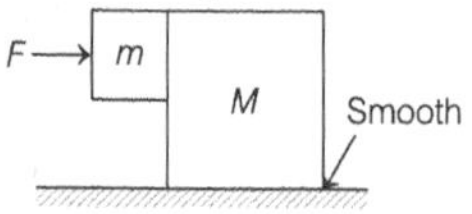

(a) 100 N (b) 50 N (c) 240 N (d) 180 N

11 A mass of 0.5 kg is just able to slide down the slope of an inclined rough surface when the angle of inclination is 60°. The minimum force (along the incline) necessary to pull the mass up the incline along the line of greatest slope is ($g = 10\ m/s^2$)

(a) 17.32 N (b) 8.66 N (c) 5 N (d) 4.33 N

12 A force of 12 N is required to start a uniform block of wood sliding on a bench for which coefficient of friction is constant. The plank is cut into three pieces and these pieces are stacked one above the other. The force F now needed to start motion will be

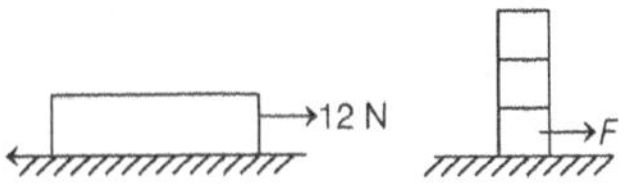

(a) $F > 12$N (b) $F < 12$N (c) $F = 12$ N

(d) depends on coefficient of friction between wooden blocks

13 A block of mass 2 kg rests on a rough inclined plane making an angle of 30° with the horizontal. The coefficient of static friction between the block and the plane is 0.7. The frictional force on the block is

(a) 9.8 N (b) $0.7 \times 9.8 \times \sqrt{3}$ N

(c) 9.8×7 N (d) 0.8×9.8N

14 Two masses A and B of 10 kg and 5 kg respectively are connected with a string passing over a frictionless pulley fixed at the corner of a table as shown. The coefficient of static friction of A with table is 0.2. The minimum mass of C that may be placed on A to prevent it from moving is

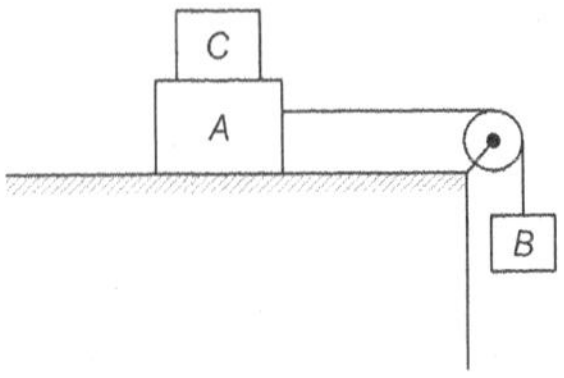

(a) 15 kg (b) 10 kg (c) 5 kg (d) 12 kg

15 If the normal force is doubled , the coefficient of friction is

(a) halved (b) doubled

(c) tripled (d) not changed

16 A uniform chain of mass M and length L is lying on a table in such a manner that a part of it is hanging down from an edge of the table. If coefficient of friction is μ , then the maximum length of the chain that can hang without sliding is

(a) $\frac{L}{\mu}$ (b) $\frac{L}{1-\mu}$ (c) $\frac{\mu L}{1-\mu}$ (d) $\frac{\mu L}{1+\mu}$

17 With what minimum velocity should block be projected from left end A towards end B such that it reaches the other end B of conveyor belt moving with constant velocity v. Friction coefficient between block and belt is μ.

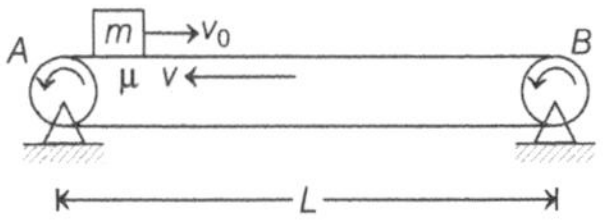

(a) $\sqrt{\mu g L}$ (b) $\sqrt{2\mu g L}$

(c) $\sqrt{3\mu g L}$ (d) $2\sqrt{\mu g L}$

18 Initially the system is at rest, find out minimum value of F for which sliding starts between the two blocks.

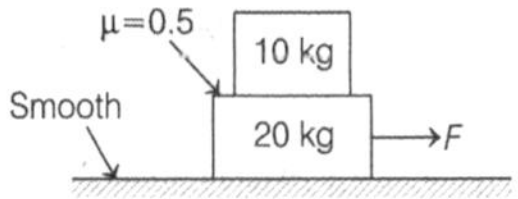

(a) 50 N (b) 100 N

(c) 150 N (d) 200 N

19 A block of mass m lying on a rough horizontal plane is acted upon by a horizontal force P and another force Q inclined at an angle θ to the vertical. The minimum value of coefficient of friction between the block and the surface for which the block will remain in equilibrium is

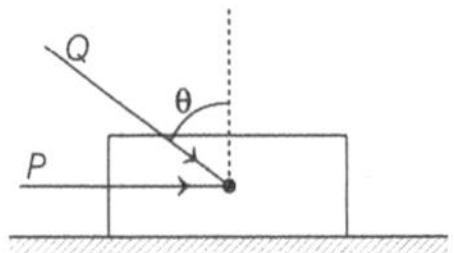

(a) $\frac{P + Q\sin\theta}{mg + Q\cos\theta}$ (b) $\frac{P\cos\theta + Q}{mg - Q\cos\theta}$

(c) $\frac{P + Q\cos\theta}{mg + Q\sin\theta}$ (d) $\frac{P\sin\theta + Q}{mg - Q\sin\theta}$

20 A bead of mass m is located on a parabolic wire with its axis vertical and vertex directed downward as in figure and whose equation is $x^2 = ay$. If the coefficient of friction is μ, the highest distance above the X-axis at which the particle will be in equilibrium is

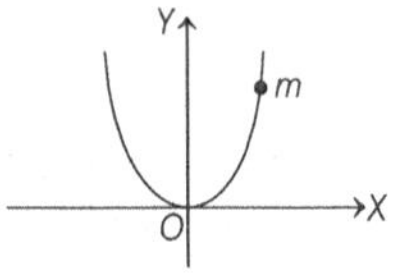

(a) μa (b) $\mu^2 a$

(c) $\frac{1}{4}\mu^2 a$ (d) $\frac{1}{2}\mu^2 a$

21 The horizontal surface below the bigger block is smooth. The coefficient of friction between the blocks is *m*. The maximum force which can be applied to keep the smaller blocks at rest with respect to the bigger block is

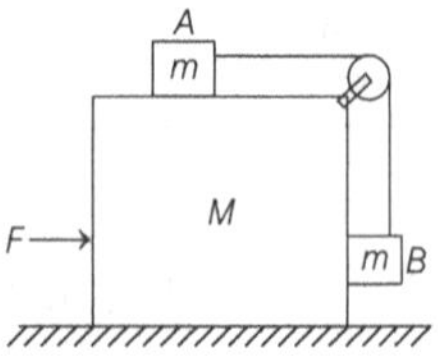

(a) $\left(\frac{1-\mu}{1+\mu}\right)(M+m)g$ (b) $\left(\frac{1+\mu}{1-\mu}\right)(M+m)g$

(c) $\left(\frac{1+\mu}{1-\mu}\right)(M+2m)g$ (d) $(1+\mu)(M+2m)g$

22 Two blocks $m_1 = 4$ kg and $m_2 = 2$ kg, connected by a weightless rod on a plane having inclination of 37° as shown in figure. The coefficients of dynamic friction μ_1 and μ_2 with the inclined plane are 0.25. Then, the common acceleration of the two blocks and the tension in the rod are

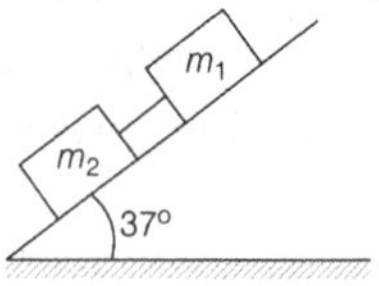

(a) $4\,\text{m/s}^2, T = 0$ (b) $2\,\text{m/s}^2, T = 5$ N

(c) $10\,\text{m/s}^2, T = 10$ N (d) $15\,\text{m/s}^2, T = 9$ N

23 A insect crawls up a hemispherical surface very slowly (see the figure). The coefficient of friction between the surface and the insect is $\frac{1}{3}$. If the line joining the centre of the hemispherical surface to the insect makes an angle α with the vertical, the maximum possible value of α is given

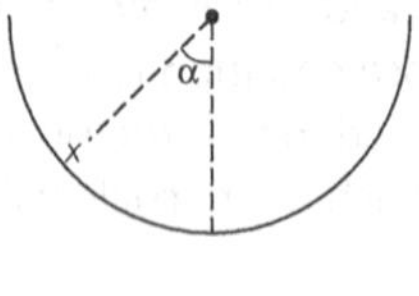

(a) $\cot\alpha = 3$ (b) $\tan\alpha = 3$

(c) $\sec\alpha = 3$ (d) $\operatorname{cosec}\alpha = 3$

24 A block of mass *M* rests on a rough horizontal surface as shown. Coefficient of friction between the block and the surface is μ. A force $F = Mg$ acting at angle θ with the vertical side of the block pulls it. In which of the following case the block can be pulled along the surface?

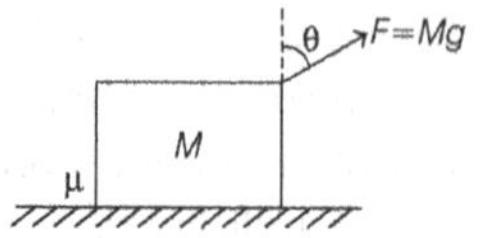

(a) $\tan\theta \geq \mu$ (b) $\tan\left(\frac{\theta}{2}\right) \geq \mu$

(c) $\cot\left(\frac{\theta}{2}\right) \geq \mu$ (d) $\cot\theta \geq \mu$

25 Two persons, pull each other through a massless rope in 'tug of war' game. Who will win?

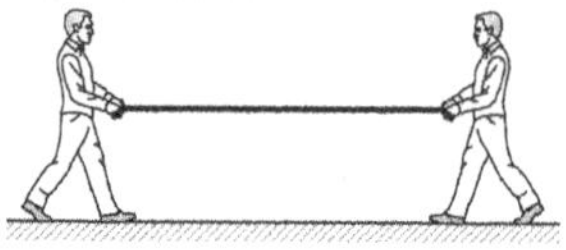

(a) One whose weight is more
(b) One who pulls the rope with a greater force
(c) One who applies more friction force (shear force) on ground
(d) One who applies more normal force (compressive force) on ground

26 Block *B* of mass 100 kg rests on a rough surface of friction coefficient $\mu = 1/3$. A rope is tied to block *B* as shown in figure. The maximum acceleration with which boy *A* of 25 kg can climb on rope without making block move is

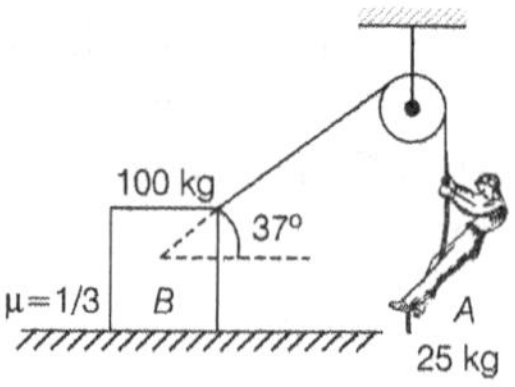

(a) $\frac{4g}{3}$ (b) $\frac{g}{3}$ (c) $\frac{g}{2}$ (d) $\frac{3g}{4}$

27 A block moves down a smooth inclined plane of inclination θ. Its velocity on reaching the bottom is *v*. If it slides down a rough inclined plane of same inclination, its velocity on reaching the bottom is v/n, where *n* is a number greater than zero. The coefficient of friction is given by

(a) $\mu = \tan\theta\left(1-\frac{1}{n^2}\right)$ (b) $\mu = \cot\theta\left(1-\frac{1}{n^2}\right)$

(c) $\mu = \tan\theta\left(1-\frac{1}{n^2}\right)^{\frac{1}{2}}$ (d) $\mu = \cot\theta\left(1-\frac{1}{n^2}\right)^{\frac{1}{2}}$

28 A block of mass 2 kg is held at rest against a rough vertical wall by pressing a horizontal (normal) force of 45 N. Coefficient of friction between wall and the block is equal to 0.5. Now a horizontal force of 15 N (tangential to wall) is also applied on the block. Then, the block will

(a) remain stationary

(b) move horizontally with acceleration of 5 m/s^2

(c) start to move with an acceleration of magnitude 1.25 m/s^2

(d) start to move horizontally with acceleration greater than 5 m/s^2

29 A car is going at a speed of 72 km/h when it encounters a 21 m slope of angle of 37°. The friction coefficient between the road and tyre is 0.5. The driver applies the brakes. The minimum speed of car with which it can reach the bottom is ($g = 10$ m/s^2)

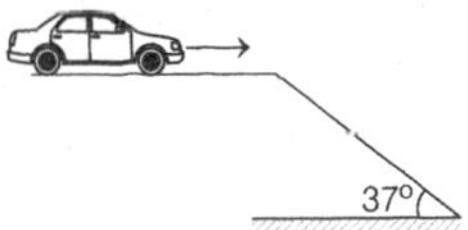

(a) 15 m/s (b) 20 m/s (c) 22 m/s (d) 25 m/s

30 A force of 100 N is applied on a block of mass 3 kg as shown in figure. The coefficient of friction between the surface and block is 1/4. The friction force acting on the block is

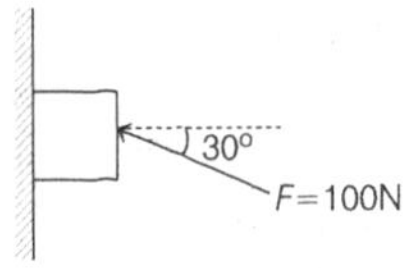

(a) $12.5\sqrt{3}$ N, downwards (b) $12.5\sqrt{3}$ N, upwards

(c) 20 N, downwards (d) 20 N, upwards

31 For the arrangement shown in figure, the tension in the string to prevent it from sliding down, is

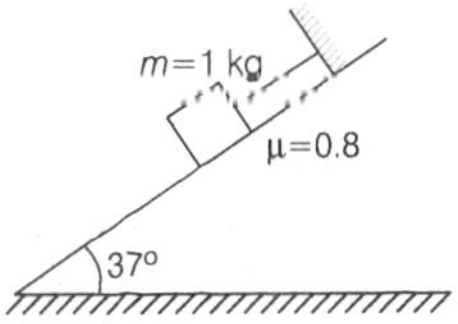

(a) 6 N (b) 6.4 N

(c) 0.4 N (d) None of these

32 If the tension in the string in figure is 16 N and the acceleration of each block is 0.5 m/s^2, find the friction coefficients at the two contacts with the blocks.

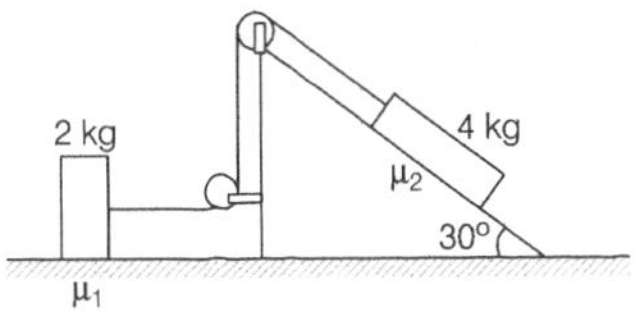

(a) $\mu_1 = 0.75, \mu_2 = 0.06$ (b) $\mu_1 = 0.5, \mu_2 = 0.05$

(c) $\mu_1 = 0.75, \mu_2 = 0.17$ (d) $\mu_1 = 0.2, \mu_2 = 0.03$

33 Two blocks *A* and *B* of masses 6 kg and 3 kg rest on a frictionless horizontal surface as shown in the figure. If coefficient of friction between *A* and *B* is 0.8 and between *A* and ground is 0.1, then the maximum horizontal force which can make them move without separation is

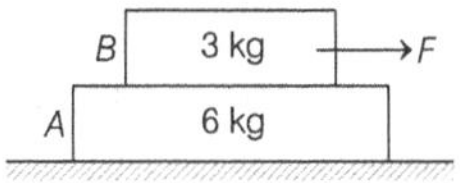

(a) 22.5 N (b) 31.5 N (c) 45 N (d) 72 N

34 If the mass of block is 1 kg and a force of $\frac{10}{\sqrt{3}}$ N is applied horizontally on the block as shown in the figure. The frictional force acting on the block is

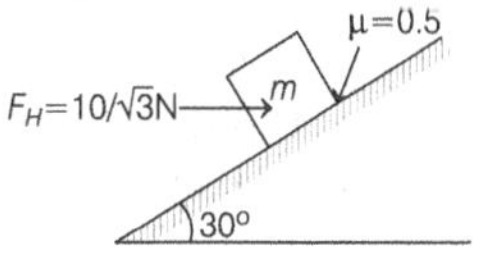

(a) Zero (b) $\frac{10}{\sqrt{3}}$ N (c) $\frac{20}{\sqrt{3}}$ N (d) 5 N

35 A heavy body of mass 25 kg is to be dragged along a rough horizontal plane $\left(\mu = \frac{1}{\sqrt{3}}\right)$. The least force required is (take, $g = 10$ m/s^2)

(a) 250 N (b) 25 N (c) 125 N (d) $\frac{250}{\sqrt{3}}$ N

36 A block slides down an inclined plane of slope angle ϕ with constant velocity. If it is, then projected up the same plane with an initial speed v_0, the distance in which it will come to rest is

(a) $\frac{v_0^2}{2g\cos\phi}$ (b) $\frac{v_0^2}{4g\sin\phi}$ (c) $\frac{v_0^2}{2g}$ (d) $\frac{v_0^2}{2g\sin\phi}$

37 A force $F = kt$ is applied to block *A* as shown in the figure. The force is applied at $t = 0$ when the system was at rest and string is just straight without tension. Which of the following graphs gives the friction force between *B* and horizontal surface as a function of time *t*?

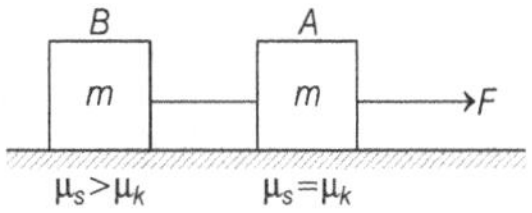

(a)

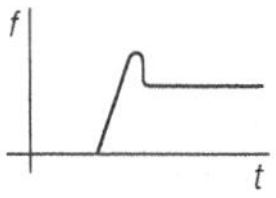

(b)

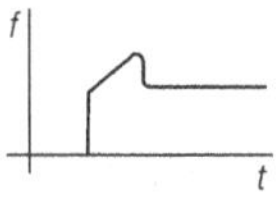

(c)

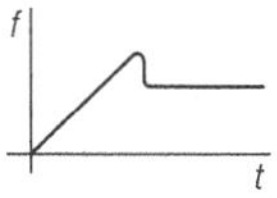

(d)

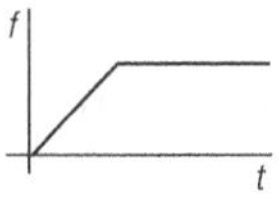

38 A 1.5 kg box is initially at rest on a horizontal surface when at $t=0$, a horizontal force $\mathbf{F}=(1.8t)\hat{\mathbf{i}}$ N (with t in seconds), is applied to the box. The acceleration of the box as a function of time t is given by

$\mathbf{a}=0$ for $0\le t\le 2.85$ and
$\mathbf{a}=(1.2t-2.4)\hat{\mathbf{i}}\,\text{m/s}^2$ for $t>2.85$

The coefficient of kinetic friction between the box and the surface is

(a) 0.12 (b) 0.24
(c) 0.36 (d) 0.48

39 A small block of mass 1 kg is placed over a plank of mass 5 kg. The length of the plank is 8 m. Coefficient of friction between the block and the plank is 0.5 and the ground over which plank is placed is smooth. A constant force F = 50 N is applied on the plank in horizontal direction. The time after which the block will separate from the plank is

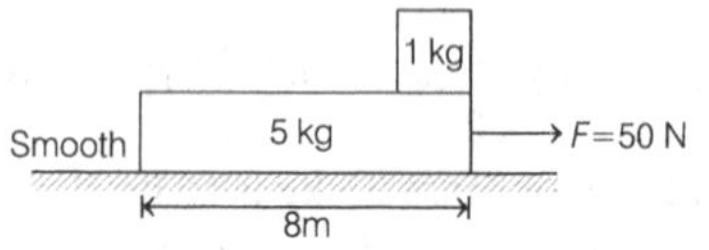

(a) 1 s (b) 2 s (c) 4 s (d) 8 s

40 Two blocks A and B of equal masses are sliding down along straight parallel lines on an inclined plane of 45°. Their coefficients of kinetic friction are $\mu_A=0.2$ and $\mu_B=0.3$, respectively. At $t=0$, both the blocks are at rest and block A is $\sqrt{2}$ m behind block B. The time and distance from the initial position, where the front faces of the blocks come in line on the inclined plane as shown in figure are (Use, $g=10\text{ ms}^{-2}$)

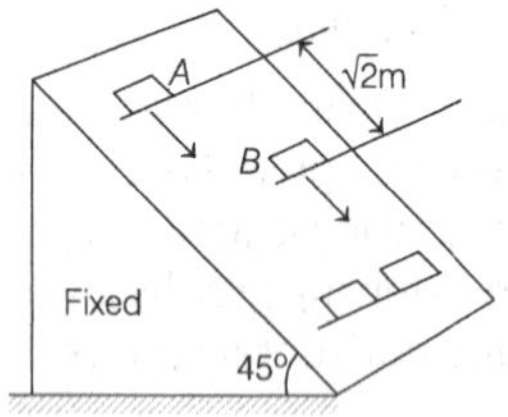

(a) 2s, $8\sqrt{2}$ m (b) $\sqrt{2}$ s, 7 m
(c) $\sqrt{2}$ s, $7\sqrt{2}$ m (d) 2s, $7/\sqrt{2}$ m

Numerical Value Questions

1 The rear side of a truck is open and a box of 40 kg mass is placed 5 m away from the open end as shown in figure. The coefficient of friction between the box and the surface below it is 0.15. On a straight road, the truck starts from rest and accelerates with 2 ms^{-2}. Find the distance (in m) travelled by the truck by the time box falls from the truck. (Ignore the size of the box).

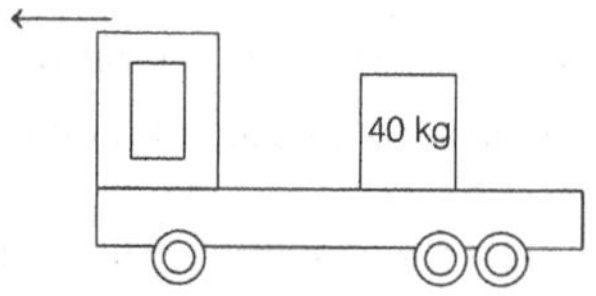

2 A block of mass m is resting on a rough horizontal ground. Minimum force required to move the block is $\frac{3mg}{5}$. Find the coefficient of friction between the block and the ground.

3 A thin rod of length 1 m is fixed in a vertical position inside a train, which is moving horizontally with constant acceleration 4 m/s^2. A bead can slide on the rod, and friction coefficient between them is 1/2. If the bead is released from rest at the top of the rod, find the time(in s) when it will reach at the bottom.

4 A 40 kg slab (B) rests on a smooth floor as shown in figure. A 10 kg block (A) rests on the top of the slab. The static coefficient of friction between slab and block is 0.75, while the kinetic friction coefficient is 0.4. The block (A) is acted upon by a horizontal force 100 N. Find the resulting acceleration (in m/s^2) of the slab(B). (Take, $g=9.8$ m/s^2)

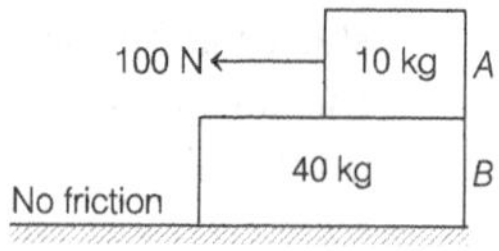

5 A wedge with a rough groove in the shape of a quarter of a circle is kept on a smooth table (see figure). A disc is placed in the groove with a small clearance. Friction exists between groove and disc. The wedge is moved with an acceleration $\sqrt{3}\,g$. If disc is to remain stationary relative to groove, the minimum coefficient of friction required is $\sqrt{\frac{18}{n}}$, then find n.

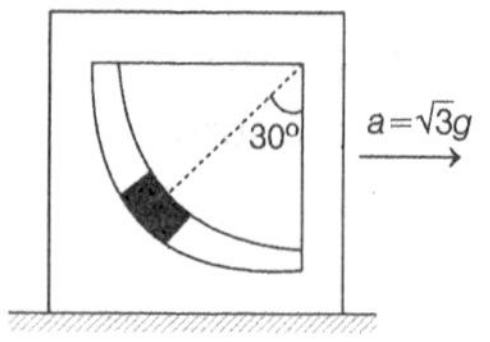

6 Blocks A and B shown each has mass 10 kg. If coefficient of static friction between A and B is 0.3 and that between B and incline is 0.4, then what is the value of force P (in N) to just start the motion of B? (g = 10 m/s^2)

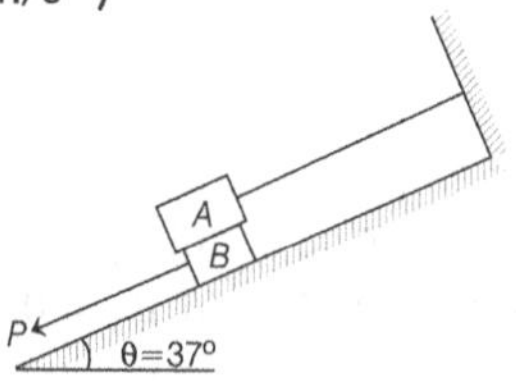

7 The conveyor belt is moving at 4 m/s. The coefficient of static friction between the conveyor belt and the 10 kg package B is $\mu_s = 0.2$. Determine the shortest time (in second) in which the belt can be stopped, so that the package does not slide on the belt.

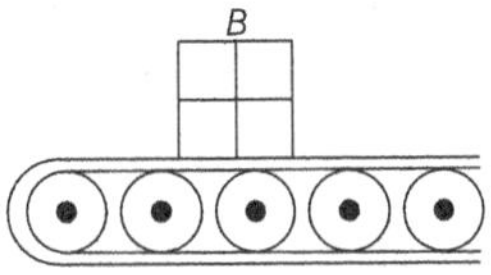

8 A box of mass 1 kg is lying on a rough horizontal floor and a horizontal force acting on box has a magnitude of $F = 3t^2$ N, where t is in seconds. If the box starts from rest, determine its speed (in m/s) when $t = 3$ s. The coefficient of static and kinetic friction between the box and horizontal floor are $\mu_s = 0.3$ and $\mu_k = 0.2$.

9 Two blocks of same mass are sliding on an incline. The coefficients of kinetic friction between the blocks and the incline are different, $\mu_1 = 0.5$ and $\mu_2 = 0.4$, respectively. Find the tension (in newton) in string. ($g = 10\ \text{m/s}^2$)

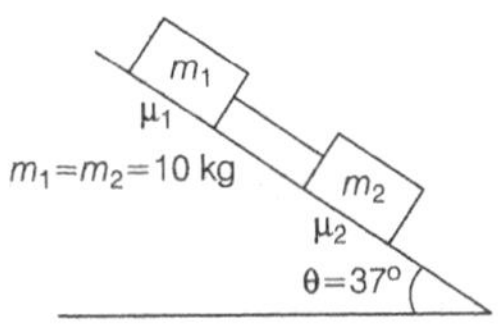

10 A crate of mass 1 kg is pulled with a force F along a fixed right angled horizontal trough as in figure. The coefficient of kinetic friction between the crate and the trough is $\mu = \sqrt{2}$ .Find the value of force F (in N) required to pull it along the trough with constant velocity.

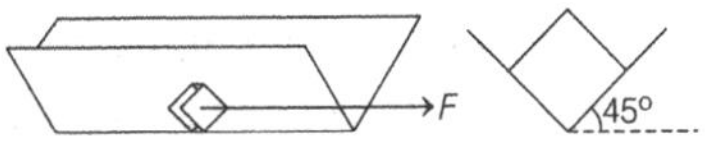

11 The friction coefficient between the board and the floor shown in figure is 0.5. Find the maximum force (in newton) that the man can exert on the rope, so that the board does not slip on the floor.

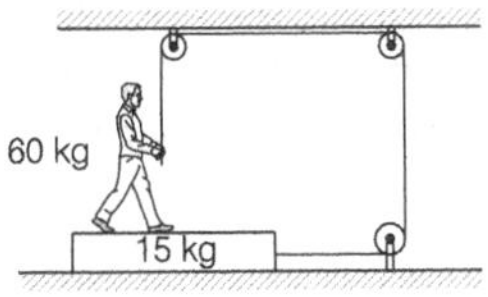

12 The following figure shows an accelerating conveyor belt inclined at an angle 37° above horizontal. The coefficient of friction between the belt and block is 1. Find the least time (in second) in which block can reach the top, starting from rest at the bottom.

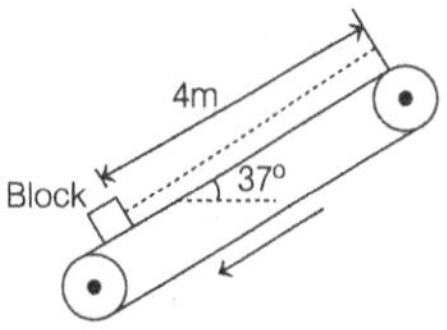

13 A man can just push a box on 37° concrete slope. When he keeps it at the point, where the angle increases to 53°, he can just hold it from sliding back. If the coefficient of friction between the box and the concrete slope is μ, find $\frac{1}{\mu}$. Assume that the man is applying same magnitude of force along the tangent to the curve only.

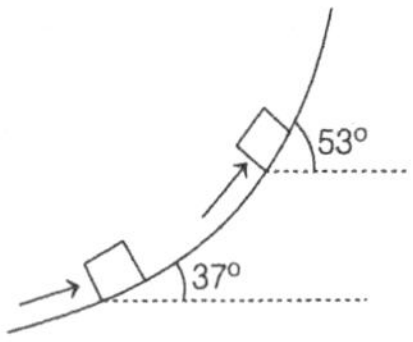

14 A cart of mass 3 kg is pulled by a 5 kg object as shown in figure. Length of cart is 40 cm and it moves on frictionless table. There is a small brick of mass 2 kg on the cart which falls at 0.8 s after the start of motion. If the coefficient of friction between cart and brick is $\frac{n}{100}$, then value of n is ($g = 10\ \text{m/s}^2$)

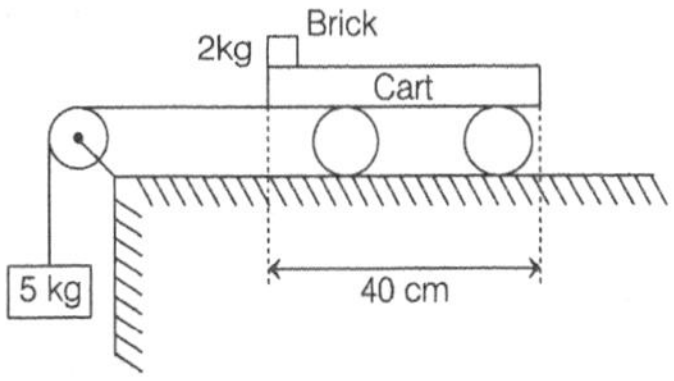

15 Block B of mass 2 kg rests on block A of mass 10 kg. All surfaces are rough with the value of coefficient of friction as shown in the figure. Find the minimum force F (in N) that should be applied on block A to cause relative motion between A and B. ($g = 10\ \text{m/s}^2$)

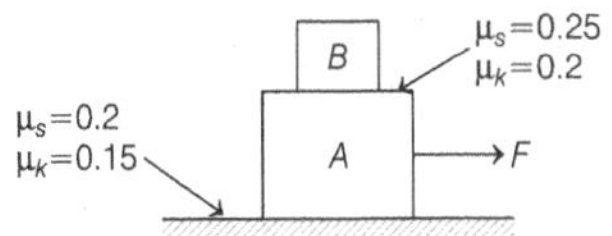

LEVEL 03 JEE Advanced Level

Single Choice Correct Questions

1 The system is pushed by a force F as shown in figure. Friction coefficient between A and B is $\frac{\mu}{3}$. Friction coefficient between B and C is $\frac{\mu}{2}$. Minimum value of F to prevent block B from downward slipping is

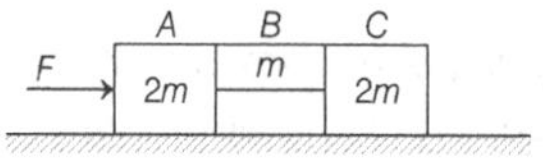

(a) $\left(\frac{3}{2\mu}\right)mg$ (b) $\left(\frac{5}{2\mu}\right)mg$ (c) $\left(\frac{2}{5\mu}\right)mg$ (d) $\left(\frac{2}{3\mu}\right)mg$

2 A block placed on a rough inclined plane of inclination ($\theta = 30°$) can just be pushed upwards by applying a force F as shown. If the angle of inclination of the inclined plane is increased (to $\theta = 60°$), the same block can just be prevented from sliding down by application of a force of same magnitude. The coefficient of friction between the block and the inclined plane is

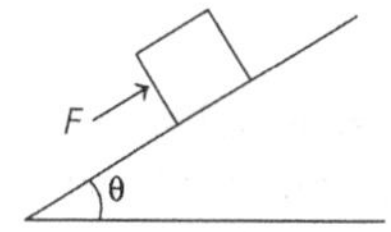

(a) $\frac{\sqrt{3}+1}{\sqrt{3}-1}$ (b) $\frac{2\sqrt{3}-1}{\sqrt{3}+1}$ (c) $\frac{\sqrt{3}-1}{\sqrt{3}+1}$ (d) None of these

3 A small body was launched up an inclined plane set at an angle $\theta = 53°$ against the horizontal. Find the coefficient of friction, if the time of the ascent of the body is $\eta = 2.0$ times less than the time of its descent.

(a) 0.5 (b) 0.6 (c) 0.7 (d) 0.8

4 In the arrangement shown in the figure, mass of the block B and A are 2 m and 8 m, respectively. Surface between B and floor is smooth. The block B is connected to block C by means of a pulley. If the whole system is released, then the minimum value of mass of the block C, so that the block A remains stationary with respect to B is (Coefficient of friction between A and B is μ and pulley is ideal)

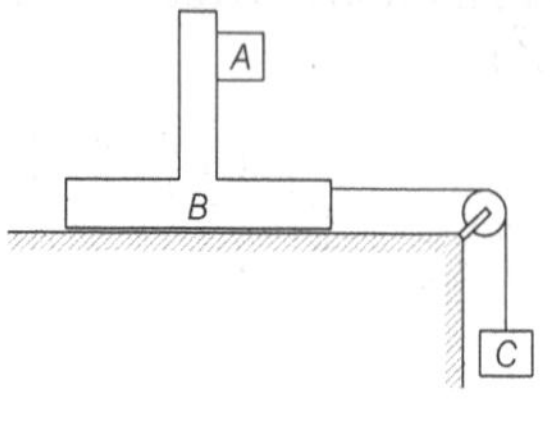

(a) $\frac{m}{\mu}$ (b) $\frac{2m}{\mu+1}$ (c) $\frac{10m}{1-\mu}$ (d) $\frac{10m}{\mu-1}$

5 Given that mass of A is 100 kg and that of B is 140 kg. Pulleys are smooth and friction coefficient between A and B and between B and horizontal surface is $\mu = 0.3$. The maximum value of mass of block C, so that neither A nor B moves is

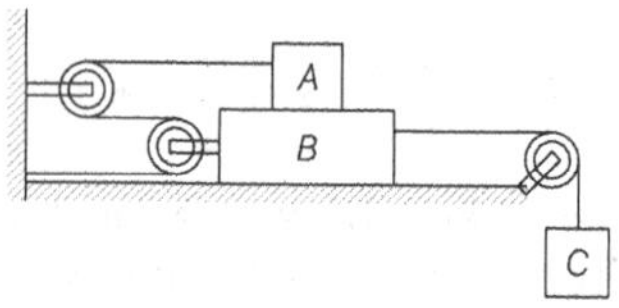

(a) 210 kg (b) 190 kg (c) 185 kg (d) 162 kg

6 In the given figure, calculate the acceleration of the block m_2, if the coefficient of friction between the blocks and the surface is 0.2. Take, $m_1 = 2$ kg, $m_2 = 6$ kg, $F = 93$ N and $g = 10\,m/s^2$, the pulley is smooth and massless.

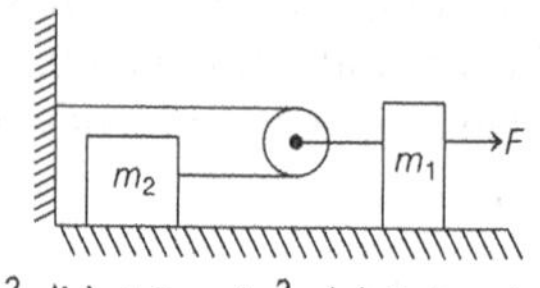

(a) $2.5\,m/s^2$ (b) $4.0\,m/s^2$ (c) $5.0\,m/s^2$ (d) $1.2\,m/s^2$

7 A block of mass 6 kg is pressed against a vertical wall (in yz-plane) with a force $\mathbf{F} = 80\hat{\mathbf{i}} + 30\hat{\mathbf{j}} + 20\hat{\mathbf{k}}$. The vertical upward direction is taken as positive Z-axis. The coefficient of friction is 0.25. The acceleration of the block is

(a) $3\hat{\mathbf{j}} - 4\hat{\mathbf{k}}$ (b) $4\hat{\mathbf{j}} - 3\hat{\mathbf{k}}$ (c) $3\hat{\mathbf{j}} + 4\hat{\mathbf{k}}$ (d) zero

8 A bead of mass m can slide on a thin vertical rod, with sliding friction coefficient between them $= \mu$. The rod is translated in the vertical plane with a constant acceleration a at an angle 37° above horizontal. For what value of a will an earth observer see equal horizontal and vertical components of the acceleration of the bead?

(a) $\frac{5g}{1+4\mu}$ (b) $\frac{5g}{1-4\mu}$ (c) $\frac{5g}{1+3\mu}$ (d) $\frac{5g}{1-3\mu}$

9 If the coefficient of friction between A and B is μ, the maximum horizontal acceleration of the wedge A for which B will remain at rest w.r.t the wedge is

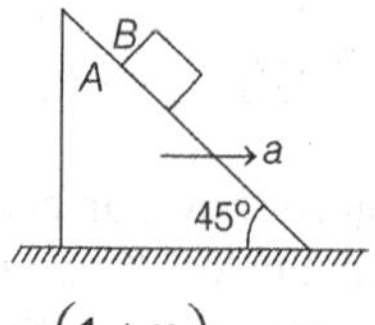

(a) g (b) $g\left(\frac{1+\mu}{1-\mu}\right)$ (c) $\frac{g}{\mu}$ (d) $g\left(\frac{1-\mu}{1+\mu}\right)$

10 Find minimum force required to applied to the trolley of mass 9m, so that blocks of masses 4*m* and *m* remain stationary with respect to the trolley. Ground is smooth. Coefficient of friction between each block and trolley is 0.2.

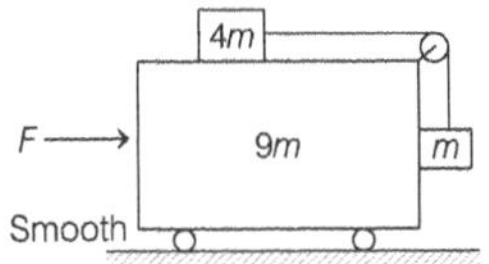

(a) $\frac{mg}{3}$ (b) $\frac{2mg}{3}$ (c) mg (d) $\frac{4mg}{3}$

11 A flat car is given an acceleration $a_0 = 2\ m/s^2$ starting from rest. A cable is connected to a crate *A* of mass 50 kg as shown. Neglect friction between the floor and the car wheels and also the mass of the pulley. Calculate tension in the cable, if $\mu = 0.30$ between the crate and the floor of the car.

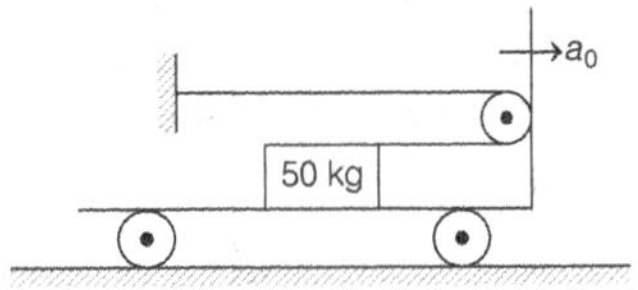

(a) 350 N (b) 250 N (c) 300 N (d) 400 N

12 A bar of mass m_1 is placed on a plank of mass m_2 which rests on a horizontal plane. The coefficient of friction between all surfaces is μ. The plank is subjected to a horizontal force *F* depending on time *t* as $F = bt$, where *b* is a constant. The moment of time t_0 at which the bar starts sliding with respect to plank is

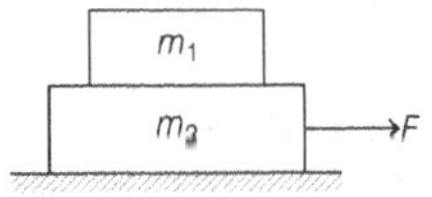

(a) $\frac{b\mu g}{m_1 + m_2}$ (b) $\frac{2(m_1 + m_2)\mu g}{b}$

(c) $\frac{(m_1 + m_2)\mu g}{b}$ (d) $\frac{2\mu b}{(m_1 + m_2)g}$

13 The given figure shows a small block of mass 20 kg kept at the left end of a larger block of mass 10 kg and length 27 m. The system is given a sharp impulse which provides an initial velocity of 10 m/s to the system (of masses). The time elapsed before the small block separates from the bigger block is

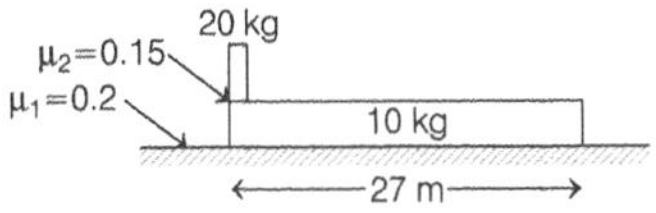

(a) 3 s (b) 5 s

(c) 6 s (d) None of these

14 A man of mass 50 kg is pulling on a plank of mass 100 kg kept on a smooth floor as shown with force of 100 N. If both man and plank move together, find force of friction acting on man.

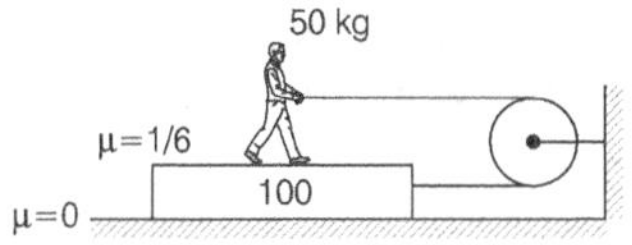

(a) $\frac{100}{3}$ N, towards left

(b) $\frac{100}{3}$ N, towards right

(c) $\frac{250}{3}$ N, towards left

(d) $\frac{250}{3}$ N, towards right

15 Two blocks, $m_1 = 2$ kg and $m_2 = 4$ kg, are connected with a light string that runs over a frictionless pulley to a hanging block with a mass *M* as shown in figure. The coefficient of sliding friction between block m_2 and the horizontal surface is $\mu_k = 0.2$. The coefficient of static friction between the two blocks is $\mu_s = 0.4$. What is the maximum mass *M* for the hanging block, if the block m_1, is not to slip on block m_2 while m_2 is sliding over the surface?

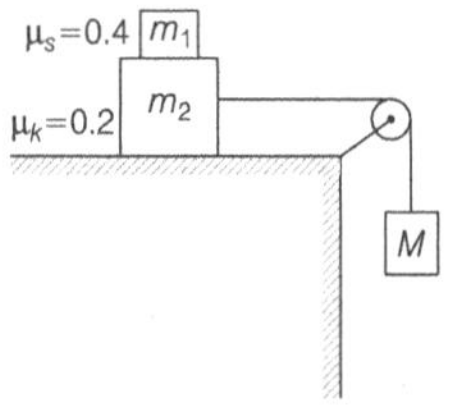

(a) 8 kg (b) 6 kg (c) 4 kg (d) 10 kg

16 In the arrangement shown in figure, coefficient of friction between the blocks of masses *m* and 2*m* is 0.75. The ground is smooth. The mass of the suspended block is 3*m*. The force of friction between *m* and 2*m* is (pulleys and strings are light and frictionless)

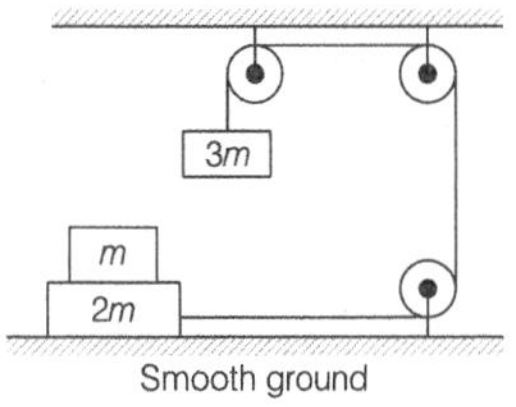

(a) $\frac{3mg}{4}$ (b) $\frac{2mg}{3}$

(c) $\frac{mg}{3}$ (d) $\frac{mg}{2}$

17 A block of mass $M = 4$ kg is kept on a rough horizontal plane. A bar of mass $m = 1$ kg is kept on it. They are connected to a spring as shown and the spring is compressed. Then what is the maximum compression in the spring for which the bar will not slip on the block when released if spring constant $k = 1000$ N/m?

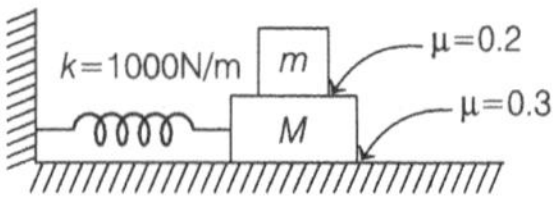

(a) 1 cm (b) 2 cm (c) 2.5 cm (d) 3 cm

18 A plank of mass $m_1 = 8$ kg with a bar of mass $m_2 = 2$ kg placed on its rough surface, lie on a smooth floor of elevator ascending with an acceleration $g/4$. The coefficient of friction is $\mu = 1/5$ between m_1, and m_2. A horizontal force $F = 30$ N is applied to the plank. Then, the acceleration of bar and the plank in the reference frame of elevator are

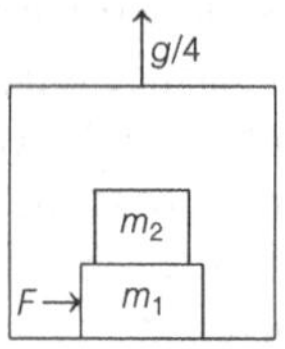

(a) $2 \text{m/s}^2, 2 \text{m/s}^2$ (b) $5 \text{m/s}^2, \frac{50}{8} \text{m/s}^2$

(c) $2.5 \text{m/s}^2, \frac{25}{8} \text{m/s}^2$ (d) $3 \text{m/s}^2, 3 \text{m/s}^2$

19 Two blocks of masses m_1 and m_2 are connected with a massless undeformed spring and placed over a plank moving with an acceleration a as shown in figure. The coefficient of friction between the blocks and platform is μ.

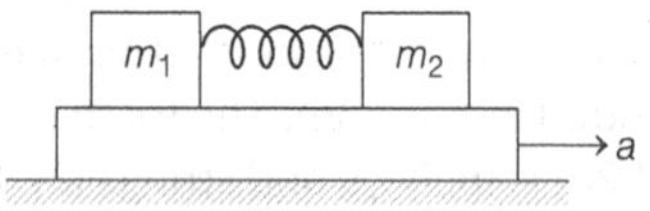

(a) spring will be stretched, if $a > \mu g$

(b) spring will be compressed, if $a \leq \mu g$

(c) spring will neither be compressed nor be stretched only, if $a \leq \mu g$

(d) spring will be in its natural length under all conditions only, if initial velocities of blocks are same

20 A block A is placed over a long rough plank B of same mass as shown in figure. The plank is placed over a smooth horizontal surface. At time $t = 0$, block A is given a velocity v_0 in horizontal direction. Let v_1 and v_2 be the velocities of A and B at time t. Then, choose the correct graph between v_1 or v_2 and t.

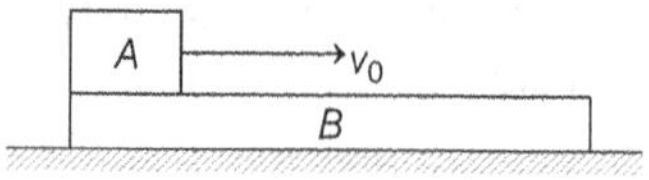

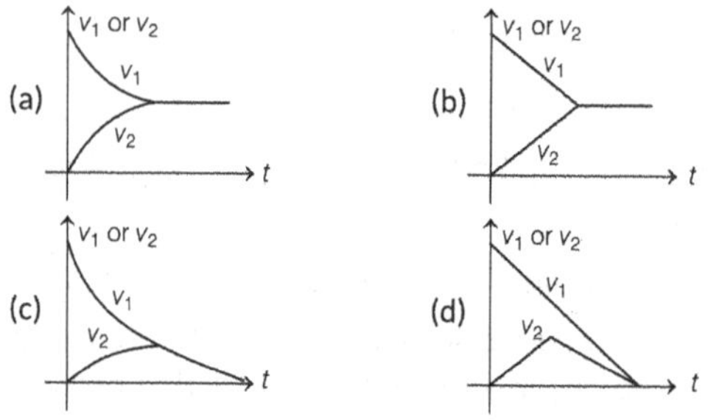

21 A plank is held at an angle α to the horizontal (Fig.) on two fixed supports A and B. The plank can slide against the supports (without friction) because of its weight Mg. With what acceleration and in what direction, a man of mass m should move, so that the plank does not move?

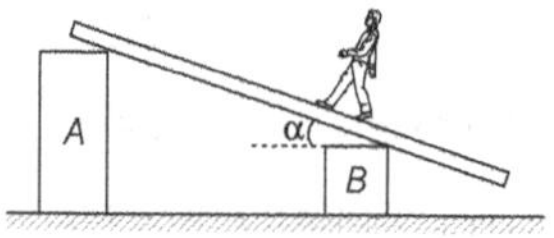

(a) $g \sin\alpha\left(1 + \frac{m}{M}\right)$ down the incline

(b) $g \sin\alpha\left(1 + \frac{M}{m}\right)$ down the incline

(c) $g \sin\alpha\left(1 + \frac{m}{M}\right)$ up the incline

(d) $g \sin\alpha\left(1 + \frac{M}{m}\right)$ up the incline

22 Three blocks A, B and C of equal mass m are placed one over the other on a rough horizontal ground as shown in the figure. Coefficient of friction between any two blocks in contact is $\frac{1}{2}$ and between C and ground is $\frac{1}{5}$. The maximum value of mass of block D, so that the blocks A, B and C move without slipping over each other is

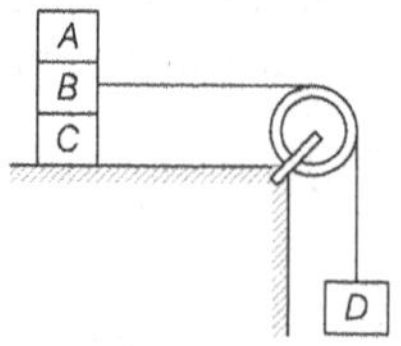

(a) 6 m (b) 5 m (c) 3 m (d) 4 m

23 A particle is at rest on a rough horizontal plane. The plane is slowly tilted until the particle starts to move and is then fixed. If the static and kinetic coefficients of friction are μ_s and μ_k ($\mu_k < \mu_s$), calculate the acceleration of the particle.

(a) $\dfrac{g(\mu_s - \mu_k)}{[1+\mu_s^2]^{1/2}}$ (b) $\dfrac{g(\mu_s - \mu_k)}{[1+\mu_k^2]^{1/2}}$

(c) $\dfrac{g(\mu_s - \mu_k)}{[1+\mu_s]^{1/2}}$ (d) $\dfrac{g(\mu_s - \mu_k)}{[1+\mu_k]^{1/2}}$

24 A wedge of mass $2m$ and a cube of mass m are shown in figure. Between cube and wedge there is no friction. The minimum coefficient of friction between wedge and ground, so that wedge does not move is

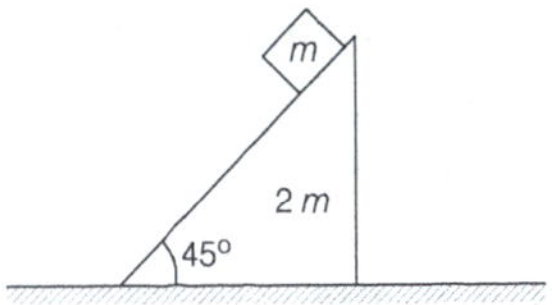

(a) 0.1 (b) 0.2

(c) 0.25 (d) 0.5

25 Consider the arrangement shown in figure. Pulleys are string are ideal. Both blocks have same mass m. The minimum coefficient of friction between the bigger block and ground for which both the blocks will be in equilibrium is

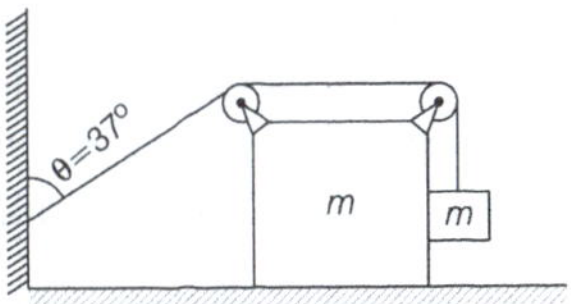

(a) $\dfrac{2}{7}$ (b) $\dfrac{3}{14}$ (c) $\dfrac{1}{2}$ (d) None of these

26 As shown in the figure, M is a man of mass 60 kg standing on a block of mass 40 kg kept on ground. The coefficient of friction between the feet of the man and the block is 0.3 and that between B and the ground is 0.1. If the man accelerates with an acceleration 2 m/s^2 in the forward direction, then

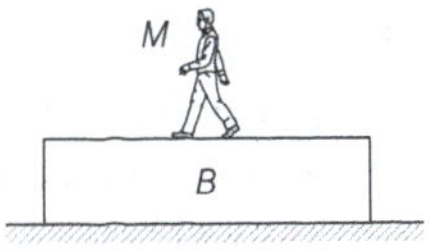

(a) it is not possible

(b) B will move backwards with an acceleration 0.5 m/s^2

(c) B will not move

(d) B will move forward with an acceleration 0.5 m/s^2

27 Wedge is fixed on horizontal surface. Triangular block A of mass $4m$ is pulled upward by applying a constant force $F = 8\,mg$ parallel to incline of the wedge as shown in the figure and there is no friction between the wedge and the block A. Find the minimum coefficient of friction between A and block B, if there is no relative motion between A and B.

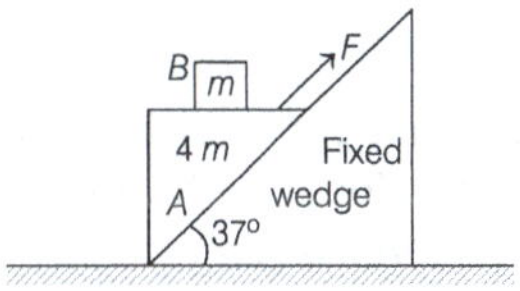

(a) $\dfrac{1}{5}$ (b) $\dfrac{1}{4}$ (c) $\dfrac{1}{3}$ (d) $\dfrac{1}{2}$

28 Four blocks are arranged on a smooth fixed horizontal surface as shown. The masses of upper blocks are m kg and lower blocks are M kg as shown in figure. The coefficient of friction between upper and lower blocks is μ. Both the upper blocks are connected by inextensible light string having initial zero tension. For all four blocks to move with same acceleration, the maximum value of horizontal force F applied to right bottom block (as shown) is

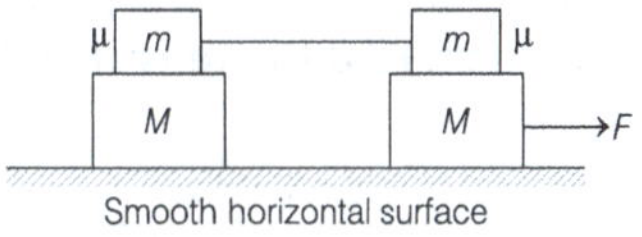

(a) $\dfrac{2\mu mg(m+M)}{2m+M}$ (b) $2\mu g(m+M)$

(c) $\dfrac{2\mu mg(m+M)}{m+2M}$ (d) $\mu g(m+2M)$

29 Two blocks A and B are placed in contact on a horizontal surface. Faces of blocks A and B, which are in contact, are inclined at 30° with the horizontal, as shown. There is no friction between block A and any surface which is in contact with this, where as friction coefficient between block B and the surface is $\dfrac{1}{\sqrt{3}}$. A force F is applied in horizontal direction on block A. What is the minimum value of F at which the block B just start moving rightwards?

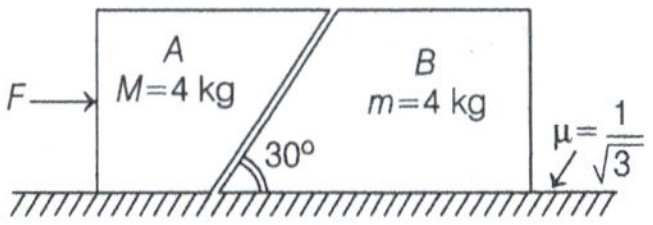

(a) $\dfrac{40}{\sqrt{3}}$ N (b) $\dfrac{80}{\sqrt{3}}$ N (c) 100 N

(d) For any value of F, motion will not start

30 A small child tries to move a large rubber toy placed on the ground. The toy does not move but gets deformed under his/her pushing force **F** which is obliquely upward as shown. Then, select correct alternative assuming that deformation is completed.

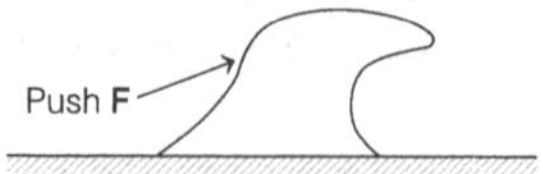

(a) The resultant of the pushing force (**F**), weight of the toy, normal force by the ground on the toy and the frictional force is zero.

(b) The normal force by the ground is equal and opposite to the weight of the toy.

(c) The pushing force (**F**)of the child is balanced by the equal and opposite frictional force.

(d) The pushing force (**F**) of the child is balanced by the total internal force in the toy generated due to deformation.

31 As shown in the figure, blocks of masses $\frac{M}{2}$, M and $\frac{M}{2}$ are connected through a light string as shown, pulleys are light and smooth. Friction is present only between block *C* and the inclined plane. System is released from rest. Find the tension in the string.

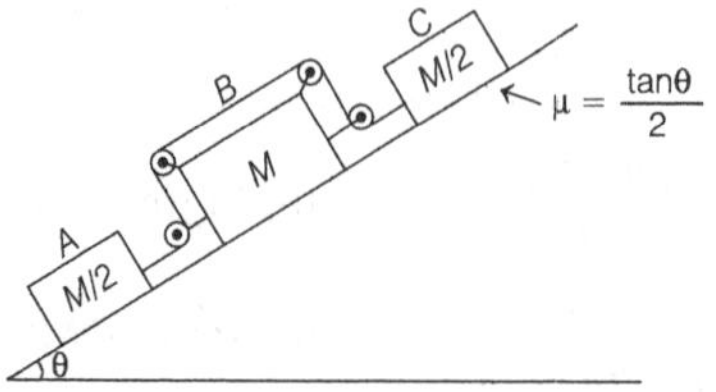

(a) $\frac{Mg\sin\theta}{4}$ (b) $\frac{Mg\sin\theta}{5}$

(c) $\frac{Mg\sin\theta}{6}$ (d) $\frac{Mg\sin\theta}{8}$

32 Given $m_A = 30$ kg, $m_B = 10$ kg and $m_C = 20$ kg. Between *A* and *B* friction coefficient $\mu_1 = 0.3$, between *B* and *C* friction coefficient $\mu_2 = 0.2$ and between *C* and ground $\mu_3 = 0.1$. The least horizontal force *F* to start the motion of any part of the system of three blocks resting upon one another as shown in figure is ($g = 10\text{ m/s}^2$)

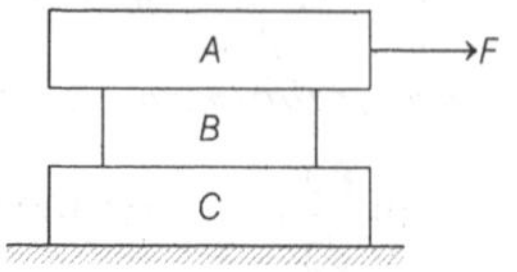

(a) 60 N (b) 90 N

(c) 80 N (d) 150 N

33 Two identical blocks of same masses are placed on a fixed wedge as shown in figure. Coefficient of friction between all the contact surfaces is μ. Choose the correct alternative.

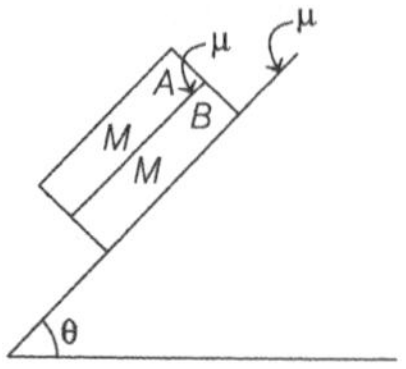

(a) For motion at any surface, $\theta \leq \tan^{-1}(\mu)$.

(b) Acceleration of block *A* will be more than acceleration of block *B* in downward direction.

(c) Acceleration of block *A* will be less than acceleration of block *B* in downward direction.

(d) Two blocks *A* and *B* move with same acceleration.

34 The system of two blocks is at rest as shown in the figure. A variable horizontal force is applied on the upper block. The maximum possible contact force exerted by the horizontal ground surface on the lower block is (coefficient of friction for both the contacts is μ)

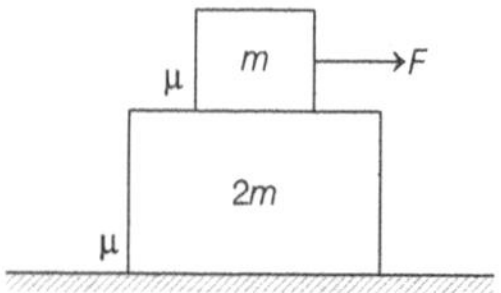

(a) $3mg\sqrt{1+\mu^2}$ (b) $3\mu mg$

(c) μmg (d) $mg\sqrt{9+\mu^2}$

35 Coefficient of friction between the two blocks is 1/3. All pulleys are massless. Then, the minimum coefficient of friction between block *B* and ground for the system to remain in equilibrium is

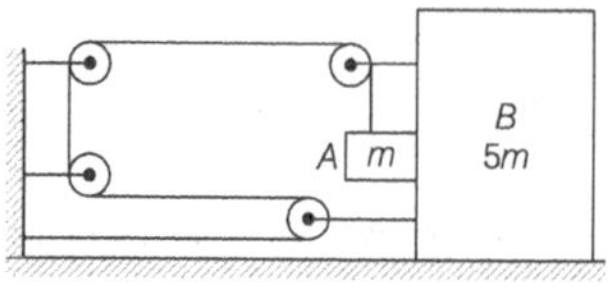

(a) $\frac{3}{5}$ (b) $\frac{1}{2}$ (c) $\frac{1}{3}$ (d) $\frac{1}{6}$

36 A wedge of mass *M* and a body of mass *m* are shown in the figure. The coefficient of friction between the wedge and the body is μ. If the masses of the pulley and threads are negligible, the acceleration of the body with respect to horizontal smooth surface on which the wedge slips will be

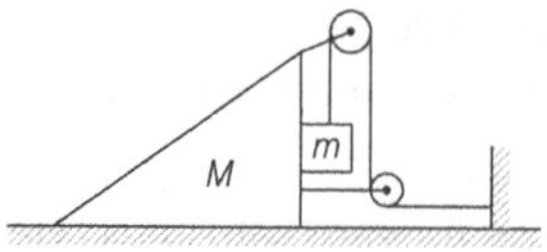

(a) $\dfrac{\sqrt{2}g}{\left(\dfrac{M}{m}+\mu+2\right)}$ (b) Zero

(c) $\dfrac{\sqrt{2}g}{\left(\dfrac{M}{m}-\mu-2\right)}$ (d) $\dfrac{g}{\left(\dfrac{M}{m}-\mu+2\right)}$

37 Two wedges, each of mass m, are placed next to each other on a flat horizontal floor. A cube of mass M is balanced on the wedges as shown in figure. Assume no friction between the cube and the wedges, but a coefficient of static friction $\mu < 1$ between the wedges and the floor. What is the largest M that can be balanced as shown without motion of the wedges?

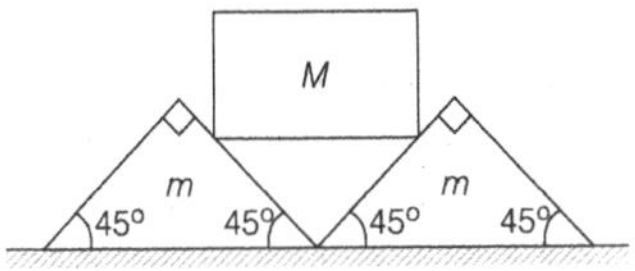

(a) $\dfrac{m}{\sqrt{2}}$ (b) $\dfrac{\mu m}{\sqrt{2}}$ (c) $\dfrac{\mu m}{1-\mu}$ (d) $\dfrac{2\mu m}{1-\mu}$

Multiple Choice(s) Correct Questions

1 A block of mass 15 kg is resting on a rough inclined plane as shown in figure. The block is tied up by a horizontal string which has a tension of 50 N. The coefficient of friction between the surfaces of contact is $(g = 10\text{ m/s}^2)$

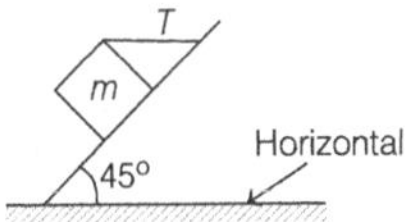

(a) 1/2 (b) 2/3 (c) 3/4 (d) 1/4

2 A block on a long table is tied by massless ropes to two hanging blocks as in figure. Initially, block C is moving downwards with non-zero velocity. The static and kinetic friction between block B and table are 0.2 and 0.1, respectively. Then,

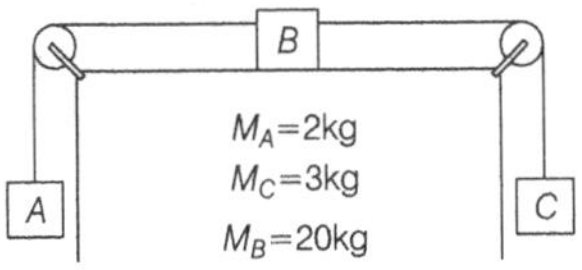

(a) acceleration of block C is 0.4 m/s^2, downwards

(b) acceleration of block C is 0.4 m/s^2, upwards

(c) block C comes to rest after sometime and thereafter it will not move

(d) acceleration of block C is zero, all the time

3 Two masses $m_1 = 4$ kg and $m_2 = 2$ kg are connected with an inextensible, massless string that passes over a frictionless pulley and through a slit, as shown. The string is vertical on both sides and the string on the left is acted upon by a constant friction force 10 N by the slit as it moves. (Use, $g = 10\text{ m/s}^2$)

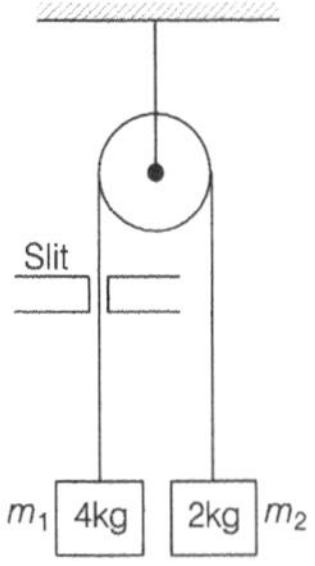

(a) Acceleration of mass m_1 is $\dfrac{5}{3}\text{ m/s}^2$, downwards

(b) Tension in the string is same throughout

(c) Force exerted by the string on mass m_2 is $\dfrac{70}{3}$ N

(d) If positions of both the masses are interchanged, then 2 kg mass moves up with acceleration $\dfrac{10}{3}\text{ m/s}^2$

4 Car is accelerating with acceleration $a = 20\text{ m/s}^2$. A box of mass $m = 10$ kg that is placed inside the car, is put in contact with the vertical wall of car as shown. The friction coefficient between the box and the wall is $\mu = 0.6$

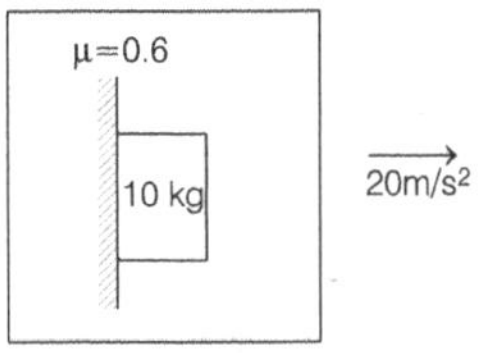

(a) The acceleration of the box will be 20 m/s^2

(b) The friction force acting on the box will be 100 N

(c) The contact force between the vertical wall and the box will be $100\sqrt{5}$ N

(d) The net contact force between the vertical wall and the box is only of electromagnetic in nature.

5 In the given figure, the value(s) of mass m for which the 100 kg block remains in static equilibrium, is $(g = 10\text{ m/s}^2)$

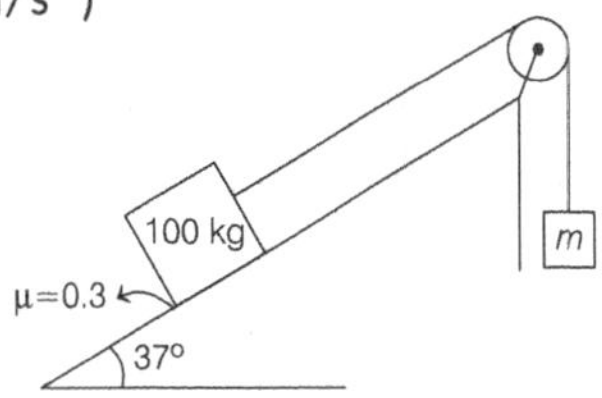

(a) 35 kg (b) 37 kg (c) 83 kg (d) 85 kg

6 A solid cube of mass 5 kg is placed on a rough horizontal surface, in *xy*-plane as shown. The friction coefficient between the surface and the cube is 0.4. An external force $\mathbf{F} = 6\hat{\mathbf{i}} + 8\hat{\mathbf{j}} + 30\hat{\mathbf{k}}$ N is applied on the cube. (Use, $g = 10$ m/s^2)

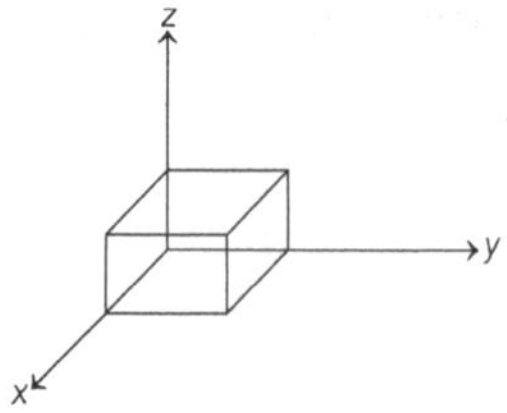

(a) The block does not start slipping over the surface

(b) The acceleration of the block is $(0.24\hat{\mathbf{i}} + 0.32\hat{\mathbf{j}})$ m/s^2

(c) The friction force acting on the block is $(-4.8\hat{\mathbf{i}} - 6.4\hat{\mathbf{j}})$ N

(d) The contact force exerted by the surface on the cube is $4\sqrt{29}$ N

7 The force F_1 parallel to inclined plane that is necessary to move a body up an inclined plane is double the force F_2 that is necessary to just prevent it from sliding down, then

(a) $F_1 = w\sin(\phi + \theta)\sec\theta$ (b) $F_2 = w\sin(\phi - \theta)\sec\theta$

(c) $\tan\theta = 3\tan\phi$ (d) $\tan\phi = 3\tan\theta$

where, θ = limiting angle of repose, ϕ = angle of inclined plane and w = weight of the body.

8 An insect of mass *m*, starts moving on a rough inclined surface from point *A*. As the surface is very sticky, the coefficient of friction between the insect and the incline is $\mu = 1$. Assume that it can move in any direction up the incline or down the incline, then

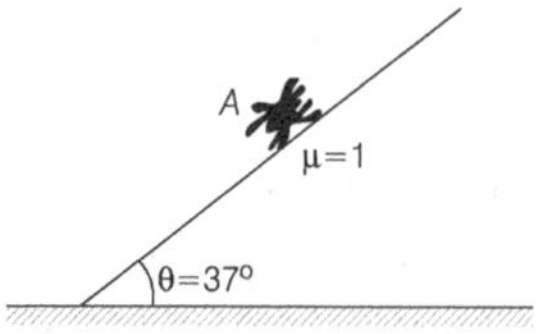

(a) the maximum possible acceleration of the insect can be 14 m/s^2

(b) the minimum possible acceleration of the insect can be 2 m/s^2

(c) the insect can move with a constant velocity

(d) the insect cannot move with a constant velocity

9 The coefficient of friction between 4 kg and 5 kg block is 0.2 and between 5 kg block and ground is 0.1, respectively. Choose the correct statements.

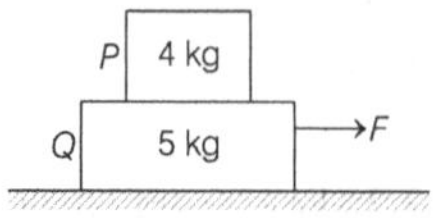

(a) Minimum force needed to cause system to move is 17 N

(b) When force is 4 N, static friction at all surfaces is 4 N to keep system at rest

(c) Maximum acceleration of 4 kg block is 2 m/s^2

(d) Slipping between 4 kg and 5 kg blocks starts when *F* is 27 N

10 1.5 kg box kept on horizontal rough ground is pushed by a horizontal force whose *F*-*t* graph is shown. Its *a*-*t* graph is also given.

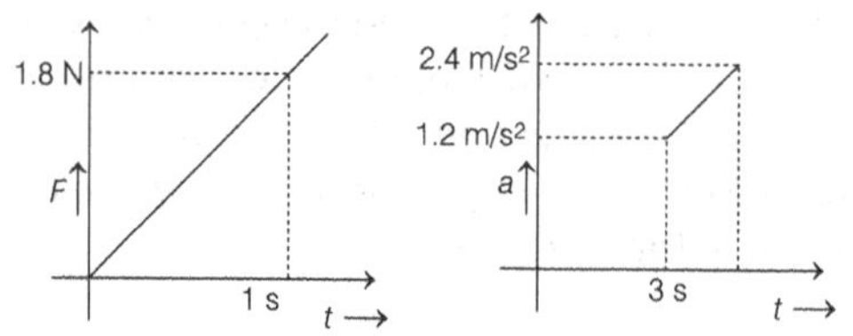

(a) Coefficient of static friction is 0.36

(b) Coefficient of static friction is 0.48

(c) Time when acceleration is 2.4 m/s^2 is 5 s

(d) Coefficient of kinetic friction is 0.24

11 An arrangement of the masses and pulleys is shown in the figure. Strings connecting masses *A* and *B* with pulleys are horizontal and all pulleys and strings are light. Friction coefficient between the surface and the block *B* is 0.2 and between blocks *A* and *B* is 0.7. The system is released from rest.

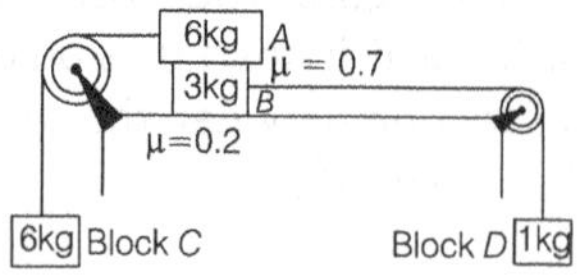

(a) The magnitude of acceleration of the system is 2 m/s^2 and there is no slipping between block *A* and block *B*.

(b) The magnitude of friction force between block *A* and block *B* is 42 N

(c) Acceleration of block *C* is 1 m/s^2 downwards

(d) Tension in the string connecting block *B* and block *D* is 12 N

12 In the arrangement shown in figure, pulley is smooth and massless and string is light. Friction coefficient between *A* and *B* is μ. Friction is absent between *A* and plane. Select the correct alternative(s).

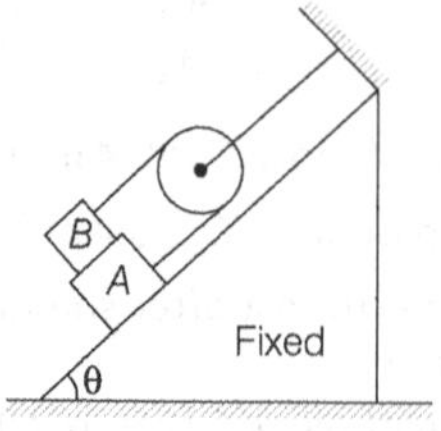

(a) Acceleration of the system is zero if $\mu \geq \frac{m_B - m_A}{2m_B} \tan\theta$ and $m_B > m_A$

(b) Force of friction between A and B is zero if $m_A = m_b$

(c) B moves downwards if $m_B > m_A$

(d) Tension in the string is $mg(\sin\theta - \mu\cos\theta)$, if $m_A = m_B = m$

13 The two blocks A and B of equal mass are initially in contact when released from rest on the inclined plane. The coefficients of friction between the inclined plane and A and B are $\mu_1 = 1$ and $\mu_2 = \frac{1}{\sqrt{3}}$, respectively. As the inclination of the inclined plane θ increases, then

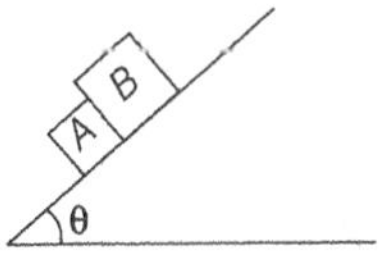

(a) there is no contact force between block A and B, if $\theta \leq 30°$

(b) there is no contact force between block A and B, if $\theta \leq 45°$

(c) acceleration of blocks is independent of θ

(d) they start moving at an angle $\theta = \tan^{-1}\left(\frac{\mu_1 + \mu_2}{2}\right)$

14 Two blocks A and B of mass 10 kg and 50 kg respectively are placed as shown in figure. Coefficient of friction between all the surfaces is 0.5. Then, ($g = 10\ m/s^2$)

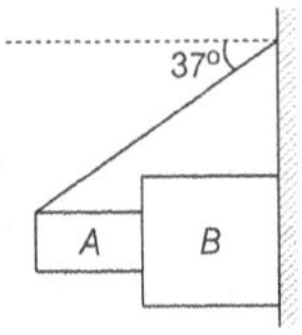

(a) tension in the string is 500 N

(b) tension in the string is 400 N

(c) acceleration of block B is $2\ m/s^2$

(d) acceleration of block B is $3\ m/s^2$

15 In the given figure, the inclined plane is frictionless and coefficient of friction between the blocks is shown. All the three blocks A, B and C are stationary. Then, choose the correct option(s).

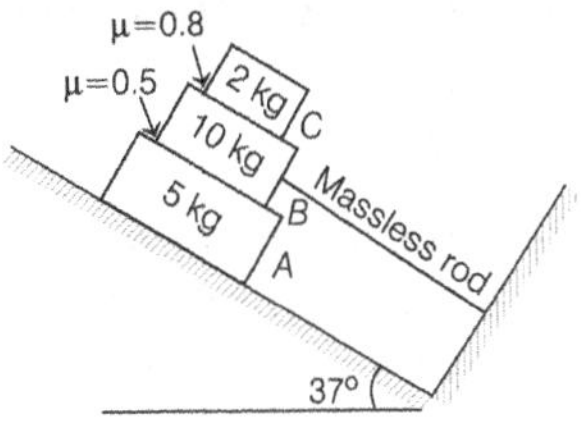

(a) Friction force on block A is 30 N

(b) Friction force on block C is 12.8 N

(c) Thrust in the rod is 102 N

(d) Block A will accelerate down

16 A 60 kg block rests on a massless very long belt which passes over a fixed pulley and is attached to a 40 kg block. If coefficient of friction between the belt and the table as well as between the belt and the block B is μ and the system is released from rest from the position shown, the speed with which the block B falls off the belt is

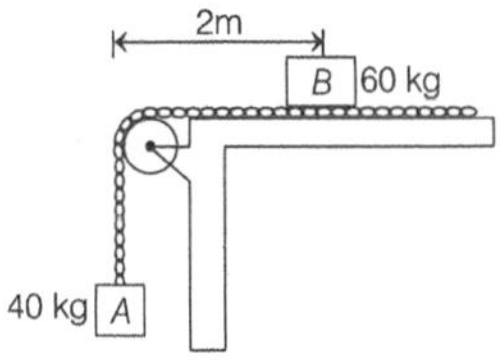

(a) $2\sqrt{2}$ m/s, if $\mu = 0.2$
(b) $\sqrt{2}$ m/s, if $\mu = 0.2$
(c) 2 m/s, if $\mu = 0.5$
(d) $2\sqrt{2}$ m/s, if $\mu = 0.5$

17 Coefficient of friction between the two blocks is 0.5 and coefficient of friction between 3 kg and table is 0.4. ($g = 10\ m/s^2$)

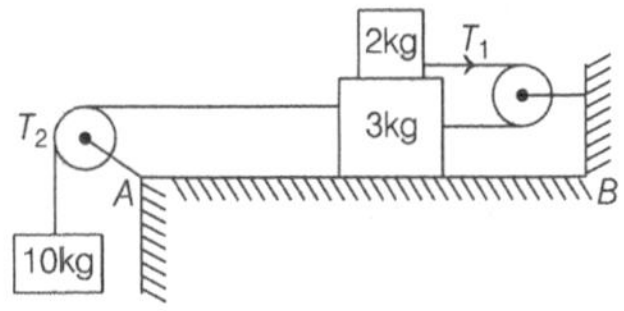

(a) Acceleration of the system of masses is $4\ ms^{-2}$

(b) Tension T_1 in the string is 18 N

(c) Tension T_2 in the string is 60 N

(d) Acceleration of 10 kg mass is $4.5\ ms^{-2}$

18 Block A is placed on cart B as shown in figure. If the coefficients of static and kinetic friction between the 20 kg block A and 100 kg cart B are both essentially the same value of 0.3.
[$g = 10\ m/s^2$]

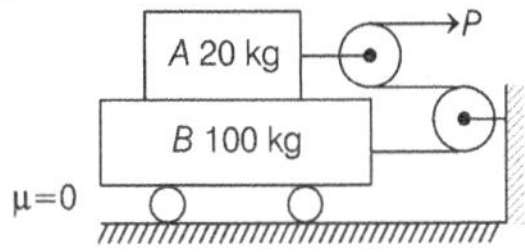

(a) The blocks A and B will have a common acceleration of $1\ m/s^2$, if $P = 40$ N

(b) Acceleration of cart A is $2\ m/s^2$, if $P = 50$ N

(c) Acceleration of cart B is $1.2\ m/s^2$, if $P = 60$ N

(d) Minimum value of P at which relative motion starts between the two blocks is 50 N

Comprehension Based Questions

Comprehension-1

A man wants to slide down a block of mass m which is kept on a fixed inclined plane of inclination 30° as shown in figure. Initially, the block is not sliding. To just start sliding, the man pushes the block down the incline with a force F. Now, the block starts accelerating. To move it downwards with constant speed, the man starts pulling the block up with the same force F. Surfaces are such that ratio of limiting friction to kinetic friction is 2. Now, answer the following questions.

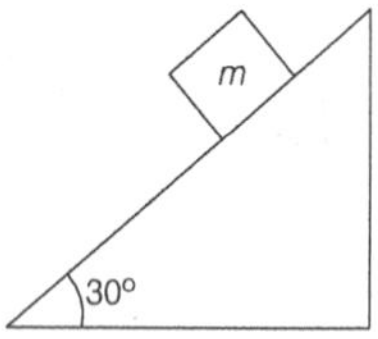

1 What is the value of F?

(a) $\frac{mg}{4}$ (b) $\frac{mg}{6}$ (c) $\frac{\sqrt{3}mg}{4}$ (d) $\frac{mg}{2\sqrt{3}}$

2 What is the value of coefficient of static friction (μ_s)?

(a) $\frac{4}{3\sqrt{3}}$ (b) $\frac{2}{3\sqrt{3}}$ (c) $\frac{1}{\sqrt{3}}$ (d) $\frac{1}{2\sqrt{3}}$

3 If the man continues pushing the block with force F, its acceleration would be

(a) $\frac{g}{6}$ (b) $\frac{g}{4}$ (c) $\frac{g}{2}$ (d) $\frac{g}{3}$

4 If the man wants to move the block up the plane, what minimum force is required to just start the motion?

(a) $\frac{2mg}{3}$ (b) $\frac{mg}{2}$ (c) $\frac{7mg}{6}$ (d) $\frac{5mg}{6}$

5 What minimum force is required to move the block up the plane with constant speed?

(a) $\frac{2mg}{3}$ (b) $\frac{mg}{2}$ (c) $\frac{7mg}{6}$ (d) $\frac{5mg}{6}$

Comprehension-2

In the arrangement shown

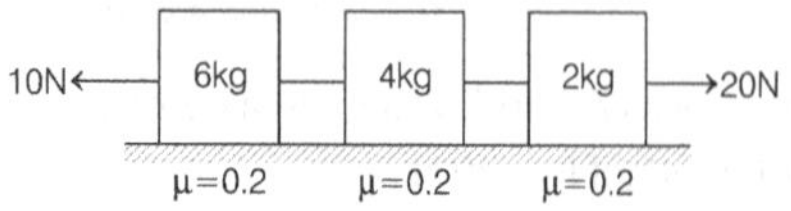

6 Tension in the string connecting 4 kg and 6 kg masses is

(a) 8 N (b) 12 N
(c) 6 N (d) 4 N

7 Friction force on 4 kg block is

(a) 4 N (b) 6 N (c) 12 N (d) 8 N

8 Friction force on 6 kg block is

(a) 2 N (b) 8 N (c) 6 N (d) 4 N

Comprehension-3

Block A of mass m and block B of mass $2m$ are placed on a fixed triangular wedge by means of a massless, inextensible string and a frictionless pulley as shown in figure. The wedge is inclined at 45° to the horizontal on both sides. The coefficient of friction between block A and the wedge is 2/3 and that between block B and the wedge is 1/3. If the system A and B is released from rest, find

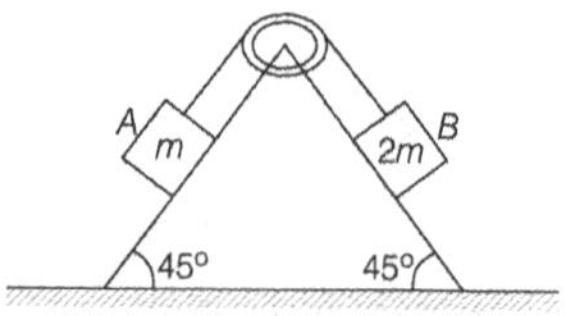

9 the acceleration of A,

(a) $\frac{g}{\sqrt{2}}$ (b) $\frac{g}{2\sqrt{2}}$ (c) $\frac{g}{3\sqrt{2}}$ (d) 0

10 tension in the string

(a) $\frac{\sqrt{2}mg}{3}$ (b) $\frac{2\sqrt{2}mg}{3}$ (c) $\frac{2mg}{3}$ (d) $\frac{mg}{3\sqrt{2}}$

11 and the force of friction acting on A.

(a) $\frac{\sqrt{2}mg}{3}$ (b) $\frac{2\sqrt{2}mg}{3}$ (c) $\frac{2mg}{3}$ (d) $\frac{mg}{3\sqrt{2}}$

Comprehension-4

Two bodies A and B of masses 10 kg and 5 kg are placed very slightly separated as shown in figure. The coefficient of friction between the floor and the blocks is $\mu = 0.4$. Block A is pushed by an external force F. The value of F can be changed. When the welding between block A and ground breaks, block A will start pressing block B and when welding of B also breaks, block B will start pressing the vertical wall

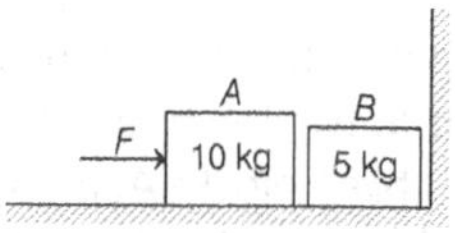

12 If $F = 20$ N, with how much force does block A presses the block B

(a) 10 N (b) 20 N (c) 30 N (d) zero

13 What should be the minimum value of F, so that block B can press the vertical wall

(a) 20 N (b) 40 N (c) 60 N (d) 80 N

14 If $F = 50$ N, the friction force (shear force) acting between block B and ground will be

(a) 10 N (b) 20 N (c) 30 N (d) None of these

Comprehension-5

A sufficiently long plank of mass 4 kg is kept on a smooth horizontal ground. A block of mass 2 kg is kept over the plank and is being acted upon by a time varying horizontal force $F = 0.5t$, where F is in newton and t is in seconds as shown in figure. The coefficient of friction between the plank and the block is given as $\mu_s = \mu_k = \mu$. At $t = 12$ s, relative motion between the plank and the block just starts.

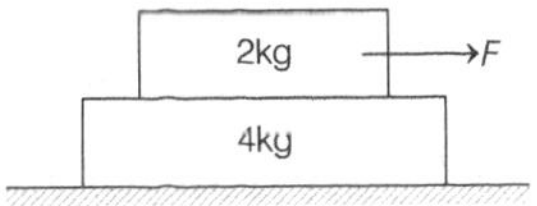

15 The coefficient of friction μ is

(a) 0.10 (b) 0.15
(c) 0.20 (d) 0.30

16 The acceleration *a versus* time *t* graph for the plank and the block shown in figures below is correct represented in

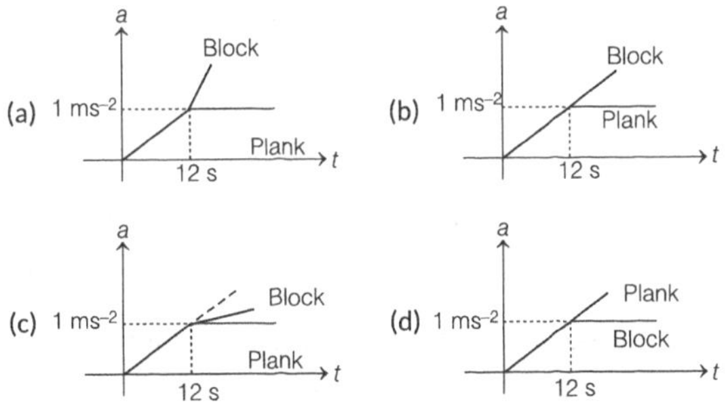

17 The average accelertion of the plank in the time interval 0 to 15 s in the figure will be

(a) $0.2\ \text{m/s}^2$ (b) $0.3\ \text{m/s}^2$
(c) $0.4\ \text{m/s}^2$ (d) $0.6\ \text{m/s}^2$

Comprehension-6

A system of two blocks and a light string are kept on two inclined faces (rough) as shown in the figure below. All the required data are mentioned in the diagram. Pulley is light and frictionless. [Take, $g = 10\ \text{m/s}^2$, $\sin 37° = \frac{3}{5}$]

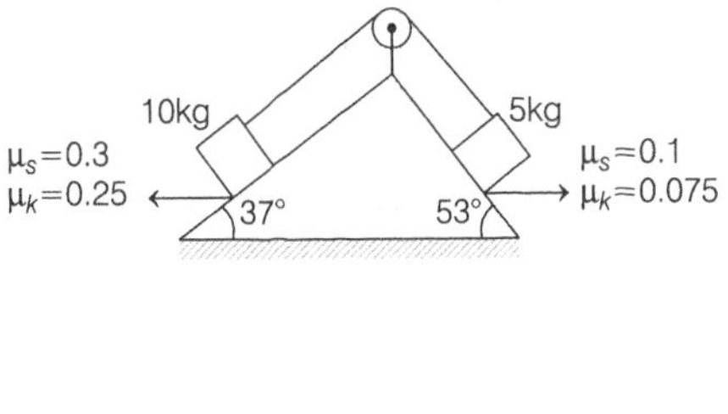

18 If the system is released from rest, then the acceleration of the system is

(a) $\frac{7}{15}\ \text{m/s}^2$ (b) zero
(c) $\frac{47}{15}\ \text{m/s}^2$ (d) $\frac{225}{15}\ \text{m/s}^2$

19 If the system is initially moving in such a way that block of 10 kg is coming down the incline with a speed of 2 m/s, then how much time the system takes to come to a stop ? (Assume the length of incline to be large enough.)

(a) 13.33 s (b) 80 s
(c) Infinite (d) Question is irrelavent

20 If 5 kg is replaced by 4 kg and the system is released from rest, the tension in the string would be

(a) 35.57 N (b) 38.25 N
(c) 40.35 N (d) 45.17 N

Comprehension-7

A monkey of mass m clings to a rope hanging over a fixed pulley. The opposite end of the rope is tied to a weight of mass M lying on a horizontal table. The coefficient of friction between the weight and the table is μ. The monkey moves downwards with respect to the rope with an acceleration b.

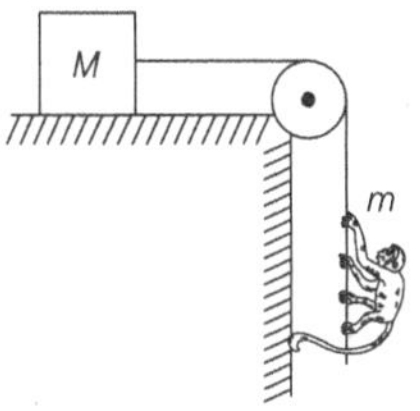

21 The acceleration of weight is

(a) $\frac{2m(g+b) - \mu Mg}{M + 2m}$ (b) $\frac{m(g+b) - \mu Mg}{2(M+m)}$
(c) $\frac{m(g+b) - 3\mu Mg}{M + 3m}$ (d) $\frac{m(g-b) - \mu Mg}{M+m}$

22 The tension of rope is

(a) $\frac{Mm(\mu g + g + b)}{M+m}$ (b) $\frac{Mm(\mu g - g + b)}{M+m}$
(c) $\frac{Mm(\mu g + g - b)}{M+m}$ (d) $\frac{Mm(\mu g - g - b)}{M+m}$

Comprehension-8

Two blocks of masses 25 kg and 5 kg are placed on a horizontal table as shown in the figure. A massless string passes over a frictionless and massless pulley whose one end is connected to 25 kg block and other end is connected to block M. The coefficient of friction between two blocks is $\mu = 0.3$ and between the 5 kg block and ground is zero. The system is released from rest. (Take, $g = 10 \text{ m/s}^2$)

Answer the following questions by selecting most appropriate alternate.

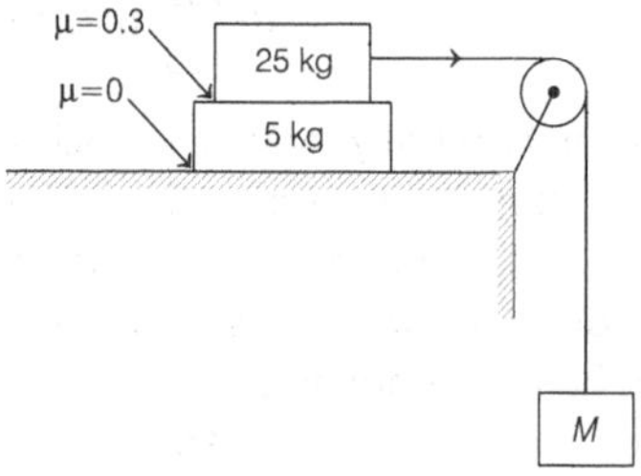

23 If $M = 45$ kg, the force of friction between two blocks will be

(a) 80 N (b) 60 N
(c) 30 N (d) 75 N

24 If $M = 45$ kg, the acceleration of the system will be

(a) 6 m/s^2 (b) 5 m/s^2
(c) 8 m/s^2 (d) 10 m/s^2

25 Find the value of M for which there will be slipping between the blocks.

(a) $M > 90$ kg (b) $M > 0$
(c) $M < 90$ kg (d) None of these

Comprehension-9

A system of masses is shown in the figure with masses and coefficient of friction indicated.

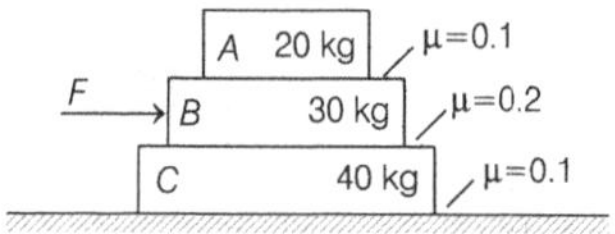

26 The maximum value of F for which there is no slipping anywhere.

(a) 90 N (b) 100 N
(c) 80 N (d) None of these

27 The minimum value of F for which B slides on C

(a) 100 N (b) 112.5 N (c) 115 N (d) 117.5 N

28 The minimum value of F for which A slips on B

(a) 125 N (b) 150 N (c) 175 N (d) 180 N

Comprehension-10

A block of mass 15 kg is placed over a frictionless horizontal surface. Another block of mass 10 kg is placed over it, that is connected with a light string passing over two pulleys fastened to the 15 kg block. A force $F = 80$ N is applied horizontally to the free end of the string. Friction coefficient between two blocks is 0.6. The portion of the string between 10 kg block and the upper pulley is horizontal as shown in figure. Pulley, string and connecting rods are massless. (Take, $g = 10 \text{ m/s}^2$)

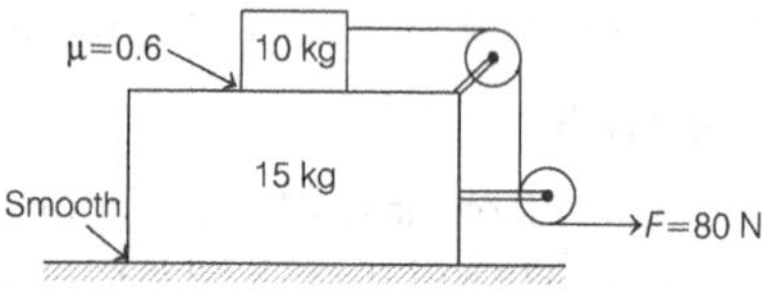

29 The magnitude of acceleration of the 10 kg block is

(a) 3.2 m/s^2 (b) 2.0 m/s^2
(c) 1.6 m/s^2 (d) 0.8 m/s^2

30 The magnitude of acceleration of the 15 kg block is

(a) 4.2 m/s^2 (b) 3.2 m/s^2
(c) $16/3 \text{ m/s}^2$ (d) 2.0 m/s^2

31 If applied force $F = 120$ N, then magnitude of acceleration of 15 kg block will be

(a) 8 m/s^2 (b) 4 m/s^2
(c) 3.2 m/s^2 (d) 4.8 m/s^2

32 Continuing with the situation, if the force $F = 80$ N is directed vertically as shown, the acceleration of the 10 kg block will be

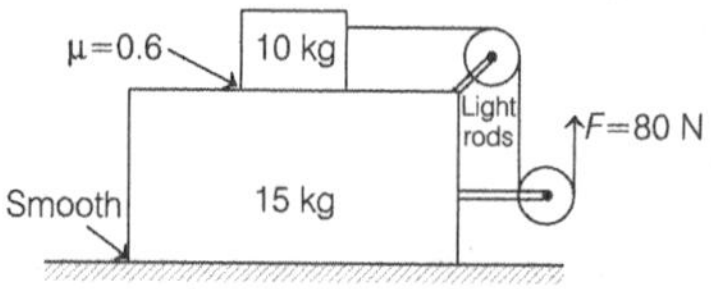

(a) 2 m/s^2, towards right (b) 2 m/s^2, towards left
(c) 6 m/s^2, towards left (d) $16/5 \text{ m/s}^2$, towards right

33 In the situation of the previous question, acceleration of the 15 kg block will be

(a) 4 m/s^2, towards right
(b) $16/5 \text{ m/s}^2$, towards right
(c) $2/3 \text{ m/s}^2$, towards right
(d) $4/3 \text{ m/s}^2$, towards left

Comprehension-11

In the figure, the coefficient of friction between the two blocks is 0.3 and that between the bigger block and the ground is also 0.3.

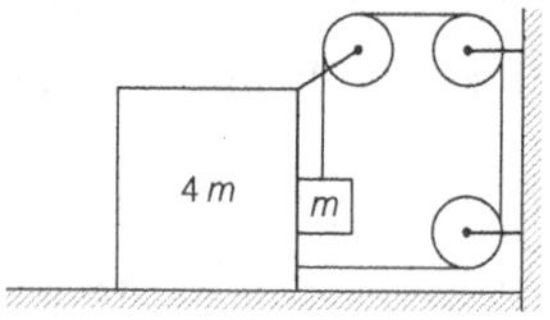

34 Find the acceleration of the bigger block.

(a) $\frac{g}{11}$ (b) $\frac{g}{13}$ (c) $\frac{g}{15}$ (d) $\frac{g}{18}$

35 If acceleration of the bigger block is a, then acceleration of the smaller block is
(a) $\sqrt{5}a$ (b) $2a$ (c) $\sqrt{2}a$ (d) $\sqrt{3}a$

Comprehension-12

A block of mass m is placed over the wedge as shown in figure. Coefficient of friction is $\mu = \frac{1}{2\sqrt{3}}$ and angle of inclined plane is 30°.

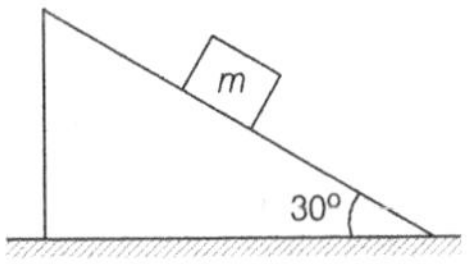

36 Minimum acceleration of wedge to keep the block stationary w.r.t, wedge is
(a) $\frac{g}{2\sqrt{3}}$ (b) $\frac{3\sqrt{3}g}{5}$ (c) $\frac{\sqrt{3}g}{7}$ (d) $\frac{g}{2\sqrt{5}}$

37 Maximum acceleration of wedge to keep the block stationary w.r.t. wedge is
(a) $\frac{g}{2\sqrt{3}}$ (b) $\frac{3\sqrt{3}g}{5}$
(c) $\frac{\sqrt{3}g}{7}$ (d) $\frac{g}{2\sqrt{5}}$

38 Acceleration of wedge towards right, so that friction does not act on the block is
(a) $\frac{g}{\sqrt{3}}$ (b) $\sqrt{3}g$
(c) $\frac{\sqrt{3}g}{2}$ (d) zero

Match the Columns Questions

1 In the given figure, find the accelerations of blocks A and B for the following cases. ($g = 10\text{ m/s}^2$)

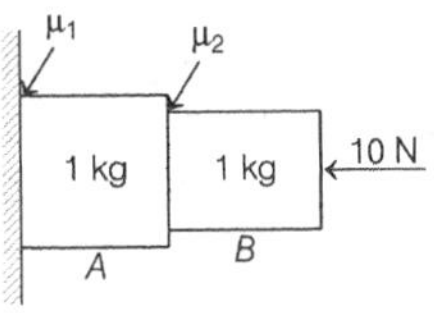

Column I	Column II
(a) $\mu_1 = 0$ and $\mu_2 = 0.1$	(p) $a_A = a_B = 9.5\text{m/s}^2$
(b) $\mu_2 = 0$ and $\mu_1 = 0.1$	(q) $a_A = 9\text{m/s}^2, a_B = 10\text{m/s}^2$
(c) $\mu_1 = 0.1$ and $\mu_2 = 1.0$	(r) $a_A = a_B = g = 10\text{m/s}^2$
(d) $\mu_1 = 1.0$ and $\mu_2 = 0.1$	(s) $a_A = 1, a_B = 9\text{m/s}^2$

2 A block of mass 10 kg is placed on a rough inclined plane of inclination 37° as shown in the figure. A force F is applied on the block along the plane. The coefficient of kinetic friction and coefficient of static friction are $\mu_k = 0.2$ and $\mu_s = 0.3$ respectively, ($\sin 37° = 0.6, g = 10\text{ m/s}^2$)

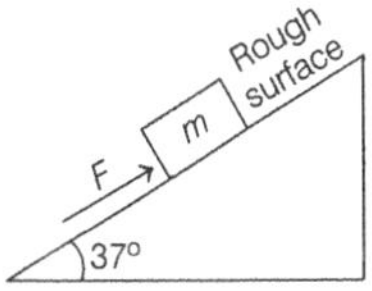

	Column I		Column II
(a)	When the value of $F = 40$ N	(p)	The nature of friction force between block and plane is static
(b)	When the value of $F = 80$ N	(q)	The nature of friction force between block and plane is kinetic
(c)	When the value of $F = 30$ N	(r)	The direction of friction is upward
(d)	When the value of $F = 90$ N	(s)	The direction of friction is downward
		(t)	Friction is zero

3 Two blocks of masses m_1 and m_2 ($m_2 > m_1$) are placed in contact with each other on an inclined plane as shown in figure. The coefficient of friction between m_1 and surface is μ_1 and between m_2 and surface is μ_2. (Take, $\tan\theta = 0.25$)

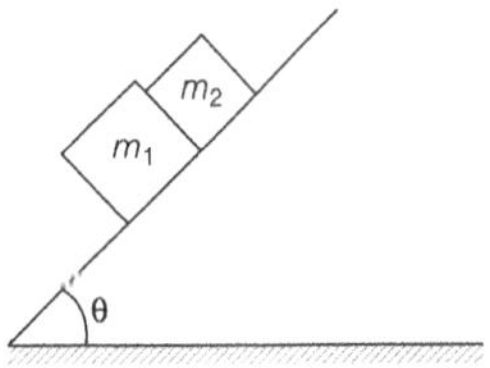

	Column I		Column II
(a)	$\mu_1 = 0.3, \mu_2 = 0.2$	(p)	Acceleration of both blocks, is different.
(b)	$\mu_1 = 0.2, \mu_2 = 0.3$	(q)	Acceleration of both blocks, is same.
(c)	$\mu_1 = 0.3, \mu_2 = 0.3$	(r)	Normal reaction between both the blocks is zero.
(d)	$\mu_1 = 0.2, \mu_2 = 0.2$	(s)	Normal reaction between both the blocks is non-zero.

4 A block placed on a rough inclined plane. Angle of inclination θ of the plane as shown is varied starting from zero. The coefficient of static friction and kinetic friction between the block and the plane are μ_s and μ_k respectively ($\mu_s > \mu_k$). Column II shows the graphs which necessarily contains θ taken on X-axis. Column I represents the quantities taken on Y-axis of Column I. Match the quantities of Column I with graphs of Column II.

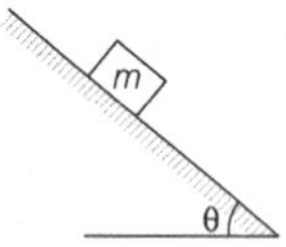

	Column I		Column II
(a)	Friction force between the block and plane	(p)	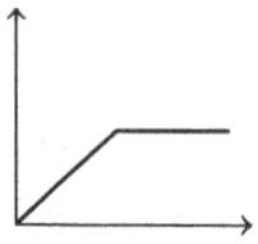
(b)	Normal force between the block and the plane	(q)	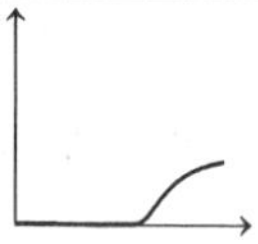
(c)	Total contact force between the block and the plane	(r)	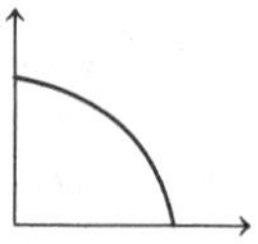
(d)	Acceleration of the block	(s)	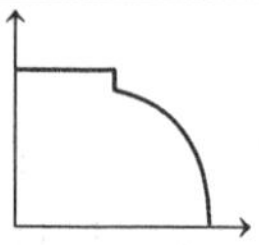
		(t)	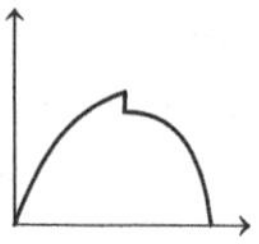

5 In the arrangement shown in figure, pulleys are small, light and frictionless threads are inextensible and mass of blocks A, B and C are $m_1 = 5$ kg, $m_2 = 4$ kg and $m_3 = 2.5$ kg, respectively. Coefficient of friction for both the planes is $\mu = 0.50$. ($g = 10 \text{ m/s}^2$)

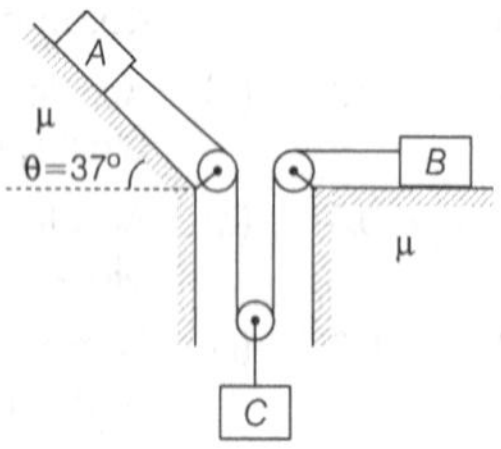

	Column I		Column II
(a)	Acceleration of block A (in m/s^2)	(p)	10
(b)	Acceleration of block B (in m/s^2)	(q)	2
(c)	Acceleration of block C (in m/s^2)	(r)	4
(d)	Tension in the string connecting A and B (in N)	(s)	0

6 For the situation shown in figure, in Column I, statements regarding friction forces are mentioned, while in Column II some information related to friction forces are given. Match the entries of Column I with entries of Column II. (Take, $g = 10 \text{ m/s}^2$)

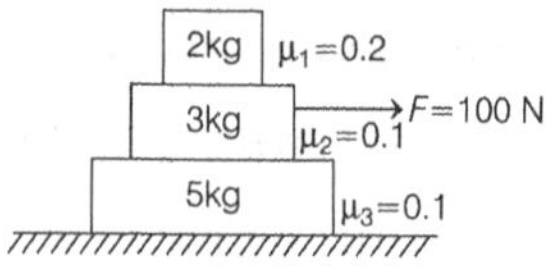

	Column I		Column II
(a)	Resultant friction force on 3 kg block	(p)	towards right
(b)	Resultant friction force on 5 kg block	(q)	towards left
(c)	Friction force on 2 kg block due to 3 kg block	(r)	zero
(d)	Friction force on 3 kg block due to 5 kg block	(s)	non-zero

Numerical Value Questions

1 A side view of a simplified form of vertical latch B is as shown. The lower member A can be pushed forward in its horizontal channel. The sides of the channels are smooth, but at the interfaces of A and B, which are at 45° with the horizontal, there exists a static coefficient of friction $\mu = 0.4$. What is the minimum force F (in N) that must be applied horizontally to A to start motion of the latch B if it has a mass $m = 0.6$ kg?

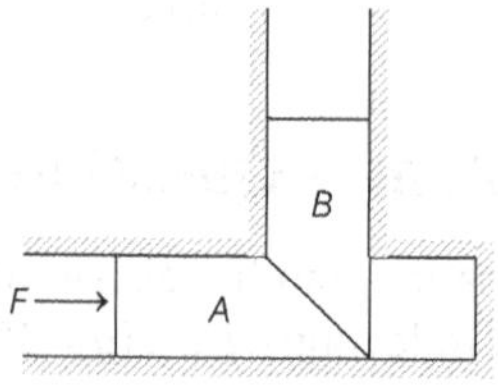

2 In the situation shown in figure for what value of horizontal force F (in N), sliding between middle and lower block will start? (Take, $g = 10 \text{ m/s}^2$)

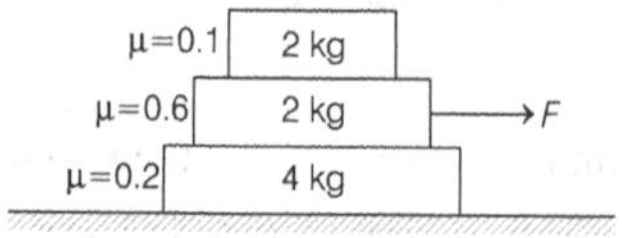

3 The three flat blocks as shown in the figure are positioned on the 37° incline and a force P parallel to the inclined plane is applied to the middle block. The upper block is prevented from moving by a wire which attaches it to the fixed support. The masses of three blocks in kg and coefficient of static friction for each of the three pairs of contact surfaces are shown in the figure. Determine the maximum value which force P (in N) may have before slipping take place anywhere. $(g = 10\ \text{m/s}^2)$

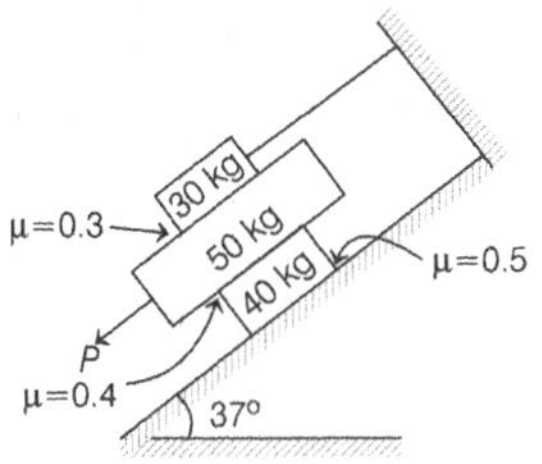

4 In the figure, the blocks A, B and C weigh 3 kg, 4 kg and 8 kg, respectively. The coefficient of sliding friction between any two surfaces is 0.25. A is held at rest by a massless rigid rod fixed to the wall, while B and C are connected by a light flexible cord passing around a fixed frictionless pulley. Find the force P necessary to drag C along the horizontal surface to the left at a constant speed. Assume that the arrangement shown in the diagram, B on C and A on B is maintained all throughout.

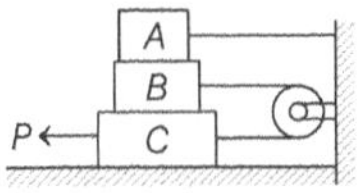

5 A car begins to move at time $t = 0$ and then accelerates along a straight track with a speed given by $v(t) = 2t^2 \text{ms}^{-1}$ for $0 \le t \le 2$. After the end of acceleration, the car continues to move at a constant speed. A small block initially at rest on the floor of the car begins to slip at $t = 1$ s and stops slipping at $t = 3$ s. Find the coefficient of kinetic friction between the block and the floor.

6 A circular disc with a groove along its diameter is placed horizontally. A block of mass 1 kg is placed as shown. The coefficient of friction between the block and all surfaces of groove in contact is $\mu = 2/5$. The disc has an acceleration of 25 m/s^2. Find the acceleration of the block with respect to disc.

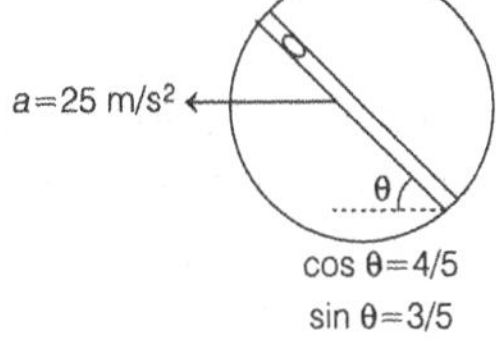

7 A vertical rod of mass 4 kg is hanging on a rope and a 3 kg cat is grasping the bottom end of the rod. The rope is cut off and the frightened cat begins to run up on the rod. While the rod is falling vertically, the cat remains at the same height, with respect to the ground. If the acceleration of the rod is $n\,(g/4)$, then what is the value of n?

8 A wedge A is resting on another wedge B as shown in figure. Both wedges have same mass $\left(\frac{21}{88}\right)$ kg. The angle θ is 37°. The coefficient of friction between the two wedges is $\frac{1}{6}$. Find the maximum value of F (in N) for which there is no sliding between wedges.

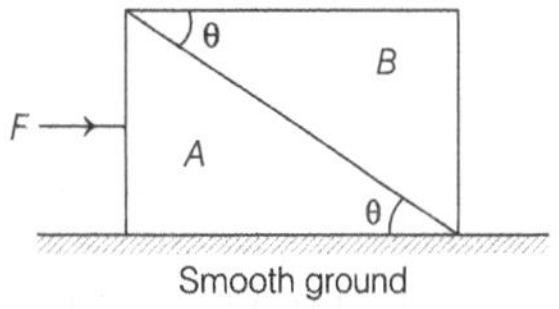

9 A 40 kg boy hangs from the midpoint of a rope, the ends of which are tied to two rings each of mass 5 kg which are free to move on a horizontal fixed rod (see figure). What is the maximum possible separation d (in m) of the rings when the boy is hanging in equilibrium, if the coefficient of static friction between the rings and rod is 4/5 ?

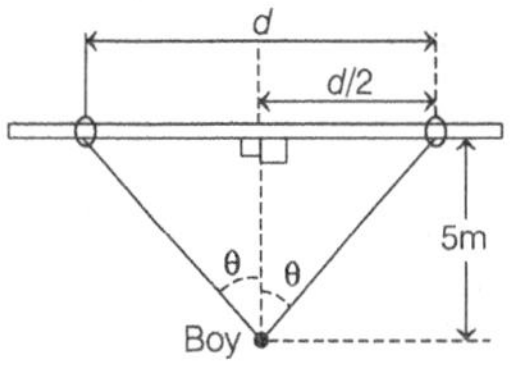

10 With two fingers, you hold a cone motionless upside down, as shown in figure. The mass of the cone is $(m = 1\ \text{kg})$, and the coefficient of static friction between your fingers and the cone is $(\mu = 0.5)$. What is the minimum normal force (in N) you must apply with each finger in order to hold up the cone? Consider only translational equilibrium.

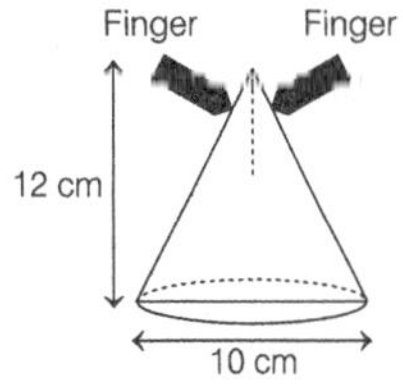

11 A uniform chain of length L has one of its ends attached to the wall at point A, while $\frac{3L}{4}$ of the length of the chain is lying on table as shown in figure. Find the minimum coefficient of friction between table and chain, so that chain remains in equilibrium.

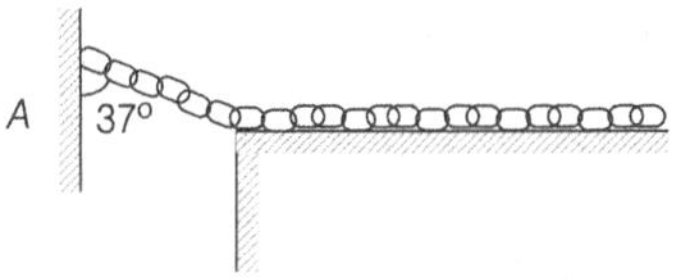

12 A block is kept on the rough horizontal surface and force acting on it as a function of time is shown by a graph. Find velocity (in m/s) of the particle at the end of 10 s.

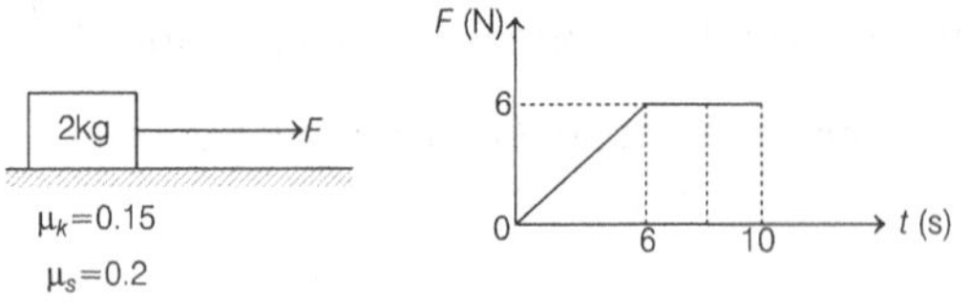

13 Two blocks of equal mass 2 kg are placed on a rough horizontal surface as shown and a force **F** is applied on the upper block. The system is initially at rest. Find acceleration of the lower block in m/s^2.

14 Horizontal force that a boy can apply on the stack of books is 120 N. Static friction coefficient between hand and book is 0.6, and between each book is 0.4. Mass of each book is 960 g. What is the maximum number of books that the boy can lift in one stack?

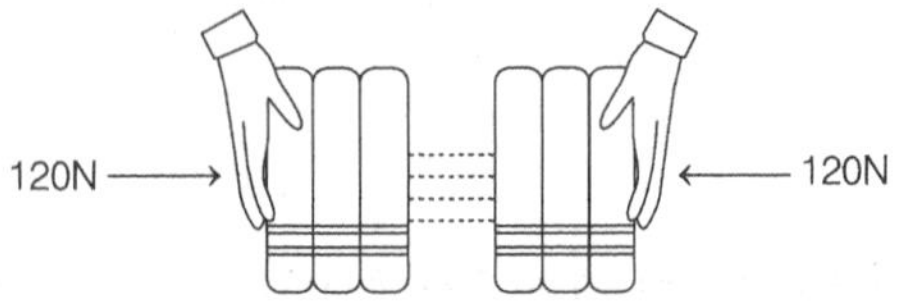

15 The figure shows the top view of a block *B* of negligible size and mass $m = 2$ kg lying on a smooth horizontal plane. The board *AC* moves with a constant acceleration $a_0 = 10 \text{m/s}^2$ in the direction shown. The coefficients of friction between the board and the block are $\mu_s = 0.6$ and $\mu_k = 0.5$. Calculate acceleration (in m/s^2) of the block relative to the board at the instant shown.

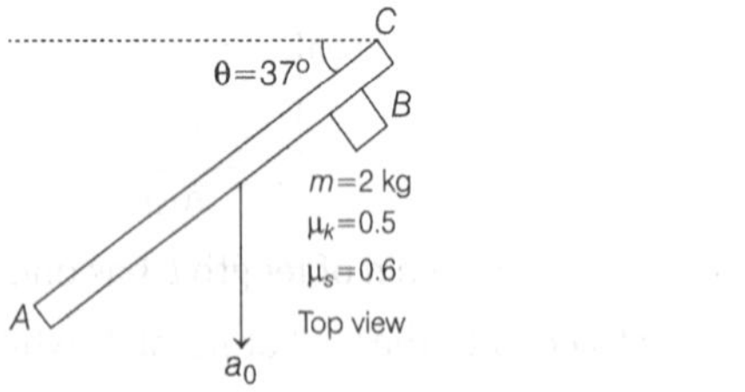

16 A force $F = 20$ N is applied to a block (at rest) as shown in figure. After the block has moved a distance of 126 m to the right, the direction of horizontal component of the force *F* is reversed. Find the velocity(in m/s) with which block arrives at its starting point.

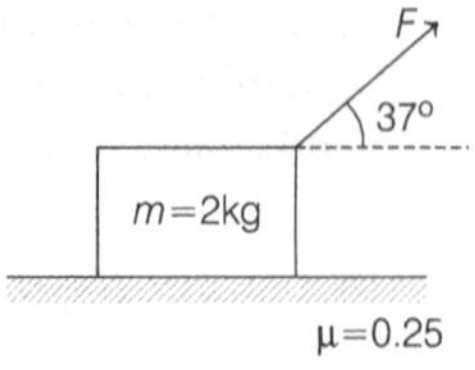

17 In the figure shown, the coefficient of friction between blocks *B* and *C* and also between *A* and *B* is 0.75, while contact between block *C* and wall is smooth. Mass of block *B* is negligible and mass of block *C* is 10 kg. Determine the minimum force *F* (in N) needed to cause upward impending motion of block *C*.

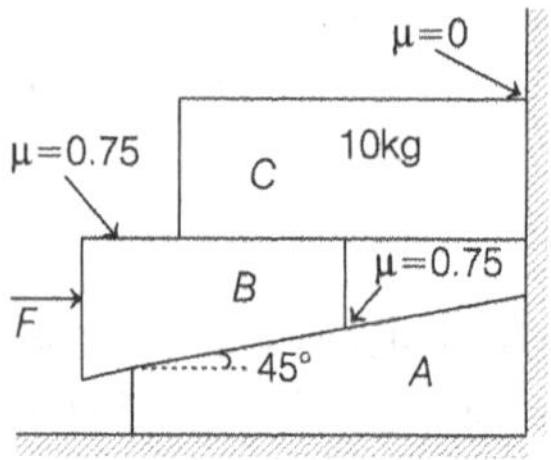

18 Two blocks each of mass *m* are connected as shown in figure. Pulleys are smooth and light. The coefficient of static friction at all surfaces is μ_s. If inclination θ is gradually increased, then θ at which the blocks begin to slide is given by $\theta = \tan^{-1}\left(\frac{100\mu_s}{p}\right)$. Find *p*.

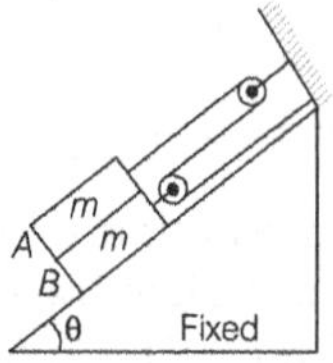

19 A cube of mass *m* slides down an inclined right angled trough as shown in figure. Two walls of the trough are equally inclined to the horizontal. If the coefficient of friction between the cube and the trough is $\frac{1}{2\sqrt{2}}$, then find acceleration of the cube in m/s^2.
($g = 10 \text{m/s}^2, \sin 53° = \frac{4}{5}, \cos 53° = \frac{3}{5}$)

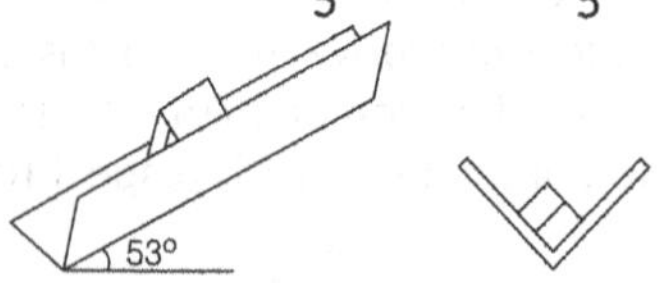

20 At what maximum mass *M* (in kg) will bars not slide over each other, if the coefficient of friction between the bars is equal to $\mu = \frac{1}{8}$, and the coefficient of friction on the plane is equal to zero? Threads are massless and inextensible, pulleys are ideal.

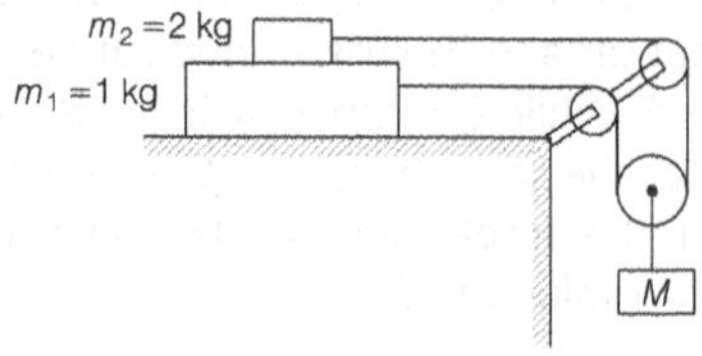

Previous Years' Questions

JEE Main

1 Given below are two statements:

Statement I The limiting force of static friction depends on the area of contact and independent of materials.

Statement II The limiting force of kinetic friction is independent of the area of contact and depends on materials.

In the light of the above statements, choose the **most appropriate** answer from the options given below [2024, 27 Jan Shift-II]

(a) Statement I is incorrect but Statement II is correct.
(b) Statement I is correct but Statement II is incorrect.
(c) Both Statement I and Statement II are incorrect.
(d) Both Statement I and Statement II are correct.

2 A block of mass m is placed on a surface having vertical cross-section given by $y = \frac{x^2}{4}$. If coefficient of friction is 0.5, the maximum height above the ground at which block can be placed without slipping is [2024, 30 Jan Shift-II]

(a) $\frac{1}{6}$ m (b) $\frac{1}{4}$ m
(c) $\frac{1}{3}$ m (d) $\frac{1}{2}$ m

3 A body of mass 10 kg is moving with an initial speed of 20 m/s. The body stops after 5 s due to friction between body and the floor. The value of the coefficient of friction is
(Take, acceleration due to gravity $g = 10\ \text{ms}^{-2}$) [2023, 31 Jan Shift-II]

(a) 0.3 (b) 0.5 (c) 0.4 (d) 0.2

4 A block of mass m slides down the plane inclined at angle 30° with an acceleration $g/4$. The value of coefficient of kinetic friction will be [2023, 29 Jan Shift-I]

(a) $\frac{2\sqrt{3}+1}{2}$ (b) $\frac{\sqrt{3}}{2}$ (c) $\frac{2\sqrt{3}-1}{2}$ (d) $\frac{1}{2\sqrt{3}}$

5 A block of mass 5 kg is placed at rest on a table of rough surface. Now, if a force of 30N is applied in the direction parallel to surface of the table, the block slides through a distance of 50 m in an interval of time 10s. Coefficient of kinetic friction is
(Given, $g = 10\ \text{ms}^{-2}$) [2023, 1 Feb Shift-I]

(a) 0.50 (b) 0.75 (c) 0.25 (d) 0.60

6 Consider a block kept on an inclined plane (inclined at 45°) as shown in the figure.
If the force required to just push it up the incline is 2 times the force required to just prevent it from sliding down. The coefficient of friction between the block and inclined plane (μ) is equal to [2023, 25 Jan Shift-II]

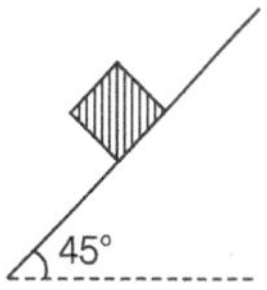

(a) 0.50 (b) 0.25 (c) 0.33 (d) 0.60

7 A bag is gently dropped on a conveyor belt moving at a speed of 2 m/s. The coefficient of friction between the conveyor belt and bag is 0.4. Initially the bag slips on the belt before it stops due to friction. The distance travelled by the bag on the belt during slipping motion is [Take, $g = 10\ \text{m/s}^2$] [2022, 27 July Shift-I]

(a) 2 m (b) 0.5 m (c) 3.2 m (d) 0.8 m

8 A block of mass M slides down on a rough inclined plane with constant velocity. The angle made by the incline plane with horizontal is θ. The magnitude of the contact force will be [2022, 27 July Shift-II]

(a) Mg (b) $Mg\cos\theta$
(c) $\sqrt{Mg\sin\theta + Mg\cos\theta}$ (d) $Mg\sin\theta\sqrt{1+\mu}$

9 A block of mass 40 kg slides over a surface, when a mass of 4 kg is suspended through an inextensible massless string passing over frictionless pulley as shown below. the coefficient of kinetic friction between the surface and block is 0.02. The acceleration of block is
(Given, $g = 10\ \text{ms}^{-2}$). [2022, 29 June Shift-II]

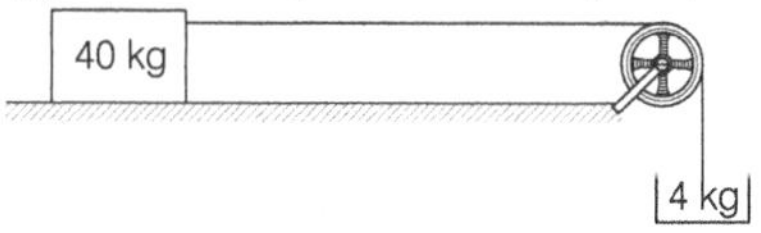

(a) $1\ \text{ms}^{-1}$ (b) $1/5\ \text{ms}^{-2}$
(c) $4/5\ \text{ms}^{-2}$ (d) $8/11\ \text{ms}^{2}$

10 A system of two blocks of masses $m = 2$ kg and $M = 8$ kg is placed on a smooth table as shown in figure. The coefficient of static friction between two blocks is 0.5. The maximum horizontal force F that can be applied to the block of mass M, so that the blocks move together will be [2022, 27 June Shift-I]

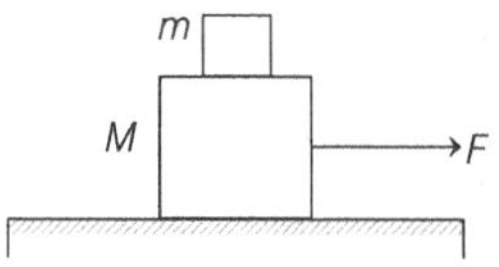

(a) 9.8 N (b) 39.2 N
(c) 49 N (d) 78.4 N

11 A block of mass 10 kg starts sliding on a surface with an initial velocity of 9.8 ms^{-1}. The coefficient of friction between the surface and block is 0.5. The distance covered by the block before coming to rest is [Use, $g = 9.8\ ms^{-2}$] **[2022, 24 June Shift-I]**

(a) 4.9 m (b) 9.8 m (c) 12.5 m (d) 19.6 m

12 A uniform chain of 6 m length is placed on a table such that a part of its length is hanging over the edge of the table. The system is at rest. The co-efficient of static friction between the chain and surface of the table is 0.5, the maximum length of the chain hanging from the table is .... m **[2022, 25 June Shift-I]**

13 A steel block of 10 kg rests on a horizontal floor as shown. When three iron cylinders are placed on it as shown, the block and cylinders go down with an acceleration 0.2 m/s^2.

The normal reaction R by the floor, if mass of the iron cylinders are equal and of 20 kg each, is ...... N. [Take, $g = 10\ m/s^2$ and $\mu_s = 0.2$] **[2021, 20 July Shift-I]**

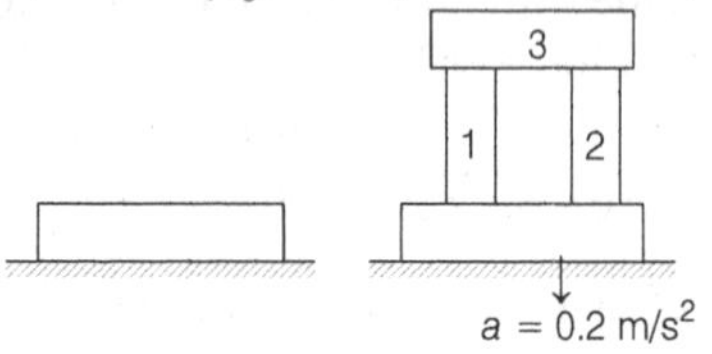

(a) 716 (b) 686 (c) 714 (d) 684

14 A block of mass m slides along a floor, while a force of magnitude F is applied to it at an angle θ as shown in figure. The coefficient of kinetic friction is μ_k. Then, the block's acceleration a is given by

(g is acceleration due to gravity) **[2021, 16 March Shift-I]**

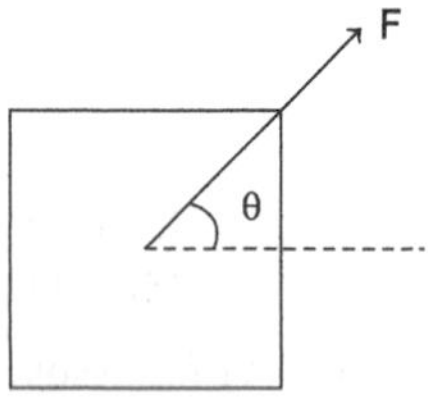

(a) $-\frac{F}{m}\cos\theta - \mu_k\left(g - \frac{F}{m}\sin\theta\right)$

(b) $\frac{F}{m}\cos\theta - \mu_k\left(g - \frac{F}{m}\sin\theta\right)$

(c) $\frac{F}{m}\cos\theta - \mu_k\left(g + \frac{F}{m}\sin\theta\right)$

(d) $\frac{F}{m}\cos\theta + \mu_k\left(g - \frac{F}{m}\sin\theta\right)$

15 A body of mass 1 kg rests on a horizontal floor with which it has a coefficient of static friction $1/\sqrt{3}$. It is desired to make the body move by applying the minimum possible force F N. The value of F will be .... (Round off to the nearest integer).

[Take $g = 10\ m\ s^{-2}$] **[2021, 17 March Shift-II]**

16 The coefficient of static friction between two blocks is 0.5 and the table is smooth. The maximum horizontal force that can be applied to move the blocks together is ....N.(Take, $g = 10\ ms^{-2}$) **[2021, 26 Aug Shift-II]**

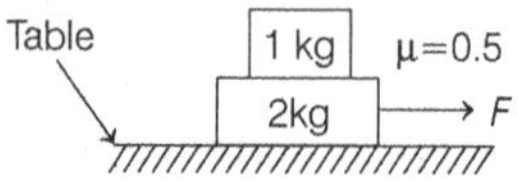

17 A body of mass 1 kg rests on a horizontal floor with which it has a coefficient of static friction $1/\sqrt{3}$. It is desired to make the body move by applying the minimum possible force F newton. The value of F will be .... (Round off to the nearest integer)

(Take, $g = 10\ ms^{-2}$) **[2021, 17 March Shift-II]**

JEE Advanced

1 A block of mass $m_1 = 1$ kg and another mass $m_2 = 2$ kg are placed together (see figure) on an inclined plane with angle of inclination θ. Various values of θ are given in List I. The coefficient of friction between the block m_1 and the plane is always zero. The coefficient of static and dynamic friction between the block m_2 and the plane are equal to $\mu = 0.3$.

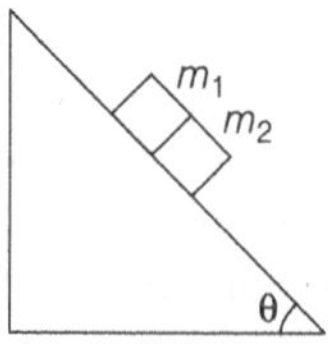

In List II expressions for the friction on the block m_2 are given. Match the correct expression of the friction in List II with the angles given in List I, and choose the correct option. The acceleration due to gravity is denoted by g.

[**Useful information** $\tan(5.5°) \approx 0.1$; $\tan(11.5°) \approx 0.2$; $\tan(16.5°) \approx 0.3$]

	List I		List II
P.	$\theta = 5°$	1.	$m_2 g \sin\theta$
Q.	$\theta = 10°$	2.	$(m_1 + m_2) g \sin\theta$
R.	$\theta = 15°$	3.	$\mu m_2 g \cos\theta$
S.	$\theta = 20°$	4.	$\mu (m_1 + m_2) g \cos\theta$

(2014 Adv.)

Codes

(a) P-1, Q-1, R-1, S-3 (b) P-2, Q-2, R-2, S-3

(c) P-2, Q-2, R-2, S-4 (d) P-2, Q-2, R-3, S-3

2 A small block of mass of 0.1 kg lies on a fixed inclined plane PQ which makes an angle θ with the horizontal. A horizontal force of 1 N acts on the block through its centre of mass as shown in the figure. The block remains stationary if
(Take $g = 10\ \text{m/s}^2$) **(2012)**

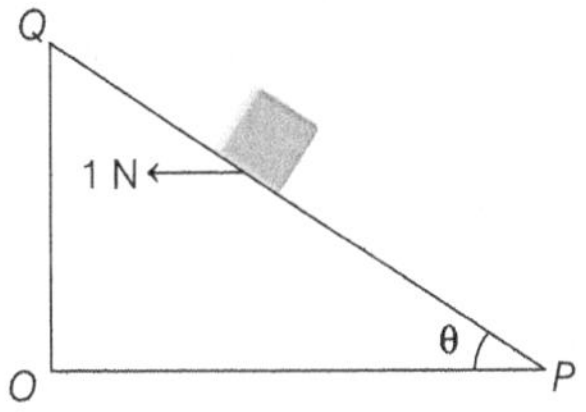

(a) $\theta = 45°$.
(b) $\theta > 45°$ and a frictional force acts on the block towards P
(c) $\theta > 45°$ and a frictional force acts on the block towards Q
(d) $\theta < 45°$ and a frictional force acts on the block towards Q

3 A block of mass m is on an inclined plane of angle θ. The coefficient of friction between the block and the plane is μ and $\tan\theta > \mu$. The block is held stationary by applying a force P parallel to the plane. The direction of force pointing up the plane is taken to be positive. As P is varied from $P_1 = mg(\sin\theta - \mu\cos\theta)$ to $P_2 = mg(\sin\theta + \mu\cos\theta)$, the frictional force f *versus* P graph will look like **(2010)**

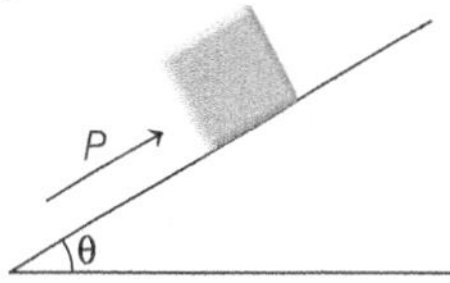

(a)
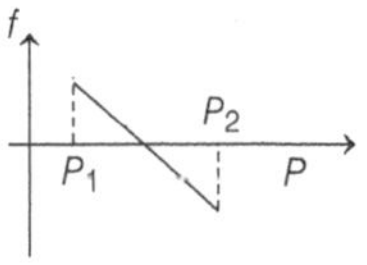

(b)
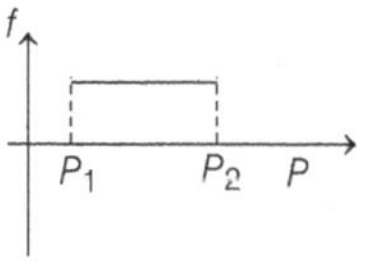

(c)
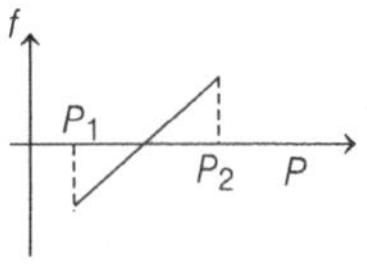

(d)
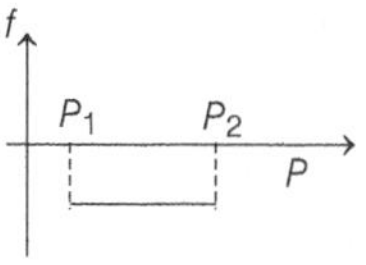

Answer Key

Level 1

1.

2.

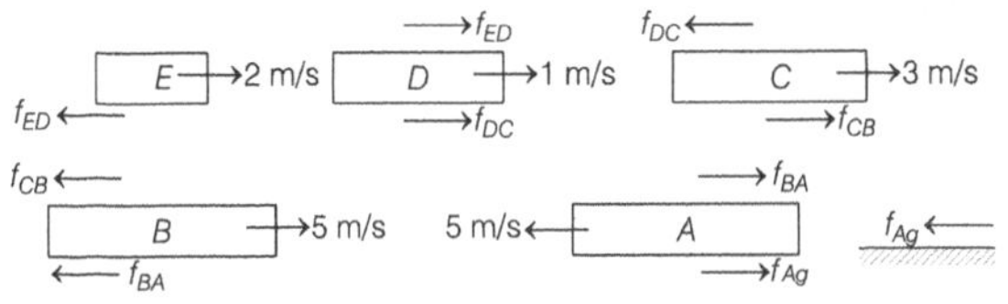

3. $s = 10$ m **4.** $s = 5$ m (b) 3.236s **5.** 20 N and $\mu_s \geq 0.5$

6. (a) $0\ \text{m/s}^2$, 0 N (b) $0\ \text{m/s}^2$, $f_s = 25$ N (c) $0\ \text{m/s}^2$, $f_L = 30$ N
(d) $1.2\ \text{m/s}^2$, $f_k = 25$ N

7. 0.4 and 0.35 **8.** (a) $0.5\ \text{m/s}^2$ (b) 0 (c) $0.1\ \text{m/s}^2$

9. (a) 0 (b) $10/3\ \text{m/s}^2$ up the wall (c) 0

10. (a) $2\ \text{m/s}^2$ down, 40 N (kinetic), up
(b) $1\ \text{m/s}^2$ down, 40 N (kinetic), up
(c) $0\ \text{m/s}^2$, 40 N (limiting), up
(d) $0\ \text{m/s}^2$, 20 N (static), up
(e) $0\ \text{m/s}^2$, 0 N
(f) $0\ \text{m/s}^2$, 10 N (static), down
(g) $0\ \text{m/s}^2$, 40 N (limiting), down
(h) $1\ \text{m/s}^2$ up, 40 N (kinetic), down

11. $F_{\min} = 60$ N **12.** $1.25\ \text{m/s}^2$ **13.** $\mu \geq 2$ **14.** $\dfrac{g}{\mu}$

15. $\dfrac{12}{19}$ **16.** (a) $\theta \leq \tan^{-1}\mu$ (b) $mg\sin\left(\dfrac{\theta}{2}\right)$

17. $\mu_k = \dfrac{1}{2\sqrt{3}}$ **18.** $\dfrac{\mu mg}{\sqrt{1+\mu^2}}$, $\tan^{-1}\mu$

19. (a) $mg\sin\theta + \mu mg\cos\theta$ (b) $mg\sin\theta - \mu mg\cos\theta$
(c) $mg(\sin\theta - \mu\cos\theta)$

20. (a) $0.4\ \text{m/s}^2$ and $2\ \text{m/s}^2$ (b) $14/15\ \text{m/s}^2$ and $14/15\ \text{m/s}^2$

21. $0\ \text{m/s}^2$ and 10 N (static) up the plane

22. 10.5 kg **23.** M/3 **24.** 0.33 **25.** 3 m/s

26. (a) $2.5\ \text{m/s}^2$, $2.5\ \text{m/s}^2$ (b) $5.1\ \text{m/s}^2$, $5\ \text{m/s}^2$
(c) $3\ \text{m/s}^2$, $3\ \text{m/s}^2$ (d) $1\ \text{m/s}^2$, $0\ \text{m/s}^2$
(e) $5\ \text{m/s}^2$, $10\ \text{m/s}^2$ (f) $1\ \text{m/s}^2$, $1\ \text{m/s}^2$
(g) $0\ \text{m/s}^2$, $3.33\ \text{m/s}^2$ (h) $20\ \text{m/s}^2$, $0\ \text{m/s}^2$

27. (a) False (b) True (c) True (d) False
(e) True (f) True (g) False (h) False
(i) True (j) False (k) False (l) True
(m) False

Level 2

Single Choice Correct Questions

1. (c)	2. (a)	3. (c)	4. (d)	5. (a)
6. (d)	7. (c)	8. (a)	9. (c)	10. (c)
11. (b)	12. (c)	13. (a)	14. (a)	15. (d)
16. (d)	17. (b)	18. (c)	19. (a)	20. (c)
21. (c)	22. (a)	23. (a)	24. (c)	25. (c)
26. (b)	27. (a)	28. (c)	29. (c)	30. (c)
31. (d)	32. (a)	33. (b)	34. (a)	35. (c)
36. (b)	37. (a)	38. (b)	39. (b)	40. (a)

Numerical Value Questions

1. 20	2. 0.75	3. 0.5	4. 0.98	5. 54
6. 28	7. 2	8. 22	9. 4	10. 20
11. 250	12. 2	13. 7	14. 0.4	15. 48

Level 3

Single Choice Correct Questions

1. (b)	2. (c)	3. (d)	4. (d)	5. (d)
6. (c)	7. (a)	8. (a)	9. (b)	10. (b)
11. (a)	12. (b)	13. (c)	14. (a)	15. (b)
16. (d)	17. (c)	18. (c)	19. (d)	20. (b)
21. (b)	22. (c)	23. (a)	24. (b)	25. (b)
26. (b)	27. (d)	28. (a)	29. (d)	30. (a)
31. (d)	32. (a)	33. (d)	34. (d)	35. (b)
36. (a)	37. (d)			

Multiple Choice(s) Correct Questions

1. *abc*	2. *bc*	3. *ac*	4. *abcd*	5. *bc*
6. *bcd*	7. *abd*	8. *abc*	9. *cd*	10. *ad*
11. *ad*	12. *ab*	13. *ad*	14. *ac*	15. *ac*
16. *ac*	17. *abc*	18. *abc*		

Comprehension Based Questions

1. (b)	2. (a)	3. (d)	4. (c)	5. (d)
6. (a)	7. (d)	8. (a)	9. (d)	10. (b)
11. (d)	12. (d)	13. (c)	14. (a)	15. (c)
16. (a)	17. (d)	18. (b)	19. (a)	20. (a)
21. (d)	22. (c)	23. (c)	24. (a)	25. (d)
26. (a)	27. (b)	28. (b)	29. (a)	30. (b)
31. (b)	32. (a)	33. (d)	34. (d)	35. (a)
36. (c)	37. (b)	38. (a)		

Match the Columns Questions

1. a → r, b → q, c → p , d → s
2. a → pr, b → ps ; c → qr ; d → qs
3. a → q, s; b → p , r; c → qr ; d → q,r
4. a → t; b → r; c → s ; d → q
5. a → r, b → s, c → q, d → p
6. a → q, s; b → r ; c → p, s; d → q,s

Numerical Value Questions

1. 14	2. 30	3. 12	4. 78.4	5. 0.30
6. 10	7. 7	8. 5	9. 10	10. 65
11. 0.25	12. 8	13. 5	14. 12	15. 2
16. 56	17. 775	18. 20	19. 5	20. 3

Previous Year's Questions

JEE Main

1. (a)	2. (b)	3. (c)	4. (d)	5. (a)
6. (c)	7. (b)	8. (a)	9. (d)	10. (c)
11. (b)	12. (2)	13. (b)	14. (b)	15. (5)
16. (15)	17. (5)			

JEE Advanced

1. (d)	2. (c)	3. (a)

SOLUTIONS

Level 1

1. (a)

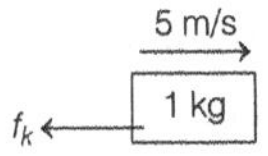

(b)

2.

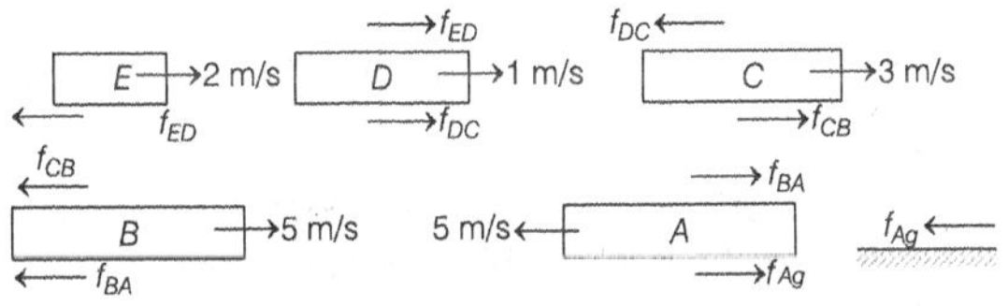

3.

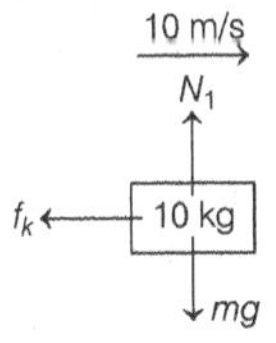

$\Sigma F_y = 0 \Rightarrow N_1 = mg = 100$ N

$f_k = \mu_k N_1 = 0.5(100) = 50$ N

$\Sigma F_x = ma \Rightarrow -50 = 10a \Rightarrow a = -5$ m/s^2

$v^2 = u^2 + 2as \Rightarrow 0^2 = 10^2 + 2(-5)s \Rightarrow s = 10$ m

4. (a)

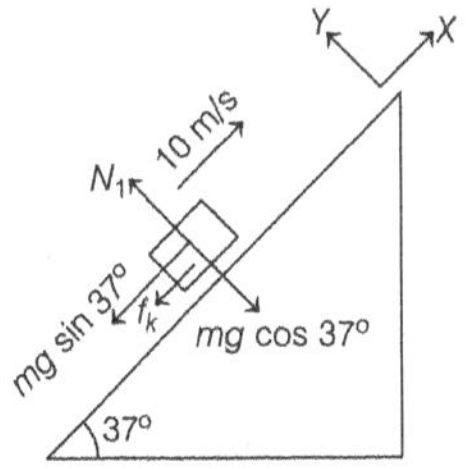

$\Sigma F_y = 0 \Rightarrow +N_1 - mg\cos 37° = 0 \Rightarrow N_1 = mg\cos 37°$

$f_k = \mu_k N = 0.5(mg\cos 37°)$

$\Sigma F_x = ma_x$

$\Rightarrow -mg\sin 37° - 0.5(mg\cos 37°) = ma_x \Rightarrow a_x = -10$ m/s^2

$v^2 = u^2 + 2as \Rightarrow 0^2 = 10^2 + 2(-10)s \Rightarrow s = 5$ m

(b) For time of ascent (t_1)

$v = u + at \Rightarrow 0 = 10 + (-10)t_1 \Rightarrow t_1 = 1$s

For time of descent,

$\Sigma F_x = ma_x \Rightarrow mg\sin 37° - \mu mg\cos 37° = ma$

$\Rightarrow a = 2$ m/s^2

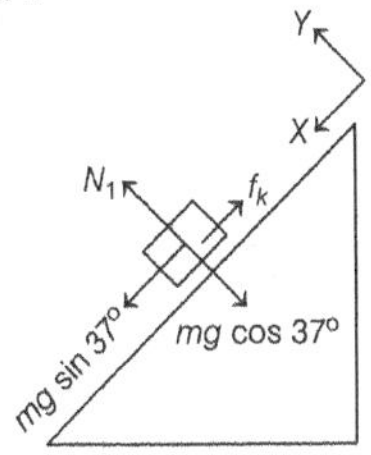

$s = ut + \frac{1}{2}at^2 \Rightarrow 5 = 0 + \frac{1}{2}(2)t_2^2 \Rightarrow t_2 = \sqrt{5}$s

Total time $= t_1 + t_2 = (1 + \sqrt{5})$s

5.

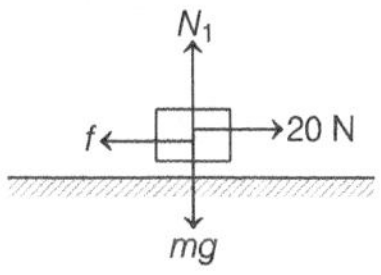

$\Sigma F_y = 0 \Rightarrow N_1 - 40 = 0 \Rightarrow N_1 = 40$ N

Since, the block is not moving.

$\Sigma F_x = 0 \Rightarrow 20 - f = 0 \Rightarrow f = 20$ N (static)

$f \le f_L \Rightarrow 20 \le \mu_s(N_1) \Rightarrow \mu_s \ge 0.5$

6. $f_L = \mu_s N \Rightarrow f_L = 0.6(50) = 30$ N

$f_k = \mu_k N \Rightarrow f_k = 0.5(50) = 25$ N

(a) Since, no force is applied, frictional force will be zero.

(b) Since, applied force is less than limiting friction, block won't move and static friction will be equal to the force applied, i.e. 25 N.

(c) Since $F = f_L$, the block is on verge of motion. So, $a = 0$ and $f_L = 30$ N.

(d) Since $F > f_L$, the block will be set into motion and nature of friction will be kinetic.

$F - f_k = ma \Rightarrow 31 - 25 = 5a \Rightarrow a = 1.2$ m/s^2

7. $f_L = \mu_s N = 8 \Rightarrow \mu_s = \frac{8}{20} = 0.4$

$f_k = \mu_k N = 7 \Rightarrow \mu_k = \frac{7}{20} = 0.35$

8. (a)

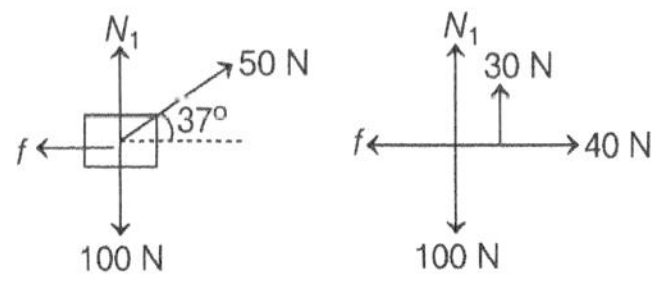

$\Sigma F_y = 0 \Rightarrow N_1 + 50\sin 37° - 100 = 0$

$\Rightarrow N_1 = 70$ N $\Rightarrow f_L = \mu_s N = 0.5(70) = 35$ N

$\Sigma F_x = ma_x \Rightarrow 40 - 35 = 10a_x \Rightarrow a_x = 0.5$ m/s^2

(b)

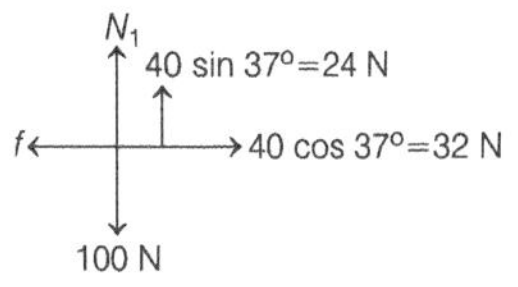

$\Sigma F_y = 0 \Rightarrow +N_1 + 24 - 100 = 0$

$\Rightarrow N_1 = 76$ N

$\Rightarrow f_L = \mu_s N = 0.5(76) = 38$ N

Since, driving force is less than the limiting friction, the block will not move. So, $a = 0$.

(c) $\Sigma F_y = 0$

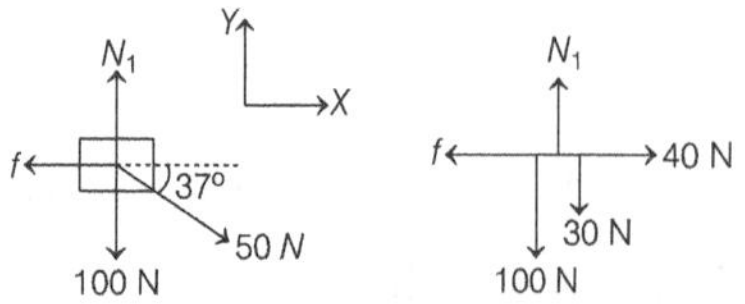

$\Rightarrow \quad N_1 - 100 - 30 = 0 \quad \Rightarrow \quad N_1 = 130$ N

$f_L = \mu_s N_1 \Rightarrow f_L = 0.3(130) = 39$ N

$\Sigma F_x = ma_x \quad \Rightarrow 40 - 39 = 10a_x \Rightarrow a_x = 0.1 \text{ m/s}^2$

9. (a)

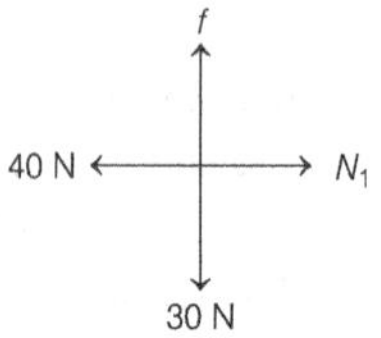

$\Sigma F_x = 0 \quad \Rightarrow \quad N_1 - 40 = 0 \quad \Rightarrow N_1 = 40$ N

$f_L = \mu_s N \quad \Rightarrow f_L = 0.8(40) = 32$ N

Since, $f_L \geq 30$ N, the block won't move.

So, $\quad a = 0$

(b)

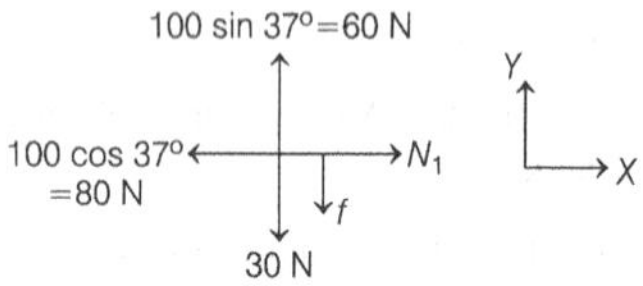

$\Sigma F_x = 0 \quad \Rightarrow +N_1 - 80 = 0 \quad \Rightarrow N_1 = 80$ N

$f_L = \mu_s N \quad \Rightarrow f_L = 0.25(80) = 20$ N

In absence of friction, driving force on the block is $60 - 30 = 30$ N up the wall which is more than the limiting friction. So, block will accelerate up the wall.

$\Sigma F_y = ma_y \quad \Rightarrow 60 - 30 - 20 = 3a_y \quad \Rightarrow a_y = \dfrac{10}{3} \text{ m/s}^2$

(c)

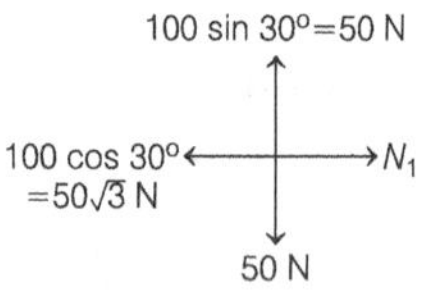

Since, driving force is zero in absence of friction, no friction will act

$\Rightarrow \qquad f = 0$ and $a = 0$

10.

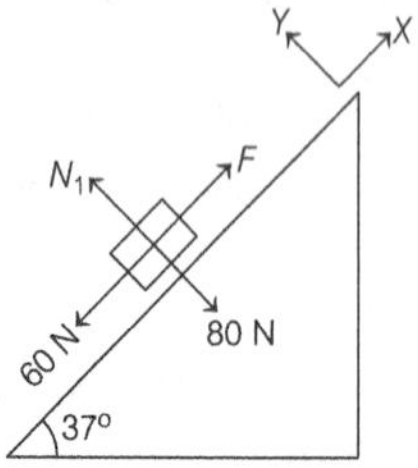

$\Sigma F_y = 0 \quad \Rightarrow +N_1 - 80 = 0$

$\Rightarrow \quad N_1 = 80$ N $\quad \Rightarrow \quad f_L = \mu_s N = 0.5(80) = 40$ N

(a) $\quad F = 0$ N

Friction will 40 N (kinetic) up the place,

$\Sigma F_x = ma \quad \Rightarrow 60 - 40 = 10a$

$\Rightarrow \qquad a = 2 \text{ m/s}^2$, down the plane

(b) $\qquad F = 10$ N

Friction will be kinetic 40 N up the plane,

$\Sigma F_x = ma \quad \Rightarrow 60 - 10 - 40 = ma$

$\Rightarrow \qquad a = 1 \text{ m/s}^2$, down the plane

(c) $\qquad F = 20$ N

Friction will be 40 N limiting up the plane.

$a = 0$

$\Sigma F = ma \quad \Rightarrow 50 - 40 = 8a \quad \Rightarrow a = 1.25 \text{ m/s}^2$

(d) $\qquad F = 40$ N

Since, driving force $(60 - 40 = 20 \text{ N})$ is less than the limiting friction, the block will not move.

So, $a = 0$ and $f_S = 20$ N, up the plane

(e) $F = 60$ N, $\quad f = 0$ and $a = 0$

(f) $F = 70$ N

Since, driving force $(70 - 60 = 10 \text{ N})$ is less than the limiting friction, the block will not move.

So, $a = 0$ and $f_S = 10$ N, down the plane

(g) $F = 100$ N, $a = 0$ and $f_L = 40$ N, down the plane

(h) $\qquad F = 110$ N

$\Sigma F_x = ma_x \quad \Rightarrow \quad 110 - 60 - 40 = 10a$

$\Rightarrow \qquad a = 1 \text{ m/s}^2$, up the plane

and $\qquad f_k = 40$ N, down the plane

11. $\qquad \Sigma F_y = 0 \quad \Rightarrow +N_1 - 100 - f = 0$

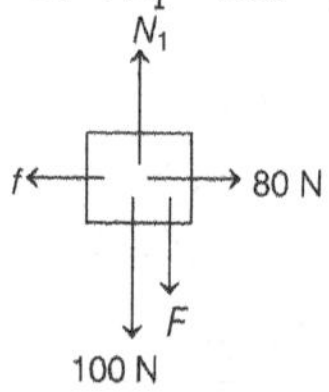

$\Rightarrow \qquad N_1 = 100 + F \quad \Rightarrow \quad f_L = 0.5(100 + F)$

For block not to move,

$80 \leq f_L \quad \Rightarrow \quad 80 \leq 0.5(100 + F)$

$\Rightarrow \qquad F \geq 60 \text{ N} \quad \Rightarrow \quad F_{min} = 60$ N

12. $\Sigma F_y = 0 \quad \Rightarrow N_1 - 80 = 0 \quad \Rightarrow N_1 = 80$ N

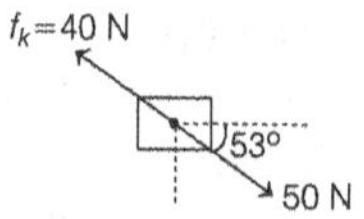

$f_L = \mu_s N = 0.5(80) = 40$ N

$\Sigma F = ma \Rightarrow 50 - 40 = 8a \quad \Rightarrow a = 1.25 \text{ m/s}^2$

13.

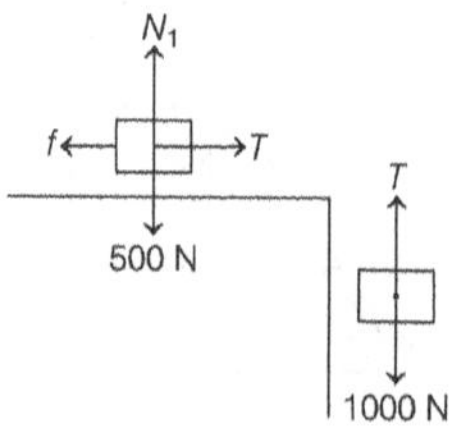

For 100 kg block,

$$\Sigma F_y = 0 \Rightarrow T - 1000 = 0 \Rightarrow T = 1000 \text{ N}$$

For 50 kg block,

$$\Sigma F_y = 0 \Rightarrow N_1 - 500 = 0 \Rightarrow N_1 = 500 \text{ N}$$

$$\Sigma F_x = 0 \Rightarrow T - f = 0 \Rightarrow f = T = 1000 \text{ N}$$

$$f_L = \mu N_1 = \mu(500)$$

$$f \le f_L \Rightarrow 1000 \le 500(\mu) \Rightarrow \mu \ge 2$$

14. Lets take acceleration of cart as a

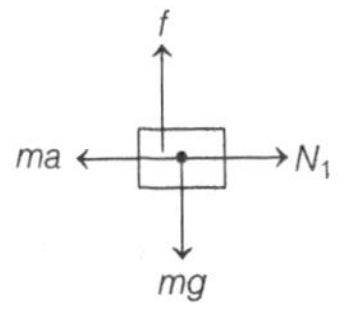

$$\Sigma F_x = 0 \Rightarrow N_1 = ma$$

$$\Sigma F_y = 0 \Rightarrow f = mg$$

and $\quad f \le f_L \Rightarrow mg \le \mu N_1 \Rightarrow a \ge \dfrac{g}{\mu} \Rightarrow a_{min} = \dfrac{g}{\mu}$

15.

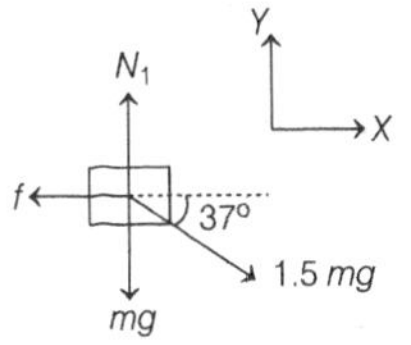

$$\Sigma F_y = 0 \Rightarrow +N_1 - mg - 1.5mg \sin 37° = 0 \Rightarrow N_1 = 1.9mg$$

$$\Sigma F_x = ma_x \Rightarrow 1.5mg \cos 37° - \mu N_1 = m(0)$$

$$\Rightarrow \mu = \frac{1.5mg \cos 37°}{1.9mg} \Rightarrow \mu = \frac{12}{19}$$

16.

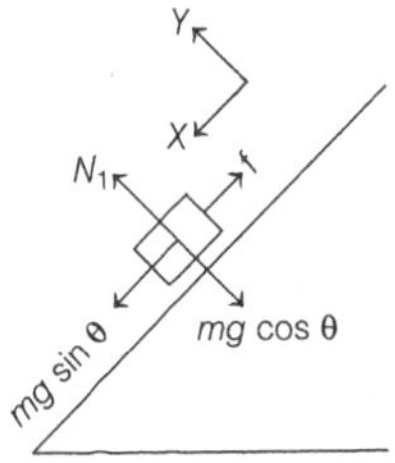

(a) $\Sigma F_y = 0 \Rightarrow +N_1 - mg \cos\theta = 0 \Rightarrow N_1 = mg \cos\theta$

$\Sigma F_x = ma_x = 0 \Rightarrow mg \sin\theta - f = 0 \Rightarrow f = mg \sin\theta$

$f \le f_L \Rightarrow mg \sin\theta \le \mu_s mg \cos\theta \Rightarrow \theta \le \tan^{-1}(\mu)$

(b) The block will not slide down.

So, the friction will be $mg \sin\left(\dfrac{\theta}{2}\right)$ (static), up the plane.

17.

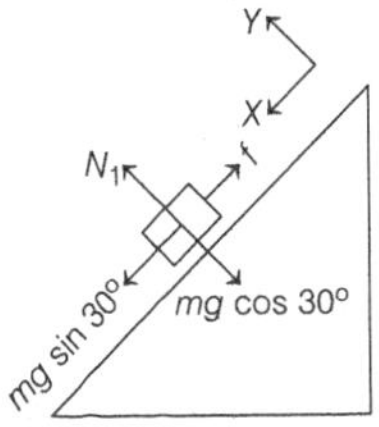

$$\Sigma F_y = 0 \Rightarrow +N_1 - mg \cos 30° = 0$$

$$\Rightarrow \quad N_1 = mg \cos 30°$$

$$\Sigma F_x = ma_x$$

$$\Rightarrow mg \sin 30° - \mu_k(mg \cos 30°) = m\left(\frac{g}{4}\right)$$

$$\Rightarrow \quad \mu_k = \frac{1}{2\sqrt{3}}$$

18.

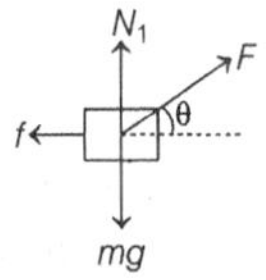

$$\Sigma F_y = 0 \Rightarrow N_1 + F \sin\theta = mg \Rightarrow N_1 = mg - F \sin\theta$$

For just moving the block,

$$F \cos\theta = \mu(mg - F \sin\theta)$$

$$\Rightarrow \quad F = \frac{\mu mg}{\cos\theta + \mu \sin\theta}$$

$$y = \cos\theta + \mu \sin\theta$$

To minimise F, we have to maximise y.

$$\frac{dy}{d\theta} = -\sin\theta + \mu \cos\theta = 0 \Rightarrow \tan\theta = \mu$$

So, at angle $\theta = \tan^{-1}(\mu)$, F is minimum

and $\quad F_{min} = \dfrac{\mu mg}{\sqrt{1+\mu^2}}$

19. (a) $F = mg \sin\theta + \mu mg \cos\theta$

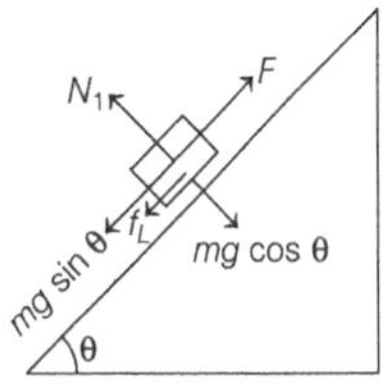

(b) $F + f_L = mg \sin\theta \Rightarrow F = mg \sin\theta - \mu mg \cos\theta$

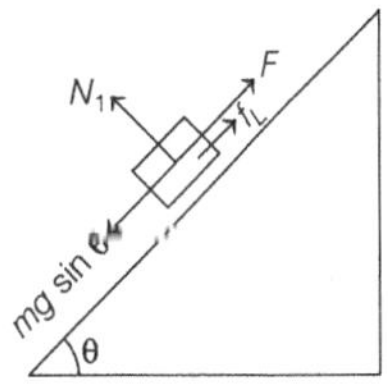

(c) $N_1 = mg \cos\theta + F$ and $mg \sin\theta = \mu(mg \cos\theta + F)$

$\Rightarrow F = mg(\sin\theta - \mu \cos\theta)$

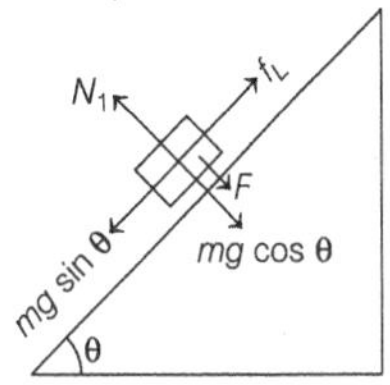

20. (a) For 10 kg block,

$$mg \sin\theta - \mu mg \cos\theta = ma$$

$$\Rightarrow \quad a = g \sin\theta - \mu g \cos\theta$$

$$\Rightarrow \quad a = 10\left(\frac{3}{5}\right) - 0.5(10)\left(\frac{4}{5}\right) \Rightarrow a = 2 \text{ m/s}^2$$

For 5 kg block,

$$a = g\sin\theta - \mu g\cos\theta$$

$$\Rightarrow \quad a = 10\left(\frac{3}{5}\right) - (0.7)(10)\left(\frac{4}{5}\right) \Rightarrow a = 0.4\ \text{m/s}^2$$

(b) For (10 kg + 5 kg) system,

$$\Sigma F_x = ma_x$$

$$\Rightarrow (m_1 g\sin\theta + m_2 g\sin\theta) - \mu_1 m_1 g\cos\theta - \mu_2 m_2 g\cos\theta = (m_1 + m_2)a$$

$$\Rightarrow (50\sin 37^\circ + 100\sin 37^\circ) - 0.5\times 50 \times \cos 37^\circ - 0.7\times 100\cos 37^\circ = 15a$$

$$\Rightarrow a = \frac{14}{15}\ \text{m/s}^2$$

21. $N_1 = 80$ N

$f_L = \mu N_1 \Rightarrow f_L = 0.5\times 80 \Rightarrow f_L = 40$ N

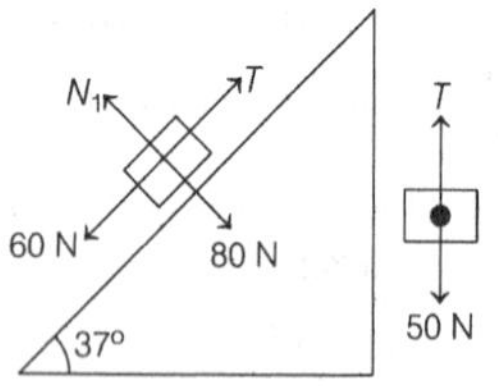

In absence of friction, driving force on the (10 kg + 5 kg) system is 10 N along the string. Since, 10 N $< f_L$, system will be in equilibrium.

So, $a = 0$ and static friction will be 10 N, up the plane.

22. For block A,

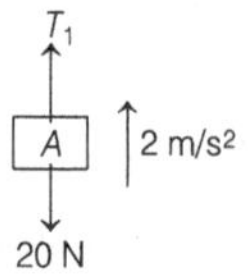

$$\Sigma F_y = ma_y \Rightarrow T_1 - 20 = 2(2) \Rightarrow T_1 = 24\ \text{N}$$

For block B,

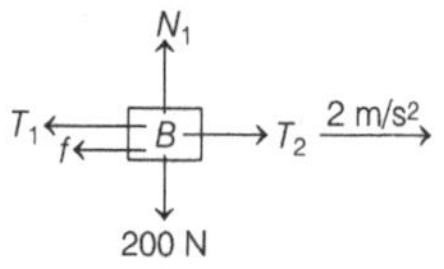

$$\Sigma F_x = ma_x \Rightarrow T_2 - T_1 - f = 20(2)$$

$$\Rightarrow \quad T_2 - 24 - 0.1(200) = 40 \Rightarrow T_2 = 84\ \text{N}$$

For block C,

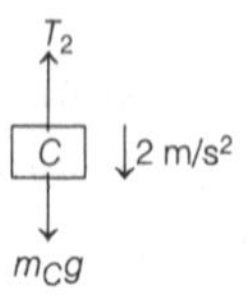

$$\Sigma F_y = ma_y \Rightarrow m_C(10) - 84 = m_C(2)$$

$$\Rightarrow \quad m_C = \frac{84}{8} = 10.5\ \text{kg}$$

23. $Mg\sin 30^\circ - \mu Mg\cos 30^\circ - T = M(0)$

$$\Rightarrow \quad T = \frac{Mg}{3} \text{ and } mg - T = 0 \Rightarrow m = \frac{M}{3}$$

24. $f = \mu\left(\frac{3Mg}{4}\right)$

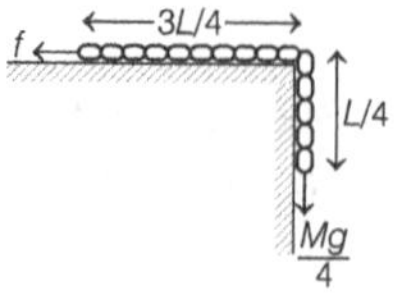

$$\frac{Mg}{4} = \mu\left(\frac{3Mg}{4}\right) \Rightarrow \mu = \frac{1}{3}$$

25. $f_k = \mu mg = ma \Rightarrow a = \mu g = 2\ \text{m/s}^2$

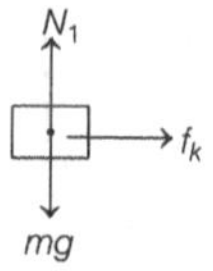

$$v = u + at \Rightarrow v = -5 + 2(4) = 3\ \text{m/s}$$

26. (a) Taking both the blocks as a system,

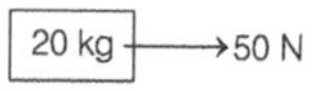

$$\Sigma F = ma \Rightarrow 50 = 20a \Rightarrow a = 2.5\ \text{m/s}^2$$

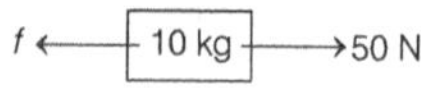

For upper 10 kg block,

$50 - f = 10(2.5) \Rightarrow f = 25$ N and $f_L = 0.5(100) = 50$ N

Since, $f < f_L$

Friction between both the blocks is static & common acceleration is 2.5 m/s^2.

(b)

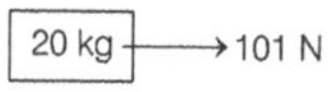

$$\Sigma F = ma \Rightarrow 101 = 20a \Rightarrow a = 5.05\ \text{m/s}^2$$

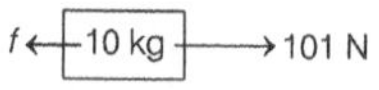

$$\Sigma F = ma \Rightarrow 101 - f = 10(5.05) \Rightarrow f = 50.5\ \text{N}$$

Since $f > f_L$; our assumption is wrong. Friction between the blocks will be kinetic.

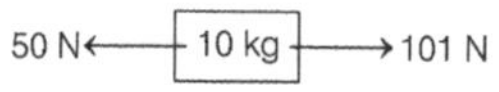

$$\Sigma F = ma \Rightarrow 101 - 50 = 10a \Rightarrow a = 5.1\ \text{m/s}^2$$

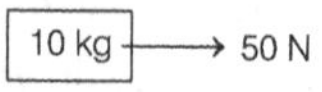

$$\Sigma F = ma \Rightarrow 50 = 10a \Rightarrow a = 5\ \text{m/s}^2$$

(c) For system,

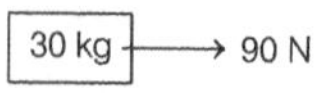

$$\Sigma F = ma \Rightarrow 90 = 30a \Rightarrow a = 3\ \text{m/s}^2$$

For 10 kg block,

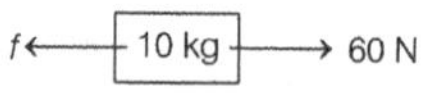

$$\Sigma F = ma \Rightarrow 60 - f = 10(3) \Rightarrow f = 30\ \text{N}$$

and $f_L = 0.5(100) = 50$ N

Since $f < f_L$; our assumption is correct.

Both the blocks will move with common acceleration of 3 m/s^2.

(d)

$f \leftarrow$ [15 kg] $\rightarrow$ 30 N

$$f_L = 0.5(150) = 75 \text{ N}$$

Since, applied force is less than the limiting friction, acceleration of system will be zero.

So, both the blocks cannot move together.

25 N $\leftarrow$ [5 kg] $\rightarrow$ 30 N

$$\Sigma F = ma \Rightarrow 30 - 25 = 5a \Rightarrow a = 1 \text{ m/s}^2$$

$f \leftarrow$ [10 kg] $\rightarrow$ 25 N

$$f = 25 \text{ N} \quad \text{and} \quad a = 0$$

(e)

75 N $\leftarrow$ [15 kg] $\rightarrow$ 200 N

$$\Rightarrow \quad 200 - 75 = 15a \Rightarrow a = \frac{125}{15} = \frac{25}{3} \text{ m/s}^2$$

[5 kg] $\rightarrow f$

$$f = 5a = 5\left(\frac{25}{3}\right) = \frac{125}{3} \text{ N} \quad \text{and} \quad f_L = 0.5(50) = 25\text{N}$$

Since $f > f_L$; our assumption is wrong.

[5 kg] $\rightarrow$ 25 N

$$\Sigma F = ma \Rightarrow 25 = 5a \Rightarrow a = 5 \text{ m/s}^2$$

25 N $\leftarrow$, 75 N $\leftarrow$ [10 kg] $\rightarrow$ 200 N

$$\Sigma F = ma \Rightarrow 20 - 75 - 25 = 10a \Rightarrow a = 10 \text{ m/s}^2$$

(f)

75 N $\leftarrow$ [15 kg] $\rightarrow$ 90 N

$$\Rightarrow \quad 90 - 75 = 15a \Rightarrow a = 1 \text{ m/s}^2$$

[5 kg] $\rightarrow f$

$$f = 5(1) = 5 \text{ N} \quad \text{and} \quad f_L = 0.5(50) = 25 \text{ N}$$

Since $f < f_L$; our assumption is correct.

Both the blocks will move together with common acceleration of 1 m/s^2.

(g)

20 N $\leftarrow$ [5 kg] $\rightarrow$ 10 N

$$\Sigma F = ma \Rightarrow 20 - 10 = 5a \Rightarrow a = 2 \text{ m/s}^2\text{, left}$$

$f \leftarrow$ [2 kg] $\rightarrow$ 10 N

$$f - 10 = 2(2) \Rightarrow f = 14 \text{ N} \Rightarrow f_L = 0.5(20) = 10 \text{ N}$$

Since $f > f_L$, our assumption is wrong.

10 N $\leftarrow$ [2 kg] $\rightarrow$ 10 N

$$\Sigma F = ma \Rightarrow 10 - 10 = 2a \Rightarrow a = 0$$

20 N $\leftarrow$ [3 kg] $\rightarrow$ 10 N

$$\Sigma F = ma \Rightarrow 20 - 10 = 3a$$

$$\Rightarrow \quad a = \frac{10}{3} \text{ m/s}^2\text{, left}$$

(h)

15 N $\leftarrow$ [5 kg] $\rightarrow$ 50 N

$$\Sigma F = ma \Rightarrow 50 - 15 = 5a \Rightarrow a = 7 \text{ m/s}^2$$

$f \leftarrow$ [2 kg] $\rightarrow$ 50 N

$$50 - f = 2(7) \Rightarrow f = 36 \text{ N} \Rightarrow f_L = 0.5(20) = 10 \text{ N}$$

Since $f > f_L$, our assumption is wrong.

10 N $\leftarrow$ [2 kg] $\rightarrow$ 50 N

$$\Sigma F = ma \Rightarrow 50 - 10 = 2a \Rightarrow a = 20 \text{ m/s}^2$$

$f \leftarrow$ [3 kg] $\rightarrow$ 10 N

$$f = 10 \text{ N and } a = 0$$

Level 2

Single Choice Correct Questions

1. For smooth inclined plane

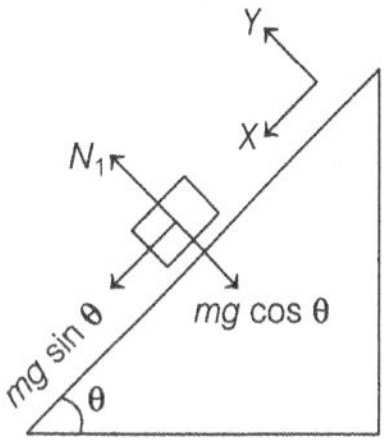

$$\Sigma F_x = ma_x \Rightarrow mg\sin\theta = ma \Rightarrow a = g\sin\theta$$

$$s = ut + \frac{1}{2}at^2 \Rightarrow d = \frac{1}{2}(g\sin\theta)t_1^2$$

$$\Rightarrow \quad t_1 = \sqrt{\frac{2d}{g\sin\theta}}$$

For rough inclined plane,

$$\Sigma F_x = ma_x \Rightarrow mg\sin\theta - \mu_k mg\cos\theta = ma$$

$$\Rightarrow \quad a = g\sin\theta - \mu_k g\cos\theta$$

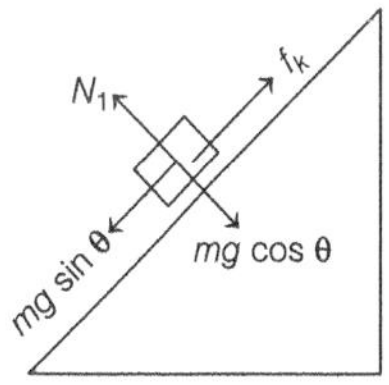

$$s = ut + \frac{1}{2}at^2 \Rightarrow d = \frac{1}{2}(g\sin\theta - \mu_k g\cos\theta)t_2^2$$

$$\Rightarrow \quad t_2 = \sqrt{\frac{2d}{g(\sin\theta - \mu_k\cos\theta)}}$$

and we are given $t_2 = nt_1$

$$\Rightarrow \quad \sqrt{\frac{2d}{g(\sin\theta - \mu_k\cos\theta)}} = n\sqrt{\frac{2d}{g\sin\theta}}$$

$$\Rightarrow \quad \mu_k = \left(1 - \frac{1}{n^2}\right)\tan\theta$$

2. For upper half,

$$\Sigma F_x = ma$$

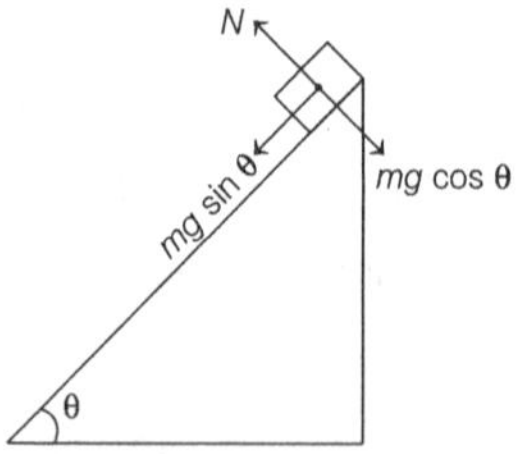

$$\Rightarrow \quad mg\sin\theta = ma \quad \Rightarrow a = g\sin\theta$$

$$v^2 = u^2 + 2as \quad \Rightarrow v^2 = 0^2 + 2(g\sin\theta)l \quad \Rightarrow v = \sqrt{2gl\sin\theta}$$

For lower half,

$$\Sigma F_x = ma_x \quad \Rightarrow mg\sin\theta - \mu mg\cos\theta = ma$$

$$\Rightarrow \quad a = g\sin\theta - \mu g\cos\theta$$

$$v^2 = u^2 + 2as$$

$$\Rightarrow \quad 0^2 = (\sqrt{2gl\sin\theta})^2 + 2(g\sin\theta - \mu g\cos\theta)l$$

$$\Rightarrow \quad \mu = 2\tan\theta$$

3. $\Sigma F_y = 0$

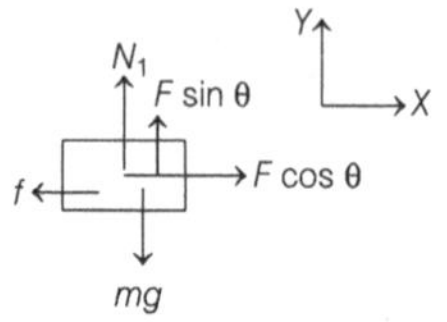

$$\Rightarrow +N_1 + F\sin\theta = mg \quad \Rightarrow N_1 = mg - F\sin\theta$$

$$\Sigma F_x = ma_x$$

$$\Rightarrow \quad F\cos\theta - \mu(mg - F\sin\theta) = ma$$

$$\Rightarrow \quad a = \frac{F}{m}(\cos\theta + \mu\sin\theta) - \mu g$$

4. $F_1 = 2F_2$

$$mg\sin\theta + \mu mg\cos\theta = 2(mg\sin\theta - \mu mg\cos\theta)$$

$$\Rightarrow \quad \tan\theta = 3\mu \quad \Rightarrow \quad \theta = \tan^{-1}(3\mu)$$

5.

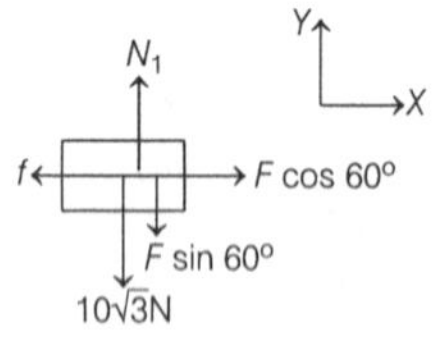

$$\Sigma F_y = 0 \quad \Rightarrow \quad +N_1 - 10\sqrt{3} - F\sin 60° = 0$$

$$\Rightarrow \quad N_1 = 10\sqrt{3} + F\sin 60°$$

$$f_L = \mu N_1 = \frac{1}{2\sqrt{3}}\left(10\sqrt{3} + \frac{\sqrt{3}F}{2}\right) = 5 + \frac{F}{4}$$

For not moving the block, $f \le f_L$

$$\Rightarrow \quad F\cos 60° \le 5 + \frac{F}{4}$$

$$\Rightarrow \quad F \le 20\text{ N} \quad \Rightarrow F_{max} = 20\text{ N}$$

6. Since, the block is at rest, $N = mg\cos\theta$

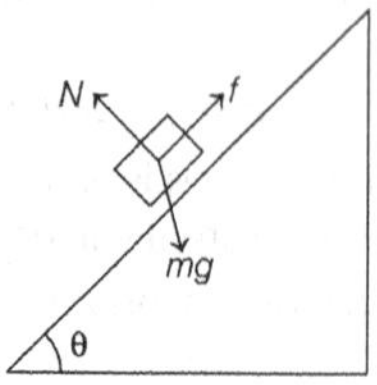

$$f = mg\sin\theta$$

$$\text{Contact force} = \sqrt{N^2 + f^2} = mg = 30\text{N}$$

7. $\Sigma F_y = 0 \quad \Rightarrow \quad +N_1 - F - mg\cos 30° = 0$

$$\Rightarrow \quad N_1 = F + mg\cos 30°$$

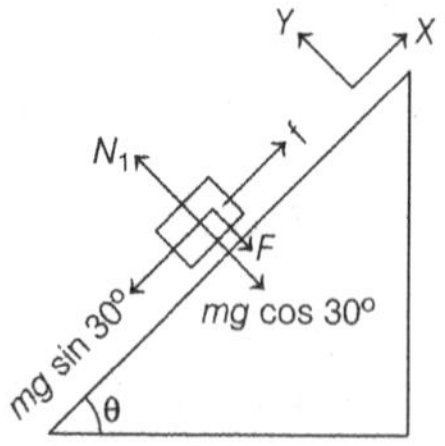

$$\Sigma F_x = 0 \quad \Rightarrow \quad f = mg\sin 30°$$

$$f \le f_L \quad \Rightarrow mg\sin 30° \le \mu(F + mg\cos 30°)$$

$$F \ge \frac{mg(\sin 30° - \mu\cos 30°)}{\mu}$$

$$F_{min} = \frac{mg}{2\mu}(1 - \sqrt{3}\mu)$$

$$= \frac{2\sqrt{3}(10)}{2\left(\frac{\sqrt{3}}{4}\right)}\left(1 - \sqrt{3}\left(\frac{\sqrt{3}}{4}\right)\right) = 10\text{ N}$$

8. $\Sigma F_y = 0 \quad \Rightarrow N_1 - mg = 0 \quad \Rightarrow \quad N_1 = 10\text{ N}$

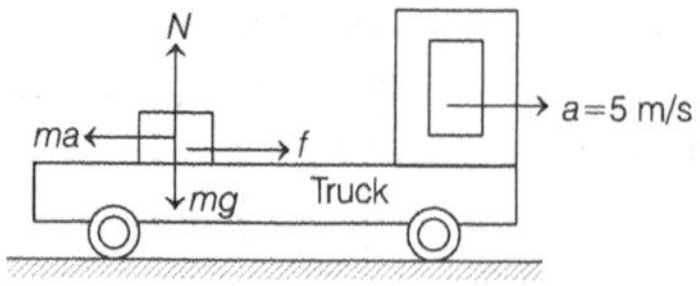

$$f_L = \mu N_1 = 0.6(10) = 6\text{ N}$$

$$\Sigma F_x = 0 \quad \Rightarrow f = ma$$

$$\Rightarrow \quad f = 1(5) = 5\text{ N (static)}$$

9.

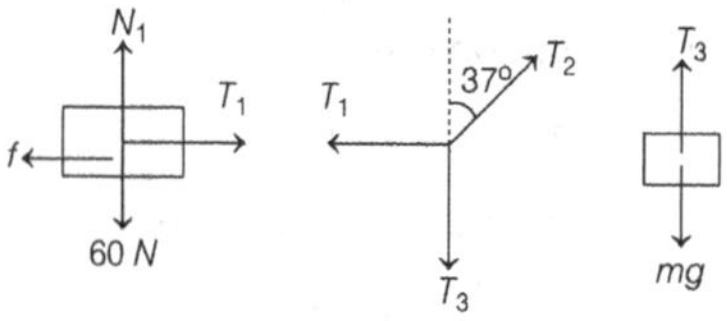

For block B,

$$f_L = \mu N_1 = \frac{1}{4}(60) = 15\text{ N}$$

To make B just start moving,

$$T_1 = f = 15 \text{ N}$$

For node,

$$\Sigma F_x = 0 \Rightarrow T_2 \sin 37^\circ = T_1 \quad \text{...(i)}$$

$$\Sigma F_y = 0 \Rightarrow T_2 \cos 37^\circ = T_3 \quad \text{...(ii)}$$

From Eqs. (i) & (ii), we get

$$T_3 = \frac{4}{3} T_1 = 20 \text{ N}$$

For block A, $\Sigma F_y = ma_y \Rightarrow m_A g - 20 = 0 \Rightarrow m_A = 2 \text{ kg}$

10. For $(M + m)$ system,

$$\Sigma F_x = ma \Rightarrow F = 60a \Rightarrow a = \frac{F}{60}$$

For 10 kg,

$$\Sigma F_x = ma_x \Rightarrow F - N_1 = 10a$$

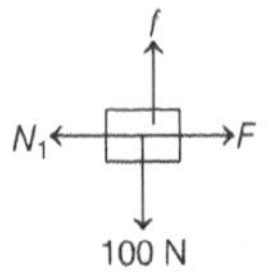

$$\Rightarrow \quad N_1 = F - 10a$$

$$\Sigma F_y = 0$$

$$\Rightarrow f - 100 = 0 \Rightarrow f = 100 \text{ N}$$

$$f \le f_L \Rightarrow 100 \le 0.5(F - 10a)$$

$$\Rightarrow \quad 100 \le 0.5\left(F - 10\left(\frac{F}{60}\right)\right) \Rightarrow \frac{5F}{6} \ge 200$$

$$\Rightarrow \quad F \ge 240 \text{ N} \Rightarrow F_{min} = 240 \text{ N}$$

11. $mg \sin 60^\circ = f$ and $f_L = \mu mg \cos 60^\circ$

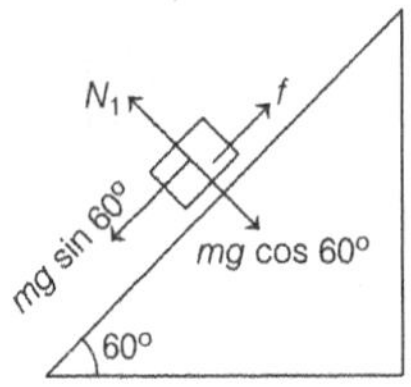

To take the block up the plane

$$F \ge mg \sin\theta + f_L$$

$$\Rightarrow \quad F \ge mg \sin 60^\circ + \mu mg \cos 60^\circ$$

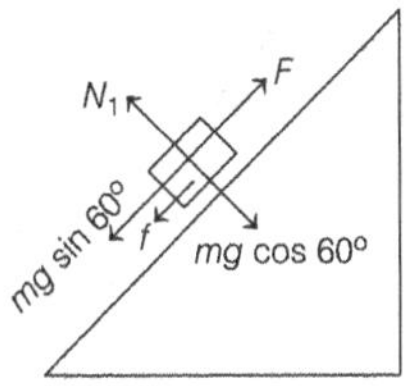

$$\Rightarrow \quad F \ge 2mg \sin 60^\circ$$

$$\Rightarrow \quad F_{min} = 2(0.5)(10)\left(\frac{\sqrt{3}}{2}\right) = 5\sqrt{3} \text{ N or } 8.66 \text{ N}$$

12. $f_L = \mu N$ & N is same in both the cases.

So, $\quad F = 12 \text{ N}$

13. $f_L = \mu N = 0.7(mg \cos 30^\circ)$

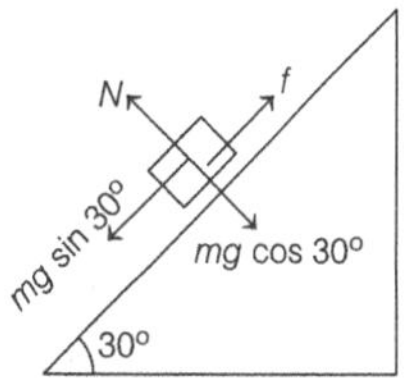

Since, the block is not sliding down, friction will be static.

$$f = mg \sin 30^\circ = 9.8 \text{ N}$$

14.

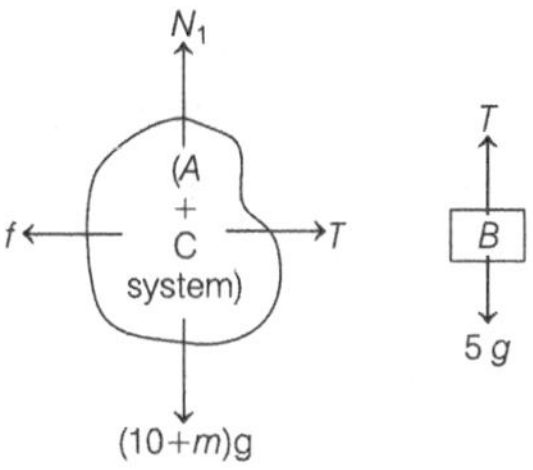

For B, $\quad \Sigma F_y = 0 \Rightarrow T = 5g$

For $(A + C)$ system,

$$\Sigma F_y = 0 \Rightarrow N_1 = (10 + m)g$$

$$f_L = \mu N_1 = 0.2(10 + m)g$$

$$\Sigma F_x = 0 \Rightarrow T = f \Rightarrow f = 5g$$

$$f \le f_L \Rightarrow 5g \le 0.2(10 + m)g$$

$$\Rightarrow 10 + m \ge 25 \Rightarrow m \ge 15 \text{ kg} \Rightarrow m_{min} = 15 \text{ kg}$$

15. Coefficient of friction depends only on the nature of two surfaces in contact. Hence, option (d) is correct.

16.

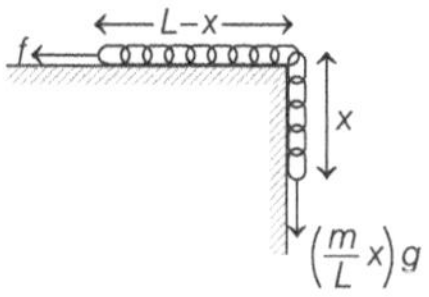

$$f_L = \mu N \Rightarrow f_L = \mu\left(\frac{M}{L}(L - x)g\right)$$

For chain not to slide, $\dfrac{M}{L} xg = \mu\left(\dfrac{M}{L}(L - x)g\right)$

$$\Rightarrow \quad x = \mu L - \mu x \Rightarrow x = \frac{\mu L}{1 + \mu}$$

17. To make the block just reach B, velocity at $B = 0$

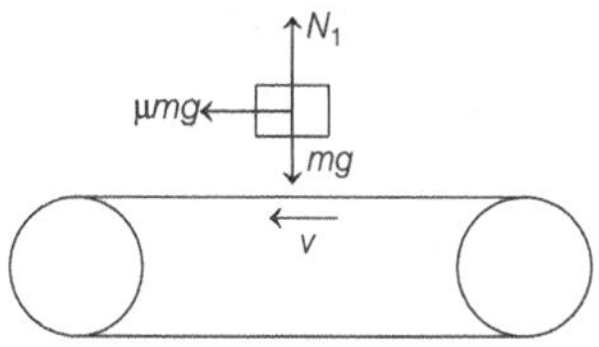

$$\Sigma F_x = ma \Rightarrow -\mu mg = ma \Rightarrow a = -\mu g$$

$$v^2 = u^2 + 2as \Rightarrow 0^2 = v_0^2 + 2(-\mu g)L \Rightarrow v_0 = \sqrt{2\mu g L}$$

18. FBD of 10 kg block,

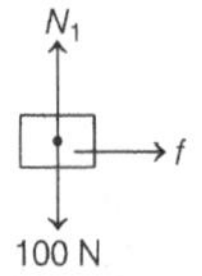

$$\Sigma F_y = 0 \Rightarrow N_1 = 100\text{ N}$$
$$\Sigma F_x = ma \Rightarrow f = 10a$$

For maximum acceleration,

$$10a = f_L = \mu(100) \Rightarrow a_{max} = 5\text{ m/s}^2$$

For (20 kg + 10 kg) system,

$$\Sigma F_x = ma \Rightarrow F = 30(5) = 150\text{ N}$$

19. For keeping block in equilibrium

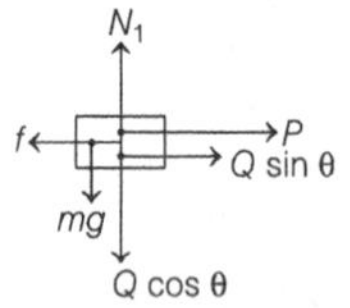

$$P + Q\sin\theta \le f_L \Rightarrow P + Q\sin\theta \le \mu(mg + \theta\cos\theta)$$

$$\Rightarrow \mu \ge \frac{P + Q\sin\theta}{mg + \theta\cos\theta} \Rightarrow \mu_{min} = \frac{P + Q\sin\theta}{mg + Q\cos\theta}$$

20.

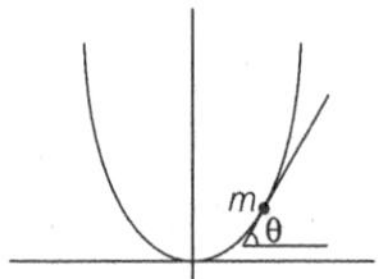

$$y = \frac{x^2}{a} \Rightarrow \frac{dy}{dx} = \frac{2x}{a}$$

Since, the particle is not sliding down,

$$mg\sin\theta < f_L \Rightarrow mg\sin\theta < \mu(mg\cos\theta) \Rightarrow \tan\theta < \mu$$

$$\Rightarrow \frac{dy}{dx} < \mu \Rightarrow \frac{2x}{a} < \mu \Rightarrow x < \frac{\mu a}{2}$$

$$y = \frac{x^2}{a} \Rightarrow y < \frac{(\mu a/2)^2}{a} \Rightarrow y < \frac{\mu^2 a}{4}$$

21.

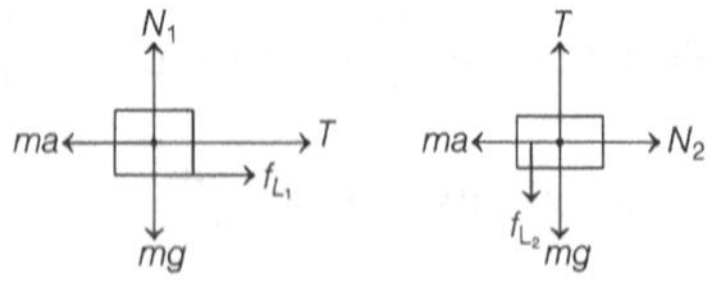

For keeping smaller blocks at rest w.r.t. the bigger block

$$ma = mg + f_{L_2} + f_{L_1} \Rightarrow ma = mg + \mu N_2 + \mu N_1$$

$$\Rightarrow ma = mg + \mu(ma) + \mu(mg) \Rightarrow a = \left(\frac{1+\mu}{1-\mu}\right)g$$

So, $$F = (M + 2m)\left(\frac{1+\mu}{1-\mu}\right)g$$

22. In absence of string both blocks have same acceleration $(g\sin\theta - \mu g\cos\theta)$ down the plane. So, $T = 0$

and $a = g\sin\theta - \mu g\cos\theta = 4\text{ m/s}^2$

23.

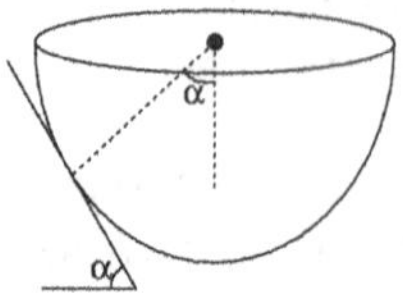

$$\Sigma F_y = 0 \Rightarrow N_1 - mg\cos\alpha = 0 \Rightarrow N_1 = mg\cos\alpha$$
$$\Sigma F_x = 0 \Rightarrow mg\sin\alpha = f$$

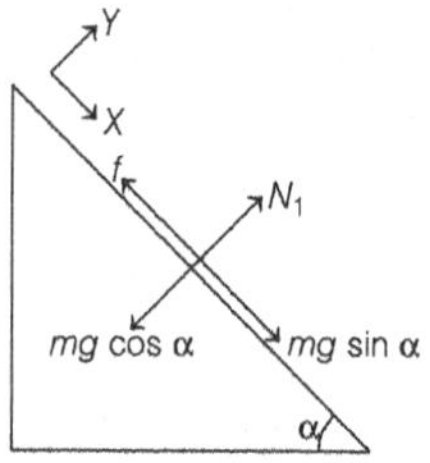

and $f \le f_L \Rightarrow mg\sin\alpha \le \mu mg\cos\alpha$

$$\Rightarrow \tan\alpha \le \frac{1}{3} \Rightarrow \tan\alpha_{max} = \frac{1}{3} \Rightarrow \cot\alpha_{max} = 3$$

24. $\Sigma F_y = 0 \Rightarrow N_1 + Mg\cos\theta - Mg = 0 \Rightarrow N_1 = Mg(1 - \cos\theta)$

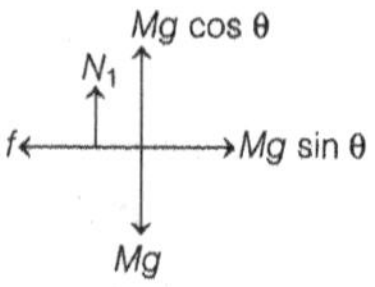

For pulling the block,

$$Mg\sin\theta \ge f_L \Rightarrow Mg\sin\theta \ge \mu N_1 \Rightarrow Mg\sin\theta \ge \mu Mg(1 - \cos\theta)$$

$$\Rightarrow \frac{\sin\theta}{1 - \cos\theta} \ge \mu \Rightarrow \frac{2\sin\left(\frac{\theta}{2}\right)\cos\left(\frac{\theta}{2}\right)}{2\sin^2\left(\frac{\theta}{2}\right)} \ge \mu \Rightarrow \cot\left(\frac{\theta}{2}\right) \ge \mu$$

25.

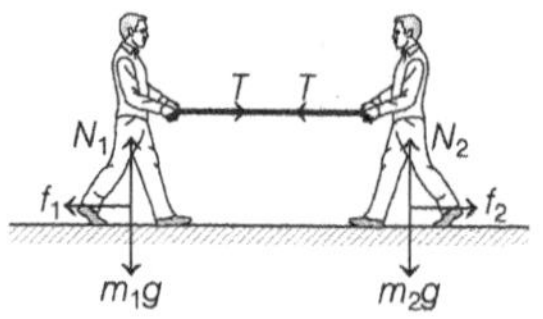

26. For block B,

$$\Sigma F_y = 0$$
$$\Rightarrow +N_1 + T\sin 37° = mg$$
$$\Rightarrow N_1 = mg - T\sin 37°$$

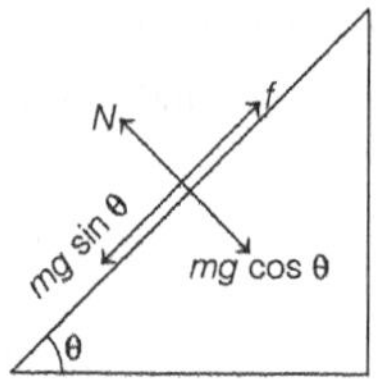

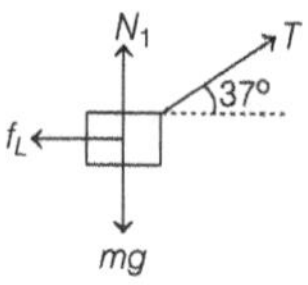

$$\Sigma F_x = 0 \Rightarrow T\cos 37° = f_L$$

$$\Rightarrow \frac{4T}{5} = \mu\left(mg - \frac{3T}{5}\right)$$

$$\Rightarrow \frac{12T}{5} = 100g - \frac{3T}{5} \Rightarrow T = \frac{100g}{3}$$

For A,

$$\Sigma F = ma \Rightarrow T - 25g = 25a$$

$$\Rightarrow \quad \frac{100g}{3} - 25g = 25a \Rightarrow a = \frac{g}{3}$$

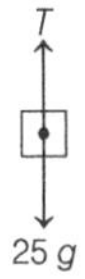

27. On smooth inclined plane

$$a = g\sin\theta$$
$$v^2 = u^2 + 2as$$
$$\Rightarrow \quad v^2 = 0^2 + 2(g\sin\theta)l \Rightarrow v = \sqrt{2gl\sin\theta} \quad \text{...(i)}$$

On rough inclined plane

$$a = g\sin\theta - \mu g\cos\theta$$
$$v^2 = u^2 + 2as$$
$$\Rightarrow \quad \left(\frac{v}{n}\right)^2 = 0^2 + 2(g\sin\theta - \mu g\cos\theta)l$$
$$\Rightarrow \quad v^2 = n^2[2(g\sin\theta - \mu g\cos\theta)l]$$
$$\Rightarrow \quad v = n\sqrt{2gl(\sin\theta - \mu\cos\theta)} \quad \text{...(ii)}$$

From Eqs. (i) and (ii), we get

$$\sqrt{2gl\sin\theta} = n\sqrt{2gl(\sin\theta - \mu\cos\theta)}$$
$$\Rightarrow \quad \sin\theta = n^2(\sin\theta - \mu\cos\theta)$$
$$\Rightarrow \quad n^2\mu\cos\theta = (n^2 - 1)\sin\theta$$
$$\Rightarrow \mu = \left(\frac{n^2 - 1}{n^2}\right)\tan\theta \Rightarrow \mu = \left(1 - \frac{1}{n^2}\right)\tan\theta$$

28. $f_L = \mu N \Rightarrow f_L = 0.5(45) = 22.5$ N

Net driving force $= \sqrt{20^2 + 15^2} = 25$ N

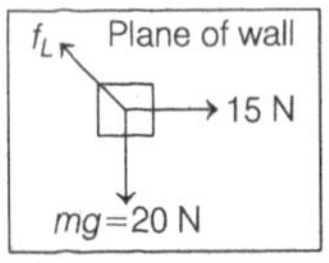

$$\Sigma F = ma \Rightarrow 25 - 22.5 = 2a \Rightarrow a = 1.25 \text{ m/s}^2$$

29. $a = g\sin\theta - \mu g\cos\theta$

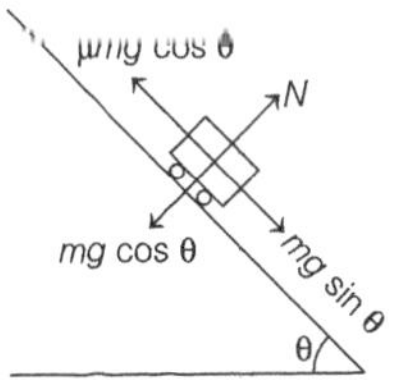

$$v^2 = u^2 + 2as$$
$$\Rightarrow \quad v^2 = (20)^2 + 2 \times 10\left(\frac{3}{5} - \left(\frac{1}{2}\right)\left(\frac{4}{5}\right)\right)(21)$$
$$\Rightarrow \quad v = \sqrt{400 + 84} = \sqrt{484} \text{ m/s} = 22 \text{ m/s}$$

30.

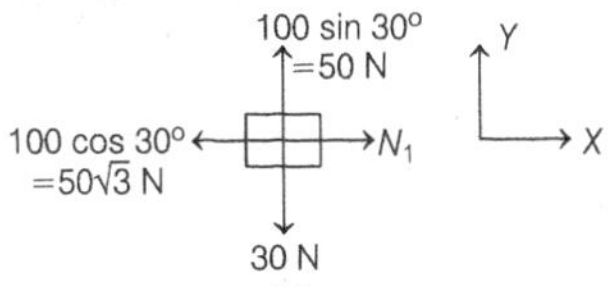

$$\Sigma F_x = 0 \Rightarrow N_1 - 50\sqrt{3} = 0 \Rightarrow N_1 = 50\sqrt{3} \text{ N}$$

$$f_L = \mu N_1 = \frac{1}{4}(50\sqrt{3}) = 12.5\sqrt{3}$$

In absence of friction, driving force on the block is

$50 - 30 = 20$ N, up the wall.

Since, $20 < f_L$

Friction will be 20 N (static) downwards.

31. $N_1 = mg\cos 37° = 8$ N

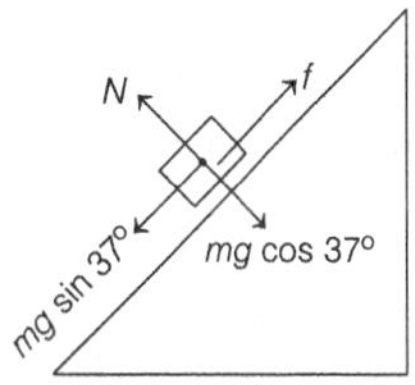

$$f_L = \mu N_1 = 0.8(8) = 6.4 \text{ N}$$

Since, $mg\sin\theta = 6 < f_L \Rightarrow T = 0$

and friction will be 6 N (static) up the plane.

32. For 2 kg block,

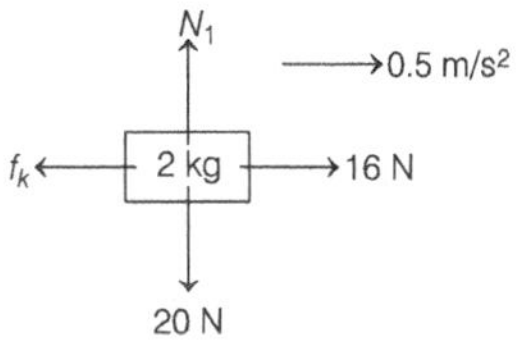

$$\Sigma F_y = 0 \Rightarrow N_1 = 20 \text{ N}$$
$$f_k = \mu N_1 = 20\mu_1$$
$$\Sigma F = ma \Rightarrow 16 - 20\mu_1 = 2(0.5) \Rightarrow \mu_1 = \frac{3}{4}$$

For 4 kg block,

$$\Sigma F = ma \Rightarrow 40\sin 30° - 16 - f_k = 4(0.5)$$

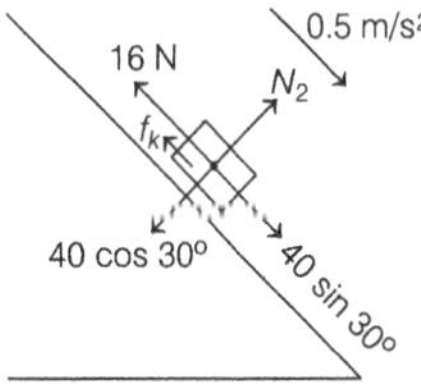

$$\Rightarrow f_k = 2 \text{ N} \Rightarrow f_k = \mu_k N \Rightarrow 2 = \mu_k(40\cos 30°)$$
$$\Rightarrow \mu_k = \frac{1}{10\sqrt{3}} = 0.0577 = 0.06$$

33. For 6 kg block,

$$\Sigma F = ma \Rightarrow 24 - 9 = 6a \Rightarrow a_{max} = 2.5 \text{ m/s}^2$$

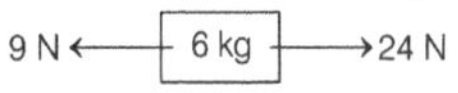

For 3 kg block,

$$\Sigma F = ma$$

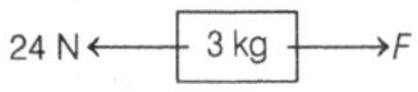

$$\Rightarrow \quad F - 24 = 3(2.5)$$
$$\Rightarrow \quad F = 31.5 \text{ N}$$

34. $\Sigma F_y = 0$

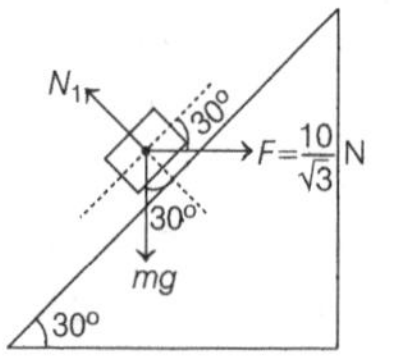

$\Rightarrow \quad +N_1 - mg\cos 30° - F\sin 30° = 0$

$\Rightarrow \quad N_1 = mg\cos 30° + F\sin 30°$

$\Rightarrow \quad N_1 = 5\sqrt{3} + \dfrac{5}{\sqrt{3}} = \dfrac{20}{\sqrt{3}}\,\text{N}$

$f_L = \mu N_1 = 0.5\left(\dfrac{20}{\sqrt{3}}\right) = \dfrac{10}{\sqrt{3}}\,\text{N}$

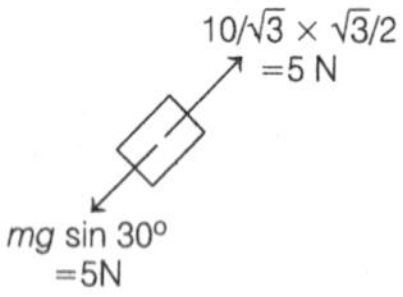

Along the inclined plane, in absence of friction, net force is zero.

So, $\quad f = 0$

35. $F_{min} = \dfrac{\mu mg}{\sqrt{1+\mu^2}} = \dfrac{\frac{1}{\sqrt{3}} \times 25 \times 10}{\frac{2}{\sqrt{3}}} = 125\,\text{N}$

36. $\Sigma F_x = ma_x \quad \Rightarrow mg\sin\phi - f_k = 0 \quad \Rightarrow f_k = mg\sin\phi$

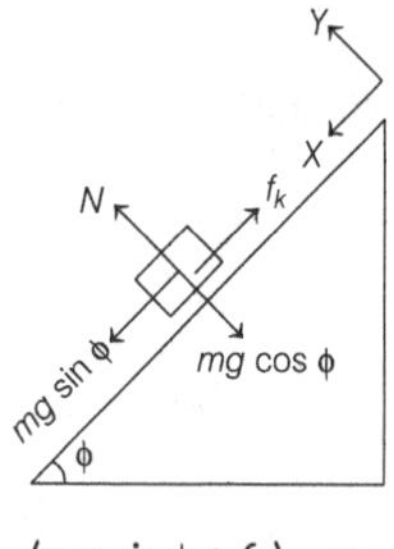

$\Sigma F_x = ma_x \quad \Rightarrow -(mg\sin\phi + f_k) = ma_x \quad \Rightarrow a_x = -2g\sin\phi$

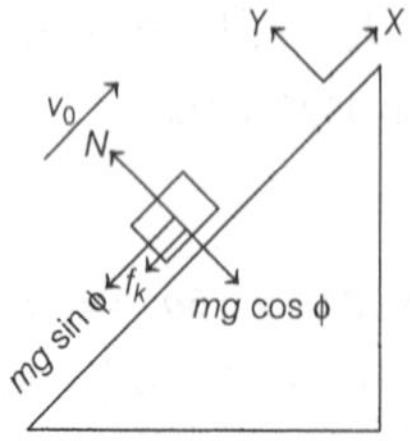

$v^2 = u^2 - 2as \quad \Rightarrow 0^2 = v_0^2 + 2(-2g\sin\phi)s \quad \Rightarrow s = \dfrac{v_0^2}{4g\sin\phi}$

37. For $F \le \mu_s mg$, tension in the string is zero. So, friction force on block B will be zero. As F further increases, friction on B will increase and when it is set into motion, kinetic friction will act.

38. For $\quad t > 2.85$

$\Sigma F = ma$

$\Rightarrow \quad 1.8t - f_k = 1.5(1.2t - 2.4) \quad \Rightarrow \quad f_k = 3.6\,\text{N}$

$f_k = \mu_k N \quad \Rightarrow \quad 3.6 = \mu_k(1.5)g \quad \Rightarrow \quad \mu_k = 0.24$

39. $f_k = \mu_k N \quad \Rightarrow \quad f_k = 0.5(10) = 5\text{N}$

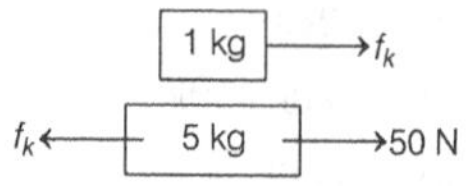

For 1 kg, $\Sigma F = ma \quad \Rightarrow \quad 5 = a_1 \Rightarrow a_1 = 5\,\text{m/s}^2$

For 5 kg, $\Sigma F = ma \quad \Rightarrow 50 - 5 = 5a \quad \Rightarrow \quad a_2 = 9\,\text{m/s}^2$

$a_{rel} = a_2 - a_1 = 9 - 5 = 4\,\text{m/s}^2$

$s_{rel} = u_{rel}t + \dfrac{1}{2}a_{rel}t^2 \quad \Rightarrow \quad +8 = 0 + \dfrac{1}{2}(4)t^2 \quad \Rightarrow$

$t = 2\text{s}$

40. $a_A = g\sin\theta - \mu_A g\cos\theta$

$a_B = g\sin\theta - \mu_B g\cos\theta$

$s_A = 0 + \dfrac{1}{2}(g\sin\theta - \mu_A g\cos\theta)t^2$

$s_B = \sqrt{2} + 0 + \dfrac{1}{2}(g\sin\theta - \mu_B g\cos\theta)t^2$

$s_A = s_B$

$\Rightarrow \quad \dfrac{1}{2}g(\sin\theta - \mu_A\cos\theta)t^2 = \sqrt{2} + \dfrac{1}{2}g(\sin\theta - \mu_B\cos\theta)t^2$

$\Rightarrow \quad \dfrac{1}{2}gt^2(\mu_B - \mu_A)\cos\theta = \sqrt{2}$

$\Rightarrow \quad t = \sqrt{\dfrac{2\sqrt{2}}{g(\mu_B - \mu_A)\cos\theta}} = 2\text{s}$

$s_B = \sqrt{2} + \dfrac{1}{2}g\left(\dfrac{1}{\sqrt{2}} - (0.3)\left(\dfrac{1}{\sqrt{2}}\right)\right)(2)^2 \quad \Rightarrow \quad s_B = 8\sqrt{2}$

Numerical Value Questions

1.

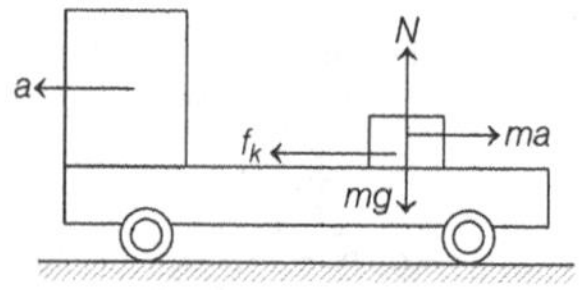

For block,

$\Sigma F = ma \quad \Rightarrow m(2) - 0.15mg = ma' \quad \Rightarrow a' = 0.5\,\text{m/s}^2$

$s = ut + \dfrac{1}{2}at^2 \quad \Rightarrow \quad 5 = \dfrac{1}{2}(0.5)t^2 \quad \Rightarrow \quad t = \sqrt{20}\text{s}$

For truck,

$s = ut + \dfrac{1}{2}at^2 \quad \Rightarrow \quad s = 0 + \dfrac{1}{2}(2)(\sqrt{20})^2 = 20\,\text{m}$

2. $F_{min} = \dfrac{\mu mg}{\sqrt{\mu^2 + 1}} = \dfrac{3mg}{5} \quad \Rightarrow \quad 25\mu^2 = 9\mu^2 + 9$

$\Rightarrow \quad 16\mu^2 = 9 \quad \Rightarrow \mu = \dfrac{3}{4} = 0.75$

3. w.r.t. train $\Sigma F_x = 0 \Rightarrow N = ma$

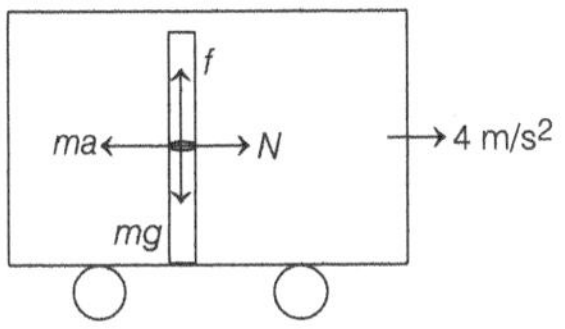

$$\Sigma F_y = ma_y \Rightarrow mg - \mu N = ma_y \Rightarrow mg - \mu ma = ma_y$$

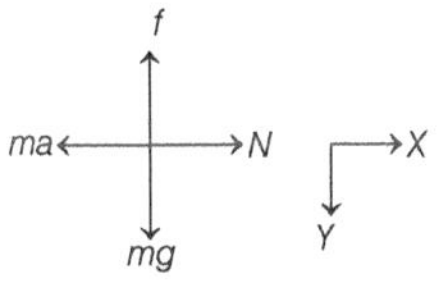

$$\Rightarrow a_y = g - \mu a \Rightarrow a_y = 10 - \frac{1}{2}(4) = 8 \text{ m/s}^2$$

$$s_y = u_y t + \frac{1}{2}a_y t^2 \Rightarrow 1 = 0 + \frac{1}{2}(8)t^2 \Rightarrow t = 0.5\text{s}$$

4. Taking $(A+B)$ system,

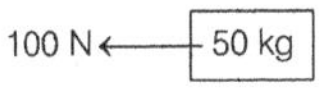

$$\Sigma F = ma \Rightarrow 100 = 50a \Rightarrow a = 2 \text{ m/s}^2$$

For B,

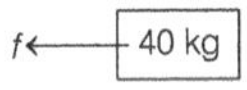

$$\Sigma F = ma \Rightarrow f = 40 \times 2 = 80 \text{ N}$$

$$f_L = \mu_s N = 0.75 \times 98 = 73.5 \text{ N}$$

Since, $f > f_L$, our assumption is wrong.

Friction between the blocks will be kinetic.

For B,

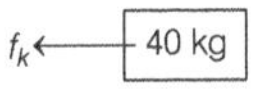

$$\Sigma F = ma \Rightarrow f_k = 40a \Rightarrow 0.4 \times 10 \times 9.8 = 40a$$

$$\Rightarrow a = 0.98 \text{ m/s}^2$$

5.

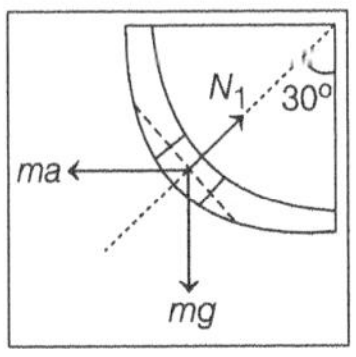

$$\Sigma F_y = 0 \Rightarrow N_1 - mg\cos 30° - ma\sin 30° = 0$$

$$\Rightarrow N_1 = \sqrt{3}mg$$

$$f_L = \mu N_1 \Rightarrow f_L = \mu(\sqrt{3}mg)$$

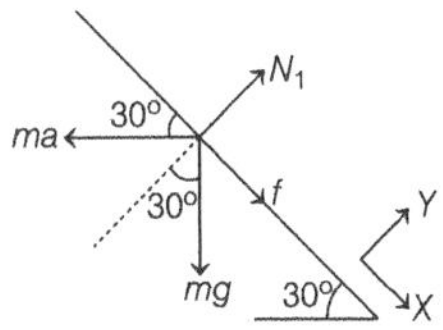

$$\Sigma F_x = 0$$

$$\Rightarrow ma\cos 30° = f + mg\sin 30°$$

$$\Rightarrow f = \frac{3mg}{2} - \frac{mg}{2} = mg$$

$$f \le f_L \Rightarrow mg \le \mu(\sqrt{3}mg)$$

$$\Rightarrow \mu \ge \frac{1}{\sqrt{3}} \Rightarrow \mu_{min} = \frac{1}{\sqrt{3}}$$

6.

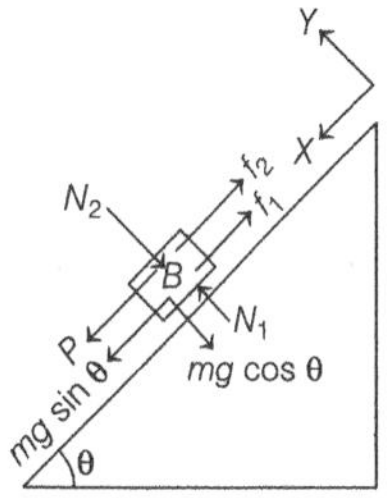

$$\Sigma F_x = 0$$

$$\Rightarrow P + mg\sin\theta = f_1 + f_2$$

$$\Rightarrow P + 100\sin 37° = \mu_1 N_1 + \mu_2 N_2$$

$$\Rightarrow P + 60 = (0.4)(200\cos 37°) + (0.3)(100\cos 37°)$$

$$\Rightarrow P + 60 = 64 + 24 \Rightarrow P = 28 \text{ N}$$

7. For B,

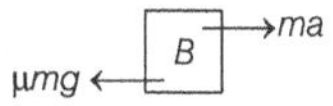

$$\Sigma F_x = 0 \Rightarrow ma = \mu mg$$

$$\Rightarrow a = \mu g = 0.2(10) = 2 \text{ m/s}^2$$

For belt,

$$v = u + at \Rightarrow 0 = 4 + (-2)t \Rightarrow t = 2\text{s}$$

8. $f_L = \mu_s N = 0.3(10) = 3\text{N}$

When the box starts moving

$$\Rightarrow F = f_L \Rightarrow 3t^2 = 3 \Rightarrow t = 1\text{s}$$

For $t > 1$s,

$$\Sigma F = ma \Rightarrow F - f_k = ma \Rightarrow 3t^2 - (0.2)(10) = 1a$$

$$\Rightarrow a = 3t^2 - 2 \Rightarrow \frac{dv}{dt} = 3t^2 - 2 \Rightarrow \int_0^v dv = \int_1^t (3t^2 - 2)dt$$

$$\Rightarrow [v]_0^v = [t^3 - 2t]_1^t \Rightarrow v = t^3 - 2t + 1$$

At $t = 3$,

$$v = 3^3 - 2(3) + 1 = 22 \text{ m/s}$$

9.

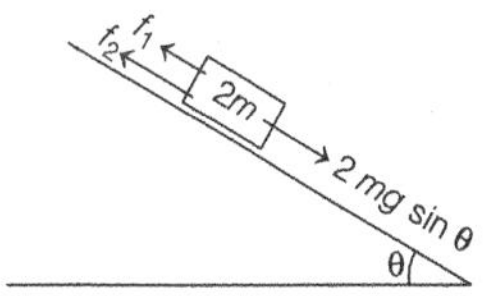

For system

$$\Sigma F_x = ma$$

$$mg\sin\theta + mg\sin\theta - \mu_1 mg\cos\theta - \mu_2 mg\cos\theta = 2ma$$

$$\Rightarrow 2a = 2g\sin\theta - 0.5g\cos\theta - 0.4g\cos\theta$$

$$\Rightarrow a = 6 - 3.6 = 2.4 \text{ m/s}^2$$

For m_2,

$$\Sigma F_x = ma_x \Rightarrow mg\sin\theta - T - \mu_2 mg\cos\theta = ma$$

$$\Rightarrow T = mg\sin\theta - \mu_2 mg\cos\theta - ma$$

$$\Rightarrow T = 60 - 32 - 24$$

$$\Rightarrow T = 4 \text{ N}$$

10.

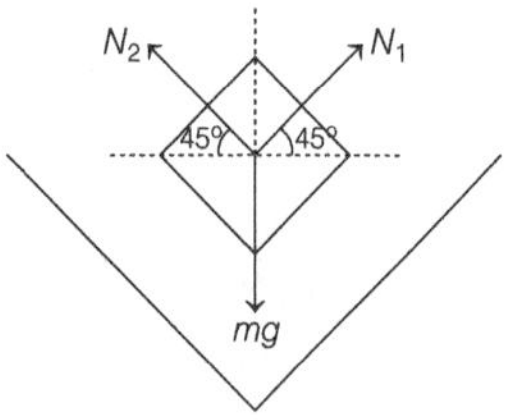

$$\Sigma F_y = 0 \Rightarrow 2N_1 \sin 45° = mg \Rightarrow N_1 = \frac{mg}{\sqrt{2}}$$

$$\Sigma F_x = ma_x \Rightarrow F - \mu N_1 - \mu N_2 = m(0)$$

$$\Rightarrow \quad F = \mu(N_1 + N_2) = \mu \frac{2mg}{\sqrt{2}} = 20 \text{ N}$$

11.

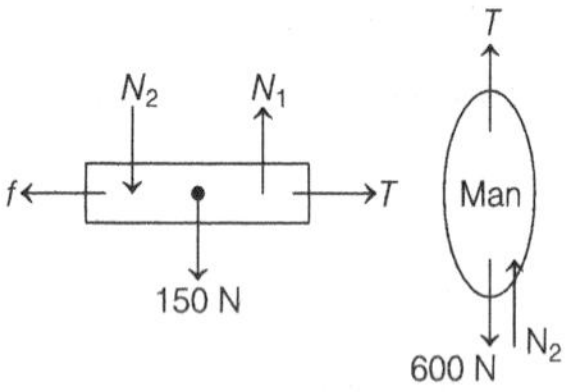

For board,

$$\Sigma F_x = ma_x \Rightarrow T - f_L = 0$$

$$\Rightarrow \quad T = f_L \Rightarrow T = \mu N_1$$

$$\Rightarrow \quad T = 0.5(N_2 + 150) \quad \text{...(i)}$$

For man,

$$\Sigma F_y = 0 \Rightarrow T + N_2 - 600 = 0$$

$$\Rightarrow \quad N_2 = 600 - T \quad \text{...(ii)}$$

From Eqs. (i) and (ii), we get

$$T = 0.5(600 - T + 150) \Rightarrow 3T = 750 \Rightarrow T = 250 \text{ N}$$

12. For block,

$$\Sigma F_x = ma_x \Rightarrow f_k - mg \sin\theta = ma$$

$$\Rightarrow \mu_k mg \cos\theta - mg \sin\theta = ma$$

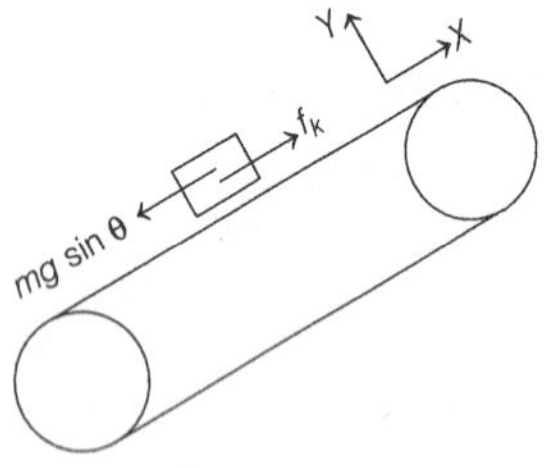

$$\Rightarrow \quad a = 2 \text{ m/s}^2$$

$$s = ut + \frac{1}{2}at^2$$

$$\Rightarrow \quad 4 = 0 + \frac{1}{2}(2)t^2 \Rightarrow t = 2\text{s}$$

13. $F_1 = mg \sin 37° + \mu mg \cos 37°$

$F_2 = mg \sin 53° - \mu mg \cos 53°$

$F_1 = F_2$

$$\Rightarrow \quad mg \sin 37° + \mu mg \cos 37° = mg \sin 53° - \mu mg \cos 53°$$

$$\Rightarrow \quad 3 + 4\mu = 4 - 3\mu \Rightarrow 7\mu = 1 \Rightarrow \mu = \frac{1}{7}$$

14. $f_k = \mu N \Rightarrow f_k = 20\mu$

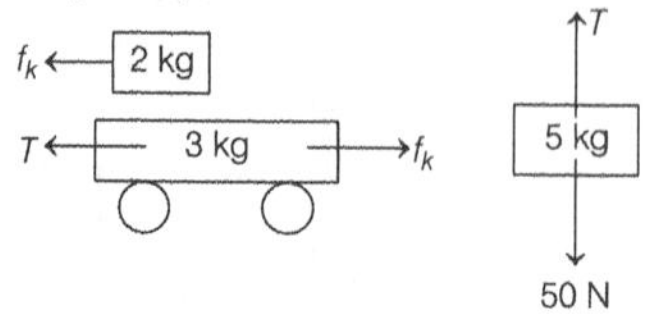

$$50 - T = 5a_1 \quad \text{...(i)}$$

$$T - 20\mu = 3a_1 \quad \text{...(ii)}$$

From Eqs. (i) and (ii), we get

$$a_1 = \frac{50 - 20\mu}{8}$$

For 2 kg block,

$$\Sigma F = ma \Rightarrow f_k = 2a_2 \Rightarrow 20\mu = 2a_2 \Rightarrow a_2 = 10\mu$$

$$a_{\text{rel}} = a_1 - a_2 = \frac{50 - 20\mu}{8} - 10\mu = \frac{50 - 100\mu}{8}$$

$$s_{\text{rel}} = u_{\text{rel}}t + \frac{1}{2}a_{\text{rel}}t^2 \Rightarrow 0.4 = 0 + \frac{1}{2}\left(\frac{50 - 100\mu}{8}\right)(0.8)^2$$

$$\Rightarrow \quad 50 - 100\mu = 10 \Rightarrow 100\mu = 40 \Rightarrow \mu = 0.4$$

15. $f_L = \mu_s N$

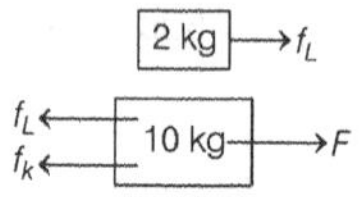

$$\Rightarrow \quad f_L = 0.25\,(20) = 5\text{N}$$

$$f_k = \mu_k N = 0.15(120) = 18 \text{ N}$$

For 2 kg,

$$\Sigma F = ma$$

$$\Rightarrow \quad f_L = 2a_{\max} \Rightarrow 5 = 2a_{\max} \Rightarrow a_{\max} = 2.5 \text{ m/s}^2$$

For $(A + B)$ system,

$$\Sigma F = ma \Rightarrow F - 18 = 12(2.5) \Rightarrow F = 48\text{N}$$

Level 3

Single Choice Correct Questions

1. For $(A + B + C)$ system,

$$\Sigma F_x = ma_x \Rightarrow F = 5ma \Rightarrow a = \frac{F}{5m}$$

For C,

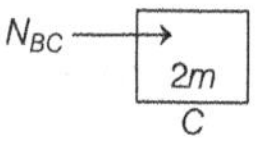

$$\Sigma F_x = ma_x \Rightarrow N_{BC} = 2m\left(\frac{F}{5m}\right) = \frac{2F}{5}$$

For A,

$$\Sigma F_x = ma_x$$

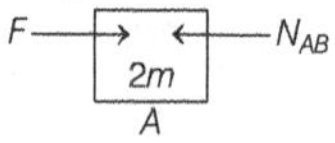

$$\Rightarrow \quad F - N_{AB} = 2m\left(\frac{F}{5m}\right) \Rightarrow N_{AB} = \frac{3F}{5}$$

For B,

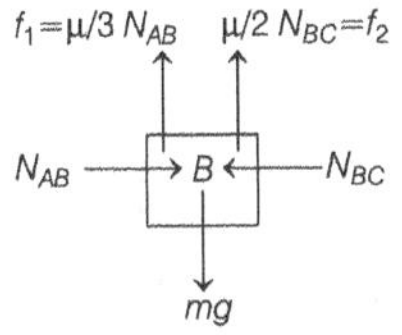

$$\Sigma F_y = 0 \Rightarrow mg - f_1 - f_2 = 0$$

$$\Rightarrow mg = \frac{\mu}{3} N_{AB} + \frac{\mu}{2} N_{BC} \Rightarrow F = 5\, mg$$

2. $\Sigma F_x = 0$

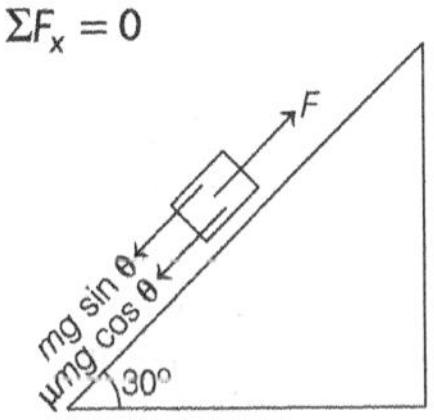

$$\Rightarrow F - mg \sin 30° - \mu\, mg \cos 30° = 0$$

$$F = mg \sin 30° + \mu\, mg \cos 30° \quad \text{...(i)}$$

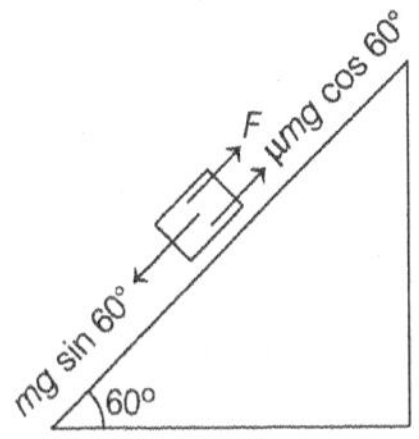

$$\Sigma F_x = 0 \Rightarrow mg \sin 60° = F + \mu mg \cos 60°$$

$$\Rightarrow F = mg \sin 60° - \mu\, mg \cos 60° \quad \text{...(ii)}$$

From Eqs. (i) and (ii), we get

$$mg \sin 30° + \mu\, mg \cos 30° = mg \sin 60° - \mu\, mg \cos 60°$$

$$\mu = \frac{\sqrt{3} - 1}{\sqrt{3} + 1}$$

3. For ascent,

$$\Sigma F_x = ma_x \Rightarrow -mg \sin\theta - \mu\, mg \cos\theta = ma$$

$$\Rightarrow a = -g(\sin\theta + \mu \cos\theta)$$

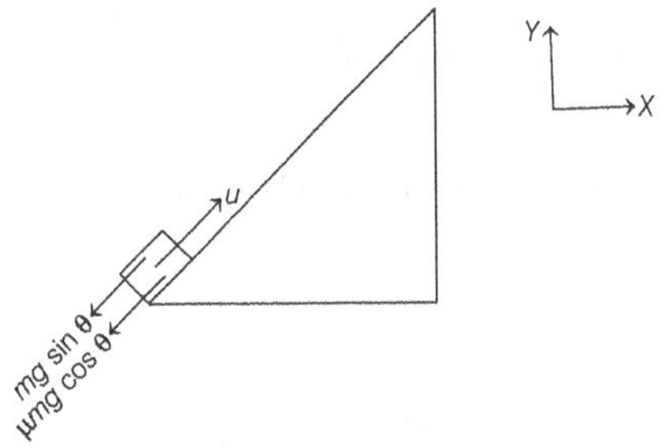

$$v = u + at \Rightarrow 0 = u - g(\sin\theta + \mu \cos\theta)\, t_1$$

$$\Rightarrow t_1 = \frac{u}{g(\sin\theta + \mu \cos\theta)}$$

$$v^2 = u^2 + 2as$$

$$\Rightarrow 0^2 = u^2 - 2g(\sin\theta + \mu \cos\theta)s \Rightarrow s = \frac{u^2}{2g\,(\sin\theta + \mu \cos\theta)}$$

For descent, $\Sigma F = ma_x$

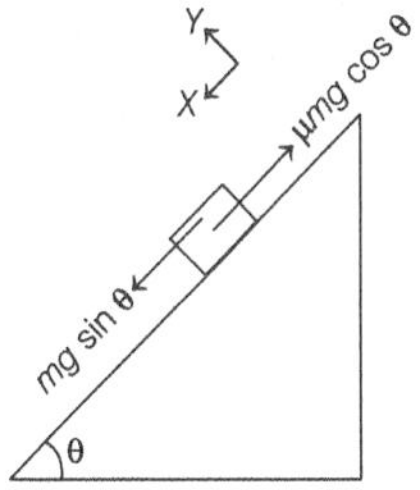

$$\Rightarrow mg \sin\theta - \mu\, mg \cos\theta = ma$$

$$\Rightarrow a = g \sin\theta - \mu g \cos\theta$$

$$s = ut + \frac{1}{2} at^2$$

$$\Rightarrow \frac{u^2}{2g\,(\sin\theta + \mu \cos\theta)} = 0 + \frac{1}{2} g(\sin\theta - \mu \cos\theta)\, t_2^2$$

$$t_2 = \frac{u}{g} \sqrt{\frac{1}{(\sin\theta + \mu \cos\theta)(\sin\theta - \mu \cos\theta)}}$$

$$\because \quad t_2 = 2t_1$$

$$\Rightarrow \frac{u}{g} \sqrt{\frac{1}{(\sin\theta + \mu \cos\theta)(\sin\theta - \mu \cos\theta)}} = 2\left(\frac{u}{g(\sin\theta + \mu \cos\theta)}\right)$$

$$\Rightarrow \frac{\sin\theta + \mu \cos\theta}{\sin\theta - \mu \cos\theta} = 4$$

$$\Rightarrow \sin\theta + \mu \cos\theta = 4 \sin\theta - 4\mu \cos\theta$$

$$\Rightarrow 3 \sin\theta = 5\mu \cos\theta \Rightarrow \mu = \frac{3}{5} \tan\theta$$

$$\Rightarrow \mu = \frac{3}{5} \tan 53° \Rightarrow \mu = 0.8$$

4. For A

$$\Sigma F_x = 0 \Rightarrow N = 8ma$$

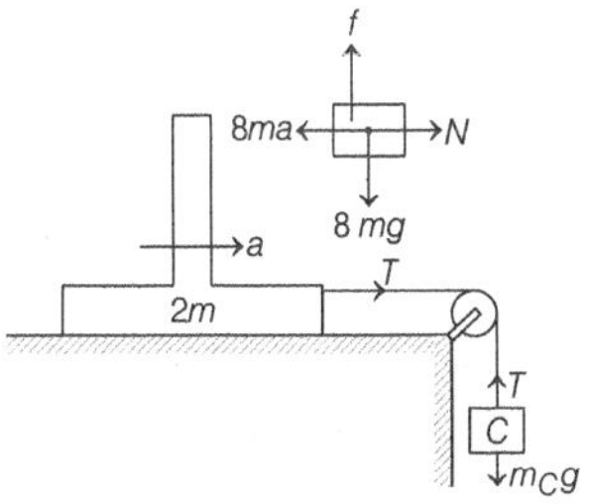

$$\Sigma F_y = 0 \Rightarrow f = 8mg$$

$$f \le f_L \Rightarrow 8mg \le \mu(8ma) \Rightarrow a \ge \frac{g}{\mu}$$

For C, $\Sigma F_y = ma_y \Rightarrow m_C g - T = m_C a$ ...(i)

For $(A + B)$,

$$\Sigma F_x = ma_x \Rightarrow T = 10ma \quad \text{...(ii)}$$

From Eqs. (i) and (ii), we get

$$a = \frac{m_C g}{m_C + 10m} \text{ and } a = \frac{m_C g}{m_C + 10m} \ge \frac{g}{\mu}$$

$$\Rightarrow \mu m_C \geq m_C + 10m \quad \Rightarrow m_C \geq \frac{10m}{\mu - 1}$$

5.

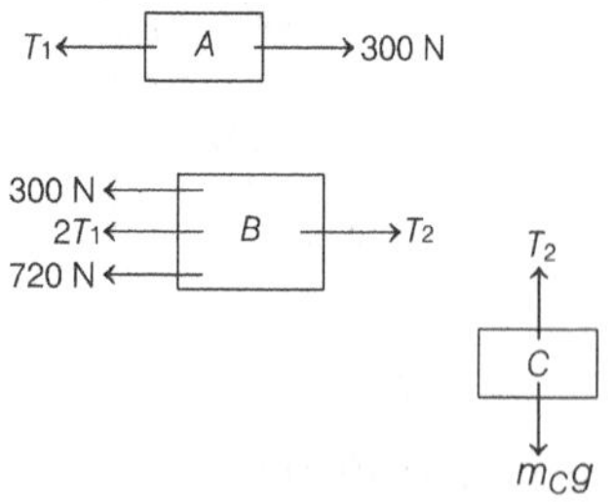

For A,

$$\Sigma F_x = 0 \quad \Rightarrow \quad T_1 - 300 = 0 \quad \Rightarrow T_1 = 300 \text{ N}$$

For B,

$$\Sigma F_x = 0 \quad \Rightarrow T_2 = 300 + 2T_1 + 720 \quad \Rightarrow T_2 = 1620 \text{ N}$$

For C,

$$\Sigma F_y = 0 \quad \Rightarrow m_C g - T_2 = 0 \Rightarrow m_C = 162 \text{ kg}$$

6.

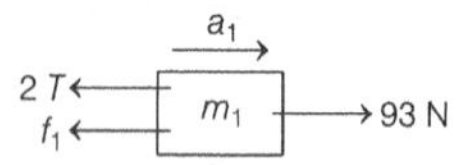

$$f_1 = \mu m_1 g \quad \Rightarrow \quad f_1 = 0.2(20) = 4 \text{ N}$$

For m_1,

$$\Sigma F_x = ma_x \quad \Rightarrow \quad 93 - 2T - 4 = 2a_1 \qquad \text{...(i)}$$

For m_2,

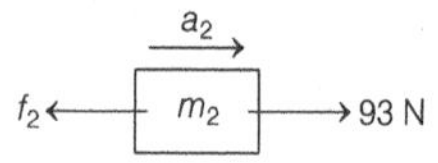

$$f_2 = \mu(m_2 g) = 0.2(60) = 12 \text{ N}$$

$$\Sigma F_x = ma_x$$

$$\Rightarrow \qquad T - 12 = 6a_2 \qquad \text{...(ii)}$$

and from string constant

$$a_2 = 2a_1 \qquad \text{...(iii)}$$

Solving Eqs. (i), (ii) and (iii), we get

$$a_1 = \frac{65}{26} = \frac{5}{2} \text{ m/s}^2 \quad \text{and} \quad a_2 = 5 \text{ m/s}^2$$

7.

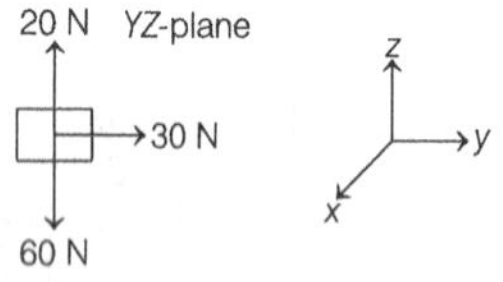

In absence of friction, net force in yz-plane

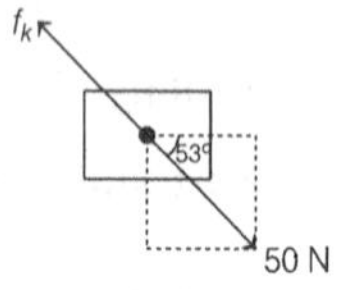

$$\mathbf{F} = 30\hat{\mathbf{j}} - 40\hat{\mathbf{k}} \quad \Rightarrow \quad F = 50 \text{ N}$$

So, kinetic friction (f_k) will act opposite to it.

$$f_k = \mu_k N = 0.25(80) = 20 \text{ N}$$

$$\Sigma F = ma \quad \Rightarrow 50 - 20 = 6a \Rightarrow a = 5 \text{ m/s}^2$$

$$\mathbf{a} = 5\cos 53^\circ \hat{\mathbf{j}} - 5\sin 53^\circ \hat{\mathbf{k}} = 3\hat{\mathbf{j}} - 4\hat{\mathbf{k}}$$

8. For bead $\Sigma F_x = 0$

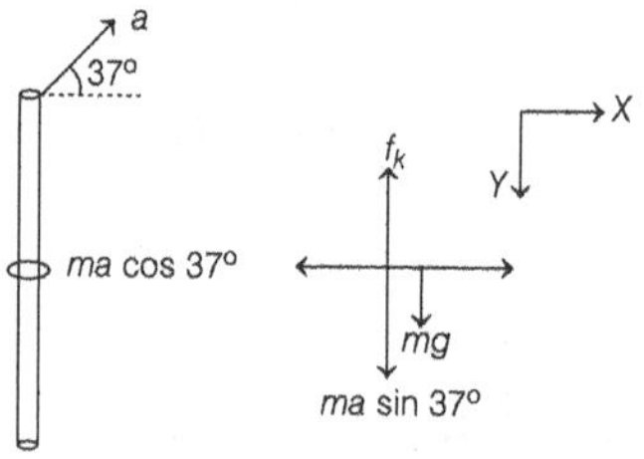

$$\Rightarrow \quad N_1 - ma\cos 37^\circ = 0 \quad \Rightarrow \quad N_1 = \frac{4ma}{5}$$

So, $f_k = \mu_k N_1 \quad \Rightarrow \quad f_k = \mu\left(\frac{4ma}{5}\right)$

$$\Sigma F_y = ma_y$$

$$\Rightarrow \quad mg + ma\sin 37^\circ - \mu\left(\frac{4ma}{5}\right) = ma_y$$

$$\Rightarrow \qquad a_y = g + \frac{3a}{5} - \frac{4\mu a}{5}$$

As seen from ground,

$$a_x = a_y \quad \Rightarrow a\cos 37^\circ = g + \frac{3a}{5} - \frac{4\mu a}{5}$$

$$\Rightarrow \quad (4\mu + 1)\frac{a}{5} = g \quad \Rightarrow \quad a = \frac{5g}{4\mu + 1}$$

9. $\Sigma F_y = 0 \quad \Rightarrow N_1 - mg\cos 45^\circ - ma\sin 45^\circ = 0$

$$N_1 = \frac{m(g + a)}{\sqrt{2}}$$

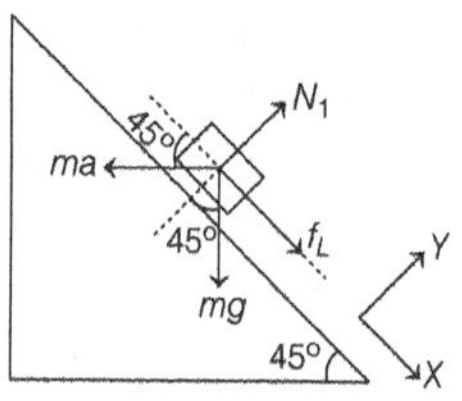

$$f_L = \mu N_1 = \frac{\mu m(g + a)}{\sqrt{2}}$$

$$\Sigma F_x = 0 \quad \Rightarrow f_L + mg\sin 45^\circ - ma\cos 45^\circ = 0$$

$$\Rightarrow \quad \frac{\mu m(g + a)}{\sqrt{2}} + \frac{mg}{\sqrt{2}} - \frac{ma}{\sqrt{2}} = 0 \quad \Rightarrow \quad a = g\left(\frac{1 + \mu}{1 - \mu}\right)$$

10. Lets take acceleration of trolley to be a.

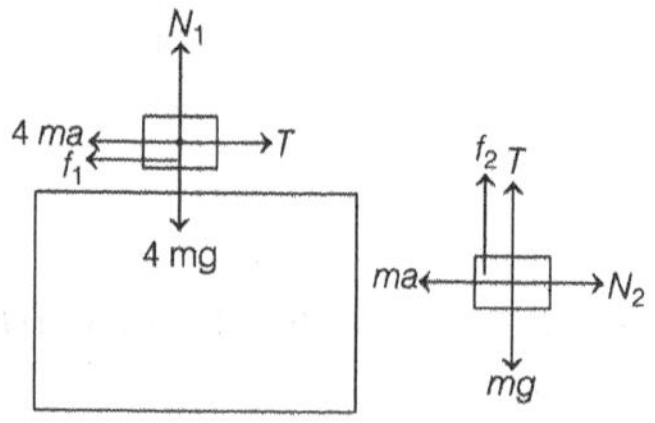

For ($4m$ and m) system,

Net force on them along the string = 0

$$\Rightarrow \qquad 4ma + f_1 + f_2 = mg \quad \Rightarrow 4ma + \frac{1}{5}(4mg) + \frac{1}{5}(ma) = mg$$

$$\Rightarrow \quad \frac{21ma}{5} = \frac{mg}{5} \quad \Rightarrow \quad a = \frac{g}{21}$$

For $(9m + 4m + m)$ system

$$\Sigma F_x = ma \quad \Rightarrow F = (14m)\left(\frac{g}{21}\right) = \frac{2mg}{3}$$

11. Lets take acceleration of crate to be a.

From string constraint

$$\Rightarrow \quad +a_0 + a_0 - a = 0 \quad \Rightarrow a = 2a_0 = 4 \text{ m/s}^2$$

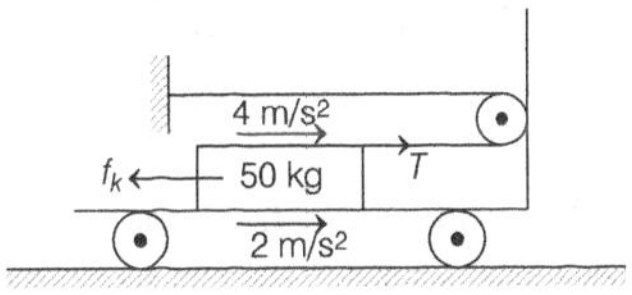

For crate,

$$\Sigma F_x = ma_x \quad \Rightarrow T - 0.3(500) = 50(4) \quad \Rightarrow T = 350 \text{ N}$$

12. For m_1,

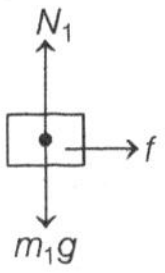

$$\Sigma F_x = ma_x \quad \Rightarrow \quad f = ma$$

So, acceleration of m_1 will be maximum when $f = f_L$

$$\Rightarrow \quad \mu m_1 g = ma_{max} \quad \Rightarrow a_{max} = \mu g$$

For $(m_1 + m_2)$ system,

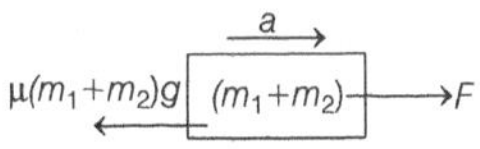

$$\Sigma F_x = ma_x \quad \Rightarrow F - \mu(m_1 + m_2)g = (m_1 + m_2)a$$

$$\Rightarrow F = \mu(m_1 + m_2)g + (m_1 + m_2)\mu g \quad \Rightarrow \quad F = 2\mu(m_1 + m_2)g$$

$$\Rightarrow \quad bt_0 = 2\mu(m_1 + m_2)g \quad \Rightarrow t_0 = \frac{2\mu(m_1 + m_2)g}{b}$$

13.

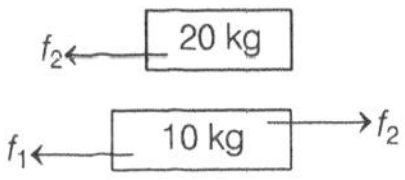

$$f_2 = 0.15(200) = 30\text{N}, \quad f_1 = 0.2(300) = 60\text{N}$$

For 20 kg, $\Sigma F_x = ma_x \quad \Rightarrow \quad -30 = 20a_2 \quad \Rightarrow \quad a_2 = -1.5 \text{ m/s}^2$

For 10 kg, $\Sigma F_x = ma_x \quad \Rightarrow +30 - 60 = 10a_1 \quad \Rightarrow a_1 = -3 \text{ m/s}^2$

$$a_{21} = a_2 - a_1 = -1.5 - (-3) = 1.5 \text{ m/s}^2 \quad \Rightarrow \quad s_{21} = 27 \text{ m}$$

$$s_{21} = u_{21}t + \frac{1}{2}a_{21}t^2 \quad \Rightarrow 27 = 0 + \frac{1}{2}\left(\frac{3}{2}\right)t^2 \quad \Rightarrow t = 6 \text{ s}$$

14. For (man + plank) system,

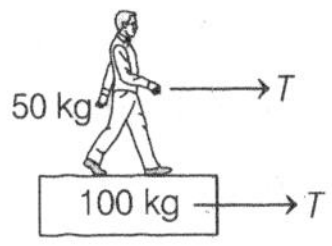

$$\Sigma F_x = ma_x \Rightarrow 2T = 150a \Rightarrow 2(100) = 150a \Rightarrow a = \frac{4}{3} \text{ m/s}^2$$

For man,

$$\Sigma F_x = ma_x \quad \Rightarrow T - f = 50a \quad \Rightarrow 100 - f = 50\left(\frac{4}{3}\right)$$

$$\Rightarrow \quad f = 100 - \frac{200}{3} = \frac{100}{3} \text{ N, towards left}$$

15. For m_1,

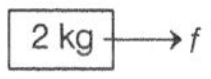

$$\Sigma F_x = ma_x \quad \Rightarrow f = 2a$$

$$f_L = 2a_{max} = 0.4(20)$$

$$\Rightarrow \quad a_{max} = 4 \text{ m/s}^2$$

For $(m_1 + m_2)$ system,

$$\Sigma f_x = ma_x \quad \Rightarrow T - 0.2(60) = 6a \qquad \text{...(i)}$$

For hanging block,

$$Mg - T = Ma \qquad \text{...(ii)}$$

Solving Eqs. (i) and (ii), we get

$$a = \frac{Mg - 0.2 \times 6 \times g}{6 + M} \quad \Rightarrow \quad a \le 4$$

$$\Rightarrow \quad \frac{10M - 12}{6 + M} \le 4 \quad \Rightarrow 10M - 12 \le 24 + 4M$$

$$\Rightarrow \quad 6M \le 36 \Rightarrow M \le 6 \text{ kg} \quad \Rightarrow M_{max} = 6 \text{ kg}$$

16. For $(m + 2m)$ system,

$$\Sigma F_x = ma_x \quad \Rightarrow \quad T = 3ma \qquad \text{...(i)}$$

For $3m$,

$$\Sigma F_y = ma_y \quad \Rightarrow \quad 3mg - T = 3ma \qquad \text{...(ii)}$$

Solving Eqs. (i) and (ii), we get

$$a = \frac{g}{2}$$

For m,

$$\Sigma F_x = ma_x$$

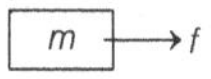

$$f = m\left(\frac{g}{2}\right) = \frac{mg}{2} \quad \Rightarrow f_L = 0.75(mg) = \frac{3mg}{4}$$

Since $f \le f_L$, friction between the blocks will be static.

$$f = \frac{mg}{2}$$

17. For m,

$$\Sigma F_x = ma$$

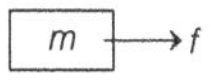

$$f = ma \quad \Rightarrow f_L = ma_{max} \quad \Rightarrow 0.2(1 \times 10) = 1\, a_{max}$$

$$\Rightarrow a_{max} = 2 \text{ m/s}^2$$

For $(M + m)$ system,

$$\Sigma F_x = ma_x \quad \Rightarrow \quad kx - 0.3(50) = 5a$$

$$\Rightarrow \quad a = \frac{kx - 15}{5} \quad \Rightarrow a \le a_{max} \quad \Rightarrow \quad \frac{kx - 15}{5} \le 2$$

$$\Rightarrow kx \le 25 \Rightarrow 1000x \le 25 \quad \Rightarrow x \le 2.5 \text{ cm}$$

18. Taking $(m_1 + m_2)$ system

$$\Sigma F_x = ma_x \Rightarrow 30 = 10a \Rightarrow a = 3\ \text{m/s}^2$$

For m_2,

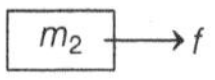

$$\Sigma F_x = ma_x \Rightarrow f = 2 \times 3 = 6\ \text{N}$$

$$f_L = \mu_s N = \frac{1}{5}\left(2\left(g + \frac{g}{4}\right)\right) = 5\ \text{N}$$

Since $f < f_L$, friction between the blocks will be kinetic.

For m_2,

$$\Sigma F_x = ma_x \Rightarrow 5 = 2a_2 \Rightarrow a_2 = 2.5\ \text{m/s}^2$$

For m_1,

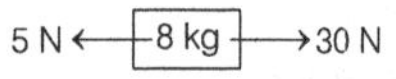

$$\Sigma F_x = ma_x \Rightarrow 30 - 5 = 8a_1 \Rightarrow a_1 = \frac{25}{8}\ \text{m/s}^2$$

19. Let the value of a be increased from zero. As long as $a \le \mu g$, there shall be no relative motion between m_1 or m_2 and platform, that is, m_1 and m_2 will move with acceleration a. As $a > \mu g$, the acceleration of m_1 and m_2 will become μg each.

Hence, at all instants the velocities of m_1 and m_2 will be same.

So, the spring will always remain in natural length.

20.

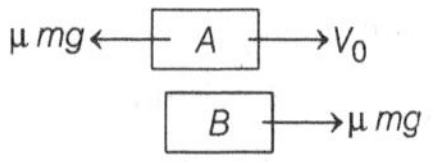

For A,

$$\Sigma F_x = ma_x \Rightarrow -\mu mg = ma_1 \Rightarrow a_1 = -\mu g$$

and $\quad v = u + at \Rightarrow v_1 = v_0 - \mu g t$

For B,

$$\Sigma F_x = ma_x \Rightarrow \mu mg = ma_2 \Rightarrow a_2 = \mu g$$

and $\quad v = u + at \Rightarrow v_2 = 0 + \mu g t \Rightarrow v_2 = \mu g t$

21.

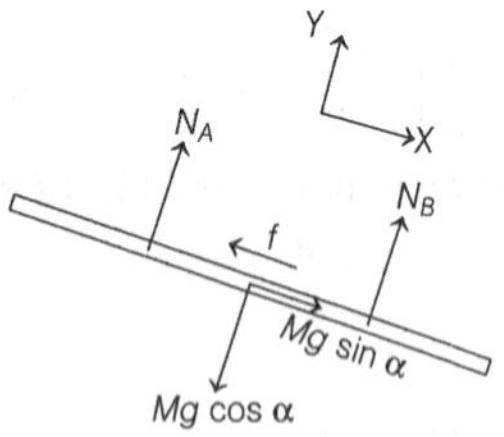

For plank not to slide

$$\Rightarrow \Sigma F_x = 0 \Rightarrow f - Mg \sin\alpha = 0 \Rightarrow f = Mg \sin\alpha$$

For man,

$$\Sigma F_x = ma_x$$

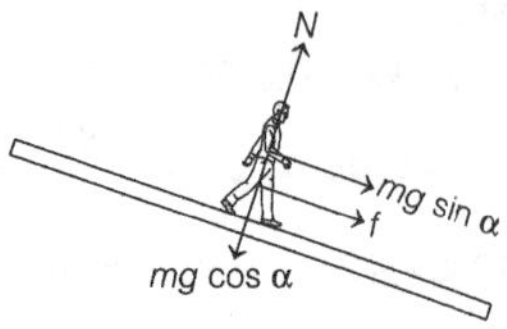

$$\Rightarrow mg \sin\alpha + f = ma \Rightarrow a = \left(\frac{m+M}{m}\right) g \sin\alpha$$

$$\Rightarrow a = \left(1 + \frac{M}{m}\right) g \sin\alpha, \text{ down the incline}$$

22. For A,

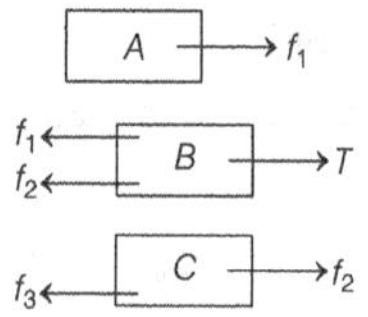

$$\Sigma F_x = ma_x \Rightarrow f_1 = ma_1$$

$$f_1 \le f_L$$

$$\Rightarrow ma_1 \le \frac{1}{2}(mg) \Rightarrow a_1 \le \frac{g}{2}$$

For C, $\quad \Sigma F_x = ma_x \Rightarrow f_2 - f_3 = ma_3$

$$\Rightarrow f_2 - \frac{1}{5}(3\ mg) = ma_3 \Rightarrow f_2 = ma_3 + \frac{3mg}{5}$$

$$f_2 \le f_L \Rightarrow ma_3 + \frac{3mg}{5} \le \left(\frac{1}{2}(2mg)\right) \Rightarrow a_3 \le \frac{2g}{5}$$

So, the maximum acceleration for which A, B and C can move together is $\frac{2g}{5}$.

For $(A + B + C)$ system,

$$\Rightarrow \Sigma F_x = ma_x \Rightarrow T - \frac{1}{5}(3\ mg) = 3m\left(\frac{2g}{5}\right) \quad \text{...(i)}$$

For D,

$$\Rightarrow \Sigma F_y = ma_y \Rightarrow m_D g - T = m_D\left(\frac{2g}{5}\right) \quad \text{...(ii)}$$

Solving Eqs. (i) and (ii), we get

$$m_D = 3m$$

23. When the block just starts to move

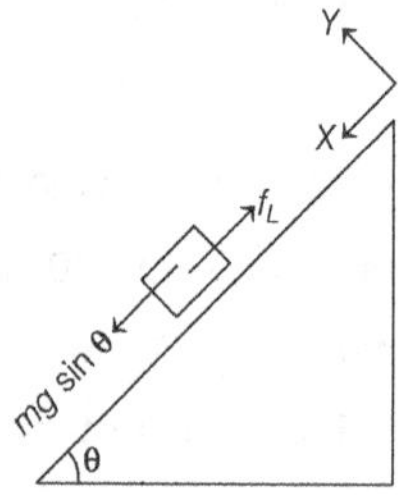

$$mg \sin\theta = f_L \Rightarrow mg \sin\theta = \mu_s\, mg \cos\theta \Rightarrow \tan\theta = \mu_s$$

Once the block starts sliding down, friction acting on the block will be kinetic.

$$\Sigma F_x = ma_x \Rightarrow mg \sin\theta - f_k = ma$$

$$\Rightarrow mg \sin\theta - \mu_k\, mg \cos\theta = ma$$

$$\Rightarrow a = g(\sin\theta - \mu_k \cos\theta)$$

$$\Rightarrow a = \frac{g(\mu_s - \mu_k)}{\sqrt{1 + \mu_s^2}}$$

24. For block,

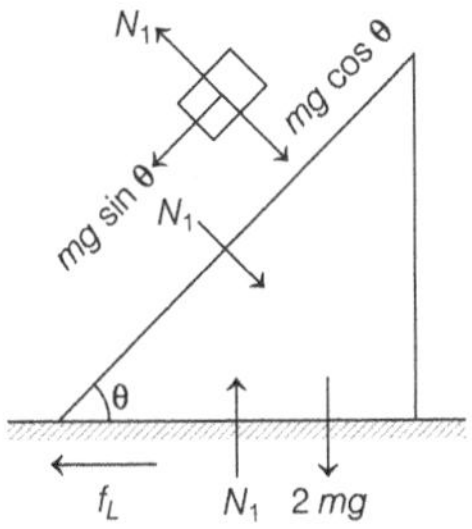

$\Sigma F_y = 0 \Rightarrow N_1 - mg\cos\theta = 0 \Rightarrow N_1 = mg\cos\theta$

For wedge, $\Sigma F_y = 0 \Rightarrow +N_2 - 2mg - N_1\cos\theta = 0$

$\Rightarrow \quad N_2 = 2mg + mg\cos^2\theta$

$\Sigma F_x = 0 \Rightarrow N_1\sin\theta - \mu N_2 = 0$

$\Rightarrow \quad mg\cos\theta\sin\theta = \mu(2mg + mg\cos^2\theta)$

$$\Rightarrow \quad \mu = \frac{\sin\theta\cos\theta}{2+\cos^2\theta} = \frac{\sin 45^\circ\cos 45^\circ}{2+\cos^2 45^\circ} = 0.2$$

25.

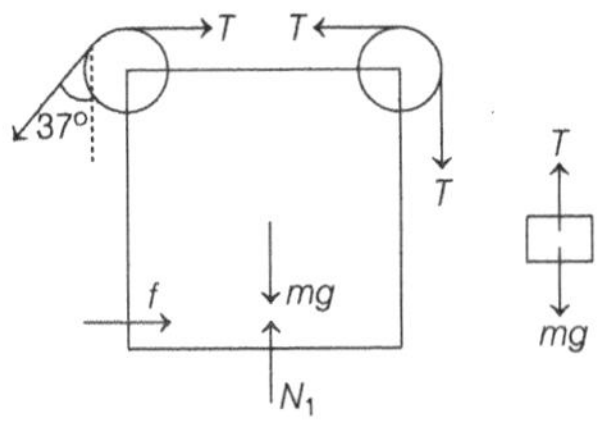

For hanging block,

$\Sigma F_y = 0 \Rightarrow T - mg = 0 \Rightarrow T = mg$

For bigger block,

$\Sigma F_y = 0 \Rightarrow N_1 - mg - T - T\cos 37^\circ = 0$

$$\Rightarrow \quad N_1 = mg + T + T\left(\frac{4}{5}\right) \Rightarrow N_1 = \frac{14mg}{5}$$

$\Sigma F_x = 0 \Rightarrow T\sin 37^\circ - f = 0$

$$\Rightarrow \quad \frac{3mg}{5} = \mu\left(\frac{14mg}{5}\right) \Rightarrow \mu = \frac{3}{14}$$

26.

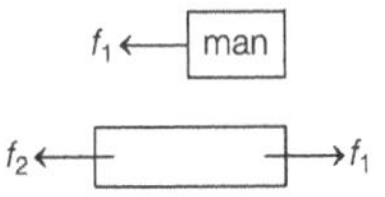

For man, $\Sigma F_x = ma_x \Rightarrow f_1 = 60(2) = 120\text{ N}$

$\Rightarrow \quad f_2 = \mu N = 0.1(100\times 10) = 100\text{ N}$

For plank, $\Sigma F_x = ma_x \Rightarrow f_1 - f_2 = ma$

$\Rightarrow \quad 120 - 100 = 40a \Rightarrow a = 0.5\text{ m/s}^2$, backwards

27. For $(M+m)$ system,

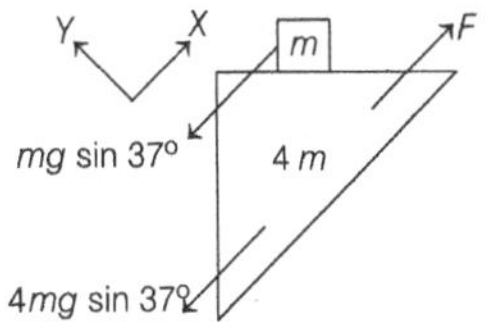

$\Sigma F_x = ma_x \Rightarrow F - 5mg\sin 37^\circ = 5ma$

$$\Rightarrow 8mg - 5mg\left(\frac{3}{5}\right) = 5ma \Rightarrow a = g$$

For block B,

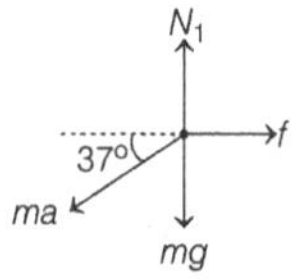

$\Sigma F_x = 0 \Rightarrow f = ma\cos 37^\circ$

$\Sigma F_y = 0 \Rightarrow N_1 = mg + ma\sin 37^\circ$

$$f \le f_L \Rightarrow \frac{4ma}{5} \le \mu\left(mg + \frac{3ma}{5}\right)$$

$$\Rightarrow \quad \mu \ge \frac{1}{2} \Rightarrow \mu_{\text{min}} = \frac{1}{2}$$

28.

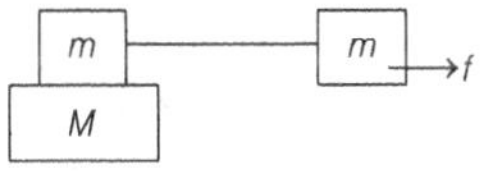

For the above system,

$\Sigma F_x = ma_x \Rightarrow f = (M+2m)a$

and $\quad f \le f_L \Rightarrow (M+2m)a \le \mu mg \Rightarrow a \le \dfrac{\mu mg}{M+2m}$

Taking all the four blocks as system,

$$\Sigma F_x = ma_x \Rightarrow F = (2M+2m)a \Rightarrow F \le \frac{2(M+m)\mu mg}{M+2m}$$

29.

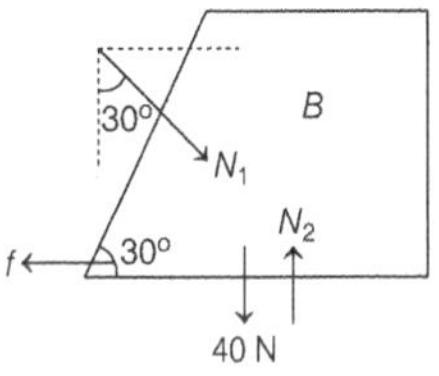

For block B,

$\Sigma F_y = 0 \Rightarrow N_2 = 40 + N_1\cos 30^\circ$

$$f_L = \mu N_2 = \frac{1}{\sqrt{3}}\left(40 + \frac{\sqrt{3}N_1}{2}\right) = \frac{40}{\sqrt{3}} + \frac{N_1}{2}$$

For B to just start sliding,

$$\Sigma F_x = 0 \Rightarrow N_1\sin 30^\circ = \frac{40}{\sqrt{3}} + \frac{N_1}{2}$$

So, B will never slide.

30. Resultant of all external forces acting on the toy is zero.

31. For B,

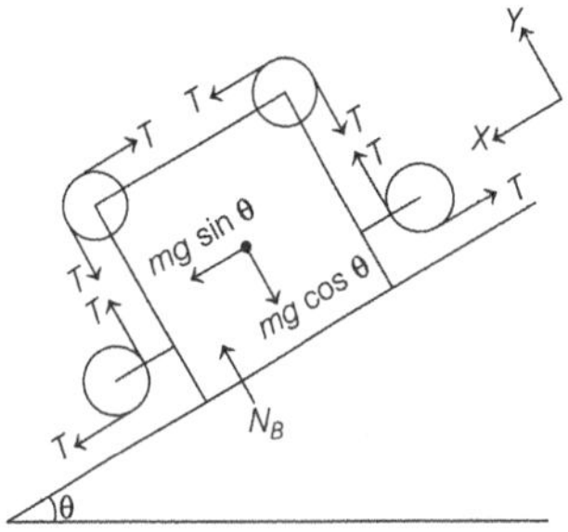

$\Sigma F_x = ma_x \Rightarrow Mg\sin\theta = Ma_B \Rightarrow a_B = g\sin\theta \quad$ ...(i)

For A,

$$\frac{M}{2}g\sin\theta - T = \frac{M}{2}a_A \quad \text{...(ii)}$$

For B,

$$T+\frac{Mg}{2}\sin\theta-\left(\frac{\tan\theta}{2}\right)\left(\frac{M}{2}g\cos\theta\right)=\frac{M}{2}a_C$$

$$T+\frac{Mg\sin\theta}{4}=\frac{M}{2}a_C \quad \text{...(iii)}$$

From string constraint

$$+a_A-a_B+a_B-a_C=0 \Rightarrow a_A=a_C \quad \text{...(iv)}$$

From (ii), (iii) and (iv), we get

$$T=\frac{Mg\sin\theta}{8}$$

32. $f_1=0.3(300)=90$ N, $f_2=0.2(400)=80$ N

$$f_3=0.1(600)=60\text{ N}$$

It $F<60$ N, none of the blocks will move. So, minimum force required to start relative motion anywhere is 60 N.

33.

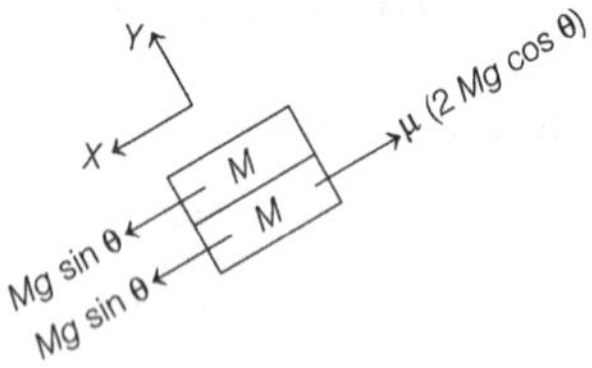

Taking both blocks as a system, $\Sigma F_x=ma_x$

$\Rightarrow 2Mg\sin\theta-\mu(2Mg\cos\theta)=2Ma \Rightarrow a=g(\sin\theta-\mu\cos\theta)$

For upper block,

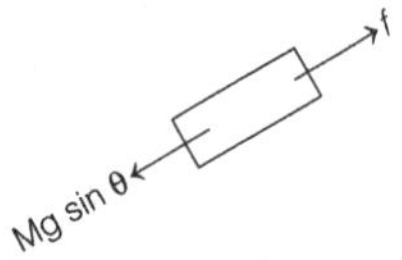

$$\Sigma F_x=ma_x \Rightarrow Mg\sin\theta-f=Mg(\sin\theta-\mu\cos\theta)$$

$$\Rightarrow \quad f=\mu Mg\cos\theta \text{ and } f_L=\mu N=\mu(Mg\cos\theta)$$

Since, $f\le f_L$ both the blocks will have common acceleration.

34.

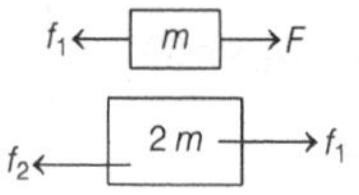

$$f_{1L}=\mu\, mg \text{ and } f_{2L}=\mu\,(3mg)$$

f_1 can be maximum μmg and when f_1 is μmg, $2m$ will not slide and f_2 will be μmg (static).

So, contact force $=\sqrt{N^2+f_2^2}$

$$=\sqrt{(3mg)^2+(\mu mg)^2}$$

$$=mg\sqrt{9+\mu^2}$$

35. No friction will act between the two blocks.

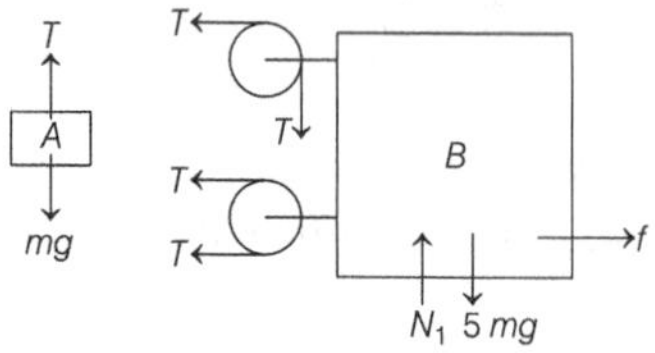

For A, $\Sigma F_y=0 \Rightarrow T-mg=0 \Rightarrow T=mg$

For B, $\Sigma F_y=0 \Rightarrow N_1=5mg+T \Rightarrow N_1=6mg$

$$\Sigma F_x=0 \Rightarrow f=3T=3mg \Rightarrow f\le f_L$$

$$\Rightarrow \quad 3mg\le\mu(6mg) \Rightarrow \mu\ge\frac{1}{2}$$

36.

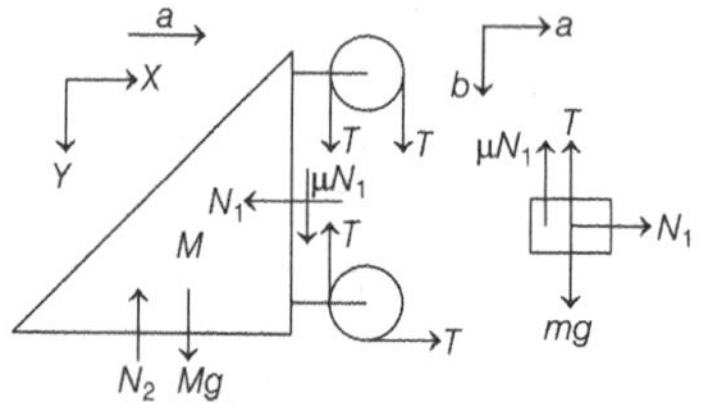

a = acceleration of wedge

and b = acceleration of block w.r.t. wedge

For block, $\Sigma F_x=ma_x \Rightarrow N_1=ma$ ...(i)

$\Sigma F_y=ma_y \Rightarrow mg-T-\mu N_1=mb$ ...(ii)

For wedge, $\Sigma F_x=ma_x \Rightarrow T-N_1=Ma$ ...(iii)

$a=b$ ...(iv)

Solving Eqs. (i), (ii), (iii) and (iv), we get

$$a=\frac{g}{\frac{M}{m}+\mu+2}$$

Acceleration of body $=\mathbf{a}=a\hat{\mathbf{i}}+a\hat{\mathbf{j}}$

$$\Rightarrow \quad |\mathbf{a}|=\sqrt{2}a$$

37. For M,

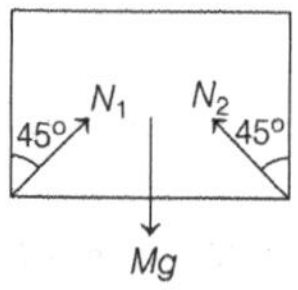

$$\Sigma F_x=0 \Rightarrow N_1\sin45^\circ-N_2\sin45^\circ=0 \Rightarrow N_1=N_2$$

$$\Sigma F_y=0 \Rightarrow N_1\cos45^\circ+N_2\cos45^\circ=Mg$$

$$\Rightarrow N_1=N_2=\frac{Mg}{\sqrt{2}}$$

For m,

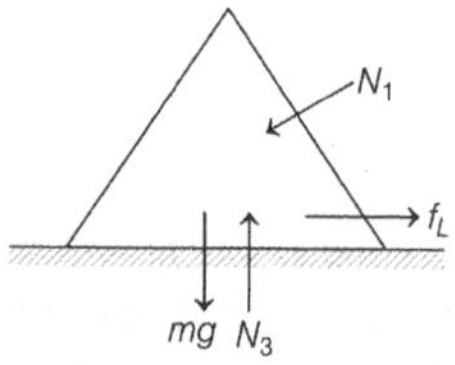

$$\Sigma F_y=0 \Rightarrow N_3=mg+N_1\cos45^\circ$$

$$\Rightarrow \quad N_3=mg+\frac{Mg}{2}$$

$$\Sigma F_x=0 \Rightarrow N_1\sin45^\circ=f_L$$

$$\Rightarrow \quad N_1\sin45^\circ=\mu\left(mg+\frac{Mg}{2}\right)$$

$$\Rightarrow \quad \frac{Mg}{2}=\mu mg+\frac{\mu Mg}{2}$$

$$\Rightarrow \quad M=\frac{2\mu m}{1-\mu}$$

Multiple Choice(s) Correct Questions

1. $\Sigma F_y = 0$

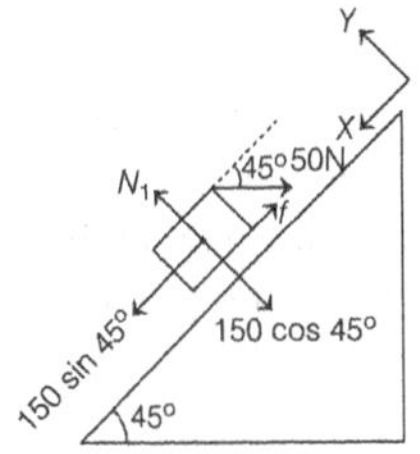

$\Rightarrow N_1 + 150\cos 45° + 50\sin 45° = 0$

$\Rightarrow \quad N_1 = 200\sin 45° = \dfrac{200}{\sqrt{2}}$ N

$\Sigma F_x = 0 \quad \Rightarrow \quad 150\sin 45° - f - 50\cos 45° = 0$

$\Rightarrow \quad f = \dfrac{100}{\sqrt{2}}$ N

$f \le f_L \quad \Rightarrow \quad \dfrac{100}{\sqrt{2}} \le \mu\left(\dfrac{200}{\sqrt{2}}\right) \quad \Rightarrow \quad \mu \ge \dfrac{1}{2}$

2. $f_k = \mu_k N = 0.1\,(20\,g) = 2g$ N

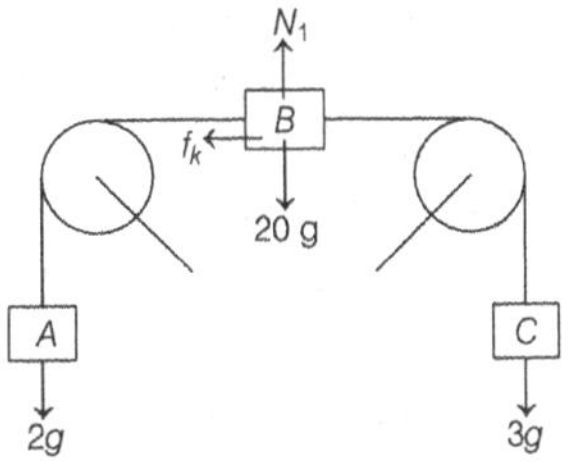

$a = \dfrac{3g - 2g - f_k}{25} \quad \Rightarrow \quad a = -\,0.4\text{ m/s}^2$

Once the system comes to rest, it will not move as driving force is less than the limiting friction.

3. A. $a = \dfrac{40 - 20 - 10}{6} = \dfrac{5}{3}\text{ m/s}^2$

B. Tension is not same throughout.

C. For 2kg, $\Sigma F_y = ma_y$

$\Rightarrow \quad T - 20 = 2\left(\dfrac{5}{3}\right) \quad \Rightarrow \quad T = 20 + \dfrac{10}{3} = \dfrac{70}{3}$N

D. $a = \dfrac{40 - 20 - 10}{6} = \dfrac{5}{3}\text{ m/s}^2$

4. w.r.t car

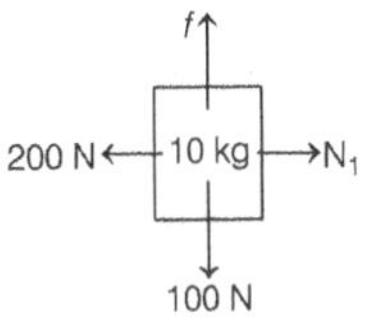

$\Sigma F_x = 0 \quad \Rightarrow N_1 - 200 = 0 \quad \Rightarrow \quad N_1 = 200$ N

So, $\quad f_L = \mu_s N_1 = 0.6 \times 200 = 120$ N

Since, mg is less than $f_L = 120$ N, friction between the box and car will be 100 N (static).

So, $f = 100$ N and the box will not slide down the vertical wall.

Contact force $= \sqrt{N^2 + f^2} = \sqrt{(200)^2 + (100)^2} = 100\sqrt{5}$ N

5.

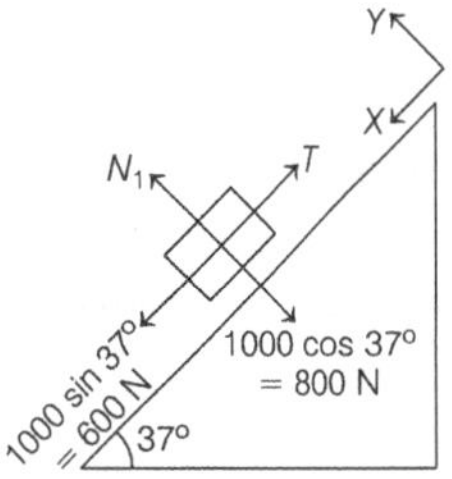

$\Sigma F_y = 0 \quad \Rightarrow +N_1 - 800 = 0 \quad \Rightarrow N_1 = 800$ N

$f_L = \mu N_1 = 0.3 \times 800 = 240$ N

To just take the block up the plane T should be $600 + 240 = 840$ N

To prevent the block from sliding down the plane, T should be

$600 - 240 = 360$ N

So, for values of $360\text{ N} \le T \le 840$ N, system will remain in equilibrium.

$\Rightarrow \quad 36\text{ kg} \le m \le 84$ kg

6. $\Sigma F_z = 0 \Rightarrow +N_1 + 30 - 50 = 0 \quad \Rightarrow N_1 = 20$ N

$f_k = \mu_k N = 0.4(20) = 8\text{N} \quad \Rightarrow \ f_k = -8\sin 37°\,\hat{i} - 8\cos 37°\,\hat{j}$

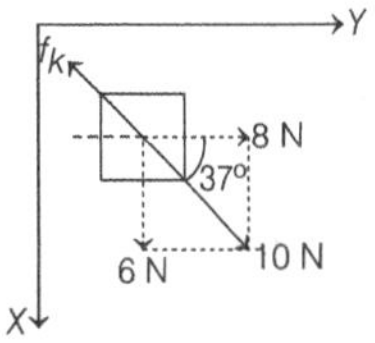

$f_k = (-\,4.8\hat{i} - 6.4\hat{j})$ N $\quad \Rightarrow \quad a = \left(\dfrac{10-8}{5}\right) = 0.4\text{ m/s}^2$

7. $F_1 = W\sin\phi + \mu W\cos\phi$

$F_2 = W\sin\phi - \mu W\cos\phi$

$F_1 = 2F_2$

$\Rightarrow \ W\sin\phi + \mu W\cos\phi = 2(W\sin\phi - \mu W\cos\phi)$

$\Rightarrow \ 3\mu\cos\phi = \sin\phi \quad \Rightarrow 3\mu = \tan\phi \quad \Rightarrow 3\tan\theta = \tan\phi$

and $\quad F_1 = W\sin\phi + \tan\theta\, W\cos\phi$

$\Rightarrow \quad F_1 = W(\sin\phi\cos\theta + \sin\theta\cos\phi)\sec\theta$

$\Rightarrow \quad F_1 = W\sin(\phi + \theta)\sec\theta$

$F_2 = W\sin\phi - \dfrac{\sin\theta}{\cos\theta}W\cos\phi$

$\Rightarrow \quad F_2 = W\sin(\phi - \theta)\sec\theta$

8. $a_{max} = \dfrac{mg\sin\theta + \mu\, mg\cos\theta}{m} = 14\text{ m/s}^2$

$a_{min} = \dfrac{\mu\, mg\cos\theta - mg\sin\theta}{m} = 2\text{ m/s}^2$

$f_L = \mu\, mg\cos\theta$

When static friction is $mg\sin\theta$ up the plane, then $a = 0$.

9. $f_{1L} = 0.2(40) = 8\text{ N} \quad \Rightarrow f_{2L} = 0.1(90) = 9$ N

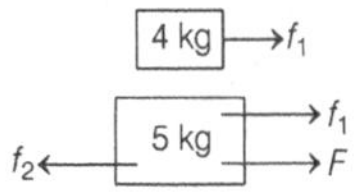

For 4 kg,

$$\Sigma F_x = ma \Rightarrow f_1 = 4a \quad \text{and } f_1 \le f_{1L}$$
$$4a \le 8 \Rightarrow a \le 2\ \text{m/s}^2 \Rightarrow a_{max} = 2\ \text{m/s}^2$$

For (4 kg + 5 kg) system,

$$\Sigma F_x = ma_x \Rightarrow F - 9 = 9a \Rightarrow F = 9a + 9$$

For slipping to take place between 4 kg and 5 kg blocks, $a \ge 2\ \text{m/s}^2$

$$\Rightarrow \quad F \ge 9(2) + 9 \Rightarrow F \ge 27\ \text{N}$$

10. From F-t graph,

$$F = 1.8t$$

At $t = 3$, block starts to move.

So, $F = f_L \Rightarrow 1.8 \times 3 = \mu_s (1.5)(10) \Rightarrow \mu_s = 0.36$

and $\Sigma F = ma \Rightarrow F - f_k = ma$

$\Rightarrow 1.8 \times 3 - \mu_k (1.5\,g) = 1.5 \times 1.2 \Rightarrow \mu_k = 0.24$

$$\Sigma F = ma \Rightarrow F - \mu_k (1.5g) = 1.5(2.4)$$

$\Rightarrow 1.8t - 0.24(15) = 1.5 \times 2.4 \Rightarrow t = 4\ \text{s}$

11. Lets assume A and B move together with acceleration a towards left.

Then,

$$60 - T_1 = 6a \quad \text{...(i)}$$
$$T_1 - T_2 - 18 = 9a \quad \text{...(ii)}$$
$$T_2 - 10 = 1a \quad \text{...(iii)}$$

Solving Eqs. (i), (ii) and (iii), we get

$$a = 2\ \text{m/s}^2, T_1 = 48\ \text{N} \quad \text{and} \quad T_2 = 12\ \text{N}$$

Now for 6 kg,

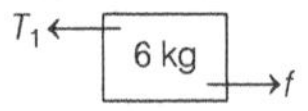

$$\Sigma F_x = ma_x \Rightarrow T_1 - f = 6(a) \Rightarrow 48 - f = 12$$

$\Rightarrow \quad f = 36\ \text{N}$ and $f_L = 0.7(60) = 42\ \text{N}$

Since $f < f_L$, our assumption is correct.

12.

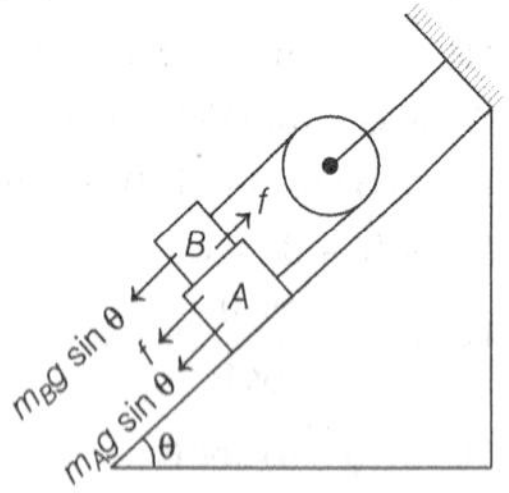

(A) $m_B > m_A$

For system to be equilibrium,

Net force along the string = 0

$$\Rightarrow \quad m_B g \sin\theta = f + f + m_A g \sin\theta$$
$$\Rightarrow \quad 2f = m_B g \sin\theta - m_A g \sin\theta$$
$$\Rightarrow \quad f = \frac{(m_B - m_A) g \sin\theta}{2}$$

and $\quad f \le f_L$

$$\Rightarrow \frac{(m_B - m_A) g \sin\theta}{2} \le \mu\, mg \cos\theta \Rightarrow \mu \ge \frac{(m_B - m_A)\tan\theta}{2}$$

(B) If $\quad m_A = m_B$, then $f = 0$

13. Angle of repose for A is $\tan^{-1}(1) = 45°$

Angle of repose for B is $\tan^{-1}\left(\frac{1}{\sqrt{2}}\right) = 30°$

If $\theta \le 45°$, none of the block has the tendency to slide down. So, contact force between them will be zero.

When they just start moving together down the inclined plane, friction between blocks and inclined plane will be limiting.

$$\Sigma F_x = 0$$

$\Rightarrow mg \sin\theta + mg \sin\theta - \mu_1 mg \cos\theta - \mu_2 mg \cos\theta = 0$

$\Rightarrow 2\sin\theta = (\mu_1 + \mu_2)\cos\theta \Rightarrow \theta = \tan^{-1}\left(\frac{\mu_1 + \mu_2}{2}\right)$

14.

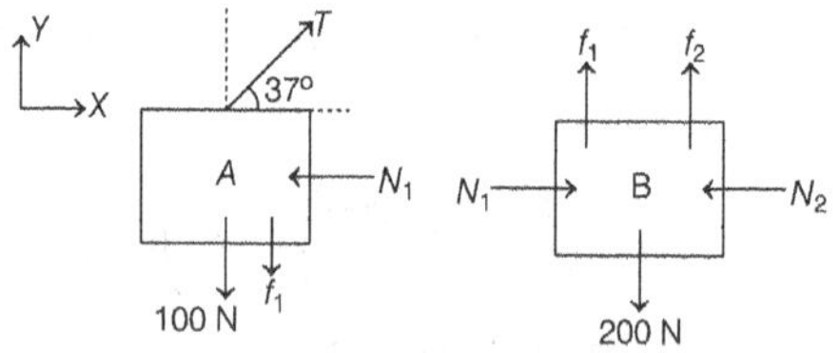

For A, $\quad \Sigma F_x = 0 \Rightarrow T\cos 37° = N_1 \quad \text{...(i)}$

$\quad \Sigma F_y = 0 \Rightarrow T\sin 37° = f_1 + 100 \quad \text{...(ii)}$

and $\quad f_1 = \mu N_1 \quad \text{...(iii)}$

Solving Eqs. (i), (ii) and (iii), we get

$$T = 500\ \text{N and } N_1 = 400\ \text{N}$$

For B,

$$\Sigma F_y = ma_y \Rightarrow mg - f_1 - f_2 = ma$$

$\Rightarrow 500 - 200 - 200 = 50a \Rightarrow a = 2\ \text{m/s}^2$

15.

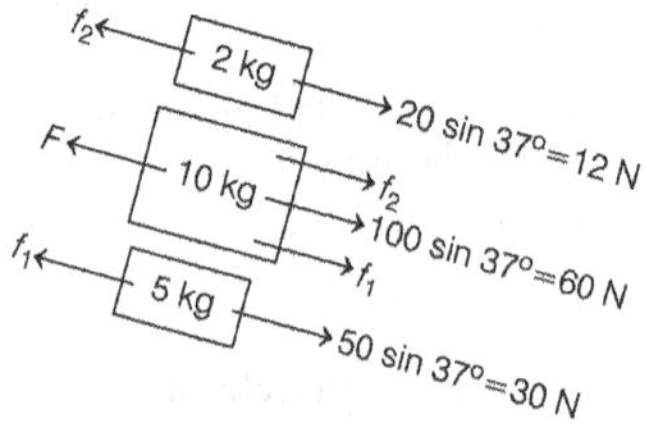

$$f_{1L} = 0.5(120\cos 37°) = 48\ \text{N}$$

So, friction between 5 kg and 10 kg will be 30 N (static).

$$f_1 = 30\ \text{N} \Rightarrow f_{2L} = 0.8(20\cos 37°) = 12.8\ \text{N}$$

So, friction between 2 kg and 10 kg will be 12 N (static).

$$f_2 = 12\ \text{N}$$

For 10 kg block

$$\Sigma F_x = 0 \Rightarrow F - f_1 - f_2 - 60 = 0 \Rightarrow F = 102\ \text{N}$$

16. If $\mu = 0.2$

Lets assume belt and block B move together with common acceleration a.

$$a = \frac{400 - 0.2(600)}{100} = 2.8\ \text{m/s}^2$$

For 60 kg block

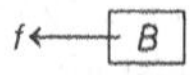

$$f = 60 \times 2.8 \Rightarrow f = 168\ \text{N} \Rightarrow f_L = 0.2(600) = 120\ \text{N}$$

So, our assumption is wrong. Friction between block B and belt will be kinetic.

$$a_B = \frac{120}{60} = 2 \text{ m/s}^2$$

$$v^2 = u^2 + 2as \Rightarrow v^2 = 0^2 + 2(2)(2)$$

$$\Rightarrow \quad v = 2\sqrt{2} \text{ m/s}$$

If $\mu = 0.5$, $a = \dfrac{400 - 0.5(600)}{100} = 1 \text{ m/s}^2$

For 60 kg block,

$$f = 60 \times 1 = 60 \text{ N}$$

Since $f \le f_L$, our assumption is correct.

$$v^2 = u^2 + 2as \Rightarrow v^2 = 0^2 + 2(1)(2) \Rightarrow v = 2 \text{ m/s}$$

17.

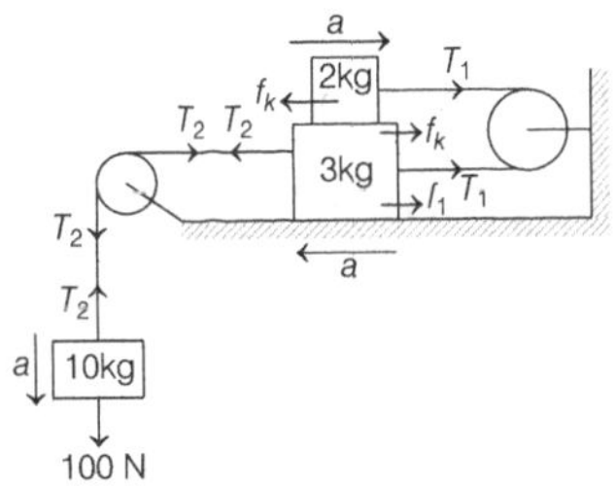

For 10 kg block,

$$\Sigma F_y = ma_y \Rightarrow 100 - T_2 = 10a \quad \text{...(i)}$$

For 3kg block,

$$\Sigma F_x = ma_x \Rightarrow T_2 - T_1 - 0.5(20) - 0.4(50) = 3a \quad \text{...(ii)}$$

For 2 kg block,

$$\Sigma F_x = ma_x \Rightarrow T_1 - 0.5(20) = 2a \quad \text{...(iii)}$$

Solving Eqs. (i), (ii) and (iii), we get

$$a = 4 \text{ m/s}^2, T_1 = 18 \text{ N}, T_2 = 60 \text{ N}$$

18. Lets assume A and B move together with common acceleration a.

$$\Sigma F_x = ma_x \Rightarrow 3P = 120a \Rightarrow a = \frac{P}{40}$$

For 100 kg block,

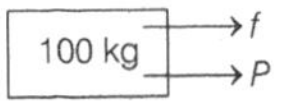

$$\Sigma F_x = ma_x \Rightarrow P + f = 100\left(\frac{P}{40}\right)$$

$$\Rightarrow \quad f = 1.5P \Rightarrow f_L = 0.3(200) = 60 \text{ N}$$

For our assumption to be correct

$$f \le f_L \Rightarrow 1.5P \le 60 \Rightarrow P \le 40 \text{ N}$$

So, If $P \le 40$ N, $a = \dfrac{P}{40}$ for both the blocks.

If $P > 40$ N $\Rightarrow a_{20\,\text{kg}} = \dfrac{2P - 60}{20}$ and $a_{100\,\text{kg}} = \dfrac{P + 60}{100}$

Comprehension Based Questions

1 and 2. $F + mg \sin 30° = \mu_s mg \cos 30°$ ...(i)

$mg \sin 30° = F + \mu_k mg \cos 30°$ ...(ii)

$\mu_s = 2\mu_k$ ...(iii)

Solving Eqs. (i), (ii) and (iii), we get

$$F = \frac{mg}{6} \Rightarrow \mu_s = \frac{4}{3\sqrt{3}} \text{ and } \mu_k = \frac{2}{3\sqrt{3}}$$

3. If the man continues to push down

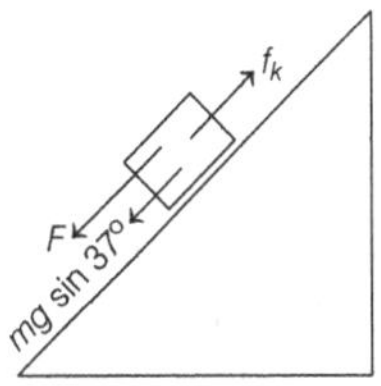

$$F + mg \sin 30° - \mu_k mg \cos 30° = ma$$

$$\Rightarrow \frac{mg}{6} + \frac{mg}{2} - \frac{mg}{3} = ma \Rightarrow a = \frac{g}{3}$$

4. $F_{min} = \mu_s mg \cos 30° + mg \sin 30° = \dfrac{7mg}{6}$

5. $F_{min} = \mu_k mg \cos 30° + mg \sin 30° = \dfrac{5mg}{6}$

6,7 and 8. Driving force on system $= 20 - 10 = 10$ N

Limiting friction for system $= 0.2 \times 60 + 0.2 \times 40 + 0.2 \times 20 = 24$ N

So, the system will be in equilibrium.

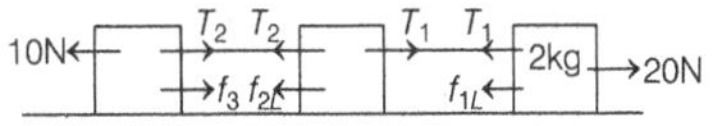

$$f_{1L} = 0.2(20) = 4 \text{ N}$$

For 2 kg, $\Sigma F_x = 0 \Rightarrow T_1 + f_{1L} = 20$

$\Rightarrow \quad T_1 = 16$ N

$$f_{2L} = 0.2(40) = 8 \text{ N}$$

For 4 kg, $\Sigma F_x = 0 \Rightarrow T_1 = T_2 + 8 \Rightarrow T_2 = 8\text{N}$

For 6 kg, $\Sigma F_x = 0 \Rightarrow T_2 + f_3 = 10 \Rightarrow f_3 = 2$ N

9. Driving force on the system along the string

$$F = 2\,mg \sin 45° - mg \sin 45°$$

$$= mg \sin 45° = \frac{mg}{\sqrt{2}}$$

Limiting friction for the system,

$$f_L = \frac{2}{3}(mg \cos 45°) + \frac{1}{3}(2\,mg \cos 45°)$$

$$= \frac{4}{3} mg \cos 45° = \frac{4mg}{3\sqrt{2}}$$

Since, $F < f_L$, system will be in equilibrium.

$$a = 0$$

10. First, limiting friction will act on B.

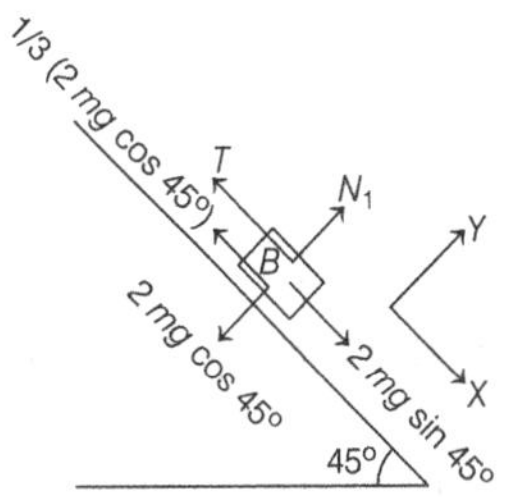

$$\Sigma F_x = 0 \Rightarrow 2mg \sin 45° = T + \frac{1}{3}(2\,mg \cos 45°)$$

$$\Rightarrow \quad T = \frac{4}{3\sqrt{2}} mg = \frac{2\sqrt{2}\,mg}{3}$$

11. For A,

$$\Sigma F_x = 0 \quad \Rightarrow T = mg \sin 45° + f$$

$$\Rightarrow \qquad f = T - mg \sin 45° = \frac{mg}{3\sqrt{2}}$$

12. If $F < f_L$ (40 N), A will not press B.

13. $F \geq (f_L)_A + (f_L)_B \quad \Rightarrow \quad F \geq 40 + 20 \quad \Rightarrow \quad F_{min} = 60$ N

14. If $F = 50$ N

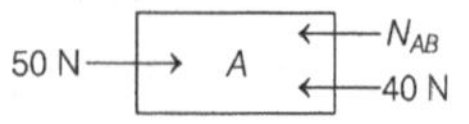

then $\quad N_{AB} = 10$ N $\quad \Rightarrow f = N_{AB} = 10$ N

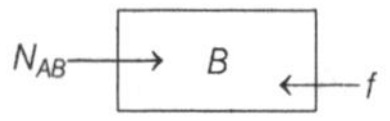

15. At $\quad t = 12$ s $\quad \Rightarrow F = 0.5t = 6$ N

For (2 kg + 4 kg) system,

$$\Sigma F_x = ma_x \quad \Rightarrow 6 = 6a \quad \Rightarrow \quad a = 1 \text{ m/s}^2$$

For 2 kg block,

$$6 - f_L = 2(1) \quad \Rightarrow f_L = 4 \text{ N} = \mu(20) \quad \Rightarrow \quad \mu = 0.20$$

16. For $t < 12$, acceleration of each of them will be

$$\frac{0.5t}{6} = \frac{t}{12}$$

For $t > 12$,

$$a_{block} = \frac{0.5t - 4}{2} \quad \Rightarrow a_{plank} = 1 \text{ m/s}^2$$

17. For $\ t = 0$ to $t = 12$ s,

$$a = \frac{t}{12} \quad \Rightarrow \int_0^v dv = \int_0^t \frac{t}{12} dt \quad \Rightarrow v = \frac{t^2}{24}$$

At $\qquad t = 12, v = \frac{(12)^2}{24} = 6$ m/s

For $\qquad t = 0$ to $t = 12$, $a = 1$ m/s^2

$$v = u + at \quad \Rightarrow \quad v = 6 + 1(3) = 9 \text{ m/s}$$

$$a_{avg} = \frac{\Delta v}{\Delta t} = \frac{9 - 0}{15} = 0.6 \text{ m/s}^2$$

18. Driving force on system along the string

$$= 100 \sin 37° - 50 \sin 53° = 60 - 40 = 20 \text{ N}$$

Limiting friction on the system

$$= 0.3(100 \cos 37°) + 0.1(50 \cos 53°) = 24 + 3 = 27 \text{ N}$$

Since, driving force < Limiting friction

$$a = 0$$

19. Driving force = 20 N

Kinetic friction on system

$$= 0.25(100 \cos 37°) + 0.075(50 \cos 53°)$$

$$= 20 + 2.25 = 22.25 \text{ N}$$

$$a = \frac{20 - 22.25}{15} = -\frac{2.25}{15} = -0.15 \text{ m/s}^2$$

$$v = u + at \quad \Rightarrow \quad 0 = 2 - 0.15\,t$$

$$\Rightarrow \qquad t = \frac{40}{3} \text{ s or } 13.33 \text{ s}$$

20. Driving force on the system $= 100 \sin 37° - 40 \sin 53°$

$$= 60 - 32 = 28$$

Limiting friction on the system

$$= 0.3(100 \cos 37°) + 0.1\,(40 \cos 53°)$$

$$= 24 + 2.4 = 26.4$$

So, the system will accelerate.

Kinetic friction on the system

$= 0.25(100 \cos 37°) + 0.075(40 \cos 53°) = 20 + 1.8 = 21.8$ N

$$\text{Acceleration } = \frac{28 - 21.8}{14} = \frac{31}{70} \text{ m/s}^2$$

For 10 kg block,

$$100 \sin 37° - T - 0.25(100 \cos 37°) = 10 \times \frac{31}{7}$$

$$T = 40 - \frac{31}{7} = \frac{249}{7} \text{ N or } 35.57 \text{ N}$$

21 and 22.

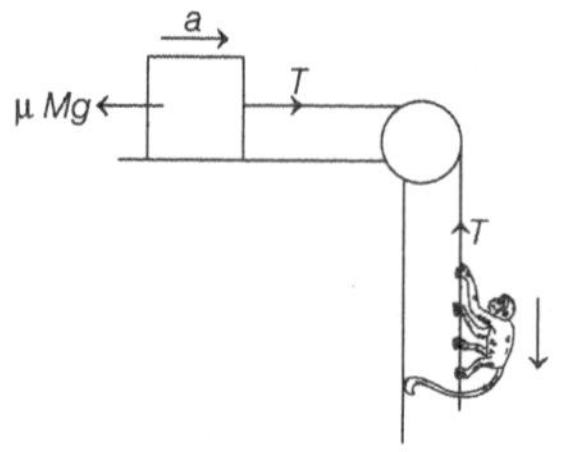

$$a_{MR} = b \quad \Rightarrow \quad a_M = b + a_R = b + a$$

For block,

$$\Sigma F_x = ma_x \quad \Rightarrow \quad T - \mu Mg = Ma \qquad \text{...(i)}$$

For monkey,

$$mg - T = m(b + a) \qquad \text{...(ii)}$$

Solving Eqs. (i) and (ii), we get

$$a = \frac{m(g - b) - \mu Mg}{M + m} \quad \text{and } T = \frac{Mm(\mu g + g - b)}{M + m}$$

23 and 24. $\quad 450 - T = 45a \qquad$ ...(i)

$$T = 30a \qquad \text{...(ii)}$$

Solving Eqs. (i) and (ii), we get

$$a = 6 \text{ m/s}^2$$

For 5 kg block,

$$\Sigma F_x = ma_x \quad \Rightarrow f = 5 \times 6 = 30 \text{ N}$$

25. For 5 kg block,

$$\Sigma F_x = ma_x$$

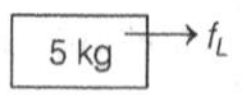

$$f_L = 5a \quad \Rightarrow \quad 75 = 5a \quad \Rightarrow \quad a = 15 \text{ m/s}^2$$

$$a = 15 = \frac{Mg}{M + 30}$$

$$\Rightarrow \qquad 10M = 15M + 450 \qquad \Rightarrow \qquad M = -90 \text{ kg}$$

which is not possible.

26.

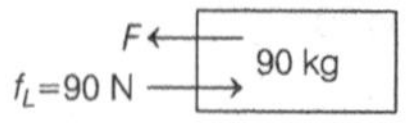

$$f_L = 0.1 \times 900 = 90 \text{ N}$$

For system not to move,

$$F \leq 90 \text{ N}$$

27.

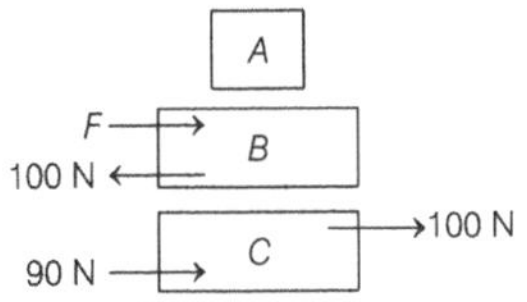

For C,

$$\Sigma F = ma \quad \Rightarrow 100 - 90 = 40a \quad \Rightarrow a = 0.25 \text{ m/s}^2$$

For sliding to take place between B and C, acceleration of B should be greater than 0.25 m/s^2.

For $(A+B)$, $\quad \Sigma F = ma \quad \Rightarrow F - 100 = 50 \times 0.25$

$\Rightarrow \quad F = 112.5$ N

28. For A,

$\Rightarrow \quad \Sigma F_x = ma \quad \Rightarrow f = 20a \quad \Rightarrow f_L = 20\, a_{max}$

$\Rightarrow \quad a_{max} = 1 \text{ m/s}^2$

For $(A+B)$,

$\Rightarrow \quad F - 100 = 50(1) \quad \Rightarrow F = 150$ N

29 and 30.

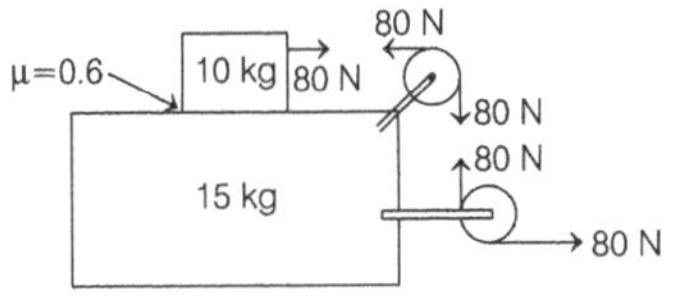

For (15 kg + 10 kg) system,

$$\Sigma F = ma \quad \Rightarrow \quad 80 = 25a$$

$$\Rightarrow \quad a = \frac{16}{5} = 3.2 \text{ m/s}^2$$

For 15 kg block,

$$\Sigma F = ma \quad \Rightarrow f = 15\left(\frac{16}{5}\right) = 48 \text{ N}$$

$$f_L = 0.6 \times 100 = 600 \text{ N}$$

Since $f < f_L$, both blocks will move with common acceleration of 3.2 m/s^2.

31. $F = 120$ N

Friction between the blocks will be kinetic.

For 15 kg block,

$$\Sigma F = ma \quad \Rightarrow f_k = 60 = 15a \quad \Rightarrow a = 4 \text{ m/s}^2$$

32 and 33.

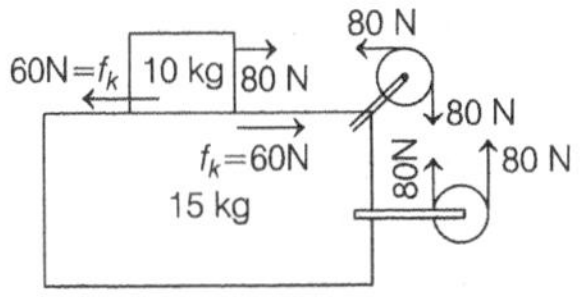

For 10 kg,

$$\Sigma F = ma \quad \Rightarrow 80 - 60 = 10a$$

$$\Rightarrow \quad a = 2 \text{ m/s}^2, \text{ towards right}$$

For 15 kg,

$$\Sigma F = ma \quad \Rightarrow \quad 80 - 60 = 15a$$

$$\Rightarrow \quad a = \frac{4}{3} \text{ m/s}^2, \text{ towards left}$$

34.

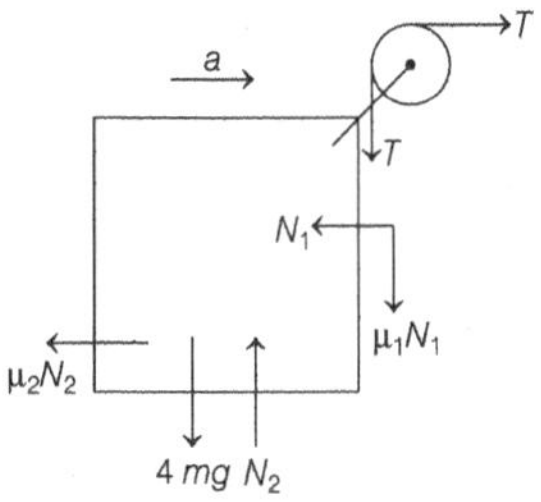

For smaller block,

$$\Sigma F_x = ma_x \quad \Rightarrow \quad N_1 = ma \qquad \text{...(i)}$$

$$\Sigma F_y = ma_y \quad \Rightarrow \quad mg - T - \mu_1 N_1 = mb \qquad \text{...(ii)}$$

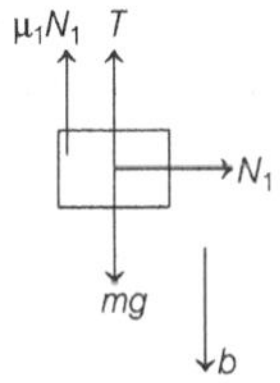

For bigger block,

$$\Sigma F_x = ma_x \Rightarrow 2T - \mu_2 N_2 - N_1 = 4ma \qquad \text{...(iii)}$$

$$\Sigma F_y = 0 \Rightarrow N_2 = 4mg + T + \mu_1 N_1 \qquad \text{...(iv)}$$

From string constraint,

$$-a - a + b = 0 \quad \Rightarrow \quad b = 2a \qquad \text{...(v)}$$

Solving Eqs (i), (ii), (iii), (iv) and (v), we get

$$a = \frac{g}{18}$$

35. $\mathbf{a} = a\hat{\mathbf{i}} + b\hat{\mathbf{j}} = a\hat{\mathbf{i}} + 2a\hat{\mathbf{j}}$

Acceleration $= \sqrt{a^2 + (2a)^2} = \sqrt{5}a$

36.

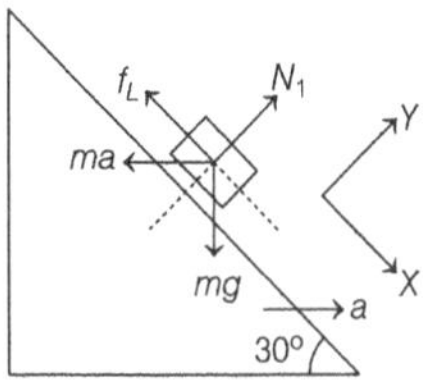

$$\Sigma F_y = 0 \quad \Rightarrow N_1 - mg \cos 30° - ma \sin 30° = 0$$

$$\Rightarrow \quad N_1 = mg \cos 30° + ma \sin 30° \qquad \text{...(i)}$$

$$\Sigma F_x = 0 \quad \Rightarrow \quad mg \sin 30° = ma \cos 30° + \mu N_1 \qquad \text{...(ii)}$$

From Eqs. (i) and (ii), we get

$$a = \frac{\sqrt{3}g}{7}$$

37.

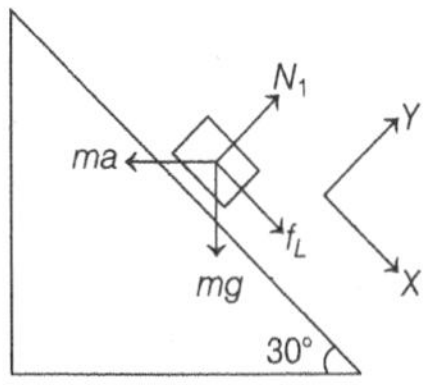

$$\Sigma F_y = 0 \quad \Rightarrow N_1 = mg \cos 30° + ma \sin 30° \qquad \text{...(i)}$$

$$\Sigma F_x = 0 \quad \Rightarrow \quad ma \cos 30° = mg \sin 30° + \mu N_1 \qquad \text{...(ii)}$$

Solving Eqs. (i) and (ii), we get

$$a = \frac{3\sqrt{3}g}{5}$$

38. In absence of friction, $\Sigma F_x = 0$

$\Rightarrow \quad ma\cos 30° = mg\sin 30° \quad \Rightarrow a = \dfrac{g}{\sqrt{3}}$

Match the Columns Questions

1. (a)

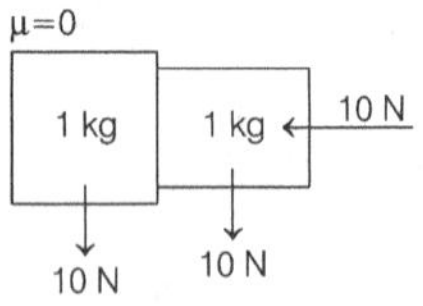

In absence of friction between the blocks, both blocks have same acceleration. There is no relative motion between them. So, friction between the blocks will be zero.

$$a_A = a_B = 10\ \text{m/s}^2,\ f = 0$$

(b) Between the blocks

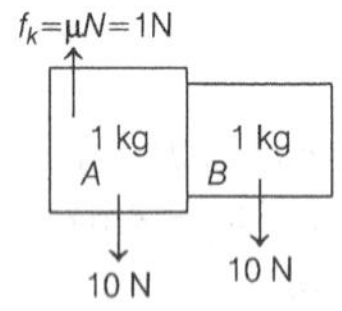

$f = 0$ as $\mu = 0$

For A,

$$\Sigma F = ma \quad \Rightarrow 10 - 1 = 1a_A \Rightarrow a_A = 9\ \text{m/s}^2$$

For B,

$$\Sigma F = ma \quad \Rightarrow 10 = 1a_B \Rightarrow a_B = 10\ \text{m/s}^2$$

(c) Taking $(A + B)$ system,

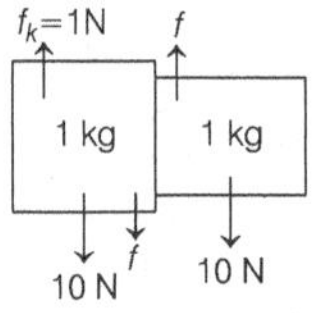

$$\Sigma F = ma \quad \Rightarrow \quad 20 - 1 = 2a \quad \Rightarrow \quad a_A = a_B = 9.5\ \text{m/s}^2$$

For B,

$$\Sigma F = ma \quad \Rightarrow 10 - f = 1(9.5) \quad \Rightarrow f = 0.5\ \text{N}$$

and $\quad f_L = \mu N = 1(10) = 10\ \text{N}$

As $f < f_L$, our assumption is correct.

(d) Taking $(A + B)$ system,

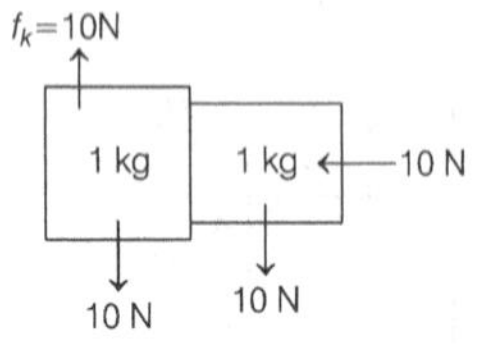

$$\Sigma F = ma \quad \Rightarrow 10 + 10 - 10 = 2a \quad \Rightarrow a = 5\ \text{m/s}^2$$

For B,

$$\Sigma F = ma \Rightarrow 10 - f = 1(5) \quad \Rightarrow f = 5\ \text{N}$$

and $f_L = \mu N = 0.1(10) = 1\ \text{N}$

So, our assumption is wrong. Friction between the blocks will be kinetic.

For B,

$$\Sigma F = ma \Rightarrow 10 - 1 = 1 \times a_B = 9\ \text{m/s}^2$$

For A,

$$\Sigma F = ma \Rightarrow 10 + 1 - 10 = 1 \times a_A \Rightarrow a_A = 1\ \text{m/s}^2$$

2. (a)

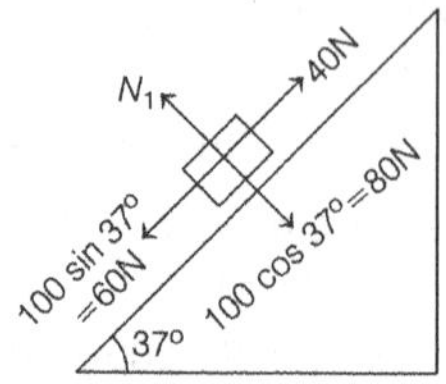

$$\Sigma F_y = 0 \quad \Rightarrow N_1 - 80 = 0 \quad \Rightarrow \quad N_1 = 80\ \text{N}$$

$$f_L = \mu N_1 = 0.3(80) = 24\ \text{N}$$

In absence of friction, driving force on the block is 20 N down the plane.

Since, 20 N $< f_L$, friction will be 20 N (static) up the plane.

(b) In absence of friction, driving force is 20 N up the plane.

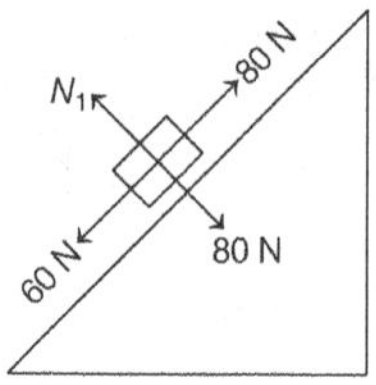

Since, 20 N $< f_L$, friction will be 20 N (static) down the plane.

(c)

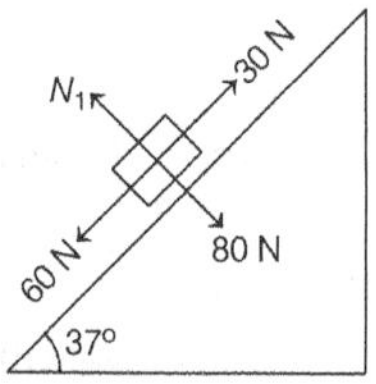

Since driving force is more than limiting friction, block will move and friction will be kinetic up the plane.

(d)

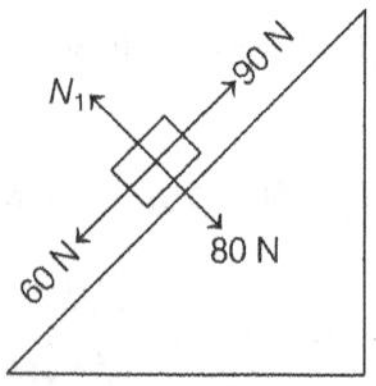

Since driving force $90 - 60 = 30$ N is more than limiting friction, block will move up the plane and friction will be kinetic down the plane.

3. (c) When $\mu_1 > \tan\theta$ and $\mu_2 > \tan\theta$, both the blocks will be at rest. Normal force between them will be zero.

(b) When $\mu_1 < \tan\theta$ and $\mu_2 > \tan\theta$, m_2 will be at rest, m_1 will slide down.

(d) When $\mu_1 = \mu_2 < \tan\theta$, both blocks will slide with same acceleration and normal force between them will be zero.

(a) When $\mu_1 > \tan\theta$ and $\mu_2 < \tan\theta$ and $m_1 g \sin\theta + m_2 g \sin\theta \geq \mu_1 m_1 g \cos\theta + \mu_2 m_2 g \cos\theta$, both blocks will slide down with same acceleration and normal force between them will be non-zero.

4. Contact force $= R = \sqrt{N^2 + f^2}$

For $\theta \leq \tan^{-1}(\mu_s)$, $N = mg\cos\theta$

$$f_s = mg\cos\theta,\ R = \sqrt{N^2 + f_s^2} = mg,\ a = 0$$

For $\theta > \tan^{-1}(\mu_s)$, $N = mg\cos\theta$

$$f_k = \mu_k mg\cos\theta \Rightarrow R = (\sqrt{1+\mu_k^2})\, mg\cos\theta$$

$$a = g\sin\theta - \mu_k g\cos\theta$$

5. Block B will not move, as tension acting on block B is less than limiting friction.

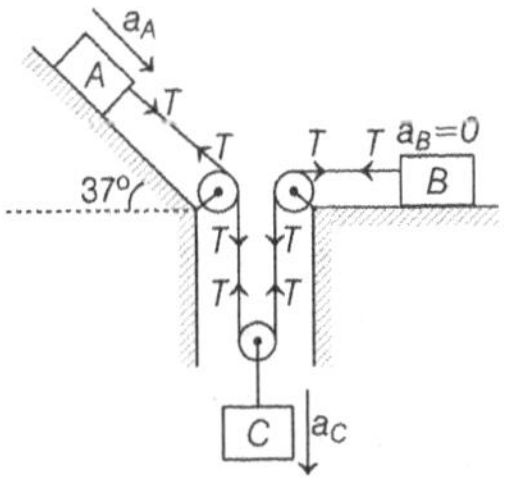

For C, $\Sigma F = ma \Rightarrow 25 - 2T = 2.5\, a_C$ ...(i)

For A, $\Sigma F = ma$

$\Rightarrow T + 50\sin 37° - 0.5(50\cos 37°) = 5a$

$\Rightarrow T + 10 = 5a_A$ ...(ii)

From string constraint,

$\Rightarrow a_A = 2a_C$ ...(iii)

Solving Eqs. (i), (ii) and (iii), we get

$$a_A = 4,\ a_B = 0$$

and $a_C = 2$ and $T = 10$

6. $f_{1L} = 0.2(20) = 4\text{ N}$

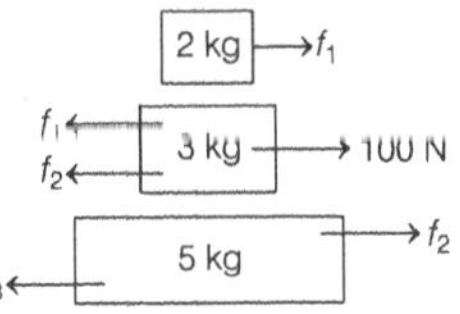

$$f_{2L} = 0.1(50) = 5\text{ N},\quad f_{3L} = 0.1(100) = 10\text{ N}$$

Acceleration of 5 kg will be zero as

$$f_{2L} < f_{3L}$$

If we take (3kg + 2 kg) as a system

$$\Sigma F = ma \Rightarrow 100 - 5 = 5a \Rightarrow a = 19\text{ m/s}^2$$

But maximum acceleration of 2 kg can be 2 m/s^2. So, friction between 2 kg and 3 kg will be kinetic.

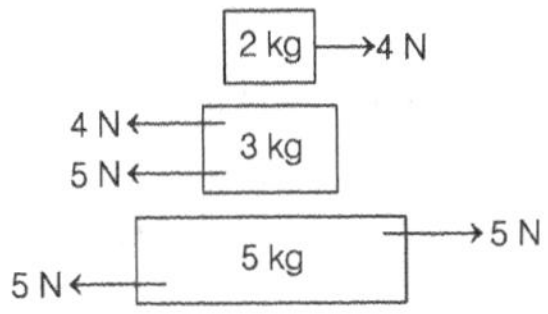

Numerical Value Questions

1. For A,

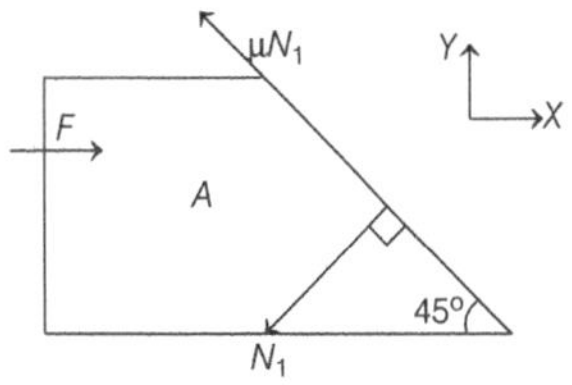

$$\Sigma F_x = 0 \Rightarrow F - N_1\sin 45° - \mu N_1\cos 45° = 0$$

$$\Rightarrow \quad F = \frac{N_1}{\sqrt{2}}(1+\mu) \quad \text{...(i)}$$

For B,

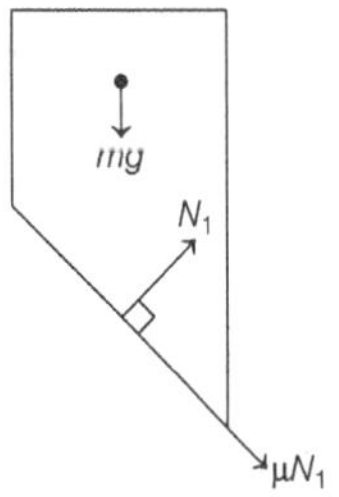

$$\Sigma F_y = 0 \Rightarrow N_1\cos 45° = mg + \mu N_1\sin 45°$$

$$N_1 = \frac{\sqrt{2}\,mg}{1-\mu} \quad \text{...(ii)}$$

Solving Eqs. (i) and (ii), we get

$$F = mg\frac{(1+\mu)}{(1-\mu)}$$

2.

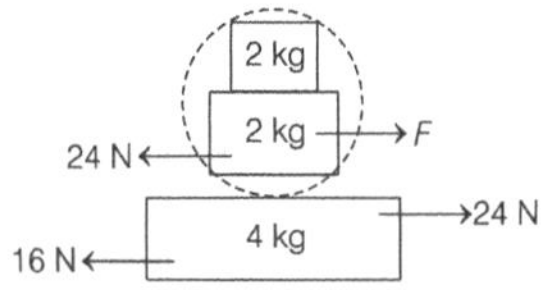

For 4 kg, $\Sigma F = ma \Rightarrow 24 - 16 = 4a \Rightarrow a = 2\text{ m/s}^2$

For sliding to occur between middle and lower block, acceleration of middle block should be more than 2m/s^2.

But maximum acceleration of topmost block is $\mu g = 1\text{ m/s}^2$.

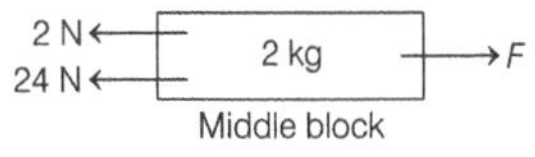

So, $\Sigma F = ma \Rightarrow F - 24 - 2 = 2(2) \Rightarrow F = 30\text{ N}$

3.

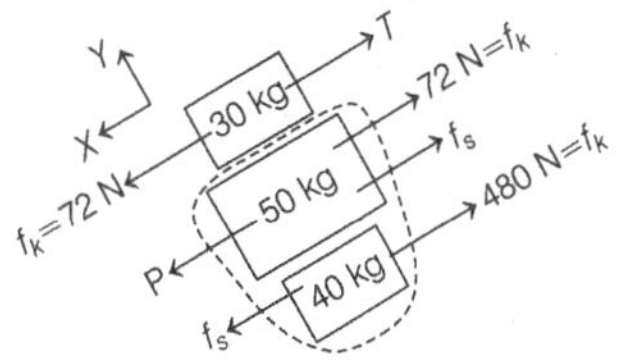

For (50 kg + 40 kg) system

$$\Sigma F_x = 0$$

$$\Rightarrow P + 500\sin 37° + 400\sin 37° - 72 - 480 = 0 \Rightarrow P = 12\text{ N}$$

4.

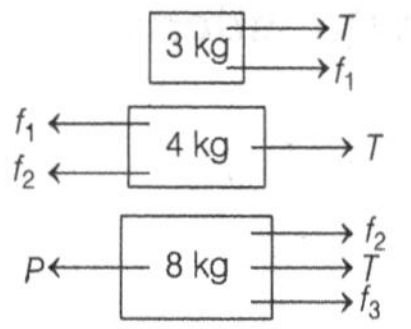

For 4 kg,

$$\Sigma F_x = 0 \Rightarrow T - f_1 - f_2 = 0 \Rightarrow T = f_1 + f_2 \quad \text{...(i)}$$

For 8 kg,

$$\Rightarrow \quad \Sigma F_x = 0 \Rightarrow P - f_2 - f_3 - T = 0 \Rightarrow P = T + f_2 + f_3 \quad \text{...(ii)}$$

From Eqs. (i) and (ii), we get

$$P = f_1 + 2f_2 + f_3 \Rightarrow P = 0.25(3g + 2(7g) + 15g)$$

$$\Rightarrow \quad P = 8g = 78.4 \text{ N}$$

5.

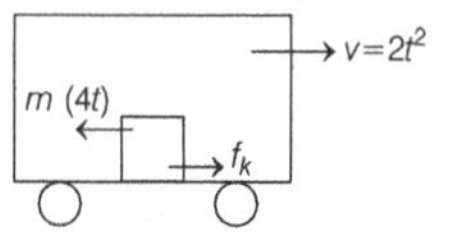

$$\Sigma F = ma \Rightarrow m\frac{dv}{dt} = m(4t) - \mu_k mg$$

$$\Rightarrow \quad \int_0^0 dv = \int_1^2 4t\,dt - \int_1^3 \mu_k g\,dt$$

$$\Rightarrow \quad [v]_0^0 = 4\left[\frac{t^2}{2}\right]_1^2 - \mu_k g[t]_1^3$$

$$\Rightarrow \quad 0 - 0 = 4\left(\frac{3}{2}\right) - \mu_k(10)(2) \Rightarrow \mu_k = 0.3$$

6.

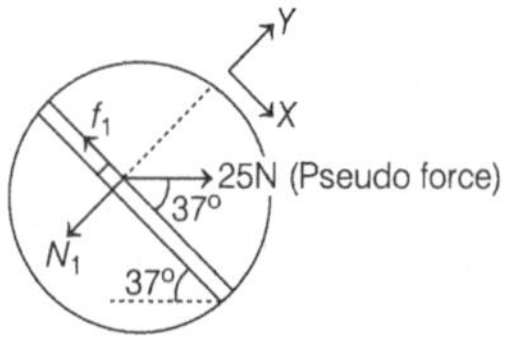

xy-plane in horizontal

$$\Sigma F_y = 0 \Rightarrow N_1 = 25 \sin 37° = 15 \text{ N}$$

$$f_1 = \mu N_1 = \frac{2}{5}(15) = 6 \text{ N}$$

$$\Sigma F_z = 0 \Rightarrow N_2 - mg = 0 \Rightarrow N_2 = 10 \text{ N}$$

$$f_2 = \mu N_2 = \frac{2}{5}(10) = 4 \text{ N}$$

$$\Sigma F_x = ma_x$$

$$\Rightarrow \quad 25 \cos 37° - f_1 - f_2 = ma$$

$$\Rightarrow \quad 20 - 6 - 4 = 1a \Rightarrow a = 10 \text{ m/s}^2$$

7.

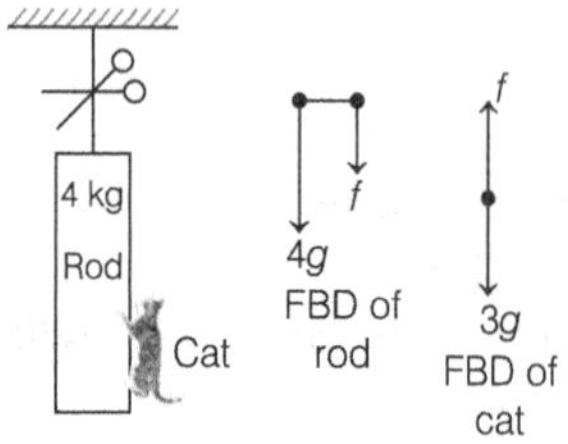

For cat, $\Sigma F_y = 0 \Rightarrow f - 3g = 0 \Rightarrow f = 3g$

($\because$ acceleration of cat with respect to ground is zero.)

For rod, $\Sigma F_y = ma_y \Rightarrow 4g + f = 4a \Rightarrow a = 7\frac{g}{4}$

8.

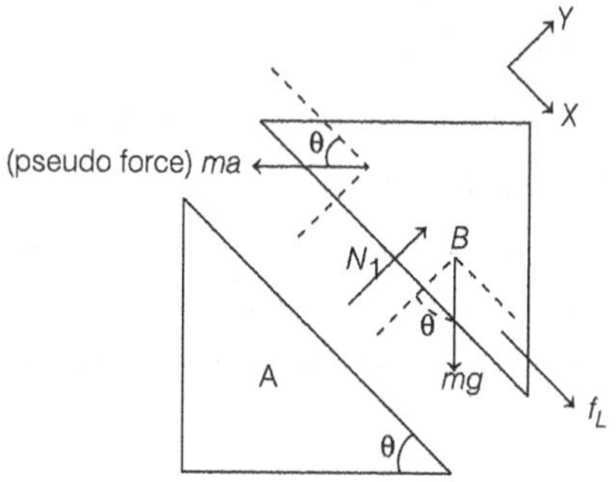

For *B*,

$$\Sigma F_y = 0 \Rightarrow N_1 - mg\cos\theta - ma\sin\theta = 0$$

$$\Rightarrow \quad N_1 = mg\cos\theta + ma\sin\theta \quad \text{...(i)}$$

$$\Sigma F_x = 0 \Rightarrow mg\sin\theta + F_L - ma\cos\theta = 0$$

$$\Rightarrow \quad mg\sin\theta + \mu N_1 = ma\cos\theta \quad \text{...(ii)}$$

Solving Eqs. (i) and (ii), we get

$$a = \frac{(\tan\theta + \mu)\,g}{1 - \mu\tan\theta} = \frac{\frac{3}{4} + \frac{1}{6}}{1 - \left(\frac{3}{4}\right)\left(\frac{1}{6}\right)} = \frac{220}{21} \text{ m/s}^2$$

For $(A + B)$ system,

$$\Sigma F_x = ma_x \Rightarrow F = \left(2 \times \frac{21}{88}\right)\left(\frac{220}{21}\right) = 5 \text{ N}$$

9.

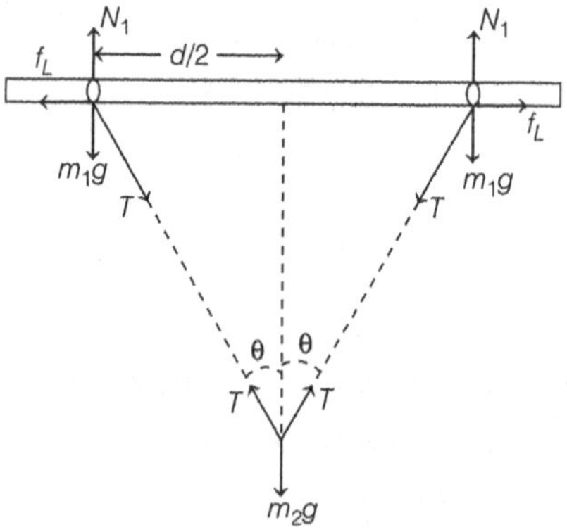

For boy, $2T\cos\theta = m_2 g$ ...(i)

For ring, $\Sigma F_x = 0 \Rightarrow f_L = T\sin\theta$ ...(ii)

$\Sigma F_y = 0 \Rightarrow N_1 = T\cos\theta + m_1 g$ ...(iii)

$f_L = \mu N_1$ ...(iv)

Solving Eqs. (i), (ii), (iii) and (iv), we get

$$\tan\theta = \frac{\mu(2m_1 + m_2)}{m_2}$$

and also $\tan\theta = \dfrac{d/2}{5} \Rightarrow d = 10 \text{ m}$

10.

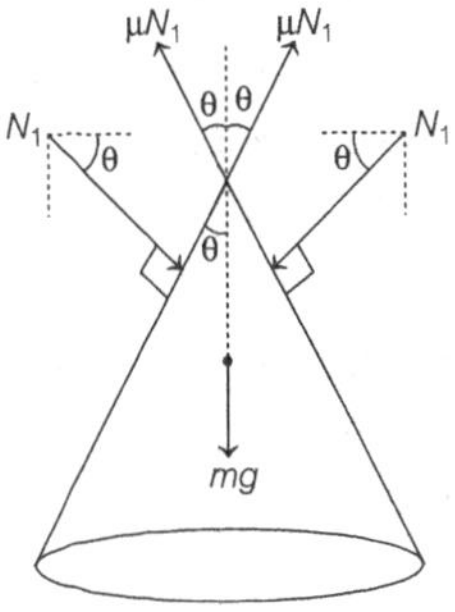

For cone to be in equilibrium,

$$\Sigma F_y = 0 \Rightarrow 2\mu N_1 \cos\theta = mg + 2N_1 \sin\theta$$

$$\Rightarrow N_1 = \frac{mg}{2(\mu\cos\theta - \sin\theta)} = \frac{10}{2\left(0.5\left(\frac{12}{13}\right) - \frac{5}{13}\right)} = \frac{130}{2} = 65\text{ N}$$

11. For part BC,

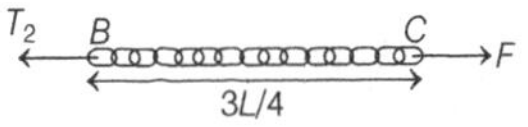

$$\Sigma F_x = 0 \Rightarrow T_2 = f = \mu\left(\frac{3Mg}{4}\right)$$

For part AB,

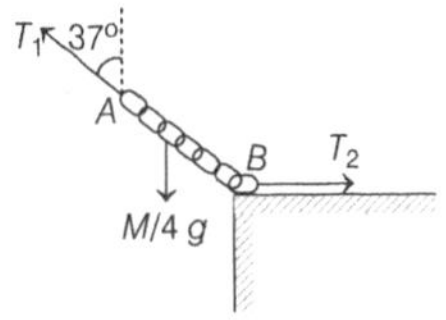

$$\Sigma F_x = 0 \Rightarrow T_1 \sin 37° = T_2$$

$$\Sigma F_y = 0 \Rightarrow T_1 \cos 37° = Mg/4 \Rightarrow \mu = 0.25$$

12. $f_L = 0.2(20) = 4$ N, $F = t$

Block will start to move when $F = f_L$,

$\Rightarrow \quad t = 4$ s

From $\quad t = 4$ to $t = 6$,

$$\Sigma F = ma \Rightarrow t - 3 = 2\frac{dv}{dt} \Rightarrow \int_0^v dv = \int_4^6 \frac{1}{2}(t-3)\,dt$$

$$\Rightarrow [v]_0^v = \frac{1}{2}\left[\frac{t^2}{2} - 3t\right]_4^6 \Rightarrow v = 2\text{ m/s}$$

From $\quad t = 6$ to $t = 10$,

$$\Sigma F = ma \Rightarrow 6 - 3 = ma \Rightarrow a = 1.5\text{ m/s}^2$$

$$v = u + at \Rightarrow v = 2 + (1.5)(4) = 8\text{ m/s}$$

13. For (2 kg + 2 kg) system,

$$\Sigma F_y = 0 \Rightarrow N_1 - 20 - 20 - 10 = 0$$

$$\Rightarrow \quad N_1 = 50\text{ N}$$

$$f_k = 0.1(50) = 5\text{ N}$$

$$\Sigma F_x = ma$$

$$\Rightarrow 25 - 5 = 4a \Rightarrow a = 5\text{ m/s}^2$$

For lower 2 kg block,

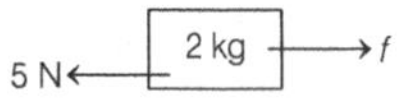

$$\Sigma F_x = ma \Rightarrow f - 5 = 2(5) \Rightarrow f = 15\text{N}$$

$$f_L = \mu N_2 = 0.6(30) = 18\text{ N}$$

Since $f < f_L$, our assumption is correct.

14. There are two possible ways for books to slip.

(a) The books lose grip at the book-hand contact.

(b) The books lose grip between each other.

(a) Find we draw FBD of all the books. Lets say there are n_1 books.

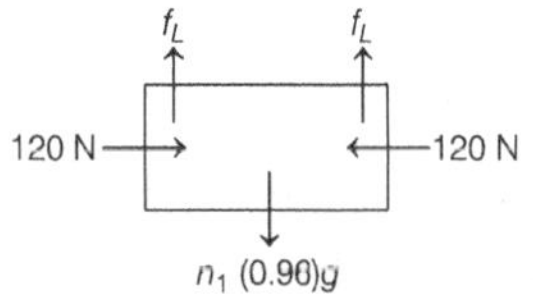

$$\Sigma F_y = 0 \Rightarrow 2f_L = n_1(0.96)g$$

$$\Rightarrow 2(120)(0.6) = n_1(0.96)g \Rightarrow n_1 = 15$$

(b) Lets say there are n_2 books.

We will draw FBD of $(n_2 - 2)$ books.

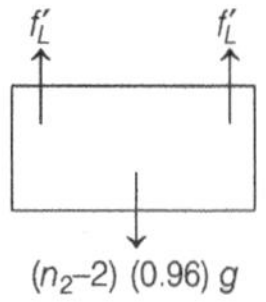

$$\Sigma F_y = 0 \Rightarrow 2f_L' = (n_2 - 2)(0.96)g$$

$$2(0.4)(120) = (n_2 - 2)(0.96)g \Rightarrow n_2 = 12$$

So, for no slipping anywhere,

number of books = 12

15.

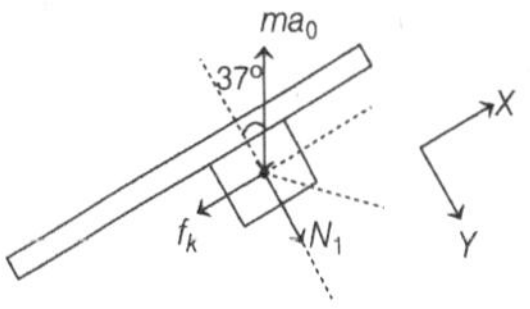

$$\Sigma F_y = 0$$

$$\Rightarrow N_1 - ma_0 \cos 37° = 0 \Rightarrow N_1 = ma_0\left(\frac{4}{5}\right)$$

$$\Sigma F_x = ma_x \Rightarrow ma_0 \sin 37° - f_k = ma$$

$$\Rightarrow ma_0\left(\frac{3}{5}\right) - \mu_k N_1 = ma \Rightarrow \frac{3}{5}ma_0 - 0.5\left(\frac{4}{5}ma_0\right) = ma$$

$$\Rightarrow \quad a = 2\text{ m/s}^2$$

16. $\Sigma F_y = 0$

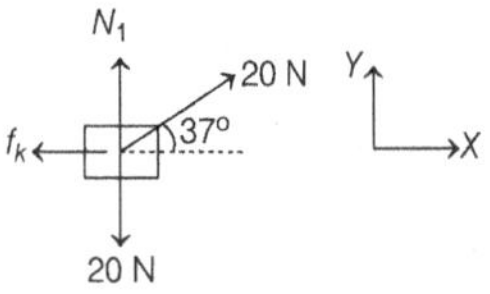

$$\Rightarrow N_1 + 20\sin 37° - 20 = 0 \Rightarrow N_1 = 8\text{ N}$$

$$\Sigma F_x = ma_x \Rightarrow 20\cos 37° - 0.25 N_1 = 2a$$

$\Rightarrow$ $a = 7\text{ m/s}^2$

$v^2 = u^2 + 2as$

$\Rightarrow$ $v^2 = 0^2 + 2(7)(126) \Rightarrow v = 42\text{ m/s}$

When horizontal component is reversed,

$$\Sigma F_x = ma_x$$

$\Rightarrow$ $-f_k - 20\cos 37° = 2a$

$\Rightarrow$ $-2 - 16 = 2a$

$\Rightarrow$ $a = -9\text{ m/s}^2$

$\Rightarrow$ $v^2 = u^2 + 2as$

$\Rightarrow$ $0^2 = 42^2 + 2(-9)s \Rightarrow s = \dfrac{42^2}{18} = 98\text{ m}$

Now, friction will reverse its direction,

$\Sigma F_x = ma_x \Rightarrow 16 - 2 = 2a \Rightarrow a = 7\text{ m/s}^2$

$v^2 = u^2 + 2as \Rightarrow v^2 = 0^2 + 2(7)(126 + 98)$

$\Rightarrow$ $v = 56\text{ m/s}$

17.

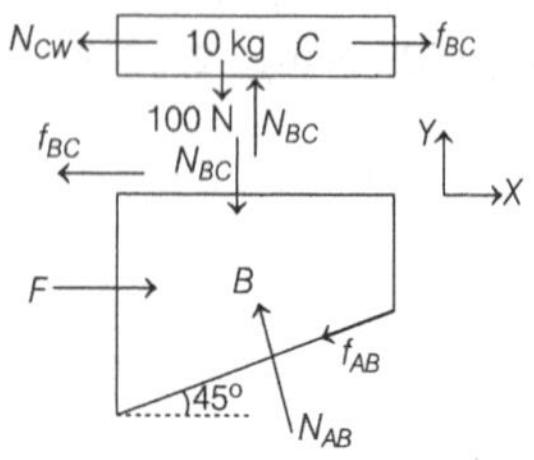

For C,

$\Sigma F_y = 0 \Rightarrow N_{BC} - 100 = 0 \Rightarrow N_{BC} = 100\text{ N}$

For B,

$\Sigma F_y = 0 \Rightarrow +N_{AB}\cos 45° - N_{BC} - f_{AB}\sin 45° = 0$

$N_{AB} = \sqrt{2}N_{BC} + f_{AB} \Rightarrow N_{AB} = \sqrt{2}(100) + 0.75 N_{AB}$

$\Rightarrow N_{AB} = 400\sqrt{2}\text{ N}$

Again for B,

$\Sigma F_x = 0 \Rightarrow +F - f_{BC} - f_{AB}\cos 45° - N_{AB}\sin 45° = 0$

$\Rightarrow$ $F = f_{BC} + \dfrac{f_{AB}}{\sqrt{2}} + \dfrac{N_{AB}}{\sqrt{2}}$

$F = 0.75(100) + \dfrac{0.75(400\sqrt{2})}{\sqrt{2}} + \dfrac{400\sqrt{2}}{\sqrt{2}}$

$F = 75 + 300 + 400 = 775\text{ N}$

18.

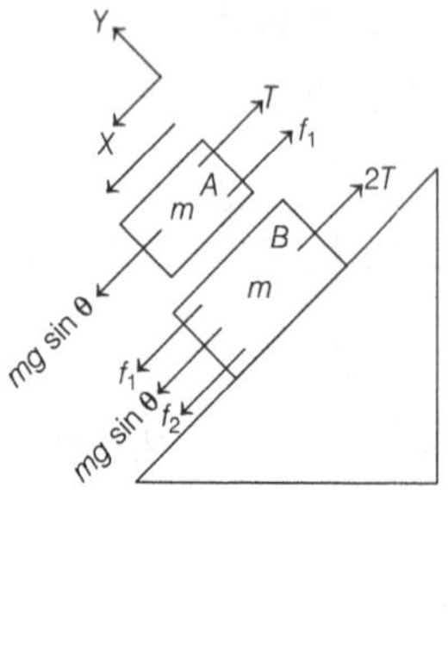

For A, $\Sigma F_x = 0 \Rightarrow mg\sin\theta = T + f_1$ ...(i)

For B, $\Sigma F_x = 0 \Rightarrow 2T = f_1 + f_2 + mg\sin\theta$ ...(ii)

From Eqs. (i) and (ii), we get

$2(mg\sin\theta - f_1) = f_1 + f_2 + mg\sin\theta$

$\Rightarrow$ $mg\sin\theta = 3f_1 + f_2$

$\Rightarrow$ $mg\sin\theta = 3(\mu_s mg\cos\theta) + \mu_s(2mg\cos\theta)$

$\Rightarrow$ $\tan\theta = 5\mu_s$

19. $N_1\sin 45° + N_2\sin 45° = mg\cos 53°$ ...(i)

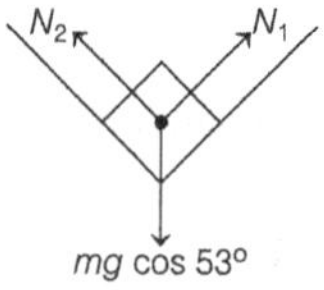

and $N_1\cos 45° = N_2\cos 45°$ ...(ii)

Solving Eqs. (i) and (ii), we get

$2N_1\sin 45° = mg\cos 53°$

$\Rightarrow$ $N_1 = \dfrac{3mg}{5\sqrt{2}}$

Along the trough, $\Sigma F = ma$

$mg\sin 53° - \mu N_1 - \mu N_2 = ma$

$\Rightarrow$ $\dfrac{4mg}{5} - \dfrac{1}{2\sqrt{2}}\left(\dfrac{3mg}{5\sqrt{2}}\right) - \dfrac{1}{2\sqrt{2}}\left(\dfrac{3mg}{5\sqrt{2}}\right) = ma$

$\Rightarrow$ $\dfrac{4mg}{5} - \dfrac{3mg}{10} = ma \Rightarrow a = 5\text{ m/s}^2$

20.

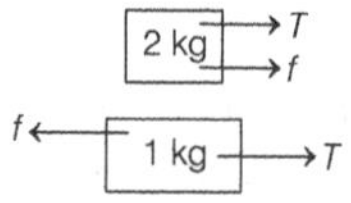

For system of (2kg + 1 kg)

$\Sigma F = ma$

$\Rightarrow$ $2T = 3a$ ...(i)

For 2 kg, $\Sigma F = ma$

$\Rightarrow$ $T + f_L = 2a$

$\Rightarrow$ $T + \dfrac{1}{8}(20) = 2a$ ...(ii)

From Eqs. (i) and (ii), we get

$\dfrac{3a}{2} + \dfrac{5}{2} = 2a$

$\Rightarrow$ $\dfrac{a}{2} = \dfrac{5}{2}$

$\Rightarrow$ $a = 5\text{ m/s}^2$

Now, $Mg - 2T = M(5)$ ...(iii)

and $2T = 3(5)$ ...(iv)

From Eqs. (iii) and (iv), we get

$M = 3\text{ kg}$

Previous Year's Questions

JEE Main

1. (a) Limiting force of static friction and kinetic friction does not depend on the area of contact but they depends on materials.

2. (b) For no slipping,

$$\mu\, mg \cos\theta \geq mg \sin\theta$$

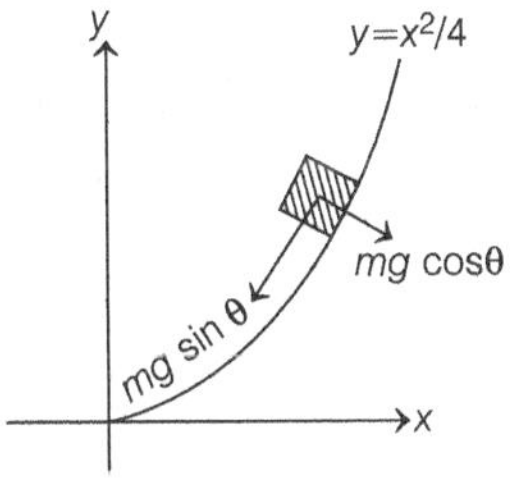

or $\quad \mu \geq \tan\theta$

$\Rightarrow \quad \mu \geq \dfrac{dy}{dx} \qquad$ ...(i)

Here, $\quad \mu = 0.5$ and $y = \dfrac{x^2}{4}$

$\Rightarrow \quad \dfrac{dy}{dx} = \dfrac{x}{2}$

So from Eq. (i),

$$0.5 \geq \frac{x}{2} \Leftrightarrow x \leq 1$$

As, $\quad x \leq 1$ or $x^2 \leq 1$ and $y = \dfrac{x^2}{4}$

So, $\quad x^2 = 4y \Rightarrow \; 4y \leq 1 \Rightarrow y \leq \dfrac{1}{4}$

$\therefore \quad y_{max} = \dfrac{1}{4}$m

3. (c) Given, $u = 20$ m/s, $t = 5$ s

Let, μ be the coefficient of friction, then R = retardation,

$$a = \mu g$$

Using, $v = u - at$

$\Rightarrow \quad 0 = 20 - \mu g \times 5$

$$\mu = \frac{20}{10 \times 5} = 0.4$$

4. (d) According to the question,

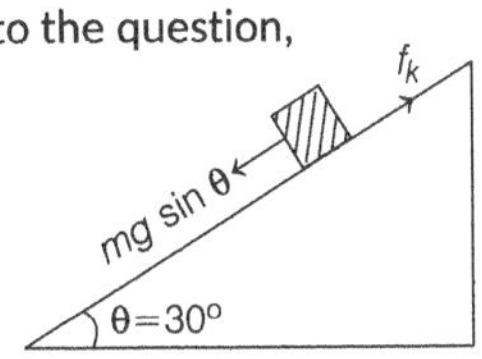

Acceleration of block

$$= \frac{mg \sin\theta - \mu_k mg \cos\theta}{m}$$

$$= g(\sin\theta - \mu_k \cos\theta) = \frac{g}{4} \qquad \text{[Given]}$$

So, $\sin\theta - \mu_k \cos\theta = \dfrac{1}{4}$

As $\theta = 30°$; we have

$$\frac{1}{2} - \frac{\sqrt{3}}{2}\mu_k = \frac{1}{4} \text{ or } \mu_k = \frac{2 \times 1}{4\sqrt{3}} = \frac{1}{2\sqrt{3}}$$

5. (a) The given situation in question is as follows.

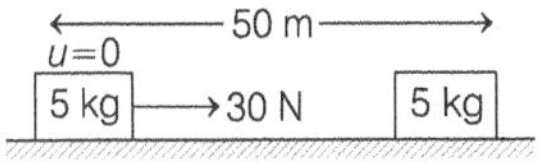

Let, the coefficient of kinetic friction be μ

Acceleration, $\quad a = \dfrac{F - f}{m} = \dfrac{F - \mu mg}{m}$

$$a = \frac{30 - \mu \times 5 \times 10}{5} = 6 - 10\mu$$

Using second equation of motion,

$$s = ut + \frac{1}{2}at^2$$

$\Rightarrow \quad 50 = 0 + \dfrac{1}{2}(6 - 10\mu) \times 10^2$

$\Rightarrow \quad 6 - 10\mu = 1.0$

$\Rightarrow \quad \mu = 0.5$

6. (c) When pushing upward, friction force would be in downward direction.

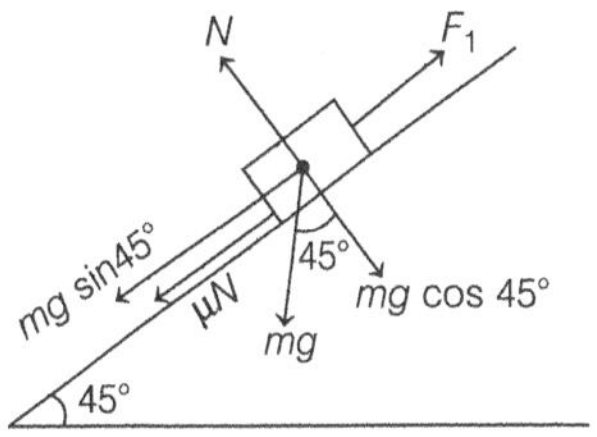

$$F_1 = mg \sin 45° + \mu N$$

$$= mg \sin 45° + \mu\, mg \cos 45°$$

$$F_1 = \frac{mg}{\sqrt{2}} + \frac{\mu mg}{\sqrt{2}}$$

When preventing it from sliding, friction force would be in upward direction.

$$F_2 + \mu N = mg \sin 45°$$

$$F_2 = mg \sin 45° - \mu mg \cos 45° = \frac{mg}{\sqrt{2}} - \frac{\mu mg}{\sqrt{2}}$$

According to given situation,

$$F_1 = 2F_2$$

$$\frac{mg}{\sqrt{2}} + \frac{\mu mg}{\sqrt{2}} = 2\left(\frac{mg}{\sqrt{2}} - \frac{\mu mg}{\sqrt{2}}\right)$$

$$3\,\mu mg = mg$$

$$\mu = \frac{1}{3} = 0.33$$

7. (b) Since, the bag is slipping on the conveyor belt, retardation due to friction will be

$$a = \frac{-\mu Mg}{M} = -\mu g$$

or $a = -0.4 \times 10 = -4 \text{ m s}^{-2}$

In the frame of conveyor, $v = 0$ and $u = 2$ m/s

Using, $v^2 - u^2 = 2as$

$\therefore \quad (0)^2 - (2)^2 = 2 \times -4 \times s$

or $-4 = -8s$

or $s = \frac{1}{2} = 0.5$ m

8. (a) Since, the block is moving with constant velocity, thus acceleration of the block is zero.

Therefore, net force on the block is zero.

$$F_{\text{plane}} + Mg = 0 \quad \Rightarrow \quad F_{\text{plane}} = -Mg$$

9. (d) The given situation is shown below,

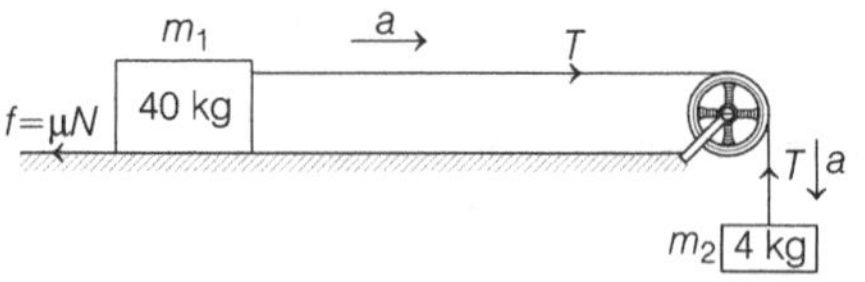

For $m_1 = 40$ kg

$$f = \mu N = \mu m_1 g = 40 \mu g = 40 \times 0.02\, g = 0.8\, g$$

and $T - f = m_1 a$

$$T - 0.89\, g = 40a \quad \text{...(i)}$$

For $m_2 g - T = m_2 a$

$$\Rightarrow \quad 4g - T = 4a \quad \text{...(ii)}$$

On adding Eqs. (i) and (ii), we get

$$3.2g = 44a$$

$$\Rightarrow \quad a = \frac{3.2 \times 10}{44} = \frac{32}{44} = \frac{8}{11} \text{ m/s}^2$$

10. (c) Since, both masses move together therefore,

$$\mu_1 = \mu_2 = 0.5$$

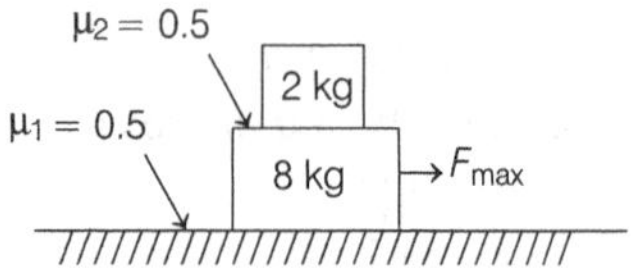

If both blocks move together, then

$$a = \mu_1 g = 0.5 \times 9.8 = 4.9 \text{ m / s}^2$$

Now, taking 2 kg and 8 kg as combined (single) mass,

$$m = 10 \text{ kg}$$

$$F_{max} = ma = 49 \text{ N}$$

11. (b) Given, mass of block, $m = 10$ kg

Initial velocity, $u = 9.8$ m/s

$$\mu = 0.5$$

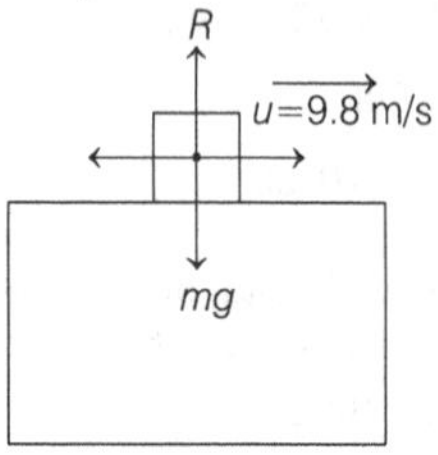

$$f = \mu R = \mu Mg \quad \text{... (i)}$$

$$\mu mg = ma$$

$$\Rightarrow \quad a = \mu g = 0.5 \times 9.8 = 4.9 \text{ m/s}^2$$

The distance covered by the block, ,

$$\Rightarrow \quad s = \frac{u^2}{2a} = \frac{(9.8)^2}{2 \times 4.9} = 9.8 \text{ m}$$

12. (2) Given,

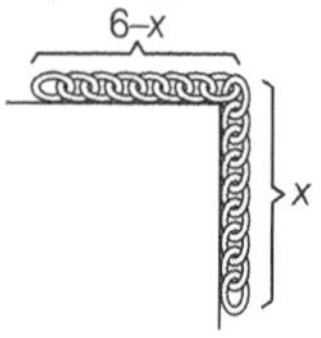

$$\mu_s = 0.5$$

Let x length is hanging, then $6 - x$ on the table Hanging mass

$$= \frac{m}{6} \cdot x$$

Mass on the table $= (6 - x) \frac{m}{6}$

For not to slide

$$\left(\frac{m}{6} x\right) g \le \mu_s \left((6 - x) \frac{m}{6}\right) g$$

$$x \le 2 \,;\, x_{max} = 2$$

13. (b) The force equation in vertical direction is $Mg - R = Ma$

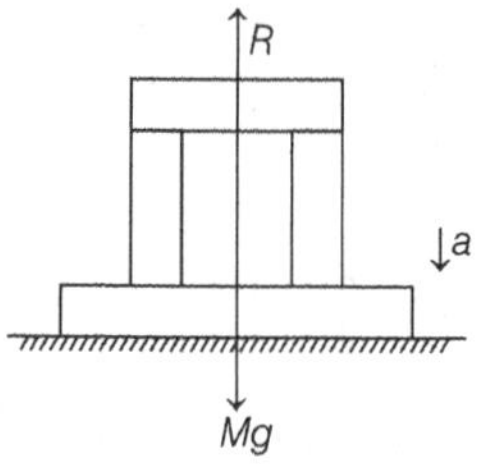

Where, M = collective mass of block and iron cylinders

$$= 10 + 3 \times 20 = 70 \text{ kg}$$

a = acceleration of block = 0.2 ms^{-2}

$g = 10 \text{ ms}^{-2}$ and $\mu_s = 0.2$

and R = normal reaction

Force along verticle axis $Mg - R = Ma$

$\therefore \quad 70g - R = 70 \times 0.2$

$\Rightarrow \quad R = 70 \times 10 - 14$

$= 700 - 14 = 686$ N

14. (b) The FBD of the block is shown below

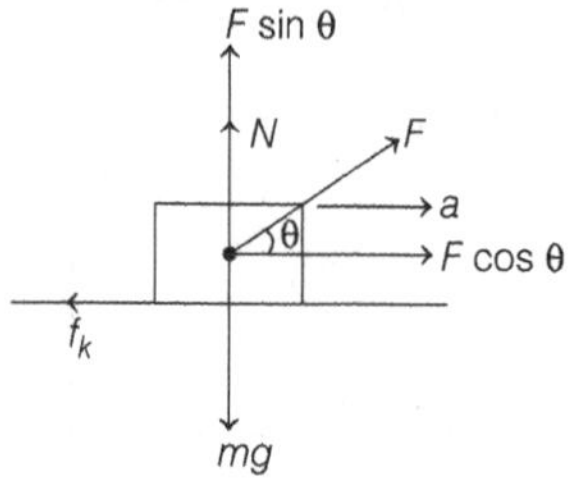

We have, $N = mg - F \sin\theta$ ...(i)

and $F \cos\theta - f_k = ma$

$\Rightarrow \quad F \cos\theta - \mu_k N = ma$ ...(ii)

From Eq. (i) and Eq. (ii), we get

$$F \cos\theta - \mu_k (mg - F \sin\theta) = ma$$

$$\Rightarrow \quad a = \frac{F}{m}\cos\theta - \mu_k\left(g - \frac{F}{m}\sin\theta\right)$$

This is the required acceleration of the block.

15. (5) Given,

Mass of body, $m = 1$ kg

Coefficient of static friction $\mu = \frac{1}{\sqrt{3}}$

Minimum force,

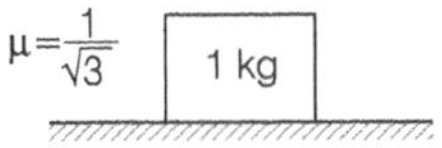

$$F = \frac{\mu mg}{\sqrt{1+\mu^2}} = \frac{\frac{1}{\sqrt{3}} \times 1 \times 10}{\sqrt{1+\frac{1}{3}}} = 5 \text{ N}$$

16. (15) Given, $\mu = 0.5$

$\because \quad F = ma$

$F = (1+2)\,a = 3a \quad$ ...(i)

From free body diagram of 1 kg block,

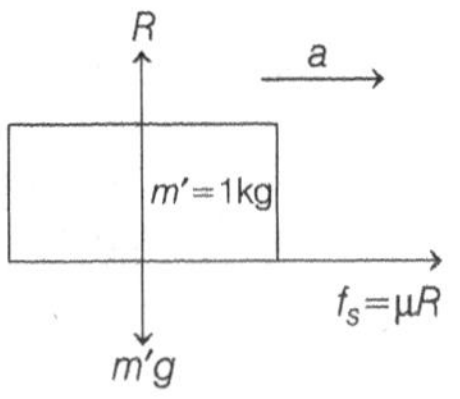

Force balance forces X-direction,

$F_s = \mu R = m'a \quad$ ...(ii)

Force balance forces Y-direction,

$R = m'g$

$\mu m'g = m'a \quad [\because R = mg]$

$\Rightarrow 0.5 \times 1 \times 10 = 1 \times a \;\Rightarrow\; a = 5 \text{ ms}^{-2}$

Put the value of a in Eq. (i), we get

$F = 3 \times 5 = 15$ N

Thus, the maximum horizontal force required to move block together is 15 N.

17. (5) Given, $m = 1$ kg $\Rightarrow \mu = 1/\sqrt{3}$

FBD of the block

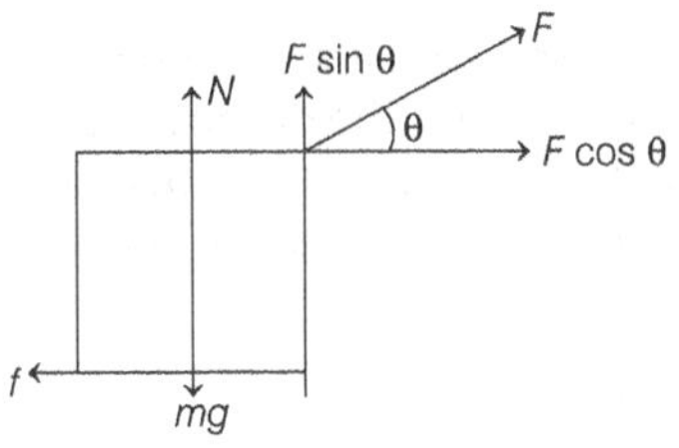

In X-direction,

$F\cos\theta = f = \phi = \mu N \quad$ ...(i)

In Y-direction,

$F\sin\theta + N = mg \quad$ ...(ii)

$\Rightarrow \quad N = mg - F\sin\theta$

On putting value of N in Eq. (i), we get

$$F = \frac{\mu mg}{\cos\theta + \mu\sin\theta} \;\Rightarrow\; F = \frac{\mu mg}{\sqrt{1+\mu^2}}$$

On putting the values

$$F = \frac{\frac{1}{\sqrt{3}} \times 10}{\sqrt{1+\left(\frac{1}{\sqrt{3}}\right)^2}} \Rightarrow F = 5 \text{ N}$$

Hence, minimum possible force 5 N.

JEE Advanced

1. Block will not slip if

$(m_1 + m_2)\,g\sin\theta \le \mu m_2 g\cos\theta$

$\Rightarrow \quad 3\sin\theta \le \left(\frac{3}{10}\right)(2)\cos\theta$

$\tan\theta \le 1/5$

$\Rightarrow \quad \theta \le 11.5°$

(P) $\theta = 5°$ friction is static

$f = (m_1 + m_2)\,g\sin\theta$

(Q) $\theta = 10°$ friction is static

$f = (m_1 + m_2)\,g\sin\theta$

(R) $\theta = 15°$ friction i,s kinetic

$f = \mu m_2 g\cos\theta$

(S) $\theta = 20°$ friction is kinetic

$\Rightarrow \quad f = \mu m_2 g\cos\theta$

2. $W = mg = 0.1 \times 10 = 1$ N

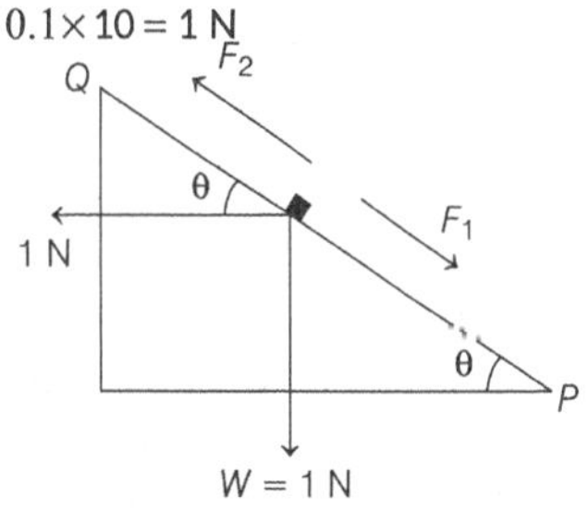

F_1 = component of weight $= 1 \cdot \sin\theta = \sin\theta$

F_2 = component of applied force $= 1 \cdot \cos\theta = \cos\theta$

Now, at $\theta = 45°$: $F_1 = F_2$ and block remains stationary without the help of friction.

For $\theta > 45°$, $F_1 > F_2$, so friction will act towards Q.

For $\theta < 45°$, $F_2 > F_1$ and friction will act towards P.

3. When $\quad P = mg\,(\sin\theta - \mu\cos\theta)$

$f = \mu\, mg\cos\theta \quad$ (upwards)

when $\quad P = mg\sin\theta;\; f = 0$

and when $\quad P = mg\,(\sin\theta + \mu\cos\theta)$

$f = \mu mg\cos\theta \quad$ (downwards)

Hence, friction is first positive, then zero and then negative.

CHAPTER~12

WORK, ENERGY AND POWER

LEVEL 01 Starter Level

12.1 Work Done by Force

1 An object is displaced from point A (2 m, 3 m, 4 m) to a point B (1m, 2 m, 3 m) under a constant force $\mathbf{F} = (2\hat{\mathbf{i}} + 3\hat{\mathbf{j}} + 4\hat{\mathbf{k}})$ N. Find the work done by this force in this process.

2 A particle moves along the X-axis from $x = 0$ to $x = 5$ m under the influence of a force F (in newton) given by $F = 3x^2 - 2x + 7$. Calculate the work done by this force.

3 An object is displaced from position vector $\mathbf{r}_1 = (2\hat{\mathbf{i}} + 3\hat{\mathbf{j}})$ m to $\mathbf{r}_2 = (4\hat{\mathbf{i}} + 6\hat{\mathbf{j}})$ m under the action of a force $\mathbf{F} = (3x^2\hat{\mathbf{i}} + 2y\hat{\mathbf{j}})$ N. Find the work done by this force.

4 A 5.0 kg block moves in a straight line on a horizontal frictionless surface under the influence of a force that varies with position as shown in the figure. How much work is done by the force as the block moves from the origin to $x = 8$ m?

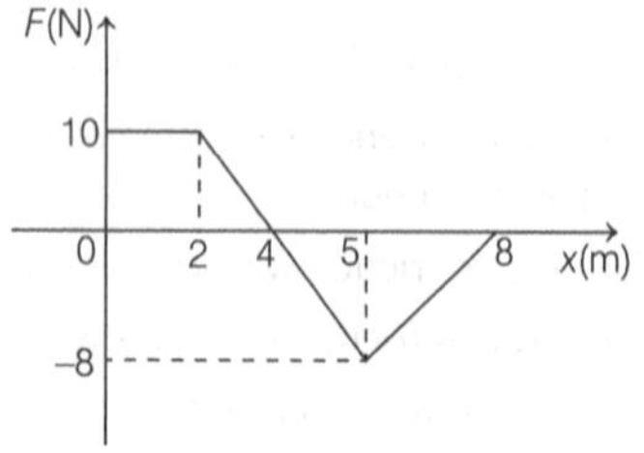

5 A chain of length L and mass M is slowly pulled at constant speed up over the edge of a table by a force parallel to the surface of the table. Assuming that, there is no friction between the table and chain, calculate the work done by force till the chain reaches to the horizontal surface of the table.

6 The figure shows a smooth circular path of radius R in the vertical plane which subtends an angle $\left(\frac{\pi}{2}\right)$ at O. A block of mass m is taken from position A to B under the action of a constant horizontal force F.

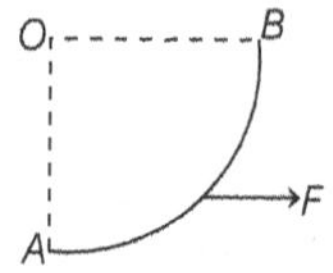

(a) Find the work done by this force.

(b) In part (a), if the block is being pulled by a force F which is always tangential to the surface, find the work done by the force F between A and B.

12.2 Work-Energy Theorem

1 A mass of 2 kg is acted upon by a single force $\mathbf{F} = (3\hat{\mathbf{i}} + 4\hat{\mathbf{j}})$ N. Due to force, mass is displaced from (1, 5) to (4, 8). If initially the speed of the particle was 2 m/s, find its final speed.

2 A body of mass 5 kg is acted upon by a variable force. The force varies with the distance covered by the body. What is the speed of the body when the body has covered 25 m? Assume that the body starts from rest.

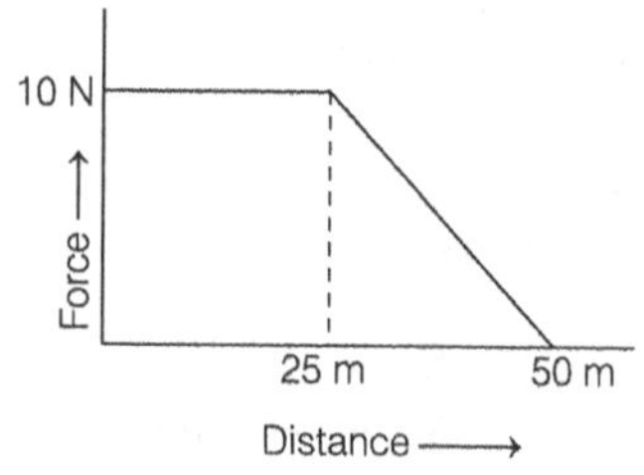

3 The graph between the resistive force F acting on a body and the distance covered by the body is shown in the figure. The mass of the body is 25 kg and initial velocity is 2 m/s. When the distance covered by the body is 4 m, find its kinetic energy.

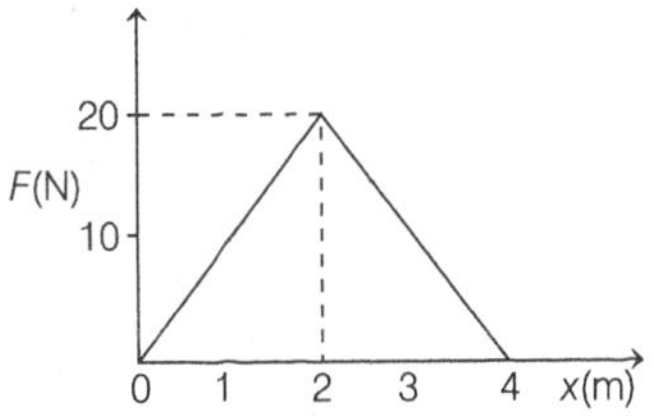

4 The displacement of a particle of mass 2 kg is given as $x = \frac{t^3}{3}$. Find work done by all forces acting on the particle during the first 2 s.

5 A particle of mass m moves on a straight line with its velocity varying with the distance travelled according to the equation $v = a\sqrt{x}$, where a is a constant. Find total work done by all the forces during a displacement from $x = 0$ to $x = d$.

6 Find the ratio of energy required to accelerate a car from 10 to 20 m/s to that required to accelerate from 0 to 10 m/s.

7 A bullet of mass 20 g is fired from a rifle with a velocity of 800 m/s. After passing through a mud wall 100 cm thick, velocity drops to 100 ms^{-1}. What is the average resistance of the wall? (Neglect friction due to air and work of gravity)

12.3 Work Done by Gravity, Normal and Friction Force

1 Calculate the work done against gravity by a coolie in carrying a load of mass 10 kg on his head when he moves uniformly a distance of 5 m in the
(a) horizontal direction (b) upwards vertical direction. (Take, $g = 10 \text{ m/s}^2$)

2 The two blocks in an Atwood machine have masses 2.0 kg and 3.0 kg. Find the work done by gravity during the fourth second after the system is released from rest. (Take, $g = 10 \text{ m/s}^2$)

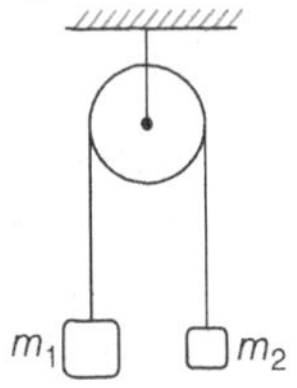

Atwood machine

3 A rigid body of mass 2 kg initially at rest moves under the action of an applied horizontal force of 7 N on a table with coefficient of kinetic friction = 0.1. Calculate the

(a) work done by the applied force on the body in 10 s,
(b) work done by friction on the body in 10 s,
(c) work done by the net force on the body in 10 s and
(d) change in kinetic energy of the body in 10 s.

4 A 1.8 kg block is moved at constant speed over a surface for which coefficient of friction is 0.25. It is pulled by a force F acting at 45° with horizontal as shown in the figure.

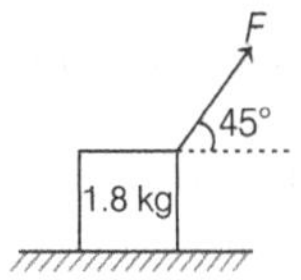

The block is displaced by 2 m. Find the work done on the block by

(a) the force F,
(b) friction and
(c) gravity.

5 A box weighing 2000 N is to be slowly slid through 20 m on horizontal straight track having friction coefficient 0.2 with the box.

(a) Find the work done by the person pulling the box with a chain at an angle θ with the horizontal.
(b) Find the work when the person has chosen a value of θ which ensures him the minimum magnitude of the force.

6 A block of mass 500 g slides down on a rough incline plane of inclination 53° with a uniform speed. Find the work done against the friction as the block slides through 2 m. [Take, $g = 10 \text{ m/s}^2$]

7 A block of mass 20 kg is slowly slid up on a smooth incline of inclination 53° by a person. Calculate the work done by the person in moving the block through a distance of 4 m, if the driving force is
(a) parallel to the incline and (b) in the horizontal direction. [Take, $g = 10 \text{ m/s}^2$]

8 A block of mass 2.0 kg is pushed down an inclined plane of inclination 37° with a force of 20 N acting parallel to the incline. It is found that the block moves on the incline with an acceleration of 10 m/s^2. If the block started from rest, find the work done

(a) by the applied force in the first second,
(b) by the weight of the block in the first second and
(c) by the frictional force acting on the block in the first second. [Take, $g = 10 \text{ m/s}^2$]

9 A rigid body of mass 3 kg is taken slowly up an inclined plane of length 10 m and height 6 m, and then allowed to slide down to the bottom again. The coefficient of friction between the body and the plane is 0.5.

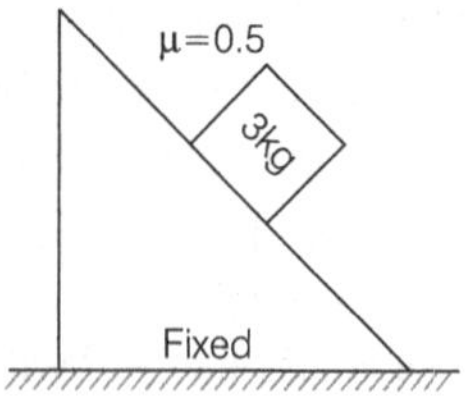

Using, $g = 10\ m/s^2$, find the

(a) work done by the gravitational force over the round trip,

(b) work done by the applied force (assuming it to be parallel to the inclined plane) over the upward journey,

(c) work done by frictional force over the round trip and

(d) kinetic energy of the body at the end of the trip.

10 A uniform chain of length L and mass M overhangs a horizontal table with its two third part on the table. The friction coefficient between the table and the chain is μ. Find the work done by the friction during the period, the chain slips off the table.

11 A block of mass 2 kg is projected with speed 10 m/s on the surface of the plank of mass 8 kg, kept on smooth ground as shown in figure.

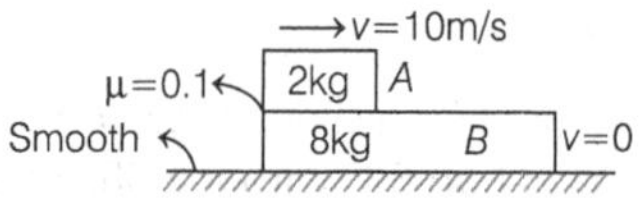

(a) Find out the velocity of two blocks when frictional force stops acting.

(b) Find work done by kinetic friction on A.

(c) Find work done by kinetic friction on B.

(d) Find work done by kinetic friction on both the blocks.

12 A small block of mass 20 kg rests on a bigger block of mass 30 kg, which lies on a smooth horizontal plane. Initially the whole system is at rest. The coefficient of friction between the blocks is 0.5. A horizontal force $F = 50$ N is applied on the lower block.

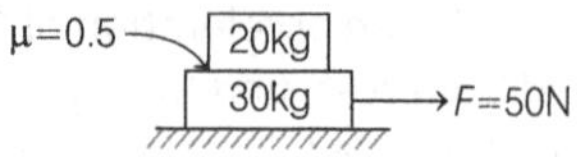

(a) Find the work done by frictional force on upper block and on the lower block in $t = 2$ s.

(b) Is the work done by frictional force on upper block converted to heat or mechanical energy or both?

13 A projectile is fired from the top of a 55 m high cliff with an initial speed of 50 m/s at an unknown angle. Find its speed when it hits the ground. (Take, $g = 10\ m/s^2$)

14 A body of mass m when released from rest from a height h, hits the ground with speed $\sqrt{gh}$. Find work done by resistive force.

15 A body of mass 2 kg slides down a curved track which is quadrant of a circle of radius 1.8 m. All the surfaces are frictionless. If the body starts from rest, find its speed at the bottom of the track.

16 Figure shows a particle sliding on a frictionless track which terminates in a straight horizontal section. If the particle starts slipping from the point A, how far away from the track will the particle hit the ground?

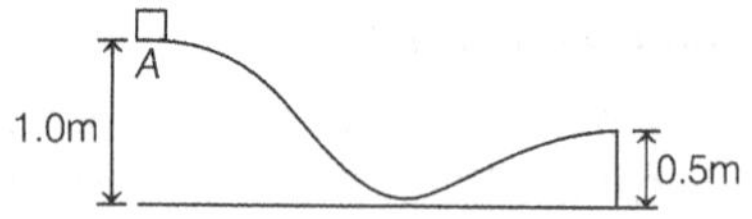

17 A 250 g block slides on a rough horizontal table. Find the work done by the frictional force in bringing the block to rest, if it is initially moving at a speed of 40 cm/s. If the friction coefficient between the table and the block is 0.1, how far does the block move before coming to rest? (Take, $g = 10\ m/s^2$)

18 In a children's park, there is a slider which has a total length of 10 m and a height of 8.0 m (figure). A vertical ladder is provided to reach the top. A boy weighing 200 N climbs up the ladder to the top of the slide and slides down to the ground. The average friction offered by the slide is three tenth of his weight.

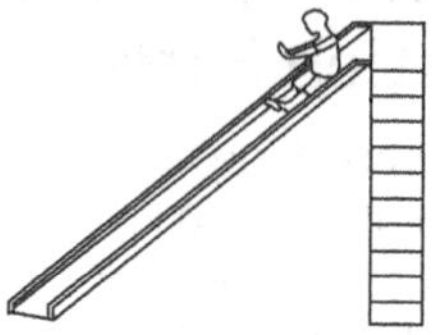

Find

(a) the work done by the ladder on the boy as he goes up,

(b) the work done by the slide on the boy as he comes down and

(c) the work done by forces inside the body of the boy.

19 A block of mass 200 g is moving with a speed of 4 m/s at the highest point in a closed circular tube of radius 10 cm kept in a vertical plane. The cross-section of the tube is such that the block just fits in it. The block makes several oscillations inside the tube and finally stops at the lowest point. Find the work done by the tube on the block during the process. (Take, $g = 10\ m/s^2$)

20 A block weighing 10 N travels down a smooth curved track *AB* joined to a rough horizontal surface (figure). The rough surface has a friction coefficient of 0.20 with the block. If the block starts slipping on the track from a point 1.0 m above the horizontal surface, what distance will it move on the rough surface?

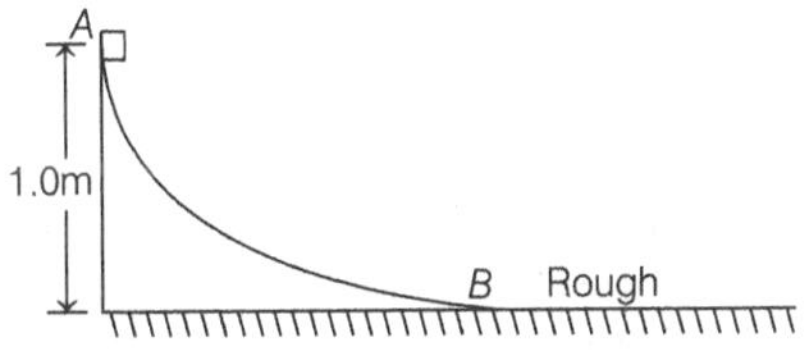

12.4 Work Done by Tension

1. The bob of a simple pendulum of length l is released when the string is horizontal. Find its speed at the bottom.
2. The bob of a simple pendulum of length l is given a velocity $\sqrt{gl}$ at its mean position. Find the maximum angle made by the string with the vertical.
3. The masses m_1 and m_2 $(m_2 > m_1)$ are released from rest. Using work-energy theorem, find out velocity of the blocks when they move a distance x.

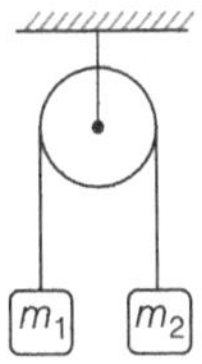

4. An object of mass m is tied to a string of length L and a variable horizontal force is applied on it which is initially zero and gradually increases until the string makes an angle θ with the vertical. Find work done by the force F.

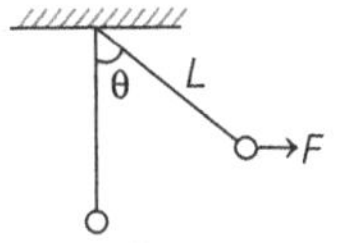

5. Two blocks are connected by a string as shown in the figure. They are released from rest. μ is the coefficient of friction between the floor and the block of mass m_1. Find their common speed after they have moved a distance L.

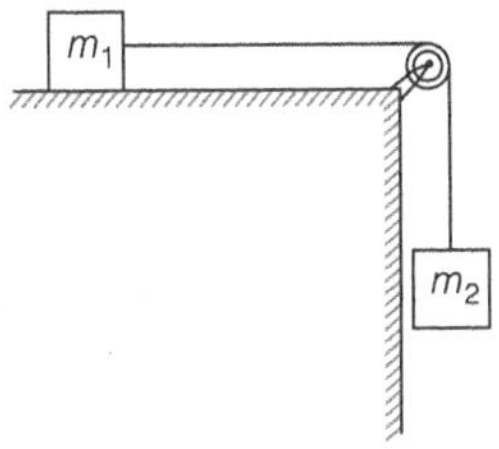

6. Consider the situation shown in figure below. The system is released from rest and the block of mass 1.0 kg is found to have a speed 0.8 m/s after it has descended through a distance of 1 m. Find the coefficient of kinetic friction between the block and the table.

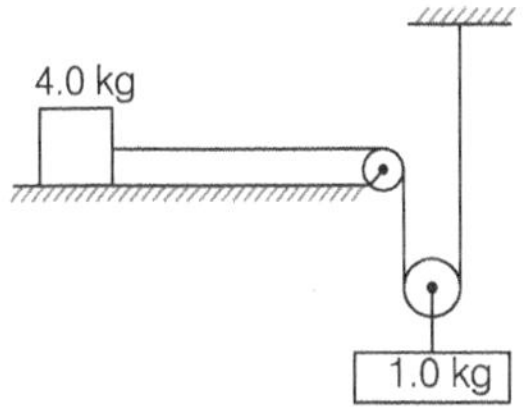

12.5 Work Done by Spring

1. A block of mass m sliding on a smooth horizontal surface with a velocity v meets a long horizontal spring fixed at one end and having spring constant k as shown in figure. Find the maximum compression of the spring. Will the velocity of the block be the same as when it comes back to the original position shown?

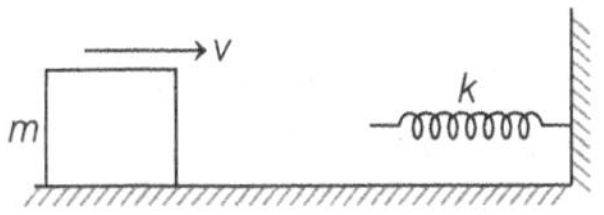

2. Coefficient of friction between block and ground is μ. Initially, spring is in its natural length.

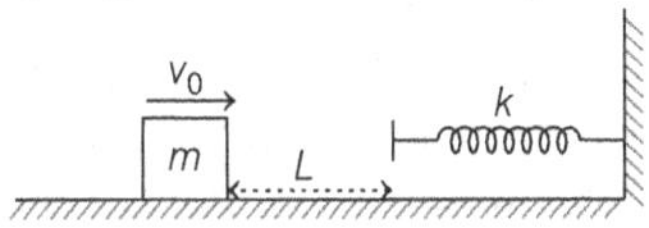

(a) Find minimum speed v_0 required to given to the block which is initially at a distance L from the spring, so that the maximum compression in the spring is L.

(b) Also find speed of the block when it gets separated from the spring.

3. As shown in figure, there is a spring block system. Block of mass 500 g is pressed against a horizontal spring fixed at one end to compress the spring through 5.0 cm. The spring constant is 500 N/m. When released, the block moves horizontally till it leaves the spring. Calculate the distance, where it will hit the ground 4 m below the spring?

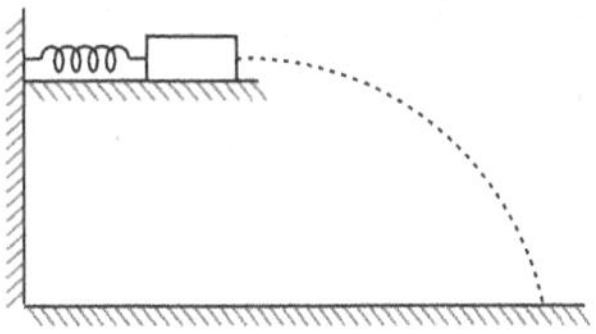

4 A massless platform is kept on a light elastic spring, as shown in the figure. When a sand particle of mass 0.1 kg is dropped on the pan from a height of 0.2 m, the particle strikes the pan and stricks to it while the spring compresses by 0.01 m. From what height should the particle be dropped to cause a compression of 0.04 m?

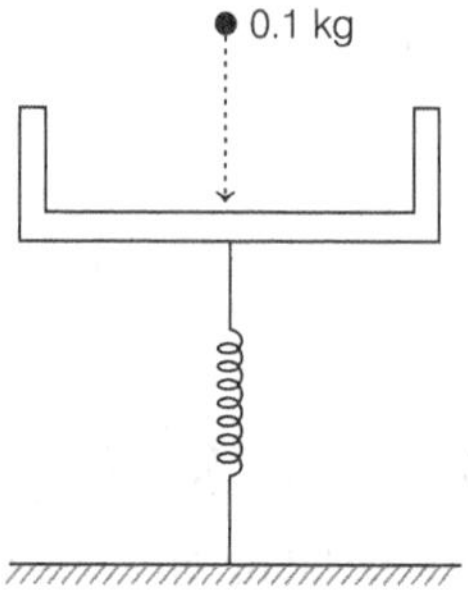

5 A block of mass 250 g is kept on a vertical spring of spring constant 100 N/m fixed from below. The spring is now compressed to have a length 10 cm shorter than its natural length and the system is released from this position. How high does the block rise? $(g = 10\ \text{m/s}^2)$

6 A spring ($k = 100$ N/m) is suspended in vertical position having one end fixed at top and the other end joined with a 2 kg block. When the spring is in non-deformed shape, the block is given initial velocity 2 m/s in downward direction. Find maximum elongation of the spring.

7 One end of a spring of natural length h and spring constant k is fixed at the ground and the other is fitted with a smooth ring of mass m which is allowed to slide on a horizontal rod fixed at a height h (figure). Initially, the spring makes an angle of 37° with the vertical when the system is released from rest. Find the speed of the ring when the spring becomes vertical.

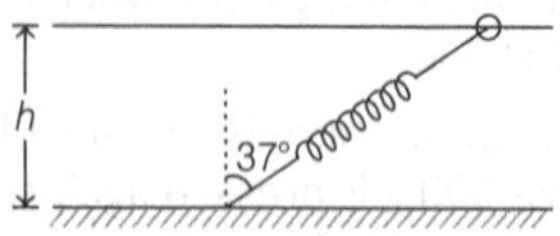

8 One end of a light spring of natural length d and spring constant k is fixed on a rigid wall and the other is fixed to a smooth ring of mass m which can slide without friction in a vertical rod fixed at a distance d from the wall. Initially, the spring makes an angle of 37° with the horizontal as shown in figure. When the system is released from rest, find the speed of the ring when the spring becomes horizontal.

$$\left[\sin 37° = \frac{3}{5}\right]$$

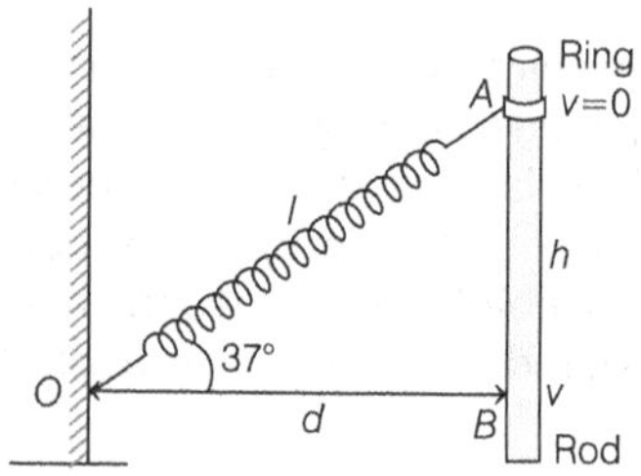

9 Figure shows a spring fixed at the bottom end of an incline of inclination 37°. A small block of mass 2 kg starts slipping down the incline from a point 4.8 m away from the spring. The block compresses the spring by 20 cm, stops momentarily and then rebounds through a distance of 1 m up the incline. Find the friction coefficient between the plane and the block and the spring constant of the spring. [Take, $g = 10\ \text{m/s}^2$]

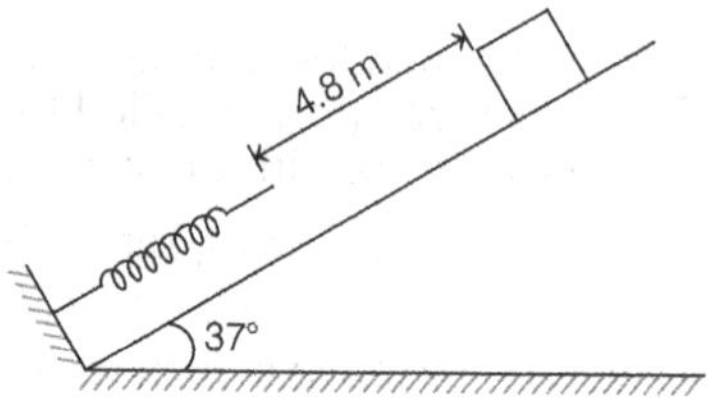

10 For what minimum value of m_1 the block of mass m will just leave the contact with surface?

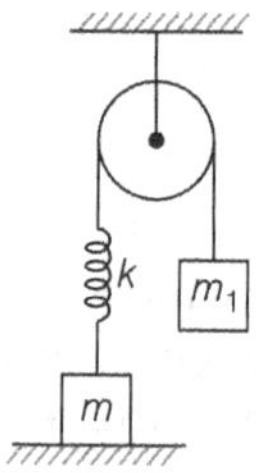

12.6 Work Done by Pseudo Force

1 A block of mass 10 kg is pulled by force $F = 100$ N. This motion is observed by three observers, A, B and C as shown in figure.

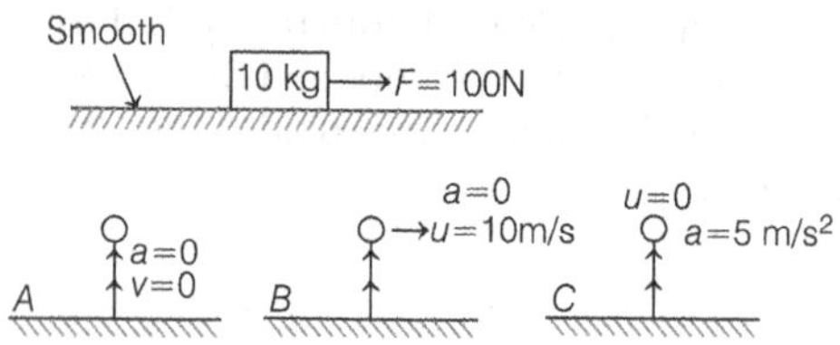

(a) Find out work done by the force F in 10 s as observed by A, B and C.

(b) Find work done by pseudo force for observer C and verify work-energy theorem for observer C.

2 The small pendulum of mass m is suspended from a trolley that runs on a horizontal rail. The trolley and pendulum are initially at rest with $\theta = 0°$. If the trolley is given a constant acceleration a, determine the maximum angle θ_{max} through which the pendulum swings.

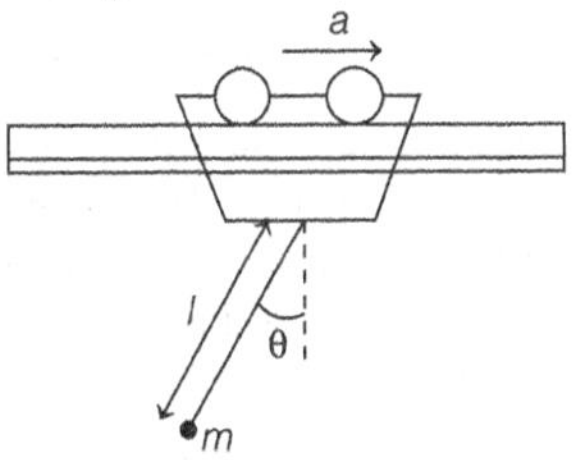

12.7 Conservative and Non-conservative Forces and Potential Energy

1 A force $\mathbf{F} = (x\hat{i} + y\hat{j})$ N acts on a particle which moves in the xy-plane.

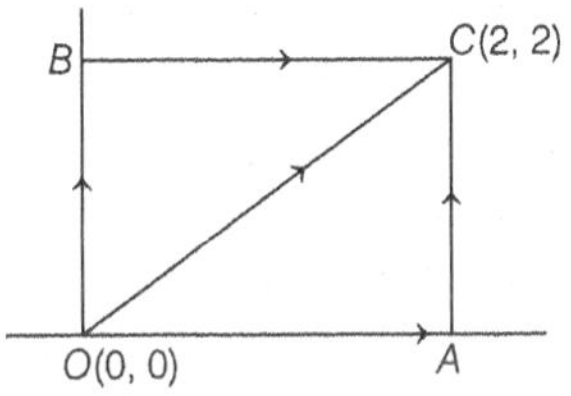

(a) Find the work done by $\mathbf{F}$ as it moves the particle from A to C (figure) along each of the paths OAB, OBC, and OC.

(b) Determine whether $\mathbf{F}$ is conservative or not.

2 A force $\mathbf{F} = (x\hat{i} + xy\hat{j})$ N acts a particle which moves in the xy-plane.

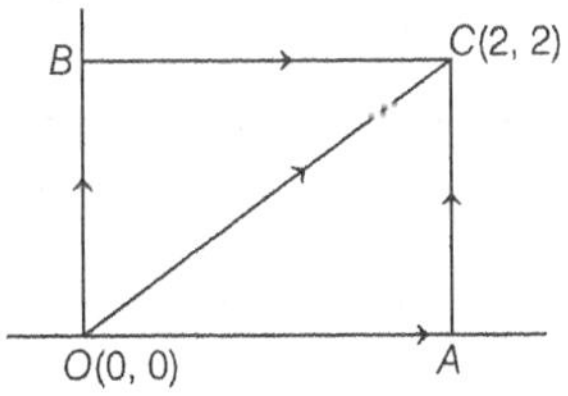

(a) Find the work done by $\mathbf{F}$ as it moves the particle from A to C (figure) along each of the path OAB, OBC, and OC.

(b) Determine whether $\mathbf{F}$ is conservative or not.

3 A force $\mathbf{F} = (y\hat{i} + x\hat{j})$ N acts on a particle which moves in the xy-plane.

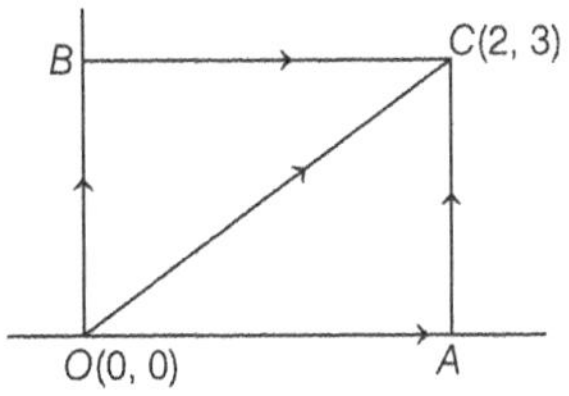

(a) Find the work done by $\mathbf{F}$ as it moves the particle from A to C (figure) along each of the paths OAB, OBC, and OC.

(b) Determine whether $\mathbf{F}$ is conservative or not.

4 Calculate the force $F(y)$ associated with the following one-dimensional potential energies.

(a) $U = -(x^2 + y^2 + z^2)$

(b) $U = -xy$

(c) $U = x^2y - x^3y^2z$

(d) $U = U_0 \sin(ax + by)$

5 The potential energy function of a particle in a region of space is given as

$$U = (2x^2 + 3y^3 + 2z)\text{ J}$$

Here, x, y and z are in metres. Find the force acting on the particle at point P (1m, 2m, 3m).

6 Force acting on a particle in a conservative force field is

(a) $\mathbf{F} = 2\hat{i} + 3\hat{j}$ (b) $\mathbf{F} = 2x\hat{i} + 2y\hat{j}$

(c) $\mathbf{F} = y\hat{i} + x\hat{j}$ (d) $\mathbf{F} = -3x^2y\hat{i} - x^3\hat{j}$

Find the potential energy function, if it is zero at origin.

7 A particle mass $m = 1$ kg lying on X-axis experiences a force given by law $F = x(3x - 2)$ N, where x is the x-coordinate of the particle in metres.

(a) Locate the points on X-axis where the particle is in equilibrium.

(b) Draw the graph of variation of force F (Y-axis) with x-coordinate of the particle (X-axis). Hence or otherwise indicate at which positions the particle is in stable or unstable equilibrium.

(c) What is the minimum speed to be imparted to the particle placed at $x = 4$ m such that it reaches the origin.

8 Potential energy of a particle moving along X-axis is given by $U = \left(\frac{x^3}{3} - 4x + 6\right)$. Here, U is in joule and x in metre. Find position of stable and unstable equilibrium.

9 Force acting on a particle moving along X-axis is as shown in figure. Find points of stable and unstable equilibrium.

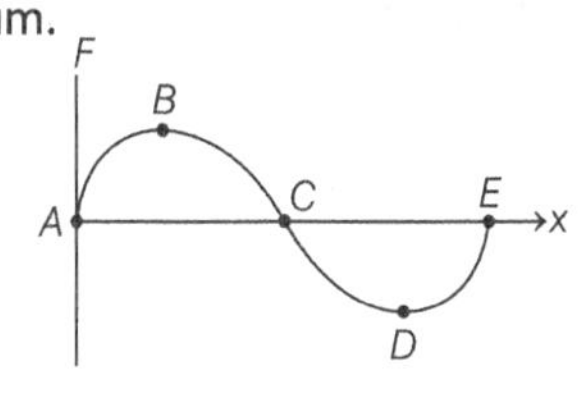

10 The potential energy (in SI units) of a particle of mass 2 kg in a conservative field is $U = 6x - 8y$. If the initial velocity of the particle is $\mathbf{u} = -1.5\,\hat{\mathbf{i}} + 2\hat{\mathbf{j}}$, then find the total distance travelled by the particle in first 2 s.

11 A 5.0 kg block is thrown up a 30° incline with an initial speed v of 6.0 m/s. It is found to travel a distance $d = 2.0$ m up the plane as its speed gradually decreases to zero. Then, what is the loss in mechanical energy of the block due to friction in this process?

12 The bob of a pendulum is released from a horizontal position *A* as shown in figure. If the length of the pendulum is 2 m, what is the speed with which the bob arrives at the lowermost point *B*, given that it dissipated 10% of its initial potential energy against air resistance? ($g = 10\ \text{m/s}^2$)

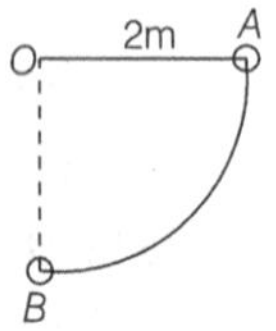

13 A rod of length 1 m and mass 0.5 kg hinged at one end, is initially hanging vertical. The other end is now raised slowly until it makes an angle 60° with the vertical. Find the required work. (Use, $g = 10\ \text{m/s}^2$)

14 A uniform chain of length *L* and mass *M* is lying on a smooth table and one-third of its length is hanging vertically down over the edge of the table. If *g* is acceleration due to gravity, what is the minimum work required to pull the hanging part on to the table.

12.8 Power

1 A force $\mathbf{F} = (3\hat{\mathbf{i}} + 4\hat{\mathbf{j}})$ N acts on a 2 kg object that moves from an initial position $\mathbf{d}_1 = (-3\hat{\mathbf{i}} - 2\hat{\mathbf{j}})$ m to final position $\mathbf{d}_2 = (5\hat{\mathbf{i}} + 4\hat{\mathbf{j}})$ m in 6 s. What is the average power delivered by the force during the interval?

2 A particle moves with a velocity $\mathbf{v} = (5\hat{\mathbf{i}} - 3\hat{\mathbf{j}} + 6\hat{\mathbf{k}})$ m/s under the influence of a constant force $\mathbf{F} = (10\hat{\mathbf{i}} + 10\hat{\mathbf{j}} + 20\hat{\mathbf{k}})$ N. Find the instantaneous power delivered to the particle.

3 A block of mass *m* is moving with a constant acceleration *a* on a rough horizontal plane. The coefficient of friction between the block and plane is μ. At time *t* from the beginning find the power delivered by

(a) gravity (b) normal force
(c) friction (d) the external agent

4 A block of mass 2.0 kg is pulled up on a smooth incline of angle 30° with the horizontal. If the block moves with an acceleration of $1.0\ \text{m/s}^2$, find the power delivered by the pulling force at a time 4.0 s after the motion starts.

5 A stone is projected with velocity *u* at an angle θ with horizontal. Find out

(a) average power of the gravity during time t.
(b) instantaneous power due to gravitational force at time *t*, where *t* is time of flight.
(c) when is average power zero?
(d) when is instantaneous power zero?
(e) when is instantaneous power negative?

6 A car of mass 1000 kg accelerates uniformly from rest to velocity of 54 km/h in 5s. What is the average power of engine during this period? (Neglect friction)

7 A water pump lifts water from a level 10 m below the ground. Water is pumped at a rate of 30 kg/min with negligible velocity.Calculate the minimum horsepower the engine should have to do this. (746 W = 1 HP)

8 Power applied to a particle varies with time as $P = [3t^2 - 2t + 1]$ W, where *t* is time in seconds. What is the change in kinetic energy of particle between time $t = 2$ s to $t = 4$ s?

9 An automobile of mass *m* accelerates, starting from rest, while the engine supplies constant power *P*, show that:

(a) the velocity is given as a function of time by $v = \left(\dfrac{2Pt}{m}\right)^{1/2}$

(b) the acceleration of the car is not constant but is given as function of time by $a = \left(\dfrac{P}{2m}\right)^{1/2} t^{-1/2}$.

(c) the position is given as a function of time by $s = \left(\dfrac{8P}{9m}\right)^{1/2} t^{3/2}$.

LEVEL 02 JEE Main Level

Single Choice Correct Questions

1 A block of mass $M = 9$ kg is moving with uniform velocity of 2 m/s on a rough horizontal surface under the action of constant force F. The force acts at an angle 37° to the horizontal. Find work done by the force F during an interval of 4 s of motion.

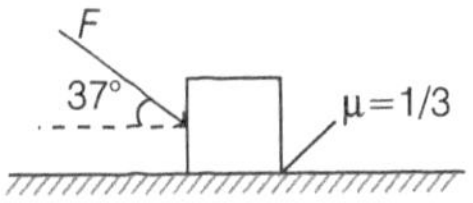

(a) 400 J (b) 300 J (c) 320 J (d) 100 J

2 A force $F = a + bx$ acts on a particle in the x-direction, where a and b are constants. Find the work done by this force during a displacement x from $x = 0$ to $x = d$.

(a) $(a + bd)\, d$ (b) $\left(a + \dfrac{bd}{2}\right) d$

(c) $\left(a + \dfrac{bd^2}{2}\right) d$ (d) None of these

3 Velocity-time graph of a particle of mass 2 kg moving in a straight line is as shown in figure. Work done by all the forces on the particle is

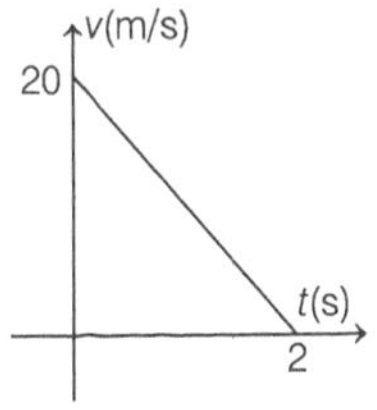

(a) 400 J (b) – 400 J (c) – 200 J (d) 200 J

4 A block of mass m is taken from A to B under the action of a constant horizontal force F. Work done by this force is

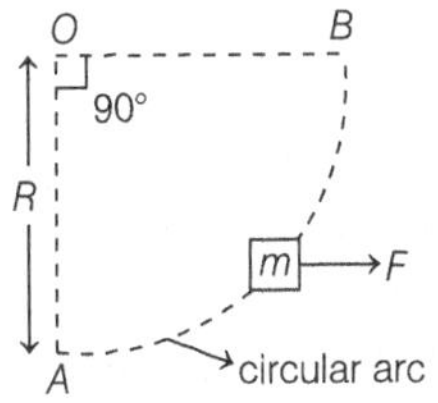

(a) FR (b) $\dfrac{\pi}{2} FR$ (c) $\dfrac{FR}{\sqrt{2}}$ (d) $\dfrac{FR}{4}$

5 A particle of mass m is projected with velocity u at an angle θ with horizontal. During the period when the particle descends, from highest point to the position, where its velocity vector makes an angle $\dfrac{\theta}{2}$ with horizontal, work done by the gravity is

(a) $\dfrac{1}{2} mu^2 \tan^2\left(\dfrac{\theta}{2}\right)$ (b) $\dfrac{1}{2} mu^2 \tan^2\theta$

(c) $\dfrac{1}{2} mu^2 \cos^2\theta \tan^2\left(\dfrac{\theta}{2}\right)$ (d) $\dfrac{1}{2} mu^2 \cos^2\left(\dfrac{\theta}{2}\right) \sin^2\theta$

6 A particle moves on a rough horizontal ground with some initial velocity say v_0. If the $\dfrac{3}{4}$th of its kinetic energy is lost in friction in time t_0, then coefficient of friction between the particle and the ground is

(a) $\dfrac{v_0}{2gt_0}$ (b) $\dfrac{v_0}{4gt_0}$

(c) $\dfrac{3v_0}{4gt_0}$ (d) $\dfrac{v_0}{gt_0}$

7 A car of mass m starts moving so that its velocity varies according to the law $v = a\sqrt{s}$, where a is a constant, and s is the distance covered. The total work performed by all the forces which are acting on the car during the first t seconds after the beginning of motion is

(a) $\dfrac{1}{8} ma^4t^2$ (b) $\dfrac{1}{8} ma^2t^4$

(c) $\dfrac{1}{4} ma^4t^2$ (d) $\dfrac{1}{4} ma^2t^4$

8 A block of mass 50 kg is projected horizontally on a rough horizontal floor. The coefficient of friction between the block and the floor is 0.1. The block strikes a light spring of stiffness $k = 100$ N/m with a velocity 2 m/s. The maximum compression of the spring is

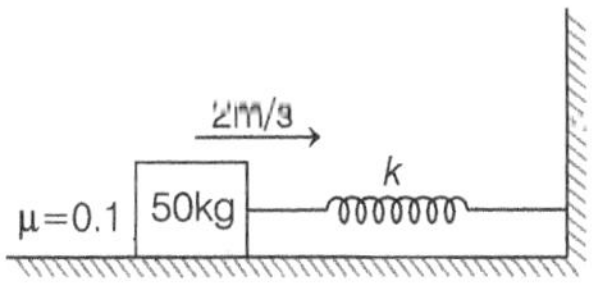

(a) 1 m (b) 2 m

(c) 3 m (d) 4 m

9 Figure shows a frictionless hemispherical bowl of radius R. A ball of mass m is pushed down the bowl from a point A. It just rises up to the edge B of the bowl. The speed with which the ball is pushed down along the bowl is

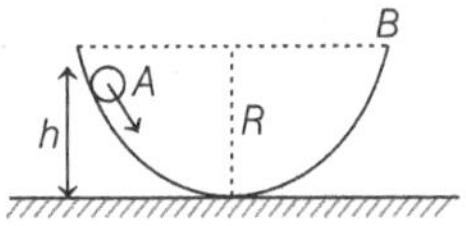

(a) $\sqrt{g(2h - R)}$ (b) $\sqrt{2g(R - h)}$

(c) $\sqrt{2g(R - 2h)}$ (d) $2\sqrt{g(R - h)}$

10 The potential energy U of a particle of mass $m = 1$ kg moving in the xy-plane is given by $U = 2x + 5y - xy$. If the particle is at rest at $(2, -2)$, its acceleration (in m/s^2) at this position is given by

(a) zero (b) 3 (c) 4 (d) 5

11 A particle moving along X-axis has potential energy $U = 2 + 20x - 5x^2$ J. The particle is released from $x = -3$. The maximum value of x will be [x is in metre and U is in joules]

(a) 5 m (b) 3 m (c) 7 m (d) 8 m

12 A rigid body is acted upon by a horizontal force which is inversely proportional to the distance covered s. The work done by this force will be proportional to

(a) s (b) $\sqrt{s}$ (c) s^2 (d) None of these

13 A man pulls a bucket of water from a depth of h from a well. If the mass of the rope and that bucket of water is m and M respectively, the work done by the man is

(a) $(M + m)gh$ (b) $\left(\frac{M+m}{2}\right)gh$

(c) $\left(M + \frac{m}{2}\right)gh$ (d) $\left(\frac{M}{2} + m\right)gh$

14 A bob hangs from a rigid support by an inextensible string of length l. It is displaced through a distance l (from the lowest position) keeping the string straight and then released. The speed of the bob at the lowest position is

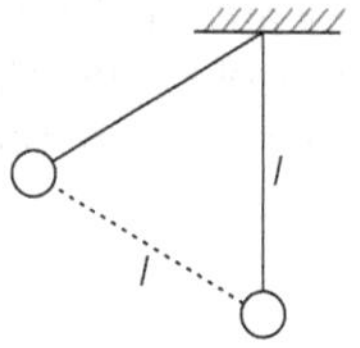

(a) $\sqrt{gl}$ (b) $\sqrt{3gl}$

(c) $\sqrt{2gl}$ (d) $\sqrt{5gl}$

15 In the figure, a block slides along a track from one level to a higher level, by moving through an intermediate valley. The track is frictionless until the block reaches the higher level. There, a frictional force stops the block in a distance d. The block's initial speed v_0 is 6 m/s, the height difference h is 1.1 m and the coefficient of kinetic friction μ is 0.6. The value of d is

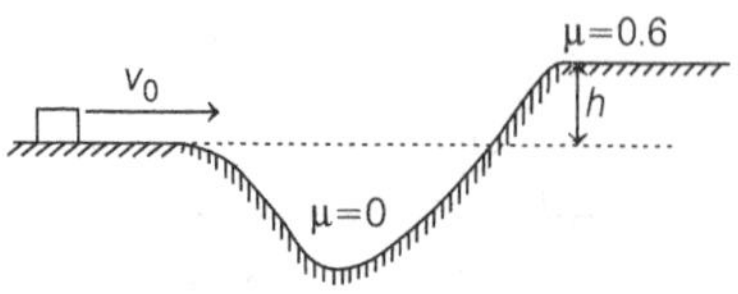

(a) 1.17 m (b) 1.71 m

(c) 7.11 m (d) 11.7 m

16 If a simple pendulum of length l has the maximum angular displacement (θ), then the maximum kinetic energy of its bob of mass m is

(a) $\frac{1}{2}mgl$ (b) $mgl \cos\theta$

(c) $mgl(1 - \cos\theta)$ (d) $\frac{1}{2}mgl \sin\theta$

17 A particle of mass m moves on the X-axis under the influence of a force of attraction towards the origin O given by $F = -\frac{k}{x^2}\hat{\mathbf{i}}$. If the particle starts from rest at a distance a from the origin, the speed it will attain to reach a distance x from origin is $(x < a)$

(a) $\sqrt{\frac{2k}{m}}\left[\frac{a-x}{ax}\right]^{1/2}$ (b) $\sqrt{\frac{2k}{m}}\left[\frac{a+x}{ax}\right]^{1/2}$

(c) $\sqrt{\frac{k}{m}}\left[\frac{ax}{a-x}\right]$ (d) $\sqrt{\frac{m}{2k}}\left[\frac{a-x}{ax}\right]^{1/2}$

18 A uniform chain has mass M and length L. It is lying on a smooth horizontal table with half of its length hanging vertically downward. The work done in pulling the chain up the table is

(a) $\frac{MgL}{2}$ (b) $\frac{MgL}{4}$ (c) $\frac{MgL}{8}$ (d) $\frac{MgL}{16}$

19 A block is resting over a smooth horizontal plane. A constant horizontal force starts acting on it at $t = 0$. Which of the following graph is correct?

(a)
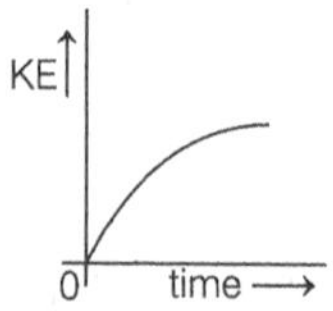

(b)
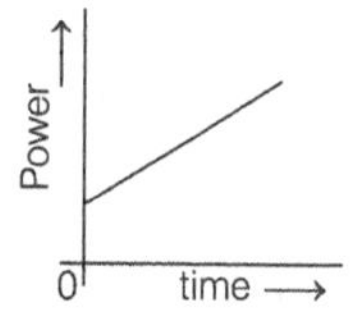

(c)
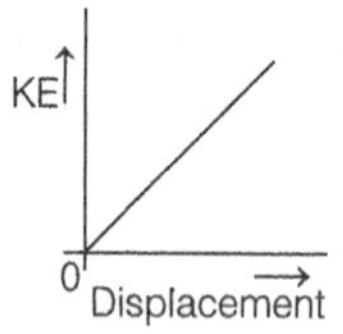

(d)
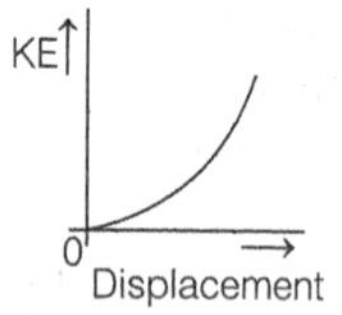

20 A body with mass 2 kg moves in one direction in the presence of a force which is described by the potential energy graph. If the body is released from rest at $x = 2$ m, then its speed when it crosses $x = 5$ m is

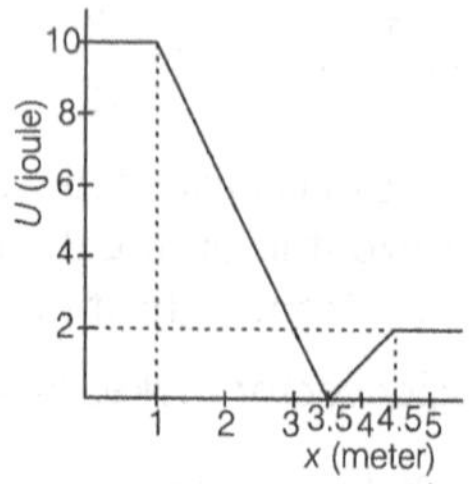

(a) zero (b) 1 m/s (c) 2 m/s (d) 3 m/s

21 System shown in the figure is released from rest. Pulley, string and spring are massless and friction is absent everywhere. The speed of 5 kg block when 2 kg block leaves the contact with ground is (take, force constant of spring $= k = 40$ N/m and $g = 10$ m/s^2)

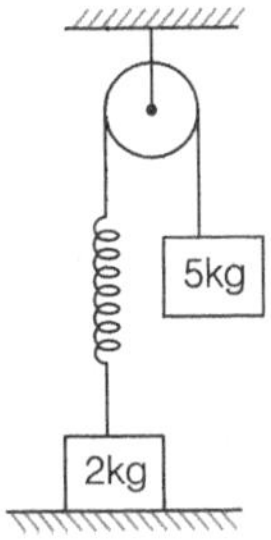

(a) $\sqrt{2}$ m/s (b) $2\sqrt{2}$ m/s
(c) 2 m/s (d) $4\sqrt{2}$ m/s

22 In the figure, 2 kg and 1 kg blocks are joined together by a massless and frictionless pulley. When the mass 2 kg is released from the height 60 cm above the floor, it strikes the floor with a speed (assume string is light) ($g = 10$ m/s^2)

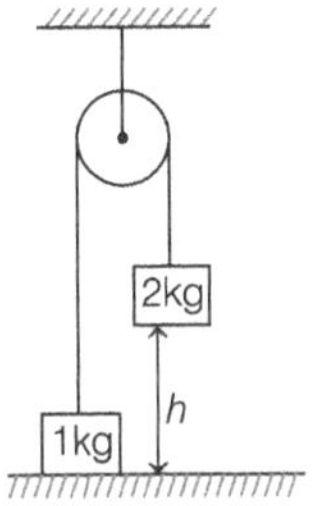

(a) 2 m/s (b) 3 m/s
(c) $\sqrt{2}$ m/s (d) $\sqrt{3}$ m/s

23 The upper one third of an inclined plane with inclination ϕ is perfectly smooth, while the rest part is rough. A body starting from rest at the top will again come to rest at the bottom, if the coefficient of friction for the rough part is given by

(a) $\frac{2}{3}\tan\phi$ (b) $\frac{2}{3}\cot\phi$ (c) $\frac{3}{2}\tan\phi$ (d) $\frac{3}{2}\cot\phi$

24 A block of mass 1 kg slides down a vertical curved track that is one quadrant of a circle of radius 1 m. Its speed at the bottom is 2 m/s. The work done by frictional force is

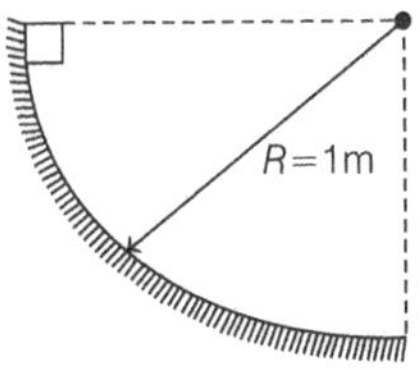

(a) 8 J (b) –8 J (c) 4 J (d) –4 J

25 A body of mass m is accelerated uniformly from rest to a speed v in a time T. The instantaneous power delivered to the body as a function of time, is given by

(a) $\frac{mv^2}{T^2}t$ (b) $\frac{mv^2}{T^2}t^2$ (c) $\frac{1}{2}\frac{mv^2}{T^2}t$ (d) $\frac{1}{2}\frac{mv^2}{T^2}t^2$

26 A particle is projected vertically upwards with a speed of 16 m/s. After sometime, when it again passes through the point of projection, its speed is found to be 8 m/s. It is known that, the work done by air resistance is same during upward and downward motion. Then, the maximum height attained by the particle is (take, $g = 10$ m/s^2)

(a) 8 m (b) 4.8 m (c) 17.6 m (d) 12.8 m

27 The potential energy (in joule) of a body of mass 2 kg moving in the xy-plane is given by $U = 6x + 8y$, where the position coordinates x and y are measured in metre. If the body is at rest at point (6m, 4m) at time $t = 0$, it will cross the Y-axis at time t equal to

(a) 1 s (b) 2 s (c) 3 s (d) 4 s

28 A vehicle of mass M is accelerated on a horizontal frictionless road under a force changing its velocity from u to v in distance s. If a constant power P is given by the engine of the vehicle, then v is

(a) $\left(u^3 + \frac{2Ps}{M}\right)^{1/3}$ (b) $\left(\frac{Ps}{M} + u^3\right)^{1/2}$

(c) $\left(\frac{Ps}{M} + u^2\right)^{1/3}$ (d) $\left(\frac{3Ps}{M} + u^3\right)^{1/3}$

29 A particle is projected with speed u in air at an angle θ with the horizontal. The graph showing the variation of instantaneous power due to gravity P with time t will be

(a)
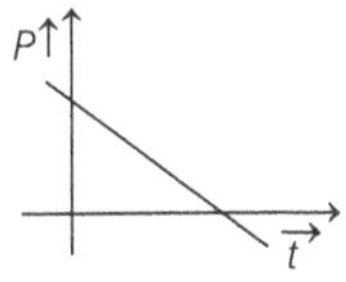

(b)
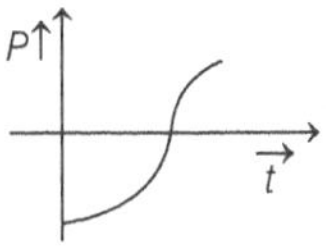

(c)
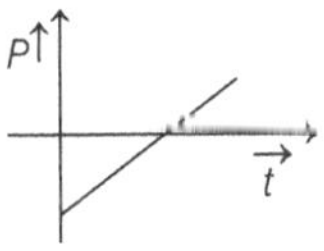

(d)
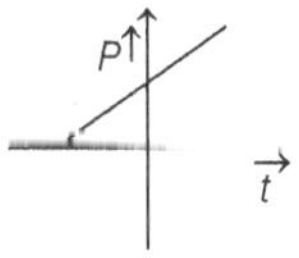

30 A block of mass 5 kg dropped from a height of 2 m above a massless spring compresses it by 0.5 m (see figure) and then rebounds. The spring constant k of the spring is

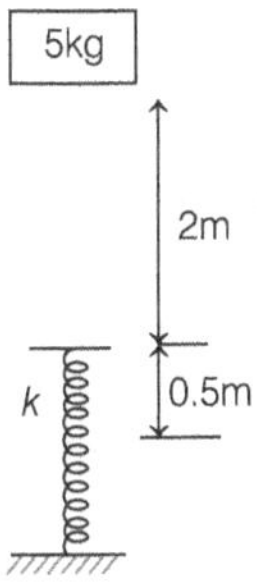

(a) 1000 N/m (b) 800 N/m
(c) 400 N/m (d) 500 N/m

31 A 15 g ball is shot from a spring gun whose spring has a force constant of 600 N/m. The spring is compressed by 5 cm. The greatest possible horizontal range of the ball for this compression is ($g = 10\ m/s^2$)

(a) 6.0 m (b) 12.0 m (c) 10.0 m (d) 8.0 m

32 Power supplied to a particle of mass 2 kg varies with time as $P = \frac{3t^2}{2}$ W. Here, t is in second. If velocity of particle at $t = 0$ is $v = 0$, the velocity of particle at time $t = 2$ s will be

(a) 1 m/s (b) 4 m/s (c) 2 m/s (d) $2\sqrt{2}$ m/s

33 An elastic string of unstretched length L and force constant k is stretched by a small length x. It is further stretched by another small length y. The work done in the second stretching is

(a) $\frac{1}{2}ky^2$ (b) $\frac{1}{2}k(x^2 + y^2)$

(c) $\frac{1}{2}k(x + y)^2$ (d) $\frac{1}{2}ky(2x + y)$

34 A man of mass m is climbing up the rope as shown in figure. Tension in string is more than mg, and there is no slipping between man and rope. Assuming, rope is massless and inextensible

(a) $W_{\text{all forces}} = \Delta K$ is not applicable on man, since $W_{mg} < 0, W_{\text{Tension}} = 0$ and $\Delta K > 0$

(b) $W_{\text{all forces}} = \Delta K$ is applicable on man, since $W_{mg} < 0$, $W_{\text{Tension}} = 0$ and $\Delta K < 0$

(c) $W_{\text{all forces}} = \Delta K$ is applicable on man, since $W_{mg} < 0$, $W_{\text{Tension}} > 0$, and $\Delta K > 0$

(d) $W_{\text{all forces}} = \Delta K$ is applicable on man, even though $W_{mg} < 0, W_{\text{Tension}} = 0$ and $\Delta K > 0$

35 A certain system has potential energy given by the function $U(x) = -ax^2 + bx^4$ with constants, $a, b > 0$. Which of the following cases is an unstable equilibrium point?

(a) 0 (b) $-\sqrt{\frac{a}{2b}}$ (c) $\sqrt{\frac{a}{2b}}$ (d) $\sqrt{\frac{a}{b}}$

36 Velocity of a body of mass 2 kg moving in xy-plane is given by $\mathbf{v} = (2\hat{\mathbf{i}} + 4t\hat{\mathbf{j}})$ m/s, where t is the time in second. The power delivered to the body by the resultant force acting on it at $t = 5$ s is

(a) 80 W (b) 160 W (c) 40 W (d) 100 W

37 A cord is used to lower vertically a block of mass M by a distance d with constant downward acceleration $\frac{g}{4}$. Work done by the cord on the block is

(a) $-Mg\frac{d}{4}$ (b) $3Mg\frac{d}{4}$ (c) $-3Mg\frac{d}{4}$ (d) Mgd

38 A chain of length l and mass m lies on the surface of a smooth sphere of radius $R (R > l)$ with one end tied on the top of the sphere. Then, the gravitational potential energy of the chain with reference level at the centre of sphere is given by

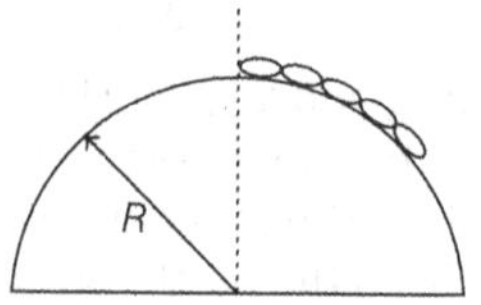

(a) $\frac{mR^2g}{l}\sin\left(\frac{l}{R}\right)$ (b) $\frac{mR^2g}{l}\cos\left(\frac{l}{R}\right)$

(c) $\frac{mR^2g}{l}\cot\left(\frac{R}{l}\right)$ (d) $\frac{mR^2g}{l}\tan\left(\frac{R}{l}\right)$

39 The force acting on a body moving along X-axis varies with the position of the particle as shown in the figure. The body is in stable equilibrium at

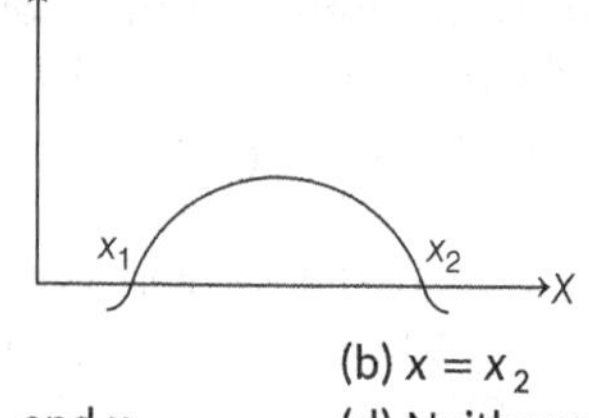

(a) $x = x_1$ (b) $x = x_2$

(c) Both x_1 and x_2 (d) Neither x_1 and x_2

40 A pump motor is used to deliver water at a certain rate from a given pipe. To obtain n times water from the same pipe in the same time, the factor by which the power of the motor should be increased is

(a) n^2 (b) n^3 (c) n^4 (d) $n^{1/2}$

41 The potential energy for a force field is given by $U(x, y) = \cos(x + y)$. The force acting on a particle at position given by coordinates $\left(0, \frac{\pi}{4}\right)$ is

(a) $-\frac{1}{\sqrt{2}}(\hat{\mathbf{i}} + \hat{\mathbf{j}})$ (b) $\frac{1}{\sqrt{2}}(\hat{\mathbf{i}} + \hat{\mathbf{j}})$

(c) $\left(\frac{1}{2}\hat{\mathbf{i}} + \frac{\sqrt{3}}{2}\hat{\mathbf{j}}\right)$ (d) $\left(\frac{1}{2}\hat{\mathbf{i}} - \frac{\sqrt{3}}{2}\hat{\mathbf{j}}\right)$

42 If v be the instantaneous velocity of the body dropped from the top of a tower, when it is located at height h, then which of the following remains constant?

(a) $gh + v^2$ (b) $gh + \frac{v^2}{2}$ (c) $gh - \frac{v^2}{2}$ (d) $gh - v^2$

43 Water is pumped from a depth of 10 m and delivered through a pipe of cross-section 10^{-2} m^2. If it is needed to deliver a volume of 10^{-1} m^3 per second the power required will be

(a) 10 kW (b) 9.8 kW (c) 15 kW (d) 4.9 kW

44 The work done by force $\mathbf{F} = x^2\hat{\mathbf{i}} + y^2\hat{\mathbf{j}}$ around the path $ABCDA$ shown in figure is

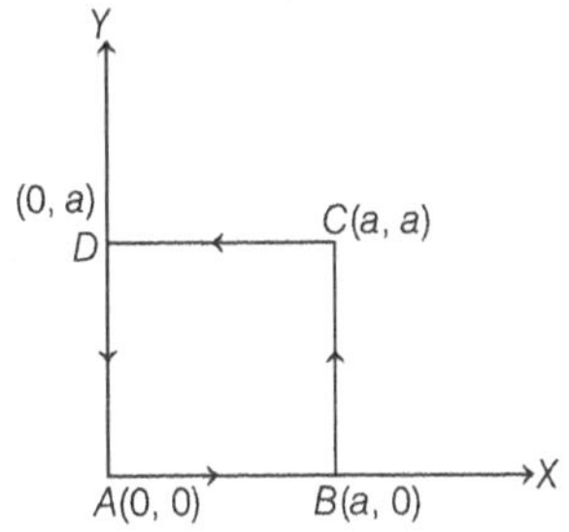

(a) $\frac{2}{3}a^2$ (b) zero (c) a^3 (d) $\frac{4}{3}a^3$

45 A small block of mass m is kept on a rough inclined surface of inclination θ fixed in an elevator. The elevator goes up with a uniform velocity v and the block does not slide on the wedge. The work done by the force of friction on the block in time t will be

(a) zero (b) $mgvt \cos^2 \theta$

(c) $mgvt \sin^2 \theta$ (d) $mgvt \sin 2\theta$

46 A force $\mathbf{F} = -k(y\hat{\mathbf{i}} + x\hat{\mathbf{j}})$ (where k is a positive constant) acts on a particle moving in the xy-plane. Starting from the origin, the particle is taken along the positive X-axis to the point $(a, 0)$ and then parallel to the Y-axis to the point (a, a). The total work done by the force $\mathbf{F}$ on the particle is

(a) $-2ka^2$ (b) $2ka^2$

(c) $-ka^2$ (d) ka^2

47 A block of mass 10 kg is acted upon by a force of 40 N parallel to the inclined plane as shown. Find work done by applied fore during first 10 s of its motion. Initially, block was at rest.

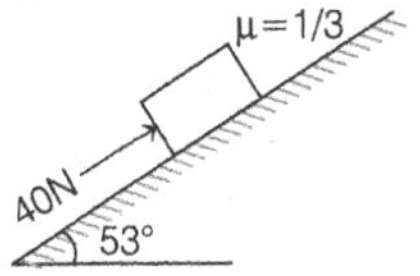

(a) – 4000 J (b) 4000 J

(c) – 8000 J (d) 8000 J

48 The minimum work done required to accelerate a truck on a horizontal road from rest to speed v

(a) is less than that required to accelerate it from v to $2v$

(b) is equal to that required to accelerate it from v to $2v$

(c) is more than that required to accelerate it from v to $2v$

(d) may be any one of the above since it depends on the force acting on the truck and the distance over which it acts

49 A man who is running has half the kinetic energy of the boy of half his mass. The man speeds up by 1 m/s and then has the same kinetic energy as the boy. The original speed of the man was

(a) $\sqrt{2}$ m/s (b) $(\sqrt{2} - 1)$ m/s

(c) 2 m/s (d) $(\sqrt{2} + 1)$ m/s

50 A body is moved from rest along a straight line by a machine delivering constant power. The ratio of displacement and velocity varies with time t as

(a)
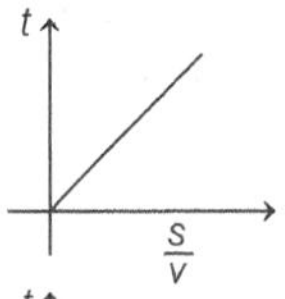

(b)
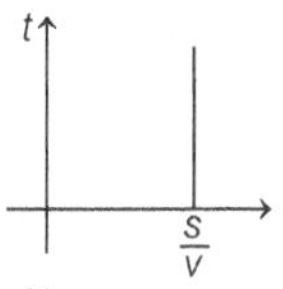

(c)
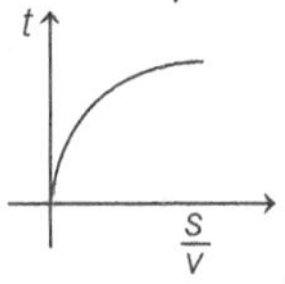

(d)
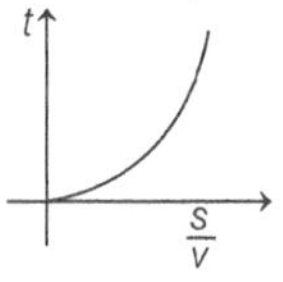

51 The net force exerted on a particle acts in the $+x$-direction. Its magnitude increases linearly from zero at $x = 0$ to 24.0 N at $x = 3.0$ m. It remains constant at 24.0 N from $x = 3.0$ m to $x = 8.0$ m and then decreases linearly to zero at $x = 13.0$ m. Determine the work done to move the particle from $x = 0$ to $x = 13.0$.

(a) 252 J (b) 216 J

(c) 196 J (d) None of these

52 In the figure shown, pulley and spring are ideal. If k is spring constant of spring, the potential energy stored in it is $(m_1 > m_2)$

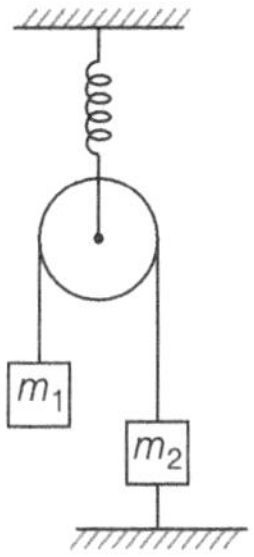

(a) $\frac{2m_1^2g^2}{k}$

(b) $\frac{2m_2^2g^2}{k}$

(c) $\frac{(m_1 + m_2)^2g^2}{k}$

(d) $\frac{1}{2}\frac{(m_1 - m_2)^2g^2}{k}$

53 A block of mass m released from rest at point A. The compression in spring, when the speed of block is maximum is

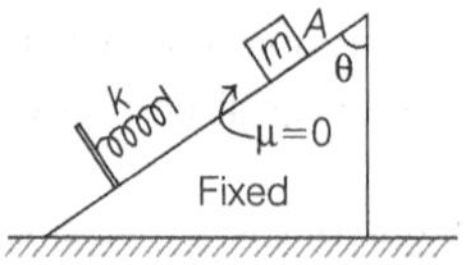

(a) $\frac{mg \sin\theta}{k}$ (b) $\frac{2mg \sin\theta}{k}$

(c) $\frac{mg \cos\theta}{k}$ (d) $\frac{2mg \cos\theta}{k}$

54 A body of mass m was slowly hauled up the hill (figure) by a force F which at each point was directed along a tangent to the trajectory. Find the work performed by this force, if the height of the hill is h, the length of its base l, and the coefficient to friction μ.

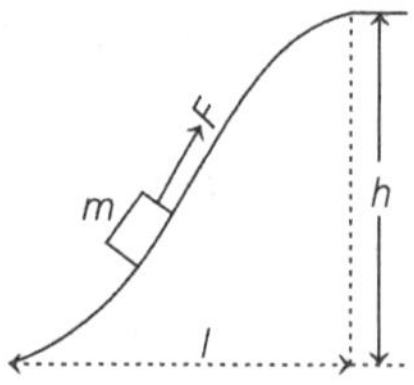

(a) $mg(h+\mu l)$ (b) $mg(\mu h+l)$

(c) $2mg(\mu h+l)$ (d) $2mg(h+\mu l)$

55 Which of the following graphs represents the graphical relation between momentum (p) and kinetic energy (K) for a body in motion?

(a) 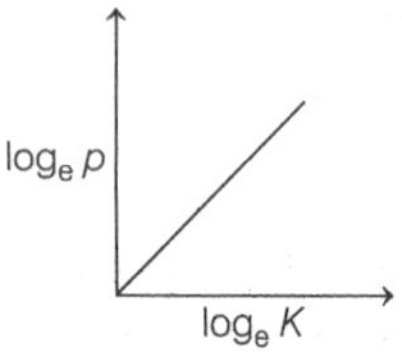

(b) 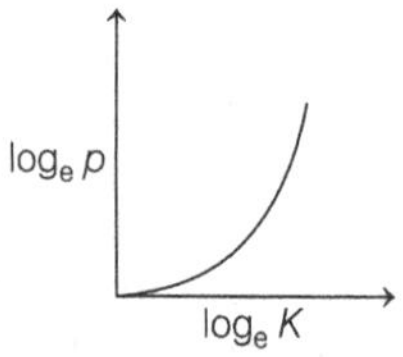

(c) 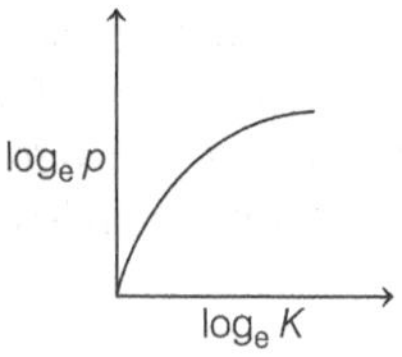

(d) None of these

56 A particle is at the origin and a force $F = kx$ is acting on it (where k is a positive constant). If $U(0) = 0$, the graph of $U(x)$ *versus* x will be (where U is the potential energy function).

(a) 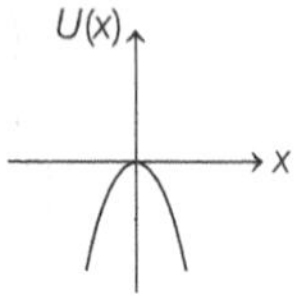

(b) 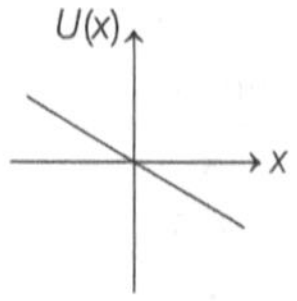

(c) 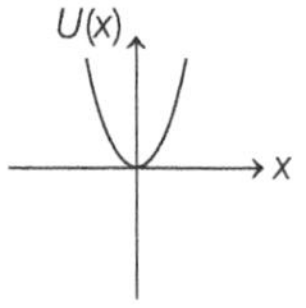

(d) 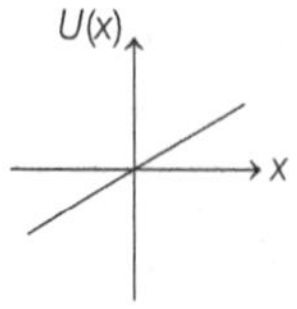

57 A ball of mass m is released in a circular tube of radius R. A spring of spring constant k which is in its natural length is placed in the tube as shown in figure. If angle made by radius vector of the ball with the vertical when ball comes at an instantaneous rest is $60°$, then the value of k is

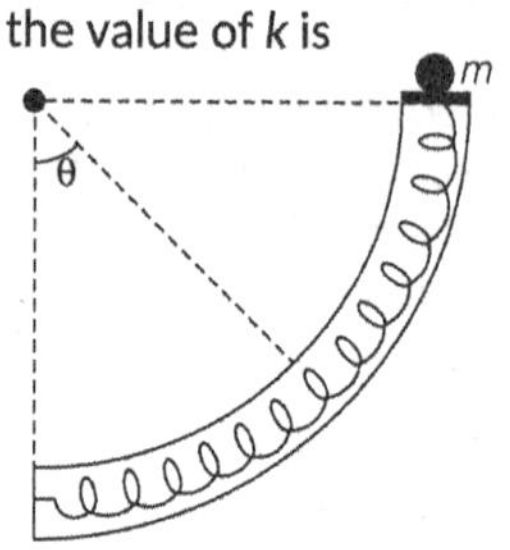

(a) $\frac{9mg}{\pi^2 R}$ (b) $\frac{18mg}{\pi^2 R}$ (c) $\frac{36mg}{\pi^2 R}$ (d) $\frac{72mg}{\pi^2 R}$

58 A block moves up a 30° inclined under the action of certain forces, three of which are shown in figure. $\mathbf{F}_1$ is horizontal and a magnitude 40 N. $\mathbf{F}_2$ is normal to the plane and of magnitude 20 N. $\mathbf{F}_3$ is parallel to the plane and of magnitude 30 N. Determine the work done by each force as the block (and point of application of each force) moves 80 cm up the incline.

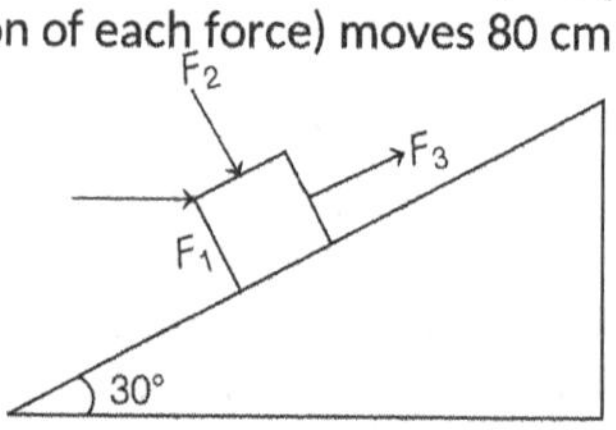

(a) 28 J, 34.6 J, 24 J (b) 28 J, 0 J, 24 J

(c) 24 J, 44 J, 15 J (d) 20 J, 0 J, 15 J

59 A block of mass m lying at point P of a wedge having a smooth semi-circular track of radius R. What should be the minimum value of a_0, so that mass can just reach the point Q?

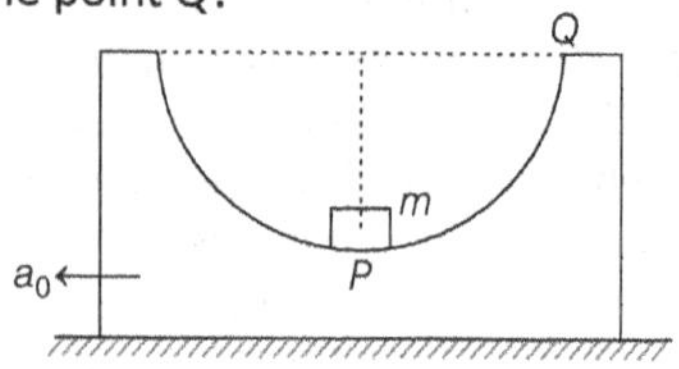

(a) $\frac{g}{2}$ (b) $\sqrt{g}$ (c) g (d) Not possible

60 An object of mass $m = 0.5$ kg when attached to a vertical spring and lowered very slowly to its equilibrium position stretches the spring by 10cm. If the same object is attached to the same vertical spring but permitted to fall instead, then the maximum speed of the mass will be (take, $g = 10\ \text{m/s}^2$)

(a) 1 m/s (b) $\sqrt{2}$ m/s (c) $\frac{1}{\sqrt{2}}$ m/s (d) $\frac{1}{2}$ m/s

61 A block of mass m is suspended by a light thread from an elevator. The elevator starts from rest and accelerates upward with uniform acceleration a. The work done during t second by the tension in the thread is

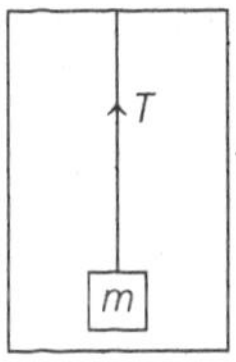

(a) $\frac{m}{2}(g+a)\,at^2$ (b) $\frac{m}{2}(g-a)\,at^2$
(c) $\frac{m}{2}gat^2$ (d) zero

62 A uniform chain of length 2 m is kept on a table such that a length of 60 cm hangs from the edge of the table. The total mass of the chain is 4 kg. What is the work done in pulling the entire chain on the table?
(a) 7.2 J (b) 3.6 J (c) 120 J (d) 1200 J

63 A body is moved along a straight line by a machine delivering constant power. The distance moved by the body in time t is proportional to ($u=0$)
(a) $t^{1/2}$ (b) $t^{3/4}$ (c) $t^{3/2}$ (d) t^2

64 A truck of mass 30000 kg moves up an inclined plane of slope 1 in 100 at a speed of 30 km/h. The power of the truck is (given, $g = 10$ m/s^2)
(a) 25 kW (b) 10 kW
(c) 5 kW (d) 2.5 kW

65 Two bodies of mass m_1 and m_2 ($m_2 > m_1$) are connected by a light inextensible string which passes through a smooth fixed pulley. What is the instantaneous power delivered by an external agent to pull m_1 with constant velocity v at any instant t?

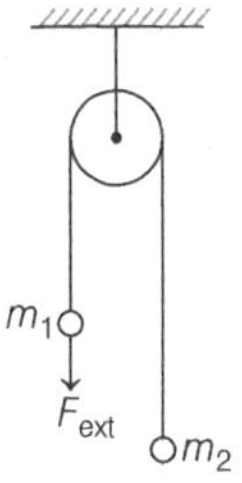

(a) $(m_2-m_1)\,gv$ (b) $(m_2+m_1)gv$
(c) $2(m_2-m_1)\,gv$ (d) $2(m_2+m_1)\,gv$

66 A machine gun is firing 60 bullets per minute with a velocity of 700 m/s. If each bullet has a mass of 50 g, the power developed by the gun is
(a) 20000 W (b) 10000 W
(c) 12250 W (d) 12000 W

67 A ring of mass m can slide along a fixed smooth vertical rod as shown in figure. The ring is connected by a spring of spring constant $k = \frac{4mg}{R}$, where $2R$ is the natural length of spring. The other end of spring is fixed to the ground at point A at a horizontal distance of $2R$ from the base of the rod. Calculate the velocity of the ring as it reaches the ground.

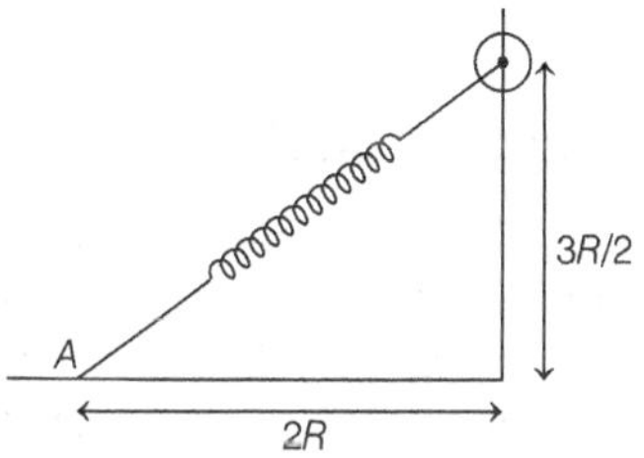

(a) $\sqrt{gR}$ (b) $\sqrt{2gR}$ (c) $\sqrt{3gR}$ (d) $\sqrt{4gR}$

68 A block attached to a spring, pulled by a constant horizontal force, is kept on a smooth surface as shown in the figure. Initially, the spring is in the natural state. Then, the maximum positive work that the applied force F can do is [given that, spring does not break]

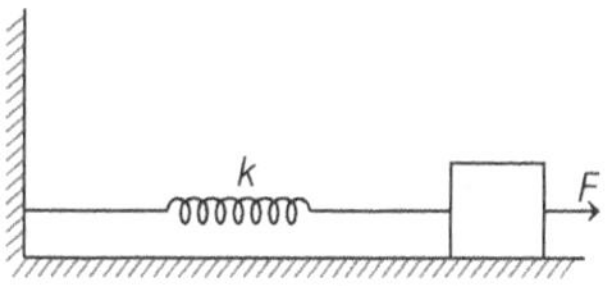

(a) $\frac{F^2}{k}$ (b) $\frac{2F^2}{k}$
(c) $\frac{3F^2}{2k}$ (d) $\frac{F^2}{2k}$

69 A small mass slides down an inclined plane of inclination θ with the horizontal. The co-efficient of friction is $\mu = \mu_0 x$, where x is the distance through which the mass slides down and μ_0, a constant. Find the distance covered by the mass before it stops.
(a) $\frac{2\tan\theta}{\mu_0}$ (b) $\frac{\tan\theta}{2\mu_0}$
(c) $\frac{\tan\theta}{\mu_0}$ (d) $\frac{4\tan\theta}{\mu_0}$

70 A block of mass m is pulled by a constant power P placed on a rough horizontal plane. The friction co-efficient between the block and surface is μ. Find the maximum velocity of the block.
(a) μmgP (b) $\frac{2P}{\mu mg}$
(c) $\frac{P}{2\mu mg}$ (d) $\frac{P}{\mu mg}$

71 An open knife edge of mass m is dropped from a height h on a wooden floor. If the knife penetrates upto depth d into the wood, the average resistance offered by the wood to the knife edge is

(a) mg (b) $mg\left(1-\frac{h}{d}\right)$

(c) $mg\left(1+\frac{h}{d}\right)$ (d) $mg\left(1+\frac{h}{d}\right)^2$

Numerical Value Questions

1 A small block slides along a path that is without friction until the block reaches the section $L = 3$ m, which begins at height $h = 3$ m on a flat incline of angle 37°, as shown. In that section, the coefficient of kinetic friction 1. The block passes through point A with a speed of 15 m/s. Find the speed (in m/s) of the block as it passes through point B where the friction ends. (Take, $g = 10\text{ m/s}^2$)

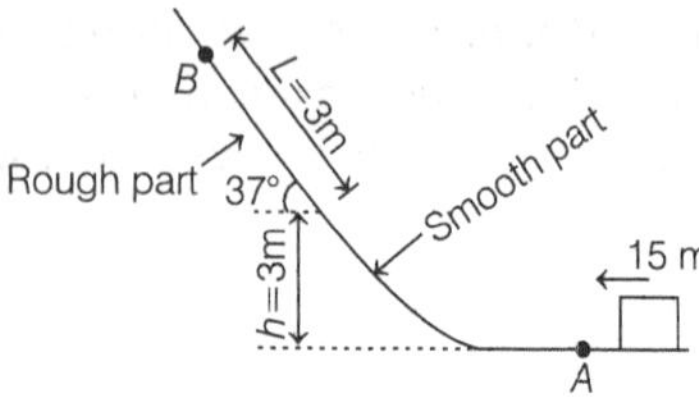

2 The potential energy of a 200 g particle free to move along the X-axis is given by $U(x) = \left(\frac{x^2}{2} - x\right)$ J. The total mechanical energy of the particle is 2 J. Then, find the maximum speed (in m/s).

3 A force $\mathbf{F} = (3t\hat{\mathbf{i}} + 5\hat{\mathbf{j}})$ N acts on a body due to which its position varies as $\mathbf{s} = (2t^2\hat{\mathbf{i}} - 5\hat{\mathbf{j}})$ m. Find work done (in J) by this force in initial 2 s.

4 A ball is released from point A as shown in figure. The ball leaves the track at B. All surfaces are smooth. If track makes an angle 30° with horizontal at B, then maximum height (in m) attained by the ball from the ground is

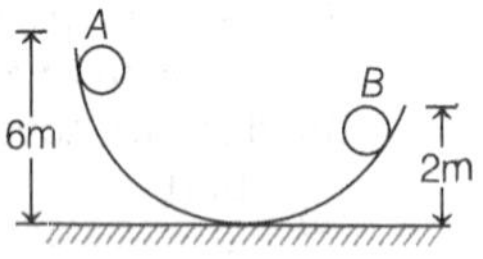

5 The spring block system lies on a smooth horizontal surface. The free end of the spring is being pulled towards right with constant speed $v_0 = 2$ m/s. At $t = 0$ s, the spring of constant $k = 100$ N/cm is unstretched and the block has a speed 1 m/s to left. Find the maximum extension (in cm) of the spring.

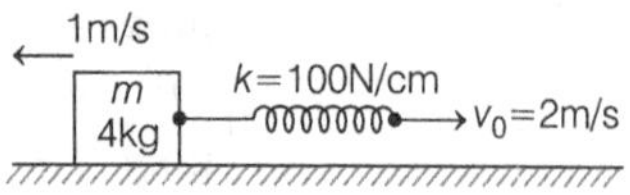

6 A spring gun has spring constant 100 N/m. A small ball of mass 0.1 kg is put in its barrel by compressing the spring through 0.05 m as shown in the figure. Find d (in m) if the ball leaves the gun horizontally at height of 2 m above the ground. ($g = 10\text{ m/s}^2$)

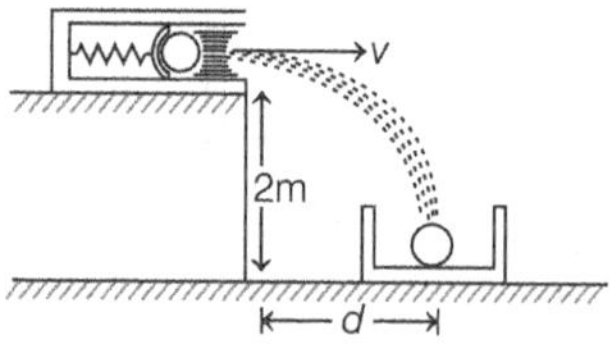

7 A particle of mass 2 kg starts to move at position $x = 0$ and time $t = 0$ under the action of force $F = (10 + 4x)$ N along the X-axis on a frictionless horizontal track. Find the power (in W) delivered by the force in watts at the instant when the particle has moved by the distance 5 m.

8 A block of mass 5.0 kg is suspended from the end of a vertical spring which is stretched by 10 cm under the load of the block. The block is given a sharp impulse from below, so that it acquires an upward speed of 2.0 m/s. How high (in cm) will it rise? (Take, $g = 10\text{ m/s}^2$)

9 Force acting on a particle moving in a straight line varies with the velocity v of the particle as $F = \frac{2}{v}$ N. Find the work done(in J) by this force in time 3 s.

10 The total mass a cyclist and her bicycle is 120 kg. While pedalling, she generates power of 640 W. Her motion is opposed by road resistance of magnitude 16N and air resistance of magnitude $8v$ N, where v is her speed in m/s. Find the greatest speed(in m/s), that she can maintain on a horizontal road.

11 A particle of mass $m = 2$ kg (initially at rest), suspended by a massless string, is pulled from position A by applying a constant horizontal force $F = \frac{mg}{3}$. Find the velocity (in m/s) at point B shown in figure.

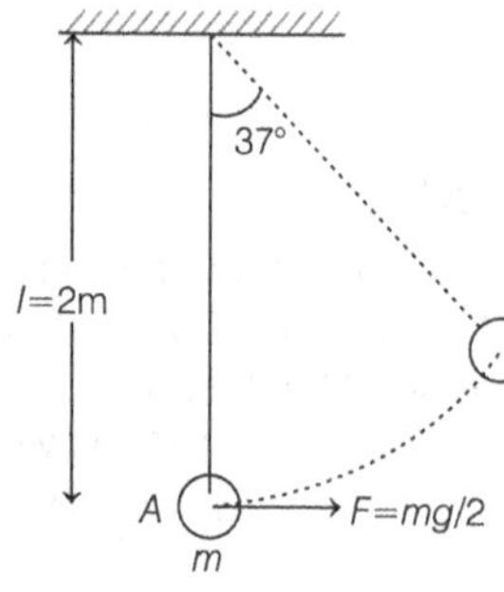

12 A block of mass 1 kg is kept on smooth inclined surface of an elevator moving up with a constant velocity of 5 m/s. Find the work done (in J) by normal reaction (as seen from ground) on the block is 10 s.

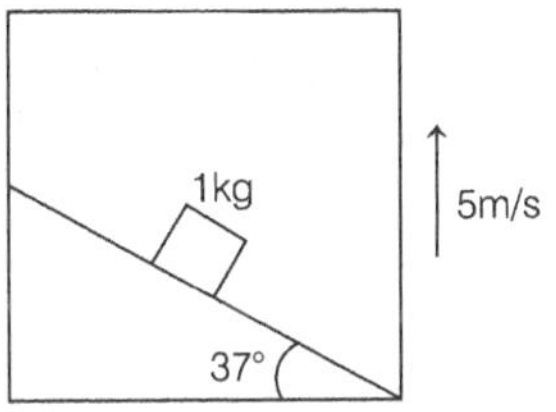

13 A block of mass $m = 2$ kg starts from rest with spring unstretched on a rough incline. Force constant of spring, $k = 8$ N/m, coefficient of kinetic friction $\mu_k = \frac{1}{8}$. What is the speed (in m/s) of the block when it has slid a distance $x = 0.5$ m down the incline?

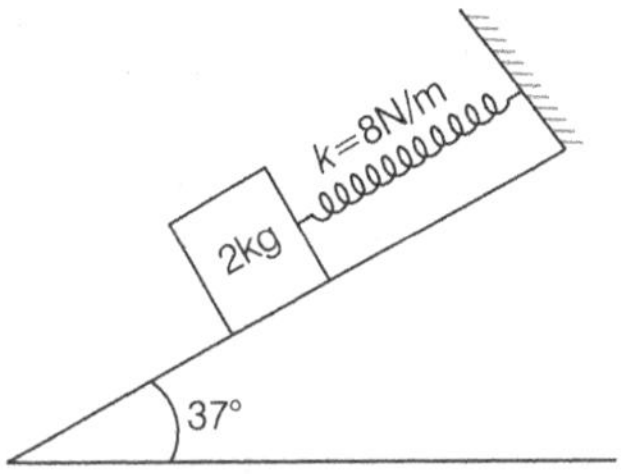

14 A block of mass 2 kg is suspended by a massless spring constant 24 N/m, block supported from (below), such that spring is relaxed. Another massless identical spring is located below it, initially relaxed and at a separation of 1 m. Now, the block is released from rest. Find the maximum extension (in m) of the upper spring.

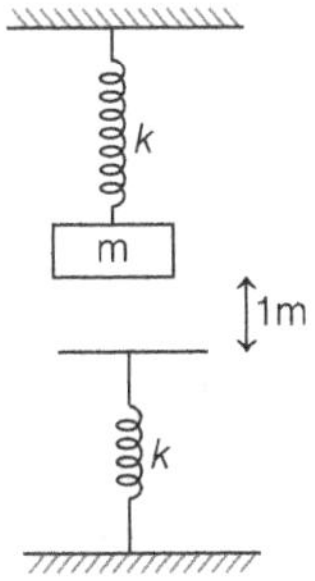

15 An object of mass 5 kg falls from rest through a vertical distance of 20 m and reaches ground with a velocity of 10 m/s. The work done by air resistance is $-n$ Joule. Find n. ($g = 9.8$ ms^{-2})

16 A 3 kg block rests on top of a 2 kg block which is attached to a spring of force constant $k = 40$ N/m. The upper block is suddenly removed. Find the maximum height (in m) reached by the 2 kg block. ($g = 10$ ms^{-2})

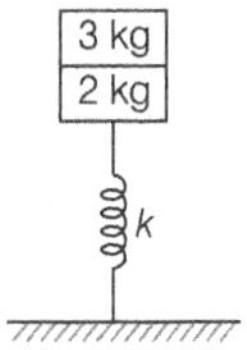

17 A 1.5 kg block is initially at rest on a smooth horizontal surface when a horizontal force in the positive direction of X-axis is applied to the block. The force is given by $F = (8 - x^3)$ N, where initial position of the block is $x = 0$. Find the maximum kinetic energy (in J) of the block between $x = 0$ and $x = 4$ m.

18 A 1.0 kg block collides with a horizontal weightless spring of force constant 2.75 N/m as shown in figure. The block compresses the spring 4.0 m from the rest position. If the coefficient of kinetic friction between the block and horizontal surface is 0.25, find the speed (in m/s) of the block at the instant of collision.

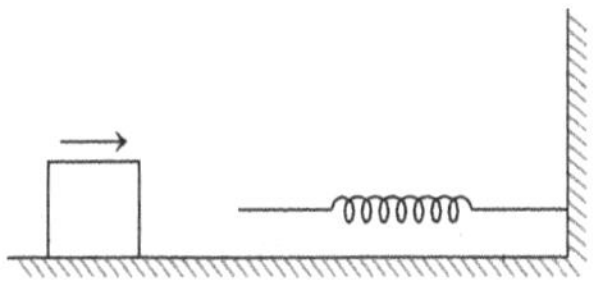

19 A car of mass m enters a region in which a resistive force acts. The speed of the car is v_0 at the origin along positive X-axis. The force is given by $F = -\alpha x^2$, where α is a positive constant.

If the distance travelled by the car before coming to rest for the first time is $\left(\frac{nmv_0^2}{4\alpha}\right)^{1/3}$, then find the value of n.

20 A body of mass 2 kg is moved from a point A to a point B by an external agent in a conservative force field. If the velocity of the body at the points A and B are 5 m/s and 3 m/s respectively, and the work done by the external agent is - 10 J, then find the change in potential energy (in J) between points A and B.

LEVEL 03 JEE Advanced Level

Single Choice Correct Questions

1 A mass 2 kg is moving along X-axis, such that its x-coordinate with respect to time is given as $x = 2t^2 + 4t$. Find the work done by a force $F = 3t\hat{\mathbf{i}} - 3t^2\hat{\mathbf{j}} + \sqrt{5}t\hat{\mathbf{k}}$ in first 2 s.

(a) 56 units (b) 44 units (c) 64 units (d) 46 units

2 A force $\mathbf{F} = (3xy - 5z)\,\hat{\mathbf{j}} + 4z\hat{\mathbf{k}}$ is applied on a particle. The work done by the force when the particle moves from the point (0, 0, 0) to the point (2, 4, 0) as shown in the figure is

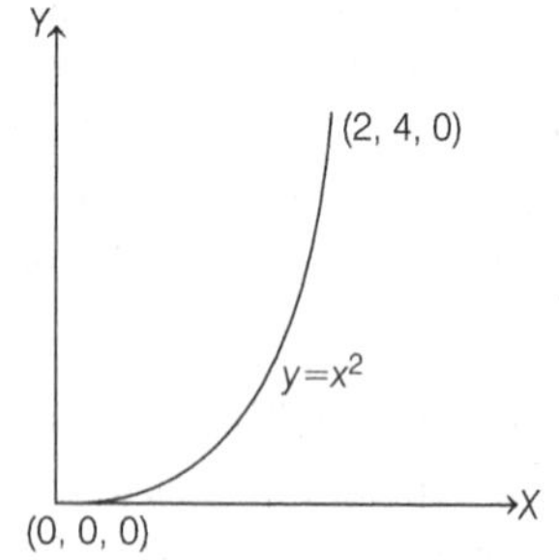

(a) $\frac{280}{5}$ J (b) $\frac{140}{5}$ J (c) $\frac{232}{5}$ J (d) $\frac{192}{5}$ J

3 A force $\mathbf{F} = (3x^2y\hat{\mathbf{i}} + x^3\hat{\mathbf{j}})$ N is acting on a particle. Find work done by the force when the particle moves from (1 m, 1 m) to (2 m, −1 m).

(a) 2 J (b) −5 J (c) 8 J (d) −9 J

4 A block of mass m is thrown with a velocity v_0 towards a spring as shown in figure. Initially, the block is at a distance L from the spring and the spring is in its natural length. The coefficient of friction between the block and the ground is $\mu = ax$, where a is a constant and x is the distance travelled. Find value of v_0 such that the maximum compression in the spring is L.

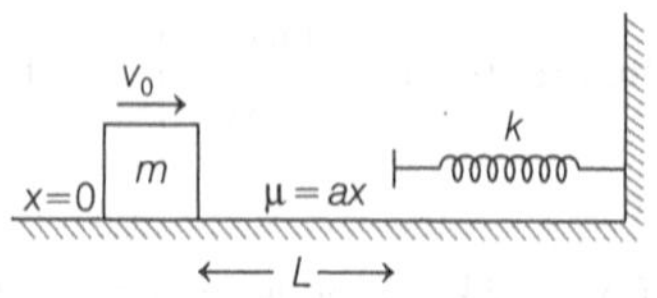

(a) $\left[\frac{kL^2}{m} + 2aL^2g\right]^{1/2}$ (b) $\left[\frac{kL^2}{m} + aL^2g\right]^{1/2}$

(c) $\left[\frac{kL^2}{m} + 4aL^2g\right]^{1/2}$ (d) $\left[2\frac{kL^2}{m} + aL^2g\right]^{1/2}$

5 In the figure shown, all the surfaces are frictionless, and mass of the block, $m = 1$ kg. The block and wedge are held initially at rest. Now, wedge is given a horizontal acceleration of 10 m/s^2 by applying a force on the wedge, so that the block does not slip on the wedge. Then, work done by the normal force in ground frame on the block in the first 2 s is

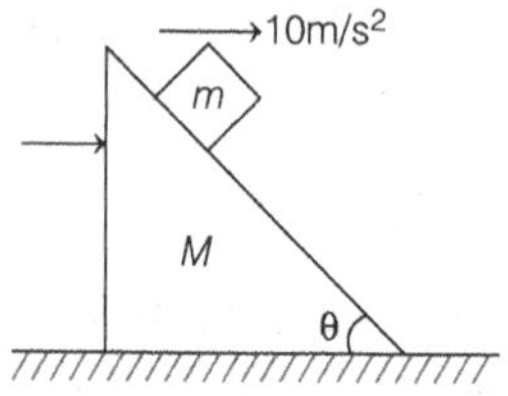

(a) 100 J (b) $100\sqrt{2}$ J (c) 200 J (d) $200\sqrt{2}$ J

6 A particle is projected along a horizontal field whose coefficient of friction varies as $\mu = \frac{A}{r^2}$, where r is the distance from the origin in metre and A is a positive constant. The initial distance of the particle is 1 m from the origin and its velocity is radially outwards. The minimum initial velocity at this point, so that particle never stops is

(a) ∞ (b) $2\sqrt{gA}$ (c) $\sqrt{2gA}$ (d) $4\sqrt{gA}$

7 A plank of mass 8 kg, length 5 m is on a smooth horizontal surface. A small block of mass 2 kg is on the plank at one of its ends. The coefficient of friction between block and plank is 0.5 A horizontal external force $F = 20$ N acts on the block at $t = 0$ as shown, then the work done by net force acting on the plank by the time the block falls off the plank is

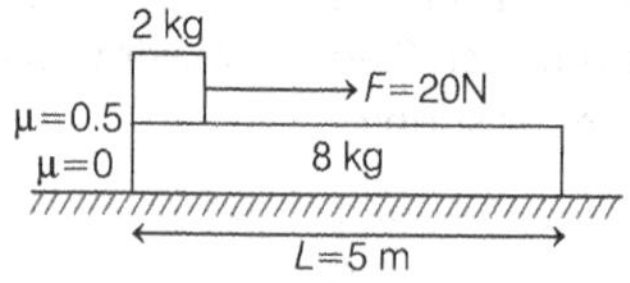

(a) $\frac{5}{3}$ J (b) $\frac{10}{3}$ J (c) $\frac{25}{3}$ J (d) $\frac{50}{3}$ J

8 A vertical spring of force constant 100 N/m is attached with a hanging mass of 10 kg. Now, an external force is applied on the mass, so that the spring is stretched by additional 2 m. The work done by the force F is ($g = 10$ m/s^2)

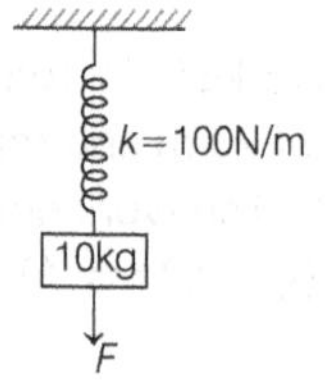

(a) 200 J (b) 400 J (c) 450 J (d) 600 J

9 Find maximum elongation in spring when system is released with spring unelongated

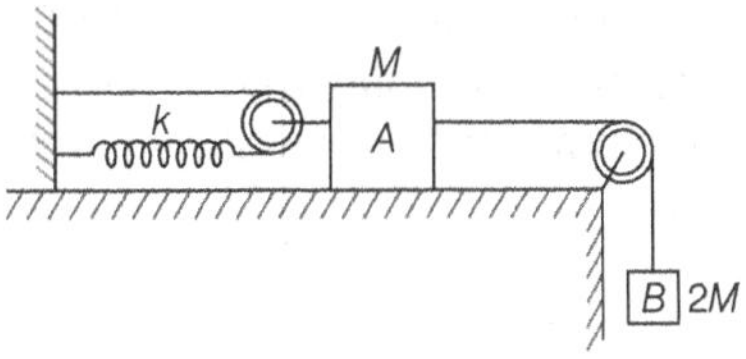

(a) $\frac{2Mg}{k}$ (b) $\frac{Mg}{k}$ (c) $\frac{Mg}{2K}$ (d) $\frac{Mg}{4k}$

10 A block of mass m is attached with a massless spring of force constant k. The block is placed over a rough inclined surface for which the coefficient of friction is $\mu = \frac{3}{4}$. The minimum value of M required to move the block up the plane is (Neglected mass of string and pulley and friction in pulley)

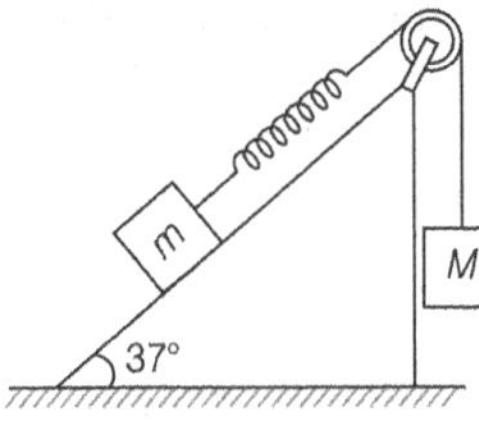

(a) $2m$ (b) $\frac{6m}{5}$ (c) $\frac{4m}{5}$ (d) $\frac{3m}{5}$

11 A block of mass m is attached with a spring in its natural length, of spring constant k. The other end A of spring is moved with a constant acceleration 'a' away from the block as shown in the figure. Find the maximum extension in the spring. Assume that initially block and spring is at rest w.r.t. ground frame.

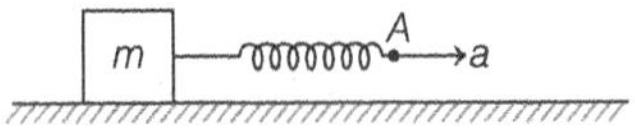

(a) $\frac{ma}{k}$ (b) $\frac{1}{2}\frac{ma}{k}$ (c) $\frac{2ma}{k}$ (d) $\frac{4ma}{k}$

12 If the work done by an internal conservative force on a system is positive in a certain process, assuming the presence of no other external forces,

(a) the kinetic energy increases and the total mechanical energy increases in the process.
(b) the kinetic energy increases, while the total mechanical energy remains constant during the process.
(c) the kinetic energy decreases, while the total mechanical energy remains constant during the process.
(d) the kinetic energy may increase or decrease, but the total mechanical energy increases in the process.

13 A block of mass m rests on a rough floor. It is pressed against a spring of force constant k and held in position A. The initial compression produced in the spring is $x_0 = \frac{4\mu mg}{k}$, where μ is the coefficient of friction between the block and the floor. The block is released at $t = 0$. Find the maximum velocity attained by the block.

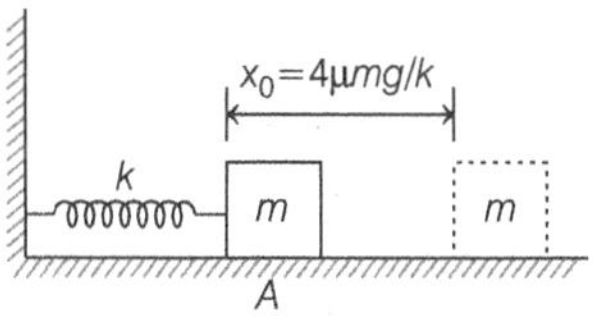

(a) $\mu g\sqrt{\frac{m}{k}}$ (b) $2\mu g\sqrt{\frac{m}{k}}$
(c) $3\mu g\sqrt{\frac{m}{k}}$ (d) $\frac{\mu g}{2}\sqrt{\frac{m}{k}}$

14 A block of mass 1 kg, kept on a frictionless ground is acted upon by a force of 10 N along X-axis. When the block reaches the position (20, 0), which of the following is not correct?

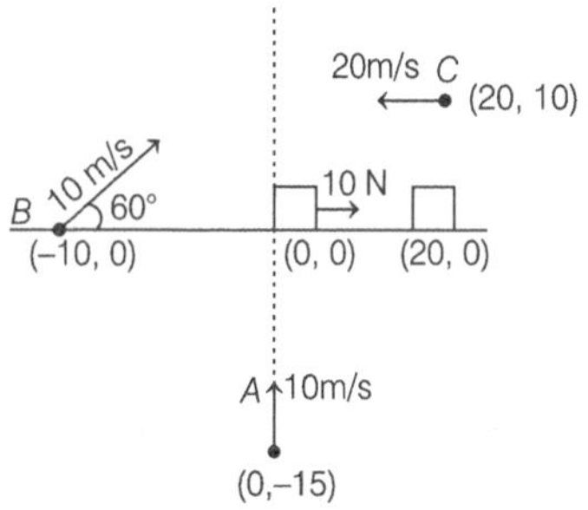

(a) Work done by the force with respect to A is 200 J
(b) Work done by F with respect to B is 100 J
(c) Work done by F with respect to C is 600 J
(d) None of the above

15 A particle slides along a track with elevated ends and a flat central part as shown in the figure. The flat part has a length $l = 3.0$ m. The curved portions of the track are frictionless. For the flat part, the coefficient of kinetic friction is $\mu_k = 0.20$. The particle is released at point A which is at a height $h = 1.5$ m above the flat part of the track. Where does the particle finally come to rest?

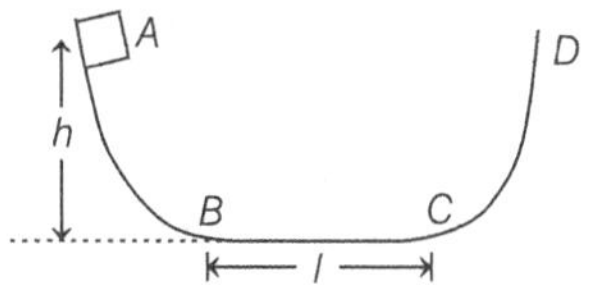

(a) At B (b) At C
(c) At mid-point of portion BC
(d) On portion BC but not at the mid-point

16 In the figure shown, a spring of spring constant $k = 100$ N/m is fixed at one end and the other end is attached to the mass $m = 1$ kg. The coefficient of friction between block and the inclined plane is $\mu = 0.25$. The block is released when the spring is in its natural length. Angle of inclination is $\theta = 37°$. Find the maximum speed of the block during the motion. $(g = 10 \text{ m/s}^2)$

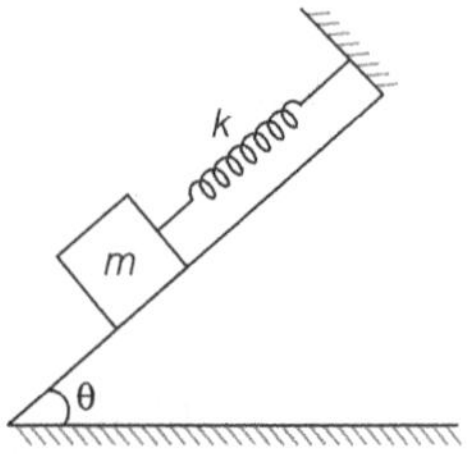

(a) 0.2 m/s (b) 0.4 m/s (c) 0.5 m/s (d) 0.8 m/s

17 AB is a quarter of a smooth circular horizontal track of radius $9\sqrt{2}$ m as shown in the figure. A particle P of mass 2 kg moves along the track from A to B under the action of a force F directed always towards point B, its magnitude is constant and equals 6 N. If the particle stars with speed of 6 m/s, what is its speed at point B?

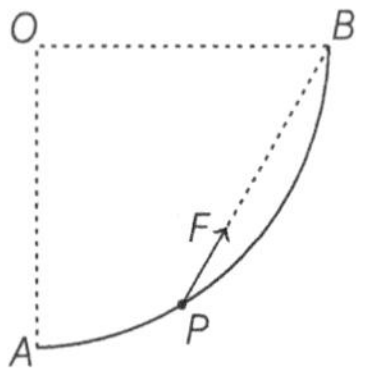

(a) 8 m/s (b) 9 m/s (c) 10 m/s (d) 12 m/s

18 An object of mass m is slowly pushed some partway up a vertical loop ending at a point a height $h < R$ above the bottom. The coefficient of friction between the object and the track is μ. Find work that has to be done against friction.

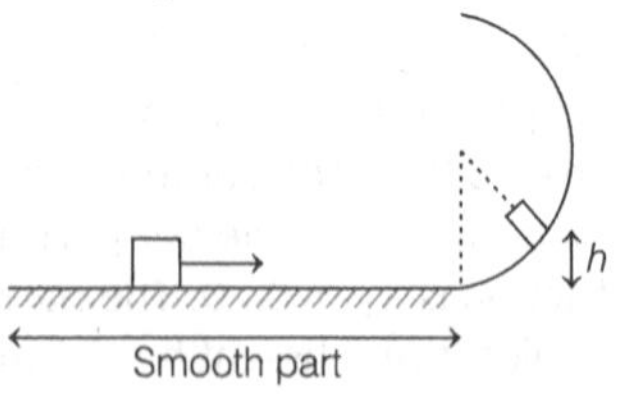

(a) $2\mu mg(2hR - h^2)^{1/2}$ (b) $\mu mg(2hR - h^2)^{1/2}$
(c) $2\mu mg(hR - h^2)^{1/2}$ (d) $\mu mg(hR - 2h^2)^{1/2}$

19 The potential energy of a particle of mass 1 kg is $U = x^2 - 4x + 14$. Here, U is in joules and x in metre. On the positive X-axis particle travels up to $x = +6$ m. The maximum kinetic energy of the particle is

(a) 16 J (b) 10 J
(c) 6 J (d) 20 J

20 A wedge of mass M fitted with a spring of stiffness k is kept on a smooth horizontal surface. A rod of mass m is kept on the wedge as shown in the figure. System is in equilibrium. Assuming that all surfaces are smooth, the potential energy stored in the spring is

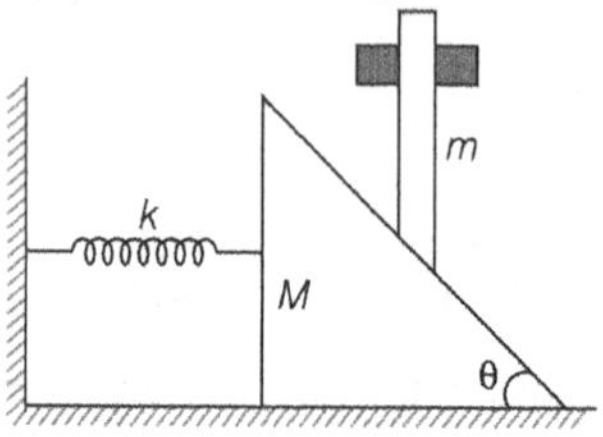

(a) $\dfrac{m^2g^2\cot^2\theta}{2k}$ (b) $\dfrac{m^2g^2\cot^2\theta}{k}$
(c) $\dfrac{m^2g^2\tan^2\theta}{2k}$ (d) $\dfrac{m^2g^2\tan^2\theta}{k}$

21 The spring is compressed by distance a and the system is released from rest. The block again comes to rest when the spring is elongated by a distance b. During this process,

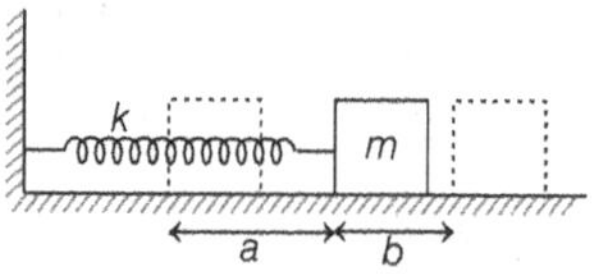

(a) work done by the spring on the block $= \dfrac{1}{2}k(a-b)^2$

(b) work done by the spring on the block $= \dfrac{1}{2}k(a^2+b^2)$

(c) coefficient of friction $= \dfrac{k(a-b)}{2mg}$

(d) coefficient of friction $= \dfrac{k(a+b)}{2mg}$

22 Potential energy curve U of a particle as function of the position of a particle is shown. The particle has total mechanical energy E of 3.0 J. Then, select correct alternative.

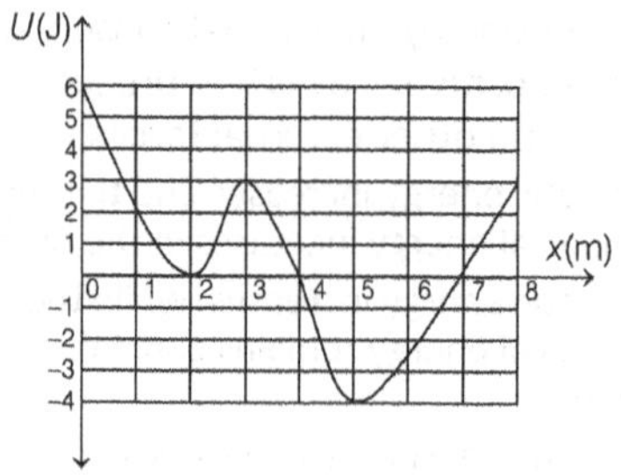

(a) It can never be present at $x = 0$ m.
(b) It can never be present at $x = 5$ m.
(c) At $x = 2$, its kinetic energy is 0 J.
(d) At $x = 1$, its kinetic energy is 3 J.

23 A particle A of mass $\frac{10}{7}$ kg is moving in the positive x-direction. Its initial position is $x = 0$ and initial velocity is 1 m/s. The velocity at $x = 10$ m is (use the graph given)

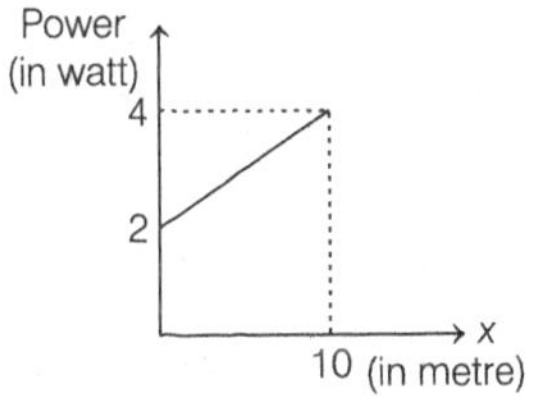

(a) 4 m/s (b) 2 m/s (c) $3\sqrt{2}$ m/s (d) $\frac{10}{3}$ m/s

24 A small body of mass m is located on a horizontal plane at the point O. The body acquires a horizontal velocity v_0. Find the maximum instantaneous power developed by the friction force, if the friction coefficient varies as $k = \alpha x$, where α is a constant, and x is the distance from the point O.

(a) $-mv_0^2\sqrt{\alpha g}$ (b) $-mv_0^2\sqrt{\frac{g}{\alpha}}$ (c) $-\frac{1}{2}mv_0^2\sqrt{\alpha g}$ (d) $-\frac{1}{2}mv_0^2\sqrt{\frac{g}{\alpha}}$

25 A ring of mass $m = 3$ kg slides over a smooth vertical rod. Attached to the ring is a light string passing over a smooth fixed pulley at a distance of $L = 8$ m from the road as shown in figure. At the other end of the string there is a mass $M = 5$ kg. The ring is held level with the pulley and then released. Determine the distance by which the ring moves down before coming to rest for the first time.

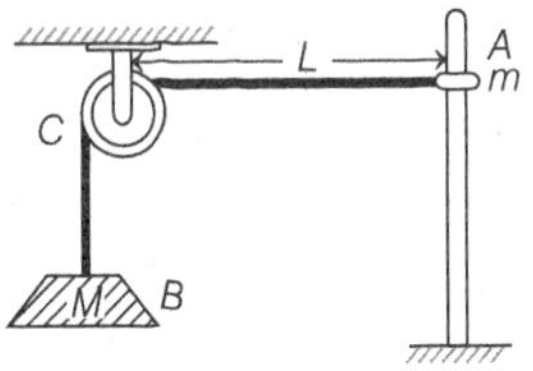

(a) 10 m (b) 12 m (c) 15 m (d) 17 m

26 The blocks A and B shown in the figure have masses $M_A = 5$ kg and $M_B = 4$ kg. The system is released from rest. The speed of B after A has travelled a distance 1 m along the incline is

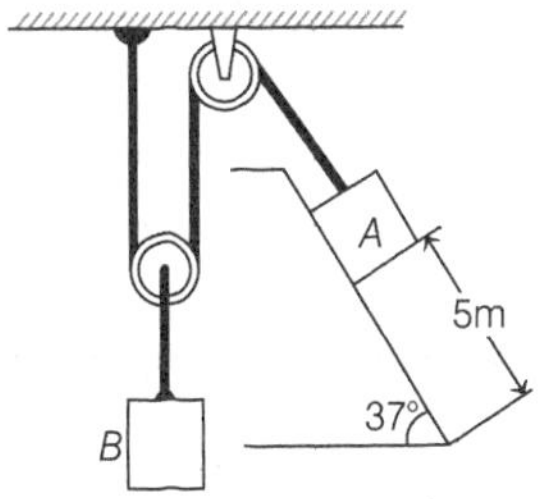

(a) $\frac{\sqrt{3}}{2}\sqrt{g}$ (b) $\frac{\sqrt{3}}{4}\sqrt{g}$ (c) $\frac{\sqrt{g}}{2\sqrt{3}}$ (d) $\frac{\sqrt{g}}{2}$

27 In the figure shown, the system is released from rest. Find the velocity of block A when block B has fallen a distance l. Assume all pulleys to be massless and frictionless.

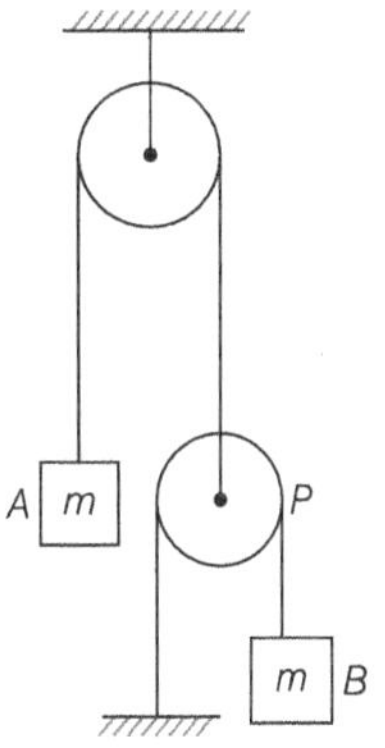

(a) $\sqrt{\frac{gl}{5}}$ (b) $\sqrt{\frac{2gl}{5}}$ (c) $\sqrt{5gl}$ (d) None of these

28 A body of mass m is pushed with the initial velocity v_0 up an inclined plane set at an angle θ to the horizontal. The friction coefficient is equal to μ. What work does the friction force perform by the time it stops for the first time?

(a) $\frac{-mv_0^2\mu}{2(\mu + \cot\theta)}$ (b) $\frac{-mv_0^2\mu}{2(\mu + \tan\theta)}$ (c) $\frac{-mv_0^2\mu}{2(1 + \tan\theta)}$ (d) $\frac{-mv_0^2\mu}{2(1 + \cot\theta)}$

29 A small ball rests at the bottom of a watch glass of radius R. It is displaced through a small distance x from this position and released. Calculate the total distance covered before it comes to the bottom and rests there. Coefficient of friction between watch glass surface and the ball is μ.

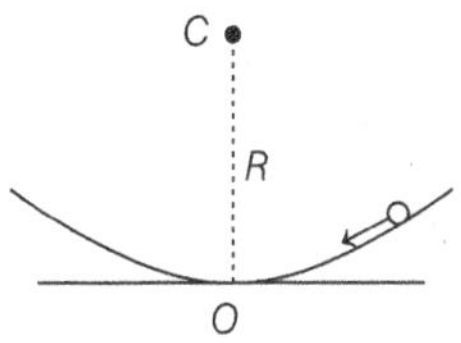

(a) $\frac{x^2}{2\mu R}$ (b) $\frac{x^2}{3\mu R}$ (c) $\frac{x^2}{4\mu R}$ (d) $\frac{2x^2}{\mu R}$

30 A force F acting on a body depends on its speed v as $F \propto \frac{1}{v^2}$. The power delivered by F will depend on displacement s as

(a) s^0 (b) $s^{1/4}$ (c) $s^{-1/4}$ (d) $s^{-2/3}$

31 Starting at rest, a 10 kg object is acted upon by only one force as indicated in figure. Then, the total work done by the force is

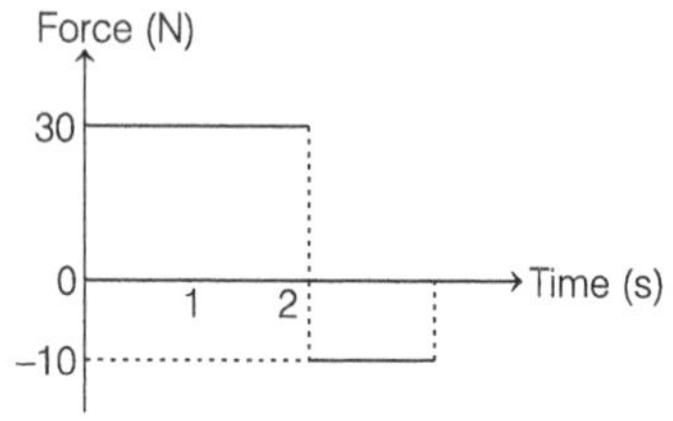

(a) 50 J (b) 125 J (c) 245 J (d) 490 J

32 Block A in the figure is released from rest when the extension in the spring is $x_0 \left(x_0 < \frac{mg}{k}\right)$. The maximum downward displacement of the block is (there is no friction)

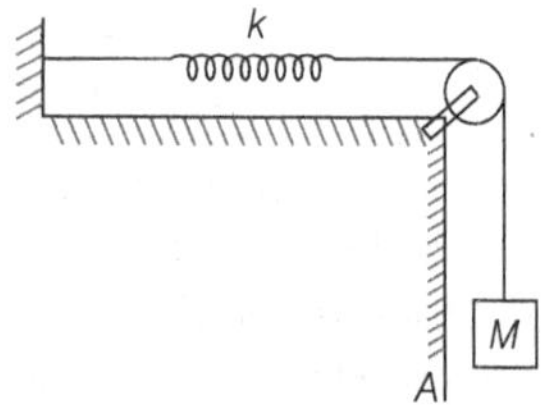

(a) $2\left(\frac{Mg}{k} - x_0\right)$ (b) $\frac{2Mg}{k} + x_0$

(c) $\frac{2Mg}{k} - x_0$ (d) $2\left(\frac{Mg}{k} + x_0\right)$

33 A block of mass 5 kg is released from rest when compression in spring is 2 m. Block is not attached with the spring and natural length of the spring is 4 m. Maximum height of block from ground is ($g = 10\ \text{m/s}^2$)

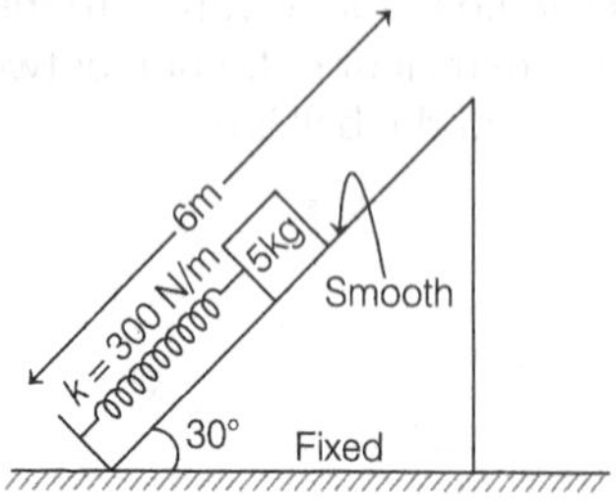

(a) 5.5 m (b) 4.5 m (c) 6 m (d) 7.5 m

34 A block of mass 3 kg moving with a speed 1 ms^{-1} collides with a spring of spring constant 100 N/m as shown. Portion AB of the surface is smooth while BC is rough. Find the minimum value of coefficient of friction for which block will not bounce back once the spring is compressed. ($g = 10\ \text{m/s}^2$)

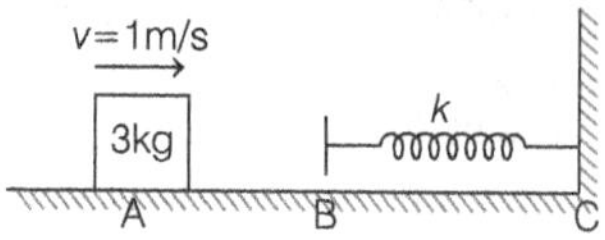

(a) $\frac{1}{2}$ (b) $\frac{1}{3}$ (c) $\frac{1}{4}$ (d) $\frac{1}{6}$

35 A block of mass m starts from rest from height h on a frictionless inclined plane. The block slides down the plane, travels across a rough horizontal surface with coefficient of kinetic friction μ, and compresses a spring with force constant k by distance x and travels total distance d on horizontal surface before momentarily coming to rest. Then, the spring extends and the block travels back across the rough surface, sliding up the plane. The correct expression for the maximum height h' that the block reaches on its return is

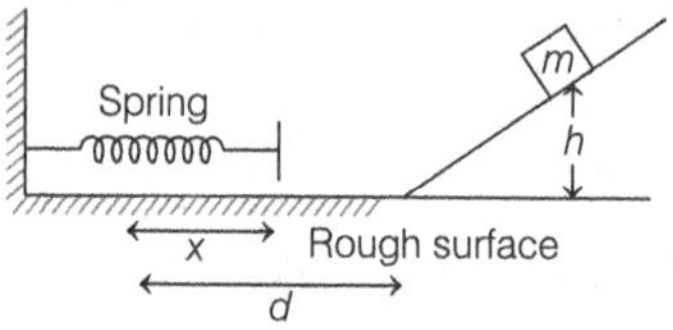

(a) $mgh' = mgh - 2\mu mgd$

(b) $mgh' = mgh + 2\mu mgd$

(c) $mgh' = mgh + 2\mu mgd + kx^2$

(d) $mgh' = mgh - 2\mu mgd - kx^2$

36 The potential energy function for the force between two atoms of a diatomic molecule is given by $U = \frac{a}{x^{12}} - \frac{b}{x^6}$, where a and b are positive constants and x is the distance between the atoms. Find the minimum energy required to break up the molecule.

(a) $\frac{2a^2}{b}$ (b) $\frac{b}{2a^2}$ (c) $\frac{b^2}{4a}$ (d) $\frac{2b^2}{a}$

37 A block of mass m is being pulled up the rough incline by an agent delivering constant power P. The coefficient of friction between the block and the incline is μ. The maximum speed of the block during the course of ascent is

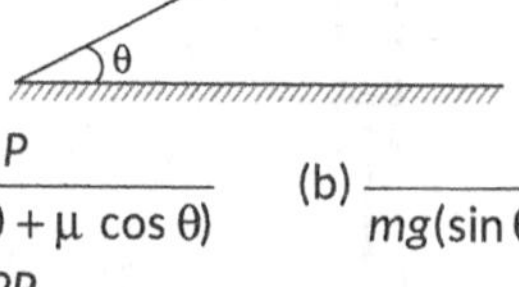

(a) $\frac{P}{mg(\sin\theta + \mu\cos\theta)}$ (b) $\frac{P}{mg(\sin\theta - \mu\cos\theta)}$

(c) $\frac{2P}{mg(\sin\theta - \mu\cos\theta)}$ (d) $\frac{3P}{mg(\sin\theta - \mu\cos\theta)}$

38 In the figure, the variation of components of acceleration of a particle of mass 1 kg is shown w.r.t. time. The initial velocity of the particle is $\mathbf{u} = (-3\hat{\mathbf{i}} + 4\hat{\mathbf{j}})$ m/s. The total work done by the resultant force of the particle in time interval from $t = 0$ s to $t = 4$ s is

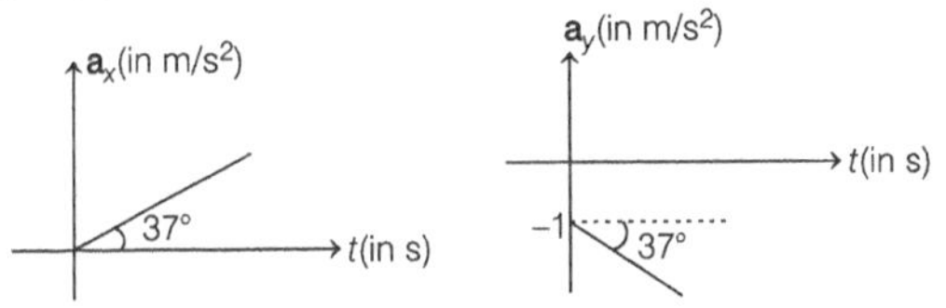

(a) 22.5 J (b) 10 J
(c) 0 (d) None of these

39 A long plank of mass M is initially at rest on a frictionless surface. A small block with mass m and initial speed u_0 slides on top of the larger plank. The coefficient of friction between the block and plank is μ. Net work done by friction if the top block falls off the plank after sliding over its length L is

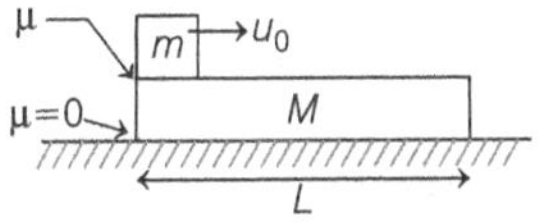

(a) $-\mu mgL$
(b) $-\mu(M+m)gL$
(c) $-\mu\left(\frac{Mm}{M+m}\right)gL$
(d) $-\mu MgL$

40 A particle of mass m moving along a straight line experiences force F which varies with the distance x travelled as shown in the figure. If the velocity of the particle at x_0 is $\sqrt{\frac{2F_0x_0}{m}}$, then velocity at $4x_0$ is

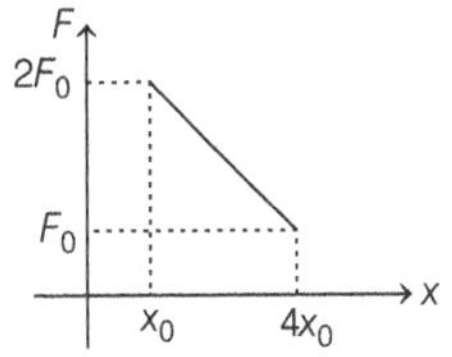

(a) $2\sqrt{\frac{2F_0x_0}{m}}$ (b) $2\sqrt{\frac{F_0x_0}{m}}$
(c) $\sqrt{\frac{F_0x_0}{m}}$ (d) None of these

41 The potential energy of a particle of mass m free to move along X-axis is given by

$U = \frac{1}{2}kx^2$ for $x < 0$ and $U = 0$ for $x \geq 0$.

(x denotes the X-coordinate of the particle and k is a positive constant). If the total mechanical energy of the particle is E, then its speed at $x = -\sqrt{\frac{2E}{k}}$ is

(a) zero (b) $\sqrt{\frac{2E}{m}}$ (c) $\sqrt{\frac{E}{m}}$ (d) $\sqrt{\frac{E}{2m}}$

42 The given plot shows the variation of U, the potential energy of interaction between two particles with the distance separating them r. Then, which of the following statement is correct?

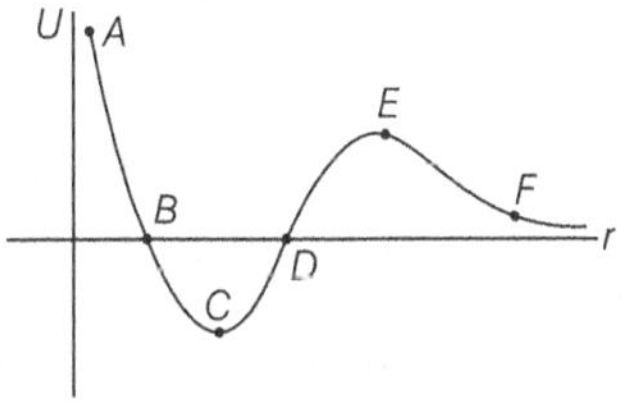

(a) B and D are equilibrium points.
(b) E is a point of stable equilibrium.
(c) The force of interaction between the two particles is attractive between points C and D and repulsive between points D and E on the curve.
(d) The force of interaction between the particles is repulsive between points E and F on the curve.

43 A particle, which is constrained to move along the X-axis, is subjected to a force in the same direction which varies with the distance x of the particle from the origin as $F(x) = -kx + ax^3$. Here, k and a are positive constants. For $x \geq 0$, the functional form of the potential energy $U(x)$ of the particle is

(a)
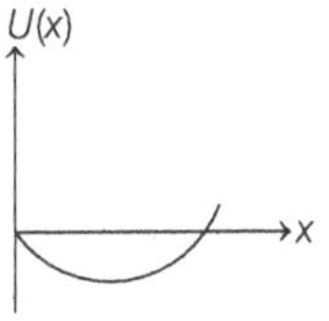

(b)
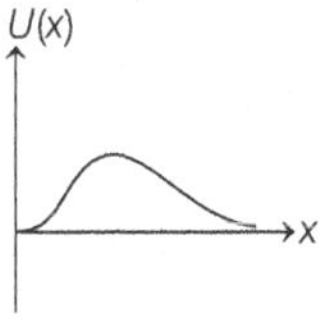

(c)
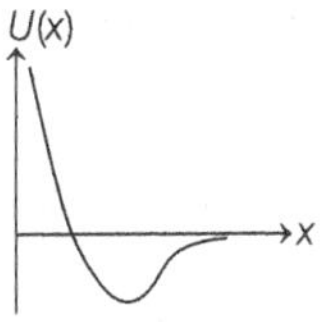

(d)

44 Select the correct alternative.
(a) Work done by kinetic friction on a body always results in a loss of its kinetic energy.
(b) Work done on a body, in the motion of that body over a close loop is zero for every force in nature.
(c) Total mechanical energy of a system is conserved in the absence of external forces.
(d) When total work done by a conservative force on the system is positive, then the potential energy associated with this force decreases.

45 Given, $\mathbf{F} = (xy^2)\hat{\mathbf{i}} + (x^2y)\hat{\mathbf{j}}$ N. Find the work done by this force when a particle is taken along the semicircular path OAB, where the co-ordinates of B are (4, 0).

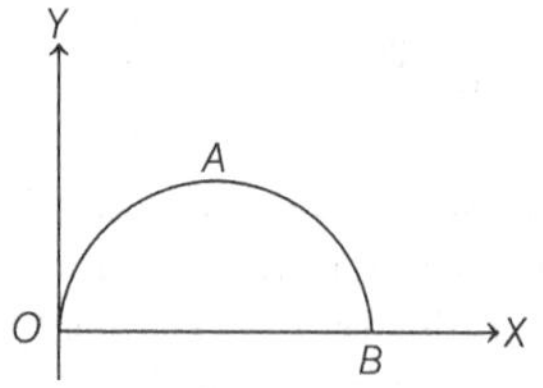

(a) $\frac{65}{3}$ J (b) 37.5 J (c) $\frac{73}{4}$ J (d) zero

46 A small object with mass $m = 0.01$ kg is attached to the free end of an ideal spring with $k = 10$ N/m. The other end of the spring is connected to a fixed frictionless pivot located at the origin O as shown in the figure. The relaxed length of the spring is 0.1 m. An unspecified force F carries the object initially at rest from point A to point B in the vertical plane. At point B, the object has the speed 5 m/s. The work done by the force F is ($g = 10$ m/s^2)

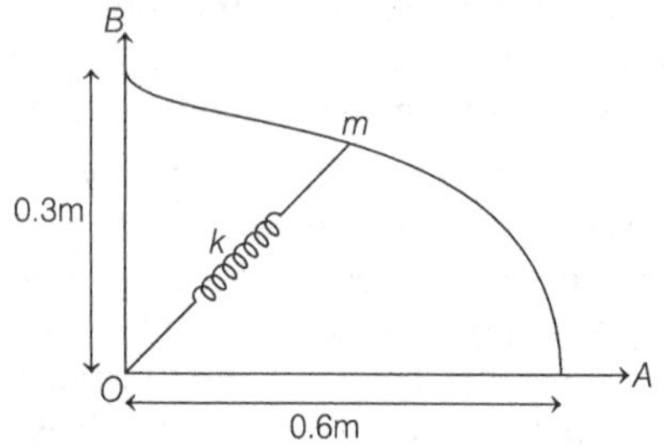

(a) – 0.895 J (b) – 1.255 J
(c) 1.255 J (d) 0.895 J

47 Block A of mass 48 kg is held at rest on a smooth horizontal floor. A light frictionless, small pulley is fixed at a height of 6 m from the floor. A light inextensible string of length 16 m, connected with block A passes over the pulley and another block B of mass 25 kg is hung from the string. Initial height of B is 5 m from the floor as shown in figure. When the system is released from rest, B starts to move vertically downwards and A slides on the floor towards right. Calculate speed of B just before it strikes the floor.

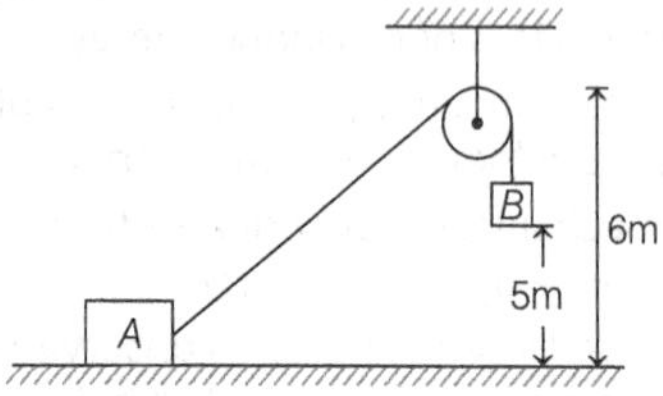

(a) 5 m/s (b) 6 m/s (c) 8 m/s (d) 10 m/s

48 A small block of mass m is released from rest from point D from slides down DGF and reaches the point F with speed v. The coefficient of kinetic friction between the block and both the surfaces DG and GF is μ, the velocity v is

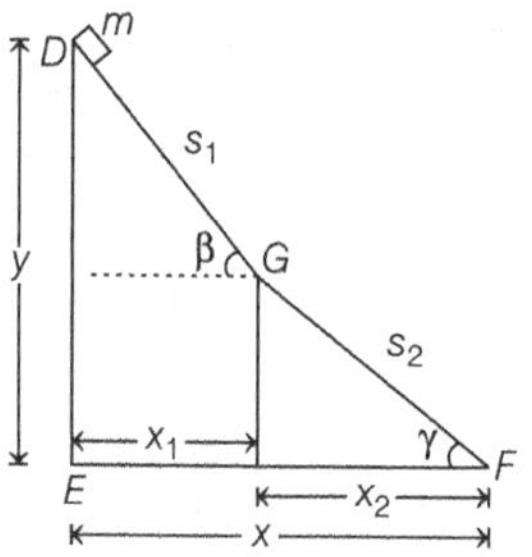

(a) $\sqrt{2g(y - x)}$ (b) $\sqrt{2g(y - \mu x)}$
(c) $\sqrt{2\mu g(y - x)}$ (d) $\sqrt{2g\sqrt{(y^2 + \mu^2 x^2)}}$

49 A block-spring system is placed on a smooth horizontal plane as shown. What initial velocity should be given to the block along a direction parallel to the force as shown in the figure, simultaneously when the force is applied, so that the maximum elongation occcured in the spring is twice of the maximum compression occured in it?

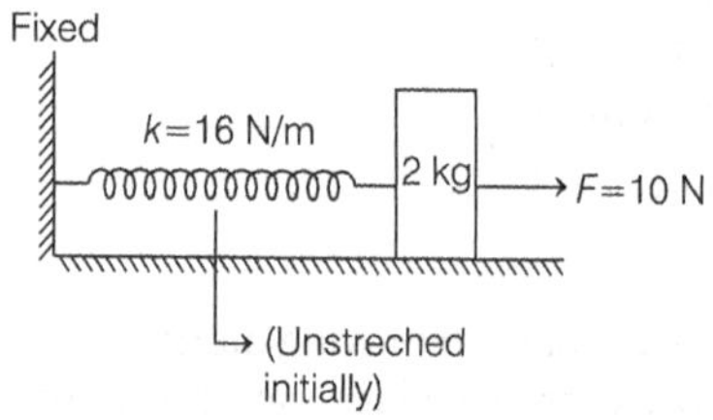

(a) 2 m/s (b) 5 m/s
(c) 8 m/s (d) 10 m/s

50 Two blocks of masses $m_1 = 1$ kg and $m_2 = 3$ kg connected by a relaxed spring. They are lying on a rough horizontal surface. The coefficient of friction between the blocks and the surface is 0.4. What minimum constant force F has to be applied in horizontal direction to the block m_1 in order to move the other block? ($g = 10$ m/s^2)

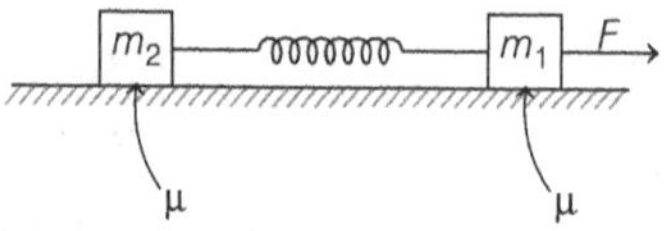

(a) 4 N (b) 10 N
(c) 12 N (d) 16 N

51 Two bodies A and B connected by a light rigid bar 10 m long move in two frictionless guides as shown in figure. B starts from rest when it is vertically below A.

Find velocity of B when $x = 6$ m. Assume $m_A = 32$ kg, $m_B = 16$ kg and $m_C = 6$ kg (use, $g = 9.8\ m/s^2$)

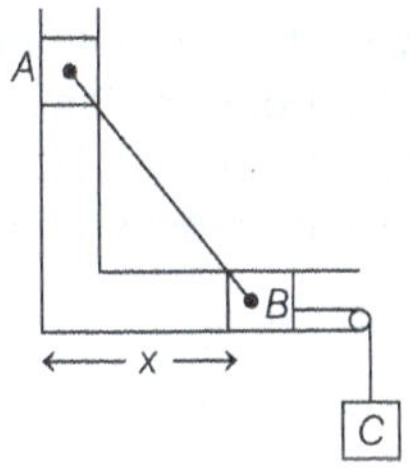

(a) 5 m/s (b) 7 m/s (c) 8 m/s (d) 10 m/s

Multiple Choice(s) Correct Questions

1 A 300 kg crate is dropped vertically onto a long conveyor belt moving at 4 m/s. A motor maintains the belt a constant speed. The belt initially slides under the crate with a coefficient of friction $\mu = 0.4$. After time t_0, the crate is moving at a speed of the belt. During the period in which the crate is being accelerated,

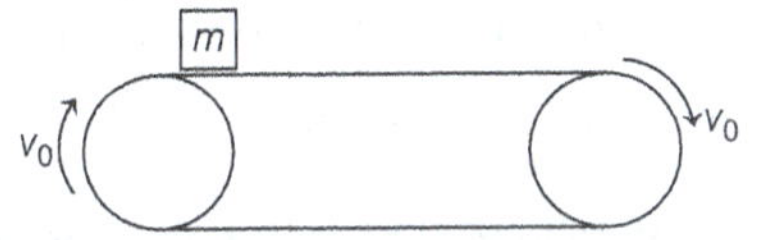

(a) acceleration of the block is $2\ m/s^2$
(b) work done by friction on the crate is 2.4 kJ
(c) work done by friction on the belt is – 4.8 kJ
(d) work done by the motor which drives the belt is 7.2 kJ

2 In the following K = kinetic energy, U = potential energy, and W = work. In using the expression $K_2 + U_2 = K_1 + U_1 + W_{other}$, we recognise that
(a) we are assuming no friction is present
(b) gravitational and elastic potential energies would be included in U_1 and U_2
(c) K and U can be either positive or negative, depending on the reference point chosen
(d) W_{other} can be positive or negative

3 A particle initially at rest is displaced by applying a non-conservative force F in a uniform gravitational field. In the process, following physical quantities associated with the particle are measured

ΔU = change in gravitational potential energy,
ΔK = change in kinetic energy,
ΔW_1 = work done by the force F,
ΔW_2 = work done by the gravitational force and
ΔE = change in mechanical energy.

(a) $\Delta W_2 = \Delta U$ (b) $\Delta K = \Delta W_1 + \Delta W_2$
(c) $\Delta K + \Delta U = \Delta W_1 + \Delta W_2$ (d) $\Delta W_1 = \Delta E$

4 The potential energy U for a force field $\mathbf{F}$ is such that $U = -kxy$, where k is a constant. Then,
(a) $\mathbf{F} = ky\hat{\mathbf{i}} + kx\hat{\mathbf{j}}$
(b) $\mathbf{F} = kx\hat{\mathbf{i}} + ky\hat{\mathbf{j}}$
(c) $\mathbf{F}$ is a conservative force
(d) $\mathbf{F}$ is a non-conservative force

5 A ball of mass m is attached to the lower end of a light vertical spring of force constant k. The upper end of the spring is fixed. The ball is released from rest with the spring at its normal (unstretched) length, and comes to rest again after descending through a distance x.
(a) $x = \frac{mg}{k}$
(b) $x = \frac{2mg}{k}$
(c) The ball will have no acceleration at the position, where it has descending through $\frac{x}{2}$.
(d) The ball will have an upward acceleration equal to g at its lowermost position.

6 Figure shows an ideal spring block system, force constant of spring is k which has been compressed by an amount x_0. If x is instantaneous deflection of spring from its natural length, mark the correct option(s).

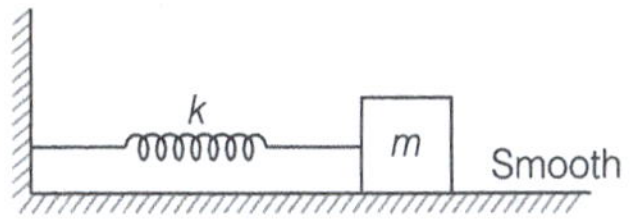

(a) Instantaneous power developed by spring is
$$P = kx\sqrt{\frac{k}{2m}(x_0^2 - x^2)}$$
(b) Maximum power of spring is $\frac{kx_0^2}{2}\sqrt{\frac{k}{m}}$
(c) Maximum power occurs at $x = \frac{x_0}{\sqrt{2}}$
(d) Maximum power occurs at $x = \frac{x_0}{2}$

7 A boy of mass m starts running on a straight road, from rest and after an interval of time t_0, he attains a speed of v_0. Then,
(a) average frictional force acting on the boy in the interval is $\frac{mv_0}{t_0}$
(b) total work done by friction in the interval is $\frac{1}{2}mv_0^2$
(c) total work done by normal reaction in the interval is zero
(d) the direction of friction on boy is in backward

8 Potential energy function along X-axis in a certain force field is given as $U(x) = \frac{x^4}{4} - 2x^3 + \frac{11}{2}x^2 - 6x$.

For the given force field,

(a) the points of equilibrium are $x = 1, x = 2$ and $x = 3$

(b) the point $x = 2$ is a point of unstable equilibrium

(c) the points $x = 1$ and $x = 3$ are points of stable equilibrium

(d) there exists no point of neutral equilibrium

9 Potential energy (in joule) of a particle of mass 1 kg moving in xy-plane is $U = 3x + 4y$, here x and y are in metre. If at time $t = 0$, particle is at rest at point P (6m, 4m). Then,

(a) acceleration of particle is $(3\hat{i} + 4\hat{j})$ m/s^2

(b) time when it crosses Y-axis is $t = 2$ s.

(c) speed of particle when it crosses Y-axis is 10 m/s.

(d) it crosses Y-axis at $y = -8$ m

10 Power of a force acting on a block varies with time t as shown in figure. Then, angle between force acting on the block and its velocity is

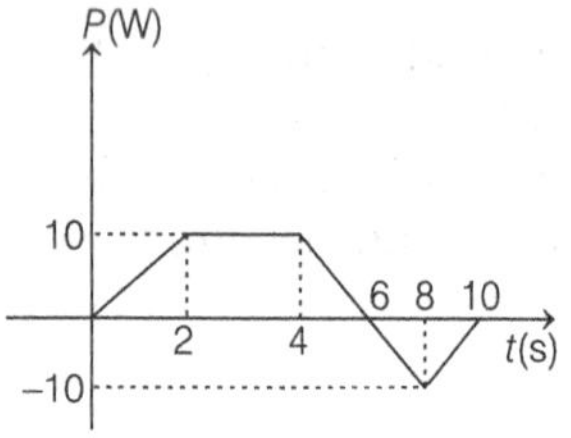

(a) acute at $t = 1$ s

(b) 90° at $t = 3$ s

(c) obtuse at $t = 7$ s

(d) change in kinetic energy from $t = 0$ to $t = 10$ s is 20 J

11 Which of the following is/are conservative force(s)?

(a) $\mathbf{F} = 2r^3\hat{\mathbf{r}}$

(b) $\mathbf{F} = -\frac{5}{r}\hat{\mathbf{r}}$

(c) $\mathbf{F} = \frac{3(x\hat{\mathbf{i}} + y\hat{\mathbf{j}})}{(x^2 + y^2)^{3/2}}$

(d) $\mathbf{F} = \frac{3(y\hat{\mathbf{i}} + x\hat{\mathbf{j}})}{(x^2 + y^2)^{3/2}}$

12 A block of mass 2 kg is hanging over a smooth and light pulley through a light string. The other end of the string is pulled by a constant force $F = 40$ N. The kinetic energy of the particle increases 40 J in a given interval of time. Then, $(g = 10 \text{ m/s}^2)$

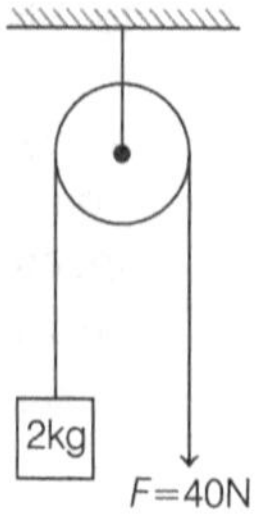

(a) tension in the string is 40 N

(b) displacement of the block in the given interval of time is 2 m

(c) work done by gravity is - 20 J

(d) work done by tension is 80 J

13 Two blocks, of masses m and $2m$, are connected to a light spring of spring constant k that has one end fixed, as shown in figure. The horizontal surface and the pulley are frictionless. The blocks are released from rest when the spring is non-deformed. The string is light. Then, select correct options.

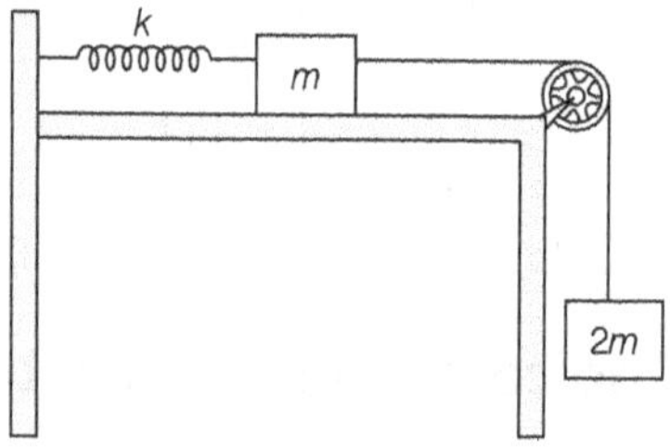

(a) Maximum extension in the spring is $\frac{4mg}{k}$.

(b) Maximum kinetic energy of the system is $\frac{2m^2g^2}{k}$.

(c) Maximum energy stored in the spring is four times that of maximum kinetic energy of the system.

(d) When kinetic energy of the system is maximum, energy stored in the spring is $\frac{4m^2g^2}{k}$.

14 Which of the following relations are always true? $\mathbf{v}$ = velocity, $\mathbf{a}$ = acceleration and $K = \frac{1}{2}mv^2$ = kinetic energy.

(a) $\frac{dK}{dt} = m\mathbf{v} \cdot \mathbf{a}$

(b) $\frac{d|\mathbf{v}|}{dt} = \frac{\mathbf{a} \cdot \mathbf{v}}{|\mathbf{v}|}$

(c) $\frac{d|\mathbf{v}|}{dt} = \left|\frac{d\mathbf{a}}{dt}\right|$

(d) $|\Delta\mathbf{v}| = \left|\int_{t_1}^{t_2} \mathbf{a}\, dt\right|$

15 Which of the following statement(s) is/are true for a system comprising of two bodies in contact exerting frictional force on each other?

(a) Total work done by static friction on whole system is always zero.

(b) Work done by static friction on a body is always zero

(c) Work done by kinetic friction on a body is always negative

(d) Total work done by internal kinetic friction on whole system is always negative.

16 Choose the correct alternative(s).

(a) When a conservative force does positive work, the potential energy of the system decreases.

(b) Work done by friction on a body always results in a loss of its kinetic energy.

(c) Work done in the motion of a body over a closed loop is zero for every force in nature.

(d) Work done by friction on a body may increase its kinetic energy.

17 Block m is released from rest when spring is in its natural length (assume pulley is ideal and block does not strike on ground during its motion in vertical plane), then

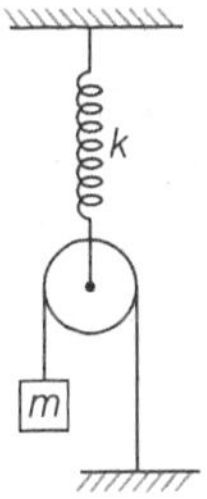

(a) maximum elongation in the spring is $\frac{4mg}{k}$

(b) maximum elongation in the spring is $\frac{2mg}{k}$

(c) maximum speed of block is $2g\sqrt{\frac{m}{k}}$

(d) maximum speed of block is $g\sqrt{\frac{m}{k}}$

18 A block of mass m is projected with velocity v_0 over a rough surface as shown in the figure, at $t = 0$. After time t_0 block stops. Consider a reference frame S, which is moving with velocity v_0 in the direction of motion of block, then work done by friction from $t = 0$ to $t = t_0$

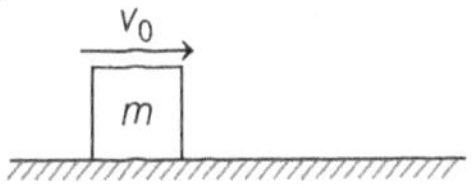

(a) on block is $-\frac{1}{2}mv_0^2$ w.r.t ground

(b) on block is $\frac{1}{2}mv_0^2$ w.r.t. S

(c) on ground is zero w.r.t. ground

(d) on ground is $\frac{1}{2}mv_0^2$ w.r.t. S

19 Figure shows net interaction force (conservative force) between two particles A and B against the distance between them, when the distance between them varies from x_1 to x_4. Then,

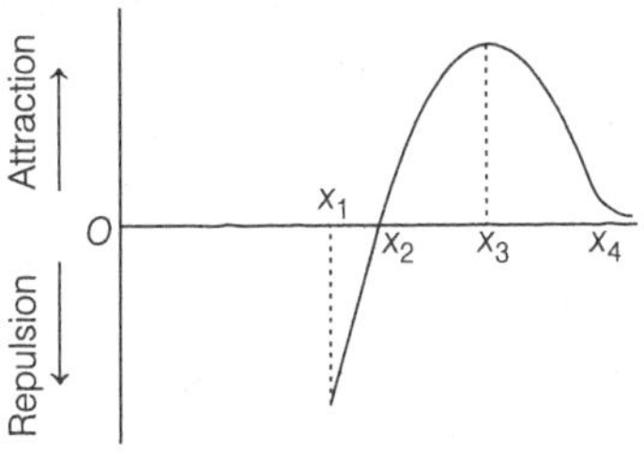

(a) potential energy of the system increases from x_1 to x_2

(b) potential energy of the system increases from x_2 to x_3

(c) potential energy of the system increases from x_3 to x_4

(d) kinetic energy increases from x_1 to x_2 and decreases from x_2 to x_3

20 Two inclined frictionless tracks of different inclinations meet at A from where two blocks P and Q of different masses are allowed to slide down from rest at the same time, one on each track, as shown in figure. Then,

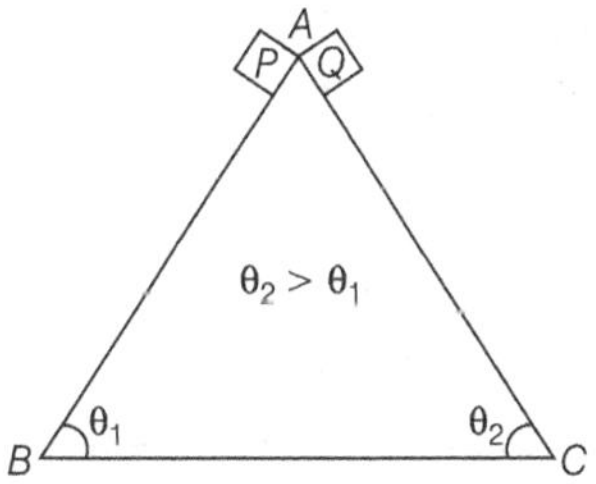

(a) both blocks will reach the bottom at the same time

(b) block Q will reach the bottom earlier than block P

(c) both blocks reach the bottom with the same speed

(d) block Q will reach the bottom with a higher speed than block P

Comprehension Based Questions

Comprehension-1

In figure shown, the spring constant is k. The mass of the upper block is m and that of the lower block is 3 m. The upper block is depressed down from its equilibrium position by a distance δ and released at $t = 0$

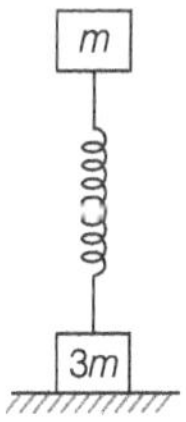

1 The minimum value of δ for which the lower block loses contact with the ground is

(a) $\frac{3mg}{k}$ (b) $\frac{2mg}{k}$

(c) $\frac{4mg}{k}$ (d) $\frac{mg}{k}$

2 The value of δ for which the minimum normal reaction on 3 m from ground is mg is

(a) $\frac{3mg}{k}$ (b) $\frac{2mg}{k}$

(c) $\frac{mg}{2k}$ (d) $\frac{mg}{k}$

Comprehension-2

A uniform rod of mass M and length L is sliding along its length on a horizontal table whose top is partly smooth and rest rough with friction coefficient μ. The rod after moving through smooth part, enters the rough with velocity v_0.

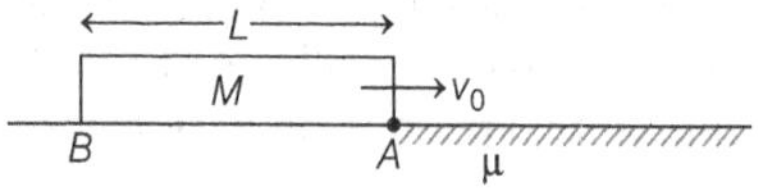

3 What will be the magnitude of the friction force when its x length ($< L$) lies in the rough part during sliding?

(a) $\frac{\mu Mgx}{L}$ (b) $\frac{\mu Mg(L-x)}{L}$ (c) μMg (d) $\frac{\mu MgL}{x}$

4 Determine the minimum velocity v_0 with which it must enter, so that it lies completely in rough region before coming to rest.

(a) $2\sqrt{\mu gL}$ (b) $\sqrt{\mu gL}$ (c) $\sqrt{\frac{\mu gL}{2}}$ (d) $\frac{\sqrt{\mu gL}}{2}$

5 If the velocity is double of the minimum velocity as calculated in Q. No 4, then what distance does its front end A would have travelled in rough region before the rod comes to rest?

(a) $\frac{3L}{2}$ (b) $2L$ (c) $\frac{5L}{4}$ (d) $\frac{5L}{2}$

Comprehension-3

A particle is moved along the different paths OAC, OBC and ODC as shown in the figure. Path ODC is a parabola, $y = 4x^2$. The work done by a force $\mathbf{F} = xy\hat{\mathbf{i}} + x^2y\hat{\mathbf{j}}$ on the particle along

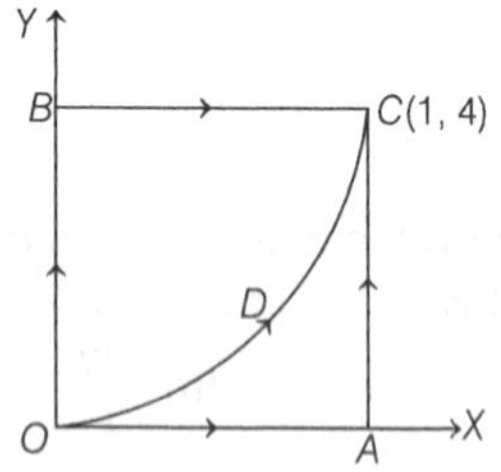

6 the path OAC is

(a) 8 J (b) 2 J (c) $\frac{19}{3}$ J (d) zero

7 the path OBC is

(a) 8 J (b) 2 J (c) $\frac{19}{3}$ J (d) zero

8 the path ODC

(a) 8 J (b) 2 J (c) $\frac{19}{3}$ J (d) zero

9 the force is

(a) conservative (b) non-conservative
(c) pseudo (d) None of these

Comprehension-4

A particle of mass m approaches a region of force starting from $r = +\infty$. The potential energy function in terms of distance r from the origin is given by

$$U = \frac{k}{a^3}(3ar - 2r^3) \text{ for } 0 \le r \le a$$
$$= \frac{k}{r} \text{ for } r \ge a$$

10 With what minimum velocity should the particle start at $r = \infty$ to cross over to other side of the origin?

(a) $\sqrt{\frac{3k}{ma}}$ (b) $\sqrt{\frac{9k}{4ma}}$ (c) $\sqrt{\frac{4k}{3ma}}$ (d) $\sqrt{\frac{3k}{2ma}}$

11 What will be speed at origin in the above question?

(a) $\sqrt{\frac{3k}{ma}}$ (b) $\sqrt{\frac{9k}{4ma}}$ (c) $\sqrt{\frac{4k}{3ma}}$ (d) zero

Comprehension-5

In the figure, the variation of potential energy of a particle of mass $m = 2$ kg is represented with respect to its x-coordinate. The particle moves under the effect of this conservative force along the X-axis.

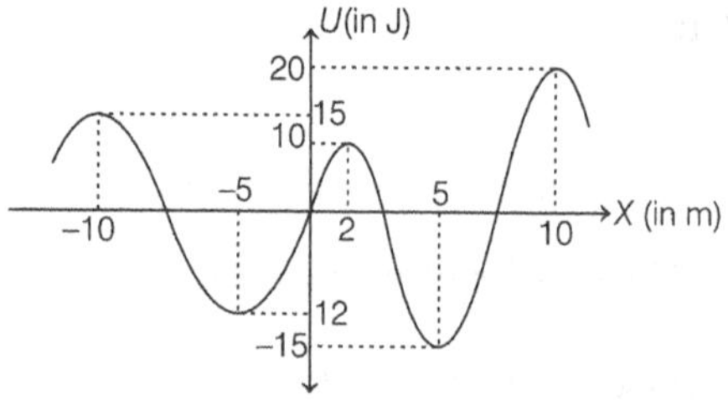

12 If the particle is released at the origin, then

(a) it will move towards positive X-axis
(b) it will move towards negative X-axis
(c) it will remain stationary at the origin
(d) its subsequent motion cannot be decided due to lack of information

13 If the particle is released at $x = 2 + \Delta$ where $\Delta \to 0$ (it is positive), then its maximum speed in subsequent motion will be

(a) 10 m/s (b) 5 m/s
(c) 15 m/s (d) 7.5 m/s

14 $x = -5$ m and $x = 10$ m positions of the particle are respectively of

(a) neutral and stable equilibrium
(b) neutral and unstable equilibrium
(c) unstable and stable equilibrium
(d) stable and unstable equilibrium

Comprehension-6

Two blocks of mass 2 kg and 3 kg are arranged as shown in the figure. The value of friction coefficient between 2 kg and 3 kg surface is 0.4 and 0.02 t between the surface of 3 kg block and ground. A time varying horizontal external force $F = 5t$ is acting on 3 kg block where t is time in seconds.

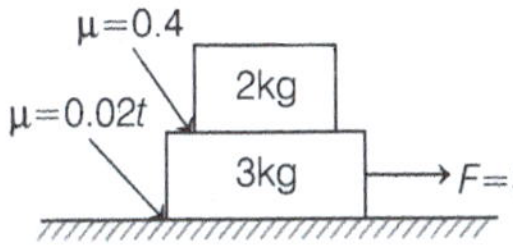

15 Work done by the friction force on 2 kg block up to 5 s with respect to 3 kg block is

(a) 100 J (b) 400 J
(c) zero (d) 160 J

16 Choose the nature of the graph of KE of block 2 kg with time

(a) 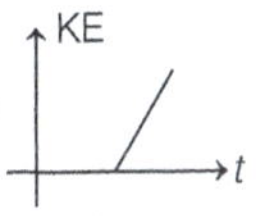

(b) 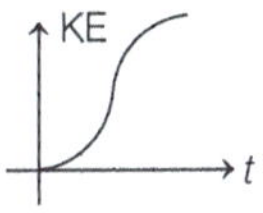

(c) 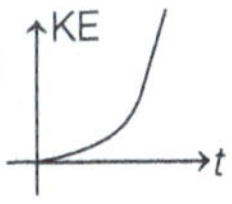

(d) 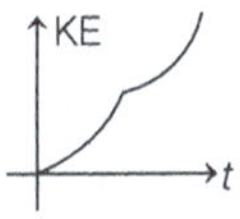

Comprehension-7

Consider the system shown below, with two equal masses m and a spring with spring constant K. The coefficient of friction between the left mass and horizontal table is $\mu = \frac{1}{4}$, and the pulley is frictionless. The string connecting both the blocks is massless and inelastic. The system is held with the spring at its unstretched length and then released.

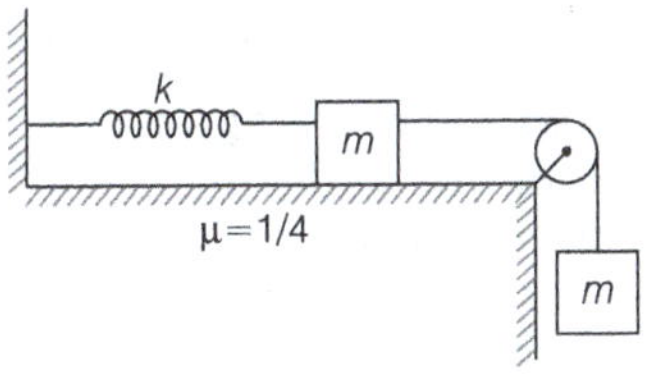

17 The extension in spring when the masses come to momentary rest for the first time is

(a) $\frac{3mg}{2k}$ (b) $\frac{mg}{2k}$ (c) $\frac{mg}{k}$ (d) $\frac{2mg}{k}$

18 The minimum value of μ for which the system remains at rest once it has stopped for the first time is

(a) $\frac{1}{\sqrt{3}}$ (b) $\frac{1}{3}$ (c) $\frac{1}{2}$ (d) $\frac{1}{\sqrt{2}}$

19 If the string connecting both the masses is cut just at the instant both masses came to momentary rest for the first time in Q. No. 17, then maximum compression of spring during resulting motion is $\left(\text{take, } \mu = \frac{1}{4}\right)$

(a) $\frac{2mg}{3k}$ (b) $\frac{mg}{2k}$
(c) $\frac{mg}{k}$ (d) $\frac{mg}{3k}$

Comprehension-8

A small bead B of mass m is free to slide on a fixed smooth vertical wire as indicated in the diagram. One end of a light elastic string, of unstretched length a and force constant $\frac{2mg}{a}$ is a attached to B. The string passes through a smooth fixed ring R and the other end of the string is attached to fixed point A, AR being horizontal. The point O on the wire is at same horizontal level as R and $AR = RO = a$.

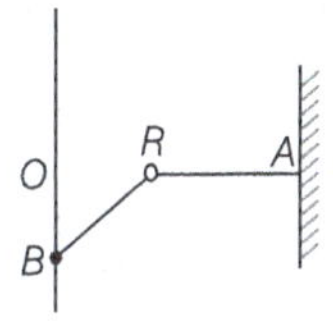

20 In the equilibrium position, find OB.

(a) a (b) $\frac{a}{4}$
(c) $2a$ (d) $\frac{a}{2}$

21 The bead B is raised to a point C of the wire above O, where $OC = a$ and is released from rest. Find the speed of the bead as it passes O.

(a) $\sqrt{4ag}$ (b) $\sqrt{3ag}$
(c) $\sqrt{2ag}$ (d) $\sqrt{ag}$

22 Find the greatest depth below O of the bead in the subsequent motion.

(a) a (b) $\frac{a}{4}$
(c) $2a$ (d) $\frac{a}{2}$

Comprehension-9

In a conservative force field, we can find the radial component of force from the potential energy function by using $F = \frac{dU}{dr}$. Here, a positive force means repulsion and a negative force means attraction. From the given potential energy function $U(r)$, we can find the equilibrium position where force is zero. We can also find the ionisation energy which is the work done to move the particle from a certain position to infinity.

Let us consider a case in which a particle is bound to a certain point at a distance r from the centre of the force. The potential energy of the particle is $U(r) = \frac{A}{r^2} - \frac{B}{r}$, where r is the distance from the centre of the force and A and B are positive constants.

23 The equilibrium distance is given by

(a) $\frac{A}{B}$ (b) $\frac{2A}{B}$ (c) $\frac{3A}{B}$ (d) $\frac{B}{2A}$

24 The equilibrium is

(a) stable (b) unstable (c) neutral (d) cannot be predicted

25 The work required to move the particle from equilibrium distance to infinity is

(a) $\frac{B}{4A}$ (b) $\frac{4B}{A}$ (c) $\frac{B^2}{4A}$ (d) $\frac{4B^2}{A}$

26 If the total energy of the particle is $E = -\frac{3B^2}{16A}$, and it is known that the motion is radial only then the velocity is zero at (here, r_0 = equilibrium distance)

(a) $\frac{r_0}{3}$ (b) $\frac{2r_0}{3}$

(c) r_0 (d) $\frac{2r_0}{5}$

Comprehension-10

A ball mass 2 kg is dropped from P at a height of 0.4 m above free end of a vertically fixed spring of spring constant $k = 200\ \text{Nm}^{-1}$. (Take, $g = 10\ \text{m/s}^2$)

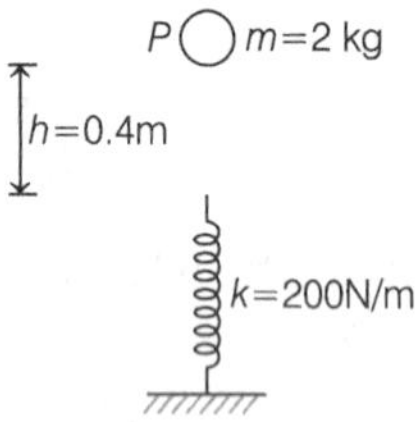

27 Find the maximum compression in the spring.

(a) 0.4 m (b) 0.5 m

(c) 0.6 m (d) None of these

28 Find the maximum speed attained by particle.

(a) 2 m/s (b) 3 m/s

(c) 4 m/s (d) None of these

29 Find the height below P, where particle attains maximum velocity.

(a) 0.4 m (b) 0.5 m

(c) 0.6 m (d) None of these

Match the Columns Questions

1 A block of mass m is slowly made to move up the incline by a force F which is directed along the tangent of trajectory. μ is the coefficient of friction between the block and the incline.

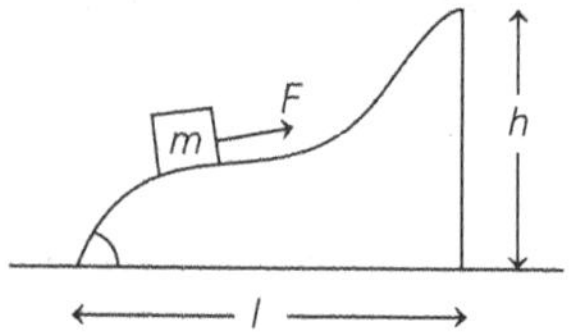

	Column I		Column II
(A)	Work done by gravity	(P)	$-\mu mgl$
(B)	Work done by frictional force	(Q)	$-mg\sqrt{l^2+h^2}$
(C)	Work done by the force F	(R)	$-mgh$
(D)	Total work done on the system (of mass m)	(S)	$mg(h+\mu l)$
		(T)	zero

2 A single conservative force acts on a body of mass 1 kg that moves along the X-axis. The potential energy $U(x)$ is given by $U(x) = 20 + (x-2)^2$, where x is in metre. At $x = 5.0$ m, the particle has a kinetic energy of 20 J, then

	Column I		Column II
(A)	minimum value of x in metre	(P)	29
(B)	maximum value of x in metre	(Q)	7.38
(C)	maximum potential energy in joules	(R)	49
(D)	maximum kinetic energy in joules	(S)	− 3.38

3 A block of mass $m = 1$ kg is at rest with respect to a rough wedge as shown in figure. The wedge starts moving up from rest with an acceleration of $a = 2\ \text{m/s}^2$ and the block remains at rest with respect to wedge. Then, in 4 s of motion of wedge, work done on block (assume angle of inclination of wedge is $\theta = 30°$ and $g = 10\ \text{m/s}^2$)

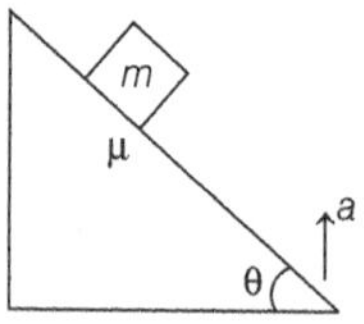

	Column I		Column II
(A)	by gravity (in magnitude)	(P)	144 J
(B)	by normal reaction	(Q)	32 J
(C)	by friction	(R)	160 J
(D)	by all the forces	(S)	48 J

4 ACB is a smooth quarter circular path of radius R. Four forces are acting at a particle placed at A. F_1 is always horizontal, F_2 is always vertical, F_3 is always tangential to path, F_4 is always directed from particle's position to point B. Magnitude of all forces are equal to F.

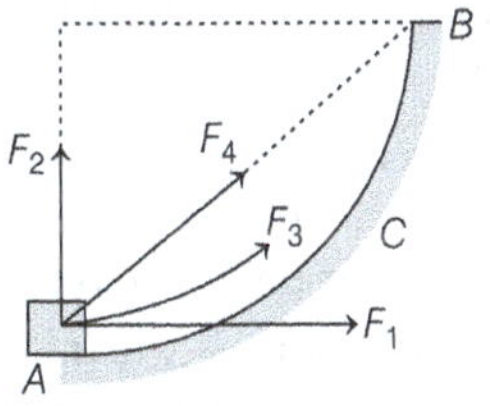

	Column I		Column II
(A)	Work done by F_1 is	(P)	FR
(B)	Work done by F_2 is	(Q)	$\sqrt{2}\,FR$
(C)	Work done by F_3 is	(R)	$\frac{\pi FR}{2}$
(D)	Work done by F_4 is	(S)	$\frac{FR}{\sqrt{2}}$

5 Match the physical situation on the left with the graph on the right. The graphs depict the variation of total energy (E), potential energy (U) and kinetic energy (KE) with time.

	Column I		Column II
(A)	A mass attached to an unstretched ideal spring. Released in vertical plane from rest until it reaches its maximum extension.	(P)	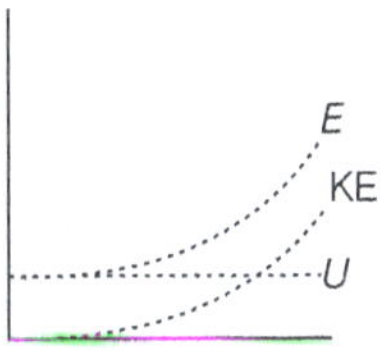
(B)	An object undergoing free fall.	(Q)	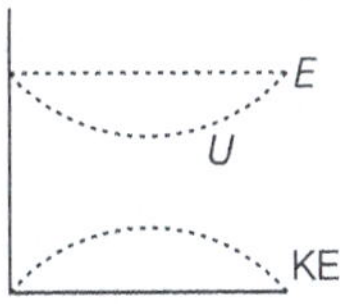
(C)	An object being pulled on a level, frictionless surface by a constant force in the horizontal direction.	(R)	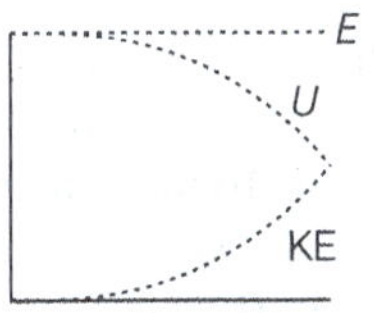
(D)	A block is coming down on a rough inclined plane with constant velocity	(S)	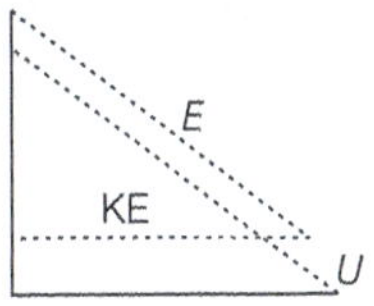

6 Acceleration a *versus* x and potential energy U *versus* x graph of a particle moving along X-axis is as shown in figure. Mass of the particle is 1 kg and velocity at $x = 0$ is 4 m/s. At $x = 8$ m;

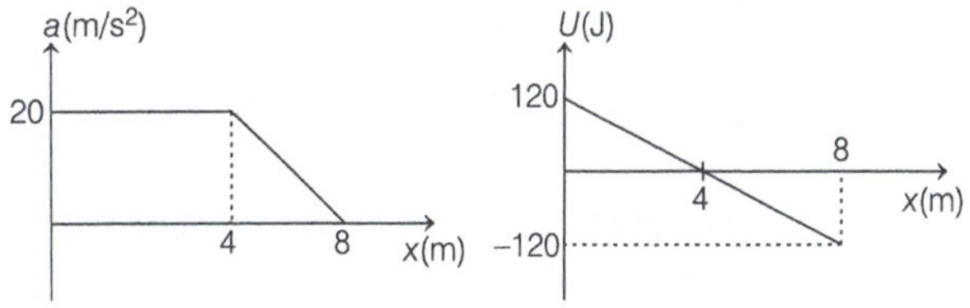

	Column I		Column II
(A)	Kinetic energy	(P)	120 J
(B)	Work done by conservative forces	(Q)	240 J
(C)	Total work done	(R)	128 J
(D)	Work done by external forces	(S)	112 J
		(T)	– 120 J

7 Match the following

	Column I		Column II
(A)	work done by all the forces	(P)	change in potential energy
(B)	work done by internal conservative forces	(Q)	change in kinetic energy
(C)	work done by external forces and internal non-conservative forces	(R)	change in mechanical energy
		(S)	None

8 F-x and corresponding U-x graph are as shown in figure. Three points A, B and C in F-x graph may be corresponding to P, Q and R in the U-x graph. Match the following:

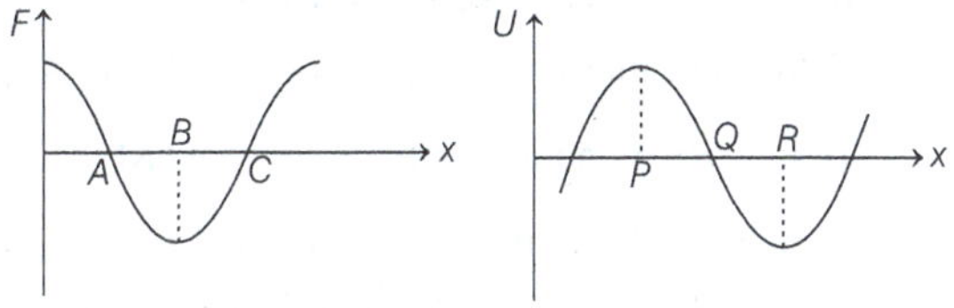

	Column I		Column II
(A)	A	(P)	P
(B)	B	(Q)	Q
(C)	C	(R)	R
		(S)	None

9. Initially, springs are in natural length. An application of external varying force F causes the block to move slowly distance x towards wall on smooth floor

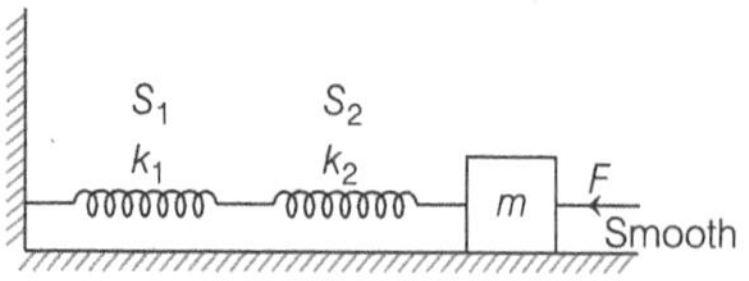

Column I		Column II	
(A)	Work done by S_2 on block	(P)	zero
(B)	Work done by S_2 on S_1	(Q)	$-\frac{1}{2}\left(\frac{k_1k_2}{k_1+k_2}\right)x^2$
(C)	Work done by F on block	(R)	$\frac{1}{2}\left(\frac{k_1k_2}{k_1+k_2}\right)x^2$
(D)	Work done by S_1 on wall	(S)	$\frac{1}{2}\frac{k_1k_2^2x^2}{(k_1+k_2)^2}$

10 In the figure shown, 1 kg block is given a velocity of 6 m/s and 2 kg plank is given a velocity of 3 m/s. Ground is smooth. Coefficient of friction between the two blocks is 0.04. When the relative motion between them stops,

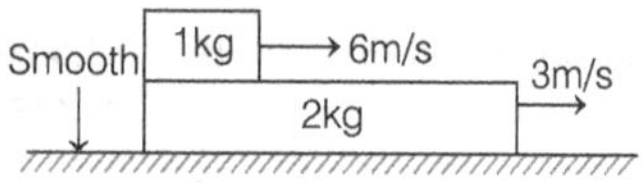

Column I		Column II	
(A)	time taken (in seconds) for relative motion to stop	(P)	– 10
(B)	work done (in J) by friction force on the block	(Q)	7
(C)	Work done (in J) by friction force on the plank	(R)	3
(D)	Loss in mechanical energy (in J) of block plus plank system	(S)	5

Numerical Value Questions

1 A block of mass $m = 4$ kg is projected with a speed $u = \frac{1}{2}$ m/s on a long platform of mass $M = 17$ kg as shown in the figure. Due to friction between the block and the platform, the block slows down and after certain moment comes to rest w.r.t the platform. Find the magnitude of average power (in watts) developed by the force of friction during the entire process? ($g = 10\ m/s^2$)

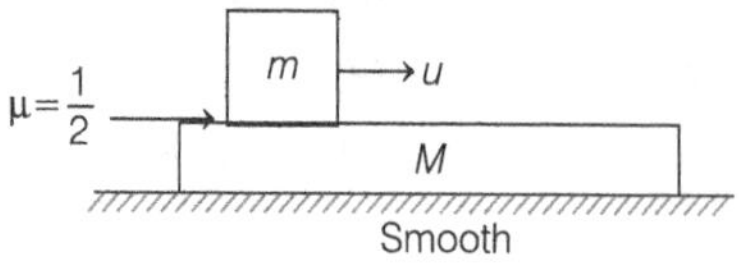

2 A particle of mass 2 kg is subjected to a two-dimensional conservative force given by $F_x = -2x + 2y$ and $F_y = 2x - y^2$ (x, y in metre and F in newton).

If the particle has kinetic energy of (8/3) J at point (2, 3), find the speed (in m/s) of the particle when it reaches (1, 2).

3 A particle of mass m moves along the quarter section of the circular path whose centre is at the origin. The radius of the circular path is a. A force $\mathbf{F} = y\hat{\mathbf{i}} - x\hat{\mathbf{j}}$ N acts on the particle, where x, y denote the coordinates of position of the particle. If the work done by this force in taking the particle from point A $(a, 0)$ to point B $(0, a)$ along the circular path is $\frac{-\pi a^2}{x}$, then find x.

4 A ring of mass $m = 2$ kg can slide over a smooth vertical rod. A light string attached to the ring passes over a smooth fixed pulley at a distance of $L = \frac{26}{3}$ m from the rod as shown in diagram. At the other end of the string mass $M = 5$ kg is attached, lying over a smooth fixed inclined plane of inclination angle 37°. The ring is held in level with the pulley and released. Determine the velocity of ring (in m/s) when the string makes an angle ($\alpha = 37°$) with the horizontal. ($\sin 37° = 0.6$, $g = 10\ m/s^2$)

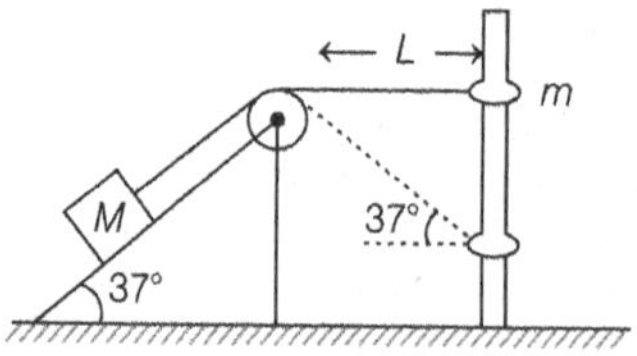

5 The block, shown in figure, is released from rest with the spring initially unstretched. The spring constant is 50 N/m and mass of the block is 1 kg. Find the maximum extension in spring (in cm).

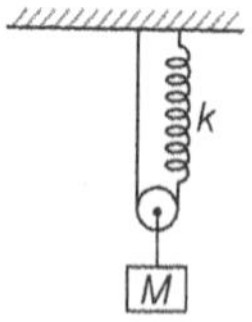

6 A block of mass 10 kg is released on a fixed wedge inside a cart which is moving with a constant velocity of 10 m/s towards right. The initial velocity of the block w.r.t the cart is zero. The work done (in J) by normal reaction(with respect to ground) on the block in 2 s is ($g = 10\ m/s^2$)

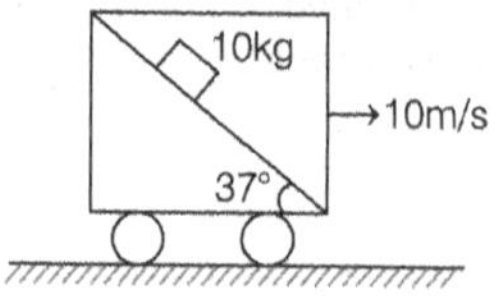

7 A spring with spring constant $k = 500$ N/m and relaxed length zero has one end attached to a wall and the other end attached to a ring with mass $m = 1$ kg. The ring is pulled to the side and is slipped over a vertical pole that is fixed at some distance from the wall as shown in the figure. The ring is held with the spring horizontal and then ring is released. Find the maximum vertical displacement of the ring (in cm). ($g = 10\ m/s^2$)

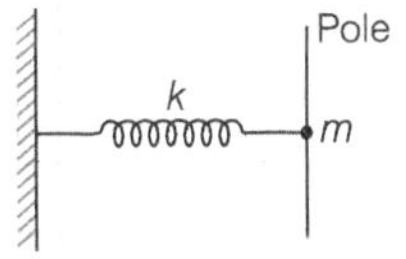

8 In the arrangement shown, the block is released from rest, i.e. $x = 0$ (when the spring was in its natural length), on an incline having $\mu = 0.5x$. Find the maximum elongation (in m) in the spring. (Take, x is in metre and $g = 10\ m/s^2$)

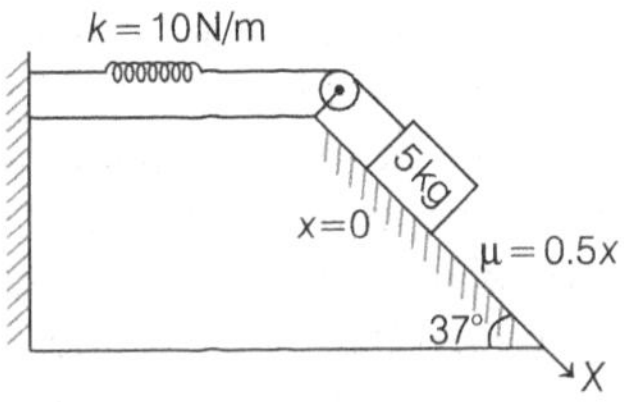

9 A block of mass m kg moving with kinetic energy 8 J on a smooth horizontal surface hits the free end of a spring, whose other end is attached to a rigid wall as shown in the figure. If restoring force applied by the spring is given by

$$F(x) = (-2x - x^3)\ N$$

Then, find the maximum compression (in m) in the spring.

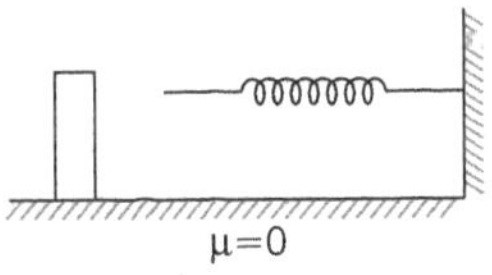

10 The blocks of mass $m_1 = 1$ kg and $m_2 = 2$ kg are connected by an ideal spring, rest on a rough horizontal surface. The spring is unstretched. The spring constant of spring is $k = 2$ N/m. The coefficient of friction between blocks and horizontal surface is $\mu = \frac{1}{2}$. Now, the left block is imparted a velocity u towards right as shown. Find the largest value of u (in m/s) such that the block of mass m_2 never moves. (take, $g = 10\ m/s^2$)

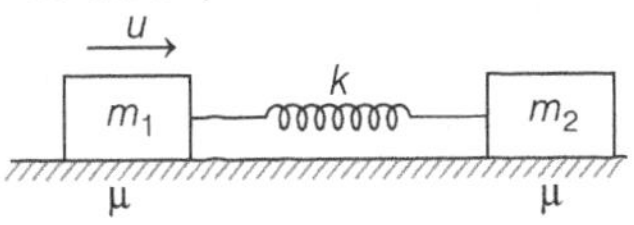

11 Two blocks A and B each having mass of 0.32 kg are connected by a light string passing over a smooth pulley as shown in the figure. The horizontal surface on which the block A slides is smooth. The block A is attached to a spring of force constant 40 N/m whose other end is fixed to a support 0.40 m above the horizontal surface. Initially, when the system is released to move, the spring is vertical and unstretched. Find the kinetic energy (in J) of the block A at the instant it breaks off the surface below it. ($g = 10\ m/s^2$)

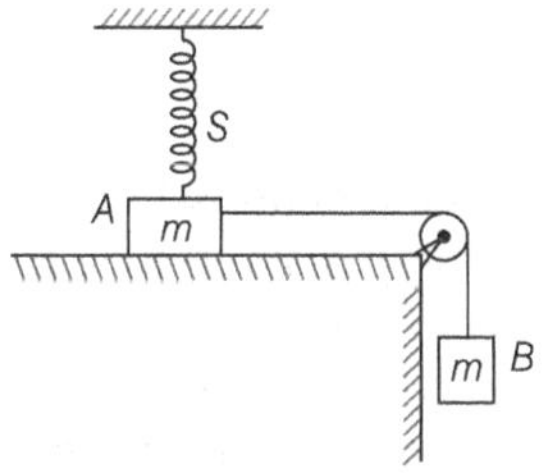

12 A 0.5 kg block slides from point A on a horizontal track with an initial speed of 3 m/s towards a weightless spring of length 1 m and having a force constant 2 N/m. The part AB of the track is frictionless and the part BC has coefficient of static and kinetic friction as 0.22 and 0.20. respectively. If the distances AB and BD are 2 m and 2.14 m respectively, find the total distance (in m) through which the block moves before it comes to rest completely. ($g = 10\ m/s^2$)

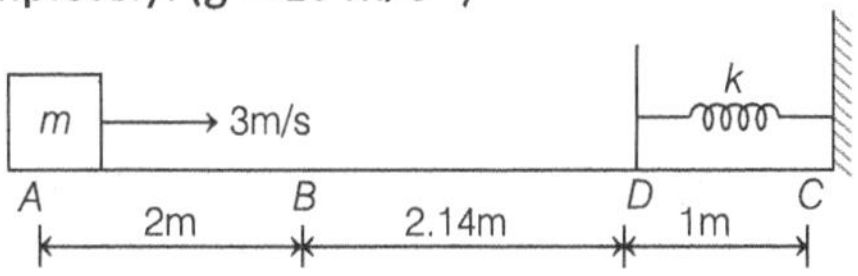

13 A cubical pit of depth $H = 1$ m is half filled with water. A very powerful centrifugal pump forces the water up onto the surface through a cylindrical pipe of radius $R = \frac{H}{\sqrt{4\pi}}$ m. What is the work done (in kJ) by the pump if it pumps out all the water in time $t = \sqrt{\frac{8H}{42}}$ s?

14 A particle of mass m is hanging with the help of an elastic string of unstretched length a and force constant $\frac{mg}{a}$. The other end is fixed to a peg on vertical wall. String is given an additional extension of $2a$ in vertical downward direction by pulling the mass and released from rest. If the maximum height reached by it during its subsequent motion above point of release is $\frac{\lambda a}{2}$, then find λ. (Neglect interaction with peg if any)

15 A block of mass 2 kg is released from rest on a spring A of spring constant 100 N/m as shown in the figure. The block compresses the spring B through a distance 10 cm. Find the spring constant (in N/m) of spring B.

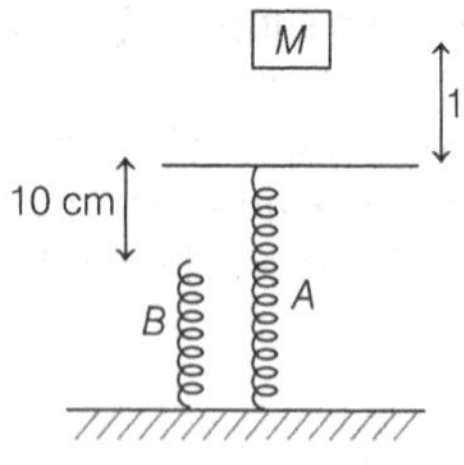

16 Two identical beads of mass 1 kg each are connected by an inextensible massless string and they can slide along the two arms AB (horizontal) and BC (vertical) of a rigid smooth wire frame in vertical plane. The system is released from rest as shown in figure. When they have moved by a distance of 0.1 m, the speed of the vertically moving bead is $\frac{x}{25}$ m/s. Find the value of x.

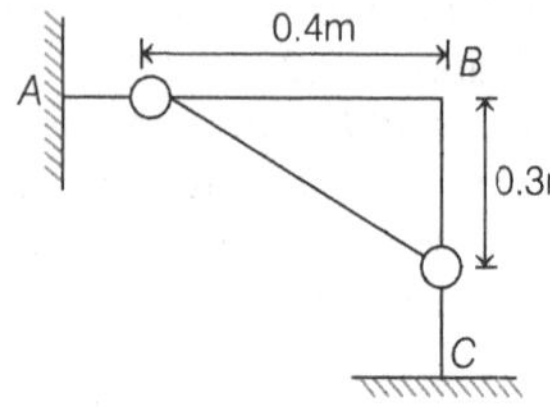

17 A light string $ABCDE$ whose mid-point is C passes through smooth rings B and D, which are fixed in a horizontal plane distance $2a$ apart. To each of the points A, C and E is attached a mass m. Initially C is held at rest at O (mid-point BD) and is then set free. If the distance OC, when C comes to instantaneous rest is $\frac{4a}{\eta}$, then find η.

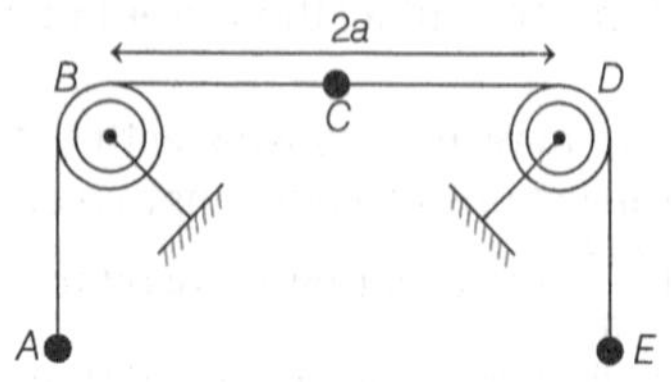

18 A ring of mass m can slide along a fixed rough vertical rod as shown in figure. The ring is connected by a spring of spring constant $k = \frac{4mg}{R}$, where $2R$ is the natural length of the spring. The other end of the spring is fixed to the ground at a point A which at a horizontal distance of $2R$ from the base of the rod. If ring is released from height $\frac{3R}{2}$ and it reaches the ground with a speed $\sqrt{3gR}$, the coefficient of friction between rod and ring will be $\frac{1}{n(3 - 4 \ln 2)}$. Find n.

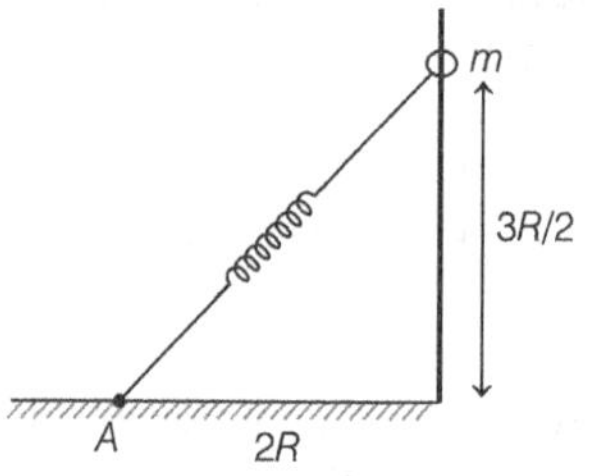

19 The axle ofa pulley of mass $m = 1$ kg is attached to the end of a spring of spring constant $k = 200$ N/m whose other end is fixed to the ceiling. A massless rope is placed on the pulley such that its left end is fixed to the ground and its right end is hanging freely from the pulley which is at rest in equilibrium. We begin to pull the endpoint A at the right end of the rope by a constant vertical force of $F = 15$ N. Friction can be neglected between the rope and the pulley. Find the maximum displacement (in cm) of point A after applying F.

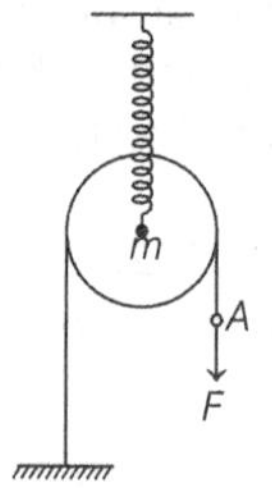

20 A block of mass 1 kg is released from top of a rough incline having $\mu = \frac{1}{\sqrt{3}}$. The initial speed of the block is 2 m/s. The incline plane is of unknown length and has a spring of constant $k = 100$ N/m connected at base as shown in figure. Find the maximum compression (in cm) of spring.

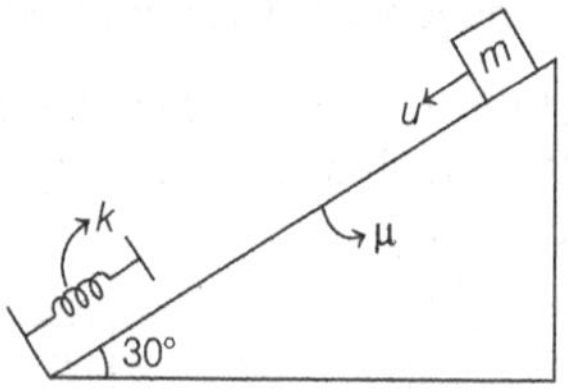

Previous Year's Questions

JEE Main

1 A block of mass 100 kg slides over a distance of 10 m on a horizontal surface. If the co-efficient of friction between the surfaces is 0.4, then the work done against friction (in J) is **[2024, 29 Jan Shift-I]**

(a) 4200 (b) 4500 (c) 4000 (d) 3900

2 The potential energy function (in J) of a particle in a region of space is given as $U = (2x^2 + 3y^3 + 2z)$. Here x, y and z are in metre. The magnitude of x-component of force (in N) acting on the particle at point $P(1, 2, 3)$ m is **[2024, 29 Jan Shift-I]**

(a) 4 (b) 8
(c) 2 (d) 6

3 The bob of a pendulum was released from a horizontal position. The length of the pendulum is 10 m. If it dissipates 10% of its initial energy against air resistance, the speed with which the bob arrives at the lowest point is [Use, $g = 10 \text{ ms}^{-2}$] **[2024, 29 Jan Shift-II]**

(a) $6\sqrt{5}\text{ ms}^{-1}$ (b) $5\sqrt{6}\text{ ms}^{-1}$
(c) $2\sqrt{5}\text{ ms}^{-1}$ (d) $5\sqrt{5}\text{ ms}^{-1}$

4 A particle is placed at the point A of a frictionless track ABC as shown in figure. It is gently pushed towards right. The speed of the particle, when it reaches the point B is (Take, $g = 10 \text{ m/s}^2$) **[2024, 30 Jan Shift-I]**

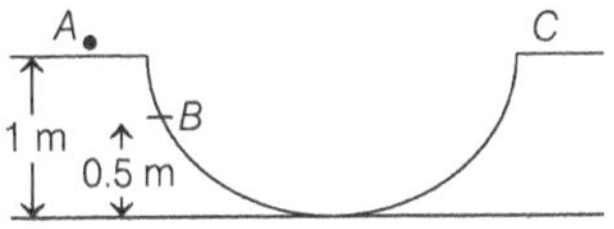

(a) $\sqrt{10}$ m/s (b) 20 m/s
(c) $2\sqrt{10}$ m/s (d) 10 m/s

5 A block of mass 1 kg is pushed up a surface inclined to horizontal at an angle of 60° by a force of 10 N parallel to the inclined surface as shown in figure. When the block is pushed up by 10 m along inclined surface, the work done against frictional force is [$g = 10 \text{ m/s}^2$] **[2024, 30 Jan Shift-II]**

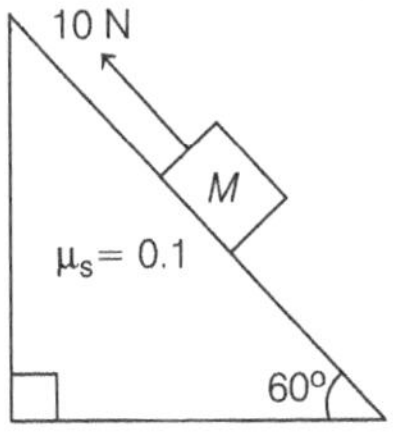

(a) 5×10^3 J (b) 5 J
(c) 10 J (d) $5\sqrt{3}$ J

6 Two bodies are having kinetic energies in the ratio 16 : 9. If they have same linear momentum, the ratio of their masses respectively is **[2023, 13 April Shift-I]**

(a) 3 : 4 (b) 4 : 3 (c) 9 : 16 (d) 16 : 9

7 Given below are two statements :

Statement I A truck and a car moving with the same kinetic energy are brought to rest by applying breaks which provide equal retarding forces. Both come to rest in equal distance.

Statement II A car moving towards east takes a turn and moves towards north, the speed remains unchanged. The acceleration of the car is zero.

In the light of above statements, choose the most appropriate answer from the options given below. **[2023, 12 April Shift-I]**

(a) Statement I is incorrect but Statement II is correct.
(b) Statement I is correct but Statement II is incorrect.
(c) Both Statement I and Statement II are correct.
(d) Both Statement I and Statement II are incorrect.

8 For a body projected at an angle with the horizontal from the ground. Choose the correct statement. **[2023, 1 Feb Shift-II]**

(a) The horizontal component of velocity is zero at the highest point.
(b) The vertical component of momentum is maximum at the highest point.
(c) Gravitational potential energy is maximum at the highest point.
(d) The Kinetic Energy (KE) is zero at the highest point of projectile motion.

9 Identify the correct statements from the following

A. Work done by a man in lifting a bucket out of a well by means of a rope tied to the bucket is negative.
B. Work done by gravitational force in lifting a bucket out of a well by a rope tied to the bucket is negative.
C. Work done by friction on a body sliding down an inclined plane is positive.
D. Work done by an applied force on a body moving on a rough horizontal plane with uniform velocity in zero.
E. Work done by the air resistance on an oscillating pendulum is negative.

Choose the correct answer from the options given below **[2023, 29 Jan Shift-II]**

(a) B, D and E only (b) B and D only
(c) B and E only (d) A and C only

10 The momentum of a body is increased by 50%. The percentage increase in the kinetic energy of the body is .... %. **[2023, 8 April Shift-I]**

11 A body of mass 5 kg is moving with a momentum of 10 kg^{-1} ms. Now, a force of 2 N acts on the body in the direction of its motion for 5 s. The increase in the kinetic energy of the body is .... J **[2023, 8 April Shift-II]**

12 A force $F = (2 + 3x)\hat{i}$; acts on a particle in the x direction where F is in newton and x is in meter. The work done by this force during a displacement from $x = 0$ to $x = 4$ m, is .... J. **[2023, 11 April Shift-I]**

13 A particle of mass 10 g moves in a straight line with retardation $2x$, where x is the displacement in SI units. Its loss of kinetic energy for above displacement is $\left(\frac{10}{x}\right)^{-n}$ J. The value of n will be .... **[2023, 6 April Shift-I]**

14 To maintain a speed of 80 km/h by a bus of mass 500 kg on a plane rough road for 4 km distance, the work done by the engine of the bus will be .... kJ. [The coefficient of friction between tyre of bus and road is 0.04] **[2023, 12 April Shift-I]**

15 A block of mass 10 kg is moving along X-axis under the action of force $F = 5x$ N. The work done by the force in moving the block from $x = 2$ m to 4 m will be .... J. **[2023, 15 April Shift-I]**

16 A car accelerates from rest to u m/s. The energy spent in this process is E J. The energy required to accelerate the car from u m/s to $2u$ m/s is nE J. The value of n is .... **[2023, 13 April Shift-II]**

17 A force $F = (5 + 3y^2)\hat{j}$ acts on a particle in the y-direction, where F is in newton and y is in metre. The work done by the force during a displacement from $y = 2$ m to $y = 5$ m is .... J. **[2023, 01 Feb Shift-II]**

18 A spherical body of mass 2 kg starting from rest acquires a kinetic energy of 10000 J at the end of 5th seconds. The force acted on the body is .... N. **[2023, 24 Jan Shift-I]**

19 A small particle moves to position $5\hat{i} - 2\hat{j} + \hat{k}$ from its initial position $2\hat{i} + 3\hat{j} - 4\hat{k}$ under the action of force $5\hat{i} + 2\hat{j} + 7\hat{k}$ N. The value of work done will be .... J. **[2023, 01 Feb Shift-I]**

20 A lift of mass $m = 500$ kg is descending with speed of 2 ms^{-1}. Its supporting cable begins to slip thus allowing it to fall with a constant acceleration of 2 ms^{-2}. The kinetic energy of the lift at the end of fall through to a distance of 6 m will be .... kJ. **[2023, 31 Jan Shift-I]**

21 A closed circular tube of average radius I5 cm, whose inner walls are rough, is kept in vertical plane. A block of mass 1 kg just fit inside the tube. The speed of block is 22 m/s, when it is introduced at the top of tube. After completing five oscillations, the block stops at the bottom region of tube. The work done by the tube on the block is .... J. (Given, $g = 10$ m/s). **[2023, 10 April Shift-I]**

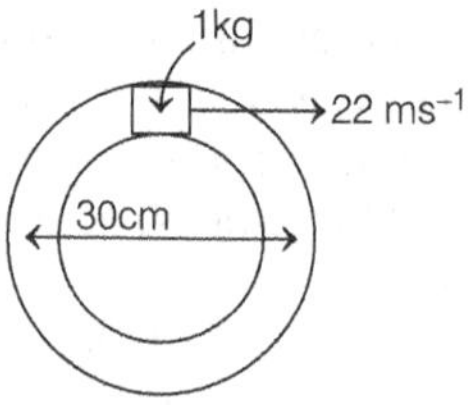

22 If the maximum load carried by an elevator is 1400 kg (600 kg - Passengers + 800 kg - elevator), which is moving up with a uniform speed of 3 m s^{-1} and the frictional force acting on it is 2000 N, then the maximum power used by the motor is .... kW ($g = 10$ m/s^2) **[2023, 10 April Shift-II]**

23 A body of mass 1 kg begins to move under the action of a time dependent force $\mathbf{F} = (t\hat{i} + 3t^2\hat{j})$ N, where $\hat{i}$ and $\hat{j}$ are the unit vectors along X and Y-axis. The power developed by above force, at the time $t = 2$s, will be .... W. **[2023, 24 Jan Shift-II]**

24 If momentum of a body is increased by 20%, then its kinetic energy increases by **[2022, 29 July Shift-II]**

(a) 36% (b) 40%
(c) 44% (d) 48%

25 A body of mass 8 kg and another of mass 2 kg are moving with equal kinetic energy. The ratio of their respective momenta will be **[2022, 26 July Shift-II]**

(a) 1 : 1 (b) 2 : 1
(c) 1 : 4 (d) 4 : 1

26 In the given figure, the block of mass m is dropped from the point A. The expression for kinetic energy of block when it reaches point B is **[2022, 29 June Shift-II]**

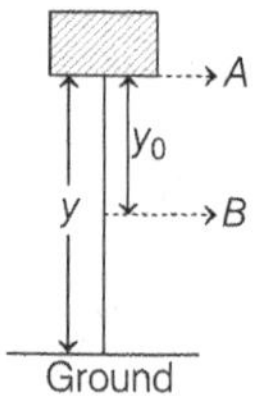

(a) $\frac{1}{2}mgy_0^2$ (b) $\frac{1}{2}mgy^2$
(c) $mg(y - y_0)$ (d) mgy_0

27 Arrange the four graphs in descending order of total work done, where W_1, W_2, W_3 and W_4 are the work done corresponding to figures A, B, C and D, respectively **[2022, 26 June Shift-II]**

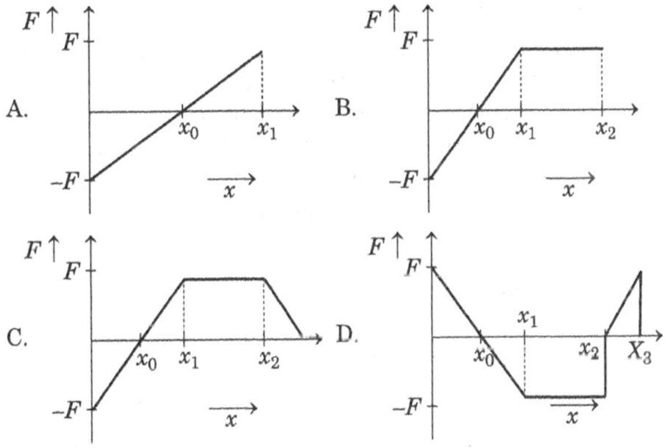

(a) $W_3 > W_2 > W_1 > W_4$ (b) $W_3 > W_2 > W_4 > W_1$
(c) $W_2 > W_3 > W_4 > W_1$ (d) $W_2 > W_3 > W_1 > W_4$

28 Potential energy as a function of r is given by $U = \frac{A}{r^{10}} - \frac{B}{r^5}$, where r is the interatomic distance, A and B are positive constants. The equilibrium distance between the two atoms will be **[2022, 24 June Shift-II]**

(a) $\left(\frac{A}{B}\right)^{1/5}$ (b) $\left(\frac{B}{A}\right)^{1/5}$ (c) $\left(\frac{2A}{B}\right)^{1/5}$ (d) $\left(\frac{B}{2A}\right)^{1/5}$

29 A 0.5 kg block moving at a speed of 12 ms^{-1} compresses a spring through a distance 30 cm when its speed is halved. The spring constant of the spring will be ... Nm^{-1}. **[2022, 25 June Shift-I]**

30 A body of mass 0.5 kg travel on straight line path with velocity $v = (3x^2 + 4)$ m/s. The net work done by the force during its displacement from $x = 0$ to $x = 2$ m is **[2022, 25 July Shift-I]**

(a) 64 J (b) 60 J
(c) 120 J (d) 128 J

31 A particle experiences a variable force $\mathbf{F} = (4x\hat{\mathbf{i}} + 3y^2\hat{\mathbf{j}})$ in a horizontal X-Y plane. Assume, distance in metre and force in newton. If the particle moves from point (1, 2) to point (2, 3) in the XY-plane, then kinetic energy changes by **[2022, 24 June Shift-I]**

(a) 50.0 J (b) 12.5 J
(c) 25.0 J (d) 0 J

32 Sand is being dropped from a stationary dropper at a rate of 0.5 kgs^{-1} on a conveyor belt moving with a velocity of 5 ms^{-1}. The power needed to keep the belt moving with the same velocity will be **[2022, 27 July Shift-I]**

(a) 1.25 W (b) 2.5 W (c) 6.25 W (d) 12.5 W

33 A porter lifts a heavy suitcase of mass 80 kg and at the destination lowers it down by a distance of 80 cm with a constant velocity. Calculate the work done by the porter in lowering the suitcase.
[Take, $g = 9.8\ ms^{-2}$] **[2021, 22 July Shift-II]**

(a) −62720.0 J (b) −627.2 J
(c) +627.2 J (d) 784.0 J

34 If the kinetic energy of a moving body becomes four times of its initial kinetic energy, then the percentage change in its momentum will be **[2021, 20 July Shift-II]**

(a) 100% (b) 200%
(c) 300% (d) 400%

35 A particle of mass m moves in a circular orbit under the central potential field, $U(r) = \frac{-C}{r}$, where C is a positive constant. The correct radius-velocity graph of the particle's motion is **[2021, 18 March Shift-II]**

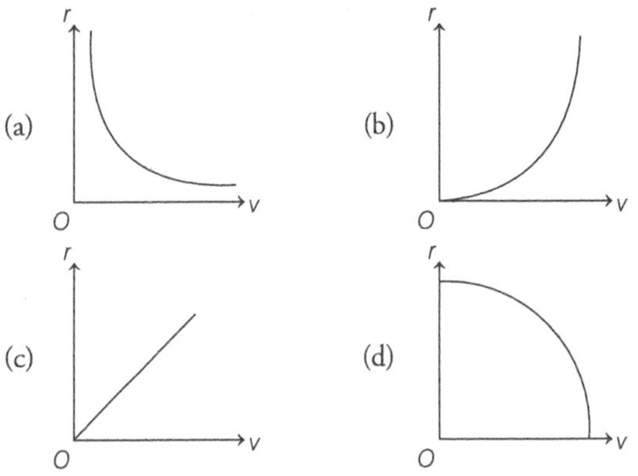

36 Two persons A and B perform same amount of work in moving a body through a certain distance d with application of forces acting at angle 45° and 60° with the direction of displacement respectively. The ratio of force applied by person A to the force applied by person B is $\frac{1}{\sqrt{x}}$. The value of x is .... **[2021, 27 Aug Shift-I]**

37 A force of $F = (5y + 20)\hat{j}$ N acts on a particle. The work done by this force when the particle is moved from $y = 0$ m to $y = 10$ m is ...... J. **[2021, 25 July Shift-II]**

38 Two particles having masses 4 g and 16 g respectively are moving with equal kinetic energies. The ratio of the magnitudes of their linear momentum is $n : 2$. The value of n will be .... **[2021, 25 Feb Shift-II]**

39 Two solids A and B of mass 1 kg and 2 kg respectively are moving with equal linear momentum. The ratio of their kinetic energies $(KE)_A : (KE)_B$ will be $\frac{A}{1}$, so the value of A will be .... **[2021, 25 Feb Shift-II]**

40 A body of mass m dropped from a height h reaches the ground with a speed of $0.8\sqrt{gh}$. The value of workdone by the air-friction is **[2021, 01 Sep Shift-II]**

(a) -0.68 mgh (b) mgh

(c) 1.64 mgh (d) 0.64 mgh

41 A block of mass m (as shown in figure) moving with kinetic energy E compresses a spring through a distance 25 cm when its speed is halved. The value of spring constant of used spring will be $nE\,\text{Nm}^{-1}$ for $n = \ldots\ldots\ldots$.

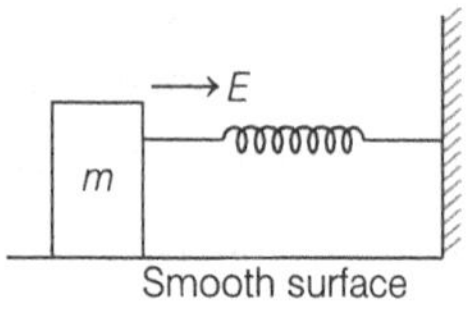

42 An automobile of mass m accelerates starting from origin and initially at rest, while the engine supplies constant power P. The position is given as a function of time by **[2021, 27 July Shift-II]**

(a) $\left(\frac{9P}{8m}\right)^{\frac{1}{2}} \cdot t^{\frac{3}{2}}$ (b) $\left(\frac{8P}{9m}\right)^{\frac{1}{2}} \cdot t^{\frac{2}{3}}$

(c) $\left(\frac{9m}{8P}\right)^{\frac{1}{2}} \cdot t^{\frac{3}{2}}$ (d) $\left(\frac{8P}{9m}\right)^{\frac{1}{2}} \cdot t^{\frac{3}{2}}$

43 A body at rest is moved along a horizontal straight line by a machine delivering a constant power. The distance moved by the body in time t is proportional to **[2021, 20 July Shift-II]**

(a) $t^{\frac{3}{2}}$ (b) $t^{\frac{1}{2}}$ (c) $t^{\frac{1}{4}}$ (d) $t^{\frac{3}{4}}$

JEE Advanced

1 A particle is moved along a path AB-BC-CD-DE-EF-FA, as shown in figure, in presence of a force $\mathbf{F} = (\alpha y\hat{\mathbf{i}} + 2\alpha x\hat{\mathbf{j}})$ N, where x and y are in metre and $\alpha = -1\,\text{Nm}^{-1}$. The work done on particle by this force $\mathbf{F}$ will be .... joule. **[JEE Advanced 2019]**

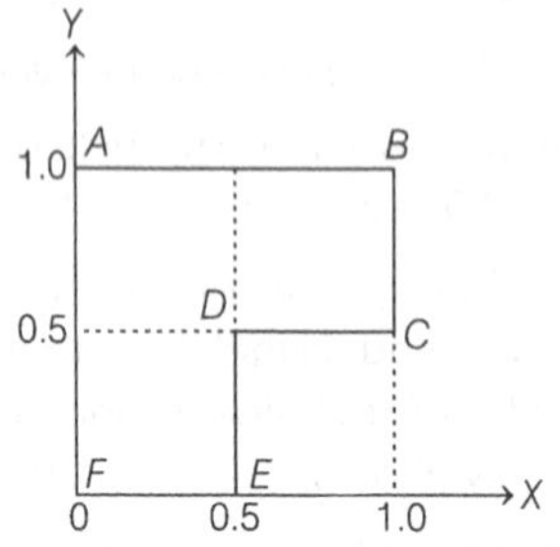

2. A particle of mass m is initially at rest at the origin. It is subjected to a force and starts moving along the X-axis. Its kinetic energy K changes with time as $dK/dt = \gamma t$, where γ is a positive constant of appropriate dimensions. Which of the following statements is (are) true? **(2018 Adv.)**

(a) The force applied on the particle is constant

(b) The speed of the particle is proportional to time

(c) The distance of the particle from the origin increases linearly with time

(d) The force is conservative

3 A particle of unit mass is moving along the x-axis under the influence of a force and its total energy is conserved. Four possible forms of the potential energy of the particle are given in Column I (a and U_0 are constants). Match the potential energies in Column I to the corresponding statement(s) in Column II. **[JEE Advanced 2015]**

Column I	Column II
(A) $U_1(x) = \frac{U_0}{2}\left[1 - \left(\frac{x}{a}\right)^2\right]^2$	(P) The force acting on the particle is zero at $x = a$.
(B) $U_2(x) = \frac{U_0}{2}\left(\frac{x}{a}\right)^2$	(Q) The force acting on the particle is zero at $x = 0$.
(C) $U_3(x) = \frac{U_0}{2}\left(\frac{x}{a}\right)^2 \exp\left[-\left(\frac{x}{a}\right)^2\right]$	(R) The force acting on the particle is zero at $x = -a$.
(D) $U_4(x) = \frac{U_0}{2}\left[\frac{x}{a} - \frac{1}{3}\left(\frac{x}{a}\right)^3\right]$	(S) The particle experiences an attractive force towards $x = 0$ in the region $\lvert x \rvert < a$.
	(T) The particle with total energy $\frac{U_0}{4}$ can oscillate about the point $x = -a$.

4. Consider an elliptically shaped rail PQ in the vertical plane with $OP = 3$ m and $OQ = 4$ m. A block of mass 1 kg is pulled along the rail from P to Q with a force of 18 N, which is always parallel to line PQ (see figure). Assuming no frictional losses, the kinetic energy of the block when it reaches Q is $(n \times 10)$ J. The value of n is (take acceleration due to gravity $= 10\,\text{ms}^{-2}$)

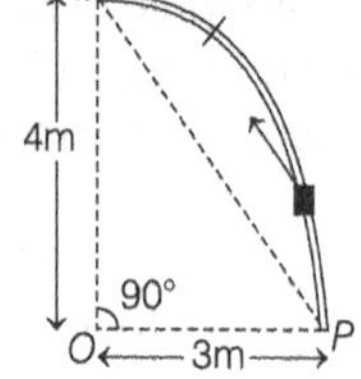

(2014 Adv.)

5. The work done on a particle of mass m by a force, $K\left[\frac{x}{(x^2+y^2)^{3/2}}\hat{\mathbf{i}} + \frac{y}{(x^2+y^2)^{3/2}}\hat{\mathbf{j}}\right]$ (K being a constant of appropriate dimensions), when the particle is taken from the point $(a, 0)$ to the point (0, *a*) along a circular path of radius *a* about the origin in the *x*-*y* plane is **(2013 Adv.)**

(a) $\frac{2K\pi}{a}$ (b) $\frac{K\pi}{a}$ (c) $\frac{K\pi}{2a}$ (d) 0

6. A particle of mass 0.2 kg is moving in one dimension under a force that delivers a constant power 0.5 W to the particle. If the initial speed (in ms^{-1}) of the particle is zero, the speed (in ms^{-1}) after 5 s is **(2013)**

7. A block of mass 2 kg is free to move along the *x*-axis. It is at rest and from *t* = 0 onwards it is subjected to a time-dependent force *F*(*t*) in the *x*-direction. The force *F*(*t*) varies with *t* as shown in the figure. The kinetic energy of the block after 4.5 s is **(2010)**

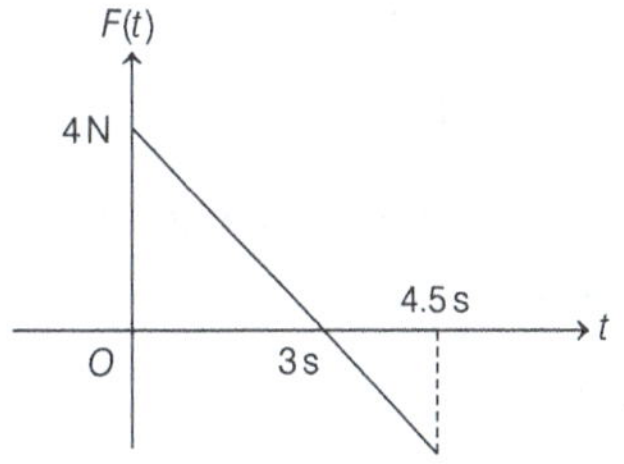

(a) 4.50 J (b) 7.50 J (c) 5.06 J (d) 14.06 J

Answer Key

LEVEL 1

12.1 Work Done by Force

1. –9J **2.** 135 J **3.** 83 J **4.** 14 J

5. $\frac{MgL}{2}$ **6.** (a) *FR* (b) $\frac{F\pi R}{2}$

12.2 Work-Energy Theorem

1. 5 m/s **2.** 10 m/s **3.** 10 J **4.** 16 J

5. $\frac{1}{2}ma^2d$ **6.** 3 **7.** $F = 6300$ N

12.3 Work Done by Gravity, Normal and Friction Force

1. (a) zero (b) 500 J **2.** 70 J

3. (a) 875 J (b) –250 J (c) 625 J (d) 625 J, change in kinetic energy of the body is equal to the work done by the net force in 10 s.

4. (a) 7.2 J (b) – 7.2 J (c) zero

5. (a) $\frac{40000}{5+\tan\theta}$ J (b) 7692.3 J **6.** 8 J

7. (a) 640 J (b) 640 J **8.** (a) 100 J (b) 60 J (c) – 60 J

9. (a) Since the gravitational force is a conservative force, therefore the work done in round trip is zero. (b) 300 J (c) – 240 J (d) 60 J

10. $\frac{-2\mu MgL}{9}$ **11.** (a) 2m/s (b) – 96 J (c) 16 J (d) – 80 J

12. (a) 40 J, – 40 J (b) Work done by frictional force on the upper block is converted to its kinetic energy.

13. 60 m/s **14.** $\frac{-mgh}{2}$ **15.** 6 m/s **16.** 1 m

17. – 0.02 J, 8 cm **18.** (a) zero (b) – 600 J (c) 1600 J

19. – 2J **20.** 5 m

12.4 Work Done by Tension

1. $\sqrt{2gl}$ **2.** 60° **3.** $\left(\sqrt{\frac{2(m_2-m_1)gx}{m_1+m_2}}\right)$

4. $mgL(1-\cos\theta)$ **5.** $\sqrt{\frac{2(m_2-\mu m_1)gL}{m_1+m_2}}$ **6.** 0.057

12.5 Work Done by Spring

1. $v\sqrt{\frac{m}{k}}$, No **2.** (a) $v_0=\sqrt{4\mu gL+\frac{kL^2}{m}}$ (b) $v=\sqrt{v_0^2-6\mu gL}$

3. 1.414 m **4.** 3.32 m **5.** 20 cm **6.** $\left(\frac{\sqrt{3}+1}{5}\right)$m

7. $\frac{h}{4}\sqrt{\frac{k}{m}}$ **8.** $\sqrt{\left(\frac{3gd}{2}+\frac{Kd^2}{16m}\right)}$

9. (a) 0.5 (b) 1000 N/m **10.** $\frac{m}{2}$

12.6 Work Done by Pseudo Force

1. (a) 50000 J, 40000 J, 25000 J (b) 12500 J **2.** $2\tan^{-1}\left(\frac{a}{g}\right)$

12.7 Conservative and Non-conservative Forces and Potential Energy

1. (a) 4 J along each path (b) Conservative

2. (a) $W_{OAB}=6$ J, $W_{OBC}=2$ J, $W_{OC}=\frac{14}{3}$ J

(b) Non-conservative as work cannot be found without knowing path

3. (a) $W_{OAB}=6$ J, $W_{OBC}=6$ J, $W_{OC}=6$ J (b) Conservative

4. (a) $\mathbf{F}=2x\hat{i}+2y\hat{j}+2z\hat{k}$ (b) $\mathbf{F}=y\hat{i}+x\hat{j}$

(c) $\mathbf{F}=-(2xy-3x^2y^2z)\hat{i}-(x^2-2x^3yz)\hat{j}+x^3y^2\hat{k}$

(d) $\mathbf{F}=-aU_0\cos(ax+by)\hat{i}-bU_0\cos(ax+by)\hat{j}$

5. $\mathbf{F}=-4\hat{i}-36\hat{j}-2\hat{k}$

6. (i) $U(x,y,z)=(-2x-3y)$ (ii) $U(x,y,z)=-(x^2+y^2)$

(iii) $U(x,y,z)=-xy$ (iv) $U=x^3y$

7. (a) $x=0$ and $x=\frac{2}{3}$

(b)

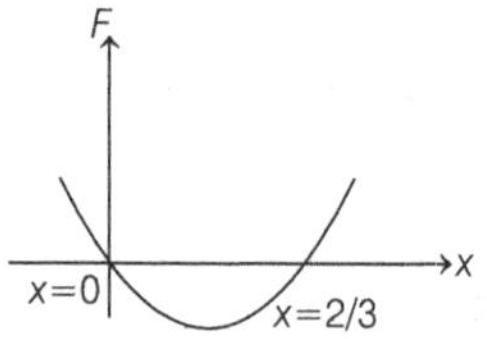

The particle is in stable equilibrium at $x = 0$ m and unstable equilibrium at $x = \frac{2}{3}$ m

(c) $v = \sqrt{\frac{2600}{27}}$ m/s

8. $x = 2$ stable, $x = -2$ unstable **9.** Stable C and Unstable A, E

10. 15 m **11.** 41 J **12.** 6 m/s **13.** 1.25 J **14.** $\frac{MgL}{18}$

12.8 Power

1. 8 W **2.** 140 W

3. (a) 0 (b) 0 (c) $-\mu mgat$ (d) $m(a + \mu g)at$ **4.** 47.2 W

5. (a) $mg\left[\frac{gt}{2} - u\sin\theta\right]$ (b) $-mg(u\sin\theta - gt)$

(c) $\frac{2u\sin\theta}{g}$ (d) at the highest point

(e) from base to highest point (f) From highest point to base.

6. 22.5 kW **7.** $\frac{49}{746} = 6.6 \times 10^{-2}$ HP **8.** 46 J

Level 2

Single Choice Correct Questions

1. (c)	2. (b)	3. (b)	4. (a)	5. (c)
6. (a)	7. (a)	8. (a)	9. (b)	10. (d)
11. (c)	12. (d)	13. (c)	14. (a)	15. (a)
16. (c)	17. (a)	18. (c)	19. (c)	20. (c)
21. (b)	22. (a)	23. (c)	24. (b)	25. (a)
26. (a)	27. (b)	28. (d)	29. (c)	30. (a)
31. (c)	32. (c)	33. (d)	34. (d)	35. (a)
36. (b)	37. (c)	38. (a)	39. (b)	40. (b)
41. (b)	42. (b)	43. (c)	44. (b)	45. (c)
46. (c)	47. (a)	48. (a)	49. (d)	50. (a)
51. (b)	52. (a)	53. (c)	54. (a)	55. (d)
56. (a)	57. (c)	58. (b)	59. (c)	60. (a)
61. (a)	62. (b)	63. (c)	64. (a)	65. (a)
66. (c)	67. (d)	68. (b)	69. (a)	70. (d)
71. (c)				

Numerical Value Questions

1. 9	2. 5	3. 32	4. 3	5. 6
6. 1	7. 300	8. 20	9. 6	10. 8
11. 2	12. 320	13. 2	14. 1.5	15. 730
16. 1.50	17. 12	18. 8	19. 6	20. 6

Level 3

Single Choice Correct Questions

1. (a)	2. (d)	3. (d)	4. (c)	5. (c)
6. (c)	7. (d)	8. (a)	9. (a)	10. (d)
11. (c)	12. (b)	13. (c)	14. (d)	15. (c)
16. (b)	17. (d)	18. (b)	19. (a)	20. (c)
21. (c)	22. (a)	23. (a)	24. (c)	25. (c)
26. (c)	27. (a)	28. (b)	29. (a)	30. (c)
31. (b)	32. (a)	33. (a)	34. (b)	35. (a)
36. (c)	37. (a)	38. (b)	39. (a)	40. (d)
41. (a)	42. (d)	43. (d)	44. (d)	45. (d)
46. (a)	47. (a)	48. (b)	49. (b)	50. (b)
51. (b)				

Multiple Choice(s) Correct Questions

1. (b,c)	2. (b,d)	3. (b,d)	4. (a,c)	5. (b,c,d)
6. (b,c)	7. (a,c)	8. (a,b,c,d)	9. (b,c)	10. (a,c,d)
11. (a,b,c)	12. (a,b,d)	13. (a,b,d)	14. (a,b,d)	15. (a,d)
16. (a,d)	17. (a,c)	18. (a,b,c)	19. (b,c,d)	20. (b,c)

Comprehension Based Questions

1. (c)	2. (a)	3. (a)	4. (b)	5. (d)
6. (a)	7. (b)	8. (c)	9. (b)	10. (b)
11. (b)	12. (b)	13. (b)	14. (d)	15. (c)
16. (d)	17. (a)	18. (b)	19. (c)	20. (d)
21. (a)	22. (c)	23. (b)	24. (a)	25. (c)
26. (b)	27. (a)	28. (b)	29. (b)	

Match The Columns Questions

1. A → R, B → P, C → S, D → T
2. A → S, B → Q, C → R, D → P
3. A → R, B → P, C → S, D → Q
4. A → P, B → P, C → R, D → Q
5. A → Q, B → R, C → P, D → S
6. A → R, B → Q, C → P, D → T
7. A → Q, B → S, C → R
8. A → R, B → S, C → P
9. A → Q, B → S, C → R, D → P
10. A → PR, B → QS, C → QR, D → P

Numerical Value Questions

1. (5)	2. (2)	3. (2)	4. (5)	5. (20)
6. (960)	7. (4)	8. (2)	9. (2)	10. (10)
11. (0.38)	12. (4.24)	13. (9)	14. (9)	15. (800)
16. (21)	17. (3)	18. (8)	19. (60)	20. (20)

Previous Year's Questions

JEE Main

1. (*)	2. (a)	3. (a)	4. (a)	5. (b)
6. (c)	7. (b)	8. (c)	9. (c)	10. (125)
11. (30)	12. (32)	13. (2)	14. (784)	15. (30)
16. (3)	17. (132)	18. (40)	19. (40)	20. (7)
21. (245)	22. (48)	23. (296)	24. (c)	25. (b)
26. (d)	27. (a)	28. (c)	29. (600)	30. (b)
31. (c)	32. (d)	33. (b)	34. (a)	35. (a)
36. (2)	37. (450)	38. (1)	39. (2)	40. (a)
41. (24)	42. (d)	43. (a)	44. (b)	

JEE Advanced

1. (0.75) **2.** (a,b,d)

3. A → PQRT, B → QS, C → PQRS, D → PRT

4. (5) **5.** (d) **6.** (5) **7.** (c)

SOLUTIONS

Level 1

12.1 Work Done by Force

1. $W = \mathbf{F} \cdot \mathbf{s} = \mathbf{F} \cdot (\mathbf{r}_2 - \mathbf{r}_1) = (2\hat{\mathbf{i}} + 3\hat{\mathbf{j}} + 4\hat{\mathbf{k}}) \cdot (-\hat{\mathbf{i}} - \hat{\mathbf{j}} - \hat{\mathbf{k}})$

$$= -2 - 3 - 4 = -9\text{ J}$$

2. $W = \int F\,dx = \int_0^5 (3x^2 - 2x + 7)\,dx$

$$= [x^3 - x^2 + 7x]_0^5 = 125 - 25 + 35 = 135\text{ J}$$

3. $W = \int \mathbf{F} \cdot d\mathbf{s} = \int (3x^2\,\hat{\mathbf{i}} + 2y\hat{\mathbf{j}}) \cdot (dx\,\hat{\mathbf{i}} + dy\hat{\mathbf{j}})$

$$= \int_2^4 3x^2\,dx + \int_3^6 2y\,dy = [x^3]_2^4 + [y^2]_3^6$$

$$= 64 - 8 + 36 - 9 = 83\text{ J}$$

4. $W = \int F\,dx$ = area under F-x graph

$$= \frac{1}{2}(4+2)(10) - \frac{1}{2} \times 4 \times 8 = 30 - 16 = 14\text{ J}$$

5. Lets say at any time x length is on the table and L-x is hanging.

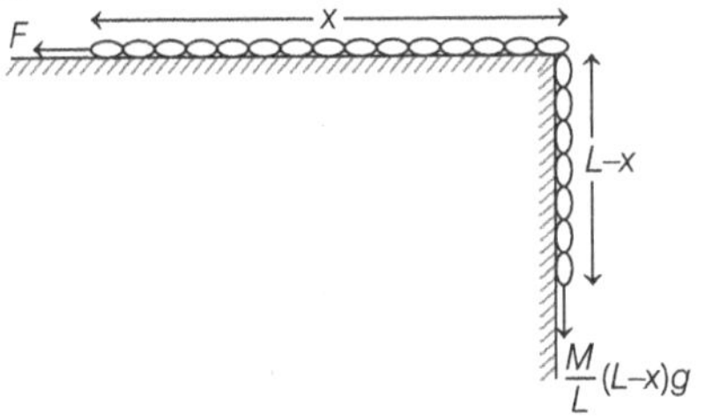

$$\Sigma F = ma \;\Rightarrow\; F - \frac{M}{L}(L - x)\,g = 0 \;\Rightarrow\; F = \frac{M}{L}(L - x)\,g$$

$$W = \int F\,dx = \int_0^L \frac{M}{L}(L - x)\,g\,dx = \frac{Mg}{L}\left[Lx - \frac{x^2}{2}\right]_0^L$$

$$= \frac{Mg}{L}\left(\frac{L^2}{2}\right) = \frac{MgL}{2}$$

6. (a) $W = \int \mathbf{F} \cdot d\mathbf{s} = \mathbf{F} \cdot \int d\mathbf{s} = \mathbf{F} \cdot \mathbf{s} = FS\cos\theta = F(R)\cos 0° = FR$

(b) $W = \int \mathbf{F} \cdot d\mathbf{s} = \int F\,ds\cos 0° = F\int ds = F\left(\frac{\pi R}{2}\right)$

12.2 Work-Energy Theorem

1. $W = \mathbf{F} \cdot \mathbf{s} = (3\hat{\mathbf{i}} + 4\hat{\mathbf{j}}) \cdot (3\hat{\mathbf{i}} + 3\hat{\mathbf{j}}) = 9 + 12 = 21\text{ J}$

From work-energy theorem,

$$W = \Delta K \;\Rightarrow\; 21 = \frac{1}{2} \times 2 \times v^2 - \frac{1}{2} \times 2 \times (2)^2$$

$$\Rightarrow\; v^2 = 25 \;\Rightarrow v = 5\text{ m/s}$$

2. $W = \int_0^{25} F\,dx$ = Area under F–x graph

$$\Rightarrow \quad W = 25(10) = 250 \quad\text{and}\quad W = \Delta K$$

$$\Rightarrow \quad 250 = \frac{1}{2} \times 5 \times v^2 - 0 \;\Rightarrow v = 10\text{ m/s}$$

3. $W = \int F\,dx$ = Area under F-x graph

$$= -\frac{1}{2} \times 4 \times 20 = -40\text{ J}$$

Negative sign as force is resistive.

$$W = \Delta K \;\Rightarrow\; -40 = K_2 - \frac{1}{2} \times 25 \times 2^2 \;\Rightarrow K_2 = 10\text{ J}$$

4. $x = \dfrac{t^3}{3} \;\Rightarrow\; v = \dfrac{dx}{dt} = t^2$

$$W = \Delta K = \frac{1}{2}mv_2^2 - \frac{1}{2}mv_1^2$$

$$= \frac{1}{2} \times 2 \times (2^2)^2 - \frac{1}{2} \times 2 \times (0^2)^2 = 16\text{ J}$$

5. $v = a\sqrt{x}$

At $x = 0$; $v = 0$

At $x = d$; $v = a\sqrt{d}$

$$W = \Delta K = \frac{1}{2}m(a\sqrt{d})^2 - 0 \;\Rightarrow\; W = \frac{1}{2}ma^2d$$

6. $W = \Delta K$

$$W_1 = \frac{1}{2} \times m\,(20)^2 - \frac{1}{2}m(10)^2$$

$$W_2 = \frac{1}{2} \times m(10)^2 - \frac{1}{2}m(0)^2 \;\Rightarrow\; \frac{W_1}{W_2} = 3$$

7. $W = \Delta K \;\Rightarrow\; -Fd = \dfrac{1}{2}mv^2 - \dfrac{1}{2}mu^2$

$$\Rightarrow -F(1) = \frac{1}{2} \times \frac{20}{1000}(100)^2 - \frac{1}{2} \times \frac{20}{1000}(800)^2$$

$$\Rightarrow\; F = 6300\text{ N}$$

12.3 Work Done by Gravity, Normal and Friction Force

1. (a) $W = Fs\cos\theta = mg(5)\cos 90° = 0$

(b) $W = Fs\cos\theta = (10 \times 10)(5)\cos 0° = 500\text{ J}$

2. $30 - T = 3a$ ...(i)

$T - 20 = 2a$ ...(ii)

Solving Eqs. (i) and (ii), we get

$$a = 2\text{ m/s}^2$$

$$s_{nth} = u + \frac{1}{2}a(2n - 1) = 0 + \frac{1}{2}(2)(2(4) - 1) = 7\text{ m}$$

Work done by gravity on 3 kg block $= 3 \times 10 \times 7 = 210$ J

Work done by gravity on 2 kg block $= -2 \times 10 \times 7 = -140$ J

Work done by gravity on system $= 210 - 140 = 70$ J

3.

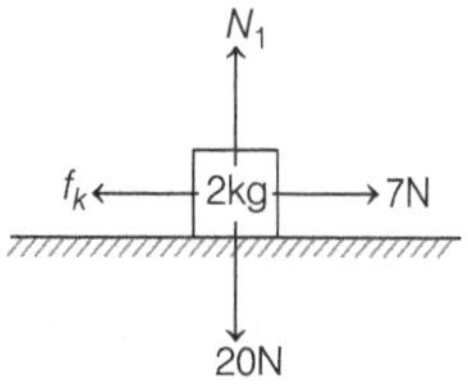

$$f_k = \mu_k N = 0.1\,(20) = 2\,\text{N}$$

$$\Sigma F = ma \quad \Rightarrow \quad 7 - 2 = 2a \quad \Rightarrow \quad a = 2.5\,\text{m/s}^2$$

$$s = ut + \frac{1}{2}at^2 = 0 + \frac{1}{2}(2.5)(10)^2 = 125\,\text{m}$$

(a) $W_F = Fs\cos 0° = 7 \times 125 \times 1 = 875$ J

(b) $W_f = Fs\cos 180° = 2 \times 125 \times (-1) = -250$ J

(c) Work done by net force $= 5 \times 125 \times 1 = 625$ J

(d) $\Delta K = W = 625$ J

4.

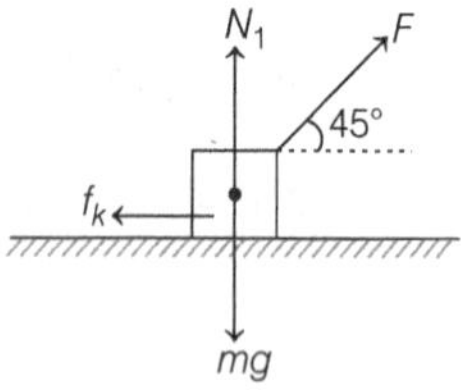

$$\Sigma F_y = 0 \quad \Rightarrow \quad N_1 = mg - F\sin 45°$$

$$\Sigma F_x = 0 \quad \Rightarrow F\cos 45° = f_k$$

$$\frac{F}{\sqrt{2}} = 0.25\left(18 - \frac{F}{\sqrt{2}}\right) \quad \Rightarrow \quad F = \frac{18\sqrt{2}}{5}\,\text{N}$$

(a) $W_F = Fs\cos 45° = \dfrac{18\sqrt{2}}{5} \times 2 \times \dfrac{1}{\sqrt{2}} = 7.2$ J

(b) $W_{\text{friction}} = f_k\, s\cos 180° = -7.2$ J

(c) $W_{mg} = mg\, s\cos 90° = 0$

5.

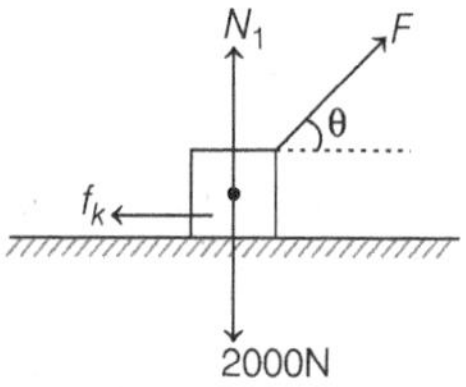

$$\Sigma F_y = 0 \quad \Rightarrow \quad N_1 = 2000 - F\sin\theta$$

$$\Sigma F_x = 0 \quad \Rightarrow \quad F\cos\theta = f_k$$

$$\Rightarrow \quad F\cos\theta = 0.2\,(2000 - F\sin\theta)$$

$$\Rightarrow \quad F = \frac{2000}{5\cos\theta + \sin\theta}$$

(a) $W = Fs\cos\theta = \left(\dfrac{2000}{5\cos\theta + \sin\theta}\right)(20)\cos\theta = \dfrac{40000}{5\cos\theta + \sin\theta}$

(b) $F = \dfrac{2000}{5\cos\theta + \sin\theta}$

To minimise F, we have to maximise $5\cos\theta + \sin\theta$

$$y = 5\cos\theta + \sin\theta$$

$$\frac{dy}{d\theta} = -5\sin\theta + \cos\theta = 0 \quad \Rightarrow \tan\theta = 0.2 = \frac{1}{5}$$

$$W = Fs\cos\theta = \left(\frac{2000}{5\cos\theta + \sin\theta}\right)(20)\cos\theta$$

$$= \frac{40000}{5 + \tan\theta} = \frac{40000}{5 + \frac{1}{5}} = 7692.3\text{ J}$$

6.

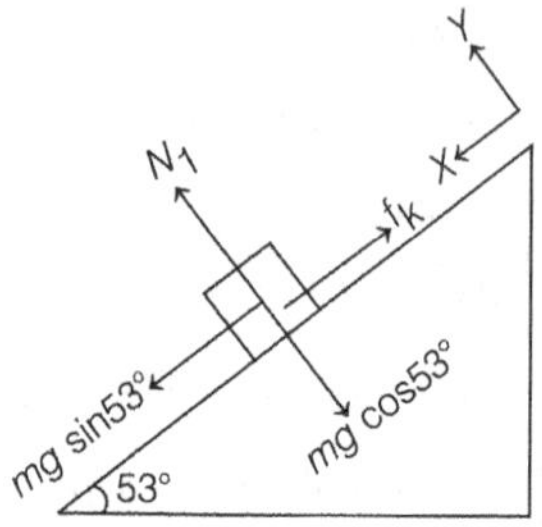

$$\Sigma F_x = 0 \quad \Rightarrow \quad mg\sin 53° - f_k = 0 \Rightarrow f_k = mg\sin 53°$$

Work done against friction $= (mg\sin 53°)\,(2)$

$$= 0.5 \times 10 \times \frac{4}{5} \times 2 = 8\text{ J}$$

7.

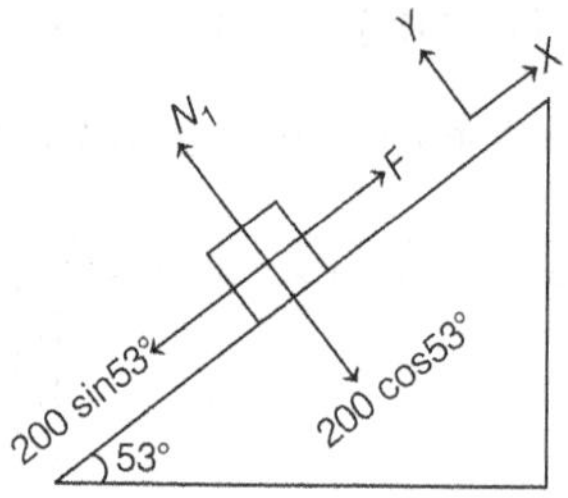

(a) $\Sigma F_x = 0 \quad \Rightarrow \quad F - 200\sin 53° = 0 \quad \Rightarrow \quad F = 160$ N

$W_F = 160 \times 4 \times \cos 0° = 640$ J

(b) $\Sigma F_x = 0 \quad \Rightarrow \quad F\cos 53° - 200\sin 53° = 0 \quad \Rightarrow \quad F = \dfrac{800}{3}$ N

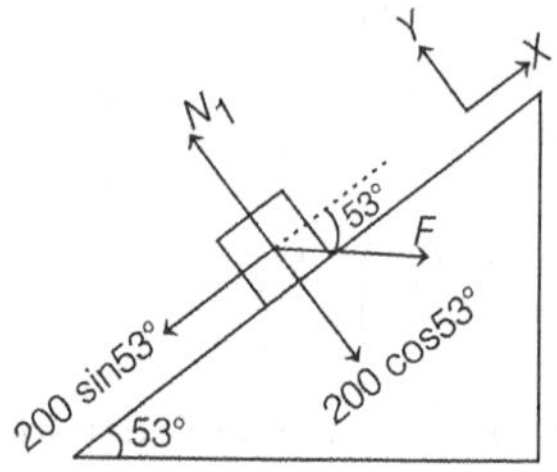

$$W_F = Fs\cos 53° = \frac{800}{3} \times 4 \times \frac{3}{5} = 640\text{J}$$

8.

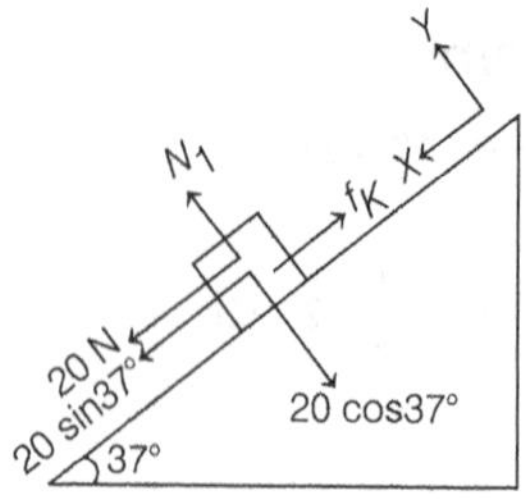

$$\Sigma F_x = ma_x \quad \Rightarrow \quad 20 + 20\sin 37° - f_k = 2(10) \quad \Rightarrow \quad f_k = 12\,\text{N}$$

$$s = ut + \frac{1}{2}at^2 \Rightarrow s = 0 + \frac{1}{2}(10)(1)^2 = 5\,\text{m}$$

(a) $W_F = Fs\cos\theta = 20(5)\cos 0° = 100$ J

(b) $W_{mg} = (20\sin 37°)(5) = 60$ J

(c) $W_{friction} = Fs\cos\theta = 12(5)\cos 180° = -60$ J

9.

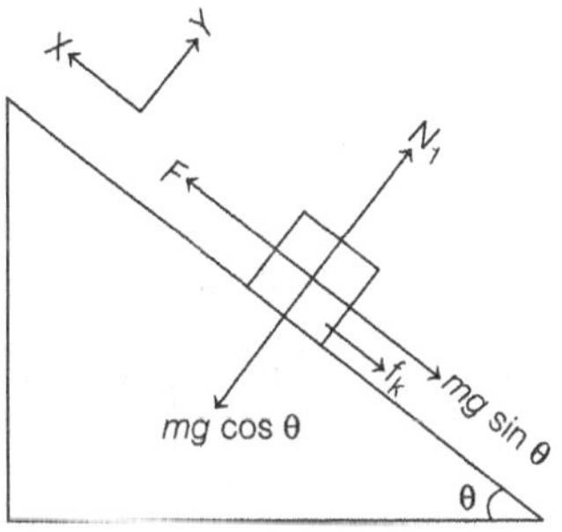

For upward journey,

$$\Sigma F_x = 0 \Rightarrow F - mg\sin\theta - \mu mg\cos\theta = 0$$

$$\Rightarrow \quad F = mg\sin\theta + \mu mg\cos\theta$$

$$\Rightarrow \quad F = 3\times 10\times\frac{3}{5} + (0.5)3\times 10\times\frac{4}{5} \Rightarrow F = 18 + 12 = 30\,\text{N}$$

(a) $W_{mg} = 0$

(b) $W_F = Fs\cos\theta = 30(10)\cos 0° = 300$ J

(c) $W_{friction} = -(\mu mg\cos\theta)(10) - (\mu mg\cos\theta)(10) = -240$ J

(d) $W_{mg} + W_F + W_{friction} = \Delta K$

$$\Rightarrow \quad 0 + 300 - 240 = K - 0 \Rightarrow K = 60\,\text{J}$$

10.

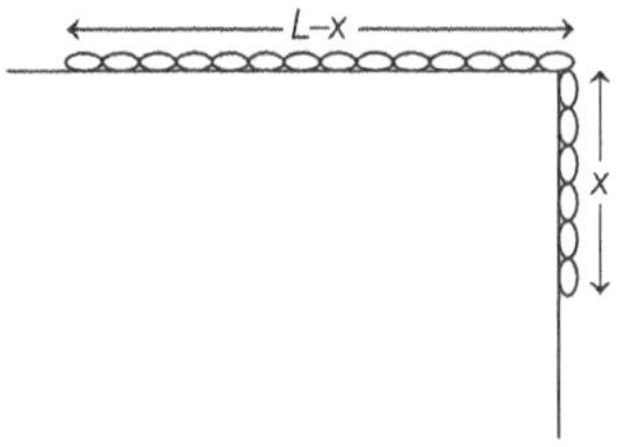

$$f_K = \mu N_1 = \mu\left(\frac{M}{L}(L-x)g\right)$$

$$W = \int F dx$$

$$\Rightarrow \quad W = \int_{L/3}^{L}\frac{\mu M}{L}(L-x)g\,dx\cos 180°$$

$$W = -\frac{\mu Mg}{L}\left(Lx - \frac{x^2}{2}\right)_{L/3}^{L}$$

$$W = -\frac{\mu Mg}{L}\left[\left(L^2 - \frac{L^2}{2}\right) - \left(\frac{L^2}{3} - \frac{L^2}{18}\right)\right] \Rightarrow W = -\frac{2\mu MgL}{9}$$

11.

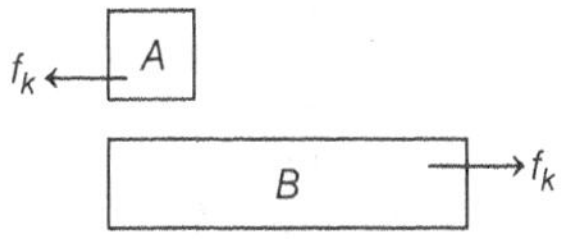

$$f_k = \mu_k N = \mu_k mg = 0.1\times 2\times 10 = 2\,\text{N}$$

For A, $\Sigma F = ma \Rightarrow -2 = 2a_A \Rightarrow a_A = -1\,\text{m/s}^2$

For B,

$$\Sigma F = ma \Rightarrow 2 = 8a_B \Rightarrow a_B = 0.25\,\text{m/s}^2$$

$$v_A = u + at = 10 - t \Rightarrow v_B = u + at = 0.25t$$

$$v_A = v_B \Rightarrow 10 - t = 0.25t \Rightarrow t = 8\,\text{s}$$

(a) At $t = 8$

$$v_A = 10 - 8 = 2\,\text{m/s}, \quad v_B = 0.25\times 8 = 2\,\text{m/s}$$

(b) $s_A = ut + \frac{1}{2}at^2 = 10(8) + \frac{1}{2}(-1)(8)^2 = 48$ m

$$W_1 = Fs\cos\theta = 2(48)\cos 180° = -96\,\text{J}$$

(c) $s_B = ut + \frac{1}{2}at^2 = \frac{1}{2}(0.25)(8)^2 = 8$ m

$$W_2 = Fs\cos\theta = 2(8)\cos 0° = 16\,\text{J}$$

(d) $W = W_1 + W_2 = -96 + 16 = -80$ J

12.

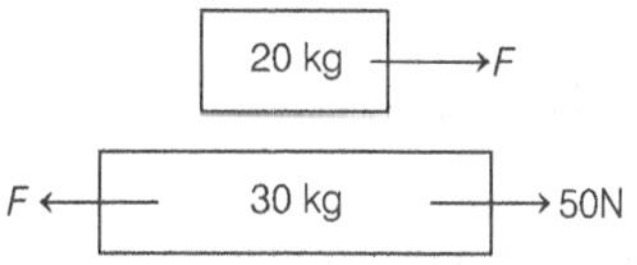

Taking both blocks as a system,

$$\Sigma F = ma \Rightarrow 50 = 50a \Rightarrow a = 1\,\text{m/s}^2$$

For 20 kg block,

$$\Sigma F = ma \Rightarrow f = 20(1) = 20\,\text{N}$$

$$f_L = \mu_s N = 0.5(200) = 100\,\text{N}$$

Since $f < f_L$, our assumption is correct. Friction between the blocks is 20 N (static).

$$s = ut + \frac{1}{2}at^2 = 0 + \frac{1}{2}(1)(2)^2 = 2\,\text{m}$$

(a) Work done by friction on upper block

$$= 20(2)\cos 0° = 40\,\text{J}$$

(b) Work done by friction on lower block

$$= 20(2)\cos 180° = -40\,\text{J}$$

(c) Mechanical energy

13. $W_{\text{all forces}} = \Delta K \Rightarrow W_{mg} = K_2 - K_1$

$$\Rightarrow +mg(55) = \frac{1}{2}mv^2 - \frac{1}{2}m(50)^2$$

$$v = \sqrt{2500 + 1100} \Rightarrow v = 60\,\text{m/s}$$

14. $W_{\text{all forces}} = \Delta K \Rightarrow W_{mg} + W_{air} = \Delta K$

$$\Rightarrow +mgh + W_{air} = \frac{1}{2}m(\sqrt{gh})^2 - 0 \Rightarrow W_{air} = -\frac{mgh}{2}$$

15. $W = \Delta K \Rightarrow W_{mg} + W_N = \Delta K$

$$\Rightarrow +mg(1.8) + 0 = \frac{1}{2}mv^2 - 0 \Rightarrow v = 6\,\text{m/s}$$

16.

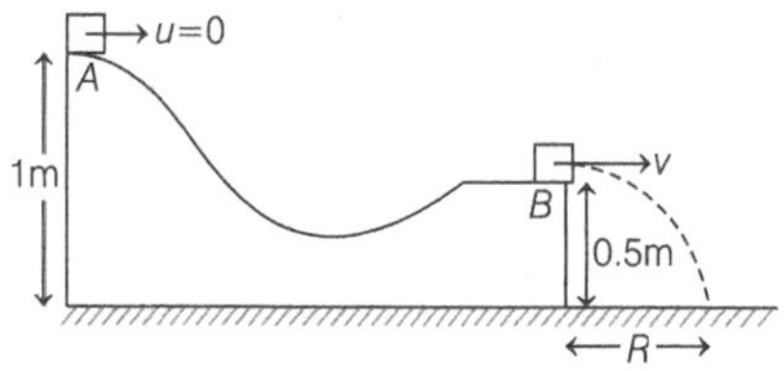

From A to B,

$$W = \Delta K \Rightarrow W_{mg} + W_N = \Delta K$$

$$\Rightarrow + mg\,(0.5) + 0 = \frac{1}{2}mv^2 - 0 \quad \Rightarrow v = \sqrt{10}\text{ m/s}$$

$$T = \sqrt{\frac{2h}{g}} = \sqrt{\frac{2(0.5)}{10}} = \frac{1}{\sqrt{10}}\text{ s}$$

$$R = vT = \sqrt{10}\left(\frac{1}{\sqrt{10}}\right) = 1\text{ m}$$

17.

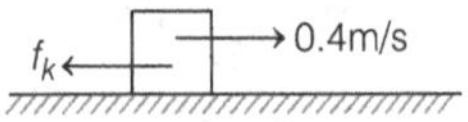

$$W = \Delta K \quad \Rightarrow \quad W = \frac{1}{2}\times\frac{1}{4}(0)^2 - \frac{1}{2}\times\frac{1}{4}\times(0.4)^2$$

$\Rightarrow \quad W = -0.02$ J,

$W = (\mu mg)(S)\cos 180° = -0.02$

$\Rightarrow \quad s = 0.08 = 8$ cm

18. (a) While climbing the ladder $W_N = 0$

(b) While sliding down,

$$W_{\text{friction}} = \left(\frac{3}{10}mg\right)(10)\cos 180° = -600\text{ J}$$

(c) While climbing the ladder

$$W_{mg} + W_N + W_{\text{internal forces}} = \Delta K$$

$$\Rightarrow \quad -200\times 8 + 0 + W_{\text{internal forces}} = 0 - 0$$

$$\Rightarrow \quad W_{\text{internal forces}} = 1600\text{ J}$$

19. $W_{mg} + W_{\text{tube}} = \Delta K$

$$\Rightarrow \quad + mg\,(0.2) + W_{\text{tube}} = \frac{1}{2}\times 0.2\times 0^2 - \frac{1}{2}\times 0.2\times 4^2$$

$$W_{\text{tube}} = -2\text{ J}$$

20.

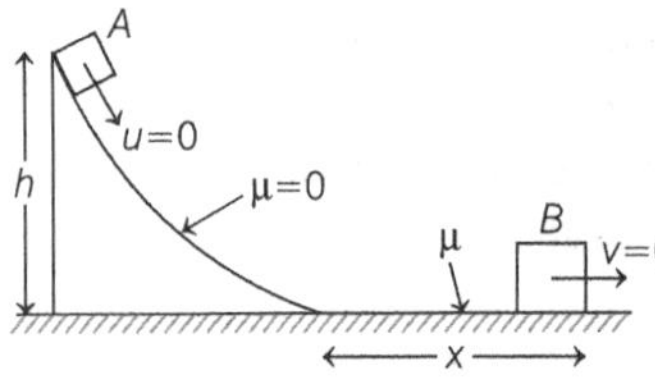

From A to B,

$$W_{mg} + W_N + W_{\text{friction}} = \Delta K$$

$$\Rightarrow \quad + mgh + 0 - (\mu mg)x = 0 - 0 \quad \Rightarrow x = \frac{h}{\mu}$$

12.4 Work Done by Tension

1. $W_{mg} + W_T = \Delta K \quad \Rightarrow \quad + mgl + 0 = \frac{1}{2}mv^2 - 0 \quad \Rightarrow v = \sqrt{2gl}$

2.

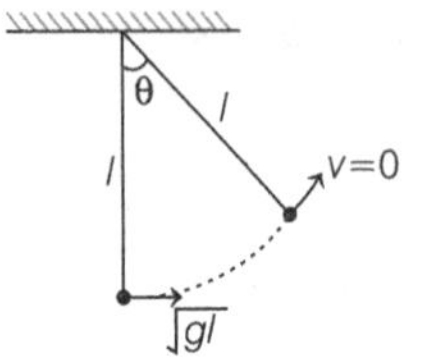

$$W_{mg} + W_T = \Delta K$$

$$\Rightarrow - mgl\,(1 - \cos\theta) + 0 = 0 - \frac{1}{2}m(\sqrt{gl})^2$$

$$\Rightarrow \quad \cos\theta = \frac{1}{2} \quad \Rightarrow \quad \theta = 60°$$

3. $W = \Delta K \quad \Rightarrow \quad W_{mg} + W_T = \Delta T$

$$\Rightarrow (m_2gx - m_1gx) + 0 = \left(\frac{1}{2}m_2v^2 + \frac{1}{2}m_1v^2\right) - (0+0)$$

$$\Rightarrow \quad v = \sqrt{\frac{2(m_2 - m_1)gx}{m_1 + m_2}}$$

4. $W = \Delta K \quad \Rightarrow \quad W_{mg} + W_T + W_F = \Delta K$

$$\Rightarrow \quad - mgL\,(1 - \cos\theta) + 0 + W_F = 0 - 0$$

$$\Rightarrow \quad W_F = mgL(1 - \cos\theta)$$

5. $W_{mg} + W_T + W_N + W_{\text{friction}} = \Delta K$

$$\Rightarrow \quad (m_2gL + 0) + 0 + 0 - \mu m_1gL$$

$$= \left(\frac{1}{2}m_1v^2 + \frac{1}{2}m_2v^2\right) - (0+0)$$

$$v = \sqrt{\frac{2(m_2 - \mu m_1)gL}{m_1 + m_2}}$$

6. $W_{mg} + W_T + W_N + W_{\text{friction}} = \Delta K$

$$\Rightarrow \quad (1\times 10\times 1 + 0) + 0 + 0 + (-\mu\,(40)\times 2)$$

$$= \left(\frac{1}{2}\times 1\times(0.8)^2 + \frac{1}{2}\times 4\times(1.6)^2\right) - (0+0)$$

$$\Rightarrow \quad 10 - 80\mu = 5.44 \quad \Rightarrow \quad \mu = 0.057$$

12.5 Work Done by Spring

1. $W = \Delta K \quad \Rightarrow W_{mg} + W_N + W_{\text{spring}} = \Delta K$

$$\Rightarrow \quad 0 + 0 + \frac{1}{2}k(0^2 - x_{\max}^2) = 0 - \frac{1}{2}mv^2 \quad \Rightarrow \quad x_{\max} = \left(\sqrt{\frac{m}{k}}\right)v$$

Magnitude of velocity will be same but direction will get reversed.

2. (a) $W = \Delta K \quad \Rightarrow W_{mg} + W_N + W_{\text{spring}} + W_{\text{friction}} = \Delta K$

$$\Rightarrow \quad 0 + 0 + \frac{1}{2}k(0^2 - L^2) - \mu mg(2L) = 0 - \frac{1}{2}mv_0^2$$

$$\Rightarrow \quad v_0 = \sqrt{\frac{kL^2}{m} + 4\mu gL}$$

(b) $W = \Delta K \quad \Rightarrow W_{mg} + W_N + W_{\text{spring}} + W_{\text{friction}} = \Delta K$

$$\Rightarrow \quad 0 + 0 + 0 - \mu mg(3L) = \frac{1}{2}mv^2 - \frac{1}{2}mv_0^2$$

$$\Rightarrow \quad v = \sqrt{v_0^2 - 6\mu gl}$$

3. First, we find the speed with which it leaves the spring.

$$W_{mg} + W_N + W_{\text{spring}} = \Delta K$$

$$\Rightarrow \quad 0 + 0 + \frac{1}{2}\times 500\left(\left(\frac{5}{100}\right)^2 - 0^2\right) = \frac{1}{2}\times\frac{1}{2}\times v^2 - 0$$

$$\Rightarrow \quad v = \sqrt{2.5}\text{ m/s}$$

$$R = uT = u\sqrt{\frac{2H}{g}}$$

$$\Rightarrow \quad R = (\sqrt{2.5})\sqrt{\frac{2(4)}{10}} = \sqrt{2}\text{m} = 1.414\text{ m}$$

4. $W_{mg} + W_{\text{spring}} = \Delta K$

$$+ mg\,(0.2 + 0.01) + \frac{1}{2}k\,[0^2 - (0.01)^2] = 0 - 0 \qquad \text{...(i)}$$

$$+mg(h+0.04)+\frac{1}{2}k[0^2-(0.04)^2]=0-0 \quad \text{...(ii)}$$

Solving Eqs. (i) and (ii), we get

$$h=3.32\,\text{m}$$

5.

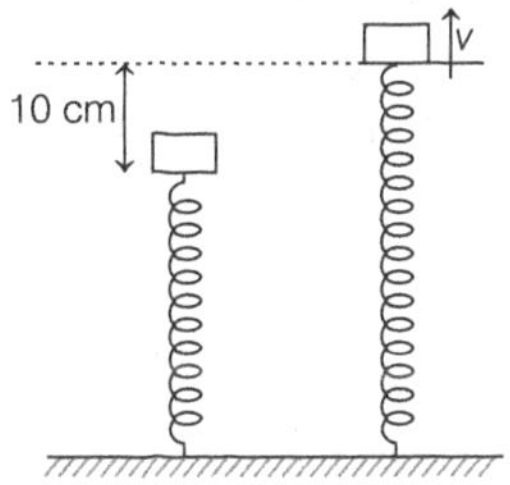

When spring acquires natural length, block will lose contact with the spring.

$$W_{mg}+W_{spring}=\Delta K$$

$$\Rightarrow\ -0.25\times10\times0.1+\frac{1}{2}\times100[(0.1)^2-0^2]=\frac{1}{2}\times0.25v^2-0$$

$$\Rightarrow\ v=\sqrt{2}\,\text{m/s}$$

$$H_{max}=10+\frac{v^2}{2g}=10+\frac{(\sqrt{2})^2}{20}\times100=20\text{ cm}$$

6. $W_{mg}+W_{spring}=\Delta K$

$$\Rightarrow +2\times10\times x+\frac{1}{2}\times100\times(0^2-x^2)=0-\frac{1}{2}\times2\times2^2$$

$$\Rightarrow 50x^2-20x-4=0$$

$$\Rightarrow \quad x=\left(\frac{1+\sqrt{3}}{5}\right)\text{m}$$

7. $W_{mg}+W_N+W_{spring}=\Delta K$

$$\Rightarrow\ 0+0+\frac{1}{2}\times k\left(\left(\frac{h}{\cos37^\circ}-h\right)^2-0^2\right)=\frac{1}{2}mv^2-0$$

$$\Rightarrow \quad v=\sqrt{\frac{kh^2}{16m}}$$

8. $W_{mg}+W_N+W_{spring}=\Delta K$

$$\Rightarrow +mg\left(\frac{3d}{4}\right)+0+\frac{1}{2}k\left(\left(\frac{d}{\cos37^\circ}-d\right)^2-0^2\right)=\frac{1}{2}mv^2-0$$

$$\Rightarrow \quad v=\sqrt{\frac{3gd}{2}+\frac{kd^2}{16m}}$$

9. Applying work-energy theorem between initial and final position.

$$W_{mg}+W_N+W_{friction}+W_{spring}=\Delta K$$

$$\Rightarrow +mg\sin37^\circ(5-1)+0-\mu mg\cos37^\circ(5+1)+\frac{1}{2}k(0^2-0^2)=0-0$$

$$\Rightarrow \quad \mu=\frac{2}{3}\tan37^\circ=0.5$$

Applying work-energy theorem between initial position and point of maximum compression

$$W_{mg}+W_N+W_{friction}+W_{spring}=\Delta K$$

$$\Rightarrow\ +mg\sin37^\circ(5)+0-\mu mg\cos57^\circ(5)+\frac{1}{2}k[0^2-(0.2)^2]=0-0$$

$$\Rightarrow \quad k=1000\,\text{N/m}$$

10. Applying work-energy theorem for m

$$W_{mg}+W_{spring}=\Delta K$$

$$+m_1g\left(\frac{mg}{k}\right)+\frac{1}{2}k\left(0^2-\left(\frac{mg}{k}\right)^2\right)=0-0 \Rightarrow m_1=\frac{m}{2}$$

12.6 Work Done by Pseudo Force

1. (a) For block $\Sigma F=ma \Rightarrow 100=10a \Rightarrow a=10\,\text{m/s}^2$

$$s=ut+\frac{1}{2}at^2=0+\frac{1}{2}(10)(10)^2=500\,\text{m}$$

Work done by F w.r.t. observer $A=100\times500=50000$ J

Work done by F w.r.t. observer B

$$=100(500-10\times10)=40000\text{ J}$$

Work done by F w.r.t. observer $C=100(500-250)=25000$ J

(b) $W_F+W_{pseudo\ force}=100\times250-50\times250=12500$ J

$$\Delta K=K_2-K_1=\frac{1}{2}\times10\times50^2-0=12500\text{ J}$$

So, $W_F+W_{pseudo\ force}=\Delta K$

2. $W_{all\ forces}=\Delta K$

$$W_{mg}+W_T+W_{pseudo}=\Delta K$$

$$\Rightarrow -mgl(1-\cos\theta)+0+ma(l\sin\theta)=0-0$$

$$\Rightarrow \quad \frac{1-\cos\theta}{\sin\theta}=\frac{a}{g} \Rightarrow \tan\left(\frac{\theta}{2}\right)=\frac{a}{g}$$

$$\Rightarrow \quad \theta_{max}=2\tan^{-1}\left(\frac{a}{g}\right)$$

12.7 Conservative and Non-Conservative Forces and Potential Energy

1. (a) $W_{OAB}=W_{OA}+W_{OB}=\int_0^2 x\,dx+\int_0^2 y\,dy=4$ J

$$W_{OBC}=W_{OB}+W_{BC}=\int_0^2 y\,dy+\int_0^2 x\,dx=4\text{ J}$$

$$W_{OC}=\int(x\hat{i}+y\hat{j})\cdot(dx\,\hat{i}+dy\,\hat{j})=\int_0^2 x\,dx+\int_0^2 y\,dy=4\text{ J}$$

(b) As work done by force can be found without having to know the path, force is conservative.

2. (a) $\mathbf{F}=x\hat{i}+xy\hat{j}$

$$W_{OAB}=W_{OA}+W_{AB}=\int_0^2 x\,dx+\int_0^2 2y\,dy=6\text{ J}$$

$$W_{OBC}=W_{OB}+W_{BC}=0+\int_0^2 x\,dx=2\text{ J}$$

$$W_{OC}=\int(x\hat{i}+xy\hat{j})\cdot(dx\,\hat{i}+dy\hat{j})=\int_0^2 x\,dx+\int_0^2 xy\,dy$$

$$=\int_0^2 x\,dx+\int_0^2 y^2\,dy \qquad (\because y=x)$$

$$=2+\frac{8}{3}=\frac{14}{3}\text{ J}$$

(b) Force is non-conservative as work done by force between initial and final states cannot be found without knowing the path taken.

3. $\mathbf{F} = y\hat{\mathbf{i}} + x\hat{\mathbf{j}}$

$$W_{OAB} = W_{OA} + W_{AB} = 0 + \int_0^3 2\,dy = 6\text{ J}$$

$$W_{OBC} = W_{OB} + W_{BC} = 0 + \int_0^2 3dx = 6\text{ J}$$

$$W_{OC} = \int (y\hat{\mathbf{i}} + x\hat{\mathbf{j}}) \cdot (dx\,\hat{\mathbf{i}} + dy\hat{\mathbf{j}}) = \int (y\,dx + x\,dy)$$

$$= \int_{(0,\,0)}^{(2,\,3)} d\,(xy) = [xy]_{(0,\,0)}^{(2,\,3)} = 6\text{ J}$$

(b) $\mathbf{F} = y\hat{\mathbf{i}} + x\hat{\mathbf{j}}$ is conservative as work done depends only on initial and final positions.

4. (a) $U = -(x^2 + y^2 + z^2) \Rightarrow \mathbf{F} = 2x\hat{\mathbf{i}} + 2y\hat{\mathbf{j}} + 2z\hat{\mathbf{k}}$

(b) $U = -xy \Rightarrow \mathbf{F} = y\hat{\mathbf{i}} + x\hat{\mathbf{j}}$

(c) $U = x^2y - x^3y^2z$

$$\mathbf{F} = -(2xy - 3x^2y^2z)\,\hat{\mathbf{i}} - (x^2 - 2x^3yz)\,\hat{\mathbf{j}} + x^3y^2\hat{\mathbf{k}}$$

(d) $U = U_0 \sin(ax + by)$

$$\mathbf{F} = -aU_0 \cos(ax + by)\,\hat{\mathbf{i}} - bU_0 \cos(ax + by)\,\hat{\mathbf{j}}$$

5. $U = (2x^2 + 3y^3 + 2z) \Rightarrow \mathbf{F} = -4x\hat{\mathbf{i}} - 9y^2\hat{\mathbf{j}} - 2\hat{\mathbf{k}}$

At (1, 2, 3)

$$\mathbf{F} = -4\hat{\mathbf{i}} - 36\hat{\mathbf{j}} - 2\hat{\mathbf{k}}$$

6. (a) $dU = -dW$

$$dU = -\mathbf{F}\cdot d\mathbf{s} = -(2\hat{\mathbf{i}} + 3\hat{\mathbf{j}}) \cdot (dx\,\hat{\mathbf{i}} + dy\,\hat{\mathbf{j}})$$

$$\int_0^U dU = -2\int_0^x dx - 3\int_0^y dy \Rightarrow U = -2x - 3y$$

(b) $dU = -2x\,dx - 2y\,dy$

$$\int_0^U dU = -\int_0^x 2x\,dx - \int_0^y 2y\,dy \Rightarrow U = -x^2 - y^2$$

(c) $\int dU = -\int (y\,dx + x\,dy) \Rightarrow \int_0^U dU = -\int_{(0,\,0)}^{(x,\,y)} d\,(xy)$

$$\Rightarrow \quad U = -xy$$

(d) $dU = -dW$

$$dU = -\mathbf{F}\cdot d\mathbf{s} = -(-3x^2y\hat{\mathbf{i}} - x^3\hat{\mathbf{j}}) \cdot (dx\,\hat{\mathbf{i}} + dy\,\hat{\mathbf{j}})$$

$$dU = 3x^2y\,dx + x^3\,dy \Rightarrow \int_0^U dU = \int_{(0,\,0)}^{(x,\,y)} d\,(x^3y)$$

$$\Rightarrow \quad U = x^3y$$

7. (a) $F = x(3x - 2) = 0 \Rightarrow x = 0$ and $x = \frac{2}{3}$

(b)

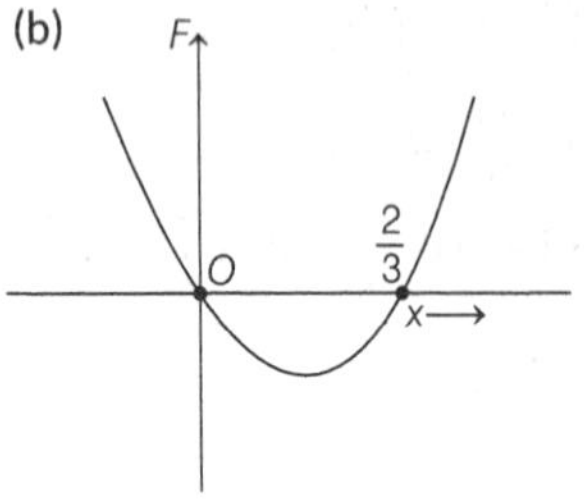

At $x = 0$, the particle is in stable equilibrium and at $x = \frac{2}{3}$, unstable equilibrium.

(c) Between $x = 0$ and $x = \frac{2}{3}$, force is directed towards negative X-axis. So, we just need to make particle reach $x = \frac{2}{3}$, after which it will go by itself.

$$W = \Delta K \Rightarrow \int_4^{2/3} (3x^2 - 2x)\,dx = 0 - \frac{1}{2} \times 1 \times u^2$$

$$\Rightarrow \quad [x^3 - x^2]_4^{2/3} = -\frac{u^2}{2}$$

$$\Rightarrow \left(\frac{8}{27} - \frac{4}{9}\right) - (64 - 16) = \frac{-u^2}{2} \Rightarrow u = \sqrt{\frac{2600}{27}}\text{ m/s}$$

8. $U = \frac{x^3}{3} - 4x + 6 \Rightarrow \frac{dU}{dx} = x^2 - 4$ and $\frac{d^2U}{dx^2} = 2x$

$$F = -\frac{dU}{dx} = -(x^2 - 4) = 0 \Rightarrow x = 2 \text{ and } x = -2$$

At $x = 2$, $\frac{d^2U}{dx^2} > 0$, so $x = 2$ is stable equilibrium.

At $x = -2$, $\frac{d^2U}{dx^2} < 0$, so $x = -2$ is unstable equilibrium.

9. If particle is displaced slightly on either side of A, it will move away from A. So, A is unstable equilibrium. C is stable equilibrium and E is unstable equilibrium.

10. $U = 6x - 8y \Rightarrow \mathbf{F} = -6\hat{\mathbf{i}} + 8\hat{\mathbf{j}} \Rightarrow \mathbf{a} = -3\hat{\mathbf{i}} + 4\hat{\mathbf{j}}$

$$\mathbf{s} = \mathbf{u}t + \frac{1}{2}\mathbf{a}t^2 = (-1.5\hat{\mathbf{i}} + 2\hat{\mathbf{j}})(2) + \frac{1}{2}(-3\hat{\mathbf{i}} + 4\hat{\mathbf{j}})(2)^2$$

$$= -9\hat{\mathbf{i}} + 12\hat{\mathbf{j}}$$

$$|\mathbf{s}| = \sqrt{9^2 + 12^2} = 15\text{ m}$$

11. Loss in kinetic energy $= \frac{1}{2} \times 5 \times 6^2 = 90$ J

Gain in potential energy $= 5 \times 9.8 \times \frac{1}{2} \times 2 = 49$ J

$$\Delta E = \Delta K + \Delta U = -90 + 49 = -41\text{ J}$$

So, loss in mechanical energy = 41 J

12. $\frac{90}{100} mgh = \frac{1}{2} mv^2 \Rightarrow v = \sqrt{1.8gh} = \sqrt{1.8 \times 10 \times 2} = 6$ m/s

13.

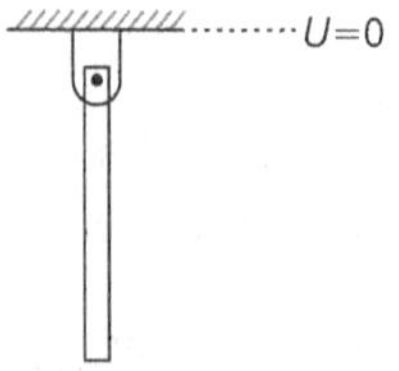

$$U_1 = -mg\left(\frac{L}{2}\right)$$

$$\Rightarrow \quad U_2 = -mg\left(\frac{L}{2}\cos 60°\right)$$

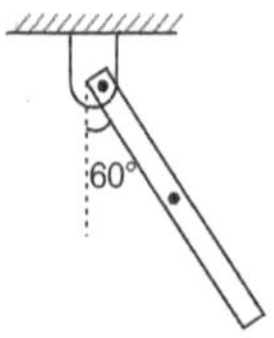

$$W_{ext} = \Delta U + \Delta K$$

$$W_{ext} = (U_2 - U_1) + 0$$

$$= \frac{mgL}{4} = \frac{0.5 \times 10 \times 1}{4} = 1.25\text{ J}$$

14.

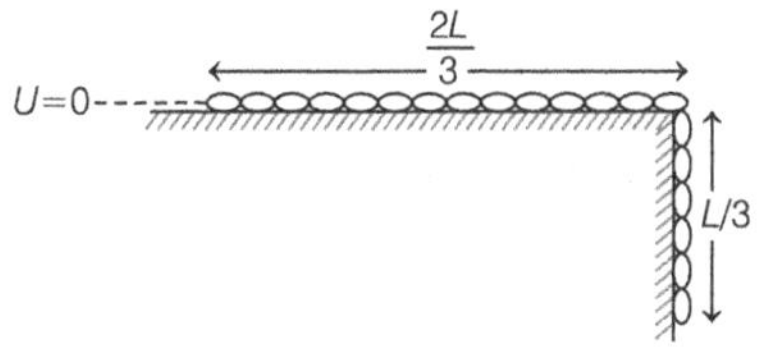

$$U_1 = -\left(\frac{M}{3}\right)g\left(\frac{L}{6}\right) \Rightarrow U_2 = 0$$

$$W_{ext} = \Delta U + \Delta K = \left(0 - \left(-\frac{MgL}{18}\right)\right) + 0 = \frac{MgL}{18}$$

12.8 Power

1. $P = \frac{W}{t} = \frac{\mathbf{F}\cdot\mathbf{s}}{t} = \frac{(3\hat{i}+4\hat{j})\cdot(8\hat{i}+6\hat{j})}{6} = \frac{48}{6} = 8\text{ W}$

2. $P = \mathbf{F}\cdot\mathbf{v} = (10\hat{i}+10\hat{j}+20\hat{k})\cdot(5\hat{i}-3\hat{j}+6\hat{k}) = 50 - 30 + 120$
   $= 140\text{ W}$

3. $v = u + at \Rightarrow v = 0 + at = at$
   (a) $P_{gravity} = (mg)\, v\cos 90° = 0$
   (b) $P_{normal\ force} = Fv\cos\theta = Nv\cos 90° = 0$
   (c) $P_{friction} = Fv\cos\theta = (\mu mg)(at)\cos 180° = -\mu mgat$
   (d) $P_{external\ agent} = Fv\cos\theta = (\mu mg + ma)\, at\cos 0°$
   $= (\mu g + a)\, mat$

4. $\Sigma F_x = ma_x \Rightarrow F - mg\sin\theta = ma$
   $\Rightarrow \quad F - 2\times 9.8\times\frac{1}{2} = 2\times 1 \Rightarrow F = 11.8\text{ N}$
   $P = \mathbf{F}\cdot\mathbf{v} = Fv\cos\theta = 11.8\times 4\times\cos 0° = 47.2\text{ W}$

5. (a) Average power of gravity $= \frac{W_{gravity}}{t}$
   $$= \frac{-mg\left(u\sin\theta\, t - \frac{1}{2}gt^2\right)}{t} = -mg\left(u\sin\theta - \frac{1}{2}gt\right)$$
   (b) $P = \mathbf{F}\cdot\mathbf{v} = (-mg\hat{j})\cdot(u\cos\theta\,\hat{i} + (u\sin\theta - gt)\hat{j})$
   $= -mg\,(u\sin\theta - gt)$
   (c) $P_{avg} = -mg\left(u\sin\theta - \frac{1}{2}gt\right) = 0 \Rightarrow t = \frac{2u\sin\theta}{g}$
   (d) $P_{insta} = -mg\,(u\sin\theta - gt) = 0 \Rightarrow t = \frac{u\sin\theta}{g}$
   (e) $P_{insta} = -mg\,(u\sin\theta - gt) < 0 \Rightarrow t < \frac{u\sin\theta}{g}$
   $P_{insta} = -mg\,(u\sin\theta - gt) > 0 \Rightarrow t > \frac{u\sin\theta}{g}$

6. Average power $= \frac{W}{t} = \frac{\Delta K}{t} = \frac{\frac{1}{2}\times 1000\times 15^2 - 0}{5} = 22.5\text{ kW}$

7. $P = \frac{dW_{ext}}{dt}$
   $$P = \frac{dU + dK}{dt} = \frac{dU}{dt} = \frac{d}{dt}(mgh) = \frac{dm}{dt}gh = \frac{30}{60}\times 9.8\times 10$$
   $= 49\text{ W} = \frac{49}{746}\text{ HP} = 6.6\times 10^{-2}\text{ HP}$

8. $P = \frac{dK}{dt} = 3t^2 - 2t + 1 \Rightarrow \int_0^K dK = \int_2^4 (3t^2 - 2t + 1)\,dt$
   $\Rightarrow K = (64 - 16 + 4) - (8 - 4 + 2) \Rightarrow K = 46\text{ J}$

9. (a) $P = Fv\cos 0°$
   $\Rightarrow \quad P = mav \Rightarrow P = m\frac{dv}{dt}v$
   $$\int_0^v v\,dv = \frac{P}{m}\int_0^t dt \Rightarrow v = \left(\frac{2Pt}{m}\right)^{1/2}$$
   (b) $a = \frac{dv}{dt} = \frac{1}{2}\left(\frac{2Pt}{m}\right)^{-1/2}\left(\frac{2P}{m}\right) = \left(\frac{P}{2m}\right)^{1/2} t^{-1/2}$
   (c) $v = \frac{ds}{dt} = \left(\frac{2P}{m}\right)^{1/2} t^{1/2} \Rightarrow \int_0^s ds = \left(\frac{2P}{m}\right)^{1/2}\int_0^t t^{1/2}dt$
   $$\Rightarrow s = \left(\frac{2P}{m}\right)^{1/2}\frac{t^{3/2}}{\left(\frac{3}{2}\right)} \Rightarrow s = \left(\frac{8P}{9m}\right)^{1/2} t^{3/2}$$

Level 2

Single Choice Correct Questions

1.

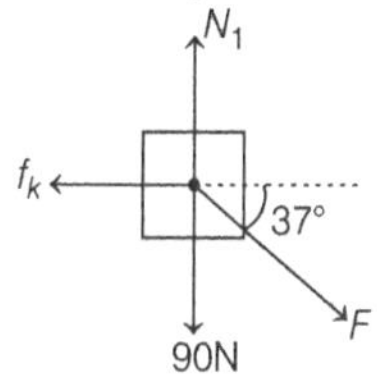

$$\Sigma F_y = 0 \Rightarrow N_1 = 90 + F\sin 37°$$
$$\Sigma F_x = 0 \Rightarrow F\cos 37° = f_k$$
$$\Rightarrow F\cos 37° = \frac{1}{3}(90 + F\sin 37°) \Rightarrow \frac{4F}{5} = 30 + \frac{F}{5}$$
$$\Rightarrow \quad F = 50\text{ N}$$
$$s = ut + \frac{1}{2}at^2 = 2(4) = 8\text{ m}$$
$$W_F = Fs\cos\theta = 50\times 8\times\cos 37° = 320\text{ J}$$

2. $W = \int F\,dx \Rightarrow W = \int_0^d (a + bx)\,dx = \left[ax + \frac{bx^2}{2}\right]_0^d = ad + \frac{bd^2}{2}$

3. $W = \Delta K \Rightarrow W = K_2 - K_1$
   $\Rightarrow \quad W = \frac{1}{2}\times 2\times 0^2 - \frac{1}{2}\times 2\times (20)^2 \Rightarrow W = -400\text{ J}$

4. $W = \mathbf{F}\cdot\mathbf{s} \Rightarrow W = Fs\cos\theta \Rightarrow W = FR$

5.

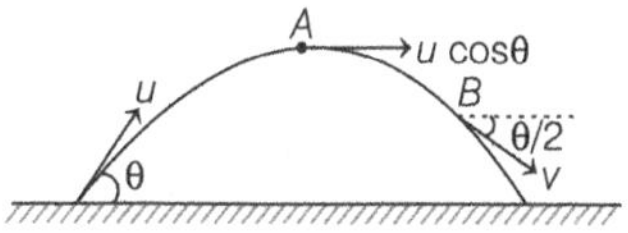

Horizontal component of velocity remains constant.

$$\Rightarrow \quad u\cos\theta = v\cos\left(\frac{\theta}{2}\right) \Rightarrow v = u\cos\theta\sec\left(\frac{\theta}{2}\right)$$

From A to B,

$$W_{mg} = \Delta K = \frac{1}{2} m \left(u\cos\theta \sec\left(\frac{\theta}{2}\right)\right)^2 - \frac{1}{2} m (u\cos\theta)^2$$

$$= \frac{1}{2} mu^2 \cos^2\theta \left(\sec^2\left(\frac{\theta}{2}\right) - 1\right)$$

$$= \frac{1}{2} mu^2 \cos^2\theta \tan^2\left(\frac{\theta}{2}\right)$$

6. $K_1 = \frac{1}{2} mv_0^2 \Rightarrow K_2 = \frac{1}{4}(K_1) = \frac{1}{4}\left(\frac{1}{2} mv_0^2\right)$

$\Rightarrow \quad \frac{1}{2} mv^2 = \frac{1}{4}\left(\frac{1}{2} mv_0^2\right) \Rightarrow v = \frac{v_0}{2}$

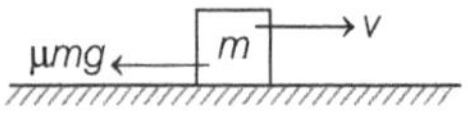

$v = u + at \Rightarrow \frac{v_0}{2} = v_0 + (-\mu g)t_0 \Rightarrow \mu = \frac{v_0}{2gt_0}$

7. $v = a\sqrt{s} \Rightarrow \frac{ds}{dt} = a\sqrt{s} \Rightarrow \int_0^s \frac{ds}{\sqrt{s}} = a\int_0^t dt \Rightarrow 2\sqrt{s} = at$

$\Rightarrow \quad s = \frac{1}{4} a^2t^2$

$$W = \Delta K = \frac{1}{2} m (a\sqrt{s})^2 - \frac{1}{2} m(0)^2$$

$$= \frac{1}{2} ma^2 s - 0 = \frac{1}{2} ma^2 \left(\frac{1}{4} a^2t^2\right) = \frac{1}{8} ma^4t^2$$

8. Applying work-energy theorem,

$$W_{mg} + W_N + W_{friction} + W_{spring} = \Delta K$$

$\Rightarrow \; 0 + 0 - (\mu mg)x + \frac{1}{2} K(0^2 - x^2) = 0 - \frac{1}{2} mu^2$

$\Rightarrow \quad -50x - 50x^2 = -\frac{1}{2} \times 50 \times 2^2$

$\Rightarrow \quad x^2 + x - 2 = 0 \Rightarrow \Rightarrow x = 1\,m$

9. From A to B, applying work-energy theorem,

$$W_{mg} + W_N = \Delta K$$

$\Rightarrow \; -mg(R-h) + 0 = 0 - \frac{1}{2} mu^2 \Rightarrow u = \sqrt{2g(R-h)}$

10. $U = 2x + 5y - xy$

$\mathbf{F} = \left(-\frac{\partial U}{\partial x}\right)\hat{i} + \left(-\frac{\partial U}{\partial y}\right)\hat{j} \Rightarrow \mathbf{F} = (-2+y)\,\hat{i} + (-5+x)\,\hat{j}$

At $(2, -2)$

$\mathbf{F} = -4\hat{i} - 3\hat{j} \Rightarrow \mathbf{a} = -4\hat{i} - 3\hat{j} \Rightarrow a = 5\,m/s^2$

11. $U = 2 + 20x - 5x^2$

At $x = 3$; $U = 2 + 20(-3) - 5(-3)^2 = -103$ J

$K = 0 \Rightarrow E = U + K = -103$ J

For maximum value of x, $v = 0$

$\Rightarrow \quad K = 0, \quad U = -103$ J

$2 + 20x - 5x^2 = -103$

$\Rightarrow \; 5x^2 - 20x - 105 = 0 \Rightarrow x^2 - 4x - 21 = 0$

$\Rightarrow \quad (x+3)(x-7) = 0 \Rightarrow x = -3$ and $x = 7$

12. $F \propto \frac{1}{s}$

$W = \int F\,ds \propto \int \frac{1}{s}\,ds \Rightarrow W \propto \ln s$

13. $U_1 = 0, \quad U_2 = Mgh + mg\left(\frac{h}{2}\right)$

$W_{ext} = \Delta U + \Delta K \Rightarrow W_{ext} = Mgh + mg\left(\frac{h}{2}\right)$

14.

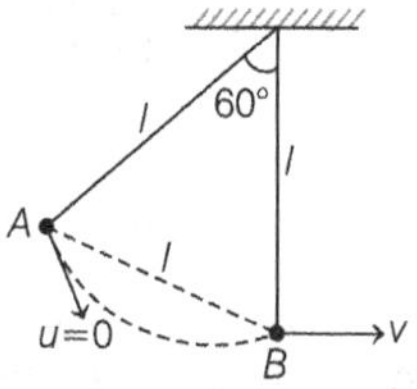

Applying work-energy theorem from A to B,

$$W_{mg} + W_T = \Delta K$$

$\Rightarrow \; +mgl(1 - \cos 60°) + 0 = \frac{1}{2} mv^2 \Rightarrow v = \sqrt{gl}$

15. Applying work-energy theorem between initial and final positions,

$$W_{mg} + W_N + W_{friction} = \Delta K$$

$\Rightarrow \; -mgh + 0 - \mu mg(d) = 0 - \frac{1}{2} mu^2 \Rightarrow d = \frac{7}{6}\,m = 1.17\,m$

16. Kinetic energy will be maximum at the lowest point.

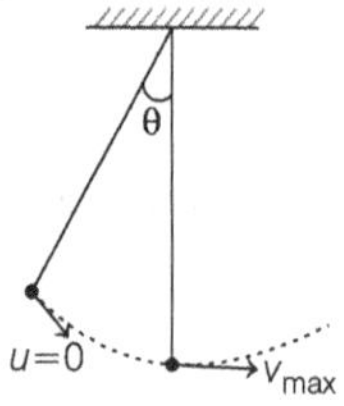

$$W_{mg} + W_T = \Delta K$$

$\Rightarrow \quad +mgl(1 - \cos\theta) + 0 = K_{max} - 0$

$$K_{max} = mgl(1 - \cos\theta)$$

17. $F = -\frac{k}{x^2}$

$W = \int_a^x F\,dx = \int_a^x \frac{-k}{x^2}\,dx = k\left(\frac{1}{x} - \frac{1}{a}\right)$

From work-energy theorem,

$W = \Delta K \Rightarrow k\left(\frac{1}{x} - \frac{1}{a}\right) = \frac{1}{2} mv^2$

$\Rightarrow \quad v = \sqrt{\frac{2k}{m}}\left(\frac{a-x}{ax}\right)^{1/2}$

18. $U_1 = -\frac{M}{2} g\left(\frac{L}{4}\right), \quad U_2 = 0$

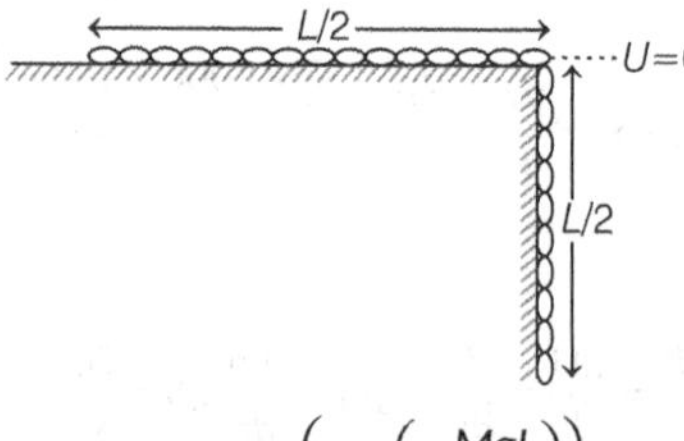

$$W_{ext} = \Delta U + \Delta K = \left(0 - \left(-\frac{MgL}{8}\right)\right) + 0 = \frac{MgL}{8}$$

19. $F = ma \Rightarrow a = \frac{F}{m} = \text{constant}$

$v = u + at \Rightarrow v = at$

$P = Fv = F(at) \Rightarrow P \propto t$

$K = \frac{1}{2}m(at)^2 \Rightarrow K \propto t^2$

and $K \propto s$ as $s \propto t^2$

20. $K_1 + U_1 = K_2 + U_2 \Rightarrow 0 + 6 = \frac{1}{2} \times 2 \times v^2 + 2 \Rightarrow v = 2\,\text{m/s}$

21. For 2 kg block

$$\Sigma F_y = 0$$

$\Rightarrow \quad Kx + N_1 = 20$

When 2 kg leaves contact ($N_1 = 0$) $\Rightarrow Kx = 20 \Rightarrow x = 0.5\,\text{m}$

Applying work-energy theorem for 5 kg block

$$W_{mg} + W_{spring} = \Delta K$$

$\Rightarrow \; +5 \times 10 \times 0.5 + \frac{1}{2} \times 40 \times (0^2 - (0.5)^2) = \frac{1}{2} \times 5 \times v^2 - 0$

$\Rightarrow \quad v = 2\sqrt{2}\,\text{m/s}$

22. Applying work-energy theorem for (2 kg + 1 kg) system

$$W_{mg} + W_T = \Delta K_{system}$$

$\Rightarrow (+2 \times 10 \times 0.6 - 1 \times 10 \times 0.6) + 0$

$= \left(\frac{1}{2} \times 2 \times v^2 + \frac{1}{2} \times 1 \times v^2\right) - (0 + 0)$

$\Rightarrow \quad v = 2\,\text{m/s}$

23. $W_{mg} + W_N + W_{friction} = \Delta K$

$\Rightarrow + mg\sin\phi \times l + 0 - \mu mg\cos\phi \times \frac{2l}{3} = 0 - 0$

$\Rightarrow \quad \mu = \frac{3}{2}\tan\phi$

24. $W_{mg} + W_N + W_{fricition} = \Delta K$

$\Rightarrow +1 \times 10 \times 1 + 0 + W_{friction} = \frac{1}{2} \times 1 \times 2^2 - 0$

$\Rightarrow \quad W_{friction} = -8\,\text{J}$

25. $v = u + at \Rightarrow v = 0 + at \Rightarrow a = \frac{v}{T}$

$P = Fv = mav = ma(at) = ma^2t = \frac{mv^2}{T^2}t$

26. Between initial and final positions

$W_{mg} + W_{air} = \Delta K \Rightarrow 0 + W_{air} = \frac{1}{2}m(8)^2 - \frac{1}{2}m(16)^2$

Between initial position and maximum height position

$$W_{mg} + W_{air} = \Delta K$$

$\Rightarrow -mgh + \frac{1}{2}\left(\frac{1}{2}m(8)^2 - \frac{1}{2}m(16)^2\right) = 0 - \frac{1}{2}m(16)^2$

$\Rightarrow \quad h = 8\,\text{m}$

27. $U = 6x + 8y \Rightarrow \mathbf{F} = -6\hat{\mathbf{i}} - 8\hat{\mathbf{j}} \Rightarrow \mathbf{a} = -3\hat{\mathbf{i}} - 4\hat{\mathbf{j}}$

$s_x = u_x t + \frac{1}{2}a_x t^2 \Rightarrow (0 - 6) = 0 + \frac{1}{2}(-3)t^2 \Rightarrow t = 2\,\text{s}$

28. $P = Fv \Rightarrow P = Mav$

$\Rightarrow \quad P = M\left(v\frac{dv}{ds}\right)v = \int_u^v v^2\,dv = \frac{P}{M}\int_0^s ds$

$\Rightarrow \quad \left[\frac{v^3}{3}\right]_u^v = \frac{P}{M}[s]_0^s \Rightarrow v^3 - u^3 = \frac{3Ps}{M} \Rightarrow v = \left(u^3 + \frac{3Ps}{M}\right)^{1/3}$

29. $\mathbf{v} = u\cos\theta\,\hat{\mathbf{i}} + (u\sin\theta - gt)\,\hat{\mathbf{j}}, \quad \mathbf{F} = -mg\hat{\mathbf{j}}$

$P = \mathbf{F} \cdot \mathbf{v} = -mg(u\sin\theta - gt)$

30. $W_{mg} + W_{spring} = \Delta K$

$\Rightarrow +5 \times 10 \times (2 + 0.5) + \frac{1}{2} \times k(0^2 - (0.5)^2) = 0 - 0$

$\Rightarrow \quad k = 1000\,\text{N/m}$

31. $\frac{1}{2}mv^2 = \frac{1}{2}kx^2 \Rightarrow v = x\sqrt{\frac{k}{m}} = 0.05\sqrt{\frac{600}{15 \times 10^{-3}}}$

$\Rightarrow \quad v = 10\,\text{m/s}$

$R_{max} = \frac{v^2}{g} = \frac{(10)^2}{10} = 10\,\text{m}$

32. $P = \frac{3t^2}{2} \Rightarrow \frac{dK}{dt} = \frac{3t^2}{2} \Rightarrow \int_0^K dK = \int_0^t \frac{3t^2}{2}dt \Rightarrow K = \frac{t^3}{2}$

At $t = 2$, $\quad K = \frac{2^3}{2} = \frac{1}{2} \times 2 \times v^2 \Rightarrow v = 2\,\text{m/s}$

33. $U_1 = \frac{1}{2}kx^2, \quad U_2 = \frac{1}{2}K(x + y)^2$

$W_{ext} = \Delta U + \Delta K = \left(\frac{1}{2}k(x + y)^2 - \frac{1}{2}kx^2\right) + 0$

$= \frac{1}{2}ky(2x + y)$

34. Work done by gravity is negative. Work done by tension is zero as point of application of force is stationary. But there will be work done by internal forces within the man. So,

$$W_{mg} + W_T + W_{\text{internal forces}} = \Delta K$$

35. $U = -ax^2 + bx^4 \Rightarrow \frac{dU}{dx} = -2ax + 4bx^3$

$\frac{d^2U}{dx^2} = -2a + 12bx^2$

For equilibrium points,

$F = -\frac{dU}{dx} = 0 \Rightarrow -(-2ax + 4bx^3) = 0$

$\Rightarrow x = 0$ and $x = \sqrt{\frac{a}{2b}}$ and $x = -\sqrt{\frac{a}{2b}}$

At $x = 0$; $\frac{d^2U}{dx^2} < 0$

So, $x = 0$ is unstable equilibrium position.

36. $\mathbf{v} = 2\hat{\mathbf{i}} + 4t\hat{\mathbf{j}} \Rightarrow \mathbf{a} = \frac{d\mathbf{v}}{dt} = 4\hat{\mathbf{j}}$

$$P = \mathbf{F} \cdot \mathbf{v} = (m\mathbf{a}) \cdot \mathbf{v} = 2(16t)$$

At $t = 5$, $\quad P = 160\text{ W}$

37. $\Sigma F = ma \Rightarrow Mg - T = Ma$

$\Rightarrow \quad T = \frac{3Mg}{4}$

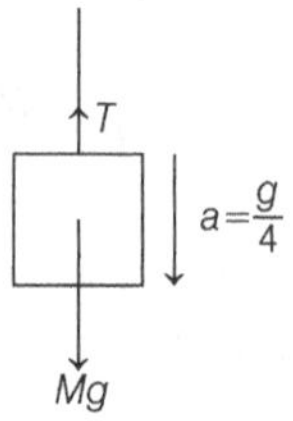

$$W_T = Td\cos 180° = -\frac{3Mgd}{4}$$

38. $dm = \frac{m}{l}(R\,d\theta) \Rightarrow dU = dm\,g\,(R\cos\theta)$

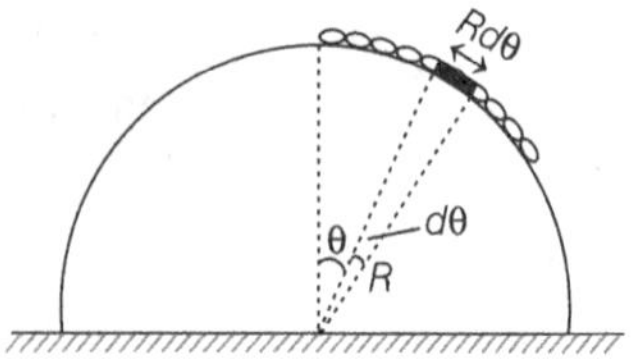

$$\int dU = \int_0^{l/R} \frac{mgR^2}{l}\cos\theta\,d\theta \Rightarrow U = \frac{mgR^2}{l}\sin\left(\frac{l}{R}\right)$$

39. Body is in stable equilibrium at $x = x_2$ as, if the body is displaced slightly on either side from $x = x_2$, it will come back to its equilibrium position.

40. $K = \frac{1}{2}mv^2 \Rightarrow \frac{dK}{dt} = \frac{1}{2}\frac{dm}{dt}v^2 \Rightarrow P = \frac{1}{2}\frac{dm}{dt}v^2$

Now, $\frac{dm'}{dt} = n\frac{dm}{dt} \Rightarrow \rho Av' = \eta\rho Av \Rightarrow v' = nv$

So, $\quad P' = \frac{1}{2}\frac{dm'}{dt}v'^2 = \frac{1}{2}n\frac{dm}{dt}(nv)^2 \Rightarrow P' = n^3P$

41. $U = \cos(x+y) \Rightarrow \mathbf{F} = \sin(x+y)\,\hat{\mathbf{i}} + \sin(x+y)\,\hat{\mathbf{j}}$

At $\left(0, \frac{\pi}{4}\right)$; $\quad \mathbf{F} = \frac{1}{\sqrt{2}}\hat{\mathbf{i}} + \frac{1}{\sqrt{2}}\hat{\mathbf{j}}$

42. $E = \frac{1}{2}mv^2 + mgh \Rightarrow m\left(\frac{v^2}{2} + gh\right) = \text{constant}$

43. $\frac{dV}{dt} = Av \Rightarrow 10^{-1} = 10^{-2}\,v \Rightarrow v = 10\text{ m/s}$

$$E = mgh + \frac{1}{2}mv^2$$

$$\Rightarrow \quad \frac{dE}{dt} = \frac{dm}{dt}gh + \frac{1}{2}\frac{dm}{dt}v^2$$

$$P = \frac{d(\rho V)}{dt}gh + \frac{1}{2}\frac{d(\rho V)}{dt}v^2$$

$$P = \frac{dV}{dt}\left(\rho gh + \frac{1}{2}\rho v^2\right)$$

$$P = 10^{-1}\left(10^3 \times 10 \times 10 + \frac{1}{2} \times 10^3 \times 10^2\right) = 15\text{ kW}$$

44. $W_{ABCDA} = W_{AB} + W_{BC} + W_{CD} + W_{DA}$

$$= \int_0^a x^2\,dx + \int_0^a y^2\,dy + \int_a^0 x^2\,dx + \int_a^0 y^2\,dy = 0$$

45.

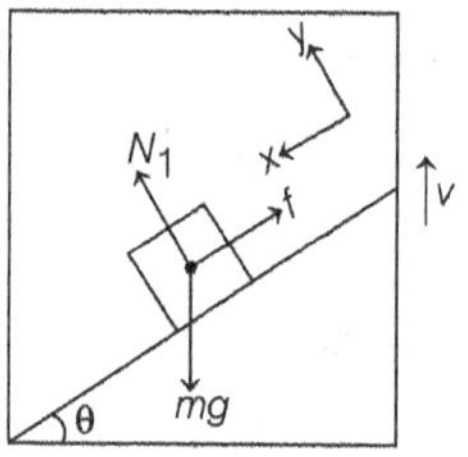

$\Sigma F_x = 0 \Rightarrow mg\sin\theta - f = 0$

$\Rightarrow \quad f = mg\sin\theta$

$$W_{\text{friction}} = fs\cos\theta = (mg\sin\theta)(vt)\cos(90 - \theta)$$

$$= mg\,vt\sin^2\theta$$

46. $W = -\int \mathbf{F} \cdot d\mathbf{s} \Rightarrow W = \int -k(y\hat{\mathbf{i}} + x\hat{\mathbf{j}}) \cdot (dx\,\hat{\mathbf{i}} + dy\,\hat{\mathbf{j}})$

$W = -k\int (y\,dx + x\,dy) \Rightarrow W = -k\int_{(0,\,0)}^{(a,\,a)} d(xy)$

$W = -k[xy]_{(0,\,0)}^{(a,\,a)} = -ka^2$

47.

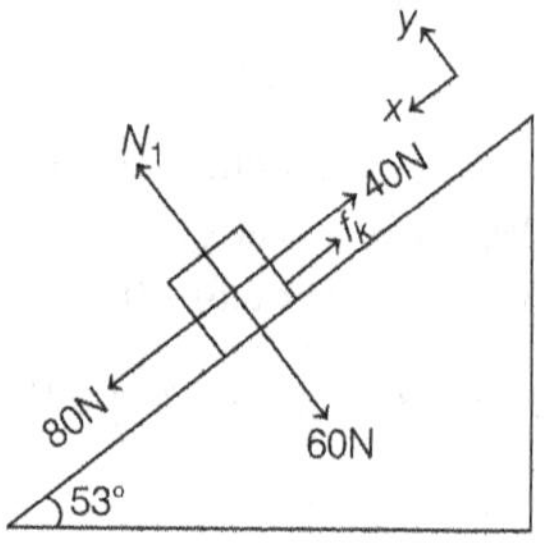

$\Sigma F_y = 0 \Rightarrow N_1 = 60\text{ N} \Rightarrow f_K = \mu N_1$

$f_K = \frac{1}{3}(60) = 20\text{ N}$

$\Sigma F_x = ma_x \Rightarrow 80 - 40 - 20 = 10a \Rightarrow a = 2\text{ m/s}^2$

$s = ut + \frac{1}{2}at^2 \Rightarrow s = 0 + \frac{1}{2}(2)(10)^2 \Rightarrow s = 100\text{ m}$

$W_F = Fs\cos\theta = 40(100)\cos(180°) = -4000\text{ J}$

48. $W = \Delta K \Rightarrow W = \frac{1}{2}m(v^2 - u^2)$

From rest to speed v,

$$W = \frac{1}{2}m(v^2 - 0^2) = \frac{1}{2}mv^2$$

From v to 2v,

$$W = \frac{1}{2}m((2v)^2 - v^2) = \frac{3}{2}mv^2$$

49. $K_{\text{man}} = \frac{1}{2}K_{\text{boy}} \Rightarrow \frac{1}{2}mv^2_{\text{man}} = \frac{1}{2}\left(\frac{1}{2}\frac{m}{2}v^2_{\text{boy}}\right) \Rightarrow v_{\text{man}} = \frac{v_{\text{boy}}}{2}$

Now, $\quad \frac{1}{2}m(v_{\text{man}} + 1)^2 = \frac{1}{2}\left(\frac{m}{2}\right)v^2_{\text{boy}}$

$$\Rightarrow (V_{man}+1)^2 = \frac{(2v_{man})^2}{2}$$

$$\Rightarrow v_{man}^2 - 2v_{man} - 1 = 0 \Rightarrow v_{man} = \frac{2+\sqrt{8}}{2} = 1+\sqrt{2}$$

50. $P = Fv = \text{constant} \Rightarrow mav = \text{constant}$

$$\Rightarrow m\frac{dv}{dt}v = \text{constant}$$

$$\Rightarrow \int v\,dv \propto \int dt \Rightarrow v^2 \propto t \Rightarrow v \propto \sqrt{t}$$

$$\frac{ds}{dt} \propto \sqrt{t} \Rightarrow \int ds \propto \int \sqrt{t}\,dt$$

$$\Rightarrow s \propto t^{3/2} \quad \therefore \frac{s}{v} = \frac{t^{3/2}}{t^{1/2}} = t$$

51.

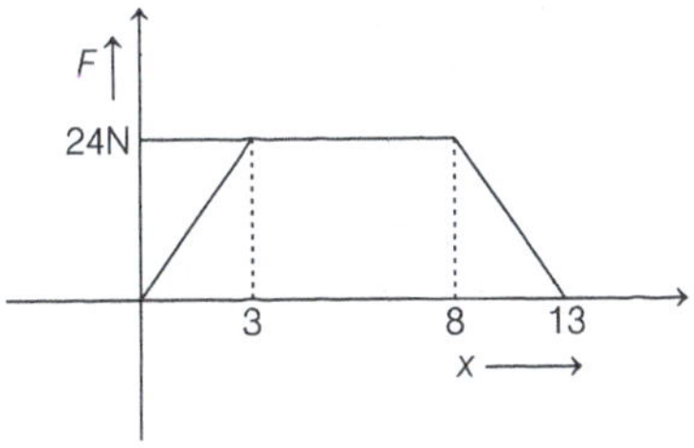

$$W = \int F\,dx = \text{Area under } F\text{-}x \text{ graph} = \frac{1}{2}(13+5)(24) = 216 \text{ J}$$

52.

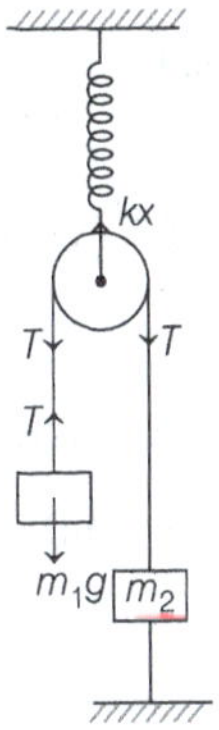

For m_1,

$$\Sigma F_y = 0 \Rightarrow T = m_1 g$$

For massless pulley,

$$\Sigma F_y = 0 \Rightarrow kx = 2T = 2m_1 g \Rightarrow x = \frac{2m_1 g}{k}$$

$$U = \frac{1}{2}kx^2 = \frac{1}{2}k\left(\frac{2m_1 g}{k}\right)^2 = \frac{2m_1^2 g^2}{k}$$

53. Speed of the block is maximum when acceleration of block is zero.

So, $mg\cos\theta = kx \Rightarrow x = \dfrac{mg\cos\theta}{k}$

54. $W_{mg} = -mgh$

$$W_{friction} = -\int(\mu mg\cos\theta)\,dl\cos 0° = -\mu mg\int dl\cos\theta$$

$$= -\mu mg\int_0^l dx = -\mu mgl$$

$W_N = 0, \quad W_F = ?$

$$W_{mg} + W_N + W_{friction} + W_F = \Delta K$$

$$\Rightarrow -mgh + 0 - \mu mgl + W_F = 0 - 0$$

$$\Rightarrow W_F = mg(h + \mu l)$$

55. $K = \dfrac{p^2}{2m} \Rightarrow \log_e K = \log_e\left(\dfrac{p^2}{2m}\right)$

$$\Rightarrow \log_e K = \log_e p^2 - \log_e 2m \Rightarrow \log_e K = 2\log_e p - \log_e 2m$$

$$\Rightarrow y = 2x - \log_e 2m$$

56. $F = kx$

$$\Rightarrow -\frac{dU}{dx} = kx \Rightarrow -\int_0^U dU = \int_0^x kx\,dx \Rightarrow U = -\frac{1}{2}kx^2$$

57.

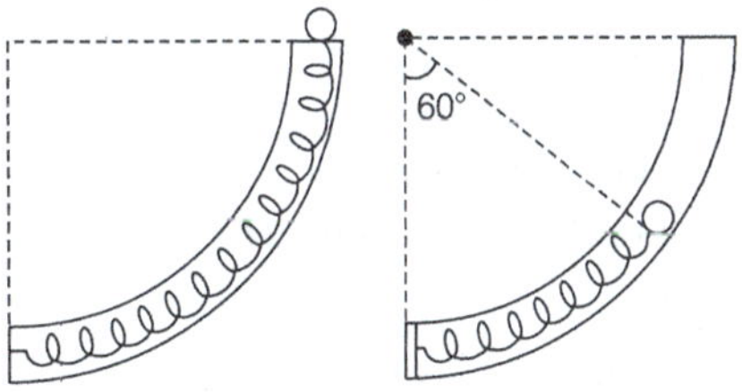

Position - 1 Position - 2

Applying work-energy theorem between position 1 and position 2,

$$W_{mg} + W_{spring} = \Delta K$$

$$\Rightarrow +mg(R\cos 60°) + \frac{1}{2}k\left(0^2 - \left(\frac{\pi}{6}R\right)^2\right) = 0 - 0 \Rightarrow k = \frac{36mg}{\pi^2 R}$$

58. $W = Fs\cos\theta \Rightarrow W_{F_1} = 40(0.8)\cos 30° = 16\sqrt{3}$ J

$W_{F_2} = 20(0.8)\cos 90° = 0, \quad W_{F_3} = 30(0.8)\cos 0° = 24$ J

59.

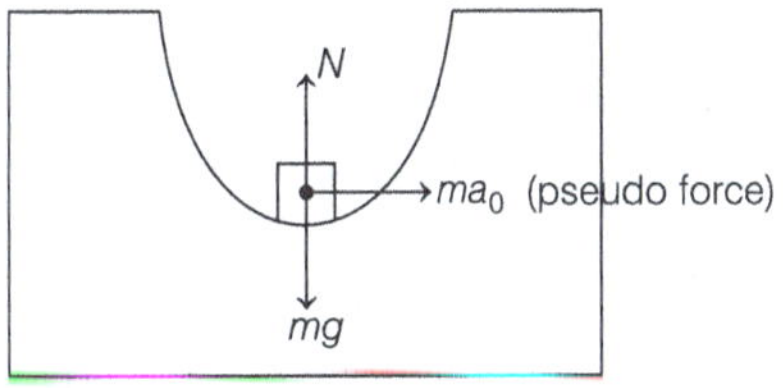

From P to Q,

$$W_{mg} + W_N + W_{pseudo} = \Delta K \Rightarrow -mgR + 0 + ma_0 R = 0 - 0$$

$$\Rightarrow a_0 = g$$

60. When the object is lowered very slowly to its equilibrium position, then at equilibrium position

$$Kx = mg \Rightarrow K(0.1) = 0.5\times 10 \Rightarrow K = 50 \text{ N/m}$$

Applying work-energy theorem,

$$W_{mg} + W_{spring} = \Delta K$$

$$\Rightarrow +0.5\times 10\times 0.1 + \frac{1}{2}\times 50(0^2 - (0.1)^2) = \frac{1}{2}\times 0.5v^2 - 0$$

$$\Rightarrow v = 1 \text{ m/s}$$

61.

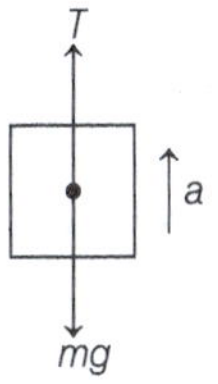

$$\Sigma F_y = ma_y \Rightarrow T - mg = ma \Rightarrow T = m(g+a)$$

$$W_T = Fs\cos\theta = m(g+a)\frac{1}{2}at^2\cos 0^\circ = \frac{m}{2}(g+a)\,at^2$$

62.

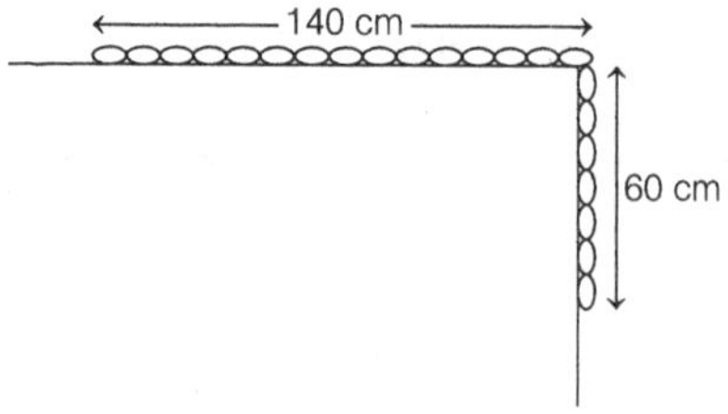

Taking table top as reference level for PE

$$U_1 = \left(\frac{4}{2}\times 0.6\right)(10)(-0.3) \Rightarrow U_1 = -3.6\text{ J}$$

When entire chain is on table $U_2 = 0$

$$W_{ext} = \Delta U + \Delta K = (U_2 - U_1) + 0 = 3.6\text{ J}$$

63. $P = Fv = \text{constant}$

$$mav = \text{constant} \Rightarrow \frac{dv}{dt}v = \text{constant}$$

$$\Rightarrow \int v\,dv \propto \int dt \Rightarrow v^2 \propto t \Rightarrow v \propto \sqrt{t}$$

Now, $v = \dfrac{dx}{dt} \propto \sqrt{t} \Rightarrow \int dx \propto \int \sqrt{t}\,dt \Rightarrow x \propto t^{3/2}$

64. $P = Fv\cos\theta \Rightarrow P = (mg\sin\theta)v\cos 0^\circ$

$$P = 30000\times 10\times\frac{1}{100}\times 30\times\frac{5}{18}\times 1 \Rightarrow P = 25\text{ kW}$$

65. For m_1,

$$\Sigma F = ma \Rightarrow F_{ext} + m_1 g - T = 0 \quad \text{...(i)}$$

For m_2, $\Sigma F = ma \Rightarrow T - m_2 g = 0$ ...(ii)

From Eqs. (i) and (ii), we get

$$F_{ext} = (m_2 - m_1)g \Rightarrow P_{ext} = F_{ext}v\cos 0^\circ = (m_2 - m_1)gv$$

66. $P = \dfrac{K}{t} = \dfrac{\frac{1}{2}mv^2}{t} \Rightarrow P = \dfrac{\frac{1}{2}\times\left(\frac{50}{1000}\times 60\right)\times(700)^2}{60}$

$$\Rightarrow P = 12250\text{ W}$$

67. Applying work-energy theorem

$$W_{mg} + W_N + W_{spring} = \Delta K$$

$$\Rightarrow +mg\left(\frac{3R}{2}\right) + 0 + \frac{1}{2}k\left(\left(\frac{R}{2}\right)^2 - 0^2\right) = \frac{1}{2}mv^2 - 0$$

$$\Rightarrow v = \sqrt{4gR}$$

68. Lets say maximum elongation in the spring is x.

$$W_{mg} + W_N + W_F + W_{spring} = \Delta K$$

$$\Rightarrow 0 + 0 + Fx + \frac{1}{2}k(0^2 - x^2) = 0 - 0$$

$$\Rightarrow x = \frac{2F}{k} \Rightarrow W_F = Fx = F\left(\frac{2F}{k}\right) = \frac{2F^2}{k}$$

69. $W_{friction} = \int -\mu\, mg\cos\theta\,dx = \int_0^S -\mu_0 x\, mg\cos\theta\,dx$

$$= \frac{-\mu_0\, mg\cos\theta\, s^2}{2}$$

Applying work-energy theorem

$$W_{mg} + W_N + W_{friction} = \Delta K$$

$$\Rightarrow (mg\sin\theta)s + 0 - \frac{(\mu_0 mg\cos\theta)s^2}{2} = 0 - 0$$

$$\Rightarrow s = \frac{2\tan\theta}{\mu_0}$$

70.

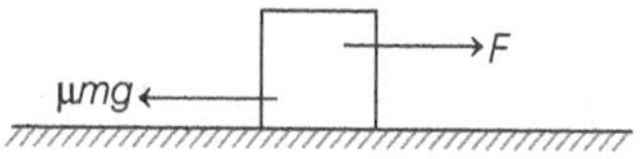

Velocity will be maximum when $a = 0$

$$\Rightarrow F = \mu mg \Rightarrow P = Fv \Rightarrow P = (\mu mg)v_{max} \Rightarrow v_{max} = \frac{P}{\mu mg}$$

71.

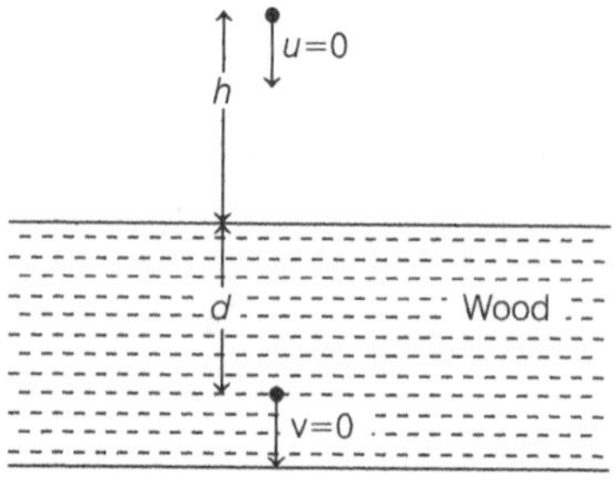

Using work-energy theorem for the knife,

$$W_{gravity} + W_{wood} = \Delta K \Rightarrow +mg(h+d) - Fd = 0$$

$$\Rightarrow F = mg\left(1 + \frac{h}{d}\right)$$

Numerical Value Questions

1. Between A and B

$$W_{mg} + W_N + W_{friction} = \Delta K$$

$$\Rightarrow -mg(3 + 3\sin 37^\circ) + 0 - (\mu mg\cos 37^\circ)(3) = \frac{1}{2}mv^2 - \frac{1}{2}m(15)^2$$

$$\Rightarrow v = 9\text{ m/s}$$

2. $U = \dfrac{x^2}{2} - x$

Speed is maximum when force is zero.

$$F = -\frac{dU}{dx} = -x + 1 = 0 \Rightarrow x = 1$$

At $x = 1$, $K + U = E$

$$\Rightarrow \frac{1}{2}\times 0.2\times v_{max}^2 + \left(\frac{1}{2} - 1\right) = 2 \Rightarrow v_{max} = 5\text{ m/s}$$

3. $W = \int \mathbf{F}\cdot d\mathbf{s} \Rightarrow W = \int_0^2 (3t\hat{i} + 5\hat{j})\cdot(4t\,dt\,\hat{i})$

$$\Rightarrow W = \int_0^2 12t^2\,dt = 32\text{ J}$$

4.

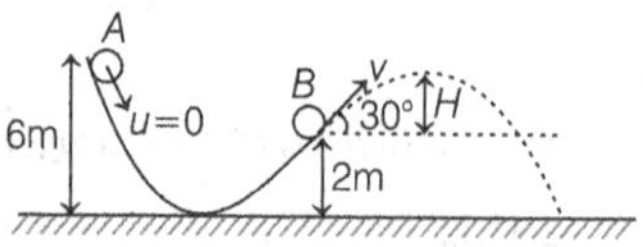

Between A and B

$$W_{mg} + W_N = \Delta K$$

$$\Rightarrow \quad +mg(6-2)+0=\frac{1}{2}mv^2-0 \quad \Rightarrow \quad v=\sqrt{8g}$$

$$H=\frac{u^2\sin^2\theta}{2g}=\frac{(\sqrt{8g})^2\sin^2 30^\circ}{2g}=1\,\text{m}$$

$$H_{max}=2+1=3\,\text{m}$$

5. With respect to free end, velocity of block is $1-(-2)=3\,\text{m/s}$ left.

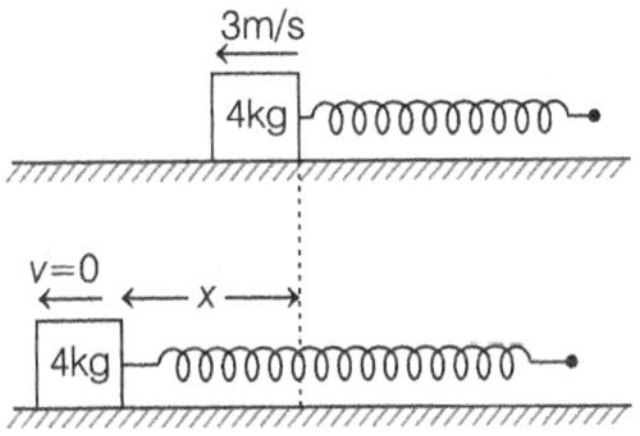

Elongation in the spring will be maximum when velocity of block with respect to free end is zero.

$$W_{mg}+W_N+W_{spring}=\Delta K$$

$$\Rightarrow \quad 0+0+\frac{1}{2}\times\frac{100}{10^{-2}}(0^2-x^2)=0-\frac{1}{2}\times 4\times 3^2$$

$$x=0.06\,\text{m}=6\,\text{cm}$$

6. Ball will leave spring when spring acquired natural length. Lets say speed of block at that instant is v.
Applying work-energy theorem,

$$W_{mg}+W_N+W_{spring}=\Delta K$$

$$\Rightarrow \quad 0+0+\frac{1}{2}\times 100[(0.05)^2-0^2]=\frac{1}{2}\times 0.1\times v^2-0$$

$$\Rightarrow \quad v=\sqrt{\frac{5}{2}}\,\text{m/s}$$

$$\text{Range}=vT=v\sqrt{\frac{2h}{g}}=\sqrt{\frac{5}{2}}\sqrt{\frac{2(2)}{10}}=1\,\text{m}$$

7. $F=ma=10+4x \quad \Rightarrow \quad a=5+2x \quad \Rightarrow \quad v\dfrac{dv}{dx}=5+2x$

$$\Rightarrow \quad \int_0^v v\,dv=\int_0^5(5+2x)\,dx \quad \Rightarrow \quad v=10\,\text{m/s}$$

$$P=Fv\cos 0^\circ=(10+4x)10=300\,\text{W}$$

8.

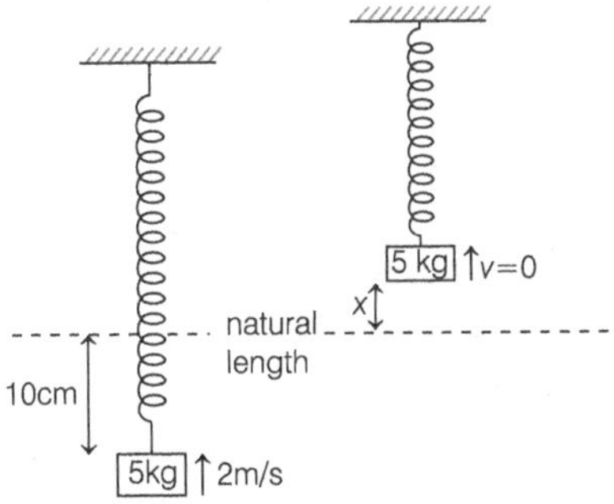

For 5 kg block

$$\Sigma F_y=0 \quad \Rightarrow 50-K(0.1)=0 \quad \Rightarrow K=500\,\text{N/m}$$

Applying work-energy theorem,

$$W_{mg}+W_{spring}=\Delta K$$

$$\Rightarrow -mg(0.1+x)+\frac{1}{2}K[(0.1)^2-x^2)]=0-\frac{1}{2}m(2)^2$$

$$\Rightarrow \quad -5-50x+2.5-250x^2=-10$$

$$\Rightarrow \quad 250x^2+50x-7.5=0$$

$$\Rightarrow \quad x=0.1\,\text{m}=10\,\text{cm}$$

Maximum height $=10+10=20$ cm

9. Given, force, $F=\dfrac{2}{v}\text{N} \Rightarrow ma=\dfrac{2}{v}$ $\quad [\because F=ma]$

$$\Rightarrow \quad m\frac{dv}{dt}=\frac{2}{v} \qquad \left(\because a=\frac{dv}{dt}\right)$$

$$\Rightarrow \quad m\int_u^v v\,dv=2\int_0^3 dt \Rightarrow \frac{1}{2}m(v^2-u^2)=2\times 3$$

$$\Rightarrow \quad \Delta K=6 \qquad \left[\because \Delta K=\frac{1}{2}m(v^2-u^2)\right]$$

So, work done, $W=\Delta K=6\,J$

10. $P=640-16v-8v^2 \quad \Rightarrow \quad Fv=640-16v-8v^2$

For velocity to be maximum, $a=0$

$$\Rightarrow F=0 \quad \Rightarrow 0=640-16v-8v^2$$

$$\Rightarrow v^2+2v-80=0 \quad \Rightarrow v=8\text{m/s}$$

11. Using work-energy theorem between A and B

$$W_{mg}+W_T+W_F=\Delta K$$

$$\Rightarrow \quad -mgl(1-\cos 37^\circ)+0+\left(\frac{mg}{2}\right)(l\sin 37^\circ)$$

$$=\frac{1}{2}mv_B^2-\frac{1}{2}mv_A^2 \quad \Rightarrow \quad v_B=2\,\text{m/s}$$

12.

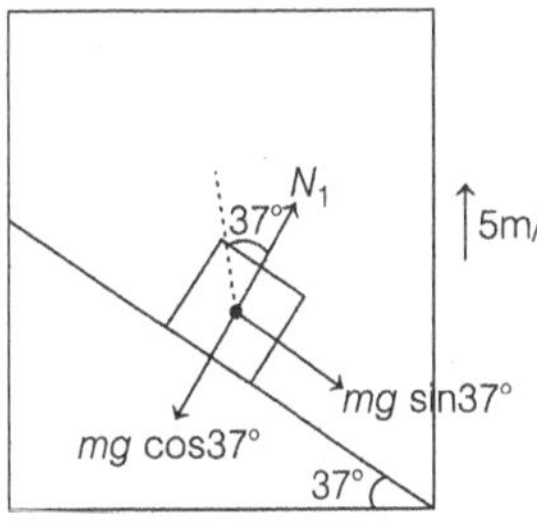

$$\Sigma F_y=0 \quad \Rightarrow N_1-mg\cos 37^\circ=0 \quad \Rightarrow N_1=mg\cos 37^\circ$$

$$W_{N_1}=Fs\cos\theta=(mg\cos 37^\circ)(vt)\cos 37^\circ=320\,\text{J}$$

13. Using work-energy theorem for block,

$$W_{mg}+W_N+W_{friction}+W_{spring}=\Delta K$$

$$\Rightarrow +mg\sin 37^\circ\times 0.5+0-\frac{1}{8}(mg\cos 37^\circ)(0.5)+\frac{1}{2}\times 8(0^2-(0.5)^2)$$

$$=\frac{1}{2}mv^2-0$$

$$\Rightarrow \quad v=2\,\text{m/s}$$

14. Using work-energy theorem for block,

$$W_{mg}+W_{spring\,1}+W_{spring\,2}+\Delta K$$

$$\Rightarrow +2\times 10\times(1+x)+\frac{1}{2}\times 24(0^2-(1+x)^2)+\frac{1}{2}\times 24(0^2-x^2)=0-0$$

$\Rightarrow \quad 6x^2 + x - 2 = 0$

$\Rightarrow \quad 2x(3x+2) - (3x+2) = 0 \quad \Rightarrow x = 0.5$

So, maximum extension in upper spring $= 1 + 0.5 = 1.50\text{ m}$

15. Using work-energy theorem for the object,

$$W_{mg} + W_{air} = \Delta K$$

$\Rightarrow \quad +5 \times 9.8 \times 20 + W_{air} = \frac{1}{2} \times 5 \times 10^2 - 0 \quad \Rightarrow W_{air} = -730\text{ J}$

16.

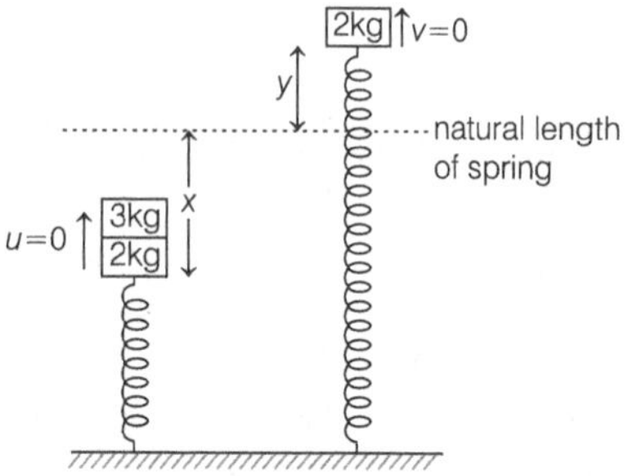

Initially lets take compression to be x.

$\Sigma F_y = 0 \quad \Rightarrow 30 + 20 - 40x = 0 \quad \Rightarrow x = 1.25\text{ m}$

After removing 3 kg block, lets take maximum elongation in the spring to be y.

Using work-energy theorem for 2 kg block,

$$W_{mg} + W_{spring} = \Delta K$$

$\Rightarrow \quad -2 \times 10(1.25 + y) + \frac{1}{2} \times 40\,[(1.25)^2 - y^2] = 0 - 0$

$\Rightarrow \quad y = 0.25\text{ m}$

So, the maximum height reached by 2 kg block

$$= 1.25 + 0.25 = 1.5\text{m}$$

17. Kinetic energy is maximum when force is zero.

$$F = 8 - x^3 = 0 \quad \Rightarrow x = 2\text{ m}$$

Using work-energy theorem, $W = \Delta K$

$$\int_0^2 (8 - x^3)\, dx = K_{max} - 0 \quad \Rightarrow K_{max} = 12\text{ J}$$

18. Using work-energy theorem for block,

$$W_{mg} + W_N + W_{friction} + W_{spring} = \Delta K$$

$\Rightarrow 0 + 0 - 0.25 \times 1 \times 10 \times 4 + \frac{1}{2} \times 2.75\,(0^2 - 4^2)$

$= 0 - \frac{1}{2} \times 1 \times v^2$

$\Rightarrow \quad v = 8\text{ m/s}$

19. $W = \Delta K$

$\Rightarrow \quad \int_0^x -\alpha x^2\, dx = 0 - \frac{1}{2} m v_0^2$

$\Rightarrow \quad -\frac{\alpha x^3}{3} = -\frac{1}{2} m v_0^2 \quad \Rightarrow \quad x = \left(\frac{3mv_0^2}{2\alpha}\right)^{1/3}$

20. $W_{ext} = \Delta U + \Delta K$

$\Rightarrow \quad -10 = \Delta U + \frac{1}{2} \times 2\,(3^2 - 5^2)$

$\Rightarrow \quad \Delta U = 6\text{ J}$

Level 3

Single Choice Correct Questions

1. $x = 2t^2 + 4t \quad \Rightarrow \quad \frac{dx}{dt} = 4t + 4 \Rightarrow dx = (4t+4)\, dt$

$W = \int \mathbf{F} \cdot d\mathbf{s} = \int (3t\hat{\mathbf{i}} - 3t^2\hat{\mathbf{j}} + \sqrt{5}t\hat{\mathbf{k}}) \cdot (dx\hat{\mathbf{i}} + dy\hat{\mathbf{j}} + dz\hat{\mathbf{k}})$

$= \int_0^2 3t(4t+4)\, dt = \int_0^2 (12t^2 + 12t)\, dt$

$= [4t^3 + 6t^2]_0^2 = 56\text{ units}$

2. $\mathbf{F} = (3xy - 5z)\,\hat{\mathbf{j}} + 4z\hat{\mathbf{k}}$

$W = \int \mathbf{F} \cdot d\mathbf{s} = \int (3xy - 5z)\, dy + \int_0^0 4z\, dz = \int 3x^3\, dy + 0$

$= \int_0^2 6x^4\, dx \qquad \left(\because y = x^2,\ dy = 2x\, dx\right)$

$= \frac{192}{5}\text{ J}$

3. $W = \int \mathbf{F} \cdot d\mathbf{s}$

$W = \int (3x^2y\hat{\mathbf{i}} + x^3\hat{\mathbf{j}}) \cdot (dx\hat{\mathbf{i}} + dy\hat{\mathbf{j}} + dz\hat{\mathbf{k}}) = \int (3x^2y dx + x^3 dy)$

$= \int_{(1,\,1)}^{(2,\,-1)} d(x^3y) = [x^3y]_{(1,\,1)}^{(2,\,-1)} = -8 - 1 = -9\text{ J}$

4. Applying work-energy theorem

$$W_{mg} + W_N + W_{friction} + W_{spring} = \Delta K$$

$\Rightarrow \quad 0 + 0 - \int_0^{2L} (ax)\, mg\, dx + \frac{1}{2}\, k(0^2 - L^2) = 0 - \frac{1}{2} m v_0^2$

$\Rightarrow \quad v_0 = \sqrt{\frac{kL^2}{m} + 4aL^2 g}$

5.

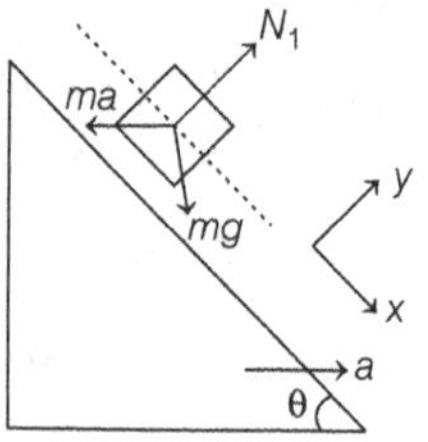

$\Sigma F_x = 0 \quad \Rightarrow mg\sin\theta = ma\cos\theta \quad \Rightarrow a = g\tan\theta$

$\Rightarrow \quad 10 = 10\tan\theta \quad \Rightarrow \tan\theta = 1 \Rightarrow \theta = 45°$

$\Sigma F_y = 0 \quad \Rightarrow N_1 = mg\cos\theta + ma\sin\theta \quad \Rightarrow N_1 = 10\sqrt{2}\text{ N}$

$s = ut + \frac{1}{2}at^2 \quad \Rightarrow \quad s = 0 + \frac{1}{2}(10)(2)^2 = 20\text{ m}$

$W_N = Fs\cos\theta = (10\sqrt{2})(20)\cos 45° = 200\text{ J}$

6. Applying work-energy theorem,

$$W_{mg} + W_N + W_{friction} = \Delta K$$

$\Rightarrow 0 + 0 - \int_1^{\infty} \frac{A}{r^2}\, mg\, dr = 0 - \frac{1}{2} m v_0^2 \quad \Rightarrow v_0 = \sqrt{2gA}$

7.

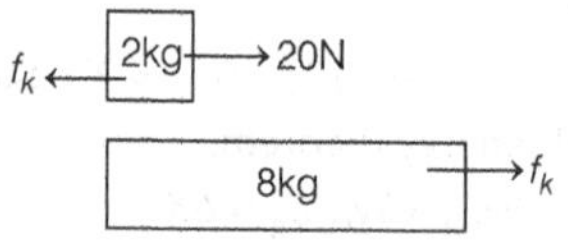

$f_k = \mu_k N = 0.5(20) = 10\text{ N}$

For 2 kg block,

$$\Sigma F = ma \Rightarrow 20 - 10 = 2a_1 \Rightarrow a_1 = 5\,\text{m/s}^2$$

For 8 kg block,

$$\Sigma F = ma \Rightarrow 10 = 8a_2 \Rightarrow a_2 = \frac{5}{4}\,\text{m/s}^2$$

$$a_{12} = a_1 - a_2 = 5 - \frac{5}{4} = \frac{15}{4}\,\text{m/s}^2$$

$$s_{12} = u_{12}t + \frac{1}{2}a_{12}t^2$$

$$\Rightarrow \quad 5 = 0 + \frac{1}{2}\left(\frac{15}{4}\right)t^2 \Rightarrow t = \sqrt{\frac{8}{3}}\,\text{s}$$

$$s_2 = u_2t + \frac{1}{2}a_2t^2 \Rightarrow s_2 = 0 + \frac{1}{2} \times \frac{5}{4} \times \left(\sqrt{\frac{8}{3}}\right)^2 = \frac{5}{3}\,\text{m}$$

$$W = Fs\cos\theta = 10\left(\frac{5}{3}\right)\cos 0^\circ = \frac{50}{3}\,\text{J}$$

8. $\Sigma F_y = 0 \Rightarrow Kx_0 = 100 \Rightarrow x_0 = 1\,\text{m}$

Applying work-energy theorem

$$W_{mg} + W_{spring} + W_F = \Delta K$$

$$\Rightarrow \quad 100(2) + \frac{1}{2} \times 100\,(1^2 - 3^2) + W_F = 0 - 0 \Rightarrow W_F = 200\,\text{J}$$

9. Lets take maximum elongation in the spring $= x$ and displacement of 2 M as y.

From string constraint

$$2y = x$$

Applying work-energy theorem for system

$$W_{mg} + W_N + W_T + W_{spring} = \Delta K_{system}$$

$$\Rightarrow \quad +2Mg\left(\frac{x}{2}\right) + 0 + 0 + \frac{1}{2}k\,(0^2 - x^2) = (0 + 0) - (0 + 0)$$

$$\Rightarrow \quad x = \frac{2Mg}{k}$$

10.

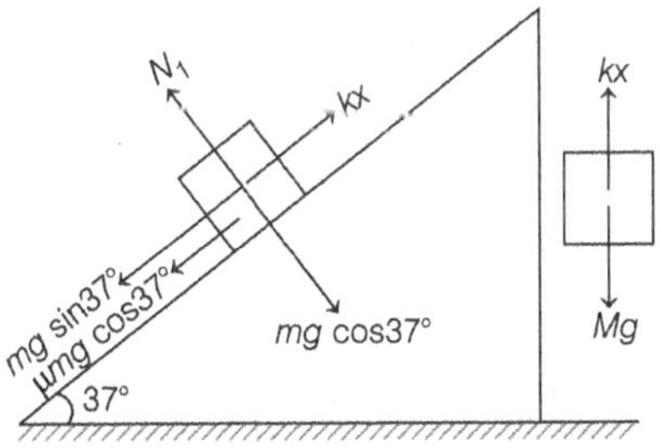

To move the block up the plane

$$kx \geq mg\sin 37^\circ + \mu mg\cos 37^\circ$$

$$\Rightarrow \quad kx \geq \frac{6mg}{5} \Rightarrow x \geq \frac{6mg}{5k}$$

Applying work-energy theorem

$$W_{mg} + W_{spring} = \Delta K \Rightarrow +Mgx + \frac{1}{2}k(0^2 - x^2) = 0 - 0$$

$$\Rightarrow \quad x = \frac{2Mg}{k}$$

$$\frac{2Mg}{k} \geq \frac{6mg}{5}$$

$$\Rightarrow \quad M \geq \frac{3m}{5} \Rightarrow M_{min} = \frac{3m}{5}$$

11.

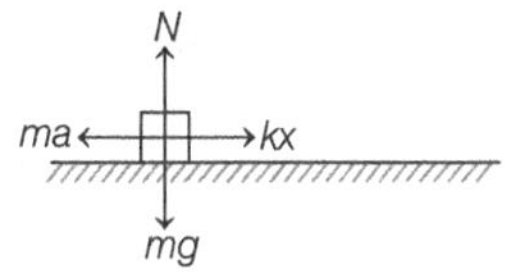

Applying work-energy theorem

$$W_{mg} + W_N + W_{spring} + W_{pseudo} = \Delta K$$

$$\Rightarrow \quad 0 + 0 + \frac{1}{2}k(x^2 - 0^2) + \text{max} = 0 - 0 \Rightarrow x = \frac{2ma}{k}$$

12. $W_{conservative} = -\Delta U$

If work done by conservative force is positive, potential energy decreases, kinetic energy increases and mechanical energy is constant.

13.

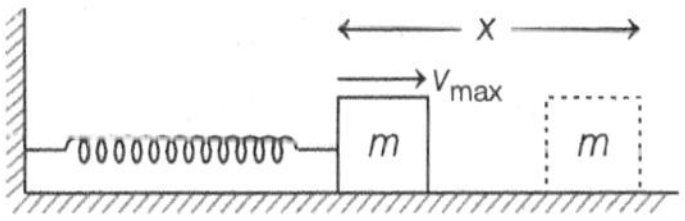

Speed of the block will be maximum when acceleration is zero.

$$\Rightarrow \quad kx = \mu mg \Rightarrow x = \frac{\mu mg}{k}$$

Applying work-energy theorem for block

$$W_{mg} + W_N + W_{spring} + W_{friction} = \Delta K$$

$$\Rightarrow \quad 0 + 0 + \frac{1}{2}k\left[\left(\frac{4\mu mg}{k}\right)^2 - \left(\frac{\mu mg}{k}\right)^2\right]$$

$$-\mu mg\left(\frac{3\mu mg}{k}\right) = \frac{1}{2}mv_{max}^2 - 0 \Rightarrow v_{max} = 3\mu g\sqrt{\frac{m}{k}}$$

14. For block,

$$\Sigma F = ma \Rightarrow 10 = 1\,a \Rightarrow a = 10\,\text{m/s}^2$$

$$s = ut + \frac{1}{2}at^2 \Rightarrow 20 = 0 + \frac{1}{2}at^2 \Rightarrow t = 2\,\text{s}$$

In 2 s,

$$\mathbf{s}_A = 20\,\hat{\mathbf{j}},\ \mathbf{s}_B = 10\hat{\mathbf{i}} + 10\sqrt{3}\,\hat{\mathbf{j}},\ \mathbf{s}_C = -40\hat{\mathbf{i}}$$

$$\mathbf{s}_{block} = 20\,\hat{\mathbf{i}}$$

Work done by F w.r.t. $A = \mathbf{F} \cdot \mathbf{s}_{block,\,A}$

$$= 10\hat{\mathbf{i}} \cdot (20\hat{\mathbf{i}} - 20\hat{\mathbf{j}}) = 200\,\text{J}$$

Work done by F w.r.t. $B = \mathbf{F} \cdot \mathbf{s}_{block,\,B}$

$$= 10\hat{\mathbf{i}} \cdot (10\hat{\mathbf{i}} - 10\sqrt{3}\hat{\mathbf{j}}) = 100\,\text{J}$$

Work done by F w.r.t $C = \mathbf{F} \cdot \mathbf{s}_{block,\,C} = 10\hat{\mathbf{i}} \cdot (60\hat{\mathbf{i}}) = 600\,\text{J}$

15. Lets take distance travelled by the block on the flat part as x.

Applying work-energy theorem for block,

$$W_{mg} + W_N + W_{friction} = \Delta K$$

$$\Rightarrow \quad +mg\,(1.5) + 0 - (0.2\,mg)(x) = 0 - 0$$

$$\Rightarrow \quad x = 7.5\,\text{m}$$

Since, the flat part is 3m long, the block will come to rest at midpoint of B and C.

16. The speed of the block will be maximum when its acceleration is zero.

$\Rightarrow mg\sin\theta = kx + \mu mg\cos\theta \quad \Rightarrow x = 0.04\text{ m}$

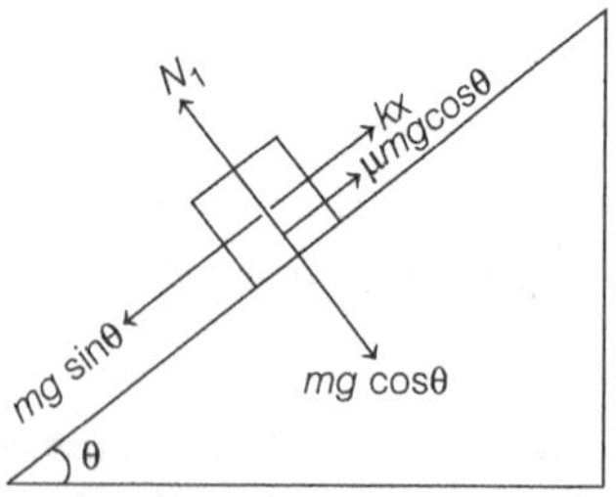

Applying work-energy theorem

$$W_{mg} + W_N + W_{spring} + W_{friction} = \Delta K$$

$$\Rightarrow +mg\sin\theta x + 0 + \frac{1}{2}k(0^2 - x^2) - (\mu mg\cos\theta)x$$

$$= \frac{1}{2}mv_{max}^2 - 0$$

$$\Rightarrow \quad v_{max} = 0.4\text{ m/s}$$

17. $dW = \mathbf{F}\cdot d\mathbf{s}$

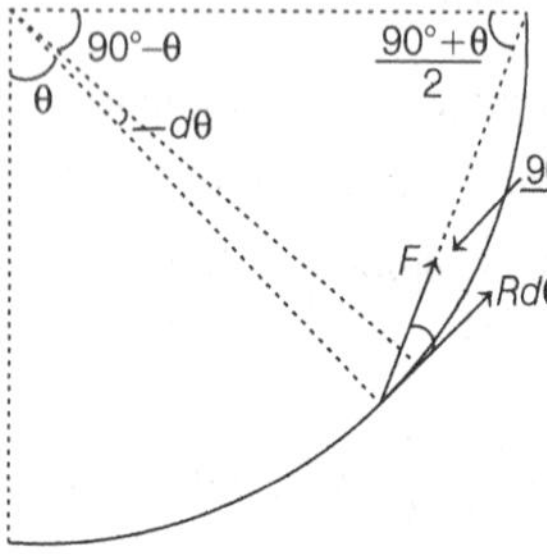

$$dW = F\,ds\cos\theta \quad \Rightarrow \quad \int dW = \int_0^{90°} FR\,d\theta\cos\left(\frac{90° - \theta}{2}\right)$$

$$\Rightarrow \quad W = FR\int_0^{90°}\cos\left(\frac{90° - \theta}{2}\right)d\theta$$

$$\Rightarrow \quad W = \frac{FR}{\left(\frac{-1}{2}\right)}\left[\sin\left(\frac{90° - \theta}{2}\right)\right]_0^{90°} = -2FR\left(0 - \frac{1}{\sqrt{2}}\right)$$

$$= \sqrt{2}FR = \sqrt{2}(6)(9\sqrt{2}) = 108\text{ J}$$

Using work-energy theorem, $W = \Delta K$

$$\Rightarrow \quad 108 = \frac{1}{2}\times 2\times v^2 - \frac{1}{2}\times 2\times 6^2 \quad \Rightarrow \quad v = 12\text{ m/s}$$

18. $W_{friction} = -\int \mu mg\cos\theta\,dl = -\mu mg\int dl\cos\theta$

$$= -\mu mg\int dx = -\mu mgx$$

$$= -\mu mg\sqrt{R^2 - (R-h)^2} = -\mu mg\sqrt{2hR - h^2}$$

19. $U = 10 + (x-2)^2$

At $x = 6$; $\quad U = 26$ J and $K = 0$

Using mechanical energy conservation

$$K_1 + U_1 = K_2 + U_2 \quad \Rightarrow \quad 0 + 26 = K_{max} + U_{min}$$

$$\Rightarrow \quad 0 + 26 = K_{max} + 10 \quad \Rightarrow K_{max} = 16\text{ J}$$

20.

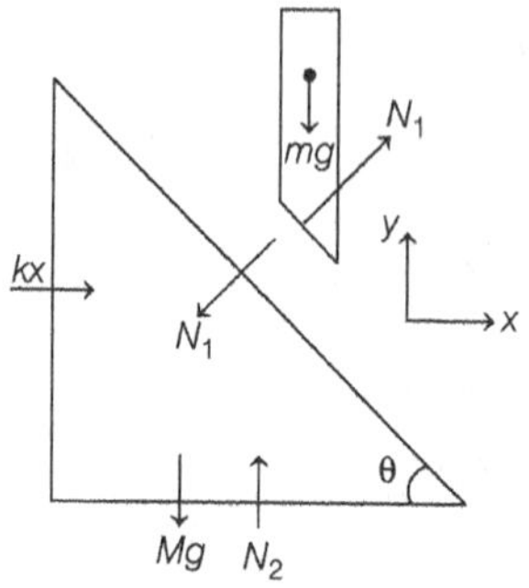

For rod

$$\Sigma F_y = 0 \quad \Rightarrow N_1\cos\theta - mg = 0 \quad \Rightarrow N_1 = \frac{mg}{\cos\theta}$$

For wedge

$$\Sigma F_x = 0 \quad \Rightarrow kx - N_1\sin\theta = 0 \quad \Rightarrow x = \frac{mg\tan\theta}{k}$$

Potential energy stored in the spring $= \frac{1}{2}kx^2$

$$= \frac{1}{2}k\left(\frac{mg\tan\theta}{k}\right)^2 = \frac{m^2g^2\tan^2\theta}{2k}$$

21. Using work-energy theorem,

$$W_{mg} + W_N + W_{spring} + W_{friction} = \Delta K$$

$$\Rightarrow \quad 0 + 0 + \frac{1}{2}k(a^2 - b^2) - \mu mg(a+b) = 0 - 0$$

$$\Rightarrow \quad \mu = \frac{k(a-b)}{2mg}$$

22. $E = K + U = 3$ J

At $x = 0$, $\quad K + 6 = 3 \quad \Rightarrow K = -3$ J

But kinetic energy can never be negative. So particle can never be present at $x = 0$.

23. From graph, $\quad P = \frac{x}{5} + 2 \Rightarrow Fv = \frac{x}{5} + 2 \Rightarrow mav = \frac{x}{5} + 2$

$$\Rightarrow \quad m\left(v\frac{v}{dx}\right)v = \frac{x}{5} + 2 \quad \Rightarrow m\int_1^v v^2\,dv = \int_0^{10}\left(\frac{x}{5} + 2\right)dx$$

$$\Rightarrow \quad \frac{10}{7}\left(\frac{v^3 - 1^3}{3}\right) = \frac{1}{10}(10^2 - 0^2) + 2(10 - 0) \Rightarrow v = 4\text{ m/s}$$

24. Using work-energy theorem,

$$W_{mg} + W_N + W_{friction} = \Delta K$$

$$\Rightarrow 0 + 0 - \int_0^x \alpha x\,mg\,dx = \frac{1}{2}mv^2 - \frac{1}{2}mv_0^2$$

$$\Rightarrow \quad v^2 = v_0^2 - \alpha gx^2 \Rightarrow \quad v = \sqrt{v_0^2 - \alpha gx^2}$$

$$P_{friction} = Fv\cos\theta = (\alpha xmg)\sqrt{v_0^2 - \alpha gx^2}\cos 180°$$

$$= -\alpha mgx\sqrt{v_0^2 - \alpha gx^2}$$

To maximise $P_{friction}$, $\frac{dP_{friction}}{dx} = 0$

$$\Rightarrow -\alpha mg\left(x\frac{1}{2\sqrt{v_0^2 - \alpha gx^2}}(-2\alpha gx) + \sqrt{v_0^2 - \alpha gx^2}\right) = 0$$

$$\Rightarrow \quad v_0^2 - 2\alpha g x^2 = 0 \quad \Rightarrow \quad x = \frac{v_0}{\sqrt{2\alpha g}}$$

$$P_{max} = -\alpha mg \left(\frac{v_0}{\sqrt{2\alpha g}}\right)\sqrt{v_0^2 - \alpha g\left(\frac{v_0^2}{2\alpha g}\right)} = -\frac{mv_0^2}{2}\sqrt{\alpha g}$$

25. Lets say 3 kg goes down by x.

5 kg will go up by $\sqrt{8^2 + x^2} - 8$.

Using work-energy theorem for (5 kg + 3 kg) system,

$$W_{mg} + W_T = 0$$

$$\Rightarrow \quad [+3 \times 10 \times x - 5 \times 10(\sqrt{8^2 + x^2} - 8) + 0] = (0+0) - (0+0)$$

$$\Rightarrow \quad 30x = 50(\sqrt{8^2 + x^2} - 8) \Rightarrow x = 15\text{ m}$$

26. When A descends by 1 m down the inclined plane, B will go up by 0.5 m from string constraint.

Using work-energy theorem for $(A + B)$ system.

$$W_{gravity} + W_N + W_T = \Delta K$$

$$\Rightarrow \quad (+5g \sin 37° \times 1 - 4g \times 0.5) + 0 + 0$$

$$= \left(\frac{1}{2} \times 5 \times (2v)^2 + \frac{1}{2} \times 4 \times v^2\right) - (0+0)$$

$$\Rightarrow \quad v = \sqrt{\frac{g}{12}} = \frac{\sqrt{g}}{2\sqrt{3}}$$

27. Using work-energy theorem for $(A + B)$ system

$$W_{gravity} + W_T = \Delta K_{system}$$

$$\Rightarrow \left(+mgl - mg\left(\frac{l}{2}\right)\right) + 0 = \left(\frac{1}{2}mv^2 + \frac{1}{2}m(2v)^2\right) - (0+0)$$

$$\Rightarrow \quad v = \sqrt{\frac{gl}{5}}$$

28.

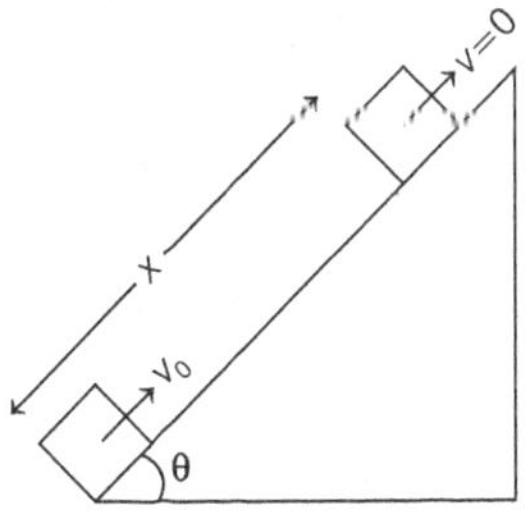

Using work-energy theorem

$$W_{mg} + W_N + W_{friction} = \Delta K$$

$$\Rightarrow -mg \sin\theta\, x + 0 - \mu mg \cos\theta x = 0 - \frac{1}{2}mv_0^2$$

$$\Rightarrow \quad x = \frac{v_0^2}{2g(\sin\theta + \mu \cos\theta)}$$

$$W_{friction} = -\mu mg \cos\theta\, x$$

$$= -\mu mg \cos\theta \left(\frac{v_0^2}{2g(\sin\theta + \mu\cos\theta)}\right)$$

$$= \frac{-mv_0^2\mu}{2(\tan\theta + \mu)}$$

29.

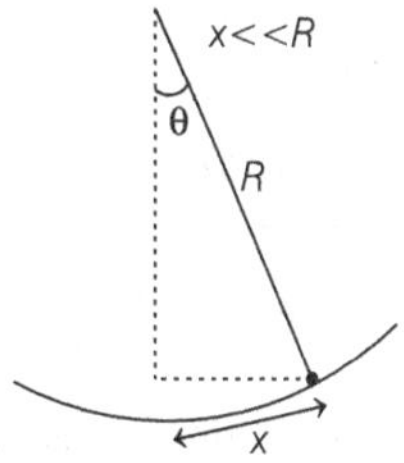

$$x = R\theta \quad \Rightarrow \quad \theta = \frac{x}{R}$$

Lets say total distance travelled before coming to rest is s.

Using work-energy theorem

$$W_{mg} + W_{friction} + W_N = \Delta K$$

$$\Rightarrow \quad + mgR(1 - \cos\theta) - \mu mgs + 0 = 0 - 0$$

$$\Rightarrow s = \frac{R(1-\cos\theta)}{\mu} = \frac{R\, 2\sin^2\left(\frac{\theta}{2}\right)}{\mu} \quad \Rightarrow \quad s = \frac{2R}{\mu}\sin^2\left(\frac{\theta}{2}\right)$$

Since, θ is small

$$\sin\left(\frac{\theta}{2}\right) \approx \frac{\theta}{2} \quad \Rightarrow s = \frac{R\theta^2}{2\mu} = \frac{x^2}{2\mu R}$$

30. $F \propto \frac{1}{v^2} \quad \Rightarrow \quad ma \propto \frac{1}{v^2} \quad \Rightarrow \quad mv\frac{dv}{ds} \propto \frac{1}{v^2}$

$$\Rightarrow \quad \int v^3\, dv \propto \int ds \quad \Rightarrow \quad v^4 \propto s \quad \Rightarrow \quad v \propto s^{1/4}$$

$$P = Fv \quad \Rightarrow \quad P \propto \frac{1}{v^2}\cdot v \quad \Rightarrow \quad P \propto \frac{1}{v} \quad \Rightarrow P \propto s^{-1/4}$$

31. $F = \frac{dp}{dt} \quad \Rightarrow \quad dp = F\, dt \quad \Rightarrow \quad \int dp = \int F dt$

Δp = Area under F-t graph $\Rightarrow \quad \Delta p = 60 - 10 = 50$

$$\Rightarrow \quad 10v - 0 = 50 \quad \Rightarrow v = 5\text{ m/s}$$

Using work-energy theorem

$$W = \Delta K = K_2 - K_1 = \frac{1}{2} \times 10 \times 5^2 - 0 = 125\text{ J}$$

32. Lets take, block further goes down by distance y.

Using work-energy theorem for block

$$W_{mg} + W_{spring} = \Delta K$$

$$\Rightarrow \quad + mg\, y + \frac{1}{2}k[x_0^2 - (x_0 + y)^2] = 0 - 0$$

$$\Rightarrow \quad + mgy + \frac{1}{2}k(2x_0 + y)(-y) = 0 \quad \Rightarrow \quad y = 2\left(\frac{mg}{k} - x_0\right)$$

33.

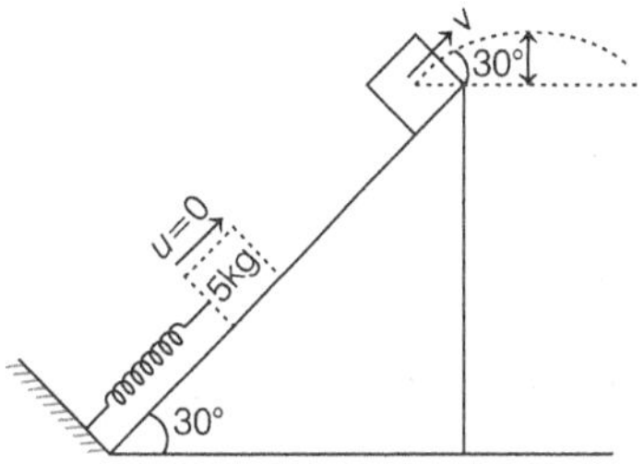

Lets take speed of block v when it leaves the wedge.

Using work energy theorem,

$$W_{mg} + W_N + W_{spring} = \Delta K$$

$$\Rightarrow -5g\sin 30^\circ \times 4 + 0 + \frac{1}{2}\times 300\times(2^2-0^2) = \frac{1}{2}\times 5\times v^2 - 0$$

$$\Rightarrow \quad v = 10\sqrt{2}\ \text{m/s}$$

Maximum height from ground

$$= 6\sin 30^\circ + \frac{v^2\sin^2\theta}{2g} = 5.5\text{m}$$

34. When the block momentarily comes to rest, then

$$kx \le \mu mg \Rightarrow x \le \frac{\mu mg}{k}$$

Using work-energy theorem

$$W_{mg} + W_N + W_{\text{friction}} + W_{\text{spring}} = \Delta K$$

$$\Rightarrow 0 + 0 - \mu mgx + \frac{1}{2}k(0^2 - x^2) = 0 - \frac{1}{2}mv^2$$

$$\Rightarrow \mu mgx = \frac{1}{2}mv^2 - \frac{1}{2}kx^2 \Rightarrow \mu = \frac{1}{2}\left(\frac{v^2}{gx} - \frac{kx}{mg}\right)$$

$$\therefore \quad \mu \ge \frac{1}{2}\left(\frac{v^2}{g\left(\frac{\mu mg}{k}\right)} - \frac{k}{mg}\left(\frac{\mu mg}{k}\right)\right)$$

$$\Rightarrow 3\mu^2 \ge \frac{kv^2}{mg^2} \Rightarrow 3\mu^2 \ge \frac{100\times 1^2}{3\times 10^2} \Rightarrow \mu^2 \ge \frac{1}{9}$$

$$\Rightarrow \mu \ge \frac{1}{3} \Rightarrow \mu_{\min} = \frac{1}{3}$$

35. Using work-energy theorem for block,

$$W_{mg} + W_N + W_{\text{spring}} + W_{\text{friction}} = \Delta K$$

$$\Rightarrow +mg(h-h') + 0 + \frac{1}{2}k(0^2-0^2) - \mu mg(2d) = 0 - 0$$

$$\Rightarrow mgh = mgh' + 2\mu mgd$$

36. $U = \frac{a}{x^{12}} - \frac{b}{x^6}$

$$F = -\frac{dU}{dx} = -\left(-\frac{12a}{x_0^{13}} + \frac{66}{x_0^7}\right) = 0$$

$$\Rightarrow x_0^6 = \left(\frac{2a}{b}\right) \Rightarrow x_0 = \left(\frac{2a}{b}\right)^{1/6}$$

$$\text{At } x = x_0;\ U = \frac{a}{\left(\left(\frac{2a}{b}\right)^{1/6}\right)^{12}} - \frac{b}{\left(\left(\frac{2a}{b}\right)^{1/6}\right)^{6}}$$

$$\Rightarrow U = \frac{b^2}{4a} - \frac{b^2}{2a} \Rightarrow U = \frac{-b^2}{4a}$$

At $x = \infty, U = 0$

$$\Delta E = U_2 - U_1 = 0 - \left(-\frac{b^2}{4a}\right) = \frac{b^2}{4a}$$

37. Speed is maximum when acceleration is zero.

$$\Rightarrow F - mg\sin\theta - \mu mg\cos\theta = 0$$

$$\Rightarrow F = mg\sin\theta + \mu mg\cos\theta \Rightarrow P = Fv$$

$$\Rightarrow P = (mg\sin\theta + \mu mg\cos\theta)v_{\max}$$

$$\Rightarrow v_{\max} = \frac{P}{mg\sin\theta + \mu mg\cos\theta}$$

38. $a_x = \frac{3}{4}t \Rightarrow \frac{dv_x}{dt} = \frac{3}{4}t \Rightarrow \int_{-3}^{v_x} dv_x = \int_0^t \frac{3}{4}t\,dt$

$$\Rightarrow v_x = \frac{3t^2}{8} - 3$$

$$a_y = -\frac{3}{4}t - 1 \Rightarrow \frac{dv_y}{dt} = -\frac{3}{4}t - 1$$

$$\Rightarrow \int_4^{v_y} dv_y = \int_0^t\left(-\frac{3}{4}t - 1\right)dt \Rightarrow v_y = -\frac{3t^2}{8} - t + 4$$

So. $$\mathbf{v} = \left(\frac{3t^2}{8} - 3\right)\hat{\mathbf{i}} + \left(\frac{-3t^2}{8} - t + 4\right)\hat{\mathbf{j}}$$

At $t = 4$

$$\mathbf{v} = 3\hat{\mathbf{i}} - 6\hat{\mathbf{j}}$$

Using work-energy theorem,

$$W = \Delta K = K_2 - K_1 = \frac{1}{2}\times 1\times(\sqrt{45})^2 - \frac{1}{2}\times 1\times(5)^2 = 10\ \text{J}$$

39. Lets say displacement of plank w.r.t. ground is x.

$$s_P = x, \quad s_{\text{block, plank}} = L$$

$$\Rightarrow s_{\text{block}} = L + s_P = L + x$$

Work done by friction on the block $= -\mu mg(L+x)$

Work done by friction on the plank $= \mu mgx$

Net work done by friction $= -\mu mg(L+x) + \mu mgx$

$$= -\mu mgL$$

40. $W = \int F\,dx =$ Area under F-x graph $= \frac{1}{2}(3x_0)F_0 = \frac{3F_0x_0}{2}$

Using work-energy theorem, $W = \Delta K$

$$\Rightarrow \frac{3F_0x_0}{2} = \frac{1}{2}mv^2 - \frac{1}{2}m\left(\sqrt{\frac{2F_0x_0}{m}}\right)^2 \Rightarrow v = \sqrt{\frac{5F_0x_0}{m}}$$

41. At $x = -\sqrt{\frac{2E}{k}} \Rightarrow U = \frac{1}{2}k\left(\sqrt{\frac{2E}{k}}\right)^2 = E$

$K = ?$ and $K + U = E \Rightarrow K + E = E \Rightarrow K = 0$

$$\Rightarrow \frac{1}{2}mv^2 = 0 \Rightarrow v = 0$$

42. $$F = -\frac{dU}{dr}$$

C and E are equilibrium points.

C is a stable equilibrium and E is unstable equilibrium point.

Between C and E, slope of U-r graph is positive, so force between C and E is negative (attractive).

Between E and F, slope of U-r graph is negative, so force between E and F is positive (repulsive).

43. $F = -kx + ax^3$

$$-\frac{dU}{dx} = -kx + ax^3$$

$$\Rightarrow \int -dU = \int(-kx + ax^3)\,dx \Rightarrow U = \frac{kx^2}{2} - \frac{ax^4}{4} + c$$

44. If internal forces are non-conservative, then mechanical energy will not conserved.

45. $\mathbf{F} = xy^2\hat{\mathbf{i}} + x^2y\hat{\mathbf{j}}$

$$W = \int \mathbf{F}\cdot d\mathbf{s} = \int (xy^2\hat{\mathbf{i}} + x^2y\hat{\mathbf{j}})\cdot(dx\hat{\mathbf{i}} + dy\hat{\mathbf{j}})$$

$$= \int (xy^2\,dx + x^2y\,dy) = \frac{1}{2}\int d(x^2y^2) = \frac{1}{2}[x^2y^2]_{(0,\,0)}^{(4,\,0)} = 0$$

46. Using work-energy theorem from A to B

$$W_{mg} + W_{\text{spring}} + W_F = \Delta K$$

$$\Rightarrow -0.01\times 10\times 0.3 + \frac{1}{2}\times 10\times[(0.5)^2-(0.2)^2] + W_F$$

$$= \frac{1}{2}\times 0.01\times 5^2 - 0 \quad \Rightarrow W_F = -0.895\text{ J}$$

47.

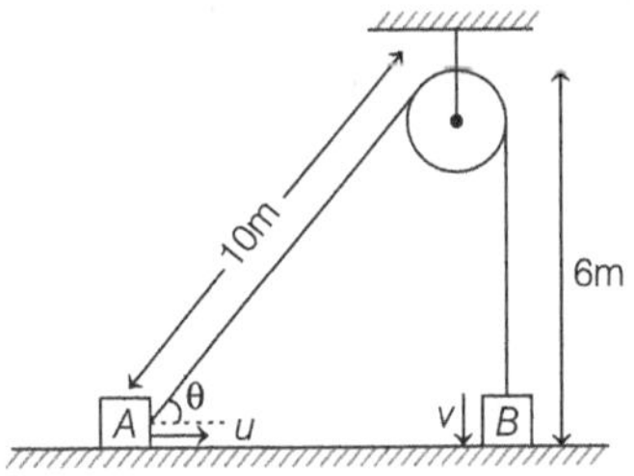

When B strikes the floor, lets take velocities of A and B as u and v respectively.

Using work-energy theorem for $(A+B)$ system

$$W_{mg} + W_N + W_T = \Delta K_{\text{system}}$$

$$\Rightarrow \quad (+25\times 10\times 5 + 0) + 0 + 0 = \frac{1}{2}\times 48\times u^2 + \frac{1}{2}25v^2$$

$$\Rightarrow 48u^2 + 25v^2 = 2500 \qquad \text{...(i)}$$

From string constraint,

$$-u\cos\theta + v = 0 \quad \Rightarrow v = u\cos\theta \Rightarrow \quad v = u\left(\frac{8}{10}\right) = \frac{4u}{5} \qquad \text{...(ii)}$$

Solving Eqs. (i) and (ii), we get

$$v = 5\text{ m/s}$$

48. Using work-energy theorem,

$$W_{mg} + W_{\text{friction}} + W_N = \Delta K$$

$$+mgy + \left(-\mu mg\cos\beta\,\frac{x_1}{\cos\beta} - \mu mg\cos\gamma\,\frac{x_2}{\cos\gamma}\right) + 0 = \frac{1}{2}mv^2 - 0$$

$$\Rightarrow \quad mgy - \mu mg\,(x_1 + x_2) = \frac{1}{2}mv^2 \quad \Rightarrow \quad v = \sqrt{2g(y - \mu x)}$$

49.

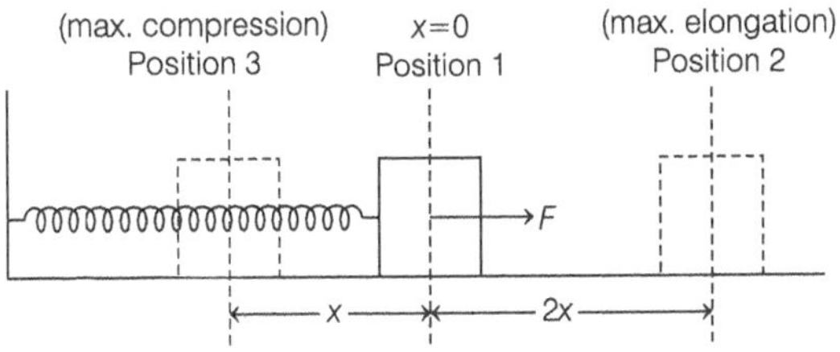

Applying work-energy theorem between 2 and 3,

$$W_{mg} + W_N + W_{\text{spring}} + W_F = \Delta K$$

$$\Rightarrow 0 + 0 + \frac{1}{2}k((2x)^2 - x^2) + F\,(3x)\cos 180^\circ = 0 - 0$$

$$\Rightarrow x = \frac{2F}{k} = \frac{2\times 10}{16} = 1.25\text{ m}$$

Applying work-energy theorem between position 1 and 2,

$$W_{mg} + W_N + W_{\text{spring}} + W_F = \Delta K$$

$$\Rightarrow 0 + 0 + \frac{1}{2}k(0^2 - (2x)^2) + F\,(2x) = 0 - \frac{1}{2}mv^2 \;\Rightarrow v = 5\text{m/s}$$

50. For m_2

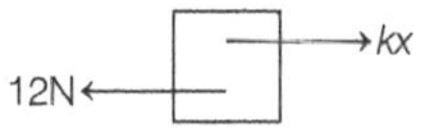

$$\Sigma F_x \geq 0$$

$$\Rightarrow \qquad kx - 12 \geq 0$$

$$\Rightarrow \qquad kx \geq 12$$

For m_1, using work-energy theorem,

$$W_F + W_{\text{friction}} + W_{mg} + W_N + W_{\text{spring}} = \Delta K$$

$$\Rightarrow \qquad Fx - 4x + 0 + 0 + \frac{1}{2}k(0^2 - x^2) = 0 - 0$$

$$\Rightarrow \quad (F-4) = \frac{kx}{2} \;\Rightarrow\; F - 4 \geq 6 \;\Rightarrow\; F \geq 10\text{ N}$$

51.

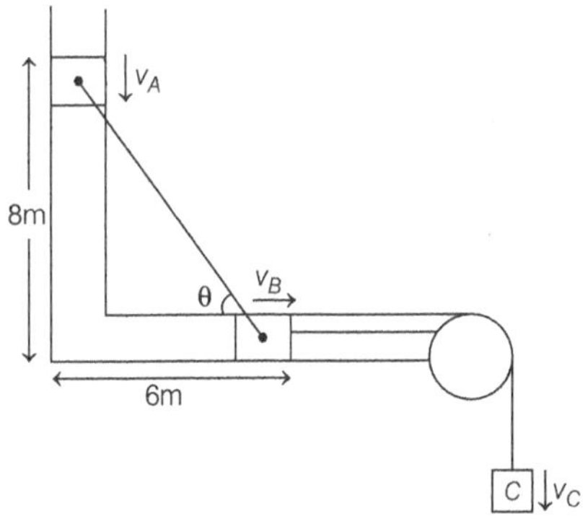

From string constraint,

$$v_B = v_C \;\text{ and }\; v_B\cos\theta = v_A\sin\theta$$

$$\Rightarrow \qquad v_A = v_B\cot\theta = \frac{3v_B}{4}$$

Using work-energy theorem for $(A+B+C)$,

$$W_{\text{gravity}} + W_N + W_T = \Delta K_{\text{system}}$$

$$\Rightarrow \quad (6\times g\times 6 + 0 + 32\,g\times 2) + 0 + 0$$

$$= \left(\frac{1}{2}\times 32\left(\frac{3v_B}{4}\right)^2 + \frac{1}{2}\times 16v_B^2 + \frac{1}{2}\times 6\times v_B^2\right) - (0+0+0)$$

$$\Rightarrow \quad v_B = \sqrt{\frac{100g}{20}}$$

$$\Rightarrow \quad v_B = \sqrt{49} = 7\text{ m/s}$$

Multiple Choice(s) Correct Questions

1.

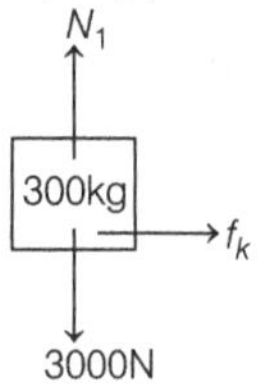

For crate,

$$\Sigma F_y = 0 \Rightarrow +N_1 - 3000 = 0 \Rightarrow N_1 = 3000\,\text{N}$$

$$f_k = \mu_k N = 0.4(3000) = 1200\,\text{N}$$

$$\Sigma F_x = ma \Rightarrow 1200 = 300a \Rightarrow a = 4\,\text{m/s}^2$$

$$v = u + at \Rightarrow 4 = 0 + 4t_0 \Rightarrow t_0 = 1\,\text{s}$$

$$s_{\text{belt}} = ut + \frac{1}{2}at^2 = 4 \times 1 = 4\,\text{m}$$

$$s_{\text{block}} = ut + \frac{1}{2}at^2 = 0 + \frac{1}{2}(4)(1)^2 \Rightarrow S_{\text{block}} = 2\,\text{m}$$

Work done friction on the crate $= (1200)(2) = 2.4\,\text{kJ}$

Work done by friction on the belt $= -(1200)(4) = -4.8\,\text{kJ}$

Using work-energy theorem for belt,

$$W_{\text{motor}} + W_{\text{friction}} = \Delta K$$

$$\Rightarrow W_{\text{motor}} - 4.8\,\text{kJ} = 0 - 0 \Rightarrow W_{\text{motor}} = 4.8\,\text{kJ}$$

2. (b, d)

3. $W_{\text{conservative}} = -\Delta U \Rightarrow \Delta W_2 = -\Delta U$

Using work-energy theorem, $\Delta W_1 + \Delta W_2 = \Delta K$

$$\Rightarrow \Delta W_1 - \Delta U = \Delta K \Rightarrow \Delta W_1 = \Delta K + \Delta U$$

$$\Rightarrow \Delta W_1 = \Delta E$$

4. $U = -kxy \Rightarrow \mathbf{F} = -\frac{\partial U}{\partial x}\hat{\mathbf{i}} - \frac{\partial U}{\partial y}\hat{\mathbf{j}} = ky\hat{\mathbf{i}} + kx\hat{\mathbf{j}}$

and **F** is conservative.

5.

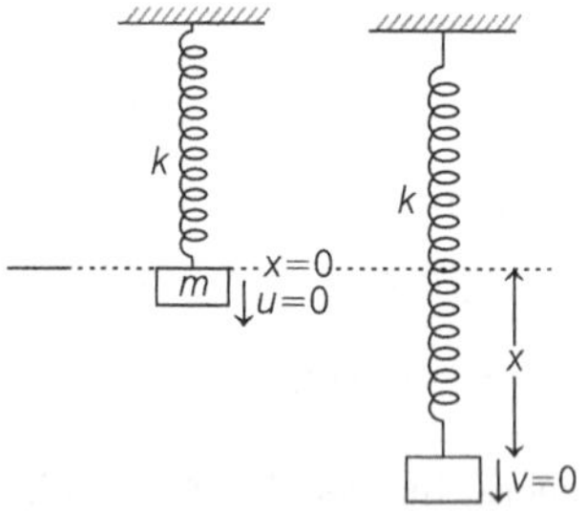

Using work-energy theorem for block, $W_{mg} + W_{\text{spring}} = \Delta K$

$$\Rightarrow +mgx + \frac{1}{2}k(0^2 - x^2) = 0 - 0 \Rightarrow x = \frac{2mg}{k}$$

At $\frac{x}{2}$,

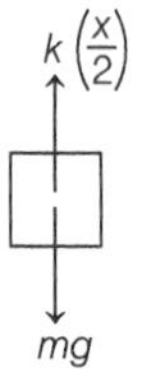

$$\Sigma F_y = ma_y \Rightarrow mg - k\left(\frac{1}{2}\frac{2mg}{k}\right) = ma \Rightarrow a = 0$$

At the lowest point,

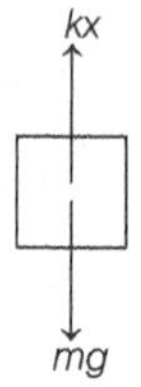

$$\Sigma F_y = ma_y \Rightarrow k\left(\frac{2mg}{k}\right) - mg = ma_y \Rightarrow a_y = g$$

6. Using work-energy theorem,

$$W_{mg} + W_N + W_{\text{spring}} = \Delta K$$

$$\Rightarrow 0 + 0 + \frac{1}{2}k(x_0^2 - x^2) = \frac{1}{2}mv^2 - 0$$

$$\Rightarrow v = \sqrt{\frac{k}{m}(x_0^2 - x^2)}$$

$$P = Fv\cos\theta$$

$$\Rightarrow P = kx\sqrt{\frac{k}{m}(x_0^2 - x^2)}\cos 0°$$

$$\Rightarrow P = kx\sqrt{\frac{k}{m}(x_0^2 - x^2)} = \sqrt{\frac{k^3x^2}{m}(x_0^2 - x^2)}$$

To maximum power,

$$\frac{dP}{dx} = 0 \Rightarrow = \sqrt{\frac{k^3}{m}}\frac{(2xx_0^2 - 4x^3)}{2\sqrt{x^2(x_0^2 - x^2)}} = 0 \Rightarrow x = \frac{x_0}{\sqrt{2}}$$

7. Frictional force on boy is static in nature.

$$W_{\text{static friction}} = 0 \Rightarrow F_{\text{avg}} = \frac{\Delta P}{\Delta t}$$

$$\text{Average friction} = \frac{mv_0 - 0}{t_0} = \frac{mv_0}{t_0}$$

Using work-energy theorem for boy,

$$W_{mg} + W_N + W_{\text{friction}} + W_{\text{internal forces}} = \Delta K$$

$$\Rightarrow 0 + 0 + 0 + W_{\text{internal forces}} = \frac{1}{2}mv_0^2 - 0$$

8. $U = \frac{x^4}{4} - 2x^3 + \frac{11}{2}x^2 - 6x$

$$F = -\frac{dU}{dx} = -(x^3 - 6x^2 + 11x - 6) = 0$$

$\Rightarrow x = 1, x = 2$ and $x = 3$

$$\frac{d^2U}{dx^2} = 3x^2 - 12x + 11$$

At $x = 1$,

$$\frac{d^2U}{dx^2} = 3 - 12 + 11 > 0$$

$\Rightarrow$ Stable equilibrium

At $x = 2$,

$$\frac{d^2U}{dx^2} = -1 < 0$$

$\Rightarrow$ Unstable equilibrium

At $x = 3$,

$$\frac{d^2U}{dx^2} = 3 > 0$$

$\Rightarrow$ Stable equilibrium

9. $U = 3x + 4y$

$$\mathbf{F} = -\frac{\partial U}{\partial x}\hat{\mathbf{i}} - \frac{\partial U}{\partial y}\hat{\mathbf{j}} = -3\hat{\mathbf{i}} - 4\hat{\mathbf{j}}$$

$$\Rightarrow \quad \mathbf{a} = -3\hat{\mathbf{i}} - 4\hat{\mathbf{j}}$$

$$s_x = u_x t + \frac{1}{2}a_x t^2 \;\Rightarrow\; 0 - 6 = 0 + \frac{1}{2}(-3)t^2 \;\Rightarrow\; t = 2\text{ s}$$

$$\mathbf{v} = \mathbf{u} + \mathbf{a}t = 0 + (-3\hat{\mathbf{i}} - 4\hat{\mathbf{j}}) \times 2 \;\Rightarrow\; \mathbf{v} = -6\hat{\mathbf{i}} - 8\hat{\mathbf{j}}$$

$$\text{Speed} = \sqrt{6^2 + 8^2} = 10\text{ m/s}$$

$$s_y = u_y t + \frac{1}{2}a_y t^2 \;\Rightarrow\; y - 4 = 0 + \frac{1}{2}(-4)(2)^2 \;\Rightarrow\; y = -4\text{ m}$$

10. $P = Fv\cos\theta$

At $t = 1$, P is positive $\Rightarrow$ θ is acute

At $t = 3$; P is positive $\Rightarrow$ θ is acute

At $t = 7$; P is negative $\Rightarrow$ θ is obtuse

$$P = \frac{dW}{dt} \;\Rightarrow\; \int dW = \int P\,dt$$

$W = \int P\,dt$ = Area under P-t graph $= 40 - 20 = 20$ J

11. as work done by these forces depend only on the initial and final positions.

12. $\Sigma F_y = ma_y$

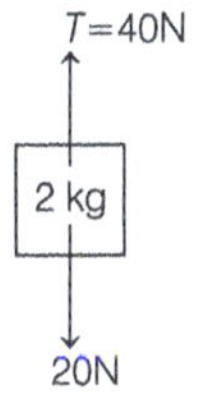

$$\Rightarrow \quad 40 - 20 = 2a \;\Rightarrow\; a = 10\text{ m/s}^2$$

Using work-energy theorem,

$$W_{mg} + W_T = \Delta K \;\Rightarrow\; -20x + 40x = 40$$

$$\Rightarrow \quad x = 2\text{ m}$$

$$W_{mg} = -20 \times 2 = -40\text{ N}, \quad W_T = 40 \times 2 = 80\text{ J}$$

13. Lets take maximum elongation to be x,

$$\Rightarrow \quad W_N + W_{mg} + W_T + W_{spring} = \Delta K_{system}$$

$$\Rightarrow 0 + (+2mgx + 0) + 0 + \frac{1}{2}k(0^2 - x^2) = (0 + 0) - (0 + 0)$$

$$\Rightarrow \quad x = \frac{4mg}{k}$$

Maximum energy stored in the spring $= \frac{1}{2}kx^2$

$$= \frac{1}{2}k\left(\frac{4mg}{k}\right)^2 = \frac{8m^2g^2}{k}$$

Kinetic energy of the system will be maximum when acceleration $= 0$

$$\Rightarrow \quad kx = 2mg \;\Rightarrow\; x = \frac{2mg}{k}$$

Using work-energy theorem for system,

$$W_N + W_{mg} + W_T + W_{spring} = \Delta K$$

$$\Rightarrow 0 + 2mg\left(\frac{2mg}{k}\right) + 0 + \frac{1}{2}k\left[0^2 - \left(\frac{2mg}{k}\right)^2\right] = K_{max} - 0$$

$$\Rightarrow \quad K_{max} = \frac{2m^2g^2}{k}$$

14. $K = \frac{1}{2}mv^2 \Rightarrow \frac{dK}{dt} = \frac{1}{2}m(2v)\frac{dv}{dt} = mva_T = m(\mathbf{v}\cdot\mathbf{a})$

$$\frac{d|\mathbf{v}|}{dt} = \text{Tangential acceleration} = \frac{\mathbf{v}\cdot\mathbf{a}}{v}$$

$$\mathbf{a} = \frac{d\mathbf{v}}{dt} \;\Rightarrow\; \int d\mathbf{v} = \int \mathbf{a}\,dt \;\Rightarrow\; |\Delta\mathbf{v}| = \left|\int_{t_1}^{t_2} \mathbf{a}\,dt\right|$$

15. (a, d)

16. (a, d)

17. Lets take maximum elongation in the spring to be x.

Using work-energy theorem,

$$W_{mg} + W_{spring} = \Delta K$$

$$\Rightarrow \quad mg(2x) + \frac{1}{2}k(0^2 - x^2) = 0 - 0 \;\Rightarrow\; x = \frac{4mg}{k}$$

Speed of the block will be maximum when $a = 0$

$$\Rightarrow \quad T = mg = \frac{kx}{2} \;\Rightarrow\; x = \frac{2mg}{k}$$

Using work-energy theorem,

$$W_{mg} + W_{spring} = \Delta K$$

$$\Rightarrow mg\left[2\left(\frac{2mg}{k}\right)\right] + \frac{1}{2}k\left[0^2 - \left(\frac{2mg}{k}\right)^2\right] = \frac{1}{2}mv^2 - 0$$

$$\Rightarrow \quad v = 2g\sqrt{\frac{m}{k}}$$

18. (A) $W_{friction} = \Delta K = \frac{1}{2}m(0)^2 - \frac{1}{2}m(v_0)^2 = -\frac{1}{2}mv_0^2$

(B) $W_{friction} = \Delta K = \frac{1}{2}m(-v_0)^2 - \frac{1}{2}m(0)^2 = \frac{1}{2}mv_0^2$

(C) $W_{friction} = \Delta K = \frac{1}{2}m(0)^2 - \frac{1}{2}m(0)^2 = 0$

(D) $W_{friction} = \Delta K = \frac{1}{2}m(-v_0)^2 - \frac{1}{2}m(-v_0)^2 = 0$

19. (b, c, d)

20.

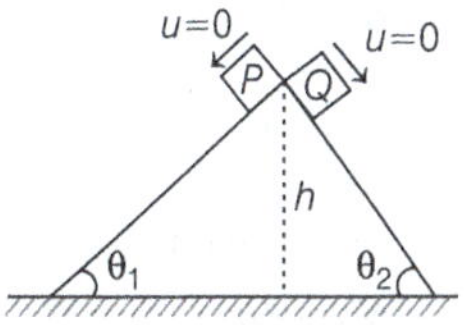

$$s = ut + \frac{1}{2}at^2 \;\Rightarrow\; \frac{h}{\sin\theta} = 0 + \frac{1}{2}(g\sin\theta)t^2 \;\Rightarrow\; t = \sqrt{\frac{2h}{g\sin^2\theta}}$$

Since, $\theta_2 > \theta_1 \Rightarrow$ Block Q will reach earlier.

Using work-energy theorem, $W_{mg} + W_N = \Delta K$

$\Rightarrow mgh + 0 = \frac{1}{2}mv^2 - 0 \quad \Rightarrow v = \sqrt{2gh}$

So, both the blocks will reach with the same speed.

Comprehension Based Questions

1. Lets say lower block will lose contact when elongation in the spring is x.

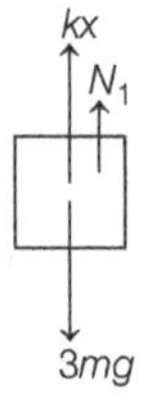

$$\Sigma F_y = 0 \quad \Rightarrow kx + N_1 = 3mg$$

For losing contact, $N_1 = 0 \quad \Rightarrow x = \frac{3mg}{K}$

Using work-energy theorem for upper block,

$$W_{mg} + W_{spring} = \Delta K$$

$$\Rightarrow -mg\left(\frac{mg}{k} + \delta + x\right) + \frac{1}{2}k\left[\left(\frac{mg}{k} + \delta\right)^2 - x^2\right] = 0 - 0$$

$$\Rightarrow \qquad \delta = \frac{4mg}{k}$$

2. For lower block,

$\Sigma F_y = 0 \Rightarrow N_1 + kx = 3mg \Rightarrow mg + kx = 3mg \Rightarrow x = \frac{2mg}{k}$

Using work-energy theorem for upper block,

$W_{mg} + W_{spring} = \Delta k$

$$-mg\left(\frac{mg}{k} + \delta + \frac{2mg}{k}\right) + \frac{1}{2}k\left[\left(\frac{mg}{k} + \delta\right)^2 - \left(\frac{2mg}{k}\right)^2\right] = 0 - 0$$

$$\Rightarrow \qquad \delta = \frac{3mg}{k}$$

3.

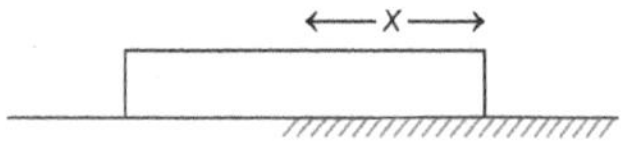

When x length of rod is in rough region,

$$f_k = \mu N = \mu\left(\frac{M}{L}xg\right)$$

4. Using work-energy theorem for rod,

$$W_{mg} + W_N + W_{friction} = \Delta K$$

$$\Rightarrow \quad 0 + 0 - \int_0^L \frac{\mu Mgx}{L}\,dx = 0 - \frac{1}{2}Mv_0^2 \quad \Rightarrow \quad v_0 = \sqrt{\mu gL}$$

5. Using work-energy theorem for rod,

$$W_{mg} + W_N + W_{friction} = \Delta K$$

$$\Rightarrow \quad 0 + 0 - \int_0^L \frac{\mu mgx}{L}\,dx - \int_L^x \mu mg\,dx = 0 - \frac{1}{2}m(2\sqrt{\mu gL})^2$$

$$\Rightarrow \qquad x = \frac{5L}{2}$$

6. $W_{OAC} = W_{OA} + W_{AC} = 0 + \int_0^4 x^2 y\,dy = 0 + \int_0^4 y\,dy = 8\text{ J}$

7. $W_{OBC} = W_{OB} + W_{BC} = 0 + \int_0^1 xy\,dx = 0 + 4\int_0^1 x\,dx = 2\text{J}$

8. $W_{ODC} = \int xy\,dx + \int x^2 y\,dx = \int_0^1 4x^3\,dx + \int_0^4 \frac{4y^2}{4}\,dy$

$$= 1 - 0 + \frac{64}{12} = \frac{19}{3}\text{ J}$$

9. Force is non-conservative as work done by the force depends on path taken.

10. $F = \frac{-dU}{dr} \quad \Rightarrow \quad F = \frac{k}{a^3}(4r - 3a)$ for $r \le a$

$$= \frac{k}{r^2} \text{ for } r > a$$

$$F = \frac{k}{a^3}(4r - 3a) = 0 \quad \Rightarrow \quad r = \frac{3a}{4}$$

For $r < \frac{3a}{4}$, force on the particle is towards origin and for $r > \frac{3a}{4}$, force is away from origin. So, we just need to make particle reach $r = \frac{3a}{4}$ and thereafter it will go by itself.

Using mechanical energy conservation between $r = \frac{3a}{4}$ and $r = \infty$.

$$K_1 + U_1 = K_2 + U_2$$

$$\frac{1}{2}mv_0^2 + \frac{k}{\infty} = 0 + \frac{k}{a^3}\left[3a\left(\frac{3a}{4}\right) - 2\left(\frac{3a}{4}\right)^2\right] \quad \Rightarrow \quad v_0 = \sqrt{\frac{9k}{4ma}}$$

11. Using mechanical energy conservation between $r = \infty$ and $r = 0$.

$$K_1 + U_1 = K_2 + U_2$$

$$\frac{1}{2}mv_0^2 + \frac{k}{\infty} = \frac{1}{2}mv^2 + 0 \quad \Rightarrow \quad v = v_0 = \sqrt{\frac{9k}{4ma}}$$

12. $F = -\frac{dU}{dx} = -$ (slope of U-x graph)

At $x = 0$, F is negative as slope is positive.

So, the particle will have towards negative X-axis after releasing it from rest.

13. Speed will be maximum where potential energy will be minimum.

Using mechanical energy conservation,

$K_1 + U_1 = K_2 + U_2 \Rightarrow 0 + 10 = \frac{1}{2} \times 2 \times v^2 + (-15)$

$\Rightarrow \qquad v = 5\text{ m/s}$

14. At $x = -5$, potential energy is minimum. Hence, stable equilibrium.

At $x = 10$, potential energy has local maxima. Hence, unstable equilibrium.

15. Maximum acceleration of upper block is

$$\mu g = 0.4(10) = 4\text{ m/s}^2$$

At $t = 5$, for lower block

$$\Sigma F = ma \Rightarrow 5t - 0.4(20) - (0.02t)(50) = 3a$$

$$\Rightarrow 25 - 8 - 5 = 3a \Rightarrow a = 4\,\text{m/s}^2$$

So, relative motion between the blocks will start at $t = 5$. So, for $t \le 5$, friction force between the blocks is static. Work done by static friction on upper block w.r.t. lower block will be zero.

16. For $t \le 5$,

$$a = \frac{5t - (0.02t)(50)}{5} \Rightarrow a = \frac{4t}{5}$$

$$\Rightarrow \frac{dv}{dt} = \frac{4t}{5} \Rightarrow v = \frac{2t^2}{5}$$

$$\Rightarrow K = \frac{1}{2} \times 2 \times \left(\frac{2t^2}{5}\right)^2 = \frac{4t^4}{25}$$

For $t > 5$, $a = \mu g = 4\,\text{m/s}^2$

$$v = u + at \Rightarrow v = 10 + 4(t - 5)$$

$$\Rightarrow K = \frac{1}{2} \times 2 \times (-10 + 4t)^2 \Rightarrow K = (4t - 10)^2$$

17. Using work-energy theorem for system,

$$W_{mg} + W_N + W_{friction} + W_T + W_{spring} = \Delta K$$

$$\Rightarrow (+mgx + 0) + 0 - \frac{1}{4} mgx + 0 + \frac{1}{2} k(0^2 - x^2) = (0 + 0) - (0 + 0)$$

$$\Rightarrow x = \frac{3mg}{2k}$$

18. Using work-energy theorem for system,

$$W_{mg} + W_N + W_{friction} + W_T + W_{spring} = \Delta K$$

$$\Rightarrow (+mgx + 0) + 0 - \mu mgx + 0 + \frac{1}{2} k(0^2 - x^2) = (0 + 0) - (0 + 0)$$

$$\Rightarrow x = \frac{2mg(1 - \mu)}{k}$$

For the block on the table, $\Sigma F_x = 0$

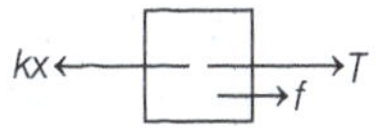

$$\Rightarrow kx = T + f \Rightarrow kx = mg + f \Rightarrow f = kx - mg$$

$$\Rightarrow f = k\left(\frac{2mg}{k}(1 - \mu)\right) - mg \Rightarrow f = mg(1 - 2\mu)$$

$$f \le f_L \Rightarrow mg(1 - 2\mu) \le \mu mg \Rightarrow \mu \ge \frac{1}{3} \Rightarrow \mu_{min} = \frac{1}{3}$$

19. Using work-energy theorem for the block on the table,

$$W_{mg} + W_N + W_{spring} + W_{friction} = \Delta K$$

$$0 + 0 + \frac{1}{2} k\left[\left(\frac{3mg}{2k}\right)^2 - x^2\right] \Rightarrow -\mu mg\left(\frac{3mg}{2k} + x\right) = 0 - 0$$

$$\Rightarrow \frac{3mg}{2k} - x = \frac{mg}{2k} \Rightarrow x = \frac{mg}{k}$$

20. For bead

$$\Sigma F_y = 0$$

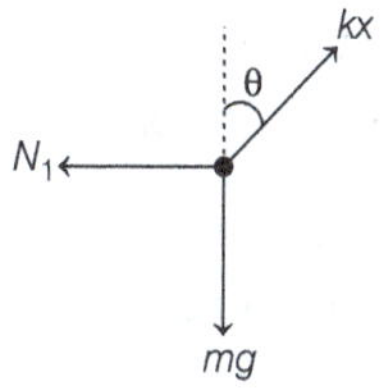

$$mg = kx\cos\theta \Rightarrow mg = \left(\frac{2mg}{a}\right)\left(\frac{OB}{\cos\theta}\right)\cos\theta \Rightarrow OB = \frac{a}{2}$$

21. Using work-energy theorem between C and O,

$$W_{mg} + W_N + W_{string} = \Delta K$$

$$\Rightarrow +mg(a) + 0 + \frac{1}{2}\left(\frac{2mg}{a}\right)[(\sqrt{2}a)^2 - a^2] = \frac{1}{2}mv^2 - 0$$

$$\Rightarrow v = \sqrt{4ag}$$

22. Using work-energy theorem for bead,

$$W_{mg} + W_N + W_{string} = \Delta K$$

$$\Rightarrow +mg(a + x) + 0 + \frac{1}{2}\left(\frac{2mg}{a}\right)[(\sqrt{2}a)^2 - (\sqrt{a^2 + x^2})^2] = 0 - 0$$

$$\Rightarrow x = 2a$$

23. $F = \dfrac{-dU}{dr} = -\left(\dfrac{-2A}{r^3} + \dfrac{B}{r^2}\right) = 0 \Rightarrow r = \dfrac{2A}{B}$

24. $\dfrac{d^2U}{dr^2} = \dfrac{6A}{r^4} - \dfrac{2B}{r^3}$

At $r = \dfrac{2A}{B} \Rightarrow \dfrac{d^2U}{dr^2} = \dfrac{6A}{\left(\frac{2A}{B}\right)^4} - \dfrac{2B}{\left(\frac{2A}{B}\right)^3} = \dfrac{1}{4}\dfrac{B^4}{A^3} > 0$

So, $r = \dfrac{2A}{B}$ is stable equilibrium.

25. $W_{ext} = \Delta U = U_2 - U_1 = \left(\dfrac{A}{\infty^2} - \dfrac{B}{\infty}\right) - \left[\dfrac{A}{\left(\frac{2A}{B}\right)^2} - \dfrac{B}{\left(\frac{2A}{B}\right)}\right] = \dfrac{B^2}{4A}$

26. $E = K + U$

$$\frac{-3B^2}{16A} = 0 + \frac{A}{r^2} - \frac{B}{r} \Rightarrow \frac{3B^2}{16A}r^2 - Br + A = 0$$

$$\Rightarrow r = \frac{4A}{3B} \text{ and } r = \frac{4A}{B}$$

27. Lets take maximum compression to be x. Using work-energy theorem for ball,

$$W_{mg} + W_{spring} = \Delta K$$

$$\Rightarrow +mg(0.4 + x) + \frac{1}{2}k(0^2 - x^2) = 0 - 0$$

$$\Rightarrow 8 + 20x - 100x^2 = 0 \Rightarrow x = 0.4\,\text{m}$$

28. Speed of the block will be maximum when its acceleration is zero.

$\Rightarrow \quad mg - kx = 0 \Rightarrow x = \frac{mg}{k} = 0.1\,\text{m}$

Using work-energy theorem,

$\Rightarrow \quad +2\times 10\times(0.4+x)+\frac{1}{2}\times 200\,(0^2-x^2)=\frac{1}{2}mv^2-0$

$\Rightarrow \quad v = 3\,\text{m/s}$

29. Height below P where particle attains maximum velocity $= 0.4 + 0.1 = 0.5\,\text{m}$

Match the Columns Questions

1. (A) Work done by gravity $= -mgh$

(B) Work done by friction $= -\int(\mu mg\cos\theta)\,dl$

$= -\mu mg\int dl\cos\theta$

$= -\mu mg\int_0^l dx = -\mu mgl$

(C) Using work-energy theorem for block,

$W_{mg}+W_N+W_{\text{friction}}+W_F=\Delta K$

$\Rightarrow \quad -mgh+0-\mu mgl+W_F=0-0 \Rightarrow W_F=mg\,(h+\mu l)$

(D) $W_{\text{all forces}}=\Delta K=0-0=0$

2. $U=20+(x-2)^2$

At $x=5, K=20\,\text{J}$

$U=20+(5-2)^2=29\,\text{J} \Rightarrow E=K+U=49\,\text{J}$

For x to be maximum or minimum velocity of the particle is zero.

$\Rightarrow \quad E=K+U \Rightarrow 49=0+20+(x-2)^2$

$\Rightarrow \quad x=2\pm\sqrt{29}$

$x_{max}=2+\sqrt{29}=7.38\,\text{m},$

$x_{min}=2-\sqrt{29}=-3.38\,\text{m}$

$E=K+U \Rightarrow 49=K_{min}+U_{max} \Rightarrow 49=0+U_{max}$

$\Rightarrow \quad U_{max}=49\,\text{J}$

$E=K+U \Rightarrow 49=K_{max}+U_{min}$

$\Rightarrow \quad 49=K_{max}+20$

$\Rightarrow \quad K_{max}=29\,\text{J}$

3.

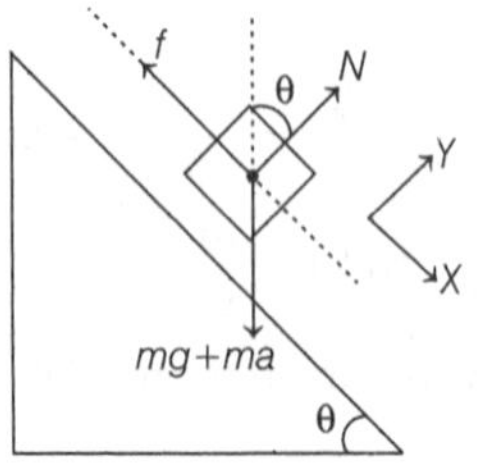

For block,

$\Sigma F_x=0 \Rightarrow f=(mg+ma)\sin\theta$

$\Sigma F_y=0 \Rightarrow N=(mg+ma)\cos\theta$

$s=ut+\frac{1}{2}at^2 \Rightarrow s=0+\frac{1}{2}(2)(4)^2=16\,\text{m}$

Work done by gravity $=Fs\cos\theta=mgs\cos 180°=-160\,\text{J}$

Work done by normal reaction $=Fs\cos\theta$

$=\{(mg+ma)\cos\theta\}\,s\cos\theta$

$=m(g+a)\,s\cos^2\theta$

$=1\,(10+2)\,(16)\cos^2 30° = 144\,\text{J}$

Work done by friction $=Fs\cos\theta$

$=[\{m(g+a)\sin\theta\}\}(s)\cos(90°-\theta)]=m(g+a)\,s\sin^2\theta$

$=1\,(10+2)\,(16)\sin^2 30°=48\,\text{J}$

Work done by all forces $=W_{mg}+W_N+W_{\text{friction}}$

$=-160+144+48=32\,\text{J}$

4. Work done by $F_1=F(s\cos\theta)=FR$

Work done by $F_2=F\,(s\cos\theta)=FR$

Work done by $F_3=\int F\,dl=F\int dl=F\left(\frac{\pi R}{2}\right)$

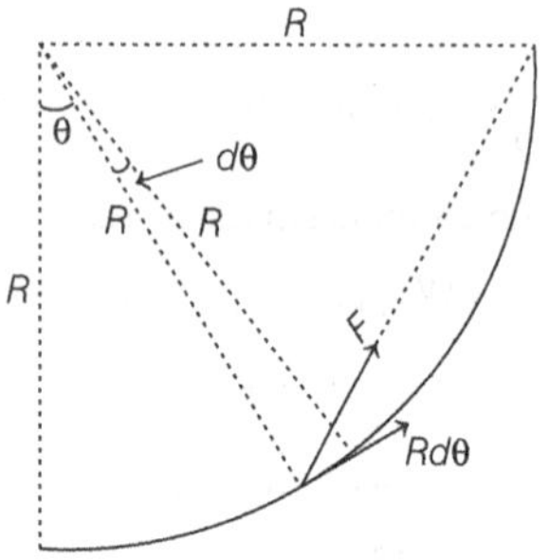

Work done by $F_4=\int_0^{90°}F\,(R\,d\theta)\cos\left(\frac{90°-\theta}{2}\right)$

$=\frac{FR}{\left(\frac{-1}{2}\right)}\left[\sin\left(\frac{90°-\theta}{2}\right)\right]_0^{90°}=\sqrt{2}\,FR$

5. (A) Object will first accelerate and then decelerate to come to rest again. Kinetic energy first increases and then decreases.

Spring potential energy plus gravitational potential energy first decreases and then increases.

Mechanical energy will be constant.

(B) Gravitational potential energy will keep decreasing and kinetic energy will keep increasing while mechanical energy will remain constant throughout.

(C) Kinetic energy will keep increasing. Potential energy will be constant. Mechanical energy will increase with time.

(D) Kinetic energy is constant with time. Gravitational potential energy decreases with time, so mechanical energy decreases with time.

6. (A) Area under a-x graph $=\frac{v_2^2-v_1^2}{2} \Rightarrow 120=\frac{v_2^2-4^2}{2}$

$\Rightarrow \quad v_2=16\,\text{m/s}$

$K_2=\frac{1}{2}mv_2^2=\frac{1}{2}\times 1\times 16^2=128\,\text{J}$

(B) $W_{\text{conservative forces}} = -\Delta U = -(-120 - 120) = 240\text{ J}$

(C) $W_{\text{all forces}} = \Delta K = K_2 - K_1 = 128 - 8 = 120\text{ J}$

(D) $W_{\text{external forces}} = \Delta E = (K_2 + U_2) - (K_1 + U_1)$
$= (128 - 120) - (8 + 120) = -120\text{ J}$

7. A → Q, B → S, C → R

8. A → R, B → S, C → P

9. Lets say compressions in S_1 and S_2 are x_1 and x_2, respectively.

$$x_1 + x_2 = x \quad \text{...(i)}$$
$$k_1x_1 = k_2x_2 \quad \text{...(ii)}$$

From Eqs. (i) and (ii), we get

$$x_1 = \frac{k_2x}{k_1 + k_2} \quad \text{and} \quad x_2 = \frac{k_1x}{k_1 + k_2}$$

For spring S_1,

$$W_{\text{ext}} = \Delta E = \Delta K + \Delta U$$

Work done by wall on S_1

+ Work done by S_2 on $S_1 = 0 + \frac{1}{2}k_1(x_1^2 - 0^2)$

$\Rightarrow 0 +$ Work done by S_2 on $S_1 = \frac{1}{2}\frac{k_1k_2^2x^2}{(k_1 + k_2)^2}$

$\Rightarrow$ Work done by S_2 on $S_1 = \frac{1}{2}\frac{k_1k_2^2x^2}{(k_1 + k_2)^2}$

For $(S_1 + S_2 + \text{block})$ system, $W_{\text{ext}} = \Delta U + \Delta K$

Work done by F on block + Work done by wall on S_1

$$= \frac{1}{2}k_1x_1^2 + \frac{1}{2}k_2x_2^2 + 0$$

$\Rightarrow$ Work done by F on block $+ 0 = \frac{1}{2}k_1\left(\frac{k_2x}{k_1 + k_2}\right)^2 + \frac{1}{2}k_2\left(\frac{k_1x}{k_1 + k_2}\right)^2$

$\Rightarrow$ Work done by F on block $= \frac{1}{2}\left(\frac{k_1k_2}{k_1 + k_2}\right)x^2$

For block,

$$W_{\text{all forces}} = \Delta K$$

$\Rightarrow$ Work done by S_2 on block + Work done by F on block $= \Delta K$

$\Rightarrow$ Work done by S_2 on block

$$+ \frac{1}{2}\frac{k_1k_2}{k_1 + k_2}x^2 = 0 - 0$$

$\Rightarrow$ Work done by S_2 on block $= -\frac{1}{2}\frac{k_1k_2x^2}{k_1 + k_2}$

10.

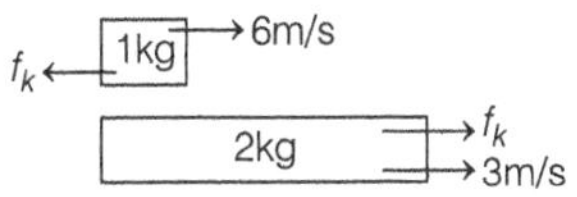

For 1 kg block,

$$\Sigma F_y = 0 \quad \Rightarrow N_1 = 10\text{ N}$$

$$f_k = \mu_k N_1 = (0.04)(10) = 0.4\text{ N}$$

$$\Sigma F_x = ma_x \quad \Rightarrow -0.4 = 1\,a_1 \quad \Rightarrow \quad a_1 = -0.4\text{ m/s}^2$$

$$v = u + at \quad \Rightarrow v_1 = 6 - 0.4t$$

For 2 kg,

$$\Sigma F_x = ma_x \quad \Rightarrow \quad 0.4 = 2a_2 \quad \Rightarrow a_2 = 0.2\text{ m/s}^2$$

$$v = u + at \quad \Rightarrow v_2 = 3 + 0.2t$$

(A) For relative motion to stop $v_1 = v_2$

$\Rightarrow \quad 6 - 0.4t = 3 + 0.2t \quad \Rightarrow t = 5\text{ s}$ and $v_1 = v_2 = 4\text{ m/s}$

(B) Work done by friction on the block

$$= \Delta K_{\text{block}} = \frac{1}{2}\times 1\times(4)^2 - \frac{1}{2}\times 1\times(6)^2 = -10\text{ J}$$

(C) Work done by friction on the plank $= \Delta K_{\text{plank}}$

$$= \frac{1}{2}\times 2\times 4^2 - \frac{1}{2}\times 2\times 3^2 = 7\text{ J}$$

(D) Work done by friction on system $= -10 + 7 = -3\text{ J}$

$$W = \Delta E \quad \Rightarrow \Delta E = -3\text{ J}$$

$\Rightarrow$ Loss in mechanical energy = 3 J

Numerical Value Questions

1.

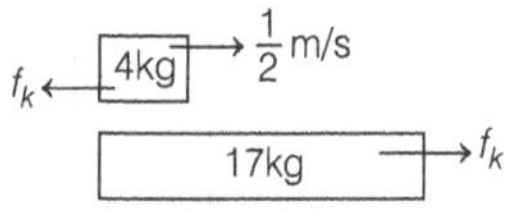

$$f_k = \mu_k N = \frac{1}{2(40)} = 20\text{ N}$$

For 4 kg block,

$$\Sigma F_x = ma_x \quad \Rightarrow -20 = 4a_1 \quad \Rightarrow a_1 = -5\text{ m/s}^2$$

$$v = u + at \quad \Rightarrow v_1 = \frac{1}{2} - 5t$$

For 17 kg platform,

$$\Sigma F_x = ma_x \quad \Rightarrow 20 = 17a_2 \quad \Rightarrow \quad a_2 = \frac{20}{17}\text{ m/s}^2$$

$$v = u + at \quad \Rightarrow \quad v_2 = 0 + \left(\frac{20}{17}\right)t$$

$$v_1 = v_2$$

$$\Rightarrow \quad \frac{1}{2} - 5t = \frac{20}{17}t \quad \Rightarrow t = \frac{17}{210}\text{ s}$$

$$v_1 = v_2 = \frac{2}{21}\text{ m/s}$$

Kinetic energy loss due to friction

$$= \left\{\frac{1}{2}\times 4\times\left(\frac{1}{2}\right)^2 + 0\right\} - \frac{1}{2}\times(17 + 4)\left(\frac{2}{21}\right)^2$$

$$= \frac{1}{2} - \frac{2}{21} = \frac{17}{42}\text{ J}$$

$$\text{Average power} = \frac{\text{Work done by friction}}{\text{Time}} = \frac{\frac{-17}{42}}{\frac{17}{210}} = -5\text{ W}$$

2. $W=\int \mathbf{F}\cdot d\mathbf{s} \Rightarrow W=\int(-2x+2y)\hat{\mathbf{i}}+(2x-y^2)\hat{\mathbf{j}}\cdot(dx\,\hat{\mathbf{i}}+dy\hat{\mathbf{j}})$

$$\Rightarrow W=-\int_2^1 2x\,dx-\int_3^2 y^2dy+2\int_{(2,\,3)}^{(1,\,2)}(y\,dx+x\,dy)$$

$$\Rightarrow W=-2\int_2^1 x\,dx-\int_3^2 y^2\,dy+2\int_{(2,\,3)}^{(1,\,2)}d\,(xy)$$

$$\Rightarrow W=-2\left[\frac{x^2}{2}\right]_2^1-\left[\frac{y^3}{3}\right]_3^2+2\,[xy]_{(2,\,3)}^{(1,\,2)}$$

$$\Rightarrow W=+3+\frac{19}{3}+2\,(2-6)=\frac{4}{3}\text{ J}$$

Using work-energy theorem, $W=\Delta K$

$$\Rightarrow \frac{4}{3}=\frac{1}{2}\times 2\times v^2-\frac{8}{3} \Rightarrow v^2=4 \Rightarrow v=2\text{ m/s}$$

3. $\mathbf{F}=y\hat{\mathbf{i}}-x\hat{\mathbf{j}}$

$$\tan\theta=\frac{F_y}{F_x}=-\frac{x}{y} \Rightarrow F=\sqrt{y^2+x^2}=a$$

$$x^2+y^2=a^2 \Rightarrow x\,dx+y\,dy=0 \Rightarrow \frac{dy}{dx}=-\frac{x}{y}$$

So, force is of constant magnitude a and is always along the tangent to the circular path and opposite to direction of motion.

$$W=\int F\,ds\cos 180°=-F\int ds=-a\left(\frac{\pi a}{2}\right)=\frac{-\pi a^2}{2}$$

4.

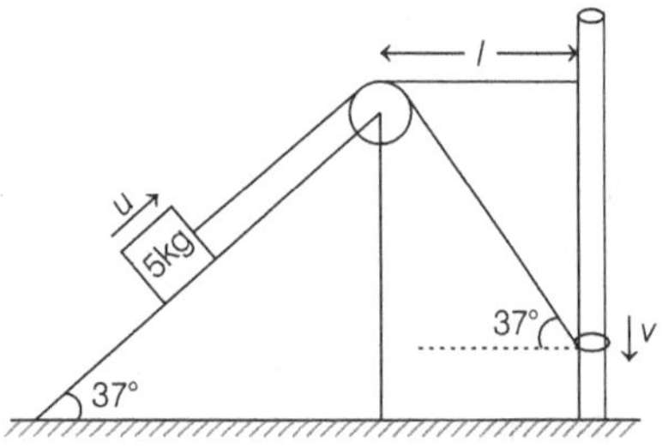

Using work-energy theorem for (block + ring) system,

$$W_{\text{gravity}}+W_N+W_T=\Delta K_{\text{system}}$$

$$\Rightarrow [+2\times 10\times l\tan 37°-5\times 10\times\sin 37°\,(l\sec 37°-l)]+0+0$$
$$=\left(\frac{1}{2}\times 2\times v^2+\frac{1}{2}\times 5\times u^2\right)-(0+0)$$

$$\Rightarrow \quad 2v^2+5u^2=130 \qquad \text{...(i)}$$

From string constraint,

$$v\cos 37°=u \Rightarrow u=\frac{4v}{5} \qquad \text{...(ii)}$$

From Eqs. (i) and (ii), we get

$$v=5\text{ m/s}$$

5. Let take maximum extension in the spring to be x.
Using work-energy theorem for system,

$$W_{mg}+W_T+W_{\text{spring}}=\Delta K$$

$$\Rightarrow 1\times 10\times\left(\frac{x}{2}\right)+0+\frac{1}{2}\times 50\,(0^2-x^2)=0-0$$

$$\Rightarrow \quad x=0.2\text{ m}=20\text{ cm}$$

6. $W_N=Fs\cos\theta$

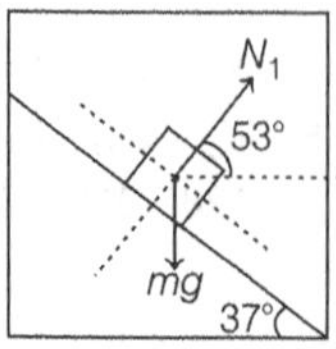

$$=(100\cos 37°)(10\times 2)\cos 53°=960\text{ J}$$

7. Using work-energy theorem for ring,

$$W_{\text{gravity}}+W_N+W_{\text{spring}}=\Delta K$$

$$\Rightarrow \quad +mgx+0+\frac{1}{2}k\,[l^2-(\sqrt{l^2+x^2})^2]=0-0$$

$$\Rightarrow \quad x=\frac{2mg}{k}=\frac{2(1)(10)}{500}=\frac{1}{25}\text{ m}=4\text{ cm}$$

8. Using work-energy theorem for block,

$$W_{mg}+W_N+W_{\text{spring}}+W_{\text{friction}}=\Delta K$$

$$\Rightarrow (+\,mg\sin 37°)x+0+\frac{1}{2}k(0^2-x^2)$$
$$-\int_0^x(0.5\,x)\,mg\cos 37°\,dx=0-0$$

$$\Rightarrow \quad 30x-5x^2-10x^2=0 \Rightarrow 15x^2=30x \Rightarrow x=2\text{ m}$$

9. Using work-energy theorem for block,

$$W_{mg}+W_N+W_{\text{spring}}=\Delta K \Rightarrow 0+0+\int_0^x(-2x-x^3)dx=0-8$$

$$\Rightarrow \left[-x^2-\frac{x^4}{4}\right]_0^x=-8 \Rightarrow 4x^2+x^4-32=0 \Rightarrow x=2\text{ m}$$

10. For m_2 to never move, $kx\le\mu m_2 g \Rightarrow x\le 5\text{ m}$
Using work-energy theorem for m_1

$$W_{mg}+W_N+W_{\text{friction}}+W_{\text{spring}}=\Delta K$$

$$\Rightarrow \quad 0+0-(\mu m_1 g)\,x+\frac{1}{2}k(0^2-x^2)=0-\frac{1}{2}m_1u^2$$

$$\Rightarrow \quad 5x+x^2=\frac{u^2}{2} \Rightarrow u=\sqrt{10x+2x^2} \Rightarrow u\le\sqrt{50+50}$$

$$\Rightarrow \quad u\le 10\text{ m/s}$$

11.

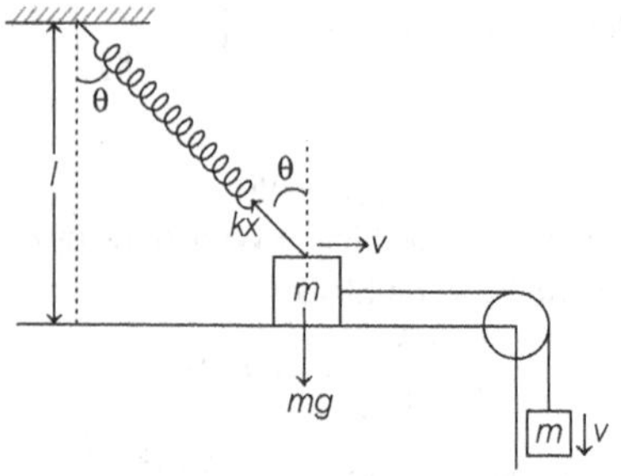

For the block on the table to lose contact,

$$\Sigma F_y=0 \Rightarrow kx\cos\theta=mg \Rightarrow k\left(\frac{l}{\cos\theta}-l\right)\cos\theta=mg$$

$$\Rightarrow kl\,(1-\cos\theta)=mg \Rightarrow 40\,(0.4)\,(1-\cos\theta)=0.32\times 10$$

$$\Rightarrow \quad \cos\theta=\frac{4}{5} \Rightarrow \theta=37°$$

Using work-energy theorem for system,

$$W_{gravity} + W_N + W_T + W_{spring} = \Delta K_{system}$$

$$\Rightarrow + mg\, l \tan\theta = 0 + 0 + \frac{1}{2}k\left[0^2 - \left(\frac{l}{\cos\theta} - l\right)^2\right]$$

$$= \left(\frac{1}{2}mv^2 + \frac{1}{2}mv^2\right) - (0+0)$$

$$\Rightarrow \quad v = \sqrt{\frac{3gl}{4} - \frac{kl^2}{32m}} = \sqrt{\frac{19}{8}}\ \text{m/s}$$

$$\text{KE} = \frac{1}{2}mv^2 = \frac{1}{2}\times 0.32 \times \frac{19}{8} = 0.38\ \text{J}$$

12. Lets take maximum compression in the spring to be x.

$$W_{mg} + W_N + W_{spring} + W_{friction} = \Delta K$$

$$\Rightarrow \quad 0 + 0 + \frac{1}{2}\times 2(0^2 - x^2) - 0.2\,(0.5)\,(10)\,(2.14 + x)$$

$$= 0 - \frac{1}{2}\times 0.5 \times 3^2$$

$$\Rightarrow x^2 + x - 0.11 = 0 \quad \Rightarrow \quad x = 0.1\ \text{m}$$

Now $f_L = \mu_s mg = (0.22)(0.5)(10) = 1.1\ \text{N}$

$kx = 2(0.1) = 0.2\ \text{N}$

Since, $kx < f_L$, the block will not move now.

So, total distance travelled $= 2 + 2.14 + 0.1 = 4.24\ \text{m}$

13.

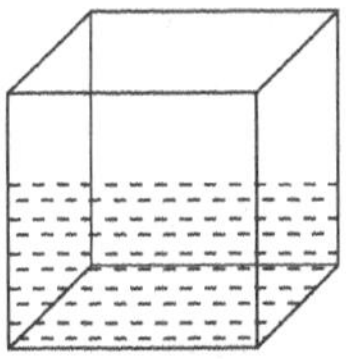

$$U_1 = mg\frac{H}{4}$$

$$U_2 = mgH$$

$$V = H\times H\times\frac{H}{2} = \frac{H^3}{2} \quad \Rightarrow \quad \frac{dV}{dt} = \frac{V}{T} \quad \Rightarrow \quad Av = \frac{V}{T}$$

$$\Rightarrow \quad \pi\left(\frac{H}{\sqrt{4\pi}}\right)^2 v = \frac{\frac{H^3}{2}}{\sqrt{\frac{8H}{42}}} \quad \Rightarrow \quad v = \sqrt{21H}$$

$$W_{ext} = \Delta U + \Delta K = mg\left(H - \frac{H}{4}\right) + \frac{1}{2}mv^2 = \frac{3mgH}{4} + \frac{21mH}{2}$$

$$= 18\ mH = 18\times 1000 \times \frac{H^3}{2}\times H = 9000\ \text{J} = 9\ \text{kJ}$$

14. Lets say extension in the string is x.

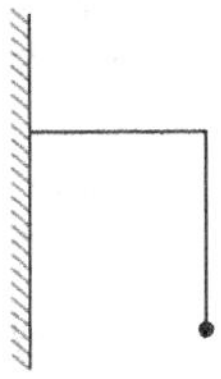

$$kx = mg \quad \Rightarrow \quad \left(\frac{mg}{a}\right)x = mg \ \Rightarrow\ x = a$$

Now, the string is given an additional $2a$ extension. When the string acquires its natural length again, it will get slack and velocity of particle is lets say v.

Using work-energy theorem for particle,

$$W_{mg} + W_{string} = \Delta K$$

$$\Rightarrow - mg\,(3a) + \frac{1}{2}\left(\frac{mg}{a}\right)[(3a)^2 - 0^2] = \frac{1}{2}mv^2 - 0$$

$$\Rightarrow \qquad v = \sqrt{3ga}$$

$$\text{Maximum height} = 3a + \frac{v^2}{2g} = 3a + \frac{(\sqrt{3ga})^2}{2g} = 4.5a$$

15. Using work-energy theorem for block,

$$W_{mg} + W_A + W_B = \Delta K$$

$$\Rightarrow + 2\times 10 \times 0.3 + \frac{1}{2}\times 100\,[0^2 - (0.2)^2] + \frac{1}{2}k(0^2 - (0.1)^2)$$

$$= 0 - 0$$

$$\Rightarrow \qquad k = 800\ \text{N/m}$$

16.

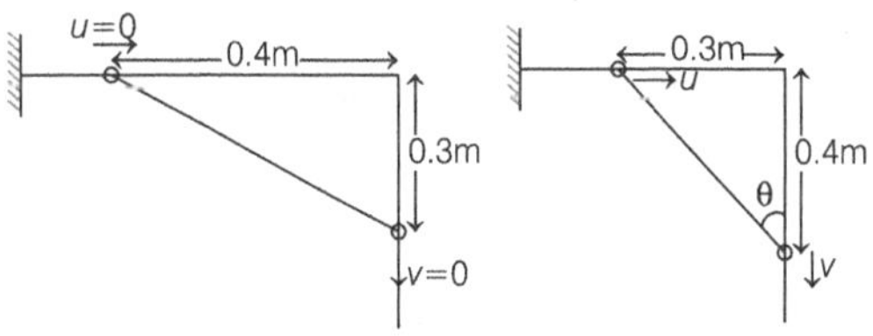

Using work-energy theorem for the two beads system,

$$W_{gravity} + W_N + W_T = \Delta K_{system}$$

$$\Rightarrow \quad (1\times 9.8\times 0.1 + 0) + 0 + 0$$

$$= \left(\frac{1}{2}\times 1\times v^2 + \frac{1}{2}\times 1 \times u^2\right) - (0+0)$$

$$\Rightarrow \qquad v^2 + u^2 = 1.96 \qquad \text{...(i)}$$

From string constraint,

$$v\cos\theta = u\sin\theta \quad \Rightarrow u = v\cot\theta = \frac{4v}{3} \qquad \text{...(ii)}$$

From Eqs. (i) and (ii), we get

$$v = \frac{21}{25}\ \text{m/s}$$

17. Using work energy for system,

$$W_{gravity} + W_T = 0$$

$$\Rightarrow \quad + mg\,(OC) - mg\,(\sqrt{(OC)^2 + a^2} - a)$$

$$- mg(\sqrt{(OC)^2 + a^2} - a) = (0+0+0) - (0+0+0)$$

$$\Rightarrow \quad OC = 2(\sqrt{(OC)^2 + a^2} - a) \ \Rightarrow\ (OC)^2 + a^2 = \left(\frac{OC}{2} + a\right)^2$$

$$\Rightarrow \ (OC)^2 + a^2 = \frac{(OC)^2}{4} + a^2 + a(OC) \ \Rightarrow \ OC = \frac{4a}{3}$$

18.

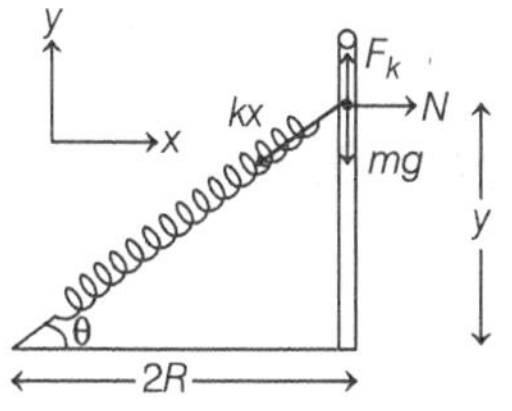

$$\Sigma F_x = 0 \quad \Rightarrow \quad N = kx\cos\theta$$

$\Rightarrow \qquad f_k = \mu N = \mu kx \cos\theta$

$W_{\text{friction}} = \int (\mu kx \cos\theta)\, dy = \int \mu k(2R\sec\theta - 2R)\cos\theta\, dy$

$$\begin{bmatrix} y = 2R\tan\theta \\ dy = 2R\sec^2\theta\, d\theta \end{bmatrix}$$

$= 4\mu kR^2 \int (1 - \cos\theta)\sec^2\theta\, d\theta$

$= 4\mu kR^2 [\tan\theta - \ln(\sec\theta + \tan\theta)]_{37°}^{0°}$

$= -16\,\mu mgR\left(\frac{3}{4} - \ln 2\right)$

Using work-energy theorem for ring,

$W_{\text{gravity}} + W_N + W_{\text{spring}} + W_{\text{friction}} = \Delta K$

$\Rightarrow \quad + mg\left(\frac{3R}{2}\right) + 0 + \frac{1}{2}k[(0.5R)^2 - 0^2]$

$-16\,\mu mgR\left(\frac{3}{4} - \ln 2\right) = \frac{1}{2}m(\sqrt{3gR})^2 - 0$

$\Rightarrow \qquad \mu = \frac{1}{8(3 - 4\ln 2)}$

19. Initially, the pulley is in equilibrium.

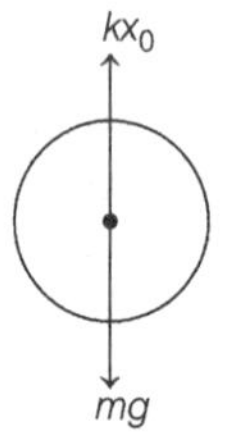

$\Rightarrow \qquad \Sigma F_y = 0 \;\Rightarrow\; kx - mg = 0$

$\Rightarrow \qquad x_0 = \frac{mg}{k} \;\Rightarrow\; x_0 = 5\text{cm}$

Lets take maximum elongation in the spring to be x.

Applying work-energy theorem for pulley,

$W_{mg} + + W_{\text{spring}} + W_F = \Delta K$

$\Rightarrow + mg(x - x_0) + \frac{1}{2}k(x_0^2 - x^2) + (2F)(x - x_0) = 0 - 0$

$\Rightarrow \qquad x_0 + x = \frac{2(mg + 2F)}{k}$

$\Rightarrow \qquad x_0 + x = 40 \text{ cm} \;\Rightarrow\; x = 35 \text{ cm}$

Displacement of point $A = 2(x - x_0) = 60$ cm

20. For the block, along the inclined plane,

$\Sigma F = ma$

$\Rightarrow mg\sin 30° - \frac{1}{\sqrt{3}}(mg\cos 30°) = ma \;\Rightarrow\; a = 0$

Using work-energy theorem for the block,

$(W_{mg} + W_{\text{friction}} + W_N + W_{\text{spring}} = \Delta K$

$\Rightarrow 0 + 0 + \frac{1}{2} \times 100(0^2 - x^2) = 0 - \frac{1}{2} \times 1 \times 2^2$

$\Rightarrow \qquad x = 0.2 \text{ m} = 20 \text{ cm}$

Previous Year's Questions

JEE Main

1. $m = 100$ kg

$s = 10$ m $\Rightarrow \mu = 0.4$

Force of friction, $f = \mu\, mg = 0.4 \times 100 \times 10 = 400$ N

Work done against friction,

$W = F \cdot s = 400 \times 10 = 4000 \;\Rightarrow\; W = 4000$ J

2. $U = 2x^2 + 3y^3 + 2z$

Given, $U = 2x^2 + 3y^3 + 2z$

$F_x = -\frac{dU}{dx} = -\frac{d}{dx}(2x^2 + 3y^3 + 2z) = -[4x]$

$F_x = -4x$

at $x = 1$, magnitude of F_x

$F_x = -4 \times 1 \;\Rightarrow\; |F_x| = 4$N

3. According to given condition,

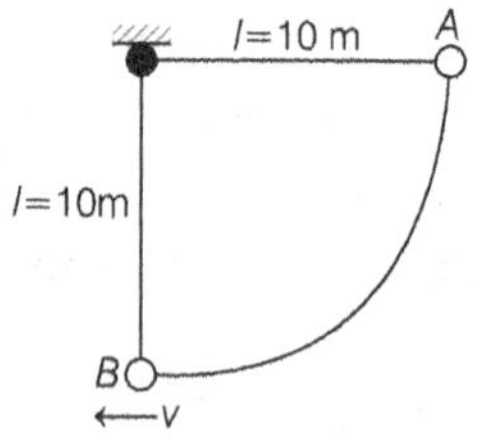

$\frac{1}{2}mv^2 = 90\%$ of $mgl \;\Rightarrow\; \frac{v^2}{2} = 0.9gl$

$\Rightarrow \qquad v^2 = 1.8gl = 1.8 \times 10 \times 10 = 180$

$\therefore \qquad v = \sqrt{180} = 6\sqrt{5}$ m/s

4. Given,

Height of point $A = 1$ m

Height of point $B = 0.5$ m

Now using conservation of mechanical energy,

$(\text{Total Energy})_A = (\text{Total Energy})_B$

$(PE + KE)_A = (PE + KE)_B$

At point A, particle is stationary ($v_A = 0$)

$mgh_A = mgh_B + \frac{1}{2}mv_B^2$

$gh_A = gh_B + \frac{1}{2}v_B^2 \;\Rightarrow\; g = 0.5\,g + \frac{1}{2}v_B^2$

$v_B^2 = g \;\Rightarrow\; v_B = \sqrt{g} = \sqrt{10}$ m/s

5.

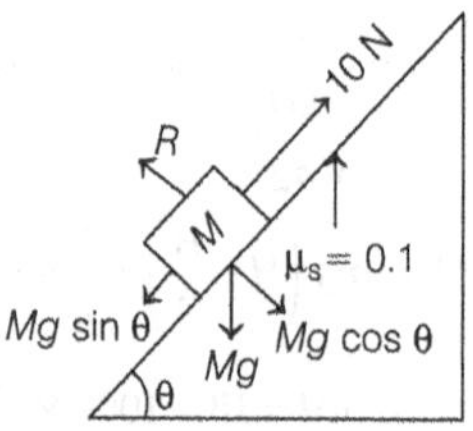

Work done against friction = Force of friction × displacement

$= \mu R \times s = (\mu\, mg\cos\theta) \times s$

Here $\quad \mu = 0.1, M = 1$ kg

$g = 10 \text{ m/s}^2, \theta = 60°, s = 10$ m

So, Work done

$= 0.1 \times 1 \times 10 \times \cos 60° \times 10 = 5$J

6. We know that,

$$KE = \frac{p^2}{2m}; \; K \propto \frac{p^2}{m}$$

$$K \propto \frac{1}{m} \text{ if } P_1 = P_2$$

$$\frac{K_1}{K_2} = \frac{m_2}{m_1} \Rightarrow \frac{m_2}{m_1} = \frac{16}{9} \Rightarrow \frac{m_1}{m_2} = \frac{9}{16}$$

$\therefore m_1 : m_2 = 9:16$

7. For statement I

Work done $= \Delta KE = -FS = 0 - KE$

$$\Rightarrow \quad KE = SF \Rightarrow S = \frac{KE}{F}$$

Hence, both car and truck will cover same distance.

For Statement II :

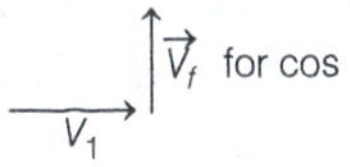

From the diagram, $\Delta \mathbf{V} = \mathbf{V}_f - \mathbf{V}_i$

$$|\Delta \mathbf{V}| = \sqrt{2}\, V$$

Thus the velocity is changing, therefore $a \neq 0$.

Hence, statement II is incorrect.

8. At highest point during projectile motion, the velocity of projectile in vertical direction becomes zero but it has horizontal component of velocity.

Because of this, kinetic energy will not be equal to zero.

Gravitational potential energy is maximum at highest point and equal to $mgH = mg\left(\frac{u^2 \sin^2\theta}{2g}\right)$

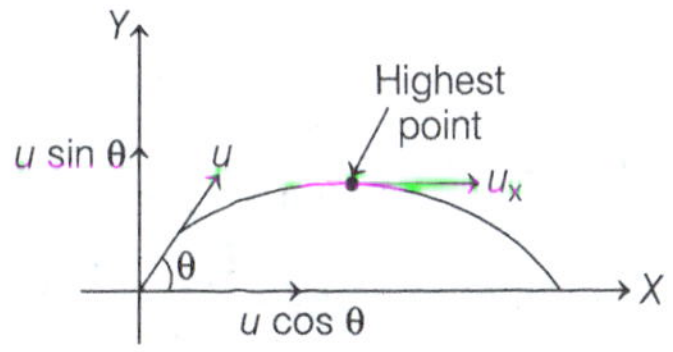

9. Work done by a force is negative when work force is acting in opposite direction of displacement. So, work of gravitational force while lifting a bucket and due to air resistance on oscillating pendulum are negative.

10. Percentage increase in kinetic energy $= \frac{K_f - K_i}{K_i} \times 100$

$$= \left(\frac{p_{f/2m}^2 - p_{i/2m}^2}{p_{i/2m}^2}\right) \times 100 = \frac{\frac{9}{4}\left(\frac{p_i^2}{2m}\right) - \frac{p_i^2}{2m}}{\left(\frac{p_i^2}{2m}\right)} \times 100$$

[Since, $p_f = p_i + 50\%$ of $p_i = 3/2\, p_i$]

$$= \left(\frac{9}{4} - 1\right) \times 100 = \frac{5}{4} \times 100 = 125\%$$

11. Acceleration of body is,

$$a = \frac{F}{m} = \frac{2}{5} \text{ m/s}^2$$

Initial velocity of body $= \frac{p}{m} = \frac{10}{5} = 2$ m/s

Final velocity,

$$v = u + at \Rightarrow v = 2 + \frac{2}{5} \times 5 = 4 \text{ m/s}$$

So, change in kinetic energy is;

$$\Delta k = k_f - k_i = \frac{1}{2}m(v_f^2 - v_i^2) = \frac{1}{2} \times (4^2 - 2^2)$$

$$= \frac{1}{2} \times 5 \times 12 = 30 \text{ J}$$

12. Given,

$$F = (2 + 3x)\hat{\mathbf{i}}$$

$$W = \int_0^4 F \cdot dx = \int_0^4 (2 + 3x)\, dx$$

$$W = \left[2x + \frac{3x^2}{2}\right]_0^4 = [8 + 24]$$

$$W = 32 \text{ J}$$

13. Given, $a = -2x$

$$v\frac{dv}{dx} = -2x$$

$$\Rightarrow \quad vdx = -2xdx$$

$$\int_{v_1}^{v_2} vdv = -2\int_0^x xdx$$

$$\Rightarrow \frac{v_2^2}{2} - \frac{v_1^2}{2} = -\frac{2x^2}{2}$$

$$\Rightarrow \frac{mv_2^2}{2} - \frac{mv_2^2}{2} = -mx^2$$

$$\Rightarrow \frac{mv_1^2}{2} - \frac{mv_2^2}{2} = mx^2$$

$$\because \text{Loss in KE} = mx^2 = \frac{10}{1000}x^2 = 10^{-2}x^2 = \left(\frac{10}{x}\right)^{-2}$$

$$n = 2$$

14. Speed of bus $(v) = 80$ km/h

mass of bus $(m) = 500$ kg

distance $(x) = 4$ km $= 4 \times 10^3$ m

For a constant speed,

Work done by engine + Work done by friction = 0

Thus, $WD_{engine} = -\, W.D._{friction} = -(-\mu\, mg\, x)$

$$= 0 \cdot 04 \times 500 \times 9.8 \times 4 \times 10^3 = 784 \text{ kJ}$$

15. Work done by variable force,

$$W = \int Fdx = \int_2^4 5x\, dx = \left[5 \cdot \frac{x^2}{2}\right]_2^4$$

$$= \frac{5}{2}[4^2 - 2^2] = \frac{5}{2}[12] = 30 \text{ J}$$

16. Given, $E_1 = \frac{1}{2}mu^2 - 0$

$$E_1 = \frac{1}{2}mu^2 = E$$

$$E_2 = \frac{1}{2}m(2u)^2 - \frac{1}{2}mu^2 = 2mu^2 - \frac{1}{2}mu^2$$

$$E_2 = \frac{3}{2}mu^2 = 3\left(\frac{1}{2}mu^2\right) = 3E \text{ J}$$

17. Given that, $\mathbf{F} = (5 + 3y^2)\hat{\mathbf{j}}$ N

Displacement is also along **Y**-axis.

So, work done, $W = \int \mathbf{F} \cdot dy$

$$W = \int (5+3y^2)\hat{\mathbf{j}} \cdot dy\hat{\mathbf{j}} = \int_2^5 (5+3y^2)\, dy$$

$$= \left[5y + \frac{3y^3}{3}\right]_2^5 = [5y + y^3]_2^5$$

$$= [5 \times 5 + (5)^3] - [5 \times 2 + (2)^5]$$

$$= [25 + 125] - [10 + 8] = 150 - 8$$

$\Rightarrow \quad W = 132$ J

18. Given, KE = 10000 J

As, $\quad KE = \frac{1}{2}mv^2$

$$10000 = \frac{1}{2} \times 2 \times v^2 \Rightarrow v = 100 \text{ m/s}$$

Now using, $v = u + at$

we have, $\quad v = at \quad$ [Given, $u = 0$]

$$v = a \times 5$$

$$a = \frac{100}{5} = 20 \text{ ms}^{-2}$$

Force on the body,

$$F = ma = 2 \times 20 = 40 \text{ N}$$

19. Force, $\mathbf{F} = (5\hat{\mathbf{i}} + 2\hat{\mathbf{j}} + 7\hat{\mathbf{k}})$ N

Displacement vector,

$$\Delta\mathbf{r} = \mathbf{r}_f - \mathbf{r}_i = (5\hat{\mathbf{i}} - 2\hat{\mathbf{j}} + \hat{\mathbf{k}}) - (2\hat{\mathbf{i}} + 3\hat{\mathbf{j}} - 4\hat{\mathbf{k}})$$

$$\Delta\mathbf{r} = (3\hat{\mathbf{i}} - 5\hat{\mathbf{j}} + 5\hat{\mathbf{k}}) \text{ m}$$

Work done,

$$W = \mathbf{F} \cdot \Delta\mathbf{r} = (5\hat{\mathbf{i}} + 2\hat{\mathbf{j}} + 7\hat{\mathbf{k}}) \cdot (3\hat{\mathbf{i}} - 5\hat{\mathbf{j}} + 5\hat{\mathbf{k}})$$

$$= (5)(3) + (2)(-5) + (7)(5)$$

$$= 15 - 10 + 35 = 40 \text{ J}$$

20. From third equation of motion,

$$v^2 = u^2 + 2as = 2^2 + 2 \times 2 \times 6$$

$\Rightarrow \quad v^2 = 28 \text{ m/s}^2$

Kinetic energy of lift, $K = \frac{1}{2}mv^2$

$$K = \frac{1}{2} \times 500 \times 28$$

$$K = 7 \times 10^3 \text{ J} \Rightarrow K = 7 \text{ kJ}$$

21. By work energy theorem

$$W_{\text{friction}} + W_{\text{gravity}} = \Delta K$$

$$\Rightarrow W_f + (10 \times 0.3) = 0 - \frac{1}{2}(1)(22)^2 \quad \Rightarrow \quad W_f = -245 \text{ J}$$

22. Given, max-load = 1400 kg

Speed of elevator $(v) = 3 \text{ ms}^{-1}$

Friction force = 2000 N

Force due to load = $Ma = mg$

$$= 1400 \times 10 = 1400 \text{ N} = 14000 \text{ N}$$

Maximum force = Force on elevator + Friction

$$= 14000 + 2000 = 16000 \text{ N}$$

$$P_{\max} = F_{\max} \times v = 16000 \times 3 = 48000 \text{ W} = 48 \text{ kW}$$

23. Given, force acting on body, $\mathbf{F} = t\hat{\mathbf{i}} + 3t^2\hat{\mathbf{j}}$

Acceleration of body, $\mathbf{a} = \frac{\mathbf{F}}{m} = (t\hat{\mathbf{i}} + 3t^2\hat{\mathbf{j}}) \text{ m/s}^2$

Velocity of body at instant t, $v = u + at \quad (u = 0)$

$\Rightarrow \quad \mathbf{v} = t^2\hat{\mathbf{i}} + 3t^3\hat{\mathbf{j}}$ m/s

Power developed by force, $P = \mathbf{F} \cdot \mathbf{v}$

$$= (t\hat{\mathbf{i}} + 3t^2\hat{\mathbf{j}}) \cdot (t^2\hat{\mathbf{i}} + 3t^3\hat{\mathbf{j}}) = t^3 + 9t^5$$

At $t = 2$ s, power is;

$$P = 2^3 + 9 \times 2^5 = 8 + 288 = 296 \text{ W}$$

24. Initial momentum of body, $p_1 = p$

Final momentum of body,

$$p_2 = p_1 + 20\% \text{ of } p_1$$

$$= p_1 + \frac{20}{100}p_1 = \frac{6p_1}{5}$$

$$p_2 = \frac{6p}{5} \Rightarrow E_K = \frac{p^2}{2m}$$

$\therefore$ Initial kinetic energy, $E_{K_1} = \frac{p_1^2}{2m} = \frac{p^2}{2m}$

Final kinetic energy, $E_{K_2} = \frac{p_2^2}{2m} = \frac{\left(\frac{6p}{5}\right)^2}{2m} = \frac{36p^2}{50m}$

$\therefore$ % increase in kinetic energy $= \frac{E_{K_2} - E_{K_1}}{E_{K_1}} \times 100\%$

$$= \frac{\frac{36p^2}{50m} - \frac{p^2}{2m}}{\frac{p^2}{2m}} \times 100\%$$

$$= \frac{11}{25} \times 100 = 44\%$$

25. We know that kinetic energy (K) of a moving body is related as its momentum (p) as given below

$$p = \sqrt{2mK} \Rightarrow \frac{p_1}{p_2} = \sqrt{\frac{m_1}{m_2} \cdot \frac{K_1}{K_2}}$$

But $K_1 = K_2$

$$\frac{p_1}{p_2} = \sqrt{\frac{m_1}{m_2}} = \sqrt{\frac{8}{2}} = \frac{2}{1}$$

$$p_1 : p_2 = 2 : 1$$

26.

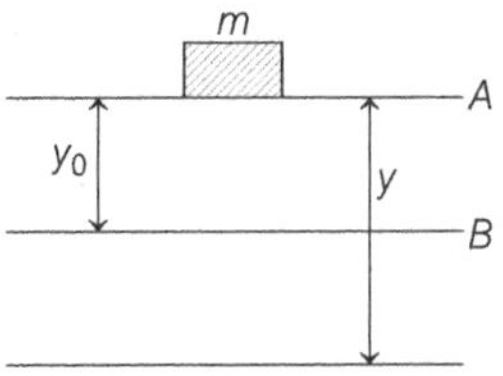

Kinetic energy at B = Potential energy at A – Potential energy at $B = mgy - mg(y - y_0) = mgy_0$

27. Work done from force-displacement (F-x) graph is equal to area enclosed under F-x curve.

The area enclosed below the X-axis is negative and area above the

X-axis is taken as positive.

From the given F-x graph in Fig. (a), Fig. (b), Fig. (c) and Fig. (d), area under F-x curve are arranged as

$(\text{Area})_{\text{Fig. (c)}} > (\text{Area})_{\text{Fig. (b)}} > (\text{Area})_{\text{Fig. (a)}} > (\text{Area})_{\text{Fig. (d)}}$

$\therefore \quad W_3 > W_2 > W_1 > W_4$

28. Potential energy, $U = \frac{A}{r^{10}} - \frac{B}{r^5}$

At the equilibrium distance between the two atoms, potential energy between the atoms should be minimum.

Hence, $\frac{dU}{dr} = 0$

$$\Rightarrow \quad \frac{d}{dr}\left[\frac{A}{r^{10}} - \frac{B}{r^5}\right] = 0$$

$$\Rightarrow \quad \frac{-10A}{r^{11}} + \frac{5B}{r^6} = 0$$

$$\Rightarrow \quad \frac{5}{r^6}\left[\frac{-2A}{r^5} + B\right] = 0$$

$$\Rightarrow \quad \frac{-2A}{r^5} + B = 0$$

$$\Rightarrow \quad B = \frac{2A}{r^5} \Rightarrow r^5 = \frac{2A}{B}$$

$$\Rightarrow \quad r = \left(\frac{2A}{B}\right)^{1/5}$$

29. Initial speed of block, $v_i = 12$ m/s

Mass of block, $m = 0.5$ kg

$x = 30$ cm $= 0.3$ m

Final speed of block,

$$v_f = \frac{v_i}{2} = \frac{12}{2} = 6 \text{ m/s}$$

According to conservation of energy,

$$U_i + K_i = U_f + K_f$$

$$\Rightarrow \quad 0 + \frac{1}{2}mv_i^2 = \frac{1}{2}kx^2 + \frac{1}{2}mv_f^2$$

$$\Rightarrow \quad \frac{1}{2} \times 0.5 \times 12^2 = \frac{1}{2} \times k \times (0.3)^2 + \frac{1}{2} \times 0.5 \times 6^2$$

$$\Rightarrow \quad k = 600 \text{ N/m}$$

30. Net work done is given as,

According to work-energy theorem,

$$W = k_f - k_i = \frac{1}{2}m(V_f^2 - V_i^2)$$

$$W_{\text{net}} = \frac{1}{2} \times 0.5[(3(2)^2 + 4)^2 - (3(0)^2 + 4)^2] = 60 \text{ J}$$

31. Given, $\mathbf{F} = 4x\hat{\mathbf{i}} + 3y^2\hat{\mathbf{j}}$

Particle moves from point (1, 2) to point (2, 3)

According to work-energy theorem,

Work done = change in KE

i.e. $\quad W = \Delta\text{KE}$

$$\Rightarrow \quad \Delta\text{KE} = W = \int\int \mathbf{F}\cdot(dx\hat{\mathbf{i}} + dy\hat{\mathbf{j}})$$

$$= \int\int (4x\hat{\mathbf{i}} + 3y^2\hat{\mathbf{j}})\cdot(dx\hat{\mathbf{i}} + dy\hat{\mathbf{j}})$$

$$= \int_1^2 4x\,dx + \int_2^3 3y^2 dy$$

$$= [2x^2]_1^2 + [y^3]_2^3$$

$$= (8 - 2) + (27 - 8)$$

$$= 6 + 19 = 25 \text{ J}$$

32. Given, rate of dropped sand,

$$\frac{dm}{dt} = 0.5 \text{ kgs}^{-1}$$

Velocity of conveyor, $v = 5$ m/s

Force applied on the belt, $F = m \cdot a$

$$= m\frac{dv}{dt} = v\frac{dm}{dt}$$

$$= 5 \times 0.5 = 2.5 \text{ N}$$

Power needed to keep the belt moving with velocity, $v = 5$ m/s, is given as

$$P = F \times v = 2.5 \times 5 = 12.5 \text{ W.}$$

33. Given, mass of suitcase, $m = 80$ kg

Let height lowered by porter,

$$h = 80 \text{ cm} = 80 \times 10^{-2} \text{ m}$$

As we know that,

Work $(W) = -\,mgh$

$\therefore \quad W = -80 \times 9.8 \times 80 \times 10^{-2} = -627.2$ J

34. We know that,

Kinetic energy, $K = \frac{p^2}{2m}$

$$p \propto \sqrt{K}$$

$$\Rightarrow \quad \frac{p_2}{p_1} = \frac{\sqrt{K_2}}{\sqrt{K_1}}$$

$$\frac{p_2}{p_1} = \frac{\sqrt{4K_1}}{\sqrt{K_1}} \Rightarrow \frac{p_2}{p_1} = 2$$

$$\Rightarrow \quad p_2 = 2p_1$$

$\therefore$ Percentage change in momentum

$$= \frac{p_2 - p_1}{p_1} \times 100 = \frac{2p_1 - p_1}{p_1} \times 100$$

$$= \frac{p_1}{p_1} \times 100 = 100\%$$

35. The central potential field when particle moves in circular orbit,

$$U(r) = -\frac{C}{r}$$

We know that,

$$F = -\frac{dU}{dr} \Rightarrow F = -\frac{d}{dr}\left(-\frac{C}{r}\right)$$

$$\Rightarrow \quad |F| = -\frac{C}{r^2}$$

$$\Rightarrow \quad \frac{mv^2}{r} = -\frac{C}{r^2} \Rightarrow v^2 \propto \frac{1}{r}$$

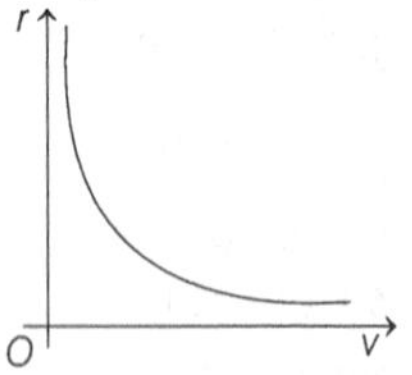

The graph between velocity and radius is hyperbolic.

36. Given, work done by both person is same, $W_A = W_B$

Direction of first force with displacement, $\theta_1 = 45°$

Direction of second force with displacement, $\theta_2 = 60°$

Ratio of force applied by person A to force applied by person B is $F_A : F_B = 1 : \sqrt{x}$.

Work done by both person is same,

$W_A = W_B \Rightarrow F_A d \cos\theta_1 = F_B d \cos\theta_2$

($\because$ distance is same for both $= d$)

$$\frac{F_A}{F_B} = \frac{\cos\theta_1}{\cos\theta_2} = \frac{\cos 60°}{\cos 45°}$$

$$\Rightarrow \quad \frac{F_A}{F_B} = \frac{\frac{1}{2}}{\frac{1}{\sqrt{2}}} = \frac{1}{\sqrt{2}}$$

$$\Rightarrow \quad \frac{F_A}{F_B} = \frac{1}{\sqrt{x}} = \frac{1}{\sqrt{2}} \quad \Rightarrow \quad x = 2$$

Thus, the value of x is 2.

37. Given, force, $\mathbf{F} = (5y + 20)\hat{j}$ N

Since, work done $(W) = \int_0^{10} F \cdot dy$

$$\therefore \quad W = \int_0^{10} (5y + 20)dy = \frac{5y^2}{2}\Big|_0^{10} + 20y\Big|_0^{10}$$

$$= \frac{5}{2}(10^2 - 0^2) + 20(10 - 0) = 450 \text{ J}$$

38. Given, mass of particle A,

$$m_A = 4 \text{ g}$$

Mass of particle $B, m_B = 16$ g

Kinetic energy of A and B is same

i.e. $\quad KE_A = KE_B$

As, kinetic energy (KE) $= p^2 / 2m$

$$\therefore \quad \frac{(p_A)^2}{m_A} = \frac{(p_B^2)}{m_B} \Rightarrow \frac{p_A^2}{4} = \frac{p_B^2}{16}$$

$$\Rightarrow \quad \frac{p_A}{p_B} = \frac{1}{2} = \frac{x}{2} \quad \text{[given]}$$

$$\therefore \quad n = 1$$

39. Given, $m_A = 1$ kg, $m_B = 2$ kg, $(KE)_A : (KE)_B = A : 1$

Linear momentum of A and B are equal.

$$\Rightarrow \quad p_A = p_B$$

$\because$ Kinetic energy (KE) $= p^2/2m$

$$\therefore \quad \frac{KE_A}{KE_B} = \frac{m_B}{m_A} = \frac{2}{1} = \frac{A}{1}$$

$$\Rightarrow \quad A = 2$$

40. The speed of the body when reached the ground, $v_f = 0.8\sqrt{gh}$

Initial velocity of the body, $v = 0$ m / s

Using the work-energy theorem,

Work done by gravity + Work done by air-friction = Final kinetic energy − Initial kinetic energy

$$W_{mg} + W_{\text{air-friction}} = \frac{1}{2}mv_f^2 - \frac{1}{2}mv_i^2$$

Here, work done by gravity $= mgh$

$$\Rightarrow \quad mgh + W_{\text{air-friction}} = \frac{1}{2}m(0.8\sqrt{gh})^2 - \frac{1}{2}m(0)^2$$

$$\Rightarrow \quad W_{\text{air-friction}} = \frac{0.64\,mgh}{2} - mgh$$

$$= 0.32mgh - mgh$$

$$= -0.68\,mgh$$

41. Given, compression in the spring,

$$x = 25 \text{ cm} = 25 \times 10^{-2} \text{ m}$$

$$v_1 = v \text{ and } v_2 = \frac{v}{2}$$

According to given situation.

Change in kinetic energy = Gain in potential energy

$$\Rightarrow \quad \frac{1}{2}mv^2 - \frac{1}{2}m\left(\frac{v}{2}\right)^2 = \frac{1}{2}kx^2$$

$$\Rightarrow \quad \frac{1}{2}mv^2 - \frac{1}{4} \times \frac{1}{2}mv^2 = \frac{1}{2}k(25 \times 10^{-2})^2$$

$$\Rightarrow E_K - \frac{1}{4}E_K = \frac{625\,k \times 10^{-4}}{2}$$

$$\Rightarrow \quad \frac{3}{4}E_K = \frac{1}{2} \times \frac{k}{16}$$

$$\Rightarrow \quad k = 24E_K = 24E \quad [\because E_K = E]$$

$$= nE \quad \text{(given)}$$

$$\therefore \quad n = 24$$

42. According to given situation energy supplied in delivering the constant power P is equal to the kinetic energy of the automobile.

$\therefore$ Energy supplied = Kinetic energy

$$\Rightarrow \quad Pt = \frac{1}{2}mv^2 \Rightarrow v = \left(\frac{2Pt}{m}\right)^{1/2}$$

or $$\frac{ds}{dt} = \left(\frac{2Pt}{m}\right)^{1/2} \qquad \left[\because v = \frac{ds}{dt}\right]$$

Integrating both sides of above equation, we get

$$\int_s^0 ds = \left(\frac{2P}{m}\right)^{1/2} \int_0^t t^{1/2} \cdot dt$$

$$\Rightarrow \quad s = \left(\frac{2P}{m}\right)^{1/2} \cdot \frac{2}{3} t^{3/2}$$

$$\Rightarrow \quad s = \frac{2}{3}\left(\frac{2P}{m}\right)^{1/2} \cdot t^{3/2}$$

$$\Rightarrow \quad s = \left(\frac{8P}{9m}\right)^{1/2} \cdot t^{3/2}$$

43. $\therefore$ Energy supply = Pt

Where, P = power and t = time taken.

$$\Rightarrow \quad \frac{1}{2}mv^2 = Pt \Rightarrow v^2 \propto t \Rightarrow v \propto \sqrt{t}$$

or $$\frac{ds}{dt} = c\sqrt{t} \qquad \text{...(i)}$$

Where, c is any constant.

Now, integrating Eq. (i), we get

$$\int_0^s ds = \int_0^t c\sqrt{t}\, dt$$

$$\Rightarrow \quad s = c\int_0^t t^{\frac{1}{2}} \cdot dt \Rightarrow s = \frac{2c}{3} t^{\frac{3}{2}} \Rightarrow s \propto t^{3/2}$$

JEE Advanced

1. $W_{AB} = \int_0^1 \alpha(1)\, dx = \alpha$

$W_{BC} = \int_1^{0.5} 2\alpha(1)\, dy = -\alpha$

$W_{CD} = \int_1^{0.5} \alpha(0.5)\, dx = -0.25\alpha$

$W_{DE} = \int_{0.5}^{0} 2\alpha(0.5)\, dy = -0.5\alpha$

$W_{EF} = 0$

$W_{FA} = 0$

$W = W_{AB} + W_{BC} + W_{CD} + W_{DE} + W_{EF} + W_{FA}$

$= 0.75$ J

2. $$K = \frac{1}{2}mv^2 \Rightarrow \frac{dK}{dt} = mv\frac{dv}{dt}$$

Given, $$\frac{dK}{dt} = \gamma t \Rightarrow mv\frac{dv}{dt} = \gamma t$$

$$\Rightarrow \quad \int_0^v v\, dv = \int_0^t \frac{\gamma}{m} t\, dt$$

$$\Rightarrow \quad \frac{v^2}{2} = \frac{\gamma}{m}\frac{t^2}{2} \Rightarrow v = \sqrt{\frac{\gamma}{m}}\, t$$

$$\Rightarrow \quad a = \frac{dv}{dt} = \sqrt{\frac{\gamma}{m}}$$

$$\therefore \quad F = ma = \sqrt{\gamma m} = \text{constant}$$

$$\therefore \quad v = \frac{ds}{dt} = \sqrt{\frac{\gamma}{m}}\, t \Rightarrow s = \sqrt{\frac{\gamma}{m}}\frac{t^2}{2}$$

3. $F = \dfrac{-dU}{dx}$

(a) $F = \dfrac{2U_0 x}{a}\left[1 - \left(\dfrac{x}{a}\right)^2\right]$

(b) $F = -\dfrac{U_0 x}{a^2}$

(c) $F = -\dfrac{U_0 x}{a^2}\left(1 - \dfrac{x^2}{a^2}\right)e^{\frac{-x^2}{a^2}}$

(d) $F = -\dfrac{U_0}{2a}\left(1 - \dfrac{x^2}{a^2}\right)$

4. From work-energy theorem

Work done by all forces = change in kinetic energy

or $$W_F + W_{mg} = K_f - K_i$$

$$18 \times 5 + (1 \times 10)(-4) = K_f$$

$$90 - 40 = K_f \text{ or } K_f = 50\text{ J} = 5 \times 10\text{ J}$$

5. $\mathbf{r} = \mathbf{OP} = x\hat{\mathbf{i}} + y\hat{\mathbf{j}}$

$$\mathbf{F} = \frac{k}{(x^2+y^2)^{3/2}}(x\hat{\mathbf{i}} + y\hat{\mathbf{j}}) = \frac{k}{r^3}(\mathbf{r})$$

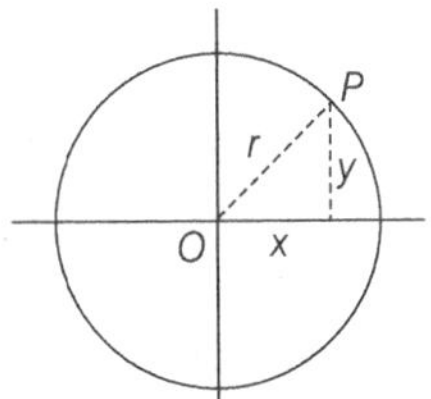

Since, **F** is along **r** or in radial direction.

Therefore, work done is zero.

6. From work energy theorem,

$$W = \frac{1}{2}mv^2$$

Since, power is constant. Therefore, $W = Pt$

$$\therefore \quad Pt = \frac{1}{2}mv^2$$

$$\therefore \quad v = \sqrt{\frac{2Pt}{m}} = \sqrt{\frac{2 \times 0.5 \times 5}{0.2}} = 5\text{ m/s}$$

7. Area under F-t graph = momentum = $p = \sqrt{2km}$

$$\therefore \quad KE = \frac{p^2}{2m} = \frac{A^2}{2m} \qquad (A = \text{net area of } F\text{-}t \text{ graph})$$

$$= \frac{\left[\left(\frac{4\times3}{2}\right) - \left(\frac{1.5\times2}{2}\right)\right]^2}{2\times2} = 5.06\text{ J}$$

CHAPTER~13

CIRCULAR MOTION

LEVEL 01 Starter Level

13.1 Kinematics of Circular Motion

1 Figure shows a circular path taken by a particle. If the instantaneous velocity of the particle is $\mathbf{v} = (2\hat{i} - 2\hat{j})$ m/s. Through which quadrant is the particle moving when it is travelling (a) clockwise and (b) counter clockwise around the circle?

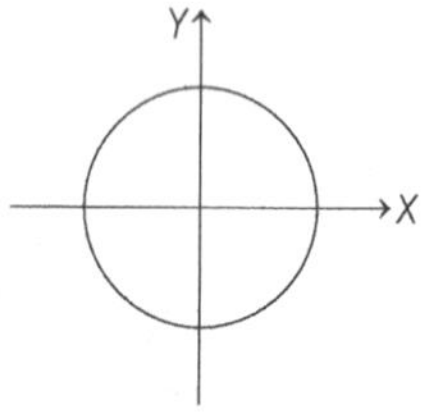

2 Find the ratio of angular speeds of minute hand and hour hand of a watch and also find the angular speed of the second's hand in a watch.

3 A wheel is subjected to uniform angular acceleration about its axis. Initially, its angular velocity is zero. In the first 2 s, it rotates through an angle θ_1. In the next 2 s, it rotates through an additional angle θ_2. Find the ratio of θ_2/θ_1.

4 A fan rotating with $\omega = 100$ rad/s, is switched off. After $2n$ rotations, its angular velocity becomes 50 rad/s. Find the angular velocity of the fan after n rotations from the beginning.

5 A fan is rotating with angular velocity 100 rev/s. Then, it is switched OFF. It takes 5 min to stop.
(a) Find the value of uniform angular retardation.
(b) Find the total number of revolutions made before it stops.
(c) Find the average angular velocity during this interval.

6 The length of second's hand in a watch is 1 cm. Find the magnitude of change in velocity of its tip in 15 s. Also find out the magnitude of average acceleration during this interval.

7 If the equation for the angular displacement of a particle moving on a circular path is given by $\theta = 2t^3 + 0.5$, where θ is in radians and t is in seconds, then find the angular velocity of the particle after 2 s from its start.

8 The angular velocity of a particle is given by $\omega = 1.5t - 3t^2 + 2$. Find the time when its angular acceleration decreases to zero.

9 The shaft of an electric motor starts from rest and on the application of a torque, it gains an angular acceleration given by $\alpha = 3t - t^2$ during the first 2 s after it starts after which $\alpha = 0$. What will be angular velocity after 6 s?

13.2 Radial and Tangential Acceleration

1 A particle moves uniformly in a circle of radius 25 cm at two revolution per second. Find the acceleration of the particle in m/s^2.

2 A particle is moving in a circle of radius 10 cm with uniform speed completing the circle in 4s, find the magnitude of its acceleration.

3 The speed of a particle travelling in a circle of radius 20 cm increases uniformly from 6.0 m/s to 8.0 m/s in 4.0 s, find the angular acceleration.

4 A car is moving with speed 20 m/s on a circular path of radius 100 m. Its speed is increasing at the rate of 3 m/s. What is the acceleration of the car at that moment?

5 A particle moves in a circle of radius 2.0 cm at a speed given by $v = 2t$, where v is in cm/s and t in seconds.
(a) Find the radial acceleration of the particle at $t = 3$s.
(b) Find the tangential acceleration at $t = 3$s.
(c) Find the magnitude of the acceleration at $t = 3$s.

6 A particle is moving in a circular path with velocity varying with time as $v = (1.5t^2 + 2t)$ m/s. If 2 cm is the radius of circular path, then find angular acceleration at $t = 2$ s.

7 A particle is moving with a constant angular acceleration of 4 rad/s^2 in a circular path. At time $t = 0$, particle was at rest. Find the time at which the magnitudes of centripetal acceleration and tangential acceleration are equal.

8 A particle begins to move with a tangential acceleration of constant magnitude 0.6 m/s^2 in a circular path. If it slips when its total acceleration becomes 1 m/s^2, find the angle through which it would have turned before it starts to slip.

9 A particle moves clockwise in a circle of radius 1 m with centre at $(x, y) = (1, 0)$. It starts from rest at the origin at time $t = 0$. Its speed increases at the constant rate of $\left(\frac{\pi}{2}\right)$ m/s^2.

(a) How long does it take to travel halfway around the circle?

(b) What is the speed at that time?

(c) What is the net acceleration at that time ?

10 Figure shows the direction of total acceleration and velocity of a particle moving clockwise in a circle of radius 2.5 m at a given instant of time. At this instant if magnitude of net acceleration is 25 m/s^2, find

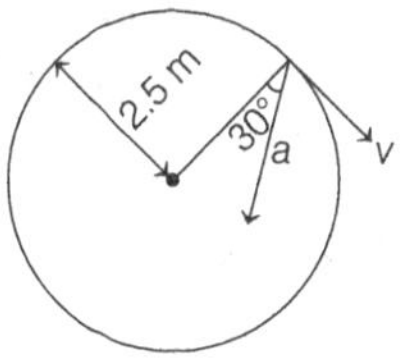

(a) the radial acceleration,

(b) the speed of the particle and

(c) its tangential acceleration.

13.3 Relative Angular Motion

1 Find the angular velocity of *A* with respect to *B* in the figure given below:

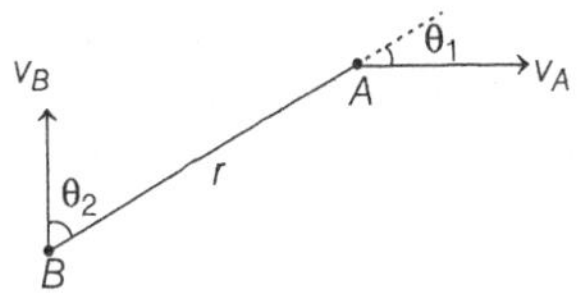

2 Find the time-period of meeting of minute hand and second hand of a clock.

3 Two particles *A* and *B* move on a circle. Initially, particle *A* and *B* are diagonally opposite to each other. Particle *A* move with angular velocity π rad/s, angular acceleration $(\pi / 2)$ rad/s^2 and particle *B* moves with constant angular velocity 2π rad/s. Find the time after which both the particles *A* and *B* will collide.

4 Particles *A* and *B* move with constant and equal speeds in a circle as shown, find the angular velocity of the particle *A* with respect to *B*, if angular velocity of particle *A* with respect to *O* is ω.

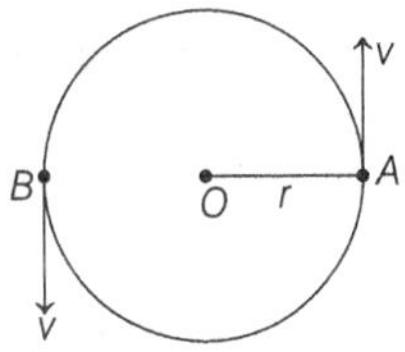

5 Find angular velocity of *A* with respect to *O* at the instant shown in the figure.

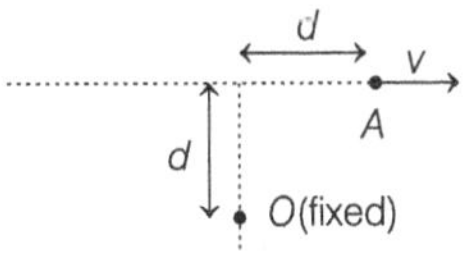

6 Find angular velocity of *A* with respect to *B* at the instant shown in the figure.

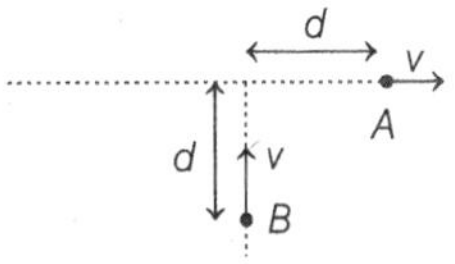

13.4 Circular Motion in Horizontal Plane

1 A block of mass 2 kg is tied to a string of length 2 m, the other end of which is fixed. The block is moved on a smooth horizontal table with constant speed 5 m/s. Find the tension in the string.

2 A mass is kept on a horizontal frictionless surface, It is attached to a string and rotates about a fixed centre at an angular velocity ω_0. If the length of the string and angular velocity are doubled. Find the tension in the string which was initially T_0.

3 A small sphere of mass 200 g is attached to an inextensible string of length 130 cm, whose upper end is fixed to the ceiling. The sphere is made to describe a horizontal circle of radius 50 cm. Calculate the time-period of this conical pendulum and the tension in the string.

4 A block of mass *m* is kept on the edge of a horizontal turn table of radius *R*, which is rotating with constant angular velocity ω (along with the block) about its axis. If coefficient of friction is μ, find the friction force between block and table.

5 A fly is sitting on a disc rotating at $33\frac{1}{3}$ revolution per minute. The distance of the fly from the centre of the disc is 10 cm. Find the minimum coefficient of friction between the disc and the fly. (Take, $g = 10\ \text{m/s}^2$)

6 A motorcyclist wants to drive on the vertical surface of wooden 'well' of radius 5 m, in horizontal plane with a minimum speed of $5\sqrt{5}$ m/s. Find the minimum value of coefficient of friction between the tyres and the wall of the well . (Take, $g = 10\ \text{m/s}^2$)

7 A block of mass m moves with speed v against a smooth, fixed vertical circular groove of radius r kept on smooth horizontal surface. Find

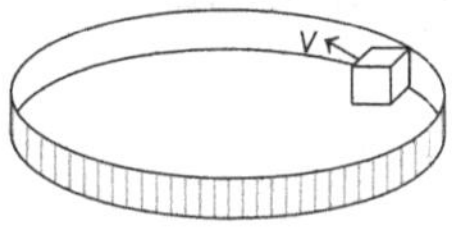

(a) normal reaction of the floor on the block.
(b) normal reaction of the vertical wall on the block.

8 A hemispherical bowl of radius R is rotating about its axis of symmetry which is kept vertical. A small ball kept in the bowl rotates with the bowl without slipping on its smooth surface and the angle made by the radius through the ball with the vertical is α. Find the angular speed at which the bowl is rotating.

9 A boy whirls a stone in a horizontal circle of radius 2 m and at height 4.9 m above level ground. The string breaks and the stone flies off horizontally and strikes the ground at a point which is 10 m away from the point on the ground directly below the point, where the string had broken. What is the magnitude of the centripetal acceleration of the stone while in circular motion? ($g = 9.8\ \text{m/s}^2$)

10 A block of mass m is kept on rough horizontal turn table at a distance r from centre of table. Coefficient of friction between turn table and block is μ. Now, turn table starts rotating with uniform angular acceleration α.
(a) Find the time after which slipping occurs between block and turn table.
(b) Find angle made by friction force with velocity at the point of slipping.

11 A car goes on a horizontal circular road of radius R, the speed increasing at a rate $\frac{dv}{dt} = a$. The friction coefficient between road and tyre is μ. Find the speed at which the car will skid.

13.5 Motion of a Vehicle

1 Find the maximum speed at which a car can turn around a curve of 25 m radius on a level road if the coefficient of friction between the tyres and the road is 0.4. ($g = 10\ \text{m/s}^2$)

2 A cyclist moving with a speed of 4.9 m/s on a level road can take a sharp circular turn of radius 7 m, then find the minimum value of coefficient of friction between the cycle tyres and road. ($g = 9.8\ \text{m/s}^2$)

3 A train has to negotiate a curve of radius 400 m. By how much height should the outer rail be raised with respect to inner rail for a speed of 72 km/h ? The distance between the rails is 1 m.

4 What should be the angle of banking of a circular track of radius 600 m which is designed for cars at an average speed of 180 km/h?

5 A circular road of radius 1000 m has banking angle 45°. Find the maximum safe speed of a car having mass 2000 kg, if the coefficient of friction between tyre and road is 0.5.

6 A turn of radius 20 m is banked for the vehicles going at a speed of 36 km/h. If the coefficient of static friction between the road and the tyre is 0.4, what are the possible speeds of a vehicle, so that it neither slips down or skids up?

13.6 Centrifugal Force

1 A particle of mass m rotates with a uniform angular speed ω. It is viewed from a frame rotating about the Z-axis with a uniform angular speed ω_0. Find the centrifugal force on the particle.

2 A ring which can slide along the rod is kept at mid point of a smooth rod of length L. The rod is rotated with constant angular velocity ω about vertical axis passing through its one of the ends. Ring is released from mid point. Find
(a) acceleration of the ring w.r.t. the rod when it is at a distance x from the axis and
(b) the velocity of the ring when it just leaves the rod.

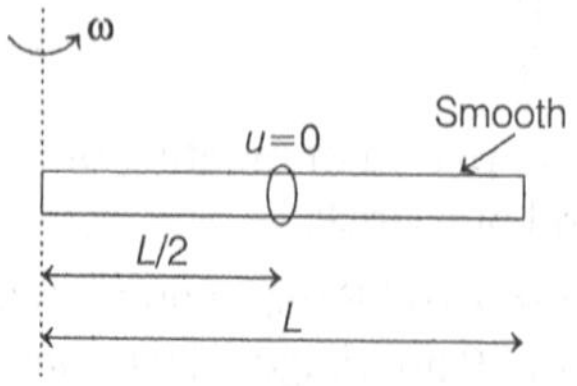

3 A table with smooth horizontal surface is placed in a cabin which moves in a circle of a large radius R. A smooth pulley of small radius is fastened to the table.

Two masses $m_1 = m$ and $m_2 = 2m$ are placed on the table connected through a string going over the pulley. Initially the masses were at rest. Find the magnitude of the initial acceleration of the masses as seen from the cabin and the tension in the string.

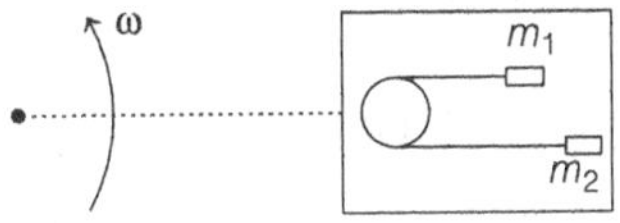

13.7 Rotation of Earth

1 A body weighs 98N on a spring balance at the north pole. What will be the reading on the same scale if it is shifted to the equator? Use, $g = GM/R^2 = 9.8\ \text{m/s}^2$ and $R_{earth} = 6400$ km.

2 A person stands on a spring balance at the equator. If the speed of earth's rotation is increased by such an amount that the balance reading is half the true weight, what will be the length of the day in this case ?

13.8 Circular Motion in Vertical Plane

1 Consider a simple pendulum having a bob of mass m suspended by string of length L fixed at its upper end. The bob is oscillating in a vertical circle. It is found that the speed of the bob is v, when the string makes an angle α with the vertical. Find

(a) tension in the string and

(b) magnitude of net force on the bob at the instant.

2 A weightless thread can support tension upto 30 N. A stone of mass 0.5 kg is tied to it and is revolved in a circular path of radius 2 m in a vertical plane. If $g - 10\ \text{m/s}^2$, find the maximum angular velocity of the stone.

3 A simple pendulum oscillates in a vertical plane. When it passes through the mean position, the tension in the string is 3 times the weight of the pendulum bob. What is the maximum angular displacement of the pendulum of the string with respect to the downward vertical.

4 A body attached to (a) a massless string (b) a massless rod, of length l describes a vertical circle such that it is just able to cross the highest point. For each case, find the minimum velocity at the bottom of the circle.

5 The bob of a pendulum at rest is given a sharp hit to impart a horizontal velocity $\sqrt{10gl}$, where l is the length of the pendulum. Find the tension in the string when (a) the string is horizontal, (b) the bob is at its highest point and (c) the string makes an angle of 60° with the upward vertical.

6 A small body of mass m hangs at one end of a string of length l, the other end of which is fixed. It is given a horizontal velocity u at its lowest position, so that the string would just becomes slack, when it makes an angle of`60° with the upward drawn vertical line. Find the tension in the string at point of projection.

7 A bucket tied at the end of a massless rod of length l is whirled in a vertical circle with constant speed. What should be the minimum speed at highest point, so that the water from the bucket does not spill, when the bucket is at the highest position ?

8 If a particle of mass M is tied to a light inextensible string fixed at point P and particle is projected at A with velocity $v_A = \sqrt{4gl}$ as shown. Find

(a) velocity at points B and C

(b) and tension in the string at B and C.

Assume that, particle is projected in the vertical plane.

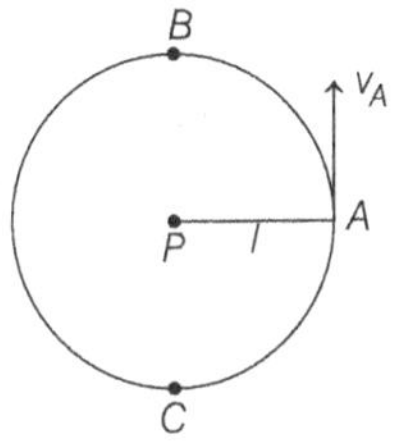

9 A nail is located at a certain distance vertically below the point of suspension of a simple pendulum. The pendulum bob is released from the position, where the string makes an angle of 60° from the vertical. Calculate the distance of the nail from the point of suspension such that the bob will just perform revolution with the nail as centre. Assume the length of pendulum to be l.

10 A small body A of mass m slides inside a large smooth hemispherical bowl of radius R as shown in figure. If the body is given a speed $\sqrt{2gR}$ parallel to the surface at point A of the hemisphere, find the normal force exerted by the small body on the hemisphere, when it is at the bottom at point B of the hemisphere.

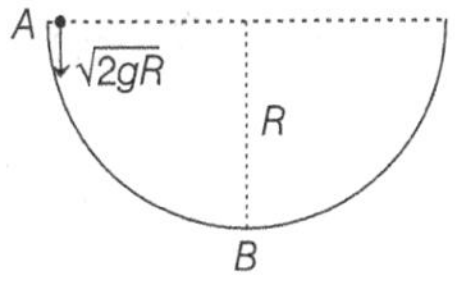

11 A car is moving with uniform speed over a circular bridge of radius R which subtends an angle of`90° at its centre. Find the minimum possible speed, so that the car can cross the bridge without losing the contact anywhere.

12 A block of mass m is released from the top of a frictionless fixed hemisphere as shown. Find

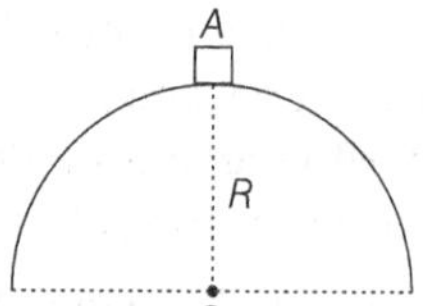

(a) the angle with the vertical, where it breaks off
(b) the velocity at the instant, when it breaks off
(c) the height, when it breaks off

13 A particle of mass m is kept on a fixed, smooth sphere of radius R at a position where the radius through the particle makes an angle of 30° with the vertical. The particle is released from this position.
(a) What is the force exerted by the sphere on the particle just after the release?
(b) Find the distance travelled by the particle before it leaves contact with the sphere.

14 A particle is projected with velocity $\sqrt{3gL}$ at point A (lowest point of the circle) in the vertical plane. Find the maximum height above horizontal level of point A if the string slacks at the point B as shown.

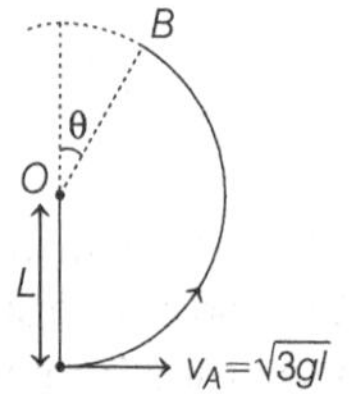

15 A block is released from the top of a smooth vertical track, which ends in a circle of radius r as shown. Find

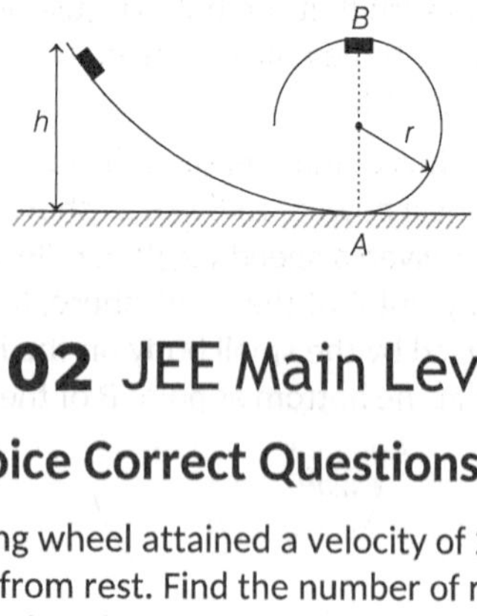

(a) the minimum value of h, so that the block completes the circle.
(b) if $h = 3r$, find normal reaction when the block is at the points A and B.
(c) if $h = 2r$, find the velocity of the block when it loses the contact with the track.

13.9 Radius of Curvature

1 A particle of mass m is projected with speed u at an angle θ with the vertical. Find the radius of curvature of the path traced out by the particle
(a) at the highest point of trajectory.
(b) at the point of projection.

2 A particle moves along the plane trajectory in the form of a parabola $y = ax^2$, where a is a positive constant with constant speed v. Find the radius of curvature of the trajectory at the point $x = 0$.

3 A track consists of two circular parts ABC and CDE of equal radius 100 m and joined smoothly as shown in figure. Each part subtends a right angle at its centre. A cycle weighing 100 kg together with the rider travels at a constant speed of 18 km/h on the track.

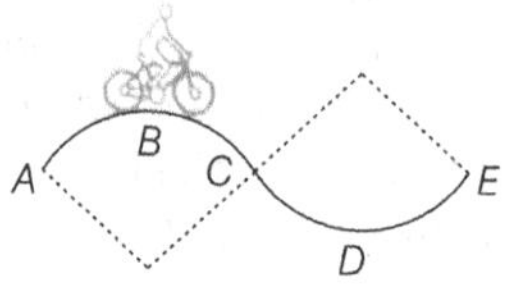

(a) Find the normal contact force by the road on the cycle when it is at B and D.
(b) Find the force of friction exerted by the track on the tyres when the cycle is at B, C and D.
(c) Find the normal force between the road and the cycle just, before and just after the cycle crosses C.
(d) What should be the minimum friction coefficient between the road and the tyre, which will ensure that the cyclist can move with constant speed? (Take, $g = 10 \text{ m/s}^2$)

LEVEL 02 JEE Main Level

Single Choice Correct Questions

1 A grinding wheel attained a velocity of 20 rad/s in 5 s starting from rest. Find the number of revolutions made by the wheel.

(a) $\frac{\pi}{25}$ revolutions (b) 50 revolutions
(c) $\frac{25}{\pi}$ revolutions (d) None of these

2 Angular position of a line of a disc of radius $r = 6$ cm is given by $\theta = (10 - 5t + 4t^2)$ rad, the average angular speed between 1 and 3s is
(a) π rad/s (b) 11 rad/s (c) 22 rad/s (d) 5.5 rad/s

3 A solid body rotates about a stationary axis so that its angular velocity depends on the rotation angle ϕ as $\omega = \omega_0 - k\phi$, where ω_0 and k are positive constants. At the moment $t = 0$, the angle $\phi = 0$. Find the time dependence of rotation angle.

(a) $k\omega_0 e^{-kt}$ (b) $\frac{\omega_0}{k}e^{-kt}$

(c) $\frac{\omega_0}{k}(1-e^{-kt})$ (d) $\frac{k}{\omega_0}(e^{-kt}-1)$

4 Two cars having masses m_1 and m_2 move in circles of radius r_1 and r_2. If they complete the circle in equal time, the ratio of their angular speeds $\frac{\omega_1}{\omega_2}$ is

(a) $\frac{r_2}{r_1}$ (b) $\frac{r_1}{r_2}$ (c) $\frac{m_1 r_1}{m_2 r_2}$ (d) 1

5 A particle is moving along a circular path of radius 6 m with uniform speed of 8 ms^{-1}. The average acceleration when the particle completes one half of the revolution is

(a) $\frac{16}{3\pi} m/s^2$ (b) $\frac{32}{3\pi} m/s^2$

(c) $\frac{64}{3\pi} m/s^2$ (d) None of these

6 A particle, moving along a circular path has equal magnitudes of tangential and angular acceleration. The diameter of path is (in metres)

(a) 2 (b) 1 (c) π (d) 2π

7 A car is moving in a circular path of radius 500 m with a speed of 30 m/s. If its speed is increasing at a rate of 2 m/s^2, the resultant acceleration will be

(a) 3.8 m/s^2 (b) 2.5 m/s^2 (c) 2.7 m/s^2 (d) 4 m/s^2

8 A particle is moving along a circular path of radius 3 m in such a way that the distance travelled measured along the circumference is given by $s = \frac{t^2}{2} + \frac{t^3}{3}$. The acceleration of particle when $t = 2$ s is

(a) 1.3 m/s^2 (b) 13 m/s^2 (c) 3 m/s^2 (d) 10 m/s^2

9 In a circular motion of a particle, the tangential acceleration of the particle is given by $a_t = 9\ m/s^2$. The radius of the circle is 4 m. The particle was initially at rest. Time after which total acceleration of the particle makes an angle of 45° with the radial acceleration is

(a) $\frac{1}{3}$ s (b) $\frac{2}{3}$ s (c) 1 s (d) $\frac{4}{3}$ s

10 A particle of mass *m* is moving in a circular path of constant radius *r* such that its centripetal acceleration a_c is varying with time *t* as $a_c = k^2 r t^2$, where *k* is a constant. The power delivered to the particle by the force acting on it is

(a) $2\pi m k^2 r^2$ (b) mk^2r^2t

(c) $\frac{(mk^4r^2t^5)}{3}$ (d) zero

11 A stone of mass of 8 kg is attached to a string 7.2 m long and is whirled in a horizontal smooth surface.The maximum tension the string can withstand is 160 N. The maximum speed of revolution of the stone without breaking it, will be

(a) $\frac{20}{\pi}$ rpm (b) $\frac{30}{\pi}$ rpm (c) $\frac{40}{\pi}$ rpm (d) $\frac{50}{\pi}$ rpm

12 A particle is kept fixed on a uniformly rotating turn table. As seen from the ground , the particle goes in a circle, its speed is 10 cm/s and acceleration is 10 cm/s^2. The particle is now shifted to a new position to make the radius half of the original value. The new values of the speed and acceleration will be

(a) 20 cm/s, 20 cm/s^2 (b) 5 cm/s, 5 cm/s^2

(c) 40 cm/s, 10 cm/s^2 (d) 40 cm/s, 40 cm/s^2

13 A coin placed on a rotating turn table just slips if it is placed at a distance of 16 cm from the centre. If the angular velocity of the turn table is doubled, it will just slip at a distance of

(a) 4 cm (b) 8 cm (c) 32 cm (d) 64 cm

14 A small block is connected to one end of two identical massless strings of length $16\frac{2}{3}$ cm each with their other ends fixed to a vertical rod. If the ratio of tensions $\frac{T_1}{T_2}$ be 4 : 1, then what will be angular speed ω of the block?

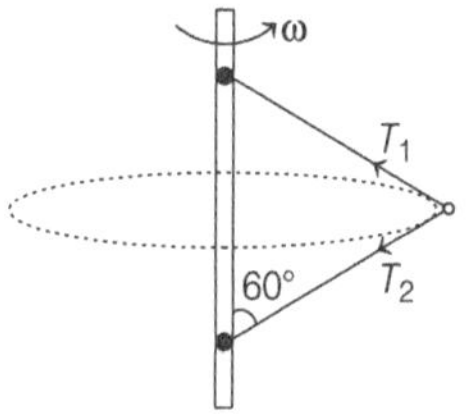

(a) 10 rad/s (b) 14 rad/s (c) 15 rad/s (d) 20 rad/s

15 A particle of mass *m* is fixed to one end of a light spring of force constant *k* and unstretched length *l*. The system is rotated about the other end of the spring with an angular velocity ω ,in gravity free space. The increase in length of the spring will be

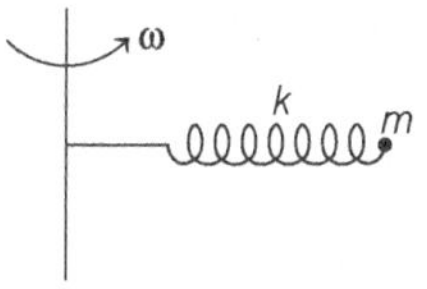

(a) $\frac{m\omega^2 l}{k}$ (b) $\frac{m\omega^2 l}{k - m\omega^2}$

(c) $\frac{m\omega^2 l}{k + m\omega^2}$ (d) None of these

16 A heavy small sized sphere is suspended by a string of length l. The sphere rotates uniformly in a horizontal circle with the string making an angle θ with the vertical. Then, the time period of this conical pendulum is

(a) $T = 2\pi$ (b) $T = 2\pi\sqrt{\frac{l\sin\theta}{g}}$

(c) $T = 2\pi\sqrt{\frac{l\cos\theta}{g}}$ (d) $T = 2\pi\sqrt{\frac{l}{g\cos\theta}}$

17 A person with a mass of M kg stands in contact against the wall of the cylindrical drum of radius r rotating with an angular velocity ω. The coefficient of friction between the wall and the clothing is μ. The minimum rotational speed of the cylinder which enables the person to remain stuck to the wall when the floor is suddenly removed is

(a) $\sqrt{\frac{g}{\mu r}}$ (b) $\sqrt{\frac{\mu r}{g}}$ (c) $\sqrt{\frac{2g}{\mu r}}$ (d) $\sqrt{\frac{g\mu}{r}}$

18 A smooth wire is bent into a vertical circle of radius a. A bead P can slide smoothly on the wire. The circle is rotated about diameter AB as axis with a speed ω as shown in figure. The bead P is at rest with respect to the circular ring in the position shown. Then, ω is equal to

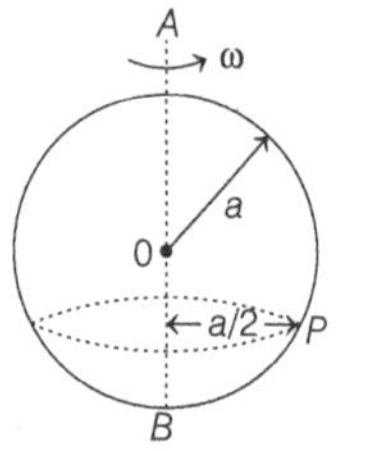

(a) $\left(\frac{2g}{a}\right)^{\frac{1}{2}}$ (b) $\left(\frac{2g}{\sqrt{3}a}\right)^{1/2}$ (c) $\left(\frac{\sqrt{3}g}{a}\right)^{1/2}$ (d) $\left(\frac{g}{2a}\right)^{1/2}$

19 A circular turn table of radius 0.5 m has a smooth groove as shown in figure. A ball of mass 90 g is placed inside the groove along with a spring of spring constant 10^2 N/cm. The ball is at a distance of 0.1 m from the centre when the turn table is at rest.

On rotating the turn table with a constant angular velocity of 10^2 rad s^{-1}, the ball moves away from the initial position by a distance nearly equal to

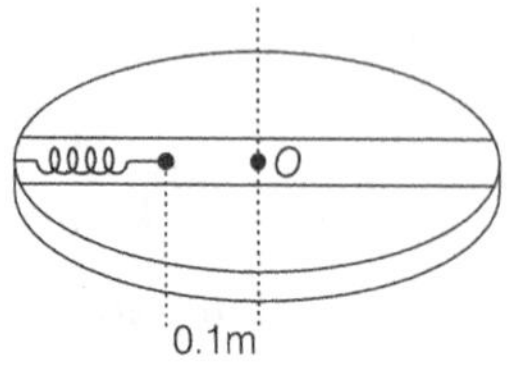

(a) 10^{-1} m (b) 10^{-2} m (c) 10^{-3} m (d) 2×10^{-1} m

20 When the road is dry and the coefficient of friction is μ, the maximum speed of a car in a circular path is 10 m/s. If the road becomes wet and $\mu' = \mu/2$, what is the maximum speed permitted?

(a) 5 m/s (b) 20 m/s
(c) $10\sqrt{2}$ m/s (d) $5\sqrt{2}$ m/s

21 A railway track is banked for a speed v, by making the height of the outer rail (h) higher than that of the inner rail. The distance between the rails is d. The radius of curvature of the track is r. Then,

(a) $\frac{h}{d} = \frac{v^2}{rg}$ (b) $\tan\left(\sin^{-1}\frac{h}{d}\right) = \frac{v^2}{rg}$

(c) $\tan^{-1}\left(\frac{h}{d}\right) = \frac{v^2}{rg}$ (d) $\frac{h}{r} = \frac{v^2}{dg}$

22 A road is banked at an angle of 30° to the horizontal for negotiating a curve of radius $10\sqrt{3}$ m. At what velocity will a car experience no friction while negotiating the curve?

(a) 54 km/h (b) 72 km/h
(c) 36 km/h (d) 18 km/h

23 A 1200 kg automobile rounds a level curve of radius 200 m, on an unbanked road, with a velocity of 72 km/h, The minimum coefficient of friction between the tyres and the road in order that the automobile may not skid is ($g = 10\ m/s^2$)

(a) 0.3 (b) 0.2
(c) 0.6 (d) 0.5

24 A circular track has radius 20 m, and angle of banking 37° with the horizontal. If $\mu_s = \frac{1}{4}$, find maximum safe speed of the car.

(a) $10\sqrt{\frac{32}{13}}$ m/s (b) $10\sqrt{\frac{13}{32}}$ m/s

(c) $30\sqrt{\frac{13}{32}}$ m/s (d) None of these

25 A simple pendulum is suspended from the ceiling of a car taking a turn of radius 10 m at a speed of 36 km/h. Find the angle made by the string of the pendulum with the vertical, if this angle does not change during the turn. (Take, $g = 10\ m/s^2$)

(a) 30° (b) 45° (c) 60° (d) 53°

26 If the apparent weight of the bodies at the equator is to be zero, then the earth should rotate with angular velocity

(a) $\sqrt{\frac{g}{R}}$ rad/s (b) $\sqrt{\frac{2g}{R}}$ rad/s

(c) $\sqrt{\frac{g}{2R}}$ rad/s (d) $\sqrt{\frac{3g}{2R}}$ rad/s

27 A car moving on a horizontal road may be thrown out of the road in taking a turn
(a) by the gravitational force
(b) due to lack of sufficient centripetal force
(c) due to friction between road and the tyre
(d) due to reaction of earth

28 A particle is acted upon by a constant force always normal to the direction of motion of the particle. It is therefore inferred that
(A) its velocity is constant.
(B) it moves in a straight line.
(C) its speed is constant.
(D) it moves in circular path.
(a) A , D (b) C, D (c) A, B (d) A, B, C

29 A train A runs from east to west and another train B of the same mass runs from west to east at the same speed with respect to earth along the equator. Normal force by the track on train A is N_1 and that on train B is N_2
(a) $N_1 > N_2$ (b) $N_1 < N_2$ (c) $N_1 = N_2$
(d) the information is insufficient to find the relation between N_1 and N_2.

30 A bead can slide along a straight rod. The friction coefficient between them is μ. At a certain moment $t = 0$, the rod starts rotating about a perpendicular axis passing through its end. At this moment, the bead is at distance 'r' from the rotation axis. The space is free of gravity. The angular velocity of the rod at any time t is $\omega = \alpha t^2$, where 'α' is a positive constant. The value of time t when the bead begins to to move is
(a) infinite (b) $\left(\frac{4\mu}{\alpha}\right)^{2/3}$
(c) $\left(\frac{\mu}{\alpha}\right)^{1/3}$ (d) $\left(\frac{2\mu}{\alpha}\right)^{1/3}$

31 A block of mass m is projected on a smooth horizontal circular track with velocity v. What is average normal force exerted by the circular walls on the block during its motion from A to B?

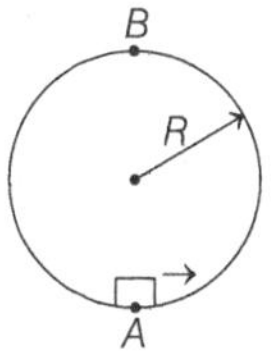

(a) $\frac{mv^2}{R}$ (b) $\frac{mv^2}{\pi R}$
(c) $\frac{2mv^2}{R}$ (d) $\frac{2mv^2}{\pi R}$

32 Two moving particles P and Q are 10 m apart at a certain instant. The velocity of P is 8 m/s making an angle 30° with the line joining P and Q and that of Q is 6 m/s making an angle 30° with PQ as shown in the figure. Then, angular velocity of P with respect to Q is

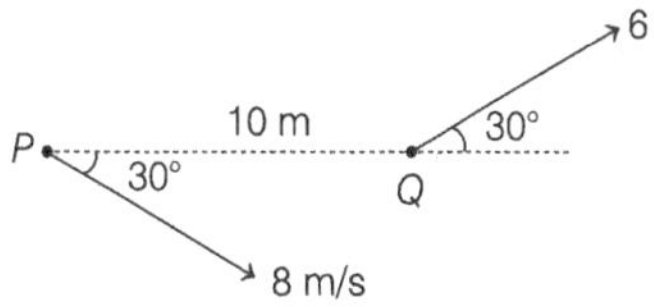

(a) zero (b) 0.1 rad/s (c) 0.4 rad/s (d) 0.7 rad/s

33 A body is thrown with the velocity $u = 10$ m/s at an angle of $\theta = 37°$ from the horizontal on a horizontal plane. Find the angular velocity of the body as observed from the point of projection at the time of landing.
(a) $\frac{5}{8}$ rad/s (b) $\frac{5}{6}$ rad/s (c) $\frac{5}{3}$ rad/s (d) None of these

34 A jet travelling at a constant speed of 432 km/h executes a vertical loop with a radius of 500 m. Find the magnitude of the force of the seat on a 70 kg pilot at the top of the loop. ($g = 10\ \text{ms}^{-2}$)

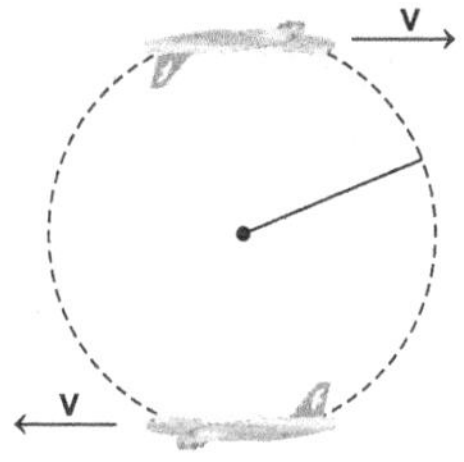

(a) 1316 N (b) 2716 N (c) 700 N (d) 2000 N

35 For a particle rotating in a vertical circle with uniform speed, the maximum and minimum tension in the string are in the ratio 5:3. If the radius of vertical circle is 2 m, then find the speed of revolving body.
(a) $4\sqrt{5}\ \text{ms}^{-1}$ (b) $2\sqrt{5}\ \text{ms}^{-1}$ (c) $4\sqrt{7}\ \text{ms}^{-1}$ (d) $2\sqrt{7}\ \text{ms}^{-1}$

36 A small body A of mass m slides inside a large hemispherical bowl of radius R as shown in figure. If the body starts from rest at the top point A of the hemisphere, find the normal force exerted by the hemisphere on the body when it is at point B of the hemisphere.

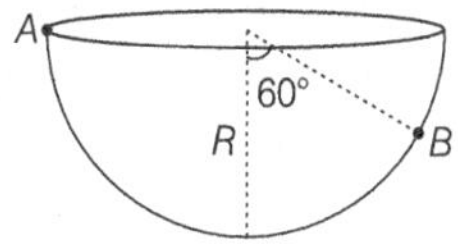

(a) $\frac{mg}{2}$ (b) mg (c) $\frac{3mg}{2}$ (d) $2mg$

37 A skier plans to ski a smooth fixed hemisphere of radius R. He starts from rest from a curved smooth surface of height $R/4$. The angle θ at which he leaves the hemisphere is

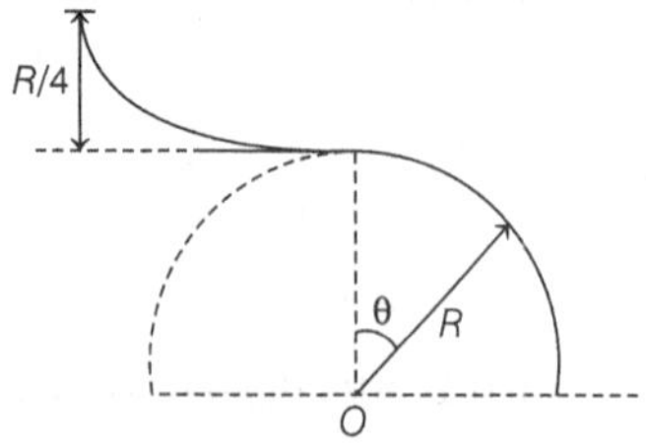

(a) $\cos^{-1}\left(\frac{2}{3}\right)$ (b) $\cos^{-1}\left(\frac{5}{\sqrt{3}}\right)$

(c) $\cos^{-1}\left(\frac{5}{6}\right)$ (d) $\cos^{-1}\left(\frac{5}{2\sqrt{3}}\right)$

38 A particle rests on the top of a hemisphere of radius R. Find the smallest horizontal velocity that must be imparted to the particle if it is to leave the hemisphere without sliding down it.

(a) $\sqrt{gR}$ (b) $\sqrt{2gR}$

(c) $\sqrt{3gR}$ (d) $\sqrt{5gR}$

39 A ball suspended by a thread swings in a vertical plane, so that its acceleration in the extreme position and lowest position are equal. The angle θ of thread deflection in the extreme position will be

(a) $\tan^{-1}(2)$ (b) $\tan^{-1}(\sqrt{2})$

(c) $\tan^{-1}\left(\frac{1}{2}\right)$ (d) $2\tan^{-1}\left(\frac{1}{2}\right)$

40 A particle suspended from a fixed point, by a light inextensible thread of length L is projected horizontally from its lowest position with velocity $\sqrt{\frac{7gL}{2}}$. The thread will become slack after swinging through an angle θ, such that θ is equal

(a) 30° (b) 135°

(c) 120° (d) 150°

41 A heavy particle hanging from a fixed point by a light inextensible string of length l is projected horizontally with speed $\sqrt{gl}$. Then, the speed of the particle and the inclination of the string to the vertical at the instant of the motion when the tension in the string equal the weight of the particle are

(a) $\sqrt{\frac{2gl}{3}}, \cos^{-1}(2/3)$ (b) $\sqrt{\frac{gl}{3}}, \cos^{-1}(2/3)$

(c) $\sqrt{\frac{gl}{3}}, \sin^{-1}(2/3)$ (d) $\sqrt{\frac{2gl}{3}}, \sin^{-1}(2/3)$

42 A stone tied to a string of length L is whirled in a vertical circle with the other end of the string at the centre. At a certain instant of time, the stone is at its lowest position and has a speed u. The magnitude of the change in its velocity as it reaches a position, where the string is horizontal is

(a) $\sqrt{u^2 - 2gL}$ (b) $\sqrt{2gL}$

(c) $\sqrt{u^2 - gL}$ (d) $\sqrt{2(u^2 - gL)}$

43 A particle is hanging from a fixed point O by means of a string of length a. There is a small smooth nail O' in the same horizontal line with O at a distance ($b < a$) from O. The minimum velocity with which particle should be projected from its lowest position in order that it may make a complete revolution round the nail without string becoming slack.

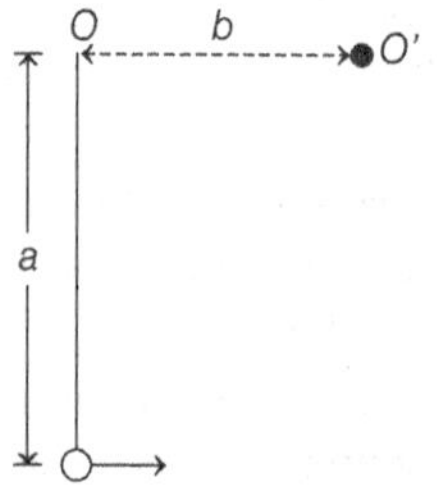

(a) $\sqrt{5g(a-b)}$ (b) $\sqrt{3(a-b)g}$

(c) $\sqrt{(5a-3b)g}$ (d) $\sqrt{(7a-3b)g}$

44 A small solid sphere is attached to one end of a string. The other end is tied to a fixed point O. Initially the sphere held in position A with the string horizontal. When the sphere is released, it swings in a vertical plane. Then, the total acceleration of the sphere at position B is

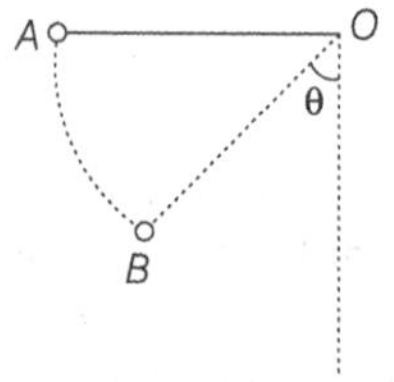

(a) $g\sqrt{3\cos^2\theta + 1}$ (b) $g\sin\theta$

(c) $2g\cos\theta$ (d) g

45 A cylindrical bucket filled with water is whirled around in a vertical circle of radius R. What can be the minimum speed at the top of the path if water does not fall out from the bucket. In this case, what normal force the bucket exerts on water at the lowest point of path?

(a) $\sqrt{Rg}$, $6mg$ (b) $\sqrt{2Rg}$, $2mg$

(c) $\sqrt{3Rg}$, $3mg$ (d) $\sqrt{Rg}$, $2mg$

46 A simple pendulum having a bob of mass m is suspended from the ceiling of a car used in a stunt film shooting. The car moves up along an inclined cliff at a speed v and makes a jump to leave the cliff and lands at some distance. Let R be the maximum height of the car from the top of cliff. The tension in the string when the car is in air, is

(a) mg (b) $mg - \frac{mv^2}{R}$

(c) $mg + \frac{mv^2}{R}$ (d) zero

47 A cube of mass M starts at rest from point 1 at a height $4R$, where R is the radius of the circular track. The cube slides down the frictionless track and around the loop. The force which the track exerts on the cube at point 2 is

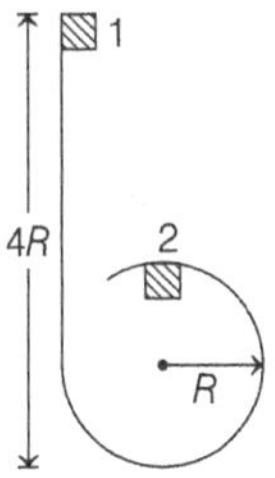

(a) 3 mg (b) mg (c) 2 mg
(d) cube will not reach the point 2

48 Figure shows the roller coaster track. Each car will start from rest at point A and will roll with negligible friction. It is important that there should be at least some small positive normal force exerted by the track on the car at all points, otherwise the car would leave the track. With the above fact, the minimum safe value for the radius of curvature at point B is (g = 10 m/s^2)

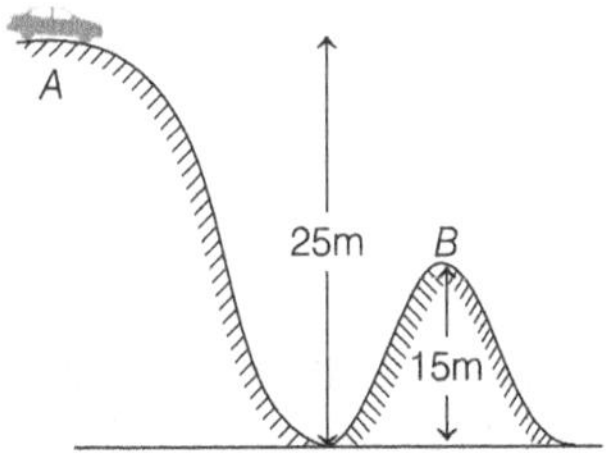

(a) 20 m (b) 10 m (c) 40 m (d) 25 m

49 The minimum speed v with which a small ball should be pushed inside a smooth vertical tube of radius R from a height h such that it may reach the top of the tube is

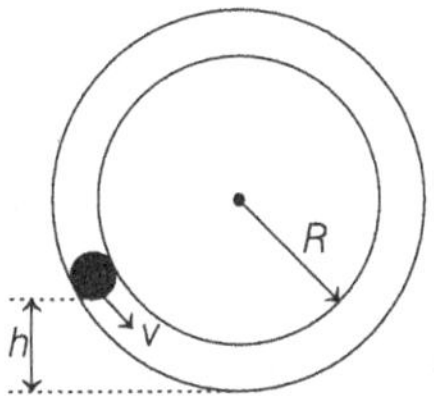

(a) $\sqrt{2g(h+2R)}$ (b) $\frac{5}{2}R$

(c) $\sqrt{g(5R-2h)}$ (d) $\sqrt{2g(2R-h)}$

50 A bead of mass m is located on a parabolic wire with its axis vertical and vertex at the origin as shown in figure and whose equation is $x^2 = 4ay$. The wire frame is fixed and the bead can slide on it without friction. The bead is released from the point $y = 4a$ on the wire frame from rest. The tangential acceleration of the bead when it reaches the position given by $y = a$ is

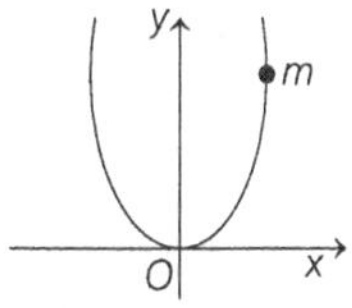

(a) $\frac{g}{2}$ (b) $\frac{\sqrt{3}g}{2}$ (c) $\frac{g}{\sqrt{2}}$ (d) $\frac{g}{\sqrt{5}}$

51 A smooth sphere of radius R is made to translate in a straight line with a constant acceleration a. A particle kept on the top of the sphere is released from there at zero velocity with respect to the sphere. Find the speed of the particle with respect to the sphere as a function of the angle θ it slides.

(a) $[2R(a\sin\theta + g - g\cos\theta)]^{1/2}$
(b) $[2R(a\cos\theta + g - g\sin\theta)]^{1/2}$
(c) $[2R(g\sin\theta + a - g\cos\theta)]^{1/2}$
(d) $[2R(g\cos\theta + a - g\sin\theta)]^{1/2}$

52 A car is moving with constant speed on a road as shown in figure. The normal reaction by the road on the car are N_A, N_B and N_C when it is at the points A, B and C, respectively.

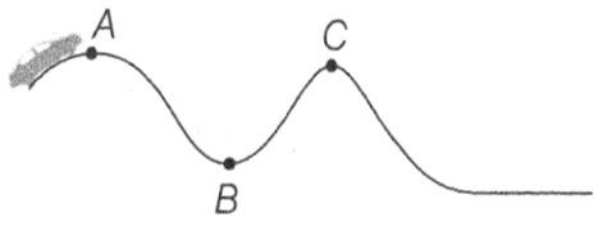

(a) $N_A = N_B = N_C$ (b) $N_B > N_A = N_C$
(c) $N_B > N_A > N_C$ (d) $N_B > N_C > N_A$

53 If the magnitude of tangential and normal accelerations of a particle moving on a curve in a plane be constant throughout, then which of the following represents the variation of radius of curvature with time?

(a) 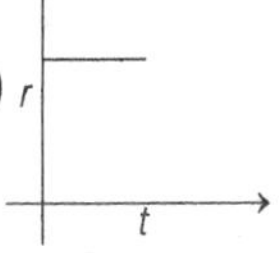

(b) 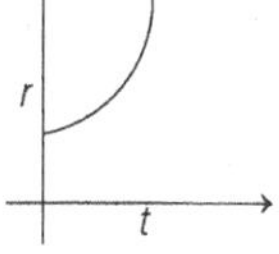

(c) 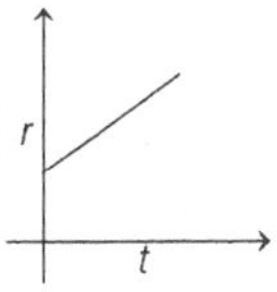

(d) 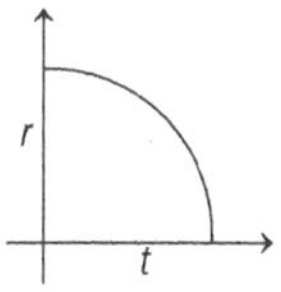

54 A particle (bob) of mass 1 kg is performing vertical circular motion. Then,

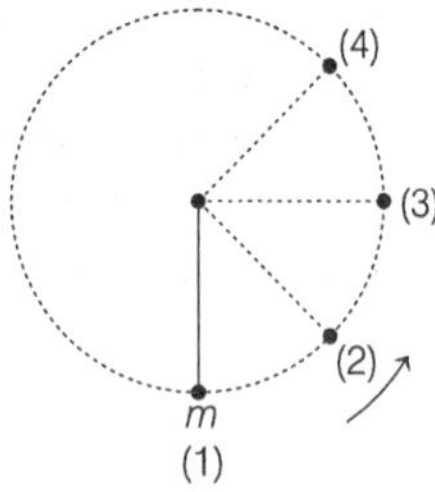

(a) power delivered by tension at point (4) is negative
(b) power delivered by tension at point (2) is positive
(c) power delivered by gravitational force at point (3) is zero
(d) power delivered by gravitational force at point (4) is negative

55 Three identical particles are joined together by a thread as shown in figure. All the three particles are moving on a smooth horizontal plane about point *O*.

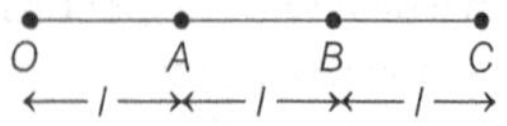

If the speed of the outermost particle is v_0, then the ratio of tensions in the three sections of the string is (Assume that the string remains straight)

(a) 3 : 5 : 7 (b) 3 : 4 : 5
(c) 7 : 11 : 6 (d) 3 : 5 : 6

Numerical Value Questions

1 A pendulum of length $l = 1$ m is released from $\theta_0 = 60°$. Find the rate of change of speed (in m/s^2) of the bob at $\theta = 30°$. (g = 10 m/s^2)

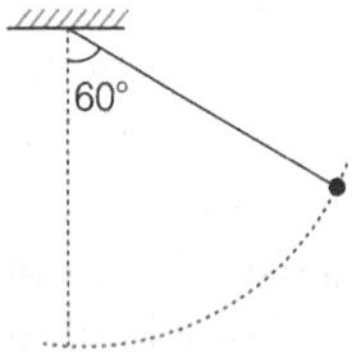

2 A particle moves along a circle of radius R = 1 m, so that its radius vector **r** relative to a point on its circumference rotates with the constant angular velocity $\omega = 2$ rad/s. Find the linear speed (in m/s) of the particle.

3 Starting from rest, a particle rotates in a circle of radius $R = \sqrt{2}$ m with an angular acceleration $\alpha = \frac{\pi}{4}$ rad/s^2. The magnitude of average velocity (in m/s) of the particle over the time it rotates quarter circle is

4 A particle *P* will be in equilibrium inside a hemispherical bowl of radius 0.5 m at a height 0.2 m from the bottom when the bowl is rotated at an angular speed $\sqrt{\frac{n}{3}}$ rad/s. Find n. ($g = 10$ m/s^2)

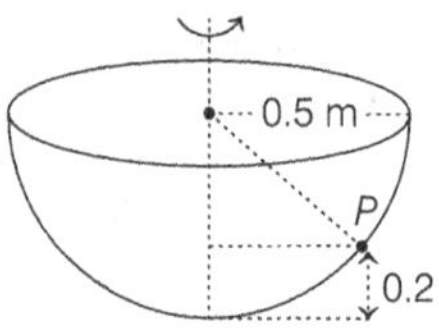

5 A bob is suspended from a crane by a cable of length $l = 5$ m. The crane and load are moving at a constant speed v_0. The crane is stopped by a bumper and the bob on the cable swings out an angle of 60°. Find the initial speed v_0 (in m/s). (g = 9.8 m/s^2)

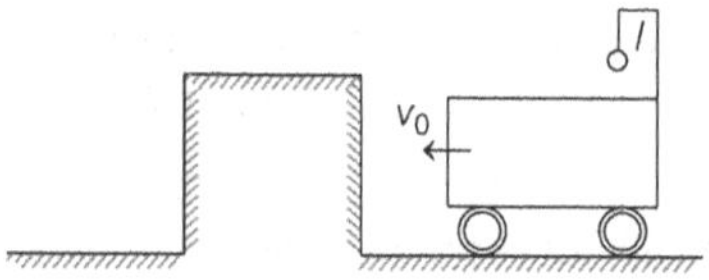

6 A particle is moving in a circle of radius 2 m such that its centripetal acceleration is given by $a_c = 2t^2$. Find the angle (in rad) traversed by the particle in the first two seconds.

7 A point moves in a circular path with a constant angular acceleration of 2 rad / s^2 starting from rest. After $\frac{1}{2}$s, the angle between the velocity and acceleration of the point will be $\tan^{-1}\left(\frac{1}{n}\right)$. Then, find the value of n.

8 A stone is attached to a light strong string and whirled in a vertical circle of radius 1 m. The tension difference between bottom and topmost point is 720 N. What is the mass (in kg) of the stone?

9 A section of fixed smooth circular track of radius R in vertical plane is shown in the figure. A block is released from position *A* and leaves the track at *B*. The radius *R* of curvature of its trajectory when just after it leaves the track at *B* is R/n. Find n.

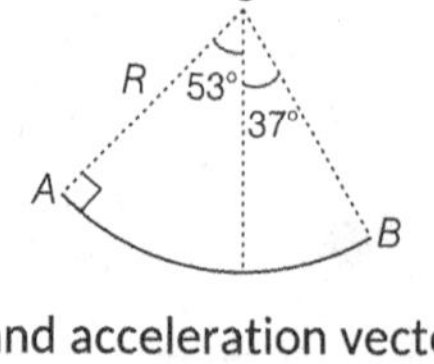

10 The velocity and acceleration vectors of a particle undergoing circular motion are $\mathbf{v} = 2\hat{\mathbf{i}}$ m/s and $\mathbf{a} = 2\hat{\mathbf{i}} + 4\hat{\mathbf{j}}$ m/s^2 respectively, at an instant of time. Find the radius (in m) of the circle.

11 A circular platform rotates around a vertical axis with angular velocity of 10 rad/s. On the platform is a ball of mass 1 kg, attached to the long axis of the platform by a thin rod of length 10 cm. Find normal force exerted by the ball on the platform (in N). ($\alpha = 30°$) Friction is absent.

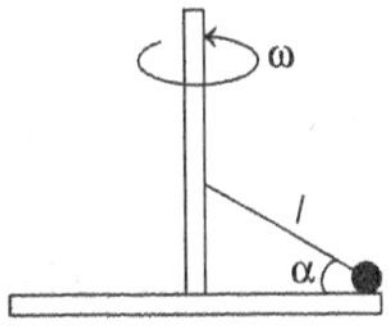

12 A heavy particle hanging vertically from a fixed point by a light inextensible cord of length $l = 54$ cm is struck by a horizontal blow which imparts to it a velocity $2\sqrt{gl}$. Find maximum height (in cm) reached by the particle from the initial position.

13 If angular velocity of a disc depends an angle rotated θ as $\omega = \theta^2 + 2\theta$, then find its angular acceleration α (in rad/s^2) at $\theta = 1$ rad.

14 A body is thrown with a velocity of 10 m/s at an angle of 45° to the horizontal at $t = 0$. Find the radius of curvature (in m) of its trajectory at $t = \frac{1}{\sqrt{2}}$ s after the body began to move.

15 Three aircrafts make a turn in the horizontal plane at uniform speed, moving along concentric circular trajectories that are shown in figure. The aircrafts move such that they are at constant distance of 600 m from each other at anytime. The aircraft closest to the center moves in a circle of radius $R = 600$m. The aircraft 2 is moving at a speed of $v_2 = 720$ km/h. Find the acceleration of third aircraft (in m/s^2).

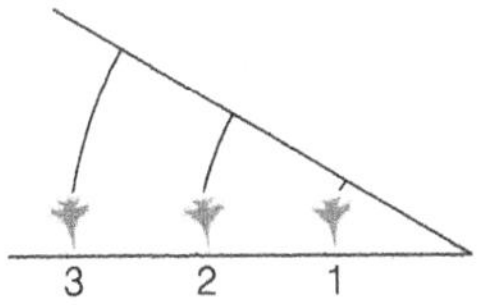

16 A particle is given an initial speed u from the lowest point inside a fixed smooth spherical shell of radius $R = 1$ m that it is just able to complete the circle. Acceleration of the particle when its velocity is vertical is $g\sqrt{n}$. Find n.

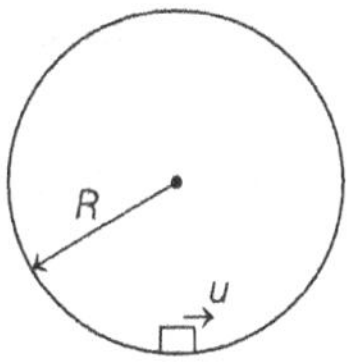

17 In the figure shown, a lift goes downwards with a constant retardation. An observer in the lift observers a conical pendulum in the lift, revolving in a horizontal circle with time period 2 s. The distance between the centre of the circle and the point of suspension is 2.0 m. Find the retardation of the lift in m/s^2. Use, $\pi^2 = 10$ and $g = 10$ m/s^2

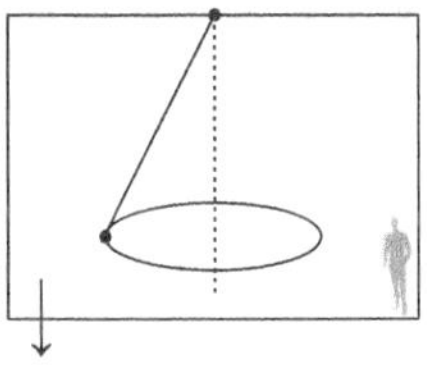

18 Figure shows a smooth track in vertical plane, consisting of two circular arcs AB and BC of the same radius $R = 2$ m. The common tangent the arcs, BD, is horizontal. A small block placed on the track at a height h above BD leaves the track at exactly at the same depth below. Determine h (in cm).

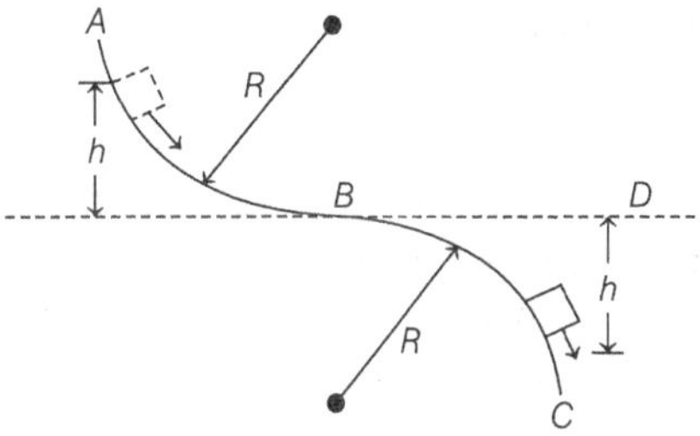

19 A stone is projected from level ground at $t = 0$ s, such that its horizontal and vertical components of initial velocity are 10 m/s and 40 m/s, respectively. Then, find the instant of time at which magnitude of tangential and magnitude of normal components of acceleration of stone are same. (Neglect air resistance) $g = 10$ m/s^2.

20 Two equal masses m each are attached by a string. One mass lies at radial distance r from the centre of a horizontal turn-table which rotates with constant angular velocity $\omega = 2$ rad s^{-1}, while the other mass hangs from the string inside the turn-table's hollow spindle (see figure). The coefficient of static friction between the turn-table and the mass lying on it is $\mu_s = 0.8$. The maximum and minimum values of r such that the mass lying on the turn-table does not slide are r_{max} and r_{min}, respectively. Find value of $(r_{max} - r_{min})$ in meter.

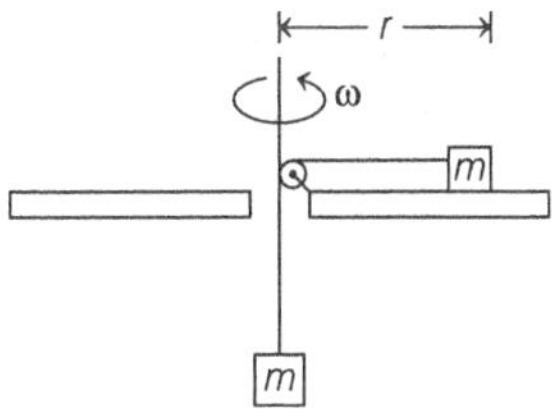

LEVEL 03 JEE Advanced Level

Single Choice Correct Questions

1 A point moves along a circle with velocity $v = at$, where $a = 0.5 \text{ m/s}^2$. Then, the total acceleration of the point at the moment when it covered $\left(\frac{1}{10}\right)^{\text{th}}$ of the circle after beginning of motion

(a) 0.5 m/s^2 (b) 0.6 m/s^2
(c) 0.7 m/s^2 (d) 0.8 m/s^2

2 Two bodies A and B rotate about an axis, such that angle θ_A (in radians) covered by first body is proportional to square of time and θ_B (in radians) covered by second body varies linearly. At $t = 0, \theta_A = \theta_B = 0$. If A completes its first revolution in $\sqrt{\pi}$ second, and B needs 4π second to complete half revolution, then angular velocity $\omega_A : \omega_B$ at $t = 5$ s are in the ratio

(a) 4 : 1 (b) 20 : 1
(c) 80 : 1 (d) 20 : 4

3 The kinetic energy K of a particle moving along a circle of radius R depends on the distance covered s as $K = as^2$, where a is a positive constant. The total force acting on the particle is

(a) $\frac{2as^2}{R}$ (b) $2as\left(1+\frac{s^2}{R^2}\right)^{1/2}$
(c) $2as$ (d) $\frac{2aR^2}{s}$

4 A particle moves along an arc of a circle of radius R. Its velocity depends on the distance covered s as $v = a\sqrt{s}$, where a is a constant, then the angle α between the vector of the total acceleration and the vector of velocity as a function of s will be

(a) $\tan\alpha = \frac{R}{2s}$ (b) $\tan\alpha = \frac{2s}{R}$
(c) $\tan\alpha = \frac{2R}{s}$ (d) $\tan\alpha = \frac{s}{2R}$

5 A particle is moving in a circle of radius R in such a way that at any instant the total acceleration makes an angle of 45° with the radius vector. If the initial speed of the particle is v_0, then the time taken by the particle to complete the first revolution is

(a) $\frac{R}{v_0}e^{-2\pi}$ (b) $\frac{R}{v_0}(1-e^{-2\pi})$
(c) $\frac{2R}{v_0}e^{-2\pi}$ (d) $\frac{2R}{v_0}(1-e^{-2\pi})$

6 A toy car revolves in a circular path of radius 1 m on a horizontal rough plane. Its' speed varies as $v = 2t^2$. It starts sliding at $t = 1$ s. Find the value of coefficient of friction between ground and the wheels of the car. (Use, $g = 10 \text{ m/s}^2$)

(a) $\frac{2\sqrt{2}}{5}$ (b) $\frac{3\sqrt{2}}{5}$ (c) $\frac{4\sqrt{2}}{5}$ (d) $\sqrt{2}$

7 A particle of mass m is moving in a circular path of constant radius r such that its centripetal acceleration a_c is proportional to t^n (where t is time). Then, the power 'P' is proportional to

(a) t^n (b) t^{n-2} (c) t^{n-1} (d) $t^{\left(\frac{n}{2}-1\right)}$

8 A particle moves in the xy-plane with the velocity $\mathbf{v} = a\hat{\mathbf{i}} + bt\hat{\mathbf{j}}$. At the instant, $t = \frac{\sqrt{3}a}{b}$, the magnitude of its tangential and normal acceleration are respectively,

(a) $\frac{\sqrt{3}b}{2}, \frac{b}{2}$ (b) $\frac{b}{2}, \frac{\sqrt{3}b}{2}$
(c) $\frac{b}{\sqrt{2}}, \frac{b}{\sqrt{2}}$ (d) None of these

9 A car moves around a curve at a constant speed. When the car goes around the arc subtending 60° at the centre, then the ratio of magnitude of instantaneous acceleration to average acceleration over the 60° arc is

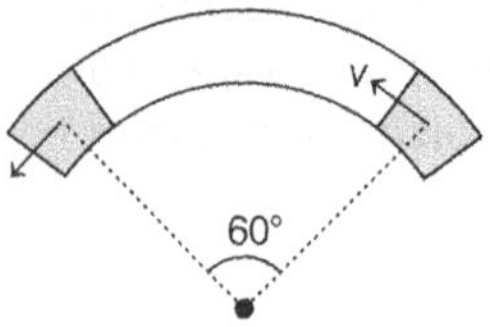

(a) $\frac{\pi}{3}$ (b) $\frac{\pi}{6}$ (c) $\frac{2\pi}{3}$ (d) $\frac{5\pi}{3}$

10 The distance r from the origin of a particle moving in XY-plane varies with time as, $r = 2t$ and the angle made by the radius vector with positive X- axis is $\theta = 4t$. Here, t is in seconds, r is in metres and θ is in radians. The speed of the particle at $t = 1$s is

(a) 8 m/s (b) 8.25 m/s
(c) 10 m/s (d) 12 m/s

11 If $\mathbf{r}$ is the position vector of a particle and $\mathbf{v}$ its velocity, then

(a) $\mathbf{v}\cdot\mathbf{r} = \frac{dr}{dt}$ (b) $\mathbf{v}\cdot\hat{\mathbf{r}} = \frac{dr}{dt}$
(c) $\mathbf{v}\cdot\mathbf{r} = 0$ (d) $\mathbf{v}\cdot\mathbf{r} = vr$

12 A racing car is travelling along a track at a constant speed of 40 m/s. A TV cameraman is recording the event from a distance of 30 m directly away from the track as shown in figure. In order to keep the car under view in the position shown, the angular speed with which the camera should be rotated, is

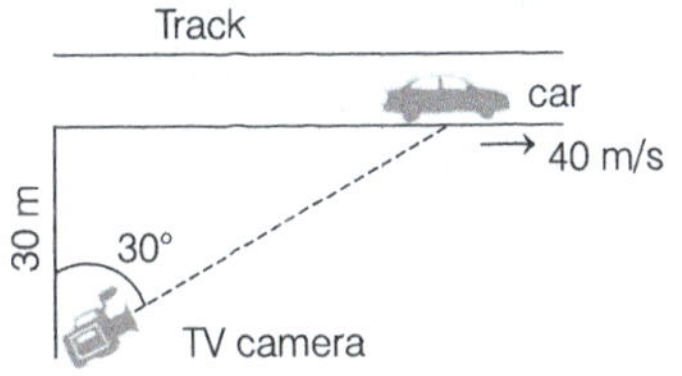

(a) $\frac{4}{3}$ rad/s (b) $\frac{3}{4}$ rad/s (c) $\frac{8}{3\sqrt{3}}$ rad/s (d) 1 rad/s

13 A body moves in a circle of radius R having centre at origin, with an angular velocity ω in the xy-plane as shown in the figure. Another body moves parallel to Y-axis with constant velocity $\frac{\omega R}{2}$. At time $t = 0$, both particles are at $(R, 0)$. The value of time t, when first body has velocity only along positive X-axis w.r.t. the second body is

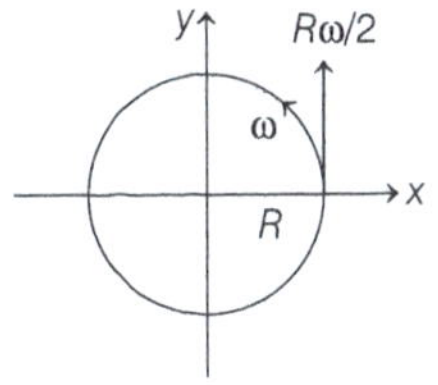

(a) $\frac{\pi}{6\omega}$ (b) $\frac{5\pi}{3\omega}$ (c) $\frac{5\pi}{6\omega}$ (d) None of these

14 Small blocks A and B connected with a string are rotated with angular velocity ω about point O as shown in the figure. Breaking strength of both the strings is 75N. The maximum angular velocity by which system can be rotated on a horizontal smooth plane

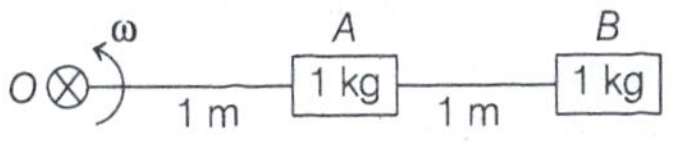

(a) 4 rad/s (b) 5 rad/s (c) 6 rad/s (d) $\sqrt{\frac{75}{2}}$ rad/s

15. The tap in a standard audio cassette has a length $L = 120$ m; the tape plays running at constant linear speed for $t = 2$ hr. As the tape starts, the full reel has an outer radius of $R_1 = 12\sqrt{2}$ cm, and an inner radius of $R_2 = 5\sqrt{2}$ cm. At some point during the play, both reels have the same angular speed. Calculate this angular speed in rad/s.

(a) $\frac{1}{500}$ (b) $\frac{5}{39}$ (c) $\frac{1}{510\sqrt{2}}$ (d) None of these

16 A single wire ACB passes through a smooth ring at C which revolves at a constant speed in the horizontal circle of radius r as shown in the figure. The speed of revolution is

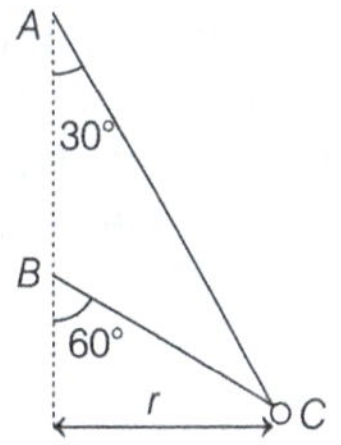

(a) $\sqrt{rg}$ (b) $\sqrt{2rg}$
(c) $2\sqrt{2rg}$ (d) $2\sqrt{rg}$

17 A 10 kg ball attached at the end of a rigid rod of length 1 m rotates at constant speed in a horizontal circle with time period 1.57 s as shown in the figure. The force exerted by the rod on the ball nearly is ($g = 10$ m/s^2).

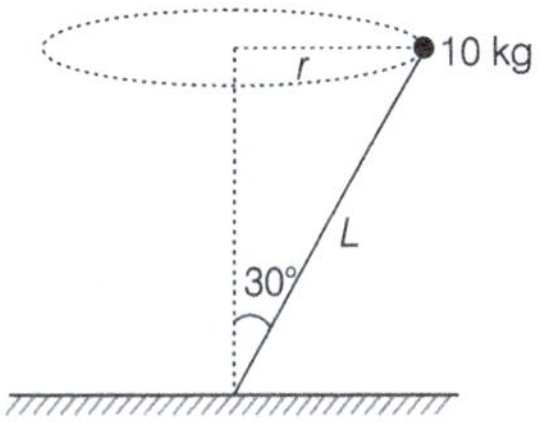

(a) 110 N (b) 158 N
(c) 128 N (d) 98 N

18 Two particles tied to different strings are whirled in a horizontal circle as shown in figure. The ratio of lengths of the strings, so that they complete their circular paths with equal time period is

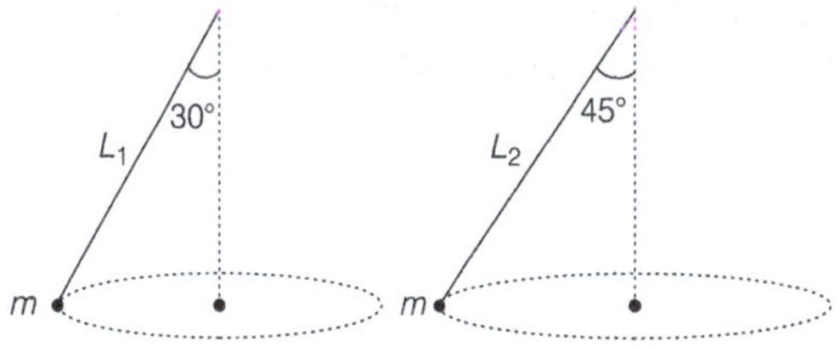

(a) $\sqrt{\frac{3}{2}}$ (b) $\sqrt{\frac{2}{3}}$
(c) 1 (d) None of these

19 A uniform circular ring of mass per unit length λ and radius R is rotating with angular velocity ω about its own axis in a gravity free space. Find the tension in the ring.

(a) $2\lambda R^2\omega^2$ (b) $\lambda R^2\omega^2$
(c) $\frac{1}{2}\lambda R^2\omega^2$ (d) $4\lambda R^2\omega^2$

20 A wet open umbrella is held upright and whirled about the handle with a unifom angular speed of 28 revolutions in 44 s. If the rim of the umbrella is a circle of diameter 1 m, and height of the rim from the ground is 2.5 m, find the radius of the circle along which the drops of water spun off the rim tangentially without any relative velocity hit the ground.

(a) $\sqrt{2}$ m (b) 2 m

(c) 1.5 m (d) $2\sqrt{2}$ m

21 A disc of radius R has a light pole fixed perpendicular to the disc at the circumference which, in turn, has a pendulum of length R attached to its other end as shown in figure. The disc is rotated with a constant angular velocity ω. The string is making an angle 30° with the rod. The angular velocity ω of the disc is

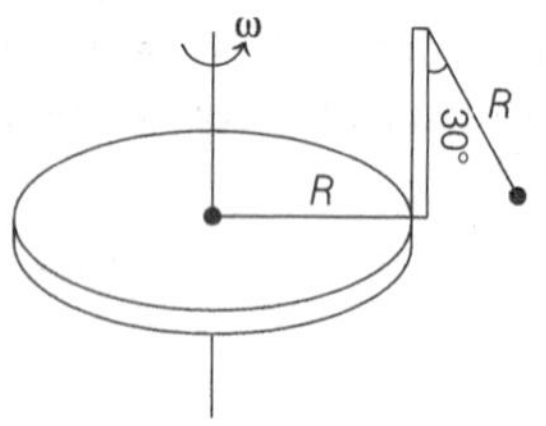

(a) $\left(\frac{\sqrt{3}g}{R}\right)^{1/2}$ (b) $\left(\frac{\sqrt{3}g}{2R}\right)^{1/2}$

(c) $\left(\frac{2g}{\sqrt{3}R}\right)^{1/2}$ (d) $\left(\frac{2g}{3\sqrt{3}R}\right)^{1/2}$

22 A small bead of mass $m = 1$ kg is carried by a circular hoop having centre at C and radius $r = 1$ m, which rotates about a fixed vertical axis. The coefficient of friction between bead and hoop is $\mu = 0.5$. The maximum angular speed of the hoop for which the bead does not have relative motion with respect to hoop is

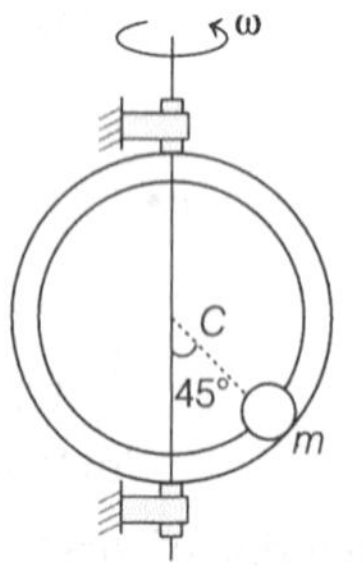

(a) $(5\sqrt{2})^{1/2}$ (b) $(10\sqrt{2})^{1/2}$

(c) $(15\sqrt{2})^{1/2}$ (d) $(30\sqrt{2})^{1/2}$

23 A small wedge whose base is horizontal is fixed to a vertical rod as shown in the figure. The sloping slide of the wedge is frictionless and the wedge is spun with a angular speed ω about vertical axis as shown in the figure. Find ω, so that the block does not slip relative to wedge.

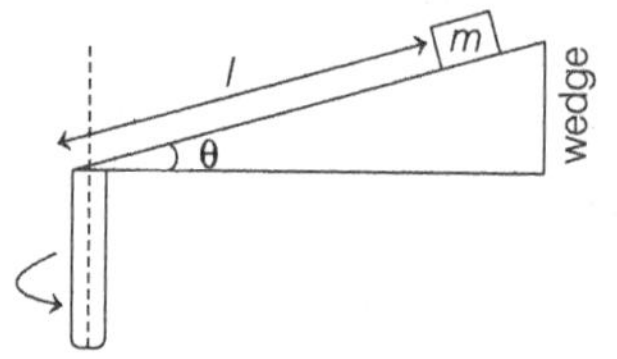

(a) $\sqrt{\frac{g\tan\theta}{l}}$ (b) $\sqrt{\frac{g\sin\theta}{l\cos^2\theta}}$

(c) $\sqrt{\frac{g\cos\theta}{l\sin^2\theta}}$ (d) $\sqrt{\frac{g\cot\theta}{l}}$

24 Two blocks A and B are connected by a cord passing around a frictionless pulley which is attached to a rotating frame. Determine the value of ω at which the blocks start sliding radially.

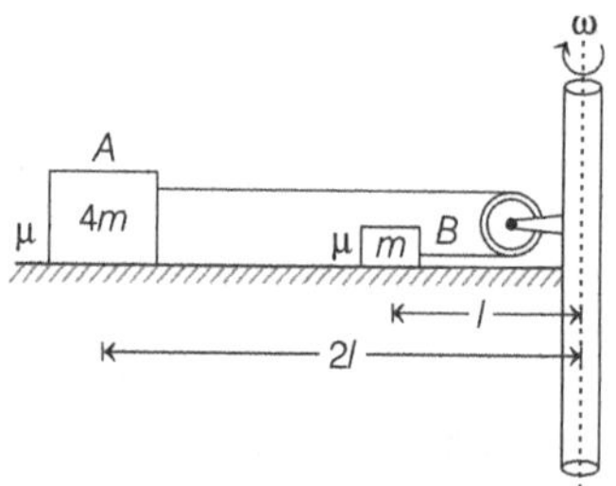

(a) $\sqrt{\frac{3\mu g}{7l}}$ (b) $\sqrt{\frac{5\mu g}{9l}}$

(c) $\sqrt{\frac{5\mu g}{7l}}$ (d) $\sqrt{\frac{\mu g}{3l}}$

25 A car is negotiating a curve of radius 150 m with a speed of 15 ms^{-1}. The angle through which the pendulum suspended from the top of the ceiling would deviate is (g = 10 ms^{-2})

(a) $\tan^{-1}\frac{3}{20}$

(b) $\tan^{-1}\frac{5}{16}$

(c) $\tan^{-1}\frac{4}{15}$

(d) $\tan^{-1}\frac{3}{16}$

26 Two cars A and B start racing at the same time on a flat race track which consists of two straight sections each of length 100π and one circular section as in figure. The rule of the race is that each car must travel at constant speed at all times without ever skidding. Then,

$$\mu_A = 0.1$$
$$\mu_B = 0.2$$
$$r_A = 100 \text{ m}$$
$$r_B = 200 \text{ m}$$

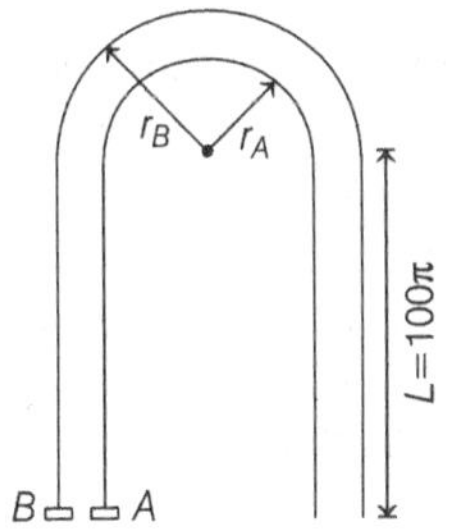

(a) car A completes its journey before car B
(b) both cars complete their journey in same time
(c) velocity of car A is greater than that of car B
(d) car B completes its journey before car A

27 The maximum tension in the string of an oscillating pendulum is thrice the minimum tension. What is its angular amplitude?

(a) 30° (b) 15°
(c) $\sin^{-1}\left(\frac{4}{5}\right)$ (d) $\cos^{-1}\left(\frac{2}{5}\right)$

28 A ball is held at rest in position A by two light cords. The horizontal cord is now cut and the ball swings to the position B. What is the ratio of the tension in the other cord in position B to that in position A?

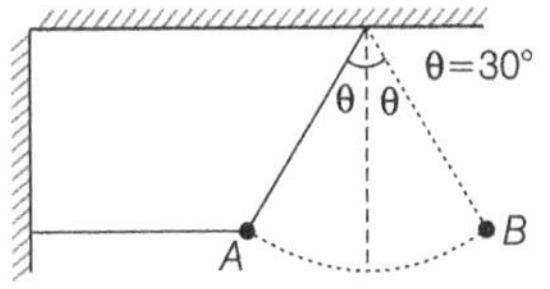

(a) $\frac{3}{4}$ (b) $\frac{1}{3}$
(c) 3 (d) 1

29 One end of ideal string tied up with fixed support and other end is tied with a bob. The string is released from horizontal position. When string makes an angle of θ with vertically downward direction, then the acceleration vector of bob is horizontal. Then, θ is

(a) $\tan^{-1}(1)$ (b) $\tan^{-1}(\sqrt{2})$
(c) $\tan^{-1}(\sqrt{3})$ (d) None of these

30 In the system shown, the mass $m = 2$ kg oscillates in a circular arc of amplitude 60°, the minimum value of coefficient of friction between block of mass 8 kg and surface of table to avoid slipping is

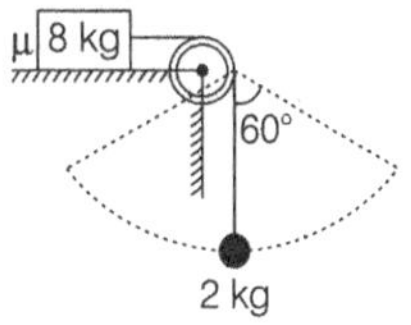

(a) 0.25 (b) 0.50
(c) 0.40 (d) None of these

31 A heavy particle hangs from a point O, by a string of length a. It is projected horizontally with a velocity $u = \sqrt{(2+\sqrt{3})ag}$. The angle with downward vertical, string makes when it becomes slack is

(a) $\theta = \sin^{-1}\left(\frac{-1}{\sqrt{3}}\right)$ (b) $\theta = \cos^{-1}\left(\frac{-1}{\sqrt{3}}\right)$
(c) $\theta = \cos^{-1}\left(\frac{-1}{\sqrt{2}}\right)$ (d) $\theta = \sin^{-1}\left(\frac{-1}{\sqrt{2}}\right)$

32 In the shown arrangement, a bob of mass m is suspended by means of a string connected to peg P. If the bob is given a horizontal velocity **u** having magnitude $\sqrt{3gl}$, find the minimum speed of the bob in subsequent motion.

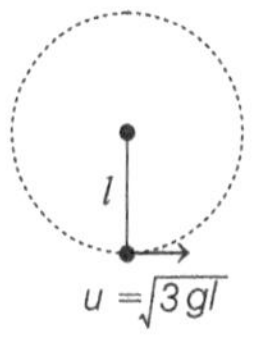

(a) $\sqrt{\frac{gl}{17}}$ (b) $\sqrt{\frac{gl}{20}}$
(c) $\sqrt{\frac{gl}{27}}$ (d) $\sqrt{\frac{gl}{25}}$

33 A small block of mass m slides along a frictionless loop inside loop as shown. The minimum value of the ratio R/r, so that the block may not lose contact at the highest point of the inner loop is

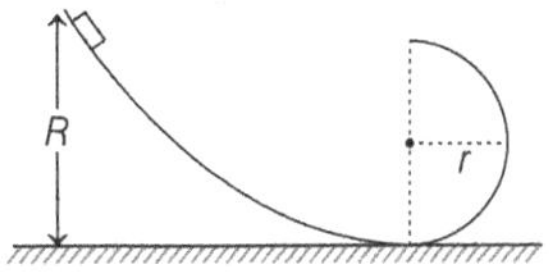

(a) $\frac{2}{3}$ (b) $\frac{7}{2}$
(c) $\frac{3}{2}$ (d) $\frac{5}{2}$

34 A point mass m connected to one end of inextensible string of length l and other end of string is fixed at peg. String is free to rotate in vertical plane. Find the minimum velocity give to the mass in horizontal direction, so that it hits the peg in its subsequent motion.

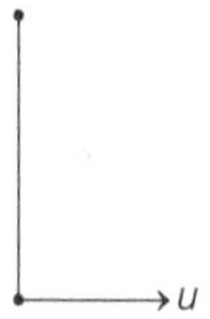

(a) $[(3+\sqrt{2})gl]^{1/2}$ (b) $[(2+\sqrt{3})gl]^{1/2}$
(c) $[(1+2\sqrt{3})gl]^{1/2}$ (d) $[(1+2\sqrt{2})gl]^{1/2}$

35 Two point masses m are connected by the light rod of length $2l$ and it is free to rotate in vertical plane as shown. Calculate the minimum horizontal velocity to be given to lower mass, so that it completes the circular motion in vertical plane.

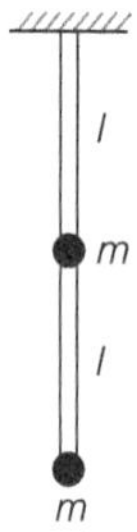

(a) $\sqrt{\dfrac{48gl}{5}}$ (b) $\sqrt{10gl}$
(c) $\sqrt{6gl}$ (d) $\sqrt{\dfrac{24gl}{5}}$

36 A collar B of mass 2 kg is constrained to move along a horizontal smooth and fixed circular track of radius 5m. The spring lying in the plane of the circular track and having spring constant 200 N/m is undeformed when the collar is at A. If the collar starts from rest at B, the normal reaction exerted by the track on the collar when it passes through A is

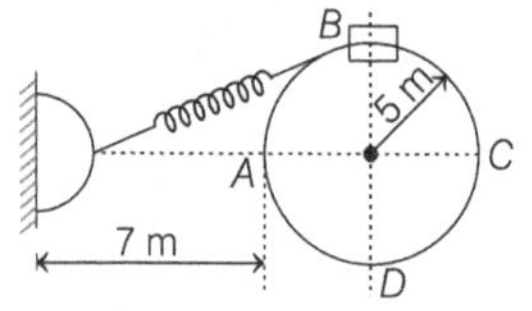

(a) 360 N (b) 720 N (c) 1440 N (d) 2880 N

37. A 2 kg block is gently pushed from rest at A and it slides down along the fixed smooth circular surface. The attached spring has a force constant $k = 20$ N/m. What is unstretched length of spring so that it does not allow the block to leave the surface until angle with the vertical is $\theta = 60°$?

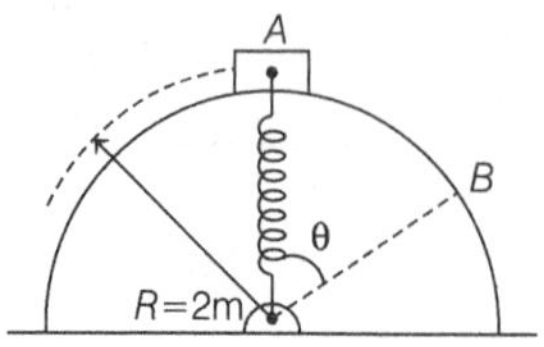

(a) 1 m (b) 1.5 m
(c) 0.5 m (d) 0.8 m

38 A particle initially at rest starts moving from point A on the surface of a fixed smooth hemisphere of radius r as shown. The particle loses its contact with hemisphere at point B. C is centre of the hemisphere. The equation relating α and β is

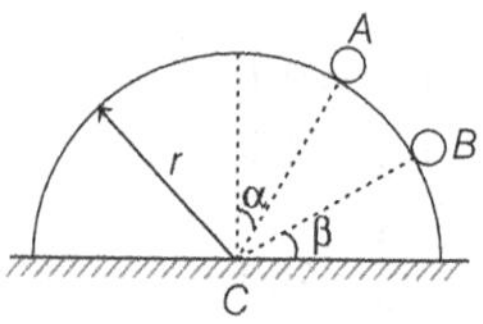

(a) $3\sin\alpha = 2\cos\beta$ (b) $2\sin\alpha = 3\cos\beta$
(c) $3\sin\beta = 2\cos\alpha$ (d) $2\sin\beta = 3\cos\alpha$

39 A person rolls a small ball with speed u along the floor from point A. If $x = 3R$, determine the required speed u, so that the ball returns to A after rolling on the circular surface in the vertical plane from B to C and becoming a projectile at C.

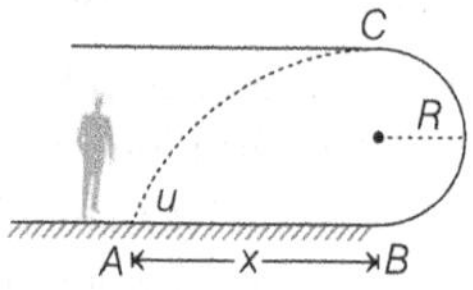

(a) $2\sqrt{gR}$ (b) $\sqrt{5gR}$ (c) $\sqrt{6gR}$ (d) $\dfrac{5}{2}\sqrt{gR}$

40 In the previous question, what is the minimum value of x for which the game could be played if contact must be maintained at point C? Neglect friction.

(a) $x_{min} = 1.5R$ (b) $x_{min} = 2R$
(c) $x_{min} = 2.25R$ (d) $x_{min} = 2.5R$

41 A small particle of mass m is released from rest from point A inside a smooth hemisphere bowl as shown. The ratio (x) of magnitude of centripetal force and normal reaction on the particle at any point B varies as

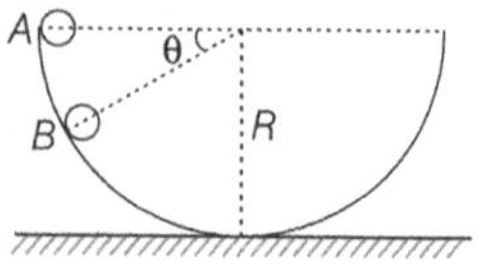

(a)
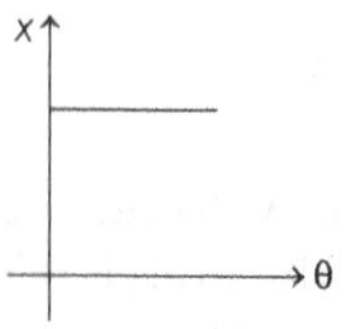

(b)
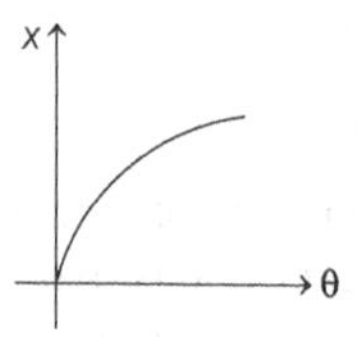

(c)
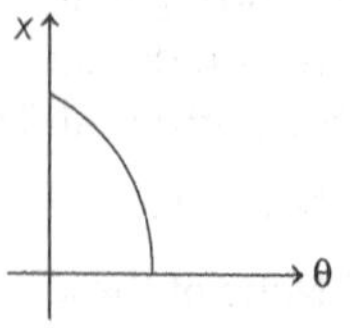

(d)
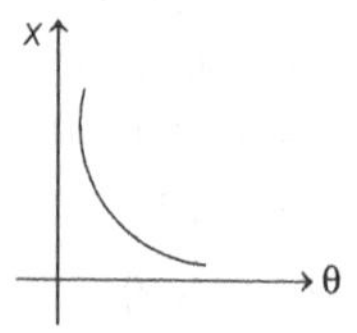

42 A bead of mass m is attached to one end of a spring of natural length R and spring constant $k = \frac{(\sqrt{3}+1)mg}{R}$. The other end of the spring is fixed at point A on a smooth vertical ring of radius R as shown in figure. The normal reaction at B just after it is released is

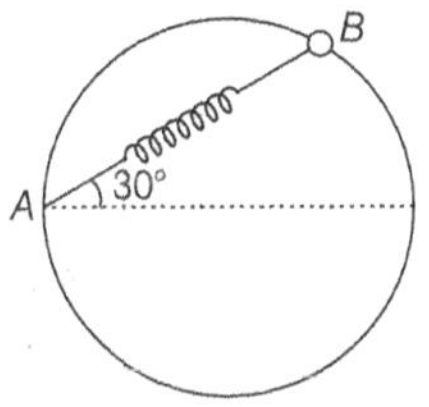

(a) $\frac{mg}{2}$ (b) $\sqrt{3}\,mg$

(c) $3\sqrt{3}\,mg$ (d) $\frac{3\sqrt{3}mg}{2}$

43 A particle of mass m is attached to the end of a light inextensible string of length $2a$, the other end of which is attached to a fixed point P. The particle is projected horizontally from the point $2a$ below P with speed v. As it comes in level with P, a peg Q at a distance a from P catches the string. In the subsequent motion,the particle can just describe a full circle about Q. Find v.

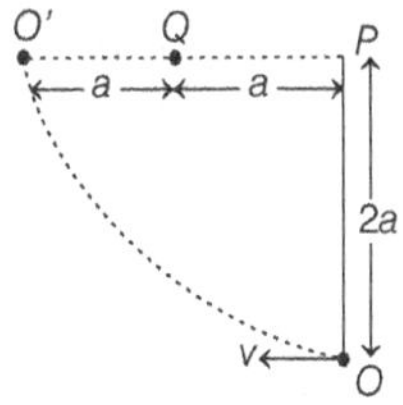

(a) $\sqrt{4ag}$ (b) $\sqrt{5ag}$

(c) $\sqrt{6ag}$ (d) $\sqrt{7ag}$

44 The sphere at P is given a downward velocity v_0 and swings in vertical plane at the end of a rope of $l = 1$ m attached to a support at O. The rope breaks at angle 30° from horizontal, knowing that it can withstand a maximum tension equal to three times the weight of the sphere. Then, the value of v_0 will be

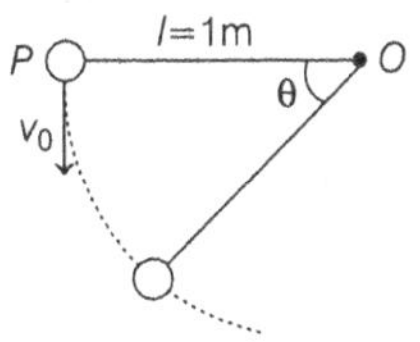

(a) $\frac{g}{2}$ m/s (b) $\frac{2g}{3}$ m/s

(c) $\sqrt{\frac{3g}{2}}$ m/s (d) $\frac{g}{3}$ m/s

45 The member OA rotates about a horizontal axis through O with a constant counter clockwise velocity $\omega = 3$ rad/s. As it passes the position $\theta = 0$, a small mass m is placed upon it at a radial distance $r = 0.5$ m. If the mass is observed to slip at $\theta = 37°$, the coefficient of friction between the mass and the member is

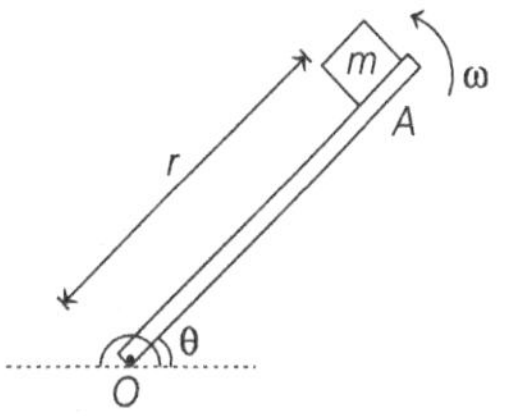

(a) $\frac{3}{16}$ (b) $\frac{9}{16}$ (c) $\frac{4}{9}$ (d) $\frac{5}{9}$

46 A circular tube of mass M is placed vertically on a horizontal surface as shown. Two small spheres of masses m, just fit in tube, are released from the top. If θ is the angle between radius vector of either ball with the vertical, then find the ratio $\frac{m}{M}$, if the tube breaks its contact with ground when $\theta = 60°$. Neglect friction.

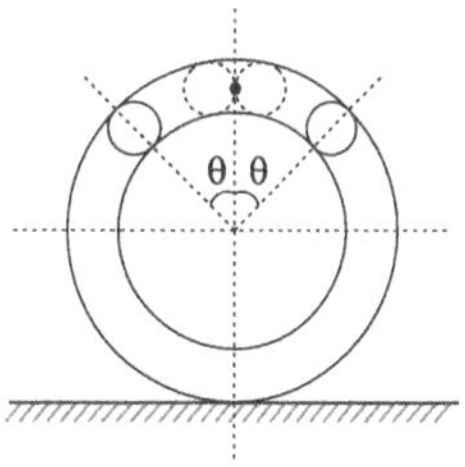

(a) $\frac{1}{2}$ (b) 4

(c) 2 (d) 6

47 An object moves counter clockwise along the circular path shown below. As it moves along the path, its acceleration vector continuously points towards S. The object

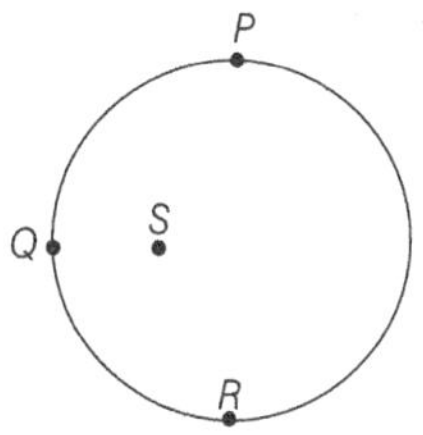

(a) speeds up at P, Q and R
(b) slows down at P, Q and R
(c) speeds up at P and slows down at R
(d) slows down at P and speeds up at R

48 A smooth track is shown in the figure. A block of mass M is pushed against a spring of spring constant k fixed at the left end and is then released. Find the initial compression of the spring, so that the normal reaction at point P is Mg.

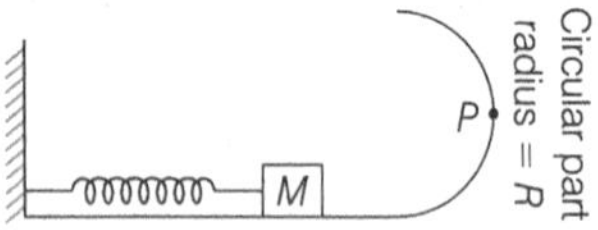

(a) $\sqrt{\dfrac{3MgR}{k}}$ (b) $\sqrt{\dfrac{2MgR}{k}}$

(c) $\sqrt{\dfrac{4MgR}{k}}$ (d) $\sqrt{\dfrac{MgR}{k}}$

49 A particle of mass m is placed on vertical fixed circular track and then it is given velocity v vertically downward at position A on track. If block moves on track with constant speed, then which of the following is incorrect?

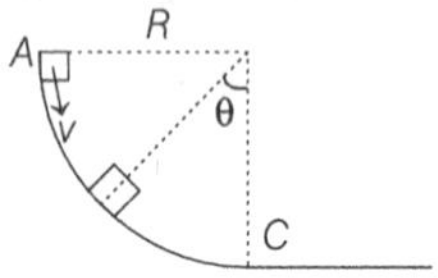

(a) coefficient of friction between block and circular track as function of angle θ is $\mu = \dfrac{\sin\theta}{\cos\theta + \dfrac{v^2}{Rg}}$

(b) Instantaneous power due to friction is $(-mg\ \sin\theta v)$

(c) Work done from A to C by friction on block will be $(-mg\,R)$

(d) None of the above

50 A collar of mass m is tied at one end of a spring of spring constant $\dfrac{mg}{R}$ and unstretched length $\dfrac{R}{2}$ and other end to fixed point O. The smooth semicircular wire frame is fixed in vertical plane. Find the normal reaction between collar and wire just before it reaches the lowest point.

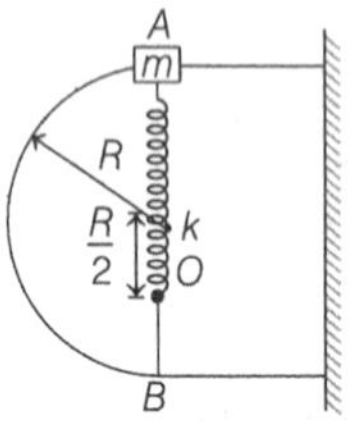

(a) 3 mg (b) 4 mg

(c) 5 mg (d) 6 mg

51 A particle is attached with a string of length l which is fixed at point O on an inclined plane. What minimum velocity should be given to the particle along the incline, so that it may complete a circle on inclined plane (plane is smooth and initially particle was resting on the inclined plane)?

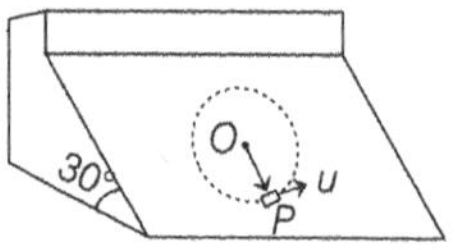

(a) $\sqrt{5gl}$ (b) $\sqrt{\dfrac{5gl}{2}}$ (c) $\sqrt{\dfrac{5\sqrt{3}gl}{2}}$ (d) $\sqrt{4gl}$

52 A bob is attached to one end of a string, other end of which is fixed at peg A. The bob is taken to a position where string makes an angle of 30° with the horizontal. On the circular path of the bob in vertical plane, there is a peg B at a symmetrical position with respect to the position of release as shown in the figure. If v_c and v_a be the minimum speeds in clockwise and anti-clockwise directions respectively, given to the bob in order to hit the peg B, then ratio $v_c : v_a$ is equal to

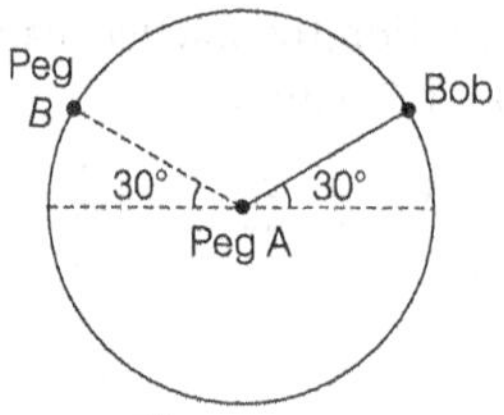

(a) 1 : 1 (b) 1: $\sqrt{2}$ (c) 1 : 2 (d) 1 : 4

53 A particle is connected to a massless rod of length R and the rod is fixed at other end with the help of smooth hinge. At lowest point, it is given a speed $\sqrt{4gR}$. Graph showing variation of magnitude of tension in the rod with the angle θ made by the rod from its initial position is

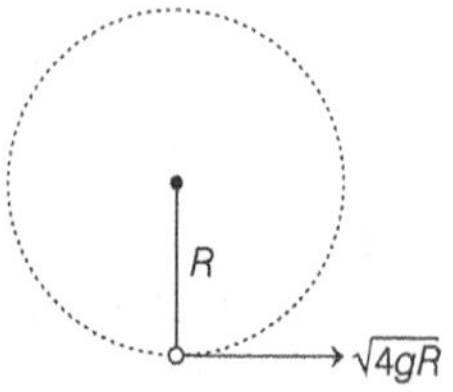

(a)
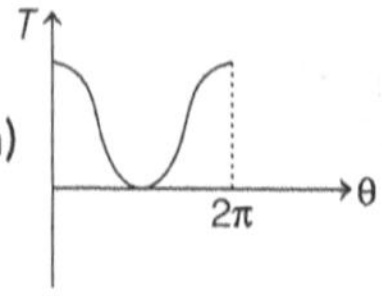

(b)
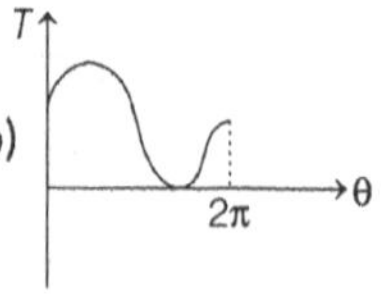

(c)
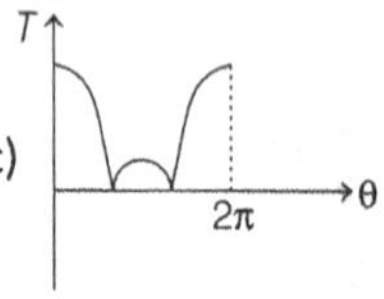

(d)
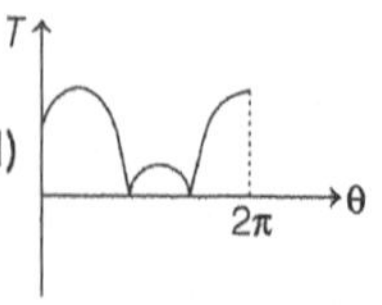

54 A particle is projected at an angle θ with horizontal. What is the radius of curvature of the parabola traced out by the projectile at a point, where the particle velocity makes an angle θ/2 with the horizontal?

(a) $\dfrac{u^2\cos^2\theta}{g\cos^3\left(\dfrac{\theta}{2}\right)}$ (b) $\dfrac{u^2\cos^2\theta}{g\sin^3\left(\dfrac{\theta}{2}\right)}$

(c) $\dfrac{u^2\cos^2\theta}{g\cos^2\left(\dfrac{\theta}{2}\right)\sin\left(\dfrac{\theta}{2}\right)}$ (d) $\dfrac{u^2\cos^2\theta}{g\sin^2\left(\dfrac{\theta}{2}\right)\cos\left(\dfrac{\theta}{2}\right)}$

55 The figure shows the velocity and acceleration of a point like body at the initial moment of its motion. The acceleration vector of the body remains constant. The minimum radius of curvature of trajectory of the body is

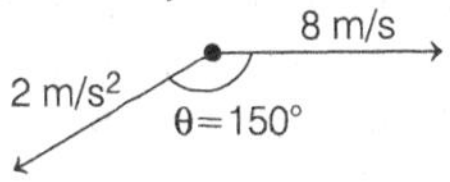

(a) 2 m (b) 4 m (c) 8 m (d) 16 m

Multiple Choice(s) Correct Questions

1 An object follows a circular path. Which of the following quantities may remain constant during the motion?
(a) speed (b) velocity
(c) acceleration
(d) magnitude of acceleration

2 A car of mass m is moving on a horizontal circular path of radius r. At an instant, its speed is v and is increasing at a rate a. Then,
(a) the acceleration of the car is towards the centre of the path
(b) the magnitude of the frictional force on the car is greater than mv^2/R
(c) the friction coefficient between the ground and the car is not less than a/g
(d) the friction coefficient between the ground and the car is $\mu = \tan^{-1}(v^2/Rg)$

3 Figure shows a rod of length L pivoted near an end and it is made to rotate in a horizontal plane with a constant angular speed. A ball of mass m is suspended by a string also of length L from the other end of the rod. If θ is the angle made by string with the vertical, then

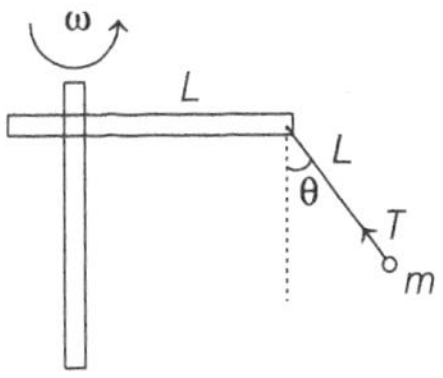

(a) $T = m\omega^2 L$ (b) $T\cos\theta = mg$
(c) $\tan\theta = \dfrac{\omega^2 L(1+\sin\theta)}{g}$ (d) None of these

4 A plank is moving along X-axis with constant velocity v_0. A pendulum having bob of mass m and length l is performing circular motion about O on the plank with speed v_0 with respect to plank as shown in the figure. At $t = 0$, particle velocity is along Y-axis, then

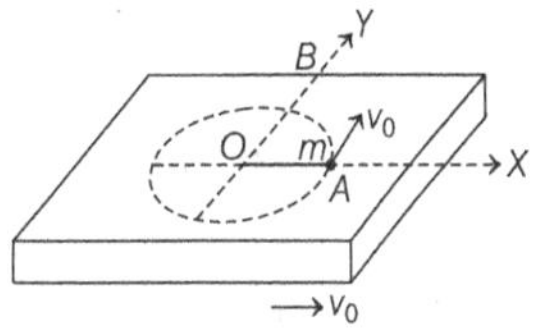

(a) Work done by tension on the particle with respect to plank is zero for any time interval
(b) Work done by tension on the particle with respect to ground in time $\dfrac{\pi l}{2v_0}$ is mv_0^2
(c) Work done by tension on the particle in time $\dfrac{2\pi l}{v_0}$ in ground frame is $-2\pi mv_0^2$
(d) Work done by tension on the particle in time $\dfrac{\pi l}{v_0}$ in ground frame is zero

5 A particle is projected horizontally with a velocity $\sqrt{\dfrac{ag}{2}}$ from highest point of the outside of a fixed smooth sphere of radius a. Then,
(a) particle will leave the sphere where contact force becomes zero
(b) particle will leave the sphere at a vertical distance $\dfrac{a}{6}$ below from the point of projection
(c) particle will leave the contact at an angle $\theta = \cos^{-1}\left(\dfrac{5}{6}\right)$ from the vertical
(d) None of the above

6 A particle P of mass m is attached to a vertical axis by two strings AP and BP of length l each. The separation $AB = l$. P rotates around the axis with an angular velocity ω. The tensions in the two strings are T_1 and T_2. Then,

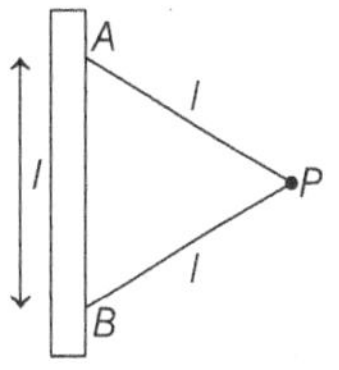

(a) $T_1 = T_2$ (b) $T_1 + T_2 = m\omega^2 l$
(c) $T_1 - T_2 = 2mg$
(d) BP will remain taut only if $\omega \geq \sqrt{\dfrac{2g}{l}}$

7 A bob of mass 2 kg is suspended from point O of a cone with an inextensible string of length $\sqrt{3}$ m. It is moving in horizontal circle over the surface of cone as shown in the figure. Then, (g = 10 m/s^2)

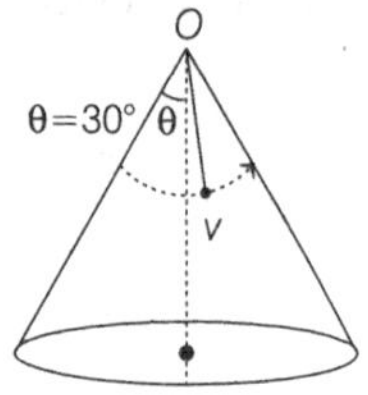

(a) bob loses contact with cone, if $v > \sqrt{5}$ m/s

(b) normal force on bob is 19 N, when $v = 2$ m/s

(c) tension in string is $\frac{38}{\sqrt{3}}$ N, when v = 2 m/s

(d) normal force on bob is $\frac{17}{\sqrt{3}}$ N, when v = 2m/s

8 In circular motion, if **v** is velocity vector, **a** is acceleration vector, **r** is instantaneous position vector, **p** is linear momentum vector and ω is angular velocity of particle, then

(a) ω and **r** are mutually perpendicular

(b) **p**, **r** and ω are mutually perpendicular

(c) $\mathbf{r} \times \mathbf{v} = 0$ and $\mathbf{r} \times \omega = 0$

(d) $\mathbf{r} \cdot \mathbf{v} = 0$ and $\mathbf{r} \cdot \omega = 0$

9 Two particles each of mass m are attached to the two ends of a light string of length L, which passes through a hole at the centre of a smooth table. One particle describes a circular path on the table with angular velocity ω_1 and the other describes a conical pendulum with angular velocity ω_2 below the table. If l_1 and l_2 are the lengths of the portions of the string above and below the table, then

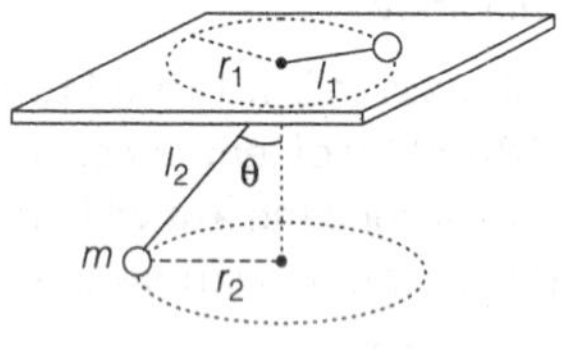

(a) $\frac{l_1}{l_2} = \frac{\omega_2}{\omega_1}$ (b) $\frac{l_1}{l_2} = \left[\frac{\omega_2}{\omega_1}\right]^2$

(c) $\frac{1}{\omega_1^2} + \frac{1}{\omega_2^2} = \frac{ml}{g}$ (d) $\frac{1}{\omega_1^2} + \frac{1}{\omega_2^2} = \frac{l\cos\theta}{g}$

10 A heavy particle is tied to the end A of a string of length 1.6 m. Its other end O is fixed. It revolves as a conical pendulum with the string making 60° with the vertical. Then, (g = 9.8 m/s^2)

(a) its period of revolution is $\frac{4\pi}{7}$ s

(b) the tension in the string is double the weight of the particle

(c) the speed of the particle is $2.8\sqrt{3}$ m/s

(d) the centripetal acceleration of the particle is $9.8\sqrt{3}$ m/s^2

11 A simple pendulum of length l and mass m is oscillating in a plane about a vertical line between angular limits $-\phi$ to $+\phi$. For an angular displacement θ when $|\theta| < \phi$, the tension in string is T and velocity of bob is v, then the conditions being satisfied are

(a) $T = mg\cos\theta$ (b) $T\cos\theta = mg$

(c) $T - mg\cos\theta = \frac{mv^2}{l}$

(d) tangential acceleration is $g\sin\theta$

12 A circular road of radius r is banked for a speed of v = 40 km/h. A car of mass m attempts to go on the circular road. The friction coefficient between the tyre and the road is negligible. Then,

(a) the car cannot make a turn without skidding

(b) if the car turn at a speed less than 40 km/h, it will slip down

(c) if the car turn at the correct speed of 40 km/h, the force by the road on the car is equal to mv^2/r

(d) If the car turn at the correct speed of 40 km/h, the force by the road on the car is greater than mg as well as greater than mv^2/r

13 One end of a thread of length l is attached to an inclined plane of angle of elevation of α. A point-like body of mass m = 1 kg is attached to the other end of the thread as shown in the figure. The body is released without initial speed, such that the thread is tight and horizontal. The coefficient of friction between the slope and the body is μ.

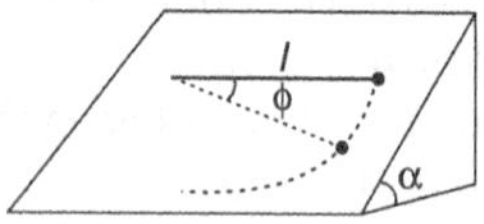

(a) The tension in the thread, when the angle between the thread and the horizontal is ϕ is $T = mg(3\sin\phi\sin\alpha - 2\mu\phi\cos\alpha)$

(b) The tension in the string will be maximum, when $\phi = 90°$

(c) The tension in the string will be maximum, when $\phi = \cos^{-1}\left(\frac{2\mu}{3\tan\alpha}\right)$

(d) The maximum speed of the particle will be, when $\phi = \cos^{-1}(\mu\cot\alpha)$

14 A particle is moving in a circle of radius 1 m with speed varying with time as $v = (2t)$ m/s. In first 2 s,

(a) average speed of the particle is 2 m/s
(b) average velocity of the particle is sin 2 m/s
(c) average acceleration of the particle is 2 m/s^2
(d) acceleration of the particle is 2 m/s^2

15 A machine, in an amusement park, consists of a cage at the end of one arm, hinged at O. The cage revolves along a vertical circle of radius r ($ABCDEFGH$) about its hinge O, at constant linear speed $v = \sqrt{gr}$. The cage is so attached that the man of weight w standing on a weighing machine, inside the cage, is always vertical. Then, which of the following is/are correct?

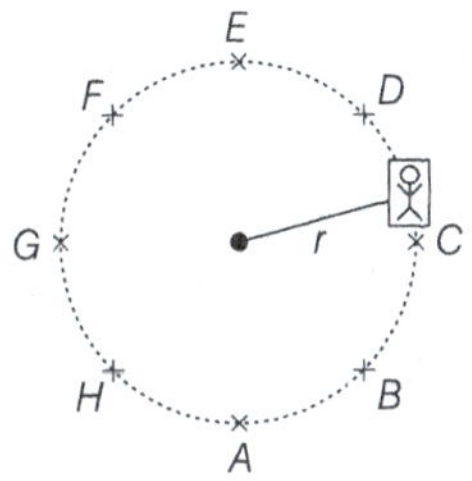

(a) The weight reading at A is greater than the weight reading at E by $2w$
(b) The weight reading at $G = w$
(c) The ratio of the weight reading at E to that at $A = 0$
(d) The ratio of the weight reading at A to that at $C = 2$

Comprehension Based Questions

Comprehension 1

A block of mass m moves on a horizontal circle against the wall of a cylindrical room of radius R. The floor of the room on which the block moves is smooth but the friction coefficient between the block and the side wall is μ. The block is given initial velocity v_0. Then, answer the following questions.

1 What is the tangential acceleration of the block ?

(a) μg (b) $-\mu g$ (c) $\mu v^2/R$ (d) $-\mu v^2/R$

2 What is the value of velocity v as the function of distance s travelled on the circumference?

(a) $v = v_0 e^{-\frac{2\mu s}{R}}$ (b) $v = v_0 e^{-\frac{\mu s}{R}}$

(c) $v = v_0\left(1 - e^{-\frac{2\mu s}{R}}\right)$ (d) $v = v_0$

3 What is the time taken by the block to complete the first revolution?

(a) $\frac{R}{\mu v_0}(e^{2\mu\pi} - 1)$ (b) $\frac{2R}{\mu v_0}(e^{2\mu\pi} - 1)$

(c) $\frac{2Re^{2\mu\pi}}{\mu v_0}$ (d) $\frac{Re^{2\mu\pi}}{\mu v_0}$

Comprehension 2

A small block of mass m is projected horizontally from the top of the smooth and fixed hemisphere of radius r with speed u as shown. For values of $u \geq u_0, (u_0 = \sqrt{gr})$, it does not slide on the hemisphere. [i.e. leaves the surface at the top itself]

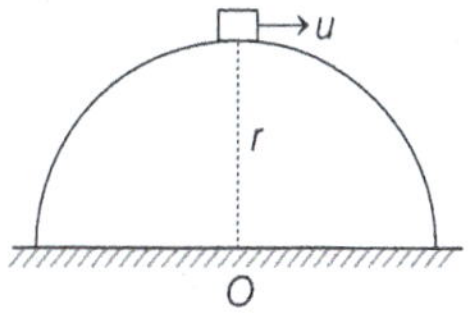

4 For $u = 2u_0$, it lands at point P on ground. Find OP.

(a) $\sqrt{2}r$ (b) $2r$ (c) $4r$ (d) $2\sqrt{2}r$

5 For $u = u_0/3$, find the height from the ground at which it leaves the hemisphere.

(a) $\frac{19r}{9}$ (b) $\frac{19r}{27}$ (c) $\frac{10r}{9}$ (d) $\frac{10r}{27}$

6 Find its net acceleration at the instant it leaves the hemisphere.

(a) $-g$ (b) $\frac{g}{2}$ (c) g (d) $\frac{g}{3}$

Comprehension 3

A small sphere of mass m suspended by a thread is first taken aside, so that the thread forms the right angle with the vertical and then released, then

7 The total acceleration of the sphere and the thread tension as function of θ, the angle of deflection of the thread from the vertical will be

(a) $g\sqrt{1+3\cos^2\theta}, T = 3mg\cos\theta$
(b) $g\cos\theta, T = 3mg\cos\theta$
(c) $g\sqrt{1+3\sin^2\theta}, T = 5mg\cos\theta$
(d) $g\sin\theta, T = 5mg\cos\theta$

8 The thread tension at the moment when the vertical component of the sphere's velocity is maximum will be

(a) mg (b) $mg\sqrt{2}$
(c) $mg\sqrt{3}$ (d) $\frac{mg}{\sqrt{3}}$

9 The angle θ between the thread and the vertical at the moment when the total acceleration vector of the sphere is directed horizontally will be

(a) $\cos\theta = \frac{1}{\sqrt{3}}$ (b) $\cos\theta = \frac{1}{3}$

(c) $\sin\theta = \frac{1}{3}$ (d) $\sin\theta = \frac{1}{\sqrt{3}}$

Comprehension 4

A bus is moving with a constant acceleration $a = 3g/4$ towards right. In the bus, a ball is tied with a rope of length l and is rotated in vertical circle as shown.

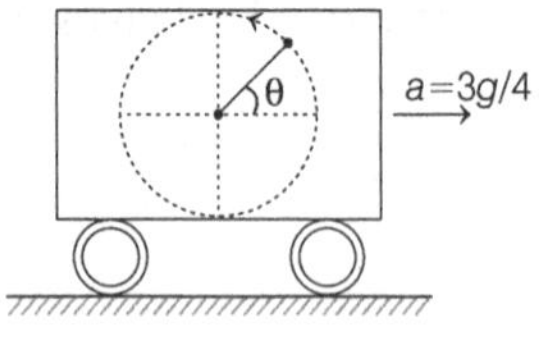

10 At what value of angle θ, tension in the rope will be minimum?

(a) $\theta = 37°$ (b) $\theta = 53°$ (c) $\theta = 30°$ (d) $\theta = 90°$

11 At above mentioned position, find the minimtun possible speed v_{min} during whole path to complete the circular motion.

(a) $\sqrt{5gl}$ (b) $\frac{5}{2}\sqrt{gl}$ (c) $\frac{\sqrt{5gl}}{2}$ (d) $\sqrt{gl}$

12 For above value of v_{min}, find maximum tension in the string during circular motion.

(a) 6 mg (b) $\frac{117}{20}mg$ (c) $\frac{15}{2}mg$ (d) $\frac{17}{2}mg$

Comprehension 5

Two identical beads are attached to free ends of two identical springs of spring constant $k = \frac{(2+\sqrt{3})mg}{\sqrt{3}R}$. Initially both springs make an angle of 60° at the fixed point N. Natural length of each spring is $2R$, where R is the radius of smooth ring over which bead is sliding. Ring is placed on vertical plane and beads are at symmetry with respect to vertical line as diameter.

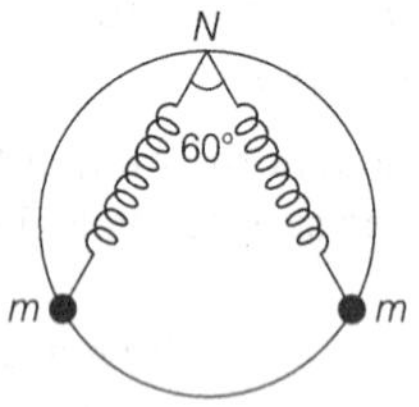

13 Normal reaction on one of the beads at initial moment due to ring is

(a) $mg/2$ (b) $\sqrt{3}mg/2$

(c) mg (d) insufficient data

14 Relative acceleration between two beads at the initial moment is

(a) $g/2$ vertically away from each other

(b) $g/2$ horizontally towards each other

(c) $2g/\sqrt{3}$ vertically away from each other

(d) $2g/\sqrt{3}$ horizontally towards each other

15 The speed of bead when spring is at natural length is

(a) $\sqrt{\frac{(2+\sqrt{3})gR}{\sqrt{3}}}$ (b) $\sqrt{\frac{(2-\sqrt{3})gR}{3}}$

(c) $\sqrt{\frac{2gR}{\sqrt{3}}}$ (d) $\sqrt{3gR}$

Comprehension 6

A particle undergoes uniform circular motion. The velocity and angular velocity of the particle at an instant of time is $\mathbf{v} = 3\hat{\mathbf{i}} + 4\hat{\mathbf{j}}$ m/s and $\omega = x\hat{\mathbf{i}} + 6\hat{\mathbf{j}}$ rad/s.

16 The value of x in rad/s is

(a) 8 (b) −8

(c) 6 (d) Cannot be calculated

17 The radius of circle in metres is

(a) 1/2 m (b) 1m

(c) 2 m (d) Cannot be calculated

18 The acceleration of particle at the given instant is

(a) $-50\hat{\mathbf{k}}$ (b) $-42\hat{\mathbf{k}}$

(c) $2\hat{\mathbf{i}} + 3\hat{\mathbf{j}}$ (d) Cannot be calculated

Comprehension 7

A small block of mass M, starts sliding down on a bigger block of mass $2M$, having a circular track of radius R. Let N_1 and N_2 be the normal reactions on the bigger block due to the wall and the floor. Do not consider the motion of the small block after $\theta = 90°$ and answer the following questions assuming all surfaces to be frictionless.

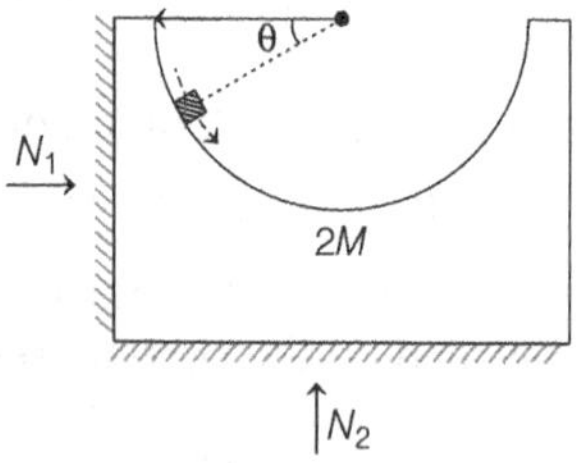

19 The value of N_1 at the instant when $\theta = 30°$

(a) $\frac{\sqrt{3}Mg}{4}$ (b) $\frac{3\sqrt{3}Mg}{4}$

(c) $\frac{\sqrt{3}Mg}{2}$ (d) $\frac{3\sqrt{3}Mg}{2}$

20 The value of $\tan\theta$ at the instant when $N_2 = 3Mg$

(a) $\frac{1}{\sqrt{2}}$ (b) $\sqrt{2}$

(c) $\frac{1}{2}$ (d) 2

Comprehension 8

A ball of mass M attached to a string of length l moves in a circle in a vertical plane as shown. At the top of the circular path, the tension in the string is twice the weight of the ball. At the bottom, the ball just clears the ground.

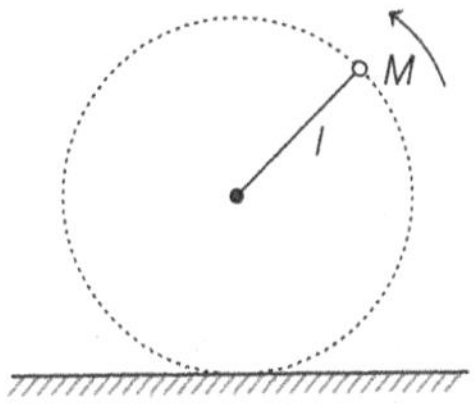

21 Determine the speed of the ball at the lowermost point.

(a) $\sqrt{3gl}$ (b) $\sqrt{5gl}$ (c) $\sqrt{6gl}$ (d) $\sqrt{7gl}$

22 If the string is cut when the ball is at the top at $t = t_0$, then the horizontal distance the ball travels before hitting the ground and after $t = t_0$ is

(a) $2\sqrt{3}l$ (b) $4\sqrt{3}l$ (c) $3\sqrt{3}l$ (d) $5\sqrt{3}l$

Comprehension 9

A vertical frictionless semicircular track of radius R is fixed on the edge of movable trolley. Initially, the system is at rest and a mass m is kept at the top of the track. The trolley starts moving to the right with a uniform horizontal acceleration $a = \frac{2g}{9}$. The mass slides down the track, eventually losing contact with it and dropping to the floor h below the top of the trolley.

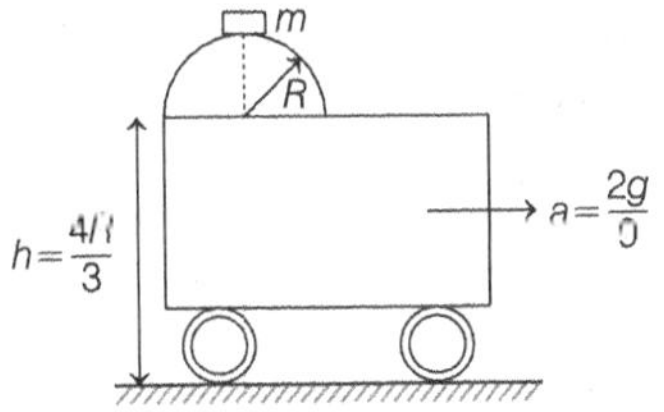

23 The angle θ with vertical, at which it loses contact with the trolley is

(a) 37° (b) 53°

(c) $\cos^{-1}\left(\frac{2}{3}\right)$ (d) $\frac{\pi}{2} - \cos^{-1}\left(\frac{2}{3}\right)$

24 The height from ground at which mass m loses contact is

(a) $\frac{4}{5}R$ (b) $\frac{17}{15}R$ (c) R (d) $\frac{32}{15}R$

25 If $R = 60$ m and $g = 10$ m/s^2, then the time taken by the mass to drop on the floor, after losing contact is

(a) 2 s (b) 3 s

(c) 4 s (d) Cannot be determined

Comprehension 10

A road of radius 20 m in banked for vehicles going at a speed of 10 m/s. The road has sufficient friction to prevent slipping. A vehicle of mass 200 kg moves on this road.

26 What is the angle of banking of the road?

(a) $\tan^{-1}\left(\frac{1}{2}\right)$ (b) $\tan^{-1}(2)$ (c) $\tan^{-1}\left(\frac{1}{4}\right)$ (d) $\tan^{-1}(3)$

27 What will be the magnitude and direction of friction on the vehicle if it negotiates the curve at a constant speed of 5 m/s?

(a) $200\sqrt{5}$ N, upwards (b) $200\sqrt{5}$ N, downwards

(c) $300\sqrt{5}$ N, upwards (d) $300\sqrt{5}$ N, downwards

28 What will be the magnitude and direction of friction on the vehicle, if it negotiates the curve at a constant speed of 15 m/s?

(a) $500\sqrt{5}$ N, upwards (b) $500\sqrt{5}$ N, downwards

(c) $300\sqrt{5}$ N, upwards (d) $300\sqrt{5}$ N, downwards

Match the Columns Questions

1 A particle is suspended from a string of length R. It is given a velocity $u = 3\sqrt{Rg}$. Match the following

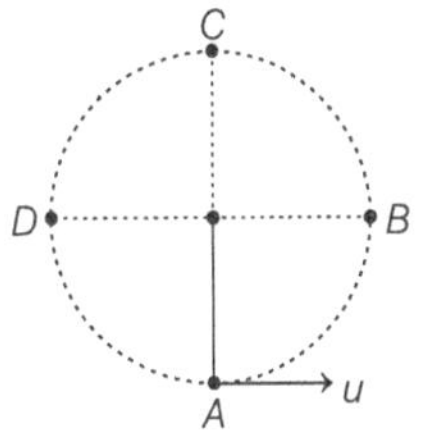

Column I		Column II
(A) Velocity at B	(P)	7 mg
(B) Velocity at C	(Q)	$\sqrt{5gR}$
(C) Tension at B	(R)	$\sqrt{7gR}$
(D) Tension at C	(S)	4 mg

2 The bob of a simple pendulum is given a velocity 10 m/s at its lowest point. Mass of the bob is 1 kg and string length is 1 m.

	Column I		Column II
(A)	Minimum tension in string (in newton)	(P)	50
(B)	Magnitude of acceleration of bob when the string is horizontal (in m/s^2)	(Q)	60
(C)	Minimum magnitude of acceleration of bob (in m/s^2)	(R)	zero
(D)	Tangential acceleration at the highest point (in m/s^2)	(S)	$10\sqrt{65}$

3 A car of mass 500 kg is moving in a circular road of radius $\frac{35}{\sqrt{3}}$ m. Angle of banking of road is 30°.

Coefficient of friction between the road and tyres is $\mu = \frac{1}{2\sqrt{3}}$. Match the following

Column I	Column II
(A) Maximum speed (in m/s) of car for safe turning	(P) $5\sqrt{2}$
(B) Minimum speed (in m/s) of car for safe turning	(Q) 12.50
(C) Speed (in m/s) at which friction force between tyres and road is zero	(R) $\sqrt{210}$
(D) Friction force (in 10^2 newton) between tyres and road if speed is $\sqrt{\frac{350}{6}}$ m/s	(S) $\sqrt{\frac{350}{3}}$

4 A bob is attached to a string as shown in the figure. At the lowest point, it is given a horizontal velocity *u*. For different values of *u*, it can have different total acceleration at different points.

For each of the points marked in Column I, match the possible direction(s) of total acceleration.

Column I	Column II
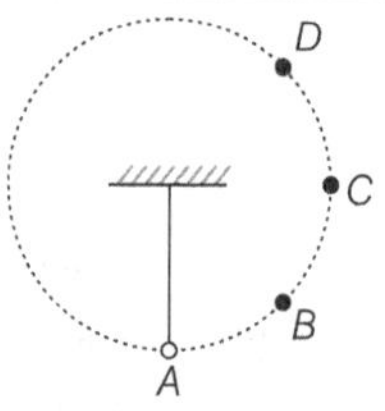	(P) 
	(Q) 
	(R) 
	(S) 
	(T) 

5 In **Column I**, a situation is depicted each of which is in vertical plane. The surfaces are frictionless. Match with appropriate entries in **Column II**.

Column I	Column II
(A) Bead is threaded on a circular fixed wire and is projected from the lowest point. 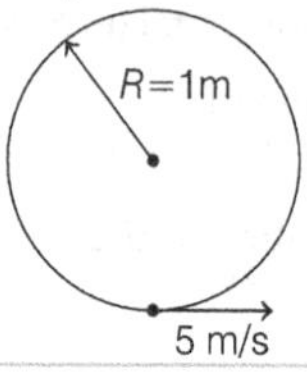	(P) Normal force is zero at top most point of its trajectory
(B) Block loosely fits inside the fixed small tube and is projected from lowest point 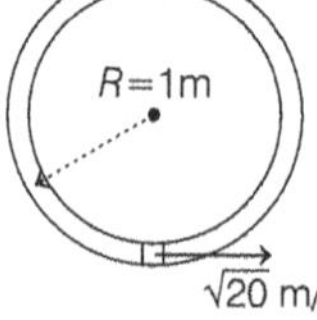	(Q) Velocity of the body is zero at top most point of its trajectory
(C) Block is projected horizontally from lowest point of a smooth fixed cylinder. 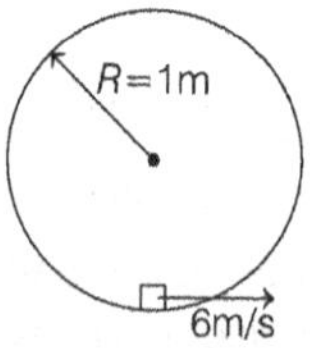	(R) Acceleration of the body is zero at the top most point of its trajectory
(D) Block is projected on a fixed hemisphere from angular position θ 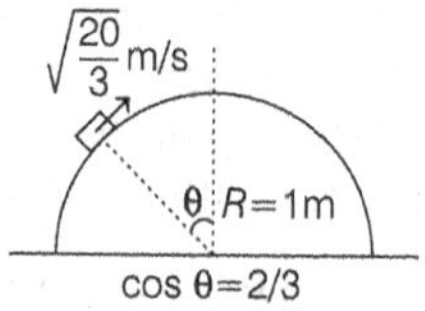	(S) Normal force is radially outward at top most point of trajectory

6 In all the four situations depicted in Column I, a ball of mass *m* is connected to a string. In each case, find the tension in the string and match the appropriate entries in Column II.

Column I	Column II
(A) 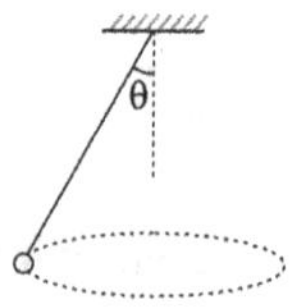 Conical pendulum	(P) $T = mg\cos\theta$
(B) 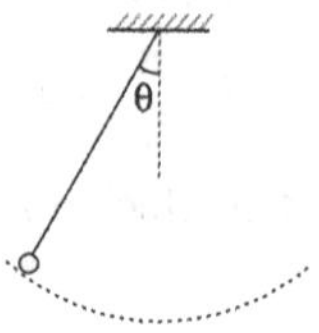 Pendulum is swinging. Angular position θ is the extreme position. *T* is tension in extreme position	(Q) $T\cos\theta = mg$

	Column I		Column II
(C)	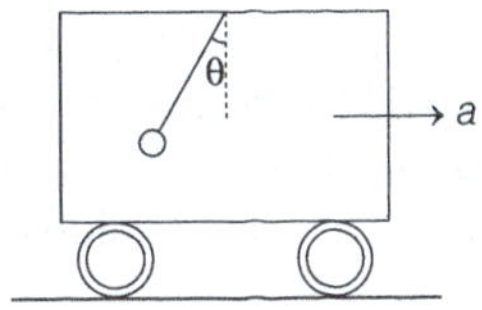 The car is moving with constant acceleration. The ball is at rest with respect to car.	(R)	Speed of ball with respect to ground is constant
(D)	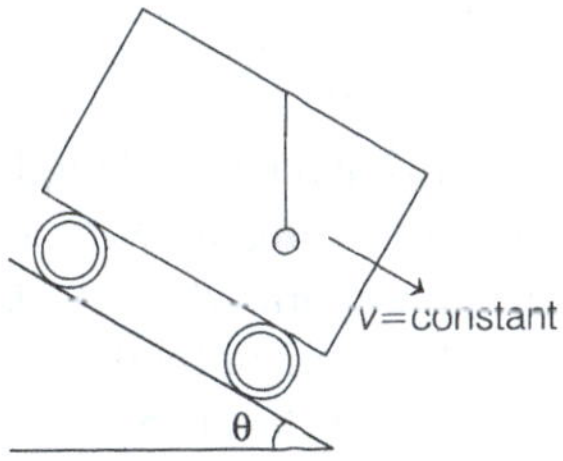 The car is moving with constant velocity. The ball is at rest with respect to car.	(S)	Velocity of ball with respect to ground is changing continuously

Numerical Value Questions

1 A stone is thrown horizontally with a velocity of 10 m/s. If the radius of curvature of its trajectory at the end of 3 s after motion began is $n\sqrt{10}$ m, then find n. (Take, $g = 10\ \text{m/s}^2$)

2 A small block of mass m rests on top of a hemispherical wedge of radius R. The wedge is given a constant acceleration $a_0 = g$ in the horizontal direction as shown in the figure. If the velocity of the block relative to wedge at the instant it breaks contact with the surface is $\sqrt{\frac{2gR}{n}}$, then find the value of n.

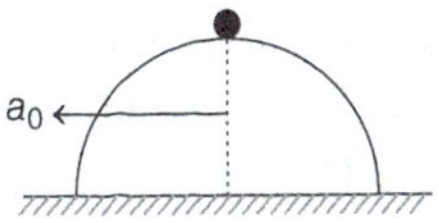

3 There is a fixed smooth hemisphere of radius R. A rod AB is placed as shown in the figure. When end A of the rod is at a distance x_1 from the centre of the hemisphere and has velocity v_A in the horizontal direction,

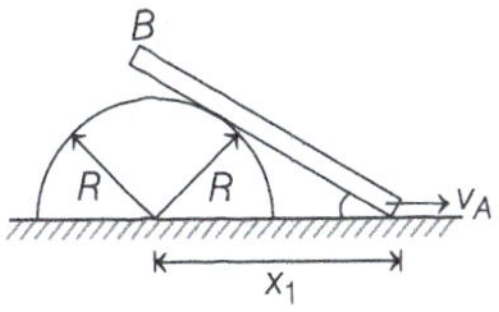

the angular speed of the rod is found as $\frac{nv_AR}{x_1\sqrt{x_1^2-R^2}}$. Find n. (Assume all surfaces are smooth.)

4 A right circular cone is fixed with its axis vertical and vertex down. A particle is in contact with its smooth inside surface and describes circular motion in a horizontal plane at a height of 40 cm above the vertex. Find its velocity in m/s.

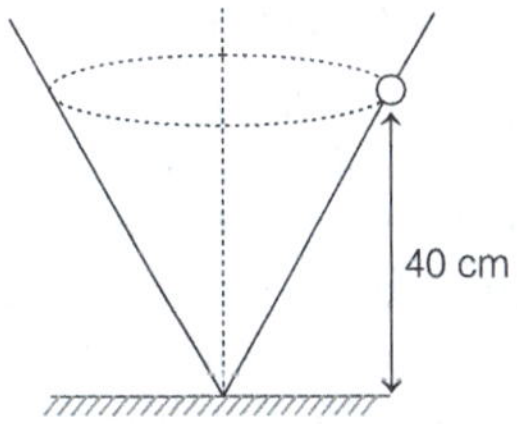

5 A small sphere B of mass $m = 1$ kg is released from rest in the position shown and swings freely in a vertical plane, first about O and then about the peg A after the cord comes in contact with the peg. If the ratio of tensions in the cord just before the sphere comes in contact with the peg to just after it comes in contact with the peg is $\frac{\beta}{10}$, then find β.

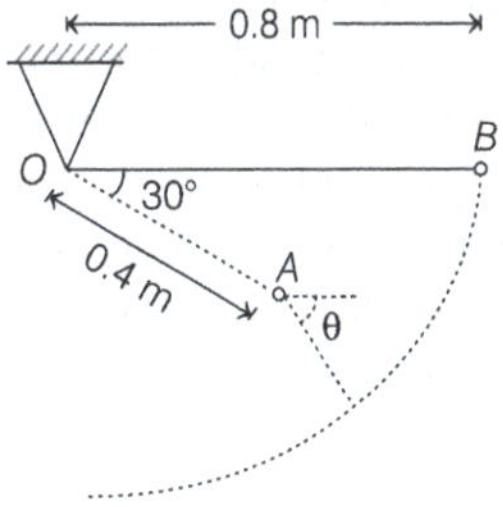

6 A large mass $M = 20$ kg and a small mass $m = 2$ kg are at the two ends of the string that passes through a smooth tube as shown in figure. The mass m moves around in a circular path, which lies in horizontal plane. The length of the string from the mass m to the top of the tube is $l = 10$ cm and θ is the angle this length makes with vertical. What should be the number of revolution per second of mass m, so that M remain stationary ($\sqrt{10} = \pi$)?

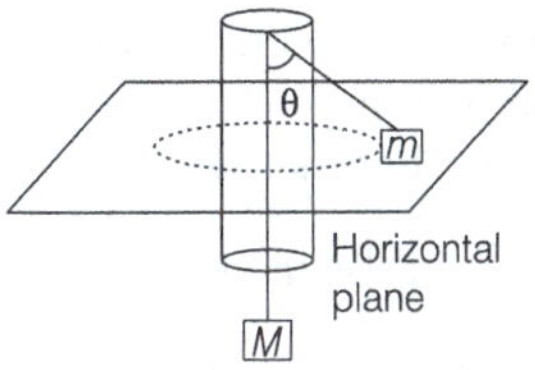

7 A particle suspended from the ceiling by inextensible light string is moving along a horizontal circle of radius 1.5 m as shown. The string traces a cone of height 2 m. The string breaks and the particle finally hits the floor (which is XY-plane 5.76 m below the circle) at point P. Find the distance OP in cm.

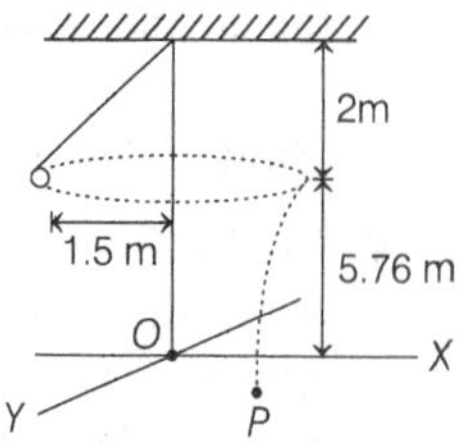

8 A rod of length 1 m is being rotated about its end in a gravity free space with a constant angular acceleration of 5 rad/s^2 starting from rest. A sleeve is fitted on the rod at a distance of 0.5 m from the centre. The coefficient of friction between the rod and the sleeve is 0.05. The time after which sleeve will start slipping on the rod is $\frac{\eta}{10}$ s, where η is

9 A rock is launched upward at 45°. A bee moves along the trajectory of the rock at a constant speed equal to the initial speed of the rock. What is the magnitude of acceleration (in m/ s^2) of the bee at the top point of the trajectory? For the rock, neglect the air resistance.

10 The drawing shows a baggage carousel at an airport. Your suitcase has not slid all the way down the slope and is going around at a constant speed on a circle of radius 2m as the carousel turns. The coefficient of static friction between the suitcase and the carousel is 0.8, and the angle θ in the drawing is 37°. How much time (in second) is required for your suitcase to go around once? (Assume limiting friction) (Take, $\pi^2 = g$)

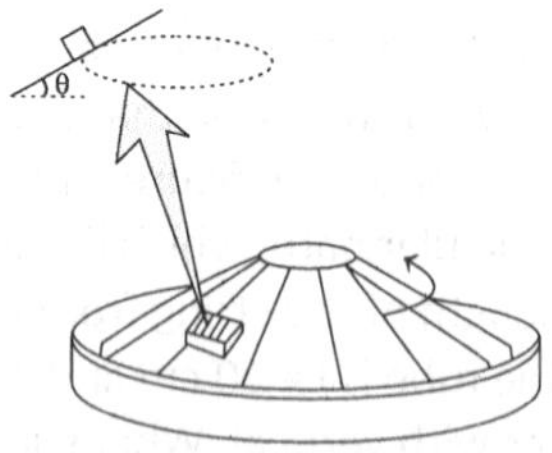

11 A particle P is moving on a circle under the action of only one force, which always acts towards a fixed point O lying on the circumference. Find the ratio of $\frac{d^2\theta}{dt^2}$ to $\left(\frac{d\theta}{dt}\right)^2$ at the moment when $\theta = 45°$. (C is the centre of circle)

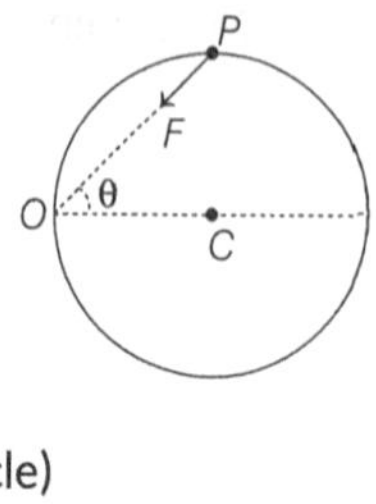

12 Tangential acceleration of a particle moving in a circle of radius 1 m varies with time t as shown (initial velocity of particle is zero). Time after which total acceleration of particle makes an angle of 30° with radial acceleration is T. Find value of T^6.

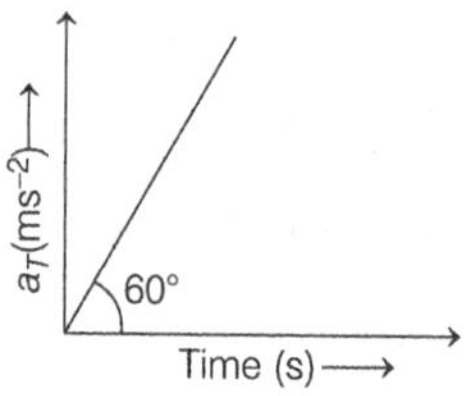

13 A block is joined to a string having a length of 25/16 m. The block is held with string horizontal and released from position shown. When the block is at C, string breaks. Find the horizontal distance (in m) from point C, where the block will land.

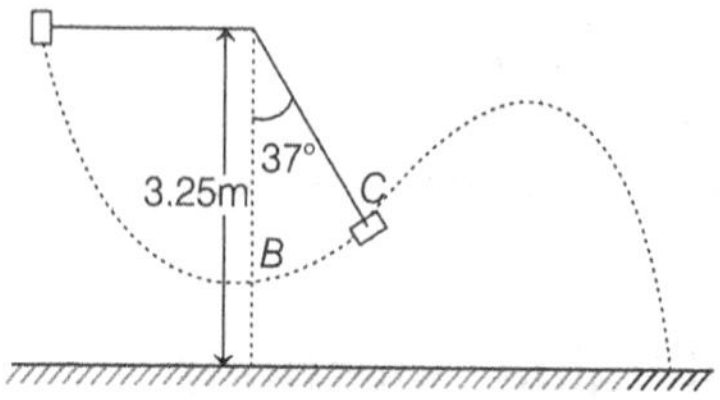

14 A particle is attached to one end of string the other end of which is fixed. The particle moves in vertical plane. The velocity at the lowest point is such that the particle can just complete the circle. If the ratio of accelerations at A and B is β, then find value of $38\beta^2$.

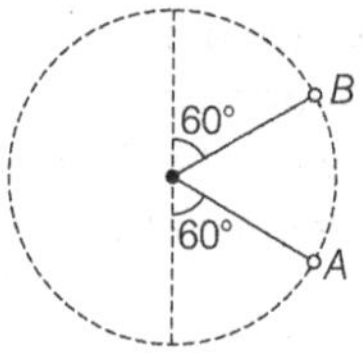

15 Two beads of mass m and $2m$ are connected by a massless rod of length R and threaded onto a smooth circular wire of radius R. When the wire rotates uniformly with angular velocity ω about a vertical diameter, the beads do not slide on it and the rod remains vertical as shown. What must be the angular velocity ω (in rad/s) of the wire? (Take $R = 15$ m)

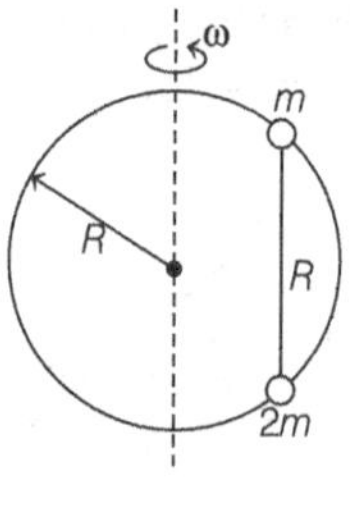

Previous Year's Questions

JEE Main

1 A train is moving with a speed of 12 m/s on rails which are 1.5 m apart. To negotiate a curve of radius 400 m, the height by which the outer rail should be raised with respect to the inner rail is (Given, $g = 10$ m/s^2) **[2024, 27 Jan Shift-I]**

(a) 4.8 cm (b) 5.4 cm (c) 6.0 cm (d) 4.2 cm

2 A ball suspended by a thread swings in a vertical plane, so that its magnitude of acceleration in the extreme position and lowest position are equal. The angle θ of thread deflection in the extreme position will be **[2024, 27 Jan Shift-II]**

(a) $\tan^{-1}(\sqrt{2})$ (b) $\tan^{-1}\left(\frac{1}{2}\right)$

(c) $2\tan^{-1}\left(\frac{1}{\sqrt{5}}\right)$ (d) $2\tan^{-1}\left(\frac{1}{2}\right)$

3 If the radius of curvature of the path of two particles of same mass are in the ratio 3 : 4, then in order to have constant centripetal force, their velocities will be in the ratio of **[2024, 29 Jan Shift-I]**

(a) $2:\sqrt{3}$ (b) $\sqrt{3}:2$

(c) $1:\sqrt{3}$ (d) $\sqrt{3}:1$

4 A stone of mass 900 g is tied to a string and moved in a vertical circle of radius 1 m making 10 rpm. The tension in the string, when the stone is at the lowest point is (If $\pi^2 = 9.8$ and $g = 9.8$ m/s^2) **[2024, 29 Jan Shift-II]**

(a) 9.8 N (b) 8.82 N

(c) 17.8 N (d) 97 N

5 A particle is moving in a circle of radius 50 cm in such a way that at any instant the normal and tangential components of it's acceleration are equal. If its speed at $t = 0$ is 4 m/s, the time taken to complete the first revolution will be $\frac{1}{\alpha}[1 - e^{-2\pi}]$ s, where α = ... **[2024, 29 Jan Shift-II]**

6 As shown in the figure, a particle is moving with constant speed π m/s. Considering its motion from A to B, the magnitude of the average velocity is **[2023, 6 April Shift-II]**

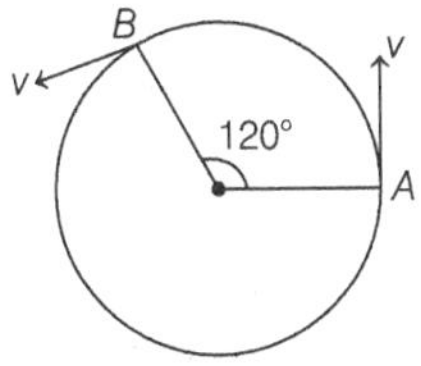

(a) π m/s (b) $\sqrt{3}$ m/s (c) $1.5\sqrt{3}$ m/s (d) $2\sqrt{3}$ m/s

7 For particle P revolving round the centre O with radius of circular path r and angular velocity ω, as shown in below figure, the projection of OP on the X-axis at time t is **[2023, 8 April Shift-II]**

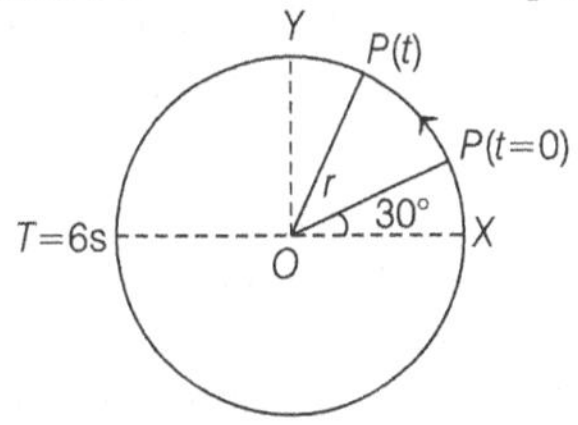

(a) $x(t) = r\cos\left(\omega t + \frac{\pi}{6}\right)$ (b) $x(t) = r\cos(\omega t)$

(c) $x(t) = r\sin\left(\omega t + \frac{\pi}{6}\right)$ (d) $x(t) = r\cos\left(\omega t - \frac{\pi}{6}\omega\right)$

8 A body is moving with constant speed, in a circle of radius 10 m. The body completes one revolution in 4 s. At the end of 3rd second, the displacement of body (in m) from its starting point is **[2023, 31 Jan Shift-II]**

(a) 30 (b) $10\sqrt{2}$ (c) 5π (d) 15π

9 A vehicle of mass 200 kg is moving along a levelled curved road of radius 70 m with angular velocity of 0.2 rad/s. The centripetal force acting on the vehicle is **[2023, 13 April Shift-II]**

(a) 560 N (b) 2240 N (c) 14 N (d) 2800 N

10 A child of mass 5 kg is going round a merry-go-round that makes l rotation in 3.14 s. The radius of the merry-go-round is 2 m. The centrifugal force on the child will be **[2023, 6 April Shift-II]**

(a) 40 N (b) 100 N (c) 80 N (d) 50 N

11 A stone of mass 1 kg is tied to end of a massless string of length 1 m. If the breaking tension of the string is 400 N, then maximum linear velocity the stone can have without breaking the string while rotating in horizontal plane is **[2023, 31 Jan Shift-II]**

(a) 10 ms^{-1} (b) 40 ms^{-1}

(c) 400 ms^{-1} (d) 20 ms^{-1}

12 A car is moving on a horizontal curved road with radius 50 m. The approximate maximum speed of car will be, if friction between tyres and road is 0.34. [Take, $g = 10$ ms^{-2}]. **[2023, 29 Jan Shift-I]**

(a) 17 ms^{-1} (b) 3.4 ms^{-1} (c) 13 ms^{-1} (d) 22.4 ms^{-1}

13 A car is moving with a constant speed of 20 m/s in a circular horizontal track of radius 40 m. A bob is suspended from the roof of the car by a massless string. The angle made by the string with the vertical will be (Take, $g = 10$ m/s^2) **[2023, 25 Jan Shift-I]**

(a) $\frac{\pi}{3}$ (b) $\frac{\pi}{2}$ (c) $\frac{\pi}{4}$ (d) $\frac{\pi}{6}$

14 A curved in a level road has a radius 75 m. The maximum speed of a car turning this curved road can be 30 m/s without skidding. If radius of curved road is changed to 48 m and the coefficient of friction between the tyres and the road remains same, then maximum allowed speed would be .... m/s. **[2022, 25 June Shift-II]**

15 A stone tied to a string of length L is whirled in a vertical circle with the other end of the string at the centre. At a certain instant of time, the stone is at its lowest position and has a speed u. The magnitude of change in its velocity, as it reaches a position where the string is horizontal, is $\sqrt{x(u^2 - gL)}$. The value of x is **[2022, 27 June Shift-II]**

(a) 3 (b) 2 (c) 1 (d) 5

16 A stone of mass m, tied to a string is being whirled in a vertical circle with a uniform speed. The tension in the string is **[2022, 24 June Shift-II]**

(a) the same throughout the motion
(b) minimum at the highest position of the circular path
(c) minimum at the lowest position of the circular path
(d) minimum when the rope is in the horizontal position

17 A pendulum of length 2 m consists of a wooden bob of mass 50 g. A bullet of mass 75 g is fired towards the stationary bob with a speed v. The bullet emerges out of the bob with a speed $v/3$ and the bob just completes the vertical circle. The value of v is ...... ms^{-1}. (If $g = 10 \text{ m/s}^2$) **[2022, 27 June Shift-I]**

18 A disc with a flat small bottom beaker placed on it at a distance R from its centre is revolving about an axis passing through the center and perpendicular to its plane with an angular velocity ω. The coefficient of static friction between the bottom of the beaker and the surface of the disc is μ. The beaker will revolve with the disc if **[2022, 25 June Shift-II]**

(a) $R \le \frac{\mu g}{2\omega^2}$ (b) $R \le \frac{\mu g}{\omega^2}$ (c) $R \ge \frac{\mu g}{2\omega^2}$ (d) $R \ge \frac{\mu g}{\omega^2}$

19 A stone of mass m, tied to a string is being whirled in a vertical circle with a uniform speed. The tension in the string is **[2022, 24 June Shift-II]**

(a) the same throughout the motion.
(b) minimum at the highest position of the circular path.
(c) minimum at the lowest position of the circular path.
(d) minimum when the rope is the horizontal position.

20 One end of a massless spring of spring constant k and natural length l_0 is fixed while the other end is connected to a small objects of mass m lying on a frictionless table. The spring remains horizontal on the table. If the object is made to rotate at an angular velocity ω about an axis passing through fixed end, then the elongation of the spring will be **[2022, 27 June Shift-II]**

(a) $\frac{k - m\omega^2 l_0}{m\omega^2}$ (b) $\frac{m\omega^2 l_0}{k + m\omega^2}$
(c) $\frac{m\omega^2 l_0}{k - m\omega^2}$ (d) $\frac{k + m\omega^2 l_0}{m\omega^2}$

21 For a particle in uniform circular motion, the acceleration $\mathbf{a}$ at any point $P(R, \theta)$ on the circular path of radius R is (when θ is measured from the positive X-axis and v is uniform speed) **[2022, 25 June Shift-II]**

(a) $-\frac{v^2}{R}\sin\theta\,\hat{i} + \frac{v^2}{R}\cos\theta\,\hat{j}$ (b) $-\frac{v^2}{R}\cos\theta\,\hat{i} + \frac{v^2}{R}\sin\theta\,\hat{j}$
(c) $-\frac{v^2}{R}\cos\theta\,\hat{i} - \frac{v^2}{R}\sin\theta\,\hat{j}$ (d) $-\frac{v^2}{R}\hat{i} + \frac{v^2}{R}\hat{j}$

22 A boy ties a stone of mass 100 g to the end of a 2m long string and whirls it around in a horizontal plane. The string can withstand the maximum tension of 80 N. If the maximum speed with which the stone can revolve is $\frac{K}{\pi}$ rev/min. The value of K is (Assume the string is massless and unstretchable) **[2022, 24 June Shift-I]**

(a) 400 (b) 300 (c) 600 (d) 800

23 A particle of mass m is suspended from a ceiling through a string of length L. The particle moves in a horizontal circle of radius r such that $r = \frac{L}{\sqrt{2}}$. The speed of particle will be **[2021, 26 Aug Shift-II]**

(a) $\sqrt{rg}$ (b) $\sqrt{2rg}$ (c) $2\sqrt{rg}$ (d) $\sqrt{\frac{rg}{2}}$

24 **Statement I** A cyclist is moving on an unbanked road with a speed of 7 kmh^{-1} and takes a sharp circular turn along a path of radius of 2 m without reducing the spee(d) The static friction coefficient is 0.2. The cyclist will not slip and pass the curve $(g = 9.8 \text{ m/s}^2)$

Statement II If the road is banked at an angle of 45°, cyclist can cross the curve of 2 m radius with the speed of 18.5 kmh^{-1} without slipping.

In the light of the above statements, choose the correct answer from the options given below. **[2021, 16 March Shift-II]**

(a) Statement I is false and Statement II is true.
(b) Statement I is true and Statement II is false.
(c) Both statement I and Statement II are false.
(d) Both statement I and Statement II are true.

JEE Advanced

1 A student skates up a ramp that makes an angle 30° with the horizontal. He/she starts (as shown in the figure) at the bottom of the ramp with speed v_0 and wants to turn around over a semicircular path xyz of radius R during which he/she reaches a maximum height h (at point y) from the ground as shown in the figure. Assume that the energy loss is negligible and the force required for this turn at the highest point is provided by his/her weight only. Then (g is the acceleration due to gravity) **(2020 Adv.)**

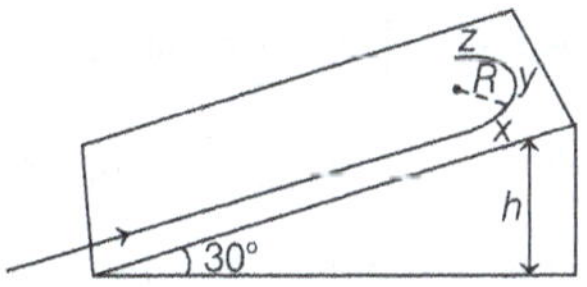

(a) $v_0^2 - 2gh = \frac{1}{2}gR$

(b) $v_0^2 - 2gh = \frac{\sqrt{3}}{2}gR$

(c) the centripetal force required at points x and z is zero

(d) the centripetal force required is maximum at points x and z

Passage 1

A frame of the reference that is accelerated with respect to an inertial frame of reference is called a non-inertial frame of reference. A coordinate system fixed on a circular disc rotating about a fixed axis with a constant angular velocity ω is an example of a non-inertial frame of reference. The relationship between the force $\mathbf{F}_{rot}$ experienced by a particle of mass m moving on the rotating disc and the force $\mathbf{F}_{in}$ experienced by the particle in an inertial frame of reference is,

$$\mathbf{F}_{rot} = \mathbf{F}_{in} + 2m(\mathbf{v}_{rot} \times \vec{\omega}) + m(\vec{\omega} \times \mathbf{r}) \times \vec{\omega},$$

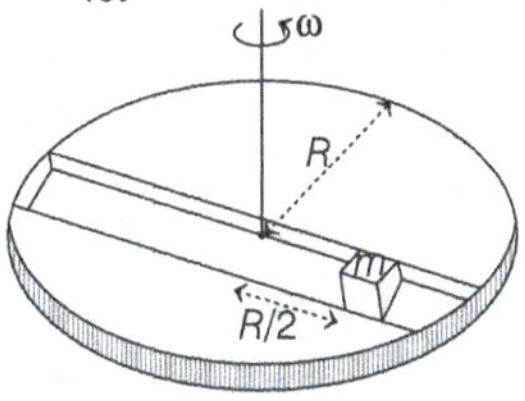

where, $\mathbf{v}_{rot}$ is the velocity of the particle in the rotating frame of reference and $\mathbf{r}$ is the position vector of the particle with respect to the centre of the disc. Now, consider a smooth slot along a diameter of a disc of radius R rotating counter-clockwise with a constant angular speed ω about its vertical axis through its centre. We assign a coordinate system with the origin at the centre of the disc, the X-axis along the slot, the Y-axis perpendicular to the slot and the z-axis along th rotation axis ($\omega = \omega\mathbf{k}$). A small block of mass m is gently placed in the slot at $\mathbf{r} = (R/2)\hat{\mathbf{i}}$ at $t = 0$ and is constrained to move only along the slot.

2 The distance r of the block at time t is **(2016 Adv.)**

(a) $\frac{R}{2}\cos 2\omega t$ (b) $\frac{R}{2}\cos \omega t$

(c) $\frac{R}{4}(e^{\omega t} + e^{-\omega t})$ (d) $\frac{R}{4}(e^{2\omega t} + e^{-2\omega t})$

3 The net reaction of the disc on the block is **(2016 Adv.)**

(a) $m\omega^2 R \sin\omega t\hat{\mathbf{j}} - mg\hat{\mathbf{k}}$

(b) $\frac{1}{2}m\omega^2 R(e^{\omega t} - e^{-\omega t})\hat{\mathbf{j}} + mg\hat{\mathbf{k}}$

(c) $\frac{1}{2}m\omega^2 R(e^{2\omega t} - e^{-2\omega t})\hat{\mathbf{j}} + mg\hat{\mathbf{k}}$

(d) $-m\omega^2 R\cos\omega t\hat{\mathbf{j}} - mg\hat{\mathbf{k}}$

Passage 2

A small block of mass 1 kg is released from rest at the top of a rough track. The track is a circular arc of radius 40 m. The block slides along the track without toppling and a frictional force acts on it in the direction opposite to the instantaneous velocity. The work done in overcoming the friction up to the point Q, as shown in the figure, is 150 J. (Take the acceleration due to gravity, $g = 10\ \text{ms}^{-2}$) **(2013)**

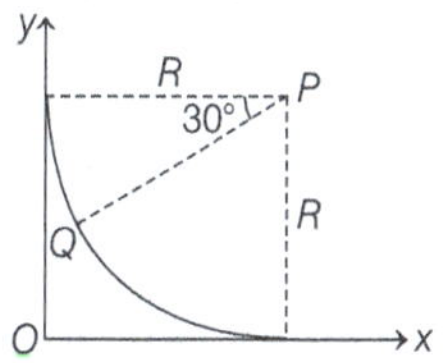

4 The speed of the block when it reaches the point Q is

(a) $5\ \text{ms}^{-1}$ (b) $10\ \text{ms}^{-1}$ (c) $10\sqrt{3}\ \text{ms}^{-1}$ (d) $20\ \text{ms}^{-1}$

5 The magnitude of the normal reaction that acts on the block at the point Q is

(a) 7.5 N (b) 8.6 N (c) 11.5 N (d) 22.5 N

6 A bob of mass M is suspended by a massless string of length L. The horizontal velocity v at position A is just sufficient to make it reach the point B. The angle θ at which the speed of the bob is half of that at A, satisfies **(2008)**

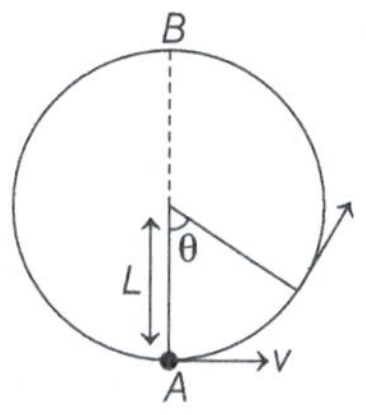

(a) $\theta = \frac{\pi}{4}$ (b) $\frac{\pi}{4} < \theta < \frac{\pi}{2}$

(c) $\frac{\pi}{2} < \theta < \frac{3\pi}{4}$ (d) $\frac{3\pi}{4} < \theta < \pi$

Answer Key

Level 1

13.1 Kinematics of Circular Motion

1. (a) first (b) third 2. 12 : 1, $\frac{\pi}{30}$ rad/s 3. 3 : 1
4. $\omega = 25\sqrt{10}$ rad/s
5. (a) $\alpha = -\frac{1}{3}$ rev/s^2 (b) 15000 rev (c) 50 rev/s
6. $\frac{\pi\sqrt{2}}{30}$ cm/s, $\frac{\pi\sqrt{2}}{30\times 15}$ cm/s^2
7. 24 rad/s 8. 0.25 s 9. 10/3 rad/s

13.2 Radial and Tangential Acceleration

1. $4\pi^2$ m/s^2 2. 2.5 π^2 cm/s^2 3. 2.5 rad/s^2 4. 5 m/s^2
5. (a) 18 cm/s^2, (b) 2 cm/s^2, (c) $\sqrt{326}$ cm/s^2 6. 400 rad/s^2
7. $t = \frac{1}{2}$ s 8. $\theta = \frac{2}{3}$ rad
9. (a) 2s (b) π m/s = 3.14 m/s (c) $\frac{\pi}{2}\sqrt{4\pi^2+1}$ m/s^2
10. (a) $25\frac{\sqrt{3}}{2}$ m/s^2 (b) $\left(125\frac{\sqrt{3}}{4}\right)^{1/2}$ m/s (c) $\frac{25}{2}$ m/s^2

13.3 Relative Angular Motion

1. $\omega_{AB} = \frac{v_A \sin\theta_1 + v_B \sin\theta_2}{r}$ 2. $t = \frac{60}{59}$ min 3. $t = 2$ s
4. ω 5. $\omega_{AO} = \frac{v}{2d}$ 6. $\frac{v}{d}$

13.4 Circular Motion in Horizontal Plane

1. 25 N 2. 8 T_0 3. $\frac{2\sqrt{3}\pi}{5}, \frac{13}{6}$ N
4. $m\omega^2 R$ 5. $\mu \ge \frac{\pi^2}{81}$ 6. $\frac{2}{5}$ 7. (i) mg (ii) $\frac{mv^2}{r}$
8. $\omega = \sqrt{\frac{g}{R\cos\alpha}}$ 9. 50 m/s^2
10. (a) $t = \left[\left(\frac{\mu g}{\alpha^2 r}\right)^2 - \left(\frac{1}{\alpha}\right)^2\right]^{1/4}$ (b) $\theta = \tan^{-1}(\alpha t^2)$
11. $v = [R^2(\mu^2 g^2 - a^2)]^{1/4}$

13.5 Motion of a Vehicle

1. 10 m/s 2. 0.35 3. $\frac{1.4}{\sqrt{101}}$ m 4. $\tan^{-1}(5/12)$
5. $100\sqrt{3}$ m/s 6. Between 14.7 km/h and 54 km/h

13.6 Centrifugal Force

1. $m\omega_0^2 r$ 2. $\frac{\sqrt{7}}{2}\omega L$ 3. $\frac{\omega^2 R}{3}, \frac{4}{3}m\omega^2 R$

13.7 Rotation of Earth

1. 97.66 N 2. 2.0 h

13.8 Circular Motion in Vertical Plane

1. (i) $T = m\left(g\cos\alpha + \frac{v^2}{L}\right)$ (ii) $m\sqrt{g^2\sin^2\alpha + \frac{v^4}{L^2}}$
2. 5 rad/s 3. 90° 4. (a) $\sqrt{5gl}$ (b) $\sqrt{4gl}$
5. (a) 8 mg (b) 5 mg (c) 6.5 mg 6. $\frac{9}{2}mg$ 7. $\sqrt{gl}$
8. (i) $v_B = \sqrt{2gL}, v_C = \sqrt{6gL}$ (ii) $T_B = Mg, T_C = 7\,Mg$
9. $\frac{4l}{5}$ 10. 5 mg 11. $v_{min} = \left(\frac{Rg}{\sqrt{2}}\right)^{1/2}$
12. (a) $\theta = \cos^{-1}\left(\frac{2}{3}\right)$ (b) $v_B = \sqrt{\frac{2}{3}gR}$ (c) $h = \frac{2R}{3}$ from the bottom
13. (a) $\sqrt{3}\,mg/2$ (b) 0.43 R 14. $H_{max} = \frac{40L}{27}$
15. (i) $h = \frac{5r}{2}$ (ii) $N_A = 7\,mg, N_B = mg$ (iii) $\sqrt{\frac{2gr}{3}}$

13.9 Radius of Curvature

1. (a) $\frac{u^2\sin^2\theta}{g}$ (b) $\frac{u^2}{g}\sec\theta$ 2. $\frac{1}{2a}$
3. (a) 975 N, 1025 N, (b) 0,707 N,0 (c) 682 N, 732 N, (d) 1.037

Level 2

Single Choice Correct Questions

1. (c)	2. (b)	3. (c)	4. (d)	5. (c)
6. (a)	7. (c)	8. (b)	9. (b)	10. (b)
11. (d)	12. (b)	13. (a)	14. (b)	15. (b)
16. (c)	17. (a)	18. (b)	19. (b)	20. (d)
21. (b)	22. (c)	23. (b)	24. (a)	25. (b)
26. (a)	27. (b)	28. (b)	29. (a)	30. (d)
31. (d)	32. (d)	33. (a)	34. (a)	35. (a)
36. (c)	37. (c)	38. (a)	39. (d)	40. (c)
41. (b)	42. (d)	43. (c)	44. (a)	45. (a)
46. (d)	47. (a)	48. (a)	49. (d)	50. (c)
51. (a)	52. (c)	53. (b)	54. (d)	55. (d)

Numerical Value Questions

1. (5)	2. (4)	3. (1)	4. (100)	5. (7)
6. (2)	7. (2)	8. (12)	9. (2)	10. (1)
11. (5)	12. (100)	13. (12)	14. (5)	15. (50)
16. (10)	17. (10)	18. (40)	19. (3)	20. (4)

Level 3

Single Choice Correct Questions

1. (d)	2. (c)	3. (b)	4. (b)	5. (b)
6. (a)	7. (c)	8. (a)	9. (a)	10. (b)
11. (b)	12. (d)	13. (b)	14. (b)	15. (b)
16. (a)	17. (c)	18. (b)	19. (b)	20. (c)
21. (d)	22. (d)	23. (b)	24. (c)	25. (a)
26. (d)	27. (c)	28. (a)	29. (b)	30. (b)
31. (b)	32. (c)	33. (d)	34. (b)	35. (a)
36. (c)	37. (b)	38. (c)	39. (d)	40. (b)
41. (a)	42. (d)	43. (d)	44. (c)	45. (a)
46. (c)	47. (c)	48. (a)	49. (d)	50. (d)
51. (b)	52. (c)	53. (c)	54. (a)	55. (c)

Multiple Choice(s) Correct Questions

1. (ad)	2. (bc)	3. (bc)	4. (abd)	5. (abc)
6. (bcd)	7. (ac)	8. (abd)	9. (bd)	10. (abcd)
11. (cd)	12. (bd)	13. (acd)	14. (abc)	15. (abcd)

Comprehension Based Questions

1. (d)	2. (b)	3. (b)	4. (d)	5. (b)
6. (c)	7. (a)	8. (c)	9. (a)	10. (b)
11. (c)	12. (c)	13. (c)	14. (d)	15. (c)
16. (b)	17. (a)	18. (a)	19. (b)	20. (c)
21. (d)	22. (a)	23. (a)	24. (d)	25. (c)
26. (a)	27. (c)	28. (b)		

Match the Columns Questions

1. A → R; B → Q; C → P; D → S
2. A → P; B → S; C → Q; D → R
3. A → R; B → P; C → S; D → Q
4. A → Q; B → P,S,T; C → R,S; D → R,S
5. A → Q,S; B → P,Q; C → P; D → Q,R,S
6. A → Q,R,S; B → P,S; C → Q,S; D → R

Numerical Value Questions

1. (100)	2. (3)	3. (1)	4. (2)	5. (6)
6. (5)	7. (390)	8. (1)	9. (20)	10. (16)
11. (2)	12. (16)	13. (4)	14. (134)	15. (2)

Previous Year's Questions

JEE Main

1. (b)	2. (d)	3. (b)	4. (a)	5. (8)
6. (c)	7. (a)	8. (b)	9. (a)	10. (a)
11. (d)	12. (c)	13. (c)	14. (24)	15. (b)
16. (b)	17. (10)	18. (b)	19. (b)	20. (c)
21. (c)	22. (c)	23. (a)	24. (d)	

JEE Advanced

1. (a,d)	2. (c)	3. (b)	4. (b)	5. (a)
6. (d)				

SOLUTIONS

Level 1

13.1 Kinematics of Circular Motion

1. (a) If the particle is moving clockwise, it will be in the 2nd quadrant as shown in figure.

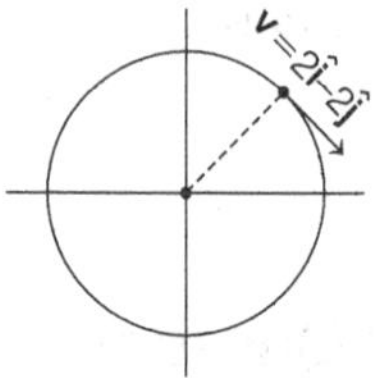

(b) If the particle is moving anti-clockwise, it will be in the 3rd quadrant as shown in figure.

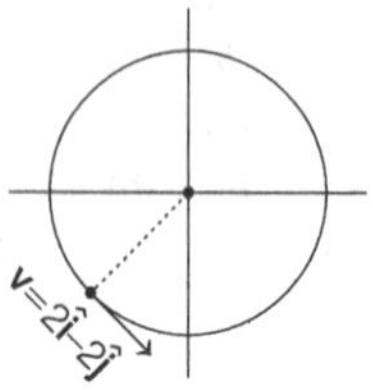

2. $\omega = \dfrac{2\pi}{T}$, where T = time period

Minute hand completes one revolution in 1 h.

So, $\omega_{\text{minute hand}} = \dfrac{2\pi}{60\,\text{min}}$

Hour hand completes one revolution in 12 h.

So, $\omega_{\text{hour hand}} = \dfrac{2\pi}{(12\times 60)\,\text{min}}$

$$\frac{\omega_{\text{minute hand}}}{\omega_{\text{hour hand}}} = \frac{2\pi/60}{2\pi/12\times 60} = 12$$

$$\omega_{\text{second hand}} = \frac{2\pi}{60\,\text{s}} = \frac{\pi}{30}\text{rad/s}$$

3. $\theta = \omega_0 t + \dfrac{1}{2}\alpha t^2$

For $t = 0$ to $t = 2$

$$\theta_1 = 0 + \frac{1}{2}\alpha(2)^2 = 2\alpha \qquad \text{...(i)}$$

For $t = 0$ to $t = 4$

$$\theta_1 + \theta_2 = 0 + \frac{1}{2}\alpha(4)^2 = 8\alpha \qquad \text{...(ii)}$$

Dividing Eq. (ii) by Eq. (i), we get

$$\frac{\theta_1+\theta_2}{\theta_1} = 4 \Rightarrow \frac{\theta_2}{\theta_1} = 3$$

4. $$\omega^2 = \omega_0^2 + 2\alpha\theta$$

$$50^2 = 100^2 + 2\alpha(2n\times 2\pi) \qquad \text{...(i)}$$

$$\omega^2 = 100^2 + 2\alpha(n\times 2\pi) \qquad \text{...(ii)}$$

From Eqs. (i) and (ii), we get

$$\frac{50^2 - 100^2}{\omega^2 - 100^2} = 2$$

$$\Rightarrow \quad \omega = \sqrt{\frac{100^2+50^2}{2}} = 25\sqrt{10}\ \text{rad/s}$$

5. (a) $\omega_0 = 100\,\text{rev/s}$

$t = 5\,\text{min} = 300\,\text{s},\ \omega = 0$

$\omega = \omega_0 + \alpha t$

$$\Rightarrow \quad 0 = 100 + \alpha(300) \Rightarrow \alpha = \frac{-1}{3}\text{rev/s}^2$$

(b) $\omega^2 = \omega_0^2 + 2\alpha\theta$

$$0^2 = (100\,\text{rev/s})^2 + 2\left(\frac{-1}{3}\text{rev/s}^2\right)\theta$$

$\theta = 15000$ rev

(c) $\omega_{\text{avg}} = \dfrac{\Delta\theta}{\Delta t} = \dfrac{15000}{300} = 50\,\text{rev/s}$

6. Speed of tip of second hand, $v = \dfrac{2\pi R}{T} = \dfrac{2\pi(1\,\text{cm})}{60\text{s}} = \dfrac{\pi}{30}\text{cm/s}$

$$|\Delta \mathbf{v}| = 2v\sin\left(\frac{\theta}{2}\right) = 2\left(\frac{\pi}{30}\right)\sin\left(\frac{90^\circ}{2}\right) = \frac{\pi\sqrt{2}}{30}\text{cm/s}$$

Average acceleration $= \dfrac{\Delta \mathbf{v}}{\Delta t} = \dfrac{\pi\sqrt{2}/30}{15} = \dfrac{\pi\sqrt{2}}{450}\text{cm/s}^2$

7. $\theta = 2t^3 + 0.5 \Rightarrow \omega = \dfrac{d\theta}{dt} = 6t^2$

At $t = 2$, $\omega = 6(2)^2 = 24\,\text{rad/s}$

8. $\omega = 1.5t - 3t^2 + 2 \Rightarrow \alpha = \dfrac{d\omega}{dt} = 1.5 - 6t = 0 \Rightarrow t = 0.25\,\text{s}$

9. $\alpha = 3t - t^2 \Rightarrow \dfrac{d\omega}{dt} = 3t - t^2$

$$\Rightarrow \int_0^{\omega} d\omega = \int_0^{t}(3t - t^2)dt \Rightarrow \omega = \frac{3t^2}{2} - \frac{t^3}{3}$$

At $t = 2$,

$$\omega = \frac{3(2)^2}{2} - \frac{2^3}{3} = \frac{10}{3}\text{rad/s}$$

For $2 < t \le 6, \alpha = 0 \Rightarrow \omega$ = constant

13.2 Radial and Tangential Acceleration

1. $\omega = 2\,\text{rev/s} = 4\pi\,\text{rad/s}$

$a = \omega^2 r = (4\pi)^2\times 25 = 400\pi^2\ \text{cm/s}^2 = 4\pi^2\ \text{m/s}^2$

2. $\omega = \dfrac{2\pi}{T} = \dfrac{2\pi}{4} = \dfrac{\pi}{2}\text{rad/s}$

$$a = \omega^2 r = \left(\frac{\pi}{2}\right)^2 10 = \frac{5\pi^2}{2}\ \text{cm/s}^2$$

3. $v = u + at \Rightarrow 8 = 6 + a(4) \Rightarrow a = 0.5\,\text{m/s}^2$

$$a = r\alpha \Rightarrow \alpha = \frac{a}{r} = \frac{0.5}{0.2} = 2.5\,\text{rad/s}^2$$

4. Tangential acceleration $= \frac{dv}{dt} = 3\,\text{m/s}^2$

Centripetal acceleration $= \frac{(20)^2}{100} = 4\,\text{m/s}^2$

Acceleration $= \sqrt{3^2 + 4^2} = 5\,\text{m/s}^2$

5. (a) Radial acceleration $= \frac{v^2}{r} = \frac{(2t)^2}{2} = 2t^2\,\text{cm/s}^2$

At $t = 3$

Radial acceleration $= 2(3)^2 = 18\,\text{cm/s}^2$

(b) Tangential acceleration $= \frac{dv}{dt} = 2\,\text{cm/s}^2$

(c) Acceleration $= \sqrt{18^2 + 2^2} = \sqrt{326}\,\text{cm/s}^2$

6. $v = 1.5t^2 + 2t \Rightarrow a = \frac{dv}{dt} = 3t + 2$

$$a = r\alpha \Rightarrow \alpha = \frac{a}{r} = \frac{3t+2}{2\times 10^{-2}}$$

At $t = 2, \alpha = 400\,\text{rad/s}^2$

7. $\alpha = 4\,\text{rad/s}^2$

$$\omega = \omega_0 + \alpha t = 0 + 4t = 4t\,\text{rad/s}$$

Centripetal acceleration = Tangential acceleration

$\Rightarrow \omega^2 r = r\alpha \Rightarrow (4t)^2 = 4 \Rightarrow t = 0.5\,\text{s}$

8. Tangential acceleration, $a_T = 0.6\,\text{m/s}^2$

Angular acceleration, $\alpha = \frac{a_T}{r} = \frac{0.6}{r}$

$$\omega^2 = \omega_0^2 + 2\alpha\theta \Rightarrow \omega^2 = 0^2 + 2\left(\frac{0.6}{r}\right)\theta$$

Centripetal acceleration, $a_C = \omega^2 r = 1.2\theta$

Total acceleration $= \sqrt{a_T^2 + a_C^2} \Rightarrow 1 = \sqrt{(0.6)^2 + (1.2\theta)^2}$

$$\Rightarrow \qquad \theta = \frac{2}{3}\,\text{rad}$$

9. (a) Tangential acceleration $(a_T) = \frac{\pi}{2}\,\text{m/s}^2$

Angular acceleration $= \frac{a_T}{r} = \frac{\pi}{2r}\,\text{rad/s}^2$

$$\theta = \omega_0 t + \frac{1}{2}\alpha t^2$$

$$\Rightarrow \qquad \pi = 0 + \frac{1}{2}\left(\frac{\pi}{2(1)}\right)t^2 \Rightarrow t = 2\text{s}$$

(b) $v = \omega r = (\omega_0 + \alpha t)r = \left(0 + \frac{\pi}{2r}(2)\right)r = \pi\,\text{m/s}$

(c) Net acceleration $= \sqrt{a_C^2 + a_T^2}$

$$= \sqrt{\left(\frac{\pi^2}{1}\right)^2 + \left(\frac{\pi}{2}\right)^2} = \frac{\pi}{2}\sqrt{4\pi^2 + 1}$$

10. (a) Radial acceleration $= a\cos 30° = \frac{25\sqrt{3}}{2}\,\text{m/s}^2$

(b) $\frac{v^2}{r} = \frac{25\sqrt{3}}{2} \Rightarrow v = \left(\frac{125\sqrt{3}}{4}\right)^{1/2}\,\text{m/s}$

(c) Tangential acceleration $= a\sin 30° = 12.5\,\text{m/s}^2$

13.3 Relative Angular Motion

1. $\omega_{AB} = \frac{(v_{rel})_\perp}{r} = \frac{v_A\sin\theta_1 + v_B\sin\theta_2}{r}$

2. $\omega_{rel} = \omega_1 - \omega_2 = \left(\frac{2\pi}{60} - \frac{2\pi}{3600}\right)\text{rad/s}^2$

$$T = \frac{2\pi}{\omega_{rel}} = \frac{2\pi}{\frac{2\pi}{60} - \frac{2\pi}{3600}} = \frac{60\times 60}{59}\,\text{s} = \frac{60}{59}\,\text{min}$$

3.

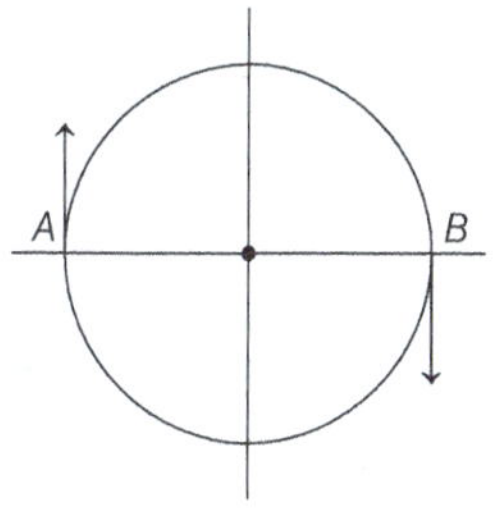

$$\omega_A = \pi, \omega_B = 2\pi, \quad \omega_{AB} = \omega_A - \omega_B = \pi - 2\pi = -\pi\,\text{rad/s}$$

$$\alpha_A = \frac{\pi}{2}, \alpha_B = 0, \ \alpha_{AB} = \alpha_A - \alpha_B = \frac{\pi}{2} - 0 = \frac{\pi}{2}\,\text{rad/s}^2$$

$$\theta_{AB} = \omega_{AB}t + \frac{1}{2}\alpha_{AB}t^2 \Rightarrow -\pi = -\pi t + \frac{1}{2}\left(\frac{\pi}{2}\right)t^2$$

$$\Rightarrow t^2 - 4t + 4 = 0 \Rightarrow t = 2\,\text{s}$$

4. $\omega_{AB} = \frac{v_{AB}}{r} = \frac{v - (-v)}{2r} = \frac{v}{r} = \omega$

5. $\omega = \frac{v_\perp}{r} = \frac{v\cos 45°}{\sqrt{2}d} = \frac{v}{2d}$

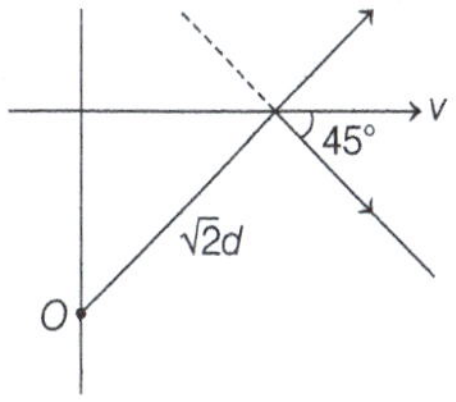

6. $v_A = v\hat{i}, \quad v_B = v\hat{j} \Rightarrow \mathbf{v}_{AB} = v\hat{i} - v\hat{j}$

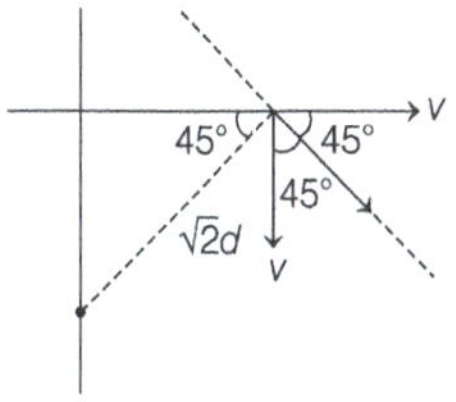

$$\omega = \frac{(v_{AB})_\perp}{r} = \frac{v\cos 45° + v\cos 45°}{\sqrt{2}d} = \frac{v}{d}$$

13.4 Circular Motion in Horizontal Plane

1. $T = \dfrac{mv^2}{R}$

$\Rightarrow \quad T = \dfrac{2(5)^2}{2} = 25\text{N}$

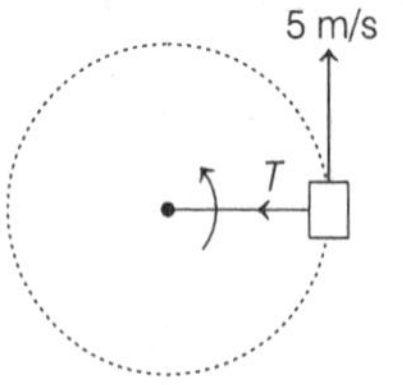

2. $T_0 = m\omega^2 l \Rightarrow T = m(2\omega)^2(2l) \Rightarrow \dfrac{T}{T_0} = 8 \Rightarrow T = 8T_0$

3. $\Sigma F_y = 0 \Rightarrow T\cos\theta = mg$

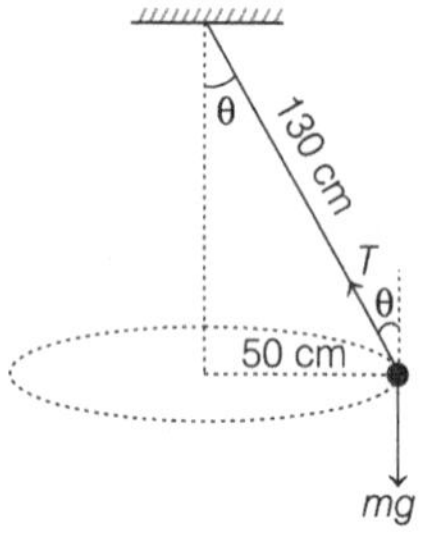

$\Rightarrow \quad T\left(\dfrac{120}{130}\right) = 0.2 \times 10 \Rightarrow T = \dfrac{13}{6}\text{N}$

$\Sigma F_x = ma \Rightarrow T\sin\theta = m(\omega^2 r)$

$\Rightarrow \quad \dfrac{13}{6}\left(\dfrac{50}{130}\right) = 0.2\omega^2(0.5) \Rightarrow \omega = \sqrt{\dfrac{25}{3}}\ \text{rad/s}$

$T = \dfrac{2\pi}{\omega} = \dfrac{2\pi}{\sqrt{\dfrac{25}{3}}} = \dfrac{2\pi\sqrt{3}}{5}\ \text{s}$

4. Friction will provide the required centripetal force for the circular motion of the block.

$\Sigma F = ma$

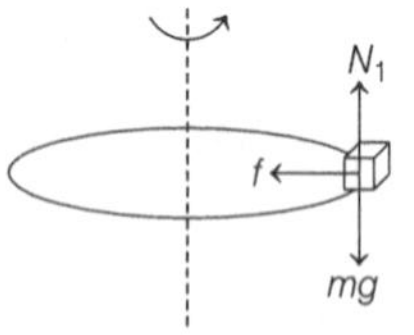

$\Rightarrow \quad f = m\omega^2 R$

5. $\Sigma F_y = 0 \Rightarrow N_1 = mg$

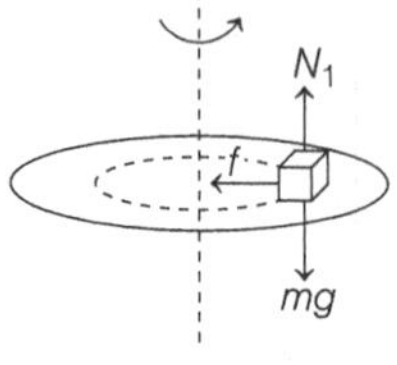

$f_L = \mu N \Rightarrow f_L = \mu mg$

$\Sigma F = ma_x \Rightarrow f = m\omega^2 r$

$\therefore \quad f \le f_L \Rightarrow m\omega^2 r \le \mu mg \Rightarrow \mu \ge \dfrac{\omega^2 r}{g}$

$\mu_{min} = \dfrac{\omega^2 r}{g} = \dfrac{\left(\dfrac{100}{3} \times \dfrac{2\pi}{60}\right)^2 (0.1)}{10} = \dfrac{\pi^2}{81}$

6. $\Sigma F_y = 0 \Rightarrow f = mg$

$\Sigma F_x = ma_x \Rightarrow N = \dfrac{mv^2}{R}$

$f \le f_L \Rightarrow mg \le \mu \dfrac{mv^2}{R}$

$\Rightarrow \quad \mu \le \dfrac{gR}{v^2}$

$\therefore \quad \mu_{min} = \dfrac{10 \times 5}{(5\sqrt{5})^2} = \dfrac{2}{5}$

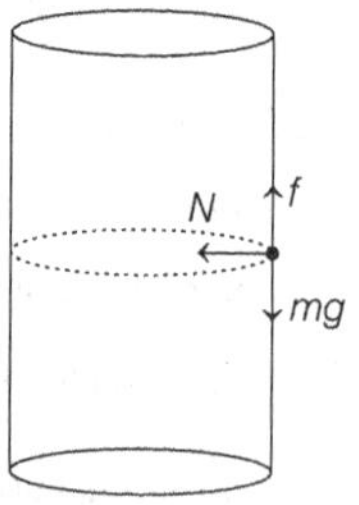

7.

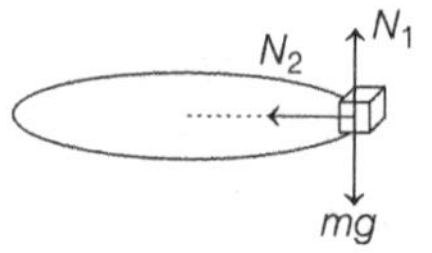

$\Sigma F_y = 0 \Rightarrow N_1 = mg$

$\Sigma F_x = ma_x \quad \therefore N_2 = \dfrac{mv^2}{r}$

8. $\Sigma F_y = 0 \Rightarrow N_1 \cos\alpha = mg$ ...(i)

$\Sigma F = ma$

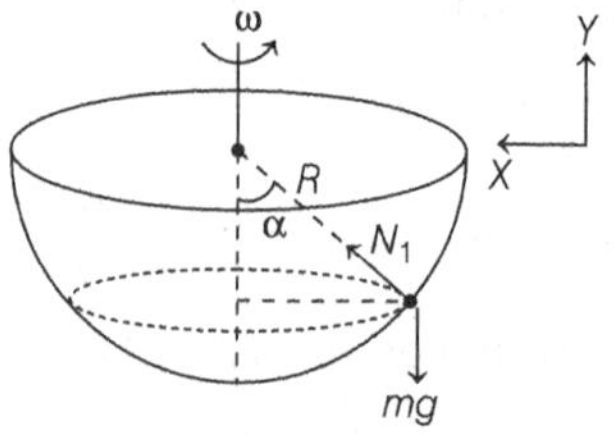

$\Rightarrow \quad N_1 \sin\alpha = m\omega^2(R\sin\alpha)$ ...(ii)

Dividing Eq. (ii) by Eq. (i), we get

$\omega = \sqrt{\dfrac{g}{R\cos\alpha}}$

9. $R = u\sqrt{\dfrac{2H}{g}} \Rightarrow 10 = u\sqrt{\dfrac{2(4.9)}{9.8}} \Rightarrow u = 10\ \text{m/s}$

Centripetal acceleration $= \dfrac{u^2}{r} = \dfrac{(10)^2}{2} = 50\ \text{m/s}^2$

10. (a) $\omega = \omega_0 + \alpha t = 0 + \alpha t \Rightarrow \omega = \alpha t$

Centripetal acceleration $= \omega^2 r = \alpha^2 t^2 r$

Tangential acceleration $= r\alpha$

Net acceleration $= \sqrt{(\alpha^2 t^2 r)^2 + (r\alpha)^2}$

$f = ma = m\sqrt{\alpha^4 t^4 r^2 + r^2\alpha^2}$

$\Rightarrow \quad f = mr\alpha\sqrt{\alpha^2 t^4 + 1}$

For slipping,

$$f = f_L \Rightarrow mr\alpha\sqrt{\alpha^2 t^4 + 1} = \mu mg \Rightarrow t = \left\{\left[\left(\frac{\mu g}{r\alpha}\right)^2 - 1\right]\frac{1}{\alpha^2}\right\}^{1/4}$$

(b) $\tan\theta = \frac{\omega^2 r}{r\alpha}$

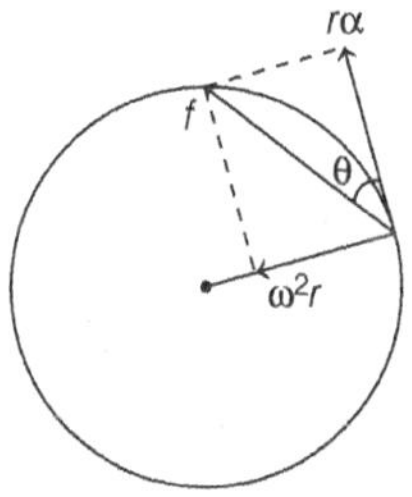

$$\Rightarrow \quad \tan\theta = \frac{\alpha^2 t^2}{\alpha} \Rightarrow \theta = \tan^{-1}(\alpha t^2)$$

11. Tangential acceleration $= \frac{dv}{dt} = a$

Centripetal acceleration $= \frac{v^2}{R}$

Net acceleration $= \sqrt{\left(\frac{v^2}{R}\right)^2 + a^2} \Rightarrow f = m\sqrt{\frac{v^4}{R^2} + a^2}$

For skidding,

$$f = f_L \Rightarrow m\sqrt{\frac{v^4}{R^2} + a^2} = \mu mg \Rightarrow v^4 + a^2 k^2 = (\mu g R)^2$$

$$\Rightarrow \quad v = [(\mu^2 g^2 - a^2)R^2]^{\frac{1}{4}}$$

13.5 Motion of a Vehicle

1. $v_{max} = \sqrt{\mu g R} = \sqrt{0.4 \times 10 \times 25} = 10$ m/s

2. $\mu_{min} = \frac{v^2}{gR} = \frac{(4.9)^2}{9.8 \times 7} = 0.35$

3. $\tan\theta = \frac{v^2}{gR} = \frac{(20)^2}{10 \times 400} \Rightarrow \tan\theta = \frac{1}{10}$

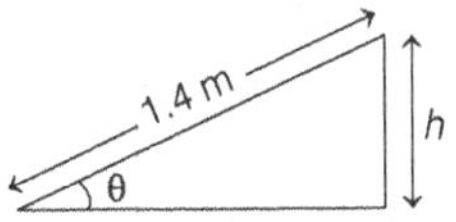

$$\sin\theta = \frac{h}{1.4} \Rightarrow h = 1.4\sin\theta$$

$$\Rightarrow \quad h = 1.4 \times \frac{1}{\sqrt{101}} \Rightarrow h = \frac{1.4}{\sqrt{101}} \text{ m}$$

4. $\tan\theta = \frac{v^2}{gR} = \frac{\left(180 \times \frac{5}{18}\right)^2}{10 \times 600} \Rightarrow \theta = \tan^{-1}\left(\frac{5}{12}\right)$

5. $v_{max} = \sqrt{\frac{g_R(\tan\theta + \mu)}{1 - \mu\tan\theta}} = \sqrt{10 \times 1000\frac{(1+0.5)}{1-0.5}} = 100\sqrt{3}$ m/s

6. $\tan\theta = \frac{v^2}{gR} = \frac{36 \times \frac{5}{18}}{10 \times 20} \Rightarrow \tan\theta = \frac{1}{2}$

$$v_{max} = \sqrt{\frac{gR(\tan\theta + \mu)}{1 - \mu\tan\theta}} = \sqrt{\frac{10 \times 20(0.5 + 0.4)}{1 - (0.5)(0.4)}} = 15 \text{ m/s}$$

$$v_{min} = \sqrt{\frac{gR(\tan\theta - \mu)}{1 + \mu\tan\theta}} = \sqrt{\frac{50}{3}} \text{ m/s}$$

13.6 Centrifugal Force

1. Centrifugal force $= m_{body}\omega^2_{observer}\, r = m\omega_o^2 r$

2. (a) With respect to the rotating rod, ring will experience a centrifugal force $m\omega^2 x$ radially outward.

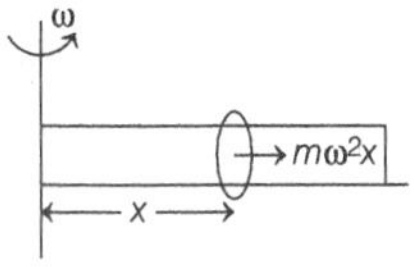

$$\Sigma F = ma \Rightarrow m\omega^2 x = ma \Rightarrow a = \omega^2 x$$

(b) $a = \omega^2 x \Rightarrow v\frac{dv}{dx} = \omega^2 x \Rightarrow \int_0^v v\,dv = \int_{L/2}^{L} \omega^2 x\,dx$

$$\Rightarrow \frac{v^2}{2} = \frac{\omega^2}{2}\left[L^2 - \frac{L^2}{4}\right] \Rightarrow v = \frac{\sqrt{3}\omega L}{2}$$

Velocity of ring w.r.t. ground $= \sqrt{(\omega L)^2 + \left(\frac{\sqrt{3}\omega L}{2}\right)^2} = \frac{\sqrt{7}\omega L}{2}$

3.

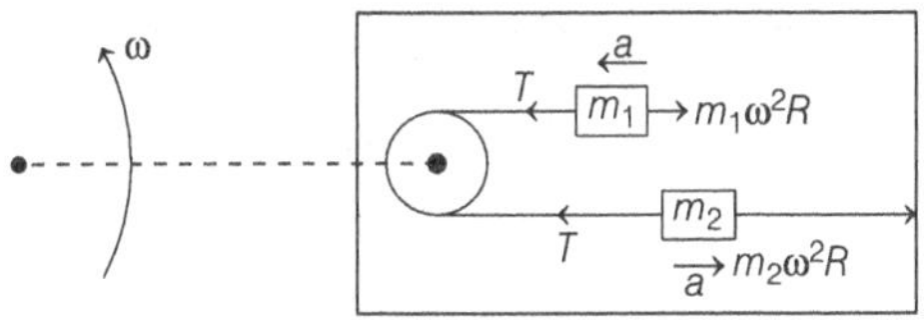

With respect to cabin, m_1 and m_2 will experience centrifugal forces $m_1\omega^2 R$ and $m_2\omega^2 R$ respectively, in radially outward direction.

For m_1,

$$\Sigma F = ma \Rightarrow T - m_1\omega^2 R = m_1 a \quad \text{...(i)}$$

For m_2,

$$\Sigma F = ma \Rightarrow m_2\omega^2 R - T = m_2 a \quad \text{...(ii)}$$

Solving Eqs. (i) and (ii), we get

$$a = \frac{(m_2 - m_1)\omega^2 R}{m_2 + m_1} \text{ and } T = \frac{2m_1 m_2\omega^2 R}{m_1 + m_2}$$

13.7 Rotation of Earth

1. At North pole $\quad w = mg$

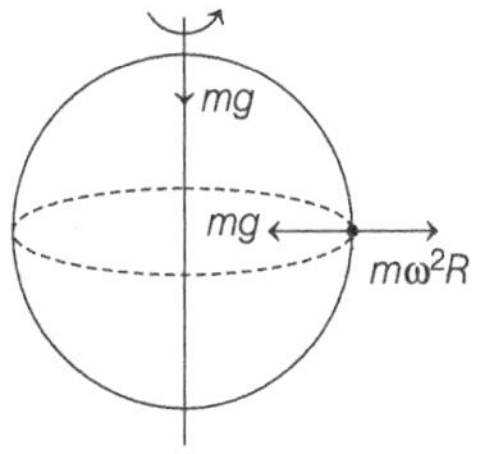

At equator, $w_{apparent} = mg - m\omega^2 R$

$$w_{apparent} = 98 - 10\left(\frac{2\pi}{24 \times 3600}\right)^2 (6400 \times 10^3) = 97.66 \text{ N}$$

2. At equator,

$$w_{apparent} = mg - m\omega^2 R \Rightarrow \frac{mg}{2} = mg - m\omega^2 R$$

$$\Rightarrow \quad \omega = \sqrt{\frac{g}{2R}}$$

$$T = \frac{2\pi}{\omega} = 2\pi\sqrt{\frac{2R}{g}} = 2\pi\sqrt{\frac{2 \times 6400 \times 10^3}{9.8}} = \frac{16\pi}{7} \times 10^3 \text{ s} = 2 \text{ h}$$

13.8 Circular Motion in Vertical Plane

1.

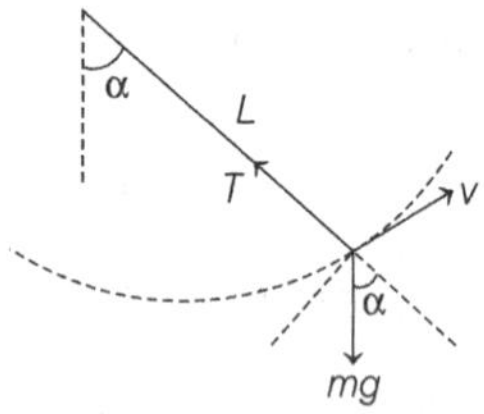

(a) $T - mg\cos\alpha = \dfrac{mv^2}{L} \quad \Rightarrow T = mg\cos\alpha + \dfrac{mv^2}{L}$

(b) Net acceleration $= \sqrt{\left(\dfrac{v^2}{L}\right)^2 + (g\sin\alpha)^2}$

$$\text{Net force} = ma = m\sqrt{\frac{v^4}{L^2} + g^2\sin^2\alpha}$$

2. Angular velocity is maximum at the lowest point,

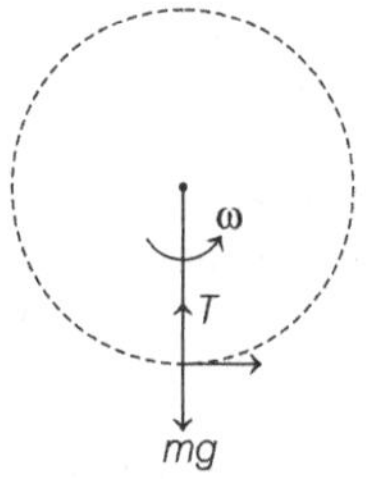

$$T - mg = m\omega^2 l \Rightarrow 30 - 0.5(10) = 0.5\omega^2(2) \Rightarrow \omega = 5 \text{ rad/s}$$

3. In the mean position, $T - mg = \dfrac{mv^2}{l} \Rightarrow 3mg - mg = \dfrac{mv^2}{l}$

$$\Rightarrow \quad v = \sqrt{2gl}$$

Using work-energy theorem between *A* and *B*,

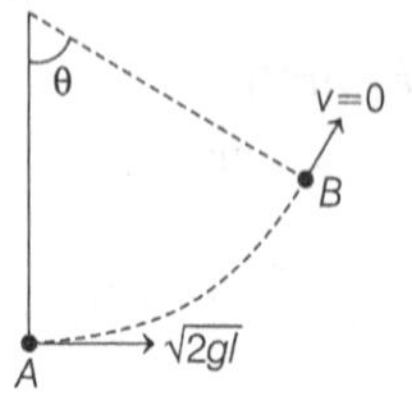

$$W_{mg} + W_T = \Delta K$$

$$\Rightarrow \quad -mgl(1 - \cos\theta) + 0 = 0 - \frac{1}{2}m(\sqrt{2gl})^2$$

$$\Rightarrow \quad \theta = 90°$$

4. (a) For massless string,

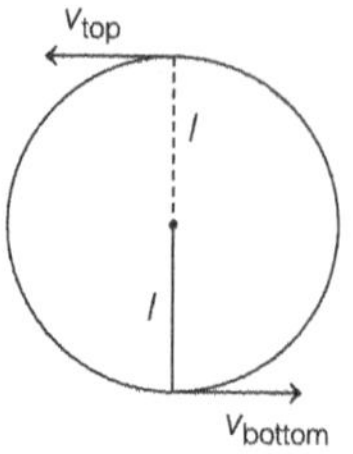

At the highest point, $T + mg = \dfrac{mv_{top}^2}{l}$

For minimum velocity, $T = 0 \Rightarrow v_{top} = \sqrt{gl}$

Using work-energy theorem betweem bottom most and top most points,

$$W_{mg} + W_T = \Delta K$$

$$\Rightarrow -mg(2l) + 0 = \frac{1}{2}m(\sqrt{gl})^2 - \frac{1}{2}mv_{bottom}^2 \Rightarrow v_{bottom} = \sqrt{5gl}$$

(b) Massless rod,

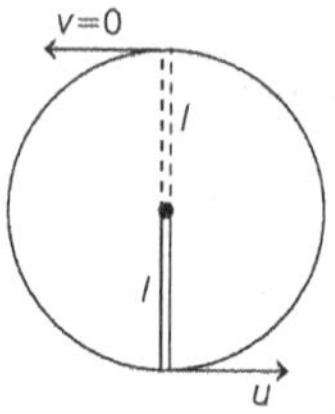

Using work-energy theorem,

$$W_{mg} + W_T = \Delta K \Rightarrow -mg2l + 0 = 0 - \frac{1}{2}mu^2 \Rightarrow u = \sqrt{4gl}$$

5. (a)Using work-energy theorem,

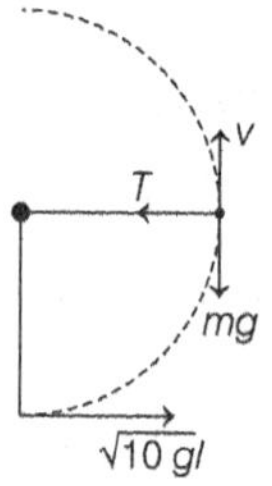

$$W_{mg} + W_T = \Delta K$$

$$\Rightarrow \quad -mgl + 0 = \frac{1}{2}mv^2 - \frac{1}{2}m(\sqrt{10gl})^2 \Rightarrow v = \sqrt{8gl}$$

Equation for centripetal force,

$$T = \frac{mv^2}{l} = \frac{m(\sqrt{8gl})^2}{l} = 8mg$$

(b) Using work-energy theorem,

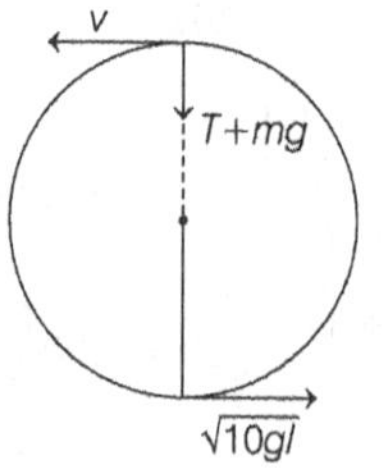

$$W_{mg} + W_T = \Delta K$$

$$\Rightarrow \quad -mg(2l) + 0 = \frac{1}{2}mv^2 - \frac{1}{2}m(\sqrt{10gl})^2 \quad \Rightarrow v = \sqrt{6gl}$$

Equation for centripetal force,

$$T + mg = \frac{mv^2}{l} \quad \Rightarrow T + mg = \frac{m(\sqrt{6gl})^2}{l} \quad \Rightarrow T = 5mg$$

(c) Using work-energy theorem,

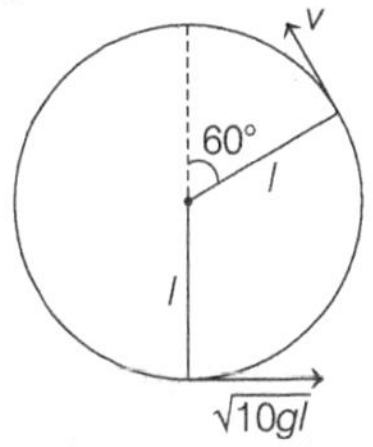

$$W_{mg} + W_T = \Delta K$$

$$\Rightarrow -mg(l + l\cos 60°) + 0 = \frac{1}{2}mv^2 - \frac{1}{2}m(\sqrt{10gl})^2 \quad \Rightarrow v = \sqrt{7gl}$$

Equation for centripetal force,

$$T + mg\cos 60° = \frac{mv^2}{l} \quad \Rightarrow T + \frac{mg}{2} = \frac{m(\sqrt{7gl})^2}{l} \quad \Rightarrow T = 6.5mg$$

6. **At point B,** $T + mg\cos 60° = \dfrac{mv^2}{l}$

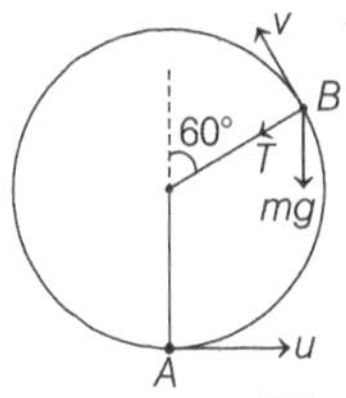

$$\because \qquad T = 0 \quad \Rightarrow v = \sqrt{\frac{gl}{2}}$$

Using work-energy theorem between A and B,

$$W_{mg} + W_T = 0$$

$$\Rightarrow -mg(l + l\cos 60°) + 0 = \frac{1}{2}m\left(\sqrt{\frac{gl}{2}}\right)^2 - \frac{1}{2}mu^2$$

$$\Rightarrow \qquad u = \sqrt{\frac{7gl}{2}}$$

At A, $\quad T - mg = \dfrac{mu^2}{l} \Rightarrow T = \dfrac{9mg}{2}$

7. For water, at the highest point,

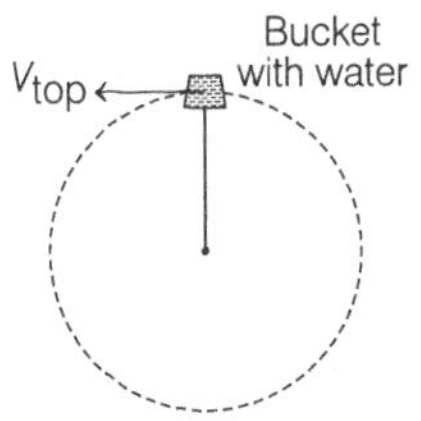

$$N + mg = \frac{mv_{top}^2}{l}$$

For v_{top} to be minimum, $N = 0 \Rightarrow v_{top} = \sqrt{gl}$

8. (a) Using work-energy theorem between A and B,

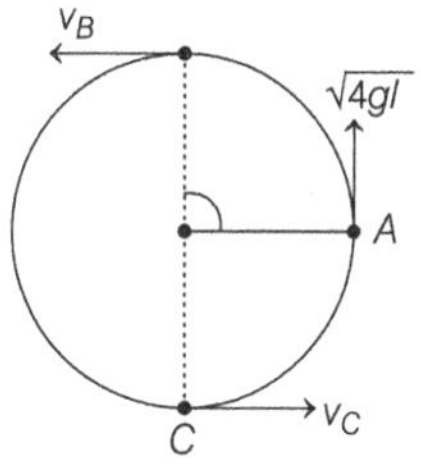

$$W_{mg} + W_T = \Delta K \Rightarrow -mgl + 0 = \frac{1}{2}mv_B^2 - \frac{1}{2}m(\sqrt{4gl})^2$$

$$\Rightarrow \qquad v_B = \sqrt{2gl}$$

Using work-energy theorem between A and C,

$$W_{mg} + W_T = \Delta K$$

$$\Rightarrow +mgl + 0 = \frac{1}{2}mv_C^2 - \frac{1}{2}m(\sqrt{4gl})^2 \Rightarrow v_C = \sqrt{6gl}$$

(b) **At B,** $T + mg = \dfrac{mv_B{}^2}{l} \quad \Rightarrow T = mg$

At C, $\quad T - mg = \dfrac{mv_C{}^2}{l} \Rightarrow T = 7mg$

9. Using work-energy theorem between A and C,

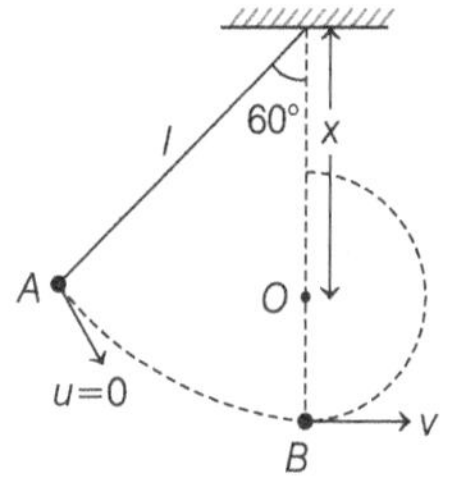

$$W_{mg} + W_T = \Delta K$$

$$\Rightarrow +mgl(1 - \cos 60°) + 0 = \frac{1}{2}mv^2 - 0 \quad \Rightarrow v = \sqrt{gl}$$

To complete vertical circle of radius $l - x$,

$$v = \sqrt{5g(l - x)} = \sqrt{gl} \quad \Rightarrow x = \frac{4l}{5}$$

10. Using work-energy theorem between A and B,

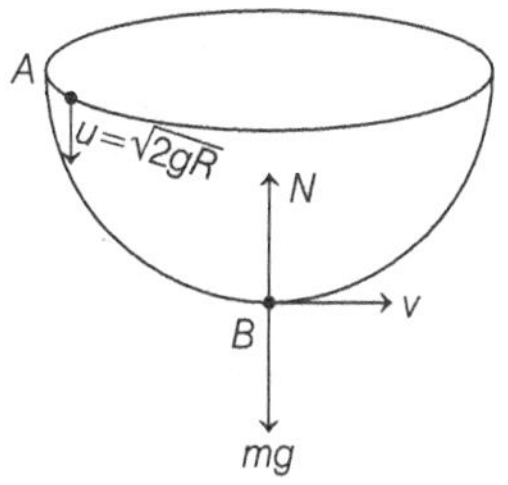

$$W_{mg} + W_N = \Delta K \quad \Rightarrow +mgR + 0 = \frac{1}{2}mv^2 - \frac{1}{2}m(\sqrt{2gR})^2$$

$$\Rightarrow \qquad v = \sqrt{4gR}$$

At B,

$$N - mg = \frac{mv_B{}^2}{R} \Rightarrow N - mg = \frac{m}{R}(\sqrt{4gR})^2 \Rightarrow N = 5mg$$

11. At initial point,

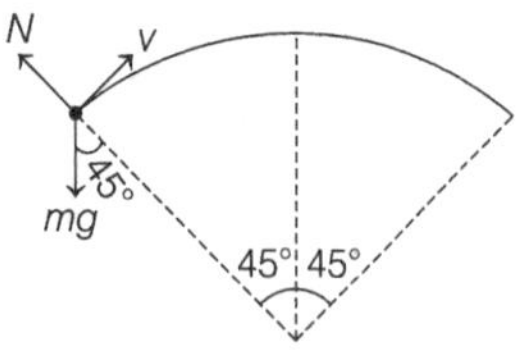

$$mg\cos 45° - N = \frac{mv^2}{R}$$

For v to be minimum

$$N = 0 \quad \Rightarrow v = \sqrt{\frac{gR}{\sqrt{2}}}$$

12. (a) Using work-energy theorem,

$$W_{mg} + W_N = \Delta K$$

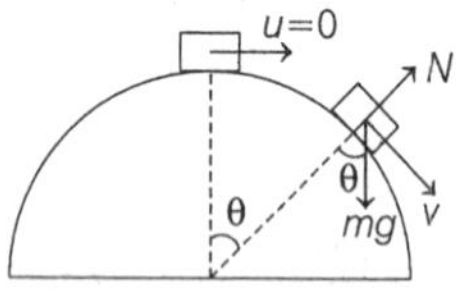

$$\Rightarrow +mgR(1-\cos\theta) + 0 = \frac{1}{2}mv^2 - 0 \Rightarrow v = \sqrt{2gR(1-\cos\theta)}$$

Equation for centripetal force

$$mg\cos\theta - N = \frac{mv^2}{R}$$

For losing contact, $N = 0$

$$\Rightarrow \quad mg\cos\theta - 0 = \frac{m}{R}(\sqrt{2gR(1-\cos\theta)})^2$$

$$\Rightarrow \quad \cos\theta = \frac{2}{3} \Rightarrow \theta = \cos^{-1}\left(\frac{2}{3}\right)$$

(b) $v = \sqrt{2gR\left(1-\frac{2}{3}\right)} = \sqrt{\frac{2gR}{3}}$

(c) Height $= R\cos\theta = R\left(\frac{2}{3}\right) = \frac{2R}{3}$

13. (a) Equation for centripetal force,

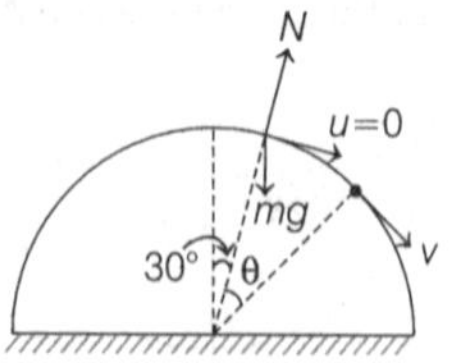

$$mg\cos 30° - N = \frac{mv^2}{R}$$

Since, $v = 0 \Rightarrow N = mg\cos 30° = \frac{\sqrt{3}mg}{2}$

(b) Using work-energy theorem,

$$W_{mg} + W_N = \Delta K$$

$$\Rightarrow +mgR(\cos 30° - \cos(30°+\theta)) + 0 = \frac{1}{2}mv^2 - 0$$

$$\Rightarrow \quad v = \sqrt{2gR(\cos 30° - \cos(30°+\theta)}$$

Equation for centripetal force,

$$mg\cos(\theta + 30°) - N = \frac{mv^2}{R}$$

For losing contact, $N = 0$

$$\Rightarrow \quad mg\cos(\theta+30°) - 0 = \frac{m}{R}[\sqrt{2gR(\cos 30° - \cos(\theta+30°)}]^2$$

$$\Rightarrow \quad 3\cos(\theta+30°) = 2\cos 30°$$

$$\Rightarrow \quad \theta + 30 = \cos^{-1}\left(\frac{1}{\sqrt{3}}\right) \quad \Rightarrow \theta = \cos^{-1}\left(\frac{1}{\sqrt{3}}\right) - 30°$$

Distance travelled $= R\theta = R\left(\cos^{-1}\left(\frac{1}{\sqrt{3}}\right) - 30°\right) = 0.43R$

14. Using work-energy theorem,

$$W_{mg} + W_T = \Delta K$$

$$\Rightarrow \quad -mgL(1+\cos\theta) + 0 = \frac{1}{2}mv_B{}^2 - \frac{1}{2}m(\sqrt{3gL})^2$$

$$\Rightarrow \quad v_B{}^2 = 3gL - 2gL(1+\cos\theta) \quad \text{...(i)}$$

Equation for centripetal force,

$$T + mg\cos\theta = \frac{mv_B{}^2}{L}$$

When string becomes slack, $T = 0$

$$\Rightarrow \quad 0 + mg\cos\theta = \frac{m}{L}(3gL - 2gL(1+\cos\theta))$$

$$\Rightarrow \quad \cos\theta = \frac{1}{3} \text{ and } v_B = \sqrt{3gL - 2gL(1+\frac{1}{3})} = \sqrt{\frac{gL}{3}}$$

Once string gets slack, the particle will become projectile motion,

$$H_{max} = \frac{u^2\sin^2\theta}{2g} = \frac{\left(\sqrt{\frac{gL}{3}}\right)^2\left(1-\frac{1}{9}\right)}{2g} = \frac{4L}{27}$$

Maximum height above A,

$$\Rightarrow \quad L + L\cos\theta + H_{max} = L + \frac{L}{3} + \frac{4L}{27} = \frac{40L}{27}$$

15. (a) Using work-energy theorem between initial position A and B,

$$W_{mg} + W_N = \Delta K \Rightarrow +mg(h-2r) + 0 = \frac{1}{2}mv_B{}^2 - 0$$

$$\Rightarrow \quad v_B = \sqrt{2g(h-2r)} \quad \text{...(i)}$$

At B, $\quad N + mg = \frac{mv_B{}^2}{r} \Rightarrow v_B = \sqrt{gr} \quad \text{...(ii)} \ (\because N = 0)$

From Eqs. (i) and (ii), we get

$$\sqrt{2g(h-2r)} = \sqrt{gr} \quad \Rightarrow h = \frac{5r}{2}$$

(b) For A,

Using work-energy theorem,

$$W_{mg} + W_N = \Delta K \Rightarrow +mgh + 0 = \frac{1}{2}mv_A{}^2 - 0$$

$$\Rightarrow \quad v_A = \sqrt{2gh} = \sqrt{6gr}$$

At A, $N - mg = \dfrac{mv_A^2}{r}$

$\Rightarrow \quad N - mg = \dfrac{m(\sqrt{6gr})^2}{r} \Rightarrow N = 7mg$

For *B*,

$v_B = \sqrt{2g(h-2r)} = \sqrt{2gr} \Rightarrow mg + N = \dfrac{mv_B^2}{r} \Rightarrow N = mg$

(c) $h = 2r$

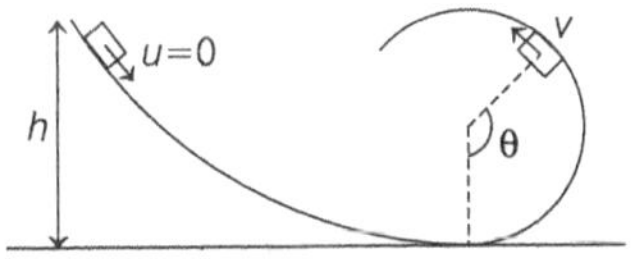

Using work-energy theorem,

$$W_{mg} + W_N = \Delta K$$

$\Rightarrow +mg(h - r - r\cos(180-\theta)) + 0 = \dfrac{1}{2}mv^2 - 0$

$\Rightarrow \quad v = \sqrt{2g[h - r(1-\cos\theta)]} \quad \Rightarrow \quad v = \sqrt{2gr(1+\cos\theta)}$

and $mg\cos(180-\theta) + N = \dfrac{mv^2}{r}$

$-mg\cos\theta + 0 = \dfrac{m}{r}[\sqrt{2gr(1+\cos\theta)}]^2$

$\Rightarrow \quad \cos\theta = \dfrac{-2}{3} \quad \Rightarrow v = \sqrt{2gr(1+\cos\theta)} = \sqrt{\dfrac{2gr}{3}}$

13.9 Radius of Curvature

1. (a)

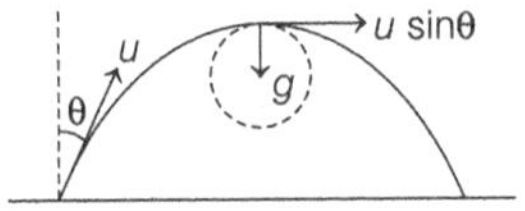

Centripetal acceleration $= \dfrac{(u\sin\theta)^2}{R}$

$\Rightarrow \quad g = \dfrac{u^2\sin^2\theta}{R} \quad \Rightarrow R = \dfrac{u^2\sin^2\theta}{g}$

(b)

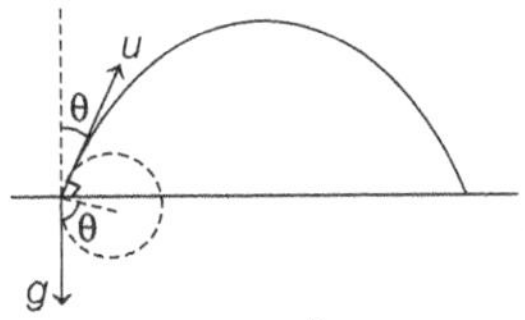

Centripetal acceleration $= \dfrac{v_\perp^2}{R}$

$\Rightarrow \quad g\cos\theta = \dfrac{u^2}{R} \quad \Rightarrow \quad R = \dfrac{u^2}{g}\sec\theta$

2. Since the particle is moving with constant speed, tangential acceleration is zero.

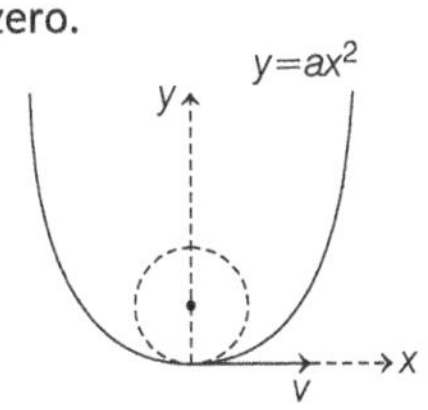

Acceleration in *y*-direction is also centripetal acceleration at $x = 0$.

$$y = ax^2 \Rightarrow \frac{dy}{dt} = 2ax\frac{dx}{dt}$$

$\Rightarrow \quad \dfrac{d^2y}{dt^2} = 2a\left(x\dfrac{d^2x}{dt^2} + \left(\dfrac{dx}{dt}\right)^2\right) \Rightarrow a_y = 2av^2$

Centripetal acceleration $= \dfrac{v_\perp^2}{R} \Rightarrow 2av^2 = \dfrac{v^2}{R} \Rightarrow R = \dfrac{1}{2a}$

3. (a) **At A,**

$mg - N_A = \dfrac{mv_A^2}{R_A} \Rightarrow 1000 - N_A = \dfrac{100(5)^2}{100} \Rightarrow N_A = 975\text{N}$

At D,

$N_D - mg = \dfrac{mv_D^2}{R_D} \Rightarrow N_D - 1000 = \dfrac{100(5)^2}{100} \Rightarrow N_D = 1025\text{N}$

(b) At *A* and *D*, since tangential acceleration is zero, friction is zero.

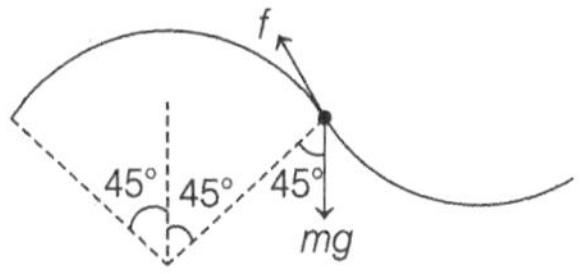

At C,

Along tangential direction,

$\Sigma F = ma \Rightarrow mg\sin 45° - f = 0 \Rightarrow f = mg\sin 45°$

(c) Just before cycle crosses *C*,

$mg\cos 45° - N_c = \dfrac{mv^2}{R} \Rightarrow 100 \times 10 \times \dfrac{1}{\sqrt{2}} - N_c = \dfrac{100(5)^2}{100}$

$\Rightarrow \quad N_c = 500\sqrt{2} - 25 \Rightarrow N_c = 707 - 25 = 682\,\text{N}$

Just after cycle crosses *C*,

$N_c - mg\cos 45° = \dfrac{mv^2}{R} \Rightarrow N_c = 707 + 25 = 732\text{N}$

(d) Maximum friction required at *C*,

$$f = mg\sin 45° \Rightarrow f \le f_L$$

$\Rightarrow mg\sin 45° \le \mu(682) \Rightarrow 707 \le \mu(682) \Rightarrow \mu \ge 1.037$

Level 2

Single Choice Correct Questions

1. $\theta = \left(\dfrac{\omega + \omega_0}{2}\right)t \Rightarrow \theta = \left(\dfrac{20+0}{2}\right)(5) = 50$ rad

Number of revolutions $= \dfrac{\theta}{2\pi} = \dfrac{50}{2\pi} = \dfrac{25}{\pi}$

2. $\theta = 10 - 5t + 4t^2$, $\omega_{avg} = \dfrac{\Delta\theta}{\Delta t} = \dfrac{\theta_2 - \theta_1}{t_2 - t_1} = \dfrac{31-9}{3-1} = 11\,\text{rad/s}$

3. $\omega = \omega_0 - k\phi \Rightarrow \dfrac{d\phi}{dt} = \omega_0 - k\phi \Rightarrow \displaystyle\int_0^\phi \frac{d\phi}{\omega_0 - k\phi} = \int_0^t dt$

$\Rightarrow \left[\dfrac{\ln(\omega_0 - k\phi)}{(-k)}\right]_0^\phi = [t]_0^t \Rightarrow \phi = \dfrac{\omega_0}{k}(1 - e^{-kt})$

4. $\omega = \dfrac{2\pi}{T} \Rightarrow \dfrac{\omega_1}{\omega_2} = \dfrac{T_2}{T_1}$

$\because \quad T_1 = T_2 \Rightarrow \dfrac{\omega_1}{\omega_2} = 1$

5. $a_{avg} = \dfrac{\Delta v}{\Delta t} = \dfrac{8-(-8)}{\pi(6)/8} = \dfrac{64}{3\pi} \text{m/s}^2$

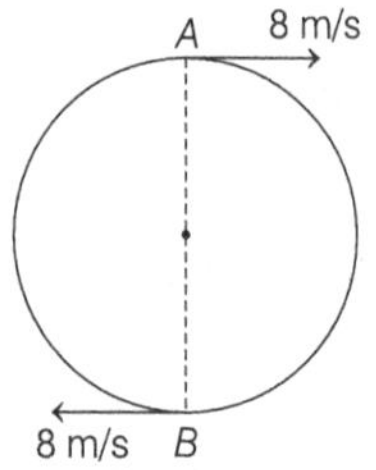

6. $a_T = \alpha \Rightarrow r\alpha = \alpha \Rightarrow r = 1\text{m}$

So, diameter = 2m

7. Centripetal acceleration $(a_c) = \dfrac{v^2}{R} = \dfrac{(30)^2}{500} = 1.8 \text{ m/s}^2$

Tangential acceleration $(a_T) = \dfrac{dv}{dt} = 2\text{m/s}^2$

Resultant acceleration $= \sqrt{a_c^2 + a_T^2} = \sqrt{(1.8)^2 + 2^2}$

$= \sqrt{7.24} = 2.7 \text{m/s}^2$

8. $s = \dfrac{t^2}{2} + \dfrac{t^3}{3} \Rightarrow v = \dfrac{ds}{dt} = t + t^2 \Rightarrow a_T = \dfrac{dv}{dt} = 1 + 2t$

At, $t = 2$

$v = 2 + 2^2 = 6 \text{ m/s}$

$a_c = \dfrac{v^2}{R} = \dfrac{6^2}{3} = 12 \text{ m/s}^2$

$a_T = 1 + 2(2) = 5 \text{ m/s}^2$

$a = \sqrt{a_c^2 + a_T^2} = \sqrt{12^2 + 5^2} = 13 \text{ m/s}^2$

9. $\tan 45° = \dfrac{a_T}{a_c} = \dfrac{9}{(v^2/4)}$

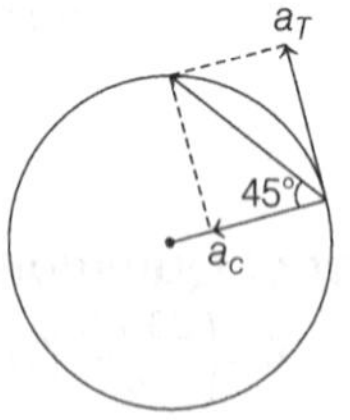

$\Rightarrow v^2 = 36 \Rightarrow v = 6 \text{ m/s}$ and $v = u + at$

$\Rightarrow \quad 6 = 0 + 9t \Rightarrow t = \dfrac{2}{3}\text{s}$

10. $a_c = k^2rt^2 \Rightarrow \dfrac{v^2}{r} = k^2rt^2 \Rightarrow v = krt$

$a_T = \dfrac{dv}{dt} = kr$

$\Rightarrow \quad P = Fv\cos 0° = (ma_T)v\cos 0°$

$= mkrkrt = mk^2r^2t$

11. $T = \dfrac{mv^2}{r} \Rightarrow 160 = \dfrac{8v^2}{7.2} \Rightarrow v = 12 \text{ m/s}$

12. $v = \omega r$ and $a = \omega^2 r$

If radius becomes half, then both v and a will become half of the original values.

13. $f_L = m\omega^2 r \Rightarrow r \propto \dfrac{1}{\omega^2}$

If ω is doubled, then r will become $\dfrac{1}{4}$ times of the original value.

14.

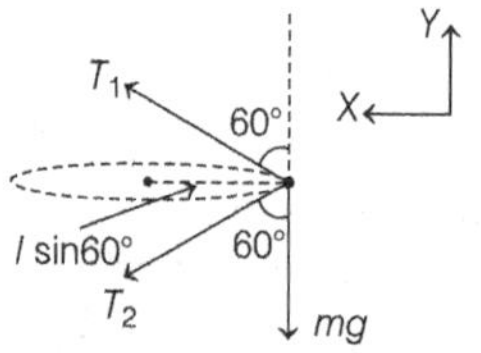

$\Sigma F_x = ma$

$\Rightarrow \quad T_1 \sin 60° + T_2 \sin 60° = m\omega^2 (l \sin 60°)$ ...(i)

$\Sigma F_y = 0 \Rightarrow T_1 \cos 60° = T_2 \cos 60° + mg$ ...(ii)

Solving Eqs. (i) and (ii), we get

$\omega = 14$ rad/s

15. $\Sigma F_x = ma_x$

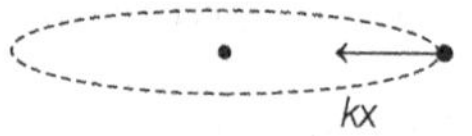

$\Rightarrow \quad kx = m\omega^2(l + x) \Rightarrow x = \dfrac{m\omega^2 l}{k - m\omega^2}$

16. $\Sigma F_y = 0$

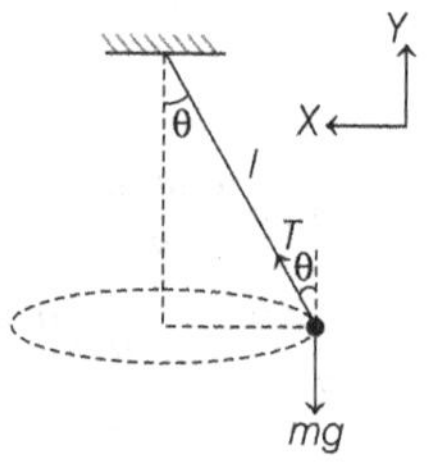

$\Rightarrow \quad T\cos\theta = mg$ ...(i)

$\Sigma F_x = ma_x \Rightarrow T\sin\theta = m\omega^2(l\sin\theta)$ ...(ii)

From Eqs. (i) and (ii), we get

$\omega = \sqrt{\dfrac{g}{l\cos\theta}} \quad \therefore \quad T = \dfrac{2\pi}{\omega} = 2\pi\sqrt{\dfrac{l\cos\theta}{g}}$

17. $\Sigma F_y = 0 \Rightarrow f = mg$

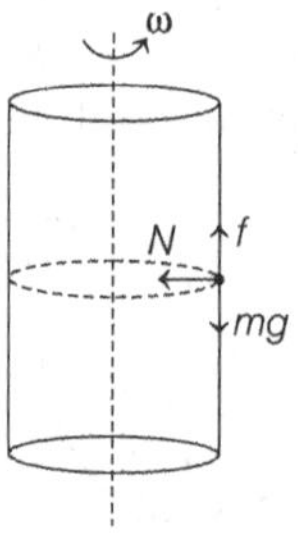

$$\Sigma F_x = 0 \Rightarrow N = m\omega^2 r \quad \text{and} \quad f \le f_L$$

$$\Rightarrow \quad mg \le \mu(m\omega^2 r) \quad \Rightarrow \omega \ge \sqrt{\frac{g}{\mu r}}$$

18.

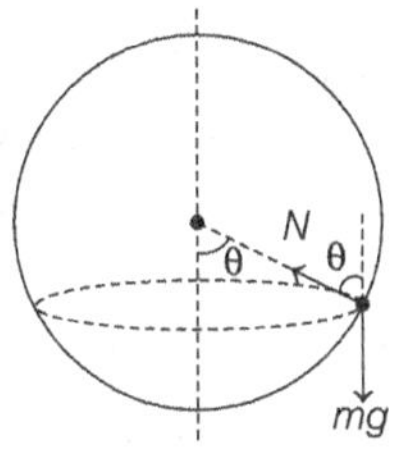

$$\Sigma F_y = 0 \Rightarrow N\cos\theta = mg \qquad \text{...(i)}$$

$$\Sigma F_x = ma_x \Rightarrow N\sin\theta = m\omega^2\left(\frac{a}{2}\right) \qquad \text{...(ii)}$$

From Eqs. (i) and (ii), we get

$$\omega = \left(\frac{2g}{\sqrt{3}a}\right)^{1/2}$$

19.

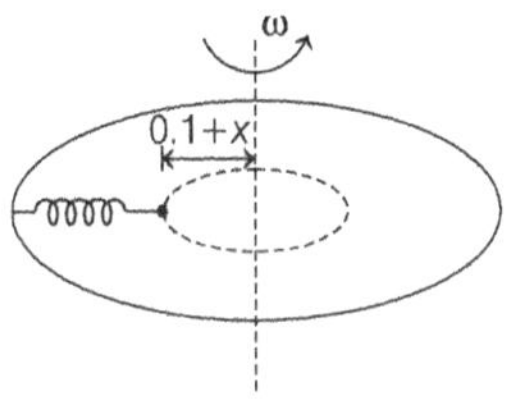

Lets take compression in the spring to be x,

$$\Sigma F_x = ma_x \Rightarrow \quad kx = m\omega^2(0.1 + x) \quad \Rightarrow x = \frac{m\omega^2(0.1)}{K - m\omega^2}$$

$$\Rightarrow \quad x = \frac{90 \times 10^{-3} \times (10^2)^2(0.1)}{10^4 - 90 \times 10^{-3} \times (10^2)^2} \quad \Rightarrow x = \frac{90}{9100} \simeq 10^{-2}\text{m}$$

20. $v = \sqrt{\mu g r}$

$$\Rightarrow \quad \frac{v_1}{v_2} = \sqrt{\frac{\mu_1}{\mu_2}} \quad \Rightarrow \frac{v_1}{10} = \sqrt{\frac{\mu/2}{\mu}} \quad \Rightarrow v_1 = 5\sqrt{2}\text{ m/s}$$

21.

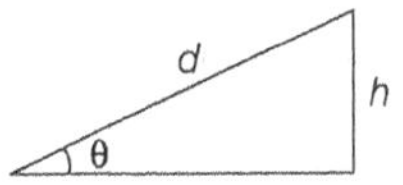

$$\sin\theta = \frac{h}{d}$$

and for banking

$$\tan\theta = \frac{v^2}{rg} \quad \Rightarrow \tan\left[\sin^{-1}\left(\frac{h}{d}\right)\right] = \frac{v^2}{rg}$$

22. $v = \sqrt{rg\tan\theta} = \sqrt{(10\sqrt{3})(10)\tan 30^\circ} = 10\text{m/s} = 36\text{km/h}$

23. $\mu_{min} = \dfrac{v^2}{gr} = \dfrac{(72 \times 5/18)^2}{10(200)} = 0.2$

24. $v_{max} = \sqrt{\dfrac{gr(\tan\theta + \mu)}{1 - \mu\tan\theta}} = \sqrt{\dfrac{10 \times 20\left(\frac{3}{4} + \frac{1}{4}\right)}{1 - \frac{3}{4} \times \frac{1}{4}}} = 10\sqrt{\dfrac{32}{13}}\text{m/s}$

25. $\tan\theta = \dfrac{a}{g} = \dfrac{v^2/r}{g} \quad \Rightarrow \tan\theta = \dfrac{v^2}{rg} = \dfrac{10^2}{10(10)} = 1 \quad \Rightarrow \theta = 45^\circ$

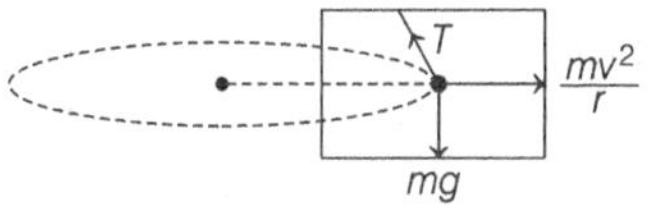

26. $w_{\text{apparent}} = mg - m\omega^2 R$

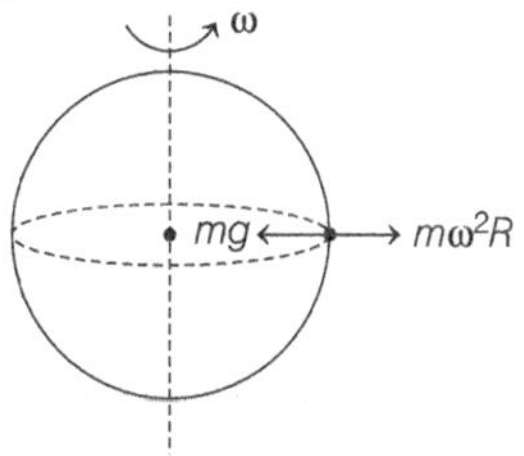

$$0 = mg - m\omega^2 R \quad \Rightarrow \quad \omega = \sqrt{\frac{g}{R}}$$

27. Due to lack of sufficient centripetal force.

28. Since, **F** is perpendicular to **v**, particle will undergo uniform circular motion.

29. Speed of both the trains is same w.r.t. the earth's surface but w.r.t. the centre of earth their speeds will be different as earth itself is rotating West to East about its own axis.

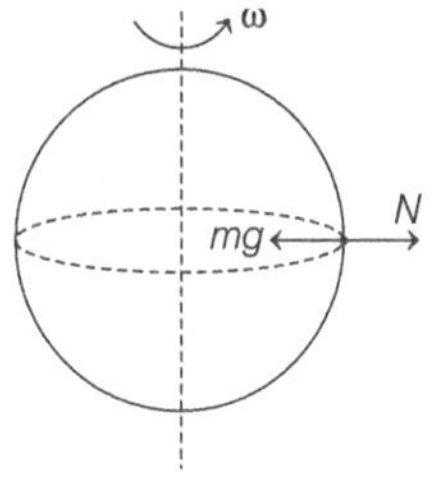

For train,

$$mg - N = \frac{mv^2}{R} \quad \Rightarrow \quad N = mg - \frac{mv^2}{R}$$

For train A, going from East to West

$$N_A = mg - \frac{m(v - \omega R)^2}{R}$$

For train B, going from West to East

$$N_B = mg - \frac{m(v + \omega R)^2}{R} \Rightarrow N_A > N_B$$

30.

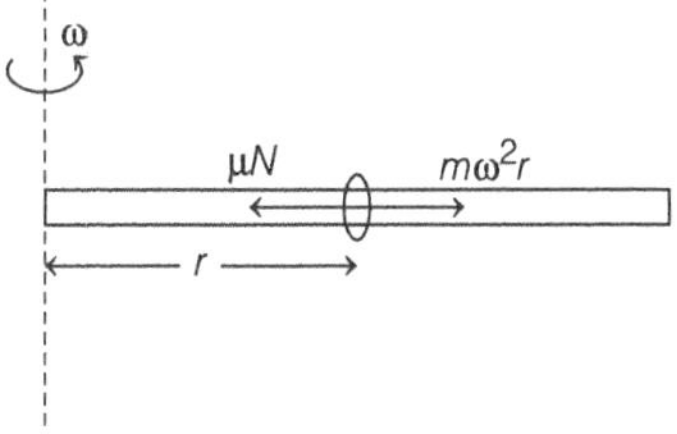

$$\omega = \alpha t^2 \quad \Rightarrow \quad \frac{d\omega}{dt} = 2\alpha t$$

$$\Sigma F = ma \quad \Rightarrow \quad N = m\left(r\frac{d\omega}{dt}\right) \quad \Rightarrow N = mr(2\alpha t)$$

Along radial direction,

$$\Sigma F = 0 \Rightarrow \mu N = m\omega^2 r \Rightarrow \mu[mr(2\alpha t)] = m(\alpha t^2)^2 r$$

$$\Rightarrow \quad t = \left(\frac{2\mu}{\alpha}\right)^{1/3}$$

31. Average normal force $= \dfrac{\Delta p}{\Delta t} = \dfrac{2mv}{\pi R / v} = \dfrac{2mv^2}{\pi R}$

32. $\mathbf{v}_p = 8\cos 30\hat{\mathbf{i}} + 8\sin 30\hat{\mathbf{j}}$

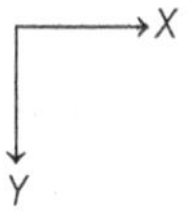

$$\mathbf{v}_Q = 6\cos 30°\hat{\mathbf{i}} - 6\sin 30°\hat{\mathbf{j}}$$

$$\mathbf{v}_{PQ} = 2\cos 30°\hat{\mathbf{i}} + 14\sin 30°\hat{\mathbf{j}}$$

$$\omega_{rel} = \frac{(\mathbf{v}_{rel})_\perp}{r} = \frac{14\sin 30°}{10} = 0.7 \text{ rad/s}$$

33. At the time of landing,

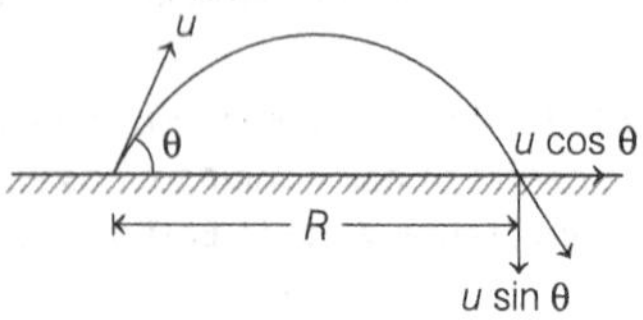

$$\mathbf{v} = u\cos\theta\hat{\mathbf{i}} - u\sin\theta\hat{\mathbf{j}}$$

$$\omega = \frac{v_\perp}{r} = \frac{u\sin\theta}{R} = \frac{u\sin\theta}{(u^2\sin 2\theta)/g}$$

$$= \frac{g}{2u\cos\theta} = \frac{10}{2(10)\left(\frac{4}{5}\right)} = \frac{5}{8} \text{ rad/s}$$

34. At the top of the loop,
FBD of pilot,

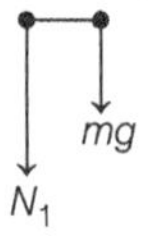

$$\Sigma F = ma \Rightarrow N_1 + mg = m\left(\frac{v^2}{R}\right)$$

$$\Rightarrow \quad N_1 + 700 = \frac{70\left(432 \times \frac{5}{18}\right)^2}{500}$$

$$\Rightarrow \quad N_1 = 1316 \text{ N}$$

35. At lowest point

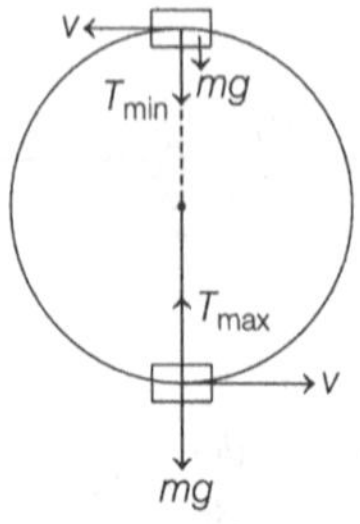

$$T_{max} - mg = \frac{mv^2}{R} \Rightarrow T_{max} = mg + \frac{mv^2}{R} \quad \text{...(i)}$$

At the highest point,

$$T_{min} + mg = \frac{mv^2}{R} \Rightarrow T_{min} = \frac{mv^2}{R} - mg \quad \text{...(ii)}$$

Solving Eqs. (i) and (ii), we get

$$\frac{T_{max}}{T_{min}} = \frac{mg + \frac{mv^2}{R}}{\frac{mv^2}{R} - mg} = \frac{5}{3} \Rightarrow 2\frac{mv^2}{R} = 8mg$$

$$\Rightarrow \quad v = \sqrt{4gR} \Rightarrow v = \sqrt{4 \times 10 \times 2} \Rightarrow v = 4\sqrt{5} \text{ m/s}$$

36. Using work-energy theorem between A and B.

$$W_{mg} + W_N = \Delta K \Rightarrow +mgR\cos 60° + 0 = \frac{1}{2}mv^2 - 0$$

$$\Rightarrow \quad v = \sqrt{gR}$$

Equation for centripetal force at B,

$$N - mg\cos 60° = \frac{mv_B^2}{R}$$

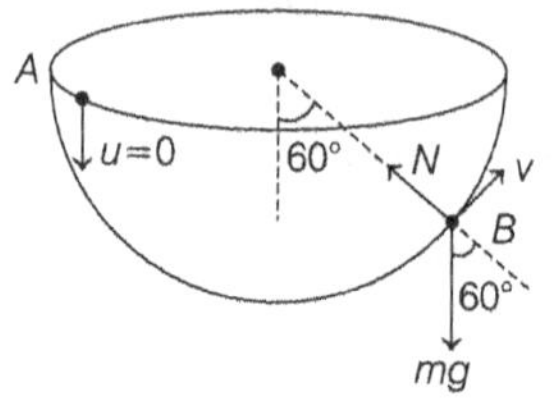

$$N = 1.5\, mg$$

37.

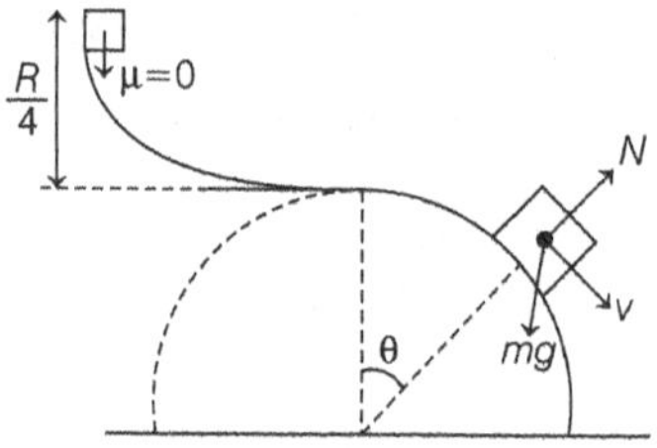

Using work-energy theorem,

$$W_{mg} + W_N = \Delta K$$

$$\Rightarrow +mg\left(\frac{R}{4} + R(1 - \cos\theta)\right) + 0 = \frac{1}{2}mv^2 - 0 \quad \text{...(i)}$$

Along radial direction,

$$mg\cos\theta - N = \frac{mv^2}{R} \Rightarrow mg\cos\theta = \frac{mv^2}{R} \quad \text{...(ii) (since } N = 0)$$

Solving Eqs. (i) and (ii), we get

$$\theta = \cos^{-1}\left(\frac{5}{6}\right)$$

38. $mg - N = \dfrac{mu^2}{R}$

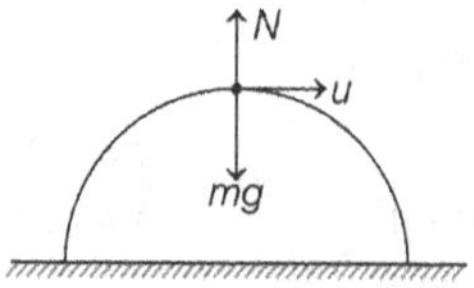

For losing contact, $N = 0 \Rightarrow mg = \dfrac{mu^2}{R} \Rightarrow u = \sqrt{gR}$

39. In extreme position, $a_{\text{centripetal}} = 0$

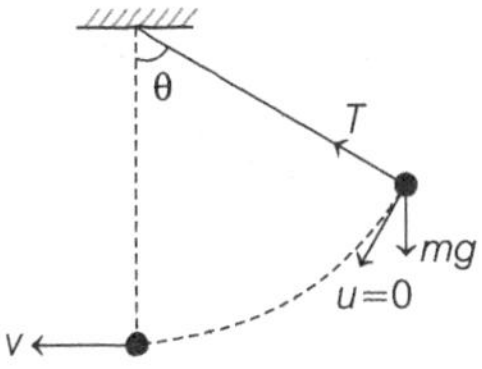

$$a_{\text{tangential}} = g\sin\theta \Rightarrow a_1 = \sqrt{a_c^2 + a_T^2} = g\sin\theta$$

Using work-energy theorem,

$$W_{mg} + W_T = \Delta K \Rightarrow +mgl(1-\cos\theta) + 0 = \frac{1}{2}mv^2 - 0$$

$$\Rightarrow v = \sqrt{2gl(1-\cos\theta)} \Rightarrow a_{\text{centripetal}} = \frac{v^2}{l} = 2g(1-\cos\theta)$$

$$a_{\text{tangential}} = 0$$

$$\Rightarrow \quad a_2 = \sqrt{a_c^2 + a_T^2} = 2g(1-\cos\theta)$$

$$\because \quad a_1 = a_2$$

$$\Rightarrow g\sin\theta = 2g(1-\cos\theta) \Rightarrow \theta = 2\tan^{-1}\left(\frac{1}{2}\right)$$

40. Using work-energy theorem between A and B,

$$W_{mg} + W_T = \Delta K$$

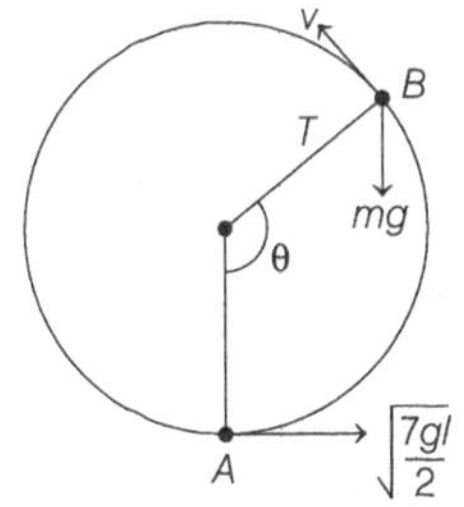

$$-mgl(1+\cos(180°-\theta)) + 0 = \frac{1}{2}mv^2 - \frac{1}{2}m\left(\sqrt{\frac{7gl}{2}}\right)^2$$

$$v^2 = \frac{7gl}{2} - 2gl(1-\cos\theta) \qquad \text{...(i)}$$

At B,

$$mg\cos(180°-\theta) + T = \frac{mv^2}{l}$$

$$\Rightarrow -mg\cos\theta + 0 = \frac{m}{l}\left(\frac{7gl}{2} - 2gl(1-\cos\theta)\right)$$

$$\Rightarrow -2\cos\theta = 7 - 4(1-\cos\theta) \Rightarrow \cos\theta = -\frac{1}{2} \Rightarrow \theta = 120°$$

41. $T - mg\cos\theta = \dfrac{mv^2}{l}$

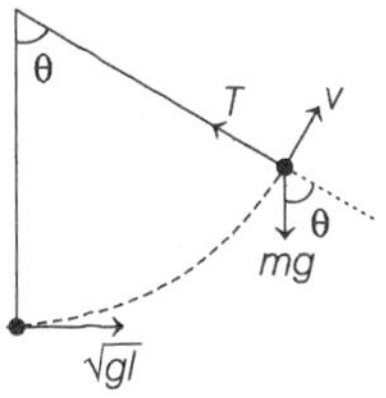

$$\Rightarrow mg(1-\cos\theta) = \frac{mv^2}{l} \Rightarrow v = \sqrt{gl(1-\cos\theta)}$$

Using work-energy theorem,

$$W_{mg} + W_T = \Delta K$$

$$\Rightarrow -mgl(1-\cos\theta) + 0 = \frac{1}{2}mv^2 - \frac{1}{2}m(\sqrt{gl})^2$$

$$\Rightarrow -mgl(1-\cos\theta) = \frac{1}{2}m\left(\sqrt{gl(1-\cos\theta)}\right)^2 - \frac{1}{2}mgl$$

$$-2(1-\cos\theta) = 1 - \cos\theta - 1 \Rightarrow 3\cos\theta = 2$$

$$\Rightarrow \quad \theta = \cos^{-1}\left(\frac{2}{3}\right) \text{ and } v = \sqrt{\frac{gl}{3}}$$

42. $\mathbf{v}_A = u\hat{\mathbf{i}}$

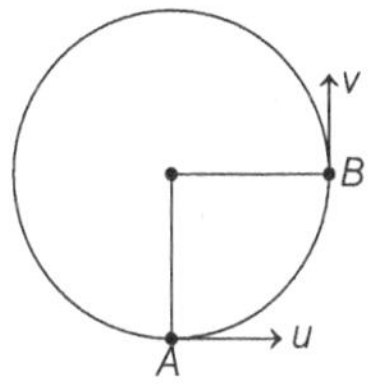

Using work-energy theorem between A and B,

$$W_{mg} + W_T = \Delta K \Rightarrow -mgL + 0 = \frac{1}{2}mv^2 - \frac{1}{2}mu^2$$

$$\Rightarrow \quad v = \sqrt{u^2 - 2gL}$$

$$\mathbf{v}_B = \sqrt{u^2 - 2gL}\,\hat{\mathbf{j}}$$

$$\Rightarrow \quad \mathbf{v}_B - \mathbf{v}_A = \sqrt{u^2 - 2gL}\,\hat{\mathbf{j}} - u\hat{\mathbf{i}}$$

$$|\mathbf{v}_B - \mathbf{v}_A| = \sqrt{(\sqrt{u^2 - 2gL})^2 + u^2} = \sqrt{2(u^2 - gL)}$$

43. Using work - energy theorem between A and B

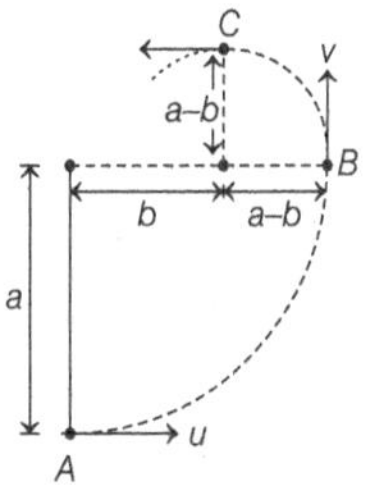

$$W_{mg} + W_T = \Delta K \Rightarrow -mga + 0 = \frac{1}{2}mv^2 - \frac{1}{2}mu^2$$

$$\Rightarrow \quad v = \sqrt{u^2 - 2ga}$$

For compeleting vertical circle around the nail at C,

$$\Rightarrow \quad T + mg = \frac{mv_c^2}{a-b} \Rightarrow v_c = \sqrt{g(a-b)}$$

[$\because T = 0$ for minimum speed]

Using work-energy theorem between B and C,

$$W_{mg} + W_T = \Delta K$$

$$\Rightarrow -mg(a-b) + 0 = \frac{1}{2}m(\sqrt{g(a-b)})^2 - \frac{1}{2}mv^2$$

$$\Rightarrow \quad u = \sqrt{5ga - 3gb}$$

44. Using work - energy theorem between A and B,

$$W_{mg} + W_T = \Delta K$$

$\Rightarrow \quad +mgl\cos\theta + 0 = \frac{1}{2}mv^2 - 0 \quad \Rightarrow v = \sqrt{2gl\cos\theta}$

At B,

Centripetal acceleration $= \frac{v^2}{l} = \frac{(\sqrt{2gl\cos\theta})^2}{l} = 2g\cos\theta$

Tangential acceleration $= \sqrt{a_c^2 + a_T^2} = \sqrt{(2g\cos\theta)^2 + (g\sin\theta)^2}$

$= g(\sqrt{4\cos^2\theta + \sin^2\theta})$

$= g\sqrt{3\cos^2\theta + 1}$

45. At the top most point,

$$T + mg = \frac{mv_{top}^2}{r}$$

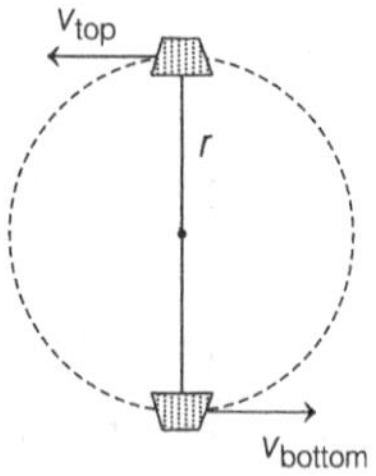

For v_{top} to be minimum

$$T = 0 \quad \Rightarrow v_{top} = \sqrt{rg}$$

Using work - energy theorem,

$W_{mg} + W_T = \Delta K \Rightarrow +mg(2r) + 0 = \frac{1}{2}mv_{bottom}^2 - \frac{1}{2}m(\sqrt{rg})^2$

$\Rightarrow \quad v_{bottom} = \sqrt{5rg}$ and $T - mg = \frac{mv_{bottom}^2}{r}$

$\Rightarrow \quad T - mg = \frac{m}{r}(\sqrt{5rg})^2 \quad \Rightarrow T = 6mg$

46. In free fall, acceleration of car is g.

For pendulum,

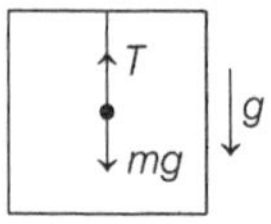

$\Sigma F = ma \quad \Rightarrow mg - T = m(g) \quad \Rightarrow T = 0$

47. Using work-energy theorem between A and B,

$$W_{mg} + W_N = \Delta K$$

$\Rightarrow \quad +mg(2R) + 0 = \frac{1}{2}mv_2^2 - 0 \quad \Rightarrow v_2 = \sqrt{4gR}$

At point 2,

$N + mg = \frac{mv_2^2}{R} \Rightarrow N + mg = 4mg \quad \Rightarrow N = 3mg$

48. Using work - energy theorem between A and B,

$$W_{mg} + W_N = \Delta K$$

$\Rightarrow +mg(25 - 15) + 0 = \frac{1}{2}mv_B^2 - 0 \quad \Rightarrow v_B = 10\sqrt{2}\,\text{m/s}$

At B,

$mg - N = \frac{mv_B^2}{R_B} \quad \Rightarrow \quad m(10) - 0 = \frac{m(10\sqrt{2})^2}{R_B}$

[$\because N = 0$ for R_B to be minimum]

$\Rightarrow \quad R_B = 20\text{ m}$

49. Using work - energy theorem between A and B

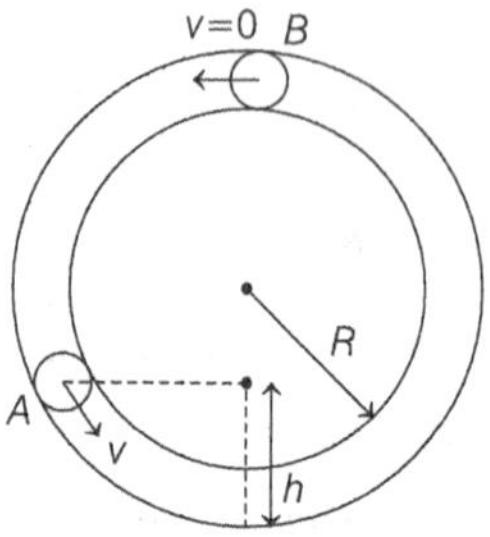

$W_{mg} + W_N = \Delta K \Rightarrow -mg(2R - h) + 0 = 0 - \frac{1}{2}mv^2$

$\Rightarrow \quad v = \sqrt{2g(2R - h)}$

50. $\Sigma F = ma \quad \Rightarrow mg\sin\theta = ma_T \quad \Rightarrow a_T = g\sin\theta$

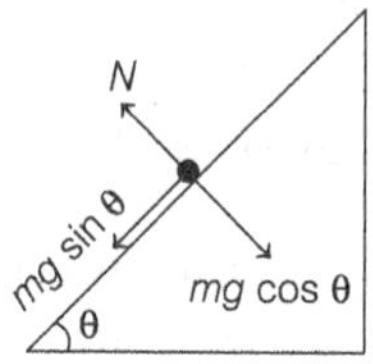

$$\tan\theta = \frac{dy}{dx} = \frac{2x}{4a}$$

$y = a, \; x = 2a \quad \Rightarrow \quad \tan\theta = \frac{2a}{2a} = 1$

$\Rightarrow \quad \theta = 45° \quad \Rightarrow \quad a_T = g\sin 45° = \frac{g}{\sqrt{2}}$

51. Using work-energy theorem,

$$W_{mg} + W_N + W_{\text{Pseudo force}} = \Delta K$$

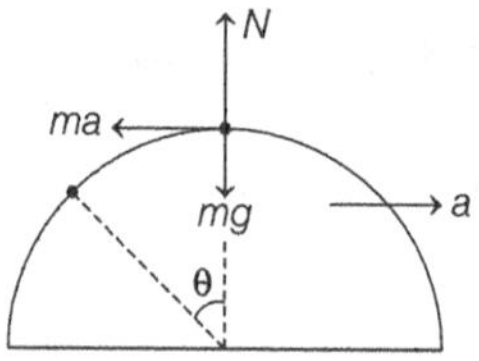

$\Rightarrow +mgR(1 - \cos\theta) + 0 + ma(R\sin\theta) = \frac{1}{2}mv^2 - 0$

$\Rightarrow \quad v = [2R(a\sin\theta + g(1 - \cos\theta)]^{1/2}$

52. At A, $mg - N_A = \frac{mv^2}{R_A} \quad \Rightarrow \quad N_A = mg - \frac{mv^2}{R_A}$

At B, $N_B - mg = \frac{mv^2}{R_B} \quad \Rightarrow \quad N_B = mg + \frac{mv^2}{R_B}$

At C, $N_C = mg - \frac{mv^2}{R_C}$

Since, $R_C < R_A \Rightarrow N_A > N_C \quad \therefore \quad N_B > N_A > N_C$

53. $a_T = \frac{dv}{dt} = \text{constant} \quad \Rightarrow \int dv \propto \int dt \quad \Rightarrow v \propto t + C$

$a_c = \frac{v^2}{R} = \text{constant} \quad \Rightarrow R \propto v^2 \quad \Rightarrow \quad R \propto (t + C)^2$

54. $P = Fv\cos\theta$

$$P_{mg} = (mg)v\cos\theta$$

At 4, angle between mg and velocity vector is obtuse

$\Rightarrow \quad P_{mg} < 0 \quad \Rightarrow P_T = Tv\cos 90° = 0$

So, power delivered by tension is zero throughout.

55.

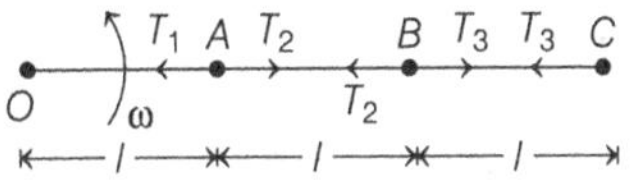

For A,

$$\Sigma F = ma_x \quad \Rightarrow \quad T_1 - T_2 = m\omega^2 l \qquad \text{...(i)}$$

For B,

$$\Sigma F = ma_x \quad \Rightarrow \quad T_2 - T_3 = m\omega^2(2l) \qquad \text{...(ii)}$$

For C,

$$\Sigma F = ma_x \quad \Rightarrow T_3 = m\omega^2(3l) \qquad \text{...(iii)}$$

Solving Eqs. (i), (iii) and (iii), we get

$$T_1 = 6m\omega^2 l : T_2 = 5m\omega l \text{ and } T_3 = m\omega^2(3l)$$

$$T_3 : T_2 : T_1 = 3:5:6$$

Numerical Value Questions

1. Along tangential direction,

$$\Sigma F = ma \quad \Rightarrow mg\sin\theta = ma \Rightarrow a = g\sin\theta$$

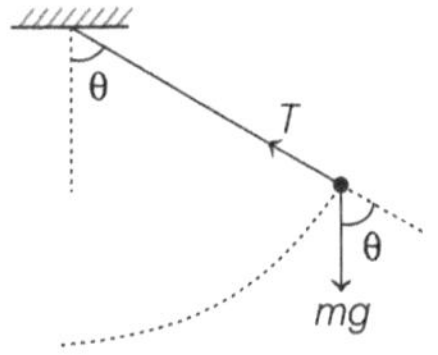

$$\therefore \qquad \frac{dv}{dt} = g\sin 30° = 5\text{ m/s}^2$$

2. $\frac{d\theta}{dt} = 2\text{ rad/s}$

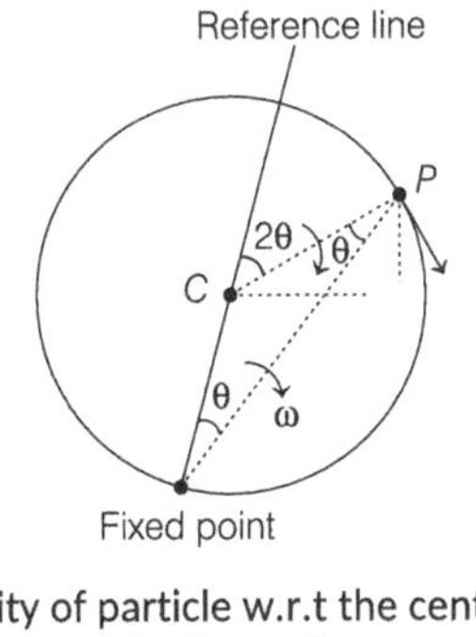

Angular velocity of particle w.r.t the centre of circle

$$= \frac{d(2\theta)}{dt} = 2\frac{d\theta}{dt} = 4\text{ rad/s}$$

$$v = \omega r = 4(1) = 4\text{ m/s}$$

3. $\alpha = \frac{\pi}{4}\text{ rad/s}^2 \Rightarrow \theta = \omega_0 t + \frac{1}{2}\alpha t^2 \Rightarrow \frac{\pi}{2} = 0 + \frac{1}{2}\times\left(\frac{\pi}{4}\right)t^2$

$\Rightarrow \quad t = 2\text{ s} \quad \Rightarrow \quad v_{avg} = \frac{\Delta S}{\Delta t} = \frac{\sqrt{2}R}{2} = 1\text{ m/s}$

4. $\Sigma F_y = 0 \quad \Rightarrow \quad N\cos\theta = mg \qquad \text{...(i)}$

$\Sigma F_x = ma_x \quad \Rightarrow \quad N\sin\theta = m\omega^2 R\sin\theta \qquad \text{...(ii)}$

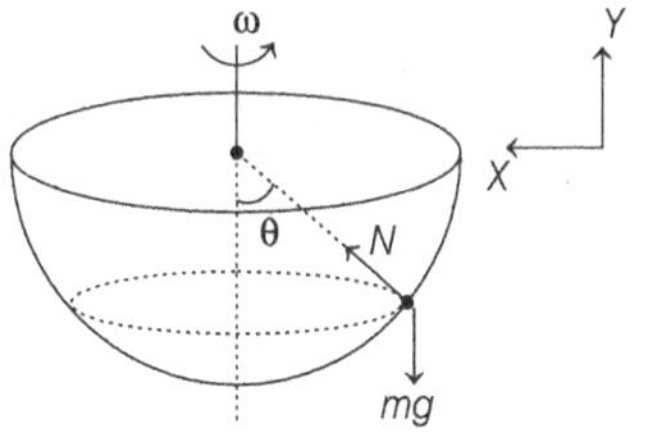

Solving Eqs. (i) and (ii), we get

$$\omega = \sqrt{\frac{g}{R\cos\theta}} \quad \Rightarrow \quad \omega = \sqrt{\frac{10}{0.5\left(\frac{0.3}{0.5}\right)}} = \sqrt{\frac{100}{3}}\text{ rad/s}$$

5. Using work - energy theorem,

$$W_{mg} + W_T = \Delta K$$

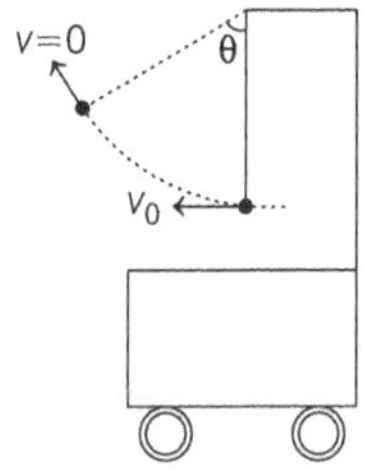

$$\Rightarrow \qquad -mgl(1 - \cos 60°) + 0 = 0 - \frac{1}{2}mv_0^2$$

$$\Rightarrow \qquad v_0 = \sqrt{gl} = \sqrt{9.8 \times 5} = 7\text{ m/s}$$

6. $a_c = 2t^2 \quad \Rightarrow \quad \omega^2(2) = 2t^2 \quad \Rightarrow \quad \omega = t$

$$\Rightarrow \qquad \int d\theta = \int_0^2 t\,dt \quad \Rightarrow \quad \theta = \left[\frac{t^2}{2}\right]^2 = 2\text{ rad}$$

7. $\tan\theta = \frac{a_c}{a_T} = \frac{\omega^2 R}{R\alpha}$

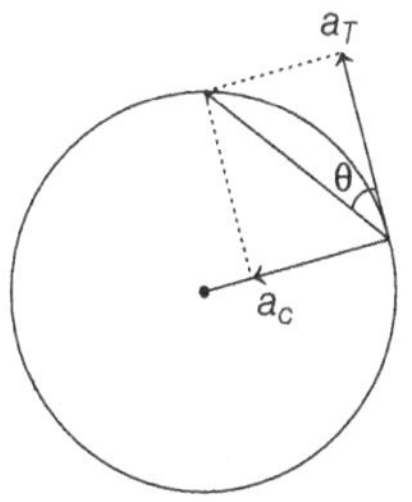

$$\tan\theta = \frac{(\alpha t)^2}{\alpha} = \alpha t^2 = 2\left(\frac{1}{2}\right)^2 = \frac{1}{2}$$

8. At the bottom most point,

$$T_1 - mg = \frac{mv_{bottom}^2}{R} \qquad \text{...(i)}$$

At the topmost point

$$mg + T_2 = \frac{mv_{top}^2}{R} \qquad \text{...(ii)}$$

Solving Eqs. (i) and (ii), we get

$$(T_1 - T_2) - 2mg = \frac{m(v_{\text{bottom}}^2 - v_{\text{top}}^2)}{R}$$

$\Rightarrow \quad T_1 - T_2 = 6mg$

$\Rightarrow \quad 720 = 6m(10) \Rightarrow m = 12\text{ kg}$

9.

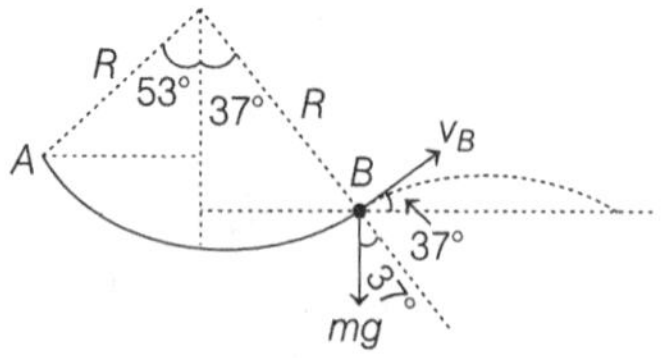

Using work - energy theorem between A and B,

$$W_{mg} + W_N = \Delta K$$

$$\Rightarrow +mg(R\cos 37° - R\cos 53°) + 0 = \frac{1}{2}mv_B^2 - 0 \Rightarrow v_B = \sqrt{\frac{2gR}{5}}$$

At B,

Centripetal accleration $= \dfrac{v_B^2}{r}$

$$\Rightarrow \quad g\cos 37° = \frac{(\sqrt{2gR/5})^2}{r} \Rightarrow r = \frac{R}{2}$$

10. Centripetal acceleration $= \mathbf{a} - \left(\dfrac{\mathbf{v}\cdot\mathbf{a}}{v^2}\right)\mathbf{v}$

$$= (2\hat{\mathbf{i}} + 4\hat{\mathbf{j}}) - \frac{4}{2^2}(2\hat{\mathbf{i}}) = 4\hat{\mathbf{j}}$$

Centripetal acceleration $= \dfrac{v^2}{r} = 4 \Rightarrow r = 1\text{ m}$

11. $\Sigma F_y = 0 \Rightarrow T\sin\alpha + N_1 = mg$

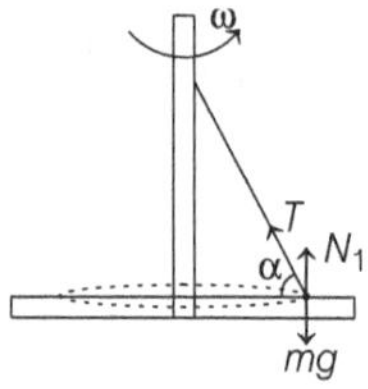

and $\quad \Sigma F_x = ma_x$

$\Rightarrow \quad T\cos\alpha = m\omega^2(l\cos\alpha)$

$\Rightarrow \quad T = m\omega^2 l = 1 \times 10^2 \times 0.1 = 10\text{N}$

$10\sin 30° + N_1 = 10 \Rightarrow N_1 = 5\text{ N}$

12. $v^2 = u^2 - 2gl(1 - \cos\theta)$

$\Rightarrow \quad v^2 = 4gl - 2gl(1 - \cos\theta) \quad$ ...(i)

$mg\cos(180° - \theta) + T = \dfrac{mv^2}{l} \Rightarrow v^2 = -gl\cos\theta \quad$ ...(ii)

From Eqs. (i) and (ii), we get

$$\cos\theta = -\frac{2}{3} \text{ and } v = \sqrt{\frac{2gl}{3}}$$

$$H_{max} = \frac{u^2\sin^2\theta}{2g} = \frac{(\sqrt{2gl/3})^2\left(\frac{5}{9}\right)}{2g} = \frac{5l}{27}$$

Maximum height from bottom,

$$= l + l\cos(180° - \theta) + \frac{5l}{27} = \frac{50l}{27}$$

13. $\omega = \theta^2 + 2\theta \Rightarrow \alpha = \omega\dfrac{d\omega}{d\theta} = (\theta^2 + 2\theta)(2\theta + 2)$

At $\theta = 1$, $\alpha = 12\text{ rad/s}^2$

14. $T = \dfrac{2u\sin\theta}{g} = \dfrac{2 \times 10 \times \frac{1}{\sqrt{2}}}{10} = \sqrt{2}\text{s}$

At $t = \dfrac{1}{\sqrt{2}}$, it will be at its highest point

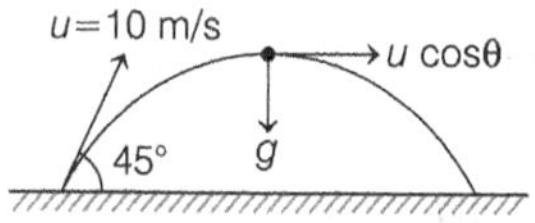

$$a_c = \frac{v_\perp^2}{R} \Rightarrow R = \frac{v_\perp^2}{g} \Rightarrow R = \frac{(10\cos 45°)^2}{10} \Rightarrow R = 5\text{m}$$

15. $v_2 = \omega r_2 \Rightarrow 720 \times \dfrac{5}{18} = \omega(1200) \Rightarrow \omega = \dfrac{1}{6}\text{ rad/s}$

$$a_3 = \omega^2 r = \left(\frac{1}{6}\right)^2 \times 1800 = 50\text{ m/s}^2$$

16. $v^2 = u^2 - 2gR(1 - \cos\theta) \Rightarrow v = \sqrt{3gR}$

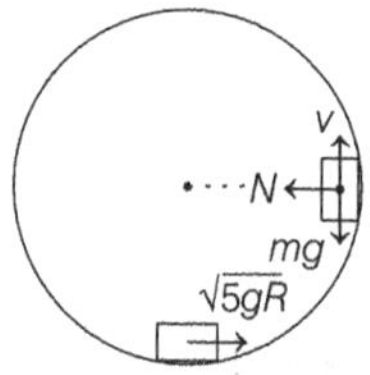

Centripetal acceleration $= \dfrac{v^2}{R} = 3g$

Tangential acceleration $= g$

Net acceleration $= \sqrt{(3g)^2 + g^2} = g\sqrt{10}$

17. For conical pendulum,

$$T = 2\pi\sqrt{\frac{l\cos\theta}{g_{\text{eff}}}} \Rightarrow 2 = 2\pi\sqrt{\frac{2}{g - a}}$$

$\Rightarrow \quad 2\pi^2 = g - a \Rightarrow g - a = 20 \Rightarrow a = -10\text{ m/s}^2$

18. Applying work-energy theorem,

$$W_{mg} + W_N = \Delta K$$

$\Rightarrow \quad +mg(2h) + 0 = \dfrac{1}{2}mv^2 - 0 \Rightarrow v = \sqrt{4gh}$

Along radial direction,

$$mg\cos\theta - N = \frac{mv^2}{R}$$

$\Rightarrow \quad mg\left(\dfrac{R-h}{R}\right) = \dfrac{m(\sqrt{4gh})^2}{R} \quad (\because N = 0)$

$\Rightarrow \quad h = \dfrac{R}{5} = \dfrac{2}{5} = 0.4\text{ m} \Rightarrow h = 40\text{ cm}$

19.

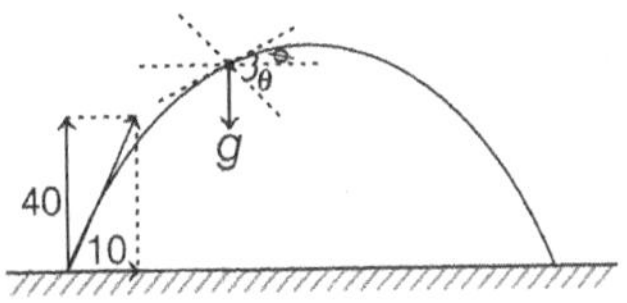

Normal component of acceleration $= g\cos\phi$

Tangential component of acceleration $= g\sin\phi$

$$g\cos\phi = g\sin\phi \Rightarrow \tan\phi = 1 \Rightarrow \phi = 45°$$

$$\tan\phi = \frac{v_y}{v_x} = \frac{40-10t}{10} = 1 \Rightarrow t = 3\text{ s}$$

20.

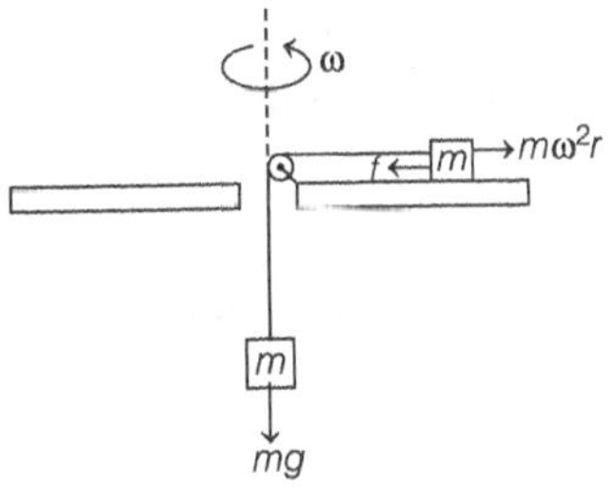

If $m\omega^2 r > mg$, then friction direction on the block on the table will be radially inwards.

So, $m\omega^2 r = mg + f \Rightarrow m\omega^2 r_{max} = mg + \mu_s mg$

$$\Rightarrow \quad r_{max} = \frac{(1+\mu_s)g}{\omega^2}$$

If $mg > m\omega^2 r$, then friction direction on the block on the table will be radially outwards.

So, $mg = m\omega^2 r + f \Rightarrow m\omega^2 r_{min} = mg - \mu_s mg$

$$\Rightarrow \quad r_{min} = \frac{(1-\mu_s)g}{\omega^2}$$

$$\therefore \quad r_{max} - r_{min} = \frac{2\mu_s g}{\omega^2} = \frac{2(0.8)10}{2^2} = 4$$

Level 3

Single Choice Correct Questions

1. $v^2 = u^2 + 2as \Rightarrow v^2 = 0^2 + 2(0.5)\left(\frac{1}{10}2\pi R\right)$

$$\Rightarrow \quad v = \sqrt{\frac{\pi R}{5}}$$

$$\Rightarrow \quad a_T = \frac{dv}{dt} = a = 0.5\text{ m/s}^2$$

$$a_c = \frac{v^2}{R} = \frac{(\sqrt{\pi R/5})^2}{R} = \frac{\pi}{5}$$

$$\therefore \quad a = \sqrt{a_T^2 + a_c^2} = \sqrt{(0.5)^2 + \left(\frac{\pi}{5}\right)^2} \approx 0.8\text{ m/s}^2$$

2. $\theta_A \propto t^2 \Rightarrow \omega_A \propto t \Rightarrow \alpha_A = \text{constant}$

$\theta_B \propto t \Rightarrow \omega_B = \text{constant} \Rightarrow \alpha_B = 0$

$$\theta_A = \omega_{0A}t + \frac{1}{2}\alpha_A t^2$$

$$\Rightarrow \quad 2\pi = 0 + \frac{1}{2}\alpha_A(\sqrt{\pi})^2$$

$$\Rightarrow \quad \alpha_A = 4\text{ rad/s}^2$$

$$\omega_A = \omega_{0A} + \alpha_A t \Rightarrow \omega_A = 0 + 4\times 5$$

$$\Rightarrow \quad \omega_A = 20\text{ rad/s}$$

$$\omega_B = \frac{\Delta\theta}{\Delta t} = \frac{\pi}{4\pi} = \frac{1}{4}\text{ rad/s}^2$$

$$\therefore \quad \omega_A : \omega_B = 20 : \frac{1}{4} = 80 : 1$$

3. $K = as^2 \Rightarrow \frac{1}{2}mv^2 = a^2 s \Rightarrow v = \left(\frac{2a}{m}\right)^{1/2} s$

$$a_c = \frac{v^2}{R} = \frac{2as^2}{mR}$$

$$a_T = v\frac{dv}{ds} = \left(\frac{2a}{m}\right)^{1/2} s\left(\frac{2a}{m}\right)^{1/2} = \frac{2as}{m}$$

$$F = ma = m\sqrt{a_c^2 + a_T^2} = m\sqrt{\left(\frac{2as^2}{mR}\right)^2 + \left(\frac{2as}{m}\right)^2}$$

$$= 2as\left(1 + \frac{s^2}{R^2}\right)^{1/2}$$

4. $v = a\sqrt{s}$

$$a_c = \frac{v^2}{R} = \frac{a^2 s}{R}$$

$$a_T = v\frac{dv}{ds} = a\sqrt{s}\frac{a}{2\sqrt{s}} = \frac{a^2}{2}$$

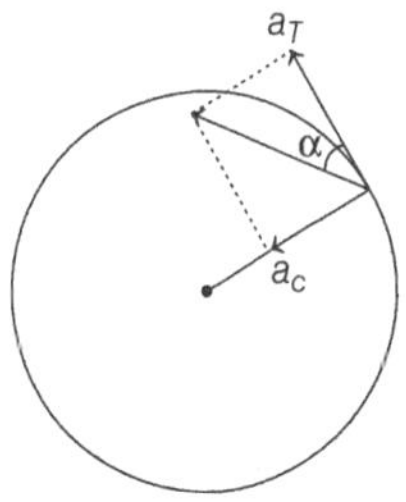

$$\tan\alpha = \frac{a_c}{a_T} = \frac{a^2 s/R}{a^2/2} = \frac{2s}{R}$$

5. $\tan 45° = \frac{a_c}{a_T} \Rightarrow 1 = \frac{v^2/R}{dv/dt} \Rightarrow \frac{dv}{dt} = \frac{v^2}{R}$

$$\Rightarrow \int_{v_0}^{v}\frac{dv}{v^2} = \frac{1}{R}\int_0^t dt \Rightarrow \frac{1}{v_0} - \frac{1}{v} = \frac{t}{R} \Rightarrow \frac{1}{v} = \frac{1}{v_0} - \frac{t}{R}$$

$$\Rightarrow \quad v = \frac{v_0 R}{R - v_0 t}$$

$$\Rightarrow \quad \frac{ds}{dt} = \frac{v_0 R}{R - v_0 t} \Rightarrow \int_0^{2\pi R} ds = v_0 R\int_0^T \frac{dt}{R - v_0 t}$$

$$\Rightarrow [s]_0^{2\pi R} = \frac{v_0 R}{-v_0}[\ln(R - v_0 t)]_0^T$$

$$\Rightarrow \qquad 2\pi R - 0 = -R\ln\left(\frac{R - v_0 T}{R}\right)$$

$$\Rightarrow \qquad R - v_0 T = Re^{-2\pi} \Rightarrow T = \frac{R}{v_0}(1 - e^{-2\pi})$$

6. $v = 2t^2$

$$a_T = \frac{dv}{dt} = 4t, \quad a_c = \frac{v^2}{R} = \frac{(2t^2)^2}{R} = \frac{4t^4}{R}$$

At $t = 1$, $a_T = 4\ \text{m/s}^2$, $a_c = 4\ \text{m/s}^2$

$$\therefore \qquad a = \sqrt{4^2 + 4^2} = 4\sqrt{2}\ \text{m/s}^2$$

$$f = ma = m(4\sqrt{2})$$

For sliding to take place,

$$f = f_L \Rightarrow m(4\sqrt{2}) = \mu mg \Rightarrow \mu = \frac{2\sqrt{2}}{5}$$

7. $a_c \propto t^n \Rightarrow \dfrac{v^2}{R} \propto t^n \Rightarrow v \propto t^{\frac{n}{2}} \Rightarrow \dfrac{dv}{dt} \propto t^{\frac{n}{2}-1}$

$$P = F_T v\cos\theta \Rightarrow P \propto a_T v \Rightarrow P \propto (t^{\frac{n}{2}-1})(t^{n/2}) \Rightarrow P \propto t^{n-1}$$

8. $\mathbf{v} = a\hat{\mathbf{i}} + bt\hat{\mathbf{j}}$

$$\mathbf{a} = \frac{d\mathbf{v}}{dt} = b\hat{\mathbf{j}}$$

$$\Rightarrow \qquad a_T = \frac{\mathbf{a}\cdot\mathbf{v}}{v} = \frac{(b\hat{\mathbf{j}})\cdot(a\hat{\mathbf{i}} + bt\hat{\mathbf{j}})}{\sqrt{a^2 + b^2t^2}} = \frac{b^2t}{\sqrt{a^2 + b^2t^2}}$$

At $t = \dfrac{\sqrt{3}a}{b}$, $a_T = \dfrac{\sqrt{3}b}{2}$

$$\Rightarrow \qquad a_c = \sqrt{a^2 - a_T^2} = \sqrt{b^2 - \left(\frac{\sqrt{3}b}{2}\right)^2} = \frac{b}{2}$$

9. Instantaneous acceleration $= \dfrac{v^2}{R}$

$$\text{Average acceleration} = \frac{\Delta \mathbf{v}}{\Delta t} = \frac{2v\sin\left(\frac{\theta}{2}\right)}{\left(\frac{\pi}{3}R\right)/v} = \frac{3v^2}{\pi R}$$

$$\frac{\text{Instantaneous acceleration}}{\text{Average acceleration}} = \frac{v^2/R}{3v^2/\pi R} = \frac{\pi}{3}$$

10. $v_R = \dfrac{dr}{dt} = 2\ \text{m/s}$,

$$v_T = \omega r = \frac{d\theta}{dt}r = 4(2) = 8\ \text{m/s}$$

$$v = \sqrt{v_R^2 + v_T^2} = \sqrt{2^2 + 8^2} = \sqrt{68}\ \text{m/s} \simeq 8.25\ \text{m/s}$$

11. $\dfrac{dr}{dt} = v\cos\theta = \mathbf{v}\cdot\hat{\mathbf{r}}$

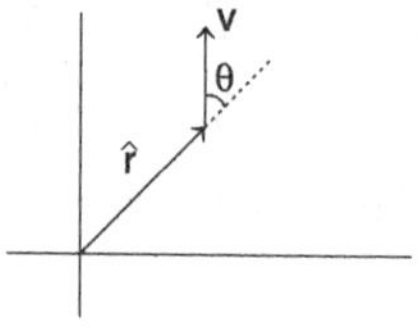

12. $\omega = \dfrac{v_\perp}{r} = \dfrac{40\cos 30^\circ}{30/\cos 30^\circ}$

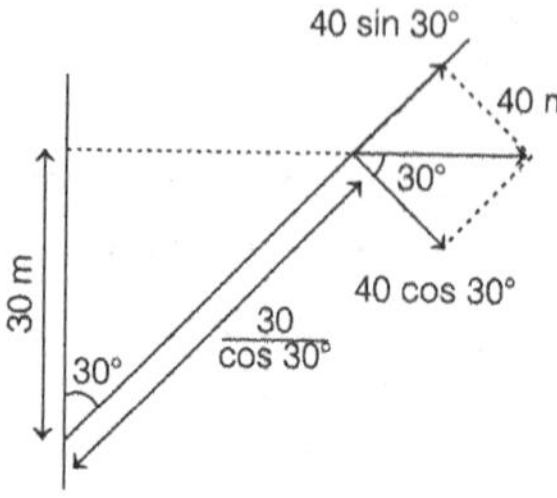

$$\omega = 1\ \text{rad/s}$$

13. $\mathbf{v}_1 = \omega R\sin(2\pi - \theta)\hat{\mathbf{i}} + \omega R\cos(2\pi - \theta)\hat{\mathbf{j}}$

$$\mathbf{v}_2 = \frac{\omega R}{2}\hat{\mathbf{j}}$$

$$\mathbf{v}_{12} = \omega R\sin\theta\hat{\mathbf{i}} + \omega R\left(-\cos\theta - \frac{1}{2}\right)\hat{\mathbf{j}}$$

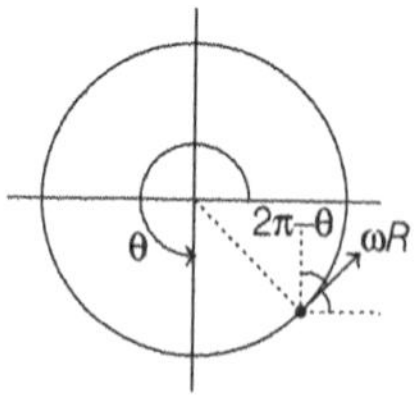

$$\Rightarrow \qquad -\cos\theta - \frac{1}{2} = 0$$

$$\Rightarrow \qquad \cos\theta = -\frac{1}{2} \Rightarrow \theta = 2\pi - \frac{\pi}{3}$$

$$\Rightarrow \qquad \theta = \frac{5\pi}{3} \Rightarrow t = \frac{\theta}{\omega} = \frac{5\pi}{3\omega}$$

14.

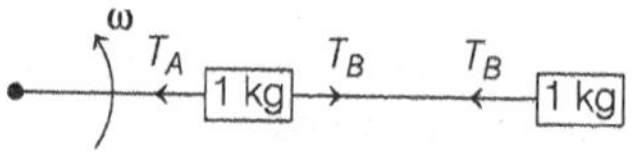

Since $T_A > T_B$; string A is likely to break first,

$$T_A - T_B = 1 \times \omega^2 \times 1 \qquad \text{...(i)}$$

$$T_B = 1 \times \omega^2 \times 2 \qquad \text{...(ii)}$$

From Eqs. (i) and (ii), we get

$$T_A = 3\omega^2 \Rightarrow 3\omega^2 = 75 \Rightarrow \omega = 5\ \text{rad/s}$$

15. Linear speed of tape $= \dfrac{120}{2 \times 3600} = \dfrac{1}{60}$ m/s

At $t = 0$, area of reel $= \pi(12\sqrt{2})^2 - \pi(5\sqrt{2})^2 = 238\pi\ \text{cm}^2$

Angular speed will be same when radius is same.

$$\Rightarrow \quad \pi r^2 - \pi(5\sqrt{2})^2 + \pi r^2 - \pi(5\sqrt{2})^2 = 238\pi$$

$$\Rightarrow \qquad r = 13\ \text{cm}$$

$$\therefore \qquad \omega = \frac{v}{r} = \frac{1/60}{13 \times 10^{-2}} = \frac{5}{39}\ \text{rad/s}$$

16.

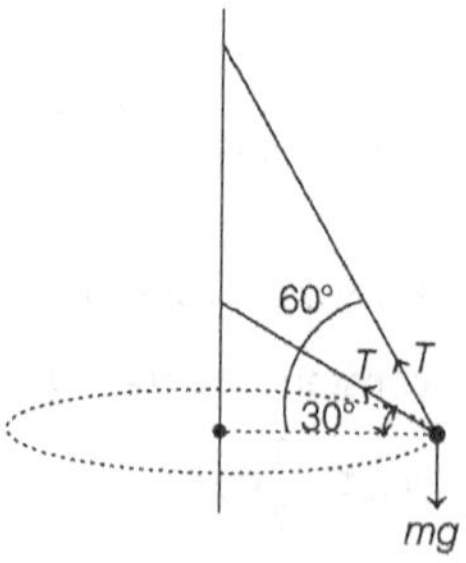

$$\Sigma F_y = 0$$

$$\Rightarrow \quad T\sin 60° + T\sin 30° = mg \quad ...(i)$$

$$\Sigma F_x = ma_x \quad \Rightarrow T\cos 60° + T\cos 30° = \frac{mv^2}{r} \quad ...(ii)$$

From Eqs. (i) and (ii), we get

$$v = \sqrt{gr}$$

17. A rod can exert force in any direction. Lets take components of force to be F_x and F_y.

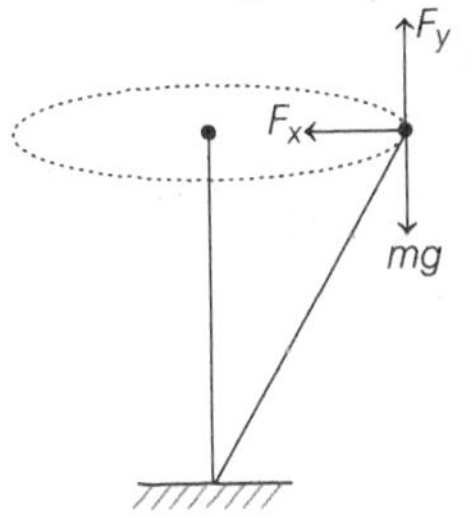

$$\Sigma F_y = 0 \quad \Rightarrow F_y - mg = 0 \quad \Rightarrow \quad F_y = mg = 100\text{ N}$$

$$\Sigma F_x = ma_x$$

$$\Rightarrow \quad F_x = m\omega^2 r = 10\left(\frac{2\pi}{1.57}\right)^2 (1\sin 30°) = 80\text{N}$$

$$\therefore \quad F = \sqrt{F_x{}^2 + F_y{}^2} = \sqrt{100^2 + 80^2} \simeq 128\text{N}$$

18. For conical pendulum,

$$T = 2\pi\sqrt{\frac{L\cos\theta}{g}}$$

Since, $T_1 = T_2 \quad \Rightarrow L_1\cos\theta_1 = L_2\cos\theta_2$

$$\Rightarrow \quad \frac{L_1}{L_2} = \frac{\cos\theta_2}{\cos\theta_1} = \frac{\cos 45°}{\cos 30°} = \frac{1/\sqrt{2}}{\sqrt{3}/2} = \sqrt{\frac{2}{3}}$$

19. Lets take an element of angular width $d\theta$ on the ring.

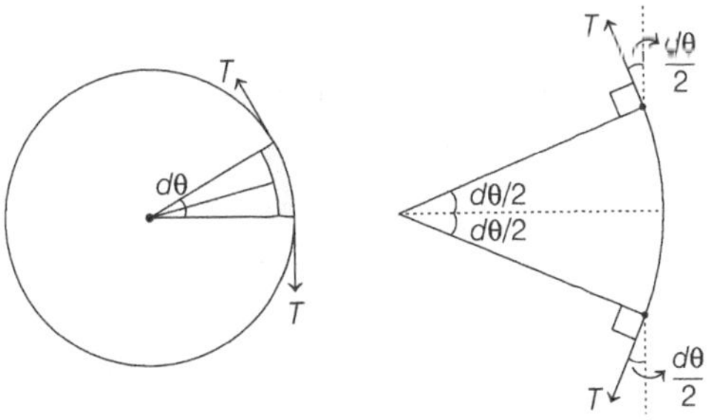

Net force on this element is $2T\sin\left(\frac{d\theta}{2}\right)$ towards the centre.

$$2T\sin\left(\frac{d\theta}{2}\right) = dm\omega^2 R$$

$$\Rightarrow \quad 2T\frac{d\theta}{2} = (\lambda R d\theta)\omega^2 R \quad \Rightarrow T = \lambda\omega^2 R^2$$

20. $\omega = \frac{\theta}{t} = \frac{28 \times 2\pi}{44} = 4\text{rad / s}$

Tangential speed $= \omega r = 4(0.5) = 2\text{m / s}$

Horizontal range $= uT = 2 \times \sqrt{\frac{2(2.5)}{10}} = \sqrt{2}$ m

Radius of circle where drops hit $= \sqrt{(0.5)^2 + (\sqrt{2})^2} = 1.5$m

21. $\Sigma F_y = 0 \quad \Rightarrow \quad T\cos 30° = mg$ ...(i)

$\Sigma F_x = ma_x \quad \Rightarrow \quad T\sin 30° = m\omega^2(R + R\sin 30°)$ ...(ii)

From Eqs. (i) and (ii), we get

$$\omega = \sqrt{\frac{2g}{3\sqrt{3}R}}$$

22. Since, we have to find maximum angular speed, bead has the tandency to slide up the hoop. So, friction will act down.

$\Sigma F_y = 0 \quad \Rightarrow \quad N\cos 45° = mg + f_L\sin 45°$ ...(i)

$\Sigma F_x = ma_x$

$\Rightarrow \quad N\sin 45° + f_L\cos 45° = m\omega^2(R\sin 45°)$ ...(ii)

$f_L = \mu N$ ...(iii)

Solving Eqs. (i), (ii) and (iii), we get

$$\omega = (30\sqrt{2})^{1/2}$$

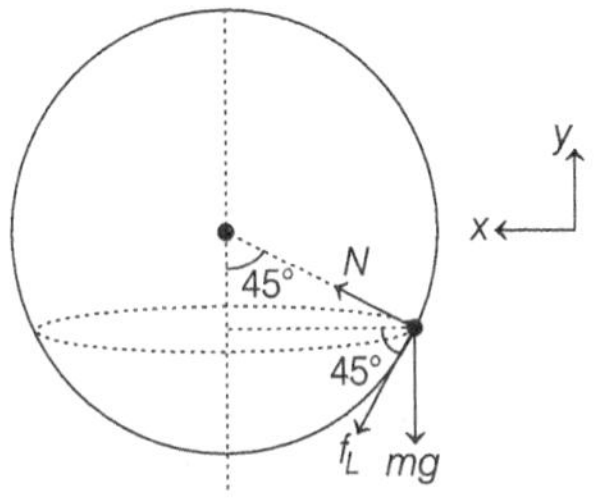

23.

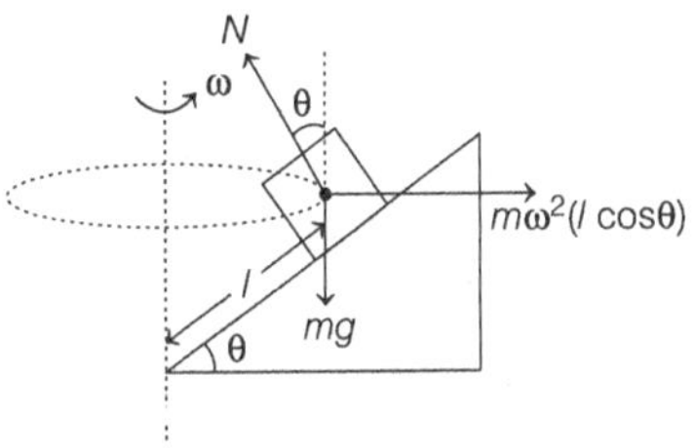

Centrifugal force on the block $= m\omega^2(l\cos\theta)$

$\Sigma F_y = 0 \quad \Rightarrow N\cos\theta = mg$ ...(i)

$\Sigma F_x = 0 \quad \Rightarrow N\sin\theta = m\omega^2 l\cos\theta$ ...(ii)

From Eqs. (i) and (ii), we get

$$\omega = \sqrt{\frac{g\sin\theta}{l\cos^2\theta}}$$

24.

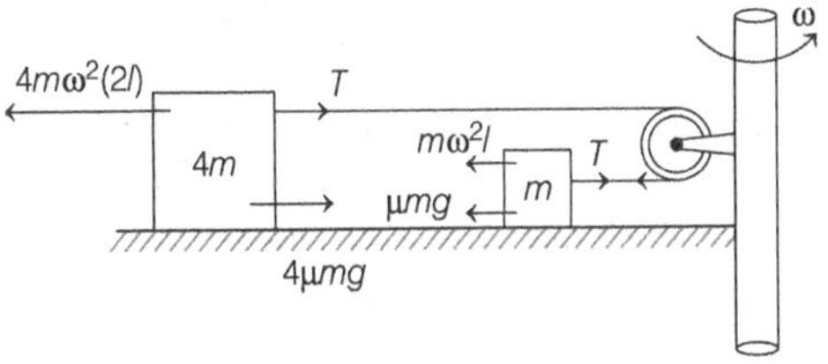

For m block,

$\Sigma F = 0 \quad \Rightarrow T = \mu mg + m\omega^2 l$ ...(i)

For 4m block,

$$8m\omega^2 l = 4\mu mg + T \quad \text{...(ii)}$$

Solving Eqs. (i) and (ii), we get

$$\Rightarrow \quad 7m\omega^2 l = 5\mu mg \Rightarrow \omega = \sqrt{\frac{5\mu g}{7l}}$$

25. $\tan\theta = \frac{v^2}{rg} = \frac{15^2}{150 \times 10} = \frac{3}{20}$

For pendulum,

$$T\cos\theta = mg \quad \text{...(i)}$$

$$T\sin\theta = m\frac{v^2}{r} \quad \text{...(ii)}$$

Solving Eqs. (i) and (ii), we get

$$\tan\theta = \frac{v^2}{gr} = \frac{3}{20}$$

26. $v_A = \sqrt{\mu_A r_A g} = \sqrt{(0.1)(100)(10)} = 10\text{m / s}$

$$v_B = \sqrt{\mu_B r_B g} = \sqrt{(0.2)(200)(10)} = 20\text{m / s}$$

$$T_A = \frac{100\pi + \pi(100) + 100\pi}{10} = 30\pi$$

$$T_B = \frac{100\pi + \pi(200) + 100\pi}{20} = 20\pi$$

27. At extreme position,

$$T_{min} - mg\cos\theta = \frac{m(0)^2}{l} \Rightarrow T_{min} = mg\cos\theta \quad \text{...(i)}$$

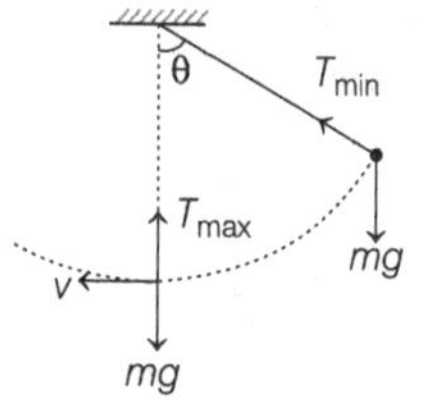

At mean position, $T_{max} - mg = \frac{mv^2}{l}$

and $v^2 = 2gl(1 - \cos\theta)$ [from work - energy theorem]

$$\Rightarrow \quad T_{max} - mg = \frac{m}{l}(2gl(1-\cos\theta))$$

$$\Rightarrow \quad T_{max} = (3 - 2\cos\theta)mg \quad \text{...(ii)}$$

Dividing Eqs. (ii) by (i), we get

$$\Rightarrow \quad \frac{T_{max}}{T_{min}} = \frac{(3-2\cos\theta)mg}{mg\cos\theta} = 3$$

$$\Rightarrow \quad \cos\theta = \frac{3}{5} \Rightarrow \theta = \cos^{-1}\left(\frac{3}{5}\right)$$

28. At position A, before cutting the cord

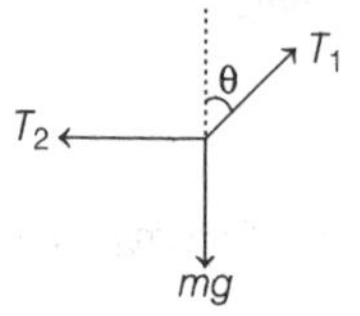

$$\Sigma F_y = 0 \Rightarrow T_1\cos\theta = mg \Rightarrow T_1 = \frac{mg}{\cos\theta}$$

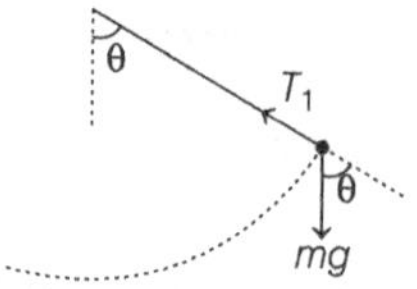

At position B,

$$T_1' - mg\cos\theta = \frac{m(0)^2}{r} \Rightarrow T_1' = mg\cos\theta$$

$$\therefore \quad \frac{T_1'}{T_1} = \frac{mg\cos\theta}{mg\sec\theta} = \cos^2\theta = \frac{3}{4}$$

29.

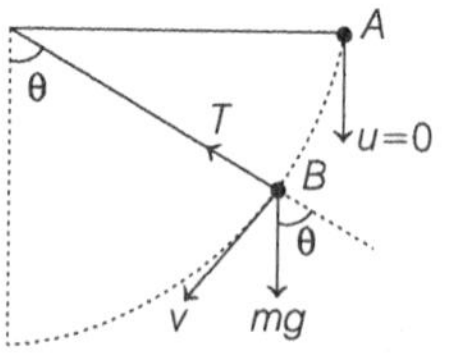

Using work - energy theorem between A and B,

$$W_{mg} + W_T = \Delta K$$

$$\Rightarrow +mgl\cos\theta + 0 = \frac{1}{2}mv^2 - 0 \Rightarrow v = \sqrt{2gl\cos\theta}$$

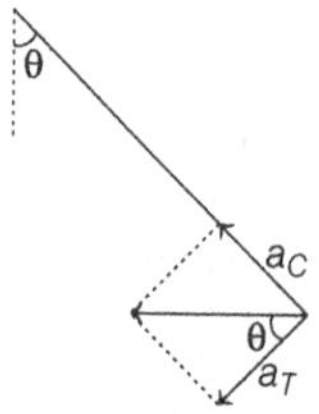

$$\tan\theta = \frac{a_c}{a_T} \Rightarrow \tan\theta = \frac{v^2/l}{g\sin\theta} \Rightarrow \tan\theta = \frac{2}{\tan\theta}$$

$$\Rightarrow \quad \theta = \tan^{-1}(\sqrt{2})$$

30. Tension in the string will be maximum, when the string is vertical.

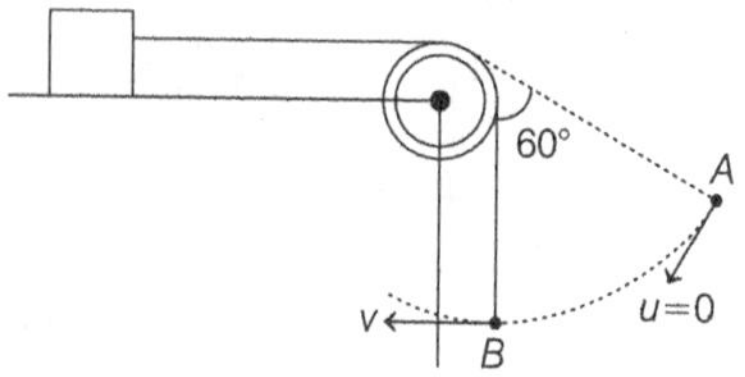

Using work - energy theorem between A and B

$$W_{mg} + W_T = \Delta K$$

$$\Rightarrow \quad +mgl(1-\cos 60°) + 0 = \frac{1}{2}mv^2 - 0 \Rightarrow v = \sqrt{gl}$$

At B,

$$T - mg = \frac{mv^2}{l} \Rightarrow T - mg = \frac{m(\sqrt{gl})^2}{l}$$

$$\Rightarrow \quad T = 2mg = 2(2)(10) = 40\text{ N}$$

For 8 kg, $\quad T = F = 40\text{ N}$

$$f \le f_L \Rightarrow 40 \le \mu(8 \times 10) \Rightarrow \mu \ge 0.5 \Rightarrow \mu_{min} = 0.5$$

31. Using work - energy theorem between A and B,

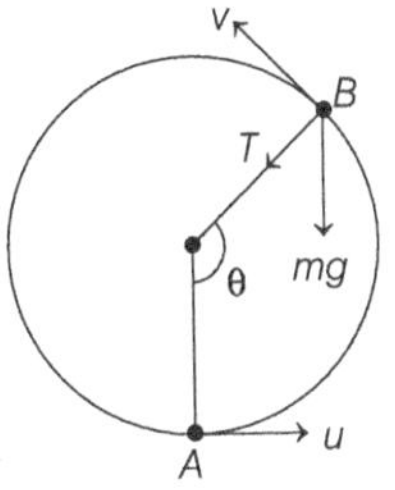

$$W_{mg} + W_T = \Delta K$$

$$\Rightarrow -mg[l + l\cos(180° - \theta)] + 0 = \frac{1}{2}mv^2 - \frac{1}{2}mu^2$$

$$\Rightarrow \quad v^2 = u^2 - 2gl(1 - \cos\theta) \quad \text{...(i)}$$

At B, $\quad mg\cos(180° - \theta) + T = \dfrac{mv^2}{l}$

For string to become slack ($T = 0$)

$$\Rightarrow \quad -mg\cos\theta + 0 = \frac{mv^2}{l} \Rightarrow v^2 = -gl\cos\theta \quad \text{...(ii)}$$

From Eqs (i) and (ii), we get

$$-gl\cos\theta = u^2 - 2gl(1 - \cos\theta)$$

$$\Rightarrow \quad \cos\theta = \frac{2gl - u^2}{3gl} \Rightarrow \theta = \cos^{-1}\left(\frac{-1}{\sqrt{3}}\right)$$

32. Using work - energy theorem,

$$v^2 = 3gl - 2gl(1 + \cos\theta) \quad \text{...(i)}$$

At B,

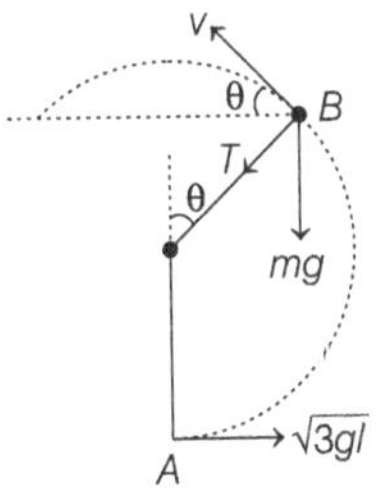

$$mg\cos\theta + T = \frac{mv^2}{l} \Rightarrow mg\cos\theta + 0 = \frac{mv^2}{l}$$

$$\Rightarrow \quad v^2 = gl\cos\theta \quad \text{...(ii)}$$

From Eqs. (i) and (ii), we get

$$gl\cos\theta = 3gl - 2gl(1 + \cos\theta) \Rightarrow \cos\theta = \frac{1}{3} \text{and } v = \sqrt{\frac{gl}{3}}$$

After string becomes slack, the particle will follow parabolic trajectory and speed will be minimum at the highest point.

$$v_{min} = v\cos\theta = \sqrt{\frac{gl}{3}}\left(\frac{1}{3}\right) = \sqrt{\frac{gl}{27}}$$

33. Using work - energy theorem between A and B,

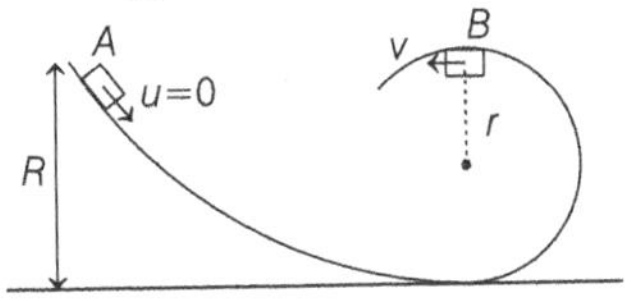

$$W_{mg} + W_N = \Delta K \Rightarrow +mg(R - 2r) + 0 = \frac{1}{2}mv^2 - 0$$

$$\Rightarrow \quad v = \sqrt{2g(R - 2r)}$$

At B,

$$N + mg = \frac{mv^2}{r} \Rightarrow 0 + mg = \frac{mv^2}{r}$$

$$\Rightarrow \quad v = \sqrt{gr}$$

$$v = \sqrt{2g(R - 2r)} = \sqrt{gr}$$

$$\Rightarrow \quad 2R - 4r = r \Rightarrow \frac{R}{r} = \frac{5}{2}$$

34. Using work - energy theorem between A and B, we get

$$v^2 = u^2 - 2gl(1 + \cos\theta) \quad \text{...(i)}$$

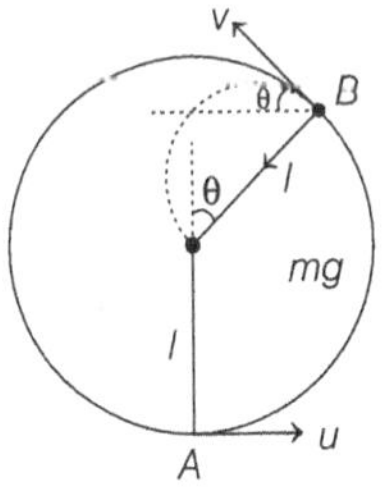

At B,

$$mg\cos\theta + T = \frac{mv^2}{l} \Rightarrow v^2 = gl\cos\theta \quad \text{...(ii)} \ (\because T = 0)$$

$$y = x\tan\theta - \frac{gx^2}{2u^2\cos^2\theta}$$

$$-l\cos\theta = (l\sin\theta)\tan\theta - \frac{g(l\sin\theta)^2}{2v^2\cos^2\theta} \quad \text{...(iii)}$$

Solving Eqs. (i), (ii) and (iii), we get

$$u = [(2 + \sqrt{3})gl]^{1/2}$$

35. Using work - energy theorem,

$$W_{mg} + W_T = \Delta K$$

$$\Rightarrow (-mg(4l) - mg(2l) + 0 = (0 + 0) - \left(\frac{1}{2}mv_0^2 + \frac{1}{2}m\left(\frac{v_0}{2}\right)^2\right)$$

$$\Rightarrow \quad v_0 = \sqrt{\frac{48gl}{5}}$$

36. Using work - energy theorem between B and A,

$$W_{mg} + W_N + W_{spring} = \Delta K$$

$$\Rightarrow \quad 0 + 0 + \frac{1}{2} \times 200(6^2 - 0^2) = \frac{1}{2} \times 2 \times v^2 - 0$$

$$\Rightarrow \quad v = 60 \text{ m/s}$$

At A,

$$N = \frac{mv^2}{R} = \frac{2 \times 60^2}{5} = 1440 \text{ N}$$

37. Using work-energy theorem,

$$W_{mg} + W_N + W_{spring} = \Delta K$$

$$\Rightarrow \quad +mgR(1 - \cos 60°) + 0 + 0 = \frac{1}{2}mv^2 - 0$$

$$\Rightarrow \quad v = \sqrt{gR}$$

At B,

$$Kx + mg\cos\theta - N = \frac{mv^2}{R}$$

$$\Rightarrow \quad 20(2-l) + 2\times 10\times\frac{1}{2} - 0 = \frac{2(\sqrt{10\times 2})^2}{2} \quad \Rightarrow l = 1.5 \text{ m}$$

38. Using work - energy theorem between A and B,

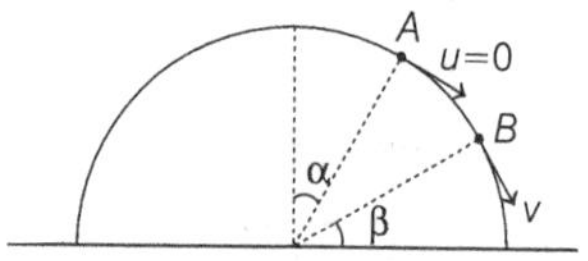

$$W_{mg} + W_N = \Delta K$$

$$\Rightarrow +mg(r\cos\alpha - r\sin\beta) + 0 = \frac{1}{2}mv^2 - 0$$

$$\Rightarrow \quad v^2 = 2gr(\cos\alpha - \sin\beta) \quad \text{...(i)}$$

At B,

$$mg\sin\beta - N = \frac{mv^2}{r}$$

$$\Rightarrow \quad v^2 = gr\sin\beta \quad (\because N = 0) \text{...(ii)}$$

From Eqs. (i) and (ii), we get

$$3\sin\beta = 2\cos\alpha$$

39. $x = v_C T = v_C\sqrt{\frac{2H}{g}}$

$$\Rightarrow \quad 3R = v_C\sqrt{\frac{2(2R)}{g}} \quad \Rightarrow \quad v_C = \frac{3}{2}\sqrt{gr}$$

and using work-energy theorem between B and C,

$$W_{mg} + W_N = \Delta K$$

$$\Rightarrow \quad -mg2R + 0 = \frac{1}{2}m\left(\frac{3}{2}\sqrt{gR}\right)^2 - \frac{1}{2}mu^2$$

$$\Rightarrow \quad u = \frac{5}{2}\sqrt{gR}$$

40. At C,

$$N + mg = \frac{mv_C^2}{R}$$

For v_C to be minimum; $N = 0$

$$\Rightarrow \quad v_C = \sqrt{gR}$$

$$x_{min} = v_C\sqrt{\frac{2(2R)}{g}} = \sqrt{gR}\sqrt{\frac{2(2R)}{g}} = 2R$$

41. Using work-energy theorem between A and B,

$$W_{mg} + W_N = \Delta K$$

$$\Rightarrow +mgR\sin\theta + 0 = \frac{1}{2}mv^2 - 0 \quad \Rightarrow v = \sqrt{2gR\sin\theta}$$

At B,

$$\Rightarrow \quad N - mg\sin\theta = \frac{mv^2}{R} \quad \Rightarrow \quad N = 3mg\sin\theta$$

$$F_C = \frac{mv^2}{R} = 2mg\sin\theta$$

$$\therefore \quad \frac{F_C}{N} = \frac{2mg\sin\theta}{3mg\sin\theta} = \frac{2}{3}$$

42. At B,

$$kx\cos 30° + mg\cos 30° - N = \frac{mv_B^2}{R}$$

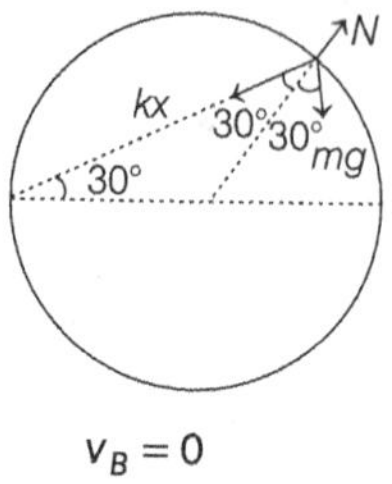

Since, $\quad v_B = 0$

$$\Rightarrow \quad N = kx\cos 30° + mg\cos 30°$$

$$\Rightarrow \quad N = \frac{(\sqrt{3}+1)mg}{R}(\sqrt{3}R - R)\cos 30° + mg\cos 30°$$

$$\Rightarrow \quad N = 3\sqrt{3}mg/2$$

43. First, we find velocity of particle when stning becomes horizontal using work - energy theorem,

$$W_{mg} + W_T = \Delta K$$

$$\Rightarrow \quad -mg(2a) + 0 = \frac{1}{2}mv_1^2 - \frac{1}{2}mv^2$$

$$v_1 = \sqrt{v^2 - 4ga}$$

Now to complete vertical circle around the peg, at the highest point, we make tension zero.

At the highest point,

$$mg + T = \frac{mv_2^2}{a} \quad \Rightarrow \quad v_2 = \sqrt{ga} \quad (\because T = 0)$$

Using work - energy theorem,

$$W_{mg} + W_T = \Delta K$$

$$\Rightarrow \quad -mga + 0 = \frac{1}{2}m(\sqrt{ga})^2 - \frac{1}{2}m(\sqrt{v^2 - 4ga})^2$$

$$\Rightarrow \quad v = \sqrt{7ga}$$

44. Using work - energy theorem,

$$W_{mg} + W_T = \Delta K \quad \Rightarrow \quad +mg(l\sin 30°) + 0 = \frac{1}{2}mv^2 - \frac{1}{2}mv_0^2$$

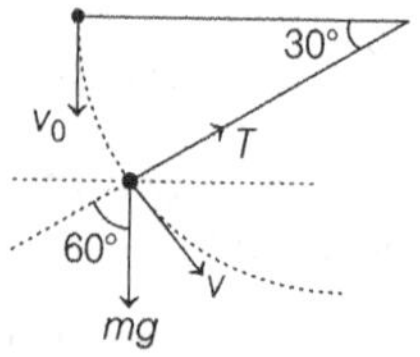

$$\Rightarrow \quad v = \sqrt{v_0^2 + gl}$$

$$\text{and } T - mg\cos 60° = \frac{mv^2}{l}$$

$$\Rightarrow \quad 3mg - \frac{mg}{2} = \frac{mv^2}{l} \quad \Rightarrow v = \sqrt{\frac{5gl}{2}}$$

$$\text{and} \quad \sqrt{\frac{5gl}{2}} = \sqrt{v_0^2 + gl}$$

$$\Rightarrow \quad v_0 = \sqrt{\frac{3gl}{2}} = \sqrt{\frac{3g}{2}} \quad (\because l = 1\text{m})$$

45. $\Sigma F_y = 0 \quad \Rightarrow \quad N = mg\cos\theta$

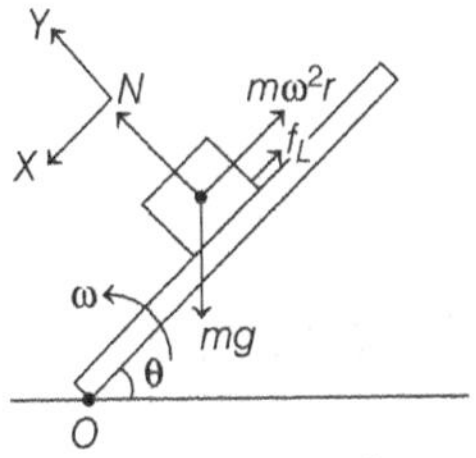

$$\Sigma F_x = 0 \quad \Rightarrow mg\sin\theta = m\omega^2 r + f_L$$

$$\Rightarrow mg\sin 37° = m(3)^2(0.5) + \mu(mg\cos 37°) \quad \Rightarrow \mu = \frac{3}{16}$$

46. Using work - energy theorem for either sphere

$$W_{mg} + W_N = \Delta K$$

$$\Rightarrow \quad +mgR(1-\cos 60°) + 0 = \frac{1}{2}mv^2 - 0 \quad \Rightarrow v = \sqrt{gR}$$

Using centripetal force equation for sphere,

$$N + mg\cos 60° = \frac{mv^2}{R} \quad \Rightarrow \quad N = \frac{mg}{2}$$

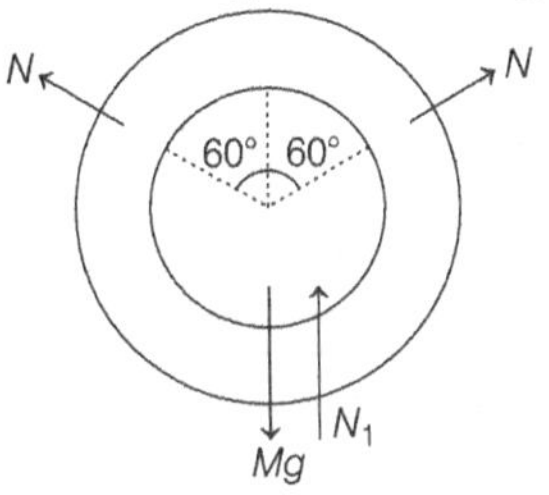

For tube,

$\Sigma F_y = 0 \quad \Rightarrow \quad 2N\cos 60° + N_1 = Mg \quad \Rightarrow N + N_1 = Mg$

For losing contact with ground $(N_1 = 0)$

$$N = Mg \quad \Rightarrow \quad \frac{mg}{2} = Mg \quad \Rightarrow \quad \frac{m}{M} = 2$$

47. At P, tangential acceleration is in the direction of velocity. So it will speed up at P. At R, tangential component of acceleration is opposite to velocity. So particle will slow down.

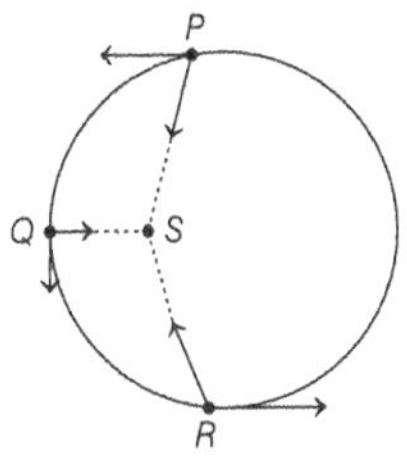

48.

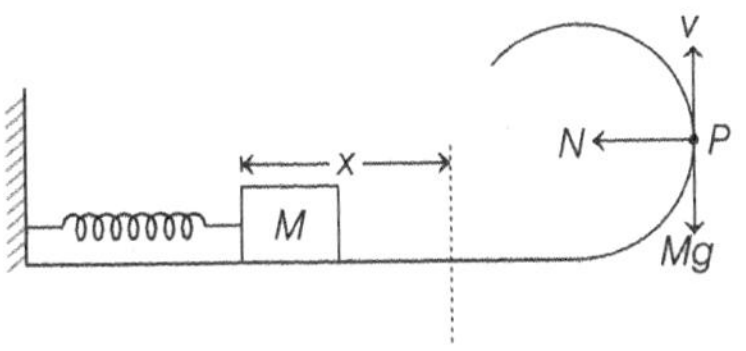

At P,

$$N = \frac{Mv^2}{R} \quad \Rightarrow \quad Mg = \frac{Mv^2}{R} \quad \Rightarrow v = \sqrt{gR}$$

Using work - energy theorem,

$$W_{mg} + W_N + W_{spring} = \Delta K$$

$$\Rightarrow \quad -MgR + 0 + \frac{1}{2}k(x^2 - 0^2) = \frac{1}{2}M(\sqrt{gR})^2 - 0$$

$$\Rightarrow \quad x = \sqrt{\frac{3MgR}{k}}$$

49. Along radial direction,

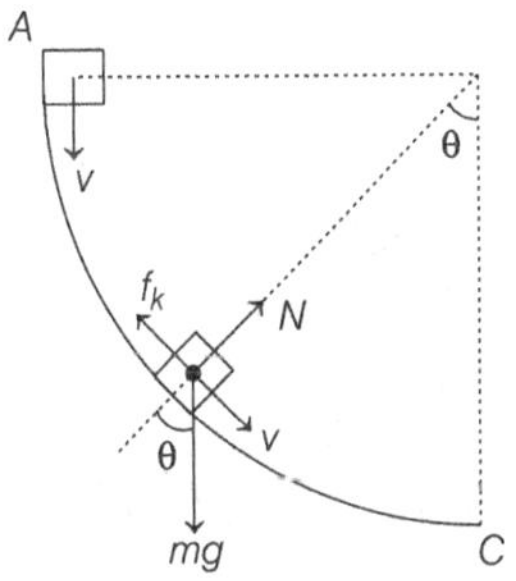

$$N - mg\cos\theta = \frac{mv^2}{R} \quad \Rightarrow \quad N = mg\cos\theta + \frac{mv^2}{R}$$

Along tangential direction,

$$mg\sin\theta - f_k = m(0)$$

$$\Rightarrow \quad mg\sin\theta = \mu\left(mg\cos\theta + \frac{mv^2}{R}\right) \quad \Rightarrow \quad \mu = \frac{\sin\theta}{\cos\theta + \frac{v^2}{gR}}$$

$$f_k = mg\sin\theta$$

$$P_{friction} = fv\cos\theta = (mg\sin\theta)v\cos 180° = -mg\sin\theta v$$

Using work - energy theorem from A and C,

$$W_{mg} + W_N + W_{friction} = \Delta K$$

$$\Rightarrow \quad +mgR + 0 + W_{friction} = \frac{1}{2}mv^2 - \frac{1}{2}mv^2$$

$$\Rightarrow \quad W_{friction} = -mgR$$

50. Using work-energy theorem between A and B,

$$W_{mg} + W_N + W_{spring} = \Delta K$$

$$\Rightarrow +mg(2R) + 0 + \frac{1}{2}\frac{mg}{R}(R^2 - (0)^2) = \frac{1}{2}mv^2 - 0 \Rightarrow v = \sqrt{5gR}$$

At B,

$$N + k(0) - mg = \frac{m(\sqrt{5gR})^2}{R} \quad \Rightarrow N = 6mg$$

51. $v = \sqrt{5g_{eff}l} = \sqrt{5(g\sin 30°)l} = \sqrt{\frac{5gl}{2}}$

52. For clockwise motion,

$$T + mg\cos 60° = \frac{mv_c^2}{R} \quad \Rightarrow \quad v_c = \sqrt{\frac{gR}{2}}$$

($\because T = 0$ for v_c to be minimum)

For anti-clockwise motion,

When string becomes vertical

$$mg + T = \frac{mv_{top}^2}{R} \quad \Rightarrow \quad v_{top} = \sqrt{gR}$$

($\because T = 0$ for v_{top} to be minimum)

Using work - energy theorem, $W_{mg} + W_T = \Delta K$

$$\Rightarrow -mgR(1 - \sin 30°) + 0 = \frac{1}{2}m(\sqrt{gR})^2 - \frac{1}{2}mv_a^2$$

$$\Rightarrow \quad v_a = \sqrt{2gR}$$

$$\therefore \quad \frac{v_c}{v_a} = \frac{\sqrt{gR/2}}{\sqrt{2gR}} = \frac{1}{2}$$

53. From work-energy theorem,

$$v^2 = u^2 - 2gR(1 - \cos\theta)$$

$$\Rightarrow \quad v^2 = 4gR - 2gR(1 - \cos\theta)$$

$$\Rightarrow \quad v = \sqrt{2gR(1 + \cos\theta)}$$

Using centripetal force equation,

$$T - mg\cos\theta = \frac{mv^2}{R}$$

$$\Rightarrow \quad T - mg\cos\theta = \frac{m}{R}(\sqrt{2gR(1 + \cos\theta)})^2$$

$$\Rightarrow \quad T = (2 + 3\cos\theta)mg$$

54. Horizontal component of velocity is constant.

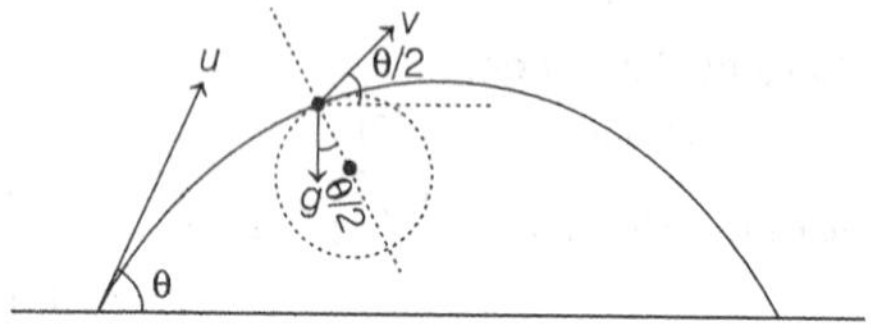

$$\Rightarrow \quad v\cos\left(\frac{\theta}{2}\right) = u\cos\theta \quad \Rightarrow \quad v = u\cos\theta\sec\left(\frac{\theta}{2}\right)$$

Centripetal acceleration $= \dfrac{v^2}{R}$

$$\Rightarrow \quad g\cos\left(\frac{\theta}{2}\right) = \left(\frac{u\cos\theta\sec\left(\frac{\theta}{2}\right)}{R}\right)^2 \quad \Rightarrow \quad R = \frac{u^2\cos^2\theta}{g\cos^3\left(\frac{\theta}{2}\right)}$$

55.

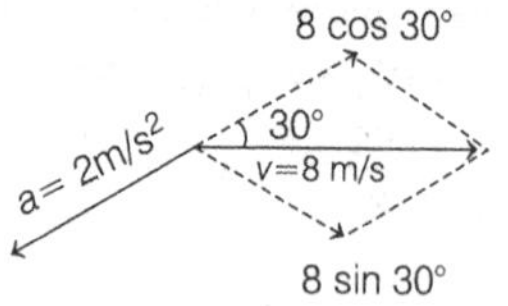

Radius of curvature will be minimum when centripetal acceleration is 2m/s^2. So, velocity along acceleration should be zero.

$$\text{Radius of curvature} = \frac{v^2}{a_c} = \frac{(8\sin 30°)^2}{2} = 8\text{ m}$$

Multiple Choice(s) Correct Questions

1. In uniform circular motion, speed and magnitude of acceleration are constant.

2. Acceleration $= \sqrt{\left(\dfrac{v^2}{R}\right)^2 + a^2}$

$$\Rightarrow \quad f = M\sqrt{\left(\frac{v^2}{R}\right)^2 + a^2}$$

$$\Rightarrow \quad f > \frac{mv^2}{R}$$

$$\because \quad f \le f_L \quad \Rightarrow m\sqrt{\left(\frac{v^2}{R}\right)^2 + a^2} \le \mu mg$$

$$\Rightarrow \quad \mu \ge \sqrt{\left(\frac{v^2}{Rg}\right)^2 + \left(\frac{a}{g}\right)^2}$$

3.

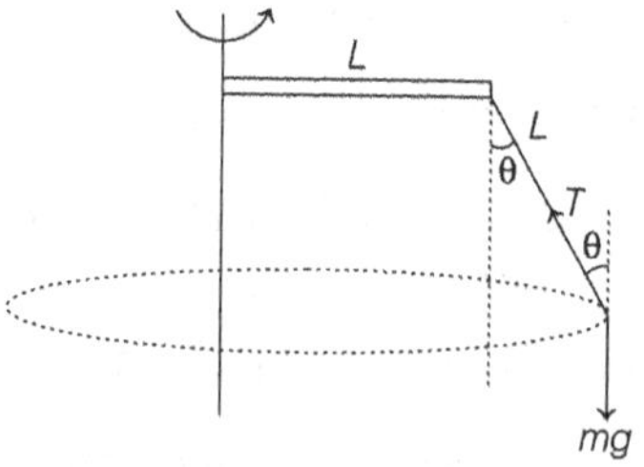

$$\Sigma F_y = 0 \quad \Rightarrow \quad T\cos\theta = mg \qquad \text{...(i)}$$

$$\Sigma F_x = ma_x \quad \Rightarrow \quad T\sin\theta = m\omega^2 L(1 + \sin\theta) \qquad \text{...(ii)}$$

From Eqs. (i) and (ii), we get

$$\tan\theta = \frac{\omega^2 L(1 + \sin\theta)}{g}$$

4. (A) With respect to plank, tension is always perpendicular to velocity. So, work done by tension is zero.

(B) In time $\dfrac{\pi l}{2v_0}$, it will complete quarter circle.

$$W_T = \Delta K = \frac{1}{2}m(2v_0)^2 - \frac{1}{2}m(\sqrt{2}v_0)^2 = mv_0^2$$

(C) In one revolution, $W_T = 0 \because \Delta K = 0$

(D) In half revolution, initial and final speeds are $\sqrt{2}v_0$.

So, $\quad \Delta K = 0 \Rightarrow W_T = 0$

5. Using work - energy theorem,

$$W_{mg} + W_N = \Delta K$$

$$\Rightarrow \quad +mga(1 - \cos\theta) + 0 = \frac{1}{2}mv^2 - \frac{1}{2}m\left(\sqrt{\frac{ag}{2}}\right)^2$$

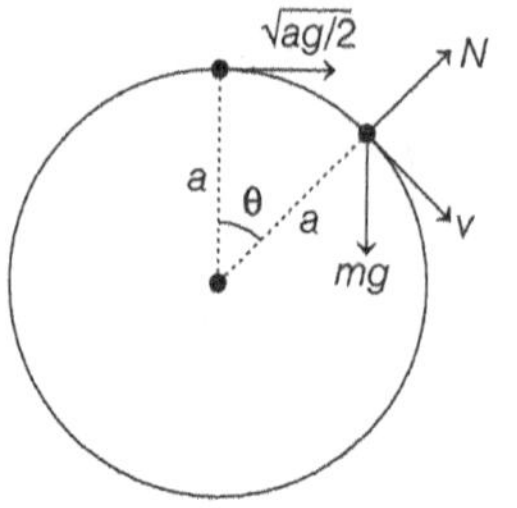

$$v^2 = \frac{ga}{2} + 2ga(1 - \cos\theta)$$

Equation for centripetal force,

$$mg\cos\theta - N = \frac{mv^2}{R}$$

$$\Rightarrow \quad mg\cos\theta - 0 = \frac{m}{R}\left(\frac{ga}{2} + 2ga(1 - \cos\theta)\right)$$

$$\Rightarrow \quad \cos\theta = \frac{5}{6} \Rightarrow \theta = \cos^{-1}\left(\frac{5}{6}\right)$$

Verticle distance below the top $= a - a\cos\theta$

$$= a - \frac{5a}{6} = \frac{a}{6}$$

6. $\Sigma F_y = 0$

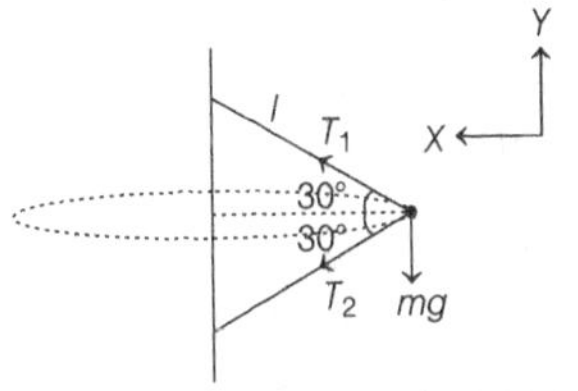

$$\Rightarrow \quad T_1 \sin 30° = mg + T_2 \sin 30° \Rightarrow T_1 - T_2 = 2mg \quad \text{...(i)}$$

$$\Sigma F_x = ma_x$$

$$\Rightarrow \quad T_1 \cos 30° + T_2 \cos 30° = m\omega^2 (l \cos 30°)$$

$$T_1 + T_2 = m\omega^2 l \quad \text{...(ii)}$$

From Eqs. (i) and (ii), we get

$$T_2 = \frac{m\omega^2 l - 2mg}{2}$$

For $T_2 \geq 0$, $\Rightarrow \frac{m\omega^2 l - 2mg}{2} \geq 0 \Rightarrow \omega \geq \sqrt{\frac{2g}{l}}$

7. $r = \sqrt{3}\sin 30° = \frac{\sqrt{3}}{2}$

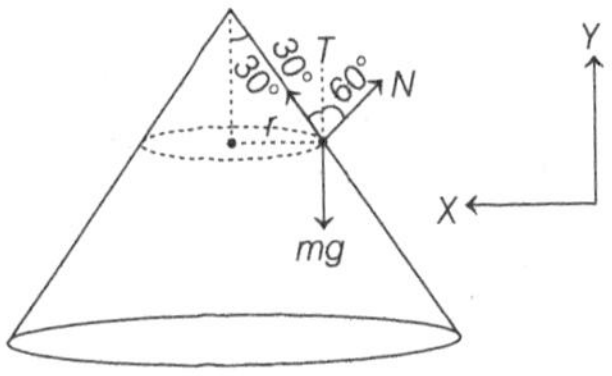

$$\Sigma F_y = 0 \Rightarrow T\cos 30° + N\cos 60° = mg \quad \text{...(i)}$$

$$\Sigma F_x = ma_x \Rightarrow T\sin 30° - N\sin 60° = \frac{mv^2}{(\sqrt{3}/2)} \quad \text{...(ii)}$$

From Eqs. (i) and (ii), we get

$$N = \frac{2mg - 4mv^2}{4} \text{ and } T = \frac{6mg + 4mv^2}{4\sqrt{3}}$$

8. **r**, ω and **v** are mutually perpendicular.

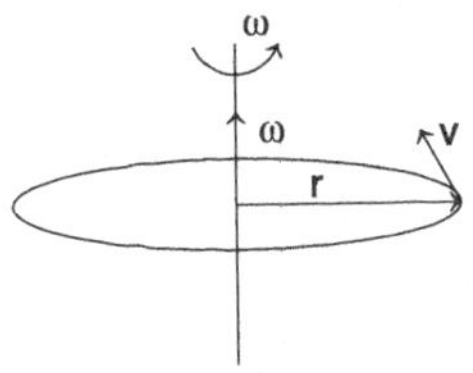

9. For the particle on the table,

$$T = m\omega_1^2 l_1 \quad \text{...(i)}$$

For the other particle

$$T\cos\theta = mg \quad \text{...(ii)}$$

$$T\sin\theta = m\omega_2^2 (l_2 \sin\theta) \Rightarrow T = m\omega_2^2 l_2 \quad \text{...(iii)}$$

From Eqs. (i) and (iii), we get

$$\frac{l_1}{l_2} = \frac{\omega_2^2}{\omega_1^2}$$

$$\frac{1}{\omega_1^2} + \frac{1}{\omega_2^2} = \frac{ml_1}{T} + \frac{ml_2}{T} = \frac{m(l_1 + l_2)}{mg/\cos\theta} \Rightarrow \frac{1}{\omega_1^2} + \frac{1}{\omega_2^2} = \frac{l\cos\theta}{g}$$

10. $\Sigma F_y = 0$

$$\Rightarrow \quad T\cos\theta = mg \quad \text{...(i)}$$

$$\Sigma F_x = ma_x \Rightarrow T\sin\theta = m\omega^2 l \sin\theta \quad \text{...(ii)}$$

From Eqs, (i) and (ii), we get

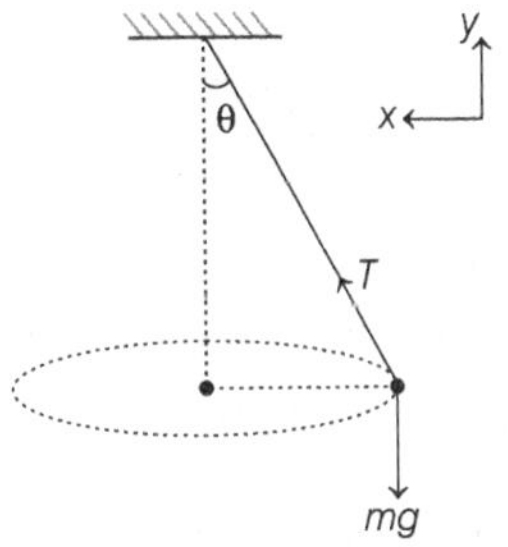

$$T = 2mg \Rightarrow \omega = \sqrt{\frac{g}{l\cos\theta}}$$

$$\text{Time period} = 2\pi\sqrt{\frac{l\cos\theta}{g}} = \frac{4\pi}{7}$$

$$v = \omega l \sin\theta = \frac{7}{2} \times 1.6 \times \frac{\sqrt{3}}{2} = 2.8\sqrt{3}\,\text{m/s}$$

$$a_c = \omega^2 r = \left(\frac{7}{2}\right)^2 \left(1.6\frac{\sqrt{3}}{2}\right) = 9.8\sqrt{3}\,\text{m/s}^2$$

11. In radial direction, $T - mg\cos\theta = \frac{mv^2}{l}$

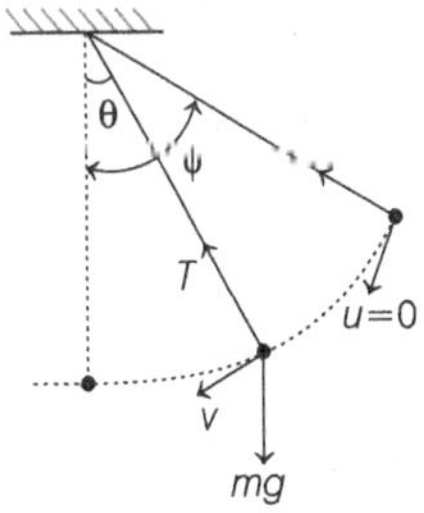

In tangential direction, $\Sigma F = ma \Rightarrow mg\sin\theta = ma_T$

$$\Rightarrow \quad a_T = g\sin\theta$$

12. $$N\cos\theta = mg \quad \text{...(i)}$$

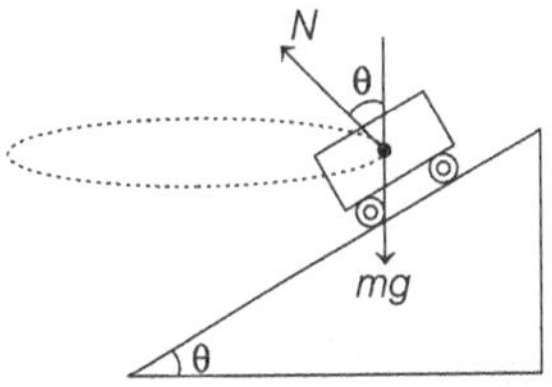

$$N\sin\theta = \frac{mv^2}{R} \quad \text{...(ii)}$$

From Eqs. (i) and (ii), we get

$$v = \sqrt{Rg\tan\theta} = 40 \text{ km/h}$$

$N > mg$ and $N > \dfrac{mv^2}{R}$

13.

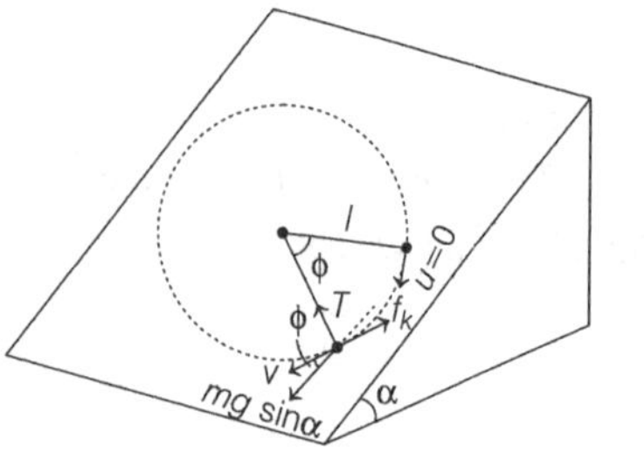

Using work - energy theorem,

$$W_{mg} + W_T + W_N + W_{\text{friction}} = \Delta K$$

$$\Rightarrow \quad (+mg\sin\alpha)(l\sin\phi) + 0 + 0 - (\mu mg\cos\alpha)(l\phi) = \frac{1}{2}mv^2 - 0$$

$$\Rightarrow \quad v^2 = 2gl\sin\alpha\sin\phi - 2\mu gl\phi\cos\alpha \quad \text{...(i)}$$

In radial direction,

$$T - (mg\sin\alpha)\sin\phi = \frac{mv^2}{l} \quad \text{...(ii)}$$

Solving Eqs. (i) and (ii), we get

$$T = mg(3\sin\phi\sin\alpha - 2\mu\phi\cos\alpha)$$

To maximise T, $\dfrac{dT}{d\phi} = 0$

$$\frac{dT}{d\phi} = mg(3\cos\phi\sin\alpha - 2\mu\cos\alpha) = 0 \Rightarrow \phi = \cos^{-1}\left(\frac{2\mu}{3\tan\alpha}\right)$$

$$v = \sqrt{2gl(\sin\alpha\sin\phi - \mu\phi\cos\alpha)}$$

To maximise v, $\dfrac{dv}{d\phi} = 0$

$$\Rightarrow \quad 2gl(\sin\alpha\cos\phi - \mu\cos\alpha) = 0 \Rightarrow \phi = \cos^{-1}(\mu\cot\alpha)$$

14. $v = 2t$

$$ds = 2t\,dt \Rightarrow \int_0^s ds = \int_0^2 2t\,dt \Rightarrow s = 4\text{ m}$$

and $\quad s = R\theta \Rightarrow 4 = 1\times\theta \Rightarrow \theta = 4$ rad

$$\text{Displacement} = 2R\sin\left(\frac{\theta}{2}\right) = 2(1)\sin 2 = 2\sin 2m$$

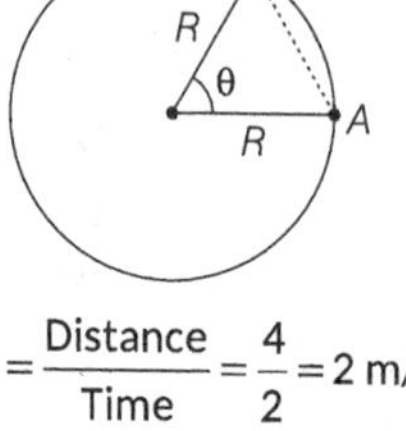

$$\text{Average speed} = \frac{\text{Distance}}{\text{Time}} = \frac{4}{2} = 2 \text{ m/s}$$

$$\text{Average velocity} = \frac{\text{Displacment}}{\text{Time}} = \frac{2\sin 2}{2} = \sin 2 \text{ m/s}$$

$$\text{Average acceleration} = \frac{|\Delta \mathbf{v}|}{\Delta t} = \frac{4-0}{2} = 2 \text{ m/s}^2$$

$$\text{Acceleration} = \sqrt{a_c^2 + a_T^2} = \sqrt{\left(\frac{2^2}{1}\right)^2 + 2^2} = 2\sqrt{5} \text{ m/s}^2$$

15. At A; $N_A - mg = \dfrac{m(\sqrt{gr})^2}{r} \Rightarrow N_A = 2\,mg = 2w$

At E; $\quad mg - N_B = \dfrac{m(\sqrt{gr})^2}{r} \Rightarrow N_B = 0$

At G; $\quad \Sigma F_y = ma_y \Rightarrow mg - N_G = 0 \Rightarrow N_G = mg = w$

At C; $\quad \Sigma F_y = ma_y \Rightarrow mg - N_C = 0 \Rightarrow N_C = mg = w$

Comprehension Based Questions

1. $N_2 = mg$

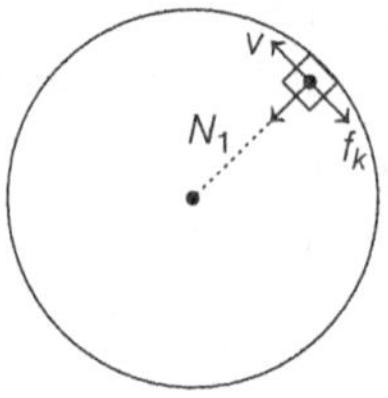

$$N_1 = \frac{mv^2}{R} \Rightarrow f_K = \mu N_1 = \frac{\mu mv^2}{R}$$

Along tangential direction,

$$\Sigma F = ma \Rightarrow -\frac{\mu mv^2}{R} = ma_T \Rightarrow a_T = -\frac{\mu v^2}{R}$$

2. $a_T = v\dfrac{dv}{ds} = -\dfrac{\mu v^2}{R} \Rightarrow \displaystyle\int_{v_0}^{v}\frac{dv}{v} = -\frac{\mu}{R}\int_0^s ds$

$$\Rightarrow [\ln v]_{v_0}^{v} = -\frac{\mu}{R}[s]_0^s \Rightarrow v = v_0 e^{-\mu s/R}$$

3. $v = v_0 e^{-\mu s/R}$

$$\Rightarrow \quad \frac{ds}{dt} = v_0 e^{-\mu s/R} \Rightarrow ds = v_0 e^{-\mu s/R}dt$$

$$\Rightarrow \quad \int_0^{2\pi R} e^{\mu s/R}ds = v_0\int_0^T dt \Rightarrow \left[\frac{e^{\mu s/R}}{\frac{\mu}{R}}\right]_0^{2\pi R} = v_0[t]_0^T$$

$$\Rightarrow \quad \frac{R(e^{2\mu\pi} - 1)}{\mu} = v_0 T$$

$$\Rightarrow \quad T = \frac{R}{\mu v_0}(e^{2\mu\pi} - 1)$$

4. $OP = uT = u\sqrt{\dfrac{2H}{g}} = 2\sqrt{gr}\sqrt{\dfrac{2r}{g}} = 2\sqrt{2}r$

5. Using work-energy theorem,

$$W_{mg} + W_T = 0$$

$$\Rightarrow +mgr(1-\cos\theta) + 0 = \frac{1}{2}mv^2 - \frac{1}{2}(\sqrt{gr}/3)^2$$

$$\Rightarrow \quad v^2 = \frac{gr}{9} + 2gr(1-\cos\theta) \quad \text{...(i)}$$

Using in radial direction,

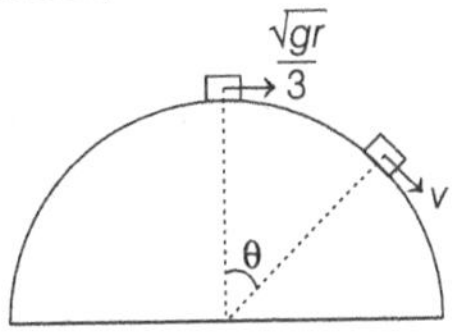

$$mg\cos\theta + N = \frac{mv^2}{r} \Rightarrow v^2 = gr\cos\theta \qquad (\because N = 0) \quad \text{...(ii)}$$

From Eqs. (i) and (ii), we get

$$\cos\theta = \frac{19}{27}$$

Height from ground $= r\cos\theta = \frac{19r}{27}$

6. After leaving hemisphere, only force acting on the block is mg. So, acceleration will be g.

7. Using work-energy theorem,

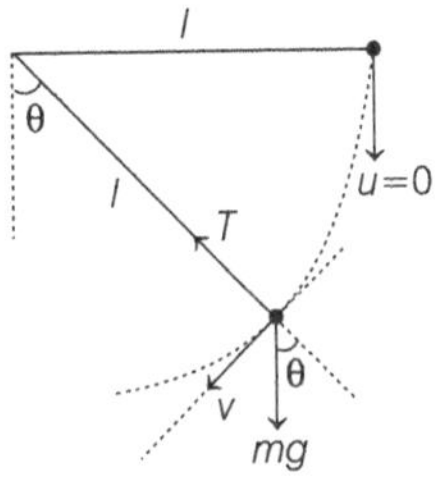

$$W_{mg} + W_T = \Delta K$$

$$\Rightarrow +mgl\cos\theta + 0 = \frac{1}{2}mv^2 - 0 \Rightarrow v = \sqrt{2gl\cos\theta}$$

Along the string, $T - mg\cos\theta = \frac{mv^2}{l}$

$$\Rightarrow T - mg\cos\theta = \frac{m}{l}(\sqrt{2gl\cos\theta})^2 \Rightarrow T = 3mg\cos\theta$$

Centipetal acceleration $= \frac{v^2}{l} = 2g\cos\theta$

Tangential acceleration $= g\sin\theta$

Net acceleration $= \sqrt{(2g\cos\theta)^2 + (g\sin\theta)^2} = g\sqrt{1+3\cos^2\theta}$

8. Vertical component of sphere's velocity will be maximum, when $a_y = 0$

$$\Rightarrow \quad \Sigma F_y = 0 \Rightarrow T\cos\theta = mg \Rightarrow 3mg\cos^2\theta = mg$$

$$\Rightarrow \quad \cos\theta = \frac{1}{\sqrt{3}} \Rightarrow T = 3mg\cos\theta = 3mg\left(\frac{1}{\sqrt{3}}\right) = \sqrt{3}mg$$

9. $$\tan\theta = \frac{a_c}{a_T}$$

$$\Rightarrow \quad \tan\theta = \frac{v^2/l}{g\sin\theta} = \frac{2g\cos\theta}{g\sin\theta}$$

$$\Rightarrow \quad \tan\theta = \sqrt{2}$$

$$\Rightarrow \quad \cos\theta = \frac{1}{\sqrt{3}}$$

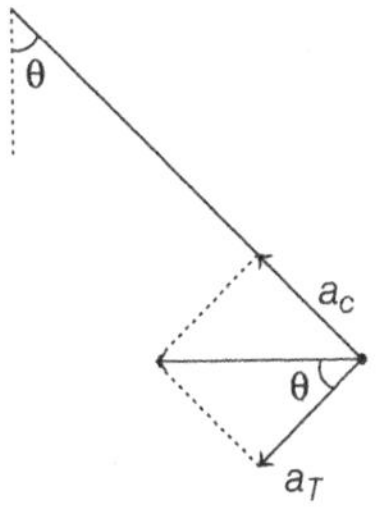

10. $\tan\theta = \frac{mg}{\frac{3mg}{4}} \Rightarrow \theta = 53°$

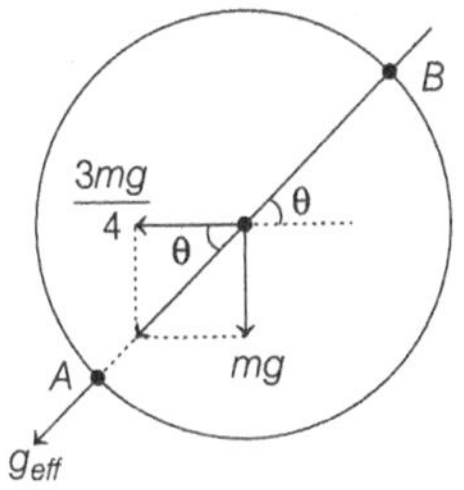

Tension will be minimum at position B.

11. $$v_{min} = \sqrt{g_{eff}l} = \sqrt{\left(\sqrt{g^2 + \left(\frac{3g}{4}\right)^2}\right)l} = \sqrt{\frac{5gl}{4}}$$

12. Tension will be maximum at A,

$$T - \frac{3mg}{4}\cos 53° - mg\cos 37° = \frac{m(\sqrt{5g_{eff}l})^2}{l}$$

$$\Rightarrow T - \frac{9mg}{20} - \frac{4mg}{5} = \frac{25}{4}mg \Rightarrow T = \frac{150mg}{20} = \frac{15}{2}mg$$

13.

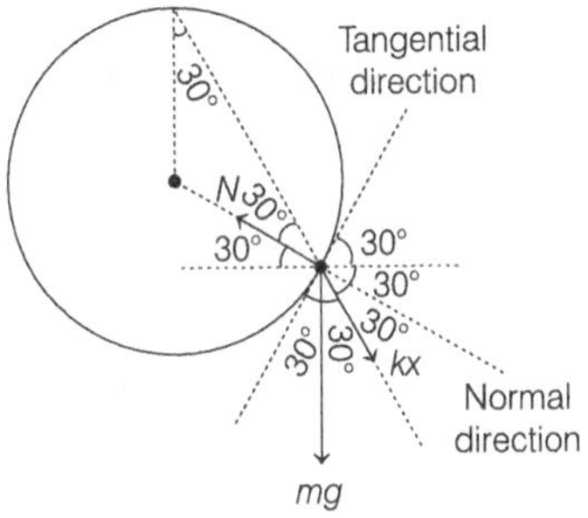

Compression in the spring $= 2R - 2R\cos 30° = (2-\sqrt{3})R$

Along radial direction,

$$N - kx\cos 30° - mg\cos 60° = \frac{mv^2}{R}$$

$$\Rightarrow \quad N = kx\cos 30° + mg\cos 60° \qquad (\because v = 0)$$

$$\Rightarrow \quad N = \frac{(2+\sqrt{3})mg}{\sqrt{3}R}(2-\sqrt{3})R\frac{\sqrt{3}}{2} + \frac{mg}{2} \Rightarrow N = mg$$

14. Along tangential direction,

$$mg\cos 30° + kx\cos 60° = ma$$

$$\Rightarrow \quad a = g\cos 30° + \frac{kx}{m}\cos 60°$$

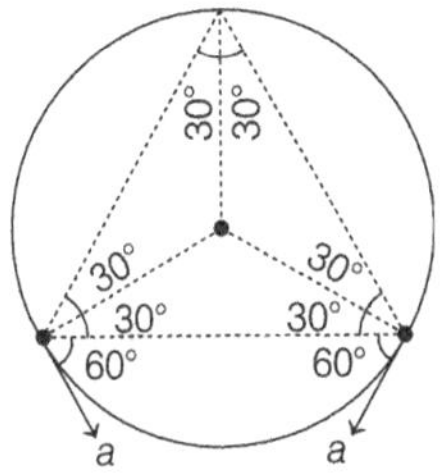

$$a_{rel} = 2a\cos 60° \Rightarrow a = \frac{\sqrt{3}g}{2} + \frac{g}{2\sqrt{3}}$$

$$\Rightarrow \quad a = \frac{2g}{\sqrt{3}} \text{ (horizontally towards each other)}$$

15.

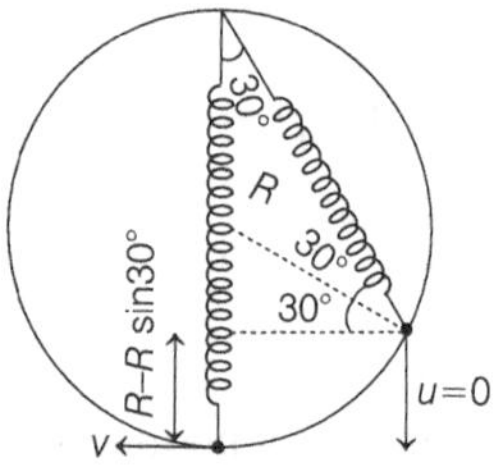

Using work-energy theorem for bead,

$$W_{mg} + W_N + W_{spring} = \Delta K$$

$$\Rightarrow +mgR(1 - \sin 30°) + 0 + \frac{1}{2}\frac{(2+\sqrt{3})}{\sqrt{3}R} mg\,\{(2-\sqrt{3}R)^2 - 0^2\}$$

$$= \frac{1}{2}mv^2 - 0$$

$$\Rightarrow \quad v = \sqrt{\frac{2gR}{\sqrt{3}}}$$

16. **v** and ω are perpendicular,

$$\mathbf{v}\cdot\omega = 0 \Rightarrow (3\hat{i} + 4\hat{j})\cdot(x\hat{i} + 6\hat{j}) = 0$$

$$\Rightarrow \quad 3x + 24 = 0 \Rightarrow x = -8$$

17. $v = \omega r \Rightarrow 5 = 10r \Rightarrow r = \frac{1}{2}$ m

18. Centripetal acceleration $= \frac{v^2}{r} = \frac{5^2}{(1/2)} = 50 \text{ m/s}^2$

19.

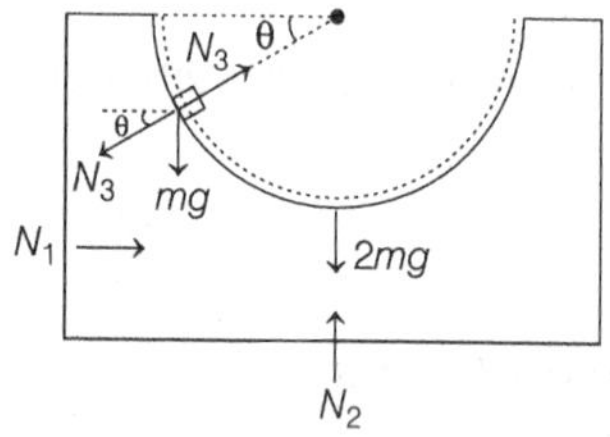

Using work-energy theorem for smaller block

$$W_{mg} + W_N = \Delta K$$

$$\Rightarrow \quad +mgR\sin 30° + 0 = \frac{1}{2}mv^2 - 0 \quad \Rightarrow v = \sqrt{gR}$$

Along radial direction,

$$N_3 - mg\cos 60° = \frac{mv^2}{R} \quad \Rightarrow N_3 = \frac{3mg}{2}$$

For bigger block,

$$\Sigma F_x = 0 \quad \Rightarrow N_1 - N_3\cos 30° = 0 \quad \Rightarrow N_1 = \frac{3\sqrt{3}mg}{4}$$

20. For bigger block, $\Sigma F_y = 0 \Rightarrow N_2 - 2mg - N_3\sin\theta = 0$

$\Rightarrow 3mg - 2mg - N_3\sin\theta = 0 \Rightarrow N_3\sin\theta = mg$

For smaller block along radical direction,

$$N_3 - mg\sin\theta = \frac{m(\sqrt{2gR\sin\theta})^2}{R}$$

$$\Rightarrow \quad \frac{mg}{\sin\theta} - mg\sin\theta = 2mg\sin\theta$$

$$\Rightarrow \quad 3\sin^2\theta = 1 \quad \Rightarrow \quad \sin\theta = \frac{1}{\sqrt{3}} \quad \Rightarrow \quad \tan\theta = \frac{1}{2}$$

21. At the highest point,

$$T + mg = \frac{mv_{top}^2}{l}$$

$$\Rightarrow \quad 2mg + mg = \frac{mv_{top}^2}{l}$$

$$\Rightarrow \quad v_{top} = \sqrt{3gl}$$

Using work-energy theorem between lower most and highest point,

$$W_{mg} + W_T = \Delta K$$

$$-mg(2l) + 0 = \frac{1}{2}m(\sqrt{3gl})^2 - \frac{1}{2}mv_{bottom}^2$$

$$\Rightarrow \quad v_{bottom} = \sqrt{7gl}$$

22. Range $= u\sqrt{\frac{2h}{g}} = \sqrt{3gl}\sqrt{\frac{2(2l)}{g}} = 2\sqrt{3}l$

23.

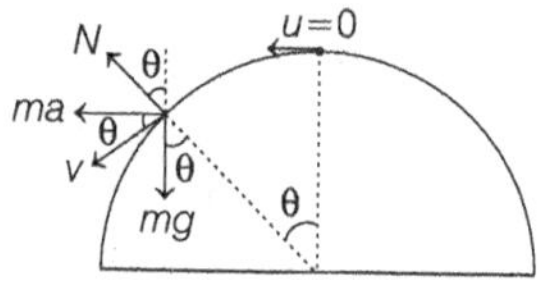

Using work-energy theorem for mass m,

$$W_{mg} + W_N + W_{pseudo\ force} = \Delta K$$

$$\Rightarrow +mgR(1-\cos\theta) + 0 + m\left(\frac{2g}{9}\right)R\sin\theta = \frac{1}{2}mv^2 - 0$$

$$\Rightarrow \quad v = \sqrt{2gR(1 - \cos\theta + \frac{2}{9}\sin\theta)}$$

Along radial direction,

$$mg\cos\theta - ma\sin\theta - N = \frac{mv^2}{R}$$

$$\Rightarrow mg\cos\theta - m\left(\frac{2g}{9}\right)\sin\theta - 0 = 2mg\left(1 - \cos\theta + \frac{2}{9}\sin\theta\right)$$

$$\Rightarrow \quad 9\cos\theta - 2\sin\theta = 6$$

$$\Rightarrow \quad (9\cos\theta)^2 = (2\sin\theta + 6)^2$$

$$\Rightarrow \quad 81\cos^2\theta = 4\sin^2\theta + 36 + 24\sin\theta$$

$$\Rightarrow \quad 81 - 81\sin^2\theta = 4\sin^2\theta + 36 + 24\sin\theta$$

$$\Rightarrow \quad 85\sin^2\theta + 24\sin\theta - 45 = 0$$

$$\Rightarrow \quad \sin\theta = \frac{3}{5} \quad \Rightarrow \theta = 37°$$

24. Height from ground $= R\cos\theta + \frac{4R}{3} = \frac{4R}{5} + \frac{4R}{3} = \frac{32R}{15}$

25. Just before losing contact,

$$v = \sqrt{2 \times 10 \times 60\left(1 - \frac{4}{5} + \frac{2}{9}\left(\frac{3}{5}\right)\right)}$$

$$\Rightarrow \quad v = 20 \text{ m/s}$$

$$s_y = u_y t + \frac{1}{2}a_y t^2 \Rightarrow 128 = (20\sin 37°)T + \frac{1}{2}(10)T^2$$

$$\Rightarrow \quad 5T^2 + 12T - 128 = 0 \Rightarrow T = 4 \text{ s}$$

26.

$$N\cos\theta = mg \qquad \text{...(i)}$$

$$N\sin\theta = \frac{mv^2}{R} \qquad \text{...(ii)}$$

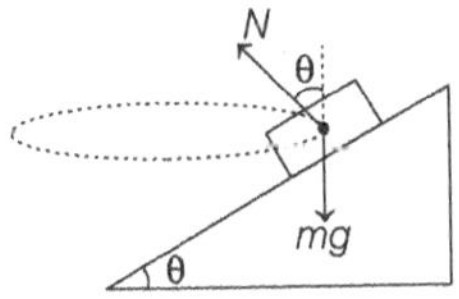

From Eqs. (i) and (ii), we get

$$\tan\theta = \frac{v^2}{Rg} \Rightarrow \tan\theta = \frac{(10)^2}{20 \times 10} \Rightarrow \theta = \tan^{-1}\left(\frac{1}{2}\right)$$

27.

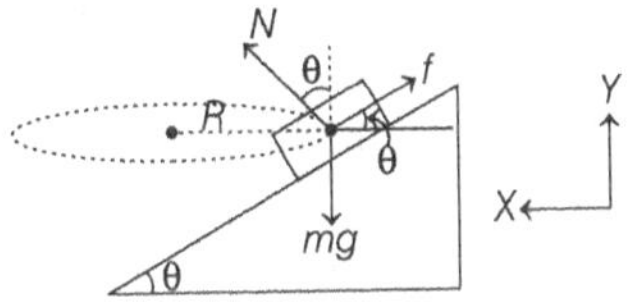

$$\Sigma F_y = 0 \Rightarrow N\cos\theta + f\sin\theta = mg \qquad \text{...(i)}$$

$$\Sigma F_x = ma_x \Rightarrow N\sin\theta - f\cos\theta = \frac{mv^2}{R} \qquad \text{...(ii)}$$

Solving Eqs. (i) and (ii), we get

$F = 300\sqrt{5}$, upwards

28.

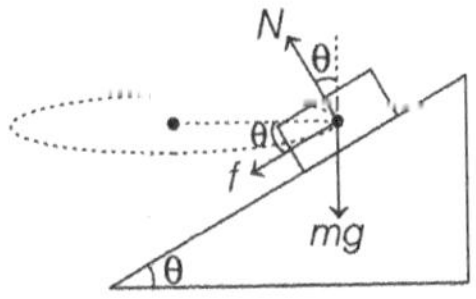

$$\Sigma F_y = 0 \Rightarrow N\cos\theta = f\sin\theta + mg \qquad \text{...(i)}$$

$$\Sigma F_x = ma_x \Rightarrow N\sin\theta + f\cos\theta = \frac{mv^2}{R} \qquad \text{...(ii)}$$

Solving Eqs. (i) and (ii),

$f = 500\sqrt{5}$ N, downwards

Match the Columns Questions

1. (A) Using work-energy theorem between A and B,

$$W_{mg} + W_T = \Delta K$$

$$\Rightarrow \quad -mgR + 0 = \frac{1}{2}mv_B^2 - \frac{1}{2}m(3\sqrt{gR})^2 \Rightarrow v_B = \sqrt{7gR}$$

(B) Using work-energy theorem between A and C,

$$W_{mg} + W_T = \Delta K$$

$$\Rightarrow \quad -mg2R + 0 = \frac{1}{2}mv_C^2 - \frac{1}{2}m(3\sqrt{gR})^2 \Rightarrow v_C = \sqrt{5gR}$$

(C) At B,

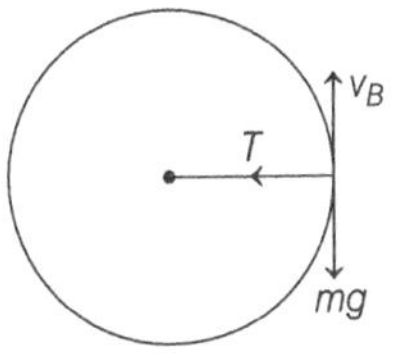

$$T = \frac{mv_B^2}{R} \Rightarrow T = 7mg$$

(D) At C,

$$T + mg = \frac{mv_C^2}{R} \Rightarrow T = 4mg$$

2. (A) Minimum tension will be at the highest point

$$T + mg = \frac{mv_{top}^2}{l}$$

$$\Rightarrow \quad T + 1(10) = \frac{1\sqrt{10^2 - 2 \times 10 \times 2})^2}{1} \Rightarrow T = 60\text{N}$$

(B) Centripetal acceleration $= \frac{v^2}{l}$

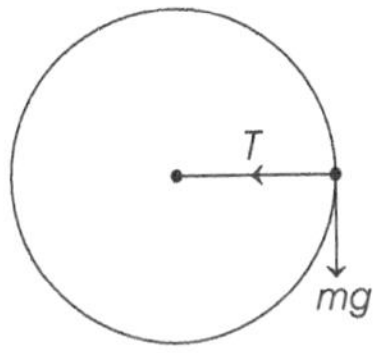

$$= \frac{(\sqrt{10^2 - 2 \times 10 \times 1})^2}{1} = 80 \text{ m/s}^2$$

Tangential acceleration $= g\downarrow = 10 \text{ m/s}^2$ down

Net acceleration $= \sqrt{80^2 + 10^2} = 10\sqrt{65} \text{ m/s}^2$

(C) Acceleration will be minimum at the highest point.

Tangential acceleration = 0

Centripetal acceleration $= \frac{v_{top}^2}{l} = \frac{(\sqrt{60})^2}{1} = 60 \text{ m/s}^2$

(D) Tangential acceleration at the highest point is zero.

3. (A) $v_{max} = \sqrt{gR\tan(\theta + \phi)} = \sqrt{gR\left(\frac{\tan\theta + \mu}{1 - \mu\tan\theta}\right)}$

$$= \sqrt{10 \times \frac{35}{\sqrt{3}}\left(\frac{\frac{1}{\sqrt{3}} + \frac{1}{2\sqrt{3}}}{1 - \frac{1}{\sqrt{3}}\frac{1}{2\sqrt{3}}}\right)} = \sqrt{210} \text{ m/s}$$

(B) $v_{min} = \sqrt{gR\tan(\theta - \phi)} = \sqrt{gR\left(\frac{\tan\theta - \mu}{1 + \mu\tan\theta}\right)} = 5\sqrt{2}$ m/s

(c) $v = \sqrt{gR\tan\theta} = \sqrt{\frac{350}{3}}$ m/s

(D)

$$N\cos\theta + f\sin\theta = mg \qquad \text{...(i)}$$

and

$$N\sin\theta - f\cos\theta = \frac{mv^2}{R} \qquad \text{...(ii)}$$

Solving Eqs. (i) and (ii), we get

$f = 1250$ N

4. $A \rightarrow Q$

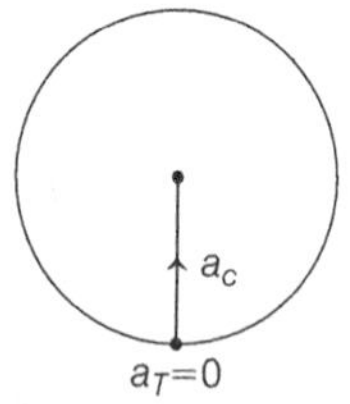

(B) a_c may or may not be zero.

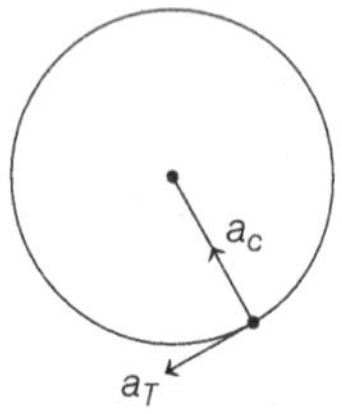

$B \rightarrow P, S, T$

(C) a_c may or may not be zero.

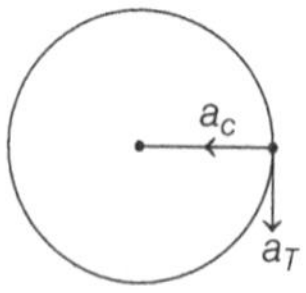

$C \rightarrow R, S$

(D) a_c may or may not be zero.

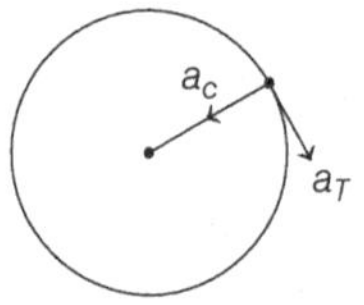

$D \rightarrow R, S$

5. (A) Using work-energy theorem,

$$W_{mg} + W_N = \Delta K$$

$$\Rightarrow -mgl(1-\cos\theta) + 0 = 0 - \frac{1}{2} \times m \times 5^2$$

$$\Rightarrow \quad 1 - \cos\theta = \frac{5}{4} \quad \Rightarrow \quad \theta = \cos^{-1}\left(-\frac{1}{4}\right)$$

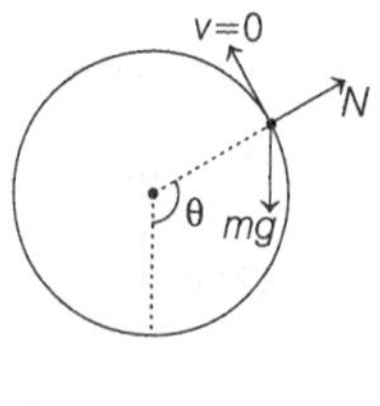

$$mg\cos(180° - \theta) - N = m\frac{(0)^2}{1}$$

$$\Rightarrow \qquad N = -mg\cos\theta \Rightarrow N = \frac{mg}{4}$$

Centripetal acceleration is zero but tangential acceleration is non-zero.

(B) Using work-energy theorem,

$$W_{mg} + W_N = \Delta K$$

$$-mgR(1-\cos\theta) + 0 = 0 - \frac{1}{2}m(\sqrt{20})^2$$

$$\theta = 90°$$

$$N = \frac{mv^2}{R} = 0$$

$$a_{\text{centripetal}} = \frac{v^2}{R} = 0$$

$$a_{\text{tangential}} = g\downarrow$$

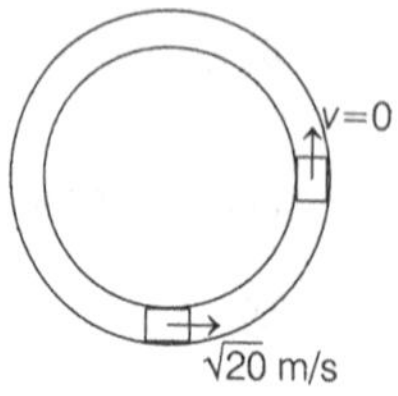

(C) Since,

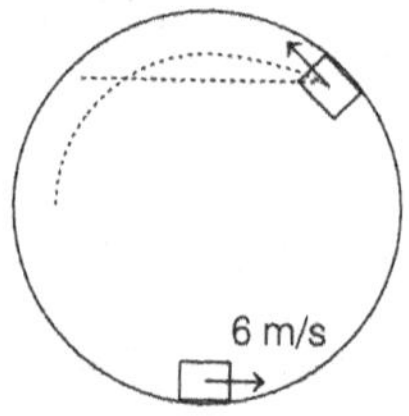

$$\sqrt{2gR} < v < \sqrt{5gR}$$

block will lose contact with the cylinder and follow parabolic trajectory.

(D) Using work-energy theorem,

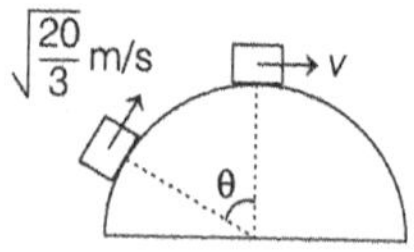

$$W_{mg} + W_N = \Delta K$$

$$\Rightarrow \quad -mgR(1-\cos\theta) + 0 = \frac{1}{2}mv^2 - \frac{1}{2}m\left(\sqrt{\frac{20}{3}}\right)^2$$

$$\Rightarrow \qquad v = 0$$

$$mg - N = \frac{m(0)^2}{R}$$

$$\Rightarrow \qquad N = mg$$

$$a_{\text{centripetal}} = \frac{v^2}{R} = 0$$

$$a_{\text{tangential}} = 0$$

6.

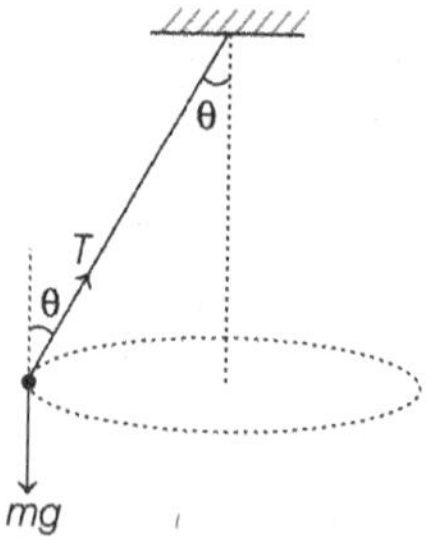

(A) $\qquad \Sigma F_y = 0 \quad \Rightarrow \quad T\cos\theta = mg$

Speed is constant but velocity is changing as direction is changing.

(B) At extreme position,

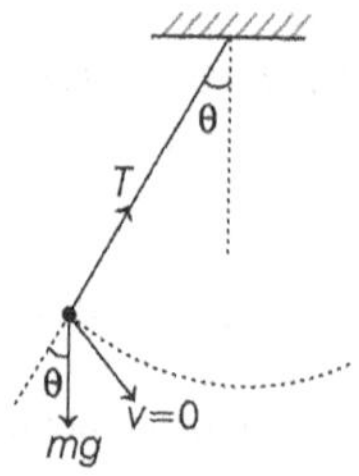

$$T - mg\cos\theta = \frac{m(0)^2}{l} \quad \Rightarrow \quad T = mg\cos\theta$$

Speed and velocity both are changing continuously.

(C) $\Sigma F_y = 0$

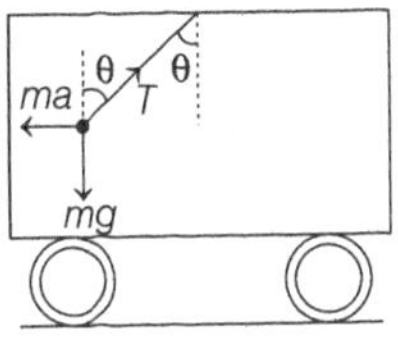

$$T\cos\theta = mg$$

Since, trolley is accelerating, both speed and velocity will change continuously.

(D) $$T\sin\phi = mg\sin\theta \quad \text{...(i)}$$

$$T\cos\phi = mg\cos\theta \quad \text{...(ii)}$$

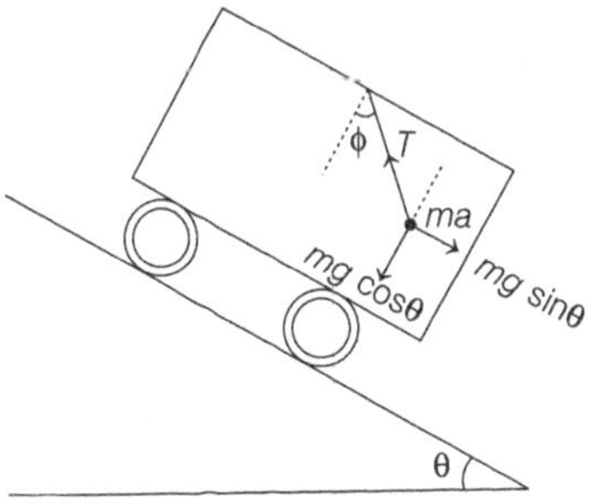

From Eqs. (i) and (ii), we get

$$\tan\phi = \tan\theta \Rightarrow \phi = \theta \Rightarrow T = mg$$

Speed and velocity are constant.

Numerical Value Questions

1.

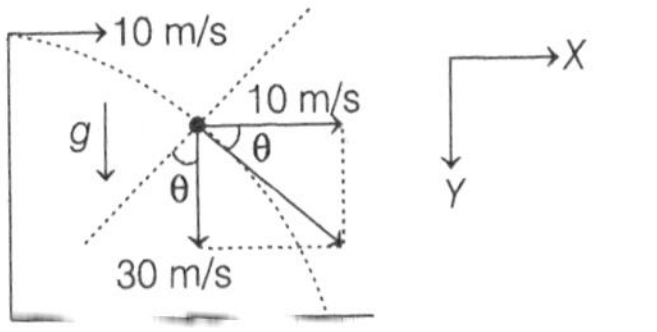

$$\mathbf{u} = 10\hat{\mathbf{i}}, \quad \mathbf{v} = \mathbf{u} + \mathbf{a}t = 10\hat{\mathbf{i}} + (10\hat{\mathbf{j}})(3) = 10\hat{\mathbf{i}} + 30\hat{\mathbf{j}}$$

$$\text{Speed} = \sqrt{10^2 + 30^2} = 10\sqrt{10} \text{ m/s}$$

$$\tan\theta = \frac{30}{10} = 3$$

$$\text{Centripetal acceleration} = \frac{v_\perp^2}{R} \Rightarrow g\cos\theta = \frac{(10\sqrt{10})^2}{R}$$

$$\Rightarrow \quad 10\frac{1}{\sqrt{10}} = \frac{1000}{R} \Rightarrow R = 100\sqrt{10}$$

2.

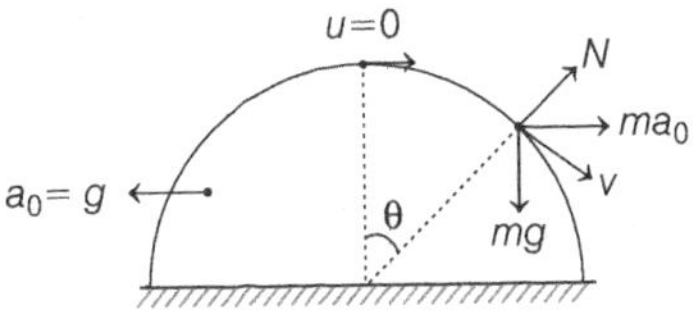

Using work-energy theorem,

$$W_{mg} + W_N + W_{\text{pseudo}} = \Delta K$$

$$\Rightarrow + mgR(1-\cos\theta) + 0 + ma_0(R\sin\theta) = \frac{1}{2}mv^2 - 0$$

$$\Rightarrow \quad v = \sqrt{2gR(1-\cos\theta) + 2a_0R\sin\theta}$$

Along radial direction,

$$mg\cos\theta - N - ma_0\sin\theta = \frac{mv^2}{R}$$

$$mg\cos\theta - 0 - mg\sin\theta = \frac{m}{R}(2gR(1-\cos\theta + \sin\theta))$$

$$\Rightarrow \quad \cos\theta - \sin\theta = 2 - 2\cos\theta + 2\sin\theta$$

$$\Rightarrow \quad 3\cos\theta - 3\sin\theta = 2 \Rightarrow \cos\theta - \sin\theta = \frac{2}{3}$$

$$v = \sqrt{2gR[1-(\cos\theta - \sin\theta)]} = \sqrt{2gR\left(1 - \frac{2}{3}\right)} = \sqrt{\frac{2gR}{3}}$$

3.

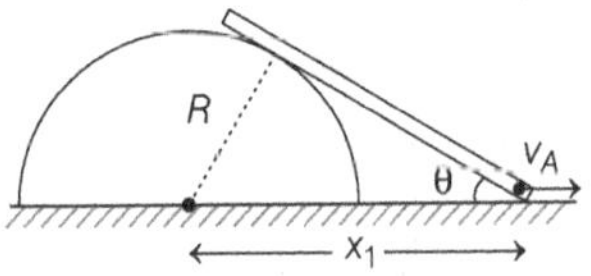

$$\sin\theta = \frac{R}{x_1}$$

Differentiating both sides,

$$\Rightarrow \quad \cos\theta\frac{d\theta}{dt} = \frac{-R}{x_1^2}\frac{dx_1}{dt} \Rightarrow \omega = \frac{d\theta}{dt} - \frac{Rv_A\sec\theta}{x_1^2}$$

$$\Rightarrow \quad \omega = \frac{-Rv_Ax_1}{x_1^2\sqrt{x_1^2 - R^2}} \Rightarrow \omega = \frac{Rv_A}{x_1\sqrt{x_1^2 - R^2}}$$

4. $\Sigma F_y = 0$

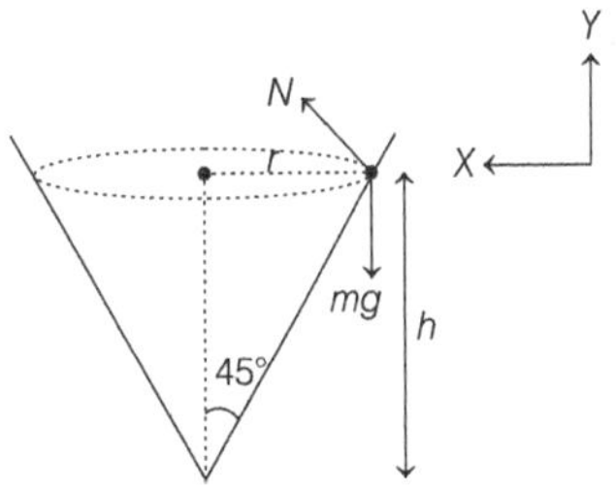

$$\Rightarrow \quad N\cos 45° = mg \quad \text{...(i)}$$

$$\Sigma F_x = ma_x \Rightarrow N\sin 45° = \frac{mv^2}{r} \quad \text{...(ii)}$$

From Eqs. (i) and (ii), we get

$$v = \sqrt{gr} = \sqrt{0 \times 0.4} = 2 \text{ m/s}$$

5. Using work-energy theorem,

$$W_{mg} + W_T = \Delta K$$

$$\Rightarrow + mg(0.8\sin 30°) + 0 = \frac{1}{2}mv^2 - 0 \Rightarrow v = 2\sqrt{2} \text{ m/s}$$

Just before coming in contact with the peg,

$$T_1 - mg\sin 30° = \frac{mv^2}{0.8} \Rightarrow T_1 = 15 \text{ N}$$

Just after coming in contact with the peg,

$$T_2 - mg\sin 30° = \frac{mv^2}{0.4}$$

$$\Rightarrow \quad T_2 = 25\text{N} \Rightarrow \frac{T_1}{T_2} = \frac{15}{25} = \frac{3}{5} = 0.6$$

6. For hanging block to be stationary,

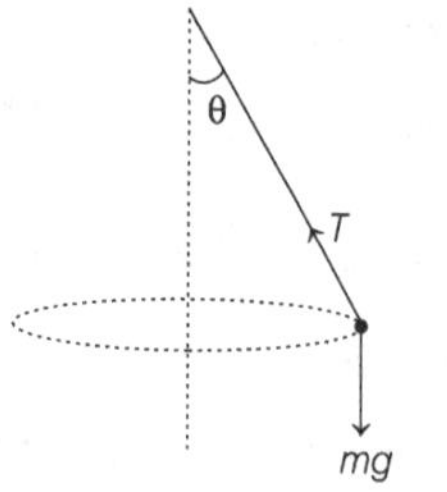

$$\Sigma F_y = 0 \;\Rightarrow\; T = mg = 200\text{N}$$

For the other block

$$\Sigma F_y = 0 \;\Rightarrow\; T\cos\theta = mg \qquad \text{...(i)}$$

$$\Sigma F_x = ma_x \;\Rightarrow\; T\sin\theta = m\omega^2(l\sin\theta) \qquad \text{...(ii)}$$

$$\Rightarrow \quad 200 = 2\omega^2(0.1) \;\Rightarrow\; \omega = 10\sqrt{10}\,\text{rad/s}$$

$$\Rightarrow \quad \omega = \frac{10\sqrt{10}}{2\pi}\,\text{rev/s} \;\Rightarrow\; \omega = 5\text{ rev/s}$$

7. For conical pendulum,

$$\omega = \sqrt{\frac{g}{l\cos\theta}} = \sqrt{\frac{9.8}{2}} \;\Rightarrow\; v = \omega r = 1.5\sqrt{4.9}\text{ m/s}$$

$$\text{Range} = v\sqrt{\frac{2h}{g}} = 1.5\sqrt{4.9}\sqrt{\frac{2\times 5.76}{9.8}} = 3.6\text{ m}$$

$$OP = \sqrt{(1.5)^2 + (3.6)^2} = 3.9\text{ m} = 390\text{ cm}$$

8. $N = ma_T = mr\alpha$

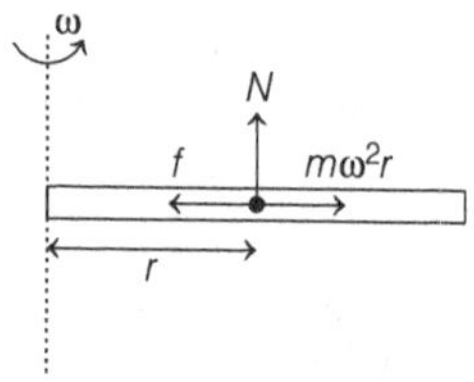

For slipping,

$$m\omega^2 r = f_L \;\Rightarrow\; m(\alpha t)^2 r = \mu N = \mu(mr\alpha)$$

$$\Rightarrow \quad t = \sqrt{\frac{\mu}{\alpha}} = \sqrt{\frac{0.05}{5}} = 0.1\text{ s}$$

9. For block, at the highest point,

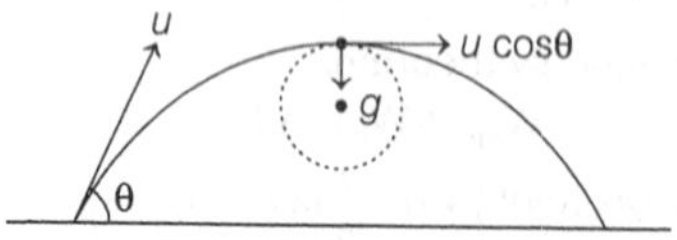

$$R = \frac{u_\perp^2}{a} \;\Rightarrow\; R = \frac{(u\cos\theta)^2}{g} \;\Rightarrow\; R = \frac{u^2\cos^2\theta}{g}$$

For bee, at the highest point,

$$\text{centripetal acceleration} = \frac{u^2}{R} = \frac{u^2}{\left(\frac{u^2\cos^2\theta}{g}\right)}$$

$$= \frac{g}{\cos^2 45^\circ} = 20\text{ m/s}^2$$

10. $\Sigma F_y = 0$

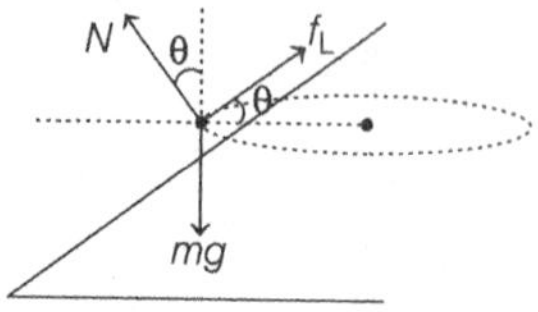

$$N\cos\theta + \mu N\sin\theta = mg \qquad \text{...(i)}$$

$$\mu N\cos\theta - N\sin\theta = m\omega^2 R \qquad \text{...(ii)}$$

Solving Eqs. (i) and (ii), we get

$$\omega = \sqrt{\frac{g}{32R}} \;\Rightarrow\; T = \frac{2\pi}{\omega} = 2\pi\sqrt{\frac{32R}{g}} = 16\text{ s}$$

11. $$\omega = \frac{d}{dt}(2\theta)$$

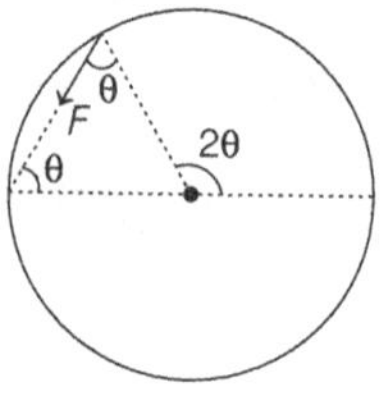

$$\Rightarrow \quad \omega = 2\frac{d\theta}{dt}$$

$$\Rightarrow \quad \alpha = \frac{d\omega}{dt} = 2\frac{d^2\theta}{dt^2}$$

Centripetal force $= F\cos\theta = m\omega^2 R$ ...(i)

Tangential force $= F\sin\theta = mR\alpha$ ...(ii)

From Eqs. (i) and (ii), we get

$$\tan\theta = \frac{\alpha}{\omega^2} = \frac{2\dfrac{d^2\theta}{dt^2}}{\left(2\dfrac{d\theta}{dt}\right)^2} \;\Rightarrow\; \frac{\dfrac{d^2\theta}{dt^2}}{\left(\dfrac{d\theta}{dt}\right)^2} = 2$$

12. $a_T = \sqrt{3}t$

$$\Rightarrow \quad \int dv = \sqrt{3t}\int t\,dt \;\Rightarrow\; v = \frac{\sqrt{3}t^2}{2}$$

$$\tan 30^\circ = \frac{a_T}{a_C} = \frac{\sqrt{3}t}{\left(\frac{\sqrt{3}t^2}{2}\right)^2 / R}$$

$$\Rightarrow \quad t^3 = 4 \;\Rightarrow\; t^6 = 16$$

13. Using work-energy theorem between A and C,

$$W_{mg} + W_T = \Delta K$$

$$\Rightarrow \; +mg\left(\frac{25}{16}\times\frac{4}{5}\right) + 0 = \frac{1}{2}mv^2 - 0 \;\Rightarrow\; v = 5\text{ m/s}$$

$$s_y = u_y t + \frac{1}{2}a_y t^2$$

$$\Rightarrow -\left(3.25 - \frac{25}{16}\times\frac{4}{5}\right) = \left(5\times\frac{3}{5}\right)T + \frac{1}{2}(-10)(T^2)$$

$\Rightarrow \quad -2 = 3T - 5T^2 \quad \Rightarrow 5T^2 - 3T - 2 = 0 \quad \Rightarrow T = 1\text{ s}$

Horizontal range $= (u\cos\theta)T = (5\cos 37°)(1) = 4$ m

14. $v^2 = u^2 - 2gl(1 - \cos\theta)$

$\Rightarrow \quad v_A = \sqrt{5gl - 2gl(1 - \cos 60°)}$

$\Rightarrow \quad v_A = \sqrt{4gl} \Rightarrow v_B = \sqrt{5gl - 2gl\left(1 - \left(\frac{-1}{2}\right)\right)} = \sqrt{2gl}$

Centripetal acceleration at $A = \frac{v_A^2}{l} = 4g$

Tangential acceleration at A = $g\sin 60° = \frac{\sqrt{3}g}{2}$

$$a_A = \sqrt{(4g)^2 + \left(\frac{\sqrt{3}g}{2}\right)^2} = g\sqrt{\frac{67}{4}}$$

Centripetal acceleration at $B = \frac{v_B^2}{l} = 2g$

Tangential acceleration atom at $B = g\sin 60° = \frac{\sqrt{3}g}{2}$

$$a_B = \sqrt{(2g)^2 + \left(\frac{\sqrt{3}g}{2}\right)^2} = g\sqrt{\frac{19}{4}}$$

15.

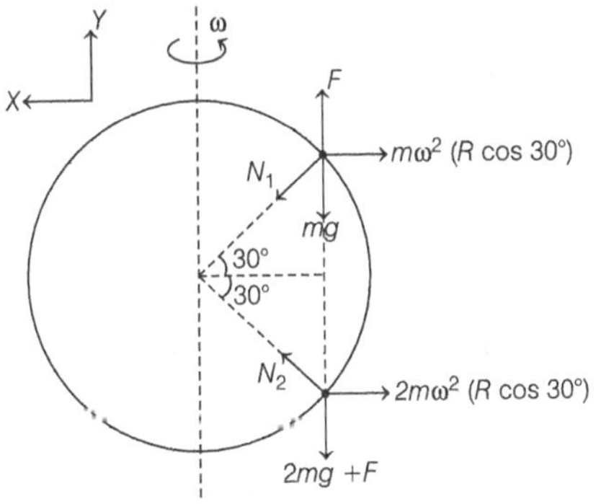

Form bead of mass m,

$$\Sigma F_x = 0$$

$\Rightarrow \quad N_1 \cos 30° = m\omega^2 (R\cos 30°) \quad$ ...(i)

$\Sigma F_y = 0 \quad \Rightarrow \quad f = mg + N_1 \cos 60° \quad$ ...(ii)

From Eqs. (i) and (ii), we get

$F = mg + \frac{m\omega^2 R}{2} \quad$ ... (iii)

For bead of mass $2m$

$\Sigma F_x = 0 \quad \Rightarrow \quad N_2 \cos 30° = 2m\omega^2 (R\cos 30°) \quad$ ...(iv)

$\Sigma F_y = 0 \quad \Rightarrow \quad N_2 \cos 60° = 2mg + F \quad$ ...(v)

From Eqs. (iv) and (v), we get

$m\omega^2 R = F + 2mg \quad$ ...(vi)

From Eqs. (iii) and (vi), we get

$$\omega = \sqrt{\frac{6g}{R}} = \sqrt{\frac{6 \times 10}{15}} = 2 \text{ rad/s}$$

Previous Year's Questions

JEE Main

1. Resolving Normal,

$N\cos\theta = mg \quad$ ...(i)

$N\sin\theta = \frac{mv^2}{R} \quad$ ...(ii)

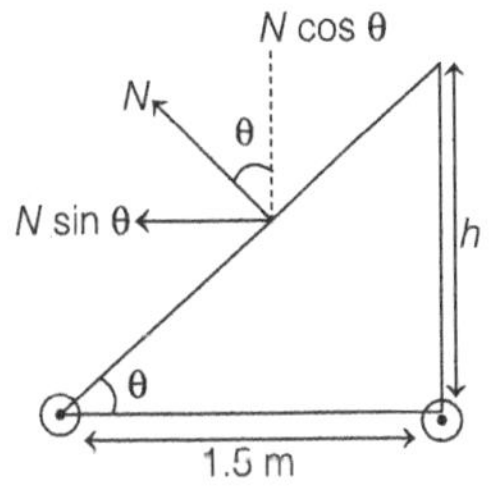

Dividing, $\tan\theta = \frac{v^2}{Rg}$

$$\frac{h}{1.5} = \frac{12 \times 12}{400 \times 10}$$

$$h = \frac{1.5 \times 12 \times 12}{400 \times 10}$$

$$= \frac{54}{1000} = 0.054 \text{ m} = 5.4 \text{ cm}$$

2.

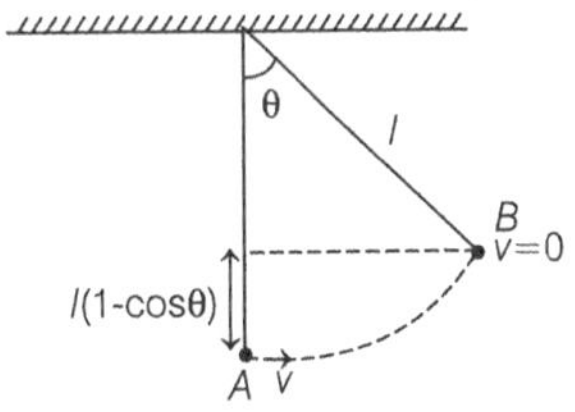

By energy conservation,

$$\frac{1}{2}mv^2 + 0 = 0 + mgl(1 - \cos\theta)$$

$$v^2 = 2gl(1 - \cos\theta)$$

Given, $\quad a_A = a_B$

$\therefore \quad \frac{v^2}{l} = g\sin\theta$

$\Rightarrow \quad 2g(1 - \cos\theta) = g\sin\theta$

$\Rightarrow \quad 2\left[2\sin^2\frac{\theta}{2}\right] = 2\sin\frac{\theta}{2}\cos\frac{\theta}{2}$

$\Rightarrow \quad \tan\frac{\theta}{2} = \frac{1}{2} \Rightarrow \theta = 2\tan^{-1}\frac{1}{2}$

3. Given, $m_1 = m_2$

and $\quad \frac{r_1}{r_2} = \frac{3}{4}$

as centripetal force, $F = \frac{mv^2}{r}$

In order to have constant (same in this question centripetal force)

$$F_1 = F_2$$

$$\frac{m_1 v_1^2}{r_1} = \frac{m_2 v_2^2}{r_2} \Rightarrow \frac{v_1^2}{v_2^2} = \frac{m_2}{m_1}\frac{r_1}{r_2}$$

$$\frac{v_1}{v_2} = \sqrt{\frac{m_2}{m_1} \cdot \frac{r_1}{r_2}}$$

$$\frac{v_1}{v_2} = \sqrt{\frac{m_1}{m_2} \cdot \frac{3}{4}}$$

$$\frac{v_1}{v_2} = \frac{\sqrt{3}}{2}$$

4. Given, Mass of stone,

$$m = 900\text{ g} = 0.9\text{ kg}$$
$$r = 1\text{ m}$$
$$f = 10\text{rpm} = \frac{10}{60}\text{rps} = \frac{1}{6}\text{rps}$$

Tension at the lowest point,

$$T = mg + mr\omega^2$$
$$= mg + mr(2\pi f)^2$$
$$= mg + mr(4\pi^2 f^2)$$
$$= mg + 4\pi^2 mrf^2$$
$$= 0.9 \times 9.8 + 4 \times 9.8 \times 0.9 \times 1 \times \frac{1}{36}$$
$$= 8.82 + 0.98 = 9.8\text{ N}$$

5. Tangential acceleration,

$$a_f = \frac{v^2}{R} = \frac{dv}{dt} \quad \text{...(i)}$$

$$\Rightarrow \frac{dv}{v^2} = \frac{1}{R}dt$$

$$\int_{v_0}^{v} \frac{dv}{v^2} = \int_0^t \frac{dt}{R}$$

$$\Rightarrow \frac{1}{v_0} - \frac{1}{v} = \frac{t}{R}$$

$$\Rightarrow t = R\left(\frac{1}{v_0} - \frac{1}{v}\right) \quad \text{...(ii)}$$

Now, $a_t = \frac{dv}{dt} = \frac{dv}{ds} \times \frac{ds}{dt} = v\frac{dv}{ds}$

$$\Rightarrow v\frac{dv}{ds} = \frac{v^2}{R} \quad \text{[From Eq. (i)]}$$

$$\Rightarrow \frac{dv}{ds} = \frac{v}{R}$$

$$\Rightarrow \int_{v_0}^{v} \frac{dv}{v} = \int_0^{2\pi R} \frac{ds}{R}$$

$$\Rightarrow \ln\frac{v}{v_0} = \frac{2\pi R}{R}$$

$$\Rightarrow v = v_0 e^{2\pi} \quad \text{...(iii)}$$

From Eqs. (ii) and (iii),

$$t = R\left(\frac{1}{v_0} - \frac{1}{v_0}e^{-2\pi}\right) = \frac{R}{v_0}(1 - e^{-2\pi})$$

Given, $R = 50\text{ cm} = 0.5\text{ m}$

and $v_0 = 4\text{ m/s}$

$$\therefore \quad t = \frac{0.5}{4}(1 - e^{-2\pi})\text{ s}$$
$$= \frac{1}{8}(1 - e^{-2\pi})\text{ s}$$

6. Given,

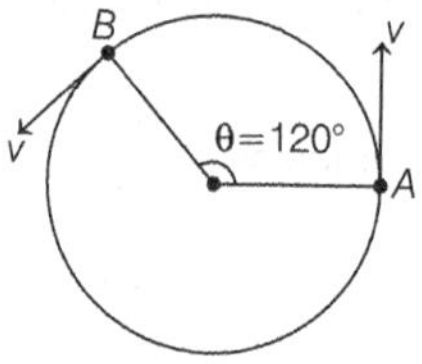

Given, $v = \pi$ m/s or $R\omega = \pi$

$$\omega = \frac{\pi}{R}\text{ rad/s}$$

Angular displacement, $\theta = 120°$ or $\frac{2\pi}{3}$

Using $\theta = \omega t$

$$t = \frac{\theta}{\omega} = \frac{2\pi/3}{\pi/R} = \frac{2R}{3}$$

linear displacement,

$$d = 2R\sin(\theta/2)$$

$$d = 2R\sin\left(\frac{120°}{2}\right) = 2R\sin 60° = 2R\frac{\sqrt{3}}{2} \Rightarrow R\sqrt{3}$$

$$\text{Average velocity} = \frac{d}{t} = \frac{R\sqrt{3}}{2R/3} = \frac{3\sqrt{3}}{2} = 1.5\sqrt{3}\text{ m/s}$$

7. Projection of particle P on X-axis is

$$x = r \cdot \cos\theta$$

or $$x = r\cos(\omega t + 30°) = r\cos\left(\omega t + \frac{\pi}{6}\right)$$

8. Time period, $T = 4$ s

Body will cover $\frac{3}{4}$th part of circle in 3 s.

The given situation can be drawn as

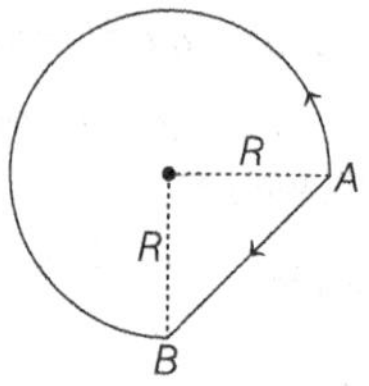

Displacement, $AB = \sqrt{R^2 + R^2} = \sqrt{2}R = \sqrt{2} \times 10 = 10\sqrt{2}$ m

9. Given,

$$m = 200\text{ kg}, r = 70\text{ m}$$
$$\omega = 0.2\text{ rad/s}$$
$$F_C = m\omega^2 r = 200 \times (0.2)^2 \times 70$$
$$= 200 \times 0.04 \times 70$$
$$= 2 \times 4 \times 70 = 560\text{ N}$$

10. Given, $m = 5\,kg, R = 2\,m$

time t for 1 rev $= 3.14$ sec or π s

θ for 1 rev $= 2\pi$ rad

Therefore $\omega = \frac{\theta}{t} = \frac{2\pi}{\pi} = 2$ rad/s

Centrifugal force, $F = mRw^2$

$$F = 5 \times 2 \times 2^2$$

$$F = 40\ N$$

11. Given, $m = 1\,kg, l = 1\,m$

Breaking tension, $T_{max} = 400$ N (breaking tension)

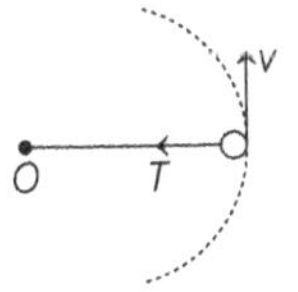

Since, stone rotates horizontally,

Thus, $T_{max} = \frac{mv_{max}^2}{l}$ or $v_{max}^2 = \frac{T_{max}\,l}{m}$

or $v_{max} = \sqrt{\frac{T_{max}}{m}\,l} = \sqrt{\frac{400 \times 1}{1}}$ or $v_{max} = 20$ m/s

12. Maximum safe speed of car over a horizontal turn is

$$v_{max} = \sqrt{\mu r g}$$

Here, $r = 50\,m, \mu = 0.34, g = 10$

So, $v_{max} = \sqrt{0.34 \times 50 \times 10} = \sqrt{170} \approx 13$ m/s

13. A bob suspended from the roof of the car by a massless string, then angle (θ) between the string and the vertical,

$$\theta = \tan^{-1}\left(\frac{v^2}{rg}\right) = \tan^{-1}\left(\frac{20^2}{40 \times 10}\right)$$

$$= \tan^{-1}(1) = \tan^{-1}\left(\tan\frac{\pi}{4}\right) = \frac{\pi}{4}$$

14. Given, $r = 75$ m, $v = 30$ m/s

$r_1 = 48$ m

Let the new speed is v_1 for curved path,

$$\tan\theta = \frac{v^2}{rg}$$

As coefficient of friction is same.

So, $\frac{v_1^2}{v^2} = \frac{r_1}{r}$; $\frac{v_1^2}{30^2} = \frac{48}{75}$; $v_1 = 24$ m/s

15. A stone has speed u at lowest position and magnitude of change in velocity when string is horizontal, is $\sqrt{x(u^2 - gL)}$.

To find x,

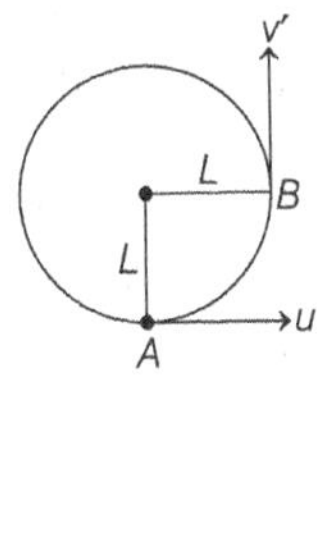

When string is horizontal, lets assume speed of stone is v'.

By conservation of energy,

$$TE_B = TE_A$$

$$PE_B + PE_B = PE_A + PE_A$$

$$mgL + \frac{1}{2}mv'^2 = 0 + \frac{1}{2}mu^2$$

$$\frac{1}{2}m(v'^2 - u^2) = -mgL$$

$$v'^2 = u^2 - 2gL$$

$$\Rightarrow \quad v' = \sqrt{u^2 - 2gL}$$

Since, v' is along Y-axis

$$\therefore \quad \mathbf{v}' = (\sqrt{u^2 - 2gL})\hat{j}$$

Initial velocity u is along X-axis. So $\mathbf{u}' = u\hat{i}$

$\therefore$ Change in velocity vector,

$$|\Delta \mathbf{v}| = \sqrt{|\mathbf{v}'^2| + |\mathbf{u}^2|} = \sqrt{(u^2 - 2gL) + u^2}$$

$$= \sqrt{2u^2 - 2gL}$$

$$|\Delta \mathbf{v}| = \sqrt{2(u^2 - gL)}$$

Equating this value with given value in question, we have

$$\sqrt{x(u^2 - gL)} = \sqrt{2(u^2 - gL)}$$

Thus, $x = 2$

16. When a stone of mass m, tied to a string is being whirled in a vertical circle with a uniform speed, then the tension in the string is maximum at lowest position and minimum at highest position of circular path.

17. From the conservation of momentum, we have

$$75 \times 10^{-3} \times v = 50 \times 10^{-3} \times v' + 75 \times 10^{-3} \times \frac{v}{3}$$

$$75 \times 10^{-3} v = 50 \times 10^{-3} \sqrt{5rg} \times \left(75 \times 10^{-3} \times \frac{v}{3}\right)$$

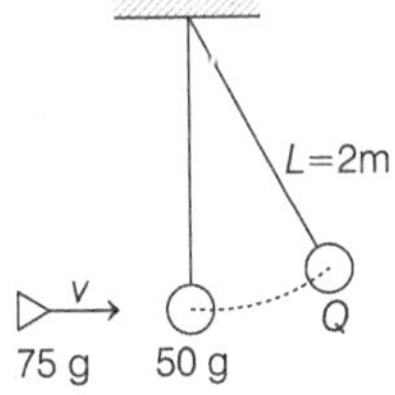

According to question, the bob completes a vertical circle of 2m radius, therefore

$$r = 2\,m, g = 10\,ms^{-2}$$

$$75 \times 10^{-3} v = 50 \times 10^{-3} \times \sqrt{5 \times 2 \times 10} + 75 \times 10^{-3} \times \frac{v}{3}$$

$$75 \times 10^{-3}\left(\frac{2v}{3}\right) = 50 \times 10^{-3} \times 10$$

$$150 \times 10^{-3} \times v = (150) \times 10^{-2}$$

$$v = 10\ m/s$$

18. Centripetal force, $F_c = mR\omega^2$

The force $\mu N \geq mR\omega^2$

$$\mu mg \geq mR\omega^2 \qquad (\because N = mg)$$

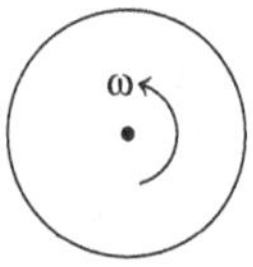

$$R \leq \frac{\mu g}{\omega^2}$$

19. The tension in the string is mg which is minimum at the highest point of circular path.

20. Given, the natural length of the spring $= l_0$

Let x be extension in the spring.

Angular speed of the mass m is ω.

The net length of the spring is $(l_0 + x)$

Thus, $kx = m(l_0 + x)\omega^2$

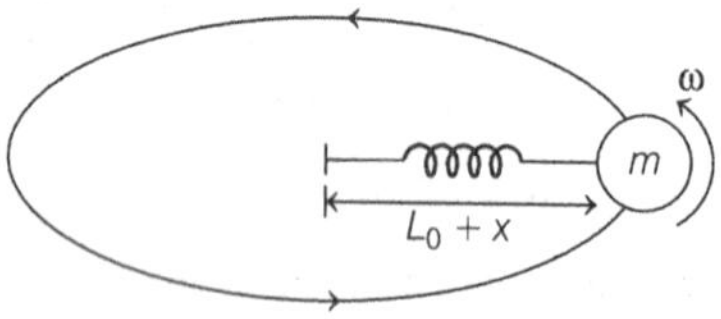

or $\quad (k - m\omega^2)x = m\omega^2 l_0$ or $x = \dfrac{m\omega^2 l_0}{k - m\omega^2}$

21. The given situation is shown below

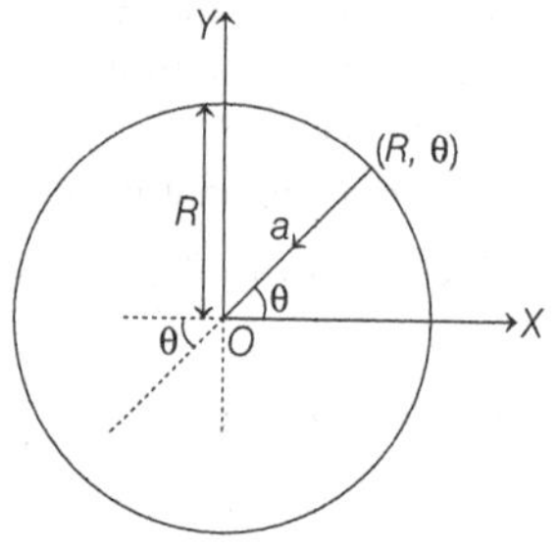

In uniform circular motion, direction of centripetal acceleration a is towards centre O, which is given as,

$$\mathbf{a} = -a\cos\theta\hat{\mathbf{i}} - a\sin\theta\hat{\mathbf{j}}$$

Since, $\quad a = |\mathbf{a}| = \dfrac{v^2}{R}$

$\therefore \quad \mathbf{a} = -\dfrac{v^2}{R}\cos\theta\hat{\mathbf{i}} - \dfrac{v^2}{R}\sin\theta\hat{\mathbf{j}}$

22. Given, mass of stone, $\quad m = 100\text{ g} = 0.1\text{ kg}$

length of string, $\quad l = 2\text{ m}$

maximum tension, $T = 80\text{ N}$

Tension in the string provides required centripetal force to the stone to revolve in circular orbit.

i.e. $\quad T = m\omega^2 l$

$$80 = 0.1 \times \omega^2 \times 2$$

$\Rightarrow \quad \omega^2 = 400 \quad \Rightarrow \quad \omega = 20 \quad \Rightarrow \quad 2\pi f = 20$

$\Rightarrow \quad f = \dfrac{20}{2\pi} = \dfrac{10}{\pi}\text{ rev/s} = \dfrac{10 \times 60}{\pi}\text{ rev/min}$

$= \dfrac{600}{\pi}\text{ rev/min} = \dfrac{K}{\pi}\text{ rev/min (given)}$

$\therefore \quad K = 600$

23. Given, radius of horizontal circle, $r = L/\sqrt{2}$

According to the question,

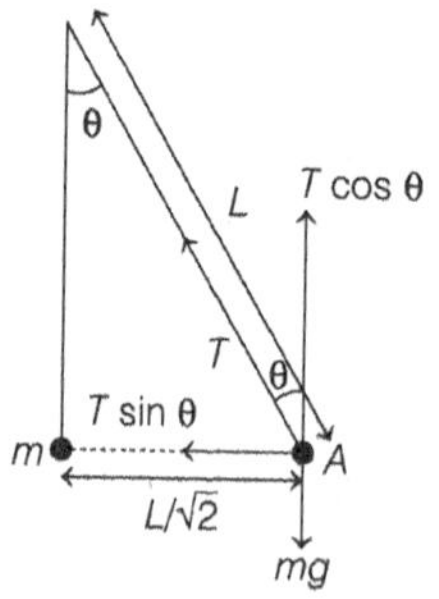

From the diagram

$$\tan\theta = v^2/rg \quad \Rightarrow \quad v = \sqrt{rg\tan\theta} \qquad \text{...(i)}$$

Now, from figure, we can write

$$\sin\theta = \frac{L/\sqrt{2}}{L} = \frac{1}{\sqrt{2}} \quad \Rightarrow \quad \theta = 45°$$

On substituting the value of θ in Eq. (i), we get

$$v = \sqrt{rg\tan 45°} = \sqrt{rg}$$

Thus, the value of speed of particle is $v = \sqrt{rg}$.

24. The maximum speed of cyclist on turn of unbanked road without slipping is given as

$$v_{max} = \sqrt{\mu gR} = \sqrt{0.2 \times 10 \times 2} = 2\text{ ms}^{-1}$$

$[\because \mu = 0.2 \text{ (given)}]$

Given, speed $= 7$ km/h

$$= \frac{7000}{3600}\text{ms}^{-1} = \frac{70}{36} = 1.94\text{ ms}^{-1}$$

As given speed is lesser than v_{max}, so the cyclist will not slip. Therefore, Statement I is true. As per Statement II, angle of banking, $\theta = 45°$

We know that for banked road,

$$v_{max} = \sqrt{\frac{gR(\mu + \tan\theta)}{(1 - \mu\tan\theta)}} \text{ and } v_{min} = \sqrt{\frac{gR(\tan\theta - \mu)}{1 + \mu\tan\theta}}$$

$\Rightarrow \quad v_{max} = \sqrt{\dfrac{10 \times 2(0.2 + \tan 45°)}{1 - 0.2\tan 45°}}$

and $\quad v_{min} = \sqrt{\dfrac{10 \times 2(1 - 0.2)}{1 + 0.2}}$

$\Rightarrow \quad v_{max} = 5.47\text{ ms}^{-1}$ and $v_{min} = 3.65\text{ ms}^{-1}$

$\because \quad v = 18.5\text{ km/h} = \dfrac{18.5 \times 1000}{5600} = 5.13\text{ ms}^{-1}$

$[\because$ given speed $= 18.5\text{ kmh}^{-1}]$

As, $v_{min} < v < v_{max}$, so the cyclist will not slip.

$\therefore$ Statement II is also true.

JEE Advanced

1. Apply energy conservation,

$$\frac{1}{2}mv_0^2 = mgh + \frac{1}{2}mv^2$$

$$\frac{1}{2}mv^2 = \frac{1}{2}mv_0^2 - mgh \quad \text{... (i)}$$

At top point y,

$$mg\sin\theta = \text{centripetal force} = \frac{mv^2}{R}$$

$$\frac{mv^2}{R} = mg\sin\theta$$

Putting this value in Eq. (i), we get

$$\frac{mgR\sin\theta}{2} = \frac{1}{2}mv_0^2 - mgh$$

$$\frac{mgR}{2}\frac{1}{2} = \frac{1}{2}mv_0^2 - mgh$$

$$\frac{yR}{2} = v_0^2 - 2gh$$

2. Force on block along slot $= m\omega^2 r = ma = m\left(\frac{vdv}{dr}\right)$

$$\int_0^v vdv = \int_{R\,2}^{r}\omega^2 rdr$$

$$\Rightarrow \quad \frac{v^2}{2} = \frac{\omega^2}{2}\left(r^2 - \frac{R^2}{4}\right)$$

$$\Rightarrow \quad v = \omega\sqrt{r^2 - \frac{R^2}{4}} = \frac{dr}{dt}$$

$$\Rightarrow \quad \int_{R\,4}^{r}\frac{dr}{\sqrt{r^2 - \frac{R^2}{4}}} = \int_0^t \omega\, dt$$

$$\ln\left(\frac{r + \sqrt{r^2 - \frac{R^2}{4}}}{\frac{R}{2}}\right) - \ln\left(\frac{R\,2 + \sqrt{\frac{R^2}{4} - \frac{R^2}{4}}}{\frac{R}{4}}\right) = \omega t$$

$$\Rightarrow \quad r + \sqrt{r^2 - \frac{R^2}{4}} = \frac{R}{2}e^{\omega t}$$

$$\Rightarrow \quad r^2 - \frac{R^2}{4} = \frac{R^2}{4}e^{2\omega t} + r^2 - 2r\frac{R}{2}e^{\omega t}$$

$$\Rightarrow \quad r = \frac{\frac{R^2}{4}e^{2\omega t} + \frac{R^2}{4}}{Re^{\omega t}} = \frac{R}{4}(e^{\omega t} + e^{-\omega t})$$

3.

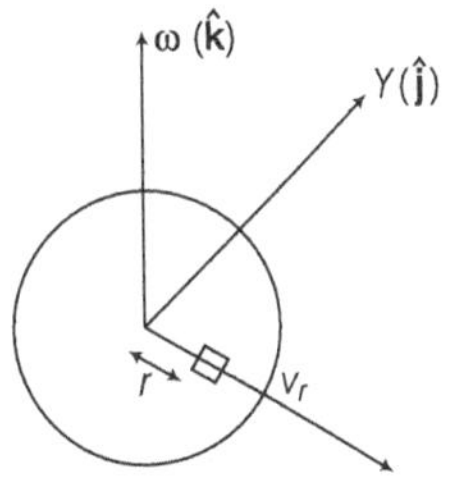

$$\mathbf{F}_{rot} = \mathbf{F}_{in} + 2m(v_{rot}\,\hat{\mathbf{i}})\times\omega\hat{\mathbf{k}} + m(\omega\hat{\mathbf{k}}\times r\,\hat{\mathbf{i}})\times\omega\hat{\mathbf{k}}$$

$$mr\omega^2\hat{\mathbf{i}} = \mathbf{F}_{in} + 2mv_{rot}\omega(-\hat{\mathbf{j}}) + m\omega^2 r\,\hat{\mathbf{i}}$$

$$\mathbf{F}_{in} = 2mv_r\omega\hat{\mathbf{j}}$$

$$r = \frac{R}{4}[e^{\omega t} + e^{-\omega t}]$$

$$\frac{dr}{dt} = v_r = \frac{R}{4}[\omega e^{\omega t} - \omega e^{-\omega t}]$$

$$\mathbf{F}_{in} = 2m\frac{R\omega}{4}[e^{\omega t} - e^{-\omega t}]\omega\hat{\mathbf{j}}$$

$$\mathbf{F}_{in} = \frac{mR\omega^2}{2}[e^{\omega t} - e^{-\omega t}]\hat{\mathbf{j}}$$

Also, reaction is due to disc surface, then

$$\mathbf{F}_{reaction} = \frac{mR\omega^2}{2}[e^{\omega t} - e^{-\omega t}]\hat{\mathbf{j}} + mg\hat{\mathbf{k}}$$

4. Height fallen up to point Q,

$$h = R\sin 30° = 40\times\frac{1}{2} = 20\text{ m}$$

Work done against friction = Initial mechanical energy – Final mechanical energy

$$= mgh - \frac{1}{2}mv^2$$

Putting the values, we get

$$150 = 1\times 10\times 20 - \frac{1}{2}\times 1\times v^2 \Rightarrow v = 10\text{ m/s}$$

5. At point Q, component of weight along PQ (radially outwards) is $mg\cos 60°$ or $\frac{mg}{2}$.

Normal reaction is radially inwards

$$N - \frac{mg}{2} = \frac{mv^2}{R}$$

or

$$N = \frac{mg}{2} + \frac{mv^2}{R}$$

$$= \frac{1\times 10}{2} + \frac{1\times(10)^2}{40} = 7.5\text{ N}$$

6. As, $$v = \sqrt{5gL} \quad \text{...(i)}$$

So, $$\left(\frac{v}{2}\right)^2 = v^2 - 2gh \quad \text{...(ii)}$$

$$h = L(1-\cos\theta) \quad \text{...(iii)}$$

Solving Eqs. (i), (ii) and (iii), we get

$$\cos\theta = -\frac{7}{8} \text{ or } \theta = \cos^{-1}\left(-\frac{7}{8}\right) = 151°$$